GARDEN WISDOM & KNOW-HOW

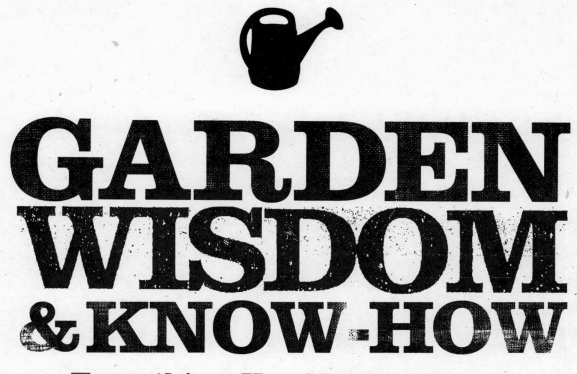

GARDEN WISDOM & KNOW-HOW

Everything You Need to Know to Plant, Grow, and Harvest

From the Editors of Rodale Gardening Books

Compiled by Judy Pray

BLACK DOG
& LEVENTHAL
PUBLISHERS
NEW YORK

Published by
Black Dog & Leventhal Publishers, Inc.
151 West 19th Street
New York, NY 10011

Distributed by
Workman Publishing Company
225 Varick Street
New York, NY 10014
Manufactured in the United States of America

Cover and interior design by Ohioboy Design
Cover illustration © Elara Tanguy

All materials in this book are published under license from Rodale Inc, with the exception
of the following illustrations:
Pages 9, 36 (top), 45, 55, 94 (bottom), 95, 96, 99, 101, 110, 162 (2 illustrations), 163 (3
illustrations), 188, 189 (3 illustrations), 190, 202 (2 illustrations), 214, 239, 251, 264
(bottom), 282, 284, 289, 296, 297, 299, 302, 305, 307, 317, 319, 329 (2 illustrations,
left), 333 (left), 374 (2 illustrations), 375 (2 illustrations), 376, 380, 381 (2 illustrations),
382 (6 illustrations), 383 (7 illustrations), 384 (5 illustrations), 407 (right), 408 (4
illustrations), 409 (2 illustrations), 410 (top), 422, 424, 425, 426 (2 illustrations),
© Elara Tanguy.

ISBN-13: 978-1-57912-837-1
h g f e d
Library of Congress Cataloging-in-Publication Data available on file.

Contents

List Your Landscape Needs

Once you've started thinking about your yard and what you want it to do, it's time to start a garden notebook. You'll find that keeping all your records in one place is invaluable as you make plans and review the progress of your garden. A good garden notebook doesn't need to be anything fancy—a loose-leaf notebook with a pocket or two to hold pencils and notes will do fine. Don't worry if it gets cluttered and messy as time goes on; you can still get what you need from it as long as you can read it and find things.

Inventory Your Site

You may think you know everything about your yard, but once you start really looking at it, you may be surprised at how many details you've forgotten. Here's a list of important facts and features you'll want to keep in mind as you take your design. As you read about them, se a page in your garden notebook to make notes about them. When you're finished, you'll have a much clearer idea of where you could put a garden or gardens in your yard.

The Vital Statistics

Before you draw up your garden plan and goals, collect some facts about your property. Doing this will help you organize your priorities and make realistic plans. You'll need to know about:

- Hardiness zone and local weather conditions
- Soil condition
- Drainage, including both wet and dry sites around your yard
- Exposure, such as areas with full sun, partial shade, or full shade
- Property dimensions, including a breakdown of the space available for gardens, recreation areas, pet runs, and other areas
- Existing insect and disease problems
- Areas to avoid, such as septic tank fields and underground utility cables or water-lines
- Locations of essential features, such as a water source, tool shed, or compost pile
- Established plants and their condition, as well as possible effects on new plants, such as shade or competition for nutrients
- How much time you have to spend on your yard and garden

Know Your Microclimates

Knowing about the microclimates on your property—places that are warmer or cooler than the rest—can be valuable when it comes to siting all your plantings. Planting a vegetable garden in a frost pocket, where frost settles late in spring and early in fall, can shorten your harvest season tremendously, for example. A sheltered, south-facing site, on the other hand, can be quite a pleasant place to sit on a cool winter day. Such sites will also encourage spring flowers to bloom earlier than in cooler parts of your yard. To verify your hunches about warmer or cooler pockets that would affect your plans, take temperature readings at different times of day throughout the year in various locations in the garden.

Use the "Landscape-Needs Checklist" to help you start thinking about what features you'd like to have in your yard. As you review the list, make sure you look at your yard from every perspective: Look out at the yard from inside the house, including the upstairs windows; look at it from the street, from down the street, from the front door, from the sides, from the back door, from the back boundary line; look back at the house from the yard. Taking a fresh look at your yard will help you identify features you'd like to hide or views you'd like to improve—such as the view out your kitchen window, for example. Date your list; you might want to add or change things later.

Then compare your wish list and landscape-needs list. Some things will probably appear on both lists. The rose hedge on your wish list, for example, may match your need to keep romping pets out of the vegetable garden. Other wants and needs may be totally incompatible. If your yard is a popular place for neighborhood football or volley-ball games, a delicate rock garden might be out of the question. Discuss the lists with your family, and decide which elements are acceptable to everyone. Also, don't forget to consider maintenance needs. A lovely perennial border can quickly deteriorate into a tangled mess if you don't have time to take care of it.

Sizing Up Your Site

Now that you've looked at what features and plantings you'd like to have on your property, it's time to take stock of what conditions you have to work with. Taking a careful look at your site—its soil, climate, and exposure—will make it easier to decide where to locate your vegetable garden, plantings of flowers or fruit, trees, hedges, or other plantings you'd like to add.

See "Inventory Your Site" to help you get a better idea of what you have to work with. Take note of wet, shady, and rocky spots, and try to take advantage of them. A wet spot may not be desirable in a play area, but it could be a good place for a group of moisture-loving plants. Also, think of the landscape as it changes through the seasons. Evergreens and berried shrubs, along with a bench in a sunny spot, can make your yard a pleasant winter retreat. A little careful planning can give the landscape four-season appeal. Don't forget details like specimen plants, interesting rocks, or sculpture to give the garden character.

How to Make a Garden Map

You don't need professional skills to draw a map of your garden. Using lined graph paper, any gardener can make a usable garden map.

Your first step should be to measure the boundary lines of your property, using a flexible measuring tape that's 25 feet or longer. It's easiest to do this with a helper to hold one end of the tape. If you work alone, stick a pencil through the loop at the end of the tape and push it into the ground to secure it. If you have a survey of your property, you can skip this step. Just use the dimensions on your survey or make a photocopy of the survey to use as a base map.

You'll also want to take measurements of the size of your house and note its location with regard to boundary lines. Make sure to note the size and location of existing garden beds and plantings as well.

Next, sit down with your list of measurements and your graph paper. Choose a scale, such as one square on paper equals 1 foot of actual space. If you have a large property, you may need to tape a few sheets of paper together to work on that scale. Or

---

you can choose a different scale, such as 1 inch on paper equals 5 feet of actual space.

Draw your boundaries, and then fill in the location of existing buildings and plantings. Make as accurate a plan as possible, and include all your garden's features—paths, trees, buildings, fences, and walkways. Double-check your counting to be sure you've drawn things accurately. With this base map, you'll have a template to use when sketching in your plans and dreams for the ideal yard and garden.

Rather than drawing your plans directly on your base map however, it's best to draw on over-lays. Use sheets of thin tracing paper as overlays to sketch in ideas and see how they fit while you work on the design. That way, you can use your master plan again and again until you decide on the best arrangement of pathways, flower beds, and other features. Then transfer the final design to your master plan.

Plan for Practicality

Whether you design your home landscape yourself or leave it to a professional, make sure that the finished plan fits your needs. Don't add a deck just because all your neighbors have them in their back-yards if what you really want is a dooryard herb garden. And while you don't want to copy your neighbors exactly, try to keep the general theme of the area in your design. A woodland garden in the Southwest would look as out of place as a cactus garden in New England. By using plants that are

---

Landscape-Needs Checklist

Here's a list of ways you can use plants and gardens to enhance your landscape, along with features you might want to add to your yard. In your garden notebook, jot down all that apply in your situation, but use this list only as a starting point. To unlock all the potential your yard has to offer, try to think about what activities you would like to have space for and what you would like it to do for you.

- Screen a patio or deck from the neighbors.
- Hide a bare foundation, or transform a dull or ugly foundation planting.
- Add a vegetable garden.
- Add interest along the front of the yard.
- Create a welcoming entrance to the house.
- Create a sitting area under shade trees.
- Add a colorful planting along the driveway,
- Make the front entrance to the house more appealing.
- Create a quiet sitting area outdoors.
- Make an area for composting or tool storage.
- Beautify a lamppost or mailbox.
- Create a boundary around the property.
- Hide an unattractive view or element (like a utility pole, laundry line, or chain-link fence).
- Make an attractive view into the yard from a prominent window indoors.
- Fill a bare spot.
- Create a place to walk to in the yard.
- Beautify a garage or outbuilding.
- Surround a bench, trellis, or arbor.
- Give a new home a more finished look.

Continued ➡

Plan before you plant. One way to reduce maintenance in the long run is to make a plan before you buy foundation plants and then choose among the many low-growing and dwarf cultivars of trees and shrubs that mature at the size you would like. Providing plants with the room they need to develop properly allows them to display their natural beauty, and you won't need to shear them into cubes or cones in an attempt to keep them in bounds. If the planting looks too sparse at first, fill in spaces with annuals, perennials, or bulbs until the shrubs develop.

best adapted to your area, your landscape will have the appropriate regional look, and your plants will be healthier, too.

There are some basic practical considerations to keep in mind while you're designing your garden. A variety of people need to have access to your property. Oil or gas delivery people need to get to the tank or inlet. Meter readers need to get to the meters. Be sure to accommodate their needs when you plan. An element as simple as a short stepping-stone path through a flower bed to a meter enables the reader to get in and out without damaging your plantings.

Electric, telephone, and cable television service people may trim trees that grow near their lines. It pays to design plantings that they will be able to work around.

Don't forget to consider your own everyday needs, either. Have you planned your paths so you will be able to get your mower and garden cart where you need to go? Is it easy to take out the garbage? What about someone delivering bulk

INFORMAL DESIGN. *Even a rectangular lot can have an informal design. Parts of the garden—terraces, lawn areas, groundcover beds, flower gardens, or plantings of shrubs and trees—all have free-form shapes that flow together in a unified, informal design.*

FORMAL DESIGN. *Because they can be unfussy and simple, formal designs are often very effective on a small lot. Rectangular beds filled with herbs and edged with dwarf shrubs, straight walks, and symmetrical design are all characteristic of a formal garden.*

garden supplies like mulch—is there a place for that?

And of course, don't plan, and certainly don't dig, before finding out where underground utilities run. Not only do you want to avoid injuring them or yourself, but you may not even be allowed to build or plant permanent features over them.

Understanding Design

Your site will determine some of your design choices. For example, the style of your home may influence the feel of the design you'd like to have. If you have a brick house, the landscape might include brick paths and clipped evergreen hedges. A house with natural wood siding lends itself to wood-chip paths and rail fencing. You'll also need to plan access areas, such as paths, steps, and ramps.

There are two general types of garden design styles—formal and informal. Formal gardens exhibit classical symmetry. Flower beds, terraces, pools, and other features are generally rectangular (or sometimes round), and walks are straight. Formal gardens are not necessarily grand; gardens designed in this manner can be unfussy and simple.

Informal gardens feature curved, free-form flower beds that sweep along the land's features. Lawns, terraces, walkways, and other features are also irregularly shaped, with one gentle arc leading to another. Natural-looking woodland wildflower gardens and free-form island beds of perennials are both examples of informal style. If the lay of your land is irregular, it will lend itself to an informal design.

BASIC DESIGN PRINCIPLES

Regardless of style, all well-designed gardens make use of three essential principles—balance, proportion, and repetition—to blend the various parts of the garden into a harmonious whole.

Balance. When elements on two sides of a central point are similar in size or visual weight, they are balanced. Balanced design gives the viewer a peaceful, restful feeling; unbalanced, lopsided design is unsettling. Balance doesn't necessarily mean symmetry; you don't need mirror-image plantings to accomplish it. Several good-sized clumps of a plant can balance one large one, for example. Symmetrical balance is a hallmark of formal gardens; and asymmetrical balance, of informal gardens.

Proportion. Garden features (plants, flower beds, terraces, and so forth) are in proportion when their scale is in good relationship to their surroundings. For example, a large clump of 9-foot-tall giant reed planted in a bed with low-growing, 2- to 3-foot perennials creates a picture that is out of proportion. Similarly, a huge shed would be out of proportion in a small yard.

Repetition. Repeating an element—color, texture, shape, or even building materials like landscape timbers—throughout a garden adds unity and harmony to a design, so the parts of the garden fit together more closely. For example, repeating the color red at intervals in a flower bed leads the eye through the design and creates a feeling of wholeness and rhythm. You can repeat the same plant, or use different species with similarly colored blooms, to achieve the same effect.

Plants and Design

The color, height, form, and texture of plants play a vital role in any garden. All plants change from season to season and year to year. They may grow taller than planned, spread too vigorously, or not

bloom when expected. Balancing and working with these changes is what makes gardening an art. Even the most carefully designed gardens are never static; their owners adjust and develop the design over time.

USING COLOR

In a garden, color can be used in many different ways. One gardener may prefer bright reds and yellows; another, soft pinks, blues, and lavenders. Color can influence the mood of a garden. Hot colors—vibrant reds, oranges, and yellows—are cheerful and bright. Cool colors—greens, blues, and purples—are more serene.

Color can influence perceived perspective. Hot or warm colors appear to bring an object or scene closer. Cool colors tend to recede and push the object farther away, so they're a good choice for making a small garden seem larger. Use them in large clumps to catch the eye, and remember that they can be easily overwhelmed by warm colors.

Use balance, proportion, and repetition to design your color scheme. Strive for balanced distribution of color. A large planting of one color can overwhelm a design. Repeating a color at intervals can unify the design. Use clumps of a single plant or several different species with the same flower color.

BALANCING HEIGHT AND FORM

Plant height and plant form should be balanced and in proportion. In a planting in front of a fence or other backdrop, plant the tallest plants in the back, the shortest in front. If the planting bed's shape is free-form, put the tallest plants at the widest parts of the border. In island beds, which can be viewed from all sides, plant the tallest plants in the center, with shorter plants around the edges.

Form refers to a plant's shape—round, vertical, creeping, or weeping, for example. It's used to describe the entire plant or just the flowers. For example, delphiniums are vertical plants with spike-shaped bloom stalks; marigolds are mound-shaped with round blooms. Intersperse different plant forms throughout a design for balance and interest. Form can be used like color, although it's more subtle. Repeating a form at intervals strengthens unity and harmony. You needn't repeat the same plant to achieve this effect; several plants with similar forms will do.

INCORPORATING TEXTURES

Plant leaves can look coarse, crinkled, glossy, fuzzy, or smooth. Flowers can be feathery and delicate or waxy and bold. Using plants with a variety of textures—and repeating interesting textures at intervals—adds interest and appeal. Like form, texture is a subtle characteristic.

Garden Size

Several factors play a role in determining the best size for the individual gardens in your design. Available space may be the main consideration, but keep in mind what landscape purpose the garden is to serve. For example, if you need a shrub border to screen an unattractive view or create a private patio space, determine the size by walking around your yard and studying where the largest plants need to be planted to accomplish your purpose. Smaller shrubs and perennials that connect these larger plants into a continuous border can be filled in later, as time and budget permit. The beauty of having an overall plan is that nothing is planted haphazardly and you'll be able to work gradually toward your goal.

For a flower garden that blooms all season, you will need enough space to accommodate a variety of

Continued ➡

plants that will provide an extended bloom period. About 125 square feet will give you enough room to mass flowers for a succession of color. For a formal garden, a 5-foot x 25-foot rectangle, two 5-foot x 12½-foot beds, or a 12-foot-diameter circle all provide about 125 square feet. In an informal garden, make the shapes free-form, or plan several related beds divided by paths. In general, don't plan gardens that are less than 4 or 5 feet wide if you want a lush effect. Don't plan them any wider if you want to be able to tend the plants without stepping into the bed, or else plan on an access path on either side.

Consider Time and Money

These last considerations are critical: How much time and money do you want to spend? You can plan for features that reduce maintenance, but any garden will require basic care—especially in the early stages. Consider how much time you want to devote to such tasks as weeding, staking, watering, and pruning. Look for tough, low-maintenance plants if you want to keep these chores to a minimum.

Plants and supplies also cost money; decide on your budget before you start to dig. If you're not realistic about what size garden you can control, it will end up controlling you. Once you have a plan, you can plant each area as time and budget permit. Plan your garden so you'll have time to enjoy it.

Installation

Once you actually have a plan, the next step is to carry it out. The first consideration in installation is often the cost. If you can't or don't want to do everything at once, consider carrying the plan out over several years. It's usually best to start with structures, such as fences and buildings. Next, add the trees and hedges. Eventually, add smaller shrubs, flowers, and groundcovers. This approach makes it fairly easy to install the landscape on your own.

If you do want to carry out the plan all at once, it may be best to hire a professional; this is especially true if the plan includes grading and drainage changes or irrigation and lighting systems. For your protection, get three bids for large projects, and make sure you have signed contracts before work begins. Also, don't forget to check local regulations and get necessary permits before starting.

Maintaining the Landscape

After you have spent all this time developing and installing your landscape, you'll certainly want to take good care of it. In new landscapes, watering is probably the most important task. Regular watering for the first year or two helps plants to settle in. After that, water your plants less frequently to encourage strong root systems. Pruning, applying mulch and fertilizer, and controlling insects and diseases are all routine maintenance tasks that keep your landscape looking its best.

Edible Landscaping

While many gardeners would like to grow their own fresh produce, not all have time or space for a separate food garden. Edible landscapes do double duty—they produce food and make our yards attractive at the same time. An edible landscape is also convenient. Slogging out to the vegetable garden on a rainy evening after work is a chore. Picking a few ripe tomatoes on your way in from the car or gathering a handful of fragrant herbs from a small garden beside the back door is a pleasure.

The concept of edible landscaping is not new. Ancient Egyptian pleasure gardens included fish ponds, flowers, grape arbors, fruit trees, and places to sit and enjoy the serenity. But by the Renaissance, gardeners began to exclude edible plants from their formal ornamental gardens. They planted separate herb gardens, vegetable gardens, and orchards. Edible landscaping concepts came to the fore in the 1980s. Gardeners recognized that many edible plants are also beautiful, and they reintroduced them to the general landscape.

Making the Transition

Only those who move into newly built homes have the luxury of designing the landscape from scratch. Most likely, your yard already has many permanent plantings. While you won't want to redesign and uproot your whole yard overnight, there are many ways to gradually transform your existing plantings into an edible landscape. Keep in mind that an edible landscape is one in which *most*, but not necessarily all, of the plantings are food-producing plants.

Start by including some edibles with your annual flowers. Remember, you don't have to plant vegetables in rows—they'll grow just as well interplanted among ornamentals and herbs. Use the same design rules you would with flowers alone. Try accenting a flower bed with deep green rosettes of corn salad, small mounds of 'Spicy Globe' basil, or crinkly red leaf lettuce.

Plant perennial herbs and vegetables in your existing ornamental borders—make room by relocating or replacing existing plants. For example, lavender and rosemary have upright forms with thin leaves and will add four-season interest to a border. Artichokes are perennial in Zones 9 and 10; their silvery, spiky foliage makes an interesting foil for other plants.

If you need to remove an existing tree or shrub that has died or outgrown its site, consider a fruit or nut tree as a replacement. A nut tree (pecan, hickory, English walnut, hazelnut—whatever is suitable for your climate) can replace a large shade tree. A full-sized fruit tree might be a good replacement for a medium-sized tree. Many of the spring-flowering pears, cherries, and crab apples used in landscaping are sterile hybrids that do not produce fruit. Their fruiting cousins are equally attractive in bloom and do produce fruit.

There are several other special ways to incorporate edibles into your existing landscape:

- Convert areas of lawn into new garden beds and include edibles in the design.

- Replace grass with food-producing groundcovers in some areas. Alpine strawberries produce fruit all summer and tolerate light shade.

- Make use of existing walls and fences, or add new ones. Train dwarf fruit trees against them, or use them to support raspberries, blackberries, or vegetables.

- Plant a fruiting hedge. Shrub roses such as rugosa roses (*Rosa rugosa*) make a lovely and intruder-resistant barrier.

- Build an arbor or trellis. Grapes are traditional, but hardy kiwi would also be a good choice for a large arbor. Vegetables like cucumbers, melons, and beans work well, too, but some need special support for the fruit.

- Add containers to your landscape. Many dwarf fruit trees are now available and can be grown in large tubs. Dwarf citrus will grow even in northern climates if the trees are moved to a cool, sunny, indoor location during the winter. Strawberry jars are good for strawberries or herbs.

Selecting Plants

When you become an edible-landscaper, you'll find that bringing vegetables and fruit trees out of hiding and into the total landscape makes your gardening even more rewarding.

There are food-producing plants to satisfy every need in your landscape. Fruit and nut trees come in a wide range of sizes and shapes, provide shade, and may provide spring blooms and/or fall color. Berry-producing shrubs, such as blueberries and wild plums, also provide flowers and fall color. Some blueberries even have attractive red branches in the winter. The flowers of certain annual and perennial flowers, such as nasturtiums and chives, are edible. Many herbs and vegetables have interesting foliage and some have showy flowers or brightly colored fruit. Fruiting vines such as grapes, melons, and climbing beans will cover fences and trellises. Some edibles, such as creeping thyme and alpine strawberries, make good groundcovers.

Your personal tastes and how much space you have available will determine what you plant. Consider these factors as you select plants:

- What foods do you like and use most? You're defeating the purpose of an edible landscape if you plant crops you won't eat.

- How big is each plant and how much will it produce? Fresh homegrown sweet corn is a treat without comparison, but those large cornstalks yield only two or three ears apiece.

- Do you have a location suitable for growing edibles? Many fruit and vegetable crops will thrive only if they have direct sun for at least six hours daily. Your choice will be limited if you have a shady yard.

- What fresh foods can you buy locally, and which are expensive or difficult to find? You may decide to plant raspberry canes and forego zucchini plants. Good raspberries are next to impossible to buy at the grocery store, while zucchini in season is cheap (or available free from friends).

A Gallery of Edibles

Almost all food-producing plants have ornamental value. The following listings are only a small sampling of the many excellent edible landscape plants.

Trees In warm climates, citrus (orange, lemon, lime, grapefruit) are versatile trees. They are large enough to provide good shade, cooling the house

Continued ➡

or an area of the garden during the heat of the day. They retain their shiny deep green leaves through the winter, and they have fruit in various stages of development and ripeness on their branches year-round. When in flower, their fragrance perfumes the air. The flowers of the orange tree are extremely sweet and can be used to flavor honey, sugar, and tea, or as a beautiful garnish.

In the East, if your flowering dogwood (*Cornus florida*) trees are in decline, replace them with Korean dogwood (*Cornus kousa*). It blooms in June (later than the flowering dogwood), the flowers are longer-lasting, and it has brilliant fall foliage. The edible fruit resembles a pale strawberry. It is tartly sweet, with a pearlike, mealy texture, and is favored by birds and wildlife. Figs make interesting foundation plants, but they need a sheltered location and winter protection in the North. Dwarf fruit trees work well in small areas.

Shrubs. A blueberry bush makes a good foundation plant but must have acid soil to thrive. Bush cherries, wild plums, gooseberries, currants, hazelnuts, and highbush cranberries (*Viburnum trilobum*) make good hedges. Tightly planted raspberries or blackberries create a living fence. Some shrub-type roses, such as rugosa roses, produce large, bright orange or red, edible rose hips with 60 times the vitamin C of an orange. The hips can be used to make tea, jam, or jelly.

Ornamentals with Edible Parts. Leaves of amaranth (especially 'Love Lies Bleeding', 'Red Stripe Leaf', and 'Early Splendor'), leaves and flowers of anise hyssop (*Agastache foeniculum*), young leaves of balloon flower (*Platycodon grandiflorus*), seeds of love, mist (*Nigella damascena*), and leaves and flowers of nasturtium and violets are edible.

Showy Edibles. The following edibles have colorful and attractive flowers: amaranth (green, purple, red), artichoke (lavender), beans (red, purple, white), cardoon (lavender), chives (lavender, white), dill (yellow-green), eggplant (lavender), garlic (white), Jerusalem artichoke (yellow), nasturtium (orange, red, yellow), okra (white, yellow), rosemary (pale blue), salsify (blue), and sugar peas (purple, white).

The foliage of edibles also comes in many interesting colors and forms. Various cultivars of artichoke, cabbage, cardoon, kale, lavender, leeks, marjoram, onion, rosemary, and sage feature shades of gray and blue. Beets, purple basil, red cabbage, red chard, pink cress, purple ornamental kale, red lettuces, and purple mustard feature pink and red shades. Carrots, endive, white ornamental kale, variegated lemon balm, nasturtiums, and thyme feature light green, yellow, and white. Asparagus has attractive green fernlike foliage.

Vines Peas are lovely trained on a fence, and they can be followed by cucumbers or squash as the season progresses. Hardy kiwi is a vigorous climber. 'Scarlet Runner' beans have bright red-orange flowers and are pretty planted with white flowering cultivars of beans. Indeterminate tomatoes can be trained on a trellis or arbor; let the side shoots grow in for maximum coverage.

Groundcovers Alpine strawberries produce tasty fruit. Many herbs are also low-growing and vigorous and can be used as groundcovers as well.

Fragrant Edibles Certain fragrances may be attractive to some people and annoying to others. The most fragrant edibles include basil, chamomile, chives, fennel, mint, oregano, parsley, sage, strawberry, thyme, and tomato. Creeping varieties of thyme and oregano are low-growing and work well planted between stepping stones, where they may be lightly stepped on, releasing their fragrance.

Budget-Stretching Ideas

There are many ways to stretch your gardening dollar. Here are a few to consider:

- Renting can be much less expensive than buying tools or equipment you may need, especially large power equipment such as shredders and tractors that you may need only occasionally. Renting also may make the difference between being able to do a job or having to hire someone to do it for you.

- For a soil-enriching boost of almost-free fertilizer and organic matter, plant a green manure crop like annual ryegrass, soybeans, or buckwheat and till it under before planting.

- Making a nursery bed is a great way to save money on plants. If your design calls for lots of groundcovers or hostas, for example, buy only a plant or two. Then systematically propagate them for a year or more by division, cuttings, or layering, depending on the species, until you have a small nursery of plants to move to your garden. A nursery bed is perfect for young seedlings, too. Keeping the young plants together ensures they get the care they need, since they're easier to water and weed en masse. Transplant to the garden when the plants are large enough to thrive on their own.

  To make a nursery bed, prepare the soil and add plenty of compost or leaf mold; a raised bed is ideal. Shade if the bed is in hot sun.

- Make shady and sunny nursery beds. Don't make the beds too small—you'll be propagating your plant and growing them on, so you'll need more space than seems likely at first.

- Don't be afraid to invest in top-quality cultivars if you can divide or propagate them.

- Look for special packages from nurseries—group offers of daffodils, hostas, and other popular perennials. You can save money with these packages, but be aware of the trade-offs: If you buy a group of unnamed plants, don't expect cultivar quality—put them on a slope or distant area that needs color rather than in a nearby bed or border. If you buy a "named, our choice" special, you won't sacrifice quality—you just won't know exactly what you're getting.

- Make compost. It saves money on purchased mulch and soil amendments, makes great fertilizer, and recycles valuable nutrients.

- Ask your local utility company who does their tree work, and call. Many will dump wood chips on your property for free mulch.

- Spend your money on the best—not necessarily the most expensive—materials possible; they will last longer and be a better investment.

- Start with smaller plants. Small plants are easier to plant and are less expensive.

- Order plants with a friend or group to take advantage of volume discounts.

- Plan before you shop, and buy only what you need. Impulse shopping is costly.

- Include some edibles in your design. You'll harvest tasty food and save money. Many edible plants are ornamental, too.

- Recycle what you have, use found materials, and make the best use of existing plants and features.

- Trade plants with neighbors. Almost everybody has too much of something, and these "extra" plants are often fast-growing—take up just what you need for quick color.

- Buy from reputable nurseries. You'll find healthier plants, often for little more than those found at bargain-basement sales. Reputable nurseries will often replace plants for free if they don't thrive.

Vicki Mattern

Gardening organically is really quite simple. Push a seed into the soil, give it sun and water, add compost, and keep down the weeds. The seed knows what to do. It will sprout, soak up nutrients, develop a stem and leaves, and before you know it, reward you with flowers, fruits, and seeds.

Your role is to nurture it along using techniques adapted straight from nature. There's nothing difficult or artificial; there are no expensive chemicals to buy. Follow this simple advice and experience the joy of growing food and flowers the healthful way—without toxic pesticides and fertilizers.

Site It Right

When choosing a new garden site or expanding an existing one, take a close look at the surrounding landscape—especially at any nearby trees. Estimate how big those trees will be in 5 to 10 years, then plan your garden so that it won't be shaded when the trees get larger.

If you are able to garden year-round, be sure to consider where the sunlight will hit your garden in winter, too. If possible, site your garden on the south side of a building to take full advantage of the winter sun.

No matter where you live, try to orient vegetable garden beds to run from north to south. That way, taller crops won't shade shorter ones however you plant them.

Raise Your Beds

The loose soil of a well-prepared raised bed allows plant roots to spread out and take in the maximum amount of nutrients and water. Raised beds also warm up faster in spring and drain better than flat beds. And because you don't walk on them (you work them from the sides), the soil never becomes compacted.

To keep plants within easy reach, make the beds no wider than *double your arm length* (about 4 to 5 feet). The length of the beds depends on the size of your garden and the lay of your land. Shorter beds can save time when weeding or harvesting, but the paths around lots of short beds can take up valuable garden space if you have a small garden. Many

Continued ➡

gardeners find 15- to 20-foot-long beds to be about the right size for convenience and efficient use of space.

If you have a structure (such as a fence or building) on one side of your garden, put a narrow bed along it rather than a path. Maneuvering a wheelbarrow down a path next to a fence or building can be difficult.

Plan Perfect Paths

When creating your garden plan, consider the width of paths you'll need to accommodate your equipment. If you plan to use a wheelbarrow, tiller, or cart, you'll need at least a few main paths that are 18 to 24 inches wide. Smaller, secondary paths can be narrower—12 to 18 inches wide.

To keep the weeds out of those paths, mulch them with a thick layer of clean straw, hay, or wood chips. Or simply make them wide enough for a lawn mower and grow grass on them. Mow the paths regularly and use the clippings to mulch the beds.

Keep the Compost Close

Compost is a must for any organic garden! It contains all of the primary nutrients, trace minerals, and beneficial organisms that plants need to grow and thrive. It also discourages plant diseases and neutralizes the chemistry of the soil. If your soil is too acidic or too alkaline, you can help put it back into balance by adding compost.

Plan to locate your compost pile or bins as close as possible to the garden. You'll be more inclined to use the compost, and you'll save time and effort because you won't need to do as much hauling. And when summers are dry, you can water the compost at the same time you water your garden.

Planning and Shopping Smart

Fern Marshall Bradley

How can you improve your garden while doing less work? Plan in advance. Many of us never seem to find the time for it, but making a garden plan can actually save time, labor, and expense, during the gardening season. Perhaps the following ideas from successful gardeners and designers on how to plan, make garden maps, and keep records can inspire you to really get organized ahead of time.

Once you've laid your garden plans, you'll be ready for one of the most exciting, yet most frustrating, aspects of gardening—the shopping. If you know exactly what plants or seeds you want, shopping is easy. But more often than not, you have to make decisions balancing what's best for the garden

---

with what's best for the wallet. In this chapter, garden professionals share hints and insights that will help you be a smarter garden shopper whether you're shopping by mail order or at your local nursery or garden center.

Planning for the Big Picture

Planning can be extra-important for gardening the organic way. Having excellent-quality soil and using preventive techniques to keep pests from getting too pesky means thinking and doing before you plant. You'll find lots of helpful tips on improving your soil in "Balancing the Soil," beginning on page OO.

But planning is a mix of the practical and the creative. We'll begin here with some of the big principles that you might want to mull over as you dream up your master garden plan.

DESIGN MANY GARDENS IN ONE

Don't be afraid to break free of traditional yard designs as you plan. Go beyond the typical rectangular plot for vegetables and fruit, flowers and shrubs around the foundation, and isolated shade trees dotting the lawn. The award-winning garden design of Kansas gardeners William and Brenda Reid mixes and blends different types of edibles and ornamentals throughout the landscape. Their corner lot produces high yields of fruits, nuts, and vegetables, has imaginative play areas for the children, provides birds and wildlife with year-round habitat and food, and is beautiful from any aspect. William Reid says, "Brenda did most of the initial design work. Essentially, she started with the perimeters and worked herself inward, always leaving pathways and walks where they naturally fell."

Here are some of the Reids' unusual design ideas:

- A border of perennial wildflowers mixed with dwarf apples, dwarf pears, raspberries, and pecans surrounds the property.
- Apples and pears espaliered against a wall form a backdrop for perennials. Other fruit trees and native pecan trees are scattered throughout the yard.
- Many plants in the landscape attract birds, including Buffalo currants, gooseberries, a pawpaw tree, persimmons, mulberries, elderberries, and an edible viburnum.
- Beans grow up and over a bean tunnel to create a special play area for children.
- Asparagus is planted in several places in the yard as a backdrop to other plantings.

PICK PLANTING SITES WITH PRECISION

The key to a successful planting is matching the plants to the site. This is especially true for plants that you are giving a more or less permanent home, like perennials, shrubs, and trees.

If you put a plant in a site that doesn't suit its growing needs, chances are it will suffer from pest problems or just not perform well. "People tend to put perennials where they want to see them, not where they will grow best," explains Dick Lighty, Ph.D., the director of Mount Cuba Center for the Study of Piedmont Flora in Delaware. "I often see people putting sun-loving plants in shade. Or if they put them in sun, as they should, they forget about whether the plants need water at the roots or not." You'll do your garden a favor if you research the needs of the plants you like. Be firm in weeding out plants that are simply not right for the site.

Cole Burrell, a Minnesota garden designer, explains that while you can't change your basic climate or the exposure of a site, you can improve soil conditions before planting to suit the plants you want to grow. "In my own garden, I brought in

---

a lot of compost and manure to improve the soil in one spot where I have lots of perennials," says Burrell. "As the garden moves out to the front, the soil gets sandy and dry." For poorer conditions like those, Burrell selects perennials that can tolerate dry soil, including rough gayfeather (*Liatris aspera*), dotted blazing-star (*Liatris punctata*), wild bergamot (*Monarda fistulosa*), and prairie coral bells (*Heuchera richardsonii*).

GO NATIVE BUT NOT WILD

There's no such thing as a *no-maintenance* landscape, but the wise use of native plants can help create a *low-maintenance* one. "Natives often have the advantage of being disease- and insect-resistant. Some are widely adaptable or tolerant of difficult landscape conditions," says Dick Bir, a North Carolina State University extension specialist. One example of a wide-ranging native tree that can be a wonderful addition to the home landscape is sourwood (*Oxydendrum arboreum*). Hardy to Zone 5, sourwood is native to the eastern and southeastern United States, has excellent form, flowers in late summer, and displays brilliant autumn color.

Bir also notes that there are as many poor-choice native plants as there are good ones. Natives, like other plants, may need fertilizing, watering, and weeding to become established. They may have occasional pest problems and require some pruning.

"And going native," Bir points out, "doesn't mean taking plants from the wild. Even when removing common plants in plentiful supply, you may unknowingly be disturbing other species that might not grow there again for a century. You also

---

Group Landscape Plants

If you have difficult soil, such as sand or clay, you've no doubt worked pretty hard to make it palatable to your shrubs and trees. "It makes sense then," says Kris Medic Thomas, a landscape manager and arborist for the city of Columbus, Ohio, "to plant other trees, shrubs, perennials and annuals in that area, too. But there's more to it than just making use of well-prepared soil." Trees, shrubs, and other plants have a better chance of survival if they share space. They are protected from mower damage, and they create microclimates for each other. For example, they shade each other's roots, lower soil temperature, and break the force of harsh winds.

Give a Child a Garden

Gardening is a great way to teach children about nature, and it provides lots of fun activities for them as well. If you'd like to include children in your garden plans, here are a few things you may want to think about:

Take the children into the garden while you work. Explain your activities, and share your feelings about gardening. Ask them questions, and encourage them to ask questions of you.

Give children simple, fun projects. Children love activity. They'll enjoy cutting pictures from seed catalogs and pasting them on a garden plan, or jumping on a bag to thresh seeds inside. Provide children with their own gardening decisions, with your guidance.

Show children the miracles of gardening. The more spectacular something is, the more it holds children's interest and encourages their willingness to learn. Help them build a vine teepee or grow giant sunflowers or huge pumpkins with their name engraved on the side. Give them tall, colorful, fast-growing, scented, fuzzy, or edible plants to grow.

Provide experiences first, and talk later. Experiences are often more memorable than words. Have children feel the soil, smell flowers, taste an herb, pull a carrot from the ground, or listen to leaves rustling. Talk to them about their discoveries after they've had the chance to explore.

Garden plot. The child-size garden should create a private world where they can play. Let them make their own.

Continued ➡

don't know what problems, such as poison ivy roots, you might bring back to your property."

Be Your Own Designer

Are you puzzled by the prospect of how to design an attractive and interesting bed of ornamentals? If you feel intimidated by the complexities of design, relax. Nancy DuBrule, the owner of Natureworks, an organic garden center in Connecticut, suggests that beginners work from four easy principles, which she explains here in everyday terms:

1. **Put plants with opposite texture, shape, and form next to each other.** "Contrasts show each other off better," says DuBrule. For example, think of the contrast between a clump of grassy-leaved Siberian iris (*Iris sibirica*) and the full form of a large-blossomed clump of peonies.

2. **Pay attention to which plants retain good foliage throughout the season, and use them.** "If you build an interesting framework of foliage, you don't notice the plants that get scraggly after they bloom," says DuBrule. She suggests that gardeners include some plants such as artemisias, meadow rues (*Thalictrum* spp.), and sages for their foliage rather than their blooms.

3. **Plan a focal point for each month.** "It can be striking in color or outrageous in shape and form. You want it to catch the eye and hold attention," DuBrule explains. For example, a bold mass of an ornamental grass such as feather reed grass (*Calamagrostis acutiflora* 'Stricta') turns a striking orange-brown in the fall.

4. **Allow adequate space for each plant.** "Leave a minimum of 1½ square feet for each plant. Some, such as daylilies, require much more," says DuBrule. "If the garden looks too sparse while you're waiting for the perennials to fill in, plant annuals between them. But even then, be careful. Annuals can grow pretty large, too."

Practical Planning Pointers

Once you've set general goals for your yard and garden, focus on specific sites. Planning for the vegetable garden, where you're worried about ease of harvest and crop rotation, is different from planning for other areas, where your biggest concern may be keeping maintenance low. Here, several of our specialists offer tips on dealing with specific planning considerations.

Fancy-Up a Front Garden with Flowers

Urban gardeners often have only a small patch of land between the sidewalk and the front of the house. Usually, a little lawn and a foundation planting fill the space, but Sarah Williams, an experienced urban gardener from Vermont, suggests that gardeners try a mixed ornamental planting instead. She offers several points to keep in mind when designing a small front garden:

Limit colors. "Too many colors in one spot are visually confusing," says Williams. "Stick to two or three—for instance, white, a range of blues, and a range of pinks—and be sure the major house color and any trim colors are repeated and complemented by the flowers in the front."

Keep plants in proportion. "You don't want to have to remove something because it has gotten too big or is giving too much shade," Williams explains.

Plan for continuous blooms throughout the season. You can have a gorgeous floral display from the first bulbs to the last chrysanthemums. Williams says, "A mixture of annuals, biennials, and perennials gives the largest visual variety and

longest bloom time. Leaving spots for annuals varies the look every year and keeps the garden exciting."

Let low-maintenance be your watchword. Front gardens are highly visible, and you don't want them to end up as an embarrassment. "Bark mulch is a lifesaver," declares Williams. "It keeps weeding chores to a minimum, and its dark color contrasts nicely with the flowers."

Reduce Renovation Woes

One daunting feature of an "inherited" yard can be an overgrown ornamental garden. If you face the task of renovating such a garden, you may appreciate these tips from Nancy DuBrule, the owner of Natureworks, an organic garden center in Connecticut. "First of all, find the plants that resist being moved," she suggests. "Design around them if possible." According to DuBrule, plants in this category include balloon flower (*Platycodon grandiflorus*) blue false indigo (*Baptisia australis*), false lupines (*Thermopsis* spp.), gas plant (*Dictamnus albus*), lupines (*Lupinus* spp. and hybrids), and peonies (*Paeonia* spp.).

Other plants will need dividing. DuBrule suggests that people lift and split plants such as daylilies, ornamental grasses, and irises. Before you replant the area, replenish the soil by adding organic matter and fertilizers. You may choose to select new plants or to replant some of the ones you lifted. "You can move them around to fit your new design. They're tough enough to take a transplant without being set back," DuBrule explains.

If the garden contains invasive plants, such as bee balm (*Monarda didyma*), coreopsis (*Coreopsis* spp.), feverfew (*Chrysanthemum parthenium*), and evening primroses (*Oenothera* spp.), now is the time to lift them, states DuBrule. You may want to keep some pieces, but think carefully before replanting or you may, in turn, pass along garden headaches to the next owner.

Dealing With Drainage Dilemmas

What can you do with wet spots on your property? "The first approach, and probably the most practical, is to choose plants that can take it, such as Japanese iris (*Iris ensata*), spotted Joe-Pye weed [*Eupatorium maculatum*], and perennial Hibiscus species," says Nancy DuBrule, the owner of Natureworks, an organic garden center in Connecticut. "The second approach is to raise the soil level." DuBrule likes to bring in topsoil when creating a raised area for a planting. "You can enclose the area with stone or wood, but you certainly don't have to," she adds. The most expensive and time-consuming approach is to correct the drainage by installing drainage tile.

DuBrule urges gardeners to be honest with themselves about the drainage characteristics of a site. In a poorly drained area, planting species that can't tolerate wet feet will just lead to headaches—and probably dead plants. So put up your umbrella, and take a long, slow walk around your yard next time it rains. Note where water settles in

your garden beds or on the lawn. Make notes on your landscape plan, and follow through to deal with those drainage problems as you put your garden plan into effect.

Think Ahead To Save Labor Later

Some simple advance planning can save precious time and energy during the rush and heat of the growing season. Oregon farming consultant Lynn Coody offers these examples of ways to plan for labor saving:

Assemble necessary supplies during the winter. You'll have more time for the catalog shopping that's needed to find many organic soil amendments and pest control supplies that aren't stocked in garden centers. It can be hard to order these materials in garden-size rather than farm-size quantities, so Coody seeks out other gardeners who are interested in placing a joint order and dividing up the materials.

Group crops by water requirements. This allows you to regulate watering needs more easily later in the season. For example, deep-rooted crops like lima beans and pumpkins need less water than shallow-rooted crops like cauliflower, lettuce, and spinach.

Divide the garden into weeding areas. Coody divides her garden into Areas 1, 2, and 3. "As soon as I plant, I begin to weed," she explains. "I thoroughly weed Area 1 first, letting the weeds grow in Areas 2 and 3. I move into Area 2 next, and finally, Area 3." Coody likes this approach because she never faces the overwhelming task of having to save her entire garden from the crush of overgrown weeds.

Made In the Shade

The shade cast by a vine-covered trellis may be just the twist that gardeners in hot-summer regions need to help their plants survive the heat. "If more people would use trellises and vines to shade some of their perennials and some of their vegetables, they'd get much longer show or yield from them," says Jim Wilson, a cohost of public television's "The Victory Garden." Wilson suggests planning for a fence on the western side of your vegetable garden or perennial beds, to block the sun from midafternoon on. "When Jane [his wife] and I were growing herbs at our farm, we had some of them backed up against the afternoon shade of trees, and they always held up two to three weeks longer than the ones in the baking sun," he says. Some shade also helps to extend the spring harvest of leafy vegetables such as lettuce.

Grow Grass In the Paths

Grass in the vegetable garden may not be a bad idea—if it's in the pathways. Janet Bachmann and partner Jim Lukens, who co-own a small organic farm in Arkansas, have discovered that keeping vegetable garden paths planted in permanent sod not only reduces maintenance but also benefits their crops. They grow vegetables in permanent beds, 4 x 50 feet. Three-foot-wide sod pathways composed of perennial ryegrass (*Lolium perenne*) and white clover (*Trifolium repens*) separate the beds. Bachmann explains the advantages of the system: "The sod provides a continuous supply of high-quality mulch material for the growing beds. When we mow, the lawn mower throws the clippings onto the beds, saving us a step. We can also concentrate our fertilizers this way; we don't spread them on the sod pathways, which don't need them. The sod allows us to walk in the garden after a rain. We don't have to worry about compacting our soils."

Bachmann and Lukens designed their beds and paths so that their tractor, which has a 7-foot span from wheel to wheel, travels on the sod when they till their beds. You may want to design your paths

Continued →

so that you can mow them in two passes with your lawn mower.

Getting the Plans on Paper

Does trying to draw a map of your yard or garden plot leave you tearing up endless sheets of paper—or tearing out your hair? If so, read the following sections for advice from the experts on hassle-free map making.

PLAY WITH POST-IT PLANNING

Those sticky squares of paper commonly known as Post-it notes are perfect for the trial-and-error process of planning the layout of your vegetable garden beds. North Carolina gardener and garden writer Bob Heitman stumbled across the idea for Post-it planning two seasons ago. "I was doing my second most favorite thing, armchair gardening, when I thought of it," Heitman remembers. "I started playing with the Post-its and found that using them was a quite pleasant and orderly way of planning my garden."

To try planning with Post-its, you'll need a smooth, hard surface to work on. Heltman made his own lap-size garden board out of a piece of tempered Masonite fiberboard. (You could also use a large erasable memo board. Decide the scale of your garden, such as 1 inch equals 1 foot. If your beds are 3 feet wide, you can use 3 X 5-inch Post-its. If they're 4 feet wide, you can snip an inch off of the 3 x 5-inch Post-its. Heitman also notes that you don't need a ruler with Post-it planning. "You can use the Post-it itself to measure spacing within and along a bed."

Try drawing on an erasable memo board when you're brainstorming garden plans or designs for flower beds and borders. You can quickly sketch in plant groupings and alter their size and shape by simply wiping them off and redrawing. Once you're satisfied with the general outlines of the plan or design, use it as a guide for creating a more detailed, formal drawing on paper.

Write each crop name on a Post-it, and go to work. You can lift and restick each crop as many times as you like until you hit the arrangement you think is best. If you succession-crop, just layer Post-its one on top of another. For example, if you plan to follow an early crop of lettuce with beans, you can use two Post-its on that plot to show the succession.

Once you have the final layout of your garden, you can draw it up on a more permanent map (Post-its do tend to lose their stickiness over time), or you can encase the Post-it board in plastic wrap to keep the Post-its intact. This will also protect them from getting dirty or wet if you take the board out to the garden with you.

MAKE MULTIPLE MAPS

Once you've drawn a general map of your property or the layout of your vegetable garden, save redrawing time by making photocopies. John Dromgoole, the host of PBS television's "The New Garden," makes 20 copies of his garden map each year and puts them in a notebook. "I try so many new things every year and do so much succession cropping that I need an efficient way to keep track of everything. The maps let me do this," says Dromgoole. He uses one map to plan out the first plantings of the year. As the season progresses, he records the placement and dates of following crops on separate copies. "I put notes on them, too," says Dromgoole. "For instance, I tried out a new kind of drip irrigation system last year. I really liked it in the beginning of the year, but by the end of the season, it developed leaks. I noted all the leaky spots on my maps."

Keeping Good Records

Keeping written notes on your garden is part of the ongoing process of making your plans a reality. Records help you know which of your new methods worked and which flopped. They help you decide which plants are best suited to your site. In the following tips, our veteran gardeners explain what they keep track of and the record-keeping styles that work best for them.

MARK THAT CALENDAR

If you're the gardener who's forever procrastinating about starting a record-keeping system, calendar record keeping may be just right for you. Stewart Hoyt, who operates a Community Supported Agriculture (CSA) operation in Vermont, says, "I've never been really good with record keeping. But now that we're doing a CSA, we have to keep track of things. So I've developed a simple system that I can stick to." Hoyt uses a calendar with "huge" daily spaces. When he comes in from the gardens each day, he notes everything he did that day along with the number of hours he spent on it. So post a calendar by the tool rack or just inside the back door, with a pencil on a string attached to it for maximum convenience. Take 3 minutes to note essentials. A calendar is a good place to record:

- Type and quantity of seed sown or number of transplants planted (including cultivar names)
- Rainfall or watering
- Areas weeded
- Pest control techniques used
- Harvest times and quantities

Then at the end of the season, sit down with the calendar and summarize the performance of your crops.

GET THE PICTURE

"Photographs are as useful as written records," says John Dromgoole, the host of PBS television's "The New Garden." "I can capture the whole garden in a few shots. I take pictures every few weeks during the growing season." Photographs refresh your memory and can answer questions about when and where things were planted if succession and inter-cropping plans get complicated.

KEEP THOSE RECORDS ON FILE

A handy way to keep track of crop performance in the vegetable garden is to make notes on file cards, as shown in the illustration below. New Hampshire organic farmer Rick Estes says, "File cards are the best record-keeping tool I've found." It's easy to separate cards into categories with dividers. Each year, you can drop in new notes just where you want them. Estes says, "I use the cards for keeping track of numbers and dates, how many of what crop I've seeded, and when." Estes also finds the cards effective for quick review and improvement of his techniques from year to year. "For example, the notes on my cards for tomatoes the year before last said 'leggy' next to the transplant date," he explains. "So I delayed seeding by a week, and last year's tomatoes weren't leggy."

IN-FIELD RECORD KEEPING

Thanks to plastic and indelible ink, you can keep year-to-year records right in your garden. Ken Ryan, an organic farmer and farm manager from New England, sticks an 8-inch plastic tag at the head of every bed as he plants it, noting the cultivar and planting date with a laundry marker. Rather than remove these tags at the end of the season or when a crop is finished, he leaves them in place. "I have years of tags at the head of every bed," says Ryan. "I have to touch up the writing every so often because it fades, but I keep up with that." Ryan likes this system because it helps him maintain good rotations if he has to deviate from his yearly plan.

Seasonal Care

Sally Jean Cunningham

Wouldn't you like to be a little bird peeking over the fence at the way other people garden? Then you could see their tricks and techniques for planting, watering, and all the other gardening chores! I certainly have plenty of quirks, shortcuts, and odd habits that are the real way I get things accomplished in my garden. Some of my methods aren't much like the directions I've read in gardening books, especially the books where the gardeners look so well-dressed and clean! I also know that lots of us garden with limited budgets and would rather make or find something rather than buy it. So I'll share an honest peek with you at how I care for my garden from winter on through the whole busy year—plus I'll add a lot of tips I've learned from some other "cleaned-up" gardeners that may make things easier for you.

Try To Remember

Try to keep a year's worth of garden records in your head, and your memory may fail you. Write it down! Be sure that you:

List crop rotations. Changing the placement of crops within your garden each year is one way to outwit pests and fungi that attack certain plant families. Using a map or chart to record where you planted each crop last year will give you a visual reference for planning this year's crop placement. This will help ensure that you don't plant crops from the same family in the same spot year after year, making them more vulnerable to diseases and insects.

Maintain soil records. Keeping track of timing, type, and amount of fertilizer applications is important in avoiding mineral imbalances. Lack of nutrients can limit plant growth, and excesses of certain nutrients can also have detrimental effects.

Keep a weather diary. Environmental disorders, such as water stress, sometimes cause symptoms that look very much like symptoms caused by insects or diseases. If you have data on weather conditions to refer to, it will help you make a better judgment about the underlying cause of the symptoms you see.

Compare cultivar records. Include jottings of how well your plants resisted heat and pests and also how well they were received on the dining room table! Perhaps you'll find some favorite cultivars or decide to choose new ones.

Continued ➡

Gardening through the Year

Deciding when the gardening year starts is a bit like deciding which came first, the chicken or the egg. Perhaps it starts when you plant seeds and plants in the spring. But perhaps it starts in the fall, since many fall activities, such as preparing compost piles and tilling the soil, are really the groundwork for next season's garden.

I'm one of those gardeners who can't get the garden out of my thoughts, even when the soil is buried under 2 feet of snow (which happens quite often here in the shadow of Lake Erie!). For me, the gardening year starts in January with indoor tasks like ordering seeds and cleaning tools, and "ends" (at least briefly) in late fall when I harvest the last of the carrots and greens.

Five Seasons of Gardening

I divide the gardening year into five seasons: winter, early spring, late spring, summer, and fall. When those seasons start and end varies according to where you live and according to the weather. For me, late spring can be mid-May, but in a cold year, it's closer to mid-June! And for a gardener in North Carolina, late spring may be late April. You'll need to decide for yourself when these seasons fall on your calendar.

In this chapter, you'll find a to-do list for each season that summarizes the garden tasks for that time of the year.

As you browse through this section, keep in mind that you can't always garden "according to plan." We gardeners are often at the mercy of the weather. For example, on the day when the soil is just right for tilling, you may not be able to borrow a tiller, and rain win be forecast for the rest of the week. In cases like this, you won't be able to garden according to your perfect plan, but perhaps you can figure out a strategy that's good enough to get you through-like hiring the teenager next door to help dig part of the garden by hand so you accomplish some planting before the downpour.

Remember, gardening is and always should be fun, so don't let my to-do lists increase your stress level. Heaven knows, I don't always have my garden in tip-top shape, but I still get a good harvest each year—of produce and of satisfaction.

Gardening in Winter

Winter is the time for make-it-yourself garden projects and tasks that you'll be too busy to accomplish once the weather turns nice. It's also the season for reading gardening books like this one and for dreaming over all those tempting catalogs while you make your seed and plant lists.

Shopping from Catalogs

Run to the mailbox and grab your pen! The arrival of garden catalogs in January creates great bursts of excitement at Wonderland Farm. But I've learned to be careful about catalog fever, because it's easy to overspend. So here are some tips for smart catalog shopping.

Read between the lines. Catalogs are sales tools, so naturally they only mention a plant's strong points. Look for what's not said. For example, if a tomato is billed as a "great keeper," but its flavor isn't mentioned, it may be pretty bland!

Compare prices. Even if you buy your seeds and plants locally, use catalogs to check typical price ranges, and watch for early- and late-season bargains on supplies.

Use regional sources. Companies that raise their plants and seeds in a climate similar to yours are more likely to sell varieties and species suited for your garden.

Order early. To be sure you get the choices you want, place your order before winter ends. Reputable companies will wait to ship your plants at an appropriate time for planting.

Making Garden Equipment

Make-it-yourself projects appeal to me because they save money, they let me turn trash and recyclables into useful items, and they're fun! You probably have your own special make-it-yourself items for the garden. Tomato cages and plant stakes are some of my favorites.

Step-by-Step Tomato Cages

I like sturdy tomato cages at least 4 feet tall. I haven't found commercial cages that really satisfy me, so I make my own out of wire fencing. I use fencing made from 14- or 16-gauge wire that has 4- by 6-inch openings. The fencing is available in 30-foot rolls, which is enough to make six or seven cages. Here's how I fashion the cages.

Step 1. Unroll the wire fencing on the floor, and use wire cutters to cut a 4-foot section of fence for each cage you want to make. Cut through the horizontal fence wires just beside one of the vertical wires.

Step 2. Line up the midpoint of the section of fence with an 8-foot-long wooden stake. Use a staple gun to fasten the wire to the stake. The pointed end of the stake should extend 18 inches below the edge of the fence.

Step 3. Bend the edges of the fencing together to form a cylinder. Wrap the cut ends of the horizontal wires around the vertical wire. Wear gloves to protect your hands from the sharp points of the wire.

These cages will support any type of tomato, even vigorous beefsteak varieties. The cages last six years or longer, depending on how heavy the fencing is and whether you store the cages inside during the winter.

Johns Cheap Stakes

My friends and I like to make our own garden stakes and markers. For example, Master Gardener John Holnbeck recycles wooden shingles into inexpensive row markers by breaking them lengthwise into pieces about 1½ inches wide and 12 inches long. He then cuts strips from white plastic bleach bottles; each strip is about 3 inches long and ¾ inch wide. He staples the strips to the stakes and uses a waterproof pen to write on the strips. They are really "cheap stakes."

I make row markers out of chopsticks that I save from my monthly excursion to my favorite Chinese restaurant. I dip the chopsticks in paint or mark them with crayons to make color-coded markers. Or you can write on the wide end with a waterproof pen.

You can also fashion plant labels by cutting up yogurt containers, detergent bottles, and plastic orange-juice containers.

Tuning Up Your Tools

I don't have enough time to take good care of my tools during the active garden season, so I work hard to clean and sharpen them well each winter.

When you bring your dull and dirty tools inside for clean-up day, first spread out newspapers or a sheet—it saves you from having to clean your floor when you're through with the tools! Using a dry steel brush, brush any dry soil off the tool blades. Then set to work with soap and water and steel wool. Next, dry the tools, and apply linseed or tung oil to the wooden handles.

The final step is sharpening. I use a #10 bastard file to sharpen my garden tools. To sharpen the edge of a hoe, shovel, or trowel, push the file hard across the blade, using the full length of the file on each pass. Be sure to sharpen the beveled side of the blade.

Gardening in Early Spring

If you live in the southern United States, you may not yearn for the change from winter and early spring to late spring. But for northern gardeners, early spring is a distinct and sometimes frustratingly long time of year. It's finally warm enough to work outside, but the soil's still too wet to dig, and there's too much danger of frost to plant most of your crops. But I manage to find plenty of early-spring fix-up projects to satisfy my need to get outside.

Building Trellises

Early spring is a good time to set up trellises for crops you want to grow vertically, like pole beans, peas, and gourds. I often use teepees for beans, and chicken-wire trellises for peas.

My friend Mary Giambra, a Master Gardener from Marilla, New York, designed a sturdy structure from PVC pipe that has several possible uses, including an arching trellis. You can also add sections to make a series of arches in order to build the framework for a hoop house. To make these arches, you'll need 36 feet of PVC pipe, six T-joints, and eight elbow joints.

Step-by-Step PVC Arches

To make a trellis out of PVC arches, prepare by using a hacksaw to cut eight 2½-foot pieces, seven 2-foot pieces and four 6-inch pieces of PVC pipe.

Step 1. Make two arches, connecting the lengths of pipe as shown below.

Step 2. Connect the arches by inserting three 2-foot sections of pipe as crosspieces in the open fittings in the T-joints.

Step 3. Sink the feet of the arches into the soil of your garden or raised beds, inserting about 1 foot of pipe into the soil. The PVC is too slippery for some plants to cling to, so cover the trellis with pea netting, or weave rough twine in a zigzag pattern back and forth between the two arches.

Unmulching

Pulling mulch off your beds on sunny spring days helps warm and dry the soil. You can re-mulch after planting (you'll have to hoe lightly to kill surface weeds before you plant). In areas with poor drainage or heavy clay, it's important to cover unmulched areas with a solid cover like plastic or a tarp when it rains to keep the soil from becoming saturated.

I don't unmulch the perennial clusters or the beds where I plan to plant hot-weather vegetables like peppers, pumpkins, and basil. The soil will warm naturally under the mulch by the time air temperatures are suitable for planting these crops, so unmulching will just lead to weed problems.

When you unmulch, leave some mulch in place at the ends or sides of beds to shelter spiders, ground beetles, and other good bugs that overwinter under mulch.

Cold-Weather Weeding

On days when your first thought is "It's too cold for gardening," try some weeding. It's good exercise, and it will help free your garden of any tough weeds later. Pull weeds whenever the ground is unfrozen but damp. The weeds usually pull out quite easily. As long as they haven't gone to seed, put the pulled weeds in a stockpile for composting.

Continued ➡

One special warning about early weeding: Don't pull out the companion plants you'll be looking for later! Your garden beds may include many weed, wildflower, and volunteer seedlings from last season's annuals and herbs. Learn to recognize the useful plants in their infancy.

Grooming Perennials

To help your perennials bloom longer in summer, take time to care for them in spring. If you left seedheads in place for the birds to feed on or for winter interest, cut them back now. Remove old leaves or plant debris, too. Remember, go lightly: Birds, beneficials, and other wild things like it wild!

When you work in your perennial beds, keep in mind that some perennials don't start to regrow until late spring. Don't dig them up in your impatience to fill the vacancy! Butterfly weed (*Asclepias tuberosa*), balloon flowers (*Platycodon* spp.), and butterfly bushes (*Buddleia* spp.) are slow starters. It's too easy to destroy the crowns of these plants by digging before the new foliage starts to emerge.

Using Simple Cold Frames

Cold frames are great for extending the growing season in spring and fall. They can help you start some crops early, harden off your trays of seedlings and transplants before planting day, and carry lots of crops into the late fall. If you don't plan to build or buy a permanent cold frame, try setting up a temporary cold frame. One method is to buy bales of straw, set them up in a rectangle, and place window glass or clear plastic across the top to form a tiny greenhouse. I rigged a protected area for trays of seedlings by suspending old storm-door glass panes across the path between two raised beds. Even an old storm window propped against your house can provide short-term protection and give you a small jump on the season.

Starting Vegetables from Seed

Many home gardeners get great satisfaction from starting their own seeds under lights. On the other hand, lots of people try it and end up frustrated, with poor results after a lot of fuss. My advice: Only start seeds indoors if you plan to set up indoor lights. (Windowsills just don't provide enough light, at least in the Northeast.)

I'm lucky to live near some great nurseries that produce high-quality transplants, so most years, I don't take time to start seeds indoors. When I do, I concentrate on the easiest seeds for indoor starting, the Cabbage Family and Squash Family crops. You can also start tomatoes, peppers, and eggplant from seeds, but they require some extra care. If you enjoy the process and have the setup, great!

Gardening in Late Spring

Although the dates you call "late spring" may vary from year to year, you know when it's arrived: Late spring is the time you can actually work the soil and do some serious gardening!

Working the Soil

To tell when your soil is ready to be worked without damaging its structure, squeeze some in your hand. If the soil crumbles, it's ready for digging. If it cakes or forms a patty, it's too wet, and you'll have to wait.

Whether you work your soil with a rotary tiller or by hand, don't overdo it. Till or fluff the soil no deeper than 7 inches about two weeks before your estimated planting day. Your purpose is simply to break the soil crust, kill the surface weed seedlings, and expose weed seeds and grubs to the birds. Then on planting day, work the surface again, no deeper than 2 inches, to kill off any new weed seedlings.

Transplanting Tips

Now's the time to set out transplants for many crops, whether you've grown them yourself or bought them at a garden center. Remember these guidelines for successful transplanting.

- Harden off your transplants for one to two weeks before planting by putting them outside during the day. At night, bring them inside, or keep them inside a cold frame.
- Transplant on an overcast, cool day—not the first hot, sunny day you have.
- Keep transplants out of the wind while you're transplanting.
- Moisten seedlings thoroughly before you plant, and water well afterward.
- Pull or cut circling or matted roots apart before you plant.
- If frost, heavy wind, or hard rain threatens, protect newly planted transplants by covering them with baskets, tin cans, milk cartons, or sheets draped over short stakes.

Preventing Pest Problems

Now is the time to start stopping pests—before they hurt your plants. In a companion garden, your most important pest-prevention tactic is in the planting. But there are some other techniques you can try in late spring that may prevent problems later on.

Using Row Covers

Floating row covers are sheets of lightweight synthetic fabric that let air and water through but keep pests out. When you drape row covers over your crops, you'll prevent problems with common pests like flea beetles, imported cabbageworms, cabbage loopers, and squash bugs.

Several brands of floating row covers are available at garden centers and from mail-order garden suppliers. I recommend that you buy row cover fabric in 5- or 6-foot widths so that you can cover your beds and still have excess fabric to bury at the edges. Choose one of the heavier-grade fabrics that don't tear easily, because your row covers can't have holes for those little pests to sneak through.

I sometimes keep crops like broccoli and cabbage covered from transplanting to harvest. I also cover vine crops like squash to keep out squash bugs. If you do this, remember to allow for pollination, or there will be no squash or pumpkins! Just remove the row covers when you see the plants in full flower.

Stopping Slugs

I don't know of any companion plant that repels slugs, but I wish I did. Slugs can be a real problem, especially when there's a wet spring. They eat a wide variety of garden crops, especially lettuce, spinach, and Cabbage Family crops.

You can fight back by handpicking and killing the slugs. It's not a fun job, but it really helps. Slugs gather under the boards that I use as garden pathways. During the day, I flip the boards over and offer the slugs as a meal for the birds. I also sink shallow dishes into the soil and fill the dishes with yeasty beer or a solution of water and yeast. The beer and yeast attract the slugs. When the slimy critters crawl into the dishes to drink, they drown.

Welcoming the Helpers

In a companion garden, spring is the season to put out the welcome mat for garden helpers. Here's a list of reminders about how to attract beneficial insects, birds, and other beneficial animals to your yard.

- Stick a tall bird perch or two in the garden, where birds can land, rest, and look around. A perch can be just a tall stake with a small crosspiece attached.
- Set up birdbaths with lots of pebbles in them.
- Allow some dandelions to bloom to provide early nectar for lady beetles, then pull the plants before they go to seed.
- To supply nectar early, sink pots of annuals into the soil, and remove them for use elsewhere when your garden has other flowers to offer.
- Make toad houses from inverted clay pots with chipped holes for doorways. Or simply pile up some rocks to provide a cool hiding spot.

Gardening in Summer

It seems to me that we spend weeks yearning for summer, but when summer gets here it's too hot to enjoy being outdoors! When summer heats up, I garden in the early morning and in the evening to beat the heat.

Watering

Even the best mulchers have to water sometimes. We don't want to use more water than necessary, but we don't want to wait until our plants have wilted to tell us they're thirsty. Here are some quick rules of thumb to help you decide when and how to water.

How often? Water when the soil feels dry to your finger about 2 inches down.

How much? Water vegetables and most flowers until the soil is damp at least 4 to 5 inches down.

What time of day? Watering in the morning is best. I avoid evening watering because it promotes fungal growth and creates perfect conditions for slugs. I avoid midday watering because the water evaporates fast, and it's not efficient. However, if the plants are stressed, *water them!* Sometimes you can't fit in watering in the morning, so it's better to water when you can than not to water at all.

We've all heard that our gardens should get 1 inch of water per week, and believe me, that's more water than you'd think. For example, it takes about 120 gallons of water to supply one inch of water for a 10- by 20-foot garden. Just one full-size tomato or pumpkin plant needs 2 to 3 gallons of water a week.

Fixing Hoses on Short Notice

If someone accidentally runs over your hose with the lawn mower, or if your hose just springs a leak, it's wise to know how to repair it fast. You can repair your hose with a simple repair kit, available at your hardware store or garden center. (It's guaranteed that hoses always rip on holidays, when the stores are closed, so I keep a basket of hose repair supplies, complete with sharp knife and all the ends and connectors I may ever need.)

Continued ➡

Step-by-Step Hose Repair

Here's my technique for fixing failing hoses:

Step 1. Use a sharp knife to cut out the leaky or damaged section of hose. Be sure to cut straight across the hose. If the weather's cold, bring the hose inside. It's hard to cut through a cold, brittle hose.

Step 2. Insert the repair coupling into the opening at the end of the intact hose and push it firmly into place. Repair couplings can be made of either metal or plastic; both types work well. Again, it's easier to do this when the hose is warm.

Step 3. Use a screwdriver to tighten the clamp in place next to the coupling. Discard the damaged section of hose.

Patrolling for Pests

In your companion garden, you should have very few serious pest problems, but it's still well worth it to inspect your plants for signs of trouble.

Walk through your garden and inspect each plant up close. Look on the undersides of leaves, at the growing tips, and down near the base of the stem—all likely spots for pests to hide and disease symptoms to show.

You may spot signs of disease here and there in your garden, but don't panic. A few discolored leaves don't mean a crop will be ruined. But if you find a plant that's seriously diseased, pull up and throw it away—you wouldn't get a worthwhile harvest from it, and it would only spread the disease throughout more of your garden.

Fertilizing

Adding fertilizer as a *side dressing* or *top dressing* isn't essential, but at times it can really help your crop. This simply means putting a little organic fertilizer on or into the soil near the plant roots. I side-dress most crops when the plants have just begun to produce fruit, tubers, or whatever I'm planning to harvest.

I use compost or alfalfa meal for side-dressing crops. I spread the material in a circle beneath the outer canopy of leaves for plants like broccoli, brussels sprouts, and tomatoes. For corn, I sprinkle the fertilizer all along a row of plants. For crops like onions that I plant in blocks, I sprinkle the fertilizer as evenly as I can around the plants.

One alternative to side dressing is to spray plants with a solution of fish emulsion or seaweed extract. These products are rich in a wide range of nutrients. They may cost more than other fertilizers, but for a small garden it may be well worth your investment. Apply the spray diluted according to the directions on the package.

I don't bother fertilizing peas, beans, most root crops, or greens like lettuce and spinach, because it doesn't seem to increase their yields.

Planting for Fall

After all the work of preparing fertile garden beds, I certainly don't want to let them sit empty. So as soon as I finish harvesting a crop, I plant something else in its place. This creates a whole new set of crops to harvest in the fall.

There are some real advantages to fall gardening. For one thing, I'm not as busy as I am in the summer, so it's easier to find time to care for the garden. There are many fewer pests to contend with. It's also a second chance for success with crops that didn't do well the first time around.

Harvesting

You've probably been harvesting since late spring, but a lot more harvesting happens quickly at the end of summer. If you're lucky, you have friends and family to help gather, store, prepare, freeze, or can your treasures. The gardener's job is to keep the harvest going.

Remember to keep things picked: Letting fruits stay on the vine can signal the crop to stop producing.

It's okay to let a few herb, broccoli, lettuce, and spinach plants go to seed, because some of them provide just the right nectar at the right time to keep our beneficial insect friends around the garden.

Gardening in Fall

In the fall, we clean up the vegetable garden and cover the soil for the winter. It's also the time to set up safe havens for beneficial insects, birds, and helpful wildlife.

Helping Beneficials and Birds

Many beneficial insects overwinter right in the garden. Cover crops and mulch protect these overwintering beneficials. Leave the water dishes in your garden filled right up until freezing weather so beneficials have a source of water. Leaving boards, stones, or cardboard in place also protects ground beetles over the winter.

Birds require water and food, either to survive in your local area or during migration, so learn about bird feeding, and keep feeders filled through the winter. In the garden, leaving the seedheads of perennials, cover crops, and weeds in place will attract many birds.

Garden Cleanup

Garden cleanup is a bit different than usual in a companion garden. You won't just make a clean sweep, because your garden neighborhoods will finish at different times. And you'll treat each bed differently, depending on which crop family and plant friends will move into the bed next spring. In some beds, you'll sow a cover crop as soon as you finish harvesting. In others you'll continue to harvest right through fall, so after clearing out the crop, you'll work the soil and then cover it with organic mulch, plastic, or a tarp. In beds where you want optimum nutrition next season you'll sheet compost by spreading a layer of manure or other high-nitrogen organic matter over the soil surface.

As you clean up, watch for annual weeds, like ragweed, lamb's-quarters, and pigweed, that have gone to seed around your garden. Snip off the stems, gather the seedheads and discard them with your household trash.

Where Cleanup Counts

Some kinds of garden cleanup are vital. If any sections of your garden suffered insect or disease problems, the damaged plants must be pulled, roots and all, in the fall. I always remove the remains of cucumbers, melons, squash, pumpkins, and all Cabbage Family crops from my garden. I burn the remains but if burning isn't allowed where you live, dispose of them in your trash.

It's also important to harvest potatoes and tomatoes thoroughly, and if you compost the plant remains, make sure they're in an active compost pile. Late blight, a serious fungal disease, and several other disease organisms can overwinter in garden debris and reappear in volunteer plants that sprout from unharvested fruits and tubers. So it is especially important to resist the temptation to take advantage of those "freebies." Instead, destroy them.

Overwintering Garden Favorites

I don't get fancy with hoop houses and cold frames, but there are a couple of simple tricks that extend my harvest of carrots and greens until Christmas. Carrots get sweeter and sweeter as the temperature drops, so cover them with a thick straw mulch, and you can harvest a snack any time you happen to be skiing by!

Lettuce, spinach, and most greens—including Chinese cabbage and Swiss chard—will tolerate several frosts. Keep them going by placing straw bales around the plants and covering the bales with a discarded storm window or a piece of heavyweight, clear plastic. You can also use the hoops that held up your row covers to support clear plastic to make a mini-greenhouse. (In warm spells, be sure to lift up the sides to avoid "cooking" the plants.)

Summing Up the Garden Year

If you ever write in a garden journal, fall is the most important time for making notes. Record the names of what you grew, what looked great, what had problems, what was too close or too far apart, and which companions worked best.

Whatever the season, remember that the less factual but more personal notes are also very important to include in your garden journal. After all, gardening is a passion for many of us—but still a hobby and not a job! So add comments on what you did and didn't enjoy doing and what was pleasing or frustrating during the season. (My notes always include "mulch more and weed less!") You may want to try drawing sketches of your garden in your journal or taping some photos of your garden to the pages. The more fun your journal is, the more likely you'll use it in all seasons.

Gardener's To-Do List

Vicki Mattern

January

Zone 3

- For an early taste of spring, grow some sprouts. Mung bean, radish, and buckwheat sprouts grow well in vented jars. Just put the seeds inside, cover them with water overnight, drain, then rinse twice a day.
- Explore seed catalogs, then send in your orders.
- Start snapdragon and pansy seedlings.

Zone 4

- Check the viability of old seeds by sprouting a few of each kind in damp paper towels enclosed in plastic bags.
- Set up your seed-starting system.
- Start a flat of hardy perennials or alpine strawberries.
- Rearrange houseplants so that all get their share of bright light. Later in the month, give them a light feeding.

Zone 5

- Gather your seed-starting equipment, then start seeds of pansies, snapdragons, and hardy perennials.
- Toward the end of the month, start onion seeds.
- Order seeds of cabbage, broccoli, cauliflower, parsley, and peas.
- Dig up a frozen chunk of chives and force them into early growth indoors.

Continued ➡

- When the snow cover is thin, check shrubs and perennials. If the roots have heaved up too close to the surface, press them back into place.
- Late this month, begin pruning apples.
- If rabbits are ravaging fruit trees and shrubs, lure them to a distant spot with corn or hay.

Zone 6
- Start hardy flowers under lights.
- In midmonth, start cabbage and onion seeds indoors.
- Order seeds for other cool-weather crops, such as broccoli, cauliflower, spinach, celery, lettuce, and peas.
- Get your coldframe ready. Mound a 4-inch layer of leaves or soil around the outside to help it hold heat.
- Check winter mulches and replenish those that have thinned.
- Wrap wire mesh around tree trunks that have been damaged by rodents.

Zone 7
- Start seeds of cabbage, onions, and hardy herbs under bright lights early this month.
- Clean out your coldframe.
- Collect plastic jugs to use as cloches.
- Late this month, mow winter cover crops.
- Direct-seed sweet peas.
- Indoors, start seeds of perennials, such as columbine and balloon flower.
- Begin dividing daylilies.
- Prune crape myrtles.
- Set out junipers, hollies, and other evergreens.

Zone 8
- Harden-off cool-weather transplants (cabbage, broccoli, etc.) that you've started indoors.
- Start lettuce indoors. When seedlings have several leaves, set them out under plastic milk jug cloches.
- Sow peas outdoors late this month.

- Set seed potatoes in a bright spot to encourage sprouting.
- Take advantage of your last chance to dig and divide crowded daylilies and daffodils.
- Dig and transplant dormant phlox, thrift, and hosta.
- Trim old leaves from liriope, but don't disturb the crowns.

Zone 9
- Sow beets, carrots, lettuce, peas, and spinach in the garden.
- Indoors, start seeds of tomatoes, peppers, and eggplants.
- Direct-seed alyssum, California poppies, nasturtium, and cornflowers.
- Prune geraniums to stimulate bushy new growth.
- Plant new persimmons, loquats, and figs.
- In the West, plant young pistachios in well-drained soil, then stake them securely.

Zone 10
- Set out transplants of onions, potatoes, cabbage, and broccoli.
- Water transplants often to keep them growing strong.
- Plant dahlias, caladiums, gladiolus, and tropical tubers, such as amaryllis and crinums.
- Set out bedding plants such as pansies, dianthus, and petunias.
- Plant young plumerias in containers.
- Trim back poinsettias and other tropicals after they finish blooming.
- Taste citrus fruits regularly so that you can harvest them at their peak of flavor.

February

Zone 3
- Garden indoors! Grow some leaf lettuce, chives, and cress beneath lights.
- Move geraniums that have been stored indoors for winter into brighter light. Slowly coax them back to life with dribbles of water and weak fertilizer.

- Late in the month, sow onion, celery, pansy, snapdragon, and viola seeds indoors.

Zone 4
- Sow seeds of onions and chives indoors under lights.
- Late in the month, start some seeds indoors of early cabbage, broccoli, cauliflower, and celery, as well as of pansies, daisies, and other hardy flowers.
- Prepare your coldframe for use next month.
- Check peonies and other perennials for signs of heaving. Press them back into place with your foot if their roots show aboveground.
- Lightly trim damaged wood from mature apple trees, but postpone heavy pruning for a few more weeks.

Zone 5
- Kick off the growing season: Start celery, onions, leeks, and hardy herbs indoors beneath lights. Toward month's end, start early cabbage.
- Outdoors, cover compost with black plastic to help it thaw.
- Start cold-hardy flowers, such as snapdragons, stocks, pansies, and lobelias, indoors beneath grow lights.
- Between snows, direct-seed poppies and larkspur outdoors.
- Order new disease-resistant apple trees such as 'Enterprise', 'Freedom', and 'Goldrush'.

Zone 6
- Indoors beneath lights, start cabbage, cauliflower, celery, and broccoli.
- Outdoors, work the soil as soon as it has dried, preparing beds for peas, potatoes, and other early crops.
- Check stored dahlias and pot up those that have begun to sprout.
- Prune back clematis vines, and sow Shirley poppies outdoors wherever you want them to bloom.

What's Your Zone?
Claire Kowalchik and William H. Hylton

The U.S. Department of Agriculture's plant hardiness zones are determined by the average annual frost-free days and minimum winter temperatures, and they're accurate in a general way. They are not specifically accurate, however. If you live on a high hill and face north, you may actually be in the next colder zone, while someone a few miles away in a sheltered, south-facing part of a valley floor could be in the next warmer zone.

Besides such local variations, there are national variations. Zone 6, for example, is as diverse as Maine and Nevada. Eastern Zone 6 is subject to lots of rain, and plants that like it moist will do well there. But the same plants may not do well at all in Nevada, where the land is thousands of feet above sea level and dry as dust.

Use the zones as a general measure of plant hardiness, rather than as a climate guide. You know your local climate, rainfall patterns, and environmental conditions better than any map.

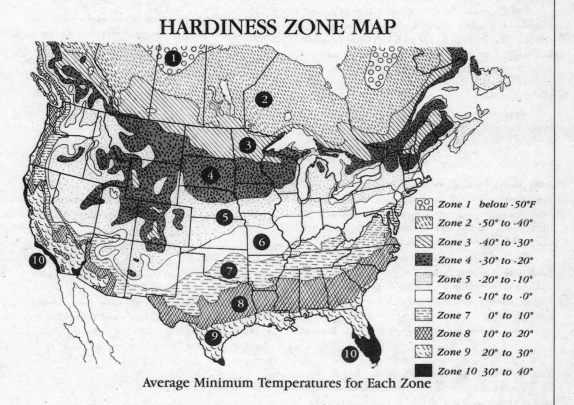

HARDINESS ZONE MAP

Zone 1	below -50°F
Zone 2	-50° to -40°
Zone 3	-40° to -30°
Zone 4	-30° to -20°
Zone 5	-20° to -10°
Zone 6	-10° to -0°
Zone 7	0° to 10°
Zone 8	10° to 20°
Zone 9	20° to 30°
Zone 10	30° to 40°

Average Minimum Temperatures for Each Zone

Continued ➡

- Start seeds of slow-growing petunias indoors beneath lights.
- Root geranium cuttings.
- Late this month, cut back ornamental grasses.
- Prune apple trees and rake the orchard floor to interrupt the life cycles of insect pests.

Zone 7

- Start slow-growing lettuce and early tomatoes indoors under lights.
- Set seed potatoes in a warm place to encourage sprouting.
- Harden-off cabbage seedlings outdoors in a cold-frame; toward month's end, plant them in the garden beneath cloches.
- Outdoors, sow peas and parsley near the end of the month.
- Mow winter cover crops and turn them under if the soil is dry enough to cultivate.
- Spread compost over beds that you will plant next month.
- Late in the month, prune hybrid tea roses hard, but give shrub roses only a light trim.
- Weed strawberries and blanket them with a row cover to encourage early bloom.

Zone 8

- Harvest asparagus spears all month!
- Plant potatoes and mulch them well. Pop onion sets or plants into fertile, well-drained beds.
- Late this month, direct-seed lettuce, endive, and other leafy greens in the garden, and prepare a bed for carrots.
- Start tomatoes and peppers indoors; as soon as the seeds sprout, move the flats or pots beneath bright lights.
- Weed and clean the garden beds where your pansies and other hardy spring flowers will soon bloom.
- Set out new roses, and heavily prune established hybrid tea roses.
- Expand your selection of small fruits! Plant figs, blackberries, blueberries, and strawberries. Also fertilize established fruits.

Zone 9

- n Finish planting cabbage, celery, peas, and broccoli early this month.
- By midmonth, direct-seed beets, carrots, and leaf lettuce.
- Mulch potato plants.
- Thin leafy greens and water them regularly. Late this month, begin planting beans, cucumbers, and early sweet corn. Also sow annual herbs, such as dill, fennel, and basil.
- Indoors, be sure to keep tomato, pepper, and eggplant seedlings beneath bright lights.

Zone 10

- Sow bachelor's buttons, nasturtiums, and California poppies outdoors.
- Cut back ornamental grasses to the point where you see new growth.
- Plant muscadine grapes and figs. Mulch them well to keep the roots evenly moist.
- Control pest caterpillars on vegetables with *Bacillus thuringiensis* (BT).

March

Zone 3

- Start cabbage, celery, brussels sprouts, broccoli, parsley, onions, and leeks indoors under lights.

- Start hardy flowers, including snapdragons and pansies, right away.
- Late this month, start petunia seeds indoors; sow poppies and sweet peas outdoors in the garden (shovel snow first, if you must!).
- Toward month's end, get a jump start on salad season by sprouting spinach and lettuce indoors.

Zone 4

- Start cabbage, broccoli, cauliflower, parsley, and celery beneath lights.
- Trim the tops of onion and leek seedlings to an inch or so high, to keep them stocky.
- Late in the month, start seeds of head lettuce, eggplant, tomatoes, and peppers indoors.
- Sprout snapdragons, pansies, and dianthus indoors, then move the seedlings to a coldframe late this month.
- Begin to prune apples and pears.
- As snow disappears, begin covering strawberries with row covers to encourage early blooming.

Zone 5

- Put seed potatoes in a warm, bright windowsill to encourage them to sprout.
- Start tomato and pepper seeds indoors.
- Plant new asparagus and rhubarb beds; fertilize established ones with a blanket of compost.
- Prepare planting beds for cool-weather crops as soon as the soil is dry enough to work.
- At month's end, move broccoli, cabbage, and cauliflower transplants outdoors to a coldframe. If a hard freeze threatens, cover the frame with an old blanket.
- Sow sweet peas, poppies, and wildflowers directly into the garden late in the month.
- Finish pruning apples and grapes, and plant new fruit trees and bushes.

Zone 6

- Start tomato, pepper, eggplant, and basil seedlings indoors under lights.
- Move broccoli, cabbage, and cauliflower seedlings to a coldframe.
- Take a soil sample and have it tested; make the necessary adjustments, using compost and organic fertilizers.
- Start planting potatoes, peas, spinach, beets, carrots, and radishes late this month.
- Plant nasturtiums, alyssum, and other half-hardy annuals indoors.
- Take cuttings from geraniums and root them in small pots indoors.
- Finish pruning fruit trees, then follow up with a dormant-oil spray.

Zone 7

- Plant peas, potatoes, and parsley right away.
- Begin a new compost pile—using leftover leaves and kitchen scraps—if you don't already have a batch going.
- After the last hard frost, transplant cabbage, broccoli, and onions to the garden. Indoors, start seeds of tomatoes, peppers, eggplant, and basil.
- Sow carrots, chard, spinach, radishes, beets, and dill in the garden.
- Start harvesting asparagus!
- Pull winter weeds from flowerbeds, then direct-seed cosmos, rudbeckias, and nasturtiums.
- Plant roses, lilies, and all types of hardy ground cover plants.

- Fertilize strawberries with compost when the first blossoms show.

Zone 8

- Mulch potatoes with straw as soon as the fat sprouts emerge from the soil.
- Thin leafy salad greens to keep them growing fast.
- Make a second sowing of carrots, beets, chard, and dill early this month.
- After midmonth, sow cucumbers, bush beans, and early sweet corn.
- Fill in empty spaces in flowerbeds with direct-seeded cosmos, nasturtiums, and lavatera.
- Set out gerbera daisies and other hardy perennials, such as roses, lilies, hardy groundcover plants, and woodland shrubs.
- Apply compost or other organic fertilizers to fruit trees and shrubs.

Zone 9

- Make your last sowings of carrots, beets, and heat-tolerant leaf lettuce, then start planting warm-weather crops.
- Start eggplant seedlings and sweet potato slips indoors.
- For quick color, sow cosmos and nasturtium seeds right where you want them to grow.
- Sow sunflowers and tithonia where their height will mesh with your garden design.
- Transplant salvias, marigolds, zinnias, celosia, gomphrena, and other annuals to flowerbeds and borders.

Zone 10

- Set out tomato and pepper transplants; plant basil, squash, corn, beans, cucumbers, and melons.
- Set out caladium corms in shady spots, or mix them with coleus in containers.
- Before slugs, snails, and pill bugs dig into your strawberries and leafy greens, defeat the pests with beer traps.
- Plant kiwi vines and avocado trees, and water new plants every few days to keep the roots from drying out.

April

Zone 3

- When weather permits, set out new asparagus and rhubarb plants.
- As soon as the soil is warm and dry enough to cultivate, begin planting onions, peas, spinach, carrots, lettuce, beets, chard, and radishes.
- Late in the month, start tomatoes, peppers, and eggplants indoors.
- Direct-seed poppies, alyssum, bachelor's buttons, cosmos, and calendulas anytime (they don't mind chilly soil).
- Remove winter coverings from peonies, then top-dress them with compost.
- Set out new strawberries.

Zone 4

- Harden-off cabbage, broccoli, and cauliflower seedlings for a week before setting them out in the garden beneath cloches.
- Sow spinach, lettuce, and radishes, then cover them with plastic tunnels to get them growing in a hurry.
- Start tomatoes, peppers, and basil indoors.
- Late this month, plant potatoes and peas.
- Set out snapdragons, dianthus, and pansies.

Continued ➜

- Divide daylilies, phlox, and other clumping perennials.
- Fertilize raspberries with compost and renew mulches beneath blueberries.

Zone 5
- Harden-off cabbage, then set out plants beneath cloches.
- Plant potatoes, peas, and spinach, followed by carrots, lettuce, and other greens.
- Start basil, tomato, and pepper seedlings.
- Plant new beds of asparagus and rhubarb.
- Set out new shrubs and trees.
- Fertilize established fruits with a thin layer of compost.

Zone 6
- Plant peas, potatoes, spinach, lettuce, and other leafy greens.
- Set out kohlrabi and broccoli under cloches.
- Between rainy spells, prepare beds for bush beans, sweet corn, and other summer vegetables.
- Weed flowerbeds, and remove protection from roses and other perennials.
- Dig up, divide, and transplant crowded daylilies, phlox, and hostas.
- Overseed sparse areas in lawns.
- Set out new fruit trees and shrubs, and fertilize established berries.

Zone 7
- Sow more carrots and lettuce early this month, and mulch potatoes with 6 inches of straw.
- Set out a few early-ripening tomato cultivars beneath cloches.
- At midmonth, sow sweet corn, cucumbers, summer squash, and bush beans, as well as herbs.
- Set out annual flowers, and plant roses, dahlias, lilies, and glads.
- Fill the backs of sunny flowerbeds with tall sunflowers or tithonia.
- Propagate ground covers and hostas in shady areas.
- Set out blackberries and strawberries, and be sure to provide plenty of water.

Zone 8
- Check the brassica patch for cabbageworms; if you spot any, handpick them or apply *Bacillus thuringiensis* (BT).
- Set out tomatoes, peppers, and eggplant, and sow sweet corn, squash, cucumbers, and beans.
- Start sweet potato slips to transplant next month.
- Replace faded lettuce with okra, peanuts, field peas, or lima beans.
- Plant annual vines to shade heat-sensitive plants from summer sun.
- Top-dress roses with compost.
- Sow easy-growing annuals such as celosia, zinnias, and sunflowers.
- Late this month, thin peaches and plums to 6 inches apart.

Zone 9
- Replace spent spring crops with okra, asparagus beans, Malabar spinach, cherry tomatoes, and sunflowers.
- Cage tomatoes, peppers, and eggplant.
- Side-dress rows of garlic, shallots, and onions with compost.
- Late in the month, sow cantaloupe, pumpkins, and squash.

- Sow hot-weather flowers such as celosias, sunflowers, portulaca, and zinnias.
- Set out bedding plants, such as asters, coreopsis, impatiens, and salvia.
- Apply mulches!
- Harvest strawberries before slugs and snails beat you to it!

Zone 10
- Pull up bolted brassicas and leafy greens, and compost them.
- Try underplanting okra with sweet potatoes.
- Keep harvesting tomatoes, cucumbers, melons, and squash to encourage continued production.
- As parsley, coriander, and dill go to seed, replace them with plants of lemongrass, Cuban oregano, and Vietnamese coriander.
- Plant allamanda and other flowering vines as shade screens for decks, patios, and windows.
- Water and remulch beds frequently.

May

Zone 3
- Plant peas and potatoes.
- Harden-off cabbage-family seedlings and set them out at midmonth.
- Direct-seed lettuce, spinach, and root crops.
- Plant asparagus, rhubarb, and celery.
- Fill flowerbeds with pansies, cosmos, and petunias.
- Set out new berry plants.

Zone 4
- Plant peas and potatoes, and direct-seed parsley and kohlrabi.
- Get busy sowing lettuce, carrots, beets, and radishes.
- Start pumpkins indoors for planting next month.
- At month's end, sow beans, sweet corn, muskmelons, cucumbers, and squash; set out tomato plants under cloches.
- Plant new perennial flowers and sow seeds of cool-weather annuals such as nasturtiums and cosmos.
- Mulch fruit trees with compost.

Zone 5
- Plant peas and potatoes right away, followed by beets, lettuce, radishes, and spinach.
- Sow carrots and early cukes around midmonth.
- Toward month's end, plant corn, beans, muskmelons, squash, watermelon, basil, tomatoes, and peppers.
- Fertilize broccoli now to keep it growing fast.
- Thin leafy greens.
- Plant sunflowers and other colorful summer annuals.
- Plant roses and perennials by midmonth.

Zone 6
- Harden-off tomato and pepper seedlings for transplanting in midmonth.
- Sow basil, sweet corn, beans, cucumbers, squash, and melons.
- Plant leaf lettuce in the partial shade of taller plants.
- Thin leafy greens and use them in salads.
- Mulch potatoes.
- Top-dress roses with compost.
- Sow sunflowers, zinnias, marigolds, and other summer annuals.

- Wait for the fading foliage of spring-blooming bulbs to turn brown before you remove it.

Zone 7
- Set out the last of your tomatoes, peppers, eggplants, and sweet potato slips.
- Be sure to harvest leafy greens often because they soon will bolt.
- Plant sweet corn, beans, melons, gourds, okra, and field peas.
- Keep mulching potatoes.
- Have *Bacillus thuringiensis* (BT) ready to apply at the first sign of caterpillar pests.
- Plant summer-blooming bulbs, such as cannas, glads, and tuberous begonias.

Zone 8
- If you expect a dry summer, install drip irrigation lines.
- Mulch everything!
- Stop watering onions, garlic, and shallots when the foliage begins to turn yellow.
- Set out sweet potato slips on a cloudy day.
- Plant okra, eggplant, peanuts, cherry tomatoes, field peas, and limas.
- Reseed sparse patches of lawn.
- Dig up and divide irises, daylilies, and Oriental poppies after they finish blooming.
- Thin fruits after the first "extras" fall from trees. Water all fruit trees and bushes during dry spells.

Zone 9
- Harvest remaining cool-season crops.
- Thin early sowings of corn and beans.
- Plant okra, melons, black-eyed peas, and jicama.
- Mulch beds if you haven't already done so.
- Begin pinching the tips of chrysanthemums and impatiens to encourage bushy growth.
- Fertilize late-blooming crape myrtles.
- Keep flowers, lawns, and roses well watered.
- When fruits begin to bloom, give them a booster feeding of fish emulsion.

Zone 10
- Plant only heat-loving edibles and ornamentals now, and water them often.
- Protect developing tomatoes and peppers from blistering and cracking by providing some shade.
- Keep tomatoes and peppers evenly moist.
- Remove faded flowers from annuals and perennials.
- Be sure fruit and nut trees receive enough water to prevent excessive fruit drop.

June

Zone 3
- Thin leafy greens and eat your thinnings.
- Harden-off and then set out melon and squash plants.
- Plant beans, cucumbers, and sweet corn.
- Get tomatoes and peppers into the ground by midmonth.
- Start brussels sprouts, cabbage, Asian cabbage, endive, and kale for fall.
- Brighten up beds with colorful warm-weather annuals such as marigolds, celosia, and impatiens.

Zone 4
- Plant the rest of your tomatoes, and set out peppers, eggplant, and basil.

Continued →

- Sow more beans, sweet corn, leaf lettuce, and cucumbers.
- Midmonth, start seeds of cauliflower, broccoli, and brussels sprouts for the fall garden.
- Sow winter squash directly in the garden for a fall harvest.
- Near month's end, sow cilantro for the salsa you will make later this summer.
- Mulch blueberries and raspberries.
- Dress up drab corners with marigolds, zinnias, and other easy-care summer flowers.

Zone 5

- Mulch your potatoes.
- Trellis peas, and stake or cage your tomatoes.
- Make second plantings of bush beans and sweet corn.
- Sow pumpkin seeds for a Halloween harvest of jack-o-lanterns.
- Plant dahlias and gladioli bulbs, then stake them right away so that you don't damage the roots later.
- Midmonth, thin apples and peaches to 6 inches apart so the trees won't carry more fruits than the limbs can handle.
- Start seeds of brussels sprouts, broccoli, and cabbage for the fall garden.

Zone 6

- Stake or cage your tomatoes, mulch them, and remove any leaves that show signs of early blight.
- Set out sweet potato slips.
- Make second sowings of squash, cucumbers, sweet corn, and bush beans.
- When spring lettuce bolts, replace it with field peas, okra, or more tomatoes.
- When your peas are finished, replace them with pole beans, cucumbers, or asparagus beans.
- Pinch back chrysanthemums to make them bushy.
- Prune spring-flowering shrubs after they finish blooming.

Zone 7

- You still have time to plant heat-loving field peas, luffas, and asparagus beans.
- Start seeds (or root cuttings) of early-maturing tomatoes for a fall crop.
- Cut and dry bunches of thyme, oregano, and mint.
- Snake a drip irrigation line through your tomato patch before the plants begin to sprawl.
- Pull up cold-loving pansies when they succumb to the heat, and replace them with annual vinca, zinnias, or celosia.
- Water all of the fruit trees and bushes that you planted this spring.

Zone 8

- Harvest, weed, and mulch!
- Replace spring peas, lettuce, and potatoes with field peas, limas, or a summer cover crop of soybeans.
- Hand-pick Colorado potato beetles and other pests.
- Plant chrysanthemums, balsam, celosia, begonias, salvia, dusty miller, geraniums, vinca, and verbena.
- Harvest blackberries and blueberries.
- Mulch figs and muscadine grapes.

Zone 9

- Replace peas with beans, substitute Swiss chard for spinach, and put in taro after harvesting early potatoes.
- Start another generation of zinnias, sunflowers, and marigolds for late-summer bloom.
- Pinch back chrysanthemums.
- Water plants in the morning so they don't become susceptible to fungus and insect infestation.
- Solarize pests and diseases in vacant beds by wetting the soil, then covering it with clear plastic for about a month.

Zone 10

- On that rare cool day, create a new bed for fall greens. Cultivate the soil, add organic matter, wet the bed down, then cover it with clear plastic for at least a month to kill weed seeds and nematodes.
- Prune cassia trees, poinciana, bougainvillea, and jasmine after they bloom.
- Prune litchi, mangoes, and other tropical fruits after the harvest this month.

July

Zone 3

- Continue to direct-sow bush beans, carrots, turnips, and beets.
- Start your first fall runs of lettuce, spinach, and other greens in the shade of taller crops.
- Mulch your potatoes!
- Gather and dry basil, mint, and other herbs before they flower.

Zone 4

- Set out seedlings of broccoli, brussels sprouts, cabbage, and cauliflower for fall harvest.
- Direct-sow some bush beans.
- Sow leafy greens such as mustard, Chinese cabbage, turnips, and lettuce, placing them where they'll get some afternoon shade.
- Plant fall spinach late this month.
- Sneak some potatoes into empty spots to harvest as "new" this fall.
- Deadhead annual flowers to keep them neat.
- Trim and repot gangly houseplants.

Zone 5

- Hurry and plant more bush beans, cucumbers, carrots, and summer squash.
- By midmonth, set out seedlings of cabbage-family members for fall harvest.
- Sow fall lettuce, oriental greens, daikons, and snap, show, or shell peas.
- Gather and dry herbs and everlasting flowers.
- Mulch your potatoes again.
- Set out asters and mums and sow some fast-growing annual flowers in the vacant spaces of flowerbeds.

Zone 6

- Direct-sow carrots, beets, and chard.
- Stretch the season with midmonth plantings of cucumbers, bush beans, and squash.
- By month's end, set out broccoli, cabbage, brussels sprouts, and cauliflower.
- Sow snap, snow, or shell peas.
- Plant any sprouted potatoes from your kitchen for a late crop of tender, new spuds.
- Water all fruits as needed through the harvest.
- Prune out old wood from raspberry and blackberry patches.

Zone 7

- Early in the month, sow a little more sweet corn and set out new tomato plants.
- Plant pumpkins and winter squash in a shady spot, but where the vines can soon run into the sunlight.
- During the second half of the month, start seedlings of broccoli, cabbage, cauliflower, and brussels sprouts indoors.
- Prepare beds for fall crops by sowing them now with a cover crop of fast-growing field peas or other legumes.
- Harvest blueberries and mulch strawberries heavily to protect them from heat and drought.

Zone 8

- You still have time to plant field peas, okra, limas, watermelon, and asparagus beans.
- Now's the time to solarize sick soil. Water empty beds, then cover them with clear plastic for at least a month.
- In the warmest parts of the zone, start tomato and pepper seedlings indoors.
- Set out chrysanthemums and pinch them back.
- Sow zinnias and sunflowers where you need late-summer color.

Zone 9

- Start tomato, pepper, and eggplant seedlings indoors for planting in fall.
- Outdoors, use old sheets or shade cloth to protect peppers and tomatoes from sunburn.
- Set out more sweet potato slips.
- In lower elevations, continue to plant corn, squash, beans, and field peas.
- In desert areas, prune back tomatoes by two-thirds.
- In humid regions, set out tropical vines and shrubs during rainy spells.
- Solarize empty beds that are infested with root-knot nematodes, or where diseases have been a problem.

Zone 10

- Direct-seed pole beans and limas, cantaloupes, collards, sweet corn, okra, southern peas, and watermelon.
- Indoors, start seeds of eggplant, peppers, and tomatoes now for the fall garden. Choose heat-tolerant cultivars, such as 'Heatwave'.
- Inspect passion fruit vines daily for caterpillars. When necessary, spray with *Bacillus thuringiensis* (BT), a natural caterpillar killer.
- Add everything you can to the compost pile. You'll need lots of humus to mix into the soil in fall.

August

Zone 3

- Finish planting your lettuce and spinach.
- At midmonth, pick off all tomato flowers so the plants' energy can be devoted to ripening fruits.
- Be ready to cover your tomatoes, peppers, and beans to protect against the first frost.
- Harvest everlasting flowers after a period of warm, dry weather.
- Renew mulches around roses, but stop feeding them.
- Prune out the oldest raspberry canes after harvest.
- Set out new strawberry plants.

Continued ➡

Zone 4

- Water the garden as needed to keep everything growing fast.
- Make a last sowing of spinach and cold-hardy lettuce.
- Dig compost into beds before setting out Chinese cabbage and fall brassicas.
- Root cuttings of perennials and herbs to grow indoors this winter.
- Dig and divide irises and daylilies.
- Sow Iceland poppies and set out pansies for fall color.
- Protect grapes and late-bearing tree fruits from birds.

Zone 5

- Sow spinach, turnips, and cold-hardy lettuce for fall.
- Water the garden if it doesn't receive at least 1 inch of rain per week.
- If you want to create a new garden bed or rejuvenate an old one for next year, cultivate the space well and sow a cover crop of oats, rye, or ryegrass.
- Sow hardy biennial flowers, such as sweet William and forget-me-nots.
- Trim ragged tops of perennials that have finished blooming.
- Prune out old raspberry canes.
- Top-dress strawberries with compost.

Zone 6

- Plant a rainbow of lettuces, multihued radishes, and colorful kales for your fall salad garden.
- Plant plenty of spinach!
- Harvest potatoes, bulb onions, beans, and squash.
- Thin fall salad greens.
- Late this month, set out pansies for fall and spring.
- Sow Shirley poppies, larkspur, snapdragons, and sweet William.
- Collect seeds of favorite annual flowers.
- Water strawberries and transplant robust new runners.

Zone 7

- Early this month, start seeds indoors for the fall garden, including broccoli, cauliflower, cabbage, Chinese cabbage, and scallions.
- Sow carrots, beets, kale, and chard in the partial shade of taller plants.
- Make your last sowings of squash and cucumbers.
- Plant fall peas by midmonth, and set out brassica seedlings for fall harvest.
- When Labor Day is near, direct-seed kohlrabi, kale, and collards.
- Keep watering fall-bearing raspberries and ever-bearing strawberries; replenish their mulch as needed.

Zone 8

- Start some basil, cucumbers, and squash indoors and set the plants out a week after they sprout.
- Direct-seed bush beans, pumpkins, and sweet corn by midmonth, followed by peas and dill.
- Start carrots in a bed of loose soil.
- Prune back okra by one-third to encourage side shoots to bear.
- Start celery, broccoli, cabbage, and brussels sprouts indoors, then set out the seedlings when they have six leaves.

- Rake the orchard floor clean to interrupt the life cycles of pests.

Zone 9

- Sow watermelon early in the month, along with limas, southern peas, and sweet corn.
- After midmonth, begin setting out your tomato and pepper transplants.
- Direct-seed cucumbers, squash, and bush beans in partial shade.
- Plant basil and dill.
- Renew fading flowerbeds by filling them with fast-growing marigolds, zinnias, and annual vinca.
- Harvest tree fruits and use spoiled fruits as bait to lure green fruit beetles into narrow-necked jar or bottle traps.

Zone 10

- Set out tomato and pepper transplants after midmonth, then cover them with shade cloth to shield them from the summer sun.
- Start seeds of hardy perennials indoors, including pansies, gaillardia, and daisies.
- Direct-sow foxglove, larkspur, cosmos, and hollyhocks.
- Pinch chrysanthemums to encourage new blossoms.

September

Zone 3

- Before the nights get too cold, pick all of your mature green tomatoes and store them indoors to ripen off the vine.
- Harvest squash, beans, and other tender vegetables.
- Cook up big batches of tomato sauce for freezing or canning.
- On freezing nights, cover lettuce, cauliflower, broccoli, and carrots to stretch the season.
- Wait 'til after frost to harvest and savor kale.
- Plant tulips, daffodils, and other spring-flowering bulbs.
- Clean and repair tools before storing them for winter.

Zone 4

- Extend the season! Plant salad greens, such as spinach, winter lettuce, and kale, in a coldframe.
- Before the first freeze, harvest tender vegetables, such as tomatoes, peppers, and melons.
- Can or freeze the last harvests of sweet corn, tomatoes, and beans.
- Prepare to cover broccoli, cabbage, and cauliflower.
- Toward month's end, dig up potatoes, onions, turnips, and carrots.
- Gather leaves and pine needles to use for winter mulching.
- Plant spring bulbs.

Zone 5

- Plant a fall salad garden of winter lettuce, spinach, and mâche in a coldframe or plastic tunnel.
- Remove the bottom leaves from brussels spouts plants to direct energy to the sprouts.
- Harvest winter squash, pumpkins, tomatoes, and peppers before frost.
- Pick apples, pears, and other late fruits, then freeze or can them to enjoy this winter.
- Prune herbs and geraniums, pot them up, then set them on sunny windowsills indoors.
- Plant pansies and spring-flowering bulbs.

- Don't cut back ornamental grasses; enjoy their feathery foliage throughout winter.

Zone 6

- Save seed from your best plants of heirloom beans, tomatoes, squash, and melons.
- Gather up and compost all of your spent garden plants.
- Harvest broccoli, cabbage, cauliflower, and kohlrabi if they're ready; if not, prepare to cover them on freezing nights.
- Harvest apples, then rake the orchard floor to disrupt the life cycles of pests.
- Weed blueberries and raspberries, then mulch them with chopped leaves.
- Plant pansies, spring-flowering bulbs, and hardy perennials such as daylilies.
- Sow a fall cover crop in vacant vegetable beds.
- Clean and repair tools before storing them for winter.

Zone 7

- Continue planting spinach, lettuce, radishes, arugula, oriental greens, kale, and collards.
- Dig up sweet potatoes and peanuts while the weather is still warm; cure them before storing.
- Late this month, plant next year's garlic crop.
- Divide multiplier onions.
- Set out new strawberry plants.
- Start pansies, snapdragons, and sweet William from seed.
- Reseed and fertilize thin areas of fescue lawns.

Zone 8

- Set out brussels sprouts, kale, broccoli, cauliflower, and cabbage transplants; check them daily for leaf-eating pests.
- Direct-seed carrots, beets, lettuce, parsley, spinach, turnips, leeks, and kohlrabi; shade the beds until seeds germinate.
- Late in the month, sow sweet William, pansies, bachelor's buttons, poppies, and snapdragons.
- Plant trees and shrubs, then water them well weekly.
- Work compost into beds; replenish mulches.

Zone 9

- If scorching temperatures have eased up, set out tomato transplants by midmonth.
- Direct-seed snap beans, sweet corn, squash, and cucumbers.
- Late this month, start seeds of broccoli, kale, and cauliflower indoors.
- Toward month's end, sow peas, beets, and carrots in the garden.
- Direct-seed cold-hardy herbs such as parsley, chives, and sage.
- Have *Bacillus thuringiensis* (BT) ready to use if leaf-eating caterpillars show up on brassicas.

Zone 10

- Plant okra early this month.
- Set out transplants of tomatoes, peppers, and onions.
- Direct-seed cucumbers, melons, and squash, as well as herbs.
- Replenish mulches and soil amendments, such as compost.
- Prune poinsettias for holiday bloom.

Continued ➡

October

Zone 3

- Clean up the garden and compost the residue.
- Finish harvesting cauliflower, cabbage, broccoli, beets, and turnips.
- Cover hardy crops, such as spinach, parsley, and kale, to keep them growing another month.
- Shred leaves, then use them for mulch.
- After the first hard freeze, cover perennials with a winter mulch of leaves, pine needles, or straw.
- Wrap the bases of fruit trees with chicken wire to protect against winter rodents.

Zone 4

- Time to harvest brussels sprouts, kale, parsley, and other hardy crops, or to prolong the harvest by covering them on cold winter nights.
- Store carrots in the garden all winter by removing the tops, then covering the bed with a foot of mulch.
- Brush white paint on young tree trunks to protect them from sunscald.
- Rake up fallen leaves, then mow or shred them. Wait until the ground freezes to use them as mulch over peonies, lilies, and other perennials.
- Scout your local garden center for bargain bulbs, then get them into the ground before month's end.

Zone 5

- Plant annual rye or winter wheat in vacant beds to prevent weeds and provide "green manure" for next season.
- Mulch carrots heavily to keep them from freezing.
- Cover salad greens with plastic on frosty nights.
- Harvest kale and brussels sprouts.
- Prune roses, rake up all their old mulch, then replace it by piling fresh straw or chopped leaves up to the lowest buds.
- Rake the orchard floor clean to interrupt the life cycles of pests and diseases.

Zone 6

- Gather up and compost all your withered garden plants.
- Harvest broccoli, cauliflower, cabbage, and kohlrabi as soon as they're ready, or be prepared to cover them on cold nights.
- Dig up sweet potatoes and harvest pumpkins and winter squash before the first hard freeze.
- Weed blueberries and raspberries, then mulch them with shredded leaves.
- Dig up and store tender bulbs and tubers, such as cannas, begonias, and caladiums, before the first frost.
- Cut back chrysanthemums and asters after the flowers fade, but wait until spring to move them.
- Plant spring-blooming bulbs.
- Set out new strawberries.

Zone 7

- Thin any spinach that you won't overwinter, and eat the thinnings.
- Cover broccoli and cauliflower on frosty nights.
- Plant garlic and multiplier onions. Set out evergreen shrubs.
- Sow seeds of poppies, larkspur, blue flax, hollyhock, bachelor's buttons, and sweet rocket.
- Plant spring-flowering bulbs.
- Set out new strawberries. Stockpile leaves and pine needles.

Zone 8

- Sow more spinach and parsley, and thin leafy greens.
- Dig up sweet potatoes and peanuts, and cure them before storing.
- Keep the roots of tomato plants constantly moist; ripening fruits are less likely to crack after heavy rains.
- Plant bunching onions, regular onions, and leeks, and prepare a fertile spot for garlic.
- Replace summer flowers with hardy annuals.
- Lift and store caladiums.
- Go wild by direct-seeding wildflowers, such as gilia, black-eyed Susan, poppies, candytuft, cone flowers, and coreopsis.

Zone 9

- Direct-seed Chinese cabbage, spinach, lettuce, and radishes.
- Set out seedlings of the cabbage-family crops you started last month, and check them daily for pests.
- Harvest sweet potatoes, cure them, then store them.
- Color-up fall flowerbeds with alyssum, calendula, dianthus, snapdragons, and ornamental kale.

Zone 10

- Thin and water fall greens and root crops.
- Fill empty spaces in the garden with Chinese cabbage, beets, cauliflower, collards, broccoli, kale, turnips, and spinach.
- Set out new strawberry plants.
- Lightly fertilize citrus trees with compost or other organic fertilizer, and water them if rainfall has been low.

November

Zone 3

- Clean up the garden and compost the remains.
- Cover empty beds with a blanket of compost.
- Dig up carrots and parsnips before the ground freezes hard.
- Cover fall-planted pansies and snapdragons with evergreen boughs.
- Trim broken branches from trees.
- Rake the orchard floor, then add a fresh layer of mulch beneath young fruit trees and grapes.
- Put chicken wire collars around the bases of fruit trees to protect them from rodents this winter.

Zone 4

- Compost spent plants.
- Dig up root crops before the ground freezes.
- After the ground freezes, cover perennials with mulch.
- Pot up some spring bulbs to force into winter bloom.
- Apply dormant-oil spray to apple and other fruit trees on a mild day.
- Paint the lower trunks of young trees to prevent winter sunscald.

Zone 5

- Harvest carrots, brussels sprouts, and cabbage and store them in a cool basement or unheated garage.
- Clean up the asparagus bed.
- If the weather cooperates, prepare a few beds now for early planting next spring, then cover them with mulch.
- Pop spring-blooming bulbs into beds if you haven't done so already.

- Mulch around pansies and other hardy flowers, but don't smother anything that's still green.
- Mow fallen leaves, then use them to mulch strawberries and blueberries.

Zone 6

- Harvest cold-weather-sweetened carrots, brussels sprouts, cabbage, and kale.
- Continue to thin lettuce and spinach.
- Hoard a mountain of leaves, then use them to cover beds for early-spring planting.
- There's still time to divide daisies and to direct-seed Shirley poppies, bachelor's buttons, and larkspur.
- Set out evergreen shrubs and trees.
- Weed strawberries and mulch bramble fruits with chopped leaves.
- Apply dormant-oil spray to fruit trees on a mild day.

Zone 7

- Start digging up winter carrots as soon as they are big enough.
- Harvest bunching onions, then plant more in a new site.
- Plant garlic.
- Gather blankets for covering lettuce and other half-hardy crops during the first hard freezes.
- Edge bulb beds with overwintering pansies for a nice look next spring.
- Trim back faded mums late in the month. Thin larkspur and poppy seedlings, and move bachelor's buttons.
- Harvest pecans.
- Use fresh pine needles to mulch strawberries and brambles.

Zone 8

- Harvest beans, tomatoes, peppers, and other tender crops before the first frost.
- Begin to harvest fall cabbage, broccoli, and brussels sprouts after cold weather arrives.
- Plant garlic, and dig and divide multiplier onions.
- Sow winter cover crops.
- Gather and bag leaves to use as mulch throughout the rest of the year.
- Lift caladium corms and store them in damp sand or vermiculite.
- Set out pansies, dianthus, snapdragons, and ornamental kale.
- Use fresh pine needles to mulch azaleas.
- Trim damaged branches from trees.

Zone 9

- Harvest squash, cucumbers, and your first fall tomatoes.
- Start planting your winter garden: Set out seedlings of cabbage, celery, and broccoli.
- Direct-seed peas, beets, carrots, lettuce, Chinese cabbage, spinach, and chard.
- Renew the herb garden with fresh plants.
- Dress up flowerbeds with some new starts of alyssum, calendula, and dianthus.
- Direct-seed bachelor's buttons, cosmos, and hollyhocks.

Zone 10

- Plant more cool-weather greens, such as lettuce, spinach, and Chinese cabbage.
- Late this month, prune back a few peppers and eggplants—they'll bear an early crop next spring.

Continued ➡

- Harvest sweet potatoes.
- Fill empty patio pots with petunias.
- Plant tropical bulbs, such as freesias and sparaxis.
- Keep citrus fruits well watered and check often for bird damage.
- Spray *Bacillus thuringiensis* CBT) on brassicas as soon as you spot leaf-eating caterpillars.

December

Zone 3
- Pot up a few more bulbs to force into bloom for early spring, and move those that already have sprouted into bright light.
- Check stored vegetables for signs of spoilage.
- Wrap the bases of fruit trees with wire mesh to protect them from hungry rodents.

Zone 4
- After the soil freezes, mulch over the crowns of perennials to keep them from heaving out of the ground during winter thaws.
- Pot up some spring bulbs to force into bloom; keep them cold (but not freezing) until they sprout.
- If whiteflies and mealybugs are attacking your houseplants, set the plants in the shower and wash your troubles down the drain.
- Inspect stored fruits, bulbs, and corms for signs of spoilage.
- Check the bases of tree trunks for mouse marks; encircle the trunks with wire mesh to prevent further damage.

Zone 5
- If you've run out of straw to cover carrots, parsnips, and salsify in the garden, dig up these root crops and store them in a cool basement.
- Harvest brussels sprouts and cabbage plants, roots and all; they'll keep for weeks that way if stored in a cool basement or root cellar.
- Cover parsley with milk jug cloches, then surround the covers with insulating leaf mulch.
- Protect overwintering spinach with row covers.
- Wrap chicken wire cages around young fruit trees to protect them from deer.
- Before the ground freezes, dig planting holes for any trees you intend to plant in late winter.

Zone 6
- Cover perennial flowers, as well as pansies and snapdragons, with evergreen boughs to protect them from ice and harsh winds.
- Harvest brussels sprouts and cabbage.
- Mulch empty vegetable beds with chopped leaves.
- To enjoy spinach throughout winter, cover the plants now with a plastic tunnel.
- Rake up all fallen apples and apple leaves to stop the spread of scab and other orchard diseases.
- On a mild day, apply dormant-oil spray to smother scale and other sap suckers.

Zone 7
- Harvest brussels sprouts, kale, cabbage, and collards.
- Mulch Jerusalem artichokes, carrots, parsnips, and other crops that will spend winter underground.
- Spread mulch over beds where early spring crops will grow.
- Turn compost one last time, then cover it with a tarp to prevent nutrients from leaching away during winter rains.

- Dig, divide, and replant crowded bulbs. Continue setting out hardy annual and perennial seedlings, then cover them with cloches.
- On a mild day, apply dormant-oil spray to smother scale and aphids.

Zone 8
- Harvest frost-sweetened spinach, kale, and collards.
- Pile compost and leaf mulch on vacant garden beds.
- Near the end of the month, start seeds of cabbage and hardy lettuces indoors.
- Plant spring-blooming bulbs.
- Direct-seed sweet peas, larkspur, Shirley poppies, and bachelor's buttons.
- Continue planting pansies, dianthus, and snapdragons.
- Prune roses, then replace their old mulch with oat straw to discourage black spot.

Zone 9
- Plant cool-season vegetables, such as lettuce and cabbage-family crops. Be patient—they grow slowly during winter's short days.
- Around month's end, start seeds of tomatoes, peppers, and eggplant indoors.
- Direct-seed poppies, bachelor's buttons, nigella, cosmos, and larkspur in well-drained beds.
- Apply a fresh layer of clean mulch to berries and grapes.

Zone 10
- Plant all sorts of greens, beets, carrots, and peas.
- Around month's end, start seeds of tomatoes, peppers, and eggplant indoors.
- Pop bedding plants, such as pansies, dianthus, and snapdragons, into both containers and empty spots in beds.
- Plant ornamental shrubs and trees.
- Enjoy your homegrown citrus fruits.

SOIL

Digging In: Creating Good Homes for Plants

Barbara Pleasant

Getting to Know Your Soil

The plants in your garden depend on the soil for their survival, because it's where they get the water and nutrients they need. You can keep plants alive in lousy soil, but why spend all your time pumping them with water and fertilizer when healthy soil can take care of a lot of that work for you?

TAKE A TEST

Whether you are new to gardening or have been at it for years, a soil test from a laboratory gives you priceless insight into your soil. Numerous factors determine a soil's basic characteristics—from the kind of rock from which it was formed, to rainfall and temperature patterns, to how the

previous owner cared for it. Bulldozers move soil around when houses are built, so it's possible that your yard includes several different types of soil. If so, you may need more than one soil test.

For a reliable test, obtain a soil test bag or box through your local cooperative extension office, or contact the soil lab of the agricultural college in your state or province. The bag or box comes with instructions for collecting a sample, which is a simply matter of digging a 4-inch-deep hole and collecting a handful-size sample. When you fill out the information form to mail in with the sample, be sure to specify that you want organic gardening recommendations. The test results will include an analysis of your soil's available nutrients, organic matter content, and pH—all of which will change as you improve your soil.

THE QUESTION OF TEXTURE

One soil characteristic that will change very slowly, and never be radically altered, is your soil's texture. Texture is determined mostly by the size of the soil particles. Sand particles are large, so sandy soil has a light, loose texture, whereas clay particles are very small, so clay soil is comparatively heavy and tight. Intermediate-size particles, such as silt or bits of organic matter, modify extremes in these two soil types. If you are lucky, your soil is either "sandy loam" or "clay loam"—meaning it's basically sand or clay with lots of silt and organic matter. Most gardeners are not so lucky and face the task of improving their soil's texture by adding organic matter. More important, understanding your soil's texture helps you tailor your gardening practices to bring out the best in your soil's hidden talents.

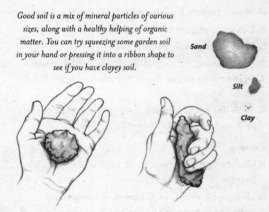

Good soil is a mix of mineral particles of various sizes, along with a healthy helping of organic matter. You can try squeezing some garden soil in your hand or pressing it into a ribbon shape to see if you have clayey soil.

Sand

Silt

Clay

The Scoop on Sand

Very sandy soil drains fast, which is generally good. At the same time, fast drainage means that dissolved nutrients may drainaway before plant roots have a chance to absorb them. Sand particles are also slippery, so nutrients don't bind to them. Because sand particles are large, the spaces between them also are quite roomy. For this reason, sandy soil does not need to be cultivated often since its air-holding capacity is already excellent. It does need to be continually enriched with organic matter, which will enhance its ability to hold onto nutrients from fertilizer. If you garden in sand, heavy mulching is so practical and useful that it should become a fundamental method in your soil care practices.

Working with Clay

Tiny clay particles pack so tightly that they trap water and stay wet, so plant roots may find it difficult to push their way through the soil, and then be dissatisfied with constant wetness. On the plus side, clay soils hold nutrients well, so rich forms of organic matter added to clay soil may nurture plants for a long time. Clay soil responds well to cultivation—which introduces much-needed air—as

Continued →

What about Manure?

For thousands of years, gardeners have used animal manure to enrich their soil with organic matter, nitrogen, and other plant nutrients. Yet modern farming methods give gardeners good reason to think twice before using manure, which may contain undesirable chemicals, weed seeds, and potentially dangerous bacteria such as *E. coli*. If you can get manure from organically raised animals, and compost it completely, manure can be a valuable soil amendment. A less risky option is to limit your use of manure to organic fertilizer (many of which contain poultry manure) that have been processed to rid them of potential contaminants.

long as you dig or till it only when it is lightly moist to dry. If you add in compost or other soil amendments each time you replant in clay soil, over time you will see a steady lightening of your soil's texture. Avoid walking on clay soil, which compacts it by squeezing out air.

Sweet and Sour Soil

In some regions, the chemical composition of the soil makes the water in the spaces between the particles acidic—think vinegar or lemon juice. In other regions, the soil is alkaline, also called sweet or basic. The measure of the acidity or alkalinity is called the pH. Distilled water, with a pH of 7, is neutral. Acidic soils have a pH less than 7, while alkaline soils are above 7.

Soil pH is important because it determines what nutrients are available to plants. Some nutrients are tied up in unavailable forms at certain pH levels, while others may be overabundant to the point of toxicity. Most plants thrive in soil with a pH between 6 and 7.5. A few, such as blueberries and azaleas, require a more acidic soil.

An inexpensive home pH test kit will give you a general idea of your soil's pH, but a soil test is more precise and reliable.

- If your soil is acidic, you can nudge it toward neutral by mixing in ground-up limestone, simply called lime. Lime is available as a powder, or in easy-to-use pellet form. Adding lime does not give instant results, so it's important to mix it in and allow rain to move it through soil crevices before planting seeds or plants.
- Alkaline soils are harder to modify, and the first step is to add acidic soil amendments such as leaf mold or peat moss. In addition, you can add elemental sulfur as a powder or granules, which will further lower the pH.

Whether your soil is acidic or alkaline, adding organic matter regularly will help bring the pH closer to the neutral mark.

Making Plant-Friendly Soil

Armed with knowledge of your soil texture and pH, you can choose wisely among the methods and materials available for improving it. When you continue the soil-improvement process season after season, it often gives amazing results. Keep in mind that it took thousands of years to form the soil, and it can take several years to transform dead dirt into dream soil. You'll begin to see some improvement right away, and your plants will reflect their satisfaction by showing steady, sturdy growth.

Regardless of your soil's type, the main way to make it better is to increase its organic matter content. Organic matter is made up of decaying plant and animal materials, such as leaves, roots,

dead insects, animal droppings, and just about anything else that was once alive and is now dead. There are four main ways to increase your soil's organic matter content: digging in soil amendments, growing green manures, using organic mulches, and recycling garden and kitchen wastes into soil-building compost. The projects in this chapter provide fun and practical ways to explore each of these options, so you can tailor your choices to suit your personal tastes.

UNDERSTANDING ORGANIC MATTER

Most natural decomposition takes place at the soil's surface, so topsoil contains more organic matter than deeper subsoil. The organic matter content of unimproved topsoil usually hovers around 3 percent, while loamy garden soil contains three times as much. Organic matter feeds a host of soil-dwelling organisms, both large and small—earthworms, insects, fungi, bacteria, and the like. The activities of these organisms enhance the soil both physically and chemically. Earthworms, for example, make tunnels that loosen the soil and improve aeration. Their excretions, called castings, are rich in readily available plant nutrients. Enzymes, acids, and other chemicals result from the biological activities of smaller soil microorganisms. These chemicals become nutrients that are used by plants.

Earthworms and other soil-borne life-forms need oxygen to do their work, so a second function of organic matter is to help hold air in the soil. When you improve soil by adding organic matter, you are creating a better home for plants as well as the organisms that form the foundation of a healthy soil community.

THE SCOOP ON SOIL AMENDMENTS

A soil amendment is a material that you mix into the soil to instantly raise its organic matter content. You can buy soil amendments in bags at garden centers, or you can buy them by the truckload. Sometimes you can scare up a local supply that's free for the taking, such as decomposed peanut shells, cocoa bean hulls, or ground, composted corncobs. Six of the most widely available soil amendments—and how to use them—are described in the "Six Inexpensive Soil Amendments" chart.

Make a Micronutrient Spray

Not all plant fertilizers come in bags, bottles, or jars. Compost is loaded with micronutrients, so it's the perfect starter material for a nutritious foliar-feed spray. Use your compost to make this nutrient-rich tonic.

1. Place 1 gallon of finished, crumbly compost in the bottom of a 5-gallon bucket. Fill the bucket to within 3 inches of the brim with lukewarm water. Stir to combine the compost and water, and cover the bucket with a piece of cloth.

2. Let the compost steep for up to a week, stirring occasionally.

3. Strain out the solids through a piece of window screening. Allow the mixture to settle, and strain again through a double thickness of cheesecloth. Add a few drops of dishwashing liquid to help the mixture stick to plant leaves, and apply it using a clean pump spray bottle.

It's convenient to buy bagged soil amendments, especially if you're in a hurry to create a new garden bed. But what exactly is in those bags of compost, humus, or soil conditioner? You may need to buy a few sample bags to find out, because what one company calls compost may be remarkably similar to what another calls humus. Here is what you are likely to find inside.

- Composted yard waste is made mostly from leaves, which are gathered in the fall and piled into huge heaps, which are turned and watered until they decompose into a soft, fluffy, dark brown to black compost. These products are an excellent choice, because the material still has a little way to go before it is completely decomposed. Purchasing them also supports the recycling of materials that might otherwise end up in landfills.

- Humus can be just about anything, but it often includes blackened chunks of nearly decomposed wood and bark—waste gathered from lumber mills that is mixed with a little soil and then composted. Chunky soil amendments often persist longer in tight clay soil, but they do not give the fast results you are likely to see with finer materials.

- Soil conditioner is a catchall term used on the labels of a range of products. They often are topsoil gathered from floodplains, where the soil is naturally high in organic matter, mixed with other types of compost.

The best advice: Experiment with various products, avoid those that smell rotten or sour, and choose products with light, fluffy textures over those that are heavy and dense.

Once you have a soil amendment, the next step is simple. Spread it over the site you want to improve, and dig it in with a spade or digging fork, lifting and turning until the amendment and the soil are nicely mixed. If you make a habit of digging in organic soil amendments each time you replant a bed or row, your soil will be well on its way to becoming a fertile, fluffy, well-drained medium that is sure to please your plants.

Keep in mind that soil amendments are not the same as fertilizers. Organic fertilizers do add organic matter to the soil as they decompose, but their primary purpose is to provide nutrients.

Health Food for Plants

Organic fertilizers contain such a huge range of ingredients that it's difficult to make generalizations as to what you will find in the package. Like synthetic fertilizers, organic fertilizers include three hyphenated numbers on the label, for example 6-4-4, which is called the fertilizer analysis.

- The first number stands for nitrogen, the main nutrient plants need to make new growth.
- The second number stands for phosphorus, an essential nutrient for vigorous root and bloom development.
- The third number stands for potassium, which supports good overall plant functioning.

Animal by-products are a good natural source of nitrogen, so organic fertilizers with a high first number tend to be based on processed manure from poultry, bats, or even crickets. Fish-based fertilizers also are often rich in nitrogen, as are fertilizers that contain ground cotton or alfalfa seeds. To boost their phosphorus and potassium content, dry organic fertilizers often include pulverized rocks, such as rock phosphate or greensand, a sedimentary, gritty silicate is rich in iron and potassium.

Continued ➡

Powdered seaweed, or liquid seaweed extract, helps to round things out by providing trace nutrients.

Using Organic Fertilizers

There is no single perfect organic fertilizer, and it can be fun to experiment with different products in search of one that is a good fit for your soil, plants, and style of gardening. Always follow the application rates given on the label, because using too much of an organic fertilizer can damage plant roots and cause unnecessary water pollution. If you have very good-quality soil, you may need less fertilizer than the product's label suggests.

When using powdered or granular organic fertilizers, it is also important to thoroughly mix them into the soil. Organic fertilizers do not dissolve rapidly, so inadequate mixing can cause "hot spots" to form around plant roots.

Organic fertilizers break down slowly when soil temperatures are cool, and release more nutrients in warm soil. Sometimes weather conditions cause the sudden release of nutrients, so it's important to watch your plants for signs that they need more or less fertilizer. Underfed plants grow slowly, show pale leaf colors, and may begin blooming while they are still quite small. Overfed plants develop lush stems and leaves, and may produce few flowers and fruits.

Supplemental Liquids

The slow, steady release of nutrients you get with blended organic fertilizers is fine for most plants. If you suspect that a plant is not getting enough nutrients, you can deliver fast relief in the form of a nitrogen-rich, water-soluble organic fertilizer, most of which are made from fish by-products.

These nutrients are immediately available to plants, so liquids are good to have on hand—especially if you are growing a "heavy feeder" like spinach or broccoli in cool soil, or when growing anything in soil that's in the early stages of improvement. Plants get 14 nutrients from the soil, but when they are in need of nutrients, they also can take them up through their leaves. For this reason, be sure to drench both the leaves and roots when giving plants a booster feeding with a liquid organic fertilizer.

Fish-based fertilizers provide abundant, ready-to-use nitrogen, but you may want to feed plants nutrients other than nitrogen in a fast-release liquid form. Kelp and seaweed-based products contain plenty of potassium, but their greatest strength lies in their ability to provide micro nutrients and other growth-enhancing substances. Seaweed sprays are increasingly popular among tomato growers, and trees and shrubs may root a little faster when soaked briefly in water with a little kelp mixed in. Pepper and rose gardeners often supplement their plants' diets with weak Epsom salt sprays (1 tablespoon per gallon of water); Epsom salt is a good source of ready-to-use magnesium and calcium.

The Whole Garden Approach

Don't let this discussion of fertilizers make you think you need to regard your garden as a giant chemistry set. Instead, simply approach soil as a living thing that needs care and nurturance. Healthy soil that contains plenty of organic matter does a superior job of retaining both nutrients and water, so the better your soil becomes, the less concerned you will need to be about the details of plant nutrition.

Getting to Know Your Soil

Soil is wonderfully alive. If you're new to organic gardening, that statement may surprise you. But beneath the surface, healthy soil is full of organisms that interact in a finely tuned living system. Explore your soil. Learn about its texture and structure, and meet the tenants that live there, too. You'll find there's a lot that your soil and its inhabitants can do for your garden—with just a little help from you.

Dig In and Learn

Unless you're the lucky owner of an old farmstead, you probably don't have great soil in your yard and garden. The soil around most modern homes is in trouble, either because of damage during construction or neglect by past owners. But how do you decide what your soil really needs? What would benefit your plants most? And where do you begin?

Get to know your soil. Once you start digging around, you'll find there's more to it than meets the eye. Healthy soil has lots of life in it, a good balance of nutrients available for plants' use, and a loose, open structure. The way you manage and work the soil affects all these aspects of soil health. This chapter introduces some of the organisms you may meet when you take a closer look at your soil. It also explains how to do a few simple tests that can tell you a lot about what's happening in the soil beneath your gardens, lawn, and landscape.

Discover which soil critters are good ones and which ones are bad news. Learn about the structure, texture, drainage, and pH of the soil that surrounds your home. Equipped with this knowledge, you can begin to make smart choices about the soil-care techniques that make the most sense for you, your gardens, your lawn, and your landscape.

The Good Guys in the Ground

As you dig into your soil and become more familiar with its characteristics, you'll undoubtedly encounter some of the many insects and other creatures of all sizes that dwell in the soil's depths. Although they make up only a minute portion of the soil by weight and volume, these living organisms play a vital role in the soil's health. When you meet any of the soil-dwellers shown on this page (and one on the next), squelch your impulse to squash, and let them go safely about their business. These are just a few of the good guys who give gardeners a helping hand in exchange for their housing in the soil.

When you see **fireflies** (*Photuris species*)—commonly called "lightning bugs"—twinkling on a summer evening, be glad for their hungry, soil-dwelling larvae. Resembling sowbugs, firefly larvae prey on slugs, snails, cutworms, and mites. The larvae live in the soil for one to two years before pupating inside a hard brown casing. Firefly adults emerge after about ten days and live for up to one week.

Many of the more than 3,000 species of ground beetles in North America prey on slugs, snails, cutworms, and caterpillars, but few are as voracious as the inch-long and extremely beneficial **fiery searcher** (*Calosoma scrutator*). Fiery searchers can live up to three years, and the adults will often climb trees in search of tent caterpillars to eat!

Millipedes (*Diplopoda* family) can range from ½ to 1½ inches long and move very slowly. Most feed only on decaying plants, breaking them down into organic matter for your soil. As predators, millipedes can eat many kinds of soil insects.

Down-'n-Dirty Soil Dwellers

Of course, not every insect you turn up with your shovel is a beneficial. And it pays to recognize the

Continued ➔

Six Inexpensive Soil Amendments

Material	What it Does	Special Attributes	Risks
Homemade compost	Increases organic matter and provides some major plant nutrients, along with many minor nutrients and enzymes that support strong growth.	The huge range of beneficial fungi and bacteria in compost made from yard and kitchen wastes can help suppress soil-borne diseases.	Weed seeds and some plant diseases can survive in compost that does not heat up as the materials rot.
Commercial compost	Increases organic matter and provides some major plant nutrients, which vary with the material used to make it.	Usually rich in beneficial fungi and bacteria. Large-volume processing creates high heat that kills most weed seeds.	Compost from community yard waste projects can contain slugs or unwanted debris, so check it carefully.
Mushroom compost	Quickly increases organic matter and overall soil fertility.	Usually made from manure-based compost, further "processed" by fungi (mushrooms), which break down potential contaminants.	Unpleasant odor disappears after several days. Working with heavy mushroom compost is often quite messy.
Spoiled hay	Increases organic matter, provides a few plant nutrients, and lightens soil texture by helping to hold in air.	Improves the way the soil handles both air and water due to the strawlike structure of grass stems, hay's main component.	Often contains dormant weed seeds, as well as fungi that can cause respiratory irritation. Wear a dust mask when handling spoiled hay.
Leaf mold	Increases organic matter, improves drainage, and lightens soil texture while enhancing water retention.	Weed free and easy to make at home. Kept moist, shredded leaves become leaf mold in 1 to 2 years.	Tends to acidify the soil's pH, which can be offset by adding lime. Clumps may need to be pulverized to make leaf mold easier to mix into soil.
Rotted sawdust or wood chips	Increases organic matter, lightens soil texture.	Very slow to decompose, which is useful in clay soils in warm climates, where more fine-textured soil amendments disappear quickly.	If not well rotted, may temporarily decrease available nitrogen in the soil. Additional fertilizer may be needed to offset this effect.

Do a Lawn-to-Garden Turnover

If your yard has too much lawn and not enough garden, turn things around by rolling up the turf like a rug.

Why not just till in the grass? Many lawn grasses can't be killed by simply turning them under, and the plant parts that do die will tie up soil nutrients as they decompose. Turf also hosts cutworms, grubs, and other insects that coexist peacefully enough with grass but can devastate tender seedlings. Removing the sod, along with a thin layer of soil, reduces these risks.

Sod is heavy, so begin by cutting the turf into smaller squares. It's easiest to peel sod from moist soil, so be sure to water the area lightly the day before you start this project. Also make appropriate plans for the sod you remove. If it's healthy, you can use it to patch thin areas in other parts of your lawn, or put it to work filling in low spots. Sentence weedy patches to your compost pile.

You Will Need

Tools:

> *Measuring tape, work gloves, garden spade, garden cart or wheelbarrow, digging fork, sturdy bucket, garden rake.*

One 2-pound bag of all-purpose flour

10 cubic feet of compost (about four 40-pound bags)

1. Use the flour to mark a 4 x 6-foot rectangle on the sod you want to remove. Mark additional lines within the space to divide it into 16-inch-wide squares. Wearing shoes with thick soles, use the spade to cut straight down through the lines of flour.
2. Starting at a short end of the rectangle, push the spade into the soil diagonally around all edges of a square of sod. Firmly grab the two outside corners of the square and flip it over toward the inside of the rectangle. Use the spade to lightly chop into the soil to loosen attached clumps. Lift the square of sod straight up, shake out the loosened soil, and then place the sod in the wheelbarrow. Repeat this procedure with the remaining 15 squares.
3. Use the digging fork to loosen the soil to a depth of 10 to 12 inches. Remove large rocks or roots and place them in the bucket.
4. Spread the compost over the soil, raking it into a 4-inch-deep layer. Use the spade or digging fork to mix the compost into the soil, breaking up clods of soil as you work. You will probably need to turn the soil over twice. Rake the enriched soil smooth with the rake, and get ready to plant.

---

bad guys when you run into them, if only because it gives you the option of tossing them out onto bare ground where a hungry bird can find them.

Cabbage maggots (*Delio rodicum*) tunnel into the roots and stems of cabbage and related crops, causing wilting and generally poor productivity. The ¼-inch-long cabbage maggots can survive the winter as pupae in the upper layers of the soil; you can make them freeze to death by cultivating the soil in late winter to expose them to the air.

Symphylans (*Scutigerella immaculata*) are pests that eat the roots of asparagus, cucumber, lettuce, radish, and tomato seedlings. Sometimes called "garden centipedes," symphylans resemble true centipedes but are only ¼ inch long with 12 pairs of legs. Fortunately, symphylan populations rarely reach damaging levels. True centipedes are larger and darker with 15 or more pairs of legs and are beneficials that prey on pest insects and mites.

The **June** or **May beetle grub** (*Phyllophaga species*) feeds on the roots of strawberries and potatoes during the spring and summer and can grow as big as 1 inch long. The grubs may remain in the ground for two years or more before emerging.

There are many different kinds of cutworms, but perhaps the most troublesome and widespread in North America is the **army cutworm** (*Euxoa auxiliaris*). At over 1 inch in length, cutworms are hefty opponents for gardeners trying to protect young plants. The cutworms feed just below the soil surface (or just above it), severing the stems of seedlings and transplants. Dig in the soil around the base of an injured plant and you're likely to find this culprit.

Down where your root crops live, you'll find the ½-inch-long adult **carrot beetle** (*Bothynus ligyrus*), which feeds on the stems and roots of beets, carrots, parsnips, and potatoes.

The small—only ¼ inch long—**subterranean termite** (*Reticulitermes* species) eats the decaying roots of plants and trees and builds tunnels in wood, which can include your house.

Northern mole crickets (*Neocurtilla hexadaetyla*) are mostly destructive, chewing up the roots of crops, eating seeds, and severing the stems of tender transplants. But these 1- to 1½-inch-long crickets also eat other insects.

Colorado potato beetle (*Leptinotarsa decemlineato*) adults and grubs feed on the leaves of potatoes, eggplant, and related crops and spend their winters underground. The adults are ⅓ to ½ inch long, and the grubs are somewhat smaller.

Lawns are the favorite feeding ground for the grubs of the **Japanese beetle** (*Popillio japonica*), so you're most likely to see the ¾-inch grubs when you turn over sod for new garden plots. Treating your lawn with milky disease spores is a safe, long-term control for these pests.

The Wonder of Worms

It's easy to take earthworms for granted because they work out of sight, deep within the soil. But in a year, an acre of worms can move 20 tons of earth. Simply by tunneling through the soil, worms break up compacted earth so that air and water can circulate more freely. They chow down on dead leaves, bits of soil, rotting plants, and other nourishing debris (collectively called organic matter), grinding the material in their gizzards. What comes out the other end is a magical elixir that increases the amount of nutrients and minerals in the soil by as much as ten times the value of the plant debris there.

Worm droppings, known as "castings," are the richest food your plants' roots will ever find. Worm action also creates great texture in soil. As the worms turn raw organic material into humus, the soil becomes moist, loose, and more like the ideal loam plants love. If your soil is healthy, it will be full of earthworms.

Worm Math

To get an estimate of the earthworm population in your soil, dig a hole 8 to 10 inches deep and a foot wide and count the number of earthworms you find in the soil you remove. More than ten earthworms is great, and six to ten indicates a moderately healthy soil, but if you have less than five you need to do some serious work on the soil! This could be an indication of low organic matter, pH problems, and/or poor drainage.

If your earthworm count is low, don't despair. Once you provide more organic material to feed them, they will return. Healthy soil can contain about 1.5 million worms per acre—even more reason not to underestimate the importance of these ambitious decomposers. And if you think that number sounds surprisingly high, consider that worms multiply extremely quickly—producing upward of 2,000 to 3,000 offspring per worm per year.

Hands-On Texture Tests

Pick up a handful of soil. Is it gritty? Sticky? Smooth or greasy? How your soil feels when you hold it in your hand is a function of its texture. Texture refers to the relative amounts of the different-size mineral particles in the soil. Clay particles are the smallest, silt particles are somewhat larger, and sand particles are the biggest.

But these different types of particles do more than make the soil feel a certain way when you stick your toes into it. The size of the particles determines how tightly they bind together and, therefore, how much space there is in the soil for air and water—and for growing roots.

Learning what texture your soil has is as easy as picking up a handful of soil and squeezing it. Start with this simple test: When the earth is moist but not wet, take a loose ball of soil about the size of a golf ball in the palm of your hand. First, squeeze the ball in your hand and release. If it crumbles, it has a reasonably balanced texture. If the soil ball holds its shape, it has a substantial percentage of clay.

Balancing the Soil

Fern Marshall Bradley

Organic gardeners should get down to ground level before they launch their planting plans. Soil care is the heart of the organic method. Fortunately, organic soil care is just a matter of following a few simple principles. The most important one is to build the organic matter content of the soil. In this chapter, you'll find expert tips on just that, as well as on evaluating the soil, cultivating, and dealing with soil problems.

Continued ➡

Sizing Up Your Soil

A good first step is to get to know the soil in your garden. Since it probably won't be too talkative, we asked the experts to explain how to get the most from professional soil tests and how to try simple do-it-yourself tests to learn more about your soil.

Take Your Best Soil Test

If you opt for a professional soil test, keep in mind that the test will only be as good as the sample you submit for testing. "Collecting a good representative soil sample isn't as easy as it looks," claims Vernon Meints, Ph.D., a co-owner of Agri-Business Consultants, a Michigan independent crop consulting firm. Here are three suggestions from Dr. Meints to help you collect the best soil sample:

1. **Divide your gardening space into sections according to what has been planted, then sample each section individually.** For example, take separate samples from areas where you grew fruits, vegetables, or ornamental crops. You may need additional samples within each crop group if you've tried different fertilizer application methods or other practices within them. Dr. Meints has found that even simple practices, such as mulching with organic materials, can alter soil test results.

2. **Sample only as deep as you till.** Dr. Meints says, "Many gardeners think they're tilling deeper than they are, since rotary tillage fluffs the soil." According to Dr. Meints, rotary tillers generally till no more than 3 inches deep, so only take a sample from the top 3 inches.

3. **Timing isn't critical.** "It's more important that the job is done," says Dr. Meints. You may find that fall is the best time to sample, because soils are generally drier in fall than in spring. Also, soil-testing laboratories are less busy in the

What's In the Bag?

While you're in the process of building up your soil, you may need to use fertilizers to help boost your plants. But how do you know if the fertilizer you're buying contains only organic products? Bill Wolf, the president of Necessary Trading Company, a Virginia company that manufactures and sells organic fertilizers, says one good way is to buy from a source you trust for good quality and service. Another good way is to look for the following clues on the fertilizer label:

The words "All-Natural Organic." Look at the fine print where the ingredient are listed. They should be natural ones such as blood meal, poultry litter, bonemeal, natural grains, seaweeds, and other organic products.

An analysis of readily available nitrogen (N), phosphorus (P), and potassium (K) that totals 15 or less. For example, the NPK ratios (listed as three numbers on the label) will be 5-5-5, 4-5-4, or 3-2-3 as a registered analysis. (Some organic lawn fertilizers contain as much as 10 percent nitrogen; the sum of their NPK ratios will be greater than 15.)

---

autumn, and you'll have several months to consider the results and plan a soil-improvement program.

Sniff For Sour-Smelling Soil

Taking a good whiff of your soil can help you judge whether or not you need to worry about having it tested. Shepherd Ogden, a co-owner of The Cook's Garden, a mail-order seed company in Vermont, uses a sniff test to monitor soil pH. Soil pH, which is a measure of the alkalinity or acidity of a soil, is important because it affects how easily nutrients in the soil can be absorbed by plant roots. Most garden plants do best when the soil is in the neutral range, at a pH between 6.0 and 7.0. "When the pH is not right, garden soil smells vinegary or sour, or the odor makes your nose tingle," Ogden explains. If the soil smells good and sweet, Ogden trusts that the pH is probably appropriate for good plant growth. When the soil smells sour, it's time to do a formal soil test.

Breaking Up (Hardpan) Is Hard To Do

Digging deep can reveal hidden problems with your garden soil. If you use a rotary tiller frequently, your soil may have developed a hardpan. A hardpan is a compacted layer of soil below the surface. Water and plant roots can't penetrate a hardpan. Plant growth may suffer, and soil won't drain well. Your soil may also have this problem if it has been driven over by heavy equipment during construction, for example.

Bill Wolf, the president of Necessary Trading Company, a Virginia company that manufactures and sells organic fertilizers, offers advice on how to detect a hardpan. "Using a trowel or shovel, examine the soil around perennial plants, in the root zone. Look for roots that suddenly turn sideways: That's where the compacted layer is," says Wolf. You can also insert a probe, such as a metal crowbar, into your garden soil. When you feel sudden pressure—it's usually at the depth of tillage—you'll know you hit the hardpan. Note the depth to compaction at several sites. If you find a hardpan layer, you can break it up by digging through it with a garden fork. For large areas with hardpans, plowing with a chisel plow is a more feasible solution.

Should You Squash or Save?

Turn a shovelful of garden soil or just scratch the surface, and you'll discover an underground living world. Thousands of insects and related creatures thrive in the dark, moist soil environment. Linda Gilkeson, Ph.D., the Integrated Pest Management Coordinator for the British Columbia Ministry of Environment, explains that soil animals can be beneficials you should save or pests you should destroy. Most beneficials either help control pests or help decompose organic matter. "Many gardeners don't know that soil-dwelling beneficials, like ground beetles, are standing guard between their garden plants and the pests," says Dr. Gilkeson.

You'll help your soil and your garden plants by encouraging a diverse population of organisms in your soil. You can encourage the good guys by minimizing soil disturbance and using organic mulches. Take the time to learn to tell pests from beneficials so you'll know which creatures to preserve and which to destroy when you're digging in the garden. Here's a short squash/save list of common garden soil inhabitants.

Squash armyworms. Armyworms are greenish brown caterpillars with white stripes on their sides and dark- or light-colored stripes on their back. They feed on garden plants at night. During the day, they hide in plant foliage or just beneath the soil surface.

Save centipedes and millipedes. These are serpentine creatures from ½ inch to 5 inches long, with many legs. Both are important predators and decomposers in the soil ecosystem. They consume dead plant materials. You'll find them among leaf litter or in any damp, dark spot.

Squash Colorado potato beetles. Adults have yellow wing covers with ten black stripes. Larvae are orangey, humpbacked grubs, with black spots on their sides. Larvae eat potato foliage, quickly defoliating potato plants. You'll find adults and pupae in soil where potatoes are grown.

Squash cutworms. These are fat, greasy-looking, gray or dull brown, 1- to 2-inch-long caterpillars with shiny heads. They are often confused with armyworms. They chew through stems of vegetable and flower seedlings at night. During the day, they rest just below the soil surface.

Save earthworms. Most garden species are less than 5 inches long. Look for red, gray, and brown worms at and beneath the soil surface. Many feed upon decomposing organic matter, transporting it through their burrows and redistributing it throughout the soil.

Save ground beetles. Adults are blue-black or brown, ¾- to 1-inch-long beetles. Larvae are dark brown or black and grublike but slender. Adults and larvae prey on other insects and pests, including slugs. Some species eat weed and vegetable seeds. Spread organic mulches to attract them.

Squash grubs. Grubs are the larvae of Japanese beetles, June or May beetles, and other beetles. They are wormlike, fat, C-shaped, and most often white with a dark-colored head. They munch on both living and dead plant roots. You'll find them in soil beneath lawns.

Save rove beetles. These resemble earwigs without rear pincers. The hard wing covers are shortened, leaving the abdomen exposed. Length ranges from $1/25$ to $1/10$ inch. Most rove beetles are insect pest predators. You'll find them under rocks, in moss or fungi, and in compost piles and organic mulches.

Squash slugs and snails. Both slugs and snails are soft-bodied and wormlike, measuring ⅛ to 8

Continued ➡

Where's the Nitrogen?

Don't be surprised if your soil test results come back from the lab without a reading for nitrogen. Even though this nutrient is essential for healthy plant growth, most soil labs don't include nitrogen as part of their basic test. That's because the nitrogen content of your soil can change dramatically and quickly. If you want a test of the nitrogen in your soil, you usually have to request it; you'll pay a few dollars more for this test.

If test results show that your soil doesn't have enough nitrogen, you can help your soil and your plants by adding more organic matter in the form of compost and appropriate amounts of nitrogen-rich fertilizers such as animal manures, bloodmeal, or alfalfa meal.

Too Much of a Good Thing

When it comes to soil nutrients, experts agree that most gardeners go too far in boosting nitrogen. The result is big lush plants but few flowers or fruits. Plants will basically take up all the nitrogen you feed them, and those overfertilized plants are also more susceptible to insect and disease problems.

So, go easy on the nitrogen. An inch or so of compost per year—a little more if you have extremely sandy soil—is enough to maintain the necessary level of organic matter you need to get good yields in most northern soils.

Down South, however, it's a different story. Organic matter in the soil just burns right up in the hot, humid conditions and long growing season. As a result, southern gardeners can apply compost and manure much more freely.

And if a soil test reveals "excessive" nitrogen, simply cut back on the organic matter, grow lots of nitrogen-hungry crops such as sweet corn, potatoes, and lettuce and let the rain and those "heavy feeder" crops take care of the problem.

inches long. Snails have a spiral-shaped shell into which they withdraw when disturbed; slugs lack a shell. Both lay clear, jellylike egg masses under stones and other debris. They feed at night on most aboveground plant parts, leaving behind a shiny trail of mucous slime.

Building Soil Fertility

An easy way to boost soil organic matter content is to spread organic materials on the soil surface and let nature do the rest. One of the best organic materials to add is compost.

You can also use living plants to add to soil fertility. Green manure crops are crops that you sow specifically to turn back into the soil to boost soil health. Living mulch is a cover crop sown among your garden crops to help suppress weeds and conserve soil moisture. We asked the experts how to get the best results from added organic material, green manures, and living mulch.

GIVE SOIL A BOOST, NOT A BLAST

Just because a little of something is good for your garden soil doesn't mean that a little more is

better. Paul Sachs, the owner of North Country Organics, a Vermont wholesale supplier of natural soil amendments, likes to remind gardeners of the saying "Everything in moderation." According to Sachs, "Everything you add to soil, including organic fertilizers and compost, has a threshold where it's not helpful anymore and possibly begins doing harm." For example, if you add too much phosphorus-rich fertilizer to the soil, the phosphorus can combine chemically with other important micronutrients such as iron and manganese, making them unavailable to your plants.

Always determine the proper application rate for soil amendments. Excess fertilizer is just another name for pollution. "Even compost will leach nitrates [soluble nitrogen compounds] into groundwater if you're not careful," reminds Sachs.

Use compost as a general-purpose garden fertilizer, but don't overapply. On bare soil, avoid spreading it more than 2 inches thick. You can apply more compost later in the season, when garden plants are established and ready to soak up nitrogen released from the compost.

PLANT A GARDEN OF BUCKWHEAT

Buckwheat is a versatile cover crop that you can use all season long. Miriam Klein-Hansen, who taught homestead gardening at the National Center for Appropriate Technology in Montana, suggests using buckwheat as a living mulch around cabbage-family plants. In spring, sprinkle buckwheat seed between broccoli, cabbage, and cauliflower transplants, leaving about 8 inches of bare soil around each transplant stem.

Klein-Hansen uses a hoe to cut the buckwheat from its roots at the midpoint of its flowering period, when bottom seeds have set. These seeds give a second buckwheat "planting" that prevents late weeds from getting established. Klein-Hansen's husband, David, turns the buckwheat under in the fall before planting winter rye over the whole garden. As they decay, the buckwheat plants feed the soil, particularly with phosphorus, which the plants accumulate as they grow. Klein-Hansen says, "I only have to weed about twice a season. After a couple of years of buckwheat/buckwheat/rye, we find almost no witchgrass [quackgrass]."

SET LIMITS WITH LIVING MULCH

Use caution with living mulch, or it can become a living nightmare. "The only good living mulch is one you've killed," says Robert F. Becker, a retired associate professor at Cornell University's New York Agricultural Experiment Station in Geneva. "Living mulches are hard to control. They can get away from you and begin competing with the crops." To avoid problems with having mulch that takes over the garden, Becker suggests waiting to seed the mulch after crops are already well-established.

Becker also recommends sowing oats as a cover crop in areas where you've harvested peas and other early crops. "The nice thing about oats is that they winter-kill," says Becker. "You don't have to deal with them in the spring. Unless, of course, it's a wet spring. The oat covering can impede drying of the soil, so I rake up the dead plants and remove them from the soil surface."

ADD NITROGEN NATURALLY

A great way to build soil fertility is to have your plants do it for you. Legumes like peas, beans, and alfalfa are plants that can transform nitrogen from the atmosphere into nitrogen compounds that can be absorbed by plant roots. Because of this, they don't need as much nitrogen added in the form of fertilizer. But to "fix" nitrogen, the legume roots

must associate with certain kinds of soil-dwelling bacteria. You can add these bacteria to the soil—a technique known as inoculating soil. In mail-order catalogs and at some garden supply centers, you can find soil inoculants specifically formulated for various cover crops and leguminous vegetable

Soil Testing—The Ph.D. Level

Many soil testing services don't provide specific organic recommendations to remedy any problem your soil test reveals, but there are a number of soil testing services that will. For a slightly higher fee than most local testing services, these labs will provide a more complete and customized package of information and instructions. They'll tell you exactly how much of which organic amendments you need to add to your soil. So if you're looking for premium, top-of-the-line organic soil testing, here are three services to consider:

Peaceful Valley Farm Supply
P.O. Box 2209
Grass Valley, CA 95945
(916) 272-4769

Peaceful Valley offers an initial soil test (which includes all the usual things like pH, organic matter, etc.) along with a 15-page booklet *Know Your Soil: A Handbook for Understanding Your Soil Test Report* written by noted organic farm adviser Amigo Cantisano. The booklet is keyed to your soil test results; once you have the booklet, your cost for soil tests in future years is reduced. The staff will be glad to answer your questions.

Timberleaf Soil Testing Services
26489 Ynez Road, Suite C-197
Temecula, CA 92591
(909) 677-7510

Timberleaf's basic soil test includes all the major plant nutrients, plus organic matter, pH, and several special tests not usually included in the lower-cost state lab packages. Your test results also include a customized report that will tell you exactly how much of any recommended soil amendments to apply, and you are entitled to one year of free consultation, as well.

Wallace Laboratories
365 Coral Circle
El Segundo, CA 90245
(310) 615-0116

Wallace Laboratories' "basic" soil test includes the usual things like NPK, pH, and salinity, plus 27 other plant nutrients. Your soil is also tested for potentially toxic elements such as arsenic, aluminum, and lead.

Quick Tip

Every bag of fertilizer has three numbers connected with hyphens on the label, such as 6-2-0. Those numbers are the NPK ratio—the percentages of nitrogen, phosphorus, and potassium in the fertilizer. Organic fertilizers have lower numbers than synthetic types because the numbers show the amount of nutrients that will be available *in the first year*. Organic fertilizers release nutrients slowly, giving your plants more nutrients in the long run.

Continued ➡

crops. However, Marianne Sarrantonio, Ph.D., the legume project coordinator for the Rodale Institute Research Center in Pennsylvania, cautions gardeners not to rely solely on inoculants to supply nitrogen for their bean crops. "Beans are poor nitrogen fixers," she explains. "They'll only fix about 30 to 50 percent of what they need."

Follow these four guidelines to get the best results with inoculants:

1. Be sure you buy the right inoculant for the legume you plan to plant. It's a good idea to buy the inoculant from your seed supplier to be sure of getting the right match.

2. Check for an expiration date. Store the inoculant in the refrigerator, and use it as soon as possible.

3. To use an inoculant, pour legume seeds in a bucket and mix them with enough water to moisten the surface. Add the inoculant and stir until the seeds are coated. You can refrigerate coated seed for short periods, but it is best to mix only enough to plant immediately. Plant as usual.

4. The bacteria can usually survive in garden soil for four years without a host. If you wait longer than that between plantings, re-inoculate.

Working with Your Soil

Is your soil everything you want it to be? Unfortunately, most of us will answer no. The organic matter content may be low, or perhaps the topsoil layer is only 3 inches thick. Or maybe your soil is so high in clay content that it is full of rocklike clods. What can you do? There aren't always easy answers, but we asked our advisers for schemes for improving problem soils. We also collected their opinions on the best ways to cultivate the soil.

CLAY CAN STRENGTHEN SANDY SOIL

Sandy soil can benefit from added clay and organic matter. "I follow the adage that 'a load of clay is like a load of manure to a sandy soil,'" explains Eliot Coleman, an organic farmer and author of *The New Organic Grower*. "If clay isn't readily available, adding organic matter is the next best alternative," You'll have to have some idea of how much clay your soil already contains and how much heavier you want it to be. For example, a sandy loam soil—considered excellent for gardening—is composed of roughly 65 percent sand, 20 percent silt, and only 15 percent clay.

Coleman figures it this way: You can boost a sandy soil's clay content 25 percent by spreading a 1-inch layer of clay over the surface of your garden and tilling it into the top 4 inches of the soil. Add less clay for a lighter effect. To keep your soil in good shape, add clay the first year, and follow it with annual applications of organic matter. Contact a local landscape supplier, who can deliver clay by the truckload. Be sure to specify that you don't want wet clay.

OUTSMART CLAY SOIL

Soils with high clay content can be heavy and hard to work. Nino Ridgway, the owner of Squeaky Green Organic Produce, who raises organic vegetables on a heavy clay soil in Wisconsin, offers three time-tested rules for dealing with heavy soil:

1. "The best way to improve a clay soil is to add organic matter. And the best way to add organic matter is to grow it in the field," says Ridgway. She sows cover crops, such as buckwheat or rye, then tills them in when they're several inches tall. Ridgway advises, "A good rule of thumb for gardeners is to keep 10 to 20 percent of their garden space in a cover crop each year."

2. Stay away when your soil is wet! If your soil is wet, don't even enter your garden. Ridgway says, "You're shooting yourself in the foot if you go ahead and work it, because it turns to concrete and requires one or more years to mend."

3. Maintain a surface mulch—even a thin layer—to break the impact of raindrops. The mulch will help prevent the crust that forms after a rainstorm. Ridgway says, "Even a light mulch of fine grass clippings is enough to improve the germination rate of fine-seeded crops like carrots, which don't like a soil crust."

IT COULD BE A SAND TRAP

Can you improve the rate at which your soil drains by mixing in sand? "That could be the wrong thing to do," says Bonnie Lee Appleton, Ph.D., an associate professor and extension horticulturist at Virginia Polytechnic Institute and State University. "A little sand impairs drainage," she says. "If you want to improve drainage using sand, it takes huge amounts—60 to 80 percent of the soil needs to be sand." For example, in order to boost the sand component of the top 5 to 8 inches of your soil by 5 to 10 percent, you would need to add 3 to 5 tons of sand per 1,000 square feet of garden. So skip the sand, and stick with a regular plan for adding organic matter, suggests Dr. Appleton.

TRY SIMPLE "SINGLE DIGGING"

If your soil is too sandy or is heavy with clay, double digging is the classic way to improve it. This method of shoveling aside the top layer of soil and loosening the subsoil improves aeration, and you can work in plenty of compost or other organic materials as you dig. However, at the Rodale Institute and Research Center in Pennsylvania, Eileen Weinsteiger, the garden project manager, found that double digging soil "wasn't worth it, because our soil was already in such good condition after many years of organic gardening." Weinsteiger explains, "Double digging improves poor soil, but it's time-consuming, so I don't recommend it unless you're gardening at an unproductive or unimproved site."

You may want to try the same simple method that Weinsteiger follows to manage soil in garden beds at the research center: Each spring, turn the soil to a depth of 1 foot. That's the depth of most garden shovels. Use your foot to push the shovel in, then turn the clump of soil. You can dig in compost or green manures at the same time.

Beds *don't* require annual digging if they're free of weeds and other vegetation or if the soil is in the fluffy condition that's best for planting. Do dig annually to bury cover crops and old vegetation, to add fertilizers, or to reshape the beds (if they need it) after a long winter.

TAKE IT EASY WITH TILLING

Frequent tillage at the same soil depth can cause the development of a hardpan, a compacted layer of soil below the surface. Hardpans prevent root penetration, and they're difficult to remedy. Paul Sachs, the owner of North Country Organics, a Vermont wholesale supplier of natural soil amendments, says, "Rotary tillage is not necessarily the soil's best friend. Overtillage really depletes soil organic matter. When you till, don't till too deeply, and alter the depth of tillage to prevent the formation of a hardpan." Sachs adds that rotating garden crops with green manure crops also helps alleviate soil compaction and maintain soil organic matter content.

Overtillage is hardest on soils with high clay content. The more clay your soil contains, the less you should till. If you're starting a new garden area, till the first year to break up sod or to work in loads of organic materials or soil amendments. In following years, continue adding organic materials or growing green manures, and work them in by hand whenever possible.

When you have to till, shallow tillage is better than deep. For example, the first tilling in spring could be to a depth of 4 inches. If you put in a second crop during the season, till only 1 inch deep to make a seedbed, or just rake the surface. Over time, you may find that your soil becomes loose and open enough that you can retire your tiller for good.

Soil-Care Secrets

If you've been piling a lot of stuff on your garden in the hopes of super-charging your soil, you could be unwittingly changing the soil's pH level or adding too much of one nutrient and not enough of another. On the other hand, if you've been largely ignoring your soil's fertility and hoping for the best, you may be cheating yourself out of optimum harvests, a lush landscape, or the best blooms. Check out the soil-care secrets in this chapter—you won't want to ignore your soil or overfertilize it anymore!

Getting Serious About Soil

Let's start with one of the best-kept secrets in gardening: the inexpensive soil tests available to most North American gardeners and farmers through their local cooperative extension offices or similar agencies. In most areas, you can get a fairly comprehensive test done for between $5 and $10—less than you'd probably spend for a bag of fertilizer. And a soil test may tell you that you don't even need to ass that fertilizer (or that you need to exchange it for something different)!

GETTING TESTED

How you go about getting your soil tested—and the kind of information you'll get back from a soil test—depends on where you live. Start with a call to your local cooperative extension office or the soil conservation service office in your area. You'll usually find these agencies listed in the government pages of your phone book. If you find that soil testing isn't readily available in your region, ask about private testing labs near you. But get your soil tested as close to home as possible so that the recommendations you'll receive make sense for your climate and soil.

Continued ➡

Exactly what's included in each area's basic test will vary because: 1) each region's system is set up differently; 2) different soil scientists attach higher significance to some things and less to others; and 3) soils and their problems really do vary from one region to the next—what might be a common problem in one locale might not even be an issue somewhere else. Take salt, for example. Because salts tend to build up in western soils from their lack of rain, western labs routinely measure a soil's salt levels. In the East, however, any salts in the soil are almost always quickly washed away by rain, so eastern labs don't routinely test for them.

Such regional differences are exactly why it pays to have your soil tested by a lab in your little corner of the world (or close to it). Some state labs even (or only) send a copy of your test results to your local county extension office; that way the agents there have immediate access to your report if you call asking for guidance.

Don't Forget to Inoculate

Some cover crops are special plants called legumes (sweet clover and alfalfa are two examples). Legumes transform nitrogen from the air into nitrogen compounds that plants can use, with the help of bacteria called nitrogen-fixing bacteria. This helps you because it means you don't have to work as hard to add nitrogen to the soil.

These special bacteria may or may not be present in the soil already. There are many different strains, and the only way to ensure that the right strain is there when you plant a legume cover crop is to put it there yourself when you plant. To do so, you'll need to buy an inoculant, a commercially produced powder that contains the bacteria. All you have to do is coat the cover crop seed with inoculant and then plant. Once you've grown a particular kind of legume in your garden, the nitrogen-fixing bacteria it needs will persist in the soil for three to five years.

A Crop that Feeds the Garden
Roger Yepsen

Even in chilly northern winters, the garden can be sown with annual rye (*Lolium multiflora*) as a cover crop that will resist erosion, control weeds, and then lend its organic matter to the soil. If done over a few winters, the result will be improved structure and aeration, and more activity by a variety of beneficial subterranean life from earthworms to fungi. Rye also contributes some nutrients, although it isn't a nitrogen builder like leguminous cover crops.

1. At summer's end, rake the beds to smooth the soil and remove plant debris.

2. Hand-sow 2 to 3 ounces of annual rye seed per 100 square feet of garden area. This will go more easily if you mix the seed with sand or friable soil.

3. Rake the seedbed.

4. In spring, from 2 to 4 weeks before you put out seeds or plants, mow the rye and turn it under.

What Soil Tests Test For

When you get a soil test kit from your extension office and mail off your soil sample, the lab runs tests to determine what your soil's pH level is and what nutrients are found. The test results usually describe whether the nutrients are present in low, medium, high, or excessive quantities. Follow the recommendations that come with the soil test results when you need to use fertilizers or amendments to build nutrient levels in the soil, or apply the amounts listed on the package. There's no advantage to overfertilizing your soil, and there is a good risk that you'll do more harm than good. Here are some of the nutrients most commonly tested for, along with tips on correcting deficiencies of these important plant "foods":

Phosphorus. Phosphorus is extremely important for healthy plant growth—without it, plants will be stunted. Sandy or shale soils that don't contain much organic matter are most likely to be phosphorus-deficient. If your soil test indicates a low amount of phosphorus, you can add bonemeal or rock phosphate to your soil and work it in to the top 6 to 8 inches. Follow the recommendations that come with your soil test results to know how much to add, and don't overdo it. Phosphorus doesn't leach out of the soil like some nutrients—once it's in the soil, it stays there. Applying too much phosphorus can throw your soil out of balance for a long time.

Potassium. Potassium helps plants fight disease, strengthens their stalks, and improves the quality of fruits and seeds. As with phosphorus, the soil most likely to be potassium-deficient is sandy with little organic matter. To help correct low levels of potassium, add manure, seaweed meal, or greensand to the soil before you plant your spring garden.

Calcium. This mineral is a major component of a plant's cell walls. The most common soil that is low in calcium is acid, sandy soil along the sea coasts. Adding limestone to this soil type helps raise the calcium level and raises the pH, too.

Sulfur. Sulfur is a major part of all living organic matter, so it's no surprise that soils low in organic matter are low in sulfur. Plants need sulfur to make proteins to survive, and nitrogen needs to have enough sulfur to feed your plants. Without sulfur your plants are in big trouble, but you can easily increase soil sulfur levels by adding manures or gypsum.

Magnesium. Magnesium helps make up chlorophyll (the stuff that makes plants green), which helps plants make food. Sandy, acid soils may be low in magnesium and will benefit from additions of dolomitic limestone (also called magnesium lime), which also raises pH.

The Ups and Downs of pH

The most common factor that labs test soil for is pH level. A soil's pH is simply a measure of its acidity or alkalinity. A pH reading of 7.0 is neutral; numbers higher than 7.0 indicate your soil is alkaline; numbers lower than 7.0 mean your soil is acidic. If a soil is extremely alkaline, it doesn't matter how rich in nutrients it is because those nutrients will be tied up and your growing plants won't be able to absorb them. The ideal pH for most plants to grow in ranges from 6.2 to 7.0. This is the range where nutrients are most available for uptake by the plant's roots.

If your soil is too acidic, your soil test report will probably tell you to add lime to raise the pH. But another portion of the test results should determine what kind of lime you choose.

If your soil's magnesium levels are okay, the lab will probably tell you to add calcitic lime. But if your soil needs magnesium, you'll probably want to add dolomitic lime (also called magnesium lime) to correct both problems.

If your soil is too alkaline, the test results may tell you to add sulfur to lower its pH. For use as a soil amendment you'll want to choose pelleted or granular sulfur, which is also known as garden sulfur. Stay away from the very finely ground sulfur that is sold to be mixed with water and sprayed onto plants as a fungicide. It's so finely ground that it can be a health hazard if you don't wear protective equipment when you handle it.

Soil Amendments

Adding the recommended nutrients to your soil will benefit your plants, whether they're flowers, herbs, vegetables, or grass. But that's only part of the picture. You also need to deal with the texture of your soil—whether it's heavy clay, light and airy sand, or somewhere in between.

If your soil texture test reveals problems with compaction, low humus, poor drainage, or poor water and air retention, the solution is to add organic matter. You can choose from a wide range of materials to help you boost your soil's condition, so make your selection based on the availability, cost, and ease of handling of the amendments you're considering.

Compost. Compost is a popular amendment because it is so cost-effective. You can buy compost or make your own. When compost is mixed into soil, the soil resists compaction and drains quickly yet still retains an enormous amount of water. Compost is very easy to spread throughout the garden.

Leaves. If you don't want to bother with making a compost pile and have a lot of extra leaves on the ground, you have the next best thing to compost. Just shred up those leaves and dig them into your soil. Most leaves are acidic but will not add enough acidity to significantly affect soil pH.

Manure. The wonder of animal manure, with its large amount of nutrients, will never cease to impress gardeners, but you should only add manure that has been aged for more than six months.

Peat moss. Another soil amendment that can help your garden is peat moss. Peat moss has a very low pH—3.0 to 4.5—which makes it good to spread around acid-loving plants such as rhododendrons, blueberries, and pines.

Mulch—It's Good for Soil and Plants

Mulching is one of the best things you can do for your gardens—whether you're growing vegetables, flowers, shrubs, or trees. Covering your soil with a thick layer of organic matter can block weed growth, keep the soil cool and moist, and—as the mulch decays—feed both the soil and the plants growing in it. But it pays to know which mulch is the right one to use in each specific gardening situation.

Grass. Freshly cut grass clippings are rich in nitrogen and other nutrients that will feed your plants as the clippings decompose. Warm-loving crops like peppers, tomatoes, and eggplants all do well with grass-clipping mulch. If your lawn can't supply enough grass clippings for your garden, check with a local lawn care service or a neighbor and see if you can get clippings.

Newspaper. Remove and recycle the slick-paper color supplements from your Sunday paper and what you've got left is a super-effective weed-suppressing mulch. Paper can keep down weeds for two summers and can be used instead of black plastic to heat up

Continued ➡

cool spring sod. Use newspaper mulch around veggies such as sweet corn, soybeans, and tomatoes. Raspberries grow well with shredded newspaper mulch, too. And the moist, dark soil under a mulch of newspaper is an earthworm paradise!

Wood chips. You can chip them yourself with a chipper/shredder, or buy them. The best place to use wood chips is in perennial beds and on garden paths. They're durable and work best where the soil isn't tilled or turned often. If you do use them in a vegetable garden, keep them on the surface. When turned under, wood chips can take up to a year to decompose and they tie up nitrogen so your plants can't absorb it.

Bark. Tree bark mulch lasts longer than wood chips because the bark sheds water rather than holding it. Bark also keeps the soil cool. Because bark has a nice appearance, use it to protect the soil in spots where you want to make a good impression—like your prized flowerbeds. Don't use bark around tomato plants; it can be harmful to them.

Pine needles. Pine needles can be a great mulch, and they're easy to get where pine trees grow. Boughs from spruce, fir, and pine trees make excellent winter mulch in northern flower gardens, protecting fall-planted pansies that you hope to overwinter and rebloom in spring.

Straw. Straw mulch has been proven to be a boon to tomatoes, preventing diseases such as anthracnose, leaf spot, and early blight from leaving their ugly marks on this favorite garden vegetable. Straw also works very well as an insulator, protecting crops such as carrots, parsnips, and potatoes that folks without root cellars leave in the ground during the cold months.

Others. Although compost, shredded leaves, and manure are most commonly used as soil amendments to add nutrients and improve soil texture, you can also use them as mulches. They provide nutrients and weed control, but many times they do more good when they're worked into the soil.

Soil Management

Care for the soil, and the soil will care for your plants. Plants growing in healthy, organically managed soil are lush, green, and vigorous. In contrast, plants growing in poor soil that lacks nutrients are often small and weak, sometimes even discolored, stunted, and deformed. Not a pretty sight!

Signs of Soil Trouble

In this chapter you'll learn to recognize some of the signals from plants that indicate nutrient deficiencies in the soil. And you'll discover how to use special plants called cover crops to build the richest soil ever.

Just as your doctor studies your symptoms to figure out the cause of an illness, gardeners learn to diagnose plant problems by looking for key signs. When nutrients are lacking in the soil, your plants will tell you. Not with words, of course, but by displaying symptoms that often point directly to the missing nutrient.

Some of these nutritional deficiencies look very similar, so to confirm your diagnosis, you may want to have your soil tested (that way you'll save the time and cost of adding nutrients that your soil doesn't need). And remember that overdoing nutrients can cause just as many problems as deficiencies can—more is definitely not better where fertilizers are concerned. Here are six deficiencies and what to do about them.

NITROGEN-DEFICIENCY SYMPTOMS

Tomatoes. Plants grow slowly and the leaves are small, light greenish and/or yellowish. Top leaves may be light green with purple veins. Flower buds turn yellow and drop off. Fruits are often small.

Corn. Leaves are light green (instead of a nice dark green) or have yellowish center streaks, and growth is stunted. The lower leaves are usually affected first; they will gradually become dry and brown and fall off.

Potatoes. The leaves and stems turn light green or pale yellow. The young top leaves may curl upward and the plant itself is stunted. At harvesttime, the tubers will be small.

Cucumbers. Leaves turn yellow. Vines don't set very much fruit, and any fruit that is produced is light in color and pointy at the blossom end (the part farthest from the vine).

NITROGEN REMEDIES

Fast fix. Scratch some alfalfa meal, composted animal manure, bloodmeal, or other high-nitrogen organic fertilizer into the surface of the soil around the plants. Or water the plants with a diluted solution of fish emulsion or spray it directly on the foliage. A warning here: If you add too much nitrogen, you'll get all plant and no fruit, especially with tomatoes. So be sure you don't overdo it.

Long-term cure. Growing and then turning under a nitrogen-fixing cover crop of clover, vetch, or peas is one of the best ways to add nitrogen to your garden. Another good way to build up the nitrogen content of your beds is with generous supplies of compost, well-rotted manure, or other nitrogen-rich organic materials, preferably added in the fall.

PHOSPHORUS-DEFICIENCY SYMPTOMS

Tomatoes. Plants grow slowly. Leaves are dark green on top but have purple undersides. Seedlings grow very slowly.

Corn. Stalks are small and the leaves turn purple at the tips and along the margins.

Potatoes. Leaves and stems are somewhat stunted and darker green than normal. Leaves may curl upward. At harvesttime, there may be irregular brown specks inside your potatoes, many radiating outward from the core. (Note: Viruses and/or extreme temperatures can cause similar specks.)

PHOSPHORUS REMEDIES

Fast fix. Foliar feed with liquid bonemeal or work dry bonemeal or rock phosphate into the soil where roots can reach it. If you had this problem last year and haven't planted yet, add these materials to your planting holes and furrows as soon as possible.

Long-term cure. Low levels of organic matter and/or extremes of soil pH (too acid or alkaline) can worsen phosphorus deficiencies. Normally, earthworms, bacteria, and other soil-dwelling organisms will break down organic matter and release its plentiful supplies of phosphorus to the plants. But extremes of soil pH will limit the activity of these creatures and thus inhibit the availability of phosphorus. So test your soil's pH—it may have to be adjusted for any long-term remedy to be effective.

If your soil is too acid, work in some limestone; if it's too alkaline, add sulfur. Build up the organic matter content of your soil. You may also need to add some rock phosphate.

POTASSIUM-DEFICIENCY SYMPTOMS

Tomatoes. Leaves become dark green, stems stay small, and leaves are bunched together (the leaves themselves may crinkle and curl upward). Older leaves become yellow, then brown at the edges. Fruits fall off the vine soon after ripening, have hard, blotchy flesh, and ripen unevenly.

Corn. Lower leaf tips and edges will become scorched and brown. Plants will grow slowly and have poorly developed root systems. Stalks will be weak, diseased, or both and often become so stressed that they snap off.

Potatoes. Growth is slow and plant growth is stunted. Leaves are very dark green in color. The leaves may turn brown at the edges and eventually die.

POTASSIUM REMEDIES

Fast fix. Scratch kelp meal or wood ashes into the soil around plants. With wood ashes, be sure to apply them only once every two or three years in any particular area to avoid creating soil imbalances.

Long-term cure. Build up potassium levels in your soil by adding some well-aged compost and/or composted manure. You can also enrich your garden beds with granite meal (a fine rock powder obtained from granite quarries)—it's a good source of slow-release potassium.

CALCIUM-DEFICIENCY SYMPTOMS

Tomatoes. Blossom-end rot (the formation of a dry, brown spot on the part of the fruit opposite the stem). Tips of new shoots are stunted and distorted.

CALCIUM REMEDIES

Fast fix. Water tomatoes evenly and regularly to allow calcium to reach the tomato flower at time of fruit formation.

Long-term cure. Add crushed eggshells (do you live close to a restaurant that serves breakfast?) to your compost or work crushed oyster shells or ground limestone into your garden beds—preferably in the fall or at least before planting.

MAGNESIUM-DEFICIENCY SYMPTOMS

Tomatoes. Older leaves turn yellow while the leaf veins stay dark green. Yellow areas eventually turn brown and die. Very few flowers and fruits form on the plant.

Beans. Older leaves turn yellow while the leaf veins stay dark green. Yellow areas eventually turn brown and die. Very few flowers and fruits form on the plant.

MAGNESIUM REMEDIES

If your soil is also deficient in potassium, work Sul-Po-Mag (mined sulfate of potash-magnesia) into the root zone of the affected plants. If your soil is acidic (pH under 6), work in dolomitic lime to raise the pH and add magnesium at the same time.

IRON-DEFICIENCY SYMPTOMS

Tomatoes. Youngest leaves turn yellow between the veins. Later, the whole leaf turns yellow, but older leaves remain green.

IRON REMEDIES

Fast fix. Foliar feed with a liquid seaweed product.

Long-term cure. Alkaline soils that are poorly aerated or over-limed can be low in iron. Add sulfur to reduce soil alkalinity. If your soil is not alkaline, use iron sulfate.

Continued ➡

Keep Soil in Shape with Cover Crops

You can help keep your soil healthy and your plants happy by planting cover crops in your vegetable and annual flowerbeds. Cover crops are crops grown to protect and enrich the soil and to control weeds. You "harvest" organic matter and nutrients from cover crops by tilling the plants back into the soil. The optimum plan is to have a vigorous cover crop growing whenever you're not growing vegetables or flowers. In most areas in the United States, that means late fall through early spring, although in some southern areas, it may mean exactly the reverse—growing your cover during summer.

Here are eight great reasons to include cover crops in your garden plans:

Cover crops provide nitrogen. Nitrogen is what puts the green in your greens. It's also the plant food most likely to be deficient in sandy soil or any type of soil that's low in organic matter.

Cover crops add organic matter. As you now know, a high level of organic matter in soil provides nutrients, helps conserve water, and improves soil structure.

Cover crops protect against erosion. The top layer of your garden soil—the most fertile part—can slip away when assaulted by the winds and rain of winter. A cover crop holds it in place.

Cover crops catch nutrients. If your area gets heavy winter rains, important plant nutrients may literally be washed out of your soil. Plant a cover crop in the fall to take up these nutrients and release them back to the soil when you turn that crop under the following spring.

Cover crops break up compacted soil. Some cover crops, such as sweet clover and alfalfa, have thick, deep taproots, which can be very effective at breaking up hard soil.

Cover crops control weeds. Planting a vigorous cover crop such as vetches and crimson clover may well be the easiest way to beat troublesome weeds.

Cover crops attract beneficials. Many cover crops provide protection and food for beneficial insects that help control pests in your garden.

Cover crops can be an effective mulch. Grow vetch, rye, or a combination of the two in your garden, mow it or let it die back naturally (either by completing its life cycle or from winter cold) and you have a ready-to-go mulch that will retain moisture as it controls weeds. Till a narrow strip through it, or punch holes right into the mulch for your transplants.

PUTTING ON THE COVER

Now that you're convinced of the advantages of growing a cover crop on your garden, here's how to go about it:

1. **Sow it.** Seeds left on top of the soil tend to dry out, wash away, or be eaten by birds. Covering the seed with a bit of soil gives it a much higher chance of success. A well-prepared seedbed is ideal, of course, but when that's not possible—if you want to sow a cover crop between established vegetable rows, for example—just rake the seed gently with a hand tool. This is especially important for large-seeded covers such as fava beans or cereal rye.

2. **Water it.** Give your garden a good soaking after planting a cover crop if there's no rain in the forecast. Another watering soon after the cover comes up will give it a competitive edge.

3. **Dig it.** What you do with your finished cover crop depends on what you plan to grow in your garden. If you've planted a legume cover to provide nitrogen for a crop such as tomatoes, turn the cover under about the time it flowers (that's when its nitrogen levels peak). Winter annual legumes typically flower between mid-April and late June.

If the cover crop hasn't flowered, but you're ready to sow or transplant some vegetables, you can turn it under anyway. You can plant right after turning under a legume—unless it has added a lot of bulky material to your soil. (In this case, let it decompose and settle a bit.)

If your cover is not a legume, wait two to three weeks after you turn it under to plant. The decomposition of nonlegumes can tie up available nitrogen in the soil for a while.

And just *how* should you turn it under? That depends on how tall it is. The average "tiller" (either a machine with tines or a gardener with a turning fork) can easily handle a low-growing cover crop such as clover.

4. **Or mow it, then dig it.** If your cover crop is a little jungle, mow it first and let it dry out for a few days before turning it under. If your lawn mower can't do the job, try using a string trimmer or a scythe.

Once the cover is cut, you can also consider setting aside the trimmings for use as a weed-smothering (and, with legumes, plant-fertilizing) mulch.

HOW AND WHEN TO PLANT COVER CROPS

After summer crops. Early flowers and vegetables such as sweet corn are generally finished producing by mid-August. If you don't intend to plant fall greens, clean up the bed and sow a cover crop by late August.

Overseeded into standing crops. If the vegetables or flowers in question will continue to produce until frost (or beyond), you can overseed the bed. Cast the seed into the standing crop in late summer as the weather starts to cool—remember, you want to have good growth before winter. Be sure that enough of it reaches bare ground to germinate and establish a cover. When you finally remove the spent crops, sow some more cover crop seed in this newly bare soil. You'll have a broader choice of cover crops—including more legumes—to choose from with earlier seeding.

In the spring. In areas with long, mild springs, sow a fast-growing cool-season cover such as a crimson clover, fava beans, or oats as soon as you can work the soil. To get your cover in earlier, you could even "frost seed"; Just spread the seed on the bare, frozen ground and let the freezing-thawing heaving action of the warming soil "pull" the seed into the soil for you.

Summer fallow. If part of your garden is temporarily bare between spring and fall crops, put those long, warm summer days to good use with a quick-growing hot-weather green manure such as cowpeas, buckwheat, or HUBAM white sweet clover. You can even overseed while growing to extend your cover crop's time in the garden.

Full-year green manure. If you feel that your garden is getting a bit worn-out in spots, it may be time to give those hard-pressed areas a rest. A one-year cover crop will build up the soil's organic matter and nitrogen reserves, interrupt disease and pest cycles, and give beneficial microorganisms, earthworms, and other helpful critters a boost. You can use perennials such as red clover and alfalfa or certain winter annuals such as crimson clover—if you remember to mow them before they flower. (If you mow after they flower, they'll die because they have completed their life cycle.)

Living mulch. Plant a low-growing perennial cover, such as white clover or a mixture of white clover and a low turfgrass, in early spring or late summer. At the proper time, turn under strips of this green growth with a hoe or tiller and direct-seed your vegetables or poke holes in it for transplants. This is not recommended for gardeners who face water restrictions because the living mulch needs a lot of extra moisture.

Your Seasonal Soil-Care Calendar

JANUARY

Work out a three-year **rotation plan** for your vegetable garden. By changing the positions of plants in different plant families from year to year, you interrupt disease and pest cycles. Plan to **alternate deep-rooted plants** with shallow-rooted plants and heavy feeders with light feeders to avoid exhausting soil nutrients.

FEBRUARY

Order seeds for your soil-building cover crops. Save money by buying a big bag of seed and splitting the cost—and the seed—with your gardening friends or neighbors.

MARCH

Find a source for **compost**. Many counties and municipalities compost leaves and yard wastes for residents' use.

APRIL

April showers bring May flowers. They also bring **erosion** and **drainage problems**. Take a walk in the rain and watch for places where the water runs off the soil surface. If it's causing soil erosion, try to figure out how you might be able to stop the runoff in the future (possibly by mulching or changing the surface grading). And when the rain stops, take a **soil sample** and have it tested by your local extension office.

- Don't be tempted to work the soil too early when it's still cold and wet.
- Begin **soil-building activities**. If spring cover crops (such as oats and clovers) are in your rotation plan, plant them now.
- If you planted a **cover crop** last fall, incorporate it as soon as you can work the soil. Get as much compost as you can carry home and dig it into your vegetable and flowerbeds.
- Low **soil temperatures** mean slow seed germination and plant growth in spring. Early planting won't save you time, and it may actually stunt the growth of your plants.
- Plant **spring vegetables** and—to give **summer crops** such as peppers, melons, and tomatoes an earlier start—lay black plastic over the planting bed for a couple of weeks to warm the soil.

MAY

If you don't have a **compost bin**, build one. (Or just make a loose pile of compostable materials.) Then begin to fill it.

- Take corrective action based on your lawn and garden soil test results, using lime or sulfur to adjust pH and **organic fertilizers** to improve nutrient levels.
- Use straw or grass clippings to **mulch** around your vegetables.

JUNE

Mulch your landscaped areas. There are good reasons to wait until your soil warms, despite the fact that your neighbors applied mulch two months ago. Your plants

Continued ➡

will get a **healthier start** and you'll be giving desirable self-sowing annual flowers a chance to get going.

- As early **vegetable crops** go to seed, you can follow them with a **summer cover** crop (e.g., buckwheat, sudangrass, millet). Don't let these summer cover crops go to seed!

JULY

Let the **decomposers** do the work this month—you've worked enough. Lend them a helping hand by turning the compost occasionally.

AUGUST

As your vegetable crops mature, clean up the debris and plant a **fall cover crop** (for example, oats, crimson clover).

- **Cut down** your summer cover crops and turn them under the soil.
- Watch your compost steam (or turn it if it stops). Monitor its health by taking its temperature!

SEPTEMBER

You can still **plant fall cover crops** (for example, annual rye, vetch, winter wheat, crimson clover).

- If you've experienced lawn or garden problems, have your soil tested.

OCTOBER

Fertilize cool-season grasses and topdress your lawn with a thin layer of compost.

- If indicated on your soil test results, add lime or sulfur to adjust the pH of your soil.
- Top off your empty vegetable beds with raked-up grass clippings and **fall leaves.** Leaving soil bare exposes it to erosion and nutrient leaching.
- **Order some worms** and start an indoor worm composting bin for your kitchen scraps.

NOVEMBER

Run over your **fallen leaves** with the lawn mower and either allow them to remain on your lawn or, if the leaf layer is too thick, drag them to your compost pile. You could also bag them to use as mulch next year.

DECEMBER

Feed the worms! Remember to make use of your **Christmas greens** by laying them over your perennials. Pine needles or shredded leaves also make good materials for a winter mulch, which helps to insulate the soil and protect your plants from frost heaving.

Soil Glossary

Aeration. The exchange of air in the pore spaces of the soil with air in the atmosphere. Good aeration is necessary for healthy plant growth.

Clay soil. Soil that is made up of very fine particles that hold nutrients well but are poorly drained and difficult to work.

Compaction. Soil condition that occurs when there is heavy traffic over an area, causing pore spaces, which normally make up about half of the soil's bulk, to collapse.

Compost. Decomposed and partially decomposed organic matter that is dark in color and crumbly in texture. Used as an amendment, compost increases the water-holding capacity and drainage of the soil, and is an excellent nutrient source for microorganisms, which later release nutrients to your plants.

Cover crop. A crop grown to protect soil from erosion while also building organic matter and controlling weeds.

Decomposers. Organisms, usually soil bacteria, that derive nourishment by breaking down the remains or wastes of other living organisms into simple organic compounds.

Double-digging. A technique used to prepare a garden bed that entails first removing a layer of topsoil, loosening the subsoil, then replacing the topsoil mixing in organic matter in the process. This raises the soil surface and improves aeration in heavy soils.

Earthworms. Beneficial soil-dwelling worms that help to break down organic matter and, in the process, both loosen and aerate the soil.

Fertilizer. A natural or manufactured material added to the soil that supplies one or more of the major nutrients—nitrogen, phosphorus, and potassium—to growing plants.

Foliar feeding. A way to give grass a light nutrient boost by spraying plants with a liquid fertilizer that is absorbed through the leaf pores. Compost tea and seaweed extract are two examples of organic foliar fertilizers.

Green manure. A crop that, before it reaches full maturity, is incorporated into the soil for the purpose of soil improvement.

Humus. A dark-colored, stable form of organic matter that remains after most of the plant and animal residues in it have decomposed.

Legume. A plant that is a member of the pea family (including clover, alfalfa, beans, and peas), whose roots host nitrogen-fixing bacteria in a symbiotic relationship. By making atmospheric nitrogen available to plants, these bacteria improve the productivity of the soil.

Loam. The best texture of soil to have; it contains a balance of fine clay, medium-sized silt, and coarse sand particles. Loam is easily tilled and retains moisture and nutrients effectively.

Micronutrient. A nutrient plants need in very small quantities. Micronutrients include copper, chlorine, zinc, iron, manganese, boron, and molybdenum.

Mulch. A layer of an organic or inorganic material—such as shredded leaves, straw, bark, pine needles, lawn clippings or black plastic—that is spread around plants to conserve soil moisture and discourage weeds. As organic mulches decompose, they help to build the soil.

NPK ratio. The ratio of nitrogen (N), phosphorus (P), and potassium (K) in a fertilizer or amendment. For example, the NPK ratio for alfalfa meal is 5-1-2.

Organic. Materials that are derived directly from plants or animals. Organic gardening uses plant and animal by-products to maintain soil and plant health, and doesn't rely on synthetically made fertilizers, herbicides, or pesticides.

pH. A measure of how acid or alkaline a substance is. The pH scale ranges from 1 to 14, with 7 indicating neutrality, below 7 acidity, and above 7 alkalinity. The pH of your soil greatly affects what nutrients are available to your plants.

Raised bed. A garden bed raised above the soil surface to remedy poor drainage problems or to improve growing conditions. This can be done by double-digging the bed, or simply by loosening the top layer of soil and adding organic material.

Rototiller. A self-powered rotary tiller that pulverizes the soil with its rapidly turning blades. It

is a useful tool for incorporating green manures and crop residues; however, overuse can damage the soil structure.

Sandy soil. Soil which contains more than 70 percent sand and less than 15 percent clay. Sandy soil is generally easy to work and well-drained, but it has poor nutrient-and water-holding abilities.

Silt. Refers to a soil particle of moderate size—larger than clay but not as large as sand.

Soil amendment. A material added to the soil for the purpose of making it more productive by improving its structure, drainage or aeration. An amendment such as compost can also be used to enhance microbial activity in the soil.

Soil dwellers. The living organisms that reside in the soil. These include decomposers such as bacteria, fungi and earthworms, beneficial parasites and predators, the larvae stages of many insects, and soil animals such as moles.

Soil structure. The physical arrangement of soil particles and interconnected pore spaces. Soil structure can be improved by the addition of organic matter. Walking on or tilling wet soil can destroy the soil aggregates and ruin the soil's structure.

Soil test kit. A set of instructions and a soil bag available through your state's Cooperative Extension Service. Test results indicate soil pH and specify what amendments and nutrients should be added to your soil to ensure success with your planned use.

Soil texture. The proportions of sand, silt and clay in a particular soil.

Symbiotic relationship. A mutually beneficial relationship between two living organisms, such as plant roots and nitrogen-fixing bacteria.

Till. To prepare the soil for planting seeds or to disturb it in order to control weeds, either with a power driven rototiller or with a hoe, spading fork or some other hand tool.

Weeds. Weeds are any plants that happen to grow where you don't want them to. Some perfectly fine plants can be considered weeds when they pop up in the wrong places.

COMPOST

The Benefits of Compost

Deborah L Martin and Grace Gershuny

Plants, animals, insects, and people are all inextricably linked in a complex web of interrelationships with air, water, soil, minerals, and other natural resources playing vital roles. Compost, too, plays an important role. There is a cycle, a continuity to life.

We are only at the very beginning of an understanding of all the parts of this cycle of life. But we are learning that upsetting the life patterns of only one kind of plant or animal, even in a seemingly minor way, can have effects on many other living things. All of the environmental problems we face are rooted in a failure to appreciate the life cycle and to keep it intact.

Continued ➡

We can use our understanding of the interrelationships of living things in active ways, too, to increase the productivity of our fields, forests, orchards, and gardens. Composting is one way to work within the life cycle in the furthering of our welfare.

Compost is more than a fertilizer, more than a soil conditioner. It is a symbol of continuing life. Nature has been making compost since the first appearance of primitive life on this planet, eons before humans first walked the earth. Leaves falling to the forest floor are soon composted, returning their nutrients to the trees that bore them. The dead grass of the meadow, seared by winter's frost, is made compost in the dampness of the earth beneath. The birds, the insects, and the animals of field and forest contribute their wastes and eventually their bodies, helping to grow food so that more of their kind may prosper. The greenness of the earth itself is strong testimony to nature's continuing composting program.

The compost heap in your garden is an intentional replication of the natural process of birth and death that occurs almost everywhere in nature. It did not take long for people to learn to imitate nature by building compost piles, as we saw in chapter 1. It is ironic that composting, the oldest and most universally practiced form of soil treatment in the world, should today be claiming so many converts. Perhaps this is nature's Restoration—a reaffirmation that people do, indeed, live best when they live in harmony with nature.

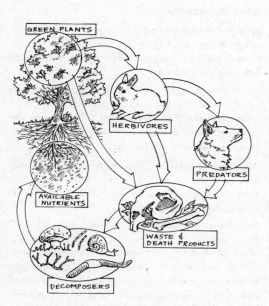

In the forest, nutrients are recycled through the natural decomposition of plant and animal waste.

Because the compost heap is symbolic of nature's best efforts to build soil, and because compost is the most efficient and practical soil builder, it has become the heart of the organic method of farming and gardening. Composting is the single most important task of the organic gardener or farmer because the health of the soil depends on the composting treatment it receives, and success in gardening and farming depends on the health of the soil.

Compost improves soil texture and structure, qualities that enable soil to retain nutrients, moisture, and air for the support of healthy crops. By increasing the soil's moisture-holding capacity, compost helps control erosion that otherwise would wash topsoil into waterways. Compost is the best recycler of biological wastes, turning millions of tons of our refuse into a food-growing asset. Compost provides and releases plant nutrients, protects against drought, controls pH, supports essential bacteria, feeds helpful earthworms, stops nutrient loss through leaching, acts as a buffer

against toxins in the soil, controls weeds, and conserves a nation's nonrenewable energy resources. Every gardener knows that compost is valuable—but, until we understand more fully all the benefits of compost, we can never understand why it must be the single most important part of gardening and farming.

Life Inside a Compost Heap

Deborah L. Martin and Grace Gershuny

The two most important aspects of a compost pile are the chemical makeup of its components and the population of organisms in it. Compost piles are intricate and complex communities of animal, vegetable, and mineral matter, all of which are interrelated, and all of which playa part in the breakdown of organic matter into humus. Composting is the result of the activities of a succession of organisms, each group paving the way for the next group by breaking down or converting a complex biodegradable material into a simpler or more usable material that can be utilized by its successor in the chain of breakdown. Generally speaking, the more "simple" the molecular structure of the material, the more resistant it becomes to bacterial attack and, hence, the more biologically stable it becomes. Whether the decomposition process takes place on the forest floor or in a gardener's compost heap, the biochemical systems at work are the same, and humus is always the result.

Humus

Humus, the relatively stable end product of composting, is rich in nutrients and organic matter and highly beneficial to both the soil and crops grown in the soil.

The advantages of humus are twofold. First, when it is mixed with the soil, the resulting combination becomes a heterogeneous, loosely structured soil mixture allowing air and water to penetrate to soil organisms and growing plants. Because of its loose texture, humus-rich soil soaks up water in its pores so that less runoff occurs. Second, humus contains a number of chemical elements that enrich the soil with which it is mixed, providing nutrients for growing plants.

The major elements found in humus are nitrogen, phosphorus, potassium, sulfur, iron, and calcium, varying in amounts according to the original composition of the raw organic matter thrown on the heap. Minor elements are also present, again in varying amounts depending on the type of compost. The N-P-K percentages of finished compost are relatively low, but their benefit lies in the release of nitrogen and phosphorus in the soil at a slow enough rate that plants can use them and they aren't lost through leaching.

Soil mixed with humus becomes a rich, dark color that absorbs far more heat than nonorganic soils, making it a more favorable environment in which to grow crops and ornamental plants.

How Compost Is Produced

The road from raw organic material to finished compost is a complex one, because both chemical and microbial processes are responsible for the gradual change from one to the other.

Decomposition of compost is accomplished by enzymatic digestion of plant and animal material by soil microorganisms. Simultaneously, the chemical processes of oxidation, reduction, and hydrolysis are going on in the pile, and their products at various stages are used by microorganisms for further breakdown.

Bacteria use these products for two purposes: (1) to provide energy to carry on their life processes and

(2) to obtain the nutrients they need to grow and reproduce. The energy is obtained by oxidation of the products, especially the carbon fraction. The heat in a compost pile is the result of this biological "burning," or oxidation. Some materials can be broken down and oxidized more rapidly than others. This explains why a pile heats up fairly rapidly at the start. It is because the readily decomposed material is being attacked and bacterial activity is at its peak. If all goes well, this material is soon used up, and so bacterial activity slows down—and the pile begins to cool. Of course, if the mass of the material is big enough, it acts as an insulator to prevent heat loss, and the high temperature may thus persist for some time after the active period is over, especially if the pile is not turned. Persistent high temperatures are the result of uneven breakdown.

The raw materials that you add to your compost heap will have to be of biological origin in order to decompose down to finished compost. Wood, paper, kitchen trimmings, crop leavings, weeds, and manure can all be included in the heap. As compost is broken down from these raw materials to simpler forms of proteins and carbohydrates, it becomes more available to a wider array of bacterial species that will carry it to a further stage of decomposition.

Carbohydrates (starches and sugars) break down in a fairly rapid process to simple sugars, organic acids, and carbon dioxide that are released in the soil. When proteins decompose, they readily break down into peptides and amino acids, and then to available ammonium compounds and atmospheric nitrogen. Finally, species of "nitrifying" bacteria change the ammonium compounds to nitrates, in which form they are available to plants.

At this stage of decomposition, the heap is near to becoming finished compost, with the exception of a few substances that still resist breakdown. Through complex, biochemical processes, these substances and the rest of the decomposed material form humus. There is some evidence that humus is largely the remains of microbial bodies.

The microorganisms of the compost heap, like any other living things, need both carbon from the carbohydrates, and forms of nitrogen from the proteins in the compost substrate. In order to thrive and reproduce, all microbes must have access to a supply of the elements of which their cells are made. They also need an energy source and a source of the chemicals they use to make their enzymes. The principal nutrients for bacteria, actinomycetes, and fungi are carbon (C), nitrogen (N), phosphorus (P), and potassium (K). Minor elements are needed in minute quantities.

These chemicals in the compost pile are not in their pure form, and certainly not all in the same form at the same time. For example, at any given moment, nitrogen may be found in the heap in the form of nitrates and nitrites, in ammonium compounds, in the complex molecules of undigested or partly digested cellulose, and in the complex protein of microorganism protoplasm. There are many stages of breakdown and many combinations of elements. What's more, microorganisms can make use of nitrogen and other elements only when they occur in specific forms and ratios to one another.

Nutrients must be present in the correct ratio in your compost heap. The ideal C/N ratio for most compost microorganisms is about 25:1, though it varies from one compost pile to another. When too little carbon is present, making the C/N ratio too low, nitrogen may be lost to the microorganisms because they are not given enough carbon to use with it. It may float into the atmosphere as ammonia and be lost to the plants that would

Continued ➡

benefit by its presence in humus. Unpleasant odors from the compost heap are most often caused by nitrogen being released as ammonia. Materials too high in carbon for the amount of nitrogen present (C/N too high) make composting inefficient, so more time is needed to complete the process. When added to the soil, high-carbon compost uses nitrogen from the soil to continue decomposition, making it unavailable to growing plants.

Affecting the interwoven chemical and microbial breakdown of the compost heap are environmental factors that need to be mentioned here.

THE CARBON CYCLE. *Green plants use carbon dioxide gas, water, and sunlight to make sugars and other carbon-containing compounds that animals use as food. Carbon compounds in plant and animal wastes provide food for decomposers in the compost pile. Materials that have passed through the decomposers' bodies and the microbial bodies themselves contain nutrients used by plants to continue the carbon cycle.*

Composting can be defined in the terms of availability of oxygen. Aerobic decomposition means that the active microbes in the heap require oxygen, while in anaerobic decomposition, the active microbes do not require oxygen to live and grow. When compost heaps are located in the open air, as most are, oxygen is available and the biological processes progress under aerobic conditions. Temperature, moisture content, the size of bacterial populations, and availability of nutrients limit and determine how much oxygen your heap uses.

The amount of moisture in your heap should be as high as possible, while still allowing air to filter into the pore spaces for the benefit of aerobic bacteria. Individual materials hold various percentages of moisture in compost and determine the amount of water that can be added. For example, woody and fibrous materials, such as bark, sawdust, wood chips, hay, and straw, can hold moisture equal to 75 to 85 percent of their dry weight. "Green manures," such as lawn clippings and vegetable trimmings, can absorb moisture equaling 50 to 60 percent of their weight. According to longtime composting advocate and researcher Dr. Clarence Golueke in *Composting*, "The minimum content at which bacterial activity takes place is from 12 to 15 percent. Obviously, the closer the moisture content of a composting mass approaches these low levels, the slower will be the compost process. As a rule of thumb, the moisture content becomes a limiting factor when it drops below 45 or 50 percent."

Temperature is an important factor in the biology of a compost heap. Low outside temperatures during the winter months slow the decomposition process, while warmer temperatures speed it up. During the warmer months of the year, intense microbial activity inside the heap causes composting to proceed at extremely high temperatures. The microbes that decompose the raw materials fall into basically two categories: mesophilic, those that live and grow in temperatures of 50° to 113°F (10° to 45°C), and thermophilic, those that thrive in temperatures of 113° to 158°F (45° to 70°C). Most garden compost begins at mesophilic temperatures, then increases to the thermophilic range for the remainder of the decomposition period. These high temperatures are beneficial to the gardener because they kill weed seeds and diseases that could be detrimental to a planted garden.

The bacterial decomposers in compost prefer a pH range of between 6.0 and 7.5, and the fungal decomposers between 5.5 and 8.0. Compost must be within these ranges if it is to decompose. Levels of pH are a function of the number of hydrogen ions present. (High pH levels indicate alkalinity; low levels, acidity.) In finished compost, a neutral (7.0) or slightly acid (slightly below 7.0) pH is best, though slight alkalinity (slightly above 7.0) can be tolerated.

Lime is often used to raise the pH if the heap becomes too acidic. However, ammonia forms readily with the addition of lime, and nitrogen can be lost.

Composting Tools and Supplies

Truth is, you can make compost without any tools or equipment. But if you want to cook up big batches of "gardener's gold," compost bins, tumblers, frames, and other gadgets can help you do the job quickly and easily.

Good Investments

Compost happens. Just pile up your grass clippings, fallen leaves, garden wastes, and kitchen scraps and the materials eventually will decompose into rich, black humus.

Although equipment isn't essential for making good compost, it can help you manage your composting operation. Here are some reasons why you might want to invest in a compost bin, frame, tumbler, or other equipment.

Appearance matters. If you have a small yard and have to make compost in full view of your neighbors, you (and your neighbors) may be happier if your compost is under cover.

Bins boost production. Compost bins can help you organize your composting so that you can be more productive. For example, with a three-bin system, you can pile slowly decomposing yard wastes in one bin, mix kitchen scraps and finely chopped materials for fast composting in another bin, and keep finished compost in the third bin. Or, use one bin for finished compost, and turn your compost-in-progress from one of the remaining bins into the other.

Get finished compost faster. By turning and aerating your pile—using a tumbler, pitchfork, and other kinds of equipment—you can speed the process and turn garbage into gold in almost no time at all.

Build-It-Yourself Bins

Whatever your composting style, there's bound to be a bin, frame, or tumbler that'll meet your needs. If you're handy, you can build your own compost bin in almost no time at all. You can use almost any durable material, including wire, wood, slats, and cinder blocks. Here are a few ideas.

WIRE CAGE

Easy does it: Start with a 10-foot length of 48-inch 12½- or 14-gauge welded steel wire fencing. Clip or wire together the ends to form a cylindrical compost bin 4 feet high and slightly more than 3 feet across. Pile your leaves, clippings, and other organic materials inside. (Use grass clippings sparingly, in layers no more than 1 inch thick, to avoid

Continued ➡

A Better Bin

Sure, you can make a simple compost bin out of a hoop of chicken wire (and you probably have!). But if you, like many gardeners, have found that composting is a cornerstone to a great yard, then you may want to build a more lasting structure. Concrete block is a humble but durable material. It's easy to make low walls of the block if they aren't going to bear a load; you just stack them up and drive metal garden stakes through the holes to keep them in place. There's no need for mortar, as is used in a foundation wall. If you want to always have some compost ready for taking and some in the process of decomposing, you can expand this bin to two or three bays. You'll only need concrete blocks (42 to build the bin as shown) and metal garden stakes to stabilize the bin.

1. Use a straight-bladed shovel to make the surface as level as possible.

2. Lay the first row of 12 blocks, taking care that the sidewalls meet the back at right angles. Leave a vertical gap of about ½ inch between blocks to allow air to circulate.

3. Lay the remaining three rows of 11, 10, and 9 blocks.

4. To stabilize the bin, use a sledgehammer to drive metal garden stakes through holes in the blocks and into the ground. If there is a chance that children will try climbing on the bin, use enough stakes to make it sturdy and pound them nearly flush with the top of the walls to prevent injury.

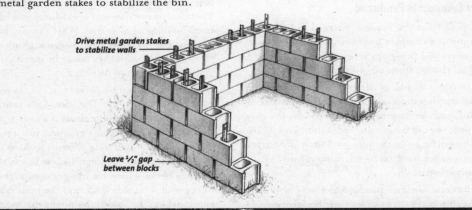

Drive metal garden stakes to stabilize walls

Leave ½" gap between blocks

matting.) When the bin is half full, drive a stake into the center of the pile. Water will run down the stake, helping to keep the pile moist.

To turn the pile, simply unfasten the bin's ends, pull the fencing away from the materials, and set the bin back up next to the heap. Then, refill the empty bin, turning the materials from the top of the original pile to the bottom of the new pile and from the outside to the inside.

WOOD AND WIRE BIN

For a bit more structure, make a wood and wire bin, using untreated 2 x 4 lumber and ½-inch mesh hardware cloth or poultry netting. (*Never use pressure-treated wood*—toxic copper and arsenic will leach into your compost and eventually contaminate your garden soil; cedar is a good choice because it resists rotting.) Use the lumber to make four 3 x 3-foot or 4 x 4-foot identical open frames. Staple the hardware cloth to one side of each frame. Next, nail three of the panels together to form a back and two sides. Use the remaining panel to make a convenient door, by hinging the edges at one corner and placing the hooks and eyes on the opposite corner. To turn the compost ingredients, just open the hooks for easy access.

A variation of this is the wire and tomato stake bin. Make a 4 x 4-foot square by driving 4-foot-long tomato stakes into the ground at 1-foot intervals. Surround the stakes with the hardware cloth or wire netting, then loop baling wire around the whole thing to secure the netting.

Set up these bins close to where you need to use compost. When you've used up the compost, move the bin to another location in need of compost, and begin a new pile.

MOVABLE SLAT BIN

Perhaps the classic compost bin is the movable slat bin (sometimes called the New Zealand box). Because slat bins are constructed entirely of wood, they hold up better than wire bins.

The sides of these bins consist of movable slats that fit inside tracks. Spacers between the slats allow air to reach the compost materials, speeding the breakdown process. The slats make access easy: When you need to work with the composting materials, you just remove as many of the slats as necessary.

Many movable slat bins have three compartments for storing compost in various stages: freshly collected materials, partially decomposed materials, and finished compost. Having multiple bins allows you to produce a continuous supply of compost for all your garden needs.

The ideal size bin for making quick compost should hold 27 cubic feet of organic material. To keep out animals like raccoons and rodents, attach hinged lids to the top of each bin. Bins like these can be made with or without a floor. Your compost will break down faster, however, without a floor—just pile the materials directly on the ground.

(Remember, use cedar or another rot-resistant wood to make a wooden bin, instead of using pressure-treated wood.)

CINDER BLOCK BIN

If durability is your chief concern, construct a permanent bin from cinder blocks (or brick) and mortar. For a bit more mobility out of the bin, use just the blocks without the mortar.

Stack the blocks three or four high to form walls. You can leave one side open to form a U-shaped bin or enclose the bin on all four sides. If you enclose all four sides, lay the blocks apart—with spaces of 1 inch or more between them—to improve air circulation. Add one or more interior walls to

create multiple bins. To turn the pile, simply remove the blocks from one side and fork the materials from one bin to another.

Cover the structure with a wooden lid or plastic tarp to keep rain out. If you make a concrete floor for your bin, make sure you slant it slightly to allow drainage. (Collect the resulting "compost tea" in a bucket and use it to feed houseplants!)

For winter protection, consider recessing the bin into a slope that has good southern exposure. A 5 x 10-foot cinder block bin can hold 2 to 3 tons of compost.

MISCELLANEOUS BINS

Compost bins come in all shapes, sizes, and materials. Feel free to use whatever you have on hand. Resourceful gardeners have been known to use such things as pallets, picket or snow fencing, and straw bales to make quality compost bins.

Pallets. Recycled hardwood pallets provide a quick, easy—and commonly free—compost bin. Just stand the pallets on end in a square, pound in fence posts to hold the corners together, and use heavy-gauge wire to fasten the pallets to the posts.

Fencing. Fencing is sturdy and allows plenty of air to circulate inside the bin. Use steel or wooden posts for the bin's corners. Attach snow, lattice, or picket fencing for the sides.

Straw bales. You can make an all-organic compost bin by using straw bales—stacked two high—for the sides. Move away a bale or two to turn and access the compost. Over time, some of the straw itself will decompose, adding more carbon to your pile.

Ready-Made Composters

Ready-made composters may cost you more than the materials for making your own bin. But commercial composters can be quite attractive and durable. They also save you the time and effort you'd spend making your own. There are two basic types—bins and tumblers—with many variations of each.

COMMERCIAL BINS

Many of these composters are made of recycled plastic, which won't warp or discolor like wood. Bins made of dark-colored plastic catch and hold the sun's heat, making them good choices for those who live in frigid climates.

Some of these bins retain moisture, too. Their sides and top cover are slanted to catch just enough rain to maintain moisture levels without drenching the compost. And while you do have to turn the compost the old-fashioned way—using a pitchfork—you don't have to uncover the composter to do so. You just insert your fork through a mixing slot near the top, loosen and turn the material, then insert the fork into one of the lower slots to mix the material on the bottom. Removable doors on the sides allow you to scoop out the finished compost. With a pliers, you can assemble the unit in about half an hour.

You can even buy an inexpensive—and "compostable"—cardboard container that will hold your compost for about a year before it's ready to become one with its contents. At that point, you can just toss it into another cardboard bin and start again!

COMPOST TUMBLERS

Tumbler or drum composters are plastic or metal containers that are usually mounted on elevated frames. Some models have gear-driven turning mechanisms; others spin on ball bearings. Another type resembles a large metal or plastic ball. To turn the contents, you just roll the ball on the ground.

Because tumblers make it easy to turn materials, they can produce compost quickly. They have at least one drawback, however. Their capacity usually isn't very large. When you've filled the tumbler to a certain level, you must stop adding fresh materials until the process has finished. During those 2 to 3 weeks, you'll need to stockpile your materials in another container or area. And because the contents rest on plastic rather than on the ground, you might want to add a few shovelfuls of soil or finished compost whenever you fill the bin. Otherwise, earthworms won't be able to get in to help the decomposition process.

DECIDING WHAT TO BUY

Don't choose a commercial composter based on its cost alone. Consider these factors, too:

Portability. Some models, especially the tumblers, are too large or heavy to move easily. Make sure you have a good site for such a bin before you buy it. Portable bins (like the ball type) allow you to make compost at several sites around the garden; they're especially good for gardeners who don't have a wheelbarrow or who garden over a large area.

Capacity. Choose a bin size appropriate to the amount of materials you expect to have for composting. Bigger isn't necessarily better if you have only small quantities of composting materials. If you have a lot of material to compost, however, two or three inexpensive cage- or open-type bins may be a better choice for you than a single large bin.

Ease of assembly. Some of the more complicated bins are sold unassembled and have dozens of pieces to screw and bolt together. If possible, read the assembly instructions before you buy.

Ease of use. If the bin has a loading door or lid, you should be able to lift or open and close it easily. The opening should be wide enough to accommodate bulky material. When considering a drum-type composter, check to see that there's enough room beneath the drum to park a wheelbarrow for unloading the finished compost.

Other Composting Tools

Besides the items in the following list, there are at least a few other tools that can help you make compost. For instance, you'll probably want a small bucket with a lid (for collecting and carrying kitchen scraps) and a pair of good-quality gloves. Many gardeners also find a chipper/shredder useful for chopping leaves and garden wastes into smaller pieces before adding them to the pile: The smaller the pieces, the faster they'll decompose.

FORKS

Use a pitchfork—which has three long, slightly rounded tines—to add materials to the pile, to turn the pile, and to transfer the finished compost to your wheelbarrow and beds. Use a straw fork (with five or six long rounded tines) for scattering light composting material.

WHEELBARROW

Of course you'll need a wheelbarrow (or garden cart) to transport your grass clippings, leaves, and garden wastes to the compost pile and to carry your finished compost to your garden. Wheelbarrows also are handy to work over when screening compost or potting up houseplants.

You'll find wheelbarrows easier to maneuver than heavy-duty garden carts because they have one wheel instead of two. And with plastic models, maintenance is minimal—they have no metal parts to rust.

Continued ➡

SCREEN

A screen is useful for separating the finer particles of finished compost from larger, less-decayed chunks. Fine, screened compost is ideal for covering seedbeds. If it's aged (6 months or more), you can even use it in potting mixes. Throw the larger stuff back into the pile for further microbial breakdown, or—if the pieces aren't too big—use it as mulch or side-dressing for plants that are already established.

You can either buy a compost screen or make your own by stapling hardware cloth or fine-gauge chicken wire to a simple wood frame.

THERMOMETER

If you want to make compost quickly (in as little as 2 to 3 weeks), you'll need a compost thermometer to monitor the temperature of your pile. The hotter the temperature, the faster the decomposition. Another advantage of "hot compost" is that it kills weed seeds and disease organisms.

Use the thermometer to check the temperature every 3 to 5 days. When the temperature drops below 120°F, aerate the pile (by turning or using a commercial aerator) to get it cooking again. You'll find compost thermometers at your garden center and in garden-supply catalogs. They're also useful for checking soil temperature.

AERATOR

The more air you get into your pile, the faster it'll break down. There may be other benefits, too: Some research indicates that aerating your pile regularly could even boost its nitrogen content and disease-fighting abilities.

Turning your pile with a fork a couple of times a week is one way to get air into it. Another is to use a tool designed specifically for this purpose. Commercially sold compost aerators come in several styles. All have a long shaft that you use to twist, turn, or bore holes into the center of the pile. Most are hand-powered, but at least one model is powered by a standard power drill.

A low-effort alternative is the compost "chimney." A compost chimney is simply a piece of PVC pipe about 4 feet in length—slightly longer than the height of your pile—with holes drilled in it. You just stick the pipe upright in the center of the pile to allow air to flow through the decaying materials.

HOSE

Moisture is essential to the composting process. Ideally, your pile should feel as moist as a damp sponge (no wetter!). When the materials begin to dry out—causing the process to slow—you'll need to remoisten the layers with a hose.

If you're buying a new hose, look for a durable rubber hose with solid brass couplings. Also, keep in mind that the more "plies" it has, the better it will hold up.

Materials for Composting

Deborah L. Martin and Grace Gershuny

Materials for composting are all around you. Many gardeners need look no further than the home grounds for a sufficient supply. Kitchen wastes, lawn clippings, weeds and plant debris, dog and cat hair, vacuum cleaner accumulations—nearly anything that once lived (and is thus organic) is a candidate for the compost heap.

After you have exhausted the home supply and still don't have all the materials you would like, you can begin to plan a series of foraging expeditions, beginning as close to home as possible and ranging

out as far as you must in order to fulfill your requirements.

Manure should be the first item on your list, since it is by far the most important ingredient in any heap. If you try, you can get it free for the hauling or at a token fee at poultry farms, riding stables, feedlots, even zoos and wild game farms—any place that holds large numbers of animals in concentration. Even a friend with one horse and no garden can supply all the manure you'll need for a backyard pile.

Your chances of getting manure at a family farm are not as good, since farmers will probably want their manure for their own fields. Even if you seem to have all the home materials your compost heap can use, try to find a source of manure. Its tremendous bacteria content will bring your heap into biological and chemical balance and aid the rapid reduction of all the other materials.

But you don't have to stop with manure expeditions. In town, you can scavenge at grocery stores, city agencies, factories and mills, restaurants, and many retail operations. Ranging farther into the country, you can find materials in fields and along roadsides, streams, and ponds, at farms and orchards, at sawmills and canneries. Nearly any organic gardener can find ample composting materials by going no further than 5 miles from home. The farmer, of course, must make composting an integral part of his or her soil management plan, utilizing every scrap of home material and adding green manure crops as necessary. Even the organic farmer—especially one who has few animals or cultivates a small but intensive area—might need to look for supplementary materials. The materials listed in this chapter can be of use to both gardeners and organic farmers seeking to enhance their composting operations.

Where to Begin

Begin, of course, at home. Are you discarding any organic matter at all? Newspapers? Tea bags? Clippings from the children's haircuts? Dishwater? With the exception of human and pet excreta (addressed later in this chapter), you can use everything. Before foraging, be sure that your home recovery program is 100 percent effective.

Once you venture outside your own yard, the best place to start is with friends, neighbors, and relatives. Some diligent composters offer to cart away kitchen scraps after every social call. This is often a valuable community service for people who would like to compost their wastes but for one reason or another are not able to do so. Recycled plastic pails with tight, fitting lids, such as those used for wallboard compound, make excellent containers for storing a week's worth or more of goodies. A layer of peat moss or sawdust on the bottom helps absorb moisture and odors. You can offer to pick up the full pail regularly, and leave a fresh, empty one in its place.

Your expeditions away from home can continue with a trip through the business directory of the phone book. Go through it slowly, listing all possible sources of materials. Your search might end when you find that you can pick up manure at the local riding stable every Saturday morning and vegetable trimmings from the neighborhood supermarket every Tuesday and Friday afternoon. After your routine is established, it usually operates like clockwork.

Here is a partial list of away-from-home materials. You will come across others in your expeditions—but do consider these for starters.

Farms and Orchards. These can provide you with spoiled hay, corn silage, eggshells, manure of every kind, feathers, barnyard litter, spoiled fruit, spent

mushroom soil, whey from dairy operations, and orchard litter.

Factories and Mills. Apple pomace is available from cider mills. Other available compostables include cannery wastes of all kinds, shredded bark, sawdust, and wood shavings from lumber mills and carpentry shops; botanical drug wastes from pharmaceutical firms; cement dust; cocoa bean hulls (good mulch); coffee chaff from coffee wholesalers; cottonseed meal; excelsior from receiving departments; felt wastes; fly ash from incinerators; agricultural frit from glass factories; grape pomace from wineries and spent hops from breweries; granite dust from cutting operations; leather dust; lignin from paper mills; spoiled meal from flour mills; peanut shells; slag from steel plants; spice marc (spent) from spice packers; tanbark from tanneries; tankage from meat-processing plants and slaughterhouses.

City Agencies. You may be able to acquire dried sewage sludge, leaf mold from parks department leaf depositories, fly ash from incinerators, aquatic weeds, and pulverized wood from tree-trimming operations.

Stables and Feedlots. Manure and stable litter of all kinds are valuable compostables.

Retail Stores. You can get vegetable trimmings from supermarkets and shops, hair from barbers and salons, pet hair from grooming parlors, food wastes from restaurants, excelsior from gift shops (used for packing breakables), plant wastes from florists, and sawdust from carpentry shops and lumber supply houses.

Roadsides, Fields, and Waterways. Old leaves, weeds, and water plants from streams, lakes, and ponds may be plentiful. A note of caution: Many native plants, even those viewed as weeds, are endangered species that are protected by law. This is especially true of plants growing near oceans or in wetlands; such areas often contain fragile ecosystems that should not be disturbed. In gathering materials in fields and wild areas, be aware of your ecological responsibility to avoid robbing natural areas of their native plants.

Regional Materials

Gardeners in certain parts of the country can avail themselves of materials abundant only in their regions. New Englanders can look for wool and felt wastes from mills, leather dust, and maple syrup wastes. Those along seacoasts can find greensand, fish scraps, and seaweed. Southwestern gardeners should look for cannery wastes, mesquite, olive residues, grape pomace from wineries, and citrus wastes. Southerners may have access to cotton gin trash, Spanish moss, peanut shell ashes, tung oil pomace, sugarcane trash, molasses residue, castor pomace, tobacco stems, rice hulls, and water hyacinth plants.

In collecting materials for your heap, not only will you be adding to your own soil's fertility and structure, but you will also be contributing to the recycling of wastes that might otherwise become pollutants in the environment. Many communities now have or are planning composting facilities for at least part of their trash. If yours is one of them, they probably make finished compost available free or at low cost to gardeners. If your town has not yet pursued this option, it may offer free delivery of leaves, shredded tree trimmings, and other compostable municipal wastes. A large poultry farm might be paying to have manure and litter hauled away. Their trash can be your treasure.

Supermarkets and restaurants will be more than happy to contribute their organic wastes to

Continued ➡

you, since it lowers their disposal costs. Most important, however, these materials, instead of being dumped, buried, or burned, will find their way back to the soil.

Materials to Avoid

Although nearly any organic material can contribute to good compost, there are some that should be avoided, and others to be used only in limited amounts. First, you want your heap to be balanced among green matter, animal wastes, manure, and soil. If you build your heap of 80 percent tankage from the local meat-packing plant, not only will you have a putrid mess, but you will attract every stray dog, cat, and raccoon within a 5-mile radius. A truckload of grape pomace or a ton of wet hops from the brewery will be equally hard to handle, as will be the neighbors if your heap's odor wafts their way. Strive, then, for a commonsense balance in the materials you select, and be sure to add a layer of soil over the heap every time you add materials that might cause odor or attract vermin.

Human feces should not be used unless they have been properly treated and permitted to age sufficiently. Even then, concerns about disease pathogens make the use of such material dubious at best for the home gardener. Urine alone can be used quite safely, however.

Wastes from pet dogs, cats, and birds should not be used on the compost pile. Although dog manure is as rich in nutrients as other manures, it is more difficult and less pleasant to handle than the mixed bedding and manure of cattle and horses. In addition, it may carry organisms parasitic to humans. Special composters designed exclusively for dog droppings offer pet owners a safe alternative.

Cat manure is even more hazardous, especially to pregnant women and small children. Cat droppings may contain *Toxoplasma gondii*, a one-celled organism that, when transmitted to a pregnant woman, may infect her unborn child, causing brain and eye disease. *Toxocara* cati is a roundworm, also common in cat feces, that causes similar problems in children. Keep the contents of the litter box away from children and the compost pile.

Bird droppings have been similarly indicated as potential disease sources. Since they are most often mixed with bedding and dropped birdseed from the bottom of the cage, bird droppings will also tend to introduce unwanted weeds into your compost.

Materials that will not decompose readily—large pieces of wood, oyster and clam shells, large quantities of pine needles, rags, brush, cornstalks, heavy cardboard—should not be used in large amounts unless they are shredded first.

Large amounts of highly acid materials such as pine needles and oak leaves should not be used without the addition of enough limestone to neutralize the acid. For acid-loving crops, however, you might wish to build acidic compost by the deliberate use of these materials.

Be very careful about diseased plants—you may be better off burning them and adding the ashes to your compost than risking inoculating your whole garden with them. Weeds can generally be composted, but be careful to ensure hot composting temperatures if they have produced seed. A few species, such as quack grass and Canada thistle, reproduce readily from the tiniest bit of surviving rhizome and should be avoided entirely.

Don't use large amounts of grease and oil, since they not only attract animal pests but also inhibit the biochemical processes necessary to successful composting. The amount of grease and oil from a normal household will cause no

problem. However, carting home tubs of spent grease from the local potato chip factory is unwise.

Do not use toxic materials. There is little sense in trying to build an organic soil by including pesticide-treated wastes in the compost heap. Plant debris from roadsides might have been subject to a broad, potent, and persistent herbicide applied by the highway department; or, if the highway is a busy one, plants might be coated with lead emissions from passing traffic. Be careful in choosing materials.

Materials for Enrichment

There are many substances you can buy to increase your compost's N-P-K content or control its pH. Although it is not necessary to add these materials to the heap, many gardeners find it worth the expense to ensure a high nutrient level in their compost.

Among the materials and products available at garden centers and through mail-order outlets are bagged manure, dried blood, limestone, cottonseed meal, greensand, hoof and horn meal, tobacco wastes, seaweed, peat moss, and other natural products that are valuable to the heap because of their nutrient levels or ability to correct pH.

Many people add lime to their compost in order to increase its pH. This is not often necessary or beneficial, and it is not a good idea if you are composting manure, since the lime reacts with the nitrates in the manure to drive off ammonia. If lime is needed, apply it directly to the soil or mix it with the finished compost for potting mixes. The microbes inhabiting your compost heap can often benefit from the calcium in lime, but other forms of calcium, such as eggshells or any marine animal (oyster, crab, clam) shells, pulverized as finely as possible, will serve as well. Bonemeal and wood ashes are also rich in calcium. Avoid all of these materials if you want compost for acid-loving plants such as rhododendrons, camellias, and blueberries, in which case you may want to use acid peat instead of soil in your heap.

Rock or colloidal phosphates are excellent materials for enriching the mineral content of your compost. Microbial action makes their nutrients more readily available than they would be if added directly to the soil. They also contain significant amounts of calcium and micronutrients. Other rock powders such as granite dust and greensand, both sources of potassium and micronutrients, are similarly made more available to plants when first consumed by compost organisms.

Specific nutrients can also be added by using plants that are especially rich in those elements in your compost. Seaweeds, such as the kelps, are rich in potassium and are also good sources of such elements as iodine, boron, copper, magnesium, calcium, and phosphorus. If available locally, seaweed should certainly be added to the compost heap. The water hyacinths that grow so abundantly in the rivers of the South are especially rich in many of the elements that are more apt to be deficient in the soil. Leaves, discussed more thoroughly later in this chapter, are a teeming source of micronutrients that are not found in upper layers of soil; use them in compost whenever possible.

Activators

A compost activator is any substance that stimulates biological decomposition in a compost pile. There are organic activators and artificial activators. Organic activators are materials containing a high amount of nitrogen in various forms, such as proteins, amino acids, and urea, among others. Some examples of natural activators are manure,

garbage, dried blood, compost, humus-rich soil, and urine.

Artificial activators are generally chemically synthesized compounds such as ammonium sulfate or phosphate, urea, ammonia, or any of the common commercial nitrogen fertilizers. These materials are not recommended.

There are two ways in which an activator may influence a compost heap: (1) by introducing strains of microorganisms that are effective in breaking down organic matter and (2) by increasing the nitrogen and micronutrient content of the heap, thereby providing extra food for microorganisms.

Those who follow the practices of biodynamic agriculture consider certain activators, made according to precise instructions, to be essential for producing the highest-quality compost. These preparations are used in minute quantities, as part of a holistic approach to working with soil, plants, and the energies of nature.

Claims have sometimes been made that special cultures of bacteria will hasten the breakdown of material in a compost heap and also produce a better quality of finished compost. Products are manufactured that are reported to be effective in improving the action of a compost heap.

Most independent tests, however—including those conducted at the Rodale Research Center—indicate that there is no benefit to be gained from the use of an activator that relies solely on the introduction of microorganisms. It seems that microorganisms will quickly multiply to the limit that their environment will permit. Since all the necessary microorganisms are already present in manure, soil, and other compo sting materials, there is no benefit to be gained from introducing strains in the form of an activator product. The best activator is a layer of finished compost from the previous heap or a generous amount of healthy topsoil.

Nitrogen Activators

The cause of most compost heap "failures" is a lack of nitrogen. Almost invariably, a heap that doesn't heat up or decay quickly enough is made from material which is low in nitrogen. Nitrogen is needed by the bacteria and fungi that do the work of composting, to build protoplasm and carry on their life processes.

In experiments conducted at the Rodale Research Center, it was shown that increasing additions of blood meal (a high-nitrogen activator) produced associated increases in the temperature of the pile, indicating increasing bacterial activity. In the tests, 3 pounds of blood meal in a 31-pound pile produced the best results.

Good nitrogen activators include not only blood meal (which is expensive when purchased commercially at garden centers), but tankage, manure, bonemeal, and alfalfa meal. Human urine, which contains about 1 percent nitrogen, also makes an excellent compost activator. Just how much you should add to the heap depends on the nature of the material you are composting. Low-nitrogen materials such as straw, sawdust, corncobs, and old weeds should have at least 2 or 3 pounds of nitrogen supplement added per 100 pounds of raw material. If plenty of manure, grass clippings, fresh weeds, and other high-nitrogen materials are available to be mixed in with the compost, no nitrogen supplement will be necessary.

Continued →

Common Materials

Here is a list of the more common—and some not-so-common—materials that can be used in composting.

Alfalfa

Alfalfa is a perennial herbaceous legume grown as livestock feed and as a green manure or cover crop. Alfalfa grows almost everywhere in the United States and is widely available as hay, meal, or dehydrated feed pellets. Its nitrogen content and absorbency make it an excellent addition to the compost pile.

In combination with leaves and/or household garbage, alfalfa serves as a good compost stimulant and activator; its 12:1 carbon/nitrogen (C/N) ratio helps bring the pile's overall C/N ratio into the desired 25:1 to 30:1 range. While expensive when sold as hay, alfalfa is moderately priced in the form of dehydrated pellets or meal, and these products can be purchased at most feed stores. Farmers and feed stores may also have rotted or spoiled bales, unsuitable as animal feed, that they will gladly give you.

Apple Pomace

Anyone who presses his or her own cider produces heaps of this sweet pulp. Yellow jackets, hornets, and bees love to zero in on the residues, so it's best to get the pomace into a working compost heap as soon as possible. Fresh pomace is wet and heavy and should be mixed well with dry leaves, hay, or other absorbent matter.

While low in nitrogen, pomace does contain valuable amounts of phosphoric acid and potash. Large numbers of seeds are also present in pomace; these storage organs contain reserves of phosphorus and nitrogen, adding to the nutrient value of the pomace.

If you collect pomace from commercial presses, look into the source of their apples and the pesticides applied to the fruit. Apple skins may contain residues of metallic sprays, especially if such sprays are used heavily. Spray residues can build up to toxic levels when large amounts of pomace are used.

Letting the Clippings Fall

Leaving grass clippings on your lawn some of the time provides the grass with natural fertilizer and saves work. It is recommended in Grasscycling, a lawn care plan promoted by the Professional Lawn Care Association of America. The low-maintenance lawn care plan is based on the highly successful Don't Bag It program originally developed in Texas. Leaving clippings does not cause thatch buildup as was once believed. Thatch is made up of dead roots, leaf sheaths, and rhizomes, not clippings. If you mow with a regular lawn mower, don't let the grass grow more than 1½ inches between mowings, and mow the grass only when it is dry. Even so, the clippings can be messy.

Mulching mowers eliminate the mess by chopping the clippings into fine fragments after they cut the grass. The fragments fall down into the lawn, where they decompose rapidly and release nutrients. Mulching mowers can also shred a few fallen leaves on the lawn while you are mowing and can be used to prepare piles of leaves for composting.

Bagasse

Bagasse is the waste plant residue left from the milling of sugarcane. Gardeners in the Deep South may have access to quantities of this valuable addition to the compost heap.

Banana Residue

The skins and stalks of this tropical fruit contain abundant amounts of phosphoric acid and potash. Banana skins also decompose rapidly, a sign that the microbes of decay are well supplied with nitrogen. Banana skins are usually a staple in kitchen scraps, and their use in a compost heap will guarantee lots of bacterial activity. Incorporate banana skins into the core of your compost pile, or cover them quickly with organic matter to avoid attracting flies.

Basic Slag

This is an industrial by-product formed when iron ore is smelted to make pig iron. The smelting process uses large amounts of limestone and dolomite that combine with impurities in the ore, rising as a sludge that coats the surface of the molten metal. Skimmed off, cooled, and hardened, the resultant slag contains numerous minerals also found in the soil-lime, magnesium, silicon, aluminum, manganese, sulfur, and iron. It also contains trace amounts of boron, chromium, copper, molybdenum, potassium, sodium, strontium, tin, vanadium, zinc, and zirconium. The exact percentage of these minerals depends on variations in the smelting process. The "Composition of Slag" table shows the main elements found in slag, the compounds in which they most often occur, and the average range of each mineral.

Composition of Slag		
Material	Compound	Percentage
Lime	CaO	38–45
Magnesia	MgO	4–9
Silica	SiO_2	33–39
Alumina	Al_2O_5	10–14
Manganese oxide	MnO	0.2–1.5
Iron oxide	FeO	0.2–0.7
Sulfur	S	1.0–2.0

Packaged slag has been pulverized into a tine black powder so it can be used as a soil builder in gardening and farming. The material is alkaline and is popular as a liming agent. Tests show that slag is better for this purpose than lime because of its greater store of minerals.

Since slag is made up of finely pulverized but insoluble particles, it can be applied liberally to soil or compost heap with no fear of overuse. It won't burn plants or roots. Beans, peas, clover, vetches, alfalfa, and other leguminous crops will benefit from its application. Slags vary in content, so check the analysis before using them. Avoid slags with low or nonexistent amounts of nutrients and minor elements. Don't use slags containing excessive amounts of sulfur.

Beet Wastes

Residues from sugar beet processing are commonly used for livestock feed, though they will compost readily. The nitrogen content averages 0.4 percent, potassium content varies from 0.7 to 4.1 percent, and phosphoric acid content ranges from 0.1 to 0.6 percent. Dried beet pulp is also available at many feed stores.

Bonemeal

A slaughterhouse by-product, the pulverized residue of bones is, along with rock phosphate, a major source of phosphorus for the farm and garden. Bonemeal also contains a large percentage of nitrogen, though the content of both minerals depends on the age and type of bones processed. Raw bonemeal usually contains 20 to 25 percent phosphoric acid and 2 to 4 percent nitrogen. Steamed bonemeal, the more commonly available variety, has up to 30 percent phosphorus and 1 to 2 percent nitrogen. Steamed bonemeal is finer than raw bonemeal, so it breaks down more rapidly in the soil or compost heap.

Bone black is charred bone that has been used as a filter for sugar refining. Bone black contains about 1.5 percent nitrogen, 30 percent phosphoric acid, and many micronutrients.

Bonemeals are most effective when mixed with other organic matter and added to well-aerated soils. They will also exert an alkalizing effect because of their lime content, so match their use to your soil's pH characteristics. Use them moderately in composting to avoid the volatilization of nitrogen to ammonia.

Buckwheat Hulls

Buckwheat is a cereal crop grown mainly in the northeastern United States and in Canada. Popular among organic farmers and gardeners as a green manure and bee forage crop, it grows well on even marginal soils. Buckwheat hulls, left after processing of the grain, are lightweight and disk shaped. They make good additions to the compost heap, though many gardeners prefer to use them as mulch. The hulls absorb water easily, stay in place once applied (a layer 1½ inches thick will suffice), and look like a crumbly loam.

Castor Pomace

Castor pomace is the residue left after the oil has been extracted from the castor bean. It is widely used as an organic fertilizer in place of cottonseed meal, because the latter is a valuable feed. The nitrogen analysis of castor bean varies from 4 to 6.6 percent, while phosphoric acid and potash have been found to be 1 to 2 percent, with greater variation occurring in the phosphorus content.

Where animal matter is unavailable, compost can easily be made with castor pomace and other plant matter. Moisten the pomace and spread it over the green matter in semiliquid form. The finer the plant matter, the quicker the bacterial action.

Citrus Wastes

Gardeners living near factories producing orange and grapefruit products should make use of this easily composted residue, though dried citrus pulp is also available in bulk from some feed stores. The nitrogen content of these materials varies according to the type of fruit and the density of the skin. The thicker the peel, the more nitrogen contained.

Orange skins contain about 3 percent phosphoric acid and 27 percent potash (surpassed only by banana skins, with 50 percent potash). Lemons are higher in phosphorus but lower in potash than oranges. Grapefruits average 3.6 percent phosphoric acid, and their potassium content is near that of oranges.

You may also use whole waste fruits (culls) in the compost pile, although their nutrient content will be lower due to the high water content. Citrus wastes will break down faster if shredded (the bagged, dried pulp sold as animal feed comes in dime-sized chips) and mixed with green matter and a source of nitrogen and bacteria like manure, lawn clippings, or garden soil.

Unfortunately, citrus crops are routinely sprayed by commercial growers. If the spray program is moderate, the chemicals should break down during the composting process without

Continued ➡

causing harm. To be absolutely sure of what you're adding to your compost, use only fruits and fruit wastes from organic growers.

Cocoa Bean Shells

These residues from chocolate factories are available in bulk from garden supply houses, but because they make such an attractive mulch, cocoa bean shells rarely find their way into the compost heap. They are rich in nutrients, though, and benefit the soil however they're used. Cocoa shell dust has 1.5 percent phosphorus, about 1.7 percent potassium, and 1 percent nitrogen—a high analysis of the latter considering the woody nature of cocoa.

If the shells themselves have been treated to extract caffeine and theobromine, the residues will have about 2.7 percent nitrogen, 0.7 percent phosphoric acid, and 2.6 percent potassium. Untreated raw shells show a higher nutrient content. Pressed cocoa cake has also been offered as fertilizer. It's higher in nitrogen, has less potassium than shells, and has a phosphorus content of nearly 0.9 percent. The nitrogen content of cake will vary according to its processing.

If you can locate a source of oil-free and theobromine—free cocoa wastes, you'll have a useful product for mulching acidic soils. The extraction process uses lime, so the shells will help raise the pH while adding moisture-retentive organic matter. Cocoa shells are also weed free and odorless.

To use them as mulch, spread the shells in a layer 1 inch deep. They are light brown, look nice around shrubs, evergreens, and flower beds, and offer excellent drought-proofing and insulative properties. Shells used in compost piles should be shredded or pulverized.

Coffee Wastes

Earthworms seem to have a particular affinity for coffee grounds, so be sure to use these leftovers on the compost pile, in your worm box, or as a mulch. The grounds are acidic and can be used by themselves around blueberries, evergreens, and other acid-loving plants. Mix the grounds with a little ground limestone for plants needing alkaline or neutral soil.

The nutrient content of coffee residues varies according to the type of residue. Grounds have up to 2 percent nitrogen, 0.33 percent phosphoric acid, and varying amounts of potassium. Drip coffee grounds contain more nutrients than boiled grounds, though the potassium content is still below 1 percent. Other substances found include sugars, carbohydrates, some vitamins, trace elements, and caffeine.

Coffee processing plants sell coffee chaff, a dark material containing over 2 percent nitrogen and potassium. Chaff is useful either as a mulch or in compost.

Apply your coffee grounds immediately, or mix them with other organic matter. They hold moisture extremely well. Left standing, they will quickly sour, inviting acetobacters (vinegar-producing microbes) and fruit flies.

Corncobs

These residues used to be available in large amounts from mills, but modern combines now shred the stalks and expel the cobs right back into the field. Cobs contain two-thirds of the nutrients found in the corn kernel, but they must be shredded before composting or their decay will take years. Let the cobs age in open piles for several months, then grind them with a shredder or lawn mower.

Cobs have superior moisture retention and make effective mulches when spread 3 to 4 inches

deep. Shredded cobs may also be used as a seed-starting medium. In longstanding, no-turn piles, unshredded cobs mixed with leaves and other dense materials will provide aeration and discourage caking and matting.

Cottonseed Meal

Cottonseed meal is made from cottonseed that has been freed from lints and hulls and deprived of its oil. Since cottonseed cake is one of the richest protein foods for animal feeding, relatively little is available for use as fertilizer. Although it is a rich source of nitrogen, most organic certification programs prohibit the use of cottonseed meal as a fertilizer. This is because cotton, as a nonfood crop, receives heavy applications of pesticides, some of which may accumulate in the seeds. Unless you have access to meal from organically grown cotton, you may choose to avoid cottonseed meal in favor of another nitrogen source for your compost pile.

Cottonseed meal is also commonly used to increase soil acidity for acid-loving specialty crops, but other materials, such as pine needles and peat moss, will serve the same purpose. Cottonseed meal has a nitrogen content of around 7 percent. Its phosphoric acid content is between 2 and 3 percent, while potash is usually 1.5 percent.

Dried Blood

Dried blood is a slaughterhouse by-product. It is high in nitrogen, about 12 percent, but its phosphorus content varies from 1 to 5 percent. Dried blood is used mainly as an animal feed, though most garden shops carry it for use as a fertilizer. The cost per pound can be quite high because it is tied to the price of meat. Dried blood can be applied directly to the soil around plants, but it should be kept several inches away from the stems to avoid burning. Dried blood may also be used in compost heaps. Sprinkled over layers of moist organic matter, its high nitrogen content stimulates decay organisms, especially when added to carbon-rich materials.

Felt Wastes

Check hat factories for discarded hair, wool, and felt. These materials may contain up to 14 percent nitrogen and will aid in making rapid, high-heat compost. Such wastes are quite dry, however, and will decompose slowly or pack down unless they are thoroughly moistened and mixed with bacteria-rich ingredients like manure or green matter.

Fish Scrap

Gardeners near oceans or fish-processing plants can usually truck home loads of this smelly stuff. It is well supplied with nitrogen and phosphorus (7 percent or above for each nutrient) and also contains valuable micronutrients like iodine. But, like all fresh residues, fish scraps easily turn anaer-

obic and are highly attractive to rodents, flies, and other scavengers.

Fish scraps must be handled carefully in the garden, either buried (covered with at least 4 inches of soil) or composted in properly built heaps enclosed by sturdy bins or pens. The trick is to use generous amounts of bulky, high-carbon materials such as shredded brush, straw, or sawdust to balance the high nitrogen and moisture of the fish, to increase aeration, and to discourage packing down.

Composting fish scraps in a pit is somewhat easier (once you've dug the pit, of course). Mix them with organic matter or soil, and cover them with enough dirt to discourage flies. The pit must also be enclosed by a sturdy fence or wall and topped with a scavenger-proof frame or lid.

Fish scrap presents difficult challenges to the composter on any scale, but it offers ample benefits when used with reasonable care and attention to providing adequate carbon and air. William F. Brinton, of Woods End Research Laboratory in Maine, has successfully demonstrated fish waste composting, with minimal odor problems, using a farm- or industrial-scale windrow method.

Garbage

Americans routinely throw away mountains of valuable food scraps, setting them out on the curb or grinding them up in disposals and flushing them into overworked municipal sewage systems. Yet kitchen scraps are truly a neglected resource, containing 1 to 3 percent nitrogen along with calcium, phosphorus, potassium, and micronutrients. The material is free, available in quantity every day, and relatively easy to handle.

Kitchen scraps may be dug directly into the garden. Alternatively, they may be composted in heaps or pits. You can conveniently save household garbage until you are ready to layer it into a new or existing compost pile. Use a plastic bucket with a tight-fitting lid, and each time you add garbage, cover it with a layer of sawdust or peat moss to absorb moisture and odors. When adding kitchen scraps to your compost pile, mix them well with absorbent matter like dead leaves or hay to offset the wetness. Use a predator-proof enclosure, and be sure to keep all scraps well into the pile's core, covering them thoroughly with dirt or additional materials to discourage flies.

Chop or shred all large pieces of matter (potatoes, grapefruit rinds, eggshells, and so on) to hasten decomposition. Do not use meat scraps, fat, or bones in compost piles, for these materials take too long to fully break down and are most attractive to scavenging animals.

Gin Trash

Gin trash is another by-product of the cotton industry. Once burned and discarded, these leaf and stem wastes are now being composted and returned to the soil. While cotton wastes contain many valuable nutrients and fibrous organic matter, their effect on soil health may not always be beneficial, depending on the type of cotton and the state in which it was produced. In some states, including Texas and Oklahoma, arsenic acid is applied as a defoliant and desiccant. Significant residues of this carcinogen are left in the gin trash, making it an undesirable addition to the compost pile. Normal arsenic levels in the soil run about 5 parts per million, but gin wastes may contain 40 times that amount.

Arsenic acid is no longer used in cotton production in California. Home composters who have access to gin trash should consider its source and the production methods used in their state

Continued ➡

before making gin trash a part of their composting program. Because of the timing of arsenic acid applications, contamination of the seeds does not occur; arsenic residue is not a concern with cottonseed meal.

Granite Dust

Granite dust is a natural source of potash that is superior to the chemically treated potash sold as commercial fertilizer. Granite dust or granite meal has a potassium content of between 3 and 5 percent, contains micronutrients, is inexpensive, and will leave no harmful chemical residues. Unlike chemically treated sources of potash, granite dust is slow acting, releasing its nutrients over a period of years. It may be used in the compost pile or added to soil or sheet compost. Use it liberally directly on the soil, applying 10 pounds to 100 square feet when spreading. Choose a windless day for application, and wear a dust mask.

Grape Wastes

Wineries produce these residues of skins, seeds, and stalks by the ton during the pressing season. Vineyards also accumulate large amounts of grapevine pieces after annual pruning. While the nutrient content of grape wastes isn't that high, the sheer bulk of organic materials involved benefits the soil by promoting aeration and microbial activity.

The residues of pressing will be wet and mushy and should be mixed with absorbent plant matter. Additional nitrogen in the form of manure or high-protein green matter may also be necessary if you desire rapid, hot compost. The prunings are tough and must be chopped into pieces 3 to 6 inches long, or shredded, if they are to break down in a season.

Grass Clippings

This is one compostable—a true "green manure"—that most gardeners can produce or obtain in abundance. Even if you don't have your own lawn, your fellow citizens do; they'll leave bags of clippings conveniently lined up along the curb sides for your harvesting every garbage collection day.

Freshly gathered green clippings are exceedingly rich in nitrogen and will heat up on their own if pulled into a pile. But, because of their high water content, they will also pack down and become slimy. This can be avoided by adding grass clippings in thin layers, alternating with leaves, garbage, manure, and other materials, thus preventing them from clumping together. If you discover a mass of matted clippings when you turn your compost, just break it up with a garden fork or spade, and layer the pieces back into the pile. Grass clippings and leaves can be turned into finished compost in 2 weeks if the heap is chopped and turned every 3 days. You can also profitably mix 2 parts grass clippings with 1 part manure and bedding for a relatively fast compost, even without turning.

Clippings that have been allowed to dry out will have lost much of their nitrogen content but are still valuable as an energy source and to absorb excess moisture. Clippings also make an excellent mulch in the vegetable or flower garden or around shrubs and trees. As a mulch, clippings look neat and stay in place, and only a light layer (3 to 4 inches) is needed to choke out weeds and seal in moisture.

If you have extra grass clippings on hand later in the season, use them as a green manure. Simply scatter them in an area that has already been harvested and turn them in immediately, along with any previously applied mulch. The fresh clippings decompose quickly in the soil and stimulate microbial activity by providing abundant nitrogen. More mulch should be added to the surface over winter to prevent exposure of bare soil to the weather. You can also use clippings as a green manure before planting a late crop, but give the soil a week or 10 days to stabilize before planting. When used this way, grass clippings greatly improve the physical condition of heavy-textured soils.

Not all grass clippings should be removed from the lawn; when left after mowing, their nutrients enrich the lawn itself, without the application of chemical fertilizers. However, most lawns do not need as much enrichment as a full growing season's clippings will provide. Collecting grass clippings also helps reduce weed growth by removing weed seeds from the lawn.

There is one environmental caution about grass clippings. Many homeowners use various "weed and feed" preparations or any of a half-dozen herbicides in striving for an immaculate lawn. The most troublesome of these chemicals is 2, 4-D, a weed killer that has caused birth defects in lab animals and may be carcinogenic.

Although this systemic, rapid-action plant hormone attacks broad-leaved plants like dandelions, literally causing them to grow themselves to death in hours, 2, 4-D doesn't affect grasses. The narrow-bladed leaves do absorb traces of the hormone but not enough to harm them. Much more 2, 4-D remains as a residue in broad-leaved plants, though even this should theoretically be broken down by soil microbes in a week. But beware of grass clippings that may have spray adhering to them from a fresh application. If used as a mulch, such clippings could cause herbicide damage to your garden plants—most of which are broad-leaved.

Ask your neighbors or whomever you gather clippings from what they used on their lawns. (If several mowings and some rains have occurred since the last application of herbicide, the clippings should be clear of 2, 4-D residue.) Use your own clippings if you have them, and look around for natural lawns showing a healthy crop of dandelions—a sign that the landowner wisely avoided using herbicides.

Greensand

Greensand is an iron-potassium-silicate that imparts a green color to the minerals in which it occurs. Being an undersea deposit, greensand contains traces of many (if not all) of the elements that occur in seawater. Greensand has been used successfully for soil building for more than 100 years. It is a fine source of potash.

Greensand contains from 6 to 7 percent of plant-available potash, but it is released very slowly when applied directly to the soil. Incorporating greensand into your compost improves the availability of its potassium and micronutrients. Good glauconite deposits also contain 50 percent silica, 18 to 23 percent iron oxides, 3 to 7.5 percent magnesia, small amounts of lime and phosphoric acid, and traces of more than 30 other elements useful to higher plant life. Unlike wood ashes, another frequently used source of potash, greensand does not have an alkalinizing effect.

Hair

Between 6 and 7 pounds of hair contain as much nitrogen as 100 to 200 pounds of manure. Like feathers, hair will decompose rapidly in a compost pile but only if well moistened and thoroughly mixed with an aerating material. Hair tends to pack down and shed water, so chopping or turning the pile regularly will hasten decay. Most barbershops or hair salons will be happy to supply you with bags of hair (though they may think your request is strange unless you explain).

Hay

Farmers often have spoiled hay available free or at low cost to gardeners. Hay is an excellent source of carbon for compost and also contains significant amounts of potassium, especially if it includes legumes such as alfalfa, clover, or vetch.

Hay is sometimes best used as mulch, especially around fruit trees. However, unless it was cut early, before seed heads began to form, it poses the hazard of introducing weed seeds into your garden. High, temperature composting will kill most weed seeds. In order to ensure that high enough temperatures (above 140°F, or 60°C) are reached, you should chop or shred the hay first, especially if it has matted in the bales. This can be done by spreading out the sections and running a lawn mower back and forth over them. You should alternate layers of nitrogenous materials such as manure with the shredded hay, to stimulate rapid heating. Make sure the materials are moist enough by giving each layer a good sprinkling. If high enough temperatures are not reached within a couple of days, the pile should be turned and relayered with an additional nitrogen source.

Hoof and Horn Meal

There are many grades of hoof and horn meal. The granular form breaks down with some difficulty unless kept moist and well covered; it also tends to encourage the growth of maggots because it attracts flies. Finely ground horn dust, which gardeners use for potting mixtures, is quite easily dissolved. The nitrogen content is from 10 to 16 pounds per 100-pound bag, or as much as a ton or more of manure, while the phosphoric acid value is usually around 2 percent. If available, this is a very handy source of nitrogen for gardeners with small compost heaps, because it can be easily stored, is pleasant to handle, and is less costly than other forms of bagged organic nitrogen.

Hops

Hops are viny plants grown and used for making beer. (Hops impart the characteristic bitter flavor.) Spent hops, the wastes left after the brewing process, are an excellent garden fertilizer, containing (when dry) 2.5 to 3.5 percent nitrogen and 1 percent phosphoric acid. They do have a strong odor when wet and fresh, but this dissipates rapidly.

Wet hops may be spread directly on the garden in fall or spring just as you would apply manure. Turn the matter under, mixing it with the top 4 to 5 inches of soil. Wet hops heat up rapidly, so keep them several inches away from plant stems to avoid burning. This tendency to heat up is, of course, desirable in making compost. Be sure to balance the sogginess of spent hops with absorbent matter.

Spent hops make a good mulch when dry. They resist blowing away and will not easily ignite if a lighted match or cigarette is tossed onto a pile. Many other mulch materials burn easily. A layer of dry, spent hops will break down slowly, staying put for 3 years or more.

Another brewery waste to inquire about is the grain left over from the mashing process. When wet, this material contains almost 1 percent nitrogen and decays rapidly.

Incinerator Ash

Incinerator ash, if available, can be a fine source of phosphorus and potash for the compost heap. Its phosphorus content depends upon what was burned but averages 5 or 6 percent; its potassium content is from 2 to 3 percent. As with many compostable materials, the source of the ash should

Continued ➡

be considered before it is added to the compost pile. Ash from apartment building incinerators may be acceptable, depending on the materials burned. It is best to avoid municipal incinerator ash, most of which is considered hazardous waste because the heavy metals and other toxic substances found in municipal solid waste often become more concentrated and soluble when burned.

Leather Dust

Available as a by-product of leather processing and as a commercial fertilizer from garden shops, leather dust contains from 5.5 to 12 percent nitrogen. Phosphorus is also present in considerable amounts. Use as a soil amendment, as a side-dressing around plants, or as a dusting over successive layers in the compost heap.

Leather dust is often contaminated with the heavy metal chromium, used in the tanning process. While one producer of leather dust fertilizer points out that the chromium in their product is in an immobile form, studies have not addressed the long-term effects of this material in the soil. Some organic certification programs prohibit the use of leather dust for this reason. Unless you have a source that produces leather dust with low or no levels of heavy-metal contaminants, it is best to refrain from using it on your compost or on soil in which food crops will be grown.

Leaves

Leaves are a valuable compostable and mulch material abundantly available to most gardeners. Because trees have extensive root systems, they draw nutrients up from deep within the subsoil. Much of this mineral bounty is passed into the leaves, making them a superior garden resource. Pound for pound, the leaves of most trees contain twice the mineral content of manure. The considerable fiber content of leaves aids in improving the aeration and crumb structure of most soils.

Many people shy away from using leaves in compost, because they've had trouble with them packing down and resisting decay. Leaves don't contain much nitrogen, so a pile of them all alone may take years to decay fully. But most leaves can be converted to a fine-textured humus in several weeks (or, at most, a few months) if some general guidelines are followed:

- Add extra nitrogen to your leaf compost since leaves alone don't contain enough nitrogen to provide sufficient food for bacteria. Manure is the best nitrogen supplement, and a mixture of five parts leaves to one part manure will break down quickly. If you don't have manure, nitrogen supplements like dried blood, alfalfa meal, and bonemeal will work almost as well. In general, add 2 cups of dried blood or other natural nitrogen supplement to each wheelbarrow load of leaves.

- Don't let your leaves sit around too long and dry out. As leaves weather, they lose whatever nitrogen content they may have had. This, combined with the dehydration of the cells, makes them much more resistant to decomposition than when used fresh.

- Grind or shred your leaves. A compost pile made of shredded material is easily controlled and easy to handle.

If you don't have a shredder, there are various other devices you can adapt to leaf shredding. Many people use a rotary mower for shredding. A mower that is not self-propelled is best and easiest to control. Two people can work together very nicely, one piling up leaves in front of the mower and the other running it back and forth over the pile. A leaf-mulching attachment on the blade will

cut the leaves finer, but sometimes it is not necessary. You will be surprised how many leaves you can shred this way in 30 minutes or so.

Of course, some people use a mower with a mulching attachment to cut up leaves right on the lawn. This does not make them available for compost or mulch somewhere else—like the garden—where they are more essential.

If you have so many leaves that you can't compost all of them—or if you don't have the time to make compost—you can make leaf mold. Leaf mold is not as rich a fertilizer as composted leaves, but it's easier to make and is especially useful as mulch.

A length of snow fencing or woven wire fencing placed in a circle makes the best kind of enclosure for making leaf mold. Gather leaves in the fall and wet them thoroughly; then tamp them down in the enclosure. Leaves are slightly acid. If your plants don't need an acid mulch, add some limestone to the leaves before tamping them down.

These leaves will not break down over the winter into the kind of black, powdery leaf mold found on the forest floor. By spring or summer they will be broken up enough to serve as a fine mulch. Some people, including nursery operators who require fine potting soil, keep leaves "in cold storage" for several years. When they come for their leaves, they find black, crumbly humus.

Leaf mold is ordinarily found in the forest in a layer just above the mineral soil. It has the merit of decomposing slowly, furnishing plant nutrients gradually, and improving the soil structure as it does so. Leaf mold's ability to retain moisture is amazing. Subsoil can hold a mere 20 percent of its weight in water; good, rich topsoil will hold 60 percent; but leaf mold can retain 300 to 500 percent of its weight.

Freshly fallen leaves pass through several stages, from surface litter to well-decomposed humus partly mixed with mineral soil. Leaf mold from deciduous trees is somewhat richer in such mineral foods as potash and phosphorus than that from conifers. The nitrogen content varies from 0.2 to 5 percent.

If you keep poultry or livestock, use your supply of leaves for litter or bedding along with straw or hay. Leaf mold thus enriched with extra nitrogen may later be mixed directly with soil or added to the compost pile.

A lawn sweeper is a good tool to use for collecting leaves. It is easier than raking and often does a better job. Hand-held leaf vacuums are also available at most lawn and garden stores.

Many municipalities are now composting leaves and yard wastes instead of dumping them into landfills. If your community has such a program, you can send in your surplus leaves with a good conscience and probably pick up finished compost in return.

Limestone

Limestone is an important source of calcium and, when dolomitic limestone is used, magnesium. It is commonly used to raise the pH of acid soils and may sometimes be appropriate when composting very acidic materials such as pine needles. However, compost made from a good variety of materials should have a pH near neutral without the addition of lime. Moreover, it is unwise to use lime with fresh manure or other nitrogenous materials, as it reacts chemically to drive off ammonia gas and thus lose some of the valuable nitrogen.

If your soil is acid, it is best to apply lime to it directly, rather than through compost. Any reliable soil test will tell you how much lime is needed. If you live in a humid region, lime should be applied every 3 or 4 years, preferably in the fall so it will become available first thing in the spring. Use a

grade fine enough to pass through a 100-mesh screen. In drier climates, where soil pH is naturally neutral or higher, liming is rarely necessary. You may want to use some lime for making potting soil with your compost—use about 1 tablespoon for 20 quarts of soil mix.

Most vegetables and garden plants prefer a slightly acid to neutral pH, so laboratory liming recommendations generally strive for a pH of 6.5 to 6.8 (a pH of 7 is neutral). Some vegetables—legumes such as beans, peas, and alfalfa, for example—do better with slightly alkaline soil, while many berries prefer acid conditions. Organic matter in the soil tends to buffer the effects of pH extremes by making nutrients available to plants regardless of soil pH. Lime, therefore, should be used to supplement soil improvement through the addition of compost.

Manure

Manure is the most valuable ingredient in the compost pile.

Molasses Residues

The wastes from sugar refining are obviously rich in carbohydrates, but they also contain some mineral nutrients. Naturally occurring yeasts in the compost will ferment these sugars rapidly. Dry molasses is also available from feed stores.

Olive Wastes

Olive pits contain phosphorus, nitrogen, and some lignin (a woody substance related to cellulose). But the pits must be ground or chopped before composting, or they'll take years to decay. Pulpy olive wastes vary in nutrient density. One analysis showed the pomace (what's left after oil extraction) having 1.15 percent nitrogen, 0.78 percent phosphoric acid, and 1.26 percent potassium. The pulp is oily and should be well mixed with other organic matter.

Paper

Many kinds of paper, even those with colored inks, can be used for compost or mulch. You can save a lot on trash collection costs, and keep the valuable carbon for your soil, by recycling paper through your compost. Although the colored inks contain various heavy metals, one study found that their concentration is low enough to be negligible, even when glossy magazines are used as a garden mulch. If only a few colored-ink items are mixed in with newsprint, there should be no cause for concern.

The secret to using paper successfully is to shred or chop it as finely as possible. Matted layers of newspaper, like hay and grass clippings, will halt the composting organisms in their tracks. Various tools will work for this process, including shredders used for brush. If you don't have a lot of paper, a sharp machete will chop it adequately. And don't forget the office paper shredder—you may even be able to recycle preshredded office paper from local businesses. Dairy farmers in various regions are being encouraged to use newspaper, which they shred using silage-making equipment, as bedding for their animals. The newspaper is very absorbent and makes an excellent compost medium when mixed with manure.

Shredded paper should be incorporated into your compost in layers, alternating with garbage or other wet materials. Because it is almost pure cellulose, it requires a concentrated nitrogen source to stimulate decomposition, but once broken down it creates a high-quality humus that will improve the tilth of any soil.

Peat Moss

This naturally occurring fibrous material is the centuries-old, partially decayed residue of plants.

Continued ➡

Widely sold as a soil conditioner, mulch, and plant propagation medium, peat's major advantages are its water retention (it is capable of absorbing 15 times its weight in water) and fibrous bulk. Dry peat will help loosen heavy soils, bind light ones, hold nutrients in place, and increase aeration. But while its physical effects on soil are valuable, peat isn't a substitute for compost or leaf mold. Expensive, relatively low in nutrients, and acidic, peat is best used as a seed flat and rooting medium or as a mulch or soil amendment for acid-loving plants.

If a distinctly acid compost is needed for certain plants, substitute peat for the soil in your compost pile. Peat compost is beneficial for camellia, rhododendron, azalea, blueberry, sweet potato, watermelon, eggplant, potato, and tomato plants—all of which prefer acidic soil conditions.

Pea Wastes

Feeding pea shells and vines to livestock and getting the waste back as manure is an excellent recycling method. Otherwise, pea wastes can be rapidly composted since they are rich in nitrogen when green. Dry vines should be shredded or chopped before or during composting, to hasten decay. Diseased vines should be burned and the ashes returned to the soil. (Pea ash contains almost 3 percent phosphoric acid and 27 percent potassium.)

Pet Wastes

As discussed earlier in this chapter, the wastes of dogs, cats, and birds are potential carriers of organisms that may cause disease in humans. Such materials should not be included in the home compost pile. Wastewater from aquariums, however, contains a certain amount of algae and organic matter that can be beneficial to plants. Use aquarium water to add moisture to your compost heap or for watering plants.

Phosphate Rock

Phosphate rock is a mainstay in organic gardens and farms because of its value as a soil and compost pile amendment. While its chemical composition varies according to the source, phosphate rock generally contains 65 percent calcium phosphate or bone phosphate of lime. A diversity of other compounds and micro nutrients important to plant development is also present.

Phosphate rock is a naturally occurring mineral, however; don't confuse it with superphosphate. The latter has been treated with sulfuric acid to increase its solubility. But many micronutrients are lost due to this processing, and the increase in the availability of sulfur stimulates the presence of sulfur-reducing bacteria in the soil. These organisms attack sulfur and also ingest a fungus that normally breaks down cellulose in the soil. Besides encouraging this microbial imbalance, superphosphate can also leave harmful salts in the soil. Furthermore, within a few days superphosphate will react chemically with calcium and other soil nutrients to become indistinguishable from the less-soluble rock powder.

Phosphate rock creates no such problems. It's slow acting, which makes nutrients available to plants for many years after a single application. Applied alone to vegetable or flower gardens, 1 pound to every 10 square feet of growing area will suffice for 3 to 5 years. It may also be sprinkled lightly over succeeding layers in a compost heap to add nutrients to the finished product. It is valuable when combined with manure and other nitrogenous materials, since it prevents loss of nitrogen in the form of ammonia. The nutrients in rock phosphate are more readily available to plants when it is added via compost, having first been incorporated into the bodies of countless microorganisms.

Pine Needles

Pine needles are compostable, although they will break down rather slowly because of their thick outer coating of a waxy substance called cutin. Pine needles are also acidic in nature, and for this reason they should not be used in large quantities, unless compost for acid-loving plants is desired. For best results, shred the needles before adding them to the heap.

Evergreen needles have been found to be effective in controlling some harmful soil fungi, such as *Fusarium* spp., when used as a mulch or mixed directly into the soil.

Potato Wastes

Potato peels are common components of kitchen scraps. They provide a valuable source of nitrogen (about 0.6 percent as ash) and minor elements for the compost pile. Rotted whole potatoes, chopped or shredded, are also worthwhile compost pile additions. The tubers contain about 2.5 percent potash, plus other minerals. Use the potato vines, too; they can be either composted or dug back into the soil. The vines, when dry, contain approximately 1.6 percent potash, 4 percent calcium, and 1.1 percent magnesium, plus sulfur and other minerals.

Rice Hulls

Often considered a waste product, rice hulls have been found to be very rich in potash and to decompose readily, increasing humus content, when worked into the soil. The hulls make an excellent soil conditioner and a worthwhile addition to the compost heap. They also make a good, long-lasting mulch that does not blow away.

Gardeners in the Texas-Louisiana Gulf Coast area can often get ample amounts of this material from rice mills; occasionally it is free. Some mills make a practice of burning the hulls, and the residue from this operation contains a high percentage of potash, making it especially valuable as a composting material.

Sawdust

Sawdust is often useful in the compost heap, although it is better used as a mulch. Some gardeners who have access to large quantities use it for both, with equally fine results. In most areas, lumberyards will occasionally give sawdust free for the hauling. Sawdust is very low in nitrogen. One of the objections against using sawdust is that it may cause a nitrogen deficiency. However, many gardeners report fine results from applying sawdust as a mulch to the soil surface without adding any supplementary nitrogen fertilizer. If your soil is of low fertility, watch plants carefully during the growing season. If they become light green or yellowish in color, side-dress with an organic nitrogen fertilizer such as alfalfa meal, blood meal, compost, or manure. Regular applications of manure tea will also counteract any slight nitrogen deficit.

Some people are afraid that the continued application of sawdust will sour their soil—that is, make it too acid. A very comprehensive study made from 1949 to 1954 by the Connecticut Agricultural Experiment Station of sawdust and wood chips reported no instance of sawdust making the soil more acid. It is possible, though, that sawdust used on the highly alkaline soils of the western United States would help to make the soil neutral, a welcome effect.

When used for compost, sawdust is valuable not only as a carbon source but as a bulking agent, allowing good air penetration in the pile. This is true only of sawdust that comes from sawmills or chain saws; the fine material that results from sanding can become packed and anaerobic. Although sawdust is slow to break down, the larger

bits you may find remaining in finished compost will not present problems when added to your soil and will improve the texture of heavy soils.

Seaweed

Coastal gardeners gather different types of seaweed by wandering the shoreline. Look for kelp (laminaria), bladder wrack (also called fucus), sea lettuce (ulva), and other varieties. Gardeners elsewhere can buy dried, granulated seaweed (kelp meal) or liquid concentrate. All these seaweed variants are rich in many types of micronutrients and are a boon to plants, soil health, and the compost pile.

Compared with barnyard manure, seaweed in general has a similar organic content. The proportions, however, vary-seaweed has more potassium than manure but has less nitrogen and phosphorus. Seaweed is perhaps most valued for its micronutrient content. An analysis of the seaweed most commonly used in seaweed meals and extracts identified the presence of some 60 elements, including all those important for plant, animal, and human health.

Use wet, fresh seaweed quickly because it deteriorates rapidly when piled haphazardly. Exposure to the elements will quickly leach out many of seaweed's soluble minerals. Dig the seaweed under, or mix it with nitrogenous and absorbent materials for rapid composting. Bacteria feast on the alginic acid found in the leaves, which makes seaweed an excellent compost pile activator. If composted with manure that is rich in litter, seaweed aids the speedy decay of the straw; very little nitrogen is lost, and all the other elements are preserved. Decay occurs rapidly.

If you have only a small amount of seaweed, chop it and soak it overnight in a gallon of hot water (160° to 180°F, or 71° to 82°C). Sprinkle this mixture over successive layers of the compost pile. The liquid can also be used as a fertilizer and as a seed-soaking solution.

Kelp meal can be used as an activator in compost, since its rich micronutrient composition stimulates microbial growth. Seaweed extract can be used to feed plants directly through their leaves, and may also be applied to compost in the course of moistening the layers. When used as a foliar feed, plant growth is also stimulated by seaweed's content of cytokinins and other plant growth hormones.

Sewage Sludge

Sewage sludge is the solid residue left after organic wastes and wastewater have been chemically, bacterially, or physically processed. Depending on how it is processed, sludge may contain up to 6 percent nitrogen and from 3 to 6 percent phosphorus.

Activated sludge is produced when sewage is agitated by air rapidly bubbling through it. Certain types of very active bacteria coagulate the organic matter, which settles out, leaving a clear liquid that can be discharged with a minimum amount of pollution. The resulting sludge is usually heat-treated before being offered as a soil amendment.

Digested sludge is formed when the solid matter in sewage is allowed to settle without air agitation, the liquid is drained off, and the sludge is fermented anaerobically. The conventional anaerobic digestion system takes from 15 to 30 days at 99°F (37°C) from the time the sewage reaches the sedimentation tank until the digested solids are pumped into filter beds for drying. The dried material is either incinerated or used for soil improvement.

Until recently, most sewage sludge was incinerated, buried in landfills, or dumped offshore. Now there's an increasing interest in using this potentially valuable material as a soil conditioner. This would be ideal if the residue were composed solely

Continued ➜

of the remains of human waste, but that isn't the case. Since industrial wastes are often treated in the same sewage plants as household wastes, sewage sludges are often contaminated with heavy metals that, when regularly incorporated into the soil, can build up to toxic levels.

All municipal sludge must be composted at high temperatures before it can be safely used as a garden fertilizer. Even then, avoid using it for edible crops, especially roots and leafy greens, since some viruses can survive hot composting temperatures. Any municipal solid waste composting operation should provide information on metals and other toxic compounds in its products if it offers them for sale to the public; most states prohibit distribution of uncomposted sludge to the public.

As restrictions on sewage waste disposal make it more difficult and costly, an increasing number of cities are establishing sludge composting programs. Gardeners who have access to the products of such programs should ask questions and get detailed answers about the content of the sludge, its chemical analysis, and how it has been processed. Unless you're absolutely sure of the chemical content of your community's sludge, don't apply it near or on food crops or anywhere that runoff might contaminate a garden, an orchard, or a well.

Soil

While not a necessity, soil is a valuable component in compost making. The thin (⅛-inch) layer called for in Indore heaps contains billions of soil organisms that consume plant, animal, and mineral matter, converting it to humus. Soil also contains minerals and organic matter, so it acts like an activator when added to compostables. You can achieve much the same results using finished compost saved from a previous batch.

There are many insects and animals that live in or near compost piles. Just like in your garden, most of these creatures are beneficial, so don't worry when you spot them—they're helping out or just enjoying the composting process.

Thin layers of dirt in the compost heap work to absorb unstable substances produced by fermentation, thereby slowing their loss to the atmosphere. And when the pile is built, a topping of several inches of topsoil will stop heat and water from leaving the pile. Don't add too much soil, however, or the finished compost will be quite heavy.

Other than your own property, sources for soil include nearby woods, fields, building excavations, and mud from streams and ponds free of industrial or agricultural pollution. Don't use pond or stream mud directly in your soil; it will have the same effect as adding raw manure. Mud is also easier to handle if you dry it before composting, by mixing it with layers of absorbent plant wastes.

Straw

Although straw will add few nutrients to the compost heap, it is widely used because it is readily available and adds considerable organic material. It is also unsurpassed as an aerating medium, as each straw acts as a conduit for air to circulate throughout the pile.

The fertilizer value of straw is, like that of all organic matter, twofold; it adds carbon material and plant food to the compost. The carbon serves the soil bacteria as energy food, while the plant food becomes released for growing crops. Where much straw is used, incorporate considerable amounts of nitrogen (preferably in the form of manures) so that the bacteria that break down the straw into humus do not deplete the soil of the nitrogen needed by growing plants.

If used in quantity, the straw should be cut up. Long pieces of straw mixed with other materials that hold water or composted with ample amounts of barnyard manure offer no trouble, though heaps cannot be turned easily. Straw compost must therefore be allowed to stand longer. For quicker compost, weigh down the material with a thicker layer of earth. This also preserves the moisture inside the heap.

If a large straw pile is allowed to stay outside in the field, it will eventually decay at the bottom into a crumbly substance. Such material is excellent for compost making and mulching. Some of the fungi it contains are of the types that form mycorrhizal relations with the roots of fruit trees, evergreens, grapes, roses, and so on, and a straw mulch will therefore benefit these plants not only as a moisture preserver but as an inoculant for mycorrhizae.

The nitrogen value of straw is so small that it need not be accounted for in composting. The mineral value of straw depends on the soils where the crops were grown. (See the table "Typical Analyses of Straws" below.)

Sugar Wastes

The most plentiful sugar-processing residue is burned bone, or bone charcoal, which is used as a filtration medium. Called "bone black" when saturated with sugar residues, this substance contains 2 percent nitrogen, more than 30 percent phosphorus, and a variable potassium content. Raw sugar residues, also known as bagasse, have over 1 percent nitrogen and over 8 percent phosphoric acid.

Tanbark

Tanbark is plant waste that remains following the tanning of leather. Its residues are shredded, heaped, and inoculated with decay-promoting bacteria. Thus composted, tanbark is sold in bulk as mulching material. Analysis shows nitrogen at 1.7 percent, phosphorus at 0.9 percent, and potassium at 0.2 percent; minor amounts of aluminum, calcium, cobalt, copper, iron, lead, magnesium, molybdenum, zinc, and boron are also present. Like peat, tanbark makes an excellent mulch but is generally too expensive to use extensively in compost.

Tankage

Tankage is the refuse from slaughterhouses and butcher shops, except blood freed from the fats by processing. Depending on the amount of bone present, the phosphorus content varies greatly. The nitrogen content varies usually between 5 and 12.5 percent; the phosphoric acid content is usually around 2 percent, but may be much higher.

Tankage, because it is usually rich in nutrient value, is especially valuable to the compost pile. However, it is also in demand as a feed additive and so is available only sporadically. Because it is an animal waste, tankage does require some special care in composting. Your compost must be kept in a secure, enclosed container, safe from four-legged scavengers. Use a good supply of high-carbon materials such as leaves, hay, or sawdust to absorb odors, with a layer of soil over each layer of tankage.

Tea Grounds

Useful as a mulch or for adding to the compost heap, one analysis of tea leaves showed the relatively high content of 4.15 percent nitrogen, which seems exceptional. Both phosphorus and potash were present in amounts below 1 percent.

Tobacco Wastes

Tobacco stems, leaf waste, and dust are good organic fertilizer, especially high in potash. The nutrients contained in 100 pounds of tobacco wastes are 2.5 to 3.7 pounds of nitrogen, almost 1 pound of phosphoric acid, and from 4.5 to 7 pounds of potassium.

Tobacco leaves are "stripped" for market in late fall, leaving thousands of stalks. Some farmers use their stalks to fertilize their own fields, chopping up the stalks and disking them into the soil. Some stalks are available for gardeners, however, and tobacco processing plants bale further wastes for home use.

These wastes can be used anywhere barnyard manure is recommended, except on tobacco, tomatoes, potatoes, and peppers because they may carry some of the virus diseases of these crops, especially tobacco mosaic virus.

Compost tobacco wastes, or use them in moderation in mulching or sheet composting mixed with other organic materials. They should not be applied alone in concentrated amounts as a mulch—the nicotine will eliminate beneficial insects, earthworms, and other soil organisms as well as harmful ones.

Water Hyacinth

Southerners who lack sufficient green matter for compost can often find quantities of the water hyacinth (*Eichhornia crassipes*) growing in profusion in southern streams. This plant is considered a serious menace to agriculture, fisheries, sanitation, and health in the South and other parts of the world where it grows with remarkable rankness. For best results, shred and mix it with partially decomposed "starter material" such as soil or manure.

Weeds

Weeds can be put to use in the compost pile. Their nitrogen, phosphorus, and potash content is similar to other plant residues, and large quantities can provide much humus for the soil. Weed seeds will be killed by the high temperatures in the compost pile, and any weeds that sprout from the top of the heap can be turned under. Be careful not to allow weeds to grow and set seed on your finished compost. Weeds can even be used for green manure, as long as they will not be stealing needed plant food and moisture. Some produce creditable amounts of humus, make minerals available, and conserve nitrogen.

There are some weeds that you are better off burning or piling separately from your garden compost, since they are extremely vigorous and hard to kill. This applies primarily to weeds that reproduce through underground stems or rhizomes, such as quack grass, johnson-grass, bittersweet, and bishop's-weed.

Wood Ash

Wood ash is a valuable source of potash for the compost heap. Hardwood ashes generally contain from 1 to 10 percent potash, in addition to 35 percent calcium and 1.5 percent phosphorus. Wood ashes should never be allowed to stand in the rain, as the potash would leach away. Wood ashes should be used very cautiously—it is not uncommon for home gardeners to create difficult nutrient imbalance problems by applying too much wood ash. It is a strong alkalinizing agent and also increases soil salinity. You should use it in the garden only if a soil test indicates acid soil and a lack of potassium.

Wood ashes can be mixed with other fertilizing materials or side-dressed around growing plants.

Continued ➡

Apply no more than 2 pounds per 100 square feet. Avoid contact between freshly spread ashes and germinating seeds or new plant roots by spreading ashes a few inches from plants. Be similarly sparing with wood ashes in your compost—use no more than a dusting on each layer, if you must. Manure and hay are also rich in potassium, and they do not pose the dangers of wood ashes.

Wood Chips

Like sawdust and other wood wastes, wood chips are useful in the garden. In some ways wood chips are superior to sawdust. They contain a much greater percentage of bark and have a higher nutrient content. Since they break down very slowly, their high carbon content is less likely to create depressed nitrogen levels. They do a fine job of aerating the soil and increasing its moisture-holding capacity, and they also make a fine mulch for ornamentals.

Generally, the incorporation of fresh chips has no detrimental effect on the crop if sufficient nitrogen is present or provided. Better yet, apply the chips ahead of a green manure crop, preferably a legume; allow about a year's interval between application and seeding or planting of the main crop. Other good ways to use wood fragments are: (1) as bedding in the barn, followed by field application of the manure; (2) as a mulch on row crops, with the partially decomposed material eventually worked into the soil; and (3) adequately composted with other organic materials. Well-rotted chips or sawdust are safe materials to use under almost any condition.

Wool Wastes

Wool wastes, also known as shoddy, have been used by British farmers living in the vicinity of wool textile mills since the industrial revolution in the early nineteenth century. The wool fiber decomposes when in contact with moisture in the soil and, in the process, produces available nitrogen for plant growth. Generally, the moisture content of the wool wastes is between 15 and 20 percent. It contains from 3.5 to 6 percent nitrogen, 2 to 4 percent phosphoric acid, and 1 to 3.5 percent potash.

C/N Ratios and Nutrient Analyses

The following tables and lists provide information about the carbon/nitrogen nutrient contents of a variety of organic materials. The presence of a material in this section does not necessarily mean it is ideal for composting; neither does exclusion of a material mean that it cannot be composted. As mentioned at the beginning of this section, the best materials for composting may be those that are in close proximity to the compost pile.

Many items are listed as ash; since it is not always desirable or possible to reduce organic matter to ash, be aware that these materials are valuable compost pile additions in their natural conditions. Burning organic matter eliminates moisture, so nutrients are much more concentrated in ashed materials than in fresh. However, the significant advantages of adding fresh materials (moisture, microorganisms, and so on) and the restrictions most municipalities place on burning make ashed materials unlikely additions to most compost piles.

Since nearly all organic material contains some amount of nitrogen, phosphorus, potassium, and micronutrients, you don't need to worry a great deal about including all the plant nutrients in your compost pile. If you incorporate a good variety of materials into your compost, the necessary nutrients will be there. Compost not only provides nutrients, it also makes soil nutrients more available to plants. Only in instances where soil analysis indicates a significant nutrient deficiency should much effort be given to boosting levels of a certain nutrient in your compost.

NATURAL SOURCES OF NITROGEN

The materials listed below are grouped into representative classifications of organic matter; each group is ordered from highest nitrogen concentration to lowest. For specific nitrogen analyses, see the table "Percentage Composition of Various Materials" on page 000.

Manure

- Rabbit manure
- Sewage sludge
- Chicken manure
- Human urine
- Swine manure
- Sheep manure
- Horse manure
- Cattle manure

Animal Wastes (other than manures)

- Feathers
- Felt wastes
- Dried blood
- Crabs (dried, ground)
- Silkworm cocoons
- Tankage
- Fish (dried, ground)
- Silk wastes
- Shrimp heads (dried)
- Crabs (fresh)
- Fish scrap (fresh)
- Wool wastes
- Jellyfish (dried)
- Lobster refuse
- Shrimp wastes
- Eggshells
- Mussels
- Milk
- Oyster shells

Meal

- Cottonseed meal
- Gluten meal
- Bonemeal (raw)
- Wheat bran
- Bonemeal (steamed)
- Bone black
- Oats (green fodder)
- Corn silage

Plant Wastes

- Tung oil pomace
- Castor pomace
- Tea grounds
- Peanut shells
- Tobacco stems
- Coffee grounds
- Sugar wastes
- Seaweed (dried)
- Olive pomace
- Brewery wastes
- Cocoa shell dust
- Grape pomace
- Potato skins (raw)
- Pine needles
- Beet wastes
- Seaweed (fresh)

Leaves

- Raspberry leaves

- Apple leaves
- Peach leaves
- Oak leaves
- Pear leaves
- Cherry leaves
- Grape leaves
- Pea (garden) vines

Grasses

- Cowpea hay
- Vetch hay
- Soybean hay
- Pea forage
- Alfalfa
- Red clover
- Clover
- Millet hay
- Timothy hay
- Salt marsh hay
- Kentucky bluegrass hay
- Immature grass

NATURAL SOURCES OF PHOSPHATE (OTHER THAN PHOSPHATE ROCK OR BONEMEAL

The following phosphate sources are listed in order from highest phosphorus content to lowest.

- Shrimp wastes
- Sugar wastes (raw)
- Fish (dried, ground)
- Sludge (activated)
- Lobster refuse
- Wool wastes
- Dried blood
- Banana residues (ash)
- Apple skins (ash)
- Orange skins (ash)
- Pea pods (ash)
- Cottonseed meal
- Hoof and horn meal
- Tankage
- Castor pomace
- Rapeseed meal
- Wood ashes
- Cocoa shell dust
- Chicken manure
- Rabbit manure
- Silk mill wastes
- Sheep and goat manure
- Swine manure
- Horse manure
- Cattle manure

NATURAL SOURCES OF POTASH

The materials in each group below are listed in order from highest potassium content to lowest.

Natural Minerals

- Greensand
- Granite dust
- Basalt rock

Hay Materials

- Millet hay
- Cowpea hay
- Vetch hay
- Soybean hay
- Alfalfa hay
- Red clover hay

Continued ➡

Kentucky bluegrass hay

Pea forage

Timothy hay

Winter rye

Immature grass

Salt marsh hay

Pea (garden) vines

Straw

Buckwheat straw

Oat straw

Barley straw

Rye straw

Sorghum straw

Cornstalks

Wheat straw

Leaves

Cherry leaves

Peach leaves

Raspberry leaves

Apple leaves

Grape leaves

Pear leaves

Oak leaves

Manure

Pigeon manure

Chicken manure

Duck manure

Rabbit manure

Swine manure

Horse manure

Sheep or goat manure

Cattle manure

Miscellaneous

Banana residues (ash)

Pea pods (ash)

Cantaloupe rinds (ash)

Wood ash

Tobacco stems

Cattail reeds or water lily stems

Molasses wastes

Cocoa shell dust

Potato tubers

Wool wastes

Rapeseed meal

Beet wastes

Castor pomace

Cottonseed meal

Potato vines (dried)

Vegetable wastes

Olive pomace

Silk mill wastes

How to Make Compost

Composting isn't difficult. All you need are some raw ingredients, a tool for handling the compost, and a place to pile it. The organisms in the pile do most of the work for you—so you end up with a great (and free) soil amendment without having to put a lot of effort into it.

Recipe Fundamentals

The basic principles of composting are simple: Combine your ingredients to provide a good nutritional balance, keep the pile well-aerated and

moist (not soggy), and let the compost microorganisms do the rest. An active compost pile, turned once a week or so, will heat up inside to a temperature as high as 160°F, but if you're willing to wait for your finished compost, you don't even have to turn it. How much easier could it get?

The compost pile has its own ecosystem, with various organisms playing a central role during different steps of the cycle. As the pile heats up, mesophilis bacteria—those that prefer some warmth—proliferate. When temperatures get above 120°F, thermophilic, or heat-loving, organisms do more of the work. At cooler temperatures, fungi and actinomycetes predominate. Earthworms and other visible macroorganisms do their jobs at cooler temperatures and on the edges of the heating pile.

You can choose from a wide selection of materials and methods to compost successfully. But the same basic principles apply to all of them. When you understand what the microbes need to flourish, you'll know what to do to help make compost happen. Before you know it, you'll have your own supply of "black gold."

Composting Basics

The aim of every composting method is simply to meet the needs of the microorganisms that do the work of turning raw organic matter into humus. Those basic needs are energy food (carbon) and protein food (nitrogen) in the right proportion; air; moisture; and warmth. A pile also needs to be a minimum size so that high enough temperatures can be maintained.

FEED THE DECOMPOSERS

The first step to successful composting is providing the right mixture of basic ingredients. Raw organic matter, the basic food for compost organisms, consists of carbohydrates (carbon) and proteins (nitrogen) in differing proportions. To keep the decomposers well-fed, you need to provide these two food groups in the right balance.

Carbohydrates, which provide energy and cell-building compounds, must make up the bulk of the diet. Protein, which is essential for growth and reproduction, is needed in much smaller quantities. A ratio of 20 to 30 parts carbon to 1 part nitrogen is ideal.

In general, carbon materials are brown or yellow and dry, bulky, or fluffy (that's why they're commonly referred to as the "dry browns"). Dry leaves, straw, hay, and sawdust are all high in carbon.

Nitrogen materials tend to be green and wet, succulent, dense, or sticky, which is why they're often called "wet greens." Fresh manure, grass clippings, fish wastes, and soybean meal are rich in nitrogen.

KEEP THE PILE MOIST

Your compost pile should be about as moist as a damp sponge. If you can squeeze water out of it, it's too wet. But the moisture level of your compost pile shouldn't be much of a problem if you're mixing the right proportions of dry carbon materials with wet nitrogen ones.

Here are some other ways to regulate the moisture level in your compost.

- For most areas, make sure your pile is in a well-drained site. For very arid regions, however, consider digging a shallow composting pit to trap more moisture.

- If your ingredients are dry, sprinkle each layer with a hose or watering can until everything is moist and has a good sheen.

- Shape your pile according to your climate. In a wet climate, round the top to shed rain. In a dry climate, make a shallow depression on top to trap water.

- To shed excess rainwater and protect the compost materials from the drying effects of the sun and wind, cover the pile with a little loose hay or straw, or use dark plastic. Or, make your compost in a container with a lid.

AERATE THE PILE

Most home compost piles depend on aerobic organisms, which require air to live. So proper aeration is critical to successful composting.

To make sure your pile is well aerated, start by choosing a well-drained site. Compost that sits in a puddle, even for a short time, will wick up the water into essential air spaces in the pile.

You'll also need to provide air passages beneath the pile. Layer brush, spent cornstalks, or other coarse materials at the bottom of the pile. Or, make a wire mesh bottom for your compost bin so that it sits a couple of inches above the ground.

The bulky carbon materials you use in your compost pile create air passages throughout the pile, improving air flow and supplying food. Straw is highly valued for this reason. But be careful about using large layers of leaves, paper, grass clippings, or other ingredients that tend to mat when wet. Before adding these materials to your pile, shred them to fluff them up a bit and to prevent them from matting together.

Turning is the traditional way to aerate compost, and frequent turning is the key to quick, hot compost. The more often you turn the pile, the faster the new materials will decompose and the higher the temperatures will become.

Easier Aeration

You can get air into the center of your compost pile without turning it at all! The trick is to run ventilation pipes—perforated PVC pipes—through the pile. (If you don't have PVC pipes on hand, you can substitute cornstalks or palm fronds—both of these plants have an open center.)

You'll need several pipes that are about 4 feet long, or a little longer than the width or height of your pile. Run one pipe horizontally through the middle of the pile. Insert parallel pipes vertically about 6 inches away, on either side of the middle pipe. As the pile heats up, withdraw a pipe and reinsert it in another part of the pile. Do this every few days, if possible.

Another easy way to open air channels without turning is simply to stab the pile with a pitchfork once a week or so.

SIZE UP THE PILE

Composting works best when the temperature inside the pile remains at about 140°F or higher. Things heat up fast with the right mix of materials, air, and water. But to keep things cooking, you need the pile to be of a certain size—at least 3 x 3 x 3 feet—to provide the necessary mass.

If the pile is smaller than that, the heat will dissipate before the pile can reach the right temperature for the thermophilic organisms. A pile that's much larger than that will be difficult for you to turn, and the interior can become anaerobic. Instead of making a pile that's too large, make two medium-sized ones.

Bacteria begin to go dormant and compost stops cooking when the compost temperature drops below

Continued →

Percentage Composition of Various Materials

The presence of a C, N, or O in the C/N column indicates whether a material's effect on compost would be carbonaceous (C), nitrogenous (N), or other (O). Rock powders, for example, do not affect the C/N ratio and are designated O. C/N ratios of ashed materials represent their effects when fresh; when ashed, they are similar to rock powders.

Material	Nitrogen	Phosphoric Acid	Potash	C/N
Alfalfa hay	2.45	0.5	2.1	N
Apple fruit	0.05	0.02	0.1	N
Apple leaves	1.0	0.15	0.4	N
Apple pomace	0.2	0.02	0.15	N
Apple skins (ash)	—	3.0	11.74	N
Banana residues (ash)	—	2.3-3.3	41.0–50.0	N
Barley (grain)	1.75	0.75	0.5	N
Barley straw	—	—	1.0	C
Basalt rock	—	—	1.5	O
Bat guano	5.0–8.0	4.0–5.0	1.0	N
Beans, garden (seed and pods)	0.25	0.08	0.3	N
Beet wastes	0.4	0.4	0.7–4.1	N
Blood meal	15.0	1.3	0.7	N
Bone black	1.5	—	—	O
Bonemeal (raw)	3.3–4.1	21.0	0.2	O
Bonemeal (steamed)	1.6-2.5	21.0	0.2	O
Brewery wastes (wet)	1.0	0.5	0.05	N
Buckwheat straw	—	—	2.0	C
Cantaloupe rinds (ash)	—	9.77	12.0	C
Castor pomace	4.0–6.6	1.0–2.0	1.0–2.0	N
Cattail reeds and water lily stems	2.0	0.8	3.4	O
Cattail seed	0.98	0.39	1.7	C
Cattle manure (fresh)*	0.29	0.25	0.1	N
Cherry leaves	0.6	—	0.7	N
Chicken manure (fresh)*	1.6	1.0-1.5	0.6–1.0	N
Clover	2.0	—	—	N
Cocoa shell dust	1.0	1.5	1.7	C
Coffee grounds	2.0	0.36	0.67	N
Corn (grain)	1.65	0.65	0.4	N
Corn (green forage)	0.4	0.13	0.33	N
Corncobs (ground, charred)	—	—	2.0	C
Corn silage	0.42	—	—	N
Cornstalks (green)	0.75	—	0.8	C
Cottonseed hulls (ash)	—	8.7	23.9	C
Cottonseed meal	7.0	2.0–3.0	1.8	N
Cotton wastes (factory)	1.32	0.45	0.36	C
Cowpea hay	3.0	—	2.3	N
Cowpeas (green forage)	0.45	0.12	0.45	N
Cowpeas (seed)	3.1	1.0	1.2	N
Crabgrass (green)	0.66	0.19	0.71	N
Crabs (dried, ground)	10.0	—	—	N
Crabs (fresh)	5.0	3.6	0.2	N
Cucumber skins (ash)	—	11.28	27.2	N
Dried blood	10.0–14.0	1.0–5.0	—	N
Duck manure (fresh)*	1.12	1.44	0.6	N
Eggs	2.25	0.4	0.15	N
Eggshells	1.19	0.38	0.14	O
Feathers	15.3	—	—	N
Felt wastes	14.0	—	1.0	N
Field beans (seed)	4.0	1.2	1.3	N
Field beans (shells)	1.7	0.3	1.3	C
Fish (dried, ground)	8.0	7.0	—	N
Fish scrap (fresh)	6.5	3.75	—	N
Gluten meal	6.4	—	—	N
Granite dust	—	—	3.0–5.5	O
Grapefruit skins (ash)	—	3.6	30.6	O
Grape leaves	0.45	0.1	0.4	N
Grape pomace	1.0	0.07	0.3	N
Grass (immature)	1.0	—	1.2	N
Greensand	—	1.5	7.0	O
Hair	14.0	—	—	N
Hoof and horn meal	12.5	2.0	—	N
Horse manure (fresh)*	0.44	0.35	0.3	N
Incinerator ash	0.24	5.15	2.33	O
Jellyfish (dried)	4.6	—	—	N
Kentucky bluegrass (green)	0.66	0.19	0.71	N
Kentucky bluegrass hay	1.2	0.4	2.0	C
Leather dust	11.0	—	—	N
Lemon culls	0.15	0.06	0.26	N
Lemon skins (ash)	—	6.33	1.0	O
Lobster refuse	4.5	3.5	—	N
Milk	0.5	0.3	0.18	N
Millet hay	1.2	—	3.2	C
Molasses residue from alcohol manufacture	0.7	—	5.32	N
Molasses waste from sugar refining	—	—	3.0–4.0	N
Mud, fresh water	1.37	0.26	0.22	N
Mud, harbor	0.99	0.77	0.05	N
Mud, salt	0.4	—	—	N
Mussels	1.0	0.12	0.13	N
Nutshells	2.5	—	—	C
Oak leaves	0.8	0.35	0.2	N
Oats (grain)	2.0	0.8	0.6	N
Oats (green fodder)	0.49	—	—	N
Oat straw	—	—	1.5	C
Olive pomace	1.15	0.78	1.3	N
Orange culls	0.2	0.13	0.21	N
Orange skins (ash)	—	3.0	27.0	O
Oyster shells	0.36	—	—	O
Peach leaves	0.9	0.15	0.6	N
Pea forage	1.5-2.5	—	1.4	N
Peanuts (seeds/kernels)	3.6	0.7	0.45	N
Peanut shells	3.6	0.15	0.5	C
Pea pods (ash)	—	3.0	9.0	N
Peas, garden (vines)	0.25	—	0.7	N
Pear leaves	0.7	—	0.4	N
Pigeon manure (fresh)*	4.19	2.24	1.0	N
Pigweed (rough)	0.6	0.16	—	N
Pine needles	0.5	0.12	0.03	C
Potato skins (ash)	—	5.18	27.5	N
Potato tubers	0.35	0.15	2.5	N
Potato vines (dried)	0.6	0.16	1.6	C
Powder works wastes	2.5	—	17.0	O
Prune refuse	0.18	0.07	0.31	N
Pumpkins (fresh)	0.16	0.07	0.26	N
Rabbitbrush (ash)	—	—	13.04	C
Rabbit manure	2.4	1.4	0.6	N
Ragweed	0.76	0.26	—	N
Rapeseed meal	—	1.0–2.0	1.0–3.0	N
Raspberry leaves	1.45	—	0.6	N
Red clover hay	2.1	0.5	2.1	N
Redtop hay	1.2	0.35	1.0	C
Rock and mussel deposits from sea	0.22	0.09	1.78	O
Roses (flowers)	0.3	0.1	0.4	N
Rye straw	—	—	1.0	C
Salt marsh hay	1.1	0.25	0.75	C
Sardine scrap	8.0	7.1	—	N
Seaweed (dried)	1.1–1.5	0.75	4.9	N
Seaweed (fresh)	0.2–0.4	—	—	N
Sheep and goat manure (fresh)*	0.55	0.6	0.3	N
Shoddy and felt	8.0	—	—	N
Shrimp heads (dried)	7.8	4.2	—	N
Shrimp wastes	2.9	10.0	—	N
Siftings from oyster shell mounds	0.36	10.38	0.09	O
Silk mill wastes	8.0	1.14	1.0	N
Silkworm cocoons	10.0	1.82	1.08	N
Sludge	2.0	1.9	0.3	N
Sludge, activated	5.0	2.5–4.0	0.6	N
Smokehouse fire-pit ash	—	—	4.96	O
Sorghum straw	—	—	1.0	C
Soybean hay	1.5–3.0	—	1.2–2.3	N
Starfish	1.8	0.2	0.25	N
String bean strings and stems (ash)	—	4.99	18.0	C
Sugar wastes (raw)	2.0	8.0	—	C
Sweet potatoes	0.25	0.1	0.5	N
Swine manure (fresh)*	0.6	0.45	0.5	N
Tanbark ash	—	0.34	3.8	C
Tanbark ash, spent	—	1.75	2.0	O
Tankage	3.0–11.0	2.0–5.0	—	N
Tea grounds	4.15	0.62	0.4	N
Timothy hay	1.2	0.55	1.4	C
Tobacco leaves	4.0	0.5	6.0	N
Tobacco stems	2.5–3.7	0.6–0.9	4.5–7.0	C
Tomato fruit	0.2	0.07	0.35	N
Tomato leaves	0.35	0.1	0.4	N
Tomato stalks	0.35	0.1	0.5	C
Tung oil pomace	6.1	—	—	N
Urine, human	0.6	—	—	N
Vetch hay	2.8	—	2.3	N
Waste silt	9.5	—	—	N
Wheat bran	2.4	2.9	1.6	C
Wheat (grain)	2.0	0.85	0.5	N
Wheat straw	0.5	0.15	0.8	C
White clover (green)	0.5	0.2	0.3	N
Winter rye hay	—	—	1.0	C
Wood ash	—	1.0–2.0	6.0–10.0	O
Wool wastes	3.5–6.0	2.0–4.0	1.0–3.5	N

*Dried manures are up to 5 times higher in nitrogen, phosphoric acid, and potassium.

Continued ➡

55°. But with a properly built compost pile, the interior temperature will stay well above that—even in freezing weather. Northern gardeners sometimes insulate their piles with leaves, straw, or even an enclosure of hay bales to keep things cooking in cold weather. Decomposition may slow for the winter but should speed up again and finish during the warmer months of spring.

5 Steps to Quick Compost

Raking up some fallen leaves in a corner of your yard and gradually adding garden wastes and kitchen scraps is a simple, low-tech way to compost. This laissez-faire method makes what's called "cool compost" because the pile literally stays cool. Just let the pile sit, and in about a year, you'll have sweet-smelling, dark brown, crumbly compost.

Screen a wire compost bin from view by planting nasturtiums or morning glories to twine up the fencing. Or plant sunflowers just outside the fence.

You may have seen your neighbors turning their compost piles and watering them. Why do they do these things? Because they want compost fast—from start to finish in just a month. So they make an active, or hot, compost pile. The microorganisms that drive the composting process need a steady supply of water and air, and the more they get, the faster they work.

There are five key steps in making a hot compost pile. The more you're willing to work with your compost, the faster it'll decompose.

1. **Shred and chop.** Shred or chop materials as finely as you can before mixing them into your pile. For example, you can chop fallen leaves by running your lawn mower over them. The same strategy applies to kitchen scraps and the like—"the smaller the better" is always the rule for compost ingredients.

3. **Mix dry browns and wet greens.** The two basic types of ingredients for making compost are those rich in carbon and those rich in nitrogen. Carbon-rich materials, or "dry browns," include leaves, hay, and straw. Nitrogen-rich materials, or "wet greens," include kitchen scraps and grass clippings (which work best when used sparsely and mixed in well so they don't mat down). Your goal is to keep a fair mix of these materials throughout your pile. (If you try to make compost solely with wet greens or dry browns, you won't have much luck.)

3. **Strive for size.** Build your pile at least 3 x 3 x 3 to 4 feet so materials will heat up and decompose quickly. (Remember, though, not to make your pile too big, or else it will be hard for you to turn.) Unless you have this critical mass of materials, your compost pile can't really get cooking. Check the pile a couple of days after you make it—it should be hot in the middle, a sign that your microbial decomposers are working hard.

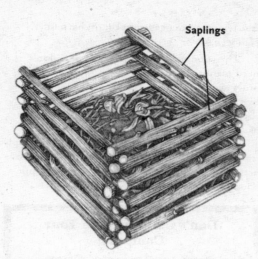

Saplings

After cutting down saplings, stack them to frame a compost pile. You can also harvest sunflower stalks—just cut off the heads and stack them log-cabin style.

4. **Add water as needed.** Make sure your pile stays moist, but not too wet (it should look like a damp sponge). You may need to add water occasionally.

5. **Keep things moving.** Moving your compost adds air to the mix. One way to add air is to get in there with a pitchfork and open up air holes. Even better, move the entire pile over a few feet bit by bit, taking care to move what was on the outside to the inside of the new pile and vice versa. Or consider getting a compost tumbler—a container that moves the materials for you. A less labor-intensive way to add air is to put a homemade "chimney" in the center of the pile.

Compost: Hot or Cold?

There's more than one way to make compost. The best method for you depends on many factors, such as the time and effort you're able to give, the space you have available, and the amount of compost you need. Composting methods range from quick, hot composting that requires more effort and attention to slow, cool techniques that are less trouble. Both hot and cold composting have advantages and drawbacks.

HOT STUFF

The biggest advantage of hot composting is its fast turnover—generally less than 8 weeks and as few as 2 weeks. To achieve that fast breakdown, the pile needs aeration: The more air it gets, the hotter it becomes (and the more hospitable to thermophilic bacteria). The object is to maintain a temperature of 113° to 158°F until decomposition is complete. You can use a thermometer to monitor the temperature or simply feel the inside of the pile with your hand. If it feels hot to the touch, you're in the ballpark. But when the temperature drops below this range, you must turn the ingredients to get the process going again.

With hot composting, you can process six or more batches in one season, even in cool climates. If you need lots of compost but have limited room to produce it, this is the way to go.

The other major advantage to hot compost is its temperature. Few weed seeds and pathogens can survive thermophilic temperatures, especially if they're maintained for several weeks.

The major disadvantage of hot composting is the labor required. Not everyone is willing or able to turn the pile every few days. Hot compost also demands specific conditions: If the moisture level or carbon-to-nitrogen ratio is wrong, you have to make adjustments. Another drawback is that you have to build the whole pile at one time. If you don't have the materials on hand to make a pile of the proper size, you must accumulate and store them until you're ready to build a new pile.

Finally, hot compost usually contains less nitrogen than cold compost. Turning allows more nitrogen to escape into the air in the form of ammonia gas.

Studies also have shown that compost produced at high temperatures is less able to suppress soil-borne diseases than cool compost. That's because the beneficial bacteria and fungi that attack pathogens can't survive the higher temperatures.

Hot Versus Cool: Compost Pros & Cons

Hot Pros
- Produces finished compost quickly
- Uses space efficiently
- Kills most weed seeds and pathogens

Hot Cons
- Labor intensive
- Requires careful control of moisture and carbon-to-nitrogen ratio
- Requires enough materials to build a 3 x 3 x 3-foot pile at one time
- May contain less nitrogen
- Doesn't contain as many disease-fighting organisms

Cool Pros
- Needs little maintenance
- Spares disease-fighting microbes
- Conserves nitrogen
- Allows for materials to be added gradually

Cool Cons
- Takes 6 months to 2 years to produce finished compost
- Doesn't kill pathogens or weed seeds
- Needs a balance of carbon and nitrogen materials to be added to the pile
- Contains more pieces of high-carbon materials that haven't decomposed
- May lose nutrients because of extended exposure to rain and sun

---

Do You Need a Compost Inoculant?

Will using one of the bacterial "compost starter" inoculants give you compost faster? No, say university researchers. According to recent tests, raw compost materials already contain more than enough bacteria to get your compost mixture cooking.

The researchers performed their tests on four compost piles, all containing a typical backyard compost mix of 2 parts leaves to 1 part grass clippings.

One pile received a standard commercial inoculant; the second, a "premium" commercial inoculant; the third, some year-old compost; and the fourth, no inoculant. All four compost piles were turned and watered weekly, and all heated up to 130°F. At the end of 2 months, all four piles contained equally finished compost. The university researchers concluded that the inoculants offered no benefit to a typical grass and leaves compost pile.

Continued ➡

THE COOL ALTERNATIVE

If you have the space but not the time or stamina to play with your compost, you can take the passive approach and make "cool compost." Cool compost will still heat up at first, but it won't reach the high temperature that actively turned compost will. The maximum temperature of cool compost is about 120°F. At that temperature, the mesophilic organisms do most of the work of making humus, which will be complete in 6 months to 2 years, depending on climate, materials, and aeration.

The advantages and disadvantages of cool composting mirror those of hot composting. Cool composting takes less work, but you'll need to wait longer to get the finished product. Cool composting also fails to kill pathogens or weed seeds but spares disease-fighting microbes.

One big plus of cool compost is that it can contain more nitrogen than hot compost. Some research has shown that "no-turn" compost contains as much as 13 percent more nitrogen than composts that are turned twice a week. In an unturned pile, microbes convert nitrogen into a stable form, so less escapes into the air as ammonia gas. To maintain that higher nitrogen level, however, you *must* cover your compost to protect it from rain. Otherwise, much of the nitrogen will leach away in the rainwater.

Another advantage of cool composting is that you can add materials a little at a time, as you accumulate them. The drawback is that you must be careful to balance carbon and nitrogen materials as you go, or you risk creating anaerobic conditions (which can cause an unpleasant odor). To prevent that from happening, keep a supply of dry carbon materials on hand to layer in when you add kitchen scraps or grass clippings.

To build a cool compost pile, follow these steps.

1. First lay a base of brush on a well-drained site.
2. Add ingredients as you accumulate them, keeping a good mix of carbon and nitrogen materials. As you add new materials, moisten them lightly, if needed, and cover them with a bit of soil.
3. When the pile has reached 3 x 3 x 3 feet, cover it with a layer of straw or leaves and let it rest for 6 months to a year, or more.
4. Before using, screen out any pieces that haven't decomposed.

The Lowdown on Manure

Farmers and gardeners have been fertilizing their soil with animal manure for centuries, and animal manure has long been recommended as a good source of nitrogen for compost piles, too. After all, animal manure is a rich source of soil nutrients, and it adds precious organic matter to soil. But for all the benefits that animal manure can offer your garden, it has a big drawback. Some may contain toxic bacteria.

KEEPING IT OUT OF YOUR PILE

If you add fresh animal manure to your compost pile, you run the risk of contaminating it with a virulent strain of *Escherichia coli* bacteria: *E. coli* 0157:H7. This bacteria lives in the intestines of cows and some other animals and appears in their manure. We humans have *E. coli* in our stomachs, too, but *E. coli* 0157 is a new, dangerous form that produces a toxin that can cause severe illness, especially in small children, the elderly, and people with compromised immune systems.

So until scientists learn more about this new strain of *E. coli*, you may want to avoid using raw manure in your home compost pile, unless you are *certain* that your compost will heat up to over 140°F

(the temperature needed to kill off harmful pathogens).

The good news, though, is that you don't need manure to make compost. Fresh grass clippings are an excellent, readily available, alternative source of nitrogen that you can add to your compost pile. Vegetable-type kitchen scraps are usually a good source of nitrogen as well. And alfalfa and soybean meals (available at farm supply stores) are just two examples of commercial products you can purchase to give your compost pile a boost of nitrogen.

> ### Don't Contaminate Your Compost!
>
> Most organic wastes make good compost fodder, but some materials are likely to contain toxic residues (herbicides, pesticides, fungicides, or heavy metals) that could contaminate your compost and your garden. Keep these out of your compost pile:
>
> · Grass clippings from neighbors or businesses that use herbicides
> · Grass clippings from golf courses
> · Highway trimmings
> · Florist shop wastes
> · Leather meal
> · Cottonseed meal (unless from an organic farm)
> · Paper mill sludge
> · Coal ash
> · Sewage sludge
> · Municipal incinerator ash

Never spread manure over vegetable gardens that have already been planted, and don't use pet feces in your pile—dogs and cats can carry parasites that, in rare cases, can be transmitted to humans (see page OO). And always wash your hands well after working in the garden—as well as any fresh produce you harvested.

What Not to Put in the Compost Pile

Although you *can* compost nearly any organic material, you should avoid or limit the use of certain materials, such as the following:

Meat scraps. These can attract unwanted animal visitors and create unpleasant odors.

Fats, oils, and grease. Large amounts of fats, oils, or grease will give your microbes indigestion, slowing down the composting process. They also may attract rodents and other pests.

Droppings from caged birds. Bird droppings may contain dangerous disease pathogens. And because they're mixed with bedding and dropped birdseed from the bottom of the cage, these droppings also can introduce weed seeds into your compost.

Droppings from dogs, cats, or other carnivores. These could contain disease organisms harmful to humans. Hot composting kills most pathogens, but some may be able to survive even prolonged heat. Cat droppings, in particular, can be hazardous to pregnant women and small children. These droppings may contain *Toxoplasma gondii*, a one-celled organism that can infect an unborn child, causing brain and eye disease. *Toxocara cati*, a roundworm common in cat droppings, can cause similar problems in children. Avoid these problems by keeping the litter box away from the compost pile and children.

Human waste. The potential for spreading disease makes the use of human waste in the compost pile too risky.

Diseased plants. Yes, hot composting kills most plant pathogens. But why risk it? Instead, burn diseased plants and add their ashes to the compost pile. Or send them to the landfill.

Weeds. Weeds that have set seed can cause trouble unless your pile is hot enough to kill the seeds. Better not to risk contaminating your whole garden with them. Certain weeds should be kept out of the compost pile entirely. Canada thistle, quack grass, couch grass, Johnsongrass, bishop's weed, comfrey, and Jerusalem artichokes can all reproduce easily from the tiniest bit of surviving root or rhizome.

Allelopathic plants. Some plants contain chemical compounds that inhibit the growth of other plants. In time, most of these compounds break down during the compost process. But to be on the safe side, you might want to avoid composting any materials from these plants, which include black walnut, sunflowers, and eucalyptus.

Large or slow-to-decompose materials. Large pieces of wood, bones, oyster and clam shells, rags, brush, cornstalks, heavy cardboard, and the like will just get in the way. If you want to compost them, shred or crush them first to speed their decay.

Highly acidic materials. If you want to use materials that are very acidic, such as fruit pomaces, add some crushed limestone to the pile to neutralize the acid. *Exception*: For acid-loving plants, such as azaleas and blueberries, you might want an acidic compost. In that case, skip the limestone.

Keeping Toxins Out

What about those widely available but questionable materials, such as floral shop waste or grass clippings from neighbors and golf courses? If the materials have been treated with herbicides or insecticides, can you poison your compost and garden by adding them to your pile?

These are good questions. Unfortunately, there are no easy answers. According to the University of Illinois Center for Solid Waste Management Research, some commonly used herbicides can remain active for a full year.

And a researcher at the Connecticut Agricultural Experiment Station says crops can take up some of these herbicides after the herbicides have been introduced to the garden. So, theoretically, you could get traces of these toxins in the food you grow.

Scientific research on how pesticides and herbicides break down in the compost pile is just beginning. But the consensus is that some of these substances may survive the composting process. Whether they do or not depends on which pesticide or herbicide was used-different chemicals break down at different rates. And the conditions within the compost pile (such as heat, moisture, and pH) also affect the rate at which they disappear.

Avoiding Tainted Compost

With all of these variables, there's just no way for the average home gardener to tell when (or if) compost ingredients that started out tainted become safe for organic food growing. So the answer for true organic gardeners is "no"—just don't do it. Don't add any herbicide- or pesticide-treated materials to your compost pile.

In case this warning comes too late and you've already added some treated golf course trimmings to your pile, don't despair. You can speed up the breakdown process and get rid of toxic residues as fast as possible (and more completely) by revving up the composting process.

According to an Ohio State University researcher, herbicide and insecticide molecules are

Continued ➡

more readily degraded under aerobic conditions. And the best way to achieve those conditions? Turn, turn, turn. The more often you turn your compost pile, the more air you add, and the faster the herbicides and pesticides will break down.

Composting Techniques and Recipes

It's no secret that there are plenty of different ways to compost. As long as you use the right ingredients—chopped or shredded "dry browns," "wet greens," air, moisture, and time—any method will work.

Here are several tried-and-true methods and a few new recipes that some ingenious gardeners concocted. Try a couple on for size, then choose the best one for you—or devise your own variation. You can't go wrong!

GOOD OLD GRASS AND LEAVES

One of the simplest techniques for making good-quality compost requires only four ingredients: dry leaves, fresh grass clippings, water, and soil.

1. Collect dry leaves and some fresh grass clippings.
2. Mix two to four buckets of clippings with 10 buckets of leaves.
3. As you work, spray the materials with a hose so that the mix feels wet, but not soggy, when you touch it. Also, add a shovelful of good garden soil as you go to introduce friendly composting bacteria to the pile.
4. Repeat Steps 2 and 3 until your pile is finished.

If you turn this mix weekly and add more water if the pile starts to dry out, you should have rich, beautiful compost in just 1 to 2 months.

GARBAGE CAN COMPOST

No space in your yard for a big compost pile? Then make compost in a can. Use a sturdy plastic or metal garbage can. Punch several holes in the bottom and sides of the can. Stand the can on bricks set in a large pan (to catch any liquid that might drain out). Layer 3 inches of soil, 2 to 3 inches of kitchen scraps, and then 2 inches of grass clippings, shredded newspapers, or chopped leaves. Repeat the layers until the can is full, finishing with a layer of soil. The finished compost will be ready in about 3 to 4 months—with no turning required! One caution: With this method, the compost may produce odors as it breaks down, so put the can in an out-of-the-way spot.

TERRIFIC TUMBLER COMPOST

The secret to success with a tumbler is to stockpile materials until you have enough to almost fill the tumbler. Here's the technique:

1. Start stockpiling kitchen wastes in a 20-gallon garbage can (put the can right by your tumbler). In about 2 weeks, you should have enough for a batch of compost.
2. Transfer the kitchen wastes to the tumbler drum, and then add equal volumes of chopped leaves and grass clippings.
3. Rotate the tumbler a few times every day for 2 weeks. (You should also be stockpiling a new batch of kitchen wastes during this time.)
4. Unload the finished compost and load in new materials to start the next cycle.

When you reach October, you can load the tumbler one final time. That batch will be ready at about the end of the following April, and you can begin the 2-week routine again.

BLENDER BOOSTER

To jump-start your compost pile, whiz up a batch of "liquid compost." As kitchen scraps accumulate, put them in a blender, add just enough water to cover them, then blend until finely chopped. Pour the resulting liquid into a bucket with a lid.

When you're ready to add it to your compost pile, dig a shallow hole into the center of the pile, then pour in the liquid. Cover the mixture with a shovelful of compost.

Or, if your gardening space is limited and you don't have room to make a traditional compost pile, pour the liquid gold directly into trenches dug in the garden. Cover with a shovelful of dirt.

For a compost bin that will stand up over the years, build it out of concrete block.

SHEET COMPOSTING

Another way to make compost without a traditional compost pile is to use the "sheet" method: Your garden beds serve as your compost pile. The idea is to clean up the bed at the end of the season, spread yard and garden waste over the bed, and then dig it all in.

By spring, your bed will be rich with compost. But because you lose the benefit of a heap's heat, you must be extra careful about the materials you use. Don't bury any diseased plants or weeds that have gone to seed. And, if you use kitchen scraps, bury them at least 8 inches deep so critters won't dig them up.

Follow these five steps to successful sheet composting in your garden:

1. Collect your yard waste. Remove large stalks and dense, fibrous matter, and then place the rest on the bed you've chosen.
2. Shred the material or run a lawn mower over it.
3. Add some high-nitrogen material, such as grass clippings or manure. Mix it all together.
4. Work the mixture into the top foot of soil, using a spade or tiller.
5. Turn the soil again in spring.

THREE-BIN COMPOSTING

If you have a three-bin composter, you can cook up a steady supply of compost for your soil. The following week-by-week schedule will help you get the most from your composter. Remember to check the moisture content when you transfer compost from bin to bin. Add dry material if it seems too soggy and water if it seems too dry.

Week 1: In the center bin, build a traditional compost pile. Spread a base layer of dry leaves or straw in the holding bin on one side; toss in kitchen wastes or garden trimmings as you collect them.

Weeks 2 and 3: Remove a few front boards from the center bin and stir the compost. Keep adding to the holding bin.

Week 4: Remove all front boards from the bins. Using a fork, transfer the compost from the center bin to the empty bin. Then transfer the contents of the holding bin to the now-empty center bin. Spread a new layer of dry matter in the now-empty holding bin. Replace the front boards.

Week 5: Check the compost in the end bin. It should be ready to use.

COLD-WEATHER COMPOSTING

When the weather turns cold in the fall, you can still keep your compost pile working by insulating it. Simply gather bags of fallen leaves from the curbsides around your town and heap them in a circle about 4 feet in diameter around a low compost pile. The bags provide some heat, the contents of the bags will decompose slightly and the center of the circle should stay unfrozen all winter, so you can keep dumping your kitchen scraps there.

You can also insulate a compost bin by piling straw bales around it and covering the whole thing with a large sheet of plastic.

Troubleshooting

Because compost is so integral to organic gardening, the creation of a "perfect" pile is a goal to which many gardeners aspire. But what if your results are less than perfect?

Don't throw in the towel. Here are some common compost problems and what to do about them.

WET, SOGGY, SLIMY COMPOST

Nothing is worse than cold, slimy compost! How does it get this way? Usually there are three contributing factors: poor aeration, too much moisture, and/or not enough nitrogen-rich materials in the compost pile.

A compost pile that is overburdened with materials that mat down when wet—such as grass clippings, spoiled hay, and unshredded leaves—can become so dense that the pile's center receives no air. If you leave this pile uncovered during prolonged rain (and don't turn it to introduce some air into the center), you'll end up with a cold, soggy mess.

Aerobic bacteria—the tiny, friendly, air-loving creatures that make compost cook—can't live in such an oxygen-poor environment. That kind of pile welcomes anaerobic bacteria, instead. These creatures will eventually make compost of your mess, but they work much more slowly than aerobic bacteria and the compost will be slimy and soggy during the 2 to 3 years it will take to decompose.

Actually, soggy compost is fairly easy to fix. If endlessly wet weather is part of the problem, cover the pile with a loose-fitting lid or tarp. You'll also need to turn the pile and fluff it up thoroughly. If you have some nitrogen-rich ingredients (such as fresh manure or shellfish wastes) and fibrous, nonmatting materials (such as shredded corncobs or sawdust), add them to help get things cooking.

DRY, DUSTY COMPOST

This opposite version of soggy, slimy compost is extremely common from May through October in areas that receive little summer rainfall. No matter what materials you pile up, the stack just doesn't get enough moisture to support the bacterial life necessary to fuel the composting process. Luckily, curing dry, dusty compost is as simple as turning on a spigot. That's right—water your compost pile until the materials feel about as wet as a damp sponge.

Put an oscillating sprinkler on top of your dry compost pile and run it for about an hour. This will moisturize the materials better than running an open hose on top—especially if the outer layers are made up of materials such as straw or grass clippings, which tend to shed water when they dry out. After sprinkling, check the center of the pile to make sure it's moist. To moisten the entire pile, you might need to turn it and water the layers as you go.

Continued ➡

No Space To Compost? Try Trenches

If you don't have room for a compost pile, you may find that trench composting is the best way to add nutrients to your soil. How do you trench compost? Just dig a hole in your garden every day, about 8 inches deep, and bury kitchen scraps. If you start along one side of a garden row, you'll actually be side-dressing or fertilizing nearby vegetables as well as boosting soil texture and fertility for next season.

You shouldn't have a problem with animals digging up what you've buried if you avoid adding meat, fat, and bones. If dogs do begin to dig in your trenches, just use a roll of chicken wire to cover your buried treasure. Roll it out over one hole at a time, along the row. Because the roll moves gradually, it also marks where you buried something last.

Compost in a Bag

Even if you live in an apartment and have absolutely no space for composting, this recipe for compost in a bag can help you recycle some of your kitchen wastes into fertilizer for your houseplants. It's also a great way to teach children about composting.

Start with a medium-sized plastic bag and a twist-tie. Watertight, self-sealing bags also work well.

Place 1 cup of shredded organic matter in the bag. Use your imagination and your available resources here—try coffee grounds, tea leaves, fruit peels, leaves, grass clippings, apple cores without seeds, carrot or potato peels, wood ashes, and so on—any kind of organic material you might normally throw-away. The more finely you can chop up or tear these items, the more effective your mini-compost bag will be.

Add ½ cup of garden soil to your bag. This is important for providing the microorganisms that will do the composting "work." Well-decomposed leaf mold or finished compost will work here, too. Don't substitute sterile potting soil; all its microorganisms have been sterilized away.

Add 1 tablespoon of alfalfa meal or alfalfa pellets (available as Litter Green cat box filler or as rabbit or hamster foods).

Pour in 1 ounce of water, and seal the bag. Shake the bag to mix all the contents thoroughly. Squeeze the bag daily to mix your compost (the equivalent of turning a compost pile).

Every other day, leave the bag open for the day to let air in. Without air, your organic matter will decompose improperly and will smell bad. If the contents of your bag smell, they may be too wet or in need of more mixing. In 4 to 6 weeks your compost should be finished and ready to use.

Turning and watering your pile should spring it to life fairly quickly. If not, you might have other problems, such as a lack of nitrogen-rich materials. If that's the case, tear the whole thing apart, add some grass clippings, manure, or bloodmeal to get it going, and pile it up again. When the pile starts cooking, don't let it dry out again. As those tiny organisms multiply, they use up a lot of water. You might have to water your compost almost as often as you water your roses during a heat wave.

Bugs!

Pill bugs and sow bugs are small crustaceans (not insects) that live on decaying organic refuse. If you turn your pile and see thousands of tiny, gray "armadillos" with seven pairs of legs each, you've discovered a nest of the primitive creatures. (Pill bugs roll up into a ball when threatened and sow bugs don't—otherwise, there isn't much difference between the two.)

These bugs won't harm your compost. In fact, they're actually helping to break it down. But if you don't remove them from the finished mixture before you spread it on the garden, you might find them snipping off the emerging roots and leaves of your garden plants.

Ants and earwigs also invade compost piles. Like sow bugs and pill bugs, they are essentially harmless to the composting process. Their presence may indicate that the breakdown process has nearly finished. Or, if you still have lots of material that hasn't broken down, these insects can simply mean that your pile is on a slow track to decomposition.

To get these bugs out of unfinished compost, raise the pile's temperature to above 120°F. Turn the pile over and rebuild it, watering it as you go. If it contains lots of slow-to-decompose materials, such as leaves or straw, mix in a nitrogen source, such as bloodmeal, manure, or shellfish wastes. It should soon start heating and, when it does, the bugs will depart for a more comfortable place.

But what if your sow-buggy compost is already finished and you want to use it on the garden without endangering small plants? Do you have to start all over again? Not if you de-bug it first! To do so, spread the compost in a thin layer on a tarp in direct sunlight and leave it there to dry.

By the way, if the dominant creature in your compost pile is the earthworm, give yourself a pat on the back! This is a sure sign that your compost has fermented, has decomposed, and is ready to spread. Transfer such worm-laden richness gently to your garden—the soil-churning activity of these organic heroes is something to encourage and be thankful for.

Bad-Smelling Compost

If your pile emits the sharp, nose-twisting stench of ammonia, it contains too much nitrogen-rich material (raw manure containing lots of urine is one likely culprit). It could also be too wet to allow aerobic bacteria to thrive. If it just "smells rotten" and there are lots of flies hanging around it, you've most likely added too many kitchen scraps or canning wastes without chopping them first or mixing them in thoroughly. For both cases, you should remake the pile to bring your stinky compost under control.

If too much "liquid nitrogen" is the problem, turn the pile and add absorbent materials—such as straw, shredded tree leaves, or sawdust—as you go. Rebuild the pile to a height of 3 feet to get it cooking again.

If kitchen scraps, canning waste, or large amounts of other mucky stuff are producing offensive odors, you can turn the pile without adding anything. As you turn, break up all that mucky stuff and mix it in well. Remind yourself that you'll avoid this unpleasant task in the future by first finely chopping these materials and then by mixing them thoroughly into the heap.

Overheating

In cold weather, an active compost pile will emit steam, causing many beginning composters to think their pile is burning. What it's really doing, though, is "breathing" it's warmth into the frosty air.

But if your compost is too nitrogen-heavy, the center can overheat and dry out, leaving visible white streaks. These white streaks are actually the dead bodies of millions of microorganisms. And, if they hadn't been cooked, they would have been busy turning your pile into finished compost!

Sometimes called "fire fanging" or "burning" by old-time gardeners, this phenomenon is quite common in piles that have been overloaded with fresh manure (especially from chickens or horses). Regular turning and watering will help you keep such a nitrogen-rich pile under control. To correct an already fire-fanged pile, rebuild it completely, adding some slow-working, absorbent material, such as shredded corncobs or sawdust. Sprinkle the new materials with water as you add them.

Raccoons, Opossums, and Other Critters

If you spot raccoons, opossums, dogs, skunks, rats, or bears at your compost pile, they're probably going after the fresh, edible kitchen scraps you recently buried.

To avoid attracting animals, remember to keep meat scraps and fat out of your pile. Mix other kitchen scraps with soil and/or wood ashes, then bury them deeply into the hot center of the pile.

If animal scavengers have grown accustomed to getting a free meal from your compost pile, you could have trouble breaking them of the habit. And unfortunately, this is one problem that can't be solved simply by turning or rebuilding the pile. You'll probably have to build or buy a covered container for your compost.

Plants Growing in the Pile

Young plants can emerge from a pile of finished, or nearly finished, compost. Invariably, a few seeds will survive the composting process (even a hot pile doesn't always heat up enough to kill all seeds). And the temperature, moisture, and fertility of the maturing compost are just about perfect for seed germination and seedling growth.

If the sprouts are weeds, just pull them out and add them to your next compost pile. (Green plants of any kind will provide nitrogen.) But if the young plants are vegetable or flower seedlings, go ahead and transplant them. Just be aware that they may be the offspring of hybrid parents and could, therefore, grow up to be something other than what you grew last season.

To avoid sprouts in future compost piles, don't add anything that contains seeds.

I Can't Turn My Compost Pile!

Most garden experts will tell you that a hot compost pile should be turned at least twice a month and as often as twice a week to keep it cooking.

But that turning can be difficult work. Seniors, disabled gardeners, and those who can garden only on weekends may be unable to do this.

If you can't turn your compost pile, relax—you can create this valuable soil amendment without turning. After all, nature doesn't need your help to decompose organic materials. And, if you build your cold pile correctly from the start, you'll avoid

Continued ➡

problems, such as bugs and unpleasant smells. Here's how.

Ensure complete breakdown of the materials that go into the pile by shredding and mixing them *before* piling them up. Put everything through a chipper/shredder, run a lawn mower over it, or use a pruning shears to cut up any large, coarse stems and stalks.

If that isn't possible, build the pile in layers—alternating "browns" (carbon-rich materials like leaves and straw) with "greens" (nitrogen-rich materials like grass clippings and kitchen scraps). Mix them together as you go.

Try to include some finished compost or rich topsoil in the mix to get things going, and water your pile as you build it. Keep the moisture level as even as possible. If the compost pile begins to dry out, water it with a sprinkler.

After 6 months to 1 year, you'll have finished compost—without ever turning the pile.

Composting with Earthworms

Deborah L. Martin and Grace Gershuny

If you let them, earthworms will do most of your composting work for you, in the garden, on the farm—or even in your basement.

Earthworms are amazing creatures, capable of consuming their own weight in soil and organic matter each day, and leaving behind the richest and most productive compost known. The castings of earthworms contain from 5 to 11 times the amount of available N-P-K as the soil the worms ate to produce those castings. How do earthworms perform this magic? The secretions of their intestinal tracts act chemically to liberate plant nutrients with the aid of soil microorganisms. And what earthworms do for the major plant nutrients, they do for the micronutrients, too. Earthworms literally tunnel through your soil, day and night, liberating plant nutrients wherever they go. Let loose in a compost heap, they will quickly reduce it to the finest of humus. Mulch your garden with organic matter of nearly any kind, and earthworms will never stop working on it until they have reduced the mulch to dark, rich humus. If you encourage earthworms to stay in your soil, or work with them in producing compost, they will virtually ensure that you produce successful compost.

The secret in producing compost with earthworms is in learning a little about earthworms and their needs. If you buy 1,000 red wigglers and thrust them into the middle of your compost pile, you will likely have 1,000 dead red wigglers the next day. Most earthworms, you see, cannot tolerate the heat of an actively working compost heap. You will also want to learn to distinguish among the various major earthworm species, since their needs are quite different, and so are their capabilities in helping you make compost.

Most of the information in this chapter comes from *The Earthworm Book* by Jerry Minnich. This chapter will suggest ways to use earthworms in composting, but the gardener or farmer who wants to learn more about the topic should consult *The Earthworm Book* for greater detail.

Most people see earthworms as a welcome natural addition to their composting efforts and also as affirmation that they are doing things right. But gardeners could make better compost if they saw the earthworm as a necessary component of the whole process, just as important as air, water, or organic matter. The earthworms can do much of the work and make composting faster-but in return, the gardener must learn to make compost

with the earthworm's needs in mind, and discover which species of worms are suitable for various composting situations.

The Right Worm

It is important to be aware of the different species of earthworms and what they can, and cannot, do:

Red worms (*Lumbricus rubellus*) and brandling worms (*Eisenia foetida*) are the species usually sold by earthworm breeders. They are commonly sold for fish bait under such names as red wigglers, hybrid reds, Georgia reds, and so on. Any name that suggests a red-and-gold or banded worm is likely to indicate a brandling worm. The others are probably red worms. These cannot survive in ordinary garden and farm soils for very long, but they will thrive in compost heaps and manure piles. They can be used to good advantage in an Indore heap and can greatly reduce the time required to produce finished compost and eliminate the need to turn the heap. However, many will be killed off or driven away when the organic matter begins to heat up from bacterial action.

Field worms (*Allolobophora caliginosa*) and night crawlers (*Lumbricus terrestris*) will attack compost heaps and manure piles from the bottom but prefer to retreat into the soil after having done so. They will not thrive in active compost and are killed by the heating process more easily than red worms and brandling worms. Night crawlers demand cool soil temperatures and will not inhabit compost and manure piles. If they are thrust into active compost, they will simply die and melt.

The data on the *Pheretimas* are still incomplete, but they seem to have requirements similar to those of the field worm and the night crawler. They are soil-living species.

Earthworms in the Indore Method

Earthworms will naturally be attracted to an Indore compost heap, attacking it from the bottom. The base layer of brush will soon become reduced in bulk and filled in with finer debris. Field worms and night crawlers will quickly infiltrate this layer, to turn and mix the earth with the organic matter. They will also reproduce quickly, increasing their population many times over. If the heap is maintained for a year or more in one location, the earth below it will become rich, friable, and loaded with earthworms. With each rain, some of the nutrients from the compost will leach deep into the soil spreading out from the actual edges of the heap. Earthworms will mix these nutrients into the soil and stabilize them for growing plants. This enrichment of the soil beneath the heap is also a good reason for changing its location every year or so. Any prized plants grown where an old compost heap was built will flourish beyond reasonable expectations.

As the materials in the heap decompose and turn to humus, field worms will advance further up into the heap. Still, they will not flood the entire heap, as will the manure-living species. The limiting factor is the high temperature; even an inactive, above-ground heap will not be attractive to field-living species. Night crawlers like even cooler temperatures but will feed at the bottom of the heap. If in autumn and early spring they pene-

trate a well-advanced heap, you know you can use it for soil improvement.

Although manure-type worms can work at higher temperatures than field-living species, even they will be killed in the intense heat of a working compost heap, where temperatures can reach 150°F (66°C). Do not introduce them until the interior of the pile has cooled down to the outside temperature. Normally this will be about 3 weeks after the last materials have been added to a well-constructed heap. At this point, dig holes at various points in the heap, and drop 50 to 100 worms in each. About 1,000 worms (a convenient number to order) will serve to inoculate a 4 by 6-foot pile. If manure-type worms and their castings were well supplied in manure that went into the heap and have survived the heat, there will be no need to introduce worms from an outside source.

In a matter of days, the worms will be consuming the organic matter, leaving rich castings wherever they go, and reproducing at a high rate. In a well-tended compost heap, 1,000 reds or brandlers can increase to 1 million in a year or two.

Manure-type worms will do much better in the Indore heap if larger quantities of manure are included in the mixture. Instead of the 2-inch layer usually recommended, add 4 or 6 inches. If no manure at all is used, the worms will still have a good chance to thrive, although their progress will be slower.

NO-HEAT INDORE COMPOSTING

A variation of the Indore method makes it possible to produce compost quickly with very little heating, using earthworms. Construct the heap so that it is longer and wider than a normal heap, but only 12 to 18 inches high. Shred all materials as finely as possible, and introduce manure-type worms immediately. They will go to work right away, and the heap will never heat up greatly because of the large surface area; the center of the heap will be too close to the cooling effects of the outside air. The major disadvantages are that it takes up more ground surface area, and the shredding of materials takes time and requires fossil energy to operate a gasoline-powered shredder or rotary mower. Also, any weed seeds present will remain viable.

MAINTAINING THE EARTHWORM POPULATION

When removing finished compost for use on garden plots or farm fields, be certain to save a good number of earthworms for future composting operations. There are several ways to do this. The easiest is to remove only half the heap at a time, spreading out the remainder to serve as the base for the new heap. If your manure worm population is not as great as you wish it to be, you can save even more by "scalping" the heap in several steps. Earthworms are repelled by light; if exposed, they will quickly dive down beneath the surface. Remove finished compost from the outer parts of the heap, to a depth where worms are exposed. Wait for about 30 minutes, then take another scalping. Continue in this manner until you have removed as much compost as you want. The earthworms will have been driven into a compact area at the bottom of the heap. At this point, spread out the remaining compost containing the earthworms, and cover it immediately with new manure and green matter. If, as so often is the case, the outer scalp of the heap has not composted fully (since it is the newest material), then set aside this first scalp and put it back after you have finished the operation. It will be the first material to be attacked in the new heap.

Continued ➡

Earthworms in Bins and Pits

Red worms and brandling worms cannot survive northern winters without some kind of protection. Further, earthworms are the favorite food of moles, which can easily penetrate an Indore heap and decimate your earthworm population in an amazingly short time. The answer to both dangers is a compost pit dug beneath the frost line and outfitted with a heavy, coarse screen on the bottom to keep out moles but allow the free passage of soil-dwelling earthworms. Manure-type worms will not migrate deep into the soil.

Often, bins and pits are combined. The earth is dug out to a depth of 16 to 24 inches (deeper in areas such as Minnesota and Maine), and boards are used to extend the pit into an aboveground bin.

For the gardener who seeks to build a compost/earthworm pit for the first time, here are some basic instructions:

1. Stake off an area 3 to 4 feet wide and as long as you wish the pit to be.

2. Excavate the earth from this area to a depth of 16 to 24 inches. (If you live where winter temperatures get to -10°F [-23°C] or colder, make it 24 inches.) Pile the excavated soil to one side, in as compact a heap as possible, for later addition to the pit.

3. Drive 2 x 4 stakes into the four corners of the pit, if you will be using boards. (Scrap lumber from old buildings is fine.) A layer of ¼-inch, rust-proof wire mesh in the bottom of the pit will protect your earthworms from moles.

4. Nail boards all around the pit. Keep one end open so you can work with the material. Use stakes to hold loose boards in this area. Add boards on top of each other, leaving about ¼ inch between each for aeration. Add boards only as the pile of materials requires them for support. The boards aboveground need never be higher than 16 inches above the ground surface; if the pit is 16 inches deep, this will mean a total of 32 inches of vertical board area. (Remember that these earthworms will not work more than 6 to 8 inches below the surface of the heap, no matter how high it is built.)

5. If you elect to use concrete blocks instead of wood, excavate the soil to a depth of one or two blocks, and add no more than two layers of blocks above the ground. At this low height, the blocks can be set in loosely, without mortar. Allow a little space between them for aeration.

Many gardeners find it helpful to divide the pit into two sections, one for new compost and the other for old. As finished compost is removed from one section, the earthworms are transferred into the newer heap on the other side, and a new heap is begun in the just-emptied side. In this way, there is always a ready supply of compost for garden use, and the earthworms are constantly maintained. An ideal setup would comprise two double pits.

Some gardeners outfit their bins with loose-fitting board lids, hinged on one side so that they swing up and open easily. This device keeps out the sun and protects the surface of the heap from excessive heat during the summer, enabling the worms to work nearer to the surface where new material is deposited. It also keeps out predators during the night and conserves moisture during hot and dry periods. When a lid is used, keep a constant check on moisture. Add water as necessary, or—better—open the lid during rainfalls if moisture is needed.

Winter Protection in the North

In the South, where winter temperatures rarely go below 20°F (-7°C), red worms and brandling worms can be maintained easily in outdoor pits with a minimum of protection. A few layers of burlap bags and a mound of straw piles over the beds will offer all the insulation needed, even if they are occasionally covered with snow. In places like Minnesota, Montana, and Vermont, however, where winter temperatures routinely dip to -20°F (-29°C), special protection is a must.

A good winter-protection system is explained fully in the booklet *Let an Earthworm Be Your Garbage Man*. It is essential reading for any northern gardener who decides to construct earthworm pits.

For winter protection, the booklet recommends digging a compost pit 16 inches deep and lining it with two layers of concrete blocks below ground, with a third layer aboveground. Pile the removed soil at the edge of the pit, and cover it thickly with straw. Line the bottom of the pit with garbage, and cover it with 2 to 3 inches of soil, then with burlap bags. Water if needed. The pit can be covered with wire mesh weighted down with bricks or concrete blocks.

In the winter, cans of garbage are added to the pit under the burlap and covered with a layer of soil.

Even in 20-below weather, the earthworms keep working and the composting process continues. By spring, the kitchen refuse added the previous autumn is ready for use in the garden.

Indoor Composting in the Winter

Earthworms can also be used indoors in the winter to produce a small amount of compost from kitchen garbage, dust from a vacuum cleaner bag, even newspapers. Generally, 1 pound of earthworms will eat 1 pound of garbage and produce 1 pound of compost each day, although this varies. There have even been a few commercial earthworm composting units placed on the market, but a simple homemade system is both easy and inexpensive and just as effective. It can be used anywhere, winter or summer, and it can be expanded into as large an operation as you wish.

This method is detailed by Mary Apelhof in her manual *Worms Eat My Garbage*. Her rule of thumb suggests that 1 square foot of surface area is needed to digest each pound of waste material generated per week. It is best to begin on a modest scale. Construct a wooden box 2 feet wide, 2 feet long, and 1 foot deep. Or get a vegetable lug box from your local supermarket, and if it has large spaces between the boards, tack in plastic screening to hold the earthworm bedding. If you construct your own box, provide for drainage and aeration by drilling a half-dozen ⅛-inch holes in the bottom and some more around the sides. A box 2 feet square and 1 foot deep will accommodate 1,000 adult worms (or "breeders," as they are called in the trade), or you can order a pound of pit-run worms (all sizes) that will do as well.

You can prepare a bedding as follows: Wet a third of a bucketful of peat moss thoroughly, and mix it with an equal amount of good garden loam and manure; add some dried grass clippings, hay, or crumbled leaves, if you wish. (Don't use oak or other very acid leaves.) Soak this mixture overnight.

The next day, squeeze out the excess water, and fluff up the material (which we will now call bedding). Line the bottom of the earthworm box with a single layer of pebbles or rocks. Then place 4 inches of the bedding material rather loosely on top of the pebbles, and wait for a day to see if any heating takes place. If initial bacterial action forces the bedding temperature much above 100°F (38°C), all the worms will be killed. Any heating that does occur will subside within 48 hours.

When you are satisfied that the bedding will present no serious heating problems, push aside the bedding material, place the worms and the bedding from their shipping container in the center, and cover them loosely with your bedding. Place a burlap bag, several layers of cheesecloth, or wet newspapers over the top of the bedding, and moisten it with a houseplant sprayer or sprinkling can.

Keep the bedding moist but never soggy. If the container begins to drip from the bottom, place some sort of container, such as a plastic dishpan, under the box to catch the drippings. Use the drippings to water your houseplants.

Start out by feeding the earthworms cautiously. If you give them more than they will eat in a 24-hour period, the garbage will sour, creating odors and attracting flies, or it will heat up, killing the worms. Begin with soft foods, such as cooked vegetables, left-over cereal (including the milk), vegetable soup, lettuce, bread scraps, soft leaves of vegetables, even ice cream. A little cornmeal will be appreciated, and coffee grounds can be added at any time. Do not use onions, garlic, or other strongly flavored foods.

Place the food on top of the bedding, and tamp it gently into the bedding. After a week or two, your earthworms should have adjusted to their new home and should be on a regular feeding schedule. You can help them along, and build better compost, if you add a thin layer of partially decayed manure from time to time (being sure that it is past the heating stage but not completely composted).

Every 2 weeks, the bedding in the box should be turned and aerated. Reduce the amount of food after such turnings, since the worms will not come to the surface as readily for a day or two after having been disturbed.

After a month, you can add another 2 inches of bedding material to handle the increased worm population, and after 3 months it will be time to start another box.

When you are ready to divide the box, prepare a second box as you did the first. Then arrange a good-sized table under a 100-watt hanging light so that the light comes to within 2 feet of the table surface. Lay a plastic sheet on the table. Dump the worms and bedding on the plastic, and heap them into a mound that peaks to within a foot of the light bulb. Pick off the pebbles and return them to the first box.

Any worms that have been exposed in turning the box will quickly react to the light by digging toward the center of the mound. This will allow you to scrape much of the bedding into a bucket. Wait another 10 minutes, then scrape away another layer of compost. After several such scrapings, all the worms will have dived into a compact ball at the bottom of the mound, where they can easily be divided and put back into fresh bedding in the two boxes.

Boxes can be stacked in tiers by affixing ½-inch-square wood strips, 14 inches high, into the four corners of each box. The strips on one box will support the box on top of it. The boxes can be watered easily with a small houseplant hose or with a portable insecticide sprayer. The drippings from all but the bottom box will fall into the box beneath it.

An even simpler method of indoor worm composting involves a plastic garbage can with some small modifications. You can make holes for ventilation and drainage with a hot knitting needle, being careful not to breathe the fumes. Air enters through holes in the lid, and water drains from holes 3 inches above the base. The bottom 6 inches should be filled with a coarse material such as gravel, sitting in 3 inches of water. A wooden barrier between this drainage area and the worms' living quarters prevents you from intermingling the materials when

Continued ➡

renewing the worms. Be sure to leave some holes to allow water to drain. Proceed to introduce worms and garbage as previously described.

Earthworms on the Farm

In the 1940s, U.S. Department of Agriculture scientists Henry Hopp and Clarence Slater found some very poor clay subsoil, containing no earthworms and virtually no organic matter, and by adding lime, fertilizers, and manure, grew a modest stand of barley, bluegrass, and lespedeza on two separate plots. On one, they left the growth untouched, while on the other they cut the top growth to form a mulch, and they added some earthworms to the soil.

By the following June, the plot containing earthworms was covered with a rich stand of all three crops, while the section without worms supported almost nothing but weeds. The total vegetation in the wormed plot was *five times* that of the wormless one. The plot with worms also had far better water-absorbing and water-holding capacity, and twice as many soil aggregates—all the result of earthworm action.

The lesson learned here is one of which every organic farmer should be keenly aware. No soil should be left unprotected over winter. Large-scale mulching and sheet composting will protect earthworm populations, and the earthworms will improve the soil structure and crop-growing capacity.

Compost Structures

Deborah L. Martin and Grace Gershuny

Gardeners have designed a host of imaginative structures for composting. Compost can be made in cages, in block or brick bins, in pits and holes, in revolving drums, in garbage cans, and even in plastic trash bags. A compost structure can be designed to be beautiful, to make compost in the shortest possible time, or to be moved from place to place with the least effort. It can be designed to make compost with no turning required, or to suit the needs of earthworms. Compost structures, in short, are designed to suit the user's needs and resources.

For most home composters, building a bin that makes use of existing or readily available materials is the most practical course. A composter in California constructed a bin using the aluminum sides of an old aboveground swimming pool. Even using bales of spoiled hay to form a temporary structure is a way to make the most of your resources in creating a composting structure, as well as the compost pile itself.

The choice of compost structure is, then, a personal decision, one that should not be made without some prior research and, perhaps even more important, some experimentation. It is experimentation that leads to new structures.

The first decision to be made is whether a structure is needed at all. The gardener or farmer with plenty of room, ample materials, and sufficient time may need no compost enclosure of any kind. In this case the traditional Indore heap is quite suitable.

If yours is a city or suburban lot, however, you might find that the open heap takes up too much room or offends neighbors and family. If space is limited, an enclosure can produce more compost in a smaller land area. It can be more attractive and keep out animals and flies. If you cannot devote a permanent spot to compost making, you will want to investigate portable structures that can be broken down and moved in minutes. If your garden is located where winter temperatures are severe, a

compost pit dug below the frost line can enable you to compost all winter long. If you want to work with earthworms in composting, then you will need to consider some special outdoor structures, and perhaps others for basement composting. Perhaps a commercially built revolving drum suits your needs because age or infirmity prevents you from turning the heap, or simply because the drum produces quick compost and attracts no pests. Perhaps you even prefer to make compost in plastic bags because of its simplicity.

It is certainly true that one compost structure is not best for everyone. It may even be that everyone needs a structure designed especially for him or her. We hope that by describing different structures, we will give you some insight into matching construction with your individual needs. If you are like most gardeners, you will take one of these suggested forms, adapt it to your needs, use it for a year or two, and then make your own adjustments until you have evolved the perfect structure for you.

Pens and Bins

By far the most common compost forms are bins and pens. To simplify, let us call a bin any container with concrete, brick, wood, or masonry sides that is fairly substantial and permanent, and pen any structure with wire or hardware cloth sides that is a less permanent installation. Not that they're that easy to classify—there are many kinds of structures called bins and pens.

In general, pens have the advantage of allowing for free circulation of air. Their disadvantage is that they also allow for free circulation of flies and four-footed pests. Bins are more stable and protecting structures, but they are often insufficiently ventilated. Neither the bin nor the pen has as great a tendency to go anaerobic as the pit, and both are easier to keep tidy than open composting forms.

A shady, sheltered spot not far from either garden or kitchen is an ideal location for either pen or bin. Often a space between house and garage or garage and shed allows the right amount of room. A three-compartment bin with tight floor and sides and with each compartment measuring a cubic yard in size makes for the neatest and easiest handling of turning. In such a structure there is at all times one batch working and one being used.

An advocate of bottom aeration claims to have made a free compost bin in 1 hour using available cement blocks and some leftover strong iron piping, plus surplus 1 by 2-inch wire mesh. The 4 by 8 by 16-inch cement blocks were laid horizontally with plenty of air between each block. Unlike other composters, this gardener preferred to have his compost bin in a sunny spot, feeling the compost would heat up faster in the sun.

The pipes were thrust across the bin from side to side over the third course of blocks, to provide the pile with a strong bed. On top of the pipes, two lengths of wide wire mesh were laid to hold a bottom layer of coarse garden debris and twigs. This layer and the mesh and pipes held back finer material and allowed for bottom aeration. The gardener never turns his compost but mixes materials together.

Lehigh-Type Bins

The Lehigh-style bin is easy to erect and disassemble. It is adjustable in size, attractive, portable, long-lasting, and it provides for proper ventilation and protection.

Construction is of alternating 2 x 4s with the corners drilled out and held together with ⅝-inch rods. Five 36-inch 2 x 4s to a side will make a bin capable of producing approximately 1 cubic yard of compost at a time.

There have been several variations of the Lehigh bin, some using logs or poles instead of 2 x 4s. However it is designed, the low cost, effectiveness, and portability of this structure has made it one of the most popular in use today.

Cage-Type Bins

Cage-type bins are simple and inexpensive to build, allow good air circulation, are portable, and allow quick turning of the heap because of a removable front panel. The Lehigh bin lacks this last feature.

There are many variations of cage-type bins, all of which require relatively little lumber, since wire screening forms most of the panels.

The wire-and-wood bin can be built using scrap 2-inch lumber covered with ½-inch chicken wire mesh. The bin is formed by two L-shaped sections held together with screen-door hooks.

To turn the pile, unhook the sides and reassemble the two sections next to the now free-standing pile. Layers can be easily peeled off with a pitchfork and tossed into the empty cage. Keep a hose handy during turning, to add moisture as needed. A properly built and maintained pile in this well-aerated bin can produce 18 to 24 cubic feet of finished compost in 14 days.

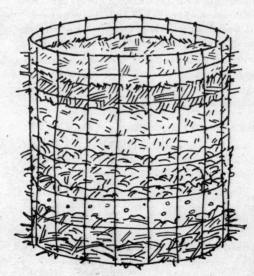

A cylinder of wire fencing can be used as a simple compost bin.

The New Zealand Bin

Perhaps the classic among compost bins is the wooden New Zealand box that was originally designed by the Auckland Humic Club to admit as much air as possible from all sides. It can be used to make several batches of compost in different stages of decomposition, ensuring a continuous supply, and it can be a very attractive structure.

There are several variations of this box, but the simplest one is a wooden structure 4 feet square and 3 feet high or higher with neither top nor bottom. The frame is held together by 2 x 4s. The wooden sides consist of pieces of wood 6 inches wide by 1 inch thick. A ½-inch air space is allowed between every two boards so that air may penetrate into the heap from all sides. The boarding in front slides down between two posts so that boards can be removed one by one when complete access to the contents is needed for turning or loading. The open side may also be built up gradually as the pen is filled. Cover the top of the pen with hardware cloth, rolled canvas, burlap, or screen.

If you are using a single bin like the New Zealand box, be sure to allow for a working space in front of the box equal to two or three times the floor area of the box. This much space is needed for turning the pile. You pile up the material

Continued ➡

outside the bin and then replace it within the bin, mixing so the outside material is placed toward the inside of the new pile.

One variation on the New Zealand box holds four separate bins for compost in different stages. The dividers between the compartments are removable to permit quick and easy shifting of compost from one bin to another.

Block and Brick Bins

Block and brick bins are permanent if mortared, but cement block bins can be constructed without mortar and can then be moved at will.

The block or brick bin is easily constructed. Usually, blocks are laid to permit plenty of open spaces for air circulation. But they can also be closely stacked, set into the ground, and mortared together, or formed into a cylindrical shape with an access gate at the bottom.

Gardeners who insist on a well-groomed compost area may prefer to have a large, rectangular, brick or block, chimneylike structure with several compartments. Use wooden hinged lids to cover the structure. In a three-bin unit, the first two bins are used in turning while the third stores finished compost. The bottom of the bin, if made of concrete, should slant one way so drainage may be caught in a gutter leading to storage cans. A combination of bricks and boards may be used, with boards set into slots along the front opening. Boards can be removed for access to the compost.

Rough stones laid with or without mortar in an open-fronted, three-fourths cylinder shape (like a larger edition of a state park barbecue pit) make an attractive rustic bin.

The Movable Slat Bin

Another type of portable bin can be constructed of wooden slats. This bin needs no hardware for support—no hooks, nails, or screws.

To make it, cut 10-foot-long 1 by 10-inch boards into 60-inch lengths. Slot each board 4 inches in from the end, 4-5/8 inches across its width, so the boards can be nested, as shown. The finished bin is 50¼ inches square and 18¼ inches high inside—perfect for even the smallest lot.

Winter Bins

Winter composting does not have to be confined to a pit. An existing compost bin, well insulated with bales of straw or hay and covered for protection from the elements, can continue the composting process during cold temperatures, although at a slower rate than during warmer weather. Structures similar to cold frames can also be used for cold-weather composting, using south-slanting glass lids to catch the rays of the sun and protect the heaps from rain, snow, and drying winds. Manure added to such bins helps to keep temperatures high enough for microbial activity.

Pens

The very simplest pen can hardly be called a structure at all. It is, however, quick to make, neat to use, and it costs little. You just buy a length of woven-wire fencing and, at the site of the compost heap, bring both ends of the fencing together to form a cylinder large enough to surround the heap. Fasten the ends of the cylinder together with three or four small chain snaps that you can find in a hardware store. Remove the cylinder to a free-standing position, and start building the heap inside the cylinder. When it is half full, drive a stake into the pile. The stake should be as long as the total desired height. You can disassemble the cylinder for easy turning by removing the snaps. You set the cylinder up again and once more turn

into it, shifting the ingredients from outside layers to inside, reversing the position of the material. The stake not only helps maintain the shape of the pile, but also aids in directing water into the heap.

A partly anaerobic version of the woven-wire cylinder is lined with a length of roll roofing that is wired to the fencing. The roofing is durable and prevents small bits and pieces from falling out of the bin.

After the bin is full, it is covered with a layer of 6-mil black plastic and left to decompose. Turning is not necessary with this system, although composting will take longer and high temperatures will not last long enough to kill weed seeds.

A refinement of the all-wire pen is the wire-and-tomato-stake pen in which ½-inch mesh poultry netting is placed inside an enclosure made by driving 4-foot tomato stakes 1 foot apart in a 10 by 5-foot rectangle and looping baling wire around the top of each stake to weave all stakes together. Small pieces of wire hold the poultry netting to the stakes. Use additional lengths of wire to reinforce the top. These pass from side to side and keep the stakes from spreading apart under the pressure of the compost. These wires are removed when the compost is turned. This type of structure is movable and reusable. However, neither pen will resist large dogs or tunneling rats.

Recycled hardwood pallets make excellent compost bins. They can be quickly assembled by driving in fence posts at the corners. A chicken wire or hardware cloth liner serves as a rodent barrier.

Garbage Can Composting

Use this system to compost kitchen scraps during the winter, or use it year-round to compost all the waste produced by a small yard and garden.

Directions

Use a hammer and a large nail to punch holes in the bottom, sides, and lid of a garbage can. Place the can on a large tray to catch draining liquid if desired.

To start the composting, place a 3-inch layer of finished compost or soil in the bottom of the can. Add finely chopped kitchen scraps followed by an equal amount of shredded newspaper, grass clippings, and/or shredded leaves. Add more material as available until the can is full, then layer new materials into another can and allow the first to finish composting—about 3 to 4 months.

Tips to Make Your Composter Work Its Best

- Protect the composter from freezing temperatures—put it in a garage or cellar.
- Start with soil or finished compost, and add a little more on top of each addition.
- Chop, shred, or even blend all additions as finely as possible.
- Add kitchen scraps before they start to smell.
- Mix the composting material after each addition and every few days. If you don't, it may produce unpleasant odors. Stir with a stick, roll the can back and forth on it's side a few times or use a "compost turning tool."
- Add water sparingly and only if your materials are very dry.

Other materials that can be used to construct pens include snow fences, lattice fencing, steel posts and chicken wire, furring strips, prefabricated picket fence sections, woven-reed or rattan fence sections, heavy window screens, storm windows with hardware cloth replacing glass, and louvered house blinds.

Pens and bins can be made to fit the contours of uneven land. One such structure consists of three bins in stair-step order going up a hill, partially cut into the bank. Composting starts in the highest bin. Turning is done by dropping the partially decomposed compost down a step, inverting it in the process. The third box receives the product of the second turning. From it the finished compost is used.

Pits

Pits for composting are dug into the ground and may be partially—or wholly—underground. The chief advantage of the pit form is its stable, secure, insulated structure. A masonry-lined, covered or coverable pit is secure from dogs, rats, clever raccoons, most flies, and wind and rain storms. Pit composting is ideal for severe winter weather because subsurface ground warmth and the heat-retaining properties of concrete enable bacteria to go on working longer. Some northern composters have a pen for summer and a pit for winter.

However, proper composting does not take place in a pit when compost becomes soggy and anaerobic. Provide some drainage to lessen the possibility of anaerobic conditions. Improper aeration and the greater possibility of anaerobic conditions remain, however, the two greatest drawbacks to pit composting. If you have the time to turn frequently and don't mind the extra strain on your back muscles in raising forkfuls of material from a lower-than-normal position, you may find ways to avoid these problems. Some pits are large and wide enough so that a person can stand at pit-bottom level while turning.

A compost pit can be built of concrete or masonry. Other materials such as tile and pressure-treated wood are also occasionally used as pit liners. A pit must have subsurface walls to prevent drainage water from entering the compost from the soil or the ground surface. Such drainage water would leach nutrients from the compost.

Some experts suggest that a concrete pit bottom is a necessity to prevent leaching, while others prefer a natural dirt bottom that serves as a source for worms and microorganisms. Some concrete-bottom proponents advise using a bottom layer of earth over the concrete, and others say the masonry walls absorb bacteria from manure and help to inoculate new compost materials as they are added.

A useful combination of a composting method and a compost, containing structure is the earthworm pit. Earthworms help aerate and mix the materials, thus eliminating some of the drawbacks of anaerobic pits. The pit, in turn, helps protect the worms from cold weather.

One gardener combined the earthworm pit with the movable-box method. He dug a rectangular hole about 18 inches deep in a flower bed. At earth level over the pit he placed a rectangular, bottomless and topless, wooden box of slightly larger dimensions than the hole. The hole was filled in layer style with kitchen garbage, manure, and green matter. When the frame was filled, too, the composter placed a board over the top and watered well. In 3 weeks, when the heat of the pile had decreased, earthworms were added.

Another successful pit is the one used by a New York State gardener. It is 4 feet wide, 4 feet deep,

Continued ➡

and 6 feet long with concrete sides and bottom. The bottom has an inset drainage grid similar to those used in basements and showers. Walls are 8 inches thick and project 18 inches above the ground. The top is made of tongue-and-groove boards nailed to 2 x 4s. A hinged lid provides access. Earthworms do the work of aeration in this pit, and garbage and leaves are the chief materials used.

An inexpensive pit may be made by digging a section of a masonry flue liner into the soil, leaving about 3 inches of it projecting above ground level. A thin layer of concrete poured into the pipe serves as the floor. A small flue liner 2 feet square may not require bottom drainage if earthworms are used, but check frequently for anaerobic conditions.

Terra cotta tiles are also useful for lining pits. These can be used for the sides in combination with a hardware cloth bottom to prevent rats from getting in from underneath. Build twin pits to make the turning job easier.

Drums

Where space limitations or offending odors are concerns, composting in drums provides an alternative to bins, pens, and pits. A metal or plastic barrel, with drainage holes in the bottom, can be raised off the ground with bricks or blocks to permit aeration. Layering kitchen wastes with absorbent materials like shredded paper or straw can help control odors; without turning or rolling, this method produces compost slowly but does provide a place for waste disposal.

Structures for City Composting

Is there any perfect form of compost making for a city gardener? Helga and Bill Olkowski, in *The City People's Book of Raising Food*, suggest a well-built two- or three-bin brick structure set between two houses. Runoff is caught in sawdust at the bottom of the bin, and the sawdust is turned with the pile. As garbage accumulates on its way to the bin, the Olkowskis layer it with sawdust in 5-gallon cans with tight-fitting lids. Sawdust is added every time fresh garbage is put into the can. The sawdust controls odor and putrefaction. In loading the bins, however, you should remember to compensate for the high-carbon content of the sawdust by using more high-nitrogen wastes.

Other city gardeners, who lack even a small space between houses, have composted successfully in garbage pails and metal drums. The danger with these methods is that they may quite easily become anaerobic and ferment. If you think it is hard enough dealing with garbage in a city, you should try to take care of a huge drum of fermented garbage. If, however, you really need to try these methods, provide aeration and drainage with holes in the bottom and sides of the drum or can. Set it in the basement or another protected area, preferably outdoors or on a flat roof. Elevate the can or drum on bricks or concrete blocks, and set a pan, larger in diameter than the drum, underneath it to catch drainage. Layer garbage with high-carbon-content materials just as you would in a regular pile. Composting is not really an indoor activity, and turning is especially hard to do in a limited space.

Trash cans can be used more readily for outdoor composting by cutting out the bottoms and setting them firmly into the ground to prevent tipping. California composter Helene Cole suggests using several of them and simply waiting 6 to 12 months for the finished product. Chopping your wastes first will speed up the process. A few air holes drilled in the lid will keep the earthworms that do most of the work in this system happy.

Another much more sensible indoor method is the earthworm box. Worms are easily raised in basements where fairly stable temperature conditions can be maintained. Worms do the turning in worm boxes, and the results of their labors are rich worm castings for compost and perhaps a little extra income for you during fishing season. If you live in an apartment, discuss composting or worm-raising plans with your landlord before launching your career.

Commercial Composters

A number of very good commercially produced composting units are now on the market. Generally built on the revolving-drum or upright-cylinder principle, these structures are designed to produce high-quality compost quickly and with a minimal effort on the part of the user. Recent articles in the *Wall Street Journal* have noted that commercial composting units represent overkill for most people, since similar composting conditions can be created without a commercial bin. Constraints on space, time, and physical ability, however, will continue to make such products appealing to many home composters.

The Green Cone, produced by Eco Atlantic, is a smaller, cone-shaped composter designed to decompose kitchen wastes. This closed, sun-heated composter features a below-ground basket for contact with the soil and a double-walled plastic cone to collect heat from the sun. Small and innocuous looking, the Green Cone can be located close to the kitchen for easy waste disposal, but according to the manufacturer, it is not meant to handle yard wastes and produces very little compost.

In general, these composters are designed for small-lot gardeners who want to make compost quickly and without offending the neighbors or attracting animals. Although such conditions can be met with a homemade bin, commercial composters offer valid alternatives to the gardener who is willing to pay $100 or more for an efficient, attractive composting unit.

The Joy of Composting

Joan Benjamin and Deborah L. Martin

Recycling your food and plant "wastes" by making compost for your garden is the single most important thing you can do to grow bountiful yields of great-tasting food and beautiful flowers. And it's easy, fun, and free! Compost provides a perfectly balanced fertilizer to feed your crops, improve the soil's structure, and protect your plants against drought, diseases, and insect pests.

This section gives you recipes for the full range of composting techniques. You can use fancy equipment or just pile ingredients directly on the ground. You can use an ultra-easy technique like sheet composting—spreading layers of grass clippings or leaves over the soil where microorganisms and earthworms will break it down. Or you can let a few bags of fall leaves decay behind the garage until they turn into dark, crumbly compost.

Since compost ingredients decompose, or "cook down," fastest when they're combined in just the right proportions, many of these recipes are formulated to help you produce rich, sweet-smelling, finished compost in as little as two weeks! Others take a more relaxed, "let-it-happen" approach that emphasizes ease over speed.

Whether your compost is made quickly or slowly, with carefully measured ingredients or whatever you have on hand, remember that turning organic matter into compost requires water and air. When you're building and tending a compost pile, it's helpful to keep this simple equation in mind:

The amount of moisture in your compost pile is almost as important as the ingredients you use. The microorganisms that do all the work in your pile need moisture to survive. But too much water can cause the compost ingredients to mat together, preventing air—another essential ingredient—from circulating.

Air is necessary because the desirable microorganisms in compost need oxygen in order to do their thing. Without air, other microorganisms will prevail (these will do the decomposition work, too, but with a lot more smell and slime). Use coarse ingredients like straw or cornstalks to keep air flowing all the time, and turn or stir things occasionally to give all the ingredients a breath of fresh air.

Combine these basic composting techniques with any of the following recipes and you'll be spreading nature's best all-natural fertilizer on your crops in no time!

Dry-Weather Compost

Your compost pile can't cook when it's dry and dusty. And it can't become the rich, crumbly soil food you seek when it's wet and waterlogged. The methods you use to keep the moisture in your pile at just the right level—it should be as damp as a wrung-out sponge—will depend on where you live. In a dry climate or during a long period of dry weather, composting in a pit in the ground or in a solid-sided bin will help keep the pile moist. Even frequent turning—with all its benefits—can cause your compost pile to dry out too quickly. Choose from among these moisture-managing methods to keep your microorganisms happy and your compost cooking.

Things to Keep Out of Your Heap

One of the most satisfying things about making compost is being able to recycle kitchen scraps and garden wastes—stuff you'd probably *throw away* otherwise—into something that's great for your garden. But that doesn't mean that every bit of household waste belongs in your compost pile. Balance the ingredients you add to your heap—you can have too much of a good thing, like grass clippings. And avoid materials that might carry diseases, materials that attract pests, and materials that slow the composting process or make it more difficult.

What to Avoid	Why
Cat droppings	May carry diseases and parasitic organisms; especially dangerous for pregnant women and young children
Coal or charcoal ashes	Contain amounts of sulfur and iron that are toxic to plants
Diseased plants	Require high-temperature (hot) composting to ensure that disease organisms are killed; otherwise may reinfect your garden when compost is spread
Dog droppings	May carry parasitic organisms; unpleasant to handle
Fish, meat, or cheese scraps	Break down slowly; attractive to foraging animals
Grease or oil	Break down slowly; inhibit composting of other materials
Weed seeds/rhizomes	Require hot composting to ensure that seeds are killed; otherwise may sprout wherever compost is applied; weeds like Canada thistle and quackgrass grow back from very small pieces of rhizome and are very hard to control

Continued ➡

Ingredients and Supplies

Pit or solid-sided bin
Compost ingredients
Pole or stake, approximately 5 feet long

Directions

1. Place ingredients in the pit or bin. Making your compost in a bin with solid sides or in a pit in the ground reduces the amount of moisture that will be lost to evaporation.

2. Spray the pile lightly with water after each addition. It's easier to start your pile with moist ingredients than to get the whole thing wet enough after it's built.

   Note: Try one—or both—of these techniques to make the most of rainfall to keep your heap moist:

   · Drive the pole or stake into the center of your compost heap to help direct rainfall into the pile.

   · Dig a shallow "well" in the top of your compost pile to catch any rain that does fall.

Wet-Weather Compost

If your weather is wet, cover your compost pile to prevent it from becoming too soggy. A soggy heap will still turn to compost, but the process is a lot smellier and messier. When steady rain threatens to make your compost pile sodden and yucky, top your heap with water-shedding ingredients or a protective tarp.

Ingredients and Supplies

Compost ingredients
Straw, hay, or plastic or canvas tarp

Directions

1. Place ingredients in a pile.

2. Cover the compost pile with a layer of rain-shedding straw or hay (later, it becomes an ingredient in your compost!) or throw a tarp over the pile.

3. Check your heap for moisture periodically. If your pile becomes too wet in spite of your efforts, turn your compost frequently to let in more air and to help return moisture to an appropriate level.

The World's Easiest Compost

"The magical thing about composting is that it happens no matter how much attention you give or don't give to your pile," explains Maria Rodale, author of *Maria Rodale's Organic Garden* and daughter of the late Robert Rodale, long-time editor of *Organic Gardening* magazine. Maria, who gardens at her home in Emmaus, Pennsylvania, just a block away from *Organic Gardening*'s editorial offices, says she thinks of her compost pile as her "home waste disposal system."

Ingredients and Supplies

All yard wastes, including weeds, spent garden plants, leaves, and grass clippings
Kitchen scraps, including peelings, seeds, rinds, cores, and cobs, but excluding fats, meats, and dairy products
Any corner in the yard, with or without a bin
A little patience

Directions

1. "Just throw everything on the pile," Maria advises. She does recommend keeping meat and dairy products and greasy or fatty foods out of the compost pile, since these break down very slowly and tend to attract pests and pets (like Maria's dog) to the pile.

2. Sit back and wait. Don't bother with measuring, chopping, shredding, turning, or other kinds of compost fussing! In time (within a month or two), dark, rich, crumbly compost will begin to form at the bottom of the pile as the ingredients decompose.

CONTAINING COMPOST-BOUND KITCHEN WASTES

Unless walking to your compost pile is your daily exercise program, you'll want a way to store up a few days' worth of kitchen scraps for less-frequent trips to the heap. In her kitchen, Maria Rodale uses a 5-gallon, lidded bucket to hold scraps for trips to the compost pile every other day or so. "A tight-fitting lid is crucial for controlling odors and fruit flies," she points out. She adds a second container when cold weather arrives: "In the winter, we also keep a medium-size garbage can with a lid outside our back door for kitchen scraps. We take this down to the pile every few weeks or so—if it's cold, there's no smell. That way, we have to take it to the main pile only when we're feeling like a walk and when the weather is cooperating!"

Simple Shovel Compost

You need nothing more than a shovel and a spot to sink it in to put this quick and easy composting technique to work in your garden, says garden writer and photographer Deb Meager of Nevada City, California. Deb's method works well when you have only small amounts of kitchen and garden waste to compost.

Ingredients and Supplies

1 bucket kitchen scraps and lawn and garden wastes
Shovel

Directions

1. Choose a spot in your garden where you want to improve the soil.

2. Dig a small hole, removing 2 to 5 shovelfuls of soil. The deeper you bury kitchen scraps for composting, the less likely it is that they'll be unearthed by foraging wild animals or pets.

3. Dump the kitchen scraps and yard wastes into the hole and chop them up a bit with the shovel.

4. Return the soil to the hole, covering the scraps and chopping a bit more with the shovel to mix some soil down into the buried scraps. The organic wastes you've put into the hole will gradually become soil-enriching compost—with no pile, no watering, and no turning!

5. Repeat this process as often as possible.

Note: In your garden, it's easy to dig a row of these holes, or a shallow trench, in the path space next to a crop row. Next year, plant your flowers or vegetables in the "compost row," and "plant" compostables where your crops once grew.

Variation: Try "Simple Shovel Compost" on your lawn, too. Use your shovel to cut loose a flap of sod, then fold it back and dig a hole. Pour in the kitchen scraps, chop them a little with the shovel, and replace the soil. Then firmly press the sod back into place. Water the spot well. Don't worry if there's a lump left behind when you're through—it will quickly disappear because the scraps shrink as they compost.

Super-Simple Straw Bale Composting

In this method, the straw bales you use to make your compost bin will become ingredients in your next batch of compost. It's recommended by Maine's master organic grower Eliot Coleman in his highly-acclaimed book, *The New Organic Grower*. Eliot says he gets consistently high-quality compost from his straw-bale bins. "I began using this straw bale method after reading about it in a book called *Intensive Gardening*, by Rachel Dalziel O'Brien," he says. "I consider it to be one of the best books ever written on market gardening."

Ingredients and Supplies

8 (or more) straw bales
Loose straw
Assorted green plant wastes
Soil

Directions

1. Stack straw bales like bricks, 2 or 3 bales high, to build a 3-sided enclosure of whatever size you want. You'll need about 8 bales to make a bin that's 2 bales high. The bales make a perfect bin because they keep all the ingredients moist and warm while still letting in plenty of air.

2. Fill the bale enclosure by alternating 2- to 3-inch layers of loose straw with 1- to 6-inch layers of green plant wastes. Make thinner layers of moist materials like grass clippings that might mat together, and thicker layers of loose, open ingredients such as tomato plants or pea vines. Sprinkle a layer of soil over each green layer.

3. Let compost happen. Eliot says he prefers to let his compost sit for about 1½ years before he uses it. The straw bales will hold together for at least 2 years. Then you can use them as ingredients in your next heap, with fresh, new bales for the enclosure.

BREATHE NEW LIFE INTO YOUR COMPOST PILE

You can get compost more quickly if you give your pile some gas—specifically that clear, breathable gas called oxygen. Air in your compost pile makes the ingredients break down faster, so you have finished compost for your garden sooner.

Adding air, by turning or using other ventilation techniques, helps when too many wet ingredients mat down and keep air from circulating through the pile. Too much air, however, can dry out a pile, so you need to be sure to add moisture even when you're turning a pile that's properly moist.

If turning your compost by moving the entire pile to a new spot seems like too much work, don't despair.

Basic Backyard Compost

Making your own compost is as easy as pie with this proven recipe from Cyane Gresham, compost specialist at the Rodale Institute Experimental Farm in Berks County, Pennsylvania. Cyane's recipe is based on her 10 years of research to identify the very best composting methods for home gardeners.

Ingredients and Supplies

1 part fresh green materials
1 part dried brown materials
1 part black materials

Directions

1. Build your pile at least 4 feet square and 4 feet high, if possible. When you make your pile this large, temperatures can quickly build up in the center to over 100°F. This rapid warm-up allows heat-loving microorganisms to rapidly turn the ingredients into finished compost.

2. Mix together the ingredients as you go and add enough water to make all the ingredients thoroughly moistened but not soggy. "Don't worry about the exact proportions," Cyane explains. "The composting process is very forgiving, and all organic matter will eventually decompose."

Continued ➡

The closer you can get to equal proportions of greens, browns, and blacks, the faster you'll get finished compost. But even if you made a pile entirely of greens, or entirely of browns, it would eventually turn into good compost. It will just probably take longer than when you mix the 3 kinds of materials together.

3. You can turn or stir the pile with a garden fork every few weeks if you want to really speed up the process, Cyane says, or you can just let it sit. Either way, make sure that the pile stays moist. If you just let it sit, "it should break down very nicely in a couple of months as long as the weather is warm." (Turning a compost pile "fluffs it up" and introduces more oxygen so that the microorganisms can multiply faster.)

Yield: 2 cubic feet of finished compost

COMPOST CHOICES

The "greens" you choose for your compost pile can include any fresh moist organic matter, like grass clippings, weeds, and kitchen scraps. Greens provide necessary nitrogen and moisture to the pile. The "browns" are older, drier, tougher materials like straw, cornstalks, sawdust, fall leaves, and dead plants. You need the browns to keep the pile loose so that air can circulate. The "blacks" can be either garden soil, manure, or chunky incompletely decomposed material from a previous compost pile. "The blacks are the great equalizer in the pile," Cyane Gresham explains. "They absorb and hold moisture, and they also introduce the microorganisms that break down the browns and greens."

Loose-Leaf Compost

If rich, soil-building compost fell from the sky every fall, there's no question that you'd gather up some for your garden, right? So why would you even think of disposing of the wealth of free, nutrient-rich leaves that fall from your trees each year?

"Homeowners should never throwaway their fall leaves," says *Organic Gardening* magazine's research editor Cheryl Long. "Tree roots draw minerals from deep in the soil in order to grow leaves and branches. If you throwaway leaves instead of recycling them, you are literally making your soil poorer and poorer every year." Fortunately leaves are very easy to compost, very good for your gardens, and often available in large quantities.

Ingredients and Supplies

Fall leaves
Lawn mower, string trimmer, or chipper/shredder

Directions

1. Shred your leaves. The benefits of shredding the leaves are threefold, Cheryl explains: "Shredding makes the volume of leaves much smaller and easier to handle. The shredded leaves are less prone to blowing away. And they decompose faster." Don't despair if you don't have a shredder—you can chop up leaves with your lawn mower. Or put the leaves in a trash can and then use a string trimmer to chop them up. Wear goggles and a dust mask with any of these methods to protect yourself from flying dust and debris.

2. Add the shredded leaves to your compost pile and mix with your other ingredients.

Variation: If you don't have time to shred your leaves, you can still compost them over the winter and add them to your gardens next spring. "All you have to do is pile 'em up, wet 'em down, and let 'em sit," Cheryl says. "If I don't have time to shred

my leaves, I just rake them into a pile and put a ring of welded wire fencing around it to keep the leaves from blowing around. Putting them in big plastic trash bags works fine, too."

You can even rescue bags of leaves destined for curbside collection and turn them into compost, Cheryl says. Just poke some holes in the bags to let air and water in and out, then wet the leaves thoroughly. Open the tops of the bags so rain can get in, and let the leaves sit for a few months or more. Like turning a compost pile, occasionally shaking the bags will help add some air to the mix.

"If I have time, I also mix a few shovelfuls of good garden soil into each pile or bag," Cheryl says, "The soil inoculates the leaves with plenty of the microorganisms and earthworms that help turn them into compost."

When your leaves reach that dark, crumbly state that's called leaf mold, you can use it as a weed-blocking, moisture-conserving mulch. Or mix the leaf mold into your garden beds to improve the soil. Either way, you'll be feeding the soil, the earthworms, and your crops with those treasures from the trees. Leaf mold also makes the perfect ingredient to add to grass clippings over the summer months. "Large amounts of fresh grass clippings alone tend to mat together and don't compost well," Cheryl explains, "If you mix in some leaf mold with the clippings, the pile will cook much better."

Halloween Leaf Compost

Transform all those brilliant red and yellow fall leaves into black gold for your garden with this recipe from veteran gardener George Weigel, garden columnist for the *Patriot-News* in Harrisburg, Pennsylvania. George's recipe includes grass clippings, which are high in nitrogen, an ingredient that speeds up the composting of the leaves.

Ingredients and Supplies

Compost bin
4 buckets fall leaves (preferably shredded)
2 buckets grass clippings, spent garden plants, or kitchen scraps
1 bucket garden soil
Sprinkling of lime or wood ashes (if available)

Directions

1. Dump the ingredients together and mix.
2. Moisten everything well as you mix.
3. Repeat with more layers until you run out of materials, bin space, or energy.

Yield: 3 buckets of finished compost

Note: Mix the finished compost into your beds. George recommends mixing in the compost about 2 weeks before planting.

Just Add Air

The tiny critters that turn your kitchen scraps and yard wastes into compost do their best work when they get plenty of oxygen. Thus, a well-aerated compost pile breaks down much more quickly than one in which the microorganisms are practically gasping for breath. The good news is, you don't have to turn your compost to keep its population of busy microorganisms breathing freely. Instead, do a little advance planning and build in a ventilation system when you build your pile.

Ingredients and Supplies

Several cornstalks, saplings, or sunflower stalks, each 4–5 feet long
String or twine

Directions

1. Use string or twine to tie the stalks or saplings into a bundle that is 5 to 6 inches in diameter.

2. Build your compost pile around the bundled stalks, so that the bundle becomes a "chimney" sticking up from the middle of the pile. Air will travel through the hollow stalks and in the spaces between them into the center of your pile.

Variation: Lay 4- to 5-foot-long perforated plastic pipes horizontally at different layers as you build your compost pile. These will also let air into the middle of the pile. As lower layers decompose, pull out the pipes at the bottom of the pile and lay them across the top before adding more ingredients.

Chicken and Chips Compost

It's a perfect compost combo—rich chicken manure mixed with wood chips or sawdust. Noted garden experts and authors Doc and Katy Abraham of Naples, New York, explain that both chicken manure and wood chips can burn plants when used alone, but when you mix the two and compost them together, you can produce a safe and effective soil amendment.

Ingredients and Supplies

1 part chicken manure
1 part wood chips or sawdust

Directions

1. Mix the 2 ingredients together thoroughly and water well.
2. Add them to your existing compost pile, or build a separate pile with them, if you prefer.
3. Let them compost for 6 months or even a year to give the wood wastes plenty of time to break down.
4. Turn the pile occasionally with a garden fork, and add water as needed to keep the material moist. (Or, if the weather is very wet, cover the pile with plastic to keep it from getting too soggy.)

Yield: 1 part of finished compost

Note: It's easy for gardeners to get wood chips or sawdust from tree-trimming companies or local sawmills, say Doc and Katy. "But when wood chips are stored in big piles, they can develop what's called sour mulch syndrome, which produces acetic acid, alcohols, and foul-smelling hydrogen sulfide," Doc explains. These compounds in sour wood mulch can damage plants. But you can prevent or cure sour mulch by combining the chips with chicken manure, which is extremely rich in nitrogen and other nutrients (so rich, in fact, that when used full strength it can damage tender seedlings). That chicken manure's nitrogen is exactly what's needed to balance the low nitrogen content of the wood chips. When the manure is mixed together with chips or sawdust and composted, the wood decomposes without producing any sour by-products, and the result is an excellent compost.

Rabbit-Powered Compost Pile

They're cute, they're cuddly, they're composting machines! More than just adorable pals, rabbits are the perfect backyard livestock, says organic gardener K. B. Laugheed of Fortville, Indiana. K. B.'s recipe for top-quality compost starts with high-nitrogen, nonsmelly rabbit manure—it keeps her compost heap hopping! K. B. says her bunnies are every bit as easy-care as the compost pile beneath their cage, and they help her process some compost ingredients, too: "The rabbits never need to be bathed, groomed, or taken for a walk," she says. "And they happily munch on your old lettuce, bruised apples, celery tips, and carrot scrapings."

Continued ➡

Ingredients and Supplies

1 or 2 rabbits
Raised hutch with wire bottom
Kitchen scraps and yard wastes

Directions

1. Lay 8 to 10 inches of kitchen scraps and yard wastes under the rabbits' hutch.

2. Let the rabbits do their thing. As more kitchen scraps and yard wastes become available, add them to the pile.

3. Add water, as needed, to keep the pile moist. In dry climates, dig a hole under the hutch to hold the pile so that it doesn't dry out quickly.

4. About once a year, rake out the finished compost and start again with a fresh base of yard wastes.

Composting by the Numbers

Knowing that the ideal ratio of carbon to nitrogen in your compost pile is about 30:1 isn't too helpful, unless you also know how to reach that ratio. But if you really want to crank up your compost pile and get it rotting hot and fast, that 30:1 ratio is a good goal to aim for. It provides a balanced "diet" that lets the microorganisms in your pile thrive.

Eric Evans, director of the Woods End Research Laboratory in Mt. Vernon, Maine, offers a few tips to help homeowners make the most of the carbon-to-nitrogen ratio. "The biggest factor in the carbon-to-nitrogen ratio is how much water is present," Eric says. "Dry materials are generally in the range of 40 to 50 percent carbon, and sloppy, wet materials are generally 10 to 20 percent carbon." So the more dry ingredients you have, the quicker you'll reach the 30:1 ratio.

Ingredients and Supplies

Pencil and paper or a calculator

Directions

1. Calculate your pile's total carbon value by multiplying the percentage of carbon of each ingredient by the number of parts (by weight) of that ingredient and then adding up the carbon totals for all the ingredients. (See "Math for Composters" below to see how to do the calculations.)

2. Do the same for the nitrogen.

3. Divide the carbon value by the nitrogen value to get the carbon-to-nitrogen ratio. If it's between 25:1 and 35:1, your pile should compost beautifully. If the ratio is higher or lower than that, adjust the proportions of ingredients to bring it into the range of 25 to 35 parts carbon for each 1 part nitrogen.

MATH FOR COMPOSTERS

Here's an example of how the carbon-to-nitrogen (C:N) ratio works when you apply the formula to real-life amounts of real-life compost ingredients:

Starting with 50 pounds of non legume hay (about 1 bale), 10 pounds of kitchen scraps, and 2 pounds of coffee grounds:

> 50 lbs. hay x 40% C = 20 lbs. C
>
> 10 lbs. kitchen scraps x 10% C = 1 lb. C
>
> 2 lbs. coffee grounds x 25% C = 0.5 lb. C
>
> 20 + 1 + 0.5 = 21.5 total carbon value
>
> 50 lbs. hay x 1% N = 0.5 lb. N
>
> 10 lbs. kitchen scraps x 1 % N = 0.1 lb. N
>
> 2 lbs. coffee grounds x 1 % N = 0.02 lb. N
>
> 0.5 + 0.1 + 0.02 = 0.62 total nitrogen value

21.5 -:- 0.62 = 34.7 parts carbon to 1 part nitrogen

Note: "The more dissimilar the materials are in terms of moisture, the bigger the error if you measure by volume and not weight," Eric adds. Even if you're unlikely to weigh every ingredient you add to your heap, this formula will give you an idea how to adjust the proportions of materials in your pile to get finished compost more quickly.

Not Your Backyard Compost

Homemade compost differs from commercial compost products in several key ways:

- Commercial compost piles are larger (commonly 8 feet tall and 16 feet wide, versus the 4 x 4-foot backyard compost pile). The size of commercial compost piles makes them difficult to mix and maintain, resulting in inconsistent quality.

- Many commercial composts are based around a single material, such as manure. (Homemade compost usually contains a mix of garden wastes, grass clippings, kitchen scraps, and leaves.) A single ingredient typically doesn't compost as well as a mix of materials. Commercial-compost makers don't always add other materials because of the extra time and cost involved.

Experts predict that we'll see more dry or dehydrated manure products marketed as compost. Many of these products claim to be fully composted, but aren't. And if you apply them at the same rate as other composts, they could burn plants because of their higher nitrogen content. If the label tells you that the product contains dehydrated manure, use it at a lower rate than mature compost.

Fast, Easy, Pest-Proof Compost in a Drum

Tumbler or drum composters make composting a breeze. They provide easy turning, super-fast compost, and no pest problems. Instead of a bin that sits on the ground, drum composters feature a large, barrel-shaped container mounted in a frame that lets you easily aerate the compost by spinning the drum. Since the tumbler is completely enclosed to keep the compost in when it spins, it's perfect for keeping foraging animals out. Drum composting works best when you shred bulky materials before you put them in the tumbler. Mike Peck, president of the PBM Group, Inc., marketers of the ComposTumbler, one of the original drum composters, offers six different recipes that work well in a drum composter.

Ingredients and Supplies

Recipe # 1

12 parts fresh grass clippings and/or kitchen scraps
3 parts sawdust

Recipe #2

9 parts fresh grass clippings
3 parts kitchen scraps
3 parts straw

Recipe #3

9 parts fall leaves, shredded
3 parts dehydrated cow manure
3 parts fresh weeds

Recipe #4

9 parts fresh grass clippings
3 parts kitchen scraps
3 parts newspaper, wet and shredded

Recipe #5

7 parts fresh or dehydrated horse manure
3 parts fall leaves, shredded
3 parts sawdust

Recipe #6

10 bushels fall leaves, shredded
2½ pounds blood meal or alfalfa meal

Directions

1. Choose your recipe and assemble your ingredients. Mike says it's best to moisten dry materials before you load them into the drum.

2. As you're loading, close the door and turn the drum several times to mix the materials.

3. Once the composter is loaded, turn it slowly once a day, and it will soon heat up to over 120°F.

4. Check the moisture level every few days and add water if needed. "The material should always be damp, like a wrung-out sponge, but not soggy," Mike says. Tumbled compost will be ready to use in as little as 2 weeks, as soon as the core temperature is no higher than the outdoor temperature during a cool part of the day. (Garden centers and garden supply catalogs sell special thermometers for measuring compost temperature, or you can just stick your hand in and make an educated guess.)

Note: Compared to other composting techniques, drum composting offers the big advantage of producing a batch of finished compost very quickly. That's because it provides the ideal conditions for fast decomposition—even moisture levels, plenty of air, and finely shredded materials. But you can use these recipes to make quick compost in a regular bin, too, because they've been calculated to have the perfect ratio of carbon to nitrogen for rapid microbial growth and decomposition. Just be sure to keep things moist and turn the pile often.

Commercial Compost

Homemade compost is the best thing you can use to feed your plants and improve your soil. But even if you make your own, there may be times when you don't have enough of it to go around. That's when commercial compost comes in handy.

Product Inequality

Your local municipal compost site or garden center is certainly an option when it comes to loading up with bulk or bagged compost. But before you do, be forewarned: Not all commercial compost is created equal. Commercial composts are highly variable in organic matter and nutrient content. Some can even harm your soil and plants. Here's how to tell the difference between safe-to-use commercial composts and the stuff you should pass on.

Municipal Compost

With landfill space decreasing and waste disposal costs rising, more communities are becoming involved in large-scale composting. In 1990, more than 1,000 municipal composting sites were operating in the United States. And new legislative limits on waste disposal and public demand for environmentally safe waste handling are sure to lead to more of these operations.

Municipal compost operations range from small leaf-composting facilities to huge systems capable of turning 800 tons of waste per day into compost. Most use mechanized turners and forced-air methods to break down the large volume

Continued ➡

of materials as fast as possible. A few are fully enclosed, automated "in-vessel" systems that take in refuse at one end and sort, grind, mix, moisten, and aerate the material as it proceeds to the other end, where it emerges as finished compost.

Many municipal compost sites offer their product to local residents at little or no cost. Even if you must pay a small fee (common if you're not a resident), you'll still probably save compared to the cost of bagged compost, which sometimes reflects the cost of transportation.

To locate a municipal composting site near you, check township or city government listings in your phone book or online. Contact the office that manages solid waste. Most states also maintain a list of operating or planned compost facilities.

(Just remember that when you visit a municipal compost site, the compost won't be bagged—meaning you'll need containers or a pick-up truck in which to haul it.)

Using Municipal Compost

Because the quality of compost from municipal operations can vary considerably, you should keep the following tips for using municipal compost in mind.

- Never use municipal sludge or compost that contains sludge. Sludge (sometimes called "biosolids") may contain toxic heavy metals, such as cadmium, nickel, and copper, which can build up in soil.
- Use municipal compost on ornamental beds—not for edible plants. Municipal compost is made from yard wastes. And some of that plant debris probably was treated with herbicides, fungicides, or pesticides.
- Gauge the quality of the compost before you load up. Some piles will be more finished than others. Choose compost that has a uniform dark brown color and sweet, earthy odor—no hint of ammonia or sourness. It shouldn't contain visible wood chips, pine needles, or other materials that still need to decompose.

Mushroom Compost

If you live near a commercial mushroom grower, you may be able to buy mushroom compost—the medium used to grow mushrooms. Mushroom compost (also called "mushroom soil") is a blend of one-third horse manure, one-third spoiled hay, and one-third ground corncobs. With a 1.4-1-1 NPK value and a near-neutral pH, mushroom compost makes an excellent soil amendment.

A bulk load of mushroom compost (about 16 tons) costs about $100-delivered. (Most places will deliver or fill a pickup truck with mushroom soil for just $5 to $10.)

Make sure you get *organic* mushroom compost, however. Organic growers use steam to kill weed seeds and competing fungi and molds—other mushroom composts may be chemically treated. One supplier of organic mushroom compost is Hawk Valley Farm in Kempton, Pennsylvania.

Eastern Pennsylvania is the "mushroom capital of the world," but mushroom growers are scattered throughout other regions, too. Check with your local Cooperative Extension office for the names of nearby growers in your area.

Bagged Compost

If you're willing to pay a bit more, you can purrchase commercial compost by the bag at your local garden center or home-improvement store. But be aware: Buying compost isn't as simple as looking for the best brand. Most commercial composts are produced and sold locally—you won't

find the same products in South Dakota and Tennessee—or even in Nashville and Memphis.

The quality of commercial composts varies because they are usually made from whatever local waste materials are available at that time. For example, one batch might be made with low-salt manure and the next with high-salt manure. That means that unless the producer monitors each batch carefully, a brand that tests at the top of the class one month could flunk the next time around.

Organic Gardening magazine and Woods End Research Laboratory in Mount Vernon, Maine, tested 30 brands of bagged compost and found the following product problems:

- **More than half of the brands tested were too old or diluted with soil,** resulting in a low organic-matter content. If the level of organic matter is too low, the compost won't improve the soil as well as a better-quality product would. (High-quality, finished compost contains 30 to 60 percent organic matter.)
- **Nearly half of the samples tested had a pH outside the preferred 6.5 to 7.5 pH range.** For optimum growth of most plants, you want a near-neutral soil pH. Nine of the samples tested too high (as alkaline as 8.3 pH), and four of them tested too low (as acidic as 4.5).
- **A quarter of the samples contained too much salt.** If compost production isn't managed properly, or if a large amount of chicken manure is used, salts can accumulate to a level high enough to injure plants—especially seedlings.
- **A quarter of the samples were sticky and wet.** These compost products would have been difficult, if not impossible, to spread.

Buying Quality Compost

Fortunately, a simple look and smell are all you need to do to find a good-quality product. If possible, ask your garden center or supplier to let you take home a few samples before you buy. Put the samples through your own round of testing, using the following criteria.

- **The texture should be loose and granular**, with little or no recognizable bark or wood. If the compost isn't loose enough for you to spread and work it easily into your garden beds, don't buy it.
- **The color should be dark brown or black-brown.** Avoid products that are light in color. They probably contain too little organic matter and too much soil. It's easiest to tell the true product color if you let the compost sample dry out.
- **The compost should be moist, not dry or soggy.** In the soil, compost can hold up to 2½ times its weight in water. But in bagged products, excess water makes the compost difficult to spread. (Plus, you'll be paying for water, not compost.) Simply lifting a bag of compost will give you a good idea of its moisture content. If it feels like a big glob, the compost probably is too wet. If it feels loose, it's probably drier.
- **Mature compost has a pleasant, earthy smell.** If you find an earthy, woodsy odor, you've probably struck "black gold"—a mature, good-quality compost. Avoid composts with a strong or unpleasant smell, indicating immature compost that could damage plants. (*Note:* Some good-quality bagged composts have a slight musty or barnyard odor when first opened. That's because the plastic bags restrict the oxygen supply to the organisms that release

the earthy odor. After a day or two, the compost should acquire that earthy aroma.)

- **Mature compost contains 30 to 60 percent organic matter.** To test the organic-matter content of any compost (commercial or homemade), spread some out on a thin layer of newspaper and let it air-dry for about a week. Then measure exactly 1 cup of the dried compost and weigh it. If it weighs between 4 and 6 ounces, it contains the desired amount of organic matter. If it weighs less than 4 ounces, it's probably immature. If it weighs more than 6 ounces, it's probably old or diluted with soil—so you shouldn't use it.

Some stores won't allow you to sample or inspect before you buy. If you buy a bag and find that it's not up to these standards, take it back and ask for a refund or dump it onto your home pile to dilute and fully compost it.

Another option is to look for bulk compost, sold at some garden centers. You'll not only be able to see what you're buying but also save some money. Many bulk composts are cheaper than bagged products: 1 cubic yard of bulk compost (the equivalent of twenty-five 40-pound bags) usually costs less than $30, while the good-quality bagged composts sell for $2 to $4 per 40-pound bag. Another advantage of bulk compost is that the garden center might be willing to deliver it right to your garden. (If they don't deliver door-to-garden, use your pick-up truck-or a neighbor's-to pick up your compost.)

Using Compost

Deborah L. Martin and Grace Gershuny

Your compost is finished. After carefully following the recommended steps for turning the year's bounty of organic materials into rich, mellow humus, you want to be certain that it's used to best advantage—that it benefits your soil most and helps to ensure a natural abundance and health in your coming crops.

It is not possible to stress too heavily the "soil bank account" theory of fertilizing. The real purpose of the organic method is to build permanent fertility into the soil by adding to its natural rock mineral reserves and to its humus content. Practically all the natural fertilizers are carriers of insoluble plant food. They start working quickly, but they don't drop their load of food all at once, as does a soluble fertilizer. An insoluble fertilizer will work for you for months and years.

So you can see that, as an organic gardener or farmer, you are adding fertilizer not only to supply immediate plant food needs, but also to build up the reserves that future crops will draw upon.

When to Apply Compost

The principal factor in determining when to apply compost is its condition. If it is half finished, or noticeably fibrous, it could well be applied in October or November. By spring it will have completed its decomposition in the soil itself and will be ready to supply growth nutrients to the earliest plantings made. Otherwise, for general soil enrichment, the ideal time for applying compost is a month or so before planting. The closer to planting time it is incorporated, the more it should be ground up or worked over thoroughly with a hoe to finely shred it. The special tools and equipment will come in handy when you wish to add compost to your soil close to planting time.

If your compost is ready in the fall and is not intended to be used until the spring, keep it in a protected place. If it is kept for a long period

Continued ➡

during the summer, water the finished compost from time to time.

For organic farmers and gardeners, it's not a bad idea to make applications of compost either in the fall or winter or in the early spring. The big advantage here is that application at such a time helps to equalize the work load. Usually this time of year is the least crowded with busy schedules, and the farmer or gardener can devote more time to doing a good job without interfering with the rest of the crop program. Also, there is less chance of damaging the soil or of injuring crops.

Just before you first work the soil in spring is a particularly good time to apply fertilizer. Then when the soil preparation is done, the fresh organic matter can be worked down into the soil to supply food for the organisms that give life to the spring soil. They become active and start to grow at about freezing temperatures. However, soil temperatures must rise to 50°F (10°C) before they really take on the dynamic action that characterizes a living organic soil. In early spring, the temperature is just about to rise to the level where the vital soil organisms can make use of it.

In summer, plants take more nutrients from the soil than they do in any other season. But perhaps you didn't realize that in summer the soil has more nutrients available to give to plants than at any other time of the year. During the summer the increased activity of bacteria and other soil microorganisms is primarily responsible for the abundance of plant food. These same microorganisms are one of the primary forces that act on organic and natural rock fertilizers to make them available to plants. The beauty of this system is that microbes are releasing nutrients to plants most quickly at just the time when plants are growing most rapidly.

Summer can be a fine time to apply compost and the natural rock fertilizers—rock and colloidal phosphate, greensand, granite dust, and diabase dust. Organic fertilizers of all types are needed even more in the summer, because they hold moisture in the soil and stimulate the bacterial activity that takes place during the warm months. However, don't count on these slow-release materials to help growing crops that suffer from deficiencies. They will not become available until the microbes have had a chance to work on them for a while. The nutrients you add in the summer will greatly benefit your plants next year and the year after.

General Rules for Applying Compost

Apply at least ½ inch to 3 inches of well-finished compost over your garden each year. There is little if any danger of burning due to overuse, as is the case with chemical fertilizers. You can apply compost either once or twice a year. The amount would depend, of course, on the fertility of your soil and on what and how much has been grown in it.

For most applications, it is important that compost be well finished—that is, aged long enough so that the decomposition process has stabilized. Unfinished compost has been found to retard germination and growth of certain plants. Some plants, such as corn and squash, seem to thrive on partly finished compost, however. In general, be most careful when applying compost shortly before planting or in seeding mixes. Fall soil preparation and mulching applications are less critical.

If you want to be certain that your compost is aged well enough, you can perform a germination test. Soak a few seeds, such as lettuce or radish, in a tea made with your compost, and soak an equal number from the same packet in distilled water. Lay each batch on a paper towel, and keep them warm and moist for a few days, until they start to sprout.

If the distilled-water-treated seeds germinate better, you know you must let your compost age longer.

When applying either half-finished or finished compost to your soil, turn over the soil thoroughly and mix the compost in with the top 4 inches of soil. If you have a rotary tiller, you can simply spread the compost on the soil surface and go over it a few times to work it in.

To improve the structure and fertility of poor soil quickly, give it a thorough compost treatment in the fall. Spade it 12 to 18 inches deep, and mix in all the half-rotted compost you have. Then leave the surface rough and cloddy so that the freezing and thawing of winter will mellow it (or plant a green manure crop that will add more fertility when it is dug or tilled under in the spring).

Putting compost down deep in the soil will also give your plants built-in protection against drought. Having humus down in the lower levels of your soil means that moisture will be held there where plant roots can get all they need in dry weather.

Also, this moisture will prevent the plants from starving during drought, since their roots can pick up food only when it is in liquid form.

The Vegetable Garden

Your vegetable garden will thrive if you give it liberal amounts of compost. (See the table "Compost Application Guide for Vegetables" on page 220.) Dig it in during the fall, bury it in trenches, put it in the furrows when you plant and in the holes when transplanting seedlings. When the plants begin to grow rapidly, mix compost with equal amounts of soil and use it as a topdressing; or mulch the plants heavily with partially rotted compost or with such raw compost materials as hay, straw, sawdust, grass clippings, or shredded leaves.

There is one rule to remember when mulching: The finer the material, the thinner the layer you will need. Remember that compost used at planting time should be well finished, especially for potatoes, which are prone to become scabby when in contact with incompletely decomposed manure. You may safely use partially finished compost only on heavy feeders like corn and squash.

For sowing seeds indoors or in a cold frame, put your compost through a ½-inch sieve, then shred it with a hoe or even roll it with a rolling pin to make it very fine. Then mix it with equal amounts of sand and soil. The ideal seeding mixture is fine textured and crumbly and tends to fall apart after being squeezed in your hand.

The Flower Garden

Finely screened compost is excellent to put around all growing flowers. Apply it alone as an inch-thick mulch to control weeds and conserve moisture, or topdress it mixed with soil. In the spring, you can loosen the top few inches of soil in your annual and perennial beds and work into it an equal quantity of compost. And use compost generously when sowing flower seeds.

Compost watering is an excellent way to give your flowers supplementary feeding during their growing season. Put a generous amount of compost in a burlap sack or other permeable container, place it in a watering can, add water, and sprinkle liberally around the plants. The can may be refilled with water several times before the compost loses its potency.

Another advantage for flower growers is that plenty of compost has been found to keep the moisture level of the flower bed too high for ants.

Your Lawn

To build a lawn that stays green all summer, has no crabgrass, and rarely needs watering, use compost liberally when making and maintaining it. Your goal is to produce a thick sod with roots that go down 6 inches, not a thin, weed-infested mat lying on a layer of infertile subsoil.

In building a new lawn, work in copious amounts of compost to a depth of at least 6 inches. If your soil is either sandy or clayey (rather than a good loam), you'll need at least a 2-inch depth of compost, mixed in thoroughly, to build it up. For northern gardeners, the best time to make a new lawn is in the fall. But if you want to get started in the spring, dig in your compost and plant annual or perennial ryegrass, which will look quite neat all summer. Then dig this green manure in at the end of summer, and make your permanent lawn when cool weather comes. Southern gardeners might be better off starting in the spring with a ryegrass cover and then over-seeding with a lawn mixture the following spring.

To renovate an old, patchy lawn, dig up the bare spots about 2 inches deep, work in plenty of finished compost, tamp and rake well, and sow your seed after soaking the patches well.

Feed your lawn regularly every spring. An excellent practice is to use a spike-toothed aerator, then spread a mixture of fine finished compost and bonemeal. Rake this into the holes made by the aerator. You can use a fairly thick covering of compost—just not so thick it covers the grass. This will feed your lawn efficiently and keep it sending down a dense mass of roots that laugh at drought.

Trees and Shrubs

Despite the attention that has been given to back-filling mixtures for the planting holes of trees and shrubs, this is one place where compost should not, as a rule, be used. Evaluations of trees planted in holes backfilled with amended materials show that this practice encourages root growth only in the original planting hole—roots don't extend out into the surrounding soil—and such plants are susceptible to waterlogging, wind throw, disease, and insect problems.

A better use of your compost for feeding newly planted trees and shrubs is topdressing the soil area surrounding the plant and watering the compost in. Small "plugs" of compost may also be augered in around the drip line; manure tea feedings are also beneficial.

Established shrubs should be fed yearly by having ½ bushel of compost worked into the surface soil, then mulched.

Continued ➡

The "ring" method is best for feeding trees: Start about 2 feet from the trunk, and cultivate the soil shallowly to 1 foot beyond the drip line of the branches. Rake 1 or 2 inches of compost into the top 2 inches of soil. Another way to feed established trees is to apply liquid compost, beginning around the base of the trunk and working out toward the drip line.

When hilling up the soil around your rose bushes for winter protection, mix plenty of compost with it—they'll get a better start next spring.

Fruit Trees

The ring method is ideal for fruit trees, too. You can work in as much as 3 or 4 inches of compost, then apply a heavy mulch that will continue to feed the trees as they rot. Some gardeners merely pile organic materials as deep as 2 feet around their fruit trees, adding more material as the covering decomposes. You can even add earthworms to speed the transformation to humus. Berry plants may be treated the same way, with lower mulches, of course, for low-growing varieties.

Another good trick for pepping up old fruit trees is to auger holes a foot apart in the soil all around the tree, and pack these with compost.

Houseplants

Lots of humus means extra-good moisture retention and air circulation in houseplant soil. A good potting mixture is composed of equal parts of loam, sand, and compost, the last put through a ¼-inch mesh. Leaf mold compost makes a fine, loose soil, while for acid-loving plants like azaleas, compost made from pine needles or oak leaves is best. Feed your houseplants every 2 weeks during their growing season with compost tea, made by suspending a cheesecloth bag of compost in water and using the liquid when it is a weak tea color. In general, compost can be added to potting mixtures as one-fourth of the total.

To rejuvenate the soil in window boxes, tubs, and indoor plant boxes, scratch an inch or so of compost into the surface twice a year. Occasional light topdressings of compost are also excellent for the soil in greenhouse benches. All of these will benefit from regular feeding with compost tea.

Soil-Compost Mixture for Starting Seedlings

You can help to ensure good germination by adding compost to seed-starting flats and beds. Make a mixture of 2 parts good garden loam; 1 part fine, sharp sand; and 1 part compost. Mix well and put 8 inches of the mixture into the hotbed, cold frame, or flat. It's a good idea to let this growing medium age for several months before seeding, especially if you are not sure that your compost has fully stabilized. Sift the soil mixture through a ¼-inch mesh screen to provide a fine-textured bed for planting. When screening the mixture, place coarse screenings in the bottom of the flats to provide better drainage.

This mixture provides adequate nourishment for young plants; you don't need to add manure or other organic fertilizers high in nitrogen. Used too soon, these fertilizers can cause the young plants to grow too rapidly, unbalancing their natural growth.

When starting plants in flats, some gardeners prefer to place a layer of sphagnum moss in the bottom quarter to half of the flat. Then after the seed has been placed in the rows, finely screened compost is sifted on top of them. When the seedlings are ready for transplanting to another flat, fill the flat with 1 part compost, 1 part sand, and 2 parts leaf mold.

Starter Solution for Plants

Starter solutions made from compost or manure can be a big help in the growing of vegetable plants. The home gardener as well as the commercial grower can benefit from the rapid and unchecked growth of young plants if the plants have reached a sufficiently advanced stage of growth and if the solution is used before they are moved to the field from the greenhouse, hotbed, or cold frame. Greenhouse operators have long made use of this method to bring their crops to a rapid and profitable production. Earlier yields have also been reported in the field.

The main benefit received from these solutions is that of providing the plant with immediately available plant food. This stimulates leaf and root growth, giving the plant a quick pickup after transplanting. These solutions are used especially on young lettuce, tomatoes, celery, peppers, melons, eggplant, cabbage, cauliflower, and all kinds of transplanted plants.

How to Use Compost Tea

The juices of compost can be the best part. Often, some of the valuable nutrients in compost are dissolved in water quite readily, and in solution these nutrients can be quickly distributed to needy plant roots.

Since plants take up nutrients along with water, the use of compost tea makes quite a bit of sense, particularly during dry periods when plants are starved for both food and water.

Many problem plants and trees can be nursed back to health by treating them with compost tea. You can use it on bare spots on your lawn, on trees that have just been transplanted, and on indoor plants that need perking up. You can even use it on vegetables in the spring to try to make them mature earlier. Compost tea is especially effective in greenhouses, where finest soil conditions are needed for best results.

It is really no trouble to make compost tea on a small scale. For treating houseplants or small outdoor areas, all you have to do is place a burlap or cloth bag filled with finished compost in your watering can and add water. Agitate it for a couple of minutes, or let it sit for a while, then pour. Nothing could be easier than that. The compost can be used several times, as one watering will not wash out all its soluble nutrients. The remaining compost is actually almost as good as new and should be dug into the soil or used as mulch. It

takes the action of soil bacteria and plant roots to extract the major value from compost.

Developing a continuous system for making compost tea for the home grounds requires a little more ingenuity and mechanical skill. One method is to attach a hose connection and an outlet pipe to a plastic bucket with a lid that will stand up under normal water pressure. The type of 5-gallon plastic pail in which primer paint, drywall compound, and a variety of commercial food products are sold can be used for this project. Create a water intake near the bottom of the bucket by drilling a hole just large enough to insert a garden hose replacement coupling. Use epoxy to attach the coupling to the bucket and to seal the edges of the hole. Make an exit for your compost tea near the top of the bucket, opposite the water intake. The water has to circulate up and through the compost before it can get out of the bucket. Epoxy a piece of PVC pipe into the exit hole to create a spout to which a sprinkler head may be attached. A second hose connection can also be used in the exit hole, allowing the bucket to remain stationary while compost tea is sprayed through a hose coming from the exit.

The operation of this compost watering can is simple. You attach the water supply to the intake connection, and the hose or sprinkling device to the exit connection. The bucket may be carried to different parts of your garden, and one charging of compost lasts for about 15 minutes of watering. A screen placed over the exit hole on the inside of the can prevents solids from escaping and clogging the sprinkling heads.

Your Seasonal Guide to Composting

Now you know the complete story about compost: how it helps your soil; the ingredients you need to make it; different methods you can use to build a pile; and how to apply it. So to help you along in your compost-making endeavors, we've put together this month-by-month calendar, which will guide you through what to do when. (Believe it or not, making compost is really a year-round project.

JANUARY

Consider starting a worm composting bucket or **bin** indoors, using newspapers as bedding material and kitchen scraps for food. Order your redworms through a garden-supply catalog.

FEBRUARY

Plan your **composting strategy**. Decide whether you want to buy a commercial bin, build your own, or just have a free-form pile. Find a shady spot on your property to place or build the bin or to build your free-form pile. Look for nearby sources of raw materials, such as pine needles or seaweed (depending on where you live).

MARCH

Find a source for finished compost (just in case your needs are greater than your means). Many **counties** and **municipalities** compost leaves and yard wastes for residents' use.

APRIL

Clean out your perennial and vegetable beds, and **add** the **winter mulch** that hadn't decomposed to your compost pile. Get those spring weeds out before they set seed and put them in your pile as well. **Dig finished compost** into your vegetable beds before planting. And **side-dress** your **perennials** with whatever compost you have left. If you

Continued ➔

have a worm bin, you can move it outside to a shady spot (but keep it covered).

MAY

With the garden in full swing, you should have plenty of raw materials (such as **spent plants**, vegetable scraps, and weeds) to add to your compost pile.

- Keep adding ingredients to your pile until it's 3 to 4 feet high, and **turn** the pile **frequently** to keep it cooking.
- When your pile gets to be a good size (a 3- to 4-foot square), **start another**.
- If heavy rains are predicted, **throw a tarp** over your compost so it doesn't get sopping wet.
- Convince your grass-bagging neighbors to call you after they mow (but **leave** your own **clippings** on the lawn to benefit the soil)—and add the clippings to your pile (as long as your neighbors don't treat their lawns with chemicals).

JUNE

If you started a compost pile back in March or April, you might have some finished compost by now.

- **Screen out** the large pieces that haven't decomposed and put them in your working pile.
- **Check the pH** of the finished compost.
- As for the unfinished stuff, turn, turn, turn.
- Also **take its temperature**. A hot (150° to 160°F) pile will be more likely to kill diseases and seeds. If it isn't as hot as you'd like it to be, **add high-nitrogen materials**, like grass clippings or vegetable peelings.

JULY

Keep your compost moist (but not wet) during the hot midsummer days. You can **trap rainwater** by making a shallow depression on top. If your pile gets very dry, rebuild it, giving each 6- to 8-inch layer a **good sprinkling**.

AUGUST

You know the routine. Build the pile; turn the pile. Keep it moist; keep it hot. **Renew the soil** between plantings by digging in finished compost. There's no such thing as too much compost.

Take photos of your compost pile and of the lush gardens that are reaping the benefits of your homemade compost.

SEPTEMBER

Spread a thin layer of compost on your lawn to keep the soil alive and healthy. As you clean out your vegetable and perennial beds and **compost** the old **stalks and stems**, remember to dispose of diseased plants and weeds that have gone to seed elsewhere.

OCTOBER

Leaves are falling!

- First, run over them with your **lawn mower**. Then you can use them on your vegetable and perennial beds, pile them in your compost bin, or bag them to mix with next summer's high-nitrogen greens. One way or the other, use your leaves.
- It's also time to clean out your worm bin. **Remove** most of the finished compost and most of **the worms**. The compost (castings) makes a high nitrogen soil additive.
- **Share extra worms** with your friends, then move your worm bin indoors for the winter.

NOVEMBER

Continue to compost your **kitchen scraps** by toting them out to your compost pile, or by feeding them to your worms if you have a worm bin.

Composting Glossary

Aeration. The exchange of air in the pore spaces of the soil with air in the atmosphere. Good aeration is necessary for healthy plant growth.

Aerobic. Describes organisms living or occurring only when oxygen is present.

Anaerobic. Describes organisms living or occurring when oxygen is absent.

C:N ratio. The proportion of bulky, dry, high-carbon materials to dense, moist, high-nitrogen materials. The ideal C:N ratio for stimulating compost organisms is 25:1 to 30:1; finished compost's C:N ratio is about 10:1.

Clay soil. Soil made up of very fine particles. Holds water and nutrients but does not drain well and can be hard to work. When dry, can become clumpy.

Cold pile. A compost pile that receives little or no turning, allowing some anaerobic decomposition to occur; composting continues at cooler temperatures over a longer period of time.

Compost. Decomposed and partially decomposed organic matter that's dark and crumbly. Used as an amendment, compost increases the water-holding capacity and drainage of the soil, and is an excellent nutrient source of microorganisms, which later release nutrients to your plants.

Decomposer. Organisms, usually soil bacteria, that derive nourishment by breaking down the remains or wastes of other living organisms into simple organic compounds.

Fertilizer. A natural or manufactured material added to the soil that supplies one or more of the major nutrients—nitrogen, phosphorus, and potassium—to growing plants.

Hot pile. A compost pile that's turned or otherwise aerated frequently, creating high temperatures and finished compost in a relatively short time.

Humus. A dark-colored, stable form of organic matter that remains after most of the plant and animal residues in it have decomposed.

Loam. The best texture for soil to have; it contains a balance of fine clay, medium-sized silt, and coarse sand particles. Loam is easily tilled and retains moisture and nutrients effectively.

Micronutrient. A nutrient plants need in very small quantities. Micronutrients include copper, chlorine, zinc, iron, manganese, boron, and molybdenum.

Organic matter. An organic soil substance that contains valuable nutrients. Can include kitchen or garden wastes, insects, sawdust, or any number of other compostable organic materials.

PH. A measure of how acid or alkaline a substance is. The pH scale ranges from 1.0 to 14.0, with 7.0 indicating neutrality, below 7.0 acidity, and above 7.0 alkalinity. The pH of your soil has a great effect on which nutrients are available to your plants.

Sandy soil. Soil that contains more than 70 percent sand and less than 15 percent clay. Sandy soil is generally easy to work with and well drained, but it has few nutrients and poor water-holding ability.

Sheet composting. A method of spreading undecomposed organic materials over the soil's surface, then working them into the soil to decompose, rather than piling them and spreading the resulting compost.

Side-dress. To apply solid (as opposed to liquid) fertilizer alongside annual plants during the growing season.

Silt. Refers to a soil particle of moderate size—larger than clay but not as large as sand.

Soil amendment. A material added to the soil to make it more productive by improving its structure, drainage, or aeration. An amendment such as compost can also be used to enhance microbial activity.

Soil structure. The physical arrangement of soil particles and interconnected pore spaces. Soil structure can be improved by adding organic matter.

Soil test kit. A set of instructions and a soil bag available through your state's Cooperative Extension Service. Test results indicate soil pH and specify which amendments you should add to your soil.

Top-dress. To apply compost or fertilizer evenly over a bed of growing plants.

TOOLS

Getting the Best from Your Tools

Fern Marshall Bradley

The notion that a tool is nothing more than a device for doing work stops at the garden gate. Anyone who has worked soil with a well-balanced fork or rake or sliced weeds effortlessly with a skillfully sharpened hoe knows that a high-quality tool not only gets the job done but also adds pleasure to the doing. Little wonder that gardeners come to think of their most effective tools as friends.

In this section, several of our experts describe the tools that they have found to be most efficient and explain why. In addition, there are tips to help you in your own search for the "perfect" tool repertoire. You'll learn how to choose and use tools, how to take care of them, and even how to improve them. You may even be inspired to come up with a new garden use for a common household item. The possibilities are endless!

Improving Tools

The tool that's sold in the local hardware store isn't always just what you need to do your best work. There's immense satisfaction in learning how to modify a tool to do its job more efficiently. Try the following expert tips for improving on standard tools, and see if they don't help lighten those gardening chores.

HACK YOUR HOE IN HALF

There's a whole slew of new, lightweight, efficient hoes on the market these days. "I'm a big fan of the Dutch scuffle hoe," says Phil Colson, the garden center manager at Highland Hardware in Georgia. "It's light and has a long handle, and the blade lays flat to the ground, so you just push and pull it back and forth through the soil to cultivate or cut weeds. Ergonomically, anything that works by pushing and pulling has a distinct advantage over the old design."

Too bad the new hoes are so expensive—and in most areas, difficult to find at the local hardware store. If you can't find (or afford) these new hoes, you can always modify a conventional hoe to act like a scuffle hoe. The conversion couldn't be

Continued ➡

simpler. Using a hacksaw, cut the hoe's blade in half from left to right. Then file the cut edge to restore the bevel at the outside bottom edge. (For directions on filing tool edges, see "Sharp Tools Save Time and Energy" on the opposite page.) Use a hammer to bend the blade inward slightly to give it a better angle for chopping weeds. "That's all there is to it," says Colson. "You'll have a hoe that's easier to use and that does a much better job of cultivating and weeding."

Colorful Tools Are Hard to Lose

You know how it is. You could swear you put that darn tool down *right there*, but somehow it walked off on its own, and you can't find it anywhere. Then, after three days of rain, you find your favorite hoe on the ground, soaking wet and sporting little orange circles of rust-to-be. Susan Sides, a North Carolina garden writer, offers this sensible solution: Paint your tool handles bright red or some other attention-getting color. "It's almost impossible to lose a tool that's painted some loud color," says Sides. It is also a not-so-subtle reminder to friends who tend to borrow tools and forget to bring them back—they'll think twice about hanging onto your hot-pink hoe or glowing yellow shovel!

Take Time to Handle the Handles

It pays to take a few minutes to work out with a new wooden-handled tool, says Phil Colson, the garden center manager at Highland Hardware in Georgia. "The first thing I do when I bring a new tool home is sand the handle smooth," says Colson. "Then I close my eyes and start feeling the surface. Instead of looking at it with my eyes, I look at it with my hands, because they're the ones that'll be grabbing it."

Use a rasp to round off any sharp edges, corners, or other places that don't feel comfortable, says Colson. Then give your hands another "look" at the handle. When the feel is just right, give the entire handle a final sanding with fine-grit sandpaper.

Then, instead of using boiled linseed oil (the usual recommendation), Colson advises that you rub tung oil into the wood. "The trouble with boiled linseed oil is that it takes forever to dry, and it's always evaporating," says Colson. And you have to keep putting more on. Tung oil, though, penetrates and sets up overnight, and it seals the wood

to keep out moisture. "To my mind," claims Colson, "it's a better way to go."

Maintaining Your Tools

Tool maintenance just isn't as much fun as using the tools in the garden. But with the size of the investment they represent, it's time well-spent. Here is advice from the experts on how to keep your tools in tip-top shape.

Sharp Tools Save Time and Energy

To give yourself an edge in the garden, grab a file and put an edge on your garden tools. "You won't believe how much easier a sharpened spade or shovel cuts through dirt," says Susan Sides, a North Carolina garden writer. "And the same holds true for almost any other garden tool with a blade. You'll save yourself a ton of work if you sharpen your digging and weeding tools and touch them up occasionally when you're out working with them in the garden."

Here are three tips for quick and easy sharpening:

1. Sharpen single-beveled tools such as spades, shovels, and traditional hoes on the beveled side only. Never sharpen the flat side.

2. Use a file that matches the contour of the surface— for instance, a flat file for a flat-faced garden spade and a half-round file for a curved shovel.

3. Sharpen the blade at whatever angle will serve you best. Generally, that means following the same angle as the original bevel. But remember that sharpening at a shallow angle gives you a sharper edge—a good choice for weed-slicing tools. Sharpening at a steeper angle produces a longer-lasting edge that's good for digging.

To sharpen, push the file forward and across the tool's blade, pressing down hard and using the file's full length on each stroke. Lift the file up off the blade on the back stroke. Keep filing until you can feel a slight burr—a barely detectable buildup of metal—along the full width of the blade's opposite side. Finish the edge by running your file lightly across the burr to remove it.

How often should you *resharpen* a tool? As often as it takes to keep the tool useful and efficient. "When I feel that the work has slowed down," says Sides, 'I'll try scraping any mud buildup off the blade. Sometimes that cleaning makes the difference. If not, I'll clean the blade with an oily rag

and give it a few swipes with the file to take the dullness off."

Straighten Those Tines

If you use a standard triangular-tined digging fork, known in most regions as a potato fork, you know that the tines tend to bend occasionally—or more than occasionally, depending on how hard the ground is (and how old the fork is). Straightening the tines can be a real bother. "But a piece of pipe makes the job really easy," says Phil Colson, the garden center manager at Highland Hardware in Georgia.

To make a tine straightener, just drive a 3-foot length of 1-inch-diameter galvanized pipe into the ground near the place where you store your tools, leaving about 1 foot of the pipe above ground. "When you're finished using your fork and you notice a tine is bent, just stick it down into the pipe and bend it back the way it's supposed to be," says Colson.

An "A-Maizing" Tool Cleaner

Garden tools have a way of repeatedly caking up with dirt and mud, and your work really slows if you don't take time to clean the stuff off. What to use? "A dry corncob makes a great in-the-garden tool cleaner," says Susan Sides, a North Carolina garden writer. "The rough surface gets all of the soil off fast, and when you're done with the corncob, you can just throw it in the compost pile."

Quick Tips for Spring Startups

Ah, spring at last, and there's work to do. You get out the old mower or tiller, yank on the starter rope—nothing. A few more useless yanks later, and you're ready to call it quits. But first, try these tips from Mike Ferrara, a senior editor for *Organic Gardening* magazine:

1. Replace any old fuel in the tank with new, fresh gas.

2. Buy and install a new spark plug.

3. Change the oil—old oil can gum up the works. Also, if it's a cool day, set the machine in the sun to warm and "thin" the oil.

4. Disconnect the spark plug and check the machine's working parts—such as tiller tines and mower blades—for tangled vegetation, twine, or the like. Clear away any obstructions, and reconnect the spark plug.

"Nine times out of ten, doing just those four things will get a sluggish engine up and going," says Ferrara.

Prevent Sprayer Clogs with Panty Hose

Spraying is enough of a chore without being stalled by a clogged nozzle. Especially if you're spraying compost or manure tea, particles clogging the nozzle can be a real problem. Michael Maltas, the garden director of the organic showpiece garden for Fetzer Vineyards in California, suggests this cheap and effective spray strainer: "Take a pair of discarded panty hose and turn one leg inside the other to form one double-thick leg. Let the toe dangle into the spray tank, and stretch the top of the hose over the opening of your sprayer tank, securing it with a rubber band. When you pour your spray into the [panty hose] strainer, the nozzle-clogging particles will be trapped." Before spraying, remove and discard the used strainer— particles and all—or rinse it out for future use.

Clues for Saving Cash

Gardeners tend to be an ingenious group, especially when it comes to saving time and money. And they're always on the lookout for ways to ease the strain on those aching backs. We asked the

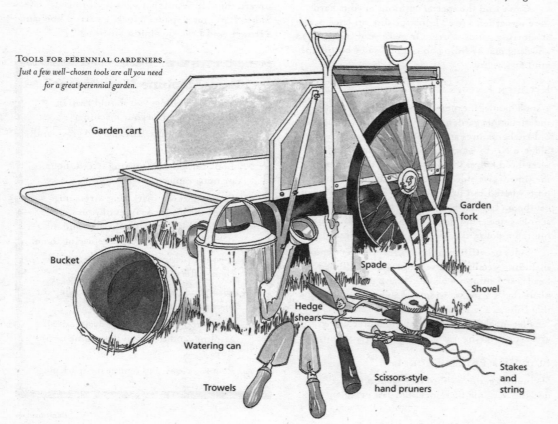

Tools for perennial gardeners.
Just a few well-chosen tools are all you need for a great perennial garden.

Garden cart

Garden fork

Bucket

Spade

Shovel

Hedge shears

Watering can

Trowels

Scissors-style hand pruners

Stakes and string

Continued ➡

experts for some of their favorite tips and techniques for stretching a dollar (and not stretching a muscle!).

TIPS FOR TROUBLE-FREE RENTALS

Renting can be the best option for tools and power equipment that you need only once or twice a year, suggests Mike Ferrara. "Chipper/shredders, heavy-duty tillers, lawn aerators, dethatchers, sod cutters, lawn rollers, stump grinders, fertilizer spreaders, and chain saws are all examples of equipment that many people don't need full-time but that are awfully useful when you do need them," says Ferrara. Some tips to keep in mind:

Most tools are rented by the day or half-day. If you think you'll need it for only a couple of hours, ask friends or neighbors if they're interested in using the tool and sharing the rental fee with you.

Try out the tool before you take it home. In the case of power equipment, start the engine, and run the machine just as if you were using it. And be sure you know how to stop it, too.

Consider hiring instead. Before you rent, check around to see if someone can do the job for you for less money. Sometimes it's actually cheaper to hire a professional with his or her own equipment than it is to do it yourself with a rental.

Shop around. The price, terms, and condition of tools can vary widely among rental stores.

Return the equipment on time. Some rental yards charge stiff penalty fees for late returns; others just call the sheriff.

PAD YOUR KNEES TO SAVE YOUR BACK

Slip-on knee pads and cushioned mats are sold at garden centers as "ground softeners" for gardener's knees. "But what knee pads really do is save your back," says Phil Colson, the garden center manager at Highland Hardware in Georgia. "Most people," he observes, "hate to get down on their knees because it's uncomfortable and often the ground is wet or muddy. So they end up bending over the whole time they're weeding or whatever, and pretty soon they've got back problems."

Can't find the special cushions at your hardware or garden store? Look for slip-on knee pads at sporting goods stores. Or make your own garden kneeling mat by filling an old hot water bottle with sand or sawdust.

KITCHEN KNIVES CUT GARDEN CHORES

Want a handy, inexpensive, multipurpose, nearly indestructible garden tool? Then shop around for old kitchen knives at flea markets, suggests Susan Sides, a North Carolina garden writer. "I have several old knives that I keep out in the garden all the time," says Sides. "I just stick them on fence posts where I can find them and where the kids can't get them. The knives don't rust because they're stainless steel—and they don't get lost as soon as you put them down, the way a pocketknife does."

Sides uses different knives for different chores, including weeding, harvesting, cutting off seed heads, and snipping twine. "I have one knife with a blade that's 2 inches wide and about 7 inches long that I use as a sort of mini-machete" she says. Smaller-bladed types, like a little butter knife, are great for pricking out seedlings for transplanting.

PICK UP A PICKLE BUCKET

"I couldn't garden without a 5-gallon bucket!" declares Virginia Blakelock, the past president of the Hobby Greenhouse Association. Blakelock loads her garden cart with buckets full of mulch, then pulls the cart to where she's working. She finds it's easy to carry a bucket of mulch into the perennial bed and spread the mulch just where she wants it. She also uses the buckets to mix up 5-gallon batches of liquid fertilizer such as fish emulsion.

Driveway sealer and other home-maintenance products are often packed in 5-gallon plastic buckets. You can also find the buckets at restaurants or luncheonettes—wherever pickles are served—often free for the asking. Clean your buckets thoroughly before relegating them to the garden.

Favorite Tools

What tools are the best? Everyone has their own special favorites. We asked our experts for their top picks in tools: Here are their answers.

WHEEL HOES FOR REAL POWER

The classic wheel hoe (a tool with long handles, a single front wheel, and a tool bar attachment behind) is generally considered strictly a weeding tool. But modern updates of the traditional high-wheel design have created a much more efficient, versatile tool, says Stewart Hoyt, a Vermont market gardener. "The wheel is smaller, and there are stirrup-style oscillating-hoe attachments in varying widths that cut just below the surface," says Hoyt.

"I'm interested in ways of working the soil as shallowly as possible," Hoyt says. "I don't see any point in destroying the good work of the worms and the frost and such. I just want to be able to incorporate a cover crop and compost into the top 1½ inches of soil. A wheel hoe does a good job of that and cuts up weeds nicely, too."

SUSAN SIDES'S FAVORITE TOOLS

During her many years as head gardener at the Mother Earth News Eco-Village, Susan Sides, a North Carolina garden writer, refined her choices of tools. Her list of favorites is sheer simplicity: a Smith & Hawken garden spade, digging fork, and trowel, and a good-quality stirrup hoe.

Sides uses the first three "because they're really well-made." As for a good stirrup hoe, she advises that you get one that pivots from the end of the handle, with a stirrup blade that bows downward toward the soil. "And that's really all I need," says Sides. "Give me a spade, a fork, a stirrup hoe, and a trowel, and I can do almost anything."

Continued ➡

Buying Used Equipment

Buying a used tiller, mower, or chipper/shredder can save you big money—or cost you big money. The first step to getting good equipment at a good price is to let dealers know that you're looking. Most name-brand power equipment dealers sell reconditioned models, but the bargains go fast. Talk to local dealers, tell them you're looking, and leave your name and phone number. Once you find a machine you are interested in, use this checklist to make sure you are getting a good deal:

Start the engine. Check to see that the engine starts easily.

Examine the spark plugs. Dark carbon deposits mean only that a tune-up is overdue. Oil-fouled plugs spell trouble.

Look at the crankcase oil. Dirty oil or a nearly empty crankcase suggests poor maintenance and serves as a warning of future repairs.

Watch for other signs of neglect. A dirty air cleaner, clogged cooling fins, or a rusty or oil-gummed throttle linkage are all signs that a machine has not been properly cared for.

If you're buying a tiller, watch out for oil leaks, low transmission oil level, unusual grinding noises, or bent or worn tines.

On chipper/shredders, look for loose welds, stress cracks, low oil, and excessive vibration when the engine is running.

For walk-behind mowers, check for rust, excessive vibrations, and faulty oil seals. Avoid mowers lacking an automatic no-operator shutoff control.

PHIL COLSON'S FAVORITE TOOLS

Few people are as knowledgeable—or as opinionated—about garden tools as Phil Colson. "I'm basically lazy," says Colson, "so my whole focus on tools is to find the most efficient implement for the job." Here are a few of his favorites:

English square-tined digging fork. "Nothing's better for separating and breaking up soil," he claims.

Floral shovel. "Most of my tools hang in the shed, but my floral shovel never gets hung because I'm always using it," says Colson. "It's about two-thirds the size of a regular shovel, with a blade about 8 inches across. You can't beat it for planting bulbs, digging, and transplanting."

A Checklist of Basic Tools

While experienced gardeners are likely to have three times this many tools in the shed, this list will give you a basic idea of the tools you'll need to have to take care of a home landscape:

- Shovel
- Spading fork
- Leaf rake
- Bow rake
- Leather garden gloves
- Pruning shears
- Trowel
- Sprayer (even if it's just a hand-held, window cleaner type)
- Wheelbarrow

Different regions of the country also have their own specialized tools. In areas with heavy clay or rocky soil, for example, it sometimes takes a pick to break through the subsoil. In the Southwest, a tool called a caliche bar (also known as a crow bar) is used to poke holes in the concrete-like caliche soil.

Quick Tip

Coffee-Can Tool Caddy

Long-handled rakes, shovels, hoes, and such have a way of "sinking" into the soil as soon as you need them. Here's a simple way to keep them organized and upright while you're working.

Cut the top and bottom from a large metal can, and nail the can to a fence post, about 3 feet up the post. Now when you're done with a tool, just slip the long handle through the metal can ring to hold it in place. A single 5-pound coffee can is big enough to hold two or

Italian grape hoe. "An incredible digging tool for jobs like planting a tree," says Colson. "You use it like a pickax; just throw it in the ground, and rock it back. You can lift soil up with its wide blade, push dirt around, and trench with it."

Dutch scuffle hoe. "I like this one because you just push the blade over the soil to weed and cultivate. And it has a long handle that lets you reach without having to take a step," says Colson.

Conventional wheelbarrow. Unlike a garden cart, a wheelbarrow doesn't require a wide path or a lot of clearance; it dumps right, left, and forward; and it's a great leverage tool for picking up heavy objects. Just lean it on its side and work the bottom edge under whatever you're trying to lift, then use your body weight to rock the wheelbarrow back up. "I've lifted 300-pound boulders that way-by myself," says Colson.

Japanese folding pruning saw. "You can carry this little 8-inch saw around in your pocket and just flip it out like a jackknife when you need it," says Colson. "It cuts on the pull stroke, and it's really sharp. It'll go through a ¾-inch branch with one pull. I hardly ever use loppers any more."

Japanese grubbing knife. "Nothing's better for getting out tenacious weeds like crabgrass and slicing off dandelions, particularly in rocky soil," says Colson.

Mason's trowel. Colson suggests this as an alternative to a high-quality garden trowel, which can be expensive. A mason's trowel is "made for lifting cement, so it's really strong, but it doesn't cost much," he says.

Felco pruners. "They give you a good, clean cut, particularly on woody material," says Colson.

Hand Tools

Barbara W. Ellis

The Basics

The range of garden tools offered today is bewildering, even for expeerienced gardeners, and a trip to the tool section of the hardware store or garden center may completely confuse the beginner. The wise gardener will start small, beginning with the basic hand tools and adding more only after learning the full use of the tools he or she already has.

You can probably get by with a few basic tools—a fork or spade for digging, a garden rake for smoothing the soil and preparing beds, a hoe for cultivating and weeding, and a trowel for working closely around plants.

The first rule of tool buying is to avoid cheap tools at all costs. The $1 trowel at the discount

store is stamped out of cheap sheet metal, poorly designed, and even more poorly constructed. Not only will it break in a short time, but it will annoy you while you use it because it won't do the job well. Do not buy cheap tools for children, either. Even children should have good tools, because they'll never learn to love gardening if the first tools they use do not work well.

The best wood for a shovel handle, as for all long-handled garden tools, is North American white ash, which is strong, light, and resilient. Hickory is stronger and is ideal for hammers and other short-handled tools. It is sometimes used for spades and forks, but is too heavy and inflexible to use for shovels and rakes. Examine the lines (rings) in the wood; they should run straight down the entire length of the handle, with no knots. Avoid painted handles, which often hide cheap wood. Also watch out for handles that are painted to look like straight-grain ash.

The attachment of the metal part of the tool to its handle is important to durability, especially for shovels. Avoid shovels of open-socket construction. The scoops are die-cut from sheet metal, then wrapped around the handle and riveted, leaving a seam. Instead, buy a shovel with solid-socket or solid-strapped construction. These are forged from a single bar of steel and completely envelop the handle, thus protecting it and greatly adding strength.

KEEPING TOOLS IN SHAPE

After making a considerable investment in good quality hand tools, it is wise to spend some time to keep them in good shape.

ROUTINE CARE

At the end of each day of gardening, clean, dry, and put away all the hand tools you used. Keep a large plastic kitchen spoon handy to knock dirt off metal blades. Do not use a trowel or other metal tool, as you could damage the blades of both tools. A 5-gallon bucket of sharp builder's sand in the tool shed or garage is useful for cleaning tools. Dip the metal blade of each tool into the sand and plunge it up and down a few times to work off any clinging soil. Use a wire brush to remove any rust that may have formed.

CARING FOR HANDLES

Wooden handles and shafts of hand tools should be kept varnished and sanded to keep them resilient and good-looking. If you buy a good-quality tool secondhand, and it has a weather-beaten handle, refresh it with several coats of varnish, sanding between each coat. You can repair split handles temporarily with tape and glue, but replace broken handles as soon as possible.

SHARPENING

Sharp-bladed hand tools will perform efficiently and with ease only if they are kept sharp. Take the time to study the angle of the bevels on all your tools, then sharpen each as needed to keep the proper bevel. And, for tools that are especially difficult to sharpen, don't hesitate to take them to a known and trusted professional.

The edge of a hoe can regain its sharpness if you run it across a grinding wheel several times. Bevel the side of the blade opposite the handle, holding the hoe at a 35- to 40-degree angle to the wheel.

The edge of a shovel need not be especially sharp, but it should be kept smooth so that dirt will readily slide off the blade. Hammer out any curls with a ball-peen hammer, and smooth out nicks with a fairly fine metal-cutting file.

On pruners, the outside of the cutting blade should be kept as sharp as possible, maintaining a

Continued ➡

fairly steep angle (10 to 15 degrees) of file to edge. The cutting edge of loppers should be filed at a similar angle.

At the end of the season, polish all the metal parts of your hand tools with steel wool, oil them to prevent rust, and store them in a dry place. Lubricate all tools that have moving parts. This is also a good time to take tools to the sharpening shop, particularly those that are tricky to sharpen at home.

Hoes

There are probably more different kinds of hoes than any other garden tool. Avid gardeners become as atttached to favorite hoes as golfers do to putters, probably because their hoe is the tool they use most frequently. With a hoe, you can layout rows, dig furrows, cultivate around plants to loosen the soil and kill weeds, create hills and raised beds, break up clods, and prepare bare spots in lawns for reseeding.

TYPES OF HOES

The standard American pattern hoe is a long-handled tool that allows you to work without too much bending. It has a broad and straight blade, a little larger than 6-by-4 inches. However, many gardeners prefer a nursery hoe, which has a shallower (2- to 3-inch) blade and is lighter to work with.

In many Third World countries, the eye hoe, with its large, heavy, and deep blade, is the standard tool for breaking new ground and digging holes and trenches, as well as for cultivating.

The oscillating hoe is a modern version of the Dutch hoe, both of which were designed to slice weeds just below the soil surface. It cuts both as it is being pushed and pulled along the ground. In modern variations, often called the "hula" or action hoe, the slicing blade moves back and forth slightly to position itself for cutting while being pulled or pushed.

An onion hoe has a thin blade 1½ inches high and 7 inches wide, and can be pulled easily along the row to cut weeds well below the soil surface. Some are short handled, for use while kneeling. The blade of the grub hoe is narrower and taller than that of the standard American pattern hoe, enabling it to work deeply in tight rows.

Very different is the Warren hoe, which has a pointed, arrowhead-like blade used to make planting furrows quickly. It is also handy for digging down to bring up stubborn weeds. The scuffle or slicing hoe is used for easy weeding in beds and borders. Its blade may be pointed or flat. A variation is the swan-neck hoe, named for the curve of the neck going into the blade. Its configuration allows the user to maintain a straight back and good balance while working. It is good for weeding in tight spaces, since the handle is held close to the body. There is also a pinpoint weeder, which has a narrow loop on the end to take up single weeds in very tight spaces.

The Canterbury hoe has three tines instead of a solid blade, and is perfect for breaking up soil, gathering up weeds and brush, and for aerating the top 4 to 6 inches of soil in rows and around plants. The double hoe has a blade on one side, tines on the other.

The grape hoe, sometimes called a hazel or adze hoe, is a large, strong tool used for weeding and general cultivation in vineyards.

SELECTING AND USING HOES

When choosing a hoe, remember that narrower blades transmit your arm power more efficiently to the tool head than wider blades. Unless you need the depth of the standard hoe blade, you will probably be better off using an onion hoe, which is lighter

and easier to use. The hoe handle should be at least 54 inches long (the traditional Dutch hoe is 64 inches) so you can work without bending over and straining your lower back muscles. In general, when working with hoes, try to remain standing upright. Run the hoe blade below and parallel to the soil surface to loosen the soil or to cut the roots of weeds. Remember to sharpen your hoe so that it will cut through weeds, which is easier than using the tool to yank the weeds out of the soil.

The blade, shank, and handle socket should be made of one-piece forged steel, attached to the handle by solid-socket construction. The handle will then be relatively easy to replace in case it breaks.

Spades, Shovels, and Forks

The standard American long-handled shovel has many uses around the home grounds, but some experienced gardeners seldom use it in actual garden work. For while a shovel is the best tool for digging rounded planting holes, most digging jobs are best accomplished with a four-tine garden fork or a spade.

SPADES

A short-handled, square-end spade is one of the most valuable and versatile garden tools you will ever own. A spade has a flat, rather than scooped blade, with squared edges. The handle is generally shorter than a shovel handle, usually ranging from 28 to 32 inches. The angle between shaft and blade is shallow, and the handle usually has a D-shaped grip for fine control.

On a good quality spade, the grip is made of wood or metal-reinforced wood that is firmly attached to or part of the handle. A spade should also have a turned edge or footrest along the shoulders of the blade to protect your feet when you step on the tool.

With a spade, you can cut easily through sod and create straight edges in soil. Spades are used for digging planting holes, prying up rocks, digging up strong roots, dividing perennnial clumps, cutting unwanted tree and shrub roots, tamping sod, hammering stakes, cutting cord, digging trenches, and moving perennials.

There are several spades deesigned for special purposes. One is the drain-tile spade, a narrow-bladed spade used for digging small trenches. It's also good for digging postholes and for transplanting in close quarters. A border spade has a short handle and a narrow blade and may be more comfortable for short people to use. The nurseryman's spade has a small, slightly curved blade especially designed for transplanting.

SHOVELS

Shovels are good for mixing cement, and for moving soil, gravel, and sand. In a pinch, you can use a shovel as a scuffle hoe to cut weeds just below the soil surface, as a garden edger, and as a posthole digger. It's a good tool for prying rocks and root clumps from the soil, although be careful not to strain the handle to the breaking point.

The standard American shovel has a handle about 48 inches long. The shovel handle should come to shoulder height or higher, to enable you to work most efficiently. Shovels should also have a turned edge or footrest along the shoulders of the blade to protect your feet when you step on the tool.

If you want to buy a shovel that will last a lifetime, ask a local building contractor for the most reliable source.

FORKS

A spading fork can cut into soil like a shovel or a spade, but usually does it more easily than solid-bladed tools can. A spading fork is handy for mixing materials into the soil, and for harvesting potatoes, carrots, and other root crops. The tines of the standard spading fork are broad and flat. Those of the English cultivating fork are thinner and square. The English version is better for cultivating and aeating the soil. Remember that forks are used to loosen soil, not to lift it.

Using Spades and Shovels Safely

When digging or lifting materials with either a spade or shovel, remember these guidelines to avoid unnecessary stress on your back.

- Push the blade vertically into the soil with your foot, using your body weight to force the blade down—don't jump onto the tool to force it into the earth.

- The angle between the blade and the handle is a design feature that helps the digging process. After you psuh the blade down, remain upright, and pull the handle (which will be tilting away from you) back, close to your body. This action will loosen the shovelful of soil, making it easier to lift.

- Use your arms to lift the tool, and if possible, support the weight of the full blade with your thigh.

- Move your feet and turn your entire body to face the spot where you will be depositing the soil, rather than twisting from the hips to move the tool.

The standard handle length for a spading fork is 28 inches. Very tall gardeners may prefer a 32-inch handle (it will be more expensive, but well worth it). Short gardeners, including children, should use a border fork, which is smaller in both handle and tine lengths. Border forks, like border spades, are also ideal for transplanting in tight spaces.

A pitchfork (three tines) and a straw fork (five or six tines) are used for picking up, turning, and scattering hay mulch, leaf mold, and light compost materials. They are also useful for spreading mulch and for cleaning up garden beds in spring.

Trowels and Cultivators

When working on hands and knees, your best friend is your garden trowel, actually a miniature version of a shovel. Use it for digging planting holes for small plants and bulbs, for transplanting seedlings, for leveling the ground, and even for digging up weeds in thickly planted beds and borders.

A well-designed trowel is efficient and comfortable to use, and does not bend or break when you exert pressure on it. Some trowels are made from forged steel and fitted with hardwood handles, but good ones are also available in unbreakable one-piece cast aluminum. When buying an aluminum trowel, look for one that includes a plastic sleeve over the handle. This will prevent your hands from blackening from contact with the aluminum.

Trowels come in a variety of blade widths and lengths. Choose one that feels comfortable in your

Continued ➡

hand. You can use a narrow-bladed trowel for planting fine seed. First use the trowel to open a small furrow, and then put seed in the trowel and let it slowly trickle out into the furrow.

A few other small tools are more suitable than a trowel for particular tasks. A hand fork is good for loosening the soil around plants and for preparing small areas for planting. A hand cultivator works well to cultivate shallowly around plants. And a daisy grubber, also called an asparagus fork, has a long shaft and forked blade which make it ideal for jabbing deep into the soil to rout out long-rooted weeds.

Rakes

The traditional metal bow garden rake so named because its head is attached to the handle with two bows, providing spring action. Popular alternatives to the bow rake include the level-head or square-back rake, which is generally narrower with shorter teeth and a shorter handle, and the landscaper's rake, which is very wide and designed specifically to level out broad areas.

These rakes are essential tools for leveling ground, creating raised beds, killing emerging weeds, gathering up debris from rows, covering furrows, thinning seedlings, working materials shallowly into the soil, erasing footprints, and pushing around mulch. Bow rakes come in many widths, with long or short teeth that are widely or closely spaced. The handle should be long, 54 to 60 inches, and the head should be heavy enough to bite into the soil easily. Wide-spaced teeth are recommended for working in rocky soil.

LAWN OR LEAF RAKES

Also called fan rakes, these are good for gathering up leaves, grass, weeds, and other debris, and for dislodging thatch from the lawn. They come in different sizes; a 19-inch head seems to be close to standard.

Metal lawn rakes last longest and are the springiest, although many gardeners prefer the action and feel of bamboo tines, and some prefer plastic or rubber. Some lawn rakes have adjustable heads that can be made narrower for raking in tight spaces such as under shrubs or in garden beds.

Scythes and Sickles

A scythe is a traditional hand tool used for mowing grain crops or tall grass and weeds. The tool consists of a long curving blade attached at an angle to a curved handle called a snath. Two short grips, called nibs, project from the snath. A sickle has a shorter blade and handle than a scythe and is used primarily for cutting back tall weeds in hard-to-reach areas.

The mechanical reaper invented in 1831 and subsequent modern machinery have made the scythe nearly obsolete. However, gardeners may still find the scythe useful for mowing grass on very steep slopes or in rocky areas. Scythes, mostly Austrian-made, are still found in many hardware stores, especially in rural areas.

A cross between the scythe and sickle is the grass hook (common names for these tools often overlap), a modern instrument with a slightly curved detachable blade that can be fastened to either a long or a short shaft. Used with two hands, it is much lighter and easier to handle than a scythe, yet has a cutting blade longer than that of a sickle.

USING A SCYTHE

Using a scythe is a tricky process that requires some strength and endurance. To mow with a scythe, stand with your feet spread moderately apart, and hold one nib of the scythe in each hand. Sweep the tool in an arc from right to left in front of you, with the blade parallel to the ground, to cut a swath. Swing the tool bak from left to right to prepare to cut the next swath. Allow your feet to take small steps as you work, in natural rhythm with the swinging blade.

Scythe blades must be sharpened frequently with a whetstone or grinding stone to work efficiently. (See "Maintaining Your Tools" on page 000 for sharpening guidelines.) Grass or weeds may be easier to mow when they are green and wet than if they are dry or dead.

USING A SICKLE

A sickle is useful wherever tall weeds must be chopped down—along fence rows, up against buildings, around trees, wherever other tools cannot reach. The curved steel blade, typically 18 to 26 inches long, is attached to a hardwood, steel, or aluminum alloy handle.

Cut weeds with a sickle by slicing with one hand in a sideways motion. Use a stick held in your other hand to hold back overhanging grass so that you can cut growth near the stem bases. If the grass is wet, you may want to hold the stick upright with one end touching the ground as a barrier between the sickle and your body, in case the sickle slips on the wet grass as you swing. As with the scythe, keep your sickle sharp at all times.

Pruning Tools

Any garden that has trees, shrubs, and hedges needs frequent snipping, trimming, cutting, chopping, and pruning. While these jobs can be arduous with the wrong tools, they are a pleasure when using proper tools that are in good condition.

PRUNING SHEARS

A pair of good quality pruning shears is essential for cutting small branches, shaping shrubs, dead-heading plants, harvesting grapes, removing raspberry canes, and cutting back tree roots. Most models will cut hardwood branches of up to ½ inch in diameter.

There are two basic types of prunners: the anvil type, in which a straight, sharp blade closes down onto an anvil or plate; and the bypass type, in which a curved cutting blade passes by a so-called hook blade, acting like household scissors. Anvil pruners are often easier to use, requiring less hand pressure to make the cut. Bypass shears make a cleaner cut, can work in tighter spaces, and can cut flush against a tree trunk or branch instead of leaving a short stump as anvil pruners do.

Many models of both anvil and bypass pruners are available, including some that have narrow blades for light trimming and working with flowers. The Japanese ikebana-style clippers have small bypass blades and large loops to fit the hand and are popular for working with flowers.

Whatever type you select, it's easiest to make pruning cuts if you work with the tool's design to get the greatest possible leverage. Position a branch between the blades as close as possible to the pivot point (the place where the two blades are attached to one another) before starting to cut, for greatest efficiency.

OTHER PRUNERS

There are other types of pruners that will make your gardening chores easier.

Pole Pruners. These are useful for reaching high tree branches or getting into the base of a thickly grown shrub. Most pole pruners operate with a lever handle or a pulley and rope mechanism.

Lopping Shears. Also called lopppers, these are heavy-duty pruners with wood or metal handles 25 to 30 inches in length. Made of either anvil or bypass construction, most can cut branches up to 2 inches in diameter. Some include ratchets or gears to increase leverage, or use several pivot points like a bolt cutter.

Hedge Shears. These tools have long blades and relatively short hardwood handles. They can cut branches up to ¼ inch thick. Most good quality shears have ash or hickory handles, although some are of metal or fiberglass. Most also have a shock absorber near the pivot point to reduce stress to the user's arm joints and to prevent knuckles from banging together. They are designed for cutting the tender new growth of hedges, and are also useful for trimming tall, coarse grass.

Electric Clippers. Power hedge clippers make short work of many trimming jobs. Some models are cordless, operating more than a half hour with a single battery recharge, and some even have small gasoline engines. The clipper blades range from 16 to 30 inches long. The shorter ones are easier to handle, the longer ones capable of doing more work.

Electric clippers seldom if ever need sharpening, since the scissor-like action of the blades keeps them sharp through use. Moderately priced clippers are dependable for cutting branches up to ¼ inch thick and will last for many years with little attention.

SAWS

Pruning saws can cut through most branches that are too thick for pruning or lopping shears. The standard seven-point (seven teeth to the inch) model has a hardwood handle and a removable curved blade 9 to 15 inches long. It can fine-cut branches up to 3 inches in diameter. For larger limbs, use a four-point saw, curved or straight-edge, with a D-grip and both cutting and raker teeth (the latter to remove sawdust as cutting takes place).

Pole saws are useful for high limbs. Some are made in combination with pole pruners. Because of their thin blades, bow saws can cut through wood very quickly. They are difficult to use when you don't have a lot of space in which to maneuver. Double-edge saws can cut both coarsely and finely, but sometimes damage other limbs when used in close quarters.

WHAT TO LOOK FOR

The difference between an inferior and a good quality saw is often in the arrangement and beveling of the teeth. The teeth should be set—bent alternately to left and right—so that the cut is slightly wider than the saw blade. This will keep the blade from getting stuck. Cheaper saws have teeth arranged like those of a rip saw and are cross-filed, making the top of each tooth flat like a chisel. Good quality saws are bevel-filed, a more expensive process than cross-filing but one that produces sharper teeth.

Wheelbarrows and Garden Carts

A wheelbarrow or garden cart can be a lifesaver if you're faced with transporting various and sundry plants, tools, flats, hay bales, compost, and other materials. Each type of garden conveyance has advantages and disadvantages; be sure to select one that meets your specific gardening needs.

The traditional garden wheelbarrow differs from a contractor's model, which is specifically designed for transporting cement. A garden wheelbarrow is made of wood and has removable straight sides, not the sloping metal sides of the contractor's wheelbarrow. Many variations of the garden wheelbarrow have appppeared over the years,

Continued →

including some with double wheels. Still, the basic design has been retained, and therein lies the major disadvantage of the wheelbarrow for garden work: the distribution of weight. Since the load lies well behind the axle and wheel, the user must share much of the load with arms, shoulders, and back.

The garden cart, on the other hand, is a large, spoke-wheeled cart that places the load directly above the axles and wheels, enabling you to move heavy loads with comparatively little effort. The large diameter bicycle-type wheels also contribute to ease of transport. They ride easily over rocks and ruts, and yet their thin tires create little friction for easy movement.

The garden cart's two wheels, placed on either side of the load, also stabilize the cart so you don't have to work to keep the load balanced and steady, as is necessary when pushing a wheelbarrow.

Another advantage of the garden cart is its large capacity. Your transplanting job will be much easier if you can load your tools, compost, and other supplies all on the flat bed of the garden cart, and wheel it easily in one trip from the tool shed to the vegetable garden.

The wheelbarrow, on the other hand, can maneuver into tight spaces where a large garden cart cannot go. It can be pushed between two rows of corn, or down a narrow path to the woodpile. But pushing most loaded wheelbarrows through soft earth is virtually impossible.

Two-wheel garden carts are bettter for most garden uses, but there are still times when a wheelbarrow is the right tool for the job. Many gardeners own both.

The classic garden cart, which comes in several sizes, has a metal-reinforced plywood body. The standard model has a nonremovable front panel, but many gardeners prefer a model with a removable front panel for easier dumping.

It is difficult to find a traditional wood garden wheelbarrow today, although they are still being made. If you buy a contractor's wheelbarrow, be sure to buy one of professional or industrial grade, not "homeowner's" or "promotional" grade. Many cheap wheelbarrows and garden carts are sold at discount and department stores every year, but most of these are litttle more than toys that will not stand up to serious garden work.

Power Tools

Barbara W. Ellis

Tillers

Rotary tillers can make short work of turning and churning garden soil, breaking new ground, cultivating, aerating, weeding, and mixing materials into the soil. The rotary tiller is a gasoline-powered machine equipped with steel blades that rotate on a central spindle. The two basic types are front-bladed and rear-bladed, terms that refer to the placement of the blades in relation to the engine. Front-bladed tillers are less expensive. The least expensive of these have no wheels at all, letting the tines themselves power the machine forward. The heaviest and most expensive tillers have rear tines and power-driven wheels, and are more comfortable to operate. Sizes range from 20-pound machines, used for cultivating in flower and vegetable beds, to the 375-pound giants designed for heavy ground moving.

Most tillers depend on four-cycle engines, running from 2 to 8 horsepower, and drive mechanisms in the form of gears, chains, or belts—all of which are about equally dependable.

If you plan to buy a tiller, learn about various models by actually using them in your garden. Borrow or rent before choosing a tiller to purchase. Remember that wheeled tillers are always easier to operate than those without wheels. Large wheels provide more maneuverability than small ones. Look for heavy, heat-treated carbon steel blades.

Some models offer optional attachments, including snow blades and throwers, log splitters, generators, shredders, blowers, sprayers, various cultivators, and even chain saws. The quality of these attachments varies widely. Garden tractors also offer tiller attachments.

CARE AND MAINTENANCE

How you operate and care for your tiller will go far in determining how long it will last and how well it will perform. The first rule is, Never try to make a tiller do more than it was designed to do. It cannot clear a meadow of rocks, turn under a field of cornstalks, or uproot a tree. When you are incorporating organic matter into the soil, work in several thin layers, one at a time, so that the tiller (and you) can work with ease. When you till new soil, don't expect to reach 8 or 9 inches in depth with a single pass. Learn the limits of your tiller and work with it—not against it.

Tiller maintenance is similar to caring for a four-cycle lawn mower. Keep the air filter clean, and change the oil every 25 hours or once a season, whichever comes first. Also check the seals of the drive system regularly, and keep debris out of the fins on the cylinder (which are meant to help cool the engine) and the grass screen over the fan. Never use gasoline that is more than two months old.

Clean your tiller thoroughly before winter. Knock out any carbon that might be plugging the portholes in the exhaust system, change the oil and filter, drain the gasoline, run the engine until all the gasoline has left the carburetor, and remove the spark plug. Then roll it into a corner and throw a blanket over the machine until spring.

Shredders and Chippers

One of the favorite large power tools of organic gardeners is often a shredder or chipper. This machine, powered with gasoline or electricity, can reduce all those leaves, pruned branches, and plant debris to beautiful mulch or compost material. Some machines are designed specifically for shredding soft plant material, others for chipping thick branches, and some have separate chutes for both functions built into the same machine.

Shredders usually operate with a spinning drum fitted with fixed hammers or swinging flails that pulverize materials. Chippers typically slice branches with one or two knife blades mounted on a metal flywheel. Shredders are better at handling weeds and other soft plant material; chipppers will handle heavier, woody materials. Large 5-horsepower moddels can chip branches up to 3 inches in diameter. Small chippers (around 2 horsepower) can take branches up to about 1 inch.

Many of these machines have trouble handling leaves. It is difficult to feed dry leaves into the machine chute quickly enough to attain any degree of efficiency—and wet leaves often clog the machine. Plus, the leaves must be collected before they are fed into the shredder. There are now string-trimmer shredders made especially for leaves, but many gardeners still find it simpler and quicker to collect leaves using a rotary mower with a bagger attached.

Electric shredder/chippers are gaining quick acceptance among gardeners. Compared with gasoline-engine models, the electrics are smaller, easier to start, quieter, and require less maintenance. However, they must be operated where there is a power source, and there is a drop in voltage when long extension cords are used.

For small amounts of garden debris, a 1- to 3-horsepower model should suffice. For a large suburban or country lot, a 5- to 8-horsepower model will both shred and chip all the waste you can produce. Sometimes neighbors will pool their resources and buy a large machine to be used by all.

CARE AND MAINTENANCE

Safety is a prime concern when using these machines. Ear pads and safety goggles are mandatory, as is common sense in feeding in materials and removing clogs. Never put your hand inside a chipper/shredder without first—every time—unplugging it or removing the spark plug. Follow all the safety precautions of the manufacturer.

Electric shredder/chippers are virtually maintenance-free. Gasoline-powered machines must have soil and filter changes according to the manufacturer's instructions. You may use this machine year-round, but if you plan to store it for the winter, drain the gasoline as you would for a tiller. For both electric and gasoline-powered machines, be sure the hopper and discharge chute are cleared of all plant debris after each use.

Mowers

Until the end of World War II, the only lawn mower common in the United States was the push reel type, in which several revolving blades move against a single fixed blade, producing a neat trim. It did a fine job on small lawns, cutting evenly and quietly. For those with small, level lawns, the push reel is probably still the ideal lawn-cutting instrument. It is inexpensive, not difficult to push, nonpolluting, still produces a neat-looking lawn—and its gentle sound of metal kissing metal is music to the ears.

The popularity of the gasoline-powered rotary mower grew with the spread of large suburban lots in the postwar period. Lawns often were too large to be cut by hand. Power real models were in favor for a while, but gradually lost out to the standard rotary mower, whose single blade revolves at a high rate of speed, literally ripping the tops off grass plants. It can easily handle rough terrain and knock down high weeds, while a reel mower cannot.

Rotary mowers have cutting widths ranging from 18 to 24 inches and can be adjusted to cut grass at different heights. Some are self-propelled, a valuable feature if your lawn is large or sloping. Electric starters are appreciated by people with physical limitations that might preclude yanking on a cord. (Newer models use an overhead valve system—OHV—which virtually guarantees starting on the first or second pull.) A bagger is a valuable option, since it can be used to collect leaves in the fall. However, if you cut your lawn frequently and depend on grass clippings for nitrogen to feed your lawn, it's best to leave clippings on the lawn, where they'll decompose and return nutrients to the soil. A mulching mower has a blade that blows finely cut pieces of grass back onto the lawn, thus building up the lawn's organic matter while obviating any raking or bagging of clippings.

Electric rotary mowers are quiet and easy to maintain, but working around the cord which supplies power to the mower is a constant annoyance. Still, many urban homeowners with small lawns prefer them over noisy and fumy gasoline-powered machines.

Gasoline-powered motors are either two or four cycle. The former, which is less common, is more efficient and likely to last longer than the

Continued ➔

latter. You must mix gas and oil each time you refuel a two-cycle engine. A four-cycle engine has a separate crankcase; you must check the oil level regularly and change the oil at least once a season. Insufficient oil is the number one cause of lawn mower trouble.

A 7-horsepower riding mower with a 25-inch deck can mow an acre of lawn in an hour. An 8-horsepower model with a 32-inch deck can mow 1½ acres of grass in the same amount of time. But if your lawn is larger than 1 ½ acres, consider acquiring a small lawn or garden tractor, which would also be useful for many other jobs around your property. These have engines in the 15 to 25 horsepower range and power take-off (PTO) capability to drive a number of optional attachments such as a log splitter, chipper, snow blower, or generator.

Care and Maintenance

Routine care of your rotary mower will greatly improve both its performance and its life. Use the oil recommended by the manufacturer and change it according to schedule. Use fresh gasoline—never more than two months old—and be sure to get the kind recommended in the owner's manual. Generally, it's unleaded for four-cycle engines, leaded for two-cycle.

After every second or third use, clean out any debris that has lodged under the housing. Cut away any string that may have wrapped itself around blades or shaft. And be sure to disconnect the spark plug or pull the electric plug before you work under the housing—every time.

Keep the air filter clean during the mowing season, following the manual directions. Clean the spark plug several times during the season, carefully scraping the tip clean and adjusting the gap to manual specifications. A plug should last two or three years and should be discarded when it becomes corroded or deformed.

Before putting the mower away for the winter, remove both gas and oil, clean it thoroughly, and sharpen the blade.

Tool Tricks and Techniques

Roger Yepsen

Every gardener starts out with a plot of ground, a shovel, and a few packets of seeds. And that's all you need, at the absolute minimum, to coax edibles and ornamentals from the yard. For most of us, however, the equipment tends to proliferate. Tools, sprayers, fencing, gadgets to scare away pests—all have the potential to make gardening easier and more productive. Some, like a good trowel or clever one-wheel cultivator, can be a pleasure to use as well.

Eventually, the well-equipped gardener may feel a bit overwhelmed by the need to clean and maintain and store this hardware. There can be a move toward simplicity, scaling back just a bit in order to get closer to the simple pleasures of collaborating with nature on a lovely day. It's a matter of balance between convenience and complexity—between time-saving equipment and finding the time to manage a garage full of stuff.

Hoe Honing

In the kitchen, you wouldn't waste your energy chopping up vegetables with a dull knife, but chances are the blade of your garden hoe hasn't gotten much attention lately. And yet if you want to efficiently deal with weeds, a sharp blade is important.

To put a keen edge on a hoe, use a mill file, a flat file with fine teeth that's available at hardware stores. Since you'll be turning your homely hoe into a weed weapon, you should wear work gloves and sharpen with care. Support the hoe, blade up, and go over the beveled edge of its blade, typically along the outer side. Hold the file at about a 45-degree angle, drawing it away from the handle as you slide it along the entire width of the blade. Repeat the stroke as needed.

A hoe does have a blade, so it shouldn't be surprising to learn that it will be a better weapon against weeds if it's kept sharp.

Replace a Handle, Spare a Shovel

If a shovel or hoe has served you well, you may be reluctant to chuck it when the handle breaks. Chances are you'll be able to replace it.

To remove an old handle, either grind the rivet down with a mill file or saw it off with a hacksaw. Drive out the rivet by tapping with a punch or a large nail. Take the shovel or hoe head to a hardware store to find a handle that will fit. A bit of filing may be necessary; use a wood rasp with coarse teeth for this part of the job. Drive the handle into place by tapping its end with a hammer cushioned with a piece of scrap wood. Secure the handle by drilling a ⅛-inch-diameter pilot hole for a wood screw.

To remove the broken handle of a shovel, file away or saw off the rivet holding it in place.

The Long and Short of Shovels

Shovels come with short D-handles and long straight handles. Which is best? That depends on you, and what you intend to accomplish in the garden. You're apt to experience less back strain with a long handle. Yet while a short handle requires you to bend a good deal more, it will make more efficient use of your energy. You might want to buy one of each, reserving the short shovel for short bursts of relatively intense digging. Chances are you'll find yourself reaching for the longer one most of the time.

Garden Tools for Women

There are female gardeners stronger and taller than some male gardeners, of course. But very generally speaking, women may find that they prefer lighter, smaller-scaled tools, as well as those that have advanced ergonomic designs to make the most of the user's strength. The advantages go beyond comfort. A properly sized tool is more efficient, will be less likely to trigger an injury, and even can give your body a superior workout.

The most obvious requirement is a pair of gloves for smaller hands, rather than settling for the usual one-size-fits-all jumbos. Several companies now market lines of tools especially for women, including trowels, pruning shears, a lightweight cordless drill for outdoor build-it projects, and a lightweight string trimmer. Women may want to look for a border spade rather than a standard shovel, because the blade is lighter and considerably smaller in area. There also are garden clogs and kneepads sized for smaller gardeners. Whatever the tool, it's a good idea to get a sense of how it feels in the hand when shopping, evaluating both weight and size.

Garden Tools for Kids

There's no better way to introduce children to chores than getting them involved in gardening. The work isn't exactly child's play, but it can be enjoyable on a lovely day and with reasonably defined tasks. And the kids can look forward to the payoff of a flavorful harvest in several weeks' time. To make sure they will really contribute and not just playact at gardening, it helps to equip them with specially made, specially sized equipment-watering can, brightly colored hand tools, shovel, rake, and hoe. There are kid-size wheelbarrows, and Troy-Bilt, the well-known garden equipment supplier, sells a serious-looking metal wagon with beefy tires and wooden sides. Don't forget little work gloves, as well as a sun hat of some kind.

Heavy Lifting with a Wheeled Friend

Don't test your back by lifting big rocks and bales of peat moss. Let a garden cart do it for you, with another person on hand. Approach the all-but-immovable object with a cart that has a removable front panel. Slide off the panel, and lift the handle of the cart to bring its front edge to the ground. Then roll or slide the payload into the cart while your helper leans on the cart handle to bring it upright.

A version of this no-lift technique works with a wheelbarrow. Tilt the wheelbarrow on its side next to the object. Then push or roll the object into the tray while also pressing on the top edge of the tray, and have a helper assist you in righting the wheelbarrow.

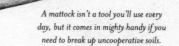

To move a heavy stone, roll it into a garden cart or wheelbarrow that's sturdily constructed and able to safely handle the weight.

Hard-Packed Soil a Headache?

There are times when a shovel just won't cut it—won't cut into dense, clay-rich soil littered with stones, that is. For tough jobs, it's good to have a mattock on hand. There are a number of different versions, but a particularly useful one has a narrow blade on one end of the head and a pick on the other. Between the two, you can effectively loosen up any kind of soil to the point that it will be receptive to a shovel. As with swinging an axe (or a golf club, for that matter), you have to make certain that no one is anywhere near the arc of the tool as you swing it.

A mattock isn't a tool you'll use every day, but it comes in mighty handy if you need to break up uncooperative soils.

Knives for Gardeners

In the same way that you find yourself reaching for a certain knife in the kitchen, you may prefer a favorite tool when working in the garden and

Continued ➡

around the yard. Serious gardeners swear by their special-purpose knives, and there are beautifully crafted models that (for a price) have the look of family heirlooms in the making.

- It's fascinating (and free) to make new plants by taking cuttings and severing layered stems, and the right knife can be a big help. A propagation or grafting knife has a short, ultra-sharp blade for making clean cuts. You can buy a model with a fixed blade, or a folding blade that makes it unnecessary to have a sheath.

- A pruning knife is sturdily built to handle the task of cutting smaller branches, and some models have a distinctively curved blade.

- For lopping vegetables in larger plots, it helps to have a lettuce or vegetable harvesting knife. The shorter edge of the blade is used to sever plants at the stem, while the longer edge is handy for trimming leaves on cabbage as well as harvesting. A plastic-handled version will cost less than one with wood.

- To keep blades at their optimal sharpest, you can carry a lightweight set of mini-hones with you in the yard. Use them for knives and pruners as you go about your work.

Special-purpose knives will make certain garden and orchard tasks go just a little more smoothly, especially if you regularly sharpen the knives with hones.

A Human-Powered Weed Whacker

For centuries, the scythe has been used to keep down brushy areas and also harvest crops. You operate it with a gently pivoting motion, feet planted securely and the upper body torqueing to and fro. It's a restful activity, and an ideal way to manage rank growth around the property, without the prep time and maintenance involved with operating a gas-powered string trimmer. They're available in beautifully curved wood, as well as in lightweight aluminum. You also can choose between blades suited for grasses and stouter steel for dealing with brush.

This isn't to say that a scythe is maintenance free. You should pause every 10 minutes or so to run a sharpening stone over the blade (and to lower your pulse rate). Over time, the blade will need to have its edge re-formed by peening with a special-purpose hammer and anvil, sold by the mail-order companies that deal in scythes.

The long, curving blade of a scythe makes short work of felling tall grasses and weeds. You'll get a workout in the bargain.

One-Wheel Wonder

Imagine a cultivating tool that's somewhere between a plain old shovel and a fume-belching tiller, one that does its work efficiently but without a noisy engine. That's a fair description of a wheel hoe, a traditional device that you push like a little plow. They've been used for more than a century, and you sometimes can find them inexpensively at yard sales and auctions. If you're willing to spend a bit more, consider buying an updated version, with a pneumatic tire to make the rolling a bit easier and attachments including a variety of hoes, hillers, and cultivators.

A wheel hoe makes efficient use of your energy, while sparing you the jarring, repetitive motions that can be involved with hoeing.

Hose-Taming Tricks

Garden hoses have a way of making trouble, side-swiping delicate plantings and getting underfoot. Here are a few ways of managing them.

- Put hose bumpers at the corners of beds, using either the commercial type that spins, the screw-in soil anchors sold for trellis wires, or large potted plants set a couple of inches into the ground.

- Get reel. Buy a hose reel, either freestanding or one intended to be mounted on a wall. There's even a model that uses the flow of the water to do the reeling for you.

- Bury hoses from the faucet at the house to individual gardens or beds.

- To avoid tripping on a hose across a walk, dig a tunnel under the walk (in an inconspicuous spot, if possible) and line it with a section of PVC pipe from the plumbing section of a home center or hardware store. It's easy to slip a hose through the plastic pipe.

PVC pipe buried beneath walk

By running a garden hose under a frequently used walk, you just might prevent a tripping accident. The hose can be pulled freely through a length of PVC pipe.

A Mindful Mower

The future is here—or at least it could be out on your lawn. The RoboMower, by Friendly Robotics, is a cute-looking automatic mower that quietly goes about taking care of that most tedious of outdoor tasks. It can operate for 3 hours on a battery charge, and it's kept from wandering off to neighboring lawns by a boundary wire that can be buried in the yard. A basic model sells for about $1,200. For a bit more, you can have a programmable RoboMower that will start mowing at a preset time and even chug on back to its docking station for recharging. And how do you keep a jealous homeowner from pirating your unattended mower? You can't, but the more-expensive model can be made to operate only when the correct four-digit code is input.

This sleek battery-operated robot mower will take over the job of trimming the lawn, freeing you up for other gardening and landscaping tasks.

Continued ➡

Gardening Techniques & Tricks

SEEDS

Seeds and Seedlings

Jeff Cox

Seeds come in an amazing variety of forms and sizes; from the dustlike seeds of begonias to the hefty coconut. But all seeds have one quality in common: They are living links between generations of plants, carrying the vital genetic information that directs the growth and development of the next plant generation. Seeds are alive. They even carry on respiration—absorbing oxygen and giving off carbon dioxide.

As long as a seed is kept cool and dry, its life processes hum along on low. Most seeds remain viable for one to three years after they ripen on a plant. Some, such as parsnip seed, can't be counted on to sprout after more than one year, but others, like muskmelon seeds, can germinate after five years or more if storage conditions are favorable. In fact, certain seeds recovered from archaeological digs have sometimes proven to be viable after many hundreds of years.

Growing your own plants from seed can be one of the most satisfying and intriguing aspects of gardening. Almost all gardeners have grown vegetables from seed. But if you're interested in a challenge, you can start your own perennials, herbs, and even trees from seed.

Seed Germination

Moisture and warmth encourage seeds to germinate. When the seed absorbs water, its internal pressure rises, rupturing the seed coat. Growth hormones within the seed go into action, directing vital compounds to where they are needed and encouraging the growth of new tissue.

All of these changes depend on temperature as well. Most garden seeds started indoors germinate best at a soil temperature of 75° to 90°F. Sprouting seeds also need air. A porous soil kept evenly moist (but not swampy) will provide enough air to support the germination process. Seeds often rot if they are submerged in water for days or if they are planted in completely waterlogged soil, so control the moisture.

After the germination process has been in action for several days (or, in some cases, for a week or more), the seed will change in ways that we can see. The root emerges and starts to grow, the stem grows longer, and then the cotyledons unfold. Once germination has begun, you can't reverse the process. If the sprouted seed continues to receive moisture, warmth, air, and light, it keeps growing. If not, it dies.

Most seeds have no specific light requirement for germination. However, some kinds of seeds need light to break dormancy and germinate, including many tiny seeds such as begonia, columbine, snapdragon, and petunia. Some larger seeds such as impatiens, spider flower, sweet alyssum, and dill are also best left uncovered. Sow light-sensitive seeds on the surface of fine, moist soil or seed-starting mix. Cover them loosely with clear plastic to retain moisture, or mist frequently.

A few types of seeds require darkness to germinate. For example, Madagascar periwinkle (*Catharanthus roseus*) will germinate far better if the flat is covered with black plastic or kept in a dark closet until seeds sprout.

Other seeds will germinate readily only if planted soon after they ripen. Angelica, hawthorn, and Solomon's-seal are three types of seed best sown soon after they are collected.

Check seed packet information to find out whether the seeds you want to raise have special germination requirements.

PRETREATING SEEDS

Some kinds of seeds require certain treatments before they'll start to germinate. No matter how ideal conditions are for germination, the seeds will remain dormant if pre-germination requirements have not been met. This characteristic, called innate dormancy, helps ensure survival in nature, because the seeds wait out the winter or the dry season before sprouting.

Certain seeds require a period of moist cold. This mechanism is common in plants native to

Continued ➜

climates with cold winters, especially perennials, trees, and shrubs. Other seeds have chemicals in their seed coats that must be soaked away before the seeds will germinate. Some seeds are slow to absorb enough water to start germination because of thick or impermeable seed coats. Plants native to areas with seasonal dry spells often have this type of dormancy. If you understand these dormancy mechanisms, you can work around them and coax the seeds to germinate.

Even seeds that don't have dormancy requirements may be slow to germinate. Appropriate pretreatment can significantly increase germination rate and reduce germination time.

Stratification Some seeds must be exposed to cold for a certain period before they will break dormancy and germinate. Stratification simulates natural conditions when a seed overwinters in cold, moist ground.

Seeds of various perennials, including wild bleeding heart, gas plant, and cardinal flower, need a cold period. You can plant them outdoors in fall, or spring plant after giving them a cold treatment. Many woody plant seeds also require stratification, including birch, dogwood, false cypress, and spruce. Some tree and shrub seeds, including arborvitae, cotoneaster, and lilac, are double-dormant, which means they require a warm, moist period followed by a cold period to germinate. If planted outdoors in fall, these seeds may not germinate for two years.

Scarification. Some seeds, such as morning-glory, sweet pea, okra, baptisias, lupines, and others, have hard seed coats that inhibit water absorption. To make a hard-coated seed absorb water more readily, nick the seed coat. Be careful not to damage the embryo inside the seed. On large seeds, use a knife to cut a notch in the seed coat, or make several strokes with a sharp-edged file. If you have only a few seeds to treat, you can scrape the seed coats with a nail file. Or, you can scarify medium-sized or small seeds by rubbing them between two sheets of sandpaper. Yet another method involves putting a sheet of medium-grit sandpaper inside a cookie sheet or rectangular metal cake pan (one you don't mind getting scraped up), putting a layer of seeds on top of the sandpaper, and rubbing over them with a sanding block to wear down the seed coats.

After scarifying, soak seeds in lukewarm water for several hours before planting.

Presoaking. Even seeds that have thin seed coats can benefit from a soak in lukewarm water for several hours before planting. Large seeds such as peas, beans, and okra will germinate faster if soaked overnight first. Before planting, drain the seeds and dry them briefly on paper towels to make them easier to handle.

Presprouting. Presprouting takes seeds one step further than presoaking. It's a good way to handle such seeds as melons, squash, and their relatives, which need plenty of warmth for germination. Because sprouted seeds can tolerate cooler temperatures, you can concentrate your population of germinating seeds in one warm place and farm out the presprouted seedlings to cooler spots where they will receive plenty of light.

Presprouted seeds are fragile; handle them with great care. Be sure to plant them before their roots grow together and tangle. Plant sprouted seeds in individual containers of premoistened potting mix. Cover them gently but firmly with potting mix and treat them as you would any container-raised seedling. Presprouted seeds may be planted directly in the garden, but it is better to keep them in containers until the roots become established.

Nancy Bubel

Security and adventure might be considered opposites in some situations, but the gardener who raises plants from seed can experience both. Security—that confidence in the future that springs from one's own ability, forethought, and preparation—and adventure—the soaring sense of "anything is possible" and "there are so many interesting things to try"—are well known to those who grow new varieties, experiment with new methods, and dabble in plant breeding and seed saving.

Skill in raising vegetable plants from seed is the very cornerstone of gardening independence. Choice of seeds and careful handling can bring you not only earlier harvests, but better vegetables. You can select varieties of food known to keep or process well so that the winter season, for which we gardeners are always planning, will be a time of abundance. Likewise, good eating will be yours all summer long from the selection of fresh vegetables you've planted for their superior quality.

Some varieties of vegetables and flowers can only be grown from seed.

The Reasons

I suspect that I'd continue to raise my own seedlings even without a good excuse, because I enjoy the process, but when I stop to think about it I realize that there are all kinds of good reasons for nurturing one's own plants from seed.

Earlier Harvests. You can get a much earlier start in the garden, and therefore put fresh food on the table sooner, when you've grown flats of cabbage, tomatoes, eggplant, and peppers indoors for setting out when the weather mellows. The sooner you can begin picking from your garden, the greater your yield for the year.

Greater Variety. Varieties of plants offered by commercial seedling vendors represent but a tiny fraction of the possibilities open to you as a gardener. Buying started plants severely limits your options for raising vegetables of special flavor, insect or disease resistance, or extra nutritional value. If, for example, you want to grow Juwarot or A+ Carrots (extra high in vitamin A) you'll have to start with seeds. Looking for special gourmet foods like globe artichokes, watercress, or Japanese melons? It's back to the seed catalogs. Peppers that are hot, but not too hot? Start your own Hungarian wax plants. Delicious, mild, sweet Golden Acre or Jersey Queen cabbage? You need to start those with seeds.

Stronger Seedlings. Seedlings you've grown yourself can be super seedlings. If you do all the right things at the right times, you'll have the best that can be grown, and you'll know that your plants have well-developed roots growing in good soil that hasn't been hyped with chemicals. You can even plant organically raised seeds to give your plants an extra start on excellence.

Healthier Seedlings. By raising your own plants, you minimize the chance of introducing soil-borne diseases to your garden. Club-root and yellows that affect cabbage, along with anthracnose, tobacco mosaic, and wilt, are some examples of plant diseases you may avoid importing if you grow your own. Of course, you must use uncontaminated soil, and, especially in the case of mosaic in pepper, eggplant, and tomato seedlings, avoid handling tobacco around the plants.

Cost Saving. You'll save money. Well, maybe. Certainly for the price of a dozen greenhouse tomato plants you can buy a small handful of seed packets, each of which will give you plants to share or to sell, or extra seeds to save for the following year. So many interesting plants can be grown from seed, though, that once you start raising seedlings you might find that you tend to put some of that saved money back into seeds of other kinds. But since you're likely to eat even better as a result, you may well consider that you're still far ahead.

Satisfaction. Creative satisfaction ought to count for something, too. From settling a well-chosen seedling in a pot of its own carefully prepared soil and watching it grow greener, sturdier, and leafier, to picking and eating the peppers, eggplant, or other nutritious food the mature plant finally bears, you've been involved all the way, and you can see that your skillful care has made a difference.

Enjoyment. At the very least, planting seeds indoors is a good cure for the winter doldrums—those bleak, cold days when February seems like a permanent condition and you feel you simply must do something to nudge the season into

Continued ➔

turning. Choose your earliest plantings judiciously, though. You don't want them to be past their prime when you set them out in the garden. Onions, chives, peppers, certain wildflowers and perennial plants, and houseplants like coleus and geraniums are good candidates for beginning the season.

First the Seeds

Nancy Bubel

You have in your hands an array of seed packets and perhaps a few jars of seeds you've saved yourself. You're anxious to plant, to get a start on the growing season that still seems far away. Take a minute now, if you will, to be aware of what the seed really is before committing it to the soil. Dry, flaky, hard, smooth, warted, ridged, powdery, or wispy, these distinctively shaped particles may look as lifeless as the February garden patch. Don't be deceived, though. Seeds don't spring to life when you plant them. Seeds are alive.

Often symbols of beginning, seeds are living guarantees of continuity between generations of plants. Inside even the most minute, dustlike grain of seed is a living plant. True, it's in embryonic form, possessing only the most rudimentary parts, but it lives, and it is not completely passive. At levels that we can't see, but laboratory scientists can measure, seeds carry on respiration. They absorb oxygen and give off carbon dioxide. They also absorb water from the air. Seeds need a certain minimum amount of moisture within their cells in order to make possible the metabolic processes by which they convert some of their stored carbohydrates into available food. Thus they maintain their spark of life—dim though it may be—until conditions are right for them to complete their destiny as germinated plants.

Begin by gathering your stored and bought seeds.

The Botanical Facts

By strict botanical definition, a seed is a ripened fertilized ovule containing an embryonic plant and a supply of stored food, all surrounded by a seed coat. In practice, though, gardeners use many seeds that are actually fruits (the mature ovary of a flower containing one or more seeds). A kernel of corn is really a seedlike fruit. Carrot, dill, and fennel seeds are, technically, dry, one-seeded fruits.

Seeds, then, are completely self-contained. Within the boundaries of the hard, dry coat that protects them, they possess enough food energy to carry them through their dormancy and into their first few days as seedlings. They have all the enzymes they'll need to convert this stored food into a form their tissues can use, and they carry within their cells the genetic information that directs what they will be and when and how.

Let's look at the bush bean as an example—not a typical seed, perhaps, but one in which it is easy to see the parts and their arrangement that are common to all seeds. The good old garden bush bean is the favorite of botanists for this purpose because its size and structure make it possible for us to see clearly how it is formed.

If you soak a bean seed in water for a few hours, the hard outer coat will slip off easily. The bulk of the bean that you now see is composed of the cotyledons, the two identical fleshy halves that comprise the "meat" of the seed. Cotyledons are rudimentary leaves. Unusually large and thick in the bean, they contain stored fat, carbohydrates, and protein. Both cotyledons are attached to a rudimentary stem, and they curve protectively over a tiny leafy bud. The root tip, at the other end of the seed, will elongate into the first root of the plant when the seed germinates. Any seed, no matter how tiny, wispy, or irregular, will possess these features: cotyledons (sometimes one, more often two), a brief stem, a leafy bud, and a root tip.

Most seed-bearing garden vegetable plants are dicots; that is, they possess two cotyledons. Beans, tomatoes, celery, cabbage, and other vegetable seedlings are dicots. When they germinate they send up two "wings." Monocots, with just a single cotyledon, are represented by the grass family (Gramineae), which includes corn, wheat, rye, and other cereal crops. These seeds send up the familiar, single grasslike spear of green.

Words to Know

Seed: A plant embryo and its supply of nutrients, often surrounded by a protective seed coat.

Seed germination: The beginning of growth of a seed.

Viable: Capable of germinating; alive.

Dormancy: A state of reduced biochemical activity that persists until certain conditions occur that trigger germination.

Seedling: A young plant grown from seed. Commonly, plants grown from seed are termed seedlings until they are first transplanted.

Cotyledon: The leaf (or leaves), present in the dormant seed, that is the first to unfold as a seed germinates. Cotyledons often look different than the leaves that follow them. In seeds such as beans, they contain stored nutrients. Also called seed leaves.

Endosperm: Specialized layer of tissue that surrounds the embryo.

Scarification: Nicking or wearing down hard seed coats to encourage germination.

Stratification: Exposing seeds to a cool (35° to 40°F), moist period to break dormancy.

Damping-off: A disease caused by various fungi that results in seedling stems that shrivel and collapse at soil level.

In many seeds, some of which are important food crops in their own right, the stored food is not contained in the cotyledons, as in the bean, but in a layer called the endosperm, which surrounds the embryo. This part of the seed varies in different species. It may consist of starch, oil, protein, or waxy or horny matter, but whatever its

form, its function remains the same—to nourish the seed from the time of its maturity on the parent plant until the beginning of the next growing season, when conditions will be favorable for its success as a plant in its own right. Often, of course, the tasty endosperm is what we're after when we raise the crop, as with buckwheat, corn, wheat, and rye.

Just to keep the record straight: Cotyledons of some plants may synthesize nourishment needed by the seed; others may both make and store food for the embryo. If you find that fact surprising, reflect that there is more—much more—that we don't yet know about seeds.

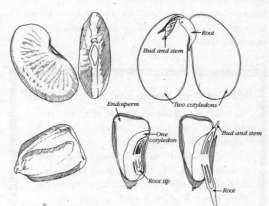

Cross sections of a bean seed, or dicot (top), and a corn seed, or nonocot (bottom).

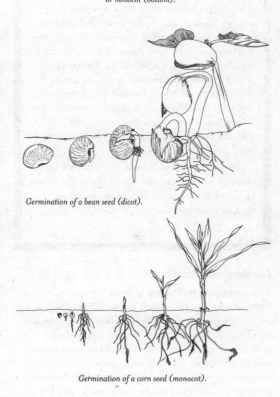

Germination of a bean seed (dicot).

Germination of a corn seed (monocot).

Dormancy

We're just beginning to appreciate, too, how much is still unknown about dormancy in seeds. If you've ever tried unsuccessfully to start a row of lettuce in midsummer heat, you have an idea of how a dormant seed behaves. It refuses to germinate, even if otherwise viable, when it lacks the right temperature, moisture, and oxygen supply that would ordinarily favor germination. Even though conditions might seem favorable for germination, such as those that occur in midsummer, they might not be right to induce germination in certain seeds.

It can be annoying to miss a seeding date for a certain crop and be unable to plant it later in the summer, however, the ability of seeds to remain dormant, in varying degrees, has contributed to the

Continued ➡

survival of seed-bearing plants as we know them. Certainly a plant that needs 90 days of warm weather to mature will be doomed to failure if it sprouts as soon as it matures at the end of the summer, shortly after the first frost. Lettuce, likewise, has less chance of success under random conditions when sown in hot, dry soil than it does in the moist, cool surroundings that promote its quick growth. Dormancy, then, is a protective device, designed to assure the continuity of the species.

A seed may be dormant because its embryo is still immature, its seed coat is impermeable to water or to gases, its coat is too unyielding to permit embryo growth (although this is rare), or because of a metabolic block within the embryo. Often, more than one of these factors operates at the same time.

Breaking Dormancy

As a gardener, it is often in your interest to try to break dormancy in certain kinds of seed. Since you intend to give the plant special care and optimum conditions, you can often do this and get away with it. For example, if you are anxious to raise a fine bed of lettuce to eat with your midsummer tomatoes—a real mark of gardening expertise—how do you give your lettuce seeds the message that it's all right for them to sprout?

Studies of seeds in research laboratories have furnished valuable clues to the interruption of dormancy. The period is relative, not absolute. In fact, there seems to be general agreement among a number of scientists who have studied this phenomenon that the whole question of seed dormancy must be considered a matter of balance between the growth-promoting and growth-inhibiting substances that are found in all plants.

So how do you tip that balance in your favor? Here is what the experts have discovered.

Temperature. Chilling the seeds often breaks dormancy.

Light. Subjecting the seeds to light—even a dim continuous light or a sudden bright photoflash—will sometimes help, especially with lettuce.

Germination depends on the total amount received. The dimmer the light, the longer the necessary exposure.

Red Light. Exposure of some seeds to red light (660 nanometers) promotes seed germination. Experiments with lettuce bear this out. However, far-red light (730 nanometers) has been found to inhibit seed germination. Practically speaking, this means that seeds that are difficult to germinate will often do better under fluorescent plant lights. Some seeds won't germinate when shaded by leaf cover, probably because the leaves filter out helpful rays while allowing the inhibiting far-red light to reach the seeds.

Dormancy is seldom a problem with vegetable seeds, except for some heat-sensitive seeds like lettuce and celery. Beans, mustard, and many other vegetable seeds never go dormant. Carrots and parsnips do need a month of afterripening following harvest before they'll germinate. Seeds you've purchased have had time, of course, to undergo any necessary afterripening in the months between collection and planting. Dormancy is not an uncommon problem when trying to germinate seeds of wildflowers, trees, or shrubs.

Choose Your Medium
Nancy Bubel

The first step in encouraging your seeds on their way to being the plants they really want to be is to prepare a starting medium that will nurture the seeds through the critical germination and seedling stages. The stuff to which you entrust your seeds should match the following description:

· Free from competing weed seeds, soil-borne diseases, and fungus spores.
· Able to absorb and hold quantities of moisture.
· Not so densely packed that vital air is excluded.
· Naturally derived and free from any substance you would not want to put in your garden.
· Noncrusting.

Since the physical conditions of their surroundings—temperature, moisture, air, and light—are more important to germinating seedlings than the nutrient content of the soil, these first mixtures in which you plant your seeds needn't be rich. In fact, it's better if they're not. But they should be light, spongy, and moist. It's a nice touch to start seeds in one of the special seed-starting media, like vermiculite, and then to transplant the seedlings into a potting soil mix that contains more nutrients. Some gardeners prefer to plant seeds directly in a potting soil mix. Many good commercial mixtures are available, or you can mix your own potting soil from the recipes listed later in this chapter.

I wouldn't recommend starting seeds in plain garden soil, because it tends to pack and crust when kept in shallow containers indoors. In addition, unsterilized garden soil may harbor fungi that cause damping-off, a disease that makes young seedlings shrivel and wilt at soil level and sometimes even interferes with complete germination. Soil in which such diseased seedlings have been grown must be pasteurized (see Heat Treatment later in this chapter) before another batch of seeds is planted in it. I find it easier to use fresh potting soil for each new seedling crop and to use the old soil for potting up young trees or rooted herbs.

Three Favorites

I've had good results planting seeds in each of the following three media.

Vermiculite. This is a form of mica which has been "popped" like popcorn by exposing it to intense heat. The resulting flakes are light and capable of holding large amounts of water. Vermiculite also absorbs nutrients from fertilizers and other soil components and releases them gradually to plants. Be sure to buy horticultural vermiculite, not the kind sold for the building trade, which is coarser, highly alkaline, and often contains substances toxic to plant roots.

A Mixture. Equal parts of vermiculite, milled sphagnum moss, and perlite combine to make another good starting medium. This provides a spongy, friable seedbed that promotes good root development. Perlite, despite its plastic appearance, is a natural product, a form of "popped"

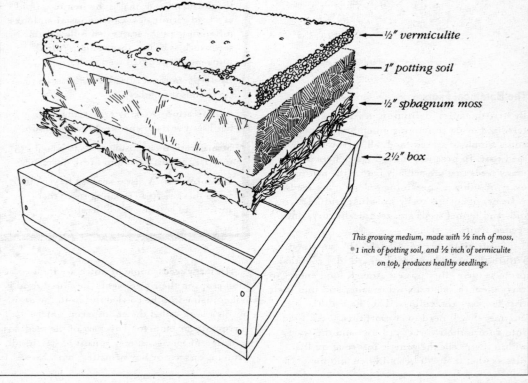

← ½" vermiculite

← 1" potting soil

← ½" sphagnum moss

← 2½" box

This growing medium, made with ½ inch of moss, 1 inch of potting soil, and ½ inch of vermiculite on top, produces healthy seedlings.

Continued ➡

volcanic ash, and while I do not like to use it alone, as I do vermiculite in some cases, it promotes good drainage in seed-starting mixes. The moss must be milled sphagnum, which is very fine, not peat moss, which is too coarse for small seeds and tends to dry and crust.

Mix these three components together thoroughly before dampening. A large old tub or bucket set on newspaper makes the job easier and spillage less of a problem. When moistening this and all other soil mixtures, I like to use warm water because it is more readily absorbed. This seems to be especially important for mixtures containing sphagnum moss, which tends to float on cold water in a dustlike layer that takes ages to soften and swell. It is also a good idea to prepare your soil mixture several hours before you intend to plant seeds. Then, if you have added too much water, you can simply pour off any that puddles on the upper surface, before planting the seeds.

A Three-Layer Arrangement. This medium is composed of a bottom layer—about one-half inch—of torn pieces of sphagnum moss that has been well dampened, then a one-inch layer of good potting soil, topped by a one-half-inch layer of vermiculite. The bottom layer of moss should not be finely milled. I use clumps of moss gathered in our woods. The air spaces trapped by the ferny fronds of the moss promote excellent root development, I've found, and the moss retains water, too. I tear up the wads of moss into small pieces so that individual plants can be removed more easily when it's time to transplant them.

You can also mix chopped sphagnum moss with other potting soil ingredients. Some evidence has shown that sphagnum moss exerts a mild antibiotic effect that helps to control bacterial diseases of seedlings. (A disease-causing fungus, *Sporotrichum schenkii*, has been found in sphagnum moss. Wash thoroughly after handling the moss, and wear gloves if you have any skin breaks on your hands.)

Alternative Media

There's nothing absolute about the mixtures that I use. Other gardeners have obtained good results with the following seed-starting media. What you choose may depend partly on what is easily available to you and on your personal reactions to the feel of the stuff.

Other options include:

- Equal parts of milled sphagnum moss and vermiculite.
- One part milled sphagnum moss and two parts each of vermiculite and perlite.
- Shredded moss alone (well dampened beforehand).
- Potting soil, either commercial or home mixed.
- A cube of sod, turned grass side down, which works well for the planting of larger seeds, like squash, melons, and cucumbers, and supports the seedling until it is planted out in the garden.

Feeding the Seedlings

Neither vermiculite, perlite, nor sphagnum moss contains the nutrients necessary to support plant growth. Seedlings growing in these substances, or mixtures of them, must be fed regularly until they get their roots in real soil.

Such liquid feeding, carried on over a period of weeks, amounts to hydroponic culture, with the growing medium serving only to hold the plants

upright and to condition the roots. Seedlings benefit from the more complex interactions taking place in real soil, so they should eventually be transplanted to a growing medium.

Potting Mixtures

A seed-starting medium provides good physical conditions for seed germination. A potting medium contributes nourishment for the growing plant. There are all kinds of potting mixture recipes from which to choose. Here are some options, along with a few hints about their suitability or limitations.

The amounts in each recipe are given in parts. A part, of course, can be any measure of volume ranging from a teacup to a bushel basket, as long as the measurement used is consistent. I'd suggest making up more soil mix than you think you'll need while you have all the ingredients assembled. Mix the components thoroughly as you go, just as if you were making granola.

Temperature Necessary to Kill Soil-Inhabiting Pests and Diseases

Pests	30 Minutes at Temperature
Nematodes	120° F
Damping-off and soft-rot organisms	130° F
Most pathogenic bacteria and fungi	150° F
Soil insects and most plant viruses	160° F
Most weed seeds	175° F
A few resistant weeds, resistant viruses	212° F

Source: George "Doc" Abraham and Katy Abraham. *Organic Gardening Under Glass* (Emmaus, Pa.: Rodale Press, 1975).

Cruso's Potting Soil

one part commercial potting soil or leaf mold
one part sphagnum moss or peat moss
one part perlite or sharp sand
This is the formula for potting soil that Thalassa Cruso recommends in her book *Making Things Grow*. For fast-growing seedlings, I like to change the proportions to two parts soil or one part soil and one part compost, mixed with one part moss and one part sand or perlite. As originally formulated, for houseplants, the mixture is a bit lean to support strong seedling growth.

Good and Simple Potting Soil

one part finished compost
one part vermiculite
Easy to mix. Moisten it well before setting plants in it.

Home-Style Potting Soil

one part finished compost
one part either loose garden soil or potting soil
one part sharp sand, perlite, or vermiculite, or a mixture of all three
This one can be made without buying any ingredients if you have access to sharp sand.

A Rich Potting Soil

one part leaf mold
two parts either loose garden soil or potting soil
one part compost or rotted, sifted manure
This potting soil is especially good for lettuce and cabbage transplants.

A Lean Potting Soil

one part either loose garden soil or potting soil
one part perlite
one part vermiculit
one part milled sphagnum moss
one part sharp sand

This is mostly physical support for the plants. Use this mixture for plants that should grow slowly, such as cactus.

Amended Potting Soil

four parts either loose garden soil or potting soil
two parts sphagnum moss or peat mos
two parts leaf mold or compost
two parts vermiculite
six teaspoons dolomitic limestone
The limestone helps to neutralize acids in the leaf mold and peat moss.

If you want to formulate your own potting mixture from what you have or can readily find, you'll probably be on safe ground if you include each of the following:

- Soil, preferably loam, for nutrients.
- Sand or perlite for drainage. Gravel may also be used in the bottom of a solid container but not as part of a soil mix.
- Compost, leaf mold, vermiculite, or moss for water retention.

Heat Treatment

Commercial potting soil should be free of harmful bacteria and fungi, but garden soil is, of course, teeming with organisms. Most of them are beneficial. I never heat-treat or otherwise "sterilize" my soil. Besides being a large nuisance, the process kills helpful soil organisms and, at temperatures above 180°F (82°C), releases dissolved salts that can be toxic to plants. Even at 160°F (71°C), some salt-releasing breakdown occurs.

If you decide to sterilize a batch of soil, the following methods will work. Plan a picnic supper or weekend trip when you do treat your soil, because the kitchen will smell awful!

Using the Oven. Before heating the soil, moisten it thoroughly so that small puddles form when you press your finger into it. Bake the soil in metal pans in a preheated 275° F (135° C) oven. Small amounts, a gallon or so by volume, should be ready within 30 to 40 minutes. Larger quantities, a half bushel or so, may need to remain in the oven for 1½ hours. It is important that the soil be wet. The steam generated by the water penetrates the spaces in the soil. Dry soil takes much longer to treat and smells much worse.

A meat thermometer inserted in the soil will indicate when it has arrived at the proper temperature to kill offending organisms. Damping-off fungi, for example, die at 130° F (54° C), and a temperature of 160° F (71° C) kills most other plant viruses and pathogenic bacteria. Avoid overheating the soil, for you want to retain as many of the more numerous helpful soil microorganisms as possible. Soil that has been baked should be rubbed through a hardware cloth screen to break up the clumps before using.

Using the Microwave. Soil poured into plastic bags can be sterilized in a microwave oven. Do this in batches of up to ten pounds. Placing the bags in the oven for 7½ minutes will kill most damping-off and root-rot fungi. Some researchers report, however, that microwave treatment changes soil pH, cation exchange capacity, and mineral content.

Using Solar Energy. An easier method recently developed at the University of California uses solar heat. Fill gallon-sized black plastic planting pots with moist soil and then place each pot in a clear plastic bag. Tie the bag closed and set the bagged pot in a sheltered location where it will

Continued ➡

receive full sun. Two weeks of direct-sun treatment in warm weather should kill most disease organisms.

Using Boiling Water. Pouring boiling water over a flat of soil does not sterilize it, but kills many microorganisms.

Helpful Hints

Perhaps the following hints will save you a bit of trouble, too.

Collect Soil in the Fall. The time to collect good garden soil for spring seed starting is in the fall, before the soil freezes solid. Even if you're lucky enough to have a winter thaw at the time you're doing your planting and transplanting, the soil is likely to be mucky, and you may not be able to dig very deeply, either.

Make Leaf Mold. There's leaf mold and there's leaf mold. Make your own seasoned pile for use in potting mixtures. One year I scraped up a bushel of lovely, crumbly, woodsy-smelling leaf mold from the edge of our woods and put it into my soil mixture. All the seedlings growing in this "special" mixture died. I'm not sure whether the stuff was too acid or if it was toxic in some other way, but from now on I test such soil amendments on a few plants rather than gambling my whole crop of early seedlings.

Avoid Peat Moss. Watch out for peat moss, too. Personally, I don't like it. It's chunky, unmercifully hard to moisten, and it crusts when it dries. I would never use peat moss in a soil mixture when I could get milled sphagnum moss. If you must use it, wet it very thoroughly several hours before you need it. I'd caution you, too, against using wetting agents (surfactants) in potting mixes or irrigation systems. They tend to reduce soil water retention, and their effect on people who handle and consume them hasn't been tested. Even mild soaps like Basic H, when mixed with soil in highly dilute solutions, reduced the growth of vital root hairs.

Use Builder's Sand. Sharp sand, specified in the soil recipes, is coarse builder's sand. Sand brought from the seashore is too fine and too salty. Don't use it for plants. Even lake sand or sand scraped up by the roadside is too fine for our purposes. It will pack into a cementlike mass that kills plant roots. I know—I used it by mistake . . . once.

Make Your Own Mix. What would I use if commercial potting mixture ingredients like vermiculite and perlite were unavailable? I would mix equal parts of compost, good garden soil, rubbed through a screen; and torn moss. I would not use garden soil alone, for no matter how good the soil, it tends to pack and harden when used indoors in small pots.

Containers

Nancy Bubel

Your seeds are ready. Your soil is mixed. Now it's time to comb closets, attic, and cellar for likely discards to hold the soil and provide a temporary home for your growing seedlings.

The ideal container for starting seeds should be no more than two to three inches deep. One that is deeper will only use up more potting soil. A shallow pan, though, will dry out quickly and limit root development. The soil holders you use for germinating seeds do not necessarily need to have drainage holes. You can prevent pooling of water around plant roots by choosing the right growing mediums to fill the containers. Long, narrow flats fit neatly under fluorescent lights; however, don't use flats that are so long that they will be heavy and difficult to handle when filled with wet soil.

Types of Containers

I've grown seedlings in all of the following kinds of containers, for different reasons and with varying results. Each has its place. Some are more useful than others. Certainly it is preferable, all else being equal, to make use of some of the many throwaways that clutter up our daily lives, but there are times when a specially prepared device will be more effective than anything else. It's silly to make do, unless you must, when with a little effort and some scrap wood you could rig up a really fine seedling-care system. At any rate, here's my list of container candidates, briefly evaluated for effectiveness, cost, and useful life.

Eggshells and/or Egg Cartons. They are inexpensive but not really much good in the trials I've run on them. Neither the shells nor the egg carton sections can hold much soil, and they dry out fast. I think it's a mistake, too, to start a child gardener with one of these cute but impractical gimmicks. The learning child deserves good equipment that will help him or her to be successful. Something about planting seeds in eggshells seems to have captured the imagination of armchair gardeners, and every spring you'll see articles in magazines suggesting the method. Go ahead and try it if it appeals to you. Just don't expect great results.

Milk Cartons. Yes, they're free, good for one growing season, and they fit together well under lights. You can either halve a half-gallon milk carton the long way or cut one side out of a quart carton. If you don't buy milk, no doubt your friends, relatives, or neighbors would save their cartons for you. Even the little pint and half-pint cartons may be used for larger individual transplants.

Aluminum Disposable Pans. The loaf pans make fine seedling trays. They last for several years, work quite well, and can be had free if you know people who will save them for you. The shiny sides of the loaf pan reflect light back onto the seedlings. One of my best generations of eggplant seedlings was raised in an aluminum loaf pan on the kitchen windowsill. Pie pans are more of a last resort for plants, for they are too shallow to hold enough soil for proper moisture retention and root development. They're fine for sprouting seeds, though, if you transplant promptly.

Peat Pots. A tray of seedlings all tucked into peat pots looks neat and satisfying, but despite the assumption that plant roots will readily penetrate the walls of the pot and find the surrounding soil, I have not found this to be true in all cases. More than once I've uprooted a plant and found its roots pretty well confined to the peat pot. Also, unless grouped closely together, peat pots dry out fast.

Peat Pellets. These compressed-soil pots in netting seem to offer less resistance to plant roots than the peat pots. If you remove the net when you plant the seedlings out. However, even though the net has air spaces, it often appears to inhibit plant roots. The soil mixture of peat pellets sometimes contains a chemical fertilizer. Peat pellets are easy to use and neat, but they are expensive and can't be reused.

Plastic Gallon Jugs. Cut-down plastic gallon jugs have worked fairly well for me, but I prefer the long, narrow cut-down milk cartons, which seem to accommodate more seedlings and waste less space under lights. Plastic jugs are free, lightweight, last two or three years, and may be further recycled by saving the cutoff top to put over seedling plants in the garden for frost protection.

Shoes. Yes, shoes. I've tried planting melon seeds in cast-off shoes on the advice of an elderly gardener whose flourishing crops indicate he must be doing something right. The shoes were fun to use and they certainly make a stir when visitors noticed them, but I can't honestly say that they made any difference in the plants that grew in them.

Bricks. For another unconventional and more widely adaptable seed-starter, use an unglazed brick set in an open frame of scrap wood that extends 1½ inches above the top of the brick. On top of the brick, put an inch-thick layer of moist sphagnum moss or vermiculite, and plant seeds in it. Then set the framed brick in a tray of water. The water should always touch the brick, but should not cover it. The continuous supply of moisture, coupled with good drainage and aeration, encourages good seedling germination.

Market Packs. These are rectangular trays made of pressed fiber. I think they are preferable to peat pots. The packs are not cheap, but they last for several years, fit together well in storage, and allow plenty of depth for root development. Also, unlike the larger flats, they may be kept on a sunny windowsill.

Clay Flower Pots. Clay pots last a long time and are fine for special transplants. They are the best containers for starting watercress seeds, because they can be kept in a tray of water so that the soil is constantly moist. As far as I'm concerned, though, they are too costly and unwieldy for most transplanting. I use small plastic pots to start cucumber and melon seedlings.

Household Discards. Chipped enamel broiler pans, rusty cake tins, or lopsided dishpans make good containers for groups of transplants. Old refrigerator crisper drawers work well, too, especially for lettuce and other leafy crops grown under lights in winter, because they hold plenty of soil.

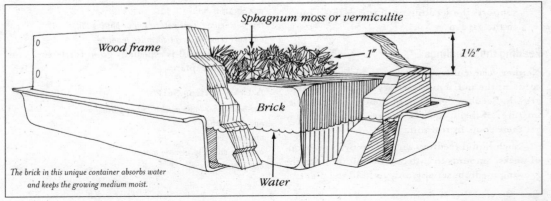

Sphagnum moss or vermiculite

Wood frame

Brick

Water

1"   1½"

The brick in this unique container absorbs water and keeps the growing medium moist.

Continued ➡

Cottage Cheese Cartons. These cost nothing and outlast at least one use. I use them primarily for give-away seedlings, because in my setup the round shape of the containers wastes space under the lights. They do fit on most windowsills, though, which can be a boon to the gardener without lights. Incidentally, if you do set them at your window, you'll probably need to provide some protection—a tray or foil liner—to prevent spills and splashes from spotting your windowsills.

Flats. My favorite. When you raise your own seedlings, there is no such thing as too many flats. A flat is nothing more than a four-sided frame made of wood, about three inches wide, with slats nailed across one open side. The slats should be spaced one-eighth to one-fourth inch apart to allow for drainage. Most flats are rectangular, because that is the most efficient shape.

Six 12- by 16-inch flats will fit on each shelf of a 26- by 48-inch, double-bank fluorescent light cart. I wouldn't recommend making flats any larger than about 14 by 18 inches, or they'll need extra bracing to hold the weight of all that soil, and then they'll be too ungainly to handle. Flats are basic. Make as many as you can find time and materials for. You won't regret it.

Plastic Trays. Commercial plastic trays 2 inches deep and 18 to 20 inches long work well and last a long time, but they are costly. Poke a few drainage holes in them with an ice-pick.

Soil Blocks. These are better than peat pots because they promote good root growth without forming a barrier. They take time and special equipment to make, though. You need a soil-block mold, a metal device with a plunger that ejects blocks of soil from a mold; a tub for mixing; soil composed of two parts peat moss that has been rubbed through one-fourth-inch hardware cloth, one part garden soil, and one part compost; water; and a tray.

To make a soil block, wet the soil mix until it forms a slurry. Then pack a four-cube block maker with the wet mix, level off the top of the mold, and eject the cubes onto a tray. Plant a single seed in each block, or plant two and cut off the extra seedling if both germinate.

Any of a variety of containers, bought or found, can be used to start seedlings.

In my experiments with soil blocks, I found that they do indeed promote good root growth. For me, though, they had two disadvantages. The first was the time and trouble necessary to make the blocks. Secondly, the blocks must be very carefully and frequently watered from above so they don't disintegrate.

Speedling Flats. A more serious competitor for my favorite plain old rectangular flat is the Speedling flat—a molded plastic-foam tray 3 inches high, 13 inches wide, and 26 inches long. The plant holding cells taper to a narrow open point at the bottom of each cell—an ingenious way to encourage a dense root ball that makes good use of the soil mix. In order to keep the roots confined to their spaces, the foam trays must be propped an inch or so above the surface to admit air. In my trials, foam trays flats produce excel-

lent seedlings, but they're a bit more cumbersome to work with than conventional flats. They're durable, though; mine is still in use after four years.

Like most gardeners who can't resist starting enough plants for the whole neighborhood, my spring seedling setup is a motley arrangement of all the flats I can muster, plus representatives of most of the other kinds of containers mentioned above, which just about sums up my advice for other seed-starters. Use what you have, buy what intrigues you, but aim for a growing supply of long-lasting, inexpensive wooden flats.

Sowing Seeds Early Indoors
Nancy Bubel

I've been starting spring plant seeds indoors in late winter for some years now, and I'm still learning—still making mistakes, too. Once in a while the cats will knock over a flat of transplants. Then I must start all over again. Quite often I experiment with a new vegetable or flower, which shakes up the routine a bit, but in general I've worked out a pattern for this yearly ritual. I no longer worry about whether the seeds will come up. I know now that they will, if I keep them warm enough. I no longer start my tomatoes in early February, because I've learned it's better to set out plants that are in active growth rather than overblown specimens I've been holding for three weeks until the weather was right. Neither do I sow seeds as thickly as I once did, although this bad habit of the amateur gardener dies hard. It has to do, I suppose, with a lurking reluctance to trust those seeds. Only time and repeated sowing and harvesting can soften that inner uneasiness and lead to the respect for each seed that gives it sufficient room to grow.

My Timetable

It is all too easy when you have a severe case of the February blues and long for an early start on spring to get out the flats and the soil mixtures and start a whole batch of spring vegetables. Now, that's perfectly all right, if you can chalk the whole project up to experience or winter indoor recreation and start another batch later at the right time. It's also all right if you live in one of those benign climates where frost won't hit after early April. However, most of us would rather try to do it right the first time. So here's a little timetable to give you an idea of safe indoor starting times for your spring-planted vegetables.

Onions—12 to 14 weeks before the safe planting-out date (which is 4 to 6 weeks before the last frost)

Peppers—8 to 12 weeks before the last frost

Eggplant—6 to 8 weeks before the last frost

Tomatoes—6 to 8 weeks before the last frost

Lettuce—5 to 6 weeks before the safe planting-out date (which is 4 to 5 weeks before the last frost)

Cole crops (cabbage, broccoli, collards, etc.)—5 to 6 weeks before the safe planting-out date (after danger of severe weather has passed, but while nights are still cold)

Cucumbers and melons—2 to 4 weeks before the last frost (but don't plant out until the weather is warm and settled)

When I raised my seedlings on sunny windowsills, I started them well within the range of traditionally recommended times given above. If anything, I started them a bit on the late side, since late-winter sun is still quite weak, and it's

not until well into March that you can expect old Sol to do much for your windowsill plants.

To make soil blocks, pack a soil block mold with wet growing medium, eject the blocks into a flat, and plant a seed in each.

The date you choose for starting your plants, then, will depend on the variety you're growing; whether you'll raise the plants in a greenhouse, on a windowsill, or under lights; and the average frost-free dates in your growing area. If you are

Continued ➡

unsure of when those dates are, check with your local county extension agent. The office is often in the county courthouse.

A Sowing Checklist

Now that we've settled the when of seed starting, let's go on to the how. Here's a checklist of seed-sowing steps:

1. **Gather your equipment.** Seek out and collect the flats or other containers, planting mix, seeds, watering can, newspaper, labels, and markers you'll need.

2. **Prepare a work space.** Choose a spot where you'll have room to knock things around. Spread a layer of newspapers over the area. It's easier to gather up and discard the papers than to mop up spilled potting soil.

3. **Review your seed packets.** Look over your packets of seeds and write out a label for each one before you plant the seeds. You won't believe, till you've done it, how easy it is to mix up different seed lots. And if you plant five kinds of pepper and eight kinds of tomato, as I do, labeling the seed flats is doubly important. A hot pepper seedling looks no different from a sweet bell pepper seedling, and you may want to plant out ten of one kind but only five of the other.

   Labels may be wooden Popsicle sticks, cut pieces of venetian blind slats, strips cut from plastic jugs, or ready-made labels from your garden supply store. I've also simply glued scrap paper labels to the sides of wood flats (glue new labels right over the old ones next year) or clipped tags to plastic containers to identify my plants. If you do any kind of experimenting with different fertilizers, kelp sprays, chilling treatments, or soil mixtures, accurate labeling and record keeping are even more important.

4. **Prepare your flats.** Spread a layer of newspaper on the bottom of each flat or container that has drainage holes or slits in the bottom to keep the soil from sifting through. If the spaces between slats are wide enough, wedge in a "caulking" of torn shreds of moss. Trim the newspaper so that it doesn't stick up above soil level, or it will act as a wick and draw off soil moisture. Fill the flats with the seed-starting medium of your choice or with potting soil if you prefer, up to about one-half inch from the top. A deep container, half-filled, will both shade the plants and interfere with ventilation of the seedlings.

   Sometimes I plant seeds in plain vermiculite, omitting the moss and soil layers. The seedlings that are started this way must either be transplanted sooner to a soil mixture containing nutrients or fertilized every four days or so.

   Finally, firm the top surface of the planting medium, preferably with a flat object like a boar or a brick. This prevents the small seeds from tumbling too far into the crevices.

5. **Prepare the seeds.** Certain seeds will germinate more quickly if given a little head start before sowing. Scarifying helps to hasten germination of hard-coated seeds like morning-glory or New Zealand spinach. Just nick the seed coats with a knife or file. Don't cut deep enough to damage the embryo.

   Presoaking cuts several days of germination time for slow-to-sprout seeds like carrot, celery, and parsley. I've had good luck planting these seeds after having poured just-boiled water over them, draining when cool,

and mixing with dry sand to avoid clumping. Some gardeners put such seeds in small muslin bags to soak overnight before planting. Other seeds like peas and beans will sprout sooner if presoaked for an hour or so in warm water. Presoaking isn't necessary for most seeds you'll be planting indoors, though. Check the listing of plants in the encyclopedia section at the back of the book to find out whether a particular seed should be presoaked.

6. **Plant the seeds.** You can either scatter the seeds over the entire surface—especially when using a small container—or you can plant in rows—usually a good idea when raising seedlings in flats. At any rate, give each fine seed at least one-eighth inch of space from its neighbor; medium seeds need one-half inch of room, and large seeds one inch.

   Getting the seeds to go where you want them can be tricky, but the knack comes with practice. To disperse fine seeds, try sowing them from a saltshaker. Medium-sized seeds like tomatoes, which may come only 20 or so to a packet in the case of some hybrid varieties, may be placed exactly where you want them with fine tweezers. According to most of the pictures you see, the real experts sow seeds by tapping them lightly directly from the seed packet. I always feel that I have better control over distribution of the seeds by taking a pinch of them in my fingers and then gently rotating thumb and forefinger to gradually dislodge the seeds. If all this is new to you, you might want to practice by sowing a few batches of seeds over a piece of white paper so that you can check to see what kind of distribution you're getting.

7. **Cover the seeds.** Except for very fine seeds, which may be simply pressed into the soil, you will need to cover the seeds with soil. The few seeds that need light for germination are noted in the encyclopedia section. These should be simply pressed into a damp seed-starting medium and covered with clear plastic or glass. The rule of thumb is that seeds should be covered to a depth of three times their size. A one-eighth-inch seed, then, would have three-eighth inch of soil over it. I hardly ever put more than one-half inch of soil over any seed, and then only for larger seeds. For indoor sowing I simply spread fine, light soil or vermiculite over the seeds. This last layer needn't be wet. If the planting medium on the bottom is well soaked, the top will soon become damp, too.

   The good thing about presoaking the growing medium is that it's then not necessary to water the planted seeds from the top. If you've ever tried this procedure, I'm sure you've found, as I have, that it's a surefire way to relocate all your carefully spaced seeds. If for some reason you do prefer to water your seedling flats from the top, either use a gentle spray from a rubber bulb sprinkler with a flat, perforated nozzle head, or spread wet burlap over the flat and water through that. In that way you'll avoid the flooding that would carry seeds willy-nilly to the corners of the flat. Be sure the top layer of vermiculite (or whatever) is pressed firmly over the seeds so that the seeds are closely surrounded on all sides.

8. **Cover the container.** You can use any one of the following materials to cover your container:
   · damp newspaper or burlap

· a scrap piece of used aluminum foil
· a plastic sheet or bag slipped around the flat
· another seed flat

   You can build a stack of seed flats if they are roughly the same size. In fact, the soil surface will receive better ventilation if the flats don't fit exactly edge to edge. Watch for mold in this case, or if you cover your containers with plastic, and provide better ventilation if mold develops.

9. **Set the containers in a warm place.** Place all planted containers in a warm place where seeds can germinate. I've found the arrangements listed on the next page conducive to good germination.

· Put flats in the corner behind a wood-burning stove, preferably not on the floor where cool air settles, but elevated two feet or so on a small stable or box.
· Set flats on a high shelf above a floor register. Watch for excessive drying, though.
· Set small batches of seeds on the pilot light on a gas stove.
· Set flats on top of a turned-on fluorescent light fixture, like a light cart setup with several tiers of lights, and they'll receive steady warmth at the ends of the tubes. Once you have the early plants (onions and peppers) sprouted and under lights, you can set the next batch of seeds that you want to germinate on the dark but warm tier above the lighted plants.

A Second Method

An alternative method of indoor seed planting, used by an accomplished gardener with whom I enjoy trading lore, goes like this. Fill a cut-down milk carton or plastic jug with starting medium, water it well, and plant the seeds. Enclose the container in a plastic bag and keep the whole shebang good and warm. After three or four days, punch drainage holes in the bottom of the container (use a pick or knife). Keep warm and covered, but allow to drain and check for mold until you see the seeds have germinated.

Presprouting Seeds

Ever since I picked up the idea from Dick Raymond's book *Down-to-Earth Vegetable Gardening*, I've been presprouting seeds of tender crops like cucumbers, squash, pumpkins, and melons. The first three are planted directly in the ground after they've germinated. Melons bear earlier if pre-germinated and then planted in individual pots for a two-week head start indoors. (Some gardeners feel that cucumbers also do, but I've not been convinced of that yet.)

   Presprouting melon and other cucurbit seeds has given me a much higher rate of germination than I was able to get when planting two seeds to a peat pot, probably because the seeds receive more constant warmth and moisture. I highly recommend presprouting seeds of those crops that need especially warm conditions during germination.

How to Presprout Seeds. To start the seeds on their way, space them evenly on a damp double layer of paper toweling (or several thicknesses of paper napkin). Be sure that no two seeds touch. Carefully roll up the towel, keeping the seeds as well separated as possible, and tuck the rolled cylinder into a plastic bag. If you label the rolls, you can put more than one variety in the bag.

   Put the bag full of damp, rolled, seed-filled towels in a warm place. I use the warm top of a

Continued ➔

fluorescent plant light fixture or the top of my insulated hot water heater.

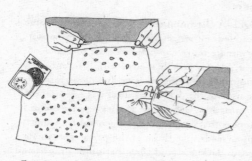

To presprout seeds, first spread them on a damp paper towel. Roll up the paper carefully and place it in a plastic bag. Set the bag in a warm place until the seeds have germinated.

Check the seeds each day. Nothing will happen for several days, but germinating seeds do need a certain amount of oxygen, and the small amount of air that wafts in when you peek at the seeds will do them good.

Signs of Life. The first sign of germination in cucurbit seeds will be the development of the root. Be sure to remove your sprouted seeds from their incubator before the root hairs grow together and tangle. If one should grow through the towel—and this often happens—just tear the towel and plant the damp shred of paper right along with the seed.

Planting Presprouted Seeds. Plant the presprouted seeds in a good rich potting mix that you've scooped into individual containers and premoistened. Cucurbits don't take kindly to transplanting, not with those fleshy, sappy, easily bruised roots, so your plants will stay right in these containers until they go into the garden. Individual half-pint milk cartons work well, since the bottom may be easily removed and the whole plant dump set in the hill. I plant my sprouted cucurbits in small plastic pots, which are easily overturned to free the seedlings when it is time to set them out. Cover the presprouted seed root lightly but firmly with soil, and set the pots under lights immediately, or put them on your sunniest windowsill.

Germination

Nancy Bubel

If you've ever lost track of a flat of germinated seeds, as I have, and discovered them too late—when the thready white stems had grown an inch before putting on pale little leaves—then no doubt you've also muttered ruefully, "Out of sight, out of mind." It is easy, in the busy spring rush, to overlook flats of planted seedlings tucked in out-of-the-way corners. For that reason, I like to keep my flats together in a place where I'll see them every day and remember to check on them.

The Process of Germination

What's going on in those flats while we wait? We commonly think of germination as being equivalent to sprouting, and it's true that the final test of complete germination is the emergence of a growing root or leaf sprout from the seed, yet the process by which a dry, dormant embryo quickens into tender, new green growth begins well before we have visible evidence of the new root or leaf.

The first step in the process of germination is the absorption of water by the seed. This is a necessary preliminary to the internal changes in the seed that trigger growth. The uptake of water by the seed (called imbibition by botanists) depends in turn on the content of the seed, the permeability of its outer layer, and the availability of the necessary amount of liquid. Seeds that contain a high percentage of protein imbibe more water than those that are high in starch. (Only under very acid or hot conditions, which don't exist in nature, will seed starch swell with water intake.) Seeds with hard coats, like morning-glories, will absorb water more readily if their hard outer shell is nicked with a file. Furthermore, the seed depends not only on the presence of moisture in the soil, but also on close contact with soil particles, to permit sufficient water uptake. The fact that a seed has absorbed water is not, by the way, proof of its viability. Even dead seeds can imbibe water.

As the seed swells with water, it develops considerable pressure, pressure that eventually ruptures the seed coat (which has already been softened by the surrounding moisture) and eases the eruption of the root. These are the physical effects of the seed's absorption of water. At the same time, internal metabolic changes are revving up life in the seed, changing its chemistry from neutral to first gear, you might say. As the seed tissues absorb water, food stored in the endosperm is gradually changed into soluble form, ready to be used as a component of new tissue.

In order, though, for the starches and proteins in the endosperm to dissolve, they must often be changed into simpler forms—the starches into simple sugars like glucose and maltose and the proteins into free amino acids and amides. The enzymes, necessary to split complex forms of stored food into simpler forms of usable food, are activated in response to the stepped-up metabolism of the seed. You will remember that even dormant seeds carry on respiration. They take in oxygen and release carbon dioxide. The rate of respiration is markedly increased in the germinating seed and both generates and supports the many interacting internal changes in the embryo.

Enzymes, then, direct the breakdown of certain useful stored foods. Hormones, also present in the seed, control both the transportation of newly soluble foods to different parts of

Soil Temperature Conditions for Vegetable Seed Germination

Crops	Minimum (°F)	Optimum Range (°F)	Optimum (°F)	Maximum (°F)
Asparagus	50	60-85	75	95
Beans, Lima	60	65-85	85	85
Beans, Snap	60	65-85	80	95
Beets	40	50-85	85	95
Cabbage	40	45-95	85	100
Carrots	40	45-85	80	95
Cauliflower	40	45-85	80	100
Celery	40	60-70	70*	85*
Corn	50	60-95	95	105
Cucumbers	60	65-95	95	105
Eggplant	60	75-90	85	95
Lettuce	35	40-80	75	85
Muskmelons	60	75-95	90	100
Okra	60	70-95	95	105
Onions	35	50-95	75	95
Parsley	40	50-85	75	90
Parsnips	35	50-70	65	85
Peas	40	40-75	75	85
Peppers	60	65-95	85	95
Pumpkins	60	70-95	95	100
Radishes	40	45-90	85	95
Spinach	35	45-75	70	85
Squash	60	70-95	95	100
Swiss Chard	40	50-85	85	95
Tomatoes	50	60-85	85	95
Turnips	40	60-105	85	105
Watermelons	60	70-95	95	105

Source: J. F. Harrington, Department of Vegetable Crops, University of California at Davis.
*Daily fluctuation to 60° or lower at night is essential.

Flower Seeds that Need Light to Germinate
(Do not cover these seeds with soil.)

Annuals	Perennials	Biennials
Ageratum	Alyssum saxatile	Bellflowers
Begonias	Balloonflower	English Daisies
Browallia	Chinese Lanterns	Foxglove
Coleus (tender perennial)	Chrysanthemums	
Godetia	Columbines	
Impatiens	Edelweiss	
Kochia	False Rock Cress	
Lobelia	Feverfew	
Mignonette	Gaillardia	
Petunias	Maltese Cross	
Portulaca	Oriental Poppies	
Scarlet Sage	Primroses (except Chinese)	
Snapdragons	Rock Cress	
Strawflowers	Shasta Daisies	
Sweet Alyssum	Sweet Rocket	

Flower Seeds that Often Germinate Best in Some Light
(Cover these seeds very lightly, if at all, with soil.)

Annuals

African Daisies	Nicotiana
Balsam	Stocks
Celosia	Tithonia (Mexican Sunflower)
Cleome	Transvaal Daisies (tender perennial)
Cosmos	Wishbone flowers
Monkey Flower (Mimulus)	

Flower Seeds that Germinate Best in Darkness
(Cover these seeds with ¼ inch of fine soil, well firmed down.)

Annuals	Perennials
Bachelor's Buttons	Delphiniums
Butterfly Flowers	Poppies (except Oriental)
Calendula	Shamrocks
Globe Amaranth	Soapwort
Nasturtiums	
Nemesia	
Painted Daisies	
Pansies (biennial)	
Phlox drummondi	
Salpiglossus (painted tongue)	
Sweet Peas	
Verbena	

Continued ➡

the seed and the building up of new compounds from the components of those that have been broken down into simpler forms. Pea seeds, for example, synthesize new compounds during the first 24 hours of the germination process.

The product of all this stepped-up activity within the seed is new tissue, originating at growing points in the root tip, the stem, the bud, and the cotyledons. This new tissue is formed in two ways: Cells already present in the seed grow longer, and cells divide to produce new cells, which then elongate.

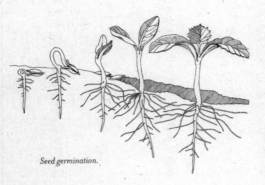

Seed germination.

Studies done on lettuce seeds, for example, show that cell division begins about 12 hours after germination has begun; the root cells show some elongation at about the same time. In corn, the first change to be observed is the enlargement of the cells, followed by cell division in the root as it emerges from the seed coat. Both kinds of tissue changes are necessary to the normal development of the seedling.

Factors that Influence Germination

Many internal and environmental conditions influence the course of germination in seeds.

The Condition of the Seed. A shriveled seed that has been stored too long or under poor conditions will have a scant supply of food stored in its endosperm. The seedling that grows from such a seed, if it germinates at all, is likely to be weak and stunted.

Mechanical injury to the seed during harvesting or drying can injure the cotyledons, stem, or root tip, or produce breaks in the seed coat that admit microorganisms, which in turn deteriorate seed quality. The hormones that promote cell elongation are produced by the endosperm and cotyledons. Any injury, therefore, that interferes with the soundness of these hormone-producing tissues is likely to result in stunted seedlings.

The Presence of Water. Water must be available to the seed in amounts sufficient to start the quickening of respiration that leads to germination. However, few seeds will sprout if submerged in water. Some air must also reach the seed for it to absorb the oxygen it needs. Water serves several purposes in the germinating seed. Initially, it softens the seed coat so the root can emerge more easily. Then it combines with stored foods to form soluble forms of nourishment for the seed. As growth proceeds, it helps to enlarge new cells, as directed by the hormones, and serves as a medium of transportation to take soluble foods and hormones to parts of the seedling where they're needed.

Sufficient Air. Even quiescent seeds in storage need a certain minimum supply of air. The requirements of a germinating seed are more critical. Our atmosphere contains a mixture of gases, with the oxygen portion fairly constant at 20 percent. (Some seeds—certain cereals and

carrots—have been shown to germinate more completely in an even richer oxygen concentration.) The oxygen taken in by the seed in respiration combines chemically with the seed's fats and sugars—a process called oxidation.

Seeds also need a certain amount of carbon dioxide in order to germinate, but they don't do well if surrounded by a considerable concentration of carbon dioxide. Cucurbits (squash, melons, pumpkins, and cucumbers) have seed membranes that admit carbon dioxide more readily than oxygen, so they are acutely sensitive to low-oxygen conditions. As gardeners, we can't manipulate the composition of the air that surrounds us, but we can make sure our germinating seeds are supplied with enough air by planting them shallowly, in a loose, friable medium, and by keeping the soil moist but not waterlogged, so some air spaces remain.

Temperature. In general, seeds need warmer soil temperatures during germination than they will need later when they've grown into plants. There *are* differences in heat and cold sensitivity, though, among the different species. Some seeds, like lettuce, celery, and peas, germinate best at low temperatures, while peppers, eggplant, melons, and others prefer more warmth. Extremes of heat and cold inhibit germination of most kinds of seed. There are, for most seeds, optimum temperatures at which they do best. This doesn't mean your seeds won't germinate at higher or lower temperatures; the drop in germination with less-than-ideal temperatures is gradual, not abrupt. Seeds that germinate best at a soil temperature of 75°F (24°C) will put forth some growth at 65°F (18°C), although it might occur later and might be less.

Some seeds, like dock, tobacco, and evening primrose, need alternating warm and cool temperatures in order to germinate. According to studies done with these plants, it's not the rate or duration of the temperature change but simply the fact of the change itself that affects them.

The most favorable germinating temperature for most garden seeds started indoors is between 75°F and 90°F (24°C and 32°C). That's soil temperature. Remember that whereas the air temperature in a room maybe 70°F (21°C), a moist flat of soil set on the floor may be cooler unless kept near a source of heat.

A soil-heating cable may be used to speed germination of some seeds that are more difficult to start. Applying bottom heat directly to the flat uses less power than heating the whole room or greenhouse. In most households, though, there is usually at least one spot—over the furnace or water heater, on top of the television set, near a

wood stove or heat register, or on a pilot light—where seed flats can be kept warm during germination.

Light. A fair number of flower seeds and some tree seeds either require light for germination or germinate more completely in the presence of light. Most vegetable seeds are indifferent to the amount of light they receive during germination. We used to think that darkness was essential to germination, but recent studies don't seem to support that conclusion as a generality. Some flower seeds, like those of the pansy, germinate best in darkness, and germination of onions and chives appears to be retarded by exposure to light. A few vegetable seeds germinate more completely under some conditions when they receive some light. In the case of lettuce and celery, for example, light promotes more complete germination only when the temperature is higher than that at which these seeds usually germinate best. At the lower temperatures they prefer, exposure to light doesn't seem to make much difference. The lesson from this is clear: When putting in a late planting of lettuce or celery when the weather is warm, press the seeds into moist soil, covering them lightly, if at all, With fine soil—although you could also spread a few dry grass clippings over the row to prevent crusting.

Vegetable seedling flats can be covered with wet newspapers, damp burlap, or used aluminum foil. Flats of seeds that need light to germinate should usually be covered with clear plastic sheets, bags, or food wrap, except for seeds that are known to germinate within a week, which may be left uncovered.

Soil Conditions. Apart from the physical conditions of friability, aeration, moisture, and freedom from waterlogging, all of which promote germination, there are other conditions in the soil that may affect the outcome of seed planting.

Organic Matter. Soils containing a high percentage of organic matter along with many microorganisms may have a higher concentration of carbon dioxide than the surrounding air. This can retard germination, depending on the permeability of the seed coat to carbon dioxide. Seeds don't need a rich mixture to start germinating.

Salt. A high salt content, found in some seaside soils, can block germination by drawing water from the seeds.

Calcium. Some seeds respond favorably to a high calcium content in the soil.

Leaf Mold. Leaf mold from the woods may contain germination-inhibiting substances. Beech tree leaves, for example, develop a compound that inhibits germination after they've been exposed for a winter. The fresh leaves do not contain this compound. Eucalyptus leaves also contain germination-inhibiting substances. I once killed a whole batch of seedlings by planting them in a mix containing some perfectly lovely leaf mold I had scraped up at the edge of our woods. Leaf mold, on the whole, is great stuff, and I use it regularly in our garden and compost pile with no ill effect. But since many of these interactions are still little understood, I no longer collect my leaf mold for seedling mixtures in the woods, but rather save maple leaves from our yard trees for this purpose.

Monitoring the Process

Keeping all these factors—water, air, temperature, light, soil conditions—in balance, while we wait for those first spears of green to show; calls for checking the seed flats at least once a day. The soil should be kept moist but not soggy. Air

Continued ➡

should be allowed to reach the soil surface at intervals, at least enough to prevent the formation of mold on the surface. Although I formerly surrounded each container of seeds with a plastic bag until the seeds germinated, I found that mold often formed on the soil because of poor air circulation. Now I simply cover the top of the flat, without surrounding it with a moisture-proof barrier. If you do find mold on the soil, chances are that exposing the flat to the air for an hour or so will take care of the problem.

Then, one day—often, in the case of peppers, just about when you'd given up hope—you'll notice little elbows of stems pushing through the soil surface.

What Seedlings Need
Nancy Bubel

The most crucial time in the life of a seedling is the period just before it has broken dormancy. Each tentative-looking little plant sprout is rather like a baby. It must have its needs met immediately. If it finds only darkness when its cotyledons break through the soil surface, it will send up a pale, weak stem in search of the light it must have. If the soil in which it is growing dries out, it can no longer enter a holding stage like the dormancy it went through as a seed. There is no going back. It has started into growth, and if it is to continue, there must be moisture within reach of the roots and light on the leaves.

Light and Temperature

As soon as the plants have germinated, then, they must be given light, either from fluorescent tubes or from the sun by way of a house or greenhouse window. I try to catch my seedlings even before the whole cotyledon has emerged, when the seed is still just a sprout. This is easier to determine when the seeds haven't been deeply buried. Then when I put them under lights I know they'll have the stimulation they need from the very beginning.

Temperature requirements of seedlings are not as critical as light, perhaps, but nevertheless are important. Once the plants are growing above ground, they need less warmth than is required for germination. The majority of vegetable plants that germinate most rapidly at 70°F to 80°F (21°C to 27°C) do well when grown at 60°F to 70°F (16°C to 21°C), with night temperatures about 10°F (5.5°C) lower. Cool growers like lettuce and onions will still flourish when temperatures drop to 50°F (10°C).

In a severe winter, seedlings kept in an unheated room must occasionally be moved or covered to protect them from freezing. Undesirably high temperatures may be a more common problem. Although I keep flats of germinating seeds in the warm corner (70°F to 80°F, 21°C to 27°C) where heat rises from our wood stove in the kitchen, I move the flats to our cool solar greenhouse as soon as the seedlings are up. Plants grown indoors in warm rooms put on weak, spindly, sappy growth that is difficult to manage under lights and to prepare for the transition to colder outdoor temperatures. Start seeds warm and grow seedlings cool.

There is, in fact, some evidence that judicious chilling of tomato seedlings, at just the right time, promotes earlier and heavier fruiting. Dr. S. W. Wittmer of Michigan State University found that tomato seedlings kept at temperatures of 52°F to 56°F (11°C to 13°C), starting immediately before the seed leaves opened and contin-

uing for 10 to 21 days, developed up to twice the usual number of flowers in the first cluster and often in the second. Since the position of the lowest group of flower buds on the plant is determined approximately a month to six weeks before blooming, the plant must be chilled during this early stage, before the opening of its first true leaves, in order to induce earlier flowering lower on the stem.

Other vegetable horticulturists report that peppers may also be induced to form early buds by chilling the plants in the seed-leaf stage. When I read these reports, it dawned on me that I'd been prechilling my pepper seedlings for years, though not through any planned program aimed at early bloom. The peppers are in bloom when I set them out in the garden in May, partly because I always start them extra early—in January—thus inadvertently chilling them at the right time.

Space

Soon after the seed leaves unfold, conditions often become crowded in the flat, unless you have spaced your seeds with mathematical precision. I know I usually need to thin mine, especially lettuce and cabbage. The best way to do this is not to yank the extra plants out of the soil, but to cut them off, using small embroidery or nail scissors. A considerable amount of root growth often takes place even before the green leaves go into operation, and the roots of plants you want to save may be damaged by pulling out neighboring roots.

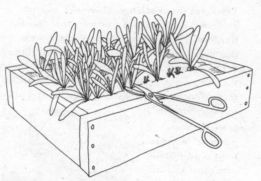

When thinning seedlings in a container, snip the tops. Pulling them can disturb the roots of nearby plants.

There is more going on in the roots of even the youngest seedling than most of us ever fully recognize. Roots not only anchor the plant and absorb nourishment, but are also responsible for maintaining the pressure that enables the plant to raise water, against the force of gravity, to its topmost leaves and stems. In many plants, roots give off exudates that help to define and sometimes defend the plant's territory. Roots of all plats synthesize many of the amino acids that control the plant's growth.

Give seedlings a little tender loving care.

Roots are examples of "being and becoming," to borrow Aristotle's phrase, used perceptively by Charles Morrow Wilson in his book Roots:

Miracles Below. Root growth is continuous. It does not stop, ever, as long as the plant lives. At the same time, root filaments are continuously dying. Root hairs, the tiny fibers that form the point of contact and exchange between the soil and the plant, constantly extend into new territory. They need moisture, but they also need air. A soil mix that is half solid matter and half pore space, with about half of the pore space filled with water, provides ideal conditions for root growth.

Superfluous seedlings are just like weeds. Thinning the seedlings, so that their leaves don't overlap, cuts down on competition for light, moisture, and nutrients and also helps to promote better circulation of air around the plant.

Transplanting into New Containers
Nancy Bubel

There comes a time shortly after your seeds have germinated when you will want to transplant them into a deeper container with a richer growing medium. Some seedlings, though, should not be moved from their original containers until you plant them in the garden (see the box in this chapter).

Why Transplant?

Those seedlings that can be transplanted benefit in several ways.

Stimulation of Feeder Roots. Some fine roots are broken in the transplanting process. As a result, a new, bushier network of feeder roots is formed. If roots are very long and thready, as in the case of onions, I often prune them to one inch or so, at the same time pruning the top growth to correspond.

Room to Grow. Crowded seedlings become weak and spindly, and the lack of air circulation around them can encourage disease. Giving them more root and leaf space promotes the health and strength of the plant and ensures that the root ball of the plant will have sufficient protective soil around it when you cut the plants apart later to set them out in the garden.

Richer Soil. Although seedlings started in soilless mixes seem to be able to subsist on liquid feedings for quite a while, I like to get my plants into a good soil mixture so that they can take advantage of the micronutrients and the beneficial interactions in the microscopic soil life, limited as these may be in the small space of a wooden flat.

Easier Selection and Evaluation. Discarding a new young green sprout is always a painful process for me. In fact, I usually keep a small container of these extra plants by the kitchen window for a week or so after transplanting, in the hope that some visitor will adopt them. Selection, nevertheless, is a necessary step in raising the best possible nursery plants. No matter how sparingly I try to sow the seeds or how carefully I thin the seedlings, I usually have more seedlings in a starting flat than I will have room for under lights or in the garden row, and so I choose, as I transplant, the seedlings that appear most vigorous.

I look for good green leaves that are symmetrical and well developed. Deformed cotyledons sometimes indicate early damage to the seed. Vegetable seeds that sprout early usually grow into vigorous plants unless they are retarded by waiting without light for the other, slower seeds to come up. There is, in fact, some evidence that early emergence is an indication of seed vigor and ultimate high yield.

Continued ➡

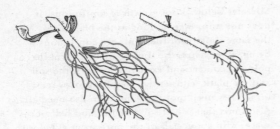

Good root growth (left) versus poor root growth (right) in a tomato seedling.

Root growth is as important as top growth in evaluating seedlings. Look for a compact, well-developed root ball. A fringe of well-branched feeder roots will do far more for the developing plant than a single, thready trailing root. It is also difficult to transplant a long, single-filament root without tangling it, bruising it, or doubling it back on itself.

When to Transplant

By the time they have developed their first true leaves, your seedlings are ready to be transplanted. It's better to get the job done before the plant has a second set of fully developed leaves, because from then on the likelihood is that the stem will be longer and more easily injured, and the roots may be lengthy and trailing and difficult to trace through the soil mix.

Some accomplished gardeners prefer to do their transplanting when the seedling is even younger, just after the cotyledons have emerged completely, and the plant is standing upright in the soil. This method does have advantages. It permits you to save almost every plant grown from expensive seed, the kind that comes ten seeds to a $2 packet, since none are lost in thinning. It puts the plants into a richer soil mix at an early age and frees your seed-planting trays and mixes for the next wave of plantings.

I have used this method occasionally for selected flower and vegetable seeds, but generally I prefer to thin my seedlings in the cotyledon stage and let them develop their first set of true leaves before transplanting. This allows me to choose the very best ones from the flat.

How to Transplant

Transplanting is more than a technique. When done well, it involves respect for the young life of the plant, even a certain empathy that can sense the thrust and direction of the tender growing roots, the reach and promise of the unfolding green leaves. The plant wants to grow. It is, you might say, programmed to grow. Having set the process in motion by planting the seeds, we now have the opportunity to give each seedling the most careful treatment so that it will continue growing smoothly on its way to producing our food.

Let's suppose that you have a flat of seedlings that you want to transplant into a larger, deeper flat of richer potting soil. The following steps will guide you through the transplanting process:

1. **Prepare the container.** Your first step will be to prepare the flat. Flats or other containers used for growing seedlings should have drainage holes in the bottom. Spread a double layer of newspaper on the bottom to keep soil from sifting through the drainage cracks. Next, arrange a one-inch layer of torn pieces of moss on top of the newspaper. This is not absolutely necessary, but in my work with young plants I've found that those planted over a torn-moss foundation develop excellent root systems. If you have no source

of fairly coarse natural moss or commercial unmilled sphagnum moss, I'd use plain potting soil, but I'd be sure to include some perlite or sand in the mix to promote drainage. Don't use a bottom layer of plain finely milled horticultural sphagnum moss. It's too fine.

Moisten the moss, pat it down flat, and fill the rest of the flat to within about one-half inch of the top with potting soil. Usually I moisten the soil thoroughly before setting the seedlings in their places, although at times I have put the seedlings into dry holes, watered them in, pulled fresh soil over the roots, and then watered again lightly. This unorthodox method has given me equally good results.

Plant Bands. Transplants may also be moved into plant bands, which should be wedged snugly together in a bowl or pan to prevent drying. To make plant bands, first take a piece of doubled newspaper about seven or eight inches long and four inches wide, and tape it around a jar two to three inches in diameter to shape it. While the paper is on the jar, fold in one end as you would a package, but don't tape it shut. Remove the plant band from the jar. Place your plant bands side by side in a pan—an old roasting pan works well—and put one-half inch of soil in the bottom of each band to anchor it in place before inserting the seedling. The folded-over bottom, if it hasn't rotted away at planting time, may simply be peeled off before setting the plant in the garden.

2. **Prick out the seedlings.** Most seed-starting gardeners soon acquire a favorite tool for this purpose. The miniature houseplant shovels that usually come as part of a set are too clumsy for most small, closely spaced seedlings. I use the slim, slightly pointed handle of an old salad fork. Wooden Popsicle sticks, pencils, and old screwdrivers can serve the same purpose. What you want is an instrument that will lift out the seedling while causing the least damage to its roots and those of its neighboring plants.

Transplanting a seedling into a new flat provides it with richer soil and more room to grow.

When seedling roots are compact enough to come up in a relatively dense cluster, it is often a good idea to water the old flat shortly before removing the seedlings from it so that enough soil will cling to the roots to help prevent transplanting shock. Seedlings raised in vermiculite, which generally falls away readily anyway, or those with long, extensive root systems, won't benefit from prewatering. By the way, it's better not to dip the roots of seedlings in water before planting them in their new location. This makes the roots cling together when, instead, they should be individually surrounded by soil.

Remove the seedlings one by one from their old quarters, planting each one before digging up another. Even a few minutes of air drying will adversely affect those delicate roots. Hold the seedlings by their first leaves rather than by the easily bruised stem, or support the root ball in your hand.

3. **Replant the seedlings.** You have several options here. You can, as suggested above, set the plants in already-moistened soil. A second option is to plant them in dry soil (over wet moss); then firm the dry soil around the seedling, and finish with a light watering to further settle the seedling.

Or, if you are putting the young plants into pots, you can tuck a wad of damp moss in the bottom, set the plant on it, half fill the pot with soil, water the plant in, and add enough additional dry soil to fill the pot.

If you're potting up a plant that has long roots, put some soil or moss in the pot and turn it on its side. Position the plant in the pot with its roots spread out on the growing medium, and gradually fill in with soil as you tilt the pot bit by bit back to its normal position. Instead of being coiled around each other, the roots will have more of their surface exposed to soil.

Plant bands, used as containers for transplants, can be made by shaping newspaper around a jar and taping the sides together.

To pot a plant with a long root, lay the pot containing some growing medium on its side and spread the roots over the medium. Gradually lift the pot to a vertical position as you fill it with growing medium.

When transplanting, set the seedlings just slightly deeper than they were in their original container. Tomatoes can be planted as deep as the root will allow. Plants that form a leafy crown, though, like lettuce and cabbage, should not have soil pulled over or into the crown. When settled into place, the first leaves of young transplants should be at about the same level as the sides of the container.

Press the soil gently but firmly over and around the roots. Roots need a certain amount of air, which should be provided by a good soil mix that is not overwatered, but they also need close and immediate contact with soil particles in order to absorb necessary nutrients.

Except for onions, leeks, and chives, which grow spears rather than spreading leaves, transplants should be spaced at least two inches apart in the flat. Three inches is better for tomatoes, cabbage, and eggplant that won't be transplanted again.

4. **Watch your seedlings.** Check for signs of wilting. If they droop, even though you've watered them well when planting them, don't pour on more water. The roots are already doing all they can. Instead, help to balance the plant's moisture supply by arranging a tent of damp newspaper over the flat or by enclosing it in a large plastic bag or covering it with a large

Continued ➡

roaster lid or other protective layer that will not rest on the plants. Keep new transplants out of direct sun for a day. I put mine back under fluorescent lights half a day after moving them, as long as they show no signs of wilting. Wilted plants should be kept shaded and cool until they perk up, which shouldn't take more than a day or two at the most.

Growing On

Nancy Bubel

Your young plants should be showing more new growth within a week after transplanting. The trick now is to keep them growing steadily until it's time to prepare them for planting outdoors.

Watering

It's important to remember, first of all, that soil in containers dries much more rapidly than the deeper, heavier soil you have in your garden. Wilting that lasts more than a day may retard the seedling, so it is best to check the flats every day to see whether they need watering. I usually water my transplants in flats about every third to fifth day, but I base the decision on the condition of the soil, not the time schedule. Short of letting the plants wilt, it is a good idea to let the soil dry out from time to time. Then the roots are stimulated to grow into the air spaces between the soil particles in search of water.

When to Water. Water is powerful stuff. It can nourish your plants, or it can kill them. Water is necessary to maintain the turgidity of the plant so that there is a continuous column of moisture in the cells. It is also indispensable to the intricate intracellular chemical processes that keep the plant growing. However, too much water ruins the soil tilth and spoils the plant. Soil that is continuously waterlogged has no air spaces to promote root growth and support helpful soil bacteria. In such a situation, other less beneficial organisms take over, rot sets in, and the roots suffer.

How do you tell when a flat needs watering? By touch, by feel, and by sight. Touch the soil. Poke your finger into a corner where it won't disturb any roots. If the soil feels powdery or dry, it needs water. When you've been handling flats for a while, you can judge by feeling the weight of the flat whether it has lost most of its water. A well-watered flat is heavier than a dry one. Other than dry soil surface, visible signs like drooping plants indicate a serious lack of water.

Water Temperature and Composition. Does water temperature and composition matter? I think it does.

Temperature. Our well water is cold, but I always use tepid water for seedlings of heat-loving plants like melons, cukes, peppers, eggplant, and globe artichokes. Water temperature is less critical for the brassicas (which include kale, cabbage, cauliflower, broccoli, and mustard), lettuce, onions, and such, which prefer a cooler environment; still, I try to temper extremely cold water to a more moderate 70°F (21°C) to avoid shocking the plant.

Chlorine. If your water is chlorinated, I'd suggest letting it stand overnight with as much surface as possible exposed to the air—in a bucket or dishpan—before using it to water seedlings. High levels of chlorine can harm plants and kill beneficial soil bacteria. Symptoms of chlorine damage include yellowing along leaf veins and, in extreme cases, curling of leaves.

Soft Water. Water that has gone through a water softener should not be used to water plants. It contains potentially toxic amounts of sodium.

Some gardeners who are good at planning ahead fill plastic jugs with water and keep them ready so that they always have room-temperature water available for their plants.

How to Water. Yes, there is more than one way to water your seedlings. Some expert seedling-raisers water their flats from the bottom. This practice supplies water quickly to the root zone and avoids excess surface dampness that can encourage damping-off disease. It is a messy business if you don't have a good setup for it, but if you have a large waterproof trough in which you can partially submerge a flat, or preferably two or three at a time, the method might be practical for you. Each flat must, of course, have drainage slits or holes in the bottom so that water can be absorbed. Leave each container of seedlings in the water until the surface of the soil starts to look dark.

Bottom watering is really more of a greenhouse refinement than it is a necessity. I've had no problem at all with top watering either seedlings or more mature plants. Watering from above carries nutrients down through the soil to the roots and makes it feasible to top-dress the plants with compost or rich soil if necessary. I often use the muddy water left from rinsing root-cellar vegetables to water my indoor seedlings.

Maintaining Humidity

Humidity—the amount of moisture in the air—is important to plants. They lose a great deal of moisture through their leaves when the air is excessively dry, as it can be in both centrally heated homes and in rooms warmed by a wood stove during cold weather. Plants suffer when humidity falls below 30 percent. They do best in the 50 to 70 percent range; higher humidity invites fungus and other disease problems. Misting plants helps, but only temporarily. The best way to increase humidity around potted seedlings is to set them in containers of damp moss or vermiculite, or in a container that holds an inch of pebbles in half an inch of water.

Potted seedlings that spend more than a month or two on this damp bed may send out roots into the moss or vermiculite. You can prevent this by setting a rack or some kind of improvised support between the damp bed and the plants.

Draping a plastic tent over the indoor garden helps to hold humidity in, although it also cuts down on air circulation. During the winter, air circulates well in a heated house, because the decrease in air pressure caused by burning fuel prompts an intake of fresh air and keeps interior air in motion.

If you notice green algae or fuzzy mold growing on the soil surface, your plants probably have more water and less air than they need. Run a small fan in

A purple coneflower seedling shows healthy growth in a flat.

the area, remove any plastic covers, and hold off on water for a few days. You might also try sprinkling some powdered charcoal over the soil surface to correct the problem.

Fertilizing

Fertilizer, like water, is a necessity that should not be overdone, or salts will accumulate in the soil to a toxic concentration. It is better to give frequent small feedings than occasional large feedings to very young seedlings. For the first three weeks, in fact, any fertilizer the seedlings receive should be half-strength rather than the full-strength mixture (1½ teaspoons to a gallon of water, for example, instead of 1 tablespoon to the gallon).

A good way to increase humidity around potted seedlings is to place them in trays containing an inch of pebbles and ½ inch of water.

When to Fertilize. Newly emerged seedlings, still in the cotyledon stage, have absorbed enough of the seed's stored nourishment to get them well off the ground. I don't fertilize my seedlings until they've begun to develop their true leaves. Seedlings growing in nutrient-free vermiculite should receive about two feedings of diluted fertilizer a week. Later, when they have been transplanted to a richer mixture containing soil and/or compost, they can go on a ten-day to two-week fertilizing schedule.

Types of Fertilizer. You can choose from a few effective fertilizers to feed your seedlings.

Fish Emulsion. I use diluted fish emulsion, a source of trace minerals as well as the three major elements, nitrogen, phosphorus, and potassium, to feed my seedling plants. The usual dilution, one tablespoon to the gallon, seems to hold true for most of the commonly sold fish-fertilizer preparations. The labels of these bottles usually become hopelessly frayed and streaked before the contents are used up, so I'd suggest jotting down the appropriate dilutions for different plants while you can still read the label.

Sprout Water. Water drained from sprouting seeds, such as that I collect from the alfalfa mung bean sprouts I raise in our kitchen, is valuable food for plants. I am convinced that sprout water helps to foster plant growth, although I can't cite any scientific studies as proof. In my one "controlled" experiment, two flats of Elite onion seedlings that I watered-in at transplanting time with sprout water grew thicker, sturdier tops than two untreated flats of the same variety in the same soil. They maintained their advantage until planting-out time. Since gibberellins (growth hormones) are known to be abundantly present in seeds, it makes sense to me to suppose that the water used to soak and rinse sprouts might well contain dissolved growth hormones.

Eggshell Water. Some gardeners save their eggshells and soak them in water until the brew develops an odor you wouldn't want in the house. (Leave them on the back porch or in the barn.) The resulting solution, diluted by an equal volume of water, is used to fertilize half-grown seedlings and other plants. Unless you're especially partial to essence of rotten egg, I'd use this on greenhouse, cold frame, and outdoor plants only, but it seems a good use of an otherwise neglected resource.

Continued ➡

Providing Light

Plants need light in order to combine airborne elements, water, and soilborne food into the raw materials of growth. There's no sense in fertilizing a plant that receives insufficient light (less than eight to ten hours a day in the case of vegetable seedlings). The plant can't make use of the food.

If, due to conditions beyond your control, your plants don't receive as much light as they should, keep the temperature low so that new growth will be less spindly. At lower temperatures, plants can tolerate less light.

Plants do a large part of their growing at night. The side away from the light adds more new tissue than the side closest to the light. This is what causes them to stretch and lean in the direction of light. Plants grown at a window should be rotated one-quarter turn each day so that no one side elongates and leans too far in any one direction.

Light

Nancy Bubel

Seedling plants may have all their other needs met—nourishment, air circulation, correct temperature, water, good growing medium, humidity—but without sufficient light, they will amount to nothing.

People are limited to using the sun's energy in indirect ways, but green plants have the ability to absorb energy from sunlight directly and to use that energy to make food they can store. Light striking a green leaf sets in motion the process of photosynthesis—the conversion, through the action of chlorophyll, of water and carbon dioxide to simple sugars and starches. Only the green parts of leaves carry on this process. White stripes, blotches, and leaf margins do not contain chlorophyll and so are not capable of photosynthesis. Red-leaved cabbage, coleus, ruby lettuce, and similar plants contain chlorophyll, but red pigment in their cells masks the green.

The Facts about Light

Light, although it may appear white to us, is actually a mixture of a rainbow of colors. A full spectrum of light includes the following color gradations, each of which has a different effect on plant life.

Green-Yellow Light. The chlorophyll in the plant reflects green-yellow light. Its effect on growth is thought to be negligible.

Orange-Red Light. This light stimulates stem and leaf growth.

Violet-Blue Light. Enzyme and respiratory processes are regulated by the violet-blue portion of the spectrum. In addition, this light encourages low, stocky growth.

Infrared (Far-Red) Light. This stimulates germination of some seeds, but can inhibit others. Its full effect still isn't completely understood.

Full-spectrum light, like sunlight, includes invisible ultraviolet rays, too. It is only the visible part of the spectrum described above, however, that provides the energy necessary for photosynthesis.

Making the Most of Natural Light

If you have a greenhouse, of course, your plants will receive the well-balanced light they need. The quality of sunlight that shines on windowsill-grown plants is the same as that in a glass-enclosed greenhouse, but the intensity is much lower, especially on cloudy and early winter days when the sun is low in the sky. You can boost the amount of light your windowsill plants receive by positioning shiny metal reflectors or boards painted with flat white paint behind the plants to bounce the light back onto their leaves. Use foil-covered cardboard, shiny cookie tins, or other household findings. The resulting arrangement may not win any interior decorating prizes, but it *does* get more light to the leaves. Try it with eggplant, a real sun and heat lover.

Another problem with raising seedlings on windowsills is that few houses have enough south-facing windows to provide a place for more than a few pots or flats. If you are limited to raising your seedlings at the window, choose the kinds of vegetables that most need an early start—main-crop tomatoes, peppers, and eggplant, for example—and sow lettuce, cabbage, and broccoli seeds in the open ground or in a cold frame. You can also raise two generations of indoor seedlings if you put your tomatoes and peppers in a cold frame about the first of May and then use your windowsills for the melons and cucumbers. Where space is limited, you can plant seeds of a hardier tomato like Sub-Arctic directly in the garden rather than raise your early tomato seedlings indoors.

Other places to put your seedlings where they will receive natural light include the following:

- A sunny corner in an outbuilding or barn; best in mid to late spring in an unheated building.
- A roof garden, protected by a plastic tent, cloches, or some other covering, which can be effective but may be cumbersome to care for. A flat, black garage roof or house roof absorbs a lot of heat.
- Cold frames.
- A solar greenhouse.

Artificial Light

A few sources of artificial light are available to choose from, but fluorescent light seems to work the best.

Sunlamps. Sunlamps might sound like a good light source for seedlings, but any gardener who tries them will find that they are death on plants. The high concentration of ultraviolet rays in the sunlamp interferes with normal plant growth.

Incandescent Light. Incandescent bulbs produce red light, which alone makes the plant grow leggy. They also produce a great deal of heat in relation to the amount of light they give off. It is not practical to try to raise seedlings under incandescent lights. In lighting supply stores, you will see special incandescent bulbs with built-in reflectors designed for raising plants. These are used as auxiliary light sources in greenhouses or for houseplants. They must always be installed in a porcelain socket, and care must be taken to prevent cold water from splashing the bulbs when watering the plants, or the blown glass may break.

Fluorescent Light. The discovery that plants do well under fluorescent light has made it possible for many more gardeners to get a good early start on the outdoor growing season and to produce plants as good as any raised in a greenhouse. Plants grown under fluorescent lights develop excellent color and stocky growth. Fluorescent light comes closer than any other artificial illumination to duplicating the color spectrum of sunlight. In varying proportions, according to the type of the bulb used, these lamps emit light from the red and blue bands of the spectrum. The tubes give off more than twice as much light per watt of power consumed as incandescent lights.

Fluorescent tubes of various kinds give off different shades of light, including warm white, cool white, natural white, and daylight. The different kinds of fluorescent powder used to coat the inside of the tube account for the range of light quality available.

Reports of results from growing plants under fluorescent light at the North Carolina State University School of Agriculture and Life Sciences and at Cornell University, as well as from experienced nonprofessional gardeners, indicate the following:

- Plants do well under a variety of tube combinations.
- Special plant-raising tubes are not necessary for starting vegetable plants.
- Best results are often obtained by mixing tube colors: For example, using one warm-white and one cool-white or daylight tube in each fixture.

Cool-white tubes emit a bright bluish white light. Warm-white tubes have a faint tan or pinkish cast. The cool-white tubes are the easiest to find, but most hardware stores will order warm-white ones for you if they don't have them in stock.

Special plant growth tubes give more blue-red than green-yellow light. Their effect on plants is mostly cosmetic: The plants look good but do not necessarily grow any better than they do under cool-white bulbs, which are the most efficient. In addition, the special-purpose fluorescent tubes are more expensive and have a shorter useful life.

In the early days of fluorescent tube experiments, incandescent lights were thought to be necessary for flowering, but it is now known that they are unnecessary. They generate so much heat that they cause rapid drying of soil and air, and they burn out much sooner than fluorescent tubes.

Using Fluorescent Light Efficiently

The effectiveness of your fluorescent lights will be influenced by the way you use and care for them.

Length of Tubes. If you are preparing a fluorescent-light setup for your plants, buy the longest tubes you can manage to fit into the space you have. Why? Light at the ends of the tubes is weaker than that in the center and falls off more as the tube ages. If my experience is any guide, you never have enough light space under the tubes. The more you have, the more plants you're tempted to start, and when they're transplanted, you'll need all the space you can muster.

Tubes are available in 12-, 18-, 24-, 36-, 48-, 72-, and 96-inch lengths. Each foot of length uses 10 watts of power. If at all possible, avoid using tubes under three feet in length; they simply don't put out as much light for the power they use. Forty-eight-inch tubes are long enough to be efficient but short enough to fit conveniently into most household arrangements.

Amount of Light. For growing seedlings, your fluorescent light setup should provide 15 to 20 watts per square foot of growing area. A single tube is, in most cases, both insufficient and inefficient, unless you have a long, skinny tray of seedlings under it. If you must use a single tube, construct a simple frame to hold foot-square mirrored tiles on both sides of the flats to reflect more light. A double row of tubes will give enough light for a flat up to about 16 inches wide,

Continued ➡

and two parallel double rows, like those attached to plant-growing carts, are even more efficient.

Types of Tube. If you are buying components and putting together your own light center or centers, you have a choice of the channel tube—a single- or double-mounted tube on a slim metal base, without a reflector—or the more common two-tube industrial-type fixture with a bent metal reflector. Channel tubes work well on shelves and undersides of cabinets, especially if surrounding surfaces are painted white to reflect more light. Industrial reflector fixtures may sometimes be obtained secondhand, but they are also widely available in lighting supply stores and from household mail-order catalogs.

High-Intensity Discharge Lamps. If price is no object, the most efficient lights you can buy today are the high-intensity discharge lamps, which—along with their fixtures—are costly to purchase but less expensive to run. There are two kinds of high-intensity discharge lamps: metal halide and high-pressure sodium. The metal halide HID lamps produce 94 lumens per watt (including ballast); cool-white fluorescent tubes produce 66 lumens per watt; and special plant-growth lights give off even less light: 37 lumens per watt for Agrilite, only 20 for Gro-Lux. The high-pressure sodium type is even more efficient (132 lumens per watt), but because its light has an unnatural yellow cast, some gardeners prefer the more natural, slightly less efficient white light of the metal halide lamps; these lose power more rapidly than sodium lamps. HID lamps cannot be mounted as close to the plant as fluorescent lights; the current limit is two feet for lights with wide-angle reflectors and six feet for those with standard mounting.

According to an industry spokesman, metal halide lamps of less than 400 watts, and those mounted in other than vertical positions, constitute a radiation hazard. Cracked bulbs can emit eye-damaging rays, much like those released by welding (according to a letter to the editor from Agrilite Company official, *Horticulture*, March 1987, p. 7).

Efficient Use. My first grow light was a 20-watt tabletop stand—a toy that helped me to get through a long northern Midwest winter when snow covered the ground until April. I raised tomato, pepper, lettuce, and pansy seedlings under that little light, and spring came after all. By then, of course, I was hooked. The following year, after moving back to Pennsylvania, to an old house full of nooks and crannies. I had a decentralized system—plant lights on every floor, from the basement to the kitchen to the bathroom, and I began raising all the seedlings we needed, racing the season to bring the earliest possible lettuce and cabbage to the table.

When we moved to our farm, we accepted a plainer, simpler house at first because we were hungry for land. In an old house that boasted not a single closet, we needed our shelves for books and canned garden produce, so I splurged on a four-shelf plant cart with four 40-watt tubes attached to three of the shelves.

I was delighted with the way my plants grew under fluorescent lights. They were stocky and green, with a special bloom to them. My only regret was that the lights consumed electric power. I tried to use them as efficiently as possible. The following tips can help you to get the most out of your lights.

1. Keep the tubes clean. Dust on the tubes decreases their efficiency.
2. Add reflecting surfaces to your setup. Use of reflecting surfaces like mirrors or aluminum foil under and around the lights gives the plants more light for the same power output.
3. Use flat white paint on shelves and reflecting boards. Flat white paint reflects more light than glossy paint.
4. Don't let the temperature drop too low. Fluorescent lamps seem to function best if the temperature doesn't fall below 50°F (10°C). Lights operated at around 40°F (4°C) may not perform as well.
5. Keep fluorescent lights turned on. To get more usable time out of the tubes, avoid turning them on and off more than absolutely necessary. A long burning time after each start is conducive to more economical operation and longer tube life. Most lamps last one to two years (10,000 to 20,000 hours) if turned on only one or two times a day. Efficiency decreases by 10 percent after a few months of use.
6. Get double use out of your lights. It is also possible, I've found, to save electric power by installing fluorescent lights for plants in spots where illumination is needed anyway. For example, we kept a fluorescent light stand on top of the refrigerator where the light it shed helped to illuminate a dark corner. We also installed a fixture on the underside of a shelf in the bathroom of our old house—light for the room and the plants. An imaginative look at your own home surroundings will no doubt suggest other possibilities.
7. Make use of the warmth of the lights. The tubes themselves give off little heat, but the ballast—the step-down transformer that makes it possible for the lights to use household current—does become warm. Most fluorescent lights have a ballast at the end of the fixture. Some recent arrangements have a remote ballast. Judicious planning of flat placement in relation to the warmer end zones of the tubes can make it possible to utilize this extra warmth to advantage, for example, in germinating seeds or starting sweet potato slips.
8. Reuse old tubes. Since light brightness decreases with the age of the tube, many gardeners routinely replace their seed-starting fluorescent tubes each year. You can still use the old tubes for general lighting purposes.

Grow-Light Setups

How you arrange your grow-light setup depends on the amount of space you have and the type of light you will be using.

When Space Is Limited. Not many of us have an entire room to devote to plants. A basement is often the most spacious area available, and that usually works very well unless furnace heat affects the plants or water is not readily at hand. Sometimes a bit of shoe horning is required to fit lights into an apartment or small home. Once, when plant space really got tight around here, I even tied a 36-inch two-tube light fixture to the underside of a piano bench so that it was suspended a few inches above a flat of plants. A crazy-looking arrangement, but it kept my tomato seedlings going until the cabbage and lettuce on the big cart were ready to graduate to the cold frame and leave room for the next wave of plants. If you're looking for ways to sneak in another light fixture or two or three, perhaps the following list will suggest some possibilities:

- Use a fluorescent study lamp you may already have.
- Install fixtures on bookshelves or storage shelves.
- Make a closet into a fluorescent light center with several tiers of lights and storage space for plant supplies.
- Install fixtures on the bottom surface of kitchen wall cabinets.
- Fit old buffet tables, radio cabinets, and other furniture with fluorescent tubes after removing interior partitions.

If your indoor seed-starting space is severely limited, you'd be wise to consider some of the following when deciding which plants to start early:

- Plants that need a long period of growth to prepare them for setting out.
- Those that are most costly or difficult to find commercially.
- Those that produce well over a long period.
- Fine-seeded plants that might get lost in the garden row.
- Vegetables you like best.

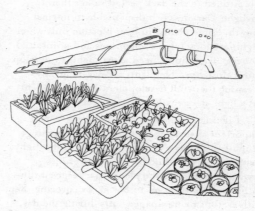

A typical grow-light setup.

Distance from Light. Seedlings, in general, need more intense light than mature plants. If they are not getting enough light, they will develop long stems before their first leaves appear. Either they're overcrowded or they are too far from the light. I keep my seedlings extremely close to the light tubes, as close as possible short of touching the leaves to the glass, and never more than three to four inches away for the first three or four weeks after germination. Then, if they are stocky and growing well, I lower them by an inch or two and continue to lower the flat placement gradually as plant height increases. Light spreads more when plants are farther from the tubes. It's also a good idea, since light at the ends of the tubes is relatively weak, to trade positions of the various flats of plants from the ends to the more fully lit center every week or so.

The shelves on my plant cart are adjustable, but I find it easier to jack up the seedling flats by using egg cartons, shallow cardboard cartons, piles of magazines, and other improvised supports that may be removed gradually as the plants grow.

Industrial reflector fixtures, the kind we once used in a basement light center, may be suspended by chains. If you leave enough slack, about 12 to 15 inches, in the chain to raise and lower the light so that it can be set at the right height for either small seedlings or taller plants, you'll have a good adjustable setup.

The Hours of Light

In my experience, seedlings do very well with 16 hours of light a day, the usual recommended time. I have made do with 12-hour light exposures under limited light space. The lights burned day and night, and the seedlings took turns

basking under them for 12 hours at a time. The tomatoes got a bit spindly, but most plants grew surprisingly well on this schedule. Sixteen hours is much better, though. Even 18 hours is not too long, but it's longer than necessary for most seedlings. Lighting time should not be increased above 18 hours. Too much light will disturb a plant, just as too much water or fertilizer will.

Providing Plants with Darkness

The light a plant receives, you remember, makes it possible for the leaves to manufacture starches and sugars, the components of growth. But a period of darkness is necessary for the plants to put these new compounds to use. Plants don't "rest" at night. They digest and grow. Both processes go more smoothly when night temperatures are 5°F to 10°F (3°C to 5.5°C) lower than daytime levels. The ideal ranges are 70°F to 75°F (21°C to 24°C) during the day and 55°F to 65°F (13°C to 18°C) at night.

Scientists have concluded that plants are actually attuned to the dark period rather than to daylight. Darkness is indispensable to normal growth. Some plants, in fact, blossom only when nights are long (chrysanthemums and poinsettia). Others, like onions, need short nights to develop fully. Most vegetable plants are day-neutral, meaning their full development isn't dependent on a light-dark rhythm of any certain pattern.

Turning off the lights at night, then, is as important as turning them on in the morning. When I shifted two batches of plants under lights that were on continuously, I was careful to provide "night" for the plants that received illumination from 8 p.m. to 8 a.m. by covering them with cartons or newspaper tents during the day.

Problems

Nancy Bubel

Fortunately, seedling plants seem to thrive within a rather generous range of conditions. If your seedlings show compact growth, plenty of good green leaves, short internodes between leaves, and slow but steady growth, all is well.

Occasionally, though, excess or deficiency in one or another of the young plant's life requirements will cause trouble. If you interpret the problem correctly and treat it promptly, you have a good chance of saving the seedlings.

Signs of Trouble

Troubled plants give clues. What should you look for? Check for the following signs.

Leaf Curl. A plant whose leaves curl under, especially in bright light, may be suffering from over-fertilization.

Solution. Naturally, you'll decrease the amount of fertilizer your plants receive if you notice symptoms of overfeeding. If the problem is severe, you might need to replant the seedlings in another flat of fresh potting soil. Be sure to leach out the extra fertilizer salts from the soil in the old flat before reusing it.

Yellowing of Lower Leaves. This is sometimes a sign of overfeeding, although it can also indicate magnesium deficiency.

Solution. Follow the same procedures as for leaf curl above.

Dropping of Leaves. Along with plant stunting, the loss of leaves may be caused by exposure of the plant to leakage of partly consumed gas from the stove or water heater. You can test for gas leaks by buying yourself a bouquet of carnations. If the

flower petals curl upward, gas has probably escaped into the air. Tomatoes will droop in the presence of gas, too. Natural gases like butane and propane don't seem to hurt plants, but manufactured gas does.

Solution. Repair the leak.

Leggy Plants. plants with long, often weak stems that have large spaces between the leaves growing from the stem may be suffering from anyone of the following conditions: insufficient light, excessively high temperature, and crowding of plants.

Solution. A leggy plant can't be reshaped to conform to the stocky, well-grown ideal form, but there are steps you can take to promote more normal growth from this point on. First, of course, remedy the cause: Supply more light, lower the temperature, or thin the plants. Plants kept at a window might need some auxiliary evening light on cloudy days. Then, if at all possible, transplant leggy seedlings. The root pruning and general mild trauma of being moved will set back their growth a bit. Set the plant deeper in the new container.

Bud Drop. Particularly with pepper seedlings, bud drop may occur if the air is excessively dry.

Solution. Try setting the flat in a tray containing pebbles and water, or mist the blossoms with a fine spray of water at least once a day.

Leaf Discoloration. Discolored leaves usually indicate a nutrient deficiency.

Pale Leaves. In seedlings that receive sufficient light, pale leaves are a sign of nitrogen deficiency. Tomato seedlings that are severely deficient in nitrogen develop a deep purple veining, especially prominent on the undersides of the leaves.

Reddish Purple Undersides. A plant deficient in phosphorus will have a reddish purple color on the undersides of its leaves. In addition, the plant will often be stunted, with thin, fibrous stems. Soil that is too acid may contribute to the unavailable of phosphorus.

Bronze or Brown Leaf Edges. Leaf edges that have turned bronze or brown may reveal a plant in need of potassium. Brown leaf edges may also appear on plants that are overwatered.

Solution. The differences among the various symptoms of deficiency are not always clear cut, especially in young plants. Your best bet, if you do notice leaf discoloration that can't be accounted for otherwise, is—in the short run—to give the plant a dose of fertilizer that contains trace minerals. In the long run, include some compost in your next soil mixture, or transplant the ailing plants to a medium that contains compost.

Discolored Roots. This is often the result of a buildup of excess fertilizer salts in the soil. Either the plant has been overfed, or overheating the soil in an attempt to sterilize it has released a high concentration of soluble salts into the soil. Water-logged roots often turn dark and may have an unpleasant odor.

Solution. Replant the seedlings in fresh soil if possible. Your second choice would be to flood

and drain the flats several times in an attempt to leach out the toxic salts. If the flat is waterlogged, either provide better drainage or replant seedlings in better aerated and drier soil.

Mold. If you see mold on the surface of the soil, it indicates poor drainage, insufficient soil aeration, possible overfertilization, and/or a lack of air circulation.

Solution. Remedy the cause and treat the symptom by scratching some powdered charcoal into the soil surface.

Insect Damage. Damage on seedling plants grown indoors most probably means that conditions are not ideal for the plant.

Solution. Control pest damage on plants grown indoors.

Damping-off. When damping-off occurs, you don't get much warning. Your first sign that the problem has hit your new plants is the total collapse of a few seedlings; the green leaves are still intact, but the stem has characteristically withered away right at soil level. Young seedlings are the most vulnerable.

Solution. Once a seedling has been attacked by the damping-off fungus (actually, there is a complex of microorganisms, any of which may cause the trouble) it can't be revived. The lifeline between root and stem has been cut off. However, you can try to prevent the problem by following these practices:

- Maintain good air circulation around seedlings by keeping the soil level high in the growing containers and thinning seedlings to avoid overcrowding.
- Avoid overwatering.
- Sow seeds in a sterile medium such as finely milled sphagnum moss or vermiculite.
- Presoak seeds in a small amount of water containing one or two crushed garlic cloves—an ancient practice that still makes sense, now that we know more about garlic's fungicidal properties. You can also treat seedlings with a garlic spray. (Blend one clove of garlic with one quart of water and strain.)
- Sprays of chamomile or nettle tea are sometimes used on seedlings to help prevent damping-off.

It is often possible to save the remainder of a flat of seedlings if only a few have died. Immediately move the flat to a more open area; make sure that it is well drained; and remove the affected seedlings. There is no sense in transplanting the others—you'd just transfer the disease to new soil. You can save the flats though. Dry them out and ventilate them. I've salvaged several

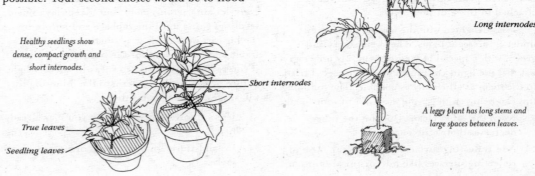

Healthy seedlings show dense, compact growth and short internodes.

Short internodes

True leaves

Seedling leaves

Long internodes

A leggy plant has long stems and large spaces between leaves.

Continued ➡

such flats and used them to produce early crops after all.

Skimpy Root Growth. This won't be evident, of course, until you transplant the seedlings. It may be caused by any one or more of the following factors:

- poor drainage
- low soil fertility
- concentration of excess fertilizer salts
- temperature too low
- insufficient air space in soil mixture

Failure to Sprout. If your seeds don't even sprout, the cause may be any one or more of the following factors:

- temperature too low or too high
- soil that was allowed to dry out
- seeds too deeply planted
- top watering that floated seeds off
- seeds that were old and poorly stored
- insufficient contact between seeds and soil
- toxic substances in soil
- damping-off disease
- lack of light for those seeds that need light in order to germinate, or lack of darkness for certain seeds, mostly flowers but also a few vegetables, that need this condition.

Hardening-Off Seedlings
Barbara Ellis

Indoors, you can control the light, water, temperature, and humidity to which your seedlings are exposed. However, seedlings need to be ready to withstand the more rigorous conditions that prevail in your garden—brighter light, wider extremes of temperature, as well as wind and rain—before they can be transplanted successfully. Sun, wind, and cold temperatures can kill succulent seedlings very quickly, or damage them enough to set them back for weeks. So, seedlings grown indoors need to be hardened off before they are moved to the garden permanently. Hardening off is a technique used to gradually introduce seedlings to their new environment. It also helps toughen them up by thickening succulent leaves and causing them to build food reserves.

Begin the process of hardening off your seedlings about a week before they're to be transplanted to the garden. If you have a cold frame, you can use it to graduate your seedlings from their cloistered conditions indoors.

1. **Slow Down Plant Growth.** Start hardening off your plants by watering them less often during the last week before transplanting and allowing them to dry out slightly between waterings. Also, don't feed them during their final week indoors. Another way to slow down growth is to keep temperatures on the cool side—if possible, a few degrees lower than what the plants have become accustomed to thus far. These steps will help thicken leaf surfaces and build food reserves.

2. **Blocking Out.** If you are growing any plants in flats, a few days before transplanting, use a knife to cut between the seedlings—a crisscross pattern from left to right and from back to front will suffice. Each plant should end up centered in a cube of soil, but leave them in the flat and otherwise undisturbed. Blocking out helps promote a well-branched root system and also cuts roots that would be broken during transplanting. Give blocked

seedlings two or three days to begin their recovery before moving them to the garden.

3. **Acclimate Plants to the Garden.** After a week of cooler temperatures, as well as reduced watering and feeding, your seedlings are ready to be gradually exposed to the conditions outdoors. Start by exposing them to filtered sun outdoors on the north side of your house, in the shade of a bush, or under some other improvised shelter. Choose a spot that is protected from wind, which can dry seedlings out very quickly and cause them to wilt. Gusty spring winds can also break stems and whip seedlings around enough to damage roots. The first day, move them outdoors for about an hour in the morning or afternoon and gradually increase the exposure until at the end of a week or ten days they can withstand a full day of direct sun.

You'll need to keep a sharp watch on your seedlings during this process. They will need watering nearly every day because sun and wind cause the shallow flats to dry out quickly. Keep the soil moist enough to avoid wilting.

There comes a day in early spring when your seedlings have been hardened off and you're ready to plant them in the garden. Although clear, breezy spring days are beautiful, they're not the best kind for transplanting seedlings. Sun and wind cause seedlings to loose large quantities of water, which newly disturbed root systems have difficulty replacing. It's a far better idea to wait and transplant seedlings at the beginning of a spell of warm, damp, cloudy weather. That way, they'll have a chance to recover and put on root growth before having to withstand sun and wind.

Try not to rush seedlings into the gardens if cold weather still threatens unless you're prepared to cover them nightly with boxes or other protective devices when the weather turns cool. Jumping the average date of last spring frost pays off some years; in others, late spring frosts take their toll of newly transplanted seedlings. Although many plants grow well in cool temperatures, others are sensitive to cold and won't begin growing until the weather (and the soil) warms up. If you can't bear to wait, be sure to hold back a few of each kind of plant as insurance against a late cold snap.

Transplanting is a stressful operation for plants, and the more you can do to ease the stress a plant suffers in being put out in the garden, the sooner it will be off and growing. Here are some tips to make your transplanting day a success.

- Dig a generous hole for each seedling so that there is ample space for the plant's roots.
- If you're planting an entire bed of plants, work plenty of compost into the soil before planting, or add a handful to each hole as you plant, mix it in, and cover with ordinary garden soil before planting.
- Water seedlings before you transplant and try to keep as much soil around the plants' roots as possible so they will not dry out. If the potting mix falls away from the roots, it's a good idea to dip them in a slurry of thick, muddy water to be sure the roots stay moist.
- As you place each plant in its hole, take time to make sure the roots fan out evenly in all directions. They shouldn't double back on each other or stick up toward the top of the hole.
- Water the seedlings as you go, rather than waiting and watering after you've finished transplanting. If the soil is unusually dry, moisten it slightly before planting, because

dry soil can quickly pull the water out of tender roots and damage them.

- To settle seedlings in their holes, fill the soil with loose, well-tilled soil, sprinkle at least a quart of water on each transplant, and gently firm the soil to eliminate large air pockets, so the roots will be in contact with the soil and there are no root-drying air spaces. A shallow, saucerlike depression will help catch rain and direct it toward the roots.
- As a general rule, set seedlings in the soil at the same depth they were growing in their pots. Tomatoes are an exception to this rule; if planted in a shallow trench on their sides with the top one or two sets of leaves above ground, the stems will grow roots and the plants will be less leggy.

Planting in Peat Pots

Seedlings grown in peat pots can be planted pot and all: That's why they are such a good choice for difficult-to-transplant species. However, keep in mind that the rim of a peat pot that sticks out of the soil will draw moisture away from the plant's roots. If this happens, the pot can become so dry it becomes a barrier that roots can't penetrate. When transplanting seedlings in peat pots, tear off the top inch or so of the pots so the remaining portion will be entirely underground. Cut slits down the sides to help roots penetrate them. Some gardeners prefer to gently tear away the entire pot if roots haven't already grown through. If you've started your seedlings in peat pellets encased in plastic netting, cut the netting off before planting. Then plant as you would any other seedling.

Don't Rush to Transplant

Although every spring gardeners rush to plant their gardens, late spring frosts and cool soil conditions can take their toll with many new plants. Many plants grow well in cool temperatures—cole crops such as cabbage, broccoli, and cauliflower, as well as peas, lettuce, spinach, and many annuals and perennials; however, others are very sensitive to cold, which can check growth or kill plants. When you begin the hardening-off process, be sure to bring your plants in each night. Seedlings that thrive in cool weather can be left out all night once they are fully hardened, but have boxes ready to cover them if frost threatens. Warm-weather plants such as tomatoes, peppers, eggplant, melons, and tender annuals and perennials also should be left out all night the last day or so of the hardening process. However, it's often best with these plants to wait an extra few days after the average last frost date before transplanting so that all danger of frost has passed and the soil has warmed.

Plant Protection

The transplanting operation doesn't end when the last seedling is in place in the garden, however. Sun and wind can still wreak havoc with your seedlings for the first week or so after transplanting, and freak, late spring frosts can reduce your carefully tended plants to mush. Be sure to keep them well watered and, if possible, screen them from heavy wind. Pale yellow leaves indicate sunscald. Cover afflicted plants promptly with screens, plastic sheeting, or anything else that will

Continued ➡

provide shade. Then gradually increase exposure to sun over several days.

Outdoor Sowing

Many kinds of seeds will germinate and grow perfectly well if sown outdoors in the garden. Vegetables such as beans, beets, corn, carrots, melons, peas, radishes, and zucchini are all direct-seeded. Annuals such as sweet alyssum, California poppies, cosmos, marigolds, nasturtiums, sweet peas, and zinnias, as well as many perennials, can also be sown outdoors where they are to grow. Plants that are difficult to transplant, including poppies, corn, cucumbers, parsley, melons, and dill, often are best sown outdoors.

Scheduling

Deciding when to sow seeds is as important for outdoor sowing as it is when you're starting seeds indoors. Check seed packets for recommended sowing dates and any other planting tips that will help improve your results. Plants that grow best when temperatures are cool, such as sweet peas, beets, carrots, and radishes, for example, can be sown as early as you can work the soil in spring. Other species, including marigolds, zinnias, squash, melons, and beans, are less tolerant of cool temperatures and should be sown after danger of frost has passed. Seed of many perennials and hardy annuals such as larkspur, poppies, and cleome, can be sown outdoors in late fall for germination the following spring.

Soil Preparation

The key to outdoor sowing success is providing seeds with a well-prepared seedbed. Seeds sown outdoors need rich, well-tilled soil in which to germinate. Before tilling in spring, make sure the soil is ready to work by squeezing a handful of it. If it forms a dense ball that doesn't crumble readily, the soil is too wet to work. Tilling wet soil can damage its structure, so if the soil is wet, wait a few days and test it again. If the soil is ready to work, use a shovel or rototiller to dig or turn it to a depth of 6 to 8 inches. Then spread a layer of compost or leaf mold over the bed and work it into the top 2 or 3 inches of soil. Compost will increase the amount of water held in the soil and will help prevent crusting after heavy rain. If you prepared your soil in the fall, you may need only to fluff up the top inch or so of soil before seeding.

When planning your garden and preparing your soil, you might consider the benefits of raised beds. Raised beds improve drainage and aeration, provide a warmer germinating area for plants, and prevent soil compaction because you can reach the center of the bed from either side and consequently don't need to walk where you planted. Raised beds can be edged by wooden boards, bricks, cement blocks, stones, or railroad ties. Structured sides make gardening easier on you because you can sit on the sides when you work on the bed rather than stooping and bending. When you are planning the dimensions of your bed, make it 3 to 5 feet wide so that you can easily reach across from different sides to work on it.

Sowing

In a vegetable garden or cut-flower garden, you can sow seeds in rows marked off with string or a board. (Rows running north-south take best advantage of the sun.) In ornamental plantings, you'll want to arrange seeds in a more free-form pattern. Whatever you do, check the seed packets

for recommended spacing and sow seeds thinly so the seedlings won't become crowded. Spacing the seeds properly from the start will reduce thinning chores later. After sowing, firm the soil in place around the seeds and water with a fine spray. Keep the bed weeded at least until seedlings can fend for themselves. Spring-sown seeds should be kept evenly moist until seedlings are well on their way. Autumn-sown annuals such as larkspur and cornflowers should be watered once when they are sown and can be left to germinate the following spring.

There are several methods for sowing seeds. Large seeds are often sown individually by hand. Smaller seeds can be planted in rows, scattered in broad strips, or broadcast over a large area.

Conventional Rows

Vegetable gardens have been traditionally planted in straight rows marked off with string or a board. After marking the row, make narrow V-shaped grooves or trenches, called furrows, for planting. Use the corner of a hoe to make furrows for large seeds or a garden tool handle to make them for smaller seeds. The rule of thumb is to sow seeds to a depth equal to 2 or 3 times the diameter of the seed. Sometimes, however, it's hard to apply this guideline with oddly shaped seeds, so check seed packets for planting depths. Packet information will also indicate if a plant requires light or darkness for germination. It's important to plant the seeds at the correct depth; they may dry out if sown too close to the surface or not be strong enough to break through the soil if sown too deeply. You can plant seeds a bit deeper in the summer if the soil is hot and dry to protect the seeds from the sun.

For small seeds, sow directly from the packet by tapping it and dropping the seeds out one at a time or drop them in pinches from your fingers. You might want to use old spice shakers to spread seeds evenly. Large seeds can be placed individually.

When you complete a row, you can pinch together soil from the sides of the furrow to cover the seed or work along the row with a hoe and tap soil from the sides of the furrow to cover the seed. Don't forget to mark each row so you will know what crop is there. Water lightly, and keep the seedbed evenly moist until germination occurs.

Seed Tapes. If you really want to ensure correct seed spacing, you can use easy-to-handle seed tapes. Many companies offer both flower and vegetable seeds that are prespaced on tape, so you just trim the tape to fit the length of the furrow. Plant the tape at the correct depth and the tape will eventually dissolve. You can find seed tapes in

well-stocked garden supply centers or through mail-order catalogs.

Broadcasting

Broadcasting is an easy method that's best for single-crop beds or broad strips of plants instead of conventional rows. It works best with fast-growing, small-seeded plants such as carrots, turnip greens, radishes, beets, and leaf lettuce. It is especially effective for sowing cover crops and lawn grasses. This method of scattering seeds lets you sow large areas quickly, but frequent weeding the first three weeks and some thinning or transplanting might be necessary.

Sling seeds outward in even motions the full width of the bed, letting seeds scatter in midair so they fall evenly on the soil. It's a bit difficult to sprinkle the small seeds evenly at first, so you might want to practice. To prevent seeds from sticking together, you can mix them with fine sand, dry coffee grounds, or dry soil and spread the mixture. White play sand, the type used in children's sand boxes, is especially useful for this purpose, because it lets you see where you've already sown. Using a mixture also makes it easier to handle very fine seeds. Next, gently press the seeds into the ground with the back of a hoe. Seeds need close contact with the soil so they can take up water necessary for germination. Gently tamp the seedbed again with a hoe and water with a gentle spray from a watering can or sprinkler. Very fine seeds do not need to be covered at all. Just rub soil between your hands, letting it lightly cover seeds, or mist with water. It's important to keep the seedbed moist until the seedlings poke up. This is fairly easy in early spring, but will be harder as the days get longer and hotter in summer.

Hill Planting

Hill planting is a good way to provide space for vines like watermelon, squash, melons, pumpkins, and cucumbers because it gives room for them to spread. It also provides them with the rich, loamy soil they require for best performance.

To build a hill, form a 6- to 12-inch-high mound of loamy, fertile soil 1 to 1½ feet square. Amend the soil with plenty of organic matter such as compost to make sure it is porous and loose. Flatten the mound on the top so water won't erode it during heavy rains. A light covering of mulch, such as salt hay, will also help prevent rains from washing the mound away before plant roots bind it together.

Plant six to eight seeds in the mound at the correct depth, spacing them along the tops and sides. Later you can thin out your plants, leaving the two or three strongest. If the soil is poor or if you'd like to provide an especially rich environment for your plants, dig a hole 12 inches deep and 12 inches square before forming each hill. Fill it with well-rotted compost, manure, or other organic material. Then build a mound on top.

Spacing and Thinning

There are many factors to consider when determining seed spacing. In the end, you have to use your judgment and experience. You can start out spacing according to packet directions, observe how much certain plants expand as they grow, and decide if you can afford to tighten up your spacing next year. If you space too closely, they'll have to compete with neighboring plants for water and nutrients. If you space too far apart, you waste valuable garden space and leave room open for weeds.

Continued ➡

Climate is a factor to consider. Wider spacing is recommended for planting in unusually dry climates, for example, because plant roots need to search farther for water. If your soil is not very fertile, heavy feeders also will benefit from wider spacing.

If your growing seedlings need more elbow room than you have allowed, you'll need to thin them. Overcrowded conditions result in competition for moisture and nutrients, which leads to weak, unhealthy plants. Try to thin as early as you can, because the longer you wait, the harder it is to disentangle roots of neighboring plants. You may have to go back and thin again as the plants grow. With many vegetable crops such as carrots, lettuce, and spinach, the thinnings are a blessing in disguise, for they make tasty additions to summer salads.

To thin, you can clip the seedling with scissors at the soil level, thus avoiding the problem of damaging entangled roots of the plants you are leaving in the row. Or you can simply use one hand to hold down the good seedlings and the other to gently pull out the extra seedling. This is easier to do when the soil is moist. You can also use a putty knife to carefully dig up the unwanted seedlings. Plants removed in this manner often can be moved elsewhere in the garden or given away.

Intensive Spacing

One way to maximize yields is to use intensive spacing. This technique involves spacing plants closer together than normally recommended on seed packets. Plants are spaced equal distances from each other so that when they mature, the leaves just touch and the entire bed is covered with foliage. Although vegetables planted in this manner will yield less per plant, because of the efficient use of space, overall yield is much higher. Intensive spacing also serves to shade the soil and help hold moisture in the soil.

Intensive Spacing for Vegetables

Here are some broad guidelines for intensive spacing. The best spacing guide is, of course, experience and knowledge of your particular climate and soil conditions. Carefully observe how well plants grow at different spacings and use that as your guideline.

Crop	Spacing (in.)	Crop	Spacing (in.)
Beans	4-9	Okra	12-18
Beets	2-6	Onions, bulb type	4-6
Broccoli	15-18	Onions, bunching	2-3
Brussels sprouts	15-18	Parsley	4-6
Cabbage	15-18	Peas	2-6
Carrots	2-3	Peppers	12-15
Cauliflower	15-18	Potatoes	10-12
Chinese cabbage	10-12	Pumpkins	24-36
Collards	12-15	Radishes	2-3
Corn	18	Spinach	4-6
Cucumbers	18-36	Squash	24-36
Eggplant	18-24	Sweet potatoes	10-12
Kale	15-18	Swiss chard	18-24
Leeks	2-6	Tomatoes	18-24
Lettuce, leaf	6-9	Turnips	4-6
Melons	24-36		

Raised beds are an essential component of intensive spacing. They provide the deep, rich, well-prepared soil required to encourage plant roots to grow down, rather than sideways to compete with neighboring plants.

As with conventionally spaced plantings, your experience and judgment are the best guidelines. Pay attention to factors like shading, companion planting, and planting combinations. For example, lettuce is a perfect choice for intensive spacing because it benefits from some additional shade. To use underground space efficiently, it's a good idea to alternate rows of leaf and root crops such as spinach and onions.

Saving Seed
Barbara Ellis

Although many gardeners depend on the annual winter deluge of seed and nursery catalogs for the seed they sow each year, there are at least two good reasons to save your own seed from year to year. First, by saving seed you can harvest, store, and replant seed of a cherished plant year after year. This is especially important when saving seed of antique or discontinued cultivars that may no longer be offered by seed companies. Second, saving seeds is the easiest way to experiment with plant breeding. You can cross-pollinate two different plants to create your own hybrid, then harvest, save, grow, and evaluate the offspring of your cross.

HARVESTING SEED

Before harvesttime rolls around, you'll need to take time to learn about and observe the plants whose seed you'd like to collect and save. The more you know about the plants from which you will be harvesting seed, the better your chances of success.

FLOWERING

If you know approximately when flowering occurs, you'll find it much easier to prepare for the harvest. You should know if the plant is an annual (produces seed in the single year of its life), a biennial (produces seed only in its second and final year of life), or a perennial (produces seed each year).

FERTILIZATION

If you wish to collect pure seed to preserve a species or special cultivar, try to find out if it is easily cross-fertilized by other species or cultivars. If so, cover the immature flower before it opens with a lightweight paper bag or other covering to prevent pollen from other plants from pollinating the flower. Then make sure the flower is pollinated with its own pollen or that from another bloom of the same type to ensure pure seed.

SEED

You'll also need to know how long it takes for the seed to ripen and the manner in which it is normally disseminated. Tiny seed can be easily lost during collection, so simply arch a seed head or pod into an envelope or other container, tap a few times to dislodge loose seed, and remove the seed head from the stem—taking seed head and seed together for cleaning afterward. Some plants dispel their seed from pods that abruptly pop or shatter and scatter the seed in all directions. For these, place an envelope around the pod or seed head before it is ripe and ready to discharge its seed. Remove the seed pod and seed from the stem once it has ripened. Seed that is difficult to harvest can often be collected easily if entire branches are removed from the plant, placed into a large paper bag, and thrashed back and forth by shaking the bag. If the seed is mature the thrashing action will dislodge it readily. Also, most plants will signal the approach of seed maturation by losing flower petals, splitting pods or capsules, and changing the color of fruit, pods, or seeds. Be aware of these signals and use them in timing the harvest.

Keep in mind that many improved cultivars sold through catalogs don't come true from seed. They may be hybrids created by crossing specific parents or color forms that must be propagated vegetatively by means such as division or cuttings.

Top 10 Tips for Storing Seeds
Vicki Mattern

If you have leftover seeds or aren't ready to plant your seeds when they arrive, you'll need to store them properly to ensure good germination.

1. Think dry and cool no matter where you store seed. Humidity and warmth shorten a seed's shelf life.

2. The refrigerator is generally the best place to store seeds.

3. Keep seed packets in plastic food storage bags, plastic film canisters, Mason jars with tight-fitting lids, or glass canisters with gasketed lids.

4. Keep your seed-storage containers well away from the freezer section of your refrigerator.

5. To keep seeds dry, wrap 2 heaping tablespoons of powdered milk in 4 layers of facial tissue, then put the milk packet inside the storage container with the seed packets. or add a packet of silica gel. Replace every 6 months.

6. Store each year's seeds together and date them. Because most seeds last about 3 years, you'll know at a glance which container of seeds might be past its prime when planting season comes.

7. When you're ready to plant, remove seed containers from the refrigerator and keep them closed until the seeds warm to room temperature. Otherwise, moisture in the air will condense on the seeds, causing them to clump together.

8. If you're gathering and saving seeds from your own plants, spread the seeds on newspaper and let them air dry for about a week. Write seed names on the newspaper so there's no mix-up. Pack the air-dried seeds in small paper packets or envelopes, and label with plant name, date, and other pertinent information. Remember, if you want to save your own seeds, you'll need to plant open-pollinated varieties. They'll come back true; hybrids won't.

9. Or dry saved seeds on paper towels. They'll stick to the towels when dry, so roll them up right in the towel to store them. When you're ready to plant, just tear off bits of the towel, one seed at a time, and plant seed and towel right in the soil.

10. Even if you're organized, methodical, and careful about storing seeds, accept the fact that some seeds just won't germinate the following year. Home gardeners will find that stored sweet corn and parsnip seeds, in particular, have low germination rates, and other seeds will only remain viable for a year or two.

Continued ➡

Feel free to experiment with these plants, but don't be disappointed at the results.

Regardless of when the harvest takes place, there are several important points to keep in mind:

- Collect seed only from healthy plants.
- Harvest on a dry, calm, sunny day.
- Use a separate container for each different type of seed.
- Clearly label each collection container with the name of the plant and the collection date.
- If you are collecting seed of wildflowers or other native plants, don't be guilty of eliminating a unique species from its native habitat. Be sure you leave ample seed behind for the continuation of the species or variety.

CLEANING SEED

Before storing seed, remove all debris that might introduce contamination during storage.

Separate seed from fleshy fruit by gently working the fruit over a fine mesh screen with your fingers, and then rinsing the resulting mixture with water. The spray will force the fruit through the mesh, leaving the seed behind.

Remove fine chaff from seed by gently dropping it onto a large sheet of paper, from a height of 4 or 5 feet. When this task is performed on a slightly breezy day or in the presence of a fan, the light chaff will be removed in the air and the heavier seed will fall onto the collection paper.

Separate fine seed from large chaff and debris by gently working the combination through a fine screen; the fine seed will fall onto the collection paper and the chaff and debris will be held behind.

DRYING SEED

Seed must be absolutely dry during storage or it might germinate prematurely. Moist conditions will also encourage mold. Air drying on newspaper in a dry, airy location works well, but often requires one to two full weeks to accomplish. This time frame can be reduced to three or four days if the seed is dried on newspaper located 6 to 12 inches below a light bulb; the air temperature around the seed should be no more than 90°F, otherwise the seed may be burned or injured. Oven drying is not recommended, since rapid drying usually results in cracking of the seed coat.

After drying, add a small amount of silica gel (equal in weight to the seed) to the storage container. The silica gel is a desiccant, and will remove additional moisture that might be introduced during storage. You can substitute powdered milk wrapped in a paper towel, but it must be replaced about every six to eight weeks.

SEED STORAGE

Seed that has been cleaned and dried should be placed in a clean, dry container. Glass jars with screw tops work well; use small jars (baby food, medicine, or spice jars are ideal) for a single type of seed, or larger jars for holding envelopes of several different types. Remember to properly label each envelope or container.

Place the containers in the refrigerator (32° to 41°F). As long as the seed remains dry, it will maintain its viability. Most seed will survive for at least a full year, and some will last for several to many years.

Upon removal from storage, allow seed to adjust to room temperatures for a few days before sowing.

Seed Projects
Roger Yepsen

If your seed packets tend to stray, and you habitually tear off the name of the plant, there is a tidy way to put whatever you're after right at your fingertips. Buy ring binder bags, place the packets in them, and use a three-ring binder to organize the packets as you see fit—by planting date, or by the type of plant. So, the tabs in such a notebook might be labeled by the weeks of the year, alerting you to the seeds that are to be started now; or, you might want to gather all the lettuces, the tomatoes, and the peppers in one section. The bags are available from office supply firms.

You can also store seed packets in three-ring binder photo sleeves. Choose sleeves that hold 3-by-5 or 5-by-7 photos, fold over the seed packet top, and insert the packets into the sleeve pockets.

Seeds are tiny, and all the more difficult to store and organize because of it. Slip seed packets into resealable plastic ring-binder pages and come up with a system for putting them in order.

Make Your Own Growing Mixes

What You'll Need

Seed-Starting Mix
>   1 part milled sphagnum moss
>   2 parts vermiculite
>   2 parts perlite

Potting Mix with Compost
>   1 part finished compost, screened through a mesh of ¼-inch hardware cloth
>   1 part vermiculite

Potting Mix without Compost
>   1 part commercial potting soil
>   1 part milled sphagnum moss

1 part vermiculite

Just about anything costs you more if you buy it in small containers, and that goes for bagged seed-starting and potting mixes. Instead, come up with your own custom blends for both in large quantities, and store them neatly in plastic garbage cans rather than floppy plastic bags that tend to spill. The one thing you don't want to do is include ordinary garden soil in your recipes, with its weed seeds, disease organisms, fungi, and insects. Not only that, but most soils are just plain too dense to get plants off to an optimal start.

To combine the ingredients easily, use a plastic tub of the sort sold for mixing cement. Or for larger volumes, spread the measured amounts of each ingredient on a tarp spread over the driveway or patio. Choose a relatively windless day to work. Even so, the dust may fly, and you may want to occasionally mist the medium with a fine spray from a hose. Use a dull hoe or a metal rake (tines up) to mix thoroughly. Then place the mixture in a new plastic garbage can—use one for seed-starting mix, and a larger one for potting mix. Keep a plastic bucket on hand in which to moisten small amounts of mix by stirring in water. Allow enough time to ensure that the medium in the bucket is completely moistened. Dry mix may dehydrate young seedlings, killing them. If you do a lot of seed starting and potting over a short period each spring, you may want to have several buckets of soaking mix on hand so that you don't feel tempted to rush the moistening process.

There are any number of recipes for seed-starting and potting mixes, so feel free to adapt the suggestions for mixes on this page. Be sure to include compost only if it is thoroughly processed, rather than half-degenerated plant matter.

Put the Damper on Damping-Off

Damping-off is a fungal disease that can rapidly lay waste to entire flats of vulnerable young seedlings. You'll know it by the afflicted stems, which may take on a water-soaked appearance or turn thin and wiry at the soil line. The unsupported seedlings topple and die. As a preventive, moisten the seed-starting medium with a mild homemade fungicide. To 1 gallon of water, stir in 1 tablespoon of clove oil (available at supermarkets and drugstores, as well as

---

Continued ➡

by mail order) and a drop or two of dishwashing soap. Among various powerfully scented herbs and spices, clove has been found to be particularly effective against two principal soil-borne pathogens.

You also can buy a fungal control agent formulated to prevent damping-off, marketed as SoilGard. It contains dormant spores of a beneficial fungus. When mixed with water, the fungus comes to life and puts off an antibiotic substance. Another product, Mycostop, harnesses a beneficial bacterium that controls or suppresses damping-off and other soil-borne troublemakers as it grows among the seedlings' roots. It too can be mixed with water for use as a soil drench.

An additional step that takes little time is to scatter a dusting of milled sphagnum moss over the soil surface. This thin layer will help keep seedling stems drier, suppressing disease, and the moss also contributes a certain antimicrobial effect. Note that this product is marketed in small bags—don't confuse it with baled peat moss. To make it easier to apply a thin layer, you can give the moss a spin in a blender to reduce the particles to a dust.

Save with Soil Blocks

Instead of buying dozens of little pots or plug trays in which to seed next year's garden, you can skip the containers altogether by using a mold to make soil blocks. These blocks are nothing more than cubes of planting mix. They encourage a healthily branching root system that sets up plants for a happy transition to the garden. (Because the blocks are relatively shallow, however, they aren't the way to go with deep growers like carrots and beets.) The steps for converting damp mixture into planting blocks are easy enough, once you buy a blocker. These devices are available from nurseries and mail-order supply companies. You'll also need trays in which to place the blocks.

You can buy blockers in two sizes, with the smaller model making many little blocks that eventually will fit nicely within a square hole in the larger blocks, which look something like square doughnuts. This system avoids disturbing the seedlings as they're moved to a larger container.

1. Stir up a batch of planting medium that will keep its shape once popped out of the blocker. Johnny's Selected Seeds (www.johnnyseeds.com) sells a mix that will work well. Here's a recipe for making your own:

    - 2 parts peat moss, screened through a mesh of ¼-inch hardware cloth
    - 1 part vermiculite
    - 1 part finished compost, also screened through hardware cloth

    Do your mixing in a flat-bottomed container that's wide enough to allow you to press the blocker into the medium; a plastic tub sold for mixing concrete is ideal, and a clean wheelbarrow will also work. Make sure you allow enough time for the medium to fully absorb the water you add to moisten the mix.

2. Press the blocker into the medium so that the squares are filled. Then push the handle to eject the row of blocks into the tray.

3. Plant seed in the conventional way.

4. You can water the blocks from the top as you would seedlings in pots or flats. Use a misting nozzle or fine rosette on a watering can to avoid causing the block to come apart. The blocks will become sturdier as roots spread through them, but to avoid the risk of crumbling them, you can deliver water from the bottom up with capillary matting.

A Plug-In Welcome Mat for Seedlings

At a cost approaching $100, a thermostatically controlled seedling mat may seem like a luxury if you're accustomed to using the secondhand heat from the top of a furnace or water heater. But assuming you start vegetables and flowers from seed each spring, you'll appreciate the convenience—and the dependable results, especially for seeds that are tricky to germinate. And because plants get off to a quicker start, they may be less vulnerable to damping-off. Small-scale greenhouses and specialty growers have discovered that seedling mats create ideal conditions, meaning less work, less reseeding, and less babying of weak plants.

A less expensive alternative is to snake a length of heating cable under the flats to provide gentle bottom heating. The cables cost roughly a dollar a foot; you can expect to pay more than that for shorter cables, and less for lengthy ones. Adding a thermostat substantially increases the price.

Heat Helps Heaps

Supplying bottom heat can make a startling difference when starting seeds. Have a look at how long it took lettuce seeds to come to life at various soil temperatures, as reported in *Knott's Handbook for Vegetable Growers*, a resource for commercial market gardeners. If you're patient—fine. But if you're anxious for that first bowl of garden-grown salad, a heat cable or seedling mat makes good sense.

77°F—2 days	50°F—7 days
68°F—3 days	41°F—15 days
59°F—4 days	32°F—49 days

Presprout For Better Results

To increase the percentage of seeds that will make it as plants, presprout them rather than trusting that garden conditions will be favorable. The germinated seeds will get off to a faster start once they reach soil or planting medium. The system works particularly well for plants that need warmth to get under way, including cukes, melons, pumpkins, and squash. Here's what you do:

1. Dampen a sheet of paper towel that's been folded over once or twice to make a blotter.

2. Arrange the seeds over the surface without allowing them to touch.

3. Place a single damp sheet of towel on top of the seeds, press down to help hold them in place, then slowly roll up the toweling.

4. Place the rolled toweling in a plastic bag. Leave the bag open and put it in a warm place, out of direct sunlight. Take a peek at the seeds each day to determine when they've begun to sprout.

5. Plant the presprouted seeds in potting mix and place them under fluorescent lights or in sunlight.

Cold Frame, Warm Plants

A cold frame might better be termed a warm frame, its purpose being to make use of heat stored in the earth as well as solar energy. You can use it at both ends of the gardening year, when the weather isn't quite so hospitable.

A variety of mail-order frame kits are on the market, typically with polycarbonate glazing and framing of cedar, redwood, or metal. If you are reasonably handy, you can assemble the frames with just a couple of hand tools.

BUILDING A WARM FRAME

A warm frame made of cedar will hold up better than those made with other woods, and there's no need to reply on preservative chemicals. (Exterior-grade plywood works well, and it slows you to make

the sides and back from a single piece rather than with two boards each.) If you are having a sheet of double-walled polycarbonate glazing cut to size, you can determine the overall dimensions of the frame. Or, to make use of an old storm window, adjust the length and width of the frame to suit it. Just make sure that the frame has a front-to-back slope to take better advantage of the sun.

1. Cut the pieces as shown, choosing the dimensions to suit the storm window, if you are using one, and your own needs. Typically, a frame will be about 3 feet deep by 6 feet wide. The front should be roughly 12 inches lower than the back, with the sides sloped accordingly, to pitch the glazing toward the sun. The front, sides, and back are from ¾-inch-thick stock; the cleats are from 2 x 4s ripped in two pieces roughly 1½ inches square.

2. Five cleats add rigidity to the frame. Assemble the back by driving 1¾-inch screws through the two back pieces into the back cleats. (For these and all screws used in the project, drill pilot holes.)

3. In the same way, attach the front piece to the front cleats.

4. Assemble the frame by attaching the sides to the cleats, front and back. Note that the top inside edge of the back will be slightly above the sloping sides. Using a hand plane, bevel this edge to the angle of the sides.

5. Install the storm window using three exterior door hinges with the screws provided, attaching them to the outside of the back and underside of the window. Or, if you are using a sheet of polycarbonate, you can keep it in place with bungee cords, attached to screw eyes driven into the sides, front, and back, as shown in the detail. Keep the front two cords loose enough that a block of wood can be inserted under the front edge of the sheet to vent the frame.

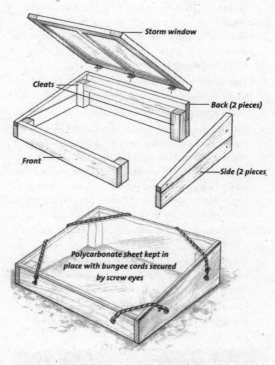

An old storm window can serve again as the lid of a cold frame. Or you can use a sheet of polycarbonate glazing.

Labels on illustration: Storm window; Cleats; Back (2 pieces); Front; Side (2 pieces); Polycarbonate sheet kept in place with bungee cords secured by screw eyes

When a Seed's Battery Runs Down

If you start plants from seed, it's good to know how long the seed of each vegetable will remain viable. Otherwise, you risk planting a row from which nothing—except weeds—will appear. While come seeds can sit around for a few years without suffering

Continued ➡

a greatly reduced germination rate, cucumbers among them, others have to be purchased each year, such as parsnips. That's especially important if you have a modest-size garden and find yourself with leftover seed at the end of each growing season. It's also apt to be a factor if you save seed from your plants and can easily collect enough to last for the next several years.

Although it's possible to give general longevity figures for vegetable seeds you may find that your seeds are considerably more or less viable because of the way in which they're stored. Ideally, seeds should be kept cool and dry and out of direct sunlight. Jars with screw-on lids are a good choice. Place them in the refrigerator, if you have the space. For legumes, however, it's best to allow the seeds to breathe by storing them in a paper or cloth bag.

Iron-Clad Seeds

Read before you reap. Catalogs, plant labels, and seed packets often alert you to any diseases to which a particular variety is resistant. The more common afflictions may be listed as abbreviations, such as TMV for tobacco mosaic virus and VFF for verticillium and fusarium wilt. Resistance to a disease means that the plant is less likely to show symptoms; it does not certify that the plant is immune. Plant varieties also may offer resistance to problems other than diseases, such as tip burn in lettuce and the effect of cold on tomatoes.

Seed Tape Simplified

This pleasant off-season gardening project is one that's suited to doing along with kids. Using an icing decorating bag and a few household materials, you can manufacture your own seed tapes with the varieties (and spacing) of your choosing. Look for decorating bags at craft stores.

What You'll Need

> Yardstick or other straightedge
> Newspaper (black-and-white sections only) or newsprint
> Wheat Flour
> Disposable icing decorator bag (or heavy-duty sandwich bag)
> Seeds
> Plastic food storage bags

1. Using the straightedge as a guide, tear off strips of newspaper about 1½ inches wide.

2. Make a paste of flour and water.

3. Fill the decorating bag or sandwich bag with paste, and cut off the very tip to make a hole. With the yardstick establishing the spacing given on the seed packets, make generous dabs of paste by squeezing the bag. (A decorating bag coupler and a star-shaped decorating tip will make the job even easier.)

4. Place one seed on each dab, tapping so that it will stay put.

5. When the paste has completely dried, gently fold or roll the strip and place it in a plastic bag along with the seed packet for identification.

6. Once it's time to plant, place the seed tape at the depth recommended on the seed packet.

Seed-Starting Glossary

Amendment Material that improves soil condition and aids plant growth.

Bolt To produce flowers and seed prematurely, usually due to hot weather.

Cotyledon Also called seed leaves. The leaf (or leaves) present in the dormant seed that unfolds as a seed germinates. Cotyledons often look different than the leaves that follow them. In seeds such as beans, they contain stored nutrients.

Damping-off A disease caused by various fungi that results in seedling stems that shrivel and collapse at soil level.

Direct-seed To sow seeds outdoors in garden soil.

Dormancy A state of reduced biochemical activity that persists until certain conditions occur that trigger germination.

Hardening off Allowing young plants to adapt slowly to wind, temperature, and light conditions outside by increasing the amount of time the plants spend outdoor each day.

Scarification Nicking or wearing down hard seed coats to encourage germination.

Seed A plant embryo and its supply of nutrients, often surrounded by a protective seed coat.

Seed germination The beginning of growth of a seed.

Seedling A young plant grown from seed. Commonly, plants grown from seeds are termed seedlings until they are first transplanted.

Stratification Exposing seeds to a cool (35° to 40°F), moist period to break dormancy.

Viable Capable of germinating.

BUYING PLANTS

Picking Perfect Plants

Fern Marshall Bradley

Do you feel overwhelmed when you page through garden catalogs or walk down endless aisles of plants at a nursery? How do you choose? We asked the experts for hints on how to get the most for your money and the best choices for your garden.

Hints For Healthy Bedding Plants

Don't make the assumption that all of the flats in the sea of plants at your garden center are equal. Inspecting plants before you buy can help you get the best quality for your money. Terry Humfeld, the executive director of the Professional Plant Growers Association, offers these four tips to help gardeners select top-quality bedding plants:

1. "Plants should have sturdy stems," Humfeld says. "Avoid any that are leggy or limp or whose leaves are curled, mottled, and yellowed. They may be infested by pests." Common pest problems for bedding plants include spider mites and aphids. Infested plants will have a harder time rebounding after being transplanted, and they may bring pest problems into your garden.

2. Stay away from plants whose lower leaves are turning yellow. It could be a sign that the flats were allowed to get too dry. Some roots may be permanently damaged.

3. Choose plants in packs that allow a larger root system and don't dry out quickly. These larger packs translate to 24 or 48 plants per flat. Flats may have as many as 72 cells per pack—an economical way to buy for large plantings. If you do choose flats with small cells, be sure to plant these plants immediately, before the roots become matted in the little cells.

4. Plants that aren't yet in bloom make a better transition to the garden than those in flower. When you have a choice, buy plants that aren't blooming. Sometimes that's not possible. Humfeld says, "If you can bring yourself to do it, pinch off the flowers and flower buds." Although most bedding plants are bred to flower in their packs, the plants will appreciate a chance to gain vegetative growth rather than flowering in their first days in the garden.

Study Your Seed Catalogs

While an impulse buy of a seed packet from a store rack might inspire you to grow a new crop or a flashy flower you've never tried before, you're best off relying on mail-order buying for seed. "Don't be carried away by the glossy package in the store," says Simon Crawford, a technical services specialist for the PanAmerican Seed Company in Illinois. "Use the store to give you some ideas, but get some catalogs. Compare prices. Do a bit of research. It's worth doing and it's quite fun!" Crawford also offers the following words to the wise:

Check the date on the packet. If you do decide to buy off the rack instead of from a catalog, be sure the current year is stamped somewhere on the envelope. If it isn't, don't risk buying it. Fresh seed germinates more reliably than old seed.

Don't confuse pelleted seed with untreated seed. Pelleted seed is coated to make the seeds easier to handle and sow. Pelleted seed packets look bulky but may not contain that many seeds. Read catalogs or seed packets carefully so you'll know whether you're buying pelleted seed, or you may feel disappointed when you receive fewer seeds than expected.

Research disease resistance. If your zinnias or other favorites always suffer from powdery mildew but you don't want to give up growing them, check for a mildew-resistant cultivar. Compare several catalog offerings to find the best choices.

Know what special labels mean. Cultivars that carry the All-America Selections Winner label have received an award for excellence after testing at trial grounds throughout the United States and Canada. This doesn't always mean that it will be the best cultivar for your garden. To receive the All-America Selections Winner label, a cultivar must perform well around the entire country; you may find that other cultivars perform better in your particular region.

Seed packets may also carry other marks of quality, such as Burpee's "Gold Ribbon Selection." This mark indicates a professional-grade product, generally a high-priced hybrid, in a small packet for home gardeners.

Crawford's bottom-line advice is: "Any seed you buy should give good results if you follow the instructions that you're given. If it doesn't, you need to complain."

Buy Bulbs Big

What makes a bounteous bulb? "'Bigger is better' is the rule," says Sally Ferguson, the director of the

Continued →

Buying Healthy Annuals

If you're buying annual flowers and vegetables, get your garden off to a good start by selecting the healthiest plants you can find. Use these pointers to make your choice:

- Look for a sales display where the plants are well cared for. Plants subjected to hot, sunny sidewalks, allowed to wilt frequently, and watered unevenly are never a bargain.

- Look at the entire group of plants being offered for sale. If some seem to be in poor health, shop somewhere else. Those that look healthy today may be diseased tomorrow.

- Look for plants with deep green leaves and bushy, compact growth. Pale overall color indicates a need for nutrients, which is easy to correct. However, distinct yellow streaks or brown leaf spots indicate presence of disease.

- Choose plants whose buds aren't yet open. If plants are already in flower, pinch off the blossoms when you set them out. Pinching will help direct the plant's energy into growing roots, so it will be better able to support more flowers and fruit later in the season.

- Don't buy by the yard. Bigger isn't necessarily better. Overgrown plants that have long outgrown their pots probably have roots circling the stem and have already had their growth severely checked.

- Buy plants that are clearly labeled, unless you're game for a gamble. Labels help you choose the cultivars you'd like to grow, and therefore flower color, bloom size, and height.

- Finally, always look carefully for signs of insect infestations or disease. Don't buy plants that show evidence of whiteflies, aphids, spider mites, or other pests. Disease symptoms to look for include rotted lesions on the stem or leaves and yellowed or spotted foliage.

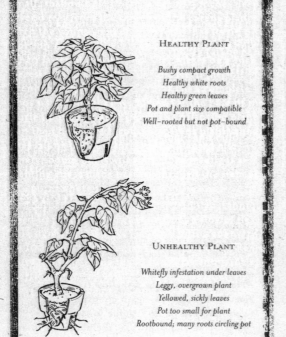

HEALTHY PLANT

Bushy compact growth
Healthy white roots
Healthy green leaves
Pot and plant size compatible
Well-rooted but not pot-bound

UNHEALTHY PLANT

Whitefly infestation under leaves
Leggy, overgrown plant
Yellowed, sickly leaves
Pot too small for plant
Rootbound; many roots circling pot

Netherlands Flower Bulb Information Center in New York. "You get what you pay for." That means that the biggest bulbs will produce the biggest flowers, and they'll generally be priced accordingly. So if you want the best show possible, buy the biggest bulbs you can afford. Ferguson also notes that many people will mistakenly reject tulip bulbs with a torn tunic (the papery skin that covers them). "A healthy tulip without a tunic will grow as well as a healthy tulip with a tunic," she says. In fact, some research shows that removing the tunic may encourage rooting after the bulb is planted. You should avoid bulbs that are soft, mushy, or spotted with disease.

Have a Root Peer

Most gardeners look carefully at the leaves before buying a plant. But Andrew Schuerger, Ph.D., a senior plant pathologist at The Land Pavilion, an agricultural display at Epcot Center in Florida, says it's important to inspect the plant much more closely, not only to determine its general vigor but also to make sure it's not going to carry disease home to your garden.

"First," says Dr. Schuerger, "look at the base of the stem. If you see any rot, any soft black lesions, or other suspicious areas, don't buy that plant."

Bonnie Lee Appleton, Ph.D., an associate professor and extension horticulturist at Virginia Polytechnic Institute and State University, also suggests that gardeners inspect the roots of potential purchases. "I drive the retailers crazy, but I suggest that people take containers off of trees and shrubs before buying," Dr. Appleton says. Sometimes, bareroot nursery stock is potted just before sale. The only way to distinguish this newly potted stock from true container-grown stock is by checking roots. The roots of a bareroot plant will have less branching and be less well-developed than the roots of a container-grown plant. Why is this important? If you buy a bareroot plant thinking it was container-grown, you may not give it the extra care it needs after planting, and you could end up with a dead plant, explains Dr. Appleton.

To check roots without harming the plant, turn it upside down while holding the soil in place and supporting the base of the stem between two fingers. Now tap gently on the side of the plant's container. In most cases, the container will slip off enough for you to examine the root structure. Also check for root disease problems. "If the roots are nice and white and you don't see any rotted splotches, you can buy the plant," says Dr. Schuerger. "But sometimes I've pulled perfectly healthy-looking plants out, and their roots have been completely rotten." Verlin Schaefer, an assistant mail-order manager for Stark Brothers Nurseries and Orchards Company in Missouri, cautions gardeners that big doesn't always mean best when it comes to fruit-tree roots. "Look for a balance between the size of the root system and the size of the tree," says Schaefer. A 4- to 5-foot-tall, standard-size young fruit tree should have 10- to 12-inch-long roots. They should be well-formed with multiple roots coming out from the taproot. If you cut through the tip of a root, the inside tissue should be white. Brown or dirty-looking tissue is diseased.

The roots of dwarf trees will be different—shorter and fibrous, like the roots of an ornamental shrub—so don't be alarmed if the roots of your small trees don't measure up to those of the big ones. They aren't supposed to. According to Schaefer, the roots of dwarf fruit trees may be only 25 percent of the size of the roots of a standard-size tree. Semidwarfs will be about 50 to 75 percent of standard size.

Steer Clear of Wild-Collected Plants

Native plants can be a wonderful choice for your yard and garden. But when you buy these plants,

---

make sure they are nursery-grown, warns Kris Medic Thomas, a landscape manager and arborist for the city of Columbus, Ohio. Many nurseries can legally dig plants from the wild—a practice that disturbs delicately balanced ecosystems. In addition, Thomas has found that the wild-collected plants often have a slim chance of survival.

Bob McCartney, a co-owner of Woodlanders, a South Carolina nursery that specializes in southeastern native plants, concurs that nursery-grown plants have a much better chance in the garden. He warns that certain species are more likely to be wild-collected than others are. "I know of no one propagating trilliums [*Trillium* spp.]," says McCartney. Others that fall into this category are native orchids such as lady's slipper orchids (*Cypripedium* spp.) and yellow fringed orchid (*Habenaria ciliaris*) and some of the native lilies (*Lilium superbum*, *L. grayi*, and *L. philadelphicum*). Others to question are native azaleas (*Rhododendron* spp.).

"One way to tell if a plant is nursery-grown is to inspect the root ball," Thomas says. "Most are planted in a clay-type soil, so the root balls will hold together well. The dirt surrounding the plants should be free of rocks and other natural debris." McCartney adds that nursery-propagated plants generally are uniform in size. "If you see odd, mixed sizes, oddly shaped plants, and native soil next to the roots, the plants probably were dug from the wild," he says.

A Check-Up For Mail-Order Arrivals

Hurray! Your plants have just arrived in the mail! Lavish your energy and excitement on your plants to make sure they're in good health. "Unpack them immediately, and set them upright," says Bob McCartney, a co-owner of Woodlanders, a South Carolina nursery that specializes in southeastern native plants. Then examine them as explained below. Be sure the soil or roots are moist. If not, water right away.

Look for flexible, green stems. Check for live wood on dormant deciduous plants by scratching the bark slightly with your fingernail. You should see a layer of green wood underneath the bark you peeled up. If you can't find green wood, you need to let the nursery know immediately.

Be sure that plants in leaf aren't wilted. If they are, soak the pot or roots in water and mist the foliage. McCartney even suggests placing the plants in a closed shower or garment bag or other location where you can fashion a cool, humid environment until the leaves become turgid again. If they don't recover, contact the shipper right away.

Examine bulbs. They should be firm and free of mold.

If you can't plant right away, store the plants in a cool place such as a basement, a garage, or the shady side of your house. If the ground is frozen when plants arrive, pot them in containers and put them in a cool, dark place until the ground thaws. Water only enough to prevent them from drying out. You don't want to encourage topgrowth.

Plant Swapping and Shopping

Fern Marshall Bradley

Once your site is prepared, it's time for one of the most exciting parts of perennial gardening—getting the plants!

Shopping for perennials, whether at garden centers or through mail-order catalogs, can be almost intoxicating. There's such a range of gorgeous plants to try, and it's so tempting to try them all. But while your first impulse may be to

Continued ➡

buy all your plants, don't overlook other sources. One of the delights of perennial gardening is swapping and sharing plants with other gardeners.

Sources of Free Plants

Gift plants. Gift plants can be a great way to enliven your landscape without spending a lot of cash. So if a plant you yearn for is growing in a friend or neighbor's garden, look it up and find out how it's propagated. Then ask boldly. Chances are she'll give you a stem cutting right now or a bit of the plant the next time it's divided.

Impassioned gardeners love to share the plants they care for. Some will whip a trowel out of their back pocket, separate a healthy chunk of the plant, and bestow it on you with a radiant smile on the slightest provocation. A friend and mentor like this is a budding perennial gardener's dream. Of course, gift plants can also become a problem if they carry disease, insect, or weed problems.

Garden clubs. Local garden club swaps or sales are also good places to pick up great deals on plants that thrive in your area. To find them, check newspaper ads or bulletin boards at nurseries and your local extension office.

The woods? You may be tempted to look to local woodlands or wild areas for free plants. *Don't do it.* When you wild-collect, you may be disturbing or destroying rare or endangered plants. You may also be collecting the seeds or roots of invasive weeds or be collecting plants that are diseased.

Plant societies. As you gain experience with perennials, you may want to become a member of a local, national, or international plant society. Many focus on a specific kind of perennial, like the Iris Society. For a reasonable membership fee, members have access to meetings, workshops, lectures, newsletters, seed exchanges, plant swaps and sales, experienced members who share information and plants, and/or garden tours.

Buying Perennials

When you shop for perennials, always take a plant list with you. Think of plant shopping like grocery shopping—go by your list or you may not end up with the ingredients you need for the results you want.

Once you have a plant list, you have more decisions to make. What size plants should you buy? And should you buy plants at local nurseries and garden centers, or via mail order from specialty nurseries? There are no universal answers to these two questions. But there are some guidelines that will help you make good choices.

Plant-buying strategies. Perennials are sold in three basic sizes: large, medium, and small. Price ranges tend to correspond to plant size.

Creating a new perennial bed or border from scratch can be an expensive proposition if you start with blooming-size plants, each of which can cost from $5 to $10 (or far more for certain desirable cultivars). You'll need to balance your need for immediate results or special cultivars against your need to stay within a budget.

Shopping in person. Buying locally offers two advantages: You can look before you buy, and you can ask questions face to face. Choose a garden center or nursery where the plants look well cared for and are clearly labeled. The staff should have answers for your questions or find answers quickly.

When you buy a perennial, what you're really looking for is a great set of roots. Tops are nice, too, but without the roots, they're just window dressing.

When you select plants, start by taking an overall look at the plants you're considering. They should have good leaf color and be perky, not thirsty and wilted. Yellowed or missing lower leaves suggest the plants haven't been cared for properly and may not do well for you. Check the undersides of leaves for signs of disease or insects. Reject any plants that don't meet the grade.

Also look at the soil. It should be moist, not dry or soggy. Potted plants should not have a gap between the soil and the pot (a gap indicates the soil has been allowed to dry out too much in the past).

Carefully turn plants out of their pots to check the roots. The roots should be white and firm. They should hold the rootball together, but they should not be circling around. Reject plants with too few or overgrown roots.

When everything else has checked out favorably, choose plants with flowerbuds rather than open flowers, especially if the plant has a limited season of bloom.

Shopping by mail. You can catalog-shop no matter where you live. It does require a leap of faith to buy plants sight unseen, but the wealth of choices offered by mail order is nearly impossible to match with local sources. Not all suppliers are equally reliable. Here are some tips to help you evaluate potential suppliers by their catalogs.

- Plant descriptions should include the botanical name. Some plants have several common names. You need to mail-order by botanical name to ensure that you get the precise plants you want.

- Be suspect of photos with bright colors that don't look natural: They've probably been artificially enhanced. Also be wary of catalogs with fanciful illustrations or grandiose claims.

- Outrageously cheap prices often mean small or poorly rooted plants—or no service.

- Check the replacement policy. Some nurseries will replace plants that die or do poorly for up to a year, perhaps asking you to pay the postage on the replacements. Others only guarantee that the plants are in good condition when shipped.

Gardening magazines also carry advertisements from mail-order companies. Another good way to find reputable mail-order sources is to ask other gardeners who their favorites are.

Order early to avoid disappointment, or call and check availability before you order. Indicate whether you want substitutions or a refund if a particular plant isn't available.

Specify a shipping date that suits your climate and schedule. Have your plants arrive on

Thursday or Friday if you plan to plant them on Saturday.

Open and examine your plants as soon as they arrive. Report to the supplier immediately. It's much easier to get replacements for plants that die a few months after planting if you've made your complaints promptly.

Buying Bare Root

Roger Yepsen

It may seem cruel and unusual to ship plants long distances without a speck of soil around their roots. But there are clear advantages to transporting them that way, for both the grower and you. You just need to make sure that the plants are treated with extra care as soon as you receive them.

Bare-Root Bonuses

Here are some advantages that bare-root stock has over potted-up plants.

- You stand to pay less, often saving from 40 to 70 percent, because these plants aren't as expensive to produce and ship.

- You can find hundreds of rare and unusual varieties not available in pots.

- Bare-root plants may adapt more quickly to your particular soil.

- The plants often arrive with more-extensive root systems.

Coddle Your Bare-Root Babies

Bare-root perennials,

To gently support tomatoes and other plants vulnerable to breaking and chafing, use strips of well-washed cotton.

shrubs, and trees look awfully vulnerable when you pick them up at the nursery or take them out of a mail-order carton. In fact, they are vulnerable and need your immediate attention, unlike plants parked in generous-size pots.

To make sure they survive in good shape, you have to take action as soon as they arrive at your doorstep. If you can't promptly pop them in the garden, there are a couple of temporary stopgap measures.

- The simplest strategy, good for a couple of days, is to allow the plants to remain in the packing material. Open the carton and pour a bit of water around any roots that feel dry to the touch. Then keep the carton in a cool, dry place until you can get into the garden.

- Pot them up. Use any old plastic pots you have about the place, and set the plants in a mixture of good soil, compost, and peat moss. Don't forget to tuck identification tags in each pot. If there is just one label for a number of plants of the same type, this is the time to make more—before you forget what's what in the rush of spring planting. Keep the pots in dappled shade where you can water them conveniently.

- Heel them in. Make a shallow trench in a partly shaded area, again choosing a handy spot that will be no trouble to visit with a hose or watering can. Lay the plants on their sides with the roots in the trench, and cover them with a mixture of good soil, compost,

Continued ➔

and peat moss. Make sure each plant or trench is identified with a label.

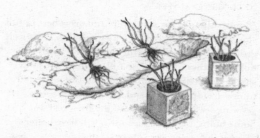

Plants with bare roots are easy to transplant but require prompt attention once you receive them. For a makeshift holding area, place their root systems in a shallow trench, fill with soil, and water as necessary.

Potting Up Purchased Plants

Barbara Pleasant

When growing your own seedlings indoors, the most difficult thinning is the last one, when you must decide which of two seedlings will be allowed to remain. Many greenhouse growers skip the last thinning, intentionally leaving two or three seedlings in a container so the consumer will see a fuller, healthier-looking specimen. When shopping for plants, it is not unusual to see pots containing several basil, parsley, or impatiens plants. Multiples also are common with cutting-grown flowers, such as hibiscus or geranium, in which three cuttings have been rooted and left to grow in one small pot. If you provide such crowded plants with roomier quarters and appropriate after-care, you can save money and end up with many more plants.

Look for pots in which the main stems of multiple plants are spaced at least 1 inch apart—a good sign that each plant will emerge from repotting with an ample supply of roots. Thoroughly water the plants, and then get ready to repot or plant them. Work in a shady place. Have clean pots and potting soil ready, or ready-to-plant space in your garden. You also will need three necessary pieces of equipment.

- A plastic fork from which the two outside prongs are broken off, leaving two prongs. This is the perfect tool for separating intertwined roots from adjoining plants.

- A sharp knife, which you can use to cut apart the roots of plants with thin, fibrous roots, such as impatiens and begonias.

- One large cardboard box with its top flaps removed, which you can set on its side and use as a temporary shade chamber for newly divided seedlings or cuttings that are moved into pots. If you are planting divided seedlings directly in the garden, be ready to cover them with small boxes or flowerpots for 3 to 5 days.

Separating Crowded Seedlings

Before you begin, pinch off any flowers or leggy stems. Pinching back the growing tips will encourage the plants to develop new branches, and reduce demands made upon injured or traumatized roots.

Remove crowded seedlings from their containers by pushing them out from the bottom, or use scissors to slice through the sides of thin plastic pots. Don't touch the main stems any more than necessary, and lay the mass of plants on its side. Use a fork or knife to separate the plants, and immediately pot them up or set them in the garden. Water thoroughly, and then provide the

divided plants with some type of shade. Don't worry that they will suffer because they are deprived of light. Instead, they will be free to concentrate on growing new roots, the plant part most needed in the days immediately following division.

PLANTING

Introduction to Planting

Jeff Cox

One of the best ways to ensure that plants will grow well is to do a good job planting them. Preparing planting areas thoroughly, so roots will quickly extend into the soil surrounding the planting holes, is time well spent.

Know Your Site

Before you dig that planting hole or plant those seeds, try to make a good match between the plant and its environment. Getting to know your soil and growing conditions—and using that knowledge to pick the right plants—is just as important as knowing the best planting techniques. So before you plant:

- Take a close look at your soil. Is it red clay or deep loam? Waterlogged or sandy and dry? Is it acid or alkaline?

- Check the amount of sunlight your site gets. Is it full sun all day or just afternoon sun? Is the shade dappled through the small, shifting leaves of a birch, or deep and heavy, as beneath a fir? A tomato plant must have six hours of direct sunlight daily for good fruit set, but the same amount of sun fades and burns ferns.

- Know your hardiness zone. Your local nurseries and garden centers generally stock only plants that are hardy in your area. But if you do any mail-order buying, knowing your zone will save you money and disappointment.

- Learn the growth rate and size of your plants. Choose a site where they won't cause problems or overgrow your garden. This is especially important for permanent plants such as trees and shrubs.

- Be aware of seasonal conditions. Is the spot you picked sheltered by a wall or windbreak, or does it get the full blast of winter winds? Is it low-lying and prone to late-spring frost?

Get Your Soil in Shape

If you set plants into poorly drained soil, the roots are likely to rot and die. If you plant seeds into poorly drained soil, they may never even germinate. Before you plant a pumpkin seed or a pine tree, be sure that your soil drains well. For very wet areas, your best bet may be to grow plants that can tolerate wet conditions.

If you till the soil for a vegetable garden or dig a hole for a tree when the soil is too wet, you'll destroy the soil's structure. Your soil will compact, causing water to run off or lie in puddles rather than penetrate. Without air, root growth suffers. If your soil is too wet, let it dry before planting.

Pick up a handful of soil and squeeze it. If it crumbles, it's perfect for planting. But if it forms a muddy ball, the soil is too wet to be worked.

Most plants pay less attention to pH than gardeners do. If your soil is fertile and well drained and not extremely acid or alkaline, most plants will do just fine. But a number of plants are more demanding. Acid-loving azaleas and blueberries, for instance, will do poorly in soil that's alkaline. If you don't know the soil pH in an area you plan to plant, it's a good idea to test it.

Enrich flower and vegetable beds with lots of aged manure, compost, or leaf mold before planting.

Seedlings

There comes a day in early spring when your seedlings have been hardened off or your bedding plants have all been purchased and you're ready to plant them in the garden. Although clear, breezy spring days are beautiful, they're not the best kind for transplanting seedlings. Sun and wind cause seedlings to lose large quantities of water, which newly disturbed root systems have difficulty replacing. It's a far better idea to wait and transplant seedlings at the beginning of a spell of warm, damp, cloudy weather. That way, they'll have a chance to recover and put on root growth before having to withstand sun and wind.

Try not to rush seedlings into the garden if cold weather still threatens, unless you're prepared to cover them nightly with boxes or other protective devices when the weather turns cool. Jumping the average date of last spring frost pays off some years; in others, late spring frosts take their toll on newly transplanted seedlings. Although many plants grow well in cool temperatures, others are sensitive to cold and won't begin growing until the weather (and the soil) warms up. If you can't bear to wait, be sure to hold back a few of each kind of plant as insurance against a late cold snap.

Ring Around the Transplant

A little ring in the soil around new transplants creates a small basin to collect water so it goes right down to the roots. "Use your finger to draw a 4-inch-diameter circle around transplants in the soil," says Bibby Moore, a registered horticultural therapist from North Carolina. The rings don't need to be deep; just draw in the soil with enough pressure to make an indentation as you do when you write in the sand at the beach. This is also very helpful when applying fish emulsion. To fertilize, Moore waters thoroughly first, then applies 2 cups of fish emulsion per transplant. The emulsion is diluted at the rate of 1 tablespoon of emulsion per 1 gallon of water.

Transplanting is a stressful operation for plants, and the more you can do to ease the stress that a plant suffers in being put out in the garden, the sooner it will be off and growing. Here are some tips to make your transplanting day a success:

- Dig a generous hole for each seedling so there is ample space for the plant's roots.

- If you're planting an entire bed of plants, work plenty of compost into the soil before planting, or add a handful to each hole as you plant, mix

Continued →

it in, and cover with ordinary garden soil before planting.

- Water seedlings before you transplant, and try to keep as much soil around the plants' roots as possible so they will not dry out. If the potting mix falls away from the roots, it's a good idea to dip them in a slurry of thick, muddy water to be sure the roots stay moist.

- As you place each plant in its hole, take time to make sure the roots fan out evenly in all directions. They shouldn't double back on each other or stick up toward the top of the hole.

- When transplanting seedlings in peat pots, tear off the top inch or so of the pot so the remaining portion will be entirely underground. Cut slits down the sides to help roots penetrate them. Some gardeners prefer to gently tear away the entire pot if roots haven't already grown through. If you've started your seedlings in peat pellets encased in plastic netting, cut the netting off before planting. Then plant as you would any other seedling.

- Water the seedlings as you go, rather than waiting and watering after you've finished transplanting. If the soil is unusually dry, moisten it slightly before planting because dry soil can quickly pull the water out of tender roots and damage them.

- To settle seedlings in their holes, fill the hole with loose, well-tilled soil, sprinkle at least a quart of water on each transplant, and gently firm the soil to eliminate large air pockets so the roots will be in contact with the soil and there will be no root-drying air spaces. A shallow, saucerlike depression will help catch rain and direct it toward the roots.

- As a general rule, set seedlings in the soil at the same depth they were growing in their pots. Tomatoes are an exception to this rule. If they are planted in a shallow trench on their sides with the top one or two sets of leaves above ground, the stems will grow roots and the tomato plants will be less leggy.

PLANT PROTECTION

The transplanting operation doesn't simply end when the last seedling is in place in the garden, however. Sun and wind can still wreak havoc with your seedlings for the first week or so after transplanting, and occurrences such as freak late-spring frosts can reduce your carefully tended plants to mush. Be sure to keep them well watered, and, if possible, screen them from heavy wind. Pale yellow leaves indicate sunscald. Cover afflicted plants promptly with screens, plastic sheeting, or anything else that will provide shade. Then gradually increase exposure to sun over several days.

Hardy Bulbs

Planting hardy bulbs is easy when you do it right. By carefully selecting a site, determining planting times, and using proper spacing and planting techniques, you'll be following the path to foolproof planting.

SELECTING A SITE

Almost all bulbs are sun lovers and grow best in full sun. However, this is only true when they're actively growing. By the time spring-blooming bulbs go dormant, they can tolerate full shade. That's why spring bulbs like daffodils and crocuses grow well under deciduous trees and shrubs—their active growing season occurs before the trees leaf out. Some bulbs, like pink daffodils, will have better color if they're grown in partial shade.

Bulbs need loose, humus-rich soil for best performance; they won't bloom well in poor, compacted soils. Most bulbs also need well-drained soil and will appreciate the addition of decomposed organic matter like composted pine bark. If you have poorly drained or compacted soil, try growing bulbs in raised beds, which will enhance drainage and make for easier planting. Of course, bulbs will thrive in beds that have been double-dug, since they thrive in well-worked soil, but in most soils this extra effort isn't essential. Bulbs prefer a pH of 6.0 to 7.0 but will tolerate slightly more acidic soils.

DETERMINING PLANTING TIMES

Plant spring-flowering and early-summer-flowering bulbs in fall so they can develop a root system and meet their cold requirements. (Hardy bulbs usually need a certain number of hours of cold temperatures to bloom.) It's best to wait until soil temperatures are below 60°F at 6 inches deep before planting. Follow these rules of thumb: In Zones 2 and 3, plant bulbs in September; in Zones 4 and 5, September to early October; in Zones 6 and 7, October to early November; in Zone 8, November to early December; and in Zone 9, December. In Zone 9, precooling may be necessary.

You can plant bulbs later in the fall, as long as they're planted before the onset of hard freezes. Late-planted bulbs tend to bloom several weeks later and on shorter stems, and there is the possibility of aborted blooms or bulbs freezing before roots are established.

Soak anemone (*Anemone* spp.) and winter aconite (*Eranthis hyemalis*) tubers overnight in warm water before planting to bring them out of dormancy. Plant anemones in fall in Zones 7 to 9, or in the spring in Zones 4 to 9. Because it is difficult to tell the top from the bottom of anemone tubers, plant them sideways.

SPACING BULBS

Place bulbs in your flower bed and space according to flower stalk height. For greatest impact, plant in clusters of ten or more rather than singly in rows. Plant large bulbs 5 to 6 inches apart and small bulbs 1 to 3 inches apart. Leave room to interplant with perennials, groundcovers, or annuals.

You can use 6-inch concrete reinforcing wire as a template to make a uniform bulb bed. Put this hardware cloth flat on the ground and place bulbs in the centers of the squares. Remove the hardware cloth before planting.

PLANTING TECHNIQUES

The general rule for planting depth is three to four times the height of the bulb. This depth will help to protect the bulbs against frost, animals, and physical damage from hoeing. Deeper planting will also help bulbs naturalize and perennialize.

The thought of planting a boxful of bulbs can be daunting, but with the right tools and techniques, bulb planting is easy. A heavy-duty

Continued ➡

Aftercare: A Timetable

How well your plants will thrive depends on the care you give them after planting. Use this care calendar to make sure you're giving your new plants what they need.

Right Away

Water: Water perennials as soon as you've planted them.

Cut back foliage: If the nursery hasn't already done this, cut off one- to two-thirds of the foliage on bareroot plants; otherwise plants will wilt. If they wilt even after you've cut them back, cut back to a few inches to give plants a chance to recover.

Mulch: Mulch your plants after watering them to maintain soil moisture and guard against wilting. Mulch will keep weeds from competing with your new plants, too.

Provide shade: Shade your newly planted perennials from direct sunlight until they've had a chance to recover from the shock of transplanting. Cover them with a sunbonded row cover like Reemay or with shade cloth, screening, or a lath cover.

The First Week

Water: Your plants' primary need will continue to be water. Check at least once a day—before and after work is even better.

Check for bugs: Check your perennials daily for signs of pests and pest damage. New plants are smaller, so they're particularly vulnerable to pest damage. Animals and birds can decimate a planting, too—if you see signs of their damage, protect your plants with screens.

Remove shade: Gradually remove your shade cover after the first few days—ideally, leave it on only during the heat of the day and remove it for the morning and late afternoon. If you can't get home to move the cover, take it off after the third day; make doubly sure that plants are well watered and mulched.

The First Season

Water: Make sure your perennials get 1 inch of water a week, from either rain or the hose.

Weed: Weeding is most important the first two years after planting; after that, plants will be large enough to shade out most weed seedlings. Mulch will help control weeds, but check for them every time you're in the garden.

Feed: If you've prepared the soil well, your perennials won't need more than an application of compost in the middle of the season, or compost (or manure or seaweed) tea once a month, to grow vigorously.

Monitor for insects and diseases: Continue to keep an eye out for pests and diseases, and apply appropriate controls.

Disbud: If you buy bareroot perennials in May or June that are late-blooming (like asters and mums), remove all their flower buds. They need to establish themselves the first growing season, not put their energy into flowering.

Deadhead: Cut off spent flowers to keep your perennials from wasting energy by setting seed.

Move things around: If plants don't look right where you've place them, don't be afraid to move them around. (Don't move perennials in bloom.) If you find you've left a gap in your bed that won't be filled in by the following season, add more plants to cover the bare spot.

Enjoy: Take time to appreciate the beautiful garden you've made.

tubular bulb planter large enough for daffodil bulbs is the ideal tool for prepared beds. It's a cup-shaped steel cylinder with a foot bar and long handle on top. Insert the bulb planter in the soil by stepping on the foot bar. Twist the planter, lift it out, then place the bulb in the bottom of the hole. Fill the hole with dirt from the planter, then repeat with the next bulb.

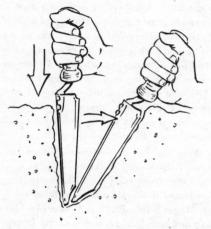

Planting bulbs in a lawn. Crocuses and grape hyacinths (Muscari spp.) brighten spring lawns and are easy to plant. Stab a bulb trowel into a soil like a dagger, and pull toward you to make a hole for the bulb. Drop in the bulb, and step on the spot to close the slot.

For planting bulbs in unworked soil, around tree roots, and in groundcovers, you need a stronger tool. Choose a naturalizing tool (a straight steel blade with a forked end, topped by a foot bar and long handle), a crowbar, or a narrow spade with a sharp cutting edge and a foot bar. Push the blade halfway into the soil and pull back, then push down hard so the blade goes completely into the soil. Push forward so the blade lifts up the soil to make a planting slot. Put in a bulb, remove the tool, step down to firm the soil, and repeat with the next bulb.

There's a special trick to planting small bulbs. Using a narrow trowel, one person can easily plant several hundred small bulbs in an hour. (See the illustration on this page for a discussion technique.)

Perennials

Because perennials live a long time, it's important to get them off to a good start. Proper soil preparation and care at planting time will be well rewarded at bloom time. Prepare your planting beds before you order or buy plants. It is best to work a season ahead and dig in early fall for a spring planting. Be sure to mulch pre-dug beds, then turn the soil in spring when you're ready to plant.

Soil Preparation

The majority of perennials commonly grown in beds or borders require evenly moist, humus-rich soil of pH 5.5 to 6.5. A complete soil analysis from your local extension office or a soiling lab will give you a starting point. For more on soils and soil testing, see Chapter 1.

Double digging is the best way to prepare a perennial bed. Despite the difficulty of the task, the rewards are unparalleled. Plants' roots will be able to penetrate the friable soil easily, creating a strong, vigorous root system. Water and nutrients will also move more easily through the soil, and the bed won't dry out as fast. As a result, your plants will thrive. Have the necessary soil amendments and organic fertilizer on hand before you start.

If you can't double dig before you plant, turn the soil evenly to a shovel's depth at planting

time. Thoroughly incorporate appropriate soil amendments and fertilizer as required. Breakup all clods and smooth out the bed before planting.

Planting

Plant perennials any time the soil is workable. Spring and fall are best for most plants. If plants arrive before you are ready to plant them, be sure to care for them properly until you can get them in the ground.

Planting is easy in freshly turned soil. Choose an overcast day whenever possible. Avoid planting during the heat of the day. Place container-grown plants out on the soil according to your design. To remove the plants, invert containers and knock the bottom of the pot with your trowel. The plant should fall out easily. The roots will be tightly intertwined. It's vital to loosen the roots—by pulling them apart or even cutting four slashes, one down each side of the root mass—so they'll spread strongly through the soil when planted out. Clip any roots that are bent, broken, or circling. Make sure you place the crown of the plant at the same depth at which it grew in the pot.

Planting bareroot perennials and transplants requires more care. Inspect the roots carefully and prune off any irregularities, then soak the roots in a bucket of lukewarm water for one or two hours to hydrate them before planting. Dig a hole large enough to accommodate the full spread of the roots. Build a mound with tapering sides in the center of the hole. Spread the roots of fibrous-rooted plants evenly over the mound, and rest the crown of the plant at its apex. Check to

be sure that the crown will end up just below the soil surface. Build up the mound to raise the crown if necessary. Do not plant too deeply!

Position rhizomes such as those of iris at or just below the surface, depending on the species. Spread the roots evenly over a mound of soil as described above. Spread tuberous roots like those of daylilies evenly in a similar fashion. Fill in the planting hole with soil, then firm it down and add more soil if necessary before you water the new plant.

Water plants thoroughly after planting so the soil is completely settled around the roots. Give your newly planted perennials a layer of organic mulch to conserve soil moisture. Provide extra water for the first month or so while plants are becoming established.

Here's one last helpful hint that's important but easy to forget: Keep the plant labels that come with your perennials, and stick them firmly in the ground next to each plant as you plant it.

Trees and Shrubs

There's no doubt about it—trees and shrubs can enhance the value of your home, both by increasing your property's monetary worth and by adding beauty and variety to your surroundings. While the cost of a well-planted property can be measured in materials, equipment, labor, and maintenance, the daily impact for most of us comes from the effects of vegetation on our physical and emotional comfort. We plant trees and shrubs because they provide welcome shade,

---

Tips for Healthy Trees and Shrubs

The key to success with trees and shrubs is to know your site. You can't choose plants that will thrive in your yard or garden until you learn about the site and how to prepare it. Here's what you, or the designer or landscape architect who is choosing the trees and shrubs for your property, need to know:

Soil: Begin learning about your site with a soil test. The results will tell you your soil's pH and fertility, two of the most important pieces of information that you must have when making a plant selection.

Also look at your soil's consistency and drainage characteristics. Is the soil loose or compacted? Is it clayey, sandy, or loamy? Is it rocky and shallow, or chalky and poorly drained? Is it elevated, depressed, or sloping? Does water stand at any time of the year? Different plants have different tolerances for these conditions, and you're best off planting a tree or shrub that will be happy in the soil you have to offer.

Soil preparation: Till the planting area before you dig. This will reduce compaction and encourage aeration and drainage. Since roots tend to stay in the top 1 foot of soil, tilling can make a real difference.

Adding soil amendments to backfill isn't necessary for typical plantings, but it may be appropriate for certain plants in particular sites. For example, if you're planting trees in raised beds or berms (mounds), adding water-holding organic soil amendments can be very beneficial, since beds and berms tend to dry out faster than ground-level plantings.

Exposure: Is the planting site sunny or shady? Buildings and nearby vegetation can limit the hours of full sun that fall on a potential planting site. Be

sure to check how many hours, and at what time of day, your plant will have direct sunlight.

Water: Note the amount of rainfall that you can expect your new tree or shrub to receive, and consider how you will water it during a dry spell. If your resources are limited select plants that can tolerate occasional drought.

Other factors: Other physical factors to watch include overhead and underground utilities (such as electric wires and water pipes); nearby buildings; actual use of the site (is it a quiet, out-of-the-way spot, or right near a path?); and the size of the area, which determines the appropriate size of the plant. Recognizing these physical limitations will enable you to make better choices. If there are overhead utilities, for example, choose plants that are naturally dwarfed or slow-growing, with an ultimate height considerably lower than that of the overhead lines and equipment. Or, if your site is near a path or sidewalk, a tree with low-hanging or pendant branches might pose a problem. Pavement and buildings may cause plants stress by reflecting heat, creating unnatural wind patterns, and limiting root space and water penetration. Finally, does the site have a vast, open, parklike scale or that of an intimate patio or enclosed backyard?

Site maintenance: It's important to maintain the planting site *after* planting, as well. If grass grows in the area covered by the mature spread of the tree's crown (the drip fine), it can compete with the tree's roots for nutrients and water. To prevent regrowth of grass after you've tilled and planted, spread mulch around the tree as far out as the drip line. Don't allow the mulch to touch the base of the tree because this can encourage disease problems.

Continued ➡

windbreaks, privacy, and—most important—beauty. Their spring flowers, lush summer foliage, autumn color, interesting bark, and variety of forms add color, texture, and appeal to the landscape.

GETTING A GOOD START

When you are buying new trees and shrubs, can avoid a lot of future problems by choosing locally adapted or resistant species. Trees and shrubs that are native to an area are often less prone to problems because they are growing in the environment to which they are best adapted. Read about the trees and shrubs you intend to buy, and avoid

very pest-prone species. Look for this information in catalogs, or ask your local nursery owner or extension agent for more information on the trees and shrubs best adapted to your area.

Once you get your tree or shrub home, some basic care will help it get established quickly. Good soil preparation will provide the ideal conditions for strong root development. Providing ample water for the first few years after planting also encourages vigorous growth. A 2- to 3-inch-thick layer of organic mulch such as wood chips helps keep the soil moist and weeds down; just be sure to keep the mulch a few inches away from the trunk or main stem to discourage animal and insect pests from attacking the base of the plant. Do any necessary pruning or staking carefully, and avoid making wounds in the trunk or stems with lawn mowers or string trimmers.

PLANTING

The trees and shrubs you buy will be bareroot, balled-and-burlapped (B&B), or in containers. Many deciduous trees and shrubs, such as apples, maples, lilacs, and roses, are sold as dormant, bareroot plants. Evergreens are usually sold B&B because even when they're dormant, they have leaves that draw water from the roots. Container-grown plants have roots established in the container (sometimes a little too well established!); these plants are easy to add to your garden, even in full growth.

Plant a barefoot tree while it is dormant, either in fall or early spring. A few trees have roots so sensitive to disturbance that you should not buy or transplant them bareroot. Your chances of success are best when these trees are container-grown: Kentucky coffee tree (*Gymnocladus dioica*), crape myrtle (*Lagerstroemia indica*), sweet gum (*Liquidambar styraciflua*), black tupelo (*Nyssa sylvatica*), white oak (*Quercus alba*), and sassafras (*Sassafras albidum*).

You can plant most B&B or container-grown trees any time of year except when the ground is frozen. There are a few exceptions, however. A few trees, especially those with thick and fleshy roots, seem to suffer less transplanting shock if planted in the spring in areas where the soil freezes deeply during the winter. Though tree roots will continue to grow until the soil temperature drops below 40°F, these trees are slow to get established and are best reserved for planting in the spring: dogwoods (*Cornus* spp.), golden-rain tree (*Koelreuteria paniculata*), tulip tree (*Liriodendron tulipifera*), magnolias (*Magnolia* spp.), black tupelo (*Nyssa sylvatica*), ornamental cherries and plums (*Prunus* spp.), most oaks (*Quercus* spp.), and Japanese zelkova (*Zelkova serrata*).

A close examination of the roots of your new tree will prevent problems that can limit growth. Trim any mushy, dead, or damaged roots. Comb out potbound roots and straighten or slice through roots that circle the root ball before you set the plant in its hole. Look carefully for girdling roots, which can strangle the tree by wrapping tightly around the base of its trunk. This stops the upward movement of water and nutrients absorbed by the roots and needed by the leaves and branches.

PREPARE A PROPER PLANTING SITE

Do you know how to dig a proper planting hole? A few minutes of extra preparation can make all the difference. Although some trees' roots may go deep, the small but all-important feeder roots forage mostly through the top 6 to 8 inches of soil. Shape the hole to accommodate the feeder roots.

Don't Coddle the Roots Traditional planting advice once called for digging the biggest hole you could dig and filling it with a rich mixture of topsoil and compost. Now gardeners have learned that the best way to plant is to dig a hole just deep enough for the roots, widening toward the top, and filled with the same soil you took out. While the "big and rich" idea did indeed get the tree off to a good start, the tree roots had no inclination to leave the hole. A hole filled with peat moss and rotted manure encourages roots to grow only in the hole instead of branching out. These pockets of overly amended soil stay too wet during rainy periods and too dry during drought. This means tree roots can suffocate from too much moisture or can be more prone to wilting during drought. Also, since the roots don't spread and anchor the plant strongly, it will be more susceptible to wind throw—being toppled during high winds.

But there may be times when soil amendments are necessary. If the soil in the root ball is significantly different from your local soil, your tree may grow better if you amend the soil before planting. Roger Funk, Ph.D., the vice president of human and technical resources at the Davey Tree Expert Company, planted B&B trees that had been grown in sandy clay loam in a landscape where the soil was a heavy blue day. He didn't amend the soil, and he found that water pooled up in the holes. "Since most nurseries are growing trees in sandy or loamy soil, and lots of gardeners have clay soils—especially in new developments, where they may have subsoil—this can be a common problem," says Dr. Funk. "It's best to evaluate the specific conditions and decide what to do on a case-by-case basis."

Encourage roots to reach out beyond the planting hole by loosening ground surrounding the hole. Plunge a garden fork in as deep as the tines allow, and wiggle it slightly to break up compacted soil. Repeat every 1 to 1½ feet to a distance of 5 feet or more on all sides.

Set It Straight After settling the plant in the hole, observe it from all angles to be sure it is positioned straight up and down. There's nothing more frustrating than filling your planting hole and then discovering that the plant is set crookedly. Once you're sure the plant is positioned properly, add soil gradually. For bareroot plants, give the tree or shrub an occasional shake as you refill the hole to sift soil among the roots. Level the soil around the base of the plant. Don't stomp all the air out of your newly filled hole: Instead of using your feet, tamp the soil with your hands or the back of a hoe to settle it and eliminate air pockets.

Water Thoroughly Water the soil thoroughly after planting. Apply a 2- to 3-inch layer of mulch to retain moisture, pulling it back a bit from the trunk. Water new plants once a week during their first year, especially if rainfall is less than 1 inch per week. By the time you notice wilting or other signs of stress, it may be too late.

STAKING

Staking is done to straighten or strengthen the trunk, or to prevent root movement and breakage before the tree anchors itself in the soil. Trees usually don't need staking if they aren't located in windy sites and are under 8 feet with small crowns.

Avoid rigid staking. Allow the trunk to flex or move slightly when the wind hits it. This movement encourages the tree to produce special wood that will naturally bend when the wind hits it. A tree that is rigidly staked will often bend over or break after it is unstaked. Given a choice, avoid

Continued ➡

buying staked, container-grown trees—you will generally be buying a weak stem.

Unstake all trees one year after planting. Any tree that had an adequate root system and was properly planted will by then be able to stand on

Settling Them In

Your new trees and shrubs may be bareroot, balled-and-burlapped (B&B), or planted in a container. For best results, follow these guidelines when planting:

Bareroot plants: As long as you plant bareroot trees or shrubs while the stock is still dormant, your chances of success are good with these generally low-cost plants. Leave a small cone of undisturbed soil in the center of the hole. Remove any circling, broken, or diseased roots from the plants, spread out the roots over the cone of soil, and fill. Water well and mulch.

Balled-and-burlapped plants: It's best to get balled-and-burlapped plants in the ground while they're dormant so the roots can get a good start before they have to supply food and water to burgeoning topgrowth. But the B&B method gives you more leeway; even actively growing trees and shrubs can be held until the weekend for planting.

The illustration on page 92 shows how to set a B&B plant in the planting hole. Remove binding ropes or twine and all nails. Leave natural burlap in place: It will eventually rot. Slit synthetic wrapping material in several places so roots can penetrate it. Try to keep the root ball intact. If the root ball is in a wire basket, cut off the loops on top to keep them from sticking up through the soil, and snip and remove the top few wires. If the tree is large, have a helper hold it in place as you fill the hole. After every few shovelfuls of dirt, add water to help settle air pockets.

Container-grown plants: Remove any labeling tags to keep the tags or wires from cutting into the stems. Support the plant while you turn it upside down and remove the pot. Even fiber pots of compressed peat or paper are best removed; exposed edges wick away moisture, and the walls slow down root growth.

Carefully snip off dead or sickly roots and use your fingers to comb out any potbound roots. Cut through circling roots. Set the plant as deep as it grew before, fill, water, and mulch.

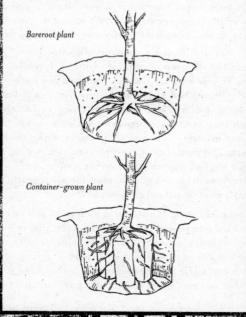

Bareroot plant

Container-grown plant

its own. If you want to leave the stakes in place to keep lawn mowers and other equipment from hitting the trunk and damaging the tree, remove the guy wires or ropes but leave the stakes for a barrier.

Finishing Touches

You don't need to prune newly planted trees and shrubs, except to remove branches that are broken, diseased, narrow-angled, or overlapping. If you cut back all the branches, you may actually slow your tree's or shrub's establishment, because buds produce chemicals that aid root growth. The exception is young fruit trees, which you must prune promptly if you plan to train them for easier harvesting and care.

A tree wrap protects the trunk from sunscald, nibbling rodents, and lawn mower nicks.

Mapping Out the Garden
Nancy Bubel

Once the soil has been prepared, it's time to find the planting plan we doodled over by the late-winter fire. Already much erased and revised, it will no doubt be changed once again as we confront the reality of freshly raked soil and extra last-minute seed purchases. Subject to revision though it may be, the planting plan is a valuable gardening tool.

Although I wouldn't presume to prescribe what form your plan should take, I *would* like to suggest several considerations to keep in mind while poring over the graph paper with seed orders and pencil in hand.

Planning Rows

If you are planning a row garden, consider the lay of the garden and the spacing of the rows.

Orientation of Rows. Your first decision, as you face that blank piece of paper, is to determine in which direction your rows will run. If possible, choose a north-south direction so that sun striking the garden from the east and west will cast a plant's shadow onto the space between the rows rather than onto the next plant.

On a sloping plot, where rain tends to carry loose soil downhill, contouring the rows so that they run parallel to the hill (and at right angles to the direction of the slope) will help to conserve much valuable topsoil. Mulching will help, too, as will terracing on a very steep slope.

Row Spacing. The space you leave between rows will be determined by the kind of plants you grow, the amount of mulch you can get, and the sort of equipment you plan to use to cultivate the garden. Rows must be separated far enough to give the plant sufficient room to grow and the gardener space to walk and often space to till or hoe.

Single rows of nonspreading plants like beets, lettuce, peas, carrots, and such are giving way, in more and more gardens, to 4- to 36-inch-wide bands of these vegetables. We've had good results with garlic, lettuce, carrots, peas, herbs, and beans planted in wide rows. Careful hand weeding between the vegetables is necessary in the early stages, but later the plants help to take care of each other by shading out weeds and keeping soil moist. Wide rows use space more efficiently than narrow drills.

On a sloping plot, rows should run parallel to the hill to prevent soil from being carried down the slope by rain.

Row middles that will be tilled should be about six to eight inches wider than the tine-to-tine measurement of the tiller. You can adapt some front-end tillers to work row spaces as narrow as eight inches by removing the two outer tines and reversing the center tines so that their blades face inward rather than outward.)

Mulched rows may be closely spaced, but if you have a lot of coarse mulch, as we do, you will want to plan your garden so that the loose, shaggy stuff will be used to mulch wide rows like tomatoes. The finer mulches like sawdust or old leaves, or neat bundles like hay, can be saved for narrow rows.

Garden Beds

Rows are customary, but not necessarily traditional. There are many good arguments for planting vegetables, herbs, or flowers, closely spaced, in small plots or blocks. Soil may be intensively improved. The beds may be raised to improve drainage. Weeding and harvesting are convenient. When well cared for, small garden beds are delightfully attractive. Many arrangements are possible. You can divide your garden area into blocks separated by paths. Each block will be solidly planted to a single vegetable or an especially chosen combination of vegetables. You might want to keep a grassy path between a double row of narrow vegetable beds. Vegetable beds may be located on the lawn, next to the house, or along a walkway.

One practical problem with garden beds bordered by grass is the encroachment of the grass into the bed. This may often be solved by sinking a thin metal edging strip between vegetable bed and grass or by building a raised vegetable bed. Some gardeners support the deeper soil with wooden boards or railroad ties, but such enclosures are not really necessary. Plant roots will hold the soil in place. When you form the beds, slope them slightly from the base to the top surface.

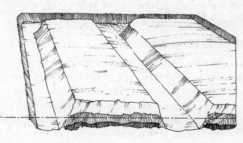

Raised beds.

Raised Beds. If I were starting a new garden today, I'd plant intensively in raised beds. Here's why:

- Raised beds are easy to work (once established).
- The deep, loose soil encourages excellent root growth.
- The absence of foot traffic prevents soil compaction.

Continued ➡

- Compost and other soil-improving additions can be concentrated where they will be effective, not wasted on footpaths.
- Raised beds warm earlier in spring.
- The solid cover of plants helps to shade out weeds and conserve soil moisture.

When starting a raised bed, remove weeds and sod and add them to the compost pile. To add humus, dig in about one bushel of manure or compost to each 25 square feet of garden. Toss on a few shovelfuls of wood ashes. Rake up all loose soil from paths and, if possible, haul in some extra soil from elsewhere on your place.

Double digging. If you double-dig your beds, you probably won't be sorry, because deeply worked soil gives plant roots more of what they need. To double-dig, remove the soil from a 1-foot-deep trench at the edge of the bed and save the dug-up soil to fill the last trench. Then, using a spading fork, loosen the packed earth in the bottom of the trench. Fill the first trench with soil dug from trench number two and continue to dig your way down the bed, trench by trench. Beds should be 3 to 3½ feet wide and any convenient length. Wider beds are hard to reach into. Leave at least one footpath between beds.

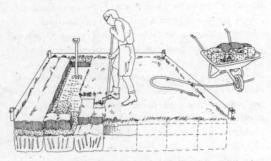

In double digging, soil is removed from one end of the bed to be placed at the other end. Successive trenches are dug, and soil is moved up the bed. During this process, the soil can be worked deeply to benefit root growth.

I've talked to a fair number of gardeners who chose not to double-dig their raised beds, and they seem to be getting good results, too. One couple first tilled their ground and then shoveled all the loose soil aside and went over the same ground again with their tiller to loosen the soil more deeply. Others have simply piled up as much soil and organic matter as they could collect to raise the beds 8 to 12 inches above ground level. All are reaping the many benefits of the raised bed. It is a trade-off of more intensive preparation and careful planning for easier care and less tilling later on.

Where to Plant What

Once you've determined the basic design and layout of your garden, you'll want to decide where to place your plants. In general, tall plants like corn or sunflowers should be planted on the north side of the garden so they don't shade adjacent vegetables. If it is necessary to put them on the south end of the garden, plant parsley, lettuce, or other midsummer shade-tolerant plants next to the corn. Placement of your crops in the garden will be partly determined by their growing habits.

Rambling Vine Crops. Squash, pumpkins, melons, and cucumbers may be planted in rows or hills. There's a certain amount of confusion surrounding the term "hill." Generally, a hill is simply a small designated area, not necessarily raised, in which a group of seeds, usually those of spreading plants, is sown. Except in very small gardens, where vines can be trained to climb fences, hills use space more efficiently than rows

when growing rambling plants. Planting vining crops in a hill rather than in rows allows for easier placement of compost and manure and simpler, quicker insect control early in the season.

Some gardeners do make hills, which are actually small elevated mounds an inch or two above the normal soil level. These small raised beds drain well and warm quickly.

Climbers. You can save space in the garden by planting cucumbers, pole beans, certain melons, Malabar spinach, and others if you put them at the edge, next to a fence or trellis, so save an end row for some of these space-takers.

Bush Vegetables. In recent years, breeders have developed space-saving bush varieties of popular long-vined vegetables like squash, pumpkins, and melons. Those shorter-vined plants also have shorter internodes—less space between the leaves. Some of them bear earlier, and some have a more determinate habit than their roaming cousins— that is, they may stop bearing and growing earlier in the season rather than continuing until frost. Most bush varieties produce full-sized fruit. Some previously developed bush-type vegetables were inferior in flavor to those grown on full-sized plants. This situation seems to be improving, though. Bush-type cucumbers seem to suffer the least loss of flavor, watermelons the most. Some of the muskmelons are so-so, but Musketeer has a fine flavor. A plant with more limited leaf area can be stressed by a large fruit load, so pinching off excess flowers and providing plenty of organic matter in the soil should help to encourage better flavor.

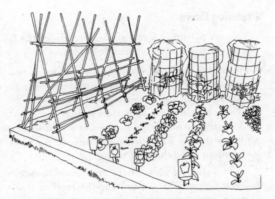

When planning a garden, try to place tall plants on the north side so they don't shade other crops. Plant climbers near an edge where they can grow up a trellis, and if you grow any perennial vegetables, give them their own bed, if you can, so they won't be disturbed.

Overwintering Crops. Parsnips, salsify, and carrots, and late-fall bearers like brussels sprouts, escarole, parsley, and collards, should be planted at the edge of the garden where they will not be disturbed if you intend to till or plow the rest of the garden in the fall.

Perennial Vegetables. Crops like asparagus, rhubarb, comfrey, and Jerusalem artichokes should, of course, be planted either at the edge of the garden where they will not be plowed up or in a separate bed.

Crop Rotation

Keep your vegetables moving! Alternating the kinds of crops you grow in a given space is just about the least expensive and least time-consuming method you can use to maintain and even improve the quality of your soil and the health of your vegetables. Each kind of vegetable that you might grow absorbs soil nutrients in different amounts. Corn and leafy vegetables need a lot of nitrogen; sweet potatoes get along

with small doses of nitrogen; root vegetables need potash; legumes (with the help of nitrogen-fixing bacteria on their roots) actually add nitrogen to the soil. By alternating vegetable families, you give the soil a chance to replenish nutrients, and you discourage the proliferation of insect pests. If you plant vulnerable food crops in a different location each year, the bean beetles won't have a ready feast waiting for them the moment they hatch. In addition, plant diseases caused by fungi and bacteria are less likely to threaten successive crops if their host plants keep hopping around. The rotation unit can be a row, half-row, a raised bed, or even a separate garden plot.

What constitutes a vegetable group? Some folks simply alternate those vegetables that are generally considered more demanding on the soil—corn, cabbage, squash, melons and their relatives, and tomatoes—with those that are satisfied with somewhat leaner soil—legumes, root vegetables, herbs, and onions. A third-year planting of a soil-enriching cover crop like buckwheat, clover, oats, or rye would be a wise addition to such a simple rotation. At the very least, you'd want to rotate corn, which is an especially heavy feeder, as well as any vegetables with which you've had serious disease and insect problems in the past.

For a more complete and effective rotation, divide your garden vegetables into seven categories: legumes; leafy vegetables; root vegetables; cucurbits; onions and their relatives; tomatoes and related peppers, potatoes, and eggplant; and corn and other grains. If you plant green manure crops, make that your eighth plant group. A sample rotation, then, might be a planting of spring peas followed by fall kale, with parsnips occupying the row the second year, squash the third year, onions next, tomatoes or related vegetables in year five, and corn the following year, after which you'd either put in a cover crop of oats or buckwheat, or begin again with legumes—perhaps soybeans—then cabbage, carrots, cucumbers, garlic, eggplant, and so on.

The most impressive garden rotation scheme I've ever seen was worked out by Vertis Bream, an accomplished Pennsylvania gardener who divided his garden into six raised beds, each 3½ feet wide, 30 feet long, and 8 to 12 inches high. The Breams plant a different group of crops in each bed every six years. For example, a bed that's growing beets, potatoes, carrots, and onions this year will be planted to wheat after the root vegetables are pulled up. After the wheat is harvested in the second year, they plant a clover cover crop, followed by corn in the fourth year, then beans, and finally, in year six, a bed of lettuce, tomatoes, and cole crops. They keep garden diagrams and move the potato row from row 1 to row 2, then 3, 4, 5, 6, and then back to row 1 as the years go by.

As these plans suggest, you will sometimes grow two different groups of plants in a certain row in a given year. Garden rotations can look complicated because we're dealing with limited areas and a large variety of plant types, and often with in-season plant successions. Don't worry about making it all come out straight, down to the letter and inch. Just do the best you can to give each kind of vegetable a different spot in the garden each year—a good reason for saving each year's mud-spattered garden plan.

Green Manure. With careful planning, you can end the season with a section of garden that is free of crops, a perfect chance to put in a soil-building crop of winter rye, or start in spring with oats to be plowed under before they head. Either way you'll add humus and nutrients to

Continued ➡

your garden. In order to have a solid block of land ready for a fall cover crop, it's necessary to group a bunch of early-maturing spring plantings together so that when they are harvested in August or September, the rye can be planted right away. (Be sure to get coarse-seeded winter rye, not the fine-seeded grass that may repeat on you in next year's garden.)

Succession Crops. To keep your garden continuously productive, plant crops in succession. They can be dovetailed in a very intricate way. All kinds of variations are possible. Here are a few examples, from my garden:

- An early planting of peas followed by a late corn planting (but use a fairly early-maturing kind of corn).
- Early cabbage followed by late beans.
- Spring lettuce giving way to fall beets.
- Early onions succeeded by fall lettuce.

Once I planted bean seeds along the row as I harvested leaf lettuce. By the time the lettuce row was used up, all the beans were up and growing. More often, I start seedlings in flats for transplanting into the garden when an early crop is finished. As I gather peas, the kale that will take their place is hardening off on the east patio. When I pull onions, I have Chinese cabbage seedlings ready to take their place.

Interplanting

When planning your garden, you might want to consider interplanting your vegetables. Interplanting saves space. It's seldom necessary, for example, to devote a whole row to spring radishes. Plant them, instead, along with your lettuce and carrots and use them as thinnings when they're ready. One year I grew a long row of bush beans between the widely spaced, just-planted rows of tomatoes and squash. By the time the vines closed over the gap, I'd harvested many meals of good green beans. Pumpkins do well at the edge of the corn patch where they have space to ramble. In studies at the University of Maryland, sweet corn and soybeans planted in the same row produced satisfactory harvests. Although individual vegetable yields were lower and corn ripened three days later, the total harvest from the row was larger.

Companion Planting

Companion planting, the pairing of plants that benefit each other in close proximity, adds yet another dimension to the juggling of rows and beds. Reports on certain vegetables sometimes vary widely; some authorities say that onions and beans do well together, while others warn that beans don't like onions. There is a firm scientific basis for the study of plant relationships, though: Plants are known to produce root exudates that do, in many cases, affect soil life and roots of other plants around them.

A whole body of companion planting lore exists that is difficult to dismiss, but difficult also, so far, to prove conclusively. Some of these protective interplanting arrangements seem to work for some gardeners but not for others. A few sound to me like myths that have simply been repeated from one writer to another without serious trial. Others have been proven effective in published studies—for example, the nematode-suppressing effect of French marigolds. Catnip oil, too, has been shown to repel 17 species of insects, but unfortunately, like the mints, it is an invasive plant that can choke out flowers and vegetables.

In my garden, I make only a few intentional companion plantings, usually radishes with cucurbits and marigolds for nematode control, but I do try to keep different plant varieties well mixed. Although I don't follow the lore closely in my garden, partly out of busyness and preoccupation with other matters, I'm no more ready to dismiss it entirely than I am to endorse without reservation the various companion-planting combinations I've heard of. One thing is certain: Growing things relate and interact in amazingly complicated and subtle ways. Much study remains to be done, and close observation by gardeners continues to be a valid source of information about the success of companion planting.

Helpful Companions. According to traditional lore, certain herbs, weeds, flowers, and vegetables have the effect of deterring insects and encouraging plant growth when planted near compatible plants. Borage, chamomile, and lovage are supposed to enhance growth and flavor in nearby vegetables. Garlic planted near roses and raspberries should deter aphids. Horseradish has the reputation of repelling potato bugs. Marjoram is said to improve the flavor of nearby food plants. Mint, sage, and rosemary are the traditional enemies of cabbage moths. Nasturtiums, which actually attract aphids and thus are useful as a trap crop, are sometimes erroneously listed as an aphid repellent. Catnip is often planted to deter flea beetles. Yarrow planted near aromatic herbs is thought to enhance their production of essential oils.

Companions for Garden Space. Another branch of companion planting pairs shallow-rooted plants like onions and celery with others, like chard and carrots, whose roots delve deeply into the subsoil. This seems to me a sensible practice that makes good use of that third dimension of garden space—depth.

Interplanting. There seems to be no question that monoculture (planting large areas to a single plant species) encourages heavier insect infestation. In repeated studies, diversified plantings have suffered less insect damage than monocultured fields. Therefore, the practice of mixing aromatic herbs and flowers with vegetables, alternating rows of different species, and interplanting various species within the row should help, at least, to confuse the

---

insects and, at best, to promote positive plant health.

Harmful Companions. Some plants, in the companion-planting tradition, harm rather than help each other. Fennel, the most notorious outcast, is said to discourage growth of most garden plants. Dill and carrots, basil and rue, sage and cucumbers, cabbage and grapes, and chives and peas or beans are all plants that reputedly make poor companions because one or both are badly affected by close proximity.

Allelopathy. The inhibition of seed germination and plant growth by certain plant-produced natural compounds is sometimes responsible for otherwise unexplained poor plant growth. Plant toxins are usually exuded by roots, but they are also generally present, in varying amounts, in stems, leaves, and fruits.

Walnut Trees and Juglone. Walnut trees release juglone, which retards many plants. I found that out the hard way in my own garden when I planted a row of beets near an English walnut tree at the edge of the garden. Beets, I have since discovered, are particularly sensitive to toxins in the soil. The beet seeds didn't even germinate. Other plants—onions and marigolds—have grown fairly well in the same spot, but most things I plant near that tree produce rather halfheartedly. Shade and competing tree roots could also be a factor, but 200 species of plants are known to be susceptible to juglone. Black walnut trees produce more of the toxin than English walnuts or butternuts.

Like beets, some crops are more vulnerable to the effect of toxins. Soybeans, tomatoes, okra, asparagus, alfalfa, lilacs, apples, peonies, and chrysanthemums, among others, have been shown to be seriously inhibited by juglone in the soil. Those plants that are resistant to juglone include red cedars, redbuds, quinces, black raspberries, corn, beans, carrots, and zinnias.

Other Allelopathic Plants. Other notorious allelopathic plants are ailanthus, artemisia, absinthium, eucalyptus, sunflowers, and sometimes sycamores.

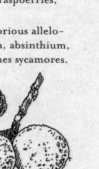

Black walnut.

Some crop plants inhibit weeds. For example, Kentucky-31 fescue grass retards growth of black mustard and trefoil. Weeds can suppress crop plants, too. In some experiments, residues of lamb's-quarters, pigweed, velvet lead, and yellow foxtail have inhibited the growth of corn and soybeans.

Although published observations of the effect of plants on the growth of other plants date back hundreds of years, scientific study of the phenomenon has only begun to scratch the surface. So many plants and variables are involved that few sweeping generalizations can be made. Allelopathy can throw a wild card into some of your planting schemes, but keep an open mind and don't let it worry you. Just try to plant your sunflowers separately and keep your garden away from walnut trees. (A distance of 1½ times the height of the tree should be safe.) If the subject interests you, conduct your own experiments, and jot down what you planted and what you observed.

Taking Pollination into Account

When laying out rows and beds, remember that corn is wind pollinated and should therefore be planted at least four rows deep, preferably six to eight. If you plant only a small amount of corn,

Continued →

make a block of four or more short rows rather than planting a single long row.

If you are planning to save seeds of wind-pollinated garden vegetables like corn and spinach, you will want to follow recommended spacing requirements to avoid crossing.

Special Problems

Perhaps you have a spot in your garden that is poorly drained, a corner that is shady, a section with hardpan, or a rocky area. Each of these special situations may be met and sometimes even partially solved by your choice of plants.

Partial Shade. Plant summer lettuce, parsley, raspberries, or rhubarb.

Hardpan. Treat the problem by planting deep-rooted vegetables like comfrey or Swiss chard to break up the impervious layer of subsoil.

Poor Drainage. Avoid planting globe artichokes, sweet potatoes, or other lovers of warm, loose soil in that spot, until you've corrected the problem by trenching to divert water and/or digging in more humus or making raised beds.

Rocks. Potatoes will do well, especially under mulch, but any crop that needs frequent hoeing and cultivating will be a challenge. If you use a tiller, get pointed tines for working around rocks. When your whole garden is rocky, you accept it and work around it (and often have as fringe benefits a lovely rock garden and several fine rock walls), but when only one part is rocky, you might as well minimize the wear and tear on your hoe by selecting crops to plant there that can be mulched early.

Short of Space. If you're short of space, make some good management decisions to get the most out of the available ground.

The Vegetable Garden. Consider some of the following criteria when deciding what to plant in your vegetable garden and how to plant it:

- Plant vegetables with the highest cash value.
- Grow vegetables that lose quality in shipping.
- Plant earlier, making use of hardy vegetables, early varieties, and plant protectors such as tunnels and cold frames.
- Stretch the harvest with continuous succession plantings.
- Grow high-yielding vegetables such as tomatoes, lead lettuce, turnips, summer squash, and edible-pod peas.

The Flower Garden. Efficient use of space allows you to grow more flowers, too. Consider the following suggestions:

- For more flowers in a small space, grow climbers like morning-glories.
- Use container plantings on patios and porches.
- Plant flowers in windowboxes.

Planting Flowers with Vegetables

There's no good reason, other than staid custom, for keeping vegetable and flower plantings segregated. More gardeners now feel free to mix flowers, herbs, and vegetables in the same plot with delightful results. Flowers brighten the patch in the backyard, and ornamental vegetables grow proudly in the front border. Not every vegetable plant assumes a pleasing form, but those that do—rhubarb chard, head lettuce, peppers, and many more—deserve their place in decorative planting.

Create lovely garden displays by growing flowers and vegetables together.

In a gorgeous display planting at Longwood Gardens in Kennett Square, Pennsylvania, vegetable and flower plants grow together in borders similar to conventional perennial beds. The plot is laid out as if it were someone's backyard, with one-third of the area in lawn and a path separating a border bed along the fence from the main vegetable bed, which curves gracefully in a long sweep down and across the yard. Where you'd expect to see masses of delphiniums and lilies, escarole, beets, and beans thrive instead, interspersed with marigolds, nasturtiums, and portulaca. A low border of alyssum sets off the arrangement. The surprising effect is that the true beauty of well-grown vegetables stands out. Boundaries between vegetables and flowers fade even more when you remember that blossoms of some flowering plants—calendula, nasturtium, and chives, for example—are edible. When planning an ornamental edible garden, keep in mind Kate Gessert's advice in her book *The Beautiful Food Garden*: "Be playful, be flexible, take risks."

Planting and Transplanting
Fern Marshall Bradley

Planting and transplanting are at the heart of gardening. To build a garden, change a garden, or move a garden, you must plant or transplant. This chapter shares the experience of expert gardeners on what works and what doesn't and presents the basics of planting and transplanting properly to ensure success. Some of what you read here may surprise you by offering a new way to look at an old practice. Try a few new techniques, and see what works best for you.

Planting the Small Stuff

In this section, the experts offer special techniques for hardening off vegetable and flower seedlings and planting them out, as well as tips on how to get perennials off to a great start in the big outdoors.

HARDENING OFF FOR THE 9-TO-5 SET

Gardeners who have an office job and also have seedlings started indoors are in a bind when it's time to harden off the seedlings to prepare them for life outdoors. Although you can move them out in the morning when you leave for work, who will take care of the seedlings an hour or two later when it's time to bring them in? Heather Will-Browne, a bedding plant specialist at Walt Disney World in Florida, has found a way to let the seedlings take care of themselves. Put the flats or pots either on the porch or under the north eaves of your house so they are protected from the sun. (You don't need much room—even the stoop outside one of your doors will do.) "It's great because they're also protected from hard rains that will destroy tiny seedlings in just a few minutes," Will-Browne says. If they're on a porch, move the flats gradually toward the outer

edge of the covered area so they'll be exposed to a bit more sun each day until they are conditioned for the garden.

A TANGLED TALE OF TRANSPLANT ROOTS

You can help bedding plants that are growing in cell packs and small pots make the transition to garden soil by untangling the roots before transplanting. "I have literally set annuals in a hole and dug them up at the end of the year to find that the roots had circled around and around in the hole. That's due to two things: the original root formation and the interface between the soil mix and the native soil," says Jim Wilson, a cohost of public television's "The Victory Garden." Plants that don't stretch roots out into the garden soil aren't going to grow well, and they're more likely to dry out. To prevent this, Wilson gently pries some of the transplants' roots loose from the potting soil at planting time to open up the root ball and keep roots from spiraling.

TEAR THE TOPS OFF PEAT POTS

Peat pots are handy, but they need careful transplanting for best growth. "We like peat pots because they make it so easy to deal with large numbers of transplants," says Christina R. J. Pey, a supervisor for the production greenhouses at the Missouri Botanical Garden. However, when planting peat pots, Pey cautions that you should tear off the top edge before planting to be sure it doesn't poke up through the soil. If the pot edge is higher than the soil surface, the peat will dry out and act as a wick, pulling moisture away from the roots. The gardeners at the Missouri Botanical Garden also break off sections of the sides and bottom of the containers to make it easier for the transplants' roots to make the transition to garden soil.

A SECOND CHANCE FOR SEEDLINGS

Most of us know the frustration of having a flat of seedlings or transplants turn out to be leggy, with stems flopping in a jumbled mess. Deep transplanting can give lanky cabbage, tomato, and other seedlings a second chance on life. "Once seedlings get leggy, they're pitiful," says Bibby Moore, a registered horticultural therapist from North Carolina. Moore revitalizes the sorry seedlings by burying their leggy stem right up to the bottom two leaves when she transfers them to individual pots. This technique works with seedlings of cabbage-family crops, as well as lettuce, tomato, and even marigold seedlings.

Moore cautions that this is not an ideal practice, it's just a salvage technique. "The next time you sow seeds, give them adequate light to begin with," she says. It's important to give the potted seedlings increased light so you don't end up with floppy transplants as well. Of course, if you do, you can resort to deep transplanting in the garden. Dig an angled planting trench, strip off lower leaves, and lay the floppy stem in the trench, as shown in the illustration below. The plant will form roots along the buried stem.

SOIL CONES KEEP ROOTS GROWING

Cole Burrell, a Minnesota garden designer, has fine-tuned a method to set bareroot perennials quickly and effectively in their planting holes. "Don't straitjacket fibrous-rooted plants into narrow holes, or they'll produce new roots at the expense of top growth while the original roots slowly die off," says Burrell. You can try his special planting technique with your perennials.

1. Mound a cone of soil inside the planting hole. The mound makes it easy to spread

Continued ➡

roots out evenly so they point in all directions.

2. Turn the plant upside down and let the roots fall open.

3. Put your hand on the roots to keep them spread out, then turn the plant over and place it on the cone.

4. Refill the hole, making sure that the plant's crown is just above ground level.

"Don't use this method for taprooted plants like purple coneflower (*Echinacea purpurea*), baptisias (*Baptisa* spp.), and butterfly weed (*Asclepias tuberose*)," says Burrell. To plant these plants, prepare the planting site by loosening and amending the soil as needed, but don't dig planting holes. Instead, insert a shovel straight down into the soil and then push it forward to open a crevice. Line up the taproot in the crevice with the crown of the plant at soil level. Remove the shovel, and firm the soil in place.

Planting the Big Guys

Trees and shrubs are a great investment. They'll add beauty, shade, and privacy to your property for many years, increasing property value as they grow. But like most things, you get what you pay for—both in the initial cost of the plants and in the care you give them at planting time. Good planting practices are critical to the good health and longevity of trees and shrubs—and recent research has shown that a lot of the timeworn advice on planting is just plain wrong. In this section, you'll find accurate techniques, tips, and advice for giving these valuable plants the best possible start.

DON'T DIG TO CHINA

Old planting recommendations had you dig a hole twice as wide and twice as deep as the root ball of the tree of shrub you were planting. New research has shown that this advice could actually harm your plants. "The best way to plant is to dig the hole as wide as possible but no deeper than the root ball," says Bonnie Lee Appleton, Ph.D., an associate professor and extension horticulturist at Virginia Polytechnic Institute and State University. If the soil is dug too deep, the root ball can sink as the soil settles, so the plant eventually becomes too deeply buried. "We've found that the majority of roots stay within the top 8 to 12 inches of soil anyway," says Dr. Appleton. "Even the roots of big trees." It's okay to set the plant an inch or two shallower than the depth of the root ball. Apply mulch to cover the top of the ball, but don't let the mulch touch the base of the trunk.

SLICK HOLE SIDES MAKE BAD ROOT BINDS

How and when you dig a planting hole can be more important than how big it is. "Rough the surface of the planting hole by slicing the sides of the finished hole with the edge of the spade, or crack some of the soil off with a fork," advises Michael Maltas, the garden director of the organic showpiece garden for Fetzer Vineyards in California. "Then the roots will be able to find a crack and take off." Maltas also points out that you shouldn't dig planting holes in wet ground with a spade, or the sides will be smeared smooth. They'll harden, forming a barrier to the roots.

SITE PREP PAYS OFF

Tree planting involves much more than just digging a hole, says Tom Ranney, Ph.D., an assistant professor at the Mountain Horticultural Crops Research and Extension Center of North

Carolina State University. "This is particularly true on urban or suburban sites where the soil is often compacted from heavy equipment and other factors," says Dr. Ranney.

Dr. Ranney recommends tilling the planting area before you dig. This will reduce compaction and encourage aeration and drainage. Since roots tend to stay in the top 1 foot of soil, tilling can make a real difference.

Adding soil amendments to backfill probably isn't necessary for typical plantings, says Dr. Ranney. But it may be appropriate for certain plants in particular sites. For example, if you're planting trees in raised beds or on berms, adding water-holding organic soil amendments can be very beneficial, Dr. Ranney says, since raised beds and berms tend to dry out faster than ground-level plantings.

It's important to maintain the planting site after planting as well. If grass grows in the area that will be covered by the mature spread of the tree's crown, it can compete with the tree's roots for nutrients and water. To prevent regrowth of grass after you've tilled and planted, spread mulch around the tree as far out as the drip line. Don't allow the mulch to touch the base of the tree, because this can encourage disease problems.

WHEN TO AMEND PLANTING RULES

"Research on whether or not to amend soil when planting has been generalized too much," says Roger Funk, Ph.D., the vice president of human and technical resources at the Davey Tree Expert Company. If the soil on your site is similar to the soil in the root ball, there's no need to amend the soil in the planting hole. But if the soil in the root ball is significantly different from your local soil, your tree may grow better if you amend the soil before planting. In one trial, Dr. Funk planted balled-and-burlapped trees that had been grown in sandy clay loam in a landscape where the soil was a heavy clay. He didn't amend the soil and found that water pooled in the holes. "Since most nurseries are growing trees in sandy or loamy soil and lots of gardeners have clay soils—especially in new developments, where they may have subsoil—this can be a common problem," says Dr. Funk. "It's best to evaluate the specific conditions and decide what to do on a case-by-case basis."

TOP SCORES FOR TREE ROOTS

Many planting recommendations suggest that gardeners slice a root ball in half from its bottom surface to about halfway through the depth of the ball. This technique may work well on bedding plants, but don't try it on trees and shrubs. "It's a harsh, destructive technique, and you face the likelihood of splitting the root ball," says Bonnie Lee Appleton, Ph.D., an associate professor and extension horticulturist at Virginia Polytechnic Institute and State University. Instead, Dr. Appleton recommends this procedure: Score roots that have grown into a meshlike mat by making shallow vertical cuts through the matted roots, cutting through the outer roots but not into the root ball. Make the cuts on two or three sides of the root mass. If woody roots are circling the root ball, cut through them in two or three places to stop the circling. Make your cuts with a knife or a pair of pruners.

AVOID THE BURLAP ROOT TRAP

Trees and shrubs with roots that are wrapped in burlap can run into problems if you don't pull off the burlap when you plant them. "Many of today's wraps are synthetic and don't decompose

like the old natural burlap did," says Bonnie Lee Appleton, Ph.D., an associate professor and extension horticulturist at Virginia Polytechnic Institute and State University. She recommends that after you set the plant into the hole, remove the rops, pins, or wires on the wrap, then drop the wrap to the bottom of the hole and *leave it there*. Don't try to slide it out from beneath the plant—you might end up cracking the root ball, which can kill the tree or shrub. If the ball is in a wire basket, either cut away the top round of loops or cut the basket down opposite sides and push the wire down into the hole.

Planting Techniques

Barbara Ellis, Joan Benjamin, and Deborah L. Martin

Planting the Low-Maintenance Way

A well-done planting job is rarely a low-maintenance enterprise. Even in the best soils, planting means at least a little bit of digging, a little removal of existing vegetation, and a little soil preparation. And the bigger the plant, the more of those things you'll have to do. In rocky, compacted, or weedy sites, planting can mean hard work, even for relatively small plants.

But planting properly pays long-term dividends. Why? Because time invested in careful planting means you'll save time later when you're not nursing sickly plants or removing dead ones. Proper planting also helps plants stay healthy and grow vigorously. Not only will your plants look great, but you also reduce your chances of having to deal with pest and disease problems down the road. Finally, if you treat your investments with care at planting time, the money you spend on plants won't go to waste. There's nothing like having to replace a newly planted tree or shrub that didn't survive a slipshod planting job to remind you that it's worthwhile to do it right the first time.

At Planting Time, Put the Weather to Work

Sunny, breezy spring days are guaranteed to set gardeners planting, but such days aren't ideal from a plant's perspective. In warm sun and drying wind, new transplants suffer because their roots can't take up enough water to replace the amount they lose through their leaves. Instead, put in your plants under gray and drizzly skies.

If you do plant on a sunny day, make sure plants are well watered before you start, and don't leave them with their roots exposed to sun and wind.

After planting, water well to help plants get growing as quickly as possible. Watering also settles the backfilled soil around the roots and forces out any air pockets that formed during planting. Save fertilizer applications until you see signs of new growth.

Cut Post-Planting Care with Seasonal Savvy

Wouldn't it be great to just stick a plant into its chosen site and be done with it? Now *that's* low maintenance! Well, you can get away with this no-care approach—and still end up with healthy plants—if you choose the right planting time. To get off to a good start, plants need moist, warm soil for good root growth, as well as ample water to support top growth. All you need to do is make the most of the weather in your region.

In most parts of the United States, spring and/or fall are ideal for establishing plants with a minimum of fuss. (In the South, late or early winter is best.) The cloudy days and cool, moist

Continued ➡

Elevated Beds for Wheelchair Gardening

Roger Yepsen

Gardeners in wheelchairs or walkers can till the soil if beds are raised to between 24 and 30 inches. Ideally, these beds should be just 2 feet wide if they will be accessed from one side, or from 3 to 4 feet wide if the gardener can work from both sides.

The beds can be an attractive addition to the garden if constructed with sturdy materials.

One approach is to stack and spike landscaping ties. Be sure to avoid using ties that have been pressure treated or preserved with pentachlorophenol. For a highly durable base, pour a concrete footer, then build low walls of concrete block, faced on the outside with a layer of brick. For better drainage, you can place a layer of gravel in the bed before adding soil.

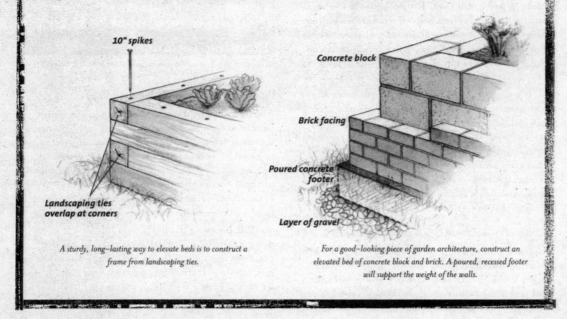

10" spikes

Landscaping ties overlap at corners

A sturdy, long-lasting way to elevate beds is to construct a frame from landscaping ties.

Concrete block

Brick facing

Poured concrete footer

Layer of gravel

For a good-looking piece of garden architecture, construct an elevated bed of concrete block and brick. A poured, recessed footer will support the weight of the walls.

---

air help reduce transplant shock by keeping moisture losses to a minimum. Here are some guidelines to help you decide which season is best for planting.

Spring planting. In spring, plants are naturally preparing for a flush of new growth, which is just what they'll need to get established in a new location. Spring rains naturally help keep new transplants well watered, too. In areas where cold weather arrives in early autumn and temperatures often fall below -10°F, early spring planting gives plants time to grow and establish themselves before harsh winter temperatures arrive.

Fall planting. Fall planting provides plants with weeks of good root-growing weather-moist soil and warm soil temperatures. Since aboveground growth slows or becomes dormant in the cooler air, the roots have a chance to catch up with topgrowth. Fall transplants also can begin growing in early spring, when the soil is still too wet for planting.

For the best root growth and winter survival, try fall planting only in areas where the soil temperature remains above 50°F for several weeks after the trees become dormant. And plant early in the fall to take advantage of good root-growing weather.

In areas with hot, dry summers and mild winters, fall planting gives new plants time to establish healthy roots before the following spring. By then, the plants' roots are also better prepared to survive the hot summer weather.

Summer planting. You can plant successfully in summer, but summer installations generally demand more watering and care than plantings timed to take advantage of the cooler weather and natural rainfall in spring and fall.

Don't Dig Down, Dig Out

Simply digging a hole and plopping a plant into it may seem like the easy way to plant, but it causes long-term problems that may come back to haunt you. Plant roots are likely to circle around in a planting hole without ever extending into the surrounding soil. Eventually, they can choke, or girdle, the plant. A planting hole can also become a "bathtub" of loose soil that traps water around roots and drowns them.

To give your plants the possible chance for a healthy, problem-free life, give them a prepared planting site. To prepare a planting site, spade or till up a planting area that's about five times the diameter of the plant's root ball. This loosens the soil so the roots can spread freely. Amending the soil over the entire area with organic matter to a shovel's depth is ideal, but it isn't absolutely necessary if you've picked plants suited to your soil conditions. When you plant, dig saucer-shaped holes, as shown in the illustration above.

Preparing planting areas for groups of trees and shrubs is a great idea. Plants growing together in a large, mulched planting area will be healthier and more vigorous than ones planted individually in the lawn.

To Plant Right, Pick Right from the Start

To save yourself hours of maintenance, pick plants that like your site from the start. By choosing plants that will thrive in your site's conditions, you'll prevent years of maintenance headaches.

It's a losing battle to plant something in a site that doesn't suit it. You can amend the soil in the sunny border between your house and driveway to get rhododendrons to grow there, but you'll tire of the extra care they'll need every year just to eke out a so-so existence. Eventually, you'll want to replace them with plants that flourish without extra effort.

Take-It-Easy Planting Tips

Although you shouldn't cut corners when it comes to proper planting, here are some tips to make planting easy.

Wheel, don't carry. Use a garden cart or wheelbarrow to carry everything you need to your site at once—plants, shovel, trowel, mulch, and any other tools you might need.

Slide, don't lift. Rather than carrying large plants, use a large tarp to slide them over rough ground. On smooth surfaces, setting plants on a dolly may do the trick.

Use professional planters. Consider having large trees and shrubs planted by the nursery where you bought them. Large plants can easily weigh over 100 pounds, so professional planting can save your back. Also, many nurseries provide replacement guarantees on plants they install.

Measure before you plant. Make sure your hole is large enough before you set your plant into it. Measuring the height and width of both the hole and the root ball will save you from having to haul the plant out of the hole repeatedly while you make it larger.

Space before you plant. If you're planting a large area of groundcovers or annuals, space out the plants you have over the area you want to plant before you dig.

Spread the roots for no-fail planting. Before you settle container-grown plants into the ground, take a minute to encourage the roots to spread out into the soil. Using a knife or trowel to quarter the root ball seems like a drastic technique, but it's a very effective way to encourage the roots to branch and spread. When you quarter a root ball, cut upward about halfway from the base.

When you plant, spread the roots out in the planting hole and backfill around them. If your planting site is newly prepared, set plants slightly higher than they grew in their pots—they'll settle in as the soil settles. Otherwise, plant them at their container-grown depth.

Bareroot Plants Make for Easy Planting

Although bareroot plants may seem strange or intimidating, they make lots of sense for low-maintenance gardeners. Since they're sold without all the soil that accompanies container-grown and balled-burlapped plants, they're easier to lift and move around your yard. If you're mail-ordering, they're also less expensive to ship. Roses, fruit trees and bushes, strawberries, and grapevines are typically sold bareroot, as are daylilies, irises, and many other perennials. Many trees and shrubs are also sold bareroot.

Fortunately, bareroot plants are easier to handle than they might seem. They're typically shipped dormant, timed to arrive at your door ready for planting. Whenever possible, plant them as soon as you can. If you can't plant right away, moisten their roots thoroughly and pack them in moist potting mix or compost. Try to hold them this way for no longer than three days.

Before you plant, soak the roots in a bucket of water for at least an hour or two. Cut off any dead or damaged roots with sharp scissors or pruning shears. Then plant them as shown above.

Check under the Burlap for Best Buys on B&B

If you buy a field-grown tree or shrub from your local nursery, chances are you'll get it balled-and-burlapped, or B&B. Before you buy, it pays to check what's under the burlap to make sure you

Continued ➡

spend all your planting efforts on a healthy plant instead of one that has been mistreated.

B&B plants are usually dug while they are dormant, and their root balls are wrapped with burlap. The biggest hazard of buying a B&B tree is that it may not have a large enough root ball.

To check the root ball size of potential purchases, use this rule of thumb: The root ball should be 1 foot in diameter for every inch of the diameter of the trunk at the base. There is no similar rule for shrubs, but bear in mind that the bigger the root ball, the faster the plant will establish itself.

Undersize root balls are a bigger hazard for trees, whose roots extend far beyond their drip lines (the point to which the tree's branches extend). The average B&B tree retains only 5 percent of its original root mass.

From Ground to Garden

If gardening were a board game, we'd all skip "start" (digging a new bed) and go straight to "win" (enjoying the results). But the old gardening wisdom is true: If you prepare the soil well in the beginning, you'll save time later on weeding, feeding, watering, and other chores. And your plants will reward you with robust health that promotes natural insect and disease resistance.

Digging In

There are as many ways to start a garden as there are gardeners. And there are also ways to make this task considerably easier. How you go about preparing your garden bed depends on a number of things, including the condition of the soil when you start and what you want to grow.

For example, double-digging is one of the best ways to build a raised vegetable bed. But if you plan to plant perennials, you can use a less work-intensive method of bed preparation, or even a no-dig method. Whatever bed preparation method you choose, remember, balanced soil that holds the right amounts of air, water, and nutrients.

Before you dig in, read on, and use your answers to the following questions to help you decide which garden-making method will work best for you:

- What do you plan to grow in your garden?
- What type of soil and soil problems do you have to begin with?
- How hard are you willing, or able, to work?
- How soon after preparing the garden do you want to plant?

Double-Digging Delivers Double-Good Beds

There's no question that it's hard work, but double-digging is still one of the absolute *best* ways to prepare a garden bed. You loosen the soil to about 24 inches deep when you double-dig, which gives your plants' roots lots of room to roam. Double-diggers who've examined the benefits of this method report that they get much higher yields from double-dug beds—in some cases, 9 to 15 *times* the yields of similar-size-but-not-double-dug plots!

1. Using a spade or sharp shovel, dig a trench about 1 foot wide and 1 foot deep across the narrow end of the bed. Put *this* soil (and only this trench's worth of soil) into a wheel-barrow. This soil will be used to fill in the last trench when you're all done digging.

2. Loosen the soil in the bottom of that trench an additional 12 inches with a spading fork. Push the tines of the fork in to their full length, then use the handle as a lever and push down to move the tines up through the soil.

3. Now dig a second trench, also about 1 foot deep and 1 foot wide, next to the first trench. Use this second trench's soil to fill the first trench.

4. When the second trench is empty, use the fork to loosen the lower 12 inches of soil in it, just as you did in the first trench.

5. Repeat these steps, trench by trench, until you reach the other end of the garden bed.

6. After you've removed the top layer and loosened the lower layer of soil in the last trench, use the soil you saved in the wheelbarrow from the first trench to fill in this trench. Rake the whole bed level from outside the bed, so you won't step on the freshly "double-dug" soil.

7. Spread a 1-inch layer of compost over the entire bed for a nutrient boost and to prevent diseases.

8. Place your plants in your newly double-dug bed! Don't step on the bed or you'll compact the loose fluffy soil. If you can't reach the center of the bed, get a sturdy board and lay it on supports resting outside the garden so it extends over the top of the bed. Stand or kneel on the board when you're ready to plant in the middle of your garden.

Another Way to Make Your Bed

Some people look at their lawn and see, well, grass. Others see spaces where new flowerbeds and mixed plantings could be. If your interest in the soil involves ways to use it to support more flowers, read on to learn the steps to follow to turn boring expanses of sod into pretty perennial gardens.

1. We've said it before, but it's worth repeating: Don't dig in wet soil. Start your bed-building venture by checking to make sure the soil is dry enough to dig.

2. To create a straight-edged bed, drive stakes into the ground and stretch a clothesline from stake to stake to mark off the perimeter of the garden. You can outline a bed with a curved edge by laying a garden hose on the ground and adjusting it to the desired shape. To mark the edges before you remove the sod, drive your garden fork into the ground along the outline of the rope or hose, and break up the sod as you go.

3. If you don't plan to use the sod in another spot in your landscape, a garden fork is a good tool for turning the sod and the soil. You can also use a sharp shovel or spade for this task, but you may find the work easier with a fork because it's easier to push the tines into the soil.

4. To lift the sod, push the fork straight down into the ground with your foot, then use the handle as a lever to pry loose a clump of sod. Grab the sod and shake the soil from the roots onto the bed. Throw the remaining grass on your compost pile and repeat until you've uncovered the soil over the entire bed.

5. If you haven't already tested the soil in this new garden bed, now is the time to take a sample to send off for analysis. It's definitely worth it to do this now, before you invest time and money

in fertilizers and amendments for your new bed.

6. Before planting, spread approximately 1 inch of compost or composted manure over the top of the bed. This is also the time to blend in any of the amendments that were recommended as a result of the soil test. Then use your fork to mix them 12 to 18 inches deep into the loosened soil.

7. When the soil is light and fluffy and the amendments are mixed in, grab a garden rake and level the surface of the soil with the tines. Then flip the rake over and smooth the soil with the backside of the rake. Now you're ready to plant.

8. Perennials of all shapes and sizes come in plastic nursery pots. The trick to unpotting them without damaging the roots is to turn the pot upside down, then cradle the soil surface and plant in one hand while gently squeezing the pot with the other until the roots and soil slide out. Untangle any roots that are circling the rootball. Then use a trowel to dig a hole deep enough to set the rootball of the plant at the same depth it sat in the pot. Make the hole wide enough so there's room to straighten out any long roots. When the plant is in its hole, firm the garden soil around the rootball. Then create a shallow trench around the root zone on the surface of the soil so water will collect and trickle down to the roots. Fill a watering can with water and soak the soil around each plant's roots.

9. When your plants are set in place and watered well, cover the ground around and between them with a 2-inch layer of compost. If you like, you can top the compost layer with an inch or two of a more attractive organic mulch, such as pine needles, buckwheat hulls, or shredded bark.

10. Edging your bed gives it a neat, finished look and has the practical advantage of keeping grass roots from taking hold in the bed's soft, fertile soil. Here's an easy and effective way to edge: Take a half-moon edger and push it straight down into the soil all along the edge of your bed. (These edging tools are inexpensive and really easy to use—the 4-inch length digs to exactly the depth of grass roots, and the curved blade is easy to push in.) Rock the edger back and forth to cut the sod.

When you've made a straight cut around the whole perimeter of the bed, make a second cut on the flowerbed side, but this time push the edger in toward the first cut at a 45-degree angle. Pull out the wedge of sod and soil, leaving a narrow, V-shaped trench around the bed. This keeps grass roots out of your beds because when the roots break through the straight side of the trench and contact air, they will turn around and grow back into the soil on the lawn side of the trench. Over time the roots will weave through and reinforce the wall of the trench, without invading your garden.

Building a Lazy Bed

If you plan to put in a new bed several months before you plant it, why not take it easy and take advantage of the time you have to create a "lazy bed"? This no-digging method is easier on your back and kinder to the soil because it preserves the existing structure, pores, and worm tunnels. And with this method you'll end up with a raised bed, which will drain well and warm up quickly in the spring.

Continued →

Start by mowing the sod or weeds or whatever is growing in your intended site as low as your mower will cut. This is the one time when it's okay to "scalp" the grass with your mower. Then completely cover the close-cropped sod with several thicknesses of newspaper. It helps to wet the newspaper to keep it from blowing away as you're laying it out.

Top the newspaper layers with 8 to 10 inches of organic matter. Be creative and thrifty and use materials that you have on hand or that are easy to come by. Shredded leaves, compost, grass clippings, wood chips, straw or hay, and even kitchen scraps are all fair game here. Just pile it on and wait for these riches to break down into healthy soil for future planting. Keep in mind that if your lazy bed is in a spot that you look at often, you'll want to top it with something that looks nice while you're waiting—choose a "pretty" mulch like wood chips or cocoa shells for the top layer. If looks are less of a concern and rich soil is the ultimate interest, tuck all that organic matter under a layer of black plastic for quicker decomposition.

If you build your lazy bed in late summer and let it "cook" until spring, it should be ready for planting when the local nurseries put their plants out for sale. While you wait, use your time to browse through glossy plant catalogs and make a map of exactly what you want to plant in the soft, rich soil of your new bed.

Raise Your Garden in Raised Beds

Few methods of gardening offer as many advantages as growing in raised beds. Raised garden beds are higher than ground level and are separated by paths. Plants cover the bed areas, and gardeners work from the paths. Typical raised beds are 3 to 5 feet across to permit easy access from the sides and may be any length. You can grow vegetables in raised beds, as well as herbs, annual or perennial flowers, berry bushes, or even small trees. Raised beds can solve problems of difficult soils; improve production; save space, time, and money; and improve your garden's appearance and accessibility. Raised-bed crops are more productive because they grow in deep, loose, fertile soil that is never walked upon. And you can grow twice as many crops in the same space: In a row garden, the crops occupy only one-third of the garden area while the paths between the rows take up two-thirds of the space. In a raised bed garden, the proportions are reversed.

First clear the site and remove weeds or sod, then use one of the following techniques to build your beds:

Mounding. This is the quickest and easiest way to make a raised bed. Simply till or fork up the soil to loosen it, then heap compost, well-rotted manure, and other organic matter on top and rake it together to create a mounded bed. If your soil is very poor or rocky, use purchased topsoil mixed with compost and amendments to build the beds from the ground up. Because a freshly built mounded bed is loose and full of air, it settles initially and can easily erode. Add more soil-compost mix if the bed loses height. Frame the bed if erosion is a problem.

Tilling and hilling. This bed-building method prepares the soil almost as thoroughly as double-digging but takes much less time.

1. With a rotary tiller, thoroughly till the entire garden area to a depth of 6 to 8 inches.

2. Using stakes, twine, and a tape measure, layout the perimeter of the beds. Be sure you leave adequate space for pathways. From this point on, walk only in those pathways, not on the marked beds.

3. Loosen the subsoil in the marked-off areas with a garden fork.

4. Next, using a spade, scoop up the top 2 to 3 inches of soil from the pathways around the beds, and add it to the beds to produce nicely raised beds.

From Companion Planting to Crop Rotation

Sally Jean Cunningham

Companion planting captivates gardeners. We're charmed by the notion that plants have "friends" who help them grow better. And as organic gardeners, we're eager to try simple, nonchemical methods that may repel pests. There's also something satisfying about learning from old-time gardeners—and companion planting certainly has deep roots in history. I've discovered that companion planting makes my garden better, but it's not the whole story of my system. I also rely on insects, birds, earthworms, and even fungi and bacteria to create a healthy, bountiful organic vegetable garden. So companion planting is only part of the picture. It's intertwined with techniques like attracting beneficial insects, building soil, and planting intensively—all vital to my companion-gardening system.

Starting with Companion Planting

I first studied companion planting on doctor's orders. I was confined to bed during a rough pregnancy—during gardening season, too! I decided that if I couldn't garden, at least I could read about it. There was plenty to read. I found books full of recommendations for pairing up vegetables with other vegetables, flowers, and herbs. There were even companion-planting suggestions for fruit trees. I tried to memorize every possible companion-planting combination, but the recommendations were sometimes confusing and very unscientific. There were even contradictions and impossibilities. For instance: One source said that bush beans grow well with cucumbers. Another recommended pairing bush beans with potatoes but said that potatoes should not be planted with cucumbers. So what's a gardener to do?

My answer was to dig hard into the research on companion planting. I sorted through hundreds of recommendations, trying to find the ones that were recommended by several sources and backed by research. Some companion-planting suggestions made lots of sense, such as planting cucumbers and broccoli together to make it harder for cucumber beetles to find the cucumber plants. Others were more like fairy tales. For example, petunias, especially pink petunias, are supposed to repel squash bugs and Mexican bean beetles. (Maybe they don't like the color pink!) And planting lettuce and squash together is supposed to put rabbits to sleep so they won't be able to eat the crops. I think I'd rather put my money on a garden fence or rely on my dogs' frequent tours around the garden to deter rabbits.

By the end of my pregnancy, I'd compiled some important reasons why companion planting works and had listed hundreds of companion-planting combinations to try. Testing those combinations and choosing the best took a few seasons of experimentation. And while I experi-mented and refined my choices, I developed my system of companion gardening.

SEARCHING FOR ANSWERS

When I decided to study companion planting, I was searching for help with my own garden. I was trying to garden organically and was failing miserably. There were horrendous holes in the broccoli leaves, the potatoes were puny, and the weeds made August a nightmare! I was even teaching organic gardening at the time, and what I did and taught were fine—as far as they went. But I made a mistake that beginning organic or "switching over" gardeners often make. I substituted organic products like bonemeal for synthetic products like chemical fertilizers—*but I gardened the same otherwise.* Somehow I thought that if I avoided pesticides, used manure, and planted my rows of vegetables, Mother Nature (knowing I'd been good to her) would keep the pests in line. So wasn't I dismayed when the Colorado potato beetles arrived in droves, every ear of corn had earworms, and there were embarrassing little green worms floating in the pot when I cooked my broccoli!

The problem was that I had a very unnatural garden: a flat rectangle of straight single rows of plants with bare soil between. This gardening style works when you rely on chemical pesticides to kill pests and chemical herbicides to wipe out weeds. But for me, the few organic products or tricks I substituted (insecticidal soaps, black plastic to kill weeds, and home remedies for pests) just wouldn't cut it. I had to rethink the whole system. I needed a garden that could take care of itself without lots of artificial help from me.

Learning from Natures "Garden"

So the season after my enforced bed rest, I started experimenting with companion planting in my garden. I was hooked on the idea of mixing and matching plants to create a beautiful garden with practically no pest problems. But I discovered that while companion planting was a great idea, it wasn't enough. I also needed to build up the diversity and richness of my garden soil and to create a diverse environment both in and around my vegetable garden. I began to study the examples of nature, paying close attention to what was happening around the pond and in the woods beside my garden.

I'd like you to imagine some of the things I saw in the woods. There were fallen leaves and hemlock needles covering the soil surface. When I bent to poke a finger under the leaves, I saw earthworms tunneling in the moist surface soil. Under a fallen tree limb, I saw centipedes and pillbugs doing some of the decomposing that turns dead plants into a rich type of organic matter called humus. There were ferns growing in the rich humus and wild blackberries clustered at the sunny edges of the woods. Both those plants thrive in the acid soil beneath the evergreens. I heard sounds, too: the hum of insects, the chattering of squirrels, and the warble of birds that were searching the woods for berries, seeds, and insects to eat.

Now, think what would happen in the woods if Joe Gardener came along with a pesticide to "get rid of those bugs?" What if he raked up the pine needles, added some lime, and planted roses or tomatoes? I'm sure you know the answer: Interfere with the links in the living chain, and the natural system starts to collapse.

So if modern human gardening styles ruin natural systems, should we move back into caves or walk around feeling terribly guilty all the time? Of course not! There aren't enough caves for all

Continued ➔

of us anyway, and feeling guilty won't make things any better. What we can do is set up gardens that take advantage of the natural processes that make the woods a successful, self-sustaining system. We can make a difference by planning gardens and landscapes that won't need chemicals to keep them looking good. And a very good way to start is by creating a more diverse environment in your own yard and garden.

Gardening with Nature

Can we re-create a natural forest or meadow in the vegetable garden? Not really—and we don't want to if we plan on producing a harvest. In our gardens, we want to choose which crops we're going to grow, after all. To mimic Mother Nature but still grow your choice of food and flowers, there are several techniques that will help.

Break up mono-crops. If you're growing a lot of one crop, plant several small plots in different parts of your garden, and mix the crop with at least one other vegetable crop.

Plant flowers and herbs. Interplanting flowers and herbs among your vegetables attracts natural predators such as birds and beneficial insects and makes it harder for pest insects to find the crop.

Shelter beneficials. Provide water, food, shelter, and breeding places for beneficial insects, toads, birds, lizards, and even snakes. Possible habitats can be hedgerows, perennial plantings, ground-covers, or rock piles. Putting out bird feeders, birdhouses, and birdbaths also helps.

Swear off pesticides. Even organic sprays like pyrethrum can kill beneficial insects. Butterflies have nearly no pesticide tolerance. And killing all the "pests" wipes out food that your beneficial insects might have eaten. Basically, if you spray, what you'll destroy is your effort to attract beneficials.

Leave some weeds. Learn which weeds or wildflowers provide habitat for natural predators, and leave a few of them in place when you weed. (Warning: Some weeds compete too well for nutrients, harbor pests or diseases, or take over too aggressively—so learn to identify weeds like Queen-Anne's-lace and goldenrod that are safe to leave in place.)

Companion Planting Creates Diversity

Creating diversity brings us right back to companion planting. My study of nature revealed the two best reasons for using companion planting in my vegetable garden, and I'll boldly state them here.

First, almost any combination of plants grown together is better than segregating crops into separate blocks. Combining plants increases biodiversity—the variety of living things in an area. And this variety is one of the big secrets of companion gardening! If you start mixing up your vegetables and adding in herbs and flowers, you'll also attract a variety of birds and beneficial insects to your garden. This alone will do a great deal to ensure a successful garden.

This leads to my second bold statement: When companion planting works to minimize pest problems, it is usually because the companion plants confuse the pest insects or attract beneficial insects. Certain plants do a good job of confusing pest insects in search of your crops. Other plants attract the beneficial insects that destroy those pests. In fact, I'll bet that many of the traditional companion plants that "repel" pests really work because the mixed-up planting confused the pest or because the companion plant harbored predatory or parasitic beneficial insects.

So either Mr. Pest never found his dinner or he was eaten before he got there!

Quick Tip

Weeds in Cracks Breaking Your Back?

Here's an easy trick for dealing with stubborn weeds that pop up between the cracks in sidewalks, patios, and paved pathways: Put ¼ cup of table salt in 1 quart of boiling water, and pour the hot liquid on the offending plants. You'll kill the weeds—and they won't come back.

Sorting Out the Companions

As I played with companion planting and increasing diversity in my garden, I still found myself searching for a way to simplify what I was doing. I didn't want to review all the companion-planting books each year and re-create my garden from scratch! I decided to create plant groupings that worked well together and to keep using those groups from year to year.

I started with the vegetable crops that I wanted to grow. I broke these up into groups I call *families*. Then I chose friends that would complement and assist the vegetables by attracting beneficial insects, confusing pests, and enriching the soil. Most of these are herbs and annual flowers, and many of them are traditional companion plants. However, I also drew from recent research on the best plants to attract beneficial insects, so my friends even include some perennial flowers, as well as cover crops, like buckwheat.

A plant family with its friends forms a *neighborhood*. I sometimes make small changes in the members of a neighborhood. For instance, one year I became very interested in fancy salad greens other than lettuce, so I added them into my lettuce neighborhood. I move my neighborhoods from bed to bed each year, a practice called crop rotation, which also plays a role in controlling insect and disease problems.

Taking Care of Your Soil

Plant neighborhoods are the heart of my system, but they're not the whole of it. My early attempts at organic gardening showed me that there's more to it than just not using chemicals, and there's more to it than mixing up your plants. Even if you plan wonderfully diverse planting beds, if your soil is in poor shape, your harvest will be poor, too. Soil is the source of food and water for my crops, so covering and protecting the soil are a big part of my companion-gardening system.

Keep Your Soil Covered

I always cover my soil. Sometimes I'm tempted not to, especially when the garden looks so fresh and orderly, with neat little seedlings pushing through the soft, raked earth. The trouble is, the garden won't look like that for long. Not only do weeds sprout, but rain and wind start to batter the soil surface. Soon that soft, raked planting bed has gullies in it where topsoil has eroded. Or if the weather's been dry, the soil surface is baked, crusty, and hard. It will be impossible for seedlings to poke through, for roots to grow, or for water to soak in. And if you cultivate to fix things, you end up stepping on the soil, and it becomes even more packed down. To prevent this destructive sequence of events, I always cover my soil.

Make the Most of Mulch

Most gardeners use mulch to cover their soil. There are many kinds of mulch. I mulch with grass clippings, straw, newspaper (shredded or in sheets), leaves, pine needles, cocoa shells, and sometimes black plastic. (I leave bark chips for the landscape plantings.) I know gardeners who use rugs, carpet runners, tarps, and shower curtains for mulch. If you don't like the looks of these "recycled" mulches, just cover them with a more attractive natural mulch. That way you can use what you have available.

Cover Up with Cover Crops

Cover crops or green manures are special crops that we plant especially to keep the soil covered. I love using cover crops in my garden because they also shelter those all-important beneficial insects, and they're prettier than many mulches.

You can choose from many grasses and grains for a cover crop, including annual ryegrass, hairy vetch, buckwheat, clover, and alfalfa. You can plant some of these in fall to cover the soil during the winter, and then turn them under in the spring to build the soil's organic content. Or you can plant them in beds that need to "rest" for all or part of the growing season. They cover and protect soil, block weeds, and add organic matter.

I think the best trick with cover crops is to plant them next to or among your vegetable crops. This is called intercropping, or interseeding. It works particularly well with legume crops like clover and alfalfa. These crops improve soil fertility by "fixing" nitrogen. This means that with the help of special bacteria in the soil, their roots can change nitrogen gas from the air into nitrogen compounds plant roots can use. (Nitrogen is a building block of protein, which plants need to live and grow, just like animals.)

Keep Crops Close Together

Still another way to cover the soil is by planting your vegetable crops dose together—intensively—in wide rows. Wide rows can be anywhere from 1½ to 4 feet wide. You can space individual plants so closely that their leaves touch or overlap when they reach full size. This leaf canopy shades the soil so weeds can't get enough sunlight to grow well, and less moisture evaporates from the soil. You can plant a single crop intensively—for example, a 3-foot-wide row of beans planted 6 inches apart in all directions. Or you can plant two or more different kinds of plants intensively for the same effect. For instance, you can plant zinnias to fill in bare spots in the broccoli bed, or plant lettuce and spinach together across a whole bed.

Be a Soil Builder

In a forest or meadow, the natural system works to continually build up the soil. Plants grow and die, then insects, bacteria, and fungi cause the dead plants to decompose, returning nutrients to the soil. Animals die, too, and their bodies also contribute nutrients as they decompose. Even rocks break down gradually and add minerals. But when we farm or garden, we use up the soil about 16 times faster than nature rebuilds it. In part, that's because we keep removing plants as we harvest, instead of letting them decompose and return to the soil. Poor agricultural practices that waste soil and cause erosion are also to blame. So we need to build the soil in our vegetable gardens all the time!

Building soil can be a lot of work, and common sense says it's easier to protect the good soil you already have. Covering the soil is a good

Continued ➡

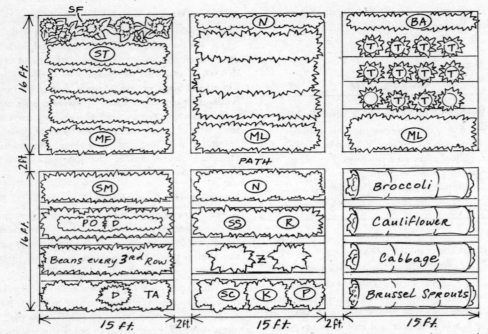

My companion garden. My garden has six blocks of beds. In each block I interplant herbs and flowers and mix my crops to create a diverse system that's full of natural pest-control power. Each year, I rotate crops from one block to another.

BA — Basil	P — Parsley	SM — Straw mulch
D — Dill	PO — Potatoes	SS — Summer squash
K - Kale	R — Radishes	ST - Strawberries
MF — Mixed Flowers	SC — Swiss chard	TA — Tansy
N — Nasturtiums	SF — Sunflowers	Z — Zucchini

start toward preventing soil loss. However, it's important not only to keep your soil but also to keep good soil structure. Soil with good structure has lots of pores, tiny openings that roots can grow through and that can hold water and air.

Once soil structure is destroyed, it can take two years or more to re-create it. Good structure, or tilth, is something that you can feel, especially as you gain experience with gardening. Good soil crumbles in your hand because it's made up of lots of little clumps of particles that contain both moisture and air.

The best way to protect soil structure in your vegetable beds is to stay off them. When we step on the soil, our body weight compresses it, crushing all those tiny openings that hold water and air. That's why I raise my beds slightly and put dear paths between them.

YOUR SOIL IS FULL OF LIVE

Imagine that you're in your garden, where you can scoop up a handful of soil and look at it. Aside from a centipede, grub, or pill bug, you might not see anything that looks alive, but that's only because your eyes aren't powerful enough to see most of the tiny organisms at work there.

In that handful of soil, there are millions of bacteria and fungi that break down organic matter, making nutrients available to plant roots. Special nitrogen-fixing bacteria work with the roots of leguminous plants to fix nitrogen. There are microscopic wormlike creatures caned nematodes—some helpful and some destructive. Root-knot nematodes infest roots of many vegetable crops and can stunt their growth, while beneficial nematodes termites, grubs, and other pest insects.

FEEDING THE SOIL

When I was a little girl, my Grandpa Harper taught me to "feed the soil and not the plant." So when I saw him put kitchen scraps into trenches in the garden, I thought he was actually "feeding" the soil! But what he was really doing was feeding the microorganisms, insects, and animals in the soil. They feed on organic matter—which can be anything from apple peels to those overgrown zucchini that you couldn't manage to give away.

For organic gardeners, getting organic matter into the soil probably takes more time than any other single gardening activity. That's because we know that our soil is our garden's gold—our most precious resource. We make and spread compost, sow cover crops, put down mulch, and dig spent crops back into the soil. One year, I used my gardening journal to jot down how I spent my time in the garden. My notes showed that I put about half my time into gathering and moving organic matter (manure, leaves, yard debris, mulch from the town), making compost, and getting the stuff into the garden!

Once we add the organic matter, the soil life takes over. The microorganisms, insects, and other soil-dwelling animals munch on it, eventually decomposing and converting the organic matter into simple forms that plants can use. Earthworms are the best-known soil-building organisms. They can process or digest their weight in organic matter daily, converting it into nitrogen, phosphorus, potassium, and other nutrients, which they leave behind in a material called castings. If you supply organic matter, you'll have a soil neighborhood of earthworms and other happy organisms that will create a rich, productive soil.

Making the Most of Your Garden

My system of companion gardening relies on some tried-and-true techniques that increase productivity and add pest-protection insurance to your garden. These methods are succession planting, relay planting, and crop rotation. Using these techniques helps make the most of garden space and also makes

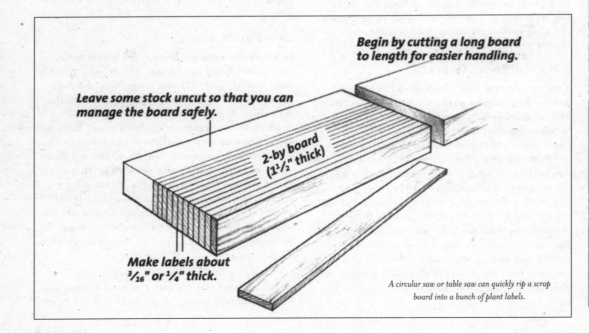

Begin by cutting a long board to length for easier handling.

Leave some stock uncut so that you can manage the board safely.

2-by board (1½" thick)

Make labels about ³⁄₁₆" or ¼" thick.

A circular saw or table saw can quickly rip a scrap board into a bunch of plant labels.

Continued ➡

the garden more diverse and naturally pest resistant. That fits right in with companion gardening!

SUCCESSION AND RELAY PLANTING

Successions and relays are two planting techniques that use space well and keep the soil covered. Succession planting is planting a new crop as soon as you pull up the plants from a crop that's finished. A typical routine would be to harvest a cool-weather crop like peas and then plant a warm-weather crop like beans or squash in their place.

Relay planting takes a bit more strategic planning. When you plant in relays, you start one crop next to, or under, an existing crop that will finish soon. For example, you may plant bush-bean seeds under broccoli plants two weeks before the broccoli harvest. That way, the beans will already be growing when you pull out the finished broccoli plants.

Another sequence I like involves overlapping plantings of early spring lettuces, onions, carrots, and more lettuce. As your harvest leaves spaces among one crop, just plant a few of the next.

CROP ROTATION PAYS OFF

For me, crop rotation is a gardening basic: It just makes sense to locate your crops in a different part of the garden each season. Crop rotation minimizes disease and insect infestations. For example, if you plant tomatoes in the same bed every year, you'll probably end up fostering a tomato disease like Verticillium wilt. The fungi that cause the disease will remain in the soil over the winter and will just start up again if you plant more tomatoes in the same spot in the spring.

On the other hand, if the tomatoes are in a new bed as little as 15 feet away, the fungi may not find their target in time to survive. The same is true for pests. How soon to repeat the same crop in one location varies by the crop and the situation. I recommend waiting at least four years before replanting a crop in the same spot, especially if a soilborne disease has been present.

Smart rotations also help make the best use of soil nutrients. That's because different crops have different nutrient needs. Some crops, such as cucumbers and tomatoes, use up lots of nutrients, while others, such as beans and potatoes, use very few or actually add nutrients. I group my vegetable crops as heavy feeders, light feeders, or soil builders when I plan rotations with soil in mind. I've built crop rotation right into my companion-gardening system, as you'll see when you create your own crop groups.

SUMMING UP MY SYSTEM

By now you know that my companion garden has a mixed-up look, and it's a real mix of gardening techniques. Companion planting is a key element, but feeding and protecting the soil are equally important. I've also worked to make special areas to attract and shelter beneficial insects and animals. And of course, I plant all my crops intensively, I plant crops in successions and relays, and I rotate crops from year to year.

The techniques themselves aren't new, but the way I've combined them is, and it adds a sense of adventure to my gardening. I'm always on the lookout for beneficial insects I might not have seen before, and I'm always thinking about new ways to make my vegetable garden even more self-sustaining. For example, one new technique I'm experimenting with is planting a hedgerow next to my vegetable garden specifically to attract and shelter those good insects and animals that prey on insect pests (I'll tell you more about that in Chapter 6, "Perennials in the Pumpkins, Shrubs on the Side").

It's easy to enjoy experimenting because my basic system works so well. As I plant cosmos with my eggplant and add compost to my intensively planted raised beds, it's nice to know that I'm part of a long tradition of gardening wisdom. The techniques and principles were always there. It's just our turn to apply them.

We'll start with garden layout and making raised beds, then move on to the nitty-gritty of setting up plant families, friends, and neighborhoods. The end result will be a successful, diverse garden, full of food and flowers and lots of life!

Plant Labels, Cheap

Wooden plant labels aren't inexpensive, and they're usually flimsy by the end of the growing season. If you have a table saw, or are handy with a handheld circular saw, you can quickly reduce a scrap length of lumber, such as a 2 x 4 or 2 x 6, into a bunch of sturdy labels. Wider boards (such as a 2 x 6 or 2 x 8) are easier to handle because you can saw off a good number of label-thickness slabs and still have some stock to hold on to. It also can help to begin by cutting boards to a manageable length that is a multiple of the desired label length. If you want 12-inch labels, for example, make cuts at 2- or 3-foot intervals.

These won't be untrasmooth, rounded pieces of art, but they'll do the job. And if they're thicker than the commercial kind, they may hold up better. Wear safety eyewear when sawing. Either rip the board by running it through a table saw, or clamp the board securely and run a circular saw along it with a ripping guide attached. Use a chop saw, table saw, circular saw, or hand saw to cut the strips to length.

Cold Frames and Hotbeds
Barbara W. Ellis

Designing and Using Cold Frames and Hotbeds

Cold frames and hotbeds are among the most useful of gardening structures, regardless of the type of gardening you do. Although most commonly used in early spring for starting or hardening-off seedlings, both can be used year-round for a multitude of purposes. Throughout much of the country, these structures can help extend the growing season by three months or more. Cold frames, and to a lesser extent hotbeds, can also be used for winter storage of container-grown plants that might not survive the rigors of winter above ground, holding over not-quite-hardy herbs or perennials, or for cold-treating spring bulbs potted up for forcing. Some models are also very useful for rooting cuttings of woody plants or perennials. Furthermore, cold frames and hotbeds—both of which are often referred to as frames for convenience—are inexpensive to build and easy to maintain.

PICKING A DESIGN

The type of frame you decide to build will depend on how you want to use it, as well as the space and site you have available. Your design can be as simple or elaborate as you wish; many cold frames and hotbeds are designed around materials on hand or ones that can be easily salvaged. Depending on the type of gardening you do, you may decide on a combination of cold frames and hotbeds, as well as permanent and portable models. There are also a variety of ready-made models for sale. Consider the following selection and design factors when making your choice.

Cold frames and hotbeds are basically rectangular, boxlike structures with glass sash on top. Most frames are designed with slanting sash roofs, with the high end toward the north, so that the sun's rays strike the glass at nearly a 90-degree angle in late winter and water and snow slide off the lids easily. Most frames are designed with lids sloping at an angle between 35 degrees and 45 degrees, which, for a 3-foot-deep model, translates to a frame that is 9 to 12 inches lower in front than in back. A slope of 35 degrees is most efficient for catching the late winter to early spring sun; a 55-degree slope catches more autumn sun, which is at a lower angle. It's possible to fine-tune your frame to catch more autumn sun by designing wedge-shaped inserts that change the angle of the glass.

The inside of the frame is usually painted white to increase the amount of light reflected onto the plants. You'll also need blocks or other props for holding the lids open to ventilate the frames.

Hot or Cold?

From a structural point of view, hotbeds and cold frames are identical, with the exception that hotbeds are supplied with some form of artificial heat. Traditionally, rotting manure served as the heat source, but today, electric heating cables are commonly used. Because hotbeds have a regular source of heat, they can be put into use earlier in the season than most cold frames and provide ideal conditions for starting most types of seeds. Also, they can be easily converted to cold frames during times of the year when heating isn't necessary.

Permanent or Portable?

There are two basic types of frames: permanent structures or portable ones. Permanent models are built over a foundation, either dug in the ground or constructed on the surface. Above-ground models provide less frost protection than ones built over a dug foundation, but both provide more reliable protection from the cold than portable frames. Permanent frames are generally sturdier and last longer as well.

Portable frames, which are basically bottomless boxes with clear lids, can be used in much the same way as permanent frames, but are not as well insulated and are therefore subject to wider temperature fluctuations. They're most often used for hardening-off seedlings grown indoors in spring, either alone or in combination with permanent frames, to help handle the spring rush of plants being gotten ready for the garden. For gardeners with limited space, one advantage is that they can be collapsed and stored during times when they're not in use. In the vegetable garden, portable frames can be used to extend the season for spring or fall crops such as lettuce or spinach, or to keep frost away from late-ripening crops such as melons that need a few more weeks to mature in autumn. In areas with mild winters, portable frames can be used to grow winter crops of cold-tolerant vegetables. They can be erected over garden beds to protect plants that might not be quite winter-hardy and will provide adequate protection for many perennials and herbs. Use them to keep rain away from plants that dislike "wet feet" in winter. In summer, use portable frames to grow seedlings in a cool, shady part of the garden.

Site Selection

Although site selection is more crucial with permanent frames than portable ones, basic considerations apply to both types of frames. Cold frames are essentially passive solar collectors, and in order to get maximum benefit from the heat and light of the sun, they should face south (southeast or southwest exposures are next best). Ideally, the site should

Continued ➡

receive full sun from midmorning to midafternoon during the winter and early spring months. Hotbeds, despite their artificial source of heat, need a full-sun exposure as well.

The site should also be fairly level and well drained. Water accumulating around a cold frame will quickly rot and kill plants, as well as damage the foundation or base of the frame. For protection from winter winds, locate your frame with a building, fence, or hedge on the north side. Although frames built right against the foundation of a house will receive some escaping heat, leaving a foot or two between frame and foundation is a good idea. That way, you can easily get behind the frame to remove the sashes. Mount a hook on the wall behind the frame for holding the lids completely open.

For the sake of convenience, select a site near a water supply and somewhere that's easy to keep an eye on all year long. Deciduous trees overhead aren't necessarily a liability; they'll provide summer shade without blocking winter sun.

Materials

Use the best materials available, especially when constructing a permanent frame. For permanent frames, a concrete block foundation topped with a frame made of decay-resistant wood painted with a nontoxic wood preservative such as Cuprinol is ideal. For portable frames, you'll need to weigh both the life expectancy of the materials and their weight. Try to use rustproof hardware in construction whenever possible.

Glass window sash are most often used to cover frames, but fiberglass, Plexiglas, or heavyweight polyethylene can be substituted. A layer of polyethylene on the underside of the glass sash can be added for extra insulation.

Proper drainage is essential, especially for permanent frames, so plan on placing at least a 6-inch layer of coarse gravel in the bottom of the frame for drainage. Incorporating drain tile into the design of the foundation is a good idea on sites where drainage may be a problem. On top of the gravel, you can add 8 inches of builder's sand in which to sink pots and other containers.

Dimensions

The size of most frames is determined by the sizes of standard window sash, and often by the sizes of salvaged or surplus windows on hand. Although 3-by-6-foot sash is traditional, smaller windows such as 2-by-4-foot or 3-by-3-foot are much lighter and easier to handle. With large sash, or in areas of heavy snowfall, plan on rafters or other supports between each sash. A bed width of about 3 feet is convenient, so you can reach the back of the frame without having to step into it. Frames can be of any length, for more than one sash can be mounted side by side. (Separate hotbeds and cold frames can also be constructed side-by-side, by dividing the foundation between heated and unheated sections and mounting a sash over each section.) Hinges at the back of the frame and handles in the front make for easy opening. Be sure the lids extend slightly beyond the frame in front so that water drains off instead of into it.

The depth of the foundation and/or the height of the frame you decide on will depend on the plants your frame is designed to accommodate. When determining how much space you'll need, take into account the maximum height (including pots) of the plants you'll be growing, as well as the distance from the top of the layer of gravel added for drainage to the lowest part of the sash. A foundation dug to a depth of 2½ feet coupled with a cement block foundation that extends 8 inches

above the ground will accommodate a wide variety of plant sizes. (Keeping the wooden portion of the frame off the ground also will reduce rot.) A deeper frame will cut out some light, but will accommodate small trees or shrubs.

Managing Your Frame

The first step toward learning to use your cold frame or hotbed effectively is to familiarize yourself with its own particular personality. A thermometer mounted inside the frame where the sun will not shine directly on it will provide useful information about temperature. Check it frequently under various weather conditions and at different times of day. A record of temperature extremes, prevailing weather, and other environmental conditions both inside and outside the frame will help you identify trends and establish schedules for your frame. For most effective light transmission, wipe away condensation each time you check the frame. Also, clean the glazing, inside and out, with clear water when it becomes dusty or splashed with mud.

Temperature Control

Controlling the temperature inside a cold frame or hotbed is of vital importance because on a bright, sunny day, whatever the outdoor temperature, inside temperature in an unvented, insulated frame can rise to 100°F or more, quickly killing plants inside. Until recently, the only way to regulate the temperature was manually—by watching it closely, propping the lid open when the temperature began to rise, and lowering the lid when it began to fall. Fortunately for today's two-career families, automatic vent openers are now available.

To control the temperature manually, you'll need to follow daily weather forecasts and use your own knowledge of local weather patterns to judge how much air to give your plants. The object is to keep the plants from cooking without chilling them. For example, if the morning sun is bright and the sky cloudless, promising continued sun, raise the lid and prop it open 4 to 6 inches. If it's windy or a bit cloudy, open the frame only slightly, so cold winds don't chill the plants. By midafternoon in late fall or early spring, or as early as noon in the dead of winter, check the thermometer inside the frame, and close the lid to conserve daytime heat. Temperature should be checked at least twice daily until you are well acquainted with your frame's personality.

If you're away from home during the day and unable to check the frame, a solar-powered automatic opener will do the opening and closing job for you. There are models with preset temperatures and ones that will allow you to select the temperature yourself. These are available through most general mail-order nursery catalogs and from local garden centers. They'll generally lift sashes up to a specified weight limit, but must be disconnected before the sashes can be opened completely. It is still a good idea to check the frame regularly, however, for vent openers will not perform the other essential chores of checking for signs of disease or insect problems.

In unusually cold weather, or if you have an uninsulated, aboveground frame, you can bank leaves, bales of hay, or soil around the frame. Be aware that this may attract unwanted rodents. Bricks or plastic gallon jugs filled with water can be stacked against the north wall to serve as passive solar collectors. You can enhance the heat absorption of either with a coat of black paint. Both will absorb heat during the day and release it slowly at night.

Containers

Although plants can be grown in a soil mixture placed directly on the layer of gravel in the bottom

of the frame, using containers has several advantages. Plants grown in pots, seed flats, or other containers can be easily added, moved about, or removed without disturbing the frame's other inhabitants. Soil mixes can be tailor-made to suit individual plants, as can watering and fertilizing schedules, so the frame can be used for plants with a variety of requirements. Using individual pots also helps control diseases, which can spread quickly in both cold frames and hotbeds. Pots can be set on the layer of gravel at the bottom of the frame, or sunk to the rim in a 4- to 6-inch layer of sand on top of the gravel.

Watering

Until you become familiar with the conditions that prevail in your cold frame or hotbed, you'll need to check plants frequently to be sure they have enough water. This is especially important in warm weather when plants are actively growing. Check the moisture of the soil between 1 inch and ½ inch deep; for most plants, it should remain moist, but not soggy, at all times. Water whenever plants look droopy, but avoid watering on cold, cloudy days. To discourage fungal diseases, water early in the day so plants and surface soil can dry out before nightfall. Use water of approximately the same temperature as the medium in which the plants are growing, because cold water can shock plants and slow their growth. If you're using your frame to store dormant plants over winter, water well before the onset of cold temperatures, and then check every few weeks through the winter. You can tailor a miniature drip system to the size of your cold frame if it's used principally for starting seedlings in spring and summer.

Pests and Diseases

During your regular visits to your frame, carefully check for evidence of disease or insect infestation. In mild climates or during mild seasons, insects, slugs, or other pests will thrive in a cold frame or hotbed if left uncontrolled. Check each pot carefully before placing it in the frame to look for hitchhiking slugs or sowbugs. The moist conditions inside a frame also are ideal for plant diseases, and the warmer the temperatures (up to a point), the greater the danger of diseases. Generous spacing and proper ventilation can help avoid disease problems. Remove and discard infested, diseased, or sick-looking leaves and plants as soon as you spot them, because problems will spread very rapidly. If serious problems develop, remove all the plants and take steps to sterilize the inside of the frame. Pour boiling water into the gravel and/or sand at the bottom of the frame, or leave the glass lids in place and tightly closed during the summer to allow heat to build up inside the frame. If you've chosen to grow plants directly in soil in the bottom of your frame, it can be treated by either method, but it is also a good idea to dig it out completely every two or three years and replace it with fresh soil.

Caring for Your Frame

Although maintenance tasks are minimal, they are essential because the moist, warm environment inside a cold frame or hotbed makes it subject to rot and rapid deterioration. Whenever paint starts flaking, repaint as soon as the frame is free of plants. Allow a newly painted frame to air for several weeks before putting it back into use, because fumes from the paint may harm plants. Recaulk as necessary to maintain airtight conditions. Watch for signs of rusted hardware and nails. Replace caulking and check regularly for places where air could leak into the frames. Keep the glass and inside of the frame clean to increase the amount of light available to plants.

Continued ➡

Year-Round Uses

How you use your frame will depend upon not only what types of gardening you enjoy, but also where you live, what exposure you have available, and what type of frame(s) you select. Experiment to discover the best way to use your cold frame and/or hotbed as well as the optimum annual schedule for your area. Keep in mind that cold frames and hotbeds can be used in much the same way, but as a general rule, you can start the season earlier or extend it longer with a hotbed. You can convert your hotbed to a cold frame during the summer or for applications where heat isn't necessary.

Spring

Spring (or late winter for southern gardeners) is the busiest season in both cold frames and hotbeds, for that is the time of year most gardeners are getting ready for the rush of spring planting.

To harden-off seedlings started indoors before transplanting them to the garden, move them to a cold frame a week or two before they're scheduled for transplanting. Gradually open the vent for longer periods each day. Shade the seedlings at first—using wood lath, burlap, or a mixture of clay soil and water painted on the glass—to keep them from burning. Expose them gradually to full sun.

Cold frames are also good places to germinate seeds in early spring—especially those of cold-tolerant vegetables, perennials, and annuals. Sow seed in flats or pots placed directly in the frame about two months before the last spring frost date. For an even earlier start, sow seeds in a hotbed or indoors and move seedlings to a cold frame after their first transplanting. This not only frees up space for more tender plants indoors, it also eliminates the succulent, rank growth that seedlings grown at warm temperatures can produce. Later in the season, more tender annuals can be sown in the frames.

In the North, where the growing season is short, cold frames can be used to start plants that require long growing seasons (such as melons) that otherwise might fail to mature. They can also be used to grow very early spring crops of lettuce or spinach.

Summer

During the summer, the glass sash that cover a cold frame are generally stored away and replaced with screens or other coverings to keep out leaves and other debris. Frames shaded with a grid of wood lath over the screens can be used in late summer to start fall crops of heat-sensitive vegetables such as lettuce. Raise seedlings in pots or flats, then transplant to the garden when temperatures begin to cool. Summer-sown perennials or biennials such as foxglove (*Digitalis* spp.) or Canterbury-bells (*Campanula medium*) can be germinated in pots or flats, held over their first winter under the protected conditions offered by a cold frame, and moved to the garden the following year. Cold frames can also be used for rooting cuttings taken any time of the year.

Fall and Winter

As the days shorten and temperatures drop, glass sash are replaced and cold frames become an ideal place to sow seed of hardy annuals, perennials, wildflowers, shrubs, or trees. With seed sown in fall or early winter, the object is not to germinate the seed immediately, but to provide a cold treatment so that it will germinate promptly the following spring. Sow seed just before the ground freezes so it won't germinate before winter arrives.

Cold frames are also ideal for growing a fall crop of lettuce or spinach. Fall is also the time to move perennials, herbs, and container-grown plants that might not be quite hardy outdoors undercover for winter protection. Semihardy herbs such as parsley can be dug from your garden and guarded in a cold frame over winter. Use your cold frame for forcing pots of hardy spring bulbs.

Making and Using a Hotbed

Hotbeds are designed and used much like cold frames, but as their name suggests, they are supplied with a regular source of heat.

Traditionally, hotbeds were heated by a layer of fresh, fermenting manure spread in the bottom of a frame. Temperatures remained high for several weeks and then slowly dropped off. To reheat the bed, the old manure had to be dug out and replaced with a fresh mixture.

Today, most gardeners use hotbeds heated with specially designed electric cables—the high-tech alternative to the manure hotbed—because of the labor involved in a manure hotbed and because fresh manure is not always easy to find and haul. Any cold frame built over a dug foundation can be made into a hotbed by adding an electric heating cable, assuming a source of electricity is available. Portable models can be used as hotbeds, although they don't conserve heat as well as permanent frames do, but a pit at least 1 foot deep needs to be dug underneath the frame to contain the heating cable.

To convert a cold frame to a hotbed, spread a 2-inch layer of vermiculite for insulation on top of the layer of gravel at the bottom of the pit. Spread the cable on the vermiculite, using long loops to provide an even source of heat. Don't allow the heating cable wires to cross, and keep loops at least 8 inches apart and 3 inches away from the edges of the frame. Cover the heating cable with an inch of sand, followed by a layer of screen or hardware cloth to keep it from being dug up accidentally. Cover the heating cable with 4 to 6 inches of coarse builder's sand in which to sink pots. A 30-foot heating cable is sufficient to heat a 3-by-6-foot frame. Cables with built-in thermostats provide an extra measure of control. Tender plants prefer a medium temperature of between 60° and

75°F; temperatures between 50° and 60°F are sufficient for more cold-tolerant annuals and perennials. Disconnect the cable during seasons when heat isn't necessary, and convert back to a conventional cold frame.

To make a manure-fueled hotbed, start with a pit 2 to 2½ feet or more deep and slightly larger than the bed that sits on top of it. Mix the manure with straw, and spread it in a 6- to 8-inch layer at the bottom of the frame. Water it lightly and cover it with soil or sand. Within a few days, the fermenting mixture will raise the temperature in the frame to 70° or 80°F. The temperature will remain high for several weeks, then drop off. To reheat, remove the old manure and straw and replace with a fresh mixture.

Gardeners who heat their homes (or a greenhouse) with steam or hot water have another option for heating a hotbed, provided it is located next to the house. A pipe system connected to the heating system in the house can be used to heat a hotbed. A single loop of pipe can be run around the inside perimeter of the bed on the surface of the soil, about 2 inches from the outside wall, or several lengths of pipe can be buried under the soil, about 16 to 18 inches apart and 8 to 10 inches from the outside wall.

Using Cloches and Row Covers

Stretching the growing season is an age-old goal of gardeners. The quest for the earliest lettuce or the first ripe tomato is universal. Like portable cold frames, cloches and row covers are designed to help extend the season by protecting plants right in the garden. You can use them to get a head start on spring by protecting germinating seedlings or young transplants from spring frost. They're also perfect for protecting maturing crops from autumn cold snaps.

Forms of these portable coverings, sometimes called season extenders, have been used for centuries to protect individual plants or shelter entire rows. In fact, nearly every gardener has devised some sort of temporary season extender when faced with an unusually late spring frost that threatens newly transplanted tomatoes or tender annuals. Everything from cardboard boxes to blankets to paper bags has been pressed into service. Today, season extenders are made from new types of plastic and other materials, which makes them versatile, easy-to-use, and inexpensive. The terms portable cold frames and cloches are often used interchangeably when referring to such structures as the double-glass frames used to cover entire rows, for example. Here, however, we've distinguished between the two by calling the heavier, mostly glass-glazed structures portable cold frames. The light, plastic- or other fabric-covered season extenders are called cloches or row covers.

The basic principle of cloches and row covers relies on the greenhouse effect. Short ultraviolet rays from the sun pass through the glass and warm the soil and the air inside. The soil collects and stores the heat, then releases it slowly. This creates a greenhouselike atmosphere and provides frost protection to plants. The warmer conditions under a cloche or row cover increase the growth rate.

By using these coverings, you can plant seed or transplants—especially of cool-weather-loving crops such as broccoli, peas, cabbage, cauliflower, lettuce, spinach, and radishes doors earlier than normal. You'll need to consider how much frost protection the type you're using provides, however, especially for cold-sensitive plants like tomatoes. Generally, row covers only provide protection from 1° or 2°F of frost.

Cloches and row covers can also be used to extend your fall growing season. They can provide warmth and frost protection to melons and other crops that need a long growing season to ripen. Or, use them to protect a late sowing of such cool weather crops as lettuce or spinach.

In spring or fall, cloches and row covers can easily be moved from crop to crop. In spring, for example, when cool-loving vegetables are well established, use them to protect tomatoes, melons, or other warm-weather vegetables.

Cloches

The first cloches (*cloche* means bells in French) were glass bell jars. They were heavy, unventilated, and breakable, but nevertheless useful in extending the growing season. Today, there are many different types of cloches, ranging from those for individual plants to those for rows. Glass models are still occasionally available, but most used today are made of plastic or fiberglass. You can make your own or buy them ready-made. You'll have to determine for yourself if the time and expense you put into buying or building cloches is worthwhile.

No matter what kind of cloche you buy or make, there are a few basic guidelines to keep in mind. Like cold frames, cloches must be ventilated to prevent overheating, so you need to pay careful attention to the temperature inside the cloche. A thermometer is helpful for keeping

Continued ➤

track of how much the area under the covers warms up. In sunny weather, you'll need to partially vent or completely remove the covers during the day. Be aware that small cloches placed over individual plants will heat up fastest. Since cloches remain in place for several weeks, be sure plants have enough elbowroom to grow. Finally, make sure the cloches are securely anchored so they don't blow away.

Homemade Cloches

The possibilities for homemade cloches for individual plants are endless. You can use plastic milk jugs with the bottoms cut out. Remove the cap to prevent overheating. To make sure they do not blow away, dig the edges of the bottoms into the soil or weight them down by tying stones or fishing weights to the jug handles. You can use wood, fiberglass, wire, or any other material to construct round, conical, or square frames to protect individual plants or entire beds. Cover them with plastic or fiberglass. Tomato cages can also be covered with plastic—even just on the sides, with the top open—to provide wind protection and a warm atmosphere. Whatever you do, be sure to anchor everything so it won't blow away, and make sure you have ventilation so the plants don't overheat.

You can use wire fencing to form a Quonset-hut-type tunnel to shelter an entire row and cover it with 4-mil polyethylene. Fiberglass also can be made into a similar structure. Take a panel of translucent corrugated fiberglass and bend it into a semicircle. Wrap stiff wire (#8 or #9 gauge) around it, making a wicket that will secure the fiberglass, and stake the wire into the ground. If you make these in 4-foot segments, you can handle them easily.

If you have glass sash left over from a house renovation project, consider making a portable cold frame/glass cloche. (For more information, see "Other Types of Frames" on page 52.) Glass frames provide more frost protection than plastic ones, but they're heavier and harder to move around.

With any cloche that covers an entire row, be sure to close up each end or the row will become a mini wind tunnel. On warm days, you can open the ends to provide ventilation. Make sure plant leaves don't touch the sides of glass cloches in cold weather.

Commercial Cloches

There is a wide variety of commercial cloches available, both for covering individual plants or for sheltering entire rows. Commercial coverings for individual plants include cone-shaped "hats," mini hothouses, and a plastic cylinder that uses water for insulation called Wall O' Water. Kits for plastic tunnel cloches are sold at most garden centers and garden supply mail-order companies. They are easy to erect. Generally you need only set wire hoops 6 or 8 inches into the ground at about 4-foot intervals along the row. Then dig trenches 6 inches deep along the edges of the row. Lay the plastic over the wires with its edges in the trenches and weigh them down with dirt or stones. Close the ends of the tunnel by tying them to stakes. Make uniform slits in the plastic for ventilation. (You can water plants without removing plastic if you have slits.)

Row Covers

Row covers are made of light permeable material, usually polypropylene or polyester, loosely laid right on top of plants or supported above them with wire hoops. They are anchored in place with stones or soil to keep them from blowing away.

Sometimes called "floating" row covers because they are so light, polypropylene or polyester covers block out about 20 percent of the sun's rays, but are permeable and let in rain and air. They can be used to extend your season and protect your crops from frost damage, but they provide only a few degrees of protection from frost. On the plus side, they "breathe," thus making overheating during the day somewhat less of a problem. (In hot, sunny weather, temperatures can rise 10° to 30°F underneath row covers, so you still need to watch for overheating.)

Row covers also can be used to protect plants from insects and birds, because they don't need to be slitted or vented unless the weather is warm. If you know from experience that an insect will start munching on your crops at a certain time, you can anticipate this and protect your plants with a row cover. Unfortunately, insects in the soil may also benefit from the nice growing environment under the cover. Crop rotation will help prevent them from attacking the same crop each year.

There are several brands of row covers made from different materials. Polyester row covers, popularly known by the brand name Reemay, were the first to be released. They are very light and permeable, but break down rather rapidly when exposed to ultraviolet light, so much so that they can only be used for one season. They are also abrasive and can damage tender plant parts. Polypropylene covers, such as Agronet, Agryl P17, and Kimberly Farms, are less abrasive to plants and last longer—from two to three seasons. All are delicate and can be ripped by the wind or torn by growing plants. Generally, they're used for about a month in spring and again in fall, then cleaned and stored until the following season.

MULCH

Mulch Better Solutions

Fern Marshall Bradley

Every organic gardener should be a mulch expert. Mulching is one of the best ways to fight weeds. It also improves the garden's appearance, reduces water loss, and protects soil from compaction and erosion. If you use an organic mulch, the icing on the cake is improved soil quality as the mulch decays.

Clear the Way with Cardboard

You can get a new site ready for planting without weeding the area and even without digging, says Susan Sides, a North Carolina garden writer. The key: cardboard.

Instead of hacking weeds away from a site and then digging or tilling, just put a layer of cardboard over the ground. Sides gets cardboard from her local recycling center. She says that chicken-feed or dog-food bags also fill the bill, as will newspaper. Once you've covered the ground, wet the cardboard and spread a layer of organic mulch, such as grass clippings, on top.

Allow at least two weeks for the grass and weeds underneath to decompose.

"I learned this trick from a woman who runs a plant nursery in Florida," says Sides. "Down there, grass and weeds are especially tough, and soil dries out quickly. But this technique takes care of both problems."

When you're ready to plant, just push a trowel through the mulch and cardboard into the moist soil, and set your seedlings in place. "After that, you can throw more mulch on top whenever you want or need to," says Sides. "The cardboard breaks down pretty quickly; worms seem to love the stuff. It only takes a few months to a year, depending on your climate, for the cardboard to decompose completely. But because weeds haven't had any chance to grow during that time, the area stays pretty much weed-free as long as you keep adding mulch."

Sour Mulch: Beautiful, But Deadly

Wood chips and shredded bark make attractive mulch, but in some cases they can spell death to your plants. Improperly stored organic mulch materials can decompose anaerobically—without oxygen—and produce chemicals including methane and ammonia gas that are toxic to plants. "Soured" mulch also tends to lower soil pH, making nutrients less available. Symptoms of mulch toxicity include yellowing of leaf margins, loss of leaves, and even dead plants.

The key to avoiding the problem, says Donald Rakow, Ph.D., an associate professor of landscape horticulture at Cornell University, is to make sure mulch gets plenty of fresh air. Mulch stored in bins or in overly large piles can't "breathe." "Mulch piles should be turned and mixed at least once a month," says Dr. Rakow. "And the pile shouldn't be higher than 8 feet or wider than 10 to 12 feet." It's also important not to let moisture accumulate in the pile.

Keep Dr. Rakow's mulch-care principles in mind not only when storing the materials but also when shopping for them at garden centers. Ask yourself these questions: If it's sold in bulk, is the mulch kept in properly managed piles? And if it comes in bags, are those bags intact, or has rainwater seeped in through rips and tears?

One sure sign of soured mulch is its odor. According to Dr. Rakow, anaerobic decomposition results in mulch that has a pungent, astringent smell, instead of its usual pleasant, woodsy aroma.

It's also important, says Dr. Rakow, to limit the layer of mulch around landscape plants to just 3 or 4 inches. "A very deep mulch increases the chance of anaerobic decomposition," says Dr. Rakow. Instead of routinely adding several inches of new mulch around shrubs and flowers each year, fluff up the material that's already there. And when you do need to add a top layer of fresh mulch, limit it to just an inch or so.

Chunky Mulch for Healthier Soil

Choose mulches for permanent plantings with extra care. "The best mulch to use is a large-chunk bark," says Jim Borland, a Colorado garden writer and consultant. According to Borland, large-chunk bark is the optimum size for allowing air to reach the soil, while still retaining soil moisture. Air is essential for soil life, such as earthworms, soil bacteria, and many other too-small-to-see creatures. Plant roots, too, need oxygen.

A mulch with small pieces can prevent oxygen from moving down into the soil. And a mulch

Continued ➡

with much larger pieces allows for air spaces that are too big, drying out the soil faster. The thickness of each particle and the way they lay together in a chunk-size mulch provides optimum air spaces. A large-chunk pine bark mulch, says Borland, is just the right size for healthy soil, and it lasts at least two or three years.

Make an Island with Mulch

One great way to boost tree health and reduce yard maintenance in one step is to link groups of trees and shrubs with a groundcover of organic mulch. "A groundcover of mulch is ideal for trees because it doesn't disturb roots and doesn't compete for nutrients and water in the soil as planted ground covers would," says Jack Siebenthaler, a registered landscape architect from Florida. The idea is to use spreads of mulch to create an "island" within a landscape, linking trees together visually the same way you would if you were planting the area with a groundcover. This is a popular solution on new building lots with a small grove of trees that were carved from existing woods.

The mulch also means no mowing or plant maintenance—just occasional weed control and remulching once or twice yearly. Bark is a handsome mulching material available throughout most of the country, while pine straw and other neat mulches are regional options. A layer about 3 inches deep is adequate for most sites.

The Lawn and Short of Grass Mulch

Generally, you should leave your grass clippings where they lay—they're an excellent source of nitrogen for your lawn, and (contrary to long-held belief) they don't contribute to excessive thatch buildup.

On the other hand, you may want to use some of those nutrient-rich clippings to mulch your vegetables and ornamentals. Eileen Weinsteiger, the garden project manager at the Rodale Institute Research Center in Pennsylvania, does just that to keep weeds down in the Research Center's growing beds. What's more, she uses a living grass mulch between the beds to smother weeds—and to provide a steady supply of clippings.

"Our growing beds are 5 x 12 feet," says Weinsteiger, "and they're separated by 2-foot-wide pathways planted in ordinary turfgrass." Nutrient runoff from compost applied to the beds in the spring helps the grass pathways thrive.

The grass pathways need weekly mowing. After the soil has warmed, in late May or June, Weinsteiger applies 4 inches of fresh, green grass clippings to the beds every six weeks. The mulch heats up as it decomposes, so she's careful not to put it too close to seedlings. "I like the idea of using something that's generated in the garden to mulch the garden," says Weinsteiger, "and the grass does an excellent job of suppressing weeds."

Matthew Cheever, the owner of Evergreen, a landscape design and maintenance company in Wisconsin, recommends grass clippings as a weed-smothering mulch for ornamentals, too—but admits the material isn't especially attractive. His solution: Apply the clippings, then top them with a layer of decorative bark mulch.

Stone Mulch Annual Beds

Most gardeners find they never have enough organic mulch to go around—particularly after they've already generously mulched the perennial beds and vegetable patch. If you still want to put in some colorful annual flowers, but you're completely out of compost, leaves, pine straw, and wood chips, what do you do?

Use stones, as shown in the illustration below. Pat Williams, a copublisher of *HortIdeas* newsletter from Kentucky, says, "By the time I get around to planting annuals, there's never enough 'real' mulch left, so I use flat stones instead. I just arrange them around the plants, and lay them close together so there are only small cracks between them. The stones keep most of the weeds out and stabilize the soil temperature, too. As the flowers grow, they more or less cover up the mulch, and the stone that's still visible blends nicely with the foliage and blossoms. And when I go to plant annuals the following year, I just lift the stones up and dig."

Mulching the Low-Maintenance Way

Barbara W. Ellis, Joan Benjamin, and Deborah L. Martin

Mulch is something of a miracle—it's a one-step way to get rid of some of the most tiresome garden chores and make time for the fun stuff. But it doesn't stop there; mulch can provide you with other benefits as well.

Organic mulches, for example, add humus to your soil as they decompose and encourage beneficial organisms and worms to grow and work in your garden. Some mulches can actually repel pests, while other unconventional mulches can save your plants from winter winds and heaving.

The materials you can round up around your home or buy locally will save you the most labor and expense. You won't have far to haul them and they're usually free (or really cheap). Take a look at everything mulch can do for you, then pick and use the materials that make your life easiest.

Haste Makes Waste with Tree and Shrub Mulching

Mulching trees and shrubs is a simple, once-a-year (or less) chore—if you take time to do it right the first time. If you get in a hurry and dump mulch around your plants any old way, you'll soon be back rearranging it to fix pest and weed problems. Here's a simple list of dos and don'ts to keep in mind.

1. **Don't heap it too high**. Deep mulch layers don't let air or water reach the soil easily so roots suffer. Four inches of mulch is plenty for good weed control, so don't strain your back or budget applying deeper amounts.

2. **Don't touch plant parts**. Keep mulch 4 inches away from tree bark and plant stems or you'll create a moist hiding place for insects and bark-eating mice and voles.

3. **Do stretch mulch to the drip line**. You'll protect your trees and shrubs best with wide mulch rings that keep lawn grass, mowers, and weeds far away from trunks and stems.

What Can Mulch Do for You?

Mulch may look pretty passive lying there in your garden, but it's constantly working to save you time and effort. Mulch offers innumerable benefits and can save you hours of time spent doing unpleasant garden chores.

Organic mulches are the most useful. They're made from once-living materials like bark, leaves, or grass clippings that eventually decompose and improve the soil. Inorganic or man-made mulches are long-lasting but don't add humus or nutrients to your garden.

Top 10 Reasons to Use Organic Mulch in Your Garden

Vicki Mattern [Au]

By applying an organic mulch to your vegetable garden or flowerbed, you'll save hours of time each year. You should spread a thin layer of wood chips, grass clippings, shredded bark, sawdust, or pine needles on your garden for the following reasons:

1. Mulch prevents most weed seeds from germinating and even makes it easier to pull those that do pop through.

2. It will hold down dirt and keep it from splashing on flowers and vegetables.

3. It will allow you to water less often because mulch keeps the soil cool and moist.

4. It decomposes slowly, releasing nutrients into the soil throughout the process.

5. Mulch encourages beneficial earthworm activity by improving the soil tilth and nutrient content.

6. It will help prevent alternate freezing and thawing of the soil in winter, which can heave plants out of the soil.

7. Mulching helps to prevent diseases by keeping water and soil from splashing onto plant leaves.

8. Compost mulches can help prevent soil erosion. Because soil that contains a lot of humus (finished compost) holds together better, rainwater permeates the soil, moving easily through the spaces between granules rather than running off the soil surface.

9. Most of the ingredients for organic mulches can already be found in your home or backyard.

10. Many types of mulch are attractive additions to the garden site.

Whichever material you choose, mulching will give you more benefits than any other single gardening chore. Here's what you can expect.

Use your lawnmower on the mulching setting to chop leaves. Then use the bagging attachment to collect them. Store the leaves in plastic bags or use them right away as mulch.

Low-work weed control. To control a minor weed problem, pull or hoe out existing weeds and bring on the mulch—at least a 4-inch-deep later of organic matter. You won't have to weed again unless seeds blow in and root. If you're coping with tough perennial weeds, see "Fight the Toughest Weeds with Ease with 'Super Mulch'" below.

Continued ➡

Fewer watering chores. A 3- to 4-inch layer of organic mulch throughout your garden can reduce the amount of water lost to evaporation by at least one-half. That means more water for your plants and less watering for you. Mulch also keeps roots cool so plants need less water.

Simple disease prevention. Rain and water droplets from sprinklers splash soil and the spores that cause fungal diseases onto plant leaves.

A cushion of mulch will keep the fungal spores and the soil off your plants.

One-step soil protection. A layer of organic mulch protects the soil from beating raindrops, which prevents crusting and soil compaction. It will also stop heavy rains from washing away valuable topsoil and plants. Mulch can also protect soil from foot traffic.

No-dig soil improvement. When organic mulches break down, they add nutrients to the soil. This gives plants a boost and saves you from fertilizing chores.

Cleaner produce. Surround vegetables and berries with mulch to keep them—and you—free of mud. You'll be able to harvest crops without lots of cleaning fuss, even in wet weather.

Protection from mower blight. A ring of mulch around the base of trees or shrubs keeps you from getting too close with your lawn mower—no more tedious trimming or bark wounds.

Safety from winter's wrath. Plants can heave out of the ground and die when temperatures alternate between freezing and thawing. Mulching after the ground freezes with loose straw or chopped leaves moderates soil temperatures and stops harmful expanding and contracting.

Fight the Toughest Weeds with Ease with "Super Mulch"

When tough perennial weeds like thistles and burdock take over your garden, fight back with "super mulch." First, mow or break off tall weeds, then cover the area with a layer of cardboard (boxes that are broken down and cut open work well) or a 1-inch layer of newspaper. Place 8 to 10 inches of spoiled hay or straw over the top. Apply the mulch in summer or fall and you'll smother the weeds in time for planting the following year. The mulch will break down into humus after a couple of seasons and make a fine planting bed.

If you're battling a particularly crafty weed like poison ivy or an invasive plant like spreading bamboo, leave the area covered for one or two years. Keep 8 to 10 inches of mulch over the area at all times, adding new mulch as the older material breaks down. Don't let the weeds get any light, and they'll give up when their food stores run out.

Mulch and Grow Better Soil

Mulch and compost can turn your poor soil into fertile ground while you grow flowers and vegetables. Follow the simple steps below in late spring, and you'll be able to plant immediately, even on clay or sandy soil.

1. Cut down any weeds or grass in your garden area with a mower and leave the clippings where they fall.

2. Cover the site with a layer of newspaper, 4 or 5 sheets deep.

3. Place 8 to 10 inches of spoiled hay or straw over the paper.

4. Top the hay with 2 inches of compost.

5. Dig some earthworms from a good garden spot and place 5 or 10 of them in 3 or 4 spots under the mulch.

6. Plant seeds of strongly rooted annual flowers or vegetables in the compost and you'll be picking flowers or harvesting crops by summer. Meanwhile, the roots and worms will break up and improve the soil texture, and the mulch and compost will break down and improve your soil's health. Try cleome, cosmos, sunflowers, amaranth, beans, and grains for the best results the first year.

Annual Flowers Make the Mulch

Does your newly planted perennial garden have more bare spots than plants? Fill in the blanks with quick-spreading annual flowers. They'll keep your planting weed-free until slower-growing perennials fill in.

Trailing annuals like sweet alyssum and Madagascar periwinkle (*Catharanthus roseus*) shade

Continued ➡

Choose Your Mulch [B]

The following are some of the best mulches to consider for your garden. Some are suitable for vegetables; others are best used in ornamental plantings. We've distinguished between biodegradable ones, which will add organic matter to the soil, and synthetic mulches like black plastic, which won't.

Material	Primary Benefits	When to Apply	How to Apply
Biodegradable Mulches			
Chopped leaves	Suppresses weeds well. Modulates soil temperature.	At planting time and as needed throughout the season.	Apply in 3-inch layers; best if chopped and composted, then allowed to sit outside for several months.
Compost	Builds tilth. Suppresses weeds. Fertilizes. Warms soil.	At planting time and as needed throughout the season.	Spread 1 or more inches as a topdressing around plants or along rows.
Grass clippings	Builds tilth. Modulates soil temperature.	At planting time and as needed throughout the season.	Apply a 1-4-inch layer around plantings. Make sure clippings are herbicide-free. May burn tender seedlings if placed too close.
Horticultural paper	Permeable to water and air. May warm soil	At planting time.	Comes in various types, such as black or with peat. Some types may crust in wet climates. Lay down in sections and anchor with soil or stones.
Newspaper	Suppresses weeds well. Retains moisture.	At planting time.	Lay down whole sections of the paper and anchor with soil or stones, or shred paper and apply 4-6-inch layers. Good to use under more attractive mulches. Do not use colored newspaper; some inks can be toxic.
Pine needles	Builds tilth. Suppresses weeds well. Some control of fungal diseases.	At planting time and as needed throughout the season.	Apply in 2-4-inch layers. Needles tend to acidify soil; don't use around non-acid-loving plants.
Shredded bark, wood chips	Retains moisture. Suppresses weeds well.	As needed around established plantings or at planting time.	Apply a 2-4-inch layer around established plantings of trees or perennials. Can tie up nitrogen in soil, so not for vegetable garden. Composted bark or wood chips are best.
Straw	Builds tilth. Suppresses weeds well. Cools soil.	At planting time and as needed throughout the season.	Lay down 8-inch layers of material around but not touching plants. Mulch heavily between rows to keep weeds at bay. May tie up nitrogen in soil; oat straw best.
Inorganic Mulches			
Aluminized paper	Suppresses weeds well. Modulates soil temperature; cools soil but warms air. May repel aphids and squash borer moths.	At planting time.	Lay down single sheets and cut slits to plant through. Make sure mulch extends at least 6 inches out from plants.
Black plastic	Warms soil. Suppresses weeds well.	At or before planting time.	Lay down single sheets of 4-6-mil plastic over whole planting area or between rows of plants. Anchor with soil or stones. Cut slits to plant through.
Clear plastic	Warms soil.	At or before planting time.	Lay down single sheets of plastic. Anchor with soil or stones. Cut slits to plant through. Weeds will grow beneath plastic.
Geotextile mulch	Suppresses weeds well. Permeable to water and air.	At or before planting time.	Difficult to cut. Lay down in single sheets and anchor with soil or stones. Cut slits to plant through.
Pebbles and stones	Suppresses weeds well. Modulates soil temperature. Retains moisture.	At planting time and as needed.	Put down pebbles (such as marble mulching trees, shrubs, and rock chips) in 1-inch layers. Good for gardens.

out weed seedlings before they can get a foothold. Even annuals that grow upright can lend a helping hand if you space them close enough so that they touch each other when they're mature.

Buy inexpensive flats of impatiens to cover bare spots in shade gardens; use French marigolds, melampodium (*Melampodium paludosum*), or narrowleaf zinnias (*Zinnia angustifolia*) as fillers in sunny areas.

Grow Your Own Mulch

Are you short on mulch materials or tired of replacing mulches every year? Instead of hauling more organic matter out to your garden, grow a living mulch. Live plants can be as effective as compost or hay at conserving moisture and reducing weeds. Living mulches are particularly good at preventing soil erosion too: They don't just protect the ground from heavy rains, they hold it in place with their roots. For tips on using plants as mulch in the flower garden, see "Annual Flowers Make the Mulch" and "Plant Once, Mulch Forever with Permanent Perennials" on this page. For vegetable gardens, read on.

Crowd out weeds with vegetables. Plant beans, cabbage-family crops, salad greens, and peas in wide rows spaced close enough so leaves touch when plants are grown. The dense growth will shade the soil so moisture doesn't evaporate. Cover bare areas so weeds can't get a toehold.

Fill in open areas with cover crops. To protect your soil over winter with very little effort, plug the bare spots in your garden with cover crops in late summer.

To plant cover crops on this schedule, as soon as you're done harvesting vegetables, cut off and compost the tops of plants. Broadcast oat, purple vetch, or hairy vetch seeds over the entire garden area for a quick protective blanket. They'll sprout, grow through the fall, and get killed back in winter.

In spring, plant right through the cover crops; they make a good mulch even when they're dead. In warm areas where cover crops survive winter temperatures, till them into the soil before planting.

Plant Once, Mulch Forever with Permanent Perennials

If you've got bare or weedy patches around trees or shrubs, plant groundcovers or other spreading perennials. They're the easiest mulch of all since they don't need refurbishing each year. They'll shade the soil, keep out weeds, and need almost no maintenance once established.

Plant daylilies, ajuga, lily-turf, and English ivy in sun or shade. For shady spots, try hostas, epimediums, lilies-of-the-valley, pachysandra, or sweet woodruff.

Weird Mulches That Work

Lots of great but unusual mulch materials are hidden away waiting for you in your house, yard, and community. See if you're overlooking any of these handy resources.

Carpet. If you just tore out some cotton or wool carpeting, take it to the vegetable garden instead of the dump. Lay strips down between the rows for a long-lasting, weedproof mulch. Only use all-cotton or all-wool carpet since synthetic ones may contain harmful chemicals.

Christmas trees. Evergreen boughs make great plant covers in winter, and you can find a plentiful supply around the holidays. Let neighbors

know you'd like their discards, or just collect them from the curb before sanitation workers do. Lop off the limbs and pile them around any perennial plants or shrubs that need protection from winter winds and freezing and thawing temperatures.

Herbs. Lots of gardeners think of herbs like mint and perilla as invasive pest plants. If you've got a large patch of rampant herbs, why fight it? Cut the plants back with hedge shears whenever you need some mulch and place the stems and leaves around your plants. You'll have fragrant weed control that helps repel insects. Other vigorous herbs for mulch include artemesia (*Artemisia* spp.), velvet sage (*Salvia leucantha*), and yarrow.

Snow. If you live in the North, don't overlook the benefits of snow mulch for winter protection. A heavy blanket of the white stuff keeps plants safe from drying winter winds and frigid temperatures. Nature often does all the work for you, but in years with little snow, you can help out by piling it up to cover perennial plants and shrubs.

Weeds. It's hard to believe, but weeds make good mulch if you're selective about what you use. For a low-maintenance living mulch, leave noninvasive weeds like chickweed in your garden if they spring up between vegetables or around trees and shrubs.

Dead weeds. You can use dead weeds as mulch, too, as long as they haven't gone to seed. Use them to anchor newspaper mulch instead of laying them on bare ground: Pulled weeds have been known to reroot in especially rainy seasons. Common weeds that make good mulches include lamb's-quarters, jewelweed, plantain, pigweed, and pokeweed. Avoid Bermuda grass, bindweed, crabgrass, nutsedge, purslane, or any other weed that can reproduce from root sections.

Wool. Nonwoven, feltlike mats made of wool and other natural fibers make a long-lasting (2 years or more) but biodegradable mulch. They're convenient (but expensive) to use since they come in squares or rolls that can be cut with scissors or a knife.

Water the soil first, then cut mats to fit, and place a single layer around but not touching plants. Or apply a layer with holes cut for plants. Anchor with soil, another mulch, wire pins, or rocks.

Look to Your Trees for Mulching Materials

Leaves make great mulch—especially if they're chopped and don't blow around like whole leaves. They're easy to come by: Just mow your yard in fall and collect the chopped leaves in a mower bag. If you don't have enough, collect bags of leaves from neighbors and put them in windows at home to mow, too. Some municipalities offer free leaves, and you can also check with lawn-care companies and your local parks department.

Move Mulch with Ease

If you're adding 4 inches of mulch to a large vegetable garden, you're in for some work. You can choose lightweight mulches, but even they can be cumbersome if you have to move large quantities around. Try these tips for getting mulch to your garden and placing it around your plants with the least effort.

Bag it or blow it. Collect grass clippings and leaves with a lawn mower bag and you'll save time raking. Dump the mulch materials directly in your garden or in a compost pile that's in or beside your garden. If you don't have a bagging mower, dump leaves in windrows near your

garden. Run your mower over the leaves to chop them, then mow in a single direction to blow the leaves into your garden or into a single row.

Get some wheels. A pickup truck or lawn tractor with a trailer makes it easy to move bulky materials like bales of straw and hay. If they aren't available, carts, wheelbarrows, and even little red wagons can save your back and make mulching easier. You can load mulch directly into these vehicles, push or pull them to your garden, then dump the materials exactly where you need them. To load up extra mulch and keep it from blowing around, fill large plastic garbage barrels, plastic bags, or washtubs, load them into a wheeled vehicle, and drop them off where they're needed.

Rob the laundry. If you don't have wheels, put plastic bags of mulch into a laundry basket. You can slide the basket over your lawn without risking a plastic bag break.

Try a tarp or stuff a sheet. It's easy to drag grass clippings or leaves to your garden if you throw them on a plastic tarp or old bedsheet.

Get double duty from mix-and-match mulches. When you're short on mulch or money, try a mixture of materials to cover your planting beds. For example, use a beautiful, decorative mulch like cocoa beans on top of an uglier, but inexpensive, mulch like grass clippings. Or sprinkle attractive shredded bark over newspaper or straw, or mix several kinds of mulch together, and top with a thin layer of decorative mulch. No one will know the difference but you and your pocketbook.

Fertilizing the Low Maintenance Way

Barbara W. Ellis, Joan Benjamin, and Deborah L. Martin

Fertilizing is certainly not on the top-ten list of favorite gardening activities. The good news: If you've been managing your soil organically by adding compost and other organic amendments regularly, your plants probably won't need very much fertilizer. Soil that's rich in organic matter generally contains plenty of nutrients that are readily available to plants. Rich soil also is biologically active, so trillions of soil organisms are hard at work breaking down even more nutrients for plants all during the growing season.

In this section, you'll learn ways to make the most of fertilizers and also cut the time and effort you spend applying them. You'll also find an explanation of what soil pH means to your plants and how to manage it efficiently.

Just the Facts: What You Need to Know about Feeding Your Plants

Nitrogen, phosphorus, and potassium (N, P, and K) are the primary nutrients plants need to grow. In addition to these three macronutrients, plants also need smaller amounts of calcium, magnesium, and sulfur—the secondary nutrients. Plants also use trace elements, also called micronutrients, in minute amounts. Trace elements include boron, chlorine, copper, iron, manganese, molybdenum, and zinc.

The good news is healthy soil that's rich in organic matter generally contains enough of all of these nutrients to keep plants healthy and growing. Fertilizing becomes necessary either when there aren't enough nutrients in the soil or when nutrients are present but are in forms plants can't take up through their roots. (A pH imbalance, for instance, will cause nutrients to be unavailable.) Of course,

Continued ➔

gardeners also fertilize to boost plant performance—to produce a bigger crop of tomatoes, for example.

KNOW HOW FOOD WILL MAKE THEM GROW

Whatever plants you want to feed, it's helpful to know how nutrients will affect them. In general, nitrogen promotes growth of leaves and stems, phosphorus encourages production of flowers and fruits, and potassium boosts root growth. Although plants need all three of these nutrients to grow, the amount of each varies according to their stage of development.

Fertilizers with different most amounts of nutrients allow you to fine-tune your feeding program. For example, plants putting out new growth benefit from fertilizers with higher ratios of nitrogen relative to the other nutrients. Plants that are flowering and setting fruits do better with an increase in phosphorus. You can make sure your plants have everything they need by applying complete fertilizers—those containing all three major nutrients—with varying ratios of nitrogen, phosphorus, and potassium. You can mix your own fertilizers by combining single-nutrient fertilizers, but if your goal is reducing the time you spend fertilizing, buying complete commercial mixes is most efficient.

Organic Fertilizers Catalog

Organic Fertilizer	Nutrients Supplied	Rate of Application	Uses and Comments
Bloodmeal, dried blood	Bloodmeal: 15% nitrogen, 1.3% phosphorus, 0.7% potassium. Dried blood: 12% nitrogen, 3% phosphorus, 0% potassium.	Up to 3 lbs. per 100 sq. ft. (more will burn plants)	Source of readily available nitrogen. Add to compost pile to speed decomposition. Repels deer and rabbits. Lasts 3-4 months.
Bonemeal	3% nitrogen, 20% phosphorus, 0% potassium, 24-30% calcium.	Up to 5 lbs. per 100 sq. ft.	Excellent source of phosphorus. Raises pH. Best on fruit trees, bulbs, and flower beds. Lasts 6 to 12 months.
Cottonseed meal	6% nitrogen, 2-3% phosphorus, 2% potassium	2-5 lbs. per 100 sq. ft. (For trees, apply 2-4 cups around drip line for each in. of trunk size.)	Acidifies soil, so it's best for crops that prefer low pH, such as azaleas, blueberries, citrus, dogwoods, hollies, and strawberries. Lasts 4-6 months.
Dolomite	90-100% MgCa (CO$_3$)$_2$(51% calcium carbonate, 40% magnesium carbonate).	To raise pH one point, use 7 lbs. per 100 sq. ft. on clay or sandy loam, 5½ lbs. on sand, and 10 lbs. on loam soil.	Raises pH and adds magnesium, which is needed for chlorophyll production and photosynthesis. Repeated use may cause magnesium excess. Also sold as Hi-Mag or dolomite limestone.
Fish meal, fish emulsion	Fish meal: 10% nitrogen, 4-6% phosphorus, 0% potassium. Fish emulsion: 4% nitrogen, 4% phosphorus, 1% potassium.	Fish meal: up to 5 lbs. per 100 sq. ft. Fish emulsion: dilute 20:1 water to emulsion.	Fish meal: Use in early spring, at transplanting, and any time plants need a boost. Lasts 6-8 months. Fish emulsion: Apply as a foliar spray in early morning or evening. Also sold as fish solubles.
Granite dust	0% nitrogen, 0% phosphorus, 3-5% potassium, 67% silica; 19 trace minerals.	Up to 10 lbs. per 100 sq. ft.	Very slowly available. Releases potash more slowly than greensand, but lasts up to 10 years. Improves soil structure. Use mica-rich type only. Also sold as granite meal or crushed granite.
Greensand	0% nitrogen, 1% phosphorus, 5-7% potassium, 50% silica, 18-23% iron oxide; 22 trace minerals.	Up to 10 lbs. per 100 sq. ft.	Slowly available. Lasts up to 10 years. Loosens clay soils. Apply in fall for benefits next season. Also sold as glauconite or Jersey greensand.
Guano, bat	8% nitrogen, 4% phosphorus, 2% potassium average, but varies widely; 24 trace minerals.	Up to 5 lbs. per 100 sq. ft.; 2 T. per pint of potting soil; 1 lb. per 5 gal. water for manure tea.	Caves protect guano from leaching, so nutrients are conserved.
Guano, bird	13% nitrogen, 8% phosphorus, 2% potassium; 11 trace minerals.	3 lbs. per 100 sq. ft. Fruit trees: 3-6 oz. per inch of trunk diameter. Houseplants: 1-2 oz. per gallon of water.	Especially good for roses, bulbs, azaleas, and houseplants. Also sold as Plantjoy.
Gypsum (calcium sulfate)	23-57% calcium, 17.7% sulfur.	Up to 4 lbs. per 100 sq. ft.	Use when both calcium and sulfur are needed and soil pH is already high. Sulfur will tie up excess magnesium. Helps loosen clay soils.
Hoof and horn meal	14% nitrogen, 2% phosphorus, 0% potassium.	Up to 4 lbs. per 100 sq. ft.	High nitrogen source, but more slowly available than bloodmeal. Odorous. Takes 4-6 weeks to start releasing nitrogen; lasts 12 months.
Kelp meal, liquid seaweed	1% nitrogen, 0% phosphorus, 12% potassium; 33% trace minerals, including more than 1% of calcium, sodium, chlorine, and sulfur, and about 50 other minerals in trace amounts.	Meal: up to 1 lb. per 100 sq. ft. Liquid: dilute 25:1 water to seaweed for transplanting and rooting cuttings; 40:1 as booster and for fruit crops.	Contains natural growth hormones, so use sparingly. Best source of trace minerals. Lasts 6-12 months. Also sold as Thorvin Kelp, FoliaGro, Sea Life, Maxicrop, Norwegian SeaWeed, liquid kelp.
Langneinite	0% nitrogen, 0% phosphorus, 22% potassium, 22% sulfur, 11% magnesium.	Up to 1 lb. per 100 sq. ft.	Will not alter pH. Use when there is abundant calcium and sulfur. Magnesium and potassium are needed. Also sold as Sul-Po-Mag or K-Mag.
Leatherdust	5.5-12% nitrogen, 0% phosphorus, 0% potassium.	½ lb. per 100 sq. ft.	2% nitrogen is immediately available; rest releases slowly over growing season. Does not burn or leach.
Manure, composted cow	2% nitrogen, 1% phosphorus, 1% potassium.	40 lbs. per 50-100 sq. ft. as soil conditioner; 2 parts to 6-8 parts loam as potting mix.	Low level of nutrients and slow release makes it most valuable as a soil conditioner. Use as winter fertilizer for houseplants.
Phosphate, colloidal	0% nitrogen, 18-22% phosphorus, 0% potassium, 27% calcium, 1.7% iron; silicas and 14 other trace minerals.	Up to 10 lbs. per 100 sq. ft.	More effective than rock phosphate on neutral soils. Phosphorus availability higher (2% available immediately) than rock phosphate because of small particle size of colloidal clay base. Half the pH-raising value of ground limestone. Lasts 2-3 years.
Phosphate, rock	0% nitrogen, 33% phosphorus, 0% potassium, 30% calcium, 2.8% iron, 10% silica; 10 other trace minerals.	Up to 10 lbs. per 100 sq. ft.	Releases phosphorus best in acid soils below pH 6.2. Slower release than colloidal phosphate. Will slowly raise pH one point or more. Also sold as phosphate rock.
Sulfur	100% sulfur.	1 lb. per 100 sq. ft. will lower pH one point. As fungicide: dilute at 3 T. per gallon of water.	Lowers pH in alkaline soil. Increases crop protein. Ties up excess magnesium. Also sold as Dispersul.
Wood ashes	0% nitrogen, 0-7% phosphorus, 6-20% potassium, 20-53% calcium carbonate, trace minerals such as copper, zinc, manganese, iron, sodium, sulfur and boron.	1-2 lbs. per 100 sq. ft.	Nutrient amounts highly variable. Minerals highest in young hardwoods. Will raise soil pH. Put on soil in spring, and dig under. Do not use near young stems or roots. Protect ashes from leaching in winter. Lasts 12 or more months.

Continued →

Keep Feeding Simple

You could easily devote all your time to formulating the right combination of macronutrients, secondary nutrients, and trace elements to satisfy the needs of each and every plant you grow. Fortunately, this is as unnecessary as it is undesirable. Use the following information about the needs of certain plant groups to help you choose the best fertilizers to use.

Leafy crops, foliage plants, trees, and shrubs, grasses. A steady supply of nitrogen gives these plants what they need to build lush, green, healthy stems and foliage. Look for products that supply from two to four times as much nitrogen as they do phosphorus or potassium.

Fruits, flowers. Phosphorus enhances the floral display in ornamental plantings and improves blossom and fruit set in fruit-producing plants, including vegetable fruits such as tomatoes, beans, and squash. A complete fertilizer for these plants has twice as much phosphorus as it does nitrogen, with an equal or lesser amount of potassium.

Root crops. As mentioned above, potassium plays a critical role in healthy root growth, so it stands to reason that root crops such as carrots, beets, and potatoes would benefit from a fertilizer ratio that's twice as high in potassium as it is in nitrogen.

Vegetables. Since a vegetable garden contains a mix of crops—root, leafy, and fruit-bearing—it's easier to supply a balanced fertilizer to all crops than to cater to a variety of different nutrient needs. To feed your whole garden select a fertilizer in which the macronutrients are in equal ratio to each other; use single-nutrient sources to satisfy specific crop needs.

Get What You and Your Plants Need— Read the Bag

When shopping for fertilizers, it's important to take time to read the bag. The label on all commercial fertilizers features a three-number NPK ratio, and also the guaranteed analysis. Some, but not all, products provide ingredient information.

The amount of macronutrients a package of fertilizer contains is expressed as a three-number ratio. The first number is the percentage of nitrogen; the second, the percentage of phosphate (the form of phosphorus plants use); and the third, the percentage of potash (the form of potassium plants use).

Commercial fertilizers—both synthetic and organic—supply one, two, or all three of the macronutrients. Some contain secondary nutrients; a few, such as seaweed and compost, also supply all of the micronutrients.

Look for fertilizers that are labeled "Certified Organic," or carefully check the ingredients to make sure all the ingredients are safe and natural. Be wary of any products labeled organic that have an NPK ratio that adds up to more than 15; these products probably have ingredients that aren't organically acceptable.

Don't Have a Feeding Frenzy

One of the best ways to save time fertilizing is not to fertilize. If you're feeding your soil regularly with compost and keeping it covered with organic mulch, most of your plants won't need any supplemental feedings. So before you haul out the fertilizer, take time to think about which plants truly need to be fertilized. Perennials, trees, shrubs, and vines that are growing well will probably continue to do fine without feeding. If they just need a boost, an annual mulching with compost will help control weeds, hold moisture in the soil, *and* feed.

Even in a well-managed organic garden, there are plants that do better when fertilized. Fast-growing vegetables tend to be more productive when they receive added nutrients. Beds of annual flowers may bloom more as well. Perennials that have been in place for a few years also benefit from fertilization to replenish the nutrients they've removed from the soil. And container plants that rely on the soil in their pots will thank you for an occasional boost. By comparison, you may choose not to fertilize your lawn. Not fertilizing has an added benefit: The grass grows more slowly and you have to mow less.

Exercise Your Application Options

Different forms of fertilizer lend themselves to different application methods. Dry fertilizers may be powdered, granular, or palletized—such products are easily applied over the soil surface. Liquid fertilizers give you the option of spraying nutrients directly on your plants as a foliar feed or watering them into the soil around plants.

1. **Foliar application.** Spray liquid fertilizer or compost tea onto plant leaves to give them a boost any time during the growing season.

2. **Side-dressing.** Apply dry fertilizer or compost in a ring around established plants or in a band next to a row of plants.

3. **Top-dressing.** A drop-type spreader lets you apply dry fertilizer or screened compost over the top of your lawn.

4. **Broadcasting.** To prepare soil for planting, you can broadcast dry fertilizer with a spreader or by hand, then rake it in.

Let Your Irrigation System Do Double Duty

If you have an irrigation system, let it fertilize for you—add a siphon attachment between the tap and the hose. Put the uptake tube into a bucket of concentrated liquid fertilizer and let the system do the rest.

With a drip system, you'll need a proportioner or fertilizer injector that will work with its lower water flow rate. To prevent clogging, filter fertilizer solutions before adding them to your irrigation system, and avoid fish emulsion. After fertilizing, flush your system with clear water for a few minutes.

Siphon attachments, proportioners, and injectors are available at well-stocked garden centers and by mail.

Cut Fertilizer Needs with Compost

If you keep only one fertilizer on hand, make it compost. The nutrient content of compost is low when compared to synthetic fertilizers (compost's NPK ratio can range from 0.5-0.5-0.5 to 4-4-4), but it does much more than just add nutrients to the soil. It promotes microorganism populations that increase the availability of nutrients to your plants. As a source of organic matter, it also helps improve soil quality, drainage, and water-holding capacity.

Once you start using compost, you'll understand why good gardeners know you can never have too much of it. See below for some of the best ways to save time and still feed your plants with compost. If you feel like you could never make enough compost to perform all these different functions, check with the agency in your local government that oversees waste collection. Chances are your municipal government, township, or local parks department has a yard waste composting facility where residents can get compost at little or no cost.

Compost mulch. Mulching perennial beds and mixed plantings with compost is enough to adequately feed most established plants. It also reduces the need to water and weed.

Top your vegetable garden in fall. Spreading a 1- to 2-inch layer of compost over your vegetable garden in late fall will protect the soil from the elements through winter and leave it ready for planting when spring arrives.

Side-dress with compost. During the growing season, you can side-dress vegetable crops with compost or use it as a mulch for the garden.

Feed your lawn. If you open your drop-type spreader to its widest setting, you can nourish your lawn with a top-dressing of compost.

Make compost tea. To make a batch of compost tea, put one or two shovelfuls of compost into a coarsely woven or burlap sack. Tie the sack shut, and steep your "tea bag" in a 5-gallon bucket of water for 1 to 7 days. Dilute the resulting liquid to a weak-tea color and use it to water your plants; strain it through cheesecloth to apply as a foliar spray or via drip irrigation. Any plants in need of a boost will respond well to a foliar application of compost tea.

Be Practical about pH

A soil's pH—the measure of its acidity or alkalinity— is important because it affects whether plants can take up the nutrients in the soil through their roots.

Soil pH varies by region and fluctuates with the previous uses of soil, such as cultivation or development. It is expressed as a number from 1.0 to 14.0: 1 is acid, 7 is neutral, and 14 is alkaline.

While some of your plants may have specific pH preferences, most tolerate a fairly wide range of soil pH. And plants that are finicky are simply expressing their need for the nutrients that are unavailable to them when the pH is "wrong."

The easiest thing to do about soil pH is nothing—as long as it's not seriously inhibiting your gardening success, leave it alone. Follow the steps below to do as little as possible about soil pH, while understanding how it affects your plants.

Know your soil's pH. Have a soil test done by a professional, or buy a home pH test kit and find out what your soil's pH is.

Know a little about pH and nutrient availability. Most nutrients plants need are available when the soil pH is between 6.0 and 7.5. When the pH is below 6.0, some nutrients, including nitrogen, phosphorus, and potassium, are less available to the plants. When the pH exceeds 7.5, iron, manganese, and phosphorus availability drop.

Know a little about plants and pH. Most cultivated plants grow best in soils with a pH in the range of 6.0 to 7.0. Common exceptions to this rule include blueberries, potatoes, and rhododendrons, all of which prefer more acidic conditions.

Choose plants accordingly. When you choose landscape plants, take pH into account. You can adjust soil pH by applying soil amendments. However, you'll be more successful if you select plants that are adapted to your soil's pH. Keep in mind that it's easier to amend cultivated soils, such as in vegetable gardens, than sodded or planted areas of the landscape.

Allow time for change. If you find your soil's pH is seriously out of kilter, or if you want to amend a limited area to make way for vegetable crops that won't tolerate existing conditions, start the amendment process early. Many factors, including soil type, organic matter content, and the type of amendment you use, will contribute to how quickly or slowly you can alter soil pH. Follow the specific recommendations you'll get with a complete soil test, and allow time for them to take effect before you plant.

Continued ➡

Discover compost. Among its many attributes, compost also includes help for gardeners struggling with unfavorable soil pH. Because compost enhances soil microorganism activity (and because soil microorganisms help make nutrients available to plants), compost serves as sort of a soil pH buffer, reducing plants' dependence on a particular pH range.

Enjoy Your Present pH

The best way to cope with soil pH is to make good use of the pH you already have. The 250-square-foot gardens shown here will produce healthy crops of vegetables (pH 7.2) and luscious blueberries (pH 5.0) with very little extra work. However, to grow blueberries in a soil where you can easily grow vegetables, and vegetables where you can grow blueberries, is another matter altogether. It takes an enormous amount of work, time, and amendments to alter soil pH. In this example, it would take 16.5 pounds of sulfur to lower the pH of the 7.2 garden to 5.0 and 30 pounds of lime to raise the 5.0 garden to 7.2. Plus, substantial pH changes must be made slowly—by amending the soil over two years or more—to avoid severely upsetting the balance of life in the soil. Few soils are in need of such dramatic amendment—be happy with what you have.

More Food Isn't Better!

Many gardeners, especially those who take a casual approach to measuring things, subscribe to the theory that if a little is good, a lot must be better. When it comes to fertilizers, they couldn't be further from the truth. With few exceptions, plants rarely take up more fertilizer than they need; the nutrients they don't use remain in the soil. Some cause imbalances in soil biology, while other more soluble products end up washing into the groundwater. So don't waste your money or your time: When you apply fertilizer, follow the label's recommendations for how much to use. If you estimate how much you need, err on the low side.

For Easy Applications, Make a Master Measure

Fertilizing your garden is easier if you don't have to spend time weighing and measuring fertilizers each time you feed. Making a master measure for the fertilizers and soil amendments you use most often will allow you to just scoop and spread—without overfeeding. To make one, first weigh the materials to determine the volume of a pound. Then pour each into a clean, dry plastic container—recycle whatever's handy; an old deli container or a modified milk jug works fine. Then mark the volume with a permanent marking pen on the outside of the container. One good general mix is 3 pounds of alfalfa meal, 2 pounds of bonemeal, and 1 pound of kelp meal for every 100 square feet of growing area.

Making and Using Organic Fertilizers

Barbara W. Ellis

What happens when you push a spading fork into your soil? Does the fork sink easily into rich-smelling earth populated by a host of well-fed earthworms? Or is your ground hard to penetrate, dry and unyielding? If the latter is true, making and using organic fertilizers is one way to turn your soil into a plant lover's dream.

The most important goal of any soil improvement program is the promotion of microbial activity, because it's the activity of microorganisms in the soil that makes nutrients available to plants. That's why adding organic matter to the soil in the form of compost or green manure is so important

to fertility. Fertilizers not only feed plants, they also feed generations of bacteria and fungi that help break down organic matter and make it available to plants. Organic fertilizers differ from chemical ones in that they tend to release nutrients more slowly and in lower concentrations than chemical fertilizers. They also tend to leach out of the soil more slowly than chemical ones. Unlike their chemical counterparts, many organic fertilizers add organic matter to the soil as well.

Whether you make them yourself or buy them prebagged at your local nursery or garden center, organic fertilizers benefit your soil and plants by slowly and gradually releasing nutrients. The organic matter present in many types of organic fertilizer also improves soil structure and tilth, as well as nutrient- and water-holding ability.

No matter what kind you choose, though, remember that fertilizers can't make up for basically poor soil. Like vitamin supplements for the body, they can help supply missing nutrients, but they can't compensate for gross deficiencies such as lack of organic matter and poor drainage. To improve poor soil, you'll need to add compost and other organic matter to the soil. Then you can count on organic fertilizers to fill in the gaps.

Selecting Organic Fertilizers

Your first goal is to supply the soil with the three major plant nutrients: nitrogen (N), phosphorus (P), and potassium (K). A soil test will tell you the amounts of each element your soil needs. Different fertilizers contain different ratios of these three basic nutrients. Choose one basic type to correct a particular deficiency or mix your own blends to suit your particular needs.

Sources of Nitrogen

ANIMAL MANURE.

Manure is a good source of nitrogen and other soil nutrients. Because of the organic matter it contains, it's also a real boon to soil structure. There are three basic ways manure is sold: fresh, composted, and air-dried. Fresh is cheapest; dried most expensive because the percentage of nutrients and humus per pound is correspondingly higher. Bagged, dried cow manure is available at any garden supply store. Some suppliers may also carry such exotic preparations as bird and bat guano.

In addition, gardeners distinguish between hot and cold manures. Although to some, hot manure means relatively fresh manure, normally the term refers to manure that contains a relatively high percentage of nitrogen. Poultry and sheep manures are examples of hot manure. Cold manures contain relatively low percentages of nitrogen. Cow and horse manure are examples of cold manures.

If you have access to a source of fresh manure, it's best to compost it for three to six months before using it near plants. Composting also kills weed seeds in manure and allows salt, which is often fed to livestock, to leach away. Applied directly to growing plants, fresh manure can burn plant tissue and even kill seedlings. The best time to apply fresh manure to your garden is in the fall, after the growing season is over. Or you can work it into the soil in spring, no less than a month before planting. You can also use it to side-dress planting rows. Never apply it directly to plants. Dried or well-rotted manure can be worked into the soil at planting time or when you're preparing your beds.

FISH EMULSION.

Fish emulsion fertilizer is a by-product of the processing of menhaden, a small, oily, bony fish related to herring. The nitrogen it contains is in the form of amino acids, which plants can take up directly. Fish emulsion isn't a complete fertilizer, though. It is low in calcium, and gardeners with soil naturally low in calcium who depend on fish emulsion exclusively may end up with deficiency disorders such as blossom end rot on tomatoes or tip bum on lettuce. Fish emulsion can be applied diluted to the soil at planting time, as a side dressing, or sprayed on as a foliar feed.

OTHER SOURCES OF NITROGEN.

Dried blood or bloodmeal and cottonseed meal are two other good sources of nitrogen. Cottonseed meal lowers soil pH as well, making it especially suitable for acid-lovers like blueberries and azaleas. Both can be added to the soil at planting time or worked into the soil during the growing season.

Leaves and grass clippings are two other free sources of nitrogen, and both also provide valuable organic matter to the soil. Chopped or whole leaves can be composted or worked directly into the soil in the fall or several weeks before planting in spring. Adding leaves directly to the soil will slightly reduce yields the first year, but as you add leaves each season, the amount of organic matter in your soil rises along with yields. Grass clippings can be composted, used as a mulch, or worked into the soil in the fall or several weeks before planting.

Sources of Phosphorus

BONEMEAL.

Bonemeal is a good slow-release source of phosphorus, which is vital for flowering, fruiting, and root development. It should be worked into the soil at planting time to get it close to the root zone. (Although it also supplies a small amount of nitrogen, bonemeal is best applied as a supplement to manure or compost, which are less expensive sources of nitrogen.) Bonemeal will raise soil pH and shouldn't be used on acid-lovers like blueberries.

Several factors influence the availability of phosphorus from bonemeal to plants. Commercial bonemeal has been steamed and crushed. The more finely ground the product, the easier it is for plants to use. The microorganisms in soil break the particles down and make the phosphorus available to plants. For this reason, bonemeal breaks down faster in a healthy soil with lots of microbial activity faster than in poor soil. Work bonemeal into the soil in spring when the soil is warming and microorganisms are active and can begin to break it down. Finally, soil pH affects availability, for if soil is too acid or too alkaline, phosphorus combines with other elements and becomes unavailable to plants. Phosphorus is most available in slightly acid soil, with a pH between 6.2 and 6.5.

Bonemeal can be used as a top-dressing or worked into the soil at planting time. It tends to be expensive and is probably best used in small applications. Add a handful to the hole when planting roses, shrubs, or trees, and a sprinkling to the holes for perennials or large bulbs such as tulips, daffodils, and lilies. Scientists have recently found that bulbs need more nitrogen than phosphorus, so be sure to provide a source of nitrogen as well.

PHOSPHATE.

Phosphate is available in two forms: colloidal phosphate and rock phosphate. Both are considerably cheaper sources of phosphorus than bonemeal. Colloidal phosphate, also called soft phosphate, is

Continued ➡

the residue left after phosphate-containing limestone has been washed. The washed, crushed limestone is then sold as rock phosphate or converted into one of the enhanced chemical phosphate fertilizers. The phosphorus in colloidal phosphate is more readily available to plants than rock phosphate, but the latter works well over the long haul.

Sources of Potassium

LANGBEINITE.

A mineral mined in New Mexico, langbeinite is an excellent source of potassium. It contains much more potassium than greensand and granite dust, which are the two most common organic sources of this essential nutrient. It's also a more readily available source of potassium than greensand, a mineral-rich sediment, and granite dust, both of which break down very slowly. Langbeinite can be worked into the soil at planting time or used as a side dressing.

OTHER SOURCES OF POTASSIUM.

In addition to langbeinite, greensand, and granite dust, seaweed is also a good source of potassium. It is most commonly available in liquid form, and in addition to potassium also contains a large percentage of essential trace minerals. It can be applied as a liquid directly to the soil or as a foliar spray. Wood ashes also contain potassium and can be mixed with other fertilizers, worked into the soil at planting time, added to the compost heap, or used as a side-dressing. Ashes tend to raise soil pH and shouldn't be used on acid-loving plants.

Applying Fertilizers

There are several different ways to apply fertilizers, and the best method will depend on what type you're using and what plants you are growing. Obviously, liquid and dry fertilizers are applied differently, and the methods and applications suitable for an intensively managed vegetable garden wouldn't be appropriate for a lawn.

How often to fertilize depends on the plants you are growing. A vegetable garden where crops are harvested and plants are removed one or more times a year will have a much greater need for fertilizer than a perennial border, for example. As a general rule plants are fertilized when they are first planted. Heavy feeders can be given supplemental feedings approximately once a month throughout the growing season. With hardy plants such as perennials, trees, and shrubs, it's important to taper off toward fall so the plant can become dormant. Fertilizing late in the growing season can trigger lush growth, which is susceptible to frost damage.

DRY FERTILIZERS

Many organic fertilizers are best applied by digging them into the soil when beds are being prepared for planting in sall or early spring. Dry fertilizers such as manure, colloidal phosphate, langbeinite, bonemeal, dried blood, and wood ashes, as well as compost, can all be incorporated into the soil in this manner. If you're preparing an entire vegetable garden, spread the fertilizer evenly over the whole bed—either by broadcasting or shoveling and raking—into an even layer. Then rake or dig it into the soil. Another alternative, especially useful with expensive materials like bonemeal, is to amend the soil along rows where the plants will be growing.

When planting perennials, shrubs, or trees, fertilizers can be added to the individual holes at planting time or worked into the soil surface around plants.

You might want to use a lawn spreader to apply rock powders over a large area. Simply put the powder into the hopper and the machine does the spreading for you. Hand-held spreaders are available for small jobs. Spreaders have the advantage of producing a consistent, even layer.

Side-dressing is an effective way to apply fertilizer, especially for supplemental feedings during the season or alongside new rows of plants. Work the fertilizer into the soil in a shallow furrow beside a row or work it into the surface around plants just outside the root zone. Plant roots grow toward the fertilizer and take it up gradually. Side-dressing is also a safe way to apply "hot" fertilizers such as fresh manure, which can burn plant roots if applied directly.

LIQUID FERTILIZERS

One of the easiest ways to apply liquid fertilizers such as manure tea or fish emulsion is to use a watering can with a perforated sprinkler head, called a rose, attached. You can also deliver liquids by means of drip irrigation systems (make sure to filter the liquid to prevent it from plugging up the system).

Foliar feeding is a quick and safe way to apply liquid fertilizer. It's nothing more than spraying dilute liquid fertilizer onto the leaves of plants, which take it up readily. Use a dilute solution of fish emulsion, liquid seaweed, or compost or manure tea, and spray it directly on the leaves of a plant. You can use a commercial sprayer of the type used to apply insecticides, but be sure to filter the liquid before spraying. You can also use a watering can with a perforated sprinkler head to do foliar feeding.

PLANT PROPOGATION

Introduction to Propagation

Jeff Cox

Learning to propagate plants—to make new plants from existing ones in your home and garden—is one of the most exciting and rewarding aspects of gardening. Many of the methods are easy, and you don't need fancy or expensive tools. Propagation is cheaper than buying large numbers of plants, so with a little time and effort you can fill your garden quickly at minimal cost. Propagating new plants will keep your house and garden full of vigorous specimens, and you'll probably have plenty to give away, too!

You can reproduce most plants by several methods. There are two major types of propagation: sexual and asexual. Sexual propagation involves seeds, which are produced by the fusion of male and female reproductive cells. Growing from seed is an inexpensive way to produce large numbers of plants. Annuals, biennials, and vegetables are almost always reproduced by seed. You can also grow perennials, shrubs, and trees from seed.

Asexual propagation methods use the vegetative parts of a plant: roots, stems, buds, and leaves. Division, cuttings, and layering are all asexual methods.

With division, you split entire plants into sections; for cuttings, you remove stem tips and root them; and in layering, you root a stem while it is still attached to the parent plant.

Select a technique by considering the plant you are working with, the materials you have, the season, and the amount of time you are willing to wait for a new plant.

Division

Division is a quick and reliable way to propagate many types of multi-stemmed plants with almost guaranteed success. Dividing—separating a plant into several smaller new plants—works well for increasing groundcovers, clump-forming perennials, bulbs, and tubers. You can also divide ornamental grasses and suckering shrubs, as well as houseplants and herbs.

The best time to divide garden plants is when they are dormant. In general, divide spring- and summer-blooming plants in the fall, and fall-blooming plants in the spring. If possible, divide houseplants in the spring as new growth starts. Divide plants with tubers and tuberous roots, such as dahlias and tuberous begonias, before planting in the spring.

The key to division is starting with a vigorous parent plant. If the soil is dry, water the plant thoroughly the day before. Whenever possible, wait for cool, cloudy weather (or at least evening), to reduce moisture loss from the plant during the process.

To divide a hardy plant, lift it from the soil with a fork or spade. Separate small clumps by pulling off the vigorous young plantlets; discard the woody center growth. Use a sharp knife to cut apart small plants. When dividing plants, make sure that each piece you remove has its own root system. Otherwise, new divisions won't grow. Replant divisions as quickly as possible, to the same depth as the original plant, and water them thoroughly. Mulch fall divisions well to protect the developing roots from frost heaving.

DIVIDING HARDY BULBS

"The easiest way to propagate hardy bulbs—especially the ones that are good for naturalizing, such as daffodils—is to dig them when the foliage yellows, separate the offsets on each bulb, and replant. You can plant them at the same depth and location as the mature bulbs, but they might reach flowering size sooner if you grow them in a nursery bed for two to three seasons first.

Propagate crocuses and other bulbs that arise from corms in much the same way: Dig them and separate the small new corms, called cormels, that form alongside the parent corm.

There are two ways to propagate lilies: Pick the small bulbils that form along the stem above the leaves or the bulblets that form at the base of the stem. Then plant them in a nursery bed, where they'll need to grow for several years to attain blooming size. You can also scale lily bulbs to propagate them. Remove the scales one at a time, and place them in a shallow flat or pot filled with moist vermiculite or peat moss. Bury the scales about halfway, and keep them moist. Small bulblets, which can be transplanted to a nursery bed, will form at the base of each scale.

Continued ➡

Division Step-by-Step

1. To start dividing a clump, cut around the mother plant with a trowel or spade (depending on the size of the plant), or loosen the soil with a garden fork. Then lift the plant from the ground, shaking enough soil from the roots so you can see what you're doing when you divide the plant. If there's still too much soil clinging to the roots, you can hose it off.

2. Use a sharp spade to divide perennials or tough clumps of ornamental grasses. Don't chop at the roots, though; try to make single, clean cuts. Another technique for separating hard-to-divide clumps is to plunge two garden forks back-to-back into the clump, then press the handles together until the clump separates into two parts. Divide each part into halves to quarter the perennial, or pull off sections for smaller divisions.

   For smaller perennials or plants with thick, fleshy roots, use a sharp knife to cut the plant apart.

3. If the center of the plant has become woody and has stopped flowering, divide the clump in half. Cut out and discard the woody center, leaving an outer ring of good plant material. Cut the ring into smaller pieces.

   Replant the divisions quickly, water them in, and cover them with damp newspaper or burlap for the first week. Pot up very small divisions until they're growing strongly, then transplant to the garden.

DIVIDING TENDER BULBS

You can increase your stock of favorite dahlia cultivars in the fall when you've dug the tuberous roots and allowed them to dry, or store the clumps whole and divide them in spring. Use a sharp, sterile knife. Make sure that each division has a piece of stem attached; new shoots sprout only from that part of the plant. Discard any thin or immature roots. Divide tubers such as tuberous begonias and caladiums in spring. Cut them into pieces, making sure each piece has an eye or bud. Let the pieces dry for two days and then plant them. Gladiolus corms produce small cormels, which you can grow to flowering size in two or three years. Dig, cure, and store the cormels the same way you treat the mature corms. In spring, plant the cormels in a nursery bed at the same time you put the mature corms out in the garden.

Cuttings

Plants have the amazing capacity to regenerate from small pieces of tissue, called cuttings. These small portions of stems, leaves, or roots will form new roots and shoots if given the right treatment.

Taking cuttings is the most common way to propagate many types of ornamental plants. Because raising plants from cuttings is an asexual type of reproduction, the new plants will look exactly like the parent.

There are several ways to make cuttings, but all types of cuttings need a medium to support them while they grow roots, plus some type of structure to protect them during the rooting period. It's also important to observe good sanitation to minimize disease problems.

The best media for taking cuttings are moisture-retentive but well drained and free of insects, diseases, and weed seeds. Commonly used media are sand, perlite, vermiculite, and peat moss. No one medium or combination is ideal for all plants, but an equal mixture of peat and sand or perlite is useful in most situations. Soil is not a good propagation medium, especially in containers. Unlike the other materials, soil is not sterile and can compact severely from frequent waterings. Only very hardy cuttings are planted directly into soil.

Some plants, such as African violets, coleus, and willows (*Salix* spp.), will root directly in water. This method is fun to try, but if you want to save the cutting, plant it in potting soil while the roots are still small. Plants may have difficulty adapting to soil if their roots are in water too long.

Cuttings need a protected, high-humidity environment while they root. Cuttings don't have roots to take up water, but they still lose moisture through their leaves. By keeping the surrounding air moist, you minimize water loss and help cuttings survive until they can support themselves.

On a small scale, plastic bags are great for protecting cuttings. Support the bag so the plastic does not rest on the cuttings and encourage rot. Provide ventilation by occasionally opening the bag for an hour or two. In most cases, you won't have to add water until the cuttings form roots. To harden off rooted cuttings, gradually open the bag for longer periods.

For large numbers of cuttings, a cold frame or greenhouse is more practical. You can set pots of cuttings on the soil or plant directly in the soil inside a cold frame. Close the frame and cover the glass with shading material, such as cheesecloth or wooden laths (like snow fencing or lattice); gradually remove the shading when roots form. Ventilate and harden off by gradually opening the cold frame for longer periods.

Use a clean, sharp tool to collect and prepare cuttings. Crushed plant tissue is an invitation to rot. Never propagate from diseased or insect-infested plants. Plant cuttings in fresh, sterile propagation mix that is stored in closed containers. Pots and propagation areas should be scrubbed clean and, if possible, sanitized by rinsing with a 10 percent bleach solution (1 part bleach to 9 parts water). Check plants often during rooting, and remove any fallen leaves or dead cuttings. Don't overwater; do provide adequate ventilation.

When Propagation Isn't a Plus
Roger Yepsen

Certain shrubs will give rise to a wealth of seedlings, more than you can use, so that controlling these freebies is added to your landscaping chores. Look for sterile hybrids of your favorite plants to keep these pests from becoming pests. For example, the Buddleia hybrids 'Lochinch' (with fragrant purple flowers) and 'Sungold' (yellow flowers) will stay politely within their bounds. Sterile Rose of Sharon cultivars, *Hibiscus mutabilis x syriacus*, include 'Tosca' (lavender flowers with a carmine eye) and 'Lohengrin' (white flowers). While winterberry euonymus (*Euonymus fortunei*) is invasive, you can go with wintercreeper euonymus 'Purpurea' and sterile variegated forms.

SOFTWOOD STEM CUTTINGS

Take softwood cuttings from succulent spring growth of woody plants such as azaleas and magnolias. Treat stem cuttings of herbaceous plants, including geraniums and impatiens, like softwood cuttings. Because these cuttings are, taken from young tissue, they form roots easily but need high humidity to prevent them from wilting.

Take softwood cuttings from April through June, when new leaves are fully expanded but stems are still soft. Take houseplant cuttings anytime.

Water the parent plant a day or two before taking cuttings. Fill a container with moist propagation mix.

Collect cuttings in the morning or on a cloudy, cool day, and keep them moist until planting. Cuttings should be 3 to 6 inches long; they usually include a terminal bud. Remove leaves from the lower half of the stem, and apply rooting hormone if desired. Insert the cutting to about one-third its length, firm the medium, and water to settle the cutting. Enclose the container in plastic, or place it under a mist system in a cold frame or greenhouse.

Ventilate plants; water to keep the medium moist but not wet. Softwood and herbaceous cuttings root quickly, often in two to four weeks. When roots appear, harden off the cuttings and plant them in the garden or in a pot.

HARDWOOD STEM CUTTINGS

Take hardwood cuttings from woody plants during their dormant period. Hardwood cuttings don't require high-humidity conditions. This method is effective for some types of woody plants and vines, including grapes, currants, willows, and some roses.

Take cuttings after leaf fall and before new growth begins in spring. Mid-autumn is often the best time to collect and plant cuttings so they can form roots before the buds begin to grow.

For potted cuttings, fill the container with moist propagation mix. If you are planting cuttings outdoors or into a cold frame, prepare a deep, well-drained nursery bed.

Collect 4- to 8-inch cuttings from vigorous, one-year-old wood, a few inches below the terminal bud. Make a straight cut at the top, slightly above a bud, and a sloping cut at the base, slightly below a bud. Stick cuttings 2 to 4 inches apart in the medium, with the top bud about 1 inch above the surface. Be sure the cuttings point upward: Double-check that you've stuck the ends with sloping cuts into the medium. Plant fall cuttings soon after they are taken, or store them upside down in moist peat moss or perlite and plant right-side up in spring. Cover fall-planted cuttings with 6 to 8 inches of mulch to prevent frost heaving; remove mulch in spring. Plant late-winter cuttings directly into pots or soil.

Keep cuttings moist. They usually root rapidly in spring, but it is best to leave them at least until fall. Transplant rooted cuttings to the garden or into pots.

EVERGREEN CUTTINGS

Broad-leaved and needled evergreens are often propagated by stem cuttings. Try this method on plants such as arborvitae, hollies, and boxwood.

Collect broad-leaved cuttings in late summer. Take needled cuttings in fall or winter; yew and juniper cuttings should have had some frost.

Fill a container with moist propagation mix, or prepare a well-drained bed in the base of a cold frame.

Continued ➡

Best Bets for Division

Dividing established perennials is a fast and sure way to fill your yard with flowers. Plants with more than one tall stem, especially clump-forming ones like garden phlox or asters, are good candidates for dividing, says Dave Bowman, who grows over 1,000 perennials as a co-owner of Crownsville Nursery in Maryland. Or keep your eye open for ones that root as they wander along the ground, such as snow-in-summer (*Cerastium tomentosum*) and creeping phlox (*Phlox stolonifera*).

The plants listed below are easy to divide by digging up a clump and separating the roots into smaller sections. Some will pull apart by hand with a bit of gentle teasing; for others, you may need a sharp knife or trowel. Replant as soon as possible, and water well. Protect from direct sun for a few days until the roots recover.

Avens (*Geum* spp.)

Bee balm (*Monarda didyma*)

Candytufts (*Iberis* spp.)

Daylilies (*Hemerocallis* spp.)

Evening primroses (*Oenothera* spp.)

Hardy ageratum (*Eupatorium coelestinum*)

Hostas (*Hosta* spp.)

Irises (*Iris* spp.)

Obedient plants (*Physostegia* spp.)

Peonies (*Paeonia* spp.)

Perennial sunflowers (*Helianthus* spp.)

Soapworts (*Saponaria* spp.)

Tansies (*Tanacetum* spp.)

Yarrows (*Achillea* spp.)

Collect 4- to 6-inch tip cuttings in the proper season. Some cuttings benefit from a piece of older wood—a heel—left at the base of the stem. To take a heel, pull sharply downward on the base of a sideshoot as you remove it from the parent plant; trim the excess with a knife.

Wounding is another way to encourage the rooting of difficult plants. Create a wound by cutting a shallow sliver on the side of the cutting near the base. This process stimulates cell division and enhances water uptake but also increases the chance of disease problems.

Before planting, remove lower leaves and sideshoots. To save space with large broadleaved cuttings, cut each remaining leaf in half. Apply rooting hormone if desired. Plant cuttings about one inch deep, firm the soil, and water to settle the cuttings. Place potted cuttings indoors in a plastic bag or in a greenhouse; alternatively, set pots in a cold frame, or plant into the frame.

Ventilate and water if necessary. Once roots appear, gradually harden off the cuttings. The new plants are best left in place until fall and then planted in the garden or in a pot.

LEAF CUTTINGS

Some plants with thick or fleshy leaves can produce roots and shoots directly from leaf pieces. This is a popular propagation method for houseplants such as African violets and snake plants.

Take cuttings any time of year. Use healthy leaves that are young but fully expanded. Thoroughly water the parent plant a day or so before collecting cuttings. Fill a container with moist propagation medium.

Cut snake plant and streptocarpus leaves into 2-inch-long pieces. Plant the pieces right-side up, about 1 inch deep. Peperomias and African violets are reproduced by leaf-petiole cuttings. Detach a leaf along with 1½ to 2 inches of its petiole. Plant vertically or at a slight angle, so the petiole is buried up to the leaf blade. After planting, water the cuttings to settle them in the soil.

If excessive condensation occurs, ventilate the cuttings. When new leaves appear in six to eight weeks, gradually harden them off. Sever plantlets from the parent leaf if it has not already withered away; transfer rooted plants to pots.

Division Dos and Don'ts

No matter which method of division you use, there are some basics that apply. Remember that division shocks your plants—treat them like the postoperative patients that they are, and follow these guidelines:

- **Do** prepare the site for your new divisions before you divide your perennials.
- **Do** take plants out of the ground before you divide them.
- **Do** make sure your tools are sharp. Sharp knives, trowels, or other tools cause fewer open wounds. Since they damage the roots less, plants are less susceptible to disease.
- **Do** card or compost the dead, woody centers of plants. Cut the remaining section of healthy plant into smaller pieces and replant.
- **Do** remove one-half to two-thirds of the foliage on your divisions so it won't wick water away from the plant, but **don't** cut off more than that or you'll slow growth and invite rot.
- **Do** replant divisions as soon as possible. Divisions are vulnerable—**don't** leave them lying in the sun.
- **Do** plant divisions ½ inch higher than they were planted originally; they'll sink a little as the soil settles. The goal is for them to end up at the same level as the original plants were growing.
- **Do** water your divisions well. Give them a good soaking as soon as you plant them, and continue to water them regularly until they're established.
- **Do** shade newly planted divisions to protect them. Cover the plants with moist newspaper or burlap held down with rocks or soil for the first week after planting.
- **Do** give divided perennials and ornamental grasses a foliar feed of liquid seaweed or fish emulsion to provide trace elements and speed establishment.
- **Do** heavily mulch plants divided in fall when the soil cools, to prevent shallow freezing and frost heaving.
- **Don't** divide perennials after early October, since the roots need time to establish themselves while the soil is warm.
- **Don't** divide taprooted perennials—start them from stem cuttings or seed. These include plants such as butterfly weed (*Asclepias tuberose*), gas plants (*Dictamnus* spp.), and rues (*Ruta* spp.).

ROOT CUTTINGS

Root cuttings are a reliable way to propagate plants with thick, fleshy roots. Slice off pencil-thick roots, and cut them into 2-inch pieces. Use a diagonal cut at the bottom of each piece so that you'll know which end is up. (They won't grow if you plant them upside down.) Pot up root cuttings in pots or cell packs filled with sterile, porous potting medium, such as half seed-starting mix and half perlite. Keep the cuttings barely moist, put them in a cold frame or an unheated room, and give them bottom heat, if possible.

These plants propagate well from cuttings of their thick, fleshy roots. Dig deep to lift the mother plant, then cut roots into 2-inch pieces for propagating.

Adam's-needle (*Yucca filamentosa*)

Baby's-breath (*Gypsophila paniculata*)

Bear's-breeches (*Acanthus* spp.)

Bugloss (*Anchusa* spp.)

Butterfly weed (*Asclepias tuberosa*)

Common bleeding heart (*Dicentra spectabilis*)

Cranesbills (*Geranium* spp.)

Mulleins (*Verbascum* spp.)

Oriental poppy (*Papaver orientale*).

Perennial salvias (*Salvia* spp.)

If you have a cold frame, unheated room, or greenhouse, you can also propagate perennials from root cuttings. The best perennials for root cuttings have fleshy roots, like Japanese anemone (*Anemone x hybrida*), grape leaf anemone (*A. vitifolia*), snowdrop anemone (*A. sylvestris*), bleeding hearts (*Dicentra* spp.), cranesbills (*Geranium* spp.), garden phlox (*Phlox paniculata*), great coneflower (*Rudbeckia maxima*), ligularias (*Ligularia* spp.), and Siberian bugloss (*Brunnera macrophylla*). Take root cuttings in the fall or winter when plants are dormant, grow them in the greenhouse or cold frame, and plant them out in a nursery bed when they are growing strongly.

Layering

Layering is a way of propagating plants by encouraging sections of stems to sprout new roots, which are cut from the mother plant and planted. This simple method produces good-sized new plants in a relatively short time.

SIMPLE LAYERING

Simple layering involves bending a low-growing branch to the ground and burying several inches of stem. It is used to propagate many types of vines and woody plants, including grapes and magnolias.

Spring is the best time to start simple layers. Choose flexible, vigorous one-year-old shoots about as thick as a pencil.

Thoroughly water the soil around the plant. The next day, bend a shoot down to the soil. Measure back 9 to 12 inches from the tip of the shoot, and mark the spot where that point on the stem touches the ground. Release the shoot, and dig a 4-inch hole at the marked point. The hole should have one side sloping toward the parent plant. Work in several handfuls of finished compost.

Remove leaves and sideshoots along the chosen stem from 6 to 15 inches behind the stem tip. Wound the stem by making a shallow 2-inch-long cut at a point about 9 inches behind the tip. Insert a toothpick or small pebble in the cut to keep it open. Dust the cut with rooting hormone. Bend the stem down into the hole, and use a wire pin to

Continued ➔

keep the wounded area in contact with the soil. Stake the stem tip if it doesn't stay upright by itself. Cover the pinned stem with soil and water thoroughly.

Keep the layered area moist and weeded. The stem may root by fall; check by uncovering the stem, removing the wire pin, and tugging lightly. If the stem feels firmly anchored, it has rooted. Sever it from the parent plant, but leave it in place until spring. Then pot it up or transplant it. If the stem is not well rooted, replace the soil and wait a year before checking again for roots.

TIP LAYERING

Shoot tips of certain plants such as black and purple raspberries root when they touch the ground. Plant tip layers in late summer, using the ends of the current season's growth. Make sure you use healthy, vigorous canes. Prepare a hole as you would for simple layers; judge the placement of the hole by the tip of the stem.

Bend the step tip down to the prepared planting hole. Lay the cane against the sloping side and place the tip against the farthest edge of the hole. Replace the soil, and water well.

By early fall, shoots will appear and roots will have formed; cut the original cane where it enters the soil. In mid-fall or the following spring, carefully dig up the rooted tip, and plant it in its new position.

AIR LAYERING

Air layering is similar to simple layering, but the stem is covered with long-fibered (unmilled) sphagnum moss rather than soil. You can air-layer upright stems of trees, shrubs, and indoor plants such as philodendrons.

Outdoors, start air layers in early fall with young wood, or in spring with the previous season's growth. Indoors, air layers can be done any time, but it's best to start when plants begin growing actively in spring.

Soak the sphagnum moss in water for a few hours or overnight. Before using, wring the excess water out of the moss, so it is moist but not dripping wet.

Start with a healthy, vigorous stem. Decide where you want the roots of the new plant to be, anywhere from 6 to 18 inches behind the tip. Remove all leaves and sideshoots for 3 inches on either side of that point. Wound the stem by making a shallow 2-inch-long cut into it. Dust the wounded area with rooting hormone. Wrap the ball of moist sphagnum moss around the wound and tie it with string. Next, cover the moss ball with a piece of clear plastic about 6 inches square. For indoor plants, tie the plastic at both ends with string or twist ties. Use waterproof tape to secure the ends on outdoor air layers; make sure the ends are completely sealed. For outdoor plants, also cover the plastic wrap with foil or black plastic and tie or tape it to the stem; this will keep the layered area from getting too hot in the sun.

Indoor plants can produce roots in a few months; outdoor plants may take one or two growing seasons. You'll be able to see the roots growing in the moss. Cut off the top of the plant below the new roots and remove the plastic. Soak the root ball for three to four hours, pot it up, and place it in a sheltered spot for a few days. Let outdoor plants grow in their pots for a few months before planting them out.

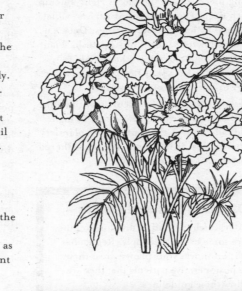

Propagating Plants
Barbara W. Ellis

One of the easiest and most economical ways to increase your plant collection is to learn how to propagate them yourself. You can start new plants in a variety of different ways—sow seed, root cuttings, layer, or divide them. Propagating plants is a fascinating hobby that requires little in the way of supplies or equipment, and the techniques involved are straightforward and relatively easy to master. Best of all, creating new plants is fun and rewarding and provides an opportunity not just to create but to share plants with other gardeners.

There are two types of propagation techniques: sexual and asexual propagation. Plants grown from seed or spores have been sexually propagated, because most seed is the result of cross-pollination and contains genetic information from two different parents. Vegetative propagation is the term used for the many different asexual ways plants can be propagated, such as division, cuttings, or layering. All vegetative techniques involve removing sections of stems, roots, or leaves from a parent and inducing them to develop into new plants by providing conditions that encourage the production of roots and shoots. Plants propagated vegetatively are genetically identical to the parent plant. For this reason, vegetative propagation is used to make exact copies of plants that have special features such as taste, color, disease resistance, size, or form. Since many cultivars do not come true from seed (because seeds resulting from cross-pollination are not genetically uniform), and others do not produce seed at all, vegetative propagation is an important way to perpetuate valuable cultivars. For example, 'Bartlett' pear was created in 1770 and is enjoyed today only because of vegetative propagation. Another benefit of vegetative propagation techniques is that they generally yield much quicker results than growing plants from seed.

Vegetative Propagation

What makes it possible for individual plant parts to transform themselves into complete plants with roots, stems, foliage, and flowers of their own? All plants have specialized clusters of cells that can divide very quickly and differentiate into all the structures a plant needs to grow. These clusters of cells, called meristem or meristematic tissue, are found in the growing tips of roots, stems, and branches. As the plant grows, it is the meristematic cells that differentiate into new stems, roots, foliage, and flowers. Meristematic tissue also lies dormant in the plant, most notably in dormant buds, which will begin to grow if given the proper stimulus. For example, the moist, humid conditions needed to root a cutting will awaken the meristem in dormant buds and cause it to begin producing roots and shoots. Plants such as orchids propagated by a specialized technique called meristem or tissue culture are grown from single cells of meristem tissue. Certain types of plant cells can also turn into meristemlike tissue, causing roots to arise on the cut surface of a stem even if dormant buds are not present.

SUPPLIES

The first task is to assemble the tools and supplies you'll need. You'll probably need the following items:

- **Propagation knife.** For taking cuttings or making cuts to encourage roots to form on a layer, you'll need knives of various sizes and shapes. Specially designed propagation knives usually have a thin, straight blade. They must be kept very sharp.

- **Pruning shears.** You'll also need one or several different sizes of pruning shears and/or scissors for cutting stems, leaves, or other plant parts.

- **Containers.** In some cases, new plants can be propagated and planted directly into the garden, but you'll need containers for rooting cuttings or potting up new plants. Many different sizes and shapes of containers will work, as long as they are deep enough to hold the base of the cuttings, provide drainage, and can be covered in some manner to maintain humidity. At least 2 inches deep is best. Try using plastic garden flats and pots or plastic food containers. Plastic shoe or sweater boxes also are very useful because cuttings can be stuck in rooting medium spread in the bottom, and with the top in place they provide the humid conditions cuttings need.

- **Rooting medium.** A good rooting medium provides enough support to hold the cutting firmly and also retains moisture, but is porous enough to drain well and allow roots to penetrate. Many mixtures will work, but a mixture of equal parts sterile, coarse sand (not builder's or beach sand) and vermiculite or perlite are recommended as the initial medium. After rooting, cuttings can be transplanted to a medium that is richer in nutrients—a mixture of one or several of the above ingredients with an equal amount of sterile potting soil is fine.

A container of water will serve as an effective rooting medium for many plants—coleus or philodendrons, for example- but this approach has drawbacks. Roots that are produced in water tend to lack the structure and strength of roots produced in other media, and they do not transplant to soil well since they tangle together and are easily damaged.

- **Dibble.** This is a pencil-like instrument that is used to make a cylindrical hole into the rooting medium for the cutting. Making a hole with a dibble (or the end of a pencil) prevents the cut end of the cutting from being damaged when it is stuck into the soil. It also prevents rooting hormone from rubbing off.

- **Atomizer.** A simple atomizer or spray bottle will make the task of increasing humidity around the cuttings quick and easy.

Continued ➡

- **Disinfectant.** Bleach or alcohol are excellent disinfectants for cleaning pruning shears and knives. Make a solution of 3 parts water to 1 part bleach or alcohol. Dip implements into a container of this disinfectant after taking each cutting to avoid transporting fungi, bacteria, or other diseases from plant to plant.

- **Heating cable.** Although this piece of equipment is optional, many kinds of cuttings will root more quickly if provided with bottom heat. You can provide bottom heat by setting propagation containers on heated surfaces, such as the top of a radiator, refrigerator, or hot water heater. Or invest in a commercial heating cable like the ones sold for speeding the germination of seeds. These are available from most mail-order nurseries or well-stocked local garden centers. They will generally keep the temperature of the medium about 5° to 10°F above the temperature of the surrounding air, and can be easily positioned along the bottom of a propagation box beneath the soil.

- **Rooting hormones.** Rooting hormones are very useful in encouraging hardwood and other difficult-to-root cuttings to form roots, but they must be used sparingly and carefully. Generally, only the tip of the cutting is dipped into the powder; in this case, more is not necessarily better. It's also important to realize that these hormones can be contaminated with fungi and other organisms. When using them, pour a small amount into a separate container, use it to treat the cuttings you're planting on a given day, then throw away the excess. It's best to store rooting hormones in the refrigerator to extend the shelf life, which ranges from six months to a year. Some formulations include chemical fungicide, but you can purchase ones that don't and use sulfur to control fungal diseases.

- **Antitranspirants.** Often used to protect evergreen foliage from water loss and windburn in winter, antitranspirants will reduce the amount of moisture lost through foliage. For this reason, they help prevent a cutting from drying out before roots have a chance to form. Antitranspirants are also quite useful when transplanting cuttings to larger pots or to the outdoors, because they reduce water loss and help plants overcome stress.

- **Propagators and mist beds.** If you're serious about getting professional results, you may want to invest in a propagation box, which is much like a miniature greenhouse. It provides uniformly high humidity, and most models come equipped with heating cables. You can also make one yourself with plastic stretched over a wood or wire frame and a heating cable spread under a layer of vermiculite or sand. You can suspend fluorescent lights over the box if necessary. Be sure to provide for ventilation to prevent excessive humidity from building up.

A mist bed is a more sophisticated piece of equipment, which is relatively expensive and is generally used in a greenhouse. A heating cable regulates bottom heat while a timer and a series of small mist nozzles spray the cuttings with a fine mist of water at intervals throughout the day. A mist bed isn't enclosed, because the frequent misting provides all the humidity the cuttings require.

Rooting Cuttings

Rooting cuttings is one of the easiest, most popular ways to propagate plants. Although there are several different types of cuttings, two basic concerns apply to all types. First, since cuttings are removed from the parent plant before roots develop, they dry out easily. To root them successfully, you'll need to provide a rooting medium that is well drained but remains moist at all times. They also require high humidity to reduce water loss. Second, it's important to provide as antiseptic conditions as possible to discourage disease organisms and fungal spores from invading the wound(s) made when taking the cutting.

Propagation Datebook

With so many options for propagating plants, it can be hard to decide what to do when. Layering can be done anytime in spring, summer, or fall. In general, divide plants either in early spring, just as new growth begins, or in summer after bloom. Take cuttings after the flush of new spring growth is over. Propagate houseplants anytime. Here are some propagation suggestions to mark on your calendar:

- In early spring, divide asters, yarrows, and other perennials. In early to midsummer, take softwood cuttings of ornamental shrubs.
- In July, take root cuttings of oriental poppies (*Papaver orientale*), bleeding hearts (*Dicentra* spp.), bugloss (*Anchusa* spp.), and other plants with thick, fleshy roots.
- In August, divide peonies (*Paeonia* spp.), digging carefully so you don't damage any more eyes than necessary. Replant with eyes not more than 2 inches below surface.
- In August, start cuttings of wax begonias, coleus, and geraniums for winter bloom indoors.
- In August, propagate groundcovers such as pachysandra and periwinkles (*Vinca* spp.) in cold frames.
- In August, start cuttings of subshrubs like lavender, santolina, sage, and thyme.
- In late summer, take cuttings of broadleaved evergreens, such as boxwoods (*Buxus* spp.), arborvitaes (*Thuja* spp.), and hollies (*Ilex* spp.).

Taking Stem Cuttings

Regardless of the type of stem cutting you're taking, it's best to start with short ones, between 3 and 6 inches in length. Remove all flowers and flower buds so that the plant's energy will go toward root rather than flower production. Also remove the bottom leaf or set of leaves so that the foliage won't touch the rooting medium.

It's important to make a clean cut without crushing the stem. Use a knife on soft and semihardwood cuttings; shears on thick stems or for hardwood cuttings. Make the cut at a 45-degree angle, so that the cut has more surface area from which the roots will grow. The top of the angled cut should be between ¼ and ½-inch below a leaf node (where leaves emerge from the stem). Be sure to sterilize your knife or shears with disin-

fectant between cuttings to avoid transporting fungi or disease organisms from plant to plant.

Fill the containers you'll be using with rooting medium, water thoroughly, and allow excess water to drain away before sticking in the cuttings. Use a dibble or the end of a pencil to make holes to insert the cuttings, spacing the holes 2 to 4 inches apart depending on the size of the cuttings. Insert the cuttings at least 1 inch into the medium, and make sure the bottom set of leaves is not in contact with the medium.

After planting the cuttings, don't let the rooting medium dry out. There are several different ways to water the cuttings. You can gently water the surface of the medium using a watering can with a fine-spray nozzle. Another method is to water from below by setting containers in a pan or tray of water and allowing water to seep upward through the drainage holes. Either way, be sure to allow the containers to drain after watering because they should not be left sitting in water. A third method is to set the propagation container atop a water-filled pebble tray, with one or several wicks running from the medium, through drainage holes in the bottom of the container, into the water. (Strips of nylon stockings work fine as wicks.) Be sure the bottom of the container doesn't make direct contact with the water.

Cuttings require high humidity (near 100 percent) in order to root without drying out. You can place a plastic bag over a single pot or group of pots and support it with thin strips of wood or heavy gauge wire to keep it from touching the foliage. Or use garden flats with clear plastic covers, sweater boxes, a cold frame or hotbed, a propagation box, or a mist bed to maintain humidity.

Ideally, the air temperature within the propagation container should be 70°F or less. Within the rooting medium, between 60° and 70°F is best. Adequate light is important, but bright light will literally cook the cuttings. Either natural, indirect sunlight or light from fluorescent fixtures is fine. Make sure fluorescent lights are suspended approximately 6 to 10 inches above the propagation container.

Types of Cuttings

Herbaceous Cuttings.

These are stem cuttings taken from herbaceous plants, meaning plants that do not develop woody tissue. Many houseplants, annuals, perennials, herbs, and vegetables can be propagated by this type of cutting. Herbaceous cuttings can be taken at any time of the year, but late spring and early summer are probably best. Most plants are in active growth at this time of year and actively growing shoots that will yield the best results.

Softwood Cuttings.

Similar to herbaceous cuttings, softwood cuttings are taken from woody plants such as ornamental shrubs, small-fruit bushes, and many trees. Softwoof cuttings should be taken from actively growing shoots in late spring or early summer. These cuttings should be 2 to 4 inches in length.

Semihardwood Cuttings.

This type of cutting is similar to softwood cuttings but is taken later in the year, when active growth has slowed down and no new leaves are being produced. The stems are becoming woody (hard) at the base, but the stem tips are still soft. Also called semiripe cuttings, these should be between 4 and 6 inches long and should be taken in late summer. They will

Continued ➡

usually require the addition of a rooting hormone for best results.

HARDWOOD CUTTINGS.

These are stem cuttings taken from outdoor deciduous trees and shrubs after the leaves have dropped. They are taken from new wood that is thoroughly ripe or woody and dormant. These are taken in late fall to early spring and should be between 5 and 12 inches long.

Because they are dormant, hardwood cuttings are treated quite differently than softwood or semi-hardwood cuttings. Place them singly (or in bundles of the same species or cultivar) in a large container filled with moist sand or vermiculite. Place the container in a cool (35° to 45°F), dark location for the winter months. When lifted in spring, the cuttings will have developed a protective callus over the cutting wound, from which roots will emerge upon planting. Dust the callus with rooting hormone and root the cuttings in a manner similar to that recommended for the other types of cuttings listed above. Bottom heat is often effective at this stage. Once rooted, cuttings will be ready for transplanting to individual pots or outdoors.

Leaf Cuttings

Not many plants will propagate from leaves, but those that do (primarily a limited number of houseplants provide a quick and easy way to increase numbers. Like stem cuttings, described earlier in the chapter, leaf cuttings require as sterile conditions as possible to discourage fungi and other disease organisms. They also need high humidity and a rooting medium that remains evenly moist.

The simplest type of leaf cutting consists of the leaf alone, without the petiole, or leaf stalk, attached. The base of the leaf is placed in the medium, which is kept evenly moist until one or more plantlets appear. Once the new plants have produced an adequate root system, the leaf can be removed and they can be potted and grown on. Jade plants (*Crassula* spp.) and piggyback plants (*Tolmiea menziesii*) are easy to propagate by simple leaf cuttings. There are several other types of leaf cuttings, which are described below.

LEAF AND PETIOLE CUTTINGS.

These consist of an entire leaf with at least ½ to 1½ inch of the petiole (leaf stalk) attached. Place the petiole into the rooting medium of a propagation container, and follow the standard procedures listed above for stem cuttings. One or more new plantlets will develop from the petiole, at which time the original leaf can be removed and the plantlets grown on in the propagation container until ready for transplanting. African violets are often propagated this way.

LEAF-BUD CUTTINGS.

As the name suggests, this type of cutting consists of a mature leaf, a dormant bud in the leaf axil, and a small amount of stem tissue (¼ to ½ inch in length) to which the leaf is attached. Place the base of the leaf into the rooting medium, covering the bud and the stem. The stem may be softwood, semihardwood, or hardwood. Then follow the same procedures described earlier in this section for leaf and petiole cuttings. The new plant will develop from the dormant bud. English ivy (*Hedera helix*) is especially easy to propagate in this manner.

SPLIT VEIN CUTTINGS.

The leaves of some plants will produce new plantlets anywhere along their undersurface where a cut vein is in contact with rooting medium. For these, remove a leaf from the plant and make slits across individual veins—one slit per vein, effectively severing a vein with each cut. Lay the leaf flat on the surface of the medium, right side up, with the underside in direct contact with the medium. You may need to tack down the leaf with hairpins or bent pieces of wire to be sure the leaf is touching the medium. Rex begonias are often propagated in this manner.

Proper Propagation

Plant propagation has it own special vocabulary. It's helpful to understand the meanings of certain terms as you read about how to propagate. Here are some of the basics:

Cutting. A cutting is part of a stem, leaf, or root that is removed from a plant and forms a new plant that looks like its parent. You can take cuttings from a wide variety of herbaceous and woody plants.

Division. Division is the separation of a multi-stemmed plant into smaller plants. It's a common way of propagating bulbs, tubers, groundcovers, and clump-forming perennials.

Layering. Layering is a technique that encourages root growth on stems that are still attached to the parent plant. Tip layering and air layering are variations on the basic layering method.

Grafting. Grafting is a method for joining a stem piece, called a scion, to a compatible plant supplying the root system, called the rootstock. The technique brings the cambium (actively growing tissue between the bark and wood) of the scion and the rootstock into close contact so that the plants will grow together as one. There are several ways to graft, including whip-and-tongue and bud grafts.

LEAF SECTIONS.

Some plants can even be propagated from small pieces of a leaf, as long as each piece includes a section of a large vein. For these, simply cut the desired number of leaf sections and place them vertically into the rooting medium. Be sure to place them right side up—with the end that was closest to the base of the plant in the medium. New plantlets will develop from the base of the primary vein. Sansevieria trifasciata, commonly called snake plant, is the plant most often propagated in this manner.

Cane Cuttings

Plants that produce canelike stems can be propagated by softwood cuttings, but one of the most productive approaches is to cut the cane into 2-inch-long sections, each of which must have a node (an old leaf scar and a dormant bud). Place each cutting horizontally into the rooting medium, with about ⅓ of the cutting (including the dormant bud) located above the surface of the medium. Use bottom heat to promote rooting, and follow the same procedures recommended for other stem cuttings. Dieffenbachias Dieffenbachia spp.) and dracaenas (*Dracaena* spp.) can be propagated in this manner.

Root Cuttings

Many fleshy-rooted plants can be propagated from the simple technique known as root cuttings. Root cuttings are taken once the plants have become dormant at the end of the growing season. Lift the parent plant and root prune it by severing several of the large, fleshy roots. Then replant the parent plant. This root pruning will not harm the plant, provided you don't remove too many roots.

Cut each root into 2- or 3-inch sections (4 to 6 inches long for trees). It's important to keep track of polarity, which end of the root was closest to the parent plant (up) and which was farthest from the plant (down). That's because the oldest part of a root cutting (generally the widest end) must be placed at the surface of the propagation medium with the youngest part of the cutting places into the medium. They won't root upside down. One easy way to keep track is to make the cut at the "top" or oldest end of the root horizontal and the "bottom" cut at a 45-degree angle. That way, each cutting will have a recognizable top and bottom for planting.

To plant root cuttings, fill a container with equal amounts of peat and ordinary sterilized potting soil. Thoroughly moisten the soil and let the water drain away. Then dust the bottom of each cutting with powdered sulfur to control fungi. Use a dibble to make insertion holes, allowing no less than 1½ inches between holes, and place the cuttings into the holes. Again, make sure that the cuttings are oriented with the oldest or top part nearest the surface. Cover the container with ¼ to ½ inch of pea gravel or coarse sand.

Crop Harvesting Schedule

When to Harvest	Crops
Daily	Beans, green and filet
	Beets
	Blackberries
	Corn
	Cucumbers
	Peas
	Raspberries
	Zucchini
Weekly	Eggplants
	Leeks
	Melons
	Peppers
	Tomatoes
As Needed	Beans, dry
	Carrots
	Brussels sprouts
	Kale
	Parsnips
	Potatoes
	Winter squash

If you are propagating hardy plants, you can place the container in a cold frame. Keep cuttings of tender plants in a frost-free place. Water only when the medium begins to become dry; too much moisture can promote the growth of fungi, which is the prime cause for loss of root cuttings. When new shoots appear, provide a mild dose of fertilizer such as manure tea. Once the plants have become established, they can be transplanted to individual pots or moved to the garden.

Division

One of the easiest ways to propagate clump-forming plants is to divide them, that not only serves to propagate, but also helps rejuvenate

Continued ➡

clumps that have spread and left an old, over-crowded center that has ceased blooming. Plants propagated in this manner are dug, separated into individual plantlets, each with its own shoot(s) and roots, and then replanted. Many perennials are divided in early spring, when plants are just beginning to awaken from winter dormancy and begin actively growing. However, spring-blooming plants are best divided in early summer, just after bloom in the case of irises, or in late summer or early fall as they approach dormancy, as in the case of such plants as peonies or hostas.

To divide a plant, dig the parent plant and either gently pull or cut apart sections of the crown. You can cut with pruners or use the sharp edge of a spade or trowel. Replant the divisions as soon as possible, and keep them well watered both until you get them back into the ground and until they become established.

A number of plants such as raspberries and lilacs produce suckers or offsets that root either before or after they are cut away from the parent plant. Use a knife to cut them away from the parent plant or use a shovel and dig the sucker or offset if it has already rooted. Make sure the cut is as close to the parent stem as possible. Replant at the same depth as when attached to the parent plant.

Bulbs can also be propagated by yet another form of division; bulbs such as daffodils that produce offsets at the base of the main bulb can be dug and separated. Once the bulb has finished blooming and the foliage is turning brown, it's a simple matter to lift the parent bulb, remove the offsets, and replant. Offsets will generally take one to several years to reach blooming size.

Layering

Most plants that have long, flexible stems are candidates for another propagation technique called layering. Layering is a method to encourage roots to develop on a section of a plant where they would not normally grow (such as on above-ground stems) while the stem is still attached to the parent plant. This process can occur naturally, such as when a forsythia branch arches downward, touches the soil and roots. It's also easy to induce the process.

To layer a plant, start with a young, vigorously growing outer stem. In mid- to late spring, dig a small, shallow hole or trench (1 to 3 inches deep) several feet from the center of the parent plant. Arch the young stem downward so that its tip or a portion near the tip can be placed into the hole. Then fasten it down with a wire wicket or a rock if necessary and cover it with soil. Keep the soil evenly moist, and by the end of fall a complete root system should have formed at the base of the buried portion of the stem. The offspring plant can then be severed from the parent plant, either that fall or the next spring, and planted else-where. Some stems will root more readily if a slanting cut is made partway through the stem at the point where it touches the soil.

Serpentine layering is a very similar technique used to produce many plants from a single, flexible stem. In this case, make a slanting cut every 8 to 10 inches along the length of the stem. Then bury the stem along the ground, fastening the cut portions into the soil in holes dug at intervals away from the plant. Leaf nodes buried underground will generate roots; those left above will grow shoots. When lifted in spring or fall, a root system should exist at each point along the stem where it was cut, and each new plant can be severed from the original parent stem and replanted.

AIR LAYERING

Some plants that do not have flexible stems can be layered in yet another way, through a technique called air layering. To air layer a plant, cut a small horizontal wedge on one side of a healthy stem, partway through the stem just below an old leaf scar (node). Dust the wound with rooting hormone, and pack a ball of moist sphagnum around the stem, thickly covering the wound. Hold the sphagnum in place by wrapping black plastic around the stem and securing it with twist ties or tape. Keep the sphagnum evenly moist until roots develop. Once the roots begin to emerge from the sphagnum, you can sever the offspring from the parent and replant. Air layering is often used to root the tops of houseplants such as dief-fenbachia (*Dieffenbachia* spp.) that have lost their lower leaves. The parent plant will usually resprout below the cut.

STOOLING.

Another form of layering, called stooling or mound layering, involves wounding each stem of a multistemmed plant about 6 inches above ground level, and then mounding soil over the base of the plant and the wounds. This is usually performed in spring. By fall, each stem will have developed its own root system from the point of the wound and can be severed from the parent plant and replanted.

Propagating Tips
Fern Marshall Bradley

Propagating is one of those gardening skills that seem a bit intimidating at first—until you try it. Once you see how easy it is to grow your own, you'll be taking snips and cuttings from plants all over your yard.

There's a method of propagating to suit any gardener's personality. You can start new plants in a downright lazy way, letting Mother Nature do the work for you through a technique called layering. Or you can experiment with soil mixes and rooting aids—even rig up a homemade fog propagator using a room humidifier.

Our experts offer innovative tips along with time-proven techniques for increasing your stock of flowers, shrubs, and fruits. If you're a beginner, start with the simple methods and the easiest plants.

Enjoy Success with Cuttings

Cut a leafy stem off of a plant, and chances are you've got a cutting to root. Taking stem cuttings can be one of the simplest ways to propagate. Rooting woody cuttings can be a little trickier, but still easy enough that nearly everyone can succeed. Try the following tips for the best results with cuttings from every type of plant from houseplants to shrubs and trees.

A SIMPLE SHORTCUT FOR MORE PERENNIALS

Save money on perennials by growing your own from cuttings. "Take cuttings of soft but not too young growth, down to about the third leaf, in early to midsummer," recommends Dave Bowman, a co-owner of Crownsville Nursery in Maryland, which specializes in perennial flowers. Put them in a nursery bed or flat, and keep them out of direct sun until they develop their own root systems. You can cover the cuttings with plastic strawberry baskets or push leafy branches into the ground around them for temporary shade.

Cuttings may show new top growth without being rooted. To be sure new roots have formed, give your cuttings a slight tug, says Bowman. If they don't let go easily, they have rooted.

REVIVE GRANDMA'S ROSE JARS

Many old-time gardeners have successfully propagated rose cuttings with nothing more than an old canning jar. "I remember, when I was a child, my grandparents used to start roses readily. They'd just snip off a piece, stick it in the ground, and cover it with a fruit jar," says Dave Dunbar, a Penn State extension agent.

In the spring, take cuttings of succulent new growth. Push a cutting a few inches deep directly into good garden soil, then cover it with an upside-down glass jar as shown in the illustration below. The jar acts as a mini-greenhouse, keeping the cutting moist and humid. A spot between other plants in the garden makes a good nursery. You won't forget about your cuttings when you see them frequently, they'll be watered along with the rest of the garden, and the taller plants will shade the sensitive cuttings from the sun. Your success rate won't be as high as with more advanced techniques, but it requires no special equipment and can be done on the spur of the moment—just like in Grandma's garden.

KEEP IT CLEAN

Diseases are hard to control in the warm, moist environment that cuttings need. To cut your losses, "start with sterile soil and sterile water," advises Steve Reynolds, a sales manager at Furney's Nursery in Washington State. "Boil the water and cool it before moistening your growing medium."

Be alert for the first signs of problems, such as curled or spotted leaves or visible fungal growth. Move quickly to remove the affected cuttings as well as neighboring cuttings. Air the flat, and try again. Reynolds takes the hard line if disease gets a toehold. "Once fungus is present, you may as well ditch it," Reynolds says. Start from the beginning with fresh medium, new cuttings, and a sterilized container. Be sure to make clean cuts to avoid ragged tissue that will decay and may cause disease problems.

TAKE CUTTINGS FROM MORE-WILLING WOOD

For the best success with cuttings, take them from young growth. "Cuttings of juvenile plants of any species root much more easily than cuttings of mature plants," states Kenneth W. Mudge, Ph.D., an associate professor of horticultural physiology at Cornell University in New York. How do you know if your forsythia or other parent plant is juvenile or mature? Flowers are the tip-off: Flowering growth is mature growth. Flowering, mature wood is usually found at the top or outside of the plant, while suckers and other low growth on the same plant are usually nonflowering, juvenile wood. As much as 90 percent of your cuttings should root if you take them from younger growth, says Dr. Mudge.

CUT 'EM LOW

Sprawling shrubs or trailing plants are usually easy to start from cuttings, but plants with a strong upright growth habit, like many shrubs and trees, can be a little trickier. That's because these plants are hormonally programmed for top growth. "Upright growers like rhododendrons and photinias are easier to root from cuttings if you

Continued →

take clippings from lower branches, where the 'straight-up' hormone isn't as concentrated," notes Steve Reynolds, a sales manager at Furney's Nursery in Washington State.

GET THE TIMING RIGHT

Most softwood cuttings are easier to root if they're made in late spring or summer, after the first flush of growth. As Steve Reynolds, a sales manager at Furney's Nursery in Washington State, explains, "Spring growth is most vigorous, but at that time a plant's hormones are geared for new top growth, not for rooting."

Individual species have their own quirks regarding timing, which you may have to discover through trial and error. For example, cuttings of bearberry (*Arctostaphylos uva-ursi*) taken in spring won't root. Reynolds says. He suggests starting bearberry cuttings in July or August.

On the other hand, cuttings of burning bush (*Euonymus alata*) taken too late aren't successful." As long as the leaves are green, it roots readily," says Kenneth W. Mudge, Ph.D., an associate professor of horticultural physiology at Cornell University in New York. "If you take cuttings when the leaves have turned pink, the cuttings will defoliate and will be hard to root."

MAKE A MINIATURE GREENHOUSE

Looking for ways to reuse clear-plastic soda bottles? You can turn them into miniature greenhouses for cuttings. John L. Creech, Ph.D., the former director of the U.S. National Arboretum, uses the improvised greenhouses to root azaleas and other plants. He cuts the bottom off of two bottles. He fills one bottom with moist sand, removes the colored-plastic bottom-rest from the other, and fits the two bottoms together.

"In July, I insert eight to ten cuttings, put the 'greenhouse' in a shady place, and keep the sand moist. It takes about six weeks for the plants to root," Dr. Creeche explains. He then transplants the baby shrubs to pots filled with soil, keeps them in a protected place, and puts them out in the garden the following year.

KEEP CUTTINGS IN A FOG

Bathing cuttings in humid air is an essential step in getting them to take root. "The whole key to starting a softwood cutting," says Steve Reynolds, a sales manager at Furney's Nursery in Washington State, "is to keep the top of the cutting humid enough so it can live until the roots get established. Keep the humidity close to 100 percent."

Commercial growers use sophisticated fogging machines to supply humidity. Home gardeners can apply the same idea on a small scale, says Kenneth W. Mudge, Ph.D., an associate professor of horticultural physiology at Cornell University in New York. Dr. Mudge suggests using an ultrasonic cool-mist humidifier as part of a home fog propagator. (See the directions below for building a home fog propagator.) You can set up a fog propagator in a cool garage, on a shaded porch, or inside a greenhouse. Be sure that the propagator box isn't exposed to bright sunlight. "Shade is vitally important anytime you're rooting cuttings," Dr. Mudge points out.

You can find the materials to build the fog propagator at any lumberyard. Nails will work fine for fastening the parts together, although construction will be a little easier and a little sturdier (as well as slightly more expensive) if you use deck screws driven with a Phillips bit in your electric drill. Galvanized screws or nails are best because they won't rust in the propagator's humid environment. Also, galvanized nails grip better than "bright"

nails. You can use untreated pine to build the frame, but it's best to coat it with flat black paint.

Here's how to construct the propagator frame:

1. **Make the base.** Cut 2 of the base sides to 34½ inches long. Cut the other 2 base sides to 21 inches long. Nail the longer pieces into the ends of the shorter pieces.

2. **Make and install the uprights.** Cut the uprights to 23¼ inches long. The key to making a sturdy propagator is to make all of the upright joints overlap the base joints. In other words, the seam where two uprights meet should never line up with the seam where two base pieces meet. Nail the uprights to the bases and then to their mating uprights. Make sure the uprights are square to the bases.

3. **Make and install the top rails.** Cut 1 top rail to 33 inches long, 1 top rail to 36 inches long, and 2 top rails to 22 ½ inches long. Again, you want to tie the top of the box together with joints that overlap the upright joints.

You'll need to set up the propagator frame on a tray or greenhouse bench containing several inches of gravel for good drainage. Set the humidifier inside the frame, and fill the remaining area of the frame with several inches of a thoroughly moistened fifty-fifty mix of peat and perlite. Add the cuttings, and cover the frame with heavy-gauge polyethylene. Be sure the plastic hangs down past the top of the base sides to create a closed chamber.

Reap the Dividends of Division

Dividing one large plant into several smaller ones is another easy technique for creating new plants. We most commonly think of dividing perennials, but you can also divide bulbs and ornamental grasses.

MUM'S THE WORD

"You can easily make 100 plants out of 1 chrysanthemum," says Dave Bowman, a co-owner of Crownsville Nursery in Maryland. "And for best growth, it's actually better to divide them every year." Go out to the garden in spring, he advises, and start pulling up shoots. Replant directly in the garden, or set out in a nursery bed until later in the season.

You can also take cuttings from potted chrysanthemums. Cut back the plant after flow-

ering, and wait for new growth. Then make as many cuttings as you can, clipping them off at the third set of leaves. Start the cuttings in a flat, cold frame, or nursery bed.

MAKE 100 DAYLILIES IN A DAY

If an established clump of daylilies is thriving in your garden, all you need is a sharp knife and a shovel to make a whole bed of these appealing perennials. "Do you know what a Ginsu knife is?" asks Chick Wasitis, laughing. Once ubiquitous on late-night television, those hard-working knives "make a terrific tool for slicing up clumps of daylilies," says Wasitis, a co-owner of Crownsville Nursery in Maryland, where he grows more than 1,000 kinds of perennials.

To divide an established daylily, lift the plant after it blooms, in mid- to late summer. Cut foliage back to 4 to 5 inches. Use a Ginsu knife, a handyman's razor-knife, or a butcher knife to separate the clump into divisions of at least a single fan with some roots attached. (Watch those fingers!)

GROW A HOST OF DAFFODILS

Shallow planting is the key to encouraging daffodils to divide. Brent Heath, a co-owner of the Daffodil Mart in Virginia, says that planting the bulbs 4 inches deep will spur bulb division. "But you're taking a risk with winter cold," Heath points out. "In winter, you may lose them."

Heath prefers to plant deep and let hybrid daffodils multiply naturally. In good growing conditions, daffodil bulbs planted deep will often double naturally in size each year, producing twice as many flowers the following season. "When you get up to 16, 32, or 64 flowers in a clump, the bulbs tend to stop multiplying. What you have is a big clump of little bulbs," Heath explains. This is the time to replant. In late May or early June, about eight to ten weeks after bloom, lift the clump, and gently shake off the dirt. Let the bulbs come apart naturally—don't pull them. Then plug the bulbs back into the soil. Plant the big bulbs 6 inches apart.

It's best to put small bulbs, called offsets, in a nursery bed until they reach maturity. Keep in mind that even under optimum conditions it will take three years until these offsets come into bloom, says Bill Kennedy, a customer representative for Van Engelen, a Dutch bulb nursery in Connecticut. Label the cultivars so it will be easy to move them into the garden as they mature. In fall of the following year, lift the bulbs, and move them to their homes in the bed or border.

SCALE A LILY BULB

If you love lilies, the good news is you can easily propagate enough of them to fill your yard. Bob and Diana Gibson, co-owners of B & D Lilies in Washington State, grow lilies by the acre, and they propagate many of their lilies by using scales from the mother bulb. The technique is shown in the illustration at right. "We sacrifice our bulbs, taking off the scales down to the pit," notes Bob Gibson. "But you can make four or five new bulbs every year by taking just the outer ring of scales. That way, you won't hurt the mother bulb at all."

Dig up the lily bulbs in fall after the foliage has nourished the bulb and died back. Mix up a bucket of potting medium for your scales. The Gibsons suggest 5 pounds of vermiculite, lightly moistened with 1 cup of water. Keep the mix barely moist so that a handful doesn't stick together. Remove the outer ring of scales from each bulb. Set the bulbs aside, and replant them in the garden as soon as possible, positioning them so that the top of the bulb is at least 6 inches below the soil surface. Let the scales dry in a shady place for one day so that a

Continued ➡

callus forms. Fill plastic sandwich-size bags with the moistened vermiculite, and use a pencil to poke several holes for ventilation in each bag. Add several scales to each bag, then store the bags in a warm (70° to 72°F), dark place.

At the end of three months, bulblets the size of green peas will have formed on each scale. Put the scales with bulblets in the refrigerator for 10 to 12 weeks, then plant out in a nursery bed, in light shade. In 3 to 4 weeks, the bulblets will put up a single leaf. By the end of the season, each plant will have three to four leaves. In another season, they'll grow a tall stem but no flowers. In fall, move them into the garden where they are to grow. At the end of the following year, they'll flower.

DON'T FEAR BOUNTIFUL BULBLETS

Lily bulbs form bulblets naturally in the garden. "A common panic of people who grow lilies in their garden," says Diana Gibson, a co-owner of B & D Lilies in Washington State, "is the sight of 'suckers' coming up around the bottom of the plant, which they fear will sap the lily's strength." But lily suckers are really young plants growing from bulblets that form on the underground part of the stem. They will do just fine left where they are and will gradually mature into full-size bulbs, expanding the clump.

Let Your Plants Layer

Layering takes advantage of the natural tendency that many plants have to sprout roots along their stems. Try our experts' suggestions for using this technique to multiply herbs and shrubs or to regenerate a leggy houseplant.

BURY A BRANCH TO MAKE NEW PLANTS

Simple layering is one technique that really lives up to its name. You can propagate many of your favorites anytime during the growing season with this easy trick. "My lavender hedge all started with one plant," says Sally Roth, a garden writer from Indiana. "All I did was push a bit of soil over a low branch here and there in the spring. By the time I had the bed ready, a dozen new lavenders were rooted and ready to be snipped away from the mother plants."

Roth says she likes the fun of experimenting to see what will root. She merely bends a low branch to the ground and scoops a handful of soil over a short section of the stem, patting it down and sometimes weighting it with a stone if the branch is inclined to spring upward.

The herb garden is a good place to start experimenting, suggests Roth. Many herbs, including absinthe, anise hyssop, artemisias, bee balm, clary sage, culinary sage, lemon balm, rosemary, scented geraniums, and thymes of all types, are especially easy to propagate just by scuffing a bit of soil over a low stem.

The perennial border, too, is full of likely candidates, such as candy tuft (*Iberis* spp.); catmint (*Nepeta X faassenii*); chrysanthemums; goldenrods (*Solidago* spp.); perennial asters; sweet William (*Dianthus barbatus*); thread-leaved coreopsis (*Coreopsis verticillata*), including the popular 'Moonbeam'; and periwinkles (*Vinca major* and *V. minor*). Vines such as English ivy, honeysuckle, jasmine, trumpet vine (*Campsis radicans*), and Virginia creeper (*Parthenocissus quinquefolia*) are also gratifyingly easy to propagate.

Herbs, perennials, and vines will usually root within several weeks, depending on the species. Even some woody shrubs can be propagated with this no-fuss method, though it may take a year or even two before they're ready to transplant. Try your hand with barberries (*Berberis* spp.), border forsythia (*Forsythia X intermedia*), rhododendrons and azaleas (*Rhododendron* spp.), rose-of-Sharon (*Hibiscus syriacus*),

common lilac (*Syringa vulgaris*), pussy willows, willows (*Salix* spp.), viburnums, and weigelas (*Weigela* spp.). But don't limit yourself to these suggestions—experiment with whatever you like.

"Starting new plants this way appeals to the skinflint in me," admits Roth. "There's no investment in supplies, and it only takes a minute. If the plant doesn't root, I haven't lost a thing. And if it does...well, there's always room for one more."

SHORTEN YOUR HOUSEPLANTS

You can rejuvenate some overgrown, leggy houseplants by air layering, a layering technique that encourages roots to form on aboveground stems wrapped in sphagnum moss. This technique works well for tall houseplants such as schefflera (*Brassaia actinophylla*), croton (*Codiaeum variegatum*), dracaenas (*Cordyline* spp.), dumb canes (*Dieffenbachia* spp.), fatsias (*Fatsia* spp.), rubber plant (*Ficus elastica*) and other Ficus species, and Swiss-cheese plant (*Monstera deliciosa*). "This is a good way to make two shorter plants from one tall plant," notes Dave Dunbar, a Penn State extension agent. Dunbar uses air layering to keep his rubber plants and scheffleras in bounds. You can also experiment with air layering on plants outdoors that don't respond well to other types of propagation. Be sure you choose a healthy, vigorous stem for air-layering. Follow this technique:

1. Using a razor blade or small, sharp knife, make a shallow, 2-inch-long slit in the stem anywhere from 6 to 18 inches behind the growing tip.

2. Sprinkle some rooting hormone on the cut, insert a wooden matchstick to keep the cut open, and then wrap with damp, long-fibered (unmilled) sphagnum moss.

3. Cover the moss with clear plastic, and secure the bundle at its top and bottom with masking tape.

4. When you see roots poking through the moss, cut off the new plant just below the new roots, and remove the tape and plastic. Soak the root ball of the new plant for 3 to 4 hours, and pot it up.

The Craft of Grafting

Many gardeners never venture to try grafting. It seems mysterious and tricky, and indeed it can be. If you'd like to try grafting, refer to a book on propagation for details on the technique. Here we've included a few hints from the experts for gardeners who have taken the plunge.

NAIL GRAFTING SUCCESS WITH PRACTICE

"Grafting is easy," says Doug Merkle, the operations manager for Indian Wells Orchard in Washington State, "but practice is the key." Merkle often uses a drywall nail to hold a graft on an apple tree together, then tightly wraps it with masking tape. Be sure that the two stems are joined cambium-to-cambium. (Cambium is a thin layer of actively growing tissue between the bark and the wood.)

"It takes manual dexterity to make good grafting cuts," says Juanita Popenoe, Ph.D., an assistant professor of plant and soil sciences at West Virginia University, "plus a lot of practice. The more you do it, the better you are at it." Inspired gardeners who are all thumbs may want to invest in a professional top-working tool, which is available from A. M. Leonard Nursery Supply Company. It's expensive, notes Dr. Popenoe, but very precise. The tool makes a V-cut in the rootstock and an exactly matching cut in the scion.

PRUNING

Pruning and Training

Fern Marshall Bradley

Pruning may seem like a mysterious art. The good news is that once you become familiar with pruning, it loses its baffling quality. If you learn how to make two basic pruning cuts—called heading cuts and thinning cuts—and understand how plants respond to those cuts, you can change pruning from a chore to a creative outlet.

Whenever you prune, evaluate which kind of pruning cuts will help control size or direction of growth, or produce better flowering or fruit production. These tips from top arborists and garden designers will get you started on a new, enlightened pruning routine.

Controlling Plant Size

We all love watching our landscape plants slowly grow and change with time. But sometimes growth can get out of hand. With regular pruning, you can prevent shrubs from turning the front walk into an obstacle course and keep that luscious fruit in the home orchard within easy reach.

PRACTICE SAFE PRUNING

With sharp shears, loppers, and a pruning saw, you can control the size and shape of most shrubs and small trees. But don't try to take on too much. Alex L. Shigo, the author of *Tree Pruning*, sets the following limits:

- If a branch is over 2 inches in diameter, don't try to cut through it.
- If you must use a ladder, the tree is too big for you to prune yourself.
- Never use a chain saw.
- Never prune near a utility line.

For limbs of large diameter or for tall trees, you can call upon another tool—a professional arborist. "If trees are of any size, the liability and safety issues are such that you'll want to have someone with experience handle the pruning," recommends Dan Neely, Ph.D., the editor of the *Journal of Arboriculture*.

RIGHT TOOL, RIGHT TASK

You wouldn't use a butcher knife to slice a loaf of bread or a paring knife to cut a watermelon in two. Likewise, you shouldn't cut tiny twigs with a pruning saw or large limbs with pruning shears. Pruning tools, like knives, come in graduated sizes and strengths for different diameters of wood. Pick the right model for whatever task lies ahead. Doing this allows you to make a clean cut every time and leave behind healthy, intact wood. Here are some suggestions on tools to choose and how to use them:

Hand-held pruners. Pruners are best for heading back or thinning out medium-size branches.

Hedge shears. Use these for manicuring formal hedges.

Continued ➡

Long-handled loppers. These work well for pruning branches up to 1½ inches in diameter.

Pruning saws. These saws are good for cutting off limbs up to 2 inches in diameter. "Look for new Japanese blades on pole saws, which have revolutionized pruning," says Alex L. Shigo, the author of Tree Pruning. "The cut they make looks like it has been shaved with a razor."

Even if your pruning tools are not high-tech, they will work well if you keep the cutting blades sharp. "They must slice, not tear the wood," says Dan Neely, Ph.D., the editor of the Journal of Arboriculture.

SELECT STRATEGIC STEMS

The key to creating a sound strategy for pruning a deciduous or broad-leaved evergreen shrub is to first figure out how the plant is constructed. Just as a person's ankle bone is connected to the knee bone, which is connected to the leg bone, shrubs are networks of interconnected pieces. Each piece of the plant can have a unique reaction to pruning.

Some parts of a plant are better targets for pruning than others. Ken Miller, a principal of Ken Miller Horticultural Consultants in Missouri, looks for medium-size stems. They resprout new growth readily, unlike larger branches or trunks. They aren't prone to producing an excess of surplus shoots, which is a common result when you shear small twigs. Usually, the best stems for pruning range from about ¼ to ⅝ inch in diameter. "They are slightly thinner than a fat Magic Marker," Miller says.

Once you find stems of the appropriate size, begin removing them one at a time. Look especially for long or overcrowded stems: Your goal is a compact shrub that maintains the original integrity and plant form of the species.

CORNER THE COLLAR

One cardinal rule in pruning woody plants is to not mess with the branch collar—the natural bulge at the base of the branch. This defies common practice of past decades, when pruning professionals routinely recommended cutting off limbs flush with the trunk. More recent research shows that cutting off the branch collar eliminates a natural barrier that keeps pests and diseases from infiltrating the core of the tree.

"Every woody plant has a collar," says Alex L. Shigo, the author of Tree Pruning. "This is true of shrubs, trees, even roses. Some people believe you can hack at will. Then cankers or other fungal diseases move in. People blame it on something else when the culprit is poor pruning."

Thus, when you see that a branch must go, prune carefully to keep the rest of the tree walled off from potential problems. Remove the bulk of the branch, leaving only a stub. Then carefully remove the stub, but leave the entire branch collar.

The branch collar swells slightly broader than the branch. It rings the branch base and protrudes slightly from the trunk. If you are in doubt about where the collar begins and ends, study wild trees that have lost branches. All that remains is the collar, perhaps enveloped in new wood or sealed with a complete, round doughnut of bark callus.

You want to achieve the same results after you prune. Cut just outside where the collar balloons out from the branch. The angle you take will vary with each tree, even with each branch. Proper cuts will heal round, not oval, and should seal by the following growing season.

TOPPING DOESN'T DO THE TRICK

One top tip that many tree professionals push is this: Don't top your trees. "A tree may respond vigorously when you whack off its head," says urban forester Dennis Lueck. "But it's an unhealthy choice for the tree and a hazard to the people beneath it."

The big cuts made when a tree is topped, Lueck explains, are an open invitation to invasion by fungi and bacteria. Rot starts at the cuts, then extends down the trunk and enters the root system, debilitating the tree. Although the flush of new growth may be vigorous, most of it grows straight up. This results in a very weak branch union, creating a joint that is likely to snap when the branches get large and heavy or when a forceful wind or load of snow comes along.

"If you do top a tree," says Lueck, "top it at ground level." Then replace the "too big" tree with a species better suited to the location. And spread the word about topping. Too many homeowners—and arborists—still resort to this tactic to reduce tree size.

Maintaining Plant Form

Pruning also helps maintain and improve plant form. Plants need shaping and thinning to help light and air penetrate to all parts of the plant. This promotes good growth and helps minimize disease problems.

Radical Pruning
Roger Yepsen [Au]

When it comes to certain shrubs, it's easy to have too much of a good thing. Buddleia, caryopteris, forsythia, kolkwitzia (beauty bush), lilac, and mock orange have an exuberance that makes them easy to grow. But if you've skipped pruning them for several years, they may have become leggy and overgrown. When plants are dormant, lop them just above the ground. If stems are too thick for lopping, go at them with a saw.

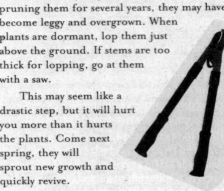

This may seem like a drastic step, but it will hurt you more than it hurts the plants. Come next spring, they will sprout new growth and quickly revive.

SELECTIVE PRUNING SIMPLIFIED

There's an art to directing the shape of trees and shrubs. Vaughn Banting, a Louisiana landscape designer and bonsai artist, has mastered that art while crafting exquisite miniature bonsai trees. He applies the same techniques to shape lush landscape plants. Simply put, he cuts stems back to a bud that will grow in the direction he wishes.

"At the base of every leaf and stem on deciduous trees and broad-leaved evergreens, there is a dormant axillary bud. If you cut the stem just beyond that area, the leaf will give rise to an axillary shoot. If the leaf points left, so will the new shoot," says Banting.

Likewise, if the leaf is under the stem, the new branch will point down. If on the top, the shoot will point up. If the plant has opposite leaves like a maple, dogwood, or viburnum, you can't predict which bud will grow after pruning. Decide which bud you want to grow out, and damage the other bud with your thumbnail.

"This kind of attention to detail is the difference between training plants and just chopping them off," says Banting.

SHAPE TREES FROM THE START

For a young tree, the leader is the core of strength that supports lesser limbs. If a second branch arises that grows strongly upright, the union of that branch with the trunk could be weak. Years later, when the upright branch has grown large and heavy or when it is weighted down by ice or snow, the union may split. Take steps while trees are young to prevent this problem, advises Richard W. Harris, Ph.D., a professor emeritus of landscape horticulture at the University of California at Davis. "There is a key to keeping attractive and safe-structured trees. On any fork in the tree structure, one side should be smaller to prevent the danger of future splitting," says Dr. Harris.

For up to five years after you plant a young tree, keep a close eye on the branches that arise from the leader. You can manipulate them to keep the tree strong and healthy for decades. Here are a few factors to juggle:

Maintain the leader. If several upright shoots arise near the top of the main trunk, encourage the strongest to become the leader by leaving it unpruned. Discourage others by removing their side branches and pinching off the top 2 inches of new growth or by heading the entire branch back by about one-quarter.

Develop strong attachments. Check all future side branches that emerge from the trunk. They should be one-half of the main limb's diameter or smaller.

Establish a branching framework. Lower on the trunk, you can pick the main framework of branches. Select branches that emerge from the trunk with a 45-degree or wider angle and radiate outward in different directions so they do not shade branches below. Be sure they are separated by 1 to 1½ feet of trunk. You can temporarily leave on other branches to strengthen the young tree, but retard their growth as detailed in "Maintain the Leader." Once the tree has a sturdy trunk and enough branches to keep the trunk shaded, begin pruning away these temporary branches. Start with the largest, and remove a few each year for a two- to three-year period to reveal the finished structure of the tree.

PRUNE A PICTURESQUE PINE

Instead of relegating pines to their usual roles as screens or green backdrops, sculpt them into focal points with character. "You can prune and pinch young pines to give them a much older look, a sense of timelessness. You can reveal their inherent beauty and character," says David Slawson, Ph.D., an independent landscape designer from Kentucky who specializes in Japanese garden design.

Pinch soft new growth on pines with your fingers rather than with pruning tools. Grasp a candle—an infant branch tipped with buds—at the point you want to pinch. (Dr. Slawson usually leaves between one-third to one-half of the total length.) Bend until the end snaps off. Thin off unnecessary candles by grasping the base between your thumb and forefinger and snapping them off. If you must remove a branch, don't just head it back—you'll be left with an ugly stump that won't regrow. Make the cut at a point where two branches join, or where the branch emerges from a main stem—this kind of cut will be much less noticeable.

When pruning pines, your window of opportunity is limited. If you want new buds to form on a candle, you must pinch it while it is immature, before the needles form. This means you must pinch during a one- to two-week period in spring. If you pinch later, the candle will develop into a single branch, but it will not sprout sideshoots.

Continued ➡

Watch for candle-break so you don't miss your chance to prune. The downy tan candles will emerge from the end of each branch and stretch out 3 to 6 inches long, or longer near the top of the tree. Pinch before the candle tissue hardens and begins to flush green with young needles. If you cut candles with pruning shears, you will remove the tips of the needles and the ends will turn brown. Which candles you remove or thin will vary according to your goals, which might include one or more of the following:

Size control. Use candling (pruning candles) to keep a pine compact without shearing. This is more subtle than shearing, because you are shaping individual branches, Dr. Slawson explains. To maintain a pine at a constant height, remove one or two of the longest candles on each branch. Then pinch the side candles back to one-third of their full height, or about ½ to 1 inch long.

More height. If you want more height, leave the longest candle on each branch tip and thin out the others. Don't pinch the remaining candles back until the tree reaches the height you want. However, continue to thin for shape.

An aged effect. If you want a gnarled tree with character, find a young tree in a nursery that has an interesting twist or S-curve to the trunk and branches. After planting, remove up to one-third of the branches to reveal the trunk line. On each remaining branch, remove the largest center candle if it emerges straight out of the branch. This will stimulate development of a zigzag branching pattern. Also remove some side candles, leaving two to three candles that point outward and one or two that point inward. Pinch those candles to create feathery clouds of foliage on the end one-third of the limb.

An Easy Espalier

If you want to get double-duty out of a narrow space, you can train dwarf fruit trees to spread lengthwise along a trellis or a series of horizontal wires. The espalier can be freestanding or against a wall or fence. You will prune and direct the trees to drench the fruit with sunlight and shape the limbs in a bold geometric design. Espalier specialist Henry P. Leuthardt says a Belgian fence, a lattice-like series of foliage-framed diamonds, is the simplest espalier to make. In this pattern, shown in the illustration below, the key is to consistently secure the branches to the trellis as they grow. "The key word here is support," says Leuthardt. "Just because the branches start growing on an angle doesn't mean they won't go back to the vertical if left to their own devices."

Creating an espalier does take some attention and persistence. If you're up to the challenge, follow Leuthardt's recommended procedure:

1. Select three to five 1-year-old whips (unbranched nursery trees) of a spur-forming tree fruit like apples and pears. Plant them 2 feet apart along your trellis or other framework.

2. Head each tree back to 15 to 18 inches. This will encourage new branches to sprout just below the cut.

3. After new branches have appeared, prune off all but two strong branches. The two you keep should be on opposite sides of the tree. Train them to a 45-degree angle as soon as they need support. As the limbs continue to grow, tie each to the trellis at 1-foot intervals using either a flexible tie or something like cloth or raffia that will rot before cutting into the swelling branch. The limbs will cross neighboring tree limbs and create a latticework pattern.

4. From the second through the fourth year, the trees will sprout vertical branches. Head them back to 4 to 6 inches long so they don't compete with the main branch. They become short spur branches.

5. After about three years, the branches will stretch diagonally to the top of the trellis. At this point, cut back upright-growing branches and thin out excess growth to maintain the open diamonds between the branches.

6. To maintain your espalier, prune at least twice a year. After the first lush growth of the growing season, thin the new green growth as necessary. You may have to prune again during the growing season if the weather encourages abundant growth, Leuthardt warns. "However, don't prune after Labor Day so you won't encourage late growth that could freeze during winter," Leuthardt says. Wait until the dormant season to clear out late summer and fall growth or to heavily prune an older espalier.

Come To Terms With Pruning

Don't prune blindly. Pruning instructions often include directions to make specific types of cuts. Be sure you know what they are before you tackle that plant!

Heading. Heading is cutting a branch back to a side bud or shoot. This makes plants shorter and bushier.

Thinning. Thinning is cutting a limb off at the base, either at ground level or at a branch collar. This technique opens the plant to air and light, and it directs growth.

Skirting or limbing up. These both mean pruning off the lower limbs of trees. Skirting or limbing up is usually done for easy passage underneath.

Shearing. Shearing is making a series of heading cuts along one plane, as when shaping hedges. When you shear, you slice through small twigs, leaving stubbed-off ends. This releases droves of dormant buds below the cut. They awaken, emerge, and flush outward in a mass of new growth.

Pinching. When you pinch, you are heading by nipping out the end bus or a short section of a twig or stem with your fingertips to make the plant more compact and bushy.

Deadheading. Deadheading is removing spent flowers, by pinching or cutting, to encourage formation of new buds. Some plants, like baptisias, won't rebloom after deadheading; others, like delphiniums, will. If you're saving seed or want the seed heads for decoration, don't deadhead.

Figuring Out the Timing

Once you've figured out *how* to prune properly, there's still the question of *when* to prune. In the sections below, our pruning specialists explain that removing part of the plant top stimulates growth at certain times of year and stifles it in other seasons.

The Whys and Whens of Pruning Well

For most landscape plants, except conifers and disease-susceptible species, you have an almost endless choice of pruning times. You can juggle your pruning schedule to make your pruning most effective. See "Prune a Picturesque Pine" on page

00 for special instructions on timing and method for pruning pines and other conifers.

"Many errors are made in timing today," says Alex L. Shigo, the author of *Tree Pruning*. "A decade ago, correct pruning meant making a flush cut and a large trunk wound. We had to set the timing to minimize injury to a tree, not to doing the best job." Now, pruning experts recommend making a collar cut, which doesn't injure the tree. So timing considerations are different. "You should know why you are pruning, and start there," says Shigo. These are Shigo's timing guidelines:

- To stunt a tree, prune it in midsummer.
- For spring-flowering shrubs or trees, prune after the floral show is over. This group includes rhododendrons and azaleas (*Rhododendrum* spp.), forsythias (*Forsythia* spp.), lilacs (*Syringa* spp.), and big-leaved hydrangea (*Hydrangea macrophylla*).
- Plants that flower on new growth should be pruned while they are dormant in early spring. This group includes most summer-flowering shrubs, everbearing raspberries, and floribunda and hybrid tea roses.
- To avoid leaving dead spots, shear a hedge after growth begins.

To Prune or Not to Prune

There are certain exceptions to your newfound pruning freedoms. Here are ways to avoid some pruning pitfalls:

Don't prune in the fall. "Avoid pruning living wood as a tree goes into dormancy. It's not equipped to produce callus until it reemerges from dormancy. The cut will remain open and susceptible much longer," says Alex L. Shigo, the author of Tree Pruning.

Watch slippery spring bark. "When trees are first breaking dormancy in spring, many have bark that is prone to slipping for a week or so. Avoid pruning at this time so you don't tear off more bark than you intended," advises Dan Neely, Ph.D., the editor of the Journal of Arboriculture.

Skip spring and early-summer pruning on disease-susceptible trees. If you grow American elms (*Ulmus Americana*), which are prone to Dutch elm disease; oaks (*Quercus* spp.), which are susceptible to oak wilt; honey locusts (*Gleditsia* spp.) that are smitten with canker; or pears, apples, quinces, crab apples, pyracanthas (*Pyracantha* spp.), and cotoneasters (*Cotoneaster* spp.), all of which can get fire blight; avoid pruning during peak infection times.

"A lot of pathogens can enter wounds, but most diseases are limited to reproducing and infecting plants during a certain time period. If the wounds are fresh during that time, there could be big trouble," Dr. Neely says. Conditions in late spring and early summer often are favorable for infection to occur. "The temperature and humidity are relatively moderate and favor fungus sporing and bacterial division. Thus, the weather encourages their spread," says Dr. Neely.

Dr. Neely suggests pruning disease-susceptible trees in late winter, just before they emerge from dormancy. You can also prune trees in late summer, he says, but you risk having trees die back if dry weather follows pruning.

Pruning the Low-Maintenance Way

Barbara W. Ellis, Joan Benjamin, and Deborah L. Martin

The absolute best way to cut down on the time and labor you spend on pruning is to avoid it altogether. And the secret to that is choosing plants that grow

Continued ➡

only as tall and wide as your space. Looking for dwarf trees and shrubs is a good start. Also keep your eye out for well-behaved fruit trees and berry bushes—there are new ones being introduced every day. Although buying on impulse is fun and easy, choosing the right plants from the start is worth the extra time it takes: It will save you pruning time and effort for the life of your plants.

But uprooting all the plants in your yard and replacing them isn't often an option. And extreme age, high winds, lightning, or diseases can also ravage plantings. What to do? Haul out the pruning saw and shears. But never fear, with the information that follows you can complete your pruning chores quickly and with confidence.

Pick Your Cuts to Prune Plants Right the First Time

Random hacking takes a lot more effort than proper pruning, and it costs a lot. These cuts come back to haunt you as rotted or diseased areas and lush, uncontrolled growth. As a first step toward reforming your pruning practices, always make proper pruning cuts that will shape your plant the way you want it to grow.

When you prune, cut just above a bud, as shown. But don't just select any bud—cut to one that's pointed in the direction you want a branch or stem to grow. Unless your plant has a bare spot in the middle, choose a bud growing away from the center to avoid crowded, crossing branches. If you're removing damaged stems or branches during the growing season, cut just above a healthy leaf to help hide the wound.

Cut Out Labor

There are two ways to prune trees and shrubs. You can thin them and save time and effort, or head them back and create more work. It's not hard to decide which technique is best for you—or your plants.

Thinning cuts. Prune selectively by cutting branches back to the next larger limb or by removing entire limbs or stems. You'll shape the plant by reducing its height and improve air circulation by opening it up. The result is a healthy, attractive plant that won't need follow-up pruning.

Heading cuts. When you cut the ends off branches, they send up a dense growth of side shoots. This type of pruning makes formal hedges look tidy and full but creates problems. It reduces air circulation and light inside the plants so inner branches are susceptible to insects or diseases; they may even get shaded out completely.

If you can't give up your formal hedge, prune it so the top is slightly narrower than the bottom so the entire plant gets light.

Use Handy Helpers to Make Pruning a Breeze

All you really need for painless pruning are a few good tools. High-quality stainless steel or forged steel blades won't snap under stress, so you'll avoid lots of wasted time and frustration. But even they have limits; treat your tools right and only tackle jobs they're designed for. If it takes lots of effort to cut, you're pruning a branch that's too big for your tool.

A set of hand pruners and a handheld pruning saw should see you through most pruning situations you're likely to encounter. If you have hedges or large plantings of flowers or brambles, a pair of hedge clippers and a pair of loppers will come in handy, too. Pick out tools that feel comfortable in your hand and are lightweight enough so pruning won't exhaust you. Clean the blades after each use, using steel wool if necessary; then wipe them with an oily cloth and they'll last a lifetime. Here's what to look for:

Hand pruners. Bypass hand pruners are kinder to fragile stems than anvil types, which tend to crush tender stems as the blade comes to rest on a flat plate. Pointed blades let you reach into tight spots and give a clean cut on stems and twigs under ½ inch thick. Ergonomic models have handles that are set at an angle to the blades so you won't have to bend your wrist as much.

Anvil pruners will cut wood with less effort than bypass pruners, though, and are a good choice if you have limited hand strength.

Pruning saws. A curved pruning saw can cut through wood with ease, especially if you select one that cuts on the push *and* pull strokes. Many models only cut on the pull stroke, so there's less pressure on the narrow blade. They're just as useful but not quite as fast. Try out models you see in local hardware stores or garden centers to find one that feels and cuts comfortably. You may find the best selection in mail-order catalogs.

Chain saws. Most people do not need a chain saw. A handsaw can handle the majority of pruning tasks with finesse. Unless you're dealing with a forest, hire a professional when you need to remove large limbs or trees. They'll have the protective gear and training to do the job safely.

Hedge shears. Nothing beats sharp hedge shears for deadheading flower plantings with great speed. They'll trim formal hedges efficiently, too—try electric models for extremely large plantings—but if you really want low-maintenance, convert your formal hedges to an informal style.

Loppers. A good pair of loppers will make short work of pruning chores for branches that are ½ to 1½ inches in diameter. The long handles give you plenty of leverage for cutting tough limbs. Ratchet-style loppers hold the blades in place while you get a better grip. Several small pulls on the handles is all it takes to slice through a stem, so you won't need Herculean strength.

Pole pruners. You'll rarely have to use a pole pruner unless you're growing fruit trees. They'll extend your reach but are awkward; it takes practice to balance and cut without injuring nearby limbs. Rent one unless you have lots of trees.

Pruning Dos and Don'ts

The way you prune plants makes a huge difference in your workload. Cut limbs correctly, and they'll recover quickly and you won't have any follow-up work to do. Cut them incorrectly, using a misguided technique like topping, and you'll create an ongoing nightmare of yearly corrective pruning. Use the dos and don'ts shown here to make your pruning jobs this year—and every year thereafter—a breeze.

1. **DO line up your pruning cuts and use three-step branch removal.** Cuts should mirror the angle of the branch bark ridge—that furrow of bark where branch and trunk meet. Your cut should closely parallel the branch collar; but not cut into it. This type of cut gives your tree the best chance to cover over the wound and keep out insects and diseases.

    Remove medium and large branches in three easy steps. First, cut part of the branch off to reduce the weight. Holding up a heavy branch while you prune it off the trunk will break your back, your pruning saw, and tear the bark. Then, undercut the remaining stub so the trunk bark won't rip when the stub falls free. Last, make the final cut from the top, beside (but not cutting into) the branch collar.

2. **DON'T make pruning cuts that are too deep or leave branch stubs.** Flush cuts injure trees so badly they can't grow over the wound; enter rot and insects. Stubs rot and give insects and diseases an opening to destroy healthy tissue.

3. **DO prune branches selectively.** Open up or lower the size of a mature tree by removing overcrowded or long branches at the point where they meet the trunk or a larger branch.

4. **DON'T top trees, ever!** This so-called method destroys a plant's natural shape and results in unhealthy, malformed trees. A host of new, weak sprouts will rise from the cuts, and they'll need constant pruning to keep them under control. Insects and diseases will find the cut wood inviting.

Do You Really Need a Chain Saw?

Sure, chain saws are fast—and great for cutting wood—but they're not so great for pruning. Before you buy, rent, or use one, consider the following:

- Unless you have lots of practice, it's hard to make a proper pruning cut without slicing into healthy tree trunks or branches.

- The only place it's really safe to use a chain saw is when both feet are planted firmly on the ground. Don't be tempted to violate this rule by climbing ladders; it's too easy to injure yourself and the tree.

- A chain saw is incredibly powerful and quick; don't give it a chance to get away from you by raising it above your head.

- Protective gear is a must when using chain saws. You'll need safety goggles, gloves, a helmet, steel-toe boots, earplugs, and heavy-duty trousers. Make it easy on yourself and hire a professional arborist with the proper gear.

Pruning Tips for Poorly Placed Plants

Plants always let you know if they're in the wrong spot by growing out of control. Get them back in shape with pruning, then take the steps necessary

Continued ➡

for a permanent cure; otherwise, you'll be doing fix-it pruning forevermore. Look for these symptoms to identify poorly placed plants.

Weak, spindly growth. Poor soil and insufficient light can cause weak, spindly growth. If you suspect poor soil, prune to reshape the plant, then use compost and organic fertilizer to restore soil fertility.

Evaluate light conditions, too; the plant may be getting too much shade. If so, prune back by one-third and transplant to a sunnier spot. Choose a shade-tolerant plant for a replacement.

Awkward shape or branching. Incorrect pruning, storm damage, and winds are just some of the reasons a plant may have an ugly or awkward shape. To correct it, lightly shape the plant by pruning out individual branches. Do not give it a "haircut" with hedge shears; you will only cause lots of additional scraggly growth and make the problem worse.

Determine why the plant grew strangely. Was it injured? Is it in an area with high winds? Storm damage probably won't recur, so pruning is a good cure. Constant, severe winds are another story; provide a windbreak or move the plant to a sheltered area. If a lawn mower caused the damage by bashing away at the base of stems, prune away the injured area and surround the plant with a wide mulch ring.

Wildly vigorous growth. Plants that smother your house or neighboring plants are definitely in the wrong place. Prune them back by one-third (more if you're dealing with an out-of-control vine) so they are manageable. Then move them to a more appropriate spot or the compost bin.

Choosing the Best Arborist

Any time you have to climb a tree or use a chain saw to prune a branch, think twice. An arborist can save you a lot of time, aggravation, and possible injury. Good ones have the training, equipment, and protective gear to do the job quickly and safely. Remember, one small slip in a tree can mean permanent injury.

Check credentials. Look for a certified arborist; they've had to pass a rigorous exam on tree care and selection. Call or write the International Society of Arboriculture, P.O. Box GG, Savoy, IL 61874; (217) 355-9411.

Consult local experts. Contact nearby botanical gardens to see if they can recommend good arborists. Extension agents, horticulture or forestry professors, or the staff at your local department of conservation may also have ideas.

Beware of incredible deals. Bargain-rate tree-pruning deals are usually a sign of inferior or incompetent work.

Check references. Ask for the names of recent clients. Call them up to see if they were pleased with the work.

Pick the Right Size and Shape to Escape Pruning Chores

Have you brought home gorgeous plants, then discovered after they engulfed your house that they were too big when full- or even half-grown? To avoid this problem, measure your planting space before you buy. That way you'll know if a 6-foot-tall, 5-foot-wide shrub will fit under your picture window. You'll save hours and hours of futile labor trying to prune oversize plants to fit. Here's how to tell what size plants will eventually reach.

Read the label. Plant labels are a great help since most list mature size and some growing hints.

Double-check the label information with garden center personnel before you buy; occasionally, labels get switched with other plants.

Check several sources. For reliable plant sizes and growth habits, head for your local library and ask for good tree and shrub books.

Cutting Dos and Don'ts

Fungal problems are the major threat to cuttings. Here are some dos and don'ts for avoiding rots and other fungal disasters:

- **Do** sterilize your knife with alcohol between cuts.
- **Do** treat each cutting with a 5 percent bleach solution (1 part bleach to 19 parts water) if you want an extra guard against fungi. If you plan to put the cuttings in a plastic propagating tent or enclosure, use chamomile tea instead of bleach solution. Dip the entire cutting for a few seconds to a minute.
- **Don't** stick cuttings deeper than 1 inch or they may rot, and **don't** let leaves come in contact with the soil surface.
- **Do** stick cuttings far enough apart so the leaves of adjacent plants don't touch.
- **Don't** let the plastic you use to enclose the flat or pot touch the cuttings.
- **Do** open the plastic on your propagating containers at least once a day—good circulation prevents fungal problems, while stagnant air encourages them.
- **Do** check your cuttings daily for mildewed or dropped leaves. Remove dropped leaves and diseased cuttings as soon as you see them to keep fungi from spreading to healthy cuttings.

The Best Time to Prune Flowering Shrubs Is When You Have the Time

Flowering shrubs aren't as choosy about pruning as you might think. Timing schemes for spring- and summer-flowering shrubs guarantee that you won't miss a season of bloom. But there's no crisis if you don't follow them; you'll still get plenty of blooms the following season. What's most important is that pruning gets done, so schedule when it's most convenient for you.

If you can't stand to miss even one bloom season, all you have to do is follow one simple rule: Prune flowering shrubs after they flower.

Spring-blooming shrubs. Trim forsythias, lilacs, sweet mock orange, and other early bloomers right after flowering. They set next year's flower buds during summer, so if you prune in fall, winter, or the following spring, you'll slice off the next season of bloom. If the plants are severely overgrown, renewal-prune by removing one-third of the stems to ground level each year.

Summer-blooming shrubs. Any time after flowering is fine for pruning hydrangeas, buddleias, rose-of-Sharon, and other summer bloomers. There's no rush as with spring bloomers, though, so take advantage of their foliage through fall and prune in late winter or early spring. Summer bloomers set flower buds on the new season's growth, so hard pruning (cutting stems back to 2 or 3 inches from the ground) will guarantee you the most flowers.

Restyle Your Shrubs to Reduce Maintenance

When it comes to low maintenance, formal, squared-off hedges and closely clipped shrubs don't make the grade. You don't have to be a slave to these maintenance monsters, which need clipping several times a year to look their best. Instead, put your hedge shears away, grab your hand pruners, and help nature rework your plants into beautiful, easy-care informal shapes.

Restyling deciduous shrubs and hedges. Use thinning cuts, not heading cuts, to open up holes in plants to let light in. (This is a good way to rejuvenate an informal hedge, too.) Make the cuts close to the ground or just above low branches; you'll encourage side buds to grow.

Remove one-third of the growth on each plant each year, taking out the most gnarled and woody branches first. Continue the process for three years until all the old growth is gone. Let new growth and suckers form the framework for your informal hedge.

Shrubs that respond well to this treatment include deutzia, forsythia, sweet mock orange, spirea, and old-fashioned weigela.

Restyling evergreen shrubs and hedges. Clean out any dead wood inside the shrubs. Poke holes in the top by reaching inside as far as you can with hand pruners and cutting branches back to larger limbs. You'll end up with an uneven but attractive look if you make sure each cut branch still has some green on it.

Broad-leaved evergreens like hollies and yews will respond to the additional light with new growth, and eventually return to their natural form. Junipers and American arborvitae may not respond at all. In that case, replacing them is the best solution.

Thin for Health

Shrubs, trees, and perennial flowers with overcrowded stems or branches are just the kind of sheltered, humid home insects and diseases like mildew prefer. Remove one-quarter to one-third of shrub or perennial stems from the center of your plants so sunlight and air can reach the inside leaves—diseases and insects hate this! Cut a few limbs out of the center of trees if they're too choked with branches for healthy growth. Take them back to a large branch or the trunk. Repeat each year until the plant has a healthy, open growth habit.

Unusually Effective Pruning Tools

Push mowers and string trimmers make good pruners for large groundcover or perennial plantings. For a fast spring cleanup, set the mower at its highest setting and run it over the plants in early spring before new growth starts. This works on level ground but not on hilly areas or plantings that have heaved out of the ground; they'll get scalped and die.

String trimmers zip through perennials, ornamental grasses, or groundcover foliage on any kind of ground. They'll leave a ragged finish, but new foliage will cover it quickly. You can't beat it when you're short on time.

Pruning and Training Glossary

Branch collar.
The bulge at the base of a branch; this part of the trunk helps hold the branch to the trunk.

Continued →

Branch crotch.

The angle at which the tree branch meets the trunk or parent stem.

Break bud.

When a latent bud is stimulated into growing out into a leaf or twig.

Cane.

A long and slender branch usually originating from the roots.

Heading cut.

To cut back a branch to a side bud or shoot.

Leader.

The main, primary, or tallest shoot of a trunk. Trees can be single-leadered, such as birch, or multiple-leadered, such as vine maple.

New wood.

A cane of the current year's growth. Some shrubs bloom only on new wood, while others bloom on the previous year's growth.

Old wood.

A cane of the previous year's growth or cane that's older.

Pinching.

To use your fingertips to squeeze off the end bud of a twig or stem to make the plant more compact and bushy.

Skirting or limbing up.

To prune the lower limbs of a tree to increase air circulation, improve visibility, or clear room underneath the tree.

Sucker.

An upright shoot growing from a root or graft union. In common usage, these are straight, rapid-growing shoots or watersprouts that grow in response to poor pruning and wounding.

Thin out.

To cutoff a limb at the base, either at ground level or at a branch collar.

Topiary.

Plants sculpted into geometric shapes or likenesses of animals or people.

SEASONAL CARE

Garden Care

Jeff Cox

After the planning and planting come the watering, weeding, and tending. While we all realize that gardening is work, it's nice to know that there are ways to make that work more pleasurable so we can spend more time enjoying our gardens rather than taking care of them. Of course, low maintenance gardens start with proper planning.

Good garden care requires the proper tools. Tools not only help you get the job done, but the right tools—used properly—will save time and effort on your part. Next on the garden-care list is weed control. Weeds can drive the most peaceful gardener to herbicidal thoughts. But we'll tell you how to keep weeds from becoming a problem in your garden—and how to control those that do appear—without resorting to dangerous chemicals.

Mulch plays another important role in the garden—it will save you time watering your plants and fighting pests. Along with mulching, you need to know the best ways to feed, stake, trellis, and water your plants. And if you feel as though all this work gets crammed into a very short time span, read on to discover ways to extend the season to get the absolute most from your garden.

Choosing Tools

The notion that a tool is nothing more than a device for doing work stops at the garden gate. Anyone who has worked garden soil with a well-balanced fork or rake, sliced weeds effortlessly with a skillfully sharpened hoe, or pruned effortlessly with a good, sharp pair of shears knows that a high-quality tool not only gets the job done but also adds pleasure to the doing. Little wonder that gardeners come to think of their most effective tools as friends.

HAND TOOLS

Whenever it's practical, use hand tools rather than power tools. Power tools are expensive and contribute to both our air and noise pollution problems. If you keep them sharp, good-quality hand tools will make your garden work go quickly and easily.

Hoes You can use hoes to layout rows, dig furrows, cultivate around plants to loosen the soil and kill weeds, create hills and raised beds, break up clods, and prepare bare spots in lawns for reseeding.

The standard American pattern hoe is a long-handled tool that allows you to work without too much bending. It has a broad, straight blade, a little larger than 6 inches wide and 4 inches deep. However, many gardeners prefer a nursery hoe, which is lighter and has a 2- to 3-inch-deep blade.

Use an oscillating hoe to slice weeds just below the soil surface. It cuts on both the push and the pull stroke. On modern variations, often called "hula" or action hoes, the slicing blade moves back and forth to cut while being pulled or pushed.

Narrow hoe blades utilize your arm power more efficiently than wider blades. The hoe handle should be at least 4½ feet long so you can work without bending over and straining your lower back muscles. In general, when working with hoes, try to remain standing upright and run the hoe blade below and parallel to the soil surface. Keep your hoe sharp so it will cut through weeds rather than yanking them out.

Shovels A standard American long-handled shovel is good for mixing cement and for scooping up soil, gravel, and sand. You can also use it to pry rocks and root clumps from the soil. You can use a shovel to dig rounded planting holes, but a garden fork or a spade generally works better for most digging.

The standard shovel handle is about 4 feet. The shovel handle should come to shoulder height or higher. Shovels should also have a turned edge or footrest on the shoulders of the

blade to protect your feet when you step on the tool.

Spades Spades have a flat, rather than scooped, blade with squared edges. With a spade, you can cut easily through sod and create straight edges in soil. Use a spade for digging planting holes, prying up rocks, dividing and moving perennials, cutting unwanted tree and shrub roots, tamping sod, and digging trenches.

A spade handle is generally shorter than a shovel handle, usually ranging from 28 to 32 inches. Like shovels, spades should have a turned edge or footrest on the shoulders of the blade.

Forks Spading forks cut into soil, usually more easily than solid-bladed tools can. A spading fork is handy for mixing materials into the soil and for harvesting potatoes, carrots, and other root crops. The tines of a standard spading fork are broad and flat; those of the English cultivating fork are thinner and square. The English version is better for cultivating and aerating soil. Remember that forks are used to loosen soil, not to lift it. Use a pitchfork (three tines) or a straw fork (five or six tines) for picking up, turning, and scattering hay mulch, leaf mold, and light compost materials.

The standard handle length for a spading fork is 28 inches. Very tall gardeners may prefer a 32-inch handle. Short gardeners, including children, should use a border fork, which has shorter tines and handle.

Trowels A garden trowel is a miniature version of a shovel. Use it to dig planting holes for small plants and bulbs, for transplanting seedlings, or for weeding beds and borders.

Some trowels are made from forged steel and fitted with hardwood handles; good ones are also available in unbreakable one-piece cast aluminum. Trowels come with a variety of blade widths and lengths. Choose one that feels comfortable in your hand.

Rakes Rakes generally fall into one of two categories: garden rakes and leaf rakes. Garden rakes are essential for leveling ground, creating raised beds, killing emerging weeds, gathering debris from rows, covering furrows, thinning seedlings, working materials shallowly into the soil, erasing footprints, and spreading mulch. Garden rakes come in many widths, with long or short teeth that are widely or closely spaced. The handle should be long (4½ to 5 feet) and the head should be heavy enough to bite into the soil easily. If you have rocky soil, choose a rake with widely spaced teeth.

Lawn or leaf rakes, also called fan rakes, are good for gathering up leaves, grass clippings, weeds, and other debris and for dislodging thatch from the lawn. Metal lawn rakes last longest and are the springiest, although many gardeners prefer the action and feel of bamboo tines, and some prefer plastic or rubber.

Pruning Tools There are two types of pruning shears: the anvil type, with a straight blade that closes down onto an anvil or plate, and the bypass type, which cuts like scissors. Anvil pruners are often easier to use, requiring less hand pressure to make a cut. Bypass shears make a cleaner cut, can work in tighter spaces, and can cut flush against a tree trunk or branch (anvil pruners leave a short stump). Most models of either type will cut hardwood branches up to ½ inch in diameter.

Lopping shears, also called loppers, are heavy-duty pruners with long handles. Both anvil and bypass loppers can cut branches up to 2 inches in diameter. Hedge shears have long blades

Continued ➡

and relatively short handles. They can cut branches up to ½ inch thick. Pruning saws cut through most branches that are too thick for shears.

Push Mowers Push mowers have several revolving blades that move against a single fixed blade, producing a neat trim. They do a fine job, cutting evenly and quietly. For those with small, level lawns, the push mower is the ideal lawn-cutting instrument. It is inexpensive, not difficult to push, nonpolluting, and quiet, and it produces a neat-looking lawn.

POWER TOOLS

In some cases, you may need the extra power of engine-driven equipment. It's tempting to use these machines on a regular basis because they get the job done quickly. Keep in mind, though, that handwork can be part of the pleasure and relaxation of gardening. If you routinely use power tools to speed through garden chores, you'll miss the opportunity to observe the growth of your plants and to watch for the beginning of disease or insect problems.

Power Mowers Gas-powered rotary mowers have a single blade that revolves at a high speed, literally ripping the tops off grass plants. Unlike push mowers, power mowers can handle rough terrain and knock down high weeds. Mulching mowers blow finely cut grass pieces back into the lawn, building up soil organic matter while removing the need to rake or bag clippings.

Tillers Rotary tillers can make short work of turning and churning garden soil, breaking new ground, cultivating, aerating, weeding, and mixing materials into the soil. The rotary tiller is a gasoline-powered machine equipped with steel blades that rotate on a central spindle.

Chipper/Shredders After a lawn mower and a rotary tiller, the favorite large power tool of gardeners is often a chipper/shredder. This machine, powered with gasoline or electricity, reduces leaves, pruned branches, and plant debris to beautiful mulch or compost material. Shredders are better for chopping up weeds and other soft plant material; chippers can handle heavier, woody materials.

TOOL CARE

After making the considerable investment in good-quality tools, it is wise to spend some time to keep them in good shape.

Routine Care Clean, dry, and put away all hand tools after each use. Keep a large plastic kitchen spoon handy to knock dirt off metal blades. Don't use a trowel or other metal tool, since you could damage the blades of both tools. A 5-gallon bucket of sharp builder's sand in the tool shed or garage is useful for cleaning tools. Dip the metal blade of each tool into the sand and plunge it up and down a few times to work off any clinging soil. Use a wire brush to remove any rust that may have formed. Keep power equipment in good repair and properly adjusted.

Handles Regularly varnish and sand wooden handles to maintain their resilience and good looks. If you buy a good-quality tool second-hand and it has a weather-beaten handle, refresh it with several coats of varnish, sanding between each coat. You can repair split handles temporarily with tape and glue, but replace broken handles as soon as possible.

Sharpening Sharp-bladed hand tools will perform efficiently and with ease only if you keep them sharp. Take the time to study the angle of the bevels on all your tools, then sharpen each, as

needed, to keep the proper bevel. If you have tools that are especially difficult to sharpen, take them to a professional for sharpening.

Winter Care At the end of the season, polish all metal parts of hand tools with steel wool, oil them to prevent rust, and store them in a dry place. Lubricate all tools that have moving parts. This is also a good time to take hard-to-sharpen tools to the sharpening shop.

Controlling Weeds

Fast, tough, and common—that's all it takes to earn a plant the name of weed. But any plant growing in the wrong place—especially if it's growing there in abundance—is a weed. Maple tree seedlings that sprout between the lettuce and radishes are weeds. So is the Bermuda grass that keeps invading your perennial beds from the lawn.

The bigger your weeds get, the more difficult they are to control. Get into the habit of a once-a-week weed patrol to cut your weed problem down to size. Using the right tools and techniques also will help to make weeding a manageable—maybe even enjoyable—task.

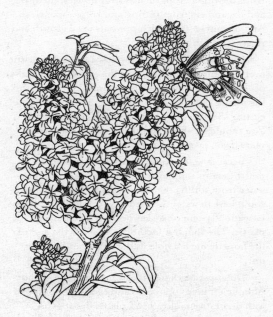

HAND WEEDING

Hand-pulling weeds is simple and effective. It's good for small areas and young or annual weeds such as purslane and lamb's quarters. Using your hands allows you to weed with precision, an important skill when sorting the weeds from the seedlings. For notorious spreaders like ground ivy, the only choice for control is to patiently hand-pull the tops and sift through the soil to remove as many roots as you can find.

Short-handled tools such as dandelion forks (sometimes known as asparagus knives), pronged cultivators, and mattocks are good for large, stubborn weeds, especially in close quarters such as among perennials. Use these tools to pry up tough perennial weeds. Hand weeders come in all shapes, and everybody has a favorite. If one type feels awkward, try another.

A hoe is the best tool for weeding larger areas quickly and cleanly. Use it to rid the vegetable garden of weeds that spring up between rows. When you hoe, slice or scrape just below the soil surface to sever weed tops from roots. Don't chop into the soil—you'll just bring up more weed seeds to germinate. Keep the hoe blade sharp. Hoeing kills most annual weeds, but many perennial weeds, such as dandelions, will grow back from their roots. Dig out these roots with a garden fork or spade.

USING MULCH

One of the best low-effort ways to beat weeds is to block their access to light and air by mulching bare soil areas. A 3- to 4-inch layer of mulch smothers out many weeds, and weeds that manage to poke through are easier to pull.

Black plastic mulch can practically eliminate weeding in the vegetable garden. Cut slits for plants and water to penetrate. Remove the plastic at the end of the growing season to let the soil breathe. You can use biodegradable materials, such as newspaper or corrugated cardboard, to temporarily suppress weeds, tilling them into the soil at the end of the season. See "Mulching Your Garden" on this page for more information on organic and black plastic mulches.

A living mulch of a low-growing grass or legume crop seeded between rows of plants in your vegetable garden can keep down weeds and improve soil organic matter content at the same time.

Even tough perennial weeds will succumb eventually to a thick layer of mulch.

Just as weeds compete with your garden and landscape plants for water, food, and growing space, your plants use the same method to crowd out weeds. As your plants grow, they will shade the ground, reducing weed germination and growth. Space vegetable and flower plants closely in beds to decrease the time until the leaves form an effective light-blocking canopy.

Reduce weed growth in your lawn by setting your lawn mower blade a notch or two higher. Taller grass is generally healthier and lets less light reach the soil.

USING HERBICIDES

In some cases, fatty-acid-based herbicides such as Safer SharpShooter can help control weeds. These herbicides provide effective spot control for annual weeds, but perennial weeds will spring up anew from the unharmed roots. Some organic gardeners have traditionally relied on vinegar or salt to kill weeds. However, these substances will affect soil balance and can harm your garden plants as well. Only use them in areas where you don't want any plants to grow, such as between cracks in a patio.

Mulching Your Garden

Every organic gardener should be a mulch expert. Mulching is one of the best ways to fight weeds. It also improves your garden's appearance, reduces water loss, and protects soil from compaction and erosion. If you use an organic mulch, the icing on the cake is improved soil quality as the mulch decays.

There are two basic kinds of mulch: organic and inorganic. Organic mulches include formerly living material such as wood chips, shredded bark, chopped leaves, straw, grass clippings, compost, sawdust, pine needles, and even paper. Inorganic mulches include gravel, stones, black plastic, and geotextiles (landscape fabrics).

Both types discourage weeds, but organic mulches also improve the soil as they decompose. Inorganic mulches don't break down and enrich the soil, but under certain circumstances they're the mulch of choice. For example, black plastic warms the soil and radiates heat during the night, keeping heat-loving vegetables such as eggplant and tomatoes cozy and vigorous.

USING ORGANIC MULCHES

There are two cardinal rules for using organic mulches to combat weeds: First, be sure to lay the

Continued →

mulch down on soil that is already weeded, and second, lay down a thick enough layer to discourage new weeds from coming up through it. It can take a 4- to 6-inch layer of mulch to completely discourage weeds, although a 2- to 3-inch layer is usually enough in shady spots where weeds aren't as troublesome as they are in full sun.

Types of Weeds

Like flowers, there are annual, biennial, and perennial weeds. Each group poses its own control problems, so you need to know which group they fall into. Here's a rundown:

Annual Weeds: Annual weeds, like lamb's quarters, wild mustard, pigweed, purslane, and ragweed, live only one season. But they produce thousands of seeds, guaranteeing success through sheer strength of numbers. Control them by pulling them before they flower and set seed.

Biennial Weeds: Biennial weeds, like Queen-Anne's-lace, form a rosette of leaves their first season. The following year, they flower, set seed, and die. Control them by removing their rosettes the first season, or pull the weeds the second season, before they set their seed.

Perennial Weeds: Perennial weeds include dandelion, Canada thistle, bindweed, dock, wild onions, ground ivy, plantain, pokeweed, and wood sorrel. Some of the worst perennial weeds are grasses, including crabgrass and quackgrass. They live for years, set seed, have deep, persistent root systems, and often have creeping stems; so a single plant can send up offspring all over the garden. The same is true for woody weeds like poison ivy. To control these difficult weeds, dig carefully to remove as much of the root system as possible. Then pull up the plants that grow from the pieces you've missed.

The best organic mulch is compost, a mixture of decomposed organic materials. For directions on making compost, see Chapter 1.

You can purchase bags of decorative wood chips or shredded bark from the local garden center to mulch your flower garden and shrub borders. A less expensive source of wood chips might be your tree-care company or the utility company. They may be willing to sell you a truckload of chips at a nominal price. Many communities are also chipping yard debris or composting grass clippings and fall leaves, then offering the result back to the community for free or for a small charge.

If you have a lot of trees on your property, shredding the fallen leaves creates a nutrient-rich mulch for free. You can use a leaf-shredding machine, but you don't really need a special machine to shred leaves-a lawn mower with a bagger will collect leaves and cut them into the perfect size for mulching.

You can spread a wood chip or shredded leaf mulch anywhere on your property, but it looks especially attractive in flower beds and shrub borders. Of course, it's right at home in a woodland or shade garden. Wood chips aren't a great idea for vegetable and annual flower beds, though, since you'll be digging these beds every year and the chips will get in the way.

Grass clippings are another readily available mulch, but they aren't particularly attractive. Some people pile the nitrogen-rich clippings under shrubs or on flower beds, but they are more appropriate on vegetable beds, where appearance is less critical. Your vegetables will thank you for the nitrogen boost!

Another great mulch for the vegetable garden is straw, salt hay, or weed-free hay. It looks good and has most of the benefits of mulches: retaining soil moisture, keeping down weeds, and adding organic matter to the soil when it breaks down. But be sure the hay you use is weed- and seed-free, or you'll just be making trouble for your garden. And don't pull hay or straw up to the stems of vegetables or the trunks of fruit trees, or you'll be inviting slug and rodent damage.

USING PLASTIC MULCH

Mulching a vegetable garden with sheets of black plastic film can do wonders. The plastic heats up in the sun, warming the soil and radiating heat during the night, effectively creating a microclimate about 3°F warmer than an unmulched garden. Because the plastic film remains warm and dry, it protects the fruits of vining crops such as strawberries, melons, and cucumbers from rotting and keeps them clean. And of course, the mulch prevents weed growth and retains soil moisture.

In raised bed gardens, lay down a sheet of plastic over the entire bed. Bury it at the edges or weigh the plastic down with rocks. Then punch holes in it for the plants. A bulb planter makes quick work of hole cutting. Sow seeds or plant transplants in the holes. You should be able to reuse the plastic for several years if you take it up and store it over winter.

Because water can't permeate the plastic, the mulch retains soil moisture but can also keep rainwater from soiling the planting bed. That means you'll have to water the garden yourself, with a drip irrigation system or soaker hoses placed beneath the plastic. The simplest method is to shove the end of the hose through a hole in the plastic and turn it on.

Don't use black plastic as a mulch under shrubs. Although it keeps out weeds and can be camouflaged with decorative mulch, black plastic destroys the shrubs' long-term health. Because water and air cannot penetrate the plastic, roots grow very close to the soil surface—sometimes right beneath the plastic-seeking moisture and oxygen. The shallow roots suffer from lack of oxygen and moisture and from extremes of heat and cold. Eventually the plants decline and die. Stick to organic mulches such as shredded leaves, bark, wood chips, or compost under your trees and shrubs.

Unlike black plastic, geotextiles—or landscape fabrics—let air and water through to the soil beneath while keeping weeds from coming up. But geotextiles have some of the same drawbacks as black plastic. If exposed to light, they degrade, so you have to cover them with a second mulch (they're ugly, so you'd want to, anyway). Some studies have found that shrub roots may grow up into the geotextile mulch, creating real problems if you want to remove it. And weeds that germinate in the mulch on top of the geotextile can send roots down into the fabric, tearing it when you pull them out.

Feeding Your Plants

Plants make their own food through the process of photosynthesis, but gardeners play an important supporting role by making sure that all the necessary raw materials are available. Organic gardeners do this primarily by enriching their soil with a wide variety of organic materials. Feeding your plants

with organic fertilizers can also help to provide them with optimum nutrition.

Organic gardeners use fertilizers like seasonings: They add the finishing touch that brings out the very best in plants. Because an organically managed soil is biologically active and rich in nutrients, organic gardeners don't need to pour on fertilizers to get good plant performance.

CHEMICAL VERSUS ORGANIC

Many organic materials serve as both fertilizers and soil conditioners—they feed both soils and plants. This is one of the most important differences between a chemical approach and an organic approach toward soil care and fertilizing. Soluble chemical fertilizers contain mineral salts that are readily available for uptake by plant roots. However, these salts do not provide a food source for soil microorganisms and earthworms, and they will even repel earthworms because they acidify the soil. Over time, soils treated only with synthetic chemical fertilizers will have decreased organic matter and altered biological activity. And as soil structure declines and water-holding capacity diminishes, a greater proportion of the soluble chemical fertilizers applied will leach through the soil. This results in ever-increasing amounts of chemicals needed to feed the plants.

Most chemical fertilizers are synthesized from nonrenewable resources, such as coal and natural gas. Others are made by treating rock minerals with acids to make them more soluble. Fortunately, there are more and more truly organic fertilizers coming on the market. These products are made from natural plant and animal materials or from mined rock minerals. However, there are no national standards regulating the content of organic fertilizers. Read labels to be sure that commercial fertilizers labeled "organic" contain only safe, natural ingredients. Look for products labeled "natural organic," "slow release," and "low analysis." Be wary of products labeled organic that have an NPK (nitrogen-phosphorus-potassium) ratio that adds up to more than 15 (one labeled 10-10-10, for example).

USING ORGANIC FERTILIZERS

If you're a gardener who's making the switch from chemical to organic fertilizers, you may be afraid that using organic materials will be more complicated and less convenient than using premixed chemical fertilizers. Not so! Commercially formulated organic fertilizer blends can be just as convenient and effective as blended synthetic fertilizers. You don't need to custom-feed your plants unless it's an activity you enjoy. So while some experts spread a little blood meal around their tomatoes at planting, then some bonemeal just when the blossoms are about to pop, most gardeners are satisfied to make one or two applications of general-purpose organic fertilizer throughout the garden.

If you want to try a plant-specific approach to fertilizing, you can use a variety of specialty organic fertilizers that are available from mail-order supply companies or at many well-stocked garden centers. For example, you can use blood meal, chicken-feather meal, or fish meal as a nitrogen source. Bonemeal is a good source of phosphorus, and kelp and greensand are organic sources of potassium.

Dry Organic Fertilizers Dry organic fertilizers can be made from a single material, such as rock phosphate or kelp, or can be a blend of many ingredients. Almost all organic fertilizers provide a broad array of nutrients, but blends are specially formulated to provide balanced amounts of nitrogen, potassium, and phosphorus, as well as micronutrients. There are several commercial blends, but you

Continued ➡

can make your own general-purpose fertilizer by mixing individual amendments.

The most common way to apply dry fertilizer is to broadcast it and then hoe or rake it into the top 4 to 6 inches of soil. You can add small amounts of fertilizer to planting holes or rows as you plant your seeds or transplants. Unlike dry synthetic fertilizers, most organic fertilizers are nonburning and will not harm the delicate roots of your seedlings.

During the growing season, boost plant growth by side-dressing dry fertilizers in crop rows or around the drip line of trees or shrubs. It's best to work side-dressings into the top inch of the soil.

Liquid Organic Fertilizers Use liquid fertilizers to give your plants a light nutrient boost or snack every month—or even every two weeks—during the growing season. Simply mix a tankful of foliar spray, and spray all your plants at the same time.

Plants can absorb liquid fertilizers both through their roots and through leaf pores. Foliar feeding can supply nutrients when they are lacking or unavailable in the soil, or when roots are stressed. It is especially effective for giving fast-growing plants like vegetables an extra boost during the growing season. Compost tea and seaweed extract are two common examples of organic foliar fertilizers.

Some foliar fertilizers such as kelp are rich in micronutrients and growth hormones. These foliar sprays also appear to act as catalysts, increasing nutrient uptake by plants. You can make your own liquid fertilizer by brewing up compost or manure in water.

With flowering and fruiting plants, foliar sprays are most useful during critical periods (such as after transplanting or during fruit set) or during periods of drought or extreme temperatures. For leaf crops, some suppliers recommend biweekly spraying.

When using liquid fertilizers, always follow label instructions for proper dilution and application methods. You can use a surfactant, such as coconut oil or a mild soap (¼ teaspoon per gallon of spray), to ensure better coverage of the leaves. Otherwise the spray may bead up on the foliage and you won't get maximum benefit. Measure the surfactant carefully: If you use too much, it may damage plants. A slightly acidic spray mixture is most effective, so check your spray's pH. Use small amounts of vinegar to lower pH or baking soda to raise it. Aim for a pH of 6.0 to 6.5.

Any sprayer or mister will work, from hand-trigger units to knapsack sprayers. Set your sprayer to emit as fine a spray as possible. Never use a sprayer that has been used to apply herbicides.

The best times to spray are early morning and early evening, when the liquids will be absorbed most quickly and won't burn foliage. Choose a cool, clear day.

Spray until the liquid drips off the leaves. Be sure to concentrate the spray on leaf undersides, where leaf pores are more likely to be open. You can also water in liquid fertilizers around the root zone. A drip irrigation system can carry liquid fertilizers to your plants. Kelp is a better product for this use; fish emulsion can clog the irrigation emitters.

Staking and Trellising

Staking plants in the flower and vegetable garden is a job that busy gardeners sometimes overlook. In most cases, however, the time you spend staking will be amply rewarded by the improved health and appearance of your garden.

Vining plants virtually require stakes or other support. Top-heavy, single-stemmed flowers like delphiniums, lilies, and dahlias benefit from support. Left unstaked, they are apt to bend unat-

tractively and may snap off during heavy storms. Staking also improves the appearance of plants with thin, floppy stems that flatten easily.

Choose stakes and supports that match the needs of the plant and of you as a gardener. They must be tall enough and strong enough to support the entire mature plant when wet or windblown, and they must be firmly inserted in the soil. A stake that breaks or tips over can cause more damage than using none at all. Take care not to damage roots when inserting a stake, and avoid tying the shoots too tightly to the stake. Install the supports as early in the growing season as possible so that the plants can be trained to them as they grow, not forced to fit them later on. When growing plants from seed, install the support before planting.

In the flower garden, choose supports that are as inconspicuous as possible. Thin, slightly flexible stakes that bend with the plant are less conspicuous and may be better than heavier, rigid ones. In general, select stakes that stand about three-fourths of the height of the mature plant. Insert them close to or among the stems so that as the plant grows, the foliage will hide the supports. Choose colors and materials that blend with the plants. Bamboo stakes tinted green are available in a variety of sizes and are a good, inexpensive choice for many plants. You can also buy wood, metal, and plastic stakes and trellises,

---

Cover Crop Closeup

Legumes

Bean, broad, fava, or field (*Vicia faba*). A winter annual legume suitable for maritime Canada and along the U.S. Pacific Coast. Must have cool weather and ample water. Can withstand temperatures to 15°F. Prefers well-drained, heavy loams high in humus and lime. Turn under when growth is succulent for fastest breakdown. Fixes 71 pounds nitrogen per acre per year; inoculate with *Rhizobium* spp. bacteria to encourage nitrogen fixation, either by dusting the inoculant along the furrow or on the seeds. Sow on 8-inch centers, covering seed ⅛ to ¼ inch deep.

Clover, crimson (*Trifolium incarnatum*). An annual legume that will grow through the winter from New Jersey south. Must have adequate soil moisture for good germination and growth. Prefers loam soils that are high in humus, but will grow on any well-drained soil except muck or extremely acid soils. Will withstand shade and low fertility. Fixes 94 pounds of nitrogen per acre per year; inoculate with *Rhizobium* spp. bacteria to encourage nitrogen fixation. Sow ½ to ⅔ ounce per 100 square feet, covering seed ½ inch deep.

Clover, white (*Trifolium repens*). A hardy perennial legume that grows throughout Canada and the United States south to the Gulf of Mexico. Thrives in cool, moist climates. Prefers humus-rich, well-drained clay, clay loam, and loam soils. Grows well in shade. Needs high lime, phosphorus, and potash. Fixes 103 to 133 pounds of nitrogen per acre per year; inoculate with *Rhizobium* spp. bacteria to encourage nitrogen fixation. Sow ¼ ounce per 100 square feet, covering seed ½ inch deep.

Lupine, large white (*Lupinus albus*). An annual legume best grown in the Deep South, Northeast, and North Central states. The most winter-hardy lupine species. Prefers sandy loam soils and acid soils. Excellent soil-builder for barren, sandy, and worn-out soil. Good for opening up heavy clay. Inoculate with *Rhizobium* spp. bacteria to encourage nitrogen fixation. Sow 6½ ounces per 100 square feet, covering seed 1 inch deep.

Pea, Austrian winter (*Pisum arvense*). Also called Canadian field pea, this legume is a winter annual. It grows all over the United States and Canada; winterkills in the North but grows through the winter in the South. Requires cool, moist conditions and grows best in loamy soils high in lime. Fixes 48 pounds of nitrogen per acre per year; inoculate with *Rhizobium* spp.

bacteria to encourage nitrogen fixation. Sow 4 ounces per 100 square feet, covering seed 1½ inches deep.

Vetch, hairy or winter (*Vicia villosa*). An annual legume that can be grown in all parts of the United States. The most winter-hardy of the cultivated vetches. Will grow on any well-drained soil, including acid soils, alkaline soils, and soils of low fertility. Will tolerate drought. Fixes 80 pounds of nitrogen per acre per year; inoculate with *Rhizobium* spp. bacteria to encourage nitrogen fixation. Sow 2½ ounces per 100 square feet, covering seed ¾ inch deep.

Grasses

Barley, winter (*Hordeum vulgare*). An annual grass that grows all over the United States and overwinters in mild climates. Well adapted to high altitudes and semiarid regions. Prefers well-drained loam soils. Tolerant of salinity and alkaline soils; does not grow well on sandy or acid soils. Sow 4 ounces per 100 square feet, covering seed ¾ inch deep.

Oats (*Avena sativa*). An annual grass that grows all over the United States and is especially good in the South where it overwinters. Prefers cool, moist climates. Will tolerate acid soil. Will grow on many soils, but does not do well on heavy clay. Provide a firm seedbed to prevent frost-heaving in winter. Sow 4 ounces per 100 square feet, covering seed 1 inch deep.

Rye, winter or cereal (*Secale cereale*). An annual grass that will grow all over the United States, but is especially well suited for the North because of its ability to tolerate extreme cold. Grows best on well-drained loams, but will grow on any soil. Will tolerate acid soil. Prefers ample moisture. Sow 4 ounces per 100 square feet, covering seed 1 inch deep.

Ryegrass, annual or Italian (*Lolium multiflorum*). A weak grass grown as an annual. Will grow all over the United States, but is best adapted to the areas from New Jersey south. Prefers loam or sandy loam soils, but will grow on any soil. Will tolerate acid soil. Makes rapid growth and holds soil well with heavy, fibrous roots. Sow 1½ ounces per 100 square feet, covering seed 3/4 inch deep.

Wheat, winter (*Triticum aestivum*). An annual grass that will grow all over the United States. Does well at high elevations. Prefers loam soils. Grows best in fertile soil, but will tolerate moderately fertile soil. Sow 4 ounces per 100 square feet, covering seed ¾ inch deep.

Continued ➡

and a wide assortment of metal rings and support systems. Using green twine or plastic-covered wire is an inconspicuous way to fasten plants to their supports.

Standard Staking Methods

Here are four ways to stake plants in the garden. Be sure to match the staking method to each plant's growth habit:

Individual stakes: Sink stake firmly near the stem when plant is 6 to 8 inches high. A loose figure-eight tie connects stem to stake securely yet maintains the plant's natural form and prevents damage to the stalk. As the plant grows, add ties every 8 to 10 inches. Two closely spaced plants can be tied to one stake if it is placed between them. Top-heavy flowers like this delphinium need stakes almost as tall as the mature plant.

Twiggy brush: For plants such as peas, coreopsis, and baby's-breath, try lengths of sturdy, twiggy brush or branches. Cut the brush to the final height of the plants, and push it 6 inches into the ground between the plants.

Wire ring supports: Bushy plants with heavy flowers, like peonies, can be grown in a wire ring. The foliage will hide the ring as the plants grow. The natural form of the plant is enhanced, not disrupted.

Stakes and strings: Insert four stakes into the corners of the bed when shoots are a few inches high. Tie string (or wire) from stake to stake to form a box about 6 to 8 inches off the ground. Add strings as needed. Run additional strings across the bed or weave them back and forth to keep plants from falling inside the bed.

In the vegetable garden, sturdiness is more important than appearance. Staking vegetables like tomatoes, peppers, and beans makes them easier to cultivate and harvest. It increases yields by preventing contamination with soilborne diseases and allowing for more plants in a given area. Choose tall, sturdy stakes or cages that can support the plant even when it is heavy with fruit, and insert stakes firmly into the ground. Use narrow strips torn from rags or bands cut from stockings to gently fasten plants to supports.

Perennial vines such as roses and grapes are commonly grown on trellises or on wires between sturdy posts.

Trees and tall shrubs are commonly staked temporarily at planting to help hold them upright until their roots become established. Fruit trees on dwarfing rootstocks may need to be permanently staked.

Using Cover Crops

Barbara W. Ellis

"Use it or lose it" is a phrase that could be applied to garden soil. Soil left without a protective covering of plants slips away like sand through an hourglass. Wind blows it away; rain washes it down hills and leaches nutrients out of the root zone. Fortunately, there is an easy way to not only stop this process but also to actually improve your soil to benefit future crops: Grow cover crops.

What exactly are cover crops? They're crops grown exclusively to feed, improve, and protect the soil. Also called green manure, cover crops—

generally legumes such as clover and grains such as rye—are sown, allowed to grow, and then tilled into the soil either with a rotary tiller or by hand before they flower and set seed. In addition to stopping erosion, cover crops also prevent nutrients from leaching out of the soil. Planted into a mature crop or immediately after the ground is cleared, they act as holding tanks, taking up nutrients and keeping them near the soil surface. In spring, after the cover crop has been tilled under, new plantings will draw on this reservoir as the cover crop breaks down. Cover crops do more for the garden, though. Those that make a fast, dense stand keep weeds from getting a foothold after the fall harvest. As they decompose, they enrich the soil with vital organic matter, which improves structure as well as nutrient- and water-holding ability. Legumes such as sweet clover also convert atmospheric nitrogen into a form that is taken up by the crop, and then released into the soil when the legumes are tilled under. Cover crops also help to retain moisture in the soil and help to moderate temperature fluctuations. Both of the effects protect earthworms and other soil microorganisms.

Planting Cover Crops

There are several different ways to use cover crops in the garden. You can sow a winter legume like sweet clover or winter rye in fall after you've harvested your vegetables and turn it under in early spring. Another option is to rotate garden beds by planting vegetables in a bed one year and a cover crop the next. You can also sow a cover crop directly under a vegetable crop, but the trick is to sow the cover crop after the vegetable crop has become well established so that they don't compete. For example, clover can be broadcast under sweet corn or other big vegetables after the last cultivation (about five weeks after corn has been sown). The clover can then be left to protect the soil in winter and tilled under in spring.

To sow a cover crop, lightly work the soil with a tiller or a spade, or just rough up open spaces between plants with a hoe, to prepare a seedbed. Then scatter the seed evenly, and rake or hoe lightly to cover it. For clovers, tamp the soil after sowing to provide a firm seed bed. If you're sowing in late summer or fall, the seeds will sprout and grow until temperatures get too cold. Some cover crops are winter-killed, others resume growing in spring. Either way, they're tilled under a few weeks before planting.

Tilling it Under

The first step in turning under a cover crop is to cut back the top growth with a sickle, scythe, or mower. This is generally done in very early spring. Make several passes with a rotary mower to chop up the plants. A layer of compost or manure spread over the top will also help speed decomposition. Then, use a rotary tiller to work the plants into the soil. You can also hand-dig the crop under, although if your garden is large this can be a daunting task. If the tops of the plants were very lush, stop after two passes with the tiller and let the soil dry out for a few days. Then till the soil again until you have a manageable seedbed.

You'll need to wait 7 to 10 days after tilling under a legume cover crop before you plant vegetables or other crops; 14 days or more after a grain crop. That's because the decomposing cover crop releases ethylene gas for the first few days, which inhibits seed germination. Also, the microorganisms breaking down the crop tie up nitrogen, and the temporary deficiency will hinder the growth of seeds or transplants.

Support Your Vegetables

Vegetables such as tomatoes, peppers, and beans need sturdy support in the garden. Try these methods to keep plants growing strong:

Lifetime Cages

The same welded steel mesh that gives reinforced concrete its strength is just the thing for making vegetable cages that will last a lifetime. You can buy it at just about any building supply center. Figure on buying at least 16 feet—enough for two cages.

The only tools you need are a small pair of bolt cutters to cut the heavy wire and a good pair of pliers. Be sure to wear work gloves to avoid cuts and blisters.

Lay the mesh strip flat on the ground. Measure an 8-foot piece by counting off 16 sections of the mesh (each section of mesh is 5¼ inches x 6 inches). In the middle of the 16th section, cut each cross wire in the middle. You'll use those loose ends later to fasten the cage together.

Next, trim off the bottom horizontal wire to create a row of 5-inch tines along the base of the cage. Now gently bend the prepared mesh section into a circle. Pull the dipped ends together, and use your pliers to twist them around each other to form the cage.

Set the cage upright around the plant, and push the tines into the ground to anchor it. Even high winds and bumper crops have a hard time toppling these cages. At the end of the season, clear off old vines and store the cages for winter, or leave the cages standing and have them double as compost bins.

Drying-Rack Trellis

For simple trellis, set up an old wooden clothes-drying rack, lay it on its side in the garden, and set your tomatoes between the rungs, which will stand about 3 feet high. As the plants grow larger, they will be supported by the rungs, and the fruit will ripen well above the ground.

Custom Stakes

Tying up tomatoes and other vegetable plants is easy with custom-made stakes. First, take a ¾-inch x 1½-inch stake and make saw cuts about ½ inch deep and about 1 foot apart staggering them on either side. Next, cut strips of panty hose 3/8-inch x 10 inches, and tie knots at each end. Put the stake in the ground, then put one end of a strip in one of the slots, using the knot as an anchor. Loop the strip around the tomato stem in a figure-eight pattern and secure it in another slot on the other side of the stake.

What to Grow

Basically, there are two types of crops that can be grown for green manure: legumes and grains. Legumes such as white clover or hairy vetch have the special ability to fix atmospheric nitrogen and add it to the soil by virtue of the *Rhizobium* bacteria that live in their root systems. The nitrogen becomes available to plants after the legume is tilled under. Grains such as winter rye, winter wheat, barley, or oats are grown for green manure because they produce lots of succulent growth that provides organic material when the plants are turned under to help build soil and boost microbial activity. They also have extensive fibrous root systems that take up and hold potassium in the soil. Buckwheat is a good source of phosphorus. Another advantage of grain crops—especially

Continued ➡

winter rye—is that they can grow quickly in the fall when temperatures are cool and rapidly absorb easily leached nutrients and hold them until spring. Rye seeds can germinate at temperatures above 33°F, and will grow in the fall until temperatures drop below 40°F. They then resume growing in the spring, providing lots of green manure for tilth- and nutrient-building. If you allow rye (especially winter rye) to grow too tall in spring, you'll need machinery to turn it under.

Combinations of grains and legumes, such as rye and hairy vetch, hairy vetch with winter barley or wheat, or clover and barley, offer the best of both worlds. They provide nitrogen fixation from the legume and organic matter from the grain. When seeded together, the fast-growing grain protects the legume until it becomes established.

Harvesting the Low-Maintenance Way

Barbara W. Ellis, Joan Benjamin, and Deborah L. Martin

A big part of hassle-free harvesting actually happens months ahead of time, when you plant your garden. For example, at planting time you could choose cultivars that are ready to pick at different times, so you don't have to harvest anything at once. But once it's time to pick, a little planning and organization go a long way toward speeding up the harvest.

The pages that follow include ideas for quick picking, as well as pointers on how and when to harvest for peak flavor. And just in case you have to harvest early, or a few crops slip past their prime before you can get to them, you'll find suggestions for fast, tasty ways to prepare non-prime produce.

Good Timing Helps You Make the Most of What You Pick

Harvesting right can be one of the most time-saving things you can do in your garden. Not only will you make the most of your gardening efforts by picking produce when it tastes the best, but letting your harvest get out of control always means extra work. And cleaning up rotten fruit, pulling bolted plants, and hauling waste to the compost pile is unpleasant work at best.

Harvesting when weather conditions favor good flavor is an easy way to make sure you get the most from what you pick. Because heat and strong sunlight make plants lose water, your produce will be the most succulent if you harvest when the weather is cool and not too bright-in the morning or evening, or on a cloudy day. As an added plus, produce that's harvested during the cooler parts of the day is cooler, so it will chill faster when refrigerated and stay fresh longer.

Try to harvest when the plants are dry so you don't inadvertently carry diseases through the garden. (Disease-causing fungi spread from plant to plant through the garden in water droplets.)

SOME DON'T LIKE IT HOT

Some crops can't take prolonged heat; it ruins their taste. Vegetables that are touchy about heat include broccoli, cauliflower, lettuce, peas, and radishes. Plan to pick them if a week or more of hot weather—temperatures higher than about 80°F—is about to set in.

Warm temperatures cause them to bolt, or send up a flower stalk. Generally it's best to send crops that have bolted directly to the compost pile. If you take the time to bring them into the kitchen, you'll find that radishes grown in too much hot weather are very hot, while bolted broccoli and cauliflower will no longer have the

crunchy heads they're grown for. Bolted lettuce leaves are bitter.

SET YOUR PICKING PRIORITIES

Good flavor can be fleeting; some crops pass their prime nearly overnight, while others stay stable for a week or two. If you are in a time crunch, first check the fruits and vegetables that won't wait, then the ones that are more patient.

You'll find harvesting at the right time means less waste—and that's good news for your plants and for your wallet.

Stretch Out Your Harvest with Simple Season Extenders

It takes just a bit of added effort to coax an extra-long harvest from many plants. What's in it for you? Sometimes weeks of harvest from plants you'd otherwise have to replace.

To get more from lettuce and other greens, for example, just remove tender outer leaves as you need them, leaving the rest of the plant to continue growing. When you harvest broccoli and cabbage, leave a few inches of stalk and a few lower leaves to encourage the plant to produce sideshoots—they'll be smaller but just as edible.

OH-SO-SIMPLE FROST PROTECTION

Protecting plants from an early frost is another way to extend your season and it doesn't have to take much more than a few minutes of your time. Providing temporary frost protection is a good way to buy time if the crop isn't ready to pick or you just don't have time to harvest. Often, a killing frost is followed by several weeks of warmer weather, so you may only have to protect plants for a night or two to extend the season by several weeks.

The quickest method is to cover the plants with sheets, blankets, or plastic on nights when frost threatens. It's primitive, but it works. Of course, you'll want to keep lightweight covers from blowing away by anchoring loose corners with rocks or bricks, or by resting dead branches over the top. Just be sure not to smash the plants in your efforts to save them. Avoid crushing especially delicate plants by placing a tomato cage over them before throwing on the cloth or plastic. Use clothespins to clip the cover to the framework.

Another method is to make a tent over a grouping of plants, using the same tent-making technique you perfected as a child: Tie a clothesline to supports on either end of the grouping—garden stakes or the backs of lawn chairs will do. Then throw a blanket, tarp, or other covering over the clothesline and anchor the corners with rocks.

For an easy but more permanent solution to frost and cold, cover cool-season vegetables like beets and greens with a 6-inch layer of loose straw or leaves. You'll have fresh produce into winter.

Become a Quicker Picker

Take a few moments during a post-planting lull to get organized. This way, once crops are ready, you can make the most out of every harvesting minute. Think about ways you can save steps and handle your produce fewer times. Here are some proven shortcuts to get you started; see how many more you can come up with.

Slip into your shoes. Keep an old pair of slip-on shoes near the door so you don't waste valuable picking time hunting for footwear. Kick them off on your way back in so you don't have to clean dirt off the floor.

Pack while you pick. Carry along plastic bags and containers and pack the produce while you're in

the garden. When you get to the kitchen, put the goods directly into the refrigerator.

Chill in the garden. If you'll be in the garden for more than half an hour, take along an ice chest and chill peas, corn, broccoli, and delicate greens and fruits; otherwise, they'll fade fast.

Sort the good from the bad. Carry an extra bucket for damaged fruits and vegetables, and toss them into it as you pick them. By sorting the good from the bad right away, you don't have to touch each piece again in the kitchen.

Clean lip outside. Wash greens or produce you plan to eat right away while outside to prevent a mess in the kitchen. Fill a bucket with cold water, or use the kids' wading pool. While you're at it, pick off and compost the inedible parts like stems and husks.

Use Basic Tools as Handy Harvest Helpers

When it comes to tools, the fewer the better. You don't want to feel like a one-man band clattering your way to the garden. For most picking jobs, your hands are sufficient—you may want to wear gloves when harvesting crops that are scratchy or smelly though.

Take along a knife for harvesting thick-stalked crops like broccoli and cabbage, as well as leafy crops like lettuce. Use scissors or pruning shears to cut the stems of peppers, okra, and other crops that don't pull off easily. If you'll be harvesting potatoes and other root crops, carry a spade or garden fork; if the soil is dry, you'll make the job easier by moistening it slightly before digging. If you have tree fruit to pick, consider investing in a long-handled fruit picker to save you from struggling with ladders.

Smart Tips for Handling Pre- or Post-Prime Produce

If you have to harvest a little early because frost threatens, or if wet weather keeps you out of the garden during a critical week, you can still make the best of your produce.

Try these not-so-tough tricks. Conquer toughness in cookable vegetables by dicing, grating, or shredding them. Then sauté, stir-fry, or add to soup, stew, or egg dishes.

Puree not-quite-prime produce. Some vegetables are well suited, either cooked or raw, to being pureed with tomato juice to make a vegetable cocktail. Which ones you use is a matter of preference; for starters, try sweet peppers, celery, carrots, and a bit of onion.

Turn them into soup. Make a soup base by boiling vegetables until they're very soft. Strain the broth and compost the vegetables. Don't use members of the crucifer family, such as broccoli and cauliflower—their flavor is too strong.

Put up jam or jelly. Make jam or jelly from berries that aren't quite ripe.

Puree post-prime fruit. Any fruit past its prime can be pureed, then served over ice cream or mixed with fruit juice and chilled for a cooling summer beverage.

Add it to the soup. Make soup from carrots, peas, potatoes—even cucumbers. Also add pureed vegetables to soup stock.

Bake it. Make breads or muffins from apples, blueberries, tomatoes, carrots, or zucchini.

Make compost. Add rotten produce to the compost pile. The rejects decompose to form great fertilizer, and you keep diseases and insects off the plant.

Continued ➡

Quick Tricks in the Kitchen

Produce is most flavorful and tender when picked at its prime—and picking produce at its peak also saves you time and work in the kitchen.

You can serve many fresh vegetables raw or give them a light steaming. By picking produce at the right time, you'll have fewer tough stems or leaves to discard, so less goes to waste and you get more food on the table.

WASHING CAN WAIT

When faced with a bushel of muddy produce fresh from the garden, you may be tempted to scrub the lot of it—using up your evening and messing up the kitchen in the process. Fortunately, you don't need to—in fact, in most cases you shouldn't. Washing most vegetables and fruits before storing makes them vulnerable to rot. It's better to wash produce right before you use it.

There are a few exceptions. Take a few moments to briskly but briefly swish greens—such as lettuce, chard, spinach, endive, and kale—in cool water, then shake off the excess and roll them in a towel before putting them into a plastic bag and then into the refrigerator. Cucumbers can be washed beforehand; so can leeks, which hide dirt in their layers.

Stretch Your Storage Time

With a little attention to how you wrap and refrigerate your produce, you'll increase its storage life. Fortunately, proper storage isn't complicated since most produce needs the same treatment: a plastic container or wrap, and a temperature of about 35°F. The few exceptions are listed in the right-hand column below. (Note that the best storage temperatures are cooler than the average refrigerator, which is generally somewhat warmer than 35°F.) Check this list to find out how to store your produce properly and how long you can expect it to last.

COLD AND MOIST

To get the maximum storage from the vegetables listed below, keep them near freezing in a refrigerator. Store in a plastic container or wrap.

Asparagus	2 weeks
Beets	1–3 months
Blueberries	2 weeks
Broccoli	3 weeks
Brussels sprouts	1 month
Cabbage (early maturing)	3–6 weeks
Cabbage (late maturing)	3–4 months
Carrots (tops removed)	4–6 months
Cauliflower	2–3 weeks
Collards	2–3 weeks
Corn	4–8 days
Kale	2–3 weeks
Lettuce	2 weeks
Onions (green)	2–3 weeks
Parsnips	2–6 months
Radishes	2–3 weeks
Turnip greens	2–3 weeks
Turnip roots	4–5 months

COOL AND MOIST

Keep the following vegetables cold but not freezing—a root cellar or basement that stays about 40°F is ideal. Keep most vegetables listed in a plastic container or wrap; potatoes store better loose so they don't get moldy—and be sure to keep them in the dark.

Beans, green	1 week
Cucumbers	10–14 days
Eggplants	1 week
Peppers, sweet	2–3 weeks
Potatoes, Irish	4–6 months
Squash, summer	7–10 days
Watermelons	2–3 weeks

COOL AND DRY

The following vegetables need cool—about 40°F—and dry conditions for best storage. Try keeping them in an attic or unheated room, and don't put them in plastic containers or wrap.

Onions	2 months
Pumpkins	2–5 months
Squash, winter	2–4 months
Tomatoes (ripe)	1 week
Tomatoes (unripe)	Up to 1 month

Season Extension
Fern Marshall Bradley

Gardeners are never satisfied with the weather. It's either too wet or too dry, too hot or too cool. Northern gardeners struggle to grow heat-loving crops like melons, tomatoes, and peppers; southern gardeners strive for sweet, succulent lettuce, crispy radishes, and tender peas. While you can't change your climate (unless you're prepared to move and face a new set of challenges!), there are things you can do to create more-favorable microclimates within your garden.

In cold-climate areas, cold frames and row covers are standard weapons in the battle against late-spring and early-fall frosts. You may also want to choose cold-tolerant or fast-maturing cultivars of your favorite crops. In hot-summer areas, gardeners use shade cloth and heat-tolerant cultivars to extend the growing season for choice cool-season crops. In this section, you'll find helpful tips from expert growers across the country on how they stretch their growing seasons.

Simple Tricks for Extending the Season

Your efforts at season extension don't have to be fancy or complicated to work. Tools as simple as a piece of plastic or a few rocks can help you get an earlier start on the season.

WARM YOUR BEDS WITH PLASTIC SHEETS

Get a head start on planting your garden by prewarming the soil. Alton Eliason, who was named Farmer of the Year in 1991 by the Natural Organic Farming Association, plants two to three weeks earlier than his neighbors. Eliason says, "In mid-February, about six weeks before my first planting date, I cover the garden with a sheet of clear plastic, right on top of the snow. Clear plastic raises the temperature by 10° to 15°F, whereas black plastic only raises it by 5° or so. The snow melts right off, and the soil's always ready a few weeks earlier than normal." Eliason gets his big plastic sheets from area greenhouse growers who replace their glazing every two or three years.

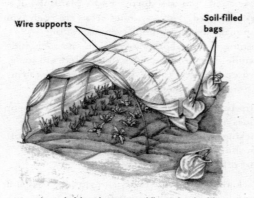

A tunnel of clear plastic protects fall crops from hard frost.

NEW WAVE PLANTING TECHNIQUES

The lay of the land in your garden beds can affect how and when soil warms. Bill McDorman, the founder of High Altitude Gardens, an Idaho mail-order seed company, finds that one of the most effective techniques for combatting cold soils is shaping the garden surface before planting.

"This is similar to making raised beds, except that you shape the beds like waves in the ocean. I make the beds 3 to 4 feet wide, and slope them to the south," explains McDorman. He plants warm-weather crop seeds, such as squash, on the south face of his waves, just below the ridge. The soil drains well there, just as it does in a raised bed. The southern exposure warms the soil, and cold air is directed by the soil configuration to fall into the "valley" beyond the wave. Other heat lovers like basil and corn also benefit from this planting technique.

GROW THEM FAST UP NORTH

Extending the growing season is an absolute necessity in places like Glover, Vermont, home of Lewis Hill, a nursery owner and the author of Cold-Climate Gardening. Hill's growing season is only 90 to 110 days, with occasional frosts in July. "This is the icebox of New England," says Hill.

How does Hill successfully produce corn, tomatoes, peppers, eggplant, pumpkins, and squash in such a harsh environment? "My favorite technique is to get intensive growth as fast as possible during the early part of summer when the days are long," explains Hill. To promote vigorous plant growth, he waters frequently and makes liberal use of liquid fertilizers, such as manure tea and fish emulsion. Standard season-extension tricks like covering seed beds and young plants with floating row covers or plastic jugs are a necessity for keeping the chilly spring and fall air from the plants. To stack the odds in favor of a good harvest, it's also smart to start with cold-tolerant and fast-maturing cultivars of normally slow-ripening crops like melons and winter squash.

TRANSPLANT TO HASTEN HARVESTS

Looking for a way to get your heat-loving crops off to a fast start? Take a tip from Jacob R. Mittleider, Ph.D., who teaches beginning farmers in Zaokski, Russia, a town about 100 miles south of Moscow (at about the same latitude as Edmonton, Alberta, in Canada). In the summer of 1991, he and his students produced more than 220 tons of food on 23 acres.

What is his secret? "I transplant everything: beans, corn, beets," says Dr. Mittleider. "I would do it with carrots, but if I do, they will never get larger than 4 inches. Transplanting gives an even harvest, not a mix of big plants and little plants."

Dr. Mittleider plants his transplants outdoors with special care so they won't lose ground during the transition. He plants in shallow trenches in raised beds and protects the young plants until they are well-established by covering them with heavy plastic supported by wire hoops.

PUTTING ROCKS INTO THE GARDEN?

Gardeners are always trying to get rid of rocks in their garden soil, but here's one tip that calls for using rocks. "I plant on the south side of rock or concrete walls wherever I can. This generally speeds plants up by as much as one month. But I don't have as much wall space as I'd like, so I import rocks into the garden," says Bill McDorman, the founder of High Altitude Gardens, an Idaho mail-order seed company.

To use McDorman's method, cover the soil around the base of each plant with a circle of whatever rocks you can find. Place the rocks close to but not touching the plants to avoid damaging the

Continued ➡

Soaker hoses and drip irrigation. For small beds, soaker hoses (left) are great, releasing water slowly and evenly to the whole bed. Cover the hoses with mulch to conserve moisture. For large beds, use a drip system (right), which delivers water through spaghetti tubes directly to the base of each plant.

tender stems. The rocks gather and store heat during the day. At night, the rocks release the heat, helping to protect the young plants from frost. The rocks also help to moderate changes in soil temperature, encouraging better root growth. You can leave the rocks in place all season, and they'll serve as a mulch to keep moisture in the soil and prevent weed growth around your plants.

Cold Frames and Other Covers

The greenhouse effect is a phenomenon that northern gardeners can take advantage of to help extend their growing season. No, not on a global scale, but by using enclosures like plastic or glass covers that trap the sun's heat and create tiny oases of warm air around growing plants.

Six bales of straw and an old window or a wooden frame covered with plastic serve well as a temporary coldframe. Use blocks of wood to vent the frame.

SLITTED TUNNELS FOR SUPER TOMATOES

Plastic covers suspended over rows of plants are a great way to protect tender crops from spring chills. But they do require regular ventilation to prevent heat from building up inside on sunny days. If you don't have the time or inclination to keep raising and lowering the sides of a solid plastic cover, try a slitted row cover instead.

A slitted row cover is "a tunnel with 6-inch openings punched through at regular intervals to ventilate the tunnel. It has been a great season extender for us," says Ward Sinclair, an organic vegetable farmer from Pennsylvania.

One year, he and his partner, Cass Peterson, planted 'Siberia' tomatoes in the field in early April and covered them with slitted row covers. "The tomatoes were flowering like crazy on Memorial Day," recalls Sinclair. "They were bursting out of the tunnels, just lifting the plastic off of the ground."

But the plants are not the only thing that tries to lift row covers at their Flickerville Mountain Farm and Groundhog Ranch. "Our main problem is wind," adds Sinclair. "You have to cover the edges of the plastic with soil along the whole length of the tunnel. You can't just put a handful of soil here and there and expect it to hold." Long metal pipes or boards also make good anchors for row covers. They are easy to move and reposition when you need to temporarily uncover the plants for maintenance or harvesting.

PROTECT PLANTS WITH PORTABLE FRAMES

If you want to protect a lot of plants with plastic row covers, try framing the row covers to make them easier to set up and take down. Robert F. Becker, a retired associate professor at Cornell University's New York Agricultural Experiment Station in Geneva, has created a design for sturdy framed covers that are easy to move around the garden. Here's how to make them:

1. Using 2 X 4's and nails or screws, make a square wooden frame, 18 inches on each side.

2. Drill four holes halfway through the frame from the top, one in each corner.

3. Make two arches of rigid wire (9- or 10-gauge works well). Position each arch diagonally over the frame, inserting the ends of the wires into the holes. This creates a dome shape as shown in the illustration below.

4. Cover the frame with a piece of clear plastic, stapling it to the wooden frame.

The wire domes sit about 1 foot above the soil surface, giving enclosed plants plenty of head room. Becker cuts a ventilation hole in the side facing south after positioning the frames. When plants need additional ventilation, Becker props up one side of the frame with a brick or rock. This extra ventilation helps harden off the plants before he removes the cap. "The only trouble with these frames is storage," admits Becker. "You need a place to keep them during the winter. I like them, though, because they're portable and inexpensive. The plastic needs to be replaced every two to three years, but the frames last for years."

KEEP PLANTS WARM WITH WATER

Wallo'Waters surround individual plants with water-filled plastic tubes, which store heat during the day and radiate it out at night to keep plants warm and toasty. Ward Sinclair, an organic vegetable farmer

from Pennsylvania, thinks they are one of the best season extenders around.

"It's a fantastic device," Sinclair declares. "It keeps peppers perfectly at 9°F." Sinclair has used Wallo'Waters to produce early tomatoes and muskmelons that blossom on Memorial Day. Once the danger of frost is past, he plants basil between the tomatoes. "I lift the Wallo'Waters off the tomatoes and set them over the basil," he says. The result? Basil a month early, to complement your early tomatoes!

One way to save some money when buying Wallo'Waters is to buy a full case of 36 and split it with your gardening neighbors, friends, and relatives. Or if you're extremely thrifty, you can follow the example of Miranda Smith, an agriculture writer and organic market gardener from Massachusetts, and build your own. Just fill 2-liter plastic soda bottles with water, set them around peppers or eggplants, and encircle the ring of bottles with a sheet of plastic.

THE WORLD'S LARGEST ROW COVER

Ever wonder what you could grow if you put your entire garden under cover? It's not as farfetched as it sounds, according to Otho Wells, Ph.D., a New Hampshire Cooperative Extension vegetable specialist. Dr. Wells calls garden-size covers "high tunnels" because they are about 6½ feet tall at the center.

"I would recommend a 14 x 36-foot tunnel for a garden," Dr. Wells suggests. "You can put an awful lot of stuff in a 14 x 36, especially when you consider companion planting." You can grow just about anything from sweet potatoes to cut flowers inside of a high tunnel. Only a few crops such as sweet corn or winter squash take up too much room.

High tunnels "give you two to four weeks head start in the spring, depending on the conditions, then take you into the fall, to Thanksgiving, and even to Christmas," says Dr. Wells. "They're like small greenhouses, but they're not greenhouses because they have roll-up sides. They give you tremendous protection against the environment: wind, rain, insects, and diseases

WATERING

Watering Your Garden

Jeff Cox

At one time or another, most of us have run into a water shortage. We couldn't wash our cars, water our lawns and gardens, or let the children play in the sprinkler. It lasted maybe a few weeks; then it rained and life returned to normal. Or so it seemed. Running on empty is becoming a way of life in state after state in the United States and in a growing number of countries around the world.

Another problem is water quality. In coastal areas with shallow water tables, for example, heavy pumping of groundwater allows salt water to seep into wells. In heavily agricultural areas, pesticides and fertilizers are tainting both surface and groundwater supplies.

Continued ➡

While we can't as individuals change patterns of water use in commercial agriculture, we can all take steps to reduce water usage in our homes and yards.

So how do you go about conserving water *and* watering your garden at the same timer One answer is drip irrigation. A drip irrigation system delivers water directly to the root zone of plants, without the waste of evaporation or runoff. Coupled with basic conservation techniques such as using mulch, selecting plants that require less water, and limiting lawn area, drip irrigation can help conserve water while ensuring a healthy garden.

Conserving Water in the Garden

With a little planning, it's possible to have good gardens, a beautiful lawn, and landscaping that need very little supplemental watering. The first step, of course, is to increase the water-holding capacity of your soil by adding organic matter. In deep, rich soil protected by mulch, plants find it much easier to develop the strong, deep root systems necessary to find water during dry periods. Cultivating the soil between row crops also helps water filter into the soil.

There are many other things you can do to reduce watering needs without sacrificing the beauty or pleasure of your yard and gardens:

· Mulch trees, shrubs, and other plants with up to 3 inches of mulch.

· Water less frequently, but water deeply, making sure to soak the root zone rather than the whole yard.

· Select native plants that require less water.

· In arid climates, follow the principles of Xeriscaping in planning and maintaining your yard. A Xeriscape (from the Greek *xeros*, meaning dry) is a water-saving garden designed for a dry region. Many municipal and state water departments publish low-cost or free guides for the beginning Xeriscaper. Check your library, bookstore, or the government listings in your phone book to read more about planning a Xeriscape. Publications on this topic are available from the National Xeriscape Council, P.O. Box 163172, Austin, TX 78751-3172.

· Limit the size of your lawn. Replace lawn with groundcovers, mulches, and shade trees to help you and your yard keep cool.

· Add a walkway, deck, or patio to help reduce water consumption while adding more enjoyment to your yard.

Using Drip Irrigation

For those situations in which you have to water, always strive for the most efficient method. When you water with the hose or an overhead sprinkler, some water is immediately lost to evaporation from plant surfaces, through surface run-off, or by falling in areas that don't need water, such as a street or walkway.

A more efficient method is a custom-designed drip irrigation system that will water all or any part of your landscape. Also called "trickle" or "weep" irrigation, drip systems are as beneficial for dryland gardeners as for those in the northern, eastern, and southern parts of the country. The water savings and increased plant growth in your garden will more than make up for the cost and effort involved in the design and installation of a drip irrigation system.

A drip irrigation system delivers water directly to a plant's root zone, where it seeps slowly into the soil one drop at a time. Almost no water is lost through surface runoff or evaporation, and soil particles have plenty of opportunity to absorb and hold water for plants. It also means very few nutrients leach down beyond the reach of plant roots. Furthermore, since drip irrigation delivers water directly to the plants you want to grow, less is wasted on weeds. The soil surface between plants also remains drier, which discourages weed seeds from sprouting. All these benefits add up to the fact that drip irrigation systems can save a great deal of water—and money in terms of reduced water bills. Studies show that well-designed drip systems use at least 30 percent, and in some cases 50 percent, less water than other methods of watering such as sprinkling.

For busy gardeners, the main benefit of installing a drip irrigation system is the savings of both time and effort. Drip systems eliminate the need to drag hoses and sprinklers around. For systems that use a timer, gardeners need only spend a few seconds to turn the system on; the timer automatically turns it off.

Plants watered with drip systems grow more quickly and are more productive, because they have all the water they need and their growth isn't slowed by water stress. (This is especially true when drip irrigation is used in conjunction with mulch.) These systems also keep water off the foliage, which helps prevent some foliage diseases such as powdery mildew.

Don't Waste Time on Water Wasters

Overthirsty plants, soil that drains too fast or too slowly, poor watering techniques, and inefficient garden plans not only waste tremendous quantities of water; they also waste your time and money. Look at your yard and garden and see which of the water wasters below are drinking you dry. Then try one or more water-saving solutions for quick relief.

Water Wasters	Water-Saving Solutions
Bare, uncovered soil. Water evaporates quickly from uncovered ground. Since wind and rain can beat at it at will, bare soil is often hard-packed or has an impenetrable crust, so water runs off it without soaking in.	Cover the ground with 2 to 4 inches of organic mulch. Use attractive mulches like bark chips or flower beds, trees, and fshrubs, or plant bare areas with groundcovers to help hold moisture in place. Use any handy mulch materials—compost, grass clippings, shredded leaves, straw—for vegetable gardens.
Poor soil. Hard-packed soil, or soil that's either high in clay or high in sand, creates watering problems. Hard-packed or clayey soils may drain so slowly that water puddles and drowns plants or runs off without soaking in. Sandy soils may drain so quickly you spend all your time trying to keep plants from wilting.	Adding organic matter in the form of compost, shredded leaves, or aged manure will improve any type of soil—it improves drainage on hard-packed and clayey soils and helps sandy soils hold water longer. Keeping your soil covered with organic mulches helps add organicmatter, but for dramatic improvement, add an inch of organic matter each year, working it into the top few inches of soil. After two to four years, you'll have a yard and garden that needs less water and less care of any kind.
Planting plans that mix moisture-loving and drought-tolerant plants. This arrangement not only wastes water but createsplant health problems, too. If you give moisture lovers enoughwater, you'll injure or drown their dry-soil companions.	Group plants with similar water needs together.Plant them in different beds if possible. If you can't, cluster them together within beds. You'll be able to water each group according to its needs without wasting water on neighbors that don't want it.
Thirsty flowers, shrubs, trees, and vegetables. Plants that droop and beg for water every time you walk by only mean more work for you.	Keep a 2- to 4-inch layer of organic mulch around plants to conserve moisture. For even more water savings, replace extra-thirsty plants with drought-tolerant ones. Native trees, shrubs, and vines are generally good choices, as are deep-rooted perennials like peonies, yarrows, daylilies, coreopsis, globe thistles, pinks, and sedums. Plant wide rows of closely spaced vegetables to protect soil moisture from evaporating.
Overhead sprinkling. Sprinklers are inefficient at delivering water to plant roots. Much of the water that's shot into the air evaporates as it falls to the ground; winds also send it in unwanted directions.	If water pressure fluctuates, sprinklers won't run efficiently or cover the areas you aim at. Switch to soaker hoses or drip irrigation so water stays on the ground. Or to reduce evaporation, choose sprinklers that create large water droplets that fall more quickly. Watering in early morning instead of during the heat of the day also reduces evaporation. Purchase a pressure regulator to ensure that sprinklers have enough water to operate effectively.
Misdirected sprinklers. Inground or overhead sprinklers that water buildings, pavement, or weeds mean big water bills; the only weeds benefit.	Adjust sprinkler heads to cover only planted areas or purchase ones with spray patterns that fit your plantings. Drip irrigation or soaker hoses spread through planting beds will deliver water exactly where you want it.
Sprinkling plants until the ground looks wet. Watering a thirsty plant just until the soil surface looks damp creates more problems than it solves.	Plants watered this way need more frequent watering and develop very shallow roots. Water less often, but water deeply each time you do it so you soak the entire root zone. This encourages plant roots to grow deep into the soil, making them more drought-resistant. After a watering session, jab your finger into the ground to see how deeply you've really watered. (Or use rain gauges to see how much water you've delivered.) You'll be amazed at how dry soil can be under a surface that "looks" soaking wet.
Lawns. Large expanses of lawn grasses are the greediest water hogs of all. They demand weekly watering to look their best in the heat of summer.	Replace the thirstiest stretches of lawn with drought-tolerant groundcovers that can fend for themselves. If you can't part with even a small bit of your lawn, replace water-demanding grasses like Kentucky bluegrass gradually by overseeding with cultivars that require less moisture. Check with your extension agent or garden center manager for good choices for your area. You can lower your water bill even more if you use drought-tolerant, low-growing grasses like turf-type tall fescue, fine fescue, or buffalograss.

Continued ➡

DESIGNING A SYSTEM

The first decision to make in designing a drip irrigation system is what you want to water. Do you want a system only for your vegetable garden or for your entire landscape? Topography is also a consideration: If your garden is hilly, you'll probably need to use emitters that compensate for pressure changes in the line.

You can design your own system, but most companies that sell drip irrigation equipment will design systems for you if provided with a scale drawing of your garden, information on what you're growing, your soil type, and garden topography. Their design will come complete with a list of parts and spacing for emitters. Whatever method you choose, start by making a fairly accurate drawing of your garden to determine how many feet of tubing you'll need.

Plants can become "addicted" to drip irrigation, because roots will concentrate in the area where the water is available. When designing a drip system to carry water along the rows of a vegetable garden or to the roots of a prized rhododendron, it's important that the water be spread uniformly throughout the irrigated area so root growth will be uniform. For example, if you are irrigating larger plants such as trees and shrubs, place emitters on two or more sides of each plant to encourage roots to grow out in all directions rather than clustering on one side. Using your system for frequent, short waterings, rather than long, slow ones, is a bad idea for the same reason; the water doesn't have a chance to spread far in the soil, and consequently the roots form a tight, ball-like mass around the emitters.

Soaker Hoses Soaker hoses are another type of drip irrigation system that provides many of the advantages of emitter drip systems at a fraction of their cost. Some ooze water over their entire length; others spurt water through tiny holes. When using soaker hoses with holes, be sure to face the holes downward so the water doesn't squirt up in the air like a sprinkler. Systems using these hoses need no assembly; it's easy to layout the hoses between small plants and along narrow rows.

Soakers save water, reduce loss through evaporation, and keep leaves dry. However, since water emerges evenly along the length of the hose, water delivery can't be directed as precisely as with an emitter system. Soaker hoses can be used for short runs (100 to 200 feet) over flat surfaces. They're useful for crops such as carrots that are closely spaced.

Also known as dew hoses, soaker hoses can be made of canvas, various types of plastic, or rubber. Hoses made of rigid plastics or rubber can be hard to lay flat and difficult to bend around corners. Plastic and rubber soakers are resistant to fungal attack and seldom develop leaks at couplings or seams, so they can be left in the beds for long periods of time without deterioration. In contrast, canvas hoses are susceptible to mold and mildew and should be drained and dried after each use.

Save Time, Save Water
Fern Marshall Bradley

In a water-conscious era, we need to be as efficient as we can about water use. But most gardens need some supplemental water. Try these tips for reducing the amount of water you apply and the time you spend doing it.

Design Around Your Downspouts

Save a few spins on your water meter by taking advantage of downspouts to irrigate plants naturally. "Pay attention to where your downspouts

---

are," advises Jim Borland, a Colorado garden writer and consultant on dryland gardening. If your downspouts lead directly to the gutter, reroute them to give your garden a boost.

Top 10 Ways to Conserve Water While Caring for Your Garden
Vicki Mattern [Au]

Water is vital to the life of your garden and yard, yet gardeners often waste this precious resource. Whether your area is suffering from a drought or not, follow these guidelines to cut down on water usage:

1. Water deeply, making sure to soak the root zone rather than the whole yard.

2. When landscaping, choose native plants that require little or no water beyond what nature provides.

3. Plant groundcovers and shade trees to help keep your yard cool.

4. Mulch your garden regularly to lock in soil moisture.

5. Use watering methods such as drip irrigation or soaker hoses to reduce evaporation by directing water to plant roots.

6. Closely space plants in your raised vegetable garden, so there is less area to water (make sure to provide enough room for root development).

7. Follow the principles of xeriscaping, a water-saving garden design method used by many gardeners in more arid climates.

8. Limit the size of your lawn by adding a deck, patio, or walkway, which also adds backyard enjoyment.

9. Connect a rain barrel to a gutter on your home to create a ready source of water for your plants.

10. Recycle household water from drinking glasses and steaming or cooking vegetables and pasta to water plants.

Plan your design to make the most of rainwater, says Borland. Shape the soil into shallow basins to catch the runoff, or construct rills of slightly hilled soil to direct water to your plants. Place water-hungry plants closest to the extra moisture. In areas with frequent rainfall, some gardeners create a miniature marsh garden near downspouts, using plants such as cardinal flower (*Lobelia cardinalis*), lesser celandine (*Ranunculus ficaria*), marsh marigold (*Caltha palustris*), yellow flag (*Iris pseudacorus*), and water-loving sedges and rushes.

Wait For Signs of Water Stress

Instead of watering your entire landscape with an inch of the precious wet stuff every week, water only when the plants need it. Generally speaking, plants in pots may need water every day, lawns every three days, and established trees every ten days, says Tom Bressan, a California irrigation specialist. But watering needs vary widely depending on the species of the plant. Stretch the time between waterings until you see signs of distress, advises Bressan.

"Eyeball it!" he urges. Look at your plants to see which ones show stress first. Stay alert to the

---

not-so-obvious signals of plant distress, such as foliage that seems dull or less glossy or shows curling edges. Watch for leaf drop, a signal that the plant is trying to conserve water. Serious wilting needs attention right away to save the plant.

Water Wisely With a Timer

Using a timer is one way to make sure your plants are getting the water they need. "Be sure your timer has separate zones for flowers, shrubs, lawn, or other areas," advises Susan A. Roth, the author of *The Weekend Garden Guide*, "so you can water them on different days for different lengths of time, according to their individual needs." Deep-rooted perennials, for instance, generally need less water than your lawn, and shaded areas stay moister than full-sun locations. You might keep lawn grass in one zone; drought-tolerant perennials, trees, and shrubs in another; and water lovers in a third.

A good timer is well worth the investment, Roth says. "Water infrequently but deeply," she urges. "Many timers can only deliver a quarter-inch of water each time they run. This is murder on your plants—and wasteful." It's also a good idea, adds Roth, to run that timer on the manual setting so you can provide water only when Mother Nature doesn't. If you set a timer on automatic, you are all too likely to end up watering your lawn during a rainstorm.

Depend on Drip

Drip irrigation is a tailor-made way of applying water just where you need it. Tom Bressan, a California irrigation specialist, recommends polyethylene tubing with emitters punched into it where you want them. Drip tapes with holes, he says, are too thin-walled for permanent plantings. It's easy to install drip irrigation in an existing bed. "Use the claw side of a hammer," Bressan advises. "Drag it along the ground to create a shallow trench for the tubing." Add extra emitters for plants that need more water. After your layout is complete, bury the tubing in mulch. (Avoid placing drip tubing on top of existing mulch, because the mulch will absorb the water intended for the soil.) Pull the mulch aside if the system needs maintenance.

In an annual bed or vegetable garden, Bressan uses the drip system without mulch. If the plantings are closely spaced, Bressan recommends using emitter lines with regularly spaced, pre-installed emitters. In an annual bed, the leaves screen the tubing, he says, and the impact of the flowers draws the eye away. And in a vegetable garden, no one objects to a visible irrigation system.

LET THIS HOSE LEAK

A leaky hose may be the best irrigation device for the vegetable garden. Arizona garden writer Lynn Tilton uses a lawn spray hose, which has holes punched all along its length, to irrigate his tomato and corn rows. The hose delivers a gentle spray of water every foot or so. Tilton mulches the beds with grass clippings and then lays out the hose. He turns on the water, and the hose sprays upward so the water falls on top of the mulch, binding it together. Then he flips the hose upside down so that the water is forced out directly through the mulch and into the soil. Tilton says, "Our sandy soil makes regular hose watering almost impossible. When I use the sprinkler hose, I get a better crop with one-third the water."

Continued ➡

Watering the Low-Maintenance Way

Barbara W. Ellis, Joan Benjamin, and Deborah L. Martin

Tired of dragging hoses and paying ever-increasing water bills? There are ways to stop spinning your wheels and your water meter. End your watering woes by using mulch or exchanging thirsty plants for drought-tolerant ones. There are tools, techniques, and watering systems that can do the work for you—and reduce your water bills—no matter what you grow.

Chances are your yard needs a water-wise makeover. In this chapter, you'll find ways to make your landscape less thirsty. Once you've added mulch and improved your soil, you'll find most established ornamental plantings need extra water only during droughts. Water is more crucial for new plantings, fruits, and vegetables, but in the pages that follow, you'll find a variety of efficient tools and techniques you can use to safely cut back on the time you spend watering them, too.

Spend Your Watering Time Wisely

Mulch can reduce your plants' water needs drastically, but there may come a time when they need a drink. When they do, you'll save time and avoid rotting roots, fungus diseases, erosion, and high water bills by applying the right amount of water when and where it's needed. Here's how.

Water only when plants are thirsty. When plants need a drink, they start to wilt, top leaves first. They droop in the heat of the day, then recover in the evening as the temperature cools down. As days pass and their thirst gets worse, leaf edges curl and leaves may take on a dull look. Eventually they don't perk up when temperatures cool, leaf edges turn brown and crispy, and, finally, they collapse.

To keep plants healthy, give them a drink when they start wilting slightly. If you wait until they are stressed, they'll be more likely to have problems.

Put water where it's needed. You'll waste less water if you use soaker hoses and drip systems to apply it to the ground directly around plants. These systems keep water off pathways, where it encourages weeds to grow, and off sidewalks and driveways, where it's wasted. You'll also have fewer disease problems with these systems since they don't wet plant leaves (which encourages fungal diseases).

Know how much is enough. The best rule is to soak the soil 1 foot deep when your plants get thirsty. Deep watering encourages deep rooting, which helps plants survive drought.

How do you know when you've soaked 1 foot deep? It depends on your soil type. Sandy soils let water pass through quickly, so ½ inch of water is all it takes to reach 1 foot down. If you have a loamy soil, ¾ inch of water will give you the desired results. Clay soils soak up water slowly, so you'll need to apply 1¼ inches of water for clay soil, spread out over several hours to keep water from pooling on the soil surface.

To measure water output for soaker hose and drip irrigation systems, follow the instructions that came with your system—their flow depends on water pressure. Use rain gauges to measure rainfall and water applied from overhead sprinklers.

Water when the time is right. If you're using an overhead sprinkler, the best time to water plants is early morning when the wind is calm and the sun is low. Water evaporates quickly during the heat of day, so much of it never reaches your plants. Plants watered in evening with overhead sprinklers or by hand tend to stay wet all night, which encourages disease. Soaker hoses and drip irrigation systems make it easy and effective to water any time, since evaporation isn't a problem and these systems don't wet the foliage.

Save Time with a Water-Saving Landscape

Do you race around your yard in the summer pouring water on every plant in sight? If so, you'll save loads of time and aggravation if you start using plants and techniques, like the ones shown here, that conserve water throughout your yard, landscape, and gardens.

It's best to start new plantings off on the right foot by selecting drought-tolerant plants. For existing gardens, though, it's often easier to change your watering methods than your plants. One good place to start cutting down on watering chores is to pick out which plants in your yard really need water and which do just fine with what they get from Mother Nature.

To decide what plants to water, determine which ones are essential to you. Do you depend on food from the vegetable garden? Do you have heirloom shrubs or flowers that you can't live without? Do you have newly planted trees and shrubs that need regular watering until they become established? Will your neighbors harass you if your lawn goes dormant? Try to limit yourself to three areas that absolutely must have additional water and let the others fend for themselves.

1. **Select drought-tolerant shrubs and plant groundcovers.** Drought-tolerant shrubs like hypericum and Northern bayberry are just as attractive in foundation plantings and flower beds as thirstier shrubs like azaleas. And groundcovers need much less water than lawn to look their best. Replacing lawn with groundcovers around trees and shrubs will cut down on the water they need—and your mowing chores as well.

When you water young seedlings, mimic light rainfall by directing the spray in a gentle arc up and out over them.

When They Need Water Most

CROP	CRITICAL TIME	BEST METHODS
Beans and peas	Germination, flowering, and while pods are developing	Drip, soaker hoses, hand-watering provided foliage is kept dry
Cabbage, broccoli, cauliflower	For 2 weeks after transplanting, and while heads are developing	Drip, soaker hoses, hand-watering if aphids are present
Carrot, radish	Germination, and while roots are enlarging; excessive water at maturity can cause roots to crack	Hand-watering or sprinkler; allow time for foliage to dry before nightfall
Corn	Germination, and from tasseling to maturity	Soaker hoses, drip, sprinklers in dry climates to increase humidity during pollination period
Lettuce, other leafy greens	Shallow roots demand constant moisture throughout life cycle.	Hand-watering, sprinkler, light mulch
Melons	Germination, and during first 3 weeks following fruit set; moderate dryness enhances flavor of almost-ripe fruits	Soaker hoses, drip
Onions, garlic	While roots are enlarging and all leaves are still green; allow soil to become dry when leaves begin to brown	Soaker hoses, drip
Potatoes	Constant moderate moisture during last month of growth	Soaker hoses, drip, hand-watering if aphids are present
Squash, cucumbers	Germination and starting 1 week after the first flowers appear until fruit has set	Soaker hoses, drip
Tomatoes, peppers	For 2 weeks following transplanting, and continuously from first flowering to maturity	Soaker hoses, drip, hand-watering of containers

Continued ➡

Play It Again

Three Good Places to Coil a Hose

You can hang a hose from a rack or buy a reel to coil it, but if you're looking for more resourceful (and less expensive) options, here are three ways to give cast-off items a second life bringing order to your hoses.

- **Garbage can coil.** Cut down an old plastic trash can for a good hose-storage spot. Using a sharp, sturdy knife, carefully cut around the circumference of the can about 2 feet from the bottom. It may be easiest to do a rough cut first, and then go back and trim the edge. Turn the cut can over, and punch several drainage holes in the bottom with a hammer and large nail. Then coil your hose inside. In winter, you can drag the container and hose into your garage, basement, or shed for neat storage.

- **Wheel rim coil.** An old automobile or truck wheel rim makes a good place to coil a garden hose. Spiff it up for garden use by sanding off any rust and then applying two coats of white, green, or black metal primer. Then simply lay the wheel on the ground and coil the hose around it.

- **Big pot coil.** If you have a large terracotta pot that's lost its looks due to cracks and chips—or a half barrel planter that's become too fragile to hold plants—you have a great item for coiling your hose. Just turn the pot over, and coil your hose around the outside of the pot. Stow the male end, or nozzle, in the pot's drainage hole.

2. **Use drip irrigation.** Install a soaker hose or drip irrigation system in your vegetable garden. Keep a thick layer of straw or other organic mulch on your garden on top of your soaker hoses so you won't lose water to evaporation or runoff.

3. **Collect free water.** Place a rain barrel under your downspout for a free water supply.

4. Mulch, mulch, mulch. Keep soil under flowers, trees, and shrubs mulched with wood chips, pine needles, or other organic mulches to hold moisture in the soil. Mulch discourages water-hogging weeds, too.

5. **Grow drought-tolerant flowers.** In flower gardens, plant drought-tolerant perennials such as coneflowers and other deep-rooted perennials like daylilies. Many ornamental grasses are drought-tolerant, too.

Make a Custom Watering System for Vegetables

Cut-to-fit irrigation systems are an easy way to make a custom system for watering vegetable gardens with parallel rows. Stretch the main supply line across the top or bottom of your garden, as shown here, and attach sections of rubber ooze hose wherever you have a row of plants. You can cut the ooze hose to any length you need. To keep moisture in the soil and discourage weeds, install the system and cover it with organic mulch.

Make Your Hoses Behave with Handy Hose Tamers

Have you ever given your hose a tug and then looked on in horror as it leveled a row of cherished plants? The hose is not your enemy—it just needs a little guidance. Use the tools and techniques shown here to make it behave.

Flip tangled hoses free. A flick of the wrist is all it takes to turn a snarled hose into a model of good behavior. Detach your tangled hose from the faucet, grasp a free end, and keep flipping and rolling the hose until all the tangles are worked out.

Connect hoses with quick-release couplers. Stop struggling with hose ends that are difficult to screw onto faucets or other hoses. Brass quick-release couplers make connecting and disconnecting hoses easy: Just screw them onto hose ends, faucets, and all your attachments, and you'll be able to snap all your watering devices together or apart as needed. They're made to swivel so hoses won't kink. Plastic couplers are cheaper than brass ones, but some won't let water out of a faucet unless a hose is attached. Buyer beware!

Hang hoses high. Hoses last longer if you keep them off the ground. Inexpensive metal hangers, which you can attach to a shed, garage, or house, keep hoses organized and ready to use. Freestanding hose hangers are an option if you want to keep your hose near a garden. They're usually made of wrought iron and have prongs that let you anchor them into the ground. They're attractive but pricey.

Take weight off your back. Wheeled carts and reels can make dragging hoses easier. A cart lets you move several hoses around your yard at once with ease; add a reel and winding and unwinding hoses becomes a simple, nonsnarling task.

Direct hoses with homemade guides. To make a simple, inexpensive hose guide, stick a piece of rebar in the soil deep enough to it's sturdy; leave several inches above ground to keep your hose in place. Cover the rebar with a piece of bamboo (if looks are important) or PVC pipe. Place the guides in front of vulnerable plants or anywhere you don't want your hose to go. Or sink wooden stakes into the ground, leaving 6 to 8 inches exposed, and cover them with plastic soda bottles.

Handy Helpers: Tools to Make Hand Watering a Breeze

You could spend the summer with your thumb hooked over the end of your hose, but it's not only uncomfortable, it's also one of the least efficient ways to complete your watering chores. For the times when hand watering makes sense, the tools shown here will help make hand watering a breeze. They'll cut down on the time you spend hand watering and reduce the amount of water you use. All the items listed are available through garden-supply catalogs and at garden centers.

1. **Bubblers and water breakers.** These attachments can turn a hard stream of water into a gentle flow or spray, so they're great for watering fragile seedlings and areas that erode easily. Lay them beside a plant and they'll water while you do other work. Move them frequently to prevent flooding.

2. **Water wands.** If you have to water plants in the middle or back of a flower bed, extend your reach and gain control of your hose end with an inflexible, lightweight aluminum or plastic wand. You'll be able to direct water at the base of a plant or along the undersides of leaves to rinse pest insects away.

3. **Watering cans.** For indoor or outdoor container plants, or for a drought emergency in the garden, watering cans are time-saving choices. They let you haul small amounts of water around quickly without lugging out hoses. Consider the filled weight of a can before you buy. Water weighs slightly more than 8 pounds per gallon, so a 2½-gallon can will weigh over 20 pounds filled. Select a smaller can or plan on filling halfway. Attachments can make your life easier, too. The oval "rose" on the spout of this can produces a gentle spray that's perfect for seedlings or new transplants.

4. **Fan sprayers, nozzles, and spray guns.** These attachments work great if you need to rinse off a dusty plant or wash off pests like aphids. They're not good for watering plants since they put out a high-pressure blast that sends mulch and soil flying.

Build a Snow Fence Windbreak

When the purpose of a windbreak is to conserve soil moisture, using a material that casts low shade while filtering wind is ideal. This simple version uses wood snow fencing, which is inexpensive, easy to install and remove, and may be attractive enough to leave up year-round.

Snow fencing is designed to let wind pass through it, and the openings between the slats also allow filtered sunlight to reach nearby plants. You can install a Snow Fence Windbreak for just the peak growing season or for high-wind periods, and put it to use again in winter to encourage snow to accumulate in places where you want it to melt in spring. Wood snow fencing, which is held together with wire, is the most attractive kind to use in your garden, but you can opt for lightweight, inexpensive plastic snow fencing if you prefer.

You Will Need

Tools: Measuring tape, sledgehammer, wire cutters, pliers
Enough 6-foot-tall steel fence posts to place a post every 8 feet along the fence
One 50-foot roll of 4-foot-tall wooden snow fencing
Plastic cable ties

1. Determine the location for your fence, which should be on the south or west side of the plants to be shaded, about 3 feet from the center of the row. Use a sledgehammer to drive posts into the ground at each end, and at any intermediate corners or bends. Install additional posts at 8-foot intervals.

2. Unroll the fencing and use the wire cutters to cut it to the length of your desired fence, allowing a few extra inches if the fence rounds a corner.

3. With the base of the fence resting on the ground, attach one end to a post with three plastic cable ties. Pull the fence tight and secure it to each successive post with zip ties.

4. Once the fence is attached to the final post, trim the excess with wire cutters and bend back any exposed wires with pliers. When it's time to remove the fencing, just snip off the plastic zip ties and roll up the fence for storage.

Collecting Rain Makes Watering Easy

Rain barrels make it easy to collect and distribute rainwater: If you already have gutters and a downspout, all you need is the barrel. You can buy plastic ones with spouts, such as the one shown here, through mail-order garden catalogs. Or make your own barrel out of a plastic trash can if you'd prefer a do-it-yourself model.

Set the barrel under a downspout as close to your garden as possible. Keep it covered to keep mosquitoes out. Then run your downspout into the barrel, attach a garden hose to the spout, and

Continued ➡

you're in the water business. Run the hose to your garden or a landscape spot downhill for automatic watering. Otherwise, use your rain barrel for filling watering cans or dip water out as needed.

Let Timers Watch Your Watering

If you don't want to spend time monitoring your soaker hoses or sprinklers—or have to ever again worry about remembering to turn them off—let a timer do it for you. Inexpensive ($10-$30) mechanical timers let you turn a dial to set the amount of water to apply. Set the dial and go about your business, and the timer will turn the water off automatically.

If you can't always be there when your garden needs you, look into the benefits of battery-operated electronic timers. They're more expensive than the mechanical models ($30-$70), but once you set the watering schedule, they'll turn the water on and off for you at the times and days you specify. These devices are particularly helpful if you're working with water restrictions that limit the days and hours you can irrigate. The only time you're likely to encounter a problem is when it rains. Unless you're home and can turn the system off, it will merrily water or overwater your plants, even during a deluge. Some timers have optional moisture-sensing probes that will turn the water off when the soil is moist and back on again when it's dry.

Easy-Does-It Watering: Fast Fill-Up for a Slow Drip

Watering new plants properly takes time and patience, but it's all-important if they're going to get a healthy start in life. You have to drizzle the water on slowly so it soaks deep into the soil. And you don't just have to water once at planting time—you're looking at a summer of weekly watering sessions. While you could set up an elaborate watering system or spend hours standing over your new plants with a hose, there's an easier and cheaper alternative: Make your own low-tech drip system from containers. Drip containers will let you leave gallons of water around a plant in a flash, and then drip it out slowly into the soil without wasting a drop. Use them for new plants or to provide extra water for particularly water-sensitive ones.

Plastic milk jugs, soda bottles, and plastic buckets make fine containers for drip-watering plants. All you need to do is punch one or two very small nail holes in the bottom of the container. Since you want the water to drip out a drop at a time, put some water in the container and start with the smallest hole you can make. Gradually enlarge it until the water drips out at the rate you want.

To water, place one or more empty drip containers beside a thirsty plant. (The number of containers you use depends on how much water the plant will need; use several containers to give large trees and shrubs several gallons of water; one or two for smaller perennials.) Then fill the container with water from a bucket or garden hose and let the water slowly drip into the soil.

Store-bought drip containers work in a similar way. One, called the Treegator, looks like a heavy-duty plastic sack that opens up so you can place it around a tree. Zip it up and fill its pouch with up to 20 gallons of water; small holes near the bottom let the water drip out at a controlled rate. Treegators are available from Spectrum Products, P.O. Box 18187, Raleigh, NC 276199-8187; (800) 800-7391.

Easy Container Watering

Potted plants can be tricky to water, especially when you're in a hurry. They flood their saucers, and water bounces off leaves and soaks your table or the floor.

You can avoid these problems by using one of the systems described above for watering large tubs and containers. Plastic soda bottles are especially handy for indoor use—their narrow shape fits even medium-size containers. Or try making your own wick-watering system and water from the bottom up. You'll avoid the fuss and muss of watering from above, and your plants can get a drink whenever they need it, even if you're away for a few days.

Let Drip Systems Water Your Ornamental Plantings

Mixed plantings of trees, shrubs, and flowers aren't made for watering with sprinklers—some plants get too much water; others, too little. You can avoid the aggravation of watering individual plants with your hose by installing a drip irrigation system. A well-planned system, like the one shown here, is versatile enough to handle a variety of plant sizes and shapes.

Run the main hose line next to the plants you want watered. Emitters set in the line let water drip out at a steady pace and are perfect for wetting closely spaced plants. For shrubs or other plants off the main line, use spaghetti tubes to send water exactly where it's needed. Use one tube for small plants, two or more for large plants. Cover the entire system with mulch to stop evaporation.

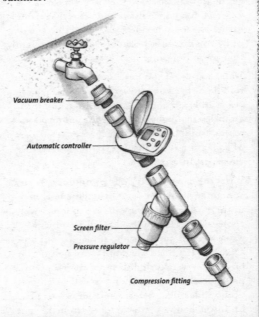

Continued ➡

- It delivers water directly to the plants you want to grow and less is wasted on weeds. And the soil surface between plants remains drier, which discourages weed seeds from sprouting.

Consider Your Options

Depending on your garden size and watering needs, you could get away with a setup as simple as a soaker hose, or you could take the plunge by investing in a full-feature professional kit. Most gardeners opt for something in between. Let's take a closer look at the possibilities.

Soaker hoses. Also known as a weeper hose or oozer hose, this simply is a length of porous hose, often made of recycled tires combined with polyethylene. Water soaks through the entire surface of the hose.

Soaker hoses generally are very durable. They aren't prone to freezing or cracking, and many brands resist the degrading effects of the sun's ultraviolet rays. Still, soaker hoses can come apart or develop leaks if the water pressure is too high—generally, above 10 pounds per square inch. If you remember to never open your faucet more than one-quarter turn, you probably won't have a problem. Or assure yourself of staying within this limit by inserting a pressure regulator disc in the female end of the hose.

Drip tubing with punch-in emitters. These drip kits feature lengths of ½-inch-diameter polyethylene hose in which you insert small plastic emitters. The emitters come in different shapes and can release water at various rates—usually from a half-gallon to 4 gallons per hour.

The main advantage of this type of system versus a soaker hose is that you can target the water so that it is delivered to very specific areas. For instance, if you have shrubs or trees or crops spaced widely apart, you can insert your emitters so that they drip only where the plants are located.

With emitters or a soaker hose, the drip rate can vary from one end of the line to the other-especially if the length exceeds 100 feet and/or your garden slopes significantly. The solution is a drip kit with pressure-compensating emitters, which are designed to put out water at the same rate regardless of the length of the hose or the slope of your yard.

Drip tubing with in-line emitters. These tubes are just like the punch-in type, except that the *emitters* are preinstalled inside the solid polyethylene tube. Typically, the emitters are spaced 12 inches apart all along the length of the hose, but 18-, 24-, and 36-inch spacing is also available.

Drip-irrigation kits. These drip systems come with everything you need—typically a soaker hose, a solid polyvinyl hose, a pressure regulator disc, end caps to close off each length of hose, and various plastic connectors. More-sophisticated systems may even include special filters and backflow preventers.

Putting It All Together

Don't go overboard by buying more watering equipment than you need. In the moderately rainy East, a simple soaker hose can do the trick. For a 5 x 40-foot ornamental border, for instance, two 50-foot lengths of hose should be adequate. Attach them to a single faucet with a twin coupler. When rainfall is scarce, turn on the faucet and let the hoses run for about an hour at a time. You can even let most types stay in place all season long, tucked beneath a couple of inches of mulch.

In drier climates, such as the interior West, you'll probably want a more complete system that can supply water to your entire property. To make the job easier, use electronic timers to turn the water on and off routinely. As the season progresses—and watering needs change—you can program the timer to keep the water running for longer or shorter periods. But if you use a timer, be sure to keep an eye on the

batteries. If they run down, you may not know there's a problem until your plants start to wither.

No matter where you live or what type of drip system you use, the key to success lies in the proper placement of the tubing. Aim to create a zone of continuous moisture below the surface of your growing beds by placing emitters 6 to 18 inches away from the stems of your plants. This will spread moisture broadly below the soil surface and promote a very wide, deep root system. And by placing the drip tubing so that it doesn't drench the very center of the plant's root system, you avoid problems such as root rot.

Another advantage of creating this zone of moisture is that you don't have to worry so much if one or two of the emitters clogs because the overall moisture present in that area of the garden will compensate for the loss of the emitters.

How far apart should you space emitters to create such a moisture zone? For loamy soils, space them 18 inches apart; for sandy soils, keep the emitters 12 inches apart; and for heavy clay soils (which hold water naturally), space emitters 24 inches apart.

Finally, there's the aesthetic question: to bury or not to bury the hoses? Packing your hoses beneath the soil line may look better, but it can cause some problems. Tunneling gophers may be attracted to the sound of the running water and leave you with a munched-through line that you won't notice until your plants begin to fail. Emitters also can clog with soil as a result of the reverse flow that occurs when the system is shut off.

The answer is to compromise. Simply cover the tubing with 1 or 2 inches of mulch. This hides the hoses and assures that your drip lines are easily retrievable at any time for repair or modification.

Drip Irrigation for Free
Roger Yepsen

An old hose, plastic cider jug, or bucket is all you need to tryout the benefits of drip irrigation without spending a dime.

A New Use for an Old Hose

If you have a vintage garden hose that loves to kink and cause trouble, use an electric drill to make tiny holes in the last several feet of its length; install a screw-on cap at that end, and you have a drip irrigation system. For a low-tech timer, set your watch to beep when the watering period is up.

One-Drip-at-a-Time Irrigation

You can use plastic jugs and weary buckets as individual plant waterers. Poke or drill small holes in the bottom, no more than ⅛ inch in diameter, and place these dripping containers next to tomato plants or shrubs. Arrange a few of them in a circle around newly established trees, rather than applying a lot of water all at once and watching most of it run off. To keep the jugs and buckets from blowing away when empty (and to make them less conspicuous), you can set them in the ground. When you make daily rounds with a hose, stop by to give the containers a fill-up.

Ingenious Ways to Water

Barbara Pleasant

Thoughtful Watering

Water is elemental to plant life, and the presence of water in the garden can be as enjoyable as sharing company with beautiful flowers. Yet water is an

increasingly precious commodity, so whether you are using it to nurture plants or treating yourself to the sound of a trickling fountain, water should be regarded as a natural treasure.

In most climates, a gardener's watering challenges change with the seasons. Sometimes there's too much water and other times there's not enough, so finding ways to even out your garden's water supply makes perfect sense.

WATERING YOUR GARDEN'S NEIGHBORHOODS

Smart gardeners understand that watering needs are rarely uniform from one end of their landscape to the other. Instead, most yards are comprised of ecological "neighborhoods"—some bright and sunny, some cool and shady. Some have rich, loamy soil that holds moisture well, while others are sandy and dry. Each district of a garden provides a suitable home for some plants, while others would feel out of place in the same spot. A good gardener is like a city planner who gets to know each neighborhood and delivers water services where they are needed most.

To promote harmony in your garden's neighborhoods, try to group plants with similar watering needs together—you'll save time and water this way, and the plants will appreciate it, too. The watering needs of vegetables should be addressed on a crop-by-crop basis in keeping with their growth cycles. With flowers, use the plant lists at right to design a colorful landscape in which plants are matched to the naturally available water supply and the amount of water you are willing—and able—to provide.

Shaping Up a Water-Wise Harden

From the earliest days of agriculture, humankind has learned to shape the land into furrows, swales, and terraces to maximize the benefits of rainfall, minimize runoff, or channel away excess water when cloudbursts bring too much of a good thing. Shifting your garden's shape to help it handle water better requires a little forethought and spadework, but it doesn't have to cost a cent and is one of the simplest ways to satisfy plants' needs for moisture.

CONTOURS THAT CONSERVE WATER

If your garden tends to need more water than nature provides, there are several ways to add contours to help move water toward plant roots, and keep it there until plants have a chance to make use of it. Here are several approaches to consider.

- Plant vegetables in furrows or shallow trenches, and dam the ends with a mound of earth. This strategy turns planting rows into shallow moats. Should rain become abundant, simply make breaks in the sides the furrows to allow excess water to drain away.

- In chronically dry climates, conserve scant water with sunken beds. To make a sunken bed, dig out the soil at least 12 inches deep, and set it aside. Mix half of the excavated soil with an equal amount of compost or other organic matter, and refill the pit with this mixture. Use the remaining soil to make wall-like mounds around the bed. In addition to channeling water toward thirsty plants, the walls above the bed will reduce water loss due to evaporation and wind.

- When setting out large plants, create a shallow basin over the root zone, enclosed by a raised ring of soil or mulch. Water will pool inside the basin and then seep down into the soil below. These basins can be 6 to 10 inches in diameter for tomatoes, roses, and small shrubs, or up to 3 feet across for larger shrubs and fruit trees.

- To slow the runoff down a slope, create natural barriers by hilling up berms across the slope.

Continued ➡

Plant them with densely rooted perennials such as daylilies or clump-forming ornamental grasses.

- Terrace hillside gardens to create a series of level tiers. Each terrace will retain water that would otherwise rush down the slope.

FLOOD-PROOFING WET AREAS

In high rainfall areas, too much water causes as many problems as does too little water in other areas. Using raised beds will go a long way toward reducing damage to plants caused by waterlogged roots. You can also use large containers to grow plants that are sensitive to flooding. To carry away the torrents of water that flow from your gutters and then wash across your lawn, incorporate a Rock Swale into your landscape's design. Even when no water is present, a curving Rock Swale suggests the fluid presence of water.

Do make sure that the water that runs through the swale ends near a storm drain, or in some other place where it will not cause damage to your property, your garden beds, or a neighbor's property. And, in some instances, it's wise to check with local zoning authorities before installing a swale that will channel water toward roadways, sidewalks, and utility areas.

Keeping the Water You Have

Conserving water makes more sense than pouring it on, week after week. You'll save time and slash water bills if you take simple steps to minimize water loss due to evaporation. You can't control the weather factors that increase evaporation—intense sun and dry air—but you can reduce water loss by taming persistent wind and by using mulches and highly efficient watering methods such as soaker hoses or drip irrigation.

MOISTURE AND MULCH

Mulch forms a physical barrier between sun and soil, and the same mulches you use to prevent weeds and add organic matter to your soil can be strong allies in your quest to conserve water. When water conservation is a priority, one of the smartest strategies is to layer coarse mulch materials over a base mulch of newspapers. By some estimates, a 3-inch layer of mulch reduces evaporation loss by 50 percent, and most mulches cool the soil, too. Mulch also traps and holds additional moisture from rain at the surface, which raises the humidity level around plants. In very dry weather, a slight increase in humidity can enhance pollination of corn, tomatoes, and several other vegetables.

If you are using a stationary watering system such as soaker hoses wait until after the watering system is in place to pile on the mulch. That way, all of the water you provide will be insulated from surface evaporation, and the mulch will protect rubber or plastic drip lines from degrading due to exposure to strong sun.

Heavy mulching does sometimes have a drawback. Moist mulches create an ideal habitat for leaf-eating slugs and snails. If you don't have slug problems in your garden, have your mulches in place before your dry season begins.

WATER-SAVING WINDBREAKS

Wind pushes evaporation into high gear, so using windbreaks is a fundamental way to conserve water. Windbreaks can serve other purposes, too, such as reducing the physical torture plants endure as they struggle to stay upright. The windbreaks described in chapter 5 are designed to turn a wind-chilled garden into a warm oasis of calm, but when your goal is to conserve moisture, it helps if the windbreak also provides filtered shade to the root zones of plants. This is exactly what happens if you use a Snow Fence Windbreak, which has saved many a tomato patch from drying to a crisp in arid Southwest gardens.

Ways to Water

There is no such thing as a garden that never needs its keeper to provide supplemental water. How much water plants need depends on soil, weather, and the plant itself. For example, established plants growing in porous, sandy soil usually need 1 inch of water per week in warm weather, while plants situated in moisture-retentive clay soils demand only half as much water. On the other hand, germinating seeds need constant moisture; shallow-rooted crops grow best when the soil never becomes truly dry; and tomatoes and some other vegetables develop physiological problems such as cracked fruits or blossom end rot when soil moisture fluctuates between wet and dry. Depending on the size of your garden, you may use one or several of the following four methods to deliver water to thirsty plants.

Hand watering is the most practical way to make sure germinating seeds and newly transplanted seedlings have adequate moisture, or to provide water to plants growing in containers, small raised beds, or other tight spots. Use adjustable nozzles to change the force of water when watering directly from a hose; a strong spray dislodges aphids and some other insects, but a softer shower is gentler to plant leaves. If you keep numerous containers, a Watering Wand is a valuable accessory when watering by hand.

Drip irrigation, in which small drips of water slowly ooze out of a drip hose or perforated container, is extremely efficient and effective when the drips are targeted to reach plant roots. If you install a large system, turn it on before you plant so you will know exactly where the puddles of moisture are located. Smaller drip buckets and bottles are an easy way to water widely spaced plants or closely planted beds.

Soaker hoses weep moisture evenly along their length, and they can be curved if needed to match the contours of your beds. A soaker hose left on for several hours at very low pressure provides excellent deep penetration of water, yet the plants' leaves remain dry. Keep soaker hoses short, to less than 50 feet long, because long soaker hoses often release more water close to the water source, and noticeably less near the end of the hose. Soaker hoses work beautifully when used beneath mulch. You can buy soaker hoses made from recycled tires at most garden centers.

Sprinklers are much less efficient than other watering methods, yet they are a practical way to water large areas of lawn or expansive plantings of flowers or vegetables. It is best to use sprinklers in the morning, or early enough in the evening to allow time for foliage to dry before nightfall. Pulsing a sprinkler by running it for 15 to 20 minutes, interspersed with 10-minute breaks, helps water to penetrate deeply into the soil.

WHEN TO WATER

How can you tell when your plants need water? Wiggling your finger into the soil is a good test. If the soil feels dry knuckle-deep in containers or between shallow-rooted plants, make plans to water. Checking the soil is often a more reliable method than simply watching your plants. Almost all vegetables and flowers wilt in the middle of a hot day, but midday wilting does not always tell a true story of what is going on below the ground. If the plants regain their perky posture by nightfall, they probably do not need supplemental water—unless they are at a life stage where any moisture shortage can lead to drought stress. The peculiar water needs of 18 popular home garden vegetables—and the best ways to satisfy those needs—are summarized below.

Working with Hoses

As time-consuming as watering with a hose can be, it's a mainstay of most gardens. When water is needed for a new planting—or to revive a plant that's unexpectedly run dry—turning on the faucet provides the fastest form of relief. The best-

equipped gardeners own two types of hoses: high-quality, heavy-duty hoses that don't kink when moved around, and a comparatively inexpensive hose with thin walls that's easy to cut and splice.

As for your good hoses, they will last for many years and be well worth their initial cost if you give them good care. Coil a hose when it is not in use, either by arranging it in a figure eight on the ground, or by winding it around a hose reel. Start with the female end (the larger fitting that screws on over a smaller one) when you coil a hose; that way, the male end (which attaches to nozzles, sprinklers, or soaker hoses) will be at the top when you need to use it. Drain hoses before storing them for winter. When storing a hose, connect the male and female ends together to keep insects or debris from getting inside.

Because bad things often happen to good hoses, it's wise to buy a few basic hose repair items when you purchase a hose. On the hose aisle at any hardware or home supply store you will also find male and female couplers, as well as splicing kits for repairing hoses that accidentally get chopped by mowers or spades. As long as these fittings match the diameter of your hose, installing them is a simple matter of trimming the hose end with a utility knife, soaking it in hot water for a few minutes to make it more pliable, and then screwing on the fittings.

HANDY HOSE ACCESSORIES

You can make life easier for yourself and increase the versatility and efficiency of a hose by installing various accessories.

- Save wear and tear on your faucet—and your back—by adding a 3- to 4-foot-long extension hose to your outdoor faucet. Then attach other hoses to this extension. To make an extension, use a utility knife to cut through the hose 4 feet from its female end, and install a male coupler to the cut end. If your outdoor faucet is hidden behind dense or prickly shrubs, add a second faucet mounted on a wood board to your hose extension.

- A splitter, often called a Y connector, allows two hoses to be attached to one faucet. With a splitter, you can keep a hose attached to one outlet and use the other for filling watering cans, rinsing produce, or washing your hands. Look for a splitter that has shut-off valves for each outlet. You also can buy four-way splitters, sometimes called gang connectors, that allow up to four hoses to run off of a single faucet. When doubling or quadrupling your outlets, bear in mind that the water pressure will be reduced by each hose you run simultaneously.

- Snap connectors take the frustration out of screwing and unscrewing hose connectors, which have an uncanny talent for going on crooked, so you end up sprayed with water when you turn on the faucet. Snap connectors screw onto the end of a hose, and you put matching connectors on nozzles, sprinklers, or other water-handling hardware.

- A simple mechanical or battery-operated timer between the faucet and the hose allows you to precisely control how long the water stays on, and makes it safe to forget that you left a sprinkler running. If you don't have a timer, other tricks to help you remember to turn off the water include using a kitchen timer, clipping a clothespin to your shirt, or slipping a hair scrunchie or big rubber band over your wrist. When you notice these odd accessories, you'll remember to turn off the water.

Extend a Hard-to-Reach Spigot

Tired of dodging spiders as you shimmy into the shrubs to turn on your faucet? Install a temporary

Continued ➡

twin faucet on the open side of the shrubs, which can be connected to the primary faucet with a short piece of hose. When winter comes, simply unscrew the hose, pull up the mounting board, and store the second spigot in your garage.

Don't be intimidated by the strange-sounding plumbing parts used to make this project. Any hardware store can provide you with the materials for a few dollars, and they will fit together like pieces of a puzzle.

You Will Need

Tools: Handsaw, drill with 7/8-inch bit, two adjustable wrenches, screwdriver, hammer
One 2-foot-long 1 x 4 pine or cedar board
1 tube of latex/silicone caulk
1 roll of Teflon plumber's tape
One ¾-inch x 1½-inch pipe nipple
One ¾-inch brass sillcock with threaded inlet (spigot made for mounting)
One ¾-inch lock washer
One ¾-inch male-female pipe-thread to hose-thread adapter
One 1½-inch-long wood screw
Small piece of scrap lumber
2 female hose couplers
Piece of ¾-inch garden hose long enough to reach between the two spigots

1. Use the handsaw to make two 45-degree cuts at one end of the 1 x 4 to form a rough V-shaped point.

2. At the other end of the board, 3 inches from the end, drill a 7/8-inch hole in the center of the board. Spread caulk around the hole on both sides.

3. Wrap a single thickness of Teflon tape around the threads on the pipe nipple, which will help to tightly seat the threads when the other pieces are screwed into place. Stretch the tape slightly as you wrap it around the pipe nipple.

4. Insert the nipple through the hole in the board. Using both wrenches, tighten the faucet into position on one end, leaving at least ½ inch of the pipe nipple exposed on the other side of the board.

5. On the back side of the board, place the lock washer over the end of the pipe nipple, and then screw on the pipe-thread to hose-thread adapter. Use two wrenches to firmly tighten the faucet and the adapter.

6. When the faucet is oriented correctly, position a wood screw in its retaining slot and screw it into the board. Place the piece of scrap lumber over the top of the mounting board, and drive the pointed end of the plank into the ground with a hammer.

7. Install female couplers onto both ends of the piece of hose. Connect the new spigot to the old one with the piece of garden hose.

Make a Long-Handled Watering Wand

After 10 minutes using a Long-Handled Watering Wand, you will feel as though your arms have grown 3 feet longer—a miraculous change that makes it much easier to water containers using a hose rather than a watering can. A Watering Wand also lengthens your reach in the garden, making the root zones of plants in the middle of a bed much more accessible. In a pinch, you can even let your watering wand do double duty as a sprinkler by slipping the end of the wood handle into a PVC pipe sleeve.

You Will Need

Tools: Utility knife, measuring tape, handsaw, screwdriver
One 4-foot piece of garden hose
One male hose coupler
One female hose coupler

1 wood broom or mop handle, or a 30-inch-long ¾-inch wood dowel
Four #20 metal hose clamps
1 small roll of duct tape
1 adjustable spray nozzle with cut-off valve

1. If needed, trim the ends of the hose with the utility knife before installing the male hose coupler at one end, and the female coupler at the other.

2. Cut the broom handle or ¾-inch dowel to 30 inches long.

3. The male (small) end of the hose will be at the head of your wand, so line it up with the dowel until it is 1 inch beyond the end of the dowel. Install a hose clamp over the dowel and the hose, ½ inch from the end of the dowel. Tighten it firmly, but don't crimp the hose wall.

4. Space the other hose clamps at regular intervals, with the last clamp 1 to 2 inches from the end of the dowel.

5. In the spaces between the two lowest clamps, wrap the hose and dowel together with duct tape to create a hand grip.

6. Screw the nozzle onto the top of the wand.

Make a Working Rain Barrel

The basic idea behind rain barrels couldn't be simpler: Just put a barrel under a downspout, and every time it rains, you'll store up water. You can tap the full barrel by opening the spigot installed near the bottom, or by dipping water out with a pail or handled saucepan. If the barrel is higher than your garden, a hose can be attached to feed the water into a drip or soaker hose system.

Keep the following safety precautions in mind as you plan this project.

- Make sure the lid is completely childproof and mosquito-resistant. If mosquitoes do get into the water, keep them from breeding by adding a doughnut of *Bacillus thuringiensis israelensis*—a safe biological pesticide often used in water gardens.

- Find a barrel that was used to store food products or soap rather than chemicals. If you can't find a used barrel, buy a feed barrel at a farm supply store, or use a plastic garbage can.

- Never drink water from your rain barrel.

You Will Need

Tools: Level, screwdriver, hacksaw, saber saw or coping saw, drill with 5/8-inch bit, adjustable wrench
Gravel
2 concrete blocks
One 50-gallon or similar-size plastic barrel or sturdy plastic garbage can
2 downspout elbows
One piece of downspout long enough to connect the elbows to the existing downspout
Twelve ½-inch No. 8 self-tapping sheet-metal screws
1 square foot of window screen
One ½-inch boiler drain (downward-facing faucet)
1 tube of latex/silicone caulk
One 9/16-inch rubber O-ring
Two ½-inch plastic basin locknuts
6 feet of ½-inch-diameter vinyl tubing
One ½-inch-to-½-inch nylon barb adapter

1. Prepare the site by leveling the ground beneath the downspout leaving a very gentle slope away from the foundation. Place 2 inches of gravel on the ground, and position the concrete blocks to support the barrel.

2. Find the seam in the downspout closest to 6 foot height. Remove the screws and then the downspout. Store these pieces so you can reinstall them in winter.

3. Assemble the downspout elbows and hold them over the barrel so the lower end is 2 inches above the barrel's top and the upper end is under the downspout. Measure and cut a piece of downspout to link the elbow assembly with the existing downspout. Screw the pieces into place.

4. Use the saber saw or coping saw to create a hole 6 inches in diameter in the top of the barrel beneath the downspout elbow. Screw the scrap of window screen over the hole to keep debris and mosquitoes away from the standing water inside.

5. To install the spigot (boiler drain), drill a 5/8-inch diameter hole in the side of the barrel 2 inches above the bottom, or just above where the side straightens vertically. Drill a second 5/8-inch diameter hole 3 inches below the top rim of the barrel, about 8 inches to one side of the lower hole. This will be the outlet for the overflow pipe.

6. Coat outside of the lower hole with caulk. Slip the O-ring over the threads of the boiler drain, and then screw on one of the basin locknuts. Push the threaded pipe part of the boiler drain through the lower hole from the outside. On the inside of the barrel, coat the edges of the hole with caulk, and then screw the second basin locknut onto the back of the boiler drain. Use the adjustable wrench to tighten both of the locknuts.

7. Coat both sides of the upper hole with caulk. Push the vinyl tubing onto one end of the barb adapter, and push the other end into the hole. Allow the sealants to dry overnight.

8. Use a hose to run several gallons of water through the gutter and into the barrel. Check to make sure it is firmly seated, and also check for leaks around the spigot. Tuck the overflow pipe behind the barrel. When heavy rains fill the barrel, position the overflow pipe to direct water away from the foundation of your house.

Make a Bucket Drip System

This simple gravity drip irrigation system is comprised of a 5-gallon plastic bucket that is raised to chest height and then connected to two drip irrigation tapes. Similar systems are widely used in underdeveloped countries, and they have a proven track record of delivering enough water to grow excellent crops when no other water is available. In your garden, a bucket drip system can save hours of watering time over the course of a growing season. Hand-watering a 25-foot row with a watering can takes about 15 minutes, but you can refill the bucket reservoir in less than 5 minutes. In addition, none of the water is lost to evaporation, and the plants' leaves remain dry while their roots receive the moisture they need.

A Bucket Drip System also can solve the problem of maintaining moist soil conditions for newly planted seeds, and may mean the difference between success and failure when you are planting carrots or broccoli for fall harvest during the hot days of summer. And, during severe droughts when water use is restricted, you can fill the bucket reservoir with slightly used water saved from washing dishes.

Don't be discouraged by the length of the supplies list for this project. All are inexpensive to buy. If you can't find irrigation tape and fittings at a local farm supply store, you can order them by mail. A 100-foot roll of irrigation tape (enough to make two bucket drip systems), plus fittings, costs only about $15. You also may want to innovate with the stand; any stand that lifts the reservoir pail at least 3 feet off the ground will work. At the end of the season, simply detach the irrigation tubes and rinse them off. When they are dry, roll them up and store them inside the bucket. With good care, they will last from 3 to 5 years.

Continued ➡

You Will Need

Tools: Hammer, spade or post-hole digger, drill, utility knife
Two 5-foot-long wood posts or 2 x 4 pine boards
Two 16-inch-long pieces of 2 x 4 pine
Eight 3-inch nails
One 5-gallon plastic pail, preferably with lid
One 5-foot-long piece of garden hose
One female hose coupler
One 2-inch square of polyester window screening
One rubber band
1 small tube of latex/silicone caulk
One male hose coupler
1 hose splitter (Y connector)
50 feet of 100-mil polyethylene irrigation tape
2 irrigation tape end caps
2 irrigation hose starter fittings

1. To assemble the stand for the reservoir bucket, place the two 5-foot posts or boards on a level surface, 16 inches apart. Six inches from the tops of the posts, nail a 16-inch piece of 2 x 4 on the side of the posts. Flip the stand over, and nail a second 2 x 4 to the other side.

2. Dig postholes and set the stand at the end of a 30-inch-wide, 25-foot-long garden row. Ideally, the row should slope very slightly away from the stand.

3. Drill a hole in the bottom of the 5-gallon plastic pail. It should be only large enough to allow the hose to pass through it.

4. Install a female coupler on one end of the hose. Place the piece of screening over the coupler opening, and secure it tightly with a rubber band.

5. Working inside the pail, pass the bare end of the hose through the hole in the bottom, and pull the hose through until the screen-covered end is just above the hole. Coat the inside and outside of the hole with silicone caulk, and seat the female coupler securely over the hole. Allow the caulk to dry.

6. Install the male coupler to the other end of the hose, and screw on the splitter. Place the bucket assembly on the stand.

7. Measure and cut two 25-foot-long pieces of irrigation tape. Place them in parallel lines down the length of the row, 10 inches apart. Install the two end caps at the far ends of the irrigation tape. Install the two hose starter fittings at the ends close to the reservoir, and attach them to the splitter.

8. Fill the reservoir pail with water, and cover it with a lid to keep out insects and debris. Observe where the water forms wet spots along the irrigation tapes. Plant seeds or plants in these wet spots. When the plants are established, weed the row and spread mulch over the irrigation tapes. Refill the reservoir pail whenever your plants need supplemental water.

Small-Scale Drippers

You can't beat the Bucket Drip System for watering closely spaced plants growing in a row, but there are other ways to drip water to widely spaced tomatoes and peppers, densely planted raised beds, or trees and shrubs scattered around your yard. Here are seven small-scale slow drippers that will save you watering time and make sure water reaches deep into the soil. When they're refilled with water from a hose or watering can, very little water will be lost to evaporation.

Flowerpot Reservoirs

Unglazed clay pots slowly lose moisture through their porous walls, and the least expensive clay pots are the most porous ones of all. To use clay pots as water reservoirs in raised beds, cover the drainage holes in several 4-inch pots with duct tape, and bury the pots almost to their rims among your plants. Fill the pots with water, and cover the tops with 4-inch-diameter disks of cardboard. The pots will empty slowly, over a period of 2 to 3 days, and are easily refilled with a hose or watering can.

Leaky Jugs

Some of the most versatile water drippers can be made from plastic milk jugs or other large drink containers. Use a hammer and a thin finishing nail to tap two holes in one side of the jug or bottle, about 1 inch from the bottom. Fill the jug with water, cap it, and carry it upside down to a plant that needs water. Place it on the ground right side up, with the holes facing the plant. You may need to loosen the cap a bit before it will start dripping. When most of the water has dripped into the soil below, the inch left behind will keep the jug or bottle from blowing away. If you live in a very windy area, you can drop several small rocks into your Leaky Jugs to give them extra weight.

Dripper Pails

If you can't reach the root zones of some plants with Leaky Jugs, or you need to water plants growing in containers, try a Dripper Pail made by inserting narrow tubing into a hole drilled into the side of a plastic pail, about one inch from the bottom. For the tubing, try the inexpensive tubing used to repair window screens, called spline. Insert the spline through the hole in the pail, caulk it into place on both sides of the pail, and place the end of the spline where you want the water to drip. As long as the pail is raised slightly higher than the outlet tube, it will slowly drip out water. If the water drips too fast, slow it down by placing a small piece of sponge over the end of the spline inside the pail.

Slow Soaker Pipes

Deep watering is sometimes a challenge, especially in clay soil. To make sure your plants receive water 12 inches below the surface, make Slow Soaker Pipes from 14-inch-long pieces of 2-inch-diameter PVC pipe. Drill several ¼-inch holes in one end of the pipe, and pound it into the soil around thirsty plants. Pull it back out, clear the plug of soil inside the pipe, and pound it back into the ground. Then simply fill the pipe with water as you water your plants.

Buried Bottles

If you know you will be faced with water shortages, plan ahead by including Buried Bottles in your planting rows. Cut the bottoms from 2-liter soda bottles or half-gallon plastic milk jugs, leaving about ½ inch of plastic intact on the "cutting" line so the bottoms form hinged lids that can be bent back. Bury the bottles spout side down between plants, with the open bottoms 2 inches above the soil line. Open the bottoms to fill the bottles, and let the water seep into the ground.

Wine Bag Waterer

The double plastic bags and attached spigots that come in boxed wine make great little water reservoirs. Cut the corner from the bag opposite the spigot, fill the bag with water, and loosely bind the cut edges together with a rubber band. Use a second rubber band to bind the top of the bag to a stake. Open the spigot very slightly, so a drip comes out every few seconds. If the bag has a push-button spigot, wedge a toothpick into the button to keep it partially depressed.

Seeping Cooler

Put an old cooler to work as a movable drip irrigator. Place the cooler near plants that need water, fill it with a hose, and partially open the drain so that water dribbles out slowly. Meanwhile, you can move on to other tasks with the hose.

Using Soaker Hoses

Unlike drip watering devices, which oftell use gravity to move water from a reservoir into the soil, soaker hoses depend on low water pressure to push water through porous hose walls, or through small holes. Purchased soaker hoses can be snaked among plants and then covered with mulch, which makes them last longer by protecting them from sunlight. When buying a soaker hose, look for brands made from recycled materials. If you accidentally run over a soaker hose with your mower and need to repair it, the same couplers or other connecting hardware used for regular hoses can be used to fix a damaged soaker hose.

A slightly different type of soaker hose, called a sprinkler hose, has thousands of tiny holes or slits that emit a fine spray when turned hole-side-up, or work like soaker hoses when turned hole-side-down. A sprinkler hose is less efficient than a soaker hose, and may cause soil erosion around plants if the pressure is turned too high.

As long as you keep them short, homemade soaker hoses made by punching small holes into regular garden hoses will often do a good job. However, be prepared to see some holes emitting lots of water, while others weep very little. You can solve this problem by making a Crybaby Soaker Hose (sidebar) or by wrapping your homemade soaker hose with strips of cloth, tightly tied in place. The fabric will help slow down water that moves through oversize holes a little too fast.

Smart Soaking

How many soaker hoses do you need, and where should you put them? Soil is a big variable, because soil type affects how water soaks into it.

- In sandy soil, water moves downward quickly, so soaker hoses should be placed closer together and run for only 1 to 2 hours. For example, if you have sandy soil, you need 2 soaker hoses to thoroughly water one 14-inch-wide row. If no rain comes, you will need to run your watering system again in a few days.

- Loamy soil takes up water more evenly, so soaker hoses can be 12 inches apart and still give excellent penetration when turned on for about 3 hours every 4 to 5 days.

- Clay soils absorb water very slowly, so it's important to give soaker hoses plenty of time, at very low pressure, in order to deliver water deep into clay soil. When left on overnight, a single soaker hose will often rehydrate a 16-inch-wide band of clay soil. Depending on weather conditions, clay soil may retain enough moisture to keep plants happy for more than a week.

Keep in mind that soaker hoses begin putting out water in the section of hose closest to the water source, so there is often a big difference in water output between the head and tail ends of very long hoses. This is seldom a problem when soaker hoses are kept to less than 50 feet long.

Continued ➡

The Flower Garden

INTRODUCTION

Planting Flower Gardens

Jeff Cox

What can brighten a yard like flowers? They add color to any yard, whether you use them along the front of your foundation planting, to line a walk leading to a patio, to brighten a shady spot, or throughout your entire landscape. A cutting garden can bring the beauty of flowers into your home—watch a winter-bare bed erupt with purple crocuses and golden daffodils, or the late autumn sun set behind a planting of purple asters and yellow goldenrod, and you won't be able to resist growing more.

In this chapter, you'll learn how to plan and grow a garden full of flowers—annuals, perennials, biennials, bulbs, and roses. You'll also learn how to maintain your garden and keep away pests and diseases, create a meadow, and grow the best flowers for cutting and drying.

Before you get started, you'll find it's helpful to learn about the different types of flowers.

Landscaping

Although you can use all types of flowers throughout your yard, there are ways to use perennials, annuals, and bulbs to best advantage. Here are some suggestions that will help you plan ways to use them in your landscape.

LANDSCAPING WITH PERENNIALS

Perennials are all-purpose plants—you can grow them wherever you garden and in any part of your garden. There's a perennial to fit almost any spot in the landscape, and with a little planning, it's possible to have them in bloom throughout the frost-free months. In addition to an endless variety of sizes, shapes, colors, and plant habits, there are perennials for nearly any cultural condition your garden has to offer.

Most perennials prefer loamy soil with even moisture and full sun. Gardeners who have these conditions to offer have the widest selection of plants from which to choose. However, there are dozens of perennials for shady sites, too.

Perennials add beauty, permanence, and seasonal rhythm to any landscape. Their yearly growth and flowering cycles are fun to follow—it's always exciting to see the first peonies pushing out of the ground in April or the asters braving another November day. Here are some ways to use perennials effectively in your yard.

Borders: If you have a fairly long area that could use some color, such as a fence, a rock wall, or the side of a building, consider a perennial border. Group plants with similar requirements for soil, moisture, and sunlight. Also plan for pleasing color combinations and arrange them by height, form, and texture to create garden pictures.

Beds: Another way to use perennials is in beds. A bed differs from a border in that it is freestanding, without an immediate background such as a fence or wall. Plant beds to add color and drama to the sides of a path, use them to define the edge of a patio or deck, or create an island bed in your lawn to relieve all that green with a bright splash of color. Plant the tallest plants in the center of the bed, using progressively shorter plants toward the edges.

Specimen plants: Larger perennials make striking specimen plants. You can use them in the landscape wherever you want an accent but don't want to feature something as large or heavy-looking as a shrub or tree. Try a large clump of peonies at the corner of the house or use a specimen plant to point visitors to a specific view of the yard or mark the beginning of a path. For example, use a bold accent like a very large-leaved hosta at a bend in a shady garden path to attract attention and pull visitors into the garden.

LANDSCAPING WITH ANNUALS

When most people think of annuals they think of color, and lots of it. Annuals are garden favorites because of their continuous season-long bloom. Colors run the spectrum from cool to hot, subtle to shocking. Plants are as varied in form, texture, and size as they are in color.

Continued →

Annuals have as many uses as there are places to use them. They are excellent for providing garden color from early summer until frost. They fill in gaps between newly planted perennials. They are popular as cut flowers. Annuals can make even the shadiest areas of the late-summer garden brighter. And since you replace annuals every year, you can create new garden designs with different color schemes as often as you would like.

You can use annuals alone or in combination with perennials or other kinds of plants. Bedding out is the traditional way of using annuals. The Victorians created extensive, colorful displays, usually with intricate patterns against emerald lawns, called bedding schemes. That's why annuals are often called bedding plants.

You can take a tip from the Victorians and create formal or informal designs in island beds or in borders. Fences, hedges, and brick or stone walls all make attractive backdrops for annual gardens. Annuals are also a good choice for outlining or edging garden spaces. Petunias, marigolds, begonias, and zinnias are ideal for beds in the sunny garden.

Many perennials are slow-growing by nature, so the average perennial garden takes up to three years to look its best. Annuals are perfect for filling in the gaps between new perennials and carrying the garden through the first few seasons. Take care not to crowd or overwhelm the permanent plants—try mid-season pruning or staking of overly enthusiastic annuals.

Landscaping with Bulbs

In spring, most gardeners' fancies turn to thoughts of bulbs—especially crocuses, daffodils, and tulips. But bulbs light up the garden throughout the year. Dahlias, lilies, glads, and many other familiar flowers are classified as bulbs. Here are some effective ways to use bulbs in your landscape.

Bulbs with groundcovers: Bulbs grow beautifully in groundcovers. There's nothing like a dark green groundcover background to make daffodils sparkle. Try them with pachysandra, English ivy, prostrate junipers, or common periwinkle (*Vinca minor*). Lawn grass is one groundcover that does not combine well with tall spring bulbs like daffodils. The reason is simple: Bulb foliage needs 8 to 12 weeks to ripen after bloom so the bulb can store enough food for the following season. By the time the daffodil or tulip foliage is ripe, the grass would be knee-high! If you enjoy the sight of blooming bulbs in your lawn, plant low-growing species like crocuses because their foliage generally matures before grass needs cutting.

Bulbs with perennials: With the exception of tender bulbs like cannas (*Canna* spp.) and dahlias that must be dug every year or treated as annuals, bulbs are perennial and should be used like perennial flowers. In fact, they're ideal companions for perennials. In spring, bulbs add color to the perennial garden when little else is in bloom, and perennials hide unsightly bulb foliage while it ripens. Peonies, hostas, daylilies, irises, and asters are especially good with bulbs.

Bulbs with trees and shrubs: Don't forget the beautiful show spring-blooming bulbs make under deciduous trees and shrubs. For best results, avoid planting bulbs under trees such as beeches and some maples that have very aggressive surface roots, which will outcompete the bulbs.

Bulbs with annuals: Annuals are perfect plants for covering dying bulb foliage or gaps in the flower border left by dormant bulbs. Marigolds, snapdragons, wax begonias, impatiens, and zinnias are all good "filler" annuals.

Bulbs with other bulbs: Don't forget about planting bulbs with bulbs. Clumps of mixed daffodils, or scatterings of other types of spring-blooming bulbs such as tulips or crocuses are well-known signs of spring.

Designing a Garden

Designing a flower garden—especially one that features perennials—may seem overwhelming at first since there are so many to choose from. But chances are your growing conditions are right for only a fraction of what's available. Let your moisture, soil, and light conditions limit the plants you choose. If you have a garden bed that gets full sun and tends toward dry soil, don't plant shade- and moisture-loving perennials like hostas and ferns. Instead, put in plants that like full sun and don't like wet feet, like daylilies and ornamental grasses. And don't forget to choose plants that are hardy in your area.

The first step in planning a flower garden is to choose the site you'd like to plant. If you're determined to grow sun-loving plants, the site should receive six to eight hours of direct sun. It's also best to select a site with good air circulation and shelter from strong winds. Take some time to examine your chosen site and learn about its soil and other characteristics so you can select plants that will grow well there.

When you've picked a site, outline the shape and size of your proposed bed right on the spot with a garden hose or string. Next, draw a rough sketch showing the shape of the bed, then measure and record the dimensions. Indicate north on your sketch with an arrow. Next, draw the shape of your bed or border to scale on a piece of graph paper. A good scale to begin with is one that assumes 1 inch on paper equals 1 foot of garden area. If your garden is extremely large, use a formula such as 1 inch equals 2 feet or 1 inch equals 3 feet. To make a plant list and draw a design, you'll also need regular and colored pencils or crayons, a tablet of paper (for plant lists), tracing paper, and a soft eraser.

To get an idea of how many plants you'll need, consider the approximate size at maturity of the types of plants you want to include in your garden. Perennial plants generally need 2 to 4 square feet at maturity; that means you can fit between 30 and 60 of them in a 125-square-foot garden. Shrubs and small trees may need 9 to 25 square feet or more.

Selecting Plants

While it's relatively easy to plan and plant an annual garden, selecting plants for a perennial garden is a challenge. There are literally thousands to choose from and a confusing array of flower colors, sizes, shapes, and textures. Start with a list of favorite plants, then add ones you've admired in other gardens, nurseries, photographs, books, magazines, and nursery catalogs. Leave plenty of

space between plants for making notes. Jot down plant descriptions, growing tips, bloom time, height, color, hardiness, and culture.

Keep an eye out for perennials with good foliage and a long season of bloom. Trees and shrubs with winter interest—like evergreens or ones with ornamental bark or branching habits—are also invaluable. Don't worry about making your list too long.

Periodically review your list and cross off plants that won't grow well in the site and don't fit your needs. If you have only shade to offer, cross off plants that need full sun. Do you want only easy-care plants? Eliminate those that need staking or deadheading to look their best. Do you want to save on water bills? Cross off any that may need supplemental watering.

Charting Your Selections

Next, make a chart to help identify plants that will add the most to your design. On a clean sheet of paper, make a column on the left labeled "Plant Name and Bloom Season." Draw lines across the page at intervals to indicate sections for each season of bloom. If you have a large garden, you can use a separate sheet for each bloom season. Write down the bloom seasons you want in the first column—early, mid-, and late summer, for example. Leave enough space under each season to list plant names.

Divide the right side of the paper into three or four columns to indicate plant heights and another three or four columns to indicate flower colors. Add an extra column to indicate plants with attractive foliage or winter interest.

Starting with the first plant on your list, enter it under the appropriate bloom season on your chart. Then indicate height and color with an "X" in the appropriate columns. Repeat this process for each plant on your list. When you finish, look the chart over to make sure you have a fairly equal representation of "X's" under each column. Will some flowers of each color be blooming in each season? Are there a variety of heights? Add and subtract plants until you have a balance in all the categories and a manageable number of plants to grow. Last, number the plants on your list. Use these numbers to fill in the spaces as you draw your garden.

Drawing Your Design

To draw your design, use tracing paper over the scale drawing of your garden that you made on graph paper. That way, you can start over easily if you need to. Begin drawing shapes on the paper to indicate where each plant will grow. Try to draw them to scale, based on the sizes you charted as described above. Instead of drawing neat circles or blocks, use oval or oblong shapes that will flow into one another.

Arrange plants, especially perennials and small shrubs, in clumps of several plants. Because of the

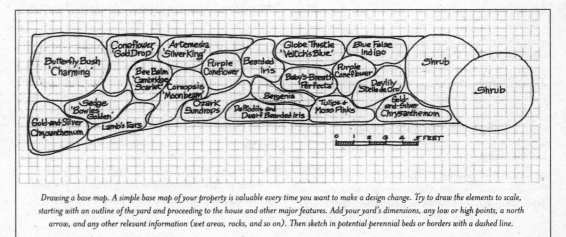

Drawing a base map. A simple base map of your property is valuable every time you want to make a design change. Try to draw the elements to scale, starting with an outline of the yard and proceeding to the house and other major features. Add your yard's dimensions, any low or high points, a north arrow, and any other relevant information (wet areas, rocks, and so on). Then sketch in potential perennial beds or borders with a dashed line.

Continued →

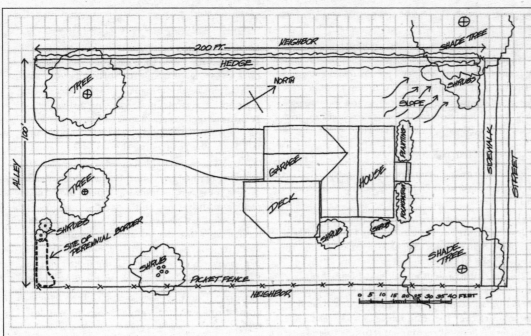

Making a bubble diagram. When you have an idea of the size and shape of your garden, draw its outline to scale on graph paper (1 inch on paper to 1 foot of ground is a good scale for most gardens). Use a pencil so you can "move" things around easily, and don't be afraid to make changes. Then draw in circles or "bubbles" to represent your perennials, making the scale of each bubble match the mature width of the plant. Write in the plant name, color, and bloom season in each bubble if you have room so you can see at a glance how good the combinations are likely to look.

basic design principles of balance and repetition, you'll want to repeat clumps of at least some species. As a general rule, you'll probably want half as many species of plants on your list as the number of individual plants you can fit in your border.

Beginning with the first plant on your list, study its "profile" and decide where you want to plant it in the garden. Transfer its name or number to the corresponding shape—or shapes if you want to repeat it in more than one spot—on your diagram. Do this with all the plants that are on your list.

As you work, you'll have to decide how many of each plant you want to grow. You may wish to follow the "rule of three" for perennials that are relatively small at maturity. Three plants will make an attractive clump when mature. For large plants, such as peonies, you may want only one plant; for others, two. Also consider color combinations as you work, and avoid large masses of single colors.

As you grapple with these problems and refine your design, be sure to make changes on both the tracing paper and your master diagram. Expect to have to redo your design several times before you feel you have it right. Each sheet of crumpled paper brings you closer to your goal of creating a beautiful garden.

When you're ready to make your garden plan a reality, it's time to head out to the nursery or pick up the plant catalogs and buy your plants.

Maintaining the Garden

Your flower garden will need basic routine care to keep it in top-notch form. If you've prepared the soil well before planting, planted carefully, and mulched your garden, you'll be well on your way to a healthy, vigorous garden. Here are some points for keeping your flowers looking their best.

START WITH THE BASICS

Weeding, watering, staking—these are just a few of the regular chores required to keep your flower garden blooming beautifully. The care you lavish upon your flower garden throughout the year will pay off with strong growth and flowering year after year. Here's a rundown on the basics of garden care.

Weeding: Weeds compete for water, nutrients, and light, so weeding is a necessary evil. Catch them while they're small and the task will seem easier. A light mulch of bark or shredded leaves allows water to infiltrate and keeps the weeds down.

Watering: Most plants need 1 inch per week for best growth. Bog and pond plants require a continual supply of water. Dry-soil plants are more tolerant of a low water supply, but during the hottest summer months, even they may need watering. Water with a soaker hose where possible and mulch to conserve soil moisture and cut down on watering.

Staking: Staking may be necessary for thin-stemmed plants such as coreopsis, yarrow, and garden phlox. Extremely tall plants such as delphiniums require sturdy stakes to keep flower spikes from snapping off. Heavy, mounding flowers like peonies may need hoop supports (circular wire supports set up on legs) to keep their faces out of the mud. You can also stake up a clump of plants by circling it with twine, then tying the twine to a sturdy stake.

Pinching: Pinching keeps plants bushy. Plants like chrysanthemums and asters have a tendency to grow tall and flop. Pinch them once or twice in the spring to encourage production of side shoots. Early pinching promotes compact growth without sacrificing bloom.

Thinning: Plants like delphiniums and phlox produce so many stems that the growth becomes crowded and vigor is reduced. Cut out excess stems to increase air circulation and promote larger flowers on the remaining stems.

Disbudding: Disbudding is another technique used to increase flower size. Peonies and chrysanthemums produce many buds around each main bud. Simply pinch off all but the largest bud to improve your floral display.

Deadheading: Removing spent flowers will help promote production of new buds in many plants. Just pinch or cut off faded flowers, or shear bushy plants just below the flower heads if the plant blooms all at once. Some perennials like baptisias and 'Autumn Joy' sedum will not rebloom, and their seed heads are decorative. Leave these for winter interest in the garden.

Winterizing: In autumn, begin preparing the perennial garden for winter. Remove dead foliage and old flowers. After the first frost, cut down dead stems and remove to the ground other growth that will die. (Leave ornamental grasses and other plants that add winter interest.) After the ground freezes, protect plants from root damage as a result of frost heaving with a thick mulch of oak leaves or marsh hay. Evergreen boughs are also good for this purpose. Snow is the best insulator of all, but most of us can't count on continuous snow cover. Mulching helps keep the ground frozen during periods of warm weather.

Dividing: Sooner or later, even the slow-growing perennials become crowded and need dividing. Divide plants in spring or fall in the North and in the fall in the South. (Some plants, such as peonies, should only be dug in the fall.) Some fast growers like bee balms, chrysanthemums, and asters should be lifted every 2 to 3 years. Other perennials such as peonies, daylilies, and hostas only need dividing when they've become overgrown. You'll know a clump is overgrown because it looks crowded, doesn't have as large or as many blooms as it used to, and may have died out in the center.

Controlling Pests and Diseases: The best way to avoid problems is with good cultural practices, good maintenance, and early detection. Healthy plants develop fewer problems. Here are a few simple tips:

- Water early in the day to enable plants to dry before evening. This helps prevent leaf spots and other fungal and bacterial problems.
- Don't overwater. Waterlogged soil is an invitation to root rot organisms.
- Remove old flowers and yellowing foliage to destroy hiding places for pests.
- Remove plants that develop viral infections and dispose of them.
- Never put diseased plants in the compost.
- Early detection of insects means easy control. Many insects can be controlled by treating the plants with a spray of water from a hose. Treat severe infestations with appropriate organic control such as a soap-spray solution. Follow label recommendations.

Growing Roses

The rose is the best-loved flower of all time, a symbol of beauty and love. Roses have it all—color, fragrance, and great shape. Many roses produce flowers from early summer until frost, often beginning the first year of planting.

The members of the genus *Rosa* are prickly stemmed shrubs with a wide range of heights and growth habits. There are as many as 200 species and thousands of cultivars, from miniatures less than 6 inches tall to rampant climbers growing to 20 feet or more. And you can find roses in gardens in just about every climate around the world.

Over the years, roses have gained a reputation for being difficult to grow. But many of the "old roses," plus a great number of the newer cultivars, are disease-resistant, widely adaptable plants able to withstand cold winters and hot summers.

SELECTING ROSES

With so many roses available, deciding on the ones you want may be the hardest part of growing them. To begin making choices, it helps to understand the differences among roses. This large, diverse genus can be divided into three major types: bush, climbing, and shrub roses.

Bush roses: Bush roses form the largest category, which has been divided into six subgroups: hybrid

Continued ➡

tea polyantha, floribunda, grandiflora, miniature, heritage (old), and tree (standard) roses. Here's a rundown:

- Hybrid tea roses usually have narrow buds, each borne singly on a long stem, with large, many-petaled flowers on plants 3 to 5 feet tall. Hybrid teas bloom repeatedly over the entire growing season.

- Polyantha roses are short, compact plants with small flowers produced abundantly in large clusters throughout the growing season. Plants are very hardy and easy to grow.

- Floribunda roses were derived from crosses between hybrid teas and polyanthas. They are hardy, compact plants with medium-sized flowers borne profusely in short-stemmed clusters. They bloom all summer long and are easily grown.

- Grandiflora roses are tall (5 to 6 feet), narrow plants bearing large flowers in long-stemmed clusters from summer through fall.

- Miniature roses are diminutive, with both flowers and foliage proportionately smaller. Most are quite hardy and bloom freely and repeatedly.

- Heritage (old) roses are a widely diverse group available prior to 1867, the date of the introduction of the first hybrid tea rose. Plant and flower forms, hardiness, and ease of growth vary considerably; some bloom only once, while others flower repeatedly. Among the most popular of the old roses are the albas, bourbons, centifolias, damasks, gallicas, mosses, and portlands; also some species roses.

- Tree (standard) roses are created when any rose is bud-grafted onto a specially grown trunk 1 to 6 feet tall.

Climbing roses: Roses don't truly climb, but the long, flexible canes of certain roses make it possible to attach them to supports such as fences, arbors, and trellises. The two main types are large-flowered climbers, with thick, sturdy canes growing to 10 feet long and blooms produced throughout the summer; and ramblers, with thin canes growing 20 feet or more and flowers borne in early summer.

Shrub roses: Shrub roses grow broadly upright with numerous arching canes reaching 4 to 12 feet tall. Most are very hardy and easily grown. Some only bloom once in early summer, while others bloom repeatedly during the summer. Many produce showy red or scarlet fruits called hips. Some species roses are considered shrub roses.

Groundcover roses: Groundcover roses are sometimes included with shrub roses. These have prostrate, creeping canes producing low mounds; there are once-blooming and repeat-blooming cultivars.

USING ROSES IN THE LANDSCAPE

To grow well, roses need a site that gets full sun at least 6 hours a day, with humus-rich soil and good drainage. If these conditions are met, you can use roses just about anywhere in the landscape. Try roses in foundation plantings, shrub borders, along walks and driveways, surrounding patios, decks, and terraces, or in flower beds and borders. Combine roses with other plants, especially other shrubs or perennials. You'll get the greatest visual impact by massing roses of a single color or cultivar.

Use climbing roses to cover walls, screen or frame views, or decorate fences, arbors, trellises, and gazebos. Grow groundcover roses on banks or trailing over walls. Plant hedges of shrub, grandiflora, and floribunda roses. For a single-row hedge, space plants 2 feet apart; for a wider hedge,

stagger rows with 1½ feet between rows and 2½ feet between plants.

You can also grow roses in containers. For all roses except miniatures, choose a container at least 14 inches deep and 1½ feet wide. You can grow miniatures in pots as small as 6 inches in diameter. Use a soilless potting mix; fertilize and water regularly. In all but frost-free climates, overwinter pots in an unheated garage or basement.

GROWING GOOD ROSES

The key to growing roses successfully is to remember that they need plenty of water, humus, and nutrients.

Soil: Prepare a new site in fall for planting the following spring, or in summer for fall planting. If you plan to grow roses with existing plants, then no special preparation is needed. For a new site, dig or till the soil to a depth of at least 1 foot. Evenly distribute a 4-inch layer of organic material such as peat moss, compost, leaf mold, or dehydrated cow manure over the soil surface. Also spread on fertilizer. A general recommendation is to add 5 pounds of bonemeal and 10 pounds of greensand or granite dust per 100 square feet. Dig or till the fertilizer and soil amendments into the soil.

Planting: For much of the West Coast, South, and Southwest, or wherever winter temperatures reach no colder than 10°F, the best time to plant bareroot roses is January and February. In slightly colder areas, fall planting gives roses a chance to establish a sturdy root system before growth starts. In areas with very cold winters, plant bareroot roses in spring, several weeks before the last frost. For all but miniature and shrub roses, space roses 2 to 3 feet apart in colder areas; 3 to 4 feet apart in warmer regions where they'll grow larger. Space miniatures 1 to 2 feet apart; shrub roses 4 to 6 feet apart.

To plant bareroot roses, dig each hole 15 to 18 inches wide and deep, or large enough for roots to spread out. Form a soil cone in the planting hole. Removing any broken or damaged roots or canes, position the rose on the cone, spreading out its roots. Place the bud union (the point where the cultivar is grafted onto its rootstock) even with the soil surface in mild climates and 1 to 2 inches below the soil surface in areas where temperatures fall below the freezing point.

Add soil around the roots, making sure there are no air pockets, until the hole is three-fourths full. Fill the hole with water, allow it to soak in, and refill. Make sure the bud union is at the correct level. Finish filling the hole with soil and lightly tamp. Trim canes back to 8 inches, making cuts ¼ inch above an outward-facing bud and at a 45 degree angle. To prevent the canes from drying out, mound lightly moist soil over the rose bush. Gently remove it when growth starts in one to two weeks.

Plant container grown roses as you would any container plant.

Water: Ample water, combined with good drainage, is fundamental to rose growth. The key is to water slowly and deeply, soaking the ground at least 16 inches deep with each watering. Water in the early morning, so if foliage gets wet, it can dry quickly. Use a soaker hose, drip irrigation system, or a hose with a bubbler attachment on the end. Roses grown in containers must be watered much more frequently. Check containers daily during the summer.

Mulch: An organic mulch conserves moisture, improves the garden's appearance, inhibits weed growth, keeps the soil cool, and slowly adds nutrients to the soil. Spread 2 to 4 inches of mulch

evenly around the plants, leaving several inches unmulched around the stem of each rose.

Fertilizing: Feed newly planted roses 4 to 6 weeks after planting. From then on, for roses that bloom once a year, fertilize in early spring. Feed established, repeat-blooming roses three times during the growing season: in early spring just as the growth starts, in early summer when flower buds have formed, and about six weeks before the first fall frost. The last feeding should have no nitrogen.

Use a commercial balanced organic plant food containing nitrogen, phosphorus, and potassium, or mix your own, combining 2 parts blood meal, 1 part rock phosphate, and 4 parts wood ashes for a 4-5-4 fertilizer. Use about ½ cup for each plant, scratching it into the soil around the plant and watering well. As an alternative, apply dehydrated cow manure and bonemeal in the spring and use fish emulsion or manure tea for the other feedings.

Pruning: Prune in early spring to keep hybrid tea, grandiflora, and floribunda roses vigorous and blooming. Many of the newer shrub-type roses need very little pruning. Heritage, species, and climbing roses that bloom once a year bear flowers on the previous year's growth. Prune these as soon as blooming is over, cutting the main shoots back by one-third and removing any small, twig growth. Remove suckers coming up from the rootstock of any rose whenever you see them.

In the first pruning of the season, just as growth starts, remove any dead or damaged wood back to healthy, white-centered wood. Make each pruning cut at an angle ¼ inch above an outward-facing bud eye, which is a dormant growing point at the base of a leaf stalk. This stimulates outward-facing new growth. Also remove any weak or crossing canes. Later in the season, remove any diseased growth and faded flowers on repeat-blooming roses, cutting the stem just above the first five-leaflet leaf below the flower.

Winter protection: In areas with winter temperatures no lower than 20°F, no winter protection is necessary. Elsewhere, apply winter protection after the first frost and just before the first hard freeze. Many shrub roses as well as some of the polyanthas, floribundas, and miniatures need only minimal winter protection. Hybrid teas, grandifloras, and some floribundas and heritage roses usually require more.

Remove all leaves from the plants and from the ground around them and destroy them. Apply a fungicidal soap spray containing sulfur. Apply ¼ cup of greensand around each plant and water well. Prune plants to one-half their height and tie canes together with twine.

Where winter temperatures drop to 0°F, make an 8-inch mound of coarse compost, shredded bark, leaves, or soil around the base of each plant. In colder areas, make the mound 1 foot deep. Provide extra protection with another layer of pine needles or branches, straw, or leaves. Where temperatures reach -5°F or colder, remove the canes of large-flowered, repeat-blooming climbers from supports, lay them on the ground, and cover both the base and the canes.

Flowers the Low-Maintenance Way

Barbara W. Ellis, Joan Benjamin, and Deborah L. Martin

Flowers can be great care consumers, but few of us would want to be without them. The instant or anticipated charm of beautiful blossoms is a big incentive for clearing space in the schedule for flower gardening. For example, who objects to taking time to plant a six-pack of colorful zinnias or petunias? Designing flower gardens may seem

Continued ➡

like an intimidating task, but in this section you'll find simple guidelines to follow that can take most of the fuss out of garden design. With forethought and smart plant choices, you can create gorgeous plantings that don't demand lots of maintenance. In some cases, planting well-designed flower beds can even reduce the amount of time you usually spend on other routine yard chores, such as mowing the lawn or trimming around trees.

A Credo for Low-Work Gardening: Don't Fight Your Site

A near-holy commandment for the low-maintenance gardener is: Match the plant to the site. Instead of trying to change difficult conditions with soil amendments or raised beds, select plants that will thrive as is. Most common garden annuals—and many herbs—are suited only for average to good soil and good drainage. But among the huge selection of flowering perennials, bulbs, vines, and grasses available, you're sure to find plants suited to any garden situation. It makes sense to use those that will thrive instead of those that will struggle for survival.

For example, broaden your garden horizons with wildflowers that are naturally suited to difficult conditions. Do a little homework before buying, and search out nearby nurseries or specialty-seed sources. Buy seeds in single-species packets, not prepackaged mixes, for better impact and to avoid later thinning.

Whether Controlled or Care-Free, Flowers Can Be Nearly Maintenance-Free

Flower gardens can have a neat, controlled look, with every plant assigned its own particular place. Or, they can run with a looser rein, creating an informal "country garden" look, with perennials spreading at will and self-sowers filling in the gaps with charming serendipity. Whether you prefer neat or nonchalant is a matter of personal choice. Either type is effective in the low-care landscape. Home landscapes often have opportunities for both types of flower garden—perhaps a disciplined, refined planting as the main display bed, and a wilder bunch out by the mailbox.

The most important thing to remember is to choose plants that suit your style. For a semiformal garden, you'll want plants like irises and hostas that know their place; if you plant self-sowers or fast spreaders, you'll spend hours on hands and knees trying to keep things under control. For the free-wheeling flower bed, focus on plants tht fill in fast, like yarrows, and that drop their seeds with abandon, like cosmos, so that the design of the garden is always an unexpected pleasure.

1. Keep formal beds manicured with mulch. Formal and semiformal gardens are unforgiving of imperfection. Weeds stand out accusatorily in a formal bed. But a controlled planting of well-behaved flowers is still within reach of low-maintenance gardeners, thanks to the miracle of mulch. Mulch smothers weeds and cuts down on watering, two big time-eaters. Plants in semiformal and formal gardens typically have a bit of open space around them, which can be an invitation to weed invasions. Make mulch your best friend, reapplying it whenever new populations of weeds crop up. Once you have a good layer of mulch down, you'll find that weeds yield easily to hand-pulling or a scuffle hoe.

2. Cultivate the country look. The informal jumble of a country garden is a good look for low-care gardeners. Combine reliable perennials, such as bee balms (*Monarda* spp.) and monkshoods (*Aconitum* spp.), with self-sowing annuals and biennials. A low-care garden should include plenty of annuals for color that lasts for weeks, often until frost. Choose annuals that resow themselves year after year. The serendipity of self-sown flowers is a part of the country garden's charm.

Invest in Plants for a Quick-Start Garden

Starting a flower garden by buying plants is more expensive than starting from seed, especially when perennials cost $3 a pot and more. But if you can afford it, it's a great time saver and a good start to a successful garden. You can install plants exactly where you want them, avoiding transplanting and thinning chores.

One-gallon pots—or even three-gallon pots—filled with healthy, vigorous perennials are mighty tempting, but your budget will be better off if you can resist the instant gratification. Four-inch starter pots of perennials may not give you as good a display their first year, but they're a great buy for gardeners on a budget. By the end of the season, the small plants will have caught up to their high-priced brothers, and by next year you probably won't be able to tell the difference.

Keep Mowing in Mind When You Design

Before you fill your yard with flowers, think about the physical layout of your beds and borders. Carefully planned flower plantings will eliminate some of that weekend drudge work behind the mower, but randomly placed beds can mean extra mowing woes.

Plan for flowering slopes. If you've been spending your Saturday mornings dragging a lawn mower up and down that bank behind the mailbox, replace that high-maintenance lawn grass with thick groundcovering perennials like daylilies (*Hemerocallis* spp.), creeping phlox (*Phlox stolonifera*), or pinks (*Dianthus* spp.). Be sure to mulch heavily until the plants are established to prevent weeds from contaminating the plot.

Size pathways to fit your mower. Keep the width of your mower in mind when designing the layout of your flower beds and borders. Allow enough space around and between beds for convenient access, according to the width of your mower deck. Few things are as frustrating—or as time-consuming—as having to add one last pass with the lawn mower to remove a final 6-inch strip of grass. If your mower cuts a 3-foot-wide swath, a 5- or 5½-foot-wide path will be just the right size, allowing some overlap between passes. A smaller 2-foot-wide cutting deck requires a path sized accordingly.

Don't make yourself cut corners. Formal, geometric beds and borders with straight edges and sharp corners are a higher maintenance design than flowing, free-form, informal shapes. Maneuvering your mower around angled turns takes more time and thought than whizzing along the edge of a curved border.

Merge beds to minimize mowing. Combining several small flower beds into one large planting is another way to finish mowing faster. Integrate isolated landscape shrubs into the planting, too, to eliminate the need for mowing around each one. If you have several rose bushes dotted along the front walk, for instance, an underplanting of lavender, alyssum, and creeping thyme will make the roses look less naked and create a small, romantic garden.

Smothering Sod Lets You Spread Your Beds

By applying a super-thick or very dense layer of mulch to the intended flower bed, you are blocking light and air from the grass plants beneath, which eventually give up and die. Eight- to twelve-page sections of newspaper are an effective smothering device. Wet the newspaper with a garden hose to keep it from blowing away as you work. Apply the sections with plenty of overlap so that desperate grass can't force its way through to the air. Then blanket the newspapers with several inches of organic mulch such as aged straw or grass clippings. Top with a thin layer of fine decorative mulch if desired, such as shredded bark or buckwheat hulls. Wet it well. Wait at least three weeks, then plant the bed with perennials or annuals from containers, pulling the mulch aside to dig a planting hole. Remove any grass roots from the backfill. Water thoroughly, and apply 2 inches of mulch around the new plants. By the time the deep mulch rots down at the end of the season, the grass should be dead. Earthworms attracted by the mulch will make the soil below loose and friable.

Like the old Roman Empire, flower gardens have a way of expanding year by year, swallowing lawn as they grow. Turning turf into flowers is one of the more daunting tasks that a low-maintenance gardener faces, but there is an easy way: Simply smother your grass.

Simple Shortcuts for Combining Colors

For most gardeners, planning isn't as much fun as doing. Figuring out color schemes and plant combinations can be frustrating and time-consuming. Dispense with complicated plans and simplify your beds and borders by planting in large blocks of color. You'll get a bigger effect by planting a dozen or more of the same plant to fill a large stretch than you will by mixing plants or colors.

Limit your beds and borders to three main colors to make selecting and placing plants easier and more satisfying. Yellow, white, pink, blue, purple, and gray or silver are effective in any threesome combination. Red and orange are often difficult to weave into the garden. Here are some other simple solutions for using color in your garden.

Settle color clashes with white. There's an easy, no-dig way to soften clashing colors in the garden—separate the clashing combatants with neutral white-flowered annuals. Here's how it works: If your brilliant pink astilbes and bright orange lilies have surprised you by blooming at the same time, fill in between them with white-flowered annuals like impatiens or sweet alyssum to soften and separate the colors. You can move one of the offending colors in the spring or fall, when it's not in bloom. Or separate them permanently with white-flowered perennials that will be in bloom at the same time. Silver-foliaged plants like dusty miller also have the same effect.

Make your yard bigger with blue. It's true, cool colors like blue make things seem farther away than they really are. A garden of blue, soft pink, and white will make your yard seem larger than one planted in red, orange, and yellow. All without having to take care of another square inch.

Start color combinations on your doorstep. Can't decide what color would be right for your garden? How about selecting a color that matches or complements your house's trim? Plant mounds of lavender-blue bellflowers (*Campanula* spp.), spiky clumps of deep violet salvia 'East Friesland', and tall purple Canterbury bells (*C. medium*) beside the stoop to accent a teal-colored door. Remember to keep things in balance—a garden the same color as the house adds nothing to the overall effect.

Continued →

Mustard siding? Yellow flowers would be too much; go with blues instead.

A Word to the Wise: Think Twice before Planting Invasives

Many of the most-expert experts scorn invasive perennials (plants that spread vigorously), but it's all a matter of perspective. If you want a balanced planting in a mixed border, or if you have a small garden, invasives can quickly become major headaches. But if you want to fill a new bed in a hurry or plant an easy-care area, they're a great choice.

When you want hurry-up-and-grow plants, look for perennials that are *stoloniferous*, which means they spread by creeping underground stems. These plants often grow so thickly that they crowd out competing weeds.

Invasive perennials vary in their rate of aggressiveness. Lamb's-ears (*Stachys byzantina*), for instance, is a fairly well-mannered spreader that expands slowly and can be easily kept in line. But a single plant of one of the fastest-spreading perennials, the native sunflower known as Jerusalem artichoke (*Helianthus tuberosus*), can colonize a 4-foot-wide area in just a single year, and its brittle tubers are nearly impossible to remove completely once it gets going.

Some invasives are easy to control by hand-pulling, but others are insistent growers that spring back no matter how often you pull. You're not doing yourself any favors by planting these eager beavers where they'll need to be brought back into bounds a few years down the line. Save them for areas that are isolated from your less-aggressive plants, or use them to create a no-care flower bed along a sidewalk fence. To preserve good neighbor relations, don't plant aggressive invasives near property boundaries.

Is Deadheading Worth Your While?

Peach-leaved bellflower (*Campanula persicifolia*) bears stalks of lovely, soft, lavender-blue flowers, but when blooms fade, blossoms brown quickly and hang on the plant like old laundry. Balloon flower (*Platycodon* spp.) is another perennial that doesn't "self clean." Many gardeners accept faded flowers in the garden, but if you prefer a neat look, you may be better off replacing these plants with those of neater habit. For example, some annuals, such as begonias and Madagascar periwinkle (*Catharanthus roseus*), drop faded flowers and bloom continuously.

On the other hand, many gardeners find deadheading—removing tired and dying flowers—an agreeable chore that doesn't take much time. Even the most dedicated low-maintenance gardener probably won't eliminate daffodils or daylilies from the garden because of their tendency to hang onto faded flowers.

When you do deadhead, suit your technique to the plant. Pinch or clip off old blooms on plants like pansies that have thin stems. Brittle stems, like those on salvia, are easy to break off with the flick of a wrist. Or deflower salvias, petunias, marigolds, and other flowers that bloom all at once in a hurry with hedge clippers.

Twiggy Support for Top-Heavy Flowers

In the formal or semiformal garden, a flower that leans with the wind or its own weight may need a little help to straighten its backbone. A twiggy clipping makes an ideal plant support for flopsy annuals such as spider flower (*Cleome hasslerana*). Such clippings are easy to handle and blend right in among the plants. Strip any leaves off the clippings and leave them to dry in the sun for a day or two. (Otherwise, they may put out roots and begin to grow when you stick them in the garden). Poke the dry branches into the soil so that they are well anchored. Put brush in place earlier in

the season for prone-to-leaning perennials, such as delphiniums, so that flower stems grow up through it.

Planting a Flowerbed: The Traditional Way
Larry Hodgson

You can start a garden the traditional way—by digging up what's already there—if there are no or few tree roots present. If so, thoroughly soak the designated area 24 hours before you begin digging, as slightly moist soil is the easiest to work with.

Start by removing whatever was growing there before. That may be lawn, an abandoned garden, brush, or weeds. If it's sod, cut into the soil about 2 inches deep with a sharp shovel, then slide the shovel under the sod and carefully lift it off. Use good-quality sod elsewhere in your yard, such as fixing a weakened section of lawn. Otherwise, simply compost it. If there is no sod, only weeds or other undesirable plants, dig them out individually. Make sure you get the weeds' entire root systems, or they will just sprout again.

Step 1. Remove brush, weeds, or lawn, making sure to get all roots.

Step 2. Add a layer of 3 to 4 inches (8 to 10 cm) of compost, peat moss, well-decomposed manure, chopped leaves, or other organic matter. Double that amount of the soil is heavy clay.

Step 3. With a garden fork or rotary tiller, work the organic matter into the soil to a depth of 8 to 12 inches (20 to 30 cm). You're now ready to plant!

Add a good layer of compost, peat moss, well-decomposed manure, chopped leaves, or other organic matter, and mix it into the top layer of soil. About 3 to 4 inches (8 to 10 cm) is probably enough in most soils, but if your soil is mostly clay, you might want to double that. Work it in thoroughly to a depth of 8 to 12 inches (20 to 30 cm). If you can use a rotary tiller in the chosen spot, you'll find it worthwhile renting one for this task, as turning over the soil and mixing it with the new amendments can be backbreaking work when done with a shovel or garden fork.

Personally, I gave up using the traditional method of starting a flowerbed years ago. I find it too much work, too slow (it takes about a full weekend just to prepare a medium-size bed), and too traumatic for the soil's microorganisms. Worse yet, turning the soil over that way inevitably leads to great masses of weeds sprouting during the following months. This is a

result of moving dormant weed seeds from under the soil and exposing them to the light, stimulating them to sprout—and of accidentally chopping up rhizomes of invasive species, thus spreading them throughout the garden. Make sure, if you do use the traditional method, you at least put down a thick layer of mulch as soon as you finish; this will bury the weed seeds again and let you get off to a reasonable start. Pull out any weeds sprouting from bits of rhizome as you see them before they begin to take over. The mulch won't stop them, but at least it will keep the soil friable and make pulling them easier.

Also keep in mind that any aggressive tree roots that are present will react to the pruning that was done as you turned over the soil by regrowing massively within a few short weeks. They'll quickly take over the bed again, much to the detriment of the plants you just put in. So if you use the traditional planting method in an area with heavy root competition, try to put in mature plants, as they are better able to cope with competition. Small or young plants are often unable to develop well under such circumstances and die out or grow only very weakly. Even years later, they'll be only a shadow of the plants that were grown using the traditional way with full-size plants or using the fast-and-easy method.

Planting a Flowerbed: The Fast-and-Easy Method
Larry Hodgson

If you have a lot of tree roots in the area where you want to plant your garden, then this is the method to use so you don't disturb tree roots any more than necessary. This is the method I prefer. It's easy to do, as there is no digging involved and no heavy rotary tiller to lug around. It takes only an hour or so to prepare and plant a medium-size garden (the traditional method takes a full weekend). And I like the fact that it resembles Mother Nature's own way of working: You never see her struggling with a rotary tiller. Instead, she simply deposits a new layer of organic material directly on the old layer. Of course, the fact that the resulting bed is weed-free and tree root-free are two more reasons why I prefer this method.

The whole point of this method is to leave the original soil intact. Be it rich or poor, rocky or organic, clay or sand—don't disturb it and don't try to improve it, just leave it as it is. Instead, you'll build a new bed on top of the old one. The old soil will simply become subsoil, and the quality of subsoil is of little importance. Instead, your new plants will be growing in a fresh layer of top-quality, weed-free soil. The microorganisms in what is now the subsoil will slowly move upward into the new layer of soil, as they would in nature when a new layer of fall leaves covers the ground. The natural microflora remain intact instead of being largely destroyed as they are in the traditional method.

Before you begin the fast-and-easy method, you'll need to save up newspaper (you'll see why in a minute). You'll need quite a bit of it for an average-size bed, so start putting it aside a good 2 to 3 weeks before you plan to start.

You'll also need to shop for soil. You don't want just any soil, but the very best. The soil you buy should be rich in organic matter, have a good structure, be perfectly friable, and be completely lacking in weeds. It should not come out of a plastic bag (living soil has to breathe), but from an open pile that has had organic matter added and been turned again and again until all weed roots and weed seeds have burned off (been decomposed). Ask your county extension agent where you

Continued ➡

can find top-quality soil locally. Have it delivered—or, if you have a pick-up or a trailer, go pick it up yourself (it's considerably cheaper that way).

PREPARING A FLOWERBED BY THE FAST-AND-EASY METHOD

Step 1. Cut back vegetation, then cover the area with a thick layer of newspaper.

Step 2. Cover the newspaper with 8 inches (20 cm) of top-quality weed-free soil...and start planting!

The day before you begin your bed, mow the area (if it is in lawn) or use a brush cutter to chop back the vegetation if the area is covered with taller plants. You don't need to remove the resulting residue: Just leave it where it lies. It will decompose and further enrich your soil. When the soil has been delivered or you've trucked it in, you're ready to begin.

On the big day, go pick out your plants from a favorite local nursery (unless you're growing them from seeds or cuttings). Make sure you've worked on your garden plan so you know exactly what you need. Bring them home, place them in a shady spot, and water them thoroughly. Of course, if you're having them delivered from a mail-order nursery, order them several weeks in advance with instructions as to the date you want them. Unwrap them upon arrival and water them well.

That same day, create a temporary barrier that will keep any weeds or other undesirable plants from pushing through the new layer of soil you are about to apply. Remember that in the fast-and-easy method you don't remove the original sod, weeds, or other growth. Instead, cover the entire bed with 5 to 10 sheets of newspaper, thus creating a barrier that efficiently controls the weeds and grasses that used to live there. Blocked under the newspaper barrier, without any access to light, the weeds will die and decompose. I've always felt that turning your enemies (in this case, weeds and invasive grasses) into compost was the best revenge of all! And this method smothers even truly nasty spreading weeds, like goutweed (Aegopodium podagraria), quackgrass (Agropyron repens), and horse-tail (Equisetum arvense). I can't say that I feel the slightest guilt at smothering goutweed! (In case you're worried about the possibility of colored newspaper ink containing lead and contaminating the soil, newspaper ink hasn't contained lead since 1986. Unless you're given to recycling truly old newspaper, there'll be no problem with lead contamination.)

Make sure your layer of newspaper is perfectly intact, with each section thoroughly overlapping the other at the edges; otherwise, the plants below will find a way through. And if you accidentally pierce a hole in your newspaper barrier, cover it up with a few more sheets of newspaper. On windy days, soak the newspaper in water before you apply it so it won't blow away. Then cover the entire newspaper barrier with 8 inches (20 cm) of soil (or 12 inches/30 cm of soil if there are no tree roots to protect) to bring it up to the proper planting depth—and you're ready to plant!

The newspaper barrier will last 6 months to a year, then begin to decompose. That's long enough to kill the undesirable plants, which can't live without light, but not enough to kill the microorganisms from the soil below—nor will it kill underlying tree roots. They'll simply bide their time until the newspaper rots away, then happily move back up into the fresh new soil. The barrier does, however, offer your plants a bit of leeway in establishing themselves. They have about a good 6 months to a year before the tree roots start to move in, and about 18 months before they are back in mass quantities. That gives your plants a deadline to meet: They must be well established, with a healthy root system, within 18 months. If so, they'll be able to compete with the tree roots as equals. If they are poorly established, the tree roots will take over and they'll likely weaken and possibly even die. So give your plants the best of care for the first 18 months, and they'll be able to grow happily for the next 18 years!

After the newspaper is in place, add the new soil on top of it. You'll want to add only a relatively thin layer of fresh soil—adding too thick a layer could smother tree roots, a they need to breathe. Eight inches (20 cm) seems to be just about the right amount. It gives you enough soil to plant in (well, at least you can plant medium-size plants), yet it isn't deep enough to smother tree roots. If there are no roots to protect, go for a full foot (30 cm) of soil: Many of the world's best soils are made up of a mere 1 foot (30 cm) of good topsoil, so why not give your shade garden plants the very best?

Planting Time

Most likely you'll want to plant your flower bed immediately after you've finished preparing the bed—and there's no reason you can't! If for whatever reason you will not be planting within the next few days, though, cover the bed with mulch. The mulch will create a barrier from above to keep weed seeds from floating in and taking over the fresh soil, and it will keep the soil light and friable. You can always push the mulch to one side when it does come time to plant.

Before planting or even unpotting, always set the potted plants out at their proper spacing to test the effect.

OUT OF THE POT, INTO THE GARDEN

Most of the time the plants you'll be using will be growing in pots, with the main exception of bulbs. They may be plants you purchased or ones you grew from seeds or cuttings. Separate the plants according to whether they are to be permanent plants (this will likely include mostly perennials, ferns, shrubs, and any hardy grasses), spring or fall bulbs, or annuals.

The first plants to put in the ground are the permanent ones. In the long run, they'll be taking up most of the space in the garden and will need the best care. Set them on the soil, but don't remove the pots yet. Instead, place them carefully according to their recommended spacing, using a ruler to measure if needed, according to your garden plan. Remember that in most cases, plants (especially smaller ones) will look best when placed together in groups of three or more. Also, stagger your plantings rather than planting in straight lines. Once you have placed all your pots on the soil, move them around and adjust them until the effect is what you want. Then you can begin planting.

For most perennials, ferns, and grasses, a simple hand trowel will be the planting tool of choice, but for larger ones you'll need a shovel. Dig a hole for each plant, about the same depth as the pot is high, and twice as wide. Place the plant, pot and all, into the hole, making sure it is deep enough, then take it out again, adding or removing soil as needed to adjust the height. Add a dusting of mycorrhizal fungi to the bottom and sides of the potting hole. Don't yank the plant out of its pot; you could damage its root system. Instead, turn the plant upside down and, slipping your fingers around the base of the plant so your palm is supporting the rootball, give a sharp rap with the heel of your hand to loosen the pot, then pull it off. If the pot doesn't want to give, you may have to cut it off.

If the rootball of the plant is lightly covered with roots or shows a lot of brown soil, plant it intact. If there are a few circling roots at the base, spread them out before planting. If the entire rootball is covered with many circling roots, that means the plant is rootbound (it's been left in its pot for too long a time). If planted as is, its own roots may remain in a circle and come to strangle it over time! To prevent this, score the rootball with a sharp knife, running it from top to bottom, about ¼ inch (6 mm) deep on all four sides. This will cut the circling roots and force the plant to form new healthy roots that will radiate outward into the fresh soil.

If the plant is rootbound (surrounded by circling roots), score the rootball on four sides to encourage new root growth with a more outward habit.

You may also have plants growing in peat pots. They don't need to be removed: Plant them pot and all. Do cut off any part of the pot that sticks up above the ground; otherwise, it may act as a wick, absorbing water from the soil and causing the plant's root system to dry out.

Continued ➡

Place the plant in its hole so it touches the mycorrhizal inoculum, and half-fill the space around the roots with soil. Water well, filling the hole and waiting until the water drains away (which it should do immediately if the soil is of good quality), then finish filling the hole with soil. Firm it down with your hand, and water well a second time. The "double watering" makes sure that both the lower and upper roots get their share of water.

Finally, don't forget to insert a plant label beside the plant—either one supplied by the nursery or one you've prepared yourself—so you can remember just what you planted and where. There is little more frustrating for a gardener than having a great plant you'd like to talk about, but not having the slightest idea what it is!

When planting, it's best to water twice: first when the planting hole is only halfway full, then when it has been filled in. That way, even the lower roots get their fair share of the water.

PLANTING BAREROOT PLANTS

Not all plants come in pots. You may have received bareroot plants through the mail or have dug up or divided plants from elsewhere. (For example, if you're overhauling an old and not-too successful flowerbed, you will probably have dug out a few survivors that you want to save and put back in the new bed.) These should be kept moist and in a shady spot until planting time. Cover their roots with burlap or landscape fiber, and spray them with water every day (more often if necessary) to prevent the roots from drying out. Don't leave bareroot plants out of the soil for too long, though. If you don't expect to be able to plant them for more than a week, pot them up temporarily in garden soil until you can get to them.

Planting bareroot plants is a bit more complicated than planting potted ones, as it's harder to judge just how deep to plant them. The idea is that, when you finish planting, the crown should be at the same depth as it was originally. You can easily see this, as the parts that were originally underground will be paler in color than those that were exposed to light. However, without a solid rootball beneath them, bareroot plants tend to sink down into the soil after watering. So I suggest digging a larger hole than for potted plants, about twice the depth and width of the roots. In the middle of the planting hole, form a cone of soil and firm it well, then place the base of the plant on this, spreading the roots all around. This cone will hold the plant at the required depth. If the cone is too short or too tall, add or remove soil from the cone and try again. Once the cone is the right height, set the plant on it, again spreading its roots out all around the cone, then sprinkle mycorrhizal inoculum directly on the

roots. Add enough soil to half-fill the planting hole, water thoroughly, then fill the hole completely with soil, tamp down, and water thoroughly a second time.

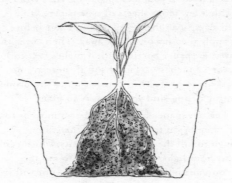

When planting a bareroot plant, create a cone of well-firmed soil and place the base of the plant on this, spreading the roots all around. This will help keep it from sinking into the soil after it is watered.

PLANTING BULBS

If you're planting in fall, before you finish your shade garden with a layer of mulch, consider planting hardy bulbs. You can plant them more easily in a bed of freshly planted perennials, grasses, and ferns than you can in a bed that is established and full of plants. Simply dig a wide but shallow hole in open spaces between plants. It should be about 3 times the height of the bulb and large enough for about 7 to 10 large bulbs (or 20 or more smaller ones), spaced about 3 times their diameter. Add mycorrhizal fungi, place the bulbs in the hole with the pointed side up, half-fill the hole with soil, water thoroughly, then fill the hole, firm the soil, and water a second time.

ANNUALS AS A "JUST BEFORE FINISHING" TOUCH

A first-year bed composed only of hardy, permanent plants like perennials, grasses, ferns, shrubs, and bulbs often looks disappointingly barren. After all, you've probably put in relatively small plants and left room for their future growth, but they probably won't reach their full size for 2 or 3 years—maybe more (plants fill out more slowly in shady spots than when they are grown in the sun). But that's easily fixed: Simply plant shade annuals in the empty spaces! They'll fill in the bed and provide abundant color the first year.

MULCH: THE TRUE FINISHING TOUCH

Of course, the true finishing touch to any shade planting will be a nice, fairly thick layer of mulch: No shade garden should be without one.

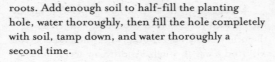

Wildflowers

Barbara W. Ellis

Anyone who has enjoyed the beauty of a spring woodland carpeted with Virginia bluebells (*Mertensia virginica*) and bloodroot (*Sanguinaria canadensis*), or a colorful autumn meadow bursting with butterfly weed (*Asclepias tuberosa*) and goldenrod (*Solidago* spp.), has felt the magic of wildflowers. These plants also hold a special fascination because they thrive in all sorts of conditions—from dry, desert soils to boggy sites, and from full sun to deep shade—all without a gardener's helping hand. Not only are there wildflowers for nearly every part of the garden, they also require little maintenance, provided they're happy with the conditions in which they've been planted.

The key to growing wildflowers successfully is understanding the conditions they require in their

native habitats. Wildflowers will grow best in locations that duplicate their native environments. Soil type, monthly rainfall, annual temperature range, and sunlight or exposure are all important. To pick the best wildflowers for your garden, try to find plants that naturally thrive in the conditions your garden has to offer. If you have a tree-shaded lot with loamy soil, for example, perhaps some of the Eastern woodland wild-flowers such as wild columbine (*Aquilegia canadensis*) or Jacob's ladder (*Polemonium* spp.) would be suitable. Or, if you have a dry, sun-baked spot, consider planting California poppies (*Eschscholzia californica*), a reseeding annual, or one of the hardy prickly-pear cacti (*Opuntia* spp.), which bear brilliant flowers followed by interesting fruit.

Tips for Success

One good way to start developing a list of wildflowers to try in your garden is to look around you. Look at the plants that spring up in vacant lots, along road-sides, or in natural areas of nearby parks or gardens. Although often thought of as mere weeds, if they are growing in conditions similar to what your garden has to offer, they might be perfect prospects. Use a field guide to identify them, if necessary, and then look for them at your local nursery or in a mail-order catalog. You'll be surprised at how many common weeds are offered for sale.

Beware of weeds that live up to that name, however. Many native plants are quite aggressive and can spread very quickly—either by abundant reseeding or by wandering rhizomes—if not kept in check. If you have an out-of-the-way corner, this might be just what you want, but keep these plants away from areas where their thuglike tendencies might pose a problem. Members of the daisy family, Compositae, such as goldenrod (*Solidago* spp.), are notorious.

Don't try to improve upon a wildflower's natural environment. Too much moisture may be stressful for a plant adapted to withstanding summer droughts, and rich soil may lead to lush foliage but little bloom if a plant is native to areas with sandy, poor soil.

Like other plants, wildflowers are sold as seeds, bare-root, or potted. Handle new plants just as you would any annual, perennial, or bulb.

Don't forget the many wildflowers that make superb additions even to formal beds and borders. In fact, many of these plants are grown in gardens so often, we forget they are actually wildflowers.

ACQUIRING WILDFLOWERS

There are several ways to obtain wildflowers to add to your garden. They're offered for sale everywhere. One sad fact to consider when purchasing wild-flowers, however, is that many plants offered for sale were collected in the wild at the expense of native populations. Virtually all of the pink lady's-slipper orchid (*Cypripedium acaule*) plants offered for sale have been wild-collected. And these beautiful native orchids have exacting requirements that nearly always doom them to death once they're dug and moved to a garden. Other plants to avoid are other native orchids; native lilies (*Lilium* species, not the popular hybrid forms); *Trillium* spp.; and carnivorous plants, such as pitcher plants (*Sarracenia* spp. and *Darlingtonia californica*).

Don't buy collected wildflowers. Ask nursery owners about the source of the native plants they sell. Do not dig plants in the wild yourself unless you are participating in an organized conservation program.

So where should you buy? Reputable nurseries are now beginning to refuse to deal in wild-collected plants and are labeling their plants as

Continued ➡

horticulturally propagated. You can also buy wild-flowers from plant sales organized by botanical gardens or local native plant societies. Or propagate your own—many are easy to grow from seed, and fellow gardeners are often happy to share plants via division.

Growing a Wildflower Meadow

For most people, the word meadow brings to mind scenes of large fields filled with grasses, daisies, and other flowering plants. Or perhaps it suggests a vast expanse of prairie with head-high grass as far as the eye can see. More recently, however, the word has been linked to gardening, and gardeners across the country are experimenting with creating their own meadows, both small and large.

MEADOW OPTIONS

There are many ways a meadow or meadow-style garden can be incorporated into the home ground. You can create a stylized meadow border with orna-mental grasses and cultivated forms of native plants such as *Rudbeckia* 'Goldsturm', purple coneflowers (*Echinacea purpurea*), and sneezeweeds (*Helenium* spp.). If you have an uncultivated area, orchard, or old field that you simply mow to keep neat, consider letting it grow up, and sow seed or plant small potted wildflowers to add color.

If you're starting from scratch, you can use a seed mix or start with potted plants. Seed is less expensive and easier to distribute than plants, so it's the choice of most meadow gardeners. The best mixes to select are ones designed especially for your region or garden.

SOWING A MEADOW

Today many seed companies, as well as the seed rack at your local nursery, offer a wide range of wild-flowers, which you can buy either as single species or in meadow mixes. Mixes are available for specific geographic (regional) hardiness ranges or for specific cultural conditions—sun or shade, dry or moist. There are also mixes selected for height and ones designed to attract birds or butterflies. Most meadow mixes will include an annual "nurse grass," which will germinate quickly and help to keep out weeds until the meadow plants have the opportunity to become established.

The key to success is in knowing what plants will do well in your specific gardening environment, and avoiding those that will not do well or that might prove invasive. Contact your local cooperative extension service or wildflower society for plant lists and other recommendations for developing a meadow in your area. Nearby botanical gardens in your area may also have demonstration meadows that you can learn from.

Compare the meadow mixes and wildflower seed offerings from several catalogs. Look at species included, the seed origin, and the price tag. Species that are native to your area will have the best chance of survival and should be tops on your list; avoid potentially invasive species. Since much of the seed offered is wild-collected, look for a statement that indicates the seed has been collected conservatively, so that collection hasn't harmed wild populations. If you collect seed yourself, be sure to do so respon-sibly: Always harvest much less than you leave behind.

Sowing Season. The next item on your agenda is to select the best time for seeding your meadow. Both fall and spring seeding are recommended, since cool daytime temperatures and not-too-cool nights are best for germinating seedlings. As a general rule, fall sowing is best if you live in the southern states (Zone 7 south); spring sowing in the North.

Site Preparation. You'll need to remove existing vegetation to prepare the seedbed. For a small area, try spreading black plastic over the entire site, secure it in place with dirt and rocks around the edges, and leave it for several months. This will kill existing weeds and cause weed seeds in the soil to germinate and die. You can also dig up existing weeds and cut out turfgrass to get ready for sowing. For a large area, you'll probably need to till the area, although deep tilling will often bring dormant weed seeds to the surface. If you do decide to till, plan on tilling several times at two- to three-week intervals to kill weeds that germinate.

Prepare the Seedbed. The next step is to lightly rough the soil's surface, so that the seeds can make good contact with the soil. If you have matched your seed mixture to the site, you shouldn't need to improve the soil unless you really want to.

Spreading Seed. Next, mix the seed with light sand (the white sand used for sandboxes is ideal), using 1 part seed to 4 or 5 parts sand. This will help you keep track of where the seed has been spread and also helps ensure that it's evenly distributed. For small meadows, you can spread by hand; use a crank seed spreader (available in most seed catalogs) for larger meadows. Look at the seed packet for the recom-mended application. Usually, 6 pounds of seed per acre or 4 ounces per 1,000 square feet are about average. Don't sow more thickly than recommended, because seedlings will become crowded and quick-to-germinate species will crowd out ones that get off to a slower start. After sowing, lightly sweep the seedbed with a broom or nearby tree branch to settle seed just below the soil surface.

Aftercare. For best results, a newly seeded meadow will require adequate moisture—either by rain or watering—to ensure that germination takes place and young seedlings have a chance to become estab-lished. A good soaking from the lawn sprinkler every several days is often the difference between success and failure in starting the meadow. Seeds will begin to germinate within seven to ten days after sowing.

ANNUAL MAINTENANCE

Once established, a meadow should require little in the way of annual maintenance. Healthy, established meadow plants don't need watering and fertilizing.

Change Is Natural

Change is a fact of life in a meadow, and in a meadow garden. New plants arrive, add new color, perhaps outcompeting other inhabitants. Some plants spread quickly via their abundantly produced seeds; others disappear because of competition from neighboring plants. Shrub and tree seedlings can move in and begin the transformation from a sunny meadow to a woodland. The changing appearance—both from season to season and year to year—is one of the fascinations of a meadow. It's also one of the reasons for annual maintenance.

You'll need to weed as the need arises. If one species takes over, reestablish a balance by weeding or even removing it altogether. You may need to resow some annuals each year to keep populations healthy. Plan on a bit of hand weeding on a regular basis to remove undesirable plants.

Your meadow also will require an annual mowing to control trees and shrubs that find their way into the meadow, before they can become estab-lished. Mow in late fall or late winter when the plants are dormant. Many gardeners prefer mowing in late winter, because they enjoy the texture and color of the winter meadow and the birds and other creatures it attracts.

The best tool for the job will vary with the size of the meadow. A weed wacker or lawn mower will prove adequate for a small meadow; you'll need a tractor and mower for large meadows. Double-cutting a tractor-mowed meadow (once at a height of 18 inches and once at a height of 6 inches) will produce an excellent seedbed mulch for all of the seed that has dropped to the meadow floor.

Stop Tiptoeing Through the Tulips

Once you've prepared garden beds to a nicely light and fluffy state, it feels just plain wrong to go galumphing over them. Instead of tiptoeing apolo-getically, or threatening your lower back by reaching over the beds to plant, cultivate, and harvest, keep a gangplank on hand—a 2-by-12-inch board of convenient length that you can lay down between rows. The board will distribute your weight, much like a pair of snowshoes. It also can be used to help plant seeds in arrow-straight lines; lightly press its narrow edge into the soil to make an indentation. To give sprouting seeds a break from the sun, support the board on a few bricks as a shade. When the board isn't in use, you can rest it across two or three stacks of cinderblocks as a garden bench.

A sturdy board or two can serve both as a handy bench and as a plank for distributing your weight when it's necessary to stand in a garden row.

Flower Glossary

Annual: An annual is a plant that completes its life cycle in one year; it germinates, grows, flowers, sets seed, and dies in one growing season. Many plants we grow as annuals, such as zonal geraniums, are actually tender perennials.

Hardy annual: An annual that tolerates frost and self-sows. Seeds overwinter outside and germinate the following year. Examples: annual candytuft, cleome.

Half-hardy annual: An annual that can withstand light frost. Seeds can be planted early. Plants can be set out in fall and will bloom the following year. Often called winter annual. Examples: pansies, snapdragons, sweet peas.

Tender annual: An annual that is easily killed by light frost. Most annuals are in this category. Examples: marigolds, petunias.

Biennial: A plant that completes its life cycle in two years, producing a rosette of foliage the first and flowers the second. Biennials can reseed and come back year after year like perennials. Examples: foxglove, sweet William.

Bulb: A diverse group of perennial plants, including true bulbs, corms, rhizomes, and tuberous roots—all structures that store nutrients to support growth and bloom.

True bulb: True bulbs have layers of food-storing scales around a flower stalk and leaves in the center. They're often covered with a papery skin,

Continued ➡

called the *tunic*. Examples: onions, daffodils, tulips, lilies, hyacinths.

Corm: A corm is a rounded, swollen stem covered with a papery tunic. Corms are solid, with a bud on top that produces leaves and flowers. Examples: crocuses, gladioli.

Tuber: Tubers are fleshy underground stems that have eyes or buds from which leaves and flowers grow. Some tubers, such as caladiums and tuberous begonias, are cormlike. Unlike corms, tubers sprout roots from the sides and top. Examples: potatoes, anemones.

Tuberous root: Tuberous roots are swollen, fleshy roots. They have a pointed bud on top; roots sprout from the bottom. Example: dahlias.

Rhizome: Rhizomes masquerade as roots, but are actually thick, horizontal stems with roots on the bottom and leaves and flowers on the top. Examples: callas, cannas, bearded irises.

Little bulbs: A general term used to refer collectively to the many species of small, hardy bulbs, especially spring-blooming ones. Examples: crocuses, snowdrops, squills, grape hyacinths.

Perennial: A plant that flowers and sets seed for two or more seasons. Short-lived perennials like coreopsis and columbines may live 3 to 5 years. Long-lived perennials like peonies may live 100 years or more.

Tender perennial: A perennial plant from tropical or subtropical regions that can't be overwintered outside, except in subtropical regions such as Florida and Southern California. Often grown as annuals. Examples: zonal geraniums, wax begonias, coleus.

Hardy perennial: A perennial plant that tolerates frost. Cold tolerance of hardy perennials is ranked by zone.

Herbaceous perennial: A perennial plant that dies back to the ground each season. Most garden perennials fall into this category.

Semiwoody perennial: A perennial plant that forms woody stems but is much less substantial than a shrub. Examples: lavender, some varieties of thyme.

Woody perennial: A perennial plant such as a shrub or tree that does not die down to the ground each year.

BULBS

Bulbs the Low-Maintenance Way

Barbara W. Ellis, Joan Benjamin, and Deborah L. Martin

Flowering bulbs are so easy and undemanding that every low-maintenance garden should include them. Hardy bulbs, such as daffodils and crocuses, are true workhorses in a low-maintenance garden. So-called tender bulbs, such as caladiums, cannas, and tuberous begonias, are pretty tough customers, too.

In this section, you'll find techniques for succeeding with a variety of bulbs and bulblike plants. After all, what could be easier than a ready-to-grow flower that comes prepackaged with its own food source and blooms over a period of years?

Let Nature Take Its Course in No-Care Bulb Plantings

In an informal landscape, an utterly easy way to use bulbs is to naturalize them. Naturalizing involves planting bulbs into your existing landscape so that they look as if they grew there on their own. For best effect, group them in drifts rather than straight rows. Best of all, once the bulbs are planted and established, your efforts are over.

Good locations for naturalizing bulbs include grassy banks, meadows, property edges, around shrubs, and open woodlands. For naturalizing in your lawn, try small, low-growing bulbs such as crocuses, glory-of-the-snow (*Chionodoxa luciliae*), grape hyacinths (*Muscari* spp.), Grecian windflowers (*Anemone blanda*), striped squills (*Puschkinia scilloides*), miniature narcissus cultivars, netted irises (*Iris reticulata*), Siberian squills (*Scilla siberica*), snowdrops (*Galanthus* spp.), and spring starflowers (*Ipheion uniflorum*).

KEYS TO SUCCESS WITH NATURALIZED PLANTINGS

- Use large quantities of small bulbs for visual impact.
- Plant in loosely defined drifts, leaving space between the bulbs; they'll fill in by naturally dividing and seeding. One way to arrange them quickly is to lightly toss the bulbs and plant them where they land.
- One kind, one color is always effective. At most, limit yourself to two or three species or flower colors in one area.
- Let the bulbs' foliage ripen. When bulbs are planted into lawn, leave the lawn uncut until the bulbs' foliage matures, or subsequent years' flowers will be diminished or even eliminated.
- Keep species' site preferences in mind when you plant. Try crocuses in sunny areas, Siberian squills and daffodils in partial shade, and woodland natives such as winter aconites (*Eranthis* spp.) and trout lilies (*Erythronium* spp.) in shadier locations.
- Match form to function. Formal-looking bulbs can seem out of place in informal plantings. Try grape hyacinths (*Muscari* spp.) instead of stiffly upright Dutch hyacinths (*Hyacinthus orientalis* cultivars); tuck species tulips into your landscape rather than their hybridized offspring.
- Top-dress naturalized bulb plantings with compost or dried manure. Apply in spring, just as the leaves start to emerge, and again in early fall to nourish future flowers.

8 Hints to Help You Buy the Best Bulbs

Starting out with healthy bulbs gets your garden off to a good start and helps keep maintenance at a minimum. Vigorous plants look better and are better able to resist pests and diseases, all with little effort on your part. Use these tips to get the best bulb buys.

1. **Consider the source.** Buying bulbs locally lets you handpick each one, ensuring that you'll get the best they have to offer. However, mail-order companies that specialize in bulbs will have a greater selection. They may offer reduced prices for large quantities of bulbs.

2. **Consider the service.** Look for local suppliers that sell bulbs at planting time, not months before. Reputable mail-order firms will ship

bulbs to you at the proper planting time for your area and guarantee bulb quality.

3. **Shop early in the season.** Placing mail orders early ensures the bulbs you want will be available and that they'll arrive at the proper time for planting. Local retailers will have the best selection early in the planting season.

4. **Select bulbs that like your locale.** Check with garden retailers and your county's extension office to learn which bulbs are right for your region. Remember that winter survival is only half the battle—some bulbs suffer when temperatures soar. Look for bulbs that will endure your local conditions.

5. **Buy the biggest bulbs.** With bulbs, you get what you pay for. Larger bulbs—often called "top size," "jumbo," or "double-nosed"—deliver the best flowers and are more likely to produce new bulbs to increase your flower planting. And they don't take any longer to plant than small bulbs.

6. **Weigh your decisions.** Buy solid bulbs that seem heavy for their size. Soft, lightweight bulbs will grow poorly, if at all.

7. **Inspect and reject.** Don't worry about small tears in the outer covering of bulbs as long as the protective skin is still there. Reject any bulbs that are moldy or showing signs of rot.

8. **Watch out for wild ones.** Collecting bulbs from their native wild habitats has endangered many species. If you buy species bulbs rather than cultivars, ask if they were nursery propagated. If you can't get a satisfactory answer, shop someplace else.

Buying Time for Your Tulips

Among the hardy bulbs, tulips tend to be short-lived perennials, sometimes producing only a couple years of bloom. Given the cost of bulbs and the effort of installing them, this gradual petering out can be a big disappointment. But not all tulips are fickle—some will return tirelessly for several years, and there are ways to encourage them.

Plant species tulips (or botanical tulips). These early-bloomers outlive their hybrid counterparts. Or select cultivars with a reputation for being long-lasting; they're sometimes sold as "perennial tulips." (Three years is perennial in hot climates; they'll last longer in cooler areas.) Plant cultivar tulip bulbs deeply, 8 to 10 inches below the soil.

Plant Combinations Bring Out the Best in Your Bulbs

In addition to keeping your bulbs healthy so they look their best, there are other ways to make the most of blooming bulbs in your landscape. By assembling some easy plant combinations, you can use bulbs to add color and sparkle to your gardens—without a lot of hassle.

Complement and contrast. In a spring garden, between the bulbs, set out low-growing flowers that bloom at the same time as your bulbs. Good bulb companions include pansies, Johnny-jump-ups, wallflowers (*Cheiranthus cheiri*), and forget-me-nots (*Myosotis* spp.). You can also combine taller bulbs like tulips with smaller bulbs like grape hyacinths.

Use flowering trees or shrubs with your bulbs to supply contrasting colors. Try blue squills (*Hyacinthoides non-scriptus*) or glory-of-the-snow (*Chionodoxa luciliae*) near yellow forsythias, or yellow daffodils near white-flowered crabapples.

Combine and cover. Plant your bulbs among spring-flowering perennials such as basketgold (*Aurinia saxatilis*), purple rock cress (*Aubrieta deltoidea*),

Continued ➡

or perennial candytuft (*Iberis sempervirens*). Since spring bulbs virtually disappear from view when their tops die back, perennials planted adjacent to the bulbs can serve as markers to remind you not to dig there later in the season.

Later-blooming perennials that emerge as your bulbs are flowering won't detract from the bulb flowers, yet they'll fill the aboveground spaces left by the bulbs and help to conceal the dying bulb foliage. Many perennials can fill this role, including daylilies, baby's-breath, hostas, and ferns.

Dig In and Double Your Bulbs

An added bulb bonus is their ability to multiply. Without your spending another penny, bulbs such as daffodils and crocuses will increase in number over the years.

If the number of flowers a bulb planting produces begins to decline over the years but there's lots of foliage evident, the bulbs have multiplied, creating a cluster of small, closely spaced bulbs.

After the foliage has faded, dig and separate the bulbs. Replant them right away, at the proper spacing. Given more space, they'll soon grow to flowering size again.

Get Maximum Impact with Minimum Effort

It's as easy to plant a garden of bulbs that blooms for months on end as it is one that blooms for only a few fleeting weeks. Why? Although most hardy bulbs flower in the spring, they don't all flower at the same time. So to make the most of your planting time, it pays to plant an assortment of different bulbs.

For example, some small bulbs like snowdrops and crocuses begin blooming in late winter, while some tulips may not finish flowering until early summer.

One good place to start is to look for the season of bloom in the descriptions of bulbs when you shop, whether you're looking in a local garden center or a catalog. You'll find ratings like "very early spring," "early spring," "mid-spring," and "late spring," for example. To get the longest bloom possible, select some from each season.

Don't just consider different species of bulbs like crocuses and tulips, either. Many bulbs, including daffodils, tulips, and lilies, have a wide variety of species and cultivars that bloom at different seasons, too. You can buy tulips, for example, that will bloom in late winter to very early spring, mid-spring, and late spring to early summer.

Also try using microclimates on your property to vary the bloom time of your bulbs—even if they're all the same cultivar. Microclimates are variations in the prevailing conditions that are caused by factors such as topography, shade, or proximity to buildings. For example, bulbs planted in a site with southern exposure will bloom earlier than the same species planted in a north-facing spot.

Tools to Make Bulb Planting a Breeze

Planting is easiest when you use the tool that works best for you and for the planting design you've chosen. For naturalizing small bulbs in a lawn or other groundcover, a narrow-blade trowel works well, as does a naturalizing tool. An auger attachment for your power drill eases the process of making individual holes for larger bulbs, while a spade is useful for digging a large hole to hold several bulbs.

Naturalizing tool. This crowbarlike tool gives you lots of leverage when planting small bulbs in your lawn. Use it much as you would a trowel, but without the bending—just use your foot to push the soil back after planting each bulb.

Trowel. Stab your trowel, daggerlike, into the soil and pull it toward you to open up a planting hole for a small bulb. Then remove it and tuck the bulb in by pressing the soil back into place.

Bulb planters. Both long- and short-handled bulb planters are useful tools for making individual holes for larger bulbs.

Auger. Turn your power drill into a bulb planter with an auger, which is also useful for digging holes for larger bulbs.

Spade. For excellent effect and a well-prepared planting site, use a classic garden spade to excavate a large hole that will hold many bulbs.

Increase Daffodils' "Face Value" with Good Site Selection

You wouldn't hang your favorite painting facing the wall. Likewise, when you plant daffodils, you want to see their faces—the open, cup-shaped sides of the flowers—not their backs.

When selecting a planting site for daffodils, it's helpful to know that their open blooms will turn toward the direction from which the strongest sunlight comes—usually south to west. Think about where you'll be when you're looking at your daffodils—at your window, perhaps, or coming up your front walk, and position plantings accordingly.

Terrific Techniques for Planting Bulbs

Whatever tool you use to prepare your site, don't skimp on the size of the hole and don't overcrowd. Bulbs planted at the proper depth and spacing live longer and are less subject to injuries from animals or cultivating tools. Try some of the tips that follow to create effective bulb displays throughout your yard.

Tuck in bulbs with single holes. To tuck bulbs between existing plants, such as in a perennial garden, use a spade, auger, or bulb planter to make individual holes.

Plant 'em together if you have the room. If you're planting lots of bulbs in an area that's free of other plants, simply dig a hole to the proper depth and space a group of them out over the bottom of the hole. This planting method maximizes the impact of their blooms and saves you from digging several individual holes.

Plant colorful beds of bulbs in planting areas. You can combine different bulbs and flower colors to create colorful designs anywhere in your yard. For best results, excavate and prepare the entire planting area all at once. Then work out your color and spacing by arranging the bulbs in the bottom of the hole before you cover them.

After planting, water thoroughly to firm the soil and to stimulate root growth. Top-dress the planting with organic fertilizer or compost. If the weeks following planting are dry, water periodically until the ground freezes. Apply mulch in late autumn to keep soil temperatures from fluctuating. Although nothing is visible above ground, vital root growth is occurring below the soil.

Try layering a planting of different-size bulbs. For a lot of pizzazz in a limited space, you can use bulbs with coinciding bloom times for a spectacular one-shot show, or with consecutive bloom for a longer-lasting display. Plant large bulbs deeply, medium-size bulbs above them, and small bulbs an inch or two below the soil surface. Choose bulbs that do not need frequent division; otherwise you may have to dig up the whole planting or put up with diminished flowering from bulbs that have multiplied.

The layered planting of crocuses, Spanish bluebells, and lilies will add color to the garden from early spring into midsummer. The lilies will

hide the fading leaves of the earlier-blooming bulbs. Be sure to offset bulbs slightly from one layer to the next and leave enough soil in between the layers for normal root growth.

Let Soil Temperatures Tell You When to Plant Hardy Bulbs

Fall-planted bulbs need time to put down roots in a new site before the ground freezes for winter. In order to bloom properly, they also need a period of cold, but not freezing, temperatures, called a chilling requirement. Here's an easy guideline you can use to make sure you satisfy both these requirements when you plant: Wait until the soil temperature 6 inches beneath the surface is below 60°F.

This means planting in September in Zones 2–3; in September to early October in Zones 4–5; in October to early November in Zones 6–7; in November to early December in Zone 8; and in December in Zone 9. In regions with mild winters, bulbs like tulips are often given a cold treatment by refrigeration before they are sold for planting in early winter.

Bulbs Bloom Best in Sites Where the Sun Shines Bright

Your bulbs will give you the greatest effect for your effort if you plant them in a sunny site. Most bulbs need strong light to grow and flower well. But if your summer yard looks shady, don't despair. Go for early-flowering spring bulbs that do most of their growing before deciduous trees and shrubs extend their leaves. These bulbs won't grow in sites with heavy, permanent shade, however, such as under evergreens.

Crocuses, daffodils, glory-of-the-snow (*Chionodoxa luciliae*), snowdrops (*Galanthus* spp.), and squills (*Scilla* spp.), as well as early tulip cultivars, are all early bloomers that are quite happy in woodland gardens and other sites with summer shade. And don't miss the chance to deck a woodland garden with these bulbs that will grow in light to partial shade: Checkered lily (*Fritillaria meleagris*), hardy cyclamen (*Cyclamen hederifolium*), trout lilies (*Erythronium* spp.), snowdrops (*Galanthus* spp.), Spanish bluebells (*Hyacinthoides hispanicus*, formerly called *Endymion hispanicus* or *Scilla campanulata*), and winter aconite (*Eranthis hyemalis*).

Help Your Bulbs Live Long and Prosper

Once hardy bulbs are in the ground, they don't need much care. However, there are a few techniques that will pay off by adding years of healthy, vigorous growth to your bulbs' lives.

- Select sound, healthy bulbs and plant them properly.
- Spread about ¼ inch of dried manure over the top of your bulb plantings in spring, just as foliage is beginning to emerge, and again in early fall.
- Mulch plantings to protect the soil, preserve moisture, and prevent weed seeds from germinating. Mulch also keeps mud from splashing on flowers.
- Remove spent flowers from bulbs before seed heads form. This enables each bulb to store food for next year's flowers instead of forming seeds.
- Plant large bulbs like tulips and daffodils at the deep end of the recommended range to slow their rate of multiplication, since the smaller bulbs that result may take several years to reach flowering size.
- Plant lilies with their roots in the shade by mulching the root zone, planting groundcovers around them, or selecting sites where other

Continued ➡

plants or structures shade the roots without blocking sun from the foliage.

- In warm-winter zones, plant bulbs at the deepest end of the recommended range to avoid soil temperature shifts and too-early warming of the soil in spring.
- Select planting sites carefully. While most spring bulbs grow well in full sun in cooler climates, they often do better in light shade in hot climates.

Simple Ways to Hide Bulb Bare Spots

Like your spring bulb garden, but dread a bare plot later in the season? Try one of these simple techniques to keep your soil covered and your garden looking its best.

Grow bulbs with annuals. Sow or set shallow-rooted annuals such as marigolds, snapdragons, or wax begonias above bulbs as they are going dormant. This gives summer cover and color to your bulb site.

Cover your bulbs with groundcovers. Before making this choice, think about how the groundcover will look when the bulbs are blooming. Will it flower at the same time? Will the flower colors complement each other? Good groundcovers to use with bulbs include bugleweed (Ajuga reptans), creeping Jenny (Lysimachia nummularia), spotted lamium (Lamium maculatum), thyme, vinca (Vinca minor), and wintercreeper (Euonymus fortunei). Or try barren strawberry (Waldsteinia spp.), English ivy (Hedera helix), pachysandra, and prostrate junipers over large, deeply planted bulbs.

Tips to Protect Your Bulbs from Beasts

Cute but pesky animals may decide that your bulb plantings are buffet tables located for their convenience. If chipmunks or voles eat up your bulbs, squirrels dig them up, or rabbits, woodchucks, deer, or birds munch on their flowers or foliage, try these techniques to end the tasting.

Plant bulbs that animals don't like. Even hungry animals leave poisonous daffodil bulbs alone; squills (Scilla spp.) and snowdrops (Galanthus spp.) are reported to be similarly unbothered. And the skunky scent of fritillaries (Fritillaria spp.) repels mice, squirrels, and voles from bulb plantings.

Put up a good defense. Take measures to prevent animal problems before they start. Put your bulbs in the ground inside a wire basket or cage—they'll still be able to send out roots and shoots into the soil, but animals won't be able to get to the bulbs. Or place sharp gravel around the bulbs at planting to discourage underground diners. Lay wire mesh on the soil surface above your bulb planting to keep squirrels from digging them up.

Take Time to Try Tender Bulbs

In comparison to their hardy counterparts, tender bulbs can hardly be considered low maintenance. However, many gardeners don't mind the extra effort it takes to grow tender bulbs. Among them are excellent plants for shady sites, such as tuberous begonias, caladiums, and calla lilies (Calla spp.). Gladiolus are tender bulbs that make great cut flowers; dahlias add valuable late-season color.

North of Zone 9, you can handle tender bulbs a couple of ways. For minimal effort, treat tender bulbs as annuals—purchase fresh stock each year and grow them for one season only. Plant them at the proper depth after the soil warms up in spring.

If purchasing them each year is too costly, save money by overwintering them—moving them to a warmer location. Bring potted bulbs indoors and allow them to rest; dig bulbs planted in the garden, then store them using one of the methods shown here. Overwintering tender bulbs takes time but saves the expense of using them as annuals in cold-winter areas.

Hang glads for good air circulation. To store gladiolus corms, shake off the soil and remove the foliage just above the corm. Break off the shriveled old corm under the new one and hang the new corms in plastic mesh bags in a dry, cool (around 45°F) spot.

Store tuberous begonias in vermiculite. After digging tuberous begonias, let the plants dry for a week or so, then cut the stems to just above the tuber. Let stem stubs dry completely, shake the soil off the tubers, and store them in vermiculite, dry peat, or sharp sand at 45° to 55°F.

Store clumps of dahlias. After frost, cut dahlias back to just above the ground, dig the clumps, and store them on their sides until the soil on the tubers dries. Store entire clumps with the soil still on them, or remove the soil and store them in barely moist peat or vermiculite in a plastic bag. Poke holes in the bag for ventilation, and store in a cool (45° to 50°F) spot. Sprinkle a little water on the peat or vermiculite during the winter if the roots wither. In spring cut the clumps up, making sure each piece has a pinkish "eye."

Storing Bulbs the Lazy Way

If you love tender bulbs but hate the bother of digging, packing, and storing them indoors through winter, try this simple technique from Ray Rothenberger, Ph.D., a professor of ornamental horticulture at the University of Missouri at Columbia. Dr. Rothenberger digs his big hybrid glads, Aztec lily (Sprekelia formosissima), Peruvian daffodil (Hymenocallis narcissiflora), and dahlias in the fall before freezing weather arrives. After digging the bulbs, he spreads them on the ground to dry in the shade or, if it's going to rain, indoors in the garage. "I leave soil on the ones that dry out easily, such as some of the dahlias—that way I don't have to fuss with storing them in vermiculite. The only dahlias I pack in vermiculite are those with very thin roots," Dr. Rothenberger says.

When the bulbs dry, he places them in plastic garbage bags, leaving the bags open. As he places the bulbs inside, Dr. Rothenberger makes absolutely sure that any soil clinging to the bulbs is dry, and he looks carefully for sow bugs. Later (when time allows), he checks them again. He flops the tops of the bags over loosely, never tying them shut, and inspects the bulbs periodically throughout the winter, throwing away any that begin to rot.

A Quick Way to Plant Bulbs

You can make quick work of planting bulbs without lifting the first spadeful of soil. "This technique will only work in deeply worked, well-amended, loose soil," says Ray Rothenberger, Ph.D., a professor of ornamental horticulture at the University of Missouri at Columbia, who likes the following technique for planting big bulbs such as Aztec lily (Sprekelia formosissima), Peruvian daffodil (Hymenocallis narcissiflora), dahlias, and hybrid gladiolus:

"The easiest way to do this is to throw down a 2 x 6 in the bed to make it easy to walk on," says Dr. Rothenberger. "Go along the edge of the board, push your spade straight down into the soil, and push it away from you to part the soil. Then you drop the bulb in behind the spade. When you pull the spade straight back out, the hole fills itself." The method (illustrated at left) works for smaller bulbs planted with a trowel, too. Dr. Rothenberger adds that you should never do this when the soil is wet, especially in clay soil, or you'll end up with a wad of concrete.

When you dig bulbs to store for winter, point your shovel straight down in the soil. This guarantees you'll miss the bulb (unless you're standing right over it, of course). Loosen the soil and scoop up the bulb as you dig. If you push the shovel or fork into the soil at an angle toward the bulb you may gash it or cut it through.

Caring for Bulbs, Corms, and Tubers

Unlike some of the prima donnas of the garden, most bulbs are not very fussy. Plant them at the right depth in the right place and you can leave them alone for the rest of the growing season, and in the case of hardy bulbs, for years. That's why you can find Madonna lilies (Lilium candidum) planted 50 years ago still blooming among the crumbled foundations of an old homestead.

But like all garden plants, bulbs will do even better with a little attention to their needs.

CARE BASICS

The bulb is a storage system, a fat underground root or stem full of stored food. These underground pantries were a defense against the harsh climates where bulbs originated. An internal "clock" within the bulb evolved, to teach it to sleep during the baking heat of an African summer or the icy cold of winter in the Chinese mountains. When rain and warmth come again, the clock signals the bulb to start growing, using the stored food. After flowering is done, the leaves make food to replenish the bulb for next year. Then the bulb goes into its dormant period, waiting out the extremes. Successfully growing bulbs is a matter of understanding this cycle of growth and dormancy.

Hardy spring bulbs are planted in fall and begin to grow roots from the time they are planted until the ground freezes. By spring, the roots are well developed and ready to support foliage and flowers.

Watering

If you have planted your bulbs at the recommended depth and given them a good drink to get them started, you will have to water only when the plants look thirsty or during a long dry spell. (Foliage that wilts and stays wilted the next day is a clue that the

Continued ➡

bulb needs water.) It's also a good idea to give your bulbs a long, thorough soaking when the flower buds show.

Don't bother with sprinklers or hand-held spray nozzles. You need to get that water to the roots of the bulb. Either lay the hose among the bulbs to soak into the ground, or use a soaker hose so the water isn't wasted in evaporation. Water long enough to be sure it soaks deep into the ground where the roots of the bulb can drink.

Fertilizing

Fertilizing is especially useful soon after planting, when the roots are beginning to form. That's why it's a good idea to add some aged, well-rotted manure and bonemeal while planting new bulbs or to give old bulbs a boost. Slow-release fertilizers such as bonemeal or special bulb food can be scratched in in the fall.

For summer bloomers, an all-around fertilizer can be used in the spring when the first shoots appear above ground. Gladioli and dahlias are heavy feeders and need regular fortification with compost and aged manure to do their best. Flowers will be bigger if fed regularly after the buds form.

Mulching

A deep mulch over winter is a good idea for hardy bulbs if your soil is susceptible to frost heaving. Unmulched bulbs may be forced out of the ground by repeated cycles of freezing and thawing. If your soil is dry, a mulch during the growing season will help retain water.

Chopped leaves make a perfect mulch and can be left in place to decompose into humus. Straw, grass clippings, or evergreen branches are other possibilities.

Don't worry about new shoots that poke up before freezing weather is over. They are unlikely to be damaged by cold or snow. Sometimes newly planted small bulbs such as grape hyacinths throw out a lot of leaves soon after planting. These leaves will not be harmed by winter weather and do not need to be protected by mulch.

Deadheading

Snip the faded flowers from your large spring bulbs as they finish blooming. If you allow the seedpods to remain, tulips, daffodils, and hyacinth bulbs may exhaust themselves with the effort of making seeds. Deadheading directs the plant's energy into producing food for next year's flowers.

Most summer-flowering bulbs also benefit from deadheading, since more of the plant's energy can go into producing food.

Removing dead flowers from the small spring bulbs like scilla and snowdrops isn't necessary, unless you don't want them to self-sow. But who doesn't want more of these first flowers of spring?

The plants flower in early spring and the flowers fade, but the foliage continues to grow and produce food for the following year. Many bulbs also produce natural divisions called offsets.

Ripening Foliage

Bulb foliage must be allowed to ripen without being cut, tied, or braided. The leaves make food to replenish the bulb for next year. Remove the leaves before they shrivel and die back, and you sap the vigor of the bulb. After the foliage has turned yellow or brown, you can cut it down and add it to the compost heap.

There are plenty of ways to draw attention from the ripening foliage, which can look unkempt and unattractive as it lengthens and then turns yellow. You can plant bulbs among ground covers such as bugleweed (*Ajuga* spp.) or wild ginger (*Asarum canadense*). Late peony-flowered tulips ('Angelique' is an ethereal pink) are lovely overplanted with ferns. Or you can interplant perennials or annuals to mask the maturing foliage. Hostas and daylilies work well to camouflage daffodil leaves.

Lifting Tender Bulbs

Bulbs that are not hardy in cold winters, such as cannas, gladioli, dahlias, and tuberous begonias, must be dug up in fall for storage. After the first light frost, when the foliage has begun to blacken, track down all of your tender summer bloomers and carefully lift them from the beds. A garden fork will do the job nicely. Be sure to dig deep enough to get beneath the bulbs, to avoid that sickening crunch of a fat tuber being sliced in half.

Replanting Stored Bulbs

The new shoots of summer-blooming bulbs such as dahlias and glads are vulnerable to frost, so wait until the weather has warmed and night temperatures stay around 50°F before you put your winter-stored bulbs back into the ground in midspring. You can plant your summer bulbs in pots or shallow boxes of damp peat to give them a head start. They can be set in a sheltered spot outdoors during the day, but be sure to protect them from frost on chilly nights.

Multiplying Bulbs

Fern Marshall Bradley

Bulbs are a lovely addition to your perennial landscape, and many of them gradually propagate themselves naturally over the years. Here are some ways to give nature a hand.

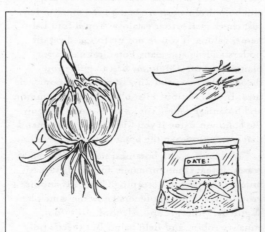

Scaling a lily bulb is a simple technique that lets you start new plants from pieces of the bulb. After your lilies flower, you can dig up the bulbs and pull off the outer scales. Given the proper conditions, the scales will produce new tiny bulbs that you can pot up.
Step 1. Gently break the scales off the bulb.
Step 2. Put the scales into a plastic bag with a few handfuls of moist vermiculite. Label and seal the bag with a pillow of air inside. Put the bag in a warm (70°F), dark place. After two months, check the scales for tiny bulbs every two weeks.

True Bulbs

Bulbs that look like onions are "true" bulbs. Daffodils, grape hyacinths (*Muscari* spp.), and snowdrops (*Galanthus* spp.) are common examples of true bulbs that multiply rapidly. The easiest way to help them spread is to divide the clumps every few years. Wait until the foliage starts to turn yellow, then dig them carefully and separate the clump. Replant them immediately at the same depth or a little bit deeper. If it's more convenient, you can store the extra bulbs in a cool, dry, rodentproof area until fall and plant them then.

Lilies

Lilies are the crowning glory of the summer garden, but the bulbs aren't cheap. They do multiply themselves slowly, but if you want to increase your lily display more quickly, there are two easy ways to go about it.

Lily bulbs aren't true bulbs: They look like a globe artichoke, with layers of scales. You can harvest scales from new bulbs before you plant them, as shown on the opposite page. A healthy bulb can donate up to six scales without any setback to its growth. If you find any small bulbs near the existing bulbs, harvest those, too. It will take about three years for each scale to grow into a blooming-size bulb. Let the potted scales grow for one year in a cold frame, transplant them into a nursery bed for a year or two, and then move them to their final home in your landscape.

Plant sprouted lily bulb scales in 4" pots. Leave the scales attached to the sprouted bulbs unless they are shriveled or rotting. Put the flats of pots in a warm, well-lit spot indoors. Move the young plants out to the cold frame in late spring.

Some lilies, including tiger lilies (*Lilium lancifolium*), make bulblets (tiny bulblike structures) cradled above each leaf along the stem. You can pit these up or poke them about an inch deep in your nursery bed in late summer. Within a few years, each bulblet will produce a blooming-size bulb to plant in your garden.

PERENNIALS

Picking the Perfect Perennials

Larry Hodgson

The secret to easy perennial gardening is simple enough: Prepare the growing area thoroughly, then pick plants that are naturally tough and well

Continued ➡

163

adapted to your conditions...and plant lots of them! In fact, if you choose the right perennials, you'll scarcely have any work to do at all. Good basic care is all your plants will need.

10 Things to Look For in a Perennial

What exactly are you looking for in a perennial? The right color is probably the first thing that comes to mind, but it's not the most important, since most perennials are available in a wide range of shades. What you really should be looking for, if you want ease of care and a garden that is always attractive, are perennials that meet my ten criteria for a perfect perennial:

1. The plant should be adapted to a wide range of general conditions (sun and shade, rain and drought, heat and cold, etc.).

2. It should be well adapted to local conditions that can be limiting factors in your choice of perennials (extremely cold winters or hot summers, particularly dry or humid air, etc.).

3. It should be long-lived.

4. It should be quick to establish. (Who wants to wait five years for results?)

5. It should be naturally resistant to insects and diseases.

6. It should grow more strongly than most weeds, yet not strongly enough to become a weed.

7. It should need little in the way of pruning, staking, division, and other fussy maintenance tasks.

8. It should remain attractive over a long period.

9. It should be easy to propagate.

10. It should be widely available.

Sounds great, doesn't it? If there were such a plant, it would truly be the perfect perennial. But it doesn't exist. In fact, some of our criteria contradict each other. For example, criterion number 3, long-lived, and number 4, quick to establish, are almost never found in the same plant. Generally speaking, perennials that are long-lived are very slow to establish, while those that reach perfection in the first season are almost always short-lived perennials that scarcely survive longer than a biennial.

Generally, the best you can do is find perennials that share seven out of ten of the desirable traits. With plants that have seven out of ten good qualities, you'll be in for an easy, beautiful ride. Plants with at least five good traits can also be quite useful. Less than that, though, and you'll probably be in for a lot of work...and more than a bit of disappointment.

How to Know What You're Looking For

The worst error any gardener can make is to buy plants without thinking, as when you go to a nursery and pick a plant because "it was the perfect shade of pink and just looked so adorable in its little pot that I couldn't resist." Trust me—looking good in a nursery pot is not a major criterion in picking a perennial. Instead, research your choices before you buy.

This doesn't mean you can never buy perennials on a whim, but if there's a plant you don't know and just can't resist buying, try to find out more about it at the nursery. (Ask around: If it's a good nursery, at least one of the salespeople will be an expert on perennials.) And when you do bring it home, read all about it before you plant it, not after it's comfortably installed in a totally inappropriate spot.

"Think Twice" Perennials

I call perennials with really major flaws—flaws that can override their best qualities and even make you wonder why you ever planted them in the first place—"think twice" perennials. But some of the plants that fall into this category are very popular with gardeners and are featured in many nurseries and catalogs, so they're impossible to ignore.

Often, "think twice" plants are particularly subject to disease or insects or are highly invasive. For example, garden phlox (*Phlox paniculata*) and bee balm (*Monarda didyma*) are both gorgeous garden plants with an unfortunate susceptibility to mildew. But the news isn't all bad—both have cultivars that are disease-resistant; you just have to know to look for them. And highly invasive plants can often be perfectly controlled just by planting them inside a root barrier...but you should know that before you plant them in your garden! In other words, think twice before you buy because you do have a choice between easy plants and difficult ones.

Regional Differences

Criterion number 2 in our list of "10 Things to Look For in a Perennial" is: "It should be well adapted to local conditions that can be limiting factors in your choice of perennials." This is a critical part of choosing a perennial because each area is different, and you need to know your local climate before you can garden with success.

For example, I live in frigid USDA Plant Hardiness Zone 3, where winters are long and cold and there are days on end when no one even expects the car to start. I often have success with plants rated hardy to Zones 6 and (occasionally) 7. Why? Because I have tremendous snow cover. Since snow stays at about the freezing point at all times, I have a thick, relatively warm blanket over my plants that keeps off the worst of winter cold and can help plants survive beyond their usual range. Plus, the snow cover lasts until well into April; by the time the snow has gone and my perennials have started to sprout, there is simply no danger of frost anymore. You can't say that for a lot of places much farther south!

Figuring Out Plant Names

It wasn't too long ago that if you so much as muttered a botanical name, your friends might label you a "plant nut." But times have changed, and botanical names are being used more widely. Just check mail-order catalogs: You'll find Latin names galore. If you're not up to speed yet on understanding and using botanical names for plants, read on. I'll do my best to guide you through the hows and whys of botanical nomenclature. In this section, I list plants by both common and botanical name. You can choose to use only the common name if you wish, but I recommend that you try to learn the botanical name as well.

Why bother with botanical names? One good reason is that common names for plants vary so much. One person's creeping Charlie is another's ground ivy. Other gardeners know the same plant as gill-over-the-ground, alehoof, cat's-foot, runaway robin, and field balm. But there's only one botanical name for this plant: *Glechoma hederacea*. Of course, if you did mention creeping Charlie to someone, they might well think you were talking about a very different plant: *Lysimachia nummularia* (a.k.a. creeping Jenny, creeping loosestrife, wandering Sally, and moneywort). There's even a houseplant, *Pilea nummularifolia*, that's called creeping Charlie.

Botanical names are composed of two parts. The first word in the name is the genus name. Many plants can share one genus name, just as many people can share the same family name. Genus names are always capitalized, and they're usually written in italics or underlined. *Hemerocallis* (daylily) is one example of a genus name.

The second word in a botanical name is the species name. It serves to identify individual plants. For example, *Hemerocallis citrina* and *Hemerocallis fulva* are both daylilies, but *H. citrina* (citron daylily) has lemony yellow flowers and *H. fulva* (tawny daylily) has tawny orange blooms. Species names are also underlined or written in italic, but they're not capitalized.

You'll notice that botanical names are always in Latin or latinized Greek: When Carolus Linnaeus developed this system of two-part names in the late eighteenth century, both languages were still in use by students of biology and botany. After Linnaeus developed his system, scientists soon found the need to separate some species into varieties or subspecies. For example, some specimens of *H. fulva* found in Japan had a more tubular flower than usual. Botanists didn't consider this difference significant enough to create a new species, so they added a third name instead—the variety name. The new plant became known as *H. fulva* var. *longituba* ("var." stands for "variety," of course) to distinguish it from *H. fulva*.

How about Hybrids?

You'll also notice the occasional use of a multiplication sign (x) in botanical names. These indicate a hybrid that has achieved species status. *Astilbe* x *arendsii*, for example, is a hybrid species that resulted from crosses between *A. chinensis* var. *davidii* and other astilbes. 'Amethyst', 'Cattleya', 'Erica', and 'Fanal' astilbes are some popular cultivars of this hybrid species.

You'll also occasionally see an x in front of a genus name, as in x *Solidaster luteus*. This indicates a hybrid genus, resulting when two different genera (the plural of genus) are crossed together. In this case, an aster (*Aster ptarmicoides*) was crossed with a goldenrod (*Solidago canadensis*), resulting in a plant intermediate between the two. (By the way, you don't need to worry about pronouncing the x. It's silent.)

Beyond Latin

When Linnaeus created his naming system, he couldn't have imagined how the modern plant breeding industry would develop. Plant breeders deliberately look for mutations or plants with special characteristics that stand out from the natural form of a plant. They also crossbreed different kinds of perennials to try to create new plants, called hybrids. These days, they're even using genetic engineering to cook up new plants. These manmade plants are called cultivated varieties or cultivars. Cultivar names are written in single quotes, as in *Hemerocallis fulva* 'Kwanso'.

Many great cultivars that we grow were developed in Europe. This can create some name confusion because German horticulturists, for example, give their cultivars German names. But some of our nurseries prefer to translate those names into English. So, you may see one nursery offering *Oenothera fruticosa* 'Fyrverkeri', while another offers *Oenothera fruticosa* 'Fireworks'. Would you guess that they're the same plant? They are! I've listed alternate cultivar names in parentheses.

Buying Perennials

In most areas, especially near urban centers, there is no lack of nurseries selling perennials. During the spring season, department stores, hardware

Continued ➡

stores, supermarkets, public markets, and even "mom and pop" shops get into the act. And there are dozens of mail-order sources. So where should you go for your plants?

ANY OLD PLACE

If you have a good eye for healthy plants, you can buy perennials anywhere. Nonspecialist sources—the department store and supermarket gang—are often (but not always) cheaper, although the selection is usually considerably more restricted than in most nurseries. On the other hand, they rarely know plants and you can't ask them questions with any expectation of a reasonable response. Worse yet, their plants can be in poor shape, as they often don't know how to care for them properly.

GARDEN CENTERS AND LOCAL NURSERIES

Garden centers and nurseries usually have a wide selection and a knowledgeable staff. You can obtain almost all the perennials that grow in your climate from a local nursery, although the nursery may not have every cultivar you're looking for.

Although retail nurseries are really set up for impulse purchases, I give them my orders ahead of time (in late winter; for example, for planting in May). I know I'll get the number of plants I want as well as the right varieties. By ordering early, I get the first choice over other customers.

Nurseries give a better guarantee on perennials than do department stores and their ilk. They don't always have a written policy, but most nurseries will guarantee perennials through the plant's first summer and some over the winter as well.

MAIL-ORDER CATALOGS

Then you have plant catalogs. Some are generalist garden catalogs, selling everything from seeds to fertilizer, with a few perennials thrown in. Others specialize in perennials, and some even specialize in a single type of perennial, such as hostas, irises, grasses, or some other specific category of plants.

The advantage of the nurseries producing mail-order catalogs is that they are generally true specialists in their field, often offering rare plants or choice cultivars of more common perennials, plants that you can rarely find locally.

I can't imagine gardening without perennial catalogs on hand. They are often a gold mine of information, and they carry all the choicest plants I hear other gardeners getting excited about; but be careful when ordering a perennial just because you've seen a color photo of it in a catalog or magazine and it just looks fabulous. Such photos often catch a plant at its very peak or in a special lighting situation that you're just not going to see in your garden. Of course, the photo will give you an idea of the plant's outline and an approximation of its color, but it won't always look that good in your garden.

Besides mail-order catalogs that sell plants, there is also a wide range of seed catalogs that carry perennial seeds. Not as many cultivars are offered by seed as in plant catalogs, since many don't come true from seed, but often rare and unusual species perennials are offered, and the prices are unbeatable. But you'll also have to grow the plant from a seedling; and that can take a year or more.

It's easiest to order plants from within your own country because no special permits are required. But it's also relatively straightforward for Americans to order plants from Canada and vice versa: At the time this is being written, import forms are no longer required for perennials, although you do have to pay for a "phytosanitary certificate," which usually costs an extra $25. Seed orders, however, cross international borders with no trouble, no paperwork, and no special fees. Use a credit card or pay by money order in the currency of the country you're buying from.

Beyond Flowers

As gardeners, we tend to be so heavily into flowers that we forget perennials can have other attributes such as an attractive silhouette, beautiful leaves, gorgeous fall colors, the ability to attract butterflies or hummingbirds to the garden, showy seedpods or berries, and so on. In fact, if you choose plants solely on the basis of showy flowers, you may end up with a garden of "one-season wonders." Once the flowers fade, you'll find yourself looking for someplace to hide them!

SHOWY FRUITS AND SEEDPODS

Besides the colorful berries of plants like baneberries (*Actaea* spp.) and ornamental strawberries (*Fragaria* spp.), there's a wide range of perennials with attractive seedheads. Seedheads range from the fluffy, flowerlike tufts of adonises and common pasque flower to pods that open to reveal brilliantly colored seeds like blackberry lily and stinking iris (*Iris foetidissima*) to the inflated blackish purple pods of baptisias, and the star-shaped capsules (perfect for drying) of gas plant (*Dictamnus albus*).

There are also perennials that bear "extended flowers" like sea hollies (*Eryngium* spp.), globe thistles (*Echinops* spp.), and most grasses. In these species, the flower just seems to go on and on—until you realize that the real blooms faded weeks ago, and what you're looking at is a cluster of maturing seedheads!

PERENNIALS WITH YEAR-ROUND INTEREST

Ornamental grasses are the stars among perennials where winter interest is concerned. Many of them are tall, rising well above even deep snow. Other perennials that add year-round interest where they aren't buried in snow include yuccas, aloes, agaves, astilbes, epimediums, hellebores, lavenders, liriopes, mondo grasses (*Ophiopogon* spp.), and sedums.

There's one important thing to remember, though: Don't cut these perennials back in the fall or you'll miss out on the winter show!

Designing Your Dream Garden

Larry Hodgson

Conventional wisdom says that you should design your garden, then choose the plants for it. But when you love plants as much as I do, you should pick your plants first, then create a design that makes them look good together. This makes especially good sense when you're planting perennials with a purpose: Choose the perennials that suit your purpose, then put them together to make your dream garden.

Basics and Beyond

Although I've planted thousands of perennials in my yard, I'm not an expert on garden design. However, I've picked up a few notions about design during my years of gardening, and I'll share these basics with you here. If I can do it, you can, too! The elements you'll work with are color, texture, and form, and I'll give you some simple guidelines for using them to create pleasing gardens.

Color and Texture

Two of the most important elements in designing a garden are color and texture. If you can get these two elements to click, you're sure to have a beautiful garden. There's a lot of theory about how to combine colors and textures to create pleasing combinations, but remember—it's theory, not law. The color police are not going to arrest you!

Most of us do a fine job choosing colors for our homes. Designing a garden isn't that different. The first color choice is made for you. It's hard to make a major mistake when you have that underlying color pulling your design together.

Keep in mind that your garden is your garden. Don't think for a minute that you have to follow anyone else's color schemes. If you combine colors in a way that seems pleasing to you, you'll be satisfied, and that's what really counts.

COOL AND WARM

When you're thinking about garden design, it's helpful to separate colors into two groups: warm colors and cool colors. Red, orange, and yellow are warm colors. They give a design more excitement and passion. Also, these colors make the garden seem closer. You might want to use warm colors to make a large garden appear more intimate or to attract attention to a distant part of the garden.

Green, blue, and violet are cool colors. They make the garden seem cooler, calmer, and more peaceful. Cool colors also seem farther away. To make a small garden seem larger, use a lot of cool colors. Cool colors will also make an unwanted view less distracting, since they'll make it seem more distant and unobtrusive.

You can plant a garden that's all warm colors, all cool colors, or a mix of both. If you mix cool and warm colors, remember that warm colors dominate. If you want a garden where warm and cool balance, plant more cool-colored perennials. A few spot plantings of warm colors in a sea of blue and green are enough.

When you mix warm and cool colors, don't put the cool colors in the background, or they'll get lost. Plant cool-colored perennials in front, with the warm-colored ones behind.

SINGLE-COLOR GARDENS

Perhaps the easiest garden to design is a single-color garden. You can create a white garden, a yellow garden, a red garden—they're all winning ideas. Choose a color that you like, and use it in various shades and tints. Choose perennials with different sizes, textures, and shapes, all in various shades of the same color, and you can have both variety and harmony at the same time.

Of course, your garden won't truly be one color because it will have a background of green foliage, and there are many shades and tints of green, too. Green leaves can range from nearly black to blue-green to chartreuse to gray or silver. And that's not counting all the variegated foliage! You can even design a green garden just using foliage. It's fun to create striking and beautiful effects with foliage, especially in shade gardens where foliage is a key factor.

COMBINING COLORS

If you want to create a garden with more than one color, you can use a color wheel to help decide which colors look good together. On the color wheel, each color is flanked by two other colors. You can move beyond a single-color garden by choosing three colors that appear side by side on the wheel.

If you like violet, for example, you could create an interesting garden using violet flowers with blue-violet or red-violet shades. Or go one step further and combine a primary color with the two secondary colors that are closest together on the wheel: orange with yellow and red, for example.

Continued ➤

Complementary Colors

Colors that are direct opposites on the color wheel are called complementary colors, and they make very vibrant combinations. Yellow and violet are complementary colors, and so are blue and orange. If these combinations strike you as too jarring, you can use tints of the main hue to prevent a clash, such as pink to soften a vibrant red. Or use white flowers or gray or silver foliage between colors that seem too strong. They'll tend to soften the blow.

Multicolor Mixes

Garden designers might call a garden of mixed colors a "polychromatic scheme," but I just call it a mixed-color garden. It can include all the colors in the rainbow. Although considered daring from a design point of view, most home gardens are color mixes, and many of them work very well indeed. A garden with many different colors often creates a light, lively atmosphere, making it a fun place to be—and that's what many people want for their garden.

I'll admit, sometimes I've created a garden of mixed colors just by randomly planting perennials in a bed. When the bed fills in, sometimes I get a rather pleasing meadow garden look, but at other times, I'm not satisfied because many of the individual colors and plants seem lost in the crowd. So now I stick with a technique that usually gives great results.

I group plants together to create spots of color, then I mix the spots together rather than sprinkling individual colors throughout the same garden. How many plants make up a "spot" of color? That varies. When you're planting small perennials like violets, you may need 15 or more to create enough color impact. But with sizable plants like garden phlox (*Phlox paniculata*), 3 plants may be enough. And some perennials are large and imposing enough to stand alone.

Texture

Although we tend to think of color as the mainstay in garden design, texture is just as important. In fact, Japanese gardens often have nothing but shades and tints of green—yet we find them pleasing and harmonious because of the careful choice of textures.

There are three basic textures: fine, medium, and coarse. Plants fit a texture category based on their leaf size and density and their flower placement. For example, bear's breeches (*Acanthus mollis*), with its large, striking leaves, is bold, while peony foliage is medium, and the feathery leaves of artemisias put them in the fine category.

When you create a garden, using a relatively even mix of fine and medium leaves with an accent of larger, bolder leaves is often the safest way to go. You can also design a striking garden using a single texture accented by a contrasting texture every now and then. One classic texture combination is fine-textured ferns with coarse-leaved hostas.

Fine textures tend to have the same effect as cool colors: They're calming and make the garden seem farther away. Coarse textures are almost as exciting and visually stimulating as warm colors and, like them, draw the garden closer. When you're combining textures, you can use the same technique of using "spots" of texture instead of just mixing textures randomly.

Featuring Plant Form

All plants have a natural form: Some plants are vertical, others are spreading, and still others are rounded, open, or prostrate. If a garden mixes too

many forms, it can appear chaotic, but repeating a limited number of forms can create a very pleasing garden.

Working with form can be more subtle than color or texture. You can create gardens with gradual changes in form, where low plants melt into spreading ones that in turn give way to vertical shapes. You can also use dramatic contrasts in form, planting a rounded perennial like "Autumn Joy" sedum right next to a vase-shaped perennial like Russian sage (*Perovskia atriplicifolia*). The typical British perennial border is a classic mixture of tall, spiky background plants (verticality with a vengeance!) with rounded plants in the middle and prostrate plants as an edging.

The Form of Flowers

Plants have an overall form or shape, and individual flowers or flower heads have a form as well. Large, bold peonies contrast with airy baby's breath blossoms, for example. There are also bell-shaped flowers, upright spikes of flowers, and daisylike blooms. My wife always complains there are too many "daisies" (rudbeckias, purple coneflowers, and perennial sunflowers) in our garden. She's right...and I'm trying to do better!

How to Handle Height

The rule of thumb concerning plant height is so simple that most gardeners follow it instinctively: Short plants go in the front of the garden, medium-sized plants in the middle, and tall plants in the back. The deeper the garden, the more varied a range of heights you can use.

This rule is perfect for very formal gardens, but if you're planning a casual garden, don't hesitate to break the rule occasionally. A few tall plants in the middle of the garden, some medium-sized ones in the front and, every now and again, a low-growing plant inching back into the bed will be more natural looking.

The Role of Repetition

Whether you're thinking about color, texture, form, or height, keep in mind that too much variety randomly tossed together can turn a garden into a total hodgepodge. The way to turn a random mix of plants into a pretty garden is through repetition. Even in a small garden, try to repeat at least three groups of the same plant, or at least the same color or texture, in different parts of the garden. You'll often find even the most unlikely plants suddenly gel perfectly!

Flowers of a Feather Bloom Together

Probably one of the most difficult things to plan for when designing a garden is getting bloom times to coincide. Although perennials can be roughly grouped into spring, summer, and fall bloomers, the actual time when a plant blooms varies from year to year, depending on the growing conditions and the weather. You just don't get guarantees on flowering time from Mother Nature.

The longer the growing season, the more difficult it is to coordinate bloom periods. In the Deep South, where Christmas rose (*Helleborus niger*) really can bloom at Christmas, each season is stretched to its maximum. The spring flowering season often lasts four months or more. By contrast, in my USDA Zone 3 garden, where spring barely lasts a month, you'll see spring and summer bloomers mingling. This makes it much easier to ensure nonstop color.

Stagger Bloom Times for Best Results

The secret to a perennial garden that always looks good is to stagger bloom times: Combine plants

with different flowering seasons so that there's always something in bloom in the garden. One thing that can help is including some everbloomers—perennials that bloom for eight weeks or more—in your design.

Staggering bloom times fits well with my "spots of color" technique. A single perennial blooming on its own might have little impact in the garden, but three or more densely flowered patches of the same plant create the impression that there's color everywhere in the garden. By having at least three different perennials in bloom in three different spots at any given time, you can have that "in full bloom" effect right through the growing season.

Of course, to do so, you'll need to know when different perennials bloom. Once you've planted your garden, you may find that there's a "hole" in it—a particular time of year when there's nearly nothing in bloom. If this happens, take a stroll through your neighborhood at that time of year and see what's blooming in your neighbors' yards. Come fall, order a few of those plants and work them into your garden.

Finally, if you can't guarantee flowering perennials throughout the season, you can count on attractive foliage at all times, so don't hesitate to get some of the color for your garden from foliage.

Beyond Perennials: Branching Out

Perennial gardens can include other plants besides perennials, and adding some annuals, bulbs, and shrubs to your perennial garden can stretch its season of color and interest. For example, while there are perennials that flower in spring, spring bulbs are the true stars of the early spring and midspring gardens. Annuals add consistent color that can tide your garden over if there are periods when perennials aren't at their best, such as during the high heat of midsummer. And shrubs will give your garden some form and interest through the winter.

Bulbs for Spring Color

From the earliest snowdrops and winter crocuses to May-blooming tulips, not to mention summer-flowering alliums and fall-blooming crocus and colchicums, bulbs ensure color when there is little else around. Spring bulbs are a perfect match for perennials because they produce their foliage in the spring when many perennials are dormant. As spring gives way to summer, the bulb foliage dies back, while the perennials sprout the new season's growth.

Because of this, you can plant bulbs and perennials quite literally in the same space. Just plant the bulbs deeply in the fall (check the bulb package to confirm the planting depth, as it does vary), then plant shallow-rooted perennials literally on top. The bulbs will come up right through the perennials—especially low-growing ones like ajugas and lamiums.

I like to plant rings of early bulbs around slow-to-sprout plants like hibiscus and balloon-flower. I've found that the bulbs serve as markers so I don't accidentally dig up the slow sprouters when I'm working in the garden preparing beds during the spring.

Adding Annuals

Annuals and perennials make a great combination, as long as you give the annuals enough room to spread without crowding the perennials. Planting patches of annuals through a bed of perennials can ensure that "always-in-bloom" look. A ratio of about one annual to five perennials works well.

Annuals also work well as edging plants for a perennial border. It's a job they do marvelously,

Continued ➨

and if the front edge of the garden—which is the first thing that catches people's attention when they enter the garden—appears to be in full bloom through the summer, the rest of the garden will seem all that much more attractive.

SHRUBS TO ANCHOR THE SCENE

Shrubs are excellent backgrounds for perennial beds, "anchoring" the garden to its landscape much better than perennials alone could ever do. Many shrubs bloom in the spring or late summer—two times of year when perennials are rather weak—so the marriage is a good one. Just make sure that each shrub has its own space.

One effective combination is shrubs with perennial groundcovers. You can let the groundcover creep under the shrubs and create a living carpet that's beautiful and easy to care for.

Of course, not all shrubs belong strictly in the background of the mixed border. Short, dense shrubs, including dwarf conifers, look great in the middle or even the front of the garden as well. Shrubs come in a wide range of forms, textures, and foliage colors, so it's easy to create beautiful combinations of perennials and shrubs. And, of course, many shrubs have beautiful blooms and colorful fruit as well.

The 10 Commandments of Perennial Design

Now that you know the basics of garden design, you can see that there are unlimited possibilities for designing and planting perennial gardens. But before you start, read my list of important lessons learned from years of gardening and designing. My "ten commandments" are some of the best practical advice I can give you, based on some of my own worst mistakes.

1. Leave room for future growth. Don't cram a new garden with perennials, or they'll have no room to spread over time. And you'll end up having to dig some up and move them. Instead, fill in with temporary plants such as annuals for the first couple of years.

2. Change your garden whenever you feel like it. It's a gardener's prerogative to change his (or her!) mind. Once you have a garden design, even one that's been prepared by a professional designer, feel free to change it. After all, it's your garden! Even professional landscapers change plans as they work.

3. Stagger your planting. Don't plant perennials in straight lines because it looks unnatural and static, except when you're planting an edging for a small rectangular or square garden.

4. Don't go with the flow. Be wary of following gardening fads too closely. True, hot pink may be the "hot" trend, but are you sure you'll be able to live with it ten years from now? Experiment with the latest trends using annuals, but make sure your perennial choices are ones you can live with for a long time.

5. Rein in the spreaders. If you plant a potentially invasive perennial in a flower bed, always plant it inside a root barrier. Nothing's harder than trying to dig out an aggressive spreader.

6. Don't be boring. Avoid mirror-image plantings on either side of a walkway or door. They may work in truly formal settings, but they often make for a boring garden.

7. Don't neglect your babies. Remember that all newly planted perennials need extra care for the first year after planting.

8. Show your plants, not your stakes. Stake perennials as discreetly as possible or use stakes that blend in with the plants' foliage. Nothing ruins a nice garden like a forest of ugly stakes.

9. Make big beds. If you're planning a perennial border, make it as wide as you can: Remember, perennials need space to grow! There's nothing more frustrating than having to divide perennials just a year or two after planting them.

10. Don't always follow the rules. Don't follow any design rule too precisely. All rules are meant to be broken, even mine!

Planting & Caring for Perennials

Taking the time to prepare the soil, follow general planting guidelines, weed, and control bad bugs will be well worth the effort. Your payoff? Loads of beautiful blooms that will grace your landscape for years to come.

Sizing Up Your Soil

Good soil is the backbone of any good garden and is key to growing lush plants. Well-prepared soil is fluffy and loose, so water, air, and nutrients can filter down easily and plant roots have room to stretch. Most soils in residential areas are loams—combinations of sand, silt, and clay. If your soil has a high percentage of sand, it's a sandy loam, whereas if your soil has a high percentage of clay, it's a clay loam.

How do you know if you have good loam soil, or too much clay or sand? Try one of these simple tests to find out what's going on down below.

THE WATERING TEST

When you're watering plants in your garden, does the water disappear so fast it looks like only the leaves have gotten wet, rather than the soil surface? And do you find you have to water frequently to keep plants from waiting? If so, you have a lot of sand in your soil.

On the other hand, if water puddles up and seems to take forever to sink into the soil, you have lots of clay. Soil with a high clay content may dry and crack apart in clods or plates between rains, and it becomes sticky or very slippery when it gets wet.

THE SOIL BALL TEST

Try this test after a rain or after you water, when the soil is moist but not soggy. Pick up a handful of soil from the site where you want to grow perennials and squeeze it. If the soil crumbles apart when you open your hand, the soil is loam. If the soil stays in a ball, it's mostly clay. If it disintegrates easily and you can see and feel gritty little crystals in it, it's a sandy soil. And if the soil crumbles but feels greasy, it's mostly silt.

UNDERSTANDING pH

Soil pH is a measure of acidity or alkalinity. It's measured on a scale from 1.0 (highly acidic) to 14.0 (highly alkaline), with 7.0 considered neutral. Most garden perennials grow best in soil with a pH of 6.0 to 7.0—slightly acidic to neutral. You can test your soil's pH yourself with a home test kit (available from garden centers and through mail-order catalogs).

Bring very acid soils closer to neutral by adding lime (often in the form of limestone); neutralize highly alkaline soils with sulfur. Adding organic matter such as leaves, grass clippings, or compost to your soil will soon bring a soil into balance—and create happier plants.

Amending Your Soil

Soil amendments benefit your garden by supplying the material (humus) that's the basis for good plant growth. Adding amendments loosens the soil, helps the soil retain water better, and improves drainage. All garden soils, even good garden loams, benefit from regular additions of organic material. And you need to apply amendments every season because organic material is constantly being broken down in the soil.

To give your perennial plants the benefits of organic matter, you must give your soil a steady supply: Add compost and mulch to established beds, or incorporate organic material into new beds.

The most commonly available soil amendments are the following:
  - Compost
  - Aged manure
  - Grass clippings
  - Shredded leaves
  - Hay and straw
  - Aged sawdust

Compost and aged manure are balanced amendments, which means that they contain a mix of nutrients and you can add them to the soil as is, at any time. Grass clippings are a good source of fast-release nitrogen, but they decompose quickly, adding little bulk to the soil. However, shredded leaves, hay, straw, and aged sawdust all need time to break down. If you want to add one of those amendments, prepare your beds in fall for spring planting or in spring for fall planting.

Putting in the Plants

You can plant perennials any time the soil is workable, although spring and fall are best for most plants. If the plants arrive or you buy them before you're ready to plant, be sure to care for them properly until you can get them into the ground. Try to plant on an overcast day, and avoid planting during midday heat.

PLANTING CONTAINER-GROWN PERENNIALS

Place container-grown plants on top of the soil according to your design. Start small, removing and planting one plant at a time rather than taking them all out of their pots and leaving them to dehydrate. And don't just grab a plant by the stem and pull it out of its pot. Instead, follow these simply but important steps:

1. Spread your hand over the surface of the soil with your fingers on either side of the plant stem.

2. Invert the pot so it's resting upside down on your hand, then pull off the pot with the other hand. (If the pot doesn't release easily, gently tap it a few times, and try again. If it's really stubborn, cut it off.) If the roots have filled the pot so tightly that they hold their shape once you've removed the pot, gently pull them loose or quarter the rootball before planting.

3. Hold the plant upside down, with your fingers on either side of the stem (as you removed it from the pot). Use a sharp knife or trowel to slice the rootball from the bottom up into four equal sections.

4. Spread out the four quarters in the planting hole to make sure the roots grow into the soil instead of remaining in a ball.

Plant container-grown perennials at the level at which they sat in the pots. If the crowns (where the roots meet the stems) are buried, the plants will have a tough time surviving.

PLANTING BAREROOT PERENNIALS

Right before you plant a bareroot perennial (they arrive with their roots in a protective substance, such as shredded wood, as opposed to actually

Continued ➡

being planted in a soil-filled container), cut off any dead, damaged, or diseased roots with a sharp knife. Mound soil in the bottom of the planting hole and spread the roots out so the crown of the plant rests on top of the mound. Then add soil around the roots to fill the hole.

Note: On a bareroot perennial, you'll have to determine the depth to which the plant was planted at the nursery or identify the crown. If you see a soil line or notice a spot where stems or leaf bases change color (green to yellow or green to white), plant it at that depth. If not, plant it so the soil comes up to but not past the point where the roots end and the stems begin.

Caring for Perennials

After you've invested time, money, and energy in your perennial garden, you'll want to keep it looking its best. That's where regular (at least a few times a week) attention to watering, mulching, weeding, and grooming comes in.

WATERING

When it comes to watering perennials, keep two rules in mind: Water deeply (really soaking the soil, not just sprinkling it), and water the roots (that is, on the ground around the plants, not into the air or onto the plants). If you break these rules, there's a good chance you'll end up with shallow-rooted, wilt-prone plants and mildewed foliage.

With a few exceptions, perennials like consistently and evenly moist soil. In general, water when the top inch or two of soil dries out and Mother Nature isn't planning on providing any rain in the near future. Also, use a hose instead of a sprinkler so you can direct the water to the bases of the plants without wetting the foliage. For best results, don't water in the evening, when the water will stay on your plants all night, encouraging powdery mildew to grow.

MULCHING

After good soil, mulch does more for plants than any technique you could use or any other product you could add to your garden. It helps maintain soil moisture (allowing you to water less often), keeps weeds at bay (giving you more time to enjoy your garden), adds nutrients to the soil (cutting down on the need to add fertilizer), and prevents erosion.

Apply organic mulch—shredded leaves, straw, bark, pine needles, or lawn clippings—around plants you've just planted, leaving about an inch of space around the stem of each plant. (Covering the crowns with mulch encourages crown rot.) If your mulch begins to break down and look thin as summer wears on, add more. After your plants have been killed by a hard frost in the fall, mulch fall transplants or put a winter mulch on your beds. The next spring, pull back the winter mulch until the soil has warmed, then pull it back up around your plants.

WEEDING

Weeding is a fact of life for every gardener, whether you're a beginner or have been gardening for 25 years. The best way to beat these less-than-desirable plants is to start weeding as soon as you see a problem. You'll have a much harder time beating weeds if you let them take over your garden and then try to bring things under control all at once. Even if you pull 'em as you see 'em, you'll still want to spend as little time as possible fighting weeds. Here are a few ways you can do just that.

- Mulch your garden. Mulch suppresses weed germination and makes the weeds that do appear easier to pull, because the soil stays soft and moist beneath the mulch.

- Remove the whole weed—roots and all—the first time. A lot of weeds can spread from a tiny piece of root or stem left in the ground.

- Don't let weeds set seed. Some perennials, such as coneflowers, self-sow so enthusiastically that they could be considered weeds. If you don't plan on starting your own nursery, cut the flower heads before the seeds ripen and drop.

- Don't compost mature weed seed heads. Although a really hot compost pile will kill weed seeds, you can't guarantee that the seeds will be in the hottest part of the pile or that your pile will get hot enough to kill all of them.

GROOMING

Grooming techniques, such as thinning, pinching, and deadheading, are fast and easy techniques that will put the finishing touches on your perennial garden.

Thinning is removing some of the stems of dense, bushy plants to let in additional light and improve air circulation. This technique helps prevent mildew on susceptible plants such as garden phlox, bee balms, and delphiniums. Thin in spring by cutting or pinching out stems at the soil level. Thin each plant to the four or five strongest shoots, leaving 2 to 4 inches between each stem.

Pinching creates more compact, bushier plants, prevents flopping, and ensures more bloom. Using your forefinger and thumb, pinch out the tips of the stems. From each pinched stem, two branches will grow. Start pinching plants in late spring or early summer. Pinch again a few weeks later to encourage even bushier plants with still more flowers, but don't pinch back after flower buds are set, or you'll discourage (rather than encourage) flowering.

Despite its gory name, deadheading, or removing spent flowers, is a very useful technique. Some perennials deadhead themselves, dropping old flowers to the ground. But the brown, papery ruins of other flowers will spoil the beauty of your garden unless you take them off regularly. Deadheading provides your perennials with more than good looks, though. It's also important for the following reasons:

- The plant can channel energy that would normally be used to produce seed back into flower, leaf, and root production.

- Invasive perennials are kept from self-sowing all over your garden.

- The bloom season often is extended because the plants will keep flowering rather than stopping after the first bloom.

For plants that have more than one flower on a single stalk and the flowers open at different times, like daylilies, carefully snap off or pinch the faded blooms between your fingers. With plants that bear one flower head on the end of each stalk, like yarrow, cut the stalks at or near the ground when the flowers fade.

Perennial Flower Finder

Ellen Phillips and C. Colston Burrell

This is a section of lists—lists that make it easy for you to see at a glance how to put perennials together. If you want to create a blue color-theme garden or just need a perennial that will add a touch of blue to your garden, turn to the list of blue-flowered perennials. Needless to say, these lists aren't meant to be exhaustive—there will always be many, many more perennials to choose from—but there are enough here to give you a strong start. You can't go wrong with these garden-worthy perennials!

Skim through the lists. Do you need perennials for clay soil, for shade, for full sun? Perennials to attract butterflies or hummingbirds? Drought-tolerant perennials? Flowers that are easy-care? Plants that can take wet feet? Think about what you want, and also see what appeals to you as you look at the lists. You might start out wanting a garden of red-flowered perennials, then decide you'd like a hummingbird garden instead because many hummingbird favorites have red flowers and you'd get the pleasure of the comical little buzzers as well. (Actually, hummingbird enthusiasts call the little birds "hummers," not "buzzers," but since they buzz loudly as they dart and hover, I can't help but call them that.) Enjoy yourself!

Perennials by Flower Color

Most of us play favorites when it comes to color. That's why color-theme gardens are so popular. If you love blue, white, and yellow, you might decide to plant a border featuring one, two, or all three flower colors. Perhaps you planted a bed that blooms in soft shades of lavender and gold, and now you feel that it needs a little pizzazz—maybe a touch of magenta or deep red. In these lists, you'll find perennials arranged by bloom color, so you can quickly check your choices for any given color.

Remember that many perennials have several—or even lots of—flower colors (irises, columbines, lupines, and chrysanthemums spring to mind), so you'll find them on many of these lists. When you don't expect a perennial to bloom in a certain color—for example, a near-white-flowered daylily—we'll give you the cultivar name as well as the genus or species.

White or Cream

Alstromeria spp. (alstroemerias)

Aster spp. (asters)

Astilbe spp. (false spireas)

Astrantia app. (masterworts)

Campanula spp. (bellflowers, harebells)

Chrysanthemum spp. (chrysanthemums)

Convallaria majalis (lily-of-the-valley)

Delphinium spp. (delphiniums)

Dianthus spp. (pinks, carnations)

Dicentra spp. (bleeding hearts)

Digitalis spp. (foxgloves)

Echinacea spp. (coneflowers)

Gaura lindheimeri (white gaura)

Geranium spp. (geraniums, cranesbills)

Gypsophila paniculata (baby's-breath)

Hedychium coronarium (butterfly ginger)

Hemerocallis cvs., such as 'Gentle Shepherd' (daylilies)

Iberis spp. (candytufts)

Iris spp. (irises)

Lamium maculatum cvs., such as 'White Nancy' (spotted dead nettle)

Leucanthemum maximum (Shasta daisy)

Leucojum spp. (snowflakes)

Lilium spp. (lilies)

Paeonia spp. (peonies)

Papaver spp. (poppies)

Penstemon spp. (beardtongues, penstemons)

Phlox spp. (phlox)

Salvia spp. (sages)

Sanguinaria canadensis (bloodroot)

Tiarella spp. (foamflowers)

Tradescantia spp. (spiderworts)

Trillium spp. (trilliums)

Continued →

Verbena spp. (verbenas, vervains)

Viola spp. (violets, violas)

Pink

Alstroemeria spp. (alstroemerias)

Armeria maritima (sea pink)

Astilbe spp. (false spireas)

Astrantia spp. (masterworts)

Bletilla striata (Chinese ground orchid)

Campanula spp. (bellflowers, harebells)

Chrysanthemum spp. (chrysanthemums)

Delphinium spp. (delphiniums)

Dianthus spp. (pinks, carnations)

Dicentra spp. (bleeding hearts)

Digitalis spp. (foxgloves)

Echinacea spp. (coneflowers)

Epimedium spp. (fairy wings)

Eupatorium spp. (Joe-Pye weeds, bonesets)

Geranium spp. (geraniums, cranesbills)

Iris spp. (irises)

Lamium maculatum cvs., such as 'Pink Pewter', 'Beacon Silver' (spotted dead nettle)

Lilium spp. (lilies)

Lobelia spp. (lobelias)

Monarda spp. (bee balms, bergamots)

Oenothera speciosa (showy evening primrose)

Paeonia spp. (peonies)

Papaver spp. (poppies)

Phlox spp. (phlox)

Salvia spp. (sages)

Thalictrum spp. (meadow rues)

Verbena spp. (verbenas, vervains)

Red and Scarlet

Aquilegia spp. (columbines)

Astilbe spp. (false spireas)

Astrantia spp. (masterworts)

Canna spp. (cannas)

Chrysanthemum spp. (chrysanthemums)

Coreopsis 'Limerock Ruby' ('Limerock Ruby' corepsis)

Crocosmia spp. (crocosmias, montbretias)

Dianthus spp. (pinks, carnations)

Gaillardia spp. (blanket flowers)

Hemerocallis spp. (daylilies)

Heuchera cvs. (alumroots, coral bells)

Lilium spp. (lilies)

Lobelia spp. (lobelias)

Monarda spp. (bee balms, bergamots)

Paeonia spp. (peonies)

Papaver spp. (poppies)

Persicaria amplexicaule (mountain fleece flower, mountain knotweed)

Salvia spp. (sages)

Silene spp. (campions, pinks)

Spigelia marilandica (Indian pink)

Veronica spicata (spike speedwell)

Purple, Lilac, Mauve, and Maroon

Agapanthus spp. (lilies of the Nile, African lilies)

Allium spp. (ornamental onions)

Alstroemeria spp. (alstroemerias)

Aquilegia spp. (columbines)

Aster spp. (asters)

Astrantia spp. (masterworts)

Callirhoe involucrata (purple poppy mallow)

Campanula spp. (bellflowers, harebells)

Chrysanthemum spp. (chrysanthemums)

Delphinium spp. (delphiniums)

Digitalis spp. (foxgloves)

Echinacea spp. (coneflowers)

Eupatorium spp. (Joe-Pye weeds, bonesets)

Geranium spp. (geraniums, cranesbills)

Hemerocallis cvs., such as 'Plum Perfect' (daylilies)

Iris spp. (irises)

Knautia macedonica (knautia)

Lavandula spp. (lavenders)

Liatris spp. (gayfeathers, blazing-stars)

Liriope spp. (lily turfs)

Lobelia spp. (lobelias)

Monarda spp. (bee balms, bergamots)

Nepeta spp. (catmints, nepetas)

Papaver spp., such as *P. orientale* 'Patty's Plum', *P. somni* (erum 'Lauren's Grape' (poppies)

Phlox spp. (phlox)

Salvia spp. (sages)

Tradescantia spp. (spiderworts)

Verbena spp. (verbenas, vervains), such as *Verbena bonariensis* (Brazilian vervain)

Vernonia spp. (ironweeds)

Veronica spp. (speedwells)

Viola spp. (violets, violas)

Blue

Agastache foeniculum, such as 'Blue Fortune' (fragrant anise hyssop)

Amsonia spp. (blue stars, amsonias)

Aster spp. (asters)

Baptisia australis (blue false indigo)

Brunnera macrophylla (Siberian bugloss, forget-me-not)

Campanula spp. (bellflowers, harebells)

Ceratostigma plumbaginoides (plumbago)

Clematis spp. (clematis)

Corydalis flexuosa (blue fumeroot)

Delphinium spp. (delphiniums)

Iris spp. (irises)

Linum perenne (blue flax)

Lobelia spp. (lobelias)

Meconopsis spp. (meconopsis)

Muscari spp. (grape hyacinths)

Phlox divaricata (wild blue phlox, woodland phlox)

Phlox paniculata cvs., such as 'Blue Paradise' (garden phlox)

Platycodon grandiflorus (balloon flower)

Pulmonaria saccharata (Bethlehem sage)

Salvia spp. (sages)

Stokesia laevis (Stokes' aster)

Tradescantia spp. (spiderworts)

Verbena spp. (verbenas, vervains)

Veronica spp. (speedwells)

Yellow

Achillea spp. (yarrows)

Alstroemeria spp. (alstroemerias)

Aquilegia spp. (columbines)

Aurinia saxatilis (basket-of-gold)

Canna spp. (cannas)

Chrysanthemum spp. (chrysanthemums)

Chrysogonum virginianum (goldenstar, green-and-gold)

Coreopsis spp. (tickseed, coreopsis)

Crocosmia spp. (crocosmias, montbretias)

Digitalis spp. (foxgloves)

Doronicum spp. (leopard's banes)

Epimedium spp. (fairy wings, barrenworts)

Euphorbia polychroma (cushion spurge)

Hemerocallis spp. (daylilies)

Iris spp. (irises)

Kniphofia spp. (torch lilies, red-hot pokers)

Ligularia spp. (ligularias, groundsels)

Lilium spp. (lilies)

Lysimachia vulgaris (yellow loosestrife)

Oenothera spp. (evening primroses)

Paeonia spp. (peonies)

Papaver spp. (poppies)

Primula auricula (aurieula primrose)

Ranunculus spp. (buttercups)

Rudbeckia spp. (black-eyed Susans, cone flowers)

Solidago spp. (goldenrods)

Viola spp. (violets, violas)

Peach, Orange, and Coral

Agastache spp. (anise hyssops)

Alstroemeria spp. (alstroemerias)

Asclepias tuberosa (butterfly weed)

Canna spp. (cannas)

Chrysanthemum spp. (chrysanthemums)

Crocosmia spp. (crocosmias, montbretias)

Diascia vigilis (twinspur, diascia)

Eremurus spp. (foxtail lilies, desert-candles)

Gladeolus spp. (gladioli, sword lilies)

Hedychium spp. (ginger lilies, garland lilies)

Hemerocallis spp. and *cvs.* (daylilies)

Iris spp. (irises)

Kniphofia spp. (torch lilies, red-hot pokers)

Lilium spp. (lilies)

Paeonia spp. (peonies)

Papaver spp. (poppies)

Schizostylis coccineus (crimson flag)

Zephyranthes spp. (rain lilies)

Green and Chartreuse

Chrysanthemum spp. (chrysanthemums)

Euphorbia spp. (spurges, euphorbias)

Helleborus spp. (hellebores), especially *H. foetidus* (stinking hellebore)

Iris spp. (irises)

Kniphofia spp. (torch lilies, red-hot pokers)

Sedum spp. (stonecrops, sedums). Note: Most sedum flower heads mature to white, pink, red, maroon, or rust, but they remain green for a very long time first, giving the presence of green flowers in your garden until they color up.

"Black"

Alcea rosea 'Nigra' (black hollyhock)

Aquilegia cvs., such as 'Black Barlow' (columbines)

Geranium phaeum var. phaeum (mourning widow hardy geranium)

Helleborus cvs. (hellebores)

Ipomoea barbatus 'Blackie' and 'Ace of Spades' (sweet potato vine)

Iris spp. (irises)

Tulipa cvs. (tulips)

Viola cvs. (Johnny-jump-ups, pansies)

Perennials for Long Bloom

Unlike annuals, perennials don't bloom nonstop from planting to frost because they need to put most of their energy into their roots so they'll live

Continued →

through the winter and have the strength to come up the following spring. Some perennials bloom for only a week or two, then the show's over until next year. Luckily for gardeners, other perennials bloom for weeks on end. (Others, like most ornamental grasses, bear showy plumes of flowers that turn into long-lasting seedheads.) If you enjoy a good show, choose from this list.

Acanthus spp. (bear's breeches)
Achillea spp. (yarrows)
Agastache spp. (anise hyssops)
Alchemilla spp. (lady's-mantles)
Armeria spp. (thrifts)
Aster spp. (asters)
Bergenia spp. (bergenias, winter begonias)
Calamintha nepeta (calamint)
Callirhoe spp. (winecups, poppy mallows)
Campanula spp. (bellflowers, harebells)
Canna spp. (cannas)
Centranthus ruber (red valerian)
Coreopsis spp. (tickseeds, coreopsis)
Corydalis spp. (corydalis, fumeroots)
Dianthus spp. (pinks, carnations)
*Diascia vigilis (twinspur)
Digitalis spp. (foxgloves)
Echinacea spp. (coneflowers)
Echinops spp. (globe thistles)
Euphorbia spp. (spurges, euphorbias)
Gaura lindheimeri (white gaura)
Geranium spp. (geraniums, cranesbills)
Gypsophila spp. (baby's-breaths)
Helianthus spp. (sunflowers)
Helleborus spp. (hellebores, Christmas roses, Lenten roses)
Hemerocallis spp. (daylilies)
Kalimeris pinnatifida (Mongolian aster)
Liatris spp. (gayfeathers, blazing-stars)
Limonium spp. (sea lavenders, statices)
Lysimachia spp. (loosestrifes)
Malva spp. (mallows)
Nepeta spp. (catmints)
Oenothera spp. (evening primroses)
Penstemon spp. (beardtongues, penstemons)
Perovskia atriplicifolia (Russian sage)
Persicaria amplexicaule (mountain fleece flower)
Phygelius x rectus (cape fuchsia)
Platycodon grandiflorus (balloon flower)
Rudbeckia spp. (black-eyed Susans, coneflowers)
Salvia spp. (sages)
Saponaria officinalis (bouncing bet)
Scabiosa spp. (pincushion flowers)
Stachys coccinea (scarlet sage)
Thalictrum spp. (meadow rues)
Tradescantia spp. (spiderworts)
Verbena spp. (verbenas, vervains)
Veronica spp. (speedwells)

*tender perennial

Perennials By Season

Knowing what perennials bloom when can be especially helpful when you're planning your garden. Maybe you want plants in bloom in every season, or you're trying to add color at a specific time—fall, for example—because you realize that you've planted all spring and summer bloomers. If you have a summer home, you may want to design a bed that blooms in a single season so you can enjoy the color while you're there. (Of course, some peren-

nials bloom from one season into the next; these lists capture the season when the plants bloom longest.) We haven't included spring-blooming bulbs or summer-blooming grasses here, but check these lists for other seasonal showstoppers.

Spring-Flowering

Amsonia spp. (blue stars, amsonias)
Aquilegia spp. (columbines)
Aurinia saxatilis (basket-of-gold)
Cerastium tomentosum (snow-in-summer)
Chrysogonum virginianum (goldenstar, green-and-gold)
Corydalis spp. (corydalis, fumeroots)
Crocus spp. (crocuses)
Dicentra spp. (bleeding hearts)
Epimedium spp. (fairy wings, barrenworts)
Helleborus spp. (hellebores, Christmas roses, Lenten roses)
Iris spp. (irises)
Lamium maculatum (spotted dead nettle)
Oenothera speciosa (showy evening primrose)
Paeonia spp. (peonies)
Primula spp. (primroses, cowslips)
Trillium spp. (trilliums)

Summer-Flowering

Achillea spp. (yarrows)
Aistroemeria spp. and hybrids (alstroemerias)
Anemone x hybrida, A. tomentosa (Japanese anemones)
Asclepias tuberosa (butterfly weed)
Aster spp. (asters)
Calamintha nepeta (calamint)
Callirhoe involucrata (purple poppy mallow)
Ceratostigma plumbaginoides (plumbago)
Coreopsis spp. (tickseed, coreopsis)
Crocosmia x crocosmiiflora (crocosmia)
Digitalis spp. (foxgloves)
Echinacea spp. (coneflowers)
Eupatorium spp. (Joe-Pye weeds, bonesets)
Geranium spp. (geraniums, cranesbills)
Heliopsis spp. (oxeyes)
Hemerocallis spp. (daylilies)
Heuchera spp. (alumroots, coral bells)
Kalimeris spp. (Mongolian asters, Japanese asters)
Kniphofia spp. (torch lilies, red-hot pokers)
Leucanthemum maximum (Shasta daisy)
Liatris spp. (gayfeathers, blazing-stars)
Lilium spp. (lilies)
Linaria vulgaris (toadflax)
Lobelia spp. (lobelias)
Monarda spp. (bee balms, bergamots)
Nepeta spp. (catmints, nepetas)
Oenothera spp. (evening primroses)
Penstemon spp. (beardtongues, penstemons)
Platycodon grandiflorus (balloon flower)
Prunella grandiflora (large-flowered self-heal)
Rudbeckia spp. (black-eyed Susans, coneflowers)
Scabiosa spp. (pincushion flowers)
Tanacetum parthenium (feverfew)
Tradescantia spp. (spiderworts)
Veronica spp. (speedwells)

Fall-Flowering

Aconitum spp. (monkshoods)
Anemone hupehensis (Chinese anemone)
Aster spp. (asters)

Boltonia asteroids (boltonia)
Chelone lyonii (pink turtlehead)
Chrysanthemum x morifolium (garden chrysanthemum)
Cimicifuga simplex (Kamchatka bugbane)
Colchicum spp. (colchicums, meadow saffrons)
Coreopsis spp. (tickseeds, coreopsis)
Cyclamen hederifolium (ivy-leaf cyclamen)
Hedychium spp. (ginger lilies, garland lilies)
Helenium spp. (sneezeweeds, Helen's flowers)
Helianthus spp. (sunflowers)
Kirengeshoma spp. (yellow bells, wax bells)
Leucanthemum nipponicum (Nippon daisy)
Lycoris spp. (spider lilies, surprise lilies)
Lysimachia vulgaris (yellow loosestrife)
Patrinia scabiosafolia (patrinia)
Physostegia virginiana (obedient plant)
Salvia spp. (sages)
Sedum spp. (stonecrops, sedums)
Solidago spp. (goldenrods)
Tricyrtis spp. (toad lilies)

Winter Interest

Acanthus spp. (bears-breeches)
Achillea spp. (yarrows)
Arum spp. (arums)
Asarum spp. (wild gingers)
Aster spp. (asters)
Astilbe spp. (false spireas)
Baptisia spp. (false indigos, wild indigos)
Bergenia spp. (bergenias, winter begonias)
Cyclamen coum (hardy cyclamen)
Echinacea spp. (coneflowers)
Eupatorium spp. (Joe-Pye weeds, bonesets)
Ferns
Galanthus spp. (snowdrops)
Helleborus spp. (hellebores, Christmas roses, Lenten roses)
Hibiscus spp. (rose mallows, hibiscus)
Hosta spp. (hostas)
Lespedeza spp. (bush clovers)
Lilium formosanum (Formosa lily)
Ornamental grasses
Rudbeckia spp. (black-eyed Susans, coneflowers)
Vernonia spp. (ironweeds)

Perennials with Showy Foliage

Attractive foliage can hold its own with flowers in the perennial garden, providing interest when plants aren't in bloom, complementing or contrasting with flower color, or enhancing a color-theme bed. Foliage can brighten shady gardens and cool down sunny ones, create tropical effects in temperate gardens, or weave a tapestry of colorful groundcover under other plantings. Some plants have such showy foliage that they can stand alone as specimen plants. Foliage is a fact of perennial life, so why not make the most of it? The choices below will get you off to a good start.

White or Silver; Solid, Mottled, or Variegated

Ajuga reptans 'Silver Carpet' ('Silver Carpet' common bugleweed)
Artemisia spp. (artemisias, wormwoods)
Arum italicum 'Pictum' ('Pictum' Italian arum)
Asarum spp. (wild gingers)
Athyrium niponicum 'Pictum' ('Pictum' Japanese lady fern)

Continued ➡

Carex morrowii 'Variegata' (variegated morrow sedge)

Cerastium tomentosum (snow-in-summer)

Heuchera americana cvs. (alumroots, rock geraniums)

Hosta cvs., such as 'Patriot' (hostas)

Lamium maculatum cvs., such as 'White Nancy', 'Beacon Silver' (spotted dead nettles)

Liriope spicata 'Silver Dragon' ('Silver Dragon' creeping liriope)

Miscanthus sinensis 'Caberet', 'Cosmopolitan' (variegated Japanese silver grasses)

Phalaris arundinacea cvs., such as 'Feesey's Variety' (ribbon grass)

Polygonatum odoratum 'Variegatum' (variegated Japanese Solomon's seal)

Pulmonaria spp. (lungworts, Bethlehem sages)

Sedum cvs., such as 'Frosty Morn' (stonecrops, sedums)

Stachys byzantina (lamb's ears)

Vinca spp. and cvs., such as V. minor 'Ralph Shuggart' (vincas, periwinkles)

Yucca filamentosa 'Variegata' (variegated Adam's needle)

Gold or Chartreuse; Solid or Variegated

Acanthus mollis 'Holland's Gold' ('Holland's Gold' bear's-breeches)

Agastache 'Golden Jubilee' ('Golden Jubilee' anise hyssop)

Arachnoides simplisior 'Variegata' (variegated holly fern)

*Canna x generalis 'Bengal Tiger' ('Pretoria') ('Bengal Tiger' canna)

Carex elata 'Aurea' (Bowles' golden sedge), C. dolichostachya 'Kaga Nisiki' (Kaga brocade sedge), C. morrowii 'Goldband' ('Goldband' morrow sedge)

Dicentra spectabilis 'Gold Heart' ('Gold Heart' old-fashioned bleeding heart)

Filipendula ulmaria 'Aurea' (European queen of the meadow)

Geranium 'Ann Folkard' ('Ann Folkard' geranium)

Hakonechloa macra 'Aureola', 'All Gold' (golden hakone grass, Japanese fountain grass)

Heliopsis helianthoides 'Loraine Sunshine' ('Loraine Sunshine' oxeye)

Heuchera 'Amber Waves' ('Amber Waves' coral bells)

Hosta cvs., such as 'Gold Standard', 'Tokudama', 'Sum and Substance' (hostas)

*Ipomoea batatas 'Margarita' ('Margarita' sweet potato vine)

Iris variegated selection such as I. ensata 'Variegata', (variegated Japanese iris), I. pallida 'Aureo-Variegata' (variegated sweet iris)

Lamium maculatum 'Aureum' ('Aureum' spotted dead nettle)

Ligularia tussilaginea 'Aureomaculata' (leopard plant)

Liriope muscari 'Pee Dee Gold Ingot' (blue lily turf)

Lysimachia nummularia 'Golden Globe' ('Golden Globe' creeping Jenny); L. clethroides 'Geisha' ('Geisha' gooseneck loosestrife)

Miscanthus sinensis 'Strictus' ('Strictus' Japanese silver grass)

*Pelargonium cvs. (zonal geraniums)

Phlox paniculata 'Goldmine' and others (garden phlox)

*Solenostemon scotellarioides cvs. (coleus)

Tanacetum vulgare 'Isla Gold' ('Isla Gold' tansy)

Tradescantia 'Blue and Gold' ('Blue and Gold' spiderwort)

Tricyrtis formosana 'Gates of Heaven' ('Gates of Heaven' Formosa toad lily)

Veronica repens 'Sunshine', V. prostrata 'Aztec Gold' (harebell speedwells)

Yucca 'Golden Sword', 'Color Guard' (varie gated yuccas)

*tender perennial

Blue or Gray-Blue

Achillea 'Moonshine' ('Moonshine' yarrow)

Corydalis flexuosa, C. ochroleuca (blue and white fumeroots)

Crambe maritima (sea kale)

Dicentra cvs. (bleeding hearts)

Festuca cinerea, such as 'Elijah Blue', 'Skinner's Blue', 'Solling' (blue fescue)

Helictotrichon sempervirens (blue oat grass)

Hosta cvs., such as 'Eatoi Blue', 'Krossa Regal', 'Blue Mammoth', 'Big Daddy' (hostas)

Panicum virgatum 'Heavy Metal', 'Dallas Blues' ('Heavy Metal' or 'Dallas Blues' switchgrass)

Ruta graveolens cvs., such as 'Blue Beauty', 'Blue Mound' (rues)

Yucca rostrata (beaked blue yucca)

Purple or Purple Variegations

Ajuga reptans 'Atropurpurea' or 'Purpurea' ('Atropurpurea' or 'Purpuea' common bugleweed)

Angelica gigas (Korean angelica, purple parsnip)

*Anthriscus 'Ravenswing' (cow parsley)

Aster lateriflorus 'Lady in Black' ('Lady in Black' calico aster)

*Canna x generalis, such as 'Pink Futurity', 'King Humpert', 'Wyoming', 'Australia', 'Intrigue', 'Pacific Beauty' (cannas)

*Colocasia esculenta 'Black Magic' ('Black Magic' elephant ear)

Corydalis flexuosa 'Purple Leaf' ('Purple Leaf' blue fumeroot)

Dahlia 'Bednall Beauty', 'Yellow Hammer', 'Bishop of Llandaff' (dahlias)

Eupatorium rugosum 'Chocolate' ('Chocolate' white snakeroot)

Geranium pratense 'Midnight Reiter' ('Midnight Reiter' meadow cranes bill)

Heuchera cvs., such as 'Palace Purple', 'Cathedral Windows', 'Velvet Night' (alumroots, coral bells)

*Ipomoea batatas 'Blackie', 'Black Heart' ('Blackie' and 'Black Heart' sweet potato vines)

Lysimachia ciliata 'Atropurpurea' ('Atropurpurea' fringed loosestrife)

Persicaria microcephala 'Red Dragon' ('Red Dragon' knotweed)

Polemonium yezoense 'Purple Rain' ('Purple Rain' Jacob's ladder)

*Ricinus communis (castor bean)

Sedum 'Matrona', 'Vera Jameson' ('Matrona' and 'Vera Jameson' sedums)

*Solenostemon scotellarioides cvs. (coleus)

*tender perennial

Glossy

Ajuga reptans (common bugleweed)

Asarum europaeum (European wild ginger)

Astilbe spp. (false spireas)

Bergenia cordifolia (heart-leaved bergenia)

Chelone spp. (turtleheads)

Colchicum spp. (colchicums, meadow saffrons)

Darmera peltata (umbrella plant)

Epimedium spp. (fairy wings, barrenworts)

Helleborus spp. (hellebores, Christmas roses, Lenten roses)

Heuchera micrantha var. diversifolia 'Palace Purple' ('Palace Purple' alumroot)

Hosta spp. (hostas)

Liriope muscari (blue lily turf)

Pachysandra spp. (pachysandras, spurges)

Paeonia spp. (peonies)

Phygelius spp. (cape fuchsias, cape figworts)

Polystichum spp. (holly ferns, sword ferns)

Stokesia laevis (Stokes' aster)

Specimen

Acanthus spp. (bear's-breeches)

Angelica spp. (angelicas, archangels)

Aralia spp. (spikenards)

Astilboides tabularis (astilboides)

*Canna x generalis (canna)

Crambe spp. (crambes, kales)

Cyathea cooperi (lacy tree fern)

Darmera peltata (umbrella plant)

Filipendula spp. (meadowsweets, queen of the meadows)

Hedychium spp. (ginger lilies, garland lilies)

Hosta spp., such as 'Great Expectations', 'Krossa Regal', 'Sum and Substance', 'Blue Mammoth', 'Big Daddy' (large-leaved hostas)

Inula spp. (elecampanes, inulas)

Kirengeshoma palmata (Japanese yellow bells)

Lespedeza spp. (bush clovers)

Ligularia spp. (ligularias, groundsels) Matteuccia struthiopteris (ostrich fern)

Miscanthus spp. (Japanese silver grasses)

Onoclea sensibilis (sensitive fern)

Osmunda spp. (flowering ferns)

Rheum spp. (rhubarbs)

Rodgersia spp. (rodgersias, Roger's-flowers)

Silphium spp. (rosinweeds, compass plants)

Symphytum x uplandicum (Russian comfrey)

Telekia speciosa (telekia)

Yucca spp. (yuccas, Adam's needles)

Perennials By Care Requirements

If you're a busy gardener or you have extensive gardens, you probably want to look for the easy-care perennials and avoid those fussy types that require tons of coddling, primping, and other maintenance. If a perennial you're considering isn't on one list or the other, consider it to require moderate care—maybe some deadheading, watering during dry spells, cutting back, or dividing occasionally—and plant or avoid accordingly.

Easy Care

Acanthus spp. (bear's-breeches)

Aconitum spp. (monkshoods)

Actaea spp. (baneberries)

Agapanthus spp. (lilies of the Nile, African lilies)

Alchemilla spp. (lady's-mantles)

Amsonia spp. (blue stars, amsonias)

Armeria spp. (thrifts)

Aruncus spp. (goat's beards)

Astilbe spp. (false spireas)

Continued ➡

Baptisia spp. (false indigos, wild indigos)
Bergenia spp. (bergenias, winter begonias)
Cimicifuga spp. (bugbanes, cohoshes, snakeroots)
Dicentra spp. (bleeding hearts)
Dictamnus albus (gas plant)
Digitalis spp. (foxgloves)
Echinacea spp. (coneflowers)
Echinops spp. (globe thistles)
Epimedium spp. (fairy wings, barrenworts)
Eryngium spp. (sea hollies, eryngos)
Euphorbia spp. (spurges, euphorbias)
Gaura lindheimeri (white gaura)
Geranium spp. (geraniums, cranes bills)
Gypsophila spp. (baby's-breaths)
Helleborus spp. (hellebores, Christmas roses,
    Lenten roses)
Hemerocallis spp. (daylilies)
Heuchera spp. (alumroots, coral bells)
Hosta spp. (hostas, plaintain lilies, funkias)
Kirengeshoma spp. (yellow bells, wax bells)
Kniphofia spp. (torch lilies, red-hot pokers)
Liatris spp. (gayfeathers, blazing-stars)
Limonium spp. (sea lavenders, statices)
Lysimachia spp. (loosestrifes)
Paeonia spp. (peonies)
Papaver orientale (Oriental poppy)
Pennisetum spp. (fountain grasses)
Perovskia atriplicifolia (Russian sage)
Platycodon grandiflorus (balloon flower)
Rheum spp. (rhubarbs)
Thalictrum spp. (meadow rues)
Thermopsis spp. (bush peas, thermopsis)
Veronicastrum virginicum (Culver's root)
Yucca spp. (yuccas, Adam's needles)

Intensive Care

Delphinium cvs. (delphiniums)
Eremurus spp. (foxtail lilies, desert-candles)
Fritillaria spp. (fritillaries, checkered lilies)
Lewisia spp. (lewisias)
Lupinus cvs. (lupines)
Meconopsis spp. (meconopsis)
Penstemon spp. (beardtongues, penstemons)
Primula spp. (primroses, cowslips)

Perennials By Preferred Conditions

Sun or shade. Hot or cool. Wet or dry. Like us,
perennials have their preferences. Check this
section to find perennials that match your garden's
conditions.

Hot and Dry, Sunny

Achillea spp. (yarrows)
Agapanthus spp. (lilies of the Nile, African lilies)
Agastache spp. (anise hyssops)
Agave spp. (agaves)
Allium spp. (ornamental onions)
Anthemis tinctoria (golden marguerite)
Artemisia spp. (artemisias, wormwoods)
Asclepias tuberosa (butterfly weed)
Calamintha nepeta (calamint)
Callirhoe involucrata (purple poppy mallow)
Centranthus ruber (red valerian)
Chrysopsis spp. (golden asters)
Delosperma spp. (ice plants)
Dianthus gratianopolitanus (cheddar pinks)

Echinacea spp. (coneflowers)
Echinops spp. (globe thistles)
Eryngium spp. (sea hollies, eryngos)
Euphorbia spp. (spurges, euphorbias)
Festuca glauca (blue fescue)
Gaillardia spp. (blanket flowers)
Gaura lindheimeri (white gaura)
Helianthus spp. (sunflowers)
Helictotrichon sempervirens (blue oat grass)
Iris bearded hybrids (bearded irises)
Knautia macedonica (knautia)
Lavandula spp. (lavenders)
Limonium latifolium (sea lavender)
Nepeta spp. (catmints, nepetas)
Oenothera spp. (evening primroses)
Opuntia spp. (prickly pears)
Penstemon spp. (beardtongues, penstemons)
Perovskia atriplicifolia (Russian sage)
Phlomis spp. (Jerusalem sages)
Phormium spp. (phormiums, New Zealand flax)
Romneya coulteri (matilja poppy)
Salvia spp. (sages)
Santolina chamaecyparissus (lavender cotton)
Schizachyrium scoparium (little bluestem)
Verbascum spp. (mulleins)
Verbena spp. (verbenas, vervains)
Veronicastrum virginicum (Culver's root)
Yucca spp. (yuccas, Adam's needles)

Moist Soil, Sunny

Agastache spp. (anise hyssops)
Alstroemeria spp. and hybrids (alstroemerias)
Amsonia spp. (blue stars, amsonias)
Anemone x *hybrida* (Japanese anemone)
Aster x *frikartii* (Frikart's aster)
Astrantia major (masterwort)
Baptisia spp. (false indigos, wild indigos)
Calamagrostis x *acutiflora* (feather reed grass)
Canna x *generalis* (canna)
Coreopsis spp. (tickseed, coreopsis)
Crocosmia x *crocosmiiflora* (crocosmia)
Digitalis spp. (foxgloves)
Geranium spp. (geraniums, cranesbills)
Hedychium spp. (ginger lilies, garland lilies)
Helianthus angustifolius (swamp sunflower)
Hemerocallis spp. (daylilies)
Heuchera x *brizoides* (hybrid coral bells)
Kalimeris spp. (Mongolian asters, Japanese asters)
Kniphofia spp. (torch lilies, red-hot pokers)
Lespedeza spp. (bush clovers)
Leucanthemum x *superbum* (Shasta daisy)
Liatris spp. (gayfeathers, blazing-stars)
Molinia caerulea (purple moor grass)
Paeonia spp. (peonies)
Patrinia spp. (patrinias)
Penstemon digitalis (foxglove penstemon)
Phlox spp. (phlox)
Platycodon grandiflorus (balloon flower)
Silphium spp. (rosinweeds, compass plants)
Solidago spp. (goldenrods)
Tanacetum parthenium (feverfew)
Veronica spp. (speedwells)

Wet Soil, Sunny

Acorus spp. (sweet flags)

Alchemilla spp. (lady's-mantles)
Asclepias incarnata (swamp milkweed)
Boltonia asteroides (boltonia)
Caltha palustris (marsh marigold, cowslip)
Canna spp. (cannas)
Carex elata 'Aurea' (Bowles' golden sedge)
Chelone spp. (turtleheads)
Darmera peltata (umbrella plant)
Eupatorium spp. (Joe-Pye weeds, bonesets)
Filipendula spp. (meadowsweets, queen of the
    meadows)
Helenium spp. (sneezeweeds, Helen's flowers)
Hibiscus moscheutos (common rose mallow)
Iris ensata, I. pseudacorus, I. versicolor, I. virginica
    (Japanese iris, yellow flag iris, blue flag iris,
    southern blue flag iris)
Juncus spp. (rushes)
Ligularia spp. (ligularias, groundsels)
Lobelia spp. (lobelias)
Matteuccia struthiopteris (ostrich fern)
Monarda spp. (bee balms, bergamots)
Myosotis scorpioides (water forget-me-not)
Osmunda spp. (flowering ferns)
Panicum virgatum (switchgrass)
Physostegia spp. (obedient plants)
Rodgersia spp. (rodgersias, Roger's- flowers)
Sanguisorba spp. (burnets)
Sarracenia spp. (pitcher plants)
Stokesia laevis (Stokes' aster)
Thalictrum spp. (meadow rues)
Thelypteris spp. (river ferns, marsh ferns)
Veratrum spp. (false hellebores, Indian pokes)
Vernonia spp. (ironweeds)
Zephyranthes spp. (rain lilies)

Dry Shade

Anemonella thalictroides (rue anemone, windflower)
Aquilegia spp. (columbines)
Arum italicum 'Pictum' (Italian arum)
Carex morrowii and cvs., such as 'Variegata'
    (morrow sedges)
Covallaria majalis (lily-of-the-valley)
Chasmanthium latifolium (Northern sea oats)
Cyclamen spp. (hardy cyclamens)
Dicentra spp. (bleeding hearts)
Dodecatheon spp. (shooting-stars)
Dryopteris spp. (shield ferns, wood ferns)
Epimedium spp. (fairy wings, barrenworts)
Euphorbia amygdaloides (wood spurge)
Helleborus spp. (hellebores, Christmas roses,
    Lenten roses)
Hepatica spp. (hepaticas, liverleafs, harbingers of
    spring)
Heuchera americana (alumroot, rock geranium)
Pachysandra spp. (pachysandras, spurges)
Polygonatum odoratum and cvs., such as 'Variegatum'
    (Japanese Solomon's seals)
Polystichum spp. (holly ferns, sword ferns)

Moist Shade

Aconitum spp. (monkshoods)
Actaea spp. (bane berries)
Arisaema spp. (Jack-in-the-pulpits)
Asarum spp. (wild gingers)
Astilbe spp. (false spireas)
Astrantia spp. (masterworts)
Begonia grandis (hardy begonia)

Continued ➡

Brunnera macrophylla (Siberian bugloss, forget-me-not)

Cimicifuga spp. (bugbanes, cohoshes, snakeroots)

Corydalis lutea (golden fumeroot)

Dicentra spp. (bleeding hearts)

Ferns

Helleborus spp. (hellebores, Christmas roses, Lenten roses)

Heuchera spp. (alumroots, coral bells)

x *Heucherella alba* (white foamy bells)

Hosta spp. (hostas, plantain lilies, funkias)

Iris cristata (crested iris)

Kirengeshoma spp. (yellow bells, wax bells)

Ligularia spp. (ligularias, groundsels)

Mertensia virginica (Virginia bluebells)

Myosotis spp. (forget-me-nots)

Omphalodes spp. (navel seeds, blue-eyed Marys)

Phlox divaricata (wild blue phlox, woodland phlox)

Polygonatum spp. (Solomon's seals)

Primula spp. (primroses, cowslips)

Pulmonaria spp. (lungworts, Bethlehem sages)

Smilacina racemosa (Solomon's plume)

Tiarella spp. (foamflowers)

Tricyrtis spp. (toad lilies)

TrilliumI spp. (trilliums)

Trollius spp. (globeflowers)

Uvularia spp. (bellworts, merrybells)

Viola spp. (violets, violas)

Perennial Favorites

With so many beautiful, dependable perennials to choose from, deciding which ones to plant in your garden can be tough. In this chapter, you'll learn about 50 outstanding plants—perennials that have been loved by gardeners for years and are just waiting to grace your flowerbeds.

Choose Carefully

Once you start flipping through the following pages, you'll probably want to plant at least one of each kind of perennial listed here. But hold on a minute before you rush gung ho to your local garden center. Take the time to read the "Plant Particulars" listed for each entry—especially the appropriate USDA Plant Hardiness Zones (see chapter 1) for each perennial that interests you. Then, consider the available light as well as the soil characteristics in each area of your yard that you want to plant. The perennials you choose should be those best suited to growth in your region and under the conditions specific to your landscape.

Plant shape, spread, height, color, and bloom time also are important factors to consider when choosing perennials. If you have limited room, rule out plants that spread aggressively, or they'll quickly invade the rest of your space. Also, make sure that the shapes, heights, and colors of your chosen plants work with the overall design you have in mind.

Express Yourself

Now go ahead—turn the page and start dreaming about the art you'll create in your garden. Remember, anyone can create a masterpiece with perennials!

Achillea

(Yarrow)

PLANT PARTICULARS

Zones: 3 to 9

Height: 1 to 4 feet

Spread: Strong spreaders; depending on species, can spread between 1 and 5 feet

Shape: Spreading clumps of stiff, upright flowerstalks

Color: White, pink, red, or yellow flowers; green or gray leaves

Bloom time: Late spring or summer to early fall

Light needs: Full sun to partial shade

Soil: Average to poor; dry but well drained

Yarrows are the perfect perennials to add some spice to your garden—literally—because their foliage has a spicy aroma. In addition to smelling good, yarrows are also attractive. Their showy, flattened flower heads are made up of many tiny, tightly packed flowers and their leaves are feathery. These extremely versatile plants work well in formal or informal borders and soften bold textures. Definitely plant yarrows along a walkway, where you'll be sure to brush against them, releasing their fragrance.

These low-maintenance plants thrive with little care. However, they do spread rapidly, so divide your plants every 3 to 5 years. In early spring or fall, dig up a clump, remove any dead stems from its center, break up the clump, and relocate the new plants.

Yarrows are excellent for cutting and for use in fresh and dried flower arrangements. To enjoy the flowers after the growing season has ended, cut the blooms before their color starts to fade; tie the stems in bunches; and hang them upside down in a dark, airy room (such as an attic) until dry.

Achillea x 'Moonshine'

Alchemilla

(Lady's-Mantle)

PLANT PARTICULARS

Zones: 3 to 8

Height: 6 to 12 inches

Spread: 1 to 2 feet

Shape: soft mounds

Color: Chartreuse flowers; gray-green leaves

Bloom time: Spring, early summer

Light needs: Sun to partial shade

Soil: Rich, moist

The leaves of lady's-mantle have an interesting feature: downy hairs. When water beads up on the leaves, the effect is an enchanting, jeweled display that's hard to beat. The plant also will reward you with clouds of lovely flowers and lush clumps of soft, fan-shaped foliage. This perennial works well at the front of the perennial border, along a wall, or edging a walk. Try pairing it with upright perennials, such as Siberian iris and astilbes. The small

variety of lady's-mantle (*A. alpina*) is perfect for rock gardens and containers.

By midsummer, the leaves of lady's-mantle can look rather tired. To perk up the plant and encourage new foliage growth, cut it back to the ground. (The plants will quickly produce a new set of leaves.) If you live in a region where the temperature really climbs during the summer, choose a partially shaded site for best growth and flowering.

Lady's-mantle will often self-sow; cut off spent flowers to prevent reseeding. Relocate new seedlings to extend an edging all along a bed. Divide overgrown clumps in spring or fall.

Anemone

(Anemone, Windflower)

PLANT PARTICULARS

Zones: 3 to 9

Height: 4 inches to 5 feet

Spread: 18 to 24 inches

Shape: Varies among species

Color: White, pink, red, purple, or blue flowers with yellow centers; deep green foliage

Bloom time: Spring, summer, fall

Light needs: Full sun to partial shade

Soil: Fertile but well drained

One of the great things about anemones is that they come in spring-, summer-, and fall-blooming varieties—which means you can have a full season of anemone color. Anemones have fragile, five-petaled flowers with fuzzy, bright yellow centers. These perennials can work well as mass plantings, in combination with spring bulbs, under shrubs, or as a groundcover, depending on the variety.

If you have room for only one anemone, make it a Japanese anemone (*Anemone* x *hybrida*). This fall-blooming beauty has single or double flowers on 3- to 5-foot stems. Combine Japanese anemones with bleeding hearts and other early bloomers; the anemone foliage will fill the space when the other plants go dormant.

To increase your anemone collection, divide spring-blooming types after flowering and summer and fall bloomers in spring.

Note: All anemones are poisonous if eaten, so you might want to avoid planting them if small children frequently visit your garden.

Aquilegia

(Columbine)

PLANT PARTICULARS

Zones: 3 to 9

Height: 6 inches to 4 feet

Spread: 1 foot

Shape: Open clumps

Color: Blue, maroon, pink, purple, red, white, or yellow flowers; blue-green to green leaves

Bloom time: Late spring to early summer

Light needs: Full sun to partial shade

Soil: Average to rich; moist but well drained

If you want to attract hummingbirds to your garden, then add columbine to your beds. Each blossom has five petals, which form a tube that holds the nectar that hummingbirds desire. These delicate-looking perennials come in shades of blue, maroon, pink, purple, red, white, or yellow that add charm to borders, woodland gardens, and rock gardens and also bridge the spring and

Continued ➡

summer bloom seasons. Combine them with late-blooming tulips to finish the spring show, and with irises and peonies to start your summer display. They also look super around the base of tall, shrubby perennials, such as baptisias and delphiniums.

In mid- to late summer, the urn-shaped seed-pods will drop lots of seed and self-sow. To prevent self-sowing, pinch off spent flowers. Otherwise, relocate the seedlings in spring.

Squiggly lines on your columbine leaves indicate that leafminers are at work. Immediately pinch off and destroy the damaged leaves, and check the plants frequently for more signs of damage. If the problem is severe, spray the plants weekly with insecticidal soap.

Artemisia

(Artemisia, Wormwood)

Plant Particulars

Zones: 3 to 9

Height: 10 inches to 6 feet

Spread: Strong spreaders; depending on species, can spread between 6 and 30 inches

Shape: Varies among species

Color: Yellowish or grayish flowers; green to silver leaves

Bloom time: Summer, fall

Light needs: Full sun

Soil: Average, dry but well drained

These aromatic plants are indispensable for adding year-round foliage interest to beds and borders. Artemisias have showy green or gray foliage and yellowish or grayish flowers, which appear late in the season. Some varieties form shrubby, mounding clumps. Plant artemisias to contrast with bright colors in your garden (especially hot pinks, reds, and oranges) or to cool pastels (such as soft pinks, purples, and blues).

If you prefer low-maintenance plants, then artemisias are the perennials for you. And once established, most of them are extremely drought tolerant. If you live in a warm, humid region, plant upright varieties instead of the mounding ones, because the mounding varieties tend to fall open from the center. All artemisia varieties should be pruned back hard if they start to lose their form.

Aster

(Aster)

Plant Particulars

Zones: 2 to 8

Height: 6 inches to 8 feet

Spread: Varies among species

Shape: Varies among species

Color: Blue, purple, red, pink, or white flowers; green leaves

Bloom time: Late summer to late fall

Light needs: Full sun to light shade

Soil: Average; moist but well drained

Bushy and beautiful, asters offer masses of showy, daisylike blooms that are ideal for edgings, containers, meadow and woodland gardens, and at the backs of beds and borders. Although you might think of asters as being primarily fall plants, many varieties begin blooming in late summer—and they come in a rainbow of colors. To create layers of texture and color, try backing pink asters with Russian sage and yellow coneflowers. Asters also pair well with ferns and wildflowers.

Tall asters probably will need staking. You also can cut them back by half in midsummer to promote sturdier stems and more branching. For bushier fall plants, pinch or shear asters in the spring or early summer. Divide plants every year or two to control their spread, rejuvenate overgrown clumps, or increase your plantings. To avoid powdery mildew, avoid wetting the leaves when watering.

Astilbe

(Astilbe, False Spirea)

Plant Particulars

Zones: 3 to 9

Height: 8 inches to 5 feet

Spread: 1 to 3 feet

Shape: Clumps of upright or cascading flowerstalks

Color: Red, magenta, rose, pink, lavender, lilac, cream, or white flowers; leaves are green or reddish

Bloom time: Late spring, summer

Light needs: Full sun to deep shade

Soil: Average; moist but well drained

If you're looking for a way to add some color to a moist, shady area of your yard, then astilbes are the perennial for you. These regal plants have airy plumes of densely packed, tiny flowers that range in color from red through all shades of magenta, rose, and pink to lavender, lilac, cream, and white. The shape of the flower clusters differs by variety; some are stiff and upright, others are open plumes, and still others cascade outward like fireworks. Astilbe leaves are fernlike and have a coppery or reddish sheen in spring.

These long-lived, low-maintenance plants are perfect companions to ferns, irises, and other moisture-loving plants. You might want to try a mass of astilbes around a water garden, where the water will reflect the flower's colorful blooms.

During the summer, snip a few of the flowers to enjoy in arrangements indoors; leave the rest to mature on the plants for winter interest.

Baptisia

(Baptisia, False Indigo)

Plant Particulars

Zones: 3 to 9

Height: 1 to 5 feet

Spread: 3 to 4 feet

Shape: Clumps of upright flowerstalks

Color: Blue, yellow, cream, or white flowers; gray-green or bluish leaves

Bloom time: Late spring to early summer

Light needs: Full sun to partial shade

Soil: Rich; moist but well drained

Plant them and forget them—that's the key to growing baptisias. These durable plants can live in the same spot for years without division, slowly forming shrublike clumps. Baptisias have colorful spikes of pealike flowers in blue, yellow, cream, and white with gray-green or bluish leaves. They're excellent border plants; use them toward the back of the border in the company of bold flowers such as peonies, oriental poppies, and irises. After flowering, baptisias make a good background for late-blooming perennials. Baptisias also produce showy gray or brown seedpods; cut them for arrangements or leave them on the plants for off-season interest.

Have patience when growing baptisias; they grow slowly at first and may require at least 5 years

to reach their full growth. In some spots, baptisias may need staking; place rounded peony hoops over the clumps as they emerge in early spring to keep the plants from toppling over.

Baptisia australis (blue false indigo)

Boltonia

(Boltonia)

Plant Particulars

Zones: 3 to 9

Height: 4 to 6 feet

Spread: 3 to 4 feet

Shape: Tall, rounded

Color: Pink, purple, or white flowers with yellow centers; blue-green leaves

Bloom time: Late spring to midfall

Light needs: Full sun to light shade

Soil: Rich; moist or dry

Add a cool touch to late summer and early fall borders and wildflowers gardens with boltonia. This elegant perennial has blue-green leaves and purple, pale pink, or snowy white flowers with yellow centers. It's easy to grow, and it will deliver blooms in poor, dry soil as well as rich, moist soil. (Just keep in mind that the plant will be smaller in dry soil than it would be in moist soil.) For an elegant, all-white combination, try 'Snowbank' boltonia with a white-variegated ornamental grass and a white-flowered Japanese anemone.

Cut back boltonias by half in early to midsummer to encourage bushiness and flowering. You can leave the stems standing after they've finished blooming to add interest and texture to your winter garden. If you want more boltonia plants, divide them in spring. Remove the dead centers and replant the vigorous outer portions.

Campanula

(Bellflower)

Plant Particulars

Zones: 2 to 8

Height: 4 inches to 5 feet

Continued ➡

Spread: Varies among species

Shape: Varies among species

Color: Purple, blue, white, or pink flowers; green leaves

Bloom time: Spring, summer

Light needs: Full sun to partial shade

Soil: Average to rich; well drained

These easy-care perennials have bell- or star-shaped flowers. They come in many different varieties, which range from low, mat-forming creepers to tall, upright plants. Choose the low-growing varieties for rock gardens and informal rock walls. The blue and purple flowers contrast well with rocks and will soften even the harshest rock surface. Use the taller varieties in beds and borders, or along walls and fences. They're also lovely in large drifts. Create stunning color combinations by grouping blue bellflowers with bright yellow yarrow, pure white peonies, and/or pretty pink astilbes.

Divide bellflowers in early spring or fall to control their spread or rejuvenate crowded clumps. Slugs are the only serious threats to bellflowers; use a dish of beer as bait to drown these pests.

Chrysanthemum

(Chrysanthemum)

PLANT PARTICULARS

Zones: 3 to 11

Height: 1 to 5 feet

Spread: Varies among species

Shape: Varies among species

Color: White, yellow, orange, red, pink, or purple; leaves various shades of green

Bloom time: Summer to fall

Light needs: Full sun

Soil: Average to rich; well drained

With so many different varieties of this perennial, you could have some sort of chrysanthemum (often shortened to "mum") blooming in your garden from early summer 'til frost. The daisylike flowers are available in shades of white, yellow, orange, red, pink, or purple. Shasta daisies and garden (hardy) mums are both types of chrysanthemums.

Mums are so varied in bloom time, color, size, and adaptability that they have a place in almost every garden. Shasta daisies, for example, are classics for the early summer garden. These white blooms create quite a pretty sight when paired with Siberian irises. And what would fall be without bright garden mums? They're perfect for tucking into bare spots in the garden left by worn-out annuals or for grouping in containers when most plants have stopped blooming for the season. Other mums work well as edging plants and at the back of beds or borders.

Coreopsis

(Coreopsis)

PLANT PARTICULARS

Zones: 3 to 9

Height: 1 to 9 feet

Spread: Varies among species

Shape: Varies among species

Color: Yellow or pink flowers; green leaves

Bloom time: Early summer to midfall

Light needs: Full sun

Soil: Average to poor; dry but well drained

Cheerful coreopsis is a dependable, easy-care plant that will bloom for months as long as you remove the spent flowers. The daisylike blooms are a welcoming sight in summer beds and borders. Coreopsis combines well with asters, irises, blanket flowers, purple coneflowers, and phlox. 'Moonbeam' (*c. verticillata*) is a particularly outstanding variety; its light yellow flowers look beautiful paired with other soft colors, such as pink, blue, and lavender. For brighter yellow blooms, look for 'Zagreb'.

Coreopsis is an especially good choice for beginning gardeners. The plants grow rapidly from seed and, once established, are quite drought-tolerant and even thrive under stress. However, they do need well-drained soil and may rot if planted in a location where water puddles. They may also flop over in soil that's too rich. Divide overgrown or declining plants in spring or fall.

Delphinium

(Delphinium, Larkspur)

PLANT PARTICULARS

Zones: 3 to 8

Height: 1 to 6 feet

Spread: Varies among species

Shape: Varies among species

Color: Blue, purple, pink, or white flowers; green leaves

Bloom time: Late spring, summer; fall rebloom

Light needs: Full sun

Soil: Rich; moist but well drained

These tall, sturdy, old-fashioned perennials are perfect for adding vertical accents to your garden. Their towers of showy flowers are traditional favorites for early summer color in beds, borders, and cottage gardens. Try placing them at the rear of a border, where their spikes can be highlighted against a wall or hedge. Create eye-catching contrasts by pairing delphiniums with bushy, mounded perennials such as peonies and baby's breath. To accent a wall or a fence, plant bold masses of mixed colors.

Encourage plants to rebloom by cutting off the spent flowers just above the top leaves. When the leafy stems begin to die back, cut them down to the new growth at the base of the plant.

Delphiniums are short-lived perennials, which means they fade out after 2 or 3 years in the garden. To propagate them, sow seeds outdoors in late summer; the seeds will grow and bloom the following season.

Dianthus

(Pinks, Carnation)

PLANT PARTICULARS

Zones: 3 to 9

Height: 3 inches to 2 feet

Spread: 8 to 18 inches

Shape: Mounds or mats

Color: White, pink, or red flowers; blue-green leaves

Bloom time: Spring, summer

Light needs: Full sun to light shade

Soil: Average; moist to dry

Pinks are beloved for their old-fashioned charm and delightful spicy-sweet fragrance. Their delicate flowers have fringed petals that complement their slender leaves. What's more, the foliage holds its color year-round, making this perennial attractive even when it's not blooming.

Most varieties of pinks are low-growing, clump-forming plants that are perfect additions to rock gardens and border edgings, and great for use as ground covers. Plant them on top of a retaining wall so you won't have to kneel down to enjoy their scent. Silvery-leaved plants, such as lamb's-ears and artemisias, make striking companions for pinks' bright blooms.

Pinks spread quickly and are often short-lived, so divide the clumps every 2 or 3 years to keep the plants vigorous. If you remove the spent flowers regularly, you'll usually be able to keep your pinks in bloom for 6 weeks or more.

Dicentra

(Bleeding Heart)

PLANT PARTICULARS

Zones: 2 to 9

Height: 8 inches to 2½ feet

Spread: Varies by species

Shape: Soft mounds

Color: Pink or white flowers; green to blue-green leaves

Bloom time: Spring, summer

Light needs: Full sun to full shade

Soil: Rich; moist but well drained

The unique flowers of this perennial, which resemble pink or white hearts with drops of blood on their tips, add splashes of color to any shade or woodland garden. Its feathery, fernlike foliage is a nice contrast to the plant's blooms. Some varieties are tall (common bleeding heart, *D. Spectabilis*) and bloom in the spring, whereas others (fringed bleeding heart, *D. eximia*) are much smaller and bloom in summer.

Because common bleeding heart often goes dormant by midsummer, pair it with bushy plants, such as asters and baby's breath, that will fill the space it leaves. Common bleeding heart also works well with daffodils, tulips, peonies, irises, and primroses. For a steady display of flowers from spring until frost, plant fringed bleeding heart with ferns, wildflowers, and shade-loving hostas.

Divide overgrown clumps of bleeding hearts in the fall or as they go dormant. The plants often self-sow; either remove spent flowers to prevent self-sowing or transplant the seedlings.

Dicentra spectabilis 'Alba'

Digitalis

(Foxglove)

PLANT PARTICULARS

Zones: 3 to 8

Continued ➔

Height: 2 to 5 feet

Spread: 1 to 2 feet

Shape: Erect flower spikes

Color: Pink, rose, white, or yellow flowers; green leaves

Bloom time: Summer

Light needs: Full sun to partial shade

Soil: Rich; moist but well drained

Here's a plant that deer seem to avoid. These stout perennials have leafy stems and tall spikes of funnel-like flowers in shades of pink, rose, white, and yellow. The insides of the plants are often spotted. Most foxgloves are either biennials (they live 2 years) or short-lived perennials (they live about 3 years).

These striking blooms perfectly punctuate the summer border, and their upright form is a welcome contrast to mounded plants such as hostas and peonies. They also look super with ferns and hostas in shade and woodland plantings. For compact, easy-care color, try perennial yellow foxglove (*D. grandiflora*). Its 2- to 3-foot spikes of soft yellow flowers combine beautifully with blues, pinks, and whites.

Common foxglove (*D. purpurea*) reaches 5 feet high when in bloom. Although it's a biennial, common foxglove acts like a perennial because it produces lots of self-sown seedlings. You can also lift the clumps after flowering, remove the bloom stalks that are spent, and replant the new rosettes in the same spot or somewhere new.

Echinacea

(Purple Coneflower)

PLANT PARTICULARS

Zones: 2 to 8

Height: 1 to 6 feet

Spread: Varies by species

Shape: Loose clumps of erect stalks

Color: Purple, pink, or white flowers; green leaves

Bloom time: Summer

Light needs: Full sun to light shade

Soil: Average; moist to dry

Butterflies love to visit purple coneflower during the blooming season, and seed-eating birds are attracted to its seedheads long after the blooms are gone. This showy perennial with daisylike flowers is also extremely heat- and drought-tolerant because the plant's thick, deep taproots store moisture in lean times. What's more, purple coneflower is about the easiest perennial to care for.

This plant is a natural choice for meadow gardens, along with ornamental grasses, goldenrods, and yarrows. In beds and borders, try pairing the bright blooms with artemisias, daylilies, coreopsis, and lamb's-ears. For a colorful late-summer display, pair purple coneflowers with black-eyed Susans.

You'll rarely need to divide purple coneflowers. (In fact, once divided, plants tend to become bushy and produce fewer flowers.) If you leave the seed-heads on for winter interest, plants may self-sow.

Epimedium

(Epimedium, Barrenwort)

PLANT PARTICULARS

Zones: 3 to 8

Height: 6 to 15 inches

Spread: Varies by species

Shape: Spreading mats

Color: White, yellow, pink, or red flowers; green, yellow, or reddish leaves

Bloom time: Spring

Light needs: Partial to full shade

Soil: Average to rich; moist to dry

These tough perennials, once established, will perform admirably in dry shade or under mature trees where nothing else will grow. Most people grow epimediums as groundcovers. However, they also work well in beds, borders, and rock gardens—even in a shade garden with astilbes, hostas, primroses, wildflowers, bulbs, and ferns.

Their heart-shaped green leaves often have red highlights; their flowers bloom in early spring before the new leaves open. Although they're often touted as evergreens, epimediums tend to look tattered by midwinter. Cut them to the ground in early spring; the plants will look neater and the dainty flowers will be more visible. New leaves will emerge with or just after the flowers.

Epimediums form spreading clumps that seldom need division. But, if you want to divide your plants, do so in late summer or early fall.

Euphorbia

(Spurge, Euphorbia)

PLANT PARTICULARS

Zones: 3 to 9

Height: 6 inches to 4 feet

Spread: Varies by species

Shape: Spreading clumps

Color: Yellow flowers; green or blue-green leaves

Bloom time: Spring, summer

Light needs: Full sun to partial shade

Soil: Average to rich; dry but well drained

If you want an outstanding foliage perennial, then euphorbia is for you. Euphorbias are succulent perennials with leafy stems and milky sap that flows freely when the leaves or stems are picked or damaged. (This sap is irritating to skin, so wear gloves while working around these plants.) Combine them with other perennials or flowering shrubs at the rear of a bed or border, or use them as container plants, as a groundcover, or in a rock garden.

Cushion spurge (*E. epithymoides*) is one of the most popular species. It forms a mound of bright yellow flowers in early spring, and the leaves turn red and orange in fall. Combine its green leaves and glowing yellow petal-like bracts with brightly colored tulips for a spectacular spring display.

Euphorbias are long-lived perennials that require little care. If you live in a zone where winters are cold but you don't get a lot of snow, provide winter protection (mulch or plant covers) to prevent leaf burn and stem damage. Divide plants in spring to rejuvenate old clumps or fill out plantings.

Gaillardia

(Blanket Flower)

PLANT PARTICULARS

Zones: 2 to 10

Height: 2 to 3 feet

Spread: Varies by species

Shape: Spreading clumps

Color: Yellow, orange, red, and brown flowers; green or blue-green leaves

Bloom time: Spring, summer

Light needs: Full sun to partial shade

Soil: Average to rich; well drained

These salt- and drought-tolerant perennials are perfect for seaside gardens and seem to thrive on neglect and heat. (Surprisingly, the only place they don't grow well is in rich, moist soil, which makes them floppy and shortens their life expectancy.) Blanket flowers produce mounds of showy daisylike flowers from early summer through fall. Plant them with other warm-colored perennials such as core-opsis, butterfly weeds, and yarrows for a harmonious display. Add interest and excitement to blanket flowers by teaming them with the spiky yellow leaves of Spanish bayonet and with purple flowers, such as sage. Gaillardia is also a great cutting flower, so make sure to add some to fresh bouquets.

Pinch off spent flowers at the tip of the stem to keep plants looking tidy and to prolong the bloom season. Blanket flowers tend to be short-lived, so divide them every 2 or 3 years in early spring to keep the clumps thriving. Sow seeds outdoors in fall or sow them indoors in winter. Seedlings may bloom the first year.

Geranium

(Cranesbill, Hardy Geranium)

PLANT PARTICULARS

Zones: 3 to 8

Height: 4 inches to 3 feet

Spread: Varies by species

Shape: Soft mounds

Color: White, blue, purple, rose, or pink flowers; green leaves tht turn burgundy-red, scarlet, or orange in the fall

Bloom time: Spring, early summer

Light needs: Full sun to partial shade

Soil: Rich; moist but well drained

Cranesbills will give you a long season of interest in the garden, thanks to their attractive foliage that turns colors in the fall. These geraniums have small, pretty flowers in shades of purple, rose, pink, white, or blue; the plants come in an array of heights that can fit into any planting scheme. (Don't confuse cranesbills with the tender bedding geraniums that you'll find at your local garden center—those geraniums won't survive a frost.)

A summer border wouldn't be complete without cranesbills. Combine them with bold colors and spiky forms or use them as "weavers" to tie together different combinations. Siberian iris, garden phlox, bellflowers, evening primroses, and ornamental grasses are all good companions.

It's nearly impossible to have too many of these versatile, easy-to-grow perennials, so divide and transplant existing plants in fall or early spring. Many cranesbills will also self-sow. If you catch the seeds before they're catapulted toward the neighbor's yard, sow them outdoors.

Helleborus

(Hellebore, Lenten Rose)

PLANT PARTICULARS

Zones: 3 to 9

Height: 10 inches to 2 feet

Spread: 10 to 18 inches

Shape: Clumps of flowerstalks

Color: Green, pink, purple, red, yellow, or white flowers; dark green leaves

Bloom time: Late winter to spring

Continued ➡

Light needs: Partial shade

Soil: Rich; moist but well drained

This perennial is what you want to plant for winter and early spring bloom and lasting foliage interest. Some hellebores have noticeable stems, and others have leaves and flowers that seem to rise directly from the ground. Their flowers come in shades of green, pink, purple, red, yellow, and white, and their leathery foliage is attractive throughout the summer, long after the blooms have faded.

Try combining hellebores with flowering shrubs that have attractive bark and early flowers; red- and yellow-stemmed dogwoods, serviceberries, and purple-leaved shrubs are good choices. The smaller bulbs, such as early crocus, reticulated iris, and species forms of daffodils and tulips are also good companions. The mottled, heart-shaped foliage of spring- or fall-blooming hardy cyclamen combines nicely with the dark green of the hellebore leaves. (Take care not to plant large floppy perennials near hellebores, which may smother the hellebores and block out the sun.)

Hellebores tend to self-sow where they are happy; transplant seedlings to other parts of the garden.

Helleborus x orientalis

Hemerocallis
(Daylily)

PLANT PARTICULARS

Zones: 2 to 9

Height: 1 to 6 feet

Spread: 1 to 5 feet

Shape: Mounds of arching leaves with clumping flowerstalks

Color: Cream, yellow, orange, red, maroon, or pink flowers; green leaves

Bloom time: Spring, summer

Light needs: Full sun to partial shade

Soil: Average to rich; dry but well drained

Tough, adaptable daylilies are easy to grow. These popular perennials have colorful flowers that each last only a day—but a profusion of new buds keeps plants in bloom for 2 to 4 weeks. These versatile 1-day wonders are great for mass plantings, especially

along walls or banks, or in combination with shrubs and trees. Use daylilies as accent plantings around foundations or with groundcovers.

Once established, daylilies spread quickly to form dense, broad clumps. Although you can leave the plants in place for years, some varieties produce so many stalks that the flowers get too crowded is the clumps aren't divided every 3 years or so. Lift the entire clump in late summer, pull or cut the thick tangled roots apart, and replant.

Heuchera
(Alumroot, Coral Bells)

PLANT PARTICULARS

Zones: 3 to 9

Height: 1 to 3 feet

Spread: 12 to 18 inches

Shape: Mounds of leaves with taller flower spikes

Color: White, pink, or red flowers; green to dark red leaves

Bloom time: Spring, summer

Light needs: Full sun to partial shade

Soil: Rich; moist but well drained

This group of perennials is made up of lovely foliage plants, many of which also have showy flowers. The evergreen leaves of heuchera are rounded, heart-shaped, or triangular and have long slender leaf-stalks. The white, pink, or red flowers hang daintily in clusters from the leafstalks.

Plant these versatile perennials in containers, in rock or woodland gardens, as groundcovers, or in a mixed border. The flower clusters add an airy look to summer beds and borders, and the mounds of green foliage are excellent for edging. Make the most of heuchera leaves by pairing them with bright flowers, like red pansies.

Prolong heuchera bloom by removing the spent flowerstalks at the base of the plants. As heucheras grow, they produce woody crowns. Divide the crowns every 3 or 4 years in spring or fall.

In warm regions, provide shade from the hot afternoon sun to keep the leaves from bleaching.

Hosta
(Hosta, Plantain Lily)

PLANT PARTICULARS

Zones: 3 to 8

Height: 6 inches to 3 feet

Spread: Varies by species

Shape: Wide mounds of leaves with taller flower spikes

Color: Lilac, white, or purple flowers; green, yellow, blue-green, and/or cream leaves

Bloom time: Summer to fall

Light needs: Light to full shade

Soil: Average to rich; moist

The bold, dramatic foliage of hostas is perfect for brightening up a shady area of your landscape. Their leafy clumps vary greatly in size, and come in a range of colors from deep green through chartreuse, yellow, and gold to blue. Leaves are oval, heart-shaped, or lance-shaped with smooth or wavy edges. Some varieties even produce spiky bloom stalks with white, lilac, or purple flowers.

Plant hostas with ferns, wildflowers, and other shade-loving perennials on the north side of your house or under the canopy of large trees. Or, inter-plant them with ferns and wild ginger for a beautiful

shady groundcover. You can also plant them with early spring bulbs. The hostas will unfurl their leaves just when the bulb foliage starts to look shabby.

Hostas grow slowly and may take 2 to 4 years to reach their full size. Allow plenty of room when you plant them to accommodate for their mature size. Small varieties spread three times as wide as they are tall. Medium-sized varieties spread twice their height, and the large ones are at least as wide as they are tall.

Iberis
(Candytuft)

PLANT PARTICULARS

Zones: 2 to 9

Height: 3 to 12 inches

Spread: Varies by species

Shape: Low creeping mats

Color: White flowers; shiny evergreen leaves

Bloom time: Early spring

Light needs: Full sun to light shade

Soil: Average; well drained

Lovely long-flowering perennials are a must for the spring garden. And that includes perennial candytuft (*I. sempervirens*), which offers tidy mounds of evergreen leaves that are covered in flat clusters of white flowers in early spring.

Candy tuft is the consummate edging plant. Its low and compact growth, early flowers, and ever-green foliage make it perfect for planting along stairs or walks, or in the front of a bed or border. In rock gardens, combine candytuft with spring bulbs, bleeding hearts, rock cresses, and purple rock cress. In a border, plant it with tulips, columbines, forget-me-nots, and spring bulbs. Planted in raised beds or atop retaining walls, it can cascade over the side.

After the plants have bloomed for the season, cut them back by about one-third to remove the spent flowers to encourage compact growth and good foliage. Prune them hard, at least two-thirds back, every 2 to 3 years to encourage new stem growth and to promote flower production. These plants seldom need division.

Iris
(Iris)

PLANT PARTICULARS

Zones: 2 to 10

Height: 4 inches to 4 feet

Spread: Varies by species

Shape: Upright spiky clumps

Color: White, yellow, orange, brown, pink, purple, or blue flowers; green leaves

Bloom time: Spring, summer

Light needs: Full sun to light shade

Soil: Varies widely by species

An iris exists for every garden situation: sun or shade, moist or dry soil, early or late bloom. In addition, you're sure to find a color to suit your taste, because bloom colors include white, pink, red, purple, blue, yellow, and brown. You can choose from a host of different species, which include bearded irises, Siberian irises, reticulated irises, and yellow flag irises. Different species bloom at different times from winter through summer, so you can enjoy this perennial practically year-round. Many irises are excellent for cutting.

Continued ➡

Bearded and Siberian irises are well suited to beds and borders with spring and early-summer perennials. Combine their strap-shaped foliage with peonies, hostas, cranesbills, and columbines. Plant moisture-loving yellow flag irises with ferns, hostas, and other lush perennials along the sides of ponds. Smaller iris species are perfect in rock gardens or at the front of a border.

If you want to divide your irises, do so after they've finished flowering in summer or early fall. Replant them immediately.

Liatris
(Gayfeather, Blazing-Star)

PLANT PARTICULARS

Zones: 3 to 9

Height: 6 inches to 3 feet

Spread: 18 to 24 inches

Shape: Clumps of upright flowerstalks

Color: Purple, pink, or white flowers; green leaves

Bloom time: Summer

Light needs: Full sun

Soil: Average to rich; well drained

Plant some of these perennials, and you're sure to attract butterflies, which love the upright, fuzzy spikes and profusion of small red-violet to purple flowers. The spikes of gayfeathers open from the top down, unlike those of most other spike-flowering perennials, which open from the bottom up.

These native American perennials are a natural choice for meadow gardens, prairie plantings, and borders. In a border, combine them with yarrows, purple coneflowers, artemisias, Shasta daisies, garden phlox, and ornamental grasses. If you want to tone down pinkish purple varieties, pair them with silvery lamb's-ears. To jazz them up, plant them with coreopsis or yellow coneflower. And don't forget to include gayfeathers in your cutting garden; they're great for fresh-flower arrangements.

You don't need a green thumb to grow gayfeathers because they're tough, low-maintenance, long-lived perennials. If you leave them alone, they'll form large clumps; if you want to create new plants, divide the clumps in the fall.

Liatris spicata 'Kobold'

Lilium
(Lily)

PLANT PARTICULARS

Zones: 2 to 9

Height: 1 to 7 feet

Spread: Varies by species

Shape: Tall, slender stalks topped with a cluster of flowers

Color: White, yellow, orange, red, or pink flowers, green leaves

Bloom time: Spring, summer

Light needs: Full sun to partial shade

Soil: Average; well drained

This large group of plants offers such a wide range of sizes, colors, and shapes that you're sure to find some to suit your garden. These perennials grow from bulbs that lack the papery brown covering (tunic) of bulbs such as tulips and daffodils. From the center of the bulb rises a tall stalk, which is clothes in leaves that may be narrow and grasslike, or wide and more swordlike. Nodding or upright flowers may be trumpet-, star-, or bowl-shaped. Lilies are available in various bloom colors, many of which have dark spots or streaks on the petals.

Combine lilies with baby's breath, hostas, asters, and other bushy perennials that will hide the bases of the lily stems. Or, plant generous groupings with ornamental grasses and vines.

If you plant tall lilies, you'll probably need to stake them. Insert a stake near the stem, taking care not to spear the bulb when you put the stake in the ground. Tie the stem loosely to the stake.

Lobelia
(Lobelia)

PLANT PARTICULARS

Zones: 2 to 9

Height: 2 to 4 feet

Spread: 1 to 2 feet

Shape: Erect spikes

Color: Red, purple, blue, white, or pink flowers; green leaves

Bloom time: Summer, fall

Light needs: Full sun to partial shade

Soil: Rich; constantly moist

Hummingbirds love these perennials, particularly *L. cardinalis*, or cardinal flower. (Butterflies love them, too.) Lobelias produce erect spikes of irregularly shaped tubular flowers that come in many colors including blue and pink.

Lobelias are best suited to gardens with moist soil, especially along ponds and streams. They are good border plants, as long as the soil doesn't dry out. Plant them in the company of Siberian and Japanese irises, astilbes, ferns, and bold foliage plants such as hostas. Combine them with other moisture-tolerant border perennials such as daylilies, spiderworts, garden phlox, and sneeze-weed. Great blue lobelia (*L. siphilitica*) has subtle blue flowers that mix well with goldenrods and ornamental grasses.

Although they tend to be short-lived, lobelias can produce many seedlings for transplanting; remove the flower spikes after blooming if you want to prevent self-sowing. Divide clumps in early fall to help plants perform well for several seasons.

Lupinus
(Lupine)

PLANT PARTICULARS

Zones: 2 to 7

Height: 18 inches to 5 feet

Spread: 1 to 2 feet

Shape: Mounds of leaves with tall flower spikes

Color: White, pink, purple, blue, or red flowers; green leaves

Bloom time: Spring, summer

Light needs: Full sun to light shade

Soil: Rich; moist but well drained

These perennials are a good choice for zones where summers are cool. (Lupines suffer in hot temperatures.) Lupines' tall, dense flower spikes produce pea-shaped flowers that come in shades of white, pink, purple, blue, and red.

Plant lupines for early summer color in cottage gardens and meadow gardens. Use them as an accent with flowering shrubs or in a border with irises, peonies, bellflowers, Oriental poppies, and annuals. They also make a wonderful accent in groundcovers such as common periwinkle.

Cut off spent flower spikes to promote possible regrowth, or let the seeds mature so plants can self-sow. For propagation, separate sideshoots from the clumps in fall. Or, if you aren't looking for a specific color (lupine seeds usually are sold in packets of mixed colors), sow seed in pots outdoors in late summer or indoors in winter. (Soaking the seed in warm water overnight can speed germination.) Place flats of seeds sown indoors in a refrigerator for 4 to 6 weeks before moving to a warm place.

Monarda
(Bee Balm, Bergamot)

PLANT PARTICULARS

Zones: 3 to 9

Height: 1 to 4 feet

Spread: 3 feet

Shape: Spreading patches of upright stems

Color: Red, pink, white, purple, or yellow-green flowers; green leaves

Bloom time: Summer

Light needs: Full sun to partial shade

Soil: Rich; moist

Put out the welcome mat for bees, butterflies, and hummingbirds with generous clumps of bee balm. This perennial has round heads of tightly packed flowers and aromatic leaves that add a splash of color to the landscape. Combine bee balms with lilies, phlox, yarrows, cranesbills, and astilbes. *M. didyma*, a wild species of bee balm, works well in the moist wild garden among bonesets, queen-of-the-prairie, hibiscus, and ferns.

Many bee balms are prone to powdery mildew, a fungal disease that appears as a dusty white coating on leaves and stems. Help avoid powdery mildew problems by planting resistant varieties, such as bright pink 'Marshall's Delight'; choosing a site with good air circulation; and thinning bee balm stems as needed.

Bee balms spread rather quickly, so you'll probably want to divide the clumps every 2 or 3 years (in spring or fall) to keep them from taking over. Relocate the new transplants, or share them with friends.

Continued ➡

Nepeta

(Catmint)

PLANT PARTICULARS

Zones: 3 to 8

Height: 1 to 2 feet

Spread: Varies by species

Shape: Soft, sprawling mounds

Color: Violet to lavender-blue flowers; gray-green leaves

Bloom time: Spring, early summer

Light needs: Full sun to light shade

Soil: Average; well drained

This perennial is simple one of the best edging plants. Its misty mounds of soft gray-green leaves and wiry stems crowned with clusters of violet to lavender-blue flowers are lovely in the garden. Catmint also offers a long season of bloom—about 2½ months.

Plant catmint along walks, as an edging for beds, as a groundcover, or in a rock garden. The gray-green leaves and lavender-blue flowers look great with pale yellow coreopsis or yarrow, or with bright yellow evening primroses and daylilies. It also works well in front of peonies and roses.

Deer and rabbits seem to avoid catmint, so try planting it as a barrier to keep these critters away from plants they do love.

After the first flush of bloom, shear off the spent flower heads to promote rebloom (they'll quickly grow back again). To propagate catmint, dig up, divide, and transplant rooted stems.

Paeonia

(Peony)

PLANT PARTICULARS

Zones: 2 to 8

Height: 1 to 5 feet

Spread: 30 to 36 inches

Shape: Loose, flower-topped mounds

Color: White, yellow, cream, pink, rose, and scarlet flowers; green leaves

Bloom time: Spring, early summer

Light needs: Full sun to light shade

Soil: Rich; moist

Peonies are prized for their variety of form and color, exceptional hardiness, and ease of care. They can have single, semidouble, or double blooms that range in color from white, cream, and yellow to pink, rose, and scarlet.

A row of peonies can make a glorious early-summer hedge. Mix several varieties (with different bloom times) together to extend the bloom season as long as possible. Classic companions include irises, foxgloves, and columbines. Hosta foliage and pink peonies make a pretty combination that's also practical: The hostas serve as natural support for the floppy peonies.

Speaking of support, taller peonies and those with double flowers usually need staking to keep their blooms out of the mud. Use hoop stakes or straight stakes and string to support floppy stalks. Single-flowered peonies generally have self-supporting stems that stand up to wind and rain.

Papaver

(Poppy)

PLANT PARTICULARS

Zones: 2 to 7

Height: 1 to 3 feet

Spread: 2 feet

Shape: Loose clumps

Color: Orange, red, pink, white, or yellow flowers; dark green leaves

Bloom time: Spring, early summer

Light needs: Full sun

Soil: Rich; well drained

These delightful flowers are wonderful for adding vibrant color to your beds. Their crepe paper–like petals come in shapes of orange, red, pink, white, or yellow. The flowers sit atop stems and open from nodding buds.

To get the most eye-popping color, plant the orange-scarlet, black-centered Oriental poppy (*P. orientale*). Bushy perennials that bloom after early summer, such as Russian sage and boltonia, make good companions. Other more subtle perennials that work well paired with bold-colored poppies include speedwells, bellflowers, baptisias, and blue stars. Use long-blooming cranesbills, perennial salvia, or spreading baby's breath to fill in the gaps after the poppies have finished flowering.

Rejuvenate crowded clumps (probably only once every 5 or 6 years) by dividing the plants just as the new leaves emerge in late summer. Lifted plants will invariably leave behind a few broken roots, which will grow into new plants. To propagate, take root cuttings while you're dividing the clumps.

Penstemon

(Penstemon, Beardtongue)

PLANT PARTICULARS

Zones: 2 to 9

Height: 4 inches to 3 feet

Spread: Varies by species

Shape: Tall spikes

Color: White, pink, rose, lavender, or violet flowers; evergreen leaves

Bloom time: Early summer through fall

Light needs: Full sun to partial shade

Soil: Average; very well drained

To bring a touch of wildflowers to your beds, try penstemon. It produces slender, single-branched spikes with tiers of irregularly shaped flowers. The flowers vary in color from white to pink, rose, lavender, and violet. This airy-looking plant has lush rosettes of evergreen leaves that form wide patches and make attractive groundcovers when the plants aren't in bloom.

Use penstemon in container plantings, as an edging, as a groundcover, in a mixed border, or in a rock garden. Combine it with cranesbills, spider-worts, yarrows, evening primroses, lamb's-ears, yuccas, and ornamental grasses.

Success with penstemon depends on choosing the right species for your growing conditions. Species native to the western mountains, for example, often cook in the heat of midwestern gardens and rot in the humidity and dampness of eastern gardens. However, many excellent eastern natives and other adaptable species are available. Good drainage is essential for all varieties except *P. digitalis*, which tolerates moist soil.

Perovskia

(Russian Sage)

PLANT PARTICULARS

Zones: 4 to 9

Height: 3 to 5 feet

Spread: 2 to 4 feet

Shape: Airy, shrublike mound

Color: Powder blue flowers; gray-green leaves

Bloom time: Summer

Light needs: Full sun

Soil: Average; well drained to dry

This tough, trouble-free perennial laughs at heat, drought, and pests. Its shrubby, branching habit supports gray-green leaves and airy sprays of tiny powder blue flowers. In addition to being tough, Russian sage earns its keep year-round by producing soft shoots in spring, flowers that bloom for more than a month in summer, and seedheads that dry in fall for winter interest.

The soft blue flowers of Russian sage complement pink, yellow, deep blues, and purples. Plant it in the middle or back of the perennial border with yarrows, phlox, balloon flowers, gayfeathers, and ornamental grasses. Also, try it as a low-maintenance landscape feature or as an accent in a cottage garden.

Cut the woody stems of this plant down to about 1 foot in late fall or early spring to promote new growth. In the North, plants often die back to the soil but resprout from the roots. Russian sage seldom needs dividing.

Perovskia atriplicifolia 'Blue Spire'

Phlox

(Phlox)

PLANT PARTICULARS

Zones: 2 to 9

Height: 4 inches to 5 feet

Spread: 24 to 30 inches

Shape: Varies among species

Continued ➤

Color: White, pink, rose, red, violet, blue, or bicolored flowers; dark green leaves

Bloom time: Spring, summer

Light needs: Full sun to full shade

Soil: Varies among species

They're favorites among perennial gardeners, and rightly so. Phlox are easy to grow, bloom prolifically, and produce a heady fragrance. Depending on the variety, phlox may produce tall, leafy stems crowned with dense, domed heads of five-petaled flower clusters, or short, creeping stems that form an attractive groundcover.

One variety gardeners prefer is garden phlox (*P. poniculoto*). Its mounded flower clusters combine well with other summer bloomers. Place garden phlox in the middle or rear of the garden, and give it ample room to spread. Combine it with perennials such as bonesets, bee balms, Shasta daisy, astilbes, meadowsweets, cranesbills, delphiniums, daylilies, and ornamental grasses.

To help prevent powdery mildew, choose a site with good air circulation, thin the stems of dense clumps, and water the plants from below to avoid wetting their leaves.

Platycodon

(Balloon flower)

PLANT PARTICULARS

Zones: 3 to 8

Height: 1 to 3 feet

Spread: 24 inches

Shape: Loose clumps

Color: Blue, pink, or white flowers; green leaves

Bloom time: Summer

Light needs: Full sun to light shade

Soil: Average to rich; well drained

Plant it now; enjoy it forever. A real showstopper, balloon flower flaunts star-shaped flowers that open from inflated round buds that resemble balloons.

These blooms look lovely with bright or pastel flowers and green or silvery foliage plants. Combine them with summer-blooming perennials such as yellow yarrows, alliums, violet sage, bee balms, and garden phlox. Use silvery foliage, such as lamb's-ears and artemisias, along with ornamental grasses to set off the bright flowers. Enjoy the blooms indoors as well as out; they last long as fresh-cut flowers if you singe the stem ends with a match to stop the milky sap from flowing.

The new shoots of balloon flowers are slow to emerge in spring, so be sure to mark their location so you don't dig into their clumps by mistake. The plants bloom for a month or more; removing the spent flowers will encourage the plants to continue blooming as well as keep them looking neat.

Polygonatum

(Solomon's Seal)

PLANT PARTICULARS

Zones: 3 to 9

Height: 1 to 3 feet

Spread: 1 to 2 feet

Shape: Arching stems with dangling flowers

Color: Greenish or white flowers; green or variegated leaves that turn yellow-brown in fall

Bloom time: Spring

Light needs: Partial to full shade

Soil: Rich; moist

For the areas of your garden in deep shade, try Solomon's seal. This graceful, arching plant has broad oval leaves and bell-shaped greenish or white flowers that hang below the foliage. In summer, it produces waxy, blue-black berries; in fall, the foliage turns yellow-brown.

Use Solomon's seal as edging, in a rock or a woodland garden, or at the back of a bed or a border. Combine it with bold foliage plants such as hostas, ferns, alumroots, wild ginger, and lady's-mantle. Most species will also do well under mature shade trees.

Although Solomon's seal prefers moist, rich soil, it will tolerate dry, stony soil. Divide plants whenever they start to outgrow their boundaries. To propagate, divide clumps in spring or fall and replant into amended soil. Or, remove the seeds from the berries in fall and immediately plant the seeds outdoors. (The seeds may take 2 years to germinate, and seedlings will grow slowly.)

Primula

(Primrose)

PLANT PARTICULARS

Zones: 2 to 8

Height: 2 inches to 2 feet

Spread: Varies by species

Shape: Rosettes of leaves with taller flowering stems or open, branched clusters

Color: Yellow, white, pink, purple, or red flowers; green leaves

Bloom time: Very early spring, early summer

Light needs: Full sun to partial shade

Soil: Rich; moist

Perky primroses have a place in every garden (they perform well in containers, too). These beloved five-petaled spring flowers bloom with flowering bulbs when the earth is reawakening, so plant them in clumps or drifts with spring bulbs such as tulips, snowdrops, and daffodils.

Some primrose varieties produce a tall stem, whereas others sport open, branched clusters close to the ground. Japanese primroses (*P. japonica*) love a spot with dependably damp soil, so combine them with irises, hostas, ferns, and lady's-mantle. If you live in a northern USDA plant hardiness zone that has erratic snowfall, mulch or cover your primroses for the winter to help them survive. In the South, provide consistent moisture and shade from the hot afternoon sun in summer; if the plants get too hot or dry, they will go dormant early—meaning you lose out on bloom time.

Pulmonaria

(Lungwort, Bethlehem Sage)

PLANT PARTICULARS

Zones: 2 to 8

Height: 9 inches to 2 feet

Spread: 1 to 2 feet

Shape: Loose clumps

Color: Pink, blue, red, or white flowers; green or variegated leaves

Bloom time: Spring

Light needs: Partial to full shade

Soil: Rich; moist

Some lungwort varieties do double duty: They not only produce pretty flowers in early spring but also sport showy silver-spotted leaves that make a bold statement the rest of the year. Some varieties of these low-growing plants have flowers that do a mid-bloom costume change: They open pink and turn to blue.

Combine lungworts with daffodils and other spring bulbs in a bed or a border or under flowering trees or shrubs. The tough and attractive summer foliage is outstanding as a groundcover. In the perennials garden, plant lungworts in drifts with hellebores, anemones, bleeding hearts, and irises. And planted singly or in groups, they brighten up shady spots under trees and shrubs.

Once lungworts are established, they are fairly drought-tolerant. However, they'll go dormant early if the soil dries out. Divide overgrown clumps after flowering or in fall, and replant into amended soil.

Rudbeckia

(Coneflower, Black-Eyed Susan)

PLANT PARTICULARS

Zones: 3 to 9

Height: 18 inches to 2 feet

Spread: Varies by species

Shape: Broad clumps of stiff, branched stalks

Color: Orange or yellow flowers; green leaves

Bloom time: Summer

Light needs: Full sun to light shade

Soil: Average to rich; well drained

Tough, adaptable coneflowers are the perfect perennials to grow if your thumb is more brown than green. Their daisylike blooms have golden yellow petals and brown or green centers that are either domed or flat.

These plants are invaluable for adding bright, long-lasting color to perennial gardens. Plant them with other summer-blooming flowers such as purple coneflowers, Russian sage, garden phlox, sedums, bee balms, and ornamental grasses, such as blue oat grass. Coneflowers also make good, long-lasting cut flowers, so you can enjoy them indoors as well as out in your garden.

Pinch off spent flowers to promote rebloom, or let the seedheads form to add winter interest to your garden. To propagate, divide clumps in spring, or dig up self-sown seedlings. You can sow seed outdoors in spring or fall.

Rudbeckia 'Goldsturm'

Salvia

(Salvia, Sage)

PLANT PARTICULARS

Zones: 3 to 10

Height: 1 to 4 feet

Continued ➡

Spread: Varies by species

Shape: Mounded to shrubby

Color: Blue, purple, pink, or red flowers; silver-gray, green, or variegated leaves

Bloom time: Summer, fall

Light needs: Full sun to light shade

Soil: Average; well drained to dry

Like coneflowers, these perennials are easy to grow and will tolerate a wide variety of conditions (although they typically prefer well-drained soil). These plants are mounded to shrubby mints with tubular blue, purple, red, or pink flowers and square stems. Many salvias also have aromatic foliage.

Spiky salvias are super mid-border or edging plants for sunny gardens. Their upright habit contrasts beautifully with mounded plants, such as cranesbills and threadleaf coreopsis. They also look great combined with yuccas, yarrows, sedums, coneflowers, daylilies, daisies, mums, and ornamental grasses.

Plant salvias in full sun or light shade; they'll get leggy and flop in too much shade. Overly rich or moist soils also encourage flopping. Cutting the spent flower stems off your salvias can promote a second bloom in late summer. In fall or early spring, cut the plants back to the ground.

Scabiosa

(Scabious, Pincushion Flower)

PLANT PARTICULARS

Zones: 3 to 7

Height: 18 inches to 2 feet

Spread: Varies by species

Shape: Clumps with long flower stems

Color: Blue, pink, or white flowers; gray-green leaves

Bloom time: Summer

Light needs: Full sun to light shade

Soil: Rich; well drained to dry

Want the perfect cutting flower? This old-fashioned perennial has fuzzy foliage and broad, flat flower heads with tiny, lacy flowers on tall stems. What's more, it blooms for a long time. The quaint look of pincushion flower makes it a charming addition to corrage gardens and informal borders. Daylilies, yarrows, and coreopsis are wonderful companions. Blue pincushion flowers and yellow heliopsis make a great pair, both in the garden and cut for indoor arrangements. To create a significant display of pincushion flowers, plant them together in groups of three or more.

Pincushion flowers will form good-sized clumps under ideal conditions but are sensitive to heat and excess soil moisture. If you live in a southern zone, place these plants where they will be shaded in the afternoon. Remove spent flowers to keep plants looking neat and encourage repeat blooms. Divide clumps in spring only if they become overcrowded.

Sedum

(Sedum, Stonecrop)

PLANT PARTICULARS

Zones: 3 to 9

Height: 2 inches to 2 feet

Spread: 12 to 18 inches

Shape: Spreading mats to upright clumps

Color: Yellow, pink, or white flowers; green, red, yellow, or silver leaves

Bloom time: Spring, summer

Light needs: Full sun to partial shade

Soil: Average; well drained to dry

Thick, succulent, waxy leaves and fleshy, often trailing stems make these perennials drought-tolerant plants. Sedums come in lots of shapes and sizes, providing interesting foliage and yellow, pink, or white showy flowers with little or no fuss. Plus, the seedheads of many varieties retain their color after flowering and hold their form when dried.

"Autumn Joy" is one popular sedum variety that looks great in several seasons. Its neat mounds are topped with green buds that open to reddish pink flowers in late summer. The flower heads hold their shape well into winter. Sedums are versatile plants for beds, borders, and rock gardens and as groundcovers under open trees. The low, spreading species works well along paths.

All sedums are tough, low-maintenance plants. Once established, they generally won't require much care from you. Just divide them in spring or fall to control their spread.

Solidago

(Goldenrod)

PLANT PARTICULARS

Zones: 3 to 9

Height: 1 to 5 feet

Spread: Varies by species

Shape: Clumps of upright stalks

Color: Yellow flowers; green leaves

Bloom time: Late summer, fall

Light needs: Full sun

Soil: Average; moist but well drained

Goldenrods are a welcome sight in the garden, blooming at a time when many other flowers are going dormant for the season. The lemon yellow or golden flowers are carried in spikelike, flat-topped, or plume-like clusters; the leafy stems may be smooth or hairy.

These easy-care perennials look as good in beds and borders as they do in meadows and wildflower gardens. Combine them with coneflowers, balloon flowers, gayfeathers, bonesets, lavender, sages, asters, and ornamental grasses. Most species of goldenrod prefer average soil (rich soils cause rampant spread and cause the flowers to flop over). All species of goldenrod hold up well under drought conditions.

Regardless of whether you choose to include goldenrod in your perennial garden, rest assured that goldenrods aren't responsible for your fall hay fever. They're mistakenly blamed for the irritating pollen that's produced by ragweed. Because goldenrod pollen isn't released into the wind (the plants are pollinated by insects), it can't be blamed for upper respiratory tract allergies.

Stachys

(Lamb's-Ears, Betony)

PLANT PARTICULARS

Zones: 2 to 8

Height: 6 inches to 2 feet

Spread: 1 foot

Shape: Spreading mats with upright flower stems

Color: Purple, pink, or white flowers; silver-gray leaves

Bloom time: Spring, summer

Light needs: Full sun to light shade

Soil: Varies among species

Delightful lamb's-ears are extremely versatile in any landscape. Their soft, fuzzy leaves just beg to be touched, and their tiny flowers add an accent of color to the silvery foliage.

Use them at the front of a border or an herb garden—or along a path, where you'll brush by them frequently. Their foliage and flower spikes are a perfect complement to green leaves and both bright and pastel flowers. Plant lamb's-ears in formal or informal gardens with irises, goat's beards, alumroots, bergenias, and lung worts.

In hot, humid conditions, the leaves may die back because the woolly foliage traps water and encourages rot. If this happens, cut the leaves and stems to the ground; new foliage should sprout when things cool off. Also, you can cut the flower stems to the ground after bloom to keep the plants looking tidy.

All species of lamb's-ears spread well when grown in the conditions they like best. Divide and replant overgrown clumps in the fall to control their spread, if you wish.

Stachys byzantina

Verbena

(Verbena, Vervain)

PLANT PARTICULARS

Zones: 4 to 10

Height: 4 inches to 5 feet

Spread: 1 foot

Shape: Varies among species

Color: Pink, purple, white, or blue flowers; green leaves

Bloom time: Summer

Light needs: Full sun to light shade

Soil: Average; well drained to dry

The popularity of these perennials stems from their different shapes, from tall upright plants to

Continued ➡

low, creeping, mat-forming ones. Surely, at least one variety will work well in your landscape. The brightly colored flowers have five flat petals that are carried in flat or spiky clusters on top of wiry stems.

The mat-forming varieties are excellent for tying together mixed plantings. Let them creep among foliage plants such as yuccas, artemisias, mulleins, and ornamental grasses. They also serve to fill in gaps between tall flowering perennials such as coneflowers, butterfly weeds, and yarrows. Contrary to usual practice, plant upright varieties at the front of a border, because the verbenas' tall, airy stems will allow you to see the plants behind.

These tough, heat- and drought-tolerant perennials bloom tirelessly throughout the summer. The creeping varieties spread quickly to form showy groundcovers, whereas the upright varieties spread slowly.

Veronica

(Veronica, Speedwell)

PLANT PARTICULARS

Zones: 3 to 8

Height: 4 inches to 6 feet

Spread: Varies among species

Shape: Varies among species

Color: White, pink, purple, or blue flowers; green leaves

Bloom time: Spring, summer

Light needs: Full sun to light shade

Soil: Average to rich; moist but well drained

Dependable, long-blooming speedwells are available in both upright and creeping varieties. The blooms are spikes of small flowers in shades of white, pink, rose, purple, and blue. Speedwells' leaves may be narrow and lance-shaped, oblong, oval, or wedge-shaped.

Practically maintenance-free, speedwells are very heat- and drought-tolerant—perfect for beds, borders, and rock gardens. You can also use them as edging, in a wildflower meadow, or along a path. Combine their colorful spiky flowers with mounded plants such as coreopsis, butterfly weeds, yarrows, cranesbills, daylilies, and ornamental grasses.

Pinch off the dead flower spikes to keep the plants blooming, and divide the plants in spring or fall for propagation or to control spread. (The creeping types tend to spread quite widely, so watch them carefully, or you may end up with plants in unwanted areas—like your neighbor's yard.)

Perennial Pest and Disease Control

Ellen Phillips and C. Colston Burrell

Effective pest and disease control is a three-step process for the perennial gardener: observe, refer, react. You'll apply the right preventives and controls at the right time if you watch your plants for signs of pests or diseases, check your references to identify pests or symptoms, and then use the recommended control for that particular problem.

In this section, you'll find out which pests and diseases attack perennials, what they look like, and what to do about them. But first, you'll learn how to prevent pests and diseases from becoming a major problem through wise plant selection and good cultural practices.

Start with Resistant Plants

Some species and cultivars of perennials are resistant to certain pests and diseases that plague similar plants. Some of these plants are naturally resistant; others were bred for resistance. Using these plants is one of the easiest ways to solve pest and disease problems. Either look for and choose resistant plants when you're starting a new garden, or replace susceptible plants with resistant species or cultivars when problems arise.

Resistant plants are the best way to solve potential garden problems like powdery mildew. Garden phlox (*Phlox paniculata*) is notoriously susceptible to powdery mildew, which disfigures the foliage with a powdery white coating and reduces plant vigor. But phlox is a staple of many summer gardens, with its tall, showy panicles of red, white, pink, or salmon flowers.

If you feel that you simply must have phlox in your perennial bed or border, you have two choices: You can battle mildew with good cultural practices and preventive spraying, or you can plant mildew-resistant cultivars like 'Bright Eyes', a pink-flowered phlox with crimson centers, or 'David', a sparkling white-flowered form. Wild sweet William (*P. maculata*), which looks like garden phlox, is also mildew-resistant and an excellent substitute; there are pink, white, and rose-colored cultivars.

Growing Plants Right

Good gardening practices result in vigorous, healthy perennials. Careful site selection and soil preparation, adequate irrigation, and preventive mulching are some of the ways you can make sure your plants are ready to resist pest and disease attacks. Just as we're less able to resist a cold when our bodies are already run down, stressed plants succumb more quickly to infection. Research has shown that weakened plants are the first to be attacked by pests.

Make sure your plants aren't water-stressed or waterlogged. Keep weeds, which are often alternate hosts for both pests and diseases, away from your garden. Add plenty of organic matter—especially compost—to your beds to enhance water and nutrient retention and fight nematodes. Space plants far enough apart for good air circulation. And grow a variety of species: Many pests and diseases are species-specific, or are confined to a few related species.

Pests in the Perennials

Pests build up most quickly when just one or two kinds of plants are grown. A bed of mixed perennials is less likely to be decimated than a bed of roses or petunias because the pests that prefer specific plants will have a harder time finding them when they're "hidden" among all those other perennials. That doesn't mean perennials are pest-free, though, as gardeners who've encountered borers in their bearded irises, Japanese beetles on their hollyhocks, or slugs on their hostas can attest.

One cause of pests in perennial beds is the nature of perennials themselves: The plants are in place a long time, giving pest populations a chance to establish themselves over many growing seasons. Fortunately, there are five ways to keep pests at an acceptable level in your garden.

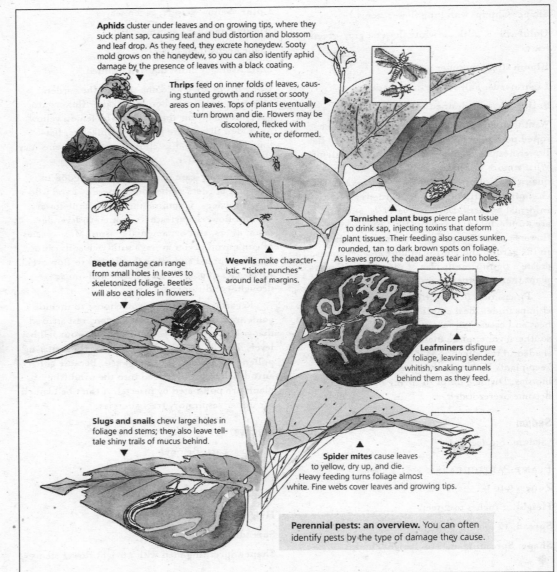

Aphids cluster under leaves and on growing tips, where they suck plant sap, causing leaf and bud distortion and blossom and leaf drop. As they feed, they excrete honeydew. Sooty mold grows on the honeydew, so you can also identify aphid damage by the presence of leaves with a black coating.

Thrips feed on inner folds of leaves, causing stunted growth and russet or sooty areas on leaves. Tops of plants eventually turn brown and die. Flowers may be discolored, flecked with white, or deformed.

Tarnished plant bugs pierce plant tissue to drink sap, injecting toxins that deform plant tissues. Their feeding also causes sunken, rounded, tan to dark brown spots on foliage. As leaves grow, the dead areas tear into holes.

Beetle damage can range from small holes in leaves to skeletonized foliage. Beetles will also eat holes in flowers.

Weevils make characteristic "ticket punches" around leaf margins.

Leafminers disfigure foliage, leaving slender, whitish, snaking tunnels behind them as they feed.

Slugs and snails chew large holes in foliage and stems; they also leave telltale shiny trails of mucus behind.

Spider mites cause leaves to yellow, dry up, and die. Heavy feeding turns foliage almost white. Fine webs cover leaves and growing tips.

Perennial pests: an overview. You can often identify pests by the type of damage they cause.

Continued ➡

1. Grow resistant species and cultivars when available.

2. Use good cultural practices.

3. Apply biological controls, which are alive and often self-perpetuating.

4. Use manual controls, including barriers and traps.

5. Use insecticidal sprays and dusts when required.

These five tactics should keep perennial pests at the "few and far between" state so your plants can bloom and thrive unmolested.

Here's an overview of biological controls, manual controls, and sprays and dusts. But first, there are two techniques that are more important than any control: monitoring and using common sense.

LOOKING FOR TROUBLE

The best and easiest way to keep pests under control is to find them when they've just arrived and there still aren't many of them, so monitor your plants. If you can start control early, your perennials will suffer minimal damage, and you can usually use a simple control. Handpicking a few Japanese beetles is far better than coping with bug sprays and stripped plants. Become a garden detective: When you're weeding, watering, or just out strolling in your garden, check your plants for pests and signs of feeding injury. Make sure you're in the garden every day—pest populations can build up fast. Try to familiarize yourself with the major perennial pests so you'll know what you're looking for, then apply appropriate controls.

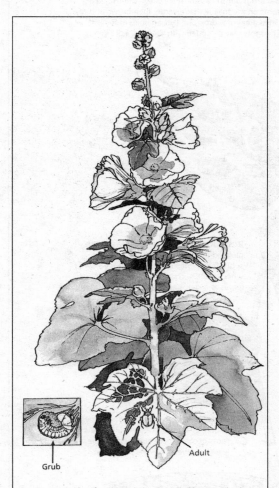

Japanese beetles. These ½-inch-long, metallic blue-green beetles consume the leaves, stalks, and flowers of many perennials. The ¾-inch-long, C-shaped grub larvae feed on the roots of lawn grasses. Handpick adults into a can of soapy water. Traps will attract these pests to your yard unless your neighbors set up traps, too. Use milky disease or parasitic nematodes on lawn areas to control beetle larvae.

USING COMMON SENSE

Don't panic at the first sight of a slug or a ragged leaf. Unless you're growing perennials for the florist industry or a flower show, a little damage is as acceptable as it is inevitable. The techniques we recommend will ensure that you have lush, healthy plants and plenty of perfect flowers. Your garden is a natural system, so be prepared for the occasional flaw. Use good sense; don't overreact.

The second time to let common sense come to your rescue is at the other end of the control spectrum. If, in spite of your best efforts, certain perennials are decimated every year, give up the fight. No matter how much you love columbines, if leafminers make them unsightly every season, it's time to throw in the trowel. There are plenty of other lovely perennials to choose from. Give it your best shot, but then let reason be your guide. Don't let pest-pocked perennials ruin the looks of your perennial garden.

If you can't live without them, remember this: You can always hide favorite but pest-plagued perennials in the cutting garden, where the colorful chaos will make pest damage less noticeable.

USING BIOLOGICAL CONTROLS

Biological controls are microscopic living organisms that infest or attack pests. They are usually pest-specific, attacking only one kind of insect, and are thought to be harmless to the environment and nontargeted species. To be effective, biological controls must be applied early because the infection takes several days to kill the pest. All are available from garden suppliers; apply according to directions.

BT. *Bacillus thuringiensis*, known as BT, is a bacterial disease that infects insect larvae. Different strains of BT have been isolated for different pests: One infects caterpillars, a second attacks the grubs of Colorado potato beetles, and a third infects mosquito and blackfly larvae. (However, the strain of BT that kills pest caterpillars will kill all caterpillars, and so on, so please don't apply a biological control unless you're sure you have or will have a problem based on past years' infestations.) Make sure you buy the strain of BT that targets your pest problem.

Milky disease. *Bacillus popilliae*, milky disease, attacks Japanese beetle grubs. Apply this bacterial disease, often sold as milky spore, to the lawn where these grubs live. Milky disease is most effective in providing grub control if everyone in your neighborhood applies it to their lawns; one application will be effective for years.

Parasitic nematodes. These microscopic roundworms parasitize and kill insect larvae, including ground-dwelling caterpillars (like cutworms) and grubs. The nematodes feed on a dead insect; about 10 to 20 days after the first infection, huge numbers of nematodes leave the carcass in search of new victims. Because nematodes perish in sunlight or dry places, they are most useful against pests in soil or hidden locations. Although the larval stage can survive for long periods in the soil, for the greatest effect you need to release more nematodes each year.

USING MANUAL CONTROLS

Manual controls are simple, low-tech methods like handpicking pests or putting barriers around plants. Some manual controls are preventive, like cutworm collars; their aim is to keep pests from reaching your plants. Others, like handpicking, come into play once pests attack. When you notice a pest problem, try these controls first; they're often all you'll need. If pest populations are too

great for effective manual control, move on to dusts and sprays.

Handpicking. This is a simple technique that merely involves plucking a pest off a plant and squashing it or drowning it in a can of soapy water. (Soap breaks the surface tension of the water so the pests can't climb out.) It's not for the squeamish, but it is highly effective when used early when populations are light.

Copper barriers. Slugs and snails get an electric shock when their slimy bodies touch copper, so these copper strips keep them out of your beds. They're easiest to use if you have wood-sided raised beds and can nail the strip around the outside of the bed. This works on a barrel garden, too. Copper strips are available from garden supply companies and are sold as Snail-Barr.

Cutworm collars. Make your own "collars" to keep cutworms from attacking your seedlings and transplants. Use cardboard cylinders like toilet paper or paper towel rolls, or roll your own. Make each collar 2 to 3 inches tall and 1½ to 2 inches wide; push them into the soil so that about half the collar is below the soil surface. Reemove the collars once plants are past the seedling stage.

Diatomaceous earth. This mineral dust is composed of fossilized diatom shells. The microscopic fossil shells have razor-sharp edges that pierce the skin of soft-bodied pests like caterpillars, slugs, and snails. The pests dehydrate and die. Diatomaceous earth also works as a repellent: Use it as a barrier on the soil around plants or around the outside of beds.

Traps. Shallow pans of beer will lure slugs and snails to a watery death. (Alcohol-free beer is even more effective, and you can use a brew of yeast and water, too.) Set the pans into the soil, placing the lip flush with the soil surface, and fill with stale beer; empty the traps daily. Snail traps are also commercially available. Other traps, like Japanese beetle traps, are available commercially but are less relevant to perennial gardeners; in fact, studies have shown that Japanese beetle traps often act as a lure, drawing pests into your garden.

USING SPRAYS AND DUSTS

The best control for a severe pest outbreak is sometimes a spray or dust. A number of sprays and dusts are harmless (like water); some are relatively harmless (like insecticidal soap); and others may be highly toxic for a short time (pyrethrins are toxic for about a day, rotenone for about a week). Don't underestimate the potential toxicity of organically acceptable insecticides like pyrethrins. If you choose to use them, wear protective clothing, a face mask, and gloves when handling or applying them. Whichever spray or dust you use, make sure you coat the undersides of the leaves; many pests congregate there, out of sight of potential predators.

Water. A forceful spray of water is often enough to control aphids and spider mites. It knocks them off the plants, and these slow-moving pests can't find their way back.

Insecticidal soap. Soap sprays are contact poisons that are effective against outbreaks of soft-bodied pests like aphids and whiteflies. You can buy insecticidal soap commercially (Safer is a commonly available brand) and dilute it according to directions, or make your own by mixing 1 to 3 teaspoons of liquid dish soap (not laundry or dishwasher detergent) in 1 gallon of water. For best control, spray plants every 2 or 3 days for 2 weeks.

Pyrethrum. Pyrethrum is made from the pulverized dried flowers of pyrethrum daisies (*Chrysanthemum*

Continued ➡

cinerariifolium and *C. coccineum*). Pyrethrum can be appplied as a dust or used as a spray and is effffective against a wide range of insects. For best control, apply pyrethrum in early evening; two applications 2 hours apart may be most effective. Because pyrethrum is not pest-specific, don't use it near water (it's extremely toxic to fish) or pets. Make sure you buy plant-derived pyrethrum, not synthetic pyrethrins or pyrethroids, which are more toxic and break down more slowly.

A Plague of Perennial Diseases

Perennials are more likely to be disease-free than annuals or vegetables because perennnial beds usually contain a mixture of plants rather than a single species or cultivar (a monoculture). Monocultures draw diseases—and the pests that often spread them—like a magnet. Good cultural practices, like adding plenty of compost and other organic matter to the soil, mulching, and cleaning up plant debris in fall, also reduce the likelihood of diseases getting a foothold in your garden.

Iris borers. In spring, borer larvae enter a fan of iris leaves at the top and burrow down to the rhizome. Pale, irregular tunnels in the leaves mark their travels. Borers also spread soft rot bacteria as they feed. To control borers, pinch and crush them in the leaves, or inject BT or parasitic nematodes into their holes. Also, remove dead leaves in fall and destroy infested fans in spring. If you've had serious borer problems, grow Siberian iris (Iris sibirica), which is usually borer-free, rather than bearded iris.

No matter how careful you are, though, you'll probably encounter diseases in your perennials from time to time. An especially hot, wet summer might provoke an outbreak of powdery mildew, a friend might inadvertently give you a peony division with botrytis blight, or an unusually high leafhopper population might spread aster yellows to your chrysanthemums. Familiarize yourself with disease symptoms so when your plants show signs of infection, you can take prompt action to save them.

There are three types of diseases that infect perennials—bacteria, fungi, and viruses—as well as a related category of pests and problems that cause diseaselike symptoms in plants. These include microscopic nematodes, nutrient deficiencies, and other disorders like herbicide drift.

PREVENTING DISEASES

Prevention is the best—and often the only—cure for plant diseases. There is no cure for viral diseases, and once your garden soil becomes infested with nemaatodes, you may have to remove all the plants in your perennial bed and solarize the soil before trying again with new plants. Even fungi like *Verticillium* can survive for 20 years in the soil. So good gardening practices and commonsense precautions can be critical in keeping diseases out or minimizing their damage.

You can start with resistant species and cultivars, especially if a disease has been a problem in the past. For example, if powdery mildew has been a plague on your bee balm (*Monarda*), try 'Marshall's Delight', which is mildew-resistant. You might have to search for disease-resistant cultivars; breeding for resistance in perennials is a fairly new phenomenon. Resistant species and cultivars are mentioned in encyclopedia entries when a disease is a particular problem for a perennial.

Site selection is also important. If you're planning a new perennial bed, site it in well-drained soil in full sun and where it will get good air circulation. Don't overcrowd plants; space them far enough apart so air can circulate between them. If you have an established bed that has become overcrowded, thin plants to improve circulation.

Fungal and bacterial diseases and nematodes can all spread by water. You can avoid encouraging infections by careful watering. Water your perennials in the morning so they'll dry before night; water the ground around the plants, not the foliage; and don't work in your perennial beds when the foliage is still wet from a rain.

Another time-honored preventive tactic is to practice good garden hygiene: Wash your hands and tools after working with diseased plants. Keep the garden clean of potentially diseased plant debris, and weed religiously to remove alternate hosts of diseases and their carriers. Cut plants to the ground at the end of the growing season. Compost healthy trimmings, but destroy any that look diseased.

CURING OR CONTROLLING DISEASE

If disease strikes in spite of your attempts to prevent it, take prompt action to curtail its development and spread.

The simplest but most painful control is to promptly remove and destroy infected foliage, flowers, or entire plants, if necessary. It's heartrending to pull out prized perennials, but sometimes that's the only alternative, especially if they have viral diseases or foliar nematodes; better to lose a plant or two than an entire bed. This technique will help control fungal and bacterial diseases as well. A more specialized technique that can be quite effective is called soil solarization.

Soil Solarization

If soilborne problems like wilts and nematodes have plagued your perennials in the past few seasons, try

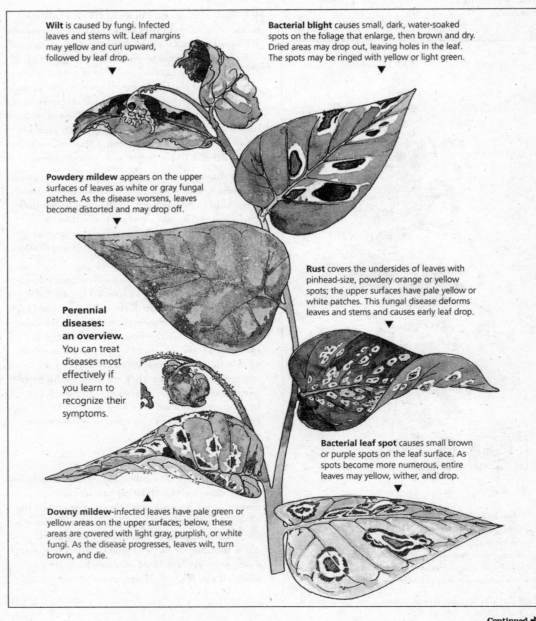

Wilt is caused by fungi. Infected leaves and stems wilt. Leaf margins may yellow and curl upward, followed by leaf drop.

Bacterial blight causes small, dark, water-soaked spots on the foliage that enlarge, then brown and dry. Dried areas may drop out, leaving holes in the leaf. The spots may be ringed with yellow or light green.

Powdery mildew appears on the upper surfaces of leaves as white or gray fungal patches. As the disease worsens, leaves become distorted and may drop off.

Perennial diseases: an overview. You can treat diseases most effectively if you learn to recognize their symptoms.

Rust covers the undersides of leaves with pinhead-size, powdery orange or yellow spots; the upper surfaces have pale yellow or white patches. This fungal disease deforms leaves and stems and causes early leaf drop.

Bacterial leaf spot causes small brown or purple spots on the leaf surface. As spots become more numerous, entire leaves may yellow, wither, and drop.

Downy mildew-infected leaves have pale green or yellow areas on the upper surfaces; below, these areas are covered with light gray, purplish, or white fungi. As the disease progresses, leaves wilt, turn brown, and die.

Continued ➡

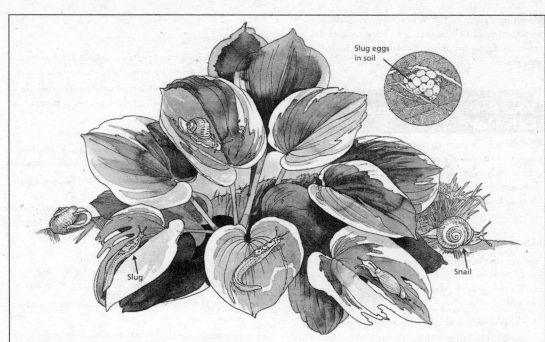

Slugs and snails. These pests thrive in the cool, moist soil preferred by many perennials like hostas. Mulches and plants with low-growing leaves provide shady hiding places from which slugs and snails emerge to feed at night. They rasp large holes in leaves and stems and leave a characteristic shiny slime trail. To control these pests, drown them in beer traps or sprinkle bands of coarse, dry, scratchy materials such as wood ashes or diatomaceous earth around plants or beds.

soil solarization. This is an easy technique, but it does require planning because it takes several months to be effective. If you're starting a new bed, prepare the bed a season before you plan to use it if you live in the North; in the South and Southwest, you can dig the bed, solarize it, and be ready to plant the same growing season.

In spring in the South and midsummer in the North, rake the new bed smooth and water it well. Dig a trench several inches deep around the outside of the bed. Spread a thin (1 to 4 mils) clear plastic sheet over the bed and press it down against the soil surface. Press the edges of the sheet into the trench, and seal the plastic by filling the trench with soil. Leave the sheet in place for 1 to 2 months.

The technique works because heat builds up under the plastic sheet, essentially cooking the top 6 to 12 inches of soil in the bed. In addition to killing nematodes and diseases, solarization will also kill weeds, weed seeds, and insect pests. The drawback is that you need bare soil; if you have a serious nematode infestation in an existing bed, you may have to dig out and discard all the perennials, solarize the soil, and replant in fall.

Battling Bacterial Diseases

Bacteria are microscopic organisms. Most are beneficial decomposers—vital to the decay cycle and to composting—and some are major pest controls, like Bacillus thuringiensis. A few bacteria cause diseases in perennials. Bacterial infections can be spread by wind, water, and contact with contaminated tools or carrier pests. Once contracted, these diseases are difficult to control. Use preventive tactics and treat signs of disease promptly.

Controlling Bad Bacteria

To control bacterial diseases, remove and discard infected plant parts. Thin plants and avoid crowding future plantings. Wash your tools and hands after handling infected plants. Avoid overhead watering. Clean up plant debris to remove overwintering sites. The most common bacterial diseases of perennials are bacterial soft rot of iris, and leaf spot, which infects a number of plants. If you live in the South, your perennials may also be infected by pseudomonas wilt, which causes leaves and stems to wilt and may kill infected plants. Keep pseudomonas wilt from spreading by digging and destroying infected plants.

Fighting Fungal Diseases

Most perennial diseases are fungal. Fungi are organisms like mushrooms that reproduce by spores, lack cholorphyll, and live on organic matter. Most fungi are beneficial, but parasitic fungi cause diseases, sapping the strength of host plants by growing and feeding on them. These fungi are microscopic, but they produce visible spores that are often easy to identify, like the white, cotttony spores of powdery mildew or the orange spores of rust.

Controlling Fatal Fungi

Fortunately, because they're the diseases you're most likely to encounter in your garden, fungal diseases are the easiest to control. Besides growing resistant species and cultivars and using cultural practices to reduce the likelihood of infection, you can choose from a number of organic fungicides to treat stricken plants. These fungicides won't cure disease on infected plant parts, but they will keep the disease from spreading to healthy parts of the plant once you've removed the infected portions. Always follow label directions. Remember that some of these sprays may leave an unattractive coating on foliage, but this is a temporary effect—and it certainly looks no worse than fungus-covered leaves. Here are some of the most effective fungicide sprays.

- **Antitranspirants.** Sprays like Wilt-Pruf that are intended to keep leaves from dehydrating have also been proven effective in preventing powdery mildew. Use one-third of the recommended summer rate and reapply to cover new growth and after rain.

- **Baking soda.** One homemade spray that tests have shown to be effective in controlling a wide range of fungal diseases, including leaf spot, anthracnose, and powdery mildew, is a 0.5 percent solution of baking soda and water. Mix 1 teaspoon of baking soda in 1 quart of water, add a few drops of liquid dish soap or cooking oil to help the mixture adhere to the leaves, and spray on infected plants.

- **Copper.** Copper is also a powerful broad-spectrum fungicide. Use copper fungicides sparingly: Repeated applications may stunt or damage plants.

- **Fungicidal soap.** Safer Garden Fungicide, which contains sulfur in a soap emulsion,

Botrytis blight. Peony shoots afflicted with this fungal disease wilt and fall over. Stem bases blacken and rot, and buds may wither and blacken. Flowers and leaves may turn brown and moldy. Remove and destroy infected plant parts. Avoid overwatering and wet, poorly drained soil. Clear mulch from crowns in spring to let the soil dry.

Crown rot. Overcrowded plants and wet, poorly drained soil are the main causes of crown rot. The leaves and stems of afflicted plants turn brown or black at the base, and black spores may appear on stems. Plants may wilt suddenly or yellow and wilt slowly. Prevention is the best control: Avoid sites with poorly drained, wet soil; divide plants regularly; don't damage crowns when digging near plants; and keep winter mulch away from the base of the plant. Remove and destroy infected plants.

Viral diseases. Perennials may be attacked by several viral diseases that cause symptoms such as spindly new growth and distorted, greenish yellow flowers and leaves. Viruses are spread by sucking insects such as aphids and leafhoppers; control these pests to limit virus problems. There's no cure for infected plants: Remove and destroy them; do not compost them. Viruses overwinter in perennials and perennial weeds, so clean up the garden thoroughly in fall if you've had problems with them. Wash any tools that come in contact with infected plants.

Continued ➡

controls fungi—including powdery mildew, leaf spot, and rust—on perennials. You can buy it in ready-to-spray or concentrate form.

- **Sulfur.** Milder than copper, sulfur still prevents fungi from growing on perennials. You can apply elemental sulfur as a dust, or spray wettable or liquid sulfur onto your plants. Apply sulfur only when temperatures will stay below 85°F; higher temperatures make sulfur toxic to plants.

VIRUSES AND VIRUSLIKE DISEASES

Even though viral diseases aren't as common in perennials as fungal and bacterial infections and nematodes, it's still important to recognize the symptoms of viral infection and eliminate infected plants before they can spread disease. There is no cure for viral infection. Symptoms can vary from plant to plant, but infected plants tend to show certain characteristic traits like greenish flowers, ring spotting (concentric rings on the foliage), and rosetting (a deformed, tight clump of leaves that resembles a rosebud). Mosaic virus and aster yellows are common.

Viruses are spread from plant to plant by direct contact rather than by wind or water. The virus must be either rubbed against or injected by pests into a susceptible plant for it to contract the disease. You can spread viral diseases to your perennials by brushing against infected plants and then healthy plants, especially when plants are wet. Smokers can transmit tobacco mosaic virus from touching cigarettes or other tobacco products and not washing up before heading out to the garden. If you inadvertently propagate infected plants, you may also be spreading viral diseases.

Controlling Vile Viruses

Because there is no cure for plants that are infected by viruses, try to keep your garden virus-free. Plant resistant species and cultivars when possible. Viruses are carried by sucking insects such as aphids, whiteflies, and leafhoppers, which spread the diseases as they feed. Control these pests by spraying plants with a mixture of insecticidal soap and 70 percent isopropyl alcohol (1 tablespoon alcohol to 1 pint soap solution) to reduce the risk of infection. Wash tools used around infected plants. Viruses overwinter in perennials and weeds such as daisies and plantains; a good fall cleanup will reduce the chances of reinfection.

Viruses infect entire plants; you can't control their spread by removing infected leaves or stems. Once perennials show viral symptoms, remove and destroy them. Do not compost infected plants.

NEMATODES: MICROSCOPIC MENACE

Nematodes are microscopic roundworms, but when they attack plants, they produce disease-like symptoms rather than the damage typical of other insects. Three types of nematodes—root knot, foliar, and stem-and-bulb—attack a wide range of perennials. Nematodes are more likely to be a problem in the South or in perennial beds that were previously used for growing susceptible vegetables.

Controlling Nasty Nematodes

Nematodes travel over wet plants on a film of water, or on garden tools and gardeners moving among plants. Promote natural nematode controls by increasing soil organic matter. You can control root knot nematodes by applying chitin (ground seafood shell wastes) or parasitic nematodes to the soil; both are available from garden-supply companies. In severe cases, remove plants, solarize the soil, and replant with nematode-free stock.

There is no cure for either stembulb or foliar nematodes. Remove and destroy infested plants and the surrounding soil; do not compost the debris.

Clean up debris in fall to destroy overwintering nematodes. Mulch in spring to keep nematodes from climbing up plants; avoid wetting leaves when watering.

Your Seasonal Perennial-Care Calendar

This month-by-month calendar is a handy reference guide to help you create and maintain your perennial garden. When using the calendar, keep in mind that these are only general guidelines. What you do specifically in your beds each month depends on what your climate and growing season are like.

JANUARY

Just because it's winter doesn't mean your landscape has to be bare and boring. Here are some things you can do this year to perk up your landscape for next winter.

- Go outside and take a look at your perennial garden (or where you'd like to put perennials).
- Are there places where shrubs, ornamental grasses, or plants with interesting winter seed pods might add structure and improve your garden's winter appearance?
- If so, make a list of those plants—or put your thoughts on paper in the form of a winter garden design to refer to later.

FEBRUARY

Read perennial gardening books and catalogs for ideas about what you want to plant and for design suggestions. Order new plants and seeds from mail-order catalogs now. Start counting down the days until spring is schedules to arrive in your zone.

MARCH

Clean up existing perennial garden beds. Rake out fallen leaves and winter mulch as spring growth begins, adding the leaves and mulch to your compost pile so it doesn't go to waste. When the soil is dry enough to dig, prepare new garden areas, amending the soil with compost.

APRIL

The arrival of spring means there's plenty for you to do to get ready for a new season of growing perennials.

- Cut back woody perennials such as Russian sage and butterfly bush as they begin to show new growth.
- Begin a garden journal; note what plants are in bloom when, what you like and don't like, and what ideas you have for changing things.
- Don't rely on plant labels to remember where everything is and what it is. (Plant labels have a habit of disappearing over time.) Instead, make a garden plan on paper or on your computer, if you don't already have one, and keep it updated as your garden evolves.

MAY

Now you can really start to go to town in your beds. Dig up and divide summer- and fall-blooming plants, and share some of your divisions with family and friends. Plant perennials, and after danger of frost has passed, fill in empty spots with annuals for all-season colorful bloom.

JUNE

Mulch the perennial garden with compost, chopped leaves, or shredded bark to help control weeds. Add new plants as desired. Continue to keep a detailed journal, noting any problem spots in your garden.

JULY

During these dog days of summer:

- Watch for signs of pests or disease, and research organic ways to prevent them in the first place.
- Look through mail-order catalogs for disease resistant varieties to replace problem plants next spring.
- Water your garden during dry spells.
- Keep things looking neat by weeding and deadheading regularly.
- Cut back plants that have finished blooming to promote new growth.
- Cut perennials to use in fresh-flower bouquets and arrangements indoors.

AUGUST

Your late-season garden can still look great during this month; you just need to stay on top of things.

- Take a good look at your beds, noting colorless areas.
- Research possible substitutions, relocations, or additions and jot them down in your garden journal.
- The end of this month is a good time to move or add plants, particularly those that bloom in spring and early summer.
- Dig up and divide early-blooming plants, keeping the new divisions well watered until they become established.

SEPTEMBER

Take cuttings of tender plants (such as salvias) and root them in moist perlite for next year's garden. Prepare new perennial beds. Amend the soil with compost; take a soil test, and adjust the pH if necessary. Cover the bare soil with a mulch of chopped leaves to prevent erosion.

OCTOBER

Clean up existing beds after the first hard frost, and throw the spent plants on your compost pile. Leave upright seedheads and pods in the garden for winter interest (the birds will thank you, too). Cover the beds with a 3- to 4-inch layer of mulch for winter protection.

NOVEMBER

Pot the now-rooted cuttings you took back in September and place them on a bright windowsill for the winter.

DECEMBER

Lay evergreen boughs over your perennials to provide an additional layer of insulation. Page through your garden journal and dream about the new perennials you'd like to try the next year.

Perennials Glossary

Acidic soil. Soil with a pH value lower than 7.0.

Alkaline soil. Soil with a pH value higher than 7.0

Amendment. Material that improves soil condition and aids plant growth.

Annual. A plant that completes its life cycle in one growing season and then dies.

Biennial. A plant that completes its life cycle in 2 years and then dies.

Bulb. An underground stem that stores energy in modified leaves, as in the bulbs of daffodils or tulips.

Compost. Decomposed and partially decomposed organic matter that's dark in color and crumbly in texture. Used as a soil amendment, compost

Continued ➡

increases the water-holding capacity of sandy soil, improved the drainage of clay soil, and is an excellent nutrient source for microorganisms, which later release nutrients to your plants.

Corm. An underground stem that stores energy in modified stem tissue, as in a crocus stem.

Crown. The part of a plant where the stem meets the roots, usually at or just below the soil line.

Cultivar. Short for "cultivated variety." Any plant that's bred for specific characteristics, such as color, fragrance, disease resistance, or other desirable qualities.

Cutting. Removing a piece of stem or root from an existing plant to grow into a new plant.

Deadheading. Removing spent flowers from a growing plant.

Disbudding. Removing some of a plant's buds to encourage the remaining buds to grow larger.

Disk flowers. The small, tube-shaped blooms located in the center of the flowering heads of plants such as asters and daisies.

Division. A method of propagation by which a plant clump is separated or split apart into two or more plants.

Evergreen. A plant that keeps its green foliage through the winter.

Hardy (*perennial*). A perennial plant that tolerates frost.

Herbaceous. A plant that dies back to the ground each year; not woody.

Humus. A dark-colored, stable form of organic matter that remains after most of the plant and animal residues in it have decomposed; the organic component of soil.

Insecticidal soap. A specially formulated solution of fatty acids that kills insect pests such as aphids, mites, and whiteflies.

Life cycle. The germination, growth, flowering, seed production, and death of a plant.

Mulch. A layer of organic or inorganic material (such as shredded leaves, straw, bark, pine needles, lawn clippings, or black plastic) that's spread on the ground around plants to conserve soil moisture and discourage weeds. As organic mulches decompose, they help to build the soil.

Neutral soil. Soil with pH of 7.0—that is, neither acidic not alkaline.

Perennial. A plant that flowers and sets seed for two or more seasons.

pH. A number from 1.0 to 14.0 that's a measure of the acidity or alkalinity: 7.0 is neutral, below 7.0 is acidic, and above 7.0 is alkaline. Soil pH greatly affects the availability of nutrients to plants.

Pinching. Removing the tips of stems to encourage more compact, bushier plants; prevent flopping; and ensure more bloom.

Propagate. To make new plants from existing ones. Some methods of propagation include saving seed from plants and then planting the seed, taking cuttings from plants, and dividing clumps of plants.

Rhizome. A horizontal underground stem modified and often enlarged for food storage.

Semiwoody. A perennial plant that forms woody stems but is less substantial than a shrub.

Succulent. Having thick, fleshy, water-holding leaves or stems.

Taproot. The central, often thickened root of a plant.

Tender (*perennial*). A perennial plant from a tropical or subtropical region that won't survive the winter outside in North America, except in subtropical regions such as Florida and southern California.

Terminal bud. The bud borne at the tip of a stem.

Thinning. Removing some stems of dense, bushy plants to let in light and improve air circulation, often to help prevent mildew on susceptible plants.

Tuber. A swollen, underground stem modified to store large quantities of food.

Variegated. Striped, spotted, or otherwise marked with a color other than green; often used to describe leaves.

Woody. A perennial plant such as a shrub or tree that doesn't die down to the ground each year.

ANNUALS

Picking the Perfect Annuals

Larry Hodgson

I have the secret to end all secrets when it comes to growing annuals: Discover which annuals are considered easy to grow under your growing conditions—then plant lots of them! There's little use trying to grow cool-weather annuals in a Florida summer, or moisture-loving annuals where summers are always dry. But if you pick the right plants for your conditions, they'll practically grow themselves!

What Is an Annual?

As the very name "annual" suggests, true annuals are plants that go through their entire life cycle—from seed to bloom to seed production to death—within one calendar year.

Actually, though, only a few of the plants we know as annuals really do go through their full cycle in just one year (on their own, at least). The other "annuals" are actually biennials, perennials, or shrubs that we can trick into blooming the first year by extending their growing season artificially. In other words, we start them indoors to encourage early bloom. We then treat them as annuals because they give the results we expect of an annual; that is, they come into bloom quickly and remain in bloom over the whole summer. When they die in the fall, it's not because they couldn't have lived longer, but because they can't take the cold or damp winters common in much of North America.

From Hardy to Tender

Since they have different origins, the plants we group together as annuals have somewhat different needs. It's easy to tell these needs at a glance if you just understand three terms: hardy, half-hardy, and tender.

- Hardy annuals are extremely fast-growing plants that you can sow directly outside in all climates. They are tough enough to sow outdoors in very early spring, before the last frost date, although you can also start them indoors a few weeks before the last frost date for even earlier bloom. Many are so tough you can sow them the previous fall for germination the following spring.

- Half-hardy annuals can be started indoors in short-season climates, 6 to 8 weeks before the last frost date. Where summers last 4 months or more, they grow fast enough that you can sow them directly outdoors. Set out transplants or direct-sow around the last frost date.

- Tender annuals are usually tender biennials, perennials, or shrubs. Unless you live in a frost-free climate, you'll sow these indoors, usually 10 or more weeks before the last frost. These plants don't like cold temperatures, so keep them indoors until 2 or 3 weeks after the last frost date.

10 Things to Look For in an Annual

Most gardeners probably first choose a particular annual for its color or flower shape—but that can be a mistake. Even the most beautiful flowers can be fleeting if you try to grow a plant in conditions it doesn't like. To get the best results, first pick out annuals that adapt well to your conditions, then look at the flower colors and forms of the plants in that group. I suggest choosing your annuals according to the following 10 criteria:

1. The plant should be adapted to a wide range of general conditions (sun and shade, rain and drought, and so on).

2. It should also be well adapted to any particularities in your climate (hot summers or humid air, for example).

3. It should bloom all summer.

4. It should grow from seed to full bloom in no more than 3 months.

5. It should be resistant to insects and diseases.

6. It should grow more strongly than most weeds, yet not strongly enough to become a weed.

7. It should need little in the way of fussy maintenance (such as pruning, staking, or deadheading).

8. It should be widely available.

9. It should come true from seed.

10. It should transplant readily at all stages of growth.

Of course, no annual meets all 10 of my criteria (wouldn't that be wonderful, though?). The best most can usually manage is 7 out of the 10, which are very good plants. And 5 out of 10 is really not that bad. However, if the plant rates less than 4, you're better off looking for something else.

Buying Annuals

There was a time when you had only two choices when purchasing annuals: Either you bought wooden boxes of ready-to-plant annuals, or you bought seed packs. Well, those wooden boxes (and the fiber ones that followed) have pretty much gone the way of the dinosaur, having been replaced by plastic containers. Seed packs still exist, of course, and in many ways, they've scarcely changed from a century ago. Let's take a quick look at the options:

Seed Packs

You'll find these for sale both in local stores and in seed catalogs, but the latter have by far the widest choice. Seed packs are relatively inexpensive, so they're a great choice if you are on a limited budget. In most cases, each annual you grow from seed costs you only a few cents! The downside of seed packs is that they do mean extra work.

Boxes, Flats, and Cell Packs

The standard containers for nursery-grown annuals include boxes, flats, and cell packs. Single pots—usually 4 inches (10 cm) in diameter for annual plants—are the most costly, and cell packs (4 to 6 plants) and six packs are the most commonly sold.

Continued ➡

In the United States, flats usually contain 8 to 12 cell packs and are the cheapest, most surefire route to a lush, full garden. Outside the states, annual containers hold anywhere from 4 to 36 plants.

The plants grown in these containers are generally raised from seed; in fact, it's the same seed you could have bought from a seed rack or a catalog, but someone else has done all the work. Container-grown seedlings can be a big plus if you're really busy; just pop the plants into the ground and water. In return, you pay a bit more, but most annuals come in at less than 50 cents a plant, so that's not exorbitant.

Annuals come in a variety of different containers. Just pop out plants from containers of peat pots, and cut through roots to separate plants if they are growing in an undivided flat.

Plugs

For years, nurseries have been buying the more-delicate annuals prestarted in trays with tiny little compartments. Normally, they pot them up into larger containers, then jack up the price. Some nurseries, however, are now selling these "plugs" (as the tiny seedlings are called) directly at greatly reduced prices. I buy all my "difficult" annuals (such as begonias and impatiens) this way. Of course, you'll have to pot up the plugs yourself, but the savings are considerable: less than one-quarter the cost of buying the same plant in a cell pack. Buy plugs early and pot them into 2½-inch (6.5 cm) pots or sectioned trays, then grow them indoors until planting-out time.

You can also buy larger plugs (in this case, starter plants) of the usually expensive annuals grown from rooted cuttings—such as Australian fan flower (*Scaevola aemula*)—once again with the idea of potting them up yourself.

Individual Pots

Rooted cuttings of container annuals are usually sold in individual pots at quite a cost: $2 or more per pot. And the larger the pot, the more you pay! If you only need a few plants for a container, though, the cost won't seem so bad. Since all these plants can be propagated by cuttings, I suggest you buy just one plant and multiply it by rooting the cuttings yourself. That will bring the price down!

Preplanted Pots and Baskets

These "finished" container plantings are the most expensive option of all. Plus, they limit your creativity since you're stuck with choosing from the available color combinations and plant choices. Personally, I prefer to plan my own mixed containers. But hey, if you find a preplanted container that you like and it's at a reasonable price, go for it!

Buying Smart

You can tell true gardeners by the annuals they purchase. Everyone around them is picking up plants in full, gorgeous-bloom, yet the true gardeners select plants with nary a blossom. Why?

They know that blooming plants kept in cramped quarters all their lives are overmature. When you put these plants in the ground, they are slow to produce new roots and tend to grow poorly

or even die back. Slightly younger plants—perhaps in bud, but not yet in bloom—react differently; put them in the garden and they immediately send out new roots in all directions, then new branches and new leaves. Soon, they are far larger, healthier, and more floriferous than the planted-when-blooming annuals will ever be.

Unfortunately, already-flowering plants sell quickest, so nurseries have no reason to set out younger, not-yet-blooming plants. If you must buy container-grown seedlings already in bloom, you can still get good results if you pinch out all the flowers and all the buds at planting time. This extra step encourages the plant to sprout new roots and shoots galore, giving you blooming plants of top quality in no time.

Going for Quality

Besides choosing annuals that are not yet in full bloom, watch out for any that have been mistreated. Yellowed leaves, leaf spots, straggly growth, wilting stems, and visible insects are not good signs. Instead, look for plants with dense, lush, dark green foliage.

Designing with Annuals
Larry Hodgson

Boy, are you in luck! There is no plant group easier to design with than annuals. For one thing, most bloom throughout the growing season. That means you don't need to account for "downtime," as you would in a perennial garden, or to plan on a color scheme that changes constantly. And annuals let you experiment! You wouldn't dare try a bold design or color combination with permanent plants like perennials or shrubs unless you're sure it will work. With annuals, though, anything goes! You don't like it? Just try something different the following year!

Design Basics

I don't consider myself an expert on design. Like most gardeners, I just follow a few basic rules and change things when I don't like them. And I confess to breaking the rules every now and then: sometimes with great results, sometimes not. Oh well, that's what I use annuals for—to experiment! Three of the basic keys to a beautiful garden are color, texture, and form. Get them to mesh and you'll be doing just fine.

Color

Of the three, color is probably the most influential factor when you choose the annuals you grow. Cool colors, like green and blue, make the garden seem calmer and more peaceful, and they can make a small garden look larger.

Warm colors, like yellow and red, stimulate the eye. They make a garden seem vibrant and alive and can make a large garden seem more intimate.

How you use warm and cool colors is up to you. You can use only one or mix the two groups. If you do choose to mix them, use about half again as many cool-colored annuals as warm-colored ones; if you use equal numbers, the warm colors will dominate. And in general, put cool colors in front of warm colors; otherwise, they'll hardly be visible.

Color Combinations

There is nothing wrong with mixing colors at random, especially if you enjoy an all-mixed-up, everything-goes appearance. If so, you'll find white flowers (and silver and gray foliage) make great moderators. You can use them to separate and soften excessively strong impacts and dilute overbearing colors.

Texture and Form

While flower color is undeniably important when planning a garden, you'll want to consider texture and form as well.

Texture can refer to either flowers or foliage. Just think fine, medium, and coarse, and you'll have a handle on it. Fine foliage creates a soft, intimate look, whereas a few spots of bold, coarse foliage can wake up a humdrum border.

Form refers to a plant's general outline; it may be vertical, rounded, open, spreading, or prostrate (practically flat). The most successful gardens usually include some of each form, with spreading or prostrate plants in the foreground, rounded plants to the middle, and vertical ones at the back or standing tall here and there as "vertical accents."

Beyond "Borders"

Most modern flower gardens feature a broad bed backed by a tall background element, such as a hedge or fence, and are laid out with plants of graduating height (shortest in the front to tallest in the back). Or if the border is to be seen from both sides, the tallest plants are in the middle with shorter plants to either side. But with annuals offering so many possibilities, why not try going beyond the border?

Carpet Bedding

This type of formal bedding is back in style. You've probably seen it in parks or in front of corporate offices: neatly trimmed, low-growing plants set out in precise geometrical patterns or even in company or municipal logos. You can adapt simpler carpet-bedding styles to the home garden. Just choose low-growing plants of contrasting colors, and set them out in relatively geometric patterns. Often a tall, upright centerpiece plant, like castor bean (*Ricinus communis*), will give carpet beds more impact.

Flower Meadows

The ultimate in informality! Best suited for vast spaces you don't have the time (or the money!) to cover with individual bedding plants, a flower meadow involves simply sowing seeds of mixed, fast-growing annuals. In fall or early spring, simply till or plow under whatever was there before. (Don't bother worrying about weeds; the nice thing about a flower meadow is that weeds fit right in!) Then sow annual wildflower seed by hand or with a spreader. Don't think flower meadows are self-maintaining, though. You'll have to till the meadow under and resow it annually; otherwise, weeds and grasses will dominate and flowers will be few.

Cut-Flower Gardens

If you're fond of gathering flowers and foliage for fresh and dried arrangements, consider growing an area of annuals just for that purpose.

The 10 Commandments of Annual Design

Over the years, I've learned a lot both from my successes and my failures. Here are the best tips I know about gardening with annuals.

1. Mix 'em up! Gone are the days when annuals had to be in a bed of their own. You can—and should—plant them among shrubs and perennials.

2. Don't plant too densely. A newly planted garden always looks barren at first, but annuals fill out in only a few weeks.

3. Plan before you plant. It's always wise to take a few minutes to make a rapid sketch of a garden plan and then pencil in a few plant names you've chosen. Next, trace the plan on the garden surface with flour or powdered lime before planting. If you make a mistake, you just have to rake the lines out and redraw. It's much easier than having to dig plants up and replant them!

4. Use annuals abundantly for new gardens. Even if you plan to have a garden mostly based on

Continued ➡

shrubs or perennials, use annuals until the permanent plants fill in.

5. Avoid straight lines whenever possible. Lines are too hard to maintain and rarely look their best; it takes only one dead plant to destroy the whole effect. Instead, go for curves and undulations when planning edges and for spots of color inside the garden. Save planting in lines for very formal styles, such as carpet bedding.

6. Repeat spots of color. You can mix any colors you like with total impunity, as long as you repeat them. One spot each of a dozen different plants will seem discordant, but if you repeat the spots (each at least twice and preferably more), the whole garden will "pull together" visually. And while you're at it, write down your successful combinations so you'll remember the following year.

7. Stake discreetly or not at all. A few twiggy branches, a bit shorter than the plants themselves, will look much nicer than a forest of upright stakes. And if possible, grow plants that don't require staking.

8. Watch out for self-sowing annuals. They have many good qualities, but that doesn't mean you should let them grow anywhere they want! Pull or dig out any annuals that appear where you don't want them.

9. Don't be afraid to experiment. One of the great advantages to annuals is that they are temporary, so you can easily replace plants that don't work with others when you replant next year.

10. Don't always follow the rules. All rules are meant to be broken, especially in design. Break or bend a few—and watch your garden come alive!

Garden Designs with a Purpose

Still not sure you're ready to design a garden on your own? I've included four annual garden designs created by professionals especially for home gardeners like you.

Look over the design layouts on the next several pages to see how the designers combine color and texture, use repetition, and choose plants that have different habits. You may find a plan that's just perfect for your yard or one that inspires you to take the plunge to design a garden of your own. Good luck and have fun!

Grandmother's Backdoor Garden

Heirloom flowers are enjoying a resurgence of popularity—and with good reason. The annuals our grandmothers and great-grandmothers knew and grew are colorful, sturdy, easy-to-grow plants. Many of these old-time favorites are also wonderful in cut-flower arrangements. Designed by heirloom-flower aficionado Sarah Wolfgang Heffner, this backdoor garden in shades of pink, blue, and lavender starts its show in late spring with larkspur and cornflowers, then keeps the color coming with cleome, ageratum, and zinnias for an abundance of bloom from midsummer through early fall (the midsummer view is shown here). This low-maintenance planting will do well in direct sun and fertile, well-drained soil.

Sowing and planting: Start ageratum seeds indoors 6 to 8 weeks before the last frost Sow cleome, cornflower, and larkspur seeds outdoors in early spring. Sow zinnia seeds doors around the last frost date, and set out dusty miller plants around the same time.

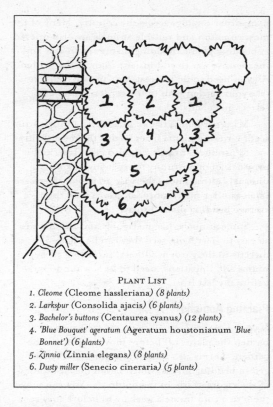

PLANT LIST
1. *Cleome* (Cleome hassleriana) (8 plants)
2. *Larkspur* (Consolida ajacis) (6 plants)
3. *Bachelor's buttons* (Centaurea cyanus) (12 plants)
4. *'Blue Bouquet' ageratum* (Ageratum houstonianum 'Blue Bonnet') (6 plants)
5. *Zinnia* (Zinnia elegans) (8 plants)
6. *Dusty miller* (Senecio cineraria) (5 plants)

An Elegant Entrance Border

There's nothing like a flower-filled garden to welcome visitors to your home. Designed by Pam Ruch, this inviting planting (shown in midsummer) combines a touch of formality loosened up by an exuberant mix of colors and heights on either side of the walk. The drought-resistant zinnias add a blast of bright color for months on end, while the Brazilian vervain adds a lively second layer of purple haze. The cool green 'Envy' zinnias provide a pleasant break for the eye. (If your 'Envy' zinnias start looking forlorn by mid- to late summer, Pam suggests pulling them out and letting the remaining plants fill the space— which they'll happily do!) The flowering tobacco offers an extra bonus of evening fragrance. Give this garden a full-sun site with average, well-drained soil.

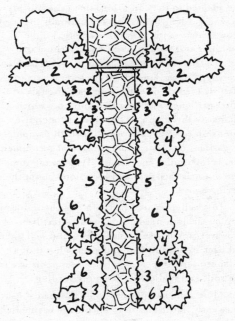

PLANT LIST
1. *Flowering tobacco* (Nicotiana sylvestris) (8 plants)
2. *'Victoria' mealy-cup sage* (Salvia farinacea 'Victoria') (72 plants)
3. *'Profusion Orange' hybrid zinnia* (Zinnia elegans x angustifolia 'Profusion Orange') (about 70 plants)
4. *'Envy' zinnia* (Z. elegans 'Envy') (12 plants)
5. *'Star White' narrow-leaved zinnia* (Z. angustifolia 'Star White') (about 70 plants)
6. *Brazilian vervain* (Verbena bonariensis) (about 30 plants)

Sowing and planting: Sow Brazilian vervain seeds outdoors in early spring. Start zinnia seeds indoors 4 to 6 weeks before the last frost date or sow outdoors around the last frost date. Sow flowering tobacco seed outdoors in late spring or indoors at the same time as the zinnias for earlier bloom. Set out mealy-cup sage plants after the last frost date.

A Regal Red Garden

This dramatic collection of rich red flowers and foliage is sure to attract plenty of attention in midsummer, whether you tuck it into an otherwise boring corner or give it a prominent spot near a sidewalk or patio. 'Lady in Red' Texas sage is even a great draw for hummingbirds. To set off the red flowers, this garden includes a variety of other complementary companions, including the char-treuse flowers of 'Lime Green' flowering tobacco, the bright green, red-veined leaves of 'Rhubarb' chard, and the dark purple foliage of 'Purple Ruffles' basil and purple fountain grass. For a more vivid effect, you might replace the purple basil with ferny, bright green parsley. Designed by Nancy Ondra, this garden works well in evenly moist but well-drained soil in either full sun or light shade.

Sowing and planting: Start snapdragon plants indoors 8 to 10 weeks before the last frost date and flowering tobacco seed indoors 6 to 8 weeks before the last frost date. Sow chard seed outdoors in early spring or indoors 6 to 8 weeks before the last frost date. Set out basil, fountain grass, impatiens, and Texas sage plants after all danger of frost has passed.

PLANT LIST
1. *'Accent Red' impatiens* (Impatiens walleriana 'Accent Red') (12 plants)
2. *'Purple Ruffles' basil* (Ocimum basilicum 'Purple Ruffles') (12 plants)
3. *'Rhubarb' Swiss chard* (Beta vulgaris cicia 'Rhubarb') (2 plants)
4. *'Black Prince' snapdragon* (Antirrhinium majus 'Black Prince') (12 plants)
5. *'Lime Green' flowering tobacco* (Nicotiana 'Lime Green') (6 plants)
6. *'Lady in Red' Texas sage* (Salvia coccinea 'Lady in Red') (6 plants)
7. *Purple fountain grass* (Pennisetum setaceum 'Purpureum') (1 plant)

A Garden with Classical Appeal

Designer Stephanie Cohen created a layout that rivals any formal perennial garden for elegance, yet it's composed entirely of easy-care annuals. Shown in midsummer, the mixture of strong spikes, billowing mounds, and cheerful climbers blooms from early summer to midfall. Full sun and average, well-drained soil are ideal for this garden.

Sowing and planting: Start snapdragon plants indoors 8 to 10 weeks before the last frost date. Sow sweet alyssum seeds outdoors in early to mid-spring. Start ageratum and hyacinth bean seeds indoors 6 to 8 weeks before the last frost date. Start zinnia seeds indoors 4 to 6 weeks before the last frost date or sow outdoors around the last frost

Continued ➡

date. Set out fountain grass, mealy-cup sage, and marguerite daisy plants, and sow morning glory seeds outdoors after the last frost date.

Plant List

1. *'Pearly Gates' morning glory* (IPOMOEA TRICOLOR *'Pearly Gates'*) *(1 plant)*
2. *Hyacinth bean* (LABLAB *purpurea* (1 plant)
3. *'Rocket White' snapdragon* (ANTIRRHINUM MAJUS *'Rocket White'*) *(6 plants)*
4. *'Splendor Pink' zinnia* (ZINNIA *'Splendor Pink'*) *(6 plants)*
5. *'Victoria' mealy-cup sage* (SALVIA FARINACEA *'Victoria'*) *(16 plants)*
6. *Purple fountain grass* (PENNISETUM SETACEUM *'Purpureum'*) *(4 plants)*
7. *'Comet Pink' and 'Comet White' maguerites* (ARGYRANTHEMUM HYBRIDS *'Comet Pink' and 'Comet White'*) *(10 plants)*
8. *'Blue Horizon' ageratum* (AGERATUM HOUSTONIANUM *'Blue Horizon'*) *(7 plants)*
9. *'Carpet of Snow' sweet alyssum* (LOBULARIA MARITIME *'Carpet of Snow'*) *(20 plants)*

Caring for Annuals

Barbara W. Ellis

Annuals are bountiful beauties loved by gardeners for their long blooming season, easy culture, and many uses. Annuals are distinguished from other flowers such as perennials and biennials because they will germinate, flower, set seed, and die, all within one growing season. Unlike most perennials, which generally bloom for only two or three weeks, many annuals flower week after week from spring until they are cut down by frost. Ageratums, fibrous-rooted begonias, marigolds, impatiens, and petunias all provide long blooming seasons.

There are many ways to use annuals in the garden. Many expert perennial gardeners fill summertime color gaps in perennial plantings with generous splashes of annuals. Annuals also can make a fine cover over a springtime bulb garden, for they are generally shallow-rooted and will hide the bulb foliage as it fades. Other gardeners prefer to use annuals alone in colorful masses. For small terraces, porches, or patios, containers and hanging baskets filled with annuals provide garden greenery and color.

Each year the newest geranium, petunia, and impatiens cultivars vie for the number one position in the bedding plant industry. Seed packets of these popular plants are available in stores and from

mail-order catalogs across the country. Many of the most common and reliable annuals are also offered as bedding plants. Bedding plants are an easy and inexpensive way to add instant color to the garden. All you need to do to create an "instant" garden is take your garden plan to the garden center and select your plants.

Many gardeners like to raise their annuals from seed. Growing plants from seed is the most thrifty way to produce annuals. It's also great fun, and it provides an opportunity to try many new or unusual cultivars not otherwise available, since seed catalogs offer many more selections than the average bedding plant display.

Some annuals, like marigolds and zinnias, are so easy to start from seed they can be planted directly in the garden. Others, including geraniums and impatiens, need to be sown indoors well before the last frost.

Planting Annuals

If you've grown annuals from seed, be sure to harden the plants off before moving them to the garden. This is also a good idea for greenhouse-grown bedding plants, which haven't been exposed to the rigors of life in the outdoors. You can move them to a cold frame a week or so before they're scheduled to go into the garden; build a simple hoop shelter out of wire and polyethylene; or move them to a sheltered spot outdoors for longer and longer periods each day.

Most gardeners transplant seedlings or bedding plants just after the last average date of frost in their area. If you put them out earlier, be prepared to cover your tender plants with burlap, news-paper, or some other protective layer if frost threatens. Listen to the weather reports during those changeable spring days. Very tender annuals such as impatiens won't really begin to grow until soil temperatures warm.

Routine Care

Once in the garden, annuals need minimal maintenance. One of the best ways to reduce the amount of work they require is to find annuals that are adapted to the conditions that generally prevail in your garden. Plants that are naturally inclined to grow in dry, sandy soil, for example, will be healthier and require less care than those that aren't. There are annual suited to every climate and every type of garden. There are several ways to identify the best ones for your garden: Talk to other gardeners, visit gardens and note which plants are thriving, call your local cooperative extension service, and look for lists in pamphlets, magazines, or other publications that recommend plants for similar conditions. Try growing some new annuals each year and keep notes about their performance.

In a well-prepared bed with enriched soil, most annuals seldom need any additional fertilizer. However, some, like petunias, respond well when cut back in midsummer and given a boost of a balanced fertilizer. Mulch helps keep moisture in the soil, and it also cuts down on weeding.

Most annuals will need to be pinched at least once early in the season to encourage branching and compact growth. To pinch a plant, use your fingernails or a small pair of shears to pinch the bud, or the bud and youngest set of leaves, off the tip of each stem. Annuals that become tall and leggy can be cut back to just above a leaf node. It's best to use shears for this purpose to make sure you make a clean cut.

Deadheading, which means removing spent flowers as they fade, prevents the plants from going to seed. This keeps the garden more attractive and

encourages the annuals to produce more flowers. It also is a way to keep annuals that will reseed prolifically in check. Only let a plant set seed if you want to save the seed.

In weeks when there is less than an inch of rain, you'll probably need to water the garden. In parts of the Southeast, Southwest, and California, where there is no rain for months at a time, traditional gardens need to be on a regular watering schedule. Using drip irrigation may be a feasible way to reduce water use.

Today, many gardeners are selecting plants able to survive with a limited supply of water. Drought-resistant annuals, such as African daisy (*Gerbera jamesonii*), sunflowers (*Helianthus* spp.), and moss rose (*Portulaca* spp.), are very useful for adding color to a garden that uses modest amounts of water.

Ending the Season

After enjoying the season of color and beauty annuals provide, there is one final job for the gardener—putting the garden to bed for winter.

Before frost threatens, consider rooting cuttings or digging and potting annuals that are actually perennials and can be brought indoors for the winter. These include wax begonias, impatiens, and verbena. You can enjoy the color they'll provide indoors and also use them to propagate new plants for next spring. You can select annuals to overwinter that have unusual flower color or other attractive features and perpetuate these characteristics for next season. Roots of four-o'clocks can be dug, dried for a few hours, and stored indoors in a cool, frost-free place through the winter.

When frost kills the impatiens, petunias, and marigolds to the ground, it's time to remove the debris from the garden. Pick up or rake off all of the spent plants and toss the remains on the compost heap where they will decompose and be returned to the garden another year in the form of rich brown compost. Leaving the garden clean during the winter is more attractive, and it minimizes insect and disease problems during the next gardening season. If you've grown French marigolds for nematode control, now is the time to till the plants into the soil.

Favorite Annuals

Larry Hodgson

They're tall or short; they're upright, rounded, or creeping; they're great in borders or in containers; they grow under a wide range of conditions; and they come in an incredible range of flower forms and colors. They're multipurpose annuals: plants that offer a bit of everything to every garden-planting scheme. You could easily design a complete annual garden around just these 13 versatile plants! Oh, but did I mention they also mingle well with bulbs, perennials, and shrubs? You simply can't go wrong when you use multipurpose annuals throughout your landscape.

Traditional Yet Ever-Changing

If you're looking for something totally new, a plant of a genus never before seen on the shelves of your local nursery, look elsewhere in this book! The multipurpose group is made up strictly of plants that have been popular for generations. Snapdragon, pansy, geranium, petunia, marigold: They're all names you've heard before, even if you've never lifted a hoe in your life. That's not to say that multipurpose annuals don't occasionally yield new characteristics: new flower forms or colors or never-before-seen growth habits. It's

Continued ➡

their tried-and-true performance, however, that you'll learn to love; just stick them in the ground and watch 'em grow. They'll bloom and bloom and bloom, making your garden look good right through the summer.

Tailor-Made to Suit Our Tastes

There are many annuals whose entire range consists of one or two cultivars. When you head to the garden center or market to buy one of these, you have little choice: just pink or white perhaps, or maybe tall or taller. Compare this sort of meager selection to nursery displays of any of the plants featured in this chapter. Even corner stores offer dozens of varieties of each in an equally wide range of colors and forms. And if you really want choice, go beyond local stores and delve into one of the larger seed catalogs: There are literally pages and pages of petunias, pansies, marigolds, and China asters, for example.

No matter what your tastes in plants are, each of the multipurpose annuals probably offers at least a few varieties that you'll just love. Of course, this wide range of plants wasn't always available. When these multipurpose annuals were first introduced a few centuries back, there was usually only one species…and it wasn't always that impressive. For example, would you believe that the original petunia, now available in such a wide range of cultivars, was a scrawny, creeping plant with tiny white flowers? None of the multipurpose annuals we grow today was any different: The original plants offered little variety and certainly didn't seem to offer much potential.

And then the hybridizers got a hold of them! Under their guiding hands; the wild species morphed into the varied plants we know and love today. Tall, ungainly plants were brought down to size, climbers and creepers became dense and compact mounders, and simple little flowers became large blooms with extra petals that bloomed in a vastly wider range of colors. The end result with each multipurpose annual has been a profusion of cultivars of each plant.

Small Is Beautiful…

One of the most remarkable and obvious changes in multipurpose annuals is that they have come down in size over the years. Most of the dense, low-growing annuals we're so used to today were once tall, rangy plants suitable only for the back of the border or scraggly spreaders that needed to be mingled with others to create a worthwhile effect. Hybridization has lead to plants with shorter and shorter internodes (the spaces between the stem leaves), resulting in dense, compact plants suitable for edging and bedding.

In fact, the entire concept of a bedding plant (and all multipurpose annuals make superb bedding plants) implies dense, short growth with abundant bloom that creates a carpet of blossoms. The shortening of annual plants over time is so universal that most gardeners would scarcely recognize the gangly ancestors of their common garden annuals. And the trend still continues, with each year bringing ever-shorter cultivars. If it never ends, I can only surmise that future generations of annuals will bloom underground!

…But Only in Plant Size

If short plants are generally seen as desirable, small flowers most certainly are not. So another major trend has been toward the development of larger and larger flowers, or at least denser clusters of flowers. Here, too, there seems to be no limit. Many modern annuals have blooms so large that they are beaten to a pulp by the slightest rain

(Grandiflora petunias, for example), but gardeners will forgive even that—as long as the plant quickly replaces its damaged blooms with new blooms.

Other trends are easy to see just by looking at what the average nursery offers. Double flowers, for example, are clearly highly prized (although that trend does seem to be abating these days). And increases in color range are a must. Is it any wonder dahlias and pansies are so popular? They are now offered in about every color of the artist's palette—and then some!

Although the trend is toward dense, short-growing annuals, don't totally rule out the more old-fashioned, taller strains of yore. Tall snapdragons, for example, can add great impact to the mid or back border-and make great cut flowers. And the old-fashioned, climbing nasturtiums look just as great on a trellis as their dwarf brethren do at the front of the border.

Annuals for Everyone

And there you have a portrait of the average multipurpose annual: dense and compact, with large, often double, flowers in a wide range of colors and forms. These versatile annuals are the wallpaper of the flower garden. There is so much choice, you can't help but find exactly what you want!

Antirrhinum

Snapdragon

Snapdragons are instantly recognizable by their terminal spikes of unique flowers. The tubular blooms with a pouting lower lip seem closed to all traffic until you lightly pinch the sides; then they quickly open to reveal a gaping maw, as if they were dragons ready to snap off your finger! Of course, the flowers are perfectly harmless, but they have fascinated generations of young and young-at-heart gardeners for decades.

PLANT PROFILE

Antirrhinum: an-tir-RYE-num

Bloom Color: Pink, purple, red, orange, yellow, white; bicolor

Bloom Time: Summer; fall through spring in mild climates

Height: 6 to 36 inches (15 to 90 cm)

Spread: 6 to 12 inches (15 to 30 cm)

Garden Uses: Container planting, cut-flower garden, edging, mass planting, mixed border, rock garden

Attracts: Bees, hummingbirds

Light Preference: Full sun or partial shade

Soil Preference: Humus-rich, moist but well-drained, neutral to very acid soil

Best Way to Propagate: Sow seed indoors in late winter or outdoors in early spring

Hardiness: Tender perennial grown as a half-hardy annual

Growing Tips

Snapdragons are easy-to-grow annuals with a long blooming season, particularly in cool summer areas. On the down side, they tend to peter out quickly in hot summer climates. If you live where summer temperatures soar, get your snapdragons into the ground early to take full advantage of their spring bloom; and plant them in partial shade, where it is naturally cooler.

You could sow snapdragons outdoors in early spring, as soon as the ground is workable, but then you'll miss half their blooming season. Instead,

start them indoors 8 to 10 weeks before your last frost date. Sprinkle seed over the surface of the growing mix—don't cover it; mist lightly and expose the tray to light to stimulate germination. Look for the first seedlings in 10 to 21 days. Snapdragons germinate readily under cool conditions, down to 50°F (10°C), but they do fine under lights at warm temperatures as well. When the seedlings have four to six leaves, pinch the stem tips lightly to encourage bushy growth. Water carefully, preferably from below; young seedlings are subject to rot if overwatered. Plant outdoors 2 to 3 weeks before your last frost date; snapdragons can take even relatively heavy frosts without complaint.

Snapdragons' excellent cold resistance makes them a great choice for winter bloom in mild-winter areas. Just sow them outdoors in August or September in an out-of-the-way spot, then transfer them to your flowerbed when nights start to turn cool.

If you're buying plants, look for healthy, dense, leafy growth. Snapdragons that are planted when already in bloom tend to fade out after their first flowering, so for the best long-term results, remove all of the flower spikes at planting time. In the garden, deadhead regularly, cutting out flower spikes when the last few flowers are opening in order to stimulate rebloom.

Although they are offered as annuals, snapdragons are actually tender perennials and occasionally survive winter even in my cold climate. When they do, though, they tend to start blooming late in the season only to suffer in summer's heat. You're best off planting new ones each spring and then yanking them out when their flowering season ends.

Good Neighbors

Snapdragons are valuable as a vertical accent in the mixed plantings of annuals and perennials. In groupings of three to six, taller cultivars can offset postbloom mounds of lady's-mantle (*Alchemilla mollis*) or perennial geraniums (*Geranium* spp.), bringing color to an otherwise green season. The range of available colors gives you all kinds of combination options, but I think the most useful of all is the cream shade, which looks great with any other color. Picking up a couple of dozen to use as filler is never a mistake.

Problems and Solutions

Rust can be a problem, especially in rainy climates. Look for resistant cultivars and avoid overhead watering. When rust has been a problem in the past, avoid planting snapdragons in the same spot 2 years in a row. Taller cultivars may need discreet staking.

Top Performer

Antirrhinum majus (common snapdragon): Originally tallish plants bearing spikes of flowers over a bushy cluster of stems, most snapdragons are now low-growing, compact plants with short, dense spikes. The original dragon's-head-like flower form is still common, but there are now many open-flowered snapdragons with trumpet-shaped blooms as well as double-flowered forms. There are dozens of cultivars, ranging in height from tall to knee-high to dwarf; and all make good garden plants, so choose according to your tastes.

Callistephus

China aster

The huge blooms of the China aster are a flower arranger's dream, and they don't look half bad in the garden either! The range of flower forms is remarkable, from single, daisylike blooms to

Continued ➡

double pompoms to those shaggy spider types that seem to be having a continuously bad-hair day. The color range is just as amazing: They've long been available in every possible shade of white, pink, red, and purple, and now there are even shades of yellow and peach. All have dark green, somewhat triangular, coarsely toothed leaves.

PLANT PROFILE

Callistephus: ka-LISS-tee-fuss or ka-liss-TEE-fuss

Bloom Color: Near blue, lavender, pink, purple, violet, peach, red, rose, yellow, white

Bloom Time: Midsummer into fall; early summer for day-neutral cultivars

Height: 6 to 36 inches (15 to 90 cm)

Spread: 12 to 18 inches (30 to 45 cm)

Garden Uses: Container planting, cut-flower garden, edging, mass planting, mixed border, rock garden

Light Preference: Full sun to partial shade

Soil Preference: Average, well-drained, slightly acid to alkaline soil

Best Way to Propagate: Sow seed indoors in late winter or outdoors after all danger of frost has passed

Hardiness: Half-hardy annual

Growing Tips

Although pretty as a picture, China asters have picked up a bad rap over the years as being difficult to grow. While that reputation isn't fully merited, I still wouldn't necessarily recommend the China aster for your first attempt at growing annuals from seed. For your first try, I suggest either buying plants or sowing the seed outdoors when all danger of frost has passed for bloom into late summer and fall.

If you're feeling adventurous, you can grow China asters from seed indoors—if you start them under lights. The problem with growing China asters indoors is that they grow poorly during short days, and because you should start them indoors 6 to 8 weeks before the last frost, the days are always short at sowing time. Giving them 12-hour days from the start, however, produces beautiful, dense, healthy plants. Just barely cover the seed; it germinates readily at room temperature in 10 to 20 days. Water lightly; soggy mix can cause seedlings to rot. Their roots are fragile, so transplant carefully, or sow in peat pots to avoid transplant shock. And prick the seedlings out with the crown at the same depth as before.

In the garden, China asters prefer full sun or only very light shade. Keep their soil moderately moist, and mulch to keep the roots cool. Cut-flower types may need staking, or you can surround them with sturdier plants to keep them upright. Individual plants bloom for only 3 to 4 weeks, so try successive sowings to prolong flowering until fall; or sow early, midseason, and late cultivars. Don't bother deadheading; China asters won't rebloom—just pull out the plants when they finish blooming.

Good Neighbors

China asters and grasses share an affinity for soil of neutral pH, which makes the two good companions. Try direct-sowing them around medium-height grasses, such as blue oat grass (*Helictotrichon sempervirens*) or northern sea oats (*Chasmanthium latifolium*). Sowing tall China aster cultivars around stiffer plants, such as *Artemisia* 'Powis Castle' or *Sedum* 'Autumn Joy', may help you avoid staking.

Problems and Solutions

Aster wilt, which causes the plants to blacken at the base and keel over, was formerly very common; but most modern China asters are now very resistant to the disease. The same can't be said for aster yellows, an incurable virus carried by insects. As the name suggests, the infected plants turn yellow, and then they die. Although leafhoppers and aphids are the main culprits, don't panic when you see them—your plants will likely have time to bloom before the disease affects them. But do destroy obviously diseased plants on sight. The real secret to controlling both aster yellows and aster wilt is to choose a different planting site for your China asters each year and to avoid replanting in the same spots for at least 4 years.

Top Performer

Callistephus chinensis (China aster): It's the only species available, but it makes up for the lack of choice by offering literally hundreds of cultivars. One important development in China asters has been the introduction of "day-neutral" plants. In the past, it was difficult to get asters to bloom early (other than under lights) because they needed the long days of summer to initiate buds, meaning they weren't in full bloom until mid-July at the earliest. Day-neutrals, on the other hand, will start to flower once they reach their adult size, regardless of day length. You won't always find the words "day neutral" noted on the seed pack, though: Look for "early blooming," "blooms within 90 days," or some other phrase that suggests the pack's contents are especially rapid from seed.

Celosia

Celosia, cockscomb

Celosia is a plant of tropical origin, and it looks every bit the part! The shiny, deep maroon or light green leaves are topped by tiny flowers clustered into plumy feather dusters or twisted brain- or coral-like masses, generally in fiery shades of red, yellow, orange, or shocking pink. Some puritanical gardeners disdain celosia's brilliant coloration and complain it stands out too much from the crowd. If it offends your tastes, try something else—but if you want to add a bit of zing to an otherwise drab landscape, this brazen beauty may be just what the doctor ordered.

PLANT PROFILE

Celosia: sell-OH-zee-uh

Bloom Color: Pink, red, orange, yellow, cream

Bloom Time: Late spring through early fall; fall through winter in mild climates

Height: 8 to 36 inches (20 to 90 cm)

Spread: 6 to 16 inches (15 to 40 cm)

Garden Uses: Container planting, cut-flower garden, edging, mass planting, mixed border

Light Preference: Full sun to partial shade

Soil Preference: Humus-rich, evenly moist but well-drained soil

Best Way to Propagate: Sow seed indoors in spring or outdoors in early summer

Hardiness: Frost-sensitive perennial grown as a tender annual

Growing Tips

Although you can sow celosia seed outdoors, you should wait until the ground has warmed up thoroughly, 1 or 2 weeks after the last frost date. You'll probably find, however, that you get better results by sowing the seed indoors, just barely covering it,

4 to 8 weeks before the last frost date. The seed sprouts in 5 to 14 days at 70° to 80°F (21° to 27°C). Celosias resent root disturbance, so for best results, start the seed in peat pots. Wait 1 or 2 weeks after your last frost date, until the night temperatures have warmed up a bit, before setting out the seedlings. When you plant them out, keep the rootball at the same depth as it was in the pot.

Slow and steady is the key to success with celosia. Abrupt changes in conditions, drought, and even just cold water from the hose can stunt its growth. Even buying plants already in bloom is risky; they often stop growing and fail to fill out. When buying celosias, look for sturdy plants not yet in flower. Failing that, remove all existing flower clusters at planting time. Six packs or cell packs are a better choice than flats because there's less root disturbance at planting time.

Good Neighbors

When planted in masses, celosia can be too much of a good thing; used judiciously, however, it can add a rich accent to a perennial bed. The dark foliage of 'New Look', a plumed cultivar with deep red flowers, makes a great foil for postbloom candy tuft (*Iberis sempervirens*) or perennial geraniums (*Geranium* spp.). Try yellow plumes around purple globe amaranth (*Gomphrena globosa*) for an interesting low border. An edging of a tightly crested cultivar can provide a fascinating contrast in front of feathery Oriental fountain grass (*Pennisetum orientale*). Wheat celosia (*Celosia spicata*) has a unique look that can be quite interesting in a naturalistic garden among grasses and meadow plants.

Problems and Solutions

The most common problem is stunted growth due to planting shock or abrupt changes in conditions, so careful planting when temperatures have warmed up is essential. Root rot is possible in soggy soil.

Top Performer

Celosia argentea plumosa (plumed celosia, feathered amaranth): This plant comes in dwarf, knee-high, and tall cultivars with green or red leaves and remarkable feathery clusters of flowers. Taller cultivars form a solid, summer-long mass of flowers at the tip of the bushy plant with smaller plumes toward its base. Dwarf cultivars produce numerous shorter clusters, all reaching much the same height. Dwarf cultivars make excellent bedding plants; taller selections are spectacular cut flowers. Height: 8 to 36 inches (20 to 90 cm). Spread: 6 to 16 inches (15 to 40 cm).

More Recommended Celosia

Celosia argentea cristata (cockscomb): Resulting from a curious mutation that comes true from seed, the flowers of the normally spiky celosia become crested like a rooster's comb. Cockscomb celosias occasionally produce normal plumed flowers; just prune these out on sight. Height: 8 to 36 inches (20 to 90 cm). Spread: 6 to 16 inches (15 to 40 cm).

C. spicata (wheat celosia): These plants are thinner, more open, and less flamboyant in both form and color than their showier cousins—and they are easier to fit into mixed plantings. The spiky flower clusters, in pale pink to deep pink, do look rather like wheat, and they take on a bicolor appearance as the lower flowers on the spike turn paler over time. Height: 28 inches (70 cm). Spread: 6 inches (15 cm).

Dahlia

Dahlia

There's no lack of choice when it comes to dahlias! There are some 20,000 different cultivars in just

Continued ➡

about every color but true blue, and they range from 1-foot (30 cm) bedding dahlias to 10-foot (3-m) border giants that fill nearly a whole flowerbed by themselves. There are so many flower forms that the American Dahlia Society has designated 16 different classes: everything from spiky cactus dahlias to fully rounded ball dahlias, formal-looking decorative dahlias, and old-fashioned single-flowered dahlias. Even the foliage ranges from dark green to deep purple!

PLANT PROFILE

Dahlia: DAH-lee-uh

Bloom Color: Near black, lavender, pink, purple, violet, red, orange, yellow, white

Bloom Time: Summer through early fall for bedding dahlias; midsummer to early fall for border dahlias

Height: 1 to 10 feet (30 to 300 cm)

Spread: 12 to 18 inches (30 to 45 cm) for bedding dahlias; 18 to 48 inches (45 to 120 cm) for border dahlias

Garden Uses: Container planting, cut-flower garden, edging, annual hedge, mass planting, mixed border

Attracts: Butterflies

Light Preference: Full sun to partial shade

Soil Preference: Average, evenly moist but well-drained soil

Best Way to Propagate: Sow seed indoors in late winter; divide tuberous roots

Hardiness: Frost-sensitive tuberous root grown as a tender annual

Growing Tips

You can start dahlias either from seed or from tuberous roots; nurseries and mail-order sources offer both in early spring. You'd think that those grown from tubers would be faster growing, but oddly enough, seed-grown dahlias usually beat the tubers to the punch. Start the fine seed indoors 6 to 10 weeks before the last frost, barely covering it, and keep it at 65° to 85°F (18° to 30°C) until seedlings emerge in 5 to 21 days. Pinch when the seedlings are about 3 inches (8 cm) tall to promote bushier growth and more abundant bloom. Wait until all danger of frost has passed and the ground has warmed up before setting them out. You can also start the seed directly outdoors, but the seedlings won't bloom until mid- to late summer.

Maintenance is simple: Water when the soil is nearly dry, mulch to keep the weeds in check, and deadhead to encourage rebloom.

I have a basic rule about whether or not to overwinter dahlias: I carefully dig up and store for the winter my favorite tuber-grown cultivars, but I let the seed-grown types freeze. It sounds cruel, but it is actually faster to grow border dahlias from seed each spring than from tubes...and just as easy. If you do want to keep your tubers, dig them up after frost has destroyed their foliage; cut off the dead leaves; and store the tubers in peat moss, vermiculite, or perlite in a cool, frost-free spot.

Check them monthly during the winter and spray them with tepid water if they seem to be shriveling. In spring, plant them directly in the garden when all danger of frost has passed, or start them indoors in pots 4 weeks before the last frost.

Good Neighbors

Shorter cultivars mound nicely and present a formal face, making them useful as edging plants, and they look great in containers, too. Combine the taller cultivars, which are excellent for cutting

but not the most generous of bloomers, with Brazilian vervain (*Verbena bonariensis*) to add continuous color for those times when the dahlias aren't in flower. The dark foliage of red-leaved selections, such as the seed-grown 'Diablo' strain, makes a handsome accent in perennial borders.

Problems and Solutions

When earwig populations are large, they do considerable damage, entirely emptying out buds before they open. Leave out boards they can hide under, then crush them underfoot. Staking is almost essential with tall dahlias. Otherwise, they are pretty much trouble-free plants.

Top Performer

Dahlia cultivars (dahlia): Almost all dahlias currently grown are complex hybrids and listed either without a species name or as *Dahlia* x *hortensis*. This category includes everything from the tiniest border types to the huge dinner-plate-flowered, back-of-the-border cultivars. Only a handful of these come true enough from seed to be sold in seed packs. Most of the latter are border-type dahlias: short, dense plants with an early-blooming, nonstop-flowering characteristic that makes them outperform even the best of the tuberous cultivars. Seed-grown dahlias do produce small tuberous roots, but they grow so quickly from seed that it is rarely worthwhile trying to maintain them over the winter.

Dianthus

China pink, sweet William

China pinks get top ratings for their incredibly long season of bloom. They're frost hardy, so you can plant them out before the last frost date for extra-early blossoms; under the right conditions, they'll still be in full bloom late the following fall! Their flat-faced, toothed or smooth-edged, 1- to 2-inch (2.5- to 5-cm) blooms are usually bicolored, with contrasting eyes or halos, and are held over mounds of grasslike, gray-green foliage. Some offer a very light clove scent.

PLANT PROFILE

Dianthus: dye-AN-thus

Bloom Color: Pink, wine purple, red, white; bicolor

Bloom Time: Early spring through late fall; fall through winter in mild climates

Height: 6 to 30 inches (15 to 75 cm)

Spread: 8 to 14 inches (20 to 36 cm)

Garden Uses: Container planting, cut-flower garden, edging, groundcover, mass planting, mixed border, rock garden

Attracts: Butterflies

Light Preference: Full sun to partial shade

Soil Preference: Average, well-drained, neutral to alkaline soil

Best Way to Propagate: Sow seed indoors in late winter or outdoors in early spring

Hardiness: Hardy perennial grown as a hardy annual

Growing Tips

China pinks are easy to grow, whether you start them from seed or buy them in six packs or cell packs. They have only two flaws: They hate hot weather (protection from afternoon sun is best where summers are hot) and they like soil on the alkaline side. Although the slightly acid soil of most gardens is acceptable, they prefer a pH of 7.0 or more; so I

suggest sprinkling a bit of powdered limestone or wood ashes into the soil at planting time.

Start China pinks indoors 8 to 10 weeks before the last frost or buy plants already in bud. You can also sow them directly in the garden 3 weeks before the last frost for somewhat later bloom; in mild climates, sow in fall for bloom the following spring. Indoors, sow at room temperature, just covering the seed. After germination, in 5 to 21 days, bring the temperatures down to 50° to 60°F (10° to 15°C). Set out these cold-tolerant plants 2 to 3 weeks before the last frost date. During summer, keep them well watered and deadheaded regularly to help maintain constant flowering.

Good Neighbors

Planted in masses, pinks create a low river of intense color that looks super edging a bed or snaking through low-growing shrubs or late-flowering mums. They can also be useful as an underplanting for roses of a complementary color range or as a filler to color the niches of a rock garden.

Problems and Solutions

When grown as annuals, pinks rarely suffer from insects or diseases, although slugs are sometimes a problem. Rust or wilt sometimes affects established plants; destroy diseased plants and set out new pinks in a different site.

Top Performer

Dianthus barbatus x *chinensis* (hybrid China pink): Almost all modern strains of so-called *D. chinensis* actually belong here. Crossing China pinks with sweet William (*D. barbatus*) has added greater frost resistance, clustered instead of solitary flowers, more fringing (true China pinks tend to have smooth-edged blossoms), and occasionally some perfume. Most modern China pinks are compact plants, which are ideal for edging and containers, although the long-stemmed cultivars seem to be coming back in style. Growing 18 to 30 inches (45 to 75 cm) tall, these taller cultivars make great cut flowers but may require staking. Height: 6 to 30 inches (15 to 75 cm). Spread: 8 to 14 inches (20 to 35 cm).

More Recommended Dianthus

Dianthus barbatus (sweet William): These plants are very similar to China pinks, but they produce clusters of more deeply fringed flowers in pink, red, white, purple, and bicolors—each stem makes a complete bouquet! Sweet Williams were originally highly scented flowers, but modern strains have lost much of their perfume. Originally biennials or short-lived perennials, sweet Williams—through careful selection—now bloom the first year from early-sown seed. Sow annual strains as recommended above; sow the biennial strains outdoors in early summer for bloom the following year. Height: 6 to 24 inches (15 to 60 cm). Spread: 4 to 12 inches (10 to 30 cm).

D. chinensis (China pink): Pure China pinks are now quite rare. Plants sold under the name *D. chinensis* are inevitably hybrids between *D. chinensis* and *D. barbatus*. Height: 6 to 30 inches (15 to 75 cm). Spread: 8 to 14 inches (20 to 35 cm).

Nicotiana

Nicotiana, flowering tobacco

Yep, this delicate summer beauty really is a close relative of the tobacco plant (*Nicotiana tabacum*). Don't try smoking any of the ornamental kinds, though; they're considered toxic! Instead, grow them for their summer-long bloom and often-exquisite perfume. Most nicotianas form a dense cluster of apple green leaves topped with spikes of

Continued →

tubular, five-petaled flowers. Be forewarned, though, that their blooms often close during the day, opening fully only in the evening, at night, and on cloudy days. If you want daytime bloom, look for cultivars labeled "open all day long."

PLANT PROFILE

Nicotiana: ni-koh-shee-AH-nuh

Bloom Color: Green, pink, salmon, red, white

Bloom Time: Late spring through early fall

Height: Varies by species; see individual listings

Spread: Varies by species; see individual listings

Garden Uses: Container planting, cut-flower garden, edging, annual hedge, mass planting, meadow garden, mixed border

Attracts: Sphinx moths, hummingbirds

Light Preference: Full sun to partial shade

Soil Preference: Evenly moist, well-drained soil

Best Way to Propagate: Sow seed indoors in late winter, outdoors in late spring

Hardiness: Frost-sensitive perennial grown as a half-hardy annual

Growing Tips

Nicotianas are adaptable, easy-to-care-for annuals that thrive in most climates and under most conditions, even alkaline soil and partial shade. They're pretty much problem-free plants with lots of visual impact in the garden.

Whether you grow them from seed or buy plants is mostly a question of how much time you have on your hands. Even raw novices will find them a snap to grow from seed. Although *Nicotiana sylvestris* is fast enough to grow from direct-sown seed (in fact, it will often self-sow), it's best to start most other types indoors 6 to 8 weeks before the last frost, at least if you want to have early bloom. Don't cover the fine seed, though: It needs light to germinate. They sprout at 65° to 85°F (18° to 30°C) in 10 to 20 days. For maximum bloom, keep the plants moist throughout the entire growing season (mulch can be a big help).

Good Neighbors

Planted in groups of six or more, the more-compact nicotianas add color and elegance to a perennial garden or a shrub border. Lime green *Nicotiana langsdorffii* looks terrific with any other color but makes an especially handsome contrast with dark foliage; try it with deep purple basil or one of the tall, dark-leafed coleus cultivars that can take a bit of sun. Tuck a plant or two of *N. sylvestris* into the back of a border for wonderful evening scent.

Problems and Solutions

Nicotianas are not particularly subject to pests, but aphids can occasionally be a problem. Knock them off with sprays of water. Reduce the chance of mildew, damping-off, stem rot, and other diseases associated with wet stems and leaves by mulching and watering from below. To help prevent tobacco mosaic virus, keep nicotianas away from other members of the Solanaceae family, which includes tomatoes, potatoes, and the like.

Top Performer

Nicotiana x *sanderae* (common nicotiana, flowering tobacco): Although often sold as *N. alata* or *N. affinis*, the common nicotiana generally belongs in the hybrid genus *N.* x *sanderae*. True *N. alata* is a tall plant, up to 5 feet (150 cm), with highly scented, yellowish green flowers that open only at night. Crossing with other *Nicotiana* species has resulted in shorter plants in a much wider range of colors.

The flowers of most modern hybrids stay open all day long, but many have entirely lost the scent that was half the charm of the species! Height: 8 to 24 inches (20 to 60 cm). Spread: 8 to 10 inches (20 to 25 cm).

More Recommended Nicotiana

Nicotiana langsdorffii (flowering tobacco): This curious plant, with small, bottle-shaped, lime green flowers dangling from upright, branching stems, is actually much more attractive than the description suggests and should be more widely grown. Its flowers remain open all day but are scentless. Height: 3 to 5 feet (90 to 100 cm). Spread: 12 to 14 inches (30 to 35 cm).

N. sylvestris (flowering tobacco): This is perhaps the most highly perfumed of the flowering tobaccos, with tall, candelabra-like stems of white flowers with extremely long tubes that half close on sunny days. Scent is faint or absent during the day but remarkable at night. Height: 3 to 6 feet (90 to 180 cm). Spread: 2 feet (60 cm).

Pelargonium X hortorum

Zonal geranium, bedding geranium

Zonal geraniums are so ubiquitous on winter windowsills and in summer containers and gardens that one could argue they need no introduction. For the benefit of true novices, though, these are the geraniums with thick, somewhat fuzzy stems and rounded, oddly scented leaves, either all green or marked with a dark, horseshoe-shaped band (the "zone" in zonal). Their main claim to fame, though, comes from their stalks of large, rounded clusters of single or double flowers, often in brilliant, eye-catching colors.

PLANT PROFILE

Pelargonium x Hortorum: pe-lar-GO-nee-um hor-TO-rum

Bloom Color: Pink, purple, salmon, red, orange; bicolor

Bloom Time: Late spring through early fall; all year indoors and in frost-free climates

Height: 10 to 36 inches (25 to 90 cm)

Spread: 8 to 14 inches (20 to 35 cm)

Garden Uses: Container planting, edging, mass planting, mixed border, rock garden, specimen plant

Light Preference: Full sun to partial shade; partial shade in hot summer climates

Soil Preference: Humus-rich, well-drained soil; tolerates alkaline soil

Best Way to Propagate: Sow seed indoors in winter; take stem cuttings at any season

Hardiness: Frost-sensitive sub-shrub grown as a tender annual

Growing Tips

These easy-care annuals have few special needs: Simply give them full sun or just a bit of shade (partial shade is a must in hot summer climates), water moderately, and you should have no problems. It's when you multiply them that geraniums become more difficult. Beginners would be wise to buy geraniums already started, skipping the seed stage entirely.

If you're adventurous, however, you can start seed indoors in early winter, 14 to 16 weeks before the last frost to get plants that will bloom by summer. That means you'll be starting seed in the dark days of winter and will probably need artificial lights. You may, therefore, prefer to start yours 10 to 12 weeks before the last frost, when days are

longer, even if that means your plants won't bloom quite as early in the season.

Seed germinates in 3 to 21 days at 70° to 85°F (21° to 30°C). Barely cover them with mix. Move the seedlings to a cooler spot—60° to 70°F (15° to 21°C)—and pinch them once when they are about 4 inches (10 cm) high to promote bushy growth.

To reproduce favorite plants by cuttings, snip off a few stem sections about 6 inches (15 cm) long and remove the lower leaves. Apply rooting hormone and insert the cut end into damp perlite or sand. Traditionally, gardeners let freshly cut stems "heal over" by setting them in a sunny spot for a week or so before inserting them into the growing mixture, but this actually does more harm than good. This is also one of the rare cases when you shouldn't cover cuttings in clear plastic because geranium cuttings tend to rot without good air circulation.

Good Neighbors

Traditionally used in garish bedding displays and in "you-can-see-it-a-mile-away" pots, geraniums have been somewhat maligned recently by garden connoisseurs who find them too brilliant for more understated modern beds. However, zonal geraniums do come in a number of subdued colors, making them suitable for softer planting schemes. Even the bright reds can be great garden accents: Tuck small numbers of them around dark-leaved neighbors, such as purple-leaved amaranths (*Amaranthus* spp.), or dot them throughout a planting of rambling nasturtiums. In containers, try combining a zonal geranium with blue lobelia and the chartreuse-gray leaves of licorice plant (*Helichrysum petiolare* 'Limelight').

Problems and Solutions

Stem rot (black leg) is common in cuttings. Increased air circulation can reduce the chance of infection. Edema, seen as raised brown patches on the undersides of leaves, is not a disease but a physiological problem resulting from excess watering.

Top Performer

Pelargonium x *hortorum* (zonal geranium): Modern hybrids tend to be dense plants that branch with little pinching: quite a contrast to Grandma's stringy geraniums! They come in a wide range of shades, including bicolors, with single or double blooms. There are dozens of categories, such as rosebuds, cactus-flowered, miniatures, and beautiful fancy-leaved geraniums with colorful foliage that's variegated with white, pink, yellow, or red. Blooms of double geraniums tend to be particularly durable, but you need to pinch them off when they do fade or they become moldy. Single-blossom types are usually self-cleaning.

Petunia

Petunia

Modern petunias are branching, semi-upright to creeping plants with sticky, hairy, spoon-shaped leaves and medium to large, trumpet-shaped, five-lobed blossoms in a wide range of colors and forms. Double, ruffled, striped, netted, picoted: There's practically no limit to their variety, and even flower colors long considered impossible, like yellow, are now common. They all bloom right through summer in most climates; although in hot, humid climates they are best considered for fall planting and winter through spring bloom.

PLANT PROFILE
Petunia: peh-TOON-yuh

Continued →

Bloom Color: Pink, violet-blue, red, yellow, white

Bloom Time: Late spring through early fall; fall through winter in mild climates

Height: 6 to 24 inches (15 to 60 cm)

Spread: Varies by species; see individual listings

Garden Uses: Container planting, cut-flower garden, edging, groundcover, mass planting, mixed border, rock garden; on slopes, in wet areas

Attracts: Hummingbirds, moths

Light Preference: Full sun to partial shade

Soil Preference: Light, evenly moist, well-drained soil

Best Way to Propagate: Sow seed indoors in late winter or spring; take stem cuttings in late summer

Hardiness: Frost-sensitive perennial grown as a half-hardy annual

Growing Tips

Petunias are among the easiest of all annuals to grow, if you buy them already started. Pinch them before you plant them, and spray occasionally during the summer with organic foliar fertilizer to stimulate continuous growth. Deadheading helps encourage more bloom and keeps the plants tidy. If your petunias get scraggly, prune them back by half, and they'll soon grow back.

Given the wide variety of petunias offered in most nurseries, it is usually not worthwhile to start them yourself from seed, unless you want a cultivar not available locally. Start them indoors 8 to 10 weeks before the last frost (12 to 14 weeks for the slower-growing doubles). Don't cover the seed; it needs light to germinate. Look for seedlings in 7 to 21 days at 70° to 80°F (21° to 27°C). After germination, drop the temperature to about 60°F (15°C). When thinning seedlings, don't methodically eliminate the smaller, weaker-looking ones; they're often the ones with the best color or most interesting forms. Plant out when all danger of frost has passed, giving the seedlings a pinch to stimulate better branching. You can also sow single-flowered petunias directly outdoors, when the soil warms up, for late-season bloom.

Petunias can be highly perfumed, especially at night, so don't hesitate to use them at nose level in flower boxes, on walls, or in hanging baskets.

Good Neighbors

Petunias are extravagant bloomers, which makes them very useful in containers. Combine them with foliage plants, such as lotus vine (*Lotus berthelotti*) or sweet potato vine (*Ipomoea batatas*), for sure success. They can also be useful in the garden as a groundcover beneath the airy clumps of gaura (*Gaura lindheimeri*) or *Artemisia* 'Powis Castle' or surrounding the blades of irises.

Problems and Solutions

Usually petunias are quite pest free, but aphids are occasional problems. Knock them off with a spray of water. Look for weather-resistant cultivars in climates with frequent heavy rains; these cultivars also tend to be less susceptible to gray mold and soft rot, which can otherwise affect both foliage and flowers in humid climates.

Top Performer

Petunia x *hybrida* (petunia): Almost all the petunias sold today are complex hybrids, which are divided into various classes. Grandifloras, with single or double flowers 4 to 5 inches (10 to 12 cm) across, come in both semi-upright and cascading cultivars; the latter are mostly used in containers. Multifloras have smaller flowers—about 2 inches (5 cm) across—but they tend to grow faster, bloom more freely, and have more weather-resistant petals. Space both types about 1 foot (30 cm) apart so they can grow together and form a carpet. Millifloras are newcomers with tiny 1- to 1½-inch (2.5- to 4-cm) flowers over mounded plants. Space them about 6 inches (15 cm) apart. Groundcover petunias, of which the 'Wave' and 'Surfinia' series are the best known, are low-growing spreaders highly popular for hanging baskets, since they can trail 3 feet (90 cm) or more. Although they are very floriferous, they need constant fertilizing to perform well. Height: 1 to 2 feet (30 to 60 cm). Spread: 6 to 36 inches (15 to 90 cm).

More Recommended Petunias

Petunia integrifolia (violet-flowered petunia): One of the rare species of petunias offered, violet-flowered petunia is a low-growing spreader that looks and behaves exactly like a groundcover petunia, of which it is a parent. It bears numerous small violet flowers throughout the growing season. Height: 1 to 2 feet (30 to 60 cm). Spread: 2 to 3 feet (60 to 90 cm).

Tagetes

Marigold

There's no denying that marigolds have sometimes been overused, but think of it this way: Their enormous popularity is a sure sign they are easy to grow. Whether you grow them from seed or buy six packs of plants, you simply can't go wrong! The way I see it, there is always room for such a workhorse, even in the gardens of the most sophisticated plant collectors! There's hardly a need to describe this common annual; the deeply cut, aromatic leaves and yellow to orange flowers are a dead giveaway.

PLANT PROFILE

Tagetes: TAH-jeh-teez

Bloom Color: Varies by species; see individual listings

Bloom Time: Summer through early fall

Height: Varies by species; see individual listings

Spread: Varies by species; see individual listings

Garden Uses: Container planting, cut-flower garden, edging, mass planting, mixed border, rock garden

Light Preference: Full sun to partial shade

Soil Preference: Not excessively rich, well-drained soil

Best Way to Propagate: Sow seed indoors in mid-spring or outdoors in late spring

Hardiness: Half-hardy annual

Growing Tips

Marigolds are a snap from seed, started either indoors 4 to 6 weeks before the last frost date, at 65° to 85°F (18° to 30°C), or directly in the garden, after all danger of frost has passed. Sown ¼ inch (6 mm) deep, they germinate quickly, usually in 4 to 14 days, and are often in bloom in less than 2 months. Of course, they are also widely available in six packs and transplant very well, even when already in bloom. Wash your hands when you've finished planting, though: When handled, marigolds give off a scented oil to which some people are allergic.

Naturally quite drought tolerant, marigolds actually do better in soil that is on the poor side. Pinch young African marigolds at least once or they may produce only one large bloom. Deadheading can help maintain continuous bloom.

Good Neighbors

Enjoy the smaller marigolds as fillers around bold plants, such as yuccas, dark-leaved cannas, or cardoon (*Cynara cardunculus*). The imposing pompoms of African marigold (*Tagetes erecta*) look super as a mass of color around evergreen shrubs. The ferny foliage of signet marigold (*T. tenuifolia*) makes a satisfying companion for more-vibrant flowers, such as zinnias.

Problems and Solutions

Leaf spot, gray mold, powdery mildew, and other leaf diseases can be problematic, especially in humid climates: Look for weather- and disease-resistant strains. Taller African marigold hybrids tend to snap off under the weight of their huge flowers; plant them more deeply than in their original cell packs so the lower part of the stem can root, providing extra support.

Top Performer

Tagetes patula (French marigold): These relatively small, bushy plants bear numerous 1-inch flowers in yellow or orange, often mixed with mahogany red. Blooms can be single, double, or crested and are often bicolored. The foliage has a vaguely unpleasant "greenery" odor. Height: 6 to 18 inches (15 to 45 cm). Spread: 8 to 12 inches (20 to 30 cm).

More Recommended Tagetes

Tagetes ereeta (African marigold): This species offers huge yellow, orange, or creamy white flowers from 3 to 5 inches (8 to 13 cm) in diameter. This species is perhaps the stinkiest of all marigolds, but fortunately the odor is emitted only if you touch the leaves or stick your nose into the bloom. Height: 10 inches to over 4 feet (25 to 120 cm). Spread: 12 to 18 inches (30 to 45 cm).

T. ereeta X *patula* (triploid marigold): This sterile plant is an F1 hybrid, a handmade cross between African and French marigolds. It is a perfect mixture of the two and usually displays pompom-like flowers 2 to 3 inches (5 to 8 cm) across. Since they produce no seed, triploids bloom up a storm and need no deadheading. Unfortunately, their germination rate is low and seed is very expensive. Height: 10 to 18 inches (25 to 45 cm). Spread: 12 to 16 inches (30 to 40 cm).

T. tenuifolia (signet marigold): A delightful but lesser-known plant with extremely fine, lacy foliage that has a pleasant lemon scent. The numerous tiny single yellow or orange flowers don't overwhelm the plant but mingle delicately with the foliage, and they attract beneficial, pest-eating insects. Height: 1 to 2 feet (30 to 60 cm). Spread: 12 to 16 inches (30 to 40 cm).

Tropaeolum

Nasturtium, Canary creeper

Nasturtiums offer both intriguing leaves and complex and colorful flowers, so they look good practically from the time they germinate. Hybridizers have worked long and hard to cut the nasturtium down to size, however; and most modern nasturtiums are "dwarf" or trailing types.

PLANT PROFILE

Tropaeolum: tro-PEE-o-lum

Bloom Color: Varies by species; see individual listings

Bloom Time: Early summer through early fall; fall through spring in mild climates

Height: Varies by species; see individual listings

Spread: Varies by species; see individual listings

Continued ➡

Garden Uses: Container planting, cut-flower garden, edging, hanging basket, mass planting, mixed border, vegetable garden; on slopes or covering trellises, fences, and pergolas

Attracts: Hummingbirds

Light Preference: Full sun to partial shade

Soil Preference: Average to poor, well-drained soil

Best Way to Propagate: Sow seed indoors in peat pots in mid-spring or outdoors in late spring

Hardiness: Tender annual or frost-sensitive perennial

Growing Tips

Nasturtiums are fast-growing annuals that seem to thrive on neglect. Sow the large seed directly outside once the ground warms up, covering it with ¼ inch (6 mm) of soil. Or get a head start on the season by starting it indoors in peat pots, in darkness, 2 to 4 weeks before planting out. It usually germinates in 7 to 12 days at 60° to 65°F (15° to 18°C). If you prefer to buy plants in the spring, cell packs are the best choice because there is less risk of transplanting shock.

The secret to great nasturtiums is benign neglect. Plant them in soils that are average to low in fertility, and don't fertilize or overwater them because rich soils can stimulate lush, rapid foliage growth with few flowers. Full sun is usually best, but partial shade is recommended in hot summer areas.

Except in mild climates (Zones 9 to 11), nasturtiums are best treated as annuals. You can, however, overwinter a particularly nice nasturtium by taking stem cuttings in late summer and growing them indoors in a sunny spot.

Good Neighbors

Always a cheerful presence in the garden, nasturtiums can be an easy answer to the problem of unsightly bulb foliage. Even the dwarfs remain distinctly rambling plants, so they are ideal for containers, hanging baskets, borders, and filling in gaps in the landscape. Attractive neighbors include sturdy plants with finely cut foliage, such as artemisias, or plants with stiff upright foliage, such as irises and blackberry lilies (*Belamcanda* spp.). Planted near a large shrub or hedge, canary creeper (*Tropaeolum peregrinum*) will wander happily among the branches.

Problems and Solutions

Aphids are a major problem. Blast them off with a strong spray of water. Caterpillars, whiteflies, flea beetles, and slugs are occasional problems.

Top Performer

Tropaeolum majus (nasturtium, common nasturtium): This is the plant most people think of when the word nasturtium is mentioned, although, in fact, the botanical name *Nasturtium* belongs to an entirely different plant—watercress (*N. officinale*). Our nasturtium bears unique, round, shieldlike leaves in deep to light green. Some cultivars, like 'Alaska' (dwarf) and 'Jewel of Africa' (climbing) are heavily marbled with cream. The 2- to 2 ½-inch (5- to 6.5-cm) flowers form wide-open trumpets and usually have a long spur at the back. The blooms come in a wide range of colors—yellow, orange, cream, red, mahogany, and cherry pink, often splotched with a contrasting color—and are commonly delightfully scented. Double types are generally sterile and must be propagated by cuttings; semidoubles are available from seed. Height: 8 to 15 inches (10 to 38 cm) for dwarfs and trailers; 10 feet (3 m) for climbers. Spread: 12 to 18 inches (30 to 45 cm).

More Recommended Tropaeolum

Tropaeolum peregrinum (Canary creeper, Canary vine): This is a very different plant with different needs. The small, gray-green leaves are divided into finger-like lobes. The curious flowers, with two large, highly fringed petals over a smaller cluster of three petals, may be canary yellow, but they actually get their name because of the plant's place of discovery. Botanists first saw this Mexican native growing on the Canary Islands. Canary creeper needs a richer, moister soil than its cousin does. Plants started indoors can bloom faster, but they also tend to peter out before the end of summer. Seed started directly in the garden blooms until fall. This superb climbing plant needs a thin support that the leaf stems can wrap themselves around. Height: 8 to 12 feet (2.5 to 4 m). Spread: 18 inches (45 cm).

Verbena

Verbena

Gardeners have more than 250 species of verbenas to choose from, and a good number of those make great garden plants. The genus includes annuals, perennials, and shrubs; and the different plants vary considerably in appearance and in care. In general, though, they are bushy to creeping plants with four-sided stems and tubular flowers with five well-spaced lobes, often notched at their tip. Although the individual flowers are small, they're held in dense clusters that will knock your socks off, both in the garden and in containers.

PLANT PROFILE

Verbena: ver-BEAN-uh

Bloom Color: Lavender, pink, purple, salmon, red, white

Bloom Time: Late spring through early fall; much of the year in mild climates

Height: Varies by species; see individual listings

Spread: Varies by species; see individual listings

Garden Uses: Container planting, cut-flower garden, edging, hanging baskets, groundcover, mass planting, mixed border, rock garden; on slopes

Attracts: Butterflies, hummingbirds

Light Preference: Full sun to partial shade

Soil Preference: Average, well-drained soil

Best Way to Propagate: Sow seed indoors in late winter; take stem cuttings in late summer

Hardiness: Frost-sensitive perennial grown as a half-hardy annual

Growing Tips

Unless you have a home greenhouse or grow under lights, you're better off buying six packs or cell packs of young verbena plants than trying to start your own from seed. If you like a challenge, though, you can save a considerable amount of money by sowing them yourself. Just don't expect high germination: With verbenas, especially the popular hybrid types, 50 percent germination is considered good; 70 percent is excellent!

Start the seed indoors, 8 to 10 weeks before the last frost. Barely cover the seed; then place in the dark until seedlings appear, usually in 14 to 28 days at 50° to 75°F (10° to 24°C). After germination, try to keep the temperatures toward the lower end of that range. Water very carefully, preferably from below to avoid damping-off, and make sure there is good ventilation.

There are fast-growing verbenas, like Brazilian vervain (Verbena bonariensis), that you can sow directly outdoors in early spring for late-season bloom. Even these are best started indoors,

though. For good germination, place the six packs or cell packs in the fridge for 2 weeks before exposing them to warmth.

Verbenas may be delicate as seedlings, but once in the garden, they are no-brainers. They prefer full sun (some shade in the afternoon is best in hot summer areas) and do well in ordinary garden soil. They are quite drought resistant, although watering in very dry weather is always wise. Avoid wetting the leaves, if possible, to reduce the spread of the fungal disease powdery mildew. If bloom becomes sparse in midsummer, shear the plants back harshly and spray them with organic foliar fertilizer; they'll soon be in full flower again.

To keep favorite plants from year to year, start cuttings in late summer and grow them indoors in bright light all winter or dig up and bring in a few plants.

Good Neighbors

Because of their cascading nature, low-growing verbenas are ideal choices for pots, but they're useful as groundcovers as well. The lacy foliage and purple flowers of 'Imagination' mingle beautifully with bold kales, yuccas, or Siberian irises (*Iris sibirica*). Combine garden verbena (*Verbena* x *hybrids*), lantana (*Lantana camara*), and tall Brazilian vervain (*V. bonaknsis*) in a large pot and you will have a long season of layered, flowering interest.

Problems and Solutions

Powdery mildew and other leaf diseases are a major problem in humid climates: Grow only disease-resistant strains, like the 'Quartz' series. Control whiteflies, spider mites, and scale insects by spraying with insecticidal soap.

Top Performer

Verbena x *hybrida* (garden verbena): This is definitely a mixed bag of plants! Some types are bushy and upright, while others are spreading, mat forming, or even trailing. The green to gray-green leaves can be simple, toothed, or deeply cut; and the fragrant or odorless flowers come in a wide range of bright and pastel colors. Many modern hybrids, like the 'Temari' and 'Tapien' series (both of which come in an astounding range of colors), are available only as vegetatively produced (cutting-grown) plants. The seed-grown strains-most either bushy or only slightly spreading-are particularly popular for garden use; the more expensive cutting-grown types—most either trailers or semi-trailers—are widely used in containers. Take your pick; they're all great plants! Height: 10 to 20 inches (25 to 50 cm). Spread: 12 to 20 inches (30 to 50 cm).

Viola

Pansy, horned violet, Johnny-jump-up

The rounded, flat-faced flowers of most pansies look just like a chubby-faced baby: How could you not love them? Garden favorites for generations, they are widely available just about everywhere and are often the first annuals to bloom. They likewise make cute little bouquets and are a standard offering in posies. If only they were a bit more heat resistant, they would be just about the perfect annual. Instead, you have to plan carefully to get the most out of them before the dog days of summer knock them flat on their faces!

PLANT PROFILE

Viola: vy-OH-luh

Bloom Color: Blue, lavender, purple, red, orange, bronze, yellow, white

Bloom Time: Early spring through summer; fall through winter in mild climates

Continued ➡

Height: Varies by species; see individual listings

Spread: Varies by species; see individual listings

Garden Uses: Container planting, cut-flower garden, edging, groundcover, mass planting, mixed border, rock garden, woodland garden; along paths

Light Preference: Full sun to moderate shade

Soil Preference: Humus-rich, evenly moist but well-drained soil

Best Way to Propagate: Sow seed outdoors in fall or indoors in winter

Hardiness: Hardy perennial or biennial grown as a hardy annual

Growing Tips

The secret to happy pansies is to remember they like things cool. In temperate climates, you'll get best results from young transplants set out in fall (for the earliest spring bloom) or in early spring, as soon as the ground can be worked. Where summers are generally cool—not over 90°F (32°C)—they bloom best in full sun and keep on going until fall. In hotter climates, look for heat-resistant cultivars and plant them in moderate shade. Where winters are mild, plant pansies in fall for bloom right through winter; then pull them up when the heat gets to them.

The easiest way to grow pansies from seed is to treat them like biennials. Sow them outdoors in midsummer, then plant them in their final home in fall, mulching well in cold winter areas. It is possible to sow pansies indoors, although it is a bit of a challenge. Sow the seed indoors 14 to 16 weeks before the last frost date, barely covering it. Place the containers in your refrigerator for 2 weeks, and then expose the seed to room temperatures; it should sprout in about 10 days. After germination, keep the temperature as low as you can; 50° to 65°F (10° to 18°C) is ideal, but room temperature is acceptable. Plant out hardened-off seedlings as soon as the soil is workable.

Outdoors, water pansies as needed and dead-head them to help maintain blooming. Cut straggly plants back severely to stimulate renewed growth.

Good Neighbors

One of the few annuals that can be planted in fall for early-spring bloom, pansies playa unique role in the garden. Let them take the spring shift in an impatiens bed or front-door planter or fill in the ground level around tall daffodils. Tuck them around plants that thrive in part shade, such as ferns or purple-leaved heucheras (*Heuchera* hybrids), and they'll bloom well into summer.

Problems and Solutions

Pansies are somewhat susceptible to leaf diseases: Choose disease-resistant strains, and rotate plantings if you notice repeated damage. Handpick slugs and snails if they become a problem.

Top Performer

Viola x *wittrocklana* (pansy): These large-flowered plants with overlapping petals are offered in an almost infinite range of colors, including a violet so deep it appears black. Most are bicolored with facelike markings, but some are all one color. Pansies are usually borderline hardy in Zone 4. Height: 6 to 9 inches (15 to 23 cm). Spread: 9 to 12 inches (23 to 30 cm).

More Recommended Viola

Viola cornuta (horned violet, viola): Horned violet is one of the parents of the pansy and is very similar to it, but with smaller flowers. The species is a long-lived plant with violet to lavender flowers, but most plants now sold under this name have been

crossed with the garden pansy. They come in a similar range of colors and tend to act as short-lived perennials or annuals. Height: 8 inches (20 cm). Spread: 6 to 12 inches (15 to 30 cm).

Zinnia

Zinnia

Bright, long-lasting, daisylike flowers are the trademark of the zinnia, a New World native that has taken the plant world by storm. Modern zinnias come in a wide range of sizes and shapes, from upright, cut-flower types to multistemmed, multi-flowered border zinnias. The flowers can be single or double, big or small, and the color range is just about complete: Only true blue is lacking. If that weren't enough, they are particularly easy to grow!

PLANT PROFILE

Zinnia: ZIN-ee-uh

Bloom Color: Varies by species; see individual listings

Bloom Time: Summer through early fall

Height: 4 to 48 inches (10 to 120 cm)

Spread: 10 to 24 inches (25 to 60 cm)

Garden Uses: Container planting, cut-flower garden, edging, mass planting, meadow garden, mixed border

Attracts: Butterflies

Light Preference: Full sun

Soil Preference: Humus-rich, well-drained soil

Best Way to Propagate: Sow seed outdoors in late spring or indoors in mid-spring

Hardiness: Half-hardy annual

Growing Tips

No doubt about it, the easiest way to grow zinnias is to sow them directly outside as soon as the ground warms up. They grow quickly, reaching blooming size in just 6 weeks. Just loosen up the soil, toss in the seed, cover lightly, and water; it'll do the rest. Nurseries often offer cell packs, but zinnias generally don't transplant well once they've reached flowering size. If you do buy plants, try pruning them back by one-third at planting time to help them make a successful transition.

You can also start zinnias indoors at 60° to 85°F (15° to 27°C). They're up like a shot (in only 4 to 7 days) and need only a 4- to 6-week head start on the season. Sow them in peat pots or cell packs to reduce transplant shock.

Full sun is a must, and good air circulation is important for preventing powdery mildew. For bushy plants with lots of bloom, pinch young zinnias when they have developed their third set of leaves. Don't put zinnias outside too early because cool air stunts their growth; wait until all danger of frost has passed and the weather warms up. Keep deadheading through summer to stimulate continuous bloom.

Good Neighbors

Combine mixed-color zinnias with tall ageratum (*Ageratum houstonianum*) for an exuberant display. Chartreuse green 'Envy' looks great with just about any other color: Tuck it among perennials in a mixed border. For an eye-catching planting that will bloom freely even through summer drought, pair mildew-resistant, narrow-leaved zinnias (*Zinnia angustifolia*) or the hybrid 'Profusion' series with mealycup sage (*Salvia farinacea* 'Victoria').

Problems and Solutions

Powdery mildew is a major problem in humid climates. Mildew-resistant cultivars are really the

only viable option under those conditions. Excessively moist soil can lead to root or stem rot. Where Japanese beetles are a problem, hand-pick and drop them into a container of soapy water.

Top Performer

Zinnia elegans (common zinnia): The most widely grown zinnia, this species has an upright habit, with opposite, bright green, broadly lance-shaped leaves and a wide range of flower colors, sizes, and forms. It is also the species the most susceptible to powdery mildew, so it's best in dry climates and well-ventilated spots in the garden. Height: 4 to 48 inches (10 to 120 cm). Spread: 10 to 24 inches (25 to 60 cm).

More Recommended Zinnias

Zinnia angustifolia, formerly *Z. linearis* (narrow-leaved zinnia): This species is a more modest plant, with smaller, simple flowers in orange to white with a yellow heart and narrower, pointed leaves. Its main claim to fame is that it seems entirely mildew resistant. The easy-to-grow 'Star' and 'Crystal' series belong here. Height: 8 to 24 inches (20 to 60 cm). Spread: 8 to 12 inches (20 to 30 cm).

Z. angustifoia x *elegans* (hybrid zinnia): This cross between the common and narrow-leaved zinnia produces plants much like the latter (and just as disease resistant) but in a wider color range, including orange, pink, red, and white. The highly popular 'Profusion' series falls here. Height: 8 to 24 inches (20 to 60 cm). Spread: 8 to 12 inches (20 to 30 cm).

Z. haageana, formerly *Z. mexicana* (Mexican zinnia): The species name is in doubt, but it's a handy place to place two old-fashioned but still popular narrow-leaved doubles, 'Old Mexico', 16 inches (40 cm) tall, and 'Persian Carpet', 12 inches (30 cm) tall. Both have multicolored blooms: orange or red flowers that are tipped in either white or yellow. Height: 12 to 18 inches (30 to 45 cm). Spread: 8 to 12 inches (20 to 30 cm).

Know Thine Enemies

Larry Hodgson

Annuals tend to be far less susceptible to pests and diseases than other plants, mostly because they don't live long. If you grow different annuals in each spot each year, the pests and diseases won't be able to build up to problem level. Ornamental annuals tend to have plentiful natural defenses against pests. That doesn't mean you will never have any problems, but the chances are reduced.

ROSES

Choosing & Using Roses

With more than 30,000 rose species and cultivars available, choosing the perfect rose isn't easy! The key is answering the question, "What do I want roses to do for my landscape?" Perhaps you want to dress up a split-rail fence, enhance a perennial garden, or add a colorful accent to a shrub border. There's a rose for almost every

Continued ➡

landscape purpose, and this section will help you decide which varieties are best suited for the project you have in mind.

All Roses Aren't Alike

Before you leap into choosing roses, it's a good idea to learn about the different classes available—what they look like and how they grow and behave. Some roses are small shrubs, while others can grow taller than you. Still other types are long and vining, while some form low groundcovers. The three major categories of roses are species roses, old roses, and modern roses. Read on to learn about these roses and how they might work in your landscape.

USING SPECIES ROSES

Species roses are tough and disease-resistant—excellent for a natural area in your yard or a shrub border. They provide a wide variety of choices of size, form, and hardiness. They bloom once, usually in early summer, and form seed-bearing rose hips in the fall.

Species roses are the original roses. About 200 different species roses exist. In general, species roses bear single, five-petaled flowers, and they self-pollinate. (So if you plant seeds from species roses, the offspring should be identical to the parent plant.)

USING OLD ROSES

Old roses are usually very fragrant, have a pleasing plant shape, and are tough, long-lasting shrubs. Common types of old roses include alba, Bourbon, damask, China, and gallica.

The drawback to planting old roses is that many bloom only once a year, usually in early summer. Although they look and small beautiful, their blooms don't last long.

USING MODERN ROSES

Unlike species roses and some old roses, modern roses bloom all summer, so you get nonstop color and landscape impact. But summer-long beauty comes with a price. Many modern roses require more maintenance than old roses or species roses because they aren't as cold-hardy or disease-resistant.

Hybrid Teas

For most people, a rose means a hybrid tea rose. These roses bear long, narrow, high-center buds, one per stem. The canes are often bare at the base, which makes hybrid teas best suited to mixed borders, herb gardens, and perennial beds where lower-growing plants can hide their gawky legs. Hybrid teas grow 3 to 5 feet high.

- Flower continually throughout the growing season
- Are available in all rose colors
- The flower form is usually semidouble or double.
- Hardiness, disease resistance, and fragrance vary greatly from cultivar to cultivar.
- Hardy only to Zone 8, so winter protection is a must
- Need rich soil, plenty of fertilizer, and ample water
- Hard pruning is required to encourage new growth and abundant flowering.

Polyanthas

Polyanthas are bushy, 2-foot-tall plants with finely textured leaves. They're sturdy, trouble-free plants,

so they're good choices for massing, edgings, and hedges.

- Produce clusters of small (1-inch) single, semidouble, or double flowers all season
- Generally hardy to Zone 5
- Bloom in shades of pink, white, red, orange, or yellow
- Need little pruning, except to remove dead or diseased wood or to shape the plants
- The Latin word *polyantha* means "many-flowered."
- Plant low-growing polyanthas around the base of taller floribundas and grandifloras for multitudes of blooms.
- Deadhead up to a month before frost for constant color.
- Good choice for small gardens

Hybrid Tea Rose

Floribundas

A result of cross-breeding polyanthas with hybrid tea roses, floribundas are bushy plants that grow 2 to 4 feet tall. They're excellent for low hedges and mass plantings as well as specimens in flower borders.

- Bear many flowers per stem throughout the growing season
- Flowers are larger than polyantha blooms and about half the size of hybrid tea roses.
- Flowers can be single, semidouble, or double and come in the entire color range for roses.
- Generally hardy to Zone 6
- Need pruning to maintain their shape; to remove weak, dead, or old wood; and to remove faded flowers
- Many of the floribundas are disease-resistant—check varieties before choosing.
- Need rich, well-drained soil

Grandifloras

A result of crossing hybrid tea roses with floribundas, grandifloras combine the classic hybrid tea rose flower form with the floriferous bloom habit of floribundas. Grandifloras generally grow 4 to 6 feet—and sometimes even taller. Because they're so tall, grandifloras work best at the back of flowerbeds or shrub borders.

- The high-centered flowers are borne singly or in clusters on long stems.
- Generally hardy to Zone 6
- Bloom continuously all season
- Flowers are generally semidouble or double and come in all rose colors; fragrance depends on the cultivar.
- A good choice for cut arrangements
- Most grandifloras are disease-resistant.

- Deadhead up to a month before frost for lots of repeat bloom.
- Cut back healthy canes by one-half to one-third for vigorous flower production.

Miniatures

Every aspect of miniature roses is reduced in size, including the stems, leaves, and flowers. The flowers can be single, semidouble, or double. Miniature roses can also be raised as houseplants, although you need a great deal of light to get them to bloom indoors.

- Bloom about one month earlier than shrub roses
- Hardy to Zone 5
- Need pruning to remove dead wood, to thin, or to improve shape
- Generally from 10 to 18 inches tall, miniatures come in a variety of forms—trailing, cascading, and climbing.
- Ideal for container plantings, hanging baskets, rock gardens, and as edging in mixed borders
- For long-blooming color in a small area, plant a group of miniatures spaced about 18 inches apart.

Narrowing Your Choices

Once you've decided whether to plant a species rose, old rose, or some type of modern rose, you've taken the first step. However, you still need to decide on a particular species or cultivar. You can narrow your selection by focusing on the flowers. Do you have favorites? Is a rose only a rose to you if it's a double red? Or do you want a particular color to go with other flowers or features? For instance, a yellow, white, or peach rose might look better in front of an orange brick wall than a red or pink rose.

COLOR AND FORM

- Species and old roses tend more toward shades of pink, white, and mauve.
- Species and old rose flowers range from flat single or semi double to many-petaled doubles that are open-cupped, globular, or quartered.
- Newer hybrids include many more reds, oranges, yellows, pinks, whites, and bicolors.
- Modern rose flowers have high centers with long inner petals forming a prominent central cone that rises from a flatter cup of outer petals.

FRAGRANCE

Fragrance is another important aspect of roses, whether you're enjoying them indoors or outside in the garden. Although it's generally true that the older types of roses seem more fragrant than newer roses, many newer cultivars have a delightful fragrance, and there are old roses without a trace of fragrance. Fortunately, fragrance seems to be back on the rose breeder's agenda, so we can look forward to more new roses that "smell like a rose."

If you'll be using your roses for potpourri or other scented crafts, alba, Bourbon, damask, moss, musk, and rugosa roses all make good choices.

Choosing Roses for Low Maintenance

Beyond their appearance and fragrance, you'll want to keep low maintenance in mind when you choose your roses. Look to the shrub roses first for trouble-free growing, especially the rugosas (species roses), polyanthas, and Meidiland roses. Then consider the hardy, pest-resistant cultivars of the old garden roses, the species roses, and the most

Continued ➡

pest- and disease-resistant of the modern hybrid teas, floribundas, grandifloras, and miniatures.

Disease-Resistant Roses

The easiest way to cut down on rose maintenance is to start by planting roses that are resistant to pests and diseases. We've divided the disease-resistant roses into groups so you can easily find the type you need for your landscaping purposes. Simply find the heading you're looking for and you'll have your roses at a glance. You don't have to limit your choices to these lists—they're just a starting point for buying disease-resistant roses.

SHRUB AND GROUNDCOVER ROSES

The term shrub rose is a catch-all designation that the American Rose Society has created to include a large variety of hardy, easy-to-grow shrubs. They range in size from groundcovers to 12-foot-tall giants! They're known as low-maintenance landscaping roses and most are attractive both in and out of bloom. Look to this group for the largest number of disease-resistant varieties. Some of the best shrub roses for garden use include David Austin roses, Buck hybrids, Meidiland roses, and the newly introduced Parkland and Explorer series from Canada. Here are just a few of the many reliable varieties of groundcover and shrub roses.

'Carefree Wonder': Clusters of double, deep pink flowers that bloom continuously on shrubs that grow 5 feet tall x 3 feet wide (Zones 4-9)

'John Davis': Large clusters of scented, double, pink flowers on arching canes that reach to 6 feet-best as a trailing shrub or tall climber; very cold hardy (Zones 3-9)

'Knock Out': Scented, deep cherry red flower clusters on a rounded shrub 3 feet tall x 3 feet wide. (Zones 4-9)

'Sarah van Fleet': Sweet, clove-scented pink flowers on upright to arching canes; reaches maximum size of 8 feet x 5 feet wide (Zones 3-9)

'Scarlet Meidiland': Mounding trailing habit; canes grow to 3 feet tall x 6 feet wide; provides good repeat bloom (Zones 4-9)

'Sea Foam': Low-spreading shrub with long-blooming clusters of double, creamy white flowers; vigorous and prostrate, plants grow 3 feet tall x 6 feet wide (Zones 4-9)

MINIATURE ROSES

Although there are many minis to choose from, many are susceptible to diseases. Here are some that are exceptionally disease-resistant. (Note: Most miniature roses are hardy to Zone 5.)

'Baby Diana': An orange bloomer

'Black Jade': Double, dark red, velvety flowers

'Jackie': Climber with fragrant, light yellow blooms

'Magic Carousel': 30-inch shrub with double, white flowers edged with red

'Rainbow's End': Readily available cultivar with yellow blooms edged with red

'Starina': Fragrant, bright red and orange flowers

RUGOSA ROSES AND THEIR HYBRIDS

Both the straight species, Rosa rugosa, and its many cultivars are known for their disease resistance. Here are some of the finest varieties and cultivars.

Rosa rugosa var. rubro: Large, single, magenta-purple flowers and large, showy hips (Zones 2-9)

Rugosa hybrid 'Blanc double de Courbet': Fragrant, semidouble, white flowers and showy hips on a 4- to 5-foot shrub (Zones 4-9)

'F.J. Grootendorst': Bears unscented, bright red, fringed flowers that resemble carnations; foliage turns orange-red in autumn (Zones 4-8)

'Frau Dagmar Hastrup': Compact shrub about 3 feet tall x 3 feet wide that produces large, single, silver-pink flowers and tomato-red hips (Zones 4-9)

'Hansa': Reaches 6 to 7 feet in height and has semidouble, purple-red flowers and orange-red hips (Zones 4-9)

POLYANTHA ROSES

The bushy, fine-textured polyanthas have a well-deserved reputation for being trouble-free. Some noteworthy choices follow.

'Cecile Brunner': 3-foot-tall bush with fragrant, pale pink flowers; also available as a climbing cultivar (Zones 5-9)

'China Doll': 2-foot-tall bush with double, pink flowers and bright green, disease-resistant leaves (Zones 5-9)

'La Marne': 5-foot-tall bush with masses of pink-and-white, cupped, and ruffled flowers (Zones 5-9)

'The Fairy': 2-foot-tall bush with abundant sprays of small, double, light pink flowers (Zones 5-9)

RAMBLERS AND CLIMBERS

'America': 8- to 10-foot climber with large, salmon-colored, hybrid-tea-type flowers and a bushy habit (Zones 5-9)

'Alchymist': 8- to 12-foot-tall arching shrub with heavy canes and large, fragrant, yellow and apricot flowers; doesn't rebloom but is very striking in early summer (Zones 5-9)

'Climbing Cecile Brunner': Can climb to 20 feet; fragrant, pale pink flowers (Zones 6-9)

'Dortmund': Showy red climber that forms clusters of large, single flowers and orange-red hips if not deadheaded (Zones 5-9)

'Dublin Bay': Repeat-blooming, large, double, red flowers (Zones 5-9)

'New Dawn': Blooms heavily in early summer with large, fragrant, pearly pink to white flowers; has a second blooming in late summer (Zones 5-9)

HYBRID TEAS AND GRANDIFLORAS

Even disease-resistant hybrid tea and grandiflora roses require a lot of maintenance compared to self-reliant shrub roses or polyanthas. However, disease resistance is a priority with breeders, so every year the organic grower has more choices.

'Crimson Bouquet': 4½-foot-tall grandiflora that bears scented, blood red blooms (Zone 4b)

'Gemini': Double, creamy pink flowers on a vigorous 5½-foot-tall bush (Zone 5)

'Keepsake': 5-foot-tall bush with very fragrant, double, high-centered, multishaded pink flowers, borne singly and in clusters, and glossy leaves on dense, sturdy canes (Zones 5-9)

'Mrs. Dudley Cross': Thornless, 3- to 4-foot-high leafy tea rose; creamy yellow, pink-edged flowers (Zones 7-9)

'Pink Parfait': 4-foot-tall grandiflora with prolific, double, pink flowers (Zone 6)

'Pink Peace': 5-foot-tall bush with very fragrant, very double, high-centered, deep pink flowers and disease-resistant, leathery leaves (Zones 6-9)

'Queen Elizabeth': Bears double, clear pink flowers continuously on 5- to 6-foot-tall shrubs (Zone 6-9)

FLORIBUNDA ROSES

When it comes to the best floribundas, here are some of the experts' picks for good disease resistance.

'Betty Prior': Continuously bears single carmine pink flowers on 4-foot-tall shrubs (Zones 5-9)

'Europeana': One of the best dark red, ever-blooming floribunda roses; bears large clusters of double, deep red flowers on dense, 3-foot-tall shrubs (Zones 6-9)

'Nearly wild': Resembles a species rose with its continuously blooming sprays of single, clear pink flowers; upright, rounded shrubs grow to 4 feet tall (Zones 4-9)

'Sunsprite': 2- to 4-foot-tall shrub with fragrant, double, golden yellow flowers (Zones 5-9)

SPECIES ROSES

Straight species roses are generally problem-free if grown in conditions that mimic their native habitat. Although not easily found in the market, they can be useful in the landscape.

Chestnut rose (Rosa roxburghii): Bears bright pink, 2-inch flowers on a 6-foot plant; has attractive peeling bark and showy hips (Zones 6-9)

Swamp rose (R. palustris): A suckering plant that produces fragrant, single, pink blooms in late June to early July (depending on region) and orange-red hips later in the season (Zones 3-7)

Virginia rose (R. virginiana): A suckering 3- to 5-foot shrub that produces single, pink flowers in June (depending on region) and red hips, which ripen in late summer (Zones 3-7)

Cold-Hardy Roses

In areas where winters are very cold, many roses won't make it to spring. Fortunately, there are choices even for the Zone 3 gardener. Species roses, such as Rosa glauco and R. rugosa are hardy to Zone 2. Many R. rugosa cultivars are also cold-hardy and can survive in Zone 3. The Explorer series and the Parkland series of roses bred in Canada are hardy to -40°F. Some choices from these series follow.

'Champlain': 3-foot-tall shrub with prolific, bright red blooms (Zones 3-9)

'John Cabot': Prolific climber with fuchsia flowers (Zones 3-9)

'Morden Centennial': Well-shaped, 5-foot-tall shrub, covered with fragrant, deep pink blooms in late June and early July (Zones 2-9)

'Simon Fraser': 2½-foot shrub with masses of semi-double, pink flowers throughout the summer (Zones 3-9)

Some rose species are also very cold-hardy. R. rugosa, R. seugera, R. spinosissima, and many of their cultivars also survive frigid winters. Here are two good examples.

'Frau Dagmar Hartopp': 3-foot shrub with large, single, silver-pink blooms and red hips (Zones 4-9)

'Wiliam Baffin': Repeat bloomer; deep pink blooms on arching, 8-foot canes (Zones 2-9)

Heat-Tolerant Roses

Many roses stop blooming and start mildewing during long bouts of humid, moist heat. Here are some roses that can take the heat.

Continued ➡

'Champney's Pink Cluster': Continuously blooming clusters of small, double, pink flowers on 4-foot shrubs (zones 6-9)

Cherokee rose (*Rosa laevigata*): Once-blooming, species rose climber with fragrant, large, single, white blooms (Zones 7-9)

China roses: Generally hardy to 0°F, these old roses are good choices for Zones 7-10; include 'Old Blush', a 6-foot bush with light pink flowers, and 'Archduke Charles', a 3-foot bush with rose red flowers

Lady Banks rose (*R. banksiae* var. *alba-plena*): Hardy to 10°F; 20-foot climber with small, fragrant, double, white or yellow blooms (Zone 8)

'Queen Elizabeth': Clear pink blooms on a 6-tall grandiflora (Zones 5-9)

Fragrant Roses

While old roses are known for their wonderful fragrance, many hybrid tea roses are also bred for fragrance. Here are a few relatively disease-resistant choices.

'Chrysler Imperial': Deep crimson flowers on a 3½-foot bush; susceptible to mildew and blackspot in cool, wet weather (Zones 4-9)

'Fragrant cloud': Repeat-blooming bush with coral-red flowers; vigorous; susceptible to disease (Zones 5-9)

'Mister Lincoln': Double, dark red, repeating blooms on erect canes (Zones 5-9)

Moss roses—named for the mossy, resinous growth covering the outside of flower buds—are usually very fragrant. Examples of these old roses follow.

'Communis': 4-foot bush with very fragrant, once-blooming, pink flowers (Zone 4)

'Henri Martin': 5-foot bush with fragrant, once-blooming, double, crimson flowers fading to deep rose (Zones 4-8)

'White Bath': 4-foot bush with very fragrant white flowers (Zones 5-9)

Selecting and Planting Roses

Barbara W. Ellis

Roses have been called the "queen of flowers." Perhaps not surprisingly, they are the oldest cultivated ornamental plant and our national flower. Although many other flowers share the word rose as part of their common names, true roses are members of the genus *Rosa*, which contains over 100 species and literally thousands of cultivars. Their showy flowers, thorny stems, and leathery green leaves are familiar to all gardeners. Blooms come in white, red, pink, orange, yellow, lavender, and all shades in between; some bear bicolored blooms. The flowers can be single or double, large or small, and may be borne singly or in dramatic

clusters. In addition, many roses also provide attractive hips that turn red in fall. Rosehips are used in jams, jellies, and teas for their high vitamin C content and tart, cranberrylike flavor.

Making the Right Choice

Probably the most important decision you'll make regarding roses in your landscape is selecting the right plant for the right place. There are so many types of roses available that choosing them requires some knowledge of each group and its distinguishing characteristics. There are roses to blend into a flower or perennial garden, or even a sunny spot in a natural garden. They make fine companions for herbs. Climbing roses are often the most suitable plant for covering a trellis or training as pillar roses on posts or old tree trunks.

The information in this section about some of the major classes of roses will help you make your selection. Rose hybridizers are constantly introducing new cultivars of roses with more attractive, longer-lasting flowers, ornamental hips, and better habit. They are also selecting for plants that exhibit disease- and insect-resistance characteristics. Although you'll find examples of cultivars listed in the sections that follow, ask your cooperative extension agent or local nursery owner for a list of the best roses to consider for your area. Since hardiness varies from class to class and cultivar to cultivar, it's also a good idea to find out which ones will survive best in your area.

HYBRID TEA ROSES

Hybrid tea roses are the most common roses grown today. The first hybrid tea, 'La France', was produced in 1867, the result of complex crosses between Chinese and European roses. Hybrid tea roses gradually gained in popularity because of their long season of bloom and the beauty of their unfurling buds. Hybrid tea roses are 3 to 5 feet tall and are primarily grown for their spectacular, many-petaled blossoms, which are borne singly or in small clusters on long, straight stems. Blooms range from 3½ to 5½ inches wide. Hybrid teas are not reliably hardy in the North and require winter protection if they are to survive in areas where temperatures routinely go below 10°F.

Hybrid teas probably require the most maintenance of any of the roses. Most hybrid teas are highly susceptible to insect and disease problems, and therefore require regular applications of insecticides and fungicides to look their best. Today, the trend is toward cultivars—both old and new—that require less maintenance and have more disease resistance. 'Miss All-American Beauty', 'Mister Lincoln', 'Pink Peace', 'Tiffany', and 'Tropicana' are all examples of hybrid tea roses. (All show resistance to black spot and powdery mildew, the two most prominent diseases of hybrid teas.) New and beautiful hybrid tea cultivars that show superior pest and disease resistance are introduced every year.

FLORIBUNDA AND GRANDIFLORA ROSES

These two classes of roses are closely related to hybrid teas. Floribunda roses, which were created by crossing polyantha roses with hybrid teas, are about 2 to 3 feet tall. The individual flowers range from 2½ to 3½ inches wide but are borne in large, many-flowered clusters. Floribundas are generally quite hardy, and can be easily grown anywhere hybrid teas are grown.

Grandiflora roses are the result of crosses between hybrid teas and floribundas. They are shrubs that can reach 6 to 8 feet in height and are about as hardy as hybrid teas. Grandifloras bear large clusters of hybrid-tea-size blooms. Both

floribunda and grandiflora roses are among the most floriferous roses in the garden. 'Europeana', 'First Edition', 'Rose Parade', and 'Razzle Dazzle' are examples of Floribunda roses. 'Queen Elizabeth' and 'Prominent' are both Grandiflora roses. (All of these cultivars exhibit resistance to black spot and powdery mildew.)

CLIMBING AND RAMBLING ROSES

Because of their tremendous versatility and adaptability, climbing and rambling roses are extremely popular. They can be trained to climb over fences, on trellises, against buildings, or up tree trunks. They're not true climbers, though, because they have no natural way to grip or hold onto supports. Instead, they must be tied in place. These roses come in many forms. Some bear clusters of small flowers; others have blooms like those of hybrid teas. Hardiness varies from type to type. Rambling roses tend to have a much more rampant and vigorous growing habit than climbers, and bloom once a season, generally on two-year-old canes. Some climbers, on the other hand, will bloom twice. 'Don Juan' and 'Improved Blaze' are examples of large-flowered climbing roses. 'Chevy Chase' is a rambling rose that is resistant to powdery mildew.

SHRUB ROSES

Shrub roses make up one of the best groups of roses to blend with other plants in a landscape. This is a catch-all class for many of the newer roses, which often are hybrids between old roses and new roses. They tend to be excellent, low-maintenance shrubs that are easy to blend into a variety of landscape settings. Many shrub roses also are highly resistant to insect and disease problems and quite cold hardy. (The shrub roses bred by Griffith Buck, such as 'Carefree Beauty', are particularly good.) 'Bonica' is a popular shrub rose that grows very well with little care. It is approximately 3 to 4 feet tall with medium-pink flowers.

OLD ROSES

Old garden roses comprise a very large group of increasingly popular roses that have been grown since long before modern roses (such as hybrid teas) came into existence. They have been subdivided into many different subgroups, including Gallica, Alba, Centifolia, Moss, Bourbon, Hybrid Perpetual, China, Musk, Noisette, and Species. Although old roses vary a great deal, they possess many unique characteristics. The plants closely resemble shrub roses and range from 2 to 8 feet in height or sometimes more. Blooms may be single or double, solid or striped, and are borne in clusters. Fragrant blooms are another feature of many of the old roses. In addition, many have attractive hips that add fall interest. Hardiness is variable. Rosa 'Mundi', 'Reine des Violettes', and 'Mary Washington' are all examples of old roses.

MINIATURES

These useful roses are excellent as edging plants, in containers, and just about anywhere you want a floriferous, low-growing plant. Often called minis, they range in height from 1 to 2 feet and are easy to grow. Although tiny, they require much the same care as their larger cousins, the hybrid teas.

Planting Pointers

Once you've made your choice, proper site selection and planting are the next steps to getting your roses off to a good start. The following pointers will help you on your way to success.

Continued ➡

SITE SELECTION

Roses absolutely require a location that has been carefully planned and prepared. Select a site that gets at least six hours of direct sunlight. Good air circulation is also important, so avoid damp, stagnant spots where there is little breeze. This will help prevent excessive problems with powdery mildew and black spot—the two most serious fungal diseases of roses. Pruning is one way to improve air circulation, but good site selection and a garden design where roses have plenty of room to grow are equally important.

Avoid spots where competition from encroaching tree roots, especially the greedy, shallow roots of trees such as silver maple, will sap the strength of your roses. However, roses are able to compete with smaller, less overpowering plants, such as many types of herbs and perennials, because their roots tend to go deep into the soil.

Soil pH should be somewhere between 6.0 and 6.5 for best growth. If the soil becomes too alkaline, you'll see chlorosis on the leaves because the plants are unable to take up the nutrients they need. Other signs of nutrient deficiencies will also appear.

SOIL PREPARATION

To prepare the soil, either double-dig the bed by hand, going as deep as possible, or use a rotary tiller. You'll need to add plenty of organic matter. Mix in generous quantities of well-rotted manure (cow or chicken are best) and/or well-rotted leaf mold. Spread a layer on top of the bed and then work it into the soil.

Excellent drainage also is a priority. Roses grow best in well-aerated soil that retains moisture but drains well. If you are gardening in heavy clay soil, consider raised beds to improve drainage. Organic matter improves soil structure and improves drainage. Chicken grit, composed of small, sharp pieces of granite, also will help to break up clay soil.

After amending the soil, carefully smooth the bed so that it's slightly higher in the center and carefully graded so that water won't form puddles in the middle of the beds after a heavy rain.

WHEN TO PLANT

Roses can be planted in early spring or in autumn. Generally, dormant, bare-root roses are shipped in autumn, and it's best to plant them as soon as they arrive. (Although bare-root roses are offered for sale in spring, it's best to buy and plant them in fall.) The roots of roses planted at this time of year will begin growing in very early spring, long before you'll be able to spot signs of growth aboveground. If you can't plant in fall (or if you can't plant right away), heeling-in and planting the following spring is the next best alternative. Dig a trench in a convenient area, lay the plants in the trench at about a 45-degree angle, and cover the roots with soil. Be sure that all the roots are adequately covered because new rose plants often dry out if exposed to cold, dry winter winds, but don't mound soil over the entire plant. It's also important to avoid overcrowding. Plants that have been heeled-in need to be moved to their permanent location before mid-spring to avoid root damage.

Container-grown roses can be purchased from garden centers in spring and planted at that time.

PLANTING

As a general rule, roses can be planted just like shrubs and trees. With bare-root plants, it's important to keep the roots from drying out. Unpack the plants as soon as possible and check to see that the packing material is damp. Make sure the roots remain damp until you are able to plant.

To plant bare-root roses, dig a hole large enough to accommodate the plant's roots and make a mound of soil in the center of the hole. Before planting, inspect the plant carefully. Remove broken or split roots or canes. Also remove weak, thin, or badly placed canes, such as those that cross the center of the plant. Most bare-root roses will be properly pruned on arrival, so if you've bought good-quality plants, you may not need to do any pruning at all. When cutting off canes, be sure to cut back to healthy wood and make cuts ¼-inch above a bud eye. Then set the plant in the hole and spread the rose roots evenly in all directions. Be sure to check the depth of the bud union, if you're planting a grafted plant, or crown, if you are planting a plant grown on its own roots. (Usually, all roses except shrub roses and old garden roses are grafted onto an understock.) Where winter temperatures fall below 0°F, the bud union should be planted 1 or 2 inches below the surface of the soil. In the South, the bud union should be planted even with the surface of the soil. Roses grown on their own roots should be planted with the crown at the surface of the soil.

Carefully fill the hole, firming the soil around the plant to eliminate pockets of air around the roots. Water thoroughly when the hole is about two-thirds full, then finish filling. To keep the plant from drying out during the first winter, mound soil up around the base of the plant to protect it. Be sure to uncover the plants in early spring.

When planting container-grown roses, remove the pot and set the plant in place with as little disturbance to the root ball as possible. Many nurseries pot bare-root roses in late winter and then offer them in pots the following spring. Unlike roses that have been grown in containers, the roots of these plants have not yet begun to grow, and it's likely the potting mix will fall from the roots if you remove the plant from its pot. To minimize transplant disturbance, dig a hole the size of the pot, cut the bottom out of the pot, and cut partway up the sides of the pot. Hold the bottom of the pot in place while you set the plant in the hole, then remove the bottom. Cut the rest of the way up the sides and remove the pot. Firm soil around the roots and water thoroughly.

MULCHING

There are several reasons for mulching roses. A layer of mulch will help conserve moisture and prevent weed growth. Mulch also looks attractive, and if applied in autumn, it can help to regulate soil temperature. Mulch can also help prevent fungal spores in the soil from splattering up onto the foliage. Use shredded hardwood bark or bark chips for mulch. Keep in mind that these materials can gradually change soil pH, so be sure to check for pH changes periodically.

WINTER PROTECTION

Protect tender roses in winter by tying up the canes and surrounding them with a burlap-covered collar of chicken wire. Stuff with leaves all around the roses. This helps prevent damage to the canes by moderating temperature changes around the plants.

Pruning Roses

If you're going to grow roses, you'll need to love—or at least like—pruning. Since the best time to prune roses is late winter, many gardeners look forward to pruning as an annual ritual of spring.

Proper pruning is vital for healthy growth—and for gorgeous flowers—so make an annual pruning appointment with your roses in late winter, just as the buds begin to swell. Annual pruning benefits plants by removing dead and diseased canes as well as crossing and weak branches. It keeps the plants well shaped and encourages vigorous growth that will lead to large, abundant flowers. On grafted plants, it's important to regularly remove any suckers that arise from the understock onto which the plant has been grafted. First- and second-year plants will need little pruning, but all other roses will benefit from some annual attention. In addition to late winter pruning, you may also need to prune in summer to keep plants from getting too tall. Remember, too, that deadheading and cutting roses for indoor bouquets is a form of pruning. Here are the supplies you'll need to begin.

- **Sharp pruning shears**. It's a good idea to dip shears in alcohol, bleach, or another disinfectant between pruning cuts to prevent spreading diseases.
- **Loppers**. Although most pruning is done with pruning shears, the larger, older branches may need to be cut with loppers to ensure a clean cut. Be very careful not to rip rose canes when cutting.
- **Wood glue or shellac and a paint brush**. After cutting back canes, paint them with wood glue or shellac in order to prevent cane borers from invading the stems.
- **Gloves**. Heavy leather gloves will help prevent too much damage to your hands and make it easier to remove large canes.
- **Garden rake**. Use this tool to rake out any debris under and around the plants after you've finished pruning. A rake also is useful for keeping the area clean and smoothing out mulch.
- **Vinyl-coated wire fencing**. This may come in handy for taller-growing roses that have problems with flopping over. After pruning, place a cylindrical cone of wire around the rose, up to around 3 feet, to support the rose during the growing season. Wire it together and use hooks of bendable wire to attach the cylinder in place.
- **Large basket or garden cart**. You'll need either or both of these to remove the prunings.

Generally, roses can be placed into one of two categories when it comes to pruning. There are the roses that bloom on old growth (also called old wood) and those that bloom on new growth produced the current season (new wood). Most roses fall into the latter category and are pruned hard in late winter, before the beginning of the growing season.

Roses that bloom on old wood include primarily old garden roses and species roses. These roses should only be pruned lightly in late winter, so that not too many of the flowers are removed. But a late-winter pruning does benefit these plants and results in larger, showier blossoms and fuller, better-shaped plants.

Roses should not be pruned in fall, because pruning at this season removes food reserves that will help the plant survive the winter. Fall pruning also encourages growth at a time the plants should be preparing for winter dormancy. The new stems produced late in the year will not harden properly before winter and will be killed by freezing temperatures.

The general guidelines for pruning vary depending on the type of roses you are growing

Continued →

and where you are growing them. Begin any pruning job by thoroughly studying the plant to decide which canes are to be removed and how the plant can be made more attractive. You should plan on removing old canes that are no longer flowering well, and any diseased or damaged wood. Also remove canes that cross the center of the plant, to improve air circulation, and eliminate any spots where canes rub and damage one another.

Pruning Techniques for Specific Roses

HYBRID TEAS

Ideally, hybrid tea roses should be pruned back to a height of 18 to 24 inches in late winter. Be sure to remove all dead, diseased, and damaged growth. Also remove any crossing branches to increase air circulation at the center of the plant. Gardeners who grow roses for exhibition often cut back more severely in order to get fewer, larger flowers for show, but this is not recommended; it will shorten the life of the plant. Remember, regular deadheading and cutting blooms is also a form of pruning. During the growing season, don't let stray branches grow so long that the plant looks straggly.

Roses that bloom on new wood, such as hybrid teas, are pruned hard in late winter. At that time, cut all dead and diseased canes back to healthy wood, remove weak, thin canes, and eliminate branches that cross the center of the plant to increase air circulation.
You can increase flowering on a hybrid tea rose by deadheading. Cut faded blooms off just below the flowers and ¼ inch above a large bud (left). Unless you're cutting fresh flowers, which will require long stems, don't cut blooms off farther down the stem, because the buds will not be as large and vigorous (right).

GRANDIFLORAS AND FLORIBUNDAS

Grandiflora and floribundas need only very basic pruning to keep them healthy. In late winter prune back all dead, diseased, and damaged growth. Also remove any crossing branches to increase air circulation at the center of the plant. These roses don't need to be cut back to reduce height. Throughout the growing season, as you remove spent blooms or cut flowers for indoor display, keep in mind that you are also shaping the plant.

CLIMBING ROSES

When pruning climbing roses, it's best to remove all ties that hold the rose to its support and lay down all canes. Then shape the plant by bringing selected canes back up and tying them in a pleasing, graceful appearance.

For best flowering, always try to have one-, two-, and three-year-old canes on the plants at all times. For example, select at least one or two three-year-old canes for training, one or two two-year-old canes and one or two one-year-old canes. All canes selected to remain on the plant should be healthy and vigorous.

Some of the more rampant climbing roses can become an impossible tangled mess if left unpruned. You can cut these back hard each winter. ('Silver Moon' or 'Dr. Van Fleet' can be treated in this manner.) Since most blooms are borne on new wood, this harsh treatment will not greatly affect flowering. Climbing hybrid teas, on the other hand, are much less vigorous than other climbers and require only a light annual pruning. On these plants, just remove dead, diseased, or damaged growth.

With tall ramblers, it's impractical to pull the whole plant down for pruning. Apply the same principles as for climbing roses—removing diseased and old, woody canes—and prune in place. Nearly all rambling roses bloom only on second-year wood, so be sure you leave young wood to encourage blooming. You can cut the ends of long canes to encourage lateral branches, which will bloom the following year. Many ramblers produce too many canes and become thick and tangled at the base; remove excess canes at the base of the plant. Rambling roses can be pruned in summer after they finish blooming.

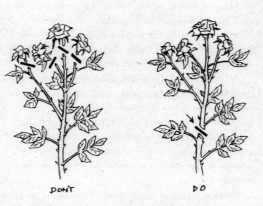

DON'T   DO

When deadheading floribundas, cut to a healthy bud just below the entire flower cluster (left) instead of simply removing the tips of the shoots just below the blooms (right).

OLD, SHRUB, AND SPECIES ROSES

There is such tremendous variation within these groups of roses that you'll need to depend on your own judgment and be sensitive to the growth habits of individual plants when pruning. Don't treat these plants as you would treat other modern roses such as hybrid teas. They don't appreciate hard pruning. Instead, it's best to leave the natural shape of the plants intact, and use pruning simply to enhance their shape and beauty, as well as to keep them under control and healthy. Restrict yourself to a late-winter pruning to remove diseased, damaged, and very old wood. Thin the growth at the center of the plant to increase air circulation, and eliminate crossing branches. You can also cut back any excessively long canes to improve the shape of the plant.

Rose Care: 1-2-3
Vicki Mattern

Many organic gardeners shy away from roses because they think these classic flowers require hours of extra work. But the truth is, you can grow beautiful roses by investing just a few hours per season. Combine careful cultivar selection, proper planting, and a few basic maintenance techniques, and you'll be rewarded with gorgeous flowers and attractive landscape plants.

Proper Planting

If you buy dormant bareroot roses, plant them either in early spring or late fall. You can plant actively growing container roses anytime during the growing season, but the earlier the better.

When you're ready to plant, select a site that receives at least 6 hours of sunlight per day. (In very hot climates, however, roses can benefit from some midday shade.) Be sure the site has good air circulation. Avoid areas close to heat-reflective surfaces, such as concrete walks or south-facing brick walls, which can attract mites. The soil should be loose and crumbly, with excellent drainage. If yours isn't, work in lots of compost or create raised planting beds.

Give rose bushes plenty of room. A good rule of thumb is to plant shrub types (old-fashioned roses, floribundas, polyanthas, and hybrid teas) no closer than 3 feet apart. Plant climbers, ramblers, and large-growing shrub roses (such as many of the David Austin English roses) 6 to 8 feet apart. Space miniature roses about 1 foot apart.

Container roses. Planting container roses is easy. Dig a hole large enough to hold the container, making sure that the top of the soil in the container is just below ground level. Tip the container and tap it to release the soil, or cut the container away from the rootball with a utility knife. Set the rose in the hole, holding onto the top of the rootball rather than grasping the rose by its stem. Fill in around the rootball with soil. Water the rose and add more soil, if necessary.

Barefoot roses. To plant bareroot roses, choose a day when the soil is relatively dry. (If conditions aren't right for planting when the roses arrive, set the plants in a bucket of water until you're ready.) Prune off any damaged or dead roots, as well as dead or damaged canes, cutting back to a healthy bud.

Dig a hole large enough for the roots to spread out naturally, then make a mound of soil inside the planting hole. The mound should be high enough that the bud union is at the proper depth.

Set the rose on the mound, spreading out its roots. Completely cover the roots with soil, tamp gently, and water well. The soil will settle and fill the hole.

Easy Maintenance

After you've got your roses planted, maintaining them organically is a simple matter of mulching, watering, feeding, and pruning. Pay attention to these basics and you should prevent most rose disease and pest problems. If diseases or pests do show up, manage them organically using the methods described on the previous pages.

Mulching. Surround the plants with a mulch to conserve soil moisture and help keep roots cool through summer. Mulching also helps prevent black spot disease by keeping the fungal spores from splashing up onto the plants from the soil. Choose mulches that will decompose and add organic matter to the soil, such as compost, shredded leaves, or shredded bark.

Depending on the material you use, the mulch layer should be 2 or 3 inches thick. (A 1-inch layer of compost, however, is all that's needed to suppress diseases.) As the mulch breaks down over time, work it into the top few inches of the soil, then add fresh mulch to bring the depth back to 2 or 3 inches.

Watering. Rugosa roses are very tolerant of dry conditions, but most other species and cultivars shine with just a bit of extra watering beyond what Mother Nature provides. Once a week, water the plants thoroughly—enough to soak down through their entire root area. Use a soaker hose or other form of drip irrigation, if possible. Overhead

Continued ➔

watering with a hose or sprinkler can promote the spread of diseases such as black spot, powdery mildew, and rust.

Feeding. Before you apply any fertilizers, it's a good idea to have your soil tested to determine any specific nutrient deficiencies. If your soil appears to be in good shape, put your roses on this simple diet regimen to keep them robust:

- About 2 weeks after spring pruning, apply a balanced organic fertilizer or a dressing of compost. (Don't feed newly planted roses until they've completed their first bloom cycle, though.)
- After roses have finished their first heavy bloom cycle in early summer, give them a second application of fertilizer.
- Feed reblooming roses again, after the second bloom cycle. (Don't use nitrogen fertilizers within 6 weeks of the first fall frost in your area, however. Late feedings encourage tender growth that frost will kill.)
- Always water your roses the day before feeding and again the day after applying fertilizer. This prevents fertilizer burn.

Pruning Basics

Don't be too nervous about pruning your roses incorrectly—they are very forgiving, even if you make a wrong cut or two. Each year, the plants produce strong new shoots, giving you beautiful blossoms and another try at pruning.

The best time to prune most roses is either late winter or early spring, about 4 to 6 weeks before the last killing frost in your area. Summer pruning is really just a matter of removing faded flowers throughout the growing season. Because pruning promotes soft new growth, discontinue it in late summer to avoid subjecting plants to winter damage.

What to Prune

The toughest part about pruning roses is deciding what to cut off and what to leave alone. As a rule of thumb, most vigorous roses can be pruned back to 6 inches tall, while others can be pruned to 10 to 12 inches without harm.

All roses. Remove canes that are dead, diseased, flowering poorly, crossed or rubbing, or growing inward. If suckers emerge from the area that's grafted, just below the ground, don't just cut them off at ground level or they'll resprout. Instead, follow each shoot underground to where it joins the stock, then use a trowel to snap it off.

Hybrid tea roses. Cut off the oldest stems at the base, leaving three to six healthy canes. Prune the remaining canes to shape the plant.

Floribunda roses. Remove the oldest stems at the base, leaving six to eight healthy canes. Prune off the top third of each remaining cane.

Climbers. Prune climbers to train and shape them, cutting back side branches to about 6 inches. Leave more canes than on other roses—about 15 or so—to get a good flush of bloom next year.

Ramblers. Ramblers bloom on first-year wood, so you should prune them more heavily each year. Cut them back to 12 to 18 inches from the ground each year.

Shrub roses. Prune off the top third of new canes and cut side shoots and older growth to 4 to 6 inches.

How to Prune

Pruning roses is a snap if you follow this advice:

- Make cuts ¼ inch above an outward-facing bud—the point where a leaf is or was attached to the stem.
- Cut at a 45-degree angle away from the bud. This promotes open growth in the center of the bush, encouraging air to circulate and preventing disease. Angling the cut prevents moisture from gathering on the bud and rotting it.
- Cut back to at least a five-leaflet node. Otherwise, the sprouting stem will be weak and spindly.
- If the inside, or pith, of the cane is discolored, cut the shoot back until the pith is white and healthy.
- If, after pruning, two or three shoots emerge from one bud, pinch off all of them but one.

Landscaping with Roses

Roses are perfect landscape plants because you can use them in so many ways. Think of them as part shrub, part perennial, and part vine. Some varieties offer season-long blooms, and many produce brightly colored hips that add a burst of color to your landscape throughout the fall and winter, too.

Use Roses Anywhere

Roses are great planted with herbs, in a cottage garden, or in a perennial flowerbed. You can also use roses as hedges or train them to climb arbors, trellises, walls, even lampposts. Your imagination is the only limit to creating a beautiful and interesting garden with roses.

A Gallery of Ideas

Once you've summed up the all the ways you can use roses in your landscape, it's time to review the possibilities in more detail. The information contained there, combined with the gallery of photos in this chapter, will help you decide exactly how and where you should use roses on your property and which roses are the best choices for your intended use.

In this chapter, you'll find ideas for different types of plantings from low-growing ground covers to 20-foot climbers. You'll also find tips to help you train climbers and ramblers, as well as suggestions for what to plant with roses to show them off to their best advantage.

The Rose Garden

The time-honored way to use roses in the landscape is to plant a rose garden—with roses in the spotlight and no supporting players. If your heart is set on a rose garden, by all means plant one, but don't grow the roses all by themselves. A bed with nothing in it but roses will attract pests and diseases, and it will look dull when the roses have finished blooming.

- Underplant your roses with herbs like lavender and catmint (*Nepeto* x *faassenii*) for a lovely contrast.
- Choose a mixture of repeat-blooming roses, including hybrid teas, floribundas, grandifloras, miniatures, shrubs, rugosas, polyanthas, and repeat-blooming old roses for a garden that will be full of blooms throughout the season.

Perennial and Shrub Borders

Roses are natural partners in the perennial garden, adding height, texture, fragrance, and even season-long bloom. Shrub, old garden, species, and grandiflora roses are all excellent choices for a perennial border.

Plant tall roses in the back of the bed, shorter ones in the middle, and minis in the front, the same way you'd use perennials. In an island bed designed to be seen from all sides, put the tallest plants in the center and work down from there.

In mixed shrub borders, where roses share the billing with other plants, multiseasonal interest isn't critical for each rose—other plants can easily take over when rose bloom is past. In both perennial and shrub borders, you can base your choice of roses on color, plant and flower form, and personal preference.

Roses with Herbs

No type of garden is more romantic or has as much historical significance than an herb garden. People have used herbs as medicines, cosmetics, seasonings for foods, and decorations throughout the ages. For many centuries, roses were an integral part of herb gardens, so selecting an old rose or two to compliment your herb garden is a wonderful choice. 'Apothecary's Rose' (*Rosa gallica* var. *officinalis*) is probably the rose grown in western gardens the longest. It has magenta, semidouble flowers that bloom in early summer—a perfect partner for lavender- and white-blooming herbs.

Don't be afraid to use culinary herbs as well as more decorative herbs to hide the base of leggy rose canes. Sweet basil, curly parsley, chives, French tarragon, 'Fern leaf' dill, and others are not only pretty to look at but are useful, too.

Roses on Structures

You may want to dress up or hide a fence, arbor, trellis, pergola, wall, building, or other structure with roses. The tall climbers, ramblers, and more aggressive shrub and old roses are ideal for this purpose. Use the shorter climbers for low fences or train them on pillars.

Miniature climbers have a powerful impact for their diminutive size. An ideal place for a miniature climber is on a mailbox or lamppost.

Combine roses with other climbers like clematis for even more beauty and bloom. Underplant with cheerful annuals in complementary colors or with cool foliage plants like hostas to create ground-level interest.

With a little guidance from you, your climbers and ramblers will create a stunning landscaping effect. Use raffia or rubber- or plastic-coated wire for the ties, making a figure-eight between the cane and the support so the tie won't put pressure on the cane.

TRAINING ROSES TO A FENCE

Ramblers are the best type of rose to train to a fence. Train the canes to grow horizontally on the fence for best bloom. When the main canes are forced to grow horizontally, they will produce more new shoots that will bear the blooms. As canes die or stop flowering well, untie them and cut them off at the base because ramblers bloom only on new wood.

TRAINING ROSES TO A TRELLIS

Train climbing roses to a trellis by starting on the outside of the plant and working across, spacing the canes evenly against the trellis as you tie them to it. The more horizontally you bend and tie the canes, the more flowers you'll have. Train climbers to an arbor in the same way, planting a rose on each side of the arbor.

Continued ➡

Roses as Groundcovers

Planting low-growing, sprawling roses is an excellent solution for hard-to-mow slopes, as long as the slope isn't too dry. Although the foliage of ground-cover roses isn't as dense as that of traditional groundcovers such as pachysandra, it's thick enough to serve the purpose. *Rosa wichuraiana*, climbing roses like 'New Dawn', and some of the Meidiland landscape rose cultivars such as 'Alba Meidiland' make colorful, effective groundcovers. They're most effective if you install them with a combination of plastic mulch and an organic mulch like bark chips, or with a thick organic mulch like shredded leaves.

Other excellent choices for groundcover roses include the following:

- 'Sea Foam', a repeat-blooming creamy white rose that grows 2 feet tall x 8 feet wide
- 'The Fairy', a repeat-blooming double pink polyantha rose that grows 2 feet tall x 3 feet wide
- Miniature roses, such as 'Snow Carpet', which grows 1 foot tall x 3 feet wide

Rose Hedges and Edgings

Shrub, old garden, and taller grandiflora roses are perfect for creating hedges as a background, screen, or barrier. Although the plants lose their leaves in winter, the thorny branches still serve as a physical barrier and also provide shelter for wildlife. Many of these roses have beautiful hips in fall and winter, so they add color to the winter landscape and attract birds to your yard. You can mix roses of similar size and compatible flower colors, or mix roses with other shrubs for a more informal, colorful hedge.

To create a thick, blooming tall hedge, you simply have to pick the right rose—one that's upright, densely bushy, and disease-resistant so it doesn't need coddling.

If you'd like a low hedge or edging, there are plenty of options. Instead of a sprawling ground-cover rose, choose one that's more upright but only reaches a mature height of 1 to 4 feet tall. Most floribundas, polyanthas, and miniature roses grow beautifully as low hedges, which are useful along walks and paths and around terraces and beds. They make a clear boundary but don't block the view.

Roses in Containers

One of the greatest pleasures of container gardening is that it's like having furniture. You can move the containers around to suit your mood or the occasion. The best arrangements of containers are in informally arranged, odd-numbered groups of different-size pots, but it's always fun to experiment with different looks and groupings.

Roses look lovely in containers. The miniature roses and shorter-sprawling cultivars are graceful in hanging baskets. You can also grow roses in containers to place on decks, terraces, porches, and patios and throughout the yard.

Smaller-growing types such as miniature roses are perfect choices for containers, as are the floribundas and polyanthas. Combine roses with annuals like ivy geraniums, annual candy tuft, sweet alyssum, and petunias for two-story color. Or create a more subtle look with herbs like prostrate rosemary or creeping thyme.

Overwintering potted roses in colder climates requires some effort, so be prepared to bring them indoors or provide protection if you live where temperatures dip below 20°F. Standard, or tree, roses are also perfect for container growing. Standard roses have a tough time surviving in winter winds, so it's best to bring them inside during the winter. When you grow a standard rose in a container, it's easy to move it in and out of your house.

Roses as Cut Flowers

There's nothing more elegant than a bouquet of roses, and when you grow your own, you can bring in armfuls of roses from the garden to enjoy without spending a fortune at a flower shop!

Make the Most of Your Roses

In this section, you'll learn how to cut and condition your roses properly so they have the longest vase life possible—nine days or more. You'll also learn how to show off your cut roses to their best advantage. You could just stick a bunch of roses in a jelly jar. But, if you arrange them in that jelly jar, you can let your creative juices produce a display that does justice to your beautiful blossoms.

Luckily, casual, simple arrangements are the style today, rather than the more stiff, formal, rule-bound arrangements of the past. Even so, to create the most satisfying arrangements, you will need to pay attention to a few guidelines regarding size, balance, color, and shape. With a little practice, you'll be able to fashion beautiful arrangements and savor the fruits of your gardening labors. But first, let's take a look at how to cut roses properly.

Wild Rose

When and How to Cut Roses

To enjoy your rose arrangements the longest, cut roses from your garden either in the evening or early in the morning. This is when the plants are most filled with water. Gather rosebuds and half-open flowers, but avoid fully open roses because they won't last long. Be sure to use pruning shears, not scissors, to cut roses because scissors don't have enough leverage to cut cleanly through the woody stems.

4 STEPS TO SIMPLY BEAUTIFUL CUT ROSES

1. Cut stems just above a five-leaflet leaf at a 45-degree angle. It's best if the leaf is facing outward because another shoot will grow from this point. Also, consider the shape and size of the bush before cutting any roses so that you don't ruin its form.

2. Once you've cut a rose, strip the foliage from the bottom 3 to 4 inches of its stem. Carry a bucket of water with you and plunge the stems into the bucket as soon as you've cut them.

3. Once you're back indoors, recut each stem underwater at a sharp angle so that the maximum area of the cut end is exposed to water. Cut off the thorns in the area where you have stripped the foliage away, using thornstrippers or a sharp knife.

4. Set the container of roses in a dark, cool, humid place (such as a refrigerator or a basement) for at least several hours, preferably overnight, in order to condition the roses before using them in an arrangement. (Cut other flowers and foliage for your arrangement at the same time as you cut your roses and put them in that same dark, humid place as your roses to condition them, too.)

Choosing Colors

Although you don't need to know a thing about color theory to arrange a beautiful bouquet, you'll have a higher success rate if you know some elementary color combinations.

- Pairings of complementary colors such as orange and blue, yellow and purple, and red and green tend to be bright and vibrant. One example is a simple arrangement of yellow roses with purple catmint (*Nepeta* x *faassenii*).
- Related colors—such as pinks, magentas, lavenders, and purples—can also make for lovely arrangements. Imagine an arrangement of pink roses, pale pink lilies, and purple lavender.
- A monochromatic arrangement is built basically around one color. For example, a bouquet of all white to creamy white flowers, such as white roses with white larkspur (*Consolida ambigua*) and white coral bells (*Heuchera sanguinea*) accented with herb foliage would be wonderful.
- A polychromatic arrangement includes a mix of many different colors. Go to your garden, gather roses and any other flowers and foliage that catch your eye, and enjoy a bounty of beauty.

Creating Your Arrangement

Styles in flower arranging are very personal, ranging from bouquets that look as though they've just been gathered from the garden to more formally arranged styles. Follow the basic principles of balance, rhythm, and scale to help guide you in making arrangements you'll love.

BALANCE

A balanced arrangement seems secure and stable. Balance your arrangement by putting the heavier-looking flowers toward the center and lower parts of your arrangements.

RHYTHM

Rhythm is how your eyes are led from the focal point (the central point of interest) throughout the arrangement. Get rhythm in your arrangements by repeating shapes and colors and by arranging branches and stems to create a continuous flow of line.

SCALE

Scale is the size relationship of the various elements. An arrangement with good scale means that the proportions of each element are pleasing and in

Continued ➡

harmony with the others. A basic guideline is that your arrangement should be 1½ times as high or as wide as the container.

Container Criteria

Containers can vary with the style or arrangement and type of roses. A hybrid tea rose with its long, stiff stem will work in a tall vase, while old-fashioned roses with multiple flowers on short stems lend themselves to small, informal, charming containers, such as a pottery bowl. The major point to keep in mind is that the container should complement the flowers, not detract from them. Containers that work best are those with the simplest designs or colors.

Live Rose Arrangements

For the simplest rose arrangements of all, grow miniature roses as houseplants and when they are at their peak bloom, put them in a decorative container and use them as centerpieces or room accents.

For miniatures to grow successfully indoors, they need at least 5 hours of bright sunlight in a south- or west-facing window. Or put them under fluorescent lights for 14 hours daily. Place the lights 3 to 4 inches above the tops of the plants.

Another important factor in indoor rose growing is soil moisture. Keep the soil evenly moist but not soggy. Feed your roses twice a month with a water-soluble organic fertilizer for indoor use. Miniature roses will bloom best at daytime temperatures of 70° to 75°F and nighttime temperatures of 60° to 65°F.

Preserving Roses with Your Microwave

Microwave oven drying with silica gel (a desiccant that resembles white sand) gives the freshest, most colorful preserved flower possible, other than freeze-drying. You can dry lots of flowers with a small amount of silica gel. The disadvantages are that you can only dry one or two flowers at a time and it can be difficult to judge the correct drying time.

1. Preheat silica gel in the microwave for 1 minute on high power.

2. Pour a 1-inch layer of the preheated gel in a small, deep, microwave-safe container or cardboard box. (Do not use the container for food preparation after using the silica gel.)

3. Place a rose with a 1-inch stem into the silica gel.

4. Microwave for 2 minutes on high power, using a turntable or rotating the container one-half turn every 30 seconds. Let the container cool for 20 to 30 seconds.

5. Carefully pour off the silica gel and check the condition of the flower. If it's too "done," cut the cooking time in half for the next rose.

6. Make a replacement stem with floral wire and floral wrapping tape. Insert a wire through the fat part of the flower just below the petals and center the wire. Gently bend the wire down on both sides and overlap the wire to form a single "stem."

7. Place the end of the floral tape against the rose and wrap the wires, twirling the wires and stretching the tape as you go. Tear off the tape at the base of the stem.

Your Seasonal Rose-Care Calendar

Now that you know the basics of good organic rose care, you need to know when to feed, mulch, water, plant, prune, and do all the other things roses need to thrive. Here's a calendar that gives you a glance of what you'll need to do each month throughout the year to keep your roses growing and blooming their best.

Also keep in mind that planting roses in Florida isn't the same as planting them in Maine because of the climatic conditions. That's why before you even start planning for roses, you need to know what hardiness zone you live in.

A plant's ability to withstand a given climate is called its hardiness. The USDA has developed a Plant Hardiness Zone Map that divides North America into ten numbered climatic zones. Zone 1 is the coldest, and Zone 10 is the warmest. Parts of Hawaii are even warmer and fall into Zone 11.

January

All climates:

- Plan your garden for the coming year, decide which roses you want to add, and order them.
- Purchase whatever new garden tools you need.
- Clean, sharpen, and repair tools you have on hand.
- Check to make sure winter protection remains in place.

Zones 8 to 10: Plant both container-grown and bareroot roses and transplant any roses you want moved.

February

All climates: Clean, sharpen, and repair any equipment you didn't get to in January.

Zones 7 to 10: Plant container-grown and bareroot roses, and transplant roses as necessary.

March

Zones 2 to 5:

- Make any adjustments to garden plans.
- Review information on roses you're planning to purchase.
- Order roses.

Zone 6: Remove winter protection from plants. Prune roses to shape, encourage new growth, or remove dead, diseased, or damaged wood.

Zones 7 to 10: Apply a balanced organic fertilizer to the soil around roses, scratching it in lightly.

April

Zones 2 to 7:

- As soon as the soil is dry enough to work, plant bare root and container-grown roses.
- Move any roses that would look better or grow better in another part of the garden.
- Prune roses to shape, to encourage new growth, or to remove dead, diseased, or damaged wood.

Zones 7 to 10:

- Remove faded flowers and remove buds on side blooms of hybrid teas for larger, longer-stemmed blooms.
- Plant container-grown roses.
- Apply balanced organic fertilizer to the soil and scratch in around roses.

May

All climates: Check for pest and disease problems and water as necessary. Apply a balanced, organic fertilizer to the soil around roses. Gather roses for bouquets for yourself and friends.

Zones 2 to 4: plant bareroot roses as weather and soil conditions permit.

June

All climates:

- Remove faded flowers and remove buds on side blooms of cutting roses.

- Continue to check for pest and disease problems and control them as necessary.
- As rose canes extend themselves, tie and peg climbers to their structures.
- Enjoy your roses!

July

All climates:

- Continue to remove faded flowers, monitor for pests and disease problems, and water as necessary.
- Apply a foliar feeding of fish emulsion or liquid seaweed.
- Apply balanced organic fertilizer to the soil and scratch in around roses.

August

All climates:

- Monitor for pests and disease and water as necessary.
- If desired, make a final application of a balanced fertilizer.
- Remove faded flowers and disbud side blooms on hybrid teas for larger, longer-stemmed blooms.

September

Zones 2 to 6: Get new beds ready for spring planting. Stop removing faded slowers.

Zones 6 to 10: Send off orders for fall planting. Plant container-grown roses. Continue to keep garden areas weeded, and water as necessary.

October

All climates: Plan new plantings.

Zones 2 to 4:

- Prune roses.
- Remove leaves from plants and from surrounding soil, and destroy.
- Apply winter mulch.

Zones 7 to 10: Send off orders for fall planting. Stop removing faded flowers.

November

All climates: Send off your rose orders for spring planting.

Zones 5 to 7:

- Prune roses.
- Remove diseased leaves and canes from plants and from surrounding soil, and destroy.
- Apply winter mulch.

Zones 6 to 10: Get new beds ready for spring planting. Stop watering.

December

All climates: Use discarded Christmas tree branches as mulch around roses.

Zones 7 to 10:

- Plant container-grown and bareroot roses as weather and soil permit.
- Transplant roses as desired
- Continue to check for pests and diseases.

Rose Glossary

Alfalfa meal. One of the most commonly recommended organic fertilizers for roses.

Aphids. Soft-bodied green, red, pink, brown, or black insects about 1/8 inch long that attack roses. Found mostly on new growth, clustered on leaf tips and buds.

Continued ➡

Axil. The angle between the cane and the upper surface of the leaf stalk.

Bareroot. A common form of shipping roses, where dormant roses are packed without pot or soil.

Beetles. Chewing insects with hard wings that eat rose leaves and flowers. Some larvae feed on the rose's roots.

Black spot. A fungal infection that forms black circles with yellow margins on leaves.

Bloodmeal. Also known as dried blood, blood meal is an animal by-product that contains 13 percent nitrogen. Sprinkled on garden beds, blood meal can repel rabbits.

Bonemeal. Finely ground bones (another animal by-product) that contains 10 to 12 percent phosphorus, 24 percent calcium, and a small amount of nitrogen.

Bud. A growth bud, or eye, found on a cane; a vegetative growing point located where a leaf joins the stem.

Bud union. The swollen point where the bud is joined with the rootstock.

Cane. A main stem, or basal shoot, of a rose, usually arising at or very near the bud union.

Clay soil. Soil that is made up of very fine particles that hold nutrients well but are poorly drained and difficult to work.

Climber. A rose that grows very tall and can be trained to grow on a trellis, an arbor, a pergola, or a wall.

Compost. Decomposed and partially decomposed organic matter that is dark in color and crumbly in texture. Used as a soil amendment, compost increases the water-holding capacity of sandy soil, improves drainage of clay soil, and is an excellent nutrient source for microorganisms, which later release nutrients to your plants.

Crown. The point on the rose where the canes sprout from the bud union.

Cultivar. Short for "cultivated variety," a cultivar is any plant that is bred for specific characteristics such as color, fragrance, disease resistance, or other desirable qualities.

Double flower. A rose that has 30 to 39 petals in four or more rows.

Eye (bud eye). A vegetative bud, or growing point, on a stem.

Feeder roots. Thin, fine-textured roots that absorb nutrients and water from the soil; also called hair roots.

Fertilizer. A natural or manufactured material that supplies one or more of the major nutrients—nitrogen (N), phosphorus (P), and potassium (K)—to growing plants.

Floribunda. Bushy roses that are a cross of hybrid tea and polyantha roses. Flowers may be single, semidouble, or double, and plants stand 2 to 4 feet tall.

Grafting. The process of joining a stem or bud of one cultivar onto the rooted stem, called the rootstock, of another cultivar.

Grandiflora. A cross of hybrid teas and floribunda roses that grow 4 to 6 feet tall. Flowers have high centers and are borne singly or in clusters.

Hip. The fruit or seedpod of the rose. Some roses have very showy hips, which add color and beauty to the fall and winter landscape.

Hybrid tea. Narrow, upright bushes that grow 3 to 5 feet high and need extra fertilizer to sustain heavy blooming. Flowers are long, narrow, and high-centered.

Lateral cane (branch). A side branch arising from a main, or basal, cane. Rambler roses, for instance, bloom on the lateral canes.

Leaf/leaflet. A rose leaf is compound and has three or more leaflets that make up the true leaf.

Loam. Textural class of soil that contains a balance of fine clay, medium-size silt, and coarse sand particles. Loam is easily tilled and retains moisture and nutrients effectively.

Main shoot. A basal or strong lateral cane.

Micronutrient. A plant nutrient needed in very small quantities, including copper, chlorine, zinc, iron, manganese, boron, and molybdenum.

Miniature rose. A rose that grows only 6 inches to 2 feet tall and all parts are miniaturized. The flowers can be single, semidouble, or double.

Modern rose. Any rose cultivar that was bred and introduced after 1867, the time when modern hybrid tea roses were first introduced.

Mosaic virus. A virus that causes leaves to develop circles of yellow or chartreuse, become streaked or mottled, or develop yellow netting. Plants may be stunted.

Mulch. A layer of an organic or inorganic material, such as shredded leaves, straw, bark, pine needles, lawn clippings, or black plastic, which is spread around plants to conserve soil moisture and discourage weeds. As organic mulches decompose, they help to build the soil.

New wood. A cane of the current year's growth. Some roses bloom only on new wood, while others bloom on the previous year's growth.

Old roses. Roses that were bred before 1867, the time when the modern hybrid tea rose was first introduced.

Old wood. A cane of the previous year's growth or older.

Own-root roses. Roses grown from cuttings, rather than being budded onto a rootstock of another plant.

Polyantha. Bushy, 2-foot plants that have narrow, finely textured leaves. Flowers are small and are borne in clusters.

Powdery mildew. A fungal disease that attacks new growth and flower buds, covering them with a thin, white, powdery substance. Growth becomes deformed.

Rambler. Similar to climbing roses, ramblers can be trained to grow on fences. They are once-blooming roses, and flowers are borne on new growth, so they must be pruned back severely each year to produce flowers the following summer.

Reversion. Suckers from the rootstock choking out or taking over from the growth of the bud graft.

Rootstock. The host plant or root portion (understock) onto which a bud of another type of rose is grafted.

Rust. A fungal disease that appears in spring as small orange spots on undersides of leaves and light yellow spots on the upper sides. Spots may also appear on canes. Most common on the Pacific Coast.

Sandy soil. Soil that contains more than 70 percent sand and less than 15 percent clay, generally easy to work and well drained but with poor nutrient- and water-holding abilities.

Scion. The technical term for the bud grafted onto a rootstock.

Semidouble flower. A flower that has 8 to 20 petals in two or three rows.

Shrub rose. A hardy, easy-to-grow plant that can grow as tall as 12 feet. The flowers can be single, semidouble, or double.

Silt. Refers to a soil particle of moderate size—larger than clay but not as large as sand.

Single flower. A flower with 5 to 7 petals in a single row.

Soil amendment. A material added to the soil to make it more productive by improving its structure, drainage, or aeration.

Soil pH. A number from 1 to 14 that is a measure of the acidity or alkalinity of soil, with 7 indicating neutrality; below 7, acidity; and above 7, alkalinity. The pH of your soil has a great effect on what nutrients are available to your plants.

Soil structure. The physical arrangement of soil particles and interconnected pore spaces. Soil structure can be improved by the addition of organic matter. Walking on or tilling wet soil can destroy the soil aggregates and ruin the soil's structure.

Soil texture. The proportions of sand, silt, and clay in a particular soil.

Species rose. Any rose that occurs naturally in nature. There are over 200 species of roses from which all other types of roses are bred.

Standard. Also called a tree rose, a standard is a rose that is grafted to a stalk (or standard), which in turn is grafted to rootstock, meaning there are two bud unions on a standard rose. These roses can be planted in the ground or used in containers as accent plants.

Stem. A branch of a cane, which emerges from a bud eye and bears leaves and at least one flower.

Sucker. A growing stem that arises from a rootstock below the bud union.

Thorn. The prickle, or sharp spine, found on the stem of roses.

Understock. The base of the plant, providing the root system, onto which the scion or bud of another rose is grafted; also called the rootstock.

Continued ➡

The Edible Garden

VEGETABLES

Introduction to the Vegetable Garden

Jeff Cox

Fresh-picked sweet corn, tomatoes, and snap peas are a taste treat you can get only from your backyard vegetable garden. The quality and flavor of fresh vegetables will reward you from early in the growing season until late fall. And when you garden organically, you know that your harvest is free of potentially harmful chemical residues.

Although the plants grown in vegetable gardens are a diverse group from many different plant families, they share broad general cultural requirements. Most will thrive in well-drained soil with a pH of 6.5 to 7.0. Some will tolerate frost; others will tolerate some shade. You should have little trouble growing vegetables successfully if you pick an appropriate site, prepare the soil well, and keep your growing crops weeded and watered.

This chapter will serve as your guide to planning, preparing, and tending your vegetable plot through the seasons.

Vegetable gardens are ideal sites for putting organic soil improvement and pest management techniques into practice. Since you're working the soil each year, you'll have lots of opportunities to add organic matter and soil amendments that help keep the soil naturally balanced.

As you make your yearly plan for planting and caring for your garden, you can incorporate techniques such as crop rotation, soil enrichment, and other cultural pest prevention methods. And there's a broad range of organically acceptable pest control methods and products for vegetable crops.

Planning Your Garden

Planning your garden can be as much fun as planting it. When you plan a garden, you'll balance all your hopes and wishes for the crops you'd like to harvest against your local growing conditions, as well as the space you have available to plant. Planning involves choosing a site (unless you already have an established garden), deciding on a garden style, selecting crops and cultivars, and mapping your garden.

SITE SELECTION

Somewhere in your yard, there is a good place for a vegetable garden. The ideal site has these characteristics:

Full or almost full sun: In warm climates, some vegetables can get by on six hours of direct sunshine each day, while a full day of sun is needed in cool climates. The best sites for vegetable gardens usually are on the south or west side of a house, where sunshine is most abundant. If part of the site you select is too shady for planting, put your compost pile there.

Good drainage: A slight slope is good for vegetable gardens. The soil will get well soaked by rain or irrigation water, and excess will run off. Avoid low places where water accumulates.

Limited competition from nearby trees: Tree roots take up huge amounts of water. Leave as much space as possible between large trees and your vegetable garden.

Easy access to water: If you can't get a hose or irrigation line to a prospective garden site, don't plant vegetables there. No matter what your local climate is, you'll most likely have to provide supplemental water at some point in the growing season, or your harvest will suffer.

Accessibility: Organic gardens need large amounts of mulch, plus periodic infusions of other bulky materials such as well-rotted manure or rock fertilizers. If you have a large garden, you should be able to drive a truck up to its edge for easy unloading. In narrow city lots, the garden access path should be wide enough for a cart or wheelbarrow.

Once you find a site that has these characteristics, double-check for hidden problems. For example, don't locate your garden over septic-tank field lines, buried utility cables, or water lines.

Continued ➡

Garden Layout

Once you've decided on a site, think about the type of vegetable garden you want. Possible lay-outs range from traditional row plantings to intensive raised beds and container gardens.

Row Planting: A row garden, in which vegetables are planted in parallel lines, is easy to organize and plant. However, it's not as space—efficient as more intensive methods, such as raised beds. You may spend more time weeding unless you mulch heavily and early between rows. Also, you'll get less yield per area than you would from an intensively planted garden. Row planting is quick and efficient for large plantings of crops such as beans or corn.

You can enhance the appearance and productivity of a row garden by making a raised bed along the front edge and planting it with herbs and flowers.

Beds: Productivity, efficient use of space, less weeding, and shading the soil are all benefits of intensively planted beds. Beds are raised planting areas, generally with carefully enriched soil, so they can be planted intensively. While they require more initial time to prepare, they save time on weeding or mulching later in the season. Because they're more space-efficient, you'll also get higher yields per area than from a traditional row garden.

Beds for vegetables should be no more than 4 feet wide so you can easily reach the center of the bed to plant, weed, and harvest.

Spot Gardens: If your yard is small, with no suitable space for a separate vegetable garden, look for sunny spots where you can fit small plantings of your favorite crops. Plant a small bed of salad greens and herbs near your kitchen door for easy access when preparing meals. Tuck vegetables into flower beds. You can dress up crops that aren't ornamental, such as tomatoes, by underplanting them with annuals such as nasturtiums and marigolds.

Containers: You may not be able to grow all your favorite vegetables in containers, but many dwarf cultivars of vegetables grow well in pots or planters. Garden catalogs include dwarf tomato, cucumber, pepper, and even squash cultivars suitable for container growing. Vegetables that are naturally small, such as loose-head lettuce, scallions, and many herbs, such as basil, also grow nicely in containers.

Crop Choices

Generally, vegetables can be divided into cool-weather, warm-weather, and hot-weather crops.

Consider the length of your growing season (the period of time between the last frost in spring and the first one in fall), seasonal rainfall patterns, and other environmental factors when choosing vegetables. There are many new fast-maturing and heat- or cold-tolerant cultivars that make it easier for northern gardeners to grow hot-weather crops such as melons and for Southern gardeners to be able to enjoy cool-loving crops such as spinach.

Have some fun when you choose plants for your vegetable garden as well. Make some of your selections for beauty as well as flavor. Beans with purple or variegated pods are easy to spot for picking and lovely to behold, for example. Look through catalogs and try some of the heirloom or other unusual cultivars they offer.

Garden Mapping

As you fill out seed order forms, it's wise to map planned locations for your crops. Otherwise, you may end up with far too little or too much seed. Depending on the size of your garden, you may need to make a formal plan drawn to scale.

Consider these points as you figure out your planting needs and fill in your map:

- Are you growing just enough of a crop for fresh eating, or will you be preserving some of your harvest? For some crops, it takes surprisingly little seed to produce enough to feed a family. You can refer to seed catalogs or check individual vegetable entries for information on how much to plant.

- Are you planning to rotate crops? Changing the position of plants in different crop families from year to year can help reduce any pest problems.

- Are you going to plant crops in spring and again later in the season for a fall harvest? Order seed for both plantings at the same time.

Preparing the Soil

Since most vegetables are fast-growing annuals, they need garden soil that provides a wide range of plant nutrients and loose soil that plant roots can penetrate easily. In an organic vegetable garden, soil with high organic-matter content and biological activity is paramount in importance. Every year when you harvest vegetables, you're carting off part of the reservoir of nutrients that was in your vegetable garden soil. To keep the soil in balance, you need to replace those nutrients. Look for every opportunity to incorporate different forms of organic matter into your soil.

Assessing Your Soil

If you're starting a new vegetable garden or switching from conventional to organic methods (or if you've just been disappointed with past yields or crop quality), start by testing your soil. Soil acidity or alkalinity, which is measured as soil pH, can affect plant performance. Most vegetables prefer soil with a pH of 6.5 to 7.0. Overall soil fertility also will influence yield, especially for heavy-feeding crops such as broccoli and tomatoes. A soil test will reveal soil pH as well as any nutrient imbalances.

Creating New Gardens

If you're just starting out, you'll probably be tilling under sod, or possibly bare ground, to start your garden. Using a rotary tiller may be the only practical way to work up the soil in a large garden. But whether you're working with a machine or digging by hand, use care. Don't work the soil when it's too wet or too dry; that would have detrimental effects on soil structure and quality.

If you're ambitious, a great way to start a vegetable garden is by double digging the soil. This process thoroughly loosens the soil so that it will retain more water and air, have better drainage, and be easier for roots to penetrate.

Depending on the results of your soil tests, you may need to work in lime to correct pH, or rock fertilizers to correct deficiencies, as you dig your garden. In any case, it's always wise to incorporate organic matter as you work.

Enriching the Soil

If you're an experienced gardener with an established garden site, you can take steps to replenish soil nutrients and organic matter as soon as you harvest and clear out your garden in the fall. Sow seed of a green manure crop in your garden, or cover the soil with a thick layer of organic mulch. Both green manures and mulches protect the soil from erosion and improve organic matter content. In the spring, you'll be ready to push back or incorporate the mulch or green manure and start planting.

If you don't plant a green manure crop, spread compost or well-rotted manure over your garden in spring and work it into the soil. You can add as much as a 6-inch layer of organic material, if you're fortunate enough to have that much on hand. The best time to do this is a few weeks before planting, if your soil is dry enough to be worked. You can cultivate with a rotary tiller or by hand, using a turning fork and rake. Never cultivate extremely wet soil, or you will be compacting it instead of aerating it. Be conservative when you work the soil. While some cultivation is necessary to prepare seedbeds and to open up the soil for root growth, excess cultivation is harmful. It introduces large amounts of oxygen into the soil, which can speed the breakdown of soil organic matter. And if soil is too wet or too dry, cultivating it can ruin soil structure.

Other opportunities for improving your soil will crop up at planting time, when you add compost or other growth-boosters in planting rows or holes, and during the growing season, as you mulch your developing plants.

Planting Your Crops

Planting season can be the busiest time of year for the vegetable gardener. Some careful planning is in order. To help you remember what you have planted and how well cultivars perform in your garden, keep written records. Fill in planting dates on your garden map as the season progresses. Later, make notes of harvest dates. If you would like to keep more detailed records, try keeping a garden journal, or set up a vegetable garden data file on index cards. With good records, you can discover many details about the unique climate in your garden, such as when soil warms up in spring, when problem insects emerge, and when space becomes available for replanting.

Getting Set to Plant

Once the soil is prepared, lay out your garden paths. Then rake loose soil from the pathways into the raised rows or beds. As soon as possible, mulch the pathways with leaves, straw, or another biodegradable mulch. Lay mulch thickly to keep down weeds. If you live in a region that has frequent, heavy rain, place boards down the pathways so you'll have a dry place to walk.

You can prepare planting beds and rows as much as several weeks before planting. However, if you plan to leave more than three weeks between preparation and planting, mulch the soil so it won't crust over or compact.

Plant Arrangement: There are practically no limits to the ways you can arrange plants in a vegetable garden. In a traditional row garden, you'll probably plant crops such as tomatoes and summer squash in single rows of single species. If you have raised rows or raised beds, you can interplant—mix different types of crops in one area—and use a variety of spacing patterns to maximize the number of plants in a given area.

Planting Combinations: Frequently you can practice succession cropping—growing two vegetable crops in the same space in the same growing season. You'll plant one early crop, harvest it, and then plant a warm- or hot-season crop afterward. To avoid depleting the soil, make sure one crop is a nitrogen-fixing legume, and the other a light feeder. All vegetables used for succession cropping should mature quickly. For example, in a cool climate, plant garden peas in spring, and follow them with cucumber or summer squash. Or after harvesting your early crop of spinach, plant bush beans. In warm climates, try lettuce followed by

Continued ➡

field peas, or plant pole beans and then a late crop of turnips after the bean harvest.

SEEDS AND TRANSPLANTS

Some vegetable crops grow best when seeded directly in place. Other crops benefit from being coddled indoors during the seedling stage and then grow robustly after transplanting.

Direct-Seeding: You can plant many kinds of vegetable seeds directly into prepared soil. But even when you follow seed-spacing directions given on the seed packet, direct-seeded crops often germinate too well or not well enough. When germination is excellent, thin plants ruthlessly because crowded vegetable plants will not mature properly. When direct-seeding any vegetable, set some seeds aside so you can go back in two weeks and replant vacant spaces in the row or bed.

Soil temperature and moisture play important roles in germination of vegetable seeds. Very few vegetable seeds will sprout in cold soil. High soil temperatures also inhibit germination. Also, be sure to plant seeds at the recommended planting depth, and firm the soil with your fingers or a hand tool after planting to ensure good contact of seed and soil.

Starting Seeds Indoors: To get a head start on the growing season or escape poor outdoor germination conditions, many gardeners start seeds indoors. Tomatoes, peppers, eggplant, cabbage, broccoli, cauliflower, brussels sprouts, onions, and celery are almost always handled this way. Cold-climate gardeners might add lettuce and members of the squash family to this list.

Some Like It Hot

Because vegetables differ so much in their preferred growing temperatures, planting the vegetable garden isn't a one-day job. Be prepared to spend several days over the course of early spring to early summer planting vegetable seeds and plants. You'll plant cool-weather crops a few weeks before the last spring frost. Set out warm-weather crops just after the last spring frost. Hot-weather crops cannot tolerate frost or cold soil. Unless you can protect them with a portable cold frame or row covers, plant them at least three weeks after the last spring frost. In warm climates, plant cool-weather crops again in early fall so that they grow during the fall and winter. Here is a guide to the temperature preferences of 30 common garden vegetables:

Cool	Warm	Hot
Beets	Cantaloupes	Eggplant
Broccoli	Carrots	Field peas
Cabbage	Chard	Lima beans
Cauliflower	Corn	Okra
Celery	Cucumbers	Peanuts
Garden peas	Peppers	Shell beans
Lettuce	Potatoes	Sweet
Onions	Pumpkins	potatoes
Radishes	Snap beans	Watermelons
Spinach	Squash	
Turnips	Tomatoes	

Keep in mind that most vegetable seedlings need sun to grow well. A sunny windowsill is adequate for vegetable seedlings, but natural sun plus supplemental artificial light is best. Also remember that vegetables started indoors receive very little exposure to stress factors present outdoors, such as wind, fluctuating temperatures, and intense sunlight. One week before you plan to transplant, begin hardening off vegetable plants by exposing them to these natural elements. Move them to a protected place outdoors, or put them in a cold frame.

If temperatures are erratic or windy weather is expected, use cloches to protect tender seedlings from injury for two to three weeks after transplanting. Remove cloches when the plants begin to grow vigorously—a sign that soil temperature has reached a favorable range and roots have become established.

In late summer, sun and heat can sap moisture from the new transplants of your fall crops faster than the roots can replenish it. Protect seedlings and transplants with shade covers instead of cloches. You can cover plants with cardboard boxes or flowerpots on sunny days for one week after transplanting, or you can cover them with a tent made of muslin or some other light-colored cloth.

Care during the Season

After the rush of planting, there's a lull while most of your crops are growing, flowering, and setting fruit. But regular plant care is important if you want to reap a good harvest later in the season. Get in the habit of taking regular garden walks in order to thin crops, pull weeds, and check for signs of insect and disease problems.

WEEDING

Start weed control early and keep at it throughout the season. Remove all weeds within 1 foot of your plants, or they will compete with the vegetables for water and nutrients. If you use a hoe or hand cultivator, be careful not to injure crop roots.

Some vegetables benefit from extra soil hilled up around the base of the plant. When hoeing around young corn, potatoes, tomatoes, and squash, scatter loose soil from between rows over the root zones of the plants. Once the garden soil has warmed (in late spring or early summer), mulch around your plants to suppress weeds and cut down on moisture loss. If you have areas where weeds have been a problem in the past, use a double mulch of newspapers covered with organic material such as leaves, straw, grass clippings, or shredded bark.

Another solution to weed problems is to cover beds with a sheet of black plastic. The plastic can help warm up cold soil, and it is a very effective barrier to weeds. If you do use black plastic, buy the thickest sheets you can find, and use them over and over again. Don't leave the plastic in place in the garden any longer than necessary, since exposure to sunlight will quickly degrade it. As soon as you remove the crop, rinse off and store plastic sheeting in a cool place.

WATERING

In the vegetable garden, some supplemental water is invariably needed, especially from midsummer to early fall. Most vegetables need ½ to 1 inch of water each week, and nature rarely provides water in such regular amounts. Dry weather can strengthen some vegetable plants by forcing them to develop deep roots that can seek out moisture. However, the quality of other crops suffers when plants get too little water. Tomatoes and melons need plenty of water early in the season when they're initiating foliage and fruit. However, as the fruit ripens, its quality often improves if dry conditions prevail. The opposite is true of lettuce, cabbage, and other leafy greens, which need more water as they approach maturity.

When to Water: How can you tell when your crops really need supplemental water? Leaves that droop at midday are a warning sign. If leaves wilt in midday and still look wilted the following morning, the plants are suffering. Provide water before soil becomes this dry.

If you don't water in time and the soil dries out completely, replenish soil moisture gradually, over a period of three days. If you soak dry soil quickly, your drought-stressed crops will suddenly take up large amounts of water. The abrupt change may cause tomatoes, melons, carrots, cabbage, and other vegetables to literally split their sides, ruining your crop.

Watering Methods: Watering by hand, using a spray nozzle on the end of a hose, is practical in a small garden but can be time-consuming in a large one. Sprinklers are easier to use but aren't water efficient. Some of the water from a sprinkler may fall on areas that don't need watering; and on a sunny day, some water evaporates and never reaches your plants' roots. Using sprinklers can saturate foliage, leading to conditions that favor some diseases, especially in humid climates. The one situation in which watering with a sprinkler may be the best option is when you have newly seeded beds, which need to be kept moist gently and evenly.

In terms of both water usage and economy of labor, the best way to water a vegetable garden is to use a drip irrigation system. You can buy several different types, including versatile systems that "weep" water into soil via porous tubing or pipes. These systems are most efficient when you install them between soil and mulch and use them at low pressure. Water seeps slowly into the soil, and there is very little surface evaporation.

Many gardeners make their own lines by punching holes into short lengths of garden hose or plastic pipe. You can also drip water to your vegetables by punching small holes in the bottoms of plastic milk jugs, filling the jugs with water, and placing them over the roots of thirsty plants.

Irrigation pipes do not take the place of a handy garden hose—you need both. Buy a two-headed splitter at the hardware store, and screw it onto the faucet you use for the vegetable garden. Keep the irrigation system connected to one side, leaving the other available for hand-watering or other uses.

STAKING

Many vegetables need stakes or trellises to keep them off the ground. Without support, the leaves and fruits of garden peas, tomatoes, pole beans, and some cucumbers and peppers easily become diseased. Also, many of these crops are easier to harvest when they're supported because the fruits are more accessible. You'll find many handy tips for staking and supporting crops in the individual vegetable entries later in this chapter.

FERTILIZING

Keeping your soil naturally balanced with a good organic-matter content will go a long way toward meeting the nutrient needs of your crops. Crops that mature quickly (in less than 50 days) seldom need supplemental fertilizer when growing in a healthy soil, especially if they're mulched. But vegetables that mature slowly (over an extended period) often benefit from a booster feeding in midsummer.

Plan to fertilize tomatoes, peppers, and corn just as they reach their reproductive stage of growth. Sprinkle cottonseed meal or a blended organic fertilizer beneath the plants just before a rain. Or rake back the mulch, spread a ½-inch layer of compost or rotted manure over the soil, and then put the mulch back in place. When

Continued ➡

growing plants in containers, feed them a liquid fertilizer such as manure tea every two or three weeks throughout the season. You can also use manure tea to feed vegetables grown in the ground.

Foliar fertilizing—spraying liquid fertilizer on plant leaves—is another option for mid-season fertilization. Kelp-based foliar fertilizers contain nutrients, enzymes, and acids that tend to enhance vegetables' efforts at reproduction. They're most effective when plants are already getting a good supply of nutrients through their roots. Use foliar fertilizers as a mid-season tonic for tomatoes, pole beans, and other vegetables that produce over a long period.

POLLINATION

You'll harvest leafy greens, carrots, and members of the cabbage family long before they flower. But with most other vegetables, the harvest is a fruit—the end result of pollinated blossoms. A spell of unusually hot weather can cause flowers or pollen grains to develop improperly. Conversely, a long, wet, cloudy spell can stop insects from pollinating. Either condition can leave you with few tomatoes, melons, or peppers, or with ears of corn with sparse, widely spaced kernels. The blossom ends of cucumbers and summer squash become wrinkled and misshapen when pollination is inadequate.

To prevent such problems, place like vegetables together so the plants can share the pollen they produce. Two exceptions here are hot and sweet peppers, and super-sweet and regular hybrid corn: Separate these by at least 25 feet to limit the amount of cross-pollination that takes place, or your harvest may not be true to type.

Tomatoes, corn, and beans are pollinated primarily by wind, though honeybees and other insects provide a little help transporting pollen about the plants. The presence of pollinating insects is crucial for squash, cucumbers, and melons. Plant flowers near these crops to lure bees in the right direction. You'll find more suggestions for helping with pollination in the individual vegetable entries later in this chapter.

PEST AND DISEASE MANAGEMENT

Pests and diseases of vegetable crops include insects, fungi, bacteria, and viruses, as well as larger animals such as raccoons and deer. Fortunately for organic gardeners, there are ever-increasing numbers of vegetable cultivars that are genetically resistant to insects and diseases. If you know that a pest or disease has been a problem in your garden, seek out and plant a resistant cultivar whenever possible.

Prevention can go a long way toward solving insect and disease problems in the vegetable garden. An important part of your continuing care for your garden is to practice the principles of organic pest management. It's important to realize that a weed-free or insect-free environment is not a natural one. If your garden is a diverse miniature world, with vigorous plants nourished by a well-balanced soil and an active population of native beneficial insects and microorganisms, you'll likely experience few serious pest problems.

Animal Pests Rabbits, woodchucks, deer, and other animals can wreak havoc in a vegetable garden. A sturdy fence is often the best solution.

Diseases Vegetable crop diseases are less threatening in home gardens than they are in farm fields, where crops are grown in monoculture. When many different plants are present, diseases that require specific host plants have a hard time gaining a firm foothold. Plus, a healthy, naturally balanced soil contains many beneficial microorganisms capable of controlling those that are likely to cause trouble.

Two of the best techniques for combating disease problems in the vegetable garden are rotating crops and solarizing the soil. Rotate crops by planting them in different places in the garden from one year to the next. When you plant the same vegetable continually in the same spot, disease organisms that feed on that plant flourish. When crops change from year to year, the disease organisms don't have a host plant and will not build up large populations. "Rotating Vegetable Families" presents many helpful suggestions for planning crop rotation in your garden.

Where diseases, weeds, soil-dwelling insects, or root knot nematodes seriously interfere with plant health, you can often get good control by subjecting the soil to extreme temperatures. Leave the soil openly exposed for a few weeks in the middle of winter. In the hottest part of summer, solarization can kill most weed seeds, insects, and disease organisms present in the top 4 inches of soil.

Harvest and Storage

As a general rule, harvest your vegetables early and often. Many common vegetables, such as broccoli, garden peas, lettuce, and corn, are harvested when they are at a specific and short-lived state of immaturity. Also be prompt when harvesting crops that mature fully on the plant, such as tomatoes, peppers, melons, and shell beans. Vegetable plants tend to decline after they have produced viable seeds. Prompt harvesting prolongs the productive lifespan of many vegetables.

Use "Days to Maturity" listed on seed packets as a general guide to estimate when vegetables will be ready to pick. Bear in mind that climatic factors such as temperature and day length can radically alter how long it takes for vegetables to mature. Vegetables planted in spring, when days are becoming progressively longer and warmer, may mature faster than expected. Those grown in the waning days of autumn may mature two to three weeks behind schedule.

In summer, harvest vegetables mid-morning, after the dew has dried but before the heat of midday. Wait for a mild, cloudy day to dig your potatoes, carrots, and other root crops so they won't be exposed to the sun. To make sure your homegrown

vegetables are as nutritious as they can be, harvest and eat them on the same day whenever possible.

Refrigerate vegetables that have a high water content as soon as you pick them. These include leafy greens, all members of the cabbage family, cucumbers, celery, beets, carrots, snap beans, and corn. An exception is tomatoes—they ripen best at room temperature.

Some vegetables, notably potatoes, bulb onions, winter squash, peanuts, and sweet potatoes, require a curing period to enhance their keeping qualities. See the individual entries on these vegetables later in this chapter for information on the best curing and storage conditions.

Bumper crops of all vegetables may be canned, dried, or frozen for future use. Use only your best vegetables for long-term storage, and choose a storage method appropriate for your climate. For example, you can pull cherry tomato plants and hang them upside down until the fruits dry in arid climates, but not in humid climates. In cold climates, you can mulch carrots heavily to prevent them from freezing and dig them during the winter. In warm climates, carrots left in the ground will be subject to prolonged insect damage.

Off-Season

After you harvest a crop in your vegetable garden, either turn under or pull up the remaining plant debris. Many garden pests overwinter in the skeletons of vegetable plants. If you suspect that plant remains harbor insect pests or disease organisms, put them in sealed containers for disposal with your trash, or compost them in a hot (at least 160°F) compost pile.

As garden space becomes vacant in late summer and fall, cultivate empty spaces and allow birds to gather grubs and other larvae hidden in the soil. If several weeks will pass before the first hard freeze is expected, consider planting a green manure crop such as crimson clover, rye, or annual ryegrass.

Another rite of fall is collecting leaves, which can be used as a winter mulch over garden soil or as the basis for a large winter compost heap. As you collect the leaves, shred and wet them thoroughly to promote leaching and rapid decomposition.

Rotating Vegetable Families

Susceptibility to pests and diseases runs in plant families. Leave at least two, and preferably three or more, years between the times you plant members of the same crop family in an area of your garden. When planning your rotations, keep in mind that some crops are heavy feeders, taking up large amounts of nutrients as they grow, while others are light feeders. Balance plantings of heavy feeders with soil-restoring legumes or green manure crops. Here are the seven family groups most often planted in vegetable gardens, plus ideas for rotating them.

Family Name	Common Crops	Rotation Relations
Cruciferae	Broccoli, brussels sprouts, cabbage, cauliflower, kale, radishes, turnips	High level of soil maintenance required for good root health. Heavy feeders. Precede with legumes; follow with open cultivation and compost.
Cucurbitaceae	Cucumbers, melons, squash, pumpkins, watermelons	For improved weed and insect control, precede with winter rye or wheat. Follow with legumes.
Gramineae	Wheat, oats, rye, corn	Plant before tomato- or squash-family crops to control weeds and to improve soil's ability to handle water.
Leguminosae	Beans, peas, clovers, vetches	Beneficial to soil and have few pest problems. Rotate alternately with all other garden crops whenever possible.
Liliaceae	Onions, garlic	Rotate with legumes, but avoid planting in soil that contains undecomposed organic matter.
Solanaceae	Eggplant, peppers, potatoes, tomatoes	Heavy feeders with many fungal enemies. Precede with cereal grain or grass; follow with legumes.
Umbelliferae	Carrots, parsley, dill, fennel, coriander	Moderate feeders. Precede with any other plant family, but condition soil with compost before planting. Follow with legumes or heavy mulch.

Continued ➡

Vegetable Harvest and Storage

Your refrigerator is one of your best storage options. If you have two available, set one at a cold temperature (32° to 40°F) and the other at a cool temperature (45° to 50°F). In a refrigerator set for normal operation, the temperature in the center storage section is usually between 38° and 42°F. The temperature just below the freezing unit is lower—often 30° to 35°F. The bottom of the cabinet is somewhat warmer than the center. Check temperatures in different parts of your refrigerator.

Your basement is another possible storage place. Temperatures in most heated or air-conditioned basements will usually be 65°F or higher in summer and 60°F or lower in winter. Create partitions to vary the temperature and humidity. You can use outdoor air, dirt floors, or wet sacks to vary the temperature and humidity needs. Unheated basements, if well ventilated, can provide good storage conditions for some vegetables.

This listing gives you the facts on when and how to harvest your vegetables for maximum flavor and how to store them properly to maintain freshness and taste:

COLD, MOIST

(32° to 40°F, 90 to 95% relative humidity)

Asparagus: Harvest by snapping 10- to 12-inch spears off at ground level. Store in plastic bags in refrigerator for up to one week. Freeze or can any surplus.

Beans, lima: Harvest when pods have filled. For tender limas, harvest when a bit immature; for "meaty" limas, harvest when mature. Store shelled limas in perforated plastic bags in the refrigerator for about one week. Surplus limas can be canned or frozen.

Beets: Begin harvest when beet is 1 inch in diameter. Tender tops make excellent greens. Main harvest is when beets are 2 to 3 inches across. Harvest spring-planted beets before hot weather; fall beets, before the first light freeze. For storage, wash roots, trim tops to ½ inch, place in perforated plastic bags, and store in the refrigerator or cold, moist cellar for two to four months.

Broccoli: Harvest terminal head while florets are still tight and of good green color. Smaller side heads will develop. Store in perforated plastic bags for up to one week in the refrigerator. Freeze any surplus.

Cabbage: Harvest when heads are solid. Store cabbage in the refrigerator, cold cellar, or outdoor pit for up to two months.

Carrots: Harvest spring crops before hot weather; fall ones, before the first light freeze. For storage, wash roots, trim tops to ½ inch, and place in perforated plastic bags. Store in the refrigerator or cold, moist cellar for two to four months.

Cauliflower: Tie outer leaves above the head when curd diameter reaches 1 to 2 inches (except purple types). Heads will be ready for harvest in about two weeks. Cauliflower may be stored in perforated plastic bags in the refrigerator for up to two weeks. Freeze any surplus.

COOL, MOIST

(45° to 50°F, 80 to 90% relative humidity)

Beans, snap: Pods will be most tender when seeds inside are one-fourth normal size. They become fibrous as the beans mature. Store up to one week in perforated plastic bags in the warm part of refrigerator. Can or freeze surplus.

Cucumbers: Harvest cucumbers when they are about 1½ to 2½ inches in diameter and 5 to 8 inches long. Pickling cucumbers will be more blocky and not as long as slicers. Store slicing cucumbers up to one week in plastic bags in the warm part of the refrigerator. Cool pickling cucumbers quickly in ice water; keep up to two days in a plastic bag in the refrigerator.

Eggplant: Harvest when fruits are nearly full grown but color is still bright. Keep in warm part of the refrigerator for about one week.

Peppers, sweet: Harvest when fruits are firm and full-sized. For red fruits, leave fruits on the plant until ripe. Store in the warm part of refrigerator in plastic bags for two to three weeks.

Squash, summer: Harvest when fruits are young and tender. Skin should be easily penetrated with the thumbnail. Store for up to one week in perforated plastic bags in the refrigerator. Surplus can be frozen.

COOL, DRY

(45° to 55°F, 50 to 60% relative humidity)

Onions, dry: Harvest when the tops have fallen over and the necks have shriveled. Remove tops, place in shallow boxes or mesh bags, and cure in an open garage or barn for three to four weeks. Store in mesh bags in a cool place. Keep ventilated during humid, muggy weather.

Peppers, hot: Pull plants late in the season and hang to dry in the sun or a warm place. Store in a dry, cool place, such as a basement.

WARM, DRY

(55° to 60°F, 60 to 70% relative humidity)

Pumpkins; Squash, winter: Harvest when skin is hard and the colors darken. Harvest before frost. Cut the fruits from the vine with a portion of stem attached. Store spread out on shelves so air can circulate.

WARM, MOIST

(55° to 60°F, 80 to 85% relative humidity)

Tomatoes: Ripe tomatoes will keep for a week at 55° to 60°F. Harvest green, mature tomatoes before frost, and keep at 55° to 70°F; for faster ripening, keep at 65° to 70°F. Mature green fruits should approach normal size and have a whitish green skin color. Keep them three to five weeks by wrapping each tomato in newspaper. Inspect for ripeness each week.

Text source: Arthur E. Gaus and Henry DiCarlo, "Vegetable Harvest and Storage," *Grounds for Gardening: A Horticultural Guide,* University of Missouri-Columbia.

You can also till shredded leaves directly into your garden soil.

Barbara W. Ellis

Designing a Companion-Planted Garden

Most of us have heard that marigolds help keep insects out of the vegetable garden or that nothing will grow near a black walnut tree. But while some of these claims seem to hold true, others do not. Just where do these horticultural maxims come from? Is there any truth to the notion that growing certain plants together can help or hinder their growth?

COMPANION PLANTING AS A TRADITION

For centuries, gardeners and farmers have cultivated different crops together in the same space to maximize available resources. American Indians, for example, used a corn-bean-squash inter-planting scheme that balanced the requirements of each crop for light, water, and nutrients. The practice of companion planting, growing two or more crops simultaneously in a given area to achieve a specific benefit, is still common among subsistence farmers and organic gardeners in many parts of the world today. On large-scale, mechanized farms, however, single-crop cultivation has been the norm for several decades.

In recent years, as the limitations and ill effects of pesticides, chemical fertilizers, and other modern practices have become more apparent, scientists have begun looking more seriously at companion planting and other "old-fashioned" methods once considered inefficient. Small-scale farmers and backyard gardeners who have kept the interplanting tradition alive now serve as a valuable source of information on the complex interactions of crops with each other and with the surrounding environment.

Yet even those who practice companion planting do not know why some interplanting methods seem to work while others don't. Only careful research, combined with the experience and intuition of practitioners, will reveal which plant combinations are most beneficial and why. In the meantime, gardeners are in a unique position to take advantage of what is already known and to try out new combinations in their own plots at home.

Benefits of Companion Planting

Not all crops respond to companion planting in the same way. In fact, some do worse when combined with other crops than if they are grown by themselves. In many cases, however, the positive effects of interplanting are striking.

Some crops, for example, show increased yields when combined with other plants. Studies suggest that different crops planted together may take better advantage of sunlight than those grown separately. Think of cool season crops such as lettuce or spinach. The intense light (and heat) of midsummer sun may damage their leaves. Planting in the filtered shade of a row of tomatoes can allow these plants to receive enough light for good growth, while preventing heat injury.

Scientists have also theorized that interplanted crops make better use of soil nutrients and water than do crops cultivated apart from others. Corn interplanted with soybeans may stimulate the beans, a legume, to fix more nitrogen in the soil. Whatever the reason, you can reap a greater harvest from many of your vegetables if you are willing to

Continued ➡

spend the extra time to learn about and practice companion planting.

By interplanting certain crops, you can also improve the quality of your soil. Many plants supply nutrients to the soil that are beneficial to crops nearby. In addition, some plants with thick roots work the soil, improving tilth and drainage.

Companion planting is particularly useful in keeping pest and disease problems under control. If you grow only one crop at a time, you are likely to attract only a small variety of insects or diseases, but these may be great in number and can wreak considerable havoc in your garden. On the other hand, if you plant two or more crops together, you may have a large variety of pests, but there will be few of each in number. In the first instance, you are creating a less stable environment where one disease or insect population can easily take over all the rest; in the latter case, the diversity of plants allows for a more stable environment in which the various pests keep each other in check.

You can also include certain plants in your interplanting scheme that will repel insects and thus prevent pest damage to other crops in the vicinity. Companion plants can even be used to attract beneficial insects to the garden.

Designing a Companion Garden

Selecting the right arrangements or combinations of plants for the companion garden can be tricky. You must aim for a balance between the benefits of mixing crops and the possible competition between those crops for space, sunlight, nutrients, and water. Lettuce interplanted with kidney beans may benefit from shading by the bean plants; this advantage will have little value if the beans compete too strongly with the lettuce for available water and nutrients, however.

Companion planting of reputedly repellent or attractant plants also requires careful investigation. Research has shown that some plants traditionally relied upon to repel pests may have other, harmful effects on companion crops or may actually attract some harmful insects. Some species of marigolds have been shown to repel harmful nematodes but may cause stunting of some vegetable crops. Tansy is an herb which may repel some insects but has been shown in some studies to attract other pests.

Every garden is different, too; what works in one may not work in another. Soil, available light, and many other factors will affect the outcome of any given planting. Even your own goals as a gardener probably differ from those of your neighbor. For example, what you consider a "high yield" may be a "moderate harvest" to others.

Nevertheless, certain companion planting arrangements that have worked for many gardeners are worth trying. Even if you do not see spectacularly increased yields or reduced pest damage, you will have gained a better awareness of how plants interact with one another and their environment. Gradually, as you gain more experience with your own particular growing conditions, you may want to experiment with new companion planting schemes.

Fencing the Garden

How many times have you carefully planted a vegetable garden, only to have the fruits of your efforts devoured by the wildlife sharing your property? While plant lovers are typically wildlife aficionados as well, the different objects of our admiration are often incompatible, especially when it comes to hungry animals and edible plants. The only solution—barring exterminating the animals, an unacceptable and generally impossible option for most of us—is to provide barriers to keep flora and fauna apart.

There are many types of fencing from which to choose. What you end up erecting will depend on the culprits doing the damage and the amount of time and money you want to spend on the project. Whatever design you select, remember that you should put up fencing before the animals have begun rummaging in your garden; if they have already munched on your lettuce, they are likely to try to return for another meal.

Chicken Wire Fences

One of the best ways to ward off midsized animals, including groundhogs and rabbits, is to erect a 3-foot-high chicken wire fence around your garden. By digging a trench and lining it with wire mesh before you set the posts, you will keep moist, if not all, of the burrowing types from entering your plot. Try spacing the posts far enough apart so that the fence is a bit floppy; animals are less likely to scale a floppy fence this size than a tight one.

Chicken wire fences are also suitable for keeping deer out of your garden. However, since

this type of fencing must be 8 to 12 feet tall to be effective, it can be both expensive and difficult to erect as well as to maintain. A high chicken wire fence is often topped with strands of barbed wire to extend its height, but this tends to be aesthetically unappealing.

Double Fences for Deer

One relatively simple and inexpensive solution to the deer problem is to erect two 3-foot-high fences made of three strings each and spaced 3 feet apart. Apparently, deer are reluctant to jump over a low fence if another fence is visible just on the other side.

If you decide to use this design, be sure to select string that is easily seen by the animals. You may want to add height to the fences in wintertime.

Another low-profile barrier that is surprisingly effective in keeping deer away is the double mesh fence. For this design, try stringing 4-foot-high, 12½-gauge mesh fencing between metal stakes spaced 5 feet apart. Allow 5 feet between the outer and inner fences. Keep the area between the two

---

Making a Scarecrow

Scarecrows have been scaring birds away—or in some cases, amusing them—for as long as man has cultivated crops. Some say these whimsical stuffed figures were first used by tribes in central or northern Europe; others claim that pre-Columbian Indians were ahead of the Europeans. Whatever its origin, the scarecrow is a common fixture in gardens and farms across the world today.

Why Build a Scarecrow?

Scarecrows are fun; no one will argue with that. With just a little straw, wood, and some old clothes, it's amazing what creative designs some gardeners come up with. Not only are they an outlet for our creativity, they're also an excellent way to involve children in the garden. Young would-be gardeners who balk at the idea of "helping" in the family vegetable plot are easily enticed by a scarecrow-making project.

Yet scarecrows serve a serious purpose, too. Each year, birds destroy millions of dollars' worth of crops including wheat, corn, sunflowers, and various kinds of fruit. Individual farmers have experienced losses of up to 75 percent or more due to the voracious appetite of birds. For the backyard gardener, too, birds pose a threat to tender young plants. Crows, blackbirds, blue jays, and many other winged creatures have been known to swoop down and snatch seedlings from the ground or to peck holes in newly ripened fruit. Thanks to scarecrows, farmers and gardeners have at least a fighting chance to save their crops from being destroyed by birds.

How Scarecrows Work

It is a common joke that scarecrows attract more birds than they frighten. Indeed, it is not unusual to see a scarecrow with at least one or two birds perched on its shoulders at any given time. If properly designed and utilized, however, these human effigies can be fairly effective in protecting your vegetable garden.

The idea behind scarecrows is simple: Put up a figure that resembles a human being (one of the birds' predators), and the birds will stay away. But there's a catch: Sooner or later, birds wise up and realize that your creative masterpiece will not harm them; in fact, it takes some

birds less than a week to figure things out. So you must try to be as ingenious as possible in the short time you have to scare them away. For example, by hanging aluminum pie plates or other shiny objects from your scarecrow's arms, you may be able to buy yourself and your plants a few days' time. Noisemakers, including pie plates banging together in the breeze, can also help to ward birds off a little longer.

The timing of your scarecrow's debut is important, too. You may want to bring your straw man out as soon as your seeds begin to germinate. Or if the birds in your area seem to go more for the ripe tomatoes or cantaloupes than for the seedlings, try putting it up in your garden just as the fruit begins to mature. The key is to use the novelty of your scarecrow's presence for all it's worth.

How to Make a Scarecrow

To build a scarecrow from scratch, you need only a few materials and a willingness to use your imagination.

1. Select two 2 x 4 stakes measuring about 4 to 5 feet long to serve as the legs. Sharpen the ends so that they can be driven into the ground easily.

2. Find an old pair of pants and put them on over the stakes.

3. Put the stakes into the ground at an angle so that they join at the top.

4. For the backbone, take a 2 x 4 measuring about 3 feet long and nail it to the top of the legs.

5. To make the arms, take a 2 x 4 measuring about 4 feet long and nail it perpendicular to the backbone, above the legs.

6. Stuff the pants with straw, then slip a shirt on over the shoulders and fill it with straw.

7. Fill an old pillowcase with straw to make the head, and tie the pillowcase opening closed around the top of the backbone.

8. For the hands, stuff some gloves with straw, then fasten them on the ends of the arms.

9. Draw a face and add any embellishments you like, such as hair, a hat, or a pipe.

Continued ➜

The Edible Garden
CHAPTER 4

Companion Planting Options

Here are some companion plantings you may want to try, with information on the type of interaction between the crops and whether the pairing has been confirmed by research studies or is simply part of companion planting tradition or folklore.

Sample Combinations	Relationship	Folklore or Fact?	Tips/Comments
For Interplanting in Neighboring Rows			
Tomatoes with cabbage	Tomatoes repel diamondback moths and flea beetles. Impoved flavor and growth.	Shown in research studies. Folklore	Tomatoes will shade transplants for fall crop from summer heat and sun.
Corn with snap beans or soybeans	Beans enhance growth of corn, possibly due to capability to fix nitrogen.	Research backs this claim in certain specific planting arrangements.	Alternate double rows of corn with double bean rows to ensure good corn pollination.
Peanuts with corn or squash	Intercropping increases yields of both crops.	Shown in research studies.	Leave plenty of space at planting for heavy vegetative growth of peanuts.
Peas with spinach, lettuce, or Chinese cabbage	Peas provide shading and wind protection for young transplants.	Traditional practice	Vining peas must be started early and trained on fence or trellis to provide good protection.
Asparagus with tomatoes, parsley, or basil	Companions help control asparagus beetles.	Folklore.	Allow 5 ft. between rows when interplanting tomatoes to avoid crowding.
For Interplanting within a Row			
Radish, onions, or beets with lettuce, beans, cabbage, or tomatoes	Various beneficial interactions including: Lettuce makes radishes tender, onions help deter weeds and repel some insects.	Mostly folklore.	Fast-growing crops can be grown around slower-growing crops. Harvest before competition between crops has detrimental effect.
Lettuce or spinach with winter squash or cucumbers	Makes better use of space and soil materials.	Traditional practice.	Lettuce and spinach are harvested before vine crops spread over bed.
Cabbage with garlic	Garlic reputedly repels many harmful insects and helps prevent disease.	Folklore; some research shows garlic contains bactericidal and fungicidal substances.	Garlic has a cold requirement for bulbing. Try as a fall planting; allow garlic to overwinter.
Corn with beans, cucumbers, melons, or squash	Makes best use of light and bed space.	Traditional practice; some research shows beans promote corn growth.	Border rows of corn with vine crops; plant beans and corn in alternating hills; 3-4 plants per hill.
Other Arrangements			
Lettuce, cabbage, bush beans, basil, seed onions, tomatoes, beets in 1-ft.-square blocks	Various beneficial interactions, good for seed-starting beds.	Mostly folklore; research shows pest repellent properties for some crops.	Block planting is best for compact, low-growing plants.
Radishes planted in a circle around a hill of bush squash or cucumbers	Radishes repel vine borers and cucumber beetles.	Folklore.	Circle planting is a way to surround crops with repellent plants.
Strips of clover or alfalfa between corn rows	Helps control weeds and conserve moisture.	Traditional practice.	Sod strips may require periodic mowing. Strip plantings of tall crops with tender low-growing plants can reduce wind damage.

fences bare if you want to watch for other, smaller intruders such as rabbits.

ELECTRIC FENCING

Electric fences are often the last resort for gardeners, yet many people swear by their effectiveness, especially in areas where wildlife has done extensive damage. The main thing to remember is that this kind of fencing must be treated with respect. If there are children in the area, be sure to spend time explaining to them exactly why the fence is dangerous and where they are permitted to play. (Of course, if the children are very young, you may want to consider another kind of fencing.) A properly designed electric fence will surprise anyone or anything that touches it, not hurt them. In fact, the barrier is more psychological than real. It gives a strong buzzing feeling that makes animals back off when they've touched it once or twice, and they'll avoid it afterwards, often even if the current is turned off. Since you have to be in contact with the ground to receive a shock, birds can safely sit on the wire.

A single strand of electric wire strung at a distance of 1 foot outside your garden's chicken wire fence will give additional protection against small animals climbing over or burrowing under the wire fence. If deer are the main nuisance in your area, try stringing the electric wire 3 feet off the ground at a distance of 3 feet from your chicken wire fence. This fence works on the same

principle as the double mesh fence and will be most effective if the chicken wire fence is at least 4 feet high.

Plants and debris that collect against the wire can drain the fence's power, so you will need to keep the area around it clean. You should also check the fence's charge periodically with a voltage tester.

Vegetables the Low-Maintenance Way

Barbara W. Ellis, Joan Benjamin, and Deborah L. Martin

If you do just a little planning before you plant and take the right steps to improve your soil, you'll find that vegetable gardening can take a lot less time and labor than you ever dreamed. This section shows you how to design food hardens for easiest care and maximum harvests.

Set Your "Sites" for Success

Before you prepare a new vegetable garden, use your head. Vegetable gardens are easiest to maintain when they have no strikes against them, like deep shade or rocky soil. Here's a checklist of what you need for success. If your site doesn't match up, choose one of the options listed for making it right.

■ **At least six hours of full sunlight.** What if you don't have enough sun? Consider growing vegetables in containers on the driveway or deck where the increased warmth will boost growth.

Otherwise, share a sunny site in a friend's yard. Vegetables simply won't be successful in the shade.

■ **Good drainage.** If your only sunny site is soggy, building raised beds will payoff big in the long run. They require some work to loosen the soil and heap it up, but once done, you'll have perfect drainage forevermore. Another choice is to build a framed raised bed using lumber or concrete blocks and fill it with good soil.

■ **Convenient access to the hose, house, and compost pile.** Think how many steps you'll save if your vegetable garden is close to your house, and your water source and compost supply are near your vegetables. It's nice to have a dry place to store tools near the garden, as well. If there is no outdoor building handy to the garden, a plastic trash can with a lid makes a quick storage bin for the essentials.

■ **Limited competition from large trees.** Trees compete with your vegetables for essential water and nutrients, so locate your garden as far as possible from hungry, thirsty tree roots. If you have only a few sunny spots and tree roots are nearby, try planting in containers or framed raised beds to keep your vegetables above the competition.

■ **Protection from marauding pets and children.** You can use fences, hedges, and even plantings of large perennials like ornamental grasses to

Continued ➡

channel children and pets away from vegetables. Or keep plants out of harm's way with raised beds.

Design Convenience into Your Garden

You can plant your garden without planning, but you'll pay for it with added effort when it's time to improve the soil, pick produce, water, or fight weeds. You don't need an elaborate plan to save labor. This garden features a variety of ideas that will make your vegetable gardening easier and more enjoyable.

Save Work by Making Smart Plant Choices

It takes most of us firm resolve (or an avalanche of zucchini) to limit the number and variety of vegetables we plant. But remember, planting decisions frame your workload for the season ahead. Bite the bullet and take these suggestions to heart.

Grow what you enjoy eating. If no one likes broccoli, why bother with it? In other words, grow the crops that are satisfying for you and your family. You may decide to grow arugula or snap peas that you couldn't otherwise afford, for example. Maybe all you really want is fresh sweet corn or tomatoes. If that's the case, don't waste space on crops that end up in the compost pile.

Forget about crops that don't do well in your garden. If you live in the cool Pacific Northwest, heat-loving cantaloupes are a struggle, whereas salad greens and beets will flourish. Likewise, if the frost flattens your 'Big Boy' tomatoes every year in Vermont, maybe it's time to switch to small tomatoes that ripen faster. You'll get big flavor with a cultivar like 'Oregon Spring,' which matures in just 60 days.

Select gourmet vegetables that aren't locally available. Why grow the same tomatoes, lettuce, and snap beans you can buy at the nearest produce stand when you can grow more flavorful choices like 'Royal Burgundy' beans, 'Lolla Rosso' lettuce, or 'Tappy's Best' tomato? Many of the tastiest types aren't grown for market because they lose quality rapidly (like baby lettuce, snow peas, or squash blossoms) or simply aren't cost-effective to grow because people don't know about them. (Ever tried mizuna, fava beans, mâche (corn salad), or "Gilfeather" turnips?) Order some seed catalogs that specialize in gourmet vegetables and choose the plants that pique your palate.

Select cultivars adapted to your growing region. There are vegetable cultivars ideal for every growing region. Instead of buying seed from big seed houses that aim for the average growing climate, patronize regional seed companies. Many focus on continuing old cultivars proven in your area and they also search out and develop new strains.

Grow only as much as you will eat. Do you really need ten tomato plants? Using tomatoes as an example, two plants per person is plenty if fresh salads are the main use. All you need are five to six plants if you want to preserve enough for year-round eating.

Select cultivars that bear throughout the season. You can avoid having to deal with one big harvest—and more produce than your family can eat—if you choose vegetables that bear fruit over a long season. If the crops you like tend to ripen all at once, plant a mixture of early, mid-season, and late-maturing cultivars to spread out the harvest.

For example, try planting a mid-season corn cultivar like 'Honey 'N Pearl' (78 days) at the same time as a later-maturing cultivar like 'Silver Queen' (92 days) to avoid a corn glut. The same technique works great for tomatoes, too.

Grow what you will be home to enjoy. If you vacation the last two weeks of August, plan your crops around your trip. Plant your corn crop so it will peak before or after your trip, for example. Likewise, if you're going to be away or super-busy when peas need to be picked, skip the peas this season.

Be realistic about putting up the harvest. These days, many time-pressed gardeners are opting to "eat what's in season" instead of spending the time it takes to manage and can or freeze large harvests. You can save time and effort if you grow only as much fresh produce as your family can eat—and not enough to fill the freezer. Consider using the extra garden space for spinach, broccoli, collards, and other hardy crops that you can eat fresh well into winter. Fresh vegetables are always tastier and more nutritious than frozen or canned.

Tuck In Your Crops

Before you dig a new garden, look for ready-made planting areas. You just might find a few places where you can tuck in some lettuce or a packet of snap beans with no more effort than clearing a few weeds and adding some compost.

You also may find spring vacancies in flower beds. Finding a place for a few "spot" gardens may allow you to grow all the salad greens, radishes, and snap beans your family can use without turning up new ground.

Make a Planting Plan That Saves Time

Before you turn a shovelful of soil in a new garden bed, take time to consider what features will make that bed easy to manage. You'll be living with your design for at least one season, so you'll certainly save enough time, energy, and aggravation to make the planning well worthwhile. Besides, you can do your planning in early spring or late fall when there aren't as many garden priorities.

Consider garden size. Keeping your garden small is the simplest way to keep it low maintenance. If you're a new gardener and don't know how much is too much, begin with an area no larger than 100 square feet. If you've been gardening a while, take a hard look at how much time you want to spend in your garden and which crops will give you the most return.

Picture your space before you dig. Rectangles and squares are the easiest bed shapes for most of us to work with. Preview your garden layout by using a garden hose to represent the perimeter of the garden. Then lay out some newspaper weighted with rocks to mark where the actual beds will be dug. What's left will be the pathways. Then stand back and look at the design and see if it looks workable. Imagine what you're going to plant where. Get out the wheelbarrow and any other garden equipment you use and see if you can reach each bed easily. Consider any hidden hazards, like the septic tank, electrical lines, or the kids' soccer field. Before you put the newspaper away, use stakes to mark the beds. It doesn't hurt to commit your plan to paper, too, before you lose any bright ideas about what you're going to plant where.

Take a look at garden length. Once you've prepared the soil in your beds, you'll have to walk around them to get from one side of the garden to the other. (Walking on the soil will compact it, destroying all your hard-earned soil improve-

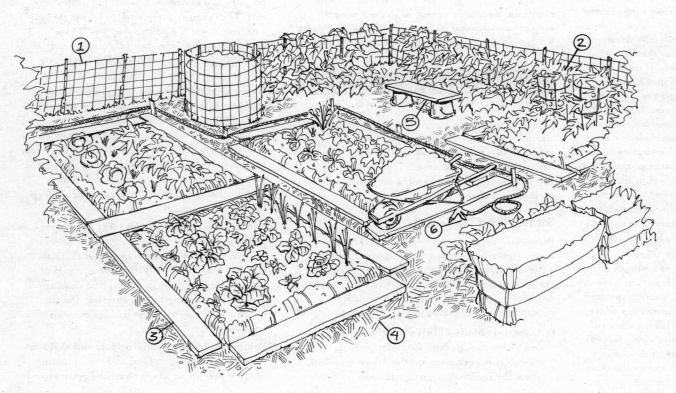

1. Train vines to save space. One way to keep vines like cucumbers from wandering is to train them up a fence. Fruits hang down for easy picking.

2. Stake tomato cages. Insert a stake inside each tomato cage to hold it in place and keep it from toppling over under heavy fruit load.

3. Use wooden planks for easy access. Wooden planks in the pathways make it easier to maneuver wheelbarrows and other equipment around raised beds.

4. Mulch to pathways to control weeds. Use bark mulch to keep pathways clear of weeds all year long.

5. Plant to rest. Make sure you take frequent breaks to keep your back in working order. A bench made out of two buckets and a wooden plank makes an inexpensive seat.

6. Keep your hoses controlled. Buy hose guides, or make ones like the bamboo guides shown here, to keep unruly hoses from hurting plants.

Continued ➡

ment.) Beds 5 to 15 feet long work well in small gardens. You can increase the length up to 30 feet in larger gardens. If you're planning framed raised beds, plank "bridges" from one edge to the other make it easy to cross from side to side in a long garden.

Keep plants within reach. You should be able to reach the middle of planting areas without trampling the beds—4 feet is a comfortable stretch for most gardeners. If you've never planted in beds before, make some sample patches before you plant; experiment with 3 feet, 3½ feet, and 4 feet and see what feels best to you.

Leave room for you! Pathways between beds need to be at least 1½ feet wide to allow for foot traffic. They should be at least 3 feet wide if you intend to take a wheelbarrow into the garden with you. In a large garden, plan for a central crossroads at least 4 feet wide to accommodate the garden cart and to allow some leeway for hauling mulch, compost, and other supplies.

Should You Grow Row by Row?

Once you've selected the best site for your vegetable garden and the crops you want to grow, you'll need to decide whether to plant in rows or beds.

GARDENING IN ROWS

Gardens planted in narrow, parallel rows or strips with paths in between are easy to plan. The soil is usually turned over each spring to clear space for new crops; it's a simple matter if you have a tiller. Row gardens are well suited to large crops like corn, pole beans, tomatoes, and potatoes.

> ### Multiple Plantings Mean Manageable Harvests
>
> By planting crops over several weeks (a technique known as succession planting) rather than all at once, you'll get a steady supply of produce instead of a one-time onslaught. How much you pick at any one time depends, of course, on how much you plant each time. The idea is to get as much as you need for a week or two, plus a little extra if you plan to store any vegetables long-term. That way, you'll never be overwhelmed. Succession planting works best with crops that ripen all at once like lettuce and other salad greens, bush beans, and corn.
>
> To plan on a continuous but not overwhelming harvest, spread out planting times throughout the season. For example, three beds of lettuce, each planted two weeks apart, will be ready for harvest about two weeks apart as well.

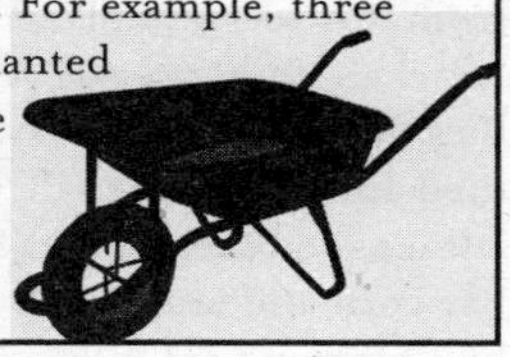

On the down side, row gardens require lots of space, and you have to spend time maintaining lots of walkways where you don't grow food. Row gardens generally have less drought resistance, and the large expanses of unplanted soil are an open invitation to weeds. Frequent cultivation also depletes soil organic matter, which increases the need for compost and fertilizer. Mechanical tillers also cause petroleum pollution.

GARDENING IN BEDS

Crops grown in beds are set out in wide areas or blocks not separated by rows. Paths between beds allow easy access to vegetables but minimize wasted space. That means you can grow more vegetables in a smaller area than with row gardens. Beds can be

tilled each season—but once you're satisfied with the location and layout, it's easier and more economical to maintain them without tilling. Because plants are spaced close together and you're not maintaining wide walkways, bed gardens need less weeding and less watering. Beds are most suitable for smaller vegetables like greens, root crops, and cole crops.

On the down side, it takes more work to prepare beds the first season. They also may be harder to design at first if you're used to planting in rows, and they aren't well suited to mechanical cultivation.

PICK YOUR STYLE

In large gardens, a combination approach works well. Plant the big crops in rows and the smaller stuff, like salad greens, cole crops, and root crops, in beds. For small gardens, beds are the obvious choice since they maximize space. Not only will you harvest more food than if you planted in rows, but grouping vegetables in blocks conserves water and reduces weeding since the leaves shade the soil between plants.

Soil Preparation without Tears

Believe it or not, sweating and straining are optional activities when it comes to making new garden beds. Try the techniques that follow for easy ways to make gardens that produce trouble-free harvests year after year.

You'll find a range of options—from beds you never dig to ones that take some effort initially but are quite easy to maintain ever after. Choose the method that fits your site and lifestyle best.

NO-DIG GARDEN BEDS

Yes, you can grow great vegetables without ever turning over the soil! Here's how.

1. Mow the area with the mower blade set as low as it will go.

2. Spread a six-page-thick layer of newspaper over the spot and water it well.

3. Cover the newspaper with at least 2 inches of compost or good soil mix. Add some balanced organic fertilizer at the rate listed on the package.

4. Rake the bed smooth and sprinkle it with water until it is evenly moist. Wait a day or two and then plant, cutting through the newspaper if setting out transplants.

Believe it or not, this method works fine the first season for everything but long-rooted crops like carrots. Plus, there's no need to dig these beds every year. Just add 2 inches of compost on top and plant.

After three years you should be able to grow anything, and you can cut back the compost you add each spring to a maintenance amount of ⅛ to ¼ inch. If you'd rather, add the compost as a side-dressing around plants in the summer.

JUST-A-BIT-OF-DIGGING GARDEN BEDS

This method requires a large supply of compost-making materials and a half-hour of shoveling per bed. The advantage is that you'll have terrific soil by the end of one season.

1. **Pile up organic matter.** Start by piling up organic matter as if you were making a compost pile. You're aiming for a pile about 4 feet wide and 2 feet high and as long as you want to make it. The combination of ingredients isn't critical, but an even mix of leafy green stuff and tougher materials like leaves and stalks is ideal. Shredded leaves are a real bonus.

Sprinkle in a little soil on the pile to start the decomposition process, and moisten the ingredients with water. They should be as wet as a wrung-out sponge.

2. **Dig a path.** Once your pile is in place, dig a path about 2 inches deep and 2 feet wide all around it, pitching the soil over the pile. You want to end up with 2 to 4 inches of soil covering the pile.

3. **Add fertilizer.** Sprinkle on a thin layer (⅛ to ¼ inch is plenty) of finished compost. Or apply a balanced commercial organic fertilizer at the rate listed on the package.

4. **Rake it smooth.** Rake the bed smooth and then sprinkle it with water until it is evenly moist.

5. **Wait.** Sit tight for a week to allow the pile to settle a bit.

6. **Plant.** That's all there is to it!

This method has two special benefits. First, it provides bottom heat early in the season from all the decomposing organic matter, a real boost in cool climates. Second, all that organic matter decomposes into an excellent foundation for your garden bed.

Finding enough organic matter to make a 4 x 2-foot base isn't as overwhelming as it sounds. Just drive around the neighborhood during leaf-raking and lawn-cutting seasons and you can rescue tons of bagged leaves and grass clippings destined for the landfill. You may want to stock up on bed-making materials in the spring and fall, too, when supplies are abundant.

LOTS-OF-DIGGING GARDEN BEDS—BUT JUST THIS ONCE

You've probably heard about the benefits of double digging, a method used to create great soil that has excellent drainage, warms early in the season, and provides perfect conditions for intensive planting. But double digging is a lot of work, isn't it?

Well, yes, but once the soil has been prepared this way, you hardly have to lift a finger again. You'll rarely need to water since double-dug beds are rich in moisture-holding organic matter. Your soil will be fertile without fertilizing, so you'll get bumper crops of vegetables—even if you plant close to make the most of your hard-earned space. Of course, close spacing means fewer weeds, so that's another task you can avoid. Plus, you'll have soil that's ready to plant whenever you're ready—even in soggy seasons.

For vegetable gardeners pressed for space or those with serious drainage problems, double-dug raised beds are ideal.

Tips for Gardening on Tough Sites

When difficult conditions make gardening seem like a lost cause, look for ways to grow around, above, or below the problem. Here are some ideas to get you started.

Grow veggies in the lawn. Is your garden site presently a lawn? If so, consider leaving the grass in place in the pathways and just digging up the growing space you'll need. This minimizes weeds and erosion, and the grass pathways are easy to keep up by mowing. Be sure to make the pathways at least as wide as your lawn mower.

Create instant raised beds. Is poor soil giving you a headache and backache? Cover the growing area with straw bales laid flat and placed end to end. Spread a 2-inch layer of compost on top and then plant. The bales will decompose within a year, creating a wonderful growing base. Good crops to try in "bale beds" include bush beans, peas, greens, okra, and

Continued ➡

eggplants. Large vining vegetables like squash, melons, and tomatoes also perform well, especially if you make a hole in the bales, pour in a bucket of composted manure and then set in transplants.

Create soil on barren sites. Are you a gardener without any soil? If you live on bedrock, or if the bulldozer that leveled your lot stole your soil, here's a solution. Make an enclosure out of lumber, stone, cinder blocks, or even straw bales. (Or buy a kid's sandbox!) The sides should be at least 8 inches high—1 foot is ideal. Put an inch of gravel or sand in the bottom to ensure good drainage. Then fill the enclosure with a mixture of good soil and compost and plant. If you want to economize on soil, fill the bottom half of the enclosure with a mix of organic matter—shredded leaves, sawdust, rotted manure, and weeds.

Save water with sunken beds. Are you gardening in the desert? Take a hint from ancient Indian tribes and plant your crops in sunken beds that capture and conserve water. To make a sunken bed, dig out a bed 1½ feet deep. Reserve the best soil in a wheelbarrow or on a tarp, and place the rest in the paths. Mix the good soil with some compost, fill the trench with 6 inches of this mix, and you're ready to plant.

Work Your Soil with Roots

Let the roots of robust seedlings cultivate the soil for you before you plant. Here's how.

1. Sow quick-growing seeds like mustard and radish by broadcasting them thickly in early spring. Several weeks later, chop the young plants out with a sharp hoe.

2. Ventilate the soil by rocking the tines of a garden fork back and forth in the soil. Or use a broadfork, which is especially designed for aerating the soil.

Easy Steps for Keeping Your Soil Healthy—and Your Vegetables Happy

Vegetables need fertile soil with lots of organic matter to grow their best and stay problem free. You can keep your soil in tiptop form by mulching and adding compost to the soil every year, but collecting, hauling, and spreading soil amendments takes work. Isn't there an easier way? Absolutely! The tips below will help you maintain your soil but let you relax the endless hunt for tons of compost and mulch-making materials.

Concentrate your efforts in beds. Instead of turning and amending your entire garden area each spring, limit your soil improvements just to your planting beds. It's a lot more economical and less time-consuming to enrich the areas where you'll actually plant crops and leave the pathways alone.

Don't till every season. As long as your soil isn't compacted, there's no need to till or dig every season. Keep your feet out of your beds, and you'll have won the battle against soil compaction.

Let plants do the tilling. Letting plants do your work is better for you and the soil. And all you need to do to accomplish this is keep something growing at all times. It's as simple as sowing seeds: As soon as one crop is finished, replace it with another. The constant action of roots and a myriad of other living processes will keep the soil loose and friable.

Grow organic matter for your soil. Instead of making tons of compost to keep your soil provided with plenty of organic matter, carry a single seed packet to your garden and grow green manures. You can plant green manure crops throughout the growing season, whenever it's convenient for you,

and they'll produce the organic matter your soil needs right where you need it.

Keep Green Manures on Hand

If you'd prefer to follow through on your intentions to plant green manures (instead of having those plants turn into good intentions), make sure you have seeds on hand year-round. Otherwise, the day that you pick to plant your crop may be the day you realize you forgot (again!) to order the seeds. Instead, order seeds like clover, hairy vetch, or soybeans when you place your next seed order. Whenever you have the time—whether it's spring, summer, or fall—you'll be ready to plant a soil-protecting cover over any garden bare spots.

Super-Simple Soil Improvement with Green Manures

Spring planting can be a snap if you grow green manure crops in summer or fall. With the simple system outlined below, all you'll need to do is rake away the winter-killed green manure and sow your seeds. Plus, you'll have a healthy, productive garden—all without digging, hauling compost, or buying fertilizer. Here's a walk through the seasonal tasks for the easiest garden you can imagine.

FIRST SPRING

A few weeks before you're ready to plant your vegetable crops, sow a mixture of seeds like radishes, mustard, or rape—any quick-growing crops that like cool weather—for an early-season green manure crop. Sow the seed thickly. A few days before you're ready to plant your vegetables, chop out these "sacrificial crops," leaving the residues to decompose.

SUMMER

Keep something growing in your garden beds at all times. If you have some empty space and you're not ready to plant a food crop, sow warm-weather green manures like buckwheat, cowpeas, or soybeans to fill the vacancies. Chop these crops down when you need the space, working the debris into the soil or using it as mulch as soon as it dries.

Don't let green manure crops get out of hand—they're easier to manage if kept small. Even if you're not ready to plant a food crop, cut them down before they get more than 8 inches tall or start to go to seed. Just plant another round of green manure to keep the process moving until you need the space.

Wait two or three days to plant vegetables after chopping down a green manure crop. (Decomposing plant material draws nitrogen from the soil, which temporarily robs it from any growing plants.) The chopped material will disappear in a day or two in warm weather; it will take a few days longer in cool weather. If you can't wait, simply rake the green manure onto the pathways. Once it dries, rake it back onto the bed as mulch.

Scrape up any mulch that has decomposed in the pathways and use it to cover vegetable crop seeds when you plant. This humus-rich blanket will keep the top of the soil from drying out and give the young seedlings a wonderful nutrient boost.

EARLY FALL

Remove the remaining summer crops and compost them. Clip the plants off at the soil level, leaving the roots in the ground to rot. In climates with cold winters, sow oats or mustard in the beds by mid-September. (Austrian winter peas are a good choice for the South.) These plants will grow until

freezing temperatures hit, and then they die back, forming a mulch blanket.

If you miss planting a fall green manure crop, be sure to cover the bed with shredded leaves. Whatever you do, don't leave the soil uncovered and open to erosion.

SECOND SPRING

About a month before your first spring plantings, push the remains of last year's green manure or any mulch you've used to cover your beds to the side, and plant the spring seed mix again. When it's time to plant early spring crops, chop out the seedlings—use hedge clippers or a string trimmer if a hoe proves difficult. You don't need to remove the roots of green manures—they should be left to rot in the ground. To aerate the bed, use a garden fork to gently lift the soil—no need to turn it over. That's all it takes! You're ready to plant.

Undersow to Grow Your Own Fertilizer

Growing a green manure crop under your main crop is a simple way to grow next year's fertilizer right where you'll need it. You'll avoid all the hassle and expense of buying soil amendments, and when used this way, green manure crops act as a living mulch, which conserves moisture and suppresses weeds.

You can undersow corn with hairy vetch, as shown here, but there are many other combinations to try, including tomatoes with oats, corn with soybeans, cabbage with cowpeas, and squash with sweet clover.

1. Plant your main crop and let it become established before broadcasting seed for your green manure crop. Corn, for example, should be about 10 inches tall before you sow.

2. To cover the green manure seed, sprinkle the area with compost or mulch it lightly with straw.

3. Let the green manure crop grow through the season and till or dig it under the following spring. It will protect the soil over the winter.

When You're Planting, It Pays to Watch the Weather

The easiest way to plant seeds and transplants in the garden is to wait until the weather is right. There's nothing wrong with trying for an early start, but you'll probably have to replant seeds that were lost to rot or replace transplants blasted by an Arctic wind. In other words, gambling on an early spring is very rarely a low-maintenance venture!

But when is the weather right? Try taking a cue from the trees and plants growing around you. Lilacs and honeysuckle grow almost everywhere, so they make good examples. When their leaves show their first green, it's safe to plant early crops like lettuce, cabbage, and peas. For warm-weather crops like corn and beans, wait until the honeysuckle or lilac blossoms are fully open.

Mix Seeds and Transplants for Speedy Planting

If spring zooms by before you finish planting, speed up the process by using both transplants and seeds. These tips will help you plant and sow your vegetables efficiently.

Tips for transplants. Use transplants for crops that take a long time to grow, like cabbage, broccoli, and tomatoes. Buy the healthiest starts you can find—this is not the place to pinch pennies on rootbound, overcrowded seedlings. Healthy transplants will get off to a faster start, bear a better crop, and crowd out weeds more effectively than sickly ones. If you don't have time to tend to young seedlings daily, use transplants for the majority of your needs. They're

Continued ➡

successful for all but long-rooted crops like carrots, radishes, turnips, and beets.

Suggestions for seeds. Buy seeds for plants that you use in quantity and that grow quickly, such as snap beans, spinach, arugula, and lettuce. Also buy seeds of plants that are so easy to handle that there's no need to spend the extra money on transplants. Examples include crops with big seeds like peas, beans, corn, and squash.

Sow Seeds Evenly to Save Time Thinning

There's no doubt about it, sowing seeds carefully is easier on the nerves than weeding extra seedlings out later. After all, what gardener likes to pull up healthy little plants? But sowing evenly is tough—especially with small seeds like carrots. Here are some simple techniques and tools that will make sowing and thinning easier for you.

Try creasing your seed packet down the middle and tapping the seeds out gently along the crease line. If seedlings still pop up in clumps, thin them out with a metal rake when they are about ½ inch high. Drag the rake across the width of the row so that the teeth dig in only about ¼ to ½ inch. The bed will look terrible for a few days, but the remaining seedlings will soon fill in the gaps. This technique works well for beets, carrots, chard, collards, kale, radishes, spinach, turnips, lettuce, and other salad greens.

If you have a large garden, consider investing in a few specialized seeding tools that make the process more efficient. A mechanical seeder makes planting lots of corn a snap and is very simple to use. These seeders have adjustable seed plates for other sizes of seeds and can be used in wide beds as well as in rows.

Crank seeders save a lot of time for crops that are broadcast—green manures, for example. This device looks a bit like a ricer only it spews out seeds instead of applesauce as you crank the handle. Most garden centers and hardware stores carry these tools.

Tactics for Timely Transplanting

Want to set out your transplants without watering them every day for a week? Let Mother Nature do the job. Sit tight until the weather is right and set in your plants when winds are calm and rain is expected. To give your plants an extra boost, soak them in seaweed solution before taking them out of their pots and give them another good drink once they are in the ground. Make a ring of soil around the base of the plant to help capture and retain water around the roots. Once transplants have been rained on, they can make it on their own unless drought sets in.

If you live in an area where rain is scarce and you have no irrigation, prick a small nail hole in the bottoms of several plastic gallon jugs, fill them with water, and space them around your plants. The water will drip out slowly, saving you from watering for at least a week.

Transplanting Tools Ease Planting Pains

Why limit yourself to a trowel or shovel when other new or familiar tools can make planting much easier? Hand-diggers shaped like mini-plows let you open up planting holes in one quick swoop. A long-handled bulb planter works as well for transplants as for bulbs (unless the soil is compacted) since you can dig holes without stooping.

Don't Make Room for Weeds

Where do weeds come from, anyway? The truth is, gardeners plant most of them. Some weed seeds blow in, but the vast majority arrive in compost and mulch. Letting weeds go to seed is another prime source of future weeding headaches. All those weed seeds lie in the soil, waiting for a chance to come to the surface where there is enough light to germinate.

Every time you turn the soil over, you bring up another crop of weed seeds. Knowing all this, what's the low-maintenance way to keep weeds out of your way? Try these tips.

Keep your beds full of growing plants. If all the space is occupied by green manure crops or vegetable crops, weeds won't have room to sprout. In addition, growing your own organic matter with green manures reduces the likelihood you'll bring weed seeds to your garden with compost.

Keep your soil mulched. If you get caught with nothing growing in your beds, keep them mulched with at least 4 inches of materials like shredded leaves, dried grass clippings, or straw. Keep a supply of these materials handy for emergencies.

Rake out uninvited sprouts. If you till up a new area or dig a new bed and don't have time to plant a green manure crop, wait a few days for the weeds to sprout. (If you can, hang in there until the first rain.) Then use a metal rake to scratch the top ½ inch of the soil, which will disrupt any germinating weeds without bringing up lots more. This tip is especially useful if you want to grow crops like carrots or lettuce, which are tedious to weed.

Cut unwanted seedlings to the quick. If a few weeds pop up early in the season, snip them off at ground level with sharp scissors while they are still small. For weeds like dandelions that have long roots, push the scissors into the soil and cut off the root as far down as you can reach. This will keep you from uprooting young crop seedlings.

Crowd out weeds with leaves. To keep weeds out of beds planted with crops, space your vegetables as closely as possible. Imagine how big your vegetables will be when they mature, and space or thin the plants accordingly. The leaves of growing plants will form a "living mulch," shading out most weed problems.

Skim the soil. To keep ahead of weeds in more open planting areas, like blocks of corn or hills of squash, chop them out while they are still small. Use a sharp hoe or a spade to skim off the weeds at soil level, and you'll avoid the hassle of digging and pulling. The only secret here is to keep the blades of your tools razor sharp. Once crops have reached full size, you can relax your weeding routine, but never let weeds go to seed!

Don't Dig Potatoes, Grow Them in Mulch!

Growing potatoes under mulch couldn't be easier. There's no digging, no tools—just a few bales of straw.

1. Place seed potatoes 1 foot apart on top of the soil and cover them with 1 foot of straw, hay, or shredded leaves. (Be sure each piece of potato has 2 or 3 eyes.)

2. Believe it or not, potato shoots and leaves will eventually poke through the mulch. When they do, add 6 more inches of clean straw mulch around the plants. (Don't cover the leaves.) Peek underneath the mulch periodically to watch the tubers develop and check to make sure they aren't turning green, which is a signal to add more mulch.

3. Begin harvesting new potatoes when the vines flower. Simply lift up the mulch and pick a few baby spuds. Harvest the main crop when the vines begin to die down.

With Beans, Peas, and Other Legumes, It Pays to Inoculate

The first time you plant legumes like peas and beans in your garden, inoculate them with the bacteria they need to fix nitrogen in their roots. Tests show that yields on inoculated crops increased up to 77 percent. To inoculate seeds before planting, moisten them in a flat pan and sprinkle on the black dustlike inoculant powder. Shake the pan to ensure good coverage.

Different legumes need different types of bacteria. The inoculant powder most commonly sold contains a mix suitable for peas, snap beans, and lima beans. If you grow other legumes, like cowpeas or scarlet runner beans, buy the proper inoculant. Once you've planted inoculated crops, you don't need to do it again. The bacteria will remain in the soil.

Which Tomato Type Is Best for You?

The type of tomatoes you plant can mean the difference between a crop that's over in a few short weeks and one that lasts throughout the summer months. That's because tomatoes are either determinate or indeterminate.

Determinate tomatoes set all their flowers and fruit at the same time, then stop growing. Choose them if you have a short growing season—since their fruits ripen all at once, you can squeeze in a complete harvest before frost. Determinate plants stay shorter, so they're easy to grow in cages and a good choice if you hate staking. Canning tomatoes, like 'Heinz' and 'Roma,' are popular determinate cultivars.

Indeterminate tomatoes continue growing and setting flowers throughout the growing season. They usually require staking, although they can be grown fairly well in extra-tall cages. On the plus side, though, they'll spread out the harvest so you aren't overwhelmed with too many tomatoes all at once. Most slicing tomatoes, like 'Beefsteak' and 'Better Boy,' are indeterminate cultivars.

Vegetable Crop Guide

Jeff Cox

Good site selection and proper soil care are the two most important steps you can take to ensure a great vegetable harvest. Knowing how to handle your crops at planting time and how to care for them through the season is icing on the cake. Use the guidelines and tips in this crop-by-crop guide to popular vegetables to ensure a bumper harvest every time.

Continued ➡

Asparagus

Asparagus officinalis (Liliaceae)

Site: At least ½ day of sun; protection from strong winds.

Soil: Evenly moist, well-drained, light, sandy loam that is rich in organic matter, pH og 6.5–7.5.

How much to plant: 20–40 plants per person.

Spacing: 1½–2' between plants in rows 3'–4' apart.

Seasons to bearing: Begin harvesting after 2–3 seasons of growth.

Asparagus is hardy in Zones 2 through 9. It thrives in any area with winter ground freezes or a dry season to provide a dormant period each year. Asparagus does best in full sun and deep, well-drained soil. Select a permanent location carefully, since plants will produce for 20 years or more. Dig out all weeds and add plenty of compost to the soil before planting. Asparagus requires high levels of nitrogen, phosphorus, and potassium. Do a soil test, and add amendments as necessary. If your soil is heavy or poorly drained, plant asparagus in raised beds.

Plant one-year-old crowns from a reputable nursery that sells fresh, firm, disease-free roots, or start your plants from seed. Soak seeds or crown in compost tea for five minutes before planting to reduce disease problems.

Most seed-grown asparagus plants eventually out-produce those started from crowns. Growing from seed also allows you to eliminate female plants. A bed of all male plants can produce as much as 30 percent more spears than a mixed bed of male and female plants. Plants grown from seed will flower their first summer. When the tiny flowers appear, observe them with a magnifying glass. Female flowers have well-developed, three-lobed pistils; male blossoms are larger and longer than females. Weed out all female plants. The following spring, transplant the males to the permanent bed.

Harvesting new plantings too soon can stress plants and make them more susceptible to pest problems. Harvest for two weeks the second season, four weeks the third season, and up to eight weeks thereafter.

Mulch with a high-nitrogen compost each spring before spears emerge, and again in fall. Leave winter-killed foliage, along with straw or other light mulch, on the bed to provide winter protection. Remove and destroy the foliage before new growth appears in the spring; it can harbor diseases and pest eggs. Over the years, the crowns will push closer to the soil surface, resulting in smaller and less-tender spears. To remedy this, mound 6 inches of soil over the rows each spring.

Bean

Phaseolus spp. (Leguminosae)

Site: Needs at least ½ day of sun.

Soil: Prefers a light, sandy soil with good drainage; pH of 5.5–6.8.

How much to plant: Bush beans: 10–15 plants per person. Pole beans: 3–5 hills per person.

Low-Maintenance Tips for Your Favorite Crops

Do you have a favorite vegetable? Check the tips and techniques below for ways to make growing it easier, faster, and more efficient.

Crop	Tips for Sure-Fire Success	Methods to Maximize Efficiency
Beans, snap	Choose cultivars with dark seeds or purple pods for early plantings; they're less likely to rot. Plant small amounts (3 plants per person) every 12 days for a continuous crop and manageable harvests.	Plant snap beans in spaces vacated by lettuce and spinach to return nitrogen to the soil. Train pole beans up a teepee made of saplings to conserve space (1 teepee serves a family of 4).
Beets	Soak seeds overnight to speed germination. Beets need thinning because each "seed" actually contains several seeds. Clip extras with sharp scissors and add to the salad bowl.	For a double crop, harvest beet leaves throughout the season. Leave two-thirds of the leaves so root harvest won't be disturbed.
Cabbage family crops (broccoli, Brussels sprouts, cabbage, cauliflower, collards, kale)	Use row-covers to prevent damage from cabbage worms. Row covers also minimize the temperature fluctuations that cause poor heading in broccoli and cauliflower.	Plant kale, collards, and Brussels sprouts for nutritious, long-season crops, sowing seeds in the spaces left from early peas or beans. These hardy greens will overwinter in many areas with minimum protection.
Carrots	For better germination, cover seeds with ½ inch of compost. Keep the compost moist until seeds are up and growing.	Sow radish seeds with carrots; radishes keep the soil loose and are ready to harvest before carrots need the space. Planting with onions reduces carrot fly infestations.
Corn	Plant when nighttime air temperatures stay above 40°F. (The soil temperature should be about 50°F.) To deter crows, cover seedbeds with row covers.	Plant a mid-season and a late-season cultivar at the same time so you won't have to remember to plant a later crop. Early cultivars aren't tasty enough to warrant the work.
Cucumbers	Use row covers to thwart cucumber beetles. Remove covers when vines blossom to allow pollination. Plant a second crop as insurance against pests when the first crop blooms.	Trellising pays off in increased cucumber yields.
Eggplant	To combat flea beetles, place white plastic buckets around eggplants. Coat the plastic with sticky Tanglefoot to capture the beetles.	Eggplants love heat—cover them with plastic jugs (remove lids and cut out bottoms) until summer nights are warm.
Lettuce	Plant many types, starting with cold-tolerant strains early in the season. Switch to heat-resistant cultivars as summer draws near.	Sow a 2½- to 3-foot block every 10 days to 2 weeks until the weather gets hot. For longer harvests, keep roots cool with mulch to retard bolting. Row covers allow harvest of many greens well into winter.
Onions	Buy sets or transplants instead of seeds for a quick, reliable harvest. Choose small (½- diameter), firm sets since they're less likely to bolt.	Onions are good companions for most crops except peas and beans. Keep a bag of onion sets in the refrigerator and use them to fill in blank spaces all season.
Peas	Soak seeds overnight to speed germination. To avoid trellising, select short cultivars and plant seeds thickly so the vines will support each other.	Interplant with radishes and early greens if space is short; avoid planting near garlic or onions. Pick daily to encourage vines to keep producing.
Peppers	To increase yields, snip off early blossoms on young plants to give them a chance to bulk out before fruiting. Boost with 1 teaspoon Epsom salts to 1 quart of water when plants set fruit.	For easy harvest, uproot hot peppers at the end of the season and hang them to dry in a warm closet. Uprooted sweet peppers will hold for a month in a bucket of water if kept in a cool location.
Spinach	Soak seeds in compost tea for 15 minutes or all night before planting. Plant heat- and bolt-resistant cultivars.	Pick outside leaves only, once they reach 3 to 4 inches long—plants stay productive longer than if you harvest the entire plant at once.
Squash	To prevent squash borer attack, use row-covers until female blossoms appear. Start another plant or two in early summer for added protection.	Pumpkins and winter squash take up a lot of space. Let them ramble over compost piles and steep slopes where other crops can't grow.
Potatoes	A month before planting, put seed potatoes in a bright, dry location, like a basement windowsill. The sprouts will grow slowly in the light. Cut them into sections with two or three sprouted eyes and plant. Crops will be ready almost a month earlier.	Why grow plain white potatoes? Specialty spuds are available in a riot of colors and shapes and are just as easy to grow. Try potatoes with yellow, pink, or blue flesh for flavors that store-bought spuds can't match.
Tomatoes	Buy the best transplants you can find. Seedlings should be bushy with sturdy stems. Choose disease-resistant cultivars. Try an assortment of single plants instead of buying a six-pack of one cultivar. Tomatoes almost always produce, but different cultivars produce better in different weather conditions.	Staking isn't necessary, but staked tomatoes have larger fruit, are easier to pick, and are less prone to rot. If you use tomato cages, buy the tallest, sturdiest ones available. To prevent cages from toppling, drive a stake inside each cage to hold it in place.

Continued ➡

Spacing: Bush beans: 4"–6" between plants in rows 1½'–3' apart. Pole beans: 6"–9" between plants in rows 3'–4' apart.

Days to maturity: Bush beans: 48–60 days. Pole beans: 62–68 days.

Beans thrive in most soil. Work in plenty of low-nitrogen compost before planting to loosen the soil. For a healthy, trouble-free crop, plant beans after soil has warmed. Optimum soil temperature for germination is 80°F. At soil temperatures below 60°F, most bean cultivars germinate poorly and are more susceptible to pests and root rot. Choose light, well-drained soil for early plantings, if possible, and cover beans with a row cover or clear plastic until they emerge. If you use clear plastic, be sure to remove it as soon as the seeds germinate to avoid "cooking" the seedlings.

Beans do best when soil pH is between 5.5 and 6.8. They don't require high soil fertility. In fact, a high nitrogen level will delay maturity. Spray young plants with seaweed extract to prevent micronutrient deficiencies and to improve overall plant health.

Soak seed in compost tea for 25 minutes before planting to help prevent disease and speed germination. Treat seed with an inoculant labeled for the type of bean you are planting before sowing to promote nitrogen fixation. Be sure to buy fresh inoculant each year, or check the date on the package for viability.

Crops That Wait for You

Few things are more frustrating than planting a beautiful garden and then not being able to keep up with the harvest. Leave your sugar snap peas on the vine for a few too many days, and you might just as well till them under as a green manure crop.

Fortunately, there are a host of forgiving crops that will more or less wait for you. They include onions, leeks, potatoes, garlic, many herbs, kale, beets, popcorn, sunflowers, hot peppers (for drying), horseradish, pumpkins, winter squash, and carrots. You can measure the harvest period for these crops in weeks or even months.

To keep your harvest from hitting all at once, stagger plantings. Make a new sowing every ten days to two weeks. Mix early, midseason, and late cultivars. Some vegetables, like bok choy and other oriental greens, can be harvested through Thanksgiving.

Never have time to pick all of your fresh snap or shell beans at their prime? Relax. Plant cultivars meant for drying, and enjoy hearty, homegrown bean dishes throughout winter.

You can pick leeks young and small or wait, the full 90 to 120 days until they mature. Leeks have excellent freeze tolerance. When protected by mulch, they can be harvested well into winter. In mild-winter areas where hard freezes are few and far between, winter is the best time to grow collards, spinach, turnips, carrots, and onions.

In all climates, be prepared to protect overwintering vegetables from cosmetic damage by covering them with an old blanket during periods of harsh weather. Or you can try growing cold-hardy vegetables such as spinach and kale under plastic tunnels during the winter months.

To avoid spreading diseases, don't touch plants when foliage is wet. Compost plants after harvest. Prevent problems by not planting beans in the same location more often than every three years.

Beet

Beta vulgaris (Chenopodiaceae)

Site: Full sun, but will tolerate partial shade.

Soil: Prefers a light, sandy loam; pH of 6.0–7.5.

How much to plant: 5'–10' of row per person.

Spacing: 4"–6" between plants in rows 12"–20" apart.

Days to maturity: 46–70 days.

Beets grow best in deep, well-drained soil with a pH between 6.0 and 7.5. Beets are cool-season plants and will tolerate temperatures as low as 40°F. However, plants will bolt, or go to flower prematurely, if exposed to two to three of temperatures below 50°F after the first true leaves have formed. Beets grow poorly above 75°F and are best grown as a spring or fall crop. Keep soil moist but not soggy, since rapid and uninterrupted growth produces the best roots. Prevent problems by not planting beets in the same location more often than every three years.

Cabbage

Brassica oleracea Capitata group (Cruciferae)

Site: Full sun.

Soil: Rich, sandy loam; pH of 6.0–6.8.

How much to plant: 5–10 plants per person.

Spacing: 15"–24" between plants in rows 2'–3' apart.

Days to maturity: 62–120 days from transplanting.

Plant cabbages in full sun in a site with fertile, well-drained soil and a pH between 6.0 and 6.8. If you have a choice of sites, spring plantings do best in lighter, sandier soils, while fall plantings do better in soils that contain more clay. Plants grow best at temperatures between 40° and 75°F.

Cabbages are biennial, and transplants exposed to cool temperatures (35° to 45°F) for ten or more days may bolt. High temperatures also cause bolting.

These plants have very shallow roots, so be sure to keep the top few inches of soil from drying out. Fluctuations in soil moisture after the heads have formed may cause them to split. Mulching helps to balance and conserve moisture. Most cabbage diseases need free water to spread, so don't water with overhead sprinklers.

To avoid problems, don't plant cabbages where members of the cabbage family (broccoli, cauliflower, brussels sprouts, or kale) have grown for at least three years. Also, avoid areas with cabbage family weeds, such as wild mustard. Destroy all crop residues, including roots, after you harvest.

If you start your own plants, soak the seed in 122°F water for 25 minutes before planting to eliminate seed-borne diseases. Once your seeds have germinated, grow seedlings at 60°F to keep them short and stocky.

Cabbages are heavy feeders and are susceptible to several nutrient deficiencies, including boron, calcium, phosphorus, and potassium.

Carrot

Daucus carota var. *sativus* (Umbelliferae)

Site: Full sun to light shade.

Soil: Deep, loose, moist, and well aerated; pH of 5.5–6.8.

How much to plant: 5'–10' of row, or 30 plants, per person.

Spacing: 3"–4" between plants in rows 16"–30" apart.

Days to maturity: 50–95 days from seed to harvest.

Carrots grow best in deeply worked, loose soils with a pH between 5.5 and 6.8. No other vegetable is as sensitive to poor soil structure. Misshapen carrots result more often from lumpy or compacted soil than from any pest problem. Carrots so well in raised beds. Work in a generous amount of compost or well-rotted manure before planting. Ciltivars with short roots will tolerate shallow or poor soil better than long, thin cultivars.

Carrots grow best when temperatures are between 60° and 70°F. They grow poorly above 75°F but will tolerate temperatures as low as 45°F. Most cultivars grow short roots at high temperatures and longer, more pointed roots at lower temperatures.

Abundant water is necessary for good root development. It is especially important to give emerging seedlings an edge against weeds. Keep soil evenly moist but not saturated.

To prevent problems with diseases and insects, do not plant carrots where carrots or parsley has grown for three years.

Carrots require moderate to high levels of potassium and phosphorus, but only a moderate level of nitrogen, so avoid high-nitrogen fertilizers. Carrots are very sensitive to salt injury and do poorly in soils with high sodium levels.

Corn

Zea mays var. *rugosa* (Gramineae)

Site: Full sun; needs wind for pollination.

Soil: Rich, well-drained loam with pH of 5.5–6.8; evenly moist but not wet.

Continued ➡

Cultivate Some Cole Crops

Cabbage, broccoli, and their less-common cousins such as kale and brussels sprouts all belong to the same family of vegetables—Cruciferae. In fact, they're all different forms of the same species, Brassica oleracea. All are grown like cabbage and are cool-weather crops that are good for planting in spring and fall.

Broccoli: Grown for its crisp green heads of flower buds. Prevent problems by planting the following improved cultivars: 'Green Dwarf #36,' 'Emperor,' and 'Mariner' are black rot-tolerant; 'Premium Crop' is resistant to Fusarium wilt; 'Citation,' 'Emperor,' 'Esquire,' 'Green Dwarf #36,' 'Hi-Caliber,' and 'Mariner' are tolerant of downy mildew; and 'De Cicco' is tolerant of flea beetles.

Transplants exposed to cool temperatures (35° to 45°F) for ten days or more may form tiny, useless flower heads prematurely. High temperatures can cause similar tiny head formation. Broccoli grows best at temperatures between 45° and 75°F. Harvest heads when buds are still tight and dark green or dusky violet, except for 'Romanesco,' which should be yellow-green.

Brussels sprouts: One of the hardiest members of the cabbage family, they can tolerate lower pH (5.5 to 6.8) than any of the other brassicas. But they are less tolerant of heat. In warmer climates grow sprouts in soil with a high clay content if you have a choice, and shade the soil around roots. Harvest sprouts when they are 1 inch in diameter or smaller and still tight. Twist them off gently, starting at the base.

Cauliflower: Grown for its dense, white heads of flower buds. Prevent problems by planting the following cultivars: 'Alpha Paloma' and 'White Rock' are tolerant of cabbage root maggots; 'Super Snowball A' tolerates flea beetles better than most cultivars.

Cauliflower is fussier about temperatures than the other brassicas. Plants only tolerate a low of 45°F and grow poorly above 75°F. Transplants exposed to cool temperatures (35° to 45°F) for ten days or more may form tiny, unusable flower heads. High temperatures can cause the same problem. Cauliflower's optimum temperature range is 60° to 65°F.

Kale: Grown for its crinkly, blue-green leaves. It is a very hardy member of the cabbage family, tolerating temperatures below 40°F. Frost improves its taste. It is less tolerant of heat than other members of the cabbage family. In warmer climates, grow kale in soil with high clay content if possible, and shade soil around roots.

How much to plant: 15–40 plants per person.

Spacing: 8"–12" apart in rows 30"–42" apart.

Days to maturity: 65–90 days from seed to harvest.

Corn does best in a rich, sandy, or well-worked soil with a pH between 5.5 and 6.8. Prepare soil by working in a generous amount of compost. Side-dress plants with alfalfa meal when they are 1 foot high and again when silk first shows at the ends of the ears. Spraying plants with seaweed extract or compost tea periodically also improves your harvest and prevents deficiencies.

Plant corn seed only after the soil is at least 60°F, or 75°F for supersweets. Seed planted in cooler soil is prone to many problems. To help speed soil warming, cover soil with clear plastic at least two weeks before planting. After planting, use row covers for about a month to give seedlings a boost.

Corn needs at least 1 inch of water a week. Keep soil moist but not soggy. Mulch plants to conserve moisture and to cut down on weeds.

Plant corn in blocks rather than long single rows to ensure good pollination. To prevent problems, do not plant corn where it has grown in the past two years. After harvest, cut or mow stalks and let them dry. Then turn them under or collect and compost them. Destroy any diseased or infested material.

Cucumber

Cucumis sativus (Cucurbitaceae)

Site: Full sun, or full morning sun and less than 3 hours of afternoon shade.

Soil: Well-drained sand or clay loam with pH of 6.0–6.8.

How much to plant: For eating fresh: 1 plant per person; for pickling: 5 plants per person.

Spacing: Grow trellised plants 6"–10" apart, or grow in hills spaced 4'–6' apart.

Days to Maturity: 55–70 days from seed, depending on the cultivar.

Cucumber seeds need 60°F soil to germinate, so wait until weather is warm to plant. Make a second planting four to five weeks after the first so you will have fruit all season. Cover plants with floating row covers to protect them from insects and late cold snaps. Remove row covers when plants begin to flower so insects can pollinate the blossoms, or you will not get any fruit.

Cucumbers do best in well-drained, loose-textured soils with lots of organic matter. They will grow in soils with a pH between 5.5 and 6.8, but they prefer a pH above 6.0. Plants need lots of water, but don't let soil become saturated. Prevent disease problems by keeping leaves dry. Mulch cucumbers to help conserve water; black plastic is a good choice for central and northern areas, but in extremely warm areas it can warm the soil too much. Organic mulches are good, too, but may provide shelter for pests like squash bugs. Foil mulches help prevent aphid problems. If rotting fruit is a problem, raise fruits off the ground by placing scraps of wood under them.

Rotate crops so that no member of the cucurbit family (squash, melon, and cucumber) is grown in the same place more often than every four years.

Caution: Cucumber leaves are easily burned by insecticidal soap and copper sprays. Use the most dilute spray recommended and use sparingly. Do not spray plants in direct sun or if temperatures are above 80°F, and don't spray drought-stressed plants.

Eggplant

Solanum melongena var. *esculentum* (Solanaceae)

Site: Full sun.

Soil: Moderately fertile, well-drained loam; pH of 6.0–6.8.

How much to plant: 2–3 plants per person.

Spacing: 20"–24" apart each way.

Days to maturity: 60–100 days from transplanting.

Eggplants do best in full sun and well-drained, fertile soil with lots of organic matter. They prefer a pH between 6.0 and 6.8 but will tolerate a pH as low as 5.5. Eggplants need a high level of nitrogen and moderate levels of phosphorus and potassium. Have the soil tested, and correct any deficiencies. They grow best at temperatures between 70° and 85°F, and poorly above 95° or below 65°F.

Eggplants need lots of water. Keep the soil evenly moist, and never let it dry out. They do well in mulched, raised beds with drip irrigation. Black plastic mulch is a good choice because it warms the soil.

Purchase stocky, insect- and disease-free plants, or start your own from seed indoors. Eggplant seeds germinate best between 80° and 90°F. Once seedlings are up, they grow best at 70°F. Do not plant out before average daily temperatures have reached 65° to 70°F. Protect transplants from wind, and water new transplants well with seaweed extract or compost tea to give them a good start. Spray plants with seaweed extract with 1 teaspoon of Epsom salts added per gallon when the first flowers open to improve fruit set.

Eggplants are susceptible to many of the same problems, pests, and diseases as tomatoes, including flower drop or misshapen fruit due to extreme temperatures, flea beetles, Colorado potato beetles, aphids, hornworms, mites, Verticillium and Fusarium wilts, tobacco mosaic virus, and anthracnose fruit rot.

Lettuce

Latuca sativa (Compositae)

Site: Tolerates partial shade; thrives in light shade in summer; does well in humid spots.

Soil: Loamy soil that is well drained and moderately rich; needs constant moisture; pH of 6.0–6.8.

How much to plant: Plant 15–20 leaf lettuce plants or 7 head lettuce plants per person.

Spacing: Leaf lettuce: 6"–12" between plants in traditional rows 1'–3' apart, or in intensive beds with 6"–9" between plants. Head lettuce: 8"–14" between plants in traditional rows 1'–3' apart.

Days to maturity: Leaf lettuce: 40 days from seed to harvest. Head lettuce: 70 days from seed to harvest, or 20–35 days from transplanting to harvest.

Lettuce grows best in rich, loose soil with a pH between 6.0 and 6.8. It likes full sun, but in hot weather it does better with light shade in the heat of the day. Lettuce needs to grow rapidly and without interruption. Provide plenty of nitrogen in both quicker-release forms, such as blood meal or soybean meal, and slower-release forms, such as compost or alfalfa meal. Spray the plants with compost tea and/or seaweed extract every other week to give them an extra boost. Spraying with compost tea may also help prevent some fungal disease problems.

Lettuce grows best at temperatures between 60° and 65°F. Most lettuce cultivars grow poorly above

Continued ➡

75°F but will tolerate temperatures as low as 45°F. Plants exposed to high temperatures will bolt. Prevent bolting by providing plants with partial shade in the heat of the summer, harvesting promptly, and planting bolt-resistant cultivars.

To grow tender, trouble-free lettuce, keep the soil moist but not soggy, and do not allow the soil to dry out. Unlike most vegetables, lettuce responds well to having its foliage sprinkled with water. Plant in raised beds to improve drainage. To help prevent disease problems, do not plant lettuce in soil where it has been grown within the last three years.

Melon

Melon, *Cucumis meto* and Watermelon, *Citrullus lanatus* (Cucurbitaceae)

Site: Full sun.

Soil: Moderately rich, well-drained soil with a pH of 6.0–6.8.

How much to plant: 1–2 plants per person.

Spacing: 8"–12" apart in rows 6'–10' apart or 2 plants per hill, with the hills spaced 2'–3' apart.

Days to maturity: 75–90 days from seed, depending on cultivar.

Melon seeds need 60°F soil to germinate. In northern areas, start plants indoors two to three weeks before the last frost date and transplant outside once weather is warm. Melons need sun and warmth—90°F is ideal. Melons are especially vulnerable to pests and cool temperatures below 50°F can be permanently injured and fail to set fruit. Cover plants with floating row covers or clear plastic tunnels as soon as they are set out. If temperatures exceed 90°F inside the tunnels, vent them with a 6-inch cut in the plastic directly over each plant. Remove covers when melons flower so insects can pollinate the blossoms, or you will not get any fruit. In the fall, temperatures below 50°F cause cold stress and rapid wilting. Cover plants on cool nights.

Melons perform best in well-drained, loose-textured soils with lots of organic matter. They prefer a pH between 6.0 and 6.8 but can tolerate a pH as high as 7.6. Melons are shallow-rooted and may wilt on hot, dry days even when they are not diseased. Keep them well watered, but do not let the soil become saturated. Wet soil can cause stems to rot at soil level. Overwatering or uneven watering can cause fruit to split. Potassium deficiency can also cause split fruit.

Prevent disease problems by keeping the leaves dry. Water carefully or use drip irrigation. Mulch melons to help conserve water: Black plastic is a good choice for central and northern areas, but in extremely warm areas it can warm the soil too much. Organic mulches are good, too, but also provide shelter for pests like squash bugs.

Caution: Melon leaves are easily burned by insecticidal soap and copper sprays. Use the most dilute spray recommended and apply sparingly. Do not spray plants in direct sun or if temperatures are above 80°F, and don't spray drought-stressed plants.

Onion

Allium cepa and other species (Liliaceae)

Site: At least ½ day of sun.

Soil: Richly organic, well-drained loam with pH of 6.0–6.5; constantly moist, but not wet.

How much to plant: About 40 plants per person.

Spacing: 1"–4" between plants in rows 1'–2' apart.

Days to maturity: Varies with cultivar and method; 100-160 days from seed to harvest. Green onions:

Harvest in 45 days from transplants or sets. Bulb onions: Harvest in 90 days from transplants or sets.

Onions grow best in full sun and deep, fertile, well-drained soil with lots of organic matter. Work in a generous amount of compost before planting. Onions need high levels of nitrogen and potassium and a moderate to high level of phosphorus, so do a soil test and amend soil as needed before planting. Onions grow well in raised beds or ridges, especially if soil is clayey.

Onions grow best between 55° and 75°F and will tolerate temperatures as low as 45° and as high as 85°F. They prefer cool temperatures early in their growth and warm temperatures near maturity.

Keep the soil moist since onions have shallow roots, but don't allow soil to become saturated because onions are susceptible to several root rot diseases. Mulching onions with composted leaves or straw is highly recommended to maintain soil organic content, help prevent disease, and keep down weeds. Wait until soil warms to apply mulch.

To help prevent populations of disease organisms from building up in the soil, avoid planting onions where onion-family members have been grown during the previous three years. In general, white onions are more prone to problems than yellow or red ones.

You can grow onions from seeds, transplants, or sets. Discard any disease sets or transplants. Transplants are seedlings started in the current growing season and sold in bunches. Sets are immature bulbs grown the previous year. Soak sets, roots, or seeds in compost tea for 15 minutes before planting to help prevent disease. Dust the roots of sets and plants with bonemeal after soaking and before planting to give them a good start.

Onion bulb formation is controlled by day length, so selecting suitable cultivars for your area is crucial. In the North choose "long-day" cultivars, and in the South choose "short-day" cultivars.

Allow tops to fall over naturally, then pull bulbs and let them air-cure for two weeks. After curing, sort out damaged bulbs and those with thick necks and put aside for immediate use. Store others at temperatures just above 32°F.

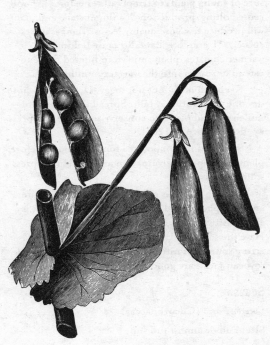

Pea

Pisum sativum (Leguminosae)

Site: Full sun; will grow in partial shade.

Soil: Well-drained soil with high organic matter is best; pH of 5.5–6.8.

How much to plant: 40 plants per person.

Spacing: Bush types: 2' between rows. Climbing types: 3' between rows. Both types: 2"–3" between plants.

Days to maturity: 56–75 days from seed to harvest.

Peas grow well in almost any soil but do best in soil with lots of organic matter and a pH between 5.5 and 6.8. A 1-inch layer of compost worked well into the soil before planting will provide sufficient nutrients for a good crop.

Peas are a cool-season, moisture-loving crop. They grow best between 60° and 75°F; they do poorly at temperatures above 75°F but will tolerate temperatures as low as 45°F. Pea foliage can withstand a light frost, but pods and flowers will be damaged unless they are covered.

Most disease problems in peas can be avoided with proper culture. Do not plant in wet soils. Plant in raised beds, and add plenty of compost to loosen the soil. Rapid germination is essential to avoid root rot problems. Choose lighter soils for earliest plantings if you have a choice, and keep soil moist but not wet. Avoid touching plants when they are wet. Dispose of vines after harvest and till soil to reduce future problems. Plant peas where no peas or beans have grown for at least three years.

Soak seed in compost tea for 15 minutes or as long as overnight to help prevent disease and speed germination. To promote nitrogen fixation, treat seed with an inoculant labeled for garden peas before planting. Be sure to buy fresh inoculant each year, or check the date on the package for viability.

Peas are susceptible to certain micronutrient deficiencies. Spray young plants with seaweed extract every two weeks to help prevent deficiencies and boost production.

Pepper

Capsicum annuum vaL annuum (Solanaceae)

Site: Full sun.

Soil: Sandy loam, or any good, well-drained soil with a pH of 6.0–6.8.

How much to plant: 3–4 plants per person.

Spacing: Plant on 1½' centers.

Days to maturity: 65–80 days from transplanting.

Peppers require deeply worked, well-drained soil with lots of organic matter. They do best at a pH between 6.0 and 6.8 but tolerate pH as low as 5.5. Peppers require a moderate to high level of nitrogen and moderate levels of phosphorus, potassium, and calcium. Have the soil tested and amend as needed before planting. Peppers grow best between 65° and 80°F. Temperatures above 85°F or below 60°F can cause blossoms to drop without setting fruit.

Peppers tolerate drought, but they do best in soil that is evenly moist but not soggy. Plant in raised beds to improve drainage, if needed. Stake peppers to keep fruit from touching the ground, and use mulch to control weeds and prevent soil-borne diseases from splashing up on the fruit.

Do not plant peppers where tomatoes, potatoes, eggplants, or peppers have been planted within the past three to five years. Also, try to plan your planting scheme to separate these crops in the garden. Compost or till under all plant residues at the end of the season, and till the soil to reduce overwintering pests.

Purchase sturdy, insect- and disease-free above 80°F. Once seedlings are up, they grow best at 70°F during the day and 60°F during the night. Wait until soil temperatures reach 65°F before setting out

Continued ➜

transplants. Spray transplants with an antitranspirant to help reduce disease problems, and water them with seaweed extract or compost tea to give them a good start. To improve fruit set, spray plants when the first flowers open with a mixture of 1 gallon of seaweed extract and 1 teaspoon of Epsom salts.

Potato

Solanum tuberosum (Solanaceae)

Site: Full or nearly full sun, with good air circulation.

Soil: Any good garden soil that drains well; pH of 5.0–6.8.

How much to plant: 5–10 plants per person.

Spacing: Leave 1' between plants in rows 3' apart, or plant in raised beds on 1½' centers.

Days to maturity: 90–120 days, depending on cultivar and climate.

Potatoes require deeply worked, well-drained soil with lots of organic matter and a pH between 5.0 and 6.8. They need moderate to high levels of nitrogen, phosphorus, potassium, calcium, and sulfur. Have the soil tested and amend as needed before planting. Gypsum is a good source of calcium and sulfur for potatoes.

Keep soil moist but not soggy, and do not allow it to dry out. Alternating dry and wet soil can cause cracked or knobby tubers. Once tops begin to yellow near harvest, you can let the soil dry out without damaging tubers.

Do not plant potatoes where tomatoes, potatoes, eggplants, peppers, strawberries, or brambles have been planted within the past four to five years. Also, try to plan your planting scheme to separate these crops in the garden. Don't plant potatoes where sod or small grains were grown the previous year: Wireworms, a common sod pest, also feed on potato tubers. Compost or till under all plant residues at the end of the season. Tilling the soil helps prevent pests from overwintering.

Potatoes are usually grown from seed potatoes (tubers) or "buds" (tiny tissue-cultured tubers), but a few cultivars, such as 'Explorer' and 'Homestead Hybrid,' are grown from true seeds. Prevent problems by planting only certified disease-free tubers. Planting true seeds or buds also helps avoid many tuber-borne diseases.

Be sure to consider the end use of your potato crop when you select cultivars for planting—the texture of a cooked potato depends on its starch content. Higher starch content yields a drier, flakier texture. New potatoes of most cultivars are 90 percent water and only 7 percent starch. At maturity, most bakers contain 15 to 18 percent starch. However, cultivars used for potato chips and french fries contain as much as 22 percent starch.

Pre-condition tubers by storing them between 65° and 70°F for two weeks before planting to encourage rapid growth. Soak pieces in compost tea for several hours before planting to help prevent disease problems. Plant them out when soil is at least 40°F.

Radish

Raphanus sativus (Cruciferae)

Site: Full sun or partial shade

Soil: Any soil; pH of 5.5–6.8.

How much to plant: A few feet of row per person per planting.

Spacing: 2" apart in rows 8"–18" apart.

Days to maturity: Spring types 21–35 days; winter types 55–60 days.

Radishes are annual and biennial vegetables grown for their crisp, peppery roots. Certain cultivars do not have fleshy roots but are grown for their crunchy seed pods. Some Daikon radishes grow 2-foot roots.

Most radishes do best in cool, moist conditions. They need a pH between 5.5 and 6.8 and light, relatively rich soil. Plant radishes as soon as soil can be worked in spring. Make small plantings weekly until early summer for a continuous supply of radishes. Temperatures between 50° and 65°F produce the best radishes; growth above 75°F is poor. Some cultivars of Daikon radishes are designed for summer planting and will flower without forming large roots if planted too early.

The secret to mild, tender radishes is rapid growth. Water heavily the first two weeks after they come up if soil is dry. A light application of compost is usually enough for a good radish crop. Radishes will not tolerate soils high in salt.

Radishes are related to cabbage and suffer from many of the same problems. Since leaves are not harvested, more insect damage can be tolerated than in cabbage plants. See the Cabbage entry on page 208 for descriptions and controls. Prevent problems with Fusarium wilt by planting resistant cultivars such as 'Fancy Red,' 'Fuego,' 'Red Devil B,' 'Red King,' and 'Red Pak.'

Spinach

Spinacia oleracea (Chenopodiaceae)

Site: Sun to partial shade; needs a cool, moist site.

Soil: Heavy, fertile loam that is moist but not soggy; pH of 6.0–7.0.

How much to plant: About 30 plants per person.

Spacing: 1'–3' between rows, 2"–6" between plants.

Days to maturity: 37–45 days from seed.

Grow spinach in well-drained soil with lots of organic matter and a pH between 6.0 and 7.0; it won't tolerate pH below 5.0. Spinach seed germinates best at soil temperatures between 45° and 75°F but will germinate as low as 35°F.

Mature spinach can survive temperatures of 20°F if gradually hardened off. However, prolonged exposure of young plants to temperatures below 45°F will cause bolting-production of a flower stalk-and plants will produce few, low-quality leaves. Temperatures above 75°F and long days also cause bolting. In warmer climates, plant spinach in filtered shade to extend its season into the warmer months.

Keep soil moist but not soggy. Do not allow it to dry out, or plants may bolt. Spread a thin layer of mulch around plants to conserve moisture, suppress weeds, and keep soil cool.

Soak seed in compost tea for 30 minutes before planting to speed germination and to help suppress soilborne diseases.

Spinach requires moderate levels of potassium and phosphorus and a high level of nitrogen. It is also sensitive to low levels of calcium and boron. Have the soil tested and amend as necessary. Fast-acting sources of nitrogen, such as blood meal and soybean meal, are good fertilizers for spinach.

Squash

Cucurbita spp. (Cucurbitaceae)

Site: Full or almost full sun.

Soil: Any good garden soil that drains well; pH of 6.0–6.8.

How much to plant: 2–4 plants per person.

Spacing: Bushy cultivars: in hills 2'–4' apart. Vining types: in hills 3'–8' apart.

Days to maturity: Summer squash: 45–50 days. Winter squash and pumpkins: 85–110 days. Squash

seeds need 60°F soil to germinate, so wait until warm weather to plant. Cover plants with floating row covers to protect them from insects and late cold snaps. Remove row covers when plants begin to flower so insects can pollinate the blossoms, or you will not get any fruit.

Squash perform best in well-drained, loose-textured soils with lots of organic matter. They will grow in soils with a pH between 5.5 and 6.8 but prefer a pH above 6.0. Squash need lots of water, but don't let the soil become saturated. Prevent disease problems by keeping the leaves dry. Mulch squash to help conserve water. Black plastic is a good choice for northern areas, but in extremely warm areas it can warm the soil too much. Organic mulches are good, too, but may provide shelter for pests like squash bugs. Foil mulches help prevent aphid problems. To prevent rot, support fruit on scraps of wood.

Rotate crops in your garden so that no member of the cucurbit family (cucumbers, melons, and squash) is grown in the same place more often than every four years.

Caution: Squash leaves are easily burned by insecticidal soap and copper sprays. Use the most dilute spray recommended and use sparingly. Do not spray plants in direct sun or if temperatures are above 80°F, and don't spray drought-stressed plants.

Sweet Potato

Ipomoea batatas (Convolvulaceae)

Site: Full sun; afternoon shade in warm climates.

Soil: Loose soil with a pH of 5.5–6.5.

How much to plant: 2–4 plants per person.

Spacing: 12" apart in rows 3' apart; 18" apart each way in beds.

Days to maturity: 70–100 days.

Sweet potatoes prefer loose, well-drained soil with a pH between 5.5 and 6.5. They require moderate amounts of nitrogen and boron, a moderate to high level of phosphorus, and a high level of potassium. Have the soil tested and amend as necessary before planting. Sweet potatoes do well in raised beds. Work in lots of organic matter before planting. Avoid topdressing after early summer, or root formation may be interrupted.

Keep soil moist, but not soggy, until the vines begin to spread. After that, water only if vines wilt. When the roots begin to enlarge in late summer, keep the soil moist until harvest. Mulch plants to suppress weeds and conserve moisture. Black plastic mulch will also warm the soil.

Plant sweet potatoes where they have not been grown for at least two years. After harvest, cut vines and let dry, then compost or till under to reduce disease buildup.

Purchase disease-free plants, or start your own from healthy, overwintered roots. Plant out when nights stay above 60°F. Soak plant roots in compost tea for five minutes before planting to help reduce disease problems. Water well with a fish emulsion or fish-meal tea after planting to give the plants a good start.

Dig potatoes gently before the first frost, after foliage starts to yellow. Dry them for two to three hours in the garden. Use any damaged or diseased potatoes as soon as possible. Cure healthy potatoes for ten days in a humid place at 80° to 85°F. Gradually reduce temperature and store them in a humid room at 55° to 60°F.

Tomato

Lycopersicon esculentum (Solanaceae)

Continued ➡

Site: Full sun or full morning sun and less than 3 hours of afternoon shade.

Soil: Moderately fertile clay or sandy loam with good drainage and a pH of 6.0–6.8.

How much to plant: Warm climates: 2 plants per person; cool climates: 4 plants person.

Spacing: Staked tomatoes: 1½'–2' apart. Unstaked, uncaged tomatoes: 3'–4' apart. Caged tomatoes: Space 2'-diameter cages 4' apart.

Days to maturity: 90–140 days from seed; 60–90 days from transplanting, depending on the cultivar.

Tomatoes require full sun and deep soil with a pH between 6.0 and 6.8. Work in plenty of compost before planting to add organic matter. Tomatoes require moderate levels of nitrogen and phosphorus and moderate to high levels of potassium and calcium. Tomatoes grow best between 75° and 90°F. Temperatures over 100°F can kill blossoms, while temperatures below 50°F can cause chilling injury.

Keep soil moist but not soggy, and do not allow it to dry out. Avoid wetting leaves when watering to help prevent diseases. Tomatoes do well in raised beds with drip irrigation and mulch. Black plastic is a good mulch in cool areas because it helps warm the soil as well as suppressing weeds and conserving water. Organic mulch helps keep the soil cooler in very warm areas while adding organic matter. Mulch also helps prevent disease by preventing the fruit from touching the ground or being splashed with soil containing disease-causing organisms.

Choose cultivars that are adapted to local growing conditions. Many of them are resistant to one or more problems. Resistant cultivars are usually denoted in seed catalogs as follows: F = Fusarium-resistant, V = Verticillium-resistant, T = tobacco mosaic virus-resistant, and N = nematode-resistant.

Do not plant tomatoes where tomatoes, potatoes, eggplants, or peppers have been planted within the past three to five years. Also, try to plan your planting scheme to separate these crops in the garden. Compost or till under all plant residues at the end of the season to reduce overwintering pests. After tilling, spread 2 to 4 pounds of blood meal or soybean meal per 100 square feet to encourage breakdown of plant material.

Purchase stocky, insect- and disease-free plants, or start your own from seed indoors. Soak seed in a 10 percent bleach solution (1 part bleach and 9 parts water) for ten minutes and rinse in clean water before planting to reduce seed-borne diseases. Tomato seeds germinate best between 75° and 90°F. Once seedlings are up, they grow best between 60° and 70°F. When plants are set out, add 1 cup each of bonemeal and kelp to each hole. Water the transplants thoroughly with fish emulsion or compost tea to give them a good start. Spray young plants with seaweed extract to help prevent transplant shock and nutrient deficiencies.

The Vegetable Plot

Roger Yepsen

When planning next year's garden, consider yourself as well as the plants. What would make this part of the yard more welcoming to you? Vegetable gardens are high-maintenance endeavors, and you'll do a better job of tilling, planting, weeding, and harvesting if you enjoy entering the place. That may mean being more generous with the paths, so that you can walk freely about the garden, with or without a garden cart in front of you or long-handled tools in your arms. You may find that cushioned paths feel a lot better underfoot than those paved with brick or stone. A mulched garden walk,

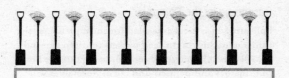

Easy Unusual Vegetables

There's always room for a new crop in most vegetable gardens. If you're looking for new tastes and textures, try some of these uncommon-but-easy-to-grow-vegetables.

- **Arugula** (*Eruca vesica ria* subsp. *sativa*). Also known as rocket. A fast-growing annual with flavorful leaves. Sow seed in rich soil in early spring and autumn. Needs cool weather and lots of water. Add young leaves to salads and soup for a distinctive nutty, spicy flavor. Use the flowers as a garnish or in salads.
- **Basella** (*Basella alba* and *B. a.* var. *rubra*). Also known as Malabar or summer spinach. A heat-tolerant, 6-foot perennial vine with thick, dark green leaves that can be harvested all season. Start plants indoors and transplant outdoors in rich soil after frost danger is past. Trellis to maximize garden space. Requires warm weather and plenty of moisture. Harvest sparingly until plants branch. Substitute the greens for spinach.
- **Elephant garlic** (*Allium ampeloprasum*). A mild, garlic-flavored ½- to 1-pound bulb closely related to the leek. Prepare a deep bed with compost or aged manure. Plant cloves 8 inches apart in fall or late summer. Mulch well in the North. Harvest bulbs the following season when tops die back. Dry in shade and store in a cool, dark, dry place. Use cloves in cooked dishes and the greens for seasoning.
- **Ground cherry** (*Physalis pruinosa*). Also known as dwarf Cape gooseberry. Low sprawling plants produce sweet, marble-sized, golden yellow fruit encased in a papery husk. Will self-sow. Start seed indoors or sow outdoors in rich soil after last spring frost. Harvest when the tan husks turn paper-thin. Add to vegetable and fruit salads for a sweet, exotic flavor. Makes delectable pies and jams. Freeze or dry to preserve.
- **Hyacinth bean** (*Dolichos lablab*). An attractive vining legume with lavender flowers and deep burgundy pods on purple stems. Start seed indoors or direct-seed outdoors in rich soil after frost danger. Grow as you would pole lima beans or on trellises in the ornamental garden. Use flowers in salads and dips. Use the young pods like string beans or fresh in salads. Cook older beans as you would green shell beans.
- **Sorrel, French** (*Rumex scutatus*). A hardy perennial with succulent, lemony leaves high in vitamin C. Start from seed or purchase plants. Plant in rich, well-drained soil in full sun or partial shade. Remove seed heads to prevent leaves from becoming bitter. Mix leaves with other greens for salads, or add them to soups or cooked dishes.

like a thickly carpeted floor, will be less jarring to your joints—and chances are your joints are already being put to the test by yard chores.

While you're giving some thought to wider paths, how about setting aside a small area for a bench? That will encourage you to indulge in a pleasure that gardeners all too seldom allow themselves—looking up from their work to enjoy the birds, the sky, or even the prim topography of the garden beds themselves. You might choose a spot that gets a bit of afternoon shade from a nearby tree. Or attach a canvas beach umbrella to a fence post next to the bench. The only trick is to remind yourself to take a break every hour or so. One way to do that is to keep an inexpensive nonelectric kitchen timer under the bench. Give it a twist to 60 minutes before you get to work, and wait for the recess bell.

All gardening and no play may not be the best way to approach your hobby. Consider setting aside a corner of the garden, and a few minutes, to enjoy the sights and sounds of your yard.

Plan a Root-Friendly Bed

Carrots, parsnips, beets, potatoes, and turnips thrive in a deep, sandy loam. If you want to be successful with them, it's important to modify heavy soil with sand and lots of organic matter—if you have access to it, 10 pounds of compost for a 10-foot-square bed. Vigorously double-digging a clay-rich soil will also help to aerate and break it up.

All of this is easier written about than done. It may seem like a Herculean task to convert the entire garden to being root-crop friendly, so concentrate on just one bed and dedicate it to deep growers. Either improve the existing soil, or build up a raised bed to establish a better growing medium from scratch. Take care to avoid walking on the bed, or you run the risk of compacting the soil. A footstep exerts between 6 and 10 pounds per square inch—and tiptoeing across the beds won't help.

A broadfork allows you to aerate the soil without bringing up slumbering weed seeds from below.

Continued ➤

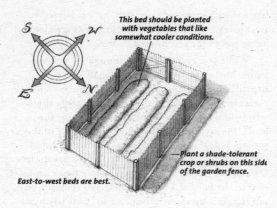

This bed should be planted with vegetables that like somewhat cooler conditions.

—Plant a shade-tolerant crop or shrubs on this side of the garden fence.

East-to-west beds are best.

Most yards have different levels of sunlight and shade, at different times of day. Try to position your plants to take best advantage of what the sun has to offer, keeping in mind the shade cast by fences and taller crops.

Gardening by the Compass

Full sunlight is recommended for most plants, as the informative blurbs on seed packets so often remind us. All-day, blazing sunshine will bring out the best in tomatoes and peppers and corn. Vegetables will reap the most solar benefit if growing in east-to-west rows. Alternatively, you can moderate light levels by planting north-to-south and arranging to have taller plants provide shade from the south end of the bed. If you are encircling the garden with a picket fence, it's also possible to use it as a light filter for lettuce and other plants that don't take to hot conditions. Grow them in the row running parallel to the south-facing side. Another such crop can be grown outside the north-facing side if it isn't vulnerable to the animal pests that caused you to put up the fence in the first place.

Gardening in Shady Places

If there are few places in your yard that offer the "full sun" requirement given for many plants, be assured that this condition isn't necessarily meant to be taken literally. After all, only desert dwellers and beachcombers are likely to be entirely free of shadows from hills and trees. Eight to 10 hours of sunlight should be sufficient, even for lumen-loving tomatoes and peppers. And if your garden is blessed with just 5 hours of sun a day, you're in great shape to grow outstanding salad greens, as well as arugula, broccoli raab, chard, collards, kale, parsley, spinach, and an enormous variety of Asian greens. You might also tuck in a few shade-tolerant shrubs for fruit, such as gooseberry, currant, and blueberry.

---

7 Secrets for a High-Yield Vegetable Garden

Vicki Mattern

Imagine harvesting nearly half a ton of tasty, beautiful, organically grown vegetables from a 15 x 20-foot plot, 100 pounds of tomatoes from just 100 square feet (a 4 x 25-foot bed), or 20 pounds of carrots from just 24 square feet.

Yields like these are easier to achieve than you may think. The secret to superproductive gardening is taking the time now to plan strategies that will work for your garden. Here are seven high-yield strategies gleaned from gardeners who have learned to make the most of their garden space.

1. **Build up your soil.** Expert gardeners agree that building up the soil is the single most important factor in pumping up yields. A deep, organically rich soil encourages the growth of healthy, extensive roots that are able to reach more nutrients and water. The result: extralush, extraproductive growth aboveground.

   The fastest way to get that deep layer of fertile soil is to make raised beds. Raised beds yield up to four times more than the same amount of space planted in rows. That's due not only to their loose, fertile soil but also to efficient spacing—by using less space for paths, you have more room to grow plants.

   Raised beds save you time, too. One researcher tracked the time it took to plant and maintain a 30 x 30-foot garden planted in beds, and found that he needed to spend just 27 hours in the garden from mid-May to mid-October. Yet he was able to harvest 1,900 pounds of fresh vegetables—that's a year's supply of food for three people from about three total days of work!

   How do raised beds save so much time? Plants grow close enough together to shade out competing weeds, so you spend less time weeding. The close spacing also makes watering and harvesting more efficient.

2. **Round out your beds.** The shape of your beds can make a difference, too. Raised beds are more space efficient if the tops are gently rounded to form an arc, rather than flat. A rounded bed that is 5 feet wide across its base, for instance, will give you a 6-foot-wide arc above it—creating a planting surface that's a foot wider than that of a flat bed. That foot might not seem like much, but multiply it by the length of your bed and you'll see that it can make a big difference in total planting area.

   In a 20-foot-long bed, for example, rounding the top increases your total planting area from 100 to 120 square feet. That's a 20 percent gain in planting space in a bed that takes up the same amount of ground space! Lettuce, spinach, and other greens are perfect crops for planting on the edges of a rounded bed.

3. **Space smartly.** To get the maximum yields from each bed, pay attention to how you arrange your plants. Avoid planting in square patterns or rows. Instead, stagger the plants by planting in triangles. By doing so, you can fit 10 to 14 percent more plants in each bed.

   Just be careful not to space your plants too tightly. Some plants won't reach their full size—or yield—when crowded. For instance, when one researcher increased the spacing between romaine lettuces from 8 to 10 inches, the harvest weight per plant doubled. (Remember that weight yield per square foot is more important than the number of plants per square foot.)

   Overly tight spacing can also stress plants, making them more susceptible to diseases and insect attack.

4. **Grow up!** No matter how small your garden, you can grow more by going vertical. Grow space-hungry vining crops—such as tomatoes, pole beans, peas, squash, melons, cukes, and so on—straight up, supported by trellises, fences, cages, or stakes.

   Growing vegetables vertically also saves time. Harvest and maintenance go faster because you can see exactly where the fruits are. And upward-bound plants are less likely to be hit by fungal diseases, thanks to the improved air circulation around the foliage.

   Try growing vining crops on trellises along one side of raised beds, using sturdy end posts with nylon mesh netting or string in between to provide a climbing surface. Tie the growing vines to the trellis. But don't worry about securing heavy fruits—even squash and melons will develop thicker stems for support.

5. **Mix it up.** Interplanting compatible crops saves space, too. Consider the classic Native American combination, the "three sisters"—corn, beans, and squash. Sturdy cornstalks support the pole beans, while squash grows freely on the ground below, shading out competing weeds. This combination works because the crops are compatible. Other

compatible combinations include tomatoes, basil, and onions; leaf lettuce and peas or brassicas; carrots, onions, and radishes; and beets and celery.

6. **Succeed with successions.** Succession (or relay) planting allows you to grow more than one crop in a given space over the course of a growing season. That way, many gardeners are able to harvest three or even four crops from a single area.

   For instance, an early crop of leaf lettuce can be followed with a fast-maturing corn, and the corn followed by more greens or overwintered garlic—all within a single growing season.

   To get the most from your succession plantings:

   · Use transplants. A transplant is already a month or so old when you plant it, and so will mature that much faster than a direct-seeded plant (one grown from seeds sown in the garden).

   · Choose fast-maturing varieties.

   · Replenish the soil with a ¼- to ½-inch layer of compost (about 2 cubic feet per 100 square feet) each time you replant. Work it into the top few inches of soil.

7. **Stretch your season.** Adding a few weeks to each end of the growing season can buy you enough time to grow yet another succession crop—say a planting of leaf lettuce, kale, or turnips—or to harvest more end-of-the-season tomatoes.

   To get those extra weeks of production, you need to keep the air around your plants warm, even when the weather is cold, by using mulches, cloches, row covers, or coldframes.

   Or give heat-loving crops (such as melons, peppers, and eggplants) an extra-early start by using two "blankets"—one to warm the air and one to warm the soil in early spring. About 6 to 8 weeks before the last frost date, preheat cold soil by covering it with either infrared-transmitting (IRT) mulch or black plastic, which will absorb heat. Then, cover the bed with a slitted, clear plastic tunnel. When the soil temperature reaches 65° to 70° F, set out plants and cover the black plastic mulch with straw to keep it from trapping too much heat. Remove the clear plastic tunnel when the air temperature warms and all danger of frost passed. Install it again at the end of the season, when temperatures cool.

Continued →

Forecasting a Freeze

Even the best computer model used by professional weather forecasters can't predict just what a cold night might hold for your garden. Learn to look for signs of frost, in the sky and on the ground.

- Look up. A clear sky means there's no cloud cover, which can serve as an insulating blanket to help keep the earth's warmth from escaping to the heavens.
- Wet a finger. If you don't detect a breeze, that favors a frost.
- Feel the lawn. If the grass is relatively dry, not dewy, frost will be more likely.
- Read the thermometers, plural—not just one, bur a few placed around the property. The temperature on your back porch may be significantly different from the reading you'd find in the garden.
- If you get a 10:00 p.m. reading of lower than 45°F and the above signs indicate trouble, cover up crops in the ground and bring in potted plants.

Foiling the Frosts of Fall

When the air gets nippy on fall nights, don't give up on your garden without trying a couple of easy ways of protecting the plants. After all, you've already done the hard labor of preparing the soil and pampering the garden.

EVENING DRESS FOR THE GARDEN

As any hibernating animal or insect could tell you, the ground remains warmer than the air as night comes on. You can take advantage of the soil's warmth by placing covers over plants in the evening. Just about anything you have hanging about the house or garage will work: old sheets and blankets, plastic tarps, newspaper, and even overturned cardboard boxes. The results aren't pretty, and you have to remember to remove the covers the following morning. Or, you can buy lightweight floating row covers of spun polyester and bump up the plant's micro-environment from 2° to 5°F. They're easy to lay down, and can be rolled up in a jiffy.

WATERING FOR WARMTH

Your neighbors might think it strange to see you out watering the garden on a cool, dark fall evening. If so, reassure them by explaining that crops can be protected from an early frost by putting more moisture in the air around them. Wet soil also is potentially able to hold considerably more heat than when it is dry.

CHEER UP CHILLY PLANTS WITH CHRISTMAS LIGHTS

The Colorado State University Cooperative Extension suggests that as fall turns frosty, you get out the Christmas lights a little early. Suspend a string of lights from the hoops of a hoop house and turn them on at dusk. Not only will the structure take on an unearthly beauty, but plants will benefit from the gentle, evenly dispersed source of heat.

Catch This Winter Flue

It used to be that gardeners routinely stored root crops in their cool basements. But that option is out if you keep this level of the home nice and cozy through the winter. If so, try sinking a section of terra-cotta flue liner in the garden and using that for storage. To ensure good drainage, place a few inches of gravel in the bottom of the hole you dig, followed by a couple of handfuls of loose straw to keep the crops clean. Then put the flue in place and carefully lower vegetables into it—beets, cabbage, carrots, kohlrabi, parsnips, potatoes,

---

Perpetual Edibles
Roger Yepsen

Until not all that long ago, you'd expect a good-size American backyard to have at least a few perennial crops: asparagus, rhubarb, and horseradish, as well as all manner of berries and a fruit tree or two. For example, a 1927 book on root crops said about horseradish that "a few clumps are found in nearly every home garden."

Landscaping and gardening fashions change, and traditional perennial vegetables are often overlooked today. But they deserve consideration. Once planted, asparagus, rhubarb, and horseradish can be counted on to perform year after year without demanding much of your time. Choose the site with care, because you're planting for the long term. As with many garden crops, this trio prefers well-drained soil with plenty of organic matter. Rhubarb leaves and the lacy tops of asparagus look attractive throughout much of the growing season, so you might give some thought to placing these plants in a relatively visible site. Horseradish is no beauty, however, and it's apt to wander intrusively, so many gardeners park it in a spare corner of the yard rather than in the garden.

Rhubarb, the Fruity Vegetable

In an era of larger backyards, rhubarb was as common as barbecue grills are today. It's still worthwhile growing, especially to provide a tart counterpoint to strawberries in pies and jams. Plant it once, and you won't have to worry about it for a decade, at which time you may want to restore its vigor by dividing the clump. Older stands of rhubarb become less productive and may send up more flowering stalks, which should be cut off as they appear to avoid sapping the plant's energy.

Choose a site that gets full sun. The plants are started from crowns because rhubarb doesn't grow true from seed. Either buy crowns from a nursery or beg a few from a gardening friend. In early spring, plant the crowns with their budding tops just 1 inch below the surface. Top dress with compost each following spring for best performance. And hold off harvesting for at least 2 years, allowing the plants to get established. Begin a normal harvest in the fourth year, cutting stalks that are at least 1 inch in diameter and allowing the rest to grow.

Planting Asparagus without a Backhoe

Well, it's not really necessary to bring in heavy equipment to make an asparagus patch. But you might not know that from reading traditional planting advice for this crop, with directions typically calling for a hip-deep trench. In the venerable *Gardening for Pleasure*, published in 1886, horticultural authority Peter Henderson recommended planting rows totaling 300 to 360 feet to feed an average family. "Pleasure" indeed! Instead, if your soil is reasonably good, you can get away with making a much more modest

trench. And in exchange for your labor, you can look forward to 20 to 25 years of harvests.

Gardeners now have their choice of all-male varieties that dramatically outproduce old standards such as 'Mary Washington'; look for 'Jersey Giant,' 'Jersey Knight,' and 'Jersey Pride,' among others. Choose a site with full sun, keeping in mind that the tall ferns will cast shade later in the season; if you are planting alongside the vegetable garden, place the asparagus bed to the west (to filter hot afternoon sun) or to the north.

Set out plants in spring, after the chance of frost is past. Typical spacing is 1½ to 2 feet between plants, and 3 to 4 feet between rows. Make the trenches 8 inches deep and 12 inches wide. Perch the crowns atop 2-inch-high mounds of soil, spreading out their roots in every direction. Cover the crowns with 2 inches of soil. Then add another 2 inches in a couple of week, and fill the trench to ground level 2 weeks after that. Every year, treat each row to a 1- or 2-inch layer of compost or aged manure and work it into the top foot or so of soil. Come the end of the season, cut down the dried foliage with a mower or scythe and distribute a layer of leaf mulch for protection through the winter.

Putting a Harness on Horseradish

Those little jars of store-bought grated horseradish tend to get lost in the refrigerator, and unfortunately, the characteristic zippy flavor doesn't last for long. You can have your own fresh supply simply by tucking a root or two in an edge of the garden. Somewhat simply, that is. Horseradish loves to roam. Once you establish horseradish, you can't very easily get rid of it.

Planting is usually in March or April. You might want to experiment with a couple of different varieties, available as small roots from mail-order sources (horseradish doesn't grow easily from seed). Or start plants with supermarket roots; they aren't treated to keep them from sprouting as potatoes tend to be. Divide the crown into four pieces, each with some root and some of the leafy top, and allow the cuts to heal for a few days. Set roots or pieces at a 45-degree angle, with the top about 2 inches below the surface. Horseradish is best harvested after a couple of good frosts have improved the flavor. You can keep the roots in the ground through the winter, digging them as needed until just before the tops begin growing again in spring.

To prepare horseradish, wash and peel the roots, then grind them in a food processor with white vinegar and salt to taste. Vinegar helps moderate the root's pungency by slowing the release of key enzymes. For a lovely magenta-tinted horseradish, toss in a bit of beet. For a creamy condiment to accompany beef, mix in mayonnaise with the prepared horseradish.

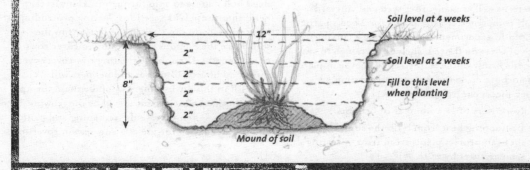

Soil level at 4 weeks
12"
2"
2"
Soil level at 2 weeks
8"
2"
Fill to this level when planting
2"
2"
Mound of soil

Continued →

rutabagas, and turnips. Add more loose straw to fill the air space. Top off the flue with a lid of wood or Styrofoam insulation, weighted with bricks or a flat stone. When temperatures drop well below freezing, you can replace the bricks or stone with a bale of straw for better insulation.

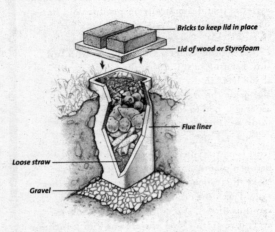

- Bricks to keep lid in place
- Lid of wood or Styrofoam
- Flue liner
- Loose straw
- Gravel

Root crops take form underground, and after harvest you can preserve their goodness by returning them to the soil. A sunken length of terra-cotta flue liner acts as a mini-root cellar, keeping vegetables at a nearly steady temperature into the winter months.

Plan a Frostbite Bed

Nothing gladdens a gardener's heart more than crops that sail right through the frosts of fall. Kale, spinach, Swiss chard, beets, carrots, potatoes, turnips, radishes, broccoli, cauliflower, Asian greens, and some lettuces—these may come into their own when the rest of the natural world is settling down for its winter-long snooze. Come spring, you'll find it easier to cultivate and plant for the new season's crops if these over-winterers are growing in their own dedicated part of the garden. So place them with a view to the year ahead.

Growing Better with Age

Here is a rundown of vegetables that go against the rule that fresh is best.

- Some winter squashes will develop their full flavor in the weeks after harvest, including butternut and buttercup.
- Carrots and parsnips may benefit from a light frost.
- Freezing temperatures may bring out the full character of many brassicas: kale, cauliflower, Brussels sprouts, kohlrabi, cabbage, turnips, and rutabagas.
- Garlic right out of the garden will taste like garlic. But if the heads are cured and stored for a time, their full flavor will have a chance to develop.

A Hoop Skirt Keeps Gardens Growing in Good Fashion

While a floating cover will indeed rest lightly on the plants below, you can trap more warm air within a row cover that's elevated by hoops. And just about the easiest hoops to erect are lengths of 9-gauge wire. You can buy coils of it from home and garden centers, as well as mail-order seed and vineyard supply companies. To size hoops for a bed's particular width, experiment with how long a curving piece of wire you'll need, including enough to sink the ends firmly in the soil. Keep the cover in place with anchors made for the purpose or simple V-shaped pieces cut from coat hangers.

Row covers offer a number of benefits.

- By trapping heat from both the sun and soil, they can protect plants from frost, elevating temperatures by 2° to 7°F.

- They warm the soil and the air in spring, getting plants off to a quicker start, which means faster germination, better root growth, and an earlier-maturing crop (beating the performance of black plastic mulch by 1 to 3 weeks).
- You may get a better yield from a number of crops, especially cukes, squash, and melons.
- The covers serve as a barrier to flying insect pests. Not only will the plants be nibbled less, but you can spare them from diseases commonly spread by bugs. Expect to have good results against such pests as cabbage moths and the cabbage root maggot fly; various flea beetle species on several vegetables; spinach leaf miner; striped cucumber beetle on melons, summer and winter squash, and pumpkins, as well as cukes; European corn borer; Colorado potato beetle on potatoes and eggplant; and potato leafhoppers.

Note that in some circumstances, a row cover can aggravate pest problems, if an insect pest manages to find its way under the cover and then reproduces freely without interference from beneficial insects on the outside. If you see this happening, consider removing the cover temporarily to admit the good bugs. A row cover may also protect pests that have over-wintered in the soil below. Again, you may need to pull back the row cover for a time. And consider rotating crops each year so that when pests come out of dormancy, they'll find a barrier between themselves and their target vegetable.

There's another sort of pest to consider when using row covers—mice. If you don't take the trouble to store the fabric at the end of the growing season, you're apt to find that mice have made good use of it for making nests.

- By placing 50-percent shade cloth over the hoops in hot weather, you may be able to grow lettuce right through the dog days of summer; the green cloth can lower temperatures by 3° to 6°F.

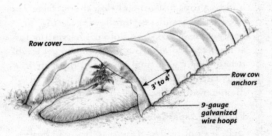

- Row cover
- Row cover anchors
- 3' to 4'
- 9-gauge galvanized wire hoops

There's nothing much to this plant protecting system—just wires and lightweight spun fabric—but the climate change within the covering is significant.

A Sturdier Hoop House

For a hoop house that gusty weather won't topple, buy a roll of concrete reinforcing screening. It's available through companies that sell concrete supplies; consult the commercial pages of your phone book. The wire is tough stuff, and you'll need bolt cutters to snip through it. Cut pieces to bend into tunnel-like sections, leaving protruding wires so that you can anchor the sections in the soil. Place the sections side by side, to cover rows of any length. Then drape floating row covers over this hoop house. Tomatoes and peppers will flourish in this environment. Coddle them for up to a month, at which point they'll be outgrowing their house. Then remove the screening and cloth and set them aside for use as a late-season coverup.

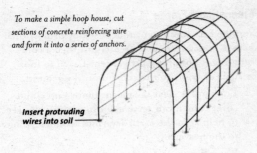

To make a simple hoop house, cut sections of concrete reinforcing wire and form it into a series of anchors.

- Insert protruding wires into soil

Grow Your Own Calcium

Garden vegetables might not look like good sources of calcium—they don't lactate, after all. But a number of crops can deliver a considerable measure of this nutrient. That's a particular plus for people with lactose intolerance. Here's a look at what a 1-cup serving of these cooked vegetables will contain. (To put these numbers in perspective, 1 cup of milk contains 300 milligrams of calcium, and 1 cup of low-fat yogurt contains approximately 400 milligrams.)

Vegetable	Milligrams of Calcium Per 1 Cup (cooked)
Rhubarb	348
Collards	266
Turnip greens	197
Kale	179
Okra	177
Beet greens	164
Pak choi	158
Dandelion	147

A Body-Building Protein Garden

For many people (gardeners included), vegetables still have the reputation of being a "good-for-you" food to be eaten dutifully along with real food—meat and dairy products, which are good sources of protein. In fact, a number of crops can pump you up with substantial amounts of that nutrient. Vegetables should figure importantly in a well-rounded, healthful diet. And as a gardener, you are guaranteed a fresh and unadulterated source.

The big surprise in this chart, unless you are a nutritionist, may be that some leafy greens pack a protein punch. All of this is good news for people who are trying to lower their intake of cholesterol-rich foods. By the way, to put the numbers in perspective, 100 grams of broiled beefsteak would give you about 22 grams of protein.

Vegetable	Grams of Protein Per 100-Gram Serving
Pumpkin seeds	29.0
Peanuts (raw, without skins)	26.3
Adzuki beans (raw)	20.0
Soybeans (dried, cooked)	11.0
Soybeans (green, cooked)	9.8
Lentils (cooked)	9.0
Fava beans (green, raw)	8.5
Peas (green, cooked)	5.4
Kale (cooked, no stems or midribs)	4.5
Brussels sprouts	4.2
Collards (cooked, without stems)	3.6
Spinach (raw)	3.2
Broccoli (cooked)	3.1

Continued ➡

Foul Air in the Fridge

The whole idea of storing vegetables and fruits in the fridge is to keep them tasting fresh, but foods in close juxtaposition may taint each other. Peter A. Ferretti, PhD, a Penn State professor of vegetable crops, has identified the most prevalent cases of flavor swapping. He suggests storing apples and potatoes in a cool garage rather than refrigerating them. Keep sensitive items as far as you can from whatever bothers them. Use up older stock first, before it can take on off flavors. And place a box of baking soda in the refrigerator to absorb odors. From time to time, skim off the top layer of powder to expose the fresher product below.

- Carrots affect celery.
- Green peppers affect pineapple.
- Onions affect apples, celery, and potatoes.
- Potatoes affect apples and pears.
- Apples affect cabbage, carrots, onions, and dairy.
- Pears affect cabbage, carrots, celery, onions, and potatoes.

SOME VEGETABLES LIKE IT WARMER

Most vegetables you bring in from the garden will have a longer storage life if kept in the refrigerator just above freezing, or from 34° to 40°F. This slows the enzyme action that results in a loss of flavor and change in texture. By the way, the chilliest section of most refrigerators is at the back of the uppermost shelf. Still, there are important exceptions to the colder-is-better rule. Crops that originated in tropical or subtropical climates don't take to being stored below 50°F, including cucumbers, squash, tomatoes, peppers, eggplant, snap beans, and potatoes. Store them in a cool place rather than the coldest part of the fridge.

Artichokes for Cool Climes

Unless you live in California, chances are you get your globe artichokes at the supermarket rather than from your backyard. But with some care, they can be grown over much of the United States. Even if the crop isn't overwhelmingly generous, there is no disputing the majesty of the plants, which can reach a height of 4 feet and will form big thistlelike blossoms if allowed to.

Globe artichokes are cultivated as perennials in warm areas, but they will be done in by winter temperatures below 20°F. If you will be growing artichokes as an annual, 'Imperial Star' is a good variety. Start plants indoors about 8 weeks before your last frost-free date. They will produce better if subjected to a bit of vernalization, or exposure to cool temperatures. Bring the plants out to the garden soon enough that they will spend at least a week in temperatures around 50°F. Although artichokes tend to get off to a slow start once transplanted, they'll need plenty of space before long; allow 30 inches between plants. By July, you can expect to begin harvesting the small buds—small, but more tender than the big commercial ones.

If you have spare room in your vegetable or flower beds, try growing a couple of globe artichokes from seed. They'll be visually outstanding, as well as producing tender, flavorful 'chokes.

Basil Rescue Mission

There's no grimmer harbinger of winter's approach than a row of frost-blackened basil. To enjoy this highly aromatic cook's friend through the winter, you might try to dig up a few of the busy plants and wrestle them into pots. But it's easier to take cuttings toward the end of summer. Remove the leaves from the lower end of the cuttings to prevent dehydration. Place the cuttings in a glass of water, then stick them in pots once they've grown roots. The clove-like scent will take you back to summer every time you touch the plants. Next spring, take cuttings from these windowsill basils and repeat the rooting process to have plants you can set out as soon as warm weather returns.

Remove lower leaves.

By taking cuttings, you can make clonal copies of your favorite plants, including those about to be done in by freezing weather.

String Climbers Along with a Maypole

Surround this pole with climbing edibles, flowering vines, or a mixture of both. To make it easier to remove the pole at summer's end and return it to the yard in spring, you can bury a length of pipe with a diameter just large enough to accommodate it, so that the top of the pipe is at ground level. Then all you have to do is slip the pole down the pipe, without needing to hammer while balanced on a stepladder.

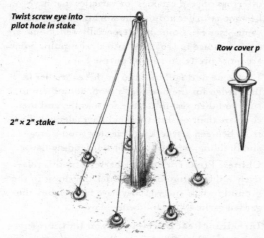

Twist screw eye into pilot hole in stake

Row cover p

2" x 2" stake

To make the most of garden real estate, think vertical. This simple pole arrangement will encourage climbers to clamber up the twines radiating down to the ground.

1. While standing on a stepladder held firmly by a helper, pound a 6- or 8-foot-long, 2 x 2 wooden stake into good garden soil. To prevent mashing the stake, you can cut an X in a tennis ball and slip it over the top before hammering.

2. Drill a pilot hole in the top of the stake and twist in a threaded eye.

3. Run lengths of twine from the eye to pegs placed 2 to 3 feet out from the pole's base. You can make pegs by cutting U-shaped hoops from coat hangers, but you'll be less likely to trip over or lose the brightly colored plastic pegs used for row covers.

4. Sow seeds or set out plants next to each peg.

AN EDIBLE ORNAMENTAL BEAN

Scarlet runner beans are a standout in the vegetable garden, producing showy blossoms that act as magnets for hummingbirds and butterflies. The large, shiny beans themselves are every bit as handsome in their own way, and they happen to taste good as well, with a flavor something like chestnuts. Even the flowers are edible, making an attractive addition to salads.

The vines need something to climb on—a maypole, trellis, arbor, or teepee of branches. Or you can snake them horizontally along a picket fence. Some gardeners even send them up tall-growing sweet corn.

Stubby Carrots for Stubborn Soil

If carrots don't care for the density of your soil, try planting short varieties that won't stick their toes in very deep. 'Parmex' is a chubby ball-type variety that's just 1½ inches long at maturity. 'Kinko' is somewhat more conventional in shape, reaching a modest length of 4 inches by the time they're ready to pull. Short, stout 'Royal Chantenay' carrots will burrow their way down into heavy soil.

If you're stuck with unyielding soil, you can skip it altogether and grow short carrot varieties in pots. While you might be able to get away with as small as a 2-gallon pot, this crop will fare better if treated to a container holding 3 or even 6 gallons of soil. Remember that potted vegetables may need more frequent watering, especially if the pots are of clay and wick moisture.

Try This Artichoke Cousin

Cardoon is an odd-sounding and remarkable-looking relative of the globe artichoke. Preparing it for harvest is an unusual process as well. The stalks of the long, jagged leaves are the edible feature, not the flower buds. To keep the stalks tender, you blanch them once they reach a length of 18 inches or so. Tie the leaves at the top to bundle them, then wrap first with newspaper and then a layer of black plastic, or with burlap. After a month or so, remove this covering and cut the stalks below the crown. Strip off the outer leaves to reveal the blanched center of the plant.

Try sautéing stalks in butter to enjoy them as Italians do. Some cooks suggest simmering cardoons first in water with a bit of vinegar to bring out their best flavor. If you allow some of the plants to mature, they will display lavender flowers that are excellent for fresh or dried arrangements. Don't allow flowers to set seed and be scattered about, or you may have a nuisance on your hands.

Cardoon has a third use, beyond being attractive and tasty. It produces an enzyme that has been used by traditional cheesemakers in Portugal as a coagulant. To try it yourself, pick the flowers, dry them, weigh out about 1 ounce, and steep in a cup of warm water. Use 1 teaspoon per quart of milk to begin with, or more if needed to cause the milk to coagulate.

A CENTERPIECE FOR THE GARDEN

Most vegetable gardens are practical affairs laid out like tiny farm fields, with parallel rows and little thought to visual drama. For something different, try arranging the beds around a central feature. A cluster of three or so tall, commanding plants will do. Cardoon is a likely candidate, spreading its jagged-edged arms over a good area as it tops off at 6 feet or so. Other handsome edibles include globe artichoke and bronze fennel. Or, you can lash together a few 8-foot-long stakes, place them right in the middle of the central bed, and train runner beans up them. Shorter plants can make a bold statement, too, if grown in a super-size urn or pot set on a stump or other base to raise it up enough to stand out.

More Cukes, Better Cukes

Cucumbers aren't a very demanding crop, but they appreciate adequate watering and prompt picking.

DON'T PLUG UP CUCUMBER PRODUCTION

It's important to keep a close eye on the cucumber patch to make sure that you harvest the cukes at their peak. If you spot a yellow one that has gone

Continued ➡

past its prime, pick it promptly. Otherwise, the vine will tend to stall, putting no more energy into growing more fruits. Another reason to pick sooner rather than later is that plants harvested late in the season tend to yield bitter cukes.

Avoiding Bitterness

Cucumbers react to stress by developing a bitter personality. There can be any of a few causes, including a run of hot days, insufficient moisture, low fertility, or foliar diseases. The off-putting taste is the work of compounds known as cucurbitacins; under difficult growing conditions, they migrate from other plant parts to the fruits. Make sure you water regularly in dry, hot spells. And look into resistant varieties; more than a half-dozen diseases can be dealt with by selecting cucumbers bred for resistance. Cucumber beetles spread pathogens as well as exercising their appetites, and they can be discouraged with a floating row cover. If you find that a particular plant is yielding bitter fruit, pull it, because its cukes won't get any milder; if the leaves show the white coating characteristic of powdery mildew, don't compost the rogued plant.

Corn: Sweet, Sweeter, Sweetest

Buying seed for sweet corn isn't quite as simple as picking up a packet of, say, Deer Tongue lettuce. That's because plant breeders have been fiddling with the genetic makeup of regular old corn, with very sweet results. These newer hybrids are classified as *normal sugary* (SU), *sugary enhanced* (SE), or *super sweet* (Sh2) varieties, as well as synergistic, which sounds frightening but only means that some kernels on each ear are SE and others are Sh2. Here are the characteristics of each group.

- Traditional sweet corn is open pollinated, meaning that you can collect seed for planting the following year—an option you don't have with the hybrids. Gardeners continue to grow old-fashioned varieties for the "corny" taste and substantial, chewy texture.

- The SUs are moderately sweet, compared to those described below. Because their sugars begin to turn into starch soon after picking, they must be eaten within a very short time. Ears have what can be called a traditional corn flavor, harkening back to a time before all these abbreviations appeared.

- Sugary enhanced varieties have a gene that raises the sugar content above that of SUs, with an excellent tenderness and a creamy texture. The ears are slower to convert sugars into starch. Small wonder that SEs are highly popular with home gardeners.

- Super sweet varieties are in fact the sweetest you can grow, and they have a crisp texture with the kernels popping as you bite into an ear. The lack of a traditional corn flavor may be a shortcoming to some people. Plantings should be isolated from other varieties that are tasseling at the same time because super sweets have weak pollen and may turn starchy and tough if pollinated by other types. A distance of at least 500 feet is necessary, because the pollen is carried by the wind.

- Each ear of a synergistic variety will have a mix of sugary enhanced and super sweet kernels to bite into, for a good blend of sweetness and tenderness. The sweetness comes on only as ears reach full maturity; otherwise they will taste watery. You can grow this variety alongside sugary and sugar enhanced rows, but quality will suffer if synergistics exchange pollen with super sweets.

Other Corn Codes

When sorting through the many varieties of sweet corn, you also should be familiar with other abbreviations. *Fl* means that the variety is a hybrid and it won't grow true from seed you collect from dried ears. Then there's resistance to common diseases: *NCLB* signifies resistance to northern corn leaf blight; *NCLB*, to southern corn leaf blight; *SM*, to smut; *SW*, to Stewart's Wilt; and *R*, to common rust.

Baby Corn for Stir-Fries

Baby corn is a novel sight in East Asian dishes—and not all that flavorful if it has been languishing in a tin can. Fortunately, it's not that difficult to grow your own. Begin with a variety that yields especially good, tender premature ears, including 'Baby,' 'Bonus,' 'Candystick,' 'Delectable,' and 'Jubilee.' Plant at a tighter spacing, from 2 to 4 inches apart, and keep a close eye on the developing ears to make sure you harvest them before they become too big. Allow no more than a couple of days after the silks first appear. By picking promptly, you also encourage the stalk to produce more ears. Keep the husks on the harvested babies until you're ready to cook them.

Grow Your Own Garlic

Garlic is undergoing a modest rediscovery, as people find out that not all varieties taste alike. Not that there's anything wrong with supermarket garlic It's cheap. It tastes garlicky, too. But it is only one color in a spectrum of garlics. Have a look at the offerings of seed catalogs for varieties that have become favorites around the world. Some are mild, some assertive. Some keep especially well. Some are a good choice for roasting into a sweet pulp. Some are quite pretty, in rosy or purple hues.

Come next fall, tuck two or three varieties in the garden for the next year's crop, allow them to cure and then rest in storage for a while, and then compare their qualities and culinary talents. Choose from between softneck varieties for good storage and braiding, or hardneck for outstanding flavor.

Chinese Pink. For an early harvest, try this relatively mild-tasting softneck. Stick the cloves in the ground in fall, and you may have fresh-from-the-garden garlic by the following May.

Inchelium Red. Discovered on an Indian reservation in northern Washington State, this softneck garlic has a mild, highly rated flavor. It's particularly suited to baking into a soft pulp.

Polish Softneck. This heirloom has been grown in the United States for a century, remaining popular because of its winter hardiness, large cloves, and sharp taste.

Chesnok Red. Originally from the former Soviet republic of Georgia, Chesnok has a flavor that stands up well when cooked. Try baking this hardneck to make a spread for crackers.

Purple Glazer. Both the bulb and cloves of this lovely hardneck variety are a rich purple embellished with gold or silver. Like Chesnok, it's from the Republic of Georgia and is a good choice for baking.

Spanish Roja. This heirloom is described as having a definitive garlic flavor, which helps to explain why it remains popular year after year.

Getting to Know East Asian Greens

Asian greens come in many shapes and sizes, with tastes ranging from mild and sweet to pungent. These varieties grow quickly with little trouble, and they may keep producing well after hard frosts have sent other vegetables reeling. Many can be harvested either early for salad ingredients and

braising mixes, or when full size for steaming and sautéing in a wok. Even the flowers, characteristically a cheerful yellow, make a pretty, edible addition to salads. The only potential problem is the confusing mix of names—English, Japanese, Thai, Chinese, Indian, and more, with a riot of different spellings. You can always go by the photos in catalogs and on seed packets.

Generally, these vegetables are sown directly into the garden from early spring into midsummer, with a second sowing when cool weather returns in early fall.

Pak choi. Also known as bok choy, this is a relatively familiar green, similar in appearance to chard, with a thick white stalk and mild flavor.

Autumn Poem. This is a flowering variety, similar to pac choi but with thick, flavorful stems and attractive flower buds.

Tatsoi. The dark green, spoon-shaped leaves grow in tidy, low-growing rosettes. You can sow this form of pac choi right into fall.

Red Giant and Osaka Purple. Grown for both salads and stir-fries, these mustards have spicy, colorful leaves. They may self-seed and reappear here and there in the garden.

Mizuna. Mizuna is a striking-looking mustard, with deeply toothed leaves and a relatively mild flavor.

Komatsuna. Sometimes listed as spinach mustard, it matures quickly, with harvesting possible just 35 days after sowing.

Gai lon. Also called Chinese broccoli, gai lon has thick, flavorful stems. Cut the main stem, and others will branch out.

Hon tsai tai. This one is worth growing for its remarkable color as well as its mildly mustardlike zip. The stems are purple, becoming more vivid in cooler weather; the leaves are dark green; and the flowers bright yellow.

Eggplants in Easter Egg Colors

Try growing slim and modest-size East Asian or Italian varieties. They come in cheerful lavender and cream colors, in solids and stripes. The fruits and the plants themselves are attractive enough to earn a place in flower beds. The taste is agreeable, too: mild, with no hint of the bitterness we associate with the familiar big boys of the produce section. And because they're slim rather than rotund, they cook up quickly in a stir-fry without sopping up a lot of oil.

Go Wild with Kale

Seed companies take pains to provide you with packets that will yield dependable results. Most of the time, that is. Some mail-order firms sell seed for open-pollinated kale that hasn't been stabilized. It's a treat to see the varied forms and colors that spring up out of those apparently identical seeds. Frilly or plain edges, smooth or crinkly, big or small, green or multicolored—it's like looking at a little forest of different trees. Pick them young to add to salads, and you'll better be able to enjoy their distinctive looks than if they're cooked. If you have a favorite couple of kales, allow them to flower and go to seed, and save the seed for the following year. When you label the seed containers, don't be shy about coming up with a fanciful name for your rare variety.

A Lettuce Explosion

There's no explaining taste, in art or in lettuce. Profound changes in the use of lettuce and other salad crops have been taking place in the United States, western Europe, and several other pans of

Continued ➡

the world. The most surprising change has been the adoption of crisphead lettuce (also known as iceberg) in countries where it was hardly used before. In England, for example, people consumed mostly butterhead lettuce until the late 1970s. At that time, only about 3 percent of the lettuce used was of the iceberg type. Then, the British discovered iceberg lettuce, and it now composes about 80 percent of the lettuce consumed in Britain. Similar changes have occurred in the Scandinavian countries and are beginning in other countries as well.

On the other hand, we in the United States have rediscovered that not all lettuce heads are round, crisp, and hard and once again are eating romaine, butterhead, and leaf lettuces, not to mention endive and escarole (*Cichorium endivia*) and spinach (*Spinacia oleraacea*). In addition, we have discovered 'Little Gem,' a Latin-type lettuce, part romaine and part butterhead, which is small, crisp, and sweet. We have also discovered radicchio, a red Italian chicory (*c. intybus* L.); mizuna, a leafy vegetable from Japan (*Brassica japonica* L.); and rocket (*Eruca sativa* Mill.), formerly found in the wild, but now known in the cultivated form as arugula. Mizuna, arugula, and spinach are often found in a salad mixture called mesclun, which is made up of tiny lettuce leaves of various shapes and colors and other salad greens.

A Chill Pill for Bitter Lettuce

When lettuce is subjected to hot summer weather or begins to bolt, the leaves are apt to take on a bitter edge. You can sweeten lettuce somewhat by rinsing it and storing it in the refrigerator for a couple of days.

Jump-Start a Salad

The reputation of iceberg lettuce has taken a hit lately because of its famous blandness. But most lettuces are relatively mild-tasting; fortunately, you can perk up a salad by including homegrown greens from the genus *Cichorium*.

- **Chicory.** These full-flavored greens look a lot like the common dandelion and are sometimes referred to as Italian dandelion. Snip them young for salads, or later in the season for braising. If you allow a few to bolt, you'll be rewarded with the familiar sky blue chicory flower seen along roadsides.

- **Belgian endive.** Also known as witloof, this unusual vegetable has a double season. It starts out in the garden, developing a root. Then it is dug up and brought into a cool basement (from 50° to 60°F) for forcing in the winter. The traditional method is to stick them in a bucket of moistened sand, leaving the crowns exposed. A lid is placed over the bucket to exclude light, which would turn the forced leaves green and cause them to be bitter. The *chicons*, as the tight pale heads are known, are ready for harvesting after 3 to 5 weeks. If given a month or two to recover, the roots may produce a second harvest. Newer varieties can be forced without this ritual.

- **Radicchio.** Similar in appearance to a small head of lettuce, the heading radicchios are bright in color and spirited in flavor. Unlike most leafy greens, they can be grilled or roasted.

- **Escarole.** This European salad green has a somewhat bitter flavor. It will taste milder if blanched for a few days or a week before harvest; cover plants with overturned bushel baskets or pots, or simple A-frames of plywood. Or, with a bit of twine, you can tie up the outer leaves to shield those within from the sun. Escarole not only adds oomph and

texture to salads, but can be braised with olive oil and a splash of balsamic vinegar.

- **Endive.** Distinct from Belgian endive (see above), this leafy green looks like a frilly lettuce but has a touch of the bitterness characteristic of this group and a more substantial texture. Those with deeply dissected leaves may be listed as frisee in catalogs.

Purples and Golds to Go with Your Greens

To visually spike a salad of greens, toss in edible flower blossoms. Some contribute mainly color, while others add a novel taste. Pick the blossoms just before using them, and either include them in the mix or scatter them over the top of the heap. Soups are famously bland-looking and also will benefit from a garnish of pretty petals. Here is a crayon box of possibilities.

Edible Plant	Color
Borage	Blue
Calendula	Gold
Chives	Purple
Dianthus	Pink
Lavender	Purple
Nasturtium	Yellow, orange
Violet	Purple, yellow, white

Lettuce as an Ornamental

You may be the sort of no-nonsense person who views the garden as a source of good food. Period. But the range of colors and shapes now available in many crops suggests laying out beds with an eye to design. Lettuces, as an example, come in cool and hot colors, and in all sorts of shapes. Instead of sowing separate blocks of this or that variety, try alternating reds and greens, or tall lettuces and round ones. Another approach is to sow a pattern, perhaps a border of 'Red Sails' or 'Outrageous' lettuce surrounding cool green 'Deer Tongue', which in turn forms a border around a speckled variety such as 'Freckles' or 'Forellenschuss'. For another pattern, divide a bed into equal-size diamonds. To keep the lines sharp between varieties, place boards along the edges of an area as you scatter seed. There's no practical benefit to planting this way—except that you may have the incentive to take more pleasure (and more care) in weeding and watering to maintain that bit if artful design.

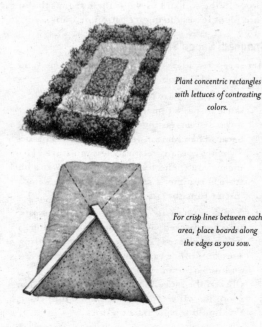

Plant concentric rectangles with lettuces of contrasting colors.

For crisp lines between each area, place boards along the edges as you sow.

A Kinder, Gentler Jalapeño

If past experiences with hot peppers have scared you off, try growing a jalapeño with good flavor but

less heat, such as Numex Primavera (supposed to pack just one-tenth the wallop), or the intriguingly named Fooled You, an F1 hybrid that looks like culinary dynamite but is devoid of heat.

And here's a tip if you've learned to be cautious around horticultural hotties. Grow truly hot varieties and milder ones in separate areas of the garden. It's all too easy to confuse the two once you have them on the kitchen counter.

Smoking Jalapeños

No, the idea isn't to light them up like ruby red cigars, but to preserve these peppers by drying gradually over a smoky, smoldering fire. The dried result is known as a chipotle. You can use a barbecue with a snugly fitting lid, starting with charcoal briquettes. Then switch to branches or chips of a hardwood such as hickory, ash, oak, or pecan, or a fruit wood such as apple. The wood can be soaked in water to help keep the fire at the moderate temperature necessary to avoid burning the peppers. Also make use of the vents to control the amount of air reaching the fire.

Rake the coals over to one side of the barbecue and place the stemmed peppers on the other side of the grill. Turn the peppers from time to time, and add wood as needed to maintain the fire. It's a slow process, taking at least several hours for the peppers to dry, so you are better off beginning early in the day. Store the cooled peppers in zippered plastic bags.

A Simple Ristra

Ornamental strings of red pepper ristras are a common sight around Southwestern and Mexican households. They're practical as well, allowing the peppers to air dry with little danger of mold forming. You'll need a lot of peppers—5 to 20 pounds of them if you want to make a 3-foot-long ristra, depending on the size of the variety. Possibilities include Anaheim, Cascabel, Cayenne, De Arbol, and Mirasol. The traditional method of stringing peppers involves tying them in bunches and then braiding individual strings along a length of twine. This version is a lot simpler: Just thread sturdy fishing line through the stems, tying the stem of the first pepper so that it will secure those above it. Make a loop at the top of the line so that you can hang the ristra. When you want to use a pepper, remove the uppermost one, rinse off any accumulated dust, and reconstitute it by dropping it in simmering water, then turning off the heat and allowing the pepper to sit for 10 minutes or so.

Pumpkins, Big and Fast

You can buy pumpkins for a song when fall comes around. But if you grow your own, the crop will lend a cheerful presence to the garden at a time of year when most plants have given up. When selecting varieties, keep in mind that some are grown primarily for their looks—color, shape, and size. Others are renowned for cooking, with sweet and flavorful flesh.

Building a Bigger Pumpkin

Gardeners like to brag about huge tomatoes and moan about huge zucchinis. And there's a particular fascination with pumpkins the size of Cinderella's coach. Here are a few tips for growing the biggest pumpkin on the block.

- Select a variety known for size. A couple of favorites are 'Prizewinner,' a hybrid; and bigger still, Dill's 'Atlantic Giant,' which is a different species from the familiar *Cucurbit pepo*. The largest pumpkin on record is an Atlantic Giant weighing in at 1,469 pounds, but chances are your best effort will be in the

Continued ➡

range of 200 to 300 pounds. To order seeds right from the developer of Dill's himself, contact him at www.howarddill.com.

- Start early, sowing seed indoors 2 weeks before planting them in the garden.
- Give them plenty of room to roam, at least an area measuring 25 feet square. A jumbo may carpet more than 2,000 square feet with its foliage.
- Anchor them. Growing vines are vulnerable to strong winds. Pile up soil at nodes along the vines; this also has the benefit of encouraging the plant to put down secondary roots. Consider putting up a length of snow fence on the side of the pumpkin patch from which prevailing winds tend to blow.
- Focus the plant's energy by cutting off all but one of the developing fruits.
- To prevent the outer skin of the developing pumpkin from hardening before it reaches full size, put up a board or a section of fence covered with fabric to block the full force of the sun.
- Position them. As a big pumpkin grows, the stem tends to meet it at an increasingly narrow angle. Gently and gradually move the fruit so that the stem remains nearly perpendicular.
- Feed and water them. It stands to reason that a living thing this big has to have a good appetite. Continue to fertilize through the season. Trickle irrigation and soaker hoses are a good approach to watering because they will be less likely than overhead sprinkling to cause mildew problems.

Toward a More Perfect Pumpkin

Pumpkins may become somewhat misshapen if allowed to just park in one place and get huge. To help ensure that they'll develop a pleasing round shape, get into the routine of rotating them about a quarter of a turn every week or so. And if you would like the pumpkins to be really big as well as really round, plan ahead for their need to sprawl by placing the hills 25 feet apart.

Punkin' Chunkin'?

Fall is that time of year when people feel like picking up a pumpkin and seeing how far they can hurl it. Or, at least some people do. Delaware hosts the annual Punkin' Chunkin' competition in which contestants use all manner of contraptions to all but put that plump orange fruit into orbit. The record now stands at an astounding 4,331 feet, accomplished with an air cannon. According to contest rules, the pumpkins must weigh between 8 and 10 pounds—no Baby Boos allowed. Pumpkins don't always fly straight and true; if it strays in flight, the competitors who fired it have 3 hours to locate it.

Edible Ornamental Winter Squashes

These brilliantly colored squashes make excellent autumn decorations—forget the fake colored leaves and the phony Halloween cobweb effect. Here's a rundown of the prettiest.

- 'Sweet Dumpling' has a brilliant patterning of dark green against warm white. Each squash has enough scrumptious flesh for one serving.
- 'Carnival' is a harlequin among dumpling-type squashes, with a riot of color. A cooler summer will help bring out the schoolbus-yellow coloring. The flavor is considered to be not quite up to the par of 'Sweet Dumpling'.
- 'Cream of the Crop' acorn squash not only is an attractive cream color on the outside but also offers creamy textured flesh within.

- 'Table Gold' acorn is a diverting golden color.
- 'Turk's Cap' is more of a novelty than a culinary favorite, but it works well in soups.
- 'Sunshine' is a Scarlet Kabocha that does seem to bring rays of sunlight into the garden and onto the windowsill.
- 'Orangetti' is a new, brightly colored version of the standard spaghetti squash. As its color suggests, this variety delivers far more beta-carotene. It also has a sweeter flavor and cooks in less time.

You don't need to buy seeds to have an interesting array of winter squashes in the garden. Supermarkets often carry a colorful selection, and you can choose the most attractive, then taste-test them at home before committing the considerable garden space that they require. Scoop out the seeds, spread them our on a few thicknesses of paper towel to dry, then store in sandwich bags on which you label the variety.

Oven-Dried Tomatoes

Rather than stand over a hot stove stirring tomatoes down into a sauce for canning, you can let the oven do most of the work of preserving them, by drying. Choose a meaty paste tomato, such as the widely grown San Marzano. Slice them in half the long way, remove the seeds, and place the halves on cake racks set on baking sheets. Sprinkle with salt. Place them in the oven, using just the pilot light if you use gas or a setting of about 150°F for an electric oven. The tomatoes will need anywhere from 8 to 24 hours to dry to a pliable state. Pack the dried halves in glass jars, pouring in olive oil to displace the air as you do so. Tuck in garlic cloves, basil, or oregano if you wish.

Fight Anthracnose on Tomatoes

Anthracnose is a soil-borne disease that causes round, sunken spots on tomatoes. These indentations eventually turn black at the center as fungal fruiting bodies are formed. Plants are especially prone to the affliction if you haven't been regularly rotating tomatoes and peppers with other crops.

Although anthracnose can be bothersome to home gardeners, you can stay a step ahead of it with a simple barrier technique. Lay two or three sheets of newspaper on the soil around tomato plants. Lightly moisten the paper, then top with 2 or 3 inches of grass clippings. This traps the disease spores in the soil and prevents them from splashing onto plant leaves during irrigation or rain.

Spaghetti Sauce Shortcuts

Here are a few ideas to take some of the time (and steam) out of the job.

- It's not necessary to have special-purpose sauce or paste tomato varieties to simmer down a great-tasting sauce. But it helps. That's because San Marzano. Roma, and other sauce favorites contain relatively less moisture. That means you spend less time standing over a hot stove at summer's end, waiting for the water in juicier tomatoes to go off as steam.
- You don't have to convert the entire harvest into hot-packed sauce for use months later. Enjoy fresh sauce right now. Begin by getting a start on dinner early enough to allow at least an hour of simmering with the lid off to thicken the sauce. You can speed things up by spooning off clear liquid from the top; reserve this liquid for use in soup stock.
- Why not do your sauce simmering when the weather isn't simmering? Run tomatoes through a strainer as you would normally, then place them in plastic containers and

freeze. Label the containers as tomato juice, rather than sauce, so that you'll know they still need to be cooked down before ladling them over pasta. When the weather turns cooler and you won't mind the added heat and humidity, take the containers out of the freezer for further processing.

Tomatoes All through the Winter

A 6-inch pot will be large enough to grow a plant, although a bigger pot will need watering less frequently and you may see more-vigorous growth. Varieties to try include 'Healani,' 'Pixie,' 'Small Fry,' and 'Tiny Tim.' Although the plants will be small, they still may need to be staked when fruits appear. Don't forget to rotate the plants so that all sides will benefit from direct sunlight.

You may have to play the role of pollinating insect once the plants develop their yellow blossoms. Just give the branches a gentle tap with your finger to help broadcast the pollen. Look for this dust around blossoms as you jiggle the plant.

Windowsill Tomatoes

You're better off with a small variety such as 'Pixie,' 'Small Fry,' or 'Tiny Tim.' Start seeds, transplant seedlings to pots placed in the window, and fertilize moderately. When watering, make sure the full depth of the pot is moist. As plants develop, support them with sticks poked into the growing medium. A fluorescent light fixture, placed just above the plants, will help to ensure that you get a crop. Rotate the plants so that all sides are treated to a sun bath. Once blossoms appear, tap the plants to help distribute the pollen.

Try These Members of the Tomato Family

Here are a couple of members of the tomato family that are easy to grow, are fun to look at, and have a hint of the flavor of their better-known relative. Their flavor is part vegetable, part fruit, and you can use them in both savory sauces and desserts.

Ground Cherries

For something completely different, experiment with ground cherries, also known as husk tomatoes and Cossack pineapple. Whatever you call them, these old-time treasures offer a novel appearance, with a husk concealing the "cherry," which is in fact a tomato relative. The berry may be yellow, orange, or red, and it's edible, with a distinctive flavor that varies from one variety to another. You might notice a suggestion of pineapple, tangerine, or even vanilla. Start them indoors a week or so before you sow tomatoes. Pick the berries when they develop full color for eating fresh or cooking down into a salsa, jam, pie filling, or ice cream topping.

Tomatillos

You may associate them with Latin American cooking, but chances are that tomatillos will thrive in your garden. They aren't very demanding, and cook down quickly into delicious homemade salsas that will put supermarket versions to shame. Start them in flats a week or two after you do tomatoes. When the husks turn thin and papery, harvest the fruits. Chop them up and simmer with onions, sauce tomatoes, bell pepper, and cilantro to make a simple sauce for use as salsa or pasta topping. You can grow familiar green varieties, or try purple ones for a special fruitlike flavor.

Personal-Size Watermelons

A big monster of a watermelon is great for a picnic or backyard party, but there may be just too much

Continued ➡

juicy goodness for a small household. Try growing one of the new modest-size melons, weighing in as low as 2 pounds and closer in size to a softball than a bread box. They not only take up less space in the refrigerator, but also hog less real estate in the garden. Pint-size varieties are available with brilliantly colored flesh in yellow, orange, even a sherbet-colored mix of yellow and pink. The rind is apt to be thinner, meaning a greater percentage of the watermelon is edible.

With tomatoes, it seems bigger is better, but that's not necessarily the case with melons. Plant breeders have come up with mini-melons that are cute, flavorful, and easy to stash in the refrigerator.

Hot Harvest Tip: Cool It!

Snip a head of broccoli or pick a snow pea, and this disconnected plant part continues to live and breathe—but not in a way that improves its quality as something to eat. Enzymes convert sugars to starch. Cells lose moisture, so that crisp becomes flaccid. The plants put off ethylene gas, which hastens the ripening of nearby harvested crops. Flavors and scents depart, too. You can't arrest these natural processes, but you can slow them down by chilling vegetables and fruit as soon as they are picked. That doesn't mean sprinting back to the house to toss your haul into the fridge. But if you'll be in the garden for any length of time, you can place a picnic cooler in a garden cart with a bit of ice, and trail that with you while harvesting. Or harvest early in the morning, before the day heats up and drying winds begin to blow. Here's how cooling helps maintain food quality.

- Slows respiration rate
- Inhibits growth of molds and bacteria responsible for decay
- Slows production of ethylene, and lowers sensitivity to ethylene's ripening effects
- Slows enzyme action
- Reduces wilting from water loss

Freezing further slows the enzyme activity in foods, but it doesn't stop the process. That's why most vegetables will hold up better in the freezer if they are first partially cooked (or blanched) to help inactivate the enzymes. This helps preserve color, texture, and flavor. Generally speaking, frozen food will maintain its quality if the blanching is at a relatively high temperature and of short duration, rather than using low heat over a longer period.

Zucchini Flowers for the Table

Just about every gardener grows zucchinis, and too many zucchinis at that. For something different, try dipping these big blossoms in a light, eggy batter and frying them in ¼ inch or so of olive oil until they turn golden brown. Just make sure you sacrifice the male blossoms, unless you don't mind reducing the yield. The females will have the telltale bulge of a developing zuke. (The males aren't useless, however; you need a few of them around to pollinate the female blossoms in order to have squash.) You'll have to go out into the garden in the early morning soon after they've opened. Unless you plan on using them right away, you can keep the blossoms perky for a few hours by refrigerating them with the base in a jar of water.

Early Pickings

While it's standard operating procedure to pick tomatoes and peppers only when they've developed their full color and sweetest flavor, you may want to try harvesting part of the crop earlier in the season. Some roadside markets sell green tomatoes well before the end of the season to suit customers who like to fry or pickle them in that immature state. Green cherry tomatoes are great when pickled. And even though peppers will turn a rich red, yellow, or chocolate brown if given the chance, you may want to pick some when green for the color contrast. Jalapeños heading for a pickling jar typically are picked when dark green and crisp in texture, and green serranos are usually the choice for making green salsa.

And of course if a frost is in the offing, you'll want to get out there and pick whatever you can, no matter what the color. Both green tomatoes and green peppers may warm up in color after you've rescued them.

Harvest Time How-To

Greens from Unexpected Sources

You don't plant broccoli, Brussels sprouts, and cabbage for their leaves, but they are nutritious and flavorful when cooked up as you would collards or kale. Pick undamaged and relatively young leaves, only when it won't compromise the main crop.

Harvest Beans When They Pass the Snap Test

If beans are rubbery and won't snap when you bend them, give a little more time before picking. But don't let them go until they show bulges from bean seeds developing within, or you'll be eating fibrous beans.

Catch Cukes at the Optimal Time

Harvest cucumbers before their seeds become half their full size. Pickling varieties should be dropped into ice water soon after picking to maintain their crispness.

With Eggplants, Bigger May be Bitter, Not Better

Many of us grew up knowing only the big black eggplants of supermarkets. With the bigness often comes a bitter taste that cooks routinely try to remove by treating with salt, but there is no compensating for an eggplant that has become spongy and seedy. To test an eggplant, press it lightly with your thumbnail. If the dent springs back, the fruit is ready to be picked; if not, you've let it go too long. Pick East Asian varieties when much smaller, still brightly colored, and glossy.

Harvesting Limas Two Ways

How do you like limas, tender or somewhat meaty? For the most tender beans, wait for the pods to fill out but pick before they are fully mature, when they will take on a more substantial texture.

The Cabbage Head Twist

Left to their own devices, certain cabbage varieties may mature and then crack toward the end of the season. To put off the harvest, try the old trick of grasping the head and giving it a gentle root-snapping twist, being careful to avoid uprooting it. With fewer functional roots, the plant may not pick up excess water from the soil.

Refrigerate Melons Only after Cutting

Melons should be kept at room temperature until you cut into them, when they will keep better in the refrigerator.

Pinch Broccoli to Get a Better Yield

Most gardeners begin to harvest broccoli by cutting the main, central head when it is full size, which then stimulates the development of the side shoots. You may be able to get more heads from each plant if you try a different approach: Earlier in the season, when the plants have grown three leaves, pinch off the growing point that would develop into the main head. This causes the broccoli to form larger side shoots than you'd expect to find.

Corn Pointers

Kernels should be plump and tender, producing milky juice when pierced with your thumbnail. The silks will be dry.

Potatoes Don't Benefit from Sweetening

Once harvested, potatoes don't react well in cold temperatures. Storing them in the refrigerator may cause some of their starch content to be converted to sugars. And while restoring them to a cool room or garage will partially reverse this process, there will be enough residual sugar to cause browning in fried potatoes.

Knocking Watermelons

It's difficult to know just when a great big watermelon is ready to eat. There are visual cues: The shaded underside will have warmed in color from whitish to a yellow tinge. If the tendril where the fruit stem meets the vine has died, that's a sign the fruit is ready to harvest. And then there's the old thumping test: An immature melon will give a metallic ring, but you'll get a dull thud if the melon is ripe.

Great Flavor from Green Tomatoes

For any number of reasons, you may find yourself at season's end with a bounty of grass-green tomatoes. Rather than toss those green tomatoes of fall into the compost bin, harvest them before the first frost and make good use of them, as gardeners have been doing for generations. Possibly because unripe tomatoes don't have the assertive taste of those that are mature, they can be used in a wider variety of recipes. Here are a few ways to convert your disappointment into good eating.

Chow-chow. Make this old-time pickled salad by chopping up green tomatoes (along with red ones, if you have them), onions, and bell peppers (green ones are just fine), and marinating in a mixture of sweetened vinegar spiced with cloves, dried mustard, allspice, and perhaps ground horseradish. Process in jars in a hot-water bath.

Dilled tomato pickles. Follow a recipe for making pickles from pickling cucumbers. Dilled green cherry tomatoes are an interesting variation on the traditional cocktail olive.

Green tomato pie filling. Combine chopped green tomatoes with chopped apples, and simmer with raisins, sugar, vinegar and lemon juice, cinnamon, nutmeg, and cloves.

Fried green tomatoes. To make this traditional favorite, dip tomato slices in a batter of flour, cornmeal, and egg before frying in oil.

Stewed green tomatoes. Sauté minced onions and sliced green tomatoes in butter, then add curry powder and salt to taste.

Toward Better Tomatoes

Raise the quality of your own homegrown fruits a notch or two with these worthwhile tricks.

Cool (Not Cold) Ripening

Tomatoes ripen best when their very last stage of ripening occurs at a moderate temperature. That's because a hot summer day can cause sugars in the fruits to turn starchy. On sweltering days, tomatoes

Continued ➜

may benefit from being picked a little early, while still somewhat pink, and then brought indoors for ripening. That's assuming your home is cooler than its surroundings. If not, then it's best to allow the fruits to remain on the vine. Whatever you do, keep tomatoes out of the refrigerator: Just 40 minutes of chilling can spoil their texture and flavor, researchers have found.

POST-HARVEST TOMATOES DON'T LIKE SUNLIGHT

You probably have heard that tomatoes don't hold up well when refrigerated. Another curious piece of their personality is that once an immature tomato is harvested, you can't speed its ripening by placing it in sunlight, as pretty as the fruits might look on a windowsill. Instead, wrap them in newsprint and place them in unsealed paper bags. Keep the bags in a cool spot where you can check on them frequently.

DECK THE RAFTERS WITH TOMATOES

Determinate varieties are likely to have a not-quite-ripe crop of tomatoes at the end of the growing season. You can pick the green fruit and cook with them. Or pull up the plants and hang them upside down from the rafters in the garage or the joists in the basement. In time, the fruits should redden up. According to the New York State Agricultural Station at Cornell University, you aren't likely to confuse this late crop with your sun-ripened tomatoes, but they'll taste better than the supermarket's off-season fare.

Your Seasonal Vegetable-Care Calendar

Obviously, planting vegetables in Florida isn't the same as planting them in Maine because of the climatic conditions. That's why before you even start planning your vegetable garden, you need to know what hardiness zone you live in.

A plant's ability to withstand a given climate is called its hardiness. The USDA has developed a Plant Hardiness Zone Map that divides North America into ten numbered climatic zones. Zone 1 is the coldest, and Zone 10 is the warmest.

This seasonal care calendar is based on gardening in Zones 5 and 6, which means you'll have to adapt it if you live in a different zone. For example, if you live in a colder zone, such as Zone 3, you'll need to push things off for a month or two (or maybe even three). Instead of starting spring broccoli seedlings at the end of February, start them at the end of March or April. If you live in a warmer zone, such as 9 or 10, you'll need to start things earlier than what's listed here because your garden will probably peter out from the summer heat by July.

January

Although the start of prime gardening season is still a few months away, here are a few things you can do now to prepare:

- Run your Christmas tree through a chipper/shredder to make mulch for your garden paths come spring.
- Look through seed catalogs to dream about what you want to plant. If you plan to start plants from seed, order the seed now!
- Inventory your garden supplies and make sure you have the essentials (such as row covers and plant cages); take a shopping trip or order from a catalog to buy items that are in short supply.

February

Map your garden, and decide when and where you'll plant each vegetable crop you plan to grow. Keep adding kitchen scraps to your compost pile, even though you may have to trudge through the snow to do it. Near the end of the month, start spring broccoli and cabbage seedlings indoors.

March

Start preparing beds by working compost into the soil as soon as the ground has thawed and dried. Start pepper seedlings eight weeks before your last frost date; start tomato and eggplant seedlings six weeks before your last frost date. Plant pea seeds directly in the garden near the middle of the month if the weather cooperates.

April

Now that the weather is warmer, you can do a lot in the garden, such as:

- Plant seed potatoes, and plant lettuce, spinach, and mesclun seed directly in the ground.
- Plant radish, carrot, and beet seeds as well as onion sets and shallots.
- Near the end of the month, plant those broccoli and cabbage seedlings that you started last month in your garden.
- Make sure to mulch your beds, or you'll spend the next five months or so weeding.

May

If you haven't started your own tomato and pepper seedlings, buy some transplants and plant them in the garden after the soil has warmed up. Place collars around the transplants' stems for protection against cutworm pests. Also plant snap beans, corn, squash, and cucumber seeds directly in your beds.

June

It's high season in the garden. Now you can:

- Harvest the peas (try not to eat all of them before you make it out of the garden!)
- Harvest salad greens such as lettuce, spinach, and mesclun before the weather gets too warm and they bolt (go to seed).
- Pull out weeds that crop up through your mulch.
- Give your beds plenty of water so they stay nice and moist, especially if Mother Nature isn't cooperating.

July

Start giving away extra zucchini. Continue watering during dry spells. Harvest onions, snap beans, summer squash, cucumbers, carrots, beets, and the first tomatoes. Pull out spring crops that are finished producing for the season, such as peas, lettuce, and broccoli. Throw the spent plants on your compost pile.

August

Can tomatoes and continue harvesting corn, peppers, snap beans, and the rest of your garden veggies. Plant a cover crop in any garden beds that are now empty. Sit in the shade and relax with a cold glass of lemonade.

September

Can more tomatoes and make salsa. Harvest pumpkins, carrots, and beets, and plant garlic for next year's crop. Pull more spent plants out of your beds, and continue planting cover crops in empty spaces.

October

Harvest the last of the tomatoes and peppers before the first fall frost. Pull all remaining spent plants out of the beds and plant cover crops. Collect stakes, temporary trellises, and row covers, and scrape off clinging soil. Carve a pumpkin or two for Halloween.

November

Rake up leaves and add them to your compost pile. Organize any notes you took from the gardening season and compile them in a binder, along with a map of what grew where.

December

Relax and enjoy some of those tomatoes you canned back in August and September. Watch the snow fly and dream about next year's garden.

Vegetable Garden Glossary

Beneficials. Helpful creatures, such as birds, bats, toads, snakes, spiders, and predatory insects, that eat pests in the garden.

Bloodmeal. Also known as dried blood, it's a slaughterhouse by-product that contains 13 percent nitrogen. Can be sprinkled on garden beds to repel rabbits.

Bolt. To go to seed. Lettuce, for example, will bolt, or go to seed, when the weather gets too hot.

Bonemeal. Finely ground bones (a by-product of animal slaughterhouses) that contain 10 to 12 percent phosphorus, 24 percent calcium, and a small amount of nitrogen.

Broadcast. To spread fertilizer evenly across an area by hand or with a spreading tool.

BT (*Bacillus thuringiensis*). A spray derived from a naturally occurring bacteria that kills certain insect larvae.

BTK. A BT variety (BT var. kurstaki) that controls cabbage loopers, cabbageworms, tomato hornworms, fruitworms, European corn borers, and pest larvae.

Cloche. Light-permeable plant covers made out of a variety of materials that are primarily used to protect plants from frost. They work much like miniature greenhouses.

Companion planting. Combinations of plants that work well together to repel pests, attract beneficial insects, or make efficient use of garden beds.

Compost. Decomposed and partially decomposed organic matter (such as kitchen scraps, leaves, grass clippings, and dead plants) that is dark in color and crumbly in texture. Used as an amendment, compost increases the water-holding capacity of the soil and is an excellent nutrient source for microorganisms, which later release nutrients to your plants.

Composting. The art and science of combining organic material so that the original raw ingredients are transformed into compost.

Compost tea. A fertilizer made by soaking a cloth bag full of compost in a watering can or barrel for several days.

Crop rotation. Rotating crops from different botanical families to avoid or reduce problems with soilborne disease or soil insects.

Cover crops. Also called green manures. A crop you plant in an empty bed that will grow rapidly and blanket the soil. Cover crops are used to hold soil in place and provide nutrients over the winter, between plantings of vegetables or between growing

Continued ➡

seasons, or as a way to rejuvenate poor soil. These crops are either harvested or tilled under into the soil. Examples of cover crops include annual ryegrass, buckwheat, and white clover.

Direct seeding. Planting seeds outside directly into the garden.

Double-digging. The process of removing a shovel full of topsoil from a garden bed, loosening the soil below, and then replacing the topsoil layer for a fertile, productive bed.

Fertilizers. A natural or manufactured material added to the soil that supplies one or more of the major nutrients—nitrogen (N), phosphorus (P), and potassium) (K)—to growing plants.

Fish emulsion. Made from filtered fish solubles, fish emulsion contains about 5 percent nitrogen. It's useful for spraying as a foliar feeding spray and to fertilize transplants.

Foliar feed. To supply nutrients by spraying liquid fertilizer directly on plant foliage.

Hardening off. Gradually exposing tender seedlings to the outdoors in a protected area for a week prior to transplanting them into the garden.

Herbicide. Substances used to kill unwanted plants. Some types are selective (they kill only a certain type of plant); others are nonselective and will kill any plants they come into contact with.

Humus. A dark-color, stable form of organic matter that remains after most of the plant and animal residues in it have decomposed.

Mesclun. A mix of salad greens such as endive, arugula, chervil, and lettuce.

NPK ratio. A recognized abbreviation that refers to the ratio of the three major nutrients—nitrogen (N), phosphorus (P), and potassium (K)—in fertilizer, such as 5-5-5 or 10-2-2.

Organic. Materials that are derived directly from plants or animals. Organic gardening uses plant and animal by-products to maintain soil and plant health, and doesn't rely on synthetically made fertilizers, herbicides, or pesticides.

Pesticide. Any substance, synthetic or natural, that is used to kill insects, animals, fungi, bacteria, or weeds.

Raised beds. Three- to five-foot-wide (on average) beds that die higher than ground level and separated by paths. Raised beds increase soil aeration and drainage and save space.

Row covers. Sheets of lightweight, permeable material, usually polypropylene or polyester, that can be laid loosely on top of plants to act as a barrier against insect pests or that can give a few degrees of frost protection at the beginning or end of the growing season.

Seed germination. The beginning of the growth of a seed.

Seedling. A young plant grown from seed. Commonly, plants grown from seeds are termed seedlings until they are first transplanted.

Sidedress. To apply solid (as opposed to liquid) fertilizer alongside annual plants during the growing season.

Soil test kit. A set of instructions and a soil bag available through your state's Cooperative Extension Service. Test results indicate soil pH and specify which amendments and nutrients should be added to your soil.

Wallo'Water. A cloche made of upright, narrow plastic tubes filled with water that can protect tomato and other seedlings from frost.

FRUITS

Introduction to Fruits and Berries

Jeff Cox

Nothing is as delicious as a mouthful of freshly picked fruit—be it a succulent, juicy peach; a tart, crisp apple; or luscious, tangy-sweet raspberries. And when that fruit comes from your own backyard, the taste is even better because you harvest your crop at the peak of perfection—you can say goodbye to the under- or over-ripe fruit found in most grocery stores. And you can grow the best-tasting cultivars, not necessarily the ones that are most attractive or ship best.

To get started, you need to determine what kinds of fruits you'd like to grow. Fruits commonly are subdivided into categories. *Tree fruits* are those that grow on trees, such as apples and peaches. *Small fruits* are either fruits that are small or fruits that are borne on small plants. Strawberries and blueberries are familiar small fruits. Some fruits, though, are difficult to place in a particular category. Mulberries and juneberries are examples of this: Both bear soft, small fruits, but they're produced on full-sized trees. Nuts are actually dry fruits with woody shells.

To develop fruit, most plants need to have their flowers pollinated. When flowers on a plant produce fruit after being dusted with their own pollen, that plant is self-pollinating. Strawberries are self-pollinating, so if you plant only one cultivar, you still get fruit. Flowers that need pollen from a plant of a different cultivar to develop fruit need cross-pollination. Apples, for example, require cross-pollination, so a 'McIntosh' tree needs a 'Golden Delicious' tree (or some other cultivar besides 'McIntosh') nearby to supply pollen. By choosing the right cultivars, gardeners all over the country can enjoy fresh fruit, beginning in spring with strawberries and going through winter with the last of the apples that ripen in cold storage.

Don't overlook the ornamental value of fruit-bearing plants. A peach tree, for example, is transformed into a cloud of pink blossoms in spring. The crimson red color of blueberry leaves in fall rivals that of the sugar maple. And strawberries make an attractive edging.

Growing Fruit Trees

Fruit trees make great landscape plants, blooming abundantly in spring and trimmed with colorful fruit in summer and fall. But unlike strictly ornamental trees, their fruit is not only attractive but also a succulent edible treat. The flavor of tree-ripened apples, peaches, and other fruits is unmatched, and you'll appreciate the savings in your grocery bills. However, to reap good-quality fruit, you must commit to pruning, monitoring, and maintaining your trees.

Before you buy, determine which fruit trees can survive and fruit in your climate. Northern gardeners should choose cultivars that will survive winter cold, blossom late enough to escape late-spring frosts, yet still set and mature fruit before the end of the growing season. Southern gardeners need cultivars that will tolerate intense summer heat and humidity. For organic gardeners, choosing disease-resistant trees is especially important. Check with local fruit growers or with your extension service office to see which cultivars have a good track record in your area. You should also do some independent research on your climate and consider your fruit needs.

Fruit trees need a dormant period during which temperatures are below 45°F. Trees that don't get sufficient winter chilling will not fruit properly. Low-chill cultivars flower and fruit with as little as half the usual cold requirement, stretching deciduous fruit production into Texas, northern Florida, and parts of California. Extra-hardy, high-chill cultivars for the far North require longer cold periods and flower a week later than most.

If winter temperatures in your area drop below -25°F, stick with the hardiest apple and pear cultivars; between -20° and 0°F, you can try most apples and pears, sour cherries, European plums, and apricots; if minimum temperatures stay above -5°F, you can consider sweet cherries, Japanese plums, nectarines, and peaches. If minimum temperatures in your area are above 45°F, be sure to select low-chill cultivars.

Freezing temperatures can kill fruit blossoms. If you live in an area with unpredictable spring weather and occasional late frosts, look for late-blooming or frost-tolerant cultivars, especially for apricots and plums.

In humid regions, select disease-resistant cultivars whenever possible. Diseases such as apple scab and brown rot are more troublesome in humid conditions.

If you are fond of baking, top your list with sour cherries and cooking apples, which make excellent pies. For canning, look for suitable cultivars of peaches, nectarines, and pears. For jellies, try apricots, plums, and quinces. If you're interested in fruit for fresh eating, think about how long the fruit will last in storage. Some apples stay good for months if kept cold, but soft fruits must be eaten within about one week or they will spoil.

Fruit trees come in shapes and sizes for every yard. Most home gardeners prefer dwarf or semi-dwarf trees, which fruit at a younger age and are easier to tend.

Standards. Standard fruit trees can reach 30 feet or taller, becoming small shade trees that can be underplanted with flowers or groundcovers. They are long-lived and hardy but can be more difficult to maintain and harvest.

Grafted Semidwarfs. Apples grafted on size-controlling rootstocks grow well. However, stone fruit trees grafted onto dwarfing rootstocks often are not long-lived. In just a few years, perhaps when the young tree is burdened with a heavy crop of fruit, the graft can unknit and the tree will die.

Genetic Dwarfs. Genetic dwarf or miniature trees are naturally compact trees grafted on standard-sized root systems. They reach about 7 feet and bear about one-fifth as much normal-sized fruit as a standard tree. Genetic dwarfs tend to be shorter-lived than standard trees and are not hardy in northern areas. They can be grown in planters and moved to a protected area where temperatures

Continued ➜

remain between 30°F and 45°F in winter, such as in an unheated storage room. Genetic dwarfs are ideal for the Pacific Northwest or the southern United States. In fact, in those areas they may be preferable to standard trees because they need less winter cold to flower.

Older genetic dwarf tree cultivars had poor-quality fruit, but modern types approach the flavor of their full-sized counterparts. However, none of the modern genetic dwarfs are disease-resistant. They need diligent thinning because foliage and fruit can become overcrowded.

Pollination requirements are another important factor to consider when selecting trees. Most apples, pears, sweet cherries, and Japanese plums are not self-fruitful. You must plant a second compatible cultivar nearby to ensure good pollination and fruit set. Peaches, nectarines, tart cherries, and some European plums are self-fruitful. Some cultivars of apples, pears, sweet cherries, and European plums are somewhat self-fruitful, but they set better crops when cross-pollinated. Fruit tree entries later in this chapter provide details about pollination requirements.

SITE SELECTION AND PLANTING

Plant fruit trees in a small traditional orchard, or intersperse them in borders, mixed beds, or a vegetable garden. You can even put a dwarf apple at the end of a foundation planting. Some will grow in lawns, but most perform better in a prepared bed.

Be certain the site you choose has the right growing conditions for fruit trees.

Sunlight Even one or two hours of daily shade may make fruit smaller and less colorful. Envision the mature size of trees and shrubs close to your planned site. If their shadow will encroach on your fruit trees in years to come, you may want to select a different site, or remove the neighboring plants. Sour cherries tolerate a bit of shade better than other tree fruits do.

Shaded soil in early spring can be beneficial. A cool soil can delay flowering, perhaps until after late killing frosts.

Soil. Fruit trees need well-drained soil. Sandy soils can be too dry to produce a good crop of fruit. Wet, clayey soil encourages various root rots.

Slope. Plant near the top of a gentle slope if possible. Planting on a north-facing slope or about 15 feet from the north side of a building helps slow flowering in spring and protects blossoms from any late frosts. Planting on a south-facing slope can hasten flowering and lead to frost damage. Sheltered alcoves on the south side of a house protect tender trees. Planting in a frost pocket, as shown in the illustration on this page, can increase the risk of spring frost damage to flowers and young fruit.

Wind. Blustery winds in open areas or on hilltops can make training difficult, knock fruit off trees early, or topple trees. Staking will help trees resist the force of prevailing winds. Where wind is a problem, you can slow it by erecting a hedge or fence. However, don't box the tree in and stifle the breeze. Air circulation is helpful for reducing diseases.

Spacing. The amount of room your trees will need depends on their mature height and width, how they are trained, their soil fertility level, and tree vigor. Give every tree plenty of space to grow without impinging on neighboring plants or spreading into shady areas. Small trees, such as dwarf peaches and nectarines, require only 12 feet between trees, while apple trees need 20 to 30 feet between trees.

Planting. To make the effort and expense of planting fruit trees worthwhile and to maximize yield and fruit quality, it pays to prepare the soil and plant them properly.

Plant fruit trees while dormant in early spring, or in the fall where winters are quite mild. Fall planting gives roots a head start, because they continue to grow until the soil freezes. However, fall planting is risky in areas where the soil freezes, because the low temperatures may kill the newly grown roots.

Most nurseries stock bareroot fruit trees. Plant the young trees as you would any bareroot tree.

You may be able to speed a young tree's establishment by dipping the roots in powdered bonemeal before you plant. Also apply compost tea or manure tea at planting. Allow the tea to sit for several days before applying, or it may burn roots.

Words to Know

Standard: A full-sized fruit tree, usually maturing to at least 20 feet in height.

Dwarf and semidwarf: Fruit trees grafted on size-controlling rootstocks. Dwarf trees often mature to 8 to 10 feet in height. Semidwarfs mature to 12 to 18 feet.

Genetic dwarf: A fruit tree that stays quite small without a dwarfing rootstock.

Rootstock: A cultivar onto which a fruiting cultivar is grafted. Rootstocks are selected for strong, healthy roots or for dwarfing effect.

Whip: A young tree, often the first-year growth from a graft or bud.

Scaffolds: The main structural branches on a fruit tree.

Pome fruit: Fruit that has a core containing many seeds, such as apples and pears.

Stone fruit: Fruit with a single hard pit, such as cherries, plums, and peaches.

Low-chill: Requiring fewer hours of cool temperatures to break dormancy.

High-chill: Requiring more hours of cool temperatures to break dormancy.

Self-fruitful: A tree that produces pollen that can pollinate its own flowers.

Compatible cultivars: Cultivars that can successfully cross-pollinate.

Crotch: The angle of emergence of a branch from the tree.

Suckers: Shoots that sprout out of or near the base of a tree.

Watersprouts: Upright shoots that sprout from the trunk and main limbs of a tree.

Caring for Fruit Trees

You can't, unfortunately, plant fruit trees and sit back and wait for them to produce. Fruit trees need your time and attention throughout the year in order to stay healthy and provide a bumper crop. You'll need to prune and train your trees, fertilize and mulch them, and protect them during the winter. Some trees may require hand-pollinating, while others need to have their fruit thinned. While there are few shortcuts to meeting these important demands, there are right and wrong ways to go about fulfilling them. Knowing the right way will

save you time and frustration and give you the best possible fruit yield.

PRUNING AND TRAINING

To grow top-quality fruit, and to have easy access for harvesting, you need to establish a sturdy and efficient branching framework. For home gardens, the two best training methods are open center and central leader. Both systems encourage the growth of branches with wide crotches that are less likely to split when burdened with a heavy fruit load.

It's important to establish the main branches while the tree is young. You'll then maintain tree shape of your bearing trees each year with touch-up pruning. Central leader trees produce more fruiting spurs, important for spur-type apple and pear cultivars. For nectarines, peaches, and Japanese plums, use open center training to maximize air circulation and sunlight penetration among the branches, which will help reduce disease.

Spread young branches so they will develop broad crotch angles. Use clothespins to hold branches out from the trunk, or insert notched boards in the crotch angle. Branches that aren't spread may develop a strip of bark called a bark inclusion in the crotch angle, making the crotch weaker and more likely to break.

In certain circumstances, it's best not to train. Some fruit trees, including apricots and pears, are particularly susceptible to disease, which can invade through pruning cuts or attack young growth that arises near the cuts. If disease is a problem in your area, you may want to limit pruning to general maintenance or renewal of fruiting wood. In the far North, keep training to a minimum, since new growth is more susceptible to winter injury. However, leave some young suckers on main scaffolds to act as renewal wood in case main branches are injured by cold.

Whether you train your trees or not, you should prune off shoots that emerge Iowan the trunk and any branches that cross and rub. Where one limb grows above and shades another, or when two branches of equal length and diameter arise at one fork, select one branch to keep and prune off the other. During the summer, remove suckers that sprout near the base, watersprouts that shoot out from the trunk or main limbs, and any dead or diseased wood.

When to prune varies with the tree type. You can prune apples and pears in early spring before the trees break dormancy. For stone fruits that are susceptible to cankers caused by disease organisms, wait until bud break, when they are less likely to be infected. Prune away dead and diseased branches on all kinds of fruit trees as the growing season continues. Stop pruning by the end of August in areas where winter injury is a concern. Late pruning can stimulate a flush of new growth that could be damaged when cold weather sets in.

FERTILIZING

Even with thorough advance soil preparation, your fruit trees may need fertilizing. Nutrient consumption varies with tree type and age, soil, and growing conditions. For instance, you will have to fertilize a fruit tree growing in the lawn more frequently than if the soil around the tree is cleared and mulched. But don't simply fertilize on a set schedule. Overfertilizing can encourage soft new growth that is susceptible to disease attack and winter injury.

Monitor tree growth to determine when trees need fertilizing. Nonbearing apple trees should grow 1½ to 2 feet per year; those producing fruit average 8 to 12 inches. Mature peach trees should grow 1 to 1½ feet each year. If your trees seem to

Continued ➡

be lagging, have the nutrient levels in the leaves analyzed. Call your local extension office for information about leaf analysis.

Fertilize only in the spring. Spread materials on the soil surface in a circle around the trunk out to the edge of the leaf canopy. If the tree is growing in the lawn, make holes with a crowbar around the perimeter of the branches and drop fertilizer below the grass roots. Avoid high-nitrogen fertilizers. The best fertilizer for fruit trees is compost because it has a good balance of nutrients. Foliar seaweed sprays improve tree health, increase yields, and increase bud frost resistance. Spray trees when buds start to show color, when petals drop, and when fruit is ½ to 1 inch.

MULCHING

Mulched trees will have access to more water and nutrients, especially if you use soil-enriching mulch such as compost or shredded leaves. Mulch also will keep down weeds that compete with trees for water and nutrients. It prevents excessive evaporation of soil moisture, a necessity around young or weak trees, in dry climates, and in sandy soils. In areas with fluctuating winter temperatures, mulch will eliminate damage from frost heaving. Mulch can keep the soil cooler in spring and delay flowering of early-spring bloomers such as apricots or peaches, hopefully beyond the threat of frost.

The drawback of mulching is that it can make heavy soils too wet and can harbor pests, especially mice and voles.

Where mulch is warranted, apply a 3- to 6-inch layer of organic mulch in an area from 1 to 2 feet away from the trunk out to just beyond the branch tips. Fluff the mulch with a spading fork occasionally so it doesn't compact. Check the soil moisture level occasionally. If the soil is staying overly wet, rake the mulch back to prevent root rot. You also may want to push the mulch out from under the tree boughs during leaf fall if disease is a problem. Afterward, rake up the fallen leaves and respread the mulch.

WATERING

Ideally, the soil around fruit trees should be evenly moist, neither dry nor waterlogged. Moisture is especially important to young trees and to trees bearing ripening crops. Thoroughly soak the root system of newly planted trees, and repeat whenever the soil becomes dry for the next few months.

After the tree is growing well, your watering schedule will depend on the weather and climate. If the weather has been dry, even during a midwinter warm spell, stick your little finger down in the soil around the drip line. If you do not feel moisture below the surface, water the tree thoroughly. A trickle irrigation system is ideal for watering fruit trees. In cold climates, stop watering by early fall to harden the plant for winter.

WINTER PROTECTION

Protect your trees against winter sunscald, frost heaving, and pest damage, all of which can injure or kill fruit trees. Sunscald occurs when sun-warmed wood is killed by nighttime cold. The damaged area becomes dry, sunken, and attractive to borers and diseases. Prevent sunscald by wrapping the tree trunk with a white plastic tree guard or painting it up to the first (lowest) scaffold branch with white latex paint diluted 1:1 with water.

To minimize frost heaving—shifting of soil when it freezes and thaws—mulch after the soil freezes to keep it frozen. This is especially important for young trees, which can suffer extensive root damage due to frost heaving.

FLOWER AND FRUIT CARE

Once your trees reach maturity, there are some extra activities involved in their seasonal care. Some trees may require hand-pollinating, others may need young fruit thinned, and all will have to be harvested.

Hand-Pollinating. Early-flowering fruit trees can suffer partial to full crop loss if the weather is not mild when the tree is in bloom. If temperatures aren't high enough for insect activity, flowers won't be pollinated and fruit won't develop. If there's a cold spell when your trees are blooming, you can save your crop by hand-pollinating. Simply collect pollen from one tree by rubbing flowers gently with an artist's brush or cotton swab, and then brush the pollen onto the flowers of a compatible cultivar.

Be sure nights are frost-free if you plan to hand-pollinate. If you expect a late frost, you can cover small trees with plastic or spray them with a frost-protecting product. As a last resort, try sprinkling water on trees all night. Use care, as the weight of ice that forms on the trees can break branches.

Thinning. Because fruit trees tend to be overburdened by young fruit, you should thin off the excess on all trees except those with cherry-size fruit. Without your intervention, the weight of the fruit may actually break limbs. The stress from the excessive fruit load may also reduce the number of flower buds the tree produces the nest year. Disease problems such as brown rot can spread quickly among crowded fruits, ruining the crop before it ripens. In addition to avoiding problems, thinning lets you channel all the tree's resources into fewer but bigger and more beautiful fruit.

Thin when the fruit is young—the smaller the better. First clip or twist off all insect-damaged or deformed fruits. Then remove the smaller fruits. Leave only the biggest and best.

If you can't reach the upper limbs of large trees, tap the limbs with a padded pole to shake loose some of the extras. On small apple, nectarine, and peach trees with big fruit, thin fruit to 6 to 8 inches apart. Plums and apricots can be more closely spaced, about 3 to 5 inches apart.

Even after thinning, fruit may become heavy enough to tear a branch. For extra support, prop branches up with a forked stick. On central leader trees, you can secure branches to the central leader with a rope or with a chain covered with garden hose.

Harvesting. Most fruit is ready to harvest when the green undercolor changes to yellow or the fruit softens and drops. Grasp the fruit in the palm of your hand and twist it off the stem carefully so you don't damage the branch. Handle the ripe fruit gently so it does not bruise.

PESTS AND DISEASES

It's not easy to grow fruit trees using only organic pest control methods. Fruit is so succulent and tasty that it attracts a wide range of pests, from mites to deer. Watch your trees diligently for pests, and control them before they damage the tree or the fruit.

Growing Fruits and Berries

Barbara W. Ellis

Planting Fruit Trees

Fruit trees are an investment that can yield bountiful, delicious interest for many years after planting. To get the best return on your investment, it's important to take extra care in selecting the right plants and picking the best site for them. There are many types of tree fruits from which to choose, and the best choices for you will depend on where you live and how much space you have available. Your local cooperative extension agent also may be able to recommend cultivars suitable for your area.

Just because you have limited space in your garden doesn't mean you can't enjoy the taste of fresh, tree-ripened fruit. Many tree fruits are grafted onto rootstocks that affect their size at maturity, and the availability of dwarf or semidwarf trees makes it possible to grow a bearing-size tree in even the smallest garden. Even if you have plenty of room available, dwarf and semidwarf plants have other advantages. Their fruit is easy to reach for picking, and it's generally easier to prune and care for smaller trees. Finally, dwarf and semidwarf fruit trees begin blooming and bear fruit sooner than standards.

SITE SELECTION

It's important to select the best possible site for your trees. For best yields, fruit trees need full sun. Avoid areas in the shadow of large ornamental trees or tall buildings. Most fruit trees prefer deep, loamy soil that is moist but well-drained and rich in organic matter, although they'll tolerate many types of soils. Heavy clay soils, however, will impede root system formation and result in poor tree growth. If you have clayey soil, plan on adding plenty of organic matter to a large area around the planting site and working it in as deeply as possible. Or consider making a large raised bed to accommodate one or several dwarf fruit trees.

Look for a site that offers good air drainage. Cold air drains downhill and settles in valleys or against barriers such as thick hedges, creating frost

Continued →

pockets. Frost can damage fruit blossoms, which appear in early spring, so try to plant trees near the top of a slope rather than at the bottom where chilly air often collects. A south- or southeast-facing slope is fine, although very early blooming trees sometimes are best planted on the side of a north-facing slope. This helps delay bloom and increases the likelihood that tender flowers will survive spring frosts. Although trees should be protected from strong prevailing winds, they should be planted in a site with good air circulation.

Heeling-In

You can buy container-grown fruit trees or field-grown trees dug and sold with their roots wrapped in burlap (called balled-and-burlapped or "b & b"). Fruit trees also are commonly sold bare-root, that is, with all the soil removed from the root system and with the roots packed in wood shavings or similar material.

It's best if you have the site all prepared so you can plant your fruit trees as soon as you bring them home or they arrive in the mail. However, if that's not possible, both container-grown and balled-and-burlapped trees can be set in a sheltered site out of sun and wind and watered regularly until you find time to plant. Bare-root trees, on the other hand, need immediate attention to keep the roots from drying out. If you can't plant them right away, you'll need to protect them with a technique known as heeling-in.

Soak the roots of bare-root trees in water for an hour or so before heeling them in. Then find a spot sheltered from direct wind and sun (the north-facing wall of a house can provide good shelter) and dig a trench with one sloping side, large enough to accommodate the roots. Lean the trees against the angled side with their roots in the trench and cover the roots with soil (or a combination of peat moss and soil), pressing lightly to pack the soil around the roots. Water thoroughly and keep the roots evenly moist but not wet until you can move the trees to their permanent location.

If your soil is frozen or too wet for heeling plants into a trench, you can use a large pot, plastic bucket, or heavy plastic garbage bag to hold moist potting soil or peat moss around the roots. Keep trees in such makeshift containers in a cool (40° to 45°F), humid garage, shed, or basement, or in a shaded outdoor area if the temperature is above freezing. If you use garbage bags, be sure to leave the top open so the roots have an air supply. Lightly water the peat moss or soil when it dries out.

It may seem reasonable to just put your new tree in a tub or pail of water. But roots can't breathe underwater and can be damaged if left this way for more than 24 hours. However, this method is fine for temporary storage overnight or for keeping the tree roots moist while you are preparing the planting hole.

Whatever method you use, remember that heeling-in is a temporary measure only. Try to move your trees to their permanent site as soon as possible.

PLANTING POINTERS

One of the best things you can do for your new fruit trees is to have the planting site ready and waiting for them. This minimizes transplant stress and helps get them off to a good start.

Site Preparation

Dig a hole that is at least 3 feet in diameter and 1½ to 2 feet deep. When in doubt, dig as wide a hole as you can, to encourage roots to spread out laterally in every direction. Remove any large rocks. Rough up the sides of the hole after you've finished

digging, to eliminate hard-packed sides that may be impenetrable to roots.

In the past, amending the soil removed from the hole with compost, purchased topsoil, or peat was considered standard operating procedure. However, recent observations indicate that filling the planting hole with rich, amended soil encouraged the roots to remain within the planting hole rather than work their way out and down into the surrounding soil. Although you may want to test the pH of your soil and adjust accordingly, or add a cup of bonemeal in the bottom of the hole, plan on filling with unamended, native soil.

Spring or Fall?

True or false. The best time to plant fruit trees is in the spring. **The answer:** It depends where you live. In areas where cold weather arrives in early autumn and temperatures often fall below -10°F, planting in the early spring will give the young tree time to grow and harden before the onset of harsh winter temperatures. Spring rains will help keep newly planted trees well watered for proper growth.

However, if your local conditions include hot, dry summers and mild winters, fall planting can give a new tree extra time to establish a healthy root system that can survive harsh summer weather. Because the tree is planted while dormant, the roots have time to become established before buds break in the spring. Fall-planted trees have a further advantage of being able to begin growth in early spring, when soil is still too wet for tree planting. Also, the soil in the fall is often drier and easier to work. For the best root growth and winter survival, fall planting should only be done in those areas where the soil temperature remains above 50°F several weeks after the trees become dormant. Plant as early in the fall as you can to take advantage of good root-growing weather.

Determining the Proper Depth

Before you plant, examine the trunk close to the roots. If your plant has been grafted, you'll find a slight knob or crook near the base of the stem. This is the graft union. Dwarf and semidwarf trees should be planted with the graft union above-ground. Covering the graft union would allow the upper part of the tree, called the scion, to root, and you would lose the effect of the dwarfing rootstock. If you live in an area with high winds, plant the tree with the top part of the graft union knob toward the prevailing wind.

Plant standard trees so the graft union is 1 to 2 inches below the ground. (Since in this case you're not worried about keeping the plant small, it doesn't matter if the scion produces its own roots.) This provides protection from severe winter weather and gives the tree better anchorage.

To see if your tree will be at the proper depth, place it in the hole you have prepared and set a broomstick or pole across the hole to help judge the depth. Make a pyramid- or cone-shaped mound of soil in the center to spread out the roots of bare-root trees. Set container-grown or balled-and-burlapped trees in the hole, container and all. If the tree is too low, add more soil to the central mound, and remove some soil if the tree is too high.

Planting

At planting time, remove containers completely—even peat or papier-mâché ones—and check to make sure that the roots aren't circling around the root ball. For balled-and-burlapped trees, cut the burlap in several places to make it easy for the roots to grow out into the surrounding soil; remove any string or wire holding the burlap in place, along with synthetic fabrics sometimes used as burlap substitutes. Cut back any broken or damaged roots without disturbing the root ball.

Soak the roots of bare-root trees for an hour or so before planting. Then cut ½ inch off broken root tips so that healthy tissue will contact the soil and more fine roots will be stimulated to grow. Prune crushed or broken roots.

If you are planting more than one fruit tree, space dwarf fruit trees 8 to 15 feet apart; semidwarf trees, 10 to 12 feet; standard trees, 25 feet. Use the larger spacing for the dwarf or semidwarf trees if your soil is deep and fertile, as each tree's root system will expand more through the years in these soils.

It's easiest to have another person hold the tree in the right position as you start to fill in the soil. Have him or her gently shake the tree as you shovel, to help settle soil around the roots. When the roots are covered by several inches of soil, you can start to press the soil down with your hands. Do this gently, taking care not to break any roots. When the hole is two-thirds filled, soak the site with a pail of water to help settle the soil around the roots. Then finish adding soil to ground level. Press the soil so that there is a bowl-shaped indentation in the ground—this will help hold water during the first growing season—and water thoroughly.

Pruning at Planting Time

It may seem criminal to cut branches off your newly purchased fruit trees, but selected pruning will ultimately lead to better tree form and growth. You'll need to remove any dead branches, which will look shriveled and blackened at planting time. If you're not sure whether a branch has life in it, carefully scrape away a small piece of bark with your fingernail. Dead wood is brown, gray, or black; healthy wood is green.

In the past, the general recommendation was to cut back unbranched bare-root trees by approximately one-third or one-half at planting time. This was thought to balance the loss of roots that occurred when the tree was dug at the nursery. Research indicates this is not necessary: Do not prune unbranched bare-root trees at planting time.

The only pruning that branched specimens need at planting time is to establish the basic framework of the tree. Remove any damaged or dead branches, along with branches growing vertically (or nearly so) against the main trunk. The narrow crotches these branches create are weak and tend to break under heavy fruit loads. The strongest branch angles are 45 degrees or greater. Choose three to five branches that are evenly spaced around the circumference of the central leader and have wide crotch angles. These will become the scaffold branches or the main branches of the tree. Prune out all the other branches.

FINISHING UP

Here are a few final steps to settle your fruit trees into their new home.

1. Cut off any wire tags to prevent them from cutting into the tree as it grows.

2. Stake the trunks of newly planted trees. (Fruit trees grafted on dwarf rootstocks will require permanent staking.) For best support, use

Continued →

Selecting Tree Fruits

Fruit trees are ornamental as well as useful, and homegrown fruit, whether eaten fresh, baked in pies, or preserved in jelly is a special treat. Before buying a tree, check with your local cooperative extension agent to find out what cultivars are best for your area. Consider planting some of the many disease-resistant cultivars available. Yields listed are for 1 year.

Fruit	Yield per Plant	Culture	Harvest Information	Comments
Apple (*Malus pumila*)	Standard: 10–20 bu. Semidwarf: 5-10 bu. Dwarf: 1–5 bu.	Full sun. Average, well-drained soil rich in organic matter; pH 5.5–7.0. Buy 1- or 2-year-old trees. Site should be protected from frost; the middle of a gentle, south-facing slope is ideal. Allow as much space between trees as their height at maturity. Water and mulch around young trees, but do not mulch near trunk. Zones 3–8.	Dwarf trees will fruit in 2–4 years after planting; semidwarfs, in 3–5 years; standards, in 5–7 years. Different cultivars ripen from early to late summer or early fall. Pick fruit when ripe but firm. Hold apple and stem and twist gently, while tilting upwards. Keep stems on apples. Do not damage spurs when harvesting.	Most apples sold today are grafted on rootstocks that affect growth rate; dwarf, semidwarf, and standard-size trees are available in most cultivars. Dwarf trees grow to be 8-12 ft.; semidwarf, 12–20 ft.; and standards, 20–40 ft. May live up to 35 years; some may fruit heavily every other year. Some cultivars are self-sterile (2 cultivars needed for pollination); others, partially self-fertile. Disease-resistant cultivars include 'Freedom,' 'Liberty,' 'Macfree,' 'Nova Easygro,' 'Prima,' 'Priscilla,' and 'Redfree.'
Apricot (*Prunus armeniaca*)	Standard: 3–4 bu. Dwarf: 3 bu.	Full sun. Deep, average, loamy soil that is moist but well drained; pH 6.0–7.0. Buy 3–5 ft., 1-year-old plants. Plant on a north-facing slope protected from cold winds if possible. Allow at least as much space between trees as their height at maturity. Avoid planting near or after member of the nightshade family, brambles, or strawberries. Prune out nonfruiting spurs. Zones 4–9.	Will fruit in 3–5 years. Fruits ripen in late summer. Harvest when fruit is almost firm and orange-yellow all over. Hold fruit and gently twist while tilting upwards.	Apricots are fast growing and may live up to 35 years. Standard trees grow 15–25 ft. high; dwarf (grafted) trees, 8–12 ft. Most are self-fertile, although a few cultivars, such as 'Moongold' and 'Sungold,' should be planted together for pollination. Thin to even out annual yield. Pink flowers open in early spring but are often ruined by frost. Disease-resistant cultivars include 'Harcot,' 'Harlayne,' and 'Harogem.'
Cherry (*Prunus* spp.)	Standard, sweet: 3–6 bu. Standard, sour: 2–5 bu. Dwarf (genetic): up to 1 bu.	Full sun. Light, moist, well-drained soil rich in organic matter; pH 6.0–8.0. Buy 1- or 2-year-old trees. A north-facing slope protected from cold winds will help delay bloom and prevent frost damage to buds. Allow as much space between plants as their height at maturity. Sweet cherries grow in Zones 5–8; sour cherries, Zones 4–8.	Sweet cherries will fruit in 3–6 years; sours in 3–5 years. Sweet cherries ripen in early summer; sour ones ripen a little later. Harvest when cherries have full color by gently twisting stems upward off of spur; ripe sour cherries are easily pulled from pits (which remain on stem).	Cherry trees may live 30–40 years. Sour cherries are self-fertile. Sweet cherries usually require compatible cultivars with overlapping blooming periods for pollination. Dwarf trees reach 6–15 ft. Standard sweet cherries grow to 20–40 ft.; sour cherries, 15–25 ft. Sour cherries are smaller than sweet ones and used for cooking. Disease-resistant cultivars include 'Hedelfingen' (sweet), 'North Star' (sour), 'Sam' (sweet), and 'Windsor' (sweet).
Citrus (*Citrus* spp.)	Depends on fruit, tree size, and conditions. True citrus can range from 150–1,000 lbs. Kumquats: 40 lbs.	Full sun. Light, loamy, moist but well-drained soil rich in organic matter; pH 5.0–7.0. Buy 1-year-old, certified disease-free trees. Planting is best done in late winter or early spring. Choose a warm, sunny, sheltered area. Space 15–35 ft. apart. Protect young trees from sunburn and cold. Water deeply and often. Require high nitrogen. Zones 9–10.	Will fruit in 3–6 years. Harvest when fruit is fully ripened, which is indicated by its mature size, color, and taste. With shears, cut ripe fruit at point it is attached to stem. Most types will keep well on the tree, so harvest only what you can use.	Includes lime, lemon, grapefruit, orange, tangerine, and kumqnat. Trees grow from 5–50 ft.; may fruit up to 100 years. Citrus trees will not grow well at temperatures below 55°F. Fruits take 7–14 months to ripen. Recommended cultivars include grapefruits 'Marsh Seedless,' 'Redblush,' and 'Rio Red;' blood oranges 'Moro,' 'Sanguinella,' and 'Tarocco;' kumquats 'Meiwa' and 'Nagami;' lemons 'Eureka' and 'Meyer;' limes 'Bearss' and 'Persian;' tangerines 'Dancy,' 'Page,' and 'Satsuma;' oranges 'Pineapple,' 'Valencia,' and 'Washington Navel.'
Peach and Nectarine (*Prunus persica*)	Standard: 2–5 bu. Dwarf (grafted): 2–3 bu.	Full sun. Loamy or sandy soil that is moist but well drained and rich in organic matter; pH 6.0–7.0. Buy 3–5 ft., 1-year-old trees. Plant on a southern slope unless spring temperatures fluctuate widely. If so, choose a north-facing slope. Allow 15–25 ft. between trees. Zones 4–10.	Will fruit in 1–3 years. Harvest fruit in mid- to late summer when it is fairly firm and no green visible; should twist off limb without much effort.	May live 10–20 years. Standard trees grow from 8–20 ft.; dwarf trees, 6–10 ft. Both come in freestone (flesh separates easily from pit) or clingstone (flesh clings to pit) cultivars. Disease-resistant cultivars include peaches 'Clayton,' 'Newhaven,' and 'Redhaven;' nectarines 'Mericrest' and 'Redchief.'
Pear (*Pyrus communis*)	Standard: 5–10 bu. Dwarf (grafted): ½–2 bu.	Full sun to partial shade. Deep, loamy soil that is moist but well drained; pH 6.0–7.0. Buy a 4-6 ft. standard, or 2½–4 ft. dwarf, 1- or 2-year-old trees. Select a site protected from harsh winds but with good air circulation. Allow 16–25 ft. between standards; 12–15 ft. between dwarfs. Zones 2–10.	Standard trees will fruit in 4–6 years; dwarfs in 2–4 years. Fruits ripen in late summer to early fall. Harvest pears when stems swell near twigs, the green skin lightens or starts to turn yellow, and they are easily separated from the twig. Fruit ripened on tree will develop brown centers and grainy texture.	Early and late-ripening cultivars available. Standard trees reach 15–25 ft.; dwarf (grafted) trees, only 8–15 ft. May live 50–75 years. Most require another cultivar for pollination; some are incompatible. Disease-resistant cultivars include 'Kieffer,' 'Monterrey,' 'Orient,' and 'Seckel.'
Persimmon (*Diospyros virginiana, D. kaki*)	50–100 lbs.	Full sun to partial shade. Well-drained soil; pH 6.0–7.0. Buy 1- or 2-year-old trees. A southern exposure is best. Space 18–20 ft. Mulch thickly. American, Zones 4–8; Japanese, Zones 7–10.	Will fruit in 3–4 years. Fruit ripens in fall. Pick when still a bit firm, keeping stem on fruit, and let ripen in warm room. Most persimmons are astringent and can only be eaten when soft. Ripe persimmons are very sweet and can be eaten fresh, dried, or used in pastries.	May live 50 years or more. American cultivars grow to 30–60 ft.; Japanese types to 20–40 ft. Most American cultivars require a pollinator; Japanese are usually self-fertile. American persimmon has yellow-orange or purple fruit, 1–2 in. wide; Japanese are orange to bright yellow, 1½–4 in. wide. Recommended American cultivars include 'Early Golden,' 'Garretson,' and 'Meader;' Japanese persimmons 'Fuyu,' 'Hachiya,' and 'Tanenashi.'
Plum (*Prunus* spp.)	Standard: 1–3 bu. Dwarf: ½–1 bu.	Full sun. Slightly heavy, moist but well-drained soil rich in organic matter; pH 6.0–8.0. Buy 3–6 ft. standard, or 3–4 ft. dwarf, 1-year-old trees. A north-facing slope will help delay bloom and prevent bud damage from frost. Space trees 18–24 ft. apart. Japanese, Zones 4–9; European, Zones 4–8.	Japanese plums fruit in 2–4 years; European plums fruit in 3–5 years. Fruits ripen in midsummer. Harvest plums when they develop a waxy white coating ("bloom"). Pick soft for eating fresh or drying, or fairly firm for cooking.	Standard plum trees reach 15–20 ft.; dwarf trees grow 8–15 ft. Japanese plums are 2-3 in. wide and usually red or yellow; European plums, 1–2 in. wide, and usually blue or purple. Plums bear fruit 25–30 years. Cultivars may require others from the same family for successful pollination. Disease-resistant cultivars include Japanese plums 'Crimson' and 'Starking Delicious;' European plums 'Count Althann's Gage,' 'Oneida', and 'President.'

Continued ➡

three stakes placed as a triangle about a foot away from the trunk. Thread a sturdy wire through an old piece of rubber hose, loop the rubber hose portion around the trunk, and attach the ends of the wire to one stake. Do the same thing for the other two stakes.

3. Wrap a spiral plastic tree guard around the tree trunk to protect it from gnawing animals and winter sunscald.

4. For spring-planted trees, place a 6-inch layer of compost, straw or other organic mulch around the tree to prevent weeds and help conserve soil moisture. In the fall, move the mulch away from the trunk, as it makes a good nesting and hiding place for mice.

Pollination and Fruit Set

Blooming fruit trees are a beautiful feature of the spring landscape, but, surprisingly, plenty of flowers doesn't always mean a plentiful harvest. Before your trees' flowers can bear fruit, they need to be pollinated and have an adequate fruit set. There are a number of factors that can stand in the way. Fickle spring weather is one of them; pollen compatibility, another. Fortunately, there are some steps you can take to ensure a bountiful crop.

FROM FLOWERS TO FRUITS

To understand the fruiting process, you'll need to know a little basic botany. Nearly everyone can identify the petals of an apple or peach blossom. Just inside the petals are a circle of slender filaments with yellow dust on top. These are the stamens, the male flower part, topped with pollen. The stamens surround the pistil, the female part of the flower. If you pull off the petals and some of the stamens, you can see the structure of the pistil. The sticky tip of the pistol, which collects the pollen, is called the stigma. The swollen part at the bottom is the ovary, which is connected to the stigma by a narrow stalk called the style. The ovary contains the eggs and develops into the fruit.

When a pollen grain lands on the stigma, it germinates and produces a long tube that grows down through the style into the ovary. This tube carries two sperm cells: One fuses with the egg to eventually form the seedling, the other fuses with a cell to form nutrient tissue for the seedling. Both must fuse, or no seed or fruit will form. In apples and pears, each ovary has ten eggs; ovaries of other fruit flowers have fewer eggs. Fruit size is linked to the number of seeds that mature, because developing seeds produce a hormone that signals the fleshy part of the fruit to enlarge.

OF WEATHER AND BUGS

All of our common fruit trees need bees or other insects for pollination—to carry pollen from stamens to stigma. However, honeybees don't fly in rainy weather and are sluggish at temperatures below 65°F. Adequate pollination is a problem in wet, cold springs. Furthermore, a spring cold snap with below-freezing temperatures can kill blossoms before bees even have a chance to pollinate them.

Even if the flower is successfully pollinated, weather still can interfere with fertilization. High temperatures can kill the ovary before the pollen tubes deliver the sperm, or cold weather (close to freezing) can delay pollen tube growth so the crucial period for fertilization is missed. In both these cases, there will be little fruit set despite a beautiful spring bloom.

Winter weather can damage fruit flowers in the bud so that they either drop before blooming or bloom but then do not set fruit. (Flower buds can be less hardy than leaf buds, so this can happen even though the tree seems otherwise undamaged.) Extreme cold can cause bud damage, but the most common cause is a winter warm spell followed by freezing temperatures. The tree loses its ability to withstand the cold during the warm spell and then is damaged in the following cold weather.

While you can't do much about the weather, you can make certain not to spray blooming trees with insecticides or other chemicals that kill or harm the all-important pollinators. Even botanical insecticides like pyrethrum and rotenone are deadly to bees; try to avoid spraying altogether or spray at dusk when bees are less active.

POLLEN COMPATIBILITY

Not only must the pollen land on the stigma for pollination to occur, it often must be the right pollen. While the flowers of many fruit tree cultivars can be pollinated by their own pollen, some have defective pollen that either does not germinate at all or simply does not pollinate effectively. Sterile cultivars such as 'Winesap' and 'Stayman' apples require pollen from another cultivar in order to produce fruit and can't pollinate any other trees. Many fruit trees don't pollinate their own flowers effectively; for a bumper harvest, you

---

Continued ➡

Pollination Requirements of Fruit Trees

There are a few basic principles to keep in mind when considering pollination requirements of fruit trees. Trees can be self-unfruitful or self-sterile, meaning they can pollinate the blooms of other trees but require pollen from another cultivar to set fruit. They can be sterile, meaning they can't pollinate their own flowers or those of any other trees. Cultivars can also be incompatible, meaning they cannot pollinate each other's blooms. Some cultivars have several different forms with different names that won't pollinate each other. For example, 'Starkspur Golden Delicious' apple won't pollinate 'Golden Delicious.' Don't be fooled by dwarfing rootstocks, either; if a cultivar is self-unfruitful, a dwarf tree won't pollinate a standard tree of that cultivar.

When selecting a pollinator cultivar, you'll need to make certain that it blooms at about the same time as the tree you want to have pollinated—a late-blooming cultivar can't pollinate an early-blooming one. You'll need to plant the trees close enough for proper pollination. Your local nursery owner, cooperative extension agent, or mail-order source will have information on bloom time and compatibility of various cultivars.

Apples

Some apples are self-fertile, although most have better fruit set if pollinated by another cultivar. Trees must be no more than 80 feet apart for pollination. Crabapples can be used to pollinate apples. 'Gravenstein,' 'Mutsu' (also called 'Crispin'), 'Jonagold,' and 'Winesap' are sterile. 'Golden Delicious,' 'Jonathan,' and 'Yellow Transparent' are self-pollinating but yield more if cross-pollinated. 'Granny Smith' and 'Tydeman Red' are incompatible and are poor self-pollinators.

Apricots

Most are self-fertile. 'Early Golden,' 'Chinese,' and 'Moorpark' are self-ertile but will produce a better crop if cross-pollinated. A few cultivars including 'Goldrich' and 'Perfection' need cross-pollination.

Cherries

Most sweet cherry cultivars require cross-pollination for best crops; sour cherries do not require cross-pollination but set heavier crops if crossed. Trees must be no more than 40 yards apart for pollination. Sour cherries aren't good pollinators for sweet cherries because they bloom later. Sweet cherries 'Bing,' 'Emperor Francis,' 'Lambert,' and 'Napoleon' (also called 'Royal Ann') are self-unfruitful and will not pollinate each other. 'Stella' and 'Lapins' are both self-fertile.

Peaches and Nectarines

Most cultivars are self-fertile. Peaches 'J. H. Hale,' 'Erlihale,' 'Indian Free,' and 'White Hale' are sterile.

Pears

Common pear cultivars need cross-pollination for best fruit set. Asian pears also require cross-pollination and will cross with common pear cultivars. Trees must be no more than 150 feet apart for pollination. 'Magness' is sterile. 'Bedford,' 'Bristol Cross,' and 'Waite' produce little pollen. 'Max Red' is a type of 'Bartlett' and won't pollinate 'Bartlett.' 'Bartlett' and 'Seckel' are incompatible.

Plums

Many European plums (and cultivars sold as prunes) are self-fruitful, although most will produce better crops if cross-pollinated. Japanese plums need cross-pollination. Japanese and European cultivars will not cross-pollinate each other.

---

will need a second cultivar for pollination. But some cultivars are incompatible and cannot cross-pollinate. (See "Pollination Requirements of Fruit Trees" for a guide to common cultivars and compatibility.)

BEATING BLOOMING PROBLEMS

There are a few things you can do when you have only one tree blooming and your pollinator cultivar isn't blooming. If a neighbor or friend has a blooming pollinator cultivar, ask to cut a few flowering branches. Place them in a bucket of water. Hang the bucket in the tree so that the bees will work both the flowers of the cut branches as well as those on the tree.

If there aren't many bees and you only have a few flowers, try hand-pollinating. With a paintbrush, touch the stamens of the flowers to collect pollen. Then brush the pollen onto the stigma of the flower to be pollinated.

Another way to satisfy the need for different pollinating cultivars is to graft a pollinator cultivar onto the tree, creating a two-in-one tree. Many nurseries offer such specially grafted trees, making it easy to grow different cultivars of fruit on one tree.

FRUIT SET AND YIELD

Flower buds of common tree fruits form during the months of August and September of the year before blooming. If the tree lacks adequate nutrients, water, or sunlight during that critical flower development phase, there will be few flowers blooming the following spring. While it is important to provide adequate water during this time, don't feed heavily—growth won't harden adequately before cold winter weather arrives. An early spring feeding—such as a 6-inch layer of compost or well-rotted manures used as mulch—will ensure that your trees are well nourished during the summer yield and flower-development periods.

Fruit trees always produce more flowers than they can possibly ripen as fruit, and some of the developing fruit drops naturally. Generally there are two periods of fruit drop, one soon after the blooming period, and then another within the month. For many cultivars, bearing a heavy crop of fruit one year will draw nutrients away from the developing flower buds, resulting in a light crop the following year. In extreme cases, the tree will develop a pattern of bearing fruit every other year. You can even out your yield by heavily thinning the fruit in the early summer of the "on" year.

Pruning and Training Fruit Trees

After the sometimes back-breaking work of digging planting holes and setting your trees, you may feel tempted to just lean back and watch them grow. But if your goal is healthy, early-bearing, heavy-yielding fruit trees, plan on pruning and training your trees rather than letting nature take its course.

If you think of your fruit tree as a solar collector, it is easy to see that proper spacing of the branches by training and pruning will allow more leaf surface area to face the sun. The more energy the leaves capture, the more flowers, fruit, and vegetative growth the tree will produce. In fact, sun must shine at least 30 percent of the time on fruiting branches or they won't develop flowers. Furthermore, fruits such as apples and cherries need light to develop proper color, which is why fruit borne on interior branches often isn't as highly colored as fruit on outside limbs. Proper training will encourage earlier fruit bearing.

Proper pruning helps control diseases, too. Fruit and foliage on properly spaced branches dry more quickly after rain or in humid weather, thus reducing the spread of fungal diseases that can ruin

Parts of a Fruit Tree

To understand where to prune, you need to know the parts of your fruit tree. The primary scaffold branches arise from the trunk to form the basic framework of the tree. The crotch angle is the angle formed between the primary scaffolds and the trunk. The primary scaffold branches divide into secondary scaffolds. The finer branches of a scaffold are called laterals. Water sprouts, foot suckers, crossing branches, and limbs that shade or rub against one another should be pruned away annually, along with diseased and damaged limbs. Also try to remove or train branches with narrow, weak crotch angles.

the ripening fruit as well as the tree. Thus, pruning and training can eliminate the need for expensive and time-consuming disease control.

Finally, pruning and training keep the tree small enough for easy harvests. Some fruit trees, particularly cherries, can become so large that, without proper care, much of the fruit becomes inaccessible. Fruit trees should be shaped to fit in with the scale of your landscaping.

For young trees, the only pruning tool you may need is a good pair of hand pruners. These cut small branches (up to ½-inch diameter) cleanly. As your tree grows and increases in diameter, you will need lopping shears, which make clean cuts through branches of up to 1¼ inches in diameter, and a pruning saw for larger branches.

It is important to clean your equipment by dipping it in a 10 percent bleach solution once you finish pruning a tree. Dip between cuts when trimming away diseased wood to prevent the spread of disease.

BASIC TECHNIQUES

The basic principles for pruning fruit trees don't differ much from those that apply to pruning ornamental trees. Proper pruning improves and promotes the health, vigor, productivity, safety, and appearance of a tree—ornamental of fruit. However, with fruit trees there are some special concerns that affect pruning and training. Fruit trees must be able to withstand the weight of heavy fruit loads. Maximum exposure to sunlight is important for fruit production and ripening.

Pruning for Strength and Yield

It's important to prune and train fruit trees so they will be able to withstand the often considerable weight of ripening fruit. Many fruit trees have branches that grow almost vertically up from the trunk, creating narrow crotches or branch angles that are more likely to break when bearing a heavy fruit crop. These branches are also more likely to break during storms. Wide branch angles—45 to 90

degrees—are the strongest, and are the goal of all pruning and training techniques. (See "Parts of a Fruit Tree" at left for more on the basic structure of a tree.)

Branch angle also affects fruit yield. Besides having a poor shape for sun-gathering, these narrow-crotched branches will be very slow to bear fruit. Branches growing at a 45- to 60-degree angle will develop more flowers and fruit.

Before you prune, it's important to know how the fruit tree bears its fruit. Many trees bear their flowers on spurs, short stubby branches that grow from the secondary scaffolds. Spurs can bear for as many as 5 to 20 years, as they do in apples, pears, European prunes, Japanese plums, and sweet cherries. Or they may bear only a few years, as in apricots and sour cherries. Try not to break off or remove spurs; the tree will have to develop new ones before fruiting again. Peaches, nectarines, apricots, Japanese plums, European prunes, and sour cherries fruit on lateral buds borne on the previous season's growth. These trees need annual pruning to ensure a constant supply of second-year wood. These plants also need pruning to keep the fruit within reach for picking and not so far out on the branches that it causes them to break under the fruit load.

Types of Cuts

There are two basic types of cuts you can make: thinning cuts and heading cuts. A thinning cut completely removes a branch, allowing sunlight to reach the center of the plant and directing energy toward the remaining branches. You can thin primary scaffold branches, which arise at the trunk, or secondary scaffold branches, which originate on the primary branches. Thinning cuts should be made at the base of the branch, but without removing the branch collar, the thickened area at the base of the branch.

Heading cuts are made in the middle of a branch to encourage branching and thicker, fuller growth. Cut just above a bud that points in the

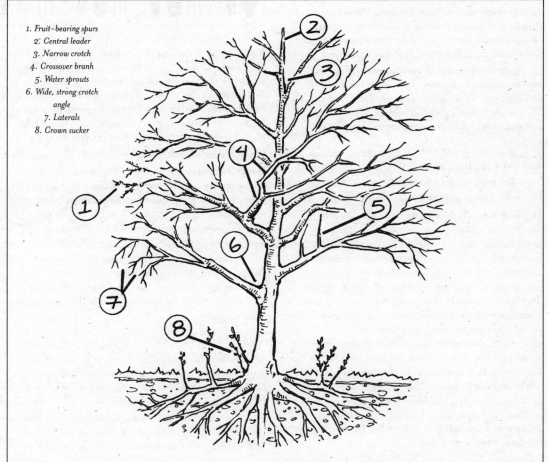

1. Fruit-bearing spurs
2. Central leader
3. Narrow crotch
4. Crossover branh
5. Water sprouts
6. Wide, strong crotch angle
7. Laterals
8. Crown sucker

Continued ➡

direction you want growth to occur. Don't cut straight across the branch; instead, cut at about a 45-degree angle across the branch, sloping away from the bud. The top of the cut should be ½ inch above the top of the bud; the bottom of the cut should be at a point above and on the opposite side of the branch from the base of the bud.

Spreading

Spreading is a training technique that is very helpful for strengthening branches by increasing narrow crotch angles. Spreading is most successful when the branch is young and supple—newly sprouted or no more than one to two years old. One of the easiest methods is to clip a clothespin between the trunk and the limb so the limb is pushed into the proper position. Another method is to cut notches in a lightweight piece of wood and wedge it between the limb and trunk. Hanging a fishing weight on the young limb until it bends to the proper position is also effective. Once the limb has grown and stays naturally in the new position, remove the spreading device.

If you need to spread a limb that is older but still can be easily bent into position, tie fabric loops around the limb and then tie a light rope to each loop. Pound a stake into the ground so that when the rope is tied to the stake, the limb is bent into position. If they can be spared, it is best to remove limbs that can't be bent easily into position.

Seasonal Considerations

A tree's response to pruning depends on the season. Late winter or early spring pruning—while trees are dormant—encourages vigorous growth, because food stored for spring growth will be shared by fewer growing points. Most fruit trees need annual dormant season pruning, though in some cases it will be only to remove any dead or broken branches. It is best to wait until just before spring growth to prune most trees. This makes the tree more resistant to winter injury and eliminates the need to reprune when a late winter storm damages or kills branches. Recent research indicates that peaches, nectarines, and apricots present an exception to this rule: Pruning them before they have finished flowering leaves them open to canker, which can invade pruning wounds. Prune these trees after they have finished flowering.

Pruning in early or midsummer results in less vigorous growth, because the stores food has already been used up by growing leaves and shoots. This is why trees trained as espaliers are often pruned in summer—to discourage vegetative growth.

Annual Pruning

To maintain healthy and fruitful trees, there are a few basic things to look for each year.

Dead or Broken Branches. The first step in pruning or training is to remove any dead or broken branches. It's easy to pick out a dead branch on a green tree, but when that same tree is dormant, live and dead wood is hard to distinguish. Dead branches are often withered or very dark when compared to living branches. An easy trick to use when dormant pruning is to start at the tip of a branch or year-old shoot, and carefully scrape a small area on the surface of the branch—it should be green just under the thin bark at the tip of the shoot. If it is black, brown, or gray, that part of the branch is dead. Move closer to the trunk or back from the tip, and continue to scrape other small areas until you can determine just where the living tissue begins. Use a thinning cut to remove dead or broken branches.

Pruning an Open Center Tree

A mature open center tree has a short trunk with three to four strong, evenly spaced scaffold branches around it. Training starts the first season after planting.

First-Year Training

The first summer, remove any branches that are less than 18 inches from the ground. The branches that grow from the top 2 or 3 buds will have narrow, weak crotch angles; cut them back to 2 or 3 buds. Then select scaffold branches from among the lower branches. Look for branches with wide crotch angles that are spaced 3 to 5 inches apart vertically along the trunk and radiate evenly around it. Don't despair if you don't have any potential scaffold branches, or only have weak-looking ones; they will develop the first summer after the top shoots are pruned away. Use spreading techniques to increase the crotch angles of the scaffold branches you select. The angles should be between 45 and 90 degrees. About a month after pruning, check the tree and cut back any new shoots growing from the top, above the scaffold branches you've selected.

Second-Year Training

The second season, make your final selection of scaffold branches; train a third or fourth scaffold if the tree did not produce enough vigorous growth the previous season. Do this in early spring for most trees; for apricots, peaches, and nectarines, prune after flowering. For the best growth, all scaffold branches should be about equal in size. If one is much larger than the others, cut it back to a lateral branch that is growing toward the outside of the tree. Cut back the shoots that have arisen at the center of the tree—where you removed the central leader last season—to short stubs above the highest scaffold branch. These will sprout again and help keep the scaffold branches growing outward rather than vertically. Use spacing techniques to further widen the crotch angles, if necessary. Thin out lateral branches growing from the scaffolds within 6 inches of the trunk, along with any branches that arise from the trunk itself. This will open up the center of the tree and encourage growth at the tips. Remove any laterals on scaffolds that cross or touch one another, along with diseased or damaged wood. During the growing season, you'll need to head back the center shoots to 3 to 5 inches so that growth continues to be directed to the side scaffolds.

Third-Year Training

By the third year, the basic scaffold arrangement should be well established. Remove completely shoots growing from the center stubs, as the scaffold branches should have attained their permanent shape. Be sure to cut away diseased branches as well as any that cross or crowd the center of the plant.

Maintenance Pruning

The branches of peaches, nectarines, apricots, European prunes, and Japanese plums need annual heading to encourage lateral bud growth and, thus, fruit production. For apricots, use heading cuts to prune away half the length of half the new growth. For peaches and nectarines, cut back all of the previous year's growth to half its length. For plums and prunes, use both thinning and heading cuts to remove approximately one-third of the previous year's growth. Head back the new growth of sour cherries by 1 to 2 inches in June to encourage the growth of lateral leaf buds that will help the tree become more vigorous. Continue to remove crossing or diseased limbs, water sprouts, and suckers.

Rubbing or Crossing Branches. When you prune, look for branches that cross or rub. Crossing branches can restrict sunlight and air circulation in the center of the plant; rubbing damages bark, creating entry points for disease organisms. Also look for branches that are parallel but simply too close together, so that one shades the other. In either case, remove the weaker branch.

Water Sprouts and Suckers. Water sprouts are fast-growing branches that arise on the trunk or branches and grow straight up, producing little, if any, fruit. They often appear at the site of old pruning wounds. Remove them as soon as you notice them, regardless of the time of year.

Suckers are sprouts that arise from the roots of the tree. Remove these as soon as you see them. If you have a grafted tree, the suckers will have the characteristics of the rootstock, not the cultivar you want to grow.

Training and Pruning Styles

Orchardists have developed several ways to train fruit trees, all based on obtaining maximum yield, sun exposure, and ease of care, and determined by the growth habits of the plants.

The ideal sun-gathering shape of a fruit tree is similar to that of a Christmas tree—with evenly spaced scaffold branches arising from around a single trunk. This is the basic shape of a central leader tree, the form most often used for dwarf apples, pears, cherries, plums, and prunes. To a lesser extent, this is also the basic shape of the modified central leader.

Open center trees have three or four main limbs that arise near where the central leader was removed. This form allows good light penetration and is most commonly used for peaches, nectarines, apricots, and standard-sized apple trees. Cherries, plums, and prunes may also be pruned as open center trees.

Whatever method you use, keep in mind that each tree presents its own particular pruning problem. Take time to stand back and examine the tree as you prune. Remember, you can always cut a questionable branch off later, but you can't reattach one cut by mistake!

Pruning a Central Leader Tree

It takes several seasons to properly train a central leader tree, but it's well worth the effort. For the first few years of training, the goals are to encourage vigorous growth and a sturdy branching structure.

First-Year Training. If you're starting with an unbranched whip, as soon as growth starts after planting, select the most vigorous shoot arising near

Continued ➡

the top of the trunk to serve as the central leader. If there is a trunk stub above this branch, remove it. To keep lower branches from competing with the central leader, prune away the next two shoots below the leader if they are less than 8 inches from the top of the tree. If you're starting with a branched tree, the procedure is the same: Select a central leader, remove the second and third shoot from the top if they are less than 8 inches from the top, if they have narrow crotch angles, or if they are growing vertically and crowding the central leader. Then remove any branches that are less than 20 inches from the ground.

The next objective is to choose scaffold branches that will form the framework of the tree. Often there are only two branches for scaffolds in the first summer after planting—more scaffolds will develop in the next few years. Choose vigorous branches with wide crotch angles that are spaced between 5 and 8 inches apart vertically and radiate evenly around the trunk. No two branches should be directly above one another. Use one of the spreading methods described earlier if the crotch angles are less than 45 degrees. If there are more branches than you need for scaffolds, cut them back to 4 inches from the trunk to encourage fruiting and to direct growth into the selected scaffold limbs. Pinch these branches monthly throughout the growing season, from June through August. (After a few seasons, once the primary scaffolds are bearing well, you can either remove the branches that you pinched or cut them back to a fruiting spur in the middle of the summer.)

Second-Year Training. Start second-year training by making a heading cut on the central leader to about 1½ feet above the highest scaffold branch. This will encourage new scaffold branches to form higher on the tree. Make a final selection for the lower main scaffold branches and spread these limbs so the branch angles are between 45 and 90 degrees. Head back these scaffold branches by pruning off the tips if they grew vigorously the year before; if growth was thin and weak, cut them back severely. Strive for a cone-shaped tree, leaving lower scaffold branches longer than those near the top. This will encourage development of secondary scaffolds and strengthen the primary scaffolds.

When growth starts, select the most vigorous shoot that arises from the tip of the central leader, and remove the second and third shoots that arise below it to ensure that it won't have to compete with other branches. Choose additional primary scaffold branches, using spreading techniques as needed. Head back any extra branches not needed for scaffolds to 4 inches as in the first growing season. Remove any suckers or water sprouts during the summer months. Continue pinching the small branches you pinched throughout last season.

Third-Year Training. Follow the directions for second-year training both early in the season and after growth starts. Remove any crossed or touching limbs. Continue spreading the scaffold branches—use the fabric tie-down method to spread these branches to a proper angle. Once growth begins, remove any water sprouts or suckers. If fruit is being borne on the leader, remove it if the leader begins to droop or stake to keep the central leader upright.

Maintenance Pruning. The fourth year, and every year thereafter, you'll need to prune to maintain the shape of the tree. A mature tree should have six to eight main scaffold branches. After the tree has reached its mature height, prune the central leader and the main scaffold branches back to weak lateral branches. Be sure to retain the cone shape of the tree, with lower scaffolds longer than higher ones.

Scaffolds that have fruited for several years will often droop downward because of the weight of the fruit. Don't remove all of these or you will reduce fruit production near the bottom of the tree. Drooping branches that have fruited for three or four years can be cut back to a side branch that points toward the outside of the tree.

Continue with standard annual pruning. Remove water sprouts and suckers, along with broken, diseased, or crossing branches.

Pruning a Modified Central Leader Tree

The modified central leader tree closely resembles one trained in the central leader style, and, in fact, for the first few years the training is exactly the same. After four or five main scaffold branches have been selected and trained, cut the central leader to just above the highest scaffold branch. This will open the center of the plant to sunlight. Cherries, plums, prunes, and some vigorous cultivars of apples and pears are often trained as modified central leaders.

Espalier

Having a small yard should not stop you from harvesting an orchard's worth of fruit. Dwarf fruit trees and decorative espalier training can greatly increase your yard's potential for fruit production. Espaliered trees, trained to grow flat rather than three-dimensionally, can be grown upon a trellis in shapes as simple as a single, nearly unbranched trunk with fruiting spurs along its length or as complex as a criss-crossing Belgian fence. Whatever the shape, this system of training and pruning has many advantages. Individual trees can be spaced 1½ to 2 feet apart when grown as a single cordon, or branch, making it easy to find room for a wealth of cultivars.

Why Grow Espaliered Trees?

Espaliered trees have much to offer the home gardener. Although they are small, their yield per space is quite high. An apple tree trained to a single branch, called a cordon, that is 6 to 7 feet tall can bear from 4 to 8 pounds of fruit. Peaches, nectarines, apricots, plums, and cherries trained in the shape of a 7-foot-tall fan and spaced 12 to 20 feet apart can each bear 12 to 30 pounds of fruit. Since the plants don't require as much space as conventionally grown trees, you'll have room for more cultivars. By selecting both early- and late-ripening ones, you can spread your harvests over a long season and grow just the right amount of fruit for your use. Espaliered trees begin to bear earlier than standard trees—within the third to fourth year from planting. The fruit colors and ripens well because it receives plenty of sunlight. Pruning, picking, and pest control are easy because everything is within view and reach. In cooler climates, espalier training can permit the growth of marginally hardy cultivars if the trees are planted next to a south-facing wall to take advantage of reflected heat.

While espalier training has many advantages, it takes more time and dedication to erect a sturdy trellis and carefully train and prune to achieve and maintain these tree shapes. As with most garden choices, perhaps the saying "Know thyself" is the best when determining whether this method is for you. For those of you who don't want to train trees into this shape, some nurseries offer pre-trained trees so all you need do is maintain the shape after planting.

Getting Started

While you can put espalier fruit trees anywhere you can place a trellis, there are some places that especially lend themselves to decorative trees. Driveway edges, borders of vegetable or flower gardens, and the outer edges of decks are good locations for espalier fruit trees. For instance, you might want to screen in your deck or patio area with artful panels of apples or pears grown in the latticed pattern of a Belgian fence. Espalier fruit trees also can be trained directly to a wall or fence, without a trellis. However, remember that it will be almost impossible to do any maintenance on the wall once the espalier tree is growing up against it. So, do not place espaliers against wood siding, wooden door frames or windows, or a fence that will require painting. If you still would like to take advantage of reflected heat but need to maintain a wooden wall, place the trellis at least 2 feet from the wall for easy maintenance access. In climates where daytime temperatures often exceed 90°F, trees should be planted away from any walls on a free-standing trellis so that trees and fruit will not be burned by excess heat reflected from walls.

Trellis Guidelines

You can support espaliers on pipe or wooden posts strung with horizontal, vertical, or diagonal strands of heavy 14-gauge wire. If your area has high winds, you might want to use plastic-covered wires so that the branches aren't injured as they rub up against the wire. Space wires 15 to 24 inches apart, with the first wire about 15 inches above ground level. On fences or walls, the highest wire should be at least 6 inches below the top of the structure for best appearance. If you choose to grow against a wall, fasten the branches to a system of wires that is spaced 2 to 4 inches from the wall.

Choosing Trees for Espalier Training

For best results, start with fruits that bear on long-lived short spurs, such as apples and pears. These can be trained relatively easily to many different shapes. Trees that bear mainly on lateral branches (one-year-old wood) or short-lived spurs, such as peaches, nectarines, apricots, plums, and cherries, are more difficult and less adaptable. In order to maintain fruit yield, you need to prune these plants to provide a constant source of new wood.

Choose trees with dwarfing rootstocks so that the shape of the tree will be easier to maintain. (For apples, trees grafted on M9 or M26 rootstocks work well on loam soil while more vigorous MM106 rootstock should be used on heavy or sandy soils. Pears should be grafted on Quince A or Quince C rootstocks.) Choose unbranched young trees for easiest training.

Espalier Shapes for Best Yields

The best shapes will be determined in a large part by the fruiting habit of the plants you are growing. For apples and pears, one of the easiest and highest yielding shapes is a simple cordon, simply an unbranched tree with fruiting spurs along its length that is either grown vertically or leaning at an angle. This style allows you to grow the most cultivars, and thus the widest variety of fruit, because the trees can be planted as little as 2 feet apart. Pears bear best when trained as a vertical cordon; apples, at an angle. Belgian fence is a form that uses branches growing on the diagonal and is suitable for apples and pears. In this form, each tree has a short trunk with two branches spread at 45 degrees in a V shape. Branches of neighboring trees are woven together to form a decorative panel.

Another way to shape apples and pears is to plant a single tree and train multiple vertical arms from the trunk, making the double-U form.

Trees trained with horizontal cordons have branches growing horizontally along a trellis. These are more difficult to maintain because they work

Continued ➡

against the plant's natural tendency to grow upward. Trees trained in this manner can have two horizontal cordons or several pairs of cordons. This form offers the advantage of more fruit production in a vertical space. Depending on the length of the horizontal cordons, space these trees 8 to 20 feet apart.

Cherries, peaches, nectarines, apricots, and plums grow best when trained in a fan shape, with permanent branches radiating from the top of a short trunk. This shape allows them the extra space they need for their fruiting wood. Space trees 12 to 20 feet apart.

PRUNING AND TRAINING ESPALIERS

Once you've selected a site, decided what trees you want to grow, and how you want to train them, it's time to plant and begin training. Plant trees just as you would any dwarf fruit tree.

Training Basics

All of the espalier styles require slightly different training, but there are some basic techniques that apply. During early training, lash bamboo canes to the trellis wires in the direction you want a branch to grow. Then train the tips of the fruit branches to the canes. This encourages growth that is ruler-straight and precisely spaced, which is especially important for the more complex designs such as the Belgian fence. Use twine, rawhide, plant ties, cloth strips, or any material that will not constrict the branches when tying them to the trellis. As you train to establish the plant's basic framework, do not simply remove all unwanted lateral branches.

Basic directions for training several popular styles of espalier are described below. Whatever shape you are making, do not let the tree fruit until training is finished, so that all the tree's resources are concentrated on fast vegetative growth. If the tree blooms, remove the fruit right after the blossoms fall.

Cordons. To train trees as simple, unbranched cordons that are vertical or diagonal, simply tie a bamboo cane to the horizontal wires of the trellis and then tie the stem of each tree to the cane. After the tree has grown to the top of the trellis, cut it above a bud at the desired height.

U or Double U. Although it takes a couple of growing seasons to train an espalier in a U or double-U shape, these are both attractive styles that are relatively easy to maintain. Once growth starts the first spring, cut the tree back to a bud just above the wire that will support the bottom of the U. Select the two best of the shoots that sprout, and train them to bamboo canes set at a 45-degree angle from the main stem. As the season progresses, lower and tie the two side arms to the first horizontal wire so they form a 90-degree crotch angle. Once they have grown long enough to form the bottom of the U, allow the tips of the stems to turn upward and train them to the top of the wire.

To form a double U, train as above and then clip each side shoot just above a trellis wire. Use bamboo canes to train two more side shoots into U shapes.

Belgian Fence and Fan. The Belgian fence and fan-shaped espalier forms are similar in design. Cut the tree back to the height of the lowest wire. For the Belgian fence design, train the top two shoots to grow in opposite directions, using bamboo cane lashed at 45 degrees to the trellis wires. As the shoots grow and intersect, the branches are woven together to form a lattice design. For the fan design, allow three to seven branches to grow from the top of the trunk and train them into a fan pattern.

Controlling Growth and Increasing Yields

Once you have the basic framework established, you'll want to begin managing the tree's growth to keep it under control and maximize fruit yields. Although conventionally grown fruit trees are pruned heavily in early spring, the best way to prune espalier-trained fruit trees is to pinch or rub off unwanted growth throughout the summer as it appears. For example, buds that will produce an unwanted or misdirected branch should be rubbed off in the early spring. If the bud opens, pinch off the growth, taking care not to damage the bark. In late summer, when shoots are longer than 9 inches and the bark is starting to turn from green to brown at the base, trim the shoot back to three leaves beyond where growth began in the spring. (There will be a rosette of smaller leaves around a circular fold in the stem where growth began in the spring.) This will encourage the development of fruit spurs at the base of the branch in the next growing season.

To encourage fruit spur formation, cut weak, year-old laterals to 4 or 5 buds during midsummer. The top buds will grow into vegetative shoots while the bottom buds are most likely to become fat fruit buds. During the next spring, before growth begins, remove the vegetative shoots, leaving only the fruit buds. When vigorous side shoots branch off the end of the cordon, control growth by bending and tying the branch into a horizontal position. If you can do this early in the season, within the first month or so of growth, fruit buds will form along the branch. Before growth begins in the next spring, cut the branch back to a fruit bud to remove the vegetative growing points and make a fruitful spur. If fruiting spurs occur unevenly along the cordon, you can often turn a dormant bud into a fruit spur by making a shallow notch ⅛-inch wide and ¹⁄₁₆-inch deep just below the bud, as soon as the tree begins to leaf out. If you place the notch above the bud, it will often turn into a vegetative branch. To prevent more vertical growth, use one of these spur-forming techniques to turn the top bud of your espalier into a fruitful spur.

On older apple and pear espalier plantings, the fruit spurs become very branched and thick with fruit buds. Thin out some of the buds so that there is space between them. For the best fruit quality, thin to one fruit per flower cluster.

Grafting Fruit Trees

Grafting is a technique used to join parts of two or more plants and cause them to grow together into a single plant. This may seem like a specialty with little relevance to home gardening, but grafting is much more common than one might think. In fact, most fruit trees sold today are grafted. In addition, grapes, modern roses, and many specialty trees and shrubs are also grafted.

Most dwarf and semidwarf fruit trees are a product of grafting. They are composed of a fruiting cultivar grafted onto a rootstock that affects growth rate and size at maturity. Grafting can also be used to add a pollinator to a tree that requires pollen from another cultivar in order to set fruit. In a technique called top working, grafting can be used to change the fruit cultivars growing on an established tree or to add fruit cultivars to a tree. (A tree can be topworked with one or several cultivars.) This technique also can be used to save a tree whose branches or top have been damaged by disease or weather.

Grafting Basics

All grafted trees consist of a stock and a scion. The stock is the plant that provides the best root system for the tree. The scion is the cultivar you've chosen for its good fruiting characteristics. In some cases, a third piece is added—the interstem—if the stock and scion aren't compatible and won't graft well with each other. The interstem is compatible with both, and is grafted between them.

The actual process of grafting involves pressing the cambium—the actively growing tissue of the stem located in a thin layer just under the bark—of the stock and the scion against one another so they grow together. There are several types of grafts, but for any of them to be successful, the cambium of stock and scion must be lined up as close together as possible. Cuts on both should be clean and fresh. After positioning stock and scion, they must be held immobile so the cambium will have a chance to join. It's important to seal any cut ends with grafting wax to make sure the tissue doesn't dry out.

Most grafting is done with cultivars of a single fruit type—grafting one or more apples onto one tree, for example. Surprisingly, different fruit tree species also can be grafted on the same plant. In this case, the compatibility of the tissues from the different stocks and scions is important; incompatible plants will fail to graft together, or they will form a weak graft that breaks easily under stress. As a general rule, nearly all grafts within a single species will be successful. Many grafts within a single genus are also successful. Plums, apricots, nectarines, and peaches all belong to the genus *Prunus*. Some potential combinations among these plants include: plums grafted onto an apricot rootstock or tree; apricots grafted onto peach rootstock; nectarines or Japanese plums grafted onto European plum stock; and apricots and nectarines grafted onto Japanese plum stock. Citrus fruits can be grafted in a similar manner, with grapefruits, lemons, and oranges grafted onto an orange rootstock. When grafting apples, use cultivars with similar growth rates, because a slow-growing cultivar won't graft well with a fast-growing one.

Obtaining Scions

Whether you are planning on topworking an existing tree or are planning to graft onto a seedling that appeared in your yard, the first step is to find scion wood of a cultivar you'd like to grow. Scion wood, the fruiting cultivar, is gathered when the tree is dormant—either in the fall or before buds swell in the spring. You can cut scions from a neighbor's tree or ask a nearby orchardist for them. However, be aware that many new fruit cultivars are Plant Variety Protected (PVP), and it is illegal to propagate them or use portions of them to graft other trees. Some mail-order nurseries offer scion wood.

Scions should be cut from narrow (about pencil width), straight wood produced in the last year. Cut the scions into 6- to 12-inch-long pieces, each with 3 or 4 leaf buds. Always cut above a bud. As you gather and cut scions, bear in mind that when you graft you'll need to align the bottom of the scion with the top of the stock; the scions will die if they are inserted upside down into the stock. An easy way to keep track of which end is which is to make a slanting cut on the bottom, a straight cut on top. Tie the scion pieces in a bundle, put them in a plastic bag with moist peat or sawdust, and store them in a refrigerator.

Types of Grafts

The grafting method you use will depend upon the size of the stock. Whip and tongue grafting is

Continued ➜

generally used to graft small pieces of wood, while cleft grafting is used for 1- to 2-inch diameter stock. Bark grafting is used when the stock is 4 or more inches in diameter. If you can, always make more grafts than necessary, so there is a better chance that some will be successful.

Whip and Tongue. Whip and tongue grafting is one method used to produce commercial fruit trees and to graft pollinator branches or add cultivars to a young tree. It is usually done in early spring while the plant is still dormant and is used to join stock and scion that are nearly the same diameter, generally less than ¾-inch diameter. Whip and tongue grafting is often called tongue grafting or whip grafting.

Cut the stock back to within a few inches of the ground if you are grafting to a planted rootstock cultivar; cut back a young branch close to the trunk if you are topworking a small tree. For the best results, the stock and scion need to be as close in diameter as possible.

Using a sharp grafting knife, make complementary long, diagonal cuts on the top of the stock and the bottom of the scion. The cut surface should be about 1½ inches long on both stock and scion. Make a second cut on each piece parallel to the first, about an inch below it, downward to the center of the stem. This forms the tongue-shaped piece on both parts. When the two pieces are fitted together, they form a tongue and groove joint. Line up the cambiums and wrap securely with a strip of rubber band, latex nursery tape, or plastic electrician's tape. If the two pieces aren't exactly the same diameter, don't just center one piece inside the other—line up the cambiums on at least one side of the graft. (Matching diameters with both sides lined up are preferable.) Cover all the cut surfaces with grafting wax or asphalt emulsion sealing compound. Once the scion begins to grow, remove the wrapping.

Cleft. Cleft grafting is a useful technique for topworking established fruit trees. You can cleft graft a new fruit cultivar onto a tree that has a damaged top or is not producing well, or add extra cultivars to the tree.

Cleft grafting should be done late in the dormant season, before the buds open. In this method, two pencil-width scions are inserted in a cleft made in a fairly upright young branch.

The ends of the short scions should be cut just above a bud and have 2 to 3 buds per piece. Shave the base of each scion so that it is wedge-shaped. The edge that is on the inside of the cleft should be narrower than the edge on the outside. There should be bark on both the narrow inside edge and the wider outside edge. The end of the scion should be blunt, not tapered to a sharp point.

The limb to be grafted, called the stock, should be between 1 and 2 inches in diameter. Cut the stock straight across with a fine-toothed saw for a smooth, even surface. Then use a hammer and chisel to split the center down 4 to 6 inches to form a cleft in the trunk or branch. The depth of the cleft will be determined by the diameter of the scion, which must fit tightly in the cleft. Using a screwdriver to keep the cleft open, insert the scion so that the side with the wider piece of bark is toward the outside of the branch. For the graft to form, you'll need to align the cambiums by pushing the scion toward the center of the cleft slightly so that the tissue just under the bark of the stock is pressing against the same tissue of the scion. Remove the screwdriver once the scion has been aligned. Wax the area and the tips of the scions as soon as the fitting is done. Wait until the following spring to cut off the weaker graft if both take.

Bark. For larger branches, bark grafting is the best technique. This can only be done in the spring, when the bark "slips," or peels easily away from the rest of the tree. Prepare three narrow scions (more if the stock or trunk is very large) about 5 inches long. Make a 2-inch downward diagonal cut on one side of the bottom of the scion and then a slightly smaller cut on the other side, making a very thin wedge. To prepare the stock, cut away the branch to be grafted—if you're replacing a broken or diseased branch cut back to healthy wood—by making a straight cut across the wood as you would for a cleft graft. Then, starting at the top of the stock, make a 2-inch slit in the bark. The bark should slip easily away, leaving the cambium exposed. Place the scion under the bark of the stock, with the longer cut side of the scion facing the inside, against the cambium. Use a small finishing nail to fix the bark and scion in place,

---

Budding Fruit Trees

Budding is a slightly different form of grafting that can be used to change or add fruit cultivars to a tree. In this case, all you need from the scion branch is a bud. The easiest technique is T-budding. Unlike grafting, T-budding is done in mid- to late summer, after the buds for next year have formed and become dormant but while the tree's bark still slips.

1. Cut a 1-foot scion from a newly grown branch. Remove the leaves, leaving the petioles (stems holding the leaf to the branch). If you can't bud right away, wrap the budstick in plastic and keep it cool. Refrigerate in a glass of water if left overnight.

2. Choose a stock branch or trunk that is pencil-sized, and make a T-shaped cut just through the bark. Using the rounded top of a budding knife (or another blunt, rounded edge such as a fingernail), gently lift the flaps of the cut, which should slip away, exposing the cambium.

3. Select a healthy bud from the middle of your budstick and make a shallow cut ½ to ¾ inch below the bud and end ½ inch above it. Slide the knife out. To release the bud, make a perpendicular cut down into the wood ½ inch above the bud. The bud is now free and looks like a little shield.

4. With the bud pointing upward just as it was on the scion, slide the shield—cut side against the wood—into the flaps of the T-cut until it is covered.

5. Press the bark over the sides of the shield and then carefully wrap the area with a strip of rubber band, leaving the bud uncovered. Rub off any buds on the stock that may compete with the grafted bud.

6. When the bud you've selected begins to grow, remove the rubber band. The following spring, after the graft has grown 2 to 3 inches, cut the stock branch above the bud, making a slanting cut back away from the bud. This will encourage bud growth. In the South, this can be done in the same growing season as budding because bud growth will start so quickly.

---

then wax the area and the tips of the scions to keep them from drying out.

Controlling Pests and Diseases

Nothing will dampen your gardening enthusiasm more than the unhappy discovery that your carefully tended trees have been damaged by pests or disease, reducing yield and possibly leaving the fruit inedible. There are steps you can take to avoid this scenario without resorting to the use of poison sprays. In considering your options for fighting pests and disease, remember to weigh your effort, expense, and any possible environmental damage against the amount of harm your trees will suffer. Some insects and diseases cause mainly cosmetic damage to trees or fruits, while others can completely kill your trees.

Watchfulness Pays. Don't forget about your trees between planting or pruning and harvest time. Check them frequently for signs of insect or disease infestation. Telltale clues include: holes in leaves; wilting; shiny coatings on leaves; holes or cuts in fruit; yellowing or brownish areas on leaves; premature defoliation; rotten spots on leaves or fruit; distorted growth; and blistering or rupturing of bark. Pheromone or sticky traps are useful for giving early warning of the arrivals of some species of harmful insects.

Know Your Enemy. Once you identify a specific problem, learn about the life cycle of the pest involved. Many trap and barrier control measures are linked to stopping a pest at a particular point in its life cycle. For example, cankerworms, which skeletonize leaves, can be combated by tying a band of sticky material around tree trunks in fall and again in February to catch wingless adult females which would climb the trunk to lay eggs in the trees.

Encourage Pest Predators. Birds eat enormous numbers of insects and insect eggs hidden under tree bark. Encourage them to visit your yard by providing birdhouses, feeders, and birdbaths. Parasitic wasps and other beneficial insects also help control many fruit tree pests.

Harvest Thoroughly. At harvest time, remove all fruit on the tree and on the ground. Windfalls or damaged fruit left on the tree are prime targets for infestation by insects or disease. Promptly prune away any branches that show signs of disease. Burn diseased fruit and prunings.

Prune Carefully. Careless pruning can leave stubs or injured wood where diseases can get a foothold. Good pruning keeps the tree open to light and air, discouraging the many disease organisms that thrive in a wet, humid environment. Disinfect pruning tools with bleach between each cut whenever you are working on potentially diseased trees.

Plant Resistant Cultivars. This is one of the most promising ways to minimize disease problems without sprays. For example, 'Madison' and 'Harbelle' peaches and 'Mericrest' nectarine are resistant to cytospora canker, and there are many scab-resistant apple cultivars available. 'Liberty' is the most disease-resistant apple cultivar produced thus far.

Use Horticultural Oil. Oil sprays coat insects on your trees, killing them by suffocation, and break down quickly in the environment. In the past, heavier grade oils, called dormant oils, were the only option available. These should only be sprayed in winter or early spring when trees are leafless. Dormant oil also smothers insect eggs hidden in bark. The new, lighter viscosity oils, called superior

Continued ➡

oils, can be sprayed during the growing season if environmental conditions are right. These sprays will suffocate spider mites and other soft-bodied sucking insects.

Be a Good Housekeeper. Bacterial or fungal spores and dormant insects can overwinter in leaf litter under fruit trees. Clean up any plant debris around your trees. Cultivating the top inch or two of soil will expose pupae of some insects to weather and predators.

Try Interplanting. As in your vegetable garden, planting different species of trees near one another may have beneficial effects. Cherry trees may form a kind of natural barrier to prevent apple codling moths from finding all your apple trees. And a mixed planting, being more diverse, may attract more birds and beneficial insects.

Spray When Critical. If faced with the choice between spraying or losing your crop or trees, remember that Bt (Bacillus thuringensis) and botanical poisons are effective against many tree pests. Botanical poisons like rotenone and pyrethrum can kill honeybees—so be extra careful if spraying at bloom time. Lime sulfur, copper and Bordeaux mixture are effective against many tree diseases and are considered low in environmental toxicity.

Making Apple Cider

What better way to celebrate your abundant harvest than by making fresh apple cider? It's an easy process that can be done with simple household appliances or hand tools—or if you have one, an old-fashioned apple cider press.

Apples needn't be picture-perfect to yield great tasting cider. You can use your windfalls if you pick them up promptly and store them in a cool area. Surface-blemished apples such as those with scab or hail marks are fine to use, too. Don't use any apples or parts of apples that have spoiled or have brown decay. Use only ripe apples, as green or underripe fruit produces flat-tasting cider. As with many juices, the best ciders are made from a mix of sweet, tart, and aromatic apples. If you grow only one cultivar of apple, you might want to trade some apples with another gardener whose varieties complement your own. Tart apple varieties include 'Winesap,' 'MacIntosh,' 'Jonathan,' 'Northern Spy,' and 'Wealthy,' while sweet apples include 'Red Delicious,' 'Golden Delicious,' 'Gala,' 'Cortland,' 'Rome,' and 'King.'

JUICING APPLES

Though yields will vary between different cultivars, a bushel of apples generally will make about 3 gallons through it, and fall into the cloth-lined of cider. Keep in mind that fresh cider only lasts in the refrigerator for a few days. However, making hard cider and freezing fresh cider are good ways to preserve this delightful beverage.

The first step in cider-making is crushing the apples. Core the apples and crush or chop them into small pieces in a food chopper blender or food processor. Put the crushed apples into a clean muslin sack—an old, clean pillowcase will do—and squeeze out as much juice as possible. Pour the juice into clean glass jugs or bottles and refrigerate, or just drink right away.

If you have a cider press its hand- or electric-powered cutting cylinder makes it easy to mince up the apples. Keep your hands and fingers away from the rotating blades. Use a large tub to hold the pulp, a smaller one to catch juice runoff, and a clean muslin sack or cheesecloth for pressing the juice out of the pulp. Once the apples are crushed, fill the muslin sack with enough pulp to fill the

---

Foiling Common Fruit Tree Pests

Apple Maggots

These pesky insects are the larvae of flies that lay eggs on fruits throughout the growing season. The larvae burrow throughout the flesh, ruining the fruit. Fortunately, it's easy to catch and kill the flies by hanging red spheres coated with an adhesive substance like Tanglefoot from the branches. The flies land on the decoys, get stuck, and die. Hang the spheres with 9 to 18 inches of open space around them. Use one trap for every 100 or so apples you expect the tree to bear.

Cankerworms

Also known as inchworms, cankerworms skeletonize the leaves of apple, apricot, and other fruit trees, weakening the tree so that little fruit matures and the tree sometimes dies. Wrap heavy paper or cotton batting around tree trunks and coat it with a sticky adhesive to stop females from climbing into the tree to lay eggs. Bt (Bacillus thuringiensis) sprays are effective against the larvae. Tilling the soil around your trees in the fall may unearth pupae, exposing them to predators.

Codling Moths

Apple codling moth larvae, which burrow into apple, apricot, peach and pear fruit, can be controlled by spraying Bt (Bacillus thuringiensis) just as eggs are hatching. Spherical red sticky traps and oil sprays also help in controlling this pest. Woodpeckers will eat eggs hidden in tree bark. Attract the birds to your trees in the winter by hanging a block of suet on the trunk.

Gypsy Moths

Young gypsy moth larvae, which feed on the foliage of many fruit trees, can be controlled with Bt (Bacillus thuringiensis) sprays. Also trap larvae with sticky bands on tree trunks, or foot-wide burlap strips tied around the trunks, with several inches draped over the string. Older larvae feed at night and hide during the day. They will nestle under the burlap, and in the late afternoon, they can be collected and destroyed (wear gloves, as touching the larvae can cause an allergic reaction).

Leafrollers

Fruit tree leafrollers are larvae that spin webs between leaves and fruits, forming a sheltered spot where they can feed on the fruits. They will attack most fruit trees including citrus. Pheromone traps will help monitor if leafrollers are entering your area. Bt (Bacillus thuringiensis) or rotenone sprays provide control.

Peachtree Borers

The larvae of these pests tunnel into the trunks of apricot, cherry, peach, and plum trees, weakening and possibly killing the trees. Kill the larvae in the holes they have made by inserting a wire and jabbing it around to spear the pests. Alternatively, spraying Bt (Bacillus thuringiensis) into the holes will work, as long as the spray directly contacts the larvae. Borers also can be blocked from entering the tree by encircling the trunk with a piece of tin. Force it down below the surface of the ground, leaving about 2 inches between the tin and trunk. Fill the space with tobacco in late spring to make a barrier against the adult moths, which try to lay eggs near the tree base in late summer and early fall.

Pear Psylla

If your pear trees appear to be covered with soot, they have probably been attacked by pear psylla. These tiny insects secrete a sweet, sticky substance. The soot is actually a fungus that grows in the secretions. Stop pear psylla before it creates a problem by spraying with dormant oil in spring. During the growing season, psylla can be controlled by dusting dwarf trees with diatomaceous earth or ground limestone or by spraying with insecticidal soap.

Plum Curculios

These pests lay their eggs in fruits of most common backyard fruit trees, cutting out crescent-shaped holes and damaging the skin. They can be trapped by taking advantage of their natural tendency to play dead when threatened. As soon as you notice damaged fruit on a tree, spread a white dropcloth under the tree and shake the tree or limbs. The insects will drop from the branches, immobile, and you can collect and destroy them.

---

press. Crank the press handle until juice no longer runs. Repeat the process with the rest of the pulp. For a clearer cider, try pouring it through a paper filter such as a coffee filter. Many cider presses are designed so that apple pieces are fed into the crusher or mincer, pass through it, and fall into the cloth-lined frame, ready for pressing.

SETTLING AND RACKING-OFF CIDER

If you prefer a cider with a slight bite to the flavor, let it stand at room temperature for three or four days before drinking. Fill clean glass jars or clear or light-colored plastic containers to just below the brim and stopper with a cotton plug (not a regular lid or cap). The plug will pop out if fermentation causes a buildup in pressure. After the cider has settled, sediment will begin to cover the bottom of the container. To "rack-off" the cider, put one end of a rubber tube (about 3 feet in length) in the cider and suck on the other end as you would with a soda straw. As soon as you feel liquid in your mouth, pinch off this end with your fingers and put the tube into an empty container that is lower than the filled one. You've created a siphon that will draw off the

clear cider. Stop the process before the sediment at the bottom of the container is disturbed.

FERMENTING CIDER

If you prefer a "dry" cider with more zip, allow the cider to stand longer at room temperature. To prevent the cider from turning to vinegar, it must not be stored in the open air. Close containers with an airlock or a curlicue glass "cork" sold by home-brew suppliers. Or tightly stretch three thicknesses of clean muslin over the bottle opening and secure it well with a rubber band around the neck of the bottle. For fermented cider, use heavy glass or plastic containers, such as those used for making homemade wine, that will withstand the fermentation pressure. After about ten days, the cider will begin frothing and may foam over the top. Clean off the sides of the container, replace the muslin if necessary, and let the frothing continue until fermentation subsides. Once this happens, the sugar in the cider has been turned to alcohol, making the flavor dry rather than sweet. This is often called hard cider. The

Continued ➡

longer the cider stands, the higher the alcohol content will be.

Storing Fermented Cider

You can store fermented cider in the refrigerator for four or five days. If you want to keep it longer, you'll need to pasteurize it to stop fermentation. Pasteurizing is simply heating the cider to 185°F. To be accurate, use a candy or jelly thermometer to monitor the temperature. Skim off the froth that will probably develop on the top of the cider and pour the hot cider into clean, heated plastic containers or glass jars (heat the containers so they won't crack when exposed to the hot cider). Refrigerate right away, as leaving it on the counter to cool down allows flavor to be lost.

An easy way to store fermented cider is to freeze it. If you plan to freeze it for more than six months, pasteurize it first.

Thinning Fruit

Once your trees begin to bear, you'll probably want to watch each and every fruit mature and ripen. But thinning by pulling off some of the immature fruit is one of the best things you can do to increase harvests and promote better tree health.

WHY THIN?

Thinning is often the most neglected task of fruit tree growing. But fruit on an unthinned tree will be smaller and less sweet. In apples, the decrease in sweetness also means a decrease in storage life. Fruit will take longer to ripen, and in the case of cultivars that are marginally hardy, the crop may not mature before the end of the growing season.

Trees that overbear also will form fewer flowers for the following season and may revert to biennial bearing—only yielding a crop every other year. Fruit trees such as peaches that have overexpended energy in ripening fruit are more likely to suffer winter damage. Furthermore, branches heavily loaded with fruit often break, ruining the tree's form and possibly its bearing potential for years.

THINNING GUIDELINES

Now that you know the importance of thinning, here are a few helpful tips.

- When thinning, use a twisting motion; don't pull. This prevents spurs from being broken or damaged.
- Thin apples, pears, and plums within two months after full bloom (the time when more than half the blossoms were open).
- Thin apricots within the first 38 to 41 days after full bloom.
- Thin peaches and nectarines before the fruit is 1¼ inches in diameter.
- Thin pears, apples, and peaches to only one fruit per cluster or spur. This keeps fruits from rubbing against one another while they are ripening.

Harvesting Tree Fruits

There's nothing better than tree-ripened fruit for fresh eating, jams, jellies, pies, or tarts. Here are some guidelines to help you decide just how and when to pick for best flavor.

WHEN TO HARVEST

Ripe sweet cherries or apricots are delectable right off the tree. It's easy to tell when these fruits are ripe—just pluck and taste one when they've reached full size and have the right color. If they are sweet, they are ripe and ready for harvest. The same applies to apples, peaches, nectarines, plums, and prunes. When ripe, most of these fruits are easy to pick. Use a slight twisting motion as you lift upwards to pick the fruit without damaging the tree.

These rules don't apply to sour cherries and pears. Sour cherries are ripe when you can pull the fruit away from the pit, leaving the pit and stem on the tree. Pears need to be picked when they are full size, but not yet ripe. If pears ripen on the tree, their flesh becomes coarse or mealy in texture. The skin of ready-to-pick pears lightens from dark green to light green and the fruit easily separates from the tree when picked with a slight upward tilting motion. To ripen pears, put them in a cool place (60° to 70°F) and cover with newspaper. Some cultivars such as 'Anjou' and 'Comice' need to be stored for a couple of months at cold temperatures (30° to 32°F) before ripening can occur. A trick that will ripen these cultivars soon after picking is putting the pears and a ripe banana or apple in a closed paper bag. The ripe fruit will release ethylene gas, which induces ripening.

HARVESTING TIPS

- Don't just drop your freshly picked fruit into a bucket—place them in gently. This will extend the storage life of fruit, particularly long-keeping apple cultivars.
- To extend the storage life of sweet cherries, leave the stems attached to the fruit you pick.
- On large trees, fruit on the outer limbs or at the top of the tree often ripen before fruit on the interior; plan more than one harvest.
- Place buckets or boxes of harvested fruit out of the sun as soon as they are filled. This is particularly important for black cherries because the dark color absorbs heat fast, making the fruit spoil quickly.
- Some fruit—plums, prunes, and apricots, for instance—continues to ripen off the tree. You can take advantage of this if your vacation is scheduled for the week these fruits will be ripening. Pick before you leave, and look forward to coming home to ripe fruit! But, peaches and nectarines soften after picking, but don't gain in sweetness—so don't pick them until the fruit is tasty.

Favorite Nuts and Fruits
Jeff Cox

Growing Nut Trees

Reliably long-lived, often gargantuan in size, and possessing many unique physical attributes, nut trees have become an important part of American culture. Grown since colonial times, nut trees are truly a multipurpose crop, providing shade, beauty, edible nuts, building materials, and wildlife habitats.

SELECTING NUT TREES

People often ask whether they should plant cultivars or seedling nut trees. Named cultivars are produced vegetatively, usually by grafting or budding, yielding genetically identical clones. The advantage of grafted trees is that you know exactly what you are going to get with respect to hardiness, cracking quality, flavor, size, and other crop characteristics. Seeds, on the other hand, are always somewhat different genetically. This genetic diversity can make a stand of seedlings less susceptible to serious insect or disease problems than a stand of genetically identical cultivars.

Where high-quality nut production is of greatest importance, as with pecan or English walnut, stick to named cultivars where available. For trees such as black walnut and butternut, where timber value may be as important as the nut quality, plant a few grafted trees and use high-quality seedlings to fill out the rest of the planting. The resulting forest will be much healthier, and the cost of seedling trees is also a fraction of that of grafted ones.

PLANTING AND CARE

These low-maintenance plants can adapt to a range of sites. They generally need very little extra care once they have been established. Keep in mind that many nut trees, including pecans and most black and English walnuts, need cross-pollination; be sure to plant more than one cultivar or seedling of each kind.

Chapters 5 and 8 include information on general care an maintenance of trees that also applies to nut tree culture.

Most nut trees have a deep anchoring taproot, making them a bit more difficult to establish than other trees. Whenever possible, start with small, young trees; they will often adjust more quickly and begin growing sooner than larger trees. Make sure you dig the planting hole deep enough to accommodate the entire taproot.

Unlike fruit trees, most nut trees don't require special pruning techniques to produce good crops. Prune nut trees as you would any shade tree, removing dead, diseased, or crossing branches regularly. If you've planted grafted trees, be sure to prune off any suckers that may arise from the rootstock. For trees that are eventually intended for timber, keep side limbs pruned off to about 12 to 16 feet up the trunk.

Most nuts are best when they are gathered as soon as they become ripe. Remove the outer husk as soon as possible to prevent mold or darkening of the nut kernel. Store the husked nuts in their shells in a cool, dry, rodent-free area. Allow the nuts to cure (dry) for one to three months. After curing, most nuts will keep in the shell for at least a year.

Growing Small Fruit

While tree fruits—apples, peaches, pears, plums, and so on—have similar cultural requirements, the small-fruit crops—blueberries, brambles, grapes, and strawberries—all require widely different care. Fortunately, they're all relatively easy to grow. In the pages that follow, you'll find details on how to plant, prune, train, and care for the most popular small-fruit crops.

BLUEBERRIES
Vaccinium spp.

Ericaceae

Blueberries are among North America's few cultivated native fruits. They have become one of the most popular fruits for home gardeners for their ornamental value, pest resistance, and delicious berries. Only their soil requirements keep them from being more widely planted.

Northerners grow two species of blueberries: *Vaccinium corymbosum*, highbush, and *V. angustifolium*, lowbush. Southern gardeners tend to raise *V. ashei*, rabbiteye blueberry. All three bear delicious fruit on plants with beautiful white, urn-shaped flowers and bright fall color. Here's a rundown:

Lowbush blueberries: Although the fruit of the lowbush blueberry is small, many people consider its flavor superior to that of other blueberries. These extremely hardy plants are good choices for the North. They bear nearly a pint of fruit for each foot of row. Lowbush plants spread by layering and will quickly grow into a matted low hedge. Zones 2 to 6.

Continued ➡

Highbush blueberries: Highbush are the most popular home-garden blueberries. Growing 6 to 12 feet or more in height, each bush may yield 5 to 20 pounds of large berried in mid- to late summer. Crosses between highbush and lowbush species have resulted in several hardy, large-fruiting plants. They grow between 1½ and 3 feet tall. Highbush blueberries vary in hardiness, but many cultivars grow well in the North if you plant them in a sheltered spot. Zones 3 to 8.

Rabbiteye blueberries: Rabbiteyes are ideal for warmer climates. They'll tolerate drier soils than highbush plants can, although they may need irrigation during dry spells. The plants grow rapidly and often reach full production in four to five years. They grow from 10 feet to more than 25 feet high and may yield up to 20 pounds of fruit per bush. Rabbiteyes do not grow well in areas that are completely frost-free, however, because they need a chilling period of a few weeks to break dormancy and set fruit. Zones 7 to 9.

Planting and Care

Blueberries require full sun and well-drained, moisture-retentive, acidic soil with a pH of 4.0 to 5.0. Of the three species, highbush blueberries are the most finicky about soil. Blueberries generally grow well in soil enriched with acidic organic material, such as peat moss, composted pine needles or oak leaves, or compost made from pine, oak, or hemlock bark. Fertilize with acidic fertilizers, such as cottonseed meal or soybean meal. Blueberries enjoy a thick, organic mulch.

Most blueberries are not entirely self-pollinating. Plant at least two different cultivars near each other for adequate cross-pollination. Blueberries grow slowly and don't reach full production until they're six to eight years old, so get a head start with two- or three-year-old plants.

Like most bush fruits, blueberries benefit from pruning as they become older. Yearly pruning helps to encourage large fruits, maintains productivity, and lets sunshine into the bushes, which aids in ripening the berries. Late winter is the ideal time for pruning.

In general, both highbush and rabbiteye plants respond to the same type of pruning. For the first three to four years, prune only to make sure each bush is growing in a strong, upright shape. If the fruit buds are too numerous, remove some of them to get fewer but larger berries. (You can distinguish fruit buds on the dormant plants because they are fatter than leaf buds.)

Harvesting

Blueberries ripen over a long season, and you don't need to pick them daily like strawberries. Different cultivars ripen to various shades of blue, so be careful not to pick them too early if you want the best flavor; taste them to determine when they're at their peak. Don't pull berries from the stem; instead, gently twist them off with your fingertips. If the berries don't come off with slight pressure, they're not ready for harvest. Blueberries keep for several days after picking if you keep them cool and dry. They are also ideal for freezing.

Preventing Problems

Although commercial growers encounter a variety of insects, home gardeners rarely have any problems. The blueberry maggot and cherry fruitworm are the most troublesome insects that are likely to appear. Reduce the chances of damage by cleaning up all the old fruit in a planting before winter.

Diseases are seldom a concern in the North but tend to be more common in the South. Botrytis tip blight kills new growth, and stem canker causes cracks in the canes. Cut away any growth that shows signs of abnormal appearance. Mummy berry makes the fruit rot and fall off. To prevent it, plant resistant cultivars, keep the berries picked, and clean up any dropped fruit. Viral diseases, such as stunt, are difficult to control and invariably result in the gradual deterioration of the plant. Buy from a reputable nursery to get disease-free plants.

Birds are unusually fond of blueberries. To prevent damage, cover the bushes with tightly woven netting before the berries begin to ripen.

Brambles

Rubus spp.

Rosaceae

Raspberries and blackberries are among the most delicious and desirable berries you can grow. They are frequently treated as gourmet fruit, but because they don't ship well, not because they are hard to grow.

Brambles can produce fruit for 10 to 25 years. It's important to choose cultivars that have the characteristics you want and that suit your climate. Here's a rundown:

Raspberries: There are two types of raspberries: summer-bearing and fall-bearing. In some areas of the country, their bearing seasons may overlap, so you can harvest raspberries from early summer until frost. Red and yellow cultivars are summer- or fall-bearers. Black and purple raspberries are all summer-bearers.

Red and yellow raspberries are the easiest raspberries to grow. Their fruit is both sweet and fragrant.

Black raspberries are not as winter-hardy as red ones, but tend to tolerate more summer heat. They also are more prone to viral and fungal diseases and have stiffer thorns. The berries are seedy but have a very intense flavor. They are good eaten fresh or in preserves.

Purple raspberries are hybrids resulting from crosses between reds and blacks. The canes are generally more winter-hardy than the black parents. They tend to be very spiny and productive with large, intensely flavored berries.

Blackberries: In general, blackberries are less winter-hardy than most raspberries. In northern areas, the roots may survive without protection, but the overwintering canes are often killed above the snow line. But because blackberries tend to be

Continued ➡

Nut Trees for Home Use

Besides producing a tasty crop, many nut trees are beautiful, long-lasting landscape specimens. You may want to try planting some of the nut trees described below in your home landscape.

Plant Name	Cultural Requirements	Size and Zone	Comments
Almond (*Prunus amygdalus*)	Rich, well-drained soil. Blossoms cannot withstand late spring frosts.	Small (20'–30'); Zones 7–9	Beautiful flowers, blooms very early, drought-tolerant; limited range.
Butternut (*Juglans cinera*)	Prefers rich, deep soil, but will tolerate a range of conditions.	Medium (40'–70'); Zones 3–7	Graceful; may be toxic to some plants; susceptible to disease; nuts stain pavement.
Chestnut, Chinese (*Castanea millisima*)	Light, upland, sandy loam soil.	Small (10'–20'); Zones 5–8	Ideal for small sites; prickly burrs surround nuts. Many Chinese-American crosses available.
Chestnut, European (*Castanea sativa*)	Rich, upland, loamy soil.	Large (50'–90'); Zones 5–8	Long-lived, stately; prickly burrs surround nuts; needs a pollinator. Mostly grown from seed.
Filbert, hazelnut (*Corylus* spp.)	Rich, light. well-drained soil	Small (10'–40'); Zones 2–8	Crimson fall foliage; husks litter ground. Grow as a hedge, multi-stemmed bush, or small tree.
Heartnut (*Juglans ailantifolia* var. *cordiformis*)	Deep, rich soil.	Medium (30'–60'); Zones 5–8	Light-colored bark, lacy foliage, fast-growing; may be toxic to some plants; nuts stain pavement.
Hickory, shagbark and shellbark (*Carya ovata* and *C. laciniosa*)	Rich, upland soil; tolerates a wide range of sites.	Large (60'–120'); Zones 3–8	Stately, long-lived; husks litter ground.
Pecan (*Carya illinoinensis*)	Deep, rich, moist bottomland is required.	Large (70'–150'); Zones 6–9	Stately, long-lived; husks litter ground. Grow strongly once established.
Walnut, Eastern black (*Juglans nigra*)	Rich, deep soil; tolerates a range of sites.	Large (60'–120'); Zones 4–8	Lacy foliage, stately; may be toxic to some plants; nuts stain pavement.
Walnut, Persian (*Juglans regia*)	Rich, deep soil.	Large (50'–90'); Zones 5–9	Stately, fast-growing; may be toxic to some plants; nuts stain pavement.

extremely vigorous, even a very short portion of surviving cane will often produce a surprising amount of fruit.

Blackberries can be divided into three general groups: erect, semi-erect, and trailing.

The erect type has strong, upright canes that are usually thorny and don't require support. They tend to be more winter-hardy than the other types and produce large, sweet berries.

Semi-erect blackberries are thornless and more vigorous and productive than the erect type. Most of them grow better if supported. The fruit is tart and large. The plants bloom and mature later than the erect type.

Trailing blackberries, or dewberries, are the least winter-hardy. They need support, are early ripening, and have large wine-colored to black fruit of distinctively good flavor.

Hybrids: Raspberry-blackberry hybrids combine the characteristics of their parents. Most of them are very winter-tender. Some are thornless. The fruit resembles blackberries.

Planting and Care

Plant brambles in a sunny site with good air circulation and well-drained soil. Start with disease-free stock, and plant in very early spring. Plant in hills or rows well away from wild or abandoned raspberries, which may carry diseases. Provide posts or a wire fence to support the canes.

Row spacing should be wide enough to allow sunlight and air to reach all plants and to allow you to walk or mow between the rows without damaging yourself or the plants. For home gardeners this means at least 5 feet between rows for raspberries and 7 feet for blackberries.

Some types of brambles produce suckers. Red and yellow raspberries spread 12 to 15 inches a year, so plant 1 to 2 feet apart, depending on how soon you want a solid hedgerow. Blacks and most purples don't sucker but form clusters of canes from their crowns. Plant them 2½ to 3 feet apart. Blackberries sucker vigorously; space them 5 to 6 feet apart in rows.

Brambles are self-pollinating. Well-maintained plantings may fruit heavily for many years, but disease often appears as plants age. Plan on establishing a new raspberry bed every ten years (less if plants begin to decline).

Pruning and Training

For black, purple, and summer-bearing red raspberries, cut off all fruit-bearing canes at ground-level as soon as harvest is over, or when growth begins in the spring. In late winter or early spring, thin out new canes that emerged the previous season; save the sturdiest ones and leave six canes per hill or 6-inch spacing between row-planted canes. Shorten lanky canes to 4 to 5 feet. Since black and purple raspberries fruit most heavily on side branches, induce side branching during the summer by pinching the growing tips of canes when they reach 2½ feet. The following late winter or early spring, shorten the side branches to about 1 foot.

For fall-bearing red raspberries, remove fruiting canes each summer as soon as the second fruiting is complete. Or sacrifice the second berry crop (which may be light anyway) and cut the entire planting to the ground as soon as leaves drop in the fall. Although this approach yields only one crop instead of two, it has several advantages. Pruning all canes to the ground eliminates winter injury to canes, results in vigorous new canes for next fall's crop, and cuts down on overwintering pests that will appear next spring.

On erect blackberries pinch the tips of 3-foot canes to force growth of lateral shoots. During the

dormant season, shorten all lateral shoots to about 1½ feet. For both types of blackberry, cut away all fruiting canes right after harvest. In winter thin out canes, leaving three or four canes per clump for erect types and eight to twelve canes per clump for trailing types.

Trellising

Though many brambles can be grown without a support system, all are best grown on a trellis. Trellising reduces disease problems, saves space, and speeds pruning and picking.

V Trellis. Summer-bearing raspberries do well on a V trellis. Construct it as follows:

1. Set a sturdy 4-inch post at each end of the row and about every 20 feet in between. Posts should be set at least 2 feet deep and extend 4 to 6 feet above ground.

2. Add a 2-inch x 4-inch cross arm, with notches cut on each arm, to hold wires. The height of the cross arms will depend on how vigorous your brambles are. Try putting them about 3 feet high, and move them if necessary.

3. Cut two lengths of 12- or 14-gauge wire or synthetic baling twine a little longer than the trellis, and fasten the ends to either side of the endpost cross arms.

4. After pruning, put the wires in the outer notches, and arrange the canes outside the wire. Tie each cane individually to the wire. Or use two sets of wires on each side of the cross arm, and sandwich the canes between them. After harvest, move the wires to the inside notch to keep the new canes upright.

Hedgerow Trellis. All types of bramble fruit do well when supported by a hedgerow-type trellising system like the one shown on the opposite page. To construct it:

1. Set a sturdy 4-inch post at each end of the row and about every 20 feet in between.

2. Hammer upward-slanting nails into both sides of each post 3 feet and 4 feet above the ground.

3. Cut four lengths of wire slightly longer than the trellis and twist the ends of the wires into a loop to fit over the end nail.

4. After pruning, lift the wires onto the nails to hold the canes upright between them. (Future pruning is easier if you can remove the wires, so don't staple them to the posts, just rest them on the nails.) Tuck new canes between the wires. A variation of this trellis uses 1-foot cross arms to hold the wires farther apart.

Harvesting

Brambles ripen in early summer. Red raspberries tend to ripen first, followed by black raspberries, and even later by blackberries. Berries do not keep ripening after harvesting. For best flavor and ease of picking, wait until they are fully ripe. Some raspberries offer a slight resistance to picking even when fully ripe. Let your taste tell you when to pick. Red raspberries vary in color at maturity from light to dark red. Some purple ones change from red to purple to almost black, with sugar levels increasing as the color darkens. Blackberries, though they also vary in color, are typically shiny black when not quite ripe and dull black when fully ripe. They come off the vines more easily when fully ripe.

Pick your berries as early in the morning as possible while they are cool. If the berries are wet, let them dry before picking. Handle them gently and place, don't drop, them into a shallow container. Refrigerate immediately.

Preventing Problems

Certain common garden pests attack brambles. Aphids can spread viruses. Japanese beetles feed on ripe fruit. Tarnished plant bugs feed on buds, blossoms, and berries. Keep surrounding areas weed-free to limit tarnished plant bugs.

Several viral diseases, which can drastically reduce yields, affect bramble crops. Raspberry mosaic stunts plants and causes yellow-blotched, puckered leaves. Blackberry sterility results in vigorous growing plants that produce only nubbins—tiny, crumbly, malformed berries—or none at all. Leaf curl causes dark green, tightly curled and malformed leaves. Since there is no cure for viral diseases, dig infected plants and dispose of them immediately.

To prevent problems with viral diseases, plant virus-resistant cultivars and purchase plants only from nurseries that sell virus-free tissue culture or certified bareroot plants. Remove all wild brambles within 500 to 1,000 feet, especially upwind, and keep aphids off your brambles because they spread viruses. Plant black raspberries away from red and yellow ones because blacks are more susceptible to viruses.

Several other diseases attack brambles, including anthracnose, powdery mildew, rust, wilts, and root rots.

Since fungi need warm temperatures and humid conditions to thrive, anything you do to keep the aboveground parts of the plants dry will be to your advantage. Select a planting site with good air circulation and drainage. Avoid overhead watering. Keep your rows narrow, and thin canes to recommended densities. Avoid excessive nitrogen. Trellis the canes for best air circulation. Keep the rows weed-free. Remove spent canes immediately after harvest. Collect and destroy all prunings. If fungal diseases have been a problem in previous years, apply lime-sulfur spray in the spring when the first leaves are ¼ to ½ inch long.

Grapes

Vitis spp.

Vitaceae

Grapes make a wonderful treat straight from the vine, or preserved as jelly, juice, or wine. They thrive in full sun, with good drainage and protection from late frosts.

There are four main types of grapes grown in North America: European, or wine grapes (*Vitis vinifera*); American, such as 'Concord' (*V. labruscana*);

Continued ➡

hybrids between European and American; and muscadine (*V. rotundifolia*).

Vinifera (European) grapes produce most of the world's table grapes, wine, and raisins. They are not as hardy as their American cousins, are much more susceptible to disease, and require more work to harvest a satisfactory crop.

American grapes have a strong grape or "foxy" flavor and slipskins, which means that the berries can easily be squeezed out of the skins. Many good fresh-eating and juice grapes have been selected from the native species.

Plant breeders have crossed and recrossed vinifera and American species and created grapes to satisfy almost every taste and use. Many of them are as hardy as their American parent, to about -10°F, and have good disease resistance.

If you grow seedless cultivars, you probably won't get grapes as large as those on bunches for sale at the market. Commercial growers dip or spray clusters with synthetic growth regulators so they'll produce big berries.

If you live in the far South, you may only be able to grow muscadine grapes. They make good jelly and juice and a sweet wine.

American and hybrid grape cultivars can be grown on their own roots. Vinifera grape roots are very susceptible to phylloxera, a sucking insect native to the eastern and southern United States and now spread throughout the world. Choose vines grafted on American rootstocks. Certain American rootstock cultivars are also resistant to nematodes and the viral diseases they transmit.

Planting and Care

Plant grapes in a sunny site with deep, well-drained, moderately fertile soil and good air circulation to promote disease resistance.

Plant dormant, one-year-old vines in the spring before their buds begin to swell and open. Soak roots in a pail of water with a handful of bone meal for one to two hours before planting. Plant muscadines 15 to 20 feet apart in rows 10 feet apart; plant other types of grapes 8 feet apart in rows 8 feet apart.

Prune each vine back to leave two live buds before planting; also cut back long roots so they'll fit easily into the hole without bending. Leave 1 to 2 inches of trunk above ground and make a shallow basin around the vine to hold water. If you are planting grafted vines, be sure to keep the graft union above ground level.

Pruning and Training

There are many ways to train grapes. One of the most common methods for home gardeners is cane pruning. If you are new to grapes, don't let talk about training and pruning scare you. Grapevines are very forgiving. You can train cane- and spur-pruned vines on an existing fence or wall.

No matter what training method you plan to use, all vines are treated the same until the second winter after planting.

First Growing Season. During their first summer, the vines need to grow a strong root system. Use drip irrigation or a soaker hose, if needed, to keep the soil damp but not soggy. From mid-August, on, water only if the leaves wilt so the vines will harden off for winter. Mulch or cultivate to control weeds.

You can let the vines sprawl on the ground the first year, or tie them loosely to a small stake to keep them out of harm's way.

First Winter. Any time from midwinter on, select the strongest, straightest shoot and prune off all

the others. Cut the chosen shoot back to two live buds. The result will look very much like the little vine you planted the previous spring. But remember, the first season is for growing roots. Go ahead and cut off all that top growth you'll have a better plant in the long run. If cold injury is a problem in your area, wait until the buds start to swell so you can see which ones are alive. You may want to select two shoots rather than one as insurance against injury.

Second Growing Season If you haven't done so already, place a stake in the ground as close as possible to the vine. When new shoots are 6 to 12 inches long, select the sturdiest, most upright shoot and tie it loosely to the stake. Break off the remaining shoots with your fingers. As the shoot grows, tie it to the stake at 12-inch intervals to form a straight trunk.

When the shoot reaches the desired height, break off the small shoots that are growing above each leaf near the base of your trunk-to-be, but don't remove the leaves. Let the sideshoots grow on the five leaf nodes just below the vine head; cut the tip off the main shoot when it grows a few inches or so above the vine head. Prune off any suckers below the soil line as close to the trunk as possible.

If your vine doesn't reach the desired height by the end of the second season, it probably hasn't developed enough roots to produce the size plant you want. Cut the vine back to two buds, and let it try again the next summer.

Fourth Growing Season. In the fourth growing season, vines are ready to bear a normal crop. For large table grapes, give vines 1 inch of water per week. In the fourth and subsequent winters, you may want to keep a few more buds on each cane for the next season. The vigor of a vine will tell you how many bugs it can support. If your wine has many spindly shoots and little fruit, try leaving fewer total buds the next winter. If it has long, thick shoots and few clusters, leave more buds the next winter.

Subsequent Growing Seasons. During the spring through mid-July, position shoots so light penetrates through the foliage. On short-trunk, trellised vines, tuck the shoots behind the catch wires above the training wire. If shoots reach the top of the trellis and hang down, they will shade the fruit and the canes where next year's flower buds are forming. Prune off the tips if they get too long. Pick off leaves and small shoots near fruit clusters to let in light. This is important because it promotes ripening and discourages pests. You may want to remove or thin clusters to increase berry size or improve quality. If you have too heavy a crop, the fruit may be slow to ripen as well.

Winter Protection

There are grape cultivars that will tolerate severe winter cold. You can grow cultivars beyond their normal northern limit by training trunks only 1 foot high and covering vines with mulch during the winter, or by bending whole vines over and burying or mulching them for the winter.

Once grape buds begin to swell in the spring, they become more frost-tender. All species are susceptible to frost damage at temperatures below 31°F. See "Growing Fruit Trees" on page 27 for more information on site selection and frost protection. Autumn frosts seldom cause damage because the high sugar content of the berries keeps them from freezing and the outer canopy protects both the foliage and fruit beneath it. If you live in an area with short seasons, plant an early-ripening cultivar.

Fertilizing

On most sites, careful soil preparation before planting eliminates the need for heavy fertilization. Mulch lightly with compost in late winter each year. Overfertilizing can cause vines to grow rampantly and produce little fruit. When in doubt, don't fertilize. Compost tea and dilute seaweed extract sprays are good general foliar fertilizers.

Harvesting

Grapevines bear by their third or fourth growing season. Harvest when the fruit tastes ripe. Support the cluster with one hand and cut its stem with pruning shears. Handle clusters gently and lay them in a basket or flat. Harvest large quantities in the morning, small amounts any time of day. Move picked fruit to a cool, protected place as soon as possible.

Preventing Problems

Grape berry moths lay eggs on flower clusters. The greenish or purplish larvae spin silver webs and feed on buds and flowers. Control grape berry moths with mating-disruption pheromone dispensers.

Many caterpillars can feed on grape leaves. Control by spraying BT (Bacillus thuringiensis). Japanese beetles are fond of grapes. A few won't hurt the vine, but complete defoliation will.

Prevention and good housekeeping are the best ways to avoid disease problems. Mulch or cultivation will help prevent spores from splashing up from the soil and infecting new growth. Keep the area under the vine weed-free to increase air movement and reduce disease problems. Fungal diseases thrive in dark, humid environments, so arrange shoots in the leaf canopy so some light falls on all foliage. Cut off any leaves that are shading clusters. Remove infected parts immediately, and collect prunings and fallen leaves and dispose of them.

Sulfur dust or spray helps prevent disease. If you've had past problems with disease, you may want to consider a regular preventive spray program. Coat all parts of the vines, including the undersides of leaves, before symptoms appear. Apply when canes are 6, 12, and 18 inches long, then every two weeks until four to six weeks before harvest.

STRAWBERRIES

Fragaria x ananassa, F. vesca

Rosaceae

Strawberries are justly celebrated each spring in festivals all over America. Fresh strawberry shortcake, strawberry ice cream, strawberry pie, and even plain, red ripe strawberries are hard to beat. The plants are inexpensive, bear a full crop within a year of planting, and are relatively simple to grow.

Continued ➡

Garden strawberry cultivars (*F. x ananassa*) are divided into three types: Junebearers, everbearers, and day-neutrals, which flower at different times in response to day length. Here's a rundown:

Junebearers: These bear fruit in June or July, or as early as April in Florida and California. They produce a single, large crop over three to four weeks. If you want to freeze lots of fruit at one time, plant Junebearers. There are early-, mid-, and late-season cultivars. Junebearers produce many runners and spread rapidly.

Everbearers: These produce a moderate crop in June, scattered berries in summer, and a small crop in late August. They are especially productive in northern areas with long summer days. The total harvest for everbearers is much less than the total harvest for Junebearers. Plant everbearers if you want berries for fresh eating all season. They produce fewer runners than Junebearers and so are easier to control.

Day-neutrals: These are unaffected by day length. They are extremely productive and bear fruit from June through frost in northern areas, or January through August in milder climates. Unfortunately, day-neutrals require pampering. They are fragile and sensitive to heat, drought, and weed competition. If you are willing to give them the care they need, they'll reward you with a generous supply of berries throughout the season from relatively few plants. Day-neutrals produce few runners, so they rarely get out of control.

Alpine strawberries: Alpine strawberries (*F. vesca*) are one of the parent species of the garden strawberry. They produce small, aromatic berries from early summer through frost. Alpines are grown from seed or divisions and produce no runners. They are care-free and make good ornamental edgings.

Planting and Care

Plant strawberries in well-drained soil rich in organic matter. The ideal location is in full sun on high or sloping ground. Avoid frost-prone, low-lying areas.

To prevent diseases associated with over-crowding, allow a square foot of space for each plant. Choose one of three different planting systems: hill, matted row, or spaced runner. For a hill system, space plants 1 foot apart each way in double rows, with 2 to 3 feet between each double row. Remove every runner so plants channel their energy into producing large berries. Since plants are well spaced, the hill system minimizes diseases associated with crowding. For a matted-row system, space plants 1½ to 2 feet apart in rows 4 feet apart. Allow the runners and daughter plants to grow in all directions to form a wide, solid row. For the spaced-runner system, set plants closer than the matted row; remove all but a few runners. Pin down runner tips so daughter plants are about 8 inches apart in every direction.

Vigilant weed control is essential to prevent aggressive perennial weeds from out-competing shallow-rooted strawberry plants. It helps to lay down a thick mulch of straw around the plants during summer.

Even well-managed strawberries will decline after a few seasons. Start a fresh bed in a new site with new plants every few years. Renovate Junebearers each year right after harvest. Cut off and rake away old leaves; dig out old, woody plants; and thin out remaining plants. Then fertilize and water.

Harvesting

Spring-planted Junebearers won't provide a harvest until a year after planting. Everbearers will produce a sizable late-summer crop, and day-neutrals will produce from midsummer through fall the year they're planted. Fall-planted berries will bear a full harvest the next growing season.

Harvest berries by pinching through the stem rather than pulling on the berry. Pick ripe berries every other day; always remove all ripe berries and any infected or malformed ones from the patch to prevent disease problems. During wet or humid weather, pick out diseased berries every day. Cull the moldy berries, wash your hands, and then pick the ripe berries. At the very least, carry a second basket or a plastic bag to put moldy or damaged berries in while you pick.

Strawberries need 1 inch of water per week throughout the growing season. Drip irrigation works best; for information on installing a drip irrigaton system, see "Using Drip Irrigation" on page 181.

After the ground has frozen, cover the plants with fresh straw, pine boughs, or spun-bonded fabric to protect them from alternate freezing and thawing, which can heave plants from the soil. (In climates were a snow cover remains through the winter, strawberries need no special winter mulch.) Pull the mulch away from the plants in early spring so the ground can warm up. Reapply fresh mulch around the plants to smother early weed. Leave spun-bonded fabric on over winter and into spring for slightly earlier harvests. Remove it when flowers open so bees can pollinate the blossoms.

Preventing Problems

Verticillium wilt and red stele infect strawberry plant roots. They are often carried in on new plants and made worse by heavy, wet soil. Remove and destroy infected plants. Replant new plants in a new location or choose resistant cultivars. Vegetables like tomatoes and potatoes are also infected by Verticillium wilt, so grow only resistant cultivars where these vegetables have grown in the last three years, and vice versa.

Gray mold rots the berries. Wet, humid weather and overcrowded beds with poor air circulation invite it. Keep rows narrow, thin out crowded plants, and remove moldy berries from the plants immediately to control gray mold.

Berries injured by the tarnished plant bug don't grow or ripen properly, but remain small and woody or form hard, seedy tips.

Apples: A Strong Start
Vicki Mattern

Yes, you can grow apples organically! If you select disease-resistant varieties (see "Organic Apple Picks" on this page) and handle your trees with care, problems should be minimal. When insect pests or diseases do show up, use organic controls such as those suggested in "Apple Pest Problem Solver." Here's how to get your apples off to a strong start:

1. **Choose the best rootstock.** First, be sure you have the best rootstock for your needs—dwarf, semi dwarf, or standard. Each rootstock has its own advantages and disadvantages. For instance, trees with certain rootstocks may require staking, be less cold hardy, or have little resistance to fire blight and other diseases. Ask a local nursery, apple orchardist, or your county extension service to recommend the best rootstocks for your site and climate.

2. **Plant it right.** Plant your apple trees in either early spring or fall. (Avoid fall planting if you live in a very cold region.) Choose a well-drained site that receives plenty of sunlight. If your soil is poor, amend the entire site—not just the planting hole—with compost and other organic materials, preferably the season before planting.

Organic Apple Picks

These reliable disease-resistant apple varieties are among the best for organic growing:

Early

'Pristine': large yellow fruit; sweet-tart flavor

'Redfree': medium-size red fruit; juicy, mild flavor

'William's Pride': large red fruit; crisp and juicy

Midseason

'Freedom': round, bright red fruit; crisp and tart

'Liberty': large, dark red fruit; crisp and juicy

'Prima': bright yellow with red blush; mildly tart

Late

'Enterprise': medium-to-large red fruit; rich, spicy flavor

'Goldrush': yellow fruit, sometimes blushed; spicy flavor improves in storage

Dig a generous-sized planting hole. Place some of the amended soil back in the hole so that the graft will be at least 6 inches above ground level. If you plant deeper, the graft could sink below the surface when the soil settles. Backfill the hole, then water the tree thoroughly.

Trees on dwarf rootstocks need staking to compensate for the vigorous roots. After planting, drive a sturdy wooden or metal stake into the ground near the tree. Tie the tree loosely to the stake. Wrap the trunk to protect it from sunscald, and install a hardware cloth sleeve to protect the trunk from rodents. Spread a layer of organic mulch over the area.

3. **Mulch matters.** Apply an organic mulch, such as straw, after planting an apple tree. Mulch helps the soil stay moist and blocks the growth of competing weeds and grasses, which could stunt the tree's growth. Keep the mulch about 2 feet away from the trunk of the tree, however, and remove the mulch in fall so that rodents don't move in for the winter.

4. **Feed lightly.** About 3 weeks after spring planting, spread a balanced organic fertilizer in a 2-foot radius around the base of the tree. Each year, spread 5 to 10 pounds of compost out to the drip line in late winter. Shoots on a well-nourished, young apple tree should grow 1 or 2 feet in a season; those on a mature, bearing tree should grow 6 to 10 inches. If growth is less than that, give them an inch or so of compost the following spring. If your tree fails to thrive, have a leaf analysis done through your extension service to identify any nutrient deficiencies.

Continued ➔

5. **Train a leader.** Train the tree to a central leader—the main trunk—so that the interior of the growing tree has access to plenty of sunlight and air.

Year 1: After planting, prune the trunk back to 2 or 2½ feet. Also head back any side branches by one-third to one-half their length.

During the growing season, when the new growth reaches 1 to 1½ feet, choose three or four main branches spaced about 4 to 8 inches apart along the trunk. Cut off all other branches on the tree, but leave the central leader alone.

Year 2: The next winter or early spring, remove any new shoots that are growing at a narrow angle and competing with the central leader. Also remove any vertical side branches. Head back each branch tip by one-third to one-half to encourage side branches to form.

When the new growth is 1 or 1½ feet long, choose another "layer" of three or four main branches about 1½ feet above the previous branches and cut off any other new branches. The remaining branches should create a spiral pattern up the trunk so that each has access to the sun.

Year 3 and after: Repeat the pruning cuts from Year 2. Each year, focus your efforts on choosing the newest layer of main branches.

Apple Pest Problem Solver

Insect pests taking a bite out of your apple harvest? Here's how to manage them organically:

Mites, aphids, and scale. If you observed infestations of these pests last year, apply dormant-oil spray very early in the season, when a quarter-inch of green shows on the flower buds.

Codling moths. Reduce codling moth numbers by wrapping trunks with corrugated cardboard to attract larvae looking for a site to pupate. Remove and destroy the wraps one month after each generation of larvae begin moving down the trunk. When apples are about 2 inches across, slip small brown paper bags over them and staple shut. Spray several applications of Surround, a kaolin clay product, beginning at petal fall.

Apple maggots. Hang red, sticky ball traps from mid-June until harvest (one trap per dwarf tree and six per standard tree).

Plum curculios. At petal fall, spray Surround. Or, reduce damage by shaking trees daily for several weeks, knocking beetles onto a tarp, then drowning them in soapy water. Clean up all dropped fruits in June and again in fall.

Fantastic Ways to Enjoy Your Fruitful Bounty

Vicki Mattern

Make the most of your fruit harvest with these two delicious recipes. Your hard work has never tasted this good!

Raspberries with Wild Rice

1½ cups defatted chicken stock
¼ cup wild rice
2 teaspoons canola oil

⅛ teaspoon dried marjoram
1 cup raspberries
2 tablespoons minced parsley

In a 1-quart saucepan, bring the stock to a boil. Transfer to the top of a double broiler. Add the wild rice, oil, and marjoram. Cover and cook over boiling water for 1 to 1½ hours, or until the liquid has been absorbed and the rice is tender. Transfer to a serving bowl. Fold in the raspberries and parsley.

Makes 4 servings

Apples and Oats Breakfast Cereal

4 cups water
1⅓ cups oat bran
½ cup raisins
1 apple, shredded
1 tablespoon maple syrup
½ teaspoon ground caraway seeds
½ teaspoon ground cinnamon
1 to 2 cups skim milk

In a 2-quart saucepan, bring the water and oat bran to a vigorous boil, stirring constantly. Reduce the heat to low and cook for 2 minutes, stirring frequently, until thick. Remove from the heat and stir in the raisins, apples, maple syrup, caraway seeds, and cinnamon. Let stand for 5 minutes. Spoon into bowls and pour the milk over the cereal to serve.

Makes 4 servings

Tips for Berries and Small Fruits

Barbara W. Ellis, Joan Benjamin, and Deborah L. Martin

A morning of maintenance once or twice a year—and a watchful eye—are all the care blackberries and raspberries need. Other small fruits are even more obliging. Small fruits bear quickly and for many years, and they are perfect in the low-maintenance garden.

This section will help you choose berries and small fruits that will give you lots of delicious fruit for little or no care in return. You'll also learn tricks for keeping overzealous spreaders in check and quick ways to boost your harvests.

Grow Berries and Small Fruits the Easy Way

Berries and small fruits are tough characters. In the wild, they grow and bear quite happily with no help from anyone. Let them grow wild in your yard if you have room—you'll get plenty of handfuls of berries for your morning cereal. Here are four simple things you can do to civilize your berry patch and increase your harvests.

Mow. Your trusty lawn mower or string trimmer is a fast and easy way to keep the weeds from overwhelming your plants. Mowing also keeps adventuring berry suckers from turning your yard into an impenetrable briar patch. Leave a few inches unmowed around the main stems so you don't damage the plants themselves.

Mulch. Cover the no-mow zone right under your plants with mulch. Straw, old carpet (preferably natural fiber) spread upside down, or even the weeds you just uprooted from the front bed will do fine. If new weeds break through, just stomp them over and dump on more mulch.

Prune. You'll get plenty of fruit from most types of berries and small fruits even if you never snip a twig. But an occasional cut or two will keep plants vigorous, thin out dead wood, and keep the fruits within reach. Only you can decide whether saving time by not pruning is worth a smaller harvest or a struggle with a tangle of thorny canes. If you decide to prune, you'll find low-maintenance pruning tips for various fruits later in this chapter.

Feed and water. Mulching your plants with organic mulch like grass clippings, chopped leaves, or pulled weeds feeds them gradually, helps control weeds, and conserves soil moisture. If you care to do more, add compost under the plants each year as an extra feeding. Watering is optional, too. In dry seasons, if you don't water, the berries will be smaller or may even shrivel up before they ripen. If you aren't content with what nature can provide, keep the plants watered from the time they flower through harvest.

Just Starting Out? Put Your Berry Best Foot Forward

Get your berry plants off to a healthy start before you plant. You'll save yourself unnecessary maintenance later on.

1. **Pick a berry good site.** Put your berries and small fruits where they will be happy. Like vegetables, they want as many hours of full sun as possible, well drained soil, and space so air can move around them.

2. **Banish pesky weeds.** It's lots easier to dig up or smother nasty perennial weeds before you plant; otherwise, you'll have to pick through a tangle of berry plants to get them out.

3. **Buy smart.** Don't be pennywise and dollar-dumb. Healthy, pest-resistant plants that are suited to your climate are a must for low-maintenance growing. To find out which types of small fruits and berries grow best in your area, call your local extension agent and ask what they have the fewest problems with. Select cultivars that are resistant to extremes (drought, cold, heat, humidity) and as many diseases as possible.

Buy plants (especially strawberries, raspberries, and blackberries) from a reputable nursery. Cheap plants are rarely a bargain in the long run and, like free plants from a neighbor, they can harbor diseases and pests.

Neglect These Care-Free Berries

It's really as easy as plant-'em-and-pick-'em with certain small fruits and unusual, delicious berries. You'll get loads of tasty fruits without pruning, staking, or other care. Here are some no-sweat possibilities.

Alpine strawberry (*Fragaria vesca* 'Alpine'). Compact plants without runners yield small, flavor-packed berries from spring through frost.

Bush cherries and native plums (*Prunus* spp.). Clouds of white flowers, then tart cherry-like fruit, cover these 3- to 10-foot bushes. Fall-bearing types thwart birds.

Currant and gooseberry (*Ribes* spp.). Tangy and translucent, red and white currants hang in clusters from 3- to 5-foot plants. Musky black currants dangle from bushes up to 7 feet tall. Try 'Crandall' for fragrant yellow spring flowers. Gooseberry fruits are larger, but the 3- to 5-foot bushes are quite thorny. Try 'Colossal' or 'Poorman' for fewer thorns.

Elderberry (*Sambucus* spp.) Clusters of creamy flowers as big as dinner plates on 5- to 10-foot stems mature into heavy crops of tart, flavorful berries.

Highbush cranberry (*Viburnum trilobum*). As much an ornamental as a fruit, these 6- to 10-foot beauties sport white spring flowers, reddish fall foliage, and tart red fruits for months.

Continued →

Juneberry (*Amelanchier* spp.). Dainty white, early-spring flowers grace these shrubs and trees. The blueberry-like pink to purple-blue fruits are also attractive.

Mulberry (*Morus* spp.). While technically a tree, the fruits are definitely berries. Shake the lower branches over a sheet to quickly gather the ripe berries. Keep trees away from walkways—dropping fruits stain.

Put Your Berries Where Your Mouth Is

To save time and enjoy more berries, plant your berries and small fruits right next to your house or driveway. That way, you won't have to hike out to the back 40 to see if they're ripe or to pick a handful.

Sound unattractive? No way! Many berries and small fruits are very good-looking plants. Some have pretty, fragrant flowers and vibrant fall color. All you need to do is think of edibles instead of ornamentals when you plan your landscape. Here are some suggestions to get you started.

Groundcovers. Strawberries fill in fast as a groundcover on sunny slopes. Mix in some pink-flowered ones for interest.

Flower beds. Alpine strawberries are as pretty an edging plant as anyone could want, and they bear all summer. Try alternating yellow and red cultivars. Red currants drip clusters of eye-catching red jewels in season.

Vines for shade. Grape- or kiwi-covered arbors make for cool outdoor sitting.

Foundation shrubs. Blueberries and highbush cranberries look wonderful behind smaller plants. They offer spring flowers, tasty eats, and fall color-things many foundation shrubs don't rise to.

Don't Sweat It—Plant a New Strawberry Patch Every Few Years

Strawberry plants are cheap; your time isn't. If you have space for two strawberry beds in you garden, try this simple approach.

Plant a new patch. Every third spring, buy new plants and plant a brand-new strawberry patch. Put it as far away from the old patch as possible to reduce the chance of pests and diseases packing up and moving on over. Harvest the berries as they ripen.

Recycle the old patch. Bid the old patch goodbye as soon as it finishes bearing that same year. Till the old plants under or mow them short and spread mulch over them to kill them.

Plant Junebearers for Jam Sessions; Everbearers for Nibbling

Sun-warmed strawberries are one of the biggest pleasures of the home garden. But too many or too few berries aren't much fun. Select the right plants to start with to tailor your harvest.

Junebearers. These are the overachievers of the strawberry family. They make lots of runners and lots of berries all at once. If that's what you want, you just can't beat Junebearers. Choose a cultivar with multiple disease resistance.

Everbearers. These produce a few runners and a modest quantity of berries spread over the whole season. Pick an old-fashioned cultivar like 'Quinalt' or go with alpine strawberries. "Day-neutral" cultivars are not a good low-maintenance choice.

Give Crowded Strawberries a Haircut and a Dose of Old News

If you grow Junebearers, your plants may seem bent on crowding themselves out of existence.

Compensate for this self-destructive trait by revving up your power mower for a once-a-year, done-before-you-know-it renovation.

Mow the tops and spread the news. After you harvest, set your mower at about 2 inches, snap on the grass catcher, and chop off all those leaves. Dump the clippings into the compost.

Cover the edges of the bed with sections of newspaper at least four sheets thick. Leave just a 6- to 10-inch-wide strip of mowed plants uncovered down the middle of the bed. Hold the paper down with handfuls of soil or compost.

Layer on compost, then mulch and water. Shovel a ½-inch layer of compost over the chopped-off plants in the unpapered strip. Then cover the whole bed (paper and compost-covered strip) with 2 inches of loose straw mulch. Finally, give the whole bed a good soaking, and you're done until next year.

Teach Your Blackberries and Raspberries to Stay Put

Blackberries and raspberries make great backyard fruit crops. Not only is their fruit delicious and abundant, the plants are also easy to grow. But they are generally thorny and can spread rampantly. Here are two things to do to make them welcome residents in your yard.

Give them enough room to start with. If you don't give blackberries and raspberries room at planting time, you'll curse them later as you try to squeeze around the plants to pick or mow. Plant raspberries and thorny blackberries 3 feet apart in a row. Plant thornless blackberries 6 feet apart in a row. Leave at least a 5-foot aisle between rows so you'll be able to get between them to mow and pick.

Show your brambles who's in charge. Curb the spreading tendencies of raspberries and blackberries right from the start. To make sure you end up with a manageable row, not an impenetrable scratchy patch, draw an imaginary 1-foot-wide strip with your new berries right down the middle. Mow the area outside that 1-foot-wide row regularly (seed it with slow-growing grass or let nature provide). Every time you mow you'll effortlessly nip off any suckers that sprout outside their designated row. No stooping, no sweat.

Take the "Ouch!" Out of Picking Bramble Fruits

If a thorny embrace isn't your idea of a good time, try one or more of these painless ideas.

Go thorn-free. Select cultivars with no or few thorns and avoid a sticky issue. Try 'Chester' or 'Navaho' for thorn-free blackberries. Boysenberries, Loganberries, and Youngberries all come in thornless versions, too. Look for 'Canby' or 'Mammoth Red' for almost thornless red raspberry harvests.

Stake it to 'em. Black raspberries and thornless blackberries don't spread much but stay in neat clumps. This is not to say they still don't try to reach out and grab you. Pound a metal fence post in right next to each clump. Tie the canes to the post with a sturdy loop of twine every year in late winter.

Round 'em up. Red and yellow raspberries spread underground to make a solid row (or patch if you let them). Avoid scratches from nodding canes with the easy-to-build V-trellis.

1. To make a V-trellis, pound pairs of 8-foot metal fence posts into the ground at an angle. They should be about 1½ to 2 feet apart at the bottom, 3½ feet apart at the top, and 6 feet high. You'll need one pair at each end of your row for rows up to 30 feet long.

2. Add a sturdy anchor post at either end of the row.

3. Use wire or plastic bailing twine to string the trellis. You'll need two wires, one 2½ feet and one 4½ feet from the ground.

4. Every year, cut off the canes that have fruited and tie the remaining canes loosely to the trellis in late winter.

Easy Pruning for Raspberries and Blackberries

Two or three short pruning sessions a year (depending on what kind of berries you have) is all it takes to tame your brambles. In return, you get easier picking with fewer scratches, and your plants will stay healthier.

SIMPLE SUMMER SNIPS

1. **Cut off used-up canes.** Bramble canes die after they make their summer fruit crop. So, after you harvest those last few fruits, pull out your trusty clippers. Clip off all the canes that had fruit on them as close to the ground as possible. Don't cut off canes that haven't made fruit yet; they hold next year's berries-in -the-making. *Fall berry pickers take note:* If your red or yellow raspberries offer you fruit in late summer and fall, don't cut off those canes. They still have a summer crop of berries in them.

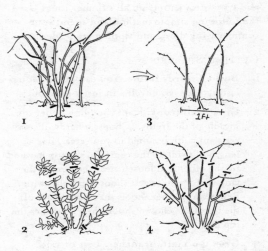

Pruning for raspberries and blackberries

2. **Pinch back thornless blackberries and black raspberries.** Left alone, these types grow long, arching canes. Pinch them back when they're young and you'll get more fruit and suffer fewer entanglements. When the canes are about waist-high, snip off the top few inches. The clipped canes will grow many side branches that will bear lots of fruit next summer.

LATE-WINTER THINNING

On a nice day in late winter or early spring, spend a few minutes with your clippers in your berry patch. Start by cutting off any fruited-out canes you didn't remove after harvest last summer. Then cut off any skinny or bent-over canes. Finally, follow the appropriate set of instructions below.

3. **Red and yellow raspberries and thorny blackberries.** Thin the remaining canes to leave four canes per foot of row. Don't snip off the tips of the canes unless they were winter-killed.

4. **Black raspberries and thornless blackberries.** Thin the remaining canes to leave five canes per plant. Shorten each side branch to about a foot long.

Continued →

Give Berry-Robbing Birds the Brush-Off

After weeks of watching them ripen, the last thing you want is bird-pecked berries. Try these tips for keeping the berries whole—and wholly for you.

Location. Plant near a door or path you use frequently. Human traffic discourages birds better than a scarecrow.

Tabby tracks. Entice a cat to lounge about in the berry patch. A puss in full view is a much more effective bird deterrent than a clever hunter hiding in the bushes.

Netting. Lightweight plastic netting keeps out birds (they will pick through it if it's too close to the fruit, though). Use a large piece and anchor it all around with boards or rocks so the winged thieves can't sneak under and have a feast. Or gather the edges around the base of a bush and tie it shut like a sack. Remove for harvest, then replace until next picking time.

Cage. Beat the netting blues by building a wooden cage frame with a door around the bush(es). Staple wire mesh or netting over it—it will last for years.

Train Grapes High and Let Gravity Do the Work

Gardeners often try to convince grapes to grow up a fence trellis, but vines don't always grow up. This means you spend your spare time tucking and tying stray shoots up all summer long. Use the following simple method and spend your summer lying down and sipping grapeade instead.

Getting Started

1. **Build a sturdy frame.** You can build a long-lasting, one-vine trellis in just a few hours.

2. **Grow a tall trunk.** Plant your vine under the middle of the trellis. (Choose a hardy, disease-resistant cultivar suited to your area.) Tie a length of twine to the center of the top bar and tie the other end loosely near the base of the vine. Let the strongest shoot climb the twine. Remove any other shoots that form. Snip off the tip of the chosen shoot when it reaches the top bar.

3. **Grow two main branches.** Lots of side branches will sprout after you cut off the tip of the upright shoot. Choose two sturdy ones near the top bar. Tie them to the top bar, with one reaching in each direction. Snip off all the other side branches. Let your two chosen branches grow until they reach the ends of the top bar. Then clip off the tips.

Growing Happily Ever After

1. **Do nothing all spring and summer.** As new shoots grow, their weight will pull them gently downward. Sit back and watch the fruit swell. Come fall, pick and enjoy. (And tell your friends how hard you worked to raise those grapes.)

2. **Do a winter haircut.** Get out your clippers on a sunny day in late winter and spend a few minutes getting your vine ready for spring. Check the ties that hold the main branches to the top bar and loosen or replace them as needed. Cut off any shoots that sprouted from the trunk below the top bar. Then cut all the hanging shoots back to leave two buds on each (the stubs will be about 4 inches long).

3. **Continue to grow happily ever after.** Alternate summer watching and winter pruning every year. As the vines age, cut off a few of the oldest stubs winter to thin things out.

This Berry Is for the Birds
Roger Yepsen

Read anything about growing elderberries, and you're apt to find a lot of grumbling about the way that birds manage to harvest the crop the day before the gardener gets around to it. You can try all sorts of stunts and devices to keep the birds away. Most practical is to toss netting over the shrubs until you're ready to pick. Or just stick a couple of plants in a relatively unused part of the yard and enjoy them and the wildlife they attract, without necessarily thinking of the elderberry pies and wine you might be making.

The plants are a bit straggly and free-growing, so they aren't the best choice for a tiny yard. Choose a site with moist, fertile, well-drained soil. Once plants are established, you can keep them vigorous by pruning 3-year-old canes. This encourages new growth and makes the overall form a little tidier.

An informal grouping of them won't attract much attention until the flowers appear—large, lacy umbrels of tiny cream-colored flowers. You can snip them for use in making fritters and pancakes, but you'll want to spare some in order to have berries. The inky berries find use in jam, pie, and wine. While the standard garden-variety elderberry remains popular, you have your choice of several that either offer generous harvests or add remarkable colors to the home landscape.

- 'Johns' is a selection of familiar native elderberry, *Sambucus canadensis*, chosen for its superior yield.
- 'Goldbeere' (*S. nigra*) produces stunning yellow berries.
- 'Black Beauty' (*S. nigra*) is just that, with purplish-black foliage setting off pink, lemon-scented blossoms.
- Variegated elderberry (*S. nigra*) has foliage patterned with cream and dark green.

Converting an Old Vine

If you already have a grapevine, it's not hard to change it over to this training method.

1. **Check the support system.** If your vine already has a sturdy trellis with a wire 5 to 6 feet high, you can use that. If not, build one over the vine as described earlier.

2. **Hack it back.** Grapevines are very forgiving, so get out a saw and some clippers on a nice day in late winter and have at it. Cut your vine back to the top of the current trunk. Or, if the current trunk is badly twisted or lying on the ground, cut it off a few inches above the soil line. Next summer train one of the new shoots as you would a newly planted vine.

Oh-So-Simple Pruning for Blueberries

You can harvest good crops of blueberries for years without ever having to prune them. But, if you'd like to boost your crop a bit or think a bit of pruning is warranted, here's what to do.

Highbush and mid-high blueberries. Cut off a few branches that are 5 or more years old at ground level each winter. Also remove any dead branches or ones that are leaning severely.

Lowbush blueberries. These ground-hugging plants spread by suckers. The easiest way to prune

---

them is to divide your patch in half and mow one half right down to the ground every winter. Alternate halves each year and you'll always have one patch busily growing back while the other patch is productively fruiting.

The Healthful Blueberry
Roger Yepsen

Blueberries aren't just for muffins and pancakes. Eaten frequently, they can have a range of beneficial health effects; in fact, in tests of some 40 fruits and vegetables, these little blue morsels ranked highest in antioxidants, including the anthocyanins responsible for their vivid color. And among blueberry varieties, 'Rubel' is a standout, with nearly double the antioxidant level. That doesn't mean they taste like vitamin pills. In fact, 'Rubel' has an excellent flavor. As a bonus, the small-size berries won't collapse in baked goods to leave the pockets created by super-size blueberries from the supermarket. 'Rubel' is a reliable producer, too, and although the small berries mean more picking, they are a relatively easy variety to harvest.

Blueberries in a Pot

Smaller blueberry varieties make handsome potted plants. And growing them in pots may be the way to go if you live in parts of the country with high-pH soils. To keep the soil cool and moist, it helps to dig a hole and sink the pot level with the ground. For the acid medium, mix 1/3 pine bark, 1/3 peat moss, and 1/3 potting soil. Stir in 1/2 ounce of sulfur for each cubic foot of soil. Fertilize with products labeled for use with azaleas. And top the pots with mulch to retain moisture and lower the temperature around the shallow roots. That's it—for the next 3 or 4 years. At that time, you'll want to replace the soil and prune back the roots, then repot.

Use a Vinegar Dressing for Sourer Soil

While there are a number of things you can do to lower the pH of soil or growing medium, the easiest way to treat potted plants or a few in the ground is to include vinegar when watering. Stir 2 tablespoons of distilled household vinegar into 1 gallon of water, and monitor the effect this has over time by testing the pH.

Plant an Edible Hedge and Throw Away Your Hedge Clippers

Need a hedge, but hate the repeated shearing it needs to stay neat? Wish you had room for some berry bushes, but can't figure out where to fit them in? Solve two problems with one low-maintenance solution: Replace your hedge with a closely spaced row of berries. Gooseberries or currants make a nice low hedge; thorny cultivars discourage trespassers. Blueberries or bush cherries make a taller, informal hedge. Raspberries and blackberries make a great narrow screen if you tie them to a fence.

Keep your hedge well back from driveways and sidewalks so dropped fruit won't land on the pavement. You may want to consult with your neighbors if the hedge will butt up against their property—offer them half the fruits, or plant away from

Continued →

the line and keep a mowed path along the actual property line to beat back wandering suckers.

HERBS

Introduction to Herb Gardens

The hardest part of herb gardening can be deciding what kind of herbs you want to grow—and then deciding where you're going to grow them. Do you want herbs for crafts or for cooking? Do you have sunny or shady sites? And what other plants grow well with herbs? Once you answer these questions, you'll be on your way to getting your herb garden off to a good start.

Herbs for Cooking

If you're just starting with herbs, or if you don't have a lot of garden space, you'll probably want to stick with basic culinary herbs. Homegrown herbs straight from the garden offer the freshest flavors—something you just can't get from store-bought herbs. It's also easy to dry herbs at home; their savory flavors will linger to add a taste of summer to midwinter meals.

A broad range of herbs is available to add flavor to everything from salad dressings to desserts. Here's a list of some popular herbs and how you can use them to liven up meals.

- Basil (with meats or vegetables, in sauces)
- Chervil (in soups or stews, or with fish or vegetables)
- Chives (in soups, salads, and sandwiches)
- Dill (with fish or vegetables; in salads or sauces; seeds used for pickling)
- French tarragon (in salads or sauces; with meats, fish, or vegetables)
- Garlic (with most anything, except desserts)
- Lovage (use like celery in soups, stews, salads, or sauces)
- Oregano (in sauces or with cheeses, eggs, meats, or vegetables)
- Parsley (with most anything, except desserts)
- Rosemary (with meats or vegetables; in soups or sauces)
- Sage (with eggs, poultry, or vegetables)
- Sweet marjoram (use like oregano)
- Thyme (with meats or vegetables)

HINTS FOR HERBAL COOKING

Fresh and dried homegrown herbs are interchangeable in most recipes. Dried herbs are more powerful, ounce for ounce, than fresh ones, so when substituting fresh herbs for dried, use two or three times more. To release the flavor of dried herbs, crush the foliage between your hands before adding it to recipes.

Most herbs don't require cooking; add them just before taking the dish off the stove. Or, for the freshest flavor, simply add a pinch of herbs to each plate at serving time. If you're using a specific herb for the first time, use restraint when adding it to a dish. If you overdo it, you might overwhelm the original flavor of the meat or vegetable that you meant to enhance.

If you do find that you've been a little heavy-handed with the seasoning, try these tips.

- Strain as much of the herbs and spices as possible out of the dish.
- Add a peeled, whole, raw potato to the pot just before serving.
- If possible, add more of the nonherb ingredients, or make a second, unseasoned batch of the recipe and combine it with the overseasoned one.
- Serve the dish chilled to blunt the taste of the overseasoning.

Herbs for Crafts

Making craft projects with herbs is a creative and delightful way to bring your garden indoors. You can work with fresh and dried herbs rich with color, texture, and fragrance to make wreaths, potpourris, and fragrant oils. The number of ways you can use herbs in crafts is really only limited by your imagination.

Many common herbs are great for craft projects. Here are a few ideas.

- Create a culinary wreath using chives, creeping sage, marjoram, oregano, or thyme.
- Braid fresh garlic heads together with bunches of herbs, then hang them to dry in the kitchen. Later, use scissors to cut away the bulbs or dried herbs as they're needed for cooking.
- Create a personalized potpourri by mixing together your favorite dried herbs, flowers, and spices. Mint, rosemary, sage, and thyme are just a few of the herbs that hold their fragrances well when dried.
- Use herbs like oregano and yarrow in fresh or dried arrangements.
- Instead of bows, add small bunches of dried and leafy herbs like thyme or sage to wrapped gifts.

Herbs for Fragrance

Flowers release their scents into the air so freely that you need only walk past roses, lilacs, or any other highly fragrant blooms to enjoy their aromas. Herbs, on the other hand, don't usually release their scents unless you rub a leaf, walk on the plant, or brush against the herb's branches. But that doesn't mean you can't grow and enjoy herbs specifically for their fragrances—and there are certainly enough fragrant herbs to choose from.

The leaves of scented geraniums, for instance, smell wonderful when you rub them. They come in a wide variety of scents, including ginger, lemon, lemon-rose, mint, nutmeg, and rose. Scented geraniums, along with lavender (floral scent), lemon balm (citrusy scent), lemon verbena (citrusy scent), and sweet woodruff (woodsy/earthy scent), are among the best-known herbs for fragrance.

You can use fragrant herbs many different ways, such as by creating these household items.

- Sachets
- Pomanders
- Herb pillows
- Essential oils
- Perfumes
- Scented candles
- Scented soaps

Herbs for Tea

Of all the things you can do with herbs, one of the most popular is making and drinking herbal tea. Historically, herbal teas were used as medicines, and many people still brew and drink them for their medicinal effects. But most people drink herbal teas because they find them soothing. You can brew a tasty pot from of any of the following herbs (use leaves only, unless otherwise noted):

- Angelica
- Bee balm
- Catnip (leaves and flowers)
- Chamomile (flowers)
- Lemon balm
- Lemon thyme
- Lemon verbena
- Mints
- Rosemary
- Sage
- Scented geraniums

Keep in mind that not all herbs are suitable for making tea. Do some research before you brew.

BREWING THE PERFECT POT OF TEA

Herbal teas are at their best when brewed lightly and delicately, and they can be made with either dried or fresh herbs. To make herbal tea, you'll need 1 teaspoon of dried herbs or 1 tablespoon of fresh herbs for each 6- to 8-ounce cup. Place the herbs in a china, pottery, or other nonmetal teapot (nonmetal pots help keep the tea pure in flavor and hot while it brews). Add boiling water and let the tea steep for 5 to 10 minutes (keep the pot covered to retain heat). Steeping time will vary, depending on what herbs you're using, so do taste checks at regular intervals until you're sure. Then strain the herbs out and serve the tea with honey, lemon, orange slices, or fresh herb sprigs.

MAKING ICED TEA

You can also make delicious iced tea using the same procedure as above, except use 3 tablespoons of fresh herbs or 2 tablespoons of dried herbs for each 6- to 8-ounce cup. (The extra amount of herbs will keep your tea from becoming diluted as the ice melts.)

For a change of pace, try freezing herb teas in ice cube trays and using the cubes to chill refreshing summer drinks, such as lemonade or punch—or to add sparkle to plain water. You can also freeze sprigs of herbs, like mint, in ice cubes for flavoring and decorating beverages.

Herbs for Healing

Herbs are also traditional ingredients in many home remedies. While natural food stores and vitamin suppliers sell all sorts of ready-made herbal medicines, it's less expensive and more satisfying to make your own remedies with herbs picked right from your garden. You can combine the herbs to fit your own needs and tastes and make just the right amounts you need. And by growing herbs organically, you can guarantee their purity because you'll know they won't have been treated with any chemicals.

Just remember that many herbs have toxic properties, and some are absolutely poisonous. That's why it's extremely important to

- make sure each plant is correctly identified before you use it;
- use all plants judiciously;
- remember that medicines that are healthful when taken in small quantities can be very harmful when taken in larger doses;
- avoid mixing herbal remedies with prescription medications; and
- consult a doctor about a serious ailment instead of trying to treat it yourself.

7 TOP HERBS

Here are seven herbs you can grow in your garden along with the conditions they cure.

Basil wastes warts. This aromatic herb contains many antiviral compounds. One widely practiced folk remedy for warts involves rubbing crushed basil leaves on the growths.

Continued ➡

Calendula treats cuts and scrapes. It reduces inflammation and heals wounds. The flowers are used externally in infusions (teas brewed for anywhere from 15 minutes to several hours), ointments, and tinctures.

Chamomile battles gingivitis. Chamomile is effective as a gargle or mouthwash for treating gingivitis. That's because its flowers contain several anti-inflammatory and antiseptic compounds.

Fennel eases asthma. The Greeks treated asthma and other respiratory ailments with fennel tea. Fennel contains a helpful chemical that helps loosen bronchial secretions.

Garlic relieves insect bites and stings. It contain enzymes that break down chemical substances that the body releases in response to pain. Interestingly enough, garlic works both internally and externally. You can make a poultice and apply it directly to insect bites and stings, or you can get a measure of relief by eating garlic.

Lemon balm alleviates migraines. The recommended dose is a tea made with 1 to 2 teaspoons of dried herb per cup of boiling water, steeped until cool.

Parsley beats bad breath. Bright green parsley is a rich source of chlorophyll, which is a powerful breath freshener.

Planning Your Herb Garden

Once you've decided what herbs you want to grow, you need to figure out where you're going to put them. If you just want to grow a few herbs, you may decide to tuck them into a flowerbed or the vegetable garden. If you really want to get into growing and using herbs, you'll probably want to create a separate garden for them. Either way, here are a few points to keep in mind.

MATCH PLANTS TO PLACE

For healthy, vigorous herbs, give your plants the best possible conditions. Although many herbs can adapt to poor, dry soil, that doesn't mean they thrive in it; fertile, well-prepared garden soil will encourage much better growth.

LEAVE ROOM TO GROW

Just like vegetables, herbs need room to spread without crowding their neighbors. For the right spacing, follow the guidelines on the seed packets or transplant labels. Crowding in lots of herbs won't give you a better harvest; instead, the plants won't grow as well, and you'll be left with lots of thinning and dividing work to keep plants healthy.

If you're growing perennial herbs that will spread—such as mint—plan some kind of containment system, or soon you'll have nothing but the spreaders. Or set aside a separate area of the garden where they can spread without endangering more delicate plants.

PICK A PRACTICAL SITE

While it's important to give your herbs the conditions they like, you'll also want to consider your needs. For example, you're most likely to use your herbs if they're close to the house. Also, plan your garden for easy care. You can do that by

- choosing a site near a water supply (for moisture-loving herbs like mint);
- allowing for paths so you can comfortably reach into all parts of the garden without stepping on the soil; and
- making at least one path wide enough so you can get into the center of a large garden with tools and a wheelbarrow.

COMPANION PLANTING

Companion planting is planting certain combinations of plants together to repel pests, attract beneficial insects, or make efficient use of garden beds. You can use herbs n companion plantings to repel or trap pests and to help other plants grow.

HERBS THAT BEAT PESTS

Try planting garlic with bush beans to repel aphids, and catnip with eggplant to repel flea beetles. A ring of chives under an apple tree is said to discourage apple scab. Other herbs used to repel pests include:

- Anise hyssop
- Borage
- Calendula
- Cilantro
- Dill
- Mint
- Rosemary
- Sage
- Scented geranium
- Tansy

You can also use herbs as traps to lure pests away from your crops. Dill and lovage can be used to lure hornworms from tomatoes, for example.

HERBS THAT HELP

Some herbs seem to enhance the growth of other plants. Try pairing borage with strawberries, chervil with radishes, sage with cabbage-family crops, and summer or winter savory with onions. Also try basil or thyme around tomatoes, and tarragon with any vegetable you're growing. (Watch out, though: Some herbs inhibit neighboring plants. Dill, for example, slows the growth of tomatoes, while garlic harms neighboring beans and peas.)

HOW TO USE COMPANIONS

You can mix and match herbs with most other plants, as long as you're meeting the growth requirements of each individual plant. Here are some guidelines to follow when choosing companions.

- Choose companion plants that have the same requirements for sunlight, water, season, and temperature.
- Plant perennial herbs with perennial crops. You can pair strawberries and Roman chamomile or lemon thyme in the same bed. Or let asparagus share space with tarragon. You can sow seeds of shallow-rooted annual herbs, such as cilantro or dill, around established perennial fruits and vegetables, but don't dig holes and set-in plants—you'll disturb the root system of the perennial.
- Avoid using invasive herbs, such as mint, as companion plants, because they'll quickly take over. Instead, grow invasive herbs in pots near the garden.

Planting an Herb Garden
Barbara W. Ellis

Herbs are among the easiest plants to grow in a garden—and the most useful. Perhaps best known for their role in cooking, where they add flavor to stews, soups, vinegars, jellies, relishes, and all types of recipes, herbs also have many other uses. They have been used medicinally and in cosmetics. In arts and crafts, they lend color and fragrance to potpourris, herb baths, wreaths, and sachets. However you use herbs in your garden, you'll find that they offer fragrance, flavor, color, a sense of history—and more.

Designing an Herb Garden

You can incorporate herbs in the garden in many different ways. Combine them with annuals and perennials in beds and borders. Plant them in a kitchen garden or perhaps a cutting garden. Grow

a more traditional herb garden—perhaps in a formal knot pattern. Or simply tuck some commonly used cooking herbs in a half-barrel or a small bed outside the kitchen door so you can dash out quickly for an easy supply of fresh herbs.

The success of any good garden is based on the quality of the design and the implementation of that design. Take time before you plant to think about what herbs you want to grow, what you'll use them for, and what sites you have that would suit their cultural needs. For example, if you want a steady supply of fresh herbs for cooking, choose a convenient place for daily harvest. If you are growing a large supply for drying, on the other hand, convenience isn't such an issue.

STYLE

Select a style that complements the house or building nearest to the garden. Herb gardens are often used for historic sites because they can be used to represent almost any time period. A dooryard garden would be suitable for a colonial-style house. This informal style of herb garden, actually a type of cottage garden, provides a warm welcome to all visitors coming to the house. This style came to America with the early colonists and was primarily utilitarian. Herbs were planted near the front door for easy access; herbs such as tansy (*Tanacetum vulgare*) also had value in keeping insects out of the house.

A Victorian garden displaying herbs in containers or in flower beds is another possibility. Although the Victorians did not grow herbs in great quantity, there was some carryover from colonial gardens. They especially loved herbs used for fragrance, as well as those with special meaning. (Perhaps the best-known herb for this purpose is rosemary, for remembrance.) A garden using herbs in the Victorian style should include some of the Hybrid Perpetual roses that were so popular during the Victorian era and are a symbol of love.

Modern herb gardens tend to blend herbs with complementary plants. Herbs can create a lovely garden at the entrance to any house or building and can be blended beautifully with other plants, particularly old roses or perennials. At long last, herbs are being recognized as important ornamentals worthy of being grown in all types of gardens—formal or informal, historic or modern. Use herbs as border plants along walkways to soften harsh edges or in containers, on balconies, rooftops, or patios. There are limitless possibilities for the use of herbs in the landscape.

HERBS IN NOOKS AND CRANNIES

Although the subject of herb lawns is often covered in gardening books, using herbs in this manner generally works better in theory than in reality. Even in the finest of English gardens, an herb lawn

Continued ➡

is something that requires a great deal of work and considerable maintenance.

That said, if you still want the challenge of a thyme or chamomile lawn, plan on starting with plants rather than seeds to avoid severe weed competition. The two best plants to use are Roman chamomile (*Chamaemelum nobile*) and caraway thyme (*Thymus herba-barona*) because they are both durable and fragrant. Plant Roman chamomile on 6-inch centers in a moderately rich, well-drained soil. Be aware that Roman chamomile sometimes dies out in spots, leaving bare areas. Caraway thyme, on the other hand, is about the toughest herb for a lawn. It will create a thick, dark green mat within one year if planted in full sun in moderately rich, well-drained soil. Because the plants attract bees when in bloom, be sure to block off the lawn during their flowering time or prune back the blossoms. You'll need to water regularly until the plants become established.

Roman chamomile and caraway thyme are also excellent to use on benches constructed so that the seat is actually a bed in which plants are grown, a tradition in many European gardens. These and other herbs can also be included for planting in the nooks and crannies between rocks in a wall or along a walkway. Some are fine for rock gardens. The best of the very small thymes to grow in between bricks or stone on a walkway is mother-of-thyme (*Thymus praecox* subsp. *arcticus*), which comes in a red-, white-, or pink-flowered form. Again, it's best to begin with plants rather than seeds because it gets the planting off to a good, quick start. In fact, many herbs such as thymes are variable when grown from seed, producing many inferior hybrids. So it's best to avoid seed-grown plants altogether.

Other herbs to consider for use as ground-covers include sweet woodruff (*Asperula odorata*), which will grow well in moist shade; wild strawberry (*Fragaria virginiana*), which is perfect for a sunny spot in a naturalized garden; pennyroyal (*Mentha pulegium*), another sun-lover hardy only to Zone 7; and golden lemon thyme (*Thymus x citriodorus* 'Aureus'), a creeping thyme grown for its attractive golden foliage.

KNOT GARDENS

A traditional knot garden is another possibility for a small, formal herb planting. Knot gardens were at their peak of popularity in Elizabethan England, when it was fashionable to include a knot as an essential component of any garden. All knot gardens featured fragrant herbs, the clippings of which were used for scenting linens and fabrics. There are a variety of knot garden styles from which to choose. (One pattern is illustrated below.)

Here are the main points to consider when thinking about and planning a knot garden.

- Place the garden where it can be viewed from above so the interlocking chains will be fully appreciated.
- Be sure the site has excellent drainage before you plant. If there is any doubt, either relocate the garden or consider adding a system of drain tiles.
- Select only plants that thrive in your area and that are completely hardy.
- Do not plan a large knot garden because when plants die, replacement plants are often hard to locate.
- Be sure to use plenty of evergreens so your knot will be interesting to look at in the winter as well as summer.
- Plan on pruning the plants in the knot from early spring through midsummer, as needed.

Don't simply shear the surface of the plants each time. Plucking some of the branches near the center of the plant allows air and light into the center, which helps avoid serious disease problems and encourages new branches and thick growth.

- Use an attractive, appropriate material, such as cobblestone or brick, to edge the bed. The edging will help accentuate the design and perhaps help drainage.

Selecting a Site and Preparing the Garden

It's important to keep a few basic points in mind when selecting a site and planting your herb garden. With the exception of shade-loving herbs, most herbs require at least six hours of direct sunlight. The soil should be slightly acid, with a pH of approximately 6.5, and should be moderately rich and well drained. It also should be free of encroaching tree roots.

To prepare a new bed for herbs, follow the steps below. You'll have to make adjustments depending on your own garden and the conditions available.

Start by laying out the bed you've designed; ideally, you'll have a detailed design on paper to follow. Remove all sod or top growth from the site. Dig the soil either by double garden digging (going two spade depths into the soil) or digging as deep as possible with a garden fork. Then apply a generous amount of organic material over the top of the area; well-rotted manure and/or well-rotted leaves are best. Adjust the pH as necessary. If the soil is heavy clay, apply generous amounts of medium-size chicken grit because this will help to break up the heavy clay and improve aeration, especially important in wet winters. The addition of gypsum will help improve the drainage in heavy clay soils. If the area is extremely wet, consider making a raised bed to help improve the drainage. The best height for a raised bed is from 12 to 18 inches. Avoid higher beds, because the soil can become too dry in winter.

Planting and Caring for Herbs

Herbs are really no different than annuals, perennials, biennials, or bulbs when it comes to planting and propagation techniques. For planting, seed sowing, or propagation information, see the appropriate sections earlier in this book for directions.

The main consideration in keeping the herbs beautiful is to keep them well pruned. For the most part, herbs love to be cut back, and they will reward you with beautiful form and habit as long as their pruning requirements are met. With cooking herbs, of course, you'll want to use the trimmings in the kitchen. For best results, prune plants on a cool, shady day so that underlying growth is not suddenly exposed to hot, baking sun.

Planting & Caring for Herbs

Once you've decided what herbs you want to grow, it's time to get your hands into the soil. In this chapter, you'll learn what you need to do when starting with plants or seeds. You'll also discover how to control herbs that grow out of bounds and how you can keep herbs thriving indoors when old Man Winter arrives.

Starting with Plants

Buying plants is the way to go if you want to start with just a few of each herb. Buying plants is also a good choice for perennial herbs. For the best

success, buy the following herbs as plants (unless otherwise indicated):

· Garlic (bulbs)	· Mint
· Scented geranium	· Oregano
· Horseradish (roots)	· Rosemary
· Lavender	· Sage
· Lovage	· Tarragon
	· Thyme

Start with only one or two plants to see how well they do in your conditions and how well you like them. You can always buy more plants next year.

SNIFFING BEFORE YOU BUY

Knowledgeable herb gardeners sniff before they buy. That's because many specialty herbs—including oregano and French tarragon—don't come true from seed. Seedlings may have no fragrance whatsoever, or they may only be a weak facsimile of the best culinary aromas. Don't buy plants hoping they'll develop fragrance and flavor as they grow because they won't. Even small plants should have the full-blown, pungent aromas the herbs are grown for. To test a plant's aroma, gently rub a leaf between your fingers and take a good whiff.

Starting From Seed

Growing herbs from seed is less expensive, but it takes more time and care than buying plants. As a general rule, growing from seed is best for annuals and biennials. It's also a good choice when you want more than just a plant or two. You can either directly sow herb seeds in the ground or sow them in pots indoors.

Herbs for direct sowing. You can sow these herbs directly in the garden: basil, borage, German chamomile, chervil, cilantro, dill, fennel, mustard, and parsley.

Herbs for indoor sowing. For an extra-early crop, start basil, sweet marjoram, and parsley indoors. For a continuous supply of fresh herbs, sow a second crop outdoors when soil temperatures warm up.

Easy perennials from seed. Catnip, chives, feverfew, and lemon balm are easy to grow from seed sown indoors or out.

Planting Herbs

Plant annual herbs just as you would plant vegetables. Since perennial herbs will grow in your garden for several years or more, take extra care to get them off to a good start. Plant them in spring or fall, when temperatures are cool and the soil has lots of moisture in it. Overcast days are best for planting because plants will have time to recover from the shock of moving from their cozy homes in pots to their new home in the garden.

Here's a three-step approach to getting your herbs in the ground.

1. **Prepare for planting.** Give your herbs a good drink before you plant by soaking them, pots and all, in a shallow tub of water, weak compost tea, or liquid seaweed solution. When you're ready to plant, pinch away any dead stems, leaves, and spent blossoms, and pull and throwaway weed seedlings growing in the pot. Then dig a hole that's deep enough so you can set the plant at the same depth it grew at in the pot.

2. **Remove plants from pots.** To remove a plant from its pot, hold one hand over the top of the pot with your fingers around the stem. Turn the pot upside down with the other

Continued ➡

hand, and tap the bottom. Then gently squeeze the plant out of the pot while keeping the ball of soil and roots intact. Loosen roots that are tightly intertwined, and cut away bent or broken ones.

3. **Settle plants in the soil.** Center the plant in the hole, making sure it is sitting at the same depth that it was in the pot. Plants planted too deeply can rot; those planted too shallowly can dry out. After setting the plant, replace the soil. Firm the soil around the stems, forming a shallow trench around the center stem to hold water and direct it to the plant's roots. Water gently and thoroughly. Apply an organic mulch such as cocoa bean hulls to keep plant leaves clean and to help retain soil moisture.

Controlling Invasive Herbs

Some perennial herbs, such as horseradish and mint, grow so vigorously that they'll engulf their better-behaved neighbors. Here are some control tactics to use on them.

- **Impermeable mulch.** Mulch around invasive herbs with a 1-inch-thick layer of newspaper. Cover the newspaper with an attractive mulch like cocoa bean hulls or bark chips. Renew this mulch combination each season to prevent the spread of invasive herbs.
- **Herbal islands.** Plant invasive herbs in island beds, surrounded by lawn. Weekly mowing around the beds will keep the spreaders in check.
- **Sunken containers.** Plant invasive herbs in large containers sunk into the soil to keep roots from spreading through the entire bed (see "Containing Creepers," below).

CONTAINING CREEPERS

If you plant an invasive herb in a bucket, the roots can't get through the bucket walls, and the bucket rim stops creeping stems that spread along the soil surface. (Trim away stems that sneak over the top.) Here's how to do it.

1. Use a hammer and nail to punch several drainage holes in the bottom of a large bucket. Five-gallon plastic buckets are ideal.
2. Dig a hole in the soil that fits the bucket. The hole should be deep enough so that when you put the bucket in the soil, the rim sticks up 3 to 4 inches above the soil surface.
3. Put the bucket in the hole and fill it with garden soil.
4. Plant the herb in the bucket, water thoroughly, and then mulch in and around the bucket to conceal its edge.

Preparing Perennials for Winter

With the end of the growing season in sight and colder weather right around the corner, it's time to start putting the garden to bed for winter. The first thing to do is stop harvesting perennial herbs in late summer or early fall, about 3 weeks before you expect the first frost. Once frosts arrive and the ground has frozen, mulch heavily to protect perennials from winter heaving (when alternate freezing and thawing of the soil pushes plants right out of the ground). When mulching, keep these points in mind.

- Straw is the ideal winter mulch. (You don't want to use leaves because they might drift over the crowns of small plants and suffocate them.)
- Draw the mulch up to, but not over, the plants.

- Gray-leaved plants that hold their leaves over winter, such as lavender and thyme, need additional protection in cold climates. Laying evergreen boughs over the plants will help ensure their survival with minimal dieback.

TENDER PERENNIALS

Tender perennial herbs, such as bay and rosemary, need protection in most parts of the United States. In zones where they're not hardy, grow them in containers and bring them indoors over winter. If you've been growing them in beds, you can still bring them indoors for the winter. Here's how.

1. Carefully dig up the plants and pot them.
2. Water the herbs and set them in a shady place outdoors for about a week, so they can gradually adjust to the dual shocks of pot culture and decreased sunlight. (If you're bringing herbs indoors that are already in pots, you'll still need to put them in shade for a week so they can adjust to the transition.)
3. Regularly check the plants, both outdoors and indoors, for pests such as whiteflies or aphids. If you find any, spray the plants with insecticidal soap.

The best time to pot most outdoor herbs is after the fall harvest and before the first frost. They should be safely indoors by the time frost strikes. Chives, however, benefit from induced dormancy before coming in from the cold. Divide the clumps, pot them, and let them stay outside until frost kills the foliage. Then bring them in, and they'll give you a new burst of lush growth.

Windowsill Herbs

Growing herbs indoors is a way to enjoy them all year long—particularly those herbs that wouldn't survive outdoors through the winter. No matter whether you decide to grow herbs as houseplants year-round or you're potting up perennials to move inside for the cold months, you'll give your plants an edge if you keep these points in mind.

Give them light. Most herbs thrive on at least 5 hours of sunlight a day. (Exceptions are the mints, parsley, rosemary, and thyme, which can take partial shade, and ginger and lemon balm, which actually like shade.)

Turn, turn, turn. Don't forget to turn the plants on windowsills regularly. Turning keeps them shapely and makes sure all sides get enough light.

Keep it cool. Most herbs like temperatures on the cool side-daytime temps of 65°F and nighttime temps of 60°F.

Give them air. Herbs are extremely sensitive to dry, stagnant air—which is what you probably have in your tightly sealed, centrally heated house. Stale air promotes fungal diseases and insect infestations. So try to keep the air moving around the plants by cracking a window in an adjoining room or by opening doors. Also, don't crowd the pots—give them plenty of space so air can circulate around them.

Mix things up. Herbs in pots need a reasonably rich soil mix with good drainage, such as 2 parts compost, 1 part vermiculite, and 1 part perlite. Or, try a mix of 1 part potting soil, 1 part sand, and 1 part peat moss.

Water regularly. Although herbs enjoy regular waterings, they're finicky plants—meaning that they don't like waterlogged soil. Water most herbs thoroughly when the soil surface starts drying out between waterings. But never let rosemary

completely dry out, or else you'll inadvertently kill it. And always use room temperature water so you don't shock the plants' root systems.

Herbs in Containers

Herbs are great container plants, which means that you can grow them even if you don't have room for garden beds. Although potted herbs won't produce the big harvests you'd reap from garden-grown herbs, a few pots in a sunny site will produce plenty of fresh herbs and some to dry, as well. And growing tender herbs such as rosemary in pots makes it easy to move them indoors for the winter.

CARE BASICS

Containers. When choosing containers for herbs, select those that have drainage holes. Also, make sure the containers are large enough to allow 1 to 2 inches of space around the rootball. If the plants becomes rootbound, move them to larger containers.

Potting mix. A good, organic potting mix is important for container plants. See "Mix things up" on the opposite page for potting mix recipes you can make yourself.

Watering. You'll need to water herbs in containers more frequently than you would if they were growing in the garden. How often to water isn't rocket science, though. If you live where it's hot and dry, you'll need to water thoroughly and frequently. If you live where it's cool and wet, you'll need to water less often. (To check to see how moist the soil is, press your finger into the top inch of soil.)

Feeding. Herbs will benefit from a seasonal spray of liquid kelp or fish emulsion.

Herb Favorites

Now that you know the basics of growing herbs, it's time to decide which ones you want to try. In this section, you'll get an overview of 27 different herbs, as well as a few specifics for growing and harvesting each one. You'll also find out how you can use the herbs you plant for cooking, or—in some cases—healing.

BE CREATIVE

Remember that you can incorporate herbs into your flower or vegetable gardens; you don't have to grow a traditional "herb garden." And if you don't have room for a garden in your landscape, grow herbs in containers on your patio or inside on a windowsill. That's one of the great things about herbs: Because they demand little, you can grow them practically anywhere—from a simple arrangement of pots on a sunny porch to a stylized formal garden.

KEEP THEM CLOSE

Even if you use herbs in your garden beds, make sure you keep a few close to your kitchen door for the spur of the moment. After all, what could be more convenient than snipping a few sprigs of lemon balm for a cup of tea at the end of a hard day at work, or gathering some oregano to add to the simmering pot of freshly made tomato sauce on the stove?

BROADEN YOUR HORIZONS

Some of the herbs in this chapter, such as parsley, are probably familiar to you, while others, such as borage and feverfew, may be new. Experiment! Plant a couple of old standbys, and then broaden

Continued ➡

your horizons by trying one or two that you've never tasted before.

Angelica

(*Angelica archangelica*)

Angelica is a plant that stands out—literally—in any herb garden, as it can grow as high as 8 feet tall. This herb sort of looks like celery; it has a round, hollow stem that's purplish in color, and it has tiny white or greenish flowers. It's a biennial, or a short-lived perennial hardy in Zones 4 to 9.

Growing Guidelines

Rich, moist, well-drained soil and partial shade are the keys to making angelica happy. Plant the seeds directly in the ground in spring, but don't cover them, because they need light to germinate. Once the seedlings are up, thin them so they're about 3 feet apart.

After frost of the first year, angelica will die back to the ground. The following year it will send up new shoots that you can harvest in early spring. If you let the seedheads develop, the plant will die after the seed ripens—but you'll get replacement plants from the seeds that have self-sown.

In the Kitchen

Angelica has a slightly sweet flavor. Although you can use the leaves to dress up green salads, fruit soups, or meat stews, the most celebrated part of angelica is its stem. Cook the stems like celery and eat them as a side dish or add them to stews. You can also candy the stem and savor it alone, or use it to decorate

- cakes
- puddings
- tarts

Harvesting Hints

As mentioned earlier, you can harvest the stems (and leaves) in the spring of the second year of growth.

Trivia Tidbits

In ancient times, angelica was supposed to ward off evil spirits and witches. Peasants would make necklaces of the leaves for their children to wear for protection. And the juice of the roots was used to make a special drink thought to ensure a long life.

Anise Hyssop

(*Agastache foeniculum*)

Anise hyssop is a sturdy and lovely plant that's as much at home in the perennial border as it is in the herb garden. The stems rise up to 3 feet tall and are topped with 3- to 6-inch spikes of lavender-blue flowers from midsummer to early autumn. You'll see a lot of bees and butterflies buzzing around this beauty, seeking its rich nectar. The leaves and flowers have a slight licoricelike scent and flavor. Anise hyssop is a perennial that grows in Zones 4 to 9.

Growing Guidelines

Although it prefers full sun, anise hyssop will also grow in light shade. A North American native, it's naturally found along lakeshores and streams in moist, well-drained soil that's very fertile.

You can buy young plants or start seeds indoors in late winter to transplant into the garden after the last spring frost—or you can sow the seeds directly in the garden a week before the last expected frost. Space seeds about 1 to 1½ feet apart. Even though anise hyssop is a perennial, the seedlings will usually reach blooming size the first year.

After a hard frost, the plants will die back to the ground. Be sure you mark the location of your plants, as they are very slow to emerge in the spring.

Plants do tend to be short-lived, so divide the clumps every year or two in spring to keep them vigorous. Even if the parent plants die out, you'll generally have plenty of self-sown volunteers to replace them.

In the Kitchen

Fresh leaves are excellent in salads. Or, chop them and add them to summer fruit cups, along with the colorful flowers. The licorice flavor of fresh minced leaves is also a nice complement to

- chicken
- fish
- pork
- rice

Fresh and dried leaves make a good tea, alone or in combination with other herbs.

Harvesting Hints

For occasional use, snip off the leaves as needed, starting from the bottom of the plant.

The fresh flowers are attractive in salads and make a nice addition to potpourri. Cut them just as they begin to open.

For tea, cut the whole stems 4 to 5 inches from the base of the plant and strip the leaves off. To air-dry whole stems, gather them early in the day and hang them in a well-ventilated, dark, dry location.

Trivia Tidbits

The botanical name, *Agostoche foeniculum*, refers to the many flower spikes on this fennel-like plant. It is just one of many unrelated plants that share the anise scent that is characteristic of fennel.

The Cheyenne called this herb "Elk-Mint" and made infusions of the leaves.

Basil

(*Ocimum basilicum*)

Basil's pungent flavor enhances any summer garden recipe. And you can choose from lots of varieties, including lemon, cinnamon, and anise-flavored types. Basil also comes in a variety of shapes and colors; you can plant varieties that are low-growing, stocky, or tall, with variegated, crinkled, purple, green, or smooth leaves. Basil is an annual that will grow in Zones 4 through 10. The plants can grow up to 2 feet tall and 8 inches wide.

In the Kitchen

Basil has a rich and spicy, mildly peppery flavor, with a trace of mint and clove. For the best flavor,

use basil fresh, rather than dried. Traditional in Italian, Mediterranean, and Thai cooking, basil is superb with

- tomatoes
- white beans
- paste
- rice
- cheese
- eggs
- fish
- lamb
- poultry
- veal

You can also pair basil with a host of mild vegetables, such as zucchini, summer squash, and eggplant. If you make your own pizza or tomato sauce, try substituting basil for oregano and see how you like the taste.

Growing Guidelines

You can grow basil in any well-drained soil amended with plenty of organic matter. Just make sure you plant basil where it will get full sun.

Start basil seeds indoors 6 weeks before your last expected frost. Plant the transplants outdoors after the danger of frost has passed and when soil temperature averages 50°F or higher. If you're growing small-leaved basil, place the plants 6 to 8 inches apart. Varieties with large leaves need 1 to 1½ feet between plants.

Mulching the area after the seedlings have shot up helps to keep the ground moist and warm and discourages weeds. But make sure you mulch after the ground has warmed up because basil roots need heat.

Harvesting Hints

Begin harvesting basil as soon as the plants have several pairs of leaves. If you harvest frequently, you'll help encourage your plants to produce new growth—which, in turn, will give you even more basil to harvest. You can keep harvesting basil up until the first frost. After harvesting, wrap dry foliage in paper towels and store it in resealable plastic bags in the fridge.

Trivia Tidbits

In Italy, basil has been and still is a sign of love. According to tradition, if a man gives a woman a sprig of basil, she will fall in love with him and never leave him. Today, he'd probably have better luck if he made her pesto and served it over pasta with salad, bread, and a little wine—and then did the dishes afterward.

Borage

(*Borage officinalis*)

Borage produces blue, star-shaped blossoms and is a nice addition to a wildflower bed or vegetable patch, as well as to your herb garden. This annual, which can grow up to 2 feet tall and 16 inches wide, attracts lots of bees, which love its flowers.

Growing Guidelines

Borage needs fairly rich, moist, light soil and full sun to grow. This herb is easy to grow from seed. Plant the seed as soon as the danger of frost has passed. (Borage will readily reseed itself after its

Continued ➡

initial planting.) When the seedlings poke their heads through the ground, thin them so they're about 2 feet apart.

Because borage likes moist soil, mulch around the plants to help contain moisture. Don't be disappointed if the pretty blue flowers don't appear on your new plants the first year; sometimes borage acts as a biennial.

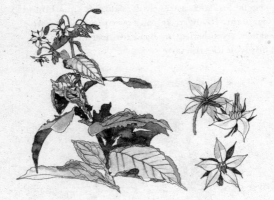

IN THE KITCHEN

Borage has a crisp cucumber flavor. You can use the leaves raw, steamed, or sautéed, as you would spinach. You can eat the flowers and stems, too; peel, chop, and use the stems like celery. The leaves and stems enhance

- most vegetables
- green salads
- salad dressings
- pickles
- cheese
- fish
- poultry
- iced beverages

HARVESTING HINTS

Harvest borage as you need it for fresh use, gathering the young, tender leaves in the morning, after the dew has dried. Always use borage fresh because it loses its flavor and color when dried.

TRIVIA TIDBITS

Borage has a reputation for invoking courage. In fact, ancient Celtic warriors preparing for battle drank wine flavored with borage to give them courage. They believed their fears would vanish and they would feel elated. (The effect was probably due to the wine, not the borage.)

Catnip

(*Nepeta cataria*)

Catnip, which many people plant for their cat's enjoyment, is a member of the mint family. Cats love this feline drug, sniffing, chewing, and rolling around in it. (Humans, on the other hand, can only feel envy at all the feline fun.) Actually, smelling catnip—not eating it—is what does the trick for cats. A happy cat may chew on the plant, but that's mostly to bruise it and release more of the magic fragrance.

Catnip is coarse-leaved and gray-green, and it produces white flowers with purple-pink spots. A perennial, catnip can grow 1 to 3 feet tall and is hardy to Zone 3 or 4.

GROWING GUIDELINES

Catnip does best in average, sandy, well-drained soil, in an area that gets full sun to partial shade (although it will be most fragrant if you plant it in full sun). The easiest way to start a catnip patch is by planting a whole plant (check out your local garden center or ask a friend with an established patch if she has any extra plants).

HARVESTING HINTS

Gather the leaves and tops in late summer when the plant is in full bloom, and dry them in the shade. Store dried leaves away from moisture.

HEALING WITH CATNIP

Some people make a tea from the dried leaves and flowering heads as a remedy for upset stomachs and insomnia.

TRIVIA TIDBITS

During the Middle Ages, catnip was thought—incorrectly—to prevent leprosy.

Chamomile, German

(*Matricaria recutita*)

Chamomile, Roman

(*Chamaemelum nobile*)

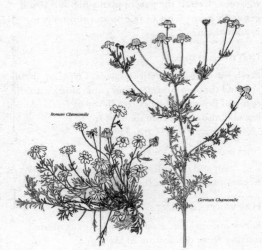

Roman Chamomile

German Chamomile

Although you're probably familiar with the word *chamomile*, you may not know that it's two different plants. German chamomile is an annual reaching 2 to 3 feet tall. It has a honey-apple fragrance and is the chamomile commonly found in tea bags. Roman chamomile is a low-growing perennial that rarely reaches more than 9 inches high-making it suitable for use as a groundcover. It's hardy in Zones 6 to 9 and normally carries a stronger fragrance than its German counterpart.

GROWING GUIDELINES

German chamomile prefers sandy, well-drained soil, while Roman chamomile does best in light, dry soil. Plant both types in full sun to partial shade.

You can sow chamomile seeds outdoors in early spring or late summer by scattering them where you want them to grow in the garden. Don't cover the seeds with soil, though, because they need light to germinate. Keep the soil evenly moist (not soggy).

When the seedlings are 1 to 2 inches tall, thin them so that they're 8 to 12 inches apart. (For a groundcover, thin Roman chamomile seedlings to 4 inches apart.)

HARVESTING HINTS

If you're going to use chamomile for tea, harvest the flowers in full bloom throughout the summer. Spread the flowers thinly on a cloth or screen to dry in the shade. Throwaway any stem or leaf parts,

and store the flowers in an airtight container away from heat, light, and moisture.

HEALING WITH CHAMOMILE

Chamomile tea helps alleviate insomnia and calm nerves. It also relieves indigestion, nausea, and flatulence. A gargle with cooled tea helps relieve mouth inflammations and sore throats.

TRIVIA TIDBITS

In the days before refrigeration, immersing meat in chamomile tea was thought to help eliminate the rancid odor of spoilage. Chamomile was also reputed to make an excellent insect repellent. And the fresh, delicate fragrance of this daisylike herb made it a popular air freshener in homes where bathing was uncommon.

Chervil

(*Anthriscus cerefolium*)

Chervil comes in two main varieties, one plain and one curly. A hardy annual, chervil looks dainty and delicate and produces small white flowers on plants that can grow to 2 feet tall.

GROWING GUIDELINES

Chervil likes a rich, humusy, slightly acid soil. Plant it in early spring or fall, since it prefers cool temperatures and bolts (goes to seed) at the first sign of heat. You can direct-seed chervil shallowly in the ground. When the seedlings reach 2 inches high, thin them to 9 to 12 inches apart.

Keep mulch away from the bases of the plants, or they may be damaged by earwigs. Also, cover small seedlings with floating row covers to protect them from rabbits, groundhogs, or other animal pests.

IN THE KITCHEN

Chervil has a subtle, tender flavor—part anise, part parsley—and is an effective seasoning in food. You can use both the leaves and the stems in cooking, and whole sprigs make a delicate and decorative garnish. Chervil enhances

- carrots
- peas
- corn
- spinach
- cream
- veal
- eggs
- fish and seafood (especially oysters)

Chervil also complements tarragon, shallots, freshly ground black pepper, shallots, freshly ground black pepper, marjoram, and lemon. Always add chervil at the end of cooking because lengthy heating turns the flavor bitter.

HARVESTING HINTS

Snip the feathery leaves 6 to 8 weeks after sowing. Use chervil fresh because dried leaves have little flavor.

TRIVIA TIDBITS

Chervil's flavor and fragrance resemble that of the myrrh brought by the wise men to the baby Jesus. Because of this and because chervil symbolized new life, it became traditional to serve chervil soup on Holy Thursday.

Continued ➡

Chives

(Allium schoenoprasum)

Chives are bulb plants, although the bulbs are so tiny that you might not realize they're there. Those plants produce beautiful, globelike, pink and lavender blossoms. A perennial, chives grow to about 18 inches high and thrive in Zones 3 to 9.

Growing Guidelines

This herb requires well-drained soil and full sun. The easiest way to grow chives is to start with young plants acquired from garden centers, by mail order, or from a friend. Plant clumps of up to six chive bulbs 5 to 8 inches apart.

Keep mulch away from the bases of the plants to improve air circulation and prevent disease problems. Chives compete poorly with other plants, so make sure to weed diligently.

You'll need to divide large clumps of chives about every 3 years. In early spring, dig up the plants and work the clumps apart with your fingers to create small clumps of four to six bulbs each. Then replant these divisions (or share them with friends).

In the Kitchen

Chives taste like mild, sweet onions. Mince the fresh, slender leaves, and use them in recipes or as a garnish. French cooking combines chives with shallots, marjoram, and tarragon. Chives also complement

- artichokes
- asparagus
- carrots
- cauliflower
- corn
- onions
- peas
- potatoes
- spinach
- tomatoes
- cheese
- eggs
- fish and shellfish
- poultry

Don't overlook chive flowers, either. Toss them in salads or add them to a dish as a beautiful, edible garnish.

Harvesting Hints

Use scissors to cut chives about 2 inches above the soil. Before the plants flower in spring, harvest from the outside edges of the clumps. After the plants flower, cut back the entire plant to remove the spent flowerstalks. Chives are best if you use them fresh.

Trivia Tidbits

Chives have been added to foods for nearly 5,000 years. Native to the Orient, they were probably first used by the Chinese and then the ancient Greeks. By the sixteenth century, they had also earned a place in European herb gardens. When the colonists came to America, they brought chives along with them.

Coriander

(Coriandrum sativum)

People have used coriander in cooking since ancient times. This cool-weather annual has pale mauve flowers that bees and other pollinators just love. (The flowers appear in spring or mid- to late summer, depending on when you sow them.) Those flowers produce seedpods that are harvested for the spice coriander. The lower leaves of the plant, commonly called cilantro, are round with slightly scalloped edges. Coriander grows 2 to 3 feet tall.

Growing Guidelines

Coriander prefers sunny sites with well-drained soil. Sow the seeds directly in the garden about ½ inch deep after the danger of frost has passed. After the seedlings appear, thin them to 4 inches apart and keep them evenly moist. Make sure you don't over-fertilize this herb because too much nitrogen in the soil will produce a less-flavorful plant.

In the Kitchen

Coriander leaves have a bold taste that combines a strong sage flavor with a sharp hint of citrus. You can mince the fresh leaves and add them to foods such as salsa, or you can use them whole as a lacy garnish.

Coriander seeds are sweetly aromatic, with a slight hint of citrus. Whole or ground seeds add character to

- salad dressings
- chili sauce
- guacamole
- marinades
- cheese
- eggs

The flavor of coriander also combines nicely with beets, onions, potatoes, clams, oysters, and sausage.

Harvesting Hints

Harvest fresh coriander leaves as needed. Coriander seeds ripen and scatter quickly, so cut the entire plant as soon as the leaves and flowers turn brown. Tie the plants in bundles, and hang them upside down with a paper bag tied securely around the flowerheads to catch the seeds as they dry.

Trivia Tidbits

Greek and Roman doctors, including Hippocrates, made medicines from coriander, but it was also prized as a spice and as an ingredient in a Roman vinegar used to preserve meat. The Chinese used coriander as far back as the Han dynasty—207 B.C. to A.D. 220. At the time, it was thought that coriander had the power to make a person immortal.

Dill

(Anethum graveolens)

Dill is simple to grow and beautiful to look at, which is why you should add it to your garden. This annual herb grows in Zones 2 through 9 and looks like a smaller version of fennel, its relative. Dill can grow up to 3 feet tall and has pretty yellow flowers and feathery, blue-green leaves.

Growing Guidelines

Dill needs moist soil with good drainage and full sun. This herb doesn't transplant well, so you'll have the best luck if you sow the seeds directly in the ground in spring, after the danger of frost has passed.

(Make sure to weed diligently because small dill seedlings don't compete well against other plants.) When the seedlings are about 2 inches high, thin them so they're 10 to 12 inches apart. If you're growing dill mostly for the foliage, you can sow the seeds just 8 to 10 inches apart; do so every 3 weeks for a constant supply of dillweed.

If you're growing dill for the seeds, keep in mind that seeds may not be produced until the beginning of the plant's second year.

In the Kitchen

Dill has a pickle flavor. You can use its feathery leaves fresh in salads and as garnishes; use the seeds whole or ground in longer-cooking recipes. Dill is delicious paired with fish (especially salmon), as well as

- cabbage
- cucumbers
- potatoes
- cheese
- cream
- eggs
- lamb
- pork
- poultry

Dillweed is easiest to handle when it's frozen on its stem. Simply snip some off with scissors as needed, and put the rest back in the freezer.

Harvesting Hints

Once the plants are well established (about 8 to 10 weeks after sowing), you can begin clipping the leaves close to the stem. You'll have to use it soon because dillweed will last only a couple of days in the refrigerator before it droops and loses its flavor. Or, you can freeze the freshly picked leaves.

Harvest the seeds when the flower matures, anywhere from 2 to 3 weeks after blossoming (the seeds will be a light brown color). When you cut the stems, make sure you leave enough of the stem on so that you can tie the plants into a bunch and hang them in a dark place for drying.

Trivia Tidbits

The name dill comes from dilla, Norse for "to lull." Dill was believed to work as a charm against witches; mystics could combat an "evil eye" spell by carrying a bag of dried dill over the heart.

Fennel

(Foeniculum vulgare)

Fennel's filigreed leaves and small yellow flowers dance in the wind. This herb stands tall (about 4 feet high) to make a good border, or, when intermittently placed among shorter specimens, creates an unusual garden skyline. Fennel is a semihardy perennial, but most people grow it as an annual. It will grow in Zones 6 through 9.

Growing Guidelines

You can plant fennel seeds directly in the ground as soon as you can work the soil in spring. Plant the seeds about 6 inches apart in a rich, well-drained bed that gets full sun. (Make sure to plant fennel away from coriander, which will prevent fennel's seeds from forming.) Cover the seeds shallowly and keep the soil moist. For a continuous crop of fennel during the growing season, keep planting seeds every 2 to 3 weeks. (Note: One or two plants will probably produce plenty of leaves

Continued ➡

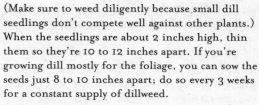

for your family so you may want to succession sow only if you're growing extra for friends.)

IN THE KITCHEN

If you like the taste of licorice, then fennel is for you. Use fresh leaves in salads and as lacy garnishes; you can eat the tender stems like celery. Use the seeds, whole or ground, to dress up breads, cakes, and cookies. Fennel also goes well with

- · beets
- · rice
- · potatoes
- · eggs
- · pickles
- · cheese
- · barley
- · fish

The leaves and seeds lend aroma and flalvor to herb butters, cheese spreads and salad dressings.

HARVESTING HINTS

Begin snipping the leaves once the plant is well established—about 8 to 10 weeks after planting the seed. Then just keep harvesting the leaves as you need them.

If you want to harvest the seeds, you'll need to keep a close eye on the plants so you'll notice when the seeds turn from yellowish green to brown. When that happens, use scissors to snip the entire seedhead and let it drop into a paper bag. Store the bag in a warm, dark place for further drying. Once the seeds are thoroughly dried, store them in glass jars.

TRIVIA TIDBITS

In medieval times, people kept a stash of fennel seeds handy to nibble on through long church services and on fast days; the seeds were considered to be an appetite suppressant.

Feverfew

(*Chrysanthemum parthenium*)

A member of the daisy family, feverfew sports small, white flowers with yellow centers. This herb looks similar to chamomile; you can tell them apart because feverfew stands up straight, while chamomile tends to bend over. Feverfew is a short-lived perennial that's often grown as an annual. It grows 2 to 3 feet tall—making it perfect for defining garden borders—and is hardy in Zones 4 to 9.

GROWING GUIDELINES

Feverfew prefers full sun and well-drained soil. In spring, after the danger of frost has passed, sow the seeds by scattering them on top of prepared soil and lightly taking them in. Once the seedlings have germinated (they do so pretty quickly), thin them to 12 inches apart. (Be on guard, though—feverfew is a profuse self-seeder and may spread beyond your garden.)

HARVESTING HINTS

Harvest feverfew's leaves before the plant blooms in summer. Pinch back or shear off the tops of the stems. Dry the leaves by spreading them in a single layer on a cloth or screen in the shade. Store dried leaves in an airtight container away from heat and light.

HEALING WITH FEVERFEW

True to its name, feverfew reduces fevers (its common name comes from the Latin word *febrifugio*, or "fever reducer") and is a mild sedative. Modern research has also shown that the regular use of feverfew reduces the frequency and severity of migraines and associated symptoms, such as nausea and vomiting. In addition, the herb's anti-inflammatory qualities may provide relief to arthritis sufferers.

TRIVIA TIDBITS

In its long history, this herb has been used as an ingredient in making sweets and wines; as an aromatic to ward off disease; and as an insect repellent. It was also used to treat infant colic, vertigo, arthritis, kidney stones, and constipation.

Garlic

(*Allium sotivum*)

Garlic's aromatic bulbs are a seasoning and a vegetable in one. Soft-neck types have tops that flop over as they dry, so they're best for braiding. Hardneck garlic has a stiff upright flowerstalk (which can grow to 2 feet high). All types of garlic are perennials grown as annuals.

GROWING GUIDELINES

Plant garlic in full sun in well-drained soil. You can plant in midfall or early spring as soon as the soil is workable. Although you can start garlic from bulbils, it's much faster and easier to plant cloves.

Set the cloves with the root end (the wider end) 1 to 2 inches deep, 6 to 8 inches apart. (If you're planting in fall, the cloves will produce shoots immediately, then become dormant until spring.) In spring, side-dress the plants with compost. Keep the soil evenly moist until the tops begin to die, then stop watering so the bulbs can mature.

IN THE KITCHEN

Garlic has a strong, oniony taste that livens up tomato sauce and pesto. (You can soften garlic's flavor by using it in recipes that require long, moist cooking, like stewing.) Other foods that are enhanced by garlic include

- · cheese spreads
- · pickles
- · meat
- · herb butters
- · poultry
- · herb vinegars

HARVESTING HINTS

Eventually, the tops of the garlic plants will begin to bend and turn brown. Garlic is ready to harvest when most (about 75 percent) of the leaves have turned brown. Pull fall-planted garlic in late June or early July; pull spring-planted garlic at the end of the season. Use a digging fork to lift garlic from the soil. Lay the whole plants in an airy, dark, dry spot for several weeks to cure. Then trim away leaves and brush off dirt.

Garlic keeps best if you store the bulbs in a cool, dark, dry spot.

TRIVIA TIDBITS

The Romans took garlic to strengthen them in battle because it was the "herb of Mars." (Mars was the Roman god of war.) European legend says that if a man chews on a garlic bulb during a footrace, no one will be able to get ahead of him. (And it's doubtful anyone would even want to draw close!)

Lavender

(*Lavandula angustifolia*)

Lavender has a classic fragrance that's reminiscent of days gone by—or at least of your grandma's house, where she had lavender sachets tucked into drawers. But despite its old-fashioned connotations, this perennial herb (it's hardy in Zones 5 to 8) is still quite popular today. And with good reason: Lavender smells great, works well in any garden setting (it can grow up to 30 inches tall), and has a myriad of uses.

GROWING GUIDELINES

This herb needs a sunny site with excellent drainage. (If your soil isn't well drained, you can amend it with compost and coarse gravel.) Lavender is difficult to start from seed because it needs a long time to germinate. So ask friends for cuttings or buy plants from your local garden center or from a mail-order supplier. Place plants 2 feet apart and water regularly for the next few weeks. Once established, though, lavender is very drought tolerant.

If you live in Zone 7 or colder, protect your lavender plants with a winter mulch of evergreen boughs to ensure strong new growth the following spring.

As it grows, lavender's stems can become woody. Keep your lavender looking its best by pruning it back by about half its height every 2 or 3 years in spring.

HARVESTING HINTS

If you're planning on drying lavender, harvest the flowers either when they first open or when they're full. To dry the flowers, spread them flat on paper or hang them in bunches in a warm, dry place, like an attic. Well-dried lavender flowers will remain aromatic for a long time.

HEALING WITH LAVENDER

In France and Spain, bruises and bites are treated with lavender compresses, while compresses of warm lavender tea are thought to relieve chest congestion.

TRIVIA TIDBITS

Up until World War I, lavender was used as a disinfectant for wounds.

Continued ➡

Lemon Balm

(*Melissa officinalis*)

Brush this perennial herb's leaves and your fingers will smell of lemon with a hint of mint. Hardy in Zones 5 to 9, lemon balm produces tiny white or light blue flowers (much loved by bees) in May or June. The flowers bloom throughout the summer, and the plant grows to about 2 feet high.

GROWING GUIDELINES

Lemon balm isn't particular about soil or site (in fact, it can become invasive if left unattended). It prefers average soil in full sun, but will make do in partial shade. Sow seed directly in the ground about 12 to 24 inches apart in early spring or fall. When the plant becomes overgrown, dig up and divide the roots, then replant the divisions in either spring or fall.

IN THE KITCHEN

Fresh lemon balm leaves make a relaxing hot tea; you can also toss a few sprigs of lemon balm into cool summer punches or iced tea. In addition to beverages, toss whole or chopped fresh leaves into

- green salads
- marinated vegetables
- fruit salads
- poultry stuffing

Lemon balm also teams well with asparagus, beans, broccoli, corn, freshly ground black pepper, olives, lamb, and shellfish.

HARVESTING HINTS

If you want to use lemon balm immediately, pick the leaves at their peak of flavor and fragrance. For later use, harvest the leaves just before the plants begin to bloom, tie the stems in small bundles, and hang them in an airy spot out of direct sunlight to dry.

TRIVIA TIDBITS

The Greek physician Dioscorides put lemon balm on scorpion and dog bites, and then he would drop some more into wine for the patient to drink. And beekeepers used to rub lemon balm inside a hive to encourage a new swarm to stay.

Lemon Verbena

(*Aloysia triphylla*)

Lemon verbena is a deciduous woody shrub that has tiny lavender flowers and attractive foliage. Simply brush by this plant and you'll release its sweet, lemony fragrance. It's only hardy in Zones 9 and 10, but it works well as a container plant—which means you can still grow it if you live where winters are cold; you just have to bring it indoors. Lemon verbena grows 10 to 15 feet high outdoors in warm climates and up to 5 feet high in cooler climates or indoors. It flowers in late summer and fall.

IN THE KITCHEN

Lemon verbena is most often used to make a delicately flavored tea. You can also use this herb wherever you want to add a touch of lemon, such as in rice, pound cake, or zucchini bread. Fresh or dried leaves also brighten the taste of

- vegetable marinades
- jams
- puddings
- salad dressings
- fish
- beverages
- poultry

Fresh lemon verbena leaves are tough, though, so be sure to remove them from marinades, beverages, and salad dressings before serving.

GROWING GUIDELINES

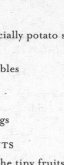

Unless you live in a very mild climate, you'll probably grow lemon verbena in a container. This plant does best in rich, moist (but not soggy) soil and full sun. Lemon verbena also likes a lot of nutrients, so feed your plant regularly with fish emulsion. (Remember: This herb is deciduous, so don't be concerned when it loses its leaves in fall.) Cut the plant back halfway in midsummer and again in the beginning of fall to keep it bushy.

You can take your container-grown lemon verbena outdoors during the warmer months. If you choose to expose your plant to the good life outside, make sure you place the container on top of a hard surface, such as tile or bricks. That way, the roots won't escape from the pot and take hold in the ground.

HARVESTING HINTS

You can harvest sprigs of lemon verbena leaves almost all year long.

TRIVIA TIDBITS

Lemon verbena hasn't figured as an important medicinal herb, probably in part due to its late introduction to Europe (it's native to Chile and Argentina). It has, however, been used in folk medicine to aid digestion and to reduce fevers.

Lovage

(*Levisticum officinale*)

This perennial herb tastes like celery, but it is a lot easier to grow. The plant can reach 5 feet tall, making it a large, dramatic specimen for your garden. Another plus for lovage is its cold tolerance; it's hardy to Zone 3.

Foliage

Seed Head

Seed

GROWING GUIDELINES

Lovage does best in moist, fertile, well-drained soil in a site that receives full sun to partial shade. Since you'll probably only want one lovage plant, purchase a seedling from your local nursery or ask a friend for a cutting. Whether you use seedlings or divisions, set them at least 2 feet apart. Wait 2 years before harvesting the roots or stems. Also, side-dress plants with a rich compost each spring, and keep them well watered during dry spells.

IN THE KITCHEN

As mentioned above, lovage leaves, stems, and seeds all taste like celery. You can use the leaves fresh in salads and fresh or dried in soups, stews, and sauces. Chop and add the stems to salads; you can also cook and puree them. The seeds, whole or ground, work well in pickling brines, cheese spreads, salads, salad dressings, and sauces. Lovage also enhances

- potatoes (especially potato salad)
- tomatoes
- steamed vegetables
- rice
- chicken
- poultry stuffings

HARVESTING HINTS

Gather seeds when the tiny fruits begin to open, which means they're ripe.

Cut the leaves or stems whenever you want to use them. To dry leaves and stems, hang them upside down in a warm, shady spot, like an attic. When dry, store the leaves and stems in tightly sealed, opaque containers because light will quickly yellow this herb.

TRIVIA TIDBITS

Lovage was very popular in the Middle Ages, when people grew it in kitchen gardens. Early herbalists recommended lovage as a diuretic, and occasionally as a cure for rheumatism, jaundice, malaria, sore throats, and kidney stones.

Marjoram

(*Origanum majorana*)

Marjoram is a gentle, subtly perfumed, calming herb whose fragrance livens recipes, potpourris, and other crafts. A tender perennial, marjoram will overwinter in Zones 9 and 10, but it is usually grown as an annual. It grows to about 1 foot tall.

GROWING GUIDELINES

This herb prefers full sun and light, well-drained soil. Because marjoram seeds are small and slow to germinate, you'll need to start them indoors 6 to 8 weeks before your last expected spring frost. When you transplant the plants to the garden, space them about 8 inches apart.

In the fall, dig plants and transfer them to containers for winter harvest indoors. Replant them again in spring.

IN THE KITCHEN

Marjoram tastes something like a mild oregano, with a hint of balsam. This herb is especially good with beef, roast poultry, green vegetables, eggs, potatoes, squash, and tomatoes. You can also add it to

- stews
- marinades
- dressings
- herb butters
- soups
- stuffings
- flavored vinegars and oils
- cheese spreads

Experiment and pair marjoram with other herbs, too. It complements basil, bay, garlic, onion, and thyme.

HARVESTING HINTS

Begin harvesting marjoram 5 to 6 weeks after transplanting into your garden, or when the plants are growing vigorously. You can keep harvesting marjoram to use fresh as you need it. You might also want to dry some; unlike some other herbs, marjoram retains a lot of its flavor when dried. Dry it away from sunlight to preserve both color and flavor. When dried, rub the stems on a screen to

Continued ➡

shred the leaves, discard the stems, and store the shredded leaves in airtight containers.

TRIVIA TIDBITS

The Greeks called marjoram "joy of the mountains" and used it at weddings and funerals and to cure rheumatism.

Mints

(Mentha spp.)

Mint seems to be a good antidote to hot summer days, when you need something cool and refreshing from your garden. And when it comes to growing mint, you have a lot of flavors to choose from: apple, lemon, orange, pineapple, peppermint, and spearmint, to name just a few. Most mints are tough perennials, so they're easy herbs for beginners. They'll grow in Zones 5 to 9, and can reach up to 2 feet high.

GROWING GUIDELINES

Plant mints in full sun or partial shade in rich, moist, well-drained soil. Mint often doesn't come true from seed, so ask a friend for cuttings or visit your local garden center for seedlings.

Although mint is an easy herb to grow, it can spread aggressively—and then you'll have a difficult time getting rid of it. To prevent mint from spreading, plant it in 5-gallon containers with holes punched in the bottom for drainage.

Frequent cutting will keep mints at their prettiest. It encourages stems to branch out and makes for lusher, healthier plants. In late fall, after your final harvest, cut your mint plants to the ground. This eliminates overwintering sites for mint pests, such as spider mites and aphids.

HARVESTING HINTS

Fresh is best when it comes to mint. And because mint is such a tough plant, you can start harvesting it almost as soon as it comes up in spring. Harvest heavily and continuously to encourage new growth, then stop harvesting 2 to 4 weeks before fall frosts.

HEALING WITH MINT

Of all the mints, peppermint is the one that has the most medicinal effects. You can use it to calm an upset stomach or relieve gas. Peppermint may also help relieve menstrual cramps.

TRIVIA TIDBITS

Beginning in the eighteenth century, mint became an important medicinal herb. Japanese mint was thought to aid fertility, while a remedy for mad dog bites called for combining peppermint or spearmint with salt and applying it to the wound.

Oreganos

(Origanum spp.)

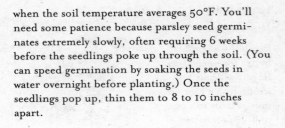

Tomatoes—and subsequently, tomato sauce— would only be half as popular without the biting flavor of oregano. This perennial herb is hardy in Zones 5 to 9 and grows to about 2 feet tall. Flavor varies with variety, so you might want to grow several different kinds to find the one (or two or three) that you like best.

GROWING GUIDELINES

Grow oregano in full sun and well-drained, rich garden soil. Starting with plants is probably the best way to grow this herb because seedlings vary in flavor. (Starting with plants also allows you to taste before planting.) Space the plants 1 to 2 feet apart, and keep mulch away from the stems to promote air circulation and prevent disease problems. Divide the plants every 3 to 5 years.

IN THE KITCHEN

Oregano has a hot, peppery flavor and enhances lots of food, including omelets, frittatas, and quiches. Oregano also adds dimension to

- eggplant
- mushrooms
- onions
- potatoes
- zucchini
- roasted bell peppers
- marinated vegetables
- beef
- pork
- poultry
- yeast breads

And, of course, oregano's flavor combines well with garlic, parsley, thyme, and olive oil.

HARVESTING HINTS

You can harvest fresh leaves all season, as long as the plants are growing vigorously. Stop harvesting 2 to 4 weeks before the first expected frost; dry the remainder of your harvest so that you can enjoy the flavor of this herb all winter long.

TRIVIA TIDBITS

Many of oregano's early uses were medicinal, rather than culinary. For example, the Greeks made dressings from oregano leaves and placed them on sores and aching muscles, while some Roman scholars recommended oregano dressings for scorpion and spider bites. And after oregano was introduced to North America by European colonists, doctors used oil of oregano to help ease the pain of toothaches.

Parsley

(Petroselinum crispum)

Parsley really has a lot more to offer than just being the token garnish on a plate of steak or fish. This herb is an excellent addition to most recipes, is rich in vitamins and minerals (A, C, calcium, and iron), and fights bad breath (the chlorophyll it contains is a natural breath sweetener). Parsley is a biennial grown as an annual; it will grow in Zones 5 through 9. You can choose from two parsley varieties: curly leaf and flat-leaved.

GROWING GUIDELINES

Parsley grows best in rich, moist, well-drained soil in full sun to partial shade. Sow seeds outdoors

when the soil temperature averages 50°F. You'll need some patience because parsley seed germinates extremely slowly, often requiring 6 weeks before the seedlings poke up through the soil. (You can speed germination by soaking the seeds in water overnight before planting.) Once the seedlings pop up, thin them to 8 to 10 inches apart.

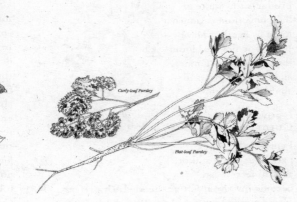

IN THE KITCHEN

Parsley has a gentle flavor and works especially well at blending the flavors around it. You can use both the curly and flat-leaved varieties in cooking, although flat-leaves parsley is more flavorful. You can add parsley to most foods (except sweets), including

- salsa
- tabbouleh
- ham
- grilled meats
- poultry

HARVESTING HINTS

You can begin harvesting parsley as soon as the plants are growing vigorously. Snip individual outer stems from the plants; they'll continue to produce new growth all season long.

Parsley dries and freezes well. If you dry it, crush it by hand after it's completely dry and store it in an airtight container.

TRIVIA TIDBITS

In ancient Greece, parsley was used in funeral ceremonies and to make wreaths for graves. Parsley was also placed in wreaths given to winning athletes because the Greeks believed that the god Hercules had chosen parsley for his garlands.

Rosemary

(Rosmarinus officinalis)

Rosemary is an herb that's not just for the kitchen spice rack. You can use rosemary to make sachets for your drawers or a rinse for your hair. And rosemary oil adds a pleasant piney scent to soaps, creams, lotions, and toilet waters.

Rosemary grows in shrubby clumps of branching stems covered with wonderfully fragrant, needlelike, green leaves. This herb is a half-hardy perennial that's an evergreen in Zones 8 through 9. In Zones 6 and 7, you can grow the hardy variety 'Arp', or you can grow rosemary as a container plant that's overwintered indoors.

Plants can reach 5 to 6 feet tall where they're hardy outdoors; container plants reach 1 to 3 feet tall.

Continued ➡

In the Kitchen

Rosemary is pungent and somewhat piney. Its flavor harmonizes with poultry, fish, lamb, beef, and pork—particularly when these foods are roasted. Gentle soups benefit from rosemary's robust character, as do marinades, salad dressings, and cream sauces. Rosemary also enhances

- mushrooms
- tomatoes
- peas
- lentils
- spinach
- cheese
- squash
- eggs

You can use both the flowers and the leaves for garnishing and cooking. Crush or mince the spiky leaves before sprinkling over or running into foods.

Growing Guidelines

This aromatic herb grows best in well-drained, sandy, or gravelly soil and full sun. Seedlings grow very slowly, so you'll want to buy plants and start with them for fastest results. Space plants 1 to 2 feet apart (if you plan to grow your rosemary as a perennial in the garden, space the plants a good 4 feet apart).

Harvesting Hints

You can continuously harvest rosemary as long as the plants are growing. Strip the needles from the stems, then chop them before using. Rosemary also dries and freezes well. Freeze whole sprigs, and when you need some leaves, slide your thumb and index finger down a sprig, taking off as many leaves as you need.

Trivia Tidbits

In ancient Greece, students wore rosemary garlands in their hair while studying for exams because they believed rosemary would help improve their memory. In the Middle Ages, men and women placed rosemary sprigs under their pillows to ward off demons and prevent bad dreams.

Sage

(Salvia officinalis)

Garden Sage

Purple Sage

Variegated Sage

If you can grow only one herb in your garden, you might want to make it sage. This shrubby perennial (about 2 feet tall) is an herb gardener's delight. The plants grow quickly without becoming invasive, and the flowers attract hummingbirds and beneficial insects. Sage is an intensely aromatic culinary herb that's hardy to Zone 5, but it will often survive in Zone 4 with winter protection.

Growing Guidelines

Sage thrives in average, well-drained soil in full sun. You can buy plants or grow your own from seed. If you grow your own, start the seeds indoors

6 to 8 weeks before your last frost date. The seeds should germinate within 3 weeks at 60° to 70°F. Transplant the seedlings outdoors after all danger of frost has passed. Space the plants 18 to 24 inches apart in the garden.

In the Kitchen

Sage leaves have a lemony, pungent taste and are the perfect complement to poultry, stuffings, and sausages, as well as

- artichokes
- potatoes
- asparagus
- squash
- eggplant
- tomatoes
- onions

You can add dried sage leaves to dishes, too. A bit of dried, crumpled sage, for example, perks up soft cheeses and lends an earthy tone to breads, especially flat breads like Italian focaccia.

Harvesting Hints

You can harvest sage leaves as long as the plants are actively growing. Sage leaves also dry and freeze well. To dry, snip the leaves from branches you've removed, discard the stems, and spread the leaves on cloth or paper in a dark, dry place. Store in an airtight container.

Trivia Tidbits

Native Americans used sage as a medicine, mixing it with bear grease for a salve they claimed would cure skin sores. They also used sage as a leafy, disposable toothbrush.

Savory, Summer

(Satureja hortensis)

Summer savory is an annual that's highly aromatic and has been used to enhance the flavor of food for over 2,000 years. It has tiny white or pale pink flowers and grows to 1½ feet high.

Summer Savory

Growing Guidelines

This herb likes full sun and average soil and is easy to grow from seed. If you start summer savory from seed, keep in mind that it germinates quickly—so plan your planting accordingly. You can sow seeds no more than ½ inch deep in flats and transplant later, or plant directly into the garden. Space plants about 10 inches apart and keep them well weeded and well watered. If the plants start to flop over, mound soil slightly around their bases.

In the Kitchen

Summer savory tastes like peppery thyme and blends well with most flavors, helping to bring them together. It's popular in teas, herb butters, and flavored vinegars, as well as with

- asparagus
- squash
- garlic
- lentils
- onions
- soups
- peas
- eggs

This herb is also a nice accompaniment to fish. You can make a fish marinade by mincing fresh savory leaves and combining them with garlic, bay, and lemon juice. Or, add minced fresh savory to mayonnaise and serve it with poached fish.

Harvesting Hints

You can begin harvesting summer savory as soon as the plants get about 6 inches tall. If you keep snip-

ping the tops of the branches, you'll be able to extend the harvest. When the plants insist on flowering, cut the whole plants and lay them on screening or paper in a warm, shady place. After they've dried (in a couple of days), strip the leaves from the stems and store the leaves in airtight jars. You can also collect the seeds as soon as they start to brown. Then place them in an airtight jar along with a desiccant (such as silica gel), and store the jar in a cool, dry place.

Trivia Tidbits

The Romans used savory extensively in their cooking, often flavoring vinegars with it. And the poet Virgil suggested growing savory near beehives because of the pleasant-tasting honey it produced.

Scented Geraniums

(Pelargonium spp.)

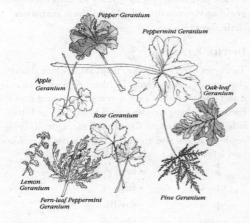

Rose Geranium

Apple, apricot, coconut, lemon, lime, peppermint, rose, strawberry—they sound like specialty lollipop flavors that you might find on a sweetshop counter. But these are just a few of the fragrances available in the amazing repertoire of scented geraniums.

These herbs aren't really geraniums at all, although their leaves look very similar to true geraniums. Scented geraniums are tender perennials that are hardy only in Zone 10. Some varieties can grow up to 3 feet high, while others are compact and work well in baskets. You can enjoy their fragrance in the garden, or dry the leaves and flowers to make sachets and potpourris.

Pepper Geranium

Peppermint Geranium

Apple Geranium

Rose Geranium

Oak-leaf Geranium

Lemon Geranium

Fern-leaf Peppermint Geranium

Pine Geranium

Growing Guidelines

You'll have the best success with scented geraniums if you start with plants or cuttings from a friend. If you choose cuttings, take them in spring or summer, using a sharp knife just below the node where a leaf grows from the stem. Place cuttings in clean sand, and allow enough space around them so that air can circulate freely. Keep them well watered (but not soggy), and in 2 to 3 weeks you should have little plants that you can transplant. Expose the plants to the outdoors only after the threat of frost is past.

In the Kitchen

You can use the leaves of rose geraniums to flavor sugar. Simply alternate layers of sugar and leaves in a mason jar, and place the jar where it will catch the sun for about 2 weeks. Then sift the leaves out

Continued ➡

and you'll have rose-flavored sugar. You can also use some varieties of scented geraniums to flavor

- tea
- jelly
- biscuits
- pound cake

HARVESTING HINTS

Pick leaves just as the flowers begin to appear—preferably on a sunny, dry, day—for maximum oil content. Dry leaves in the shade to preserve their fragrance.

TRIVIA TIDBITS

Scented geraniums arrived in America during the colonial days and became popular rather quickly. Thomas Jefferson, in fact, brought several varieties to the White House with him.

Tarragon

(*Artemisia dracunculus* var. *sativa*)

Gardeners grow this aromatic, hardy perennial for its distinctively flavored leaves. Although tarragon isn't what most people would consider a visually stunning plant, it's definitely worth growing because it's such a versatile culinary herb. Tarragon reaches 2 feet tall and will grow in Zones 4 through 8.

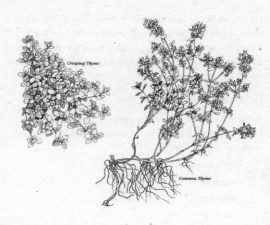

GROWING GUIDELINES

French tarragon needs full sun or partial shade and loose, rich, well-drained soil. Start by buying plants (French tarragon doesn't produce viable seed), or get divisions or cuttings from established herb gardens. Space the plants 1 to 2 feet apart. To get the best flavor from the foliage, remove the flower stems when they form. Divide plants every 3 to 5 years to keep them growing vigorously and to help them maintain their flavor.

IN THE KITCHEN

Tarragon offers a strong, unusual licorice flavor that stands out in cooked dishes. As a general rule, don't add this herb with a heavy hand, and don't cook it too long or else you'll bring out its bitter side. (For maximum flavor, add tarragon to long-cooking soups and stews during the last 15 minutes.) Just a few of the foods tarragon enhances are

- artichokes
- beef and pork
- leeks
- fish
- peas
- shellfish
- potatoes
- poultry
- rice

HARVESTING HINTS

Harvest the foliage continuously as long as the plants are actively growing. If you want to store fresh tarragon, freeze it or preserve it in white vinegar (tarragon doesn't dry well).

You can also use this herb in flavored vinegars, herbed butters, cream sauces, and soups and with cheeses, eggs, sour cream, and yogurt.

TRIVIA TIDBITS

Tarragon was thought to prevent fatigue, so pilgrims of the Middle Ages put sprigs of it in their shoes before beginning long trips on foot.

Thyme

(*Thymus vulgaris*)

Thyme is an incredibly useful herb. You can use it in recipes or as a cough suppressant; it attracts beneficial insects, like bees; and it grows just as well on a windowsill as it does in your garden beds.

This perennial herb will grow in Zones 5 through 9 and reaches about 1 foot high. Although thyme comes in both upright and prostrate forms, you should choose upright varieties for using in cooking because low-growing types are often gritty with rain-splashed soil.

GROWING GUIDELINES

A well-drained site with sandy soil in full sun to partial shade is ideal for thyme. Because thyme seed is rarely true to type, your best bet is to start with plants or divisions. Space new plants 12 inches apart.

Once established, thyme is easy to keep looking good and producing well. Prune it lightly as needed to maintain its attractive shape.

IN THE KITCHEN

The bittersweet taste of thyme seems right for almost any dish, from vegetables and meats to soups and casseroles. Specifically, thyme works well with

- corn
- rice
- peas
- cheese
- sweet peppers
- eggs
- tomatoes

Its flavor also blends well with lemon, garlic, and basil.

HARVESTING HINTS

For fresh use, pick individual leaves or small sprigs as needed. If you want to dry thyme, strip the leaves from the stems and place them on a thin screen to dry before storing. Thyme also freezes well—just make sure you use an airtight container.

TRIVIA TIDBITS

From the fifteenth through the seventeenth centuries, thyme was used to combat the plagues that swept over Europe. And as recently as World War I, thyme's essential oil served as an antiseptic on the battlefields.

Herbs the Low-Maintenance Way

Barbara W. Ellis, Joan Benjamin, Deborah L. Martin

Herbs are naturals in your low-maintenance garden. Whatever your yard is like—hot and dry, or moist and shady—there are tough herbs just waiting to go to work for you. And herbs don't just stand around looking great—nothing puts life into food like your own freshly snipped herbs.

So stop struggling with finicky plants and set your sights on herbs instead. This section gives you some no-nonsense tips for succeeding with herbs and suggests specific herbs for challenging landscape sites. You'll also find suggestions for where to plant herbs for minimum maintenance and easy ways to start your own plants.

No-Nonsense Tips for Growing Herbs

It's hard to imagine plants that are easier to grow than herbs. All they ask for is six or more hours of sun per day and average to good garden soil, and they're on their way. Hardy perennial herbs, like garlic chives, mint, and thyme, are probably the easiest herbs to grow. Once planted, they come back year after year and eventually establish large attractive clumps. Annual herbs must be replanted each year but are well worth the effort. Use these tips to get your herb garden off to a great start.

Start with transplants. If you only need one or two plants (which is plenty for most herbs), transplants are your best bet. They'll have a head start on weeds, and you won't have to spend time thinning seedlings.

Well-drained soil means no-fuss herbs. If there's one key to growing healthy herbs, it's providing them with well-drained soil. Whatever type of soil you have, before you plant turn plenty of compost or other organic material into the planting site. Organic matter will improve drainage in waterlogged clay soils and hold water in sandy ones. You can also grow your herbs in raised beds or containers.

1. Bee balm (*Monarda didyma*)
2. Rose geraniums
3. Purple sage
4. Lemon thyme
5. Parsley
6. Basil
7. Yarrow (*Achillea* x 'Moonshine')
8. Garlic chives
9. Calendulas

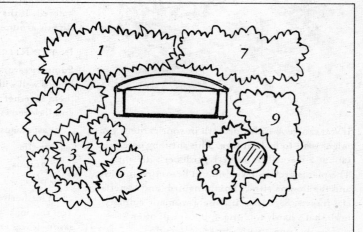

Continued →

Hold the manure. Herbs don't need rich soil or fertilizer to grow well. In fact, too-rich soil just encourages rampant, less flavorful growth. A little compost mulch every few years is all the feeding most herbs require.

Use your herbs. Regular trimming keeps new tender growth coming, so clip all season. If you have more herbs than you can cook with, use the aromatic clippings as mulch.

Give perennials a fall haircut. Regular harvesting should take care of all the pruning perennial herbs need. If they look scraggly at the end of the season, cut them back by about a third and remove old or dead wood. Check again in spring and remove any dead wood. After three to five years, many perennial herbs lose vigor and should be divided or replaced.

It Pays to Be Choosy When It Comes to Culinary Herbs

Not all herb plants are created equal. Use these suggestions so you don't get burned with a tasteless look-alike.

Grow from seeds. Annual herbs are easy to grow from seed, and you can expect good results from most any seed packet. Growing perennials from seed is more of a gamble; in general, it's easier and more reliable to start with transplants. Don't try to grow tarragon or oregano from seeds at all since these seed-grown plants are usually flavorless.

Sniff before you buy. Put potential purchases to the rub-'n'-sniff test. Rub a leaf between your fingers; if it doesn't have a good, strong aroma like the herb you're looking for, don't waste your time and money on it. This test also works for seedlings: When you thin, leave the most fragrant plants.

Buy smart. For the best selection, look for specialty growers in your area. Or order from one of the many mail-order herb nurseries.

Grow an Easy-Care, Elegant Herb Garden

A formal herb garden can take hours of fussing and trimming to keep it looking its best. With a little planning, you can keep all the elegance and eliminate all the work by trading in tightly clipped shapes for soft, natural ones. This garden features fragrant herbs that will stay neat and create waves of color with little or no pruning. To create your own fragrant refuge, select and arrange plants by height to create wavelike clumps.

This planting mixes annuals and perennials in a variety of heights and forms. Bee balm and yarrow provide a backdrop for the bench. Calendulas and garlic chives bloom under the birdbath, while rose geraniums, parsley, purple sage, lemon thyme, and piccola basil make a pleasant tapestry of color and form on the opposite side.

Don't Fuss with an Herb Garden, Grow Your Herbs with Vegetables

Why take care of two separate gardens when one will do? A super-easy way to grow annual herbs is to simply plant them in rows with your annual vegetables. There's room in most vegetable gardens for perennial herbs such as sage and chives, too: Plant them with your other perennial crops such as asparagus or rhubarb, away from the path of the tiller.

Plant a Drain Tile Herb Garden

Large ceramic drain tiles are great containers for herbs. Mix and match heights for a multi-tiered effect, or select all one height. Like any other type of container, they're a great way to grow herbs on a poorly drained site. Or consider planting invasive herbs such as mint in them to keep them out of everything else.

For best results, bury the base of each drain tile about 6 inches in the soil. For an easier and faster result with tiles under 1½ feet tall, just set the tiles directly on the soil. Be sure to level the site so each tile is stable.

Next, fill the tiles with potting mix and plant. Choose a mix designed for large containers or mix equal parts houseplant soil and perlite or vermiculite. Stir in a cup of compost per tile and water well to settle the potting mix. Leave 1 inch of headroom below the rim to make watering easy. Since containers dry out more quickly than inground plantings, water often so the mix never dries out. Monthly feeding with 2 tablespoons fish emulsion and 1 tablespoon seaweed per gallon of water will keep your drain tile garden growing strongly.

Simple Steps for Propagating Herbs

Propagating herbs is easy and rewarding, whether you need to divide a clump of herbs that's gotten too large or want to share a plant with a neighbor. For no-fuss propagation, stick to division and layering. Here's what you need to know to master these easy techniques.

Easy herb division. The best time to divide herbs is in early spring just before plants start to grow, but you can also wait until fall. To make replanting easier on your herbs, wait for a cloudy, windless day to work. Plants will be less stressed and will recover quickly. It helps to protect the newly divided plants from strong sunlight and provide extra water for a few days.

When you divide, dig up the entire clump with a garden fork or spade. Plants like oregano and mint form dense mats that are easiest to divide with a sharp shovel. For clump-forming herbs like chives, lift and water the clumps well. Then pull them apart with your hands and replant; each new clump should have three to five small bulbs to make a strong plant.

For an easy, no-dig approach to division, look for rooted sections around the edges of a clump, slice them off with a trowel, and pot them up or transplant them.

Layering. An easy way to root woody herbs like sage and lavender is to encourage them to form new roots through a process called layering. In early summer, select two or three branches near the base of the mother plant that are long enough to lay on the ground. Bend them over and strip the leaves off where the stems touch the soil. Press each stem firmly into the soil, anchor it with a U-shaped metal pin made from a piece of clothes hanger, and cover the pinned stem with soil. Keep the covering soil moist all season and you should have rooted plants to dig up, cut off the mother plant, and transplant in the fall.

Easy Ways to Hold Onto Just-Picked Flavor

Stocking your kitchen with garden-fresh herbs for the winter doesn't have to take much of your precious time. Just use the tips below.

Strip the leaves later. Dry bunches of herbs through the season in a warm, dry place. Use rubber bands to bundle the bunches. Straightened-out paper clips make handy hangers for bundles. Stuff dry bunches of herbs into large airtight containers and label them. You can strip the herbs from the stalks in the fall when you have more time. To retain flavor, don't crumble the dried leaves until ready to use in cooking.

Make herb cubes for next-to-fresh flavor. Juicy leaves like basil freeze easier than they dry. Basil retains better flavor when it's frozen, too. To make herb cubes, puree leaves in the blender with enough water to make a slurry. Pour the slurry into ice cube trays and freeze. Pop out the cubes and store in plastic bags. Add herb cubes to soups and stews as needed.

Freeze leaves whole for fast flavor. If you're really short of time, strip leaves from stems, pack them in self-closing bags, and freeze. Be sure to label frozen herbs—they'll all look the same once they're frozen.

Quick and Tasty Salads

Herbs look as good as they taste, so why hide them in the backyard? For an ornamental and edible salad bar right outside your door, try growing sage, garlic chives, basil, marjoram, tarragon, and other herbs next to greens like lettuce, chard, and arugula.

Edible flowers such as nasturtiums add color to the design—and your salads, too. To make your garden as convenient as it is attractive, choose a handy location, such as just outside the front door. That way you can easily step outside and harvest salad greens and herbs just minutes before mealtime.

Sit Back and Watch These Herbs Plant Themselves

Instead of direct seeding, thinning and fussing every year, let herbs replant themselves. Plant them once in an out-of-the-way place and each year let some of the flowers go to seed.

To get your reseeding patch started, wait until the soil warms up and prepare a seedbed outdoors where the plants are to grow. Then sow the seed and keep the area moist until the seeds pop up.

Each year, let some of the plants go to seed for a crop in fall and/or the following spring. Don't pile a lot of mulch over the seeds or they won't germinate when the weather cools off in late summer. This technique is also good for fussy herbs like angelica that only grow from just-ripened seed.

Cooking with Herbs

Claire Kowalchik and William H. Hylton

If the secret to your favorite recipe for tomato sauce is a predominance of basil and your neighbor swears only by oregano, which recipe is correct? Both, of course, because the seasoning and flavoring of food with herbs and spices is mostly a matter of personal taste. We choose harmonious flavors by tasting and smelling as we cook. The choice between basil and oregano can depend on the sweetness of the tomatoes; whether they're fresh, frozen, or canned; if the sauce will be served hot or cold; what food will be served with the sauce; and what sort of mood you're in.

So if seasoning is in the taste buds of the beholder, why bother at all with a culinary section? Because of basics. By acquainting yourself with or refreshing your knowledge of how to use herbs, classic combinations, storage methods, and individual flavor personalities, you'll become a more skillful and creative cook.

General Techniques and Preservation

The following tips and suggestions shouldn't be regarded as the last word on using herbs in cooking. Be sure to check the entries on individual herbs for additional ideas and tips.

Continued ➡

Using fresh herbs: Some say it started in California at restaurants like Spago and Chez Panisse. New Yorkers claim it began in the Village and spread from there, and others say James Beard had been doing it for years.

Regardless of where it started, any red-blooded lover of food has realized that there's a new culinary aroma in the air, and that aroma is herbal. In restaurants, markets, and in the home, fresh herbs are becoming commonplace. They're being sprinkled, pureed, and sautéed with everything from appetizers to desserts.

In fact, in many recipes, fresh herbs are taking center stage. For instance, press fresh marjoram into the flesh of fish before a quick grilling and the beautiful pattern, aroma, and taste that the marjoram offers will outperform any sauce.

Or think of pesto, the popular herb paste. We used to make it for pasta and only when we could gather enough fresh basil. Now we create pestos with oregano, dill, or coriander leaf and the medium with which we use them (chicken, fish, pasta, or vegetables) gets second billing.

Because fresh herbs are inspiring, they will continue to sprout up in a variety of recipes and cooking styles. And because cooking is an ongoing, creative process, fresh herbs will continue to be enjoyed by a growing and eager audience.

Grating, Grinding and Crushing

An electric spice grinder is very handy for grinding whole spices. Small spice graters for whole nutmeg or allspice are useful and also come in handy for grating lemon and orange peel. For crushing herbs and spices and blending them into other ingredients, a mortar and pestle are very efficient.

If you use a blender to grind spices and herbs, try this method: A pint canning jar with a standard-size mouth will fit perfectly into many blender bases. Just put the spices in the jar, place the blade, rubber, and screw bottom of the blender container onto the jar as you would a lid. Turn the jar upside down, place in the blender base, and proceed with grinding the spices.

To serve four people with a sauce, soup, stew, or sauté, use about 2 teaspoons of minced fresh herbs. To reach the fullest aroma, rub the leaves between your hands, then mince them using a sharp knife or by snipping them with kitchen shears. Mince large amounts of herbs in a food processor.

Whole fresh leaves should be rubbed between your hands before adding to marinades, soups, stews, and punches. The amount of leaves to add will vary depending on their size, but use the 2-teaspoons-for-4-servings rule and try to visualize how many whole leaves will make that amount.

For the best flavor in long-cooking foods like soups and stews, add fresh herbs during the last 20 minutes or so of cooking.

Conversely, fresh herbs may not have a chance to release their flavors in uncooked foods like salad dressings and marinades or during microwaving. Be sure to taste these foods before serving since it may be necessary to add more herbs.

Tips for keeping fresh herbs fresh: Bouquets of fresh herbs can be set into jars filled with an inch or two of water, covered loosely with plastic wrap, and refrigerated. They'll last this way for about two weeks.

Smaller sprigs of herbs should be wrapped in paper towels, sealed in plastic bags, and placed in the crisper drawer of the refrigerator, where they'll last for about two weeks. Be sure the leaves are completely dry, or brown spots may develop.

Using dried herbs: Although this is the most common condition for culinary herbs, the common *collection* is changing. Where once our staples were bay leaves, dried oregano, and cinnamon, our culinary exploration is encouraging us to reach out.

We now own saffron for our fiestas and file for our gumbos. Dried seeds like coriander and cardamom and dried roots like ginger and horseradish are now the norm for the well-stocked, creative cupboard.

Herbs preserve most flavorfully when they're picked (1) before they flower, and (2) early in the morning just after the dew has dried. Always use plants that are healthy and free from dark spots and other imperfections.

Generally use about 1 teaspoon of dried herbs to serve four people, or about half the amount you would use of fresh. Smell the herbs before using them to make sure they're aromatic. Then rub them between your hands or grind them coarsely in a spice grinder, coffee grinder, or with a mortar and pestle. Use them immediately. Dried herbs can also be steeped in warm stock or other liquid, to cover, before adding them to recipes. This will enhance their flavors. Remember to taste, and, if necessary, adjust the flavor before serving.

Tips for drying herbs: Herbs may, of course, be dried in commercial dryers. But if you don't have one, there are lots of alternatives. For starters, use your oven on its lowest setting. Spread the herbs on cookie sheets, set the sheets in the oven, and leave the oven door ajar to help encourage circulation. Stir and check the herbs occasionally. They're dry when the leaves crumble when pinched and rubbed.

Bouquets of herbs can be hung to dry. Choose an airy, dry place like an attic, and hang the herbs upside down. Tie a paper bag over the bouquet to keep it from the light and to catch falling herbs. The bouquet may take up to two weeks to dry, but check its progress daily.

Microwaving is another alternative. Start with a clear, sunny day, because in humid weather the herbs may reabsorb moisture when removed from the microwave. Brush soil from the leaves and stems with a stiff paintbrush. Then place about a cup of herbs in a single layer between paper towels, and microwave on high for about three minutes. (Delicate herbs like thyme should be turned every 30 seconds.) If the herbs aren't completely dry after three minutes, reset the timer for 20 seconds, and start the microwave again. Don't let the herbs get too hot, or they'll taste scorched. They're ready when they feel brittle and rattle when you shake the paper towels, or when the leaves pull easily from the stem.

Herbs like parsley, coriander leaf, and rosemary dry well in the refrigerator. Simply place an unwashed bouquet in a paper (not plastic) bag. Close the bag and leave it in the refrigerator for about a month. The bouquet will be surprisingly green, but dry and aromatic.

To store herbs, remove the leaves from the stems. Make sure they're completely dry, or mold could occur. Then scoop the herbs into tightly covered glass jars away from the light and heat, and they'll be flavorful for about a year. Don't make the easy mistake of storing them above or next to your stove, for the heat will dissipate their flavors.

Roots and thick stems can be dried in a commercial dryer, your oven, or a microwave. For faster drying, chop them into pieces first. Store them in tightly covered glass jars away from the light and heat, and always try to grind them as you need them, using a coffee grinder, spice grinder, or mortar and pestle.

To dry seeds, gather ripe flower heads and lay them out in an airy, dry, dark place. When the seeds are dry, you'll be able to shake them right out of the flower heads.

Pods like chilies and peppers are dried whole in a commercial dryer, in the oven, or by stringing them together and hanging them in a dry, airy place. Store them in jars or by hanging. Grind as needed in a coffee grinder, spice grinder, or mortar and pestle for use in chili powder or paprika.

Garlic cloves and onion pieces can also be dried using a commercial dryer or your oven. Store the dried pieces in a tightly covered glass jar. Grind as needed for garlic powder or onion powder.

Using frozen herbs: Clever chefs are learning that the herbal pantry is not limited to fresh or dried herbs. The freezer provides a hospitable environment for many herbs and spices because its low temperature helps them keep their flavors longer.

Continued ➔

What Herbs Go Best With…

The question usually comes up just after "What's for dinner?" While it is true that most herbs go with most foods, there are some pairings that are especially successful. Listed below are common foods and some of the herbs that best flatter them. While the table isn't the final word, it can be a starting point for your own culinary experiments.

Asparagus

Chives	Savory
Lemon balm	Tarragon
Sage	Thyme

Beans, dried

Cumin	Parsley
Garlic	Sage
Mint	Savory
Onions	Thyme
Oregano	

Beans, green

Basil	Mint
Caraway	Sage
Clove	Savory
Dill	Thyme
Oregano	

Beef

Basil	Onion
Bay leaf	Oregano
Caraway	Parsley
Cumin	Rosemary
Fenugreek	Sage
Garlic	Savory
Ginger	Tarragon
Marjoram	Thyme

Broccoli

Basil	Marjoram
Dill	Oregano
Garlic	Tarragon
Lemon balm	Thyme

Cabbage

Basil	Fennel
Caraway	Marjoram
Cayenne pepper	Sage
Cumin	Savory
Dill	

Carrots

Anise	Ginger
Basil	Marjoram
Chervil	Mint
Chives	Parsley
Cinnamon	Sage
Clove	Savory
Cumin	Tarragon
Dill	Thyme

Cauliflower

Basil	Marjoram
Caraway	Parsley
Chives	Rosemary
Cumin	Savory
Dill	Tarragon
Garlic	

Chicken

Anise	Lovage
Basil	Marjoram
Bay leaf	Onion
Borage	Oregano
Chives	Parsley
Cinnamon	Rosemary
Cumin	Saffron
Dill	Sage
Fenugreek	Savory
Garlic	Tarragon
Ginger	Thyme

Corn

Chervil	Saffron
Chives	Sage
Lemon balm	Thyme

Eggplant

Basil	Onion
Cinnamon	Oregano
Dill	Parsley
Garlic	Sage
Marjoram	Savory
Mint	Thyme

Eggs

Anise	Marjoram
Basil	Oregano
Caraway	Parsley
Cayenne pepper	Rosemary
Chervil	Saffron
Chives	Sage
Coriander	Savory
Dill	Tarragon
Fennel	Thyme

Fish

Anise	Marjoram
Basil	Oregano
Borage	Parsley
Caraway	Rosemary
Chervil	Saffron
Chives	Sage
Dill	Savory
Fennel	Tarragon
Garlic	Thyme
Ginger	

Fruit

Anise	Lemon balm
Cinnamon	Mint
Clove	Rosemary
Ginger	

Lamb

Basil	Marjoram
Bay leaf	Mint
Cinnamon	Onion
Coriander	Parsley
Cumin	Rosemary
Dill	Saffron
Garlic	Sage
Ginger	Tarragon
Lemon balm	Thyme

Mushrooms

Coriander	Rosemary
Marjoram	Tarragon
Oregano	Thyme

Parsnips

Basil	Parsley
Dill	Savory
Marjoram	Thyme

Peas

Caraway	Savory
Chervil	Tarragon
Chives	Thyme
Rosemary	

Pork

Anise	Oregano
Caraway	Rosemary
Cardamom	Saffron
Dill	Sage
Garlic	Tarragon
Ginger	

Potatoes

Basil	Marjoram
Caraway	Oregano
Chives	Parsley
Coriander	Rosemary
Dill	Sage
Fennel	Tarragon
Lovage	Thyme

Rice

Basil	Saffron
Fennel	Tarragon
Lovage	Thyme

Spinach

Anise	Cinnamon
Basil	Dill
Caraway	Rosemary
Chervil	Thyme
Chives	

Squash

Basil	Marjoram
Caraway	Dill
Cardamom	Oregano
Cinnamon	Rosemary
Clove	Sage
Ginger	Savory

Stuffing

Garlic	Rosemary
Marjoram	Sage
Onion	Thyme
Parsley	

Tomatoes

Basil	Oregano
Bay leaf	Parsley
Chives	Rosemary
Coriander	Sage
Dill	Savory
Garlic	Tarragon
Lovage	Thyme
Marjoram	

Turkey

Basil	Saffron
Garlic	Sage
Marjoram	Savory
Onion	Tarragon
Oregano	Thyme
Rosemary	

Veal

Basil	Onion
Bay leaf	Parsley
Chervil	Rosemary
Chives	Sage
Ginger	Savory
Marjoram	Thyme
Mint	

What's more, if you need to grind your dried spices ahead of time, freezing will preserve their flavors longer than keeping them at room temperature.

Many frozen herbs can be used as you would fresh—about 2 teaspoons to serve four people. Take the herbs from the freezer and toss them (without defrosting) into soups, stews, and sauces. If you're using frozen herbs in salads or other uncooked foods, drain them first. (Frozen minced herbs will need more draining than sprigs.) Note that flavors can change during freezing, so be sure to taste and, if necessary, adjust before serving.

Tips for freezing herbs: Tough stemmed herbs like basil, tarragon, and sage should have their leaves removed for freezing. Brush off the soil with a stiff paintbrush rather than washing because too much water may dilute flavors. Once the leaves have been brushed and removed, lay them out flat on a cookie sheet and freeze them for several hours. Then place them gently into freezer containers or bags, and they'll be easy to remove individually as needed.

The big question when freezing herbs is whether or not to blanch. Although the color of the herbs will usually stay greener if they're blanched, flavor and aroma will often be sacrificed.

Basil is an exception: It should be blanched, or it will turn black. Most other herbs will freeze well unblanched for up to six months if it is done just after harvesting. After that time, blanched or unblanched, they'll begin to deteriorate.

To blanch, simply place the leaves in a strainer and pour boiling water over them for one second. Then lay them on paper towels and let them cool in the air before freezing. Don't be tempted into cooling the leaves by plunging them into ice water, because it could dilute their flavor.

Delicate herbs like thyme and dill freeze well in sprigs. Simply arrange them in freezer containers or bags and seal. Use whole frozen sprigs or snip them as needed.

Herbs can also be minced by hand or with a food processor and frozen in ice cube trays. When the cubes are frozen, transfer them to plastic bags and use as needed.

Another way to freeze minced herbs is by making herb pastes. Add fresh leaves or sprigs to a food processor and begin to mince. While the motor is running, add oil, a bit at a time, until the mixture has formed a paste. Freeze the paste in ice cube trays or in tablespoon amounts wrapped in plastic.

Making herbed vinegars: Herb-flavored vinegars add magic to any recipe that asks for vinegar. They offer aroma to foods just as rhythm adds excitement to music, without overpowering the harmony of the recipe.

Choose white vinegar, white wine vinegar, red wine vinegar, apple cider vinegar, or rice vinegar, depending on the herbs you're adding. Heat the vinegar but don't boil it; then pour it into a glass jar to which you have added fresh herb sprigs or leaves. Use about three 2-inch sprigs for each cup of vinegar. Garlic, shallots, or chilies can be used, too, by adding one for each cup of vinegar.

Let the vinegar cool, then cover it, and store in a cool, dark place for up to a year. Use the vinegar in salad dressings and marinades and to deglaze pans.

Making flavored oils: Flavored oils can be a dieter's dream. The secret is that you can use less

Continued ➡

because the oil is more flavorful. For example, on a salad to serve four people, you might make a dressing using 2 tablespoons of oil. But if you use a flavored oil, you can cut the amount in half, and the dressing will be so flavorful, nondieters will be jealous.

Gently heat olive oil, peanut oil, or other vegetable oil until it's warm and fragrant. This will take three to five minutes, depending on how much oil you're heating. Then pour the oil into a glass jar to which you have added fresh herb sprigs, herb leaves, garlic, or chilies. Use about three 2-inch sprigs, one clove of garlic, or one chili for each cup of oil. Let the oil cool, cover, and store it in a cool, dark place for about six months. Use the oil to sauté and in marinades and salad dressings.

Making herb butters: Like flavored oils, herb butters allow calorie counters to use less because there's more flavor. They also jazz up a breakfast table or an appetizer tray with wonderful colors and tastes. Try serving herb butters in tiny ramekins (crocks), shaping them in butter molds, or cutting them with a butter curler.

Combine about 1 tablespoon of minced fresh herbs with ½ cup softened sweet butter. Wrap the mixture in plastic and store it in the refrigerator for about a month or in the freezer for about three months. Use the butter on warm biscuits or toast, steamed vegetables, poached chicken, or fish. Use it to sauté.

Classic Herb and Spice Combinations

Our tastes are expanding and as they do, the flavors of many countries are finding their way into our kitchens. When we use a pinch of Indian curry powder to spike a sauce or a dash of Spanish saffron to spice a soup, we are enriching ourselves with the classics of other cultures.

Bouquets garnis are the little bundles of aromatic herbs and spices used to flavor soups, stews, and sauces. The idea behind a bouquet garni is to keep the herbs contained so that flavor, but not flecks, will permeate the food. The little bundles can be made up of several fresh herb sprigs tied together with string; fresh or dried herbs tied in a cheese-cloth bag; fresh or dried herbs placed in a tea ball; or fresh or dried herbs tucked between two pieces of celery and tied with string. When using a bouquet garni that is tied together with string, make the string long enough that you can tie the loose end to the pot handle. Then when you need to remove the bouquet, it will be easy to find.

Classically, bouquets garnis contain parsley, thyme, and bay with occasional additions of whole peppercorns, whole allspice, whole cloves, celery leaf, tarragon, or marjoram. Be encouraged to expand on the bouquet concept by creating your own removable bundles. For instance, combine cinnamon stick, orange peel, lemon peel, and nutmeg to flavor warm apple cider. Or use lemon peel, whole peppercorns, and garlic together to spice up simmering vegetables.

Bouquets garnis can be made ahead in cheese-cloth bags and frozen. Add them to simmering food directly from the freezer.

Fines herbes are a combination of chervil, parsley, thyme, and tarragon, freshly minced and added to omelets, sautés, cheese sauces, and other recipes at the very last minute of cooking. The allure of fines herbes is in the freshness of the herbs and the satisfying flavor they create when combined.

Quatre epices simply means "four spices" and is used in French haute cuisine to flavor roast meats, poultry, hardy vegetables, or desserts. The four spices are a ground combination of any of the following: cloves, mace, nutmeg, ginger,

cinnamon, black pepper, or white pepper. Without the peppers, quatre epices become good old American pumpkin pie spice.

Curry powder does not grow on trees. Instead, it is an aromatic combination of many ground spices that can include coriander seed, cumin seed, nutmeg, mace, cardamom seed, turmeric, white mustard seed, black mustard seed, fenugreek seed, chilies, ginger, white peppercorns, black pepper-corns, garlic, allspice, cinnamon, cayenne, and fennel seed. Curry powder is famous in East Indian cooking where, depending on the spice combina-tion, it is called garam masala. It is also imported to Southeast Asian cuisines, especially Thai. Note that Thai curries (except for Thai Muslim curry) omit the sweeter spices like cinnamon, ginger, nutmeg, and mace and include lots of fresh basil. Thai curry powders are commonly combined with a liquid and used as pastes.

To enliven its exceptional aroma, curry powder should always be heated before eating.

Chili powder is a combination of ground spices and herbs that always contains dried chilies plus a selection of garlic powder, oregano, allspice, cloves, cumin seed, coriander seed, cayenne, black pepper, turmeric, mustard seed, and paprika. As with all dried spice and herb combinations, chili powder is best when ground as needed and heated before eating. If you must make chili powder ahead, store it in a tightly covered glass jar and keep the jar in a cool, dark place.

Chinese five-spice powder is a dried, ground combi-nation of Szechuan peppercorns, cinnamon, cloves, fennel, and star anise. It's used as a seasoning for pork and chicken and as a condi-ment. Five-spice powder is most flavorful ground as needed and heated before serving. If you're using five spice powder as a condiment, toast it first in a dry sauté pan. If you must store five spice powder, keep it untoasted in a tightly covered glass jar in a cool, dark place.

Pickling spice often includes dillweed and/or dill seed plus a choice of dried chilies, mustard seed, bay, allspice, white peppercorns, black pepper-corns, cinnamon, cloves, coriander seed, turmeric, cardamom, ginger, celery seed, garlic, mace, and nutmeg. Sound confusing? Simply choose your spices according to what you're pickling. For instance, for cucumber pickles, use dillweed, dill seed, mustard seed, celery seed, garlic, and black peppercorns. Now imagine that you're pickling carrots. Think about what flavors enhance them. You could choose cinnamon, nutmeg, bay, and peppercorns.

Salt-Free Blends

Are you one of the millions who monitor salt intake for health reasons? Don't despair! You aren't doomed to a tasteless diet.

The four basic tastes we perceive are sweet, salty, sour, and bitter. Imagine what can happen if one of those tastes, in this case salt, is removed. If you're thinking "bland," you're right. But you can achieve high flavor levels without salt. By raising the flavor levels of sweet, sour, and bitter, you can create wonderful blooms of flavor that will stimu-late your taste buds. Here are some salt-free flavor combinations for marinades, sauces, and for sprinkling.

For beef:
- lemon juice, minced fresh rosemary, and freshly ground black pepper
- minced fresh thyme, ground cloves, grated orange peel, and freshly ground black pepper

- garlic, herbed vinegar, and freshly ground black pepper
- mashed green peppercorns, minced onions, and minced fresh marjoram

For poultry:
- minced fresh ginger, freshly grated orange peel, and minced fresh sage
- minced fresh marjoram, minced fresh thyme, and apple cider vinegar
- minced fresh tarragon, minced shallots, and lemon juice
- minced fresh basil, white wine vinegar, and garlic

For fish:
- minced fresh dill, lemon juice, and mustard seed
- minced fresh lovage, celery seed, lemon juice, and freshly ground black pepper
- fennel seed, mustard seed, bay, and grated lemon peel

For green vegetables:
- minced fresh savory, minced fresh chives, and minced onions
- minced fresh dill, bay, and rice vinegar
- minced fresh basil, freshly grated nutmeg, and minced fresh marjoram

For yellow and orange vegetables:
- cinnamon, nutmeg, orange juice, and minced fresh thyme
- minced fresh ginger, cinnamon, apple cider vinegar, and minced fresh lovage or celery leaf
- minced fresh beebalm and minced fresh thyme

For cheese and eggs:
- minced fresh dill, minced fresh chives, minced fresh parsley, and paprika
- freshly grated nutmeg, dry mustard, and freshly ground black pepper
- minced fresh oregano, garlic, and minced fresh thyme

For beans, rice, and other grains:
- chilies, cumin seed, minced fresh oregano, and garlic
- saffron, garlic, and minced fresh parsley
- minced fresh mint, minced fresh parsley, grated lemon peel, and caraway seed

Sweetness Enhancers

Many herbs and spices sweeten the foods around them without adding calories. Use them alone—a pinch of cinnamon to sweeten tomato sauce—or in combination with traditional sweeteners— cardamom adds extra sweetness to cakes and cookies, for example. Experiment with these natural sweeteners:

- angelica stem in salads
- bee balm in beverages
- costmary and mint in sparkling waters
- lemon balm and lemon verbena in frozen desserts
- violet and rose in condiments
- vanilla (just a drop) in savory sauces
- rosemary in fruit salads, fruit compotes, and fruit tarts

Edible Flowers

Many flowers can add color and an outdoorsy, perfumelike flavor to your cooking. They are frequently used as floating garnishes for beverages

Continued ➡

and soups and to add color to trays and individual plates. But their flair reaches far beyond. For example, edible flowers can be minced and added to cheese spreads, herb butters, or to pancake, crepe, or waffle batter. Use them whole in salads, stuffed, or fried in a light cornmeal or flour batter.

The key word here is *edible*, which is a nice way of saying nontoxic.

Crafts from Herbs

Claire Kowalchik and William H. Hylton

Herbs invite but don't intimidate. Nearby, abundant. Rich in textures, colors, and fragrances. There's a special satisfaction from turning such homey materials into an elegant piece of craftwork.

The pleasure is not all in the result; the process itself soothes and refreshes. There are no acid baths, no deafening machinery with finger-eating blades. Herbs are quiet and fragrant, and the herb crafter's hands smell of rosemary and thyme.

But the greatest charm of herb crafts may perhaps be described as their quirkiness. A finished project shows immediately what's growing by your garage or roadside or what a neighbor happened to plant too much of. Each piece becomes absolutely personal, local, and distinctive, a refuge of the individual spirit in a formularized, mass-produced world.

Living Herb Wreaths

Wreaths make year-round pleasure for Peggy Armstrong, an herb crafter from Ohio. Peggy starts her living wreaths in the spring when she has lots of young plants and is ready to start her other herb plantings; the wreaths become circular herb gardens she happens to hang on the wall. During the summer they thrive hanging against the cedar boards on the outside of her house. When they come inside for a visit, lying on a tray of stones, a hurricane lamp in the center, they make a fragrant centerpiece for a table. One of her favorite wreaths is a treat for the palate as well as the eye, a perfect gift for a good cook:

1. Soak several handfuls of sphagnum (not milled) in water until wet throughout, about 15 minutes. Cut a strip of ½-inch-mesh chicken wire 3 inches wide and 14 to 18 inches long. Bend the long sides of the wire, so they curl up to form a trough. Squeeze enough water out of the sphagnum, so it won't drench the table while you work; then pack it tightly into the trough. (A good dense mass of sphagnum will give the plants a firm base and will hold water well.)

2. Bend the trough sides together until they overlap slightly and you have a long wire sausage stuffed with sphagnum. Fasten the ides together by bending the loose prongs (sticking out where the mesh was cut) to form little hooks that can catch in the mesh hole on the opposite side of the seam.

3. Make five to seven little wells in the sphagnum, evenly spaced about the wreath, by poking through the wire. Plant a young herb in each, anchoring wayward runners with hairpins, if necessary. Peggy uses plants from 3-inch pots whose creeping stems are about 6 inches long. She encourages wreath makers to choose plants boldly in hopes of discovering striking effects. She has certainly not been timid or tradition bound; some of her wreaths include a bright cascade of petunias.

4. Hang the wreath in strong but indirect sunlight. Peggy puts hers on the west side of her house. When the moss starts to dry out, she soaks the whole wreath for 15 minutes in a tub of water with a dash of plant fertilizer. If herb tendrils start growing in odd directions, prune them back or wire them into shape. In about six weeks, you should have a fully covered wreath.

Plants for Living Wreaths

For culinary wreaths:

chives (plant at the bottom center if the wreath is to be hung)

creeping sage

marjoram

oregano

thymes, especially creeping wooly thyme

For fragrant wreaths:

lavender

prostrate rosemary

santolina

scented geranium

To add color:

marigold

petunia

Living Christmas Balls

These little globes have some of the same magic as ships in a bottle. Fortunately they're easier to make. They can hang near windows (but out of direct sun) or on Christmas trees, and they make unusual holiday gifts.

1. Find glass Christmas balls 2½ inches in diameter with chimneys at least ½ inch in diameter. Pull off the metal tops and save them. Soak the balls overnight in a half-and-half solution of bleach and water. Then, wearing rubber gloves, swirl each ball in the solution, letting the bleach slosh around inside. Rinse them with plain water. The color should wash off easily. If any trace remains of the color or the cloudy inside coating, rub it off with a paper towel. To reach the inside, use a long-handled cotton swab or a bit of paper towel stuck on the end of a pencil.

2. Mix crumbled charcoal (available wherever aquarium supplies are sold) into a soilless potting mixture (half sphagnum and half perlite, for example). You'll need about 1 teaspoon of charcoal and ¼ cup of potting mixture per ball. Rest the ball in a cup to keep it from rolling around while you work on it. Form paper into a funnel, insert it into the ball's chimney, and pour in the charcoal-soil mix. It should fill a quarter to a third of the ball.

3. Push bits of trailing moss through the opening, and position them with a pencil or needle-nosed tweezers to form a loose carpet over the soil.

4. Take a 1¾-inch-long cutting of partridgeberry, preferably including some berries (the red will make the final ball more festive), and remove the bottom pair of leaves. Using tweezers, poke the cutting through the chimney and into the soil. Make sure at least one node is below ground. Put the point of a long-necked squeeze bottle into the ball and mist the soil.

5. Put the cap and hook back on the ball and if the mood strikes, tie a ribbon around the ball's chimney. Hang it in indirect light and mist the soil when the moss begins to look faded. The ball will make a perfect rooting chamber for the partidgeberry and the moss.

Tussie-Mussies: Bouquets with Meaning

"Making things that are pretty is one thing, but making them meaningful is another," says Lane Furneaux, a master of both arts. From her herb garden in Dallas, she's reviving enthusiasm for tussie-mussies, pretty bouquets of herbs and flowers. What is special about a tussie-mussie is that each plant in it has a meaning.

These little nosegays have been familiar British accessories for centuries, but the Victorians raised them to the level of language, particularly the coy exchanges of flirtation. A young dandy might reassure a distant lady with a tussie-mussie of forget-me-nots (for true love) and rosemary (for remembrance) and perhaps southernwood (for constancy). If she didn't find the bouquet convincing, she might send back yellow roses (for infidelity) and larkspur (for fickleness). He'd best rush for the white violets (innocence) or a lot of rue (repentance). After laying waste to several flower borders, they might get the matter sorted out, or perhaps she would finish the liaison with one scorching handful of fumitory (for hatred).

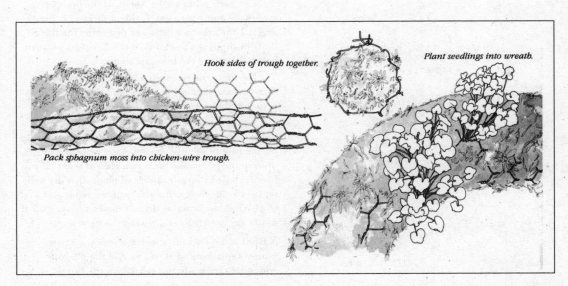

Hook sides of trough together.

Plant seedlings into wreath.

Pack sphagnum moss into chicken-wire trough.

Continued ➡

Today's revival of tussie-mussies seems to have sidestepped the lovers' quarrel (an herb patch is unlikely to replace the telephone) and concentrated on creating pretty and meaningful—and fragrant—bouquets for brides, new mothers, departing friends, new neighbors, or anyone in need of a kind word. The little bouquets have even entered politics. As legislation to form the National Herb Garden wobbled through Congress, various legislators received pleas for support in the form of tussie-mussies. The legislation did pass, which might give pause to anyone inclined to dismiss the power of a handful of flowers. To create your own flower power, here is Lane Furneaux's advice.

Selecting the plants: "Tussie-mussies are something you make with what you have," Lane emphasizes. Using only the plants from the backyard or a nearby field makes the bouquets absolutely distinctive and expressive of the maker. She describes seeing a tussie-mussie in *National Geographic* whose maker was not identified. She wrote to ask about the maker, commenting that the style didn't look American to her, and if she had to guess, she would say that it had been made in England, at Claverton in Bath. Several weeks later, she received an astonished phone call from the staff; she had guessed exactly right. She urges newcomers to relax: "Every garden has what it needs for a tussie-mussie."

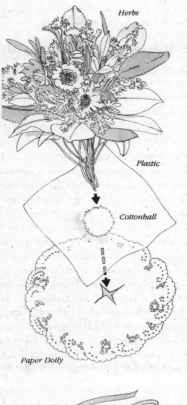

Herbs

Plastic

Cottonball

Paper Doily

Ribbon

The plant that represents the main message is Lane's starting point. This is the flower that will go into the center. She strolls through her garden searching for plants that express her theme, preferably something colorful. Perhaps opal basil flowers for good wishes, a rose for love, or a pair of roses for an anniversary bouquet. She selects other plants with complementary meanings, and finally she just picks anything that is in particularly good condition or would make a good combination for the flowers. These last plants she looks up on returning indoors, and often she discovers that their sentiments would be perfect for the occasion. She has made tussie-mussies with as few as 2 kinds of plants and as many as 36. (The 36 went into a tussie-mussie for Nancy Reagan to whom Lane had a lot to say.)

Arranging the plants: According to Lane arranging the plants is like writing a letter. It's an activity so intuitive and personal that rules become irrelevant. Here is her approach:

Starting with the plant symbol for the main sentiment, the one that will go at the center, she surrounds it with a little frame of foliage, perhaps some kind of mint for fragrance. Next a ring of something wispy is added for contrast. With a strongly symmetrical center, Lane arranges little bunches of the remaining plants asymmetrically around the outer part. (Some tussie-mussie makers use only one sprig for each sentiment, but bunching the sprigs makes a more dramatic display.) In this outer section, Lane looks for ways to accent the center color. The bouquet is finished with an outer rim of leaves, perhaps from different kinds of scented geraniums. Lane will alternate a triangular leaf with a round one, for example. Or perhaps make two rings of contrasting leaf shapes.

Assembling the bouquet: Put the sprigs in water, and then wash them, in Lane's words, "just as if they were something to eat." Groom them, cutting off spent blossoms or chewed leaves, until each sprig is perfect. Lane strips the lower leaves, although this is a matter of personal style. At Claverton, for example, tussie-mussie makers retain the leaves, crushing them together when the stems are wrapped. It makes for a bulkier base but more fragrance.

For a bouquet that will be carried, spread out a square of plastic wrap and put a little puff of moist cotton in the center. Then fold up the square so that it engulfs the stems of the bouquet, twisting it around the stems like the flaps of a folded umbrella. Cover it with a spiral of florist's tape.

Tussie-mussies are often set in a paper doily. Cut an X in the middle of the doily, fold down the points, and put the stems through the hole in the doily. Lane secures them with a ¼-inch florist's pin through each point of the X-cut. If the bouquet is eventually going into water, the doily can get pretty soggy. Lane creates a little wax protector for the doily by dipping the points of the X-cut in paraffin before inserting the bouquet stems.

Decorate the assembly with ribbon. Lane uses three colors to spiral up the stem and tie over the pins. She lets long ends trail down.

A tussie-mussie should stay fresh for several hours when wrapped this way. To keep it longer, snip off the base of the plastic container, or better yet, unwrap the stems. Set them in a glass of water. If you have included a large number of plants that dry well, set the tussie-mussie in a glass without water and wait. When the bouquet dries, remove any sprigs that didn't dry gracefully and rewrap the stems.

A final note. Include a message with the tussie-mussie explaining what you intend the plants to symbolize. Even a fellow speaker of the floral

language might appreciate clarification on plants that have several meanings. And never give anyone unlabeled basil, which can mean either love or hate.

Woven Herb Baskets

The easiest way to make these unusual craft baskets is to start with plenty of fresh herbs, weave them while they're at their most pliable, and then let them dry. These highly textured baskets with a heathery blending of colors make a dramatic container for any number of displays—pinecones, glass balls, rag dolls, or dried flowers.

Weave herbs into a wire-frame basket.

Add a handle by wiring each end to a rib of the basket.

The following design comes from the irrepressibly creative herb crafter Peggy Armstrong:

1. Start with a moss basket (the wire frame baskets that florists stuff with sphagnum moss and plant with hanging plants). Garden centers carry several sizes, particularly in the spring. Collect herbs with long stems and, ideally, feathery foliage but with few pronounced branches. Leave flowering stalks on, but break off any part of the stem that's too woody to bend.

2. To weave the first row, select one or two leafy stems. Anchor one end of the bunch by poking it very far down into a crack between two ribs at the base of the basket frame. Weave the herb stem(s) over and under the wire ribs. Press the stem(s) down against the base as firmly as possible. The stem(s) will probably go all the way around the base with a bit left over. Then just use the same stem(s) to start the next row. Weave under the ribs you went over the first time and vice versa.

3. When the first stem(s) have been completely woven in, select another one or two stems. To

Continued ➡

anchor, lay the stem(s) over the previous row so they overlap about an inch, going under and/or over the same ribs as the previous row. Then continue weaving around the basket. When you reach the beginning again, start the third row, passing the herbs under the ribs you have just gone over and vice versa. That's the basic pattern; you'll just keep repeating it until you reach the top. The most important part of the process is packing down the layers firmly. Otherwise large holes will appear in the basket as the stems dry and shrink. As you weave higher on the frame, one bunch of stems will not reach all the way around. Don't worry. Just select another bunch, let it overlap, and go on weaving.

4. After you have woven about an inch of the basket, increase the size of the herb bundle by one stem. Thus you might be weaving with three stems instead of two. About every inch up, increase the size by another stem. (The thicker bunches will give a sturdier, more dramatic basket, but it's impossible to use them near the base. There the ribs are so close together that thick bunches can't bend sharply enough to get around them.) In selecting these thick bunches, don't waste the prettiest stems by burying them in the middle. Put them where they will show on the basket's outside or inside. By composing the stem bunches carefully, you can streak colors from the top to the bottom of the basket, or give the basket's inside a different character from the outside.

5. When you've woven three-quarters of the way up the frame, add a handle. Peggy makes a semicircle of grape vines or plaited herb stems and wires each end against a rib with florist's wire. Continue weaving herb bunches through the ribs, going over or under the handle-and-rib if it were just another rib.

6. When you come to the top, fasten southernwood around the top edge with florist's wire to hide the metal rim.

7. Prop the basket upside down, perhaps on jars so it can dry.

Drying Herbs and Flowers for Decoration

In drying flowers we play a trick on Mother Nature—and discover the laugh is on us. At first a dried arrangement seems like such a magnificent way to break the rules: When everything turns dry and brown for the winter, we can have tufts of silvery, fuzzy leaves, tiny blue petals, clumps of tawny flowers, hundreds of echoes of summer. But consider the "unnatural" trick: The principal way of drying herbs and flowers is just a matter of warm air, a light breeze, and a couple of days. It's Mother Nature's trick after all.

AIR-DRYING—FOR THE RIGHT FLOWERS

Colonial Williamsburg, a sort of carnival of preservation technology, preserves its herbs and flowers in the simplest way possible. staff members tie them in bunches, hang them in a dark attic with a dehumidifier, and wait. There are other ways to dry plants, says Libbey Oliver, who supervises Williamsburg's flower arranging, but air-drying produces a look appropriate to the colonial atmosphere. (Silica drying—described later—she considers more Victorian.) Air-drying is certainly the simplest drying technique, but like any other simple task, it can be refined into an art.

Here, step-by-step, is how to do it:

1. **Choose plants that work.** The most common mistake that beginners make, says Libbey, is to try to air-dry the wrong things. The technique just doesn't work on some plants, particularly those with large petals that shed (like tulips or full-blown roses) or those with delicate structures that shrivel (like Queen Anne's lace).

2. **Pick flowers at the right stage.** Some do best when picked half open; they open more as they dry. Others do best when left to dry as much as possible on the vine (see the accompanying list, Flowers for Air-drying).

3. **For flowers, strip the leaves:** the less plant material on each stem, the faster the piece will dry. Of course, no stripping is necessary in drying foliage.

4. **Tie 8 or 10 stems in a bundle and hang them upside down.** Libbey uses a rubber band to make a slipknot around the bundle and then hooks the open loop around a clothespin on a clothesline in her drying attic.

   The drying area should be dark and well-ventilated. Air movement is the key. Heat won't be much help if the moisture has no place to go. Williamsburg's drying attic has dark paper over the windows and vents at each end. During the summer flowers dry in an average of 10 days.

5. **As soon as the flowers are dry, pack them in boxes.** Libbey adds a few mothballs. The important rule here is to arrange the flowers so you'll never have to dig through a heap to find the ones you want. Therefore, put only one kind in a box and label each box clearly.

DRYING POWDERS—FOR FINICKY FLOWERS

If hanging flowers in the attic just produces a drift of petals on the floor, try one of the powder methods. The slowest method is to bury the flower in fine sand in an open box. The sand holds the bloom open and the petals in shape while the air dries the flower. Borax, clean sand mixed with borax, plain kitty litter, and numerous other powders will do this. Flowers dry in this mixture in two to five weeks.

One powder—silica gel—actually draws water out of the plant. Finding it may be a challenge. Try drugstores, hobby shops, and florists. Silica gel costs perhaps $6 per pound, but after each batch of flowers, the powder, which looks like a laundry detergent, can be dehydrated in a warm oven and then reused. Flowers dry in this mixture in two to seven days. Afterward they may be particularly sensitive to humidity and may reabsorb moisture

Cut

Wire

Flowers for Air-Drying

Flowers to pick before fully open:

delphinium (spike should be half open, half in bud)

goldenrod

peony (dry the buds)

pokeberry

safflower (pick when some flowers are still in bud; let top leaves remain)

strawflower

Flowers to pick when fairly open:

celosia (before seeds appear)

chive flowers

marigold (will dry into dark gold pompoms)

salvia

Flowers to leave on stalk until very dry:

globe amaranth

pearly everlasting

tansy

yarrow (yellow is best)

Foliage to pick in prime condition:

artemisia

Pods to let dry on plant:

love-in-a-mist

rue seed heads (pick either green or dried)

Continued ➡

and droop if placed in a humid part of the house. The ideal way to display them in such a case is under a Victorian bell jar.

Whatever the drying powder, the method of packing is the same:

1. Pick flowers for powder drying when they're not quite fully open. Cut off the stem right under the blossom. Poke a piece of florist's wire into the center of the flower, and pull it through until it forms a wire "stem." Bend one end of the wire into a little nubbin so it won't pull through the stem and out the bottom. (The flowers will be too fragile to wire once they're dried, but the wire is essential if you want to stand the flowers in a vase.)

2. Cover the bottom of a wide, low container with a thin layer of drying powder, and nestle the flowers into the powder, with the wires curling around them. Don't let the blossoms touch. Gently pour in the remaining powder, completely burying the flowers. If the powder is silica gel, seal the container tightly. For other powders, leave the container open.

3. Try to catch the flowers when they're dry enough to hold their color, but not so dry that they fall apart. Flowers with thin petals may dry in two days, while fleshier flowers like snapdragons may take a week. Don't leave flowers in silica gel "an extra day," because they can overdry. Excavate them from the powder very gently because they'll be extremely brittle. If a petal breaks off, reattach it with a spot of white glue.

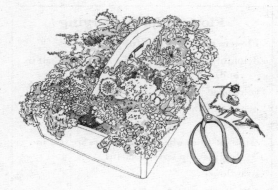

Dried Herb Wreaths

Pastels. Little pinpricks of color. Airiness, softness.

Dried herbs have opened up thousands of possibilities for wreaths. The herbs may not be evergreen, but they're practically ever ready. Instead of discarding the wreath in January, add a Valentine's Day bow and use it as a centerpiece. Hang a hatchet in it for George's birthday....We are just beginning to glimpse the decorative possibilities of wreaths.

We are also just beginning to glimpse the range of techniques. Here are two approaches from skilled herb workers; you can invent at least a dozen more.

Eileen Weinsteiger's dried herb wreaths: Eileen Weinsteiger takes care of the display herb and vegetable gardens at the Rodale Research Center. Create your own wreath following Eileen's instructions:

1. Select a wreath base of straw or Spanish moss. These are available at garden centers or can be made by bending heavy gauge wire into a circle and lashing a filling material to it with florist's wire.

2. Pick a "background" plant—something that you have tons of and that will go well with all the flowers you intend to use in the wreath. The pale fluff of Silver King artemisia, for

example, makes an excellent background. Insert it in the straw, stem by stem, until the whole wreath is covered.

3. Now add the accents, perhaps little bouquets of colorful dried flowers, spaced around the wreath connected by stretches of more neutral flowers. Or perhaps a whole circle of harmonious dried flowers with a few contrasting colors stuck here and there. You might wire in several florist's tubes so you can add fresh flowers, replacing them when they fade.

Peggy Armstrong's dried herb wreaths—any shape: Your imagination and flower supply are your only limitations in making this wreath:

1. Cut a long strip of heavy-gauge wire for the spine of the wreath or garland, and bend a hook into each end.

2. Assemble a bunch of dried flowers, perhaps 3 inches across, representing a balanced arrangement of the foliage and color accents you want in the wreath. Using fine florist's wire, bind the stems to the big wire.

   Just keep adding bunches until you've covered the wire. The most important part is keeping the bunches close to each other. Otherwise there will be gaps when the wire is bent. (Peggy prefers to keep the composition simple. She advises people to use no more than three basic colors.)

3. When you have filled the wire or run out of flowers, bend the garland into whatever shape you want. You can have a wreath, a heart, a circle with Mickey Mouse ears, or whatever. Peggy has even wound herb garlands around the poles of umbrellas at a poolside party.

Herb Garden Designs
Claire Kowalchik and William H. Hylton

There are two ways to landscape with herbs: Work them into the overall design as decorative elements, or feature the herbs in special period or theme gardens. If you don't have the room or desire for an herb garden, herbs can still make a valuable contribution to your landscape.

A low hedge of lavender or rosemary can set off a fence or wall or line a path, perfuming the air when anyone walks through. If you're tired of mowing grass, a colorful lawn of creeping thymes, chamomile, and/or pennyroyal requires almost no maintenance. (Remember, though, that an herb lawn won't hold up under heavy traffic—if you want to walk on the lawn, it's best to set down stepping stones.) On a smaller scale, creeping thymes, with their pleasantly pungent fragrance and pink, white, rose, or lilac flowers, can be planted between the bricks or stones of a path, spreading to form a colorful ground cover.

Ground covers for shady sites need not be limited to ivy or pachysandra, either. Plant sweet woodruff, with its starry white flowers, mint-scented pennyroyal, or heavenly sweet violets under your shade trees. If part of your yard is heavily shaded, angelica, lemon balm, sweet cicely, evening primrose, valerian, chervil, goldenseal, lungwort, and the hellebores will add color and texture. Reclaim a swampy site with lovage, marsh mallow, mint, elecampane, queen of the meadow, and beebalm.

Herbs can also be worked into a flower border or vegetable garden. Bright-flowered bee balm; gold, white, or cherry yarrow; garlic chives with its clusters of star-shaped, rose-scented flowers and handsome straplike foliage; variegated sage; daisy-flowered feverfew; blue-green rue; blue-spired aconite; and foxglove with its majestic spikes of flowers in shades of red, pink, yellow, and white are particularly suited to the mixed border. So much variety to choose from makes it easy to design a striking border.

In the vegetable garden, annual and biennial herbs like nasturtiums, basil, parsley, anise, dill, borage, chervil, coriander, calendula, and summer savory add diversity and possibly protection from insects. But to avoid grief at tilling time, confine the perennial culinary herbs, such as sage, thyme, and their like, to a site of their own at one end of the garden, just like those other perennial crops, asparagus, strawberries, rhubarb, and artichokes.

Landscaping

If you use herbs on a larger scale or feature them in a design or garden, good commonsense land-

Continued ➡

scaping rules apply, as they do in any type of garden design. Before you start to design, remember that all gardens involve work. The more formal the design and the larger the scale, the more weeding, clipping, mulching, and watering you'll need to do. Scale down those visions of grandeur until they reach manageable proportions.

When you begin the actual design, bear in mind that it's a lot easier—to say nothing of cheaper—to make mistakes or changes on paper than in the garden. Measure the garden site, then transfer the outline to graph paper, making the layout to scale. Mark down trees, buildings, and other obstructions, and note the direction north. Make sure to leave enough space for comfortable paths, and keep beds narrow enough to work in—4 to 5 feet is about maximum—but wide enough to look effective. Once you have the basic design down, choose the herbs that will bring it to life. The choice can be based on color, height, climatic conditions, or type of plant—for example, those suitable for a colonial or dye garden.

It's wise to keep basic rules in mind when choosing plants. First, always plant groups of a given herb together. Individual plants will get lost, creating a blurred, jumbled effect, while masses of plants will stand out and create a unified design. Second, plant in descending order of height. If your design features a border backed by a wall or fence, plant the tallest herbs in back, the lowest herbs in front. If you're planning an island bed, put the tall plants in the center, the low plants around the edge. Third, keep perspective in mind. If you're planting a knot garden, make sure the garden "floor" contrasts with the knotted "cord," or the pattern will be lost. If your design is meant to be viewed from a distance, use plants that will show up—large ones with bright flowers or silver foliage.

Finally, a word about maintenance. Herb gardens, like any others, look best when the plants are full and lush. This is vital when an herbal hedge or solid block of plants is integral to the design. It's good gardening practice to grow extra plants in a nursery area or corner of the vegetable garden, so you'll always have spares to fill in gaps.

Period Gardens

Period gardens are complex because they are limited to the designs, materials, techniques, and plants of a given historical era. Before embarking on a historical design, read everything you can on

the period of your choice, as well as on garden design in that period. An Elizabethan knot garden design is included here as a starting place. But there are other possibilities.

A medieval garden is a delightful refuge. It should be walled, if possible, and include a fountain. Surround the fountain with an herbal lawn studded with flowers—irises, clove pinks, lilies, daisies, primroses, sweet violets, and columbines.

If you have a tree in the garden, you can build a circular seat around it. But the most traditional seating arrangement is a turf seat under an arbor. The turf seat—a medieval inspiration—is an earth-filled rectangular box surfaced with a creeping herb such as one of the prostrate thymes or creeping chamomile. Its walls can be brick, stone, wood, or plaited wicker (wattling).

The vigorous formality of a colonial garden may seem far removed from the enclosed tranquility of a medieval bower, but the symmetry of a successful colonial garden is soothing. To make a colonial herb garden, layout raised, board-sided beds along a central walk. The two sides of the garden should be identical. The walk should lead to something—a sundial, bench, or view. If possible, fence the garden, or hedge it with santolina, lavender, rosemary, or southernwood.

Colonists often planted herbs randomly with vegetables and flowers. An all-herb garden should be planted informally within the rigid framework of the design. Colonial herbs include burnet, comfrey, dill, basil, clary sage, lemon balm, parsley, nasturtiums, rue, madder, woad, mint, fennel, saffron, coriander, chamomile, angelica, caraway, borage, chervil, tarragon, licorice, lovage, tansy, sweet cicely, catmint, and calendula.

One thing to bear in mind when attempting a historical recreation is to limit yourself to materials available in the period you're reproducing. For example, wood, wattling, stone, gravel, brick, and clay were the usual building materials used in the colonial days. Local materials were usually used in garden construction, down to sheep-shank edgings for beds. This sort of attention to detail, combined with a sound design and diligent maintenance, will guarantee you a successful herb garden.

Theme Gardens

A theme garden is one in which the plants are unified by a common feature, such as flower color or function. Five such garden designs are included here to inspire you—a medicinal garden, dye

garden, fragrance garden, everlasting garden of ornamental plants for drying, and kitchen garden. Other possibilities include a white garden, with silver-foliaged and white-flowering herbs; a seasonal garden, with herbs that bloom in your favorite season; an herb tea garden; and a "meaningful garden," with message herbs so popular in Victorian bouquets (such as rosemary for remembrance or borage for courage).

Theme gardens can also have literary significance. There are Shakespearean gardens all over this country, featuring plants mentioned by the bard. Biblical gardens, featuring wormwood, rue, hyssop, aloe, anise, mint, dill, coriander, mustard, saffron, cumin, and roses—all herbs mentioned in the Bible—are popular. Some include plants associated with the Virgin, such as rosemary, costmary, lady's mantle, and lady's bedstraw.

Plants for a Knot Garden

Because a knot garden is basically an indulgence, you can play with it in whatever way you wish. You could emphasize the formal geometry of this pattern by using a single plant throughout. You could use all one plant for the central accents and keep three kinds in the borders. Or you could reduce the borders to two kinds—one for the square and a second for the "loops" of the knot. You can play with the background, too. A single mulching material—cocoa bean hulls—is used here to accent the greens, blues, and grays of the herbs. You could use different stone chips to make a mosaic-white marble chips in some sections, black in others, and gray-blue crushed granite in others. Or you could use brilliantly colored fish, tank gravels to create patterns that would have thrilled the Elizabethans.

Another option is to simplify and reduce the size of the knot garden. A striking knot can be made in a 9- or 10-foot square. The thing to bear in mind is that knot gardens were originally intended to be viewed from above—as when one looked from one's terrace or castle window. The narrower and lower the herb borders, the closer you'll have to get to the knot for it to be effective—and the more maintenance it will require to keep those herbs in bounds.

The plants:

1. GREEN SANTOLINA (*Santolina virens*): A perennial, to 2 feet tall, with rich green, aromatic leaves and yellow flowers in early summer. Plan on one plant per foot of border. Keep plants clipped

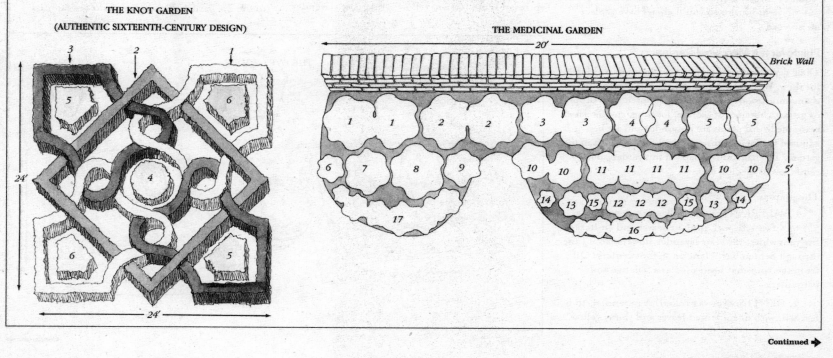

THE KNOT GARDEN
(AUTHENTIC SIXTEENTH-CENTURY DESIGN)

THE MEDICINAL GARDEN

Brick Wall

Continued ➡

back to about a foot—a hard clipping in early spring, followed by a light trim every two weeks from late May through July should keep them looking neat.

2. MUNSTEAD LAVENDER (*Lavandula angustifolia* spp. *angustifolia* 'Munstead'): A compact perennial, only 1 foot tall, with aromatic gray foliage and bright lavender flower spikes in summer. Plan on one plant per foot of border. Trim only if needed to keep plants in bounds during the growing season, but prune back hard in early spring for bushy growth. Will probably need winter protection, such as a covering of evergreen boughs.

3. GERMANDER (*Teucrium Chamaedrys*): A perennial, to 2 feet tall and wide, with dark green foliage and pink flowers in midsummer. Plan on one plant per foot of border. Clip it as you would green santolina.

4. LAVENDER COTTON (*Santolina chamaecyparissus*): A perennial, to 32 inches tall and wide, with finely cut, aromatic silver-gray foliage and yellow cottonball blooms in summer. Plant as a specimen. Prune back hard in spring to keep it from becoming woody, then shear lightly for a mounded effect.

5. HYSSOP (*Hyssopus officinalis*): A perennial, to 3 feet tall, with aromatic green foliage and white, blue, or pink flowers in summer. Plant on 2-foot centers. Shear to desired shape.

6. BLUE BEAUTY RUE (*Ruta graveolens* 'Blue Beauty'): A perennial, to 2 feet tall, with blue-green, ferny, aromatic foliage and yellow flowers in summer. Plant on 2-foot centers. Shear to desired shape.

Other plants that make handsome knot borders include dwarf and edging box, American germander, 'Hidcote' lavender, mother-of-thyme, lemon and golden lemon thyme, gray Roman and fringed wormwood, sage, winter savory, sweet marjoram, rosemary, and southernwood. Creeping thymes can be used in place of sand, stone, or mulch to fill in the design between the borders. The entire knot garden can be framed in brick or stone (preferably set no wider or higher than the borders).

Knot gardens are not low-maintenance propositions. Besides requiring constant pruning, winter protection, and standard good cultural practices, they need a supply of backup plants. Nothing looks quite as dreadful as a ratty knot garden border, with brown or empty patches where herbs didn't make it through the winter. Keep a nursery of "squares" of all the plants you use in the knot in an out-of-sight border so you'll always have replacements ready.

Plants for the Medicinal Garden

These days, plants for the medicinal garden are chiefly for show. While you may make a cup of comfrey or chamomile tea, or try your hand at horehound drops, or gather a bouquet of aconite, foxglove, and feverfew, many medicinal plants are poisonous and are best admired for their historical significance and left in the garden. The half kidney shape of this garden subtly reinforces its medical theme.

The plants:

1. VALERIAN (*Valeriana officinalis*): A perennial, 3½ to 5 feet tall, with pinnate leaves and clusters of fragrant white, pink, or lavender flowers from June through September. Plant on 2-foot centers. Oil from the roots has been used as a sedative and painkiller.

2. GENTIAN (*Gentiana lutea*): A perennial, to 6 feet tall, with deep-veined leaves and showy yellow flower clusters in late summer. Plant on 2-foot centers. The root has been used as a digestive aid, vermicide, and antiseptic wound treatment.

3. MULLEIN (*Verbascum thapsus*): A biennial, 3 to 6 feet tall in flower, with a basal rosette of large, woolly leaves and a large spike of lemon yellow flowers from June through September. Plant on 2-foot centers. The flowers have been used to treat coughs, congestion, and tuberculosis and were smoked to soothe pulmonary diseases.

4. ELECAMPANE (*Inula helenium*): A perennial, to 6 feet tall and 3 feet wide, with large basal leaves, smaller upper leaves, and yellow daisylike flowers in summer. Plant on 2-foot centers. The rhizome has been used to treat respiratory diseases.

5. AMERICAN HELLEBORE (*Veratrum viride*): A perennial, to 7 feet tall, with broad, ribbed leaves and a spike of yellow-green flowers in midsummer. Plant a 2-foot centers. The rhizome has been used as a sedative, emetic, and to treat hypertension. All plants are poisonous.

6. COMFREY (*Symphytum officinalis*): A perennial, 3 to 5 feet tall, with large, hairy basal leaves and white, rose, purple, or yellowish bell-shaped flowers from May through frost. Plant on 1½-foot centers. The root has been used to reduce inflammation and to heal broken bones.

7. LOBELIA (*Lobelia inflata*): An annual, to 3 feet tall, with toothed leaves and blue or white flowers in July and August. Plant on 1½-foot centers. The entire plant has been used to treat asthma, as a nerve stimulant, and as a tobacco substitute.

8. FEVERFEW (*Chrysanthemum parthenium*): A perennial, to 3 feet tall and wide, with aromatic, fingered foliage and creamy white, buttonlike flowers midsummer through fall. Plant on 1½-foot centers. The flowers have been used as a sedative and tonic.

9. BETONY (*Stachys officinalis*): A perennial, 2½ feet tall in flower, with a basal rosette of round-lobed leaves and spikes of white, pink, or reddish purple flowers from mid- to late summer. Plant on 1½-foot centers. The leaves have been used as a poultice, emetic, tonic, nervine, and sedative.

10. ACONITE (*Aconitum napellus*): A perennial, to 3 feet tall, with deep green, finely divided leaves and dark blue hooded flowers in large spikes in July and August. Plant on 1½-foot centers. The rhizomes have been used as a sedative, painkiller, and to treat rheumatism. All parts are poisonous.

11. FOXGLOVE (*Digitalis purpurea*): A biennial, 3 to 4 feet tall, with large, wrinkled leaves and huge spikes of white, cream-yellow, pink, rose, lavender, or purple bell-shaped flowers, often with speckled throats, which bloom in June and July. Plant on 1½-foot centers. The leaves have been used as a heart stimulant and to treat dropsy. All parts are poisonous.

12. ARNICA (*Arnica montana*): A perennial, to 2 feet tall in flower, with a basal rosette of long leaves and yellow daisylike flowers in midsummer. Plant on 1-foot centers. The flowers have been used as a compress for bruises, wounds, and inflammation. All parts are poisonous.

13. ECHINACEA (*Echinacea angustifolia*): A perennial, to 2 feet tall, with long, narrow leaves and lavender daisylike petals curving back from tall orange cones; plants flower in mid- to late summer. Plant on 1-foot centers. The roots are still used by some herbalists as an anti-infective.

14. MANDRAKE (*Mandragora officinarum*): A perennial, to 1 foot tall, with a basal rosette of wrinkled leaves and greenish yellow bell-shaped flowers borne singly in late spring. Plant on 1-foot centers. The root has been used as a painkiller and sedative. All parts are poisonous.

15. WHITE-WOOLY HOREHOUND (*Marrubium incanum*): A perennial, 2 to 3 feet tall and 15 inches wide, with hairy leaves and whorls of white flowers in summer. Plant on 1-foot centers. The leaves and flowers have been used for coughs and colds.

16. ROMAN CHAMOMILE (*Chamaemelum nobile*): A perennial, 1 foot tall in flower; with 2- to 4-inch-tall mats of feathery, fruit-scented foliage and white daisylike flowers from June through August. Plant on 6-inch centers. The flowers have been used as a sedative and hair rinse.

17. AUTUMN CROCUS (*Colchicum autumnale*): A perennial bulb, to 1 foot tall and 3 to 4 inches wide; strap like leaves wither in summer and are followed in September by rose-purple flowers. Plant on 6-inch centers. The seeds and corms have been used to treat gout and rheumatism. All parts are poisonous.

Plants for the Dye Garden

Even though dye plants formed an integral part of most dooryard gardens before the invention of chemical dyes, they were never "domesticated" like their more civilized culinary and fragrant cousins. As a result, they retain a rustic, meadow-plant feel and should be given a simple setting. Ours features half-barrel and rectangular, board-sided raised beds, with the framing staked in place. A split-rail fence or dry-stone wall makes the perfect backdrop to the dye garden. Some dye plants are familiar

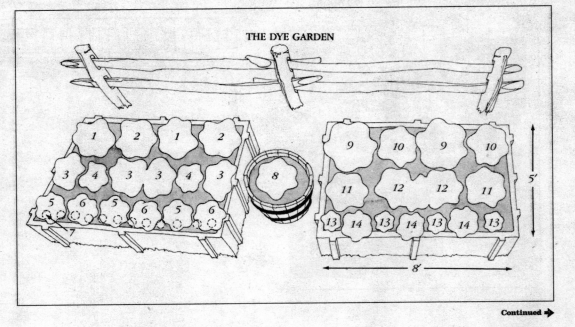

THE DYE GARDEN

Continued ➡

annual flowers—marigolds, zinnias, and calliopsis—and these have been incorporated in the design for added color until the herbs fill in. In subsequent years, they can be removed or space left for them, as desired.

The plants:

1. QUEEN OF THE MEADOW (*Filipendula ulmaria*): A perennial, to 4 feet tall, with large, bright green, lobed leaves, and fragrant, white, feathery plumes in June and July. Plant on 2-foot centers. The roots yield a black dye; the leaves and stems, harvested when the plants are just coming into bloom, yield a greenish yellow with alum used as a mordant.

2. WELD (*Reseda luteola*): A biennial, 5 feet tall in flower, with a basal rosette of long, slender, lance-shaped leaves and long, slender, yellow flower spikes in summer. Plant on 2-foot centers. The whole plant in full flower yields a lemon yellow dye with alum used as a mordant; a golden yellow with chrome; and an orange with alum and tin.

3. GOLDEN MARGUERITE (*Anthemis tinctoria*): A perennial, one of the most ornamental herbs, 2 feet tall and white, with aromatic, feathery green leaves and masses of 2-inch, yellow daisylike blooms from June through August. Plant on 15-inch centers. The flowers yield a yellow dye with alum used as a mordant; a gold dye with chrome.

4. MARIGOLD (*Tagetes* spp.): An annual, with deep green, aromatic, feathery foliage and single to double flowers in yellow; gold, orange, burgundy, and rust; also bicolors and white. Choose bushy plants in the 2-foot range, and plant on 15-inch centers. They'll bloom summer through frost. The fresh or dried flowers yield yellow, gold, orange, brown, gray, or green without a mordant; yellow with alum used as a mordant.

5. LADY'S BEDSTRAW (*Galium verum*): A perennial, to 3 feet tall, but often creeping, with whorls of narrow, pale green leaves and small yellow flowers in panicles in July and August. Plant on 15-inch centers. The roots yield light red with alum used as a mordant; purplish red with chrome. The flowering tops yield yellow with alum or chrome used as a mordant.

6. MADDER (*Rubia tinctorum*): A perennial, to 4 feet tall, but often prostrate, with whorls of leaves and greenish yellow, inconspicuous flowers in early summer. Plant on 15-inch centers. The 3-year-old roots, dried, yield a rose-red or lacquer red with alum used as a mordant; garnet red, orange, or rust with chrome; bright red or Turkey red (on cotton) with tin. The fine reds of old quilts and oriental rugs were created with madder dyes.

7. SAFFRON (*Crocus sativus*): A perennial bulb, saffron is indicated by dotted lines, as it sends up 1½-foot-long, thin, straplike leaves in spring, which die in midsummer. In September saffron bears 2-inch, lilac cup-shaped flowers with bright orange stigmata. Plant on 4- to 6-inch centers. The stigmata yield yellow with alum used as a mordant; gold with chrome. Because the tiny stigmata must be hand-harvested in great quantity to yield dye, saffron dyes have always been the property of the elite and the stuff of legend.

8. SOAPWORT (*Saponaria officinalis*): A perennial, domesticated varieties 1 to 2 feet tall, with 2- to 3-inch, lance-shaped leaves and large pink blooms in panicles from July through September. Plant on 15-inch centers. Soapwort is not a dye plant but is included in the dye garden for authenticity's sake, as the roots were used to make a soapy lather in which the yarn was washed before dyeing.

THE FRAGRANCE GARDEN

9. SAFFLOWER (*Carthamus tinctorius*): A perennial, to 3 feet tall, bushy plants with toothed, bright green lance-shaped leaves and striking scarlet-orange-yellow thistle-shaped flowers in summer. Plant on 2-foot centers. The fresh or dried flowers yield yellow with alum used as a mordant; red in an alkaline solution. It is often called poor man's saffron.

10. GOLDENROD (*Solidago* 'Goldenmosa'): A perennial, to 3 feet tall, with erect stems, slender, spear-shaped leaves, and handsome golden yellow plumes in August and September. Plant on 2-foot centers. The flowers and leaves yield yellow, gold, tan, yellow-green, avocado, olive green, bronze, brown, and khaki; yellow with alum used as a mordant; old gold with chrome. This much-maligned plant is not the source of hayfever (the real villain is ragweed). It is one of the most attractive dye plants. While 'Goldenmosa' is suggested, try any of the tall, domesticated varieties.

11. WOAD (*Isatis tinctoria*): A biennial, 3 feet tall in flower, with a basal rosette of 1-foot-long blue-green leaves and large panicles of cloudlike yellow blooms in May and June, followed by clusters of black berries that can be used in dried arrangements. Plant on 2-foot centers. The young leaves, picked fresh and fermented, yield blue; mature leaves treated in the same manner yield blue-black; weak solutions yield green. The only temperate-climate source of blue dye (tropical indigo also yields blue), woad is indisputably the most stunning dye plant in flower. It's also one of the most historic, having been used by the Picts of England as a styptic for battle wounds, causing them to appear in what was taken by the disconcerted Roman invaders as blue war paint.

12. ST.-JOHN'S-WORT (*Hypericum peiforaturn*): A perennial, to 2 feet tall, with yellow flowers in July and August. Plant on 2-foot centers. The flowering tops yield yellow and gold; the whole plant yields yellow-green with alum used as a mordant; gold with chrome; bronze with blue vitriol; yellow-green with iron and tin.

13. ZINNIA (*Zinnia elegans*): An annual, 6 to 36 inches tall, with opposite, spear-shaped leaves and double blooms to 7 inches across, with quilled, pointed petals, in white, pink, orange, red, green, purple, yellow, and multiples, from summer through frost. Plant one of the Biz-foot cultivars

on 1-foot centers; remember to choose a color or colors compatible with the reds, yellows, and golds of the rest of the bed. The flowers yield yellow with alum used as a mordant; bronze with chrome; bright gold with tin; gray-green with iron; khaki with blue vitriol.

14. CALLIOPSIS (*Coreopsis tinetoria*): An annual, 8 to 48 inches tall, with spindly, needlelike leaves and yellow, purple-red, or bicolor daisylike blooms summer through frost. Plant on 1-foot centers. The fresh flowers yield bright yellow with alum used as a mordant; bright orange-yellow with tin; rusty orange with chrome. If picked after frost, the flowers yield dull gold with alum; brown with chrome and iron; dull rust with chrome and tin.

Plants for the Fragrance Garden

The bloom season in the fragrance garden extends from the first sweet violets in April until the nasturtiums are killed by late fall frosts. Summer is a blaze of color—blue, white, lavender, apricot, and gold. But fragrant flowers are only half the story. The delightfully scented foliage of rosemary, scented geranium, lemon balm, lavender, catmint, the thymes, and nasturtiums can be enjoyed all season. The design brings the plants to nose level for a heady feeling when you're sitting on the bench; the violets form a soft carpet underfoot.

The plants:

1. SWEET VIOLET (*Viola odorata*): A perennial, 6 inches tall in spreading clumps; blooms in April and May with the classic violet fragrance. Violets prefer partial shade so they are planted under the bench and in the shelter of the brick wall. Plant all violet 'Royal Robe,' or mix them with 'Red Giant,' 'White Czar,' and 'Rosina.'

2. SNOW WHITE BEEBALM (*Monarda didyma* 'Snow White'): A perennial, 3 feet tall; blooms in July and August. Give these plants a 2-foot circle; they will spread. Both the tubular flower clusters and the leaves are fragrantly lemony.

3. HIDCOTE LAVENDER (*Lavandula angustifolia* subsp. *angustifolia* 'Hidcote'): A perennial, 1½ feet tall and up to 1½ feet wide; blooms in June and July with deep violet-blue flower spikes. Both the flowers and the silver-gray foliage are highly fragrant, with the intensely pungent lavender scent. Place 1 foot apart to form a solid "hedge."

Continued ➡

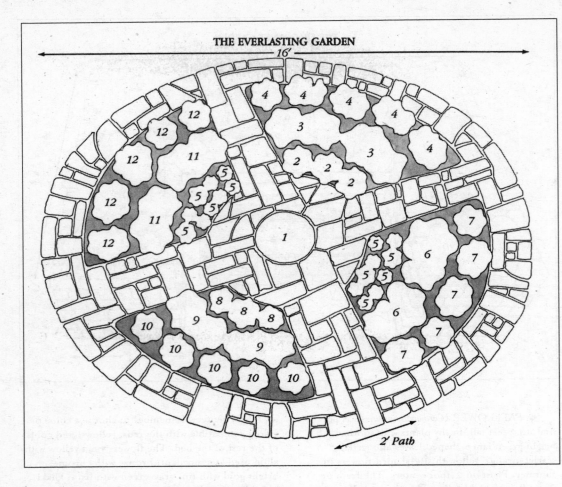

THE EVERLASTING GARDEN

16'

2' Path

herbs. They include the green flowers and foliage of ambrosia; the white, pink, mauve, rose, and purple flowers of statice; the reds, yellows, oranges, and purple-blacks of strawflowers; the silvery foliage of 'Silver King' artemisia; the white flowers of pearly everlasting; the aromatic, gray-green foliage of eucalyptus; and the handsome mauve and green pods of love-in-a-mist. Other herbs that are handsome dried include camphor-scented artemisia, beebalm, dill, elecampane, sage, and hops.

The plants:

1. LAMBROOK SILVER WORMWOOD (*Artemisia absinthium* 'Lambrook Silver'): A perennial, to 3 feet tall, with finely dissected, metallic silvery foliage, which emerges green in spring, and stalks of tiny, yellow, fluffy flowers in midsummer. The foliage is used in arrangements.

2. HIDCOTE LAVENDER (*Lavandula angustifolia* subsp. *angustifolia* 'Hidcote'): A perennial, 1½ feet tall and up to 1½ feet wide; blooms in June and July with deep violet-blue flower spikes. Plant on 1-foot centers. Both the flowers and the silver-gray foliage are highly fragrant and can be dried for arrangements.

3. GOLDENROD (*Solidago* 'Golden Baby' or *S.* 'Goldenmosa'): A perennial, 'Golden Baby' grows 2 feet tall, while 'Goldenmosa' can reach 3 feet; both have erect stems, slender, spear-shaped leaves, and handsome golden yellow plumes borne profusely in August and September. Plant on 2-foot centers. The flowers are used in arrangements; pick them early or they'll turn to loose fluff.

4. YARROW (*Achillea millefolium*): A perennial, 2 feet tall, with aromatic, feathery foliage and flat clusters of creamy white flowers from June through September. Plant on 1½-foot centers. The flowers are used in arrangements.

5. SWEET MARJORAM (*Origanum majorana*): A perennial, 1 foot tall and 4 to 6 inches wide, with small, rounded leaves and showy, deep purple flower heads. Often acts like an annual in temperate areas. Plant on 6-inch centers. The flowers are used in arrangements.

6. TANSY (*Tanacetum vulgare*): A perennial, 3 feet tall, with feathery foliage and yellow button like flowers from July through September. Plant on 2-foot centers. The pungent foliage is used in arrangements.

7. CORONATION GOLD YARROW (*Achillea jilipendulina* 'Coronation Gold'): A perennial, to 2 feet tall with fernlike foliage and flat clusters of golden yellow flowers in summer. Plant on 1½-foot centers. The aromatic flowers are used in arrangements.

8. MUNSTEAD LAVENDER (*Lavandula angustifolia* subsp. *angustifolia* 'Munstead'): A perennial, 1 foot tall, with aromatic, gray foliage and bright lavender flower spikes in summer. Plant on 1-foot centers. Both flowers and foliage can be used in arrangements.

9. FEVERFEW (*Chrysanthemum parthenium*): A perennial, to 3 feet tall and wide, with aromatic, fingered foliage and ivory buttonlike flowers midsummer through fall. Plant on 1½-foot centers. The flowers are used in arrangements.

10. CERISE QUEEN YARROW (*Achillea millefolium* 'Cerise Queen'): A perennial, to 2 feet tall, with aromatic, feathery foliage and flat clusters of bright cherry red flowers from June through September. Plant on 1½-foot centers. The flowers are used in arrangements.

4. MOTHER-OF-THYME (*Thymus serpyllum*): A perennial, creeping ground cover 3 inches tall; bears tiny lavender flowers in June and July. The small, shiny evergreen leaves are fragrant, with the pungent, salty smell of thyme. Plant 1 foot apart; plants will trail over the brick edging for a cascade effect.

5. LEMON THYME (*Thymus* x *citriodorus*): A perennial, clumping herb 4 inches tall; bears small rosy blooms in June and July. The light green leaves have a wonderful lemon fragrance. Give them 1-foot circles.

6. SCENTED GERANIUM (*Pelargonium* spp.): A perennial in Zones 9 and 10, where it may reach 3 feet tall. In colder areas cuttings or pot plants must be set out after all danger of frost has passed; plants will probably reach 1½-foot height and width in one growing season. Pink through lavender flowers are borne in summer. The soft, fuzzy green or bicolored foliage is highly fragrant. There are hundreds of scented geraniums; plant all of one kind or mix them. Favorites include lemon-scented geranium (*P. crispum*), with tiny crinkled leaves; *P. crispum* 'Variegatum', with creamy white leaf margins; rose-scented geranium (*P. graveolens*), with large, fingered leaves; and peppermint-scented geranium (*P. tomentosum*), with downy, maplelike leaves. Give plants 1½-foot circles.

7. LEMON BALM (*Melissa officinalis*): A perennial; may reach 2-foot height and width in flower; blooms July through September. Flower heads should be cut back to keep plants from wantonly self-sowing. Scalloped green foliage is strongly lemon scented. Plant in 1½-foot circles.

8. BLUE WONDER CATMINT (*Nepeta mussini* 'Blue Wonder') A bushy perennial, 12 to 15 inches tall, which covers itself with 6-inch blue flower spikes in spring and early summer. Fuzzy foliage smells minty. Shear plants back after flowering for rebloom in fall. Give plants 1-foot circles.

9. GARLIC CHIVES (*Allium tuberosum*); A perennial, to 2 feet tall; spreads in clumps. Strap like blue-green foliage contrasts nicely with the more leafy

herbs. Plants cover themselves with rose-scented clusters of starry white flowers in late summer. Cut the bloom stalks before the seeds ripen, or you'll have a forest on your hands in subsequent seasons. Plant garlic chives on 1½-foot centers.

10. NASTURTIUMS (*Tropaeolum majus*): An annual; 1 foot tall by 2 feet wide; will cascade over the brick edging. Sea green leaves are succulent and shaped like inverted umbrellas. Both leaves and flowers, which are borne summer through frost in saturated shades of red, apricot, orange, and gold, are strongly scented, with a unique, nose-pinching, pepper-perfumy smell. Sow after all danger of frost has passed. Plant on 1½-foot centers.

11. WHITE-FLOWERED ROSEMARY (*Rosmarinus officinalis* 'Albiflorus'): A perennial in Zones 8 through 10; otherwise, sink pots in the bed or plant out and pot again in fall. Can reach hedge proportions, but won't north of Zone 8, where it is unlikely to reach 2-foot height. There are several good white-flowered varieties, blooming in early summer. The main attraction, however, is the graceful branches of deep green needles with their delightfully pungent, piny scent.

Plants for the Everlasting Garden

This garden is everlasting in two senses: first, it is composed of perennials; and second, all of the plants may be dried for everlasting arrangements. To dry the flowers or foliage for bouquets or wreaths, cut the stems on a dry day after the dew has evaporated. Because flowers will continue to mature as they dry, cut them before they are fully open. Unless the foliage is ornamental when dried, strip off the leaves; otherwise, you face increased drying times and the danger of mildew. Tie the stems in loose bunches (but make the ties tight—stems will shrink as they dry). Hang the bunches upside down in a dark, warm, well-ventilated room (such as an attic or pantry) for a couple of weeks. Flowers with woody stems can be placed upright in a glass.

Many other plants can be chosen to add color and texture to an everlasting garden. Most of these are considered ornamental flowers rather than

Continued ➡

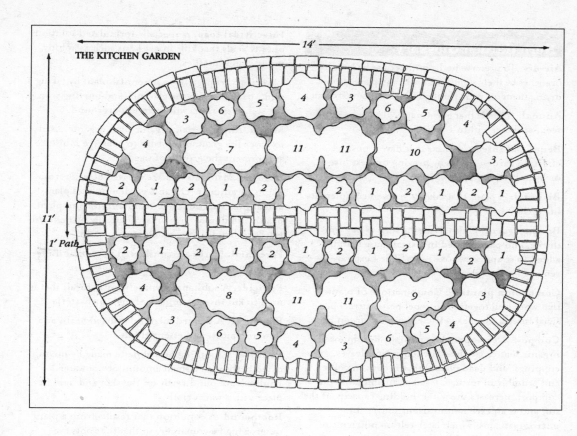

THE KITCHEN GARDEN

14'

11'

1' Path

itable spearmint scent. Confine the roots. Shear before flowering. Plant on 2-foot centers.

10. PEPPERMINT (*Mentha x piperita*): A perennial, to 3 feet tall, with long, dark green, purple-tinged leaves and purple stems, lilac-pink flowers in midsummer, and the strong, incomparable peppermint fragrance. Confine the roots. Harvest or shear back to the desired height. Shear before flowering. Plant on 2-foot centers.

11. BORAGE (*Barago officinalis*): An annual, 2½ to 3 feet tall, with strong, hairy, large green leaves and star-shaped, drooping, predominantly blue flowers (though they may also be pink and lavender) in midsummer. Flowers and leaves are edible; both are used in salads and fruit salads, while the flowers are refreshing in drinks. The flavor is reminiscent of cucumber. Plant on 1½-foot centers.

Your Seasonal Herb-Care Calendar

Now that you know the basics of growing herbs organically, you'll need to know when to start seeds indoors, direct-sow seeds outdoors, mulch, and prune to give your herb plants conditions in which they can thrive. This calendar gives you, at a glance, what you'll need to do each month.

Also, keep in mind that because of climatic conditions, planting herbs in Florida isn't the same as planting them in Maine. Before you even start planning for herbs, you need to find out what hardiness zone you live in.

January

Although the weather outside may be snowy and cold, you can warm up with thoughts of your garden to come.

- Spend some time paging through gardening magazines and herb books to collect ideas for the upcoming season. Or check out the Web site www.organicgardening.com.
- Read about all the different ways you can use herbs (in cooking, as medicines, and in cosmetics and crafts).
- Inventory your garden supplies to make sure you have the essentials, such as a trowel, a cultivator, and plant markers.

February

With spring around the corner, now is the time to start getting your garden plans together.

- Finalize which herbs you want to plant, and then decide where to grow them—in pots on your patio, on a kitchen windowsill, or in your vegetable garden or flowerbeds.
- Keep in mind that most perennial herbs like well-drained soil, so cluster water lovers (such as basil and parsley) together.
- Buy seeds for fast-growing annual herbs (like borage) to sow directly.

March

Now you can start to get your hands dirty!

- Remove protective winter mulch as you begin to see new growth on your perennial herbs.
- If you're planning on starting annual herbs from seed, now is the time to plant those seeds in flats.
- This month is also a good time to select and prepare a site for a new herb garden. An ideal place would be an area close to your house that gets at least 6 hours of full sunlight each day.

April

Plant new perennial herb plants. Trim woody herbs like lavender as they begin to show new growth. Start basil seedlings indoors for an earlier harvest.

11. BLUE BEAUTY RUE (*Ruta graveolens* 'Blue Beauty'): A perennial, 2 feet tall, with aromatic, blue-green, ferny foliage and yellow flowers in summer. Plant on 2-foot centers. The aromatic seed heads, which can be picked in the green or brown stage, are used in arrangements.

12. MOONSHINE YARROW (*Achillea jilipendulina* 'Moonshine'): A perennial, to 2 feet tall and 1½ feet wide, with fernlike foliage and flat clusters of cream-yellow flowers in summer. Plant on 1½-foot centers. The flowers are used in arrangements.

Plants for the Kitchen Garden

This kitchen garden is designed to be ornamental, but it is composed—with the exception of borage—of the most common culinary herbs. The borders of the central path are undulations of purple, green, and pink (if you let the 'Dark Opal' basil flower). Plants in the outer borders are on 1½-foot centers so each can be shown to best advantage. A mulch of bark chips or cocoa hulls will accent form and foliage color, as well as keep dirt off the bricks. Mints are invasive. Control them by sinking metal edging strips, preferably a foot deep, around their planting area, or by planting them in sunken bottomless buckets. In either case, leave an inch or so of rim or edging above the ground to control prowling stems. The focal point of the garden is the borage, with its fuzzy foliage and lovely star-shaped blue, pink, or lavender flowers.

The plants:

1. DARK OPAL BASIL (*Ocimum basilicum* 'Dark Opal'): An annual, to 15 inches tall, with dark purple leaves and pink flowers in July and August. For heaviest production of the spicy, fragrant leaves, clip off the flower heads; leave them for the most ornamental effect. Plant on 1-foot centers.

2. PURPLE SAGE (*Salvia officinalis* 'Purpurascens'): A perennial, 12 to 30 inches tall, powder green older leaves, new leaves powder purple, with purple flowers in June. The foliage has a hearty, sausage like smell; let it grow in subsequent years to fill the borders, or keep it cut back to leave space for the 'Dark Opal' basil. Plant on 1-foot centers.

3. CURLY PARSLEY (*Petroselinum crispum*): A biennial, treated as an annual. Bushy 1-foot-tall plants with dark green, moss-curled leaves. Remove after the foliage dies back at the end of the first season—the following year, the plants' energies will be directed toward producing 3-foot stalks of yellow-green umbels in summer, rather than the flavorful, vitamin-rich leaves. Plant on 1½-foot centers.

4. CHIVES (*Allium schoenoprasum*): A perennial, forming spreading clumps 1 to 1½ feet tall of tubular, deep green leaves, with striking balls of pink to pale lilac flowers in June. Plants do tend to spread, but are easily controlled by division. Plant on 1½-foot centers.

5. COMMON THYME (*Thymus vulgaris*): A perennial, shrubby plant, to 14 inches tall, with small, deep green leaves and tiny mauve flowers in June and July. The name may be common, but the fragrance and fine, salty, pungent flavor are unbeatable. Plant on 1½-foot centers.

6. SPICY GLOBE BASIL (*Ocimum basilicum* 'Spicy Globe'): An annual, rounded mound of tightly packed, pungent, light green foliage to 1 foot tall. Bears light green flower heads in July and August. The most visually appealing basil; you want to pet it. A similar variety is Burpee's 'Green Globe'. Plant on 1½-foot centers.

7. BERGAMOT MINT (*Mentha x piperita* var. *citrata*): A perennial, 2 to 3 feet tall, with long, deep green, purple-tinged leaves, purple flowers in midsummer, and a strong citrus scent. Confine the roots. Harvest or shear back to the desired height. Shear before flowering-mint is invasive enough without encouraging seeding. Plant on 2-foot centers.

8. APPLE MINT (*Mentha suaveolens*): A perennial, to 4 feet tall, with rounded, gray-green, hairy leaves, lavender flowers in midsummer, and a rich fruity scent. Confine the roots. Harvest or shear back to the desired height. Shear before flowering. Plant on 2-foot centers.

9. SPEARMINT (*Mentha spicata*): A perennial, to 2½ feet tall, with spear-shaped, bright green leaves, pink, white, or lilac flowers, and the inim-

Continued →

May

You'll have plenty to do this month in your herb garden.

- Plant annual herbs outdoors after your last frost date.
- Direct sow seeds for fast growers like dill and cilantro. To extend your harvest, sow seeds successively every 2 weeks.
- You can also plant tender perennial herbs, such as scented geraniums and rosemary, outside, either in the ground or in pots.
- Dig up and divide large clumps of perennial herbs as necessary.
- Mulch between plants with compost, shredded bark, or another organic material.

June

Continue to sow fast-growing annual herbs such as borage every 2 weeks. Harvest fresh herbs to add flavor to summertime dishes. Pull out weeds that crop up between your herbs.

July

During these lazy, hazy dog days of summer, you should:

- Water as necessary.
- Hang sages and lavender in a dry, dark place for later use in herbal wreaths.
- Make lots of pesto with your basil, cutting off flowerstalks as you harvest.
- Sit in the shade and enjoy a refreshing glass of mint iced tea (or a mint julep) made with mint you picked from your own plants.

August

Use your bounty of herbs to make flavored vinegars and oils. Sow seed for a later harvest of dill and cilantro. Continue to harvest, freezing or drying what you can't use now for use in winter.

September

Dig up and pot tender herbs such as scented geraniums and rosemary. Let them adjust outdoors in their pots before bringing them in. Or take cuttings to root for next year's garden if you don't have space for whole plants.

October

Fall signals the time to begin winding down. This month:

- Clean up the garden after Jack Frost has made his appearance.
- Pull out spent annual herbs and cut back any perennial herbs that need it.
- Organize notes you took from the gardening season and compile them in a binder, along with a map of where each herb grew.

November

Before the ground freezes, add a protective winter mulch of shredded leaves to perennial herbs. Enjoy the season's bounty by using your dried herbs for seasonings in recipes, creating potpourris, and making wreaths.

December

Use evergreen boughs as additional winter protection by laying them over your perennial plants. Give friends and family gifts of potpourris, scented sachets, wreaths, and herbal vinegars that you made with herbs from your garden.

Herb Garden Glossary

Air-dry. To preserve herbs for later use by hanging branches by their stems in a dark, airy place, or by drying them on racks through which air can circulate.

Annual. A plant that germinates, flowers, sets seed, and dies within 1 year.

Beneficial insects. Insects that have a positive effect on garden plants by preying on pest insects or by pollinating plants.

Biennial. A plant that takes 2 years to complete its life cycle.

Bouquet garni. Culinary herbs such as bay leaf, thyme, and parsley, tied in a small bunch and added to soups, stew, or sauces. The herbs are removed before serving.

Companion planting. Combinations of plants that work well together to repel pests, attract beneficial insects, or make efficient use of garden beds.

Compost. Decomposed or partially decomposed organic matter (such as kitchen scraps, leaves, grass clippings, and dead plants) that is dark in color and crumbly in texture. Used as an amendment, compost increases the water-holding capacity of the soil and is an excellent nutrient source for microorganisms, which later release nutrients to your plants.

Compost tea. A fertilizer made by soaking a cloth bag full of compost in a watering can or barrel for several days.

Culinary herbs. Herbs used in cooking.

Cutting. A 3- to 5-inch clipping of healthy green growth that is cut from the parent plant and placed in potting mix to root.

Direct seeding. Planting seeds outside directly into the garden.

Division. A way to propagate perennial herb plants by dividing established plants at the roots to form several new plants.

Dormancy. A resting phase for plants that enables them to survive conditions of cold, drought, or other stress, during which they may have no leaves or flowers.

Essential oils. Highly concentrated aromatic oils of plants that are used in cosmetic preparations.

Fish emulsion. An organic liquid fertilizer, made from fish solubles, that contains 4 to 5 percent nitrogen. It is used most often for foliar fertilization (where fertilizer is applied to and absorbed through the plant's leaves).

Full sun. Plants that thrive in full sun need a minimum of 6 hours of direct sun each day. Most herbs prefer a sunny location.

Hardening off. Gradually exposing tender seedlings to the outdoors in a protected area for a week prior to transplanting them into the garden.

Hardiness. Plants are able to tolerate varying levels of cold temperatures and still survive. Plant hardiness zones help gardeners determine which perennials will survive the winter in a specific area.

Herbaceous. A perennial plant that dies back to the ground at the end of each growing season.

Herbicide. A substance used to kill unwanted plants. Some types are selective (they kill only a certain type of plant); others are nonselective and will kill any plants they come into contact with.

Herb standard. A perennial or tender perennial herb plant that is trained to be a single stem with branches only at the top.

Insecticidal soap. A specially formulated solution of fatty acids that kills insect pests such as aphids, mites, and whiteflies.

Layering. Propagating a perennial plant by taking a stem, bending it to the ground, and burying it in the soil. New roots will form underground.

Mulch. Any material, organic or inorganic, used to cover the ground in order to preserve moisture and prevent the growth of weeds.

Organic. Materials that are derived directly from plants or animals. Organic gardening uses plant and animal byproducts to maintain soil and plant health and doesn't rely on synthetically made fertilizers, herbicides, or pesticides.

Perennial. Herbs are considered perennial if they last for 2 or more years.

Pesticide. A substance, synthetic or natural, that is used to kill insects, animals, fungi, or bacteria.

Potpourri. A scented mixture of dried herbs and flowers, spices, and essential oils.

Poultice. A soothing herbal paste made by mixing dried herbs with a small amount of hot water. Poultices are put directly on the skin and held in place with a warm cloth.

Rootbound. A condition that results from a plant outgrowing its container, so that the roots are densely crowded and often coiled around the inside of the pot.

Sachet. A fragrance bag made with a combination of dried herb leaves and (frequently) rose petals, crumbled or ground.

Seedling. A young plant grown from seed. Commonly, plants grown from seed are termed seedlings until they are first transplanted.

Self-sow. Herbs such as German chamomile, cilantro, and dill that will reseed themselves if left to go to seed.

Tender perennial. A perennial plant that is treated as an annual because it is being grown outside of its hardiness zone.

Umbels. Flowers, such as Queen Anne's lace, that all have stalks that are the same length and that emerge from the same place on the stem and form a flat-topped cluster.

Volunteers. Plants that grow spontaneously in the garden from a previous year's seeds.

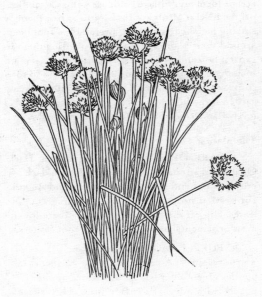

Lawns

Groundcover

Trees and Shrubs

Vines

The Landscape Garden

LAWNS

Lawn Care Basics

Jeff Cox

The goal of most homeowners is to have a lush, green lawn that's free of weeds and, at the same time, easy to maintain. In addition, most of us also want to keep the environment cleaner by cutting down on the use of gasoline-powered lawn mowers, and keep our lawns and our families healthy by avoiding the use of lawn chemicals. An ideal way to cut down on lawn maintenance is to turn some of that green grass into a richly textured bed of easy-care groundcovers.

Whether you're looking for ways to make your lawn healthier, seeking solutions to lawn problems, or looking for alternatives to lawns, this chapter will provide you with a wealth of lawn care and groundcover tips and techniques.

Healthy green turf makes everything near it look better. A carpet of green grass also makes a great place to play or relax, while preventing soil erosion and enhancing the value of your home. A good lawn is the result of conscientious gardening practices, whether you're starting a new lawn with a carefully selected cultivar or rejuvenating an existing one.

Build a strong lawn by using grass species adapted to your climate. Encourage healthy growth naturally by letting light grass clippings remain where they fall and by applying compost or other organic material. Relying on high-nitrogen chemical fertilizers can lead to problem-prone, shallow-rooted turf that needs mowing more often. These are some of the most widely grown lawn grasses:

- Bermuda grass (*Cynodon dactylon*), a fine-textured, drought-resistant grass popular in warmer climates. Becomes buff brown in the winter. Numerous runners create a wear-resistant turf. Open-pollinated strains are extremely aggressive; modern hybrids are much easier to keep from invading flower beds.
- Buffalo grass (*Buchloe dactyloides*), a creeping, warm-season grass. Tolerates drought and will grow in alkaline soil. Good wear tolerance. Brown in midsummer and fall.
- Centipede grass (*Eremochloa ophiuroides*), a coarser-leaved, warm-season, creeping grass with good drought tolerance. Plant in areas that receive little wear.
- Fine fescues (*Festuca* spp.), dark green, fine-textured, creeping, cool-season grasses with good shade tolerance, often mixed with Kentucky bluegrass.
- Kentucky bluegrass (*Poa pratensis*), a lush, dark green turf grass with narrow blades that requires substantial sunshine. Favored cool-season lawn grass. May become dormant during summer droughts or during winter freezes. Creeping stolons knit a tough turf.
- Turf-type tall fescue (*Festuca arundinacea*), a coarse, medium green grass good for sun or shade, increasingly popular in the central United States. Updated cultivars remain green most of the year. Drought-resistant. Grows in low clumps and doesn't creep, so is often mixed with other grasses.
- Zoysia grass (*Zoysia* spp.), a medium green, creeping, fine-textured grass for full sun. Green in warm weather, tan in winter.

Fertilizing Your Lawn

You don't need to know every grass plant in your yard by name to grow a healthy lawn. The most important thing to note is the time of year when the grass begins to grow rapidly. This is the ideal time to apply a good organic fertilizer. In the North where cool-season grasses have a growth spurt in spring and another in fall, plan to fertilize twice. For warm-season grasses, fertilize in late spring, just as your lawn greens up, and again a few weeks later.

Choose a finely pulverized, weed-free organic fertilizer, such as processed manure or sifted compost, and spread evenly over the lawn just before rain is expected. Mow the grass about a week

Continued →

after you fertilize. Let the nitrogen-rich clippings remain on the lawn.

Maintaining Your Lawn

Lawn maintenance involves more than just proper watering techniques. You also must mow, dethatch, and aerate your lawn regularly to keep it at its best.

Mowing. Sharpen your mower blade at the beginning of each season to make sure the grass blades are cut, rather than torn, when you mow. Remove only one-third of the grass's top-growth. The exact height for mowing depends on the species of grass. Cut low-growing grasses, such as Bermuda grass and zoysia grass, no shorter than 1 inch. Cut taller grasses, such as bluegrass and tall fescue, no shorter than 2 inches. Mow high during summer droughts. To cut very tall grass, set your mower blade at its highest setting. In the course of the next two mowings, lower the blade until you are cutting at the usual height.

If you mow regularly, let your grass clippings lie where they fall. They will eventually rot and add organic matter to the soil beneath. But don't let large clumps of clippings sit on your lawn—they block sunlight and promote disease. Gather them up and use as mulch in other parts of your yard.

Dethatching. All lawns have thatch, a layer of clippings and stems that gradually decomposes and feeds the roots. There's no need to remove it if the layer is no thicker than about ¼ inch. Thatch problems often start with overuse of synthetic chemical fertilizers, which make grass grow fast and lush. As clippings build up into a thick layer of thatch, grass plants are unable to get enough air for healthy growth. Use a thatch rake to break up thatch in a small lawn; rent a vertical mower to dethatch a larger area.

Aerating. Since lawns often bear heavy foot traffic, the soil below them becomes compacted over time. Grass roots have trouble growing down and out and instead concentrate their growth at the surface. Prevent or fix compacted lawns by aerating every two or three years. Aerating a lawn consists of poking tiny holes through the turf into the soil below. Use a step-on core cultivator for small areas; rent a power aerator machine for larger lawns. Mow the lawn and spread a thin layer of organic fertilizer. Aerate in one direction; repeat crosswise. Water the lawn deeply.

Repairing Lawns

Ruts left by heavy vehicles or scars created when shrubs or trees are removed call for prompt spot repairs. If damage occurs in winter, prepare the soil and cover it with a mulch until spring.

Loosen the soil in the damaged site, setting aside any grass plants that seem healthy. Keep them damp and shaded as you work. Add a ½-inch layer of compost or peat moss to condition the soil, along with enough good topsoil to raise the level of the damaged area 1 inch above the soil level of the surrounding turf. Lightly walk over the spot, and fill in any holes or low places. Reseed or replant, matching the primary species in your yard. Water regularly for a month.

Planting a New Lawn

All lawn grasses require at least 4 inches of good topsoil in which to stretch their roots. If your new yard has been scraped down to the subsoil, you will have to spread new topsoil. Site preparation is the same whether you plan to begin with seed or sod: Cultivate new or existing topsoil thoroughly, adding a 1-inch layer of peat moss, compost, or other organic matter. Rake out all weeds and roots, cultivate again, and rake smooth. Use a roller to evenly compact the site and make it level.

Be picky when shopping for grass seed. Improved cultivars of the best lawn grasses cost more than their open-pollinated cousins, but they offer superior performance. Choose named cultivars that have been specially bred for drought tolerance, insect and disease resistance, adaptability to shade, or other traits. Use a mechanical seeder for even distribution. Roll after seeding. Keep constantly moist for two weeks. Start mowing three weeks after seeding.

Sod is the fastest way to an attractive lawn, though the cost is higher than seed. It's ideal for spot repairs, especially in high-traffic areas or on slopes. Plant cool-season species in early spring or from late summer to early fall; plant warm-season grasses in late spring to early summer. Use only fresh, green strips. Keep them shaded and damp until planted. Work crosswise along slopes. Roll or walk on the strips after planting to push the roots into the soil. After planting, water newly laid sod every two or three days for three weeks.

Planting Options

Whether you're starting a new lawn or repairing one you've already got, you have several grass-planting options:

Spreading seed: If you're seeding a lawn area, use a spreader to distribute seed evenly. A broadcast-type spreader throws the seeds in a wide swath, so it does the job faster than a drop-type spreader will. When working near flower beds or other nonlawn plantings, the drop type is preferable because it won't cast the seed into your flower beds. Make two passes when seeding an area. On your second pass, walk at a 90-degree angle to the first pass.

Planting grass plugs: Plugs can restore a damaged lawn area. Begin by raking the area to level it and remove debris. Water thoroughly the night before you plan to plant. Use a plugger, auger, or spade to make 3-inch-diameter planting holes in a checkerboard pattern. For good establishment, place 1 teaspoon of blended organic fertilizer in each hole before planting. Plant a plug in each hole. The spacing you use will determine how long it takes for

the grass to fill in and form continuous cover. Water again after planting and regularly for the first few weeks. Fertilize your new lawn six to eight weeks after planting.

Laying sod: When laying sod, fit the strips as close together as possible. Be sure to stagger the seams between strips so that they do not line up from row to row. Use a sharp knife to cut sod to fit around walks, edgings, or other obstacles. Rolling sod after laying it improves contact between the roots and the underlying soil and gets the sod off to a good start. On a slope, always lay the rows of sod across the slope, not up and down.

Do any sod patching on the inside. Pieces along the periphery should be whole. If you're patching here and there as part of a renovation (perhaps to cover where a tree has come down or to resod a patch lost to weeds), you should use whole blocks of sod, even if the spot in need is smaller than that. The smaller the piece, the harder it is to keep alive, so cut out a spot big enough to lay in an entire block of sod.

Making spot repairs: Where weeds or lawn pests have caused damaged patches, a partial lawn renovation will usually solve the problem. Clean out weeds and dead grasses with a shovel and rake, till the soil, and amend it with an organic fertilizer. The cultivated patch of soil will compact and settle over time, so rake it into a flat-topped mound slightly higher than the surrounding turf. Plan on planting seed or sod that matches the rest of your lawn, unless you've decided on shade- or drought-tolerant lawn grass for a particularly troublesome area. After sowing or sodding, be sure to firm the soil to ensure good soil contact. Water repaired spots as necessary until the new grass shows strong new growth.

Coping with Problems

A healthy lawn is naturally more resistant to weed, insect, or disease problems. A tight cover of vigorous grass will outcompete weeds. Loose, well-drained soil helps prevent disease problems. Proper fertilization goes a long way toward preventing lawn problems since it encourages growth of strong, healthy turf. Most updated turfgrass cultivars offer genetically improved resistance to diseases and some insects. If you have lawn areas that are chronically problematic, consider replanting them with an improved cultivar or trying an alternative to lawn grass.

Continued ➡

There are a few simple steps to take if your lawn develops weed or pest problems. Use a small, sharp knife to slice off any established weeds about 1 inch below the soil surface. If more than half of the plants in your lawn are weeds, it is best to completely renovate the lawn by replanting.

Subterranean insect laevae, such as white grubs, occasionally cause serious damage when they feed on grass roots. Apply milky disease spores for long-term control of these pests. Biological insecticides that utilize parasitic nematodes control numerous insects likely to feed beneath your lawn.

Selecting Lawn Grasses

Barbara W. Ellis

One of the best ways to enhance the overall beauty of your yard is to cultivate a healthy lawn. Whether your lawn is large or small, the first step toward creating a lush green carpet is to choose a lawn grass—or, better yet, a grass mixture—that fits your climate. There are many lawn grasses available today, varying in heat and drought tolerance, active growing season, shade tolerance, and general cultural conditions under which they grow best. For this reason, experts recommend different grass species for different parts of the country. Whether you're planning to sow seed or plant sod, keep in mind that a mixture of grasses rather than a single species or cultivar is best. (Both seed and sod are generally available as mixtures.) That way, you can take advantage of the best characteristics of several grasses when planting a new lawn or renovating an old one. By choosing a mixture of grasses that are adapted to your climate, soil, and site, you'll be well on your way to a healthy green carpet.

Cool, Warm, or In Between

Grass experts recognize two major groups of lawn grasses—cool season and warm season. Cool-season grasses, which grow best in the northern half of the country, include Kentucky bluegrass, perennial ryegrass, and fine fescues. The fine fescues are further divided into red or creeping fescues, Chewings fescues, and hard fescues. Cool-season grasses typically make their strongest growth in spring and fall but may remain green all winter. They tend to become brown and dormant in midsummer.

Warm-season grasses, which are suitable for the desert Southwest and Sun Belt, include low-maintenance centipedegrass, luxurious-looking zoysiagrass, shade-tolerant St. Augustinegrass, and the incredibly tough, improved cultivars of bermudagrass. These grasses are much more heat-tolerant than cool-season grasses. They are dormant in winter and do not begin to green up until early summer. All tolerate drought better than cool-season grasses.

Gardeners in the transition zone between North and South—as well as in the West and Great Plains—can use a mixture of both cool- and warm-season grasses, commonly called transition-zone grasses. In fact, in the transitional zone, the combination of grass species found in seed or sod mixtures can become quite complex. In the East, the most important grass in the mix is often improved tall fescue, often called "turf type" tall fescue, along with small amounts of other grasses such as bluegrass and annual ryegrass. Improved tall fescues do not creep, so the other grasses in the mix help knit an otherwise tufted lawn into a smooth turf. Buffalograss and blue gramagrass, both warm-season grasses native to this country, are good choices in the western part of the transitional zone, especially in lawns that are not watered. Crested wheatgrass is probably the best choice for lawns that will not be irrigated.

The overwhelming favorite among cool-season grasses is Kentucky bluegrass, a lush, sod-forming turfgrass now available in dozens of named cultivars. The best bluegrass lawns include a blend of four or five updated cultivars that have been selected for such characteristics as color, drought tolerance, disease resistance, and ability to stand up to heavy wear. As the individual grass plants intertwine, the lawn benefits from the collective talents of the different cultivars in the mix.

Choosing the Best Grasses

When choosing any lawn grass, always avoid "common" strains in favor of the newest improved named cultivars. For example, plain Kentucky bluegrass, Kentucky-31 tall fescue, and common bermudagrass are acceptable for roadsides and meadows, but in home lawns they grow too vigorously and become invasive. Named cultivars of lawngrasses often show superior disease resistance, cold hardiness, or shade tolerance. Although many cultivars are available as seed or sod, some of the newest ones—especially of bermudagrass and centipedegrass—are only available as sod, plugs, or sprigs.

Lawn Grasses That Resist Pests

Some grasses, such as zoysiagrass and bermudagrass, are bothered by very few insect pests. But aphids, armyworms, pillbugs, and cutworms can seriously damage succulent stems and stolons of cool-season grasses. In the last decade, scientists have found that some lawn grass cultivars, including 'Repell' perennial ryegrass and 'Rebel' tall fescue, host a type of fungi that protect them from any insect predators. Where insect populations are high, introduction of these pest-resistant cultivars can greatly enhance the health of the lawn.

In Florida and Texas, the southern chinch bug frequently injures lawns. The old St. Augustinegrass cultivar 'Bitter Blue' is extremely susceptible to this pest. Two St. Augustinegrass cultivars, 'Floratam' and 'Floralawn', show good resistance to this pest.

The following lawn grass cultivars earn high ratings for pest resistance, beauty, and adaptability.

- Kentucky bluegrass: 'America', 'Midnight', 'Baron', 'Glade', 'Challenger'
- Perennial ryegrass: 'Manhattan II', 'Repell', 'Gator', 'Citation II', 'Palmer'
- Fine fescue: 'Pennlawn', 'Ruby', 'Dawson', 'Atlanta', 'Jamestown'
- Hard fescue: 'Reliant', 'Spartan', 'Scaldis'
- Turf-type tall fescue: 'Hawk', 'Rebel', 'Mustang', 'Houndog', 'Apache'
- Bermudagrass: 'Tifway II', 'Tiflawn', 'Midiron', 'Vamont', 'Texturf 10'
- St. Augustinegrass: 'Floratam', 'Floralawn', 'Floratin'

Lawn Grass Pest Patrol

When your lawn starts to show yellow or brown patches, you can be sure that lawn pests are living in your green carpet. Here's a look at the four most common lawn pests and what you can do to combat them.

Sod webworms: Webworms sever grass blades and cause irregular dead patches in the lawn. Hot, dry conditions and thatch buildup encourage the pests.

Control webworms by saturating infested areas with a soap drench (2 tablespoons liquid dish soap to 1 gallon water) to drive the larvae to the surface. Rake the pests into a pile and dump them into a bucket of soapy water. Apply BTK (*Bacillus thuringiensis* var. *kurstaki*) or drench the soil with parasitic nematodes when pests are in their larval stage (usually about 2 weeks after moths appear). Spray severely infested areas with pyrethrin if all other attempts at control fail.

White grubs: These curved, fat, whitish larvae of Japanese beetles and other beetle species chew on grass roots, leaving sections of lawn that appear burned. Lift out damaged turf.

A check for white grubs. Use a blunt-ended spade to cut through three sides of a square-foot flap of lawn. Gently pry up the roots, and roll the flap back to look underneath. Count the grubs in the ground, and then tamp the turf back down. Ten or more grubs per square foot is a serious infestation. Give the flap a little extra water for a week or two to be sure it reroots.

Walk the turf in spiked sandals (available through mail-order catalogs) that will pierce and kill the grubs. For a large lawn, apply milky disease spores according to package directions; this treatment will eliminate Japanese beetle grubs over a few seasons. Or apply predatory nematodes. Water the soil well before and after application to improve results.

Billbugs: Billbug larvae are white grubs with yellow-brown heads that feed on grass stems, causing shoots to turn brown and die. In warm weather the grubs tunnel into the soil and feed on roots and rhizomes. Billbugs are brown or nearly black ¼- to ½-inch weevils. Control grubs by aerating the lawn, watering deeply, removing thatch, and adding organic matter. Reseed or overseed with resistant cultivars.

Chinch bugs: Chinch bugs and their larvae are common lawn pests virtually everywhere except the Northwest and Plains states. The bugs and the larvae are about 1½ inches long. The bugs have a distinctive inverted-V pattern on their wings.

If your lawn shows ragged yellow or brown patches, you may have a chinch bug problem. Treating problem areas with insecticidal soap is generally effective.

A check for chinch bugs. Cut both ends from an empty coffee can and push the can halfway into the lawn. Pour soapy water into the can and wait 10 to 15 minutes. Then count the number of chinch bugs and/or larvae that float to the top. If you see more than 12, you need to take steps to control the pest.

Continued ➡

In most mixes, the shortcomings of bluegrass—its inability to grow in heavy shade and the tendency of some cultivars to germinate slowly—are dealt with by adding other cool season grasses to the lawn's plant population. Fine fescues are the top choices for lawns growing in shady spots in cool climates. Fast-germinating perennial ryegrass is added to bluegrass mixtures to provide short-term cover while the bluegrass becomes established.

Several older lawn grasses have lost popularity in recent years. Bentgrasses have earned a well-deserved reputation as high-maintenance, disease-prone grasses. In the South, many homeowners have become disenchanted with zoysiagrass because it requires too much care and is often invaded by winter weeds.

A few lesser-known grasses are making their way into lawns. Selected hard fescues, native to the Canadian Rockies, grow so slowly in the cool climates that they hardly need mowing. Breeders have developed perennial ryegrasses that are very dark green; a few of these new cultivars even creep a little. In warm climates, bahia grass is sometimes used near salt water since it tolerates salt spray.

Measuring the Lawn

Whether you are planting a new lawn or rejuvenating an old one, an accurate measurement of your lawn's surface area can help you estimate how much seed, sod, or fertilizer you will need. In lawn grass lingo, materials estimates for seed or soil amendments are usually given per 1,000 square feet of surface area. Sod is sometimes sold in square yards. To measure the surface area in square yards, first determine your square footage and divide that figure by 9 for your square yard measurement.

Most houses are square or rectangular, and lawns mimic this design. To measure, divide the lawn into adjoining squares and rectangles, and measure the length and width of each. Multiply the length by the width of each unit to find the area of each section. Add these numbers together to find your lawn's total surface area.

Round or triangular-shaped sections of lawn may be measured using standard geometric formulas. To obtain the surface area of a circle, measure the distance from the center to the edge (the radius). Multiply this number by itself (for example 10 x 10); then multiply the answer by

3.14. The result is the surface area. To find the area of a triangular section of lawn, multiply the length of the base by the length of the height; then multiply the resulting number by .5.

You can calculate the surface area of irregularly shaped lawns by dividing them into their component parts—triangles, half-circles, or rectangles. Determine the area of each part; then add the figures together to find the total surface area.

How to Measure an Amoeba

To measure odd shapes with curved edges, find the approximate center of the space. Then measure a line drawn between opposite edges through the center. Divide this line into 10-foot sections. Then, at each 10-foot mark, determine the width of each 10-foot section by measuring the distance between opposite edges (perpendicular to the original axis line). To obtain the surface area, add all the widths together and multiply the total by 10. If your yard includes island beds within the lawn, use this procedure to measure the surface area of your beds, and subtract them from the total lawn area.

Sowing Grass Seed

Even the highest quality grass seed will result in a spotty, sunken lawn if it is sown into rough, unimproved soil. Preparation for seeding a lawn may be a laborious process, but is well worth the effort, for a properly planted lawn will thrive for many years.

In general, warm-season grasses are best seeded in late spring, while transitional and cool-season grasses are seeded in early spring or early fall. If you must do something with your bare yard but the time for planting expensive seed is months away, do some preliminary leveling and sow the site lightly with annual ryegrass. The cover crop can be tilled into the soil along with other soil amendments a few weeks before planting.

Preparing the Seedbed

A raw site around a new home generally requires considerable grading before it's ready to sow. You'll need to fill in low spots and even out high ones. Don't be in a rush to get started, for it will take several heavy rains to settle in loose dirt and reveal the true contours of your new yard. Once your yard is settled, fill in the low spots with excess topsoil from high places, or buy a load of topsoil for this purpose.

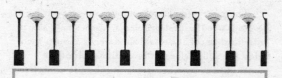

How High to Mow

As a general rule, cut grass at the high end of the range during hot weather; lower when weather is cool or plants are growing in shade. At the end of the growing season, cut the lawn back one last time at the lowest recommended height.

Grass Cutting	Height (in.)
Annual ryegrass	2–2½
Bermudagrass	1–1½
Centipedegrass	1–1½
Fine fescue	1½–2½
Kentucky bluegrass	2½–3
Perennial ryegrass	1½–2½
St. Augustinegrass	2–3
Tall fescue	2½–3½
Zoysiagrass	1–1½

Incorporate weed-free, humus-rich organic material, like compost, well-rotted sawdust or manure, peat moss, or leaf mold, into the soil by spreading a 2- to 3-inch layer and using a rotary tiller to work it in. Organic matter will improve the drainage of heavy clay soils and the nutrient-holding capacity of sandy ones. Add organic fertilizers such as bonemeal, cottonseed meal, greensand, and ashes. Add lime, if indicated by a pH test.

Rake out debris, and smooth out the surface once more. Do not attempt to seed lawn-quality grasses on steep slopes. Plant sod instead, or use the slope to achieve some other landscape effect. For example, you might plant the slope with low, spreading shrubs, or create a small rock garden around a stone retaining wall.

When the site of the future lawn is raked smooth, the soil should be firmed into place. You can rent a lawn roller, or you can use a large metal barrel, turned on its side. Roll over the area twice, until your feet leave only shallow prints in the seedbed.

Spreading Seed

You can use a mechanical seeder, available from rental centers, or spread seed by hand. The best way to ensure even distribution of seed is to make two applications. Take half of the seed and spread it while walking back and forth across the plot in parallel lines or strips. Make a second application with the rest of the seed by walking and sowing strips that are perpendicular to the first seeding. Rake lightly to barely cover the seed, and roll the area one last time to firm in the seeds and make sure there is good seed-soil contact. A light covering of weed-free straw (not hay, which contains weed seeds) will help retain moisture and keep the seed from washing away. If the site slopes more than a little, use burlap or cheesecloth to keep the soil and seed in place.

Aftercare

Grass seed needs good light and constant soil moisture for strong germination. Keep leaves and other debris off newly seeded lawns, and use a sprinkler to keep the soil evenly moist at all times for two to three weeks. Most grass seed germinates within two weeks, but bluegrass, buffalograss, and

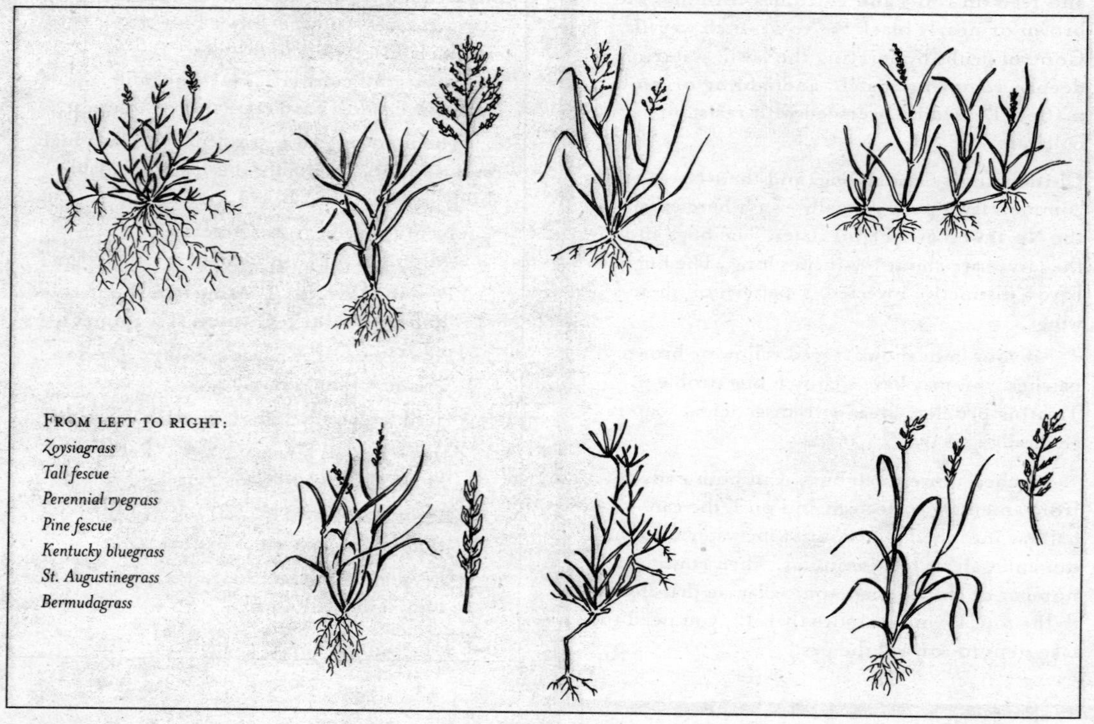

Continued ➜

FROM LEFT TO RIGHT:
Zoysiagrass
Tall fescue
Perennial ryegrass
Pine fescue
Kentucky bluegrass
St. Augustinegrass
Bermudagrass

A Guide to Selected Lawn Grasses

One of the best ways to develop a low-maintenance lawn is to select the right grass for your region. Cool-season grasses are best for the northern part of the country; warm-season grasses for the Southwest and Sun Belt. Transition zone gardeners should use a mixture of both warm-and cool-season grasses for best results.

Name	Description	Culture	Rate of Establishment	Nitrogen Needs
Cool Season				
Kentucky bluegrass (*Poa pratensis*)	Lush, green with fine texture. Good wear tolerance.	Moderate drought tolerance. Plants become dormant during periods of drougt; require regular irrigation to stay green in summer. Fertile, nearly neutral soil with plenty of aun.	1 year from seed; 6 months from sprigs; 3 weeks from sod.	Average; fertilize in early spring and early fall.
Fine fescue (*Festuca spp.*)	Dark green color and fine texture. Blends well with Kentucky bluegrass. Very good wear tolerance.	Good drought tolerance, especially in shady spots. Grows best in fertile, slightly acid soils.	1 year from seed; 6 months from sprigs; 3 weeks from mixed-species sod.	Below average; fertilize in early spring and early fall.
Perennial ryegrass (*Lolium perenne*)	Very dark green grass with fine leaves. Somewhat clumpy unless blended with bluegrass or creeping fescue. Very good wear tolerance.	Good drought tolerance. Plant in slightly acid soil in full sun.	2 months from seed, but expect 2 years for mixed-species lawn to assume mature appearance.	Average; fertilize in early fall.
Transition				
Blue gramagrass (*Bouteloua gracilis*)	Medium-fine grass with bunching habit. Forms dense sod. Good wear tolerance.	Warm-season grass often planted in transition zone and Great Plains. Drought tolerant. Good for cool, dry regions. Alkaline soil. Turns brown in severe drought.	2 years from sod.	Below average; fertilize in late spring and early summer.
Buffalograss (*Buchloe dactyloides*)	Native American grass with fine leaves and creeping stolons. Good wear tolerance.	Warm-season grass good for Great Plains and transition zone. Excellent drought tolerance. Will grow in full sun, clayey soil, and alkaline conditions. Turns brown in midsummer and again in fall.	2 years from seed, 1-2 years from plugs.	Below average; fertilize in late spring and early summer.
Fairway created wheatgrass (*Agropyron cristatum*)	Vigorous bunchgrass with deep, spreading root system. Good root system. Good wear tolerance.	Cool-season grass good for transition zone and Great Plains. Drought and cold tolerant.	About 1 year from seed.	Below average; fertilize in early spring and early fall.
Turf-type tall fescue (*Festuca elatior*)	Medium green grass, with coarse leaves. Noncreeping habit. Good wear tolerance.	Cool-season grass often grown in transition zone. Good drought tolerance. Will grow in many soils and tolerates a wide pH range.	3 months from seed.	Average to below average; fertilize in spring or fall.
Warm Season				
Improved bermuda-grass (*Cynodon dactylon* hybrids)	Medium to dark green grass with fine, stiff leaves. Excellent wear tolerance.	Excellent drought tolerance. Plant in fertile, well-drained soil with full sun.	2-3 months from sprigs; 3 weeks from sod. Seeding not recommended	Above average; fertilize in late spring and midsummer.
Centipedegrass (*Eremochloa ophiuroides*)	Medium green grass with somewhat coarse leaves. Thick creeping stolons. Fair to poor wear tolerance.	Excellent drought tolerance. Will grow in moderately fertile, acid soils. Plant in full sun.	1 year from sprigs; 2 years from seed.	Below average; fertilize once a year and supplement with iron sulfate improves color and vigor.
St. Augustinegrass (*Stenotaphrum secundatum*)	Dark green grass with creeping stems and broad, flexible blades. Fair wear tolerance.	Average drought tolerance. Plant in fertile, well-drained, sandy, neutral to slightly acid soil. Can grow in shade.	3 months from sprigs or plugs. Not available as seed.	Above average; fertilize in early spring and fall to improve color and vigor.
Zoysiagrass (*Zoysia* spp.)	Medium green, creeping grass with fine, stiff leaves. In the north, turns brown in winter. Very good wear tolerance if thatch is removed every few years.	Average drought tolerance. Plant in full sun with fertile, well-drained slightly acid soil.	2 years from sprigs; 2 months from sod. Seeding not recommended.	Below average; fertilize once a year in late spring.

centipedegrass are slower to start. In bluegrass/perennial ryegrass lawns, cut the lawn for the first time about two to three weeks after sowing to help the bluegrass compete with the more vigorous perennial ryegrass.

Planting Sod

Sod may be the perfect solution for high traffic areas, slopes, and other problem areas. Although it costs more than seed, sod is attractive from the start and becomes established quickly. In some cases, the best grass cultivars are available only as sod. Another advantage is that sod can be planted nearly any time of year, although it is sensitive to drought and must be watered faithfully until it's established. Late summer to early fall is the best time to sod cool-season grasses in the North; late spring to early summer is best for warm-season grasses.

When buying sad, look for fresh, green slabs that have been kept constantly moist. Like seed, sod is available in mixtures of cultivars suitable for different regions. Buy only from nurseries that label the mixture and certify that it is free of weeds, insects, and disease, or arrange to buy freshly dug sod from a reputable nearby sod farmer. It's important to keep the sod moist once it's been delivered to you. It's best to prepare the soil before your sod is delivered so it can be planted as quickly as possible.

To plant sod, begin by preparing the site as if you were planting seed. Level it, add soil amendments, and rake away all debris. Sod cannot be planted over an old lawn. Where grass, weeds, or any plant material is present, dig it out or till it under before planting your sod.

The day before you plan to plant, roll the prepared site and water it lightly. Firm contact between soil and sod roots is essential, so check to make sure all weeds and other debris are cleared away.

Laying Sod

Begin laying the sod against any straight edge, such as a sidewalk or a string stretched between two pegs. Lay the sod in strips, end to end, and fit them together as tightly as you can without overlapping. To prevent erosion, stagger the seams or edges of the pieces to achieve a bricklike pattern. Trim away excess sod along curved or uneven edges with a sharp knife or shovel. You can use the pieces you cut away to fill in elsewhere or to rejuvenate dead spots in another part of your lawn.

Once the sod is in place, roll it to firm the roots into the soil. Fill crevices between sod pieces with weed-free topsoil—use a broom or the back of a wooden rake to do the spreading—and turn on the sprinklers. All types of sod should be thoroughly soaked right after planting, then twice a week for three to four weeks thereafter.

Continued ➤

Planting Plugs and Sprigs

Some creeping grasses are planted as small pieces of sod called plugs or sprigs. Plugs are small, container-grown pieces of sod; sprigs are individual rooted grass stems made from shredded sod. Unlike conventional sodding, plugs and sprigs are spaced from 6 to 12 inches apart, with bare areas in between. This technique is most often used with warm-season grasses such as St. Augustinegrass, bermudagrass, centipedegrass, and zoysiagrass. Any type of sod can be cut into chunks and planted as plugs. For most grasses, this isn't a recommended practice for large areas because they spread less quickly than the species commonly planted in this manner.

Plugs and sprigs are best used for planting lawns that are level and in low-traffic places. When planting a lawn in this manner, keep in mind that several months may pass before the grass plants grow together completely. On slopes, heavy rains will wash away the soil between the plugs or sprigs, and the end result will be a spotty, uneven lawn. Weeds often appear in the areas between the plugs or sprigs and must be hoed out or pulled by hand.

For best results, plant plugs or sprigs in spring. Prepare the planting area as you would for seed or sod, but leave the soil loose instead of rolling it. Both plugs and sprigs dry out quickly, so keep them in a shady place and sprinkle them with water frequently until you are ready to plant them.

Plugs should be planted at their normal growing depth, 6 to 12 inches apart. With sprigs, lay the pieces in shallow furrows at an angle so that two-thirds of each sprig is buried and only a tuft of grass shows above the ground. An alternate way to plant is to drop the sprigs at intervals on the surface of the planting area, and push them into the soil with the heel of your shoe. After planting, roll the area to make sure the soil is firm and level and roots are in good contact with the soil. Then water the area thoroughly, and keep it damp for at least three weeks. Hoe out weeds as soon as they appear, and topdress with a good organic fertilizer when rapid growth commences.

Mowing the Lawn

Each time you mow your lawn, you actually are pruning back thousands or millions of grass plants. Mowing does much more than make it possible to walk to your car in the morning without getting your feet wet. When properly done, it helps expose the crowns of the plants to sunlight and encourages the development of tillers, or creeping stems.

The rule of thumb is to remove one-third of the grass's top growth each time you mow. Mow too high and you'll need to mow again in a few days; mow too low and you may send the grass into a state of shock by exposing the crowns of the plants to sun and cutting off too much of the leaf blades, which manufacture food for the plants. Close cutting also helps create places between grass plants where weeds can become established. Adjustments may be made to mowing heights, depending on the season. In midsummer, it's a good idea to mow higher than normal since long blades help insulate the plant's crowns from moisture loss. In early fall, warm-season grasses are sometimes cut very low and overseeded with annual rye for better winter color.

Always mow when the grass blades are dry. Sharpen mower blades at least yearly so that they slice off the tops of the grass cleanly instead of chewing it up. Rotary mowers (the most popular kind) are fine for most lawns. Reel-type mowers

are recommmended for very dense, fine-bladed grasses like zoysiagrass and hybrid bermudagrass.

Thick clumps of grass clippings may be gathered and used as mulch or added to the compost pile. Let light layers rot where they fall; they are a good source of nitrogen, and nature will take care of recycling the nutrients in the clippings.

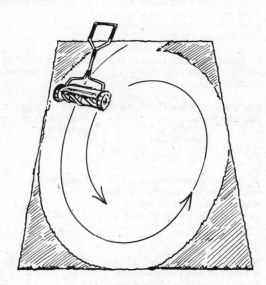

Mowing in a round or oval pattern saves time and effort, because you don't waste energy turning sharp corners.

Rejuvenating Lawns

Sooner or later, most lawns need a facelift—either of the entire lawn or of small patches that have been damaged by insects, weeds, or diseases. Many old lawns can be renovated in a weekend, though more work is in order if weeds are running rampant (in which case, it is probably best to start again from scratch) or if the soil is badly compacted as a result of heavy use.

The first step in any lawn rejuvenation project is to dig out the weeds—roots and all. For an all-over facelift, once weeds are under control, the next step is to rent a vertical mower, also called a dethatcher. Healthy lawns have about ¼ inch of thatch, the undecomposed organic matter on top of the soil, which acts as a mulch and helps conserve moisture. Heavily fertilized lawns can build up thick layers of thatch that smother the plants and create ideal conditions for insects and disease. A vertical mower cuts small slits in the turf and brings dead plant parts to the surface where they can be raked up and composted. Dethatching gives old grass new room to grow and opens little places in the turf where new grass seed can germinate.

If the soil appears hard and lifeless, some type of aeration also is in order. You can rent power aerator machines that poke holes in the turf or other machines that cut out small cores of soil. In addition, a generous topdressing with a good organic fertilizer will aerate the soil in the most natural way, by encouraging the proliferation of soil microorganisms. Fertilize after dethatching and aerating. This is also the time to apply lime, if indicated by a soil test.

Seeding or Patching

The lawn is now ready for overseeding or for patching with small pieces of sod. In bluegrass lawns, simply overseed the old, reconditioned lawn with a mixture of updated cultivars, and keep the area moist for three weeks. Fescues, perennial ryegrass, and other seed-sown lawns also may be overseeded in this way.

Grasses that cannot be sown from seed, such as zoysiagrass and the new hybrid bermudagrasses,

often respond to reconditioning so dramatically that no further planting is necessary. However, bare spots formerly occupied by weeds should be planted with pieces of sod taken from the outer edges of the lawn.

Starting from Scratch

If you want to completely renovate your old lawn and plant a new type of grass, the entire site should be tilled up and raked clean, a major job that you may want to hire someone to do. To get rid of the old grass, you can slice it away and pull it up in strips, or till it under. (You may need to till two or three times to be sure the old grass won't come back.) In hot weather, it is sometimes possible to heat-kill areas of unwanted grass by covering them with clear plastic for several days. Decrease the chances that the grass will survive by mowing it as low as possible before tilling it under. Whatever you do, don't rush to replant; be sure the old grass is dead before proceeding. Expect to wait several weeks before the site is ready for replanting.

The Organic Lawn
Roger Yepsen

You can eliminate or greatly reduce the synthetic fertilizers and pesticides used on your lawn. And that will mean one less source of worry about the health of your family, pets, and the home environment. While chemical-based lawn care treats the soil as a passive blotter, the organic approach focuses on improving the lawn from the ground up. Good soil gives rise to healthy lawns, with less trouble from pests, diseases, and adverse weather conditions. You also may find that the lawn has a reduced need for watering and fertilizer.

Working With an Existing Lawn

Unless you're moving into a new home, or are expanding your lawn into what had been a field or garden beds, you probably are looking at a reasonably well-established lawn. You can bump up its appearance a couple of notches by core aeration, adjusting mowing height, and top-dressing with a fine, sifted compost.

Increasing the level of organic matter will improve the soil's structure, with a few benefits. The soil will be better able to hold on to moisture and nutrients, while promoting good drainage. Roots will grow more easily, so that the grass will hold up better against an assault from weeds. Finally, organic matter contributes to nitrogen fixation and helps resist soilborne plant diseases.

All of this won't take place overnight. While chemical approaches can have an almost immediate effect, organic improvements are gradual. And you'll be a happier homeowner if you don't expect a totally weed-free lawn. A yard that is a bright, flawless green throughout the year is probably a lawn heavily reliant on chemical help and a lot of irrigation. The organic way involves a more relaxed perspective.

Keep Sharp

The whirling blade of a mower is out of sight, and it tends to be out of mind as well. But if it has become dull, it may be beating the grass into submission rather than cutting it cleanly. Inspect the ends of a few clippings. If they are frayed, that's a sign that the blade needs attention. The entire lawn may take on a somewhat brownish tinge. A dull blade also puts a greater load on the mower, consuming more gas and contributing to wear and tear. Shredded grass may be more susceptible to

Continued →

lawn diseases. Finally, the blade has to be sharp in order to cut damp grass without serious tearing.

Sharpening a blade isn't an easy task, no matter what the operating manual for your mower may suggest. You have to make sure the engine won't start up while you're removing the blade, and that means knowing where the spark plug is and how to remove the wire running to it. Getting at the blade is a challenge if you have a riding mower. And even a dull blade can cut you, meaning you need to be mindful when removing it. Finally, a blade may need routine balancing as well as sharpening, and that's a job beyond the skills and aptitude of most homeowners. The easiest solution is to have the mower dealer pick up the machine and do the sharpening, as well as balancing the blade if necessary. Second easiest is for you to deliver the mower. If you have no way of transporting a riding mower and the pickup charge is prohibitive, you can follow the operating manual's directions for removing the deck, then take it to the dealer.

Lawns the Low-Maintenance Way

Barbara W. Ellis, Joan Benjamin, and Deborah L. Martin

Lawn grasses and groundcovers go hand in hand in the low-maintenance landscape. Nothing beats a lawn for a durable place to play or a smooth, green swath to set off flower beds. But lawn grasses perform best in full sun on fertile, well-drained soils. That's where groundcovers come in. Nothing beats them for care-free plantings on tough-to-mow sites—or to reduce high-care grass.

In this section, you'll learn how to reduce the time you spend on your lawn by examining your equipment, grass choices, and routine care. You'll also find out how modifying old habits will help you cut lawn care. Finally, you'll learn to recognize parts of your landscape better suited for groundcovers than for turf grasses.

Keep Grass in Check with Edging and Mulch

A vigorously growing lawn will grow right into your flower beds and up to the bases of trees and shrubs if you don't control it. Neither your trees and shrubs nor your lawn benefit from the resulting competition. A combination of an edging barrier and mulch around plants and plantings will keep the grass where you want it. It will also protect other plants from too-close encounters with mowers and trimmers.

To install edging strips, start with thick, good-quality edging; you'll find a variety of edging strips at local garden centers and nurseries. Thick edging is easier to install and will last the longest. Deeper edging stays in the ground better. Here's how to go about installing your edging.

1. Use a garden hose, rope, or a line drawn with sand or lime to outline the area you want to edge. Keep curves gentle and avoid sharp corners.

2. Use straight pieces of plastic edging if possible. Warm coiled edging in the sun for easier straightening.

3. Dig a straight-edged trench that's as deep as your edging. To save yourself work on a large installation, consider renting a power trencher.

4. Working from one end, loosely install the entire length of edging with the rounded edge just above the soil line. Backfill just enough to hold the edging in place. The edging should stay in the trench without any pressure. Tight curves or forced fits will pop out later.

5. Inspect the installation, make any minor adjustments, then backfill and firm the soil

around the edging. Water the area thoroughly for uniform settling and firming.

6. Check edging strips annually to make sure spreading weeds or grass haven't grown over them. Mow over the top of the strip, with one wheel in the bed and one in the lawn. This lets you mow and trim at the same time. Keep the garden mulched to control spreading weeds.

Methods to Help You Tame the Mowing Monster

Most of us give up far too much of our limited free time to cutting grass. But if you want a traditional-looking lawn, mowing is a necessary evil that can consume large portions of your time from spring to fall. Short of giving up your lawn entirely, there are ways to make mowing easier, quicker, and more efficient.

The amount of time you spend mowing is a direct result of the vigor and layout of your lawn, as well as the kind of mower you use. Since a healthy, vigorous lawn can grow fairly aggressively, you're more likely to reduce mowing time by mowing more efficiently than by mowing less often. Try any or all of the following tips to make your mowing quicker and easier.

Repair or replace awkward spots. Level out rough spots in your lawn to allow your mower to travel more easily. Keep grassy areas at least three times the width of your mower to allow for easy turning. Fill smaller or tough-to-mow sites with groundcovers.

Mow frequently. Mow often enough to remove no more than one-third of the leaf blade at one time. Frequent mowing reduces clipping clutter, snips of germinating weeds, grinds leaves, and promotes dense turf. The mower will move quickly over the lawn, too.

Mow high. Set your mower blade to a height of about 2½ inches for most grasses; higher for fescues and St. Augustine grass. Tall grass smothers prostrate weeds, captures more sunshine, and roots more deeply to reach nutrients and water.

Use the proper tool. A properly sized mower with adequate power will speed up the mowing process. It's also a pleasure to use equipment that performs a chore quickly and easily.

Let clippings lie. Save yourself work and return moisture and nutrients to your lawn: Let cut grass lie where it falls.

Add water during dry spells. Water enough to keep the grass alive during droughts without bringing it out of heat-induced dormancy. Drought stress makes lawns susceptible to invasion by weeds, diseases, and pests. When watering is necessary, apply 1 to 2 inches by recording the time it takes for your sprinkler to fill a pan to that depth. Select sprinklers that adjust for complete coverage and distribute a large quantity of water quickly. Use programmable timers to water late at night when water pressure is high and winds are minimal.

Avoid overfertilizing. The lush new growth that results from generous applications of nitrogen is disease-prone and requires frequent mowing. A healthy lawn may get by with little more than the clippings produced when you mow, plus one or two top-dressings with compost or other organic fertilizer each growing season.

Accept and encourage diversity. Diseases, insects, and other stresses have less impact on lawns that have a mixture of grasses, along with weeds like clover.

Eliminate obstacles and trimming. Shape plantings and borders so you can guide the mower around them without excessive turning or stopping.

Consolidate plantings. Plant shrubs and trees in groups and mulch or plant beds of ground. covers

around them. It's much easier to mow around the edge of a group of plants than to mow around each plant individually.

Prune offending branches. Ducking and dodging as you mow slows your progress and is dangerous—you're not paying attention to your mower if there's a tree branch in your face. Keep trees and shrubs pruned appropriately to give you access with the mower, or plant no-mow plants beneath obstructing limbs.

Make follow-up trimming obsolete. Use perennials and groundcovers that hang over the edge of the lawn around tree trunks or along buildings. Let your mower's deck slip under the overhanging leaves to cut the grass right to its hidden edge. Install mowing strips around plantings to eliminate trimming after you mow.

Minimize Frustration with Regular Mower Maintenance

Few things are as frustrating as having a lawn in need of mowing and a mower that won't work. Performing regular maintenance on your mower or having a mechanic maintain it for you is a small investment that can prevent major mowing headaches.

Check the oil. Do this while the mower is on level ground, before you start the engine. Fill to the appropriate level for your mower's engine. Change engine oil when it's warm—contaminants are suspended and the oil will flow easily.

Keep filters clean. Clean foam filters in warm, soapy water. When they're dry, squeeze enough oil through them to lightly coat the entire filter. Gently tap and blow dirt out of pleated paper filters. Replace them when the paper discolors significantly.

Keep belts and chains snug. Check belts for cracks or glazing. Keep spares on hand even if you don't change them yourself so you don't have to wait for parts to be ordered and shipped.

Keep the mower clean. Use a leaf blower or shop vacuum to remove dust and debris from the mower deck and engine compartment. While you wash the mower, look for loose hardware or other potential problems. Avoid getting water on ignition parts, or the mower will have to dry before it will start.

Lubricate chains, bearings, and bushings. Check the owner's manual for locations and lubricant specifications.

Keep blades sharp. Sharp blades cut cleaner with less power. Removing the blades frequently for sharpening will keep them from becoming stuck on.

Speed Mowing Time with a Bigger Mower

If you have a large lawn to cut, buying a bigger mower is a straightforward way to reduce the time you spend mowing. And a larger mower with a larger engine will do the job more efficiently than a small machine that's running for a longer time.

When shopping, consider overall mower size, deck size and location, maneuverability, engine size, comfort, and cost. Mower features to consider as you shop include cutting deck placement, the power source that moves the mower (you or the engine), pull start vs. electric start, the engine's capacity relative to the work it has to do, and overall comfort and ease of use. Use this list of mower types to help you find the mower that's right for you and your lawn.

Mulching mowers. Mulching mowers (or mulching modifications to bagging mowers) chop clippings and leaves into fine pieces, reducing grass residue and allowing easier cleanup. They don't work well in grass that is too tall or wet.

Continued ➡

Bagging mowers. These machines pulverize grass, leaves, and debris while vacuuming the lawn. Bagging takes more time than allowing the clippings to fall back on the lawn, but it provides a useful material for mulching or composting. Look for bags that are large, easy to put on and take off, and easy to empty. Find a mower that bags when necessary, but also mulches or discharges effectively.

Intermediate mowers. Sized between homeowner models and mowers used by maintenance crews, some intermediate mowers offer a sulky option and may be used either as a large walk-behind or a rider.

Riding mowers. Riding mowers generally have larger decks than their walk-behind counterparts and travel faster than a comfortable walking speed. Riders come in different sizes and configurations, so find one that meets your specific needs.

Quit Vacuuming Your Lawn and Feed Your Soil Instead

Leaves or clippings can smother lawn grasses; but you don't have to spend hours vacuuming or raking them up and hauling them away. Instead, use your mower to grind them up into small particles so they can settle into the soil and decompose. You'll not only eliminate most raking, but you'll also be enriching the soil with organic matter.

You can actually treat your lawn like a giant sheet composting site. Throw anything the lawn mower will handle onto the lawn, then pulverize it. Rake up resistant material when you're finished and remove it to the compost pile. Use these tips to make the most of your mower as a soil-enriching power mulcher.

Mow often. Take care of leaves before they build up and clog the mower. The added mowing time is minimal, and you'll no longer have leaf disposal.

Keep the blade sharp. A sharp blade pulverizes effectively.

Clean the air filter frequently. Dry, dusty leaves will plug the filter quickly. Make sure that you clean your filter often, especially after mowing leaves, which produce more dust.

Circle inward. Use a side-discharge mower to blow leaves into a row, then mow the row to grind the leaves into tiny pieces and disperse them to the outside over the lawn.

Circle outward. For heavy leaf cover, start in the middle of an area and discharge the leaves to the outside for dispersal or pickup around the edges.

Make light work of leaf lifting. If you need to rake up leaves, rake them onto a large tarp for easy transport. Leaves are light when dry; grab the corners of the tarp to tote large quantities.

Keep Weeds at Bay by Reseeding

Keep weeds from colonizing your lawn by reseeding bare or sparsely covered patches. For best results, seed in late summer when soils are warm and weed seed has already germinated. Here's how.

Remove existing vegetation. Remove weeds and existing grass with a sharp spade, sod lifter, or scuffle hoe. Rough the soil to a depth of at least 1 inch, using a rake or cultivator for small areas and a rotary tiller for large ones. Level the soil with the surrounding area, then rake from several directions to make many crossing furrow lines. Grass seed germinates best in grooves, so make plenty of them.

Sow your grass seed. To increase germination, protect the seed from hungry birds, and prevent it from washing away in rain, lightly mulch the area with straw. Or tack a floating row cover over the seeded area with rocks or bent lengths of wire until the grass begins to sprout. Water gently to wet the top ½ inch of soil, then keep the area moist, but not soggy, until your seedlings are ready for mowing.

Mow when most of the area needs it. Don't wait too long to mow or taller grass will shade the remaining new seedlings. After three mowings, treat the newly seeded area like an established lawn.

Grow Grasses You Can Count On

Whether you are installing a new lawn or renovating an existing one, use the following tips to select the best grass for your lawn.

Suit your local growing conditions. Northern, cool-season lawns are commonly composed of bluegrass, ryegrass, or fescues. Warm-season lawns most often contain zoysia, St. Augustine, centipede, bahia, and bermuda grasses. Check with your county's extension office or garden centers to get up-to-date recommendations on the best grasses for your area.

Pick the best cultivars. Look for lawn grass cultivars with drought tolerance, disease resistance, and other low-maintenance characteristics. There are also dwarf or slow-growing cultivars that need less mowing.

Plant endophyte-enhanced grasses. For a lawn that resists pests, try a grass that contains endophytes, fungi that live in plants without causing harm. In grasses, these fungi confer resistance to leaf-eating pests like chinch bugs, sad webworms, and armyworms. Cultivars of fine fescues, tall turf-type fescues, and perennial ryegrasses are currently available. Choose seed mixes that contain at least 50 percent endophyte-enhanced seed for maximum protection; buy fresh seed to ensure that the fungus is viable.

Your Seasonal Lawn-Care Calendar

JANUARY

Cool Grass:

Check out the reel mowers in your local hardware store. (If the store doesn't carry them, tell somebody in charge that they should!) Winter's also a great time to think about how you use your yard and plan a project to convert some lawn to another use such as a meadow, island bed, or outdoor entertaining area.

Warm Grass:

Add lime or sulfur to correct pH, if recommended by soil test. Also, winter is a great time to think about how you use your yard. Why not plan a project to convert some lawn to another use?

FEBRUARY

Cool Grass:

Sharpen your mower blades, or take them to a nearby shop to have them sharpened. Now's a good time for a mower tune-up, too—you can beat the crowds. A properly working mower will generate less pollution. While you're at it, set your mowing height at 3 inches or higher.

Warm Grass:

If you have a power mower, take it in for a tune-up ahead of the spring crowds. Sharpen your mower blades, and consider buying a spare blade so you'll always have sharp blades on hand.

MARCH

Cool Grass:

Clean up any debris left on the lawn after the winter.

Warm Grass:

Your first mowing should be in early spring. The mowing height depends on the type of grass you're growing.

APRIL

Cool Grass:

As the grass begins to grow, you can begin to mow—but don't remove more than one-third of the height of the grass blades at each mowing. You might want to bag or rake up the clippings after the first mowing to add a good dose of nitrogen to your compost pile. But after that, leave the clippings on your lawn!

Warm Grass:

Warm-season grasses are actively growing now, so water as necessary during this season of growth, and keep on mowing.

MAY

Cool Grass:

Spread organic fertilizer. There's not much point in doing this before mid-month, as it won't begin to act until the soil warms. Water as necessary during the grass's active growing season. Deep watering, enough to wet 6 inches down into the soil, encourages healthy roots. Mow weekly or even every five days if your grass is growing rapidly.

Warm Grass:

In addition to mowing, spread organic fertilizer. Different grasses have different nitrogen requirements.

JUNE

Cool Grass:

Mow and water—but only as needed. Watch for changes in your lawn. If it changes from green to yellow, that means it's entering semidormancy. Don't worry—this is normal! You shouldn't try to revive it by watering or fertilizing. Your grass will come back in the fall—it's only resting.

Also, examine your lawn for clues about your soil. For instance, clover is a sign that your soil lacks sufficient nitrogen.

Warm Grass:

Continue to mow and water as necessary. Make mowing easier on yourself by resharpening your mower blades. Bahiagrass especially requires sharp blades. Plug or sod bare areas.

JULY

Cool Grass:

Sharpen your mower blades—yes, again! A sharp blade causes less stress to the grass. Besides, your lawn is growing so slowly that you can mow as infrequently as every three weeks (especially if the

Continued ➡

weather is dry), so you'll have plenty of time to devote to sharpening.

Warm Grass:

Continue to mow and water your lawn as necessary.

AUGUST

Cool Grass:

Test your soil, especially if you think your lawn needs help. How much topsoil do you have? Check and see: 4 inches is good—6 is better. Continue mowing, but only as needed.

Warm Grass:

Make a second application of organic fertilizer. If you're waiting for plugs or sprigs to fill in your lawn, get out the hoe and take care of any weeds that are filling in faster than your grass. Mow and water as necessary.

SEPTEMBER

Cool Grass:

This is a busy month! Look at all you can be doing to care for your lawn.

- If your lawn has bare spots, seed them now.
- If your lawn is sparse or if you'd like to overseed with a pest- or disease-resistant grass species, reseed now.
- Spread organic fertilizer or a thin layer of sieved compost.
- And of course, mow and water as necessary as your grass is actively growing.

Warm Grass:

Don't stop now! Continue to mow and water as necessary.

OCTOBER

Cool Grass:

If your soil test indicated that you need to raise the pH, add time. If your pH is too high, consider adding sulfur. Mow only as needed, the growing season is nearly over.

Warm Grass:

Warm-season grasses are entering dormancy, and you can begin to slow down, too. Cease irrigation as the growth stops.

NOVEMBER

Cool Grass:

Mow over fallen leaves to chop them up. Rake the chopped leaves if the cover is very thick (for example, under a Norway or sugar maple) and save them to use next spring as mulch. Often you can get away with just leaving them on the lawn, where they'll decompose and add nutrients. When you mow for the last time this season, mow your lawn shorter than usual.

Warm Grass:

Test your soil to determine pH and soil deficiencies. Then take a break from lawn care!

DECEMBER

Zzzzzzzzzzzz.

Whether you grow cool- or warm-season grass, your lawn is reating, so you can too!

Lawn-Care Glossary

Aeration. Boring holes in the soil with a special tool or a spading fork to open up spaces in it so that oxygen, water, and nutrients can reach grass roots. It is generally ineffective and unnecessary in a healthy lawn, although it may help lawns growing in heavy clay soil.

Clay soil. Soil that is made up of very fine particles that hold nutrients well but are poorly drained. Clay soil is heavy and difficult to work.

Compost. Decomposed and partially decomposed organic matter that is dark in color and crumbly in texture. Used as an amendment, compost increases the water-holding capacity and drainage of the soil and is an excellent nutrient source for microorganisms, which later release nutrients to your plants.

Cool-season grass. Any grass species that grows well in spring and fall (such as Kentucky bluegrass or fescue) but grows slowly or goes into a dormant state in the heat of summer.

Dethatching. Removal of excessive thatch with a dethatching machine or rake. Thatch buildup is caused by overfertilization, which can result in lawn grass growing at a faster rate than the soil organisms can break it down, and by the use of pesticides that kill earthworms, important decomposers of thatch. With good organic lawn-care practices, most lawns shouldn't need dethatching.

Endophyte. A naturally occurring fungus that lives inside some grass plants. It doesn't harm the grass, and endophyte-infected grasses are more resistant to insects and have better drought tolerance. Note: Endophytes are harmful to livestock, so don't plant endophyte-infected grasses in grazing areas.

Fertilizer. A natural or manufactured material added to the soil that supplies one or more of the major nutrients (nitrogen, phosphorus, and potassium) to growing plants.

Foliar feeding. A way to give grass a light nutrient boost by spraying plants with a liquid fertilizer that is absorbed through the leaf pores. Compost tea and seaweed extract are two examples of organic foliar lawn fertilizers.

Grubs. Larvae of beetles and other insects that overwinter in the soil, feeding on grass roots early and late in the season. You can recognize grubs by their white, C-shaped bodies; control them with milky disease spore.

Herbicide. A substance used to kill unwanted plants. Some types are selective (they kill only a certain type of plant); others are nonselective and will kill any plants they come in contact with. Corn gluten meal is one of the very few effective organic herbicides.

Humus. A dark-colored, stable form of organic matter that remains after most of the plant and animal residues in it have decomposed.

Hydroseeding. Establishing a lawn area by spraying a slurry, which is a mixture of grass seed, fertilizer, fiber mulch, and water.

Loam. The best texture of soil to have. It contains a balance of fine clay, medium-size silt, and coarse sand particles. Loam is easily tilled and retains moisture and nutrients effectively.

Named variety. A subdivision of a plant species that has been selected for its improved vigor, fine texture, or other desirable characteristics and then bred and named by the industry to ensure a standard of quality.

Nematodes. Microscopic, slender, translucent roundworms, many of which act beneficially as decomposers and pest parasites. Other nematodes feed on and damage plant roots.

Nitrogen. An element that promotes vigorous growth and healthy color and is one of the three main nutrients in a complete fertilizer. Plants can't use nitrogen directly from the air—it's converted naturally by soil microbes into a form that plants can absorb.

NPK. A recognized abbreviation that refers to the ratio of the three major nutrients—nitrogen (N), phosphorus (P), and potassium (K)—in fertilizer, such as 5-5-5 or 10-2-2.

Organic. Materials that are derived directly from plants or animals. Organic gardening uses plant and animal by-products to maintain soil and plant health and doesn't rely on synthetically made fertilizers, herbicides, or pesticides.

Overseeding. Renewing a lawn area by sowing seeds over an existing lawn without first clearing away existing sod. Overseeding is used to spruce up a weary lawn or to introduce disease-resistant grasses or a different grass species.

Pesticide. Any substance, synthetic or natural, which is used to kill insects, animals, fungi, bacteria, or weeds.

pH. A measure of how acidic or alkaline a substance is. The pH scale ranges from 1 to 14, with 7 indicating neutrality, below 7 acidity, and above 7 alkalinity. The pH of your soil has a great effect on what nutrients are available to your plants.

Plugs. Small pieces of sod of creeping types of grasses, or seedlings or cuttings of a groundcover. Plugs are generally planted 6 to 12 inches apart, depending upon how quickly they will grow together to cover an area.

Sandy soil. Soil that contains more than 70 percent sand and less than 15 percent clay. Sandy soil is usually well drained and easy to work with, but it has poor nutrient- and water-holding abilities.

Silt. Soil particles of moderate size—larger than clay but smaller than sand.

Sod. Strips of living grass held together by matted roots that can be laid on a prepared soil bed to create an instant lawn.

Soil test kit. A set of instructions and a soil bag available through your state's Cooperative Extension Service. Test results indicate soil pH and specify what amendments and nutrients should be added to your soil to ensure success with your planned use.

Spreader. A bin on wheels with an adjustable opening for spreading grass seed, fertilizer, or amendments evenly, usually over a lawn. Drop spreaders drop seed and fertilizer directly on the ground as you push them; broadcast spreaders spew the material in a radius up to 10 feet from the spreader.

Thatch. A layer consisting of the roots, stolons, and rhizomes of grass plants that fail to decompose. Thatch can accumulate to excess if the lawn has been overfertilized, or if earthworm populations have been reduced by the use of pesticides.

Topdressing. Covering the lawn surface with a thin layer of a soil amendment, such as finely screened compost, to improve or maintain soil health.

Transition lone. The geographical area where both warm- and cool-season grasses will grow, but where neither type is at its best.

Turfgrass. Grass varieties selected and bred for best performance as lawn grasses.

VNS. On a package or grass seed, VNS stands for "variety not stated" and indicates unspecified varieties of lawn seed. Grass grown from VNS seed is inconsistent in quality.

Warm-season grass. Any species of grass, such as bermudagrass or zoysiagrass, that grows well in summer, even in hot, dry climates, and is usually dormant in winter.

Continued ➔

Weeds. Any plants that happen to grow where you don't want them to. Some perfectly fine plants can be considered weeds when they pop up in the wrong places.

GROUNDCOVER

Groundcover Basics

Jeff Cox

Groundcovers are the original landscape problem solvers. Where lawn grass won't grow easily or well, groundcovers come into their own. You can use plants like pachysandra to cover bare spots in the dense shade and dry soil under trees. Choose tough, deep-rooted groundcovers like daylilies to stabilize slopes. Plant Chinese astilbes (*Astilbe chinensis*) or Japanese primroses (*Primula japonica*) in wet, boggy sites instead of mowing a quagmire.

For weed control and reduced yard maintenance, groundcovers can't be beat. But they're also excellent for covering up plants that are past their peak. For example, hostas will mask dying daffodil foliage so it can ripen in peace without becoming an eyesore. You can also use groundcovers like periwinkle (*Vinca* spp.) under spring bulbs, ferns, and perennials—its uniform green will set off taller and more colorful plants.

You can use any low-growing plant as a groundcover as long as it meets certain requirements: It should look attractive all season, spread quickly to carpet the ground, require a minimum of maintenance, and keep down weeds. Don't limit your choices to the obvious ivy, pachysandra, and periwinkle, though all three make excellent evergreen groundcovers. Wildflowers, perennials, ornamental grasses, annuals, and low shrubs can all be used as groundcovers. For most situations, choose plants that hug the ground or grow up to 3 feet tall; the most useful groundcovers are generally 6 to 18 inches tall.

Using Groundcovers

Why use groundcovers when you can just grow grass? For adaptability, resilience, and uniformity, you can't top lawn grasses. They withstand heavy foot traffic, rough play, and all the abuse a family can muster. However, it can require a lot of effort to keep lawn grasses healthy and attractive. They won't grow well under trees and shrubs or in wet sites. You'll save yourself time and work—and create a more dynamic landscape—if you reduce your lawn to the smallest size you need for outdoor activities and turn the rest of your yard over to groundcovers, decks, patios, and ornamental plantings.

Another good way to use groundcovers is to grow them in islands under trees. With a planting of groundcovers around your trees, you won't injure the trunks by scraping them with the lawn mower or waste precious gardening time hand-trimming around each trunk. A mixed planting of hostas, with their beautiful leaf patterns and colors, looks wonderful under trees. So do ferns and astilbes (*Astilbe* spp.), or try blue-green lilyturf (*Liriope* spp.) for a cool contrast to the lighter lawn grass.

Underplanting trees with groundcovers makes your landscape more interesting, too. You can tie individual plants together by surrounding them with an island of groundcover plants, or tie separate groups of plants together by underplanting them with the same groundcover. Try uniform or mixed plantings of groundcovers under shrubs and next to lawn areas, too. You'll find that your yard looks more appealing when everything looks connected—suddenly it will look like a landscaped garden, and all because of a few groundcovers!

You can also grow groundcovers instead of lawn grass where you want to limit water use. As anyone who's spent evenings or weekends holding a hose knows, lawns are very thirsty. Xeriscaping, a landscape philosophy based on water conservation and minimizing damage to the landscape, uses extensive plantings of tough, drought-resistant groundcovers. These adaptable plants reduce environmental impact, save water, and cut maintenance time.

Groundcovers also can perk up the landscape in the off season. Think about fall and winter in your garden. Many groundcovers take on beautiful hues as cool weather returns. Some, like lilyturf and bearberry (*Arctostaphylos uva-ursi*), display colorful fruits. Seed heads of ornamental grasses are loveliest late in the season. Evergreen foliage shines again light light snowfalls.

Don't forget to go beyond problem solving when you're using groundcovers—after all, you have to look at them, too. A yardful of pachysandra may get the ground covered, but it's not nearly as appealing as a combination of groundcover plant. Think about mixing shape, texture, and color in exciting combinations. Feathery ferns with white-variegated hostas and low, glossy-leaved European wild ginger (*Asarum europaeum*) will make a shady site much more interesting than anyone of the three alone. A mix of ajugas (*Ajuga reptans*)—perhaps 'Pink Beauty' (a pink-flowered, green-leaved cultivar) with the bronze-leaved 'Bronze Beauty' and large-leaved, blue-flowered 'Catlin's Giant'—will add more sparkle to a sunny spot than a single cultivar.

Don't be afraid to try something new if a combination falls flat. If a plant doesn't work where you've put it, just move it: Your best design tool is you shovel.

Choosing Groundcovers

The cardinal rule in gardening is to match the plant to the site. To get the best performance from a groundcover, you must give it the growing conditions it needs. Plant shade-loving, shallow-rooted Bethlehem sage (*Pulmonaria saccharata*) to cover a bare area in the shade of a maple tree, and sun-loving, deep-rooted yarrows (*Achillea* spp.) to stop erosion on a dry, sunny bank.

Don't forget maintenance. Plant rampant growers like ivies or sedums where you need dense cover to control weeds, not in a small space where they would quickly get out of control. For a small space that's not weed-prone, choose airy plants like Allegheny foamflower (*Tiarella cordifolia*) or chamomile (*Chamaemelum nobile*) that won't be in a hurry to overgrow the site. In both cases, a well-chosen groundcover will reduce your yard work, while a badly chosen groundcover will pitch you into a losing battle.

When you're looking for a good groundcover, let your needs limit your choices. Focus on the plants that suit your garden and your design. First, define your needs by asking yourself a few key questions:

- Is your site shaded, partially shaded, or in full sun?
- Is your site moist or dry?
- Do you need a ground-hugging plant for the site, or would a taller plant look better?
- Do you want bold or fine texture?
- How important are flowers? Flower color?
- Can you use variegated foliage to brighten things up?
- Should the plant you choose be evergreen or deciduous?

You'll find lists of groundcovers for special situations at the end of this section.

Planting and Maintenance

When you're trying to grow a good groundcover, thorough soil preparation is essential, especially in difficult sites. Plants will tale off and grow faster if you give them a head start, so you'll have less trouble with weed competition. If you haven't had a soil test, consider it; you'll learn a lot about your gardening conditions.

First remove existing sod or undesirable growth from your site. Double dig the soil to a minimum depth of 18 to 20 inches. Spread a generous layer of compost, shredded leaves, or other organic matter over the soil. Add an organic fertilizer and other amendments as needed. Turn the soil again, incorporating all the amendments thoroughly. Level the soil surface with a garden rake. Break up any remaining clods. Water to settle the soil, and you're ready for planting.

Space plants according to their growth rate and size at maturity. Plant fast-growing perennials, ornamental grasses, and other herbaceous plants 1 to 3 feet apart, depending on the mature size of the plant. Plant junipers and other large woody plants 3 feet apart. Plant slow-growing woody plants like wintergreen (*Gaultheria procumbens*) 1 foot apart.

Arrange the plants within the bed according to your design. For each plant, dig a hole large enough to accommodate the loosened root ball. If you're using container plants, make sure the plants are positioned at the same level at which they grew in the containers. Soak the roots of bareroot plants for several hours before planting. Remove the plants from the water one at a time and spread the roots evenly over a dome of soil in the bottom of the planting hole. Check the level of the crown to make sure it's at the right planting depth.

Mulch the site after planting to control weeds and reduce moisture loss. Water newly set plants thoroughly. Groundcovers need regular watering until they are well established—an entire growing season for woody plants. Pull weeds early to avoid competition.

Groundcovers as a group are tough, trouble-free plants. But some pest and disease problems are inevitable in any garden situation. Prevention is the best control. Keep plants healthy, well watered, and mulched. Remove weeds that can harbor pests.

Growing Groundcovers

Groundcovers are diverse group of plants. Propagation techniques vary according to whether you're dealing with a shrubby, vining, or perennial groundcover. Most groundcovers can be grown from seed started indoors or direct-seeded outdoors. But you'll get quicker results from fast-growing groundcovers if you take cuttings or divide them.

Take cuttings from perennial groundcovers like English ivy (*Hedera helix*), spotted lamium (*Lamium maculatum*), leadwort (*Ceratostigma plumbaginoides*), pachysandra, periwinkle, and sedum in early to midsummer. You can divide groundcovers in spring or fall. If the plant is a vine or creeper like ajuga, creeping phlox (*Phlox stolonifera*), English ivy, Allegheny foamflower, periwinkle, or winter-creeper (*Euonymus fortunei*), sever rooted plantlets

Continued ➡

from the parent stem. Lift clumps of perennials like astilbe, bergenia (*Bergenia* spp.), blue fescue (*Festuca caesia*), crested iris (*Iris cristata*), daylily, and hosta, and separate the crowns.

A slow but easy method of propagating woody groundcovers like cotoneasters (*Cotoneaster* spp.) and junipers is layering—encouraging branches to root where they touch the ground.

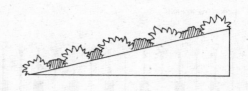

Planting groundcover on a gentle slope. Where the ground slopes gently, you can plant groundcovers directly in the bank, then mulch around them until they're established. Planting groundcovers on a steep slope. On a steep slope, plant from the top down. Put up a wooden barrier where you want a plant, pile soil behind the barrier, and plant. Once the plants are established, remove the barriers.

Beyond the Traditional Lawn

Nothing beats a lawn for playing catch, and a smooth, green swath of lawn sets off flowerbeds perfectly. But too much lawn can be boring to look at and time-consuming to mow. Why not convert some of that grass into a beautiful bed of groundcovers or an island of colorful flowers?

The Best Use for Your Backyard

How much lawn you really need depends on how you use your yard: Parties and picnics? Ball playing and swing sets? Sunbathing and strolling? Once you decide, you can determine exactly how much of the high-maintenance green stuff you need, and how much space you can devote to other, less labor-intensive landscape options. Here's a sampling of your choices:

- Low-maintenance groundcovers with attractive foliage or flowers
- Aromatic herb lawns that are pretty and useful
- Beautiful butterfly garden or meadow
- Tree and shrub borders or island beds for shade and beauty

Get to Know Good Groundcovers

Many groundcovers, such as moss pink (*Phlox subulata*) and mother-of-thyme (*Thymus serpyllum*), tolerate mowing and foot traffic. Flowering groundcovers, such as spotted lamium (*Lamium maculatum*), will add color to your landscape, and berry-bearing groundcovers, such as wintergreen (*Gaultheria procumbens*), will attract wildlife.

When it comes to care-free plantings on tough-to-mow sites, groundcovers are the answer. Review this handy checklist before you buy:

- Match plant choices to your site conditions— sun, shade, water, soil type, heat and cold, and foot traffic, and ask at the nursery for those that have a proven track record in your area.
- Mowing tolerance is important if you'll routinely be mowing around the groundcover area.

- Plants that spread by runners or stolons (underground stems) will fill an area more quickly than clump-forming plants.
- Evergreen groundcovers look good year-round and offer protection from soil erosion.
- When it comes to appearance, choose groundcovers based on leaf texture and color. Flowers are merely a short-term bonus.
- Plants with dense growth habits discourage weeds.

Getting Ready for Groundcovers

Beautiful, thick, weed-smothering areas of groundcover start with thorough soil preparation, especially in difficult sites. Preparing the soil helps get your groundcovers growing quickly and gives them a head start over weeds.

You'll need to remove the sod, then prepare the soil, tilling deeply and adding organic amendments.

Tackle Tough Sites with Terrific Groundcovers

Dry, shady sites, such as the areas under shade trees and shrubs, beneath eaves, and on shaded slopes, are some of the toughest challenges a gardener faces. Constantly wet areas are trouble spots, too. And sunny slopes are awkward to mow. Before you despair of ever having anything grow in these areas, try a groundcover that's partial to those conditions.

5 Great Groundcovers for Dry Shade

Lawn grasses have a hard time growing in shade, especially dry shade. Instead of struggling to maintain a lawn under these conditions, replace it with groundcovers that will thrive.

- Ajuga (*Ajuga reptans*): Green, purple, or variegated leaves with blue, white, or pink flowers; 4 to 6 inches tall. Zones 4 to 8.
- Epimediums (*Epimedium* spp.): Evergreen or semievergreen, heart-shaped foliage; 6 to 12 inches tall. Zones 3 to 8.
- Wintercreeper (*Euonymus fortunei*): Glossy evergreen leaves; 4 to 6 inches tall; will climb trees. Zones 4 to 8.
- Lilyturfs (*Liriope* spp.): Green, grasslike foliage with purple or white flower spikes; 18 inches tall. Zones 5 to 9.
- Common periwinkle (*Vinca minor*): Trailing, evergreen plant with shiny, dark green foliage and lavender-blue or white flowers; 4 to 6 inches tall. Zones 4 to 9.

4 Groundcovers for Soggy Sites

Even if you get grass to grow in a soggy area, the spot is usually too wet to mow. Instead, fill in the moist spots with groundcovers that enjoy the dampness. The plants below will thrive in moist to wet soil in sun or shade.

- Lady's-mantle (*Alchemilla mollis*): Pale, gray-green foliage that is velvety soft to the touch with sprays of yellow-green flowers; 12 inches tall. Zones 3 to 8.
- Astilbes (*Astilbe* spp.): Fernlike foliage with white, pink, or red flowers; 1 to 4 feet tall, depending on species. Zones 3 to 8.
- Hostas (*Hosta* spp.): Bold and beautiful heart-shaped or lancelike leaves in many sizes and shades of green; many variegated types, with white or lavender flowers in summer; 6 to 48 inches tall, depending on species. Zones 3 to 8.
- Creeping Jenny (*Lysimachia nummularia*): Small rounded leaves with yellow flowers; 2 to 4 inches tall. Zones 3 to 8.

5 Sunny-Slope Contenders

If pushing and pulling a lawn mower up slopes isn't your idea of fun, put a stop to steep-site mainte-

nance with fast-growing plants and a cover of mulch to conserve moisture.

Save Time, Mulch First

Trying to lay mulch between plants in a newly planted expanse of groundcover can be a long, tedious task. You can save yourself some time by laying the mulch first. This is especially helpful when planting groundcover plugs or plants in small pots. After laying the mulch, you can easily plant through it with a trowel without pulling up too much soil on top of the clean mulch.

- Maiden pinks (*Dianthus deltoides*): Narrow, blue-green leaves; pink or white flowers; 6 to 12 inches tall. Zones 3 to 9.
- Wintercreeper (*Euonymus fortunei*): Trailing or climbing evergreen plant; many types with variegated leaves; 1 to 2 feet tall. Zones 4 to 9.
- Perennial candytuft (*Iberis sempervirens*): Dark, evergreen leaves; flat, bright white flower clusters in spring; 6 to 12 inches high. Zones 3 to 9.
- Junipers (*Juniperus* spp.): Needle-leaved evergreen available in many forms, from prostate, 6-inch-tall types to large trees. Select a variety that matures to a height that's best for your site. Zones 3 to 9, depending on species.
- Thymes (*Thymus* spp.): Creeping, fragrant-leafed herbs with tiny white or pink flowers; foliage may be variegated; 1 to 12 inches tall. Zones 5 to 9.

5 Tough Plants for Shady Slopes

If you have a shady slope, replace the hard-to-mow grass with one of these easy-care, shade lovers.

- Ajuga (*Ajuga reptans*): Green, purple, or variegated leaves with blue, white, or pink flowers; 4 to 6 inches tall. Zones 4 to 8.
- Epimediums (*Epimedium* spp.): Spreading plant with evergreen or semievergreen leaves; small yellow, pink, bronze, or white flowers in early spring; 5 to 12 inches tall. Zones 3 to 8.
- English ivy (*Hedera helix*): Evergreen vine; 6 to 8 inches high when creeping on the ground; will climb trees to 50 feet. Zones 5 to 9.
- Japanese pachysandra (*Pachysandra terminalis*): Glossy green leaves; plant spreads by runners; white flowers; 6 to 9 inches tall. Zones 5 to 9.
- Common periwinkle (*Vinca minor*): Trailing evergreen plant with shiny, dark green leaves and lavender-blue or white flowers; 4 to 6 inches tall. Zones 4 to 9.

Sweetly Scented Herb Lawns

While many people think grass is a must in high-traffic areas, there are other plants that work just as well under fairly heavy foot traffic. Low-growing herbs such as dainty-but-tough thymes and free-ranging mints can make excellent groundcovers. And herbs offer bonuses that grass lacks. Tread on them or nick them with trimmers, and they'll perfume the air for you. Many herbs are also perfect when you're in a pinch for something to season tonight's dinner! Here are some great-smelling choices:

Roman chamomile
(*Chomomelum nobile*)

Forms a soft, dense carpet of fine yellow-green foliage that resembles Irish moss.

- Unlike Irish moss, chamomile is sturdy enough to be walked on.

Continued ➡

- Undisturbed, chamomile can reach 9 inches tall, but light foot traffic keeps it low enough to make mowing unnecessary.
- It's a fast spreader—individual plants that are planted 6 inches apart will fill in solidly in a single season.
- The yellow-centered flowers that rise above the mat add an attractive touch.
- It's not a good choice if you're allergic to ragweed, as Roman chamomile and ragweed are related.

SWEET WOODRUFF

(*Galium odorotum*)

A shade lover with a light, sweet fragrance that registers differently with different people—some smell vanilla, others new-mown hay.

- Sweet woodruff is well suited as a groundcover under trees.
- It grows rapidly and covers quickly, continuing to spread by self-seeding once established.
- Its tiny white flowers look delicate, but sweet woodruff is hardy to at least 30°F (Zone 4).

MINTS

(*Mentha* spp)

Legendary for their invasiveness, but if it's a lawn you want, mints make a tough, dense groundcover.

- Weeds don't stand a chance of competing when up against established mint.
- Grow mint where it can spread at will without causing harm or where it can be easily confined.
- Hardiness varies with variety from subtropical all the way up to Zone 3.
- Corsican mint (*M. requieni*) is tiny and too tender to walk on, but it makes a very tight, low-growing mat only 1 inch or so high that looks great between stepping stones, or as a filler in beds.
- Pennyroyal (*M. pulegium*) makes a good groundcover—either by itself or planted into an existing lawn. It's tough enough for light traffic and is easy to keep low by mowing.
- Peppermint (*M. x piperitum*) mixes nicely with grass. Mowing keeps it low, and the grass helps cushion it from heavy foot traffic. Don't use it to replace grass; it's a complement that has a wonderful scent that makes mowing more pleasant.

---

7 Reasons to Get Rid of Some Lawn

1. To conserve water
2. To stop mowing
3. To attract beneficial insects so you won't need pesticides
4. To attract butterflies
5. To feed and provide habitat for birds and other wildlife
6. To use your yard to restore native plants
7. To increase your home's energy efficiency

THYME

(*Thymus* spp.)

Not just for the kitchen anymore. Creeping woolly thyme is a good groundcover choice, but other creeping varieties are also available.

- Creeping varieties grow low and spread quickly.
- Thymes sport colors ranging from light lemon yellow to deep grayish green.
- Originally native to dry regions, most thymes grow well in dry, poor soil, and they actually require such hardships to develop their best flavor.
- Many thymes are hardy down to -30° to -40°F.

Enjoy the Beauty of a Wildflower Meadow

Creating a meadow, as more and more people are discovering, is a way to make part of your lawn area more inviting to birds, butterflies, and other wildlife. Each part of the country has native wildflowers that are favorites of the birds of that region. Wherever you live, a wildflower meadow will provide food and cover for all sorts of birds and butterflys, such as goldfinches, hummingbirds, indigo buntings, and monarch butterflies.

START SMALL

If you're considering planting a meadow garden, the best advice is to start small. Removing sod to prepare the site for a new planting involves a bit of work, so you won't want to dig up your entire yard at once. Select a section of your backyard where you'll have the opportunity to observe the planting through all the seasons before you make over your entire lawn.

THINK BIG

Keep in mind that a meadow looks distinctly different from a closely cropped lawn. Whether you choose groundcovers or a mix of native grasses and wildflowers, the look will be more tufted and will change through the seasons. Some native prairie or meadow plants can even grow as tall as 4 to 8 feet!

What you decide to plant is based on what you want and where you live. For example, if you live in the Midwest, you could instill a prairie planting. But if you're in the Southwest, the environment is too dry and hot for those plants; a more appropriate choice would be desert groundcovers or a blend of native grasses and groundcovers.

Don't skimp when it comes to selecting plants and buying seed. Your meadow will be a thing of beauty for years to come, so you won't want to waste time or money on plants that won't thrive. If your budget is tight, increase the percentage of grasses. They're a little less costly than some of the native prairie flowers. Besides, grasses form the backbone of the meadow.

6 STEPS TO A GREAT MEADOW

1. **Prepare the soil.** First you'll need to remove the grass or whatever is growing in the area where you want a meadow. Mow the grass low, and then turn under any remaining vegetation with a rotary tiller, which can be rough going, or rent a sod cutter to remove the sod completely. Then till the soil and add organic amendments.

2. **Plant.** The best time to plant in Zone 3 and warmer is about one month before the first killing frost in fall. In colder zones, plant as soon as the soil can be worked in spring.

   Broadcast the seed, walk on it to press it into the soil, and cover with straw to keep the soil from drying out. As an alternative, you can set transplants in the soil, rather than starting from seed.

3. **Water.** Keep seedlings or transplants moist until they're established—about four to six weeks.

4. **Mulch.** When the seedlings are large enough to identify as flowers and not weeds, apply 3 to 4 inches of organic mulch.

5. **Weed.** Walk through the meadow occasionally during the first year and pull out unwanted plants.

6. **Mow.** Starting the year after planting, your meadow will need to be mowed once a year in early spring. Use a string trimmer or scythe and cut 4 to 6 inches above the ground so you won't disturb the plant crowns. You can hire someone with the proper equipment to mow large meadow areas.

Calculate Your Coverage

When planting groundcovers, you can choose just one or use a combination. If you use a mixture, it's best to group each type separately rather than mixing them together. In general, space plants 6 to 10 inches apart (measuring from their centers) in staggered rows.

To get quicker and more uniform coverage, buy plants in 4-inch or bigger pots, and pull apart the individual plantlets in each pot. Plant the pieces a little more closely, and the sections will fill in the spaces quickly.

To determine how many plants you'll need, multiply the number of square feet of the area to be covered by the number of plants you plan to use per square foot. For instance, if you want to use 3 plants per square foot and the groundcover garden area is 6 feet square, you'll need 18 plants.

Liven Up Grassy Areas with Colorful Bulbs

Spring bulbs are often our first sign of spring—they can sprout even before the first robins show up! But bulbs aren't just for flowerbeds. They look great naturalized in grassy areas, too. Each spring they can give your lawn a colorful meadow look, then when mowing begins, you'll never know they were there.

Small bulbs are best for naturalizing—they're easier to plant and they bloom reliably year after year. You can even plant them under deciduous trees, because they'll be up and blooming before the trees leaf out and create their summer shade. Here are some to try:

- Grecian windflower (*Aneomone blanda*)
- Crocuses (*Crocus* spp.)
- Common snowdrops (*Glanthus nivalis*)
- Summer snowflake (*Leucojum aestivum*)
- Grape hyacinth (*Muscari armeniacum*)
- Daffodils (*Narcissus hybrids*)
- Siberian squill (*Scilla sibirica*)

To create a carpet of springtime bloom in an existing lawn, simply make a hole in the grass with a narrow trowel, dandelion digger, or garden knife. For small bulbs, you can just wiggle your tool back and forth to create a small hole and slip the bulb in place. For larger bulbs, you may have to actually lift the sod and soil, insert the bulb, and put the flap of turf back in place.

If you have a lot of large bulbs to place, use a spade or shovel and remove larger areas of turf—about 1 foot square. Loosen the soil, plant the bulbs, replace the turf and water.

Creating Islands of Beauty

Another way to cut back on lawn care while increasing the value and enjoyment you get from

Continued ➡

your landscape is to start with existing features, like a tree or shrub in your lawn, or a fence along the edge of your lawn, and create a garden around the feature.

DEALING WITH TREE ROOTS

Instead of struggling to grow and mow grass under trees, plant shade-tolerant shrubs and ground-covers under trees, then mulch for a low-maintenance planting you'll enjoy for years to come. If you have shallow-rooted trees such as maples and beeches, there will be lots of fibrous roots to work around. Deep-rooted trees such as oaks have more root-free places to plant. Whichever type of tree you have, take care not to damage large roots, and don't remove more than 5 percent of smaller roots while planting.

Add just enough compost to fill your holes and bring new plants up to the original soil level. Never bury the crown of a tree or it will decline; oaks and sugar maples are particularly vulnerable.

WHEN ALL ELSE FAILS, MULCH

Some shady areas defy gardening attempts, and that's when mulch makes the easiest groundcover of all. A layer of bark mulch can give you a care-free, weed-free surface instantly; it's especially good for unsociable sites like under black walnut trees or the heavy shade of southern magnolias. Spread mulch all the way out to the drip line for easier mowing, no weeding, and happy trees.

MOWING STRIPS EASE MAINTENANCE

Use edging strips around island beds to keep lawn grass from overtaking your islands. You can mow around them with a single pass and won't have to trim by hand. To install a brick mowing strip, use a sharp spade to dig a brick-size trench around your bed. Starting at one end of the trench, lay the bricks in side-to-side, butting them snugly against each other and leveling them as you go. Backfill as necessary and sweep dry soil into the spaces between the bricks.

Got a Fence? Eliminate the Hassles

Plantings of trees, shrubs, groundcovers, and easy-care perennials can eliminate tedious weeding or trimming along a fence. Select plants suited to the site, then plant and mulch. No more snagging the mower on the fence or coming back later with a trimmer.

Tips for Meadow Success

Set the stage for success by choosing the right kind of meadow plants.

- **Choose a regional mix.** Most seed companies and nurseries offer both wildflower mixes that are designed for specific parts of the country.
- **Avoid "instant meadow" mixes.** They are mostly annual flowers or inexpensive generic wildflowers.
- **Save on weeding with aggressive wild-flowers.** A mix of vigorous wildflowers won't give you the variety a more carefully planned and developed meadow will provide, but it will get you a flower-filled meadow fast. Try perennials like common yarrow, Queen-Anne's-lace, dame's rocket, oxeye daisy, and evening primrose. In two to three years, they'll take over and choke out any other plants with very little help from you.

If you need to be able to paint your fence occasionally or need access to plants from the back, leave a 2-foot-wide, mulched maintenance path between the fence and the plants.

Ornamental Grasses

Barbara W. Ellis, Joan Benjamin, and Deborah L. Martin

It's time to get to know the grasses you cut only once a year: the ornamental ones. They don't need supplemental watering once established, the more vigorous types can hold their own against weeds, and they're rarely troubled by diseases or insects. Best of all, ornamental grasses are truly plants for all seasons. In autumn, many dry to beautiful shades of tan and ochre. Others are evergreen or semi-evergreen.

Some ornamental grasses quickly grow to the size of large shrubs, making them great choices for quick landscape effect. Yet as vigorous as they are, the best of them don't need dividing. And no pruning headaches—just cut them down to the ground once a year in early spring.

With Grasses, It Pays to Know When They Grow

Most ornamental grasses will grow nearly anywhere, but knowing a little about their likes and dislikes will help you select the best ones for your site and situation. For gardeners, grasses fall into two general groups, as determined by their season of active growth: Warm-season grasses grow during the summer; cool-season ones during cooler months.

Although both groups include great low-maintenance plants, warm-season grasses require even less work to grow than cool-season ones. Here are some general characteristics of each group to keep in mind as you select grasses for your landscape.

WARM-SEASON GRASSES

Late spring and summer are the main growing seasons for warm-season grasses. They bloom from June through September, depending on the species. In winter, their foliage turns attractive shades of buff and tan. Generally, they are more tolerant of clay soils and poor drainage and rarely need dividing. Once a year in early spring, they need to be cut to within a few inches of the ground.

COOL-SEASON GRASSES

These grow actively during the cool seasons of the year—primarily spring and fall, winter in mild areas. Their foliage is often evergreen or semi-evergreen, and they bloom in spring or early summer. As a result, they provide landscape interest when warm-season grasses are least effective. Cool-season

grasses are fussier about soil, though. In general, they need better drainage and are less tolerant of heavy clay than warm-season grasses.

Cool-season grasses generally aren't cut back completely in early spring, as warm-season ones are. Instead, they need more selective trimming and cleaning up at winter's end. Because they tend to die out in the center of the clump, they need dividing every two or three years.

Corralling Aggressive Spreaders

Keep bamboos and ornamental grasses that spread aggressively under control by planting them inside a concrete culvert, a large garbage can with the bottom cut out, or another type of "container." The container should extend to a depth of 2 to 3 feet. Leave a 2-inch rim above the soil to control wandering aboveground stems.

Dividing Grasses Large and Small

The good news about dividing ornamental grasses is you may never need to do it. Cool-season grasses need dividing every two to three years, as new growth begins to appear in fall, winter, or early spring. Warm-season grasses almost never need dividing, but if you want more plants or need to improve the spacing in an overcrowded planting, tackle the project after you've given them their annual haircut in spring.

Get-tough division for large grasses. You'll need to use an ax, or a wedge and a small sledgehammer, to divide large warm-season grasses. Cut the crown into several hunks, then pry the hunks out with a shovel and transplant them. If you only need a division or two, pry them off the side of the clump.

Dividing large clumps of ornamental grasses isn't a job for the faint-hearted. The easiest way to tackle the task is to do it right in the ground. If you want to separate the clump into small divisions with three to five growing points each, however, you'll need to dig out the clump and wash off the soil so you can see what you're doing. Although it's more time-consuming, you won't believe how many grass plants you can get from a clump this way.

Simple division for smaller grasses. Dividing cool-season grasses and small clumps of warm-season ones is relatively easy. Use a spade to lift small clumps of grasses from the soil, then rinse the roots clean with a hose. Slice away dead areas and divide the actively growing sections with a sturdy knife or a spade. Then replant or pot up the divisions.

Grasses as Groundcovers

Grasses with spreading habits are generally too invasive for a perennial garden, but they make excellent groundcovers. Grow them alone or combine them in beds with other aggressive groundcovers. It's best to plan a site that will help you keep them in bounds without extra work. Regular mowing around a planting of them will help as well. For example, groundcover grasses are perfect for island beds surrounded by lawn, or sites with lawn on one side and a road or pond on the other. Or plant them in containers sunk in the soil.

You can also use clump-forming grasses as groundcovers; just plant them on even centers as you would a vegetable garden that's been planted intensively. On shady sites, try this technique with the grasslike sedges (*Carex* spp.) and woodrushes (*Luzula* spp.). On sunny ones, try quaking grass (*Briza media*), fescues (*Festuca* cultivars), tufted hairgrass (*Deschampsia caespitosa*), blue oat grass (*Helictotrichon sempervirens*), and fountain grass (*Pennisetum alopecuroides*).

Continued ➡

Basic Grass Care for Bountiful Results

Ornamental grasses have a plant-it-and-forget it quality that assures them a place in the heart of every gardener. Once you've chosen grasses suited to your site conditions and landscape, planting and care are simple matters. Soil preparation is largely unnecessary, particularly if you stick with the warm-season grasses. Except for requiring full sun, these grasses really don't care where you put them. Below, you'll find what little you need to know to grow a landscape full of lush, healthy, low-maintenance ornamental grasses.

PLANTING GRASSES

About the only thing you need to do to prepare an area for grasses is remove any existing vegetation and plant. Since most ornamental grasses don't ever need to be divided, planting them properly the first time really pays off. You can plant containerized grasses any time from spring through fall, but you'll minimize watering chores if you plant early or late enough for your new grass to catch spring or fall rains.

Dig your grasses a good home. Plant your grasses in holes that are about twice as wide as the containers. Spread a mixture of soil and compost in the hole, then settle the plant so its crown is about 1 to 2 inches above the soil line. Refill the hole with soil and compost, and water thoroughly to settle the plant in place.

Planting pot-grown grasses. After removing an ornamental grass from its pot, use a knife to score the roots around the outside of the root ball. Or tease them out with a screwdriver. This encourages the roots to branch and spread out in all directions.

Handling bareroot grasses. If you've ordered bareroot grasses from a mail-order nursery, unpack and inspect them as soon as they arrive from the nursery. Each plant should have at least two or three culms (growing points). Do not accept plants consisting of a single culm; they have a high failure rate. The root system should look husky. Scratch the skin of a root with your fingernail; the tissue beneath should appear whitish, not brown or black. Blackened tissue means the roots are dead. If anything looks bad, notify the nursery immediately. Cool-season grasses, especially, are prone to arrive in poor condition.

Ornamental Grasses for Special Sites

To find the best ornamental grasses for your garden, look through the list below. (You'll find true grasses and related grasslike plants listed.) For each, you'll find the season of growth, height, hardiness, and suggestions for special uses. Grasses grow well in full sun with average to rich well-drained soil, but many grasses can also grow well in problem sites—like heavy clay soil. Ornamental grasses make great additions to low-maintenance landscapes since they're so easy to care for, and because they'll grow in sites where other plants might need special pampering or special advance soil preparation in order to thrive.

Name	Description	Special Uses
Andropogon gerardii (big bluestem)	Warm-season grass. Blue-green to silvery foliage; purplish flower spikes. Height: 4–7+ feet. Zone 4.	Clump-forming habit. Will grow in heavy clay soil; tolerates drought.
Bouteloua spp. (grammagrass)	Warm-season grasses. Gray-green, fine-textured foliage; interesting, one-sided flower heads. Height: 1–2 feet. Zone 4.	Clump-forming habit. Withstand mowing. Will grow in heavy clay or sandy soil; withstand drought.
Briza media (quaking grass)	Cool-season grass. Evergreen foliage with attractive seed heads. Height: 1–1½ feet. Zone 4.	Clump-forming habit. Will tolerate a wide range of soils provided it has moisture.
Calamagrotis arundinacea 'Karl Foerster' (Foerster's feather reed grass)	Cool-season grass. Arching foliage with tall, brown to golden flower spikes; evergreen in mild climates. Height: 2–4 feet. Zone 5.	Clump-forming habit. Will grow in heavy clay soil and poorly drained or wet sites.
Carex spp. and cultivars (sedges)	Cool-season growers. Fine-textured, arching foliage in blue, green, silvery, or variegated; many are evergreen. Height: 6 inches–3 feet. Many species hardy to Zone 5.	Clump-forming habit. Will grow in shade, heavy clay soil, and poorly drained or wet sites. *C. morrowii* (Japanese sedge) and *C. sylvatica* (forest sedge) withstand drought.
Chasmanthium latifolium (Northern sea oats)	Warm-season grass. Bamboolike foliage with attractive seed heads. Height: 2–3 feet. Zone 5.	Clump-forming habit. Will grow in shade, sandy soil, and poorly drained or wet sites; withstands drought.
Erianthus ravennae (Ravenna grass)	Warm-season grass. Gray-green foliage with silvery flowers. Height: Foliage 4–5 feet; flowers 8–12 feet. Zone 6.	Clump-forming habit. Will grow in poorly drained or wet sites; withstands drought.
Festuca cinerea (blue fescue)	Cool-season grass. (Formerly F. ovinia 'Glauca'.) Blue-green foliage; evergreen. Height: 8–18 inches. Most to Zone 4.	Clump-forming habit. Will grow in sandy, well-drained soil; withstands drought.
Glyceria maxima 'Variegata' (variegated manna grass)	Warm-season grass. Foliage striped creamy yellow. Height: 2–3 feet. Zone 5.	Vigorous spreading habit. Will grow in poorly drained or wet sites.
Helictotrichon semperfirens (blue oat grass)	Cool-season grass. Blue-green foliage; evergreen. Height: 12–18 inches. Zone 4.	Clump-forming habit. Will grow in sandy soil; withstands drought.
Juncus spp. (rushes)	Cool-season growers. Semi-evergreen foliage; many have attractive seed heads. Height: 1–4 feet, depending on species. Some to Zone 4.	Clump-forming habit. Will grow in poorly drained or wet sites.
Luzula sylvatica (greater woodrush)	Cool-season grower. Mounds of matlike evergreen foliage. Height: 8–12 inches. Zone 4.	Clump-forming habit. Will grow in shade, heavy clay soil, and poorly drained or wet sites.
Miscanthus sinensis (maiden grass)	Warm-season grass. Dense clumps of arching foliage; attractice seed heads. Height: 5–6 feet. Zone 5.	Clump-forming habit. Will grow in heavy clay soil and poorly drained or wet sites; 'Gracillimus' withstands drought.
Panicum virgatum (switch grass)	Warm-season grass. Green to gray-green foliage; showy seed heads. Height: 4–7 feet. Zone 5.	Clump forming habit. Will grow in heavy clay soil and poorly drained or wet sites; withstands drought.
Pennisetum alopecuroides (fountain grass)	Warm-season grass. Mounds of arching foliage; showy seed heads. Height: 2–3 feet. Zone 6.	Clump-forming habit. Will grow in heavy clay soil; withstands drought.
Phalaris arundinacea var. *picta* (white-striped ribbon grass)	Warm-season grass. Foliage striped with green and white. Height: 2–3 feet. Zone 4.	Spreading habit. Will grow in heavy clay soil and poorly drained or wet sites; withstands drought.
Schizachyrium scoparium (little bluestem)	Warm-season grass. Light green foliage topped by fluffy seed heads. Height: 2–3 feet. Zone 3.	Clump-forming habit. Will grow in sandy soil; withstands drought. 'Blaze' has especially vibrant fall color.
Sorghastrum nutans (Indian grass)	Warm-season grass. Medium green foliage ith attractive seed heads. Height: 2–3 feet. Zone 4.	Clump-forming habit. Will grow in heavy clay or sandy soil and poorly drained or wet sites.
Spartina pectinata 'Aureomarginata' (golden-edged prairie cord grass)	Warm-season grass. Green foliage edged in yellow. Height: 3–6 feet. Zone 4	Spreading habit; can be invasive in moist soil. Will grow in heavy clay soil and poorly drained or wet sites.
Sporobolus heterolepis (prairie dropseed)	Warm-season grass. Fine-textured foliage; attractive seed heads. Height: 2–3 feet. Zone 3.	Clump-forming habit. Will grow in sandy soil; withstands drought.

Continued ➔

Plant bareroot grasses immediately. If you can't plant right away, settle them temporarily in containers of potting soil, water thoroughly, and keep them in a shady place. When you plant them permanently, dig a hole wide and deep enough to accommodate the roots. Fan out the roots over a cone of soil, and plant them so the crown is about an inch below the soil surface. After planting, water thoroughly and mulch.

Fern Affairs
Roger Yepsen

If you're considering what to do with a shady area of the yard, give the hostas and pachysandra a rest and investigate the many shapes and textures and personalities to be found among ferns. That's not to say they make a visual splash. Ferns mostly come in shades of green, and these so-called primitive plants don't produce flowers. Still, once you begin noticing ferns, their individual personalities can be very charming. For a quick introduction to these plants, here are three very different forms.

- The ostrich fern (*Matteuccia struthiopteris*) is an eager grower, quickly reaching 4 to 6 feet, and it looks like what you'd expect of a fern. It will succeed in either sunny or shady spots if the soil is moist.
- The dainty Japanese painted fern (*Athyrium nipponicum*) is shaped like a fern, but its coloration is mildly outrageous. The stems are deep red, and the leaves are frosted with silver. To bring out the best color, place them in light shade with perhaps some morning sun. They also tend to be brighter in areas with cooler summer temperatures.
- The maidenhair fern (*Adiantum raddianuma*) is conventional ferny green (except for the contrasting black stems), but its form is strikingly different. The delicate fronds are low-growing fans, making this species a good choice for the front of beds and for easing the edges of a shady path. Maidenhairs do best under bright filtered light rather than in deep shade.

Install a Stumpery

Most yards have at least one unloved and all but unredeemable spot, where low light, so-so soil, and inaccessibility seem like unsolvable issues. These odd nooks are candidates for a stumpery, a modest-size landscape feature arranged around one or more stumps for a woodsy, picturesque effect.

Farmers and contractors routinely yank stumps of felled trees from the ground when clearing land, and you may be able to pick them up for no charge. If you can't find stumps, sections of log will do. Either way, you'll have a centerpiece around which to grow ferns and woodland plants, just as Victorian gardeners did during the stumpery fad (yes, there really was one) of more than a hundred years ago.

To make the stumps or logs look as though they've been moldering for decades, use a blender to process moss, yogurt, and water into a slurry, then spread it on these objects. If there's room enough, install a rustic bench on which to contemplate your romantic woodland niche.

Caring for Your Grasses

Once they're established, your grasses will thrive almost in spite of you. Except for the first couple of months after planting or during prolonged drought, they will do fine without any additional water.

Fertilizing is entirely optional. If you're feeling extravagant, give your grasses a spring feeding with a high-nitrogen fertilizer, such as blood meal, or anything you would use on your lawn. Apply the fertilizer around the clump, not on top of it, and water it in thoroughly.

The only other care your grasses need is their once-yearly trimming. Cool-season grasses are evergreen and don't need a dramatic spring clean-up like warm-season grasses. Just clean them up each spring by cutting off browned foliage. Give warm-season grasses a spring crew cut to clear the way for new growth and get the most landscape interest from your grasses.

Give 'Em Room to Grow

Grasses form big clumps, and one of the most common mistakes is planting them too close together. When planting warm-season grasses, be sure to pick a site large enough to accommodate their size at maturity. That way, you'll only need to divide them if you want more plants for another part of your landscape. Here's a useful rule of thumb: Allow as much space between grasses as their mature height. For example, leave 5 feet of space between a grass that grows 5 feet tall and its neighbors.

Another common mistake is to plant clumps of grasses as individual specimens in the lawn. Not only does this create a spotty-looking design, it also creates more obstacles to mow around. To simplify your mowing and get more visual impact from your grasses, group them together or combine them with perennials or shrubs. When combining grasses with other plants, remember the rule of thumb about spacing. Resist the temptation to crowd other plants around them; you'll only have to move them in a year or two.

Bamboos Are Low-Maintenance Grasses, Too

Bamboos are among the most versatile, beautiful, and low-maintenance plants in the grass family. They are pest- and disease-free, too. Their only drawback—one that can be used to advantage in some situations—is that many of them are aggressive spreaders. Keep them in bounds by planting them inside an underground barrier. Or select a site with natural barriers. For example, use bamboo as an erosion-controlling ground cover on a slope between a pond and a lawn, or between a lawn and a road. Mowing will control bamboo shoots on the lawn side. Another simple solution is to plant bamboo as a specimen in your lawn and just contain it by mowing around it. But watch out if there is an unmowed zone beyond the lawn; bamboo stolons can travel 20 to 30 feet.

Following is a list of recommended spreading bamboos.

Black bamboo (*Phyllostachys nigra*): 25 feet tall; Zone 6, Zone 5 in sheltered location.

Dwarf green-stripe bamboo (*Pleioblastus viridi-striatus*): 2 feet tall; Zone 5.

Dwarf white-stripe bamboo (*Pleioblastus variegatus*): 1–2 feet tall; Zone 5.

Kuma bamboo (*Sasa veitchii*): Plant in shade; 3 feet tall; Zone 5.

Pygmy bamboo (*Arundinaria pygmaea*): Excellent low ground cover; Zone 5.

Yellow-groove bamboo (*Phyllostachys aureosulcata*): 25 feet tall; Zone 5.

Or choose a nonspreading bamboo, especially cultivars of the clump-forming fargesias (*Fargesia* spp.), which are evergreen and hardy to Zone 5.

Grow a Grass Windbreak

For quick shelter on the windy side of a perennial planting, ornamental grasses are an easy answer. A row of clump-forming grasses like maiden grass (*Miscanthus sinensis*) behind a perennial planting will shield your perennials from wind and look great, too.

TREES AND SHRUBS

Trees and Shrubs Basics

Jeff Cox

Trees, shrubs, and vines form the foundation, framework, and walls of a landscape. They can focus our attention on lovely views or shut out ugly ones. Trees also help to modify the microclimate in our yards by casting shade or serving as a windbreak. They can act as barriers to block the noise and commotion of street traffic.

While trees and shrubs can be expensive, they are true investments that can raise the value of your property. Before you spend money buying trees and shrubs, though, spend time learning about the best plant choices for your site and about how to care for the plants you select. Consult books, local gardening organizations, and county extension agents. Find a reliable nursery, and ask the owner or manager for advice. And for a dose of inspiration, visit public gardens and arboretums.

In this section, you'll find advice on selecting and caring for trees and shrubs, as well as how to use trees, shrubs, and vines for best effect in the home landscape.

Types of Trees and Shrubs

Trees are woody perennials, usually with a single trunk, ranging in height at maturity from 15 feet to giants exceeding 100 feet. A plant thought of as a tree in some parts of the country may be considered a shrub in others. Crape myrtle (*Lagerstroemia indica*) exceeds 15 feet in the South, where it is grown as a small flowering tree, but in the mid-Atlantic area, it may die back to the ground after cold winters and only reach shrub height.

Some of the most familiar and beautiful plants around our homes are shrubs. The graceful sweep of forsythia and the stately form of a privet hedge show the diversity of these woody perennials, Shrubs have multiple stems and range in height from a few inches to approximately 15 feet at maturity, although individual shrubs may grow as high as 30 feet. A shrub trained to a single stem, called a standard, resembles a miniature tree. Here's a look at the types of trees and shrubs most commonly found in home landscapes.

Continued ➡

Deciduous trees: These drop all of their leaves at the end of the growing season and grow new leaves the following spring. They are good choices for fall color. Once they drop their leaves, with the exception of some limited root growth, they generally are dormant for the entire winter.

Evergreen trees and shrubs: These hold most of their leaves year-round. Although many people think "Christmas tree" at the mention of evergreens, all plants that retain their green color throughout the year can properly be called evergreens, and there is a broad range of shapes and sizes. Evergreen can mean a 60-foot fir tree—or the diminutive rug junipers used as groundcovers.

Evergreens are divided into two groups according to the general shape of their leaves. Narrow-leaved or needle evergreens include plants such as junipers, pines, and yews. Most needle evergreens are very hardy and can be successfully grown over much of the United States. Some of these, like pines and spruces, are also known as conifers because they bear cones. But not all coniferous trees are evergreen: Larches (*Larix* spp.) and bald cypress (*Taxodium distichum*) are deciduous conifers.

Broad-leaved evergreens usually have showy flowers or fruit, and are generally not as cold-hardy as other evergreens. But some types, such as azaleas and rhododendrons (*Rhododendron* spp.), hollies (*Ilex* pp.), and Japanese barberry (*Berberis thunbergii*) are widely adaptable. Tender evergreens, such as gardenias (*Gardenia* spp.), are grown only in the warmest regions of the country. Broad-leaves evergreen trees include southern magnolia (*Magnolia grandiflora*) and live oak (*Quercus virginiana*).

If you live in a warm area, you may be able to select a third type of "evergreen" tree. Palms are categorized as evergreens, although they are monocots, not dicots like other trees. A dicot forms annual growth rings that increase the trunk's diameter, and their crown is formed of branches. Palms don't form annual growth rings, and they generally don't branch, either—their crowns are made up entirely of their large leaves.

Semi-evergreen trees and shrubs: These keep at least part of their leaves well into the winter. Shrubs such as glossy abelia (*Abelia* x *grandiflora*) are evergreen in the South and semi-evergreen farther north. And certain cultivars of Chinese or lacebark elm (*Ulmus parvifolia*) keep many of their leaves well into the winter. They may be fully evergreen in the South.

Selecting Trees and Shrubs

Your trees and shrubs will be a part of your life for a long time. Choose them with care. Think about what you want from a tree or shrub. In a design sense, trees and shrubs have a variety of uses. They can be used to screen and filter views, soften hard edges, enclose spaces, and visually connect buildings to the ground. In a good design, they also create an atmosphere that is comforting and restful.

Landscape plants provide visual interest, a catchall term that not only refers to flowers, fruit, fall foliage, and bark, but also to the interesting patterns, textures, and contrasts they create. And a cherished plant that might have been part of childhood, or reminiscent of a favorite place or time, is a soul-satisfying presence.

Trees, shrubs, and other vegetation soak up noise and glare, filter atmospheric impurities, and offer shelter from winds. They also invite wildlife and bring coolness by casting shade, by transpiration, and by wind channeling. These benefits should offer inspiration to gardeners to plan and plant their home landscapes with loving attention and to give them the best possible year-round care.

Words to Know

Clump: A tree grown with several closely growing trunks. Birches are often sold as clumps.

Vase-shaped: A tree with upswept branches, narrower in silhouette near the base than at the top, such as American elm.

Globe-shaped: A tree with a rounded, usually low-growing silhouette, such as crab apple.

Oval: A tree with branches that form an oval silhouette, such as 'Bradford' flowering pear.

Columnar: A tall, somewhat narrow form, such as 'Columnare' Norway maple.

Pyramidal: A cone-shaped tree, such as spruces or American arborvitae.

Conical: Cone-shaped, but with a narrower profile than a pyramidal tree, such as 'Wichita Blue' juniper.

Weeping: A tree with branches that droop toward the ground, such as a weeping willow.

Before you head to the nursery or garden center to buy shrubs, make a list of desired features. What should your trees and shrubs do—form a windscreen, complete your foundation planting, shade your house, serve as an accent for a flower garden, provide food for wildlife, or serve as a specimen? Would you rather have a display of flowers in spring, brightly colored leaves in fall, showy bark, or persistent fruit in the winter? How big can the shrub or tree get, how often will you have time to prune it, and what showy features do you want? Here are some suggestions for ways to use trees and shrubs in your landscape:

- Use groups of trees and shrubs to block unwanted views or accent desirable ones, both on and off your property, and to give privacy. Evergreens provide year-round concealment. Privet (*Ligustrum* spp.) is a classic hedge plant, but many others also make good hedges. A low-growing hedge, such as common boxwood (*Buxus sempervirens*), can direct traffic around walkways and define borders of flower and herb beds. Plant larger shrubs, such as spireas (*Spiraea* spp.) and viburnums, singly or in groups. They can frame outdoor spaces, provide privacy, hide unsightly views, and buffer against wind and noise.

- A unified group of trees and shrubs in a single bed looks better than a widely separated planting, and the arrangement helps protect the trees from lawn mower nicks and gouges.

- Specimen or accent plants are used alone to call attention to an attractive feature such as the finely cut leaves of full-moon maple (*Acer japonicum*), or the showy flowers of saucer magnolia (*Magnolia* x *soulangiana*). Unusually textured bark, bright fall color, or an interesting shape are other good reasons to showcase a tree or shrub as a specimen plant.

- Use ground-covering shrubs, such as rock-spray cotoneaster (*Cotoneaster horizontalis*) or shore juniper (*Juniperus conferta*), to control erosion and ease maintenance on steep banks.

- Low-growing Japanese hollies (*Ilex crenata*) or abelias (*Abelia* spp.) make good foreground plants for foundation plantings. Medium and tall shrubs, such as yews (*Taxus* spp.) and Chinese junipers (*Juniperus chinensis*), serve as background plants for foundation plantings, as well as for perennial beds.

- Be sure to learn the mature height and spread of the foundation plants you are considering. The rule is patience: Allow time for your new small plants to mature and fill the space you have planned. If you make the mistake of planting cute little arborvitaes (*Thuja* spp.) under the window, or a white pine close to the house, you'll be continually pruning or cutting them down when they outgrow their space.

- Many medium and tall-growing shrubs have naturally occurring or cultivated forms that are smaller and slower-growing. These dwarf and miniature forms, such as dwarf nandina (*Nandina domestica* 'Nana') and dwarf mugo pine (*Pinus mugo* var. *mugo*), generally do not grow more than 3 feet tall. Use them when your planting site is small, or when you want less pruning maintenance.

- Trees supply food, shelter, and nesting sites for birds and other wildlife. Those with berries or other fruits are especially welcome.

- You may want to add trees and shrubs to your landscape that will provide food for you, not just for wildlife and birds. Many common fruit trees, such as apples, pears, peaches, and plums, are available in dwarf sizes that fit neatly into a small corner or even a large container. See Chapter 4 for more on growing fruit.

- For fleshy fruit to be eaten fresh or cooked, try pawpaw (*Asimina triloba*), common persimmon (*Diospyros virginiana*), and Japanese persimmon (*D. kaki*).

- For small, fleshy fruits for jams and jellies, try blueberries, cornelian cherry (*Cornus mas*), crab apples (*Malus* spp.), and wild cherries and plums (*Prunus* spp.).

- For nuts, try hickories (*Carya* spp.), walnuts and butternuts (*Juglans* spp.), pecans (*Carya illinoinensis*), filberts (*Corylus* spp.), and chestnuts (*Castanea* spp.).

- For beekeepers interested in a new taste to their honey, try sourwood (*Oxydendrum arboreum*), lindens (*Tilia* spp.), and water tupelo (*Nyssa aquatica*).

Be realistic about the amount of maintenance you're willing to do. Do you want to plant trees and forget them, or do you enjoy pruning and raking up baskets of leaves on a brisk fall day? For some gardeners, the beauty of the tree or the bounty of the crop outweighs the extra work.

Continued ➡

Matching Plant to Site

Consider the characteristics of your site before you head for the nursery. For healthy, vigorous trees and shrubs, match the cultural requirements of the plants you buy to the conditions of your site. While most nurseries stock plants that are hardy in their area, borderline-hardy plants are sometimes offered with no warnings. It's always a good idea to ask. Remember to check catalogs for hardiness information.

Know your soil—its pH, fertility, and consistency. Take a close look at drainage; choose another site if you see standing water at any season. Check the amount of light the plant will receive.

If you're planting trees, be sure to scout out overhead wires, nearby walkways, or other limiting factors. Think about the size of your tree or shrub in 5, 10, or 20 years.

Also remember that as a tree grows, so does the area of ground that it shades. Some trees, such as thornless honey locust (*Gleditsia triacanthos* var. *inermis*), produce only light or filtered shade; grass and other plants generally have enough light to grow under or in the shade of these trees. Other trees, like the sugar and Norway maples (*Acer saccharum* and *A. platanoides*), produce very dense shade in which even shade-tolerant grasses have trouble growing. You'll need to use shade lovers such as ivy, hostas, or ferns—or a mulch—to cover the ground beneath such trees.

Even shade-tolerant plants may have difficulty growing under or near a tree, particularly a large one. If the crown of the tree is dense, as with maples, most rain is shed off the canopy of the tree. The ground immediately below may be dry even after a rain and tree roots absorb much of the available water.

Make a second list of the conditions of your site—soil, water, and exposure. For healthy, vigorous shrubs, match the plant to the site. Combine your two lists to discover the shrubs that best fill your needs.

With your list in hand, you're ready to buy. Remember that shrubs are a long-term investment. It's well worth your time and money to seek out and buy good-quality shrubs. Don't base your selection on price alone.

Growing Hedges

Plant a hedge for a privacy screen to block out unwelcome views or traffic noise or to add a green background to set off other plantings. Hedges also provide excellent wind protection for house or garden. Thick, tall, or thorny hedges make inexpensive and forbidding barriers to keep out animals—or to keep them in.

A formal hedge is an elegant, carefully trimmed row of trees or shrubs. It requires exacting and frequent pruning to keep plants straight and level. The best plants for formal hedges are fine leaved and slow growing—and tough enough to take frequent shearing. An informal hedge requires only selective pruning and has a more natural look. A wide variety of plants can be used, many of which have attractive flowers or berries.

PLANTING AND PRUNING HEDGES

It's best to plant young plants when starting a hedge. Full-grown specimens are more apt to die from transplanting stress, and finding an exact replacement can be difficult. It's easier to fill a gap in an informal hedge.

For an open, airy hedge of flowering shrubs, allow plenty of room for growth when planting. For a dense, wall-like hedge, space the plants more closely. You may find it easier to dig a trench rather than separate holes. To ensure your hedge will be straight, tie a string between stakes at each end to mark the trench before digging.

Broad-leaved plants used as a formal hedge need early training to force dense growth. For a thick, uniform hedge, reduce new shoots on the top and sides by one-third or more each year until the hedge is the desired size. Cutting a formal hedge properly is a challenge. Stand back, walk around, and recut until you get it straight—just like a haircut. Shear often during the growing season to keep it neat.

Needled evergreens require a different technique. Avoid cutting off the tops of evergreens until they reach the desired height. Shear the sides once a year, but never cut into the bare wood.

Prune informal hedges according to when they bloom. Do any needed pruning soon after flowering. Use thinning cuts to prune selected branches back to the next limb. Heading cuts that nip the branch back to a bud encourage dense, twiggy growth on the outside. To keep informal hedges vigorous, cut two or three of the oldest branches to the ground each year.

For fast, dense growth, prune in spring. This is also a good time for any severe shearing or pruning.

Care and Maintenance

The most important thing you can do for your trees and shrubs is plant them in the right spot and with great care. Carefully selected and planted trees and shrubs need only occasional attention, especially once they become well established.

During the first year after planting, water each week when less than 1 inch of rain falls, especially in summer and fall. Water to thaw the ground, and provide water for the leaves of evergreen trees during warm winter weather.

The mulch you applied at planting time will gradually decompose. Replenish it as needed, but only use a few inches. To avoid rodent problems and to encourage good air circulation, keep the mulch away from the trunk.

Small, yellow leaves, premature fall coloration, stunted twig growth, or too few flowers or fruits often indicate a nutrient deficiency. Your trees will generally receive enough fertilizer if they are located in a lawn that you regularly fertilize. If your trees are located in isolated beds, in areas surrounded by paving, or in containers, you may need to apply compost or a balanced organic fertilizer. Simply broadcast the needed fertilizer on the soil surface.

Most trees are too large for you to provide them with special winter protection such as a burlap enclosure. If snow or ice loads bend the trees' branches, avoid vigorously shaking the branches to remove the ice or snow. Frozen, brittle branches can easily break. Either allow the ice or snow to melt away naturally or very gently sweep it off.

Pruning and Training

Pruning is both a science and an art—and probably the least-understood gardening practice. A properly pruned landscape shows off each plant at its best. Well-pruned trees and shrubs produce more or better fruit and flowers. Pruning can improve the health of an ailing shrub, make trees stronger and safer, channel growth away from buildings or traffic, and restore a sense of order to an overplanted or overgrown yard.

Prune young trees at planting time and as they grow, to correct structural problems and improve their form. Training a young tree with several years

---

Showy Trees and Shrubs

Trees and shrubs can add color and diversity throughout the year. Flowering trees bring the beauty of flowers to your landscape, while many shrubs add four-season interest with their attractive foliage, colorful berries, or unusually colored or textured bark.

Small Flowering Trees

The list that folio s is arranged by time of bloom, beginning with trees that flower in early spring and progressing through summer-blooming trees. The plant name is followed by flower color.

Serviceberries (*Amelanchier* spp.): white

Cornelian cherry (*Cornus mas*): yellow

Eastern redbud (*Cercis canadensis*): pink

Chinese redbud (*Cercis chinensis*): magenta

Star magnoli (*Magnolia steflata*): white to pale pink

Saucer magnolia (*Magnolia x soufangiana*): white to wine

Flowering do wood (*Cornus florida*): white, pink

Callery pear (*Pyrus calleryana*): white

Crab apples (*Malus* spp.): white, pink, red

Carolina silverbell (*Halesia carolina*): white

Kousa dogwood (*Cornus kousa*): white

White fringe tree (*Chionanthus virginicus*): white

Japanese snowbell (*Styrax japonicus*): white

Golden-chain tree (*Laburnum x watereri*); yellow

Japanese tree lilac (*Syringa reticulata*); white

Golden-rain tree (*Koelreuteria paniculata*); yellow

Japanese pagoda tree (*Sophora japonica*): creamy white

Crape myrtle (*Lagerstroemia indica*): white, pink, lavender

Sourwood (*Oxydendrum arboreum*): white

Japanese stewartia (*Stewartia pseudocamellia*): white

Franklinia (*Frankfinia alatamaha*): white

Showy Shrubs

To add year-round interest to your home landscape, try planting a few of the plants from this list. The plant name is followed by features and seasons of interest.

Barberries (*Berberis* spp.): summer and fall foliage, flowers, fruit; all seasons

Blueberries (*Vaccinium* spp.): flowers, fruits, autumn color; summer, fall

Burning bush (*Euonymus alata*): fall foliage, winged bark; fall, winter

Crape myrtle (*Lagerstroemia indica*): flowers, fruits, bark; all seasons

Harry Lauder's walking stick (*Corylus avellana* 'Contorta'): leaves, flowers, twisted stems; all seasons

Mahonias, Oregon grapes (*Mahonia* spp.): evergreen leaves, flowers, fruits; all seasons

Oakleaf hydrangea (*Hydrangea quercifolia*): leaves, flowers; all seasons

Pieris (*Pieris* spp.): flowers, evergreen foliage; all seasons

Red-osier dogwood (*Cornus sericea*): flowers, bark; spring, winter

Rockspray cotoneaster (*Cotoneaster horizontalis*): flowers, fruit, growth habit; all seasons

Rugosa rose (*Rosa rugosa*): flowers, fruits; spring, summer, fall

Smoke tree (*Cotinus coggygria*): leaves, flowers; all seasons

Viburnums (*Viburnum* spp.); flowers, fruits; spring, fall

Continued ➡

of judicious pruning leads to a structurally sound, well-shaped mature tree.

After a few years, begin the limbing-up process if the tree is planted where passersby will walk below it. Remove the lowest branch or two by sawing through the limb just before the branch collar. Repeat every year until the lowest branches are high enough to permit easy passage. About five or six years after planting, thin to open up the canopy, reducing wind resistance and allowing light to reach the interior. If your tree is intended to block an undesirable view, use heading cuts to encourage denser branching.

As your shrubs grow, you'll need to prune them to control their size, rejuvenate old plants, repair damage, remove pests, and control flowering and fruiting.

Maintain the natural form of your shrubs by pruning back to outward facing buds or removing whole branches. Shearing is faster than naturalistic pruning, but it destroys the natural beauty of the plant—and you'll need to do it often. Learn to read the natural shape and type of a plant and prune accordingly. Many plants combine characteristics and may need more than one pruning technique.

Pruning Cuts

Many gardeners think pruning is a complicated task; however, most pruning comes down to making one of two kinds of pruning cuts: thinning cuts and heading cuts.

Thinning Cuts Thinning cuts remove branches totally. They open up a plant but don't make it shorter. Thinning directs growth into alternate patterns. Use thinning cuts to establish good structure of young trees and shrubs, to allow sunlight to reach the plant interior, to remove wayward branches or those that block a view, and to make a plant less likely to break under a heavy snow load.

Heading Cuts Heading cuts shorten plants and stimulate latent buds behind the cut to grow, making the plant more dense. Nonselective heading is the technique used to shape formal hedges and topiary. Branches are cut back partway along the stem, resulting in rapid, bushy regrowth just below the cut. Nonselective heading is often misapplied—resulting in forlorn, lollipop-shaped shrubs or trees that would look more attractive, and would likely be healthier, if pruned to follow their natural form.

Selective heading, on the other hand, reduces overall size or height of a plant without changing its natural shape. The plant suffers less stress and doesn't regrow as vigorously. Selective heading combines the best of thinning and heading, but it can't be applied to all plants. The older, larger, and woodier the plant, the fewer selective heading cuts should be used.

Pruning Dos and Don'ts

Before you grab your pruning shears and head out the door, be sure you understand basic pruning dos and don'ts—the techniques that work and the mistakes to avoid.

Proper Technique Prune from the bottom up and, in the case of large plants, from the inside out. Prune out all dead wood first—an important step for health and good looks. Dead wood is easiest to spot in the summer because the branches have no green leaves.

Next look for a few of the worst rubbing, crossing branches. Leave the best-placed one of any pair. Try to keep any branches that head up and out from the center, as well as ones that fill an otherwise empty space.

Prune to open up center areas and to clean up the base of shrubs. This improves plant health by admitting light and increasing air circulation. It also has a large impact on the beauty of a plant.

Selectively thin or head back misplaced branches: those that touch the ground, lay upon or crowd other plants, or come too close to the house, windows, and walkways.

Save any heading cuts until the end of a pruning job. Locate the longest, most unruly branch first, follow it down inside the shrub, and cut it off to a side branch inside the shrub, and cut it off to a side branch or a bud. Next year's new growth will be channeled into the bud or side branch.

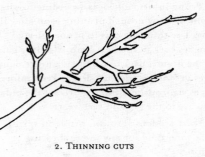

1. SELECTIVE HEADING CUTS

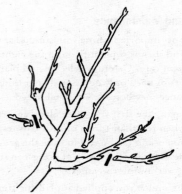

2. THINNING CUTS

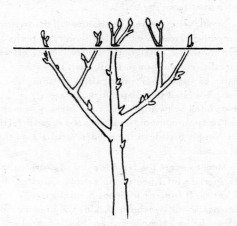

3. NONSELECTIVE HEADING CUTS

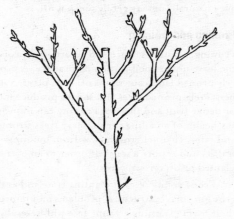

4. REGROWTH AFTER NONSELECTIVE HEADING

Pruning Mistakes. The most common pruning mistake is to cut back everything in the yard in an ill-fated attempt to make it all smaller again. This stimulates an upsurge of messy regrowth, making the final solution more difficult. Tree topping, indiscriminate shearing, and overthinning are the three major or forms of "malpruning."

The cure for badly pruned plants is time. Most will reestablish their natural habits given a few years to recover. Rehabilitative pruning can hasten the process and make plants look better. Meticulously prune all dead wood, removing all stubs. Use thinning cuts to simplify tangled branch ends. Take out entire canes. If treelike shrubs have rampantly produced suckers because of heading cuts, slowly remove the worst of them over a period of years. Let the strongest and best-laced suckers grow back into branches. Some cane-growers, like weigela, can be radically renovated by cutting them entirely to the ground. In about three years they'll regrow to mature size and bloom again. Many lovely but rampant vines, such as autumn clematis, are treated this way.

The majority of needled evergreens will not green up once they are cut back to unneeded wood. This makes their size difficult to control and radical renovation impossible.

Pruning Timetable

Plan your pruning schedule depending on what you want to accomplish. General thinning can be done in any season. Follow these seasonal guidelines:

- Spring pruning stimulates the most rapid regrowth, so it's a good time for heavy pruning. Prune evergreens in spring, but avoid pruning deciduous trees as they leaf out. Prune spring-flowering shrubs such as azaleas, daphnes, and forsythias when they finish blooming so they'll have time to grow and set new buds during summer. This is essential if you are heading back all the branches to force more blooms.

- Summer pruning has a less stimulating effect on growth. Hot or dry weather is extremely stressful for plants, so avoid heavy pruning. This is a good time to tidy up plants and remove suckers and to prune summer-flowering shrubs after they bloom.

- In mid- to late fall, make only thinning cuts. Heading cuts made late in the season can stimulate soft new growth that is easily damaged in fall freezes. Don't prune plants during the period when their leaves are falling.

I Know You, Bud!

When pruning trees and shrubs grown for flowers or fruits, it's important to be able to distinguish vegetative buds from flower buds. Vegetative buds—those forming leaves—are usually sharper, thinner, and longer than the plump flowering buds.

Terminal or apical buds, found at the tip of a twig, can be vegetative, flowering, or mixed, and they are usually plumper than lateral or axillary buds, which are found farther down the twig.

For correct timing of pruning, it's important to know where flower buds form and when they open.

Continued ➔

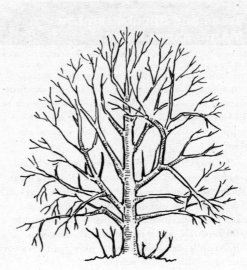

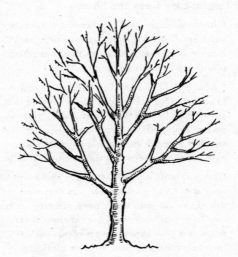

PRUNING A MATURE TREE.

If you've inherited a mature tree, some judicious pruning can make it better looking and healthier. If you're not an experienced tree-climber, hire an arborist to rejuvenate your tree. Before: Dead and diseased branches, waterspouts, tight crotch angles, and rubbing or crossing branches weaken the tree's structure and make it look neglected. After: The tree has been rejuvenated and thinned out, and branches have been headed back to encourage dense new growth.

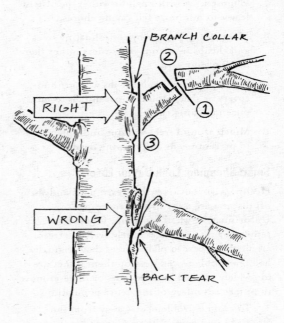

PRUNING LARGE LIMBS.

Sawed from above, a large branch will tear bark from the trunk at it falls. Use the three-cut method to prevent damage. (1) About 1 foot out from the trunk, cut halfway through the branch from underneath. (2) A few inches in from the first cut, saw off the branch from the top. (3) Remove the stub by cutting along, but never into, the branch collar. On tight crotches, saw from the bottom up.

· Late winter is the traditional time to prune dormant plants; leaves have dropped and it's easy to see plant form. Winter pruning stimulates growth, but the results are delayed until spring. This is a good time to prune fruit trees, brambles, grapes, roses, and summer- blooming shrubs, such as butterfly bushes and hydrangeas, that form flowers on the current year's wood.

Good Tools for Good Cuts

Choose pruning tools that cut cleanly and easily. Keep the cutting edges sharp. You'll probably need only three pruning tools: pruning shears for stems and twigs, lopping shears for branches that are finger-size and larger, and a pruning saw for larger branches and crowded areas.

Pruning shears are available in two types. Anvil pruners cut with a sharp blade that closes against a metal plate, or anvil; bypass pruners work like scissors. A leather holster is a wise investment: Your hands are free, but the shears are always handy.

Lopping shears have long handles that extend your reach and give you leverage for more cutting strength. A small rubber shock absorber is a welcome addition on some models. Folding pruning saws fit nicely into a back pocket. New ARS-type saws have multifaceted blades and cut twice as easily as traditional blades. Pole pruners can be used for overhead work, but be careful of overhead wires.

The pruning head can consist of either a saw or a cord-operated hook-type shear, or some combination of the two. You may find that hedge shears are extremely useful for keeping your formal hedges neat.

Pruning Evergreens

Evergreens that are the proper size for their location need very little pruning. Their natural growth habit is interesting and attractive. To remove unhealthy or errant growth, use a thinning cut, pruning off branches nearly flush against the branch from which they originate.

Unlike broad-leaved evergreens, needle-leaved evergreens aren't quick to reprout after pruning. Take care to prune them properly. Follow these steps when pruning evergreens:

· Thin evergreens by removing branches any time of the year. Cut stray branches far enough to the inside to hide the stub. Branches cut back beyond the green needles will not sprout new growth.

· Don't cut the central leader at the top of the tree—an evergreen without its central leader will have a drastically different shape.

· Prune arborvitae, hemlocks, junipers, and yews throughout the growing season.

City-Smart Trees

City trees must contend with constricted root space, compacted soil, wind tunnels between buildings, limited moisture and nutrients, high temperatures, and pollutants.

Trees used along streets, in raised planters, in median strips, or in parking lots must survive in the harshest most stressful of all landscape environments. These often-neglected trees face all the hazards of city trees and must put up with drought, paving heat, and human vandalism. Despite relentless pruning to make them fit under overhead utility lines or within narrow corridors, and even when main branches are whacked off to permit people and cars to pass by, street trees manage to survive. But all these stresses take their toll: On average, street trees live only 10 to 15 years.

In addition to resisting insects and disease, good street trees also share other characteristics. They should be "clean" trees with no litter problems, such as dropping large leaves or fruit, although sometimes, as with sycamores (*Platanus* spp.) and oaks, the litter is overlooked because of other good qualities. Avoid trees with dangerous horns or spines, such as hawthorns (*Crataegus* spp.); shallow-rooted trees that buckle paving, such as silver maples (*Acer saccharinum*); and thirsty trees, like weeping willows (*Salix babylonica*), whose roots seek water and sewer lines. Trees with branches that angle downward, such as pin oaks, also don't make the best street trees, unless they are limbed up high enough for pedestrians and traffic to pass easily. Here's a list of city-smart trees to consider. These trees are tough enough to tolerate the difficult growing conditions of city streets. All will tolerate poor soil, pollution, and droughty conditions.

Small Trees

Amur maple (*Acer ginnala*)

Flowering pears (*Pyrus calleryana* 'Aristocrat' and 'Red Spire')

Golden-rain tree (*Koelreuteria paniculata*)

Hedge maple (*Acer campestre*)

Japanese tree lilacs (*Syringa reticulata* 'Ivory Silk' and 'Summer Snow')

Sargent cherry (*Prunus sargentii*)

Tatarian maple (*Acer tataricum*)

Thornless cockspur hawthorn (*Crataegus crusgalli* var. *inermis*)

Trident maple (*Acer buergeranum*)

Medium to Large Trees

Bald cypress (*Taxodium distichum*)

Chinese or lacebark elm (*Ulmus parvifolia*)

Hackberry (*Celtis occidentalis* 'Prairie Pride')

Japanese pagoda tree (*Sophora japonica*)

Japanese zelkovas (*Zelko va serrata* 'Green Vase' and 'Village Green')

London plane tree (*Platanus* x *acerifolia* 'Blood good')

Sawtooth oak (*Quercus acutissima*)

Silver linden (*Tilia tomentosa*)

Sycamore maple (*Acer pseudoplatanus*)

Thornless honey locusts (*Gleditsia triacanthos* var. *inermis* 'Skyline' and 'Shade master')

Upright English oak (*Quercus robur* 'Fastigiata')

Upright European hornbeam (*Carpinus betulus* 'Fastigiata')

Upright ginkgo (*Ginkgo biloba* 'Fastigiata')

Willow oak (*Quercus phellos*)

Continued ➡

- Trim your evergreens gradually. If you cut off more than one-third of the total green on the plant, it may die.
- One good idea is to hold off pruning your evergreens until a few weeks before Christmas. Then use the trimmings from arborvitaes (*Thuja* spp.), boxwoods (*Buxus* spp.), cedars (*Cedrus* spp.), firs (*Abies* spp.), pines (*Pinus* spp.), rhododendrons (*Rhododendrons* spp.), and other evergreens for holiday wreaths and decorations.

Avoiding Pests and Problems

Frequent inspection of your trees will help minimize problems. Your best defenses are to buy good-quality, pest-free trees to avoid introducing pests or disease; to plant your trees in proper environments to encourage vigorous growth; to use good maintenance practices; and to minimize environmental stresses.

Biotic or pathological problems are caused by living organisms—insects, mites, fungi, bacteria, viruses, nematodes, and rodents. Abiotic or physiological problems are caused by nonliving things—improper planting and maintenance, poor soil conditions, air pollution, injury, compacted soil, construction damage, and lightning. Far more tree problems are caused by abiotic problems, which weaken trees, allowing boring insects and decay fungi to attack. If your tree shows signs of ill health, check for poor conditions that may have allowed the pest or disease to get a foothold.

The plant family bothered by the greatest number of insect and disease problems is the rose family. This large family includes such trees as crab apples, flowering pears, cherries, peaches and plums, hawthorns, serviceberries, and mountain ash. Crab apples are particularly susceptible to problems; buy only those cultivars that are resistant to the diseases rust, scab, powdery mildew, and fire blight. Other trees, such as flowering dogwood, maples, sycamores, birches, elms, locusts, and oaks, may also have numerous pest or disease problems. Ask your nursery owner for advice before purchasing.

Whenever a disease or insect problem is seen, try to control it by removing the pest or the affected plant part. Don't compost or burn infected plants. Remember to sanitize tools after pruning infested or infected wood by cleaning them with a 10 percent bleach solution (1 part bleach to 9 parts water).

Insects Most insect problems of trees are caused by a relatively small number of insects and mites (technically classed as arachnids). These pests have their preferences: Some primarily damage leaves, and others primarily damage branches and trunks.

Insects eat leaves and suck plant sap from them. The larvae of moths and butterflies, such as bagworms, cankerworms, webworms, tent caterpillars, and gypsy moths, are especially voracious leaf-eaters. Highly noticeable webs of Eastern tent caterpillars and fall webworms protect the larvae from predators while they munch your leaves. Although the nests are unsightly, trees usually recover from infestations. Remove and destroy any webs you can reach.

Gypsy moth populations rise to a peak in cycles of several years, causing almost complete defoliation in areas of heavy infestation. Handpicking and spraying BT (*Bacillus thuringiensis*) are the best defenses against severe attacks of gypsy moths. In winter, check your trees for the light brown egg masses, and scrape them off into a container of ammonia.

Other major insect pests that damage leaves are aphids and adelgids, various beetles and bugs, miners, scales, and spider mites.

Insects are always present on trees. Populations must be extreme before the tree suffers any real damage. Don't rush to the sprayer as soon as you spot a caterpillar or two. Remember, the goal is a healthy tree, not complete insect annihilation. Learn to recognize harmful pests and the signs of infestation: curled leaves, stunted growth, deformed flowers.

Try handpicking and pruning off affected branches before you reach for other controls. Even BT is not innocuous. It does kill gypsy moth larvae, tent caterpillars, and other undesirables—but it will also kill any other caterpillar that happens to eat a tainted leaf, including the beautiful luna moth, giant silk moths, and dozens of others.

Stems are damaged when insects such as borers and scales either bore into them or feed on them. Cicadas cause stem damage when they lay their eggs into slits in twigs. Microscopic wormlike nematodes also cause problems on the roots of many trees.

Diseases Tree diseases occur on leaves, stems, and roots. Many pathological diseases are difficult to distinguish from physiological problems. For instance, while fungi and bacteria can cause leaf spot diseases, spots on tree leaves can also be caused by nutrient deficiencies, improperly applied pesticides, road salts, and even drought. Be careful to properly identify a tree problem before you look for a control or corrective measure.

Most tree diseases are caused by fungi, although a few major diseases, such as fire blight on pears and other members of the rose family, are caused by bacteria. Flowering peaches and plums are also bothered by viral diseases.

Diseases of tree leaves are generally spots, anthracnoses, scorches, blights, rusts, and mildews. You will see them on your trees most frequently during moist weather and when plants are under environmental stress. Diseases of tree stems are generally cankers, blights, and decays. You will see these diseases when trees have been damaged by improper pruning, mechanical injury, and other maintenance and environmental factors. Root rots occur when soils are poorly drained and may be intensified if roots have been injured by such things as construction damage and trenching.

Physical Damage You can damage a tree by nailing items to it or gouging it with a lawn mower. Animals also damage trees. Birds may occasionally break branches or drill branches, looking for sap or insects. Moles damage your trees by cutting the roots as they tunnel, and voles actually feed on the roots. Mice and rabbits damage trees by feeding on the bark. Deer damage trees by browsing on young branch tips and by rubbing their antlers on the trunks and branches.

Handle your trees gently. Avoid lawn mower damage by using mulch or beds of groundcovers to surround the trunk. A cat that patrols outdoors now and then is one way to control rodents. Fence to keep out deer.

Trees and Shrubs the Low-Maintenance Way

Barbara W. Ellis, Joan Benjamin, and Deborah L. Martin

Few landscape options require as little maintenance as a planting of well-chosen and carefully planted trees and shrubs. But before you rush to fill your yard with trees and shrubs, note those important qualifiers: Well-chosen and carefully planted.

In this chapter, you'll learn how to choose healthy trees and shrubs that will thrive in your landscape. Since trees and shrubs are a long-term investment that can either be carefree or add loads of maintenance nightmares, it pays to do a little research, ask questions, and choose carefully. You'll also learn how to plant and care for your trees and shrubs properly.

10 Tips for Easy Trees and Shrubs

1. Choose disease- and pest-resistant species and cultivars. Check with nursery owners and your county's extension office to find out which plants are best for your area.

2. Choose plants adapted to your site's soil, exposure, and other conditions. A tree that is stressed by factors such as drought, poor soil, or not being adapted to the site you've selected is more susceptible to pests and diseases that otherwise might not trouble it.

3. Choose plants whose mature size and form fit your spot. A tree whose size and shape are suited to your spot won't need pruning. A large tree in a small space will overwhelm the landscape and pose expensive problems such as limbs overhanging your roof or blocking windows.

4. Buy from reputable nurseries. Plants from grocery and hardware store lots are usually inferior and poorly cared for.

5. Give your plants room to grow. Space them far enough apart to allow them to reach full size without crowding.

6. Choose drip irrigation where watering is required.

7. Choose trees with small or winter-persistent leaves to minimize fall raking chores.

8. Make mowing easier by consolidating trees and shrubs in islands or borders rather than dotting your yard.

9. Underplant trees and shrubs with groundcovers or shade-tolerant perennials to minimize mulching chores.

10. Mulch around trees without underplantings to prevent weeds and mowing hassles.

Smart Shopping: Look Out for Losers

Healthy, vigorous trees that resist pests and shrug off diseases are a joy in any landscape. Unfortunately, when you shop, it pays to remember that the most widely available trees aren't always best to plant. Trees that originally had few problems can develop them if they are too widely planted because pests or diseases move in to take advantage of the dense populations.

To avoid a problem, stay away from the "losers" listed here. Although some have appropriate uses, their troubles largely outweigh their benefits.

American mountain ash (*Sorbus americana*)
Cockspur hawthorn (*Crataegus crus-galli*)
English oak (*Quercus robur*)

Continued ➡

Trees (and Shrubs) to Go: Have Them Your Way

You can buy woody plants in the following three forms: bareroot, containerized, or balled-and-burlapped (B&B). Each option offers advantages and disadvantages in terms of its effect on planting and aftercare. Use this table to help you choose how you'd like to purchase your plants and to guide you in caring for any plants you buy, no matter how they arrive.

Form	Advantages	Disadvantages
Bareroot	Least expensive; cheapest to ship via mail order.	Need immediate planting or heeling-in; may arrive with insufficient root mass to allow growth; careful packing and shipping required to ensure plants don't dry out; for spring or fall planting only.
Containerized	Established root mass; easy to maintain if you can't plant right away; can plant any time during growing season if aftercare is adequate; less expensive than same size plant balled-and-burlapped.	Some plants slow to root out into soil; soilless mix around roots resists watering even after planting; more expensive than bareroot.
Balled-and-burlapped (B&B)	Usually heartier than comparably sized containerized plants; already hardened to outdoor conditions; permits planting of larger plants; usually establish more quickly.	Heavy and more difficult to transport and handle; most expensive; if wrapped in rotproof burlap (usually dyed green), must be unwrapped; large size of plant in relation to rootball may necessitate staking.

European mountain ash (*Sorbus aucuparia*)

European white birch (*Betula pendula*)

Flowering crabapple (*Malus cultivars*). Disease-resistant
  crabapples are available, but disease-prone
  cultivars are sold.

Lombardy poplar (*Populus nigra* 'Italica')

Purple plums (*Prunus cerasifera cultivars*)

Russian olive (*Eleagnus angustifolia*)

Siberian elm (*Ulmus pumila*)

Silver maple (*Acer saccharinum*)

Thornless honey locust (*Gleditsia triacanthos* var. *inermis*)

White ash (*Fraxinus americana*)

White poplar (*Populus alba*)

Save Work with Wise Buys

Woody plants are the durable goods of your landscape. Each one represents a long-term investment that helps determine how attractive and how easy to maintain your property is. With a healthy start and a small, but consistent, amount of care, the trees and shrubs you plant in your yard will become an enduring source of shade, shelter, and beauty.

Because trees and shrubs are such long-term investments, it makes sense to shop carefully when you choose them. Taking time to make smart selections not only ensures that you're satisfied with the plants you've chosen, it also helps reduce the amount of care you'll need to provide over their long lives.

Start with the Seller

Your low-maintenance tree or shrub begins its life in a nursery. Make sure the nursery you buy from, whether mail-order or local, has a reputation for quality plants and intelligent service.

Figure out just what and how many plants you need before you buy. This clear idea is your best protection against impulse buying. Before you shop, call around to find which nurseries have the plants you're looking for, what size they are, how they've been grown, and how much they cost.

Inspect and Detect

At the nursery, inspect each prospective purchase thoroughly. Here's what to look for.

- Examine leaves, stems, and bark for signs of disease or insects.
- Choose plants with foliage that's turgid and green, not drooping or yellowed.
- Inspect the roots, too. If the plant is in a container, tip it out carefully or ask nursery personnel to do this for you. No soil should fall away from the root ball, and a vigorous mass of roots should be visible at the soil surfaces that were covered by the pot.
- Check the moisture of the growth medium. An extremely dry root ball may mean that the plant has been poorly cared for and unnecessarily stressed.
- Finally, make sure the individual plant you've chosen has good form. A misshapen plant will at least require more pruning and shaping, and at worst may never outgrow its homeliness.

Make Sure Roots Measure Up

Balled-and-burlapped (B&B) trees and shrubs are field grown, usually dug while dormant, and their root balls wrapped with burlap. The biggest hazard of buying a B&B tree is that it may have an undersize root ball. The rule of thumb is that the root ball should be 1 foot in diameter for every inch of the trunk's diameter at its base. There is no comparable rule for shrubs, but the bigger the ball, the faster the plant will establish. Undersize root balls are a bigger hazard for trees, whose roots extend far beyond their driplines. The average B&B tree retains only 5 percent of its original root mass.

Look for Signs of Life

If a B&B plant is dormant, scratch its bark in a few places to make sure that it is alive throughout. Live bark scratches easily to reveal green tissue beneath. Ask nursery personnel to pull back the burlap to let you check for root girdling, a condition in which a plant's own circling roots can choke it to death. Inspect the root ball for signs of cracking, and touch the soil to see that it's moist. Don't buy a plant with a cracked or crumbled root ball.

If the root ball is wrapped in rotproof burlap, ask if the nursery will remove it and rewrap the ball in untreated burlap. This will allow you to plant without removing the wrapping.

Stay Away from Strangers

Girdling roots can cause your trees and shrubs to mysteriously decline and die. Check new tree and shrub purchases for signs of circling roots. As a plant grows, such roots can tighten around its stem, gradually cutting off its supply of water and nutrients.

Make Your Trees Work Harder: Look for 4-Season Appeal

Real landscape workhorses don't just sit there and grow, they also add visual appeal—with flowers, fruits, fall color, form, and/or attractive bark. Their blossoms or unusual foliage may allow you to spend less time tending annuals or perennials as sources of color. Their fruits may lure birds or other wildlife to brighten your yard and entertain your family.

Paint a cheery tableau outside a window with a combination of evergreen and fruit-laden shrubs. Shrubs with persistent fruits add color and attract birds to the winter landscape. An added bonus: Many make great cutting materials for holiday wreaths and arrangements.

Hedge Your Bets against High Hedge Maintenance

Lowering the amount of maintenance your landscape needs doesn't mean giving up on hedges. It simply requires you to give up on the notion that a hedge must be closely clipped and geometrical—pruned to within an inch of its life—to keep it under control and tidy. In addition to the huge amount of maintenance they require, clipped, formal hedges all too often end up top-heavy, their shaded lower foliage dropping off to reveal the unsightly, knobby knees beneath.

Instead of slipping into this time-worn, high-maintenance groove, give yourself an attitude adjustment and plan on an informal, low-maintenance hedge. The plants listed below make excellent informal hedges; they maintain a natural unshorn shape that is upright to mildly arching with little or no pruning.

For evergreen hedges, consider one of the new hybrid boxwoods—*Buxus* 'Green Gem', 'Green Velvet', or 'Green Mountain', which are all hardy from Zones 5 to 8. Hollies also make fine evergreen hedges. Consider *Ilex glabra* 'Nordic' ('Nordic' inkberry), hardy in Zones 5 to 9, or one of the blue hollies, especially *Ilex* x *meserveae* 'Blue Prince' and 'Blue Princess', hardy in Zones 5 to 8. (Plant one 'Blue Prince' for every several 'Blue Princess' plants to get berries.)

Maintaining a formal hedge requires careful pruning to keep it looking its best. It's especially important to keep the top of the hedge narrower than the bottom to prevent shading out of the lower branches. To eliminate this type of tedious maintenance, plant an informal hedge of loosely arching shrubs like forsythia or Japanese kerria (Kerria japonica), and put your hedge clippers away for good.

Continued ➡

PLANTS FOR DECIDUOUS HEDGES

'Brilliantissima' red chokeberry (*Aronia arbutifolia* 'Brilliantissima'). Zones 4-9.

Korean barberry (*Berberis koreana*). Zones 3-8.

Mentor barberry (*Berberis x mentorensis*). Zones 5-9.

Nanking cherry (*Prunus tomentosa*). Zones 3-5.

Regel privet (*Ligustrum obtusifolium* var. *regelianum*). Zones 4-8.

Rugosa roses (*Rosa rugosa* cultivars). Zones 3-7.

Summersweet (*Clethra alnifolia*). Zones 5-9.

Winter honeysuckle (*Lonicera fragrantissima*). Zones 5-9.

'Winter Red' winterberry (*Ilex verticillata* 'Winter Red'). Zones 4-9.

Keep Maintenance in Mind at Planting Time

Plant islands for easy maintenance. Instead of scattering plantings, group trees together into freeform islands in the lawn. Underplant with shade-tolerant shrubs and groundcovers, then mulch for low-maintenance planting you'll enjoy for years to come. Use edging strips to keep lawn grass from overtaking your islands, and mow around them with a single pass of the mower.

You can plant a yard full of easy-care, low-maintenance trees and shrubs and still end up with a maintenance nightmare. That's because the design you choose for your plantings can have a big effect on how much work they'll take to maintain. Keep these design principles in mind when you're deciding where to plant new trees and shrubs.

Eliminate fenceline hassles with mixed plantings. Plantings of trees, shrubs, groundcovers, and easy-care perennials can eliminate tedious weeding and trimming along fences. Just select plants suited to the site, then plant and mulch. If you need to be able to paint your fence occasionally or need access to plantings from the back, leave a 2-foot maintenance path between fence and plantings.

Prudent Planting Pays Off

Planting properly will save you scores of hours of maintenance in the future. It can also save you money replacing plants that perish because they were poorly planted. Follow the suggestions below to get your trees and shrubs off to a great start.

Whether you're planting bareroot, containerized, or balled-and-burlapped (B&B) stock, prepare the planting area before you dig your hole. Remove all unwanted vegetation and turn and loosen the soil. Soil requirements of different trees and shrubs vary widely. Whenever possible, match the plant to your existing soil. If your soil is inadequate for the plant you've chosen, incorporate soil amendments over the entire planting area, not just in the planting hole. When planting a single shrub, renovate an area at least 3 feet in diameter. For a tree, renovate an area at least 5 feet in diameter.

PLANTING BAREROOT STOCK

Mail-order trees and shrubs are usually shipped bareroot in spring. Here's how to plant them.

Inspect your plants as soon as they arrive. Bareroot plants should be carefully packed in moist materials, and their bark should show no signs of shriveling. The roots should look husky and healthy. If the root mass looks extremely small for the size of the plant, contact the nursery immediately and register your dissatisfaction.

Take care before planting. After unpacking them, soak your plants in a bucket of water or weak compost tea for 12 to 24 hours. If you can't plant immediately, bury them almost completely in a shady spot for no more than a week (a process called "heeling in"). Trim all broken or damaged roots, and prune back the top by one-third to one-half before you plant. Never allow the roots to dry out, even for a few minutes.

Plant well. Spread the roots of bareroot plants over a mound of soil in the bottom of the planting hole. Look for a soil line on the stem and use it as a planting depth guide, as shown. Backfill carefully with unamended soil, making sure that finely crumbled soil is in contact with the roots. Pat the soil down firmly around the roots, form a basin around the plant, and water several times after planting, plunging the hose end underground to fill air pockets. Apply a 2-inch layer of mulch around the plant to conserve water and weeds.

PLANTING CONTAINERIZED STOCK

Use these tips to get container-grown trees and shrubs off to a good start.

Soak before planting. Plunge each container into a bucket of water until the root ball is saturated.

Score the roots. Use a knife or screwdriver to cut the roots to a depth of ½ inch at intervals around the container. This encourages the roots to grow outward into the soil.

Dig the right hole. Dig a planting hole about twice as wide as the container, deep enough so that the surface of the root ball will be just below soil level. If drainage is poor, make the hole shallower so you have to mound the soil around the plant to cover it. Place the root ball on a slightly elevated platform of soil in the bottom of the hole. The surrounding moat will collect water to be wicked up from the bottom of the root ball-water tends to flow around the soilless mix used in most containers.

PLANTING BALLED-AND-BURLAPPED STOCK

Here's how to get B&B plants in the soil and off to a good start.

Always support the root ball. Never move a B&B plant by grasping the trunk or stem. Doing so requires the roots to support the weight of the soil and will break them. Use a dolly or a cart to move B&B plants too heavy to carry easily. Make sure the root ball is moist, but not wet, before you plant.

Check the burlap. Check to see if your plant is wrapped in a plastic burlap material or true burlap, which is biodegradable. Remove plastic burlap entirely; it can restrict root growth. Also cut away planting "cages" that may contain the roots. Real burlap will wick moisture away from the roots if it's exposed, so pull it partially away from the ball and bury it when you backfill.

Study the roots to dig the right hole. Dig a hole two to three times as wide as the root ball, and deep enough so that the uppermost roots emerging from the stem are just below soil level. Open the burlap slightly and pull away enough soil to locate these roots. In the process of digging the plant, additional soil is sometimes thrown on top of the ball. For this reason, it's easy to inadvertently plant B&B stock much too deeply. Especially in heavy soils, this is one of the most common causes of death in B&B plants. In very heavy soils, dig the hole shallow enough so that you must mound the soil around the upper third of the root ball.

Roll or gently lower the bail into the hole. Dropping B&B stock can fracture the root ball and seriously compromise the plant.

Plan for Post-Planting Care

Your new tree or shrub is most vulnerable in its first year of life. Use this simple post-planting care checklist to get your plants off to a vigorous start.

Water, water, water. Inadequate watering is the number-one cause of new plant death. Most new plants need about an inch of water per week during the first growing season.

Mulch. Keep an adequate layer of mulch around your new plant to prevent weed competition.

Feed. When the plant puts out new growth, feed it with some weak manure tea or compost tea. Or just pull back the mulch and apply a layer of compost or rotted manure around the root zone. Replace the mulch over it.

Minimal Maintenance Methods

A well-chosen, carefully planted tree or shrub will need little maintenance beyond its early years. In most cases, your plant will flourish surprisingly well with benign neglect. But you may occasionally need to intervene. Here's a rundown of the care you can expect and tips for minimizing it.

WATERING

After the first year, your trees and shrubs should not need supplemental watering, except during periods of unusual drought. The exceptions are azaleas and rhododendrons, which need steady moisture to look their best. If you can't keep them well watered, you'll be better off without them.

If you want to plant in a dry spot, choose plants adapted to drought. If your spot is boggy, choose wet-tolerant plants.

If you want to install an irrigation system for your trees and shrubs, stay away from overhead irrigation. Opt instead for one of the many drip irrigation systems available.

PRUNING

The best way to minimize pruning maintenance is to put yourself through an attitude adjustment. Forget about closely shorn globes, cones, and gumdrops. Focus instead on the graceful beauty of a shrub's natural form and learn to appreciate it. Disabuse yourself of the notion that all plants need pruning to make them look "neat" or to keep them under control. Choose shrubs and trees whose ultimate form and size are suited to the spot you have in mind.

Stop, don't top! Never, ever perform—or have performed—on your trees the disgraceful disfigurement known as "topping." This practice causes dangerous, weak-wooded trees that decline gradually and eventually die. If a tree is interfering with power lines, remove individual limbs, transplant the tree, or cut it down.

Leave limbing in limbo. Forget about "limbing up" your evergreens. This practice of removing the lower limbs of evergreens spoils their graceful form and creates more mowing for you. Let those branches sweep the ground and they'll provide their own mulch zone around the tree.

Occasionally, of course, the need to do some light pruning will arise.

FERTILIZING

Most trees and shrubs will grow just fine—albeit more slowly—without any fertilization. Applying 3

Continued ➡

to 4 inches of compost to the root zone once or twice a year is helpful. Occasionally, in very lean soil, more help is needed. Manure tea gives a quick boost to starving plants; a mulch of grass clippings provides a more slowly released nitrogen supply.

Grow them lean and mean. Too much nitrogen fertilizer promotes lush growth that is very tender and disease susceptible. Even resistant trees and shrubs can fall prone to diseases like fire blight on a nitrogen-rich diet. In Zones 3 through 7, withhold nitrogen fertilizer from your woody plants after the 4th of July to give new growth from the spring a chance to "harden" and to curtail additional lush, tender growth.

Think Small

Instead of planting a full-size tree, consider the trees listed here. They range from 10 to 25 feet tall—just right for filling in a limited-space landscape with little or no pruning.

You can screen an area quickly and easily with multi-stemmed plants. In this list, trees with multi trunk tendencies are marked with an asterisk (*).

Callery pears (*Pyrus calleryana cultivars*, especially 'Aristocrat' and 'Autumn Blaze'). Zones 4–8.

Chinese dogwood (*Cornus kousa* var. *chinensis cultivars*). Zones 5–8.

Crape myrtles (*Lagerstroemia indica* hybrids and cultivars)*. Zones 7–9.

Downy serviceberry (*Amelanchier arborea*)*. Zones 4–9.

Eastern redbud (*Cercis canadensis*). Zones 4–9.

Flowering crabapples (*Malus cultivars*). Zones 3–8.

Japanese snowbell (*Styrax japonicus*). Zones 5–8.

Japanese stewartia (*Stewartia pseudocamellia*). Zones 5–8.

Japanese tree lilac (*Syringa reticulata*). Zones 3–7.

Mountain silverbell (*Halesia monticola*)*. Zones 5–9.

Pagoda dogwood (*Cornus alternifolia*). Zones 3–7.

Star magnolia (*Magnolia stellata*)*. Zones 3–8.

White fringe tree (*Chionanthus virginicus*)*. Zones 3–9.

The Secret's in the Soil: Rhododendrons and Azaleas Demystified

There's no denying the beauty and versatility of rhododendrons and azaleas. Their bountiful, beautiful flowers and attractive, often evergreen foliage make them a welcome addition to nearly any landscape. It's no wonder that so many gardeners are willing to struggle against less-than-ideal conditions to grow them.

If rhododendrons and azaleas are must-have plants in your landscape, pay close attention: Rules about careful siting go doubly for these plants. Although they are neither more tender nor more difficult to grow than many other landscape plants, rhododendrons are very particular about the conditions they grow in. Success is a matter of choosing plants appropriate to your area, preparing the soil adequately, and supplying adequate moisture.

In the mid-Atlantic, the South, or the Pacific Northwest, soil and weather conditions make it relatively easy to grow just about any and all rhododendrons and azaleas. Gardeners in other regions need to exercise more care in selecting plants and sites. In northern zones, for example, it's important to steer clear of selections whose flower buds are not hardy enough to withstand the cold. After all, what's the use of growing a rhododendron that never blooms?

Choose a site in partial shade for your rhododendrons and azaleas. Shelter them from drying winter winds benefits evergreen types. But don't try to grow rhodies under maples; their greedy roots won't give timid rhododendrons a chance.

Dig in for Success

If you want to grow rhododendrons and azaleas in anything less than their native moist, rich, woodland soil, there's no getting around doing some soil preparation. If you have clay soil, add equal parts of coarse sand and organic matter (leaf mold, compost, pine bark, rotted manure, or rotted sawdust) and incorporate thoroughly. Add plenty of amendments, so that the resulting area is mounded up a few inches. Test the soil pH. If it's above 6.0, incorporate sulfur to bring it down into the 5.0 to 6.0 range. Plant your rhododendrons and mulch with 3 to 4 inches of pine bark, rotted sawdust, or pine needles. Spread out the roots on the surface of the root ball to stimulate them to grow outward, something rhododendrons' roots are very slow to do.

In sandy soils, forget about adding sand, but double up on the organic matter. Avoid creating a mound that will contribute to the already rapid drainage. Sandy soils are often acidic; don't routinely add sulfur without checking the pH.

Have a source of water handy, as rhododendrons need pretty constant moisture throughout summer. Drip irrigation is best. And remember to water evergreen rhododendrons thoroughly before the ground freezes to help ward off winter desiccation.

For Problem-Free Evergreens, Heed These Tips

Needled evergreens are among the most widely planted trees and shrubs. As with many popular plants, they have been heavily overplanted and often badly used. Use the tips below to minimize problems.

Choose carefully. Pines, in particular, have become host to a plethora of pests. Minimize problems by consulting with experts on the most durable evergreens for your area. Also ask about evergreen alternatives to the most commonly planted spruces and pines.

Avoid streetside sites. Many pines and most spruce cannot tolerate salt spray from vehicles whooshing along a salted street in winter. Browning fooliage on the street side of a planting is a surefire sign of salt damage.

Shelter plants from winter winds. Pick a site that is sheltered from prevailing winter winds, which can shrivel evergreens' foliage. And place them away from south-facing windows so they don't block welcome winter sun.

Consider size at maturity. Whether you're planting spruces, pines, yews, or junipers, don't be fooled by their cute, compact forms in containers. It's all too easy to take a small plant home, plop it in place next to your foundation, and end up shearing and hacking at it to keep it in bounds for the rest of its life. To avoid future pruning nightmares, look at height and spread, and space plants accordingly. Fill in between small plants with perennials or groundcovers for a finished look while you wait for plants to grow.

Buy plants that behave. If you need a low-growing or compact plant for a special site, don't depend on pruning—look for cultivars of evergreens that will

mature at the height you want. Cultivars of creeping juniper (*Juniperus horizontalis*) and western red cedar (*J. scopulorum*) mature at heights from several inches to 1½ feet. Low-growing pines, spruces, and yews are also available, so don't settle for what's most commonly available.

Adding Shade Trees and Shrubs

Larry Hodgson

The first thing most gardeners consider when they want to add more shade is planting trees. The very name "shade tree" says it all: They are trees purposely planted to create shade.

Adding trees to any landscape is often seen as the finishing touch, but landscape planners tend to see trees and large shrubs not as final details but as the actual "bones" of the garden—the structure around which it will be based. A large home, especially, can look as if it had been dropped from the sky by extraterrestrials when it sits on a bare lawn or is surrounded only by low flowerbeds or a knee-high hedge. Some height is needed to integrate it into its surroundings, and the most logical and least expensive way of adding height is by planting trees. Even on smaller lots with limited yard space, trees are essential—although the choice of trees will likely be radically different, and there will probably be fewer of them.

Studies show again and again that trees add financial value to your home, something you may want to consider if you intend to sell your home some day. You can spend $10,000 renovating the bathroom and barely recuperate the cost when you sell, yet planting a $50 tree can add 10, 20, 50—or more!—times that amount to the value of your home.

There was a time when a shade tree meant a huge, spreading 50-foot silver maple (*Acer saccharinum*) or European beech (*Fagus sylvatica*), but times have changed. Smaller lots mean that there is rarely enough room for a 50-foot monster in suburbia—or, if there is, there may be room for only one. Instead, smaller trees have come into the fore. Crabapples (*Malus* spp.) and saucer magnolias (*Magnolia* x *soulangeana*) are considered fine shade trees even though they rarely reach more than 25 feet in height. The important thing about a shade tree is that you should be able to set a lawn chair under it to enjoy the shade. Narrow, columnar trees, like upright English oak (*Quercus robur* f. *fastigiata*), don't cast much usable shade: You'll have to put your lawn chair on wheels and chase after the shade as it moves over the lawn. For good shade, look for trees with spreading or arching branches or a rounded top. You'll find that some of the smaller ones will need "limbing up" (having their lower branches removed) as they grow to make good shade trees, or the only way you'll get under them is by crawling!

Shading with Shrubs

Shrubs can create shade, and they have added benefits: They grow and fill in faster than trees, yet their roots are not so aggressive as to choke out lower plants. Also, their shade is not dense enough to create problems, largely because sunlight reaches both around and over them to ensure some sun to the plants they protect.

Fast and Easy Shade

Growing your own shade by planting trees and shrubs is wonderful but takes time. If you just can't wait, you can also build your own shade structure. This usually costs considerably more than planting trees and tall shrubs, but it does produce fast results.

Continued ➤

Although you can use a durable wood such as cedar for the frame of the structure and attach lattice or fencing as screening, there is practically an unlimited number of possible materials to use for both structures and coverings (including metal, plastic, fiberglass, and resin). You can design the structure to let in a little light or a lot, depending on your needs. And you can add climbing plants to provide further seasonal shade as needed.

FENCES AND TRELLISES

These comparatively inexpensive structures can provide localized shade for plants to their north. The shading effect of fences may be limited by municipal height regulations (6 feet is a common maximum), so check with your town's planning department before proceeding. Trellises tacked onto walls provide little shade, of course, but you can stand them upright to provide interest in the landscape or link them together for more impact.

ARBORS AND PERGOLAS

An arbor is usually a rather modest lattice structure, often covering a path or walkway, sometimes incorporating a bench, with an open or lattice roof. It was originally designed as a support for climbing plants, but it is now often used as an ornamental structure in its own right. It becomes a pergola when it is taller and more elaborate, with parallel colonnades supporting an open roof of girders and rafters. Both supply fairly good shade from the start, depending on the density of the rafters and lattice, and can provide deep shade when they are covered with climbing plants.

GAZEBOS, LANAIS, AND SHADEHOUSES

More elaborate shading structures can incorporate a raised or patio floor and an open or closed roof and are often used for relaxation or entertaining.

The original gazebo was often a six-sided outbuilding designed for gazing out over the garden in poor weather, but it has evolved to encompass a wide range of garden pavilions. Some have screen or latticework sides used for climbing plants, and they often contain a host of potted plants summering outdoors.

Lanais are like vast screened-in porches and may house a swimming pool and container gardens. They're very popular in hot climates where indoor living without air conditioning is next to impossible, and they become a sort of indoor-outdoor living room. Modern ones often feature shade cloth and trellising to support climbing plants.

A true shadehouse is generally a greenhouselike structure, but it's covered in shade cloth and is designed to cover an outdoor garden space. The shade cloth filters the sun and heat while it lets rain in. It can incorporate cooling mist systems and automated watering, creating what is essentially an artificial backyard jungle—and it will even protect plants from light frost in winter. It is popular in hot, humid climates and may cover much of the yard.

Pruning Trees and Shrubs

Barbara W. Ellis

Pruning is an art and a science, but it need not be a mystery. The skillful pruner is one who combines a solid understanding of the basics with an eagerness to learn the specific needs of the plants in his or her care and the courage to make the first cut. With these skills, you can regard

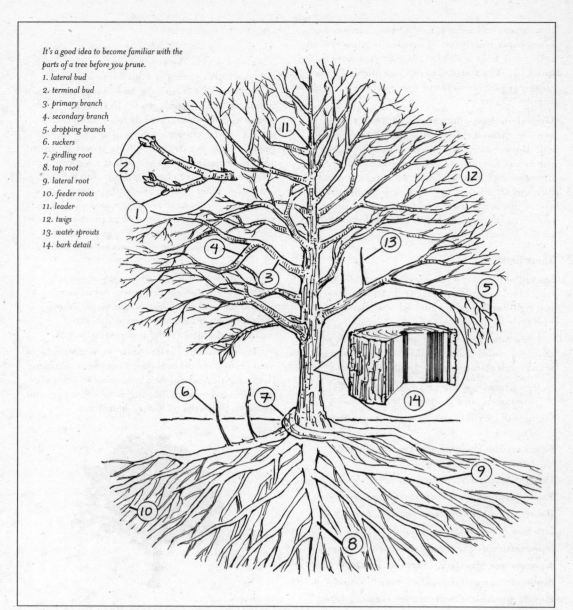

It's a good idea to become familiar with the parts of a tree before you prune.

1. lateral bud
2. terminal bud
3. primary branch
4. secondary branch
5. dropping branch
6. suckers
7. girdling root
8. tap root
9. lateral root
10. feeder roots
11. leader
12. twigs
13. water sprouts
14. bark detail

pruning with the same fondness ascribed to most other jobs in the garden. Moreover, pruning can be a source of learning and accomplishment.

Pruning with a Purpose

Rare is the landscape plant that wouldn't benefit from some purposeful pruning now and again; some species seem to need it more than others. The trick is to recognize and respect the natural growth habit of the particular tree or shrub and prune with a goal that honors the plant's natural inclinations.

Pruning in general improves and promotes the health, vigor, productivity, safety, and appearance of a tree or shrub. You will want to prune a young tree to give it a favorable root-to-top ratio and to promote its structural soundness and appearance as it matures. You will want to remove dead, dying, or diseased wood, along with crossing or rubbing branches. As the tree grows, you will want to prune away water sprouts, suckers, or wood infested by insects that may appear.

If you find you want to prune a tree or shrub to force an unnatural shape, question that plant's appropriateness for the location—or the method of pruning. From flowerless, ball-shaped forsythias to dehorned sycamore trees, tragic examples everywhere prove that no amount of pruning can salvage a poor plant or site choice.

You may be tempted to prune a tree or shrub in order to keep it in bounds, a practice that should be used only on those plants—and by those gardeners—best suited for such discipline. As most plants will eventually attain the mature size

appropriate for the conditions, try to make realistic choices when selecting plants. For example, if you have a small area that could be overrun by a large tree or shrub, you may want to consider the many dwarf and slow-growing landscape plants available today.

Another common but noble reason for pruning is to correct some kind of misshapenness or to rejuvenate a plant. The need for this is often created by crowding, mechanical mishaps, poor pruning in the past, or some form of neglect (benign or otherwise) usually attributed to the former resident of the property.

Another purpose for pruning is what might be called specialty pruning—things you might do after pruning has become a skill that you own completely. Topiary and espalier fall into this category.

Anatomy of a Tree

Knowing the various parts of a tree will be a great help not only when you prune but also in understanding how a tree grows. The tree has water sprouts, narrow crotch angles, suckers, and a broken branch that should be removed. The drooping branches near the base should also be removed. Also illustrated is the spreading root system of a well-anchored tree along with a girdling root around the base of the trunk that could eventually strangle the tree.

The phloem layer just under the bark carries food down from the leaves. Just beneath is the all-important cambium layer, a one-cell-thick layer that gives rise to all new wood. These layers,

Continued ➡

which are close to the surface, are easily damaged by girdling roots as well as lawn mowers. Inside the cambium is the sapwood, which carries water and nutrients to the foliage, and the heartwood, which is inactive sapwood that provides structural support.

PRUNING PHYSIOLOGY

The reluctant pruner should bear in mind that pruning almost always is an invigorating process for the plant. Especially if the tree or shrub is pruned while dormant, topgrowth can be reduced while much of the plant's energy is still stored in the roots. When spring comes, the root-to-top ratio is favorable and the stored carbohydrates are more than adequate to support the rapid flush of growth on top. In fact, research has shown that young trees cut back at planting time tend to outgrow those that aren't.

In specific circumstances, pruning can be debilitating for the plant. If the tree or shrub is heavily pruned while actively growing, particularly after a rapid flush of growth, it loses tissue in which it has just invested a lot of energy, without getting any return from that foliage. Pruning can also be debilitating when it is done so late in the growing season that it brings on a flush of growth that gets damaged by the first fall frost.

Skillful pruners pay close attention to the season, the plant's condition, and its response to the weather. They are fully conscious of the annual rise and fall of sap and work according to that physiology. They avoid pruning during periods of active growth unless that's called for; they avoid spring pruning of tree species that are inclined to "bleed" sap heavily.

Ten Pruning Myths

1. All pruning should be done during the dormant season.

2. A tree can bleed to death if you prune it at the wrong time.

3. A large shade tree and an overhead utility line can usually coexist peacefully.

4. All large cuts should be treated with a wound dressing.

5. Pruning will keep a tree or shrub in bounds.

6. Pruning slows growth.

7. A good pruning job should be obvious.

8. Needle evergreens can be cut back hard, just like deciduous plants.

9. Large limbs should be cut so that they are flush with the trunk.

10. Plant diseases cannot be spread through pruning tools.

Basic Techniques

Regardless of the type of pruning you are performing, you will be drawing from a repertoire of two basic cuts: thinning and heading.

THINNING

A thinning cut is one which follows the branch to be removed back to the branch where it originates. The cut is made at the branch collar,

almost flush, but leaving the collar and never leaving a stub. A thinning cut encourages the remaining limbs to continue to grow naturally and in their normal direction. A thinning cut also opens up the plant, reducing wind, snow, or rain load, and allowing sunlight to reach the ground or the innermost branches. In the same manner, thinning can be used to open a view without removing the tree.

HEADING

A heading cut, on the other hand, is one that takes the branch back to a bud or a pair of buds, rather than to the next limb. When a tree or shrub is headed back, some of the newest growth is cut away. Heading removes terminal buds, causing the buds behind the cut to break and begin to grow. Where thinning opens up the plant, heading causes it to branch and become more dense.

Shearing is a form of heading often used on hedges and in topiary culture, as well as on millions of ball-shaped shrubs in yards nationwide. Heading is often used and abused where thinning is really what's called for. The topping and dehorning of large trees are extreme, and often unnecessary, forms of heading.

When to Prune

Dead, damaged, decayed, or infested wood can be removed almost any time. If disease is involved, be sure to disinfect your pruners before you move on to the next plant. (Isopropyl alcohol is a good disinfectant and it won't corrode your pruners.) In almost every case, damaged or diseased wood is removed with a thinning cut.

Suckers, water sprouts, and crossing, rubbing, or out-of-control branches also can be removed with a thinning cut almost any time. However, the job will be easiest when the plant is dormant and the leaves have fallen away, because you can then get a good look at the tree's structure.

The timing of almost all other pruning is determined by the season of flowering. Spring-flowering shrubs, such as forsythia (*Forsythia* spp.), quince (*Chaenomeles* spp.), and most rhododendrons and azaleas (*Rhododendron* spp.), should be pruned immediately after flowering. Other spring-blooming plants include viburnum (*Viburnum* spp.), daphne (*Daphne* spp.), pieris (*Pieris* spp.), and deutzia (*Deutzia* spp.). Don't procrastinate—next year's flower buds begin to form shortly after the flowers fade, and late pruning will remove them. The only dormant-season pruning appropriate for spring-blooming plants is rejuvenation, thinning, or the removal of dead, dying, diseased, or unruly wood. Head back a spring bloomer in fall or winter and you've lost your flowers for that year.

Summer-blooming plants usually form their flower buds on the current season's wood. Therefore, plants such as crape myrtle (*Lagerstroemia indica*), hibiscus (*Hibiscus* spp.), and abelia (*Abelia* spp.) can, and should, be pruned in the winter. Also included in this list are chaste-tree (*Vitex* spp.), butterfly bush (*Buddleia* spp.), blue-beard (*Caryopteris* spp.), hydrangea (*Hydrangea* spp), and some species of rhododendron such as the late-blooming native azaleas *Rhododendron prunifolium* and *R. arborescens*.

Winter-bloomers such as some daphne species, winter jasmine (*jasminum nudiflorum*), and winter honeysuckle (*Lonicera fragrantissima*) can be treated essentially as spring-bloomers, and pruned after blooming.

Special recommendations for pruning young and mature shade trees, evergreens, shrubs, and hedges are given in the sections that follow.

Pruning and Training Young Trees

Get any young tree off to a good start with some judicious pruning at planting time. Use thinning cuts to eliminate dead, diseased, crossing, or rubbing branches, along with suckers, water sprouts, and branches with narrow crotch angles. Once these basic concerns are attended to, give some thought to the tree's intended purpose and devise a strategy to attain that goal. Will the tree be used for shade, to screen an unsightly view, or to frame or filter a pleasing one? Will it be expected to hold up one end of a hammock? Plan to prune accordingly.

The first five to seven years of a young tree's life will be its training period for a future as either an asset or a liability. Assuming that you removed all troublesome growth at planting time, make an appointment with the tree each winter to look for more of those same signs of trouble.

If the tree is to be walked under, consider removing the lowest limb or two after about the third or fourth year. Continue this annually until the lowest branches are at an appropriate height. This technique is called limbing up and, on a young tree, should be done gradually over several years. This is part of your tree's training; by leaving limbs and removing them gradually you allow them to contribute to the girth and taper of the trunk.

During this time, also give some attention to the scaffold branches, those growing directly from the trunk. Thin them to ensure that they are evenly spaced and not crowding one another. Also watch for narrow crotch angles and thin in favor of wider ones, which are structurally stronger. Feel free to remove the errant branch that heads for the roof of your house or threatens to ruin the natural silhouette of the tree. Also watch the central leader of your young tree and thin out any branches that compete directly with it.

After about the fifth year, consider thinning the crown to reduce loads from wind, snow, ice, or rain. If the plant is destined to become a large shade tree, you will eventually need to hire an arborist for this job. Remove no more than about one-third of the crown at a time.

If your tree has been planted to screen an unsightly view, retain its lower branches and prune it for fullness. To do this, use thinning cuts to attain a sound structural framework, and follow with judicious heading cuts to promote branching. The earlier you begin with this sort of training, the better the eventual results.

If you wish to have your tree filter rather than screen a view, thin it regularly without heading back the branches.

Pruning a Mature Tree

The ongoing training you provide your trees will determine their form and strength as they mature; at maturity, the form and structural strength of a tree, which is maintained by proper pruning, can be a life-and-death matter. Training a young sapling is serious business—just ask any nursery operator. Nursery owners know that uniformity and predictability are important factors in mass production and sales.

Continued ➡

When to Use an Arborist

In caring for a mature tree, it is critical to recognize your limitations and know when and how to hire an arborist. Without appropriate climbing, safety, and technical skills, removing even one errant branch can be risky business for a home gardener. Entrust your mature trees to a professional arborist.

Following are some of the services provided by professional, accredited arborists.

Large Pruning Cuts— To Paint or Not?

The work of Alex Shigo and other leading tree-watchers has revealed that the use of tree wound dressing is, for the most part, unnecessary. Decay of the tissues related to the cut will occur with or without treatment. The function of the tree paint as a barrier for moisture has been refuted by the discovery that there is plenty of moisture that actually needs to escape at the wound site. Thus, wound dressing serves as a barrier in a nonproductive way.

Tree wound dressing also has been shown not to be a formidable barrier to insects. When there has been mechanical injury (such as an auto or mower mishap), or if the aesthetic condition of the tree is under close scrutiny, tree wound dressing can and should be used in a cosmetic manner. It usually makes everybody feel better.

- **Plant management.** A management program will ensure that your trees will be examined, and corrected or treated if necessary, on a regular basis. Fertilizing, soil aeration, and pest control are other routine services that might be provided under a management program.
- **Regular pruning.** Structural correction and thinning are regular pruning services offered by arborists.
- **Storm-proofing.** This includes thinning to reduce snow, rain, or wind load; removal of weak branches; and balancing the crown so that, should it fall, it would cause the lease human hazard or property damage.
- **Grounding.** For old and valuable trees, especially on a high spot, cables can be installed that will minimum the damage of a lightning strike.
- **Cabling and bracing.** This is for trees that are structurally weakened in some way. Like grounding, cabling and bracing is worth considering for mature trees considered to be extremely valuable.
- **Topping.** Consider replacing either your arborist or your tree if this is recommended. Topping is the removal of most of the crown of the tree and usually results in horrible disfigurement. It is considered a necessary evil, especially where mature trees and overhead utility lines coexist. Still, few trees are worth having once topping has been done; consider replacing the tree with something more compatible with the reality of the site.
- **Removal.** The ultimate pruning job. If the task calls for equipment that you don't already have or don't have the training for,

such as a chain saw, consider hiring an arborist.

Choosing an Arborist

When shopping for an arborist, look around your own neighborhood, or a neighborhood with mature trees in it. You should be able to identify good work and sloppy work after some looking: The good work is practically invisible. Ferret out happy customers and ask for a referral.

If scouting around isn't for you, look up your nearest chapter of the International Society of Arboriculture in the telephone directory, and ask for a list of accredited arborists. Your nearest arboretum or botanical garden may also have such a list.

Be sure that your arborist is bonded or insured in some fashion. Don't be fooled by an impressive assortment of chain saws and a truck with a chipper. Ask for accreditation, insurance, and a look at some of the individual's previous work. A professional will be happy to show you those things. Your investment of time and effort will be well worth it.

Pruning Shrubs

As with trees, your first concern when pruning shrubs should be to preserve structural stability and health. This includes removing crossed or rubbing branches, water sprouts, and suckers, along with dying, diseased, or infested wood. Such pruning can be done during any month of the year. A thinning cut is the cut to use.

The rest of the pruning work is done according to the season and the plant's physiology and bloom time. Most spring-blooming shrubs are pruned soon after they bloom, before they set flower buds for the following year. Winter-bloomers are handled in the same manner. Shrubs that bloom in summer usually can be pruned in the winter while they are dormant.

Pruning Objectives

There are several other reasons to prune shrubs beyond the basic structural concerns. Shrubs are pruned to reduce or limit their size, to keep them vigorous and flowering, and to thin them so that sunlight can penetrate the interior of the plant. For seriously overgrown plants, all of these processes are combined into one technique called rejuvenation.

LIMITING SIZE

One of the best ways to reduce or limit the size of a shrub is to use thinning cuts to prune away branches to the next side shoot, allowing the shoot to camouflage the cut. In this case, thinning will allow light to reach the interior of the plant and encourage new growth near the interior of the plant. Thinning works much better in the long run than shearing or heading back with pruners. Heading back new growth causes the shrub to have lots of dense growth around the tips, which shades the interior of the plant and makes it hollow. Many are the azaleas and forsythias that have been shorn rather than thinned and languish as round balls, hollow shells of their former selves. Prune with the understanding of how the plant would like to look.

OPENING UP

Many shrub species respond well to being opened up on a regular basis. This is a form of rejuvenation done while the plant is dormant. With this method, you remove two or three of the oldest (and usually least healthy) branches each year. Lilacs (*Syringa* spp.), forsythia (*Forsythia* spp.), abelia

(*Abelia* spp.), heavenly bamboo (*Nandina domestica*), and Oregon grape (*Mahonia* spp.) do well with this approach. In addition to effectively reducing the height of the plant, keeping it in bounds, opening up also keeps the shrub well supplied with new wood. By rotating out old branches by cutting them back to the ground, you expose the innermost sections of the plant to sunlight, thus stimulating new, vigorous growth.

REJUVENATION

Frequently, new homeowners are faced with assortments of neglected, overgrown shrubs; occasionally, longtime homeowners are faced with a shrubby jungle if they don't stay on top of maintenance. Rejuvenation by thinning is effective on many such overgrown shrubs.

The first step is to decide whether the specimen is worth keeping, as your rejuvenation effort will require considerable commitment of time and energy. If a plant is horribly misshapen from competition with other plants, crowding, or mechanical mishaps, think twice and perhaps opt to remove it. If it's just an overgrown shrub with plenty of room and lots of appeal, determine if it can be rejuvenated and have at it.

As with the shrub where you removed old growth on a rotational basis, begin the first winter by removing—to the ground—two or three of the oldest limbs. Then come back the next year and do the same, being careful not to remove too much at one time, since full sun can be quite a shock to the innermost reaches of a plant. This process must be gradual. Eventually, the removal of the old growth will stimulate and make room for new growth and the plant will assume a new life.

Another form of rejuvenation involves the complete removal of the top of the plant during the dormant season. Although this can be done on some overgrown plants, the best results are with young, vigorous, annually-renewed specimens that bloom in the summer on new growth. Dwarf crape myrtles (*Lagerstroemia indica*), bluebeard (*Caryopteris* spp.), and abelia (*Abelia* spp.) are good candidates for this rather radical act of faith. Spring bloomers such as forsythia (*Forsythia* spp.) also can be rejuvenated this way, but, because the buds are already set, you will lose the spring bloom. Sometimes the sacrifice is worth getting the plant back under control.

One final method of rejuvenation pruning is a thinning process in which you transform an overgrown shrub into a comparably sized—but tamer—tree. Remove water sprouts and suckers; then begin limbing up and thinning back to a single or multiple trunk, selecting your scaffold branches as you go. This method works well for crape myrtle (Lagerstroemia indica), some viburnums (Viburnum spp.), and red buckeye (Aesculus pavia).

Pruning Hedges

Hedges can be short or tall, narrow or wide, formal or informal, depending on the plants you have chosen or inherited, the care required, and their natural growth habit.

With a new hedge, follow the same general strategy at planting time as described for other shrubs. The only pruning needed initially will be thinning to remove dead, diseased, or damaged branches.

Once the planting becomes established, pruning time and strategy will be determined by the hedge's level of formality. Prune an informal flowering hedge according to its flowering time—

Continued ➡

for example, prune forsythia for shape, if necessary—after flowering. Thin informal hedges to rejuvenate them during the dormant season. This helps keep the growth thick and lush and opens up the interior of the plant to encourage a steady supply of new shoots. Never shear an informal hedge.

Glossy abelia (*Abelia* x *grandiflora*), barberry (*Berberis* spp.), forsythia (*Forsythia* spp.), Chinese holly (*Ilex cornuta*), winter honeysuckle (*Lonicera fragrantissima*), and shrub roses (*Rosa* spp.) are all fine prospects for informal hedges. For a large informal hedge, consider hedge maple (*Acer campestre*) or Canada hemlock (*Tsuga canadensis*).

Treat a formal hedge much like a lawn, and trim or shear frequently throughout the growing season. As with grass, the best strategy is to cut as often as you can stand it, removing only a small bit of growth at a time. This frequent shearing is a form of heading back and encourages dense growth and the filling-in of holes. Among the plants that lend themselves to formal hedges are Japanese holly (*Ilex crenata*), yews (*Taxus* spp.), privet (*Ligustrum* spp.), and arborvitae (*Thuja* spp.).

Whether formal or informal, hedges should always be shaped so they are wider at the bottom than at the top, if only slightly. Failure to do this results in a hedge with bare ankles, then calves, knees, and so forth, because the top quickly shades the bottom and the plants become leggy. This is especially a problem with formal hedges. By making the top slightly narrower than the bottom, you allow sunlight to reach the bottom of your hedge and you are likely to have an enviable hedge...full to the ground.

VINES

Venture into Vines

Fern Marshall Bradley

You may not realize how versatile and useful vines can be in the home landscape. Train them up walls and trellises to provide shade or a privacy screen, or use them as groundcovers in difficult sites.

Use Natural Trellises

Vines make a great cover-up for some of those less-attractive features of a yard, such as a chain-link fence. They can also add an extra-special touch of beauty to the trees and shrubs in your landscape. Simply choose a shrub or tree in your yard, and plant a favorite climbing vine at its base. The vine will climb up and through the plant's branches as shown in the illustration at left. When you plant the vine, be careful not to damage the roots of the tree or shrub. Try these experts' suggestions for easy natural trellises.

Richard Hutton, the chairman of the board at the Conard-Pyle Company, a wholesale nursery in Pennsylvania, recommends growing a clematis (*Clematis* spp.) vine up a large yew tree (*Taxus* spp.). "Because of the dark green of the yew, it's a most

effective display!" says Hutton. Roger Gossler, a co-owner of Gossler Farms Nursery, an Oregon nursery that specializes in magnolias, gets a similar effect by combining clematis with the dark green of magnolias (*Magnolia* spp.). He particularly likes to combine pink cleematis flowers with the hot pink seedpods of *M. sieboldii*.

Karen Jennings, a senior vice president of Geo. W. Park Seed Company and Wayside Gardens in South Carolina, likes her clematis supported by viburnum (*Viburnum* spp.) bushes and dogwood (*Cornus* spp.) trees. Dark blue clematis flowers particularly provide a lovely contrast when mixed with the white viburnum or dogwood blossoms.

North Carolina garden writer Peter Loewer admires pest-resistant Virginia creeper (*Parthenocissus quinquefolia*) growing in old apple trees or gnarled, dead trees. The vine's magnificent red fall color lights up leafless branches. "If it starts to choke a living tree or if you simply decide you don't want it, unhook the Virginia creeper and spread it on the ground where it makes an excellent groundcover," he says. Loewer also uses a clematis such as 'Madame Bruchard' with eastern white pine (*Pinus strobus*). The pine provides the base shade needed by clematis roots and shows off the clematis's purple-blue flowers. Try this clematis cultivar with camellias (*Camellia* spp.), too.

James W. Kelly, a New York plant taxonomist, finds climbing hydrangea (*Hydrangea anomala* subsp. *petiolaris*) particularly attractive in sugar maples (*Acer saccharum*). It is pest-free, has beautiful flowers, prefers light shade, and won't harm trees.

However, rampant vines such as wisteria (*Wisteria* spp.), bittersweet (*Celastrus* spp.), wild grape (*Vitis* spp.), and honeysuckle (*Lonicera* spp.) can kill trees. So can poison ivy (*Rhus radicans*). These vines reach high into the tree and spiral around branches, blocking light and reducing the tree's food supply. The best way to get rid of these overexuberant climbers is to cut them off at the roots. But don't rip down the vines; let them wither and fall off naturally. Otherwise the tree trunk will undergo a sudden change from being shaded to being exposed to the sun and may suffer sunscald damage.

Turn Old Vines Into Trellises

For an unusual trellis, try training a vine over old vine prunings. If you have a brick garage or outbuilding, use mortar nails to create a pattern on one of its walls, suggests Bonnie Lee Appleton, Ph.D., an associate professor and extension horticulturist at Virginia Polytechnic Institute and State University. Garden centers carry special nails, called wall anchors or vine nails, that also work well. They have a strip of soft metal that can be bent around a vine's stem to hold it in place. After the nails are in place, weave prunings from grape or kiwi vines around them, then plant a flowering vine at the base of the trellis. As the flowering vine grows, train it to climb over the woody prunings. "The trellis looks nice even before a vine covers it," says Dr. Appleton.

You can also make a rustic-looking free-standing trellis by tying and weaving—and even stapling—vine prunings around two or more large, straight branches stuck in the ground. For lightweight vines like clematis (*Clematis* spp.), two branches set 1 foot deep in the ground should be sufficient. For heavy vines like wisteria (*Wisteria* spp.) or grape (*Vitis* spp.), add more straight branches for support, and set the branches 1½ to 2 feet deep or deeper if you have sandy soil.

Climbing Hydrangeas Start Slowly

Don't become discouraged if you plant a climbing hydrangea (*Hydrangea anomala* subsp. *petiolaris*) and it

seems just to sit there for a couple of years. After a slow start, climbing hydrangea will "take off like a house afire, growing from 12 to 20 feet," says Bonnie Lee Appleton, Ph.D., an associate professor and extension horticulturist at Virginia Polytechnic Institute and State University. "The wait is worth it. This vine has exfoliating bark, which makes it extremely pretty, even when naked." Make sure, though, Dr. Appleton warns, that you put climbing hydrangea where you intend to keep it, because this clinger will really latch onto whatever support you give it, and it won't let go easily.

Climbing hydrangea, which is hardy to Zone 4, likes a rich, moist but well-drained soil. It can tolerate semishade but blooms best in full sun, except in extremely hot climates.

Encourage Clingers to Cling

An occasional overhead watering will encourage a clinging vine, like climbing hydrangea (*Hydrangea anomala* subsp. *petiolaris*), smilax (*Smilax* spp.), coral vine (*Antigonon leptopus*), or trumpet vine (*Campsis radicans*), to cling by its roots, says Karen Jennings, a senior vice president of Geo. W. Park Seed Company and Wayside Gardens in South Carolina. "Once clingers are established, pinch off the tips just above the uppermost buds to make their growth denser, and prune out dead and weak wood before it blooms," says Jennings. "Cut back any over-long tendrils to two or three leaves."

Make Recycled Trellises

A tuteur is a fancy plant support for vines that's sometimes found in old French gardens. Tuteurs are elegant but expensive—unless you create your own. "You can make your own version of a tuteur. Just stick a long metal or plastic pipe in the ground and insert the framework of an umbrella into it," says North Carolina garden writer Peter Loewer. You can use any old umbrella that no longer has any fabric covering it. This umbrella trellis, shown at right, is particularly good for vines that grow by twining.

And if you're hooked up to a cable service, consider using that unneeded television antenna as a space-age-looking trellis. Stick it in the ground and train a flowering vine up and around it. Or try growing gourds or pole beans up it for an easy harvest.

Growing Vines

Jeff Cox

Versatility is the hallmark of vines. All scramble or climb, but that's where their similarity ends. You can grow vines for shade, for food, or for beauty of foliage, bloom, or fruit. Vines range from tough,

Continued ➡

woody grapes and wisterias to annuals like morning-glories and garden peas. Other favorite vines include climbing roses, clematis, Boston and English ivies, Virginia creeper, climbing hydrangea, bittersweet, and passionflowers.

You can find a vine for almost any kind of site—sun, shade, loam, or sand; boddy or dry; fertile or poor soil. You're better off matching the vine to the situation than trying to alter the environment to suit the specific plant. In general, most vines are tolerant of a wide range of cultural conditions. It is the exception, such as clematis (which requires cool soil around its roots), that has specialized requirements. Be sure to check the specific needs of any plant before adding it into your garden.

Landscaping with Vines

Vines' growing habits let you merge boundaries and soften harsh edges. Planting annual vines on fences, gates, an other structures quickly brings an established look to a young garden where the plants have yet to fill in. Use vines to define a garden room: Create green walls by covering fences, mark an entrance with a covered arbor, or provide overhead shade with a pergola.

From Seed to Vine

You can have beautiful vines for the cost of a seed packet. Try the following five beauties for color from spring until fall.

Black-eyed Susan vine (*Thunbergia alata*) produces 1- to 2-inch-wide orange, yellow, or white blooms with black eyes. Try planting them in hanging baskets, window boxes, and trellises.

Moonflower (*Ipomoea alba*) grows 8 to 10 feet long and has fragrant, white, night-blooming flowers. Soak seeds overnight or notch them with a knife or file to break through the seed coat and encourage germination.

Morning glories (*Ipomoea* spp.) will grow up to 25 feet long. They produce red, purple, pink, white, or blue flowers. Treat seeds as you would moonflower seeds for best germination.

Ornamental gourds (*Lagenaria siceraria*, *Cucurbita pepo* var. *ovifera*, and *Luffa aegyptiaca*) grown on a trellis will produce straight gourds in a variety of colors and sizes. Soak seeds overnight to promote germination.

Sweet pea (*Lathyrus odoratus*) bears fragrant pea-shaped flowers in every color but yellow in spring and early summer.

Vines soften and connect the hard edge between the structures and the plants in a garden. Plant Boston ivy or wisteria to climb up a wall of your home, and you'll link the house and garden. Vines also make the house wall more attractive, provide seasonal interest (in our example, Boston ivy has fall color and berries, and wisteria has early-summer bloom), and if planted on the south side of the house, the vines will help cool it.

Plant vines to screen unsightly walls or views. A planting of wintercreeper will make an ugly concrete wall into feature rather than an eyesore. A chain-link fence can become an asset if you cover it with trumpet vine (*Campsis radicans*) with its showers of brilliant red-orange blooms in midsummer.

Versatile vines have many other uses as well. Clematis or other vines planted next to lampposts and pillars add interest to any garden. Make the

most of a small garden or terrace by "growing up." Grow vines over railings and along windows and door frames to create a magical hideaway. Annual vines can be grown in window boxes and are useful on terraces. Morning-glories (*Ipomoea* spp.), scarlet runner beans (*Phaseolus coccineus*), and black-eyed Susan vines (*Thunbergia alata*) are good window-box choices. And don't forget attractive vines with edible parts such as cucumbers, pole beans, and peas.

Pruning and Training Vines

Pruning is your opportunity to train and control a vine. Look hard at the plant before cutting. The first step in any pruning operation is removal of dead, damaged, and diseased wood. Always use a sharp tool—a hand pruner, lopper, or saw—and make th cut just above a live bud or nearly flush with the stem. Only after "cleaning up" the plant should you start working on the live wood.

Prune live wood after the vine has finished blooming for the season. This means you'll prune spring bloomers in early summer, summer bloomers in early fall, and fall bloomers in winter or early spring. Remove dead wood anytime. Shape and control annuals by pinching early in the season. Pruning depends on the growth habit of the plant. Clinging vines like English ivy (*Hedera helix*), winter-creeper (*Euonymus fortunei*), and Virginia creeper (*Parthenocisms quinquefolia*) merely need trimming to keep them in bounds. Other vines like wisteria, clematis, and grapes will need annual pruning.

Vines the Low-Maintenance Way

If you'd like to spruce up your landscape in a hurry, try planting vines. Whether you want an easy-to-erect privacy screen, a simple way to hide a landscape eyesore, or just a quick burst of color, vines offer easy solutions to a host of landscaping challenges. Not only are they easy to grow, but their vigorous spreading nature also means they'll provide spectacular effects with little help from you. All they need is the right site and something to climb up, cling to, or scramble over. For an especially effective display—without any extra work—plant vines that offer colorful flowers, fruits, or bright leaves for autumn interest.

This section will help you choose easy-care, pest-free vines. You'll also learn easy ways to help them climb and thrive. Worried about having to build elaborate support structures for vines? Stop worrying! You'll find ideas for easy trellises, too.

Ask What Vines Can Do for You

Have you been struggling with landscape bugaboos like an unmowable lawn area, a garden the size of a postage stamp, or spots that are plagued with too much sun or shade? Forget about costly landscape renovations; let vines solve site and exposure problems for you.

Add height to small gardens. Vines are a great way to add height in gardens large or small. They can also provide an alternative to expensive, slow-growing trees. They're great for providing an ever-green backdrop without adding too much shade. And their interesting leaf shadows and colorful blooms can add a whole new care-free dimension to small gardens. They can scale trellises, walls, or the trunks of existing trees to draw the eye up. Or let them drape over entryways and porches to create a sense of mystery.

Light up shady areas. To brighten a dark spot without trimming all your trees back, try vines with variegated foliage. Look for English ivy and winter-

creeper with gold or white borders or streaks. Hardy kiwi (*Actinidia kolomikta*) has white and pink flushed leaves; variegated Japanese honeysuckle (*Lonicera Japonica* 'Aureoreticulata') has leaves marked with yellow. For best color, provide a spot with partial sun. Depend on the flowers of climbing hydrangea to brighten up very shady areas.

Replace lawn grass. If you have an area where grass won't grow or where you just don't want to have to mow, consider using a vine as a groundcover. English ivy works well in such a situation, as does winter-creeper and climbing hydrangea.

Shade a porch, pergola, or summerhouse. What if you need cool shade and privacy fast during the lazy days of summer, but you want sunshine for warmth in winter? No problem! Choose a vine that loses its leaves in winter, such as Dutchman's-pipe, hardy kiwi, or grapes. Or, choose an annual vine that will die back with the first hard frost, such as one of the morning glories.

Plant Vines to Hide Eyesores Fast

Is there an object in your landscape that you'd like to have disappear in a hurry? Vigorous vines can work magic when it comes to screening ugly architectural or landscape features quickly and painlessly. So to put your eyesore out of sight and out of mind, choose the vine vanishing act you like best.

Cover a chain-link fence. If your backyard is surrounded by a bare chain-link fence, why not dress it up with vines? Perennial vines, like trumpet honeysuckle, will hide it from view but may take a while to get established. As a "quick fix," plant fast-growing annual vines, such as hyacinth beans or morning glories, to add cover the first year.

Hide a hideous air conditioner. You can make an ugly air conditioner disappear with a screen of trel-liswork and a mix of evergreen and annual vines. (Be sure to keep the trellis and vines 1 foot away from top discharge models; 6 feet away from side discharge ones.) The annuals will give you an almost instant screen and even some colorful flowers; the evergreens will give long-lasting cover.

Make a tree stump—or tree—disappear. Instead of paying to have a dead tree or tree stump removed, just make it disappear with vines. Hiding a tree stump is easy—just plant an evergreen trailing vine such as English ivy or wintercreeper around it. Within no time the stump will be history. To turn a dead tree into an attractive addition to the landscape, use it as a support for trumpet honeysuckle or wisteria.

Vines Thrive When the Site Is Right

Do a little site research before you plant if you want to grow vines that will make your landscape look marvelous. For the best results with the least work, choose vines that are adapted to the site and soil conditions in your garden. That way, your vines will have the conditions they need to thrive, and you won't spend any extra time improving or changing the site. Use the questions below to help you evaluate your site and narrow your hunt for the perfect vine.

What's your light like? The amount of light a site receives helps dictate which vines will grow best there. Morning glories and black-eyed Susan vines need a site with full sun, while silver lace vine requires only a half-day of sun. Boston ivy, grapes, trumpet vine, and Dutchman's-pipe are equally happy in sun or shade. (Flowering types will bloom less in shade, though.) And English ivy and climbing hydrangea prefer shady spots.

How does your soil stack up? Before you decide what vines to plant, find out if the soil on your site

Continued ➡

is rich or poor. Then select a vine that will thrive in the soil you have. That way, you won't have to fertilize and amend your soil to match the needs of a particular vine. Vines such as five-leaf akebia, porcelain vine, and grapes need fertile soil and will languish in poor sites. Others, such as hardy kiwi, grow too vigorously in rich soil and are best grown in infertile soil. Trumpet vine, English ivy, Boston ivy, and wintercreeper are not so particular and will take almost any soil type.

Does your dirt drain? Drainage is another soil characteristic to consider. Wisteria and some hybrid clematis must have good drainage to perform well; five-leaf akebia and hardy kiwi are more tolerant.

Where's your water? Most vines are drought-tolerant, but you may need to think about the moisture needs of a vine before choosing it for your site. For example, grapes need enough moisture during their growing season to form plump fruits. Clematis also needs large amounts of water. Use these vines if you have a moist, well-drained site, or make sure you have easy access to a water supply in case of drought.

Quick and Painless Pruning for Vines

Don't let the thought of pruning strike fear into your heart; perennial vines only look hard to prune. In fact, it only takes a few cuts once a year to maintain their shape, curb excess growth, and remove damaged or unhealthy shoots. One rule to remember when you're giving your vines their annual trim is to always cut back to a bud, a lateral branch, or the main trunk. Be careful not to leave stubs—they may die back and cause decay in the healthy branch.

PRUNE WHEN THE TIME IS RIGHT

For most flowering vines, the right time to trim is when you have the time. Unless you're doing drastic pruning, which is best done when plants are dormant, you can shape your plants in any season.

If time isn't a concern and you want the most flowers you can possibly get, arrange your pruning schedule to suit your vines. Prune all early spring flowering vines-including wisteria, Carolina jessamine, clematis, and trumpet honeysuckle—just after they finish blooming. If you prune before they bloom in early spring, you'll snip off flowers along with the branches.

Vines that flower in late spring to summer bloom on the current year's growth, so prune them in the spring. This early pruning will encourage new growth, which leads to more flowers. Examples are American bittersweet and silver lace vine.

Grapevines need yearly pruning in mid- to late winter before the sap rises. Merely cut each shoot of last year's growth back to one or two buds.

Give New Vines a Quick Trim

To get newly planted woody vines off to a good start, give them a haircut at planting time. Start by cutting the topgrowth back by half. This gives the roots a chance to develop sufficiently to support the top growth. When you prune, always make a slanted cut just above a bud, as shown at left. Trimming topgrowth stimulates side branches to grow more vigorously, so you'll get a sturdier framework to support future growth.

Restyle an Old Vine

It takes drastic action to rejuvenate and reshape an old or neglected vine, but it doesn't have to take lots of effort. Simply spread the process out over three or more years.

Year one. Don't do any pruning in the first year. Instead, observe your vine carefully during the

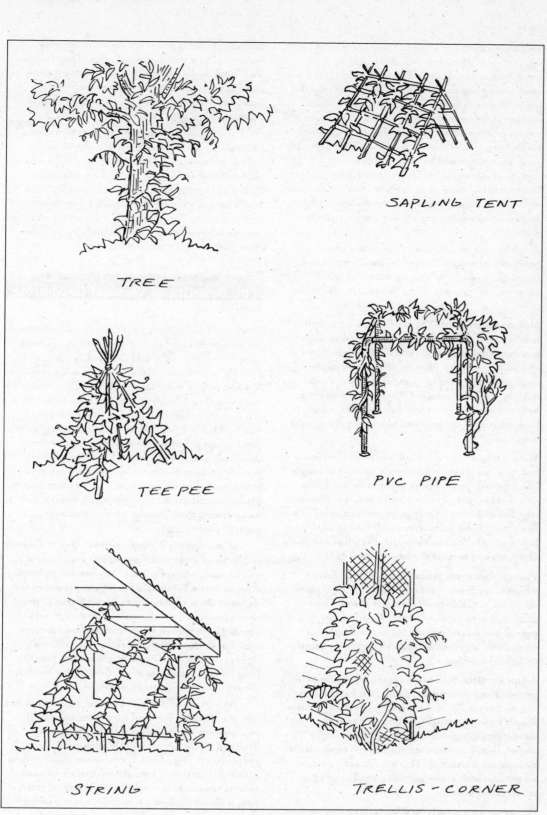

TREE

SAPLING TENT

TEE PEE

PVC PIPE

STRING

TRELLIS - CORNER

growing season and decide which parts should go. Remove dead, diseased, and overgrown branches. To make pruning easy, tie colored tape or string around branches you plan to remove. These markers make it easy to find unwanted branches when pruning season arrives.

Year two. Start the pruning portion of your renovation when the plant is dormant, in late winter or early spring. That way, it's easy to see what you're doing because there aren't any leaves—at least on deciduous vines. It's also easier on the vine since it isn't growing actively. Thin out a few of the oldest, toughest stems first by cutting them back to 6 to 12 inches above the ground, New shoots will sprout in spring; when they reach 6 to 12 inches long, prune the tips to encourage branching.

Year three. Prune again the following late winter or early spring. Remove a few more of the remaining unruly stems as you did in year two. You can continue renovation pruning into a fourth year or until you bring the vine back to the size and shape you want.

Pruning Mature Vines

You can do light pruning to shape a mature vine whenever you have the time. Snip back the straggly shoots that give your plant a messy look, and thin out any dead, broken, or diseased wood. If your vine needs lots of pruning, wait until it's dormant before tackling the task.

Easy Ways to Help Your Vines Climb

Before you invest time and money constructing elaborate trellises and arbors, look around your yard. Plants already growing in your yard can make perfect vine supports. You can also use inexpensive pipes—either metal or PVC—along with a variety of found materials to make great-looking, easy-to-build trellises.

For example, interlace a framework of pipe with saplings, or rope it together with twine or vines. (You may need to tuck the vines in and out a bit as they grow to get the desired effect.)

Continued ➡

Train up a tree. Let's face it, there are ways to support vines that are as easy as pie. Just look around when you drive in the country and you'll see vines scrambling happily up tree trunks all over the place. Why not give it a try at home? Just plant a climber at the base of a favorite tree, give it some strings or a temporary trellis to help it get up to the lowest branches, and sit back and watch it go. Some good examples would be clematis trained up a fruit tree, or climbing hydrangea in an oak. Or let light-weight trailing vines, such as black-eyed Susan vine or clematis, drape themselves over shrubs in your garden or meander their way among your perennials.

Stick with annual vines or well-mannered perennials if you try this technique. Evergreen vines, like English ivy, and extremely vigorous growers, like trumpet vine, can smother plants they cover.

Make a sapling tent. You'll need about 20 saplings, bamboo poles, or extra-long tomato stakes. Lash pairs together at the top. Add a "ridge pole" on top and lash it in place. Then tie crosspieces in place down the sides, parallel to the ridge pole, to add stability and help the vines climb. Have someone help you stand the tent up, then spread the legs, push them into the soil, and plant your vines at the base.

Make a teepee. For a vertical accent in a border or bed, you can make very attractive trellises or teepee-like supports from slender saplings or tree limbs. Cut them in 3- to 6-foot lengths and lash them together with mature grapevine cuttings or raffia (a fiber made from palm trees you'll find at your local hobby shop). You can make them as tall as you like and just plant vines at the base of the limbs.

Put together some pipes. You can make strong supports for heavy vines from metal or PVC pipes, which are available from hardware stores. Use 1-inch-diameter pipes or larger. An advantage of PVC pipe is that it can be easily cut to the length you want, fitted together with elbows and other joints, and glued together.

Adapt a trellis. When you want to cover a specific eyesore like a downspout, a standard flat trellis may not do the job. To make it hide more than one side, simply take two strips of cedar trellis as long as the downspout is high, nail them together at right angles, then butt them against the wall to which the downspout is attached. This way, you can cover a downspout with a vine without actually having it climb directly on it.

String up an annual. Slender twining annual vines, such as morning-glories and black-eyed Susan vines (*Thunbergia alata*), can be trained on sturdy twine as their sole support. Or give them some twine so they can work their way up to an awning or a piece of latticework. Just put a stake in the ground and attach the twine to it, then attach the other end of the twine to the farthest point you want the vine to reach.

Grow Your Own Awning

You can easily turn your hot, sunny porch into a cool retreat. All you need is a vigorous vine. Salvage an old awning frame as shown, or attach a metal bar to your porch. Cover the framework with chicken wire and train a Boston ivy (*Parthenocissus tricuspidata*) or Dutchman's-pipe (*Aristolochia durior*) up it to create a beautiful, shady nook. Or use a silver lace vine (*Polygonum aubertii*) and watch your framework vanish in a froth of foliage and blossoms.

Create a Quick Wildlife Garden

Vines make a perfect centerpiece for a garden designed to attract birds, butterflies, and other wildlife. Hummingbirds are drawn to colorful blooming vines with tubular flowers. They're especially fond of the color red, so they adore cypress vine (*Ipomoea quamoclit*) and trumpet honeysuckle (*Lonicera sempervirens*). They also favor orange trumpet vine (*Campsis radicans*).

For attracting butterflies, try planting cypress vine, sweet peas (*Lathyrus latifolius*), wisteria, or Japanese honeysuckle (*Lonicera japonica*). Plant wild passionflower (*Passiflora incarnata*), too, since it's a food plant for the caterpillar of the gulf fritillary. You'll see quite a show as the adult butterfly lays its eggs and caterpillars hatch out. You can expect some munched leaves, but it's a small price to pay for a front row seat at a butterfly drama.

The Benefits of Vertical Gardening
Barbara Pleasant

Good soil and healthy plants form the foundation for a successful garden, but where do you go from there? Most vegetables and flowers stay close to the ground, so trellised vines are unique in their ability to add a vertical dimension to any outdoor scene. In the vegetable garden, growing plants up rather than out pays off by increasing yields and improving plant health. Trellised pole beans, for example, typically produce 40 percent more beans per square foot than bush beans, and tomatoes must be trellised to prevent problems with diseases. With cucumbers and other small-fruited cucurbits, a trellis often coaxes plants to produce more leaves, which in turn gather more energy from the sun, resulting in larger, higher-quality crops.

As landscaping devices, trellises offer an easy way to block out unwanted views, create beautiful focal points, and enhance privacy. You can use trellised vines to create living walls for a lush, private retreat, or locate them so they will throw a curtain of shade over a hot spot on your patio, or give your deck plants much-needed relief from intense summer sun. But the best part of working with trellised flowers is the plants. From fragrant sweet peas to long-limbed miniature roses, flowers that reach for the sky always get plenty of attention.

Taking care of plants at eye level rather than in a bed is a bit easier for most gardeners, but you'll probably see fewer problems in the first place. Trellised plants dry off quickly after rain, which reduces their risk of leaf-spot diseases. Controlling insect pests is simple because you can see unwanted visitors as soon as they appear, and early intervention is the secondbest way to limit insect damage—right after prevention. Even your body benefits from vertical gardening, since you can tend, pick, and enjoy your plants with much less bending over.

Getting Started

Once you decide you want to grow a plant that is willing to scramble up a trellis, there are several types of structures to consider, from lightweight string trellises to wood or wire panels to triangular teepees. But before you start building, look around and see what you already have.

- An ordinary chain-link fence makes a fantastic trellis for most vining vegetables and flowering vines.
- You can easily add a wire trellis to the back side of a wood fence that will provide easy moorings for curling tendrils or twisting stems.
- Deck railings can be put to work as a ready-made trellis for container-grown vines, and you can transform entryways by using porch posts—or your front-step handrail—to support a well-behaved vine.

- Get double duty from wood posts that are already serving another purpose, whether they are holding up a mailbox or birdhouse or are part of an existing fence. Add a few nails and screws, attach some strings or wire, and create an instant pillar for edible or ornamental vines.

Choosing the Right Site

Before you decide where to place a new trellis—or how you will make use of a structure you already have—consider the site from the vine's point of view. Of course you want to pick a spot where a trellis will look good or block your view of an eyesore next door, but you should make sure your plants will grow well in their new home, too. Begin by digging an exploratory hole. You can amend poor soil to improve its fertility, but make sure the soil can be dug deeply enough to accommodate new posts that may need to be set in place. If you encounter a buried boulder, you will need to look for an alternate site. Underground utilities also may restrict where you can dig deep holes for posts.

TRACKING SUN AND SHADE

Sun exposure will affect your choice of sites, too. The sun rises in the east and sets in the west, and in the Northern Hemisphere, it always arcs a little to the south as it moves across the sky. The sun's angle matters little to low-growing plants, but it causes tall plants and trellises to cast shadows. To minimize the shade created by trellised plants, try to locate trellises on a north-south axis when growing plants that need abundant sun. This means that one side will face east while the other faces west. The west (afternoon) side will get more intense sun than the east (morning) side, but the difference will be less than it would be if the trellis faced north-south.

If you want to use a trellised vine to create shade, this will happen naturally if you locate a trellis on the south or west side of a hot spot in your landscape, or if you build an overhead arbor. For example, if your goal is to be able to sip tea on your deck on a summer afternoon while hummingbirds dart in and out of a lush screen of scarlet runner beans, locate the trellis on the west side of your favorite sitting spot, because intense afternoon sun always comes from the west.

You can take the confusion out of studying a site's exposure by pounding a wood stake into the ground and watching it for a few days, making mental note of where its shadows fall. Don't worry about the shade that is created at the base of a trellis, because most vines thrive when they have their roots shaded and their heads in the sun.

PLAN FOR EASY REACH

Whether you are planning to support cucumbers or a clematis, you'll also need to position the trellis so you can get to the plant for watering, pruning, and harvesting. It is usually best to allow vines to run no higher than you can reach. Choose vines that fit the space you have to offer and your notions of reasonable maintenance, and keep in mind that a vine capable of growing 10 feet tall does not necessarily require a 10-foot trellis. Once vines reach the top of their support structure, they usually turn back toward the ground, creating a cascade of foliage, flowers, and fruit.

Sizing Up Structures

The projects in this chapter provide an array of trellising options, including tied-together teepees, versatile wire panels, wood pillars and

Continued ➡

trellises, and simple techniques for using plants to support other plants. Most are quite easy and inexpensive to build or make and require little or no carpentry experience. If you can hammer a nail or install a screw, you can make these projects.

Regardless of size, the sturdiness of any trellis depends on how well it is anchored. In some situations, you may want to set a post as securely as possible, which will require anchoring it in concrete. Concrete is messy but not especially difficult to handle. Still, before you decide that concrete is needed, consider simpler solutions.

Some trellises need no posts at all. The pyramid shape of teepee trellises often makes them self-anchoring. With trellises that do depend on buried posts to hold them upright, keeping posts as close to each other as possible can enhance the structure's sturdiness. Post size affects sturdiness, too. Stout posts can bear more weight than narrow ones, but they are heavier to handle and more troublesome to move. Posts only 2 inches square, installed 18 inches deep and 4 feet apart, do a good job of supporting tomatoes, peas, and beans in the vegetable garden, and they are easily moved by wiggling them a bit before pulling them up. Moderately heavy, long-lived plants such as climbing roses and clematis will be better served with a trellis that's attached to sturdier 2 x 4-inch posts. Permanent landscape structures call for 4 x 4 or larger posts.

Safe and Sturdy Posts

When selecting posts for your garden trellises, do not use pressure-treated lumber or wood treated with creosote if edible plants or herbs will be grown nearby. Whenever possible, use weather-resistant wood such as cedar, redwood, or locust as your first choice. Chemicals leaching from pressure-treated or creosote-coated wood can contaminate the soil. Several of the hundreds of chemicals in creosote are known carcinogens that can leach into the soil and be taken up by plants. Similar problems exist with the chemicals that have been used for the last 20 years to make treated wood posts more resistant to rot and termites, so grow only ornamental plants on posts made of treated wood.

Once you've taken stock of the trellising potential of structures that you already have, you can start having fun with vines and add to your collection of supportive plant structures. You should have no trouble finding just the right vine for any spot in your yard. Study what various sites have to offer because vines differ in their needs for sun, moisture, and the sturdiness of their support.

Guy Wires

If a trellis is not as sturdy as you think it should be, you often can fix the problem by installing guy wires attached to nearby stakes, in much the same way that camping tents are secured in place. Two guy wires that pull on a trellis post from opposite directions work better than one, especially when the stakes are installed at angles that are diagonal from the trellis itself. Install the stakes at an angle, with their tops tilted away from the trellis. You also can use guy wires to attach a trellis to a nearby structure such as a building or fence.

Guy wires need not be actual wires at all. You can use whatever you have on hand to tie the trellis to stakes, including string, twine, or hemp cord. The main disadvantage of using stakes and guy wires is that they are easy to trip over, but this is less likely to happen if you paint them a noticeable color. Tying a few colorful ribbons to guy wires also makes them easy to see.

Matching Plants with Trellises

Posts serve as a trellis's legs, but most trellises also have a body made of wood, string, wire, or some type of fencing. The projects in this chapter show how you can use several versatile, inexpensive trellising materials, but there are loads of other ingenious possibilities. Creative gardeners often fashion unique trellises from flexible copper tubing or bent twigs and even tie together plastic six-pack holders to support their peas.

You can use whatever suits your taste and the needs of the plants you decide to grow. Vines are never snobbish about the support they receive as long as it matches the "growing equipment" they use to twine from point A to point B. These ingenious plant structures may be curling tendrils, curving stems, or sticky rootlets.

Curling tendrils reach out and wrap around whatever is available: Wire, string, branches, and woven-wire fencing all are fair game. Tendril-producing plants, such as peas and cucumbers, also wrap tendrils around their own leaves and stems. Young plants may need a little guidance to find their trellis, but once they get growing, they know what to do. Plants that produce curling tendrils often do best with a wire or mesh trellis.

Twining stems spiral around their support, and twining species vary in whether they twine clockwise or counterclockwise. Twining vines like pole beans and morning glory grow best when supported by poles, taut cords, or other trellising materials that resemble tree limbs or upright plants. Teepee trellises are ideal, and with a little encouragement, twining plants will cover a chain-link, wire-mesh, or lattice fence. When they run out of trellis, twining plants will twist around themselves.

Tethered vines, such as tomatoes and climbing roses, have no way to attach themselves to a support structure, so they must be fastened to their trellis. String or wire can damage the stems, so it is best to use strips of soft, stretchy cloth or discarded panty hose to tie them in place. You also can use green, plastic-coated wire twist ties. In addition, you often can train some stems manually by weaving them between the slats of a sturdy wooden trellis. Choose a solid, stationary trellis that does not move when pushed by strong wind.

Clinging vines, such as Virginia creeper, Boston ivy, and English ivy, have special holdfast roots that grow from the stems and attach themselves to surfaces (including tree trunks and wood, siding, or brick walls). The holdfast roots and the vines'

foliage retain moisture, which can damage buildings. These vines should be watched closely and pruned as needed to control their spread. Although popular and beautiful, English ivy becomes aggressive when it is abandoned by the gardener who planted it. It is easiest to control when grown in containers.

Beware of Invasive Vines

When vines are perfectly suited to their site and soil, some reseed so successfully that they become weedy pests. A prime example is morning glory, which seldom causes problems in the North, but can become so weedy in warmer climates that it is listed as a noxious weed in Arkansas and Arizona. And, even though it is a native plant, love-in-a-puff (*Cardiospermum*) is on the noxious weed lists of six southern states.

If you want to grow a vine with a questionable reputation, start with a small planting, and locate the trellis near a walkway, driveway, or other paved surface. Or, place it where you can mow around it on all sides. Unwanted seeds can't sprout in concrete, and those that sprout in mowed grass can quickly be clipped into submission.

Avoid These Unsocial Climbers

Nicknamed "unsocial climbers" by botanists, a number of once-popular perennial vines have proven so invasive that they should not be planted at all. Even though you may be able to control the behavior of one of these vines in your yard, you cannot guess where a bird may drop a seed or what will become of the vine if you move away. Fortunately, there are plenty of safe native plants to take the place of these exotic invaders. Vines to avoid planting include:

- Climbing euonymus (*Euonymus fortunei*)
- English ivy (*Hedera helix*)
- Japanese honeysuckle (*Lonicera japonica*)
- Oriental bittersweet (*Celastrus orbiculatus*)
- Porcelain berry (*Ampelopsis brevipedunculata*)

List of Climbing Plants for Shade

Larry Hodgson

Climbing plants (also known as vines, climbers, lianas, and so on; the words are pretty much interchangeable) are curious plants. Almost all other land-dwelling plants use their own internal structure (mostly a cell component called lignin) to hoist themselves upward on their own through solid, tough stems, branches, and trunks. Even annuals and perennials use lignin to solidify their stems, but woody plants are masters of the art. Wood is full of lignin and that is why trees are able to grow so tall. Without lignin, they'd flop over like rubber. However, building a strong structure out of lignin is a slow process requiring a great deal of energy, and often the tallest plants of the forest are the slowest-growing ones.

Climbing plants, though, have little use for huge quantities of lignin: They've found a way around that constraint. They hook or wrap themselves around host plants that do produce abundant lignin and use their host's hard-won structure to reach for the sky. So climbing plants are essentially profiteers, almost parasites, taking advantage of other plants and giving them little if anything in return.

We ought to find the actions of climbing plants reprehensible; instead, we very much take advantage of their sneaky ways. Climbers, you see, are the ideal plants for "filling in" open spaces. They hoist themselves up walls and fences as readily as they do trees,

Continued ➤

Seven Vines for the Vegetable Garden

Plant Name	How It Climbs	Description	Ideal Trellis
Cucumber (*Cucumis sativus*)	Curling tendrils	Fast and productive, cucumbers often need to be tied to their trellis because cucumber tendrils are sparse and weak.	Try a 3-foot-tall teepee or a diagonal trellis made with wire mesh or plastic hardware cloth.
Lima Bean (*Phaseolus lunatus*)	Twining stems	Heat tolerant and pest resistant, heirloom varieties often run 10 feet and produce beans with maroon markings. Limas grow best where summers are long and warm.	Provide a teepee-type trellis 8 feet tall or grow on a wire-mesh fence.
Malabar Spinach (*Basella rubra*)	Twining stems	A vigorous grower in hot weather, this plant's glossy young leaves taste like Swiss chard when cooked. Unpruned vines grow to 15 feet and often reseed in warm climates.	Grow three plants on a single sturdy teepee or pillar.
Pea (*Pisum sativum*)	Curling tendrils	Short varieties of snow, shell, or snap peas grow to only 18 inches, but taller ones reach 5 to 6 feet. Plant first thing in spring because peas love cool weather.	A light net or string trellis is sufficient for peas.
Pole Bean (*Phaseolus vulgaris*)	Twining stems	Easy to grow, with a huge selection of varieties. Some have purple or yellow pods, and vine length varies with variety, from 4 to 10 feet.	Provide a teepee-type trellis 4 to 8 feet tall, or grow pole beans on a wire-mesh fence.
Scarlet Runner Bean (*Phaseolus coccineus*)	Twining stems	Young pods are edible and so are the flowers. Vines run 6 to 8 feet and grow best where summers are not extremely hot.	Adapts to many types of trellises, from teepees to rustic twig fences to old stumps.
Yard-Long Bean (*Vigna unguiculata*)	Twining stems	Vigorous plants grow fast in hot weather, often growing to 10 feet. Harvest the beans when they are less than 18 inches long for best flavor.	A pair of tall, sturdy teepees connected at the top.

Nine Annual Flowering Vines

Plant Name	How It Climbs	Description	Ideal Trellis
Asarina (*Asarina scandens*)	Twining stems	Dainty, well-behaved vine usually grows to 6 feet, laden with jewel-toned snapdragon-like flowers. Grows best where summers are not extremely hot.	Choose an attractive wood, wire, or string trellis. Can be grown in containers.
Black-Eyed Susan Vine (*Thunbergia alata*)	Twining stems	In addition to the common yellow varieties, there are others that bloom white and coral pink. Vines run to 8 feet and can be grown in containers.	Use wire or sturdy string to train up a mailbox post or other pillar; excellent cover for chain-link fence.
Cup and Saucer Vine (*Cobaea scandens*)	Curling tendrils	A robust grower with stems to 20 feet long, this wine makes a good shade screen where summers are quite warm. Flowers emerge greenish white and ripen to purple.	A sturdy wood or wire trellis is required because vines become lush and heavy by late summer.
Gourd (*Lagenaria* or *Cucurbita* species)	Twining stems and tendrils	Small-fruited egg or spoon gourds mature fast enough to be grown in any climate, and the vines grow to only 10 feet. Large-fruited varieties grow to twice that size.	Grow small-fruited varieties on a pillar, diagonal, or teepee trellis. Large-fruited varieties become very heavy and need a sturdy support made of wood or wire.
Hyacinth Bean (*Dolichos lablab*)	Twining stems	Sometimes called ornamental butter bean, this plant's 10- to 20-foot-long violet stems produce lavender flowers, followed by glossy purple seedpods.	One or two plants can be supported by a string trellis, but a larger planting needs sturdy wood or wire support.
Morning Glory (*Ipomoea* species and hybrids)	Twining stems	Easy to grow and widely adaptable, morning glories come in numerous colors. Vines run 10 feet or more. Often invasive in warm climates.	Grow on a sturdy wire trellis, pillar, teepee, sunflower stalks, or a chain-link fence.
Purple Bells (*Rhodochiton atrosanguineum*)	Twining stems	Tender perennial grown as an annual, this vine likes rich soil in partial shade. Grows to 10 feet and produces exotic two-tones purple flowers.	Choose an attractive wood trellis. Can be grown in containers.
Spanish Flag (*Mina lobata*)	Twining stems	Sprays of tubular blossoms open red and ripen to yellow. Vines run to 15 feet, and seeds germinate best when soaked for a day or two before planting.	Grow on a sturdy wire trellis, teepee, or wood pillar.
Sweet Pea (*Lathyrus odoratus*)	Curling tendrils	Beautiful and often fragrant, most sweet peas climb to about 5 feet. Grow in cool weather, and nick the seeds to help them germinate faster.	A string or net trellis is sufficient for sweet peas. Can be grown in containes.

Six Long-Lived Perennial Vines

Plant Name	How It Climbs	Description	Ideal Trellis
Clematis (*Clematis* hybrids)	Twining stems and tendrils	Gorgeous flowers in a wide range of colors with attractive green foliage on 10-foot vines. Adapted in Zones 4 to 9, pruning times vary with variety.	Can be trained to grow into small shrubs or trees or on a wood or wire support.
Climbing Rose (*Rosa* hybrids)	Curved thorns, requires tying	Stiff arching canes bloom heavily in late spring, and often repeat bloom. Adapted in Zones 4 to 9, canes must be tied or wired to a stiff trellis.	Choose an attractive wood trellis to accompany the classic beauty of a climbing rose.
Cross Vine (*Bignonia capreolata*)	Curling tendrils	Improved varieties of this native evergreen vine bear orange or red flowers that attract hummingbirds. Vines grow to 20 feet in Zones 5 to 9.	Choose a sturdy wood or wire trellis that needs little maintenance since the plants are never fully dormant.
Grape (*Vitis* species)	Curling tendrils	Woody plants may live for decades. Adapted in Zones 4 to 9, grapes bear sweet fruit, and you can use the pruned branches for other projects.	Provide a very sturdy wood and wire trellis, or grow grapes over an arbor.
Hardy Kiwi (*Actinidia arguta*)	Twining stems	Large, woody plants become quite massive, mature female plants produce flavorful fruits. Adapted in Zones 4 to 9, hardy kiwis need periodic pruning.	Provide a very sturdy trellis constructed of wood and wire.
Passionflower (*Passiflora* hybrids)	Twining stems	Exotic blossoms followed by green egg-shaped fruits on 10-foot vines. Hardy in Zones 7 to 9, but can be grown as an annual farther north.	Best grown on a post, pillar, or stump or combined with annual vines on a larger trellis.

Continued ➡

and our gardens usually have lots of such barren spots to cover. So we plant them to cover up unwanted views and to add interest to otherwise dull structures: You can use them to cover up an old stump or even bring a dead tree back to life by letting vines cover it. In fact, we purposely add structures just for climbing plants to grow on: trellises, arbors, and pergolas. After all, what are they if not fast-and-easy supports for climbers?

As climbers reach ever upward, they don't take up a lot of space on the ground. Perennials and annuals need large flowerbeds, shrubs and conifers have spreading branches that just eat up space, and trees, with their thick trunks and massive root systems, are true space hogs. Climbers need only a small space-a single planting hole-to reach out in all directions…but uniquely vertically. If fact, you can usually cover an entire fence or wall with just one climber, using little horizontal space indeed. Where gardening space is rare, such as in small urban gardens, climbing plants allow you to have abundant greenery without losing virtually any usable space. So with climbers, you can have the patio, the swing set, the sandbox, and the pool…and still garden!

Born to Climb

Botanists believe climbers evolved from nonclimbing ancestors that "learned" a faster way to reach the sun. They began as tall but weak-stemmed plants that started to lean on their neighbors rather than put too much of their own energy into building a solid structure. Over time, they became so good at leaning they abandoned all other means of vertical growth. As generations passed, different climbers evolved different and often more effective means of taking advantage of their host. Here are the main ones.

Scandent climbers: These are also called clamberers; they are the least specialized climbers. They still essentially lean on their neighbors, but as their stems reach upward they manage to mingle with the branches of their host and thus gain extra support. They have no special structures to aid them in climbing, nor do they twist around their host. Where they find no host nearby to lean on, they usually contain enough lignin to grow as arching shrubs. In the garden, you'll have to either attach scandent climbers to their support or wind them through lattice or nearby branches to get them off the ground. Winter jasmine (*jasminum nudiflorum*) is a well-known scandent shrub.

Hook climbers: They're also fairly primitive and are also called clamberers. They don't twist or stick to their host, only lean and mingle like scan dent climbers, but they have the added advantage of thorny stems that can hook onto their hosts. In the garden, they too usually have to be attached to their supports; otherwise they'll grow as tall, arching shrubs. The best-known clamberer is the climbing rose.

Weavers: Just a step up from scandent climbers, weavers mostly lean on their host but also undulate as they grow and thus manage to work themselves in and out among the branches they grow through. In the garden, they may still need some help from the gardener in getting started (you may have to attach them to their supports initially) but will usually weave their way in and out of a trellis or chain fence on their own once they get going. Without a support, they simply flop, not having enough lignin to hold themselves upright. Confederate jasmine (*Trachelospermum jasminoides*) is a weaver.

Twining climbers: Also called twiners, they don't just undulate, they twist around their host, with stems that grow in a spiral. Depending on the species, they may grow clockwise or counterclock-wise. They are very efficient climbers—if you don't supply a support, they'll creep along the ground until they find one. They don't make good ground-covers, though, as they keep reaching up in search of a support, so they appear irregular. Often several branches will twist around each other and attempt to grow upright, usually flopping back down again, as they don't contain enough lignin to go very far. Morning glories (*Ipomoea* spp.) and wisterias are well-known twiners.

Root climbers: These are called rooters for short. Actually, they are officially called "adventitious root climbers," but "rooters" is so much easier to say. They produce specialized roots called holdfasts on the underside of the stem; these cling to bark, wood, brick, stone, and so on. Unlike other twiners, they are able to climb flat surfaces like stone walls without a trellis or grid. On the other hand, they won't climb up open fences (such as chain link): They seem to need broad surfaces on which to take root. Rooters usually make good groundcovers, as they hug the ground when they can find no support. The best-known rooter is English ivy (*Hedera helix*).

Clinging climbers: Also called clingers, these climbers have specialized appendages that attach them solidly to their host. The best known are tendrils, such as seen on grape vines: They are special growths that twist as they grow, wrapping around their support. Sometimes it is the leaf petiole that twists around objects, or the leaf tips. In general, tendrils can wrap around only fairly thin objects: They'll grow around string, wire, or thin branches but may need to be attached to heavier supports, such as thicker lattices and trellises.

The most specialized of the clingers are Virginia creeper and its relatives (*Parthenocissus* spp.). They bear adhesive disks at the tips of their tendrils: They'll wrap themselves around thin objects like other clingers but can also climb flat surfaces, like walls and trunks. Many clingers make good groundcovers where there are no nearby objects to cling.

Nature, of course, hates man's attempt to neatly package its species into convenient groupings, so not all plants stay in their assigned categories. Many climbers are not climbers all their lives, for example. English ivy and its relatives (*Hedera* spp.), for instance, are typically climbing plants in their youth but change into shrubs at maturity. That is, when an ivy has grown high enough up into the tree canopy to get the light it needs, it suddenly starts producing woody branches complete with larger, rounder leaves instead of climbing stems. It is only the woody form that flowers and fruits. Oddly, once an ivy matures, it will never again produce climbing stems, and even cuttings taken from mature growth will grow as shrubs, never as climbers.

Climbing hydrangea (*Hydrangea anomala* subsp. *petiolaris*) does just the opposite: It starts off as a shrub with solid woody branches and may grow that way for years. Then suddenly, for reasons unknown, it decides it is time to climb and sends out stems that stick to nearby surfaces. Still other climbers, winter jasmine for one, will start producing woodier branches if pruned regularly and will then happily live the rest of their life as a shrub. And who hasn't seen a wisteria changed, by harsh pruning, into a small tree?

Don't be stunned if your climber starts behaving in a very unvinelike fashion: Climbers are full of surprises!

Herbaceous or Woody?

Climbers can be either herbaceous or woody. Herbaceous climbers, like herbaceous perennials and annuals, die to the ground at the end of the season. Some die entirely (there are many annual climbers!); others resprout from underground roots the following season. Practically by definition, herbaceous climbers tend to be comparatively short: There is a limit to how much growth they can put on in a single season. Even so, some reach 20 feet (6 m) or more in just one season and are among the fastest-growing plants known.

Woody climbers have perennial stems that become tough and fibrous. Because they don't die to the ground each year, they can build on the previous year's growth and thus grow taller and taller over time. Some reach well above 50 feet (15 m) in height over the years. In general, woody climbers are slower-growing than herbaceous ones and may take years to reach their maximum height. Note that "woody" is used in the sense of permanent: Not all "woody climbers" produce stems covered with bark that look woody to the eye.

Of course, herbaceous and woody are terms most appropriate to temperate climates. Many tropical vines that grow as annuals in the North are actually long-lived tropical vines in their native land, with stems that grow taller from year to year. Some morning glories (*Ipomoea* spp. and *Convolvulus* spp.), for example, are true annuals, but others are tropical climbers grown as annuals. And in extremely cold climates, many woody climbers will die to the ground most winters and sprout anew in spring, as if they were herbaceous.

For the most part, shade-tolerant vines are woody: In adapting to poor light, they found it simpler to grow slowly upward over time, putting on a bit more height each year. Starting from scratch each season takes lots of energy! In this section you'll find mostly woody climbers.

Shade and Climbers

Many of the climbers described in this chapter are equally well adapted to both sun and shade…and that's because of their unique growth cycle. They're adapted to germinating in deep shade where the competition for space is less intense. From there, they either slowly build up energy or ramble about, looking for a host to climb on. Even when they find support, they are still in shade, but climbers persevere, reaching up and up through the host's dense foliage until they finally begin to pierce its crown. In general, it is only when climbers reach full sun that they begin to bloom.

Most of the "shade-tolerant" climbers described here are therefore actually sun lovers who are just biding their time. They can grow for decades in very deep shade…as foliage plants. But many of them rarely bloom there. You'll notice that most of the plants described here are grown for their attractive growth habit and beautiful leaves rather than for their flowers.

Actinidia

Kiwi vine

Plant Profile

Actinidia: ac-ti-NID-ee-uh

Bloom Color: White

Bloom Time: Varies by species; see individual listings

Length of Bloom: 2 to 3 weeks

Height: Varies by species; see individual listings

Spread: 17 to 20 feet (5 to 6 m)

Garden Uses: Arbors and trellises, background, container planting, specimen plant, woodland garden; edible fruits

Light Preference: Full sun to shade

Soil Preference: Humus-rich, evenly moist, well-drained soil

Best Way to Propagate: Take cuttings in midsummer

Continued ➡

USDA Plant Hardiness Zones: 3 to 8

The kiwis described here are not the subtropical ones that supply the large fuzzy fruits that are seen in supermarkets, but hardier species grown mostly for ornamental use. Most are vigorous woody vines that climb by twining about a support: If none is available, they'll grow as large, arching shrubs. The spring flowers are often numerous and usually creamy white and highly scented, although inevitably partially hidden by the foliage. Their main claim to fame is their beautifully variegated foliage. Small, sweet, grape-size fruits are produced on female plants in fall on mature specimens: They are not fuzzy like their large-fruited cousin and can be popped into the mouth and eaten as is.

Touchy-Feely Plants

Everyone realizes plants react to light, but did you know they also have a sense of touch? Twining vines twist about at random until they make contact with a vertical support, then they wrap themselves tightly around it. Their "sense of touch" tells them whether they need to draw tight circles, such as around a cord or thin branch, or much larger ones, as around a thicker support. If they make contact with a horizontal branch, though, they don't tighten at all but continue to twist openly. It's as if they examine the object they touch and then decide whether it is worth wrapping around or not.

Rooting climbers likewise show their touchy-feely side: They produce no roots unless the stem is pressed against an object—and even then they produce their roots only on the side touching the object.

This response of plants to touch is called thigmatropism, in case you just had to know.

Growing Tips

Kiwis prefer full sun for best blooming and fruiting, but are very ornamental in partial shade and grow well in shade, although often losing their leaf variegation. Any well-drained soil will do.

If you want to enjoy their fruit, make sure you plant both male and female plants (one male will pollinate eight or more females). Although plants may flower fairly young, it often takes 7 or 8 years before they manage to produce their first fruit.

Prune in early spring for better foliage; for fruit production, prune after flowers drop. These are vigorous, shrubby vines taking up considerable space in their youth until they begin to climb, and so are not for small gardens.

Warning: Be forewarned that cats adore *Actinidia kolomikta* and *A. polygama*, reacting to them as if they were catnip, and may not always content themselves with just rubbing against them: They'll often chew young *A. polygama* plants to death. Surround them with chicken-wire fencing for the first few years until they've grown enough that they are largely out of kitty's reach!

Problems and Solutions

Cats chew stems and leaves. Few serious pests and diseases.

Top Performer

Actinidia kolomikta (variegated kiwi vine): A very dense-growing vine, especially appreciated for the coloration of its leaves. They are purple-tinged at first, then the lower half turns silvery pink in spring and eventually silvery white in summer. Not all the leaves are variegated, and the coloration is highly variable: Cooler growing conditions and sun to partial shade help bring out the color. Several cultivars with more highly variegated foliage, such as 'Arctic Beauty', are available, though many of those grown mostly for their fruit are not very colorful. Blooms early, in late spring. Sweet yellow-green fruits are produced in fall. Height: 15 to 35 feet (4.5 to 10 m). Spread: 17 to 20 feet (5 to 6 m). USDA Plant Hardiness Zones 2 to 9.

More Recommended Kiwi Vines

Actinidia arguta (hardy kiwi): This summer-blooming species has entirely green leaves and is grown more for its small but abundant fruit than as an ornamental, although its dense cover, dark green bristle-edged leaves, and scented white flowers make it very useful for decorative purposes as well. 'Issai' is a self-fruitful variety (it produces both male and female flowers on the same plant), ideal for smaller spaces. It is not a particularly prolific cultivar, though: There are dozens of better fruit producers. Height: 20 to 30 feet (6 to 9 m). Spread: 20 to 30 feet (6 to 9 m). USDA Plant Hardiness Zones 3 to 9.

A. polygama (silver vine): This summer-blooming species is a decidedly less vigorous grower than the others and can easily be accommodated in a small space. It is grown especially for its green leaves with silvery white tips, although the small yellow-green fruits are edible. Beware: This species is especially subject to cat damage. Height: 5 to 15 feet (1.5 to 4.5 m). Spread: 8 feet (2.4 m). USDA Plant Hardiness Zones 4 to 9.

Akebia

Chocolate vine, akebia

Plant Profile

Akebia: ah-KEE-bee-uh

Bloom Color: Purple

Bloom Time: Early spring

Length of Bloom: 2 to 3 weeks

Height: 20 to 40 feet (6 to 12 m)

Spread: 20 to 40 (6 to 12 m)

Garden Uses: Arbors and trellises, groundcover, woodland garden; on slopes

Light Preference: Full sun to shade

Soil Preference: Humus-rich, moist, well-drained soil

Best Way to Propagate: Take cuttings in early to midsummer

USDA Plant Hardiness Zones: 4 to 10

This is a vigorous, dense, semi-evergreen, twining vine: Grown on a fence, it will create a perfect wall of green, and as a groundcover it makes a smooth carpet. The palmate leaves are curiously notched at the tips, as if a tiny bird had taken a bite out if each one. They attempt to be evergreen, turning purplish in fall and clinging to the plant until early winter, but are eventually frosted off below Zones 7 or 8. The hanging, cup-shaped flowers are deep purple, sometimes even nearly chocolate-colored (whence "chocolate vine") but have little impact in the garden: You have to be right up close to notice them. Curious sausage-like fleshy purple fruits are produced and are edible, but insipid. Hanging on until winter, they are much more visible than the flowers but rarely produced.

Growing Tips

Here is a nice "grow-anywhere" vine, adapting equally well from sun to shade (although partial shade to shade is preferable in hot-summer climates) and almost any soil except ones that are extremely dry or extremely wet. Its growth is rampant: Plant it at the base of its future support so it can grow straight up, or it will go wandering all over your yard looking for a host. It makes a superior groundcover about 6 to 12 inches (15 to 30 cm) tall for spots where there is nothing for it to climb on. As a groundcover it is often best established among tall trees—it climbs by twining and can't manage thick trunks.

Pruning is well accepted; indeed, it will die to the ground in colder climates and still reach a good 20 feet (6 m) the following spring. Many gardeners prefer to cut it back each year to prevent it from getting out of bounds: After all, if left alone it will readily leave its original fence or trellis and invade neighboring trees, especially in mild-winter areas. Major pruning is usually done in early spring (late fall in the North). Wayward or invasive branches can be cut off at any season.

The male and female flowers are borne together in clusters on the same plant. (Hint: The female flowers are larger and darker and borne at the base of the clump; males are smaller and found at the tip.) Where fruits are produced, fall-sown seed germinates readily the following spring, but usually chocolate vine is multiplied by softwood or semiripe cuttings.

Problems and Solutions

Chocolate vine seems virtually immune to insects and disease but may die back severely in cold winters.

Top Performer

Akebia quinata (chocolate vine, fiveleaf akebia): This is by far the most common species, with very attractive, schefflera-like leaves with five leaflets. They are dark green above, bluish green below. This species has scented flowers, said to smell of vanilla or cinnamon. There are a few cultivars, among which is the outstanding 'Variegata', with pale pink flowers and leaves marbled white. Height: 20 to 40 feet (6 to 12 m). Spread: 20 to 40 feet (6 to 12 m). USDA Plant Hardiness Zones 4 to 10.

More Recommended Chocolate Vines

Akebia x *pentaphylla* (hybrid chocolate vine): This is a cross between *A. quinata* and *A. trifoliata*, looking much the same as *A. quinata*, with four or five leaflets (occasionally six or seven), but the leaves are paler green and the flowers likewise not as dark purple, with a much fainter scent. Height: 20 to 40 feet (6 to 12 m). Spread: 20 to 40 feet (6 to 12 m). USDA Plant Hardiness Zones 4 to 10.

A. trifoliata (threeleaf akebia): As the name suggests, it's easy to tell this akebia from the other species by its leaflets, borne only three per leaf. They are also different in color: emerald green. The distinctly paler purple flowers are scentless but produce the same purple sausage-shaped fruit as the other chocolate vines. This species is deciduous in all climates and, although no hardier in actual survival rate than the others (Zone 4), its branches are more cold-hardy so it makes a better choice for garden use in Zones 4 to 6 than the others. Height: 20 to 40 feet (6 to 12 m). Spread: 20 to 40 feet (6 to 12 m). USDA Plant Hardiness Zones 4 to 10.

Ampelopsis

Porcelain berry, ampelopsis

Continued ➡

Plant Profile

Ampelopsis: am-pel-OP-sis

Bloom Color: Green

Bloom Time: Summer

Length of Bloom: 3 to 4 weeks

Height: Varies by species; see individual listings

Spread: Varies by species; see individual listings

Garden Uses: Arbors and trellises, container planting, groundcover, hanging baskets, houseplant, specimen plant, woodland garden

Light Preference: Full sun to shade

Soil Preference: Humus-rich, evenly moist, well-drained soil

Best Way to Propagate: Layer in summer

USDA Plant Hardiness Zones: Varies by species; see individual listings

The genus *Ampelopsis* is made up of about 25 species of climbing plants very much like grape plants, although with smaller berries. They climb vigorously by tendrils and readily ascend fairly thin supports like small branches and chain-link fence. The foliage varies in shape, but is usually deeply lobed and maplelike. The leaves are deciduous on most species but usually make up for that by turning brilliant fall colors. Although they are perhaps best seen as foliage plants (certainly their clusters of greenish flowers lack impact), their berries are also very attractive, changing color as they mature and often showing several colors in the same cluster.

GROWING TIPS

Like many woody climbers, porcelain berry usually starts off its life in shade and works its way upward into sun; thus it is readily adapted to almost any light condition, although it will bloom and fruit heavily only in partial shade or sun. It is likewise adapted to most soil conditions except soggy soil. Irrigation during times of drought is certainly appreciated.

Opposite each leaf is a tendril that readily twists around objects of modest size, allowing the plant to grow to great heights over time. The tendrils are not very efficient at wrapping around thick objects, though: Even latticework is a bit much for them. You'll often find you have to attach this plant to its support or weave its stems through fencing or trelliswork to allow it to climb. The stems also look quite elegant when allowed to cascade down from a support, such as from the roof of a pergola. Where no support is available, it makes a wonderful groundcover, spreading indefinitely because the branches self-layer wherever they touch the soil.

Pruning is mostly done to control wayward stems and can be done at any time of the year.

The most obvious way to multiply ampelopsis is by layering: Most produce dangling branches that can easily be fixed to the ground. Cuttings also work well, and seed-grown plants come fairly true to type.

PROBLEMS AND SOLUTIONS

Leaf diseases are frequent but rarely serious enough to need treating. Flea beetles and Japanese beetles are major annoyances: Spray with insecticidal soap to treat the former; handpick or spray the latter.

TOP PERFORMER

Ampelopsis brevipedunculata (porcelain berry, porcelain vine): A charming and elegant climber with dark green three- to five-lobed leaves that look much like maple leaves. The fruits are the most attractive element of this plant, changing color from green to turquoise-blue to purple as they mature, often with all three colors visible at the same time. They are shaded with a crackled effect much like porcelain (whence the common name). Height: 10 to 30 feet (3 to 9 m). Spread: 10 to 30 feet (3 to 9 m). USDA Plant Hardiness Zones 4 to 9.

MORE RECOMMENDED PORCELAIN BERRIES

Ampelopsis aconitifolia (monkshood vine): There are dozens of interesting species of *Ampelopsis*. This one has leaves much like those of monkshoods (*Aconitum* spp.): very deeply and elegantly lobed and dark, glossy green. They turn beautiful shades of orange, yellow, and red in fall. The small yellow-orange fruits are also attractive in fall. 'Chinese Lace' is a new cultivar with very lacy foliage. Height: 10 to 40 feet (3 to 12 m). Spread: 10 to 30 feet (3 to 9 m). USDA Plant Hardiness Zones 4 to 9.

A. brevipedunculata var. *maximowiczii* 'Elegans' (variegated porcelain berry): This gorgeous cultivar has deeply cut leaves that are highly mottled white and pink, and bright pink new shoots. It has often been used as a houseplant. It bears the same green, turquoise, and blue berries as the species. Height: 3 to 10 feet (1 to 3 m). Spread: 3 to 10 feet (1 to 3 m). USDA Plant Hardiness Zones 6 to 9.

Euonymus

Wintercreeper

Plant Profile

Euonymus: yew-ON-i-mus

Bloom Color: Greenish white; insignificant

Bloom Time: Summer

Length of Bloom: 3 or more weeks

Height: 4 inches to 70 feet (10 cm to 21 m)

Spread: Indefinite

Garden Uses: Arbors and trellises, container planting, edging, groundcover, hedge, mass planting, mixed border, rock garden, wall covering

Light Preference: Full sun to shade

Soil Preference: Humus-rich, evenly moist, well-drained soil

Best Way to Propagate: Take cuttings in summer

USDA Plant Hardiness Zones: 4 or 5 to 10

Wintercreeper is truly a triple-purpose plant: It is abundantly used as a groundcover, makes a great small shrub, and will also climb beautifully. It's a beautiful foliage plant, with glossy, dark green, oval leaves, usually with a serrated edge, with paler veins and purplish in winter. Most cultivars commonly available are highly variegated in shades of white and yellow. The leaves are fully evergreen, making this plant attractive in all seasons and one of the hardiest evergreen climbers. The flowers are insignificant, but the fruits, which open whitish to reveal a bright orange-red interior, are very attractive.

GROWING TIPS

Wintercreeper is most adaptable when grown as an evergreen groundcover. It adapts to both full sun and deep shade, rich soils and poor ones—all it really needs to be sure of is evenly moist soil (it will need irrigation during periods of drought) and good drainage at all times.

Some wintercreeper cultivars are quite shrubby, but most will grow up walls or tree trunks if given a chance to do so. They climb via holdfast roots: Plant them where you want them to climb and let them make their own moves.

Wintercreeper will not find trellises, latticework, or thin fences at all attractive for climbing. It prefers much broader surfaces, such as posts, trunks, and walls, where its roots will find something solid to sink their tips into.

Although hardy to Zone 5 (some cultivars to Zone 4), it will not climb well when exposed to harsh, cold winds, so it can be trusted to climb to any great height only in Zone 7 and above. In a well-protected spot, though, it will climb modestly, reaching up to 15 feet (4.5 m) or so even at the northern limits of its range. In mild climates it can reach up to 70 feet (21 m).

For groundcover use, plant smaller plants about 1 foot (30 cm) apart; up to 3 feet (90 cm) for well-developed plants in large containers. Wintercreeper is a fairly slow grower, so mulch well to prevent weeds from taking over while it spreads.

This is one climber not known for its exuberant growth! Not that it is weak—it simply grows slowly and densely, sticking tight to its host, without the long "whips" common to other vines. Pruning is therefore mostly a question of cutting out any winter damage, trimming back leading stems when they reach the limits of the plant's desired territory, and removing any reversions (some of the variegated types are not very stable). Prunings can be used to make cuttings: Those taken from lateral branches will climb more readily than those taken from vertical ones. When used as a groundcover, wintercreeper readily self-layers and the resulting "rooted cuttings" can be dug up and moved to other spots.

Warning: Wintercreeper berries are poisonous, though so rarely produced they aren't a major threat.

PROBLEMS AND SOLUTIONS

Mildew and fungal problems can be treated on a case-by-case basis. More serious are scale insects: Carefully inspect all wintercreepers before buying them, as this pest doesn't get around well on its own. Control it with horticultural oil.

TOP PERFORMER

Euonymus fortunei (wintercreeper): This is the only common wintercreeper that climbs (the others are shrubs or small trees) and also one of the rare evergreen species, so it really is in a class of its own. There are dozens of cultivars, including *E. fortunei* var. *radicans*, the most commonly available running/climbing variety, with dark green leaves. It is extra-hardy (to Zone 4). Most of the variegated types have an upright habit at first but will produce lateral branches that, if planted near a wall or trunk, will soon begin to climb. Examples are 'Emerald Gaiety' (white-margined green leaves with a pinkish tinge in winter) and 'Emerald 'n Gold' (similar but with yellow-margined leaves).

Hedera

Ivy

Plant Profile

Hedera: HEAD-er-uh

Foliage Color: Green and variegated

Foliage Time: Year-round

Length of Foliage Interest: Year-round

Height: 50 feet (15 m)

Spread: Indefinite

Continued ➡

Garden Uses: Container planting, edging, erosion control, groundcover, rock garden, wall covering, woodland garden

Light Preference: Full sun to shade

Soil Preference: Humus-rich, moist, well-drained soil

Best Way to Propagate: Divide rooted sections in any season; take cuttings in spring or fall

USDA Plant Hardiness Zones: 7 to 9 (some cultivars to Zone 5)

A true triple-purpose plant, ivy can be used as an evergreen climber, a creeping groundcover, or a trailing container plant. In all cases, though, the dark, leathery leaves are evergreen, making the plant attractive year-round. Few plants are as variable as ivy, with literally hundreds of cultivars, most with star-shaped or maple leaf-shaped foliage, but there are also curly, fringed, or lacy leaves. Many ivies have white to yellow variegation, another plus.

GROWING TIPS

Ivies are tough, no-nonsense plants. They don't need any care, really-except pruning to keep them in check. They will tolerate almost any conditions except constant drought. Their degree of shade tolerance is legendary: Ivies will often grow in spots so dark they're otherwise totally devoid of vegetation. Not that they can't tolerate sun (they can, especially in cooler climates), but they do prefer shade or partial shade.

Ivy leaves and berries may be somewhat poisonous to humans. While the foliage is not terribly attractive to children, the black berries can and should be pruned off.

In colder climates, ivy can be grown outdoors only as a ground cover. Surrounding a bed of groundcover ivy with a footpath is enough to keep it within bounds; ivy won't stand much foot traffic.

If you want an ivy to climb, choose a species that is sufficiently hardy for your region, then plant it near a wall or tree trunk and let it grow. It will start to grow upward all on its own, hoisting itself thanks to numerous adhesive roots that will cling to almost any surface.

PROBLEMS AND SOLUTIONS

Ivies are not immune to insects and disease problems, including aphids, mealybugs, caterpillars, leaf spot, and powdery mildew, but they rarely seem to cause major problems.

TOP PERFORMER

Hedera pastuchovii (Russian ivy): This ivy grows over the widest range of any ivy, so almost any reader of this book can grow it. A cold-hardy ivy, it will make a good groundcover nearly everywhere and will climb even in Zone 5 (and warmer parts of Zone 4). The leaves are more rounded than English ivy, even heart-shaped, with paler veins, and they turn burgundy-red in winter. Height: 40 feet (12 m) or more. Spread: Indefinite. USDA Plant Hardiness Zones 3 to 9 (as a groundcover); 5 to 9 (as a climber).

MORE RECOMMENDED IVIES

Hedera canariensis (Canary Island ivy, Algerian ivy, Madeira ivy): This is a very large-leaved ivy grown as a groundcover or climber in Zones 8 to 10. The heart-shaped leaves with three to seven lobes are very shiny and measure up to 6 inches (15 cm) in diameter. 'Gloire de Marengo' (also sold as 'Variegata'), with leaves edged silvery white, is the most common cultivar. Height: 40 feet (12m) or more. Spread: Indefinite.

H. helix (English ivy): This is by far the most popular true ivy in culture and is offered in a bewildering choice of cultivars—some all green but many variegated white or yellow. Hardiness varies enormously from one cultivar to the next, with most not fully hardy beyond Zone 6, and some only to Zone 8. 'Baltica', 'Wilson,' and 'Thorndale'; though, are hardy enough to be used as groundcovers in Zone 5 and as climbers in warmer parts of Zone 6. They have dark green leaves. Irish ivy (*H. hibernica* 'Hibernica', often sold as *H helix* 'Hibernica') is very similar but not as hardy (Zones 8 to 10). Irish ivy can be invasive and is banned in some areas. Height: 40 feet (12 m) or more. Spread: Indefinite.

Hydrangea

Climbing hydrangea

Plant Profile

Hydrangea: hy-DRAIN-gee-uh

Bloom Color: White

Bloom Time: Early summer

Length of Bloom: 2 to 3 weeks

Height: Varies by species; see individual listings

Spread: Varies by species; see individual listings

Garden Uses: Arbors and trellises, groundcover, specimen plant, wall covering, woodland garden; along paths, on slopes

Light Preference: Full sun to shade

Soil Preference: Humus-rich, evenly moist, well-drained soil

Best Way to Propagate: Sow ripe seed

USDA Plant Hardiness Zones: Varies by species; see individual listings

This is a most unusual and attractive deciduous climber, both in and out of bloom. It produces huge domed flowerheads, up to 10 inches (25 cm) in diameter, composed of a cluster of fairly modest, highly scented, whitish fertile flowers surrounded by a ring of much larger pure white sterile ones. They dry to a nice beige and last much of summer, adding to the plant's interest. The glossy dark green leaves are charming as well and turn a nice golden color in some climates (elsewhere they fall green). In winter the naked branches show off their bark: thick, flaky, and a rich cinnamon brown. It produces two types of shoots: climbing ones that cling to vertical surfaces, but also outward-growing ones. Thus, unlike most climbing plants whose leaves cling to their host like shingles, climbing hydrangea fills

up plenty of aerial space. It's quite the show plant!

GROWING TIPS

Like so many woody vines, climbing hydrangea is adapted to a wide range of conditions, from deep shade to full sun (at least in cooler climates) and to most types of soil. For best results, though, give it a good, rich soil with even moisture and good drainage. It is only moderately drought-resistant, so it will appreciate a good mulch and occasional watering. In colder climates, plant it on the north or east side of a house or large tree for protection from the harsh winter sun.

This is the slowest of the vines described in this chapter. Plants grow like shrubs for the first few years and you begin to wonder whether someone hasn't sold you the wrong thing. After 3 to 5 years, though, it starts showing its true colors and sends out climbing shoots. Growth is ever so slow: It easily takes a decade for this plant to start to look good, and two or more for it to be at its best!

Warning: Don't try to force climbing by tying its woody branches to a support: They're not flexible like most other vines, and you're likely to damage them. Just let it do its own thing and it will climb when the time comes.

This is not a plant that needs a lot of pruning. Remove branches that are heading in unwanted directions whenever you notice them. If you want to cut an overgrown one back, do so over a period of several years, pruning as the blooms fade.

Although climbing hydrangea is easy to grow, it is also very difficult to multiply. Cuttings of semigreen wood are possible, but the failure rate is high. It may self-layer eventually and you could remove the resulting plants, but in general, either grow it from seed (if you're incredibly patient!) or buy new plants.

PROBLEMS AND SOLUTIONS

It's not usually subject to insects or diseases.

TOP PERFORMER

Hydrangea anomala subsp.*petiolaris* (climbing hybrangea): This is the usual form sold in nurseries, with beautiful heart-shaped leaves. You may find it sold under the name *H. petiolaris*. It differs most notably from the true species, *H. anomala*, because its leaves are heart-shaped while the latter has pointed leaves. *H. anomala* is just as attractive as *H. anomala* subsp. *petiolaris* but rarely available. Height: 9 to 50 feet (3 to 15 m). Spread: 9 to 35 feet (3 to 10 m). USDA Plant Hardiness Zones 3 to 9.

MORE RECOMMENDED CLIMBING HYDRANGEAS

Hydrangea seemannii (evergreen climbing hydrangea): This is a much rarer species and is only for those who have mild winters. It has similar blooms to *H. anomala* subsp. *petiolaris*, although smaller, and long, dark, glossy evergreen leaves. Similar, but with larger flower clusters lacking sterile blooms, is *H. serratifolia*. Both grow in shade but need some sun to bloom. Height: 10 to 50 feet (3 to 15 m). Spread: 7 to 17 feet (2 to 5 m). USDA Plant Hardiness Zones 8 to 10.

Menispermum

Moonseed

Plant Profile

Menispermum: men-ih-SPUR-mum

Foliage Color: Green

Continued ➡

Foliage Time: Spring to fall

Length of Foliage Interest: 3 months or more

Height: 15 feet (4.5 m)

Spread: Indefinite

Garden Uses: Climbing plant, groundcover, hanging basket, woodland garden

Light Preference: Full sun to shade

Soil Preference: Humus-rich, moist, well-drained soil

Best Way to Propagate: Divide offsets at any time

USDA Plant Hardiness Zones: 3 to 9

I'm always surprised that moonseed is not better known. True enough, its small greenish flowers are not showy, but the leaves are very beguiling—large and oval to heart-shaped, often with intriguing lobes—and they totally cover the plant, meaning it can completely hide even the most annoying view. The only explanation for this plant's surprising lack of popularity is that it is a native plant, and unfortunately we tend to look down on our native varieties and praise importees instead. I suggest doing an about-face and taking a second look at this unusual home-grown beauty: You won't regret it.

Growing Tips

As with many climbing plants, moonseed can be used as either a groundcover or a vine. As it climbs by entwining, it will need a support it can wrap itself around, such as a thin trunk, a post, a wire, or a trellis. Otherwise it will run across the ground and form a carpet of greenery.

It is native to the eastern third of North America, from Quebec and Manitoba down to the Deep South, so it is widely adapted to a nearly complete range of climates. It does best in rich, well-drained soils and is fairly drought-tolerant once established, though it thrives if mulched and watered regularly. In the wild it grows about equally well in sun and fairly dense shade and will do the same in your garden.

Like many vines, actually growing moonseed is a snap—it requires just about nothing from you to remain in top shape—but what it may well need is a bit of selective pruning. Given the chance, it will gladly leap from the trellis you choose for it to a nearby shrub or tree (or even telephone pole), then take that over, too. It also spreads by offsets produced by underground rhizomes, so be ready to cut it back whenever its stems outstep their bounds. As for the invasive roots, ideally you should always plant this vine within a root barrier so it can never escape and cause any problems. Otherwise you will find it popping up here and there, such as in your lawn.

Multiplication is usually done by digging up offsets appearing in the ground near the mother plant (if you used a root barrier) or anywhere within 10 feet (3 m) if you didn't. This can be done at any time the plant is not dormant. Fresh seed is rarely available unless you have wild moonseeds growing in your area. If so, harvest the seed when the grapelike berries are ripe (in early fall), remove the pulp, and plant the seed without delay. Germination will then take place the following spring, after the seeds have been exposed to winter's coolness. Stored seed, such as that offered in seed packs, often goes into prolonged dormancy and may need more than one period of cold in order to germinate. Seed-grown moonseed plants put on only modest growth the first year or so but, after that, quickly do their duty as a carpeting groundcover or object-concealing vine.

Problems and Solutions

Moonseed is reputed to be essentially insect- and disease-free.

Top Performer

Menispermum canadense (moonseed, Canada moonseed): This is the only species with much of a commercial distribution and even then, it is quite rare in nurseries. Since there is a considerable amount of variety in the shape and size of the leaves, it's a shame that special cultivars are not available. Height: 15 feet (4.5 m). Spread: Indefinite. USDA Plant Hardiness Zones 3 to 9.

More Recommended Moonseeds

Menispermum dauricum (Asian moonseed): Much rarer in culture, Asian moonseed is very similar to its North American cousin, varying mostly in the number of flower clusters found at each axil (two instead of the single cluster found on *M. canadensis*). Since the flowers are insignificant anyway, there is no reason to prefer one species over the other: Choose whichever is the most readily available in your area. Height: 15 feet (4.5 m). Spread: Indefinite. USDA Plant Hardiness Zones 5 to 9.

Parthenocissus

Parthenocissus, Virginia creeper, Boston ivy

Plant Profile

Parthenocissus: par-then-oh-SIS-us

Bloom Color: Greenish white

Bloom Time: Early summer

Length of Bloom: 2 to 3 weeks

Height: Varies by species; see individual listings

Spread: Varies by species; see individual listings

Garden Uses: Arbors and trellises, background, container planting, groundcover, mass planting, wall covering, woodland garden; on slopes

Light Preference: Full sun to shade

Soil Preference: Humus-rich, evenly moist, well-drained soil

Best Way to Propagate: Take cuttings from spring to fall

USDA Plant Hardiness Zones: Varies by species; see individual listings

Parthenocissus will grow on almost anything. Trellises, fences, stumps, rusting cars: It does it all. In nature, it is famous for scrambling up the tallest trees, then leaping from one to the next, leaving dangling woody stems that would leave Tarzan's lianas in the dust. In the garden, people love the way it climbs vertical walls then drips down, creating a dancing green curtain. Don't look for attractive flowers: They're greenish and hidden by the leaves, but the deeply cut foliage is stupendous with its brilliant display of fall colors. When the leaves drop, they reveal blue or black berries that draw hordes of hungry birds in winter. No wonder parthenocissus is the queen of the hardy vines!

Growing Tips

These vines are among the most adaptable of all, seemingly immune to sun or shade, and any type of well-drained soil will do. They'll even grow in cracks in pavement!

Perhaps the nicest thing about parthenocissus is that they grow so quickly. Most woody vines take a few years to get going, but these babies are already well up your wall within a few months. Their tendrils are equipped with holdfasts that allow them to climb walls, tree trunks, or any vertical surface, yet the tendrils still twist so they can also mount trellises, latticework, fences, and the like.

Fast growth has a price, though, and that's likely to mean some pruning. Cutting back stems that try to work their way into the gutter or cover the window is likely to become an annual tradition if you grow them on a house. They can overwhelm an arbor or pergola in just a few short years—and did you really want them to completely cover that tree? It's best to learn to cut them back every few years, or even annually: They resprout quickly from the base and can easily grow back 20 feet (6 m) in a single summer.

Don't neglect parthenocissus as a groundcover either—most species create a superb green carpet in shade or in sun.

If you need more plants, just take cuttings: Both green, semi-green, and woody cuttings root readily. Plus, they self-layer where their stems touch the ground. You can also extract seeds from the fruit in fall: Sown outdoors, they'll sprout in spring. Of course, cultivars will not come true to type.

Problems and Solutions

Mildew has an annoying habit of showing up in late summer but does little real damage, nor do other diseases. Leaf-eating insects are another story: Grape flea beetle, Japanese beetle, and leaf skeletonizer may require a few sprays with insecticidal soap.

Top Performer

Parthenocissus quinquefolia (Virginia creeper, woodbine): This ubiquitous climber is native to middle and eastern North America, from Mexico to Canada, but is now grown around the world, from the tropics almost to the Arctic Circle. Its compound leaves with five leaflets are reddish in spring, dull dark green in summer, and brilliant red in fall. The bluish black berries are evident only in fall and winter. 'Star Showers', with leaves green-and-white in summer then pink-and-red in fall, is a weaker grower, ideal for spots you don't want to see overwhelmed. Englemann ivy (*P. virginiana* var. *engelmannii*), with smaller leaves, is commonly grown; *P. henryana* (Zones 7 to 9) has similar leaves but with a spectacular silver overlay. Height: 40 to 50 feet (12 to 15 m). Spread: 30 feet (9 m). USDA Plant Hardiness Zones 2 to 10.

More Recommended Parthenocissus

Parthenocissus tricuspidata (Boston ivy): A shiny-leaved version of the previous, with variable leaves, mostly maple-shaped but sometimes trifoliate. It conveniently dies to the ground each winter in cold climates, saving you a lot of pruning! There are several cultivars, including 'Veitchii', with smaller leaves and purple fall color instead of scarlet; and 'Fenway', with golden leaves. Height: 50 to 70 feet (15 to 21 m). Spread: 20 feet (6 m). USDA Plant Hardiness Zones 4 to 10.

Trachelospermum

Confederate jasmine, star jasmine

Plant Profile

Trachelospermum: tra-key-lo-SPUR-mum

Bloom Color: White

Bloom Time: Mid-spring to early summer

Length of Bloom: 6 weeks or more

Height: Varies by species; see individual listings

Spread: Varies by species; see individual listings

Garden Uses: Arbors and trellises, container planting, groundcover, hanging baskets, house-

Continued ➡

plant, mass planting, wall covering, woodland garden; on slopes

Light Preference: Full sun to shade

Soil Preference: Humus-rich, evenly moist, well-drained, acid soil

Best Way to Propagate: Take cuttings in spring or summer

USDA Plant Hardiness Zones: 9 to 10; frost-sensitive perennial grown as a tender annual

This vine gets its common name, Confederate jasmine, not from its home country, Asia, but from its great popularity in the southeastern United States. It is now just as popular in Southern California as well. It's a twining vine with shiny, dark green, oval leaves, tinted purple in winter, that are attractive in their own right. This plant's best attribute, though, are its beautifully creamy white flowers, with five petals slightly twisted to one side like a pinwheel. They are so highly scented, especially at night, it is most likely you'll smell it before you see it. This plant can reach considerable heights—or it can be grown as an evergreen groundcover or even as a houseplant. You choose!

GROWING TIPS

Confederate jasmine can be grown outdoors year-round only where temperatures don't drop much below 23°F (-15°C). It prefers a rich, moist, acid soil and is not very drought-tolerant; keep it well watered in times of drought. Although full sun is fine when it's summering outside in the North, elsewhere it does best in shade or partial shade: The starry flowers truly brighten up the darkest corners. Indoors, grow in a medium-size pot on a small trellis, or train it to run around a hoop made from a wire coat hanger. Outdoors it will grow up arbors and pergolas, cover stumps, and even climb into trees.

For use as a groundcover, space the plants about 2 to 3 feet (60 to 90 cm) apart under tree or shrub cover or to the North of walls or buildings. It grows quite quickly, forming a dark green carpet about 10 to 16 inches (25 to 40 cm) tall.

Although Confederate jasmine is a fairly strong climber, it does have trouble getting started, so it is permissible to fix it to its support to start. With time, its twining, weaving stems will manage to work themselves in among the crossbars of a trellis or through latticework. Don't be afraid to prune back the excessively long shoots it sometimes produces. Otherwise, prune to shape it after it finishes blooming.

This plant roots readily from stem cuttings taken spring through fall outdoors, or year-round indoors. The cuttings exude a sticky white sap called latex. Plunge their tips into water to cause the sap to congeal before inserting them in moist growing mix.

PROBLEMS AND SOLUTIONS

Insects and disease are infrequent.

TOP PERFORMER

Trachelospermum jasminoides (Confederate jasmine, star jasmine): This is the most common species, with snow white flowers. Although very popular, it is not the hardiest species: Where it is borderline hardy outdoors, consider *T. asiaticum*, described below. 'Variegatum' has leaves beautifully marbled white with a pinkish tinge in winter. 'Madison' is a hardier selection, said to do well in protected spots of Zone 7. Height: 3 to 30 feet (1 to 9 m). Spread: 10 to 17 feet (3 to 5 m). USDA Plant Hardiness Zones 9 to 10.

MORE RECOMMENDED STAR JASMINES

Trachelospermum asiaticum (Japanese star jasmine): This is a hardier plant than the previous one and worth trying where Confederate jasmine is suffering. It has smaller leaves and similar but dangling flowers, creamy white at first, more yellow after a few days. Height: 3 to 20 feet (1 to 6 m). Spread: 10 to 17 feet (3 to 5 m). USDA Plant Hardiness Zones 8 to 10.

Working with Living Trellises

Barbara Pleasant

Any plant that grows lean and tall can be used to support twining vines. In spring, short peas are often happy to cling to clumps of ornamental wheat, and in the summer garden, you can use amaranth, corn, Jerusalem artichokes, or okra to support pole beans or long-vined limas. Single-stemmed sunflowers make great support plants in either a vegetable or a flower garden, where they can be used as living trellises for dainty asarina or more muscular purple-podded hyacinth beans.

There are a few things to keep in mind when using plants as trellises. Drenching rain combined with wind can cause tall plants to fall over, which becomes even more likely if the plant is top-heavy with the added weight of a vine. Giving the support plant a 2-week head start on the vine is important, too, because once vines get growing, they seldom slow down. Should a plant being used as a living trellis start to look like a leaning tower, tying it to a tall, slender stake may provide a temporary remedy.

Using an Unemployed Stump

When a treasured old tree must be removed, leaving a stump about 3 feet high instantly creates a great trellis for perennial vines such as passion-flower or trumpet creeper. Tree roots often dominate the soil around a stump, so you may need to use a short rebar stake to probe about in search of a suitable planting pocket for a vine. If the stump is too short to provide vertical growing space for a vigorous vine, perhaps you can drill holes into the top that will support upright stakes. A single sturdy stake topped with a small weather vane or piece of metal sculpture can transform a vine-covered stump into a beautiful garden focal point.

Another option is to hollow out the top of the stump to create a planting space for cascading flowers or annual vines. If this seems like too much work, grow your vines in a large, heavy container placed on the stump. As the vines sprawl, they will cover both the container and the stump.

Plant Partners for Clematis

One of the most beautiful vines you can grow, clematis also makes a great team player when trained to wind its way through a small tree or shrub. The host plant provides support for the clematis, which in turn furnishes a bit of shade for its living trellis. In most cases, the clematis will bloom after its support plant has leafed out, so each blossom floats on a sea of lush foliage.

Clematis vary in color, bloom season, and ideal pruning times, but because there are hundreds of varieties to choose from, it is not difficult to coordinate them with exactly the right host plants. Don't worry that the host plant will shade out the clematis, because the vine will seek out sunny pockets in the tree or shrub's canopy and eagerly fill them in. The "Six Sure-Fire Clematis Combos" chart lists several proven partnerships between clematis varieties and widely adapted host plants.

To begin one of these lovely liaisons, plant a clematis 2 feet from the base of the host plant. Clematis need rich, fertile soil with a near-neutral pH, so be sure to mix in some lime if your soil is naturally acidic. As the clematis grows, secure a slender stake between the vine and a low branch of the tree or shrub to help the clematis find its way. When pruning clematis trained this way, you can avoid future training sessions by pruning it back only to where it threads into the lowest branches of its host plant.

Continued →

Gardening Indoors

HOUSEPLANTS

Living with Houseplants

Barbara W. Ellis

Raising houseplants provides year-round gardening pleasure. Foliage and flowering indoor plants are generally easy to care for, and species can be found that will grow well in almost any part of your home. Houseplants are a great medium for experimenting with propagation techniques and satisfying the urge to garden, no matter what the weather.

Your first task in caring for a houseplant fresh from the greenhouse or plant store may be to repot it in a larger or more decorative container. Many gardeners assume that a plant should subsequently be repotted every few months. Actually, a plant should be repotted only if its roots fill its container, or if you prefer a different pot or type of soil mix for the plant. Spring is usually the best season to repot a houseplant. Wait until a plant finishes blooming before changing its container. Before repotting a plant, always check to see if its roots have run out of growing space.

To check the condition of a houseplant's roots, water the plant well and wait a few minutes for the moisture to soak in. Then turn the plant upside down, holding your palm flat against the soil with the stem between your fingers. Tap the edge of the pot lightly against the hard edge of a counter or workbench. The root ball should fall free of the container. If the plant will not come loose, run a kitchen knife around the inside edge of the container and then tap it again.

A layer of broken crockery at the bottom of the pot will keep soil from sifting out of the container, but will not help improve drainage. Be sure the crockery does not block the drainage hole. In this illustration, a pot shard is blocking the hole and will impede drainage.

Rootbound plants have a mass of tangled white roots which fill the pot and may even protrude through the pot's drainage holes (if your plant is not rootbound, you can simply set it back into its pot). Healthy roots are usually creamy white and plump. Dead roots are brown or black and shriveled. Remove any dead roots before putting the plant in a new container.

How to Repot

Repot a houseplant in a container one size larger than its present pot. For example, if your plant is growing in a 6-inch pot, move it into an 8-inch container. Soak empty clay pots in water for several hours before placing a plant in them. Make sure that the plant's soil is thoroughly moist before transplanting.

You can fill the bottom of a new pot with a shallow layer of broken crockery so soil won't sift out.

Next, put in a layer of fresh soil, and insert the root ball so the old soil line is just below the new soil level. Make sure that the stem sits symmetrically in the middle of the pot. Fill in the edges with soil medium and compact it with your fingers or a pencil. Water the plant generously after repotting and keep it in a shady spot for several days.

Soil Mixes for Houseplants

Whether you mix your own potting soil or buy one of the many formulations offered in plant

Continued ➜

stores and garden centers, there are a few things all potting soils have in common. Although certain plants are grown in pots filled with a single ingredient—some orchids can be grown in fir bark, and bromeliads are often grown in sphagnum moss, for example—most plants grow best in a medium that combines several ingredients. Some of the ingredients in potting soil provide nutrition; others improve texture, enhance drainage, or aid water retention. For example, peat moss soaks up water, and sand ensures that the soil doesn't remain soggy; compost and other organic matter add texture and provide nutrition.

For handsome and healthy houseplants, you'll need to match the conditions a particular plant prefers with the right soil mix. For example, while all potting soils retain water for the plant, some plants require more soil moisture than others. Most cacti are grown in mixtures that drain quickly and retain little moisture; most ferns, on the other hand, grow best in a mixture that remains moist but not soggy.

Soil pH affects how plant roots absorb both water and nutrients. The pH scale runs from 0 to 14, with the lower numbers reflecting acid conditions and the higher numbers, alkaline conditions. Most houseplants prefer to grow in a neutral to slightly acid soil with pH between 6.2 and 6.8. There are a few exceptions—gardenias (*Gardenia* spp.), hydrangeas (*Hydrangea* spp.), and acacias (*Acacia* spp.) are popular houseplants that will not thrive unless they are grown in an acid soil mix. Adding iron chelate to the soil will effectively acidify the medium. Store-bought mixes are usually carefully balanced to provide plants with a neutral pH. If you are making your own soil mix, be sure to check its pH.

INGREDIENTS

A good potting soil should start with soil and/or compost. Whatever you use, it's important that it

be free of fungi, soilborne diseases, insects, and weed seeds. Also, it should be well drained. Don't use plain garden soil—it is usually much too heavy when used in containers and tends to pack and crust. Also, unsterilized garden soil harbors fungi and insects. You can start with good garden loam or purchased topsoil, then sift it through a screen to remove rocks and large clods and sterilize it at temperatures of 150° to 180°F for 30 minutes. Sift and sterilize compost or composted manure before you use it, as well.

Sharp sand, also known as builder's sand, is another basic ingredient. It increases drainage, allowing soil aeration around the roots. Perlite and vermiculite are common ingredients that add no nutritional value but increase the air- and water-holding capacity of the mix. Peat moss is a good source of organic matter to hold moisture in the soil. Leaf mold is another common ingredient that offers nutrients and water-holding capacity and contributes to the structure of a mix. Leaf mold is not generally commercially available, but it can easily be homemade by composting autumn leaves.

To these main ingredients, you can add soil amendments such as lime, which neutralizes soil pH and provides calcium. Bonemeal is an excellent source of phosphorus and nitrogen. Wood ash is a source of potassium, but should be used sparingly as it has a potent effect on soil pH.

Commercial Potting Soils

Commercial potting mixes have a variety of ingredients, and not all manufacturers list the contents of their mixes. Choose a mix that specifies its contents on the package. Try to find a mixture that closely matches the components in the recommended homemade mixes below. Avoid mixes that contain chemical fertilizers.

RECIPES FOR POTTING MIXES

Potting mixes can be as simple or as complex as you wish. Here are a few that are suitable for a wide range of houseplants.

All-Purpose Houseplant Mixes

· One part peat moss, compost, or leaf mold; 1 part sterilized garden loam or purchased potting soil; and 1 part sharp sand or perlite.

· One part peat moss; 1 part sterilized garden loam or purchased potting soil and sterilized, composted manure mixed half-and-half; and 1 part sharp sand.

· Two parts sterilized garden loam or purchased potting soil; 1 part peat moss, compost, or leaf mold; and 1 part sharp sand or perlite.

Rich Houseplant Mix

Humus-loving plants grow better in a somewhat richer mixture.

· One part sterilized garden loam or purchased potting soil; 2 parts compost or leaf mold; and 1 part sharp sand or perlite.

Epiphyte Mix

Epiphytes are plants that grow on other plants—such as in the crotches of trees—without parasitizing them. They grow in leaf litter and other organic matter that collects around them. Several common houseplants, including some ferns, orchids, and bromeliads, fall into this category.

· One part sterilized garden loam or purchased potting soil; 2 parts leaf mold, peat moss, osmunda fiber, or shredded fir bark, or a mixture of all these ingredients; 1

part sharp sand or perlite; and ½ part crushed clay pot, brick, or gravel.

To each peck (roughly 2 gallons) of the above recipes, add ½ cup of bonemeal and ½ cup of lime.

Dividing Houseplants

Houseplants can be propagated in many different ways. Division is one of the easiest ways to produce new plants. The method varies slightly depending on the type of plant you are propagating.

PROPAGATING WITH OFFSETS AND SUCKERS

The easiest and most successful method for propagating houseplants is to divide off runners or offsets. Any plant that multiplies by producing "pups" can be divided. Episcias (*Episcia* spp.), African violets (*Saintpaulia* spp.), aloes (*Aloe* spp.), and mints (*Mentha* spp.), along with ferns, bromeliads, and many succulents, are among the many popular plants that can be successfully propagated by this method.

Separating a side shoot from its parent is as simple as it sounds. First, turn the plant out of its pot and examine the roots. For this method to succeed, all the separate divisions must have individual root systems. You'll probably find that each offset has vigorous roots which are intertwined with the parental root system.

Take the base of each crown in your hand and tease the roots free by pulling them slowly apart. Try not to damage any roots, and never pull at the foliage. When they're completely untangled, pot each plant separately, providing fresh soil for both the parent and its progeny. Keep the newly potted plants in a cool, shady spot for several days.

Some plants such as African violets, saxifrages (*Saxifraga* spp.), and episcias send out aerial runners with new plantlets dangling from the tips. Those plantlets won't send down roots until they can sink their feet into soil. To encourage root development, take a U-shaped hairpin and secure the plantlet firmly on top of a pot filled with loose, humusy soil (rich houseplant mix is fine). Leave the plantlet attached to its parent and keep the soil moist for two to three weeks while it develops roots. Then cut the runner. The dangling offsets of spider plants (*Chlorophytum* spp.) will even begin to initiate roots while hanging in the air. These can be removed from the parent plant and rooted in water or rich houseplant mix.

DIVIDING RHIZOMATOUS PLANTS

Many common houseplants spread by underground rhizomes, which will send up new plantlets that can be cut and potted up. Rhizomatous begonias (*Begonia* spp.), snake plants (*Sansevieria* spp.), and many gesneriads form underground rhizomes that send up new plantlets. If left undivided, the plant will form an expanding cluster of growth, eventually choking itself into starvation. One solution is to keep repotting the growing plant. Another remedy is to divide the plant into two or more smaller specimens.

Turn the root ball out of the pot and use a sharp knife to cut the rhizome and its accompanying section of roots. The easiest method is simply to cut the root ball in half. You can divide it into small sections if you have many rhizomes sending up growing shoots. Repot all the divisions in separate containers, adding new soil around the sliced root systems. Put the plants in a shady

Continued ➡

spot and water them generously while they recover.

DIVIDING BULBS, CORMS, TUBERS, AND TUBEROUS ROOTS

Tuberous begonias (*Begonia x tuberhybrida*), oxalis (*Oxalis* spp.), achimenes (*Achimenes* spp.), dahlias (*Dahlia* spp.), and caladiums (*Caladium* spp.) are among the many popular houseplants that sprout from bulbs, tubers, or corms. Although each of these underground structures is different, they all store food during growth in preparation for dormant periods. And they usually produce new bulbs, corms, or tubers during their growing cycle, which can be divided when the plants go dormant.

To divide these plants, wait until the foliage dies back completely, and withhold water until the soil is dry. Turn the plant out of its pot and remove excess bulbs. They can be potted up right away or stored in a cool, dark, dry place until their growing season arrives. When stored bulbs begin to grow, pot them with growing ends up and begin supplying sun and water.

Increasing Humidity

Low humidity is one of the greatest problems encountered by indoor gardeners. During the winter, when furnaces and wood stoves are pouring out dry heat, indoor humidity is especially low. In extreme cases, homes can have as little as 10 percent humidity during the heating season.

If you suffer from chapped lips, dry skin, and clogged sinuses in the winter, you can imagine how uncomfortable your tropical plants must feel. Most tropical species require 40 to 60 percent humidity to thrive. When the air is dry, indoor plants lose water continuously through their leaf pores. The leaves look dehydrated, leaf edges turn brown, and leaves fall.

The easiest method of increasing humidity is to purchase a humidifier or vaporizer. However, there are less expensive methods of raising humidity for plants. When you group plants together, especially in a recessed bay window or window greenhouse, leaf transpiration increases the moisture in their immediate area. Setting pots on pebble trays filled with an inch of pebbles and ½ inch of water (remember to refill the tray as the water evaporates) also raises humidity for clustered plants. Simply putting a pan of water near a radiator, heat register, baseboard heater or on a woodstove can help increase the humidity in a room.

Misting plants is not an efficient way to combat a humidity deficit. Misting may raise humidity for a few moments, but only continual misting significantly increases moisture in the air around your plants. And, constantly moist leaves can develop fungal problems.

Pruning and Training Houseplants

If left to their own devices, most plants send a single stem shooting straight upward. A skillful gardener counteracts that tendency and coaxes the plant to bush into a handsome, shapely specimen. The secret is pruning.

Actually, although the scale is quite different, the principles of pruning houseplants differ little from those used for pruning trees. Early pruning can be used to shape and train a plant into an attractive shape. Heading cuts can be used to encourage bushy growth; thinning to remove unsightly branches and open up the center of the plant.

A saucer or tray filled with pebbles and water will provide much-needed humidity for houseplants.

Houseplants that Love High Humidity

Although nearly all houseplants benefit from increased humidity, the following require high humidity for best performance.

Allamanda spp. (common allamanda)

Begonia spp. (begonia, especially rex)

Bougainvillea spp. (bougainvillea)

Calathea spp. (calathea)

Gardenia spp. (gardenia)

Mandevilla (mandevilla)

Maranta spp. (maranta, including prayer plant)

Gesneriad-family members such as African violets (*Saintpaulia* spp.), columnea (*Columnea* spp.), episcia (*Episcia* spp.), lipstick plant (*Aeschynanthus* spp.), gloxinia (*Gloxinia* spp.), and many ferns also thrive in high humidity.

Pruning techniques vary depending on how severely you plan to prune. If your plant is young and has only a few sets of mature leaves, merely pinch the growing bud. Pinching is a type of heading cut that doesn't require knives or shears. Simply grasp the growing stem and snip off the terminal bud, with or without the top pair of leaves, using your thumb and forefinger. After pinching, the stem is not noticeably shorter, but the side shoots receive a "growth message" and immediately begin to develop. Regular pinching encourages branching and dense growth.

If your plant is too tall, use a pair of sharp pruning shears and cut the growth to the desired height. Cut to either softwood or hardwood, and always cut just above a bud or a set of leaves. When judging the target height, remember that the plant will probably branch out just below the cut. Many older houseplants can be completely rejuvenated with a stern hardwood pruning. Use sharp, heavy-duty pruning shears to cut the stems back close to the base. New, fresh growth will shoot out within a few weeks.

ROOT PRUNING

If a plant is potbound, repot when you prune to provide nourishment for the new growth. This is especially important when pruning hardwood plants. If you don't want to move the plant to a larger container, prune the roots as well and pot the plant back into the same container.

To root prune, turn out the roots and, with a sharp knife, carve off an inch (or more for large plants) around the entire surface of the root ball. Work quickly, and cut the roots cleanly. Put the roots back in the pot, and add fresh soil. Keep the plant in the shade and water frequently until new roots grow.

Give Each Houseplant the Light It Needs

Roger Yepsen

Plants rely on light energy to drive the metabolic machinery of photosynthesis. With too little light, the machine slows and a houseplant performs poorly and may die. If the light is too intense, foliage may be burned. And one variety's sunlight requirement can cause another variety to drop all of its leaves. Plants are sensitive not only to the brightness of the light they receive, but to its duration and even the colors from which it is composed. For healthy windowsill greenery, you need to pay as much attention to light levels as to fertilizer and water.

A Grow-Light Like the Sun Itself

For years, greenhouse growers have relied on high-intensity discharge (HID) lamps for a blaze of light to supplement sunshine. For commercial operations, that supplemental light is especially important in northern states and in the winter. Most of us homeowners make do with too little light for many of the plants we'd like to grow indoors, but now HIDs are available in lower wattages. The smallest of them aren't terribly expensive, although powerful ones rated at 300 watts or so require a ballast (transformer) and are something of an investment. On the positive side, the bulbs last for 10,000 hours or more. And the quality of light resembles the sun's own, covering much of the spectrum. If you're serious about having a grouping of houseplants perform at their best, consider the purchase of an HID.

A Light Mover

Unless you can afford a bank of HIDs, you'll be limited to focusing a single fixture on one or a few plants that need a lot of light. Or, you can install a nifty automatic light mover that slowly propels the high-powered fixture along a ceiling track, increasing your growing area by 30 to 60 percent. There's no need to go up onto a stepladder to adjust a light this way and that—a 5-watt-motor does the work. Check the Internet for a supplier.

Use a Mirror for Nicely Groomed Plants

If you have a spare dressing mirror, you can use it to reflect the sun's energy and bathe the dark side of seedling flats placed by windows or large potted plants (especially ones in heavy clay pots). You not only make better use of the solar energy trickling in through the panes, but also distribute it more evenly so that plants will grow symmetrically rather than leaning into the light. Painting adjacent walls and trim a semigloss white wall will also help bump up light levels. And you can cover the windowsill or window-side table with shiny Mylar, serving both to protect the surface below and to bounce light back up at the plants.

Continued ➔

Make the sun do double duty by placing a space mirror behind large house-plants that aren't easily turned or moved. The plants will be more likely to grow to a well-rounded form because there is more than one light source.

Add a Shelf

Light levels drop off quickly inside a house so plants needing high light levels should be placed as close to the window as possible. If your windowsills are narrow, consider adding a plant shelf to the sill for your houseplants. You can find a shelf kit (attach it just below your sill) or build your own sill extender (be sure to support the extension with a bracket). Or place a table right in front of the window so plants get direct light. Tie back any curtains (even sheer curtains) and be sure to keep windows clean to allow in the brightest light.

Getting It Right

If your houseplant isn't thriving, it may not be a case of too much or too little water or fertilizer. It may be that it isn't getting the right light. If plants develop white or brown patches or take on a yellow tone, the light level may be too strong. Move the plant farther from the window or move it to a different, lower-light window.

Most plants that show signs of stress actually need more light. If a plant is leggy, if the leaves yellow and drop, or if the plant isn't growing at all, move the plant to a brighter location and see what happens.

Plants do drop leaves when you move them to a lower light situation or just bring them home from the store. Your indoor light conditions are probably lower than those in the store. Keep the plant in a higher light window and the plant will adjust to your conditions in a few weeks.

Harvesting and Using Flowers

Barbara W. Ellis

When the flower garden you've planned and nurtured finally bursts into bloom, you'll want to enjoy the blossoms to their fullest. Bouquets of cut flowers are the perfect way to bring the delicious fragrances and glorious colors of the garden indoors. Although flowers last longest when left in the garden, with just a little special care you can lengthen the life of cut flowers—adding days of enjoyment from floral arrangements. Longer vase life begins with something as simple as how you cut the flowers. There are a number of conditioning techniques that will also help lengthen vase life. Although the additional treatments listed below may seem like too much bother, many flowers will benefit from them. Try them, and you'll find they make a difference. Treat blooms immediately after cutting, before you soak them overnight.

Cutting

Scissors and fingers are not the tools of choice for harvesting flowers. Picking flowers by pinching them off with your fingers tends to tear the stems or uproot the plants. It also generally crushes the stem rather than severing it cleanly. Even scissors can bruise stems and close off the channels that carry water to the bloom. For best results, use a very sharp knife to cut flowers. As a general rule, cut across the stem at an angle to provide as wide a cut surface for water uptake as possible. This also prevents the stem from resting squarely on the bottom of the container, which would prevent water uptake. It's a good idea to have a bucket of water handy to receive your freshly picked flowers. Lukewarm water (100° to 110°F) is best; icy-cold water is a bit of a shock for the cut blooms.

Good timing also makes a difference in the vase life of flowers. Don't cut flowers during the heat of the day, when they may already be drooping. Instead, cut them during the cooler hours of early morning or in late afternoon or evening when they are not under stress from the sun.

Flower maturity is also an important consideration. Mature blooms that are full of pollen will not last as long as newly opened flowers. Choose blossoms that are just about to open fully. With some happy exceptions (daffodils and forsythia, for example), tightly closed buds will not open after they've been cut; they'll simply wilt when cut and put in water. Roses generally will open if cut once one outside petal has unfurled. Daisies last longest if picked when the flowers are fully open but the centers are still firm and slightly green. Spiky flowers like gladiolus, lupine, and delphinium will have the longest vase life if you select stems with lower flowers in full bloom and upper buds just on the threshold of opening. Snip off lower flowers as they wilt.

Conditioning

You can lengthen the vase life of flowers by conditioning them properly. That means allowing them to absorb as much water as possible as soon as they've been picked. Immediately after cutting and before arranging, stand flowers in deep water for six to eight hours—or, even better, overnight—in a cool, dark place. Immerse the foliage, but be sure to keep the flowers dry. Most flowers will take up warm water (around 100°F) more quickly. Conditioning will let the flowers drink in the water and be at their sturdiest for you to work with them. If the flowers have been out of water, recut the stems at an angle before plunging them in tepid water.

Surprising as it may sound, some flowers benefit from a hot bath immediately after cutting. Flowers that benefit from this treatment include windflower (*Anemone* spp.), broom (*Cytisus* spp.), bellflower (*Campanula* spp.), rose campion (*Lychnis coronaria*), columbine (*Aquilegia* spp.), (daphne (*Daphne* spp.), hellebdre (*Helleborus* spp.), lobelia (*Lobelia* spp.), beard-tongue (*Penstemon* spp.), primrose (*Primula* spp.), and periwinkle (*Vinca* spp.).

To give your flowers a hot water bath, start by cutting the stems at an angle. Pour 1 inch of boiling water into a heat-resistant container. Protect the blossoms from steam with a collar of newspaper, then submerge the tips of the stems in the water for about one minute. Then plunge the stems up to the base of the flowers into tepid water (100° to 110°F) and give the flowers a good deep soak.

There are specific techniques suitable for different types of flower stems. Stems are generally classified as woody, milky, hollow, or soft.

Woody Stems

The blossoms of flowering trees, shrubs, and some vines have woody stems that have difficulty taking up water unless they are specially prepared.

To increase water uptake, strip off the bark 1 inch above the cut, then lightly crush the tip of the stem to break down the fibers so they can more readily take up water. A wooden rolling pin or mallet will do the job with a few gentle taps; use a sturdy block of wood or a chopping board to save your countertop. An alternative method is to cut a series of slits up through the center of the base of the stem—again, to about 1 inch. After splitting the stems, soak them in tepid water for several hours. Dogwood (*Cornus* spp.), mountain laurel (*Kalmia* spp.), forsythia (*Forsythia* spp.), honeysuckle (*Lonicera* spp.), and fruiting trees such as apples and crab apples all benefit from this treatment.

Some other types of flowers have fibrous stems that also benefit from splitting before soaking. These include thistle (*Cirsium* and other genera), mallow (*Malva* spp.), and chrysanthemum.

Milky Stems

Stems that exude milky sap when cut must be sealed at the tip before they are arranged. To condition poppies (*Papaver* spp.), hydrangea (*Hydrangea* spp.), poinsettia (*Euphorbia pulcherrima*), or any other milky-stemmed flower, singe the stem tips immediately after picking for a second or so over a match or candle flame. With a sizzle, the cut will be sealed. You can also seal the ends with a hot water bath. Return flowers to water until time for arranging. If you need to cut the stems to length for the arrangement, you'll need to seal them again.

Hollow Stems

One of the secrets of flower show winners is filling the hollow stalks of plants such as dahlias, delphinium, and lupine with water, then plugging the opening. Hold each stalk upside down to receive water from a medicine dropper or narrow-spouted watering can. Release any air bubbles by tapping the stem firmly with your finger. Use a tightly twisted wad of absorbent cotton as a stopper. Then stand flowers upright in deep water before arranging.

Soft Stems

Hyacinths, daffodils, and other soft-stemmed flowers last longer if you recut their stems under water to avoid the formation of an air lock. A basin or wide, shallow bowl full of water is perfect for dunking the stem while you cut it with your sharp knife. Be sure to cut stems at an angle. Then condition these flowers in cold water before arranging. When picked, the stems of daffodils exude a runny, clear sap that can clog the stems of other flowers arranged with them. To avoid this, soak daffodils in a separate container of cold water for two to three hours after cutting and before arranging. Try to cut the stems to the length you'll need in the arrangement before soaking them, to avoid recutting them.

Flower Arranging

Flower arranging doesn't have to be difficult. In fact, probably the hardest part is overcoming the fear of designing your first bouquet. Arrangements can be as simple as daisies in a milk jug or as elaborate as a mixed bouquet for a buffet table, but if you're a beginner, it's best to start simple and work up. Just remember, flowers are always beautiful—it's hard to make them look ugly!

All good arrangements start with a few basic materials—fresh, properly conditioned flowers and foliage, tools, and containers. Knowing a few

Continued ➡

simple styling principles will help steer you in the right direction and encourage you to experiment.

MATERIALS

Take a tip from nature to inspire your designs and help you select the plant materials you use in arrangements: Your garden and the fields and forests nearby contain a wealth of colors, textures, and fragrances. Don't be afraid to try to recreate this natural beauty in your arrangements. Mix several types of flowers or foliage, select a variety of colors, or try new color combinations. Experiment with many types of materials to blend texture, color, and fragrance. For example, when selecting flowers, consider combinations of wildflowers, perennials, annuals, flowering shrubs and trees, roses, and herbs. Look to trees and shrubs, ferns, perennials, grasses, and herbs for foliage to add to your arrangements. Don't overlook the showy heads of ornamental grasses, seedpods, or shrubs with berries for unusual color and texture. Bring fragrance indoors with sweet-smelling blooms, but don't overlook pungent herbs—many of them make wonderful additions to bouquets. Crush a leaf between your fingers now and then to release their fragrance. Using flowers in varying stages of development will enrich the texture of an arrangement—combine unopened buds with fully blown flowers, for example.

Containers

The choices for a container are almost limitless. Just remember tat the container and flowers must complement each other to form an artistic unit. Often a container in a neutral color with simple lines is most effective, since it doesn't compete with your plant material for attention. That doesn't mean you should avoid a container with some individuality. Consider baskets, handmade pottery, and vessels of wood, pewter, or brass. Even seashells and rocks can hold flowers, especially in oriental or contemporary arrangements. All of these containers have the advantage of being opaque and will hide the mass of stems and any mechanical support system you've used.

A clear glass container lets the flowers take center stage. Stems showing through a transparent bowl make the flowers appear larger. Glass—cut crystal particularly—reflects light and makes flowers glow.

Some containers are so ornate that putting many colors in them creates confusion. But a monochromatic arrangement in one of these could be stunning—an all-white bouquet in an oriental vase, for example.

Tools

The tools you need for flower arranging aren't numerous, nor difficult to find. In addition to plant materials and containers, you'll need tools for cutting flowers, as well as mechanics, the tools used to hold flowers in place in their containers. Mechanics such as floral foam, pinholders, or chicken wire provide much-needed stability. They allow you to place stems exactly where you want them and hold flowers in position for best effect.

Mechanics

Experiment with some or all of the following mechanics in future arrangements.

Floral Foams. Perhaps the most widely used mechanic, floral foam bricks come in two forms, for either fresh or dried flower arranging. The bricks used for arranging fresh flowers absorb water and stems can be stuck in place anywhere in the brick for support. You can cut the bricks to fit any container. Use waterproof floral tape fastened to the edges of the container and across the top of the foam to hold it in place. (The container must be dry when you fasten the tape to it.) For best results, soak the foam for several hours in water before arranging flowers; it takes time for water to soak in, and sticking stems in dry foam can cause them to wilt.

Floral foam can be reused, so don't throw it away after a single use. After your arrangement has passed its prime, remove the spent flowers, taking care not to break the foam apart. Then store foam wet in a plastic bag if you'll be using it within a few days; otherwise, store it dry. When reusing, don't place new flowers in old stem holes in the foam. Air pockets there could stop the flow of water up the stem.

Pinholders. These are small, heavy implements that have round, oval, square, or rectangular metallic bases with many closely set pins molded into them. They're used primarily in low or flat containers such as those used in Japanese and contemporary arrangements, because they can be concealed in small containers. Secure the pinholder to its container with waterproof floral clay. Remember that container, pinholder, and clay must be dry when you fasten them together, to remain tightly in place.

Grid Mechanics. Chicken wire, the best known grid mechanic, is often used to hold flowers in position in large vases. To use chicken wire, cut a square of wire and fold the edges to fit tightly inside the mouth of the vase. Hold wire in place with waterproof floral tape. (The container must be dry when you fasten the tape to it.) You can also use waterproof floral tape to create grids over wide-mouthed vases, helping flowers to stay more upright.

Other Mechanics. Use marbles, pebbles, gravel, shells, or sand as mechanics by filling the container and using them to support flowers. These materials can provide interesting highlights to arrangements when used in clear or colored glass containers. Use clear marbles if you don't want mechanics to be so easily seen.

You can also design arrangements without mechanics. Flower and foliage stems, along with twiggy branches stuck in the mouth of the container, will hold flowers in their artistic poses.

Wiring

For most arrangements, wiring isn't necessary, but for some styles—especially formal ones—you may want to strengthen or bend a stem so it stays in position. To wire a bloom, insert the end of a piece of floral wire into the flower head. Then loosely wrap the remaining wire down around the stem. An alternative method used with some types of flowers is to guide the wire from the head down through the stem; this technique hides the wire and does not deter water flow.

STYLING PRINCIPLES

Whether you're planning a flower garden or making a flower arrangement, there are some basic design principles that will help you create a pleasing design.

Balance

Flowers have visual weight of size and color that must be balanced in a pleasing manner if an arrangement is to be attractive. For example, the visual weight may be distributed evenly throughout the bouquet or may be used at the base of an arrangement to provide a stable foundation. Balance is important in designing an arrangement regardless of the shape or style you've selected. Even though some styles are not symmetrical, all should be balanced. Otherwise, the arrangement will look top-heavy or lopsided. In applying these principles, the general rule is to place flowers with more visual weight closer to the focal point of the arrangement. Other, less weighty flowers can be used to lead out and away from the center.

Flower Color. Generally, dark and bright colors carry more weight than light colors. Dark colored flowers, such as maroon tulips or deep purple bearded iris, or bright colors, such as brilliant orange marigolds or flaming pink peonies, have more weight than blooms of equivalent size in light colors such as white, lilac, or pale yellow. Try to balance the distribution of each throughout the arrangement. An arrangement with large, brilliantly colored blooms at the top and white or other light flowers at the bottom will look top-heavy; one with dark flowers all to one side will look lopsided.

Dark colors can also be used to add visual weight to the base of an arrangement to add stability. Intersperse light colors throughout a bouquet to reflect more light and add an airy effect. This will also break up heavy masses of color.

Flower Size. Of course, large flowers have a heavier appearance, or visual weight, than small flowers. Try to avoid the top-heavy look of an arrangement with large flowers at the top and smaller, more delicate-looking flowers beneath. (If you want to repeat the color of a large flower at the very top of an arrangement, use a bud or partially opened flower that won't "weigh" as much.) You can use several small flowers to balance a larger one. Large flowers are effective when used to create visual weight near the center of an arrangement. Increase the visual weight of small flowers by allowing them to protrude farther from the center of the arrangement than large flowers. Small flowers often are used as fillers in arrangements—they're interspersed throughout the arrangement to add a feathery touch and delicate color.

Flower Shape. You'll also want to balance the many different shapes of the flowers in the arrangement. Use tall, spiky flowers to direct the eye outward, by placing them around the outside of a bouquet. Or use them to make a flourish at the tips of a design, making the arrangement "reach." Round, denser flowers draw the eye toward the center of the arrangement.

Flower Texture. Finely textured flowers add an airy quality to bouquets; coarser flowers give the arrangement a more solid appearance. In most cases, it's best to intersperse the various textures you're using so that they are distributed evenly throughout the bouquet. However, you can also use texture to create an accent. For example, seed heads of ornamental grasses can be used to create an attractive plume in an arrangement.

Proportion

An arrangement is said to be in proportion when its scale is in good relationship with its surroundings. This means that the different elements of an arrangement—flowers, foliage, and container—should all go well together and create a harmonious composition. A huge bouquet in a tiny container would be out of proportion just as would an arrangement mixing only 3-inch-wide zinnias with tiny tufts of baby's-breath. Mix a variety of sizes of flowers and foliage, and choose a container that is appropriate in size and style to the flowers you're using.

Repetition

Repeating one element in a design helps unify an arrangement and create a cohesive whole. You can

Continued ➡

repeat particular flowers—red zinnias, for example—or repeat a color using many different flowers all of the same or closely related colors, such as yellow marigolds, yarrow, and chrysanthemums. You can also repeat specific combinations of flowers throughout a bouquet, or repeat lines in a geometrical arrangement.

Styles and Shapes

Floral designers use many different styles and shapes of arrangements to suit various tastes. An arrangement can have an airy, informal style, with flowers gathered in a loose bouquet—a handful of mixed wildflowers placed in a vase, for example. Formal arrangements tend to have a more compact and regular style—such as a low composition for the center of a dining room table.

There are eight traditional shapes for arrangements: round, triangular, L-shaped, crescent, horizontal, contemporary vertical, traditional vertical, and Hogarth or S-curved. Some shapes are particularly suitable for certain kinds of occasions. The horizontal arrangement, for example, is the best choice for a centerpiece on a formal dining table. This low arrangement won't interfere with conversation across the table.

Whatever shape arrangement you're making, start by deciding where to put the center of your design. This will be the imaginary source from which the flowers appear to grow. When you place flowers in the container, aim stem tips at this focal point to give the bouquet a more natural appearance. As you work with the flowers, be sure to remove foliage that would be below the water line.

How to Make a Flower Arrangement

A simple round arrangement makes an excellent centerpiece for informal dining. You can create a compact, formal Colonial-style mound of flowers, or a colorful, loose, informal array of your garden favorites. Whatever the style, the round arrangement is a good choice for learning floral design. Just follow the steps listed here.

1. Begin by preparing the container for designing. Cut a piece of wet floral foam to fit snugly in the container you've selected. Then fix it in place with two strips of floral adhesive tape. (Or use a pinholder secured with clay instead.) Fill the container with water. Place the container on a lazy Susan so that you can rotate it with ease while designing to view the arrangement from all sides.

2. In a round arrangement, the focal point is the center of the foam block or pinholder. Aim your stem tips toward this point. Start by placing some of the foliage you've gathered to cover the foam base.

3. Place the largest flowers next. Position some very close to the focal point and some farther away at various distances out and up from the center, roughly outlining the round shape of the arrangement. Check to make sure the arrangement is balanced, with visual weight evenly distributed throughout the bouquet.

4. Create contrast by adding linear material such as tall, spiky flowers, seed heads of ornamental grasses, and twigs or berry branches alongside the first few flowers placed in the center.

5. Define the roundness further by filling in large gaps with medium-size flowers and foliage.

6. Check to make sure the floral foam is covered with foliage.

7. Round out the bouquet by filling any spaces with small, dainty flowers. Baby's-breath (*Gypsophilia* spp.) makes a good filler for this purpose.

Making a Dried Arrangement

The steps are almost reversed in making a dried arrangement. You may need to use floral wire to strengthen the stems of dried flowers, or wire small clusters of flowers together and insert them all together. First, cover the mechanics with sheet moss, which is available from floral suppliers. Then define the round outline with small filler material such as dried baby's-breath or statice. Build the arrangement by adding medium-size flowers and then large flowers. Last, carefully place the linear material such as ornamental grass seed heads or dried spikes of lavender for accents to soften the edges.

How to Press Flowers

Pressing is one of the best ways to preserve flowers and retain them as treasured keepsakes, whether they're from your wedding bouquet or a child's walk in the woods. You can use pressed flowers to make a variety of decorative items such as pictures, candles, frames, stationery, cards, and bookmarks. These items can hold their color and artistic value longer than dried flower arrangements, wreaths, or potpourri.

Selecting Plant Material

You can gather an abundance of materials for pressing in meadows and forests, or you may already have plenty of flowers and foliage in your garden. Choose flowers with heads that will flatten well. Flowers with simple shapes such as violets are easier to press than large, trumpet-shaped lilies, for example. Various leaves, skeletonized or fresh, take nicely to pressing and add a fine contrast to colorful flowers. You can also press grasses, herbs, tree leaves, and ferns. Try pressing plants and flowers in different stages of growth: fronds and fully developed ferns; flowers and their buds. For large, double flowers such as peonies or roses, try pressing individual petals and recreating the "flower" by arranging the separate petals in your compositions. Don't be afraid to experiment. In addition to the materials listed above, try mosses and lichens or even slices of fruits and vegetables. With any new material, it's a good idea to jot down notes about what steps you take as you discover what works for you.

Harvest plant material when it is dry and stems are full of water. The best picking time is on a dry day in the late morning. Press your gatherings shortly after cutting, or keep them in a container of water until you're ready to press them. Remember not to press flowers when wet or wilted.

The Flower Press

You don't need any elaborate supplies to experiment with pressing flowers. Start with a heavy, hardcover book or a telephone directory for a press. Place the materials you're pressing between sheets of blotting paper (available in art stores) to prevent ink from staining the flowers—and moisture from the flowers from staining the book—then insert them between the pages of the book. Stack heavy books or bricks on top of the book press for extra weight.

You can construct a sturdier press from plywood. A plywood press enables you to apply more pressure to the flowers, quickening the entire process and giving better results. Cut two pieces of heavy gauge plywood to equal dimensions; rectangles that will accommodate a folded sheet of newspaper—about 14 by 16 inches—are ideal. Drill a hole in each corner, then use long bolts with wing nuts to connect the two boards at each of the four corners. Use the wing nuts to tighten and loosen the press to adjust pressure.

Plant material is pressed between the plywood boards in sandwiches of absorbent paper such as recycled paper or newsprint and blotting paper.

First, place a layer of absorbent paper on the board—several folded sheets of newspaper are ideal. Next, put down a layer of blotting paper. Arrange your flowers on the blotting paper. Try to use as much space on the blotting paper as possible when spreading out the flowers, but don't overlap the specimens—they'll stick together. Arrange flowers so that you'll end up with a variety of stem curves, as well as open flower faces and profiles, so you'll have plenty of choice for your compositions. It's best to keep all of the same type of flower, or at least all of the same color, in one layer, so you'll be able to find them easily. You may even want to label the layer. After you've arranged the flowers, add another piece of blotting paper, several more sheets of newsprint or absorbent paper, and then more blotting paper and another layer of flowers. Make as many layers as you want, as long as the corner bolts that hold the plywood pieces together will span the depth.

For best results, keep your press in a warm, dry place, because too much moisture in the environment may promote mold to form. After the first few days of pressing, change the absorbent paper between layers, but leave the blotting paper intact so you don't disturb your flowers. Check for wetness periodically for the remainder of the pressing process. Keeping the paper dry and pressure strong will quicken the drying process for most plant materials and yield more vivid colors. (Very succulent materials, however, require less pressure but more frequent paper changes.)

Materials are dry when they're crisp to the touch—this should take at least two weeks. Store your dried flowers in the press until you're ready to use them.

Making a Pressed Flower Picture

Creating a pressed flower picture is like painting one. Use the flowers as brushstrokes of color and texture; leaves as background. You can create bouquets or depict scenes with dried flowers, and it's easy to rearrange the dried materials until you have a composition that pleases you.

1. Begin your picture by choosing a paper or fabric background. The background should be simple and not overpower your picture—a sheet of mat board is fine. The background should contrast with the flowers to play up

Continued ➡

their colors. For example, use a dark background if you'll be working with mostly light flowers.

2. Cut the background to the size and shape of your frame. If you're using paper or fabric, mount it with spray adhesive on a piece of mat board or foam core. Spray adhesive, unlike regular white glue, won't leave bumps on the background surface.

3. Start building your picture by putting down the larger backdrop flowers and leaves. These can be skeletonized leaves, fern fronds, long flowers, and leaves. Move the delicate plant material carefully with forceps or tweezers.

4. Next, arrange the bolder, more colorful flowers that will form the center of your arrangement. Layer some of these over the stems of backdrop elements. (Don't forget, unless you plan to frame with a mat, the finished picture must be flat. You may need to cut away the plant parts that won't be seen.)

5. Position small, dainty flowers for accent, and cover any unsightly stems with pressed leaves, lichens, or moss.

6. To assemble the picture permanently once you've created an arrangement that pleases you, turn the arrangement upside down or sketch it so you'll remember how all the elements were arranged. To turn upside down, cover it with a piece of heavy cardboard, hold tightly, and turn. Then fasten down the elements of your design one at a time, starting with the background material. Use rubber cement or water-soluble white craft glue that dries clear. Use a toothpick to dab tiny amounts on the backs of flowers and foliage. Let the glue dry overnight. Then cover your picture with glass and frame it.

Drying Flowers

Arrangements, wreaths, and other projects made from dried flowers have nearly universal appeal. Fortunately, drying flowers is easy and requires little more than adequate storage space and an abundance of plant materials. Many gardeners only think of drying annual flowers such as cockscomb (*Celosia* spp.), strawflower (*Helichrysum bracteatum*), and gomphrena (*Gomphrena globosa*) in the late summer or fall. But there are flowers suitable for drying all seasons of the year, in your garden and in the meadows and forests around your home. For example, daffodils and tulips dry well in desiccants such as silica gel. Pussy willow is another early spring feature that is easy to dry. In spring and summer, try drying blooms of ornamental onions (*Allium* spp.), astilbe (*Astilbe* spp.), and yarrow (*Achillea* spp.), all of which are easy to air-dry. In fall, ornamental grasses make wonderful additions to dried bouquets. Also try ripened seed heads from weeds, perennials such as blue false indigo *Baptisia australis*), twigs, and vines. Don't be afraid to experiment with many different types of plant materials.

The traditional way to dry flowers is to air-dry them in bunches. The fragrance and nostalgic charm of flower bunches suspended from a drying rack are just as enjoyable as the dried blossoms and grasses will be in an arrangement later. Although air-drying is still popular, desiccants have widened the range of flowers that can be dried successfully and microwave drying has shortened the process to a matter of minutes or hours, not days or weeks. Regardless of the technique you choose, there are a few pointers that apply to all of them.

TIPS FOR SUCCESS

- Don't harvest flowers or other plant material when the weather is cloudy and damp or the plants are wet. If you should find a few hidden drops of dew on material you've harvested, use the edge of a paper towel to gently absorb the water before drying.

- Don't harvest plant material that is wilted. If you can't dry cut material immediately, stand it in water in a cool, dark place until you can get to it.

- Select the most perfectly formed flowers you can find; drying will accentuate any flaws.

- Experiment with flowers at various stages of development—blooms often open further as they dry. But don't pick flowers which have been fully open for several days, as they're more likely to turn brown and shatter.

- Keep a notebook to jot down what works and what doesn't—what you harvested, what stage of development it had reached, how you dried it, and other methods you'd like to try to improve your results.

- If you've a specific arrangement in mind, dry perhaps twice as much material as you think you'll need. Then you'll not be caught short if some flowers do not dry perfectly or are damaged in storage.

- To protect plant material from shattering or reabsorbing moisture from the air, spray after drying with matte-finish plastic craft sealer or hair spray.

- Flowers dried with silica gel can reabsorb moisture. You'll need to display them in an airtight container, such as a Victorian bell jar, or store them until the air is less humid, such as during the winter heating season.

- If you're not using them right away, store flowers in flat boxes in one or two layers separated by tissue paper so they can be easily located later without damaging your handiwork. Add a few mothballs to repel rodents and moths. Silica-gel-dried flowers should be stored in an airtight container with silica gel or dry sand in the bottom.

AIR-DRYING

Air-drying is a simple method for preserving large quantities of plant material. Results differ from plant to plant. Some such as cockscomb (*Celosia* spp.) will dry nearly perfectly, with attractive form and brilliant color. The colors of some blossoms will fade, but these can be used to impart an antique aura to nosegays or arrangements.

Flowers with fat, moist blossoms or many petals such as peonies (*Paeonia* spp.) generally do not air-dry well. They drop their petals, fade, or shrivel past recognition. (See "Plants for Air-Drying" below for a list of the flowers to start with for each of the methods described below. You can

---

Plants for Air-Drying

There are several ways to air-dry plant material, and some plants are better suited to one method than another. Here are lists of plants suited to each method.

Plants to Hang Upside Down

   Achillea spp. (yarrow)

   Allium spp. (ornamental onions and chives)

   Ammobium alatum (winged everlasting)

   Armeria maritima (thrift)

   Artemisia spp. (artemisia or wormwood)

   Carthamus tinctorius (safflower)

   Celosia spp. (cockscomb)

   Delphinium spp. (delphinium or larkspur)

   Limonium spp. (statice)

   Lunaria annua (money plant or honesty)

   Salvia spp. (sage)

   Sedum spectabile (sedum)

   Solidago spp. (goldenrod)

   Tagetes spp. (marigold)

Other materials that can be dried hanging upside down include seed heads of *Clematis* spp., Oriental poppies (*Papaver* spp.), and coneflowers (*Echinacea* spp. and *Rudbeckia* spp.); seedpods of many plants including blue false indigo (*Baptisia australis*); rosebuds; cattails (*Typha* spp.); and branches of pussy willow and knotweed (*Polygonum* spp.). Blooms of globe amaranth (*Gomphrena globosa*), strawflower (*Helichrysum bracteatum*), and everlasting (*Helipterum* spp.) are best wired before they're hung to dry for the stems aren't strong when dry and tend to droop.

Plants to Dry Right Side Up

In addition to the plants listed here, grains and ornamental grasses also can be dried right side up.

   Echinops spp. (globe thistle)

   Gypsophila paniculata (baby's-breath)

   Physalis alkekengi (Chinese-lantern plant)

   Cotinus coggygria (smoke tree)

Dry the following plants right side up, but set the stems in ½ inch of water: *Calluna* spp. (heather), *Hydrangea* spp. (hydrangea), and *Moluccella laevis* (bells-of-Ireland). Florist's proteas (*Protea* spp.) and other related florist's flowers, including *Banksia* spp., *Hakea* spp., and *Grevillea* spp., can also be dried in this way.

Dry with Support

Slip the stems of the following plants through screens or hardware cloth to provide support for the flower heads.

   Anethum graveolens (dill)

   Daucus carota var. *carota* (Queen-Anne's-lace, wild carrot)

   Foeniculum (fennel)

   Heracleum spp. (hogweed)

   Leontopodium alpinum (edelweiss)

Dry Flat on a Screen

Many plant materials can be spread on screens or layers of absorbent paper for drying. These include dock (*Rumex acetosa*), bamboos and grasses (which can also be dried by hanging or upright), fungi, twigs, and sprigs of lavender (*Lavandula* spp.).

Continued ➡

experiment with other flowers as you become more experienced.)

The ideal spot for air-drying is a dark room with warm, dry, gently moving air. The dryness of the air will affect whether the process takes a week or three weeks. Consider an attic, dry basement, garage, shed, or closet.

Many flowers can be hung upside down to dry. Strip foliage from their stems and make small bunches of them. Put no more than five in a bunch, and stagger flower heads so they don't touch. Make a slip knot with a string or rubber band down toward the stem ends to hold them tightly together. Then hang them from hooks, pegs, coat hangers, or racks that are either suspended from the ceiling, along walls, or free-standing.

Some flowers and plants dry better when placed right side up in a widemouthed container. Spread the stems out so they aren't crowded or crushed, and so you'll be able to separate them easily. Try drying some of the plants you normally hang to dry, to create a pleasing curve in the stem. Other plants should be dried in a similar container, standing in ½ inch of water.

Round, flat flower heads need support to dry flat. Slip stems through a screen, such as ¼-inch hardware cloth, letting heads rest faceup on the screen. Some materials are best laid flat to dry on a wood-framed screen that lets air circulate beneath. Or use an absorbent surface such as newspaper; turn occasionally during the drying process.

DESICCANTS

Drying agents, or desiccants, not only speed dry as they absorb water from petals and leaves but also expand the range of flowers that you can preserve. The flowers dried by this method much more closely resemble fresh flowers in color and form.

Of the commercially available desiccants, silica gel works fastest. It now comes very finely ground for use with flowers and can be sifted into blooms to encourage them to dry quickly without leaving bumps from coarse grains on the petals. Silica gel is available from hobby or craft stores, florists, and garden centers, as well as mail-order suppliers. Although it's expensive, it can be reused indefinitely. It usually comes with blue "color indicator" crystals that change color when the silica gel is saturated with moisture. To reactivate it by drying it out, spread it on a flat baking pan and heat it in a 250°F oven until the original color returns.

Drying flowers with desiccants such as silica gel is easy. Just follow these steps.

1. Select an airtight container, such as a cookie tin. Since different flowers dry at different rates, plan on using a separate container for each type of flower.

2. Gather flowers and cut stems to 1 inch or so in length. If you expect to need wire stems for arranging, it's a good idea to wire them now. To wire a bloom, insert the end of the wire into the flower head. Loosely wrap the remaining wire down around the stem. An alternative method used with some types of flowers is to guide the wire from the head down through the stem.

3. Spread a ½-inch layer of silica gel on the bottom of your container. Then set the blossoms on the silica gel, bending wired stems out of the way as needed. Set daisy like flowers facedown; complex, many-petaled flowers like

roses or carnations faceup. Space the blossoms so they don't touch one another.

4. With a spoon or measuring cup, gently pour silica gel around the blossoms, first filling in support underneath each bloom and then making sure all crevices in the bloom are filled. Cover with another ½-inch layer of silica gel. You can make additional layers of flowers if the container is deep enough.

5. Tightly close the container and label it with date and contents.

6. If you're drying simple flowers such as small daisies, open the container in about two days and gently shake it until a few petals appear. If they feel like crisp paper, carefully pour off silica gel into another container and remove flowers. For fleshy or more complex, many-petaled flowers, wait several days before checking.

7. After the flowers have dried, partially refill the container with a layer of silica gel and insert flower stems up to, but not covering, the petals. Close the container and leave for another two to four days to finish drying. This is especially necessary with more complex, many-petaled flowers, like roses.

8. Check the blooms regularly, and remove them when they are fully dry. With a small camel's hair paintbrush, dust off any clinging silica gel. Protect blooms from shattering with a drop of clear-drying glue at the flower's center and base.

9. Keep a record of drying times you use for each flower type so you develop a sense of what works best. Flowers immersed in silica gel for too long will become overly dry and be very brittle, so you'll want to get it just right.

MICROWAVE DRYING

Microwave drying is not only speedy for flowers, it also solves the problem of how to preserve foliage, which shrivels or changes color when dried by any other method.

You can dry autumn leaves, fern fronds, or other foliage in your microwave. First, to protect the microwave, put a cup of water at the back of the oven. Replace the water each time you run the microwave. Fold a paper towel in half and put the leaves to be dried inside it. They should not overlap. Place the paper towel in the microwave and place a microwaveable dish on top to prevent the leaves from curling. Cook two minutes on high power, then remove the leaves. If they are dry and crisp, they are done. If they seem almost dry, overnight air-drying will most likely finish them. If they've lost color or appear too dry, try a new batch and less cooking time. Use a dry paper towel for each new batch of leaves.

You can also dry flowers in the microwave using silica gel. Dry one flower at a time, using a small microwaveable container that is about 3 inches taller than the flower. Put in a layer of silica gel, insert the blossom, then carefully cover the flower, filling in all nooks and crannies with the silica. (Don't wire blooms before putting them in the microwave. If you need to wire them, do it immediately after they're done, before they cool.) Add a layer on top, leaving about 2 inches of space between the top of the gel and the top of the container.

Place a cup of water at the back of the microwave, and replace the water each time you do a new flower.

To eliminate guesswork, place a microwave thermometer in the silica so it does not touch

sides or bottom of the container. Put the container in the microwave and heat on high for 30 to 60 seconds at a time, until the thermometer reads 200° to 220°F. Use a rotating rack or turn the container every 30 seconds. Remove the container from the microwave with thermometer still in place. Allow silica to cool until the temperature reads 70° to 80°F before removing the flower. Keep a record of cooking times and results for various flower types so you can make adjustments if needed. If flowers turn beige, reduce cooking time the next try.

After the flowers have dried, carefully sift away the silica gel. Insert flower stems up to, but not covering, the petals, in another larger container with a fresh layer of silica gel. Close the container and leave the flowers for another two to four days to finish drying. Then clean the flowers with a small paintbrush and spray with sealer.

Making a Dried Flower Wreath

Wreaths are a delightful way to decorate doors or bring nature into your home. They also make treasured gifts or keepsakes, especially when the flowers are from your own garden.

There are a variety of ways to make a wreath, partly because of the many choices for wreath bases. You can start with a wire frame and cover it with small bunches of dried baby's-breath (*Gypsophila* spp.), statice (*Limonium* spp.), or dried 'Silver King' Artemisia (*Artemisia ludoviciana* var. *albula*) for filler. Wrap floral wire around the stems of the bunches and wire them to the frame. Continue adding and wrapping bunches until the entire frame is covered. For a quick wreath, intersperse small bouquets of mixed dried flowers for the bunches of base material as you go.

You can also start with a base made of straw or Spanish moss, both of which can be purchased at craft stores or garden centers. Start with a background filler—as with a wire frame, baby's-breath, statice, or Artemisia are fine—and insert it stem by stem until the entire base has been covered. Then add accent flowers to dress it up. Small bouquets of colorful dried flowers wired together—plus dried herbs for fragrance—are easy to add by poking them in place. Or you can fasten them with hairpin-shaped floral pins or bent pieces of wire. You can add just a few bright accents and intersperse them with stems of more neutral colors. Keep in mind that you want a harmonious composition of color and texture.

You can also make a wreath base from trailing vines, such as grapevine and trumpet vine. Harvest the vines in summer or fall when they are pliable, and use them immediately so they don't become brittle. Trim off leaves and green growth. Begin the wreath by looping a circle with the vine in the desired size for your wreath. Continue making circles, weaving the ends in and out around the initial loop. Once you've woven one vine in place, you can add another until the wreath is as thick as you desire. Tuck the ends in when you're finished. If you like the look of dried grape tendrils poking out in all directions, save some lengths of vine with attractive tendrils until the end, then weave or wire them in place. Once you've created the vine base, add accent materials by wiring or using hot glue to fasten them in place. Don't plan on covering the entire base with dried flowers, since the vine wreath adds an attractive, woodsy touch.

Attaching Flowers

There are several ways to attach flowers to a wreath. It's generally easiest to wire small bunches of filler or background material together and

Continued ➡

The Best Herbs for Indoors

Basil (*Ocimum Basilicum*): annual, to 2 ft. tall. Needs full sun; 6.0 optimum pH. Give basil well-drained soil, and water whenever the soil surface begins to dry. Harvest by snipping the growing tips frequently to keep plants bushy and prevent flowering. Prefers daytime temperatures in the 70s and nighttime temperatures in the 60s. Don't let the temperature drop below 50°F. Plants will remain productive for three to six months if prevented from flowering. Try handsome compact cultivars such as 'Spicy Globe' and 'Green Globe'.

Bay (*Laurus nobilis*): perennial tree or shrub, to 40 ft. tall (though not indoors). Needs full or part sun; 6.2 optimum pH. A slow grower, bay will take years to reach 2 ft. in a pot. Allow the soil to dry between waterings. Pot up one size in the spring. Prefers daytime temperatures in the 60s and nighttime temperatures in the 50s, but can take temperatures in the low 40s. Allow plants plenty of room for good air circulation. Harvest by cutting off individual older leaves as needed or to dry.

Chives (*Allium Schoenoprasum*): perennial, to 1½ ft. tall. Needs full sun; 6.0 optimum pH. Prefers daytime temperatures in the 70s and nighttime temperatures in the 60s, but can take temperatures in the low 40s. Water when the soil begins to dry, and give plants room for good air circulation. Repot whenever plant looks crowded (you can divide clumps and pot up individually as well). Plants will live several years in pots. Harvest by cutting off individual leaf blades to within 1 inch of the soil surface. Because chives makes such slow growth from seed, it's best to buy a pot that's already established. Or divide and pot up a clump outdoors in the fall; leave the pot outside until the foliage has been killed back by frost, then bring the pot inside where it will make vigorous new growth.

Dill (*Anethum graveolens*): annual, to 3 ft. tall. Needs full sun; 6.0 optimum pH. Prefers daytime temperatures in the 60s and nighttime temperatures in the 50s, but can take temperatures in the mid-40s. Give plants room for good air circulation, and water whenever the soil surface begins to dry. Sow directly and thin to three seedlings per 6-in. pot or five per 8-in. pot; plants may need staking. Productive for two to four months indoors; harvest by cutting individual lower leaves once plant reaches 1 ft. tall. Dill is a difficult plant indoors. The best cultivars for pot culture are 'Aroma' and 'Bouquet.'

Garlic chives (*Allium tuberoosum*): perennial, to 2 ft. tall. Needs full sun; 6.0 optimum pH. Culture as for chives. A beautiful plant, with straplike, dark green foliage and dusters of pure white star-shaped flowers that smell like roses.

Ginger (*Zingiber officinale*): perennial, to 3 ft. tall. Needs shade. Ginger enjoys high temperatures, high humidity, and moist soil. Plant a fragment of rhizome—underground stem—with "eyes" on it in a roomy, shallow pot. When the rhizomes fill the pot, harvest by lifting them.

Marjoram (*Origanum Majorana*): perennial, to 1 ft. tall. Needs full sun; 6.9 optimum pH. Prefers daytime temperatures in the 70s and nighttime temperatures in the 60s, but can take temperatures in the high 40s. Marjoram needs good drainage and can be kept on the dry side. Allow plenty of room for air circulation. Cut plants back often to maintain bushy habit, as they are rapid growers. Potted plants remain productive for one to two years; after they become woody, root new 4-in. tip cuttings. Heavenly fragrance is pervasive—use sparingly in cooking.

Mints (*Mentha* spp.): perennial, to 2 ft. tall. Needs full or part sun; 6.5 optimum pH. Mints prefer daytime temperatures in the 60s and nighttime temperatures in the 50s, but can take temperatures in the low 40s. Give them good air circulation and high humidity, and water when the soil surface begins to dry. When crowded, repot into a container wider than it is deep, or divide into sections and pot each section. Mints remain productive for six months or more in pot culture. Harvest by trimming or cutting individual stems. Peppermint (*M. X piperita*), spearmint *M. spicata*), and pineapple mint *M. suaveolens* 'Variegata') make good pot plants.

Oregano (*Origanum vulgare*): perennial, to 1½ ft. tall. Needs full sun; 6.8 optimum pH. Prefers daytime temperatures in the 70s and nighttime temperatures in the 60s, but can take temperatures in the high 40s. Give plants good drainage and keep them on the dry side. Cut back often to contain spreading habit and improve air circulation. To insure getting culinary oregano, buy plants or take 4-in. tip cuttings. Plants will remain productive in pots for one to two years. When they become woody, replace them.

Parsley (*Petroselinum crispum*): biennial, to 1½ ft. tall. Needs full or part sun; 6.0 optimum pH. Grows best between 60° and 65°F, but can take temperatures in the low 40s. Can be grown from seed; germination takes 9 to 21 days. Cover seed with ¼ in. of soil. Sow in late spring in a big container—a 3-gallon bucket is ideal. Set the pot outdoors and keep it watered until fall. Bring it indoors before the first fall frost, giving it cool temperatures and plenty of sun. Plant several to have plenty through spring. Harvest parsley by cutting the outer leaves, leaving the central rosette to produce new growth. The fine flavor of flat-leaf (Italian) parsley is stronger than that of curly parsley, but both make handsome pot plants. Parsley remains productive for six to nine months in pot culture.

Rosemary (*Rosmarinus officinalis*): perennial, to 6 ft. tall. Needs full or part sun; 6.8 optimum pH. Prefers daytime temperatures in the 70s and nighttime temperatures in the 60s, but can take temperatures in the low 40s. Don't let plants dry out completely or they'll die. Prune or pinch back frequently to maintain bushy habit. Propagate by 4-in. tip cuttings. Rosemary needs good drainage. If the needlelike evergreen leaves turn brown, the plant is being overwatered. Woody growth and yellowed leaves are signs that the plant is pot-bound.

Sage (*Salvia officinalis*): perennial, to 2½ ft. tall. Needs full sun; 6.4 optimum pH. Common culinary sage has spear-shaped, pungent, pebbly, gray-green foliage and blue flowers. Purple sage, with purple foliage; tricolor sage, with purple, white and green variegated foliage; and pineapple sage (*S. elegans*), with pineapple-scented foliage and red flower spikes, are also handsome pot plants. Sage must have good drainage but can withstand infrequent waterings. Prefers daytime temperatures in the 70s and nighttime temperatures in the 60s, but can take temperatures in the low 40s. Allow plenty of room for air circulation. Sage remains productive for one to two years in pots. Grow from tip cuttings. Prune regularly to maintain bushy shape. Be sure to have enough on hand for stuffing the Thanksgiving and Christmas turkeys!

Savory, winter (*Satureja montana*): perennial, to 1½ ft. tall. Needs full sun; 6.7 optimum pH. Winter savory prefers daytime temperatures in the 70s and nighttime temperatures in the 60s, but can take temperatures in the low 40s. Water when the soil surface begins to dry, and give plants plenty of room for air circulation. Prune regularly to keep plants productive. Winter savory will remain productive in pots for one to two years.

---

then insert them. If you're using a straw or Spanish-moss-based frame, you can wire flowers to wooden floral picks, which come with a short piece of wire attached just for this purpose. Just gather a few stems together, wrap the wire around them, and poke them in place.

To wire with floral wire and corsage tape, first fold a piece of floral wire alongside the stem with the fold at the base of the flower head. Wind half of the wire around the stem to secure it. The second half of the wire remains long, to serve as the stem. Finish by wrapping corsage tape down the length of the wire, beginning at the flower head. Corsage tape will seal in place as you stretch and twirl it as you wrap. Be sure to cut wire stems

to appropriate lengths so they will be held tightly in the base without protruding.

You can also glue flowers in place with either white craft glue that dries clear or hot glue. Nuts, berries, herbs, seedpods, and other materials may also be glued in place to accent your wreath.

Herbs as Houseplants
Claire Kowalchik and William H. Hylton

Herbs work hard as houseplants. They're not content to be merely decorative, like a fern or an ivy. In addition to good looks, herbs give you flavor, fragrance, or both. Running your hand

over a piny rosemary or pungent, clove-scented thyme as you pass by can bring a room to life. And nibbling a leaf of fresh mint, basil, or chives can bring you to life.

Visually, there's an herb for every taste. Some are downright cute—a little mound of 'Spicy Globe' basil or a mat of fluffy lemon thyme covered with pink flowers. Others are more stately, like a potted bay shrub with its dark, glistening leaves and dignified carriage. Some, like spearmint, with its ramrod stems and crisp, toothed foliage, and chives, with its clump of tubular stems, are positively architectural. And then there are those like rosemary, with fuzzy, white, arching branches covered with dark ever-

Continued ➡

green, needlelike leaves, and parsley, with its mossy curls of foliage, which are simply beautiful.

But why grow herbs indoors? There are plenty of convincing reasons if "because I like them" isn't good enough. If you're an apartment dweller, your home is probably your garden. If you want to grow herbs well, there's no place like home. For those of us who live outside the Deep South, winter puts an end to outdoor herb growing but not to our craving for fresh herbs. The plants may go dormant until spring, but our taste buds don't! And some perennials simply wouldn't make it over the winter in most of the country. Bay, for example, is expensive, slow-growing, and very temperature-sensitive. Rosemary, lemon verbena, tricolor sage, marjoram, and scented geraniums are other finicky—but wonderful—herbs. Unless you have more money than sense, you'd be well advised to pot them up and bring them in over the winter or to grow these in pots year-round.

If you have some extra space and a fluorescent light setup, winter is also an ideal time to root cuttings for spring transplanting. You can increase your stock of lemon verbena, rosemary, lavender, thyme, and scented geraniums. By spring, you'll have the makings of a whole herb garden—or a border or edging. No need to wonder if the mail-order plants will arrive all right or if the local nursery has that cultivar you particularly like.

To simplify things, we can divide "house-plant" herbs into two categories: herbs grown indoors all year, which are basically decorative and fragrant plants; and herbs grown indoors in winter, which are usually food plants.

Herbs All Year

If you're going to have a plant in your house all the time, it's got to look good. And it helps if it's not too demanding. If you're going to grow herbs indoors and you want them to look good, you've got to stop thinking of them as herbs—for a minute, anyway. Think of them as houseplants. How will they look together? Do some make a particularly effective grouping? How will they look in flower? What are you going to put them in? And where are you going to put them?

The first rule of thumb is: If you're growing a plant for its ornamental appeal, it must look nice. One way to do this is to put them in an attractive container—a window box, ornamental tub, or planter box. Trailing varieties often look well in hanging baskets. Another technique is to plant them individually in similar containers. Groups of plain clay pots or dark Japanese-style planters are visually effective and focus attention on the plants—their colors, shapes, and textures—rather than on the container. Carefully chosen baskets can add another dimension of texture without distracting from the herbs. But if you've always wanted to plant herbs in that huge brass pot with nymphs and mermaids all over it, do it. Just put it in another place, so the spotlight is on the planter, not on the clash between the planter and the clay pots all around it.

Another way to play with herbs is to group them according to some unifying characteristic: herbs with white or blue flowers, gray-leaved herbs, fragrant herbs. It's better to mix herbs of different growth habits, rather than having a forest of tall herbs in one corner, trailing herbs on the sideboard and end tables, and a cluster of miniatures across the room on a table by themselves. Mixing lets you see more of the plants.

You can also train myrtle and some cultivars of scented geranium into standards: dwarf "trees" with a single "trunk." Myrtle and other herbs also lend themselves to topiary and espalier; however, before you start turning out thyme turtles, you'd do well to read up on the techniques and make sure you're willing to devote the time and care needed to maintain these high-tech plants. It would be good, too, if you prepared a spot to showcase the results.

There's one more thing to bear in mind: Potted plants don't have to stay indoors forever. You can move your bay, lemon verbena, and rosemary onto the patio for a summer breather, or sink them and your scented geraniums—pots and all—into the flower bed. They're a snap to unearth again in the fall, without root loss or transplant shock. Just make sure they haven't gained a few bugs before you bring them back inside!

Herbs in Winter

If you're growing herbs specifically for winter, chances are some of those herbs will be culinary herbs. You may be bringing in a clump of chives or a rosemary, or a spring-planted pot of parsley or ginger. Or you may be rooting cuttings of perennials like mint, sage, and oregano in midsummer for the winter windowsill. Or you may be sowing seeds of dill, basil, and marjoram in late August for the plant table. But a goal every gardening cook probably has in mind is: fresh herbs for winter salads, stir fries, and sauces, right at your fingertips.

When growing herbs for the winter kitchen garden, there's one cardinal rule: Make sure you grow enough. One perky little parsley or bright green basil may cheer you up on a snowy morning, but it is unlikely to go far toward perking up winter salads or spaghetti. Here's where a plant table comes in handy. Most herbs need strong sunlight to grow and produce well, and space at south-facing windows is usually at a premium. Setting up fluorescent lights over a shelf or table adds more growing space, so you can grow a more realistic number of high-use plants: parsley, basil, dill, chives, oregano, and the mints. If you enjoy cooking and don't have an attached greenhouse, a winter plant table is practically indispensable. And it lets you save the pretty plants—marjoram, thyme, rosemary, and lemon balm—for the windows!

Culture

Growing herbs indoors means dealing with seven major aspects of plant culture: light, temperature, air circulation, soil, fertilization, water, and pests. There are also the techniques for bringing plants in and propagation. Because herbs are less tolerant than most houseplants—they insist on conditions being "just so"—it helps to review their needs before heading out to the nursery or garden. Nobody wants a winter's worth of pale, spindly, spider-mite-infested herb plants.

Light: Most herbs thrive on light—at least five hours of direct sunlight a day. (Exceptions are the mints, bay, parsley, rosemary, thyme, myrtle, and santolina, which can take partial shade; and ginger and lemon balm, which actually like shade.) Natural sunlight can be supplemented or replaced with fluorescent light. A two-tube, cool white fixture hung 6 to 8 inches above the herbs and left on for 14 to 16 hours a day will keep your plants bushy and productive. You can maximize natural exposure by putting shelves in your south-facing windows, but don't crowd plants in or you'll have circulation problems.

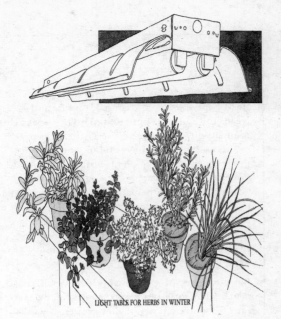

To make sure that windowsill plants get sufficient light, you can supplement the sun's energy with a fluorescent fixture mounted on wall brackets.

Don't forget to turn the plants on windowsills regularly. Turning keeps the plants shapely and makes sure all sides get enough light.

Temperature: Most herbs like temperatures on the cool side—daytime temperatures of 65°F and night temperatures of 60° or even 55°F. Bay, dill, and the mints are the most insistent on daytime temperatures in the 60s and night drops to the 50s, and parsley does best between 60° and 65°F day and night. The other common household herbs do fine with daytime temperatures in the 70s and night lows in the 60s. If your house is cool, most herbs can survive temperatures in the mid- to low 40s (though scented geraniums and basil can't take it below 50°F). Obviously, foliage pressed against a frozen windowpane will freeze and die. Move the plants away from the glass in freezing weather, or slip a sheet of paper between the plant and the pane.

Air circulation: Herbs are extremely sensitive to dry, stagnant air—the kind, unfortunately, in many tightly sealed, centrally heated houses. Stale air promotes fungal diseases and insect infestations. On the other hand, a blast of crisp winter air may be bracing to us, but it (or a constant draft) is anathema to herbs. Try to keep the air moving around the plants by cracking a window in an adjoining room or by opening doors for better cross-ventilation. Another preventive measure is to give the plants plenty of space so air can circulate around them. Don't crowd the pots, and don't let the foliage from neighboring plants touch! Finally, if the air is very dry, you can set the pots on pebble-lined trays filled with an inch or less of water. But make sure the pots are over—not in—the water.

Soil: Herbs in pots need a reasonably rich soil mix with good drainage. Some successful mixes are:

2 parts compost, 1 part vermiculite, and 1 part perlite
1 part sand and 1 part peat moss
1 part compost, 1 part sand, and 1 part perlite
7 parts loam, 3 parts peat moss, and 2 parts coarse sand
1 part potting soil, 1 part sand, and 1 part peat moss.

Experiment until you find a mix you're happy with. One word of warning: If you habitually have problems with plant diseases, you might be best off not using soil in your mixes. Or add sterilized soil if there's a source at hand.

On the subject of soil, be sure your plants have enough of it. No herb should be grown in a pot less than 4 inches in diameter; 6 inches is even better.

Continued ➔

For plants that spread by underground stems, like the mints and ginger, wide, shallow pots are ideal. And for herbs with long taproots, like bay and parsley, a deep pot or bucket is a necessity.

Fertilization: Fertilizing potted herbs involves a balancing act. You want to fertilize them enough to keep them productive but not so much that they get leggy and begin to lose their flavor. Once-a-month applications of seaweed or fish emulsion (which can smell pretty foul in a closed house, remember!) at half-strength should give them enough nutrients to keep growing.

Water: Herbs like regular waterings, but they're finicky. Waterlogged soil and pots standing in water tend to bring on root rot and other fungal diseases. Hence the need for a well-drained potting mix (leave the clay in the yard). Water most herbs thoroughly when the soil surface starts drying out. Let bay, marjoram, oregano, sage, and thyme dry out between waterings. But never let rosemary completely dry out—just one "dry spell" can kill it. The mints, lemon balm, ginger, and scented geraniums enjoy more moist conditions than their brethren. Always use room-temperature water so you don't shock the plants.

Pests: Herbs aren't attacked by pests often, but close, dry, indoor conditions can bring on infestations of spider mites, whiteflies, and aphids in succulent species, and scale on woody plants like bay, rosemary, and lemon verbena. Soap sprays can control spider mite, whitefly, and aphid attacks. To make such a spray, dissolve 1 to 2 tablespoons of a mild flaked soap like Ivory or Oxagon in 1 gallon of warm (not hot) water. Spray diligently once a week until the pests are brought under control. Be sure to coat the undersides of the foliage. Needless to say, wash the soapy residue off the leaves before adding them to food! Yellow sticky traps work well for whiteflies. Scale can be controlled by scraping off the insects or by daubing them weekly with alcohol-dipped cotton swabs. Isolate any infested plants, and if you can't control the infestation, get rid of them. This may seem drastic, but it's preferable to having an entire houseful of insect-ridden plants.

Bringing plants in: Perennial plants that won't survive the winter outside in most of the United States and Canada—rosemary, bay, lemon verbena, oregano, marjoram, camphor, and scented geraniums—must be brought indoors over the winter if they're to see another summer. Other perennials, such as chives, garlic chives, thyme, the mints, winter savory, and lavender, make the transition to indoor conditions fairly easily. When preparing to move plants inside for the winter, remember to acclimatize them first.

Dig the plants, causing as little root damage as possible, and pot them carefully. Then water the herbs and set them in a shady place outdoors for three days to a week so they can gradually adjust to the dual shocks of pot culture and decreased sunlight. Check the plants vigilantly for pests, and isolate them for a couple of weeks before mixing them in with your other houseplants, just in case an infestation has slipped by you. This shading-and-checking routine is necessary even when moving in plants that have spent the summer outdoors in their pots, like bay, rosemary, parsley, and lemon verbena.

The best time to pot most outdoor herbs is after the fall harvest and before the first frost. They should be safely indoors by the time frost strikes. Chives and garlic chives, however, benefit from induced dormancy before "coming in from the cold." Divide the clumps, pot them, and let them remain outside until frost kills the foliage. Then bring them in for a new burst of lush, stocky growth.

Propagation: Start annual seeds (such as basil and dill) as well as parsley and perennials that will come true from seed (marjoram and thyme, for example) in the same mix you plan to pot them in. Sow the seed in late August or early September, water the flats, cover them with plastic wrap, and put them where temperatures will drop no lower than 60°F. (The top of the refrigerator is warm and out of the way) When the seeds sprout, remove the plastic and move the flats into full sun. Keep the soil moist but not soggy. When seedlings have their second set of true leaves, transplant them to 4-inch pots, and when the first pots are outgrown, move the plants to 6-inch pots.

For cultivars that will not come true from seed or herbs like lemon balm that are difficult to germinate, start with plants or take cuttings. Rosemary, the mints, thyme, lavender, lemon verbena, scented geraniums, culinary oregano, and sage can be propagated by taking 4-inch tip cuttings, stripping off the lower leaves and sticking the stems in moist perlite. Take the cuttings two to three weeks before the first fall frost (or earlier; they take two to three months to root). If your home has especially low humidity, you can cover the flats with glass or plastic to promote higher moisture levels. Again, be sure to keep the perlite moist but not soggy.

CONTAINERS AND POTS

Container Gardens

Barbara W. Ellis

Growing Vegetables in Containers

Container gardening is more popular today than ever—and for good reason. It is a boon for apartment dwellers, a necessity for rooftop gardeners, and just plain fun even for those of us blessed with ample garden space. Raising flowering plants in containers has long been a favorite activity, and more and more gardeners are discovering the challenges and rewards of container vegetable gardening.

Vegetables and flowers can readily be grown in tubs, crocks, pots, barrels, sacks, baskets—nearly any vessel that is nontoxic and large enough to accommodate the plants and allow sufficient drainage. Containers may be decorative—half-barrels and wood planting tubs are both popular—or strictly practical. Some containers are especially designed for vegetable growing.

You can make a simple container by slitting plastic bags of soil mix and setting transplants directly into the bag. Or consider recycling baby bathtubs, leaky buckets, plastic milk jugs, and other containers that otherwise would help to clog a landfill. Whatever you choose, be sure there are holes in the bottom so that excess water drains away. Otherwise, your plants can easily become waterlogged and drown. Drainage holes also are important for flushing water through the soil to dissolve accumulated salts.

Almost any vegetable can be grown in containers, but the most popular are the salad vegetables, including lettuce, radishes, onions, cucumbers, and peppers. Carrots, beets, and other root crops will do well in containers as long as you provide sufficient rooting space. Cucumbers are particularly suited to hanging baskets; peppers and eggplant can be interplanted with flowering annuals. In response to the increasing popularity of container gardening, breeders have developed dwarf or compact cultivars of most common vegetables. Even watermelons can now be raised in 5-gallon containers.

Herbs grow well in smaller containers. Parsley and thyme are well suited for hanging baskets, where they may be interplanted with flowering annuals. Two-gallon tubs or baskets are large enough to support vigorously growing perennial herbs such as mint and rosemary. Eight- to 12-inch pots are sufficient for basil and lavender. And even 4- to 6-inch pots will support chives, dill, parsley, and thyme. A box planter under the kitchen window is a convenient place to grow chives, parsley, and other low-growing herbs so you can snip quickly while cooking.

A word to the wise: Be sure to pick a container that will be large enough to handle the mature plant. Transplanting can stress a plant, which will affect your harvest. Again, be sure that your containers have drainage holes.

KEYS TO SUCCESS

The keys to successful container vegetable growing are a good soil mix, adequate soil moisture, and a steady nutrient supply, along with some good basic gardening practices.

Trellised peas

Decorative pots of flowers screen buckets

Salad greens

Continued ➡

Soil

The soil mix should be light, airy, capable of holding moisture and nutrients, yet quick to drain. A common mixture is 1 part potting soil, 1 part compost, and 1 part sharp sand, with a little added bonemeal. A moe expensive variation of this mix substitutes vermiculite for the sand, producing a mix that weighs less but holds more moisture.

Water

Adequate soil moisture is critical. Summer heat dries soil mix in containers rapidly. Soil in wood and unglazed clay containers dries out more quickly than that in plastic or other nonporous containers. If your area has intensely hot summers, don't use dark-colored containers, which absorb heat more readily than those made of light colored materials. Wooden containers have an insulating effect and may help to keep roots cooler.

In general, you'll need to water all container plants daily in hot weather, not only to keep roots moist, but to help cool your plants and wash away accumulated salts.

Food

Vegetables in containers need more frequent feeding than those grown in the open garden. The most popular fertilizer is ordinary fish emulsion, although liquid seaweed is also suitable. Mix according to label directions and apply once a week. You can also feed container vegetables with home-made manure tea.

Training Standards

Visitors to formal gardens are often impressed upon seeing container-grown roses, geraniums, lantanas (*Lantana* spp.), and other woody shrubs that have been specially trained into treelike forms called standards. You can train standards for your own garden and enjoy them indoors or out, all year around, depending on your climate. The training takes patience and care, but is by no means a task for experts only.

The perfect candidate to be trained as a standard is a fast-growing woody shrub that produces many small-sized leaves. If the shrub blooms freely, so much the better. Geraniums, roses, and lantanas are often trained into standards. But there are many other candidates—figs (*Ficus* spp.), fuchsias (*Fuchsia* spp.), citrus trees (*Citrus* spp.)—nearly any woody shrub that appeals to you. Even woody herbs such as lavender (*Lavandula* spp.) sweet bay (*Laurus nobilis*), and rosemary (*Rosmarinus officinalis*) may be trained to tree form. Plants with small leaves are best because when the standard has grown to 3 to 4 feet in height, the crown of small leaves atop the single "trunk" helps to create the impression of a real tree in miniature.

Standards can be grown in garden beds, but container growing is preferred because the plants can then be moved indoors or outside, depending on the season, the weather, and the hardiness of the plant. Some standards are produced by grafting compatible plants—a favorite tea rose scion grafted or budded onto a *Rosa multiflora* rootstock, for example. The following directions are for turning an ordinary shrub into a miniature tree, without grafting.

STEPS FOR TRAINING

1. Start your standard with a small, rooted cutting, but choose a strong and straight one. You may also use a small plant if it has a single, strong leader that is growing upward. Plant it into a 3-inch pot and begin the training immediately.

2. Insert a 10-inch stake next to the plant to train the leader to grow perfectly vertical. Tie the main stem to the stake using soft cord, and remove any side shoots that appear.

3. As the leader grows, continue to tie it every 2 to 3 inches—or even more closely if it threatens to stray. Continue removing any side shoots that appear. Leaves that grow directly from the leader may be kept temporarily, since they help to manufacture food for the plant's growth. They will be removed after the tree is trained.

4. When the plant reaches about 12 inches in height, transplant it to a larger pot, if necessary, and insert a new stake that will be nearly as tall as the eventual height of the standard. Continue to grow the plant in this manner, repotting as necessary when the plant becomes rootbound, until it reaches the desired height.

5. When it has grown as tall as you wish, stop the plant's vertical growth by pinching the terminal bud. This will force the growth of lateral branches. Allow these to grow for about an inch, then pinch these back, also, to encourage still more lateral branches to form. By encouraging lateral branching and removing side shoots from the trunk, you are forcing the plant to form a globular head or top.

6. To maintain the standard at the desired height and shape, you'll need to pinch and prune it regularly. In several years, the main trunk or stem will become thick and sturdy enough so that the supporting stake can be removed.

7. For continued health, be sure to meet all the other requirements—light, humidity, temperature, seasonal rest—of the species you have chosen.

Creating a Tub Garden

If a full-sized lily pond is not in your immediate gardening future, you can at least experience a bit of the aquatic gardening world with a tub garden of your very own. Lily ponds are certainly lovely, but tub gardens also have advantages. They're easy to set up and maintain, may be moved about if necessary, and can be used on porches, patios, decks, and terraces. Be sure to pick a site in full sun—at least five hours of direct sun daily—for best bloom of water lilies.

GETTING STARTED

Almost any large container at least 20 inches deep and 12 inches wide may be used for a tub garden, as long as it is watertight. If you have an attractive container that is not watertight, then look for a suitable plastic liner. Wooden half-barrels are commonly used for tub gardens, as are large ceramic tubs. If you choose to sink the container into the ground, then, of course, outward appearance is not important. Be sure that there are no residues of toxic substances in the container you choose. Wooden half-barrels used for aging whiskey can be toxic to fish. Fresh barrels will smell of whisky. Age them several months until they no longer smell before you try adding fish or plants.

Selecting Plants Potting Plants for Tub Gardens

Water lilies (*Nymphaea* spp.) are the most popular plants for tub gardens. Since water lilies need ample growing space, most tubs are capable of handling no more than one full-sized plant. Your best bet is one of the dwarf water lilies; that way, you'll have room for one or more of the fascinating bog plants available. For visual interest, consider adding a plant that will provide a vertical accent. For the latter, consider pickerel weed (*Pontederia cordata*), bog rush (*Juncus effusus*), elephant's-ear (*Colocasia* spp.), or arrowhead (*Sagittaria* spp.). Water poppy (*Hydrocleys nymphoides*) is a floating-leaved plant with showy yellow flowers. European water clover (*Marsilea quadrifolia*) has bright green, floating leaves shaped like four-leaf clovers. Other aquatic plants may be found in mail-order water garden catalogs.

To provide clear water and a proper habitat for fish, each tub should have at least one pot of submerged oxygenating plants, such as elodea (*Elodea* spp.) or hornwort (*Ceratophyllum demersum*).

Potting Plants

Once you've selected the container for your tub garden and chosen a site in full sun, you're ready to pot up your plants. It's best to pot the plants and set them in place before filling the tub with water. Wait a week or two for the plants to become established before introducing fish.

Each plant should be grown in its own pot. In this case, it's not necessary to use pots with holes in the bottom; plastic dish tubs are ideal. The best soil for tub plants is ordinary garden loam that has been sieved to remove rocks, pieces of roots, and other organic matter. Manure, compost, peat moss, and raw organic matter such as roots or leaves will foul the water.

Position the roots and fill the containers. Leave enough room at the top of the pot for a 2-inch layer of pea gravel on the surface of the soil. This will help keep the water clear and discourage fish from digging in the soil and muddying the water.

Filling the Tub

Set the plants in place in the tub. The amount of water that should cover the pots varies from plant to plant. Pots of oxygenating plants rest on the bottom. Full-sized water lilies can rest on the bottom, generally. Miniatures or bog plants must be positioned closer to the surface. Use bricks under pots to adjust them to the proper depth. Then fill the tub slowly by trickling in water.

It will take a few weeks for your tub to become balanced. Once the soil has settled to the bottom and the plants begin to grow, the water should clear. If the water turns very green before the plants have had a chance to grow, empty the tub and refill it. Once the leaves of water lilies and other floating-leaved plants appear, they will shade the water. This will not only keep it cool during the hot summer months, but will also help reduce free-swimming algae in the water. Plants and fish prefer water temperatures in the 65° to 75°F range. When you are ready to introduce fish, float them on the surface of the water in a water-filled plastic bag for an hour to equalize the temperature, before opening the bag and releasing them. (Remove fish immediately if they begin gulping air at the surface.)

In the fall, unless you live in an area where temperatures do not fall below freezing, you'll need to drain and clean the tub. Fish can be moved indoors into an aquarium or other container; goldfish can be kept through the winter at temperatures between 40° and 45°F. Tropical lilies grown in temperate climates are best discarded at this time. Hardy lily tubers may be stored in moist sand over winter and replanted the following spring.

Making Mix and Choosing Containers

Fern Marshall Bradley

After you've decided what plants you want to grow, your first priority is choosing the right containers and potting soil. You can match your containers to your house style, personal taste, or the type of plant you're growing. (For example, a tropical-looking bamboo or vine would look at home in a wicker basket.) You'll be amazed at the variety of containers available—from standard clay and plastic to half-barrels and "found objects" like old teapots or watering cans. Here are some great tips for finding or making good soil mixes and containers.

Continued →

Do You Have Soil Savvy?

If your garden soil produces luscious tomatoes or stunning roses, you may wonder whether it would work just as well for your potted plants. Definitely not, says Rita Buchanan, a Connecticut garden writer. "I think one of the most common mistakes container gardeners make is digging up soil from the garden and putting it in a pot," she says. "A pot is so little compared to the garden—moisture just doesn't drain through a pot like it does in the ground." That means you need a soil that won't pack down too easily or stay wet too long. Buy a commercial potting soil mix or make your own. Buchanan suggests mixing equivalent amounts of loamy garden soil, screened compost or peat moss, and perlite or coarse sand.

Coarse Mix Is Fine For Pots

Check the heft on that bag of potting mix before you lug the sack home. Jim Wilson, a cohost of public television's "The Victory Garden," feels that the single most important thing about growing plants in containers is using a coarse-textured growing mix and avoiding dense, heavy potting soil. Wilson suggests that when you're buying potting soil in retail outlets you judge bags of similar volume by weight, because the label usually provides little information about contents. (Potting mixes don't have to list ingredients.) "If the bag is heavy, don't buy it," he says. "Some mixes contain sand to add weight, so you'll think you're getting more; if it's river sand of varying particle size, it just packs down in the pot. The other thing to watch for is bags where the soil is [made] wet to make it heavier and give it a rich, black color."

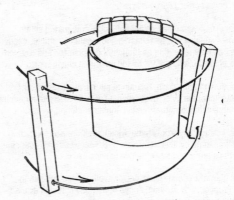

Plastic pots are unquestionably useful because they're lightweight and reusable. But they don't make much of a show on the patio or deck. One alternative to repotting in a decorative container is to hide the plastic pot in an attractive "cover-up." This handsome wooden pot is really a shell of 1 x 1's. To make one, cut the 1 x 1's to the right length to cover your pot. Drill holes through each piece about 1 inch from the top and bottom, as shown. String the pieces together with copper wire.

Pick a Perfect Pot

Not all containers are created equal—that's the word from Holly H. Shimizu, the acting assistant executive director at the U.S. Botanical Garden in Washington, D.C. If you're trying to decide which kind of container to use, she suggests keeping these points in mind:

- Clay and terra-cotta pots are porous, so you'll probably need to water plants in them more often than if you used plastic containers. But soil in these types of pots stays cooler than in plastic—a benefit in sunny sites and hot weather.
- Plastic pots hold heat and water better than clay pots. They're also lighter and less expensive, but they have a tendency to crack or break with age.
- Stone and concrete containers are extremely durable, but they're very heavy and relatively expensive.

Whatever kind of pot you choose, remember that any container used for plants should have holes for adequate drainage. Shimizu says that using old pots is fine, as long as you care for them properly. "When you recycle your pots, it's very important to make sure they're clean. A lot of people neglect to do that—and the pots can carry diseases that way," she says. She recommends removing old soil and plant debris, soaking the pot in water, then scrubbing it with a mild liquid detergent. Rinse the pot thoroughly, and dry it. Your container is now ready for a new plant!

Continuing Care

Choosing a pot and potting soil mix gives your plants a good start, but you can't stop there. Container plants need ongoing care—watering, feeding, grooming, watching for signs of pests and diseases, and if they stay outdoors all year, winterizing. Surprisingly, the biggest hurdle for most plant owners is watering. Here are some expert tips and tricks for handling watering and other routine chores.

Help! They Can't Swim!

Overwatering is the number one problem in container gardening, according to Tovah Martin, the staff horticulturist at Logee's Greenhouses in Connecticut. "When you're living with a plant intimately, you tend to baby it, and that usually means watering it too frequently," she says. "You have to remember that the soil does not go down to China." When you overwater, you are actually suffocating the roots, which can eventually die from lack of oxygen.

So when should you water? "When the soil is dry to the touch," says Martin. She suggests sticking your finger about ½ to 1 inch down into the soil; if it feels dry, it's time to get out the watering can. Don't let the soil become parched, however. If it gets too dry, it won't be able to absorb moisture, and the water will simply run down the sides of the container.

Sometimes the plant itself is your best moisture barometer. Martin lets her plants go into a slight wilt before watering them. "It usually does no harm to let plants wilt slightly," she says. "As a matter of fact, with many plants, such as bougainvilleas, it will promote bud formation."

How much water is enough? Martin recommends leaving about ¼ to ½ inch between the soil surface and the rim of the container when you're potting a plant. Then, each time you water, fill the pot to the rim once. Don't succumb to the temptation to refill it again and again, or you'll drown the roots.

The Root of the Problem

When's the last time you looked at the roots of your potted plants? The last time you repotted them? Never? If your plants are looking peaked, inspect their root balls. Taking your plants out of their pots from time to time to inspect the roots won't hurt them. Simply turn the pots upside down and gently lift the plants out. If the roots look bright and shiny, you'll know they're healthy. But if they look soft, rotted, or discolored or if they smell bad, that's a sign of trouble. Cut away diseased or discolored roots and repot in a sterile soil mix.

Put Panty Hose In Your Pots

Old panty hose can be part of a handy system for watering houseplants and hanging baskets. Some houseplants, such as African violets, wood sorrels, and ferns, need more water than others. If you have trouble remembering to make those extra watering trips, try using a hidden water reservoir for passive irrigation. Barbara W. Ellis, the managing editor of garden books for Rodale Press, has rigged up a system using a plastic freezer container under each extra-thirsty plant in her office, as shown in the illustration below. She pots up the houseplant in a shallow container, such as an azalea pot or bulb pan, that has a 1-inch-wide strip of panty hose inserted through the bottom drainage hole. The panty hose strip hangs down into the freezer container and wicks water up to the soil mix. She conceals the whole setup inside a larger decorative pot. "It's a really convenient system for plants that need more-frequent watering," says Ellis.

Rocks In Your Pots?

Contrary to what some gardeners may think, putting a layer of gravel or other similar material in the bottom of a container does not improve drainage. In fact, it can decrease plant growth, since the space occupied by rocks could hold soil and roots instead.

There is still a valid reason for putting rocks in pots, however: Pebbles, rocks, gravel, stone chips, or broken pottery can keep pots from blowing over.

Winterizing Potted Trees

If you garden in the North, take special precautions to make sure your hardy containerized trees and shrubs survive the winter outdoors. According to Christina R. J. Pey, a supervisor for the production greenhouses at the Missouri Botanical Garden, the most important thing is to check the size of the plant's root ball. "If the root ball is almost touching the container sides, chances are the plant will be affected by the cold and may even die," says Pey.

If the roots of any of your trees or shrubs are too near the sides of their container, consider moving the plant to a larger pot. If your plant is already in as large a pot as you want or have room

Continued ➡

Selecting Plants for Container Gardens

Container gardening is a great way to brighten up a deck or patio—or just a corner of your backyard where you're tight on space. Any of the following plants will thrive in containers such as tubs, old wheelbarrows, pots, urns, troughs, sinks, or hanging baskets—just make sure there are holes for adequate drainage. Position your container before you fill it—it may be too heavy to move later. It is very important to feed and water plants regularly. After a couple of months in their containers, plants will need about a pint of liquid fertilizer, like manure tea or fish emulsion, every two weeks during the summer.

Name	Height	Description	Culture
Achimenes spp. (Achimenes)	8–12 in.	Flowering African violet relatives with scaly rhizomes and flat-faced, tubular flowers in pink, blue, purple, red, orange, yellow, or white. Blooms spring to frost.	Tender perennial usually grown as an annual from scaly rhizomes. Partial to deep shade. Light, well-drained soil rich in organic matter. Water and feed heavily. Propagate by division, cuttings, seeds. Rhizomes can be dried and overwintered indoors.
Begonia X *semperflorens-cultorum* hybrids (Wax begonia)	6–12 in.	Compact, fleshy plants with waxy single or double flowers that are pink, red, or white. Foliage is fleshy and green, maroon, or bronze. Blooms spring to frost.	Tender perennial usually grown as an annual. Full sun to partial shade. Moist, well-drained soil rich in organic matter. Best propagated by cuttings. Or sow seed indoors 12–14 weeks before last frost. Almost continuous bloom. Can be brought indoors in fall and overwintered as a houseplant.
Browallia speciosa (Browallia)	12–15 in.	Attractive plant with bell-shaped flowers in blue or white. Leaves are narrow and dark green. Blooms spring to frost.	Tender perennial usually grown as an annual. Full sun to partial shade. Moist, well-drained soil rich in organic matter. Propagate by cuttings or sow seed indoors 6–8 weeks before last frost. Can be brought indoors in fall and overwintered as a houseplant. Attractive when combined with other annuals.
Caladium spp. (Caladium)	9–30 in.	Genus grown for its showy, many-colored leaves marked and patterned in combinations of white, pink, red, or green.	Tender perennial grown as summer-flowering bulb from tuber-corms. Partial to deep shade. Moist, well-drained soil rich in organic matter. Remove flowers as they appear. Propagate by division. Hardy only in Zone 10; dig tuber-corms and store in a cool, dry spot over winter. Many cultivars available.
Calendula officinalis (Pot marigold)	6–24 in.	Daisy-family member with yellow, cream, white, or orange daisylike flowers and bright green leaves. Blooms spring to frost.	Annual. Full sun to partial shade. Rich moist soil. Sow seeds in the containers where the plants are to grow. Excellent cut flower. Best where summers are cool.
Catharanthus roseus (Rose periwinkle)	18–24 in.	Low-growing, summer-blooming plant with showy, flat-faced flowers in white, rose, pink, or mauve. Leaves are glossy green. Sometimes sold as *Vinca rosea*.	Tender perennial usually grown as an annual. Full sun to partial shade. Will tolerate most soils, including dry ones. Hardy in Zone 10. Prefers warm temperatures.
Celosia cristata (Cockscomb)	6–36 in.	Unique-looking, summer-flowering annual with crested or plumed flower heads in yellow, orange, red, and purple.	Annual. Full sun. Sandy, well-drained soil rich in organic matter. Sow seeds indoors 4–6 weeks before last frost, or sow outdoors. Good cut flower. Blooms can also be dried. Attractive when combined with other annuals.
Chrysanthemum X *morifolium* (Hardy chrysanthemum)	12–48 in.	Popular, fall-blooming perennial with yellow, purple, scarlet, orange, pink, or white daisylike flowers that may be single or double.	Hardy perennial. Full sun to partial shade. Rich to average, moist, well-drained soil. Pinch back stems in early part of season to encourage branching. Zones 3–10; often grown as annual. Good cut flower. Many reclassified as *Tanacetum* or *Leucanthemum*.
Coleus X *hybridus* (Coleus, flame nettle)	6–36 in.	Shrubby plant grown for its ornamental foliage, which is variegated in combinations of chartreuse, white, bronze, gold, copper, yellow, pink, red, purple or green.	Tender perennial usually grown as an annual. Full sun to partial shade. Moist, well-drained soil rich in organic matter. Propagate by cuttings, seeds. Pinch off flowers as they form. Can be brought indoors in fall and overwintered as a houseplant. Excellent plant to add color to a shady spot.
Crocus spp. (Crocus)	3–6 in.	Early spring-blooming plants with purple, lilac, blue, cream, yellow, white, or orange chalice-shaped flowers and grassy leaves.	Hardy perennial grown from a corm. Full sun to partial shade. Sandy or gritty, well-drained soil. Propagate by cormels, seeds. Zones 3–8. Useful for adding spring color to large containers that remain unplanted during winter.
Hemerocallis hybrids (Daylily)	12–48 in.	Summer-blooming, clump-forming plants with sword-shaped leaves and trumpet-shaped flowers in yellow, orange, red, pink, or lavender. Each bloom opens for only a day.	Hardy perennial. Full sun to partial shade. Moist, well-drained soil rich in organic matter. Propagate by division. Zones 3–8. Many cultivars available; miniature selections are especially effective in containers.
Hosta spp. (Plantain lily)	6–36 in.	Sturdy, clump-forming perennials grown for their attractive foliage, which may be blue-green, green, or patterned with yellow and/or white. Spikes of violet or white, bell-shaped flowers produced in summer or fall.	Hardy perennial. Partial to deep shade. Moist, well-drained soil rich in organic matter. Propagate by division. Zones 4–9. Many cultivars available. Underplant with crocuses or daffodils for spring color.
Impatiens wallerana (Busy Lizzy, patient Lucy)	6–30 in.	Mound-shaped, fleshy plant covered with single or double flowers of white, pink, orange, salmon, red, or lavender. Flowers may be a solid color or bicolor. Blooms appear spring to frost.	Tender perennial usually grown as an annual. Partial to dense shade. Moist, well-drained soil rich in organic matter. Prefers warm weather. Can be brought indoors in fall and overwintered as a houseplant.
Lantana camara (Yellow sage)	12–36 in.	Shrubby plant with many clusters of tiny flowers that are usually yellow or pink on opening and change to red, orange, or lavender. Blooms appear spring to frost.	Tender shrub usually grown as an annual. Full sun. Rich, loamy, well-drained soil. Propagate by softwood cuttings. Seed takes 8 weeks to germinate; sow indoors 12–14 weeks before last frost. Zones 8–10; has become a weed in areas where it is hardy. Can be brought indoors in fall and overwintered as a houseplant.
Lobelia erinus (Edging lobelia)	4–8 in.	Trailing, summer-blooming annual with many small fan-shaped flowers in deep blue, pale blue, red, or white.	Annual. Full sun to partial shade. Rich, sandy, moist soil. Sow seed indoors 10–12 weeks before last frost; do not cover, seed requires light for germination. Pinch plants to promote bushiness. Attractive when combines with other annuals.
Lobularia maritime (Sweet alyssum)	6–12 in.	Ground-hugging, spring- to summer-blooming plant with abundant clusters of fragrant white, pink, or purple flowers.	Perennial usually grown as an annual. Full sun. Average well-drained soil. Shear back plants occasionally to encourage repeat bloom. Can be brought indoors in winter for further bloom. Attractive when combined with other annuals.
Muscari spp. (Grape hyacinth)	8–12 in.	Low-growing, spring-blooming bulbs with dense grapelike clusters of bluish purple or white, bell-shaped flowers. Grasslike leaves.	Hardy bulb. Full sun to partial shade. Sandy, well-drained soil rich in organic matter. Zones 5–8. Good for cutting. Many cultivars available. Useful for adding spring color to large containers that remain unplanted during winter.
Nicotiana alata (Flowering tobacco)	18–30 in.	Summer-flowering plant with white, lime, lavender, pink, or red, trumpet-shaped flowers that are very fragrant at night.	Full sun to partial shade. Moist, well-drained soil rich in organic matter. Sow seed indoors 6–8 weeks before last frost.

Continued ➡

Name	Height	Description	Culture
Pelargonium spp. (Geranium)	12–36 in.	Large genus grown for ornamental flowers and/or foliage. Bedding or zonal geraniums grown for their 3–5-in.-wide flower clusters in pink, salmon, red, or white. Other species grown for their scented foliage. Blooms appear spring to frost.	Tender, shrubby perennial usually grown as annual. Full sun. Loamy to sandy, well-drained soil rich in organic matter. Propagate by cuttings. Remove flowers as they fade. Hardy in Zone 10; can be brought indoors in fall and overwintered as a houseplant. Many cultivars available.
Petunia spp. (Petunia)	10–18 in.	Popular, sprawling annuals with trumpet-shaped blooms in many forms and colors. Blooms may be violet, pink, salmon, rose, red, yellow, or white, either solid colors or bicolors. Blooms may be single or double and appear spring to frost.	Full sun. Rich, light, sandy soil with very good drainage. Pinch branch tips after first flush of bloom to encourage branching. Attractive when combined with other annuals.
Portulaca grandiflora (Rose moss)	4–8 in.	Fleshy, mat-forming plant with red, gold, yellow, cream, rose, white, or salmon flowers that open in sunny weather. Blooms appear spring to frost.	Annual. Full sun. Sandy, dry, well-drained soil. Withstands heat, drought. Attractive when combined with other annuals.
Thunbergia alata (Black-eyed Susan vine)	48–120 in.	Vining plant with orange, buff, or apricot flowers that have a purple or black throat and dense, dark green leaves. Blooms appear spring to frost.	Tender perennial usually grown as an annual. Full sun to partial shade. Light rich, moist, well-drained soil. Provide a trellis or allow to trail over edges of pot or hanging basket. Sow seed indoors 6–8 weeks before last frost.
Tulipa spp. (Tulip)	6–30 in.	Popular spring-blooming plants with cup-shaped blooms in many colors including red, yellow, pink, white, maroon, and orange.	Hardy bulb. Full sun. Sandy, well-drained soil rich in organic matter. Propagate by offsets. Zones 2–9. Can be grown as an annual, or, when leaves yellow, lift and store bulbs in a cool, dry spot and replant outdoors in fall. Useful for adding spring color to large containers that remain unplanted during winter.
Viola spp. (Violet, pansy)	4–6 in.	Attractive, spring-to-summer blooming plants with purple, blue, red, yellow, white, or ivory flowers. Many are bicolored with large, facelike patches.	Annual and perennial species. Full sun to partial shade. Moist, rich soil. Best in areas with cool summers. Pinch back plants in midsummer to encourage further bloom. Mulch in summer to keep soil moist and cool. Good for adding early spring color to containers left outdoors; attractive when combined with other annuals.

for, you can prune the roots back. (When you root-prune, prune the top growth in the same proportion.)

Another way to winterize container-grown trees and shrubs is to move them to a protected site—against the side of a building or in a garage that gets lots of light. Clumping your plants together also provides protection against the cold. For larger containers that can't easily be moved, Pey suggests piling mulch up around them.

Tropicals Take the Heat

Temperature has a critical effect on growth of tropical plants in containers indoors. Fred Saleet, the owner of The Banana Tree, a Pennsylvania company that specializes in uncommon tropical seeds, recommends the following temperature regimes:

- *Heliconia* spp. (heliconias): daytime— 80°F or higher; nighttime—not below 70°F
- *Musa* spp. (bananas): daytime—75°F or higher; nighttime—at least 67°F
- *Strelitzia* spp. (bird-of-paradise): daytime—80°F or higher; nighttime— not below 68°F
- *Theobroma cacao* (chocolate-tree): daytime and nighttime—at least 70°F

Keep in mind that temperature requirements vary according to which species you're growing.

Creative Containers

Containers aren't just for houseplants or annual flowers. You can grow dwarf fruit trees, shrubs, flowering perennials and bulbs, ornamental grasses, vines, and just about any other plant in a container. You can have a container vegetable

garden, herb garden—even water garden. So stretch your limits, and try something different. Here, the experts offer us some ideas for branching out into new areas with container gardening.

Theme Gardens, Container-Style

The sky's the limit when it comes to container garden ideas. For something a bit out of the ordinary, try a garden with a lemon-fragrance theme, like the one on display one summer at the U.S. Botanic Garden in Washington, D.C. "All of the plants had some lemon flavor or golden flowers," says Holly H. Shimizu, the acting assistant executive director at the U.S. Botanic Garden. To start a similar container garden of your own, she suggests planting lemon-scented marigolds (*Tagetes tenuifolia*), golden lemon thyme (*Thymus* X *citriodorus* 'Aureus'), lemongrass (*Cymbopogon citratus*), lemon balm (*Melissa officinalis*), and lemon basil (*Ocimum basilicum* 'Citriodorum'). Don't forget lemon-scented geraniums (*Pelargonium crispum*), including 'Prince Rupert' and 'Mabel Gray,' "the most lemony of all," according to Shimizu. "It's so lemony, your mouth waters," she says.

If a more formal design appeals to you, try a container knot garden. Shimizu recommends a figure eight composed of clipped fragrant herbs and topiary—for example, silver and golden thyme to form the eight and a myrtle (*Myrtus communis*) topiary to fill the center of each of the circles. "The topiaries we used in our display had twisted stems and round heads, like lollipops," she says. "You can use any number of complementary plants—any other kind of topiary, if you want height, or another little filler in the middle of the eight. It depends on whether you like the open look or the closed look."

Try These Four Tropicals

If you're thinking about growing exotic plants indoors, you'll need to tend to their needs year-round, says Fred Saleet, the owner of The Banana Tree, a Pennsylvania company that specializes in uncommon tropical seeds. According to Saleet, four tropical plants that are relatively easy to grow and have the same general cultural requirements are bananas (*Musa* spp.), cacao or chocolate-tree (*Theobroma cacao*), the exotic bird-of-paradise (*Strelitzia* spp.), and heliconias (*Heliconia* spp.)

My, How Small You've Grown!

The next time you start a bonsai, plant a seedling of the same species in the ground at the same time. Within a few years, you'll be amazed at the difference in size between your miniature containerized specimen and that shady tree outside.

Top Ten Herbs to Grow Indoors

Here are ten herbs that are excellent for indoor growing, recommended by Christina R. J. Pey, a supervisor for the production greenhouses at the Missouri Botanical Garden:

Basil	Oregano
Dill	Parsley
Fennel	Sage
Marjoram	Tarragon
Mint	Thyme

All four of these plants need a combination of warmth, bright light, and high humidity—and not just when it's sunny and warm outside. Says Saleet, "Many people grow them very well in the spring and summer. Then, in the winter, they ask, 'Why is it dying? It was growing so well!'" He suggests using a high-intensity light (100 watts or higher) when the weather turns dark and cold. "You want consistency in the climatic conditions," he says. "You don't want a break in the action."

Keep in mind that these tropical plants, particularly the banana, also require frequent fertilization. "If a plant is pushing out one flower after another, that means it's in need of a supply of nutrients," says Saleet. Don't make the mistake of fertilizing the plant if it looks sick, however. Although there's a chance that it's suffering from

Continued →

nutrient deficiency, more than likely there's something else, such as spider mites infestation, that's causing the problem.

Double Your Bulbs, Double Your Bloom

Ever wonder how exhibitors at flower shows get so many tulips or daffodils to bloom in one container? "The bulbs are planted one on top of the other," says Raymond J. Rogers, the garden editor for Dorling Kindersley in New York. "That's why the pots look like they're jam-packed—they are jam-packed." When the bulbs bloom, you'll have a pot that's bursting with color—a real showstopper on a gray winter day.

According to Rogers, who has won many awards for his bulb entries at the Philadelphia Flower Show, it's best to start with a soil mix composed of 2 parts good garden soil, 2 parts potting mix, 1 part perlite, and 1 part #3 grade (coarse) sand. Here's the method.

1. Put the soil mix in the bottom one-third of the pot, then put in a layer of bulbs pointed-side-up. (How much mix you add depends on bulb size. For example, plant long-necked daffodils deeper than short-necked daffodils.)

2. Add mix until the tops of the bulbs just poke through the surface, then position a second layer of bulbs in between the tops of the first layer.

3. Add another layer of mix until you can barely see the tops of the bulbs poking through.

This method works best with tulips and daffodils, though some people have had success planting reticulated iris (*Iris reticulata*) in double layers. Rogers doesn't recommend double-planting for hyacinths, which tend to push each other out of the soil. Your potted bulbs will require an initial cold treatment and proper subsequent care to force them into bloom.

Be Bold With Bonsai

"People don't realize how easy bonsai is," says John Lennon, the owner of J. Lennon Landscaping in California. "Everybody's afraid of them and they shouldn't be." Lennon feels that cultivating the exotic-looking dwarfed trees can be every bit as easy as growing any other trees in containers.

Lennon suggests starting with Japanese maples (*Acer japonicum* and *A. palmatum*) or junipers (*Juniperus* spp.), both of which are "forgiving." You can buy the starters sold in nurseries or simply start them from seedlings yourself. Japanese maples like to be kept moist, so be sure to water them frequently. They'll need a fair amount of sun, too. Junipers like more light (preferably full sun) but less water than maples do.

According to Lennon, one of the secrets of bonsai success is repotting the plant on a regular basis, as you would any containerized tree. It's best to perform this task during the plant's dormant stage, usually in winter. Every year or two, pull the bonsai tree out of its container, and knock off about one-third of the root ball with the three-pronged claw or other hand tool, as shown in the illustration below. (You can also use pruning shears to cut the excess roots.) "You've got to be brutal," says Lennon. "If you aren't vigorous with them, they won't come back vigorously." Repot the plant using fresh soil, then fertilize. The plant should eventually respond with plenty of new growth.

Pruning is, of course, central to bonsai care. "That's where practice comes in," says Lennon. He suggests taking off about one-third of the plant each time you repot it. Keep in mind that maples usually send out lots of new growth after they're pruned, so you'll need to prune the shoots regularly to keep the shape you have established.

Junipers tend to produce most of their new growth all at once, so they won't need constant pruning.

According to Lennon, how you prune depends on the effect you want to achieve. For instance, if you want your maple to look as natural as possible, you'll need to round out the crown of the plant. Removing most of the branches from one side of a juniper can give it a kind of windswept look. Regardless of the style you choose, it's best to keep the center open to allow for good air circulation and prevent problems with pests.

Best For Hanging Baskets

For attractive indoor hanging baskets, try these plants recommended by Tovah Martin, the staff horticulturist at Logee's Greenhouses in Connecticut:

Aeschynanthus spp. (lipstick plants)

Begonia 'Tom Ment 1' 'Orange Rubra', and 'Elaine' (angel-wing begonia cultivars)

Columnea spp. (columneas)

Kalanchoe pumila, K. uniflora (kalanchoes)

Pelargonium peltatum (ivy geranium)

Container Plants the Low-Maintenance Way

Barbara W. Ellis, Joan Benjamin, and Deborah L. Martin

Whether you're growing tubs of herbs and vegetables on the deck or houseplants in a sunny window, growing plants in containers adds a dimension to gardening that's hard to pass up. Growing plants in pots lets you move plants at will: You can easily bring a cherished tender herb like rosemary indoors to protect it from winter cold or grow an ever-changing display of flowers on a deck or patio. It also puts you in control of the growing conditions. You can garden if the soil is lousy, plant when you have the time, and use every available space. With containers, you can take advantage of light and moisture wherever you find them—in sunny stairwells and steamy bathrooms, under trees, or out front beside your driveway.

In this chapter, you'll find tips and techniques for making container gardening even more enjoyable than it already is.

Simple Steps to a Successful Container Garden

It doesn't take much to keep container plants happy. Since you control the soil, water, and light, it's easy to provide perfect growing conditions. For the best results and the least hassle, group plants with similar needs in a single container. If you mix sun-loving flowers with shade lovers, or mix plants that need lots of water with those that don't, you'll drive yourself crazy trying to keep all of them happy and healthy.

GROW GREAT PLANTS WITH THE RIGHT SOIL MIX

Choose a commercial container mix or make your own to get potted plants started right. A good mix drains well, retains moisture, and provides support for your container plant. Experiment with a few to find the one that's right for your plants. Or buy a mix and doctor it.

For a good do-it-yourself mix, combine 1 part potting soil and 2 parts organic matter—compost, shredded bark, leaf mold, or any material large enough to improve drainage and lend stability. Sharp sand, used by masons (available at most lumberyards), is another good option.

You can tailor it to fit your watering habits, too. If you like to water often, use sharp sand to increase drainage in your mix; if you grow on the dry side, add organic matter like compost to hold moisture between waterings.

LET THERE BE THE RIGHT AMOUNT OF LIGHT

You can make any container plant happy. Move pots to the shade if the sun gets too bright, or set them in the sun if that's what your plants prefer. Cluster sun lovers together in a hot spot so you can water them with a quick once-over. Let shade-tolerant combinations grace bare spots under trees and in dark corners.

ADD WATER AND LET THE PLANTS GROW

Once plants are potted and placed in an area with adequate light, all they need is water. Give them the right amount when they need it, and you'll have healthy plants and few maintenance chores.

Use the knuckle test to know when to water clay or plastic containers. Stick your finger into the soil down to the first knuckle. If your fingertip is dry, it's time to water. How much is enough? Irrigate every pot until water flows out the bottom. If your plant drains into a saucer, throw out the excess.

Because container-grown plants have restricted root space, they're often nutrient-stressed. To keep your container garden growing vigorously, plan on feeding regularly. Compost tea, liquid kelp, or fish emulsion are all fine fertilizers for container plants that you can apply when you water. As a rule, water at half the strength recommended on the container twice as often.

Container Options

The sky's the limit when it comes to choosing containers for your plants to grow in. Of course, there are hundreds of conventional containers to choose from. Explore as many as you can think of.

But don't just stop there. Container gardening means recycling. Plant in leftover pieces of pipe from plumbing projects, drain tiles that have been stood on end, rusty wheelbarrows, used tires, old bird cages—anything can become a planter/conversation piece in your garden. Where openings can't hold soil, make a liner of burlap or plastic screen.

Build a Space- and Labor-Saving Vegetable Box

Wooden fruit or vegetable crates from the grocery store—or their plastic equivalent, milk or storage crates—make great no-till vegetable garden boxes. If you grow in these handy containers, you won't have to wait for soil to warm up or for the weather to improve; whenever you're ready to plant, the conditions are right.

Start your crate garden with burlap. Before filling your crates with your favorite soil mix and amendments, line them with burlap to keep soil from escaping. Then moisten the soil and start planting.

Just plant and grow. Small plastic milk crates are great for plants like lettuce and basil. For tall tomatoes or climbing cucumbers, use a wooden vegetable crate with a wire support. To make a simple support, after planting staple a 6-foot-tall section of hog wire (fencing with 4-inch squares) around the outside of the box. Attach it to itself for extra strength. Plants can lean or climb on the wire.

Continued ➡

What Plants Need

When conditions aren't right, plants let you know—all you have to do is take a look at their leaves. A few commonsense cultural practices will cure most container plant problems.

Pale, stretched-out, spindly plants. Give these plants a brighter spot. If lower leaves turn yellow, water less often and feed with fish emulsion or another soluble fertilizer at a half-strength rate for two waterings to get them going again.

Plants that wilt even with adequate watering. Plants with this symptom may have root problems. Pull the plant out of its pot and take a look at the roots. If roots have filled all available space, divide the plant, repot it in new soil, and resume routine care. If roots are few or rotting, repot and let the soil dry between waterings.

Keep Herbs Close at Hand

When you're cooking, the last thing you have is time to waste. The sauce simmers, pasta's ready to serve, and you need some parsley. You don't have time to change shoes and tromp out to the garden. Turn instead to a convenient half-barrel filled with your favorite fresh herbs. A traditional strawberry pot works great, too; plant separate herbs in pockets on the jar's sides and they'll all have enough room to grow. Be sure to water from both the top and sides. When you need an herb, just snip off a sprig with scissors.

Take to Wheels for Easier Plant Care

Mobile gardening may not be an automotive trend, but putting containers on wheels lets you move them easily. Three-wheel steel dollies from your local hardware store make it easy to wheel huge pots about—whether you need to bring tender tropicals inside when seasons change or move large houseplants where you can water or spray safely away from carpets and furniture. Or bolt casters on a circle of plywood or other material. A wagon makes a great tool for rolling sun-loving annuals out to your shady patio to quickly decorate for a party. Or use it to move pot-grown tomatoes to safety when frost threatens.

Wick Away Indoor Water Cares

Containers with built-in reservoirs and wicks, and soil additives designed to conserve moisture, are modern technology's answer to tedious watering chores. Lots of "self-watering" pots work quite well. You can also make your own wick system, as shown here.

Some plant care professionals use encapsulated moisture products to conserve water in container plantings. These water-absorbing polymers swell up to hold extra moisture and release it later. Other less expensive substances, like peat moss,

vermiculite, and perlite, do the job as well or better in home environments.

Insert wicks when you pot. Cotton wicks, pieces of wool or cotton yarn, and strips of panty hose all make fine wicks. Insert them halfway up the container, through the drainage hole, when you pot.

Buy wick waterers. Many companies offer pots with built-in wick-watering systems. These have a reservoir, a tube to fill it, a wick that runs up into the medium, and often a water-level indicator.

Watering made easy. To water, just fill the reservoir. Until you're sure your wick system is working properly, also check the soil regularly to make sure it's damp enough.

Use Household Items to Keep Plants from Drowning

A saucerful of water can mean root rot or death for plants like rosemary that demand well-drained soil. Try these tips for getting rid of that water without breaking your back.

Best Bets for Least-Work Potted Plants

Successful container gardens start with plants that like container life. Use these tips to find the best plants for your potted garden.

Look for drought-tolerant plants. Drought-tolerant herbs, ornamental grasses, annuals such as geraniums and marigolds, and many perennials, including daylilies, sedums, and hardy cacti (*Opuntia* spp.), make fine container residents. Fleshy leaves are a good clue to go by when you're looking for drought-tolerant plants: Plants that have them, like sedums, can hold on to water better than plants with thin, papery leaves.

Select dwarf shrubs and trees. You'll find a wide variety of dwarf shrubs and trees to choose from at well-stocked nurseries and garden centers. Dwarf cultivars generally have smaller root systems, grow slowly, and keep pleasing proportions for years. Those qualities translate into less work for you since they'll rarely need pruning or repotting.

Grow fruits, vegetables, and herbs. You can grow dwarf fruit trees, herbs, and a wide variety of vegetables (compact cultivars are best) on a sunny site in a variety of tubs and pots. Lettuce and other salad greens will perform well in a half-day of sun.

Try tropicals. Shallow-rooted tropical foliage plants seem to defy gravity. The huge leaves that emerge from small root systems make them ideal for growing in pots.

Plant groundcovers. Groundcovers provide living mulch beneath potted trees, suppress weeds, and often deliver bonus blooms. Try annual groundcovers like sweet alyssum, evergreen ones like creeping junipers, or flowering perennials like creeping thymes, sedums, or hen-and-chicks.

Grow flowers to keep your garden colorful. Perennials and annuals keep container plantings blooming nonstop until frost. If you're growing a potted tree that blooms in spring, put summer and fall-flowering perennials in the same container to extend the bloom. Or grow several smaller pots of perennials and bring them front and center while they're flowering. Annuals have shallow root systems that make them terrific companions to any container plant. Try sweet alyssum, coleus, impatiens, petunias, or marigolds, just for starters.

Plant sprawlers to dress up containers. Quick color and instant cover change even worn or stained containers into flower-filled beauties. Any plants that cascade or sprawl, like petunias, vinca, creeping thyme, and trailing junipers make good choices since their foliage drapes and decorates any

Indoor Herbs Aplenty
Roger Yepsen

A pot of carefully pruned rosemary or spicy bush basil makes an attractive windowsill plant, but you'll probably be reluctant to snip off much for cooking. And chances are that if you love plants, your south-facing windows are already filled to capacity. So, if you really like to cook with fresh herbs year-round, consider arranging a light table for them. This involved setting up fluorescent shop lights over a sturdy table or shelf that won't be marred by water. It's almost like having an attached greenhouse—on a far more modest scale, of course.

For most plants, provide at least 12 hours of light a day from a two-tube fixture suspended about 6 inches above the plants. You can hang the lights from two or three sturdy brackets. Place the brackets over studs in the wall above the windows and drive screws to anchor them securely. To locate the studs, you can use a magnetic or electronic stud finder. Or, look at the baseboard or chair rail trim and note where it has been nailed; if these locations are 16 inches on center, they indicate the studs' positions within the wall.

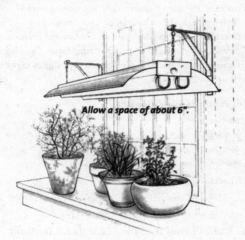

Allow a space of about 6".

Give Indoor Herbs a Boost

If you bring your favorite herbs indoors for the winter rather than sacrificing them to the frosts of fall, they may not reward your kindness with lush growth. They are apt to go dormant, performing sluggishly. Here's a way to goose them into growing with youthful energy.

1. Pot up the plant and boldly cut back the top growth to just 2 or 3 inches.

2. Place the plant in a clear plastic bag with the opening on top and seal it.

3. Create a false winter by placing the potted plant in the refrigerator for 2 weeks, subjecting it to another 2 weeks in the freezer, and then moving it back to the refrigerator for a final 2 weeks.

4. Place the plant on a sunny windowsill with the bag open and look for new growth.

Continued ➡

pot. And don't forget annual vines like black-eyed Susan vine (*Thunbergia alata*). Plant a pot of each, or mix and match.

Make friends with invasive plants. Put unmanageable mints and intrusive bamboos in half-barrels on a patio or in plastic pots or bottomless buckets set in the ground. Sink pots of bog plants into the sides of water gardens; they'll get needed moisture without troubling fish and filter systems.

Grow Patio Pots for Year-Round Interest

It doesn't take lots of space, plants, or bother to decorate your deck, patio, or porch with nonstop color. Fill a large, sturdy container with a variety of plants chosen for their hardy habits, successive seasonal color, contrasting textures, and eye-pleasing forms. It can stay outside all year to brighten your landscape in every season.

Select a small tree or shrub with attractive winter twigs, evergreen foliage, or colorful berries, add bulbs to bloom in spring, a perennial plant to flower during the summer, and an evergreen groundcover to complement the planting and keep weeds away.

Ultra-Light Potting Mix

Joan Benjamin and Deborah L. Martin

You can still move even really big containers if you fill them with this ultra-light mix developed by New Yorker Linda Yang, author of *The City and Town Gardener*. The mix's lightness comes from the large proportion of perlite, a porous, very lightweight soil amendment.

Ingredients and Supplies

5 parts perlite
1 part soil
5 parts peat or compost
Organic fertilizer or dehydrated cow manure

Directions

1. Moisten the perlite to reduce the dust, then mix all the ingredients together.

2. Add a handful of granular organic fertilizer or a trowelful of dehydrated cow manure to each 3 gallons of mix.

3. Use this light mix to fill hanging baskets, windowboxes, and balcony or rooftop garden containers. Keep an eye on moisture—this mix drains quickly.

If you're planting shallow-rooted annuals in a large, deep container, reduce the weight by filling the bottom part of the container with empty plastic bottles of Styrofoam "peanuts." A layer of burlap will save you from picking lightweight fillers out of your potting mix when it's time to repot.

Super-Simple Potting Mix

What could possibly be simpler than this two-ingredient container mix recipe from Connie Beck, who teaches vocational horticulture in San Diego County, California. You can buy perlite—a very lightweight natural mineral—at garden centers.

Ingredients and Supplies

1 part perlite
1 part compost (sifted)

Directions

1. Moisten the perlite before you start mixing—it's usually very dusty.

2. Mix the perlite into the compost, and you're ready to plant!

Note: Connie says that this mix is so good at preventing diseases that she lacks examples of plant problems to show her students.

Overhead Herbs
Roger Yepsen

It may be ornamental rather than strictly practical, but a kitchen seems to look more like a no-nonsense workplace if there are bundles of herbs hanging to dry from joists. Or, if you don't have an old farmhouse with authentic exposed joists, simple hooks on a wall will do. Cut the stems just above ground level to facilitate tying bundles with twine. The less-humid air of fall may help the herbs to dry. But unless your house is unusual, kitchen oils and dust will conspire to coat these herbs with an unappetizing fur. So either use them fairly promptly or treat them as nonfunctional decoration, something like wax fruit in a glass bowl.

Plant a Potted Kitchen Herb Garden

Barbara Pleasant

Think you don't have room for a kitchen garden? Think again! Planting culinary herbs in pots lets you dress up your deck, porch, or patio with plants that are pretty as well as productive. Plus, it's easy to move them around or replace plants that are past their prime, so they'll always look their best.

Herbs can grow equally well in individual pots or grouped into larger planters. Even for gardeners who have plenty of garden space, single pots are ideal for herbs that spread rampantly by creeping roots or stems, such as mints. Containers also make it easy to bring herbs indoors in fall and extend your harvest into winter. On the down side, individual pots have limited space for roots, so they tend to need frequent watering and fertilizing. Larger planters provide more rooting room, but they also tend to be heavy and difficult to move. Consider using a mix of container sizes to enjoy the advantages of each.

There's no one best type of container for kitchen herbs—anything that can hold potting soil will do the job, as long as it has holes in the bottom for drainage. If your potted garden is in a highly visible spot, set the herbs directly into decorative planters, or grow the herbs in plastic nursery pots and slip them into prettier planters. Fill your chosen containers with an all-purpose potting soil, but not regular garden soil, which can compact tightly with regular watering.

During the growing season, water regularly to keep the soil evenly moist; small pots may need to be watered as often as once a day during dry, windy weather. Also, fertilize once every 2 to 3 weeks with diluted fish emulsion or a commercial organic liquid fertilizer to keep the plants healthy and vigorous. Herbs normally aren't bothered much by

pests or diseases, but if you notice any problems, pinching off the affected parts is an easy way to stop them from spreading.

The possible combinations of plants and pots is limited only by your imagination, but to get you started, here's a simple plan for a basic container herb garden comprised of three containers. Once you get the hang of growing herbs, personalize the planting plan for your particular needs!

You Will Need

Tools: Watering can, hand trowel
1 round container, 14 inches in diameter
1 rectangular window box container
1 hanging basket container
One 40-pound bag of potting soil (more for larger containers)
Container-grown herb plants

For the large round planter:
1 clump of chives
1 fennel plant
1 sage plant
1 French tarragon plant

For the window box:
1 basil plant
2 parsley plants
1 spearmint plant

For the hanging basket:
1 Greek oregano plant
1 creeping rosemary plant
1 English thyme plant

1. Thoroughly water the purchased herbs, and trim away any yellowed leaves or damaged stems.

2. Fill all three containers to within 2 inches of the top with purchased potting soil. Push the herbs from their pots by squeezing on the bottoms and jiggling the plants free. Set the plants in place as shown, beginning with the largest plant in each group.

3. Add potting soil to fill in spaces between the herbs. Tap or gently shake the containers to help settle the soil in place. Add additional soil until the tops of the root balls are barely covered.

4. Set the containers in place, and water thoroughly with room temperature water. Wait several hours or overnight, and water the containers again.

Welcoming Wildlife

Butterflies and Bees

Birds and Small Animals

Welcoming Wildlife

WELCOMING WILDLIFE

Wildlife and Birds

Jeff Cox

While you're planning and dreaming about your yard and garden, don't overlook the joys of attracting wildlife and birds. Your yard can become a veritable Noah's ark if you provide the basics for nature's creatures: food, water, shelter, and a safe place in which to reproduce and raise the next generation. With careful planning, you can develop even a tiny yard to attract a surprising array of wildlife and birds. Small occupants, such as rabbits, squirrels, and birds, can become near-permanent breeding residents. Animals with larger territories, such as deer and foxes, may appear for a visit as their travels come to include your backyard as a regular stop.

Attracting Wildlife

Although wild birds have been welcome backyard and garden visitors for decades, other forms of wildlife have generally been greeted with much less warmth. But growing numbers of gardeners across the country are developing a new attitude toward squirrels, rabbits, mice, toads, salamanders, crickets, and all the rest that the neighborhood ark might hold.

Look at your backyard from a new perspective— one of wildlife in search of food, water, cover, and a safe place for their young. When viewed in this light, tangled brush, tall weeds, and dead trees take on a much more essential role than manicured lawns and rows of flowers.

More on Wildlife

In 1991, the National Wildlife Federation registered its ten-thousandth backyard habitat. That number represents only those gardeners who took the time and trouble to officially register the wildlife-friendly habitats they had developed. Millions of others—the Federation estimates more than 12 million—are enjoying the fruits of attracting wildlife into their backyards without any official recognition whatsoever. For information on registering your backyard, write to Backyard Wildlife Habitat Program, National Wildlife Federation, 1400 16th Street NW, Washington, DC 20036-2266.

Food To make your sanctuary attractive to a number of species, you'll need to include a variety of plants. The cottontail rabbit, for example, eats herbaceous plants such as grasses and clovers for much of the year and in winter adds the twigs and bark of young trees and shrubs. The eastern gray squirrel is most decidedly a nut eater—primarily acorns, hickory nuts, and beechnuts—but corn is also a great attraction. Birds depend on insects as their mainstay, adding seeds, berries, and fruits.

Raccoons relish crayfish, grasshoppers, frogs, and birds' eggs, but almost any living creature that is smaller and slower than a 'coon will find its way into its diet. Acorns, corn, and fleshy fruits also are favorite raccoon foods. Most of the diet of the red fox is small rodents, such as mice, voles, and rabbits. In summer and fall, fox diets also include as much as 25 percent fleshy fruits. The browsing diet of the white-tailed deer consists largely of twigs from trees and shrubs but is supplemented in spring and summer by many of the same herbaceous plants cottontail rabbits eat.

Shelter Tall and mid-sized trees, shrubs, tall herbaceous plants, grasses, and groundcovers all provide for varying needs of different species. Weeds and wildflowers also play their part where local ordinances and neighbors will allow.

Continued ➡

Consider seasonal diversity, too. Different plants produce their buds, fruits, and seeds at different times of the year. Some plants, such as evergreens, supply shelter year-round. The brambly interior of a blackberry patch makes a good escape route for small animals such as rabbits, even in winter.

You'll attract the most wildlife by mimicking the plantings of nature. Wild animals stay safe from predators by moving from place to place through protective cover. An isolated berry bush may attract a migrating group of cedar waxwings, but a grouse who tries to reach it could soon become hawk food. If you add another few bushes, and perhaps a hemlock (*Tsuga* spp.), and front the shrubs with meadow grasses and wildflowers, you'll make the planting attractive to a variety of wild creatures.

To this living landscape add snags, logs, brush piles, and rock piles to provide places for smaller creatures to hide and to rear their young. You can camouflage these elements by planting vines like wild grapes or Virginia creeper (*Parthenocissus quinquefolia*) to trail over them. In the process, you'll provide additional food sources.

Water Water is the most overlooked aspect of backyard wildlife habitats. Food and cover preferences vary widely, but nearly all creatures need water. A birdbath will serve many birds, many insects, and some mammals. A ground-level fountain will provide for even more drinkers and might also attract some amphibians. A small pond of varying depth will find use by nearly every creature that you can expect to draw into the backyard and can even provide a permanent home for frogs and turtles.

Attracting Birds

Birds are most gardeners' favorite visitors, with their cheerful songs, sprightly manners, and colorful plumage. Birds are also among nature's most efficient insect predators, making them valuable garden allies. In an afternoon, one diminutive house wren can snatch up more than 500 insect eggs, beetles, and grubs. Given a nest of tent caterpillars, a Baltimore oriole will wolf down as many as 17 of the pests per minute. More than 60 percent of the chickadee's winter diet is aphid eggs. And the swallow lives up to its name by consuming massive quantities of flying insects—by one count, more than 1,000 leafhoppers in 12 hours.

Unless your property is completely bare, at least some birds will visit with no special encouragement from you. Far more birds, however, will come to your yard and garden if you take steps to provide their four basic requirements: food, water, cover, and a safe place in which to raise a family. Robins, nuthatches, hummingbirds, titmice, bluebirds, mockingbirds, cardinals, and various sparrows are among the most common garden visitors.

Landscaping for Birds

Feeders, birdbaths, and birdhouses play important roles in attracting birds. But trees, shrubs, and other vegetation can do the whole job naturally. Plants provide food, cover, and nest sites, and because they trap dew and rain and control runoff, they help provide water, too.

When adding plants to your landscape, choose as many food-bearing species as possible, with enough variety to assure birds a steady diet of fruit, buds, and seeds throughout the year. Mix plantings of deciduous and evergreen species in order to maintain leafy cover in all seasons. Species that are native to your region are generally best because the local birds evolved with them and will turn to them first for food and cover. Combine as many types of vegetation as possible: tall trees, shorter trees, shrubs, grasses, flowers, and groundcovers. The greater the plant diversity, the greater the variety of birds you will attract to your yard.

Hummingbirds have their own landscape favorites. Preferred trees and shrubs include tulip tree (*Liriodendron tulipifera*), mimosa (*Albizia julibrissin*), cotoneasters (*Cotoneaster* spp.), orange-eye butterfly bush (*Buddleia davidii*), flowering quinces (*Chaenomeles* spp.), and rose-of-Sharon (*Hibiscus syriacus*). Favored perennials include columbines (*Aquilegia* spp.), common foxglove (*Digitalis purpurea*), alumroots (*Heuchera* spp.), cardinal flower (*Lobelia cardinalis*), penstemons (*Penstemon* spp.), torch lilies (*Kniphofia* spp.), sages (*Salvia* spp.), and delphiniums (*Delphinium* spp.).

Of course, there is the flip side to landscaping for the birds, especially if you grow berries for your family. Bird netting may be a necessity if you don't want to share your cherries and blueberries with your feathered friends.

Providing Feeders

Food is the easiest of the four basic requirements to supply. Even if you live in a city apartment, you can attract birds by putting a feeder filled with seed on your balcony. If your landscape is mostly lawn and hard surfaces, you can use feeders as the main food supply while you add plantings of fruiting trees and shrubs. And if your yard is a good nature habitat, where plants are the primary food source (as they should be), feeders can provide crucial nourishment during winter, drought, and other times when the natural food supply is low. Besides, carefully placed feeders allow you and your family to watch and photograph birds.

Some birds, including juncos, mourning doves, and towhees, feed on the ground, while others, including finches, grosbeaks, nuthatches, titmice, and chickadees, eat their meals higher up. In order to attract as many different birds as possible, use a variety of feeders—seed tubes, broad platforms, and shelf and hanging types. Place them at varying heights, widely separated from one another, and near the protective cover of a tree or shrub if possible. No matter what the style, the feeder should resist rain and snow, should be easy to fill and clean, and should hold enough birdseed so that you don't have to refill it every day, but not so much that the food spoils before it can all be eaten.

Water All Year

Under normal conditions, most birds get all the water they need from the food they eat, from dew, and from rain. Nonetheless, a reliable water source makes life easier for birds—and can be critical during drought or in arid regions.

A birdbath or shallow pan set in the open and at least 3 feet off the ground, with shrubs or overhanging branches nearby to provide an escape route from cats or other predators, is ideal. The water in the bath should be no deeper than 3 inches. Birds are particularly attracted to the sound of moving water, so it helps to hang a dripping hose (or a leaky can or jug, filled with water daily) from a branch over the bath.

Birds need water in winter, too. Commercial immersion water heaters will keep the water in birdbaths thawed in winter. They are available from stores and mail-order supply houses that sell bird supplies. You can try to keep water from freezing by pouring warm water into the baths as needed, but on very cold days this requires a lot of pouring.

Cover and Nest Sites

Cover is any form of shelter from enemies and the elements. Different bird species favor different kinds of cover. Mourning doves, for example, prefer evergreen groves; others prefer the refuge of densely twiggy shrubs. Likewise, most species require a particular kind of cover in which to raise a family. Some birds, including red-winged blackbirds, nest in high grass; others, such as cardinals, nest in dense foliage; and still others, such as woodpeckers, need wooded land.

You can add more nest sites and attract many types of birds to your yard with birdhouses. Different species have different housing requirements, but there are ready-made birdhouses and build-your-own plans for everything from bluebirds to barn owls. Whichever birdhouse you choose, make sure that it is weather-resistant, that its roof is pitched to shed rain, and that there are holes in the bottom for drainage and in the walls or back for ventilation. A hinged or removable top or front makes cleaning easier. Position birdhouses with their entrance holes facing away from prevailing winds, and clean out the nesting materials from the boxes after every nesting season.

Why Welcome Wildlife?

Barbara Pleasant

From the buzz of insects to the trill of bird songs, wild creatures of all shapes and sizes help connect us to the natural world. Their natural rhythms—migrating, hibernating, raising young—help free us from the unnatural rhythms our own lives sometimes follow. Their beauty rests our eyes, while the intricate behaviors of wild things are as amazing as the most complex technology. And the very presence of wildlife tells us about the health of our environment. An abundance of wild creatures, from microscopic to massive, is a sign that our surroundings are as healthy for our families as they are for theirs.

Welcoming Wildlife Back

Wherever you live, there's little doubt that it once was home to a much greater number and variety of wild animals than it is today. By adapting our landscapes to make them more inviting to wildlife, we are welcoming nature back to its old haunts. Before you set out feeders and houses, sow butterfly-magnet plants, or install a natural pond, take a look at your current gardening practices. Some things may need to change before your yard is ready to host buntings and bunnies.

Keep your landscape pesticide-free.

Most songbirds eat insects at some stage in their lives, so spraying poisons on bugs is like feeding it to the beautiful birds you hope to attract. And, because butterflies *are* insects, it makes little sense to spray pesticides if you enjoy seeing butterflies flutter through your yard.

Curb your pets.

Even well-fed house cats love to hunt, so if you're luring birds to your yard with food, make sure you're not luring them to their deaths. Keep Kitty indoors, or make her wear a bell that warns wildlife when she is near, and ask your neighbors to do the same with their cats. Dogs also hunt instinctively and will harass any critters that catch their attention. If you're serious about making wild animals feel at home at your place, set some boundaries with your pets.

Continued →

GIVE UP YOUR MANICURE.

A bare expanse of closely cropped grass punctuated with a small tree and tightly pruned shrubs is about as uninviting to wildlife as an acre of asphalt. Wildlife thrives along landscape edges, where grasses and flowers give way to the shelter of shrubs and trees. Be as orderly as you like close to your house, but enhance your yard's edges to make it more hospitable to wildlife.

Wildlife-Friendly Landscaping

As you lure in wildlife, don't worry that your yard will turn into a wild jungle—and you certainly don't have to sacrifice your vegetable garden. Instead, take a positive approach by stocking your yard with wildlife-friendly plants, arranged in ways that are pleasing to you and to your wild visitors.

Trees and Shrubs for Birds

To attract birds to your landscape, look at plants from a bird's point of view. Do they provide food and shelter? Nest sites? Try to plant a variety to provide birds with protective cover and a varied diet throughout the year. The following trees and shrubs are excellent food sources—producing berries, nuts, or seeds that birds will flock to. Evergreen species provide food but are also especially important for winter cover. These species will grow in most regions of the country.

Evergreen Shrubs

  Chinese holly (*Ilex cornuta*)

  Cotoneasters (*Cotoneaster* spp.)

  Japanese yew (*Taxus cuspidata*)

  Oregon grape (*Mahonia aquifolium*)

Deciduous Shrubs

  American elder (*Sambucus canadensis*)

  Bayberries (*Myrica* spp.)

  Blueberries (*Vaccinium* spp.)

  Common buckthorn (*Rhamnus cathartica*)

  Japanese barberry (*Berberis thunbergii*)

  Pyracanthas (*Pyracantha* spp.)

  Raspberries and blackberries (*Rubus* spp.)

  Red-osier dogwood (*Cornus sericea*)

  Sand cherries (*Prunus pumila, P. besseyi*)

  Viburnums (*Viburnum* spp.)

Evergreen Trees

  American holly (*Ilex opaca*)

  Canada hemlock (*Tsuga canadensis*)

  Douglas fir (*Pseudotsuga menziesii*)

  Eastern red cedar (*Juniperus virginiana*)

  Pines (*Pinus* spp.)

  Spruces (*Picea* spp.)

Deciduous Trees

  American beech (*Fagus grandifolia*)

  Cherries (*Prunus* spp.)

  Common persimmon (*Diospyros virginiana*)

  Crab apples (*Malus* spp.)

  Flowering dogwood (*Cornus florida*)

  Hackberries (*Celtis* spp.)

  Hawthorns (*Crataegus* spp.)

  Hickories (*Carya* spp.)

  Oaks (*Quercus* spp.)

  Serviceberries (*Amelanchier* spp.)

  White ash (*Fraxinus americana*)

• Look for ways to create pathways for wildlife to travel through your landscape.

• Plant a hedge that includes berry-producing shrubs and evergreens for year-round shelter and winter food.

• Work with your neighbors to form connected greenways for birds and animals.

Balancing Benefits

It's natural that the pleasure you find in gardening should lead you to an interest in your landscape's wild side. Yet when it comes to wildlife, cute is in the eye of the beholder. Chipmunks are fun to watch until they uproot an entire planter full of pansies while digging for seeds. Deer appear elegant until they eat a patch of expensive tulips you've waited all winter to see bloom.

Gardening to attract wildlife is a balancing act between your commitment to preserve and protect nature and your desire to create a landscape that satisfies your family's needs for food, recreation, and beauty. You can achieve both goals by taking a strategic approach to sharing your landscape with wildlife.

Successful Sharing

The old saying about good fences making good neighbors is practical guidance when it comes to sharing your landscape with wildlife. As much as human development allows, wildlife live, roam, and eat according to their instincts. Most of the wild creatures that enter your domain will show little interest in your gardens, but it takes only one or two troublemakers to take the pleasure out of playing host to your wild neighbors. A little planning—and some sturdy fencing—can help keep wildlife from raiding your garden and spoiling your fun.

• Place feeding stations away from your vegetable garden, fruit trees, and berry patch.

• Provide desirable alternatives. Plant a mulberry tree to give fruit-eating birds something other than your blueberries and cherries to dine on; sow a patch of "bunny" lettuce far from your garden and close to sheltering shrubbery.

• Use fences, netting, rowcovers, passive scare devices, and other techniques to keep your food from becoming their food.

Give 'Em Shelter

Providing shelter is the best way to attract different kinds of wild creatures to your landscape. Every creature needs a place to hide from predators, rest, and perhaps raise their young. More than shortages of natural food or water, a scant supply of suitable habitat is responsible for the shrinking populations of many wild species. Giving wildlife a place to live and reproduce in your landscape can be a treat for you, too. You'll have the chance to see species that don't visit feeders, and you may enjoy the rare pleasure of watching fledgling birds testing their wings in first flight, or the remarkable sight of a mother opossum with her babies clinging to her back.

HEDGE YOUR BETS

Creating shelter for wildlife is relatively simple. While you might think first about building houses for birds and animals, most wild animals—even the cavity-nesters that houses are meant for—prefer natural sites for nesting and cover. With a little planning, your landscape can include the sorts of natural shelter that wild birds and animals like best and need most. A well-placed evergreen windbreak, for example, can help lower your heating costs by sheltering your house from winter winds, and at the

---

same time provide roosting and nesting places for birds, as well as cover for many small mammals.

Who's at Home in Your 'Hood?

Where you live determines, in large part, what species of wildlife are likely to appear in your yard. A visiting armadillo is an improbable (at best) guest in a Minnesota garden, and a Stellar's jay (a western species) would be a surprising rarity in South Carolina. Visit your local library, talk to wildlife-minded neighbors, or join a bird-watching group to learn more about what kinds of birds, reptiles, and mammals call your region home. Then take steps to provide the types of food and shelter that will make them feel welcome in your landscape.

Like an evergreen windbreak, a hedge of mixed evergreen or deciduous shrubs creates superb shelter for wildlife. By providing a long row of unbroken shelter, a hedge lets small animals move through their habitat unseen by predators. It offers safe nesting spots for songbirds, and a place where they can dash for cover when a hawk flies overhead. Hedges that include fruit-producing plants serve as a food supply, too.

A wildlife hedge need not be carefully pruned, and will probably be more attractive to you, and to wildlife, if it is comprised of a tangle of evergreen and berry-bearing deciduous shrubs. The plants listed below are easy to grow and can be woven into a wildlife-friendly hedge. If you don't have room for a long hedge, try mixing shelter and food shrubs together by grouping several along the outer edge of your landscape.

12 TERRIFIC SHELTER AND FOOD SHRUBS

  Barberries (*Berberis* spp.)

  Bayberries, wax myrtles (*Myrica* spp.)

  Cranberry bush (*Viburnum trilobum*)

  Elderberries (*Sambucus* spp.)

  Hollies (*Ilex* spp.)

  Junipers (*Juniperus* spp.)

  Lilacs (*Syringa* spp.)

  Mahonia (*Mahonia aquifolium*)

  Manzanitas (*Arctostaphylos* spp.)

  Ninebark (*Physocarpus* spp.)

  Rugosa rose (*Rosa rugosa*)

  Yews (*Taxus* spp.)

STAND UP FOR SNAGS

A dead, decaying tree, which is called a snag, may not fit your vision of landscape loveliness, but it's an ideal home for many cavity-nesting birds and animals. The most adorable birdhouse you can imagine won't get a second look from chickadees, nuthatches, titmice, woodpeckers, and wrens if there's snag space available. Kestrels and owls often move into holes created by woodpeckers, as do squirrels and raccoons. In addition to spaces for nesting and roosting, snags often host wood-eating insects, so they are also a food source for insect-eating birds and mammals.

Whenever possible, leave room in your landscape for this perfect wildlife refuge. If you find yourself confronted by a landscape tree that is dead or dying, consider your options before firing up the chain saw.

Continued →

- Is it a hazard to people or property? Sometimes trimming off a few limbs reduces the likelihood that the tree might cause damage.
- Can you leave a significant part of it? A 12- to 20-foot trunk is better than no snag at all.
- Is it attractive? With the addition of plants, feeders, or drilled nesting holes, a dead tree may become the liveliest focal point in a wildlife lover's landscape.

If the top of the remaining trunk is at a reasonably accessible height (for you, not for the birds), top it with a birdbath or a hopper feeder. Drill holes into the trunk and stuff them with suet or peanut butter. Drive a few long nails into the trunk and use them to serve halves of apples or oranges. Mount a hanger arm and hang a tube feeder from it. Birds will flock in to enjoy the treats you provide.

Don't worry, by the way, about the insects that arrive to chomp and chew through the decaying wood of a dead tree—they're not about to attack other plants in your landscape. The insects that feast on dead trees are specifically there for that purpose, and healthy landscape plants are not their cup of tea.

However, insect-eating birds regard wood-chomping insects as a delicacy. Snags often attract woodpeckers and other birds for whom wood-eating insects are dietary staples.

Your Backyard as a Wildlife Habitat
Sally Roth

When I decided to turn my front yard into a wildlife haven, I started with a budget of $100—not much in landscaping dollars. I knew it wouldn't stretch to let me do the whole front yard, so I started small, focusing on a grouping of berried shrubs. I planted three deciduous winterberry hollies in a single group, curving them around a flat-topped rock that held a clay saucer—an impromptu bird and chipmunk watering hole that served for years until I got around to putting in the stone recirculating basin on my master plan.

That was almost a garden all by itself, but I added wildflowers and spring bulbs around their feet for spring interest, then mulched with lawn mower—chopped oak leaves. I was pleased with the first step, and so were the birds. Bluebirds and thrushes arrived within weeks, feasting on the berries and splashing in the bath. When the berries were gone, the protective branches of the shrubs gave the birds at my nearby feeders a new place to perch.

Lay Down the Log

If a standing snag isn't feasible in your landscape, consider a log instead. You can turn a section of a fallen tree trunk or even a substantial branch into a "horizontal snag" by simply placing it on the ground. Once it's in place, wildlife will discover the log and move in. Small mammals like chipmunks and rabbits will nest under it, as will toads, snakes, salamanders, and lizards. Woodpeckers will fly in to hunt for insects during the day, and skunks may make nighttime visits for the same reason. To find a suitable piece of dead-wood, ask permission to search in local woods, particularly after a storm has moved through the area. Utility companies, tree services, and parks departments are other potential sources for a nice log.

The following spring, when my wallet was a little fatter, I added on to my original planting. I created a second planting near the first, but based it on blueberries and viburnums. By extending the planting of wild blue phlox (*Phlox divaricata*) and other wildflowers from one group of shrubs to the next, the two pieces merged into a single garden.

Gardening bit by bit lets me extend my garden whenever the time is right. Each new piece is a satisfying garden in itself, and the whole thing expands gradually. Best of all, it looks good right from the start. I keep it from looking schizophrenic by repeating colors and plants throughout. Spicebushes, for example, are a repeating theme that helps tie things together.

Bringing in the Good Guys
Sally Jean Cunningham

When you use my companion-gardening system, you group your crop families and their plant friends together in garden neighborhoods. That means they'll live and grow together in peace and harmony, right? Not always! Now the outsiders start to arrive—insects and animals, invited or not. They come flying, crawling, digging, and marching right into your happy plant community. But most of them will be welcome guests, those wonderful beneficial insects that you've attracted by planting flowers and herbs. They're your main line of defense against the pests insects that will also inevitably drop in. In this section, you'll learn all about the "good guy" insects: how they control pests, what they look like, where you'll find them in your garden, and more special techniques you can use to help them thrive.

Taking a Bug's Eye View

Insects fascinate me. When I first studied organic gardening, I was delighted to discover that most of the insects in my garden are my allies in fighting pests. But many people find it hard to believe that most insects are beneficial, because long ago somebody taught them to be afraid of insects and say "Eeeuuuw" when they saw a spider or an ant. Most of those in the insect-fearing crowd will concede that a few insects do good things—but don't let those "bugs" get too close!

Those folks would be surprised to learn about the major roles insects play in the survival of our planet. For example, without insect pollination, there would be food shortages, because about one-third of the food we eat comes from plants pollinated by insects. Insects are critical to the decay cycle that returns nutrients to the soil. They're also an important part of the food chain for birds, fish, frogs, and other animals.

INTRODUCING THE GOOD GUYS

So who are all the "good guys"? Lady beetles probably top most people's lists, followed by praying mantids and honeybees. Of course, spiders are helpful, and so are pest-eating lightning bugs, and then there are earthworms—certainly worth their weight in gold, even if they're not insects. But they're just the beginning. Believe it or not, 95 to 99 percent of all insects are beneficial or harmless to human life and endeavors.

There are four main job descriptions for beneficial insects: predator, parasitoid, pollinator, and soil builder/garbage collector. Whether you see them at work or not, you can bet your companion garden employs thousands of beneficial insects carrying out these four important jobs.

Blooming with Ideas

There's no need to consult a professional designer to learn about good combinations—unlimited possibilities are right in front of your nose. Think about the spring wildflowers, a summer meadow, or the last hurrah before frost. How can you improve on wild blue phlox and Dutchman's breeches with a few trilliums thrown in for good measure? What could be more beautiful than madder-purple fall asters and a sweep of goldenrod, decorated with filmy plumes of virgin's bower vine? If you want a beautiful combination, borrow from nature.

I've learned to jot down companion possibilities when I see them. No matter how often I think, "Oh, I'll remember that," I never do unless I write it down. I'm not organized enough to keep a nice neat notebook, but even a scrap of paper in the pocket of my jeans serves the purpose.

Like all insects, beneficials have distinct stages in their life cycles. Some types of insects undergo a process called complete metamorphosis. These insects emerge from eggs as larvae, such as caterpillars, which look completely unlike the adults. A larva feeds and grows, then forms a pupa (a resting stage in which the insect covers itself with a hard shell). After resting awhile in the pupa, the adult emerges.

Other types of insects have a lifestyle known as incomplete metamorphosis. These insects emerge from eggs as nymphs, resembling tiny adults. The nymphs feed and molt several times before reaching adult size and form. All stages in the life cycle of a beneficial insect can be helpful to gardeners.

INSECT PREDATORS

The most familiar beneficial insects—lady beetles and praying mantids—are predators. They hunt down and eat their prey just as the lion hunts the antelope. Predatory insects are usually larger than their prey, and often they hunt in the larval (caterpillar or grub) stage as well as in the adult stage.

Predatory insects usually prey on several kinds of insects. The praying mantis, for example, captures and eats just about anything it can wrestle to the ground—including another praying mantis! Many predators have names that are clues to their behavior: assassin bugs, ambush bugs, soldier beetles, and tiger beetles. Other colorful names describe the insect's appearance, like big-eyed bugs, dragonflies, and lacewings. Delicate lacewings can actually be fierce hunters. Certainly the larvae are voracious eaters—that's why they're nicknamed aphid wolves!

Paper wasps are also fine insect hunters. People are often afraid of these wasps, but they are rarely aggressive toward humans unless their lives are threatened. What paper wasps seek are full-size caterpillars, such as gypsy moth larvae and imported cabbageworms which the wasps feed to their young.

INSECT PARASITOIDS

Parasites are organisms that live their entire lives directly on the bodies of their *hosts*. Mistletoe is a well-known plant parasite that develops special rootlike structures that puncture tree bark and absorb water and nutrients from the trees. Fleas and lice are insect parasites.

Continued ➡

A Backyard Wildlife Habitat

Think like a bird or a rabbit and you'll have a ready idea of what's needed to make a landscape appealing to wildlife—protective cover, food, and water. Supply these basis, and your backyard will soon be a fascinating place alive with birds, bugs, and animals.

You can adapt this plan according to how much space you have available in your own yard. Just adjust the size of the various elements.

Develop the plan one part at a time, if you like. You'll most likely want to start with the birdfeeding area, which will give you an immediate payoff.

Make permanent features like arbors and rock walls the first step of each section, to give it structure you can build around. Plant shrubs and trees as soon in your long-range plan as you can, because they will take the longest to fill in.

Features

1. Street
2. Driveway
3. Hummingbird garden
4. Patio with potted fuchsias and geraniums
5. Shade garden
6. Bird feeding area with assorted feeders and a few shrubs
7. Corridor of mixed shrubs and trees, mostly deciduous with a few evergreens
8. Birdseed garden
9. Meadow or prairie garden
10. Sitting place
11. Rock wall (piled or unmortared)
12. Pond and bog garden
13. Naturalistic woodland
14. Brush pile
15. Shallow drinking/bathing station for birds that is made from rock and recirculating pump, including small waterfall for sound of water to attract birds
16. Butterfly garden
17. Grape arbor
18. Berry bushes: thimbleberries, blueberries, viburnums, and elderberries
19. House
20. Huckleberry, lowbush blueberry, and bearberry
21. Evergreen woodland of conifers, rhododendrons, azaleas, and hollies

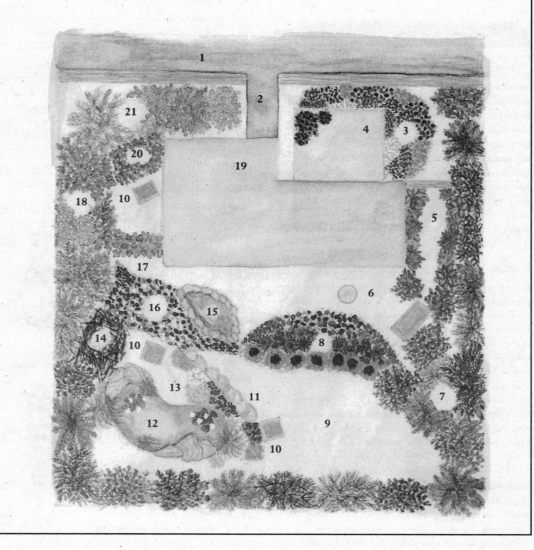

Parasitoids, a special kind of parasite, live on the body of their hosts for only a part of their lives. Parasitoid insects lay eggs on or inside the body of a host insect, larva, or egg.

When the parasitoid larvae hatch, they feed on the host. The most common parasitoids are wasps and tachinid flies. Braconid wasps lay eggs in the bodies of tomato hornworms, and the larvae feed on the caterpillar. If you grow tomatoes in your companion garden, you will probably see tomato hornworms with little white bumps or growths attached, which are the wasp's pupae. The pupae develop when the hornworm is near death. More adult wasps will emerge from the pupae, ready to hunt down still more tomato hornworms.

INSECT POLLINATORS

Bees pollinate about 75 percent of the world's food-crop plants. Most gardeners have no idea of the wonderful variety of bees—over 4,000 species of bees in North America alone. Bumblebees and a large group called "solitary bees," which includes mason bees, leafcutter bees, and squash bees, actually do much more pollinating than honeybees.

Flies are the second most important pollinators. Other pollinators include butterflies, beetles, moths, wasps, and even thrips. For the sake of pollination alone, never kill a bee, fly, or wasp in the garden—unless you're allergic to the stings, or unless it's a deerfly or horsefly that's about to bite you!

SOIL BUILDERS AND GARBAGE COLLECTORS

There is so much to praise about the insects and other creatures that build soil and break down decaying matter in nature and in our gardens. Anyone who has a compost pile has met some of these creatures, including millipedes, centipedes, beetles, sow bugs, and earwigs. They turn yard waste into "black gold."

Keeping Your Good Guys Happy

Once you've planted your beds with a mix of those flowers, herbs, and groundcovers, you can pretty much sit back, relax, and watch the garden happen. The beneficials will control the pests, and your role will be to orchestrate, watch for situations that need extra help, and fine-tune the whole arrangement.

There are some extra things you can do to take care of the beneficial insects in your garden. Beneficials need the same things that all living creatures must have: water, food, shelter, and protection (particularly for breeding). Your garden will provide the food, and it's easy to make sure your beneficials can find water and shelter.

A Changing Landscape

A natural garden is a work in progress, not a finished masterpiece. Its life is interesting, and its face is beautiful, but even when you step back and say "Ahhh," the picture doesn't hold for long. Even the slowest-growing desert landscapes are always changing. Seeds drop and sprout, roots reach out and shoulder neighboring plants aside, voles uproot the groundcovers, birds strip the bark for nest-building—the cycle never ends. Relax and enjoy the process instead of fighting to capture a particular moment. With a natural landscape, instead of a static scene, you can look forward to a lifetime of surprises.

Continued ➡

WATER FOR BENEFICIALS

Your companion garden should have water available at all times and at two levels. For flying insects, a waist-height water dish like a birdbath works well. However, while water a few inches deep is perfect for birds, tiny insects may drown in such "deep" water! Give beneficials plenty of places to land by adding rocks and pebbles. (Think of it as providing a beach and towels for your guests.)

For insects that live at ground level, put out a few shallow pans, and add water to them whenever you water your garden. Any container will do, from old pie tins and plastic dishes to nice ceramic bowls. Choose a container with sloping sides and pebbly surfaces so that tiny beneficials have places to alight. If you're concerned about standing water allowing mosquitoes to breed, just stir up the water or refill it often with a vigorous stream of water from the hose.

Other beneficial animals will visit your bug baths too, including frogs, toads, birds, and maybe even a lizard or salamander. All of these will also dine on insects.

FOOD FOR BENEFICIALS

Most beneficial insects need two types of food sources. One is pest insects, so we need to be sure there are some aphids, leafhoppers, plant bugs, slugs, and all kinds of caterpillars around our gardens. This can be tough for gardeners to accept, because who wants bugs in their produce? But if there are *no* pests in your garden, there won't be any beneficials either, and that can leave your crops vulnerable to attack. You'll need to be patient and trust in your unseen army.

To survive when the pest pickings are poor, beneficials will dine on nectar and pollen. The flower and herb "friends" in your companion garden win provide that in plenty.

SHELTERING BENEFICIALS

Be sure that beneficials have places to hide themselves and their eggs around your yard and garden all year. During the garden season, include some permanent plantings in your garden, like a cluster of perennials around a birdbath. Having permanent mulched pathways also shelters many insects like ground beetles.

The tough times to provide shelter for insects are fall and winter, when you want to pull out the spent crops and cut down the dead foliage. Leave some of the perennial foliage standing over winter—it may harbor beneficial insect eggs. You can also create a special mulch boundary around the edge of your garden that won't be dug or tilled. Many beneficial insects will overwinter under mulch or in the soil, and this boundary will give them a place to hide.

BUYING BENEFICIAL INSECTS

Raising beneficial insects for sale to farmers and gardeners is a booming business. You'll see insects for sale in many garden-supply catalogs and at some nurseries. Should you buy beneficial insects to release in your garden? I say no! I believe on a home-garden scale, we can attract all the helpers we need by planting the right attractant plants and supplying water and shelter.

One case where buying beneficials may help is in home greenhouses or large sunrooms. Gardeners who have indoor gardening areas like these can buy many effective pest controllers. One type is a lady beetle called a mealybug destroyer (*Cryptolaemus montrouzieri*). The larvae of these beetles look like giant mealybugs themselves, with a white, waxy cottonlike coating.

Both the shaggy-looking larvae and the adult beetles dine on mealybugs. They are active only in temperatures above 56°F, and they prefer humid conditions.

CHECKING OUT YOUR BENEFICIAL BUDDIES

How can you tell whether beneficial insects are at work in your garden? One way to tell is by what you don't see. If no holes appear in your plant leaves, it's probably because beneficials are keeping caterpillars, beetles, and other pests at bay.

Another way is to go on a beneficial-insect exploration tour in your garden.

"Backyard Garden Beneficials," is a rundown of 31 kinds of the most common beneficials found in backyard gardens. In this section, you'll find pictures of the insects, tips on identifying them, including their most distinctive features, and the likely spots where they hide in or near your garden. Pick a day when there's not much wind, grab this book or an insect field guide, a magnifying glass or lens (at least 10 power), and perhaps your reading glasses for close-up work.

You may want to keep a notebook to record what insects you see, and on which plants. You can also jot down any questions you have about the insects. One warning here: You may get less "gardening" done if you're like me. The more I look, the less I weed. But then so many of the beneficials are on those "weeds" anyway!

Backyard Garden Beneficials

Once you've planted a companion garden, there will be beneficial insects in it—whether or not you know who they are. In this section, you'll find information and illustrations to help you identify these small, hardworking gardening helpers. You'll also discover how they're helping out in your garden. Check the "Did You Know?" feature for my somewhat nonscientific interpretations of insect behavior and other tidbits of information I've discovered, plus a few of my own experiences with treasured insect guests. I've grouped the insects by family (like "Beetles" and "Wasps") to make it easy to look up the type of insect you're interested in.

Beetles

Beetles are the largest group of insects—about one-third of all the insects on earth are beetles. Lots of them are beneficial predators and pollinators. Beetles lay eggs that hatch into larvae (an immature stage). After feeding, the larvae pupate, and adults, emerge from the pupae. You can often identify a beetle by the straight dividing line that appears to run down its back from head to tail. The line is formed by the folding of the wings. Beetles have two pairs of wings, and both adults and larvae have chewing mouthparts. Beetles may be vegetarians, scavengers, predators, or parasites.

FIREFLIES (*Lampyridae*)

Distinctive features: While they are also called "lightning bugs," fireflies are really beetles. The adults are brown or black, long and flat, with a luminous, blinking organ on the tip of the abdomen. Larvae also glow, and they resemble flat beetles with impressive jaws. Adults are about ½ inch long.

Life cycle: Fireflies lay eggs in the soil, and the larvae hatch and overwinter there. The flashing of fireflies is part of their mating behavior, and there are different blinking patterns for different species.

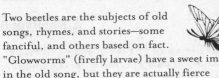

Two beetles are the subjects of old songs, rhymes, and stories—some fanciful, and others based on fact. "Glowworms" (firefly larvae) have a sweet image in the old song, but they are actually fierce hunters. They climb onto the backs of snails. When a snail pops its head out, the glowworm attacks, secreting an enzyme that paralyzes the snail so the glowworm can digest it.

On the other hand, the old poem about the ladybug (really a lady beetle) who's supposed to "fly away home" because her house is on fire and her children are burning is not so far from the truth. It refers to the practice of burning fields to prepare them for replanting. Undoubtedly, lady beetles and lots of other creatures have been destroyed in those fires.

No one's written a song yet about the multicolored Asian lady beetle, but she does have a nickname—the "Halloween Ladybug." That may be because she wears lots of disguises. These beetles can be yellow, orange, or red, with or without spots!

Where to find them: Firefly larvae favor moist places under bark or debris. The adults are easy to spot flashing on summer evenings, usually at the edge of woods or a field, in your hedgerows, or even in lawn areas under trees.

How they help you: Adult fireflies don't feed, but the larvae are active predators of other insects, slugs, and snails. They hunt at night—just when slugs are also out attacking your garden.

Special notes: Of course, firefly larvae don't really have little lightbulbs inside their bodies. The light they produce is the result of a reaction of special chemical substances in the organ located at the tip of the abdomen. Perhaps it's the inspiration for those glowing plastic cartridges that children love to play with!

GROUND BEETLES (*Carabidae*)

Distinctive features: Ground beetles are shiny and black or brightly colored. Some have prominent eyes, long antennae, and distinct "waists." Ground beetles hide under stones and run quickly when disturbed. Their larvae have distinct segments, strong legs, and visible "jaws" for grasping prey. Some give off strong odors. Adults are ¾ to 1 inch long.

Ground beetle

Life cycle: Some ground beetles lay eggs in small cells made of mud, twigs, and leaves. The larvae may be active predators for about a year, and adults often live from two to three years.

Where to find them: During the day, look for ground beetles under rocks, logs, or boards. If you find them, don't disturb them. They are also attracted to goldenrod, pigweed, groundcovers, and brush. This large beetle family includes over 3,000 species in North America.

Ground beetle larva

How they help you: Adults and larvae are valuable predators of Colorado potato beetles, root maggots, imported cabbageworms, diamondback moth larvae, cutworms, cabbage loopers, asparagus beetles, aphids, flea beetles, gypsy moth larvae,

Continued ➡

spider mites, tent caterpillars, and many other garden pests.

Special notes: The best way to encourage ground beetles is to maintain perennials, hedgerows, or a small woodpile near the garden. It's best not to handle ground beetles for reasons beyond their fierce-looking jaws (yes, they do nip!). For example, the bombardier beetle (*Brachinus* spp.) emits a little cloud of toxic liquid that can stain your skin. And when disturbed, the green pubescent ground beetle (*Chlaenius sericeus*) gives off an odor that smells like leather.

Lady Beetles (*Coccinellidae*)

Distinctive features: Also called ladybugs and ladybird beetles, these beetles are dome-shaped and round or oval. They may be red, orange, beige, or yellow, and many have black spots. Many species, such as the 11-spotted lady beetle, have a specific number of spots on their backs. The larvae are dark with orange or yellow marks and have six legs. They're sometimes called "alligators" because they look like alligators in miniature. The pupae are usually dark with orange marks. Adults are $1/16$ to $3/8$ inch long.

Life cycle: Lady beetles overwinter as adults, usually under leaf or woodpiles or in garden debris. Adults lay clusters of pointed, yellow eggs. The larval stage lasts 20 to 30 days, and the pupal stage, 3 to 12 days.

Where to find them: Every spring, I find handfuls of lady beetles in debris under my tansy and in the groundcover around my lilacs. In early spring they thrive on pollen from dandelions and other flowers. You'll also find them on yarrow, alfalfa, goldenrod, scented geraniums, and all types of daisies. There are over 450 species of lady beetles in North America.

How they help you: Lady beetles are general predators of aphids and many other insects, including thrips, mites, mealybugs, and scale. They also eat the larvae or eggs of many pests. Depending upon the species, adults may eat from 50 to hundreds of aphids per day, and larvae often eat more. (The larva of the common convergent lady beetle, *Hippodamia convergens*, eats its weight in aphids daily.)

Special notes: Lady beetles will often disappear if all the aphids in the area are destroyed, so don't be too quick to spray aphids—even with mild organic controls such as insecticidal soap. To tide them over when insect prey is sparse, maintain permanent plantings of tansy, angelica, and spring-flowering shrubs.

Rove Beetles (*Staphylinidae*)

Distinctive features: Rove beetles have short antennae and prominent, pinching jaws used to seize other insects. You might have mistaken them for earwigs. They move rapidly, carrying the tip of their abdomens high above the ground. The gold-and-brown rove beetle is noted for its shiny golden hairs over the abdominal tip. Adults are $1/10$ to 1 inch long.

Life cycle: Rove beetles overwinter as larvae, pupae, or adults. They lay eggs in soil or decomposing organic matter such as leaf litter. There can be several generations a year.

Where to find them: Rove beetles seek shelter in dark, damp places, such as compost piles or under leaves, stones, or boards. My garden's wooden pathways offer them a covered bridge for happy hunting. Planting dense groundcovers and providing mulched areas will also help to shelter them. Up to 2,900 species occur in North America.

How they help you: Both adults and larvae are active scavengers, dining on whatever insect larvae and soft-bodied insects they find. They are especially appreciated for consuming root maggots and other fly maggots. (One species studied gobbled up 80 percent of the cabbage maggots in the test plot.) Some species are also parasitoids.

Special notes: These beetles have very sharp jaws that look rather threatening and may be used to pinch you if you handle them. A few also have an extra defense: They can spray a strong, smelly liquid in the direction their tails are pointing. So appreciate these hungry maggot-hunters when you spot them, but don't get too close!

Soldier Beetles (*Cantharidae*)

Distinctive features: These beetles resemble fireflies (without the glow). They are elongated, usually brownish yellow or tan, and display long antennae. The Pennsylvania leatherwing (*Chauliognathus pennsylvanicus*) has a long dark spot at the base of each wing, and the head and area behind the head also have black spots. The downy leatherwing (*Podabrus tomentosus*) is a bluish gray beetle named for its fuzzy, hairy appearance. Adults are $1/3$ to $1/2$ inch long.

Life cycle: Adults lay eggs in clusters in the soil, and the larvae live in the soil. There are one or two generations per year.

Where to find them: Milkweed, goldenrod, hydrangeas, catnip, and many other flowers will attract soldier beetles to your garden. You'll spot the beetles frequently on flowers in late summer. The pupae need permanent plantings (perennials, cover crops) where they will not be disturbed. The Pennsylvania leatherwing is found only east of the Mississippi, but many other species are common throughout North America.

How they help you: Adults and larvae are usually predators, feeding on many kinds of insects, including cucumber beetles, grasshopper eggs, caterpillars, root maggots, rootworm larvae, and most soft-bodied insects.

Special notes: If you've had bad cucumber beetle problems in your garden, make a special effort to attract soldier beetles to your cucumbers. Try planting catnip, or let milkweed or goldenrod spring up among your cukes.

To buy and release lady beetles in your garden, thoroughly wet the area where you plan to release the beetles, and release them in the evening. Try putting out a sponge spread with commercial beneficial insect food (available from suppliers of beneficial insects), and release some of the insects under a damp straw mulch. This will maximize the chances that the lady beetles will stay in your garden instead of flying away.

Tiger Beetles (*Cicindelidae*)

Distinctive features: These big-eyed beetles have long antennae and vary in color from bronze, green, and blue to black. Some have yellow markings. They have long legs and can run fast and fly well. The larvae are noticeably S-shaped, with strong hooklike projections on their abdomens that they use to anchor themselves in the soil while they grab their prey. Adults are $1/2$ to $3/4$ inch long.

Life cycle: Adults and larvae overwinter in the soil. Females lay eggs singly in burrows in the soil. The larvae dig burrows in open areas from which they hunt. Each generation takes two to three years to complete its cycle.

Where to find them: Tiger beetles move fast, but you may spot them flying or running after predators in sunny, open areas or napping in the sunshine on bare, sandy or dusty spots on pathways or beaches. They also swarm around lights at night. There are about 100 species of tiger beetles throughout North America.

How they help you: Adult tiger beetles eat ants, flies, caterpillars, grasshoppers, aphids, and any other insect that they can catch. The ferocious larvae seize grubs or insects, sometimes even chasing after the prey and then dragging it back to the den for dinner.

Special notes: These beetles and their larvae could star in fast-action movies and exciting chase sequences—if only we could catch up with them! They are rather violent, however. The adult grabs its victim with sharp, sickle-shaped jaws and then whacks it against the ground until it stops moving. As predators go, this one is a real ally for gardeners—but quite a brute! To give tiger beetles a safe spot to overwinter, maintain some perennials, groundcovers, and undisturbed areas around the garden.

Bugs

This group of insects is often referred to as "true bugs" because many people call all insects "bugs." True bugs have shield-shaped bodies with a triangular area on top, above the point where the wings cross. Bugs have mouthparts designed for sucking—some are spearlike, carried under the insects' bodies, but pointed straight out for feeding. Predatory bugs impale their prey and suck out the body fluids. The life cycle includes egg, nymph, and adult stages. The nymphs are often different colors from the adults but change gradually as they molt several times, shedding their outer skins until they emerge as winged adults.

Ambush Bugs (*Phymatidae*)

Distinctive features: These aggressive predators have pale yellow or greenish yellow bodies and a wide, dark band across the abdomen. Their well-developed front legs are especially strong for seizing prey. Adults are less than $1/2$ inch long.

Life cycle: Not much is known about ambush bug life cycles. Adult bugs attach their black oval eggs to leaves; nymphs emerge through the tips of the eggs.

Where to find them: These bugs are masters of camouflage, but I've spotted many on New England asters in the field near my garden. Also look in goldenrod. Ambush bugs are found throughout the United States.

How they help you: Ambush bugs eat flies, butterflies, day-flying moths, and other bugs. Beekeepers consider ambush bugs pests because the bugs eat bees.

Special notes: Ambush bugs get their name from their behavior of lying in wait in flowers and snatching victims that fly near. An ambush bug

Continued ➔

injects its prey with saliva, which paralyzes the victim so the bug can feed without struggle.

ASSASSIN BUGS (*Reduviidae*)

Distinctive features: These long, oval bugs have thin heads that look stretched out. They have large eyes and spiny front legs that are very powerful—they use the legs to grasp prey. The adult bugs have curved mouthparts that are carried under their heads. There are several kinds in several colors, from dull brown through yellow, green, or black. The nymphs are often brightly colored, in shades of red. The adults are usually ½ to ¾ inch long.

Life cycle: Assassin bugs overwinter as adults, nymphs, or eggs in garden litter, fields, or beneath perennial plantings. Depending upon the species, the complete life cycle takes one year or more.

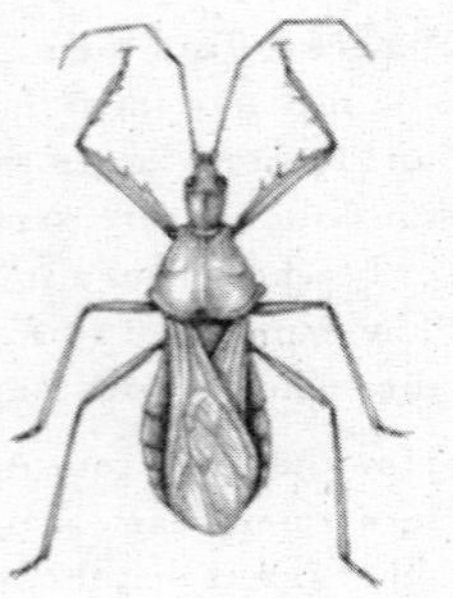

Where to find them: Assassin bugs frequent meadows, fields, and gardens. Watch for them in your hedgerows, perennials, or groundcover plantings. You may spot their eggs—rusty-colored bundles topped with white caps—on leaves or in the soil. Assassin bugs are common throughout North America.

Assassin bug

Assassin bug nymph

How they help you: Assassin bugs eat aphids, leafhoppers, flying insects (including bees), asparagus-beetle eggs and larvae, and other beetle larvae.

Special notes: Assassin bugs are fun to spot but not to handle. They can inflict a nasty bite that really hurts!

BIG-EYED BUGS (*Lygaeidae*)

Distinctive features: These tiny oval bugs are named for their huge eyes that point sideways. They are off-white through tan, gray, and brown, with small black spots on head and thorax. The bugs drop to the ground when disturbed. The eggs have distinctive red spots and are laid singly. Adults are ⅛ to ¼ inch long.

Assassin bugs come in a variety of colors and shapes. Some are long and stretched out like walking sticks; others are oval or rectangular. The wheel bug (*Arilus cristalus*) is huge (1⅛ to 1 3/8 inches long) and can capture and devour large caterpillars such as tomato hornworms. Wheel bugs also eat Japanese beetles and European chafer beetle larvae. They are found east of the Rocky Mountains. A small assassin bug, called the bee assassin, is more common in the western United States. It is generally red with black or brown markings, or brown with yellow marks. It's not popular with beekeepers, because it attacks honeybees along with a variety of other insects.

Life cycle: Adults overwinter in garden litter. They eat nectar and seeds when prey isn't available. There are several generations per year.

Where to find them: Look for big-eyed bugs under potato plants, clover, and other low-growing groundcovers or cover crops. The best-known species (*Geocoris* spp.) of big-eyed bugs is common in southern states north to Maryland, and in California.

How they help you: Big-eyed bugs prey on insect eggs, aphids, blister beetles, leafhoppers, and spider mites. Nymphs and adults can eat several dozen spider mites per day. Effective control for corn earworm eggs.

Special notes: The big-eyed bug isn't found where I live in western New York, but many of its relatives are found here. The big-eyed bug belongs to the insect family called "seed bugs." Its members eat seeds—hence the name—but many are also predators. If you have a butterfly garden with milkweed in it, you are sure to find the small eastern milkweed bug (*Lygaeus*), which has a bright red X on its black body.

DAMSEL BUGS (*Nabidae*)

Distinctive features: Damsel bugs are fast-moving, thin, gray or brown insects with curving, needle-like beaks, powerful forelegs, and threadlike antennae. The wingless nymphs look similar to but are smaller than adults. Adults are ⅜ to ½ inch long.

Life cycle: Adults overwinter in weeds, alfalfa, or grain fields and lay eggs in spring. Nymphs emerge after one week and dine on other insects. There are one or two generations per year.

Where to find them: Look carefully under groundcovers or cover crops, especially alfalfa and clover, for these small, nondescript insects. The only place I've found them is in my neighboring farmer's alfalfa field. Damsel bugs are found throughout North America.

How they help you: These little hunters are not frail "damsels in distress." In fact, they cause distress to aphids, caterpillars, thrips, leafhoppers, treehoppers, mites, redheaded pine sawflies, and plant bugs.

Special notes: If you find damsel bugs in nearby fields, try moving them into your garden—perhaps to beds of tomato plants underplanted with clover. Handle them carefully! These not-so-ladylike damsels can inflict a painful bite.

MINUTE PIRATE BUGS (*Orius* spp.)

Distinctive features: To the unaided eye, these tiny bugs just look like black dots. With a magnifier, you'll see their oval black bodies with a black-and-white pattern of triangles, and very small heads. Nymphs are pinkish, yellow, or tan and have red eyes. Adult bugs are ¼ inch long.

Life cycle: Adults overwinter under perennials or groundcovers. Females lay eggs on stems and leaves. Nymphs feed on insects for two to three weeks. There are three or four generations per year.

Where to find them: Minute pirate bugs like the shelter of corn, alfalfa, clover, and vetch. Try looking for them on white flowers because it's easy to spot the black bugs against the white flowers. I found them gobbling thrips on daisies in my garden. Minute pirate bugs are found throughout North America.

How they help you: One research study counted over 50 varieties of prey for these active predators! Both adults and nymphs kill large numbers of

---

aphids, thrips, leafhoppers, corn earworm eggs, and spider mites.

Special notes: Minute pirate bugs are sold commercially for greenhouse use in Europe and the United States, especially for thrips control.

SPINED SOLDIER BUG (*Podisus maculiventris*)

Distinctive features: These shield-shaped bugs may be yellow, beige, or brown, with black speckles. They have long snouts that point straight forward. Their pointed shoulders—like a soldier's uniform with epaulets—distinguish them from a pesty relative, the stink bug. Adults are ½ inch long.

Life cycle: Adult spined soldier bugs overwinter under permanent plantings and lay eggs on leaves in spring. Nymphs start out eating plant juices or water but soon become predators. After six to eight weeks, they reach adult stage and continue feeding for another month or two. There are up to two generations per year.

Spined soldier bug

Where to find them: In my garden, spined soldier bugs are easy to spot on, around, and under tansy! Also look for them on other flowering perennials. Spined soldier bugs are found throughout North America.

How they help you: These busy predators eat lots of pests, especially larvae of Mexican bean beetles and Colorado potato beetles. (Commercial growers even use them.) Other prey include European corn borer larvae, corn earworms, armyworms, imported cabbageworms, sawfly larvae, and—unfortunately—even a few beneficials, such as lady-beetle larvae.

Special notes: You can buy a special attractant substance called a pheromone to lure spined soldier bugs to your garden—but I'll bet you won't have to in your companion garden. Tansy does the job just fine.

TWO-SPOTTED STINK BUG (*Perillus bioculatus*)

Distinctive features: This bug is also called the conspicuous stink bug, and it's easy to see why. This fellow really stands out with his shield-shaped, black body with a wide, curved, orangey band across the back. Nymphs are red and black. Adults are ⅜ to ½ inch long.

Life cycle: Females lay gray eggs in clusters on the undersides of leaves. There are two or three generations per year.

Where to find them: Look for two-spotted stink bugs in weedy areas, where they feed on plant juices to supplement their diet of insects. You may also spot them in your asparagus bed. These bugs occur throughout the United States.

How they help you: Nymphs and adults consume eggs or larvae of Colorado potato beetles, Mexican bean beetles, asparagus beetles, and cabbage loopers.

Special notes: One study on two-spotted stink bugs showed that they reduced Colorado potato beetle populations by up to 60 percent. It would be especially helpful to lure two-spotted stink bugs to your potato patch, asparagus bed, or cabbage neighborhood.

Dragonflies

Dragonflies are long, slender insects with large, compound eyes that nearly cover the head or

Continued ➡

bulge out to the side. They have sharp, biting mouthparts and can eat their prey while in flight. All have four strong wings that move independently and can propel the insects forward or backward. Immature dragonflies, called *naiads*, are powerful predators that capture aquatic insects—and even small fish—by using a bristly lower "lip" that emerges at lighting speed to grasp the prey. This group of insects also includes damselflies. There are about 5,000 species worldwide and about 450 in North America.

DARNERS (*Aeschnidae*)

Distinctive features: Darners are the fastest, largest dragonflies. They are usually green, brown, or blue, and have large, clear, finely netted wings that can span up to 5 inches in some species. Their large compound eyes meet on top of their heads. Their wings remain outstretched at rest. Adults are 2¾ to 3⅛ inches long.

Life cycle: Females hover above water and thrust their eggs below the surface, usually into slits in the stems of submerged plants. The nymphs, or naiads, live in water and crawl out in early spring or late summer to transform into adults.

Where to find them: Darners may lay their eggs in small ponds or even backyard water gardens. You may find the nymphs under stones or debris near water gardens or small streams. Brown darners (*Boyeria vinosa*) occur throughout most of the eastern United States. Green darners (*Anax junius*), also called darning needles, are common throughout most of North America.

How they help you: Darners prey on mosquitoes, bees, and many flying insects. Larvae eat mosquito larvae and other aquatic life.

Special notes: You may have a chance to witness the transformation of a darner naiad into an adult. The naiads emerge from the water—sometimes traveling only 1 foot from the edge—and split their skins down the center of the body so the adult can emerge. If you're interested in attracting darners, be sure your water garden has an appropriate open "shore" where the nymphs can emerge.

NARROW-WINGED DAMSELFLIES
(*Coenagrionidae*)

Distinctive features: Narrow-winged damselflies are brightly colored, often shiny blue or blue-green. They have two pairs of wings that taper to a narrow stalk at the base. They hold their wings vertically over their bodies when at rest. The nymphs, or naiads, live in water, using their fish-like gills to propel themselves. Adults are 1 to 2 inches long.

Life cycle: Females deposit eggs on plants above or below the water surface. The nymphs capture aquatic insects and tadpoles until fully grown. Adults of many species emerge from the water in July or August.

Where to find them: A backyard pond, water garden, or bog garden will attract damselflies. Since they are not strong fliers, adult damselflies usually stay close to a water source. You'll find nymphs of many species in quiet or slow-moving water.

How they help you: Naiads dine on many aquatic insects, including mosquito larvae. Adults are general predators who eat many other insects. They are especially effective at controlling aphids. Most North American damselflies belong to this family.

Damselflies and dragonflies mate in flight, and you may spot mating pairs flying together near ponds and water gardens. The males may also assist the females when it's time to lay eggs. The male holds the female while she dips her abdomen into the water to deposit the eggs. Then, like a helicopter, the male lifts the female straight up and away from the water's surface. In another species, the male and female submerge themselves in the water for up to 30 minutes in order to lay eggs.

Special notes: Some familiar damselflies are nicknamed for their colors. Doubleday's bluet (*Enallagma doubledayii*) has a bright blue body. The red bluet (*Enallagma pictum*) has a bright red, reddish yellow, or brown and yellow body. If you live in the Northeast, you might have met it personally, as it often alights on a person's shoulder to nibble gently and harmlessly on clothing.

Lacewings

The scientific name for this group of insects, *Neuroptera*, comes from the network of veins in the transparent wings of its members. There are over 300 species in North America. The ones we meet most often are lacewings, mantidflies, and antlions. Brown and green lacewings are generally considered the most valuable predators of garden pests. Insects in this order have two pairs of long, oval wings, which they hold like a tent over their bodies when at rest. They have chewing mouthparts, and the larvae are mostly predators.

BROWN LACEWINGS (*Hemerobiidae*)

Distinctive features: These delicate insects have brown, transparent, netted wings covered by fine hairs. Their eggs are cream-colored ovals laid directly on the undersides of leaves. The larvae often camouflage themselves with debris, earning them the nickname of "trash collectors." Adults are ¼ to ⅜ inch long.

Life cycle: In the spring, females lay hundreds of eggs on the undersides of leaves. The larvae scavenge under organic matter for one to three weeks. Some species have several generations in a year.

Lacewings have a funny-looking relative known as the "antlion" or "doodlebug" (family *Myrmeleontidae*). Adult antlions are about 1½ inches long and resemble dragonflies. The bug's whimsical name may be due to the appearance of the larvae, which have an oversized head, short legs, and a bristly body. They also walk backward. This fellow is not funny to an ant, however, as its long spiny jaws are lethal. Antlions make pits in the sand, where they lie in wait for ants or ticks. When the ants pass by or fall in, the antlion consumes them. They are found mainly in dry, sandy soil in sheltered spots in the southern and southwestern United States.

Where to find them: Adult brown lacewings fly in the evening and night, mostly in woods, orchards, or fields. Try poking under some leaves in these areas, and you may find the spindle-shaped larvae, fuzzy with organic "trash," just trundling along. Brown lacewings occur throughout North America.

How they help you: Both adults and larvae are generalists, eating aphids, mealybugs, nymphs of scale insects, and other soft-bodied insects. A single lacewing larva consumes 100 to 600 aphids in the course of its development.

Special notes: Brown lacewings are often described as shy or secretive, and not much is known about how effectively they control pests in gardens. However, they are effective aphid predators and are beneficial wherever they occur.

GREEN LACEWINGS (*Chrysopidae*)

Distinctive features: These pale green to bright green insects have transparent wings, which they hold upright over their small bodies. They also have golden or copper-colored eyes. The larvae have prominent pincers, and their bodies are patterned in pinkish brown and cream spots. Adults are ⅜ to ⅝ inch long.

Life cycle: From spring into summer, females lay eggs on leaves near aphids. When the larvae emerge, they eat anything in reach. After two to three weeks, they pupate in round silken cocoons attached under leaves. New adults emerge one to two weeks later. Most overwinter as adults, often in clusters, in dry, dark, protected places. There are two or three generations per year.

Where to find them: You may spot green lacewings flying about in the evening in late spring or late summer, especially around meadows or forest edges. Try looking in your corn patch, too. You will recognize the creamy pinhead-sized eggs the moment you see them—with the help of a magnifying glass. Each egg is suspended on a delicate filament attached to a leaf or twig. Lacewings supplement their insect diet with nectar, so you may also find them on yarrow, angelica, Queen Anne's lace, sunflowers, and scented geraniums. Green lacewings occur throughout North America.

How they help you: Some research counts show that lacewing larvae eat 100 to 600 aphids before reaching the adult stage. They eat thrips, mites, whiteflies, and eggs of many pests, including leafhoppers, cabbage loopers, Colorado potato beetles, and asparagus beetles. They also eat small caterpillars and beetle larvae. They are used commercially in greenhouses, vineyards, and fields.

Special notes: There are pros and cons to aggressive predators like the lacewing larvae. For one thing, they emerge from their eggs ready to eat everything—including each other. That must be why Mother Nature designed lacewing eggs on isolated filaments. It gives each nymph a chance to eat some aphids before a "sibling" gobbles him up! For commercial sale, each lacewing egg is packed in an isolated cell to prevent cannibalism if the eggs hatch en route.

Flies

Swatting flies may be fine in your kitchen, but don't kill any flies in your garden! With the exception of a few biters like horseflies, deerflies, and mosquitoes, most garden flies are either valuable pollinators, predators, or parasitoids—and several are all of the above. Flies have only two wings (one pair). Their life cycle includes egg, larval, pupal, and adult stages. Predatory flies have piercing mouthparts for attacking their prey and feeding on their body fluids.

Continued ➡

Aphid Midges (*Cecidomylidae*)

Distinctive features: These tiny flies, also called gallflies, resemble mosquitoes. They have long spindly legs, long antennae, and fragile bodies. The larvae are bright orange. Adults are $1/16$ inch long.

Life cycle: Aphid midges overwinter as larvae in little cocoons in soil, emerging in late spring to search for aphids. Female midges lay up to 250 tiny orange eggs on leaf surfaces near aphids. There are several generations per year.

How they help you: One species of aphid midge (*Aphidoletes aphidimyza*) is widely used in the greenhouse industry in Europe, Canada, and parts of the United States to combat many kinds of aphids. One larva alone can eat 10 to 80 aphids before pupating. In gardens, aphid-midge larvae eat cabbage aphids and many others. Related species also attack mites, mealybugs, and other soft-bodied insects.

Where to find them: Look for tiny, bright orange larvae all over the flowers that aphids like most, including roses, especially in mid- to late summer. The adults fly at night, perhaps seeking pollen and nectar, so go searching for them with a flashlight. You may even catch a glimpse of "the mating dance," which looks like a tight little cluster of bodies just suspended in midair. Aphid midges occur throughout North America.

Special notes: Since there are many generations of aphid midges in a season, you must keep the "honeydew" coming. Choose a variety of long-flowering herbs and flowers, including Queen Anne's lace, dill, thyme, and wild mustard. The pupae need undisturbed soil or groundcovers, so provide permanent plantings such as wildflowers, perennials, and shrubs. Aphid midges thrive in high humidity and temperatures from 60° to 80°F.

Hoverflies (*Syrphidae*)

Distinctive features: These flies are often mistaken for bees because they have black- and yellow- or white-striped bodies. You can tell the difference by the pattern of movement; hoverflies hover outside of flowers and dart quickly in and out, while bees alight on flowers and stay awhile. Larvae are pale, greenish brown, sluglike maggots. They leave a dark, oily excrement behind. Hoverflies are also called flower flies or syrphid flies. Adult hoverflies are $1/2$ to $5/8$ inch long.

Bug zappers are marketed as control devices for mosquitos, gypsy moths, blackflies, and other pest insects. However, what they *really* kill are lots of innocent night-flying insects. Scientists at the University of New Hampshire who conducted "zapper counts" found dead lacewings as well as parasitic wasps that control gypsy moth and other caterpillars. They also found predatory beetles that prey on pest caterpillars. Other victims were caddis flies (an essential link in the ecology of ponds and streams) and beautiful large moths such as luna and cecropia moths that burned their wings in the zapper and were left flopping helplessly on the ground.

Ironically, bug zappers do little or nothing to decrease mosquito or gypsy moth populations. So zappers have no place near your garden—or anywhere else!

Life cycle: Hoverflies overwinter as pupae, attached to plants or hidden in soil. The female hoverfly lays individual eggs on leaves near aphid colonies. Larvae emerge about three days later. There may be five to seven generations per year, depending upon availability of aphids.

Where to find them: You can find the sluglike larvae wherever aphids are abundant. Hoverfly adults require nectar and pollen and are attracted to a variety of flowering plants and herbs, such as yarrow, Queen Anne's lace, wild mustard, horseradish, and feverfew. Hoverflies occur throughout North America.

How they help you: The adults are important pollinators, and the larvae are effective predators of aphids, leafhoppers, scale, mealybugs, thrips, corn borers, and corn earworms. One larva can consume aphids at a rate of 1 per minute, or up to 400 aphids in its larval stage, depending upon the species.

Special notes: Hoverfly larvae may be scavengers, parasites, or plant eaters. One type, the narcissus bulb fly (*Merodon equestris*), produces larvae that damage spring bulbs. However, the rest of the family make up for this troublesome relative. Larvae of the American hoverfly (*M. americanus*) and the flower fly (*Toxomerus* spp.) are probably as important as lady beetles in controlling aphids.

Robber Flies (*Asilidae*)

Distinctive features: Some species of robber flies resemble bumblebees, and others look like damselflies. All have strong legs with which to hold their prey. They also have bearded faces with a hollowed-out area between the eyes. Many are gray and very bristly or hairy. The long, cylindrical larvae taper at each end. Adults are $1/2$ to $3/4$ inch long.

Life cycle: Robber flies overwinter as larvae. The larvae pupate in the soil. When the adults emerge, they must feed on both nectar and insects before they can reproduce. There is one generation per year.

Where to find them: Check in decaying wood or in the soil for robber fly larvae. When you're working in your garden, watch for flying insects that drop down on other insects from above—they're robbers! Robber flies are found throughout North America.

How they help you: Robber flies are aggressive predators of all kinds of insects, including beneficial ones. They attack butterflies, grasshoppers, wasps, bees, and flies. Larvae in the soil attack grubs, root maggots, and insect eggs.

Special notes: Robber flies were surely named by somebody under the influence of old Robin Hood stories who imagined the flies as daring, bearded robbers leaping down on unsuspecting passersby. These flies really look like robbers! Some are short and stocky, and others are thin with narrow "waists"—and they all have that hairy-looking face. The indentation between the eyes (they have *three*) definitely gives them a villainous look. Add to that the tendency to jump on their victims, and you indeed have a drama with a well-cast robber—only *we* know he's good!

Tachinid Flies (*Tachinidae*)

Distinctive features: Flies from this large family are usually stocky, with coarse bristles around the abdomen. They resemble large houseflies with mottled black, grayish, tan, or reddish brown bodies. Adults are $1/3$ to $1/2$ inch long.

Even if you never studied entomology in school, you can figure out lots of things about insects and their behavior just by taking a close look. For example, some predatory flies (especially hoverflies) look rather like bees because they have black-and-yellow stripes. But it's easy to separate the flies from the bees by counting their wings.

Flies have only two wings, while bees and wasps have two *pairs* of wings. (Counting the number of wings on a flying insect is tough when the insect's in flight but quite easy when it's resting on a leaf or flower.)

As for insect behaviors, I think one of the most interesting beneficials to watch in action is a tachinid fly. I often spot these flies searching for a host on which to lay eggs—walking rapidly, and with what seems like great determination, over soil and plants. When the sly spots its target, the fly signals its intent by hopping and circling around its prey.

The caterpillars and beetles that the fly attacks also enact their individual dramas clearly. They make agitated movements to try to avoid the fly's attack and will also try to remove fly eggs by wiping their legs along their bodies.

Life cycle: Adults lay eggs on the bodies of other insects. The larvae feed inside the host insects, usually killing them. The larvae then drop to the soil to pupate. (Some pupate inside a host body.) Adults feed on nectar and usually fly from late spring to late summer. There may be several generations per year.

Where to find them: Look for white eggs on caterpillars or true bugs; these eggs are a clue that tachinid flies or other parasitoids have been there. You'll often spot adult tachinid flies on wildflowers and herbs in meadows and fields. I've seen them on tansy and Queen Anne's lace in my garden. Tachinid flies occur throughout North America.

Tachinid fly

How they help you: Many kinds of tachinid flies are effective parasitoids of vegetable crop pests, including European corn borers, corn earworms, imported cabbageworms, cabbage loopers, cutworms, armyworms, Colorado potato beetles, stink bugs, squash bugs, tarnished plant bugs, and cucumber beetles.

Special notes: Some flies are fairly general in their choices of targets, while others have specific hosts. Studies on pest control using tachinid flies show varying success rates. As with many efforts at natural pest control, one beneficial insect or pest-management strategy may not be enough—but collectively, tachinids are part of a winning team.

Mantids

There are 11 species of mantids in North America, and 1,800 around the world, but we are most familiar with the praying mantis. All mantids have long bodies and "praying" forelegs with spines that help to capture prey. Mantids have necks that seem to rotate so that the insect can look behind itself.

Continued ➡

They can be as small as ⅜ inch or as large as 6 inches.

PRAYING MANTIS (*Mantis religiosa*)

Distinctive features: These familiar garden insects get their name from their tendency to hold their forelegs up "in prayer." They are about 2 inches long, are green or tan, and fly very well. They are experts at camouflage, often matching their choice of habitat plant to their bodies.

Life cycle: Females attach flat egg masses, which resemble papier mâché, to twigs or fence posts, where they overwinter. Up to 200 nymphs hatch in the late spring and proceed to eat everything in sight—including each other! The lucky ones blow off on a breeze and take over a new territory, which they dominate for their one-year life cycles.

Where to find them: Since they are territorial, you won't usually see more than one praying mantis in your garden. I've spotted a praying mantis on borage and goldenrod, but they may choose any garden or meadow plants as hunting grounds. Praying mantids are found in the southern and eastern United States and north into Ontario.

How they help you: Mantids are voracious hunters and truly undiscriminating predators of anything they can catch in their powerful forelegs. While you can buy praying mantis egg cases, I think they're a dubious purchase. However, naturally occurring mantids probably help to control pests in the garden, especially if there's a serious outbreak and the pest is abundant.

Special notes: The common praying mantis is from Europe, accidentally introduced in 1899 on nursery stock. The Chinese mantis was also introduced in 1896, and is found in the eastern United States. The narrow-winged mantis was brought in from southern Asia in 1933 and has naturalized in Delaware and Maryland. All are considered beneficial.

Mites

Mites are not insects, but they are another type of tiny creature that plays important roles in the garden. Some are plant pests, but many are also important predators of garden pests. Mites are eight-legged, flat-bodied organisms that look somewhat like very small spiders. There are about 30,000 named species of mites in the world—and lots more still to be named! One way to tell a spider from a mite is that the spider appears to have a "waist"—actually a division between the upper body and abdomen. With mites, you can't distinguish the two body parts.

Mantids would surely win gold ribbons in the Insect Olympics. A praying mantis can make two strikes with its forelegs in a fraction of a second. A mantis's jaws are strong enough to crack the hard shells of most insects. Some mantis species have even captured small frogs, lizards, and hummingbirds! Luckily, those are not the species you'll find in your garden. In the United States, the biggest mantis is the Chinese mantis—only about 3 inches! By the way, although mantids won't wrestle us to the ground, they will nip—so proceed with appreciative respect!

PREDATORY MITES (*Phytoselidae*)

Distinctive features: Predatory mites are nearly invisible to the naked eye. Even with a magnifying glass, all you'll see are tear-shaped, pale or reddish brown dots.

Life cycle: Adult mites hibernate in debris or under bark. Predatory mite species complete their entire life cycle in only a few days, so there are many generations per year.

Where to find them: You probably won't see mites around your garden because they're so small. Pollen-rich plants may help to maintain some predatory mites, and one study shows that bell peppers (which have pollen-rich flowers) maintained one species.

How they help you: Predatory mites attack spider mites, thrips, or fungus gnats. They may attack adults, nymphs, larvae, or eggs. Predatory mites are found throughout North America.

Special notes: Several kinds of predatory mites are sold for pest control. One success story is *Amblyseius fallacis*. This all-purpose mite preys on many harmful spider mites and can be released in strawberries, raspberries, orchards, bedding plants, and in ornamental plantings. If you buy garden plants at a greenhouse this year, ask the manager if she has worked with any "mighty mites" lately.

Spiders

Many people are scared of spiders, but in the garden, they're nothing to fear—unless you're an insect looking for plants to munch on! Spiders belong to a group of organisms called arachnids, having eight legs and two body parts. Most spiders have eight simple eyes. There are about 3,000 species of spiders in North America. Studies of spiders in agricultural crops show their pest-control value in crops as diverse as potatoes, rice, and cotton. Home gardeners can encourage them by providing mulch—especially straw—and a diversity of flowers. Although they have jaws, very few spiders bite people. In fact, even the most dreaded spiders, such as tarantulas and black widows, attempt to avoid and escape from humans rather than attack.

CRAB SPIDERS (*Thomisidae*)

Distinctive features: These small spiders skitter sideways, backward, or forward, like crabs. They are usually short and wide, with the second pair of legs longer than the others (also giving that "crab-claw" appearance). There are 200 North American species, so crab spiders come in many colors, many of them camouflaged to match their preferred plant hiding places. Adults are ½ inch long.

Life cycle: Crab spiders don't spin webs. Instead, they search out their prey on plants, both day and night. They usually wait for prey on flower heads. The female produces eggs in silken sacs, which she protects until she dies, usually before the spiderlings emerge.

Where to find them: These spiders often hide in flower heads, waiting for flying insects. Many species prefer yellow and white flowers, such as cosmos, daisies, and goldenrod. Crab spiders are found throughout North America.

How they help you: Crab spiders are generalists and will capture any insect that passes by them.

Special notes: Some crab spiders are named for their looks. The goldenrod spider (*Misumena vatia*, sometimes called "flower spider" or "red-spotted crab spider") often hides out on goldenrod or daisies, changing its color to yellow for camouflage. The thrice-banded crab spider (*Xysticus triguttatus*) is brown, black, and white, with dashed lines across its lower abdomen.

In the fall, thinking about pest control is usually low on our list of priorities. Your attitude may be "what's done is done," and you'll tackle next year's pest problems next year. But fall garden cleanup can make a big difference in next year's pests. I'm not just talking about raking and cleaning up garden debris. This time, I mean hiring—actually *buying*—some beneficial mites to do the job for you.

If you've had problems with spider mites in your garden, especially in your strawberries, you can get help from *Amblyseius fallacis*, a beneficial mite that is used widely in commercial crops. When released in the fall, the mite will also wipe out mites in your home garden. It will overwinter, too, and become active in spring.

ORB WEAVERS (*Araneidae*)

Distinctive features: Orb weavers may be various shades of brown and orange, with dark brown bands and markings. They hang head downward in large webs (up to 20 inches across). They often have a cross-shaped mark on the abdomen, inspiring the common name "cross spider." Orb weavers have eight eyes in two horizontal rows with four eyes in each row. Adults are 1/16 to 1 1/8 inches long.

Life cycle: Orb weavers make symmetrical five- or six-sided webs every night, eating the remains of the previous night's web. Females attach egg masses to plants at the sides of the webs.

Where to find them: You'll find orb weavers stretching webs between plants in your garden or between foundation shrubs and your house. This huge family includes several hundred species in North America, among them our familiar garden spider (*Araneus diadematus*) of the northeastern United States.

How they help: Garden spiders and other orb weavers catch all sorts of flying and jumping insects, including grasshoppers, flies, and moths.

Special notes: Some orb weavers are recluses, hiding in caves and dark places. One of these is the barn spider (*Araneus cavaticus*), which spins its webs in barns, caves, or other shady locations. Another spider that is quick to hide is the black-and-yellow argiope (*Argiope aurantia*), which drops to the ground when disturbed. It likes sunny, quiet places with no wind. I've spotted them on warm afternoons in my sunny perennial border.

Spiders are remarkably ingenious at spinning webs suited to their style of hunting and self-protection. Sheet-web weavers (*Linyphiidae*) make flat or dome-shaped "sheets." One species is called a hammock spider because it stretches its sheet between fence posts or branches. Funnel web weavers (*Agelenidae*) make webs that "funnel" the prey down to the hungry spider at its base. No matter the style, if you see a web, just let it be—you have a garden helper somewhere nearby.

Continued ➡

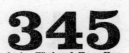

WOLF SPIDERS (*Lycosidae*)

Distinctive features: These brown or gray spiders are called wolf spiders because of their coloration and hunting technique. They have eight dark eyes arranged in three rows, the first row having four eyes. Depending on species, adults are from $1/8$ inch to $1^1/8$ inches long.

Life cycle: Not web spinners, wolf spiders live mostly on the ground, some digging burrows for retreat. Females carry or drag their egg sacs or transport their young on their backs.

Where to find them: I see these spiders regularly when I move mulch under flowers or vegetables. I sometimes disturb a mother with her egg sac. You will also see wolf spiders basking in the sun or sitting with egg sacs in the "doorways" of burrows. There are 200 species ranging throughout North America.

How they help you: These general predators hunt at night, eating all kinds of insects, including aphids, mites, flies, moths, and beetles.

Special notes: Thin-legged spiders (*Pardosa* spp.) are the largest group of wolf spiders (about 100 kinds in North America), and only a specialist can tell them apart. The clue to identifying a spider as a wolf spider is its long-legged, thin look, dark color, and long pale and dark stripes running from head to abdomen.

Wasps

Wasps belong to an insect group that also includes bees, ants, and sawflies. All wasps have a narrow "waist" and two pairs of membranous wings. Adult wasps have chewing mouthparts and some have tonguelike structures they use to drink nectar. Females of most species have a stinger. Their life cycle includes eggs, larvae, pupae, and adults. Most wasps are beneficial as pollinators or as predators or parasitoids of insect pests. There are thousands of species of wasps in North America, so just a few of these outstanding beneficials are listed here!

APHIDIID WASPS (*Aphidiinae*)

Distinctive features: These wasps are tiny and black, with long antennae. Adults are $1/8$ inch long.

Life cycle: Most species lay hundreds of eggs, each in the body of an aphid. The larvae eat the contents of the aphid and pupate inside the dead aphid's body. The new adult wasp cuts a hole in the aphid body and emerges, leaving a shell behind. Adults live one to three weeks, and there are several generations each year.

Where to find them: Aphidiid wasps show up wherever there are aphids and supplemental nectar and pollen, but they may be hard to spot. Look for the empty shells of dead aphids, called "mummies," on plant leaves—they look like beige, papery sacs. Aphidiid wasps are found throughout the United States.

How they help you: Scientists report that aphidiid wasps are effective controls for summer and fall aphid infestations, more so than early-season aphids. Females of some species can parasitize hundreds of aphids a day. Most of those aphids then die before reproducing. Studies show significant success in controlling pea, bean, melon, potato, cabbage, and green peach aphids.

Special notes: Many aphidiid wasps are sold commercially and are one of the best success stories in greenhouse organic pest management in the United States and Europe. *Aphidius colemani* and *A. matricariae* can prevent problems with up to 40 kinds of aphids. Best of all, the wasps are able to establish themselves in most regions of the United States and can overwinter. To encourage them in your

garden, maintain wildflowers and perennials, including herbs of the carrot family such as dill, Queen Anne's lace, fennel, and coriander.

> One little wasp has really earned star billing for over 60 years of greenhouse heroism. It's *Encarsia formosa*, the terror of greenhouse whiteflies. This pinhead-sized wasp isn't native to the United States, but it's now being raised commercially and has become established in some areas of the United States. These wasps need warm, humid climates, cannot tolerate any pesticides, and require a ready supply of whiteflies—something that many greenhouses have all too often!

BRACONIS WASPS (*Braconidae*)

Distinctive features: These small black or brown wasps look like flying ants. The wasps have a long, tubelike protrusion beneath the body called an ovipositor (it's used to place eggs.) The cocoons look like white bumps on the bodies of parasitized caterpillars. Adults are up to $3/8$ inch long.

Life cycle: Adult wasps insert eggs into a host egg, larva, pupa, or adult. The larvae develop inside the host's body and then form cocoons. The whole life cycle may be from 20 to 50 days.

Where to find them: When you see white cocoons attached to caterpillars, beetle grubs, and fly larvae, it's evidence that braconid wasps are at work in your garden. It's estimated that there are over 1,900 species of braconids in North America.

How they help you: Studies of braconid wasps in corn and cabbage crops show that they're effective against European corn borers, cabbage maggots, and diamondback moths. Other prey include tent caterpillars, gypsy moth caterpillars, tomato hornworms, and armyworms. Some species of braconids are commercially available.

Special notes: Braconid wasps benefit from flowering plants beginning in spring, such as sweet alyssum.

CHALCID WASPS (*Chalcididae*)

Distinctive features: Chalcid wasps are tiny black wasps. Through a magnifying glass, they may be metallic blue, green, or yellow. The tubelike structure called an ovipositor is not visible in chalcid wasps, so that's one way you can distinguish them from braconid wasps. Some chalcid wasps "play dead" if they are disturbed. Adults are $1/16$ to $3/8$ inch long.

Life cycle: Female wasps lay one or two eggs in the skin of a caterpillar. The larvae feed inside the caterpillar, pupate, and emerge. Some species lay eggs that develop into up to 1,000 larvae each. Adult wasps feed on nectar or honeydew (a secretion given off by aphids and some other insects).

Where to find them: You may spot chalcid wasps anywhere around your garden or in permanent plantings. Chalcid wasps are found throughout North America.

How they help you: Chalcid wasps feed on a wide range of pests, including aphids, whiteflies, leafhoppers, caterpillars, and scale.

Special notes: Some experts regard chalcid wasps as more significant controls for pests than braconid or ichneumonid wasps because chalcids can produce so many larvae from just one egg. It's

an unusual asexual type of reproduction called hypermetamorphosis!

ICHNEUMONID WASPS (*Ichneumonidae*)

Distinctive features: This is one parasitoid you can see easily! The females often have a huge, dangling, tubelike structure for laying eggs (an ovipositor) that is even longer than her long antennae and legs. Colors vary through reds and browns. Adults vary in size from $1/8$ inch up to an impressive $1^5/8$ inches.

Life cycle: Female wasps inject eggs into hosts—usually caterpillars. The wasp larvae slowly consume the host until the adult wasps emerge.

Where to find them: I have seen ichneumonids on window screens or around the porch light on a summer evening (another good reason to ban bug zappers!). You may also find a dried-up caterpillar or cocoon with another cocoon inside. The inner cocoon harbors an ichneumonid. The adults need nectar and water. They'll frequent your bug bath as well as parsley family plants like tansy, lovage, dill, and sweet cicely. There are over 3,300 species in North America.

How they help you: Ichneumonids target many vegetable- and fruit-crop pests. Commercially, they're used to control pests such as diamondback moths, European corn borers, and cabbage moths.

Special notes: In nature's systems, insects are not "good" or "bad," but simply living things that have a niche and a unique way of surviving. Ichneumonid wasps may parasitize the caterpillars of some of our favorite moths and butterflies, as well as spider egg sacs. However, these wasps target so many more of our problem insects that we clearly call them "beneficial."

Trichogramma WASPS (*Trichogramma* spp.)

Distinctive features: These are very tiny, about the size of a pencil point. If you viewed a *Trichogramma* wasp through a microscope, you would see a squat, yellowish or brown wasp with red eyes and short antennae. Adults are about $1/50$ inch long.

Fear of wasps is nearly paralyzing to some people. They avoid picnics, shun the porch, and invest in can after can of toxic sprays just to rid the house of a wasp nest. But most wasps are beneficial, although a few stings can make the friendliest human wary!

It may help you to know that none of the small parasitoid wasps described here sting people or pets at all. Even most large parasitoids like ichneumonid wasps are nonstinging. Their long ovipositors (egg-laying tubes) look threatening, but they're only a danger to insect pests. One species, the giant ichneumonon (*Magarhysa macrurus*), can insert its ovipositor a full inch into wood and lay an egg on its victim (which is usually an insect larva in the tree).

If you find a nest of wasps near your house where you can't tolerate it, remember this: Wasps are most likely to be agitated and sting you if they're disturbed during hot, humid weather. Remove the wasp nest only on a cool, dry, dark evening, and place it where the wasps can escape unharmed.

Continued ➡

Hornets are a type of wasp, and believe it or not, some hornets are beneficial insects! Many people are afraid of hornets, but the European hornet is a predator that attacks grasshoppers, horseflies, and yellowjackets. Giant hornets and bald-faced hornets also destroy many insects. So leave hornets in peace as much as possible, both to avoid being stung and to allow them to carry out their beneficial duties.

Life cycle: Female wasps lay eggs in the eggs of another insect. The young pupate within the host egg, and one or several adults will emerge within a week. Several generations may develop each season. They overwinter as pupae in the host egg.

Where to find them: *Trichogramma* wasps are so small that you won't see them in your garden. However, they probably are there, frequenting plants with delicate flowers, such as Queen Anne's lace, tansy, coriander, and parsley. *Trichogramma* wasps are found throughout the United States.

How they help you: These wasps are one of the most widely used biological controls for commercial agriculture. They're released for control of imported cabbageworms, corn borers, corn earworms, cabbage loopers, and many other pests. They're effective only when released over a wide area, and the timing of the release has to be just right. In your home garden, rely on native *Trichogramma* wasps for pest duty.

Special notes: Biological controls like attracting or buying beneficial insects for pest control are rarely effective as single measures. (Instead, the smart gardener does several positive things at once—including arranging for many beneficials to be around at all times.) *Trichogramma* wasps are a good example: Since some of these wasp species emerge in warm weather, they're not very effective for early season pests, but growers can release them to help with pest problems later in the season.

BUTTERFLIES AND BEES

Attracting Butterflies and Moths

Sally Roth

I've never been a butterfly catcher, but I'm definitely a butterfly collector. One recent morning, I added three cloudless sulphurs, a red admiral, ten common blues, a red-spotted purple, and "the prize"—four gorgeous, great, spangled fritillaries—to my collection. Not to mention a dozen or so dainty white cabbage butterflies.

I do my "collecting" through the window at my desk, watching the butterflies that dance over the flowers outside. My new butterfly garden is in its first full summer and already it's a lively place. As more and more flowers come into bloom, the garden invites a visit from these colorful nectar-seekers.

Butterfly season can be as short as six weeks in the far North or in high mountains, but in mild southern Florida, butterflies fly all year. They begin to appear in numbers once the average daily temperature stays above 60°F, but in most areas, hot summer is when butterflies are at their peak. So a summer-blooming garden is a great way to attract butterflies to your natural landscape. An open, sunny spot is the best place to put a butterfly nectar garden.

You'll see the largest number of butterflies on warm, sunny days when the wind is calm or only a light breeze is blowing. When the sun clouds over, they disappear like magic.

Start with Flowers

Making a butterfly garden couldn't be easier. Flowers are the place to start. You'll want an abundance of them. Luckily, most of the best nectar plants—zinnias, for instance—are super-easy to grow and fast to bloom, and seeds and plants are available everywhere.

A new garden needs color in a hurry, so when I started my butterfly planting, I scattered seeds of fast-blooming annuals—old standbys like sweet alyssum, cosmos, and zinnias. Most of the packets I bought at ten-for-a-dollar seed racks, so I could use a liberal hand without counting pennies.

In the flower bed along the road, I sprinkled seeds I'd saved from an old garden. Of course, I hadn't labeled them. They turned out to be garden catchfly, or none-so-pretty, an old-fashioned wildflower that fell out of favor because of its hot-pink color, but which often turns up in butterfly or wildflower seed mixes. A neighbor from the farm down the road offered all the bachelor's-buttons I wanted: They'd snuck into her soybean fields. They transplanted nicely, making airy clumps of cornflower blue that bloomed for weeks. Any bare spots filled in fast with wild chamomile and white daisy fleabane.

The garden is a jumble of colors and plants, and the butterflies love it. This morning, cabbage whites and yellow sulphurs were dancing over the wild daisies. And the golden-brown spangled fritillaries, which get their name from a spangling of silver dots on the undersides of their wings, were feeding on the vivid pink catchfly.

Herbs for Nectar Collectors

Almost any plant that offers clusters of small, tubular flowers will be eagerly sought by butterflies. That description suits a lot of herbs: mints, rosemary, lavenders, and hyssops, just to name a few.

On the steep, stony hill beside our house, I planted lavender, thyme, and oregano, hoping they'd tumble down the slope in a pleasing mix of soft colors and textures. They did fill in well, and they brought a bonus: Their plentiful flowers are a super draw for butterflies.

The herbs are especially popular with little blue butterflies. I didn't realize how popular at first. When I glanced at the hill, I'd see a few small butterflies fluttering about, and I thought that was it. But then I discovered that when the blue butterflies fold their wings, their silvery undersides are perfectly camouflaged against the gray foliage. Only when they flutter to another flower or open their wings to bask for a moment do I get a glimpse of lovely lavender-blue like a summer sky.

Hosting Future Generations

Along with flowers and herbs, you'll want to make sure that your natural garden includes plenty of good host plants for butterflies to lay their eggs on. When future generations begin hatching in your garden, they'll tend to linger if there's plenty of nectar and host plants for subsequent broods. My own garden—and not only the "butterfly garden" part of it—sustains populations of spicebush swallowtails, black and tiger swallowtails, coppers, metalmarks, little blues, admirals, red-spotted purples, hackberry butterflies, and emperors. I like to look for caterpillars almost as much as I love to watch butterflies.

Irresistible Oregano

If you grow herbs, you already know how attractive those tiny flowers are to butterflies. The myriad blooms on a single plant of oregano can keep butterflies busy for half an hour.

I grow oregano as an ornamental. One of my seed-started plants blooms with white flowers rather than the usual mauve flowers. It's a novelty in the garden that I enjoy for its own sake as well as for its nectar abilities. But any kind of oregano is tops with butterflies.

In two years, my single plant has spread into a tumbled mound that covers a good 3 square feet. I cut it back to the ground in winter, and it regrows with a vengeance, spreading by rooting branchlets. It begins to bloom in early summer and keeps going until frost. For months, it's a favorite stopping place for butterflies of all descriptions. The dainty hairstreaks find it particularly appealing, but big yellow tiger swallowtails and bold black-and-white zebra swallowtails also partake.

Having a patch of oregano is like having a living laboratory of insect life. More than butterflies visit my planting. I see wasps of all descriptions, from giant cicada killers to elegant, slim blue hornets. And a million other insects, give or take a few, are also drawn to the plant, providing me with hours of viewing pleasure.

Continued ➡

Butterflies are pickier than a four-year-old when it comes to food for their larvae. They look for very specific plants. Monarch caterpillars eat only milkweed. Most others are just as selective: Hackberries lay eggs on elm; spicebush swallowtails go for (what else?) spicebush; zebra swallowtails look for pawpaws. When the eggs hatch, the first meal is right under their feet. Many caterpillars spend their entire lives on a single plant, never leaving unless the food runs out.

It's amazing how fast butterflies will find your garden if you offer suitable host plants. If you've ever grown broccoli, you've seen this in action. Those white butterflies flirting over your veggie garden are checking out a future home for their caterpillars.

Look closely at an Eastern black swallowtail to see the cloud of powdery blue and bright orange eyespot on its outer hind wing. Lure them to your garden with parsley, dill, Queen Anne's lace, or carrot plants for the caterpillars and nectar sources such as phlox and milkweed.

THE DANGERS OF PESTICIDES AND HERBICIDES

Pesticides and herbicides are the number one enemy of beautiful butterflies. Pesticides kill off adults and caterpillars. (Ever stop to think what that creepy green caterpillar on your roses might turn into?) And herbicides take care of future generations by destroying the "weeds" that butterflies lay their eggs on. Even the natural control *Bacillus thuringiensis* (BT) is deadly to butterflies and moths. It kills "leaf-eating caterpillars," and that includes just about every single one. Spray BT on your young oak to protect against gypsy moths, and you wipe out future lunas, cecropias, and everything else on the leaves, along with the pests.

Our American penchant for tidiness has eliminated too much prime butterfly habitat. Every highway roadside that's mown like lawn grass could be supporting hundreds of butterflies if it were left to grow naturally.

Nasturtium is a sprawler, not a true climber, but you can coax it along a fence or up a trellis to bring the bright flowers, and the butterflies that visit them, into easy view.

To be a friend of the butterflies, you'll have to overcome any neatnik urges in your own garden. The easiest way to boost butterfly numbers in your garden is to let a corner get a little weedy. You don't have to grow thistles—unless you want your neigh-

bors to be really fond of you—but you can nurture clover, asters, sandvine, milkweeds, and seedling trees. Whatever crops up is likely to become home to one kind of butterfly larvae or another.

The Fine Art of Puddle-Making

If anybody ever saw me driving down the dirt road by our house, they might put in a call to the county sheriff: I weave from one side to the other like a drunken fool. It's not because I've been tippling, though. I'm trying to avoid the butterflies congregating at the mud puddles in the road. Yellow, white, and orange sulphurs; little blues; red-spotted purples; big, gorgeous swallowtails; and other beauties cluster around the edges of the puddles, drinking from the mud. Their delicate proboscis probes the mud, drawing up water and minerals like a portable drinking straw.

I use the same idea to draw butterflies to my garden. My installation methods are primitive: To create a mud puddle, I simply run the hose for about five minutes at about 11 A.M. each morning on a bare, somewhat gravelly patch of earth. For true puddle butterflies, it's not necessary to have standing water. Mud is what they're after.

If you make a mud puddle a feature of your garden, you'll attract more than butterflies. Chances are you'll also find toads if you look for them at night. They wait for earthworms to leave the saturated soil, then gulp them down. Usually a few gulps is all it takes to get a wriggler down the hatch, but once I saw a small toad using his "hands" to help shove the worm in. Robins will look for worms at your puddle, too, and they'll collect mud for nest-building. (By the way, if you see a robin with a balding breast, it has already built its nest: Smoothing out the cup of mud causes wear and tear on the feathers.)

Literate butterfly lovers appreciate the comma butterfly and its close relative, the question mark, which carry distinctive marks of punctuation on their outer hind wings. Look for commas in clearings, glades, and open woods.

Water in a Saucer

For the butterflies that prefer to drink water rather than mud, I fill a large, shallow, clay saucer with coarse gravel and pour in water. This stays wet all day, even in hot summer, and draws some of my favorite butterflies.

Usually the first to arrive are the fluttery brown-gold hackberry butterflies and the angle-wings, mostly commas and question marks. Anglewings are a common type of butterfly that looks like a leaf when its wings are closed: Not only is the color right, but the edges of the folded wings are scalloped like the margin of a dead leaf. And question marks' closed wings boast punctuation marks that look like they've been painted on with Wite-Out. Like a bunch of impatient chickadees at the feeder, the golden-brown butterflies brush against my ankles as soon as I pull out the hose.

Red admirals stop by for a drink at the saucer, too. They're bigger butterflies, with dark brown

wings slashed with a brilliant red stripe and a dash of white. Like the hackberry tribe, they're completely unafraid of me. They often ride on my shoulder or my hat while I work in the garden or walk to the mailbox.

I'm always delighted when a red-spotted purple shows up at my butterfly watering saucer. These elegant creatures seem like they should be rarities, but they're as common as starlings around here. Like most butterflies, the undersides of their wings aren't as pretty as the tops. In fact, they look like two different species altogether, depending on which side you're looking at. Underneath, they're drab brownish blue spotted with Chinese red, but seen from above, they're as gorgeous as the blue morpho butterflies of the Tropics. Their velvety, matte-black wings are overlaid with a sheen of cobalt blue and powdered with vivid turquoise along the edge.

Saved by the Computer

Black swallowtail caterpillars eat only plants in the carrot family, like dill, parsley, and Queen Anne's lace. I used to think that any particular black swallowtail caterpillar would eat all of those plants, but I learned differently when I found a group of five swallowtail caterpillars on my very last stalk of dill in the garden.

At the same time, I was also hosting a brood of swallowtails on parsley in the vegetable garden, and there was a third brood working on Queen Anne's lace near the driveway.

Wanting to raise a few butterflies, as I do every year, I took the dill stalk and its inhabitants indoors to a sunny windowsill. I filled their jar with fresh-picked parsley and waited for them to chow down. But they weren't interested. I tried Queen Anne's lace. Same deal. My caterpillars were hungry, but they wanted dill. Those caterpillars on the other plants must have come from different stock.

I made a quick trip to the supermarket and came back with a tiny $2 bunch of dill. When I put it in the jar, they fell upon it like wolves. They were hungry—much too hungry. That expensive dill wouldn't last long. I scoured friends' gardens and begged whatever dill I could find, but it was the end of summer and all I ended up with was a paltry bunch. Maybe it would hold them for the next week, I thought, and then they'll go into the chrysalis stage.

No luck. They ran through it in three days and were even bigger and more voracious. Every greengrocer for 40 miles around was out of dill. I was desperate. So I put out a message on CompuServe, the electronic communication service. The next morning, a fat package arrived by Federal Express, sent by an electronic friend. I could smell it as soon as I opened the door—fresh, fragrant dill! My caterpillars were saved. (And my very curious FedEx man felt like a hero.)

In two days, the caterpillars went into the chrysalis stage, transforming into elegant, pointed sarcophagii that hatched in another two weeks into fabulous, velvety black swallowtail butterflies. They clung to my fingertips as I carried them outside to release them, blissfully unaware of how close to oblivion they'd come.

Continued ➡

More Than Nectar

Nectar isn't the only thing on the menu for butterflies. Some species have truly disgusting eating habits. Roadkill and other carrion are big favorites with hackberry butterflies, red-spotted purples, and admirals. Dead snakes are a particular delicacy, and in summer, I stir up clouds of butterflies every time I drive past a flattened opossum or raccoon. Though it seems incongruous to see butterflies eating carrion, it's just part of the natural foodchain.

Manure is manna for some butterflies, too, and the fresher, the better. They're quick to find any deposits left by our dogs, and I've also seen them sipping delicately at bird droppings. Some entomologists say that the manure of carnivorous animals is best. One butterfly collector in Africa turned to civet cats, the ordure of which he collected and placed at appropriate points in the forest paths. He was richly rewarded by obtaining many butterflies that he hadn't been able to get any other way.

Tree sap is another butterfly delight. When loggers toppled an old oak at our boundary line, the seeping trunk became a feeder for dozens of butterflies, including commas, question marks, hackberries, red-spotted purples, and monarchs. At night, when the beam of my headlights caught the stump, I saw dozens of teeny red eyes glowing in a perfect circle. When we walked up with flashlights, we found the stump was ringed with feeding moths, including many of the stunning underwings, whose usually concealed hind wings are striped vivid red or orange and black.

The monarch is the only butterfly that regularly migrates north and south as birds do. Hawk-watchers at mountaintop lookouts often see monarchs floating by along the same path as hawks and eagles.

Fruit Feeders

One year, our little 'Seckel' pear tree bore a bumper crop, way too many for us to use, so I let some of the fruit hang on the tree. We noticed a few butterflies fluttering around the tree one afternoon and walked over for a closer look. It took me a minute to realize the tree was hosting scores of butterflies. They were clustered on the pears, their wings closed, and only the dull-colored, well-camouflaged undersides were showing. It was like one of those hidden-picture puzzles: "Can you find 50 butterflies in this picture?"

Most of the butterflies were my favorite red-spotted purples. The rest were mostly anglewings. Several kinds of anglewings roam my area, but the ones on the pear tree were commas and question marks. Though you can hardly see an anglewing when its wings are closed, the butterflies are glorious when they open, a flash of golden orange deepening into brown. The question mark, the bigger of the two species, sometimes shows a thin edging of lilac around its wings—a beautiful accent to its tawny

color. Red admirals, hackberry butterflies, and tawny emperors made up the rest of the crowd.

I did a rough count of 40 butterflies on the 6-foot-tall tree, but it wasn't easy to get an exact number because some of them were pretty feisty. They'd shove each other off the fruit or battle in the air.

After a few minutes of watching, it occurred to me that the butterflies might be drunk. The most favored pears were also the most rotted, and I could clearly smell fermenting pear juice. Some of the butterflies were so besotted that they sat on my finger in order to keep drinking.

Raising Butterflies and Moths

Tending caterpillars through their metamorphosis into the adult form is one of the most rewarding nature studies I know. And to a kid, it's like magic. If you want easy results, stick with butterflies. A newly emerged butterfly is a creature of wonder. Fresh from its chrysalis, it pumps life into wrinkled wings, expanding them to perfect beauty. Every year, I try a new kind, as well as a couple of my standards—the monarchs and black swallowtails I've been raising since I was a child. These two are almost always a success. *

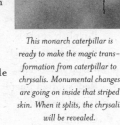

This monarch caterpillar is ready to make the magic transformation from caterpillar to chrysalis. Monumental changes are going on inside that striped skin. When it splits, the chrysalis will be revealed.

Be a Caterpillar Detective

Once you start looking for their calling cards, you'll find caterpillars all over your garden. Check your plants for any of these three telltale signs that say a caterpillar is at home.

- Chewed leaves. Look for holes and bare ribs in leaves. Or look for totally denuded stems. When I noticed that almost every leaf was missing from a bur marigold, I thought I was too late to catch the caterpillar. Then I noticed that one of the "twigs" was actually a brown-green pillar. He was clinging with his hind feet, his body sticking out from the stem at exactly the same angle as the rest of the bare branches.

- Frass, or caterpillar droppings. Watch for collections of tiny pellets, usually dark brown or black, on leaves or in leaf axils at a stem. When a new brood of question marks hatches in the oak tree over our driveway, I follow their growth by watching the frass on the roof of our white car: At first it looks like ground pepper, then coarse ground pepper, then peppercorns.

- Web shelters. Some caterpillars, such as the red-spotted purple, draw a leaf together with webbing to make a shelter. Be careful, though—spiders do the same thing. Don't poke your finger in and get caught unawares.

Once you find a caterpillar, it's fun to figure out just what it is. Check photos or drawings in field guides. You can narrow down the possibilities by identifying the host plant it's eating—many caterpillars have favorite food plants.

It's easy and fun to raise your own butterflies from caterpillars. Just follow these simple steps.

1. When you spot a caterpillar feeding, put it into a clean, dry jar (18-ounce peanut butter jars fit on a windowsill nicely). Include a handful of whatever plant it was dining on and a bare stick that reaches from the bottom to near the top. Cover the jaw with a circle of cheesecloth held in place by a rubber band. Try to identify the caterpillar; if it's a moth, you may need to add soil to the jar.

2. Add fresh greenery every day, and remove the old stuff.

3. Every few days, carefully remove caterpillar, stick, and leaves, and dump out any droppings. Wipe out the jar with a damp paper towel, dry it, and then return the caterpillar, food, and perch.

4. Many butterfly caterpillars take about two to three weeks to go from hatching to chrysalis. Others may take a month or more, and some hibernate as caterpillars. They grow incredibly fast, shedding their skin as they get larger. If your caterpillar sits in one spot without eating or hangs from the stick, looking half-dead, don't despair; it's most likely getting ready to molt.

5. When your caterpillar is ready to pupate, it will anchor itself in a patch of silk, then hang. Many caterpillars loop a line of silk around their bodies to hold themselves at an angle from the support.

6. One day, probably when you aren't watching (caterpillars seem to have a knack for this), your lowly worm will transform itself into a magical chrysalis. Many chrysalises are camouflaged in drab browns; others are full of odd knobs. The monarch has the most beautiful chrysalis: It's a translucent green with gold dots that hangs like a Chinese lantern of jade.

7. Many chrysalises hatch in about two weeks; others may take months or may wait until next year. When your butterfly emerges, it will sit quietly in one place while its wings enlarge and harden. Carry it outside without jostling those fragile wings, and set it on a plant to take its first flight.

The chrysalis of the monarch butterfly is an ethereal, pale jade green, studded with gold. The plump chrysalis has a lid whose opening is marked with a delicate row of gold and black dots.

Host Plants for Moths

To boost the population of moth caterpillars in your garden, and thus the adult moths (which will come to the host plants for egg-laying), nurture the native plants of your region. Many of the most common shade trees are popular host plants for pretty, harmless moths. (Pest moths usually seek out the leaves of vegetables or food crops.) Trees like acacia, alders, apple, ashes, birches, cherries, elms, fringe-tree, hickories, honey locust, maples, oaks, pawpaw, plums, poplars, sweet gum, tulip tree, walnuts, and willows are favorites for moth caterpillars. They also like shrubs like ceanothus, sassafras, and spicebush, as well as perennial plants like milkweeds, mints, and plantains.

Continued ➔

Regional Butterfly Checklist

Butterflies vary by region, just as birds and wild-flowers do. The following species occur in all regions:

Orange sulphur
Coral hairstreak
Mourning cloak
Common sooty wing
Clouded sulphur
(yellow sulphur)
Gray hairstreak
Red admiral
Tawny-edged skipper
Common wood nymph
Painted lady
Checkered skipper
European cabbage white
Monarch
American painted lady
Spring azure
Viceroy
Silver-spotted skipper

In addition, you might see any of those listed below, depending on where you live. I like to keep an informal checklist each year. It's my own version of the Xerces Society's annual butterfly census, and it helps me gauge population changes and new visitors.

New England and the Mid-Atlantic

Zebra swallowtail
Giant swallowtail
Tiger swallowtail
Black swallowtail
Spicebush swallowtail
Eastern tailed blue
Banded hairstreak
Red-spotted purple
Pearl crescent
Comma
Question mark
Great spangled fritillary
Dun skipper
Southern golden skipper

Southeast and South

Pipevine swallowtail
Zebra swallowtail
Giant swallowtail
Tiger swallowtail
Black swallowtail
Spicebush swallowtail
Sleepy orange
Cloudless sulphur
Great purple hairstreak
Eastern tailed blue
Reakirt's blue
Banded hairstreak
Gulf fritillary
Common wood nymph

Queen
Buckeye
Snout butterfly
Red-spotted purple
Pearl crescent
Comma
Question mark
Great spangled fritillary
Dun skipper
Southern golden skipper

Midwest

Zebra swallowtail
Giant swallowtail
Tiger swallowtail
Black swallowtail
Spicebush swallowtail
Eastern tailed blue
Purplish copper
Banded hairstreak
Coral hairstreak
Red-spotted purple
Pearl crescent
Comma
Question mark
Great spangled fritillary
Dun skipper
Southern golden skipper

Northwest

Pale swallowtail
Two-tailed swallowtail
Western swallowtail
Anise swallowtail
Purplish copper
Lorquin's admiral
Field crescent
Great spangled fritillary
West Coast lady
Woodland skipper
Sandhill skipper

Arizona, California, and Nevada

Pipevine swallowtail
Giant swallowtail
Pale swallowtail
Two-tailed swallowtail
Black swallowtail
Western swallowtail
Anise swallowtail
Sleepy orange
Cloudless sulphur
Great purple hairstreak
Eastern tailed blue
Reakirt's blue
Purplish copper
Gulf fritillary
Queen
Buckeye
Snout butterfly

Lorquin's admiral
Weidemeyer's admiral
Field crescent
Pearl crescent
Great spangled fritillary
West Coast lady
Dun skipper
Woodland skipper
Golden skipper
Sandhill skipper

Mountain West

Pale swallowtail
Two-tailed swallowtail
Black swallowtail
Western swallowtail
Anise swallowtail
Great purple hairstreak
Eastern tailed blue
Purplish copper
Banded hairstreak
Lorquin's admiral
Weidemeyer's admiral
Field crescent
Pearl crescent
Question mark
Great spangled fritillary
West Coast lady
Dun skipper
Woodland skipper
Golden skipper
Sandhill skipper

New Mexico and Texas

Pipevine swallowtail
Giant swallowtail
Tiger swallowtail
Two-tailed swallowtail
Black swallowtail
Western swallowtail
Spicebush swallowtail
Sleepy orange
Cloudless sulphur
Great purple hairstreak
Eastern tailed blue
Reakirt's blue
Banded hairstreak
Gulf fritillary
Queen
Buckeye
Snout butterfly
Red-spotted purple
Weidemeyer's admiral
Pearl crescent
Question mark
West Coast lady
Dun skipper
Golden skipper
Sandhill skipper

Continued ➡

A Well-Meaning Death Trap

Commercially made butterfly feeders are big sellers, but I have yet to find one that I like. Last year I bought a yellow plastic contraption that was as poorly designed as it was ugly. It looked like a giant yellow daisy, as gaudy as a pink flamingo in the garden.

A plastic cover with grids for feeding spots covers the reservoir of sugar water. Butterflies liked the sugar water all right, and so did honeybees, yellowjackets, and bald-faced hornets. But the stinging insects weren't the real problem. The main reason I pitched the feeder was because it was a death trap.

The moat in the center is supposed to stop ants, but instead it trapped small butterflies, which managed to get in but couldn't climb out. Panicked, they battered their wings in the narrow space until they were broken wrecks. Every time I walked by the feeder, I had to free damaged butterflies or scoop dead ones out of the moat.

You can make a better, safe feeder yourself. Just put a piece of metal screening over a small saucer of sugar water. I set my sugar feeders on top of a post for easy viewing.

Can't Fail Concoctions

When I saw how butterflies, moths, and big, interesting beetles flocked to oozing sap on the bark of our very old, very decrepit oak tree, it gave me an idea. Why not try to replicate that sap and paint a tree with it?

Actually, the idea wasn't original. I vaguely remembered reading about such concoctions in one of the old turn-of-the-century butterfly books in my collection. The first old book I checked had a guaranteed-to-work recipe, but I wasn't sure where to locate one of the crucial ingredients: "one rank-smelling snake, dead four days or longer." Fortunately, the next book suggested a mixture of beer and sugar. I mixed it up, but it was so runny it wouldn't stick, maybe because I used granulated white sugar.

Finally I came up with my own recipes, which work like a charm:

> 1 bottle flat beer (open the bottle and let it sit the day
>   before you make up the recipe)
> 2 boxes dark brown sugar
> 4 mashed bananas

or:

> 1 bottle molasses
> ½ cup cheap rum
> 1 cup water

I slosh the stuff together with a wooden spoon in a plastic bucket, then use a big paintbrush to apply it to tree trunks, fence rails, and an old stump along the paths in my woodland garden. Butterflies gather as soon as an hour after application, and at night, moths and beetles come to feast. I reapply the bait every day for about a week, then weekly after that.

Moths are more difficult to raise because most of them pupate in the soil. If I find a moth caterpillar, once I've figured out what kind of caterpillar I have, I supply suitable habitat in an aquarium: a couple of inches of moist soil on the floor covered with a layer of dead leaves and debris. Some moth caterpillars refuse to pupate in captivity, at least for me. I've never had luck with the big pink-and-yellow imperial silk moths. Their giant hairy caterpillars are restless in captivity and won't go underground. Yet when I set them free, they seem to know they're outside and will walk a few inches, then burrow immediately.

Moths: Creatures of the Night

Have you ever wondered why some flowers are night-scented, saving their sweetest fragrance for the dark? Those flowers are sending a come-hither call to pollinating moths, which home in on the scent.

On languid summer evenings, when the smell of honeysuckle hangs in the heavy air, I often walk over to the hedgerow to watch the moths at work. Sometimes six or more sphinx moths will be feeding at the vine, setting the clusters of flowers quivering from the motion of their wings.

It may not warm your heart to learn that many of the moths that come to drink at the flowers in your night garden are Jekyll-and-Hyde characters: While they add grace to the night garden, their caterpillars (including tomato hornworms, tobacco hornworms, sweet potato hornworms, cutworms, and armyworms) can be detested garden pests. Not to worry, though: In the well-balanced state of a natural landscape, these caterpillars rarely reach threatening numbers. Birds, mice, shrews, and other predators will soon pick them off.

Moonflowers are another night delight. I wouldn't go a summer without them. I grow the vines in a wooden half-barrel on my deck, where they climb almost to the peak of the roof, aided by a tracery of strings. These big morning-glory relatives open at dusk, unfurling their petals while you watch. Like evening primroses (another night-garden plant that I wouldn't be without), the flowers release a delicious whiff of scent when they twirl open. Sit nearby, and it smells like you've been spritzed by the atomizer of a perfume bottle.

Pristine and perfect, the large blossoms of moonflower vine release a heady perfume when they unfurl at dusk. They self-sow, with restraint, even in cold-winter areas.

As soon as night-blooming flowers open, moths are there to greet them. Unlike butterflies, many moths extend their proboscis while flying to suck up nectar from the flower. That tomato hornworm you despise in your garden turns into a five-spotted hawkmoth, a dusky flier with a 4- to 5-inch wingspan and an extra-long sipping straw—its proboscis may extend 6 inches or more!

Butterfly Shelter

Butterflies need the same basics as other wildlife—food, water, and shelter. Though it may take them a while to use the butterfly "house," they'll soon make use of a fruit feeding station and a water dish with wet sand or gravel and stones for safe landing. Other garden visitors will also be drawn to a butterfly feeding station, including wasps and hornets. There's no need to run scared, however: the thread-waisted insects will be so intent on their feeding that they usually don't mind a bit if you stand and watch. Just be sure to keep a respectful distance.

Odd as it seems to us, many moths lack functioning mouthparts. Once they have wings, these insects never eat. They live only for love, emerging from their cocoons for the sole purpose of propagating the species. Their lives may be as short as a few days; at most, they live a couple of weeks. Some of the most beautiful moths meet this fate. Among them are two groups of familiar moths:

Cecropia moths are as richly patterned as an antique paisley shawl. Look for the large red and white crescents on the hind wings. Wingspread can reach 7 inches.

- Giant silk moths, which include the pink and brown cynthia moth, the Chinese-red and brown cecropia and Glover's moths, the rusty orange ceanothus and polyphemus moths, and the ethereal, celadon-green luna. Their wings can reach from 4 to 6 inches across.
- Tiger moths, including the dalmationlike leopard moth, the highly colored garden tiger and virgo tiger moths, and the clymene moth, whose wing markings form a fleur-de-lis when closed. The familiar brown and black woolly-

Continued ➡

bear caterpillar grows up to be a rather plain-Jane tiger moth, with golden-tan wings.

Moths give you a great reason to spend time in your garden at night, when you're home from work and can really enjoy it. Nectar-drinking types will visit your night-blooming or light-colored flowers, and others will seek mates and host plants in the hospitable habitats you've created. Just one glimpse of a luminous luna or a majestic cecropia will make you a moth gardener for life!

Bringing in the Beautiful Butterflies

Joan Benjamin and Deborah L. Martin

Want a garden that's colorful, healthy, and free of major pest problems? Just make sure that your yard is inviting to insect-eating birds, pest-destroying beneficial insects, and pollinating bees and butterflies.

The recipes in this chapter provide food for your invited guests. But butterflies and beneficial insects have some other needs too—specifically, water, shelter, and living space. These essential items are easy to provide, and because water and sheltering plants are attractive, you'll enjoy them as much as the beneficials.

Start with water. Butterflies and beneficial insects can't survive or thrive without it. Mud puddles and a shallow pan of water that's filled with small stones will give butterflies and beneficial insects a place to land and drink. Change the water in containers frequently—daily if possible—so that butterflies and beneficial insects can always get a fresh, clean drink.

A Fluttery Butterfly Garden

Butterflies can't live on nectar alone. If you want to attract lots of butterflies and get them to stick around, try this three-part recipe from LuAnn Craighton, a naturalist with the education department at Callaway Gardens in Pine Mountain, Georgia. LuAnn says the first step is to pick a place with the right living conditions. Next, grow a variety of plants. And third, care for the plants organically.

Ingredients and Supplies

10 nectar-producing flowers for adult butterflies

10 host plants for butterfly caterpillars

1 (or more) 3 x 3-foot sunny garden spots sheltered from strong winds

1 or 2 flat stones (for warming spots)

Shallow puddle or terra-cotta saucer filled with wet sand and laced with a few dashes of Epsom salts

1 seat (for butterfly watching)

Directions

1. In a spot that gets at least 6 hours of sun each day, plant a variety of plants that attract butterflies and provide food for their young.

2. Add 1 or 2 flat stones where the butterflies can warm themselves.

3. Provide a puddle or other shallow water source so that your butterflies can drink or search for salts.

4. Site a bench where you can enjoy the show!

FLUTTERY FACTS

· Butterflies are cold-blooded and don't get moving until their body temperature reaches about 80°F.

Enjoy your garden in a whole new light by planting light-colored and white flowers that show up prettily at night. Delight all your senses by including flowers with fabulous evening fragrance, too.

If you like to entertain without a lot of fuss, a moonlight garden is the perfect place for a party on a balmy summer's eve. Your guests can have the fun of watching night-bloomers like the moonflower vine open their flowers, and no one will ever notice if you've been less than perfect about weeding.

Watch for night visitors in your moonlight garden. Bats may swoop down to scoop up insects at flowers, and big sphinx moths will hum at blossoms like night-flying hummingbirds.

Plant List

1. Honeysuckle (*Lonicera japonica* or *L. fragrantissima*)
2. Sweet alyssum (*Lobularia maritima*)
3. Pale evening primrose (*Oenothera pallida*)
4. Night-scented stock (*Matthiola bicornis*)
5. Petunias (*Petunia integrifolia*)
6. Tobacco (*Nicotiana rupestris*)
7. Lemon lilies (*Hemerocallis flava*)
8. Moonflower vine (*Ipomoea alba*)
9. Yucca (*Yucca filamentosa*)
10. Evening primrose (*Oenothera biennis* and other spp.)
11. Madonna lilies (*Lilium candidum*)
12. White-flowered Japanese wisteria (*Wisteria floribunda*)
13. Formosa lilies (*Lilium formosanum*)
14. 'Ida Miles' daylilies (*Hemerocallis* 'Ida Miles')
15. 'Eenie Weenie' daylilies (*Hemerocallis* 'Eenie Weenie')

· When butterflies gather in groups around puddles, they're after salts in the mud, not just the water.

· Larvae chew holes in the leaves of host plants, but seldom harm the plant.

· The organic caterpillar killer BT (*Bacillus thuringiensis*) controls cabbage loopers and other vegetable-eating larvae. But it will also kill butterfly larvae if it drifts to their host plants. Avoid BT and hand-pick problem caterpillars, or be *extremely* careful if you use BT.

· In hot, dry climates, butterflies appreciate dappled shade in the heat of the day.

A Bee-ootiful Garden

Be a friend to bees by growing plants that will attract them to your garden. A mixture of perennial herbs and self-sowing annuals attracts bees and adds beauty to your garden too, says Rose Marie Nichols McGee, president of Nichols Garden Nursery in Albany, Oregon. The plants in this mix are so easy to grow that "it's hard to go really wrong with it," she adds.

Ingredients and Supplies

1 seed packet sweet alyssum

1 seed packet catmint (or buy small transplants)

1 seed packet coriander

1 seed packet dill

Moonlight Garden Design

16. Moonflower (*Datura inoxia* spp. *inoxia*, also sold as *D. meteloides*)
17. Flowering tobacco (*Nicotiana sylvestris*)
18. 'Mt. Fuji' phlox or other white cultivars (*Phlox paniculata* 'Mt. Fuji')
19. Flowering tobacco (*Nicotiana alata*)
20. Night phlox (*Zaluzianskya capensis*)
21. Four-o'clock (*Mirabilis jalapa*)
22. Night-blooming cereus (*Selenicereus*, *Hylocereus*, *Peniocereus*, and other genera)

1 seed packet tansy phacelia

1 seed packet poached egg flower or meadow foam

1 seed packet corn poppies

1 seed packet single-flowered sunflowers

1 seed packet white yarrow (or buy small transplants)

Organic fertilizer (optional)

Directions

1. In early spring, prepare planting areas on the borders of your garden. A band of flowers 1 foot wide will bring bees and all kinds of other beneficial insects. Depending on the amount of seed per packet, this mix covers between 100 and 200 feet of border.

2. Sow small amounts of each type of seed on prepared ground that's moderately fertile and free of weeds. (In areas with mild winters, you can plant seed in the fall if you prefer.)

3. Gently water the seeds in and keep the ground evenly moist while the flowers are getting established (the first month or so after planting).

4. Once the seeds are up, water them with a diluted organic fertilizer, such as a weak solution of fish emulsion or liquid seaweed. If your soil is good and fertile, you can skip the additional fertilizer.

Continued ➡

Butterfly Nectar Garden Design

A wealth of nectar plants is an invitation that's impossible for butterflies to decline. They'll flock to your garden for the sweet nectar in this long-blooming garden, which offers food all season but hits its peak in summer, just when butterflies are most numerous.

Many of the plants in this garden will also attract egg-laying butterflies, boosting your butterfly population by doing double duty. Asters, for instance, will attract pearl crescents; butterfly weed may host monarchs; and turtle-head may draw Baltimore checkerspots.

It's fun to keep a logbook noting which butterflies visit, how many, and when. Butterflies have their season, just like flowers do. Spring brings little blues; summer, the swallowtails; and monarchs peak late in the season.

By keeping track of who's who, you can learn the butterflies as they appear, and you will build a record of butterfly populations in your garden. You may want to jot down notes on the weather, too, so you can compare your log year by year: Does a rainy spring mean more or fewer butter-flies in the garden? Does an extra-cold winter foretell a shortage of butterflies next spring?

A butterfly garden is simply full of pleasures and possibilities.

Plant List

1. Spicebush (*Lindera benzoin*)
2. Common milkweed (*Asclepias syriaca*)
3. Joe-Pye weed (*Eupatorium maculatum*)
4. Ironweed (*Vernonia noveboracensis*)
5. Mexican sunflower (*Tithonia rotundifolia*)
6. Seckel pear tree (*Pyrus communis* 'Seckel')
7. Azure aster (*Aster azureus*)
8. False sunflower (*Heliopsis helianthoides*)
9. Pink turtlehead (*Chelone lyonii*)
10. Small black-eyed Susan (*Rudbeckia triloba*)
11. Oregano (*Origanum vulgare*)
12. Swamp (pink) milkweed (*Asclepias incarnata*)
13. Purple New England aster (*Aster novae-angliae*)
14. Garden phlox (*Phlox paniculata*)
15. Mistflower (*Eupatorium coelestinum*)
16. Butterfly weed (*Asclepias tuberosa*)
17. Catmint (*Nepeta mussini*)
18. Sawtooth sunflowers (*Helianthus grosseratus*)
19. Heart-leaved aster (*Aster cordifolius*)
20. Purple coneflower (*Echinacea purpurea*)
21. 'Goldsturm' black-eyed Susans (*Rudbeckia fulgida* var. *sullivantii* 'Goldsturm')
22. Butterfly bush (*Buddleia davidii*)

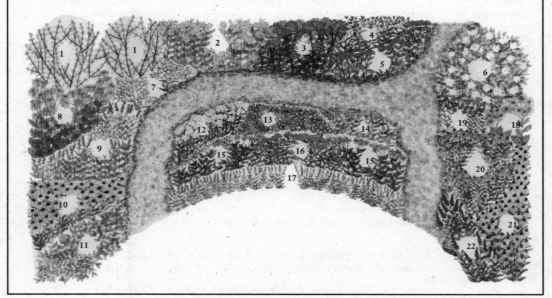

Moth or Butterfly?

Almost all moths fly at night, but that's not a surefire way to tell the two apart. Some moths fly during the day, and others are crepuscular, coming out in late afternoon or early evening.

If you're in doubt, check the antennae. Butterflies have "clubbed" antennae, with visible thickening at the tips. The antennae are thin, and if you look very closely, you'll see they're segmented.

Moth antennae lack the club at the tip, tapering to a point instead. Their antennae are often feathery, sometimes extravagantly so. And moth bodies are plumper and furrier than those of butterflies.

Fruit Plate for Butterflies

If you don't have a pear tree in your garden, you can set up a mini-version with a couple of ripe pears from your supermarket. Here's how:

1. Nail a plastic dinner plate (check a thrift shop for one in an unobtrusive color) to the top of a post. I like to keep my butterfly feeder at waist level, where it's easy to watch.

2. Let two or three pears ripen until they're very soft, then slice them in half and set them on the feeder. Overripe watermelon is also a big draw, especially for monarchs.

3. It may take a few days for the butterflies to discover the fruit, but they will come. So will wasps, so keep the feeder out of the line of traffic to avoid mishaps.

4. You'll see that the fruit remains attractive—to the butterflies, that is!—even when it's unap-pealing brown mush. In fact, that's when it's most attractive to them. Butterflies eat by sucking up liquids through their proboscis (say "pro-BOSS-iss"), and the more rotted a fruit is, the easier it is for them to feed on it. Lean close and you can watch a butterfly unroll its coiled proboscis and insert it like a straw.

Best Shrubs for Butterflies

Shrubs	Description	Conditions	Comments
Blue spirea (*Caryopteris* spp.)	Open, small-foliaged, gray-leaved, woody perennial or shrub with filmy clusters of light to medium blue or blue-purple flowers in late summer. Grows 3–5' tall and 3' wide.	Full sun. Loose soil with excellent drainage. Most species, Zones 5 to 9.	Late-blooming flowers are highly attractive to butterflies.
Butterfly bushes (*Buddleia* spp.)	Deciduous or semievergreen shrub to 10' or more with conical spires of flowers at each branch tip in summer. Grows 4–5' wide.	Full sun. Ordinary soil. Zones 5 to 9, depending on the species.	Flowers are sweetly fragrant. Many cultivars are available.
Ceanothus (*Ceanothus* spp.)	Deciduous or evergreen shrubs with dense form and abundant clusters of tiny, usually blue or blue-purple flowers in spring and summer. Grows 1–6' tall or more; width varies.	Full sun. Average to dry soil. Most are hardy only to Zone 8, except for white-flowered New Jersey tea (*C. americanus*) and western snowbrush (*C. velatinus*), which are hardy to Zone 4. Most thrive to Zone 10 (maximum)	Blooms last for weeks.
Privets (*Ligustrum* spp.)	Deciduous or evergreen shrubs or small trees with small leaves and highly scented, small, white flowers in summer. Grows 3–15' and 4' wide.	Full to partial sun. Average to poor soils. Hardiness depends on species; common privet (*L. vulgare*) is hardy to Zone 4. Other species, Zones 5 to 7.	An old-fashioned standard that's not often used in today's gardens. Privet is unbeatable as a dense, fast-growing hedge. The fragrant flowers attract many butterflies.

Continued ➡

Fruit Feeder Attracts Butterflies

Ripened fruit attracts many species of butterflies, says David Roth-Mark of New Harmony, Indiana. He offers butterflies all kinds of fruit buffets, and has discovered that they seem to like pears and bananas the best, "especially when the fruit is really soft and brown."

David surmises that the butterflies are more easily able to pierce the flesh of the fruit with their proboscis when it's overripe. He peels the bananas and slices the pears in half lengthwise before putting them on his feeder. "One pear can last for a week," he says, "so it doesn't cost much to keep them happy."

Watermelon Magnet for Monarchs

Watermelon on the patio is a regular part of summer life—a slice of summer that butterflies, especially monarchs, enjoy, too, says nature lover Pauline Hoehn Gerard of Henderson, Kentucky. "I keep a chunk of watermelon on the deck rail just for butterflies," says Pauline. "In late summer, there might be a dozen butterflies eating at the same time." She adds that the butterflies seem to enjoy the watermelon most when it's overripe.

Swallowtails Think Purple

Many backyard butterfly enthusiasts have noticed that big swallowtails seem to prefer the color purple, and Jim Becker, co-owner of Goodwin Creek Gardens, agrees. "It seems that purple and swallowtails go together," he says. "Brazilian vervain (*Verbena bonariensis*) is absolutely excellent for attracting butterflies."

This tall, bare-stemmed perennial offers its clusters of tiny, sort purple flowers for months, until frosts stop it for the season. It's easy to plant anywhere in the garden, but be sure to keep some near the front of the bed, where you can watch the butterflies that come to visit. Jim also recommends another verbena, a sprawling hybrid called 'Homestead Purple' that grows so fast you can use it as a groundcover.

Nature Versus Nurture

Sometimes Mother Nature's haphazard plantings teach the most useful lessons about gardening. "I planted all the flowers the books said in order to attract butterflies," says Pauline Hoehn Gerard, "but I still didn't have many." Then she remembered how many butterflies she saw fluttering over the milkweed (*Asclepias* spp.), ironweed (*Veronia noveboracensis*), and asters along the dirt lane to her house when she was a girl. She brought home some of these "weeds" from her mother's land, and she quickly found that butterfly visitations increased dramatically. It turns out that Pauline's old "weed" favorites are all-American natives that bloom from the middle of summer on, when butterfly populations are at their peak.

Barbara Trick, office manager for Aullwood Audubon Center and Farm, uses native trees to attract butterflies. Tulip trees, hackberries, maples, oaks, and white ash are nurseries for swallowtails, giant silk moths, and other winged beauties.

"Beefsteak" for Butterflies

When her Beefsteak tomato crop swelled and cracked one year in the heat, Deborah Burdick, of Mt. Vernon, Indiana, discovered that the cracked, leaking fruits turned out to be butterfly attractors. "I was walking out for my mail when I saw motion at the tomato plants. There were a bunch of butterflies—beautiful golden ones that I learned were hackberry butterflies, and some beautiful black and blue red-spotted purples! Now I leave some of my cracked tomatoes on the vine just for the butterflies."

Pick the Right Nectar Plants

You don't have to resort to trial-and-error to find out which plants attract butterflies. Ann Swengel, a vice president of the North American Butterfly Association (NABA), suggests growing some of these nectar and host plants as a starting point for attracting a variety of butterflies. For a much longer list, write to NABA at 4 Delaware Road, Morristown, NJ 07960.

Plant	Description	Hardiness Zones
Black-eyed Susan (*Rudbeckia hirta*)	Yellow and brown daisylike blooms; 2- to 3-foot-tall hairy-leaved plant	Annual
Purple coneflower (*Echinacea purpurea*)	Rose-pink daisylike blooms; 2- to 4-foot-tall perennial	Zones 3 to 8
Yellow cosmos (*Cosmos sulphureus*)	Yellow, orange, or red daisylike blooms; 2- to 3-foot-tall bushy plants	Annual
Goldenrods (*Solidago* spp.)	Plumelike clusters of golden or yellow blooms; 1- to 5-foot-tall perennial	Zones 3 to 9
Impatiens (*Impatiens wallerana*)	Flat, spurred blooms in lavender, pink, red, orange, or white; 6- to 24-inch-tall, neatly mounded plants	Annual
Joe-Pye weeds (*Eupatorium* spp.)	Substantial clusters of fuzzy rose-purple flowers; bold 3- to 12-foot-tall perennials	Zones 3 to 8
Lantanas (*Lantana* spp.)	Flat-topped clusters of red and yellow or pink blooms; 18-inch- to 4-foot-tall shrubby plant	Zones 8 to 10 (treat as an annual farther north)
Lupines (*Lupinus* spp.)	Dense 2-foot-long spikes of pealike flowers in shades of pink, white, blue, purple; bushy perennials grow 2½ to 3½ feet tall	Zones 3 to 6
French marigold (*Tagetes patula*)	Daisylike to rounded red and yellow blooms (choose single-flowered cultivars instead of doubles—butterflies can reach the nectar more easily); 6- to 20-inch-tall plant with strongly scented leaves	Annual
Mints (*Mentha* spp.)	Spikes of small, 2-lipped purple, pink, or white flowers bloom at top of plants; bushy, spreading perennials grow to 2 feet tall	Zones 5 to 9
Pineapple sage (*Salvia elegans*)	Small bright-red 2-lipped blooms; 2- to 3-foot-tall herb with fragrant leaves	Annual
Rose verbena (*Verbena canadensis*)	Rounded clusters of purple, rose, or white blooms; 8- to 18-inch-tall perennial	Zones 4 to 10 (treat as an annual farther north)
Brazilian vervain (*Verband bonariensis*)	Rounded clusters of tiny violet blooms; 3- to 4-foot-tall perennial	Zones 7 to 9
Zinnia (*Zinnia elegans*)	Round, flat, or mounded blooms in every color but blue; 6- to 36-inch-tall plants grow low and mounded or upright and bushy	Annual
Glossy abelia (*Abelia x grandiflora*)	Clusters of small pinkish purple or white blooms; 3 to 6 feet tall and wide; rounded, semi-evergreen shrub	Zones 6 to 10
Azaleas (*Rhododendron* spp.)	Lavender, orange, pink, red, white, or yellow funnel-shaped blooms; 1 to 20 feet tall (depending on species); evergreen and deciduous shrubs	Zones 4 to 9
Orange-eye butterfly bush (*Buddleia davidii*)	Pink, purple, red, or white fragrant lilaclike blooms; 5- to 15-foot-tall arching plant that flowers best if cut back to the ground each spring	Zones 5 to 10
Lilacs (*Syringa* spp.)	Large, very fragrant blue, lavender, pink, or white bloom clusters; 4- to 20-foot-tall upright plants look loosely rounded over time	Zones 3 to 7

Best Vines for Butterflies

Vines	Descriptions	Conditions	Comments
Honeysuckles (*Lonicera* spp.)	Various species of evergreen or deciduous vines, some highly invasive, with red, yellow, white, pink, coral, or bicolor tubular flowers, usually fragrant and rich with nectar. Bloom summer through fall.	Sun to partial shade. Most soils. Most species. Zones 4 to 9	Try coral honeysuckle (*L. sempervirens*), a beautiful, red-flowered species that attracts hummingbirds as well as nectar-seeking butterflies.
Honeyvine (*Synanchum leave*)	Long, heart-shaped leaves and rounded clusters of extremely fragrant, small, creamy white flowers on a deciduous vine. Blooms in summer.	Full sun to partial shade. Widely adaptable. Zones 6 to 9.	This milkweed relative smells as sweet as honey and attracts nectar-seeking butterflies as well as egg-laying monarchs. Self-sows freely and can become pesty if you don't keep after seedlings.
Passionflowers (*Passiflora* spp.)	Intricate flowers of mythic religious symbolism dot these deciduous vines, followed by showy, often edible fruits. Blooms in summer.	Full sun to shade. Ordinary soil. Many are tropical, maypop (*P. incarnate*) is hardy to at least Zone 6. Most species, Zones 6 to 9.	In southern states, the Gulf fritillary lays eggs on the leaves of passionflower vines.

Continued ➡

All Around the Butterfly Bush

The single butterfly bush (*Buddleia davidii*) in the back of Janice Ostock's garden in Bethlehem, Pennsylvania, drew a steady stream of butterflies, but it was hard to get a glimpse of the butterfly visitors close up. So she created her own butterfly visitors' center by adding a path that circled the bush. The butterflies often retreat to the back of the bush when an observer comes near, says Janice, but the new walkway puts the nectar sippers in full view.

Early Bloomers for Early Butterflies

When a few days of unseasonably warm weather late in winter coax early butterflies from their sheltered niches beneath bark, not many flowers are waiting to greet them. Nature lover Pauline Hoehn Gerard, felt sorry for the early butterflies because there was no nectar to sip, so she planted early-blooming autumn-flowering cherry (*Prunus subhirtella* 'Autumnalis'), which she notes blooms not only in fall but also in late winter, whenever the weather turns mild for just two or three days.

Pauline also recommends winter-flowering witch hazel (*Hamamelis* x *intermedia* 'Arnold Promise'), whose ribbony-petaled flowers offer sustenance until real spring arrives. Pussy willow is another great food source for butterflies. When early butterflies such as the tiny blue spring azures and the elegant, understated mourning cloaks emerge from winter slumber, there's a banquet of rich nectar waiting for them.

Butterflies Think Lavender Is Lovely

Barbara Trick, office manager for Aullwood Audubon Center and Farm in Ohio, loves her patch of lavender. When the sweet blue-purple flowers bloom, "it's absolutely covered with butterflies and bumblebees," she says. "There are so many honeybees and bumblebees at it that the plants practically vibrate." Jim Becker, co-owner of Goodwin Creek Gardens in Oregon, concurs with Barbara about lavender. "Lavender has proven to be an excellent butterfly flower for us," he says, noting that his visitors include masses of skippers and western swallowtails.

Spritz the Bricks for Butterflies

As David Roth-Mark of New Harmony, Indiana, was watering the potted plants on the family deck one July, he noticed that butterflies were attracted to the wet spots on the bricks. So a couple of times a day, he wets down the bricks with the hose to give butterflies a drink. Many butterflies are puddle-sippers and seek out hospitable wet spots to congregate and drink. If you don't have bricks to wet with the hose, you can keep a spot of gravel wet or make a butterfly drinking station out of an old cookie sheet or big clay saucer lined with gravel or river stones.

But there still may be a missing piece needed to turn your yard into a good butterfly habitat: plants that larval butterflies (caterpillars) like to eat. Most caterpillars grow up on a diet of wild tree, shrub, or weed leaves, but a few prefer herbs and other garden plants. Plant a few extra carrot family herbs, and you can watch the drama as tiny green and black-striped caterpillars gain size daily, and eventually become black swallowtail butterflies.

The small, fragrant flowers of many herbs also attract wild and domestic bees, which provide their pollination services free of charge. Also expect to see a huge range of beneficial buzzers that help keep peskier insects under control.

Chives (*Allium schoenoprasum*)
Garlic chives (*Allium tuberosum*)
Dill (*Anathum graveolens*)
Lavender (*Lavandula* spp.)
Oregano (*Origanum* spp.)
Parsley (*Petroselinum crispum*)
Rosemary (*Rosmarinus* spp.)
Pineapple sage (*Salvia elegans*)
Creeping thyme (*Thymus serphyllum*)

BIRDS AND SMALL ANIMALS

A Gardener's Best Friends

Vicki Mattern

The best garden aid you could ever invest in is probably sitting outside your window right now, ready to work for peanuts—or sunflower seeds. See that chickadee out there—the one with the bright black eyes and friendly cocked head? No doubt he's one of your feeder favorites. Now take a look at those starlings lurking nearby, ready to drop down by the dozen, scaring off your small feeder guests. You've probably wondered what you could do to discourage them. Big mistake. Every bird in your yard is valuable, especially in winter. That's when future populations of pests get stopped dead—literally—by the sharp eyes and quick beaks of the feathered army.

No Such Thing as Eating Like a Bird

Watch a bird when it leaves your feeder and you'll see that it constantly is searching out bits of food from every part of your garden. Finches sway on the stems of lamb's-quarter and ragweed, devouring seeds that would otherwise sprout in your beds. Sparrows, juncos, and towhees scratch beneath plants, vacuuming up fallen seeds and any insects that cross their path. Even the common house sparrow helps out, eating thousands of seeds of crabgrass, chickweed, purslane, and other weeds. Chickadees tear open cocoons of bagworms and other pests, munching the tasty morsels inside.

Nuthatches scour trees top to bottom in a comical upside-down posture that gives them a great vantage point for picking insects and their eggs out of cracks in the bark. The brown creeper covers niches that nuthatches overlook, spiraling from bottom to top of the same trees. Woodpeckers whack their way into tree bark and plant stems, ferreting out hidden larvae and harmful ants and beetles. Even those scorned starlings earn their stripes, patrolling your lawn with sharp, stabbing beaks for Japanese beetle grubs.

Consider that a single chickadee—maybe the very one who's entertaining you outside the window right now—can down a thousand or more scale insects, aphids, codling moths, pear psyllas, pine weevils, and other delicacies in just one day, and you get some idea of the immensely positive potential of a bird's appetite. That's why it makes such great gardening sense to invite more birds to your yard. Fewer pests mean healthier flower gardens, bigger and better vegetables, long-lived trees and shrubs, and less work for you.

In a single day, one diminutive house wren can consume 500 beetles, grubs, and insect eggs. More than half of a chickadee's winter diet is aphid eggs. And a swallow can consume incredible numbers of flying insects—by one researcher's count, a single swallow ate more than 1,000 leafhoppers in less than a day.

A Delectable Landscape

Unless your property is barren of trees, shrubs, and flowers, you'll be delighted with bird visitors who regularly stop by to check out your offerings. But you can attract far more birds by offering a few bird amenities, such as berry-producing shrubs and fruit trees, water for drinking and bathing, and nesting spots in trees and birdhouses. Your first visitors will undoubtedly be robins, nuthatches, hummingbirds, titmice, cardinals, and sparrows, but with a little extra enticement, you can welcome special birds, such as bluebirds, goldfinches, and juncos.

Feeders, birdbaths, and birdhouses playa vital part in bringing birds to your backyard garden. But trees, shrubs, and flowering plants can fill the same role without extra effort from you! Plants provide food, cover, and nesting sites, and because they trap dew and rain and control runoff, they help provide water, too.

When choosing plants, look for food-bearing species that will provide fruits, buds, and seeds throughout the year. Mix deciduous and evergreen varieties in order to provide cover and shelter all year-round. Native species are usually the biggest bird attractant, and local birds will turn to them first for food and cover.

Doing Your Part

In winter, a feeding station is the best way to lure the anti-pest squad to your yard. It takes a lot of fuel to keep those hyperactive bodies humming, so easy pickings are always welcome. But don't worry about your feeder birds getting lazy. Maybe bugs and weed seeds taste better than birdseed, or maybe it's just in the genes, but birds will still glean your garden no matter how delicious a banquet you spread.

For results right now, all you need are a few dollars' worth of seed, a simple cylindrical or open tray feeder, and a plastic mesh onion bag stuffed with suet (or freebie beef trimmings). If you like, add a source of water or a discarded Christmas tree for shelter to make your yard an even better place for birds to linger. Within a week or two, you'll have a host of garden helpers for pest control at its finest. You'll also enjoy the pleasure of their company. When your garden is alive with birds, even the grayest winter day can be a delight.

Holiday Feast

Winter birds love a Christmas feast even after the holiday. Set your Christmas tree outside where it's sheltered from the wind, then gather leftovers from holiday baking to make garlands of raisins, nuts, and dried fruit slices. For "ornaments," fill citrus rinds with peanut butter and fruit.

Winter Berries for the Birds

Vicki Mattern

Bird watching can be habit forming. The chair by the bird feeder window is often the most popular seat in the house. But not all birds live on feeder

Continued ➡

meals alone. Some simply will not eat from a feeder, no matter how tempting the treats are. To attract the largest variety of birds into your backyard in the cold months, you must also plant the right shrubs, bushes, and trees for them.

The best bets are those plants that produce plenty of berries and hold them on their branches into winter, when other food sources become sparse. These plantings can provide not only food but also shelter for your wild, feathered visitors all year long. Additionally, many of these bushes can serve as foundation plantings and bring birds close to your viewing window.

Birds are gluttons when it comes to berries: They can't eat just one. Flocks of robins or tanagers will return day after day until every berry on your dogwood is history. And once the berries are gone, so are the birds.

You can extend the season by planting different cultivars and types of berries. A combination planting of shining sumac, elderberry, and winterberry holly, for example, will ensure a steady level of bird activity around your yard.

Going Native

When choosing trees and shrubs for the birds, always try to use native varieties no matter where you plant. Natives will thrive naturally in your soil and climate. And you rarely need to fuss with soil improvements, fertilizer, or extra watering.

Also, research shows that foraging birds seek out the familiar over the exotic species. Putting native plants into your garden and yard will give you an edge in attracting birds. So instead of planting a hedge of forsythia, which has little bird value, try a food-providing hedge of bayberry, blueberry, elderberry, or sumac. It can work as a border planting or hedgerow, and will supply tasty morsels for many birds.

Birds don't care how good your landscape design skills are, but a yard with bird appeal should also look good to your eyes. Whether you like straight edges, right angles, and controlled plantings of a formal style, or the casual plantings and curving lines of an informal or naturalistic garden, you can take steps to build bird appeal. Remember that birds are more likely to take up residence in an area that has little traffic. If you can keep at least part of your yard undisturbed, or nearly so, with low-maintenance or naturalistic plantings, birds will soon build nests in the hedges, shrubs, and trees.

There are many attractive berry bushes for the birds, but here are four genera—dogwood, holly, sumac, and viburnum—whose varieties and cultivars are adaptable to a wide range of soil conditions and climates.

Dogwoods

Dogwoods (*Cornus* spp.) are always a big hit with fall- and winter-feeding birds. Many of these birds are accustomed to seeking out dogwoods because so many of the native species bear fruit. Bluebirds, grosbeaks, tanagers, thrushes, vireos, waxwings, woodpeckers, and a host of other birds adore the dogwoods' red, shiny berries.

Most of the North American varieties are shrubs with casual growth habits. Flowering dogwood (*Cornus florida*) is a superb small tree for a partly shaded site to Zone 5. Other, lesser-known dogwoods are just as popular with birds, although they seem to be a well-kept secret among gardeners. Many species are available, including pale, or silky, dogwood (*C. obliqua*) and red osier dogwood (*C. sericea*), two shrubs that make fine windbreaks or cover habitat at feeding stations; they bear clusters of stemmed fruits that are eagerly stripped by birds.

The native gray dogwood (*C. racemosa*) has attractive blue-green foliage, white flowers, and whitish berries, and it makes an excellent shrub for either a landscape border or naturalized area.

Include These Vines in Your Wildlife Garden

Vines make a perfect centerpiece for a garden designed to attract birds, butterflies, and other wildlife. Hummingbirds are drawn to colorful blooming vines with tubular flowers, such as cypress vine (*Ipomoea quamoclit*), trumpet honeysuckle (*Lonicera sempervirens*), and orange trumpet vine (*Campsis radicans*). Butterflies are attracted to cypress vine and sweet peas (*Lathyrus latifolius*).

Native dogwoods may be sold at extremely reasonable prices by your state department of natural resources or through county extension offices. You also can check with a nearby nature center or native-plant specialist to get recommendations for your region.

Hollies

When holly berries are ripe, every day is Christmas for the birds. Many varieties of birds will come and visit continuously until all the berries are gone. The berry-laden branches of the deciduous variety 'Winter Red' can be stripped bare in just minutes! Hollies attract at least 12 species that eat its berries, including cedar waxwings, eastern bluebirds, and northern mockingbirds.

Most of us think "evergreen" when we think of hollies, but deciduous types hold great appeal for birds, too—especially for bluebirds, which seem to find holly berries irresistible. Unlike evergreen hollies, some of which can grow to 100 feet tall, deciduous hollies (*Ilex verticillata* and hybrids) are shrubby plants that grow only about 6 to 9 feet tall. 'Winter Red' produces huge amounts of gorgeous, bright red berries on 9-foot-tall plants. If you have a small yard, choose 'Red Sprite,' which grows to just 3 to 5 feet in height.

All of the hollies are perfect for planting in groups or in a mixed border outside the window of your favorite easy chair. Hollies are pollinated by insects rather than wind, so be sure to plant at least one male tree nearby. A nursery center employee may be able to identify the sex of the tree before you buy. Evergreen hollies are hardy to Zone 5; deciduous types are even tougher, thriving as far north as Zone 3.

Sumacs

Sumacs (*Rhus* spp.) get short shrift in most home landscapes, probably because they are such common wild plants. They become part of the backyard scenery, hardly drawing a second glance.

Only in autumn, when sumac leaves become burnished with crimson or orange, and in winter, when their branches stand bare and stark with a candelabra of deep red fruits, can sumacs be considered eye-catching and landscape worthy.

Sumacs flourish from Zones 2 to 10, depending on the species, and in an assortment of conditions. Most grow best in full sun to light shade and are very drought tolerant.

Winter is when sumacs become standouts with birds. Although sumac berries aren't a preferred food, as are acorns or nuts, they are very much

appreciated by birds as a meal of last resort. Those spires of fuzzy fruits provide long-term food in the leanest months of the year, when little else is available. Some of the best winter bird watching often can be had from spots that overlook a stand of gangly sumacs.

Viburnums

Viburnums are a diverse group of more than 150 shrubs and small trees. They bear plentiful blooms, and some have fall foliage that's as brilliant as that of a sugar maple. They are fast growing, too, making them fine for a hedge or shrub grouping.

Viburnums differ greatly in hardiness, although most adapt to a range of soil types, moisture levels, and light conditions. Two American natives, nannyberry viburnum (*Viburnum lentago*) and downy arrowwood (*V. dentatum*), are among those that flourish as far north as Zone 2. Others, including many Chinese species and cultivars, are far more tender, surviving only to Zone 9. In general, however, most species are hardy to at least Zone 6.

The berries come in red, blue, and orange, as well as the blue-black of nannyberry and arrowwood. Plant breeders have developed dozens of garden-worthy viburnum cultivars, but the berries of some have lost their appeal to birds. If you want surefire berries for birds, stick to native species, which will thrive naturally in your garden.

More Trees and Shrubs to Attract Birds

Vicki Mattern

These lesser-known landscape plants also are excellent for attracting birds to your yard in winter. Check mail-order catalogs that specialize in native plants.

Manzanitas (*Arctostaphlyos* spp.): Striking, smooth red bark characterizes many of the shrubby species of this western and southwestern genus, which also includes ground-hugging bearberry (*A. uva-ursi*). The red or brown berries are prime food for grouse, grosbeaks, jays, and mockingbirds. (Zones 2 to 6)

Hackberries (*Celtis laevigata*, *C. occidentalis*, and other species): These lovely shade trees have interesting warty gray bark and a multitude of small fruits that ripen in late fall to early winter. Hackberries are a source of food for flickers, jays, mockingbirds, orioles, sapsuckers, thrashers, thrushes, titmice, woodpeckers, and wrens. (Zones 5 to 9 for *C. laevigata*; Zones 2 to 9 for *C. occidentalis*)

Bring In the Birds

Besides providing food for birds this winter, try these additional tips for making your yard a year-round haven for them:

- Offer water. Provide a birdbath or other source of drinking water.
- Make a home. To attract wrens, hang a house with a 1-inch-diameter hole from a branch in a fruit tree 5 to 10 feet above the ground. Bluebirds prefer a house with a 1 1/8-inch-diameter hole mounted on a post 4 to 6 feet above the ground. Robins and swallows prefer an open nesting shelf 6 to 10 feet above the ground.
- Plant a hedgerow. A naturalistic hedgerow will attract those nesting birds that don't use bird boxes.

Continued ➡

California dogwood (*Cornus californica*): This dogwood is a deciduous western native shrub with dark red bark and white berries. It is considered a hybrid of western dogwood (*C. occidentalis*) and red osier dogwood (*C. sericea*) by some taxonomists. Its berries are eaten by songbirds, crows, grouse, quail, and partridges. (Zones 4 to 8)

Persimmons (*Diospyros virginiana, D. texana*): Persimmons are native trees with large, simple leaves and bark that's checkered like an alligator hide. The astringent orange or orange-red fruits are fleshy and turn soft and sweet when ripe. They are beloved by bluebirds, catbirds, mockingbirds, robins, sapsuckers, starlings, and waxwings. (Zones 4 to 9 for *D. virginiana*; Zones 7 to 9 for *D. texana*)

Greenbriers (*Smilax* spp.): These evergreen or deciduous native climbers, some thorny stemmed, are absent in parts of the West but abundant in the southeastern United States. Berries may be yellow, black, blue, or green and are devoured eagerly by many birds. Bluebirds, catbirds, fish crows, flickers, mockingbirds, fox sparrows, white-throated sparrows, thrushes, and pileated woodpeckers are among the prime customers. (Zones 3 to 8)

American cranberry (*Viburnum trilobum*): An eye-catcher in fall, this native bears heavy crops of glowing red fruits. The upright shrub grows to 9 feet in height. Its white spring flowers may have some fragrance; fall color can be striking or muted, in shades of yellow to red. The fruits are attractive to eastern bluebirds, cedar waxwings, bobolinks, cardinals, and mockingbirds. (Zones 2 to 8)

Attracting Songbirds and Hummingbirds

Sally Roth

Birds have a special place in the natural landscape. I can't think of any other wild creatures that will conduct their lives while we watch, but with songbirds, you can share the whole cycle. In spring, you get to welcome them back from migration and watch them in their most colorful plumage as they begin courting and nesting. In summer, there are nests to find and fledglings to enjoy. In autumn, it's feast time as birds stock up for the long flight south.

Birds are a delight any time of year, but it's in winter that I appreciate their presence the most. There's not much to look at in the garden during the bleak, bitter days. Even the clumps of ornamental grass add only a little life, rustling in the cold wind that knifes across the fields. Yet the view out the window isn't all bleak. All I have to do is look over near the bird feeders, under the shrubs, or in the weedy patch beyond the meadow. The garden is sleeping—but the birds sure aren't.

The edges of my big tray feeder are lined with goldfinches in winter, 20 of them at a time, and they're none too polite. They squabble constantly, threatening each other with open wings and open beaks. All in winter plumage now, their soft, green-gold feathers tell the season as sure as any calendar. Right about the time the pussy willows turn from sleek silver to yellow fluff, the goldfinch males will begin to sport an odd blotchy look as their sunny breeding plumage returns.

Along the roof edge, I can see chickadees hanging, waiting for an opening at the feeder. Meanwhile, a pair of white-breasted nuthatches in dapper dress take turns swooping from the oak to the feeder, then back again. Hitching down the trunk in their odd upside-down way, they wedge sunflower seeds into crevices in the bark.

The red-mesh suet bags that hang like cheerful Christmas ornaments from a dozen sturdy shrubs

are popular this cold morning. The suet is frozen too hard to dent it with my fingernail, but the woodpeckers hammering away have the perfect chisel-like beaks for the job.

In the brushy part of the garden, where asters and grasses offer seeds and shelter, sparrows and juncos are scratching away, kicking up clods of frozen-together leaves as they search for morsels. I turn away to freshen my coffee and come back to find a male bluebird on the holly, carrying the sky on his back, as Thoreau said, though today the real horizon is drab gray instead of azure. The bluebird is soon joined by his mate and the three youngsters from this year's brood. They pick off one berry after another, methodically stripping the stems. I catch myself thinking, Hey, don't eat so fast!, and then I laugh. That's what they're there for, after all.

Flowers with long spurs are tailor-made for hummingbird bills.

Meeting a Birds' Needs

It's easy to attract birds to your garden. All you have to do is put up a feeder. But feeder birds zip in, eat, and zip back out. To keep them in your garden, you'll have to fill more than one basic need.

Food, water, and shelter are the big three. In addition, your birds will need corridors of cover to move safely from one part of the garden to another. Birds are too close for comfort to the bottom of the food chain, and without adequate cover, your guests will still be eat-and-run types. You'll have to think like a bird if you want to make them feel at ease in your garden.

The downy woodpecker is common in farm country and suburbs throughout North America, wherever large trees are found. In the wild, they nest in cavities in dead branches on otherwise live trees, but they'll quickly accept a loglike nest box with a handful of sawdust on the bottom.

Creating Cover

You'd be surprised by how little cover many birds need. A split-rail fence provides no shelter, but if you let grasses and wildflowers grow up around the bottom of it, birds can use that thin strip to travel at will. Instead of isolating your feeders, surround them with sheltering shrubs that let birds move safely to berry bushes or to the water garden.

Often in winter, our feeder becomes a regular stopping point for a Cooper's hawk, a slim, steel-gray songbird-eater that used to go by the old nickname "blue death." Evidently, these predators, which usually keep to the forests, have learned about the easy pickings a feeder attracts. I see them even in cities, patrolling neighborhoods for a likely feeder.

Without cover, songbirds at a feeder are sitting ducks. Cooper's hawks are swift and agile, and a chickadee is no match for them. To even the game, I always park our discarded Christmas tree on its

side next to the feeders for the duration of the winter. It may not be pretty, but to the birds, it makes the difference between life and death.

More than once, I've watched the hawk perch on the Christmas tree and carefully extend a claw down into the branches to try to nab its prey. If the birds sat tight, they were safe. But sometimes a sparrow or junco became unnerved and fled in terror, becoming an instant dinner for Mr. Hawk.

Watch a flock of native sparrows or wood warblers fly across open ground, and you'll see that they don't fly in a straight line. The birds fly as fast as they can, twisting and dodging in flight. It's as difficult to follow a single bird with your eyes as it is a snowflake in a blizzard. That indirect flight is for a good reason: It's just as hard for a hawk to pick out or pick off a single individual as it is for your eyes to follow them.

The best way to provide cover for birds is to provide connected plantings so birds never need to come out in the open. Plan your garden as a series of linked sites, joined together by protective grassy or weedy patches or by brush or evergreens. Think of the corridors of plants in your garden as bird paths. They're essential to making feathered visitors feel at home.

Food for All Seasons

Since food is the primary attraction, the first thing you'll want to do is provide an assortment. Like us, different birds prefer different types of food. I keep my feeders well stocked year-round, but I also fill my garden with live, growing bird treats.

What's on the Menu?

I keep the menu simple at my bird feeding station: Sunflower seeds, white millet, and suet are the staples. Sunflower seeds will appeal to most of the customers, and millet will bring in the smaller seedeaters who can't crack the big sunflower seeds. The suet takes care of woodpeckers and others that prefer soft food.

I also keep tube feeders filled with niger, the tiny black seed that used to be called thistle, but which is actually *Guizotia abyssinica*, a sunflower relative with small yellow flowers. For high nutrition and high fat, I serve peanut butter straight from the jar, smeared on the roofs of the feeders. (Contrary to popular belief, there's no danger of suffocation from birds eating straight peanut butter, according to ornithologists at Cornell University.)

Like any good restaurateur, I offer frequent specials at the bird café. Sometimes hulled sunflower chips are on the menu. Occasionally there's expensive canary seed, a real treat for finches, or a handout of peanuts, walnuts, or pecans picked up along the road here where the trees grow wild. In winter, when the cardinal customers swell from the 10 regulars to a horde of 70 or more, I start hauling in hundred-pound sacks of cracked corn. Starlings love it, too, but it's cheap enough to share.

I grow lots of berried shrubs, but I also plant a lot of grasses and flowers for the birds. Grains and sunflowers are staples in the bird garden, just as at the feeder. In spring, I scratch up sunny ground and scatter white millet, straight from the birdseed sack. I plant extra-thick, so the millet looks like a lush bed of green grass. By midsummer, the seed-

Continued ➡

heads are showing. Goldfinches and others begin nibbling long before they turn golden. Foxtail grasses, wild oats, and other natives sprinkle the garden and fill in the gaps between shrub plantings. They do double duty—no, triple duty—by supplying cover and nesting material as well as food.

Sunflowers are another item that's perennially on the garden menu. When I moved to the Midwest, I discovered dozens of perennial species of sunflowers, native prairie flowers that are equally at home in a naturalistic garden. Most perennial sunflowers are spreaders, but that's okay with me—and with the birds. The tasty seeds of Maximilian sunflower, sawtooth sunflower, and others attract birds well into late fall.

I tried to plan for all-year good taste when I selected berry bushes for my garden. Some fruit ripens in late summer, just in time to catch the eye of refueling migrants. Other berries are at their peak in fall, and some are ignored by birds until winter hunger drives them to search out the last fruits left on the trees and bushes.

At the Feeder

Watching birds at a feeder is a great way to spend an hour or an afternoon. It's so soothing that some institutes use it as a meditative therapy for their clients. Enjoying the birds at my feeders is as much a part of my morning routine as a cup of coffee. I can't imagine starting the day without either one.

A feeding station is also a great way to learn to identify birds. Instead of a hundred or more species flitting through the leaves in a May woods, there's only a handful, and they're in plain view. Be sure to establish your station close to a window where you can easily watch sitting in your favorite chair—I can see my feeders from my kitchen table.

My first bird feeder was a simple open tray, knocked together out of scrap lumber. Twenty years later, the most-used feeder in my collection is one of that same simple design.

A tube feeder, whether it's stocked with niger seed or sunflower, will attract finches. Here a trio of species—house finches, goldfinches, and pine siskins—dine together.

The more aggressive birds can monopolize a feeder, so I keep several filled. If blue jays take over one of the feeders, the shyer chickadees and titmice can visit another.

Golden Bounty

The best sunflower I've ever found for birds is the tickseed sunflower (*Bidens aristosa*). Despite its name, it isn't an annoyance to socks or dogs because the seeds lack the stick-tight prongs of other members of the genus.

This is an annual plant native to eastern North America, and it's a beauty. It grows into a 4-foot-tall plant, branched and bushy, with ferny leaves that look a little too much like marijuana. (Just ignore your neighbors' funny looks.) It blooms late, about August, and cloaks itself in hundreds of small golden daisies. The flowers have a delicate look and texture, more like cosmos than traditional sunflowers. They smell sweet and attract even more butterflies than butterfly bush.

But it's the abundant seeds that are the real pay-off. From September through spring, my stand of tickseeds attracts sparrows, juncos, titmice, chickadees, goldfinches, and other small birds. The birds hang on the seedheads like parrots or scratch the ground beneath for dropped crumbs. The plants seed themselves with abandon, but I don't mind. Unwanted seedlings are easy to pull out or smother with mulch.

Plant tickseed sunflower where it can sow itself freely for a bounty of golden bloom, or grow it in a big pot with morning glories or cypress vine.

You can get as fancy as you like with feeders, from copper-roof cupolas to white-column palaces that would cost more than my birdseed budget for a year. But before you succumb to a fancy feeder, think about how you'll fill and clean it. A pretty cedar pagoda dangles from a post in my yard, but it's almost always empty. To fill it requires me to balance a cup of birdseed in my teeth while I slide open a glass door with one hand and try to keep the whole shebang from tipping over with the other. Pretty is as pretty does, as your grandma probably told you.

Many birds prefer an open tray, perhaps because their exits are unimpeded and they have a good view of approaching predators. You can make one easily—it's a great project for kids. Use hardware cloth for the bottom, so rainwater can drain easily. I keep the sides on mine as low as possible, so I can see the birds better. A low tray feeder that stands on the ground with short feet will serve ground-feeding birds like doves and sparrows and keep the seed off the wet ground. A tray attached to a tree trunk will attract everything from jays to juncos.

Finches, siskins, titmice, and (sometimes) chickadees visit hanging tube feeders, which offer a limited number of perches but conserve seed and protect it from moisture. Don't go the cheap route when you buy a tube feeder: You'll pay for it in

spilled birdseed. Those with heavy metal bases and seed-cup holes are more stable in the wind, and that means less seed wasted on the ground. If house finches have overrun your tube feeders, buy one with perches above the holes. Acrobatic goldfinches will have no trouble reaching them, but house finches will be stymied.

Water—It's Essential

If you provide clean water, you'll give birds another reason to linger in your garden. Birds love a birdbath all year long, even in the coldest days of winter. It removes dust and parasites from their feathers, and it probably feels good, too—they revel in splashing as much as any two-year-old.

A shallow, rough-bottom container is a perfect choice, but birds can make do with just about anything. I keep a bucket of water filled outside for our dogs, and I've seen house finches, chickadees, and other birds using it, too. Up the road at the horse barn, bluebirds line up on the edge of a deep metal trough, sipping daintily.

The traditional birdbath is still a good design, but after two pedestals were broken by my rowdy dogs, I switched to using only the tops. I have three basins in the garden, each set on a flat rock about 6 inches tall. The one that gets the most use is almost hidden from view, beneath an exuberant arch of boltonia stems. In spring, when the vegetation is cleared away, the birds are more wary about bathing.

A naturally hollowed-out stone that's cupped to form a shallow basin makes a good birdbath. Another birdbath alternative is a simple large clay saucer, if you set a flat, rough stone into it to provide better footing. Of course, a garden pond or stream is better yet.

Once the birds discover their bath, they'll be regulars. It's my guess that that's why pedestal-type baths attract birds so quickly: Like red plastic hummingbird feeders, the birds are used to seeing them—they know what that shape means.

If you have an outdoor electrical outlet, you can use an immersible water heater to keep your birdbath in use all winter. They cost as little as $15 at pet- and pool-supply stores and are simple to install: Lay the heater in the birdbath, plug it in, and you're set. If you need an extension cord to get from outlet to birdbath, be sure to buy a heavy-duty cord suitable for outdoor use.

The sound of splashing water will catch the ear of passing migrants who might otherwise overlook your birdbath. You can rig up a slow-dripping bucket from a branch and set your birdbath under it, or you can invest in a recirculating pump (about $50) and spend a few hours creating a gentle murmur of water.

Birds especially appreciate a source of fresh water in winter, when natural ponds and puddles are frozen over. Simply lay an electric heater in your birdbath to keep it ice-free.

Continued ➡

Giving Your Birds Shelter

Shelter from the wind and weather and from predators is the last element of the bird garden. Evergreens are ideal bird shelters. An eastern red cedar that stands at the corner of my garden is home to dozens of birds every night. If you stand close to it, you can hear their sleepy twitters as they settle down for the night, safe from predators who won't risk its prickly branches.

A single evergreen will offer some shelter, but a group planting is better for cardinals and other birds that flock and roost together in winter. Many of the plants that you choose for food value will do double duty as shelter. Plant for diversity, mixing plant types and heights as they would be in nature. But remember to keep some open areas between shrub groupings so that you can still watch the birds!

Nest Boxes—Instant Homes

It's exciting to put up a nest box and watch to see who moves in. You can buy nest boxes or nest box kits, but they're also a fun project for families to build together from scratch. Birds are pretty forgiving when it comes to carpentry mistakes. They won't mind the crooked nail or the slightly off-center hole. Nest boxes also provide winter shelter. Or you can make a roost box for birds seeking shelter in winter—it looks like an elongated nest box with the entrance hole at the bottom. Birds that don't nest in cavities won't nest in your boxes, but they may turn to your trees and shrubs as a safe haven to build their nests. Try to avoid the temptation to take a peek—your scent leaves a clear trail for predators.

Recipe for Bluebirds

I'm not much of a cook, but for birds, I pull out all the stops. Last winter, when deep snow hit the lower Midwest, bluebirds came in to my feeders in droves. They'd never visited the feeders before, though they had come for berries in the garden. I was stunned by their beauty—such an intense blue against the fresh snow.

Ransacking the pantry, I pulled out cornmeal, a jar of chunky peanut butter, and a bottle of corn oil. I mushed it up to crumbly cookie-dough consistency, then took it outside. The bluebirds moved off only a few feet. When I scattered the dough on the porch where it would be protected from the snow, they immediately returned, fluttering down right at my feet. What a magic day, standing in the midst of bluebirds and falling snow.

Here's my "magic bluebird" recipe:

Peanut-Butter Dough
6 cups yellow cornmeal
18-ounce jar chunky peanut butter
6 small boxes of raisins, chopped with a floured knife (optional)
1 cup corn oil

Mix by hand. Adjust proportions of cornmeal and peanut butter if needed until dough reaches a lumpy but crumbly consistence.

Fruit for All Seasons

To plant a larder that will sustain birds for months, plan your fruit-bearing plantings around these seasonal treats.

Spring

Birds are looking for soft foods in spring, and they're abundant. Caterpillars and insects fill the bill nicely (and literally), with no assistance from you. A well-planted garden, full of young trees and a diversity of shrubs, will naturally attract insects, and that's what will draw the birds.

You can supplement the insect diet with strawberries. Plant a bed or a border of them just for the birds. Wild strawberries provide the perfect-size fruits for birds, and the plants make an appealing groundcover. The familiar wild strawberry that I gathered and made into bouquets of berries as a child is ideal. Alpine strawberries, which grow in self-contained tuffets, are a good choice, too, and so are Western beach strawberries. They're native to the West Coast, but they grow well in other regions, and their shiny leaves are as ornamental as wild ginger.

Summer

Summer kicks fruit season into high gear. Anything you like to eat, birds do, too. Sour cherries, pin cherries, and other cherry trees are great for the bird-friendly garden. Plums, apricots, and peaches are also good bird attractors. When our peach tree surprised us with a bumper crop one summer, the house finches made short work of the fruits at the top of the unpruned tree. They puncture the fruit to drink the sweet juice.

Add some raspberries and blackberries to your hedges, and plant river grapes, fox grapes, or Concords to clamber up trees and over trellises. Blueberries are superb bird fruits. Elderberries offer dinner plate–size heads of delectable, tiny berries, relished by waxwings, thrushes, robins, and other birds. Try blue or red elders for a change of pace. The bushes are more substantial than common elderberry, and the crop sustains birds for weeks.

Fall

Fall is viburnum time! There are dozens of species, and the fruits of all of them are appreciated by birds. I find that the birds pick the berries off the arrowwood first; then they turn to gray dogwood and American cranberrybush viburnums. Sumacs are welcomed, too. I prefer the look of shining sumac in the garden. Its winged stems hold glossy leaves that turn fire-engine red in autumn and shine like a beacon

until they drop. Bluebirds are especially fond of sumac fruits.

If you don't mind its self-sowing tendencies, and if you have birds visiting your yard, you probably already have some pokeweed. The stems turn Day-Glo purple in fall, and the clusters of black berries disappear fast when migrating birds discover them.

Winter

Now the birds turn to the last of the berry crop. They seek out the hanging, ¼-inch berries of hackberry trees, and they clean the clusters of showy orange fruits from the pyracantha that climbs the chimney. Cotoneasters also draw them in. And hollies of all kinds are eaten with relish. Roving flocks of waxwings visit the garden, searching out the last of the pokeweed and any remaining viburnum or sumac berries. Hawthorns shine like an "Eat at Joe's" sign. Crabapples, ignored by most birds until winter, become a fruit of choice. Hybrid varieties are often passed over by birds (my guess is that they just don't taste good), but the shriveled fruit that hangs from the wild crabs in my garden draws house finches, bluebirds, tufted titmice, mockingbirds and other fruit-eaters.

Mockingbirds thrive in areas with few trees, dense shrubbery, and lots of edible fruits like these bittersweet berries.

Nesting Materials

Bird-feeder traffic drops off dramatically in spring, when birds begin nesting. Instead of trying to entice birds to your yard with food, offer them some tempting nesting materials.

Scatter the items on an open area or drape them over shrubs. I like to tease the orioles by tying butcher string onto twigs. They're as adept as Boy Scouts at undoing the knots.

Here are some nest-material options, in order of their desirability:

- White duck or goose breast feathers (cannibalize an old bed pillow, ask at a farm, or check a duck pond)
- Other colors of breast feathers (breast feathers are the curled ones, wide and soft at the end)
- Goose or duck down
- Short lengths of white butcher string (no longer than 8 inches to prevent mishaps)
- Short lengths of other string or yarn
- Horsehair from mane or tail
- Rabbit and opossum fur (check a thrift shop for an old fur coat or collar, nail a strip to a board, and mount on a tree)
- Dog fur

You can also offer dried grass blades, fine twigs, bark strips (grapevines are a great source), and spaghum moss, but birds often prefer to collect their own.

There's another trick you can use to attract nesting birds: Keep a mud puddle fresh and wet. Nest-building swallows, robins, and other birds can travel for great distances to collect mud in times of drought.

Continued →

Songbirds in Your Garden

I didn't realize how different birdlife can be until I moved from the East to the Pacific Northwest and set up my first bird feeder. There was nary a blue jay in sight, though the elegant midnight-blue Steller's jay was a fine substitute. Cardinals, which I'd taken for granted, never managed to cross the Rockies. But I did host varied thrushes, like robins but dressed in gorgeous golden orange and blue, and a throng of ruddy brown western fox sparrows. It was an education.

The songbirds you find in your garden will depend on where you live, what kind of habitat you provide, and what kind of habitat is nearby. Here are some of the birds that may turn up in your garden.

Hermit thrush (above), Purple finch (below)

EAST

Northern bobwhite
Mourning dove
Golden-shafted flicker
Red-bellied woodpecker
Downy woodpecker
Hairy woodpecker
Eastern phoebe
Blue jay
Black-capped chickadee
Tufted titmouse
White-breasted nuthatch
House wren
Mockingbird
Gray catbird
Brown thrasher
Robin
Veery
Eastern bluebird
Blue-gray gnatcatcher
Wood thrush
Hermit thrush
Cedar waxwing
White-eyed vireo
Red-eyed vireo
Warbling vireo
Yellow warbler
Yellow-rumped warbler
Black-throated green warbler
Ovenbird
Common yellowthroat

Kentucky warbler
Eastern meadowlark
Red-winged blackbird
Common grackle
Brown-headed cowbird
Baltimore oriole
Scarlet tanager
Cardinal
Rose-breasted grosbeak
Indigo bunting
House finch
Goldfinch
Rufous-sided towhee
Chipping sparrow
Field sparrow
Swamp sparrow
Song sparrow

In winter:

Red-breasted nuthatch
Brown creeper
Golden-crowned kinglet
Ruby-crowned kinglet
Purple finch
Dark-eyed junco, slate-colored race
White-throated sparrow
White-crowned sparrow
Tree sparrow
Fox sparrow
Evening grosbeak
Purple finch
Pine siskin

SOUTH

Northern bobwhite
Mourning dove
Golden-shafted flicker
Red-bellied woodpecker
Downy woodpecker
Hairy woodpecker
Eastern phoebe
Blue jay
Carolina chickadee
Tufted titmouse
White-breasted nuthatch
Brown-headed nuthatch
House wren
Winter wren
Carolina wren
Mockingbird
Gray catbird
Brown thrasher
Robin
Eastern bluebird
Wood thrush
Hermit thrush

Blue-gray gnatcatcher
Cedar waxwing
White-eyed vireo
Red-eyed vireo
Northern parula warbler
Yellow warbler
Yellow-rumped warbler
Pine warbler
Common yellowthroat
Kentucky warbler
Eastern meadowlark
Red-winged blackbird
Rusty blackbird
Brewer's blackbird
Common grackle
Brown-headed cowbird
Baltimore oriole
Scarlet tanager
Summer tanager
Cardinal
Blue grosbeak
Indigo bunting
Painted bunting
House finch
Goldfinch
Rufous-sided towhee
Chipping sparrow
Field sparrow
Song sparrow

In winter:

Red-breasted nuthatch
Brown creeper
Dark-eyed junco, slate-colored race
White-throated sparrow
White-crowned sparrow
Swamp sparrow
Fox sparrow
Evening grosbeak
Purple finch
Pine siskin

MIDWEST

Northern bobwhite
Mourning dove
Golden-shafted flicker
Red-shafted flicker
Red-bellied woodpecker
Downy woodpecker
Hairy woodpecker
Golden-shafted flicker
Eastern phoebe
Say's phoebe
Blue jay
Black-capped chickadee
Tufted titmouse
White-breasted nuthatch

House wren
Bewick's wren
Carolina wren
Mockingbird
Gray catbird
Brown thrasher
Robin
Eastern bluebird
Wood thrush
Blue-gray gnatcatcher
Cedar waxwing
White-eyed vireo
Bell's vireo
Red-eyed vireo
Warbling vireo
Yellow warbler
Yellow-rumped warbler
Ovenbird
Common yellowthroat
Kentucky warbler
Eastern meadowlark
Western meadowlark
Yellow-headed blackbird
Red-winged blackbird
Rusty blackbird
Brewer's blackbird
Common grackle
Brown-headed cowbird

Common yellowthroat (above), Red-bellied woodpecker (below)

Continued ➡

Baltimore oriole
Western tanager
Scarlet tanager
Summer tanager
Cardinal
Rose-breasted grosbeak
Black-headed grosbeak
Blue grosbeak
Indigo bunting
Lazuli bunting
Painted bunting
House finch
Goldfinch
Dicksissel
Rufous-sided towhee
Grasshopper sparrow
Chipping sparrow
Field sparrow
Swamp sparrow
Song sparrow

FAR NORTH
Northern bobwhite
Mourning dove
Golden-shafted flicker
Red-shafted flicker
Downy woodpecker
Hairy woodpecker
Eastern phoebe
Blue jay
Gray jay
Black-billed magpie
Black-capped chickadee
Boreal chickadee
White-breasted nuthatch
Red-breasted nuthatch
Brown creeper
House wren
Winter wren
Gray catbird
Brown thrasher
Robin
Wood thrush
Hermit thrush
Swainson's thrush
Veery
Eastern bluebird
Mountain bluebird
Golden-crowned kinglet
Ruby-crowned kinglet
Bohemian waxwing
Cedar waxwing
Solitary vireo
Red-eyed vireo
Warbling vireo
Orange-crowned warbler
Yellow warbler
Yellow-rumped warbler
Black-throated green warbler
Blackburnian warbler
Blackpoll warbler
Ovenbird
Common yellowthroat

Wilson's warbler
American redstart
Eastern meadowlark
Western meadowlark
Red-winged blackbird
Rusty blackbird
Brewer's blackbird
Common grackle

Dicksissel (above), Golden-crowned kinglet (below)

Brown-headed cowbird
Baltimore oriole
Bullock's oriole
Scarlet tanager
Western tanager
Rose-breasted grosbeak
Evening grosbeak
Indigo bunting
Lazuli bunting
Purple finch
House finch
Pine grosbeak
Common redpoll
Pine siskin
Goldfinch
Red crossbill
White-winged crossbill
Rufous-sided towhee
Dicksissel
Dark-eyed junco
American tree sparrow
Chipping sparrow
White-crowned sparrow
White-throated sparrow
Fox sparrow
Swamp sparrow
Song sparrow

WEST
Scaled quail
California quail
Gambel's quail
Mourning dove
Red-shafted flicker
Acorn woodpecker
Downy woodpecker
Hairy woodpecker
Golden-shafted flicker
Black phoebe
Say's phoebe
Steller's jay
Scrub jay
Pinyon jay
Magpies
Black-capped chickadee
Mountain chickadee
Chestnut-backed chickadee
Plain titmouse
Bridled titmouse
Verdin
Bush tit
White-breasted nuthatch
Red-breasted nuthatch
Pygmy nuthatch
House wren
Bewick's wren
Winter wren
Cactus wren
Mockingbird
Gray catbird
Sage thrasher
Curve-billed thrasher
Robin
Varied thrush
Hermit thrush
Western bluebird
Mountain bluebird
Blue-gray gnatcatcher
Golden-crowned kinglet
Ruby-crowned kinglet
Bohemian waxwing
Cedar waxwing
Phainopepla
Solitary vireo
Bell's vireo
Warbling vireo
Orange-crowned warbler
Lucy's warbler
Yellow warbler
Yellow-rumped warbler
Townsend's warbler
Black-throated gray warbler
Common yellowthroat
Western meadowlark
Yellow-headed blackbird
Red-winged blackbird
Brewer's blackbird
Great-tailed grackle
Common grackle
Brown-headed cowbird

Scott's oriole
Bullock's oriole
Western tanager
Summer tanager
Cardinal
Black-headed grosbeak
Evening grosbeak
Blue grosbeak
Lazuli bunting
Purple finch
House finch
Pine grosbeak
Rosy finch
Pine siskin
American goldfinch
Lesser goldfinch
Rufous-sided towhee
Brown towhee
Black-throated sparrow
Dark-eyed junco
Chipping sparrow
Brewer's sparrow
White-crowned sparrow
Golden-crowned sparrow
Fox sparrow
Song sparrow

Continued ➡

A Birdseed Garden

Seed-eating birds will forage for months in a garden full of naturally appealing foods. Let the stalks stand in winter—birds will continue to glean seeds and insects through the seasons, and sparrows will scratch around beneath the plants for any morsels that may have dropped. Many of the best birdseed plants are those we're used to thinking of as weeds. But if you've ever scared up a batch of sparrows from a weedy field, you know how attractive these plants are. That's because they're chock-full of seeds—and that's exactly why they're weeds. The prodigious seeds spread the plants throughout farm fields, roadsides, and other disturbed ground. As far as the birds are concerned, it's all easy pickin's. This garden uses some of the prettier self-sowing plants, and the birds should clean off the seeds well enough to keep them from being too "weedy."

Plant List

1. "Russian Mammoth" sunflowers (*Helianthus annuus* "Russian Mammoth") with false climbing buckwheat (*Polygonum scandens*) and grain buckwheat (*Fagopyrum esculentum*)
2. Foxtail millet (*Setaria italica*)
3. Tickseed sunflowers (*Bidens aristosa*)
4. Zinnias (*Zinnia elegans*)
5. "Autumn Beauty" and "Music Box" sunflowers (*Helianthus annuus* "Autumn Beauty" and *H. annuus* "Music Box")
6. Lamb's quarters (*Chemopodium album*)
7. "Sensation" cosmos (*Cosmos bipinnatus* "Sensation")
8. Amaranths (*Amaranthus* spp.)

Installing a Bubbling Spring for Birds

One of the prettiest birdbaths I've ever seen was a simple homemade "spring"—a collection of rounded river stones set on a bed of gravel, piped with a recirculating pump. Water bubbled up through the stones just like a real spring, spreading out between them to create shallow places for birds to sip or splash. A semicircle of larger rock surrounded the spring and sheltered ferns.

The trick to the arrangement was a small plastic trash can buried at the center of the stones, which sloped slightly downward to a center depression above the can. Topped with a sturdy metal grid, that can held the pump and the pipe that carried the water in the can to the surface. A layer of pond liner under the gravel beneath the stones collected the water and returned it to the buried can.

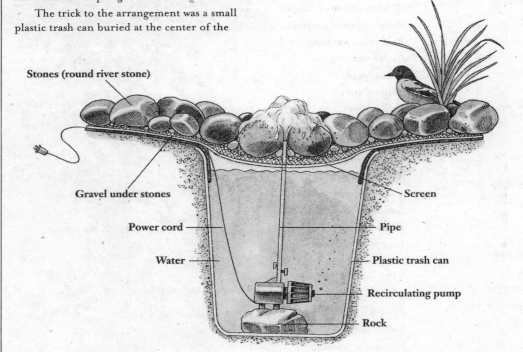

- Stones (round river stone)
- Gravel under stones
- Power cord
- Water
- Screen
- Pipe
- Plastic trash can
- Recirculating pump
- Rock

Hummingbirds in Your Garden

Hummingbirds are easy to bring to your garden, even if you live right in the middle of a city. These little zippers come to our yards for one big reason: to eat. It takes a lot of sugar to keep a hummingbird's energy up.

The ruby-throated hummingbird is the only species that makes its home east of the Mississippi, though strays of other species may turn up from time to time. Go west, and you'll find hummers with pink, purple, blue, and orange feathers. That iridescent flash of color comes from tiny feathers called gorgets.

If you're planning a camping trip to Texas or west of the Great Plains, take along a hummingbird feeder and a couple of packets of instant nectar. Hang it at your campground, and you're in for a treat.

I remember babbling to a ranger in the southwestern mountains about a hummingbird I'd seen in the pines. It was just gorgeous, I said, all green and purple and blue. What was it?

"That's a magnificent hummingbird," the ranger replied.

"Sure is," I agreed enthusiastically. "But what is it called?"

The ranger laughed. "That's its name," he said, "the magnificent hummingbird."

The ruby-throated hummingbird, which ranges across the eastern half of the country, is attracted to orange or red flowers like this trumpetvine. Its rapid wingbeats—up to 75 times per second—make it an avian helicopter.

SEEING RED

Red is the key to attracting hummers. They can't resist investigating anything red or orange, from the handles of my favorite pruners to the jumpsuits worn by scientists on Mount St. Helens after the volcano. (The hummingbirds probed the grommets, trying to figure out how to get nectar out of the protective suits.)

If you haven't had hummingbirds in your garden before, start by making a big splash of red. Put out a dozen zingy geraniums and a plastic hummingbird feeder—the gaudier the better. Once you have hummers coming regularly, you can switch to a more subtle feeder design. But for starters, go for something good and tacky, like a big, red plastic strawberry.

A HUMMINGBIRD GARDEN

Hummingbirds are fast eaters, and they usually zip in and out pretty quickly at the feeder. To get them to linger, you can plant a hummingbird garden.

Think of that beak when you choose flowers: Hummingbirds naturally prefer flowers with long tubes, where sweet nectar awaits. Tubed blossoms (think of a trumpetvine or honeysuckle flower) or spurred flowers (think of a columbine) are great enticements. It's a win-win thing for both bird and blossom: The hummer gets the nectar, and the flower gets pollinated. Sometimes I see hummers with their heads dusted yellow with pollen. Hummers will notice tubular blossoms before you

Continued ➡

do. You've probably never thought of the herb sage as having a tubular flower, but take another look. Hummingbirds certainly do—they enjoy both culinary sage and its ornamental relatives, the salvias. Bee balm is another hummingbird favorite, and, of course, the hummers like the reddest varieties best.

Hummingbirds often make a garden their home if it includes a good-size tree where they can mount their tiny, cuplike nest of spider silk and lichens. If you see a hummer going from one spiderweb to another in your garden, watch to see whether it's picking out tiny insects or whether it's collecting silk. Then good luck trying to follow it with your eyes to a nest site!

Hummingbirds are beautiful, but they're also bullies. Not only do they claim breeding territories, but they also claim food sources—a feeder, a fuchsia, or a pot of geraniums—as their own. And they'll guard them from anybody, including humans and dogs.

I once watched a single hummingbird drive away a flock of 30-plus cedar waxwings. The waxwings were flycatching over a stream; the hummer was drinking nectar from the orange jewelweed flowers along its edge. Every time a waxwing flew out, the hummingbird zoomed to the attack, chasing the much larger bird out of sight. After several such forays, the waxwings gave up and retreated en masse.

On migration, hummingbirds follow a path of red flowers when they head north. When my flowering quince comes into bloom, I hang out the feeder. In the Pacific Northwest, it was the blossoming of the red-flowering currant, a sinuous, lovely, native shrub, that told me when to expect the first tiny guests. Of course, in mild climates such as the Southwest or Southern California, hummingbirds are a year-round pleasure. I'll never forget drinking a New Year's Day toast while watching hummers zip around the flowers of a blooming bottlebrush tree in a Los Angeles backyard. It was just another part of the everyday magic that happens when you garden for the birds.

Brilliant Bird Gardens
Joan Benjamin and Deborah L. Martin

Discover wonderful ways to bring more color and life into your gardens (and a little creature company, too!) From far-out feeders to flower favorites, find out how to entice your favorite birds to your backyard and provide food, water, and cover for your feathered friends. You'll discover that the right selection of plants is the easiest way to attract an interesting array of birds. To lure eye-catching butterflies to your flower garden, follow these gardener-tested tips and techniques that will bring flutters of brilliant color all season long.

Compass Plants Have Impact

"Birds love the seeds of the compass plant," says Jim Becker, who gardens with birds in Oregon. The compass plant looks something like a giant yellow hollyhock from a distance, with a spire of golden daisy flowers that can grow to reach 8 feet tall. An imposing clump makes a grand statement beside a garden gate—but make sure it's in easy view of an indoor window so that you can enjoy the parade of finches, juncos, sparrows, downy wood-peckers, and other seed-eaters who will be stopping by all fall and winter. Compass plant (*Silphium laciniatum*) grows best in moist, well-drained, humus-rich soil in full sun.

Christmas Celebrations

Winter birds love a Christmas feast even after the holiday. Set your Christmas tree outside where it's sheltered from the wind, then gather leftovers from holiday baking to make garlands of raisins, nuts, and dried fruit slices. Fill citrus rinds with peanut butter and fruit for ornaments.

Birds Love Love-Lies-Bleeding

Let things go to seed in your garden and you'll be surprised at the birds you attract, says Jim Becker, co-owner of Goodwin Creek Gardens in Williams, Oregon. "We grow amaranth and a decorative millet and sell the seeds, and we have to cover the plants when the seeds are ripe to fight off sparrows and juncos. But the birds love the seeds so much that we always leave some for them when we're done harvesting," says Jim.

Jim and his wife, Dottie, grow love-lies-bleeding (*Amaranthus caudatus*), an annual with long strands of deep pink flowers that look like thick, soft yarn, and 'Hopi Dye' amaranth, an upright, plumey type. "Both amaranths are great for dried flowers as well as for birdseed," Jim says.

Sow seeds outdoors after all danger of frost has passed and the soil is warm. Amaranth will ripen most of its grain 90 days after sowing.

With Bird Feeders, Bigger Is Better

When you're hosting a lot of backyard birds, a feeder can empty quickly as hungry beaks snatch up sunflower seeds and other morsels. Save time refilling feeders by choosing large-capacity feeders that hold more seed. One ingenious option is hopper feeders that refill themselves as the seed level drops. Hopper feeders prevent waste, too, because windy, rainy weather doesn't soak the whole buffet, only the portion that's in the tray of the feeder.

Betsy Colwell, president of Droll Yankees, a company that's been making high-quality bird feeders for decades, says her favorite feeder is a large hopper model called the Jagunda. "I'm busy all week," she says, "so I can fill it up at the beginning of the week and not have to refill it until the weekend." When birds are depending on your banquet, a big feeder means they won't go away hungry when supplies run out and you're not home.

An A-maize-ing Hedge for Birds

Pauline Hoehn Gerard of Henderson, Kentucky, wanted to keep alive her memories of her childhood farm, so she planted a triple row of corn along her property line. "I planned to pick the ears for decorations, but the birds beat me to it. We had cardinals galore, blue jays, blackbirds, even woodpeckers feasting on our corn hedge," she says.

Pauline says she loves watching corn grow, and she needed a quick-growing hedge for privacy at her new home. Her corn grew quickly to towering heights, giving her home a farmlike feel, along with protection from prying eyes, and brought with it the added bonus of fun-to-watch birds at harvest-time.

Back-to-Back for Bluebirds

Bluebirds often face very stiff competition for birdhouses, especially from tree swallows. Since bluebirds aren't aggressive, the swallows usually end

---

Building a Bluebird Nest Box

Bluebird boxes are popular with backyard birdwatchers for one very good reason: They work. Bluebirds like open spaces, with woods or hedgerows nearby. They like farmland and suburban areas, and are partial to golf courses and cemeteries. If you have a suitable bluebird habitat in your yard or nearby, the chances of a box attracting a nesting pair are very good.

Building birdhouses is a great family activity, and you don't need to be a master carpenter to be successful at it. All you need is a saw, a drill, a hammer, and some nails. A pair of hinges and a hook and eye attached to one side will let you open the box for easy cleaning. Affix the floor 3" from the bottom of the nest box back, and mount the box by drilling two holes through the "apron" of wood left at the bottom.

If your workshop is really minimal, you can have the boards sawed to size at a home building supply store. However, an electric saw is fairly inexpensive and worth it if you're building more than one house.

Other birds, including titmice, nuthatches, and chickadees, may also be interested in your bluebird house. Why not make several?

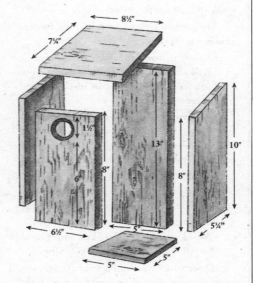

You can vary the dimensions of a bluebird box somewhat, but don't change the size of the hole. Any bigger, and it will allow entrance to starlings. Mount the box 4–8' above the ground.

Nectar Recipe

Instant nectar, available wherever hummingbird feeders are sold, is fast and easy to make. But it's super-expensive when you compare it with the cost of making your own, and the red dye often used is unnecessary and unhealthful. (Use red on the feeder, not in the nectar, to attract your hummers.)

Nectar is nothing more than sugar water. For every 4 parts water, add 1 part sugar. For easy refills, mix up a gallon jug and store in your fridge.

My feeders hold about 2 cups of nectar. When they need refilling, I measure out ½ cup of white granulated sugar, then pour 2 cups of boiling water over it. I stir to mix and let it cool before filling.

Don't add red food coloring, and don't use honey. Both can cause health problems for your hummers.

Superfine white sugar, which you can find at some supermarkets and at bar-supply stores, dissolves instantly even in cold water, but it costs more than granulated sugar.

Continued ➡

A Hummingbird Garden

No hummingbird can resist a splashy display of brightly colored flowers and nectar-rich blossoms. This garden will bloom from spring to frost, so visiting hummers will always find something to feast upon. Wild columbine and flowering quince start the season, offering their blossoms to the first of the migrants. Rose-of-Sharon, petunias, and many other flowers are in full tilt right at nesting time, so there's plenty of high-energy food. Late-bloomers like pineapple sage make sure there's still an abundance for fall migrants.

Long-blooming annuals and tender perennials like impatiens and geraniums are a staple in the hummingbird garden, because their flowers keep going for months without letting up. Plant your favorite color of garden-center petunias the first year. Then let them self-sow. They'll revert to the species form, a vigorous plant with simple, fragrant blossoms of white, lavender, and pink-purple.

Red flowers in this garden act as a hummingbird magnet. Once the tiny birds have found your special spot, tubular blossoms will encourage them to linger.

Plant List

1. White-flowering rose-of-Sharon (*Hibiscus syriacus*)
2. Cypress vine (*Ipomoea quamoclit*) with white- and blue-flowering morning glories (*Ipomoea tricolor* 'Pearly Gates' and 'Heavenly Blue')
3. Potted red-flowered geranium (*Pelargonium* x *hortorum*)
4. Pineapple sage (*Salvia elegans*)
5. Blue-flowered delphinium (*Delphinium belladonna*)
6. Flowering tobacco (*Nicotiana sylvestris*)
7. Self-sown (species) petunias (*Petunia integrifolia*)
8. 'Grandview Scarlet' bee balm (*Monarda didyma* 'Grandview Scarlet')
9. Anise hyssop (*Agastache foeniculum*)
10. Salmon-rose 'Picasso' geraniums (*Pelargonium hortorum* 'Picasso')
11. Golden columbine (*Aquilegia chrysantha*)
12. Hardy fuchsia (*Fuchsia magellanica*)
13. Red buckeye (*Aesculus pavia*)
14. White-flowered impatiens (*Impatiens wallerana*)
15. 'Homestead Purple' rose verbena (*Verbena canadensis* 'Homestead Purple')
16. California fuchsia (*Zauschneria californica*)
17. Apple-scented geraniums (*Pelargonium odoratissimum*)
18. Red- and salmon-flowered Texas sage (*Salvia coccinea* species form or 'Lady in Red' for red flowers and *S. coccinea* 'Cherry Blossom' for salmon flowers)
19. Great blue lobelia (*Lobelia syphilitica*)
20. Blue-flowered larkspur (*Consolida ambigua*)
21. Wild columbine (*Aquilegia canadensis*)
22. Coral bells (*Heuchera sanguinea*)
23. Flowering quince (*Chaenomeles speciosa*)

up with possession of the houses, but David H. Drake, president of Coveside Conservation Products, a birdhouse manufacturing company, says the solution is simple.

"Mount two bluebird houses back to back or very close together, and tree swallows and bluebirds will live happily as neighbors."

The key to this idea's success is knowing that birds of the same species, like two families of tree swallows, won't nest in adjoining apartments, even though they will nest as nearby neighbors. By putting the houses back to back, you play on the tree swallows' natural instinct not to share space. Birds of different species, however, will coexist contentedly even if their homes are very close together.

Feature the Food Chain

Prairie wildflowers, like coneflowers (*Echinacea* and *Ratibida* spp.), Joe-Pye weed (*Eupatorium* spp.), and many others, not only produce edible seeds for birds but are also unparalleled at attracting insects—the foundation of the food chain, notes Neil Diboll, chairman of Prairie Nursery, Inc., in Westfield, Wisconsin.

"Insects are the number one food for baby birds, so plant the prairie plants, attract the bugs, and feed the birds!" says Neil. When you plant perennial wildflowers that attract insects, you're bound to attract the birds that dine on them. If you buy large plants, you'll get flowers the first year you plant. After the flowers are finished, sparrows, finches, and other songbirds will enjoy the seeds from fall right through winter.

Choosing a Hummingbird Feeder

Hummingbird feeders have come a long way in the last ten years or so, but designers still don't have the message that form follows function. A feeder must be easy to refill and easy to clean, since you'll be doing both frequently. If your garden is graced with hummingbirds, you can count on refilling the feeder at least once a week.

Molds are unhealthy to hummers, so keeping your feeder clean is a must. I use a bottle brush to clean the main body of the feeder and an old toothbrush to get at the gook in holes and crevices.

Before you buy a hummingbird feeder, check out these features:

- Examine how the feeder comes apart. Will you be able to clean it easily, or will you have to work blindly in tight, hard-to-get-at crannies?

- Beware of feeders that require you to turn them upside down to remove and reinsert the reservoir; spilled sugar water is an annoyance on hands and clothes.

- Make sure your feeder has a decent-size reservoir that won't need refilling every day. Small feeders are cute but impractical.

- Avoid opaque feeders. You won't be able to tell if the inside needs cleaning.

Once you have chosen your feeder, you'll need to hang it up. I've found that a black iron shepherd's hook is a fine place to hang a feeder.

Continued →

Plants That Attract Hummingbirds

You can grow a beautiful hummingbird garden by choosing a selection of the following plants. Or plant one or a mix in a hanging basket for head-high hummingbirds.

All grow well in full sun, with average soil, unless otherwise indicated.

Hardy Perennials

Bee balm (*Monarda didyma*)
Unusual whorled flowers in pink, red, white, and red-purple. Fast spreader. Zones 4 to 10.

Catmints (*Nepeta* spp.)
Loose, mounding clumps of silvery leaves with abundant, small, lavender-blue flowers. Most hardy in Zones 3 to 10.

Columbines (*Aquilegia* spp.)
Long-spurred flowers are held on bare stems above a rosette of pretty, lobed foliage. Most hardy in Zones 3 to 10.

Coral bells (*Heuchera sanguinea*, x *H. brizoides*)
Rosettes of scalloped leaves bear many long-blooming stems of tiny red, pink, or white blossoms. Go for the zingy colors to attract hummers. Zones 3 to 10.

Delphiniums (*Delphinium* spp.)
Beautiful spikes in all shades of blue, purple, and white rise above rosettes of foliage. Best in cooler climates. Zones 3 to 10.

Hyssops (*Agastache* spp.)
Densely packed, narrow spikes of tiny flowers, often with fragrant foliage, are more familiar to herb gardens but beloved by hummingbirds. Zones 4 to 10.

Penstemons (*Penstemon* spp.)
Midheight perennials with abundant tubular flowers in blue, white, and purple. Best in West. Many are difficult to grow and short-lived, but worth trying. Must have perfect drainage. Hardiness depends on species; varying from Zones 3 to 9.

Phlox (*Phlox paniculata*)
Old-time garen favorite with often fragrant flowers in pink, red, white, and lilac. Zones 3 to 9.

Pineapple sage (*Salvia elegans*)
Large bush with fragrant foliage and late-blooming, bright red flowers. Zones 8 to 10; grow as annual in cold regions.

Salvias (*Salvia* spp.)
Salvia coccinea (Zone 8, but grow as annual elsewhere) has brilliant red flowers. Red sage (*S. splendens*) cultivars are hummingbird magnets. Many are hardy in Zones 5 to 10, others only in Zone 9 or 10. Many of the tender salvias can be grown as annuals in all zones.

Annuals and Tender Perennials

Grow in a sunny spot, in well-drained average garden soil. Many will self-sow.

Cleome (*Cleome hasslerana*)
Spidery whorls in pink, white, and purple on 4' plants. Annual; all zones.

Four-o'clocks (*Mirabilis jalapa*)
Bushy, tuber-forming tender perennials with flowers in red, yellow, white, and pink—sometimes more than one color on a single plant! Blooms in late afternoon. Perennial in Zones 9 and 10; grow as annuals in all other zones.

Geraniums (*Pelargonium* x *hortorum*)
Familiar container plants with pink, salmon, red, or white flowers. Perennial in Zones 9 and 10; grow as annuals in all other zones.

Geraniums, scented (*Pelargonium* spp.)
A wonderful assortment of leaf shape and scent. Flowers are much less showy than common gerniums but highly attractive to hummers. Perennial in Zones 9 and 10; grow as annuals in all other zones.

Impatiens (*Impatiens wallerana*)
Indefatigable bedding annual with red, white, pink, lavender, and mixed colors. Perennial in Zones 9 and 10; grow as annuals in all other zones.

Nicotianas (*Nicotiana* spp.)
Sweet-smelling tobacco relatives with tubular blossoms. Avoid 'Nikki' hybrids. Nearly all are annuals. *N. alata* is a perennial hardy in Zones 9 and 10.

Petunias (*Petunia* spp. and hybrids)
Popular annuals with sprawling plants and a variety of colorful flaring trumpet flowers. All petunias will attract hummers. Annual; all zones.

Tithonia (*Tithonia rotundifolia*)
Huge, bushy but single-stemmed branching plant, to 8' high and 4' wide with a multitude of brilliant orange-red daisylike flowers in late summer. Also attracts butterflies galore. Annual; all zones.

Shrubs and Vines

Butterfly bush (*Buddleia davidii*)
Bush with fragrant, lilac-purple flowers held in conical spires at each branch tip. Zones 5 to 9.

Flowering quince (*Chaenomeles speciosa*)
Red, pink, or salmon flowers early in spring catch the first wave of migrating hummingbirds. Use dwarf cultivars such as 'Nana' in masses, as groundcovers; taller varieties are fine shrubs for mixed borders. Zones 5 to 10.

Fuchsias (*Fuchsia* spp.)
Earring-drop flowers in fabulous color combinations of red and purple, pink and white, and others. Grow as shrubs in warm climates; annuals elsewhere. Zones 8 to 10.

Mandevilla (*Mandevilla splendens*)
Hot pink tubular flowers on a tender vine that grows fast enough to be enjoyed as an annual. Zone 8 or 9.

Trumpetvine (*Campsis radicans*)
Fast-growing, extremely vigorous vine with rich orange tubular flowers. Give it a very sturdy support. May become a problem, but hummingbirds love it. Similar crossvine (*Bignonia capreolata*) is less aggressive. Zones 5 to 9.

Slip-Sliding Away

"I love squirrels," says Heidi Doss, "but sometimes they get into my birdhouses and destroy the nests." So Heidi made simple baffles for her birdhouse posts out of 30-inch lengths of PVC pipe. She slips the pipe over the post and lets it slide to the ground, then she mounts the house on top of the pipe. The squirrels can't get a climbing grip on the slippery plastic barrier.

"My wrens are much more relaxed," says Heidi, a teaching naturalist at Wesselman Woods Nature Preserve. "It's as if they know the squirrels won't be able to reach their eggs or babies."

Benefits of Bayberries

Bird lovers should try planting bayberry (*Myrica pensylvanica*), recommends Mike Hradel, owner of Coldstream Farm in Michigan. This easy-to-grow shrub not only offers evergreen shelter year-round, providing what Mike calls a "visual shield" to keep birds safe, but it also provides a winter banquet for birds. "It's unusual to find food and cover on the same bush in winter," he says.

Bayberry is tops with just about every bird that's around in winter. "More than 20 kinds of birds eat the berries," Mike notes, including pheasants, wild turkeys, flickers, downy woodpeckers, chickadees, Carolina wrens, and yellow-rumped warblers. "The one I could hardly believe is the tree swallow," he says. "I thought they ate only insects. But they love bayberries!"

The native shrub thrives in many soil conditions, including acid soils and poor, sterile, sandy soils, and is salt tolerant. Plant bayberry shrubs in full sun to partial shade in Zones 2 to 7.

The Cupboard Gourmet

Cleaning out the cupboards used to yield nothing more than a trash can full of stale food, so bird-watcher Deborah Burdick of Mount Vernon, Indiana, decided to make a special recipe for her backyard birds. "I emptied the last inch or two of all the cereal boxes, added some raisins that were hard as rocks, and mushed in the leftover oatmeal from breakfast," she relates. "Then I spooned out dabs of the stuff right onto the ground." Sparrows arrived before she even got back in the house, and they were soon joined by the local mockingbird and a bunch of noisy blue jays.

Now she crumbles stale crackers by hand so the pieces are smaller, and sometimes she treats her birds to a dollop of peanut butter for a tastier mix. Deborah says that natural cereals (without a lot of added sugar or preservatives) are best for the birds because they supply healthy calories that provide longer-lasting energy. Cereals with nuts or berries in the mix are always surefire favorites, too.

A Mix of Millets Suits Sparrows

Small seed-eaters like sparrows, juncos, buntings, and finches love the tiny, round seeds of millets, a group of annual grasses. Any type of millet is perfect for feeding birds from summer through winter because the birds pick every seed clean, says David A. Kester, owner of Kester's Wild Game Food Nurseries. Some millets shed their seeds and provide a banquet for sparrows and other ground-feeding birds. Other millets keep their seedheads intact on the plants, making sturdy landing pads for the finches who feed on the seeds.

David's company sells a millet mix that includes the familiar birdseed proso millet (*Panicum millaceum*), which has an arching, branching seedhead that ripens in only 65 to 70 days. Siberian millet (*Setaria italica*), also called German millet, is

Continued ➡

another member of the mix. *S. berian* millet has interesting solid seedheads that "droop like a long finger," according to David. Seedheads like cattail pokers are the trademark of pearl millet (*Pennisetum glaucum*), another good bird plant. Japanese millet (*Echinochloa crusgalli*), with seedheads shaped like a turkey's foot, and several other types, round out the menu.

Plant a Food Patch for Birds

Tempt pheasants, quail, bobwhites, doves, and dozens of smaller birds with a patch of food plants just for them. David A. Kester, owner of Kester's Wild Game Food Nurseries in Omro, Wisconsin, encourages bird lovers to plant a special bird garden that includes both perennials and annuals. He recommends clovers, including bird's-foot trefoil (*Lotus corniculatus*), which sports clusters of sunny yellow blossoms, and bush clovers (*Lespedeza* spp.), which have small pink or purple pealike flowers. For fast payoff, include annuals like sorghum, buckwheat, and small-seeded soybeans and peas. Prepare a small planting bed, mix together a handful of seeds, and sow the seeds over the bed. Water generously until the seeds germinate, then take the low-maintenance approach—just wait for the bird visitors to arrive.

Some Like Their Gardens Wild

Find a discreet part of your garden and let it go wild, and you'll get all kinds of pleasant bird surprises, says Jim Becker, co-owner of Goodwin Creek Gardens in Williams, Oregon. Birds love weed seeds even better than birdseed. "Let some weeds stand, and you'll have birds visiting until every seed is gone," he says, pointing to chicory and wild lettuce as two favorites of feathered friends. Goldfinches are particularly fond of both plants, he adds.

Lamb's-quarters, dock, and ragweed (if you don't have allergies) are top-notch, too. Jim says that even a small patch of weeds (about 3 x 3 feet), will provide plenty of great edibles for feathered friends. If you have room, let an even larger patch go wild, and you'll be on your way to creating a natural bird habitat. Be sure to keep your wild patch well away from your vegetable garden, though, so that stray seeds don't sow a crop of heavy labor for next season.

Warm Water in Winter

Second-story condo resident and bird lover Elizabeth Castaldi of Washington, D.C., says supplying fresh water in the winter to birds is a challenge. On cold days, she fills a clay saucer with warm water in early morning. "The birds have learned my schedule," she says. "They're already in line for baths when I bring the water outside." When she heads to work, she brings the saucer indoors until the next morning's birdie bath time.

Plant a Birdseed Garden

When bird-feeder traffic drops off in late spring, Heidi Doss of Evansville, Indiana, has an ingenious solution for getting rid of the last few inches of birdseed. "I know whatever's left won't last until fall, when feeding season picks up again, so I use it to plant a garden for my birds. Heidi prepares a bed just she would for planting annuals, then she scatters the leftover seed and covers it lightly with soil.

Plant mixed seed so that you can learn what kind of plants grow from birdseed. "Buckwheat really surprised me—I had no idea it was so pretty," says Heidi. Let the birdseed plants mature in place so that the birds can enjoy the seeds just as they grow. Birds will come and go in the patch all winter long, says Heidi.

Appreciating the Ordinary

Starlings, pigeons, and English sparrows were just "city birds" to Gretchen Harrison of Boston, but that changed when her two-year-old daughter, Erica, discovered the "birdies." Looking at the city bird life through fresh eyes, Gretchen found these birds as fascinating as any songbirds.

She and Erica feed their little troupe of feathered friends just what cosmopolitan birds like most—slices of sourdough bread, leftover French pastries, scraps of cream-cheese Danish, and the remnants of corned beef sandwiches. As the birds linger over the feast, Gretchen and her daughter learn their habits and personalities, and now they bird-watch daily on their sojourns through the city.

Once you change your outlook on city birds, you'll find they can be very interesting to watch. "Now I see how tender the pigeons are with their mates, and I love to watch the feathers on the starlings change colors in the sun, and listen to them sing," Gretchen says, "Even the English sparrows are pretty darn cute—especially if they're all you have!"

Wreath of Welcome

As soon as bird enthusiast Janice Ostock of Bethlehem, Pennsylvania, moved into her new home, she hung a grapevine wreath beside her front door. "I was still unpacking boxes when I noticed a house finch bringing sticks to the porch, and when I checked, I found a pair of them were making a nest in my wreath!" she exclaims. Since finches, robins, and other songbirds often nest near human haunts, wreaths and hanging baskets located near the doorway all make great nest sites.

Janice's birds built their deep cup-shaped nest on the bottom of the wreath. "It looked just like the wreaths you see in the shops," she says, "except instead of an artificial nest, mine was real—and had birds in it."

Birds Aren't Bread Snobs

If you're baking and things don't turn out quite right, put the "failures" out for the birds. Like Janice Ostock of Bethlehem, Pennsylvania, you may find that you end up baking just for the birds. When Janice experimented with her new electric bread maker, the first loaves were rejects, so she tossed them outside for the birds. "When I finally gave up on baking, I saw the birds were still coming for the leftovers—except there weren't any. I couldn't let them down, so I still bake—just for them! They aren't fussy at all about how the bread turns out," she says.

A loaf of her dense, chewy bread, chock-full of nuts and raisins, probably costs more than the day-old bread she could buy at a bakery outlet, but Janice says she doesn't mind. She likes baking for an appreciative audience who relishes even the mistakes.

View Vines As Opportunity

With their tangle of stems and often luxuriant leaves, vines are favorite hiding places and home-sites for many songbirds. Learn to look in vines and you'll discover lots of bird nests, says Marie Bedics, whose Pennsylvania farmhouse has a wall covered with Boston ivy (*Parthenocissus tricuspidata*). The ivy shelters neighborhood wrens, sparrows, and robins at night, and its thick growth also provides a home for a catbird that has lived in her yard for well over a decade.

Other vines favored by birds include: Virginia creeper (*Parthenocissus quinquefolia*), English ivy (*Hedera helix*), autumn clematis (*Clematis terniflora*), anemone clematis (*Clematis montant*), and grapevines. All are excellent bird homes and hideouts.

Marie says the best part of the ivy-covered nests is that you never know there are any birds there. "But at night, just before dark, I can hear them twittering as they settle down to sleep," she says. "And I watch the catbirds coming and going with food for their babies."

Keep the Neighbors Happy

Natural-looking gardens make birds and butterflies happy, but they may stir up trouble in a neighborhood of traditionally groomed lawns. Jean Hadley, whose natural landscape covers acres in Solitude, Indiana, suggests a couple of simple tricks to keep neighbors content. "That feeling of the yard being out of control seems to be what bothers neighbors most," she says. "If you're making the transition from grass to plants in your yard, make sure you have nice, neat, wide paths going through it. That gives it a planned look that signals the plantings are intentional and not just noxious weeds left to roam."

Jean says that a fence helps too—not to hide the gardens, but just to give them a civilized feel. A jumble of plants along a split-rail fence looks a lot better to most people than a so-called weed patch, she says. Even though you could have the same plants with either scenario, adding the fence can make a huge difference in how the garden is perceived.

Winter Fruit for Wild Birds

Most trees drop their fruit in fall, says Mike Hradel, owner of Coldstream Farm in Free Soil, Michigan, when there's more than the birds can eat. But in winter, when they really need it, there's little available. Good bird plants for wintertime, he suggests, are dogwoods and crabapples; he also recommends small-fruited crabapples like 'Sargent' and 'Zumi,' which bear perfectly bite-size fruit for avian visitors.

Paint Is for People

"Birds would much rather be in a birdhouse that's made as inconspicuous as it could be," says David H. Drake, president of Coveside Conservation Products in Maine. "Otherwise it's easier for predators to find them." He recommends leaving nesting boxes au naturel, with no paint or decorations, so that they blend in with the landscape as easily as tree bark.

A coat of paint won't deter birds, but David adds, "Paint is for people—the birds don't care!" Sometimes paint can be a good thing, he says. If your spring weather swings from warm to cold, a dark-painted birdhouse will soak up heat and keep it cozy. If you put a birdhouse in full sun, a coat of white paint will keep it cooler inside by reflecting those warming rays.

Best Bets for Nest Building

Indian hemp (*Apocynum cannabinum*) and the very similar-looking dogbane (*A. androsaemifolium*) supply perfect nest-building materials for orioles and vireos, says Jean Hadley of Solitude, Indiana. Colonies of these plants grow at the wood's edge and in the meadow on Jean's property. All winter long, the stems of the plants weather in the rain and snow to become bird magnets by late spring. That's when Baltimore orioles, vireos, and the occasional yellow warbler descend to pull apart the old stems, stripping off thin, soft strings that are as tough as dental flow—just the thing for weaving

Continued ➡

nests. Plant dogbane and Indian hemp where the plants have room to spread naturally into a colony.

Get Wild with "Wild Ones"

If joining together with other nature lovers for seed exchanges, chats with kindred spirits, nature hikes, field trips, excursions, and tours of backyard wildlife gardens sounds like your cup of tea, get in touch with Wild Ones—Natural Landscapers, Ltd., a nonprofit group dedicated to educating and sharing information among "regular people" who love to learn about wildlife.

Members share information about gardening with native plants, attracting birds to their gardens and flower beds, and generally creating wildlife-friendly, ecologically sound backyards. For more information, write to Wild Ones—Natural Landscapers, Ltd., P.O. Box 23576, Milwaukee, WI 23576.

Keep the Peanut Eaters Happy

Peanuts are a big draw for woodpeckers, blue jays, chickadees, titmice, and nuthatches, but the nuts disappear fast when you offer them in an open feeder. The perfect solution is a tube feeder of stainless-steel wire mesh with ¼-inch holes, says Betsy Colwell, president of Droll Yankees. The mesh holes are too small to let birds grab whole peanuts, but plenty big for woodpeckers and others to hammer through and get pieces.

The big draw for the peanut feeder is the woodpeckers, says Betsy. "They love peanuts! They'll bang away, just like they do on trees." Squirrels don't bother the feeder, she says, because they can't chew through the mesh.

If you're the handy type, you can make a homemade peanut feeder by replacing the plastic tube of an existing tube feeder. Here's how:

1. Measure the circumference and height of the tube of the existing feeder. (For example, some tubes measure 11 inches around and 12 inches high.) Buy a piece of stainless-steel, ¼-inch wire mesh to correspond to the measurements you took. If you can't find stainless steel mesh, use hardware cloth.

2. Roll the wire mesh into a tube shape to fit the feeder's top and bottom, then bend the mesh over itself to anchor the edges together.

3. Fasten the feeder top and bottom to the mesh. Usually, the bottom of the feeder will hold tight when inserted into the mesh, and the top is held in place with the wire hooks at the ends of the handle.

4. Insert the bottommost perch of the feeder.

5. Fill with shelled whole peanuts, and hang the feeder in a spot where you can watch the visiting birds.

Faking It

Many gardeners use red flowers to lure hummingbirds to their garden, where they'll stay to sample flowers of other colors, too, but natural-garden lover Jean Hadley of Solitude, Indiana, had trouble fitting fire-engine red into her romantic pastel color scheme. So she turned to subterfuge—a quick trip to the local discount store gave her an armload of red silk flowers that she wired to nearly everything in the garden. "It worked like a charm!" says Jean laughing.

Now she has hummingbirds every summer, returnees who remember her garden of nectar-filled flowers, even though the red silk deception is long gone.

Shape Is What Matters

If you love hummingbirds, plant a garden specifically for them. Jim Becker, co-owner of Goodwin Creek Gardens, says flower shape, not color, is what matters most when planning a hummingbird garden. Tubular flowers, whether they're tiny mint flowers or 8-inch datura blossoms, are what hummingbirds seek. Their long, skinny beaks are exactly right for reaching the nectarines at the base of these flowers. "Red gets their attention, but they really like deep purples and blues, too," he notes.

Hummingbirds will go to just about any flower, Jim says. If it proves to be a good nectar source, they'll return to it over and over. One of Jim's favorite hummingbird flowers is a white-flowered

selection of normally bright red cardinal flower (*Lobelia cardinalis*), which he selected from a batch of seed-grown plants.

Natural Nectar

Hummingbirds are hungry after migratory flights, so treat them to nectar-rich early bloomers, Jim Becker, suggests planting red flowering currant (*Ribes sanguineum*), a graceful shrub or small tree native to the Pacific Northwest that's also at home in Zones 6 through 8. A buffet table in a bush, dangling clusters of red-to-pink fragrant flowers decorate the branches very early in spring.

High-Rise Hummingbirds

Hummingbirds have such an eye for red that they'll go to great lengths—or heights—to investigate, says Elizabeth Castaldi of Washington, D.C. Trying to brighten her small second-story balcony, she added a pot of bright red zonal geraniums (*Pelargonium* spp.) that could take the all-day sun and heat. Within days, she noticed a male ruby-throated hummingbird at the flowers. When migration time came in early fall, she had a constant stream of tiny winged visitors humming with delight at her bright container garden.

Bring on the Hummers

"Hummingbirds return from migration in early spring, when there's not a lot blooming in the garden," says Jim Becker, who co-owns Goodwin Creek Gardens with his wife, Dottie. Luckily, the long-spurred, nectar-filled blooms of native American columbines are just hitting full stride when the zippy little birds return to the scene. Jim and Dottie grow both the eastern and western wild columbine (*Aquilegia canadensis, A. formosa*). Both are great garden plants as well as hummingbird plants. Columbines bloom for weeks, sustaining the birds until other plants come into flower.

Advantages of Agastaches

Their Latin name may be a mouthful, but perennials from the genus *Agastache* are sure-fire hummingbird attractors. Most plants have foliage with a delicious licorice scent, which has given more than one species the nickname licorice plant, or anise hyssop. But it's the whorled spikes of small tubular flowers that are the prime attraction for hummingbirds.

Many gardeners are familiar with anise hyssop (*Agastache foeniculum*), but there are many more to be discovered, says Jim Becker. Native mostly to the American Southwest and Mexico, agastaches include many plants of surprising cold hardiness, usually to Zone 6.

Agastache species and hybrids offer a variety of flower color, including blue-purple, salmon, rosy orange, pink, and pale blue. Hummingbirds love all of them. Jim recommends 'Apricot Sunrise,' whose beautiful orangey apricot flowers light up perennial gardens. 'Firebird' is a vivid orange-salmon-flowered hybrid that creates a full, branching plant.

Richly fragrant rock anise hyssop (*Agastache rupestris*) has gray-green foliage and rich, rosy orange flowers; hardy to Zone 5, it blooms for almost two months straight. Plant in lean, well-drained soil in full sun.

Perch-Free Means Predator-Free

Perches on birdhouses are so common that it doesn't occur to most people that perches allow predators access to baby birds. If you're building new birdhouses, eliminate the predator threat by

---

Continued ➡

┌───┐

Annual Flowers for the Birds

These annuals produce seeds that birds like to eat. All of these flowers thrive in full sun, so choose an open spot for your bird-garden planting.

Sweet alyssum (*Lobularia maritima*)
Pink, purple, or white blooms appear in ¾-inch-wide clusters on 6- to 12-inch-tall mounds of foliage

Grain amaranth (*Amaranthus hypochondriacus*)
Spiked flower heads grow 1 foot tall and are red, green, or marbled red and green; the seed heads are beautiful; plants grow 6 feet tall

China aster (*Callistephus chinensis*)
Blue, rose, or white blooms are 2½ inches wide; plants grow 2 feet tall.

Bachelor's buttons (*Centaurea cyanus*)
Blue, pink, purple, red, or white blooms grow 1 to 2 inches wide on 12- to 30-inch-tall plants

Black-eyed Susan (*Rudbeckia hirta*)
Daisylike yellow blooms have brown centers and grow 2 to 3 inches wide; plants grow 1 to 3 feet tall

Cosmos (*Cosmos bipinnatus* and *C. sulphureus*)
Blooms are 1 to 2 inches wide; *C. bipinnatus* has

pink, white, or crimson ray flowers with a yellow center; plants grow 4 to 6 feet tall; *C. sulphureus* has yellow, red, or orange daisylike blooms on 2- to 3-foot-long stems

Flax (*Linum usitatissimum*)
Blue or white delicate ½-inch-wide blooms grow on 3- to 4-foot-tall stems

Larkspur (*Consolida orientalis*)
Blue, rose, violet, or white blooms are 1½ inches long and grow on long spikes; plants grow 1 to 2 feet tall

Pincushion flower (*Scabiosa atropurpurea*)
Rounded 2-inch-wide blooms come in blue, cream, lavender, maroon, pink, and white; plants grow 2 to 3 feet tall

Corn poppy, Shirley poppy (*Papaver rhoeas*)
Four-petaled 2-inch-wide blooms come in deep purple, red, or white; plants grow 2 to 3 feet tall

Sunflower (*Helianthus annuus*)
Yellow, red, and rust-colored blooms grow 3 to 12 inches wide on plants that are 1 to 12 feet tall (size depends on the variety)

└───┘

attracting seeds. "Because these are annual plants, you can grow them in any region," explains horticulturist Linda Harris of Ferry-Morse Seeds.

Ingredients and Supplies

Metal garden rake

1 seed packet sweet alyssum

1 seed packet grain amaranth

1 seed packet China aster

1 seed packet bachelor's buttons

1 seed packet black-eyed Susan

1 seed packet cosmos

1 seed packet flax

1 seed packet pincushion flower

1 seed packet corn poppy or Shirley poppy

1 seed packet sunflower

Directions

1. Prepare the site by digging or tilling to loosen the soil if needed.

2. Scratch the soil surface about 1 inch deep with a metal garden rake. Then use the back of the rake to smooth the soil.

3. After your area's last spring frost date, mix the seeds together. Each seed packet contains about 100 seeds, which will cover a bed that's about 10 x 20 feet (200 square feet). You may need to combine only a portion of the seed in each packet. You can save the leftover seed or share it with your friends.

4. Broadcast the seed over the bed by hand. You may want to add some sand or potting soil to the seeds first to make it easier to distribute evenly.

5. Press the seed into the soil surface by walking gently on the bed or by dragging a board over the bed.

6. Keep the seeds moist until the seedlings are about 2 inches tall.

Note: Linda points out that most of the plants will reseed, so you don't have to replant every year. But if you want to make sure that a particular flower always appears, scatter more of those seeds over your planting area each spring.

SITE YOUR BIRD GARDEN RIGHT

This planting has a very informal, wildflower-meadow look, according to Linda Harris, so choose a site that's not too close to the house but still close enough to enjoy. To make the planting look less wild and more gardenlike, she suggests growing three different sunflower varieties of different heights. The similar flowers will help tie the planting together for a more coordinated look.

Make a Cagey Fruit and Suet Feeder

Barbara Pleasant

Serving fruit to tempt orioles, mockingbirds, catbirds, house finches, Carolina wrens, thrashers, and other fruit-loving birds is as easy as impaling an orange half on a sturdy nail and waiting to see who flies in for a sweet meal. Unfortunately, the birds may lose out on this treat when squirrels, raccoons, and other varmints discover that they can make off with the fruit. Capable of doing

Setting the Table for Birds

Just like relatives, birds and other wild creatures will beat a path to your garden if they can find a free meal there. Many songbirds love sunflower and other seeds, while woodpeckers and nuthatches prefer a high-fat diet of nuts and suet. Several of the showiest birds prefer fruit. To attract the widest variety of birds, provide special feeders stocked with different foods in different parts of your yard. In addition to the fruit feeder, you can make a "Goldfinch-Getter" tube feeder, turn a fruit box into a tray feeder, or make a stone landing trimmed with fragrant herbs for the area where you offer tempting seeds.

If you're just getting started feeding birds and other wildlife, do a little research to see who's likely to visit, and at what time of year. Check with your neighbors or your local cooperative extension office to get the scoop on the birds and other critters that live in or migrate through your area. Then set the table accordingly, putting out only a little food at first, so there's less wasted if it goes uneaten. When you start to get takers, increase the supply to match the demand. With a little patience, you'll be amazed at the variety of wildlife that shows up looking for breakfast in your yard. Different species may show up at dusk for an early dinner.

double duty as a box for purchased suet cakes, this simple feeder lets birds enjoy halves of oranges or apples while deterring greedy starlings, raccoons, and squirrels.

You Will Need

Tools: Measuring tape, pencil, saw, drill with ¼-inch bit, wire cutters, hammer, screwdriver

One 22-inch-long piece of 1 x 2 furring strip

1 wire clothes hanger

Eight 2-inch nails

1 scrap board or shingle, 8 to 12 inches long and 6 to 8 inches wide

One 6-inch-square piece of wire hardware cloth with ½-inch mesh

One 2-inch-long piece of thin scrap wood or wood craft stick

One 3-inch nail

2 screws

1. Saw the furring strip into two 6-inch pieces and two 5-inch pieces. Lay them on a flat surface to form a square frame. Use the drill to make matching holes through the lower sides of the frame 1 inch from the bottom of the side pieces. Use the wire cutters to cut the straight bottom from the clothes hanger, and check to see that it easily passes through the drilled holes in the sides. Set the hanger wire aside.

2. Use 6 of the 2-inch nails to nail the frame pieces into a square on the scrap board or shingle base.

3. Cut a square of hardware cloth to match the size of the frame. Weave the hanger wire through the bottom of the hardware cloth, and then push the ends through the holes in the sides of the frame. Use wire cutters to bend them back toward the base.

4. Turn the feeder over, and drive a 2-inch nail through the back of the baseboard, so that its tip protrudes through the center of the wooden frame.

5. Loosely nail the 2-inch-long piece of scrap wood or craft stick to the top of the frame to hold the hardware cloth door closed. Drive a 3-inch nail into the base of the frame to serve as a perch.

6. Drill guide holes for the mounting screws, and securely attach the feeder to a sturdy post or dead tree. Stick it with a halved apple, orange, or a cake of suet.

Make an "Oh My Darling" Tray Feeder

Barbara Pleasant

Providing meals for birds and other wildlife doesn't have to be a budget-buster—and your wild guests won't groan "not this again" like your family does when they find leftovers on the table. Foods such as bread or pizza crusts, crushed crackers, leftover pasta, fruit pieces, and crumbled suet work best when offered on a tray feeder's flat feeding surface. In addition, these freebies can help to draw bossy crows, jays, magpies, pigeons, and starlings away from your seed feeders, redx an sorts of seed bill and giving...

Wildlife That Preys on Insect Pests

Beneficial insects and birds aren't the only kinds of beneficial animals. Several other kinds of wildlife are predators of pest insects or problem rodents. Take a few simple steps to attract and assist these helpers.

Bats. The common brown bat can eat 3,000 insects (including lots of mosquitoes) in one night. You can build houses especially for bats to roost in. They're also attracted by ponds.

Lizards and salamanders. These creatures eat vast numbers of insects and do no harm to anyone. They're attracted by cool, damp places like rock piles.

Snakes. Dangerous snakes are rare—there are only four species in the United States—and not likely to visit the garden. The ones you see control rodents, insects, even slugs and snails! Snakes like the shelter of rocks, woodpiles, or brush near the garden.

Toads and frogs. Just one toad can consume well over 10,000 insects (slugs too!) in one year. Make a cool, dark toad shelter out of rocks or inverted clay pots that have "doors" chipped out.

Moles. Even these maligned marauders of spring lawns have a garden benefit. Moles eat huge numbers of grubs, like Japanese beetle grubs. They even cultivate parts of my garden but have moved on to deeper or damper locations by planting time! So before you act to "get rid of" any of nature's living gifts, consider the big picture—how everything relates to everything else. Maybe you'll find you have lots more friends than you knew!

Continued ➔

feeders, so they're the perfect place to serve bird-friendly leftovers. A tray with a wire mesh bottom will let some crumbs sift through, but it also lets water drain away, so foods on the tray don't get soggy (and moldy) if they sit for a couple of days. Even so, keep an eye on treats that you put on your tray feeder. If birds don't gobble them up in a day or two, empty the tray and try offering your feathered friends something else.

Making a tray feeder is easy. Treat yourself to a box of the sweet little oranges known as clementines, and then transform the lightweight wooden box into a feeder. If you don't have a fruit box, use an old picture frame with its back removed as a tray feeder frame.

You Will Need

Tools: Tin snips, staple gun, drill

One 24-inch-square piece of aluminum screening

1 open-topped fruit box

4 small screw eyes

4 yards of nylon cord or lightweight chain

One 12- to 18-inch piece of wire

1 S hook

1. Cut a piece of aluminum screening to match the outside dimensions of your wooden box. Staple the aluminum screening to the bottom of the box to keep feeder foods from falling through the cracks and corner holes.

2. Drill a small pilot hole at each corner of the top (open side) of the box and insert a screw eye in each hole. Fasten a piece of cord to each screw eye. Join the other ends at the top, so the feeder hangs parallel to the ground.

3. Loop the wire over a tree limb, fasten the ends securely, and use the S hook to attach the feeder to the wire.

Pave the Way to Bird-Feeding Ease

Barbara Pleasant

The favorite food of seed-eating birds, sunflower seeds meet with less approval from lawn-lovers trying to tend the turf below the feeder. In places where birds dine and sunflower shells fall, sparse grass and anemic flowers are a common result, because sunflower shells—and constant bird pecking—inhibit the growth of other plants. Paving the area beneath a seed feeder solves the problem and makes feeder maintenance easier, too. Your paved feeding station will serve as a beautiful landscape focal point even when no birds are present.

Installing pavers involves a bit of heavy lifting, but it's an otherwise easy project that produces long-lasting results. Doing the math to figure out how many flagstones or pavers you need is simple multiplication, but you may get confused when estimating how much paver base and sand to buy. These materials are sold in 40- to 60-pound bags, which contain a specified measurement in cubic feet (this information is printed on the label). One cubic foot is 12 inches wide and deep, so a cubic foot of crushed stone will cover 6 square feet when spread 2 inches deep (12 divided by 2 equals 6).

You Will Need

Tools: Stakes and string, shovel, wheelbarrow, tamping tool, carpenter's level, mallet, broom

Flagstones or brick pavers

Crushed stone, sometimes called paver base

Coarse sand, also called builder's sand

A Place for Snakes

Sally Jean Cunningham

When I find rocks in my garden beds, I stack them in piles and leave them there. Rock piles help to welcome and shelter toads and lizards, as well as some other pest eaters that have a bad reputation—snakes! Snakes give many people the creeps. But most snakes are not poisonous. And they aren't slimy or sneaky or interested in you at all. (Where I live in western New York, virtually no snakes are dangerous—certainly *not* the ones we see around our gardens.)

I was lucky to learn as a child that snakes are great to have around. My grandpa Harper taught me how to pick up snakes behind the head and showed me that they are dry and cool to the touch—and very interesting. I've taught my daughter, Alice, about snakes too.

Country homes need snakes to control rodents in outbuildings and basements. Snakes are very valuable around the garden, where they eat insects as well as rodents. Snakes like the shelter of rock piles, brush piles, woodpiles, and sometimes black plastic or boards, so I purposely set up a few such snake-friendly locations around the garden.

Whooo's There?

Birds and squirrels will visit a tray feeder by day, but after dark, your tray feeder may host a different clientele, including some who come to dine on the other diners!

Flying squirrels are seed-eaters like their chipmunk and squirrel cousins, but they're active at night. Just because you don't see them doesn't mean they aren't around. Feeders that seem to empty overnight are a clue that these small squirrels are gliding into your feeding station while you sleep.

Mice are quick to find seeds and other morsels on the ground below bird feeders, and they'll quickly adopt a routine of visiting your feeding station for a nightly buffet. Keep the area around your feeders tidy to avoid attracting mice (and their larger rodent relatives).

Opossums eat a wide range of foods, and these curious-looking marsupials may stop by your feeders after dark for a late-night snack. Splay-footed star-shaped tracks around your feeders may be the first sign you see of opossums in your yard.

Owls don't eat seeds, but these efficient predators may fly in on muffled wings to hunt mice that are feasting on fallen bits of food. Since people rarely get to see these carnivorous cavity-nesters, owls can be a good reason to tolerate mice around your feeders.

Raccoons may become nightly regulars, especially if you have a water source nearby for their well-known "washing" rituals. Intelligent and persistent, raccoons can become unwelcome garden raiders, so locate feeders as far as possible from your cultivated crops.

---

1. Mark off the area you wish to pave. For straight-edged shapes, use stakes and string to mark the space; for irregular or curved shapes, mark the border with flour, flexible garden hose, or rope.

2. Measure the space you've marked, then dust off your math skills and determine its area by multiplying its length by its width. Get enough pavers or flat flagstones to cover the area.

3. Shovel out the soil to a depth of 4 inches. Use the excavated soil to fill raised beds or for other garden projects. To improve drainage, dig the foundation so that it has a very slight slope of about ¼ inch per 2 feet of space, slanted downward to the edges.

4. Fill the excavated area with 2 inches of crushed stone. Tamp it down firmly with a flat tamping tool or with the end of a 4 x 4 landscaping timber.

5. Top the crushed stone with a 1-inch layer of coarse sand. Tamp it down firmly.

6. Starting with the straightest edge, lay your stones or pavers in place, leaving ¼ inch between them. Leave larger crevices near edges where you'd like to grow herbs or other crevice plants. Use the carpenter's level to make sure adjoining stones or pavers are even.

7. Take a moment to look at the layout of your pavers. If you're happy with how things look, use the mallet to tap each paver into its spot. If your pavers appear uneven or crooked, remove them and re-level the crushed stone and sand base.

8. Toss sand onto the paved area and sweep it into the spaces between the pavers. Sprinkle the area lightly with a hose to help settle the sand into the joints, and add more sand if needed to fill in the crevices.

Make a Gourd Birdhouse

Barbara Pleasant

Bulb-shaped hard-shell gourds are fun and easy to grow, and they make wonderful houses for birds. Birds don't mind if their house has a natural finish, or you can scrub the gourd with a copper dish scrubber, allow it to dry, and then paint it to create a birdhouse that's pretty and functional. Do be careful to gauge the size of the entry hole to the type of bird you hope to attract, because birds prefer a hole that's so small that predators can't get in to rob the cradle. Some of the most common birds that like gourd houses—and living near people—include wrens, chickadees, titmice, and sparrows. Tailor the house to suit wrens or chickadees by making the entry hole only 1 to 1 1/8 inch wide. Titmice and sparrows prefer a 1 ½-inch-wide entry hole.

You Will Need

Tools: Disposable dust mask, drill with ⅛-inch bit, keyhole saw, long-handled fork or spoon

1 dry gourd, 8 to 10 inches in diameter

2 feet of sturdy, flexible wire

1. Shake the gourd to loosen the seeds inside it. Put on a dust mask (many people are allergic to gourd dust). Holding the gourd on a steady surface, use the drill to start the entry hole: Drill 3 small holes, ¼ inch apart, just above the widest part of the gourd. Enlarge the hole to its finished size with the keyhole saw.

Continued ➡

2. Turn the gourd upside-down, and make three small holes in the bottom. Should rain blow into the house, it will drain out through these holes.

3. Shake the loose seeds and membranes out through the entry hole. Then use the fork or spoon to scrape out any remaining loose material. If desired, sand the gourd and then paint it with light-colored exterior enamel paint (dark colors will cause the house to overheat on hot days).

4. Drill 2 small holes on either side of the stem, 1½ inches from the top. Run flexible wire through the holes and twist it over the top of the gourd to form a hanger.

5. Choose a spot to hang the house where your new tenants will be in plain view, but far enough from open windows so you won't be bothered by the chirping of hungry chicks.

Building a Small Mammal Shelter
Sally Roth

The antics of rabbits, chipmunks, and other small mammals are a delight to watch. By supplying an abundance of natural foods and a safe place where they can hide from predators, you can easily encourage these interesting creatures to take up year-round residence in your garden.

Create an inviting home for small mammals like chipmunks and ground squirrels with a loose pile of stones. Add sections of PVC pipe in the pile as you build, making sure that the ends of the pipe are left open. Those holes and tunnels are mighty inviting to small mammals.

Life at the bottom of the food chain isn't easy. Hungry hawks, owls, housecats, and other predators are always on the prowl for small mammals. Give these endearing creatures a fighting chance by constructing safe havens here and there in your garden. A loose pile of rocks will give them plenty of crevices for fast getaways.

Create a Hummingbird Haven
Barbara Pleasant

Hummingbirds don't eat seeds, suet, or fruit, but a combination of resting places, red flowers, and nectar feeders makes an inviting haven for jewel-like hummingbirds. A single sugar-water feeder will attract these zippy flyers to your yard, but they're more likely to stick around your landscape if they also find plenty of tubular flowers to supply them with natural nectar. Fortunately, many of the same flowers that attract hummingbirds also attract butterflies, and the two creatures coexist quite peaceably.

Meanwhile, use a feeder stocked with sugar water to lure hummingbirds close enough so you can see them easily by looking out of your windows. Wait until mid-spring or later, because hummingbirds migrate south in the winter. Setting up an appealing hummingbird site is remarkably simple, and once the tiny birds make a habit of visiting, they will return daily until nature calls them to fly to the tropics in fall.

1. Stretch a thin wire between two posts—such as on a porch or beneath an arbor—and hang one or more nectar feeders from it. Decorate the wire with a few red ribbons or red silk flowers to get the hummers' attention and to keep unsuspecting humans from accidentally running into it. Hummingbirds will sometimes perch on the wire between visits to feeders and flowers.

2. Include flowers that bloom red, and others with tubular blossoms, in your garden, or in pots or hanging baskets. Red petunias, impatiens, or geraniums will attract hungry hummers, as will any color of salvia or lantana. Grow beautiful blue morning glories up the support posts next to the feeders. Hummingbirds find the color red irresistible, but you will often see them sipping nectar from lavender hostas or pink geraniums. Hummingbirds don't read plant lists, and once they find a flower they like, they will return to it again and again.

FEEDER FEATURES AND FILLING
Hummingbird feeders are easily found in supermarkets, chain drugstores, hardware stores, and specialty bird centers. They come in a wide range of prices and styles. Choose a feeder that suits your needs, as well as the birds'. It should be easy to clean and refill, and have a translucent nectar reservoir that lets you see when it needs cleaning or refilling. Also look for guards over the feeding ports, which keep wasps and bees from becoming a nuisance. If the feeder you like best is not made of bright red plastic—the color that catches a hummingbird's eye—just fasten a red artificial flower to it the first few times you put it out. Hummingbirds will quickly figure out that it's the feeder, not the flower, that merits their attention.

Perches aren't necessary on a hummingbird feeder, because these tiny dynamos hover while they drink by lapping with their long tongues. But hummers sometimes will use perches between sips, as will woodpeckers and songbirds that discover the sweet treat. If the competition for nectar at your hummingbird feeder becomes too intense, consider removing the perches or switching to a perchless model.

There's no need to spend money on commercial nectar mixes. To make nectar for your feeder, combine 1 part sugar with 4 parts water—for example, ¼ cup of sugar to 1 cup of water—and bring the mixture to a boil. Do not add red food coloring, and don't use honey in place of sugar. Food coloring is unnecessary, and honey poses a hazard to hummingbirds' health. Let the "nectar" cool, then fill your feeder. Store any extra nectar in the refrigerator for up to a week. To keep mold from growing in the feeder, clean out any remaining nectar every 2 or 3 days, wash the reservoir and feeding ports, and refill it with fresh sugar water.

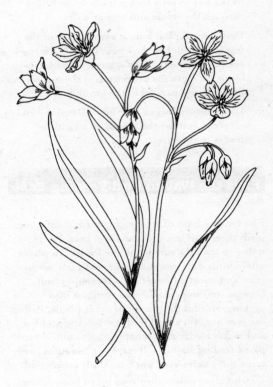

Continued ➡

Garden Design and Landscape

DESIGNING GARDENS

Designing a Companion Garden

Sally Jean Cunningham

It's easy to have fun with a companion garden. After all, you're not just planting vegetables. You're also planting fragrant herbs and colorful flowers, and you're attracting birds, butterflies, and other wild friends to double the fun! As you've learned, the herbs and flowers do serve a serious purpose. But once you've done the work of grouping your crops and choosing plant friends for them, designing your garden layout and watching your garden grow can be a real pleasure.

Simple garden projects can add new zip and excitement to your garden. Try projects that are both fun and practical, like a toad shelter or a homemade trellis for growing gourds or flowering vines. Fix up a colorful and creative scarecrow. Even if it doesn't scare any animal pests, it will make you smile!

Dream Up a Garden Theme

There are so many ways to play with companion gardens. I like to create gardens with exciting color schemes, just as if I were designing a perennial bed or border. You can also give a garden a regional theme or use lots of trellises and supports to make a vegetable jungle. Once you start, you're bound to come across some great new ideas. Here are a few suggestions to get you started.

A chili-sauce garden. My grandma made a terrific sweet/hot chili sauce, and even in a tough gardening year, I always grow the ingredients for the chili, including onions, sweet peppers, chili peppers, and tomatoes. You may have your own family heirloom chili recipe begging for garden-fresh ingredients. If not, do a little experimenting, and create your own!

A cool cabbage combo. I like to end the gardening season in style with some bright, bold color in my garden. For a great mix of red, blue, and purple, plant red cabbages in a 3-2-3 pattern, and substitute dainty blue cupflowers (*Nierembergia* spp.), love-in-a-mist (*Nigella damascena*), and rocket larkspur (*Consolida ambigua*) for some of the heads of cabbage. At each end of the bed, plant purple garden mums. I don't know whether all the flowers in this combination are helpful companions, but they certainly help lift my spirits on a sunny fall day!

Stir-fry flair. Chinese vegetables are mostly cool-weather crops, so you can create a bed just for fan and early winter salads, stir-fry, or Chinese specialties. Some of the Chinese vegetables to try include Chinese cabbage, celery cabbage, daikon radish, Chinese broccoli, mizuna, and Chinese spinach.

Some like it hot! There are some wonderful hot colors in both flowers and vegetables that you can combine to make a sizzling "hot garden." Try planting a bed of tomatoes and peppers with bright red salvias, Mexican sunflowers, and tall, red-orange marigolds. Scatter tall red cosmos throughout. Mix in some red cabbage, red basil, and scarlet runner beans. Then give it all a border of bright red petunias.

A festive fence of beans. Grow a multicolored bean fence using a combination of dry beans, purple beans, and yellow wax beans. Just plant each seed in sequence, spacing them 7 inches apart along a fence or trellis. If you use varieties that have a similar number of days to maturity, you can harvest your own colorful three-bean salad all at once!

Three Fun and Fanciful Designs

I think vegetables have as much right to be in the front yard as any other kind of garden, so one of my designs is for a salad garden to highlight the foundation and front walkway of a suburban home.

Vegetable gardens can be very pretty, especially when we mix in flowers to create companion gardens. And successful vegetable gardeners want to show off what they've grown (especially if the garden says "Look what you can grow organically!"). Plus, the front yard is often the place with the right sun or soil for a vegetable garden.

The garden includes all the vegetables and herbs you need for a terrific salad, and even the flowers in it are edible.

Just one note when you're planting edibles in your front yard. Keep them away from the edges of

Continued ➡

driveways or streets where they can be contaminated by road salts or automobile exhaust.

The second design is a circular garden that I've called the wheel garden because the plan looks like an old-fashioned wagon wheel with paths for spokes. Between the spokes, there are wonderful combinations of vegetables, herbs, and flowers.

My third special garden design is a great choice for gardeners with limited space. I call it the Small TALL Garden because it uses lots of trellises, arbors, and towers to maximize production in small beds.

All of these gardens meet the basic definition of companion gardens: The crops are grouped in families, the garden includes lots of flowers and herbs, and everything's intensively planted in raised beds. I did make some concessions, perhaps adding a few more flowers than I would have in a garden where production was the primary goal. And in some cases, rotating crops is a bit harder. But making these adjustments is worth it to me for the extra excitement these gardens provide.

Choosing Varieties

In most cases, I haven't specified what varieties of crops or flowers to grow, except for a few specific varieties that have special qualities. For example, 'Siam Queen' basil has lovely purple flowers that add excitement, and 'Purple Wave' petunias have a spreading habit that makes them a wonderful groundcover. For the vegetable crops, it's important for you to choose varieties that grow well in your local area and that have flavors you like! Don't be afraid to substitute for crops that you wouldn't eat. For example, I frequently use Swiss chard in my gardens because I really like it. But I know lots of people who'll politely pass it by at the table. If you're in the "no Swiss chard" crowd, just substitute another leafy crop that you enjoy eating.

Here's the layout for my front-yard salad garden. The garden has four beds, each 3 feet wide and 20 feet long (the equivalent of a conventional 15- by 20-foot garden). Here, they're arranged to flank a pathway leading to the front door. You can arrange the beds in any way that suits your front yard. For example, if you have a curving walkway that leads from your driveway to your front door, you can lay out the beds on either side or both sides of the walk.

To make this garden extra-special, I used *only* edible flowers, so anybody can go out to harvest supper. The edible flowers include pansies, violets, petunias, and daylilies. (In this garden, we *do* eat the daisies!)

Planting the Garden

In the plant list on the opposite page, numbers in parentheses indicate how many transplants, bulbs, or sets to plant. Plant other crops from seed; one packet should be plenty.

Plants for a Front-Yard Salad Garden

Vegetables

Beans (pole varieties)	Onions (24 to 36)
Carrots	Peas (tall varieties)
Cherry tomato (1)	Radishes
Cucumber (1)	Romaine lettuce
Kale	Spinach
Leaf lettuce	Swiss chard
Mesclun (mixed salad greens)	Tomatoes (4)
	Zucchini (1)
New Zealand spinach	

Herbs and Edible Flowers

Basil (3)	Johnny-jump-ups (12)
'Siam Queen' basil (3)	Garden mums (2)
Bee balm (10)	Nasturtiums
Borage (2)	Pansies (20)
Calendulas (10)	Parsley (2)
Chives (2)	'Purple Wave' petunias (2)
Daylilies (2)	Rose, 'The Fairy' or other shrub type (2)
Dill	
Gladioli (6 to 12 bulbs)	Salad burnet (1)
Hollyhocks (5)	Sweet William (8)
	Violets (9)

Any round garden is a perfect place to practice crop rotation. In this case, I've planted a circular garden 20 feet in diameter with a 4-foot-wide "hub" or center circle. The garden is divided into six wedge-shaped beds with 18-inch-wide paths in between. To reduce or enlarge the garden, just make the beds shorter or longer.

Managing the garden. The best management strategy for this garden will be to work the soil well before you first shape the beds and not to till after that. Keep the soil covered with mulch or cover crops, and create permanent wood-chip paths between the beds. You can till the garden by tilling in a spiral from the center out, but only if you use a temporary path covering like grass clippings or straw. Even in a fanciful garden like this, I suggest planting a cover crop like buckwheat every few years to rebuild the soil.

The garden hub. Your round garden doesn't have to have a plain circle of grass or mulch at its hub. Use the space for a fun garden project. I can picture a comfortable lawn chair next to a birdbath or a tall ornamental grass like maiden grass (*Miscanthus sinensis*). You could even plant a small apple tree for shade.

Other possible "centerpieces" include a water garden in a tub or a large pot of Jerusalem artichokes surrounded by mint. (Let the plants tussle for space while you breathe in the mint scent and harvest some crunchy tubers.) Just be sure to leave enough space around the center planting for weeding, watering, and harvesting.

Planting the garden. In the plant list below, numbers in parentheses indicate how many transplants or sets to plant. Plant other crops from seed; one packet should be plenty.

Plants for a Wheel Garden

Vegetables

Beans (bush variety and pole variety)	Potatoes (16)
Broccoli (9)	Radishes
Cucumber (2)	Spinach
Kale	Summer Squash (1)
Lettuce (leaf variety)	Swiss chard
Peas (tall variety)	Tomatoes (4)
Peppers (12)	Cherry tomato (1)
	Zucchini (1)

Herbs

Basil (12)	Dill	'Siam Queen' basil (8)

Flowers

Buckwheat	Gazanias (2)
Calendulas (10)	Ornamental kale (7)
Cleome (3)	Nasturtiums (5)
Cosmos (3)	Sweet alyssum (12)
Yellow cosmos (5)	Zinnias (9)

If you read gardening magazines, you've probably noticed that it's often city gardeners who have the most creative small gardens in their tiny yards or on their balconies and rooftops. I lived in New York City many years ago, and I remember how small city lots can be. So I designed a small-space companion garden to grow maximum crops in a minimal space. The design includes lots of trellises and arbors (that's why I call it the Small TALL

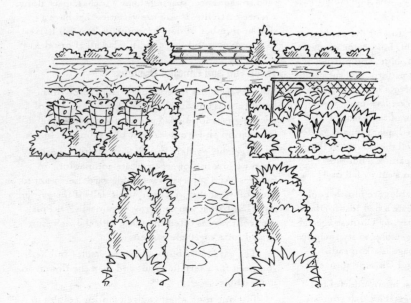

A front-yard salad garden. If you have a sunny lawn in your front yard, liven it up with raised beds full of salad fixings, including edible flowers.

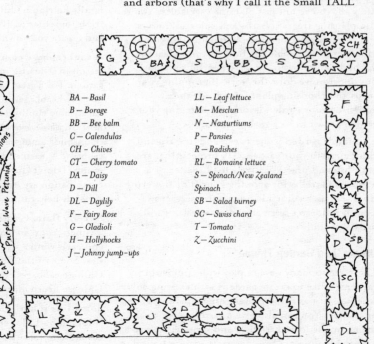

BA — Basil
B — Borage
BB — Bee balm
C — Calendulas
CH — Chives
CT — Cherry tomato
DA — Daisy
D — Dill
DL — Daylily
F — Fairy Rose
G — Gladioli
H — Hollyhocks
J — Johnny jump-ups

LL — Leaf lettuce
M — Mesclun
N — Nasturtiums
P — Pansies
R — Radishes
RL — Romaine lettuce
S — Spinach/New Zealand Spinach
SB — Salad burney
SC — Swiss chard
T — Tomato
Z — Zucchini

Continued ➡

Garden). It's great for anyone who wants lots of production in a small space, whether in the city, suburbs, or country.

There are six beds, each 3½ by 7 feet. Arching arbors connect pairs of beds across a center path. The center path is 4 feet wide (but you can adjust the width to suit whatever arbors you build or buy).

Plant supports. You can use many kinds of cages, trellises, or fences to grow pole beans, tomatoes, and vine crops like cucumbers and winter squash. In this design, the vine crops grow over a "tent" made of heavy wire mesh that is nailed over a hinged frame.

You'll also notice a strawberry tower in one bed. I think the price of the tower is worth it for the luxury of harvesting fresh strawberries from a small garden!

Planting the garden. In the plant list below, numbers in parentheses indicate how many transplants, crowns, or sets to plant. Plant other crops from seed; one packet should be plenty.

PLANTS FOR A SMALL TALL GARDEN

Vegetables

Asparagus (5)	Onions (24 to 36)
Beans (pole varieties)	Peas (tall varieties)
Carrots	Radishes
Cucumbers (3)	Spinach
Daikon radishes	Summer squash (1)
Gourds (4)	Strawberries (16 to 20)
Kale	Swiss chard
Lettuces (mixed varieties)	Tomatoes (3)
Melons (3)	Zucchini (1)
New Zealand spinach	

Herbs

Basil (7)	Fennel (3)
Chives (2)	Parsley (2)
Coriander (3)	Italian parsley (6)
Dill (3)	

Flowers

Calliopsis (6)	Mexican sunflowers (5)
Love-lies-bleeding (3)	Sunflowers
Marigolds (5 to 9)	Swan River daisies (2)

Ornamental Climbers

Climbing rose
Silver lace vine (*Polygonus aubertii*)

TWO SPECIAL CLIMBERS

Two special flowering ornamentals, a climbing rose and silver lace vine, are beautiful and easy to grow.

Climbing roses. When I look for a climbing rose, I want one that's disease tolerant, pest-free, and hardy to the colder side of Zone 5 (preferably Zone 4). Not too many roses fill the bill. I've selected 'Henry Kelsey' as one of those few, reported by many rosarians as the best climbing rose for northern areas. It produces vigorous shoots laden with blooms that have deep red petals and contrasting gold stamens. 'Henry Kelsey' blooms from summer through the first frosts.

Other candidates for this situation are 'William Baffin' (deep pink, hardy to Zone 3), 'Leverkusen' (medium yellow, hardy to Zone 4 or 5), and 'John Cabot' (medium red, hardy to Zone 3).

Silver lace vine. If you plant silver lace vine, you may end up with a vine 25 to 30 feet long by the end of the summer. In areas with cold winters, silver lace vine may die back in winter and "only" grow 15 feet the following year. This vigorous vine likes full sun or partial shade and prefers dry, well-drained soil.

If silver lace vine sounds too aggressive for your taste, there are other easy climbers to try. Dutchman's pipe (*Aristolochia macrophylla*) can grow to 15 to 20 feet but is easy to control by cutting back each winter. It sports huge heart-shaped leaves and delicate, 3-inch, tubular, yellow flowers. Ever-blooming or climbing honeysuckle (*Lonicera sempervirens*) is fragrant and long-flowering and likes rich, well-drained soil and full sun or partial shade.

Creating Your Own Designs

I hope my fun designs and ideas trigger your creativity. Just remember, you don't have to make huge changes in your gardens all at once. You can start with something as simple as planting one bed in a new location or in a new shape. Try an oval or triangular bed. Or create a small companion-garden bed as a highlight in your front lawn. Why not, when you're mixing so many colorful flowers and herbs among the vegetables!

Gardening and Landscaping Design

Fern Marshall Bradley

Becoming Your Own Designer

Is your yard exactly the way you'd like it to be? Few of us can answer that question with an unqualified "Yes!" Perhaps you live in a new development where the yards are 95 percent lawn. Or, if you live in an established neighborhood with plenty of gardens and shade trees, you probably have some landscape problems—especially in those shady spots.

If you'd like to improve your yard's appearance, you may want to try designing your own landscape plan. You may feel intimidated by the thought of creating your own design. It seems like a huge undertaking that requires special skills and training. But the truth is, you can easily improve your yard using some basic ideas and techniques that are also used to professional designers. Choose a project you can feel confident trying. You can give your whole yard a face-lift, redesign the backyard only, or just redo the area around your patio.

Be creative. Whatever the scale of your project, you'll find that landscaping especially with perennial flowers, is a great chance to be creative and have fun. Perennials can express your personality—your likes, dislikes, and style. For example, if you're a collector at heart, you'll aim to grow as many different plants as you can, not worrying about the fine points of design. Or, you may find that perennials bring out the artist in you. You'll thrive on plotting borders and rearranging plants to present an exquisitely planned garden picture every season of the year.

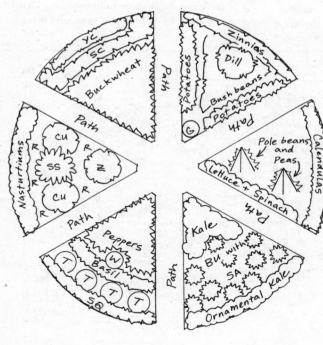

BU — Broccoli underplanted	R — Radish	T — Tomato
C — Cleome	SA — Sweet Alyssum	W — White Cosmos
CT — Cherry tomato	SC — Swiss chard	YC — Yellow cosmos
CU — Cucumbers	SQ — 'Siam Queen' basil	Z — Zucchini
G — Gazania	SS — Summer Squash	

A — Asparagus
BA — Basil
C — Chives
CA — Carrots
CO — Coriander
CP — Calliopsis
CU — Cucumbers
D — Dill
DR — Daikon radish
F — Fennel
GO — Gourds
IP — Italian parsley
K — Kale
LE — Lettuce
LLB — Love-lies bleeding
M — Marigold
ML — Mixed Lettuce
MS — Mexican Sunflowers
NS — New Zealand Spinach
O — Onions
P — Parsley
R — Radish
S — Swan River daisy
SC — Swiss chard
SF — Sunflowers
SP — Spinach
SS — Summer squash
ST — Strawberry Tower
SW — Strawflowers
T — Tomatoes
Z — Zucchini

Continued →

As with any creative process, there's more than one way to tackle designing a landscape project. If you're a natural organizer, you'll enjoy mapping your project and developing plant lists. If you're a spur-of-the-moment sort, you may never get the details on paper. But whatever your style, take some time to read or browse through the process of developing a landscape plan presented here. You're sure to find tips and examples that will help you shape your ideas. Then take a walk and look at gardens. You'll find ideas for garden styles as well as plants that are well-adapted to your local climate. Take snapshots of appealing plantings—they'll be reminders when you're drawing up designs.

Trust yourself. As you develop ideas, remember that there are no wrong answers when it comes to landscaping with perennials, just different ones. Experiment! Grow plants that appeal to you. Don't worry too much about following rules. Talk to other gardeners and look at their gardens. Try to learn from their successes and failures. But above all, have fun.

Using Design Terms

A perennial garden isn't just one kind of garden. That's one of the things that makes them so fun and exciting to plant. But the terms used to describe the different categories of perennial gardens can be confusing. Understanding the terms is useful in developing landscape ideas, though, so it's worth your while to sort them out.

Mass plantings. Mass plantings are group plantings of a single kind of plant. Easy-care, low-maintenance plants are the best choice for mass plantings. For a low-maintenance garden on a sunny, dry site, masses of 'Autumn Joy' sedum, black-eyed Susans (*Rudbeckia* spp.), daylilies, or ornamental grasses would be spectacular.

Mixed plantings. Mixed plantings are a variety of plants growing together in one garden. They combine herbaceous perennials with trees, shrubs, vines, annuals, and other plants. They're a perfect choice for a site that needs year-round interest—they don't leave a bare expanse of ground in winter.

Perennial beds. A garden along a patio or foundation or at the edge of the lawn is usually called a bed. Island beds are plantings—perennials alone, or a mixed planting—surrounded by a sea of lawn.

Beds are designed to be seen from more than one side. Because beds are for viewing close up, plant them with perennials that have long flowering periods and attractive foliage.

Perennial borders. Borders are longer than beds and generally are planted along a fence or at the boundary of a yard. Borders can also edge one or both sides of a walk or driveway. They're usually designed to be seen from one side only. A garage, fence, or hedge behind a border provides an excellent backdrop. Masses of asters, 'Autumn Joy' sedum, chrysanthemums, daylilies, peonies, Siberian iris (Iris sibirica), and ornamental grasses all make fine plants for a sunny border.

The Possibilities of Perennials

Perennials make any yard a special place to be. Whether they're arranged in practical, low-maintenance plantings or jumbled together in cheerful confusion, perennials add color, fragrance, texture, and movement to the landscape. As shown in the sample landscape on this page, perennials are multipurpose plants that can reduce maintenance, create mystery, welcome visitors, attract wildlife, and much more. Keep the possibilities of perennials in mind as you launch your own plan for redesigning some or all of your property.

Sizing Up the Views

Imagine living in the middle of a garden. Flowers and foliage surround you. Patterns of sunlight and shadow play upon the ground, and pleasant fragrances waft by on the breezes. A flower-lined path leads off in one direction, beckoning you to follow it into a shady clump of trees. A glance in another direction reveals a bench surrounded by herbs and sun-loving perennials. Why not put your house in the middle of that garden?

All too often, we think of gardens as out in the yard somewhere—completely separate from the house. But the most satisfying home landscapes surround the house with the garden.

Think for a minute. How often do you look out your kitchen window? If it's 10 times a day, that's 3,600 times each year. What could be nicer than to see beautiful flowers outside every window? That's what putting your house in a garden means.

This isn't as difficult to accomplish as it might seem. Fortunately, you don't have to plant flowers

on every square inch of your yard. You will need to spend some time thinking about the placement of your perennial plantings in relation to your house.

It's all too easy to make spur-of-the-moment choices and end up with flowerbeds scattered randomly around your yard. But for gardens that give maximum pleasure, begin by discovering what parts of your yard are visible when you're inside, looking outside. Once you know that, you can plant perennials to fill the spaces framed by your windows and create views that will put a smile on your face every time you see them.

START INDOORS

Gather up a pencil and a sketchbook or notebook, and spend a few minutes looking out each window of your home. Linger longer in front of windows that are most important to you—the kitchen or living room windows, perhaps.

Draw an outline of each room and indicate where the windows are. Make notes or pictures of what you see—flowerbeds, trees, the patio, the garbage cans, the neighbor's pool, a park across the street, mountains in the distance.

Plan for "Face" Value

To give your house an appealing public face, take a look at it from the street, too. An effective design will add a neat, welcoming look to a house. It creates attractive views for your neighbors, and will delight you every time you return home. Here's an added bonus: Studies show that when you sell your home, you'll realize a return on investment of 100 to 200 percent on money spent on landscaping.

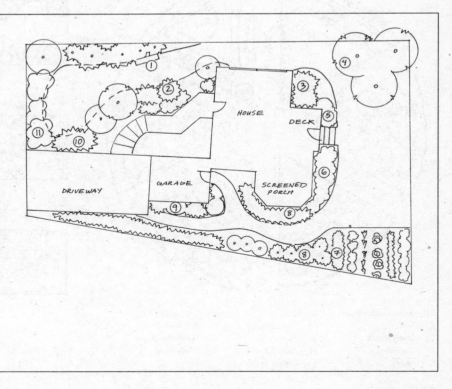

Next, write down your ideas for improving the view, or any other ideas that pop into your head. Would a cluster of shrubs make the patio seem cozier and more appealing? How about adding flowerbeds along a walkway? What about planting herbs and flowers under the window in the breakfast nook?

If trees and shrubs have obliterated the view from a window, try to look past them and think

---

1. *Create an outdoor retreat. A garden bench surrounded by perennials is a wonderful spot to relax, relieve stress, and enjoy the beauty of nature.*

2. *Add eye appeal. One of the best reasons to plant perennials is simply that they're beautiful. They'll add appeal to your yard whether they're planted in the lawn, around a patio, along a walkway, at the edge of your yard, or in front of a fence.*

3. *Direct traffic. Sweeps of perennials planted along walkways help guide visitors. And large clumps of perennials, ornamental grasses, and shrub roses will discourage people from taking shortcuts you'd rather they not try.*

4. *Eliminate maintenance monsters. Replace scraggly grass and eliminate tedious trimming under trees by planting hostas and other shade-loving perennials.*

5. *Furbish your foundation. Low-growing perennials and evergreen groundcovers make great easy-care foundation plantings. Best of all, they don't need all the trimming typical foundation shrubs do.*

6. *Bring the outdoors in. Surround a deck or patio with a flower garden you can see from the inside as well. Or plant a colorful and fragrant bed you can enjoy every day from your kitchen window.*

7. *Hide the uglies. Ornamental grasses and tall perennials, like 8-foot tartarian asters (Aster tataricus), can screen the view of a vegetable garden that's past prime or hide the neighbor's garbage cans. Combine them with shrubs for year-round screening.*

8. *Frame a fabulous view. Plant perennial gardens you can see from inside your house, especially from dining and living room windows.*

9. *Dress up ho-hum features. Surround an otherwise plain garage or edge dull-looking steps with cheerful perennials to dress up your landscape in one easy step.*

10. *Transform trouble spots. There are perennials that will grow in nearly any kind of soil and in conditions from full sun to full shade. Sedums and many herbs will thrive in hot, dry sites, like the area along this paved driveway. Moisture-loving perennials like hostas, astilbes, and ferns will transform a wet site from an ugly quagmire into a garden.s*

11. *Greet them with flowers. Why grow lawn in the front yard when flowers will dress up your house and welcome visitors, too? For a bed that's attractive year-round, mix in plants with long bloom seasons and foliage that evergreen or remains attractive after plants finish blooming.*

Continued ➡

what you might see. If the window overlooks the neighbor's house or a busy street, you may want to leave things as they are. But if a shrub or tree branch blocks an otherwise beautiful view of your garden, consider doing some selective pruning to improve the view.

CHECK THE BIG PICTURE

After you've checked all your window views, go outside and look from your garden back to your house. Walk around the edges of your yard and follow paths you normally travel. Then, get off the beaten track so you have a fresh view of your house and the surrounding yard.

Again, jot down your ideas as you walk. Look at the "fit" between the house and the landscape. Is it a rambling, comfortable-looking house that seems surrounded by stiff, uncomfortable-looking plantings? Does the house look "plopped down" on the lot—a huge structure surrounded by scattered gardens that seem too small?

Don't worry about solving these problems now. We'll get to that in the coming chapters. For now, just record your impressions so you can refer to them later.

Evaluating Your Yard

What details of your yard can you picture in your mind's eye? Does it have walkways, raised beds, steps, or terraced slopes? How big are they and what do they look like? What are the problem spots that need improvement? These details are the foundation of your landscape. As you create your new landscape, you'll use perennials to improve these features and also to ass new features.

If you're someone who thinks on paper, it's best to make a written site assessment of your yard's features. (Visual thinkers may do this more informally, with just a few jotted notes.) Taking snapshots is also a great way to record the features of your yard.

Take a tour of your front, back, and side yards. As you go, sketch your yard and make notes about what you have to work with. Your goal is to collect as much information as you can, and also to begin cooking up landscape ideas that might appeal to you. Use the list below to help you decide what to record.

Your house. Describe the exterior of your house from all angles. Include distinctive details, the style and mood of the architecture, and the materials the house is made of.

Solid features. These include walks, walls, fences, terraces, lampposts, decks, and outbuildings (such as sheds). Note the materials they're made of and the style or mood they suggest. Also make notes about whether their style seems compatible with your house.

Plants and gardens. Note the locations of individual large trees and shrubs, shrub borders, wooded areas, or foundation plantings. Also include the outlines of flower and vegetable gardens.

Utilities. Your design will need to accommodate underground cables, septic fields, and other utilities, so don't forget to record their approximate locations.

Water. Mark streams and ponds if you have them, as well as water spigots, rain barrels, or other water sources.

Traffic patterns. Formal walkways aren't the only traffic routes in your yard. Record unofficial paths

as well—your route to the garage or compost pile, and the cut-through to the neighbor's yard. Make a note if paths need to accommodate a garden cart or wheelbarrow, and record areas where cars are occasionally parked or driven.

Shade and sun. Observe your yard at several times of day to see which parts are shady or sunny, and which receive sun or shade for only part of the day.

Problem spots. Challenging sites like slopes, wet spots, rock outcrops, and areas with compacted soil will figure prominently in your design, so mark them down.

BUT DO YOU LIKE IT?

It's all too easy to get caught up in visual details—like walkways and lampposts—at this stage. After you've dealt with what you see, try to write down your feelings about your yard. What areas appeal to you? What are the eyesores you'd like to hide or redo?

You'll probably end up with a jumble of sketches and notes. Later on you'll sort them and figure out what you really have time and room to do. For now, dream happily, get to know your yard, and reach for as many ideas as you can imagine.

What's Your Style?

Understanding your personal style—whether you are quiet and contemplative or exuberant and colorful, for example—is an enormously powerful design tool. It will help you figure out what you want and need in your garden, as well as what kinds of garden features *aren't* suited to your personality.

Think about the way you like to do everyday tasks such as setting the table or keeping house. The way you accomplish them can say a great deal about the kind of garden you'd enjoy most. For example, when you set a table, do you prefer the cheerful confusion of mismatched tableware, or the quiet simplicity of matched pieces? Your answer says something about whether you would feel more comfortable in a riotous cottage garden where flowers tumble over one another, or in an elegant formal garden with orderly beds of flowers.

Is your house comfortably "lived-in," or is it neat and orderly, with everything in its place? The answer to this question will not only help you discover the right garden style for you, it may help you avoid maintenance nightmares. For example, if you prefer the everything-in-its-place approach, a garden with bold, clean lines and wide, easy-to-maintain paths is probably a good choice. You'll also probably be less able to tolerate the sight of faded flowers, flopping stems, and scruffy foliage than someone who loves the lived-in look. To keep maintenance manageable, choose plants that need minimal deadheading, stand tall without staking, and remain attractive through the season.

FORMAL OR INFORMAL?

If you like well-organized flowerbeds in regular patterns, you prefer formal gardens. If fluid, free-form beds are more your style, informal gardens will appeal to you. Nearly all gardens are either formal or informal in style, although some use elements of both styles. Here are some characteristics that distinguish the two.

Formal style. Gardens with a formal style look peaceful and balanced. They feature rectangular, oval, or round beds; sheared, geometrically shaped hedges and evergreens; and stone, brick, concrete, or gravel walkways. Materials, shapes, or plantings—such as boxwood hedges—are repeated throughout the garden. You'll often see statues, sundials, and simple water features in formal gardens.

Informal style. Informal gardens are more dynamic and exciting to look at than formal ones. Natural, organic-looking shapes predominate. Instead of brick walkways, you'll see mulched paths and rustic features like split-rail fences. And instead of matching beds of perennials, an informal garden might feature two free-flowing beds with unmatched mixtures of flowering shrubs and perennials.

SPECIAL STYLES

The existing conditions in your yard will also influence the style of your gardens. Your yard may have a grove of mature trees that cries out to be underplanted with an informal garden of shade-loving hostas, wildflowers, and azaleas. Perhaps your yard already has some formal rectangular beds and clipped hedges. You may decide to add your personal touch by planting some of your favorite perennials in the existing gardens. Incorporating existing "hardscape," like brick pathways, is usually a good idea, too.

The style of your house can and should affect the landscape you plan. You'll be most satisfied if they harmonize with each other. For example, if you have a single-story ranch house, a large, free-spirited cottage garden filled with tall perennials could overwhelm the front yard. Or, if you have a home with period architecture—Colonial or Victorian, for example—you may want a garden that features plants from that era.

Regional style also can determine the kind of gardens you plant. Mediterranean-style gardens are classic California choices; an informal planting of prairie plants might be a good Midwestern choice.

Here are some of the most popular special styles for American gardens.

Colonial style. This style can be quite formal, with boxwood hedges or knot gardens of clipped lavender cotton (*Santolina chamaecyparissus*). But Colonial gardens can also be informal mixed beds filled with herbs, like lavender and thyme, and old-fashioned flowers, like cranes bills (*Geranium* spp.), peonies, pinks (*Dianthus* spp.), and violets.

Country style. Rustic and relaxed looking, country-style gardens are generally informal, although they may have formal features like square beds or weathered brick terraces. The plants are a joyful jumble: herbs, salad greens, and old-fashioned perennials like daisies, hollyhocks, irises, and peonies.

Cottage style. Plants take center stage in a cottage garden. These informal, even wild-looking gardens feature old-fashioned perennials, like primroses (*Primula* spp.) and pinks (*Dianthus* spp.); fragrant roses and other flowering shrubs; herbs; and reseeding annuals like sweet alyssum. Narrow paths allow plants to be enjoyed up close.

Mediterranean style. Sunbaked terraces, fragrant herbs, and formal, rectangular pools are classic features of Mediterranean gardens. Shady sitting areas under trees, awnings, or umbrellas provide relief from the sun. Paved areas—and the containers that decorate them—often feature terracotta and various ceramics.

Modern style. Formal or informal in style, modern gardens feature bold, simple shapes and strong contrasts. Mass plantings create striking groups with different colors and textures, using plants such as ornamental grasses, yuccas, showy stonecrop (*Sedum spectabile*), and large-leaved hostas.

Continued ➡

Natural landscapes. These informal gardens are inspired by nature's gardens. They feature plants that are native to the region—or at least look as if they are. Natural materials (native stone walls, for example) and areas designed to attract butterflies and other wildlife are also characteristic of natural landscapes.

Putting Your Ideas Together

You've probably discovered by now that you've gathered an exciting array of ideas for your landscape. You have views to improve, features to highlight and others to screen from sight, garden styles to try, and an impressive list of "must grow" perennials.

There are any number of ways to sort through your ideas. If you have a computer, you can type them all in and organize them with the stroke of a key—or move them around with a mouse, for that matter. If you're a list maker, sheets of lined paper and a pencil may suffice. An easy, low-tech way to organize your ideas is to write them out on 3 x 5 cards.

SORT YOUR IDEAS

Gather all your notes, sketches, and snapshots, and spread them out on a table. (An out-of-the-way spot where you can leave them for several days is ideal.) You'll also need a pack of 3 x 5 index cards and/or some lined paper, as well as a couple of sharp pencils. Depending on how fancy you want to get, colored pens, pencils, or markers may come in handy, too.

To turn the 3 x 5 cards into a handy system for sorting out all the ideas you've gathered, write each of your major ideas onto a card. Start with the ideas you came up with when checking views out windows and around your yard. If that's an overwhelming number of ideas, just make cards for the most important ones. For example, you may have imagined a mixed bed of perennials and flowering shrubs around the terrace in front of the living room window.

Next, make cards for each of the major features of your yard. You'll want ones on both good and bad features—major trees and shrubs, existing plantings, hardscape features like concrete walkways and walls, utility areas, and problem sites like slopes or wet spots.

Finally, look over your notes about the garden styles that appeal to you. Make a card for each type of individual garden and planting you'd like to have. For example, you may want an herb garden, a country garden, and a planting that attracts butterflies.

Now you have a neat stack of cards. Look through them and think about what you've missed. Ask yourself—and other family members—what you want and need your landscape to do. Nongardening family members will have definite opinions, too: You may need an area for playing ball, working on a car, or placing a swing set. Or you may want a spot for growing divisions of your great-aunt's peonies or a frog pond—make cards for them, too. (You also may want to use colored markers to color-code the different kinds of cards or to rank the importance of the ideas.)

PLAY THE GARDEN GAME

It's time to transform your ideas into garden projects. Have you already started to see links between your ideas? For example, would raised beds or terraces on the sunny slope turn it from a problem into the perfect spot for the herb garden you've always wanted? If so, put those cards together in a pile. Could you position the herb garden so it provides a pleasing view from the kitchen window? If so, add that card to the pile, and so forth.

As you sort your cards, look for ways to combine different ideas into a single garden or planting. For example, many of us would love to have a perennial border, an herb garden, a rose garden, room for a peony collection, and a bird garden. But most of us don't have enough space or time to devote to so many different gardens. Try combining all those ideas: A perennial border easily could include herbs, low-maintenance shrub roses, the peony collection, and flowers that attract hummingbirds. Rosehips and seed from perennials and flowering shrubs would provide food for seed-eating birds; a birdbath or small rock-edged pool would provide water.

You'll have cards that don't fit easily into any of your piles. Some you'll have to discard. With others, you may just have to look for the best fit. If you want a private outdoor retreat but don't quite know where to put it, you may want to write "Outdoor retreat?" on several cards and put it into several of your piles to serve as a reminder that you want to include that feature.

When you finish, each pile represents a project to tackle. Keep the cards! When you get ready to design your bed or border, your pile of idea cards will help you decide what kinds of plants to include. Cards on views and problem spots in the same pile will remind you of important issues, such as the need to make your border visible from the living room and the path to the neighbor's yard that must be maintained.

Mapping and Planning

Fern Marshall Bradley

Make a Working Map

A working map of your yard will help you get from the idea stage of landscaping to the *doing* stage. You'll use your working map as the base sketch for drawing landscape plans, calculating how much space you have, determining how many plants you'll need to buy, and much more. Your map doesn't have to be an artistic accomplishment. Think of it as a picture of what you're starting with.

The first thing you need to do is gather materials: one standard and two colored pencils, a ruler, a clipboard, scrap paper, some large sheets of graph paper and tracing paper, and a compass.

If you have a survey map of your property, dig it out, too. You can draw your working map on a photocopy of the survey map, or just refer to it to draw the outline of your property. If you don't have a survey map, you can locate your property corners as you make your map.

You'll also need something to measure with, such as a 100-foot measuring tape, along with a helper to hold one end. Or you can make a homemade measuring device fashioned from stakes, string, and tape. First, tie one end of a long (200 to 250 feet) piece of string to a stake. Then measure and mark 10- or 20-foot intervals along the string. Wrap the marked string around the stake and tie the free end to a second stake.

To use the measurer, stake it at the point you're measuring from, then stretch it to the feature you want to locate. Count up the marks along the string, multiply by your interval (10 or 20 feet), and that's the distance.

Next, make a list of features in your yard to include on your map. Include the property corners (unless you're using a survey), existing plantings, and all other features.

Step-by-Step Mapping

There's a simple mathematical technique that will help you draw an accurate map. It's called triangulation. But before you start drawing, you must measure the distances to all the features on your list from a set of reference points. Here's what to do:

1. Sketch your property on a piece of scrap paper. Use this to record measurements.

2. Pick two reference points to measure from, such as the two corners on one side of your house. Measure the distance between the two reference points and write it on your sketch.

3. Circle each reference point with a different color pencil—say red and blue. You'll record all the measurements made starting from the red reference point in red and from the blue reference point in blue (this will help you keep things straight later on when you're drawing your working map).

4. Measure the distance from one of your reference points to a feature on your property that you want to map, such as a tree or the corner of a perennial border. (If you want to map the boundaries of your yard, the first measurements you should take are the distances from your reference points to the corners of your property.)

5. Measure the distance from the other reference point to the same feature. (Be sure you're using the right color pencil to record the distances!) Record these measurements either on your features list or on your map, whichever is more helpful to you as you work.

6. Repeat steps 4 and 5 for all other important features in your yard.

7. Go inside and start drawing your map on graph paper. Choose your scale, and pencil in your reference points.

8. Using triangulation, mark the location of each feature you measured onto your map.

If your yard has lots of features to record, you may want to alternate measuring and mapping, plotting just three or four features at a time. Or if you're good at keeping notes and numbers organized, you may be able to do all your measuring in one outdoor session. Either way, work carefully because accuracy is the most important feature of a working map.

If you don't have a helper when you're measuring, try this variation on the technique. Pound in a stake at one reference point and attach your measuring string or tape to it. Then measure the distance between that reference point and several features, moving the free end of the tape or string from feature to feature. Then switch and measure from the other reference point to the same features.

You may need to pick new reference points when you switch from measuring your front yard to your backyard, or to map features that are unreachable from your first set of reference points.

You'll bring your personal style to the map you make. The detail-oriented among us probably will enjoy drawing an accurate scale map; others may find it tedious and end up with a looser rendition.

Whatever you think of the process, consider it a one-time investment in your landscape design. Once you've drawn it, you can lay sheets of tracing paper over the map to sketch endless design variations. Or, you can make a set of photocopies of the original map and sketch directly on them. Either way, you can draw to your heart's content and never have to redraw your working map.

Continued ➡

Read on for more features that you'll want on your working map before you begin designing.

Get Personal with Problem Sites

You know where they are—those nasty sites that bog down your mower, turn into raging rivers during rainstorms, or sprout lush crops of weeds no matter what you do. An important part of planning your landscape is finding solutions for those problem sites. To design a plan that does away with problem sites forever, you need to get to know them "up close and personal." As you find the problem sites in your yard, mark them on a copy of your working map for reference.

RAMBLE IN THE RAIN

There's no better way to figure out what to do about surface water drainage than to get an umbrella, put on a pair of galoshes, and go outside during a rainstorm. You'll see firsthand where water cuts runoff paths across your property, as well as where it puddles up. Don't plan to simply direct this water off your property and into the storm sewer as quickly as possible. Instead, look for ways to slow or redirect its flow and help it soak into the soil.

Solving runoff problems. You may be able to redirect water that flows across your yard or puddles next to your foundation by bringing in soil to build up a berm. Treat the berm like a raised bed and plant it with shrubs, ornamental grasses, and perennials.

Another option is to plant the site with perennials like daylilies that will tolerate the runoff. Or, you can double-dig the soil and/or add terraces to slow the flow of water. Double-dug soil will hold a considerable amount of water, especially if you cover it with a heavy layer of mulch.

Solving puddling problems. Sites where water tends to puddle are perfect for moisture-loving perennials like hostas, ferns, and Japanese iris (*Iris ensata*). Another option is to dig a water garden—but before you do, check whether the site collects water from neighboring yards as well as your own. If any of your neighbors use garden chemicals, those chemicals may end up in your yard, possibly killing the fish or plants in your water garden.

SCRUTINIZE YOUR SHADE AND SUN

Take time to look for sunny and shady pockets in your yard. Knowing where they are will help you pick the right plants for your landscape. To really figure out your sun and shade patterns, you'll need to observe your yard several times during the course of a day. Some sites never get any direct sun—on the north side of your house next to an evergreen, for example. Others are sunny or shady only in the morning or afternoon. Note patterns on a copy of your working map, using slashing lines in one direction to indicate morning sun and another direction for afternoon sun.

CHECK THE TRAFFIC

Check your yard for compacted soil and scraggly grass—the signs of unofficial pathways. Accommodate these paths rather than fight them. For example, if an unofficial path to the neighbor's house runs through a site you covet for a perennial border, plan to install stepping-stones through the border.

MULL OVER YOUR MOWING

During your next few mowing sessions, notice what your mowing problems are. Are there awkward spaces around shrubs or trees? Slopes that leave you panting? Rough areas of scraggly grass that are hard on the mower—and you? Target these areas

for planting with groundcover or mass plantings of perennials.

SEARCH FOR SAD SOIL

Stunted plants—or no plants at all—are one clue that your soil is less than wonderful. Problem soil areas may need cultivation or generous enrichment with organic matter. Or, you may just need to figure out what types of plants would be happy in those conditions. You'll learn more later about matching plants to soils. For now, just make note of problem areas.

Draw Your Dream Landscape

Now that you've brainstormed ideas, mapped your property, and made special note of problem sites, you're ready to create a landscape plan. Drawing a landscape plan is something like putting together a jigsaw puzzle. The objective is to blend all your ideas and the existing features of your landscape into a picture that will please you. It's a fun and creative process, as well as a challenge. But don't worry, you don't have to be an artist to create a workable design. And remember, you don't have to make a plan for your whole property. You may want to draw a plan for just your front yard, for example.

SKETCH YOUR IDEAS

To start, gather the 3 x 5 cards or other notes that summarize your ideas. You'll also need the working map of your landscape, pencils, a ruler, sheets of tracing paper, and any ideas you've collected from books or magazines.

Put a piece of tracing paper over your working map. You'll sketch ideas on the tracing paper, which is usually called an overlay. (You can use photocopies of your map instead if you prefer.) You may want to pencil in some reference points (like the outline of your house) on each overlay before you start sketching. This will help you realign the overlay if it shifts position while you're sketching.

Review the pile of cards that has your most important ideas in it. For example, you may want a perennial garden in a sunny spot that you can see from both the kitchen and the living room. You may have a specific site in mind—the only spot that's in full sun and visible from both rooms, for example—or there may be more than one site that would work.

Next, start sketching ovals or rectangles on those sites to represent the garden. At this point, stick to general concepts. You'll work out detailed bed shapes and plant choices later. Landscape plans of this sort are often called "bubble diagrams," and one is shown on this page.

When you're done with the first pile of cards, move on to the next one. As you work, look for connections between spaces—you may find activities that seem to fit together. For example, if you position an herb and flower garden next to a sitting area, you'll get extra enjoyment from your garden when you sit outdoors.

Whenever you have too many ideas on an overlay, cover the overlay with a new sheet of tracing paper. Trace the parts of the design you like, and continue drawing. (Since you may want to refer back to previous overlays, don't throw any of them away until you have a finished design.)

You probably will run out of landscape space before you run out of ideas. If you do, try to incorporate leftover ideas into areas you've already assigned. In the end, you may have to discard some ideas. Just be sure they are the ones that are least important to you. If they aren't, go back and rework your design to fit them in.

MAKE A PRACTICALITY CHECK

Before you draw up a final plan, take a minute to step back and look critically at your plan. Two important practical considerations are installation costs and required maintenance. For example, say your rough design features a brick walkway flanked by two 100-foot perennial borders. Do you have the money to buy all those plants and bricks, and the time to maintain such large plantings? Perhaps two smaller borders of mixed groundcovers and a crushed stone walk would be more practical and economical. You could design a smaller perennial garden at another site.

If you're planning on stone walls or brick walkways, make a few phone calls to find out approximate costs of materials. This safeguards you from getting stuck in an overly ambitious project.

FORMALIZE YOUR DRAWING

A final, detailed drawing of your plan will help you calculate your material needs for walls and walkways, tally how many plants you'll need, and figure out the best way to install your new landscape.

Start with your working map, your bubble diagram, and a new sheet of tracing paper. You may want to collect some tools that will help you draw shapes: A compass and a triangle may be helpful, especially for formal designs. For drawing informal sweeping curves, experiment with a set of French curves and/or a flexible curve (a flexible wire coated with plastic that has one flat side you can trace against). Both of these drawing tools are available at craft and office-supply stores.

You'll use these tools to create customized shapes in place of the simple ovals or rectangles on your bubble diagram. It's easiest to start with a defining feature in your plan—perhaps a sweeping bed around a clump of trees or a long, low wall along a slope. Draw that feature in first; it will help you figure out how the rest of the elements will fit. For example, you may want to echo the shape of the bed you drew around the trees on the other side of your yard.

Another excellent option is to use a grid to structure your design. Using a grid helps ensure that your plan puts your house at the center of your garden.

THE FINISHING TOUCHES

There's a saying that "good bones make good gardens." Although gardens don't seem the least bit bony when they're in the full flush of summer bloom, well-designed gardens do have a structure that holds them together to create a unified picture. These bones (structure) are the shapes, colors, textures, and materials repeated throughout a garden. The bones of a garden are especially important in winter: When perennials are dormant, the bones are still there to make your landscape pleasant to look at. The bones of a garden also often help guide visitors from one part to another.

Create a structure. Using a certain material throughout your garden creates its bones. Stone, brick, or flagstone in walls, terraces, and walkways become garden bones. Trees and shrubs, especially evergreens, also serve as garden bones, as do evergreen groundcovers. Hedges and fences also can play a role in the bones of your garden.

Plan to use several materials or types of plants to create the bones of your garden. For example, you may want to use rug junipers to edge crushed stone walkways throughout your garden, and then set off your perennial plantings with a backdrop of mixed evergreens and an edging of blue fescue (*Festuca cinerea*) in front to echo the color of the evergreens. In summer, the structure of your garden could take

Continued ➡

on a whole different dimension if you use yellow- or blue-flowered perennials throughout.

Connect the spaces. As you look at your plan, imagine how visitors will walk from one area to the next. For example, if you plan a flowerbed around your patio, how will your visitors know not to tramp across your perennials in winter? You may want a low fence or hedge to separate the patio from the garden, as well as a pair of evergreens or stone pilings on either side of the designated path.

Repeat shapes. Repeated shapes create harmony. Use rectangles, ovals, or sweeping curves that echo one another—such as the edges of mixed plantings along either side of a yard.

Simple is effective. For small yards, a simple, formal garden is often most effective. Or plan on a design with strong structure—like a path that winds into the backyard between beds of mixed flowers and shrubs.

Balance garden and open space. Take an extra look at the shapes defined by areas of lawn, patios, or mass plantings of groundcovers. Designers call this the negative, or open, space in a design. Open spaces should have clean, pleasing shapes. A central oval- or hourglass-shaped lawn is much more visually pleasing than a lawn that has complicated zigzag edges. Strive to balance the negative space and positive (filled-in) space, which you'll plant with perennials, shrubs, trees, or mixed groundcovers.

Look for outdoor room. Try to enclose some areas, at least partially, with shrubs and perennials or hedges. Add easy-care shrub roses, ornamental grasses, and perennials around a patio to screen it from neighboring yards.

Include surprises. Paths that wind out of sight, stepping-stones that lead visitors through a garden, or unexpected clumps of color in an otherwise green landscape create surprise and fun in your garden.

VISUALIZE YOUR DESIGN

It's tough to imagine what your rough drawing will look like as a finished landscape. For a test, try to imagine yourself actually doing things in your planned yard. Are there paths to follow, sitting areas to enjoy? Does your yard have spaces for all the activities you enjoy?

To get an idea of how large you'd like your plantings to be, try piling up plastic bags filled with leaves or arranging lawn chairs on a proposed site to get an idea of the total volume of plants. If you're trying to either screen a particular view or make sure you don't cover one up, have a helper hold up a pole to estimate how tall you'll need your plantings.

Snapshots of your house are a good visualizing tool. Sketch in rough shapes of the proposed plantings on the photos (or photocopies of the photos).

Prioritize Your Projects

Once you've polished your plan on paper, it's time to inject a little dose of reality. Much as you'd like to plant your entire dream landscape right now, undoubtedly you don't have enough time, money, and muscle to do so. You need to take a hard look at your plan and pick the project or projects that you want to implement first.

One way to choose is to start with the site you see most clearly from the house. Or, you may decide to start with the project that will be the most enjoyable, such as planting the shady wildflower garden you've always wanted. Solving your worst maintenance nightmare often comes out as top priority.

When you're choosing your "do-first" projects, try to include one simple project on your list: The reward of seeing one finished, lovely spot in your unfinished yard is worth it.

MAKE A PRACTICAL PLAN OF ACTION

In most cases, you'll install your priority projects over time. Simple projects may take only a weekend or two. But depending on your budget, how ambitious your projects are, and the time you have to spend, others may take as long as several years to complete. That's one of the reasons having a simple project high on your list is so important. You can plant a small bed around a lamppost or on either side of a short set of steps in a single weekend, giving you pride in accomplishment and readying you to tackle more complicated projects over a longer span of time. Here are some suggestions to help you with scheduling.

Plan around hardscape. If your plan calls for adding a patio, house addition, walls, or walkways, don't plant around those sites until the building project is complete. Otherwise, you'll spend time repairing plantings after construction.

Consider a Grid

A grid is nothing more than a series of squares drawn on a piece of tracing paper and placed over the working map of your landscape. The secret is that the size of the squares and their placement relate directly to your house, and the garden is designed around the grid squares. This helps to create a landscape plan in which the gardens and other features are proportional to your house.

Pick a prominent feature to base the grid on. In this example, each grid square is the same size as the existing patio. Major plantings generally take up one or more individual grid squares.

Don't select a grid square that's too small. It leads to a fussy, overcomplicated design. After you draw in your grid, fill in landscape features, working out from your house. This will ensure that the landscape unfolds from the house and the house is at the center of beautiful gardens.

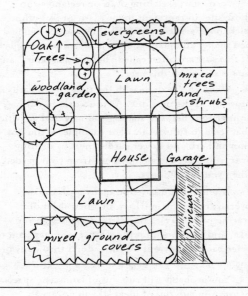

Plant woodies first. Give trees and shrubs a head start by planting them first, especially if shade is at a premium in your yard. As they're growing, you can add perennials and groundcovers as time and budget allow. If you're planning an island of trees and shrubs, mulch them well after planting to control

weeds. Then gradually plant perennials among the mulch.

Mulch and grow. You can avoid digging on some sites by trying no-dig soil improvement. Scalp all weeds on the site, then cover it with a newspaper layer 12 to 15 sheets thick. Then spread 4 to 5 inches of straw, and top it off with 2 inches of decorative mulch. If you have it, add 1 inch of compost under the mulch. You can make planting holes right in the mulch, fill them with purchased soil, and plant them with annuals to cover the site in the summer. Keep the site mulched for a year, then plant with perennials.

COST-CUTTING TIPS

There's no doubt about it, installing a landscape can be expensive. Sometimes doing it yourself is the best option; other times it's not. Here are some tips to help you keep your pocketbook under control.

Learn a skill. Check books out of your local library or attend a workshop to learn a landscape skill like bricklaying or building stone walls.

Rent, don't buy. You can rent nearly any kind of equipment or tool to make landscape installation easier. Instead of hiring someone with a tractor or buying one yourself, rent one to move soil or accomplish other tasks that your landscaping plan requires.

Use nursery services. If your plan calls for large trees and shrubs, having the nursery plant them may pay off in the long run. Many nurseries will guarantee specimens they plant, but extend a more limited warranty for specimens you plant yourself.

Opt for local materials. Consider a variety of materials for each project, then select the one that's least expensive in your area. Limestone paving slabs may be much cheaper than bluestone in some areas, for example. Also keep an eye out for used materials you can acquire—used brick, for example.

Before You Plant

So you've settled on your top-priority project and you're ready to go! But as one last step, check out the microclimate and soil on your project site. The information in selecting the right plants for the site.

CLIMATE ON A SMALL SCALE

The amount of shade or sun a site receives is just one factor in the microclimate of a site. If you haven't already determined how much sun and/or shade your site receives, read "Scrutinize Your Shade and Sun" on the previous page. Also evaluate the wind, exposure, and slope conditions.

Wind. Prevailing winds can wreak havoc with perennial plantings—drying plants out, ruining blossoms, and blowing them over. If your site is windy, consider making a windbreak part of the project. A fence is a quick solution, but barrier plantings will last longer and provide better protection.

Exposure. South-facing sites along a building or wall are generally warmer and more exposed in winter than north-facing ones. And the extra heat given off by the wall or fence behind a south-facing site warms these sites in spring. For this reason, they're a good place to plant spring bulbs. But broad-leaved evergreens can suffer from leaf scorch on a south-facing site both in summer and on unusually warm winter days.

Plants on a north-facing site are protected from both winter and summer sun. And west-facing sites

Continued →

that receive afternoon sun tend to be hotter than east-facing ones.

Slope. Perennial groundcovers are fairly easy to establish on slopes. But if you plan to plant a mix of perennials, you'll need to build terraces and level planting beds.

Planning terraces requires a little mathematical figuring. The first step is to measure the rise and run of the slope. From that, you can figure out how many terraces you'll need.

LOOKING AT WHAT'S DOWN UNDER

Complete your site examination by taking a look at the soil. Dig a few test holes with a garden fork or spade. Poorly drained soil, compacted soil layers, and too-sandy or too-clayey soil are some of the common problems you may face. Certainly, you can work to improve your soil before you plant. But in the long run, your plants will do best if you match their needs to the soil. For example, if you have very light, sandy soil, perennials like ligularias (*Ligularia* spp.) that need rich, moist soils just won't grow well.

If you strike rocks repeatedly while you're digging, consider building a raised bed over the area or planting shallow-rooted groundcovers around the rocks. Another option is to dig up some of the larger rocks and stack them in a low wall.

Roots are another matter. If you hit roots at every turn, you are dealing with a shallow-rooted tree.

Secrets of Successful Combinations

Putting perennials together in great combinations is easy and fun. What's more, creating combinations of perennials is the first, most important step in designing an entire perennial garden from scratch.

In the preceding section, you've worked through the process of deciding where you want to plant perennials in your yard and what styles of gardens you want. Now you're ready to try designing beautiful combinations of perennials.

In this section, you'll find a series of perennial combinations with explanations of how color and design principles were used to choose the plants. You'll learn how to work with attractive foliage, plant forms, and other features in perennial combinations. Once you understand how to put plants together in attractive combinations, you'll find it a natural progression to design an entire perennial garden.

DESIGNING WITH COLOR

Many gardeners find designing with color intimidating. They're afraid they'll make a mistake and combine flowers that don't look attractive together. Or they're simply overwhelmed by all the plants to choose from—each more beautiful than the last!

The key to comfort with combining colors is to get out there and experiment. Tryout some of the combinations you see in this book, or design some of your own. Granted, you may end up with a dreadful combination or two. But that's what shovels are for—you can always move one of the offending plants somewhere else and try a new combination the next year.

Using the color wheel

In elementary school art classes, you probably learned about the primary colors—red, yellow, and blue—and how to mix them to make other colors. Those early experiences playing with paints are similar in some ways to combining colors in gardens.

The color wheel can provide the basis for choosing good perennial combinations if you know how to use it. It can also help you look at color more critically and figure out what's working in a particular combination and what isn't.

For example, *complementary* combinations—blue and orange, red and green, yellow and violet—have lots of contrast and are bright and exciting to look at. Colors that harmonize share the same pigments—yellow, yellow-orange, orange, and orange-red, for example. You can make stunning combinations by starting with complementary colors—violet and yellow, for example—and then adding harmonizers, such as blue-violet and red-violet, to the picture.

Flowers usually don't come in the pure colors you see in the wheel. Instead, you'll be dealing with colors like peach, lemon yellow, apricot, burgundy, deep purple, or lilac. Sometimes surrounding colors can influence our perception of color. To determine a flower's true color, try holding a solid white card behind the bloom to neutralize the influence of nearby foliage.

You'll find that light also influences color. Combinations that are so-so in the early morning can literally glitter in late afternoon sun. Ornamental grasses are particularly spectacular when backlit.

GETTING STARTED

Besides color, when you design combinations you'll also want to consider things like plant height and form, leaf shapes, and bloom time. It can get complicated! Try not to get lost in the "rules" of garden design. If you do, you may forget what's really important-filling your yard with plants that appeal to you and grow well together. That's not to say you should throw all design principles out the window. If you look closely at great-looking combinations and gardens, you'll see that flower shapes, heights, forms, and textures all play a role in the design. And repeating certain elements—like color or texture—throughout a design helps it become a unified, visually appealing picture.

As you look at the plant combinations that follow, keep in mind that color preferences are highly subjective. You may not like all the color combinations you see here. Figuring out what you do like is most important. In fact, you're sure to like the combinations you design if you use your favorite colors.

Don't get caught up in trying to apply all these principles at the same time—there's simply too much to remember. Just use them as well as you can. And remember, a shovel is your plant eraser. You can always add new plants or move some if your combinations don't turn out quite right at first. You'll find out that's half the fun!

Contrasts Create Excitement

This lush perennial garden uses contrasts between plants to form a dynamic picture. At the same time, it also uses repetition—plants that look alike in some way—to pull the garden together. The rounded mound of 'Autumn Joy' sedum, which echoes the shapes of its individual blooms, provides a solid, clean-looking anchor for the planting. It balances the exuberant and unruly explosion of New York ironweed above it. The white-striped foliage of the variegated Japanese silver grass, echoed in miniature by the creeping lilyturf in the front of the border, provides color and texture contrast to the sedum. And the ribbonlike shape of these two plants repeats in contrasting colors both in the rough-stemmed goldenrod blossoms and the ironweed leaves.

DESIGN KEY

1 'Autumn Joy' sedum (*Sedum* 'Autumn Joy')

2 Rough-stemmed goldenrod (*Solidago rugosa* 'Fireworks')

3 New York ironweed (*Veronia noveboracensis*)

4 Variegated Japanese silver grass (*Miscanthus sinensis* 'Variegatus')

5 Purple coneflower (*Echinacea purpurea*)

6 'Moonbeam' coreopsis (*Coreopsis verticillato* 'Moonbeam')

7 Smoke tree (*Cotinus coggygria*)

8 Creeping lilyturf (*Liriope spicata*)

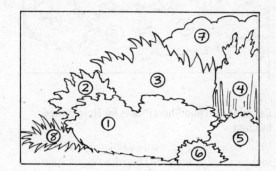

Mass Plantings Make a Bold Statement

In mass plantings, blocks of color and texture take precedence over the shapes of individual flowers. This planting features flowing drifts of color, which is more effective than hard-edged rectangles of plants. Note that the heights of the plants vary so each mass of color shows to best effect.

A mass planting is especially effective from a distance, where the bold blocks of color would be most dramatic. Planting at a distance has another advantage: You can enjoy all the color without having to worry about picking off spent blooms.

DESIGN KEY

1 Shining coneflower (*Rudbeckia nitida* 'Herbstsonne', also called 'Autumn Sun')

2 Spotted Joe-Pye weed (*Eupatorium maculatum* 'Atropurpureum')

3 Feather reed grass (*Calamagrostis acutiflora* 'Stricta')

4 Brazilian vervain (*Verbena bonariensis*)

5 Feathertop grass (*Pennisetum villosum*)

6 Russian sage (*Perovskia atriplicifolia*)

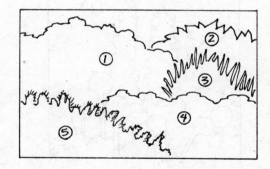

Use Foliage for 4-Season Color

Great gardens are more than just flowers! As perennials come in and out of bloom, foliage is fundamental for keeping a garden looking its best. That's why it often makes sense to mix evergreen shrubs in perennial beds and borders.

This mixed planting will have foliage interest year-round. The dwarf eastern white pine and 'Blue Star' juniper will provide winter color. In summer, the Chinese astilbe foliage will remain green and attractive all season, while the fine foliage of 'Moonbeam' coreopsis provides a colorful skirt for the garden.

DESIGN KEY

1 Drawf eastern white pine (*Pinus strobes* 'Nana')

2 Chinese astilbe (*Astilbe chinensis* var. *pumila*)

3 'Blue Star' juniper (*Juniperus squamata* 'Blue Star')

4 'Moonbeam' coreopsis (*Coreopsis verticillata* 'Moonbeam')

Continued ➡

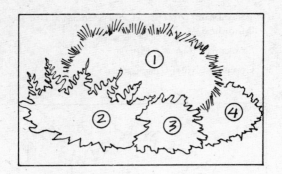

Combine Tall and Short Plants for Heightened Interest

Vines clambering on trellises add a casual country look to a bed or border. They're a perfect solution if you need nearly instant height in a newly planted bed, or if you have space for only a narrow border. In a deep border, you can create contrasts in height by planting clumps of 5- and 6-foot-tall perennials at the back, and scale down to 1-foot mounds at the front. But in tight spaces, tuck a vine like this Jackman clematis at the back of the border to add height. (Since vines grow up, not out, they don't need the space that larger perennials require.)

Clematis like to grow with their heads in the sun and their feet in the shade, so this type of site is ideal. If you need extraquick results, try annual vines like morning glories trained in a similar manner.

DESIGN KEY

1   Jackman clematis (*Clematis jackmanii*)

2   Hybrid delphinium (*Delphinium elatum*)

3   Persian onion (*Allium aflatunense*)

Choose Plants That Suit Your Site

Matching plants that will grow well together is the secret to planting an attractive garden that stays that way. Once you've selected several plants that you think would look nice together, check out the cultural conditions they require. You'll have the best results, if you stick to plants that all need the same type of site and soil. In this garden, even though the 'Autumn Joy' sedum is much more drought-tolerant than the 'Montgomery' Colorado spruce, both will grow well in rich, well-drained soil. Note that these garden companions will also make an arresting winter picture. Both sedum and 'Goldsturm' black-eyed Susan have attractive seed-heads that persist through winter, and the spruce will add a spot of silver-blue.

DESIGN KEY

1   'Goldsturm' black-eyed Susan (*Rudbeckia fulgida* 'Goldsturm')

2   'Autumn Joy' sedum (*Sedum* 'Autumn Joy')

3   'Montgomery' Colorado spruce (*Picea pungens* 'Montgomery')

Use Dramatic Plants to Accent Your Landscape

Specimen plants like August lily are the exclamation points of garden design. Technically, a specimen plant is one that is grown alone in the landscape so its shape and form can be appreciated from all sides. Use one to mark the entrance to a garden path or set off one part of your yard from another. But be judicious: Too many exclamation points can create confusion—and lots of obstacles to mow around.

The best specimen plants are attractive for much or all of the growing season. Shrubs or small trees are an obvious choice, but large hostas or heucheras (*Heuchera* spp.) also make great specimen plants in a shady garden. For a sunny site, you might use variegated yuccas or large ornamental grasses.

DESIGN KEY

1   August lily (*Hosta plantaginea*)

2   English ivy (*Hedera helix*)

Match the Shape of a Garden to the Site

Shapes, texture, and movement play important roles in the design of this lush foliage garden. The fountain sets the shape of the bed and the plantings in it. Water pouring from the jug in the child's arms seems to cascade out into the garden to create ripples of plants. The net effect is a sculpture integrally linked to the setting: It's hard to imagine it without the surrounding plants.

DESIGN KEY

1   'Palace Purple' heuchera (*Heuchera micrantha* 'Palace Purple')

2   'Silver Carpet' lamb's-ears (*Stachys byzantina* 'Silver Carpet')

3   Artemisia (*Artemisia* sp.)

4   'Goldmound' spirea (*Spiraea* 'Goldmound')

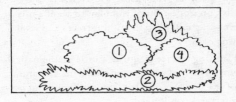

Watch for Great Combinations That Happen by Chance

You can blanket your yard with blocks of annuals and be able to predict with some certainty that it will look the same in June, July, August, and September, but what fun is that? Perennials create their own combinations, and those combinations change all the time. One plant may spillover onto another, as these Japanese anemones have toppled onto asters. Or, one year a perennial may bloom earlier or later than normal, creating a combination you hadn't planned. As the years go by, perennials also reseed and spread to make their own combinations—some good, some bad. Your job as the master color coordinator is to guide your plants with a gentle hand toward color combinations you find appealing, however long they last.

DESIGN KEY

1   Japanese anemone (*Anemone x hybrida*)

2   Aster (*Aster* sp.)

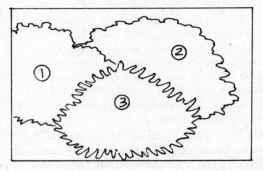

Combine Complementary Colors

One way to start a design is with complementary colors like yellow yarrows and lavender-blue cranesbills. Select the complements you want to use and then build around them by picking different flowers in similar colors.

When you try to select perennials of a particular shade, you'll find that flower color isn't always easy to define. For example, if you check descriptions in several mail-order catalogs for *Geranium* 'Johnson's Blue', you'll find it described as brilliant blue, clear blue, lavender-blue, and blue. Because flower colors are difficult to capture on film and in print, photographs of it vary as well—you'll see depictions from brilliant blue to lilac. In the end, the only true test is to grow the plant in your own garden and decide for yourself what color it is.

DESIGN KEY

1   'Johnson's Blue' cranesbill (*Geranium* 'Johnson's Blue')

2   'Moonshine yarrow' (*Achillea* 'Moonshine')

Continued ➡

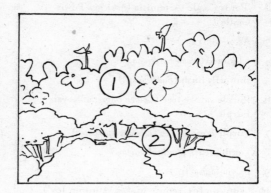

Plant Ribbons of Hot Color for Maximum Impact

When subtle just won't cut it, bright, cheerful hot colors may be the answer. Hot colors are the color of fire—red, orange, and yellow. They pop out in the landscape and make things look closer than they really are. Notice how the bright clumps of color at the back of this landscape seem to pop out in front of the green foliage that surrounds them.

DESIGN KEY

1   Bee balm (*Monarda didyma*)

2   Coneflower (*Rudbeckia* sp.)

3   Threadleaf coreopsis (*Coreopsis verticillata*)

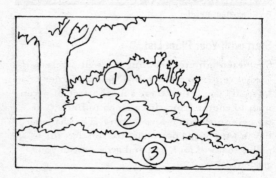

Use Cool Colors for Calming Effects

Rows of cool colors are at the forefront of this elegant spring scene. Cool colors are the color of water—blue, green, and violet, as well as silver, gray, blue-green, and gray-green. They create a garden with a serene feeling, and they also appear to make things recede. A small garden planted with blues and purples, for example, will look larger because everything seems farther away. Pale pink is also considered a cool color, while hot pink is a hot color.

DESIGN KEY

1   Blue atlas cedar (*Cedrus atlantica* 'Glauca')

2   Bearded iris (*Iris* bearded hybrid)

3   Juniper (*Juniperus* sp.)

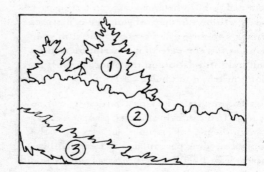

Startling Color Contrasts Can Make Stunning Combinations

Although pink and orange aren't high on many gardeners' lists of plants they'd like to see growing together, they work beautifully together in this garden. The pink plumes of 'Superba' fall astilbes,

set off against dark green foliage, set the tone for this scene. Beyond the fence, the lilies act as an exclamation point that foreshadows more excitement in the border beyond. Yellow lilies alone would have worked, but the garden would lack that "Look at me!" excitement.

DESIGN KEY

1   Lilies (*Lilium* spp.)

2   'Superba' fall astilbe (*Astilbe taquetii* 'Superba')

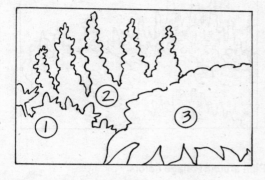

Use a Color Theme to Unify Your Garden

Gardens that celebrate a passion for a certain color like yellow, blue, or white have a long tradition in perennial gardening. Whether you plant just a corner of your yard with your favorite color or use it to fill an entire garden, it's great fun sleuthing out all the color possibilities. For example, there are hundreds of yellow-flowered perennials to choose from.

Yellow tulips, daffodils, irises, and primroses would extend the summer color scheme of this planting into the spring. Plants with variegated leaves, such as golden-striped ornamental grasses or *Yucca filamentosa* 'Bright Edge', or gold-colored foliage, such as golden oregano (*Origanum vulgare* 'Aureum'), are also a great option.

DESIGN KEY

1   'Statuesque' daylily (*Hemerocallis* 'Statuesque')

2   'Coronation Gold' yarrow (*Achillea* 'Coronation Gold')

3   'Moonbeam' coreopsis (*Coreopsis verticillata* 'Moonbeam')

Don't Forget the Power of White Flowers and Foliage

White is actually a strong color that can hold its own against more brightly hued garden residents. In this garden, white plumes of delphiniums and steely

silver flowers of giant sea holly are every bit as bright as the yellow daisylike flowers of heartleaf oxeye. White is also useful for mediating disputes between clashing colors in a border. For example, a white bank of baby's-breath between clumps of orange-red lilies and pink cranesbills (*Geranium* spp.) can do wonders. Silver-leaved plants like 'Powis Castle' artemisia also make effective moderators. In an emergency, you can also add clumps of annual dusty miller between color combatants.

DESIGN KEY

1   Giant sea holly (*Eryngium giganteum*)

2   Delphinium (*Delphinium* hybrid)

3   Heartleaf oxeye (*Telekia speciosa*, also known as *Buphthalmum speciosum*)

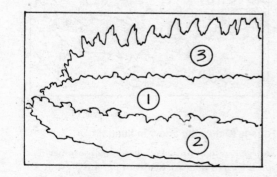

Design with Rivers of Color

One look along a country roadside during the height of summer will confirm that nature isn't subtle about painting colors across the landscape. You can take a cue from nature and plant your garden in meadowlike drifts of color. This technique is especially effective in large borders that you'll view from a distance. In a small garden, you can get a similar effect by planting a few clumps of each perennial. Either way, planting color drifts reduces the hodgepodge effect that can result when a garden has too many small dabs of color.

DESIGN KEY

1   'Goldsturm' black-eyed Susan (*Rudbeckia fulgida* 'Goldsturm')

2   'Autumn Joy' sedum (*Sedum* 'Autumn Joy')

3   Foerster's feather reed grass (*Calamagrostis arundinacea* ('Karl Foerster')

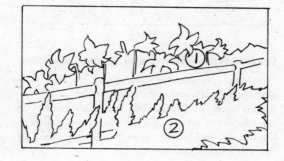

Include the Backdrop in Your Design

This border has it all. Clumps of soft color march across the garden providing height and a sense of movement. It also has something that's easily missed: a deep green hemlock backdrop that sets off the soft colors of the perennials. The color scheme of this border would fade away against a light backdrop.

Before you plan a garden, take a minute to figure out what you'll see it against. If you are planning a

Continued ➔

perennial bed or island that you'll usually see silhou-etted against the lawn, consider brighter colors that would stand out against grass green. And while perennials will show effectively against a solid board fence or dark siding, consider your colors carefully if your house is white, yellow, or pastel-colored.

Design Key

1   Mullein (*Verbascum* sp.)
2   Penstemon (*Penstemon* sp.)
3   'Autumn Joy' sedum (*Sedum* 'Autumn Joy')
4   Speedwell (*Veronica* sp.)
5   Clary (*Salvia sclarea*)

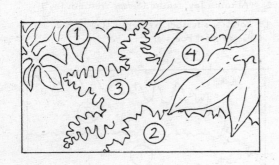

Plan around Foliage Colors

Since most perennials bloom for only a few weeks in summer, foliage is often the real workhorse that keeps a garden looking great day in and day out. The spring green hosta leaves light up this shady garden as much as the fleeting pink flowers of dame's rocket. The clump of lady fern makes an especially inter-esting companion: Although it is the same green as the hosta, its lacy leaves stand out against the dark forest floor, creating a stunning textural contrast.

Design Key

1   Pagoda dogwood (*Cornus alternifolia*)
2   Dame's rocket (*Hesperis matronalis*)
3   Lady fern (*Athyrium filix-femina*)
4   'Piedmont Gold' hosta (*Hosta* 'Piedmont Gold')

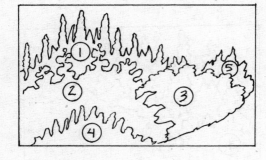

Foliage Makes the Show in Shade

Foliage can light up a shady garden all summer if you'll let it. There are plenty of perennials with variegated leaves that will add color and interest to even the darkest spot. In addition to the ones shown here, hostas, hardy cyclamen (*Cyclamen hederifolium*), and variegated Solomon's seal (*Polygonatum odoratum* 'Variegatum') will bring whites, golds, yellows, and greens to your garden. All add flowers for at least a few weeks. In this small corner of a garden, the mazus provides a carpet of white flowers and the lungwort bears rosy wine blooms to herald spring.

Design Key

1   'Excalibur' lungwort (*Pulmonaria* 'Excalibur')
2   White-flowered mazus (*Mazus reptans* 'Albus')

3   Persian ivy (*Hedera colchico* 'Dentatovariegata')

Combine Plants with a Goal of Season-Long Color

One of the challenges of working with colors in a perennial garden is that the colors of individual flowers come and go. One way to plan a summer-long display of color is to take a spring combination like this one and look for later-blooming perennials that will repeat it in other seasons.

Try peonies with Siberian iris (*Iris sibirica*) or maiden pinks (*Dianthus deltoids*) with bellflowers (*Campanula* spp.) for early summer bloom. Follow it up with balloon flowers (*Platycodon grandiflorus*) and bee balm (*Monarda didyma*) for summer. Sum up the year with hot pink and blue asters.

Design Key

1   Tulip (*Tulipa hybrid0*)
2   Forget-me-not (*Myosotis* sp.)
3   Lamb's-ears (*Stachys byzantina*)

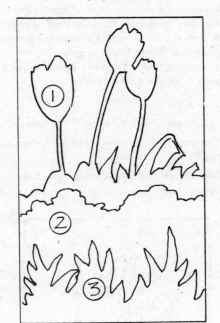

Perennials Can Provide Great Fall Color

Colors can signify the season as clearly as the weather. Fall brings silvers, bronzes, yellows, and golds to gardens as surely as it puts a nip in the air. Fall's colors are more subtle than those of the early spring and summer garden, but they are no less beautiful. This late fall garden won't be finished with the first frost of the season. And many of the plants here will continue to provide color and interest through the winter. Ornamental grasses will turn a lovely beige, adding color and texture until they're cut to the ground in early spring. Seedheads of sedums, which turn paler bronze, and cone-flowers, which turn dark brown, will stand through the winter as well.

Design Key

1   'Sarabande' Japanese silver grass (*Miscanthus sinensis* 'Sarabande')

2   'Powis Castle' Artemisia (*Artemisia* 'Powis Castle')
3   Aster (*Aster* sp.)
4   Cleome (*Cleome hasslerana*)
5   Butterfly bush (*Buddleia* sp.)
6   Purple smoke tree (*Cotinus coggygria* 'Royal Purple')
7   Purple coneflower (*Echinacea purpurea*)
8   Lamb's-ears (*Stachys byzantina*)
9   Salvia (*Salvia* sp.)
10 'Autumn Joy' sedum (*Sedum* 'Autumn Joy')

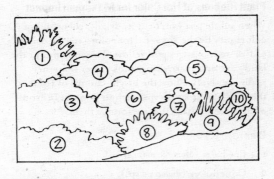

Planning A Perennial Garden

Fern Marshall Bradley

Start with Your Plant List

Spend ten minutes browsing at a well-stocked garden center or paging through mail-order cata-logs, and you'll find there's no shortage of peren-nials to choose from. It's a cinch to find 50 or 60 perennials you'd love to grow. The challenge lies in winnowing down that list to select the plants that will look best and grow best in your garden.

If you're like most gardeners, you love the annual onslaught of catalogs with their tempting offerings. But it's easy to get caught in the trap of buying everything that looks and sounds appealing. Making a plant list is the best way to ensure that you buy wisely. It takes time but allows you to evaluate each plant, as well as make comparisons between plants.

You're not a list maker? Are you prone to impulse purchases? Or are you simply over-whelmed when you visit a garden center or try to wade through catalogs? Don't despair. Try one of these suggestions for developing a list of plants.

Start with your site. Choose plants with your site conditions in mind. If you have a hot, sunny site, consider only plants that will thrive under those conditions and eliminate all the others. If you're tempted to buy whatever looks interesting or new, take a written summary of your site conditions with you to the garden center. Hold it in your hand as you compare your description to the cultural information on the plant labels. If they don't match, don't buy!

Review your style. Picking a garden style or color scheme first can help you pick plants. A cottage garden theme, for example, suggests old-fash-ioned reseeding perennials and biennials like peach-leaved bellflower (*Campanula persicifolia*) and foxgloves (*Digitalis* spp.).

Start your design with classic plants that epit-omize your style. If you have a particular color scheme in mind—yellow and blue, for example—that narrows your choices as well. And if you like cutting and arranging flowers, you may want to choose perennials with bloom colors that will

Continued ➡

match the colors of the furniture or wallpaper in your dining or living room.

Build on combinations. Select a perennial combination and check whether it will grow well on your site. If it will, use that combination as the basis for your design. This will focus your search.

Keep in mind that gardens don't have to contain lots of different kinds of perennials to be beautiful and satisfying. You can also create a perfectly lovely garden simply by making mass plantings of the two or three plants in one combination.

Include some sentiment. Planning beds and borders around plants that provide special memories adds a wonderful dimension to any garden. Perhaps there are specific plants that remind you of happy childhood experiences, dear friends or relatives, or a neighborhood where you used to live.

For example, if plants have been passed down through generations—like peonies that grew in a grandmother's garden—they can be the center-piece of a family memory garden.

Start with a professional design. You may want to contract the task of creating a specific garden to a professional garden designer. If you do, tell the designer as much as you can about the site, and the style of garden you want. Make a list of favorite plants that you'd like included in your garden, and discuss it with your designer. Another alternative is to adapt an existing design and plant list to suit your site. For ideas, turn to the previous section, where you'll find designs for a color theme garden, butterfly garden, perennial herb garden, and many others.

Chart Your Plants

Making an organized plant list can seem like a chore. It's easier and more fun to circle plants that catch your eye in a catalog, or to scribble down a quick list of choices. But once you discipline yourself to make a formal list, you'll never regret it. An organized list—actually a chart—is invaluable when you design a garden. If you take time to record some basic facts about each plant, you can use it to evaluate your overall list of choices at a glance.

To generate a plant chart you need graph paper and a clipboard, a pencil, a ruler, a 3 x 5 card, and a packet of colored pencils or markers. You'll also need reference materials, mail-order catalogs, and possibly a perennials encyclopedia.

First, write a very brief summary of the conditions at your site on the 3 x 5 card. A few words will do, such as "Dry shade" or "Full sun, hot, well-drained soil." Clip this card on your clipboard, sticking out from behind the graph paper. Each time you see a plant that appeals to you, check whether it will grow in the conditions you've listed. If it won't, put it on a wish list of plants for another site.

Line the graph paper and begin listing plants. Use colored pencils or markers to make the color bar that indicates bloom season and color. Don't worry if the bloom color isn't exact. You'll use it to make overall judgments, such as: Are there too many yellows and not enough pinks? Does anything on the list bloom in early fall?

In the "Comments" column, list the general shape of the plant first. Then note suggested combinations (many catalogs provide them), or notes about special care.

Once you've finished, evaluate your list. Start crossing plants off, eliminating ones with bloom seasons that are too short, foliage that isn't attractive for most of the season, or that aren't quite suited to the site. Also be sure you have a good assortment of heights and shapes. You may want to eliminate plants that need special care like staking or frequent division.

How Many Kinds of Plants?

Perennials need anywhere from 2 to 4 square feet of space per plant at maturity. So, to fill a 120-square-foot garden, you'll need between 30 and 60 plants. That doesn't mean you'll need 30 to 60 different species or cultivars; for an effective design, you'll want to plant drifts of some plants and repeating clumps of others throughout the garden to unify it. You probably actually need 15 to 30 different kinds of plants.

It's easy to let the collector's instinct take over and order one of everything. But you'll design a far better-looking garden if you steel yourself and limit your list. It's possible to have a fabulous-looking garden with only a handful of carefully chosen plants. And once you get your main perennials established, you can experiment with other plants that appeal to you.

Make a Planting Plan

Once your plant list is trimmed to size, it's time to turn it into a garden. To do that, you'll experiment with planting plans—arrangements on paper of your carefully chosen perennials.

Start by drawing your garden site to scale on a piece of graph paper. A good scale to start with is 1 inch equals 1 foot. For a large garden, you may need to try 1 inch equals 3 or 4 feet, or tape several sheets of graph paper together.

To position plants, begin drawing circles, ovals, or other shapes to represent clumps of plants. Start with one of the more important plants on your list—one that will provide color over a long season or that you want in a prominent place, for example. Then add others around it. Try to keep the shapes to scale. If you are planning a drift of a single perennial, be sure your bubble accommodates two, three, or more plants. It's easiest to number the plants on your list, and use the numbers (rather than writing out names) to identify each bubble on your diagram.

If you're designing a perennial border, draw the taller plants in the back and add layers of shorter plants in front. For an island bed, position the tallest plants in the center and add layers of shorter plants around them. For a formal rectangular garden, you may want to plant rows of a single plant along the edges with a contrasting plant in each corner. Here are some other tips to help you position plants and evaluate your design.

Plant in clumps. Design dramatic clumps of perennials, with three or more plants in each clump. A design filled with single plants will make an unsatisfying, spotty-looking garden with random bits of color here and there.

Repeat colors and textures. Place clumps of perennials with outstanding foliage or especially long bloom seasons throughout the garden. This helps unify the design and ensures you'll have attractive foliage and flowers to look at much of the time.

Move the color around. Arrange colors evenly throughout the site. If all your pink- or yellow-flowered plants are in one place, you'll end up with a lopsided garden.

Vary heights. Keep most of the tallest plants at the back (or in the center for an island bed), bringing a few forward a bit to create depth and variety. Bring some medium-height plants into the front row as well. Avoid a soldierlike lineup of plants of equal height.

Think season to season. Spread the bloom for each season through the whole border.

Try planting on centers. One technique that works effectively for meadow and prairielike gardens is to divide the site into 1-foot squares and plant a perennial or grass in each square. (Small plugs or 2½-inch pots are used for this technique.) Arrange the plants in drifts, with three, four, or more perennials planted in adjacent squares. Then let the plants spread and fill as they will.

Limit your plant list. If you run out of space on your plot plan before you run out of plants on your list, resist the temptation to squeeze in each and every plant. Instead, check the list of leftover plants against the plan. If some favorites are still on the list, substitute them for a plant that's on the plan. After you double-check, set the list aside. Keep those leftover plants in mind for replacement possibilities in the event that ones you've selected don't grow as well as you had hoped.

Creating Woodland and Shade Gardens

Sally Roth

I've always liked surprises, and my woodland garden is full of them. Long before my perennial borders wake from winter slumber, I begin haunting the paths of my woodsy front yard. No wildflowers are chancing the weather yet, but the birds know spring is coming. This February morning, a pair of Carolina chickadees are courting, offering each other love songs in high, thin voices.

There's so much to watch in a woodland garden that the first wildflowers usually manage to take me by surprise. I know spring is here for sure when I come across a nosegay of dainty purple hepatica or a cluster of bloodroot flowers, their wide white stars held flat in the warmth of the sun. Once the wildflowers get going, there's something new every week. Watching them emerge from winter slumber into bud and bloom rejuvenates my spirit. As the flowers awake, the insects do, too. A humming noise leads me to a bevy of fat, slow bees bumbling about the pussy willows. They're right at nose level, but they're interested in pollen, not in me. At this height, it's easy to watch as they clean their dusty legs.

My woodland garden is so full of life that I sometimes forget what it looked like just a few short years ago. When we moved into our little log house, the front yard was a lovely sweep of green lawn beneath old oaks and elms. (And yes, they're American elms—this area seems to be one of the last bastions against Dutch elm disease.)

Most passersby would have said our front yard was pretty, and it was, in a parklike way. But to me, that green perfection was boring. Except for a scattering of robins and an oriole nest swinging from the tulip tree, I couldn't find much life to look at in my own front yard. The sunny side yard had plenty of room for playing ball with the dogs and catch with the kids. Who needed a front yard that was just for show?

Continued →

The Making of a Woodland Garden

Little by little, I replaced the greensward with a woodland garden. I started with a single bed, smothering the grass with an ankle-deep layer of chopped leaves and putting in a few special plants from my local garden center. I tried to limit my choices to berried shrubs for the birds (though I splurged on a star magnolia, which the dogs promptly chewed off to a nubbin).

When October came around, I took advantage of the bounty of fallen leaves and chopped them into bits with a few passes of the lawn mower. Then I piled them into new beds along a tentative web of paths. When I liked the look of things, I moved in young trees and shrubs—redbuds, sugar maples, wild hydrangeas, viburnums, and my favorite, spicebush—from the natural woods behind our house.

In just a few short years, my woodland garden is looking like a real woods. Young oaks, maples, and hickories have sprouted in the blanket of humus, and wildflowers are multiplying happily. Last year I had a spread of self-sown, sky blue phacelia that rivaled my favorite wild spot down the road. The "exotic" plants I added—Japanese painted ferns, a few azaleas, and some favorite Oregon wildflowers—don't seem out of place here because I chose them to fit the feeling of the natural landscape.

The Nature of a Woods

In eastern Pennsylvania, where I grew up, the woodland was mostly deciduous trees (hardwoods), with occasional stands of hemlock, white pine, or spruce (softwoods) to add variety and contrast. In fall, the hillsides blazed with red and orange maples and the clear yellow of birches and tulip trees, accented by the deep green of the conifers. Because the trees and shrubs of the understory aren't dense and can be easily pushed aside if need be, you can enter an eastern woodland just about anywhere, whether or not there's a deer trail to guide your feet. In spring and summer, the air is rich and earthy with humus; in fall, there's a delicious crunch of dry leaves underfoot. Sunlight slants through the branches and beneath the canopy, creating patterns on the woodland floor.

Not until we moved to the Pacific Northwest did I find out that all woods are not created equal. The forests in Oregon are almost entirely coniferous. I was stunned to find, not to mention two or three times taller than eastern hardwood forests. Gigantic firs and spruces loom like somber giants, their branches interwoven to create a constant twilight on the forest floor. It's a good thing hiking trails are so common in the Northwest, because these woods are nearly impenetrable. The underbrush of wiry huckleberry, leathery-leaved salal, and waist-high ferns makes travel difficult except on paths. Instead of humus, the woods are aromatic with cedar and fir. Your footsteps are soundless on the thick, spongy carpet of needles.

Just about the time I got used to the deep, quiet cathedrals of the Northwest woods, we moved to southwestern Indiana–back to the hardwoods. We were so busy settling in and exploring our new surroundings (prairie flowers and grasses were a great distraction!) that it wasn't until my first Christmas in Indiana that I noticed that these woods, too, were different from my old Pennsylvania stomping grounds.

I like to cut my own greens for holiday decorations. But as I pulled on my boots that winter morning, I couldn't quite recollect where any

evergreens were. Surely there must be a white pine in the woods behind our house, I thought, but after a morning of hiking, I found that everything was indeed deciduous. This was new to me, so I got in the car to reconnoiter on the gravel backroads that run through the farm fields. Whenever I saw a conifer on the horizon—and you can see for miles in this flat land—I'd head toward it. Each time, the pine or spruce turned out to be in someone's front yard. Oddly enough, our corner of Indiana is bereft of conifers, except for the deciduous bald cypresses that dot the river bottoms.

Shaking my head in wonderment, I ended up clipping boughs from a prickly eastern red cedar along the hedgerow, missing those soft Oregon firs and Pennsylvania pines more and more with every "Ouch!"

Woodland or Shade Garden?

I call my front yard a woodland garden because I intended it to look like a natural woods. A little disorganization is fine with me: After having set the garden's foundation in place, I'm letting the garden go pretty much where it wants to.

Like other natural gardens, creating your own woodland is a learning experience. In the first year, you'll lay out beds and paths and settle plants into place. You may fool yourself into thinking that's your garden. But someone else's ideas are always at work in a naturalistic woodland—the best gardener of all, Mother Nature.

At the head of my driveway is a more controlled planting, and that one I call a shade garden. Each plant is carefully chosen and placed in a design I planned for texture and all-season color. No one would ever call it formal, but it has a more groomed look than my woodland garden, where plants mix and match among a free-form blanket of leaves. My shade garden is an ornamental planting, but it has a lot to offer wildlife, too: Myrtle warblers feast on the waxy bayberries, bees and other insects visit the coltsfoot when it blooms in early spring, and native sparrows tug off pieces of dried ornamental grass for their nests.

In years past, a shady yard used to be something to complain about. Most gardeners have wised up, although even today, I still hear people talking about how they can't grow anything in the shade. More than once, I must admit, I've found myself grabbing them by the arm while I evangelize about the pleasures of a shady garden.

Whether your style leans toward a densely textured planting of quiet evergreens or a blatant copy of Mother Nature's grand scheme, you can create a beautiful natural landscape in the shade. In both shade and woodland gardens, you'll enjoy the play of color and texture, the song of wind through the branches, and the trilling calls of courting birds.

The Shady Side of Gardening

If you're dreaming of a woodland or shade garden, you probably already have some shade. Maybe the garage casts a daylong shadow along a strip that you've tried to brighten with impatiens. Maybe your front yard boasts a beautiful old maple, with roots so thick and thirsty that nothing grows beneath it. Or perhaps the street side of your place is bordered by a tall hedge or fence that shelters you from traffic but casts quite a shadow.

Not all shade is created equal. Under a grove of firs, the shade is deep and constant. In my former woodland garden in Oregon, beneath firs and spruces, the wildflowers are true shade-lovers,

Footpaths are a must in the old-growth forests of the Pacific Northwest, where giant conifers can top 300 feet and the understory is thick with a tangle of vine maple, ferns, and young trees. A carpet of fallen needles muffles every footfall and soaks up the soft rain like a sponge.

Hardwood trees like these paper birches make a deciduous forest glow with glorious color in autumn. Common in northern forests from Alaska to Maine, they were "canoe birch" to Native Americans, who sewed the strong white bark over frames of cedar for their watercraft.

adapted to the all-season dimness beneath the evergreens. They included tall white fairybells, wide parasols of incredibly fragrant vanilla leaf, lacy tangles of rosy pink fumitory, and a carpet of wood sorrel.

Light is dimmed under an oak or Norway maple, too, but it's a seasonal effect. When the tree bares its branches come autumn, whatever is beneath it will be in the sun.

In springtime, when the warming rays of the sun reach through bare branches of oaks and poplars, my favorite wildflowers wake into bloom. These are the so-called spring ephemerals, like snow white bloodroot and creamy Dutchman's breeches, pink-tinged spring beauties and toothwort, and wild blue phlox and dwarf delphinium. These plants need sun to bloom and form flowers

Continued ➡

for next year, which is why they grow naturally in deciduous woodlands. By the time the trees' and shrubs' leaves grow in, throwing the garden into shade, the spring ephemerals have gone dormant until the next year.

One of the most unsettling sights I've ever seen was a spring woods in full bloom—in August. Hordes of gypsy moths had completely defoliated the trees, and when the sunlight reached the forest floor, it woke the spring ephemerals. Rose-breasted grosbeaks and wood warblers were moving through the trees in their drab fall plumage, while beneath them blood-root was blooming and mayapple was pushing up. It was downright weird.

The quality of shade, as well as its season, also varies. Beneath alders or birches, shade is dappled, with sunlight glancing through the leaves to speckle the ground in changing patterns. In the shadow of a garage or a neighboring building, however, shade is solid and unchanging.

If you're the type of person who loves details, you can keep a calendar that charts when your planned garden spot is in sun or shadow. And you can think about how the shade changes through the seasons, as the sun charts a higher or lower course through the sky.

A spot that gets morning sun in high summer, when the sun is northward and nearly overhead, may be in shade all day in autumn, when the sun slinks along close to the horizon. And vice versa, of course.

When you're planning a shade garden, there's no need to spend a year measuring the way the light shifts. Summer sun is the important factor. That's when the earth is tilted toward old Sol and the rays are most intense. Site your shade garden so that it will be out of the reach of the hot summer sun when it's at its peak, from 10 A.M. to 2 P.M.

But unless you're new to the neighborhood, chances are you already know where and when the shade falls in your yard. That's where you hang the hammock in summer, where you can't grow vegetables or grass, or where the last bit of snow lingers.

Shade-loving plants are adapted to lower levels of light. Their foliage will burn in the sun, and their growth will suffer if the sun is too direct or lasts too long. But except for a few absolute "shademasters," most shade-loving plants will adapt to partial shade as long as they're protected from the most brutal rays of the sun.

Shady soils can be moist or dry, just like those in other parts of the garden. Tree roots can soak up an enormous amount of moisture, especially if it's been a while since the last rain—even an inch of rainfall can leave the soil under a tree barely moist after the roots wick it away. And where rainfall is scarce, the soil may be bone-dry. You can handle dry shade in several ways: Choose plants that will thrive in dry, shady conditions; use mulches to help slow evaporation; and dig in organic matter to help your soil retain more water. Columbines, hostas, impatiens, and astilbe all prefer moist soil, but many shade-lovers will thrive in dry conditions. Try stout, spiny bear's breeches (*Acanthus mollis*), tall, blue American bell-flower (*Campanula americana*), fringed bleeding heart (*Dicentra eximia*), the invasive but beautiful plume poppy (*Macleaya cordata*), and two hellebores, Corsican and fetid (*Helleborus lividus* var. *corsicus* and *H. foetidus*).

Shade Garden or Woodland Garden?

The line between shade and woodland gardens is easily blurred, but there are distinctions that make your garden a shade garden as opposed to a woodland garden or vice versa. These general ideas will help you decide which direction is right for you.

Shade Garden

- Can be created in a small or large space. Even a 2-foot-wide strip can be made into an appealing shade garden.
- Is generally more controlled in look and feel, although the degree of control is up to you.
- Usually consists of low-growing, low-maintenance plants, including lots of ground-covers and evergreens, so it looks good and green year-round.
- Is in shade almost all the time, in every season.
- Can be created anywhere you have part or full shade: where a tree or a building casts a shadow, between your house and your neighbor's, or on the north side of your home.
- Includes more "exotic" plants that wouldn't naturally grow in your area.
- Attracts birds and small mammals seeking food and shelter.

Woodland Garden

- Needs plenty of elbowroom to look natural. Fifty square feet is about the minimum, although you might create a strip of woodland garden (10 x 30 feet or more) along a walk or drive.
- Is more naturalistic in look and feel. At its finest, it looks like a piece of natural woods transplanted to your yard.
- Has a seasonal look that mirrors the natural woodland of your area.
- May change in sun or shade exposure, depending on the season.
- Needs trees for an underpinning. If your yard is graced by shade trees, or even a single good-size tree, you have the perfect foundation for a woodland garden. If you don't already have trees, you can add them.
- Includes many native species, but can also be rounded out with ornamentals that maintain the effect.
- Attracts nesting birds and mammals.

Start with Structure

Once you have your shady site picked out, it's time to do a little planning. As with any garden, you'll want to start by laying out the basic structure.

Paths in any garden are a major part of the garden framework, and they're what I always start with. Then I plan for height and "hardscape" elements like walls and structures, the other things that give a garden some backbone. The last thing I do is plant evergreens to help the garden hold its shape in winter.

In my Indiana woodland garden, once I had an idea where the paths would go, I started planning the understory. I didn't want the three old shade trees to stick out like sore thumbs. I needed to step them down with a second layer of shorter trees, to provide a transition between the shade trees and lower-growing plants.

Adding an Understory

The layer of shorter trees and shrubs that surround mature trees in a natural woods is called the understory, and it's a vital part of a woodland—and a woodland garden. Many understory trees are actually understudies—youngsters of the dominant forest species that come into their own when an old patriarch keels over, creating an opening for more sun. These trees typically grow tall and spare, concentrating their energy on pushing upward toward the sun, not on growing side branches.

The more attractive understory plants for a woodland garden are shade-tolerant, midheight species that will grow and branch normally, even in the shadows. There are plenty of good choices, from eastern deciduous woodland natives like American persimmon and eastern redbud, to western species such as vine maple and Pacific yew, to foreign, shade-tolerant species, including China's golden-rain tree, the signature tree of the former Utopian community here at New Harmony and one of my favorites for landscaping.

The easiest way to choose understory trees for a woodland garden is to spend an afternoon looking at different stretches of nearby woods. The first thing you'll notice is that much of the understory is made up of youngsters—10-, 20-, or 30-year-old trees waiting to take the place of their elders. But you'll find lots of midheight possibilities, too.

In our Indiana woods, I jotted down my favorites: persimmon, sassafras, redbud, dogwood, Kentucky coffee tree, and blue beech. If you don't know the names of your local trees, take a field guide with you, or collect leaves to identify later.

Beneath the layer of midheight trees come shrubs of all sizes, including those that cross the line to small tree status, such as fringetree and spicebush. I always run out of space long before I run out of possibilities—there are so many good choices, it's hard to stay focused. Choose those that personally appeal to you, but try for a mix of fall foliage, flowering, and evergreen plants, while keeping an eye out for those with good winter form. If a plant incorporates more than one good trait, hallelujah.

Between and beneath the shrubs go the herbaceous plants: perennials, annuals, ferns, and groundcovers. I don't mind admitting that I blatantly copy many of my planting combinations directly from Mother Nature. When I saw a patch of white violets mingling with pale blue Jacob's ladder, punctuated by spikes of blue camas lilies and surrounded by a ruff of spring green fragile ferns, I claimed the combination for my own and went home to order the plants from my stash of specialty catalogs. If it works in the wild, it will usually work in your garden, as long as you can offer the plants similar conditions.

Grow Your Own Trees

As you stroll the paths of your woodland or shade garden in spring, watch for the first unfolding

Continued ➡

leaves of baby trees. Even if there's no nearby natural woods, seedlings will sprout in your woodland garden from berries or seeds brought in by birds or on the wind or from nuts and acorns buried by squirrels.

Not only is it fascinating to watch the first tiny growth spurts of a tree, but it's also a good way to add to your garden. Try to leave the young seedling in place; it will grow faster and sturdier if its roots aren't interrupted. If you must move it, transplant as soon as possible and take a giant-size scoop of earth with the seedling to avoid disturbance.

In just four years, my woodland garden had sprouted an impromptu nursery of sugar maples, tulip trees, elms, beeches, hickories, four kinds of oaks, sassafras, wild cherries, hackberries, redbuds, dogwoods, and even two prized hawthorns—not one of them planted by me.

It sounds like such a bonanza would overwhelm the garden, but I've found that the young trees take care of themselves. Many of them die out naturally. Others grow so vigorously you can't believe it. Did you know that a two-year-old tulip tree can reach 4 feet tall? One of my three-year-old redbuds is taller than me.

It's incredibly satisfying to watch a tree grow from a seedling sprout to a sturdy specimen. I appreciate my garden-center trees well enough, but I have a definite fondness for the trees I watched sprout their first leaves.

Foliage Favorites

Designing a garden for a shady site will quickly move your focus from flowers to foliage. Though there are plenty of flowers that bloom in shade—lamiums, hellebores, and American bellflower are three of my favorites—much of the show is carried by the foliage of the plants you choose for your garden.

Except for a cherished planting of golden hakone grass, my shade-garden colors are pretty much basic green during the growing season. Autumn brings wonderful warm colors from shrubs and perennials and long-lasting impact from the miscanthus, spodiopogon, and other ornamental grasses, which mellow to tan and beige. Groundcover conifers acquire a tinge of red, gold, or silver with cold weather and shorter days.

I've learned that when I stick to a plain green color scheme, I can concentrate on textural effect rather than on color. My shade garden is like a needlepoint tapestry—it's rich with variations in color and texture, but they blend together into a cohesive whole.

In my shade garden, I use ground-hugging plants like bearberry and European wild ginger to add a change of height and some gloss to the planting. Because I want the shade garden to look good year-round, I use a lot of evergreen groundcovers in it.

In my woodland garden, I plant more casual groundcovers, including deciduous types. I like the spiky texture that white foamflower adds, and I choose the running type not the ones that stay in neat clumps.

I discovered one of my favorite groundcovers by accident. On one side of my woodland garden, where hardy geraniums bloom in spring, a wine of Virginia creeper sprouted from a seed probably brought in by birds. I had no place for the vine to climb, so I let it creep—and that's what it does best. Its interesting, five-part leaves provide greenery

Woodland Garden Design

Create a shady haven with a combination of shrubs, trees, and perennials that offer structure and beauty year-round.

Many of the plants in this garden offer colorful flowers as well as richly textured foliage. This garden offers all-season beauty, from earliest spring, when the star magnolias burst into bloom, to the glories of fall, when your shady spot will be glowing gold and orange.

In winter, the graceful forms of the deciduous shrubs and the weight of evergreens will give it structure until the seasons roll around again and the warming sun coaxes the ephemeral spring wildflowers into bloom.

Plant List

1. Deodar cedar (*Cedrus deodara*)
2. Flowering dogwood (*Cornus florida*)
3. American holly (*Ilex opaca*)
4. Hemlocks (*Tsuga canadensis*)
5. Spicebushes (*Lindera* benzoin)
6. Existing deciduous shade tree
7. Hazel (*Corylus avellana*)
8. Eastern white pine (*Pinus strobus*)
9. Thimbleberry (*Rubus parviflorus*)
10. Serviceberry (*Amelanchier laevis*)
11. Lowbush blueberry (*Vaccinium angustifolium*)
12. Waterleaf (*Hydrophyllum macrophylla* or *H. canadense*)
13. Rhododendrons (*Rhododendron* spp.)
14. Beaded woodferns (*Dryopteris bissetiana*)
15. Yellow birch (*Betula lutea*)
16. Heathers and heaths (*Calluna* and *Erica* spp.)
17. Log bench
18. Orange-flowered witch hazel (*Hamamelis* x *intermedia* 'Diane', 'Orange Beauty', or 'Copper Beauty')
19. American persimmons (*Diospyros virginiana*)
20. Virginia creeper (*Parthenocissus quinque folia*)
21. Winterberry (*Ilex verticillata*)
22. Christmas ferns (*Polystichum aerostichoides*)
23. Black pussywillow (*Salix gracilistyla* var. *melanostachys*)
24. American bellflowers (*Campanula americana*)
25. Hearts-a-bustin' (*Euonymus americanus*)
26. Bottlebrush grass and fall Japanese anemone (*Hystrix patula* and *Anemone japonica*)
27. Dead tree
28. Golden hakone grass (*Hakonechloa macra* 'Aureola')
29. Whipoorwill azaleas (*Rhododendron periclymenoides*)
30. Star magnolias (*Magnolia stellata*)
31. Dutchman's breeches and bloodroot (*Dicentra cucullaria* and *Sanguinaria canadensis*)
32. Japanese painted ferns (*Athyrium goeringianum* 'Pictum')
33. Pottery bird bath (basin only) set on a rock
34. Bench

Note: All shrubs and planting areas can be underplanted with spring ephemeral wildflowers, such as wood anemone, rue anemone, mertensia, erythroniums, mayapple, Jack-in-the-pulpit, bloodroot, and others.

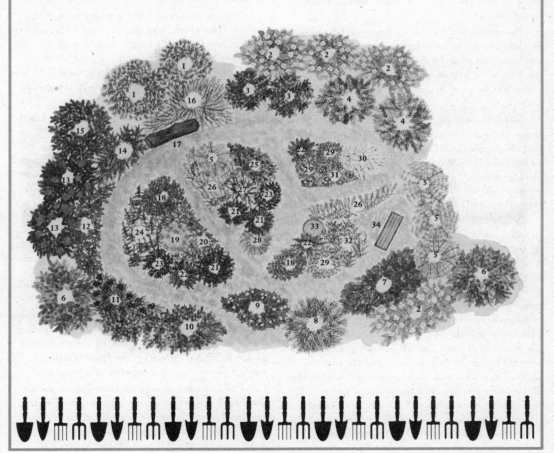

Continued ➡

through spring and summer, but in fall they literally shine. The foliage turns brilliant red and crimson, winding through my garden like a river of fire. As a bonus, mature vines bear deep blue berries that are eagerly sought by downy woodpeckers.

Fabulous Ferns

Ferns add a lush touch to a shady garden, even if you plant just a single clump. Beware of where you buy them, though—some unscrupulous suppliers dig them up from the wild to sell. If I'm ever tempted by the often bargain-basement prices of wild-collected stock, I think about what was destroyed so somebody could make money from it. Unless it says "nursery propagated," I don't buy it.

My friend Bill was transplanted to a new house after 70 years in the old one, and though he tried to make up for lost time, he never could re-create the gardens he'd worked on for half a century. What he missed most of all, he often said, was the fern grotto. Delicate, black-stemmed maidenhair ferns sprang from cracks in the granite, he told me, and misted like an angel's hair when the water sprayed over the rock. He planted maidenhair above a small pool at the new place, but it didn't have the same magic for Bill.

I thought the new planting was beautiful. Bill's ferns thrived above the water as if they'd always grown there. In my heart, I wondered what it was that he was really missing. Was it his position? His fortune? His youth?

It wasn't until years later that I found out just what Bill had given up. I was hiking along a spongy-soft trail in a stand of hemlocks when I came upon a real fern grotto. It was so beautiful that I fell to my knees without thinking, in absolute awe of such grace. Silvered with a fine mist, the rippling tresses of maidenhair fern bowed from every crevice in the wet rock wall. A fine thread of icy water dropped to a pool below, its depths so clear that I shook my head to try to clear my eyesight when a ripple spread across.

Maidenhair fern looks as ethereal as its name, but it's as tough as forsythia. Many other beautiful ferns will also adjust easily to life in a shade garden. If you've never explored the world of ferns, a shade garden is a great excuse to dig in.

Finishing Touches for Your Woodland Garden

For most gardeners, the finishing touches in a shade or woodland garden would be paths, benches, and the like. But for me, they're the first step—part of the essential bones of the garden. My finishing touches are mushrooms, moss, and other materials that make the garden seem real. But luring these humble plants into your yard isn't as easy as you might think.

The Marvel of Mushrooms

When I was a kid, I used to try to plant flowers. Literally, I mean. I'd stick dandelions and roses and whatever else I could find into the soil stem first. Naturally, lacking roots, every one died.

It's just as useless trying to transplant a mushroom. No matter how big a scoop of earth you take, you won't come close to collecting all of the many miles of the nutrient-gathering mycelial threads that keep the mushroom alive. A mushroom is only the "flower" of the fungus; it sprouts to spread spores for reproduction.

You can try collecting mushrooms for sowing spores (though I've never had any luck at it). Or you can just wait and see what comes up naturally. Shaggy mane mushrooms sprout every year in my front yard.

Can't-Fail Ferns

The ferns listed here will thrive in the shade in rich, moist, well-drained soil. Many other species and varieties are available, but these are among the easiest to grow.

To keep your ferns happy, mulch them well with chopped leaves and let fallen autumn leaves remain in place. The emerging fronds have a lot of lift power. In spring the new fiddleheads will push up right through last year's leaves.

Beaded wood fern (*Dryopteris bissetiana*). This unusual fern has dark green, leathery, 1- to 2-foot-tall fronds that are divided into round segments, which give the plant a beaded appearance. The arching fronds stay green all winter; the plant doesn't send up new fronds until summer. USDA Plant Hardiness Zones 5 to 8.

Christmas fern (*Polystichum acrostichoides*). Common throughout eastern North America, this classic evergreen fern settles easily into the garden. The clump of deep green, leathery fronds stays fresh all winter. Early settlers supposedly used it for Christmas decoration, but I find that the fronds dry out and curl soon after picking. Zones 3 to 9.

Cinnamon fern (*Osmunda cinnamomea*). Mighty clumps of 3- to 5-foot-tall fronds surround upright spikes of bright cinnamon-color fertile fronds. This plant makes a great punctuation mark with groundcovers or among perennials, and it makes red-orange or white impatiens look new again. In autumn, cinnamon fern turns a rich, rusty brown color. Zones 2 to 10.

Fragile fern (*Cystopteris fragilis*). This little charmer usually stays under 12 inches tall and may not even clear 6 inches. It unrolls its tiny fiddleheads very early in the season and is beautiful with ephemeral spring wildflowers. The lacy fronds are a clear spring green and go dormant by summer. Fragile fern spreads into colonies but is never a pest. Zones 2 to 9.

Hay-scented fern (*Dennstaedtia punctiloba*). This airy fern grows in light shade or sun; it's a good one to plant where woodland garden meets lawn. It spreads rapidly by creeping roots to form large colonies. Brush against the delicate fronds, and you'll smell the wonderful fragrance of newly mown hay. In fall, it turns soft primrose yellow. Zones 3 to 8.

Japanese painted fern (*Athyrium goeringianum* 'Pictum'). This is the showgirl of the big lady fern genus. She comes tarted up with silver and burgundy, but it's a wonderful effect in a shady garden. The clump of 1- to 2-foot fronds can expand to bushel-basket size in moist, rich soil. Just slice through it with a spade to multiply your collection. Zones 4 to 9.

Lady fern (*Athyrium angustum*, *A. asplenioides*, and *A. filix-femina*). The first two lady fern species named are native to America; the last is from Europe. All grow in a clump of fresh, medium green, erect fronds that grow 18 to 30 inches tall. "Crested" forms of European lady fern are much in vogue among fern fanciers; their fronds are sometimes so distorted that they look like curly parsley. I prefer the species *A. angustum*, Zones 2 to 8; *A. asplenioides*, Zones 4 to 9; *A. filix-femina*, Zones 4 to 8.

Maidenhair ferns (*Adiantum pedatum*, *A. aleuticum*). Native to eastern and western North America, these delicate ferns have fronds that radiate from a crescent-shaped axis at the top of a bare, blackish stem. Maidenhair fern gradually expands into a colony and looks beautiful on a slope, where its Rapunzel effect can be best appreciated. Zones 2 to 8.

Sensitive fern (*Onoclea sensibilis*). This was the first fern I knew, which is probably why I'm still partial to it. It is widespread in the eastern half of the country. It spreads like crazy, which can be an asset of not, depending on where you put it. Keep in mind that it will swamp all but the most stalwart plants. If you're tired of pachysandra, add this fern to the planting—they look great together. Fronds have wide segments, giving the plant a bolder appearance than the typical "ferny" fern. Sensitive fern turns brown in autumn. Zones 2 to 10.

One of my favorite fungi sprouts liberally in my wood-chip paths. It's the tiny bird's-nest fungus, a ¼-inch cup that holds minute brown "eggs." I like to put the "nests" into plastic specimen boxes with a tight-fitting, magnifying lid as a quick gift for young friends.

Moss Makes Your Woods Look Old

Moss is a lot easier to move into the garden, but, like fungi, it will often appear spontaneously if conditions are right. You can move small pieces of moss from other places on your property and press them into bare soil or on moist, decaying logs. Or you can buy a bag of prepared "moss bits" from a commercial supplier and follow the instructions for sowing. Don't decimate a natural spread of moss in the wild. Mosses are slow-growing plants, and it takes them many years to recover from even one afternoon's thoughtless collecting.

The Value of Deadwood

Collecting the final finishing touch, deadwood, can become habit-forming. Deadwood may not sound too appealing at first, but it's a great way to give your woodland garden structure and make it more appealing to wildlife.

Dead trees are prized by woodpeckers, and they make a fine foundation for a feeding area. You can smear peanut butter on them, wire suet to them, or hang feeders from them. A dead tree is also a favorite perch for birds approaching the feeder.

You say you have no dead tree? No problem. You can make one.

Unless your nickname is Samson, you're probably going to have more luck erecting a dead limb than an entire dead tree. Here's how to do it:

1. Choose a limb at least 4 inches thick and at least 6 feet tall. Stab a fingernail into it to make sure the wood is firm, not decayed.

2. For a short-term, one- or two-season "tree," simply plant your limb into the soil. Dig a hole at least a foot deep (deepen the hole if the "tree" is taller), insert the thick end of the limb, and firm up the soil around it.

3. For a longer-lasting "tree," you can fill the hole with quick-setting concrete before you

Continued

"plant." Mound the concrete around the limb so that it slopes downward, allowing water to drain quickly. But keep in mind that when the tree eventually falls, you'll be left with a block of concrete in the ground.

As with any dead tree, you'll want to avoid getting beaned if the thing topples. I give my dead "trees" an occasional medium-force push every now and then to make sure they're still standing firm.

Logs, stumps, and even sizable branches are heavy and awkward and hard on the back. Don't take on more than you can carry. Enlist a friend to share the labor. I sometimes amaze myself by balancing such heavy objects across my old metal wheelbarrow, holding them in place with a hoe, and finagling the barrow through the garden. But I don't recommend this procedure.

Deadwood is just as useful lying down as it is standing up, and it's often more decorative. An interesting log or branch can add a very artistic touch to a shade garden or that final bit of realism to the woodland garden. Add a good-size log (8 inches or better) to your woodland garden, and you hand an invitation to all kinds of interesting creatures. Fascinating click beetles, which pop and flip in your hand like Mexican jumping beans, will work on and below the bark. Engraving beetles will mark the trunk with hieroglyphics, and wood-boring beetles of all kinds will work on the wood. After bugs come birds, especially woodpeckers.

A log or stump also offers shelter for animals beneath it. When I dragged a toppled aspen into a previous garden, settling it between a couple of thickets of berry bushes, a cottontail rabbit dug a warren beneath it in less than a week. The stump in my current garden sheltered a cottontail this year, too. Actually, it sheltered six of them. If I lean down and peek at just the right angle, I can still see the soft bowl of grasses and fur that was their nursery. Mice and other small mammals will also make use of a fallen log. So will toads, salamanders, snakes, and lizards.

Another interesting character that may show up to investigate your deadwood is a skunk. Skunks are interested in the grubs that hide in the decaying wood, and like woodpeckers, they're adept at digging them out. Don't fret if a skunk turns up in your garden. If you treat it with plenty of respect and give it a wide berth, it will have no reason to spray.

I've appreciated skunks ever since one helped me out by excavating and destroying a colony of yellowjackets that had moved into my garden. I saw him sniffing near the wasps' nest-hole in the moonlight one night, and the next morning, the paper hive was strewn around the yard and nothing was left of the nest but an empty crater. I still don't know how he avoided getting stung.

Wildlife in Woodland Gardens

Deadwood isn't the only thing that will attract wildlife to your shady gardens. They'll also come to seek fruit, berries, nuts, and other foods and to seek shelter. Shrubs with berries and trees that bear nuts or acorns will draw birds and small mammals. Insects will move in to seek a niche and so will the creatures that eat them: mice, moles, voles, shrews, and other small furry types. Hawks and owls may scout your gardens hoping to catch the rodents unawares.

An unexpected bonus of my woodland garden is that it swiftly became a corridor of safety for the birds that live in the real woods several hundred yards away. Towhees, rose-breasted gros-

beaks, and scarlet tanagers now feel comfortable visiting my feeders, and wood thrushes and veeries scratch about in the leaf litter of my woodland garden. Vireos and wood warblers move from the tall sugar maples in the woods to the young redbuds and spicebushes in the garden, gleaning insects from the foliage. If there were less human and canine traffic in the garden, I have no doubt these birds would come to nest as well as dine.

Seasonal Pleasures

A shade or woodland garden is a wonderful respite from the summer sun. Even the dogs seek a haven there in summer, flopping on their sides beneath a favorite bush.

But it's a pleasure through all of the other seasons, too. In autumn, after the asters and goldenrod have finished the season in the meadow garden, my woodland garden is still a place of unexpected delights. Berries of spicebush and hollies ripen into shining red, as polished as the bowl of apples on my kitchen table. Leaves blaze with color, then sift down from the canopy into a wonderful crunchy blanket that's as much fun to kick through now as when I was a kid.

By the time winter settles in, chickadees, titmice, nuthatches, white-throated sparrows, and dozens of other birds have taken over the garden, gleaning the last seeds and berries, scratching aside the leaves, and scouring bark and branches for insects. Their quiet chips and call notes sound like a conversation among friends. There's always life and motion outside my window, even on the dreariest days (especially on the dreariest days—that's when the birds really come to forage). And snow in a woodland is one of nature's most beautiful sights. What a difference from a few years ago, when all I had to look out upon was a boring expanse of perfect grass.

Creating Water and Bog Gardens
Sally Roth

Water makes a garden a special place. Being around water, whether it's a pond, a brook, an ocean, or a fountain, refreshes and energizes us. Looking into water inspires both serious contemplation and idle daydreaming. And when you have water, you'll have all kinds of surprises. You may see regal great blue herons, slick-furred muskrats, iridescent dragonflies that flit about like living jewels, lotuses with flower centers that dry into huge salt-shaker pods, frogs perched on lily pads just like in cartoons—and that's just above the water.

Surface tension creates a thin film of water that is truly walkable, if you have the right equipment. Look on for water striders, which skate about like long-legged spiders, or whirligig beetles, which zip around in circles too fast for human eyes to follow. Catch one in a paper cup for a close-up look.

The submerged world holds even more curiosities. Turn over a few rocks in a streambed, and you'll get an inkling of what sorts of oddballs await in the water world. One summer, I enjoyed myself thoroughly introducing my sophisticated, well-traveled neighbor to the weirdos underwater. We crouched in the shallows, examining the primitive-looking, spike-tailed insects flattened beneath every rock. We fished out the vicious giant-jawed creatures that turn into jeweled dragonflies. And we peered at naked caddis-fly larvae hiding inside portable homes of cemented debris. Even in Rome, said my worldly

neighbor, he'd never seen anything to match this gallery.

Water also brings all kinds of gardening opportunities. Now you can consider wonderful water-loving plants, from classic water lilies opening their waxen cups to the sun, to tiny white flowers of starwort (*Callitriche hermaphoditica*) spangling the water like a handful of stars, to the striking lances of golden club poking up from cool, blue-green leaves. You can plant stalwart yellow and blue flag irises that wave like French banners, or you can indulge in extravagant Japanese irises, which grow to huge, ruffled perfection in boggy places. Before you know it, you'll be wishing for more space in your water garden, just as you do in your perennial borders.

I've been lucky enough to have natural water at or near every place I've lived, so I've never had to excavate for a pond. But I've lent my back and my advice to friends putting in ponds, pools, and fountains, and I've seen the transformation that water can work on a garden. It's magic!

Water Music

A still pool offers serenity and multiplies the impact of plants and sky reflected in its mirrored surface. But it's water music that brings a garden alive. The quiet burble of a fountain, the splash as water spills over a rock ledge, a silver thread of water tinkling into a fern-lined pool—our eyes follow our ears to the sound, and we are drawn to water as instinctively as any bird or other wild creature is.

Before you reach for that shovel, though, think about what qualities of a water garden are most important to you. Start by thinking about the water itself. A quiet pool has a much different personality than a rippling brook. If the sound of water is important to you, you'll want to add a small fountain or a recirculating stream. Or you can allow one side of the pool to lead off to a short drop, where falling water will play its music. If you opt for a fountain, there's a wide variety of possible effects, from a gentle shower to an arching spray to a thin trickle.

Besides the ephemeral pleasures of water music, there are more tangible aspects to consider, too. The kinds of plants we think of as typical water-garden plants—water lilies, lotuses, pickerelweed, and many others—thrive in still waters. You'll need a pool or pond area for these to do well.

Look at the lay of your land, too, when you're planning a place for a water feature. If you have a slight slope, that's a natural beginning for a waterfall or handmade stream. A recirculating pump and buried tubing will carry the water back to the starting point.

The size of your garden or yard is another thing to keep in mind. Of course you can't dig a huge farm pond in a typical subdivision or on a city street. But a small pond can fit in any garden.

Water Garden Visitors

If you build it, they will come. Birds, animals, bugs, and butterflies, that is. The traffic at your birdbath is nothing compared to the visitors you'll see at a pond. I love to check the guest register in the soft mud at the edge of the pond. Because many of your visitors will come in the night, you'll soon want to add a field guide to animal tracks to your collection. I look for the perfect pairs of half-moon deer prints, the widespread stars of skunk feet, the thumbed handprints of raccoons, and the big, turkey-like marks and white-lime splashes of herons.

Continued ➡

Best Trees for Woodland Gardens

Trees	Description	Conditions	Comments
Flowering dogwood (*Cornus florida*)	Small tree with graceful layered habit and beautiful white or pink flowers in spring. Reaches to 10'.	Partial or light shade. Moisture-retentive, organic soil. Zones 5 to 9.	Unfortunately susceptible to fast-spreading dogwood blight; call your extension agent about the extent of the problem in your area before planting.
Oaks (*Quercus* spp.)	Many species of medium- to large-size trees, all bearing acorns. Grows 100' or more.	Partial to full shade. Zones 3 to 9, depending on species.	Many oaks are widely adaptable, but it's fun to get to know your native oaks, like white oak and red oak in the East, Midwest, and North; Gambel oak in the intermountain states; and blackjack oak in the Southeast.
Redbuds (*Cercis* spp.)	Small trees with tiny pink or white blossoms thickly studded along the branches before the leaves appear in early spring. Reaches to 40'.	Partial to light shade. Average, well-drained soil. Hardy to Zones 5 to 8, depending on species.	Redbuds are ideal for planting under tall shade trees. Eastern redbud (*C. canadensis*) is a trouble-free small tree, hardy to Zone 5. In the West, try Western redbud (*C. occidentalis*), a shrubby, multitrunked species with excellent drought tolerance, hardy to Zones 8 to 9.
Spruces (*Picea* spp.)	Large, evergreen conifers with dense, short, stiff needles. Reaches to 150'.	Sun to partial shade. Average, well-drained soil. Zones 2 to 4.	Spruces have dense branches that make excellent protection from the elements for birds. Norway spruce (*P. abies*) and Colorado spruce (*P. pungens*) are widely adaptable.
Sugar maple (*Acer saccharum*)	Large tree with graceful form and superb orange and gold fall color. Reaches to 130'.	Sun to light shade. Rich, moist, organic soil. Zones 3 to 5.	Excellent shade tree. Outstanding red, yellow, and orange fall color, even on young seedlings.

Best Shrubs for Woodland Gardens

Shrubs	Description	Conditions	Comments
Flame azalea (*Rhododendron calendulaceum*) and pinxterbloom azalea (*R. periclymenoides*)	*Deciduous native azaleas with loose clusters of pink or white (pinxter) or red, orange, or yellow (flame) flowers in spring reaches to 9'.*	*Partial to full shade. Rich, moist, acid soil. Flame azalea, Zone 5. Pinxterbloom azalea, Zones 4 to 8.*	*These adaptable eastern natives are like manna to hummingbirds. Pinxterbloom azalea flowers are wonderfully fragrant, while flame azalea offers vivid, unusual flower color.*
Hearts-a-bustin' (*Euonymous Americana*)	Deciduous shrub to 8' with intriguing fruit capsules that split open when ripe in fall, revealing the red "heart" inside. Excellent fall color. Reaches to 5'.	Partial to moderate shade. Average garden soil. Zones 6 to 9.	This relative of the common landscape shrub burning bush is a quieter presence in the garden, though it still offers brilliant crimson fall color as well as decorative fruits appreciated by birds.
Pussy willow (*Salix discolor*)	Deciduous shrubs with charming furred catkins in spring, before the leaves emerge. Reaches to 20'.	Sun to partial or moderate shade. Average soil. Also thrives in wet soil. Zones 4 to 9.	Good for early foraging honeybees. A favorite for coaxing a bouquets in late winter.
Spicebush (*Lindera benzoin*)	Graceful, open, deciduous shrub with attractive form. Dark-barked branches are studded with tiny yellow blooms in very early spring. Reaches 4-15'.	Partial to full shade. Average soil. Also thrives in wet soil. Zones 4 to 10.	An underused American native. All parts have a pleasant spicy fragrance. Red oval berries are a favorite of thrushes and don't last long on the bush.
Thimbleberry (*Rubus parviflorus*)	Deciduous shrub with maplelike leaves, white flowers in spring, and red raspberrylike fruit in summer. Reaches to 6'.	Partial to moderate shade. Humus-rich acid soil, but also adapts to average soil. Zones 4 to 9.	Shredding bark adds to winter appeal. The similar purple-flowering raspberry (*R. odoratus*) is also good for the woodland garden.

It's a toss-up between frogs and birds as to who will find your water first. When my children were toddlers, a frog often moved into their shallow inflatable swimming pool overnight! But frogs aren't nearly as plentiful today as they were ten years ago, for reasons that aren't clear yet but may have a lot to do with ozone depletion. Frogs may still move into your pond quickly, usually within a few weeks, but chances are that your first visitors will be birds. A reliable source of clean, fresh water is a powerful draw for songbirds, especially if the area is planted with sheltering grasses and shrubs.

I love to watch birds reveling in their baths. Robins, goldfinches, blackbirds, native sparrows, and bluebirds are especially fond of bathing, but I have also been privileged to spy on evening grosbeaks, cardinals, chickadees, warblers, and, once, a scarlet tanager at the bath. But even starlings and English sparrows are fun to watch as they go through the motions.

At first they duck their heads tentatively, but before long, they're thrashing about with fluttering wings, as uninhibited as a toddler in the tub. When the bird is thoroughly soaked and looking as pathetic as a wet cat, it'll look for a place to preen and perch out of harm's way while its feathers fluff and dry. On a hot, dusty summer day, you know how good that bath must feel. But they'll also bathe in weather so chilly that brittle ice decorates the water's edge. It makes me shiver just to see them, even if I'm watching through a window.

Container Water Gardens

It's amazing how satisfying even a tiny water garden can be. If you only have room for one plant, grow a water lily. They may seem pricey when you compare the cost to perennials, but even the most common types are exquisite. A single water lily, partnered with a glimpse of dark, shining water, is a delight to the soul.

When space and time (not to mention money) were really tight one summer, I made a water garden in a big plastic tub—one of those "muck buckets" sold at discount stores. I chose a black tub, which looked surprisingly good when filled with graceful rushes, a single pink water lily, and the wonderful textures of water lettuce and ferny milfoil. (I can't resist those rosettes of ruffled, pleated water-lettuce leaves.)

My tub wasn't ultraviolet (UV)-light resistant, and it only held up for three years before the UV rays degraded the plastic and leaks appeared. But then again, it only cost $7. Large, sturdy, UV-resistant plastic tubs and pots are now made in appealing shapes and matte finishes and are widely available at garden centers. Or you can go the cheapskate route like I did and shop the housewares department.

Some gardeners use oak half-barrels, lined or unlined. I tried filling a half-barrel with water without using a liner, hoping the staves would swell and stop any leaks. It was a little tricky keeping the metal barrel bands evenly horizontal as the wood expanded, and the wood never became totally watertight, but the barrel did hold water. My half-barrel never did become a successful water garden, unfortunately, because my dogs claimed it as their own watering hole. After a few weeks of mourning over broken stems and damaged plants, I gave up on the water garden and let the dogs have their way. But I did get a nice bog garden out of it, thanks to the constant slopping of water over the edge of the tub and the slow leakage through the staves. Around the barrel's muddy base, moisture-loving plants, including forget-me-nots and even watercress, grew in beautiful profusion.

Continued ➡

Best Wildflowers for Woodland Gardens

Wildflowers	Description	Conditions	Comments
American campanula (*Campanula Americana*)	Spikes of azure blue open-faced stars appear summer through fall on a branching 3-5' plant.	Sun to full shade. Annual. Self-sows. Average, well-drained soil. All zones.	Unusual color for the shade. Scatter seed generously in fall; may not germinate until second spring. Let plants self-sow.
Bloodroot (*Sanguinaria canadensis*)	White stars and large, blue-green lobed leaves. Plants reach 8". Blooms in early spring.	Partial to full shade. Average, well-drained soil. Zones 3 to 9.	Reliable very early spring wildflower. Naturalizes well. Roots "bleed" red sap.
Dutchman's breeches (*Dicentra cucullaria*)	Mounds of lacy gray-green foliage and arching stems of little creamy "pantsloons." Appear in spring. Plants reach 8-12".	Partial to full shade. Humusy, well-drained soil. Zones 3 to 9.	Charming but tough. Spreads into colonies.
Fringecups (*Tellima grandiflora*)	Stems of tiny fringed green, white, or pink bells appear above rosettes of rounded, hairy leaves. Blooms in spring. Reaches 12".	Partial to full shade. Average, well-drained soil. Appreciates humus. Zones 4 to 9.	A northwestern native that combines beautifully with other shade perennials. Foliage persists after blooming, like heuchera, which it resembles. Spreads by thick rhizomes and will form a groundcover in loose, organic soil.
Jack-in-the-pulpit (*Arisaema triphyllum*)	Unusual peek-a-boo flower with hooded spadix over erect spathe, the "Jack." Plants have two three-lobed leaves. Blooms in spring. Reaches 2-3'.	Partial to full shade. Average, well-drained soil. Zones 4 to 9.	Tight clusters of bright red berries are relished by chipmunks and other wildlife.
Mayapple (*Podophyllum peltatum*)	12" high umbrella of usually one rounded, multipart leaf; Some plants branch into two leaves, hiding a single waxy white flower at their juncture. Blooms in spring. Reaches 1-2'.	Sun to full shade. Average, well-drained soil. Zones 3 to 9.	Watching the furled umbrellas of mayapple push through the soil and then open over a few days is a simple pleasure. Rhizomes spread freely in loose, organic soil to form colonies.
Wild sweet William (*Phlox divaricata, P. stolonfera*)	Semi-evergreen creeping perennial with beautiful blue-lavender flowers produced in great abundance in spring. Reaches to about 12" when in bloom.	Sun to full shade. Average, well-drained soil. Zones 3 to 8.	A beautiful companion to spring bulbs. Both species spread into large, loose mats. Several cultivars in various colors are available, but the species are worthy as is.

Best Groundcovers for Woodland Gardens

Groundcovers	Description	Conditions	Comments
Canada mayflower (*Maianthemum canadense*)	Also known as false lily-of-the-valley, a more descriptive name, this 6" native bears a single stem with two or three leaves topped in spring to summer by a cluster of small white flowers.	Partial to full shade. Loose, humusy soil; also thrives in poor soils. Zones 2 to 9.	Spreads by slender, creeping roots. Slow to establish at first. Nice as a textural accent with other ground covers.
Foamflower (*Tiarella cordifolia*)	Clumps of 1" or taller foliage like heucheras, with feathery spikes of tiny, creamy white flowers rising above the leaves. Spreads rapidly by stolons. Blooms in spring.	Partial to full shade. Moist, humusy; does not tolerate drought. Zones 3 to 9.	Beautiful with wild phlox and other native wildflowers. Allow fallen leaves from overhead trees to remain in place as a mulch. Don't be fooled by the variety collina (*T. wherryi*), which looks just like the species but doesn't spread.
Green-and-gold (*Chrysogonum virginianum*)	Rosettes of triangular, dark green leaves topped with short-stemmed bouquets of bright gold daisy flowers; plants grow to 6-23" tall. Blooms in spring.	Partial to full shade. Average garden soil; very adaptable, but not drought-tolerant. Zones 5 to 9.	Nice as an underplanting to shrubs. Long period of bloom, with sporadic flowers through summer.
Waterleaves (*Hydrophyllum* spp.)	Beautiful silver-splashed leaves grow from knotty, fast-spreading rhizomes. White or blue spring or summer flowers have fuzzy stamens. Reaches 1-1½'.	Partial sun to full shade. Widely adaptable. Zones 3 to 9.	Large-leaved (*H. macrophylla*) and broad-leaved waterleaf (*H. canadense*), shorter species with wide, silver-spangled leaves, are my favorites.

Best Shrubs for Shade Gardens

Shrubs	Description	Conditions	Comments
Korean azalea (*Rhododendron mucronulatum*)	Deciduous shrub to 8' with rose-purple flowers in early spring.	Partial to moderate shade. Acid, organic, humus-rich soil. Zones 5 to 8.	Blooms extremely early. Beautiful with emerging ferns.
Rhododendrons, evergreen (*Rhododendron* spp.)	Many cultivars. Evergreen shrubs with large, oval, glossy leaves and big trusses of flowers, often fragrant. Reaches 6-12' or taller.	Sun to full shade. Zones 4 to 8.	The sheltering leaves of evergreen rhododendrons give structure to the winter garden and offer birds protection in inclement weather. Flowers are visited by hummingbirds.
Red-flowered currant (*Ribes sanguineum*)	Deciduous shrub to 12' with very graceful form and dangling clusters of unusually fragrant deep pink or red flowers in early spring.	Partial to full shade. Humus-rich, moist, acid soil. Zones 5 to 6 (7).	This pretty shrub offers very early spring bloom for hummingbirds and berries for other wildlife.
Witch hazels (*Hamamelis* spp. and hybrids)	Deciduous shrubs or small trees with odd flowers like scraps of bright ribbons in spring or fall. Some are winter blooming.	Partial to full shade. Average soil; vernal witch hazel (*H. vernalis*) and Virginia witch hazel (*H. virginiana*) also thrive in moist soil. Zones 5 to 8.	Carefree shrubs with flowers just when you need them most—the doldrums of late winter. Vernal witch hazel (*H. vernalis*), to 10', has attractive, vase-shaped habit and blooms in very early spring. Virginia witch hazel (*H. virginiana*) is larger and blooms in fall and winter. Chinese witch hazel (*H. mollis*) is a Chinese species with yellow flowers in late winter. Hybrid witch hazel (*H. x intermedia*) has several cultivars.
Hollies, evergreen (*Hex* spp. and hybrids)	Evergreen shrubs and small trees with prickly leaves and showy red berries. Reaches to 50'.	Partial sun to shade. Average, well-drained soil. Hardy to Zones 4 to 9, depending on species.	Good evergreens for winter interest and shelter. Abundant berries are favorites of robins and other birds.

Continued ➡

Tubs and pots are heavy enough even before adding water, so decide on the location of your container water garden before you move it into position. A sunny spot is good for water lilies, but a partly shaded site will cut down on evaporation and algae. You'll need to collect a few flat stones or bricks to help boost plant pots to proper height inside the tub. I like to perch a rock in my container water garden as a sipping spot for birds or a landing pad for dragonflies. I set it on top of a submerged piece of clay drainage pipe so that the surface of the rock breaks the water but the underpinnings aren't exposed.

The biggest problem with container water gardens is that they're too small. Water plants move faster than Napoleon, and their aim is the same—to expand their empire. Even if you choose well-mannered plants, you'll soon run out of room for more than a few. What to do with the rest? If you're still not ready to install a pool, try a metal horse trough. These are long and narrow, shaped like a throat lozenge with rounded corners, and they have plenty of room in which to create a good garden. You can buy them new at farm-supply stores, or check country auctions. I found an old one at a farm auction for a few dollars; I gave it a once-over with a can of black,

matte-finish spray paint, and it did the job perfectly.

Natural Water-Garden Style

It's not difficult to put in a pond, but it takes some thinking to make it look natural. I love ponds and pools, but I wince at the unnatural stone edging I see all too often, even in the pages of the best water-garden-supply catalogs. Rubber and polyvinylchloride (PVC) liners have made it easy for pools to hold water, but the trouble is that the ponds too often end up looking artificial. They're surrounded by an edging of flat stone, laid as carefully as a flagstone walk. No matter how many water lilies grace the surface, the hand of a human is all too apparent in these gardens. I prefer my water gardens a little wilder, so they look like something that might have been there forever, not like something that was built from a kit and a truckload of stone.

For a natural look, you'll want to start with an irregularly shaped pool. Leave the rectangles and circles to formal gardens; their lines are too rigid to blend into a natural landscape. If you should happen to have a pool with a regular outline, you can disguise it with plantings that spill over its edges and merge naturally into nearby gardens.

Japanese maples, which dip their weeping branches down to the water's surface, can soften almost any pool.

Pool Options

In years gone by, if you wanted a water garden, you had to mix cement and mortar and tackle an enormous project that makes me tired just thinking about it. But water gardens are getting easier every year. With the advent of PVC and butyl rubber liner sheets, installing a pool is well within the reach of even mechanically challenged gardeners.

It's perfectly possible to install a backyard pool in one weekend of intensive labor, but I prefer to do it in three easy steps: I devote one weekend to planning and shopping, one to digging and installing, and one to planting and filling.

You'll save yourself some time and trouble if you call on your friends when it's time to put in the liner. They can help position the liner and hold the edges in place while you secure them. Liners are heavier than you'd think, and without several pairs of hands, it's easy for part of the liner you've just positioned to slip down into the hole. Also, it's a good idea to install the liner on

Best Trees for Shade Gardens

Trees	Description	Conditions	Comments
Kousa dogwood (*Cornus kousa*)	Small tree with layered branches and white bract "flowers," similar to flowering dogwood. Blooms in spring. Reaches to 20'.	Sun to moderate shade. Moist, organic soil. Zones 5 to 8.	This appealing tree and the related hybrid Stellar dogwoods (*C. x rutgersensis*) are vigorous and trouble-free. The red fruits are supposedly attractive to birds, but go ignored on my tree.
Cornelian cherry (*Cornus mas*)	Small tree with shrubby, multitrunked habit and cheerful yellow bumbles of tiny flowers along the bare branches in early spring. Reaches to 20'.	Sun to moderate shade. Average, well-drained soil. Drought-tolerant. Zones 4 to 8.	A tough little tree, undemanding and adaptable. Looks great underplanted with Virginia bluebells and muscari. Red berries follow flowers and are eagerly sought by birds.
Japanese plume cedar (*Cryptomeria japonica* 'Elegans')	An elegant evergreen conifer with soft clouds of green foliage shading to red and blue. Reaches to 150', grows to about 50' in a garden setting.	Sun to partial or light shade. Average, well-drained soil. Zones 6 to 9.	Adaptable and trouble-free. Needles look sharp, but are soft and springy to the touch. Foliage becomes tinged with plum purple in cold weather.
Red buckeye (*Aesculus pavia*)	Small tree or large open shrub with candelabras of tubular red flowers in spring. Foliage resembles that of horsechestnut. Reaches to 12'.	Sun to full shade. Average, well-drained soil. Zones 6 to 9.	One of the first trees to unfold its foliage in spring. Flowers are much sought by hummingbirds.
Serviceberries (*Amelanchier* spp.)	Small trees or shrubs with delicate, white, cherrylike blossoms in spring and blue-black fruits that are tasty to man and beast. Reaches to 5-20'.	Sun to moderate shade. Well-drained, acid soil. Zones 4 to 9, depending on the species.	The native serviceberries are enjoying a new popularity among gardeners, so more cultivars are appearing in catalogs and garden centers.

Best Wildflowers for Shade Gardens

Wildflowers	Description	Conditions	Comments
Heucheras (*Heuchera* spp. and hybrids)	Rosettes of pretty scalloped leaves with graceful 12-18" stems of white, pink, or red flowers. Blooms in spring or summer.	Sun to partial or moderate shade. Average, well-drained soil. Zones 3 to 9, depending on the species.	Many newer hybrids have gorgeous foliage. 'Pewter Veil' has dark-veined silvery leaves.
Trout lilies (*Erythronium* spp.)	Mottled or clear green leaves arising from a deep-set bulb, bearing a pretty nodding, six-petaled flower in yellow, white, purple, or varied colors. 6-24" tall, depending on the species. Blooms in spring.	Light to full shade. Moist, humusy soil. Hardy to Zones 2 to 8, depending on species.	Trout lilies get their name from the leaves, which are often speckled with brown or purple like the belly of a trout. They are long-lived and multiply, but may be slow to bloom after planting.
Virginia bluebells (*Mertensia virginica*)	An ethereal early spring beauty with light green oval leaves and 1-2' stems of dangling bells of rain-washed blue. Buds are pink. Blooms in spring.	Partial shade. Moist, humusy soil, but will also grow in clay. Zones 3 to 9.	Dies back completely after blooming, so plant among groundcover that can later camouflage the bare spot, or overplant with other shade-loving annuals.
Wild bleeding heart (*Dicentra Formosa*, *D. eximia*)	Lacy, gray-green foliage in shaggy 18" clumps with arching stems of pink hearts strung along a bare stem in spring.	Partial to full shade. Moist, humusy soil. Zones 2 to 9.	Wild bleeding heart (*D. eximia*), the native eastern species, does better in humid summer heat than the swestern species. Western bleeding heart (*D. Formosa*), which is more drought-tolerant.
Wild columbine (*Aquilegia canadensis*, *A. chrysantha*)	Intriguing, long-spurred blossoms above rosettes of lacy, gray-green foliage. Yellow-flowered *A. chrysantha* grows to 3½'; red and yellow *A. canadensis*, usually about 2'.	Partial sun to full shade. Average, moist garden soil. Zone 3 to 9.	Favorites of hummingbirds. Long period of bloom.

Continued →

Best Groundcovers for Shade Gardens

Groundcovers	Description	Conditions	Comments
European wild ginger (*Asarum europacum*)	Glossy, leathery, heart-shaped leaves appear in spring and spread in mats about 6" high. Evergreen.	Light to full shade. Well-drained, moist soil. Zones 4 to 7.	The shiny leaves are eyecatching among other textures in the garden.
Lungwort or Bethlehem sage (*Pulmonaria saccharata*)	Pretty pointed oval leaves are generously splashed and dotted with silvery white, an effect that subtly adds light to the shade garden. The 12-18" tall plants gradually spread to about 2 feet.	Light to full shade well-drained moist soil. Zones 3 to 8.	The spring-blooming flowers are similar to Virginia bluebells: they open pink from pink buds, then age to light blue. Pink and white cultivars are also available. If your summers are hot and humid, try long-leafed lungwort (*P. longifolia*), with extremely long, slim leaves spotted silvery gray and clusters of purple-blue spring flowers.
Western beach strawberry (*Fragaria chiloensis*)	Mat-forming strawberry with very shiny, deep green leaves. White flowers and red berries shine among the foliage.	Sun to partial or light shade. Very adaptable. Does best in loose soils and thrives in sand. Hardy to at least Zones 3 to 9.	A beautiful, low-maintenance ornamental. Birds, turtles, and toads appreciate the fruits.
Wintergreen (*Gaultheria procumbens*)	Creeping, prostrate evergreen shrub with small, shiny leaves and scarlet fruits in summer and fall.	Partial to full shade. Moist, humusy, acid soil. Zones 4 to 7.	Does best in cool climates. An old favorite for glass-bowl gardens.
Yellow, corydalis (*Corydalis lutea*)	Lacy, pale blue-green foliage, 8-15" high, looks good all season. Dainty, spurred yellow blooms held on wiry stems. Most abundant in spring, the flowers show up sporadically until frost.	Light to full shade. Well-drained, moist soil. Zones 5 to 7.	Self-sows, with a charming habit of showing up in niches of rock walls or brick paths. A fine-textured companion for hostas. Tricky to start from seed; buy plants instead.

This water garden evoked memories of the old oaken bucket. A pair of variegated irises draws attention to the always-trickling pump.

a sunny day—let it warm up in the sun first, so it's flexible and easier to handle.

Remember that smoothing out a liner isn't as fussy as making a bed. Don't worry about pleats and wrinkles in the liner; they'll soon be hidden by algae and the slight natural cloudiness of the water.

Edging Your Pool with Rocks

Liners and preformed pools are easy to install, but their plastic edges will stick out like a sore thumb unless you hide them. Rocks are the best choice for the job because soil alone will soon wash into the pool with the next good rain.

However, there's no law that says the rocks that hold the liner in place or disguise the edge of the pool must be all the same size. Incorporate several large rocks (or boulders if you can manage them) into the edging. Group them together naturally, varying the height by using rocks of different sizes or by layering them. Bury the bases of larger rocks partway into the soil to make them look natural. Extend the rocks into surrounding garden, blending them in with grasses and shrubs.

Be sure to use rocks that occur naturally in your area. Chunks of lava, for example, will look out of place in a limestone region. Keep in mind that quarried stone will also look different from weathered rock. The retaining wall of bright white quarried limestone in my garden stuck out like a spotlight until time added lichens, mosses, and natural stains to its surface.

Mottled or medium- to dark-colored rocks will blend into surrounding vegetation more easily than light-colored limestone or sandstone. But beware of a higgledy-piggledy effect of mixed colors. For a natural look, choose your rocks so that the colors blend with each other.

Sandstone will absorb water, which makes it a great place for mosses to start colonizing. Algae will colonize the rock first, giving it a green patina that makes it look like it's been part of the garden for a long time. Then mosses and lichens will move in. The drawback with sandstone is that much of the water it absorbs is lost through evaporation, so you may have to refill the pool more often.

Granite and slate don't suck up water like porous sandstone, and they're less hospitable to

Continued ➡

Water Garden Options

These days, when it's time to put ib your pool, you have several choices of water garden or pond liners. Concrete is still an option, but there are better materials available, including plastic and rubber sheet liners, preformed plastic pools, and an old farm-pond standard, packed clay. Here are the pros and cons of each.

Type of Pool	Pros	Cons	Recommendations
Concrete	Long-lasting. Reasonable price.	Messy, hard work. May crack from thawing ice. Alkalinity from lime may affect water balance.	Not recommended.
Packed clay	Cheap. Good for large-size pond in area with naturally heavy soil or where water naturally accumulates.	Heavy labor. Requires pounding with a rammer or sledgehammer or by repeated rolling. Large equipment may have to be brought in, which can damage lawn and garden.	Not recommended except for very large ponds. If you have a naturally boggy site, it's easiest to plant a bog garden there and install a lined pool elsewhere.
Plastic or rubber sheet liners	Can follow any shape or contour. Less expensive than a preformed pool. Can be extended beyond pool to create bog garden. Allows quick growth of algae on bottom and sides to disguise artificial nature of pond lining. Forgiving of excavation irregularities because it drapes easily.	Must be carefully installed to avoid sharp objects and leaks. Edges must be held in place with rock, timbers, or brick. Be sure to buy a liner that resists damage from ultraviolet light (sunlight). Butyl rubber lasts up to 50 years; less-expensive PVC lasts for 5 to 15 years.	Best choice for pools and ponds. Also good for streams and waterfalls, and excellent when used in combination with preformed sections in waterfalls and streams.
Preformed	Easy to install. Small sections can be linked together to form streams or waterfalls. Rigid pools will last for up to 50 years. Often include built-in shelves for plants.	More expensive than other options. May not be size or shape desired. If you want a bog garden nearby, it will have to be created separately. Most are too small for an effective natural pond. Many are too shallow (less than 2 feet) to accommodate overwintering fish and plants. Can crack without proper soil support. Edge looks unnatural and must be disguised.	Small units are excellent for creating waterfalls and streams, either alone or combined with lined sections.

Water Garden Visitors

Water gardens are rich with wildlife. Some will come to live there, some will come to drink, and others will come to dine. Here are some you might encounter.

Beavers, mink, otters: They may move to an isolated pond or stream, or you may see them eating or fishing.

Bitterns: You'll spot them looking for food or standing with beak stretched to the sky among the reeds. Watch for the least bittern, a tiny heron the size of a robin.

Cedar waxwings: They'll be flycatching—grabbing insects while in flight over the water.

Dragonflies and darners: Larvae are aquatic; adults are beauty on the wing in colors of silver, turquoise, cobalt, brilliant tropical green, and red.

Ducks: Only a big pond will draw ducks. If your pond is in the woods and away from human activity, you may be lucky enough to land a wood duck, the beauty queen of the duck world. Wood ducks are more reclusive than Howard Hughes. Unless you're very sneaky; you're more likely to see them fleeing than swimming.

Frogs: They'll move in fast and become summer-long residents.

Herons: You'll see them fishing for dinner.

Hummingbirds: Watch for hummers sipping from jewelweed near the water or collecting spider silk for nest.

Mayflies: Flat "bugs" with 3-pronged tails on submerged rocks are mayfly larvae. They hatch all at once, take to the air, and live only hours.

Minnows and other fish: Fish are brought in as eggs on bird feet.

Muskrats: They may be eating cattails or burrowing into walls.

Northern harriers (marsh hawks): These hawks will be patrolling for mice and rodents.

Nutria: Nutrias like to nibble on reeds and vegetation. They look like giant hamsters on steroids.

Opossums and skunks: These nocturnal critters will be scouting for food or looking for a drink.

Predaceous diving beetles: Big, black, and mean, those jaws mean business to unlucky aquatic insects or larvae.

Raccoons: You may see one washing up before dinner or catching frogs and fish.

Red-winged blackbirds, swamp sparrows, song sparrows: They may nest in reeds or other vegetation.

Robins and other songbirds: Look for these busy birds bathing and drinking, as well as nesting in nearby vegetation.

Spring peepers and chorus frogs: They'll call for mates in early spring, then disappear. These are tiny, thumbnail-size guys with a voice as big as Maria Callas's.

Tadpoles: Look for them on submerged decaying vegetation or on the bottom in the shallows.

Turtles: They'll be basking on logs or swimming. Look for black dots breaking the surface of a pond, and watch to see if they suddenly disappear or move: Those are turtle heads.

Voles: Voles may set up den tunnels in the banks.

Water striders: Watch them skate on the surface film. These are resident, spiderlike insects.

Whirligig beetles: You can see them whizzing in circles on the water surface, in tight groups of dozens or hundreds. They look like tiny silvery bumper cars at high speed.

Yellow warblers: Warblers may nest in willows and other shrubs near the water.

tiny rock plants. Their surfaces remain mostly bare until they're colonized by lichens. Use these rocks as accents or anchors around your water garden. If the rocks you're using are already weathered, remember your nature lore when you situate them: Moss grows on the north side.

Consider the angles of the sides of the rocks when you position them. If your rocks slant in all different directions, your pool won't be a restful place. The clashing angles will jangle your view.

Try to include one or two substantial, flat-surface rocks near the pool as sitting spots. But keep them back from the lined edge to avoid collapsing the edge into the water when you sit on them!

A cobblestone "beach" makes an appealing approach to a small section of your pond or stream. Place rounded river stones closely together, leading from shallow water to a grassy or boggy area near the water garden. (I always wondered where cobblestones got their name until I walked the Oregon beaches, where smooth, round stones of basalt cover the sand. As the waves washed in and then receded, the stones knuckled against each other with a wonderful, low-pitched "cobble-cobble-cobble" song.) Animals and birds are quick to take to a cobbled beach, where the stones give them a feeling of safety as they drink and bathe.

Plants are the best tool for softening the stony edges of a lined water garden. After you get your rocks in place, plant sprawlers, weepers, and creepers that will insinuate themselves over and between the rocks.

Planting a Pool

Planting a pool is not like planting a garden. Most water gardeners plant containerized plants rather than transplanting the roots into the soil, unless they have an unlined pond with a clay bottom. "Planting" is mostly a matter of moving pots around. Some suppliers sell plants already in pots; others sell bareroot plants that you pot yourself.

For the most pleasing view of your water garden, keep at least half of the water free of plants. Otherwise, you may begin to feel like you're in some plant-choked inland canal.

Continued ➡

Installing a Pool

Call on a friend or two to help make the work go faster and easier when you install a preformed pool. Many preformed pools come with a stepped edge, which allows you to grow plants that like shallow water near the edges.

Step 1: The old carpentry adage, "Measure twice, cut once," also holds true for digging. Hold the preformed pool right side up to mark its outline with stakes and rope or string.

Step 2: When the hole is dug, insert the pool and check for levelness and fit. Be sure the performed ledge, if there is one, is well supported by soil beneath it.

Step 3: Laying in a liner is easier with a helper. Lap the edges into pleats to ensure a smooth fit, but don't worry too much about wrinkles, which will be invisible once the pool fills.

Step 4: Line the edge of the pool with rocks to hold the liner in place. Vary the size and shape of the stones, and pile some in groups to mimic Mother Nature's freeform arrangements.

Step 5: Plants are the finishing touch. Lilies and other water plants can spread surprisingly fast. Be sure to keep some water clear as your plants mature; the view of water is one of the pleasures of a pond.

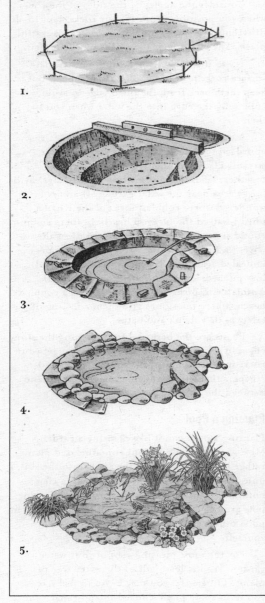

1.
2.
3.
4.
5.

Fill the pool to a depth of at least 1 foot, or below the level of your knees, before planting. Deeper water makes it harder for you to maneuver while planting. Plant from the center outward.

Start with aquatics, like water lilies and lotus, which do well in deep water. Aquatic plants are usually planted in containers with slatted sides that are open to the water. Because they are rampant growers, they'll need dividing when growth shows signs of becoming stunted. Tie a "handle" of plastic string across the top of the basket before you settle it into the pond. That makes it easy to lift later, to reposition or repot the plant. All you do is slip the handle of a hoe under the plastic handle and lift the pot out of the water.

Position young water lilies about 6 inches beneath the surface, by stacking shallow blocks or bricks beneath the pot, so that they don't exhaust themselves trying to reach the surface. As the plant gets stronger, you'll see more leaves appearing on the surface. That's when you can begin removing the blocks gradually, one at a time, until the pot is resting on the bottom of the pond.

After you place the aquatics, add a few oxygenating plants here and there; these fast growers will quickly fill in. Include two or three species of oxygenating plants, either planted separately or combined, but always in a container to control their rampant growth. Cover the soil surface of the pots with coarse gravel to prevent the soil from muddying the water when you submerge the containers.

Scatter a few floating plants, such as water lettuce, which dangle their roots into the water instead of getting nutrients from the soil. Place the floaters where they'll look pretty and have a bit of elbow room.

Moving outward toward the pool edges, add marginals like arrowhead and pickerelweed, which thrive in shallow water. Then finish your planting with moisture-loving bog plants such as irises and marsh marigold in the wet soil around the pond's edges. You may notice in some books and catalogs that there's not a clear distinction between many bog plants and marginals. Most of these plants will flourish happily in either shallow water or boggy soil conditions—and some will adapt to life in an average garden bed!

Examine all plants for duckweed before you put them in the water. This tiny aquatic plant has leaves barely 1/8 inch long, but it can cover a pond with a film of green in no time.

Unless you live in a cold-winter area, where they grow as annuals, do not plant water hyacinth, water lettuce, or other aquatics that have achieved noxious weed status. If you're not sure what's welcome and what's not, call your county extension office or the Nature Conservancy.

Adding Fish

Fish in a pond are fun to watch. I prefer minnows and other small, dull-colored species to the bright ornamental goldfish or koi that populate many pools, but that's a matter of personal taste. Some gardeners become avid collectors of koi, which can cost as much as a purebred dog (or a car!). To me, koi look as out of place in a natural garden as a plastic flamingo would look in a meadow. (Of course, if I lived in China, where golden carp do appear in wild waters, or in Florida, where live flamingos stalk the grassy flats, I'd have a different outlook.)

Pond fish are available at the same places where you buy plants and water-garden supplies, or you can buy goldfish at any pet store. They'll grow to amazing proportions once they're in a pond. Check a bait shop for live minnows and small fish.

Wait a couple of weeks after you fill your pool before you add fish to allow the plants time to get rooted. Fish may dislodge even established roots as they poke around looking for food. Your mosquito population will nosedive once you have fish; wigglers (mosquito larvae) are a prime fish food. Fish also eat algae, so they'll help keep your water looking clear. And goldfish love to eat duckweed.

Sometimes simple is best. This water-lily garden mirrors the shapes of the flat rocks that rim the pool, lending a sense of serenity to the garden. Plants in the stone crevices soften the effect without hiding the architecture of the rocks.

Continued ➡

Plants to Soften a Pool's Edge

Try these plants to disguise the edge of your pool. Some, like ivy and ajuga, trail over the water's edge. Others, like the ferns, astilbes, and heavenly bamboo, add a feathery look to the water garden. All will make the transition from water to land look more natural.

Astilbes (*Astilbe* spp.): Stalwart perennials with divided foliage and plumy spires of flowers, either arching or erect, in shades of red, pink, pink-purple, and white. Zone 4.

Brooklime (*veronica beccabunga*): Beautiful, true-blue flowering tender perennial. The fast-spreading 1-foot-tall plant has sprawling habit and succulent stems. Zone 8.

Bugle (*Ajuga reptans*): Familiar mat-forming groundcover with ground-hugging leaves and spikes of blue (sometimes pink) flowers. Zone 3.

Buttercups (*Ranunculus* spp.): Many species of buttery-yellow-flowered perennials. Aggressively invasive, which may be a positive trait in your water garden edging. Most to Zone 3.

Forget-me-nots (*Myosotis* spp.): Perennial and annual delicate pale or true blue flowers on scrambling, low-growing plants. A beauty. Most to Zone 3, but self-sow abundantly and often bloom first year, so can be grown as annuals.

Heavenly bamboo (*Nandina domestica*): Shrub with airy, bamboo like foliage. Many good cultivars, from dwarf groundcovers with flaming red foliage to 5 feet and taller. Zone 6 or 7.

Ivy (*Hedera helix*): Find interesting ivies in the houseplant section; small-leaved or lacy-looking types are pretty along water. Hardiness depends on cultivar; experiment.

Japanese maple (*Acer palmatum*): Shrubs or small trees with graceful shape and lacy leaves. Zone 5.

Kenilworth ivy (*Cymbalaria muralis*): Delicate perennial vine with scalloped leaves and tiny lilac-blue flowers. Great in crevices of rock. Zone 6.

Maidenhair ferns (*Adiantum* spp.): Fine-textured queen of ferns with beautiful fronds on wiry stems. Easier to grow than it looks. Hardiness depends on species.

Marsh marigold (*Caltha palustris*): Glossy round leaves with waxy yellow flowers are a cheerful sight in early spring. Spreads fast. Zone 3.

Meadowsweets (*Filipendula rubra, F. ulmaria*): Tall plants with compound leaves and airy clusters of pink flowers; almost shrublike in stature. Spread into large stands. Zone 3.

Ornamental grasses: Many species and cultivars, all with grace. Hardiness varies.

Sedges and rushes (*Juncus* spp.): Many species and cultivars. Choose the ones that appeal to you most. Hardiness varies.

Watercress (*Nasturtium officinale*): Deep green, shiny leaves with tiny white flowers. Leaves have excellent spicy taste before flowering. Zone 5.

Even if you don't introduce them, fish may show up in your pond. I used to puzzle over this mystery—were they falling from the sky?—but then I learned that they come in as eggs on the feet of ducks, herons, and other water-visiting birds.

Great blue herons, merganser ducks, green herons, and other fish-eaters will make short work of your finny friends once they discover your pond. You can prevent predation by stretching netting across the pool or by weaving monofilament fishing line across the water at intervals and among the edging plants. Water plants and rocks will provide some protection for fish, but catching these slippery creatures is a heron's job, and they are masters at waiting for the right moment. If a determined bird finds your pond, only mechanical means can save your finny friends.

If you've stocked your water with dime-store goldfish that you don't mind losing to birds, think of your water garden as a glorified bird feeder. (It's also a good way to avoid winter guilt when fish are trapped in ice.) It's a treat to watch herons and other birds fish. Great blues often flip their catch into the air, then swallow it head or tail first. Kingfishers take their prize to a nearby tree limb and bash it into submission by slapping it against the branch.

At Hawk Mountain, a Pennsylvania observation point on the migration route of hawks, I once saw an osprey come flapping along, its talons firmly gripping a nice, plump, bright orange and white koi. As the bird flew past the lookout, it delighted us watchers by casually reaching down and tearing off a bit of sushi on the wing.

Bringing Water to Life

A waterfall or stream can add a delightful element to your natural landscape. Water runs downhill, but that doesn't mean you need a steep hillside to create a waterfall or stream in your garden. A stretch of falling water needs only a very slight incline to be successful. Even in my flat midwestern garden, there are several good sites where water would naturally run downhill. If you can't tell the lay of your land by simply looking, layout a garden hose, turn on the tap, and watch where the water goes.

A streambed or waterfall can be as long and elaborate or as short and simple as you have room and muscle to build. The basic idea boils down to this: You need an upper pool, or "top pool," where the water originates, and a lower pool, or "bottom pool," which contains the hidden recirculating pump that will return the water to the top pool.

I find that a simple design with a few broad shelves of rock where water can spill over is more restful than a tumbling, complicated streambed, but in this, as in all other garden matters, suit yourself. If you have a slope with a drop of several feet, a series of rock ledges will make a wonderful, natural-looking waterfall.

Both streams and waterfalls are easiest to make by using a flexible PVC or butyl rubber liner. The liner edges are easy to hide, and you can design the twists and turns in any way you like. Preformed sections can also be joined together to make a bed. Alter the angles between them to create meandering curves like those a real stream would carve out.

Because streams are free-form, with bends and variations in width from one pool to

---

Plants for Every Niche

Water lilies are the first plants that come to mind when we think of a water garden, but there are lots of other possibilities. In fact, there are plants that are ideally suited to every part of your water garden, from deep pools to shallow edges and boggy areas. For a large pond to look good, you'll need a mix of plants from all of the following niches. A small pool can get by with only aquatics and floating plants, if they're what you really like. A bog garden, of course, needs only bog plants.

- Aquatics must have their roots submerged, so they should be planted in water that's 1 to 3 feet deep. Don't go overboard with aquatics; their big leaves can hide too much of the water. Aquatics include the familiar water lilies and lotuses, plus other less well-known plants like golden club, water hawthorn, and water violet.

- Floaters are surface plants like water lettuce and duckweed, which float on top of the water. They reduce algae by blocking sunlight and competing for nutrients, but they can also conceal the water. Floaters can overwhelm a pond because they reproduce so quickly. An occasional raking to remove the extras will keep the water visible. To remove duckweed, stretch a piece of cheesecloth over the tines of your rake or use a net to gather it.

- Oxygenating plants are mostly submerged, though their tops may be visible. They grow incredibly fast and help keep the water clear because they compete with algae for nutri-

ents. They also add oxygen to the water, which is some thing your fish will appreciate. These plants have exotic names like cabomba, anacharis, vallisneria, and myriophyllum. But they've become familiar to us because they're commonly sold in aquarium shops to oxygenate fish tanks. A newly planted pool will probably horrify you in a week or two, when the water turns green from algae. Be patient, though, and soon your oxygenating plants will starve out the scum.

- Marginals grow in the shallower water along the pond edge or in the very wet soil nearby. They're further divided into deep marginals, which like water about 12 inches deep, and shallow marginals, which grow well in shallow water (6 inches or less) or in wet soil. They include cattails, forget-me-nots, many sedges and rushes, and my personal favorite, western skunk cabbage.

- Bog plants are moisture-lovers that thrive in soggy soil. Once you see cardinal flower in full glory in a wet spot, you'll feel a little guilty about relegating it to a mixed border. Irises and sweet flag, royal fern, and astilbes also shine in boggy soil, along with a host of other interesting plants. Try buttonbush, with its fuzzy globes of white flowers and persistent seedheads. Or start a collection of willows. I'm partial to pussy willows, but any of the family are glorious in winter and early spring, when their bare branches flush with color.

Continued ➡

another, it's easiest to use separate pieces of liner for each section of stream, overlapping them at the ledges. A single liner is mighty unwieldy when you're working on a stream, but if you prefer to use one piece, round up a couple of patient friends to make the work go more smoothly.

Make your streambed wide—at least 2 feet—so that you can span it with a bridge and plants can spill over the edges without totally obscuring the watercourse. A stream can be much shallower than a pond because it won't be sheltering fish and water plants that need the protection of deep water from winter cold. Six to 12 inches is a decent depth for a stream.

A section of stream looks very odd if it ends abruptly. Disguise the terminus of your recycled stream by hiding it with shrubs or by extending the water garden into a bog. You can also stretch a streambed of dry rocks from the end of the water garden.

FALLING WATER FINESSE

Waterfalls have impact no matter what their size. Even the narrowest sliver of water can make a big splash, figuratively speaking.

Remember that all the water channeled into the fall will be pouring over the brink. To make a thin veil of water, you can widen a stream at the

Cross-Section of a Lined Pool

In nature, the plants you'll find at the edge of the water are bog plants that thrive in the wet or very moist soil naturally found there, But in a garden pond, the soil at water's edge is usually ordinary garden soil of average moisture, because the water is held strictly in place by the pond liner. To make bog plants happy there, you'll have to fool them by creating a mini-bog with an earthen dike and the pond liner.

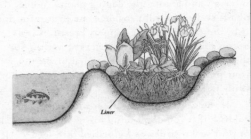

Mound the soil at the edge of your pond as shown here to create a catch basin of sorts where bog plants will get the moisture they need. Rocks on the ridge help keep the liner in place.

Making a Streambed

Create the illusion of a natural stream by piecing together several preformed ponds or stream sections. Layout the arrangement of the stream with a pair of garden hoses or with strips of cloth ripped from an old bedsheet. Start with a pool at the highest point. Move the outline around until you have a pleasing course. For a more graceful look, end the stream in a pool that is wider than the top pool.

Plan your stream in sections. When you dig out the streambed, leave a ledge of soil between sections of the stream. That way, the water won't all drain down to the lowest pool when your pump isn't running.

Dig out a narrow trench a few inches from the streambed to carry the hose for the recirculating pump from the lowest pool back to the top pool. Remove any rocks or other sharp objects from the streambed and rake it smooth. Spread a layer of sand ½ inch deep over the bottom, or layout a polyester padding liner in each section of stream. Lay the first piece of liner in the bottom pool, draping it over the sides and up the ledge to meet the second pool. Repeat as needed, overlapping the next liner on

top of the previous one at the ledges between stream sections.

After installing the pump and pipe, lay stone around the edges of all sections to hold the liner in place and to cover the hose trench. Allow the liner to extend outward beyond the stones. For the most permanent results, set the stones into a mortar of fast-setting concrete, like Quikrete. Build waterfalls at the ledges if desired. (See "Building a Waterfall" on the next page.) Lay the liner in the small top pool. After you've put in the liner, lay stone around the outlet pipe of the recirculating pump, which will spill into the small top pool, to hide the pipe from view.

Scoop the reserved soil onto the exposed edges of the liner, filling in between the rocks at the sides of the stream and burying the bases or the rocks partway so they look well rooted in the ground. Walk on the soil to firm it down. Add plants to the banks of the stream, planting them into the soil beyond the liner. It won't take long before they creep to the water's edge, giving your creation the look of a natural stream. Be sure to set some water plants close to the edge so they can blend with the edging plants.

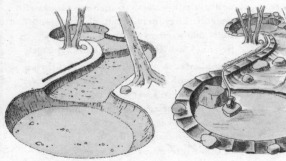

Dig out the stream, leaving a shallow ledge along the sides for anchoring the liner. Reserve the soil to cover the liner edges when your stream is complete.

Set the pump into the bottom pool on a flat stone base about 3 inches high. Site it close to the last ledge so that you don't have to run more pipe than necessary. Run the hose through the trench, along the stream, to the top pool. Fill in the trench with soil.

A leaky stream is aggravating, so check for leaks before you do the final touches. Fill the pools with water, and run the pump for about two hours to check for leaks. If water spills through the rocks and past the liner, mound soil under the liner at that point to raise it higher so that water can't escape.

Calendar for Pond Cake

Once your pond is planted, you'll want to watch for algae buildup, diseases or pests on pond plants, and leaks. If your winters turn cold and the water in your pond freezes, you'll have to make some allowances for tender plants and seasonal chores. If you garden in a warm-winter area, you'll need to control the growth of plants so that they don't overwhelm the water. Here are some season-by-season guidelines for good pond care.

Spring

Add marginal and aquatic plants. Rearrange plantings along the edge of the pool if needed. Clean out collected dead leaves and other debris from the bottom of the pool. Reconnect the submersible pump that was removed for winter storage. Bring aquatics out of winter storage and put them back into the pool. Collect rainwater in a wooden barrel for topping off the pool during the season; rainwater has fewer minerals than tap water, so it's less likely to cause algae growth. If snails begin devouring water-lily leaves, float some pieces of lettuce and skim them off with a net when they are full of snails. Listen for the chorus of courting frogs. Watch for migrating songbirds stopping by.

Summer

Refill the pond as water evaporates. Use collected rainwater, which won't change the chemistry in the pond. Rake or net off excess floating plants as needed to expose the water. Lift and repot any aquatic plants with stunted leaves or plants that produce lots of leaves but few flowers. Watch for green water, caused by excessive algae growth; add oxygenating plants to control. If long strands of algae form a blanket in the pond, rake them out and pile them on the compost heap. Protect fish from herons. Watch for leaks (dropping water level, wet soil) and repair with patches. Look for tadpoles and baby fish.

Fall

Put netting over the pool to block falling leaves. In cold-winter climates, remove the submersible pump. Remove yellowing foliage of water plants before it falls off into the water. Cut back oxygenating plants. Lift pots of tender water lilies and other tender plants before the weather turns cold. Overwinter tender floaters in a saucer of water in bright light, perhaps on a windowsill. For water lilies, slice off all growth to the crown and overwinter them in galvanized tubs in a cool garage. Or store the plants out of water for the winter by wrapping the pots in wet newspaper and storing in plastic bags in a cool but nonfreezing location. An old refrigerator, set to stay at about 35° to 38°F, is perfect.

Winter

Remove netting with fallen leaves. Adjust positions of rocks as needed. Check frequently to be sure water remains unfrozen if you have fish. Don't break the ice by hitting it; the shock waves can harm or kill fish. Install an electric pool heater if needed. Do not feed fish in winter in cold-winter areas; their metabolism slows as the temperature drops.

Continued ➡

point of drop with a shelf of thin rock. If the edge is fairly even, the water will fall in a single sheet of silver. A jagged, irregular front edge of the rock will break the fall into sections. You can also train the water over the face of a boulder for a whole different look.

I've always liked the surprise of delicate ferns peeking out from behind a waterfall. You can allow for a little planting like this by building a pocket of soil into the ledge, behind the face of the jutting shelf of rock that creates the fall. You can also fake it by setting a potted fern behind the curtain of water, hiding its container with extra rocks.

You won't have to fake it for long, though. One of the most gratifying things about creating a water garden is seeing how plants find their own niches. Places where you'd never think to plant are apt to be the spots where plants will pop up by themselves, their roots snaking into rock crevices to find the cool, moist soil below.

I love to watch mosses and lichens take hold on rocks by the water. Their textures and colors are beautiful, but in a subtle way that demands a close-up, unhurried look to appreciate the russets and olives, the incredible chartreuse and lime green.

Add a dead branch or log beside your streambed, and you'll be surprised how quickly it becomes softened by mosses. When mosses are silvered with fine spray, I can't resist running my fingers over them—but with only the lightest touch.

BRIDGING THE WATER

Bridges are more than a way to cross the water. They're a great place for dreaming and thinking, and they add physical beauty to the natural landscape. They also let you sneak up on things you otherwise couldn't get to, like that frog in the middle of the pond or the fish that hide out in deep water.

Keep your bridge as unobtrusive as you can. If a tree won't cooperate and fall in just the right place, you can use two unfinished wooden planks,

at least 2 inches thick, to span the water. If the spread is wide, brace the boards partway across with a support of rocks. You can also build or buy a graceful bow bridge or a simple flat-plank crossing, with or without a rough handrail of saplings.

Stepping stones can also get you out into and across the water. Settle them firmly so that a teetering stone doesn't surprise anyone into an unplanned dip.

The Bog Garden

I've always laughed when reading garden books that explained how to fix the drainage of a soggy spot. Shovel in sand and leaf mold, build raised beds, install drainage tile—why bother? That wet spot is a place to put in treasures that won't grow anywhere else.

My mother taught me how to turn problem sites into gorgeous gardens. When a place at the foot of a hill held water long after the rest of the yard dried out, she didn't frustrate herself by trying to grow bearded irises, dianthus, and daffodils that would have rotted in a single season. Instead, she brought in stately yellow flags (*Iris pseudacorus*) and partnered

them with a clump of shorter sky blue irises (*Iris versicolor*) that swiftly grew into a wide-spreading mat. At their feet was a cloud of blue forget-me-nots (*Myosotis sylvestris*). My mother didn't know the lingo for landscaping, but her natural artist's eye told her what looked good together.

It was my mother who taught me to look at natural swampy spots and see what thrived and then to translate the best of those plants into a garden. I loved the wildness of cattails, but she knew they were rampant growers that would quickly swallow the rest of the planting. So she helped me plant their tubered roots in old galvanized buckets, where they'd stay put. Thirty years later, I'm still a cattail lover, but I've learned about other species more in keeping with the scale of my garden: a Japanese species (Typhus minima) that grows cute, roundish balls instead of long, thick tails, and a native American species, T. angustifolia, which has long, slim cattails and narrow leaves that look as graceful as an ornamental grass.

If you like Japanese irises—those exquisite, veined blooms held wide open like angel wings, in soft purples, blues, and pinks—you'll love the way

---

Build a Dry Stream

If you like the look of a flowing stream but don't want to pipe water into your garden, you can mimic a natural watercourse with a bed of stones. Look for a natural depression for your stream of stone. If the area is dry all year, start by laying down a blanket of thick black landscape plastic to block weeds. Then pour sand over the plastic and set in smooth, rounded river stones.

Some gardeners put a dry stream along a swale where water already drains. If the water comes fast and furious, the stones will be dislodged, so it's best to set at least a foundation course into mortar. Landscape the edges of your "stream" with clumps of ornamental grasses that imitate the look of reeds along a natural stream, but don't obscure the water. Keep it visible from a distance.

A dry stream may fool a casual human visitor, but wildlife won't be tricked into thinking it's water. Insects and spiders, however, will love your new landscape feature. Hunting spiders that spring upon their prey, rather than orb weavers, will move into the crevices among the stones.

Building a Waterfall

A lovely, splashing waterfall can add more to your natural landscape than any other feature. And it's not much harder to build than a water garden. Once you've selected your spot, which should of course slope downhill, dig out a top and bottom pool, as described in the directions for making a streambed on the previous page. Line the pool, then take a look at your rock collection to pick out suitable pieces for the waterfall.

Choose a relatively thin, flat rock that spans the stream to serve as the waterfall rock. A piece of slate or shale will work well, but pick one that isn't too flimsy-looking. Fill in around the main rock as described in the step-step directions below, then install a submersible pump in the base pool. Place it on a flat rock base about 2 to 4 inches high, close to the waterfall. Lay the outlet pipe into the trench along the pools, so that it exits at the upper pool. Fill in the trench.

Finish the edges of the pools with rock. Fill the pools with water, run the pump, and check for leaks. If you've built carefully, all you should hear is the refreshing gurgle of the water as it spills over your falls.

Step 1: After you have lined the top and bottom pools, drape another piece of liner over the face and ledge for the waterfall. This will protect the bottom liner from being cut by rocks.

Step 2: Settle the rock into position so that it juts out over the supporting face of the fall and anchor it between large supporting rocks at each side. Work mortar in between the waterfall rock and the liner so that water won't sneak through underneath it.

Step 3: Fill in behind and under the waterfall rock with smaller rocks, to create a seal that directs the water over the falls. Mortar these stones into place to prevent them from being dislodged by the force of the water.

Step 4: Fill in soil around the edges and between the rocks. Add plants. Then pat yourself on the back and bring your friends and family to the garden to see your new waterfall.

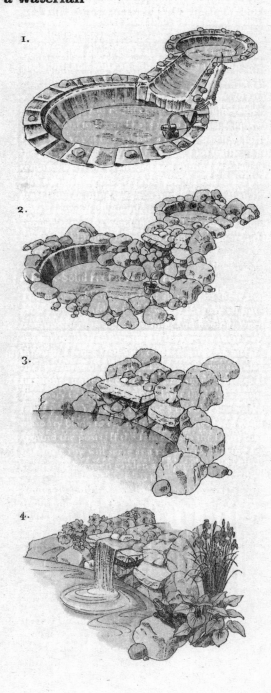

1.

2.

3.

4.

Continued ➡

Best Poolside Plants for Water Gardens

These plants are appealing near water. They thrive in moist to wet soil.

Poolside Plants	Description	Conditions	Comments
Astilbes (Astilbe spp.)	Easy to grow perennial with feathery plumes, either upright or arching, in shades of pink, red, or white above ferny clumps of divided leaves.	Sun to shade. Moist soil. Zones 3 to 8, depending on species.	Most astilbes are hybrids (A. x arendsii); the cultivar selection is enormous, from diminutive 1"-tall 'Glow' to 'Purple Blaze,' which can reach almost 5'.
Feather reed grass (Calamagrostis acutiflora)	Upright, 1-2' tall arching grass with showy panicles of flowers held well above the foliage.	Sun. Moist soil. Zones 5 to 9.	The cultivar 'Stricta' is deservedly popular.
Forget-me-nots (Myosotis spp.)	Annual and short-lived perennial species of low-growing, mounding habit with myriads of delicate sky blue or true blue tiny flowers.	Sun to moderate shade. M. scorpioides and M. sylvatica, two of the best, are hardy to Zones 3 to 8, depending on the species.	Longest-lived in cooler climates, but self-sow abundantly to renew and expand the planting.
Horsetails (Equisetum spp.)	Cylindrical, jointed, leafless stems grow in spreading colonies.	Sun to light shade. Moist to wet soil. Will also grow in average garden soil. Zones 3 to 11, depending on species.	Scouring rush (E. hyemale) is a common, widely adaptable species. The stems are banded with ash-color stripes.
Monkeyflowers (Mimulus spp.)	Several species of perennials with tubular flowers in various colors, including clear red, yellow, and blue.	Sun to part shade. Moist soil. Hardiness depends on species. Blue-lavender M. ringens, to Zone 3; red M. cardinalis, to Zone 7; yellow, often red-speckled M. guttatus, Zone 6.	An underused perennial with pretty and abundant bloom that lasts for a long time. Many self-sow, but never to the point of pestiness.

Water Garden Design

A natural pond, like almost every planting in nature, is incredibly diverse. Once you start to count the types of plants that grow in, on, and around the water, you'll find you get into double digits fast. While there's something to be said for the serenity of a water garden that holds just a few kinds of plants, I like to mimic nature with a grand jumble.

Shrubs and trees anchor this four-season planting. Bushes and irises add vertical exclamation points that play against the horizontal water. Of course the garden is filled with flowers, too, from the earliest pussywillows to the glorious lotuses of high summer and the unusually shaped turtlehead that closes out the season. In fall, baldcypress adds soft russet color, and grasses hold the spotlight into winter.

Plant List

Fill in nooks and crannies between perimeter stones around a liner pond and between larger plants with spreading or creeping plants that appreciate moisture such as:

Marsh marigolds (white and yellow) (*Caltha palustris*)

Primroses (*Primula* spp.)

Forget-me-nots (*Myosotis* spp.)

Moneyworts (*Lysimachia nummularia*)

Manna grass (*Glyceria maxima*)

Horsetails (*Equisetum* spp.), including contorted horsetails (*E. scorpioides var. contorta*)

Youth-and-old-age (*Tolmeia menziesii*)

Sweet white violets (*Viola blanda*)

Monkey flowers (*Mimulus lutea* and other spp.)

Dwarf sedges (*Carex* spp.)

Buttercups (*Ranunculus acris, R. repens,* and other spp.)

Iris pallida and other small irises

Use small water plants to add textural contrast on water surface:

Water lettuce (*Pistia stratiotes*)

Water clovers (*Marsilea quadrifolia*)

Parrot feather (*Myriophyllum aquaticum*)

Water buttercups (*Ranunculus fiabeliaris*)

'Pygmaea Alba' dwarf water lilies (*Nymphaea* 'Pygmaea Alba')

Fairy moss (*Azolia caroliniana*)

Note: Integrate the pond/bog garden with other plantings; don't isolate it in the middle of a lawn. Plant outward from at least one side of the bog garden, using other plants as the soil becomes less moist.

Water and Bog Garden

1. 'Flamingo' Japanese silver grass (*Miscanthus sinensis* 'Flamingo')
2. Umbrella plant (*Peltiphyllum peltatum*)
3. Tall moor grass (*Molinia caerulea* ssp. *arundinacea*)
4. 'Flame' red willow (*Salix alba* 'Flame')
5. Rocks
6. 'Zebrinus' banded bulrush (*Schoenplectus tabernaemontana* 'Zebrinus')
7. Sweet flag (*Acorus calamus*)
8. Goatsbeard (*Aruncus dioicus*)
9. Japanese irises (*Iris ensata*)
10. Cardinal flowers (*Lobelia cardinalis*)
11. Feather reed grass (*Calamagrostis acutifiora*)
12. Joe-Pye weed (*Eupatorium fistulosum*)
13. Pink turtlehead (*Chelone lyoniz*)
14. Cotton grass (*Eriophorum latifolium*)
15. Royal ferns (*Osmunda regalis*)
16. Blue pickerel weed (*Pontederia cordata*)
17. American lotus (*Nelumbo lutea*)
18. Papyrus (*Cyperus papyrus*)
19. Water lilies (*Nymphaea* spp.)
20. Large decaying stump
21. Yellow skunk cabbages (*Lysichiton americanum*)
22. 'Bowles Golden' sedge (*Carex data* 'Bowles Golden')
23. Golden club (*Orontium aquaticum*)
24. Yellow flag (*Iris pseudacorus*)
25. Scarlet rose mallow (*Hibiscus coccineus*)
26. Hooker's pussywillow (*Salix hookeriana*)
27. New Zealand hair sedge (*Carex comans*)
28. 'Kleine Fontains' Japanese silver grass (*Miscanthus sinensis* 'Kleine Fontains')
29. Soft rush (*Juncus effusus*)
30. Baldcypress (*Taxodium distichum*)

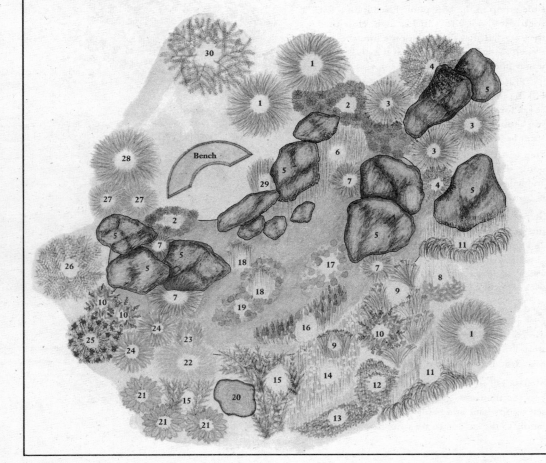

they flourish and spread in wet soil. They're one of the more expensive perennials, and I never had enough to satisfy me until I planted three of them at the end of our driveway, where water always puddled. I put in a weeping willow at the same time, with thirsty roots that helped soak up a lot of the standing water but left the ground moist. The irises outdid themselves in that problem spot, and for the first time in my garden, they began to multiply at a visible speed, almost as fast as daylilies.

Another plant that will adapt to ordinary soil but which shines in wet soil is the winterberry, or deciduous holly. The berries are fatter, shinier, and more plentiful on my bushes in a boggy spot than they are on the twin plants I placed in the "normal" garden. I planted them among a stand of soft rush (Juncus effusus) with deep black-green color that sets off the red berries. When the rush bleaches to tan in winter, it still provides good background texture and color for the dark-stemmed, red-berried holly bushes.

MAKING A BOG

Ponds and streams in nature have wet, boggy edges, where water-loving plants thrive. Gardener-built water features, however, are a different story. If you use a liner or a preformed pool, the water is kept inside so that it doesn't seep out into the sur-rounding soil (unless you intentionally install it that way). The plants outside the pool itself will have their roots in normal, dry soil.

Best Marginal Plants for Water Gardens

These plants are called "marginal" because you grow them in wet soil at the water's edge or in shallow water.

Marginal Plants	Description	Conditions	Comments
Arrowheads (*Sagittaria* spp.)	Glossy, arrow-shaped leaves in dense stands with spikes of white flowers accented with a purple blotch.	Sun to light shade. Zones 4 to 11, depending on the species.	Tubers of *S. latifolia* were once used as food by Native Americans.
Banded bulrush (*Schoenplectus tabernae-montant* 'Zebrinus')	Upright, cylindrical green stems striped with horizontal yellow bands.	Sun to partial light shade. Zone 7.	This spreading rush makes striking colonies at a pond's edge and in shallow water.
Cattails (*Typha* spp.)	Strappy, erect leaves with stiff pokers of packed brown flowers, like cigars atop bare stems.	Sun. Wet soil and shallow water. Zones 2 to 11, depending on species.	Cattails are a fast-growing plant for the waterside, but they can take over small spaces in a hurry. *Dwarf T. minima*, a Japanese species hardy to Zone 4, has short, fat, brown spikes instead of long "tails," and is much less invasive.
Papyruses (*Cyperus* spp.)	Umbrellas or pompons of leafy green atop tall stems.	Sun to partial shade. Wet soil or shallow water. Zones 9 to 11.	Grow as pot plant and bring indoors for winter in cold climates.
Soft rush (*Juncus effuses*) and other rushes (*Juncus* spp.) brown in cold weather.	Upright or arching, grasslike clumps with tufts of soft brown flowes.	Wet soil or shallow water. Zones 4 to 9, depending on species.	Soft rush is a widely adaptable beauty with dark green foliage and showy flowers. Hardy to Zone 4, it turns
Sweet flags (*Acorus gramineus*)	Fans of irislike leaves that rarely bloom.	Sun to light shade. Moist soil or shallow water. Zones 4 to 11, depending on the species.	Foliage has a lovely, sweet fragrance when bruised. Once used medicinally.

Best Plants for Water Gardens

Aquatic Plants
These aquatic plants are for the dee-water part of your pond.

Plants	Description
Golden club (*Orontium aquaticum*)	Broad, strappy, velvety leaves with a showy stalk of golden flowers, 3-5' tall. Can also be grown as a marginal plant. Zones 6 to 11.
Lotus (*Nelumbo* spp.)	Many cultivars and species with wide, round leaves held above the water's surface. Showy, water-lilylike flowers, often fragrant. Tropical species survive only in mild-winter areas. Cold-hardy species including the American lotus (*Nelumbo lutea*) grow as far north as Zone 2 or 3. Most species are hardy in Zones 4 to 11.
Water buttercup (*Ranunculus aquatilis*)	Forms large spreading mats of small, three-lobed, floating leaves (and ferny submerged leaves) dotted with small, white, yellow-centered flowers that look like buttercups. *R. flavatilis* is similar, with yellow flowers. Zones 6.
Water lilies (*Nymphaea* spp.)	Many cultivars and species with wide, flat leaves that float on the water's surface. Beautiful flowers, usually fragrant. Some night-blooming. Most are tropical species that must be taken inside in cold-winter areas. Hardy types vary in their tolerance for cold; refer to nursery catalogs to find out which will grow in your zone. Zones 3 to 11, depending on species and cultivar.

Oxygenator Plants
These plants float or grow in the water. All spread rapidly and may need occasional thinning. A rake does the trick.

Plants	Description
Hair grass (*Eleocharis acicularis*)	Very skinny leaves like fine blades of wiry grass. Actually a water rush in the Cypress family. Grows in small tufts. Zone 4.
Milfoils (*Myriophyllum* spp.) including parrot feather (*M. aquaticum*)	Several species of beautiful feathery-foliaged plants that add soft, lush texture. Hardiness varies with species; beautiful light green parrot feather, to Zones 7; others grow in Zones 3 to 11, depending on the species.
Pondweeds (*Elodea* spp.)	Familiar aquarium plant with curled whorls of small, narrow-pointed leaves. Hardiness depends on species; common *E. canadensis* and *E. nuttallii* hardy to at least Zones 5 to 11, depending on the species.
Starworts (*Callitriche* spp.)	A dense mass of small plants with fine, whorled leaves and clusters of tiny, white, star flowers. Sometimes called water chickweed, which it resembles. Several similar species. Hardiness depends on species; generally to Zone 5.

Floater Plants
These plants aren't rooted in the ground. They float in the water, usually forming mats.

Plants	Description
Frogbit (*Hydrocharis morsus ranae*)	Looks like small white water lilies, with leaves only one inch across. Many similar species, generally hardy to Zones 5 to 9.
Water chestnut (*Trapa natans*)	Interesting rosettes of diamond-shaped leaves with serrated edges on reddish stalks. White flowers followed by 1- 1¼" hard, black fruits that can be eaten. Naturalized in America as far north as New York. Zone 5.
Water hyacinth (*Eichhornia crassipes*)	An unwelcome pest in warm areas, where you should avoid planting it. In cold-winter areas, makes an attractive accent with bulbous-stemmed glossy leaves and pretty clusters of lavender flowers. Fish appreciate the cover formed by the abundant roots and runners. Only for cold-winter areas, where it will die after frost. Zones 8 to 11.
Water lettuce (*Pistia stratiotes*)	Another nuisance plant in warm areas, this pretty floater produces rosettes of pale green, wedge-shaped leaves like a tight-packed crop of garden lettuces. Do not plant in mild climates; in cold-winter areas, it will die with hard frost. Zones 8 to 11.

Continued ➡

Many bog plants are adaptable and will flourish even without constant moisture. You can create the effect of a bog garden beside a pool by using plants such as Japanese irises, which grow well in average soil as well as in true bogs, or by using plants with lush foliage.

But if you want a real bog, you can have a great deal of fun playing in the muck. If you're also installing a lined pool, you can make room for bog plants by leaving a stepped ledge along the top of the pool, anchoring the liner on the ledge with rocks. Then extend the liner from the ledge, allowing for a pocket of soil before sloping it upward above the water level. Bog plants will flourish in the saturated soil in the lined pocket.

You can create a bog garden without a pond by installing a liner at a depth of about a foot. Punch holes into the liner every 3 feet or so to provide slow drainage. A child's rigid swimming pool makes a good underpinning for a small bog garden. As with the liner, open some holes in the bottom so that you don't end up with a mud puddle. I've always loved royal ferns, but my site wasn't right for these native American bog plants. Until, that is, I dug a hole and "planted" a $10 kid's plastic swimming pool. Then I filled it with leaf mold, sand, and compost, soaked it until it was as sopping as a wet sponge, and grew fantastic ferns.

Whether it's a ferny bog garden, a stream and waterfall, a lush pond, or a simple container water garden, nothing lights up a natural landscape like water. Try it and see. And water gardening is addictive—you may not be able to stop with just one garden. That's because water—and water plants—are so delightful. Your local birds, butterflies, and other wildlife will agree.

DESIGNING STRUCTURES

Special Features for Every Garden

Sally Roth

The human touches you add to your natural landscape do as much to set the mood as the plants you choose to fill your gardens. Man-made elements like fences, walls, and path materials are major attention-grabbers in a garden. If they blend in gracefully, looking like something that might have occurred naturally, they'll reinforce the relaxed attitude of the garden. But if they clash with the style of the plantings, your garden will never look right, no matter how you shift the plants around.

Natural Fence Options

When I needed to fence part of my woodland garden to keep my dogs from wandering onto the road, I started by picturing the scene in my mind. I take a seasonal approach when I do these visualizations, imagining the garden with spring wildflowers, then cloaked in summer greenery, then mellow with autumn color, and finally in the bareness of winter.

I started my imaginings with a picket fence. How would a white picket fence look around my woodland garden? Way out of place, was the instant answer: Not only would the white paint draw attention like a beacon, but it would also emphasize the rigidity of regularly spaced pickets.

But I like picket fences, so I wasn't ready to give up on the idea altogether. In my mind, I gave the fence a coat of green-gray paint—now there's a job that's much speedier in the mind's eye than it is even for Tom Sawyer!—and tried the picture again. Spring and summer were fine because the fence was hardly visible. Fall wasn't bad. But in winter, the color looked artificial.

Best Flowers for Bog Gardens

Flowers	Description	Conditions	Comments
Cardinal flower (*Lobelia cardinalis*)	Stunning spikes of vivid red flowers rise to 4' above a basal clump of foliage. Blooms in summer.	Sun to partial or light shade. Wet soil, but also grows well in average garden soil. Zones 2 to 9.	A hummingbird magnet. May self-sow with restraint, but more plants are always welcome.
Great blue lobelia (*Lobelia siphilitica*)	Bushy clumps of foliage topped by branching spikes of blue to blue-purple tubular flowers in summer. Reaches 2-3'.	Sun to partial shade. Wet soil or average garden conditions. Grows well in heavy clay. Zones 4 to 9.	Beautiful blue color and a long period of bloom. Cut back spent flower spikes to promote branching and rebloom until frost.
Japanese iris (*Iris ensata*, Higo strain)	The royalty of the iris clan, with 2-4" tall plants and stalks of two to four glorious, flat flowers in summer. Blue, purple, white, or reddish violet.	Sun to partial shade. Wet, rich soil. Also grows well in shallow water or in moist garden soil. Zones 8 to 9.	For best effect, plant several of a single cultivar instead of a hodge-podge. Magnificent flowers.
Marsh marigold (*Caltha palustris*)	Low-growing, mat-forming plants with glossy, round leaves and gleaming, butter yellow flowers.	Partial sun to full shade. Wet or boggy soil. Also does well in moist garden soil. Zones 3 to 10.	Fast spreading, good for disguising the edges of artificial ponds. "Alba" has white flowers.
Western skunk cabbage (*Lysichiton americanum*)	An arum with clumps of huge oval, pointed leaves and unusual callalike waxen yellow flowers with heavy, sweet-musky scent. Blooms in spring and summer. Reaches 1-2'.	Sun to shade. Wet soil. Zones 3 to 9.	Another native beauty saddled with an unfortunate name. Treasured in British gardens. Naturalizes well.
Yellow flag (*Iris pseudacorus*)	Statuesque 5' clumps of scrappy irislike foliage with fleur-de-lis-shaped yellow flowers in summer.	Sun to light shade. Moist soil to shallow water. Zones 5 to 9.	A beautiful plant for poolside. Spreads into a significant clump and may self-sow.

Best Ferns for Bog Gardens

Ferns	Description	Conditions	Comments
Cinnamon fern (*Osmunda cinnamomea*)	Robust clumps of erect fronds reach as tall as 5', and sprout clusters of cinnamon-color fertile fronds in the center of the clump.	Partial sun to shade. Widely adaptable. Thrives in wet, lime-free soil but also grows well in average, humusy soil. Zones 2 to 10.	Easy to grow and statuesque. Beautiful golden color in fall.
Maidenhair ferns (*Adiantum* spp.)	Many species of delicate-looking ferns with lacy texture, from 8-30" tall depending on species.	Partial sun to full shade. Very adaptable. Need moisture but also do best with good drainage; give them a spot on the rocks in a bog garden or create a pocket of soil among the poolside rocks. Hardy to Zones 2 to 8, depending on species.	Maidenhair ferns look beautiful near water and are worth the bit of extra trouble it takes to elevate their roots out of the wet soil. They naturally grow in woods woods, ravines, on waterfalls and cliffs, and at streamsides. Most have creeping roots that expand to form colonies. Although maidenhair ferns look incredibly delicate, they are tough and adaptable.
Royal fern (*Osmunda regalis*)	Airy but good-sized, forming clumps as tall as 10'.	Partial sun to light shade. Wet soil. Zones 2 to 10.	Easy to grow in the right place, and a beauty. Stays in a compact clump.
Silvery glade fern (*Athyrium thelypteroides*)	Creeping fern with erect, arching fronds to 4' tall. Silvery undersides.	Partial sun to shade. Damp, rich soil. Zones 4 to 9.	Easy to grow. The silvery color of the frond's undersides comes from the whitish immature spore-bearing sori, which are attached in rows beneath each leaf.

Continued ➔

Back to the mental paint bucket. This time I went with a deep black-green, and I modified it further by making the pickets narrower and a little more rustic in design. In my mind, I planted shrubs against the fence here and there on both sides to create pockets of vegetation that occasionally obscured the wood. It was better, but still off.

Then I had a flash of insight: How about a weathered, unpainted fence? I kept the pickets narrow, stretched the fence a little taller, and tried it out. Perfect.

Of course, your choice of fence style is also mightily influenced by the thickness of your bill-fold. Luckily, compromise works well with fencing. You can use your desired, more expensive materials in short stretches, where they're most visible, and finish the job with inexpensive rolls of wire fence. Fast-growing shrubs and vines make good camouflage for the utilitarian parts of your fence. New plastic net fencing on the market, such as that sold for deer-proofing or construction, also makes a serviceable choice for fence-builders on a budget.

Make a Twig Fence

"Twig" fences are made of saplings or branches, not twigs. The name describes the style, not the materials. These fences have a rough, rustic charm that looks great in a natural landscape, and they're a good family project. Even a small section of twig fence lends immense appeal to the garden. You might use it to define the back border of your bird feeding area or to back up a bench.

To make one, you'll need a supply of branches that are about 1 to 2 inches thick and as tall as you want your fence to be. You'll also need some thicker wood, about 3 to 4 inches thick, for the horizontals and the section posts. If you don't have your own tree clippings, watch for work crews clearing utility right-of-ways or call a tree service.

Gather your branches while they're still green, and trim them to size with a hatchet. Strip off most of the smaller twigs, but leave some on to give your fence more personality. A simple picket-style fence is easy to construct. Nail the uprights to the horizontals at whatever spacing suits your fancy. Try to keep the spacing even, but don't be too rigid about it: Part of the charm of this kind of fence is its homemade imperfection. You can also lash the uprights together, using plastic twine for durability, followed by a wrapping of raffia for artsiness. If you want to experiment with a more complicated design, sketch it out on paper first. I've seen these fences done in rectangular sections, like a simple frame, with a crossed X of two pieces in each box.

Living Fences

If you're not trying to keep animals in or out, a hedgerow makes a good fence. If you want to discourage traffic from canines and others, you can plant prickly pyracantha or barberries to discourage passing through. You can also hide a simple wire fence in the bushes if needed to keep critters where they belong.

Choose plants that provide food and cover for wildlife when you plant your hedge. Viburnums, roses, brambles, and other fruiting plants are ideal candidates.

Slope Solutions

I don't know about you, but I don't have very much mountain-goat blood in me. I'd much rather amble along level paths on a hillside than try to keep my footing on a slope. Terracing is a sensible solution that will let you get more out of your slope—not only will you be able to enjoy the garden more comfortably but you can also get a better view of it. And most important, a terraced hillside is

less prone to erosion, as ancient farmers discovered millennia ago.

Making terraces is a matter of digging out soil from part of the hill and spreading it into a lower "raised bed," which you'll build out of wood or stone. I use landscape timbers, which are widely available, reasonably priced, and fairly easy to move around. Railroad ties are great, but they weigh a ton and are usually coated in creosote, which will

make your whole garden smell like tar on hot days. (In addition, there is the possibility that toxins from the wood could leach into the soil.)

Like the rest of my gardens, my terraces were built in a free-form way. I didn't measure or calculate feet and inches; I worked by eyeballing as I went. My technique went like this: "Hmmm, let's put a path along here, now another step of the terrace, a little higher, a little higher there,

Simple lines and weathered wood look best in a natural garden. They set off the plants without calling undue attention to the manufactured elements in the garden.

Natural Touches

It's always easier to play "what's wrong with this picture" than it is to decide what's right. The right garden bench can make a garden look great; the wrong furniture will stick out like a sore thumb and call attention to itself rather than to your garden. Here are some tips on choosing accessories that will match the mood of your natural garden rather than competing with it.

- Solid wood fences that create a wall seem to fade into the background.
- Fences with pickets or uprights are attention-getters. Their spaced lines create a rhythmic pattern that draws the eye. If you can't live without a picket fence, keep the pickets taller and slimmer than usual and more closely spaced.
- Think rustic when you're choosing a fence. Roughly split rails and posts that lean a little out of kilter are better than smooth, round, sanded rails and perfectly upright posts.
- Any painted objects in the garden will shout to be noticed, unless you choose a color that blends into the greenery. Muted, grayed midrange greens, black-green, and tans or browns are possibilities.
- Unpainted, weathered wood is least distracting.
- A patina of moss or lichens helps stone and concrete hardscape become a part of the garden. Instead of faking it with spray-on recipes, let the natural process of weathering be an education in another kind of plant succession.

perfect." If this method fills you with dread, follow the formula below.

Designing Paths

I depend on my dogs, my kids, and my own feet to show me where the paths should go. If the backyard traffic takes a shortcut through a flower bed, they're trying to tell me something. Unauthorized shortcuts are a clear message that the established path misses the mark. Unless they're in the mood for aimless wandering, animals and humans want a path that's the quickest route from one place to another. If you try to force their feet onto a winding, curving detour that wastes steps, they'll outvote you and create their own switchbacks.

When I'm planning a new garden, or a new path through an old garden, I follow different guidelines for different paths. If the path is from the house to the mailbox, from the house to the driveway, or leading to any other clear destination, I plan it as a utilitarian path—an express route. If it's a path for pleasure, then I let it meander. Of course, if human or animal footprints show me that a shortcut is needed, I make sure to include a straightforward route at that point, while still giving garden visitors the alternative of a slower, less direct trail.

Utilitarian Routes

When you want to keep your paths on the straight and narrow, use these tips. They guarantee that your family and friends will stay on the path and out of your gardens.

- Keep them straight, avoiding curves if possible.
- Make the path at least 3 feet wide for easy travel when carrying packages.
- Keep the surface level and "fast," as they say at the racecourse: Don't use loose gravel that will be hard to tread; instead, use packed material that will spur your steps. Wood chips will soon pack into a dense layer that makes solid footing.

Continued ➡

· Be sure the path is easy to see, both during the day and at night.

GARDEN PATHS

When it's not necessary to get quickly from point A to point B, plan your paths so that you get the most you can out of your garden. You can weave your paths in curves and cross them back and forth over each other to make the stroll a longer one.

One continuous loop through the garden is the minimum when it comes to paths. A single, dead-end path that makes you retrace your footsteps coming and going isn't nearly as much fun as a path that loops around and lets you keep going without doing an about-face. I avoid dead ends unless there's a sitting area at the end of the path.

To guide family, friends, and visitors to the main paths through the garden, mark these paths with a simple ornament. Anything that draws attention to the beginning of the path will work. These are great spots to use special favorites from your own collection or any of the garden ornaments sold in shops and catalogs. Here are a few suggestions:

· A pair of rocks flanking the entrance.

· A metal ornament with black, brass, or verdigris finish. I like to use a metal stick hummingbird, butterfly, or other natural subject. Many artists are beginning to turn out wonderful, whimsical designs, like oversize praying mantids and dragonflies, made of copper that will weather beautifully.

· A small metal or concrete frog, turtle, or other animal, perched on a rock or settled in mulch.

· A special rock or a small grouping of specimens: agate, crystal, volcanic lava, or whatever you've collected.

· A cast stone or concrete Japanese lantern straddling a thick, flat rock.

The width and shape of your paths have great psychological effect. A narrow path flanked by shrubbery will make passersby hurry through. Though we may not realize it consciously, our animal instincts sense danger in such close quarters. Widen a path, and footsteps slow like magic.

To make your garden seem larger, curve the paths. Sketch your plan on paper first, and you'll be surprised at how much mileage you can get out of a curving trail.

I like to allow plenty of options as to which way to go, so I include intersecting paths to give a choice of direction. Human feet don't turn corners easily, so instead of making paths meet at right or sharp angles, I widen the inside corners at intersections into curves to allow easy travel in either direction. Curved corners can be useful, too, if you want to

Build a Terrace

Before you begin digging, mark the outline of your terrace with string and stakes. Cut timbers for the sides of the beds to the length you've determined is your desired depth for each bed. Lay the first timber as shown below, then dig out the sides of the first bed, level with the bottom of the front trench and as deep as you have planned the bed. Lay in the first side timber. Repeat for the other side. Lay another front, overlapping it onto a side, then lay the sides and spike in place. Dig the soil out from the hill above to fill the bed you just made, and level it smooth. Add a back timber above the last course of sides, to form the front base of the second bed.

If this sounds like more work than you want to tackle, you might try a more informal approach. I've had good luck adding simple terraces, like a series of very broad, shallow steps, up a slope,

using just a front timber or two for each step, and letting the sides of the bed roll into the natural hill. I hold the timbers in place by pounding in two stakes outside the wall. I fill in the slopes on either side of my "steps" with daylilies, butterfly bushes, and perennial hibiscus, and use the terraced steps for shorter, trailing plants, leaving a clear pathway to walk up and down.

You can also use flat, fairly thin rocks or slate or even broken pieces of paving concrete as a retaining wall for terraces. Dig a thin trench about 3 to 6 inches deep and set the stones in vertically, leaning backward, with their faces turned outward. You might think this would look artificial, but if you plant alyssum, creeping veronica, and other sprawlers to spill over the edges of the slabs, it looks almost as good as a stone wall.

Dig a shallow trench to lay the timbers for the front of the first (the lowest) bed. It only needs to be a couple of inches deep. Settle the first timber into the trench.

Lay the timbers so that their ends overlap. Spike the front and sides in place with 10-inch galvanized nails, then lay the back timber of the bed, which actually forms the bottom timber of the front of the next bed.

Continue building and filling your course of beds up the hill, measuring to make sure the depth and height are going according to plan. Dig into the hill as needed to set the sides of each bed.

Plant in the beds and along the sides, to disguise the timbers and create the illusion of a hillside of flowers. Add some low-growing plants along the front, to spill over the edge.

Continued ➡

turn traffic in a certain direction: By curving just one inside corner, you encourage travelers to move in that direction.

When I have a plant I want to show off, I widen the path into a bulge at that point. That's an effective way to slow feet, and it lets my special plant get more attention. Intersections also get a lot of attention, so they're a good place to plant your favorite specimens. Of course, I look at every plant in my garden every morning, so these machinations are more for visitors than they are for me.

I find a path of carefully laid stone a distraction, but I like to keep a sense of fun in my garden by using log rounds or stepping stones to leapfrog short distances. Stepping from one to the other makes me remember my days in the woods as a kid, when I'd squeak through bushes and undergrowth by stepping from one rock or log to another. These types of stepping stone paths are often less obtrusive than full-scale trails, so they don't interrupt the integrity of the planting design or affect the mood of the garden.

Installing Low-Level Walkway Lights

A series of restrained, low-level pathway lights will make your steps surefooted after dark and show off your plants, too. Strands of electric path lights are available at any discount store. They're easy for even a novice to install, but you'll need an outdoor electric outlet within easy reach for plugging them in.

Step 1: Dig a shallow trench along the path where you want to install the lights.

Step 2: Measure the distance to the outlet, then lay in the cord and insert the lights at appropriate spacings. Cover the trench with soil and walk on it to firm it.

Step 3: Add plants around lights, being very careful not to dig into the trench where the wire is laid. Be sure the lights are unplugged until the planting is finished, so that you don't get a jolting surprise.

1.   2.   3.

Garden Paths Design

Multiply the pleasure of your garden by letting paths meander wherever there's room. Include a few intersections so that garden visitors can have choices of where to go next. Use shrubs to create a sense of mystery and anticipation of what's around the next bend.

You can adapt the ideas in this design to fit your own yard and your own plants. Work the paths around the existing trees and shrubs that anchor your garden. You can start with a basic framework of paths to get you to the mailbox, house, and car, and then add others as the garden evolves. I find that paths often suggest themselves—if I keep stepping into the groundcover to get a closer look at the caterpillars on the spicebushes, I add some stepping stones up to and around the shrubs so that I have easy access.

Path Design Key
Landscape Elements

1. Driveway	7. Bird feeding area
2. Front door	8. Sitting area
3. Utility meter	9. Water garden
4. Mailbox/news-paper box	10. Small tea table with two chairs
5. Privacy fence	11. Shrub
6. Street	

Paths
Often-Used Routes:

P-1 Path from driveway to front door: Should be as direct as possible for fast, sure-footed route.

P-2 Path from front door to mailbox: Should be straight and direct for those occasions when a quick route is desired.

P-3 Connecting route from P-1 path to utility meter: Should be clearly defined for meter readers.

P-4 Connecting route from front door to bird feeding station: Should be simple and direct with good footing and wide enough to haul supplies as needed.

Optional Paths:

P-5 Alternate route back to house from mailbox: A curving path makes the garden seem larger.

P-6 Curve the path around shrubs to create a sense of mystery and anticipation.

P-7 Widen the path to slow footsteps; a narrow path makes people walk faster.

P-8 Vary materials for different feeling: Flagstones around a water garden mimic stepping stones in a pond for a casual, fun approach.

P-9 Avoid dead ends unless there is a sitting area at the end of the path. Plan paths so that there are plenty of options as to which way to go.

P-10 Instead of making paths meet at right or sharp angles, curve the corners widely to allow easy travel in either direction. Curve only one corner if you want to direct traffic toward that side.

P-11 Place a particularly interesting specimen plant at wide intersections in the path. Wide places naturally invite lingering, so spice them up with something neat to look at.

P-12 Log rounds can bridge a short distance between paths—without interfering with garden planting design. They unobtrusively guide visitors to "squeak through" a place.

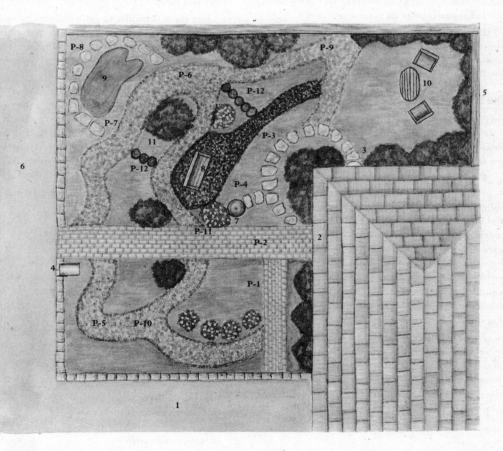

Continued ➡

PATH MATERIALS

Some years back, a friend brought two natives of Hong Kong to visit us. The girls were high school teenagers who'd lived in the city all their lives. As we led our guests out to the table in our shady yard, they began giggling and talking excitedly to each other, meanwhile walking very oddly, with high, bouncing steps.

Was something wrong? We wanted to know. They were extremely shy, but finally they explained. Never before, they said, had they walked on grass. All they knew beneath their feet was the concrete of city life.

I tried to give them a word to describe what they were feeling, but everything I thought of—springy, spongy, firm but with a give—failed miserably. What English word can convey that delicious feeling of walking on natural grass? For that matter, how could you describe all of the sensations of walking a forest path, or a river trail, or a sandy beach? You can't come close to summing up all of the things that make an ordinary day in nature such an incredible experience. It's not just the feel of humus or turf beneath your feet, but the scents in the air, the sounds of birdsong, the play of sun and shadow.

Why surface a path at all? You may not need to. *Au naturel* paths of fallen leaves, pine needles, softly packed earth, or sand are perfectly suitable. But in my area, rains can turn an earthen path or fallen leaves into slippery city. I like sure footing beneath my feet, so I use wood chips on my paths. In a meadow garden or other sunny area, you can use wide mown grass trails as paths, or you can plant traffic-tolerant groundcovers like clover or chamomile.

Natural materials are best for natural landscapes. Wood chips are my path surface of choice for a woodland or shade garden. In these settings, they look as natural as a deer trail. They're low-cost (or free), and they only need to be renewed once every couple of years in most cases. Installation is simple: Just rake them into a layer 4 to 6 inches deep. They'll pack down under foot traffic. And maintenance couldn't be easier: Just renew them as needed—usually once or twice a year.

If you're not fond of wood chips, or if you live where trees are scarce, turn to other natural materials. Your choices will vary depending on where you live and what the terrain is like.

The Fragrant Path

Forgiveness, an old saying goes, is the sense of the violet that clings to the heel that crushed it. I find walking on flowers a little sadistic but I don't have any compunction about walking on fragrant herbs.

Creeping thyme is hardy and easy to grow, and it spreads like mad. Roman chamomile is almost as obliging. (Don't confuse the mat-forming perennial Roman chamomile with German chamomile, a kneehigh, airy annual.) Both plants are great to work into an existing grass path. Or you can put down a wood-chip path and transplant starts of the herbs here and there along it. Walk carefully for a season, and the herbs will fill in nicely. Both release a delicious fragrance when you tread on them, and they quickly bounce back if traffic isn't too heavy.

Don't try herbs on the main path to your house because their leaves will quickly get worn off. But even on the busiest thoroughfare, you can plant chamomile, thyme, or creeping pennyroyal at the edges, where they can send aromatic tendrils out into the traffic.

Building a Stone Wall

Having grown up in the Northeast, where stones are a natural harvest every time you turn the soil, my attitude toward them was as objects of annoyance rather than objects of beauty. I remember reading a national columnist's advice for naturalizing a yard full of daffodils: Loosen the soil to a depth of 2 feet, she advised, so that you could plunge your arm into the soil up to the elbow. Right, I scoffed, thinking of the skinned knuckles and broken wrist that would result if I tried to do that. Planting bulbs for me was more likely to be a matter of working with a dandelion digger and making narrow slits into the earth to nestle the bulbs into.

I admired stone walls, of course, but it never occurred to me to try to make one until we bought the old quarrymaster's house at a former slate quarry. Suddenly I had tons of rock to play with, big slabs of charcoal-colored slate 6 inches thick or better.

"With such a ready supply just a short wheelbarrow's drive from my garden, I planned my first stone wall, a 30-inch-high, curved retaining wall for a raised bed of herbs and perennials.

I couldn't believe how easy it was to make. Though I boned up by reading step-by-step how-to books, the actual process was as instinctive as building with my then-two-year-old's set of wooden blocks.

BEFORE YOU BEGIN

If you're not blessed (or cursed) with an abundance of natural stone on your own place, you'll have to order it. Check the Yellow Pages under "Stone-Natural" to find dealers. Before you order, plan a visit to the dealer's yard to see samples of the rock. You can expect to pay about $100 or more a ton for natural stone. You'll want flat stones for easy stacking.

I was lucky to have my own rock quarry because I seriously underestimated how much rock I'd need. A couple of formulas from professionals will make it easy for you to get a handle on how much stone you need.

Use these formulas to get a ballpark estimate to see if the project fits your budget, then double-check your needs with your stone supplier. The final amount will vary somewhat depending on the type and size of the stone you select.

If your dealer sells stone by weight, your figuring is simple. Allow a ton of stone for every 25 square feet of the wall's face. To figure square feet, multiply the height of the wall times its length. A 20-foot-long wall that's 3 feet tall equals 60 square feet of face (60 ÷ 25 = 2.4 tons of stone). Allow a little extra for waste, and order 2.5 tons of stone.

If your rock yard sells by the cubic yard, you'll need to do a bit more calculating:

1. Measure the length of your intended wall in feet. Let's say 20 feet, as an example.

---

2. Multiply by the intended height and width. We'll make our imaginary wall 3 feet high and 12 inches wide, so 20 feet x 3 feet x 1 foot = 60 feet.

3. Divide by 27 to get the number of cubic yards, which is the measure by which stone is often sold by the truckload. In our case, 60 ÷ 27 = 2.222.

4. Add 5 percent to your cubic yard total to allow for waste—those stones that you can't gracefully fit into the wall. 2.222 x 0.05 = 0.111.

5. Add your totals from Steps 3 and 4 together: 2.222 + 0.111 = 2.333, or rounded up, 2.5 cubic yards of stone.

Garden Accents

Along with the gardening renaissance has come an explosion in art for the garden. No longer do you have to search out ornaments from antique shops. Now anybody with a phone can order all kinds of finishing touches, from Victorian gazing globes to resin gargoyles that look like they just dropped in from Notre Dame.

Remember that garden ornaments are like jewelry: It's better to have one great piece than it is to pin a dozen cheap sparklers to your bosom (though there are times, I admit, when I'm in the mood for flash). Instead of lining the edges of your pond with a dozen facsimile frogs, turtles, and bunny rabbits, why not invest in a statuesque, life-size heron?

Of course, part of the fun of a natural garden is that you can hide ornaments for visitors to come upon unawares. A concealing curve in the path is a great approach to a special piece of garden art. I have a small collection of concrete frogs (some not in the best of health) that I like to move around during the season. My son likes to discover their new hiding places. Sometimes I lose track of one or another of them myself, and then it's fun to come upon them again.

Keep in mind that any object made by human hands is automatically an attention-getter in the garden. Birdhouses, butterfly shelters, and bat houses are often focal points in the natural landscape. So use them sparingly but well—you, your visitors, and wildlife will all enjoy them.

Edgings

Fern Marshall Bradley

Edgings are picture frames for your landscape. They accent individual sections and help tie sections together into a unified whole. They also reduce mowing and trimming by preventing lawngrass from creeping into your perennials and by giving you a clean edge to trim up to.

Decorative edgings. Garden centers offer diminutive picket fencing, rustic log ends, terracotta tile roping, and other attractive edgings. Collectors may enjoy making their own edgings from large seashells, river pebbles, or salvaged bricks. If you're patient, try the timeless elegance of a miniature clipped box hedge. For a quicker version, try a hedge of tiny-leaved bush basil plants, or an edging made of willow shoots.

Hard-working edgings. For quick results, use a commercial black plastic edging made up of interlocking 8-inch-wide pound-in sections. It's easy to install, but you'll need to push it back in each spring because it tends to frost-heave. Roll edgings work well also. Spend a little extra when you buy plastic edging and get one guaranteed not to crack in heat or cold.

Back-Saver

You've heard it before, and it's still good advice: Lift with your legs, not your back. Bend your knees and crouch to pick up stone, boosting its weight with your heavy-duty thigh muscles when you lift. Don't bend at the waist, even though that seems easier, unless you want a long vacation at the chiropractor's office.

Continued ➡

Build a Hundred-Year Wall

Building a stone wall can sound more intimidating than it really is. Keep in mind that even a petite wall can carry a lot of weight, both visually and literally. But it's really not hard to build. I revamped my mother's always-eroding front garden one year by carving a path at the bottom of her steep bank and setting in a stone wall about 18 inches high to hold the soil. I added a second retaining wall about halfway up the slope, making it just two stones high and one stone thick. The whole project took only an afternoon, and the stone "walls" set off her collection of ferns and wildflowers beautifully.

Take your time when building—you want this to last forever. The only tools you'll need are a chisel and a stonemason's hammer to whack off occasional protruding bumps that keep the stones from lying smoothly. A level is optional, but don't forget safety goggles and a long-sleeved shirt and pants so that you don't get nicked by flying chips.

Step 1: Mark off the area for the wall with stakes and string, then dig out existing soil and turf to a depth of 6 to 12 inches. If your wall will have soil behind it, angle the back edge of this foundation so that it slants backward. Fill with coarse gravel.

Step 2: Pick out some of your biggest, most level stones, and lay them on the gravel. If your stones are rectangular, lay them endwise so that the short ends are at the face. Make sure they're solid and level. You can eyeball the horizontal lay of your wall by using a piece of string tied to two stakes, raising it after each course of stone. Or you can use a carpenter's level. You're not aiming for perfect flatness, just a general impression of horizontal trueness. In other words, you don't want your wall to look like it's crooked. Fill in chinks between stones with small broken pieces or gravel. Ram them in with the end of a hoe. Pour 2 inches of soil over the base layer of stone so that it's easier to level the next layer.

Set the next course of stone, working by the one-over-two rule. This time, you can set rectangular stones so that their longest side is toward the face, except at the ends of the wall. At both ends of the wall, set a rectangular stone with the short end facing front, as on the bottom layer, digging it into the earth behind the wall for extra stability. It also adds strength to set in a stone this way about every 6 feet along the wall. If your stones are wobbly, shim them with small pieces of rock until they feel solid.

Step 3: If your wall is built against a slope, fill in behind the wall after each layer with broken stone and soil, packing it in solidly with your trusty hoe handle. Continue laying courses in this manner. Put aside pretty, flat, large stones as you find them to save for the top layer.

Step 4: For the top layer, lay the stones as you did for the foundation, with their short ends facing the front. Finish packing the space behind the wall, and fill in with soil around the wall as you like.

1.

2.

3.

4.

Cast-in-place concrete edging with a mowing strip and a decorative edge of brick or stone, like the one shown on the opposite page, is very convenient and durable. The concrete base prevents the bricks or stones from falling over and from frost-heaving. Choose bricks or pavers designed to be walked on. If your ground freezes in the winter, choose severe-weathering brick.

Mixing your own ready-mix concrete isn't hard; just follow the instructions on the bag. To decide how many bags you'll need, multiply the width of your edging by its depth and length. This will give you its volume in cubic inches. Each ½-cubic-foot bag of concrete mix will fill 864 cubic inches.

When you work with concrete, wear tough gloves. Wash off any concrete that gets on your skin right away to prevent chemical burns. Don't pour more concrete base at one time than you can finish before it hardens.

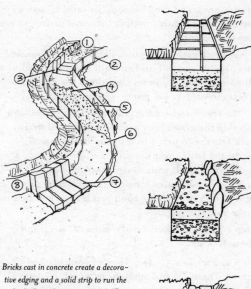

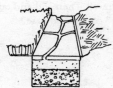

Bricks cast in concrete create a decorative edging and a solid strip to run the wheel of your lawnmower over. The edging takes some work to install, but you'll recoup all that work and more in saved maintenance time.

Step 1. Dig a 9"-deep, flat-bottomed trench. The trench should be 8" wider than the width of the edging.

Step 2. Hammer in wooden stakes and fasten 8"-high hardboard strips to them to make a form for the edging. Check with a measuring tape as you work to be sure forms are parallel.

Step 3. Set a few loose bricks in place to check that the form is correct. Pack soil into low spots to level the bottom of the trench.

Step 4. Pour a 4" layer of fine gravel into the trench between the forms, and use your feet or the end of a 2 x 4 to pack it smooth.

Step 5. Grease inside edges of forms with vegetable shortening so they'll be easy to remove after edging is laid.

Step 6. Pour 2" of prepared ready-mix concrete over the gravel; smooth it with a leveler.

Step 7. Set bricks in still-soft concrete; slant flat bricks slightly outward to shed water. Coat the forward edge of each brick with a ¼"-thick layer of ready-mix mortar. Use a putty knife to remove excess mortar and to cut a groove in each joint.

Step 8. Wait a few hours once bricks are in place. Then take off forms, fill in soil, and replace turf. Wait a few days before putting weight on the edging.

Continued ➡

Note: You can also make edgings from patio blocks, river rocks, or slate.

Paths
Fern Marshall Bradley

The minimum width for a foot path is 18 inches. For a path that's used daily, 3 or 4 feet is a more suitable width. On a 5-foot path, two people can walk abreast even if plants drape romantically over the path's edges.

Choosing materials

Paths that will take daily use should be smooth, solid, and nonslip. Poured concrete, asphalt, or large slabs of quarried stone are your best choices. Firmly set bricks or pavers or wooden walkways will also do but are harder to keep free of snow.

Loose material such as gravel, crushed shells, or sand makes a fine path for more leisurely strolling. Wood chips, bark chips, sawdust, mown grass, stepping-stones, and even bare soil in some climates serve well for lightly traveled, informal paths and are easy on the budget.

A brick path set in sand, like the one shown on this page, is easy to build and will stand up to all climates. If you live in an area where the ground freezes in winter, use severe-weathering bricks.

In regions where the ground never freezes, you can skip the gravel layer as long as your soil drains well. Dig the trench 4 to 6 inches deep, spread landscape fabric over the soil base, and add 2 to 4 inches of sand. If your design involves cutting bricks, get the professionals at the building-supply center to show you what tools you'll need and how to make cuts safely.

Step 1. Dig a flat-bottomed trench 12" deep and about 5' wide.

Step 2. Pack in a 5"-deep layer of compactable gravel. Then add and tamp more gravel to create a 9" compacted base.

Step 3. Spread landscape fabric over the gravel, overlapping the pieces.

Step 4. Lay two strips of rigid plastic edging along the sides of the trench, and use galvanized spikes to anchor one strip in place.

Step 5. Test-lay some bricks to determine exactly where to position the second edging strip. Anchor the second edging strip, keeping the two strips parallel.

Step 6. Spread 1" sand, water it well, and tamp it solid. Smooth out the surface with a leveler (a second person helps here). If the brick pattern involves straight lines, stretch a string guide now as a starting point.

Step 7. Begin laying bricks. Tap each brick sharply with a rubber mallet to set it firmly in place. Press bricks tightly against edging strips. Leave ⅛" gap between bricks.

Step 8. Use a leveler to check whether bricks are even. Tap down any high ones. Brush loose sand into the gaps until they are ¼" short of being full. Water with a fine spray. From this point on, you can walk on the bricks.

Step 9. Fold fabric over bricks and backfill the remaining gap with soil. Snip off the excess fabric ½" below the path surface.

Stone Retaining Walls
Fern Marshall Bradley

By building a stone retaining, wall, you can turn a tough-to-maintain slope into a productive and beautiful garden. A dry-laid (mortarless) stone wall is an excellent project for a beginning wall builder.

It's best not to try building a wall more than 3 feet high. If you have a slope that would require a high wall, you have two options: Either split the slope and build two walls with a level planting terrace between them, or hire a professional to build one high stone wall.

Step-by-Step Wall Building

If you don't already have an abundance of stones on your property, you can buy natural and quarried stone, or even manmade interlocking building blocks. To find sources, look under "Stone" in the yellow pages of your telephone directory. If you have stone delivered, have it dumped as close to the worksite as possible, preferably with about half of the load on the uphill side of your wall and half downhill.

Take it easy when you're working. Always lift with your legs, not your back; and if you can't lift a stone easily—don't lift it. Use a couple of stout iron bars to roll and pry stones that are too big to lift, and use sturdy wooden ramps to get them up onto the wall as you build.

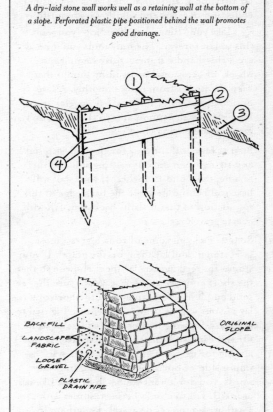

A dry-laid stone wall works well as a retaining wall at the bottom of a slope. Perforated plastic pipe positioned behind the wall promotes good drainage.

BACKFILL
LANDSCAPE FABRIC
LOOSE GRAVEL
PLASTIC DRAIN PIPE
ORIGINAL SLOPE

Step 1. Pound posts into the ground in a line along the area you want to terrace. Leave 9" exposed at the top.
Step 2. Nail two rows of 1 x 4 boards along the tops of the posts.
Step 3. Dig the soil out downslope and pile it above the wall to expose another 9" of post.
Step 4. Nail two rows of 1 x 4s to the newly exposed parts of the posts.

Here's how to build a stone retaining wall.

1. Use a spade or shovel to dig out a flat area at the base of the slope. Cut out a flat area equal to the thickness of the planned wall, plus 1 foot more. Pile the excavated soil up slope, or somewhere else out of your way.

2. Mark the outline of the outside face of your wall in the dirt. (Keep in mind that there's no law that walls have to be straight.) Then mark a second line behind the first, one foot back from the rear edge of the wall. For example, if your wall will be 1½ feet thick, mark the second line 2½ feet back from the first. Two flexible hoses work well for marking out smoothly curving walls.

3. Dig a 12-inch-deep, flat-bottomed trench between the two guidelines you marked. Don't dig deeper than 12 inches-your wall should be built on undisturbed soil.

4. Line the trench and 2½ feet up the exposed earth face with strips of landscape fabric, overlapping adjacent strips 6 inches. Anchor the fabric temporarily to keep it in place.

5. Pour a 6- to 8-inch layer of compactable gravel into the trench and tamp it down well. Fold the

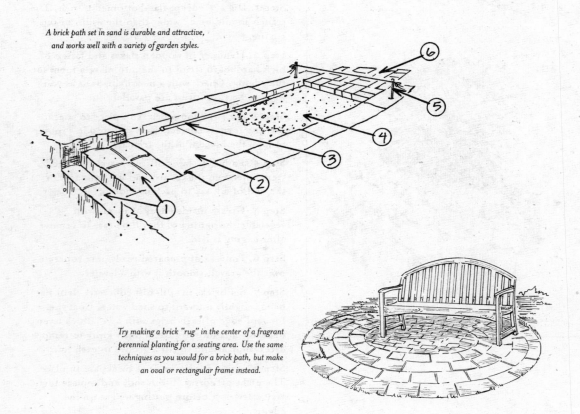

A brick path set in sand is durable and attractive, and works well with a variety of garden styles.

Try making a brick "rug" in the center of a fragrant perennial planting for a seating area. Use the same techniques as you would for a brick path, but make an oval or rectangular frame instead.

Continued ➡

fabric in over the gravel at the outside edge of the trench.

6. Spread out all the stones so you can see what you have to work with. Then, start laying up your wall. Place the largest stones first, following the outer contour of the trench. Adjust the underlying gravel so the stones sit firmly.

7. Continue adding layers, choosing the stones carefully. Ideally, each stone should span the joints in the layer below it, from front to back and/or from side to side. Overlapping the stones strengthens the wall. Also, make sure the stones sit firmly. If necessary, slip small, flat stones under the larger ones to remove any wobble.

8. When the wall is about 1 foot high, lay a length of 4-inch-diameter perforated plastic pipe on the gravel behind it for drainage. The pipe will exit the wall at a corner. Or, if your wall will not have exposed corners, use an elbow to direct the pipe out through the front of the wall. Cover the pipe with 1 foot of loose, coarse gravel and fold the landscape fabric over the gravel toward the wall.

9. Lay more layers of stone, making the wall a little narrower with each layer (about 2 inches for every foot of height). Keep the back of the wall vertical, and taper the outside. Use large, flat stones for the top layer, then backfill in behind the wall with the soil you dug out of the slope.

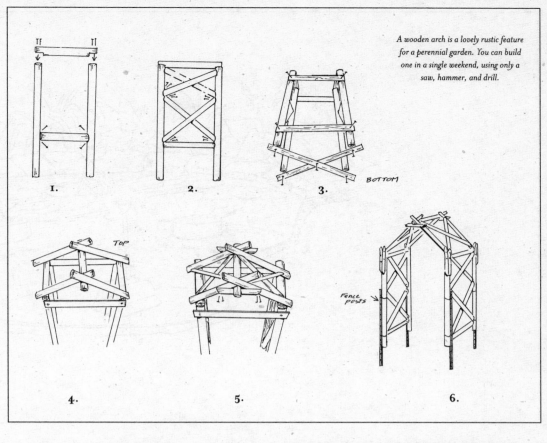

A wooden arch is a lovely rustic feature for a perennial garden. You can build one in a single weekend, using only a saw, hammer, and drill.

I.   2.   3.   BOTTOM
TOP
4.   5.   FENCE POSTS   6.

Adding Height with Trellises and Arbors

Fern Marshall Bradley

A yard full of perennials can look like a flat sea of plants. To give your landscape depth, variety, and some soothing shade in the long term, you'll want to include shrubs and trees in your design. You can also use arbors, pillars, and other vertical features like those shown here.

A rustic arch. It's easy to add height with a rustic arch made from cut saplings, like the one illustrated above. You can use hickory, oak, or maple saplings. Cedar or locust would be even better because they are more rot-resistant.

To build the arch, you'll need 4-inch-diameter saplings for the uprights and crossbars. Cut the four uprights 6½ feet long; cut two 18-inch crossbars and two 12-inch crossbars.

For the ridge pole and rafters, use 2½-inch-diameter saplings. The ridge pole is 18 inches long; the four rafters are each 5 feet long.

Last, you'll need 1½-inch-diameter saplings for the lattice; cut 12, each 4 feet long.

The arch is held together with 8-, 10-, and 12-penny common nails.

Step 1. Assemble the two side panels. Drill two holes through the uprights at each joint, insert 12d nails, and hammer them firmly into the crossbars.

Step 2. Add lattice braces. Lay a lattice piece across the panel. Mark where to cut and trim with a saw. Drill two holes through each end, insert 10d nails, and hammer them firmly into the uprights.

Step 3. Brace the side panels. Nail scraps of lumber between the side panels to hold them 4 feet apart, as shown. These braces stay on until the arch is installed.

Step 4. Add the rafters and ridge pole. Drill and nail two rafters to the uprights and each other. Position the ridge pole, and drill and nail it firmly to the rafters. Then attach the second pair of rafters.

Step 5. Attach the roof lattices. Use the same procedure as for the side lattices. Use the scrap ends of the lattice pieces to reinforce the arch joints. Drill and nail them on firmly with 8d nails.

Step 6. Set the arch on concrete pavers (to keep the wood dry and prevent rot). Anchor the arch with 4' metal fenceposts driven into the ground next to each of the uprights.

To add height quickly while you wait for newly planted trees and shrubs to grow, try using simple pillars, arbors, and fast-growing vines and grasses.

Lighting Your Landscape

Fern Marshall Bradley

If you have a busy lifestyle, you may rarely see your perennials during the workweek. Wouldn't it be nice to sit outside and enjoy your flowers long after the sun sets? You can do it by adding lighting to your perennial plantings. You can position lights to illuminate a bed from either the front (spotlighting) or above (downlighting), or you can create special, subtle effects by backlighting or lighting them from below (uplighting).

With a simple do-it-yourself 12-volt lighting system, it's surprisingly easy and affordable to light up your landscape. You can buy simple kits with a transformer that plugs into a regular household outlet. In some systems the lights even snap on or off the wire with no tools, so you can move them around to create different effects.

Outdoor Rooms of Green

Some folks like to set up folding chairs on the front lawn and watch the traffic go by. But most of us find ourselves hanging out in a more private part of the yard, one that offers some sense of enclosure. A traditional porch does that splendidly, of course, and with a little planning and planting you can do the same somewhere on your property. This spot is apt to catch the sun at the appropriate time of day, along with shade when necessary. It could offer a view to the front of the house so that you can keep an eye out for arriving visitors, or to the backyard so that you can monitor the kids' activities. And you might want to create the effect of walls with hedges, rock walls, or even just a row of potted plants. Add comfortable seating (a bench without a back might not qualify) and move right in.

Continued ➡

*A cross-section of a water garden reveals
the plastic liner that holds the water in, and
a submersible pump that creates the fountain at the water's surface.*

A Straight and Simple Stone Path

What You'll Need

Rectangular flagstones of three or more different lengths
String and stakes
Square-bladed shovel
Work gloves
Work shoes

Much of the challenge of installing a flagstone path is getting those odd-shaped puzzle pieces to fit. They're heavy, sharp-edged, and seem to resist snuggling close to one another. You can make matters easier for yourself by visiting a home and garden center or stone dealer and buying rectangular stones. Be equipped with the overall length you need, so that you can order pieces of varying lengths that will do the job. If you have the choice of different thicknesses of stone, the thinner stuff is easier to move and less expensive, but it may be more prone to cracking over time.

Because rectangular stones are cut with some precision, the cracks between them are smaller and weeds have less of an opportunity to establish themselves along the walk. In fact, you can skip the usual step of laying down a bed of sand before putting the stones in place, although it may be easier to provide a level layer with sand than with stony or clumping soil.

1. Layout the walk with string stretched between two stakes tapped into the ground. If you place the string outside of where the walk will go, it'll be less likely to get in your way as you dig the trench. Alternately, you can layout the string along both edges of the path's intended course and make lines with aerosol paint.

2. Dig a trench for the walk so that the top of the stones will be at ground level.

3. Wearing work gloves, put the stones in place. Vary their lengths randomly along the walk. If the last stone isn't the right size for the length of the walk, you can ask your supplier to saw it. Or do the job yourself with a circular saw and masonry blade, wearing safety glasses.

4. Put your weight on the walk to test it for stability. Tuck small stones and soil under the stones as necessary to level them. Finally, place soil along the outside edges and tamp it down. In time, grass will spread into this new strip of soil, making the walk look like it has been there for years.

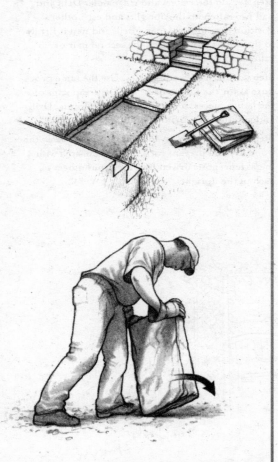

Plant Projects

Garden Structures

For the Home

Garden Projects

PLANT PROJECTS

Build a Super Compost and Soil Sifter

Vicki Mattern

For starting seeds and filling pots, you need "screened compost." That's where a compost sifter comes in handy. The sifter is a screening box that is designed to fit right on top of your wheelbarrow or garden cart, so that you can fill it with fine-textured compost and then toss the larger remnants back into the compost pile for further cooking. You can construct this useful gadget in just an hour for a cost of less than $15.

MATERIALS

2 untreated 1" x 12" x 8' boards

2-inch galvanized deck screws, or 2-inch galvanized or aluminum nails

?-inch or ?-inch metal hardware cloth

Heavy-duty staple gun and staples

1. Measure the inside distance between the sides of your wheelbarrow or cart—this measurement will determine the size of your sifter's opening.

2. From each board, cut one 24-inch-long piece and one 36-inch-long piece. From each of the 26-inch leftovers, cut one ?-inch-wide retaining strip to help hold the screen in place.

(Use a jigsaw to cut handholds. Use a router or sandpaper to smooth the edges of the holds.)

3. Screw or nail the four sides together at the corners.

4. Using the staple gun, staple the hardware cloth to the bottom edges. (For potting soil, use ?-inch hardware cloth; for other garden uses, ?-inch cloth is fine.)

5. For the bottom of the sifter, cut two 24-inch-long filler pieces from the leftover boards to cover the parts of the box that will extend beyond the sides of your wheelbarrow or cart. (Use the measurement from Step 1 to determine the size of the pieces.) Also cut ?-inch-wide guide strips from the leftover pieces to hold the sifter tightly in place on your cart. Screw or nail the filler boards into place and then staple the screen to them. Now screw or nail the ?-inch pieces; attach the retaining strips to the long edges of the box; and attach the guide strips to the edges of the filler boards so they will rest against the facing sides of your wheelbarrow or cart and hold the sifter in place.

Making a Barrel Composter

Barbara W. Ellis

For small composting operations, the barrel composter is ideal. The composter is easy to build and use. The compost is easy to turn by rotating the drum.

TOOLS REQUIRED

Electric drill

Saws (saber saw with metal-cutting blade and handsaw or circular saw)

Screwdriver

Pliers

Paintbrush

MATERIALS

Lumber-Cut List

You'll need to cut lumber into the following lengths. Use pressure-treated lumber or, if you prefer, untreated pine painted with a preservative or flat black paint. It's best to measure and then cut the pieces as you assemble them to be sure they fit together correctly.

4 pcs. 2 x 4 x 40" (legs)

4 pcs. 2 x 4 x 29?" (frame horizontals)

2 pcs. 1 x 3x 40-⅝" (cross braces)

4 pcs. 1 x 3x 23?" (corner braces)

2 pcs. ? x 7?"-diameter wood circles (bearings)

2 pcs. ? x 2?"-diameter wood circles (bearings)

Hardware

1 55-gallon drum (composter)

2 pcs. 1? x 2" hinges

1 small hasp

Continued ➔

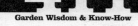

I pc. ? x 40?" steel rod

8 pcs. ? x I?" stove bolts

12 pcs. ? x I" stove bolts

28 pcs. I?" #10 wood screws

I pint black rust-retardant paint

1. Obtain a 55-gallon drum that has not been used for toxic chemicals. (Paint barrels are ideal.)

2. Drill a ?-inch hole in the exact center of both ends of the drum to accommodate the ?-inch steel rod. Make a simple gauge to find the center by cutting a 6-inch diameter circle out of heavy cardboard or wood. Mark the exact center of the circle and cut out a 90-degree wedge. Attach a piece of wood so that one edge bisects the cut-out wedge. Hold the gauge with the cut-out edge against the edge of the drum. Draw a line where the piece of wood bisects the end of the drum. Move the gauge 90 degrees and draw another line. The intersection of these lines will be the exact center.

3. Draw the lines for the barrel opening, rounding the corners slightly. Drill a ?-inch hole on one line to make a starting place for the saber saw. Cut through the barrel, following the line. If the barrel has ribs, cut a I-inch vee notch on each rib to facilitate opening the door. Attach the hinges and the hasp to the barrel and lid with ?-by-I-inch stove bolts.

4. From ?-inch pine, cut two 7?-inch-diameter circles (bearings) and two 2?-inch-diameter circles. Drill a ?-inch hole in the center of each and apply glue to the 2?-inch circles. Glue each 2?-inch circle to a 7?-inch one. (It's a good idea to temporarily slip them over the ?-inch steel rod and clamp them.) After the glue has dried, remove the bearings, insert the rod through the barrel, and assemble. Use four ?-by I?-inch stove bolts in each bearing to bolt them to the drum.

5. To build the support frame, use a corner lap joint to fasten the legs to the horizontal pieces. (To make a corner lap joint, remove one-half the thickness of the stock to a length comparable to the width of the stock on the ends of both pieces to be joined.) Use two I?-inch #10 wood screws in each joint. Cut grooves (dadoes) on the legs 23 inches from the bottom to fit the I-by-3-inch cross braces. Cut 45-degree angles at both ends of the 23?-inch- long corner braces and attach across corners with I?-inch #10 wood screws. Cut a ?-inch notch in the center of each top horizontal piece to accommodate the rod.

6. Drill several rows of ?-inch holes along the bottom of the barrel underneath the door opening to eliminate excess moisture. Paint the barrel unit inside and out with black, rust-retardant paint.

Making a Three-Bin Composter

Barbara W. Ellis

Tools Required

Electric drill

Saw (circular saw or handsaw)

Hammer

Pliers

Materials

Lumber-Cut List

Cut lumber into the following lengths. Use pressure-treated lumber or untreated pine painted with a preservative or flat black paint. Measure and cut the pieces as you assemble them to be sure they fit together correctly.

For Bins

I pc. 2 x 6 x 108" (center joist)

2 pcs. 2 x 6 x 30" (headers)

2 pcs. 2 x 6 x III" (outside joists)

2 pcs. 2 x 6 x 14?" (brace blocks)

4 pcs. I x 6 x 33" (short floor boards)

8 pcs. 2 x 6 x 41?" (corner posts)

24 pcs. I x 6 x 36" (partition boards)

6 pcs. 2 x 2 x 34" (inside door tracks)

2 pcs. 2 x 2 x 35?" (outside door tracks)

I pc. 2 x 6 x 96" (cut to fit for post blocks)

14 pcs. 2 x 6 x 34?" (floorboards)

6 pcs. I x 6 x III" (backboards)

18 pcs. I x 6 x 35?" (door slats)

3 pcs. I x 3 x 35?" (door slats)

For Lids

18 pcs. I x 6 x 37" (lid boards)

3 pcs. I x 2 x 36" (front battens)

3 pcs. I x 2 x 34" (back battens)

2 pcs. I x 2 x II?" (hatch battens)

2 pcs. I x 2 x 22" (header batten)

Hardware

For Bins

22 pcs. ? x 3?" carriage bolts with nuts and washers

galvanized nails 16d

galvanized nails 8d

For Lids

6 strap hinges 8" (lids)

2 strap hinges 4" (hatch)

4 lengths jack chain, approximately 36" each

8 heavy eye screws

4 snap hooks

I box I?" #6 galvanized screws

Building the Bins

1. **Base.** Nail a header to each end of the center joist, using 16d nails. Nail the outside joists, front and back, across the ends of the headers. Nail the brace blocks in place between the joists. Locate the nail the four short floor-boards across the joists where the partitions will be located, using 8d nails.

2. **Partitions.** For each of the four partitions (two outside and two inside), nail six partition boards to connect two corner posts, spacing them evenly. Nail the inside door tracks to the partition boards, I inch back from the corner posts. Nail the outside door tracks flush with the front of the two interior partitions.

Position the assembled partitions—one on each end of the base and one on each side of the interior compartment; drill and bolt the corner posts to the outside joists.

3. **Post Blocks.** Cut the 2 x 6 x 96" post block board in three pieces, to fit snugly between the bottoms of the front corner posts. Bolt the post blocks in place, flush with the floor surface.

4. **Floor.** Space the floorboards evenly across the joists and nail them in place. There will be five for each of the two end compartments and four for the middle compartment.

5. **Back.** Nail the backboards in place, covering the back corner posts.

6. **Front.** Feed door slats horizontally into the door track.

Building the Lids

1. **Lids.** Construct two of the three lids. Using a drill and galvanized screws, fasten six lid boards to the front and back battens; allow about ? inch between boards. Each lid will measure 36 inches across. Construct the third lid in the same manner, but leave out the two middle boards.

2. **Hatch.** Fasten the hatch battens to the two remaining lid boards, one batten about 2 inches from the end of the boards and one batten 18 inches from the same end. Fasten the header batten to the boards, 20 inches from the end, just behind the back hatch batten. Cut between the header batten and the back hatch batten to separate the hatch. Fasten the two remaining boards and the header batten to the partially constructed lid. Hinge the hatch to the lid.

3. **Finish.** Attach the three lids to the bins with the 8-inch hinges, so that they are centered over the compartments. Use eye screws to attach a chain to the bottom of the lids of the two end bins. Attach the chains on the inside edge at about the middle of the boards, on the side near the center partition. Attach chains underneath both sides of the lid of the middle bin. Mount snap hooks on the ends of the chains. Use pliers to attach eye screws to the bin partitions.

Build a Combo Composter

Barbara Pleasant

This easily assembled compost bin gives you a place to throw withered plants and food scraps, *and* you can use it to store your digging fork, spade, and other tools you reach for every day. Sturdy enough to resist invasions by the family dog, the Combo Composter is made from wooden pallets—also called skids—which are usually free for the asking at lumberyards or home improvement stores. Open spaces between the pallets' slats allow air to circulate freely, and the front comes off in seconds for easy access. By orienting the pallets so that the outer slats are parallel to the ground, you can slip tool handles through the open spaces at the top edge—or use them to hold one of the Easy Aerators. The finished bin is quite heavy, so it's best to assemble it near its permanent location. To get this bin to perform a fast disappearing act, paint it dark green or brown, and locate it in a shady spot.

You Will Need

Tools: Work gloves, marker, drill and bits, screwdriver, hammer, measuring tape

Continued ➡

4 wooden shipping pallets

6 galvanized corner brackets

Twenty-four 1-inch wood screws

Four 4-inch-long pieces of scrap wood or furring strips

Eight 2-inch nails

Two 12-inch bungee cords (utility tie-downs)

1. Place the pallets that will be the sides of the bin on the ground, with the outer slats horizontal.

2. Attach a corner bracket to the edge of the top cross-board, another to the middle cross-board, and another to the second board from the bottom. To attach each bracket, hold the bracket in place with the bend in the bracket aligned with the outside edge of the pallet. Mark the screw holes, drill guide holes, and then screw the brackets in place. Repeat this procedure as you attach 3 brackets to the other side.

3. To attach the sides, rest the back pallet against a wall or tree, or have a helper hold it for you. Beginning with the center bracket, attach the side pallets to the back pallet the same way you did in Step 2.

4. To make compartments for tools, nail short pieces of scrap wood across the top of the back pallet at 6-inch intervals.

5. Position the bin in its permanent location. If necessary, dig out or add soil beneath the base to make the bin sit solidly on the ground.

6. Fill the bin with kitchen scraps, yard waste, and refuse from your garden. When you are not working the heap, close up the bin by securing the fourth pallet to the front with the bungee cords.

Make a Flip-Flop Compost Corral

Barbara Pleasant

This circular compost corral is incredibly easy to put together, yet it still gives you the versatility of a two-compartment bin. Gradually fill one wire-enclosed side with compostables, and when you're ready to dig in and begin some intensive turning to finish off the composting process, simply flip the bin to the other side of the central post, and start all over again.

The most challenging part of this project is installing the post. As long as the soil is moist, you should be able to pound a metal fence post into the ground by placing a piece of scrap lumber over the top and pounding away. If you prefer, install a wood post in a narrow posthole dug 18 inches deep. When installing either type of post, make sure there is 2 feet of free space on both sides. You can use the leftover lawn fencing for other projects, such as the Portable Trellis on page 8.

You Will Need

Tools: Wire snips, staple gun, hammer, pliers

1 roll of 3-foot-wide vinyl-coated 2 x 3-inch mesh lawn fencing

Two 48-inch-long 1 x 2 furring strips

One 6-foot-long metal fence post.

1 small piece of scrap lumber

8 to 10 plastic cable ties

Two 6-inch lengths of 2-inch-diameter PVC pipe

1 thick rubber band

1. Use the wire snips to cut one 6-foot-long piece of fencing. To keep the fencing from rolling up as you try to cut it, it helps to have a helper

hold the roll. Snip off protruding pieces of wire to create clean edges.

2. Use the staple gun to attach the furring strips to the cut ends of the fencing. Center the fencing so that about 6 inches of wood extends beyond the top and bottom of the fencing.

3. Cover the top of the fence post with the piece of scrap lumber, and pound it into the ground until the protruding metal wings near the base of the post are just below the soil's surface. To land sound blows, you may want to stand on a sturdy stool.

4. Using the plastic cable ties, attach the midpoint of the fencing to the fencepost at several points, with the bottom of the fencing flush with the ground.

5. On one side of the post, form a circle with the two sides of the fencing and mark the ground where the furring strips meet. Pound one of the pieces of pipe 5 inches into the ground, and then use pliers to pull it back out. Push a stick through the plug of soil to clear the center of the pipe, and then pound it back into the hole again, leaving the top ? inch above the soil line. Install a second pipe sleeve the same way on the other side of the post.

6. On the first side you want to fill with compost, bring the two furring strips together and insert the bottom ends into the PVC pipe sleeve. Secure the top ends of the furring strips together with a thick rubber band.

Construct a Garbage Can Compost System

Barbara Pleasant

Contained compost systems are more challenging to manage compared to open piles. They are harder to aerate; they tend to be smaller (and thus slower to decompose); and it's easy to overwater the materials, so they become slimy. But if your town requires closed compost containers—or your dog likes to dig in an open pile—an enclosed system may be your best choice.

This easy system consists of two modified garbage cans with snap-on lids—an upright can for collecting materials, and a second can that sits on rolling casters for easy turning. To facilitate drainage, the bottom is removed from the collecting can. The rolling can includes interior baffles that help to mix the materials each time the can is turned. Having two containers that serve differing purposes helps to avoid the most common pitfalls of closed compost systems, and it makes the composting process more enjoyable, too. A bag of packaged compost is used to help get the compost off to a good start, or you can use compost you have made yourself.

You Will Need

Tools: Drill with bits, utility knife, hammer, measuring tape, screwdriver, adjustable wrench, garden hoe

Two 32-gallon plastic garbage cans with locking lids

One 20-quart bag of finished compost

Sixteen 2-inch nails

Two 36-inch-long pieces of 2 x 4 lumber

Two 15-inch-long pieces of 2 x 4 lumber

Two 18-inch-long pieces of 2 x 4 lumber

4 heavy-duty casters with wood screws

Four 30-inch-long pieces of 1 x 2 furring strips

Twelve 3-inch-long bolts with washers and nuts

One 18-inch bungee cord (utility tie-down)

1. To enhance aeration and drainage in the collection can, drill approximately 30 holes all over the sides of the can. Turn the can upside-down, and use the utility knife to cut out the bottom, leaving the curved bottom edge and 1 inch of the can's bottom intact.

2. Set the can in place and fill the bottom 6 inches of the can with loose material such as straw, pruned branches, or spent plants pulled from your garden. Cover with a 2-inch layer of damp, finished compost. Close the can and lock on the lid. You can now begin using the can to collect kitchen trimmings and yard waste, alternating with 1-inch layers of finished compost.

3. To make the base for the rolling bin, build a frame by nailing the 36-inch-long 2 x 4s and the 15-inch-long 2 x 4s together into a rectangular frame. Place the frame on a level surface, and nail the two 18-inch-long 2 x 4s over the top, with their outer edges 12 inches in from the edge of the assembled frame. Mark the centers of each crosspiece, and make four more marks 6 inches from the center marks. Use wood screws to attach the casters to the cross-pieces at each mark.

4. Turn the second can on its side. Hold one of the 1 x 2 furring strips against the outside of the can, and use the drill to make 3 guide holes for the bolts that go through the furring strip and the can. Switch the furring strip to the inside of the can, and install the bolts by threading on washers, inserting the bolts from the outside so they go through the can and the furring strip and extend into the interior of the can. Then screw on and tighten the nuts. Repeat with the 3 remaining furring strips.

5. Use the drill to make approximately 30 aeration holes in the sides and bottom of the second can. Snap on the lid, and place the can on the casters.

6. Whenever the collection can is halfway full, transfer its contents to the rolling can. The easiest way to do this is to lay the collection can on its side, and pull batches of material into the lid with a hoe. Then dump them into the rolling can.

7. Secure the lid of the rolling can with a bungee cord. Roll the can several times to mix the materials, and add water if needed to lightly dampen the contents. Roll the can every few days. In 3 to 5 weeks, the compost should be ready to use in your garden.

Make an Indoor Worm Farm

Barbara Pleasant

Remember the ant farm you had as a kid? You can have as much fun growing worms, which will reward you with rich fertilizer for your garden. Specifically, the worms create worm castings—excretions high in nitrogen, phosphorus, and potassium, as well as micronutrients and enzymes. Castings are slightly more acidic than garden compost and are a more concentrated source of plant nutrients. You can add them directly to the garden, sprinkle them over the soil's surface of your potted plants, or mix them into potting soil.

Vermicomposting can be done indoors year-round, and it is not stinky when you have the right balance of bedding, water, worms, and food scraps. Bad odors are a sign that you're overfeeding or the bedding is too wet. Fortunately, vermicomposting is

Continued ➡

easy to do correctly, and it gives you an alternative use for kitchen scraps in winter, when outdoor compost often freezes. It also makes a great science project for kids.

For best results, use red worms (*Eisenia foetida*), which are also known as red wrigglers. They are raised commercially for fishing bait, so you often can buy them by the pint at fishing supply stores. For this project, you will need 1 pound of worms, which is roughly equal to 3 pints of fishing worms. The worms can process about 3 pounds of kitchen waste per week.

This project uses a plastic storage bin, modified to meet the needs of the worms. Keep the bin in a dimly lit place where the temperature stays between 55°F and 77°F. Place it on bricks above a sheet of plastic, and use newspapers to catch any liquids that drain from the bottom. Newspapers enriched with "worm juice" make great garden mulch.

You Will Need

> Tools: Drill and ?-inch drill bit, bucket, pump spray bottle, hand trowel
>
> One 12-inch-deep 50-quart plastic storage bin with lid
>
> Shredded paper for bedding; enough to fill the bin ? full
>
> 1 quart peat moss
>
> 1 cup cornmeal
>
> 1 pound of red worms (*Eisenia foetida*)

1. Drill 30 evenly spaced ventilation holes in the bottom and sides of the bin.

2. Place the bedding material and peat moss in the bucket and moisten it uniformly until it is as damp as a wrung-out sponge. Mix in the cornmeal. You may need to prepare the bedding in bucket-size batches.

3. Dump the prepared worm bedding into the plastic bin. Fluff the bedding gently to create air pockets. Mist bits of paper that remain dry.

4. Add the worms to the top of the bedding. Begin adding small amounts of food scraps at first, burying them just beneath the surface. Increase the amount of food as you learn how much your worms can consume.

5. Mist the bedding as needed to keep it slightly damp. Soggy bedding causes odors.

6. After 2 to 3 months, when the worms have converted most of the bedding to castings, use a hand trowel to move the compost and worms to one side of the bin. Add fresh bedding and food scraps to the empty side of the bin. Give the worms a few days to move to the fresh side and then remove the compost. Fill the empty side with fresh bedding.

Make These Nifty Sifters

Barbara Pleasant

Soil sifters separate the big stuff from the little stuff, whether that stuff is the rocks from your garden soil or undecomposed broccoli stalks from your compost. Use different sifters for different jobs; the Rock-Removing Roll is great for sifting out rocks, while the Cheap Seat Sifter will make quick work of turning chunks of compost into fine crumbles.

Rock-Removing Roll

You Will Need

> Tools: Heavy-duty gloves, wire snips, pliers, wheelbarrow

> One 6-foot-long piece of 36-inch-wide chicken wire (poultry netting)
>
> 6 feet of insulated wire

1. Cut the chicken wire to length, and roll it into a cylinder. Crimp and fold the side edges to close it.

2. Close one end of the cylinder by bending in 12 inches of the chicken-wire on all sides. Thread the insulated wire through the side edge seam and through the closed end to keep them closed. Use pliers to wrap the ends of the insulated wire through the mesh to keep them from coming loose.

3. Fill the wire roll with rocky soil, and shake it vigorously to remove soil while retaining rocks. Dump the rocks in the wheelbarrow, and use them for another garden project.

Cheap Seat Sifter

You Will Need

> Tools: Utility scissors, staple gun, bucket
>
> One 14-inch-wide cardboard box
>
> One 16-inch square of aluminum window screening
>
> 1 old wood chair without seat
>
> Duct tape

1. Remove the flaps from one end of the box, and cut two of them into 1-inch-wide strips.

2. Place the screening over the seat area of the chair, and trim the edges if needed to make them the proper size. Staple the edges in place, sandwiching the cardboard strips between the staples and the screening.

3. Open out the flaps on the other end of the cardboard box, and place it over the screening. Tape the opened flaps to the chair.

4. Place a bucket of compost in the cardboard hopper, and then place the bucket under the Cheap Seat Sifter. Use a hand trowel or gloved hand to stir and scrape the compost across the screen.

Barbara Pleasant

Raise your garden to new heights and get an up-close experience with direct-sown seeds by planting lettuce, bush beans, and trailing flowers in a straw bale bed. You won't have to bend far to tend your plants or contend with weeds, and at the end of the season you can use the decomposing straw as mulch. Get extra mileage from this project by positioning three beds in a semicircle, which creates a protected pocket for hardening off tender seedlings started indoors. If you have a new bed planned for the next season, the bale beds will smother weeds and grasses, so the spot will be ready to dig by fall.

The decomposing straw creates gentle bottom heat, so straw bale beds also are a good way to get a head start on spring. On cold nights, simply cover them with plastic or old blankets, held aloft with sticks stuck into the bales. Bale beds need frequent watering, so keep a hose or watering can handy. In rainy weather, don't be surprised to see mushrooms sprouting from the bottoms of the bales. These "weed" mushrooms are not edible, but their appearance is evidence that naturally occurring fungi are busy promoting decomposition within the bales.

> ### Bale Bed Banquets and Bouquets
>
> You can grow any plants that are not heavy feeders in a straw bale bed. If there is still time left in the growing season, follow lettuce and bush beans with quick crops of fall radishes, turnips, or baby bok choy. If you'd rather grow flowers, stud the middle of the bale beds with upright zinnias, and flank them with cascading petunias. For fall, fill bale beds with bright chrysanthemums, and add a few pumpkins, gourds, or winter squash to complete the display. Keep in mind that wet bales of straw are heavy, so it's best to put them in their permanent places before you plant them. They also become fragile as the straw begins to decompose, so the bales should not be moved until you're ready to tear them apart to use the straw as mulch.

You Will Need

> Tools: Scissors, garden hose, handheld digging fork
>
> 3 bales of wheat straw
>
> 20 yards jute or hemp string
>
> Water-soluble organic all-purpose plant food
>
> Three 20-pound bags of compost
>
> 1 packet each bush bean, lettuce, and nasturtium seeds

1. Place the straw bales in a sunny spot, with the cut ends of the straw facing up. The bailing twine or wire should be parallel to the ground. To reinforce the baling twine, tie string around the sides of each bale to help hold them together as the straw begins to decompose.

2. Thoroughly dampen the bales, which may require you to water them 3 days in a row. On the third day, drench the moistened bales with plant food, mixed according to label directions.

Continued ➡

3. Wait 1 week. Wet down the bales again, wait a few hours for the straw to soften, and then use the small digging fork to chop into the top of the bales. Leave a 2-inch margin of intact straw around the edges. Pry out enough straw to create 6-inch-deep bowls inside each bale.

4. Place half of the compost in the hollowed-out bales, and lightly chop it in with the digging fork to sift it down into the straw. Spread the rest of the compost over the top.

5. Nick the nasturtium seeds with a nail clipper. Soak the nasturtium and bean seeds overnight. Plant the beans 1 inch deep down the center of each bale, and water well. Scatter lettuce seeds down either side of the bean row, and firm them in by patting lightly with the palm of your hand. Poke the nasturtium seeds into the compost 2 inches inside each corner.

6. Keep the compost moist until the seeds germinate, and then thin the seedlings if they are too crowded. Every 2 weeks, give your straw bale beds a thorough drench with liquid plant food.

Grow a Wagon Garden
Barbara Pleasant

That little red wagon that's a little too unsteady for the children or grandchildren is great for moving seedlings indoors and outdoors, so it makes hardening off a breeze. When most of your seedlings are in the ground, use the wagon as a novel container for a compact patio tomato, grown in the company of robust nasturtiums. In the fall, simply clean out the wagon and put it back to work moving plants or other gardening supplies. You can use an old wheelbarrow for this project, too.

You Will Need

Tools: Hammer and nails, tape measure, wood saw, watering can, garden trowel, strips of stretchy cloth

An old child's wagon

One 48-inch-long wood tomato stake

Newspapers

One 20-pound bag of potting mix (more for a large wagon)

1 patio tomato plant

1 packet of nasturtium seeds

All-purpose water-soluble organic plant food

1 stout stick, 2 inches longer than the width of the wagon (optional)

1. Wash and dry the wagon, and use the hammer and a nail to make 10 drainage holes in the bottom of the wagon.

2. To prepare a stake to support the tomato, measure the width of the wagon between the inside edges. Use the saw to cut off the bottom of the tomato stake at exactly this length. Place the long piece of the tomato stake on a flat, solid surface, and center the short piece across the bottom edge to form a T. Nail the two pieces together.

3. Cover the bottom and sides of the wagon with 4 thicknesses of newspaper. Twelve inches from the front of the wagon, install the stake by pushing the base inside the wagon. If it fits very tightly, use the hammer to tap it into place. If the fit is so loose that the stake falls over, shim the ends of the base with squares of folded newspaper.

4. Thoroughly dampen the newspapers before filling the wagon with potting soil. Plant the tomato near the base of the stake, laying its roots and lowest section of the stem at a diag-

onal angle. Nick the nasturtium seeds with nail clippers before planting them 4 inches apart in the rest of the wagon. Water well, and move the wagon to a place that gets at least 6 hours of full sun each day.

Play It Again
Creative Containers

From old work boots to discarded Easter baskets, perhaps your storage room is a treasure trove of whimsical containers for just the right plants. When using boots or shoes as planters, use a hammer and nail to make a few drainage holes in the soles, and stick with plants that don't mind dry conditions, such as sedums or other succulents. To turn porous baskets into containers, simply line them with a piece of cloth before filling them with soil.

Look for ways to use old pieces of furniture, too. The phrase "garden bed" takes on a whole new meaning when an old bed frame is sunk into the garden and filled with colorful pansies or petunias. And few planters are more charming than an old seatless wooden chair that's been retrofitted to hold a large container of small-fruited cucumbers, or a frothy pot of verbena. Making a sturdy platform for the container is usually a simple matter of cutting two wood slats that can be laid over the chair's rungs.

5. To keep the soil from drying out, cover the soil's surface with damp newspapers until the nasturtium seeds germinate. After the nasturtium seeds sprout and begin to grow, thin them to 4 plants. If desired, lift the extra seedlings and transplant them to your garden.

6. Water your Garden as often as needed to keep the soil lightly moist. Topping the soil with mulch will help retain moisture. Every 2 weeks, give the soil a deep drench with a water-soluble organic plant food, mixed according to label directions.

7. As the tomato grows, tie it loosely to the stake with strips of stretchy cloth. When the tomato vine becomes heavy with fruit, reinforce the upright stake by placing a stout stick across the top edges of the wagon, if necessary. Tie it snugly to the stake.

GARDEN STRUCTURES

Build a Simple Potting Bench
Vicki Mattern

Planting doesn't happen only in the garden. Most gardeners also plant flowers, veggies, and herbs in pots for the deck or patio or to enjoy year-round as houseplants. This easy-to-build portable bench is perfect for all of your potting, transplanting, and seed-starting work. Because it's made from

cedar, it looks good, weathers well, and is naturally rot-resistant. You can set up the bench wherever you need it—it's lightweight and easy to carry. When you're not using the bench, just fold it and hang it on a wall in a shed or the garage.

Materials
1" x 3" x 8' cedar boards (11)
5/16" x 3" carriage bolts (4)
2" galvanized deck screws (40)
?" galvanized deck screws (12)

1. Cut seven of the 8-foot 1 x 3 boards to the following lengths: eight 48-inch pieces; two 42?-inch pieces; two 20-inch pieces; three 18?-inch pieces; and two 10-inch pieces.

2. Form a 42?-inch x 20-inch rectangle by fastening two of the 18?-inch lengths between both 42?-inch pieces with the 2-inch screws; this is the apron.

3. Use the 2-inch screws to fasten the third 18?-inch piece between the sides in the center of the rectangle; this is the center batten.

4. Fasten the two 20-inch pieces across the ends of the rectangle, using the 2-inch screws at the ends and the 1?-inch screws in the middle.

5. Fasten the 10-inch pieces in opposite corners of the rectangle, using the 1?-inch screws; these are the spacers that allow the legs to fold properly.

6. Fasten the eight 48-inch pieces to the top of the apron, using 2-inch screws, to complete the tabletop.

7. Turn the tabletop over and attach the 18?-inch center batten to it with 1?-inch screws.

8. To make the legs, cut two 8-foot 1 x 3 boards into four pieces, 29?-inches long and tapering from 3 inches at one end to 1? inches at the other. Round off the wide end and drill a 5/16-inch diameter hole through the center point at that end.

9. Drill four 5/16-inch diameter holes through the apron and spacers, then bolt the legs to the tabletop.

10. For leg braces, cut the remaining 8-foot boards into two 20-inch and two 17⅝-inch pieces. With the legs open slightly past 90 degrees, use 2-inch screws to attach the 20-inch braces to them so that the braces act as stops against the apron.

11. Fold the legs up against the table and attach a 17⅝-inch brace across each pair of legs at the point where they just clear the opposite legs when folded; use 2-inch screws.

Build a Raised-Bed Hoop House
Vicki Mattern

Materials
Frame: Untreated 6" x 6" landscape timbers (two 8' pieces and two 4' pieces)

Hoops: ?" diameter flexible conduit (four 10-inch pieces)

Ridgepole: One 8' 2 x 2 stud

Cover: One 10 x 25' roll of 6-mil greenhouse-grade plastic (cut four 52"-square pieces and one 8? x 12?" piece)

Side anchors: Two 8' 2 x 2 studs

Also: Small wooden stakes, staples, sheet metal screws, cardboard

A hoop house is an inexpensive, portable structure for extending the growing season. For extra frost

Continued →

protection, you can cover it with an agricultural foam "blanket" on cold nights. Here's how to build a simple 4-foot-high hoop house:

1. Build a raised-bed frame (about 4 feet wide x 8 feet long) using untreated landscape timbers. Drill four equidistant 1-inch-diameter holes into the tops of both long sides, drilling all the way through the wood. These holes will anchor the hoops.

2. Create a template for the hoops by driving wooden stakes into the ground, forming a 4?-foot-high arch. The two bottom stakes should be about 4 feet apart, with the curved section beginning about 21 inches from the bottom of each side. Arch and form the hoops using the ¾-inch-diameter metal conduit sold to protect electrical wires. Gently bend the conduit around the stakes.

3. To raise the roof, drill four equidistant 1-inch-diameter holes in the ridgepole to match the four pairs of holes in the frame. Run each hoop through a hole in the pole, securing it by running a sheet metal screw down through the pole and into the hoop. Insert the hoops into the frame.

4. Trim the plastic squares to be about 1 inch bigger all around than the area of the end hoops. At each end, put one piece on the inside of the hoop and one on the outside, then staple the edges together all around the hoop.

Center the large piece of plastic over the ridgepole, then staple it to the pole. (To keep the plastic from tearing, cut thin cardboard into long strips and place these over the plastic before stapling.)

On each side, anchor the plastic by stapling the bottom to the two remaining pieces of lumber. When ventilation is needed on warm days, simply roll up the sides.

Get a Greenhouse
Vicki Mattern

Want to extend your growing season to include all four seasons? Buy or build a greenhouse. Many sizes and styles are available, ranging from simple, unheated structures that you fit on a porch or patio to freestanding, climate-controlled conservatories. No matter what type of greenhouse you use, paying attention to these factors will maximize your chance of success:

1. Get the light right.
The quantity and quality of the light that enters a greenhouse from the outside can vary tremendously depending on the type of see-through material—

known as *glazing*—that is used for the ceiling and walls. Corrugated polyvinyl chloride (PVC), for example, lets in 84 percent of the available light, while Plexiglas lets in 93 percent. That may not seem like a big difference, but it is to your plants!

As a rule of thumb, every 1 percent increase in light transmission of your glazing material increases plant growth 1 percent during winter. So, that 9-percent difference between PVC and Plexiglas could well prove to be the difference between success and failure—especially if your greenhouse will be located in an area with a lot of winter cloud cover. There, greenhouse owners need to make the most of every bit of sun they get.

Cleanliness counts, too. If your greenhouse covering is dirty or dusty, wash it. Then establish a regular schedule of window washing.

If your greenhouse is covered with a flexible plastic film that has yellowed, replace it with a greenhouse-grade plastic designed to take the sun (available from greenhouse supply companies). The newer greenhouse plastics contain ultraviolet inhibitors that can extend the life of the plastic 4 years; infrared inhibitors, which reduce heat loss at night; and wetting agents so that condensation runs down the sides of the greenhouse instead of dripping onto your plants.

How you arrange plants inside the greenhouse can make a difference too. The area of brightest light is next to the glazing. At the end walls, where the framing interferes with light transmission, the lower light levels are better for shade-loving plants like impatiens.

2. Keep it hot, hot, hot
Greenhouses are like growing zones. They contain micro climates of cold and hot spots. If you learn where these areas are, you can satisfy the needs of both heat lovers (such as tomatoes, peppers, eggplants, and cucumbers) and cool-clime plants (such as lettuce)—all in the same greenhouse.

Place several thermometers throughout your greenhouse to learn the best place for growing specific plants. Shade-tolerant azaleas, for instance, may do best under the bench, where the temperature is a bit cooler and the light is indirect. Tropical orchids and bougainvillea are likely to thrive near the ceiling, where it's hotter and brighter.

Just be aware that the warmest spot by day—next to the glazing—becomes the coldest spot at night. You can stabilize indoor temperatures by incorporating heat-storing masses, such as brick floors and water barrels, in your greenhouse's design.

You may also want to add some supplemental heat to your greenhouse. If the greenhouse is attached to your home, you can tie it into your home heating system. If you choose to use a natural gas or propane heater, be sure to spend the extra money to vent the heater outside. Both of these gases produce sulfur dioxide and ethylene gas, which can harm plants. The sulfur dioxide, for instance, combines with the water that condenses on the inside of glazing to form sulfuric acid (acid rain!). Be careful, though, that you don't melt the glazing with the heater's surface.

3. Keep the air moving.
Warming a greenhouse is important, but keeping it cool can be crucial! In many parts of the country, too much heat is the biggest problem greenhouse growers must prepare for. As the sun beats down on your greenhouse during the unpredictable weather of spring, the air trapped inside can quickly heat up to 110°F or more. Ceiling vents that let hot air escape from the top of the greenhouse are the best protection, particularly in hot

or sunny climates. Second best are vents and fans located on the end walls to bring in cool air from outside.

If you aren't around during the day to control the ventilation yourself, spend a bit more to get automatic vents. Most are gas-filled cylinders that push the vent open as rising heat expands the gas inside. You also can get thermostatically controlled exhaust fans that run when the mercury reaches a preset temperature.

Air circulation is important even when you aren't venting excess heat. Having a fan running continuously inside a sealed greenhouse, for instance, is nearly a necessity. It can lessen the chance of plant diseases taking hold and help prevent depletion of the carbon dioxide (CO_2) that plants need for photosynthesis.

Individual plants tend to totally deplete the CO_2 in a tiny envelope of air that surrounds each leaf. But the CO_2 in these tiny pockets can be replenished somewhat by simply moving the air around with a fan. To completely replenish the CO_2, you'll need to open a vent to bring in fresh air.

4. Gauge the humidity.
Buy a humidity gauge (you can find them in hardware or home supply stores) so that you can maintain a relative humidity level of 40 to 50 percent inside your greenhouse. Most times, this means adding a little moisture to the dry winter air. In that case, either run a humidifier or try venting your electric clothes dryer into the greenhouse.

But you could need to *lower* the humidity, instead. If you overwater (especially in winter), the excess will go right into the air, raising the humidity level to as high as 95 percent. And high humidity coupled with poor air circulation can set off an explosion of root rot or powdery mildew on your plants.

To prevent such problems, water only when the soil in your greenhouse containers is dry—and watch that humidity gauge. You can also run an exhaust fan or just open a window on a warm winter day to decrease the humidity.

Stoop-Free Potting Bench
Roger Yepsen

You can make this potting bench in about a weekend, if you have basic woodworking skills. If not, show the drawings and general construction steps to a carpenter or woodworker and have them do the job. This design includes a few optional features: a tool shelf below the work surface, and a seed packet shelf and herb-drying bar above. The bench is made from 5/4 pine, which typically measures just over 1 inch thick. You can paint, stain, or varnish the piece, or leave it unfinished.

A standard height for a work surface is 36 inches, but that may not be right for you. If your kitchen counters are comfortable to work at, measure their height and use this dimension for the bench. Overall, the bench measures 72 inches high, 48 inches wide, and 28 inches deep.

The bench is put together with both screws and water-resistant polyvinyl acetate glue (such as Titebond II). Parts are assembled with glue on their mating surfaces, then clamped before driving the screws.

What You'll Need
96 feet 5/4 x 6 pine
#6 x 2-inch galvanized screws
#8 x 3-inch galvanized screws

Continued ➡

A potting bench puts pots and labels—as well as many common tasks—right at your fingertips. It also helps keep you organized because there's one central spot for gardening odds and ends.

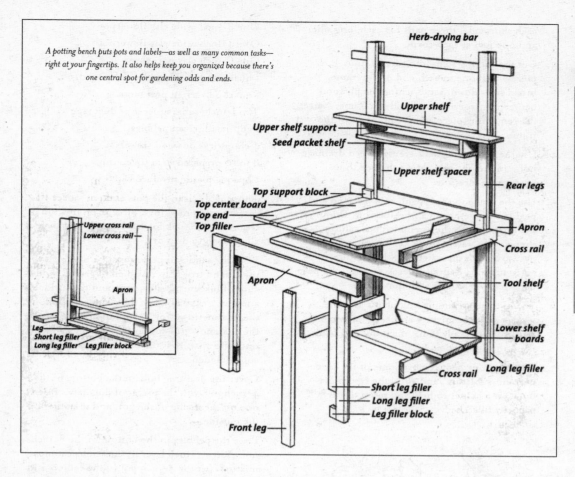

Herb-drying bar

Upper shelf

Upper shelf support
Seed packet shelf

Upper shelf spacer

Rear legs

Top support block
Top center board
Top end
Top filler

Apron

Cross rail

Upper cross rail
Lower cross rail

Apron

Tool shelf

Leg
Short leg filler
Long leg filler
Leg filler block

Lower shelf boards

Apron

Long leg filler

Cross rail

Short leg filler
Long leg filler
Leg filler block

Front leg

Creative Fence Posts

As you plan a garden fence, consider having at least a couple of posts extend higher than usual. These extra-tall posts can do double duty, providing a place to hang a birdhouse where you can enjoy the occupants (as they help you control plant-eating worms). Shy birds might not take to such a public spot, but wrens seem to put up with having humans nearby, even though they show their irritation by chattering a good deal. Or, string wire between a pair of tall posts for training sweet peas, runner beans, or honeysuckle.

You Will Need

Tools: Measuring tape, handsaw, pencil, drill with ?-inch bit, hammer

One ?-inch-diameter wooden dowel

One 36-inch-long piece of 2 x 4 lumber

Five 2-inch-long finishing nails

1. Use the saw to cut five 3-inch pieces from the dowel.

2. Mark 6-inch increments down the middle of the broad side of the 2 x 4.

3. Drill holes through the board at each mark. Insert a piece of dowel into each hole.

4. Place the assembled planting bar on a solid surface, narrow edge down. Nail through the edge of the bar and into each dowel piece to secure them in place.

5. To use the bar, place it on prepared soil and jiggle it back and forth to make 5 perfectly spaced planting holes. When planting a broad bed, pick up the planting bar and, with the end dowel still in the first planting hole, pivot the bar to make a perpendicular set of holes. Then make a row at each end hole, and so on down the row.

2?-inch galvanized finishing nails

1. The legs are "sandwiches" of several pieces, which allows you to make sturdy joints without the need for tricky cuts. Assemble them as shown in the detail view, together with the apron and cross rails.

2. Construct the rear legs, attaching them to the cross rails and then slipping in the rear apron.

3. Nail the boards for the lower shelf, with a little space between them to allow the wood to expand and contract. Attach the narrow tool shelf to the underside of the cross rails with screws.

4. Make the tabletop, with the boards running front to back rather than the usual lengthwise configuration. This allows you to make use of short scrap pieces and also will make it easier to brush off the surface. Attach the small support blocks to the rear legs, then nail the narrow fillers. Next come the end boards, and finally the boards in the middle. Nail the boards into the aprons.

5. Assemble the upper shelves, fitting the upper shelf spacers into the slot between the rear legs. Attach the upper shelf supports to the rear legs with screws. Trim the back of the upper shelf to fit between the rear legs, then nail it in place. Nail the upper shelf front onto the supports. Also nail the seed packet shelf onto the bottom of the shelf supports, and the herb-drying bar between the rear legs.

Fashion Your Own Fence
Roger Yepsen

You can buy all sorts of fencing material at a home and garden center, including preassembled panels in various woods or plastic. To set your garden apart, give some thought to designing your own pickets. The least expensive option is to saw them to length from bundles of 1 x 3s. You can even cut decorative top ends on each picket—a time-consuming project, but one that will set your garden apart. A few ideas are shown here. Make

straight cuts with a circular saw or saber saw; a saber saw will negotiate any curves; and a drill will make the holes. To drill the half-circle cutouts in adjacent pieces, place them side to side in a simple jig that, along with a couple of clamps, will hold them securely. A *forstner* bit in an electric drill will make a neater bore. If you put a sharp point on the pickets, the fence will be that much more formidable to climbing and leaping animals.

Make a Planting Bar
Barbara Pleasant

When you're planting lots of garlic or onions, or dropping large seeds into the ground, a planting bar can save time and help you get spacing perfect. When you're not using the planting bar for planting, hang it from a wall and use it to hold bunches of herbs or flowers as they dry.

Make a Handy Sink Screen
Barbara Pleasant

On busy gardening days when you're constantly washing out pots or grooming plants, you will

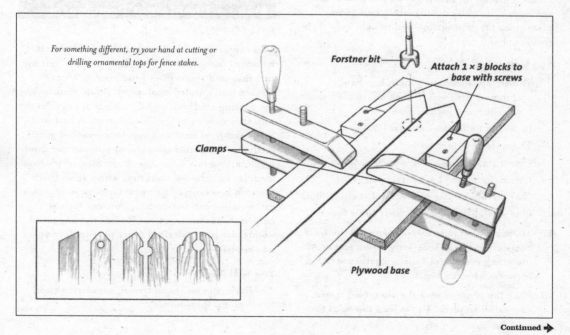

For something different, try your hand at cutting or drilling ornamental tops for fence stakes.

Forstner bit

Attach 1 × 3 blocks to base with screws

Clamps

Plywood base

Continued ➡

417

spend less time cleaning up after yourself with the help of a sink screen. Keep your sink screen in a cabinet between uses, or let it do double duty as a drying rack for kitchen herbs. This 12 x 12-inch version fits perfectly into a standard-size kitchen sink.

You Will Need

Tools: Tape measure, handsaw, hammer, scissors, staple gun

One 6-foot-long 1 x 2 furring strip

Sixteen 1?-inch nails

1 small roll of polyester window screening

1. Cut the furring strip into six 12-inch-long pieces. Place two of the cut pieces on a flat surface, broad side down, and partially drive 2 nails into each end, ? inch from the outer edge. Position two pieces at right angles to the first two, overlapping the corners, and nail them together to form a box.

2. Cut a piece of screening 12 inches wide and 12 inches long. Staple it to the frame.

3. Place the remaining two pieces of 1 x 2 along the high sides of the frame, flat side down, so they cover the edge of the screening. Nail them in place.

Build a Propagation Bed
Barbara Pleasant

The more you garden, the more you need a holding bed for plants you're not quite ready to plant, as well as those that need some growing time before they are set out in the garden. As temporary quarters for perennials you've divided, or plants given to you by a generous friend, a quickly constructed propagation bed is hard to beat. Locate it in a spot that gets afternoon shade, so plants with skimpy roots won't have to struggle against the demands of hot sun. Reinforced by a sturdy plywood bottom, this bed can be moved if needed to give plants exactly the exposure they prefer. When the bed is left situated in one place, the bottom serves as a barrier to tree roots and soil-dwelling insects, and keeps the propagated plants from settling in too deeply as well.

This bed measures 2 x 4 feet, which is the same size as a quarter sheet of plywood. Most home supply stores carry precut pieces, so the only sawing required is cutting the frame pieces, which can be done with a handsaw. The light, loose texture of the sand—peat moss mixture promotes fast root development, discourages soil-borne diseases, and makes it easy to lift plants when their new homes are ready. You also can sink container—grown plants into the propagation bed to help keep their roots cool and moist.

You Will Need

Tools: Tape measure, pencil, handsaw, hammer, drill with ?-inch bit, garden spade, wheelbarrow, garden hose

12 feet of 1 x 8 pine or cedar lumber

Thirty-four 2-inch nails

One 2 x 4-foot piece of ?-inch plywood

One 6-foot-long 1 x 2 furring strip

One 50-pound bag of play sand (1 cubic foot)

One small bale of peat moss (1 cubic foot)

1. To make the frame, measure and cut the 1 x 8 boards into two 4-foot-long pieces and two 2-foot-long pieces. Nail them together at the corners to form a box.

2. Place the plywood over the assembled frame, and nail it in place. Use at least two nails for

each short side, three nails for each long side, and one nail at each corner.

3. Cut the furring strip into three 2-foot-long pieces. Nail one to each end of the frame, broad sides down, sandwiching the plywood between the furring strip and the frame. Nail the remaining piece across the center of the frame.

4. Use the drill to make 12 evenly spaced drainage holes in the plywood. Move the bed to its permanent location.

5. Use the spade to thoroughly mix the sand and peat moss together in a wheelbarrow. Dump the mixture into the assembled bed, and drench with water. Wait a few minutes for the peat to absorb the water, stir the mixture, and water it again. Repeat if necessary until the peat particles appear dark with moisture.

6. To use the bed, simply sink plants into the sand—peat moss mixture and keep them moist until you are ready to lift them out and plant them in your garden.

7. To move your bed, remove some of the sand—peat moss mixture, and allow the rest to dry out. Get a helper to help you move the dry, partially filled bed.

Make a Double Pot Propagator
Barbara Pleasant

This easy system, which makes use of the porous nature of inexpensive terra-cotta clay pots, sets up in a snap and always gives good results. Water poured into a sealed small pot is slowly absorbed by the rooting medium, and a plastic tent provides the humidity needed by rootless cuttings. A half-and-half mixture of sand and peat moss makes a good medium for rooting cuttings, or you can use damp seed-starting mix or perlite. Regardless of which medium you choose, start over with a fresh batch for each new crop of cuttings. Develop your propagation skills with fast-rooting cuttings such as chrysanthemums, or coleus, before moving on to woody plants, which need more time to develop new roots.

You Will Need

Tools: Bucket, hand trowel, measuring cup, pump spray bottle

One 8-inch-wide clay flowerpot

One 4-inch-wide clay flowerpot

One 6-inch clay pot saucer

1 quart clean sand (such as play sand)

1 quart pulverized peat moss

Two 1-inch-square pieces of duct tape

1 cup small, clean pebbles

4 chopsticks or wood skewers

8 to 10 prepared stem tip cuttings

1 opaque plastic produce bag

1. Thoroughly clean the pots and pot saucer. If you are using new ones, place them in a tub of clean water to soak for 10 minutes, and then allow them to drip dry.

2. Place the sand and peat moss in a bucket, and use a hand trowel to mix them together. Add 2 cups of lukewarm water, mix, and then add another 2 cups of water. Mix again, and allow the mixture to sit for 10 minutes. If pieces of the peat moss still appear dry, add more water until the mixture is the consistency of raw cookie dough.

3. Cover the drainage hole in the bottom of the 4-inch pot with the pieces of duct tape. Place one on the inside of the pot, and the other on the outside.

4. Place the pebbles in the bottom of the 8-inch pot. Add a 2-inch layer of the sand/peat moss mixture. Set the 4-inch pot in the center, and press lightly. Add more of the sand/peat moss mixture if needed to raise the top rim of the smaller pot ?-inch above the top rim of the larger pot.

5. Fill the space between the two pots with the sand/peat moss mixture. Spray lightly with water, and add more sand/peat moss mixture if needed until the space is filled to within ?-inch of the top of the 8-inch pot. Gently lift and rinse out the smaller pot, and then put it back into place.

6. Use one of the chopsticks or skewers to make 8 to 10 evenly spaced holes in the sand/peat moss mixture for cuttings. Stick the prepared cuttings into the holes, and use your fingers to make sure they are in firm contact with the rooting medium.

7. Insert the chopsticks or skewers along the outside of the 4-inch pot. Place the Double Pot Propagator on the saucer, and position it in a warm place out of direct sunlight. Pour 1 cup of lukewarm water into the small pot, and then cover the Propagator with the plastic bag, arranging the folds so the plastic is held above the cuttings by the chopsticks or skewers.

8. After 2 days, remove the plastic bag and use your finger to see if the sand/peat moss mixture is still moist. If it feels dry, add ? cup water to the small pot. Replace the plastic cover.

9. Check the moisture level again every other day, and add ? cup water to the small pot whenever it becomes empty. Remove any cuttings that have wilted. Leave the plastic cover off at night, but put it on during the day.

10. Three weeks after setting the cuttings to root, pull gently on cuttings that show evidence of new growth. If you feel slight resistance, use a fork to lift them and transplant them to small individual pots. Keep the transplanted cuttings in a shady place outdoors, or indirect light indoors, and keep moist. Increase light as new growth appears.

Continued ➡

Make a Portable Trellis

Barbara Pleasant

As handy as a pocketknife, a portable trellis made with chicken wire attached to 1 x 2s can work as a freestanding support in an open vegetable or flower garden, or you can place it next to a wall or wood privacy fence. You can change its shape, too, so the same trellis that supports a straight row of peas in spring can be changed into a circular cage for summer tomatoes. When winter arrives, simply pick off the dead vines and roll up the trellis like a scroll for storage, or use it as a collection bin for leaves. Best of all, this trellis comes together so quickly that you can make several in one afternoon.

Farm supply stores often stock chicken wire (also called poultry netting) in 36-inch or wider widths, but most home supply stores sell the 24-inch-wide version. Plain galvanized wire is fine, but many gardeners prefer chicken wire that has been covered with a vinyl coating because it looks better and is easier to clean at the end of the season. Both types are inexpensive to buy, and you will find plenty of uses for small leftover pieces. A 12-inch square piece, crumpled into a ball and placed in a teapot, is a flower arranger's best friend.

You Will Need

Tools: Thick gloves, tin snips, staple gun, hammer, spade, scissors, carpenter's level

10-foot roll of 24-inch-wide 20-gauge chicken wire (poultry netting)

Four 5-foot-long pieces of 1 x 2 cedar lumber

Eight 1?-inch galvanized finishing nails

Cord, twine, or wire for use as guy wires

Four 18-inch-long wood stakes

1. Wearing gloves, use the tin snips to cut two pieces of chicken wire 4 feet long.

2. Set two of the 1 x 2s on a flat surface, 4 feet apart, with their broad sides down. Use the staple gun to attach the chicken wire to both 1 x 2s, beginning at the top edge and allowing a ?-inch margin between the outer edge of each 1 x 2 and the chicken wire. Attach a second piece of chicken wire below the first one.

3. Top each 1 x 2 with another, sandwiching the edges of the chicken wire between them. Nail them together with the finishing nails.

4. Dig two 12-inch-deep holes for the trellis legs. Set the trellis in place, and refill the holes. Firm in the soil around one leg, and stabilize it with two guy wires attached to two stakes. Use the level to make sure the trellis stands up perfectly straight.

5. Adjust the position of the second leg, stretching the trellis tight as you work, before installing the last two stakes and guy wires. Check to make sure the trellis is straight before firming the soil around both legs.

A Trellis That Suits to a "T"

Barbara Pleasant

The T-bar trellis offers grapes and other fruiting vines what they need for better health and higher yields—maximum exposure to light and a permanent place to ramble. You can use it for hardy kiwis or long-handled dipper gourds, too, or make a shorter version for raspberries. Consisting of two T-shaped posts set 12 feet apart and connected with three runs of galvanized wire, this trellis is meant to last for many years, so the posts are permanently set in concrete. This is a heavy trellis that requires the joint efforts of two people to build and install.

If you dream of a shady sitting place near a too-sunny garden, you can use two T-posts to support a small pergola. Set the posts 6 feet apart and top them with wood slats or a panel of cedar or redwood lattice, nailed into place.

T-trellises do not have to work in pairs. To use a single T-trellis to support a vigorous climbing rose, install diagonal wires between the ends of the crosspieces and the base of the post, and tie new canes to these wires with strips of soft, stretchy cloth. A single T-trellis also makes a great structure for supporting a collection of hanging baskets, which can be hung from the crosspieces as well as the main post.

You Will Need

Tools: Measuring tape, power saw, drill with ?-inch extension bit, ratchet wrench, post-hole digger, level, wheelbarrow, spade, wire snips

One 6-foot-long 4 x 4

Two 8-foot-long 4 x 6 posts of rot-resistant wood (cedar or locust)

Two 5-foot-long 4 x 6 crosspieces

Four 10-inch-long ⅜-inch-diameter lag screws

20 flat metal washers

Eight 5-inch-long ⅜-inch-diameter lag screws

Eight 7-inch-long ⅜-inch-diameter lag screws

6 large screw eyes

2 bags premixed concrete

42 feet of galvanized, high-tensile, 12-gauge wire

Three 5?-inch turnbuckles

1. To make the braces, measure and saw four 16-inch pieces from the 6-foot 4 x 4. Then cut 45-degree angles at the ends of each piece.

2. Lay the two 4 x 6 posts on a flat surface, broad sides down. Place 5-foot-long crosspieces at the tops of each post, measuring to make sure they are perfectly centered. Drill guide holes for two 10-inch lag screws 2 inches apart on the tops of the crosspieces. Thread washers onto the 10-inch lag screws. Use the ratchet wrench to attach the crosspieces to the posts with lag screws.

3. To attach braces to each T-post, position the braces and drill guide holes at each junction for one 5-inch and one 7-inch lag screw. Install the screws with washers as you did in Step 2, placing them at horizontal and vertical angles.

4. Mark the center of each crosspiece. Then mark spots 4 inches inside each outside edge. Drill guide holes for the screw eyes, and securely screw them into place.

5. Dig 24-inch-deep postholes 12 feet apart. Set each assembled T-section in the holes, and use a level to make sure they are plumb. Mix concrete according to label directions, and shovel it into the holes. Allow the concrete to set for at least 48 hours.

6. Cut three 14-foot lengths of the 12-gauge wire. Screw a turnbuckle to its maximum length, and hook one end into a screw eye. Thread the end of a piece of wire into the other end of the turnbuckle, loop the end through the eye twice, and then loop it around itself. Attach the other end of the wire to the opposite T-post, stretching the wire as tightly as you can. Twist the turnbuckle to further tighten the wire. Cut off the excess wire, leaving a 3-inch-long tail.

7. Repeat Step 6 to install the remaining 2 wires.

Get Creative with Cloches

The historical version of a garden cloche was a glass bell jar, but in more recent times, resourceful gardeners turned to cloches made from plastic milk jugs with their bottoms removed. To help hold a milk carton cloche steady in the wind, push a stick through a V-shaped cut made in the top of the handle. Leaving the top off of a milk jug cloche creates an instant vent.

To cloche a plant that's too big for a milk carton, use bubble wrap to make an insulated teepee. Place four or more 24-inch-long sticks around a plant, tie them together at the top, and enclose the base of the teepee with a 16-inch-wide band of bubble wrap (available in the office supply section at discount stores). Secure the wrapping in place with clothespins, and be sure to leave an opening at the top through which hot air can escape.

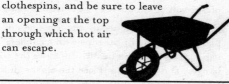

Make a Tube Hoop Cloche

Barbara Pleasant

If you want to get a head start growing widely spaced hills of potatoes, squash, or melons, or protect a drift of flowers from late freezes, you need a cloche that can cover some ground. A Tube Hoop Cloche covers a 20-inch-diameter circle, and it's easy to move from place to place. Made from easily scavenged materials, this cloche looks like a giant shower cap. An opening in the top makes it easy to vent on sunny days, or you can close it up tight when the weather turns cold. When the vent is open, a coat hanger attached to the stake keeps the plastic from falling down onto the plants below.

You Will Need

Tools: Heavy-duty scissors, measuring tape, utility knife, office stapler, felt-tip marker, pliers

1 bicycle inner tube

One 7-foot-long piece of old garden hose

One 4-foot-square piece of 4- or 6-mil clear plastic

1 wire coat hanger

One 20-inch-long piece of ?-inch PVC pipe

2 thick rubber bands

1. Use the scissors to remove the air valve from the inner tube by cutting across the tube on either side of the valve. Use the utility knife to trim the garden hose to 2 inches shorter than the length of the tube, or about 70 inches.

2. Slip the hose inside the tube. Overlap the ends of the tube about ? inch. Pinch together the overlapped edges of the tube on the outside of the hoop, and staple them together.

3. Spread out the plastic, and lay the prepared tube on top. Use the scissors to cut a circle of plastic 12 inches wider than the hoop on all sides (about 46 inches in diameter). Make 8 equally spaced marks along the outside edge of the plastic circle with a felt-tip marker.

4. Pull the loose plastic up through the center of the hoop, and staple the edge of the plastic to the outside of the hoop at equal intervals by pinching the inner tube, folding the edge of the plastic over the pinched rubber, and

Continued →

stapling it in place. Using the marks on the plastic as guides, begin by stapling 4 opposite points around the edge of the tube. Then install staples at midpoints between the first 4 staples. Between the 8 stapled points, gather the loose edges of plastic into pleats. Fold the pleats over and staple them to the tube.

5. Use the pliers to bend down the hook of the coat hanger. Hang the coat hanger in the top of the stake, and secure it in place with a rubber band. Push the PVC pipe stake into the ground near the plant you want to protect, and center the Tube Hoop Cloche over the stake.

6. Use scissors to cut a 6-inch-wide X in the top of the plastic. Hold the cut edges together above the top of the stake and secure them with a rubber band. On sunny days, remove the rubber band so hot air can vent out of the top of the cloche. When open, the top edges of the plastic will be supported by the clothes hanger.

7. To move the cloche, secure the top edges of the plastic to the top of the pipe with a rubber band, grasp the pipe firmly just above the coat hanger, and pull it up. Place the cloche in its new place, and push the pipe into the ground.

Build an Isolation Box
Barbara Pleasant

If you want to protect an individual plant from insect or animal pests, a simple frame that can be covered with rowcover or another lightweight fabric will do the trick. This is a great way to keep Japanese beetles away from a treasured rose during their 6-week feeding period, or to safeguard a tomato from the moths whose larvae become tomato hornworms. An isolation box can serve other purposes as well:

- If you plan to save seeds from a certain plant, you can use your isolation box to exclude pollinating insects (unless the plant is self-fertile, you will need to distribute pollen between different flowers by hand).

- When you decide that you must use an organic pesticide, you can use the box to exclude beneficial insects for a day or two after the plant is sprayed.

- Use the frame to support bird netting if berries or tomatoes need temporary protection.

- Cover the frame with an old sheet to turn the box into a shade cover for seedlings set out in hot weather or for newly seeded beds of slow sprouters such as carrots, parsley, or onions.

This lightweight model goes together in minutes, and because the joints are not glued together, it can be taken apart and stored when not in use. Simply pop the pieces apart, hose them down, and bind them together with string or a large rubber band. Don't hesitate to alter the size of the frame to fit your needs. To raise the frame's height, simply attach additional pieces of PVC pipe to the legs.

You Will Need

Tools: Measuring tape, handsaw, pruning shears or loppers
Two 10-foot pieces of ?-inch PVC pipe
Four ?-inch-diameter 3-way (90 degree) elbow connectors
Four ?-inch-diameter male connectors
Four 18-inch-long straight sticks or bamboo stakes
One 10-foot-square piece of rowcover

Rowcover Alternatives

Rowcover fabric made for home gardens doesn't have holes in it, so it blocks only a little light, and tiny flea beetles can't get through to damage plants. There are other fabrics that make good stand-ins for purchased rowcover fabric, such as flexible polyester window screening, discarded sheer draperies, or mosquito netting. Another great option is tulle, the polyester net fabric used to decorate ballet tutus, bridal veils, and party tables. Inexpensive and widely available at fabric and craft shops, tulle even comes in festive colors. The openings in the net are less than $1/16$-inch wide, so tulle is best used as a barrier for medium to large-size insects, such as various beetles and moths.

Tulle is usually 59 inches wide, which is not wide enough to completely cover a tunnel or box. When using any alternative material that's too narrow to give good coverage, simply sew pieces together with a needle and thread, or use a sewing machine. Rowcover can be cut and sewn, too. If you know how to sew, try creating unique garden fashions from rowcover or alternative fabrics, such as a quick slipcover, for the Isolation Box.

1. Saw the pipe into four 30-inch-long pieces—four for the top of the frame and four for the legs.

2. Arrange four of the cut pieces into a square on a flat surface. Firmly push the ends into the elbow connectors to form a box. With the open ends of the connectors facing up, screw in the male connectors until tight. They may not screw in all the way. Firmly twist the legs into the open end of the connectors.

3. Carry the frame to where you want to use it, and adjust the position of the legs to make the frame square. Mark the places where the legs touch the ground.

4. Use the pruning shears to trim sticks or stakes. Push the sticks or stakes into the ground 10 inches deep at the places marked for the legs, making sure they are perfectly straight. Lift the frame, and slip the legs over the sticks. Push the legs into the soil 3 inches deep.

5. Cover the frame with rowcover, and secure the bottom edges with bricks, stones, or pieces of scrap lumber.

Fashion a Flashy Scarecrow
Barbara Pleasant

Most gardeners enjoy the sight and sound of birds in the landscape—until those feathered friends take a liking to newly planted seeds, tender seedlings, and just-ripened berries. Songbirds are most likely to visit the garden in search of caterpillars and other tasty bugs, but crows, mockingbirds, jays, and a few other species sometimes become "beaks gone bad." Before these clever creatures learn that your garden is a great place for lunch, put a scarecrow or two on patrol.

Anyone who's ever done battle with crows or jays knows that the term "bird-brained" is less of an insult than most people think. These birds are bold and intelligent, and they quickly recognize the difference between genuine threats and our feeble attempts to chase them off. You can make a traditional scarecrow

stuffed with straw, but this flashier version is more likely to do a good job of spooking birds. Birds quickly become accustomed to stationary stuffed scarecrows and will eventually use them as perches. They are much less likely to cozy up to a scarecrow that flashes in the sun, flaps in the wind, and has brightly colored dangling hands. A successful scarecrow may not win a prize in the fall porch-decorating contest, but its features will make it scarier to birds than any benign straw-stuffed dummy.

You Will Need

Tools: Wood saw, scissors or wirecutters, pliers, stepladder, rubber mallet
1 sturdy bamboo pole or tall fence post
3 yards of string or thin, pliable wire
1 metallic compact disc (or aluminum pie pan)
1 wire clothes hanger
Two 18-inch-long wood stakes
8 wood or plastic clothespins
1 suit of old clothes, including a long-sleeved shirt and pair of baggy pants or billowy skirt
1 pair of brightly colored rubber gloves

1. Use the saw to cut a shallow 1-inch-deep V-shaped notch in the top of the bamboo pole or fence post. Use string or thin wire to hang a shiny compact disc or a pie pan from the top of the pole, running the string through the notch to keep it from slipping. This forms the scarecrow's "head." If desired, use a waterproof marker to draw eyes on the scarecrow's face.

2. Attach a second piece of string or wire to the top of the pole, and pull a loop through the center hole of the disk (or through a hole punched near the lowest rim of the pie pan). Hook the clothes hanger through the loop. Use pliers to close the hanger's hook to help keep it on the loop.

3. Use the rubber mallet to drive the prepared pole in place in your garden. Pound 2 stakes into the ground on either side of the pole, and secure it with guy wires tied or wired to the stakes.

4. Use clothespins to fasten the pants or skirt to the hanger's cross bar. Slip the shirt over the hanger. Don't worry about stuffing the clothes—it's better if the scarecrow's "body" flaps in the slightest breeze.

5. Fasten the rubber gloves to the ends of the sleeves with clothespins. If the weight of the gloves makes the sleeves too heavy to move freely, slip a long branch, a straight piece of wire, or a yardstick into the sleeves to hold them out from the scarecrow's "body."

6. Let your scarecrow blow in the breezes. If necessary for stability, use string or fine wire to loosely attach the clothing to the pole. Keep birds guessing by moving your scarecrow around in the garden. The best time to change its location is in the evening. The next morning's early birds will be surprised to find it in a different spot.

Weave a Rustic Homegrown Fence
Barbara Pleasant

Kids and dogs rarely mean to trample the dahlias or break the begonias, but the damage they cause while chasing errant balls or neighborhood cats can be severe.

Here's a pretty yet practical handmade fence that can save your garden from destruction and save your family from stressful discord.

Continued ➡

This version is 12 feet long and 3 feet high, but you can make a smaller version if you want to create a low edging around flower beds. If you live near woods, you can gather your materials as you thin out unwanted undergrowth. Or, grow your own wood for weaving. If your own property lacks a supply of wattle-worthy wood, check with a local tree-trimming business or your local parks department to see if you can acquire what you need from them. The misguided pruning practice of "topping" trees causes them to produce a gold mine of growth that's perfect for wattle fence construction—loads of long, straight, whippy branches. If your neighbor is inclined to this type of arboreal abuse, offer to prune the afflicted tree of its resulting suckers (those long, straight stems) and put them to good use in your fence.

You Will Need

Tools: Pruning saw, loppers, pruning shears, hatchet, measuring tape, hammer, scissors

One 18-inch-long rebar stake

Small piece of scrap lumber

Five 4-foot-long, 2-inch-diameter posts

Thirty-two 4-foot-long flexible branches

Jute or twine

1. Use the pruning saw and loppers to gather your materials. Trim off stubs and leaves with pruning shears. Shape one end of each post to a point with a sharp hatchet.

2. Mark places for posts 3 feet apart. Use the rebar stake, topped with a piece of scrap lumber, to make guide holes for the posts. Pound the posts into the guide holes 12 inches deep. They may be slightly wobbly.

3. Starting at each end, weave flexible branches between the posts, alternating the position of each branch on either side of the posts. Use at least four horizontal rows of branches to make the fence sturdy enough to work as a barrier. As you weave, adjust the posts as needed to keep them upright. The fence will become sturdier as each row of horizontal branches is added.

4. When you are satisfied with the woven pattern of the branches, use jute or twine to tie the ends of protruding branches to adjacent horizontal branches to hold them in place. Trim off any awkward ends.

5. Weave jute or twine through the ends of the horizontal branches on both outside edges of the fence, lashing them to the outermost posts to keep them from sliding up and down. Trim the ends of the branches on the outside of the fence to make them even.

Grow a Living Fedge

Barbara Pleasant

What do you get when you cross a fence with a hedge? The answer is a fedge, which you can make by weaving fresh willow branches together, with their bases nestled into moist soil so they take root and grow. You can start a fedge with willow or other woody cuttings gathered from woods or roadsides. Or, use whatever green branches you have on hand, including those pruned from fruit trees, grapes, or forsythia or other flowering shrubs. As long as you make the fedge in spring, when deciduous plants are just emerging from dormancy, many of them will take root and leaf out.

In traditional fedges, branches are arranged diagonally, so they cross each other within the structure. However, you also have the option of setting branches into the ground vertically, so they grow straight up. A fedge can be temporary—lasting only a few years—or you can make it a permanent part of your landscape. If your goal is to establish a permanent coppice plot, you can plant your first cuttings in a fedge, and then cut all of the plants back to the ground after 2 years. In subsequent seasons, the plants will regrow into a hedge that will produce a steady supply of young branches to use in garden projects made of weavable woods.

You Will Need

Tools: Spade, handsaw, wire snips, staple gun

Three 5-foot-long wood posts

30 feet of 10-gauge wire

Twelve 8-inch-long willow stem tip cuttings (or cuttings from other deciduous plants)

Mulch for a 12-foot-long row

1. Prepare the soil in a 12-foot-long row by digging in organic matter and removing weeds, roots, and rocks. Set the posts in the ground, 12 inches deep and 4 feet apart.

2. Install 2 tiers of wire between the posts, with the bottom tier 12 inches from the ground and the top tier 36 inches from the ground. Wrap the ends of the wire around the end posts before snipping off the ends. Staple the wire to all three posts.

3. Push half of the cuttings into the ground 2 feet apart and 3 inches deep, setting them at a diagonal angle. Push the remaining cuttings into the soil 6 inches from the first set, crossing the cuttings so they form right angles. Water well.

4. As the cuttings begin to leaf out, remove any weeds and then mulch over the soil. Train the new growth to twine in and out between the wires.

Sweet 'N' Sour Codling Moth Trap

Roger Yepsen [Au]

For a nontoxic way of catching codling moths around fruit trees, mix up a brew of household ingredients.

1. Pour 1 cup of cider vinegar, ⅓ cup of dark molasses, ⅛ teaspoon of ammonia, and 5 cups of water into a plastic gallon jug. Put on the cap and shale well to mix.

2. Cut two or three 2-inch holes just below the shoulders of the jug.

3. Hang the jug from a fruit tree, passing a strip of cloth through the handle so that the holes are canted downward and won't admit rainwater.

4. Monitor the trap and replace the brew from time to time.

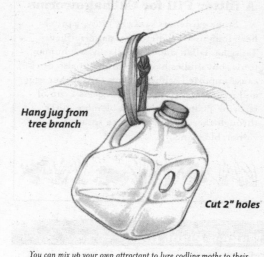

Hang jug from tree branch

Cut 2" holes

You can mix up your own attractant to lure codling moths to their deaths in this trap.

A Detachable Window Box

Roger Yepsen

Winter weather is tough on wooden window boxes, shortening their serviceable lives. In particular, the planting medium will expand as it freezes, possibly causing the joints to fail. This design is easy to build, is light enough to manage easily, and can be lifted off of its support come cold weather. There's no need to paint (and scrape and repaint) the box because it's made of cedar and assembled with stainless-steel screws.

1. From 1 x 6-inch cedar boards, cut the sides, ends, and bottom to length. You'll also need to cut two mounting pieces, one that will be attached permanently to the windowsill and the other for the box itself. Note that one long edge of each piece has a 45-degree angle; you can make both pieces with a single angled cut down the middle of a 1 x 6.

2. Assemble the box by drilling pilot holes, then driving the screws. Drill the drainage holes in the bottom. Attach the other mounting piece to the windowsill, bevel side up as shown.

3. Line the box with a piece of plastic sheet, tucking in the corners. Punch drainage holes through the plastic over the holes in the bottom.

4. Mount the window box and either add a potting mixture or use individual potted plants.

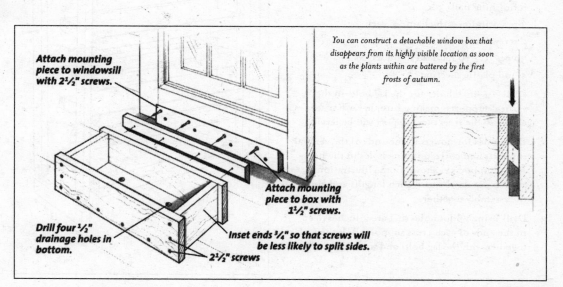

Attach mounting piece to windowsill with 2½" screws.

Attach mounting piece to box with 1½" screws.

Drill four ½" drainage holes in bottom.

Inset ends ¾" so that screws will be less likely to split sides.

2½" screws

You can construct a detachable window box that disappears from its highly visible location as soon as the plants within are battered by the first frosts of autumn.

Continued ➜

A Bitter Pill for Cabbageworms

Some gardeners swear by tansy, a bitter herb long used medicinally as a vermifuge. Tansy has fallen out of popularity as a human tonic, but studies have shown that it also can cause imported cabbageworms to lay fewer eggs and to develop more slowly. Process 1 cup of tansy in 3 cups of water in a blender, filter through cheesecloth, and then spray on vulnerable plants.

Make a Plant Rack
Barbara W. Ellis

If you're sold on the benefits of starting seedlings under lights but need to conserve space in your basement or plant room, building a plant rack may be the solution. Ours is inexpensive and relatively easy to build.

Tools Required

Electric drill
Saw (circular saw or handsaw)
Hammer
Pliers

Materials

Lumber-Shopping List

4 pcs. 2 x 4 x 8'
3 pcs. 2 x 3 x 8'
5 pcs. 1 x 3 x 8'
1 sheet (4 x 8') ?" A-C grade exterior plywood

Lumber-Cut List

You'll need to cut the lumber you've bought into the following lengths.

4 pcs. 2 x 4 x 63?" (vertical supports)
4 pcs. 2 x 4 x 18" (horizontal supports)
6 pcs. 2 x 3 x 48" (cross supports)
3 pcs. ? x 3 x 47?" plywood (tray bottoms)
6 pcs. 1 x 3 x 47?" (tray sides)
6 pcs. 1 x 3 x 16?" (tray ends)

Hardware

2 dowels, 5/16" x 48"
3 double-tubed, 48" fluorescent light fixtures with hangers
12 lag bolts 5/16" x 3?" with flat washers
3 broom handles or 1" dowels, 48" long
6 finishing nails 3d
2 pcs. window sash chain, 4' each
2 screw hooks
36 pcs. 1?" #6 flathead wood screws
4-mil plastic sheeting

1. Drill 5/16-inch holes for the lag bolts in the vertical supports, making sure they are spaced evenly so the trays they support will be level.

2. Drill holes for dowels in the ends of the vertical supports and corresponding holes in the horizontal supports as shown in the illustration above. Cut dowels to 4-inch lengths and glue the assembly together.

3. Drill ?-inch pilot holes that are 2 inches deep in the ends of each cross support. Bolt the rack together with the lag bolts and washers.

4. To make the tray bottoms, drill and countersink pilot holes through the tray bottoms into the tray sides and ends. Fasten tray bottoms to sides with flathead wood screws. For a waterproof liner, spread 4-mil plastic on the tray bottoms and up the sides, and staple or tack it in place. Slide the finished trays onto the rack.

5. To mount the fluorescent lights, first twist screw hooks into the underside of the horizontal supports at the top of the rack. Hang a 4-foot piece of window sash chain from each hook. Drive finishing nails partway into the ends of three broom handles, slip the broom handles through the hangers on the light fixtures, and insert the nail ends into loops of the sash chain. Adjust the lights up or down by moving the nails to higher or lower loops.

The three lights combined use about 260 watts per hour (40 watts per tube plus ballast).

For quick germination, start your seeds on the rack's top level, where the soil can be warmed by heat rising from the lower lights. Once the seedlings have sprouted, move them to a lower level and start a fresh seed tray on top.

Making a Portable Cold Frame
Barbara W. Ellis

This simply designed cold frame is tried and true—as well as easy and inexpensive to build. Its dual window-positioning system is a convenient feature; rods attached to both sides of the frame can be raised to any of three positions to hold the glazing open wide when full ventilation is desired or while tending the plants inside. When only a small amount of ventilation is needed, wooden cams attached to the front adjust to hold the lid open from 1 to 3 inches.

This frame is designed to use an old storm window measuring 32? by 62⅜ inches as the glazing. If you have a window with different measurements on hand, adjust the width and length of the frame accordingly. The width of the frame should be 1 inch less than the width of your window; the length of the frame should be 1⅛ inches less than the length of your window. When adjusting the design, retain the height of the front and rear walls used here, but allow the slope of the window and the width of the box to change as necessary.

This frame can be easily dismantled for storage. The only maintenance it should need is periodic repainting and caulking.

Tools Required

Electric drill
Saw (table or circular)
Hammer
Pliers
Screwdriver

Materials

Lumber-Shopping List

1 pc. 1 x 4 x 10'
1 pc. 1 x 2 x 5'
1 sheet (4 x 8') ?" A-C grade exterior plywood

Lumber-Cut List

You'll need to cut the lumber you've bought into the following lengths. Use pressure-treated lumber or untreated pine painted with a preservative. It's best to measure and then cut the pieces as you assemble them to be sure they fit together correctly.

2 pcs. 1 x 2 x 18?" (rear vertical cleats)
2 pcs. 1 x 4 x 58?" (front and rear horizontal cleats)
2 pcs. 1 x 2 x 6" (front vertical cleats)

Hardware

2 hardwood dowels ⅝" x 36"
1 wood-frame storm window 32?" x 62⅜"
10 pcs. 1?" #8 flathead wood screws
2 carriage bolts 5/16" x 2" with flat washers and wing nuts
3 pcs. 3" tee hinges with fasteners
4 pcs. 1?" eye screws
12 finishing nails 4d
1?" aluminum nails
? pint waterproof glue
1 quart exterior-grade primer/sealer
1 quart exterior-grade enamel
1 quart copper nephthenate wood preservative

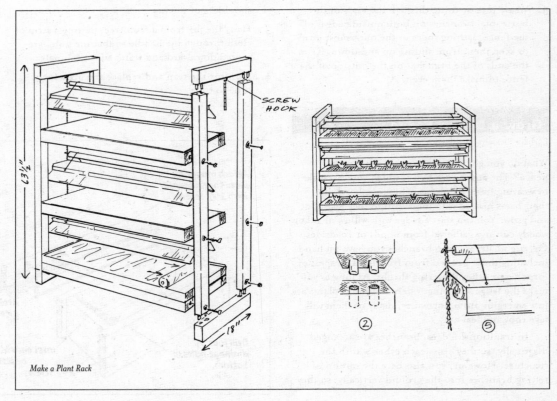

Make a Plant Rack

Continued ➡

1. Lay out the front-, rear-, and side-wall panels on the sheet of plywood. Cut out all four pieces. The rear-wall panel will be ? inch wider than its final size, so its upper edge can be beveled (see step 4).

2. Fasten the vertical cleats across the ends of the rear-wall panel using waterproof glue and 1?-inch aluminum nails. Avoid nailing at the three points on each end where screws will be inserted to hold the side panels in place in step 7.

3. Fasten the horizontal cleat to the upper edge of the rear-wall panel, between the two vertical cleats and flush with the top of the rear wall, using waterproof glue and 1?-inch aluminum nails. Avoid putting nails in areas where hinges will be attached in step 9, or near the upper edge of the panel, which will be trimmed away in step 4.

4. To bevel the top edge of the frame, start by laying the rear-wall panel down with the cleats facing up. Position one of the side panels against it, overlapping the edge and making sure the bottom and back edges of each panel are aligned flush. Scribe or draw a line across the end of the rear-wall panel and vertical cleats where they are crossed by the upper edge of the side-wall panel. Do the same using the other side-wall panel on the opposite end. This establishes the angle of the bevel. Now connect the two slanted lines by scribing or drawing across the length of the rear-wall panel on the front and back. Using a table saw or portable circular saw, rip and bevel the top edge of the rear panel.

5. Attach the front vertical cleats to the front-wall panel using waterproof glue and 1?-inch aluminum nails. Avoid nailing where screws will be inserted from the side in step 7.

6. Attach the front horizontal cleat to the front-wall panel, flush with the upper edge of the panel, using waterproof glue and 1?-inch aluminum nails.

7. Temporarily fasten the side-wall panels to the rear- and front-wall panels using 4d finishing nails or small brads. Drive the nails only partway into the wood for easy removal later. Drill a pair of 3/32-inch-diameter pilot holes centered 13/16 inch from the front edge of each side panel. Drill the first hole 1? inches above the base of the panel and the second 5 inches above. Center and drill three pilot holes of the same diameter through the back edge of each side panel. Install 1?-inch #8 flathead wood screws in the holes; then remove all temporary fasteners.

8. Cut the two window-positioning cams out of ?-inch plywood. Drill a 5/16-inch-diameter hole through each cam. Center and drill two 5/16-inch-diameter holes each 4? inches above the bottom edge of the front panel and 15 inches from the ends to accept the bolts for fastening the cams. Attach the cams to the outside of the front panel, using 5/16- by 2-inch carriage bolts with flat washers and wing nuts. Install the bolts from inside the panel.

9. Position the window on top of the cold frame so the rear edges of each are flush. Center the window over the frame so both edges hang slightly over the outer edges of the frame sides. Fasten the window to the frame using three 3-inch tee hinges. Attach a hinge 4 inches from each end and one in the center. Check to make sure the window opens and shuts properly.

10. To attach the dowel support rods, fasten the 1?-inch eye screws into two linked pairs. Install one end of each pair into a front panel vertical cleat, 4? inches above the base of the cold frame.

Then drill a 1/8-inch-diameter pilot hole into one end of each 36-inch wooden dowel. Screw the remaining eye screws into the dowels to fasten them to the frame.

11. Drill six 1 1/16-inch-diameter holes into the window frame, on the underside about halfway through the wood. You'll need three holes on either side. Locate one pair of holes 16 inches from the rear edge of the window; space the other two pairs on 4-inch centers toward the front. Drill the holes at an angle (approximately 65 degrees) to accommodate the dowel support rods when the window is in the open position.

12. Dismantle the cold frame to prepare it for planting. Sand all sharp edges and coat all bare wood surfaces with copper naphthenate wood preservative. After allowing the preservative to dry completely, paint the entire frame and, if necessary, the window frame with an exterior-grade primer/sealer.

13. Reglaze the window if the glazing is loose. Fill in any cracks or holes in the window or frame with caulk. Paint the wooden parts of the cold frame with two coats of good-quality exterior-grade enamel. Reassemble the cold frame when you are ready to use it.

Build a Planter

Barbara W. Ellis

This 8-cubic-foot planter is versatile, durable, portable, and protective for both ornamentals and container food crops. It can be used to grow a tree rose, a dwarf fruit tree, or a mixture of vegetables and flowering annuals on porch, patio, balcony, or deck. Fitted with casters, it can easily be rolled indoors in the fall to grow by a bright kitchen window or in a greenhouse over the winter, and then rolled back outdoors in the spring. It will last for many years.

Tools Required

- Screwdriver
- Electric drill
- Miter box and saw
- Saw (crosscut or electric)
- Paintbrush

Materials

Lumber-Cut List

Use redwood, cedar, or pressure-treated wood.

6 pcs. ? x 7? x 21?" (base)
12 pcs. ? x 7 3/8 x 23?" (side slats)
4 pcs. ? x 1? x 25?" (band)
4 pcs. ? x 2 x 26?" (cap)
16 pcs. ? x 1? x 22?" (battens)

Hardware

#6 x 1?" galvanized wood screws
12 to 16 pcs. #6 x 1 5/8" galvanized wood screws (for side corners only)
4 pcs. 3?" corner braces
4 heavy-duty casters
Clear wood finish for exterior wood or other ultraviolet inhibitor

1. **Base.** The 22?-inch-square base consists of two layers, with three boards per layer, running in opposite directions. The ?-inch gap between each board allows for drainage; four drainage holes are created in the center of the planter, as well as a hole near each of the four corners. To assemble the base, screw the two layers together, drilling from the bottom layer of boards into the top layer. Attach the casters to the base. Throughout the construction, predrill all holes.

2. **Sides.** Screw individual side slats into the base, allowing the sides to completely cover and extend about ? inch below the base, depending on the size of the casters. The sides of the planter should be 1? inches above the ground. For added strength, use three or four #6 1 5/8-inch screws on each side corner.

3. **Band.** Use the miter box to cut the ends of the four band pieces to join at corners. Notch corners of the four pieces 1/16 x 3? inches to accept corner braces. Screw the bands into the sides. Attach the corner braces to band corners at top.

4. **Cap.** Use the miter box to cut the ends of the four cap pieces. Screw the cap pieces into the top of the planter so the cap covers the top edges of the side slats and braced band. The inside edge of the cap is flush with the inside of the planter. The outside edge of the cap extends slightly beyond the band. Predrill all holes.

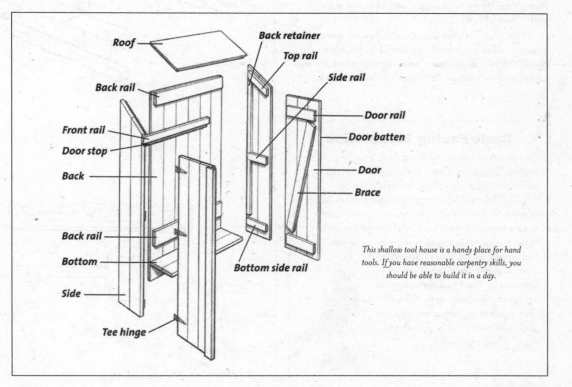

Roof
Back retainer
Top rail
Back rail
Side rail
Front rail
Door rail
Door stop
Door batten
Back
Door
Brace
Back rail
Bottom
Bottom side rail
Side
Tee hinge

This shallow tool house is a handy place for hand tools. If you have reasonable carpentry skills, you should be able to build it in a day.

Continued ➡

5. **Battens.** Screw the battens into the sides, four battens per side, so the side slat seams are covered. The corner battens are flush with the side edges. Stagger the screw holes on either side of the seams.

6. **Finish.** If you've used redwood or cedar, paint the outside of the planter with a clear finish. It is not necessary to paint the inside of the planter. Add 1 inch of gravel to the inside bottom of the planter for additional drainage. Indoors or on a wooden deck, be sure to use a drip tray beneath the planter.

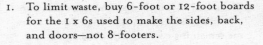
A Tool House
Roger Yepsen

What You'll Need
32 feet 1 x 2 pine
16 feet 1 x 4 pine
16 feet 1 x 5 pine
96 feet 1 x 6 pine
1/6 sheet ?-inch CDX plywood
#6 x 1?-inch galvanized screws
#6 x 1⅝-inch galvanized screws
#6 x 2-inch galvanized screws
Six 4-inch galvanized tee hinges
One 3-inch barrel bolt

Gardening requires enough labor without making repeated trips between wherever you stash implements and the garden itself. An attractive tool house, just deep enough to hold a row of commonly used hand tools, can be a great convenience. The structure is just a box, basically, with a little shed roof. It can be attached to the wall of your house or garage, or anchored to a sturdy garden post. To keep the wood from rotting at the lower edge of the tool house, the sides rest on either bricks or concrete blocks. The inside of the structure measures 9 inches deep, 34 inches wide, and 6 feet high. Although you can make all the cuts needed for the project with a handsaw, the work goes much more quickly with a circular saw. The construction is of solid wood, capped by a plywood roof, and assembled with both screws and water-resistant polyvinyl acetate glue. Parts are put together with glue on their mating surfaces, then clamped before driving the screws. Each door is hung with three tee hinges, and they are secured with a barrel bolt.

The instructions and drawing given here offer general ideas on how to go about building a tool house. If you don't have basic carpentry skills and tools, you can ask a carpenter to do the work.

Basic Paving Installation
Paving materials vary a great deal from region to region, based on what's available, but installation techniques for most materials are very similar. In areas where the ground freezes in the winter, lay paving on 2 inches of leveled sand over a base of 4 to 6 inches of tamped gravel. Where the ground does not freeze, you can install paving on a layer of leveled sand without the layer of gravel beneath it. Pour concrete directly on sand, eliminating the gravel. Stone patterns, tiles, and edgings are usually set in a 1-inch-deep mortar bed over sand.

1. To limit waste, buy 6-foot or 12-foot boards for the 1 x 6s used to make the sides, back, and doors—not 8-footers.

2. Begin by constructing each side, attaching the three rails to its inside surface. Cut the roof pitch at the top of the side, using the top rail as a guide. Attach the back retainers to each side, placing one above and one below the middle rail.

3. Make the back, attaching its two rails to the back boards. Leave a little space between each of the back boards to allow them to expand and contract with changes in the weather.

4. Attach the back to the sides.

5. Make the bottom by attaching two boards into the bottom side rails.

6. Make the front rail, which ties the top of the tool house together.

7. Add the roof, attaching it by driving screws into the pitched sides.

8. Make each door from three boards, attaching its two rails and the diagonal brace to the back surface.

9. Hang each door with three tee hinges, then make the door stop, which closes the gap at the top of the doors and gives you a place to mount the *strike* (or top component) of the barrel bolt. Attach the door stop to the back of the front rail.

10. Make the door batten and attach it to the outside edge of one door. The batten acts as a lip to hold the other door closed.

11. Mount the barrel bolt at the top of the door with the batten. Mount the strike on the door stop.

Barbara W. Ellis, Joan Benjamin, and Deborah L. Martin

Although most gardeners prefer plants to paving, there are many places in the landscape where paving is useful, appropriate, and labor saving. Installing a paved path once, for example, is a much better use of your time than repeatedly working to maintain part of your lawn that's trampled by traffic.

Find the Right Paving for Your Project
Start your paving project with a mental design. Consider how you'll use the paved area. As a patio? A lightly traveled path? How big is the area you want to pave? Choose paving that harmonizes with your home and is appropriate for the intended uses. You can install some paving materials, such as bricks, in different ways to create varying visual effects. For a large paved surface, you might choose to combine different materials to make it look more interesting.

Asphalt, bricks, concrete, stones, tiles, and wood are all types of paving that may find a place in a home landscape. While you can install most paving options yourself, you may choose to hire a contractor to install some types, such as asphalt and large-scale concrete projects. One advantage of brick and precast concrete pavers is that you can install paving at your own pace. You can finish your project in a day or gradually, as you have time to work on it.

Concrete. Concrete is a familiar and inexpensive paving. It is durable, needs little or no maintenance, and is more versatile than most people realize. You can vary its color, or seed it with stones to change its texture. It is unforgiving, however, and preparation before pouring is critical since you can not stop once you have begun.

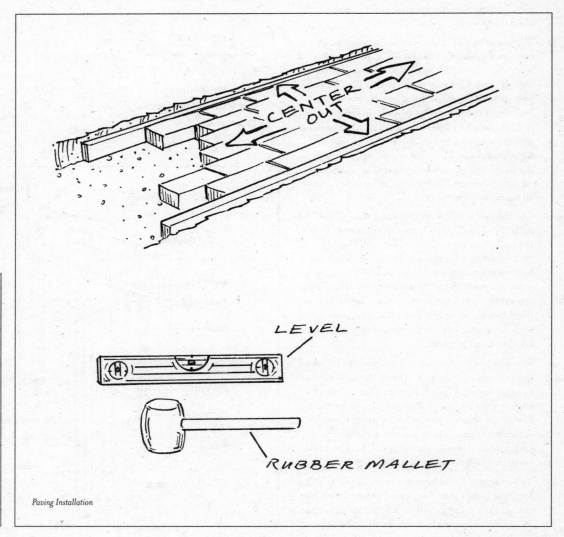
Paving Installation

Continued ➡

Concrete requires sturdy forms to hold its weight in place while it hardens, and you must have tools, such as edgers and floats, to give the surface the proper finish. You can mix concrete in a wheelbarrow or trough, or you can rent a portable motorized mixer.

Brick. Brick paving is one of the best choices for do-it-yourself home projects. Bricks come in a variety of colors and textures, and they are easy to plan with. Brick paving absorbs moisture so it dries quickly after a rain, doesn't become slippery, and stays cool in summer.

It is relatively simple to estimate the amount of material and cost because of the uniform size (about 2 x 4 x 8 inches), which is compact and easy to handle. You can lay bricks in many patterns; mixing patterns adds interest to large paved areas and helps define borders.

Precast pavers. Precast concrete pavers offer another easy-to-install paving option. They come in many colors and shapes, and are dense, durable, and of uniform size. Some styles fit together in interlocking geometric patterns. Install precast pavers on a base of sand over gravel, with sand joints between pavers. Some styles are shaped with holes in them that allow you to grow grass or other groundcovers over the paved area.

Add a Layer of Prevention

If you're laying pavers over sand rather than setting them in mortar, it's worth your time to put a weed-blocking barrier over the sand. You can use landscape fabric, cardboard, layers of newspaper, or any other light-excluding materials, as long as you keep the surface level. Although it adds a step to your paving installation, it will keep weeds from coming up through your pavement for years to come.

Paving Installation: Careful Planning Smooths the Way

1. **Outline the area you plan to pave.** Use a string stretched between stakes to outline the area and serve as a digging guide. It also will help you determine the amount of material you'll need. Use a hose to design curved edges or draw them on the ground with lime or bonemeal. Measure frequently with your tape measure to maintain equal distances between edges.

   If you're installing a walkway, skip to Step 5 and install edging strips to serve as your digging guide.

2. **Stretch a string as a reference point.** Stretch your string a few inches to a foot above the ground and use a line or carpenter's level to level it. The string will serve as a reference point as you dig out the bed for your paving and base materials. If you're installing a paved area next to your house, slightly slope the strings away from the house for drainage—about 1? inches for every 8 feet.

3. **Excavate the site.** Measure down from your strings to help keep the bed level as you dig. Remove enough soil to accommodate the depth of your base materials plus your paving. Stretch a string diagonally across the area and measure down from it to check the depth of the bed in the middle of the site. Add more stakes and stretch more strings as needed.

4. **Level the bed and add gravel.** Use a rake to level the bed, then add gravel. Use a hand tamper or mechanical compactor to firm it and remove air pockets.

5. **Add sand and level it.** Lay 2 inches of coarse sand over the gravel and level it with a *screed*, a straightedge that you pull across the sand at a constant height. It knocks down high spots and lets you see where to fill in low spots.

   Screed bars work like rails that the long, straight screed slides over. For wide areas like patios, lay lengths of 2 x 2s on the gravel base to provide screed bars for the sand. If you are installing a path that has an edging, it can serve as the screed bars. Nail a board that fits between your edgings to a longer board that will lay across them to smooth the sand base in a path.

6. **Set the pavers.** Once the sand is level, begin setting your pavers, leaving about ⅛ inch of space between each of your bricks, precast concrete pavers, or tiles. Work the pattern from the middle out toward the edges, so any discrepancies are less noticeable or can be accounted for if cutting is necessary. Measure frequently to ensure the pattern is straight. It's easy to pry up stones, bricks, or pavers and reset them as needed. A rubber mallet for easing the pavers into position and a level for ensuring their evenness are handy at this stage.

7. **Install edging.** An edging will hold your paving in place and define the paved area. You can use a redwood 2 x 4 set on edge and staked firmly in place, a row of bricks set on edge, or heavier paving units made specifically to serve as edging. The edge paving can be set in a mortar base to help hold the entire project together.

   Edging usually completes the installation, but for a walkway it may come at the beginning. Set with the top at final grade, it serves as both a digging guide and as screed bars for leveling the sand. Maintain exact measurements between edgings in this case so paving units fit. A temporary, moveable edging set on grade can also serve as screeding.

8. **Spread fine sand over the finished paving.** Sweep it into the cracks until they are full. Sprinkle the paving with a garden hose, then repeat with more sand.

Tools Needed for Paving Installation

Broom
Rubber mallet
Carpenter's level
Saw
Hammer and nails
Shovel
Hand or machine compactor
String and stakes
Rake
Tape measure
Wheelbarrow

Step-by-Step Steps

Barbara W. Ellis, Joan Benjamin, and Deborah L. Martin

To transform a slippery slope into easy-to-use steps, you'll first need to know the *rise* and run of the slope. To measure the rise, hold a 2 x 4 or a long pole horizontal and level, with one end resting at the top of the slope. Measure the distance straight down from your pole to the bottom of the slope. To measure the *run*, place a pole upright and level at the bottom of the slope, and measure the horizontal distance to the top of the slope.

Now do some simple math to see how many steps you'll need. Divide the rise of the slope by the desired height of each step. The result is the

number of steps. Now divide the run of the slope by the number of steps to find the length of each tread. Check the table to see if your treads and risers are properly proportioned; if not, adjust your numbers until you achieve the right balance.

Tread-to-Riser Relationships

Use these recommendations to design steps that will be easy to negotiate.

Tread (inches)	Riser (inches)
19	4
18	4?
17	5
15	5?
14	6
13	6?
12	7

Steps Can Ease Your Ups and Downs

Steps add an inviting aspect to the landscape and create transitions from one part of your yard to another. They also save you the hassles (and hazards) of scrambling up and down slopes and offer a solution for steep, hard-to-mow areas. Well-planned steps are safe and easy to use because they maintain the right proportions between treads (the part you walk on) and risers (the vertical parts). Steps on gentle slopes work best with low risers and wide treads, while steeper slopes need taller risers and narrower treads. Use the method shown on this page to find the total rise and run for your slope. With that information, you can work out how many steps you need and how much material it will take to build them.

Let your steps conform generally to the slope rather than trying to shape the slope to fit the steps. It means less work for you and a more comfortable climb. To make your steps easier to use, plan for a width of at least 4 to 5 feet, if your site and materials will allow it. Be flexible with your design, letting the treads extend over flat areas to form short pathways where the slope flattens, then rises again.

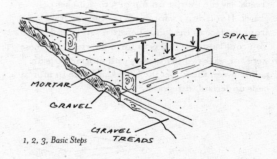

1, 2, 3, Basic Steps

1, 2, 3 Basic Step Installation

Follow these steps to install yours.

1. **Mark the rises.** Use stakes to mark both ends of each riser. Use a shovel to shape the slope into rough soil steps, using the stakes as guides. You may need a pick or mattock to accomplish this task.

   The tread of each step is just a short section of paving. Leave enough space between risers for the necessary gravel and/or sand base, in addition to the depth of the tread material.

2. **Install the steps.** Work from the bottom to the top of the slope. Alternately set risers and treads in place. Use a carpenter's level to keep them horizontal.

3. **Grade the site.** After the steps are installed, grade the soil on either side to slope naturally down to the steps. Border your steps with stones

Continued ➡

or plantings of perennials, herbs, groundcovers, or low shrubs to give them a finished look that's easy to maintain.

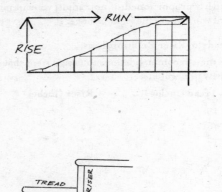

Step-By-Step Steps

Step Options

Timber steps. Steps constructed with 4 x 6 timbers for risers are the simplest to build. You can stack two 4 x 4 timbers together to make risers for steeper slopes. Drill into the timbers and tie them to the soil with galvanized metal stakes or spikes (basically huge nails).

Brick or concrete steps. You could also make the risers from bricks or from concrete poured into simple forms. Pave the treads with brick, gravel, wood chips, or groundcovering plants. If you choose to make brick treads, set them in a base of 1? to 2 inches of mortar over 3 to 4 inches of gravel. Treads of gravel and other loose materials will require edging to keep them in place.

Stone steps. Fieldstone steps with risers of smaller stones look natural in informal landscapes. This type of step can wind more easily because of the varying size of the components. To make wider steps, set two or more fieldstones side by side on a wider bed of small stone risers. For stability, set the small stones a mortar bed with at least ? inch of mortar between the small stones and the fieldstone cap. As with brick treads, lay the mortar on top of 3 to 4 inches of gravel. If you don't want to see the mortar, rake it from the face of the joints before it sets completely. You could also use bricks to form the risers for these steps, or stack two fieldstones with mortar beneath and between them. Set the bricks and slate in mortar beds underlaid with gravel.

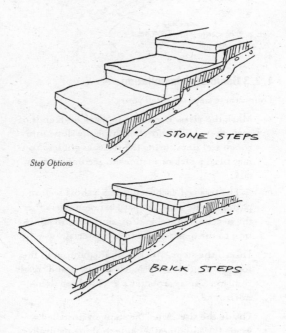

STONE STEPS

Step Options

BRICK STEPS

Make certain the layout of your deck is rectangular. From one corner stake (stake A), measure 3 feet out along the outlining length of string toward another stake (stake B); fold a piece of masking tape over the string to mark that point. From stake A, measure 4 feet along the string toward the stake at the other corner (stake C); mark that point with a second piece of tape. Measuring from tape mark to tape mark across the hypotenuse of the triangle, the distance should be exactly 5 feet. If it is not, adjust the position of stake B or C until the measurement is 5 feet and your deck is a true rectangle.

Low-Care, Easy-to-Build Deck

Barbara W. Ellis, Joan Benjamin, and Deborah L. Martin

Building a deck is not automatically a major investment involving a contractor. You can add a simple deck to your landscape in about a weekend, using tools you probably have at home. Size and place the deck to suit your needs—since it's freestanding, it can go anywhere. Precast concrete piers support the deck's 4 x 4 beams; these are topped by a deck of 2 x 6s.

Begin by deciding where you want your deck. Check the site for sun, drainage, and slope of the land. It's okay if the site slopes slightly, but the more level it is the better. If you're building your deck next to your house, any slope should be away from the house.

Decide on the size of your deck and make a plan to help you figure out how many beams, piers, and deck boards you need. Space your beams (the distance the deck boards must span) no more than 3 feet apart on center (from the center of one beam to the center of the next). Keep the space between the piers, along the length of beams, no more than 5 to 6 feet on center. If your deck is next to your house, leave a ?- to 1-inch gap between the deck and the house.

Simple Steps to an Easy Deck

1. **Layout your deck with stakes and string.** Use two stakes to mark each corner; place one about 6 inches out on a straight line with one side and the other stake 6 inches out on a line with the other side. When you stretch strings between the stakes, the strings will cross at the corners of the deck and form its outline.

   Stretch string between the stakes and level it with a carpenter's level or, preferably, a line level. The string helps you visualize the deck, determine where you need to add or remove soil, and level the piers. Remove all sod in the deck area.

2. **Lay out the piers.** Working from your drawing, measure in from the strings and lay out the piers. Drive a stake to mark the center of each pier position. Set the piers back from the edges of the deck to keep them out of sight.

3. **Dig a hole for each pier.** Dig deep enough to accommodate a 6- to 8-inch gravel base plus most of the height of the pier. Stretch additional strings, as needed, to help you position

your holes and measure the depth to dig. Remove the soil in a wheelbarrow, add gravel to each hole, and tamp the gravel to remove any air pockets. If you don't have a good tamper handy, use the end of one of your 4 x 4 beams. In areas where the ground does not freeze in the winter, you can set your piers in smaller holes with just a 2-inch layer of sand in the bottom.

4. **Set the precast piers onto the gravel.** Adjust the height, level, and exact alignment according to string lines and a carpenter's level. Backfill with soil around the piers. Check the accuracy of your work with a tape measure from time to time to make sure the piers are spaced properly.

5. **Spread landscape fabric.** To prevent grass and weeds from growing up between the deck boards, spread landscape fabric or other light-blocking material over the area. Cut an X in the fabric over each pier and pull it down snugly around them.

6. **Saw the 4 x 4 beams to length.** Lay them across the piers and nail them in place. Each pier will have a wooden nail block or metal hardware precast in it for nailing the beam. Align the ends of the beams with a string or a straightedge, or by careful measurement.

7. **Nail on the decking.** Laying out the decking can be tricky, but with a small deck you can lay out the boards before nailing them. Snap chalk lines as nailing guides, then attach each 2 x 6 deck board to the beams with two 16d galvanized nails at each beam. You can use ring-shank or twist nails for stronger hold. Use a 16d nail to space between the boards as you nail them. Let the first and last deck boards overhang the ends of the beams about an inch. You can adjust this somewhat, or adjust the spacing between the boards to make them fit evenly. If necessary, you can narrow the width of one board to fit the width of the last space.

As you work, use a straight edge to align all the deck boards on one end; let the other end extend slightly long. After all the boards are nailed in place, measure from each side of the deck and snap a chalk line to mark the edge of the boards. Cut along this line with a portable circular saw to even the ends. Soften up this hard edge with a rasp. Stain and/or seal the cut ends and your deck is complete.

FOR THE HOME

Make a Grapevine Wreath

Barbara Pleasant

When gathering vines from wild or cultivated grapes for making wreaths, use pruning shears to nip off the leaves (save pretty young leaves for cooking). Leave the curled tendrils intact. If you will not be using the vines right away, wind them into a coil in a large washtub or laundry basket, and cover them with a wet towel.

Continued ➡

You can make grapevine wreaths freehand, but it's easier to use a form made from a piece of scrap plywood. Decorate your wreath after it has dried.

You Will Need

Tools: Measuring tape, pencil, hammer, pruning shears

One 2-foot-square piece of scrap plywood

Four 4-inch nails

4 or more pieces of grapevine at least 4 feet long

Several 8-inch-long pieces of string

1. Draw an 18-inch-wide circle on the plywood, and hammer four 4-inch nails at equal intervals around the circle. Hammer them only as deep as needed to hold them secure.

2. Holding the thickest end of a cut piece of vine, wind it loosely around the nails, and then tuck in both of the ends. Repeat with as many vines as you like.

3. To help hold the wreath tight, tie it together with pieces of string before slipping it off of the form.

4. Lay the wreath on a flat surface to dry, and expect it to shrink a little. Should a wreath begin to warp as it dries, weight it with a board held in place with a brick.

Make a Woven Wheat Good Luck Charm
Barbara Pleasant

For thousands of years, people in different parts of the world have captured and preserved the fertility of summer by making woven wheat charms, which were hung in the kitchen through winter as a blessing for the house. The following spring, many rituals involved burying the woven wheat in the garden as a good luck charm for a bountiful season.

You Will Need

Scissors

9 stems of wheat, with the seed heads intact

Three 10-inch-long pieces of waxed dental floss

2 heavy books

1. Gather almost-mature wheat stems, with the whiskered heads attached, and hang them upside down in a bundle to dry. If you don't grow your own wheat, ask permission to gather some stems from a farm field, or look for dried wheat stems in craft stores.

2. When you're ready to weave, soak 9 dried wheat stems in warm water for 15 to 30 minutes to make the stems pliable.

3. Working on a flat surface, tie the wheat stems together with dental floss just below the seed heads. Separate the stems into three sections. Tie the middle three stems together three inches below the cluster of tops.

4. Braid the 3 stems on one side of the cluster, and then braid the other 3 stems. Curve the ends of the braids together to form a heart shape, and tie them tightly to the center bunch of stems. Trim off the ends.

5. Arrange the seed heads the way you want them, and place the weaving between two books to dry for at least 3 days. Hang your finished weaving on a wall or over your kitchen door.

Make a Broomcorn Whisk Broom
Barbara Pleasant

Making a perfect broom requires practice, but anyone can make a pretty yet primitive whisk broom. The secret is to bind the stems together as tightly as you can, which is best done with the help of a handy doorknob. You can use a straight stick or dowel for the handle, or turn your broom into an art piece by using a curved branch of rhododendron or other gnarled wood.

You Will Need

Tools: Ruler, drill, hammer, wire snips, scissors

About ? bushel of cleaned broomcorn tops

One 18-inch-long stick, 1 inch in diameter, or an old wooden broom handle

One 2-inch-long finishing nail

One 36-inch-long piece of flexible wire

One 24-inch-long piece of cotton string

1. Harvest the seed-bearing tops from mature broomcorn, and hang them in small bundles to dry for several days. To remove the seeds, lay several stems on a flat surface and pull a ruler over them until the seeds break free.

2. Drill a small hole through the handle, one inch from the end. Tap the finishing nail through the hole, so that ? inch (or more) of the nail extends on either side of the handle. Attach one end of the wire around one end of the nail, leaving 3 inches of wire extending outward from the nail. Attach the other end of the wire to a post, doorknob, or other stationary fixture.

3. Arrange a handful of broomcorn stems around the nail, with the tops of the stems one inch above the nail. Pull the wire taut, and rotate the broom to wrap the wire around the stems.

4. Repeat Step 3 twice, until the broom is full and tight and the nail is completely covered. Wind the two wire ends together tightly, and trim the ends.

5. Tie the string around the bundle, just above the nail. Wind it around the bundle tightly several times, and tie off the ends. Use scissors to trim the tops and bottoms of the broomcorn stems.

Make a Batch of Potpourri
Barbara Pleasant

Why spend money on artificial air fresheners when you can create your own right at home? Making potpourri is a great way to use up odds and ends of dried herbs and flowers, and you can add little pinecones, seeds, or even dried bits of fruit if you like. There's no one set recipe for potpourri, so it's easy to tailor the look and fragrance of each batch to make one-of-a-kind creations.

To pump up the fragrance of potpourri, you will need one or more small bottles of pure, organic essential oil—highly concentrated extracts made from fragrant plants, which are available at health food stores. Most retail displays include tester bottles, so you can sniff before you buy. If you can't decide, choose essential oils based on where you plan to use your potpourri. Lavender oil is quite popular for closet sachets and active living areas; some people like rose oil for

Great Things to Do with Dried Flowers

- Press individual blossoms within the pages of a heavy book. Enclose the dried blossoms in plastic laminating sheets to create beautiful bookmarks, or glue them inside homemade greeting cards.

- Decorate a Grapevine Wreath with dried flowers and foliage; change the dried materials every few months to fit the seasons.

- Make a seasonal table display by combining dried flowers, seed heads from grains and grasses, and ornamental gourds in a large oval platter.

- If dried blossoms break off from their stems, use a hot glue gun to attach them to gift-wrapped boxes, baskets, wreaths, and other decorative objects.

- Turn a perfect dried blossom into a unique accessory by tucking it into your hair barrette or ponytail holder.

- Use short-stemmed dried flowers to make a tiny arrangement in a pretty teacup. Place an inch of dry sand in the teacup to help hold the stems in place.

potpourri kept on bedside tables; and various citrus scents are always welcome in the kitchen.

Your potpourri will hold its scent longer if you use a fragrance fixative such as orris root, which is made from a type of iris. Craft stores sell other fixatives, too, such as calamus (which has a mild fruity scent) and spicy-smelling benzoin. However, orris root is widely available and works well in any type of potpourri.

You Will Need

Tools: Measuring spoon, wooden spoon, scissors

1 package of orris root crystals or other fixative

1 small bottle of pure, organic essential oil

1 pint-size glass jar with lid

6 cups of dried flowers, herbs, and seedpods

One 2-quart airtight glass or plastic container

1. Place 3 tablespoons of fixative and 15 to 20 drops of essential oil in a glass jar. Mix lightly with a wooden spoon and screw on the lid. Set aside for 2 days.

2. Select materials for your potpourri that include colors and scents to complement the room where you'll display your potpourri. Use scissors to cut them into small pieces. Place the materials in an airtight glass or plastic container.

3. Add the infused fixative to your dried materials, and toss everything together lightly with the wooden spoon. Put on the lid, and place the container in a dry, dark place for 2 weeks.

4. Place your finished potpourri in an open bowl to use as an air freshener, or tuck it into cloth pouches to use it as drawer or closet sachets.

Continued ➡

Making More Light

The more seedlings you grow indoors, the more light you will need. Ordinary fluorescent shop lights work well and are widely available in 24- and 48-inch lengths. Look for a model that includes a reflective hood, and suspend it from the ceiling with hooks and chains. In addition to providing the light your plants need to grow, an illuminated group of seedlings brings a cheery note to any room.

Make a Bottle Gourd Candle Holder
Barbara Pleasant

You can make a candle holder from any size of bottle gourd, but it's a great use for very small ones. Remember that gourds are flammable, so do not leave your candle holder unattended or allow the candle to burn very low.

This is a good starter project to introduce you to gourd crafting. Be as creative as you like with the outside finish. Plain shoe polish or furniture wax are all you need to give your gourd a natural finish, or you can use paints, leather dye, or a coat of clear polyurethane.

You Will Need

Tools: Pencil, dust mask, craft saw, knife, sandpaper, paint and paintbrushes, brown shoe polish

I small bottle gourd, cured and cleaned

I broad candle

12-inch piece of velvet ribbon that matches the candle

1. Place the gourd on a soft surface, such as a foam pad or old pillow, and use the pencil to mark 2 parallel cutting lines on either side of the gourd's waist. One will be the bottom of the candle holder, and the other will be the top.

2. While wearing the dust mask, use the craft saw to remove the top and bottom from the gourd. Scrape away loose material from inside the gourd with the tip of the knife. Sand the cut edges and inside surfaces until they are smooth.

3. Paint the interior surfaces of the gourd, allow them to dry, and then apply a second coat.

4. If desired, paint the outside of the gourd. If you prefer a natural look, finish the gourd with two coats of brown shoe polish.

5. Set the candle holder on a level surface and insert a candle. If needed, use the knife to shape the bottom of the candle so that it sits firmly in place. Tie the velvet ribbon into a bow around the middle of the candle holder.

Make a Light Box from a Drawer
Barbara Pleasant

Providing ample light is often the most challenging aspect of growing your own seedlings. An inexpensive fluorescent light can do the job—provided you keep the bulb 2 to 3 inches from the seedlings' topmost leaves, and paint all nearby surfaces bright white to reflect every last light ray. This light box, made from an old drawer, can accommodate about a dozen seedlings at a time, and you can raise or lower the lights in keeping with the size of your plants. Between seed-starting seasons, simply take it apart for easy storage.

To make sure seedlings get as much light as they need, leave the lights on for about 14 hours a day (fluorescent lights give off very little heat, so don't worry about "cooking" your plants). If you like, add a timer to turn the lights on and off automatically. If the seed-starting mix dries out quickly (indoor air in late winter can often be quite dry), cover the box and lights with a sheet of clear plastic at night, after the lights are turned off. Be sure to remove it before turning the light back on, because it could pose a fire hazard.

You Will Need

Tools: Measuring tape, handsaw, drill, marking pencil, screwdriver

I wood dresser drawer at least 19 inches wide

One 24-inch-long piece of poplar, ?-inch thick and 4 inches wide

One 24-inch-long piece of poplar, ?-inch thick and 3 inches wide

I can of bright white spray enamel paint

Four 32 x I bolts with matching wing nuts

One 18-inch-long under-counter fluorescent light fixture

8 small ?-inch screw eyes

1. To make the frame for the lights, measure the exact width of the drawer between the outside edges. Cut the 4-inch-wide piece of poplar to this length to form the top piece. For the sides, cut the 3-inch-wide piece of poplar into two 12-inch-long pieces.

2. In a well-ventilated place or outdoors, paint the cut pieces and the inside of the drawer with white enamel paint.

3. Drill 2 holes in the lower section of each side piece for the bolts, with the holes about 2 inches apart and diagonal rather than straight across. Check to make sure the bolts will barely pass through the holes. Center one of the side pieces upright against the outside of the drawer, and use the pencil to mark where you should make matching holes in the side of the drawer. Drill holes through the pencil marks, and loosely attach the side piece to the drawer with bolts and wing nuts. Repeat on the other side.

4. Check to make sure the top piece fits correctly between the two side pieces. Follow the manufacturer's directions to attach the light fixture to the top of the light frame.

5. Unscrew the wing nuts to disassemble the sides. Use a small drill bit to make guide holes for the screw eyes in matching sets of two, which will support the lights at two different heights. Install one set of screw eyes 2 inches from the tops of the side pieces, and another set 2 inches below the first set.

6. Reassemble the side pieces, and firmly tighten the wing nuts. Slide the top into place at either of the two heights, so the ends rest on the screw eyes. Plant your seedlings in the drawer, and turn on the lights. Or, place seedlings started in small containers inside the drawer.

Continued ➡

Weeds, Pests & Diseases

WEEDS

An Overview of Weeds

Jill Jesiolowski Cebenko and Deborah L. Martin

What makes a weed a weed? For some people, it's a plant out of place or a plant that competes with crops. Some weeds are poisonous or may cause allergies in livestock or people, while others may harbor insect pests and plant diseases.

But weeds can also be beneficial. Many weeds are excellent food sources for butterflies, bees, and the many beneficial insects that control pests. Handled correctly, they can make good green-manure crops. Some break up heavy soil and other-wise improve soil texture, and others bring up nutrients from the subsoil. Many birds and other wildlife depend on weedy areas for food and shelter. Some weeds are beautiful, some protect soils from erosion, some stabilize steep banks, and some are good food in their own right. As indicator plants, weeds can also tell you about your soil and growing conditions.

Weed Seeds

Soils contain millions of weed seeds. Researchers in England once sifted through the top few inches of soil on a hectare (2.47 acres) of land. They counted 1.33 million prostrate knotweed seeds, 1.73 million shepherd's purse seeds, 3.21 million chickweed seeds, and 16.6 million annual bluegrass seeds. This isn't surprising when you consider the number of seeds a single weed plant can produce. For example, curly dock sets an average of 29,500 seeds per plant, purslane sets 52,300, and redroot pigweed sets 117,400.

Not all seeds survive, of course, and many are eaten by birds and other animals. The ones that do survive don't germinate all at once. In many cases, environmental conditions inhibit sprouting and growth. The seed may be buried so deeply that the level of oxygen in surrounding soil is too low or the level of carbon dioxide too high to allow them to germinate. Temperature, light, day length, or moisture levels may not be right. Seeds can remain dormant for many years, waiting until conditions become right for germination (for example, being brought up to the surface when the soil is disturbed). Some seeds are "innately" dormant. They must go through the alternate freezing and thawing cycles of winter or some other process to break their dormancy.

Annual, Biennial, or Perennial?

Annual weeds live only one season. They usually germinate in spring, grow to maturity, produce seed in summer, and die in fall. They guarantee their sur-vival by producing a significant number of seeds. Most weeds in your garden are annuals. They gener-ally sprout quickly and grow rapidly. Common annuals include chickweed, knotweed, lamb's-quarters, pigweed, purslane, ragweed, and smartweed.

Winter annuals act almost like biennials (see below). They usually germinate in late summer and grow into a small rosette of leaves on the soil surface during their first year. The leaves may die back with heavy frosts, but they grow again in spring of the following year along with the flowering stalks. Flowering and seed production occur in spring or early summer, then the plant dies. Shepherd's purse is an example of a winter annual.

Biennials live for two seasons, producing leaves the first year—typically in the form of a low-lying *rosette* of leaves—and flowering and setting seed in the second year. Common biennials are burdock, mullein, Queen-Anne's-lace, and teasel.

Perennials have lifespans of 3 years or more. They produce seeds, and they also spread by their roots or bulbs. Many grow long, tenacious *taproots* that make them almost impossible to pull out. Some have long runners or underground roots that can send up new plants yards away from the parent plant. Common perennial weeds are bindweed, chicory, dandelion, goldenrod, and plantain.

Some of the most invasive and troublesome weeds are *woody perennials*. These include Japanese honeysuckle, kudzu, multiflora rose, and poison ivy. Birds enjoy the nutrient-rich seeds of woody perennials and are one of the main ways these

Continued ➔

noxious weeds spread—they ingest the seeds and deposit them elsewhere in their droppings. The stems of some of these plants can root wherever they touch the soil, so they multiply rapidly.

Grasses may seem like the worst weeds because they produce so many seeds and the plants are hard to uproot. Some perennial grasses, such as quackgrass, can produce new plants from underground stems yards away from the original plant. Most perennial grasses reproduce from rhizomes (creeping underground roots) as well as from seeds. Even some annual grasses, such as crabgrass, can send up new plants from stem joints that contact the soil.

7 Secrets of Weed Warriors

Vicki Mattern

Experience is often the best teacher, as every gardener who has ever let a weed go to seed knows. To find out the very best ways to prevent and eliminate garden weeds, the editors of *Organic Gardening* magazine asked readers for their most successful weed-beating strategies, tips, and techniques. Here are their top secrets:

1. **Timing is everything.** Don't think that you have to eradicate each and every weed the moment you see it. If weeds are too small, you may not be able to grasp them well enough to pull them out completely. On the other hand, waiting until weeds mature to control them isn't effective, either. By then, the wind may have carried their seeds throughout your garden, or their roots could have grown deeper than your cultivation tools will reach.

   Each weed has a certain size that's most responsive to your tug. When the soil is slightly moist and friable and the weed reaches that ideal in-between size, give a pull—it should come out with little resistance and without snapping off.

2. **Hot water works.** Many gardeners say that pouring boiling water on weeds is the most foolproof eradication method. Most weeds are killed within a day of receiving such treatment. Thistle and other tenacious types, however, may need to be scalded several times before they'll surrender.

3. **A little sodium may do the trick.** To keep weeds from growing between the paving stones of walkways or patios, *Organic Gardening* readers often pour ordinary table salt (sodium chloride) in the cracks. Weeds rarely grow back, they report.

   As an alternative to using salt, one reader sprinkled baking soda (sodium bicarbonate) directly on several weeds in his lawn. He found that the baking soda was more effective than hand pulling at killing such deep-rooted species as hairy cat's ears, dandelion, and broadleaf plantain.

   After experimenting with various application methods and amounts, he came up with the following recommendations:

   • Apply 1 teaspoon of baking soda per weed. Using less than a teaspoon won't kill the weed, but using more than that isn't necessary.

   • Sprinkle the baking soda over the entire weed. Placing the whole dosage on the center of the stem of each plant is less effective than covering the leaf surface.

   • Apply a second dose, if necessary. Although a single application of baking soda killed about 80 percent of the cat's ears plants, a second application was needed to control the plantain.

   • Apply the baking soda at any time during the growing season. It seems to be equally effective whether applied in wet spring weather or during a summer drought.

   Note: If you live in a dry climate where the soil may be naturally high in salt, be careful about using salt or baking soda to control weeds. Too much sodium could kill not only your weeds but also your garden plants.

4. **You can sprout them out**…If removing weeds one by one is too big a task in your garden, try managing their life cycle to suit your plans. In Europe, some gardeners and farmers spray beer on newly tilled land to stimulate the germination of weed seeds in spring. Two weeks later, the farmers till again, turning the weeds into instant green manure.

5. **…or crowd them out.** Speaking of green manure, be sure to try cover cropping, a classic technique for controlling weeds organically. One *Organic Gardening* reader moved to a new home that had no mulch materials for blocking weeds, so she planted a mixture of soybeans and buckwheat in vacant garden beds. The cover crops grew beautifully, shading out all but the most stalwart weeds. And because the soil was moist beneath the crops' leafy canopy, the surviving weeds came out with ease. As a bonus, the cover crops enriched the soil when she turned them under.

   Buckwheat is an especially appealing cover crop because it grows fast and matures in just 30 to 50 days. What's more, its white flowers attract pollinating bees to your garden. You might also consider one of the many types of vetch or clover, both of which help increase the soil's nitrogen content while they shade out weeds. Cover-crop seeds usually are sold at farm supply stores.

6. **When in doubt, mulch.** Mulch is a very effective way to control weeds, as many gardeners have known for years.

   Newspaper mulch makes a particularly good weed barrier. Here's what to do. When your plants are at least 2 or 3 inches tall (or just after you have transplanted them to the garden), surround them with a layer of newspaper, two sheets thick, and cover the paper with grass clippings. The clippings will keep the soil moist, while the paper prevents light from reaching weed seeds waiting to germinate. The newspaper and clippings will even yield benefits for your garden long after the weeds cease to be a threat. By fall, the paper will decompose and you'll be able to turn everything into the soil.

   If you'd rather leave those clippings right on the lawn to fertilize the grass, use a thicker layer of six to eight sheets of newspaper and anchor it in place with pine needles, bark chips, or another organic mulch.

7. **Action must follow planning.** Armed with the previous ideas, you might be tempted to lay back and contemplate which approach is best for your garden. Before you do, consider this caution sent by another reader: "Every year I plan to conquer the weeds in my garden, but that's about as far as I go. I'm sorry to say that my method of planning—without follow-through—has proven ineffective. I don't recommend it to amateurs."

10 Easy Ways to Beat Weeds

Vicki Mattern

A single weed as many as 250,000 seeds. Though some seeds are viable for only a year, others can lie dormant for decades, just waiting for their chance to grow. Buried several inches deep, the lack of light keeps them from germinating. But bring weeds to the surface, and they'll germinate right along with your flower and vegetable seeds.

Even if you're diligent at hoeing and pulling weeds, more seeds arrive—by air, by water runoff, and in bird droppings. You may accidentally introduce weeds by bringing seeds in on your shoes, clothing, or equipment or in the soil surrounding the roots of container-grown stock.

If you had more weeds then seedlings last year or are already feeling defeated by the number of weeds choking out your favorite plants, don't worry! These surefire tips will help you keep down weed populations during the growing season:

1. **Know your enemy.** Before you can determine your best defense strategy against weeds, you need to know what you're up against. Some weeds, such as miner's lettuce, chickweed, purslane, and dozens of grasses, are shallow-rooted annuals. Others, such as dock, comfrey, thistles, and certain runner grasses, are deep-rooted perennials. The two types require different control methods. Arm yourself with a good field guide, then identify and inventory your weeds. After that, you can…

2. **Assault annual weeds when it's dry.** Wait for the weather to be hot and dry for several days, then attack young annual weeds with a rake, hoe, or trowel. That way, the drought-stressed weeds are sure to shrivel and die, even if your cultivation doesn't remove the entire root of the plant.

3. **Give perennial weeds a shower.** The long taproots of perennial weeds cannot be pulled out when the soil is dry. To remove these weeds, wait for wet soil—either from rainfall or from your hose. If the soil is wet and loose, even pesky thistles should come out with their roots intact—which means they won't grow back!

4. **Comb that grass right out of your beds.** If invasive grasses, such as Johnsongrass or bermudagrass, threaten your garden, use a pitchfork to "comb" your beds before you plant in spring, suggests an Organic Gardening reader. Work the soil until it's sufficiently loose for planting, then go over the entire area with a pitchfork, stabbing into the ground and levering it back toward the soil's surface. The tines of the fork will catch any buried grass roots, which you can then remove by hand. This technique has removed about 90 percent of the grasses from a reader's market garden in Texas.

5. **Become a mulching maniac.** Deprive weeds of the light they need by covering bare soil with a thick layer of grass clippings, shredded leaves, pine needles, or other organic mulch. Any survivors that do manage to penetrate the mulch usually are so weak that you can easily remove them by hand.

6. **Cook 'em.** If you've got a large-scale weed problem, bake the plants beneath a sheet of clear plastic. For best results, wet the soil before you cover it with the plastic. Leave the plastic in place for at least 3 weeks—ideally, when the weather is hot and sunny. This method is especially effective against cool-season weeds and annual grasses.

Continued →

7. **Let lettuce help your peas.** Peas and other shallow-rooted crops can be damaged easily by cultivating the surrounding soil. That's why broad-leaved weeds can easily overtake them. So why not establish an edible, living mulch to fight the weeds and provide an extra early-season crop? Sow seeds of a fast-growing leaf lettuce thickly between young pea plants. The lettuce will outperform the weeds, and you can harvest the lettuce thinnings as you pick your peas.

8. **Squash pigweed.** If you're faced with a pugnacious patch of pigweed, fight back by planting a mixture of squash and buckwheat. The vigorous squash and quick-growing buckwheat will easily overtake the weeds. At the end of the season, harvest the squash, pull out the vines, and turn under the buckwheat. The buckwheat will add organic matter and nutrients to the soil for next year's crops.

9. **Berry your weeds.** Use strawberries to smother weeds! These perennial fruits spread by runners and are vigorous enough to overcome many weeds—even in light shade. In mild-winter areas, such as Zone 9, they'll grow (and hold off weeds) all year long. Try growing them as a groundcover beneath blueberries and roses.

10. **Till 'em two times...** In Maine's chilly Zone 5, organic market gardener Eliot Coleman uses a tiller to battle redroot pigweed, the seeds of which can remain viable in the soil for years. Coleman runs the tiller through his beds as early as possible in the spring to bring the weed seeds closer to soil's surface, where they can germinate. That's right: Coleman encourages the weed seeds to sprout! Then, a week or two later, he tills a second time to clear the area of the young weeds before he plants his vegetables.

Rules for Reading Weeds
Vicki Mattern

Before you draw any conclusions about what your weeds say about your soil, consider the following.

- Look for large populations of the same weed rather than just a few individual plants.
- Look for more than one type of "indicator weed." Two or more weeds that like the same conditions are stronger evidence that your soil provides those conditions.
- Consider the health of the weeds. Robust plants are good indicators; weeds that look pale or weak don't tell you much about your soil.
- Weeds that keep coming back year after year are especially good indicators of soil conditions. Their environment must be hospitable for them to survive (or reseed) from one year to the next.

Spring Ahead in Fall
Never allow weeds to set seed, or you'll face an even bigger weed problem next year. It pays to be especially vigilant in late summer to fall, when daylight-sensitive annual weeds mature and produce seeds before they are killed by frost. No matter how busy you are with the harvest, take the time to pull out those weeds *before* they set seed—or you'll be hoeing forever next spring.

Outsmart Lawn Dandelions

If you see dandelions in your lawn, it probably means that the surface soil has become too acidic due to a loss of calcium through the removal of grass clippings. Under these conditions, dandelions get a foothold because their long taproot can reach into the subsoil for calcium, while the short roots of lawn grasses cannot. With the grasses too weak to crowd out the dandelions, the resourceful weeds thrive.

What to do? First, contact your cooperative extension office and find out how to have a soil test taken. (It usually costs less than $10.) Then, if the soil test confirms your suspicions, dust your lawn with lime according to the recommendations on the test. In milder cases you can use compost to replace the calcium. Also, set your lawnmower to cut the grass 3½ inches high (no lower), and allow the clippings to remain on your lawn. By taking these simple steps, you'll deprive dandelions of their competitive advantage.

Weeds Can Be Good Guys, Too

You may find it hard to believe, but having a few weeds here and there is actually good. Weeds can attract and provide shelter for beneficial insects (those that eat the pesky insects that damage plants). Weeds can help protect gardens and especially lawns from disease attacks, too. Because many diseases attack particular plant species, having more than one species of grass in the lawn ensures that your entire lawn won't succumb to a single disease. And some weeds offer other benefits: For example, dandelions are edible, and white clover provides nutrients for the soil.

Guide to Weeds
Jill Jesiolowski Cebenko and Deborah L. Martin

Weeds in this section are listed alphabetically by common name within groups divided according to their growth habits. They are grouped into annuals, biennials, perennials, woody perennials, and grasses. Scientific names are also given.

Prevention and Control

Weeds must be controlled in gardens because they compete for light, water, and food with desired plants. It's most important to keep weeds down when crop plants are small. Later, however, when crops are well established, an understory of low-growing weeds usually doesn't harm the crops. Crops may even benefit if the weeds attract beneficial insects or make it harder for pests to find their foods plants.

Whether or not you should try to control weeds in nearby areas around the garden depends on the situation. Weeds that produce windblown seeds and those that are spread by birds feeding on the fruit have the potential to spread the farthest. This means that preventing them from going to seed in nearby areas could help reduce the number of weeds falling on your garden. For common weed species, however, there are usually so many growing in the area that it would be impractical to try to control them. Also, because many weeds are important food plants for bees, butterflies, and other beneficial insects as well as birds and other wildlife, it might be more important to leave the weedy hedgerows and ditches undisturbed. Where a new, invasive species is showing up, controlling the weed as it appears can be an effective way to slow its spread.

Learning about the life cycles of weeds can help you manage them effectively and can stop you from unintentionally making a weed problem worse. For example, tilling up quackgrass only makes it

multiply faster. In general, annuals are managed by preventing them from setting seeds, whereas managing perennials means you also need to remove or kill the roots. It may take 3 years or more to completely eradicate some woody perennials.

Because many garden weeds are most simply dealt with by hoeing or pulling them as early as possible before they flower, the hardest part can be to tell weed seedlings from crop seedlings. With experience you'll be able to recognize younger weeds. At first, however, you may want to sow seeds in rows (rather than broadcast them randomly over a bed) so that you can safely pull plants that grow between the rows. A trick that helps is sowing a few radish seeds in each row—these germinate quickly, marking the row before the intentionally planted crop and weeds come up.

PREVENTION

Soil conditions. Although many weeds seem to able to grow anywhere, some thrive only in certain conditions. By altering the conditions, you can make it harder for the weeds to grow, while at the same time improving conditions for garden plants. Examples include remedying poor drainage, which would inhibit the growth of weeds that like wet conditions, or adding lime to correct a low soil pH, which would discourage weeds that like acidic soils. In heavy soils, weeds are difficult to pull; but if you add compost and turn in organic matter, the soil becomes lighter, and weeds are easier to pull when they do sprout up.

CULTURAL CONTROLS

Smother crops. Growing green-manure crops can be used to smother some types of weeds while also benefiting the soil. Sow the smother crop thickly, and turn it under before any weeds that might have sprouted have a chance to set seed. When using green manure to control weeds, it's better to turn under two or three crops in quick succession during the season than to leave the cover crop to grow longer.

Closely seeded garden crops, such as leaf lettuce and other leafy greens, can also smother weeds or prevent their germination by shading the soil. Interplanting tall crops, such as corn, with crops that run over the ground, such as squash, can also reduce the amount of light reaching the weeds.

BIOLOGICAL CONTROLS

Research into biological controls for weeds has resulted in economical, long-term control of various introduced weeds. Most such weed control programs involve finding insects that fed on the weeds in the region they originally came from. The insects are extensively tested to make sure that they don't eat any desirable plants, and then they're released to attack the target weed.

Biological control insects have been released in North America for purple loosestrife, tansy ragwort, spurges, St.-John's-wort, various thistles, and others. Some plant disease fungi have also been developed as biological controls. Government agencies usually release these controls to benefit a whole region; they aren't something a home gardener would buy. An exception to this would be several fungi that are being developed to control dandelions in lawns.

PHYSICAL CONTROLS

Simply hoeing and pulling weeds are tried-and-true weed-control methods that most gardeners use. Many well-designed weeding tools are available to help make this task easier and more efficient. Most annual weeds, if pulled before they flower, can be left in the garden to mulch the soil or can

Continued ➡

be composted. Annuals that readily sprout roots from stem joints and most perennial weeds should be removed from the garden and allowed to dry thoroughly before being composted. Here are a few more ideas for physical controls:

Cultivation. Repeated cultivation can greatly reduce the number of weed seeds in the soil. Allow the weeds to germinate, then destroy them by tilling or cultivating the soil. Allow the weeds to germinate for another 2 weeks, then cultivate again. If you have time to allow several cycles of germination and cultivation before sowing garden plants, you can considerably reduce the number of weeds that come up later in the crop.

Mulches. With respect to managing weeds, mulches have several advantages. First, the soil under mulches stays moist and loose, so it's easier to pull any weeds that grow. The thicker the mulch is, the more it will shade the soil and smother germinating weed seedlings. A 2- to 4-inch layer is usually enough to control most annual weeds if applied early in the season. Make sure the mulch is free from weed seeds, however, so that it doesn't cause more weed problems. Shredded leaves, clean straw, compost, and other organic materials help suppress weeds as well as provide other benefits to garden plants.

Extremely dense, light-excluding materials—such as black plastic, landscape fabric, or thick layers of newspaper or cardboard—can be used to smother all vegetation under them. These are commonly used to kill sod or smother established patches of weeds so that the soil can be used for a garden the following season. The heavy mulches may be needed for several years to control extremely vigorous woody perennials.

Mowing. For annual weeds, periodically mowing or cutting off the tops so they can't set seed will eradicate them in 1 year because the roots die in fall. For perennials, close cutting or mowing at 2- to 4-week intervals can also eventually kill the plants, because the roots become exhausted from sending up shoots.

Applying heat. There are several ways to apply heat to weeds to kill them-but heat is more useful for weeds on driveways, patios, and sidewalks than in gardens because the heat can also kill the garden plants. Pouring boiling water on weeds is an effective control for seedlings growing in crevices in bricks and pavement. Soil solarization (described on page 135) can heat the soil enough to kill weed seeds in the top layer of soil. Handheld flamers and infrared weeders can also be used to control weeds.

HERBICIDES

Although home recipes using salt, vinegar, or other household substances can be used to kill weeds, they're also very harmful to other plants and organisms in the soil. Salt, for example, is highly soluble and moves through the soil, damaging roots of trees and other desirable plants. In the garden setting, there's little use for herbicidal products because of the risk of harming desirable plants. Two organic herbicides that have some limited uses are as follows:

Fatty acids. A commercial nontoxic herbicide (Safer's) is made from fatty acids, which are naturally occurring ingredients used in making soap. It kills the leaves of plants but not the roots; therefore, it's most effective on annual weeds and on seedlings of perennials. Because a fatty-acid spray can also kill garden seedlings, it's best used in hard-surfaced areas or in garden areas before seeds are sown. There's no residual effect, so seeds can be planted immediately after using the fatty acids.

Corn gluten meal. A substance in corn gluten meal (a byproduct of animal feed) has been found to suppress germination of seeds without affecting growing plants. Several products are available for use on lawns, where they can both prevent weed seeds from germinating and provide some nutrients such as nitrogen. Corn gluten meal can also be used in garden areas where transplants, not seeds, are being planted.

ANNUALS

Annuals Sow Thistle

Sonchus oleraceus

Range: Throughout the United States and southern Canada; particularly troublesome in coastal regions.

Description: Plants grow 1 to 6 feet (30.5 to 183 cm) tall. Stems are erect and branched and ooze a milky sap when cut. Leaves are alternate on the stem and more numerous toward the base of the plant. The largest leaves are deeply cut into irregular lobes on each side, with an arrow-shaped tip and toothed, spiny leaf margins. Flower heads are pale yellow and rounded and resemble dandelions. Seeds have tufts of long hairs that allow them to be carried on the wind. Blooms June to October.

Life Cycle: Annual, reproducing by seeds.

Prevention and Control: Hoe or pull plants or apply a thick mulch to prevent germination and to smother seedlings. Watch waste places for blooming sow thistles, and mow them before seedheads begin to form.

Notes: Sow thistles are common in both cultivated and uncultivated areas with good light exposure. Perennial sow thistle, a troublesome weed in northern areas, looks like annual sow thistle, but the leaf is less prickly, and the flower is a more vivid yellow. The perennial species spreads from both the rootstock and the seeds and must be dug up to be eradicated. Both sow thistles are a source of food for hoverflies and other beneficial insects.

Black Nightshade

Solanum nigrum

Range: Eastern half of the United States and southeastern Canada.

Description: Plants grow 1 to 2 feet (30.5 to 61 cm) tall. Plants are low and spreading and branch prolifically. Leaves are alternate on the stem and are wide at the base of the leaf and narrow at the tip, with wavy edges. The star-shaped, five-petaled flowers are white and grow in clusters. Small green berries turn black upon maturity and contain numerous seeds. Seeds are wrinkled, flattened, and a dull yellow to brown color. Blooms from July to September.

Life Cycle: Annual, reproducing by seeds.

Prevention and Control: Nightshade is rarely present in large numbers, so it's effective to pull or hoe any plants that take root in the garden. Prompt removal is advisable because nightshade can host pests that attack other tomato-family crops, such as Colorado potato beetle, and the bacteria that cause blackleg of potato, which survives on nightshade roots.

Notes: Nightshade is especially common in disturbed soils.

Carpetweed

Mollugo verticillata

Range: Throughout the United States (except north-central areas) and southern Canada.

Description: Stems grow to 1 foot (30.5 cm) long. Plants are bright green and prostrate and spread outward from a central taproot. They branch profusely at the base, making a flat, carpetlike mat. Leaves are smooth and narrow and taper to a point. They grow in clusters of five or six leaves in whorls from stem joints. Two to five small, white, five-petaled flowers also grow from stem joints. Seed capsules are tiny and three-lobed and hold numerous orange-red, ridged seeds. Blooms from June to September.

Life Cycle: Annual, reproducing by seeds.

Prevention and Control: Pull carpetweed immediately because it grows, flowers, and sets seeds rapidly. Hoeing it off just below the soil line is effective. Apply dense mulches to smother seedlings.

Notes: Carpetweed tolerates a wide range of soil conditions.

Catchweed Bedstraw, Cleavers

Galium aparine

Range: Throughout the United States and southern Canada.

Description: Stems grow from 8 to 60 inches (20.3 to 152 cm) long. They lie on the ground or over other plants and are jointed, slender, and tough, with four lengthwise ridges. Short, downward-pointing bristles grow along the ridges. Leaves are lance-shaped, with a central vein and sharp bristles on the top surface and edges; they grow in clusters of six to eight leaves in a whorl at each stem joint. Flowers are small and white with four lobes joined into a tube; they grow in groups of one to three, on stalks that arise from leaf axils. Seedpods are round and bristly and are divided into two chambers. Blooms from May to July.

Life Cycle: Annual, reproducing by bristly seeds that stick to passing animals and people.

Prevention and Control: Hoeing and pulling will eradicate bedstraw from the garden. When removing the weed, dig down to get all roots because it readily sprouts again. Apply dense mulches to smother seedlings. Remove seeds from shoes and socks after working in infested areas, such as along edges of fields and pastures.

Notes: Catchweed bedstraw prefers moist, rich soils with moderately good drainage. It's commonly found in soils that once formed creek or river beds, on the edges of woodlands, and in slightly shaded areas formed by hedgerows and fences. Flowering occurs fairly early in the season, so remove plants as soon as you notice them.

Common Chickweed

Stellaria media

Range: Throughout the United States and southern Canada.

Description: Stems usually grow 4 to 12 inches (10.2 to 30.5 cm) long, but they can reach up to 18 inches (45.7 cm) long. Plants are bright green and grow in a loose mat on the soil surface. Stems branch profusely from the central crown, which grows from a fibrous, shallow root system. Leaves are small and oval, are pointed at the tip, and are opposite each other on the stem. Flowers are white, with five split petals, giving the appearance of ten petals. Sepals are green and hairy and extend beyond the petals. Seed capsules are oval and hold

Continued ➡

many red-brown, ridged seeds. Blooms from early spring to early winter.

Life Cycle: Annual or winter annual, reproducing both by seeds and by rooting along stems. Typically sets seed in fall and can grow vigorously during winter in mild climates.

Prevention and Control: Pull or hoe plants before they set seed. Because stems root easily, remove plants from the garden, and allow them to dry in the sun before composting them. Use dense mulches to smother seedlings.

Notes: Though this plant likes rich soil, it tolerates high acidity. It makes the most vigorous growth during cool weather when soil moisture is high and can serve as a protective groundcover over garden soils in areas with mild winters. Edible.

Common Cocklebur

Xanthium strumarium

Range: Throughout the United States and southern Canada (except in Quebec and northern New England).

Description: Plants grow 1 to 4 feet (30.5 to 122 cm) tall. Stems are erect, ridged, and hairy, some with reddish spots; stems are so branched that established plants look like a bush. Leaves are large, triangular to heart-shaped, and slightly lobed, with toothed edges. They're alternate on the stem and rough on both sides. Male flowers grow in short terminal spikes and drop soon after the pollen has been shed. The female flowers grow in clusters in leaf axils. Burs develop from the female flowers; they have two larger, sharp, incurved hooks at the top and are covered with hooked bristles, which attach to passing people or animals. Burs are light green, turning brown and woody as they mature. Blooms in August and September.

Life Cycle: Annual, reproducing by seeds.

Prevention and Control: Hoe or pull plants in the garden. Use dense mulches to smother seedlings. In fields, mow before the plants flower, repeating as needed during the season to prevent plants from flowering.

Notes: Cocklebur seedlings are poisonous to livestock. Cocklebur grows well in wet soils. Cocklebur can be confused with common burdock, but the former has elongated burs, whereas burdock has round burs.

Common Mallow

Malva neglecta

Range: Throughout the United States and southern Canada.

Description: Stems grow 4 to 12 inches (10.2 to 30.5 cm) long. They branch at the base, appearing nearly erect or spreading close to the ground. Leaves are wide, rounded, slightly hairy, and sometimes slightly lobed, with softly toothed edges and long, slender petioles. Flowers are white to pale purple, have five petals, and are borne singly or in clusters from leaf axils. Seedpods are round and flattened and split into many pie-shaped segments. Blooms from April to October.

Life Cycle: Annual or biennial, reproducing by seeds.

Prevention and Control: Pull or hoe plants in the garden. Apply dense mulches to smother seedlings. Mow or cut larger plants in nearby areas to prevent them from setting seed.

Notes: Common mallow will grow in a wide range of soil conditions.

Common Ragweed

Ambrosia artemisiifolia

Range: Eastern and north-central United States, and central and eastern Canada.

Description: Plants grow 1 to 3 feet (30.5 to 91.4 cm) tall. Stems are erect, unbranched or branched toward the top. Leaves are smooth, deeply lobed, and fernlike. They're sometimes opposite on the stem at the base of the plant, but they're more commonly alternate for the entire length of the stem. The flower heads are greenish spikes that grow at the tips of the branches and from the leaf axils. Seeds develop inside a brown woody husk with spines along the top. Blooms from July through September.

Life Cycle: Annual, reproducing by seeds.

Prevention and Control: Because ragweed is shallow-rooted and reproduces only by seed, hoeing and pulling are effective. Use dense mulches to smother seedlings. Mow nearby roadsides and other weedy spots before the plants bloom to prevent flower and seed formation.

Notes: Ragweed is a source of irritating pollen and is the most common cause of hay fever in fall. In some states and provinces, ragweed is considered a noxious weed and falls under weed-control ordinances. Ragweed grows in poor, dry soils but is adaptable to a wide range of conditions.

Corn Cockle

Agrostemma githago

Range: Throughout the United States and southern Canada.

Description: Plants grow 1 to 3 feet (30.5 to 91.4 cm) tall. Stems are erect are covered with soft hairs, and bulge slightly at the leaf joints. Leaves are lance-shaped, hairy, and opposite on the stem. Flowers are purplish pink and 1 to 2 inches (2.5 to 5.1 cm) wide, with five petals that have dark veins; they're borne one per stem and have long, narrow, green sepals. Seed capsules are puffy, with the sepals at the top; they hold many small, black, spiny seeds. The stems grow from a shallow taproot. Blooms from May to September.

Life Cycle: Winter annual, reproducing by seeds. Usually germinates in fall and sends up flowerstalks the next spring.

Prevention and Control: Pull or hoe plants before seeds set. Apply thick mulches to smother seedlings. Seed is rarely viable for more than a year if it's buried to a depth of 6 to 8 inches (15.2 to 20.3 cm).

Notes: Seeds are poisonous. Livestock and poultry must be kept off fields with corn cockle.

Corn Spurry

Spergularia arvensis

Range: West coastal United States and Canada; most of eastern United States; also Colorado.

Description: Stems are 6 to 18 inches (15.2 to 45.7 cm) high and slender and branching. Leaves are threadlike, ½ to 1 inch (1.3 to 2.5 cm) long, with grooves on the underside; they're arranged in whorls on the stems. The small, white, five-petaled flowers are carried at the ends of stems, which bend down as the seedpods ripen. The seedpods are longer than the sepals and split into five sections. The seeds are dull black, circular, and flattened, with a pale narrow wing around the outer edge.

Life Cycle: Annual; flowers all summer; spreads by seeds.

Prevention and Control: Hoe or pull plants before seeds set. Use dense mulches to smother seedlings.

Notes: Corn spurry grows best in light, sandy soils or gravelly areas. The flowers are attractive to beneficial insects such as parasitic wasps (page 26), so a moderate number of corn spurry plants among tailor vigorous crop plants can be desirable.

Devil's Beggar-Ticks

Bidens frondosa

Range: Throughout the United States and southern Canada.

Description: Plants grow from 2 to 5 feet (61 to 152 cm) tall. Stems are usually smooth and are almost square; they grow in groups from a shallow, branched taproot. Leaves are opposite on the stem and are divided in three or five leaflets with pointed tips and toothed edges. They may have short hairs on the undersides but are always smooth on the upper surfaces. Flower heads are yellow-orange, with five petal-like outer flowers on each head. The seed is long and wedge-shaped, with two barbed spikes at the top. Blooms from July to October.

Life Cycle: Annual, reproducing by seeds.

Prevention and Control: Hoe or pull plants. Use dense mulches to smother seedlings. Mow or cut plants in nearby areas before they set seed.

Notes: Devil's beggar-ticks prefer rich, moist soil but will grow along roadsides, in waste places, and in damp areas. Animals may carry seeds into the garden. This weed can be an alternate host for Mexican bean beetle (page 43).

Field Dodders

Cuscuta spp.

Range: Throughout the United States south of Vermont and the Great Lakes, with the exception of much of the Pacific Coast states. Also found in prairie provinces in southern Canada.

Description: Stems may reach 7 feet (2.1 m) long, but because they grow in tangled masses on the host plant, the height is variable. Stringlike, yellowish, pinkish, or orange stems emerge from the ground. Dodders lack leaves because they don't produce chlorophyll. Instead, they have tiny suckers that attach to host plants. Once attached, the stem breaks from the root. The small, white, five-lobed flowers are produced in loose, rounded clusters. The calyx is large relative to the petals. Seeds are numerous, fairly small, and yellow to reddish brown. Blooms from July to September.

Life Cycle: Annual, reproducing by seeds.

Prevention and Control: Dodder seeds can be spread to gardens and fields mixed in small-seeded grains, with cover-crop seed or in hay used as mulch. If flowers haven't yet formed, immediately pull both the dodder and the host plant and compost them. If flowers have formed, pull both the dodder and the host plant and burn or dispose of them in the garbage. If necessary, solarize the soil for the summer months where dodder has been a serious problem. If you can't remove the host plant, continue to remove and destroy all visible dodder several times a season for up to 2 years. If dodder is mixed in with a cover crop, keep the area mowed for the season to make sure it doesn't set seed.

Notes: Field dodder is a parasite. It prefers open, dry sites.

Continued ➡

Giant Ragweed

Ambrosia trifida

Range: Throughout the United States, with the exception of Pacific Coast areas, and into southern Canada from southwest Quebec to British Columbia.

Description: Plants can grow to 12 feet (3.7 m) tall, but are usually 2½ to 6 feet (76.2 to 183 cm) tall. Stems are erect branched toward the top, covered with coarse hair, and rough. Leaves are hairy and divided into three or five deep lobes, with a border of leaf tissue along each side of the petiole. Flowers are greenish and grow on spikes at the tip of stems and in the leaf axils at the top of the plant Blooms from July to September.

Life Cycle: Annual, reproducing by seeds.

Prevention and Control: Hoe or pull ragweed that appears in the garden. Apply dense mulches to smother seedlings. Frequently mow any ragweed that's growing in waste places to prevent the formation of flowers and seeds.

Notes: Ragweed is a source of irritating pollen and is the most common cause of hay fever in fall. In some states and provinces, ragweed must be controlled by law. Giant ragweed prefers moist soils but will grow in less ideal conditions. It's common in hedgerows and along the edges of fields and roadsides.

Jimsonweed

Datura stramonium

Range: East, Midwest, Southwest, and along the Pacific Coast of the United States and southern Canada.

Descriptions: Plants may grow to 5 feet (1.5 m) tall. They're bushy with spreading leaves, which are oval to triangular in shape with toothed edges. Stems are sometimes slightly purple. Flowers are white to pink and are a deep, funnel shape. Seed capsules are distinctly spiny and have four lobes. Seeds are kidney-shaped, flattened, and slightly pitted. Blooms from June to September.

Life Cycle: Annual, reproducing by seeds.

Prevention and Control: Pull and compost jimsonweed before seed capsules start to form; wear gloves when handling plants because they can cause skin irritation. Use dense mulches to smother seedlings.

Notes: Jimsonweed resembles eggplant and thrives in rich soil and full sun. It can harbor diseases and pests common to other tomato-family crops. The seeds are poisonous.

Lamb's-Quarters

Chenopodium album

Range: Throughout the United States and southern Canada.

Description: Plants grow 1 to 3 feet (30.5 to 91.4 cm) tailor more in rich soil. Stems are upright and branched, typically with grooves of lighter green or red running lengthwise. Leaves are egg-shaped or roughly triangular with toothed edges. They're alternate on the stems and generally wider on the bottom than the top of the plant. Green or reddish green, petal-less flowers grow in irregularly shaped spikes at the tops of branches. Blooms from early summer through fall.

Life Cycle: Annual, reproducing by seeds. In fall, very young plants can flower and set seed before frost.

Prevention and Control: Pull or hoe lamb's-quarters when they're young because they grow rapidly. In hot dry weather, pulled seedlings can be left in the garden as mulch. Otherwise, compost them. Use dense mulches to smother seedlings.

Notes: Lamb's-quarters with a reddish purple sheen can indicate that the soil is nitrogen-deficient. Young leaves are edible, raw or cooked.

Marshpepper Smartweed

Polygonum hydropiper

Range: Throughout southern Canada and the United States (except for southern Georgia and Florida).

Description: Plants are 6 inches to 2½ feet (15.2 to 76.2 cm) tall. Stems are prominently jointed, erect, smooth, and sometimes reddish. Leaves are alternate on the stem, narrow, lance-shaped, and pointed at the tips; they're smooth to slightly hairy. Petioles are small or absent. Flowers are small, four-lobed, and greenish white with pink edges; they grow in terminal spikes that droop in arches. The calyx, which sometimes has slightly reddish margins, protects the dull brown, lens-shaped or triangular fruit that contains a single seed. Blooms from June to November.

Life Cycle: Annual, reproducing by seeds.

Prevention and Control: Apply dense mulches to smother seedlings. Hoe or pull the plants. Remove pulled plants from the garden to prevent re-rooting from the stem nodes; dry in the sun before composting. Improving drainage helps to discourage the growth of smartweed.

Notes: Marshpepper smartweed prefers moist or boggy areas and is usually found in ditches, along shorelines, or in other low, poorly drained soils. Birds like the fruit and spread it to new ground. Stems and leaves are edible (they have a peppery flavor).

Mayweed

Anthemis cotula

Range: Throughout the United States and southern Canada.

Description: Plants can reach 12 to 18 inches (30.5 to 45.7 cm) tall. The multi-branched stem is erect and either smooth or covered with soft hairs. Leaves are alternate on the stem, light yellowish green, and finely divided into narrow segments. They have a distinctly bad odor when crushed. Small, white ray flowers surround a center of yellow disk flowers. Blooms from May to September.

Life Cycle: Annual, reproducing by seeds. In some climates, mayweed is a winter annual, germinating in late fall, overwintering, and sending up flower-stalks the following spring.

Prevention and Control: Hoe or pull plants in the garden. Use dense mulches to smother seedlings. Mow or cut plants in nearby areas to prevent formation of seeds.

Notes: Common names for this plant include stinkweed, fetid chamomile, dog fennel, and stinking daisy, all referring to the highly unpleasant odor that the leaves give off. Despite these names, it's attractive to beneficial insects and provides them with pollen and nectar. It's adapted to a wide range of soil conditions.

Mile-a-Minute

Polygonum perfoliatum

Range: Southern New England, New York to Virginia, and west to Ohio; it's expected to spread over a wider eastern and southern range.

Description: Plants grow as a long, trailing vine, with a delicate, reddish stem bearing hooked barbs. Leaves are light green, alternate on the stems, and nearly perfectly triangular in shape, with hooks on the undersides. Distinctive cup-shaped, leafy structures circle the stems at intervals; this is where the small, white flowers (and later the fruit) emerge. Fruit are metallic blue and segmented; there's one shiny black seed in each segment. The vine grows very rapidly into a thick wave of vegetation that covers and smothers other plants, including trees. It produces many seeds continuously from June to October.

Life Cycle: Tender annual, killed by the first frost. Birds (and possibly other animals) feeding on the berries may spread seed over long distances. The seeds are also spread along streams because they can remain afloat in water for days.

Prevention and Control: Pull plants before flowers form. This task is easier before the barbs harden on the stems and leaves, but it can be done later (wear thick gloves and protective clothing because the tough barbs can seriously scratch skin). Check frequently for emergence of new seedlings. Repeatedly mowing or trimming plants to prevent them from flowering and setting seed will eventually control them as the vines die over the winter.

Notes: A native plant from Asia, it has been spreading from the original introduction site in Pennsylvania since the 1930s. It prefers extremely wet soils and full sun, but it can survive on drier sites and in part shade; it colonizes fields, stream banks, roadsides, and natural areas.

Morning Glories

Ipomoea spp.

Range: *I. purpurea* grows in the eastern half of the United States and Pacific Coast areas; *I. hederacea* grows in the eastern half of the United States (except in the most northern states).

Description: Stems grow from a few feet up to 10 feet (3 m) long, are slightly hairy, and twine around plants and objects in their path. Leaves are alternate on the stems with smooth edges and obvious veins arising from the midrib. Leaves of tall morning glory (*I. purpurea*) are heart-shaped, whereas leaves of ivy-leaved morning glory (*I. hederacea*) are three-lobed. Flowers are trumpet-shaped and pink, blue, purple, or white. They normally grow in groups of three to five from each flower-stalk. Blooms from July to September.

Life Cycle: Annual, reproducing by seeds.

Prevention and Control: Morning glories can become troublesome in warm regions. Pull every shoot in and around the garden, and allow the plant material to dry thoroughly to kill the vines before composting them. Use dense mulches to smother seedlings.

Notes: Watch for bird-sown morning glory vines growing in hedges and along fencerows. Don't let plants that spring up in nearby waste places flower or set seed.

Pennsylvania Smartweed

Polygonum pensylvanicum

Lady's Thumb

Polygonum persicaria

Range: *P. pensyivanicum* is found in eastern and central United States as far west as Wyoming, and in southeastern Canada; *P. persicaria* has a similar range, including the northern half of the western United States into southern Canada.

Description: Plants grow up to 3 feet (91.4 cm) tall. Stems are erect, somewhat tough, and swollen at the stem joints. Leaves are alternate on the stem and long and pointed at both ends, and many of

Continued ➡

them have a darker splotch in the middle. The leaf has a short petiole extending from a sheath that encircles the stem. As the plant matures, lower sheaths dry and falloff; on *P pensyivanicum* these papery sheaths have bristles. Flowers are pink or purplish, borne on short spikes, and are densely packed. Seeds are shiny and black. Blooms from late May to October.

Life Cycle: Annual, reproducing by seeds.

Prevention and Control: Pulling and hoeing are effective controls for these annual plants. Apply dense mulches to smother seedlings. Mow plants in ditches and roadsides to prevent them from setting seeds near your garden.

Notes: Pennsylvania smartweed can tolerate wet or compacted soils, shade, acidity, and low-nutrient levels. If it becomes a serious pest in the garden, it may indicate poor drainage or other problems with the soil. As the soil improves, smartweed populations will decrease.

Prickly Lettuce

Lactuca serriola

Range: Throughout the United States and southern Canada.

Description: Plants may grow to 5 feet (1.5 m) tall. Stems are pale green and spiny, especially toward the bottom; they ooze a bitter, milky sap when cut. Leaves are alternate on the stem and sometimes blue-green, with short spines along the wavy or toothed margins. They clasp the stem tightly and have two lobes that project beyond the attachment point. The taproot is thick and deep. Flowers are numerous, small, and yellow. Seeds have a white tuft of hair at the end that enables them to be blown in the wind. Blooms from July to September.

Life Cycle: Annual, winter annual, or biennial, reproducing by seeds. The wind carries the seeds. Can sprout from the crown if only the foliage is removed.

Prevention and Control: Hoe or pull plants as you see them, cutting below the crown before they set seed. Apply dense mulches to smother seedlings. Prickly lettuce is rarely present in large numbers on cultivated land, but it can be a problem in old pastures or neglected fields. Mow or cut before flowering and again every 2 to 3 weeks thereafter to deplete the plant's reserves.

Notes: Most commonly found on light soils with good drainage. Prickly lettuce is an excellent plant for attracting beneficial insects; therefore, it could be left undisturbed in surrounding areas. However, because it can carry some of the same diseases as cultivated lettuce, it may help to remove it in surrounding areas if disease has been a continuing problem.

Prickly Sida

Sida spinosa

Range: Throughout the eastern two-thirds of the United States.

Description: Plants are 8 to 38 inches (20.3 to 96.5 cm) tall. Stems are erect, hairy, and many-branched. Leaves are alternate on the stem and lance-shaped with toothed margins. Two spiny projections grow from the base of each stem joint below the leaf petiole. The light yellow, five-petaled flowers also grow on short stalks from the stem joints. The calyx of the flower encloses the bottom of the seedpod. This also has five sections, each topped by two sharp beaks and containing a single seed. The plants grow from a long taproot. Blooms from June to October.

Life Cycle: Annual, reproducing by seeds.

Prevention and Control: Apply dense mulches to smother seedlings. Prickly sida is easy to pull when it's young and small (wear gloves to protect your skin from the spines). It grows a long, tenacious taproot early in the season, so the most effective control is cutting stems from the root with a very sharp hoe. Don't let plants flower and set seed in waste areas or along fence rows or roadsides.

Notes: Prickly sida thrives in the climate and soils of southern states.

Prostrate Knotweed

Polygonum aviculare

Range: Throughout the United States and southern Canada.

Description: Stems are 6 to 24 inches (15.2 to 61 cm) long and lie flat on the soil surface, forming wiry mats. Slender, ridged stems arise from thin taproots and branch in all directions; the joints of the stems have a papery covering. The stems may rise upward slightly at the flowering tips. Leaves are alternate on the stem, smooth-edged, and elongated, with somewhat pointed tips. Flowers are small and white or yellow and bloom where they join the stem. Seeds are dull brown and triangular. Blooms from midsummer to late fall.

Life cycle: Annual, reproducing by seeds.

Prevention and Control: Pulling when the plant is young is the best control. Hoeing is effective on older plants, as long as the crown of the plant just at or slightly below the soil surface is severed from the roots. If knotweed is a serious problem, apply a dense mulch to smother weeds, and add organic matter or dig deeply, turning in compost or aged manure to aerate soil.

Notes: Prostrate knotweed grows where soils are hard and compacted. It's more likely to reside in permanent pathways than in the garden beds. Eliminate it from these areas by aerating with a spading fork and then covering with a deep mulch.

Prostrate Pigweed

Amaranthus blitoides

Range: Throughout southern Canada and the United States except the southernmost areas of Texas, Florida, and California.

Description: Stems are 8 to 24 inches (203 to 61 cm) long. Pigweed branches from the base and at nodes along each stem, spreading over the ground in a low mat. The reddish stems are smooth and commonly erect at the growing tips. Leaves are small and oval. Flowers are inconspicuous, lack petals, and are clustered in clumps that feel prickly to the touch. Seeds are lens-shaped and shiny black. Blooms from July to October.

Life Cycle: Annual, reproducing by seeds.

Prevention and Control: Smother seedlings with dense mulches. Hoe or pull plants. Because seeds are so plentiful and flowers so inconspicuous, be careful to remove plants early in the season. Don't leave pulled weeds in the walkways if the plants have flowers because the earliest seeds can mature on the pulled plants.

Notes: Prostrate pigweed prefers dry, sandy soils; however, it will grow in any garden soil that has good drainage.

Purslane

Portulaca oleracea

Range: Throughout the United States and southern Canada.

Description: Stems grow to 1½ feet (45.7 cm) long, are smooth and succulent, and branch to form dense mats on the soil surface. The stems are usually tinged with red. Leaves are alternate or almost opposite on the stems and are rounded to oval in shape with smooth edges. Leaves may grow in a cluster at the tip of stems. Flowers are pale yellow and small and grow singly. The calyxes are green and enclose the petals, forming seed capsules that contain numerous tiny seeds. Blooms from July to September.

Life Cycle: Annuel, reproducing by seeds.

Prevention and Control: Apply dense mulches to smother seedlings as they sprout. Purslane doesn't germinate until soils have warmed, so seedlings may germinate after the garden has been cultivated in spring. Pulling and hoeing are effective controls. Pulled plants shouldn't be left in the garden because little bits of stem can take root.

Notes: Stems and leaves of purslane are edible, raw or cooked.

Redroot Pigweed

Amaranthus retroflexus

Range: Throughout the United States and southern Canada.

Description: Plants can grow to 6 feet (1.8 m) tall, but they're usually much shorter. Stems are slightly reddish, rough or hairy, upright, but sometimes branching at the top. Leaves are alternate on stems, dull green, and oval with pointed tips. Leaf edges are slightly wavy. Flower clusters look more like green bottle brushes than blooms; they grow in spikes. Seeds are shiny black or red-brown. The tough, deep taproot is distinctly red at the soil line. Blooms from July to October.

Life Cycle: Annual, reproducing by seeds. Plants germinating in spring grow 1 to 3 feet (30.5 to 91.4 cm) tall before blooming, but plants that germinate in late summer and early fall can produce seed when they've grown only a few inches. A single plant can produce thousands of seeds, which can remain viable in the soil for years.

Prevention and Control: Apply dense mulches to smother seedlings. Pull or hoe seedlings. Remove pulled plants from the garden and dry them in the sun before composting because they root easily. For severe infestations, cultivate the soil and leave it open for up to 2 weeks to allow seeds to germinate, then cultivate to kill the seedlings; repeat the cycle several times. Heavy infestations can also be choked out by growing cover crops.

Notes: Redroot pigweed grows in any garden soil.

Shepherd's Purse

Capsella bursa-pastoris

Range: Throughout the United States and southern Canada.

Description: Plants grow 8 to 18 inches (20.3 to 45.7 cm) tall. A basal rosette of lobed leaves commonly appears in late summer or fall, but it can also grow in spring or summer. After the rosette has overwintered or is well established in spring or summer, erect stems grow from the crown. Stems are branched and typically covered with tiny, grayish hairs. Leaves growing from the stems are smaller and narrower than those in the basal rosette. They clasp the stem and have slightly toothed edges with an overall arrow shape. Four-petaled white flowers grow in long stalks at the ends of branches. Seedpods develop at the ends of the long stalks and are triangular in shape. Blooms from March to November.

Continued ➡

Life Cycle: Annual or winter annual, reproducing by seeds.

Prevention and Control: Use dense mulches to smother seedlings. Hoe or pull plants before they flower or set seed. Shepherd's purse roots easily, so remove pulled plants from the garden and compost them.

Notes: Shepherd's purse is present in almost all gardens, fields, and roadways. Its flowers are a rich source of nectar for beneficial insects; therefore, allow it to remain in waste areas and roadsides.

Spanish Needles

Bidens bipinnata

Range: Throughout the eastern United States south of upper New York state, and west to Kansas.

Description: Plants grow 1 to 3 feet (30.5 to 91.4 cm) tall. Plants have a square stem that's sometimes hairy. Leaves are opposite on the stem and are fernlike leaflets with toothed edges. Flower heads are carried singly on long, leafless branches, toward the top of the plant. Pale yellow ray flowers surround darker yellow disk flowers in the center of each flower head. The long, slender seeds have three or four barbed spikes at the ends. Blooms from August to October.

Life Cycle: Annual, reproducing by seeds.

Prevention and Control: Apply dense mulches to smother seedlings. Hoe or pull plants. Watch waste places and areas along woods, walls, fences, and hedgerows for Spanish needles, and mow before flowers form.

Notes: Spanish needles grow in sandy or rocky soils, open fields, and slightly wooded areas. The barbed seeds stick to clothing and to the fur of passing animals, ensuring seed dispersal over a wide area.

Spotted Spurge

Euphorbia maculate

Range: Eastern two-thirds of the United States, and the Pacific Coast region north of central California; also areas in the eastern half of southern Canada,

Description: Plants are 1 to 2 feet (30.5 to 61 cm) long. The purplish, multi-branched stems form a mat that lies flat on the ground. Stems have milky sap. Leaves are hairy, opposite on the stem, and oval with serrated edges. There's a reddish area near the base of the leaf that gives the plant its name. Flowers are tiny and have petals fused together to form a cup; they're carried at the tops of branches on long stalks. The seed capsule is usually three-sided and contains small, pitted, triangular seeds. Blooms June to October.

Life Cycle: Annual, reproducing by seeds.

Prevention and Control: Apply dense mulches to smother seedlings. Hoe or pull plants. Spotted spurge germinates only in warm soils; look for seedlings in late spring and early summer.

Notes: Spotted spurge can grow well in slightly dry, gravelly, or sandy soils. It doesn't grow in shade; therefore, the dense canopy of an intensively planted garden bed helps inhibit growth of any spotted spurge that germinates later in the season.

Velvet Leaf

Abutilon theophrasti

Range: Throughout the United States except northern Maine, Michigan, Wisconsin, and the southeastern states.

Description: Plants grows 4 to 6 feet (1.2 to 1.8 m) tall. Stems are erect and covered with velvety hairs. Leaves are also covered with short, velvety hairs. They're alternate on the stem and heart-shaped with tapering, pointed tips. Flowers are borne on short stalks near the top of the plant. They're cream- to yellow-colored, about ¾ inch (19.1 mm) wide, with five yellow petals and many visible stamens around the taller pistils. Seedpods are 1 inch (2.5 cm) wide and cup-shaped, with stiff, prickly spikes around the edge; each pod contains as many as 15 prickly seeds. Blooms in midsummer, and seed sets in late summer to early fall.

Life Cycle: Annual, reproducing by seeds.

Prevention and Control: Apply dense mulches to smother seedlings. Pull or hoe plants. Mow plants in nearby waste places or along fencerows before seeds form.

Notes: Velvet leaf prefers rich, somewhat sandy soils in warm climates. Because the plant is so distinctive and grows only from seed, it's easy to eliminate from the garden.

Wild Mustards

Brassica spp.

Range: Throughout the United States and southern Canada.

Description: Plants grow up to 2 feet (61 cm) tall, depending on the species. Stems are erect and branched near the top. Leaves toward the bottom of the plant are lobed or deeply toothed; they become smaller toward the top. Small, bright yellow, four-petaled flowers are loosely clustered at the ends of branches. Seedpods are long and cylindrical and develop quickly. Seeds are dark brown or black. Blooms from early summer to late fall.

Life Cycle: Annual or winter annual, reproducing by seeds.

Prevention and Control: Use dense mulches to smother seedlings. Hoe or pull plants before seeds form. Seeds remain viable for many years in the soil. Mow plants along roadsides and field edges before seeds form.

Notes: Mustard flowers are an excellent source of nectar for beneficial insects, so allowing mustard to bloom in nearby areas can be useful. To avoid spreading seeds, pull plants immediately around the garden before the lower (earliest) flowers start to form seedpods; thoroughly dry the pulled plants before composting them. Leaves are edible.

BIENNIALS

Common Burdock

Arctium minus

Range: Northern two-thirds of the United States; southern Canada.

Description: Plants grow from 1 to 5 feet (305 to 152 cm) tall. During the first year, the stems are short and hairy and grow from a crown, forming a dense rosette of large, somewhat fuzzy, heart-shaped leaves with noticeable veins. The second year, the stems are elongated, erect, and branched, and the leaves are alternate on the stem. The bottom leaves can be 1 foot (30.5 cm) or more long; leaves are smaller toward the tops of the stems. Flowers are small, reddish, surrounded by spiny bracts, and clustered. Seeds are round, spiny burs, about ½ inch (12.7 mm) wide. Blooms from July to October.

Life Cycle: Biennial, reproducing by seeds.

Prevention and Control: Pull or hoe seedlings and first-year plants. Dig up second-year plants, ensuring that as much of the large, deep taproot is

removed as possible; burn any plants that have developing burs. Cut or mow down flowerstalks of burdock along roadsides and nearby areas before they set seed; repeated mowing will eventually kill established plants.

Notes: Burdock prefers fertile soil in undisturbed areas such as fence rows or unused farmland. Burs stick to anything, so seed is easily spread by animals and people.

Common Teasel

Dipsacus fullonum

Range: Eastern United States, from central Maine to North Carolina and westward in a narrow strip to Utah; northern Pacific coast south to central California.

Description: Plants may grow to 6 feet (1.8 m) tall. First-year plants grow in a rosette of narrow, scallop-margined, prominently veined, spiny leaves. Second-year plants grow tall, erect stems. Stems are sturdy, angled, and prickly and usually branch toward the top of the plant. The leaves are opposite along the stems and commonly form a bowl-like structure where their bases join around the stem. Leaves are narrow, toothed, and prickly at the edges and on the underside of the midrib. Flowers are white or purple with four petals and bloom in a large egg-shaped head that later becomes a prickly brown seedhead. Sharp, long bracts extend well beyond the central flower and become stiffly hooked at maturity. Blooms from July to October.

Life Cycle: Biennial, reproducing by seeds.

Prevention and Control: Apply dense mulches to smother seedlings. Pull or dig plants in the garden, taking out as much of the taproot as possible. If necessary to control plants in other areas, cut or mow before plants set seed, repeating until no more shoots appear.

Notes: Dried flower heads of teasel were once used to card wool. Today, the distinctive seedheads are used in dried flower arrangements.

Garlic Mustard

Alliaria petiolata

Range: From eastern Canada south to Virginia and west to Kansas and Nebraska.

Description: Mature plants reach 2 to 3½ feet (61 to 91.4 cm) tall. First-year plants form a low-growing rosette of leaves that remains green during winter. In the second year, erect, flowering stems form in early spring. Leaves are triangular to heart-shaped with toothed edges; they smell distinctly of garlic when crushed. Flowers are small, white, buttonlike, with four petals and are borne in clusters at the tops of stalks. Seedpods are short, narrow, and four-sided and stand erect from the plant; they contain shiny black seeds. Blooms in early spring, with seeds forming as early as mid-May; by late June most stems have dried up; however, the seedpods remain through summer. Seeds can remain viable for 5 years or more.

Life Cycle: Biennial, reproducing by seeds.

Prevention and Control: Apply dense mulches to smother seedlings (seedlings appear in fall). Hoe or pull plants anytime, making sure you remove the whole root because the plant can sprout from root pieces. Mow larger plants very early in the year before they set seed. Check for new shoots in a couple of weeks and mow again, repeating until no more shoots appear.

Notes: Garlic mustard tolerates poor, dry soil but thrives and is invasive in shaded and moist sites. It's commonly seen along roadsides and edges of

Continued ➔

woods. In some areas, this plant smothers native wildflowers—such as hepatica, trilliums, and wild ginger—that complete their life cycle in spring. The whole plant is edible, raw or cooked.

Henbit, Dead Nettle

Lamium amplexicaule

Range: Throughout the United States and southern Canada (except for the Dakotas, Montana, and part of Utah).

Description: Plants grow 4 to 16 inches (10.2 to 40.6 cm) tall. Stems are four-sided, branching, and upright. They tend to root where the lower joints of the stem come in contact with the soil. Leaves are opposite on the stem, hairy, and round, with deeply scalloped edges. Flowers are small and pink or purplish, with two lips and a long, tubular neck (corolla); they grow in whorls where upper leaves attach to stems. Blooms from April to June and again in September.

Life Cycle: Biennial or winter annual, reproducing by seeds and by rooting stems.

Prevention and Control: Apply dense mulches to smother seedlings. Hoe or pull plants, making sure that all pieces of roots are removed. Look for henbit early in the season, and control it before it drops seeds in the garden or adjacent areas. Remove pulled plants from the garden to prevent them from re-rooting; allow them to dry in the sun before composting.

Notes: Henbit prefers good soils and high-moisture levels. It prospers in cool, moist weather and is most troublesome in early spring and fall.

Poison Hemlock

Conium maculatum

Range: Throughout the United States and southern Canada (except for the north-central states and Canadian prairies).

Description: Plants grow to 2 to 7 feet (61 to 213 cm) tall. First-year plants form a low-growing rosette of leaves. Second-year stems grow tall, erect and branched. The stems are ridged and typically spotted with small purple splotches. More leaves appear at the base than at the top of the stems. Leaves are compound and fernlike, with finely cut leaflets arranged along a central stalk; they're triangular in overall outline. The tiny white flowers appear in umbrella-shaped heads at the ends of branches. Fruit is small and round and divides down the center into two sections, each containing one seed. The plant has a long, white taproot. Blooms from June to September.

Life Cycle: Biennial, reproducing by seeds.

Prevention and Control: Wear gloves, long sleeves, and pants while handling this plant; all parts are poisonous and can cause skin irritation. Pull or dig the plants early in the season before seeds begin to form, taking as much of the deep taproot as possible. Dispose of the pulled plants by throwing them in the garbage or by burying them deeply. Infestations on cultivated ground are rare, although the plant sometimes migrates onto the edges of fields.

Notes: It's believed that Socrates was poisoned with a tea made from the poison hemlock plant. Whether the story is true or not, all parts of poison hemlock are fatally poisonous.

Queen-Anne's-Lace, Wild Carrot

Daucus carota

Range: Throughout the United States and southern Canada (except for areas in the north-central states and Canadian prairies).

Description: Plants grow to 3 feet (91.4 cm) tall. First-year plants grow in a rosette of leaves from a white, fleshy taproot. Second-year plants grow tall, with erect, hollow stems that are ridged and hairy. Leaves are slightly hairy, compound, and fernlike. Leaves are alternate on the stems and attached to the stem by sheaths at their bases. Tiny white flowers form in flat, umbrella-shaped heads at the top of the plant. A single purplish flower commonly appears in the center of the flower head. As the flower heads mature, they cup inward. The light tan, seedlike fruits are ribbed and prickly. Blooms from June to September.

Life Cycle: Biennial, reproducing by seeds.

Prevention and Control: Apply dense mulches to smother seedlings. Pull or dig plants in the garden, making sure you remove as much of the taproot as possible. Mow or cut down plants in other areas before seeds set, repeating until no more new shoots form. If the disease aster yellows has been a problem in garden plants, it may be helpful to control Queen-Anne's-lace in areas around the garden. Otherwise, it's such a valuable plant for attracting beneficial insects that it would be better to leave as much of it growing in nearby areas as possible.

Notes: Queen-Anne's-lace provides pollen and nectar for parasitic flies and wasps, minute pirate bugs, lady beetles, and many other beneficial insects that feed on pests of garden plants. The plant is common in dry soil, along roadsides and edges of fields.

Tansy Ragwort

Senecio jacobaea

Range: Atlantic coast from Maine to Rhode Island; Maritime Provinces of Canada; Pacific coast from British Columbia to northern California.

Description: Plants grow to 4 feet (1.2 m) tall. First-year plants grow in a low rosette from a taproot. Second-year plants send up tall, erect stems. Stems are coarse and usually branch only at the top below the flowers. Leaves are deeply cut and lobed, with toothed edges. At the base of the plant the leaves may be hairy on the undersides. Upper leaves are alternate on the stem but clasp the stem. Flowers are round, bright yellow, and buttonlike and up to 1/2 inch (12.7 mm) across; they grow in wide clusters. Blooms from July to September.

Life Cycle: Biennial or winter annual, but can be a short-lived perennial. Reproduces by seeds and by root pieces.

Prevention and Control: Dig or pull plants in the garden, removing as much of the taproot as possible. In fields and waste places, mow early and often enough to prevent flowering and setting seed. In some western and eastern regions, watch for beneficial insects that have been released as a biological control for ragwort. These include the cinnabar moth, which has yellow-and-black-striped caterpillars that feed on the foliage, and a species of flea beetle and a large weevil, both of which have larvae that bore in the roots and kill the plants.

Notes: This plant prefers dry soil. It produces an alkaloid in the foliage that's toxic to horses and cattle.

White Campion, White Cockle

Silene alba

Range: Eastern and north-central United States; Pacific Northwest United States, south to the middle of California; southern Canada from coast to coast.

Description: Plants grow 1 to 2½ feet (30.5 to 76.2 cm) tall. Stems are hairy, sticky, erect, and somewhat branching with an open habit. Leaves grow on stems in opposite pairs. They're hairy, light green, up to 4 inches (10.2 cm) long, and narrow with pointed tips. Flowers are held on long stems and are white to pink and fragrant, with five, deeply notched petals. They have a green-striped, bulbous tube below the petals. The seed capsule is toothed at the top and contains many flat, round, gray, bumpy seeds. Blooms from June to August.

Life Cycle: Biennial or short-lived perennial, reproducing by seeds and rootstock.

Prevention and Control: Apply dense mulches to smother seedlings. Hoe or pull plants, ensuring that the entire root is dug out. Mow or cut down plants before they set seed. Repeat the mowing until no shoots appear, or apply a dense mulch for one growing season.

Notes: This plant likes rich, well-drained soil and is commonly found along roadsides and bordering fields. It's an attractive plant for hoverflies and other beneficial insects, so it should be left to bloom in waste areas.

PERENNIALS

Broadleaf Plantain

Plantago major

Range: Throughout the United States and southern Canada.

Description: Plants are 6 to 18 inches (15.2 to 45.7 cm) tall Leaves grow in a flattened rosette of rounded, waxy, green leaves, 3 to 4 inches (7.6 to 10.2 cm) long. Leaves are thick and rough, with prominent parallel veins from the tip to the base. The leaf stems are stiff and wide and cup upward into a trough shape. Stems that carry flower and seed spikes are wiry and grow from the center of the rosette of leaves. Flowers are tiny and green, and seed capsules are brown or slightly purplish. They contain as many as 15 seeds each. Plantain can be much shorter and flatter in areas where it's mowed or trampled (such as in lawns). Blooms from May to September.

Life Cycle: Perennial, reproducing by seeds.

Prevention and Control: Dig or pull plants from gardens and lawns, ensuring that the entire root is removed. Where it is difficult to remove the root, repeatedly cut off the plant at the soil line until the root stops sprouting. Where plantain continues to invade lawns it is often a sign of compacted soil; therefore, aerate the lawn and spread a thin layer of compost to increase organic matter.

Notes: Plantain thrives in dense, compacted soils and shaded areas.

Buckthorn Plantain

Plantago lanceolata

Range: Throughout the United States and southern Canada.

Description: Flowerstalks are 6 to 24 inches (15.2 to 61 cm) tall. Stems are wiry, erect, and leafless, bearing only the flowering spike. Leaves grow in a low rosette of narrow, lance-shaped, dull green leaves up to 1 foot (30.5 cm) long. Leaves narrow at the base and have three to five prominent veins that run lengthwise. The flower spikes are oval to elongate and are held considerably above the leaves. Flowers are tiny, greenish, and numerous and have distinctive long, yellowish or pale stamens that stick well out from the spike. Seed capsules grow in rows along the spike, and each contains two smooth seeds. Plants can be much shorter where they have been mowed or trampled. Blooms from May to October.

Life Cycle: Perennial, reproducing from seeds.

Continued ➤

Prevention and Control: Dig or pull plants from gardens and lawns, ensuring that the entire root is removed. Where it's difficult to remove the root, repeatedly cut off the plant at the soil line until the root stops sprouting. If plantain continues to invade the lawn, the soil may be compacted, so aerate and increase organic matter.

Notes: Plantains prefer dense, compacted soil. Problems with plantain decrease as hardpan is broken up and aerated.

Canada Thistle

Cirsium arvense

Range: Northern United States and southern Canada from Quebec westward.

Description: Plants grow from 2 to 5 feet (61 to 152 cm) tall. The stem is thin and erect, with branches at the top. Leaves are 4 to 5 inches (10.2 to 12.7 cm) long, alternate on the stem, and deeply lobed with toothed, spiny edges. They're silvery and hairy on the underside. Flower heads are pink to purplish, are ¾ inch (19.1 mm) wide, and are borne in loose clusters at the top of the plant. Bracts beneath the flowers have weak bristles, but there are no spines on the stems bearing the flower heads. The seeds are flattened, ribbed, and oblong, with tufts of white hairs that allow them to be carried in the wind. Roots are deep, wide-spreading rhizomes. Blooms from July to October.

Life Cycle: Perennial, reproducing by creeping roots (rhizomes) and seeds. Seeds have a long period of viability, and roots sprout prolifically.

Prevention and Control: Wear thick gloves and pull or dig plants, removing every piece of root possible. Dry out root pieces in the sun before composting. After removing plants, sow a thickly planted cover crop to smother shoots and prevent seeds from germinating; apply a dense mulch to smother new shoots, or cut down new shoots monthly. Mow or cut nearby plants in field edges or waste areas before they flower; continue mowing monthly for several growing seasons to deplete roots. (This step may not kill plants but will prevent patches from spreading.) Apply dense mulches (cardboard, newspaper, plastic) for at least one and possibly up to three growing seasons to smother shoots. Corn gluten meal herbicides are effective at killing seeds before they emerge (but not shoots or roots). Sheep and goats will eat the thistles.

Notes: In some regions, biological control insects have been released to combat Canada thistle.

Chicory

Cichorium intybus

Range: Throughout the United States (except areas south of North Carolina and the Texas panhandle, as well as portions of north-central states); southern Canada from Nova Scotia to British Columbia.

Description: Plants grow from 1 to 6 feet (30.5 to 183 cm) tall. Stems are erect, branched, and hollow and ooze a milky juice when cut. Leaves at the base of the plant form a rosette of roughly lance-shaped leaves with deeply toothed to lobed edges. Leaves are alternate on the stem, smaller and less lobed than lower leaves; toward the top of the plant, they clasp the stem. Flowers are round and blue (occasionally white), with many petals and up to 1½ inches (38.1 mm) wide. Up to three flowers appear on each long stem arising from the uppermost leaves. Two rows of bristly bracts at the flower base are quite visible. Flowers close each evening. Plants have a deep taproot. Blooms from June to October.

Life Cycle: Perennial, reproducing from seeds and by spreading roots.

Prevention and Control: Pull or hoe plants, making sure to remove as much of the root as possible. Apply dense mulches to smother seedlings or shoots sprouting from roots. Repeatedly cut plants below the crown to eventually kill established roots. If it's necessary to control chicory in nearby areas, mow or cut plants before seeds form; otherwise, leave plants growing to attract beneficial insects.

Notes: Chicory prefers soil with a neutral to slightly alkaline pH and is most troublesome in limestone areas. It's most common along roadsides, fences, and unused land. It attracts beneficial insects. Roots are used as a coffee substitute or additive.

Coltsfoot

Tussilago farfara

Range: Northeastern United States as well as southeastern Canada; eastern areas west to Minnesota as well as eastern areas in Canadian prairies.

Description: Flowerstalks reach 6 inches (15.2 cm) tall and appear in early spring. They're erect scaly, leafless, and somewhat woolly, with a purplish tinge. Leaves are heart-shaped, are 4 to 8 inches (10.2 to 20.3 cm) wide, and appear at the end of the flowering season. They have long petioles, and the undersides are covered with whitish hairs. Flowers are light yellow and up to 2 inches (5.1 cm) wide and resemble dandelions, with many narrow petals. Seeds have a tuft of hair that allows them to be spread by the wind. Blooms from April to May.

Life Cycle: Perennial, reproducing by seeds and roots.

Prevention and Control: Apply dense mulches to smother seedlings. Pull or dig plants, taking care to follow the spreading roots and dig them out entirely. Dry them in the sun before composting pulled plants. For serious infestations, apply dense mulches for a growing season to smother plants or mow plants every few weeks until roots stop sending up shoots.

Notes: Coltsfoot is adapted to a wide range of conditions and is commonly seen along roadsides and waste areas.

Common Milkweed

Asclepias syriaca

Range: Eastern half of United States (except for the Gulf Coast); southern Canada from New Brunswick to Saskatchewan.

Description: Plants grow 2 to 5 feet (61 to 153 cm) tall. Stems are upright, stout, fuzzy, and not branched. When cut, stems ooze a milky sap. Leaves are 4 to 8 inches (10.2 to 20.3 cm) long, opposite on the stem, broadly oblong and rounded, thick, and tough, with prominent veins; they're smooth on top, downy on the underside. Flowers are borne in large clusters from the upper leaves and stem tips. The star-shaped blooms are waxy, pinkish white to darkish pink and fragrant. Seedpods are large, teardrop-shaped, green, and spiny; they ripen into dry, grayish brown husks that split down one side to release seeds. Seeds are flat, brown, and oval and tipped with many feathery, silky white hairs. Plants have an extensive creeping root system (rhizomes). Blooms from June to August.

Life Cycle: Perennial, reproducing by seeds and by rhizomes.

Prevention and Control: It's usually sufficient to pull plants found in the garden, as long as underground rhizomes are also removed. Apply dense mulches to smother seedlings or shoots sprouting from roots. Don't let pods ripen on plants near your garden. Where the caterpillars of monarch butterflies are present, manage milkweed in nearby areas by cutting off flower heads before the pods start to ripen, and leave the leafy part of the plant for the caterpillars.

Notes: Common milkweed is found in old pastures, woods, roadsides, and gardens. Milkweed grows in many conditions but is most common in drier soils. It's the only food plant for the caterpillars of monarch butterflies.

Common Pokeweed

Phytolacca Americana

Range: Throughout the United States from Maine to Minnesota, and southward, including the area between Florida and the eastern two-thirds of Texas.

Description: Plants grow 3 to 9 feet (91.4 to 274 cm) tall. Stems are thick, upright, and reddish. The stem is usually branched near the top. Leaves are alternate on the stem and oval, getting smaller toward the top of the plant. They're smooth, with alternate veins from the central midrib. The flowers grow in narrow, drooping, 4- to 6-inch (10.2 to 15.2 cm)-long strands, arising from stalks opposite upper leaves. The tiny, white flowers have five petals. They drop quickly and are followed by drooping clusters of dark purple berries, each containing 10 seeds. Plants grow from a large taproot. Blooms from June to September.

Life Cycle: Perennial, reproducing by seeds.

Prevention and Control: Use dense mulches to smother seedlings. Using gloves, pull or dig young plants before the large root develops. Large plants must be cut below the crown with a sharp spade, and as much of the root must be removed as possible. To clear ground of pokeweed, cut off and remove each group of stems, then continue to cut or mow the area every few weeks until they stop sprouting. Alternatively, after cutting down established plants, cover the entire area with a dense mulch (newspaper, cardboard, or plastic) for a growing season.

Notes: Pokeweed likes deep, rich, well-drained soils, but it doesn't survive long in a garden that's regularly cultivated. The entire plant is poisonous, except for young shoots.

Common Yarrow

Achillea millefolium

Range: Throughout the United States (except areas in the Southwest) and southern Canada.

Description: Plants grow 1 to 2 feet (30.5 to 61 cm) tall. Stems are erect and usually simple but may branch toward the top. Stems may be smooth or slightly hairy. Leaves are delicate and feathery and give off an aromatic scent when crushed. They're covered with soft gray hairs and arise almost directly from the stem. Flowers are carried in flat, compound clusters and are usually white or yellow (rarely pinkish). Blooms from June to October.

Life Cycle: Perennial, reproducing by seeds and roots.

Prevention and Control: Pull plants in the garden before the they set seed, making sure that all roots are removed. Apply dense mulches to smother seedlings or shoots growing from roots. It usually isn't necessary or desirable to remove yarrow from nearby areas because the plants provide pollen and nectar for beneficial insects, particularly hoverflies, lady beetles, and parasitic wasps.

Continued ➡

Notes: Yarrow grows in various conditions but is particularly common in thin, poor soils. Flowers dry well for winter arrangements.

Common Yellow Wood Sorrel

Oxalis stricta

Range: Throughout the United States and southern Canada.

Description: Plants grow 4 to 18 inches (20.3 to 45.7 cm) tall. Young stems are generally erect but are thin and weak. As the plant grows, the stems branch in all directions and tend to spread low over the ground. Stems are light green and somewhat hairy. Leaves grow on long, thin petioles and are divided into three, heart-shaped leaflets with an obvious vein running down the center of each leaflet. Flowers are clear yellow with five petals. Seedpods are cylindrical and slightly hairy, with pointed tips. Seeds are tiny and are ejected quite a distance from the pod when it bursts. Blooms from May to October.

Life Cycle: Perennial, reproducing by seeds.

Prevention and Control: Hoe or pull plants before they set seed, removing all of the root. Plants can root readily from joints in the stem, so remove pulled plants from the garden and dry in the sun before composting. Use dense mulches to smother seedlings or shoots from pieces of root remaining in soil.

Notes: Wood sorrel is common with acid soil and in neglected areas, dry lawns, and bare soil. It grows quite well in shade.

Curly Dock

Rumex crispus

Range: Throughout the United States and southern Canada.

Description: Plants grow from 1 to 4 feet (30.5 to 122 cm) tall. A dense rosette of thick, 6- to 12-inch (15.2 to 30.5 cm)-long leaves grows first from a thick, branching taproot. Later, flowering stalks grow from the rosette; stems are hairless and ridged, with enlarged joints; stems turn reddish brown in fall. Leaves are lance-shaped, with curly or wavy margins. Leaves growing on the stems are alternate, with short petioles growing from a papery sheath just above each leaf joint. The flower head has many branches with small, narrow leaves interspersed among the flowers. The small, greenish flowers become reddish brown as they age. The seeds are shiny, brown, and triangular, with a papery, winged covering. Blooms from June to September.

Life Cycle: Perennial, reproducing by seeds.

Prevention and Control: Pull or dig plants, making sure that the entire large, branched taproot is dug out of the soil. Removing dock is easiest when it's young, before the taproot has had a chance to grow deep. Apply dense mulches to smother seedlings or shoots arising from root pieces.

Notes: Curly dock is tolerant of poor conditions, but it's most common in moist soils. It commonly grows along roadsides and ditches, at the edges of fields, and in waste places.

Dandelion

Taraxacum officinale

Range: Throughout most of the United States and southern Canada.

Description: Flowerstalks grow to 1 to 12 inches (2.5 to 15.2 cm) high. Plants grow a basal rosette of lobed or toothed leaves arising from a deep, fleshy taproot. When leaves or stems are cut, they ooze a milky sap. Flower buds are nestled into the leaf rosettes at first, then grow above the leaves. Flower heads are bright yellow, 1 to 2 inches (2.5 to 5.1 cm) across; the flowerstalks are hollow, smooth, and pale on the outside. Seeds have tufts of hairs that allow them to drift in the wind. Plants can grow and flower as flat, low rosettes where they're repeatedly mowed or trampled. Blooms from March to December.

Life Cycle: Perennial, reproducing by seeds and from root crowns.

Prevention and Control: Where dandelions aren't desired, dig or pull plants before the seeds set, removing as much of the taproot as possible. For lawns, use a sharp, forked dandelion cutter to sever the taproot as deeply as possible, disturbing the soil as little as possible. (The larger the opening in the soil, the more likely it is that weed seeds will germinate in the opening.) Persistent plants may require digging several times to remove new shoots developing from roots. Dandelions provide a vital source of early pollen for bees and many other beneficial insects that feed on garden pests; therefore, it's neither necessary nor desirable to eradicate them from nearby areas.

Notes: Dandelion flowers can be used to make wine, the leaves can be cooked or eaten fresh, and the roots can be roasted for a coffee substitute.

Field Bindweed

Convolvulus arvensis

Range: Throughout the United States (except for Florida and the extreme southern areas of Texas and the Southwest) and southern Canada.

Description: Stems are long, twining vines growing 2 to 7 feet (61 to 213 cm) long. They're smooth and thin, and they lie prostrate on the ground or climb up vegetation and objects. Leaves are alternate, simple, and smooth-edged, and many of them flare into two lobes at the base. Flowers are trumpet-shaped with a wide, round mouth; they're white or pink and 1 inch (2.5 cm) wide. The dark seeds have a rough, pebbly texture. Blooms from June to September.

Life Cycle: Perennial, reproducing by seeds and creeping roots.

Prevention and Control: Bindweed is difficult to eradicate because roots can extend for many feet in the soil. Dig or pull plants, making sure that the entire root is removed. Don't let it remain in the garden long enough to gain a foothold. For severe infestations, apply a dense mulch (newspaper, cardboard, or plastic that's well weighed down) to the area and to a wide area around the infestation to control spreading roots; leave in place for the entire season. Mow or cut plants in waste areas to prevent seeds from forming.

Notes: Bindweed likes rich soil, good drainage, and bright light conditions.

Field Horsetail

Equisetum arvense

Range: Throughout the United States (except in the Southeast) and southern Canada.

Description: Plants grow up to 18 inches tall (45.7 cm). Stems are stiff, erect hollow, jointed, and very tough. They're either vegetative (which means they don't produce flowers) or fertile (which means they produce flowers). Fertile stems appear first in spring. They aren't branched; they have prominent, swollen joints and what looks like small oval pinecones (the fruiting heads) at the tips. The stem dies back after the fruiting heads shed their spores. Later the vegetative stems appear; these have whorls of long, thin branches arising from each leaf joint. The roots are strong rhizomes that can grow many feet deep in moist soils.

Life Cycle: Perennial, reproducing by spores and by creeping roots.

Prevention and Control: Pull or dig plants, removing as much of the root as possible; this is a temporary measure because shoots eventually grow back from the pieces of root left in the soil. Repeated removal, combined with keeping the soil cultivated and open, discourages horsetail sufficiently for the season to allow garden crops to grow. Smothering plants with dense mulches (cardboard, newspaper, or plastic) can provide temporary control; however, shoots can eventually penetrate even asphalt surfaces. Where possible, for long-term prevention of horsetail invasions, dry out the site by improving drainage, and enrich the soil with compost and organic matter; make sure that the soil is well drained over winter.

Notes: Horsetail thrives in moist, sandy, or gravelly soil, especially along edges of woods and fields and in ditches.

Goldenrods

Solidago spp.

Range: Many species throughout the United States and southern Canada.

Description: Plants grow from 2 to 5 feet (61 to 152 cm) tall. Stems are generally solitary, but they may be clustered. Leaves are numerous and crowded, especially toward the middle to the top of the plant. They're narrow and lance-shaped and have prominent, parallel veins and sharply toothed margins. Leaf undersides may be slightly hairy. Basal leaves usually die and drop as the season progresses. The many-branched flower heads are carried at the top of stems. Flowers are yellow to yellow-green and bloom on long spikes that droop in graceful arcs. Blooms from July to October.

Life Cycle: Perennial, reproducing by seeds and creeping rhizomes.

Prevention and Control: To remove plants from the garden, hoe or dig plants, removing as much of the root as possible. It may be necessary to dig established roots several times throughout the season whenever new sprouts appear. Apply a dense mulch to smother seedlings or shoots. It usually isn't necessary or desirable to control goldenrod in nearby areas and roadsides because it's an important source of pollen and nectar for bees and many beneficial insects.

Notes: Goldenrod can grow in any type of soil, but it does require good light. It's an important source of pollen and nectar for honeybees and other beneficial insects, such as minute pirate bugs and hoverflies. Contrary to popular belief, goldenrod doesn't cause hay fever; that's because it isn't pollinated by spreading pollen in the wind.

Ground Ivy

Glechoma hederacea

Range: Throughout the eastern half of both the United States and southern Canada, except for Florida and southern Georgia.

Description: Stems grow 15 to 30 inches (38.1 to 76.2 cm) long, usually spreading along the ground. Stems are four-sided and branching and commonly root at the stem joints. Leaves are round or kidney-shaped, bright green, and opposite on the stem, and they have scalloped margins. Flowers are blue or purplish and grow from the point where the leaf meets the stem on upright

Continued ➡

branches. They're small and trumpet-shaped, with two lips. Blooms from April to July.

Life Cycle: Perennial, reproducing by seeds and creeping stems.

Prevention and Control: Hoe or pull plants, making sure to take all roots and connecting stems. Remove pulled plants from the garden and dry them in the sun to prevent stems from sprouting roots when they're composted. Apply dense mulches to smother seedlings and shoots developing from fragments of stems left in the garden or to smother dense patches on lawns.

Notes: Ground ivy, a mint relative, prefers rich soils that are somewhat moist. It grows well in shade and typically tries to form a groundcover under trees.

Heal-All

Prunella vulgaris

Range: Throughout the United States (except for regions in the north-central states) and southern Canada.

Description: Stems are up to 24 inches (61 cm) long; they're four-sided and can be erect or prostrate on the soil. Leaves are opposite on the stems, hairy when young, and smooth as they mature; they have smooth or slightly toothed margins and are spaced widely along the stems. Flower spikes are thick, grow at the tips of branches, and have a pair of visible bracts below them. The small, tube-shaped flowers have two lips and are blue, purple, or pink (rarely white) with green or purplish calyxes. Where plants are mowed or trampled, they grow into dense, prostrate mats. Blooms from May to October.

Life Cycle: Perennial, reproducing by seeds and runners (stolons) that root at the joints.

Prevention and Control: Apply dense mulches to smother seedlings and young plants. Dig or pull plants, removing all of the connected aboveground runners and roots. Remove pulled plants from the garden and allow them to dry in the sun to prevent stems from sprouting roots before composting them.

Notes: Heal-all thrives in moist areas and is common in lawns and along roadsides.

Hedge Bindweed

Convolvulus sepium

Range: Eastern and northwestern United States and southern Canada.

Description: Stems grow 3 to 10 feet (91.4 to 305 cm) long and trail on the ground or twine up plants and over objects. Stems are usually smooth, but they may be covered with small hairs. Leaves are alternate on the stem and arrow- or heart-shaped, with pointed tips and squared-off lobes at the base. Flowers are trumpet-shaped, white or pinkish, and 1 to 2 inches (2.5 to 5.1 cm) wide. Roots are very long and shallow. Blooms from June to August.

Life Cycle: Perennial, reproducing by seeds and creeping underground stems (rhizomes).

Prevention and Control: Removing this invasive plant from gardens requires persistence in pulling it every time a shoot appears. Pull out roots and shoots, remove the pulled plants from the garden, and dry them in the sun before composting them. To remove a large patch of bindweed, apply a dense mulch (cardboard, newspaper, or plastic that's well weighed down) to the affected area and to a wide border around it; leave the mulch for the entire growing season and watch for roots spreading from under the mulched area. Limiting the area of moist soil in the garden by using a drip irrigation system

helps prevent bindweed roots from re-colonizing garden beds because dry soil deters them. To control bindweed in hedges, cut the stems near the ground to kill tops and prevent seeds from forming.

Notes: Hedge bindweed can climb nearby plants or fences, but without a support it will trail along the ground. It's quite invasive, and it will quickly cover the edges of roadways or fields, choking out less-vigorous plants. Bindweed likes rich, moist soils and good light. It grows quickly in the cool conditions of spring and fall, and in coastal areas it may continue to grow all winter.

Hoary Vervain

Verbena stricta

Range: Midwest, the Great Plains, Texas, and along the Pacific coast in the United States.

Description: Plants grow 1 to 4 feet (30.5 to 122 cm) tall. Stems are erect and simple or branched toward the top, and they're covered with soft, white hairs. Leaves are opposite on the stem and oval, with toothed edges. They have a coating of soft, white hairs that makes them look almost downy. Flowers grow in slender, upright spikes of small purple, pink, or white blooms; flowers open in succession from the bottom to the top of the spike. Seeds are dark brown. Blooms from June to September.

Life Cycle: Perennial, reproducing by seeds and by creeping underground roots (rhizomes).

Prevention and Control: Apply a dense mulch to smother seedlings. Pull or dig plants in the garden, removing the whole root system. Remove pulled plants from the garden to prevent them from rooting again, and dry them in the sun before composting. Cut or mow plants in nearby areas before they flower.

Notes: Hoary vervain likes dry, gravelly soils and grows well where fertility is low. It's unlikely to infest garden areas that are well tended and have high levels of organic matter.

Horse Nettle

Solanum carolinense

Range: In the eastern half of the United States, in the West from Idaho and Arizona to California (except the state of Washington), and in southern Canada.

Description: Plants grow 1 to 3 feet (30.5 to 91.4 cm) tall. Stems are stout, erect, and branched or unbranched, with yellowish spines. Leaves are up to 5 inches (12.7 cm) long, alternate on the stem, and oblong or oval, with wavy or lobed edges. The leaves also have prickly, yellow spines along the veins and the leaf stem. The flowers are star-shaped, 1 inch (2.5 cm) wide, and white, pale blue, or violet. They bloom in small clusters, and each flower has a green calyx with five sepals at its base. Numerous seeds develop within a round, yellow-orange berry, which is ½ inch (12.7 mm) wide; the berries wrinkle as they mature. Blooms from June to September.

Life Cycle: Perennial, reproducing by seeds and creeping underground roots (rhizomes).

Prevention and Control: Wearing gloves, pull or dig plants before they flower and dig up the entire root system; remove the plants from the garden and dry them in the sun before composting. Cut or mow nearby plants in fields and along roadsides before they flower; repeat mowing as new shoots appear. To clear a heavily infested area, dig plants and then apply a dense mulch (newspaper, cardboard, or plastic) to smother new shoots for the growing season.

Notes: Horse nettle grows best in sandy soil in full sun. It's poisonous.

Purple Loosestrife

Lythrum salicaria

Range: Northeastern United States to Virginia and Missouri and western Washington state; eastern Canada and southern British Columbia.

Description: Plants grow 2 to 4 feet (61 to 122 cm) tall. Stems are stout and erect. Like the leaves, they may be smooth or have small, downy hairs. Leaves are opposite each other on the stem or arise in three-leaved whorls that clasp the stem. They're smaller and more lance-shaped toward the top of the plant; leaves at the base are more heart-shaped. Flowers are a clear purple color and very showy. They have six petals, grow in slender, upright, tapering spikes that are wider at the base, and are interspersed with leafy bracts. Blooms from June to September.

Life Cycle: Perennial, reproducing by seeds.

Prevention and Control: Loosestrife—along with its entire root system (which isn't extensive)—must be dug out to be eliminated, preferably before plants flower. Apply a dense mulch to smother seedlings. Cut or mow established plants and continue to mow every few weeks until plants stop sending up shoots, or mulch with newspaper, cardboard, or plastic for a growing season. Where loosestrife continues to be a problem, improve the drainage of the site if possible.

Notes: Loosestrife can grow in a range of conditions, but it thrives in moist, swampy conditions. It's an invasive weed that has become a serious pest in wetlands, where it chokes out native plants needed to sustain wildlife. The seeds float and are readily carried by flowing water to new sites. Although once considered an ornamental, it's now recognized as a serious problem and shouldn't be planted.

St.-John's-Wort

Hypericum perforatum

Range: Throughout the eastern half of both the United States and southern Canada; also southern British Columbia and Pacific Northwest states.

Description: Plants grow 1 to 2 feet (30.5 to 61 cm) tall. Stems are smooth, erect and multi-branched with a woody base. The numerous leaves are each 1 inch (2.5 cm) long, oblong, and dotted with tiny pinhole spots that let light through. They're opposite on the stem and attached directly to the stem. The stems carrying the blooms are quite leafy. Flowers have five yellow-orange petals with dark dots at the edges of the petals. The flowers are 1 inch (2.5 cm) wide and have noticeable, long stamens growing in three distinct groups. The seedpods are round with pointed tips and contain three chambers with numerous seeds. Blooms from June to September.

Life Cycle: Perennial, reproducing by seeds and creeping roots.

Prevention and Control: Apply a dense mulch to smother seedlings. Using gloves, pull or dig plants, removing the entire root. To clean a heavily infested area, cut or mow the plants and continue to mow every few weeks until the roots stop sprouting, or apply a dense mulch (cardboard, newspaper, or plastic).

Notes: St.-John's-wort prefers dry, gravelly, or sandy soils; it won't grow in damp areas. It contains a compound that irritates the mouths of livestock that graze on it. It can also cause an allergic reaction and severe burns on skin with exposure to

Continued ➡

sunlight In some regions, insects that eat St.-John's-wort are being released as a biological control.

Sheep Sorrel

Rumex acetosella

Range: Throughout the United States and southern Canada.

Description: Plants grow up to 6 to 18 inches (15.2 to 45.7 cm) tall. Young plants form a rosette of leaves, which are 1 to 3 inches long (2.5 to 7.6 cm) and arrow-shaped. Thin, erect, flowering stems grow from the center of the rosette; they branch toward the top of the stem. Leaves growing from stems are narrower than those in the rosette and have two distinct basal lobes. Stems and flowerstalks are reddish. Small, red or yellowish flowers grow on branching, upright spikes. The fruit is shiny, triangular, and yellow or reddish brown. Plants have widely spreading root systems. Blooms from May to October.

Life Cycle: Perennial, reproducing by seeds and extensive creeping roots (rhizomes).

Prevention and Control: Apply a dense mulch to smother seedlings. Pull or dig plants, along with the roots. Remove plants from the garden to prevent them from rooting, and dry them in the sun before composting. Improve soil fertility and add lime to raise the soil pH, which inhibits the growth of sorrel.

Notes: Sorrel typically indicates poor fertility. It grows on acidic, shallow, dry, or gravelly ground.

Stinging Nettle

Urtica dioica

Range: Eastern half of the United States (except Florida), eastern Washington state, Idaho, Colorado, northern Texas, and southern Canada.

Description: Plants grow 2 to 6 feet (61 to 183 cm) tall. Stems are erect and ridged and covered with hairs that sting bare skin, leaving red welts. Leaves are also covered with stinging hairs; they're opposite on the stem, rough, dark green, oval to heart-shaped with coarsely toothed margins. Tiny green flowers bloom in clusters on drooping spikes originating from points where leaves meet the stem and at the tips of stems. Fruits are tiny, grayish brown, and lens-shaped. Blooms from June to September.

Life Cycle: Perennial, reproducing by seeds and creeping roots (rhizomes).

Prevention and Control: Wear boots, thick pants, and tough gloves, and use a sharp spade to dig stinging nettles. Follow the spreading roots through the soil and lift them. Let the plant dry in the sun before composting (continue to wear gloves when handling the wilted plant material). Cut or mow plants and continue to mow every few weeks when shoots reappear, or apply a dense mulch (cardboard, newspaper, or plastic) for a growing season.

Notes: The leaves are edible as steamed greens.

Tall Ironweed

Vernonia altissima

Range: Eastern half of the United States south of Vermont and New Hampshire.

Description: Plants may reach 10 feet (3.1 m) tall. Stems are smooth and branch widely toward the top. Leaves are alternate on the stem, lance-shaped with pointed tips, and up to 10 inches (25.4 cm) long, with small, pointed teeth at the margins. They usually point upward, rather than horizontally from the stem. Flowers are reddish purple and ½ inch (12.7 mm) wide; they grow in loose, open clusters. Green, sharply toothed, leaf-like structures enclose the base of the flower heads. Blooms from August to October.

Life Cycle: Perennial, reproducing by seeds and creeping roots (rhizomes).

Prevention and Control: Dig or pull plants, along with the roots. Mow or cut plants in the late summer before they set seeds. Apply dense mulch (cardboard, newspaper, or plastic) to smother seedlings or shoots developing from roots of plants that have been mowed down. Improve the drainage of garden soils to discourage tall ironweed.

Notes: Tall ironweed prefers very moist rich soils. It's an attractive food plant for bumblebees, so you may not want to eradicate plants in areas near the garden.

Wild Garlic

Allium vineale

Range: Throughout the United States

Description: Plants grow 1 to 3 feet (30.5 to 61 cm) tall. Stems are stiff and erect, with leaves growing only from the lower half. Leaves are hollow with a basal sheath that encircles the stem. In some areas, wild garlic will flower and set seed. The flower head is umbrella-shaped and made up of whitish green, pink, or purplish red flowers on a short stock; plants set seeds in early spring. The plant produces small, grain-sized, aerial bulblets on the top of the stem and larger bulblets underground toward the end of summer. Blooms from May to June.

Life Cycle: Perennial, reproducing from seeds, aerial bulblets, and bulbs.

Prevention and Control: Dig up every plant, removing as many underground bulbs as you can find. Cultivate regularly to control developing shoots; this is most effective in dry soil. If wild garlic is a serious problem, apply a dense mulch (newspaper, cardboard, or plastic) to heavily infested areas for an entire season, Improving the soil drainage helps discourage the growth of the weed.

Notes: Wild garlic tolerates almost any environment but it grows best in heavy, fertile soil. Leaves smell like garlic.

Yellow Rocket, Winter Cress

Barbarea vulgaris

Range: Northeastern United States south to Arkansas, areas in the north-central states, and Pacific Northwest; southeastern Canada.

Description: Plants grow 1 to 2 feet (30.5 to 61 cm) tall. During the first year, a rosette of leaves forms close to the ground. Leaves are glossy and lobed; the rounded terminal lobe is so large that lower lobes look more like smaller individual leaves than portions of the same leaf. In spring of the second season, stems grow from the crown. The stems are hairless and may be ridged. Leaves are alternate on the stems and lobed at the base; they become less lobed and shorter toward the top of the stem. Flowers are bright yellow, have four petals, and grow in loose clusters at the end of each branch. They're followed by 1-inch (2.5 cm)-long seedpods with tiny yellow seeds. Plants have a deep taproot. Blooms from April to August.

Life Cycle: Short-lived perennial, reproducing by seeds; in some areas it grows like a winter annual.

Prevention and Control: Hoe or pull plants, removing the deep taproot. Cut or mow heavily infested areas before plants set seed, repeating

mowing every few weeks until they stop sending up shoots, or apply a dense mulch (newspaper, cardboard, or plastic) for the growing season. It may not be necessary or desirable to control rocket in nearby waste or weedy areas because it's an excellent source of food for bees and beneficial insects.

Notes: Rocket likes rich soils with good moisture levels and quickly colonizes newly cultivated areas. It provides some of the earliest pollen and nectar in spring for beneficial insects and bees. It's edible.

WOODY PERENNIALS

Japanese Honeysuckle

Lonicera japonica

Range: Eastern half of the United States north to Michigan.

Description: Plants grow up to 30 feet (9.1 m) long. Stems are woody and trail or climb over vegetation and objects. Stems lying on the soil surface sprout roots at the leaf joints. Leaves are opposite on the stem, slightly hairy, and oval. Paired, highly fragrant, and white, pink, or yellow flowers arise from each side of the leaf joints just above the leaf. The five petals form a long tube with two uneven lips. Berries are purplish black and shiny. Two or three seeds are enclosed in each berry. Blooms from June and July.

Life Cycle: Perennial, reproducing from seeds, trailing stems, and underground rhizomes.

Prevention and Control: Pull seedlings as soon as they appear. Dig deeply to remove established rhizomes and rooting stems; continue to watch for new shoots, and remove them as they appear. This job takes several seasons; honeysuckle is vigorous and spreads rapidly. To slow the spread of plants, cut or mow plants in uncultivated areas before they set fruit (which is spread by birds), and continue to mow periodically for several seasons, or pasture goats in the area.

Notes: Honeysuckle twines up fences or nearby trees, or if it doesn't have support, it trails along the ground. Berries are a favorite food of many seed-spreading birds. In the southern states, leaves remain on the plant all winter.

Kudzu

Pueraria lobata

Range: Southeastern half of the United States and mid-Atlantic states.

Description: Plants reach to up 60 feet (18.3 m) long in one season, smothering vegetation and growing over objects. When young, the stems of the vine are slightly hairy, but as they age, they become woody and smooth. Leaves are divided into three leaflets; they're usually lobed and alternate along the stem. Flowers are small, reddish purple, and grape-scented and resemble pea flowers; they're borne in clusters. The large, upright petal is bright yellow at the base. Seedpods grow up to 4 inches (10.2 cm) long and look like hairy pea pods. Kudzu grows from a large, deep, starchy, tuberous root. Blooms from late August to September.

Life Cycle: Perennial, reproducing mainly by runners and stems that root at the leaf joints; also may sometimes spread by seeds.

Prevention and Control: Cut vines and dig out as much of the deep roots as possible. Because each piece of root can sprout, continue to watch for shoots, cutting or digging them as they appear or mowing closely every month for two growing seasons. Apply a dense mulch (newspaper, cardboard, or plastic) for one or more growing seasons

Continued →

to smother shoots—it may take 2 to 3 years to eliminate established vines.

Notes: The branching stems of kudzu twine around upright supports or trail long distances across the ground.

Multiflora Rose

Rosa multiflora

Range: Throughout most of the United States except the Rocky Mountain, desert, and southeastern coastal plain areas; parts of eastern Canada.

Description: Plants grow to 10 feet (3.1 m) tall. Stiff thorns protect the stems. The deciduous leaves are compound, divided into seven to nine oval leaflets, with sharp-toothed edges; they're arranged along a central stalk with a single middle leaflet at the tip. Leaves are fuzzy on the undersides. The flowers are white or light pink, fragrant, and about 3/4 inch (19.1 mm) wide; they grow in clusters. Flowers are followed by bright red, pea-sized hips that can persist on the canes until spring. Blooms from May to June.

Life Cycle: Perennial, reproducing by seeds and from cane tips that root where they touch the soil.

Prevention and Control: Dig out plants invading gardens, removing as much of the roots as possible (wear heavy gloves to handle the canes). To clear thickets of rose, cut stems at the soil line, then continue to mow at monthly intervals, or apply a dense mulch (newspaper, cardboard, or plastic) for at least one growing season. Eliminating this rose may take several seasons.

Notes: A full-grown multiflora rose is a huge shrub, with long stems that stand erect for 4 to 5 feet (1.2 to 1.5 ml, then arch back to the ground. The hips are an excellent source of vitamin C and are relished by birds, which help spread the seeds.

Poison Ivy

Toxicodendron radicans (Rhus radicans)

Range: Throughout the United States (except for Alaska and California) and southern Canada.

Description: Poison ivy grows either as a shrub or as a climbing vine. All parts of the plant contain an oil that causes painful and itchy skin blisters. Each leaf is made up of three leaflets, 2 to 4 inches (5.1 to 10.2 cm) long, with pointed tips borne on long petioles. Leaves may be hairy or shiny, with smooth or slightly toothed edges. Shape and characteristics of the leaves vary; however, the leaves do turn red in fall. Flowers grow in clusters and are tiny and yellow-green, with five petals. Flowers are followed by small, hard, dry, white or grayish white fruit. Blooms from late May to July.

Life Cycle: Perennial, reproducing by seeds and creeping roots that grow from joints in the lower stems.

Prevention and Control: Wear protective clothing (gloves, long-sleeved shirt, pants, and boots) when working around this plant. Dig out roots as soon as you notice the characteristic three leaflets. In fall, about a week after the first hard frost, look for the leaves turning reddish orange, and dig out the plants. Put pulled plants and roots into heavy plastic bags, then discard them in the garbage, or allow pulled plants and roots to dry in the sun, then bury them. Don't compost poison ivy, and don't burn it because it produces toxic smoke. Note that some people are extremely sensitive to poison ivy and shouldn't attempt to control it until winter when leaves have fallen from the stems. Cut stems off at ground level, then apply a dense mulch (newspaper, cardboard, or plastic) for at least one growing season.

Notes: The toxic oil can remain for years on tools that come in contact with this weed. If you come in contact with poison ivy, immediately wash your skin thoroughly with soap and lots of water for 15 minutes; wash clothing with strong detergent.

Poison Oak

Toxicodendron toxicarium (Rhus tocicodendron)

Range: Southeastern United States from New Jersey to Florida, west to Missouri, Oklahoma, and Texas; related species in California

Description: Plants grow to 4 to 6 feet (1.2 to 1.8 m) tall. All parts of the plant contain an oil that causes painful and itchy skin blisters. Stems are slender and woody. Unlike poison ivy, poison oak doesn't grow roots from stem joints, nor is it a climber. Leaves have soft hairs and are divided into three leaflets. Leaflets are also hairy and are variously shaped. Many have deep teeth or lobes and are shaped like maple or oak leaves. Flowers grow in clusters and are small and whitish with five petals. Green to light tan berries form in fall. Blooms from May to June.

Life Cycle: Perennial, reproducing by seeds and underground roots.

Prevention and Control: Wear protective clothing (gloves, long-sleeved shirt, pants, and boots) when working around this plant. Dig out roots as soon as you notice them. Put pulled plants and roots into heavy plastic bags, then discard in the garbage, or allow pulled plants and roots to dry in the sun, then bury them. Don't compost poison oak, and don't burn it because it produces toxic smoke. Cut stems off at ground level, then apply a dense mulch (newspaper, cardboard, or plastic) for at least one growing season.

Notes: The toxic oil can remain for years on tools that come in contact with this weed. If you come in contact with poison oak, immediately wash your skin thoroughly with soap and lots of water for 15 minutes (contrary to myth, this won't cause the rash to spread); wash clothing with strong detergent.

GRASSES

Bermudagrass

Cynodon dactylon

Range: Southern two-thirds of the United States; hardy only south of Pennsylvania.

Description: Stalks grow up to 1⅓ feet (40.6 cm) tall, but the rest of the plant is prostrate and creeping, forming dense sod. Rooting stems (stolons) lie along the soil surface, branching, rooting, and carrying the wiry stems. Leaves are fine, narrow, short, and gray-green, with a fringe of hairs just above the sheath where they attach to the stem. The flower head is divided into three to seven 1- to 2-inch (2.5 to 5.1 cm)-long spikes that radiate from the ends of erect stalks. Two rows of deep orange, prickly seeds develop along each spike. Roots are thin, scaly rhizomes. Blooms from June to August.

Life Cycle: Perennial, reproducing by rhizomes, stolons, and seeds.

Prevention and Control: Pull or dig plants, removing all roots and stolons. Allow pulled plants to dry in the sun before composting. In gardens with heavy infestations, apply a dense mulch (newspaper, cardboard, or plastic) for a growing season. In southern areas, solarizing the soil for the hottest part of the season can kill the roots. On the northern edge of its range, fall plowing to expose roots to heavy frosts can kill the plant.

Notes: Bermudagrass can be used as a lawn or pasture grass in dry, sandy soils. If lawn plants are creeping into gardens, establish a mowed strip between the lawn and the garden or install an edging strip as a barrier to keep bermudagrass in bounds.

Crabgrasses

Digitaria spp.

Range: Throughout the United States and southern Canada. Large crabgrass (*D. sanguinalis*) isn't found in North Dakota; smooth crabgrass (*D. ischaemum*) isn't found in southern Florida, west Texas, or parts of the Southwest.

Description: Plants grow 15 inches (38.1 cm) (smooth crabgrass) to 3 feet (91.4 cm) (large crabgrass) tall. Stems can be erect or spread on the ground. They can root from joints of the stem lying on the soil, so crabgrass commonly forms a dense mat. Leaves of large crabgrass are hairy, narrow (¼ inch [6.4 mm] wide), and elongated. Leaves of smooth crabgrass are smaller and smooth, with a blue to purplish cast. Crabgrass flower heads grow in terminal spikes on upright stems. Tiny hairs grow both from the areas where leaves arise from their sheaths and on the bracts below the florets. Blooms from July to September.

Life Cycle: Annual, reproducing by seeds or from roots growing from stem joints.

Prevention and Control: Pull or dig plants before they set seed, removing all stems and roots. In lawns, fertilize in early spring to promote the growth of desired grasses and decrease the openings in the turf that allow crabgrass seed to germinate. Corn gluten meal herbicides can be used on lawns to stop crabgrass seeds from germinating (this has no effect on growing grasses). Repeated mowing only encourages crabgrass to grow in a spreading mat; because they can continue to flower and set seed, mowing isn't a control method.

Notes: Crabgrass is most common 'In dry and sandy soils, but it will grow in other conditions.

Foxtails

Setaria spp.

Range: Throughout United States and southern Canada.

Description: Green foxtail (*S. viridis*) grows 1 to 3 feet (30.5 to 91.4 cm) tall. It has erect or ascending stems that branch close to the base. Leaves are hairless but rough, and there's a fringe of hairs around the base of the leaf where it meets the stem. Flower heads are long, bristly, green spikes, 1 to 3 inches (2.5 to 7.6 cm) long with tips curving downward. Seeds are green and ¹/₁₆ inch (1.6 mm) long. Yellow foxtail (*S. glauca*) is shorter, growing 1 to 2 feet (30.5 to 61 cm) tall, and usually grows in clumps. The leaves have a few long hairs at the base where they attach to the stem. Its seeds are larger than green foxtail's and are yellowish. Foxtails may be shorter and more spreading in habit where they have been mowed or trampled. Blooms from June to September.

Life Cycle: Annual, reproducing by seeds.

Prevention and Control: Apply dense mulches to smother seedlings. Pull or dig plants in the garden as early as possible to ensure that no seeds have set. If renovating a field, mow before seeds form, and repeat if necessary; the following spring, cultivate several times before planting a cultivated crop. Several years of cultivating to control foxtail before it can set seed is usually enough to deplete the supply of viable seeds in the soil

Notes: Foxtails tolerate a wide range of conditions and are commonly found along roadsides and in

Continued ➡

waste areas. They don't reproduce by underground stolons or rhizomes as many grasses do, so digging up scattered clumps is relatively easy.

Johnsongrass

Sorghum halepense

Range: Southern two-thirds of the United States and areas in Washington State and Oregon.

Description: Plants grow 1½ to 6 feet (45.7 to 183 cm) tall and have strong, erect stems. They look somewhat like slender corn plants. Leaves are 6 to 20 inches (15.2 to 50.8 cm) long and smooth, with a white vein down the center. Flowers are loose, upright, hairy, and purplish. The seeds are red-brown. Roots are fleshy, scaly rhizomes that may grow quite deep from established plants. Blooms from June to October.

Life Cycle: Perennial, reproducing by seeds and roots.

Prevention and Control: Dig Johnsongrass out of the garden, removing all roots. Apply a dense mulch (newspaper, cardboard, or plastic) for at least one growing season. The mulch may have to stay in place for two seasons. For serious infestations in fields, frequent mowing or close grazing is necessary to deplete the deepest growing roots.

Notes: Because established Johnsongrass clumps are very difficult to kill, remove small plants as soon as they're seen throughout the season.

Quackgrass, Couchgrass

Agropyron repens

Range: Throughout southern Canada and the United States except the southernmost states.

Description: Plants grow to 2 to 3 feet (61 to 91.4 cm) tall. Stems are smooth, with three to six joints. Leaves are narrow, with pointed tips; they're ribbed and rough to the touch on the upper surface, smooth on the undersides. A distinguishing characteristic of quackgrass is the pair of clawlike appendages clasping the stem at the base of each leaf. Flowers are 2- to 6-inch (5.1 to 152 cm)-long spikes, with two opposite rows of tiny flowers arising from sharp and tiny bracts. The seeds are tiny, yellow-brown, and grain-shaped. Roots are tough, fibrous rhizomes, with many scaly joints. Blooms from late May to September.

Life Cycle: Cool-season perennial, reproducing by seeds and rhizomes.

Prevention and Control: Pull or dig plants from gardens, following along the lengths of roots to remove as much as possible. Dry pulled roots in the sun before composting. Continue to hoe or pull plants as shoots reappear. To clear infested areas, mow closely, then apply a dense mulch (newspaper, cardboard, or plastic) to smother shoots; or seed a smother crop (such as successive crops of buckwheat, followed by winter wheat or rye). Mulch heavily for several feet around all garden areas to prevent quackgrass from invading from nearby areas. Quackgrass roots are easiest to remove from deep, friable garden soils, so lighten heavy soils by digging in compost and green-manure crops.

Notes: Quackgrass is adapted to many soil conditions but prefers full sun; it's commonly seen in gardens, lawns, pastures, and neglected areas.

Weed Problems for Vegetable Gardeners

Fern Marshall Bradley

The secrets to success with weed control are simple: Stop weeds early, keep the soil covered as much as possible, learn how to fight persistent weeds, and never let weeds set seeds.

Do weeds have a positive aspect? Weeds do increase the diversity of a garden, and some produce deep roots that mine the subsoil for nutrients. However, the benefits of weeds usually don't outweigh the negatives: They compete with crops for water and nutrients, they host pest insects and diseases, and they restrict air movement. Perhaps the best way to view these plants as a benefit is to consider them an ever-present reason to enjoy a half hour in your garden, doing a little light weeding.

Sidestepping Weed Problems

Almost all gardeners lose a crop sooner or later because they fail to weed during a critical stage, or they till a weedy bed that they shouldn't, or they let weeds go to seed. These are easy mistakes to make, especially when your garden is just one of the many activities that fill your life.

The good news is there are strategies that help busy gardeners cope with weed problems, so that you never face the depressing task of trying to uncover young vegetable plants hidden under a jungle of weeds. You'll combine the following tactics:

- Limiting the food supply for weeds
- Pregerminating and killing weeds before you plant a crop
- Cultivating quickly and shallowly when weeds are small
- Mulching and planting cover crops to suppress weeds

CONTROL THE FOOD SOURCE

Standard soil preparation instructions for organic gardeners often read something like this: Spread 2 inches of compost over the surface of the bed and work it into the top few inches of soil. This technique creates a beautiful soil environment for extensive root growth. However, if your soil contains a large bank of weed seeds, it's also an invitation to weeds to sprout en masse because you're turning the soil—which brings weed seeds near the surface—and putting food (compost) within easy reach.

If you know that your soil is heavily stocked with weed seeds, try an alternate approach. Don't spread compost far and wide. Instead, disturb the soil surface as little as possible. If you plan to sow seeds, sow in narrow rows rather than wide rows or by broadcasting. Open a fairly deep furrow (2 or 3 inches), and fill it with compost to the depth at which you want to sow the seeds. Put your seeds in the furrow, and cover them with compost to soil level. This concentrates the nourishment right where the seedling roots can reach it and keeps it away from the perennial weed population. If you're planting transplants, dig the planting hole extra deep and wide, and mix in compost as you plant and refill the hole. (If the plant ends up on a little hill, that's fine—just mold a low berm around it to retain water. This also helps prevent weed competition by keeping the bed surface dry—all the water soaks in right around your plants.)

With this approach, you'll need to side-dress every few weeks as the crops grow because the limited supply of compost won't last too long. Or, once the soil is warm enough, spread compost on the soil surface and top it with a weed-seed-free mulch such as chopped leaves.

WEED FIRST, SOW LATER

Once the weed seed bank is at a more reasonable level in your garden, you can return to the soil preparation method of spreading compost and working it in. Be smart, though, and outwit weeds with a trick called the stale seedbed method. After you've prepared the bed, water it well, then let it sit for 2 weeks. A hearty crop of weed seedlings will sprout. At that point, you can kill the weeds by hoeing gently just below the soil surface or by using a flame weeder. Your goal is to disturb the soil as little as possible. After the hoed or flamed weed seedlings are dead, remove them from the soil surface and plant your crop seeds. Since you've already defeated the main flush of weed competition, your crop will have a much better chance to establish itself.

CULTIVATE WHEN IT COUNTS

In spring, to encourage the soil to warm up and dry out, we deliberately leave the garden uncovered. What happens when soil is bare? Weed seeds germinate and rhizomes sprout, and many of them establish themselves more quickly than crop plants will. There's a critical window of competition between crops and weeds that starts about a week after a crop emerges and lasts about 1 month. During that month, if you don't handicap the weeds, chances are good that they'll outpace your crop, and the crop will never attain its full size and productivity.

Add compost to each planting site for transplants. A low berm around the transplant blocks water from running off, and that reduces weed seed germination.

Fast and Easy Cultivation

If you love to hand-weed, you'll enjoy early season weed control. Invest in a thick kneeling pad or a gardening stool to increase your and gently remove small weeds in crop rows and around seedlings. Be sure that the plants are dry before you weed (to avoid the risk of spreading disease spores), but to ease the job, weed when the soil is moist. If necessary, water the area the day before you weed.

If possible, weed in the morning on a sunny day, and leave the seedlings to wilt and die on the soil surface. Come back later or the following day and rake up the seedlings for your compost pile (seedlings left in the garden sometimes attract critters and diseases that feed on dying plant tissue, and then they may also spill over and attack your crop seedlings).

Take along an old screwdriver on your hand-weeding forays. It's handy for plunging into the soil to loosen up weeds with minimal disturbance to nearby crop seedlings.

Using a Weeding Tool. For weeding, try to find one long-handled hoe for clearing out weeds quickly, and also a short-handled tool for fine work closer to plant stems. Preferences vary when it comes to the design of a hoe blade, but it's worth it to buy a quality tool, whatever style you choose. And if back problems or arthritis in your hands bother you, investigate tool handle extensions that allow you to work without bending, and tools with padded handles that put less stress on your hands.

Continued ➡

When you use a hoe or hand weeder, keep the blade parallel to the soil surface. Mentally picture a line half an inch below the soil surface, and pull your hoe blade gently down the bed following that line. Your goal is to cut through weed stems or pull weed roots loose from the soil without flipping or tossing soil. That's because when you disturb the surface soil, you expose more weed seeds to light and stimulate them to germinate.

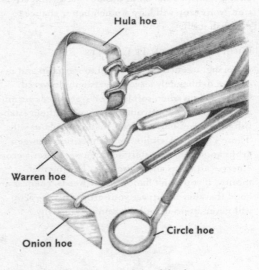

Hula hoe

Warren hoe

Onion hoe

Circle hoe

Try a variety of hoes to see which works best for you.

Flame Weeding. A flame weeder can be a useful part of your weed control efforts. You can use a flame weeder to kill weeds between rows or hills of seedlings, but it takes precise technique to avoid singeing crop seedlings. Safety is always the most important considerations when using a flame weeder. Your goal is to pass the flame very lightly over the bed—the flame needs to come in contact with a weed seedling for just one-tenth of a second to kill it. You shouldn't see the weed seedlings turn black as you work; if you do, you're applying too much heat. The flame could be heating the soil, too, which damages soil organisms and crop roots. If you've done the job right, the weeds will begin to droop and wither about 24 hours after being flamed, and a day after that they will be dead.

Observe these precautions when you use a flame weeder:

- Always station a 5-gallon bucket of water or a hose nearby (be sure the water supply is turned on—use a breaker at the nozzle so you can release the flow in an instant).
- Never use a flame weeder on a garden bed that is covered with mulch.

- Never use a flame weeder near any garden bed that is covered with dry mulch such as news-paper or wood chips.
- Never use a flame weeder near beds that contain dried-up plant residues.
- Never use a flame weeder on a windy day.

COVER THE SOIL

A good layer of mulch can very effectively prevent the return of weeds once you've prepared a garden bed (or after you've weeded). There are plenty of choices of mulch, from materials you have on hand—such as newspaper and grass clippings—to purchased plastic or organic mulches.

In some regions and circumstances, mulching the garden can lead to pest problems, providing hiding places for such undesirables as squash bugs and earwigs. And at the start of the season, leaving the soil uncovered to warm the soil is the most important consideration. But as soon as you can, put mulch in place. See the Mulch entry for details on mulch materials and how to manage mulch.

Another way to cover bare soil is to plant cover crops. These crops not only deny weeds the opportunity to grow but they also build soil structure, prevent erosion, and more. If you haven't been planting cover crops in your garden, start today.

Covering the soil with clear plastic to cause heat to build up and kill weed seeds is another way to fight weeds. This technique is called solarization and is discussed in detail on page 186.

KEEP AFTER SEED HEADS AND HOST PLANTS

Weed control is less critical at the height of the gardening season because most crops are large enough to withstand some weed competition. However, don't forget about weeds. Throughout the season, be on the watch for weeds that are going to seed and weeds that host serious vegetable crop diseases (particularly weeds in the cabbage and tomato families).

Weeds are prolific seed producers. A single pigweed plant can bear up to 250,000 seeds. Stopping deposits to the seed bank in the soil is one of the most effective ways to reduce future weed problems. Weeds also wreak havoc if they break out in a nasty disease that can spread to crop plants. For example, nightshade can suffer from late blight, a devastating fungal disease that can wipe out tomato and potato crops.

Summer is not always a fun time to weed, but at the least, tour your garden every few days with a garbage bag and sharp garden clippers in hand. Cut flowerheads of weeds directly into the garbage bag (don't risk composting them, in case some seeds are already maturing in the flowerheads). You can come back later in the season when it's cooler to dig out the foliage and roots. If you spot weeds that are disease hosts, cut them off at ground level and stick them in the bag, too. (Never work around disease hosts when the garden is wet because disease spores spread easily in wet conditions.)

Battling Bigger Weeds

When weed seedlings escape your notice, they grow up to become full-size weeds. In most, but not all, cases it's a good idea to pull out such weeds, roots and all. But getting rid of big weeds can be tricky, depending on the type of roots they have. If a particular type of weed is fairly widespread in your garden, first pull up one to see what the roots are like.

Taproots. For weeds with a long, sturdy central root, such as dandelion, insert a dandelion fork or a narrow trowel vertically into the soil alongside the weed. Pull gently on the top and jab with the tool. You should feel the release as the root breaks or is cut well below the soil surface, and the root will pull

freely from the soil. It's easiest to pull taprooted weeds a day or two after a soaking rain or watering.

Fibrous Roots. When the soil is moist, it can be fairly easy to pull out fibrous-rooted weeds simply by grasping the plant at the crown, where roots and topgrowth meet, and pulling upward. Use a hand fork to loosen the clump first if it resists—don't injure your hands or wrists by overpulling.

Bulbous Roots. Uproot these (wild onion, or onion grass, is an example) as you would fibrous-rooted weeds, but don't try to shake the soil free. The clump may include small bulblets that would fall free and then resprout in the bed. Carefully put the weeds, roots, and clinging soil into a hot compost pile to kill weed seeds. The heat will kill the bulbs, too. Otherwise, put these weeds into a discard pile or throw them out with household trash.

Rhizomes. If your problem weed has lots of long, somewhat fleshy roots that run horizontally at or below the soil surface, like those of many grasses, proceed with caution! These roots are specialized stems called rhizomes. Even a small piece of rhizome left behind in the soil when you pull the plant has the ability to resprout roots and leaves. Sometimes the best course of action with rhizomatous weeds is to repeatedly cut back the tops at ground level, leaving the roots undisturbed. It's a long process, but eventually you can starve out the roots and rhizomes by removing the weed tops.

Weed Emergencies

Sometimes weeds take over the garden much more quickly than you expect. Perhaps you had an extra busy week at work, or came down with a summer cold that kept you out of the garden entirely. If that particular week happens to be warm and wet, by the time you return to the garden, the weeds have taken over—everywhere. When a weed emergency like this happens, how do you get your garden back?

DECIDE WHAT TO SAVE

First, decide which crops are most worth saving. These may be crops such as melons or peppers that take the longest to produce. Or you may choose the vegetables you most like to eat. Weed out those beds (refer to the guidelines above to see which roots to uproot and which to cut off at ground level). Next, put down mulch without delay. An ideal choice is newspaper topped by straw or chopped leaves, to ensure that you smother any weeds that resprout from roots left in the soil.

SACRIFICE TO SAVE

Next, take stock of how much time and energy you have to deal with the rest of your garden. If you can't save the whole garden, don't try. Choose a bed or two for sacrifice to the garden gods. In these beds, you'll quickly cut everything to ground level—weeds and crops—and then cover the bed (as described below) while the plant material breaks down.

Before you bring in the lawn mower or string trimmer, though, check the beds for weeds that are going to seed. Use garden clippers to snip off all seed heads and discard them in plastic bags with your trash.

As you work, if you notice that a particular weed seems to dominate in a bed or throughout your garden, take time to identify it precisely. Refer to "Ten Weeds Worth Recognizing," below, for specific recommendations for bringing that weed under control, because you're bound to see it again in your garden in the future.

With weed seeds removed, cut all plants down to ground level. Cover the bed with black plastic, heavy cardboard, or an old wool (not synthetic) blanket, and weight down the edges. Later in the season,

Continued ➡

About Organic Weed Killers

Insecticidal soap sprays that kill soft-bodied insects can also damage plant tissue, and garden product manufacturers have come up with herbicidal "soap sprays" as well—formulations of fatty acids that are strong enough to kill tender plants. Other organic herbicides have a vinegar base.

These herbicides work well for controlling weeds in the cracks along walkways and at the edges of patios, but they're not a good choice for the food garden. And of course, never use chemical herbicides in the vegetable garden. To safeguard your crops, your soil, and your health, stick with hoeing, mulching, and hand-weeding.

when you have time, you can uncover the bed and turn under the plant debris. Then wait a couple of weeks and if there's time left in the season, you can plant a fall crop.

Ten Weeds Worth Recognizing

In many gardens, one or two species of weeds are predominant. It's worth it to identify these dominant weeds to the species level so that you can plan the most effective approach for bringing them under control.

BERMUDAGRASS (*Cynodon dactylon*)

Range: Southern two-thirds of the United States, occasionally a problem farther north

Description: Also called wiregrass and devilgrass, bermudagrass grows fast and is a particular problem in Southeastern gardens. This perennial grass has a network of creeping stems with thin, gray-green or bluish green leaves.

Control Strategy: Dig out bermudagrass early and late in the season when you can search out and pull up its extensive roots without damaging crop roots. Let the plants dry in strong sun and then compost them. Solarizing a bed infested with bermudagrass will weaken the root system. Follow up by planting a cover crop to overwinter, and that will further reduce, although not eliminate, the problem. Mulching around crops helps, but bermudagrass often finds a way to pop up through mulch and then spread across the mulch surface.

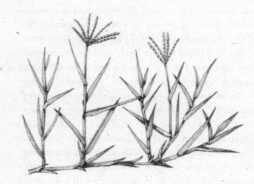

BINDWEEDS (*Convolvulus* spp.)

Range: United States and Canada

Description: The pretty trumpetlike flowers and heart-shaped dark green leaves of bindweed, or wild morning glory, might tempt you to allow it to ramble in your garden, but don't be fooled. With roots that plunge down 10 feet and spreading vines, bindweed can be a nightmare in the garden.

Control Strategy: Pulling bindweed seedlings is okay because the full root will come up when you pull it. However, once a plant has more than five leaves, the brittle roots will probably break as you pull them out, and pieces left behind will regrow. Mulching will help to weaken bindweed but won't control it fully. Solarizing and tilling aren't effective; flaming may weaken a stand over time.

If only one bed or area of your garden is infested with bindweed, you can eradicate the weed by covering the area tightly with black plastic for 2 years.

Another approach is to weaken the stand first, then mulch to suppress regrowth. Let the bindweed grow until it's about to flower, then use a string trimmer to cut it back to ground level. New shoots will sprout. Let these grow for 3 weeks, then cut them back to the ground. After that, dig in the bed and pull out as many roots as you can. Dispose of these roots in the trash or burn them.

Next, cover the bed with cardboard or several thicknesses of wet newspaper, overlapping pieces well. Top that with a few inches of chopped leaves or other dense organic mulch. Check it occasionally.

Bindweed shoots will find their way up through the mulch covering. Cut them off.

The following season, you can try cutting holes through this covering to set transplants in place. Renew the top mulch covering. Water the transplants directly at the base, and watch carefully for any bindweed shoots that try to grow out through these openings.

By the following season, the bindweed should have died out. This is more work-intensive than black plastic, but it's kinder to the soil.

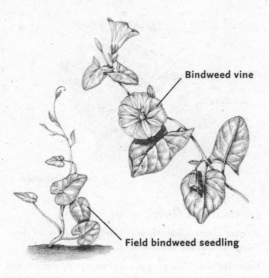

Bindweed vine

Field bindweed seedling

CANADA THISTLE (*Cirsium arvense*)

Range: Northern half of United States, Canada

Description: Sharp spines along the edges of the crinkled, silvery leaves make this tough perennial weed hard to handle. Upright stems up to 5 feet tall sport pink to purple flowers from midsummer through fall.

Control Strategy: Wear thick gloves to cut back plant tops. Use a shovel or other tool to loosen roots before trying to pull out thistles. Let the roots dry thoroughly in the sun before composting. Never till this weed. Cutting back plant tops repeatedly will weaken the stand enough to allow successful gardening (but stay on the lookout for occasional shoots). When an area is seriously infested, though, try the mulching technique described for bindweed. If you don't take steps to weaken a strong thistle population, it could take over your entire garden.

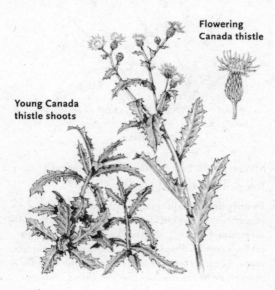

Flowering Canada thistle

Young Canada thistle shoots

CRABGRASS (*Digitaria* spp.)

Range: United States and southern Canada

Description: This spreading annual grass sends out many thick, round stems from the base. Two common weed species are large crabgrass and smooth crabgrass. Large crabgrass leaves have white hairs along the edges. Smooth crabgrass leaves are smaller, with a purplish hue.

Control Strategy: Pull crabgrass by hand, removing all roots as well as stems. Don't compost plants if seeds have started to form. After clearing an area, mulch it well to prevent regrowth.

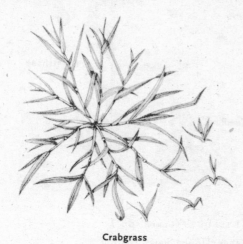

Crabgrass

LAMB'S-QUARTERS (*Chenopodium album*)

Range: United States, Canada

Description: Lamb's-quarters is a pretty, bushy weed with slightly toothed, medium green leaves. Later in the season the stems become woody, and dead stems last into winter.

Control Strategy: It's easy to kill lamb's-quarters seedlings by hoeing and hand weeding, but watch for each new wave of plants. Young plants are edible, so you can add young, tender leaves to salads. Mulch beds once the soil is warm to prevent to set seed, and be mindful that plants produce multiple seed stalks; it doesn't help to cut back only the top of the plant. Don't compost any plants that have gone to flower.

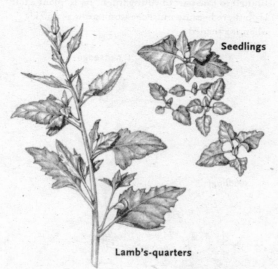

Seedlings

Lamb's-quarters

NIGHTSHADES (*Solanum* spp.)

Range: Various species across the United States and Canada

Description: Nightshade rarely takes over a garden, but it's an important annual weed to control because it can host diseases and pests of the tomato family, including Colorado potato beetles. Nightshade has broad, wavy-edged leaves with narrow tips. The leaves are purplish underneath. White star-shaped flowers (they look very similar to pepper flowers) appear from midsummer to late summer. Later, flowers turn into green berries that mature to black.

Control Strategy: Hoe and hand-pull seedlings and young plants to minimize the chance for the weeds to become hosts for insect pests and diseases. Never allow nightshade plants to reach the stage of producing seeds. Mulch areas infested with nightshade seeds to suppress germination.

Continued ➜

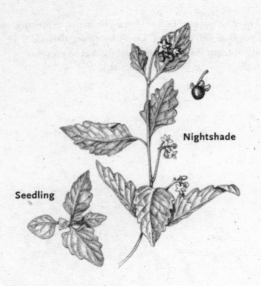

Seedling

Nightshade

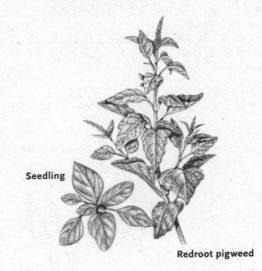

Seedling

Redroot pigweed

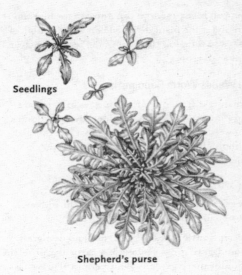

Seedlings

Shepherd's purse

smaller plants well in the sun before composting, or they may rejuvenate in the pile and keep growing. Dense cover crops do a good job of smothering pigweed. Solarizing the soil will kill pigweed seeds in top few inches of soil, which should give year's reprieve from battling this weed.

Nutsedges (*Cyperus* spp.)

Range: United States, Canada

Description: Sedges are grasslike plants with thick, yellowish green or dark green leaves that are V-shaped in cross section. The flowerheads are tufts of light-colored flower spikes at the top of the stems.

Control Strategy: The best strategy for controlling nutsedge is to pull out small plants, but only small plants, by hand. Once plants have more than six leaves, stop pulling them. Otherwise, as you pull the plants, you will knock loose tubers that have formed in the soil, and each tuber will produce a new plant. You can cut the plants back to soil level (they will resprout), and be sure to cut off tops if flowerstalks begin to appear.

Mulching and solarization won't provide thorough control (but they won't hurt). If nutsedge is limited to one part of your garden, try to plant a tall crop there because nutsedge won't grow as quickly when it's shaded.

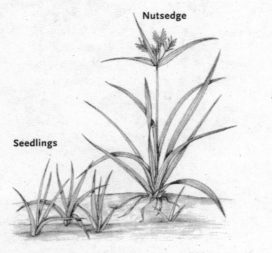

Nutsedge

Seedlings

Pigweeds (*Amaranthus* spp.)

Range: United States, southern Canada

Description: These annuals begin to appear in gardens in late winter and continue germinating through summer. Redroot pigweed is the most common type, with oval leaves on upright, rough stems. Prostrate pigweed grows as dense, ground-hugging mats. It has a fleshy root that is hard to pull—pieces left behind in the soil will resprout. The flowers are hard to spot; they form in small clusters in the leaf axils.

Control Strategy: If pigweed grows past the seedling stage, uproot the plant as soon as you spot any flowers because these plants are highly prolific seed producers. Large pigweed plants develop a deep taproot, and you'll need to sever the taproot with a tool before you can pull out the plant. Don't compost plants that are in flower or bear seeds. Dry

Quackgrass (*Elytrigia repens*)

Range: United States, except for some areas of the Deep South and Southwest; Canada

Description: This perennial grass has upright stems with long, narrow leaves. Leaves feel rough on the upper surface but smooth on the underside. Also called couch grass and wheat grass, quackgrass produces long rhizomes that sprout fibrous roots at the nodes.

Control Strategy: Pull out individual plants, uprooting as much of the rhizomes as you can find. Bits of root will resprout, so work carefully. Let roots and rhizomes dry well before putting them in a compost pile. Never till a garden bed that's infested with quackgrass.

Quackgrass

Shepherd's Purse (*Capsella bursa-pastoris*)

Range: United States; Canada

Description: Seedlings of shepherd's purse resemble those of radishes and turnips, which isn't surprising because this annual weed belongs to the cabbage family. Shepherd's purse won't outcompete crops, but it's a weed to know and remove because it hosts some of the diseases that can infect cabbage and related crops, as well as the beet leafhopper, which transmits curly top virus.

Control Strategy: Cultivate to uproot young plants; when they dry, add them to the compost pile. When the soil warms, mulch the soil to prevent more plants from germinating.

Roger Yepsen

While the automatic response of some homeowners is to wage an all-out herbicide attack, there are many less-drastic control measures—strategies that worked efficiently in the centuries before synthetics existed and that still do the job. And there are a few new wrinkles in weed control, as well.

Weeds aren't completely without redeeming values. Many of them produce food, including nectar and seeds, for wildlife (the monarch butterfly couldn't manage its well-known migration without weeds). You can get an idea of a weed's worth by taking the time to observe a forgotten patch of wild plants. It's likely to be a lively spot on every level—high and low, from afar and when viewed through a magnifying lens. Hawks hover overhead. Songbirds flit from one seedhead to another. Bees, butterflies, and many other insects flock to flowers no less attractive than those in carefully cultivated beds. Spiders spin their webs to harvest some of the bug life. Succulent plant growth is apt to be crawling with sap suckers of all sorts—not a sight to warm a gardener's heart, but these insects will help attract beneficial parasites and predators. There likely will be warm-blooded critters on the ground, as well.

The weeds you pull or mow can make an important contribution to the compost pile, so long as the temperature of your compost pile is high enough to inactivate seeds. And a healthy patch of weeds will even serve as a diagnostic tool, telling you something about the quality of your soil.

Compost Your Weeds

When you yank weeds or hoe them from the garden, the task will seem a little lighter if you see these unwanted plants as material for the compost pile. By only a slight stretch of the imagination, future crops will spring from the energy embodied in these unwanted visitors to the yard. You can even *encourage* certain weeds to grow for composting. Not every wild plant is a good candidate, but try permitting certain manageable annuals to leaf out—chickweed, lamb's-quarters, purslane, and ragweed are commonly seen choices. Just be sure to keep an eye on these weeds so that you harvest them for composting before they set seed. While a steaming-hot compost pile may inactivate weed seeds, it's best not to take a chance.

Pickle Your Weeds

Vinegar may preserve pickles, but it's devilishly tough on garden weeds. Studies by the USDA's Agricultural Research Service found that vinegar containing 15 to 20 percent acetic acid could knock out 95 to 100 percent of the weeds in its trail. But

Continued ➡

before you rush into your pantry for a bottle of apple or distilled vinegar, note that household vinegars typically run from just 5 to 8 percent. While this concentration may work well enough on younger weeds, you'll need to buy super-sour "horticultural vinegar" to get a near-complete kill. Check with local gardening centers. This natural herbicide is thought to work by breaking down cells in the leaves and desiccating the plant.

The vinegar is applied to foliage with an ordinary spray bottle. But do so with care. Horticultural vinegar can irritate the skin and eyes. It also is indiscriminate in what it kills, so make sure that the spray doesn't drift over to garden plants.

Annual Weed Bake-Off

You've felt the intensity of the midsummer sun on your back when gardening. Well, you can harness that energy to combat weeds, bacteria, fungi, and nematodes. All you need is a sheet of clear 1-mil plastic—and a good, long stretch of sunny weather. Also, keep in mind that while a bed is in the process of being *solarized* under that sheet, it will be out of commission for the 4 to 6 weeks that it takes the soil to cook. That may leave you enough time to plant early- and late-season crops.

1. Preceding the hottest 4 to 6 weeks of the growing season, groom the bed to be solarized, removing all garden waste and weeds.

2. Water the bed, soaking the soil well so that the sun's heat will penetrate deeper. (If the soil dries out in the weeks that follow, peel back the plastic in the early morning or evening, soak it again, then re-cover.)

3. Place the clear plastic over the bed. Use clear wrapping tape as necessary to seal any seams. Seal the perimeter of the area with a berm of soil.

4. You may need to leave the plastic on for the full 6 weeks, depending on your climate and also on how sunny the weather has been. Also, if this period has been unusually cloudy, temperatures under the plastic may be insufficient to do the job.

BRUSH HOGGING

There's an aggressive sound to the term "brush hogging," and this is a high-powered task as landscaping chores go. It involves taking on a patch of ground that has gone beyond the weedy stage and is host to shrubs and young trees. In many parts of the country, this is the natural fate of any area that's left to its own devices. Don't attempt to tame the woody stuff with your lawn mower. Instead, buy or rent a brush hog—either a dedicated walk-behind machine, or a self-powered unit that is towed behind a good-size lawn tractor. Some hogs can handle sapling trunks up to 2 inches in diameter.

Eat Your Weeds

A number of all-too-familiar garden weeds can be eaten fresh, steamed, or sautéed. That continues to be a tradition along the Mediterranean, with families going out to forage each spring. In the United States, we seem to have lost the knack, even though there's no shortage of wild edibles. You may find yourself fond enough of certain weeds that you dedicate a part of the garden to them, allowing your favorites to go to seed for the next year's crop. Try sautéing wild greens with garlic in olive oil. Add them to bean-and-pasta soup. Tuck them into calzones or layer them in lasagna.

- Purslane (*Portulaca oleracea*). A bright-colored variety, 'Goldberg,' is marketed for its hue and its more generous size, but the wild version is also fine, holding up well with cooking.

- Dandelion (*Taraxacum officinale*). This is perhaps the best-known wild green, and some people go off into the countryside in spring to harvest them. Get them young, before they become bitter. A traditional recipe from the Campagna region of southern Italy combines wild dandelion greens, sausage, and cannellini beans.

- Lamb's-quarters (*Chenopodium album*), The somewhat spinachlike young shoots can be used in salads and soups.

- Pigweed (*Amaranthus hybridus*), A relative of the amaranth you see in seed catalogs, this wild cousin offers leaves that are good steamed.

- Garlic mustard (*Alliaria petiolata*). This spring visitor catches your eye with its white flowers and your nose with its garlicky scent. Garlic mustard is an invasive nonnative species, but you can keep it in check by processing the leaves and taproots in a blender to make pesto, a novel idea suggested by Steve Brill in **The Wild Vegetarian Cookbook** (Harvard Common Press, 2002). Or simply toss a few leaves in a salad to give your greens an edge.

- Shepherd's purse (*Capsella bursa-pastoris*). The young leaves of this common weed are mild enough to use in salads. Collect the heart-shaped seeds for use as a peppery addition to soups.

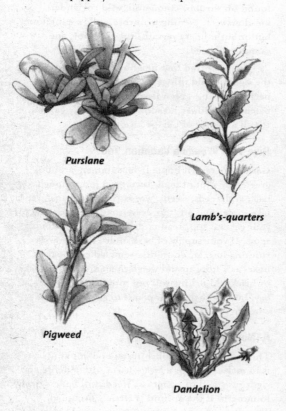

Purslane

Lamb's-quarters

Pigweed

Dandelion

KNOW WHAT YOU'RE PICKING

Before taking advantage of this no-plant, no-till, no-mulch harvest, take a few precautions. First, be familiar with what you're about to put on your plate. Educate yourself with a field guide or accompany a knowledgeable forager. Second, avoid plants that may have been sprayed with an herbicide, particularly along roadsides. Third, be cautious about having children seeing you forage, or they may do the same on their own—and some weeds, wild berries, and fungi are poisonous.

Weed Barriers for Walkways

There is no one perfect way to banish weeds from garden paths, except perhaps for laying down blacktop, and even paving can give way to certain aggressive growers. Most of us would prefer something soft and yielding underfoot, at any rate. A layer of mulch looks good, breaks down into a valuable soil amendment over time, and allows water to quickly perc through. But it won't be impervious to

A Bouquet of Weeds

What could be easier than amassing a bouquet of roadside weeds? Focus less on brilliant blossoms than on texture and movement, and you'll find yourself appreciating all sorts of grasses, stems, and seedpods that once escaped your notice. Just make sure you check with landowners before harvesting what you *assume* to be up for grabs—you might not be the only one to treasure that patch of goldenrod or milkweed.

weeds, requiring a second out-of-sight layer to squelch them. Here are a few choices.

- Newspaper is free, if a bit lumpy. And unless you keep it well covered, it can be unsightly and—worse still—become airborne in a strong wind.

- A roll of plastic or landscape fabric goes down quickly, but it may not hold up more than one season and is not biodegradable.

- A roll of brown kraft paper, available at office and art supply stores, also goes down in a jiffy, and it will biodegrade.

- Corrugated cardboard, recycled from large boxes, is stouter stuff than paper, and it also biodegrades.

- Roofing paper, with its coating of tar, is rugged stuff, and you can roll out more than one thickness for lasting effect.

If you've been unhappy with past efforts to tame garden paths, you might convert those vulnerable strips of soil to lawn. That's not a magical solution. First, you've got to establish a healthy patch of turf if the grass is to stand up to frequent foot traffic. That requires watering as needed and cutting regularly with a mulching mower. And you'll need to keep the grass from turning the beds into lawn. For that, install strips of plastic edging that extend deeply enough that grass won't migrate. This edging can have the additional benefit of helping to shore up the sides of raised beds.

A Rock-Solid Fix for Weedy Fences

The most stubborn weeds of all must be those that grow along a garden fence, where they are all but immune to mowing, shoveling, and hoeing. Weeds are particularly infuriating if they weave their way up through a fence clad with chicken wire. An attractive, permanent cure is to lay a row of rectangular flagstones under the fence, using smaller pieces as necessary to bring this stone layer flush up against fence posts. You even can use a circular saw with a masonry blade to cut notches in stones for a good fit around the posts. If the fence abuts the lawn, the flagstone row will serve as a mow strip, making a crisp edge between garden and yard.

Continued ➡

Holding a Torch for Weeds

A surefire way to kill weeds is with a flamer, a type of propane torch with an extended wand. The goal isn't to burn the unwanted plants, but to heat them to the point that their cell walls are destroyed, leading to a gradual death. Flamers of various sizes are sold by mail-order garden supply firms. The smallest are handheld, of the sort used for removing paint. To take out weeds on a large scale, you can buy a backpack flamer with a 3-gallon propane cylinder. At a weight of more than 30 pounds and a price over $200, this amounts to all-out weed warfare.

Flaming is particularly useful in killing stubborn weeds along brick paths and in clearing newly turned beds in which weed seedlings are just beginning to show their heads. To deflect heat from garden plants, hold the blade of a shovel alongside the flame. Keep the garden hose handy if there is combustible brush nearby.

Not all weeds are equally susceptible to flaming. Purslane resists it. So do grasses, because much of their activity is belowground and out of reach of the flames. Perennials that grow up from a fleshy root system may require repeated treatments.

A Savage Little Hoe

The hoe is such a simple tool that you might not be all that curious about various models. But a swan's-neck hoe really is something improved in the gardener's arsenal. That graceful crook in its neck positions the blade so that you can make weed-killing slices without killing your back. You can stand erect, rather than stoop. The blade's sharp edges are particularly suited to poking out stubborn weeds and getting into cracks between bricks and flagstones.

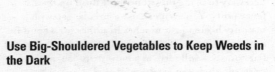

Use Big-Shouldered Vegetables to Keep Weeds in the Dark

You've probably noticed that there isn't a lot of weed activity beneath the jumbo leaves of squash, for example. Whenever possible, try to use vegetable foliage to block out weeds, both by choosing big-leaved crops and by planting on a tighter spacing. Fast-growing vegetables also can help by getting a jump on weeds. And you yourself can help the vegetables compete, by seeing to it that you've given them adequate water and nutrients. Here's a list of weed suppressors.

Beans	Squash, pumpkins, and melons
Cucumbers	Sweet corn
Kale	Sweet potatoes
Lettuce	Swiss chard
Potatoes	Tomatoes

The Importance of Being Shallow

A weed seed buried beneath a foot or so of dirt isn't able to cause you much grief. And the soil in your garden is likely teeming with these potential specks of trouble. That—and not laziness—is the reason stated by some gardeners for preferring to cultivate shallowly. You might experiment with letting sleeping weed seeds lie by doing the same. Over the next few growing seasons, the seeds in the top few inches of soil will sprout. Assuming you take care of them before they can set and broadcast seed of their own, you're then home free—or at least weed free, relatively speaking.

Worthwhile Weeds

If your local government allows it, you might allow a patch of weeds to flourish somewhere in your yard. One nice thing about a weed patch is that it's zero maintenance—the weeds are growing there because they're happy, so there's no need for you to get involved. Second, these plants likely will provide meals and lodging to a number of beneficial insect species. Helpful predators and parasites are apt to be found in wild carrot, wild daisies, dandelions, stinging nettle, goldenrod, common sorrel, and tansy, among others. In a Michigan State University study, five or more beneficial insect species were found on shrubby cinquefoil, wild coriander, meadowsweet, evening primrose, yellow coneflower, buttonbush, hoary vervain, culver's root, and swamp milkweed.

You may find that neighbors feel threatened by the sight of wild things growing so close to their perfect putting-green lawns. If so, try calling the patch a wildflower meadow or a butterfly garden. It's all a matter of perspective.

Give Your Weeds a Vacation, Too

Gardeners return home from summer vacations greeted by a lot of mail, lawn grass long enough to bale, and weeds, weeds, weeds. To ensure that weeds take some time off, too, leave time while packing for your getaway to spread mulch in the yard's trouble spots. If your supply of bark mulch and straw is running low, lay down disassembled cardboard boxes as a stopgap and weigh them down with rocks or bricks. Mulching will not only keep the weeds at bay, but also help allow plants to get by with less watering.

A (Nearly) Weed-Free Lawn

The first step in establishing a good-looking lawn is to make sure it is a *healthy* lawn, with a dense and vigorous stand of turfgrass. Weeds will be less likely to move in if the ground is already occupied. There are a number of things you can do to keep the grass growing thick and green.

- Remove no more than one-third of the blade length when you mow, to avoid slowing plant growth.
- Keep weeds from spreading by mowing before they can set seed.
- Water deeply, rather than sprinkling often and only superficially.
- Allow mulched clippings to stay in place and fertilize the lawn.
- If necessary, periodically remove thatch either with a rake or a rented dethatcher.
- Make sure you are growing an appropriate mix of turf grass species for your region, as well as for the light conditions of your own yard. For information, check with your county agricultural extension agent or your state's agriculture department Web site.

Flaming a Stale Bed

Creating a "stale bed" sounds like a bad idea, but it's a technique used by large-scale growers to make their soil relatively free of weeds. You begin by tilling the soil as you would normally but then allow the beds to sit idle during the predictable flush of new weeds. Some growers will even water the beds to encourage weeds to appear now, rather than later in the season when they will be intermingled with crops. The weeds are flamed before they go beyond the seedling stage, and the way is then clear for sowing seed or putting out transplants. You even can flame weeds that appear after sowing seed, as long as your seedlings haven't pushed aboveground.

Reading Your Weeds

You don't necessarily need a soil test or rain gauge to diagnose the problems underlying a lousy lawn. The weeds may tell the story.

- Quackgrass does well on thin, poorly watered lawns.
- Ground ivy is apt to trouble lawns that get too little sunlight and have poor drainage.
- Knotweed shows up in lawns with compacted soil.
- Crabgrass suggests you've been mowing too short or watering too often.
- Clover is a sign that the lawn has insufficient fertility.
- If you spot chicory's sky blue blossoms, that's a sign that the soil is high in clay and also relatively fertile.
- Buttercups signal wet hardpan soils.
- Acid clay soils are apt to host a good crop of dandelions.
- Horsenettle flourishes in sandy soils high in nitrogen.
- Fumitory favors soil high in potassium.
- Eastern bracken tells you the soil likely is low in potassium and high in phosphorus.
- Wild mustard moves in to acidic hardpan soils.
- All (or a few) of the above? Then your lawn likely has a number of shortcomings that are preventing the grass from looking its best.

The Weed-Zapping Two-Step

Most of the troublesome weeds in the garden have sprouted from seeds in the top 2 to 3 inches of soil. If you cultivate the beds, then take a break for at least a couple of weeks to allow these weeds to come to life, you can nip them in the bud with a second tilling. That will mean a relatively clean slate for your seedlings or transplants. The technique works best if the soil is warm enough for the weed seeds to sprout readily, so try it when preparing the garden for fall crops. And make that delayed tilling relatively shallow, to avoid stirring up more trouble.

Continued →

448

Weeds, Pests & Diseases
Chapter 10

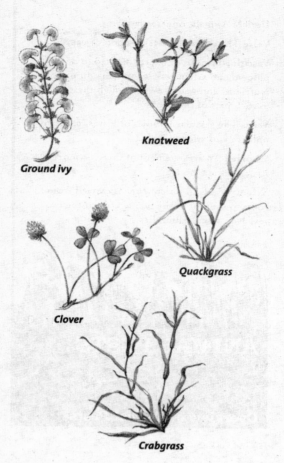

Knotweed

Ground ivy

Quackgrass

Clover

Crabgrass

LET SLEEPING SEEDS LIE

It seems that really working the soil to a good depth would have to be a good thing. But it ain't necessarily so. Some aggressive weeds just love having their belowground parts chopped up. Take quackgrass, for an infamous example. This weed is trouble, as suggested by its other names: devil's grass, witch grass, and dog grass. The underground rhizomes are mighty enough to grow right through asphalt, and just a single plant can send out 300 feet of them in a year. You only make matters worse by going over quackgrass with a rototiller, because this creates thousands of pieces that each can grow into a new plant. So disturb only the very top layer of soil. Take a sharp hoe to shoots that appear, and eventually the rhizomes will be starved.

Be Wary of These Wild Ones

Some weeds and wild plants can be worse than an annoyance if they are poisonous or are armed with itch-producing chemicals.

Even if you are sympathetic to weeds, there are several common species that shouldn't be welcomed to the yard because of their potential hazards to health. That's especially true if you have inquisitive children who like to roam the grounds. Here are several of most notorious weeds you're apt to encounter.

Poison ivy (*Toxicodendron radicans*). No surprise here. This vine supposedly was once imported to England as an ornamental—it does have glossy foliage and red berries, after all—but that sounds like horticultural folklore. If you can't eradicate the plant, teach your kids how to identify the leaves. Be cautious about embracing a pet that has been cruising an area rich in PI.

Deadly nightshade (*Solanum dulcamara*). This perennial woody vine attracts attention with small star-shaped purple flowers and berries that turn lipstick red when ripe. Its toxin is at its most concentrated in the unripe berries, and small children are particularly vulnerable because of their lower body weight.

Butterfly Weeds

Weeds attract not only helpful insects, but also beautiful ones. The caterpillars that will turn into butterflies like to feed on clovers, milkweed, nettle, Queen Anne's lace, common sorrel-and butterfly weed itself (*Asclepias*). So allow a weed-prone edge of the lawn to go wild, and see what develops.

Poison hemlock (*Conium maculatum*). Attractive enough to be mistaken for a garden plant, poison hemlock resembles anise or wild parsley. The entire plant is poisonous to humans: the leaves, the stems (children may become ill if they use them as straws), the roots, and especially the seeds.

Pokeweed (*Phytolacca americana*). This weed is a standout, sending up thick stems to a height of 5 feet or more. The inky berries ripen to a rich purple, and if digested they can bring on headache, abdominal pain, and severe diarrhea.

American bittersweet (*Celastrus scandens*). This woody vine finds its way into wreaths and dried flower arrangements, where it shows off its yellow-orange berries. The berries can cause stomach upset and diarrhea if ingested.

Holly (*Ilex* spp.). It's rarely thought of as an unwanted plant, but holly is worth mentioning for its attractive, yet poisonous berries. Eating them can lead to nausea, vomiting, and diarrhea.

Weeds Glossary

Acheme A dry, one-seeded fruit that does not open readily. The seed is distinct from the fruit. Common among members of the composite family.

Acute Sharply pointed.

Alternate An arrangement of leaves, branches, or flowers in which each is placed singly at different heights along the stem.

Annuals Plants that live from seed to maturity, reproduction, and death in only one growing season.

Anther The part of the stamen that bears pollen.

Apex The uppermost point; tip.

Awn A bristlelike appendage. Found most commonly on grass flowers.

Axil Upper angle where a leaf or branch joins the stem.

Axillary Situated in an axil.

Barb A rigid bristle or point, usually reflexed.

Beak A long, prominent point.

Berry A fleshy fruit containing two or more seeds, such as a tomato and a grape.

Biennial Living two growing seasons, usually flowering during the second.

Bipinnate Twice-pinnately compound.

Blade The flat, expanded part of the leaf.

Bract A small, rudimentary or underdeveloped leaf. Often found in flower clusters.

Bristle A stiff, hairlike growth.

Bulb An underground bud with fleshy scales or bracts.

Bulblet A small bulb borne on the inflorescence or stem.

Calyx All the sepals of a flower cluster considered collectively; the outer perianth whorl.

Capsule The dry, dehiscent fruit of two or more carpels.

Carpel One of the ovarian portions of a compound pistil.

Chlorophyll The green pigment necessary for photosynthesis, developed in the chloroplasts of plant cells.

Clasping Applied to leaves that partly or completely surround a stem, as seen in grasses.

Compound leaf Leaf in which the blade is divided into two or more sections, or leaflets.

Cordate Heart-shaped, with the point away from the base.

Corolla The inner set of floral leaves, or petals. Sometimes fused, as in morning glories.

Corymb A raceme with the lower flowerstalks longer than those at the tip, so that the head gives a flattened appearance. Outer flowers open first.

Culm The stem of a grass. Usually hollow except at the nodes.

Decumbent Lying flat, with the tip pointing upward.

Decurrent Extending along the sides of another, as in leaves where the blades extend as wings along the petiole or stem.

Dehiscent Opening by valves or slits, as in a seed capsule. Poppy capsules are dehiscent.

Dentate Toothed, with outward-pointing teeth.

Dioecious A plant bearing only one sex on a plant; male and female flowers are on separate plants.

Disk flower The tubular flowers in the center of the head of many composites. The yellow center of the daisy is composed of disk flowers.

Divided Separated to the base.

Drupe A single-seeded fruit with a fleshy outer part. Stone fruits such as peaches and cherries are drupes.

Elliptic Oval in shape.

Entire Describes a smooth leaf margin. Not toothed, lobed, or serrated.

Fibrous Fine adventitious roots, usually in a mass.

Floret An individual flower of a cluster, head, or spike.

Fruit The ripened ovary or ovaries with attached parts.

Grain Fruit of grasses particularly; seed coat and ovary walls fused into one body.

Habit The general growth pattern of a plant or its mode of growth, such as shrubby, trailing, or erect.

Poisonous to Pets

Dogs and cats occasionally munch on weeds, for whatever reason. And if they chew on certain toxic species, they can become very ill—without the ability to tell you what they've tangled with. Generally, if a plant is classified as poisonous for humans, it will have the same effect on pets. And some plants that don't trouble us are noxious to them. Dogs are adversely affected by onion, garlic, heavenly bamboo, schefflera, and dracaena. Cats can't handle calla lily, philodendron, pothos, and scindapsus.

Continued ➤

Habitat The environmental conditions of a specific place in which a plant grows.

Head A short, compact flower cluster of sessile or nearly sessile florets.

Herbaceous Not woody

Imperfect Describing flower lacking either stamens or carpels. It is "imperfect" because it has only one sex.

Indehiscent Applied to a seedpod or capsule that does not readily open at maturity.

Internode The part of a stem between two nodes.

Involucre A whorl of small leaves or bracts just under a flower or flower cluster. Generally protects reproductive structures.

Lanceolate Lance-shaped, several times longer than wide, and tapering to a pointed apex.

Leaflet One part of a compound leaf.

Legume A member of the family Leguminosae. Characterized by a fruit that splits readily along two sides at maturity, such as a pea pod.

Lobed Divided to about mid-point.

Mericarp One of the two carpels of a fruit of the parsley family.

Midrib The central rib or vein of a leaf or other organ.

Monoecious Having both male and female flowers on the same plant, such as many kinds of squashes.

Netted Applied to veins, meaning they form a network pattern.

Node The part of a stem where leaves or branches emerge.

Nut A hard, indehiscent, one-seeded fruit.

Obovate Ovate, but with the narrower end at the bottom.

Opposite Two leaves or buds at a node.

Ovary The part of the pistil bearing the ovules.

Ovate Egg-shaped, with the broader end at the bottom.

Ovule An undeveloped or immature seed.

Palmate Radiating from a central point like a fan or the fingers on a hand.

Palmately compound Leaflets radiating from a central point.

Panicle An inflorescence. A branched raceme with each branch bearing a cluster of flowers. Overall, a panicle is shaped like a pyramid.

Pappus A ring of fine hairs developed from the calyx. A pappus often acts as a dispersal mechanism, as in dandelion seeds.

Peduncle Stem of a solitary flower or flower cluster.

Perennial Growing three or more seasons.

Perfect Applied to flowers having both stamens and carpels.

Perianth The floral envelope, the calyx and corolla together. Most often used to describe flowers without clear divisions between calyx and corolla, such as lilies.

Petal One of the leaves of the corolla, usually colorful.

Petiole The stalk of a leaf.

Phloem The vessels in the plant that carry dissolved sugars from leaves to the rest of the plant. One of the two vessels in the vascular bundle.

Pinnate Similar in appearance to a feather, having leaflets along each side of a common axis.

Pinnately compound Leaflets arranged on each side of a common axis.

Pinnatifid Leaflets cleft to the middle or beyond.

Pistil The seed-bearing organ with a style (a tube bearing the stigma at its apex), stigma (the part of the pistil that receives the pollen grains), and ovule.

Pistillate Having pistils and no stamens. Female.

Pod Usually describes a dry, dehiscent fruit.

Pollen The spores or grains borne by the anther, which contains the male element.

Prickle A stiff, pointed outgrowth from the epidermis or bark.

Procumbent Trailing on the ground without rooting.

Prostrate Lying flat on the ground. Some prostrate stems can root.

Pubescent Covered with short, soft hairs.

Raceme An inflorescence composed of pedicled florets growing from a common axis. Flowers open from the base upward.

Ray flower A flower growing on the margin of the disk flowers, strap-shaped. The white petals of the daisy are ray flowers.

Rhizome Underground or barely superficial reproductive stem.

Rhombic Shaped like an equilateral parallelogram, usually having oblique angles.

Rib A primary vein in a leaf or flower.

Rootstock Roots that can develop adventitious buds. Often used to mean underground reproductive stems as well.

Rosette A cluster of leaves, usually basal and shaped like a rose, or radiating from a center.

Runner A slender, trailing stem that takes root at the nodes.

Sepal One of the divisions of a calyx.

Serrate Having sharp teeth that point forward.

Sessile Without a petiole or stalk.

Sheath A long structure surrounding an organ or part.

Simple leaves Leaves in which the blade is in one piece, not divided.

Spike A flower spike with sessile or nearly sessile flowers.

Stamen The pollen-bearing, or male organ, of a flower.

Staminate Having stamens and no pistils. Male.

Stipule A basal appendage of a petiole.

Stolon A stem that bends to the ground and takes root at the tip or nodes.

Succulent Fleshy tissues storing much water.

Taproot A central, tapering, main root with smaller lateral roots. A carrot is a taproot.

Tendril A slender organ, leaf, or stem with which a plant clings to a support.

Terminal At the end of a stem or branch.

Thorn A stiff, sharply pointed, and somewhat degenerate branch.

Toothed Dentate. Having pointed edges along the margins.

Trifoliate A compound leaf with three leaflets, such as poison ivy.

Tuber A modified underground stem that usually stores food. Reproductive. A potato is a tuber.

Umbel A flower cluster that is shaped like an umbrella, such as dill flower heads.

Utricle A small, one-seeded fruit.

Valve The separate parts of a pod or capsule.

Vascular bundle The term applied to describe phloem and xylem vessels, or veins, in plants. Nutrients and water travel through these vessels to each part of the plant.

Veins The vascular bundles of leaves, containing phloem and xylem vessels.

Whorled An arrangement of three or more structures at a node.

Xylem Vessels in which water is carried from roots to the rest of the plant. One of the two vessels in vascular bundles

ANIMAL PESTS

Overview of Animal Pests

Jeff and Liz Ball

The depredations of animal pests like moles, gophers, and deer can be so discouraging that they might make you consider giving up on your property altogether. Unfortunately, there are no quick, surefire solutions to any serious animal-pest invasion. You have three basic choices in almost all cases: You can trap the pest to kill or remove it; you can set up a barrier of some kind that will effectively deny the pest access to your yard or garden; or you can put repellents on or around your plants to keep pests away from them. This section will focus first on the most effective control measures available for your use, and then it will address various preventive measures. The section ends with a pest-by-pest description of the most effective management methods.

Controlling Animals

Effective animal pest control depends on three prime factors: timing, persistence, and diversity.

TIMING

In managing animal pests, good timing is crucial. Install barriers before you expect an animal to make its appearance, and start control measures at the very first indication of damage. Unlike most insects, animals can wipe out an entire planting or even the whole garden in a very short time if the problem is left unattended.

PERSISTENCE

Some animals, such as squirrels and deer, are ingenious in foiling your attempts to thwart them. A single try at establishing a barrier may not do the job. You will have to keep trying until you come up with a control or combination of controls tht finally outsmarts the wily marauders.

DIVERSITY

No single control method or preventive step is always satisfactory, even if it worked last year. Typically, a variety of strategies and devices are required, often used in combination. Placement of traps and barriers must be shifted frequently to ensure success against persistent pests.

Continued ➡

In many cases, the only realistic option you have in controlling a pest after it has discovered your yard is trapping. Biological controls have limited effectiveness, and poisons pose hazards to the environment, pets, and children. In this section, we present control steps ranging from those with the least impact to those with greater impact on the environment.

Traps

Most people are unhappy about having to kill any living creature, so they prefer to use what are called "live traps," which catch the animal without harming it. Once caught, the culprit is brought out to the countryside and released.

Live-trapping animal pests isn't the best control, simply because the animal might not survive in its new environment. Any given area already has an established population of wildlife, and adding a new member puts a little more demand on the available food, water, and habitats. Using barriers to prevent pests from getting to your plants in the first place is perhaps the best solution, but if it doesn't work effectively in your backyard, you may have to resort to trapping if you want to protect your landscape.

Box traps are the safest design for live-trapping garden pests. The leg-hold design and the snare design are nonspecific, and will trap and kill pets as well as pests. Also, these traps can maim an animal instead of killing it. Box traps are available for many of the most troublesome animal pests, including chipmunks, gophers, groundhogs, mice, moles, rabbits, and squirrels. (See the box, "The Best Traps for the Worst Pests," for recommended sizes.)

Of course, you can also set traps and snares that will kill animal pests, such as the mousetrap. When dealing with the prolific rodents such as gophers, mice, and moles, this is often the best method of control.

Using Traps

Set the trap in some sheltered area near or around where you have spotted a pest in action. Do not set the trap out in the open. Conceal it with leaves, sticks, and/or grass clippings so that it looks a bit more natural. To avoid raising the suspicion of the animals you want to catch, try not to leave your own scent on the trap any more than you have to. You can boil traps with pine cones, dried leaves, or other natural materials to mask your scent. Handle the traps and the bait with gloves—preferably rubber gloves just out of the package. Follow the directions that come with the trap to set it up correctly with bait in place. After that, check the trap every day to renew the bait and see if you have trapped the culprit. Once you have trapped the animal, consult your local County Extension agent for advice on where to take it.

Biological Controls

Compared with the wide range of predators and parasites available for insects, there aren't many biological controls available for animal pests. While badgers eat gophers and mountain lions eat deer, people do not generally have these natural predators in their backyard. However, a couple of biological controls may already be waiting in your yard.

Many homeowners have found that animals pests tend to be less troublesome when there are dogs or cats outside much of the time. Most rabbits, for example, do not feel very comfortable eating while a dog or cat is on the prowl. Male dogs and cats will mark their territories with scent, and these boundary marks can sometimes keep rabbits from venturing onto your lawn. If you let your pets

play or stay in the yard, make sure their rabies shots are up to date.

Poisons

There are no poisons that are not in one way or another potentially dangerous to pets and children. Do not use poisons to control animal pests in the landscape.

Preventing Pest Problems

Over the years, desperate homeowners and gardeners have resorted to a number of ingenious tactics in the battle against animal pests. Here are some of the most successful preventive measures, from fences to bars of soap.

Barriers

If you know from past experience that one of more animal pests are likely to attack your backyard, then the best approach to controlling them is to deny them access in the first place. There are a number of techniques for preventing access, some more effective than others. If you want to use a barrier, that usually means building some kind of fence.

Fences

Here you have a choice: You can put up a temporary fence that is designed to be movable and easily erected, or you can take the time and go to the expense of building a permanent fence to solve the pest problem once and for all. There are any number of fence designs in both categories designed to keep animals out of a garden bed or stand of shrubs, and there are just as many stories about how some of those animals, especially raccoons and deer, overcame the barrier and still entered the garden sanctuary.

Fencing off a small, garden-sized section of your property is relatively easy; or you can fence around the entire yard. Remember that various animals can jump, dig, and squeeze through small places. The size of the fence depends on which pest or pests you are trying to thwart: Make sure your fence is high enough to be effective. To keep deer out, it must be at least 7 to 8 feet high. A 3-foot fence will keep out gophers, groundhogs, and rabbits. Even if burrowing pests are not currently a problem, if you are going to the trouble of erecting a permanent fence, it is a good idea to bury at least 6 inches of it in the ground to forestall any future subterranean invasions. Finally, be sure your fence is a solid barrier—spacings between boards or other materials should be less than 2 inches. The actual design of your fence and the materials you use will ultimately depend on how much time and money you wish to spend.

Repellents

For many years, gardeners have been trying to find substances that will repel animals from their yards and gardens. There are now on the market a number of products that promise to successfully ward off various animal pests, including birds, rabbits, raccoons, and deer. In addition, there are dozens of home remedies invented by frustrated gardeners under siege from some troublesome animal. These products work better for some gardeners than others, and no one product seems to be foolproof all of the time in all areas of the country. If you prefer not to rig a barrier, then you may wish to experiment with one or more of these repellent products; however, you must not be too confident about their effectiveness in your particular landscape.

The Best Traps for the Worst Pests

Chipmunks
5" x 5" x 15" box trap. Bait with peanuts or other nut meats.

Gophers
Standard wooden-based rat traps, a two-pronged pincher trap (called the Macabee trap), or a squeeze-type box trap. Bait with a large amount of grain, sunflower seeds, peanuts, or other nut meats.

Groundhogs
12" x 12" x 36" box trap. Bait with nut meats or pieces of fruit.

Mice
5" x 5" x 15" box trap, standard wooden-based mouse traps, or glue boards especially designed for mice. Bait with nut meats, dried fruit, or bacon.

Moles
Choker or harpoon-type trap. No bait needed.

Rabbits
10" x 12" x 30" box trap. Bait with fresh greens, carrots, or fresh clover.

Squirrels
8" x 8" x 24" box trap. Bait with peanuts, sunflower seeds, walnuts, almonds, oats, or melon rind.

Repellents come in two general forms—those that repel by odor and those that repel by some visual, tactile, or audible characteristic.

Using Scent to Repel Pests

Various animal repellents are sold commercially in many garden centers and through mail-order catalogs. Big-Game Deer Repellent, Hinder, and Ro-Pel are a few examples. The success of the scent repellents is quite spotty. Some homeowners swear by them; others find they don't work at all. Dozens of home remedies have been reported in garden magazines, and several scent repellents seem to be particularly popular.

Cat Litter. Many gardeners find that used cat litter repels rabbits when it's sprinkled on the lawn and around ornamentals, and repels moles and gophers when it's buried. The advice is to sprinkle well-used litter around vulnerable plants, replacing it each week and after each rain. For moles and gophers, dump the litter right into the holes of the active burrows. But use caution when handling and distributing litter: Cat feces may contain toxoplasmosis parasites, which can infect humans. Do not use litter around edible plants.

Hair. Lots of homeowners report that they have kept deer away by hanging human hair from the trees around their landscape. Use mesh bags with a ⅛-inch or smaller mesh. Place at least two large handfuls of hair in each bag and hang them from the branches of trees and shrubs at a height of about 30 inches. They should be no further than 3 feet apart. This method works best if you replace the hair every four days, which means that you really need to be friends with a barber or hairdresser to make this system work.

Continued →

Soap. Deer are also repelled by strongly scented soap. Use bars of deodorant soap, keeping them in their wrappers so they'll last longer. String them on wires and hang them about 4 feet above the ground (deer-nose height) on the branches of the trees or shrubs to be protected. Space them no farther than 3 feet apart. Ornamenting your trees and shrubs with soap in late winter provides protection throughout this season, when hungry deer cause widespread damage to tender new shoots.

While gardeners have tried many other materials, such as ammonia, vinegar, blood meal, and manure from zoo carnivores to repel animals through noxious odors, none have been proven uniformly effective. That is why we hesitate to recommend them as repellents for animal pests.

Using Tactile and Audio Tricks

A host of audio, visual, and tactile tricks that keep pests away have been tried and recommended. The following two techniques are frequently recommended. Though no scientific research supports their effectiveness, their popularity suggests that they might be worth a try.

Pepper Technique. Pepper is organic, so it doesn't harm the soil, and it's very inexpensive. Sprinkle black or hot pepper all over and around plants. It reportedly repels rabbits and squirrels. Reapply the pepper after rain.

High-Tech Vibrations. The Rodent-Repelling Garden Stake is a commercial device from West Germany. It is battery-powered and vibrates at 60-second intervals to repel burrowing rodents and moles over as much as ⅓ acre. Technology like this has its price, and this gadget carries a hefty price tag (over $75). It is carried by Hammacher Schlemmer.

These schemes just scratch the surface of the long list of home remedies for animal pests. In the rest of this chapter we will look at individual animal pests and the best prevention and control measures for each. Keep in mind that if you have neither the time nor the inclination to experiment, or lack the patience to try multiple approaches, then the most reliable control device is a trap, and the best prevention is an effective barrier.

Guide to Animal Pests

Jeff and Liz Ball

People create lovely landscapes for their pleasure and enjoyment. However, a property with a lovely lawn and a variety of healthy trees, shrubs, vines, and ground covers will also, inevitably, attract pest animals. While many of these animals are appealing in nature, they are seldom welcome in the yard. As they go about raising a family, eating, and sleeping, they inadvertently damage plantings. What follows in this section are profiles of the most troublesome pests and options for controlling and preventing problems. Some of these solutions have been proven more effective than others; you'll need to try them to see how they work in your landscape.

Chipmunk

Chipmunks are territorial animals. Males and females live apart rather than in communal burrows. They have a keen sense of smell and a strong sense of curiosity. In the course of gardening, your scent is transferred to plants, bulbs, or seeds that may be planted in the chipmunk's territory. The chipmunk feels its territory has been invaded; curiosity overcomes caution, and the animal digs up the plant

SIGNS OF CHIPMUNK DAMAGE

Plants and bulbs are dug up, especially just after they have been planted in the soil.

BEST CONTROL STRATEGY

Traps are about the only effective control for chipmunks. Use a 5" x 5" x 15" box trap, baited with peanuts or other nut meats.

STEPS TO PREVENT CHIPMUNK DAMAGE

Repellents

Ro-Pel repels chipmunks by odor and taste. Spray it on bulbs, seeds, and landscape plants before planting them. Be sure to wear gloves and a mask; the label warns that you should avoid skin contact and inhalation of the fumes. Ro-Pel is available from Burlington Scientific Corporation and Ringer Corporation.

Barriers

Once any type of plant that has previously been bothered by chipmunks is in the ground, cover it with a piece of screening or fencing. Ordinary window screening or fence with a mesh of up to 1 by 2 inches will suffice. Place the screening on top of the plant, securing it with stones. The plant may be slightly flattened, but will recover in a few days. On bigger plants, place the screen flat on the ground around the base (fencing that is heavier need not be secured). The screening discourages the chipmunks from coming near the plant. Leave it in place for about a week, until your scent dissipates and the plant had established itself. Screening works over bulb beds as well.

Antitranspirants

Recent research suggests that spraying bulbs with an antitranspirant spray (usually applied to the foliage of broad-leaved evergreens to keep them from dehydrating and wilting in winter) masks the human scent, so the chipmunk will overlook them. Commonly available antitranspirants include Wilt-pruf, Pro-Tec, and VaporGard. These products are widely available in garden centers and nurseries.

Deer

Deer can spell disaster for a landscape. They usually feed in the late evening or early morning, when no one is around. One or two deer can virtually destroy an ornamental or vegetable garden in one night. Far from finicky eaters, they devour almost everything found in the flower and food garden, as well as foliage and bark from trees and shrubs. Various species of deer thrive throughout the United States and Canada.

SIGNS OF DEER DAMAGE

Deer can chew young plants to the ground. On fruit trees and other ornamental trees and shrubs, deer will eat leaves, flower buds, shoots, fruit, and even bark.

VULNERABLE PLANTS

Deer will eat almost anything: fruits, vegetables, flowers, and foliage. On small trees, especially fruit trees, they relish the growing tips in summer and the buds in winter.

BEST CONTROL STRATEGY

The most effective way to control deer is with a wall or fence.

STEPS TO PREVENT DEER DAMAGE

Barriers

A 6-foot solid wood or masonry wall will deter deer even though they could jump over it, because they are less likely to bother a yard or garden they can't see. For small areas, homeowners have had success with a double woven wire fence 8 to 10 feet tall.

Don't skimp on fence height—a wire fence *must* be that tall to be effective. If you don't care about looks or are desperate enough to try anything, a double fence of string has also been proven effective. The second fence should be 3 feet inside the first; both should have three strings and be 3 feet tall. The double fence confuses the deer and they won't try to jump. Make sure the string is easy to see.

Repellents

Many times a particular odor repels deer. However, it must be kept fresh to be effective. One handy trick is to mix your repellent agent with an anti-transpirant such as Wilt-pruf, Pro-Tec, or VaporGard to give it season-long effectiveness.

Soap

For the orchard or any newly planted trees, string bars of deodorant soap on wire and hang them on outer tree branches about 30 inches from the ground and no farther than 3 feet apart. Leave soap wrappers on so the soap will last longer.

Eggs

Another effective control is an egg spray. Louisiana researchers found that a spray of 18 eggs in 5 gallons of water protected an acre of soybeans from deer. The deer were repelled by the smell of decomposing eggs, which in that dilution was too faint for humans to detect.

Hair

Human hair, available from beauty parlors and barber shops, provides some protection if the deer aren't desperate for food. Use mesh bags with 1/8-inch or smaller mesh, and fill each with at least two large handfuls of hair. Hang them from outer tree branches about 30 inches from the ground and no more than 3 feet apart.

Hot Sauce Spray

Another effective remedy is a homemade hot sauce or spray of Tabasco sauce. Mix 1 to 2 tablespoons Tabasco sauce and 2 tablespoons antitranspirant in 1 gallon water. Spray vulnerable shrubs and plants with this mixture. Be sure to respray after it rains.

Garlic

Recent research has shown that selenium, which gives off a garlicky odor, prevents deer from eating tree shoots and seedlings. Since the selenium in garlic is the component responsible for the notorious "garlic breath," spraying a garlic solution on trees might have a similar repellent effect. Like hot sauce, it would have to be reapplied after rains. And remember, you might be repelled by your garlicky trees too! An alternative is planting a time-release garlic capsule (available at health-food stores) at the base of each tree or shrub.

Commercial Repellents

If home remedies don't work, there are many commercial products that may be worth a try.

Big Game Repellent (Deer Away). This product repels by odor and is made from eggs, which repel deer as they decompose. It's a highly effective repellent. Apply it according to package directions and reapply after rains.

Bonide Rabbit-Deer Repellent and Bulb Saver. One taste of this stuff and rabbits and deer should walk away. Spray, brush, or dip branches. Use it for shrubs, evergreens, trees, and fruit trees. Bonide

Continued ➡

Repellent will last three to six months. It is available from Bonide Chemical Company.

Chew-Not. This product also repels by taste. Spray, brush, or dip branches in the solution. It is primarily used on fruit trees and some varieties of evergreen. Chew-Not's disadvantage is that it leaves an unattractive white residue on the plants due to its eggwhite consistency. It is available from Nott Manufacturing Company.

Hinder. This is a soap-based formulation that repels by odor. It must be reapplied after heavy rains. It comes as a spray, and is available from Uniroyal-Leffingwell Chemical Company.

Ro-Pel. Both the odor and taste of this product repel pests. Spray it on both sides of the leaves of landscape plants. Be sure to wear gloves and a mask when using it. Ro-Pel is available from Burlington Scientific Corporation and Ringer Corporation.

Gopher

Gophers range in length from 6 to 12 inches. They have a thick body with small eyes and ears. Their sense of smell is excellent. They seldom are found aboveground. Once gophers arrive in your yard, they resemble a small invasion force. One acre can feed and house 16 to 20 gophers, so it is easy to see why they can be a very serious problem. Gophers range from Indiana west to the Pacific Ocean. The most common is the pocket gopher (*Geomys bursarius*).

Signs of Gopher Damage

Gophers push soil out of their holes, creating distinctive fan- or crescent-shaped mounds on the surface of the ground. After digging a mound, they may close up the entrance hole with a soil plug. One gopher can create several mounds a day. Gopher tunnels, about 2 inches in diameter, follow no pattern, running from a few inches to 2 feet below the soil. You know you have gophers when your plants are damaged in areas where there are fan-shaped mounds. Sometimes plants simply disappear—one morning you'll look out and find that a gopher has yanked your pansies down into its tunnel.

Vulnerable Plants

Gophers eat the underground parts of garden crops and a wide variety of roots, bulbs, tubers, grasses, and seeds. They can damage lawns, flowers, vegetables, vines, and trees. Their mounds sometimes smother small plants, and they can girdle and kill young fruit trees.

Best Control Strategy

A sure way to drive this pest away is to determine the location of all the entrances to its tunnel system and then fumigate. Find a piece of hose material that can be attached to the exhaust of a power lawn mower. Stick one end of the hose into the gopher's tunnel, then seal the opening with soil. Next, drop some oil onto the inside of the hot exhaust pipe to create smoke, and attach the other end of the hose to the smoking pipe. After a few minutes, you should see smoke coming from all other entrances to the tunnel system. You may see gophers emerging as well.

Once you identify all the entrances to the tunnel system, you have several choices. You can seal them with piles of soil and continue to blow exhaust from the power mower into the tunnel, killing the inhabitants with poisonous carbon monoxide fumes, or you can put sulfur into the holes and seal all the entrances. The cheapest source of sulfur is one of the emergency highway flares that come with auto safety kits or are found in auto supply stores. Cut through an emergency flare with a sharp knife (not a saw). Dig into the runway, then pour the flare powder directly into the tunnel. Cover this hole, as well as all the exit holes that you have discovered. The more airtight the tunnel system is, the more anxious the gophers will be to leave. Once you are sure that the gophers are gone, seal the tunnels securely with soil. You'll know the gophers are gone when you no longer see fresh mounds around your property.

Another option is to place small ammonia-soaked sponges into each gopher hole and then seal them all. Gophers will abandon their burrows in a hurry. The best time to use this control is in early spring.

Other Options for Controlling Gophers

Flooding

Set up traps over the openings of the gopher tunnels, then locate the main gopher burrow by probing the soil with a long screwdriver or similar probe. When the probe hits the main tunnel, it should suddenly drop about 2 inches. Once you've located the main tunnel, insert a garden hose into it. When you turn the water on, it will flow in both directions throughout the tunnel system. The gopher will try to escape by exiting from one of the mounds. It can then be trapped.

Traps

Trapping can effectively eliminate gophers. Place standard wooden-based rat traps in shallow pits near burrow entrances. Cover the trap trigger with a thin layer of dirt and lure your victims to the traps by sprinkling grain on the dirt.

You can also trap gophers with a Macabee or other pincher trap, or with a box trap such as the Gopher Getter. You'll need two or more traps. Set them with special care. Wear gloves to prevent human scent from contaminating the devices. If you inadvertently touch the traps, you can wash them in soapy water. Open up the main burrow enough to allow you to insert two traps, one facing in each direction. The gopher will run over the trigger mechanism, regardless of the direction in which it is moving. Attach strong twine or rope between the trap and a stake driven into the ground. This prevents the rodent from pulling the trap deep into the burrow. Use a wooden board, cardboard, or other sturdy material to cover the traps, and be sure to sift dirt around the edges of the covering to exclude light. If the gopher sees light, it will push soil toward it, tripping the trap without being caught. If you don't catch any gophers within three days, pull out the traps and reset them in a new location.

Steps to Prevent Gopher Damage

Barriers

Bulb beds and individual shrubs or trees can be protected with ½-inch-mesh wire if it is laid on the bottom and sides of the planting hole. Be sure to place the wire deep enough so that it does not restrict root growth.

Gophers occasionally feed on the bark of certain trees, particularly stone fruits such as peaches and cherries. It is wise to protect the trunks of vulnerable trees with cylinders of ½-inch galvanized hardware cloth sunk 12 inches underground and rising 12 inches above the surface.

Repellents

Cat Litter

Dump several scoops of well-used cat litter right into each burrow entrance. As mentioned at the beginning of this chapter, do not use this trick in the food garden. It is an option for the flower garden and general landscape, if children won't be playing in the soil.

Ro-Pel

A commercial product, Ro-Pel can be used to keep gophers away. Both the odor and taste of this product repel these rodents. Spray it on both sides of the leaves of landscape plants. Be sure to wear gloves and a mask when using it. Ro-Pel is available from Burlington Scientific Corporation and Ringer Corporation.

GoPherIt

GoPherIt is a battery-powered sound-emitting device that you can insert into the lawn or garden. It emits sound waves every 15 seconds, and will keep gophers out of areas of up to 100 feet in diameter. The sound waves cannot be detected by humans or nonrodent pets. GoPherIt is available from Ryans Company and Ringer Corporation.

Mole

Moles do not eat plants, but they do eat lots of grubs, beetles, earthworms, and other soil dwellers. Moles cause trouble because they harm the root systems of young plants when they tunnel through the soil in search of food. This damage is compounded by the fact that they can spread disease from plant to plant. In addition, other pests that are more harmful, like field mice, use mole runs. Several mole species are known; they are found throughout the United States.

Signs of Mole Damage

In their search for food, moles make an extensive network of tunnels, many of which are used only once. They are solitary animals, and it is likely only one or two moles are responsible for all the damage to your lawn or garden. Moles are active all year long. When cold weather comes, they follow the earthworms deep into the soil below the frost line. Mole tunnels can be distinguished from gopher tunnels by the fact that they do not have the characteristic fan-shaped mound at the entrance that gopher tunnels have.

Vulnerable Plants

Lawns rich in grubs and earthworms are most likely to be riddled with molehills. Young seedlings in the early spring can be harmed by moles tunneling in search of grubs and other insects.

Best Control Strategy

Traps can be effective, but you have to be persistent. The best time to trap is in early spring when the first mole ridges appear. To find out which runs are used as "travel lanes," step lightly on a small section of several tunnels so that you disturb but do not completely collapse them. Mark these sections with stones or garden stakes. In two days, note which ones are raised—those are active runs and good locations for setting a trap. You can restore the turf over unused tunnels with a lawn roller or by treading on them.

Choker traps (such as the Nash mole trap), scissor-jawed traps (such as the Out O' Sight), and harpoon traps (such as the Victor mole trap) do catch moles when used properly. Install these traps according to instructions that come with them. They all basically work by springing when a mole

Continued ➡

sets off the trigger-pan as it attempts to raise a flattened portion of its run.

OTHER OPTIONS FOR CONTROLLING MOLES

Digging

As an alternative to trapping you can try digging out moles. Because moles may be active at any time of the day, it is often possible to see the soil ridging up as the mole moves along. Put a shovel into the soil right behind the mole, and flip the animal out into a bucket, which you can then fill with water to drown the culprit.

Flushing

A technique that's effective when mole runs are short is to flush the little animals out with water. Just open the main run, insert a garden hose, and turn on the water. When the water spreads through the tunnels, adult moles will try to escape through other exits, where you can kill them with a shovel. If you flood the runs in spring, you will also drown the young in their nest.

STEPS TO PREVENT MOLE DAMAGE

Get Rid of Grubs

Beetle grubs feed on plant roots and in turn are eaten by moles. Remove the grubs and your lawn will be less attractive to moles. Kill Japanese beetle grubs in your soil with applications of *Bacillus popilliae* (commercially available as Doom and Grub Attack, among other brand names). Other beetle grubs can be controlled with parasitic nematodes (sold as Bioquest).

Repellents

Cat Litter

You might achieve success with the strong odor of well-used cat litter. Dump several scoops of litter right into the mole's burrow. A sprinkling of tobacco or red pepper into each burrow may also deter moles.

Mole Evictor

The Mole Evictor is a battery-operated vibrating device that you set in the soil. The vibrations emanating from it supposedly drive moles away for good. For information contact Ryans Company.

GoPherIt

Like the Mole Evictor, GoPherIt produces battery-powered vibrations that clear moles within a 50-foot radius. It is available from Ryans Company and Ringer Corporation.

Windmills

Another vibration trick is to set windmills (available commercially through garden supply catalogs) in mole runs. These windmills create vibrations that seem to deter moles. A less expensive alternative is to insert a child's pinwheel into the tunnel ridge. Empty glass soda bottles work along the same principle. Set a bottle straight down into the mole run, open end up. The wind blowing across the opening of the bottle creates vibrations that spread along the mole tunnel.

Rodent Rocks

Rodent Rocks are porous lava stones that have been soaked in an organic repellent containing onions and garlic. When the rocks are buried 6 inches deep and 2 to 4 feet apart, their odor is claimed to effectively repel moles for 4 to 12 months. Circle the lawn with rodent rocks for best effectiveness. You can buy a package of about 60 Rodent Rocks from Gardener's Supply Company.

Barriers

Moles will avoid hard, stony soil, which is difficult to dig through. You can create an effective barrier by digging a trench 2 feet deep and 6 inches wide around vulnerable areas. Fill the trench with heavy clay and stony and/or compacted soil and keep it dry. You can pave or mulch the barrier to create an attractive path around the lawn or garden.

NATURAL PREDATORS

Cats are natural predators. They'll kill moles, but they won't eat them because of their bad taste.

NOTES AND RESEARCH

No evidence exists to support claims that castor beans (sometimes called mole plants) keep moles away, or that daffodil bulbs or dandelions work either.

Mouse

A number of different types of mouse may nibble on your landscape plants. The field mouse (also called the meadow vole) is chunky in build, with small ears that are almost concealed in fur. They are white underneath and gray-brown on top. The house mouse, which is less likely to damage your landscape plants, is gray all over, with large, distinct ears. The white-footed mouse and related deer mouse range over most of the continent. They have whitish underparts like the field mouse, as well as whitish legs and feet and tails over 2 inches long.

SIGNS OF MOUSE DAMAGE

Mice are known to move into mole tunnels and use them to gain access to plant roots. They create surface trails through long grass, weeds, and brush, and can also burrow underground. They are most damaging in winter, when they gnaw the bark of young shade or fruit trees, sometimes girdling and killing the trees. Because of their tunneling habits, mice can chew bark from trunks several inches underground, girdle trees at ground level, or reach higher branches by digging through snow. Orchardists report that voles can kill scores of fruit trees in an orchard during a single winter. Tree-girdling usually occurs between October and April. Mice may also overwinter in the mulch placed around strawberries or perennial flowers, where they chew on the roots. They are generally active all year round.

VULNERABLE PLANTS

Roots of vegetable and flower plants in the garden are fair game for mice. These rodents also gnaw on roots of young trees and shrubs, as well as on bark buried under the snow during the winter months.

BEST CONTROL STRATEGY

The traditional mousetrap still works. The most effective way to reduce mice through trapping is to buy a large number of snap-traps and plan a one- or two-night massacre. Buying a few traps to catch mice over a long period of time does not work as well. Bait the traps with a tiny dab of peanut butter or bacon, or a 50=50 mix of peanut butter and uncooked oatmeal. A good technique is to bait the traps for two or three nights without setting them. Then when you finally do set the traps, you'll catch the mice by surprise.

A steel drum with bait inside makes a very simple homemade mousetrap. The mice scramble into the standing drum, and once they are inside, they can't climb out. You'll have caught them red-handed.

OTHER OPTIONS FOR CONTROLLING MICE

Glue Board

Besides the basic mousetrap, there is also a product on the market called a glue board. This is a sheet of extremely sticky material that literally stops mice in their tracks when they try to run across it. Once you've caught a mouse, dispose of both the glue board and the pest. J. T. Eaton & Company carries glue board traps.

Vitamin D Bait

A vitamin D-pelleted bait causes a calcium imbalance in the mouse's blood. Mice stop feeding after eating the pellets and die in two to four days. This bait is toxic only to rodents. It is available from Necessary Trading Company and Natural Gardening Research Center.

STEPS TO PREVENT MOUSE DAMAGE

Ro-Pel

Mice do not like the taste of Ro-Pel. Spray it on both sides of the leaves of landscape plants. Be sure to wear gloves and a mask when using it. Ro-Pel is available from Burlington Scientific Corporation and Ringer Corporation.

Barriers

Plastic Guards

Commercial plastic wrap-around guards placed around the base of trees will prevent mice from chewing on bark, but these guards must be installed each fall and removed each spring. If they are left on year-round, the trunks become more vulnerable to borer attack and the bark remains tender and slow to harden off.

Hardware Cloth

Galvanized hardware cloth makes a durable mouse-proof guard that can be left on all year. Buy 14-inch mesh in a 24-inch width. Cut the hardware cloth wide enough to completely encircle the tree. If you plan to leave it on year-round, allow plenty of room for the trunk to expand as it grows. Make a cylinder around the trunk, fastening the edges securely. Bury the cylinder at least 2 inches deep to keep mice from digging under it. Make sure the top of the cylinder extends above the snow line.

Other Options

Good sanitation is one way to discourage mice from visiting your yard. Clean up all possible food sources, such as vegetables left in the garden at season's end and fallen apples, crabapples, or other fruit. Be sure to use rodent-proof containers of metal or glass to store seeds and birdseed, and keep birdseed swept up.

Always pull mulch away from the base of young shade and fruit trees in the winter. Don't mulch perennials or strawberries until the ground freezes hard. Putting mulch down early invites the mice to set up housekeeping and gives them easy access to roots in unfrozen soil.

Keep an area of at least 3 feet clear around trees, removing tall grass, weeds, and shrubby growth. Mice do not like to come out in the open and will hesitate to cross that bare space to gnaw on the trees.

Natural Predators

Any owls and snakes on your property will help keep the population of mice under control. Of course, one of the best rodent controls known is the house cat.

Rabbit

Rabbits have shown themselves to be extremely adaptable to human environments. Cottontails are active mainly from dusk until midmorning and spend the warmer part of the day in shaded areas. They may hide under thick shrubs or beneath garden sheds. The Eastern cottontail is the species usually found nibbling in the yard and garden, but various species of rabbit are found throughout the United States and Canada.

SIGNS OF RABBIT DAMAGE

Herbaceous plants, especially young ones, will be nibbled down to the base. In winter, rabbits

Continued →

remove a considerable amount of bark from young trees, and they chew the new shoots.

Vulnerable Plants

Rabbits' favorite foods include carrots, geraniums, grasses, lettuce, marigolds, peas, strawberries, tulip shoots, raspberry canes, weeds, and the bark of young shrubs and trees, particularly euonymus, honey locust, and sumac. They especially relish young bean growth and the bark of young fruit trees (apple trees are the all-time favorite). Rabbits don't like corn, cucumbers, or squash, and will only eat evergreen bark if they're really desperate.

Best Control Strategy

Trapping is the most effective way to control rabbits. Commercial box traps measuring 10" x 12" x 30" are recommended. Rabbits are more likely to enter a dark trap than one that's well lighted, so put a tarpaulin over the trap.

Steps to Prevent Rabbit Damage

Barriers

Ordinary chicken-wire fence can rabbit-proof the flower garden, but it isn't very attractive. Bury the fence 6 inches into the soil and extend it at least 2 feet aboveground. Make sure the holes in the mesh are smaller than 2 inches—1 to 1½ inches is ideal.

Tree Guards

Commercial Wrap and Alternatives

Tree guards are an essential piece of equipment in the war against rabbits. When preparing newly planted trees or an orchard for the winter, wrap the lower portion of trunks with commercial tree wrap, burlap, aluminum foil, or a piece of metal window screen. The wrapping should be 2 feet above the height of the deepest expected snow cover—rabbits can walk on top of the snow. In winter, tramp down the snow around your trees so rabbits can't chew on low limbs. Remove protective wrappings each spring to prevent the trunks from becoming tender and to avoid attracting borers.

Wire Guards

You can put wire guards around individual plants, shrubs, or trees if you have the time and patience to make them. Make a cylinder around each plant with hardware cloth, attaching it to stakes to keep it upright. Make the guards higher than 18 inches so a rabbit can't stand up on its hind legs to reach its lunch. If you use wire around tree trunks, extend it 2 feet above the projected snow depth.

Repellents

Repellents may help you reduce rabbit damage. As mentioned in the beginning of the chapter, these vary in effectiveness. In the case of rabbit control, taste repellents are often more effective than scent repellents.

Scent Repellents

You can choose from a wide range of scent repellents to keep rabbits away from your plants. Rabbits tend to avoid anything that smells of blood. Sprinkling dried blood meal on the soil around vulnerable plants may keep rabbits away, but you'll have to reapply it after each rain.

Some gardeners have reported that vinegar wards off rabbits. Save a few corn cobs after a meal and cut the cobs in half. Soak them in vinegar for 5 minutes, then scatter them throughout the flower or vegetable garden. Two weeks later, soak them again in the same vinegar. You can keep reusing this vinegar; just keep it in its own labeled bottle.

Other rabbit repellents reported effective by some homeowners include lion and tiger manure (sold by some zoos as ZooDoo); a solution of cow manure and water applied as a spray; onions inter-planted among crops; fish tankage and bonemeal; and soybeans planted adjacent to the garden. Sprinkle or place repellents immediately around the target plants.

Taste Repellents

You can purchase commercial taste repellents or make one at home. During the growing season, discourage rabbits by spraying nicotine sulfate on your garden. Prepare the spray by mixing ½ teaspoon 40 percent nicotine sulfate in 1 quart water. An even easier repellent to use is black or hot pepper. Simply sprinkle it all over and around plants.

Ro-Pel is a taste repellent. It can be dusted on plants, or you can follow the package instructions to make a spray. Ro-Pel is available from Burlington Scientific Corporation and Ringer Corporation.

A combination antitranspirant and pest repellent is Bonide Rabbit-Deer Repellent & Bulb Saver, available from Bonide Chemical Company. The branches of shrubs, evergreens, trees, roses, fruit trees, ornamentals, and nursery stock should be sprayed or brushed with or dipped into this product. The effect will last three to six months.

Visual Repellents

Inflatable or cast plastic snakes and owls look lifelike and are readily available from most mail-order garden catalogs. These pseudo-predators will frighten rabbits away from the tree or garden area they're placed in. Move them every few days so the rabbits won't catch on.

Eliminate Daytime Cover

One way to reduce the rabbit population in the yard is to remove brush piles, one of their favorite daytime resting places. Clear out overgrown walls, fences, and ditches. Lack of cover will discourage rabbits from hanging around. Anything you can do to eliminate sanctuaries will help solve the rabbit problem; however, if you live next to a wooded area, there may be too many hiding places to deal with in this manner. Fortunately, nearby big trees may help, since they will encourage predators such as owls and hawks.

Squirrel

Eight species of squirrel live in the United States. The most common are the eastern gray squirrel and the fox squirrel, which can make nuisances of themselves at bird feeders and cause occasional problems in the landscape.

Signs of Squirrel Damage

Squirrels eat crocuses and other bulbs. They often make holes in the lawn or garden as they search for nuts buried earlier in the season.

Vulnerable Plants

Squirrels eat nuts (including green and ripe walnuts and almonds), fruits (such as oranges, apples, and avocados), buds, bulbs, and bark. They love birdseed.

Best Control Strategy

You can catch a squirrel in a medium-sized box trap baited with fruit, nuts, or peanut butter.

Steps to Prevent Squirrel Damage

Scent Repellents

Ro-Pel, a commercial product, smells and tastes awful to squirrels. Soak bulbs in Ro-Pel before planting them, and squirrels will leave them alone. This repellent is available from Burlington Scientific Corporation and Ringer Research.

Sticky Repellents

The Squirrel, also commercially available, is a sheet of paper coated with gel. The unpleasant sensation of gel on their feet discourages squirrels from encroaching on the protected area. This paper is available from J. T. Eaton & Company.

Squirrel Baffles

To keep squirrels out of bird feeders, put a baffle on the pole beneath the bird feeder or on the wire it's strung on. Baffles are available from the same companies that sell bird feeders and supplies. You can also make your own from stovepipe.

Preventing Damage from Animals

Barbara Pleasant

A hungry raccoon, deer, squirrel, or rabbit can do more damage in an hour than most insects can do in a week, so they can be formidable garden pests. Prevention or early intervention is crucial, because once hungry animals discover good food in your garden, they become much more difficult to manage. Hunger and the availability of other foods are important variables, because starving animals will often eat plants they normally leave alone.

Try Scent Fences

In landscape situations where an actual fence is not practical, you may have luck deterring animals with various scents. Odor repellents are useful when you have just a few plants in need of protection, and in situations where the pest animals have plenty of other places to go in search of food.

If you choose this "scents-ible" approach to plant protection, be prepared to keep raising a stink as long as animal pests pose a threat. Most repellents need to be refreshed as their aromas fade, especially if they're exposed to the elements. Here are some widely used repellents with reputations for success in keeping plant-munchers at bay.

- **Deodorant soap.** Popular for protecting fruit trees from deer browsing, aromatic bars of soap hung 3 to 4 feet above the ground often are effective. Place a bar in a mesh bag, or drill a hole through the middle and hang on a piece of twine. Each bar will protect an area of about 1 square yard, so large trees and shrubs may need more than one bar. This is a great use for the small bars of soap often provided by hotels.

- **Predator scents.** Rabbits and deer instinctively avoid areas that seem to be frequented by predators. Hang the blanket your dog has been sleeping on over the garden fence, or tuck tufts of dog hair (or human hair) into mesh bags and hang them around your garden or on your favorite shrubs. Put small amounts of used cat litter into the bottoms of coffee cans that have several holes punched in their sides and set them around the outside of your garden (never allow used cat litter inside your garden).

- **Hot stuff.** All mammals can taste the fire in hot peppers, so dousing plants with a spicy spray will often deter casual munchers. Combine 2 cups of water, 2 tablespoons of Tabasco sauce, 1 teaspoon of hot chili powder, and a squirt of dishwashing liquid, and spray or sprinkle it liberally over plants that are being bothered by squirrels, rabbits, deer, or other four-legged creatures. Reapply this spicy cocktail after heavy rains, which usually wash plant leaves clean.

- **Castor oil.** A powerful repellent for moles, castor oil also has proven useful in repelling squirrels, chipmunks, and gophers. If these varmints are rooting around in your flower

Continued ➡

beds or containers, a castor oil solution is an easy-to-apply deterrent. In a glass jar, combine 1 ounce of castor oil with 1 tablespoon of dishwashing liquid and 1 cup of warm water. Shake the jar to mix the solution. Pour this mixture into a watering can and add 1 gallon of water. Sprinkle onto containers and flower beds where animal damage is occurring, or pour it directly onto mole tunnels. Reapply after heavy rains.

Planning an Animal-Resistant Garden

Barbara Pleasant

If you are one of the thousands of gardeners who live in an area where deer and rabbit populations are high, you know too well the heartbreak of looking out your window in the morning to find that your garden has been ravaged during the night. You cannot control what wild animals do while you sleep, but can design a landscape that offers little in the way of attractive foods. As for those plants that rabbits and deer love—such as most fruits and vegetables—the best solution is to fence in the area where you plan to grow your own produce.

Where rabbits are the primary problem, you can install a dependable rabbit fence in a matter of hours. Deer, in comparison, have no trouble leaping over a 6-foot-tall fence, and if they are hungry enough, they will barrel through an electric fence as well. Still, electric fencing is relatively inexpensive and easy to install. Do check your local zoning laws before you start; for safety reasons, some communities restrict electric fence use by homeowners. If you do install an electric fence, post appropriate warning signs and make your neighbors aware of the fence's location.

There is another option—7½-foot-tall black plastic mesh fencing, which is sold by companies that specialize in deer-resistant garden supplies. Plastic mesh fencing's light weight makes it easy to install, and it requires few fence posts to hold it in place. The mesh is nearly invisible at even a relatively short distance, so it doesn't impede landscape views. Deer have a hard time seeing it, too, and are usually so spooked when they run into it that they don't return for a second encounter.

Working with Animal Resistant Plants

You can fence in your food garden, but what about the rest of your landscape? Although rabbit and deer appetites vary with season and region, the plants listed on the next page in "60 Animal-Resistant Plants" are generally unattractive to rabbits, deer, and even squirrels. If you use large numbers of these plants, animals will gradually lose interest in your yard, and you can begin slipping in favorite plants here and there, where their presence will be camouflaged by plenty of neighboring plants animals find distasteful.

For best results, plant nothing but animal-resistant plants around the perimeter of your yard. If you know the direction from which animals tend to enter your property, barriers of thorny blackberries and unpalatable plants may turn them away.

Many of the plants that resist deer and rabbits are also poisonous to people, so take this into consideration if you share your garden with curious kids. Fencing in your edible plants and growing herbs in their own special area make it easy to teach kids the difference between safe and toxic plants.

Build a Fence That Bugs Bunnies

Bunnies frolicking in your yard on a summer evening make a charming sight, but it's much harder to romanticize their company when you find your lettuce nibbled down to nubbins, and nothing but stubs where your beans used to be. Scent repellents may have some effect in keeping Peter Cottontail and pals out of your garden, but you have to be rigorous in refreshing them after every rainfall. Even then, they may not do the trick once critters have discovered the goodies in your garden.

It's easy to install a basic fence that will keep rabbits—and groundhogs—from using your garden as their own personal salad bar. The fence doesn't have to be tall—18 to 24 inches is usually enough—but it does need to extend underground. There is also good reason to allow the top of the fence to remain loose and somewhat floppy. Should a raccoon or other climbing animal try to scale the fence, the wire will naturally curl backward toward the animal, making the fence much more difficult to climb. Leaving the top edge unattached also makes it easier to step over when you're carrying tools or harvested vegetables. Although this fence does include a section that can be opened when you need to get inside with a wheelbarrow, you will usually come and go by simply stepping over the fence.

If you want to camouflage the fence, you can do so with handmade wattle panels. Or, you can use a low picket fence, which is easy to install using preassembled panels.

You Will Need

Tools: Garden spade or trenching spade, mallet, hammer, sturdy gloves, wire cutters
48-inch-tall wood or metal fence posts, 1 for each corner, plus one for every 4 feet of fencing
36-inch-wide chicken wire (also called poultry netting) to enclose the perimeter of your garden
Wire or plastic cable ties for fastening chicken wire to posts, 3 for each post
Two 24-inch-long pieces of 1 x 2 furring strip
Four 1½-inch nails
Two short bungee cords (utility tie-downs)

1. Dig a 6-inch-deep trench around the perimeter of your garden using the garden spade or trenching spade.

2. Use the mallet or hammer to set the posts in the trench, first at the corners of the garden and then at 4-foot intervals in between. Pound them in 8 inches deeper than the bottom of the trench. If necessary, make guide holes for the posts with a rebar stake.

3. Unroll the chicken wire and stretch it between the posts along one side of the garden, aligning the bottom edge of the wire with the bottom of the trench. Use wire or plastic cable ties to fasten the chicken wire to the posts in three places—1 inch, 13 inches, and 25 inches above the soil. Do not attach the top edge of the chicken wire to the posts.

4. Repeat Step 3 with the remaining sides of the garden. When you reach the section between the last post and corner, cut the chicken wire to the proper length, and reinforce the cut edge with the furring strips. Lay the cut edge on the ground, and sandwich the edge of the chicken wire between the two furring strips, with the tops of the furring strips 6 inches from the top edge of the chicken wire. Nail them together.

Make an Animal Tracking Box

You know you have an animal pest making secret visits to your garden, but you have yet to catch a glimpse of your wild visitor. Many animals are nocturnal, but you don't have to stay up all night waiting to see who shows up. Instead, make a simple tracking box, and study the footprints the animal leaves behind.

You Will Need

Tools: Utility knife, scissors, watering can
1 waxed cardboard box
1 roll of duct tape
3 gallons of clean sand

1. Use the utility knife to cut around the sides of the box, removing all but the bottom and 3 inches along all four sides. Use the duct tape to reinforce the box by taping across the bottom in both directions. Also wrap tape around all of the sides and corners of the box.

2. Fill the prepared box almost to the top with clean, dry sand. Place it where animal activity is likely, and sprinkle the sand with water until it is lightly moist. Pat the surface level with your hand. Press your hand lightly to see if it leaves a print. If needed, add more water to the sand and smooth it again.

3. Check the box for prints first thing in the morning. Use the toe-counting method to narrow the field of possibilities.

   - Four toes on both the front and back feet, with a fifth central pad, are signs of an animal in the dog, cat, or rabbit family. Dog tracks usually include claw marks, while those of cats do not. Rabbit tracks are elongated, with toe marks barely visible.

   - Four toes on the front feet and five toes on the back suggest some type of rodent, such as mice, squirrels, chipmunks, or woodchucks.

   - Five toes on all four feet are evidence of the raccoon family, which includes weasels, skunks, opossums, and raccoons. The tracks resemble the shape of a small human hand.

   - Two elongated toes are proof of a visit by deer, elk, or moose

5. To make a convenient opening in the fence, make an 8-inch-long vertical cut in the chicken wire 4 feet from the last corner post. Roll up the lowest 6 inches of chicken wire between the cut and the furring strips so it will not be buried. Fasten the reinforced end of the fence to the last corner posts with bungee cords.

6. Before refilling the trench, angle the bottom edge of the chicken wire outward, so that any animal trying to dig under the fence will be almost standing on top of the wire as it digs. Refill the trench with soil, and pack it down firmly.

Make a No-Dig Barrier

Whether you want to foil cats intent on digging up newly planted carrots or squirrels after your tulip

Continued ➡

bulbs, a wire barrier will do the trick. As long as these and other animals can't get their paws into soft, freshly dug soil, your work won't be ruined. You can leave the barriers in place as long as you like. If digging mice and squirrels are a problem all winter, it's best to provide protection for bulbs until spring, when other foods become available. You can hide the wire barriers from view by covering them with a thin layer of chopped leaves or other organic mulch.

You Will Need

Tools: Sturdy gloves, wire cutters or tin snips, scissors

Chicken wire (also called poultry netting)

1 wire clothes hanger

1 yard of colorful ribbon or yarn

1. Wearing gloves to protect your hands, use the wire cutters or tin snips to cut a piece of chicken wire large enough to cover the area where your seeds or bulbs are planted. Lay it on top of the soil, and bend the edges down so they stick into the soil.

2. To make staples to secure the chicken wire in place, use the wire cutters or tin snips to cut off the two corners of the clothes hanger, 5 inches from the corners. Bend the ends in until the sides are parallel.

3. Bend the two wires attached to the hanger's hook downward until the ends are parallel. Bend the remaining straight piece of wire into a U-shape.

4. Pin down the four corners of the chicken wire with the wire staples. Tie a 9-inch piece of ribbon or yarn to each staple to make them easy to find.

Bird-Deterrent Basics
Barbara Pleasant

Most gardeners regard birds as friends rather than foes, but large numbers of crows, blackbirds, jays, and even mockingbirds can become a nuisance when they discover your seeds, seedlings, or almost-ripe berries. Birds are quick to grow accustomed to the devices gardeners use to try to scare them away, so success at protecting your garden from bird damage requires a multifaceted approach.

Use Motion. Whirligigs, wind socks, compact discs dangling on strings, or other devices that wiggle or wave will help keep birds wondering if the objects are alive and, therefore, if they should avoid them. Relocate these devices regularly, before birds figure out that they are actually harmless. Reflective foil tape moves in the wind, so it makes a good deterrent for tomatoes, berry bushes, and other plants that need protection for several weeks.

Use color. Put brightly colored pinwheels and flags around your garden to take advantage of birds' color vision. Some gardeners use colorful stuffed animals, purchased at yard sales, to populate their gardens with curious, colorful "predators."

Use sound. Things that make noise help to keep birds away, too. Just be careful to avoid noise-makers that drive you and your neighbors bonkers in the process. Try wind chimes or similar unobtrusive and unpredictable sound sources. One old-fashioned method that works well in windy areas is to bury empty soda bottles around the garden, with their open mouths 2 inches above the soil line. As wind blows over the bottles, it creates an eerie song that spooks birds. You can also try playing a battery-operated radio in the part of your garden you want to protect. Change the station each day so birds don't become too accustomed to the sound.

---

60 Animal-Resistant Plants

15 Perennials Rabbits and Deer Usually Don't Eat

Butterfly weed (*Asclepias tuberosa*)
Coral bells (*Heuchera americana*)
Ferns (many species)
Foxgloves (*Digitalis* spp.)
Goat's beard (*Aruncus dioicus*)
Goldenrods (*Solidago* spp.)
Hardy geranium (*Geranium macularum*)
Hellebores (*Helleborus* spp.)
Irises (*Iris* spp.)
Joe-Pye weeds (*Eupatorium* spp.)
Lamb's ears (*Stachys byzantina*)
Penstemon (*Penstemon digitolis*)
Purple coneflower (*Echinacea purpurea*)
Solomon's seal (*Polygonarum biflorum*)
Spiderwort (*Tradescantia virginico*)

15 Animal-Resistant Flowers and Herbs

Ageratum (*Ageratum houstonianum*)
Anise hyssop (*Agastoche* spp.)
Bee balm (*Monarda didyma*)
Begonia (*Begonia* spp.)
Catnip (*Nepeta* spp.)
Dusty miller (*Senecio cineraria*)
Lantana (*Lantana* spp.)
Lavender (*Lavandula* spp.)
Mealycup sage (*Salvia forinacea*)
Mint (*Mentha* spp.)
Nicotiana (*Nicotiana alara*)
Oregano (*Origanum* spp.)
Rosemary (*Rosmorinus officinalis*)
Strawflower (*Helichrysum bracteatum*)
Thyme (*Thymus* spp.)

12 Animal-Resistant Flowering Shrubs

Abelia (*Abelia grandiflora*)
Blue mist shrub (*Caryopteris clandonensis*)
Bridal wreath spiraea (*Spiraea* spp.)
Butterfly bush (*Buddleia davidii*)
Currants (*Ribes* spp.)
Daphne (*Daphne* spp.)
Forsythia (*Forsythia x intermedia*)
Grape holly (*Mahonia* spp.)
Holly (*Ilex* spp.)
Lilac (*Syringa* spp.)
Rose of Sharon (*Hibiscus syriacus*)
Viburnum (*Viburnum* spp.)

8 Deer-Resistant Evergreen Trees and Shrubs

Chinese holly (*Ilex cornuta*)
Common boxwood (*Buxus sempervirens*)
Fraser fir (*Abies fraseri*)
Junipers (*Juniperus* spp.)
Mountain pine (*Pinus mugo*)
Norway spruce (*Picea abies*)
Scots pine (*Pinus sylvestris*)
White spruce (*Picea glauco*)

10 Bulbs Squirrels (Usually) Won't Bite

Autumn crocus (*Colchicum* spp.)
Crown imperial, checker lilies (*Fritillaria* spp.)
Daffodils, narcissus (*Narcissus* spp.)
Glory of the snow (*Chionodoxa* spp.)
Grape hyacinths (*Muscori* spp.)
Grecian windflower (*Anemone blanda*)
Hyacinths (*Hyacinthus* spp.)
Ornamental alliums (*Allium* spp.)
Squills, scillas (*Scilla* spp.)
Surprise lilies (*Lycoris* spp.)

Use danger. Scarecrows and other things that look like threats—including rubber snakes, plastic owls, or reflective balloons—will make birds think twice about dining in your garden. Be sure to change the location of your scare devices often enough to convince birds they are real.

Use netting. Birds that are too smart or persistent for other methods can be kept from raiding the garden with plastic bird netting. Some birds will reach through netting that is draped over plants, so it's best to attach the netting to posts to create a few inches of space between the netting and the plants. Use clothespins to gather the edges of the netting together, and to secure it to strings tied between the posts.

Five Fine Pest Barriers
Barbara Pleasant

Faced with unexpected pest problems, creative gardeners have come up with a long list of easy-to-make barriers. The more you garden, the more you will probably invent solutions to pest challenges. Like the ones described here, they may surprise you with their simplicity—and with how well they work.

Milk Jug Melon Cradles

Protect developing melons from mice and mold. Cut a 1-gallon plastic milk jug in half vertically, and then use an ice pick to punch three or four drainage holes in each half. Slip a prepared cradle beneath a growing melon or winter squash. The plastic cradle will create enough of a barrier to protect the fruit from nibbling mice and other determined varmints, and it will also reduce the risk of rot due to soil-dwelling fungi and bacteria.

Bag Up Your Corn

If you think that raccoons or crows are watching your sweet corn for signs of ripening, beat them to the punch by covering almost-ripe ears with small paper bags (such as lunch bags) fastened in place with clothespins or rubber bands.

Make Flea Beetle Teepees

If you grow eggplant, you've seen the tiny jumping flea beetles that chew hundreds of holes in eggplant leaves. Flea beetles often move to eggplant from early potatoes, or from horse nettle, a common host weed. To keep them off your eggplant, make a teepee around the plants with several sticks fastened together at the top with string, and cover the structure with scraps of rowcover or a piece of cheesecloth. Either can be held in place with clothespins.

Bubble Wrap Barrier

Broccoli, cauliflower, and other cabbage family cousins often thrive in the fall garden—if you can keep them safe from cabbage root maggots, the larvae of a fast-moving fly. To frustrate these flies, surround each seedling with a mat that covers the root zone and fits snugly around the stem. Tar paper is a popular choice, or you can use bubble

Continued ➡

wrap. Cut either material into a 10-inch-wide circle, cut a slit from one edge to the center, and place it around seedlings right after transplanting.

Stick Squirrel Barrier

In a good acorn year, squirrels are eager to hide their treasures everywhere, including in large containers left outdoors through the winter. Keep hardy plants safe from squirrel digging by covering your pots with a simple barrier woven from sticks. Collect a dozen or so sticks a few inches longer than the diameter of your pot, and weave them together, waffle-style, on a flat surface. Then go back and tie the joints together with string. Place the barrier over the soil in your containers.

Your Seasonal Pest-Fighting Calendar

Now you've learned all about the different types of insect and animal pests that might visit your garden and how to control them. Here's what you should be doing each month of the year to help protect your garden from these creatures and critters.

That's where this handy calendar comes in. It lists helpful hints that you can use even during the months when you're not growing anything in your beds—so that you get the better of pests, and not the other way around.

January

Winter isn't too early to start thinking about pest control. You can:

- Figure out a rotation plan for your vegetable beds so that you're not growing the same plant family in the same location each year.
- Make a list of pollen- and nectar-providing plants, such as alyssum and goldenrod, that you can incorporate into your beds to attract beneficials.
- Research what pest problems are common in your area and how you can control them organically.

February

Finalize what you want to plant this year. If you're buying seeds or plants through mail-order catalogs, try to choose varieties with resistance to pests that are common in your area. Consider fencing your garden if you have a serious problem with groundhogs and rabbits.

March

With warmer weather just around the corner, now is the time to

- Check out the condition of your garden soil; healthy plants are much less likely to be attacked by pests.
- Add compost to your beds, and make sure they have good drainage.
- Choose appropriate sites for your plants (for example, make sure shade lovers aren't growing in full sun) to give them the opportunity to thrive.
- Put up birdhouses and bat houses around your property to encourage these pest-eating creatures.
- Prune diseased wood out of fruit trees and shrubs to make them less inviting homes to pests.

April

Mulch garden beds with grass, hay, wood chips, or other organic materials to suppress weeds. Begin patrolling your garden to learn what pests and beneficials are residing there. Give that cracked clay flowerpot a second life as a toad house in your garden. Inspect any plants you buy to make sure they're free of insects.

May

Put row covers on seedlings after you plant them to prevent insect pest damage, such as flea beetles on eggplant and cabbage loopers on broccoli and cabbage. Sink shallow dishes of beer into the soil around your beds to lure slugs to their demise.

June

Although you may take vacation time during summer, pests stay hard at work. So this month:

- Time your vegetable plantings to avoid the worst pests.
- Watch for aphid colonies on lush young growth, and use a heavy stream of water or a soap spray to reduce their populations.
- Handpick pest insects.
- Pick up damaged fruit off the ground so it's not inviting to insect and animal pests.
- Use a summer oil spray if spider mites, scale, or mealybugs are a big problem on trees and shrubs.

July

Your garden is in full swing now, producing juicy tomatoes and luscious peppers—inviting snacks for insect and animal pests. Remember to:

- Continue patrolling your garden and hand-picking insect pests.
- Spread ground black pepper or chili powder around your beds to repel hungry rabbits. If you have a dog, let him police your garden to help scare rabbits away.
- Hang old nylon stockings filled with cat or dog hair around plants that deer like to eat.

August

Continue to patrol the garden for pest problems and pull out weeds and diseased plants. Enjoy the harvest as summer starts to fade away.

September

Take notes on which varieties did well in your garden and which were prone to pest problems. Also make notes on which beneficials visited your garden; that way, you can be sure to grow plants next year that will attract them.

October

Remove mulch from around the base of fruit trees to discourage mice from nesting there and nibbling on root systems. Put hardware cloth tree guards around young trees to prevent mice and rabbits from eating the bark.

November

Now that the growing season is pretty much over, it's time to ready your garden for winter.

- Clean up any remaining spent vegetable plants for the winter and compost the debris (except for diseased plants, which you should dispose of).
- Be sure to leave spent perennials in your beds so overwintering beneficials will have someplace to live during the cold months.
- Mulch perennial and strawberry beds with a layer of straw to prevent winter injury.

December

Hang strong-scented soap bars in trees and shrubs to deter deer. Put up feeders for your feathered friends. Relax by the fire with a good book, and dream about warmer days ahead.

Terrify Them with Technology
Roger Yepsen

The surest weapon for scaring off the animals that prey on the garden is you, the gardener. But you can't be out there waving your arms at all hours of the day and night. And while the folksy form of a scarecrow is a quaint sight, it's not apt to be intimidating to animals for long. Instead, consider buying a Scarecrow, a clever battery-powered device that's attached to the end of a garden hose. It detects movement (caution: any creature's movement, gardener included) and directs a blast of water in that direction.

Pest Glossary

Abdomen. The last section of an insect's body, following the head and thorax. Digestive and reproductive organs are found in the abdomen.

Antenna. Paired, segmented structures, also called feelers. One on each side of the head. Aid sensory perception. Plural antennae.

Bacteria. A single-celled microorganism that reproduces by simple cell division. Beneficial bacteria can help control insect pests, but some bacteria species can cause serious plant diseases, like bacterial wilt and fire blight.

Beak. Long mouthpart used by sucking insects to pierce the surface of a plant or animal. Hollow and jointed. One or more tiny needles in the beak pierce the tissue.

Beneficials. Helpful creatures—birds, bats, toads, snakes, spiders, and predatory insects—that eat garden pests.

Biological controls. Pest-control measures that use living organisms to fight other living organisms. Examples include releasing and attracting natural insect predators and parasites and using microbial sprays to control insects and diseases.

BT. *Bacillus thuringiensis.* A spray derived from naturally occurring bacteria that kill certain insect larvae.

BTK. A BT variety (*B. thuringiensis* var. *kurstaki*) that controls cabbage loopers, cabbageworms, tomato hornworms, fruitworms, European corn borers, and pest larvae.

Caterpillar. Larval stage of a butterfly or moth. Segmented or wormlike, with a distinct head, 12 simple eyes, a pair of very short antennae, and usually six well-developed legs, as well as two to five pairs of prolegs.

Chrysalis. The tubular, hard pupal shell of a butterfly.

Cocoon. The silken pupal case of a butterfly or moth.

Companion planting. Combinations of plants that work well together to repel pests, attract beneficial insects, or make efficient use of garden bed space.

Compost. Decomposed and partially decomposed organic matter (such as kitchen scraps, leaves, grass clippings, dead plants) that is dark in color and crumbly in texture. Used as an amendment, compost increases the water-holding capacity of the soil and is an excellent nutrient source for microorganisms, which later release nutrients to your plants.

Continued ➡

Composting. The art and science of combining organic material so that the original raw ingredients are transformed into compost.

Compost tea. A fertilizer made by soaking a cloth bag full of compost in a watering can or barrel for several days.

Compound eye. Eye of an insect, composed of separate, close-fitting hexagonal lenses. Sensitive to movement and color. Larvae lack compound eyes.

Crop rotation. Rotating crops from different botanical families to avoid or reduce problems with soilborne diseases or soil insects.

Cultural controls. These are gardening practices that reduce pest problems and include building organically enriched, biologically active soil, selecting well-adapted disease-resistant varieties, keeping the garden clean, and practicing crop rotation.

Dormant. Inactive; in suspended animation; hibernating. Dormancy occurs in winter.

Dormant oil. A heavy petroleum oil that can be sprayed on dormant orchard trees and ornamental plants to control overwintering stages of mites, scales, aphids, and other insects. See also Summer oil.

Exoskeleton. The hard outer covering or skeleton that protects an insect's body like armor. Forms a jointed frame.

Frass. The sawdustlike excrement of borers, such as the peachtree borer and squash vine borer.

Fungi. A generally beneficial spore-producing organism that helps the decomposition process. Fungi also cause many common plant diseases such as powdery mildew and late blight.

Grub. The larva of a beetle. Grubs are plump, flat, or wormlike, with well-developed heads and 3 pairs of legs. They pupate in the soil or other protected sites.

Hibernation. A winter period of suspended animation passed by many insects that live more than one season. Usually spent in soil or garden debris.

Honeydew. A sweet, sticky substance secreted by aphids as they feed. Honeydew allows sooty mold to grow on leaves.

Horticultural oils. See Dormant oil; Summer oil.

Host. A plant or animal that a parasite or pathogen depends on for sustenance.

Insecticidal soap. Specially formulated solutions of fatty acids that kill insect pests like aphids, mites, and whiteflies.

Instar. The form of an insect between each molt. Most insects pass through three to six instars.

Larva. An immature stage of an insect.

Maggot. The larva of a fly, usually a small, white, legless worm without an obvious head. Mouthparts are hooked.

Milky disease spores. A microbial insecticide that kills Japanese beetle grubs.

Molt. A shedding of the exoskeleton so that an insect can grow. The old skin splits after a new one has formed beneath it.

Nematode. A microscopic, unsegmented, thread-like worm; some nematodes are beneficial, while others can harm plants.

Nymph. An immature stage of an insect that doesn't form a pupa.

Organic matter. Materials that are derived directly from plants or animals. Organic gardeners use plant and animal by-products to maintain soil and plant health and don't rely on synthetically made fertilizers, herbicides, or pesticides.

Organic pest management. An approach to pest control that combines cultural, biological, and physical measures to prevent problems or to keep them in check.

Parasite. An insect that lives and feeds in or on another insect or animal for at least part of its life cycle.

Pathogen. An organism that causes disease. Pesticide. Any substance, synthetic or natural, that is used to kill insects, animals, fungi, bacteria, or weeds.

Pheromone. A chemical substance, such as a sexual attractant, secreted by an insect to create a response in others of its species.

Pheromone traps. Insect traps that work by attracting male insects to the scent of breeding female insect. These traps are available for a variety of flying pests, including cabbage loopers, Japanese beetles, and peachtree borers. The traps work best in large areas or orchids.

Pheromone traps. Insect traps that work by attracting male insects to the scent of breeding female insects. These traps are available for a variety of flying pests, including cabbage loopers, Japanese beetles, and peachtree borers. The traps work best in large areas or orchards.

Physical controls. Control measures that prevent pests from reaching your plants or remove them if they do. Barriers, traps, and hand-picking are physical controls.

Predator. An insect that feeds on another live insect or animal.

Pupa. A hardened shell formed by a larva, within which the adult stage develops.

Row covers. Sheets of lightweight, permeable material, usually polypropylene or polyester, that can be laid loosely on top of plants to act as a barrier to insect pests or that can give a few degrees of frost protection at the beginning or end of the growing season

Scavenger. An insect that feeds on dead plants, animals, or decaying matter.

Spiracle. One of many tiny holes in the thorax and abdomen of an insect that serve as breathing pores.

Summer oil. A light petroleum oil that controls aphids, mealybugs, spider mites, scales, and some caterpillars. For use on ornamentals. See also Dormant oil.

Thorax. The center section of an insect's body, between the head and the abdomen. Wings and legs are attached to the thorax.

Trap crops. Plants you grow to lure pests away from other crops in your beds. For example, dill lures tomato hornworms away from tomatoes.

Virus. Microscopic organisms that must be inside the living cell of a host to reproduce. Viruses can be transmitted by insects, mites, and nematodes as well as through contact with garden tools and plant cuttings.

Viviparous. Bearing live young. Aphids can be viviparous.

INSECTS AND MITES

Insects

Jeff and Liz Ball

Most of the insects you see in the flower garden are either harmless, adding a little color and diversity to the garden without threatening your plants, or beneficial, pollinating your flowers or eating pests. However, pest insects do visit the flower garden. Most of the time, their damage level is acceptable—you'd have to crawl within inches of your plants to see the few holes in the leaves. In these cases, the best policy is live and let live: Spraying would just disrupt the natural balance (which, after all, is keeping things under control) and waste your time and money. If you're threatened with an invasion, however, or if pests are making your garden look ragged and unsightly, it's time to reach for the controls.

Fortunately, flower gardeners have a variety of safe and effective controls for insect pests in the backyard. New botanicals, biologicals, and traps are being researched, tested, and marketed on a regular basis. Because more and more of these controls are effective only on one pest or a related group, and even broad-spectrum botanicals often work better on some pests than others, "know thine enemy" is the relevant commandment here. Identify your problem pest—then choose the appropriate control. An understanding of insects in general and how they identify and feed on various flowers will give you a better idea of how to use natural pesticides most effectively. (If it's a stomach poison, for example, you'll have to apply it to parts of the plant that the pest will eat.)

Of course, many of the pest problems you face in the flower garden can be prevented before they develop. The first line of defense is the plant's own built-in protections. If certain pests become problems almost every year, choose resistant cultivars whenever they're available. (Catalogs usually mention pest or disease resistance in their plant descriptions, and you can often get a listing from your cooperative extension agent.) By following good gardening practices and giving plants the care they need, you'll encourage all your plants' natural resistance to pests.

Insects themselves—the beneficial allies that prey on or parasitize pests—are your second line of defense. For that reason, there is no need to kill off every last pest insect on your property. The beneficial predators need some food to encourage them to stay around. A healthy balance of beneficial and pest insects tends to keep outbreaks under control.

Despite our best preventive efforts, however, occasionally pest insects appear in overwhelming numbers. At such times, the third line of defense is an environmentally safe pesticide. Many biological and botanical pesticides, as well as organic controls such as insecticidal soap and diatomaceous earth, are now available at garden centers and through mail order.

The best approach to pest control in the flower garden is a well-rounded strategy that includes good garden practices, prevention, and, when needed, safe controls. With such an approach, your

Continued ➜

garden can be beautiful and comparatively problem-free year after year.

Identifying the Pest

Obviously, identification of invading insect pests is the key to successful prevention and control. Develop the habit of observing the leaves and buds of your flowering plants closely. As you become familiar with the look of the plant, you will be able to see symptoms of pest infestation as soon as they develop. Knowledge of characteristic symptoms will make it easier to identify the insect culprit. Then you can plan a control strategy.

Look for Symptoms

The signs of insect attack are easily recognized, although a few may resemble disease symptoms. Some of the most common symptoms of insect pest attack include the following:

- Leaves chewed from the outside edge
- Holes chewed in the leaves
- Complete defoliation of the plant
- Leaves wilted and discolored
- Discolored speckles on the leaves
- Leaves curled or puckered

Once you are alerted to the possibility of insect pest problem, examine the affected plant for the culprit itself. In most cases, insect pests attack the plant's tender new growth, so look there first. Check the upper leaf surfaces, then the undersides of the leaves (where most insects and their eggs are located), and finally, the point where leaves attach themselves to the stem. Examine the buds and flowers. Although pests can also strike roots, and many pests—such as the dreaded slug—work at night, this daytime search will reveal most of the common culprits.

There are a number of good books for identifying pest insects. *Rodale's Color Handbook of Garden Insects*; *Rodale's Garden Insect, Disease, and Weed Identification Guide*; *The Healthy Garden Handbook*; and *The Golden Guide to Insect Pests* are particularly easy to use.

Controlling Insect Pests

When you have found a pest or its damage, the next step is determining an effective control. Your goal is to suppress pest populations before they do measurable harm to the flower garden.

Traps and Mechanical Controls

Before you reach for sprays or dusts, even though they might be comparatively harmless botanical or biological controls, consider trapping or some other physical means of removing insect pests from plants. Often these solutions to the problem are the safest, surest, and least expensive.

Cover Traps

Some pests seek protection from the hot sun during daylight hours. Trap them by offering a simple piece of board or a length of empty garden hose for shelter. Slugs happily crawl under boards, and earwigs readily crawl into a piece of garden hose. Check these traps twice a day and discard any inhabitants in a can of water containing a little kerosene or soap.

Handpicking

Handpicking, though not for the squeamish, is one of the oldest methods of safe and effective insect control. Used in the early stages of infestation, it can forestall a population explosion. Pick off pests and squash them between your fingers, or just drop them in a can of kerosene or soapy water. Wear tight-fitting rubber gloves if you don't like the idea of handling insects.

Locating insects and then handpicking them is slow work. To speed things up, spray water on the plants. Disgruntled pests will crawl from their wet hiding places to the tops of the plants, where it's easier to pick them.

Sticky Traps

Sticky traps can be used to cut down on aphid and whitefly numbers. You can purchase them or make your own. To make a trap, take a 10" x 10" piece of Masonite or other sturdy material that is colored school bus yellow and cover it with something sticky such as Tangle-Trap, TackTrap, Stickem, glycerine, motor oil, or petroleum jelly. Hang the traps so that they are adjacent to, but not above, susceptible plants, or attach them to stakes. Clean and recoat them periodically.

Water Spray

A forceful water spray will take care of some pests by itself. Drench infested plants with a hose, targeting the undersides of leaves where many insects live and lay their eggs. Aphids and spider mites can be controlled this way. Spraying plants with water several days in succession will disrupt the pests' breeding and hatching cycles and can eliminate the population altogether.

Spray plants early in the morning. Use a hose with a nozzle that emits a fine spray of water. Turn the water on high and thoroughly spray the infested plant. Spray at least twice more, either three days in a row or every other day. This will wash off the pests that are already feeding on your plants and eliminate their eggs.

Natural Sprays and Dusts

If handpicking and mechanical controls are not effective, try a spray or dust to get rid of insect pests. Most products can be applied in either form, but sprays are a little easier to use and generally provide more thorough and even coverage than dusts. You can use virtually any type of sprayer, from a plastic, hand-held bottle to a large garden sprayer, depending on the size of the plant or the garden area you need to cover. Listed below are several different types of sprays and dusts, with details on how to use them.

Insecticidal Soap

Insecticidal soaps, such as Safer's, are now widely available commercially. They have been specially formulated to kill certain pest insects, while sparing beneficial insects. Insecticidal soap is biodegradable and breaks down within 7 to 14 days, so it does not harm plants or the environment. It is safe to use around animals and people. While homemade soap sprays might be effective, only commercial soap spray is recommended for uniform performance. It is easy to use and is effective against many insect pests, including aphids, spider mites, and whiteflies.

If you are dealing with a heavy infestation, spray affected plants every two to three days for two weeks. Set the sprayer for medium droplet size and strong pressure to thoroughly wet all surfaces of the plant from top to bottom. Insecticidal soap is a contact insecticide, so it must directly contact the insect to be effective. Take care to spray the undersides of leaves, where you will find most of the pests.

Insecticidal Soap and Alcohol

Increase the effectiveness of insecticidal soap by mixing it with isopropyl alcohol. Make this mix by adding a tablespoon of alcohol of each pint of insecticidal soap solution. Alcohol alone can burn plants, but diluted in the soap spray, it penetrates an insect's waxy protective coating and carries the pesticide with it, bringing it in direct contact with the insect's body.

Garlic Spray

We're all cautious about eating garlic or onions when we're in the company of others, fearful that those we're talking with will turn and walk away at the smell of garlic breath. Apparently garlic has that effect on pest insects, too. Homemade sprays from garlic, onions, or chives have been found to effectively repel certain insect pests. To make the spray, mix ½ cup of finely chopped garlic cloves, onions, or chives with 1 pint of water; then strain out the particles and spray.

Researchers are working on a more potent brew made by soaking 10 to 15 finely minced garlic cloves in a pint of mineral oil for at least 24 hours. The oil is then strained. Two teaspoons of the oil are mixed with a quart of insecticidal soap solution and applied to infested plants. Some tests show the soap spray's effectiveness has been greatly improved by the garlic oil, even on pests not normally killed by the soap alone. However, the true effectiveness of this spray is still undetermined.

Diatomaceous Earth

Diatomaceous earth (often called D.E.) keeps pests from plants in the same way that hot coals would prevent most people from walking up to something. Diatomaceous earth is a powder made from the fossilized skeletons of diatoms—microscopic sea creatures composed primarily of silica. The granules of this fine powder are soft to us, but to insects they are very sharp; they cut the bodies of soft-bodied pests such as caterpillars on contact, causing them to dehydrate and die. D.E. is effective against aphids, caterpillars (including cutworms), fly maggots, grubs, mites, slugs, and the like. It does not harm earthworms.

When you buy D.E., make sure that it's designated for agricultural use, not for use in swimming pool filters. To apply, dust D.E. around the base of plants in the late evening, ideally after a light rain or after plants have been sprayed with a fine mist of water. Dust progressively upward from the ground, covering stems and leaves, especially the undersides of leaves. You can also spray it on plants. Put ¼ pound D.E. in a 5-gallon sprayer. Add 1 teaspoon of flax soap (available from paint supply stores) or insecticidal soap concentrate in a quart of warm water, then add more water, enough to make 5 gallons. Mix the solution well. Reapply after rain.

Biological Controls

The variety of beneficial insects, bacteria, and viruses that already reside in your yard will help protect your flowering plants from pest insects. Perhaps the best known of the biological controls are the predatory and parasitic insects that attack and destroy pests. There are also microscopic creatures—the viruses and bacteria—that are more than willing to enlist in your war against the troublesome insects in your flower garden. Two that are readily available for use against flower pests are Bt (*Bacillus thuringiensis*) and milky spore disease (*Bacillus popilliae*).

Bt (*Bacillus thuringiensis*)

Bt is a naturally occurring parasitic bacterium that attacks leaf-eating caterpillars. It invades their digestive systems and kills them within 24 hours. You can purchase commercially prepared Bt under a number of trade names, including Bactur, Biotrol, Dipel, and Thuricide. Bt is sold in both powder and liquid forms. The powder may be applied as a dust or diluted with water and sprayed on plants. The liquid is usually concentrated and should be diluted with water according to package instructions. The liquid Bt can only be stored for a year; in effect, you need to replace it each season. Stored in the container in a cool, dark place,

Continued ➡

powdered Bt will remain viable for three to five years.

Because Bt kills all caterpillars, it's important to make sure that you've got a problem before you apply it. Otherwise, you could kill the beautiful butterflies and lovely nocturnal moths that add such delight to the summer garden. Try to identify the moths and butterflies hovering over your flowers; most are colorful and harmless. Make sure you're not destroying the parsleyworm that tomorrow might be a gorgeous black swallowtail. If caterpillars are causing unsightly damage—say, if corn earworms are eating holes in your ageratum foliage or leaf tiers are rolling your forget-me-not leaves—try handpicking before resorting to Bt. If you're confronted by a major infestation or have too many plants to handpick, Bt is an effective control.

The timing of Bt applications is critical because it must be eaten by the caterpillars to be effective. Generally, caterpillars are most active in the spring and late summer. Observe your plants closely during these times, and as soon as you see destructive caterpillars beginning to feed, spray or dust plants with Bt. Thoroughly cover all parts of the plant leaves, especially the undersides. When using the powdered form of Bt, wet plants before you dust them. Dusting the undersurfaces as well as the top surfaces of leaves keeps Bt active longer because the bacteria survive longer out of direct sunlight. Reapply the dust after each rain.

To make a foliar spray from powdered Bt, follow the directions on the container. Spray infested plants every 10 to 14 days until the pest is under control. To help the diluted powder adhere to plant leaves, add 1 tablespoon of fish emulsion to each gallon of spray. A little commercial insecticidal soap or light horticultural oil also works as an adherent. The liquid concentrate formulation of Bt adheres well to plants.

Keep in mind that Bt breaks down in sunlight. The powdered form remains viable for only seven days after application, and the liquid spray form for just 24 hours. Apply Bt each year as the pest caterpillars emerge.

Milky Spore Disease (*Bacillus popilliae*)
Like Bt, milky spore disease is a bacterial disease. It is applied to lawns to control beetle grubs—specifically, the white grubs of the Japanese beetle, a major pest of roses and other flowers. Milky spore takes 2 to 3 years to provide complete control of grubs, but it continues to be effective for up to 20 years, so that a single application provides long-term control. It is sold as a dust, in granular from, or as a wettable powder under the trade names Doom, Grub Attack, and Japidemic. Apply in spring or fall, when grubs are most active. Because beetles can emerge from surrounding lawns and migrate to your flowers, you'll get best control if your neighbors apply milky spore to their lawns when you treat yours. Unused milky spore remains viable for several years.

THE LAST RESORT—BOTANICAL POISONS
In spite of every precaution, sometimes pest insects overwhelm a flower bed. In these cases, the traps, sprays, and other methods discussed above can't control the situation fast enough and prized flowers are threatened. Under these rare circumstances, it may be necessary to resort to the last line of defense—the botanical poisons. These products include pyrethrum, rotenone, ryania, and sabadilla. Although these poisons have been extracted from various plants and are, therefore, natural substances, they are deadly to all insects. They'll kill off the pest insects that infest your plants, but they will also kill nearby beneficial insects, including honeybees. These products require careful handling for user safety, as well. Use them as a last resort in situations where there is no alternative. Because these products do break down quickly, they do not pose a significant threat to the environment.

Minimize the impact of botanical poisons by using them carefully. If a botanical poison is necessary while honeybees are pollinating, use pyrethrum rather than rotenone, and spray at dusk, when bees are least active. Even though it's more toxic to bees, pyrethrum breaks down more quickly—within 6 hours if the temperature is 55°F or higher. Foliar sprays of either pyrethrum or ryania are less toxic to bees than dusts. If a heavy dew is predicted, do not spray; the insecticide will not break down before the bees begin feeding in the morning.

Pyrethrum
Made from the crushed dried flowers of the painted or pyrethrum daisy (*Chrysanthemum cinerariifolium*), pyrethrum paralyzes many insects on contact. It acts quickly, passing directly through the skin of the insect and disrupting its nerve centers. The insect becomes disoriented and stunned. However, if an insect receives less than a lethal dose, it will revive completely. Pyrethrum residues do not persist in the environment, and their impact on pests lasts only 6 hours. It must contact the insect directly to be effective. Usually, two applications to the threatened plant, three to four days apart, will successfully control a pest problem. Apply pyrethrum in the evening to avoid killing bees, and don't use it near streams or ponds—it's toxic to fish.

Do not confuse this botanical insecticide with synthetic pyrethrins, like allethrin, or with the synthetic pyrethroids, which are altogether more complex and persistent types of chemicals and have a much more devastating effect on beneficial insects and the environment.

Pyrethrum plus Alcohol
We've already seen that alcohol boosts the effectiveness of insecticidal soaps; it can also make pyrethrum more effective. Again, it penetrates an insect's waxy protective coating, allowing the pyrethrum to paralyze and kill the pest more quickly. To make this solution, mix 2 parts alcohol with 1 part water, then add the pyrethrum in the concentration called for on the bottle. Do not get this mixture on your skin. If you do, wash immediately with soap and water.

Pyrethrum Blends
In crisis situations, when the life of an important plant is seriously threatened by insect infestation and no other control has worked, you can raise the ante even higher. Potent blends of poisons are available that combine pyrethrum with rotenone, ryania, or both. In a typical blend, the pyrethrum serves as the immediate knockdown agent, while the rotenone or the ryania kills insects over a longer period. Apply these blends at dusk, after honeybees have returned to the hive.

Timed-Release Pyrethrum
For longer term effectiveness, purchase pyrethrum that has been encapsulated so that it functions as a time-released insecticide when sprayed onto plants. It adheres to the leaves of plants and remains potent for up to a week.

Rotenone
Rotenone is refined from the roots of several tropical plants, including derris, cube barbasco, and timbo. Rotenone is a stomach poison. When used properly, it doesn't harm humans, wildlife (except fish), or pets, but it is a very powerful insecticide and should be used with respect. It will kill beneficial insects, including ladybugs and honeybees, as well as pests. You can apply rotenone as a dust; however, less is needed if you dilute it with water and spray it on plants. Use it only at dusk, after the bees have returned to the hive. A 1 percent solution will take care of most insects. If you are dealing with Japanese beetles or weevils, or if the 1 percent solution doesn't seem to be effective, increase the concentration to 5 percent. Rotenone remains potent for two to three days. Spraying once every three days, making two or three applications, should control most troublesome insect pests. Because it is very toxic to fish, do not spray it around bodies of water.

Sabadilla
The seeds of a lily from South America and the Caribbean are the source of sabadilla. One of the safer botanical poisons, it has little effect on mammals, but it is toxic to bees. It is available only as a dust. Wet plants before applying for better coverage. Apply it weekly on the undersides of the leaves of infested plants until the target pests are under control. A contact poison, it controls such pests as aphids, blister beetles, squash bugs, stink bugs, and caterpillars. Sabadilla isn't easy to find, but it is available through mail-order catalogs. One brand name is Red Devil. Unlike most pest controls, sabadilla actually becomes more effective in storage.

INSECT PREDATORS AND PARASITES
As mentioned earlier in this chapter, many species of resident beneficial insects devour thousands of insects each day. Learn to recognize these "good" insects and make them welcome in your landscape.

Because many beneficial insects emerge later in the season than pest insects do, gardeners may be more aware of pest problems early in the season than they are later. When the beneficials arrive, they must have a steady food supply, so resist the temptation to eradicate all insect pests immediately. Beneficial predatory insects will stay in your yard and police it only if there is something for them to eat. Your goal should be to maintain a balance of "good" and "bad" insects, so use pesticides sparingly early in the season before beneficials come on the scene.

Create the Best Environment
While you can buy beneficial insects and introduce them into your garden, it is far cheaper and probably more effective to simply encourage the beneficial species native to your area. Create the kind of environment they like. The more diverse the plantings in and around your yard and garden, the more attractive it will be to a wide variety of helpful insects. The more permanent plantings you have around the yard—perennial beds, woodland gardens, groupings of shrubs—the more stable the habitat you offer for beneficials to reside in year after year. Some homeowners go so far as to set aside a special nursery, or insectary patch, where weeds, brambles, and wildflowers are encouraged to thrive, providing a haven for "good" bugs. (A wildflower meadow would provide the same environment) These special plantings are most effective within 25 to 50 feet of the plants you are trying to protect, but they provide some protection up to 150 feet away. Hedgerows, windbreaks, and wooded patches also serve as nurseries for beneficials.

As for specific plants, trichogramma wasps find food and winter shelter on buckwheat, dill,

Continued →

mustard, and tansy. Parasitic wasps and flies are especially fond of black-eyed Susans, daisies, goldenrod, and related flowers. General favorites include Queen Anne's lace and other members of the parsley or carrot family (Umbelliferae)—herbs like angelica, anise, caraway, chervil, dill, lovage, and parsley—plus flowers such as asters, bachelor's buttons, milkweed, and yarrow. Some evergreens provide a haven for all sorts of helpful insects. Ample supplies of nectar and pollen provide food for predators when pest populations are low and for many beneficial adult parasites.

Clyde Robin Seed Company offers a wildflower mixture, Border Patrol, which is specially designed to attract and support beneficial insects. This mix produces an attractive wildflower garden with a secret agenda of supporting a beneficial insect population in your landscape. It contains seeds of angelica, baby-blue-eyes, bishop's flower, black-eyed Susan, candytuft, evening primrose, nasturtium, strawflower, wild buckwheat, and yarrow. Border Patrol is also available through Gardener's Supply.

Entomologist Linda Gilkeson has observed in her research that water is as important to maintaining a beneficial insect population as food and shelter. Consider placing two birdbaths in the yard—one for insect-eating songbirds, the other for beneficial insects. To make a birdbath attractive to insects, stack several piles of small stones in it to allow the insects to drink water without the danger of drowning. Place this bath in among the flowers where birds are less likely to land. You don't want them eating the beneficial insects you are trying to attract. Put the other birdbath out in the open. Birds prefer to land in open areas so they can see cats or dogs approaching. Don't forget a dish of water for your other garden ally, the toad. A sunken dish, perhaps shaded by a low shelter of rocks and/or boards, will keep this companionable, long-lived amphibian eating pests in your garden throughout the season.

Beneficial Insects and Nematodes Available Commercially

If you don't want to plant a wildflower patch or set up a birdbath to attract beneficials, you can still purchase beneficial insects and release them in your backyard. While it is not quite as simple as it sounds, this is an effective alternative when time or space limits your ability to attract naturally occurring beneficial insects. It is important to follow directions carefully, lest your newly purchased insects promptly fly away. Make the effort to determine the right time to release these pest fighters and follow the technique correctly so commercial beneficial insects will settle down in your garden.

Timing is critical. Introduce predatory and parasitic insects before pests get out of hand, but not prematurely. There must be sufficient numbers of pests to keep the beneficials busy and well fed. Unless they find insects to eat and the right plants to shelter them, beneficials will go elsewhere. Consider the type of environment needed by the beneficials you plan to purchase. Alter your backyard habitat to make sure that water is available and to provide the types of flowers mentioned above. Following are descriptions of the various predators and parasites that might be able to help you control the insect pests in your flower garden, along with information on how to introduce them into your backyard and keep them there.

Beneficial Nematodes

Not all nematodes are plant parasites. Certain species will help you control pests. These soil-dwelling, microscopic worms burrow inside pest grubs, soil-dwelling caterpillars (like cutworms),

and maggots. They release bacteria, which usually kill the host insect within 48 hours. The nematodes then feed and reproduce within the dead insect.

Beneficial nematodes (the best known is *Neoaplectana carpocapsae*) attack black vine weevils, chinch bugs, cutworms, fall armyworms, fire ants, fungus gnats, Japanese beetle grubs, mole crickets, pine weevils, root maggots, rose chafers, sod webworms, strawberry weevils, white grubs, wireworms, and the larvae of cucumber beetles, flea beetles, gypsy moths, and squash vine borers. They will not harm beneficial insects or earthworms.

Beneficial nematodes are sold in packages of 1,000,000 and up. (Ten million—the amount in a box of BioSafe, one trade name for the nematodes—will treat up to 225 square feet.) They look like powder and can be stored in your refrigerator from two to six months. Mix them with water and use a sprayer or watering can to introduce them into the soil. Apply as soon as plants are up. An application of 50,000 nematodes per plant, for example, will control iris borers. To treat container-grown plants, apply roughly 5,000 nematodes to each gallon of soil. Water the nematodes into the soil around the base of your plants in the early spring. You should see effects within five days, but allow two months for maximum control.

Nematodes will overwinter in the soil as far north as Minnesota, but their survival rate is not high enough to provide effective insect control the following season, so reapply each year. Only the infective juvenile stage of the nematode is functional as an insect control.

Green Lacewing Larvae

Of all the beneficial insects you can buy through the mail, green lacewings (Chrysopa spp.) are probably the most effective all-purpose controls. Various species occur naturally throughout North America, but all have a slender body and long, delicate, transparent green wings. They are ½ to ¾ inch long and lay their tiny white eggs on threadlike stalks on the undersides of leaves. The adults eat pollen, nectar, and honeydew. It's the larvae, known for their voraciousness as aphid lions, that feed on pest insects. They are alligator-shaped, yellowish gray with brown marks and tufts of long hair, and they grow to about 3/8 inch long. Their most distinctive feature is a pair of long, thin jaws, which curve together like ice tongs. Three or four generations are produced each year. Lacewings pass the winter in the pupal stage in cocoons.

The insects lacewing larvae attack include aphids, leafhopper nymphs, mealybugs, mites, scale, whiteflies, and the eggs of caterpillars, mites, thrips, and other small pests. Ravenous little creatures, they can eat up to 60 aphids an hour. By boosting the natural lacewing population in your flower beds in the early summer, you can get a jump on these insect pests. Lacewings cannot bear the cold, so wait until the average air temperature is at least 70°F.

You can purchase lacewings in egg or larval form, although eggs are trickier to handle. Approximately 5,000 lacewing larvae will cover an area of about 2,500 square feet. They like to eat each other, so release them as soon as you receive them by placing them in different areas of the yard. Unlike other beneficial predators, lacewing larvae tend to stay in the area where they're released. But because their effective period is short—they become adults in one to three weeks—your best bet for control is to make three releases, one every five to seven days.

If you've ordered eggs, don't be surprised to find some larvae in the container; the eggs may have hatched in shipment. The eggs must be lodged gently in leaf and stem crevices, in spaces between petals, or in flower centers.

To encourage continued residence of newly introduced lacewings, place Wheast around the yard and garden. This is a sweetened dairy product sold as food for beneficial insects. Lacewing adults will also eat a honeydew-like mixture made from 1 part sugar and 1 part brewer's yeast in water and such commercially available versions as Bug Chow and BugPro, which should be mixed with enough water to give a molasses-like consistency. Put drops of this mixture on plants that are vulnerable to the pests you want lacewings to control. And don't forget to include nectar-rich flowers like oleander, Queen Anne's lace, and yarrow in your flower beds-adult lacewings will feel right at home.

Ladybugs

Ladybugs (*Hippodamia convergens*) are the beneficial insects that first come to mind for most of us. We learned in childhood that these rather endearing little orange-colored beetles with black spots are welcome in the garden. The reason is that both the larvae and the adults eat small insects. They can eat up to 40 aphids an hour—one adult may consume 5,000 aphids—and will also make meals of chinch bugs, mealybugs, scale, spider mites, thrips, whiteflies, and other soft-bodied pests, as well as various small larvae and insect eggs.

Ladybugs reverse their coloring from larval to adult stage. The ¼-inch-long beetles are orange to red with black spots, and the larvae are black with orange spots. The larvae are about ½ inch long and are usually covered with spines. The cylindrical eggs are yellow-orange. There is only one generation each year. In the East and Midwest, ladybugs overwinter in weedy areas or garden trash; in the West, they migrate to the mountains each fall.

Estimates differ, but plan on releasing about one ladybug per square foot—2 to 3 gallons of them per acre. Released too early in the season when their food supply is low, ladybugs will be forced to seek food in other yards. If you're not sure whether the pest population in your yard will support all the ladybugs you've bought, release only some of them and store the rest in the refrigerator, where they'll survive for up to three weeks. Release them late in the evening when the air has cooled off and dew has

Beneficial Insects and the Plants That Attract Them

To attract beneficial insects to your garden and encourage them to stay, grow the plants they prefer.

Lacewings. Members of the carrot family, oleander, and wild lettuce.

Ladybugs. Alfalfa, angelica, coffeeberry, evergreen euonymus, goldenrod, Mexican tea, morning-glory, oleander, and yarrow. Ladybugs also like ragweed, but you probably don't want to plant this hayfever source in your garden!

Parasitic wasps. Members of the carrot family, members of the daisy family, buckwheat, buttercup, goldenrod, oleander, strawberries, and white clover.

Syrphid flies and hover flies. Members of the daisy family.

Continued ➡

settled on the grass. If the ground is dry, lightly water the yard and garden. When releasing ladybugs, gently place handfuls of beetles at the base of your pest-ridden plants. Cover them immediately with damp straw or hay. They will soon climb the plant and begin to hunt for food. Walk 20 to 30 paces and release another handful near another group of infested plants. Handle ladybugs gently so as not to excite them into flight. Under normal conditions, they will mate within 48 hours and produce aphid-eating offspring in two weeks.

To encourage ladybugs to stay in your yard, grow pollen- and nectar-producing plants such as alfalfa, angelica, coffeeberry, evergreen euonymus, goldenrod, Mexican tea, morning-glory, oleander, and yarrow. Commercially available food attractants such as Bug Chow and BugPro, which should be mixed with water until molasses-like, then placed in droplets on the plants, also help newly released adults settle down.

Parasitic Wasps

These tiny insects, though a danger to insect pests, do not sting gardeners. They willingly attack a variety of aphids and caterpillars. A few different types are available commercially through mail-order catalogs.

The adults of each of these parasites feed on nectar, which they obtain from weeds and wild-flowers, particularly those in the daisy and carrot families. By planting some of these in your yard, you will encourage beneficial wasps to stay. Perhaps the best plant for all wasps is fennel. It seems to attract a large number of beneficial insects all season long.

Braconid Wasps

These wasps lay their eggs in the bodies of aphids, cucumber beetle grubs, cutworms, gypsy moths, hornworms, tent caterpillars, and various other larvae. The larvae hatch and grow inside their hosts, weakening and often killing them. Then they pupate on the backs of the hosts. These pupae are the "wasp eggs" so often seen on the backs of parasitized tomato hornworms.

Braconid wasps are sold commercially as eggs. The adults, which can be black, red, or yellow, are just $^1/_{16}$ to $^5/_8$ inch long. They prefer warm, humid, conditions with temperatures above 59°F.

Chalcid Wasps

Chalcid wasps seek out aphids, asparagus beetles, leafhoppers, scale, whiteflies, and various caterpillars and other beetles. They lay their eggs in or on the pest. The larvae grow inside the pest, weakening and eventually killing it. Some adults also feed directly on the host. The adult chalcid is just $^1/_{16}$ to $^3/_8$ inch long, so you'll probably not see them unless you take pains to do so. Chalcid wasps are found throughout North America. Like the braconid wasps, chalcids prefer warm, humid conditions. One chalcid wasp of interest to flower gardeners, the trichogramma wasp (see below), is available commercially.

Ichneumon Wasps

Species of ichneumon wasp range in size from $^1/_8$ to 3 inches long and in color from yellow to brown and black. Adults lay eggs in borers, cutworms, eastern tent caterpillars, fall webworms, sawflies, and other larvae. Ichneumon wasps are not commercially available, but are found naturally throughout North America.

Trichogramma Wasps

The tiny ($^1/_{45}$-inch-long) trichogramma wasps kill the eggs of insect pests. The female wasp lays her eggs in the pest egg, and when the trichogramma

Beneficial Insects Available Commercially

Beneficial nematodes
Green lacewing larvae
Ladybugs
Parasitic wasps
   Braconid wasps
   Chalcid wasps
   Ichneumon wasps
   Trichogramma wasps
Praying mantids
Predatory mites

egg hatches into a larva, it consumes its host. Among the 200 species of pest that trichogramma wasps parasitize are aphids, armyworms, cabbageworms, cutworms, fall webworms, gypsy moths, hornworms, leafrollers, loopers, mealybugs, scale, whiteflies, and various beetle larvae.

The release of trichogramma wasps is more effective when coupled with a spray of Bt (*Bacillus thuringiensis*) on infested plant leaves (see page 000); a sequence of three smaller releases is more effective than one large release. Make the three releases at two-week intervals so the wasps can parasitize host eggs as they're laid. The most effective species for protection of ornamentals is *Trichogramma minutum*, while the best species for general garden use is *T. pretiosum*. Trichogrammas are widely available commercially. Shipped in the egg, 20,000 will control host species on ½ acre.

Praying Mantids

These fearsome-looking creatures, the Darth Vaders of the insect world, are known for their voracious appetites for insects, including flies, mosquitoes, and moths. Various species are found throughout North America. They may be green or brownish and are about 2 inches long. They have papery wings and enlarged front legs adapted for grasping. Mantids overwinter in the egg stage. They deposit their eggs on twigs and grass stems in an egg case that looks like it was made from papier-mâché. Each case contains 200 or more eggs. One generation of mantids occurs each year.

When you buy praying mantis egg cases, you may get more than you bargained for. Unlike most of the other beneficials, the mantids prey on all insects, including each other. Each egg case may produce a couple of hundred hungry little mantids, but they will probably eat each other before they start working on your pest problem. The few that do survive will establish territories and drive off others of their kind. Regardless of how many egg cases you set out, by midsummer there will be only two or three mantids in a 20-by-40-foot flower garden. At this rate, those mantids will have cost you a couple of dollars each, and it is likely that you already have some in your backyard anyway.

If this hasn't discouraged you, and you still want to purchase mantids, try about three egg cases for 5,000 square feet of garden. To increase the young mantids' survival rate, put the egg cases in a screen-covered box. Check them every day after the trees begin to leaf out. Provide them with water, and, after two days, separate the newborns before they start eyeing one another. Scatter them around the garden. They will still drive off many of their brothers and sisters, but coverage should be fairly good, and you may even have a generation that will reproduce and help provide control next year.

Predatory Mites

Predatory mites will attack other mites, including spider mites and greenhouse mites. One release per season should provide continued control, since some mites will remain in the garden after the pest outbreak is stopped. You'll only need two predatory mites for each square foot or plant less than 2 feet tall; for larger plants, release two per large stem or branch. Mites flourish in warm weather with temperatures averaging between 68° and 86°F. If daytime temperatures are too low, their reproductive rate slows.

ANIMAL PREDATORS

In addition to naturally occurring spiders and beneficial insects like assassin bugs, ground beetles, robber flies, rove beetles, soldier beetles, and others that will police your yard for pests, you can count on help from larger beneficial creatures. Among these allies are bats, toads, songbirds, and lizards, all of which will eagerly gobble up grubs or binge on beetles. Of course, some of these animals can make pests of themselves, as well. For instance, skunks are voracious eaters of grubs and larvae, but they may inadvertently tear up your seedlings while looking for them. A few seasons of experience will indicate which ones are most valuable for your pest control problems and which ones need to be denied entry.

This inventory of pest-eating insects and animals that reside in a balanced, active backyard ecosystem provides a persuasive argument against the use of garden chemicals that might harm these friends of the garden. If you attract and encourage beneficial insects and predatory animals, you will find that most of your insect problems will be reduced considerably. The process may take a few years, but the results will be worth the effort. Once you have achieved a flower garden where a variety of plants, insects, and animals are in balance, no pest problem should get out of control. Remember, too, that when you have a system in which all the elements are balancing and controlling each other, you'll have less work to do.

Bats

Bats suffer from bad press. Stories of vampires, bites in the neck, and, lately, rabies obscure the ways in which bats offer very real benefits to the gardener. These unobtrusive mammals do not bother humans unless they are cornered or provoked. They venture out in the early evenings to make a meal of insects. A single bat can eat over 1,000 mosquitoes a night. And they produce bat guano, an excellent source of organic nitrogen. So, if you have a multitude of night-flying pests, you'd be better off putting up bat houses (now readily available from suppliers that offer a wide selection of birdhouses and feeders) than putting out the garlic.

Birds

Songbirds are seldom credited for all their help in controlling flower garden pests. Although many adult songbirds eat seeds, they also harvest tens of thousands of insects during the weeks when they raise their young. Baby birds cannot digest seeds and must be fed fresh insects. Increase your yard's bird population and you'll reduce the pest population.

Feeding birds during the winter months contributes significantly to maintaining a good-size bird population in your area. To encourage them to stay around over the summer, continue supplemental feeding at the feeder. Put out less food, less often. This will encourage them to stay in your yard without making them entirely dependent on the feeder.

Continued ➜

Provide an inviting backyard habitat for birds. Landscape with plants that offer tasty seeds and berries. *Echinacea* and *Rudbeckia* are favorite seed producers, and roses that produce large hips are good for winter nourishment. In addition, provide trees and shrubs where birds can take shelter and hide from the neighborhood cats and dogs. A supply of water year-round is a necessity: Sometimes water is more important than food. Remember to put the birdbath or water dish in the open where birds can see cats and dogs coming. Consider providing birdhouses and nesting platforms; then you'll be sure to have many parent birds collecting insects for their young.

Some of the best pest patrollers are house wrens, northern (formerly Baltimore) orioles, and chickadees, but many other birds will help you control insect pests. Even the lowly starling and the pugnacious English sparrow devour literally thousands of pest insects or insect larvae each season.

Frogs and Toads

Frogs and toads are princes when it comes to pest control. In a toad's eight-month active season, it can eat 24,000 insects—think of its 30-year lifetime average! Unfortunately, they don't discriminate between pests and beneficial insects. They'll happily gobble up large numbers of cutworms or potato beetles, but they're just as likely to eat helpful spiders or ladybugs. Frogs are particularly fond of sow bugs, and toads will devour ants, aphids, caterpillars, cutworms, grasshoppers, slugs, spiders, and squash bugs, but in general, what they eat depends on what happens to be in your yard. Unless you have a pond or water garden, you shouldn't attempt to keep frogs, but a half-buried water dish and a few hiding places will spell home to a toad. You can encourage toads to stay by leaving the door or driveway light on at night—they'll relish all those moths and beetles on the screen door.

Lizards

If you live in the southern or western states, the lizards you see lolling about on some sunny rock or warm patch of ground will help keep the insect population down. Lizards prefer stony, open terrain. Vertical surfaces like trees, stone walls, fences, and walls of abandoned buildings are favorite haunts, though anoles (our American chameleons) seem to like hedges, and beautiful, blue-lined skinks enjoy sunning on patios and chimneys. Lizards are harmless, amusing reptiles that can provide hours of leisurely observation as you go about your garden chores or indulge in a bit of sunning yourself. They should be encouraged to call your yard their home.

Skunks

Skunks eat a wide variety of food, including chicken eggs, mice, snakes, and yellow jackets, but their favorite fare is plant-eating insects and larvae lurking in flower beds and lawns. They are particularly good at rooting out grubs and cutworms. Of course, they also love fruit, but they usually gather pieces that have fallen to the ground. So, if you see a skunk waddling across the lawn, don't chase it, especially since it will probably spray you with a fragrance you won't enjoy wearing.

Snakes

While certain parts of the country are plagued by genuinely dangerous snake species, most snakes that find their way into your backyard only represent a threat to garden pests. Garter snakes and the like prey on rodents and snap up bugs and beetles. Try to overcome any antipathy you may harbor toward these creatures and permit them to hunt in and around your flower beds. They will return the

courtesy by consuming pest insects for you and curbing the population explosion of bulb-eating voles and mice.

Preventing Pest Damage

Of course, keeping insects pests away from your plants means even less work for you. You can discourage pests by following good gardening practices. Take a few precautionary steps before and after the growing season to foster plant vigor, because healthy plants are less susceptible to attack. Just a little more effort up front will save hours of labor later on.

Yard and Garden Cleanup

Perhaps the most important step you can take to maintain a pest-free and disease-free garden is to keep the yard and garden neat and clean. Fallen, decaying leaves and twigs shelter slugs, snails, and other pests that hide out during the day. Rotting weeds and plants, as well as soggy leaves and twigs, harbor pest insects and disease spores over the winter. Keeping your yard free of clutter and plant debris is essential to keeping down populations of insect pests next season.

Fall Cleanup

Clean up thoroughly in the fall. When all leaves and twigs have dropped from the shrubs and trees, and annuals and perennials have faded and died, collect all this organic material and compost it. However, refuse from diseased plants, as well as organic mulch that has been used during the growing season and may harbor disease, should be trashed. Get down to bare soil in all your gardens where annuals have been, around perennials, and under all shrubs.

Once your garden soil is cleared, cultivate it by raking thoroughly, if possible. In perennial beds and under shrubs, cultivate only 1 or 2 inches to avoid damaging the shallow root systems. This fall cultivation buries those insects that normally overwinter on the surface of the soil and brings to the surface those that prefer to snuggle a little deeper in the earth. The former suffocate; the latter will be eaten by birds.

This is also a good time to improve soil texture by incorporating humus-rich materials like shredded leaves and compost, and to add amendments like lime, greensand, or fresh manure that need a season to break down. By spring, the nutrients will be available to your plants.

About two to three weeks after that first deep cultivation, shallowly rake cleared gardens and bare areas again. This exposes more larvae to birds and other predators. Then leave the soil bare until it freezes hard.

Once the soil has frozen hard, lay a 2- to 6-inch layer of organic mulch over all the bare soil in the garden and around the shrubs. In those areas of the South where there is no freeze, leave the soil bare for at least a month before mulching it. Leaves chopped in a shredder, or shredded by running the lawn mower back and forth over them, are ideal mulching material. In the fall, leaves are plentiful and make excellent composting material next spring when they are removed before planting.

Spring Cleanup

After a major fall cleanup, spring preparation is simple. Remove the winter mulch from any areas where spring bulbs and early-blooming perennials have been planted. Leave the mulch around the shrubs and supplement it later in the season.

Barriers

Barriers are effective in preventing pest infestations in flower beds. There are a variety of barriers that will

discourage pests from attacking ornamental plants by denying them access throughout the season.

Mulch

Among its other benefits, mulch can block some insect pests from reaching your plants, especially those that overwinter just under the surface of the soil. At the very least, it controls weeds, which may harbor pests. Black plastic mulch or any of the new agricultural fabric (geotextile) mulches laid on bare soil will prevent many larvae from emerging. Agricultural or landscape fabric mulch effectively prevents soil-dwelling insects like weevils from climbing up from the soil and attacking the foliage of flowering plants. Cut a circle of material wide enough so that it extends half again wider than the width of the plant all the way around. Fit the fabric mulch snugly around the stem of the plant and fasten it firmly to the soil. This makes a barrier, preventing the weevils from emerging from the soil.

Flexible Copper Sheeting

If your flowers are regularly raided by slugs and snails, bar their path, with Snail-Barr, a 3-inch-wide band of thin, flexible copper sheeting. You can wrap it around the outside edge of a window box or planter, or around the lip of a barrel or flower pot. If you grow flowers in raised beds that are edged with boards or railroad ties, attach Snail-Barr around the outside. Slugs and snails get an electric shock when their slimy bodies encounter the copper, and they don't stay around to prolong the encounter.

Diatomaceous Earth

The needle-sharp crystals of diatomaceous earth act as an effective barrier to soft-bodied insects, like slugs and snails.

Resistant Plant Varieties

One of the best ways to prevent pest problems is to grow plants that simply aren't bothered by insects. Over the years, researchers have developed flower cultivars that are resistant to specific insect pests. There aren't yet as many insect-resistant ornamentals as there are vegetables, but researchers are breeding new insect- and disease-resistant flowers every season. Keep your eye on the market for new developments, and check seed catalogs for the resistant cultivars that will grow best in your area.

Learn Insect Emergence Times

Learn when a specific pest insect is likely to appear in your garden. Timing is crucial. If you are prepared at the right time with the right control, you can stop a problem before it has begun. Each species of insect has its own fairly predictable pattern of birth, feeding, maturity, reproduction, wintering, and death. If you can learn these patterns and how they coincide with your yard and garden calendar, you'll be able to predict when problems might arise. To facilitate preventive measures, it's especially important to know when overwintering pests are due to emerge in your flower garden.

The emergence times of insects vary from region to region, even neighborhood to neighborhood. Air temperature, moisture, and the availability of food all affect an insect's schedule. Check with your cooperative extension agent for a rough idea of when the problem insect typically appears, then record these times. More important, observe your garden and mark down the date when you begin to see each pest arrive. To make these emergence times easier to remember, connect them with some other garden-related event, such as the budding or blooming of lilacs in the spring, or jot them down in a garden diary.

Continued ➡

Bad Bugs

Distinguishing bad bugs from the good guys can be difficult, especially since bad bugs don't carry tiny flags with the word "pest" written on them. But while lots of insects may reside in your garden, most of them aren't harmful. That's why you should use the following guide to help you identify a suspected pest before you decide to do it in.

Light Snacking Is OK

Even when you find pests in your garden, keep in mind that most of their snacking doesn't particularly endanger your vegetables, flowers, or landscape plantings. As we mentioned back in Chapter 1, your plants can tolerate some damage. For example, holes in the leaves of a potato plant or an apple tree only affect the crop's yield if quite a bit of damage is done. For this type of pest, you might not need to do anything, or you may need to do something only in years with particularly heavy outbreaks. Many insect populations rise and fall over a period of years, so outbreaks over a few years may be followed by several years without damage.

PLANNING AHEAD

Although you'll find descriptions of more than 20 pests in the following list, don't be intimidated! They won't all reside in your garden. Only a few are a problem for any given plant or region of the country. Once you find out which pests are regular problems where you live, the best thing you can do is to plan ahead to prevent the problems next year. Preventing pest damage is easier and more effective than treating your plants or trying to control the pests after the damage occurs.

Aphids

Aphids are soft, pear-shaped, and very tiny ($1/16$ to $3/8$ inch long). Two short tubes project backward from the tip of their abdomen. Aphids have long antennae. Some types of aphids have wings, which are transparent, longer than their body, and held like a roof over their back. Aphids may be green, pink, yellowish, black, or powdery gray. Nymphs resemble adults but are smaller and wingless.

WHERE THEY LIVE

You'll find aphids throughout North America.

THEIR LIFE CYCLE

Aphids reproduce like there's no tomorrow. Female aphids can reproduce without mating, giving birth continuously to live nymphs. Nymphs mature in 1 to 2 weeks and start producing offspring themselves.

When days become shorter in the fall, both males and females are born. They mate, and then females lay eggs on stems or in bark crevices. The eggs overwinter and hatch the following spring. In very mild climates and in greenhouses, aphids may reproduce year-round.

PLANTS THEY ATTACK

Aphids feed on most fruit and vegetable plants, flowers, ornamentals, and shade trees.

WHY THEY'RE A PROBLEM

Both adults and nymphs suck plant sap, which usually causes distorted leaves, buds, branch tips, and flowers. Severely infested leaves and flowers may drop. As they feed, aphids excrete a sweet, sticky honeydew onto the leaves below. This allows a sooty mold to grow, which, in addition to being ugly to look at, blocks light from leaves. Also, some aphids spread viruses as they feed.

ORGANIC DAMAGE CONTROL

- Drench plants with strong sprays of water from a garden hose to kill aphids. (A hard, driving rainstorm will have the same effect.)
- Keep your plants as healthy as possible, and spray dormant oil to control overwintering eggs on fruit trees.
- Attract predators by planting pollen and nectar plants such as yarrow and sweet alyssum.
- Control ants that guard aphid colonies in trees from predators by placing sticky bands around the trunks.
- Spray aphids with insecticidal soap, summer oil (on tolerant plants), and homemade garlic sprays.

Black Vine Weevils

Adult weevils are oval, brownish gray or black, and $1/3$ inch long. They have a pattern of small yellow patches on their backs. Their larvae are fat, white grubs that are up to $1/2$ inch long with yellowish brown heads.

WHERE THEY LIVE

You'll find black vine weevils in the northeastern United States, as well as from California to the Pacific Northwest.

THEIR LIFE CYCLE

For weevils, reproducing is solely women's work, as there are only female weevils—no males. The adults emerge from the soil in June and feed for several weeks before laying eggs in the soil around host plants.

The eggs hatch in about 10 days and the larvae immediately burrow into the roots to feed for the rest of the season. They stay in the soil over the winter, then resume feeding on roots the following spring. The larvae pupate in early spring, completing the cycle.

PLANTS THEY ATTACK

Black vine weevils most commonly attack blackberry, blueberry, cranberry, and strawberry plants, as well as some ornamentals, particularly azaleas, camellias, rhododendrons, wisterias, and yews.

WHY THEY'RE A PROBLEM

Weevils chew along leaf edges, leaving small, scalloped bite marks. Adults rarely cause serious damage, but larvae can be very damaging because they feed on plant roots. Their feeding stunts plant growth and may indirectly kill plants by allowing disease organisms to enter injured roots.

ORGANIC DAMAGE CONTROL

- At night, when they feed, knock weevils off plants onto a sheet on the ground and destroy them. (If you don't want to squish them, you can just drop them in a bucket of soapy water and drown them.)
- Lay boards under plants and check for weevils hiding under them during the day.
- Plant resistant rhododendron and azalea varieties that have rolled leaf edges, which prevent weevils from grasping an edge to feed.
- Intercept weevils as they climb shrubs by tying a 6-inch-high band of plastic wrap painted with sticky trap glue around the trunk.
- Add bird-friendly shrubs, birdbaths, and feeders to your landscape—birds and other predators find black vine weevils delicious.

Cabbage Loopers

Cabbage looper adults are mottled gray-brown moths with a silvery, V-shaped spot in the middle of each forewing. Their wingspan is $1\frac{1}{2}$ inches. Because they fly late in the evening, you rarely see them. Their larvae are green caterpillars with pairs of wavy, white or light yellow lines down their backs and one line along each side.

WHERE THEY LIVE

Cabbage loopers are found throughout North America.

THEIR LIFE CYCLE

Adult moths emerge in May from their overwintering cocoons to lay eggs. The eggs hatch in 3 or 4 days and the larvae feed for 2 to 3 weeks. They pupate for up to 2 weeks in thin silk cocoons attached to the stems or undersides of leaves. Three or four generations of cabbage loopers may appear in a year, depending on where you live.

PLANTS THEY ATTACK

As you might expect, cabbage loopers attack mainly cabbage and cabbage-family plants. They'll also feed on beets, celery, lettuce, peas, spinach, tomatoes, and flowers, including carnations and nasturtiums.

WHY THEY'RE A PROBLEM

Cabbage looper caterpillars damage plants by chewing large holes in leaves. If you have lots of them, they can ruin whole plants. Larvae are most damaging during the last few days of their development.

ORGANIC DAMAGE CONTROL

- Handpick caterpillars several times a week and spray *Bacillus thuringiensis* var. *kurstaki* (BTK) as well.
- Attract predatory and parasitic insects to the garden with pollen and nectar plants.
- If you live in the North, start your cabbage indoors and put the plants out in the garden very early to avoid peak populations.
- At the end of the season, bury spent cabbage plants to destroy cocoons before adults emerge in spring.
- Many native parasites and predators attack cabbage loopers. Invite these helpers into your garden by planting flowers for them to feed on when loopers are not prevalent. Beneficial insects prefer tiny flowers like those that make up the large, flat umbels of parsley, dill, fennel, and coriander. Alyssum and tansy are also known to attract beneficials.

Cabbage Maggots

Adult cabbage maggots are nondescript gray flies, $1/4$ inch long, with long legs. The white, tapering larvae (which you will probably see much more often than the adult flies) burrow into the roots of plants, where they cause serious damage.

WHERE THEY LIVE

Cabbage maggots are found throughout North America.

THEIR LIFE CYCLE

In warmer regions, adult flies begin emerging in late March. The females lay eggs in the soil beside the plant roots. After they hatch, the larvae feed on the fine roots, then tunnel into the taproots, feeding for 3 to 4 weeks. They pupate, and adults emerge in 2 to 3 weeks. In most areas, cabbage maggots produce two to four generations a year. The fall generation of pupae overwinters several inches deep in the soil.

Continued ➜

PLANTS THEY ATTACK

Cabbage maggots attack all cabbage-family plants.

WHY THEY'RE A PROBLEM

In the early stages of infestation, plants wilt in the midday heat. Young plants often die, either directly from maggot feeding or because the injured roots become diseased and rot. Older plants may survive but may produce only a small crop. Cabbage-family root crops, such as turnips and radishes, may be ruined. Maggots do the most damage early in the season when the weather is cool and moist. In hot, dry summers, most eggs from later generations never hatch.

ORGANIC DAMAGE CONTROL

- Avoid the most damaging early generation of flies by planting radishes very early.
- Cover seedlings and small plants, such as radishes and Chinese cabbage, with floating row covers, burying the edges under soil well.
- Set out transplants through slits in 6-inch squares of tar paper to prevent flies from laying eggs near stems, or wrap stems with paper 1 to 2 inches above and below the soil line before planting.
- Burn or destroy roots of cabbage-family plants as soon as you harvest the crop.
- Try repelling egg-laying flies by mounding wood ashes, hot pepper, or ginger powder around your plant stems.

Colorado Potato Beetles

Adults are yellowish orange, with 10 lengthwise black stripes on their wing covers and black spots on their middle section. They are 1/3 inch long. The larvae are dark orange, humpbacked grubs, ranging from 1/16 to 1/2 inch long. They have a row of black spots along each side. The beetles lay bright yellow eggs on end in upright clusters on the undersides of leaves.

WHERE THEY LIVE

Colorado potato beetles are found throughout most of North America.

THEIR LIFE CYCLE

In spring, the beetles emerge from the soil to feed on potato plants as soon as the first shoots are up. After mating, the females lay up to 1,000 eggs each during their several-month life span. The eggs hatch in 4 to 9 days, and the larvae feed for 2 to 3 weeks. They bury into the soil to pupate for another 2 to 3 weeks, and adults emerge in 5 to 10 days. These beetles may produce up to three generations a year. Adults and sometimes pupae overwinter several inches deep in the soil.

PLANTS THEY ATTACK

Colorado potato beetles are major pests of potatoes and, in some areas, damage tomatoes and eggplants, too. They may also attack related plants, such as petunias.

WHY THEY'RE A PROBLEM

Both adults and larvae chew on leaves and stems of potatoes and related plants. Young plants may die, while older plants can be severely defoliated, which can leave you without any spuds. A moderate amount of feeding, though, doesn't harm plants or reduce yields.

ORGANIC DAMAGE CONTROL

- Choose plant varieties that have some resistance to potato beetles.

- Mulch plants deeply with straw, and trap over-wintered beetles in plastic-lined trenches around the potato patch. (The beetles have an easy time crawling or falling into the trench, but they just slip on the plastic when they attempt to crawl back out.)
- Cover susceptible plants with floating row covers until midseason.
- To control larvae, spray *Bocillus thuringiensis* var. *san diego* (BTSD) as soon as eggs are present.
- In the fall, till the soil to kill overwintering beetles.

Corn Earworm/Tomato Fruitworm

Adults are large, yellowish tan moths with a wingspan of 1½ to 2 inches. The larvae are light yellow, green, pink, or brown caterpillars, 1 to 2 inches long, with white and dark stripes along their sides. Eggs are round and light green, with a ribbed pattern, and are laid singly on undersides of leaves or on corn silks.

WHERE THEY LIVE

This pest is found throughout North America.

THEIR LIFE CYCLE

Adult moths emerge in early spring in the south to lay eggs, which hatch in 2 to 10 days. Some moths migrate northward, flying long distances before laying eggs later in the season. Caterpillars feed for 2 to 4 weeks, then pupate in the soil. New moths emerge 10 to 25 days later. Pupae overwinter in the soil, although earworm pupae aren't hardy enough to survive the winter in the northern United States and Canada. Corn earworms produce up to four generations a year.

PLANTS THEY ATTACK

Corn, peppers, and tomatoes are the main plants that earworms/fruitworms attack, but the pests have also been reported on beans, cabbage, okra, peanuts, squash, and sunflowers.

WHY THEY'RE A PROBLEM

The caterpillars feed on fresh corn silks, entering the ear from the tip, then moving down the ear, eating kernels as they go. In tomatoes (which is why they're also called tomato fruitworms), the cater-pillars eat the flower buds, chew large holes in leaves, and burrow into ripe fruit. They also chew leaves of other plants.

ORGANIC DAMAGE CONTROL

- Plant corn varieties with tight husks to prevent larvae from entering.
- Attract native parasitic wasps, lacewings, and minute pirate bugs by interplanting with pollen and nectar plants.
- Avoid attracting moths to your garden by keeping nearby lights off at night.
- Inspect plants frequently and handpick caterpillars.
- Apply several drops of vegetable oil to the tip of each ear of corn 3 to 7 days after the silks first appear.

Cucumber Beetles

Spotted cucumber beetle adults are greenish yellow, about ¼ inch long, with 12 black spots on their wing covers. The larvae are ¾ inch long, slender, and white with reddish brown heads. Striped cucumber beetle adults are yellow, ¼ inch long, with black heads and three wide black stripes on their wing covers. Their larvae look the same as **spotted** cucumber beetle larvae.

WHERE THEY LIVE

Both types of cucumber beetles are found throughout most of North America.

THEIR LIFE CYCLE

Spotted cucumber beetles spend the winter under crop debris and clumps of grass, emerging in spring to lay eggs in the soil close to plants (particularly corn). When the eggs hatch, larvae feed in roots of plants for 2 to 4 weeks, then pupate, producing up to three generations a year. (These larvae are a real problem in southern regions, where they're known as corn rootworms.) Striped cucumber beetles overwinter in dense grass, emerging from April to early June. **Striped** cucumber beetles feed on weed pollen for 2 weeks, then lay their eggs. After the eggs hatch, the larvae burrow down to feed on roots for 2 to 6 weeks, after which they pupate. They produce up to four generations a year.

PLANTS THEY ATTACK

These pests eat corn, cucumbers, melons, pumpkins, and squash.

WHY THEY'RE A PROBLEM

Larvae tunnel into the base of stems and feed on roots, often killing young plants. Adult beetles eat holes in leaves and chew on fruit skin. Cucumber beetles are also thought to transmit bacterial wilt and mosaic viruses, which can cause more damage than the beetles' direct munching.

ORGANIC DAMAGE CONTROL

- Plant wilt- and mosaic-resistant cucumber, squash, and melon varieties to avoid the main damage from these beetles.
- As soon as the seedlings emerge, cover your plants with floating row covers and secure the sides by covering them with soil. When the plants begin to flower, lift the covers for a few hours each morning so bees can pollinate the plants.
- After harvest, pull out and destroy infested spent plants to eliminate overwintering sites.

Cutworms

Adult cutworms are large, brownish or gray moths with 1½-inch wingspans. The larvae (which do the damage) are fat, greasy gray or dull brown caterpillars with shiny heads.

WHERE THEY LIVE

You can find cutworms throughout North America.

THEIR LIFE CYCLE

Adult moths emerge from the overwintering pupae and lay their eggs on grass stems or in the soil from early May to early June. After the eggs hatch (in 5 to 7 days), the cutworms feed on grass and other plants for 3 to 5 weeks, then pupate into the soil. Moths emerge from late August to early September, producing the second generation of the year.

PLANTS THEY ATTACK

These pests attack most early vegetable and flower seedlings, shoots, and transplants.

WHY THEY'RE A PROBLEM

Cutworm caterpillars feed at night on young plants, usually cutting the stem at or just below the soil line so that the plant topples over. They may completely eat seedlings.

Continued ➡

Organic Damage Control

- Protect transplants by putting collars around the stems. You can cut empty paper-towel or toilet-paper rolls into sections to make collars, or use small empty tin cans with the ends removed. Press the collars about 1 inch into the soil.
- Dig around the base of damaged transplants in the morning and destroy hiding larvae.
- Avoid the main population of cutworms by planting later in the season.

European Corn Borers

Adult females are pale, yellowish brown moths with 1-inch wingspans. They have dark, zigzag patterns across the wings, male moths are smaller and darker. Larvae are gray or beige, about 1 inch long, with brown heads. They have small brown dots on each segment. Corn borer eggs are white to tan. You'll find them on undersides of leaves in masses of 15 to 20 overlapping eggs.

Where They Live

You'll find European corn borers throughout the Midwest to eastern North America.

Their Life Cycle

Moths generally emerge from dead cornstalks and plant stems (left from last year's garden) in June. They lay eggs from late June to mid-July. The eggs hatch in a week and the larvae feed for 3 to 4 weeks before spinning a delicate cocoon inside a stalk. The protected cocoons can survive over winter. There are several different strains of corn borers, and they differ in the number of generations a year (from one to three).

Plants They Attack

Corn is the major victim of the borers, and in some regions it is the only vegetable they attack. In other areas, borers may also damage beans, peppers, potatoes, and tomatoes.

Why They're a Problem

Young caterpillars feed on the first whorls of corn leaves, on corn tassels, and beneath the husks of ears. Older larvae burrow into cornstalks and also feed in tassels and ears. Boring weakens stalks, causing them to break easily.

Organic Damage Control

- Start by planting corn varieties with strong stalks and tight husks.
- If you have lots of European corn borers, remove the tassels from two-thirds of your corn plants before the pollen sheds. This eliminates many larvae in the tassels, while leaving enough tassels for pollination.
- Spray Bacillus thuringiensis var. kurstaki (BTK) twice, a week apart, on leaf undersides and into the tips of corn ears.
- European corn borers overwinter in cornstalks and plant debris, so clean up your corn patch in the fall. Shred and compost the stalks or dispose of them immediately after harvest.

Flea Beetles

Adult flea beetles are very tiny—just 1/10 inch long. They're black, brown, or bronze with enlarged hind legs. They jump like fleas when they're disturbed. The larvae live in the soil and are thin, white, legless grubs with brown heads.

Where They Life

Flea beetles are found throughout North America.

Their Life Cycle

Adults emerge from the soil in spring to feed and lay eggs on the roots of plants. They die out by early July. The eggs hatch in about a week, and the larvae feed for 2 to 3 weeks. They pupate in the soil, and the next generation of adults emerges in 2 to 3 weeks. These pests produce up to four generations a year before the final generation of adults settles down for overwintering.

Plants They Attack

Flea beetles attack most vegetables, particularly cabbage-family plants, potatoes, and spinach. They also feed on flowers and weeds.

Why They're a Problem

You can recognize flea beetle damage by the small, round holes the adults chew through leaves. These beetles are most damaging in early spring, when heavy infestations can actually kill seedlings. Larger plants usually survive and outgrow the damage, unless they were infected with a plant virus spread by the beetles. Larvae feed on plant roots.

Organic Damage Control

- Plant susceptible plants as late as possible to avoid the most damaging generation.
- Cover seedlings and potato shoots with floating row covers until adult beetles die off.
- Flea beetles prefer full sun, so interplant crops to shade susceptible plants.
- Lightly cultivate the soil around plants before and after planting to destroy any flea beetle eggs and larvae in the soil.
- Flea beetles like to hide in cool, weedy areas. Prevent them from hopping onto your susceptible crops by surrounding the crops with a 3-foot-wide strip of frequently weeded bare ground.
- Confuse the beetles by mixing up your plantings. Surround their favorite food plants with flowers and herbs like Queen Anne's lace, dill, and parsley, which attract beneficial insects.

Imported Cabbageworms

Adult cabbageworms are the common white butterflies you see in everyone's garden. Their wings are white with black tips and one or two small black spots on the forewing. They have a wingspan of 1½ inches. Cabbageworm larvae are velvety green caterpillars with a fine, light yellow stripe down the back. The eggs are tiny yellow cones laid on undersides of plant leaves.

Where They Live

Imported cabbageworms are found throughout North America.

Their Life Cycle

Adult butterflies emerge in spring to lay eggs on cabbage-family plants. When the eggs hatch, the caterpillars begin feeding on the undersides of leaves for about 2 to 3 weeks before pupating in garden debris on the soil surface. The butterflies emerge from the pupae in 1 to 2 weeks. Last-generation pupae overwinter in garden debris. These pests produce three to five overlapping generations a year.

Plants They Attack

Imported cabbageworms like to eat nasturtiums, as well as all cabbage-family plants, including broccoli and cauliflower.

Why They're a Problem

Cabbageworm caterpillars bite large, ragged holes in cabbage leaves and chew on cauliflower

---

A Home for Mr. Toad

Toads eat lots of pest insects, including cucumber beetles, cutworms, grasshoppers, and slugs. But to attract them to your garden, you'll need to provide shelter for them, as well as garden organically. (The porous skin of a toad is very sensitive and will absorb toxins from chemical sprays.)

Here are some things you can do to make sure that the toads that visit your garden have someplace to call home (or at least a place to hide during the day):

- Use lots of mulch. Toads like to burrow into it.
- Turn a broken clay flowerpot upside down; clay absorbs moisture and stays damp and cool, just the way toads like it.
- Arrange rocks so that there's a hollow space inside.
- Grow a fern grove. Ferns do well in moist, shady spots and their leaves create a great foraging spot for toads while providing protection from predators.

---

and broccoli florets. They also soil plants with their dark green droppings and tunnel inside heads of broccoli and cauliflower—where they sometimes go unnoticed until (gulp!) it's too late.

Organic Damage Control

- Plant purple cabbage varieties, which are less often attacked by cabbageworms.
- Cover small plants with floating row covers to prevent butterflies from laying eggs on plants.
- Place yellow sticky traps among host plants to catch female butterflies.
- If you don't have too many caterpillars, try handpicking them.
- If you have a severe cabbageworm infestation, spray Bacillus thuringiensis var. kurstoki (BTK) at 1- to 2-week intervals.
- Clean up all spent plant debris in the fall and dispose of it in order to thwart cabbageworms the following season.

Japanese Beetles

Japanese beetle adults are blocky, metallic blue-green beetles ½ inch long. They have bronze-colored wing covers and their legs are relatively long, with large claws. Beetle larvae are fat, dirty white, C-shaped grubs with brown heads, up to ¾ inch long.

Where They Live

These pests are found throughout the Northeast.

Their Life Cycle

Adult beetles emerge from late June to July. The beetles feed on plants until late summer, then burrow under grasses to lay eggs. The eggs hatch into larvae that feed until cold weather arrives. As fall approaches, the larvae burrow deeper into the soil to avoid freezing during winter. They move toward the surface again in spring to resume feeding on roots. They pupate in the soil in May and June, so it takes 1 to 2 years for the full life cycle to play itself out.

Continued ➡

PLANTS THEY ATTACK

Japanese beetles feed on a variety of vegetables, including beans, corn, and tomatoes, as well as on trees, shrubs, vines, fruits, and flowers. Their larvae damage turfgrass and other grasses.

WHY THEY'RE A PROBLEM

The beetles chew on flowers and skeletonize leaves, which wilt and drop. If you have lots of beetles, they may completely defoliate plants. Beetle larvae feed on roots of lawn turf and other grasses.

ORGANIC DAMAGE CONTROL

- If you notice a lot of beetles during midsummer, cover smaller or more valuable garden plants with floating row covers.
- In the early morning, handpick beetles or shake them from plants onto sheets, and then drown them in a bucket of soapy water.
- Destroy beetle eggs in your lawn by allowing it to dry out well between waterings in midsummer, or stop watering and allow the grass to go dormant for the summer months.
- Aerate the lawn with spiked sandals to kill grubs while they're close to the soil surface in late spring and early fall.
- Apply parasitic nematodes to the lawn in early spring or early fall when the white grubs are in the soil.

Leafhoppers

Adult leafhoppers are mostly wedge-shaped and slender, and range from $1/10$ to $1/2$ inch long. Most leafhoppers are either brown or green; some have bright bands of color on their wings. All have well-developed hind legs and can jump rapidly into flight when disturbed. The nymphs are similar to the adults, but paler in color and wingless. They can't fly, but they do hop rapidly when disturbed.

WHERE THEY LIVE

Leafhoppers are found throughout North America.

THEIR LIFE CYCLE

Female leafhoppers start laying eggs when leaves begin to appear on trees. The eggs hatch in 10 to 14 days and the nymphs develop for 1 to 4 weeks before reaching maturity and laying more eggs. The first fall frosts usually kill any remaining nymphs. Adults usually spend the winter on wild host plants; some species overwinter as eggs. Most species have two to five generations a year.

PLANTS THEY ATTACK

Leafhoppers attack flowers, fruit trees, and vegetables, especially apple trees, beans, eggplant, grapes, peanuts, potatoes, and squash-family plants.

WHY THEY'RE A PROBLEM

Both adults and nymphs suck juices from stems and undersides of leaves, giving leaves a light, mottled appearance. Their toxic saliva distorts and stunts plants and causes tip burn and yellowed, curled leaves. If you have a lot of leafhoppers, they may stunt the growth of entire plants. Leafhoppers also spread viruses.

ORGANIC DAMAGE CONTROL

- Control nymphs while they're still small by spraying them with insecticidal soap or by washing them from plants with strong sprays of water.
- Cover plants with floating row covers.
- Grow pollen- and nectar-producing plants like goldenrod and yarrow to attract beneficials, such as lady beetles.

- Healthy plants can often tolerate some leafhopper feeding, so keep a watchful eye on susceptible crops and action may not be necessary.
- When possible, grow resistant varieties. For example, certain species of leafhoppers avoid beans and potatoes with fuzzy leaves.

Leafminers

Leafminers are mostly black or black and yellow flies. They're incredibly small ($1/10$ inch long), so you've probably never even seen one. Their larvae are pale green, stubby, translucent maggots, found in tunnels between the upper and lower surface of leaves. The eggs are white and cylindrical, and they lay side by side in clusters on leaf undersides.

WHERE THEY LIVE

These pests are found throughout North America.

THEIR LIFE CYCLE

Adult flies emerge from overwintering cocoons in early spring and lay eggs on leaves. The larvae mine in the leaf tissue for 1 to 3 weeks, then pupate for 2 to 4 weeks. Most species of leafminers have two or three generations a year.

PLANTS THEY ATTACK

Leafminers attack beets, cabbage, chard, lettuce, peas, peppers, spinach, and tomatoes. They're also a problem on trees, ivy, and flowers—especially chrysanthemums and nasturtiums.

WHY THEY'RE A PROBLEM

Larvae tunnel through leaf tissue and may damage the leaves enough to destroy seedlings. On older plants, though, leafminers are often more of a nuisance than a serious problem. Leafminer damage is also unsightly on ornamentals.

ORGANIC DAMAGE CONTROL

- Cover seedlings with floating row covers to prevent adults from laying eggs.
- Keep row covers on all season on small plants, like beets and chard, where leafminers really like to hang out and eat.

Natural Predators

Spined soldier bugs, green lacewings, and syrphid flies all enjoy snacking on the small larvae or eggs of imported cabbageworms. Here are some things you can do to attract each of these good guys.

Spined soldier bugs. Grow pollen-providing plants (adults like to hang out on the flowers of goldenrod, hydrangeas, and milkweed). Maintain undisturbed areas near your garden.

Green lacewings. Grow angelica, caraway, cosmos, dandelion, dill, goldenrod, sunflowers, and sweet alyssum. Provide water in a pan filled with gravel—especially during dry spells—so the delicate insects can alight on the gravel and drink without drowning.

Syrphid flies. Grow pollen and nectar plants, especially sweet alyssum and wild mustard. Allow some broccoli to flower. Landscape with tall plants like sunflowers that break the wind so syrphid flies can hover undisturbed.

- Remove any nearby dock or lamb's-quarters, which are wild hosts for the beet leafminer.
- In spring, handpick and destroy damaged leaves and egg clusters, which will help reduce later generations.
- Tiny parasitic wasps help to keep leafminer populations under control. Attract these beneficial predators into your garden by making sure that you have lots of flowers blooming throughout the season.
- Keep plants well watered throughout the growing season. Plants suffering from inadequate moisture are more susceptible to leafminer damage.

Mexican Bean Beetles

Adults are oval, yellowish brown to copper-colored beetles, $1/4$ inch long. They have 16 black spots arranged in three rows across their wing covers and look a lot like lady beetles (which are good guys). The beetle larvae are fat, legless, yellowish orange grubs up to $1/3$ inch long. They have six rows of long, branching spines on their body. Eggs are bright yellow ovals laid on end in clusters of 40 to 60 on undersides of leaves.

WHERE THEY LIFE

These pests are found throughout North America, except in the Pacific Northwest.

THEIR LIFE CYCLE

Adult beetles start to emerge about the time the first bean leaves are up, and more continue to straggle out of hibernation over the next few months. The beetles feed for a couple of weeks before the females lay eggs on bean plants. After the eggs hatch (in about 5 to 14 days), the larvae feed for 2 to 5 weeks, pupate, and then the beetles emerge about a week later. Mexican bean beetles produce up to four generations a year, with adults overwintering in garden debris or leaf litter.

PLANTS THEY ATTACK

Bean beetles damage all kinds of beans, including cowpeas, lima beans, snap beans, and soybeans.

WHY THEY'RE A PROBLEM

Larvae and adults skeletonize leaves, leaving behind a characteristic lacy appearance. Attacked plants may produce fewer pods and may be completely defoliated and killed in July and August when beetles are most numerous.

ORGANIC DAMAGE CONTROL

- If you notice Mexican bean beetles in your garden, don't panic. Experts have found that bean plants can tolerate up to 50 percent defoliation and still produce a good crop.
- Plant resistant bean varieties.
- In the South, plant early-season bush beans to avoid damage.
- Cover young plants with floating row covers.
- Leave a few flowering weeds between rows, or interplant your garden with herbs and flowers to attract native predators and parasites.
- Remove or dig in crop debris after harvest to remove overwintering sites.
- Handpick larvae and adults daily.
- Toads love to eat bean beetles. Attract these hungry bug eaters into your garden by providing areas of moist shade.

Peachtree Borers

These unusual moths have narrow, clear wings with $1\frac{1}{4}$-inch wingspans. They have a blue-black body,

Continued ➡

and males have narrow yellow bands around the body. The larvae are white grubs, up to 1 inch long, with dark brown heads.

Where They Live

Peachtree borers are found throughout North America.

Their Life Cycle

Peachtree borers have an unusual life cycle. In July and August, female moths emerge from the soil to lay eggs on trees or soil close to the trunk. The eggs hatch in 12 days and larvae bore under the bark at ground level, where they overwinter before resuming feeding in the roots in spring. The larvae pupate in silken cocoons in the soil by late June or July, usually within a few inches of the trunk.

Plants They Attack

These borers attack mainly peach trees; they also occasionally attack apricot, cherry, nectarine, plum, and prune trees.

Why They're a Problem

Because peachtree borer larvae bore beneath the bark at the base of trees and into the main roots near the surface, they often girdle trees. Their entrance holes are filled with a gum mixed with sawdust. Young or weakened trees may be seriously damaged or killed, whereas older and more vigorous trees that are better established are less likely to be adversely affected.

Organic Damage Control

- Avoid injuries to tree bark from lawn mowers and other pieces of equipment, as adult moths are attracted to injured trees.
- Inspect tree trunks in late summer and remove soil several inches deep around the base of each trunk to look for borer holes containing larvae. Dig out the larvae with a sharp knife or kill them by working a flexible wire into the holes.
- Cultivate the soil shallowly around the trunk to destroy pupae.
- Studies have shown that parasitic nematodes can reduce borer damage by as much as 66 percent. Spray these microscopic beneficials around the trunk of the tree near the soil line in late April. The nematodes will seek out the peachtree borers and parasitize them, releasing a lethal bacteria as they feed.

Soft Scales

Female soft scales are tiny oval or round, legless, wingless bumps. Males are minute, yellow-winged insects. The youngest larvae are tiny crawlers resembling minute mealybugs, while older larvae settle and become sedentary.

Where They Live

You'll find scales throughout North America.

Their Life Cycle

Females of some species lay as many as 2,000 eggs, while others give birth to several nymphs per day. Nymphs move around on the plants for a short time, then settle in place to feed. Scales residing outdoors may produce one or two generations a year, while indoor populations may produce up to six generations.

Plants They Attack

Soft scales attack citrus and other fruit trees, as well as ornamental shrubs, trees, and many types of houseplants.

Why They're a Problem

All stages of scales weaken plants and cause leaves to yellow and drop by sucking sap from them. If you have a severe infestation, your plant may die. Soft scales also secrete a sticky substance called honeydew on leaves and fruit as they feed. (Certain species of ants feed on the sticky honeydew—and these ants will actually protect the scale to preserve their food supply.) Sooty mold, a black fungus, grows on the honeydew.

Organic Damage Control

- Attract native parasites and predators to your garden. Tiny parasitic wasps and lady beetles are particularly helpful in controlling scale. So if you have infested houseplants, move them outside for the summer, and let these beneficials clean them up for you.
- Scrub scales gently from twigs with a soft brush and soapy water, or a cloth dipped in insecticidal soap, then rinse well.
- Spray affected plants (including fruit trees) with horticultural oil. (Spray during dormant season when beneficial insects aren't active.)
- Prune and destroy branches and twigs that are significantly infested.
- Wash scale off plants with a strong spray of water from your garden hose. Be sure to hit the undersides of leaves, too.
- Keep your plants healthy. This includes enriching the soil with compost and watering adequately.

Slugs and Snails

Snails carry coiled shells on their backs, while slugs have no shells. Common species of slugs and snails are 1/8 to 1 inch long. (Banana slugs found in coastal areas stretch from 4 to 6 inches long.) Slugs and snails are gray, tan, green, or black, and some have darker spots or patterns. They leave a characteristic slimy trail of mucus behind. Their eggs are clear, oval, or round and are laid in jellylike masses under stones in the garden.

Where They Live

You'll find these slimers throughout North America.

Their Life Cycle

Adults lay eggs in moist soil, and the eggs hatch in 2 to 4 weeks. Slugs can grow for up to 2 years before reaching maturity.

Plants They Attack

Slugs and snails attack any tender plants, although slugs in particular have a taste for vegetables. Snails can be a serious problem on citrus.

Why They're a Problem

Both slugs and snails feed primarily on decaying plant material. But they also eat soft, tender plant tissue and make large holes in foliage, stems, and even bulbs. They may completely demolish seedlings and severely damage young shoots and plants. They may also crawl up trees and shrubs to feed. Both are most numerous and damaging in wet years and in regions that receive lots of rain.

Organic Damage Control

- Garden organically so that your landscape is a welcome home for many natural enemies of slugs, including birds, garter snakes, toads, and lizards.
- Maintain permanent walkways of clover, sod, or stone mulches to encourage predatory ground beetles.

- Repel slugs and snails with copper strips fastened around trunks of trees or shrubs.
- Edge garden beds with copper flashing or screening (make sure you've removed all the slugs first).
- Protect seedlings temporarily by spreading wide bands of cinders or wood ashes on the soil.
- Set out traps such as pots, boards, or overturned grapefruit rinds; check the undersides of the traps every morning and destroy the slugs you find.
- Bury tin cans with the lip flush to the soil surface and fill the traps with beer to attract slugs. The slugs will fall into the beer and drown.
- Encircle tender young seedlings with a protective barrier of crushed eggshells.

Spider Mites

Spider mites are incredibly tiny—less than 1/75 to 1/50 inch long. Adults have eight legs and are reddish, pale green, or yellow and have fine hairs on the body. Some have a darker patch on each side. Most species spin fine webs on plant leaves and shoots. Spider mite eggs are minuscule pearly spheres found on webbing or on leaf hairs.

Where They Live

Spider mites make their homes throughout North America.

Their Life Cycle

Eggs hatch in 1 to 8 days, and nymphs develop into adults in 5 to 10 days. Outdoors, eggs or adults overwinter in crevices in bark or in garden debris. These pests have a short life cycle and may reproduce year-round on indoor plants.

Plants They Attack

Many vegetables, fruits, and herbs fall prey to spider mites.

Why They're a Problem

Both adults and nymphs suck the juice from plants on the undersides of leaves. If you have a lot of spider mites, their feeding weakens plants, causes leaves to drop, and results in stunted fruit. The first signs of damage are yellowed speckled areas on

Oriental Fruit Moth

Adult oriental fruit moths are small, dark gray moths that lay eggs on fruit trees in spring. Their larvae are white to pinkish gray caterpillars with brown heads. The caterpillars bore into twigs of fruit trees early in the season, causing them to wilt and die. In midsummer, caterpillars bore into developing fruit. Late-summer caterpillars enter the stem end of maturing fruit and bore into the pit.

The larvae overwinter in cocoons on tree bark or in weeds or soil around the trees. They pupate in early spring, and the moths emerge from early May to mid-June to lay eggs.

You can help prevent the oriental fruit moth from getting the better of your fruit trees by planting peach and apricot varieties that bear fruit before midsummer. To destroy overwintering larvae, cultivate the soil 4 inches deep around unmulched trees in early spring. Pick and destroy immature, infested fruit, and spray summer oil to kill eggs and larvae.

Continued ➡

leaves. In severe infestations, leaves become bronzed or turn yellow or white with brown edges. The webs may cover both sides of the leaves and eventually cover the tips of branches. Spider mite outbreaks can be sudden and severe in hot, dry conditions. When humidity is low, spider mites feed more to avoid drying up, which drives them to lay more eggs, speeding up their development.

ORGANIC DAMAGE CONTROL

- Knock off spider mites with a strong spray of water. Be sure to spray the undersides of leaves, which is where the mites like to feed.
- Maintain high humidity around houseplants and plants in greenhouses.
- Spray dormant oil on fruit trees to kill over-wintering spider mite eggs.
- Keep plants well-watered throughout the growing season; moisture-stressed plants are more vulnerable to spider mite attacks.
- Spray infested plants with horticultural oil.

Squash Bugs

Adults are oval, dark brown to black, and very tiny. Their abdomen is flattened and covered with fine, dark hairs. They give off an unpleasant smell in self-defense. The youngest nymphs are pale green, while the older ones are covered with what looks like a grainy gray powder. Squash bug eggs are shiny yellow, turning brick red as they mature, and are laid in groups on the undersides of leaves.

WHERE THEY LIVE

You'll find squash bugs throughout North America.

THEIR LIFE CYCLE

Female bugs lay eggs in spring. The eggs hatch in 1 to 2 weeks, and the nymphs take 4 to 6 weeks to develop. Adults overwinter under garden debris, vines, or boards. Squash bugs produce one generation a year.

PLANTS THEY ATTACK

These pests prefer cucumbers, melons, pumpkins, squash, and gourds.

WHY THEY'RE A PROBLEM

Both adults and nymphs suck plant juices, which causes leaves and shoots to blacken and die. Severely attacked plants may not produce any fruit.

ORGANIC DAMAGE CONTROL

- Plant resistant squash varieties.
- Handpick eggs, nymphs, and adults from the undersides of leaves.
- Support vines off the ground with trellises.
- Place boards on the ground next to plants in early summer and destroy adults found under the boards every morning.
- Tachinid flies will parasitize up to 80 percent of squash bugs in a given area. The flies, which are found throughout most of the United States, lay their eggs on the squash bugs, then their larvae emerge inside the body of the squash bug. Don't kill any squash bugs that you notice carrying little white eggs since the eggs will hatch into more tachinid flies. Attract the adult flies by planting dill, parsley, sweet clover, fennel, buckwheat, goldenrod, wild carrot, or amaranth.
- Remove overwintering sites by cleaning up the garden in fall.
- Protect young seedlings with row covers until the plants are large enough to sustain some damage and still produce a crop.

Tarnished Plant Bugs

Tarnished plant bug adults are quick-moving, oval bugs that are ¼ inch long. They're a mottled light green to coppery brown and their top wings have a black-tipped yellow triangle on each side. Nymphs are yellowish green with five black dots on the body, similar to adult bugs, but wingless. Tarnished plant bugs lay their eggs into plant stems or leaves.

WHERE THEY LIVE

These bugs make their homes throughout North America.

THEIR LIFE CYCLE

Adults emerge in early spring to feed on fruit buds and other early foliage. They move to garden plants or weeds, such as clover, chickweeds, and dandelions, to lay eggs. The eggs hatch in 10 days; nymphs feed for about 3 weeks, then molt to adults. Tarnished plant bugs produce up to five overlapping generations a year; the adults overwinter under fallen leaves.

PLANTS THEY ATTACK

Most flowers, fruits, vegetables, and weeds are food for tarnished plant bugs.

WHY THEY'RE A PROBLEM

Both adults and nymphs suck the juice from leaves, buds, and fruit. Their toxic saliva causes buds and pods to drop and distorts leaves and shoots. Parts of plants wilt or are stunted, and branch tips blacken and die back. Feeding on tomatoes and other fruit causes pitted catfacing on the fruit, while feeding on broccoli and cauliflower leaves dead spots on florets.

ORGANIC DAMAGE CONTROL

- Cover plants with floating row covers, especially if you have a lot of tarnished plant bugs.
- Keep your garden free of weeds and dead plant debris, and make sure to remove spent plants at the end of the season.
- Grow pollen and nectar plants, such as sweet alyssum, daisies, and cosmos, to attract native predatory bugs such as big-eyed bugs and minute pirate bugs, which feed on nymphs.
- In vegetable gardens, plant cool-season cover crops like subterranean clover. These cover crops attract big-eyed bugs, one of tarnished plant bugs' natural enemies.

Thrips

Adult thrips are minute—about $1/50$ to $1/25$ inch long. They're yellowish brown or black and have narrow, fringed wings. They move quickly and like to hide in tight crevices in plant stems and flowers. Nymphs are light green or yellow and look similar to adults, but smaller.

WHERE THEY LIVE

You'll find thrips throughout North America.

THEIR LIFE CYCLE

Adults become active in early spring and lay eggs in plant tissue. The eggs hatch in 3 to 5 days, and the nymphs feed for 1 to 3 weeks before molting to the adult stage. Thrips produce many generations a year and breed year-round in greenhouses; adults overwinter in sod, debris, or cracks in bark.

PLANTS THEY ATTACK

These bad bugs attack asparagus, cabbage, lettuce, onions, peas, flowers, and fruit and shade trees.

WHY THEY'RE A PROBLEM

Both adults and nymphs suck the contents of plant cells. In severe infestations, they leave plants stunted and distorted and flowers damaged. Some species spread tomato spotted wilt virus.

ORGANIC DAMAGE CONTROL

- Plant pollen and nectar plants and provide a water source in your garden to attract predators such as lacewings and lady beetles.
- Spray dormant oil in early spring to control thrips attacking fruit trees.
- Use bright blue or yellow sticky traps to catch adults in greenhouses.
- Wash thrips off with a strong spray of water from your garden hose.

Whiteflies

Adult whiteflies are tiny, powdery-white insects, $1/20$ inch long. Although their name suggests that they're related to flies, they really aren't—they're related to aphids. Whiteflies rest on the undersides of leaves and fly up when they're disturbed.

Squash Vine Borers

Another pest that attacks squash family plants is the squash vine borer, which is found throughout North America (except for the West Coast). Adults, which are narrow-winged, olive brown moths, lay eggs on stems near the bases of plants. The larvae are white grubs with a brown head and bore into squash vines. The vines wilt suddenly, and girdled vines rot and die. The larvae may also feed on fruit later in the season.

Squash vine borer larvae or pupae overwinter in the soil. Adults emerge as squash vines begin to lengthen and then lay their eggs on stems and leaf stalks. The larvae burrow into stems for 4 to 6 weeks, then pupate in the soil for winter. These pests usually produce only one generation a year.

Control borers by planting early or late to avoid the main egg-laying period. Also fertilize plants to promote vigorous growth so the vines are better able to tolerate borer attacks.

Scales of Armor

Armored scales are similar to soft scales, except that they are mostly found in the Deep South, Southwest, and California—and they have waxy armor. Adults are tiny round or oval hard bumps, with no visible head or legs. These scales secrete an armor of wax in an oyster shell or circular shape. Depending on the species, they can be ashy gray, yellow, white, reddish, or purplish brown. The early stage nymphs are mobile crawlers, while later stages are legless and hardly move. In the South, armored scales are serious pests of citrus, but they also attack palms, roses, and tropical ornamentals. In the North, they infest fruit and shade trees, currants, grapes, raspberries, and ornamental shrubs. To combat armored scales, apply dormant oil sprays during winter. You can also try summer oil on plants that tolerate it.

Continued ➡

Nymphs are tiny, flattened, translucent scale also found on the undersides of leaves. The eggs are gray or yellow cones the size of a pinpoint.

WHERE THEY LIVE

Whiteflies are a pest throughout North America.

THEIR LIFE CYCLE

The complete whitefly life cycles takes only 20 to 30 days at room temperature. The eggs hatch in 2 days into tiny scales; the scales feed on plant juices before molting to adults. These bugs produce many overlapping generations a year, continuing all winter in greenhouses and warm climates. In cold winter areas, whiteflies can't survive outdoors in winter. However, they can reinfest gardens each spring if they're brought in on infested transplants from commercial greenhouses and nurseries.

PLANTS THEY ATTACK

Whiteflies attack citrus plants and many vegetable crops, especially squash and tomato family plants.

WHY THEY'RE A PROBLEM

Both nymphs and adults suck plant juices, weakening plants. They can spread plant viruses through their feeding. They also exude honeydew, which supports the growth of sooty molds on leaves and fruit.

ORGANIC DAMAGE CONTROL

- Capture adult whiteflies on yellow sticky traps.
- Use a handheld vacuum to suck up adults from the undersides of leaves (you can do this if the infestation isn't too severe).
- Control nymphs with insecticidal soap.
- Wash the sticky coating from leaves with water.
- Smother whiteflies with a spray of horticultural oil. Spray during the cool times of the day since the oil can react with sunlight and damage plant leaves.
- Attract wasps that parasitize whiteflies into your garden by providing food and shelter. Parasitic wasps feed on the nectar of parsley, dill, Queen-Anne's lace, daisies, sunflowers, and coneflowers. Grow tall plants like corn and sunflowers to protect these tiny fliers from the wind.

Potions and Practices for Organic Pest Control

Joan Benjamin and Deborah L. Martin

On any warm summer day, your garden is filled with flying, crawling, and jumping insects. But very few of these creatures are plant pests. Most of them—including spiders, lady beetles, and many wasps and flies—are more interested in capturing other insects than in aggravating gardeners. So controlling the few insects that are pests really isn't hard. Organic gardeners have devised lots of useful sprays, barriers, and traps for controlling pests without chemical pesticides.

Pest insects usually have specific food requirements. Many of the pest control formulas in this chapter work by tricking pests into thinking that they are on the wrong plant or making them eat something that they can't digest.

You'll also find formulas in this chapter for bigger pests, like squirrels, deer, cats, and dogs. These pesky animals can frustrate gardeners by eating or trampling plants. But, although we don't want animals to hurt our gardens, we also don't want to hurt the animals, so all of the formulas you'll find here are strictly nonpoisonous. They

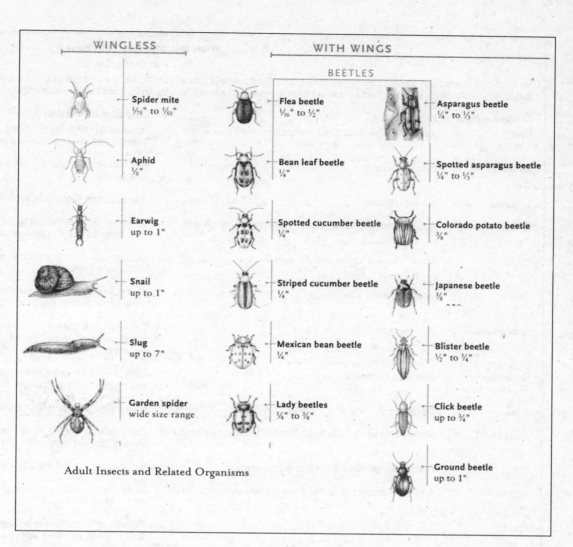

Adult Insects and Related Organisms

WINGLESS

- Spider mite 1/75" to 1/50"
- Aphid 1/8"
- Earwig up to 1"
- Snail up to 1"
- Slug up to 7"
- Garden spider wide size range

WITH WINGS

BEETLES

- Flea beetle 1/16" to 1/2"
- Bean leaf beetle 1/4"
- Spotted cucumber beetle 1/4"
- Striped cucumber beetle 1/4"
- Mexican bean beetle 1/4"
- Lady beetles 1/4" to 3/8"

- Asparagus beetle 1/4" to 1/3"
- Spotted asparagus beetle 1/4" to 1/3"
- Colorado potato beetle 3/8"
- Japanese beetle 3/8"
- Blister beetle 1/2" to 3/4"
- Click beetle up to 3/4"
- Ground beetle up to 1"

work by conditioning animals to look elsewhere for dinner.

Use these same approaches when developing your own formulas to solve unusual pest problems in your garden. For example, if you have a problem with an insect that eats one type of plant but is never seen on another, try planting the two types of plants close to each other to confuse the pest and lessen the damage. Or you might brew a tea from leaves of the plant the pest ignores and use it to drench the plant that the pest likes. It just might fool them!

Pest Patrol Bucket Blend

No insect prisoners can escape when you hand-pick pests and toss them into this easy-to-mix

---

Discover the World's Safest Insecticide: Water!

It may be tempting to bring out the arsenal when you find your favorite rosebush infested with aphids, but a safer and less-expensive solution is as close as the end of your hose—water! Researchers at Texas A&M University have been able to knock out 70 to 90 percent of aphid infestations by spraying water through a specially designed hose. A strong shot of water will wash away spider mites and thrips, too! You don't necessarily need a high-tech wand on the end of your hose, though; you can achieve good results using an ordinary watering wand. Just make sure to spray both the upper and lower sections of the leaves. Once those pests hit the ground, it's very difficult for them to make it back onto your plants.

---

blend of soap, oil, and water. In her garden near Fenelon Falls, Ontario, Mary Perlmutter, author of *How Does Your Garden Grow...Organically?*, takes this blend along on pest patrol every morning to dispatch any pesky insects like Japanese beetles, Colorado potato beetles, and tomato hornworms that she finds attacking her plants.

Ingredients and Supplies

    1 quart water (approximately)
    1 small bucket or pail
    1 teaspoon dishwashing liquid
    2 tablespoons cooking oil (any type)

Directions

1. Put 2 to 3 inches of water in the bucket or pail.
2. Add dishwashing liquid and oil and mix. The oil will float to the top, where it will remain as small droplets.
3. Gather unwanted insects from your garden, tossing the pests into the mixture as you go.

Yield: About 1 quart of pest-killing mixture

Note: "The oil means they have no hope of being able to crawl back out," Mary reports. Caterpillars quickly sink to the bottom of the soap-oil mix, and Colorado potato beetles swim for only a few seconds. The dishwashing liquid in this blend helps keep the oil mixed into the water. By breaking down an insect's outer covering, or cuticle, it also speeds the demise of the pests you toss into your bucket.

Mary often uses the same mixture for several days. When she's finished with the liquid, she pours it onto her slow compost pile (where she puts tree prunings and other organic materials that break down slowly).

Continued ➡

Plants That (May) Keep Pests Away
Sally Jean Cunningham

Here's a listing of companion plants reputed to repel garden pests. Choose some of them as plant friends for your vegetable families. Many of these recommendations are based on tradition and folklore alone, so don't rely too heavily on them for pest protection. Experiment for yourself. You may find that some of these plants do a great job in your garden.

Companion Plant	Pests Repelled	Companion-Garden Uses
Basil	Aphids, asparagus beetles, mites, mosquitoes, tomato hornworms	Plant next to paths where you'll brush it often, releasing the aromatic oil that may confuse pests; try it along the edge of asparagus beds and among tomatoes and eggplants
Borage	Tomato hornworms	Plant with tomatoes, and let it self-sow throughout the garden to attract beneficial bees and other insects
Calendula	Asparagus beetles	Definitely attracts beneficials, so plant throughout the garden as well as by your asparagus
Catnip	Aphids, asparagus beetles, Colorado potato beetles, squash bugs	Catnip's repellent qualities are backed by research; can spread uncontrollably, so plant in pots and place them near or among peppers, potatoes, tomatoes, and vine crops
Chives	Aphids, Japanese beetles, probably many insects	Excellent perennial herb to place around roses, raspberries, grapevines—or wherever Japanese beetles are a problem
Garlic	Japanese beetles, many other pests	Plant around roses or other flowers that suffer from Japanese beetles, especially in a cutting garden; or mix a spray from crushed garlic and water
Zonal geraniums	Japanese beetles	Tests show these flowers, especially white-flowered types, repel and even kill Japanese beetles; try among roses or other crops that Japanese beetles favor; may also work as a trap crop by attracting the beetle
Horseradish	Colorado potato beetles	Not a practical companion for potatoes, because it's a spreading perennial; plant among other permanent plantings, such as asparagus, raspberries, strawberries, and perhaps rhubarb
Hyssop	Cabbage moths	Some studies back this claim; try planting among broccoli, brussels sprouts, cabbage, and cauliflower
Marigolds	Mexican bean beetles, root-knot nematodes, root lesion nematodes	Strong evidence supports repellent qualities for nematodes; plant a solid block in nematode-infested areas; at flowering, chop and turn under entire crop
Mints	Aphids, cabbage moths, possibly other pest insects	Very invasive; surround with a solid root barrier or grow in pots
Nasturtiums	Aphids, Colorado potato beetles, Mexican bean beetles, squash bugs	Studies show conflicting evidence; plant with vine crops to protect ground beetles and spiders and to act as a pretty living mulch
Onions	Carrot rust flies	Research backs interplanting with carrots to repel rust flies; intermingle the crops or plant clusters or strips of onions and carrots side by side
Parsley	Asparagus beetles	Plant on the edges of asparagus beds; it often survives over winter; let some go to flower to attract beneficials
Radishes	Cucumber beetles	There's some evidence that radishes do confuse cucumber beetles; plant three to five seeds in every "hill" or cluster of cucumber plants; also plant among squashes and pumpkins
Rosemary	Cabbage moths, carrot rust flies, Mexican bean beetles	Plant among beans and cabbage family crops, or beside lettuce and carrot combinations
Rue	Japanese beetles	Traditional reports also list rue as a growth inhibitor for some plants; not practical except among plantings of perennials; caution: touching the foliage may cause allergic reaction
Sage	Cabbage moths, carrot rust flies, others	Include in a perennial herb or flower border
Savory	Mexican bean beetles	Plant on the edges of tomato/bean plantings or in perennial herb areas around the garden
Southern-wood and wormwood	Flea beetles, mosquitoes	Plant in perennial clusters or herb borders near or beside the garden, and use them near areas where people congregate (we rub them on our skin as mosquito repellents)
Tansy	Colorado potato beetles, squash bugs	Some tests support tansy as a repellent, but the best reason to plant is to attract beneficial insects
Thyme	Cabbage moths	Studies back this claim: plant near cabbage family crops or in any perennial/herb combination near the vegetable garden; creeping thymes are excellent groundcovers for permanent plantings

Your First Defense Against Pests

If you spot insect pests on a plant, simply pick them off! Then dispense with the pests using two flat rocks or whatever squashing method you can think up.

If the pests are too small, fast, or numerous for hand-picking, take action right away with an appropriate pest control formula. Pest populations tend to build up very quickly, and it's always easier to control a pest problem the day you discover it than to wait for another day—by then, you may face double the problem.

HATE TO HAND-PICK?

Many gardeners are squeamish about handling insects with their bare hands. If you're averse to plucking pests with your fingers, try using disposable latex gloves when you go on pest patrol. Your hands will stay clean, and you'll still have enough dexterity to nab the pests. Another option when your prey is slow-moving, like slugs, is to pick up the pests with chopsticks. You can also shake pests like Colorado potato beetles and Japanese beetles off of plants and directly into your bucket of oily soap mixture.

Paralyzing Pest Salsa

Paralyze pests with salsa that's only a little stronger than you might eat on your chips. The creator of this formula, Santa Barbara gardener and author Kathleen Yeomans, uses it to control pests ranging from ants to black widow spiders.

"This is my favorite all-purpose insect spray," Kathleen says. According to Kathleen, the spray will make ants pass out cold, and it has actually killed a black widow spider.

Ingredients and Supplies

2 pounds ripe, blemished tomatoes

1 large onion

1 pound fresh chili peppers

2 cloves garlic

Food processor or blender

1 cup vinegar

½ teaspoon pepper

Cheesecloth or coffee filter

Pump spray bottle

Directions

1. Roughly chop the tomatoes, onion, peppers, and garlic.

Continued ➡

2. Place the chopped vegetables in a food processor or blender and blend until liquefied.

3. Add vinegar and pepper to the mixture.

4. Strain the mixture through several layers of cheesecloth or a disposable coffee filter.

5. Pour the strained liquid into the pump spray bottle.

6. Spray the liquid directly on pests that you spot in your garden.

Yield: About 3 cups of insect-knockout salsa

Note: Crushed garlic contains allicin, the smelly compound that confounds the sensory receptors of insects in search of a tasty plant feast. Hot peppers are loaded with fiery capsaicin, which gives a chemical burn to marauding mammals and some soft-bodied insects. Onions help give the salsa an extra aromatic kick, and the sulfur in them may suppress some fungal diseases. Many pests avoid tomatoes, so the unmistakable tomato odor signals them to look elsewhere.

Caution: This salsa can be highly irritating if it gets in your eyes or mouth, so spray it only on a windless day.

Pest-Puzzling Garlic Extract

Garlic has a perplexing effect on a wide range of garden pests, from aphids to Mexican bean beetles. This formula for garlic extract comes from David Stern, an organic farmer and director of the Garlic Seed Foundation in Rose, New York. Garlic extract probably works by confusing insects in search of their favorite host plants, so for maximum effectiveness, spray before any pests have become a serious problem.

Ingredients and Supplies

¼ pound garlic (2–3 whole garlic bulbs)

1 quart water

4-5 drops dishwashing liquid

Blender or food processor

Cheesecloth

1-quart glass jar

Directions

1. Separate the garlic bulbs into cloves but do not peel them.

2. Place the whole garlic cloves in a blender or food processor with 1 cup of the water. Chop well. If you have lots of garlic plants, you can use garlic leaves instead of cloves. The chopped leaves also contain allicin, one of the pest-repelling ingredients in garlic.

3. Add the rest of the water and the dishwashing liquid. Blend until liquefied. (This usually takes several minutes.)

4. Strain the mixture through cheesecloth to remove bits of garlic that might clog the sprayer. It's a good idea to strain a second time if any debris remains in the concentrate.

5. Store the strained concentrate in a glass jar with a tight fitting lid until you are ready to use it.

Yield: About 1 quart of concentrated garlic extract

Note: To make a spray from the concentrated extract, dilute 1 part extract with 10 parts water (¼ cup concentrate to 2½ cups water). Put the diluted extract in a pump spray bottle or pressure sprayer and apply to plants that are under pest attack or that you suspect are likely targets, like young bean and potato plants. David points out that you can also apply the garlic extract to the soil to discourage nematodes.

Good Bugs Don't Like Garlic

Be selective when you spray your plants with garlic extract. Even though it's organic, it can disrupt or even kill helpful insects like syrphid flies and lacewings which prey on pest insects.

Citrus Killer for Aphids

Pesky insects go into convulsions when doused with citrus oil extract. This mixture quickly neutralizes aphids and other soft-bodied insects in the California garden of Kathleen Yeomans, author of *The Able Gardener*. She also uses it to deter ants. "The spray will keep ants away for a while, but they may come back," Kathleen observes. But since this mixture has such a refreshing smell, you'll probably enjoy using it often.

Ingredients and Supplies

1 pint water

Rind from 1 lemon, grated

Cheesecloth

Pump spray bottle

Directions

1. Bring the water to a boil. Remove from heat and add the grated lemon rind.

2. Allow the mixture to steep overnight.

3. Strain the mixture through cheesecloth, and pour into the pump spray bottle.

4. Apply the mixture to plant leaves that are under attack by aphids or other soft-bodied insects. The mixture must come in contact with the insects' bodies to be effective.

Yield: About 1 pint of citrus oil extract

Citrus Substitutes

Lemon isn't the only source for a citrus spray. You can make a similar spray using orange or grapefruit rinds. Richard Merrill, director of horticulture at Cabrillo Community College in Santa Cruz, California, has tried several kinds of citrus sprays on aphids. "Citrus fruits with pungent rinds work best, since they probably include more limonene and linalool, which are the active ingredients," he says. For example, a navel orange with a mild, sweet rind would probably not carry the punch of a spray made from the rind of a sour orange, grapefruit, or lemon.

Hot Spray for Flea Beetles

Shoo away pesky flea beetles by dousing plants with a potent mixture of garlic and hot pepper. Pennsylvania market gardener Cass Peterson uses this mixture to keep flea beetles from feeding on her spring broccoli and cabbage.

Ingredients and Supplies

6 cloves garlic

Hammer

1-quart glass jar with lid

1 tablespoon powdered or crushed hot pepper

1 quart warm water

Cheesecloth

Pump spray bottle

Directions

1. Smash unpeeled garlic cloves with a hammer.

2. Put the crushed garlic in the glass jar.

3. Add the hot pepper and warm water. Screw on the lid.

4. Shake up the mixture.

5. Set the jar in the sun to steep for 2 days or longer. "If you pop off the lid to take a sniff and your eyes water, it's ready," Cass says.

6. Strain the mixture through the cheesecloth and pour the liquid into a pump spray bottle.

Yield: About 1 quart of garlic pepper spray

Note: Apply the garlic pepper spray as soon as you see flea beetles, and reapply it after rains or heavy dew. Since flea beetles feed on both sides of plant leaves, make sure that the plants are thoroughly drenched. As with any water-based spray, this mixture can damage plant leaves if applied in the middle of a hot, sunny day.

Cass suggests starting a new batch of spray every few days in late spring, when flea beetles are at their worst. Work outdoors, where you won't mind the mess and smell. If a hammer isn't handy, Cass smashes the garlic with a brick, piece of wood, or the palm of her hand.

Variation: You can use any type of pepper for this mix as long as it's really hot. Since Cass grows a variety of hot peppers, she picks whatever type is plentiful. Cayenne pepper or crushed pepper flakes, available on the spice shelf at the supermarket, work equally well and make a convenient substitute for crushed whole pepper.

New York–Style Slug Bait

Stop slugs dead with a do-it-yourself slug saloon. At Cornell University in Ithaca, New York, Dr. Marvin Pritts has studied beers, nonalcoholic beers, and various yeast-sugar mixtures to trap slugs in strawberries. In the strawberry fields where he conducted his research, beer attracted many more slugs than the other mixtures did. The slugs didn't care for plain sugar and water; they wanted beer—nonalcoholic as well as regular beer—and they weren't fussy about the brand! "We looked at many different brands, and there really wasn't much difference," Marvin says.

Ingredients and Supplies

2 roofing shingles

1 heavy knife or utility shears

6 shallow containers such as quart jar lids

1 can or bottle of any brand of beer, nonalcoholic or regular

1 pail or bucket

Directions

1. Cut roofing shingles into three 1-foot-square pieces.

2. Fold the squares in half to form covers for your slug traps.

3. Settle the edges of the covers into the mulch or soil near plants that are being damaged by slugs.

4. Fill containers to the rim with beer. Slide the containers under the covers and leave them in place.

5. After 1 or 2 days, empty the trapped slugs and old beer into a pail or bucket.

6. Refill the traps with more beer.

Yield: 6 slug traps

Note: Marvin says to check the undersides of the covers, too. Slugs may be hiding there, waiting for their chance at the beer. All of the slugs that actually make it into the traps will be dead, but the late arrivals may still be alive.

Ailing Slug "Ale"

If there's one pest that every gardener loves to hate, it's a slug. Slugs can ruin tender young vegetables and beautiful flower gardens in just a few nights' feedings. But slimy slugs will drink themselves to death when you offer them this aromatic brew concocted by Carl Elliot, garden coordinator for Seattle Tilth's demonstration garden.

Continued ➡

Any time is a good time to get rid of garden slugs, but Carl says to be especially vigilant in the fall. That way, there will be fewer slugs around in the spring, when your garden is brimming with the young, tender plants that slugs like best.

Ingredients and Supplies

I quart unpasteurized beer

I tablespoon sugar

I teaspoon baking yeast

Plastic milk jug or large glass jar

15 I-quart plastic yogurt containers

Directions

1. Mix ingredients together in the milk jug or jar. If you're not sure whether the beer you have is unpasteurized, check the bottle label.

2. Let the mixture sit in a warm (70°F) place for a few days, until you see bubbles form.

3. While the mixture is brewing, make some of Carl's Seattle-style slug traps by cutting openings I inch high x 2 inches wide in the sides of the yogurt containers, as shown in the illustration at right.

4. Pour the beery brew about ½ inch deep into the yogurt containers and replace the lids. 5. Bury the yogurt containers around your garden so that the openings in the sides are about ¼ inch above the soil line.

Yield: Enough brew to fill about 15 slug traps

Note: When setting the traps, make sure that the windows in the traps are just a little higher than ground level to keep ground beetles from falling in. Ground beetles eat slug eggs, so the more of them you have, the better. Empty, clean, and refill the traps every 3 days, Carl advises. "Slugs like fresh beer. They won't go in there if it smells like bacteria," he says.

A Low-Profile Slug Trap

Here's an inconspicuous beer-baited slug trap that's perfect for high-visibility flower beds. Save some I-liter soda bottles. Cut the bottles in half, and insert the top half of the bottle upside down into the bottom half. This will create a funnel effect. Pour ½ cup of beer into each funnel and sink the bottles partway into the soil. The slugs will crawl in and drown. To clean out the traps, remove the funnel part, and pour the contents of the traps on your compost pile. Then you can add fresh beer, put the funnels in place again, and put the traps back in the garden.

Slug-Dissolving Spray

Fry baby slugs alive when they're hiding in the crowns of daylilies and other perennials in the spring. For slugs that are too small to handpick or be attracted to traps, Marianne Binetti uses this recipe in her Washington State garden.

Ingredients and Supplies

1½ cups nonsudsing ammonia

1½ cups water

I-quart pump spray bottle

Directions

1. Pour the ammonia and water into the spray bottle.

2. Shake gently to mix.

3. Spray the mixture in areas where small slugs appear to be active.

Note: "It fries the skin off the slugs, but it doesn't hurt the plants, and the ammonia breaks down into nitrogen," Marianne says. She keeps a spray bottle filled with this solution by the back door so that it's always ready to use when she discovers slimy slugs slinking around in her garden.

Flower Pot Death Traps for Slugs

Some people eat snails, but nothing eats slugs except other slugs. All slugs are cannibals, so you can trap them using fellow slugs as bait. Marianne Binetti, a garden columnist and television personality from Enumclaw, Washington, came up with an attractive but deadly way to deal with slugs that reside near her raised beds.

Ingredients and Supplies

Clay pots of various sizes

Directions

1 Put clay pots on the frame of your raised beds, upside down, with ½ inch of the lip extending out from the frame.

2. After a few days, check each of the pots for slugs.

3. Knock any slugs that you find out of the pots. Smash the slugs on the top of bed frame, and rearrange the pots so that they cover the dead slugs. The dead slugs attract more slugs to the pots, so you can kill more slugs every few days. "I know it sounds horrible, but it works," Marianne says.

Burlap Bag Booby Trap

Slay slippery little milk slugs before they shred young lettuce or other spring seedlings. Seattle Tilth demonstration garden coordinator Carl Elliot lays down old burlap bags all around his lettuce bed.

In the morning, when the slugs have retreated under the bags to hide for the day, Carl crushes them with his feet. He leaves the dead slugs under the bags to lure more slugs.

Mealybug Death Drench

Melt mealybugs from the stems of orchids and sensitive tropical houseplants with this cheap and easy spray. Bob Thompson, an orchid hobbyist who lives near Daytona Beach, Florida, says this formula will control mealybugs on any plant, including citrus and poinsettias. The soap kills some of the mealybugs right away as it penetrates their protective coating, Bob says. Survivors are then suffocated by the thin coating of corn oil. "It's horribly effective," Bob reports. "Within days, every mealybug is gone."

Ingredients and Supplies

I gallon water

Pressure sprayer

2 tablespoons corn oil

2 tablespoons dishwashing liquid

Directions

1. Place the water in a clean pressure sprayer.

2. Mix in oil and dishwashing liquid.

3. Apply thoroughly to plants infested with mealybugs. Make sure the mixture coats the insects well. The mixture will not harm sensitive orchid foliage, but to be effective, it must contact the insects directly.

Yield: I gallon of mealybug-killing drench

Note: Bob usually makes a gallon-size batch of drench for his greenhouse full of orchids. For smaller jobs, just make a quart of drench and use a pump spray bottle.

Recheck your plants about 2 weeks after treatment because some mealybug eggs may have survived. If you find only a few mealybugs, either repeat the treatment or follow up with an alcohol spray (see "Massacre Mealybugs with Rubbing Alcohol" at right).

Massacre Mealybugs with Rubbing Alcohol

If you have only one plant infested with mealybugs, don't mess with a soap spray. Just spritz the mealybugs with rubbing alcohol. Bob Thompson keeps a small spray bottle filled with alcohol in his orchid greenhouse and uses it to neutralize any mealybugs he finds on isolated plants. Bob uses rubbing alcohol straight from the bottle (it's usually a mixture of 70 percent alcohol and 30 percent water).

Steam Treatment for Fire Ants

If you share your garden space with fire ants, you know how painful their stings can be. Gwen Snyder and Phil Strniste, owners of Bee Natural Farm in Fairhope, Alabama, keep fire ants at bay by steaming the mounds with hot water to kill the queen ants and disperse the colonies.

Ingredients and Supplies

I-2 gallons water

Large pot (such as a canner)

Cooking thermometer

Directions

1. Put the water into the pot. Be sure that you can carry the pot comfortably. If a large pot filled with water is too heavy, use smaller pots. (The last thing you want to do is burn yourself by spilling the hot water.)

2. On the stove, heat the water to between 160° and 170°F. Gwen and Phil find that this temperature is hot enough to kill fire ants and safer to handle than boiling water.

3. Quietly carry your pot or pots of water outdoors and set them near the fire ant mound.

4. Douse the mound quickly with I to 2 gallons of hot water. Your objective is to kill the queen, so don't disturb the colony before pouring on the water. The worker ants will quickly spirit the queen away when the mound is disturbed. The queen is most likely to be active on a warm day between 11:00 A.M. and 2:00 P.M.

Note: By the time you return to the ant colony on the second day, the surviving ants will have built a new home. To really be effective against large colonies, the treatment may need to be repeated for 3 consecutive days, Gwen and Phil say. If the colony disappears after I or 2 applications, look around to see if the ants have moved to a new spot. Continue to steam out any small colonies as soon as they appear, provided that they are far enough away from plants that the hot water will not injure the plants' roots.

Fire Ant Sticky Traps

In their garden, Gwen Snyder and Phil Strniste find that hot water never gets rid of every last fire ant. They use a different method for keeping ants from chewing on okra flowers and pods, which fire ants are especially fond of. Phil paints the main stems of his okra plants with a sticky substance used to trap insects, such as Stickem or Tangle-Trap. The fire ants either get stuck or won't try to cross the sticky barrier, so they never reach the flowers and pods.

You can also use a band of sticky goo to protect citrus trees from fire ant feeding. Fire ants chew on the bark and growing tips of citrus trees and also feed on the fruit.

Continued ➡

TRY A DUSTY FIRE ANT DETERRENT

Disturbing an active fire ant mound is certainly no picnic for you or your pets, and it's all too easy to do in an area infested with these pests. Although they're small—¹/8- to ¼-inch long—fire ants inflict a painful sting, and they often attack by the hundreds when their territory is invaded.

Fire ants are pests in the garden, where they may damage eggplant, corn, okra, strawberries, and potatoes. They can also become household pests, entering through small cracks near the soil line and building nests inside walls, around plumbing, and under carpeting.

If you live in an area where fire ants are active, use a dusty barrier of diatomaceous earth (DE) to help keep these pests from moving into your garden or your home. DE is a natural material made from the fossilized remains of diatoms.

When insects come in contact with DE, it damages and dries their waxy outer skeleton, and they die of dehydration.

To keep fire ants out of your house, caulk openings, especially near the soil level. Then apply a 2- to 3-inch band of DE around the foundation. Use a similar DE band around your garden to exclude fire ants from your crops. Wear a dust mask and goggles when applying DE to avoid inhaling the dust or getting it in your eyes.

---

10 Fast Ways to Control Pests
Vicki Mattern

Did insect pests get the best of you and your garden last year? Were you witness to overnight attacks on your veggie crop? Are you a bit worried that this year might bring a repeat performance? Never fear! Here are 10 timely, timesaving tips to help you take charge of your garden's bad bugs *now*:

1. **Mix your signals.** A confusing mix of sights and scents can help deter certain insect pests. So try to increase biodiversity and avoid monoculture by mixing plants from different families. Instead of planting long rows of a single crop, plant onions alongside broccoli, tomatoes with basil and chives, and peas with carrots. Better yet, interplant edibles with ornamentals. Add a few hot pepper plants to your flowerbeds, or edge your vegetable beds with low-growing annual flowers, such as alyssum and dwarf marigolds.

2. **Attract an airborne defense squad.** One of the best ways to short-circuit an onslaught of pests is to attract an airborne cavalry charge of beneficial insects. Many beneficials—including the small wasps that prey on pest caterpillars—will gratefully take advantage of the flat-topped floral landing platforms offered by members of the umbel family, which includes dill, Queen-Anne's-lace, parsley, and carrots. (You have to allow the parsley and carrot plants to overwinter and grow into their second year to get those umbrella-shaped flowers that beneficials find so attractive.) other plants beloved by beneficials include sweet alyssum, all kinds of mints, and chamomile.

3. **Negate nematodes.** Marigolds can greatly reduce the damage caused by root-ravaging nematodes—those tiny soil-dwelling worm-like pests—but only if you use them correctly. For the best effect, grow a thick stand of marigolds as a cover crop for a season, then turn them under the soil. The next year, plant whatever you like in that area—nematodes won't be around to cause trouble underground.

4. **Grow your own decoy (#1).** Try allowing a single weed to grow as a decoy among your cultivated crops. Decoy crops may attract pests and help to keep the bad guys away from your other crops. Striped blister beetles, for instance, seem to prefer redroot pigweed to tomato plants growing nearby. To keep the insects from moving to your tomatoes, check the pigweed each morning and shake off any beetles into a bucket of soapy water.

5. **Grow your own decoy (#2).** You can trap flea beetles in a similar manner using arugula, the spicy salad green. Pesky flea beetles—a voracious pest of eggplants, brassicas, and potatoes—will flock to the arugula first. Use a handheld vacuum to suck the beetles off the decoy plants before they can make their way to your main crops. You may have to repeat the vacuum cleaner escapade a few times each season to keep ahead of the invading flea beetle army.

6. **Grow your own decoy (#3).** Knowing that aphids are attracted to all things yellow, the staff of Ecology Action in Willits, California, have learned to plant yellow nasturtiums at the base of tomato plants to lure aphids away from the tomatoes. Monitor the nasturtiums closely, they urge. After the flowers have drawn in the aphids—and before the aphids reproduce—pull out the decoy plants and destroy their load of insects.

7. **Set up traps!** Earwigs, sow bugs, pill bugs, slugs, and snails all have one thing in common: They like to hide out in damp, shady places during the heat of the day. To take advantage of this trait, lure them with attractive "trap nests"—boards, pieces of paper, seashells, broken crockery, etc. Get out early every morning to check each lure, then dump the trapped critters into a bucket of soapy water.

8. **Pull back the mulch.** Organic mulches such as straw and leaves prevent weeds, maintain soil moisture, and improve soil quality. Unfortunately, under certain conditions they also can provide a home for insects that feed on tender young plants, such as slugs, sow bugs, and pill bugs. If these pests typically pose a problem in your garden, pull your mulch at least 2 inches away from the stems and stalks of transplants and young seedlings.

9. **Pull up those covers.** Sometimes the best way to head off insect trouble is to stretch some row covers over your crops. Besides keeping out pests, such as cucumber beetles, squash bugs, and cabbage maggots, row covers speed crop growth by trapping a blanket of warm air around new seedlings and established plants.

10. **Take out the apples and the trash...** Cleaning up garden debris may not be the flashiest method of controlling pests, but it is certainly one of the most effective and, by far, the easiest. By allowing insect larvae to overwinter in your garden and orchard, you are locking yourself into a cycle of repeated infestation. To break the cycle, promptly clean up all faded flowers, spent crops, and fallen end of the season.

Chigger-Chasing Sulfur

If you live in the Southeast, you probably know the unpleasant aftereffects of an encounter with chiggers. Take heart! You can conquer the chiggers lurking in your lawn with two well-timed applications of soil sulfur, a concentrated sulfur product available at some garden centers that is used to lower soil pH. Trisha Shirey, grounds manager at Lake Austin Spa Resort in Austin, Texas, says this remedy is especially effective in soft swaths of Bermuda grass.

Ingredients and Supplies

> 5 pounds powdered soil sulfur
> Drop or broadcast spreader
> Rubber gloves
> Dust mask
> Oscillating sprinkler

Directions

1. Early in the morning when the grass is wet with dew, use the drop or broadcast spreader to apply the sulfur, taking care to apply it as evenly as possible. Sulfur is a natural chemical dust, so wear rubber gloves and a dust mask to protect your hands and lungs while you work.

2. Immediately water the area for about 20 minutes using an oscillating sprinkler. Be sure that the sulfur is completely washed down into the grass.

Yield: Enough sulfur to treat 100 square feet of lawn

Note: For best results, Trisha suggests following this procedure twice each summer—once in late spring and again in late summer. Trisha thinks that the sulfur treatment can also help control fleas in the lawn.

SULFUR SIDE EFFECTS

Sulfur not only chases chiggers away but it also tends to lower soil pH (makes the soil more acidic). So if you're applying sulfur on soils that tend to be alkaline, you're probably doing yourself a double favor. But if your soil is naturally acidic, check the pH in the fall if you used soil sulfur during the summer. If the pH has fallen below 5.3, you'll need to apply lime to raise the pH. Ask your local Cooperative Extension Service for recommendations on how much lime to apply.

Rub Out Pests with Rubbing Alcohol

Houseplants bothered by pests? Rub them out with rubbing alcohol. Gardener Dominique Inge of Granbury, Texas, finds this recipe effective against mealybugs, whiteflies, red spider mites, aphids, fungus gnats, and scale. She cautions that it may cause leaf burn on some plants and doesn't recommend it for African violets.

Ingredients and Supplies

> ½–1 cup rubbing alcohol
> 1 quart water
> Pump spray bottle

Continued ➜

Directions

1. Mix ingredients in a pump spray bottle.
2. Test spray on a leaf to check for burning.
3. Wait 1 day and check for damage before treating the entire plant.
4. Treat at 3-day intervals for 10 days or as needed. Don't use this in the heat of the day.

Yield: 4½–5 cups of alcohol spray

Wash and Vacuum Pests Away

Ordinary water is a great weapon for dispatching houseplant pests. If your houseplants are infested with spider mites or aphids, try putting the plants in your kitchen sink and running a strong stream or spray of cool water over the foliage and stems. The force of the water can literally wash whiteflies, mites, and aphids right off the plants. Check the plants a few days later. If you find pesky pests that survived the treatment, wash the plants again. (Note that African violets dislike having their foliage washed, so don't try this technique on your violets.)

For plants that you can't wash, try vacuuming instead! Get out your handheld vacuum cleaner. With one hand, move the vacuum lightly over the plants, and with the other hand, support or hold the foliage so that the suction of the vacuum won't tear the leaves. Keep in mind that the insects you vacuum up may be only stunned, not killed. When you're finished pest-vacuuming, move away from your plants before you open the vacuum. Dump the pests into soapy water to kill them. This treatment works well for whiteflies, but may not be strong enough to suck off aphids or all spider mites.

Tomato Stake Whitefly Trap

Trick whiteflies with the color yellow. Whiteflies are attracted to yellow surfaces, and you can buy commercially produced traps that have sticky yellow surfaces where whiteflies land and get fatally stuck. In Brooklyn, Ohio, tomato lover Katherine Jarmusik came up with a nifty way to recycle some household items into a sticky whitefly trap at a cost that is much lower than the price of commercial traps.

Ingredients and Supplies

4 (6-foot-long) tomato stakes
4 (48-ounce) juice cans, each with 1 end removed
Yellow paint
Paintbrush
12 yellow or clear plastic bags (like the ones used to cover newspapers on rainy days)
Petroleum jelly

Directions

1. Use the stakes to support growing tomatoes. Or, if you're already using another type of support for your tomatoes, pound in the stakes alongside the plants. Four stakes set every 2 feet will protect a row of 10 tomatoes.
2. Paint the juice cans yellow.
3. Place the painted cans over the tops of the tomato stakes.
4. Cover each can with a yellow or clear plastic bag.
5. Smear petroleum jelly on the outside of the bags.

Yield: 4 super-sticky whitefly traps

Dealing with Dead Whiteflies

Whiteflies are so attracted to her yellow traps that the whole bag is soon covered, Katherine Jarmusik says. When the whiteflies get too thick on the bags, she removes the old bags, throws them away, and replaces them with new ones that are coated with fresh petroleum jelly.

Katherine finds that 4 cans, with 2 or 3 bag replacements per can, are enough to protect her 20 x 30-foot garden plot from whitefly damage. Yellow is the key to success with these traps, Katherine points out. "If you have enough yellow plastic bags, you can skip the step of painting the cans."

Vinegar Foils Fungus Gnats

Lure fungus gnats and fruit flies to a watery death with a simple cider vinegar trap. Christine Haugen, director of Green Horizons International, who specializes in earth-safe pest control, uses this formula when fungus gnats or fruit flies invade her Virginia home. "The gnats will find the jar within a few minutes and land on the rim to investigate," Christine says. "Then they will continue on in and drown."

Ingredients and Supplies

1 small wide-mouth jar (a baby food or bouillon jar works well)
1 tablespoon cider vinegar

Directions

1. Fill the jar about 7/8 full with water.
2. Add the vinegar.
3. Place the jar on a kitchen counter or table, especially near ripening fruit. You can also place the traps near houseplants if they're infested with fungus gnats. Leave the trap undisturbed.

Yield: About ⅔ cup of fungus gnat attractant

Note: In most situations, all the fungus gnats and fruit flies in your house will die in the trap within a few days. If you have a severe problem, you may need to replace the mixture in the jar after a week or so.

Fighting Fungus Gnat Larvae

Fungus gnats look like tiny fruit flies with beige wings. The gnats may lay eggs in the soil of houseplants, and their larvae may suck juices from the roots of the plants. Since the cider vinegar traps attract only adult fungus gnats, Christine Haugen suggests using neem to control the larvae in the soil. Neem is an organic pest control product extracted from the neem tree; it's available at garden centers and from mail-order garden suppliers.

Confuse Cuke Beetles with Rattails

Confuse cucumber beetles and other garden pests by planting rattail radishes in and around your vegetables. After Master Gardener Carol Kelly of Saltsburg, Pennsylvania, heard other gardeners talking about interplanting radishes with pest-plagued crops, she decided to try rattail radishes, a special variety of radishes that have edible pods. She especially recommends planting this tasty deterrent around your summer squash plants to repel cucumber beetles.

Carol thinks that regular radishes will discourage cucumber beetles, too, but the rattail radish plants grow bigger—often 18 inches tall—and she likes the flavor of the edible pods, which appear after the flowers. "I pick them when they're still young and tender and chop them into salads," Carol says. Rattail radishes develop a thick taproot, but it's not edible like other kinds of radishes.

Ingredients and Supplies

1 packet summer squash seeds
1 packet rattail radish seeds

Directions

1. After danger of frost has passed, plant squash seeds or transplants directly in the garden.

2. Sow a few rattail radish seeds in between the rows or around the hills of squash and at the ends of the rows. Rattail radish seeds are available in seed catalogs—check the listings for oriental vegetables.

Onion Rings for Cabbage Loopers

Confuse cabbage loopers and cabbageworms by surrounding your broccoli, cabbage, and cauliflower plants with onions. In both spring and fall, Charlotte, North Carolina, gardener Jeff Davis sees very few loopers when he uses this easy companion planting method.

Ingredients and Supplies

20 assorted cabbage, cauliflower, broccoli, kohlrabi, or brussels sprout seedlings
100 onion sets

Directions

1. In the spring, set out the seedlings in the normal manner, spacing them at least 18 inches apart.
2. As you settle in each plant, surround it with a ring of onion sets, spacing them 4 inches apart. The idea, Jeff says, is to encircle the cabbage family plants so that they're hidden by a screen of onions.

Note: Jeff inspects his plants often in search of cabbage loopers, but rarely finds one of the leaf-eating visitors. On 20 cabbage plants surrounded by onions, he may find 3 loopers at the peak of their season.

Some of the onions eventually grow into bulbs, but Jeff harvests most of them for use as green onions.

Beetle-Busting Potato Planting

Outsmart Colorado potato beetles before they stage a feast in your potato patch. Cynthia Connolly, an organic market gardener in Monticello, Florida, uses a companion planting plan to confound the beetles. Her not-so-secret weapons are garlic and onions. "The year we first tried this, Colorado potato beetles devastated our other potatoes, but the ones grown with the garlic had hardly any damage at all," Cynthia explains. Potato beetle adults looking for host plants upon which to lay eggs apparently are confused by the barrier of onions and garlic that guards the spuds.

Ingredients and Supplies

30 garlic cloves or plants
40 onion plants or sets
Seed potatoes for a 20-foot-long row (about 5 pounds)

Directions

1. In the fall, dig or till a garden bed or row in an area of your garden where potatoes have not been grown for 2 years.
2. Plant sprouting garlic cloves (or set out garlic plants) in a line down the outside of one side of the row or bed.
3. In early spring, plant seed potatoes down the middle of the prepared row or bed.
4. Plant onion plants or sets down the side of the row or bed opposite from the garlic, so that the potatoes are surrounded on all sides with garlic and onions.

Gummy Grasshopper Flour Formula

Stop grasshoppers from eating your plants by making them eat all-purpose flour. When you use this simple flour dust, grasshoppers, blister beetles, and

Continued ➡

other chewing insects will end up with their mouthparts so gummed up that they can't eat another thing, reports Trisha Shirey, grounds manager at Lake Austin Spa Resort in Austin, Texas.

Ingredients and Supplies

3 cups plain all-purpose flour
Garden duster or salt shaker
Ice pick or carving fork
Garden hose with spray nozzle

Directions

1. Put the flour in the garden duster. (If you're treating only a small area, use less flour and put the flour in a salt shaker.)

2. Go out in your garden and jiggle the plants upon which grasshoppers or blister beetles are feeding (this gets the insects moving).

3. Dust the insects and the leaves with flour.

4. After 2 days, rinse off the flour using a fine spray from a hose. On plants with hairy leaves, such as tomatoes, you may need to rinse twice to clean off the flour.

Note When the grasshoppers eat dusted leaves, they ingest so much flour that they become sick and stop eating, Trisha says. Since the success of the method hinges on getting plenty of flour on the leaves that the bugs are eating, it's best to apply the dust in the morning, while the plants are damp with dew.

As long as you rinse off the flour after 2 days, you won't harm your plants. But don't use self-rising flour, because the salts in that type of flour may injure plant leaves and aren't good for your soil.

PAPER BAG DUSTER

If you don't have a commercial garden duster, save yourself the investment by improvising a duster using a simple brown paper lunch bag. With an ice pick or carving fork, punch about a dozen small holes in the bottom and lower sides of the bag. Put flour in the bag. Then, when you want to apply the dust, hold the bag closed with one hand and tap the bottom of the bag with your other hand to release a cloud of floury dust. Empty powder containers, grated cheese jars, or discarded spice jars with shaker lids are other good prospects for recycling into a duster. Anything with a shaker top works well for this type of non measured application.

Insect Glossary

Abdomen The last section of an insect's body, following the head and thorax. Digestive and reproductive organs are found in the abdomen.

Antenna Paired, segmented structures, also called feelers; one on each side of the head. Aids sensory perception. Plural is *antennae*.

Beak Long, stylus-like mouthpart used by sucking insects to pierce the surface of a plant or animal; hollow and jointed. One or more tiny needles in the beak pierce the tissue.

Brood All the insects that hatch from eggs laid by a given mother, or those that hatch and mature at the same time. Commonly used to refer to bees.

Caterpillar Larval stage of a butterfly or moth. Segmented or wormlike, with a distinct head, 12 simple eyes, a pair of very short antennae, and usually six well-developed legs, as well as two to five pairs of prolegs.

Chitin A hornlike substance that forms a layer of the exoskeleton.

Chrysalis The tubular, hard pupal shell of a butterfly.

Class The largest subgroup of a phylum. Insects belong to the class Insecta or Hexapoda (meaning "six-legged").

Cocoon The silken pupal case of a butterfly or moth.

Compound eye The eye of an insect, composed of many separate hexagonal lenses fitted closely together; sensitive to movement and color. Larvae lack compound eyes.

Crawler The first active instar of a scale.

Cuticle The outer layer of the exoskeleton.

Dormant Inactive; in suspended animation; hibernating. Dormancy occurs in winter.

Elytra The hard, opaque wing covers of which meet in a straight line down the insect's back and cover most of the thorax and abdomen, giving an armored appearance.

Exoskeleton The hard outer covering or skeleton that protects an insect's body like armor. Forms a jointed frame.

Family The largest subdivision of an order, Each family contains a group of related genera (see Genus). Family names end in "-idae."

Frass The sawdust-like excrement of borers such as the peachtree borer and the squash vine borer.

Genus The largest subdivision of a family. Each genus is made up of a small group of closely related members. Plural is *genera*.

Gregarious Living in groups, as in ants, aphids, and honeybees.

Grub The larva of a beetle. Grubs are plump, flat, or wormlike, with well-developed heads and three pairs of legs. They pupate in the soil or other protected sites.

Hibernation A winter period of suspended animation passed by many insects that live more than one season. Usually spent in soil or garden debris.

Honeydew A sweet substance secreted by aphids, which is relished by ants. Also produced by mealybugs, scales, and whiteflies.

Host plant The plant on which an insect feeds, lives, or lays eggs.

Instar The form of an insect between each molt. Most insects pass through three to six instars.

Larva Immature form of an insect that is more or less wormlike; may be legged or legless; may be smooth or covered with spines or tufts of hair. They have chewing mouthparts. Plural is larvae.

Maggot The larva of a fly, usually a small, white, legless worm without an obvious head. Mouthparts are hooked. Maggots tend to feed inside the host plant or animal.

Mandibles The strong chewing jaws of arthropods.

Maxillae Second pair of jaws just behind the mandibles.

Metamorphosis A form change during which an insect molts and passes through nymph to adult stages (incomplete metamorphosis) or through larval to pupal and adult stages (complete metamorphosis).

Molt A shedding of the exoskeleton so that an insect can grow. The old skin splits after a new one has formed beneath it.

Nymph An immature adult with undeveloped wings and, in some cases, different markings from the adult.

Ocellus The simple, single-lensed eye of an insect. It perceives light but produces no image. Insects usually have them as well as compound eyes. Found at the base of the antennae or on top of the head. Larvae rely on them entirely. Plural is ocelli.

Order The largest subgroup of a class. Insects are divided into 26 orders. Each order contains a large group of insects that share similar wing structures.

Oviparous Egg-laying

Ovipositor The egg-laying organ in female insects.

Parasite An insect that lives and feeds in or on another insect or animal for at least part of its life cycle.

Pheromone A chemical substance, such as a sexual attractant, secreted by an insect to create a response in others of its species.

Phylum A major division of the animal kingdom. Insects belong to the phylum Arthropoda (meaning "joint-legged").

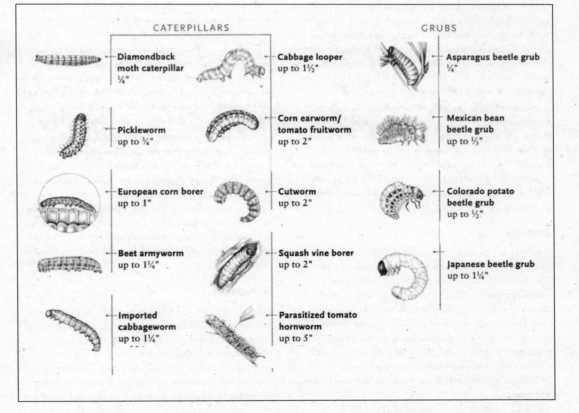

CATERPILLARS

Diamondback moth caterpillar ¼"

Pickleworm up to ¾"

European corn borer up to 1"

Beet armyworm up to 1¼"

Imported cabbageworm up to 1¼"

Cabbage looper up to 1½"

Corn earworm/ tomato fruitworm up to 2"

Cutworm up to 2"

Squash vine borer up to 2"

Parasitized tomato hornworm up to 5"

GRUBS

Asparagus beetle grub ¼"

Mexican bean beetle grub up to ⅓"

Colorado potato beetle grub up to ½"

Japanese beetle grub up to 1¼"

Continued ➡

Predator An insect that feeds on another live insect or animal.

Proboscis Long, retractable sucking tube through which nectar is syphoned by insects such as butterflies and moths.

Proleg A plump, fleshy, false leg that enables larvae to move more easily. Caterpillars may have up to five pairs, which are sometimes hooked to enable them to hang from a host plant.

Pubescent Downy; covered with short, fine hairs.

Pupa An inactive stage between larva and adult in which adult features develop. The pupa may be encased in a chrysalis or cocoon, or it may roll itself in a leaf. Plural is *pupae*.

Pupate To turn into a pupa.

Scavenger An insect that feeds on dead plants, dead animals, or decaying matter.

Sessile Incapable of movement; immobile. Some female scales are sessile.

Species The fundamental unit in classification. The species refers to a single insect that may be distinguished from others in its genus by a particular feature or habit. Plural is *species*.

Spiracle One of many tiny holes in the thorax and abdomen of an insect that serve as breathing pores.

Thorax The center section of an insect's body, between the head and the abdomen. Wings and legs are attached to the thorax.

Vector A disease carrier.

Viviparous Bearing live young. Aphids can be viviparous.

DISEASES

Overview of Diseases

Jill Jesiolowski Cebenko and Deborah L. Martin

Plant diseases can be hard to diagnose compared to insect problems. After all, potato beetles are quite visible, but it takes a microscope to see a virus or most fungi and bacteria. Diagnosing a disease is also difficult because symptoms can look like those that excessive cold or heat, sun scald, high salt levels, nutrient deficiencies, waterlogged soils, low light levels, and other problems can cause.

If you maintain well-drained fertile soil, enriched with compost, and take sensible precautions, such as cleaning up crop debris after harvest, you won't see many diseases in the garden. If, however, a disease problem recurs year after year or is especially damaging, you would be wise to learn what it is, how it spreads, and how to manage it and prevent it in the future.

Bacteria

Bacteria are microscopic, single-celled organisms. Each bacteria cell reproduces by dividing in two. The bacteria that attack plants produce toxic compounds that kill the plant cells; the bacteria then use the contents of the plant cells for their own growth. Plants react to such attacks by triggering the death of cells around the bacterial infection, which isolates the bacteria colony from the rest of the plant and causes the characteristic spots, or shothole appearance, in leaves as the dead tissue drops out.

Bacteria enter plants through openings such as pores and wounds. Some cause wilting, as the multiplying bacteria kill the cells in the vascular system or plug it with masses of bacteria. Others cause spots, rots, and blights, which are all symptoms of dying plant tissue. Some bacteria cause plant tissue to grow abnormally into galls.

Fungi

Fungi cause the majority of plant diseases. As a group, these microscopic organisms are distinguished by their lack of chlorophyll, which means that they can't make food for themselves and so must rely on getting their nutrients from other organisms or organic matter. Some fungi, called *saprophytes*, live only on dead organic matter. They break down organic material in compost piles and soils into forms that other organisms can use. Most pathogenic (disease-causing) fungi parasitize living plant tissue, but some can live off of both living and dead plant material. Many live all summer in plants, then they overwinter on dead crop debris.

Fungi have cells made up of branching filaments, or minute tubes, called *hyphae*. A group of hyphae form a *mycelium*, which typically looks like a velvety spot or coating on a leaf. Some fungi reproduce asexually from sections of hyphae called *sclerotia*, whereas others make reproductive units, called *spores*. Sclerotia are generally quite easy to see, whereas spores are usually microscopic.

Most fungi can make different types of spores to guarantee their survival in almost any situation. In general, asexual spores are produced in the best growing conditions. They are released from a special structure, generally called a "fruiting body." They're carried by wind, rain, animals, and sometimes people to new sites, where they germinate if temperature and humidity are right. Furthermore, pathogenic fungi that spend most of their life cycle on roots and debris underground commonly produce swimming spores, or zoospores. Fungi that attack plant parts above ground may also produce swimming spores that navigate through dew and rain on the leaves.

Spores that can remain dormant until they encounter good germinating conditions and an appropriate host are called *resting spores*. Fungi typically produce them in fall in preparation for winter. Some dormant spores can remain viable, or capable of germination, for years.

When spores germinate, they send out a tube, or *hypha*. This usually enters the plant through a wound or natural opening. Some pathogenic fungi are also capable of forcing their way into plant cells by exuding enzymes that kill the cells or by using a strong hypha tip that can bore into plant tissue.

Fungi cause wilting when mycelium plugs the plant's vascular system or destroys the cell walls. They also cause rots and blights as they release toxins that break down cells in seeds, roots, and fruits. Infected plants can appear *chlorotic* (yellowed) or have other discolorations caused as the plant cells die and as photosynthesis and other metabolic activity is restricted. Some fungi cause *galls* and *smuts*, which are abnormal growths of plant tissue.

Nematodes

Nematodes are actually a group of unsegmented roundworms. They range in size from microscopically small to several inches long. Some species break down organic matter, some attack insects, and others attack plants. The plant-feeding species are usually discussed with plant diseases because their mode of action and ways to control them are similar. Like fungi, some species of nematodes have a dormant state that can remain in the soil for many years.

The mouthparts of nematodes pierce plant tissue. Some species excrete a digestive juice that rots cells before they feed. Others exude substances that stimulate nearby plant cells to enlarge or multiply abnormally. They also carry many viral diseases. But even when they don't carry disease, the small holes they make allow other diseases to enter the plant.

Although they can move, nematodes are so tiny that they rarely travel more than a foot (30 cm) through the soil. They're usually introduced to a piece of land by infected planting stock, infested soil, or running water.

Viruses

Viruses are minute parasitic bits of genetic material (DNA or RNA) with a protein casing. Their genetic material causes host cells to make more viruses. Viruses can multiply only in a living host. Some viruses can remain inactive but viable for as long as 50 years in dead plant material.

Many viruses are carried by insects, which are then called *vectors*. Seeds may carry viruses, and infected propagating stock is certain to produce infected plants. Viruses can also be spread from one plant to the next on knives, equipment, and tools.

Three symptoms of viral infection are yellowing or other discoloration, stunting, and malformations. Mosaic patterns, ring spots, and a uniform pale color are all symptoms of infection. Stunting can affect a whole plant or one part, such as a leaf, branch, ear, or other part. Malformations include leaf rolls, puckering, and "shoestring" leaves (extremely narrow, twisted leaves).

The Spread of Disease

Plant pathogens spread in various ways. Spores and bacteria may be blown on the wind or carried on splashes of water. Many pathogens can be moved from plant to plant mechanically, meaning that animals, tools, equipment, and even gardeners that have come into contact with infected plant material can spread the pathogens. Insects can also spread some diseases by carrying the pathogens in their saliva from one plant to the next. As they feed on the sap, they release the pathogens into the new host. For any disease, knowing the life cycle of the pathogen and the way it spreads can help you avoid bringing it into your garden and spreading it further.

DISEASE RESISTANCE

Plants are immune to many diseases because the pathogen simply can't attack a particular host. For example, potatoes are immune to attack from corn smut fungi and corn is immune to late blight. In contrast, resistance means that the plant may have some degree of susceptibility to the pathogen, but it's able to fight against it. Many varieties of garden vegetables have been bred for resistance to certain common diseases.

Resistance can be *genetic*, meaning it's an inherited characteristic of the plant, or *induced*, meaning that the plant's immune system has been activated to fight off infection. Plants that have been bred for resistance may have physical characteristics, such as a thicker leaf cuticle (the exterior surface of the leaf) or woodier stems, which repel the action of germinating spores.

Plants can also be selected for their strong immune response that helps them tolerate diseases well enough to produce a useful crop. Some plants can quickly mobilize a cell response that neutralizes

Continued ➡

invading pathogens. This response causes the cells around an infected area to die. The layer of dead cells isolates the infection from the rest of the plant and causes the corky spots or holes in leaves that are characteristic symptoms of some diseases. Other plant responses to infection are uncannily like our own immune system because exposure to a pathogen activates genes that cause the plant to become resistant to later attacks.

The environmental conditions a particular plant is growing in also helps determine whether or not it can resist infection. For example, a variety with cuticles thick enough to repel germinating spores when it's growing in good conditions might still be infected in low-light conditions when the leaf growth is weaker and the cuticle thinner. Plant nutrition, watering, light levels, and other conditions also contribute to disease resistance.

PREVENTION AND CONTROL

Before any disease can occur, the three elements of the "disease triangle" must be present: a susceptible plant, the disease-causing agent (pathogen), and favorable environmental conditions for growth of the pathogen. A disease can't develop if even one of these elements is absent. Most prevention and control measures for managing plant diseases are based on removing one or more of these elements.

For example, susceptible plants can be removed from the equation by planting resistant or immune crops. Pathogens can be removed from the equation by removing infected plants from the garden. Although gardeners can't control the weather, they can make environmental conditions unfavorable for pathogens by avoiding overhead watering, pruning to promote good air circulation, and taking other precautions.

Prevention

Healthy plants. Start with certified disease-free seeds, tubers, and plants where possible, and give them the best care. Of course, fertile soil, fed with compost and enriched with high levels of organic matter, is the key to growing healthy plants that resist infection. It's important to correct any problems with soil drainage. Reduce the length of time plant leaves are wet by installing drip irrigation, watering only at the base of the plant, or using sprinklers only in the morning so that leaves have a chance to dry before evening. Pruning and spacing plants to increase air circulation between plants also allows leaves to dry faster and thwarts the spread of many fungi. Plant the right plant in the right spot—for instance, a shade-loving plant won't do well in full sun and in such a weakened state will be more susceptible to attack.

Resistant varieties. Whenever possible, choose disease resistant or tolerant varieties when buying seeds, tubers, transplants, and nursery stock. Read descriptions in seed catalogs to find varieties that have disease-fighting characteristics. Tomato varieties are commonly labeled with V, F, or N (sometimes all three): The "V" means verticillium-resistant, "F" means fusarium wilt-resistant, and "N" means root-knot nematode-resistant. For other types of plants, look for descriptions such as "resistant to powdery mildew," "tolerant of anthracnose," or "scab-resistant."

Preserve natural enemies. Finished compost is a rich source of beneficial soil fungi, bacteria, and other organisms that help protect plants from disease. These naturally occurring microorganisms are invisible, but they're vital in protecting plants. Some suppress pathogens in the soil by producing compounds that inhibit their growth. Others actively attack pathogens and some colonize plant roots, which keeps pathogens out. Airborne fungi,

yeasts, and other microorganisms also live on the surface of leaves and protect them from attack. Because sprays aimed at controlling pathogens can also kill these beneficial microorganisms, it may be good to avoid using such sprays unless they're absolutely necessary.

Cultural Controls

Remove alternate hosts. For example, some rusts can't complete a life cycle without a specific, alternate host plant, such as cedar for cedar-apple rust or juniper for pear-trellis rust. If there are a few of the alternate host plants in the area, removing them can reduce or eliminate the disease locally. If there are many alternate hosts in the area, then it may be hard to have an effect.

Crop rotation. A way to reduce the spread of soil-borne pathogens is to avoid planting susceptible plants in infected soil until infective spores die off. Because some pathogens can live in the soil for a couple of years, it's necessary to grow nonsusceptible plants in those soils during that time. Crop rotation is also a preventive measure to ensure that pathogens that might be present at low levels don't have a chance to build up to damaging levels.

With that in mind, though, crop rotation in a home garden is less effective than in a larger area because it's hard to rotate the susceptible crop a great distance from the initial site of infection. It helps to use permanent raised beds, especially if coupled with careful sanitation measures. Where the whole garden is plowed or tilled at one time, infected soil is spread around.

To rotate crops effectively, it's important to know which plant belongs in each family so that you don't mistakenly plant related crops one after the other. For example, tomatoes, potatoes, eggplant, and peppers are all in the same family (Solanaceae), and cabbage, cauliflower, broccoli, mustard, radishes, turnips, Chinese cabbages, and brussels sprouts are all related (Cruciferae). When planting herbs and annual flowers in the garden, they should also be considered in the crop rotation because many belong to the same families as garden vegetables. For example, sweet alyssum is a member of the cabbage family (Cruciferae), and dill and coriander are in the same family as carrots and celery (Umbelliferae).

Physical Controls

Sanitation. The sources of disease infection (inoculum) around the garden can be reduced or eliminated by cleaning up crop debris and pulling out infected plants. Where allowing infected plants to remain could jeopardize the whole crop, it's advisable to pull the whole plant, including roots and sometimes the surrounding soil, and remove it from the garden. Whether or not infected plant material can be composted depends on what the organism is and how hot the composting process is likely to be. In some cases it's advisable to burn, bury deeply, or discard infected plants in the garbage rather than compost them.

Cleaning tools and implements, as well as shoes and hands, is an especially important sanitation measure when moving from infected plants or soils to uninfected areas. Also, avoid moving from plant to plant when humidity is high enough to leave a film of moisture on leaves, as diseases can be spread quickly this way.

Removing weeds in the garden and from nearby areas can help manage some diseases if the weeds are likely to harbor diseases affecting crop plants. This is most effective if there are very few such disease host plants in the area. Some plant diseases are spread so widely on the wind that host plant removal doesn't contribute to control.

Barriers. If a disease is spread by sucking insects, such as aphids or leafhoppers, screening out the insect carrier can exclude the disease. Sprays of kaolin clay can be used to coat leaves and fruit with a fine barrier of clay, which foils the leafhoppers and other insects and prevents some pathogenic fungi from attacking.

Hot-water treatments. Hot-water treatments can be used to kill some pathogens carried in certain types of seeds. Some commercial seeds are already heat treated; gardeners can also use hot water to treat their own seeds. Follow recommendations given under the disease entries for exact temperatures and timing.

Solarization. Solarization involves covering soil with clear plastic during the summer months to heat it 6 to 8 inches deep to temperatures that kill pathogens. Solarization has been shown to keep soil-borne pathogens—such as verticillium, fusarium, southern blight, and nematodes—in check for 2 to 3 years. First, remove all vegetation, rake the soil smooth, soak it well with water, then cover with clear plastic stretched tight over the surface. A clear plastic tarp or 4-mil-thick plastic sheeting can be used. Bury the edges of the plastic 6 inches deep to achieve a good seal. Leave in place for 6 to 14 weeks in the hottest part of the summer. This works best in the warmest regions. In northern regions, use two layers of plastic with a thin air space between them to increase the heating effect, and leave the soil covered for the maximum length of time.

Biological Controls

Fermented compost tea. The many beneficial microorganisms found in compost can be used effectively as a disease treatment by steeping compost in water to make a tea. It has been found that the tea is more effective as a disease control when it's allowed to ferment. Use finished compost and steep 1 part compost to 5 to 8 parts water for 3 to 7 days (2-week fermentations may be more effective on some diseases). Strain the liquid and filter it through a fine screen before putting it in the sprayer. Apply the tea to the lower part of the plant stem and around the roots for soil-borne diseases or onto leaves for powdery mildews.

Commercial **products.** Various naturally occurring fungi (e.g., Ampelomyces quisqualis) and bacteria (e.g., Bacillus subtilis, Pseudomonas spp.) are becoming increasingly available to buy. Depending on the product, they're applied to leaves, roots, or branches to suppress plant diseases. However, these products are probably more useful for commercial growers than home gardeners, who may find them too expensive for use on the few plants that might benefit.

Fungicides

As with any type of treatment, it's important to make sure that the problem is correctly identified and that treatment is really necessary before using sprays or dusts. Unfortunately, these must be applied before pathogens infect plants to provide a protective barrier—once plants have been infected, they can't be cured by such treatments (though healthy plants can fight some types of infections). Most sprays and dusts can also harm beneficial microorganisms that help protect plants from pathogens. Fermented compost tea sprays are an exception because they actually add beneficial microorganisms.

Water. In the case of powdery mildew, the presence of water on the leaf stops spores from germinating. Spraying leaves thoroughly on both sides with plain water in midday several times a week can provide satisfactory control. This isn't a useful method

Continued ➡

Common Disorders of Vegetable Crops

Condition	Crop	Symptoms	Cause
Black heart	Beet, turnip	Darkening in center, sometimes hollow	Boron deficiency; sometimes potassium or phosphorus deficiency
	Potato	Same	Lack of oxygen
	Celery	Same	Fluctuating soil moisture; calcium deficiency
Blasting	All flowers	Buds or flowers drop prematurely	Soil too wet or dry
	Onion	Leaf tips bleach, brown, and wither	Bright light after cloudy, wet conditions
Blossom-end rot	Tomato, pepper, cucurbits	Dark, sunken area at blossom end of fruit	Dry conditions after wet; calcium deficiency
Cracked stem	Celery	Stem cracks	Boron deficiency
Hollow heart	Crucifers	Hollow stem	Boron deficiency
Sunscald	Tomato, pepper	White area appears, blisters before secondary rotting occurs	Excessive loss of foliage; heavy pruning or trellising of tomatoes
Tipburn	Lettuce, potato	Leaf tips brown	Bright light after cloudy, wet conditions; potassium deficiency; calcium imbalance

where plants are also susceptible to other diseases that would develop in wet conditions.

Milk. Fresh milk sprays made from 1 part milk and 9 parts water and sprayed twice a week have been shown to suppress powdery mildew of cucumber and zucchini. It's thought that the milk may work by preventing the fungus from invading, or it may boost the plant's immune system by providing nutrients.

Oils. Narrow-range oils are mainly insecticidal, but they can be used to control plant diseases such as powdery mildew. Mix according to product instructions for use on plants during the growing season.

Botanical extracts. Garlic sprays and essential oils from some plants have some disease-suppressing properties. These are becoming increasingly available in commercial products.

Baking soda. Homemade baking soda sprays are typically recommended to control powdery mildew. A common recipe calls for mixing 1 teaspoon of baking soda, 1 drop of liquid soap, and 2 quarts of water. A spray of baking soda and oil can also be used to control powdery mildew: Mix 1 tablespoon baking soda, 1 tablespoon narrow-range oil, 1 drop of detergent, and 1 gallon of water. Commercial baking soda sprays are also available.

Sulfur. Both sprays and dusts containing sulfur are available to control plant diseases caused by fungi. Sulfur binds with the spores to prevent them from germinating. To be effective, the sulfur must be present on all susceptible leaves before the fungi invade; therefore, it must be used at 7- to 14-day intervals during damp weather to protect new foliage. Sulfur harms the beneficial mites that live on leaves of fruit trees and other plants; therefore, it should be used with caution. It also shouldn't be used when temperatures are over 80°F (27°C) because it can damage leaves. Because some plants can't tolerate sulfur, always check labels before using it.

Copper. Sprays containing copper (fixed copper, Bordeaux mixture) are sold to control bacterial diseases and some fungal diseases. Copper sprays can damage leaves and must be used according to instructions on the package. Copper is also a heavy metal and can build up in the soil if used continually. Where frequent spraying with copper is required to control a disease, it would be better to concentrate on finding ways to prevent the problem in future.

A Word of Encouragement

In your garden, you probably won't have the chance to get to know more than a few diseases that are common problems in your region. Organic gardeners know that diseases aren't very common. Healthy plants growing in a healthful environment are resistant or tolerant to most pathogens. They have a lot of unseen help from beneficial fungi and bacteria, in the air and in the soil, that suppress the pathogens. A balanced, organic garden is your best insurance against disease problems.

The most common diseases are listed here, with a brief description of the most obvious symptoms. Several diseases have similar symptoms; this table is meant as a guide to help you narrow down the possibilities. You will need to read the detailed descriptions given in the disease entries to make a final diagnosis.

Defeating Plant Diseases the Organic Way

Joan Benjamin and Deborah L. Martin

Whether it's rust on your roses or powdery mildew on your pumpkins, the ugly symptoms and disappointing crops caused by plant diseases have no doubt resulted in suffering for you (or rather, your plants). All kinds of plants, from mighty oaks to dainty annual flowers, are susceptible to the bacteria, fungi, and viruses that cause plant diseases. But that doesn't mean that you're doomed to diseased plants. You have lots of solutions, from disease-prevention planting plans to homemade remedies that can help you keep your vegetables, flowers, lawn, trees, and shrubs healthy.

Prevention is the best defense. It's easier to keep your plants disease-free than to try to cure them once they're infected. The best way to ensure your plants' health is to provide a healthy, fast-draining soil and appropriate growing conditions. Organic matter is the key to soil health and good drainage, so make sure that your soil has plenty.

The right plants can make disease prevention much easier. Choose disease resistant varieties whenever possible and match plants to the conditions in your garden.

Adopt a disease prevention routine. When you walk through your garden, always be on the lookout for discolored leaves or other symptoms that just don't look right. If you see diseased leaves, pluck them off of your plants to prevent the disease from spreading. If necessary, remove a sickly plant before it infects its neighbors.

If you're growing fruits and vegetables, be sure to clear out plant debris after your harvest so that you don't give diseases a place to camp out, waiting for spring to strike again. (Don't work in the garden when plants are wet because water is a great disease conductor.) Compost any healthy material you remove from your plants, but be sure to throw any diseased leaves or stems into the garbage.

Doctor plants with care. In some cases, you can use sprays, powders, and other treatments to discourage disease or prevent it from spreading. When treating plants with a spray or powder, keep these simple rules in mind:

- **Test your treatments.** Try both homemade and store-bought cures on one leaf first to test your plant's sensitivity. It's like trying out a stain removal product on a small area before going whole hog. Wait a day to see if any problems turn up before you treat the entire plant.

- **Stick sprays in place.** If your spray rolls off your plants' leaves, it isn't going to do much good. Try adding a drop of liquid soap (with as few additives as possible) to your sprays to break up surface tension on leaves and help the mix stay in place.

- **Get started early.** First thing in the morning is the best time to spray. Don't use sprays late in the day when humidity is building up or dew is settling since these are prime conditions for some diseases to spread.

- **Watch the weather.** Don't apply treatments in windy or rainy weather. If it rains after an application, plan to reapply.

- **Keep cool.** Don't treat plants when temperatures are above 90°F. Some sprays can burn leaves at high temperatures.

- **Cover up.** Remember to use any spray or powder with caution, no matter how harmless it may seem. Wear long sleeves, goggles, gloves, and long pants. Use a dust mask with powders and a respirator with sprays that may irritate your throat or lungs.

- **Store disease-control products carefully.** Always label containers and keep them out of the reach of children and pets. Do not expose sprays or powders to light or heat.

PLANT DISEASE PRIMER

How can you tell when your plants are sick? Common symptoms include yellow or blotchy leaves, distorted growth, patches of mold, and dying leaves or plants. But other problems, like a nutrient deficiency or lack of water, may cause these symptoms too. Making the right diagnosis can be tricky.

If you think your plants are diseased, compare their symptoms to those described below for some common plant diseases. Then, check the symptoms caused by lack of nutrients. Chances are, you'll figure out what's troubling your plants. If you're stumped, take a sample of the plant to your local Cooperative Extension office and ask for help in diagnosing the problem.

Blights. Spreading brown spots or patches on leaves can be a clue that your plants have a fungal blight. The fruits may shrivel and rot. Other types of blight may look like a white or gray growth on the flowers.

Downy or powdery mildew. If your plants have a white powdery coating on the leaves, the problem is powdery mildew. If the fuzzy coating is on the undersides of the leaves, downy mildew may be the

Continued ➡

cause. Various fungi cause these diseases, which can affect a wide range of plants.

Mosaic. Mosaic is a viral disease that causes a range of symptoms including mottled leaves, twisted growth, and stunted plants.

Rust. If your plants look as if they're covered with rust, the cause is rust fungi.

Stem, root, and crown rots. These fungal diseases cause stems, crowns, and/or roots to become soft. Affected parts often turn brown or black or look water-soaked. Plants may be stunted or wilted.

Wilts. Both bacteria and fungi can cause wilt diseases. The common symptoms are yellow leaves and wilted plants. Suspect wilt diseases especially if plants wilt suddenly even when the soil is fairly moist.

Compost Tea Cure-All for Plants

To blast away blight in the vegetable garden, start your plants off with a few sips of compost tea. That's the advice of Steve Peters, agricultural planning associate for Seeds of Change, an organic seed company. "I have used compost tea as a preventive measure—it's pretty remarkable," says Steve, who says he's been pleased with the success even with plants like tomatoes and potatoes that are susceptible to the fungal diseases early blight and late blight.

Ingredients and Supplies

    5-gallon bucket
    Good-quality, finished compost
    Fine-screened strainer
    Backpack or pump sprayer

Directions

1. Fill the bucket halfway with compost, then add an equal amount of water, and stir.

2. Continue to stir the mix every other day with a large stick or branch, letting the stuff steep for about 1 week or until the liquid is mahogany colored.

3. Let the solid material settle to the bottom of the bucket and run the liquid through a fine screen. "You're basically decanting it," Steve says. "You've got a lot of solid material in there and if you're not careful, it can clog your sprayer. With careful pouring, it should be okay."

4. Pour the strained mixture into a backpack sprayer. Or pour it into a spray bottle and store the remainder in the bucket. Make sure that you label the bucket.

5. Spray young plants about once a week. The tea has a double benefit, Steve says. "It also acts as a foliar (leaf) fertilizer."

Yield: About 2½ gallons of compost tea.

Seedling-Ease Chamomile Tea

It's sad to watch beautiful little seedlings suddenly wilt and die—cut down before their time by a disease called damping-off. There is no cure for this soil-dwelling fungal disease, but according to Penny King, an herbal educator, you can prevent damping-off with chamomile tea. Penny saw her share of damping-off when she grew herbs commercially as the owner of Pennyroyal Herbs in Georgetown, Texas. She found that she could prevent damping-off losses simply by watering her seedlings with chamomile tea.

Ingredients and Supplies

    1 cup water
    2 teaspoons dried chamomile flowers
    Strainer

Symptoms of Disease

The following list of symptoms and causes will help you decide whether you have a cultural disorder; fungal, bacterial, or viral disease; or if your plants may be infested with nematodes.

Cultural Disorders

A variety of conditions can cause cultural disorders, including nutrient deficiencies, improper pH, poor soil drainage, under-or-overfertilization, and improper light exposure. The symptoms of these problems generally cause chlorosis, or yellowing, of the leaves. Chlorotic areas in most cases eventually turn brown or die. Look closely to see if the yellowing affects all of the leaves or only the youngest or oldest ones. Cultural disorders can also result in yellowed or browned leaf edges, yellowing between the veins of the leaves, or in irregular or mosaic spots or patterns.

Fungal Diseases

Plants infected with fungi can develop a variety of symptoms, depending on the type of disease involved. Look for pale patches on the leaves that mayor may not be associated with rust-colored, powdery-looking patches on the upper or lower surface; round or irregular spots or blotches of chlorotic (yellowed) tissue that darken with time and dead spots or blotches on leaves are other signs of fungal diseases. Also look for water-soaked or greasy-looking spots on leaves or stems, or black, rotted-looking streaks or blotches. In this case, once the fungi have rotted all the way around the stem (girdle it) the afflicted stem will wilt and die. Seedlings that die suddenly, rotting at the soil surface and falling over, probably have been afflicted with a common fungal disease called damping-off.

Bacterial Diseases

Plants that exhibit the following may have a bacterial disease of some kind: rotted leaves, stems, branches, or tubers, often accompanied by a foul odor. When cut, afflicted plant parts often exude sticky-looking, yellowish or whitish masses of bacteria. Other symptoms of bacterial diseases include wilted leaves or stems, or large, irregularly shaped galls near the soil line on roots and stems.

Viral Diseases

There are many different viral diseases, all of which cause slightly different symptoms. Look for some or all of the following symptoms if you suspect your plants may be infected with a viral disease. Virus-infected plants generally exhibit overall poor plant performance, specifically, small, stunted plants, leaves, and blossoms. Blossoms and leaves may be disfigured, or the plant may develop shoots that branch abnormally, creating witches'-brooms. Many viral diseases cause a yellow-and-green mottling pattern on leaves, stems, or even blossoms. Also look for puckered, rolled, or extremely narrow ("shoestring") leaves and chlorosis (yellowing of leaves), specifically irregular yellow spots on leaves, often accompanied by leaf curling or excessive branching.

Nematode Infestation

Nematode-infested plants are stunted and grow poorly. Root knot nematodes form galls or swellings on plant roots, which you will find if you dig the plants to examine the roots. Other species cause deformed leaves or stems. Put nematodes at the bottom of your list of suspects. If no other explanation seems to fit, check the possibility that your plants have nematodes.

Directions

1. Bring the water to a boil, then remove from heat and stir in the chamomile flowers. Cover and allow the mixture to come to room temperature.

2. Strain the liquid and use full strength. Dampen potting soil mixtures with the tea before you plant your seeds. And then water with the tea blend, spraying the soil lightly each day with the chamomile tea instead of water.

Yield: About 1 cup of Seedling-Ease tea

Note: You can also use chamomile tea to water cuttings and to soak seeds prior to planting.

Variations: For a slightly stronger antifungal tea, add 2 teaspoons of dried horsetail (*Equisetum arvense*) to the water and chamomile flowers. (You can buy dried horsetail from many mail-order herb suppliers.)

Use this stronger tea solution on established plants that exhibit signs of fungal disease. Repeated applications of the tea can cure many fungal problems. Be sure to spray both sides of the leaves thoroughly.

"Hot" Compost Helps, Too

Adding "hot" compost to your seed-starting mix also helps protect your seedlings from disease, says compost-and-disease expert Harry Hoitink, Ph.D., professor of plant pathology at the Ohio State University. Just amend a standard peat/vermiculite starting mix with at least 5 percent mature compost, preferably from a pile that has recently

---

been heated. Any disease organisms in the compost materials are killed in the hot pile. Then, as the compost cools, beneficial disease-preventing microbes reproduce quickly and get the upper hand.

More Chamomile Tea for Seedlings

"Chamomile tea definitely works," says Steve Peters, agricultural planning associate for Seeds of Change, an organic seed company. Even broccoli and other brassica seedlings, which often fall prey to the low light and lack of air circulation in greenhouses, will survive with a dousing of strong chamomile tea.

Steve mixes 1 cup of dried chamomile flowers with 1 quart of water to make his tea. He suggests steeping the brew for at least an hour, explaining that "the stronger it is, the more effective it is." He adds that the taste of this strong tea, should you try it, would probably be too bitter to drink.

Spray the seedlings as soon as they appear. Continue spraying daily until the seedlings are past the danger point (about two weeks).

Using sterile soil for seed-starting, rather than garden soil or potting soil that has already been used, should be your first step in preventing the damping-off fungus, Steve advises. And keeping soil moist, rather than soaked, is also important.

Andy's Simple Alfalfa Solution

Try giving your flowers and vegetables a shot of alfalfa for a nutritional boost that makes plants stronger and more able to fight off diseases. You

Continued ➡

can prevent most types of fungal diseases if you spray your plants with alfalfa tea early in the season, says Andy Lopez, founder of the Invisible Gardeners of America. And what if you don't have a field of alfalfa growing nearby? Don't worry—alfalfa is available as a powdery meal that you can buy from farm or organic garden suppliers.

Ingredients and Supplies

    1 cup alfalfa meal
    1-gallon bucket
    Cheesecloth
    Biodegradable dishwashing liquid
    Backpack or pump sprayer

Directions

1. Add the alfalfa meal to a bucket of water. Let it sit for a few hours, then strain the mixture through cheesecloth.

2. Add a dash of biodegradable dishwashing liquid to help the tea stick to plant leaves.

3. Fill the spray bottle with the mixture and spray plants.

Yield: About 1 gallon of alfalfa solution

WELL-FED LEAVES RESIST DISEASE

Just as people take a daily vitamin to keep from getting sick, plants stay healthier when they get occasional doses of nutrient-rich organic sprays like Andy Lopez's alfalfa solution. Applying foliar (leaf) sprays may not prevent disease organisms from attacking your plants. But well-nourished plants are more likely to keep growing and producing even if they are suffering from disease. You may not notice the disease symptoms until very late in the season.

When you spray nutrient solutions to help prevent disease, it's best to spray in the early morning, especially if you live in a humid climate.

Rhubarb Spray to the Rescue

For a garden rescue straight from the garden, try Mary Perlmutter's recipe for a rhubarb spray that destroys fungal diseases as well as aphids and June bugs. "If I see signs of a disease that's just starting, I give it a shot of the rhubarb mixture," says author and organic gardener Mary, who has experimented for years with using plants like rhubarb and garlic for solving disease problems in her rural Canadian garden.

Ingredients and Supplies

    ½ cup rhubarb leaves (about 6 leaves), crushed
    3 quarts water
    Pot (for boiling)
    Blender (optional)
    Cheesecloth or fine-mesh sieve
    Pump spray bottle

Directions

1. Cut or tear rhubarb leaves into small pieces. Mary uses rhubarb from her garden, but if you need to buy some, you may find rhubarb with its leaves intact at a farmers' market. Most supermarkets sell it with the leaves removed.

2. Place the leaves in the water and bring it to a rolling boil.

3. Steep the leaves for at least an hour. Mary says she likes to steep them overnight.

4. Shred the boiled leaves further in a blender, if desired. Strain the solution through the cheesecloth or sieve and pour it into a spray bottle. Add the leaf residue to your compost pile.

5. Spray affected plants thoroughly.

Yield: About 3 quarts of rhubarb-leaf spray

Note: Mary suggests making a new batch of rhubarb spray each time you want to spray. "I have been known to strain it and put it in the freezer," she says, "but I prefer a fresh mixture." She adds that you can also keep leftover spray—carefully labeled—in the refrigerator; for a freshness check, be sure that it doesn't have an off odor. Or, if you have a spot where you'd like to lower the pH in your garden, just pour the excess rhubarb spray into your compost or soil for a slightly acidic boost.

Hello Jell-O Seed Starter

To get her flower and vegetable seeds off to a disease-free start, organic gardener Marion Hess of Northville, Michigan, believes in a sweet approach. She sprinkles her seeds with Jell-O powder. She also feeds her young plants with Jell-O as they grow.

Ingredients and Supplies

    Peat pots
    Potting soil
    Seeds
    1 package Jell-O powder, any flavor with sugar
    Powdered skim milk, in amount equal to Jell-O (optional)
    Salt shaker or other sprinkling device
    Newspaper

Directions

1. Fill the peat pots with potting soil and place 2 seeds in each pot.

2. Fill the salt shaker with the Jell-O powder (and powdered skim milk, if desired, for extra calcium) and sprinkle the powder lightly on top. Gently press down the powder and cover lightly with soil.

3. Moisten the soil and cover it with damp newspaper.

4. After 4 days, remove the newspaper and keep the seeds in a warm area with temperatures of 55° to 65°F.

Note: Should your friends snicker about your plant's snacking habits, just tell them that it makes sense when you think about what's in Jell-O, Marion says. "The gelatin helps the plant hold water, and the sugar feeds the organisms in the soil."

JELL-O DIET PLAN FOR PLANTS

Even after your plants are up and running, Jell-O can still help keep them healthy, Marion Hess says. "In any organic, liquid fertilizer, such as compost tea, I always add Jell-O," she reveals. Add ½ to 1 teaspoon of Jell-O powder to 1 gallon of fertilizer in a bucket. Mix well and use the mixture immediately to prevent thickening. Pour directly on the soil. Because of possible thickening, you don't want to use a spray bottle with this mixture, Marion warns.

Many adventurous gardeners use Jell-O for their houseplants, but Marion says it's just as great at fighting off fungal diseases in outdoor plants. And, she adds, while any flavor will do, lemon's her top choice, because she thinks the citrusy odor repels some bugs.

Compost Your Lawn Problems

Looking for a magic pill to cure all your lawn ills? Compost comes mighty close—it will feed your lawn, improve the soil structure, and prevent diseases! And it doesn't take very much compost to do all this, according to Cornell University plant pathologist Eric Nelson, Ph.D., who has been

researching compost's ability to prevent lawn diseases. Here's his recommendation, based on the latest research.

Ingredients and Supplies

    Composted poultry manure
    Cyclone or drop-type fertilizer spreader

Directions

1. If you have chickens, you can make your own poultry compost. If a flock of hens isn't for you, buy composted poultry manure bagged at nurseries and garden centers. Why poultry manure? Eric says that of all the composts Cornell has tested on lawns, composted poultry manure seems to work best for suppressing diseases.

2. Apply 10 pounds of compost per 1,000 square feet of lawn about once a month during the growing season. Regular applications of this "black gold" can prevent a whole host of diseases that strike both cool and warm season grasses, including snow mold, brown patch, dollar spot, pythium blight, necrotic ring spot, red thread, and summer patch.

Note: If you use homemade compost, screen it to remove any chunks before applying it with the spreader. The compost will go through the screen and the spreader best if you let it dry out a little before you try to screen it.

DISEASE-PROOF YOUR GARDEN WITH A DOSE OF COMPOST

Lawn grass isn't the only plant that gets healthier when you treat it with compost. According to renowned compost-and-disease expert Harry Hoitink, professor of plant pathology at the Ohio State University, extensive international research has now proven that you can protect your garden crops from diseases by applying compost regularly. To get maximum disease-preventing power, Harry says to "use a surface mulch of slightly immature compost in your garden beds."

Spicy Garlic Garden Spray

Get the best results from garden sprays by catching problems right away, advises Mary Perlmutter, author of *How Does Your Garden Grow...Organically?* Mary vigilantly patrols her garden each morning for signs of distress. If she spies any trace of fungal disease (rust on a hollyhock or blackspot on a rose, for instance), she prepares this potent garlic cure, applies it, and sees improvement almost immediately.

Ingredients and Supplies

    3 cloves garlic, crushed
    1 onion, peeled and minced
    1 teaspoon Jalapeño pepper, crushed
    Fine-meshed sieve or cheesecloth
    Pump spray bottle
    1 drop dishwashing liquid or 2 tablespoons vegetable or horticultural oil (optional)

Directions

1. Steep garlic, onion, and pepper in 1 quart of warm water for 1 hour or longer.

2. Strain the mix through a sieve or piece of cheesecloth and retain the liquid.

3. In the spray bottle, dilute 1 part of the strained liquid in 4 parts warm water and add the soap or oil, if desired. (Adding oil will help the mixture remain on the plants longer; adding soap will improve spray coverage on leaves and stems.)

4. Mist plants lightly.

Continued ➡

Yield: About 1 quart of spicy spray concentrate

BE WARY, SAYS MARY

You may not have five hours each morning to survey your vegetables, flowers, perennial plants, and fruit trees, as Mary Perlmutter does. But, she points out, it would be a shame not to take a quick walk through your yard at least once a day to find out how your crop is growing. That way, you can nip problems in the bud before diseases turn into death sentences.

"I check the plants," Mary explains. "I don't touch every single plant; but if I see a plant that's looking sad, I will examine it. Usually, it's from lack of water." Mary's biggest problem may be summer drought, but she keeps an eye out for other problems, too. She looks for yellowing, white powder, strange patterns on leaves, dull leaves that should be shiny, curling leaves, and any other symptoms that suggest illness or other problems.

Early action, whether it's spraying to stop disease from spreading or careful pruning of diseased leaves, can keep small problems small. "You have to be in touch with all parts of the garden," Mary says.

MORE GREAT GARLIC IDEAS

If the idea of garlic in the garden grabs your interest, try these variations. Horticulturist and organic gardener Howard Garrett recommends the first two sprays for fighting diseases and insects:

Garrett's garlic/pepper blend. Liquefy two garlic cloves and two hot peppers in a blender that is half-filled with water. Strain out the garlic and pepper bits, then mix the remaining liquid with enough water to make 1 gallon of spicy concentrate. For the final spray, use ¼ cup of the concentrate for each gallon of water. Two tablespoons of molasses will help the mixture adhere to leaves.

Plain and simple garlic juice. For a plain garlic juice, use three garlic cloves and follow the directions above—it makes a great additive for any garden-disease or insect-pest spray.

For extra garlic power in his garden, Andy Lopez goes a different route. Andy is the founder of the Invisible Gardeners of America, an organization which provides education on organic gardening techniques to its 6,000 members. Here's his recipe for a fungus-free garden.

Get growing to fight fungus. Andy grows the pungent herb around vulnerable plants, explaining that the garlic aroma provides a fungus-free environment. Andy adds that "garlic has been around for centuries as a fungal control."

Garlic has so many uses that you'll want to have lots of it around. Growing your own garlic is an easy and economical way to keep a steady supply of this useful bulb on hand, and it lets you try different kinds of garlic for cooking and for pest and disease control.

Start with whole bulbs from a local grower. Separate the individual cloves and plant them in mid-fall in full sun and well-drained soil. Set the cloves 1 to 2 inches deep and 6 to 8 inches apart. Harvest in early July when most of the leaves have turned brown, and lay the plants in a dark, dry spot to cure for several weeks. Trim leaves and roots and brush away excess soil, then store in cool, dry conditions.

Mighty-Milk Tomato Blight Cure

To ward off common tomato diseases, like early blight, try a sprinkling of powdered milk when you set out the tomato transplants. This simple suggestion comes from organic gardener Marion Hess, who is a special contributor for Prodigy's on-line gardening

newsletter *Prodigy Gardens Newsletter*. Marion credits milk with her amazing tomato track record of no diseases, ever. "I have never even had to rotate my crop," she marvels. And the technique is gentle, Marion assures. "It won't hurt anything in your yard."

Ingredients and Supplies

¼ cup plus 2 tablespoons powdered nonfat milk

¼ cup Epsom salts (optional)

1 shovelful of compost (optional)

Salt shaker or other sprinkling device

Hand trowel

Directions

1. Prepare your garden site or planting container for planting by digging a hole.

2. Use the shaker or your hand to sprinkle the powdered nonfat milk into the planting hole. Add the Epsom salts and compost or composted manure, if desired. The Epsom salts and compost will boost your plant's overall growth and disease resistance, Marion says.

3. Mix the ingredients into the soil with the hand trowel.

4. Set your tomato plant in place and refill the hole with soil.

5. Sprinkle about 2 tablespoons additional powdered nonfat milk around the plant, then mix the milk into the soil with the trowel.

6. Add more powdered milk every few weeks throughout the growing season by sprinkling about 2 tablespoons of the powder on top of the soil. When you use your trowel (or a spade or garden fork) to mix the powder into the soil, take care not to damage roots that are growing near the soil surface.

MULCH TOMATOES IN TO KEEP DISEASE OUT

A layer of mulch doesn't just keep moisture in the soil; it also can protect your tomatoes from diseases, says Dr. Frank Killebrew, extension plant pathologist at Mississippi State University. "The mulch provides a physical barrier between soil and plant surfaces and reduces the amount of disease inoculum that is splashed onto foliage, stems, and fruits during rainy periods," explains Dr. Killebrew. Mulching can prevent tomato (and cucumber) rot diseases. He suggests using black plastic or organic materials such as bark, composted sawdust, oat straw, or pine needles for mulch.

Wipe Out Black Spot with Tomato Leaf Tonic

When black spot attacks her roses, organic gardener and author Mary Perlmutter uses ingredients that are plentiful all summer long: tomato leaves and onions! Mary steeps the leaves and onion in alcohol. The sharp-smelling solution not only discourages the black spot fungus but aphids, asparagus beetles, and scale insects as well.

Ingredients and Supplies

10 tomato leaves

1 medium-size onion, finely chopped

½ cup rubbing alcohol

Cotton batting

Stick, about the size of a chopstick

Directions

1. Pick 10 tomato leaves from a healthy tomato plant and chop them into small pieces.

2. Combine the onion with the tomato leaves in the rubbing alcohol. Steep the mixture overnight.

3. Make a cotton swab by wrapping a piece of the cotton batting around the stick. The idea is to make a swab that is large enough to let you apply the mixture easily.

4. In the morning, remove any diseased leaves from your roses. Dip the swab in the tomato-onion solution and wipe the entire plant, including the tops and undersides of all the leaves.

Yield: About ½ cup of black spot-stopping Tomato Leaf Tonic

BEATING BLACK SPOT

Black spot (*Diplocarpon rosae*) is a disfiguring fungal disease that infects roses during warm, wet weather. The disease causes black spots ringed with yellow on rose leaves. While black spot is rarely fatal, a severely infected plant may drop all of its leaves.

Luckily, you can thwart black spot with good gardening practices. Every time you visit your garden, clean up fallen leaves and organic debris to remove places where black spot spores collect. While you're there, prune off and destroy infected leaves and seriously infected canes.

You can also keep black spot off plants by being careful not to splash spore-laden, muddy water on them when watering. A mulch of disease-fighting compost actually kills spores in the soil and keeps them from splashing onto plants.

Good air circulation also prevents black spot spores from taking hold. To open the center of rose bushes to air and sun, carry pruners on garden visits and cut out any inward-growing shoots. Growing roses in full sun and spacing them far enough apart for adequate air circulation can stop black spot troubles before they start.

Baking Soda Blitz

For a disease fighter that's cheap, easy, and proven effective, look no further than your kitchen cabinet. This recipe, offered by Dr. Thomas A. Zitter, a professor in the Cornell University Department of Plant Pathology, includes lightweight oil that acts as a spreader-sticker to help the baking soda stay on leaves. By keeping the baking soda on the leaves, the oil makes the spray more effective.

Use this recipe when you have to spray only occasionally—some plants may be injured by repeated applications of oil.

Ingredients and Supplies

1 tablespoon baking soda

1 tablespoon horticultural oil

1 gallon water

1-gallon backpack or pump sprayer

Directions

1. Mix the baking soda, oil, and water in the sprayer.

2. Spray each plant completely, including the tough-to-reach spots like the undersides of leaves, says Dr. Zitter. "Some of these things (fungi) do very well on the underside of a leaf. If you spray only the top, you will reduce the population by half—if you're lucky—and you will have a new set of spores."

Yield: About 1 gallon of fungus-fighting spray

Variation: Dr. Zitter points out that while baking soda is great, its near relation, potassium bicarbonate, performed even better in studies and the Environmental Protection Agency (EPA) has approved it as a commercial home and garden product. (Look for potassium bicarbonate at garden centers.)

Continued ➡

Deluxe Baking Soda Spray

Instead of mixing separate sprays for diseases and insects, consider using Dennis Glowniak's deluxe combo spray, which works for both. Spray weekly and it's "good-bye pests!" promises Dennis, president of the California Organic Garden Club.

Ingredients and Supplies

    1½ tablespoons baking soda

    1 tablespoon insecticidal soap

    1 tablespoon canola oil

    1 cup plus 1 gallon water

    1 tablespoon vinegar

    Backpack or pump sprayer

Directions

1. Mix the baking soda, soap, and oil with 1 cup of water.

2. Add the vinegar. Don't mix the vinegar in until last or the mixture may bubble over.

3. Pour the mixture into the sprayer and add 1 gallon of water. Shake or stir to combine the ingredients.

4. Spray plants, covering the tops and bottoms of the leaves.

Yield: About 1 gallon of baking soda spray

BAKING SODA'S BEST AS A PROBLEM PREVENTER

You should always keep a simple solution of 1 teaspoon baking soda to a quart of water mixed and ready for action in your garden, states Dorothy Read, editor of *The Garden Sampler* magazine, which is based in Peru, Vermont. The spray stops fungal diseases on everything from roses to pumpkins, Dorothy claims.

Dorothy's recipe is simple and effective at combating fungal diseases such as black spot and powdery mildew, but there are other versions you can try as well. No matter which recipe you use, be snappy about it, Dorothy urges, because while bicarbonates stop the spread of fungi, they can't clean up a diseased mess. Dorothy explains that baking soda works best as a preventive—if you've had trouble with fungal diseases in the past, start spraying susceptible plants before disease symptoms start and continue at weekly intervals to prevent the problem.

Powdery Mildew Solution

Here's a new twist on the popular baking soda-and-oil mix for controlling powdery mildew. Iowa-based garden writer Veronica Fowler offers this version that uses Murphy's Oil Soap. "The baking soda alters the pH of the leaf, making it more difficult for powdery mildew to form," Veronica explains. "The oil soap serves as a spreader-sticker, so that the mix spreads more evenly and doesn't wash off as readily."

Ingredients and Supplies

    1 gallon warm water

    3 tablespoons baking soda

    1 tablespoon Murphy's Oil Soap

Directions

1. Mix all ingredients well.

2. Spray plants when you spot the very first sign of powdery mildew—a grayish coating on leaves. Coat both sides of leaves thoroughly. Spray every 7 to 10 days until daytime temperatures start getting into the 70s.

Yield: About 1 gallon of Powdery Mildew Solution

Note: On plants with chronic powdery mildew problems, use this spray as a preventive. Spray once or twice in very early spring before any sign of

disease appears. If you notice powdery mildew, take action to stop its spread. Remove all affected leaves and spray with a baking soda solution. Prune or thin to improve air movement around the foliage. Finally, make sure the plant isn't stressed by drought or other problems; stressed plants seem more susceptible to infection.

PLANTS PESTERED BY POWDERY MILDEW

The fungal disease powdery mildew is ugly but it seldom does serious harm. If you're growing a plant that's susceptible to the fungus—check the list below—and don't like how it looks, keep baking soda and Murphy's Oil Soap handy for a quick preventive spray.

Trees and Shrubs

    Crabapples (*Malus* spp.)

    Crape myrtle (*Lagerstroemia indica*)

    English oak (*Quercus robur*)

    Euonymous (*Euonymous* spp.)

    Hackberries (*Celtis* spp.)

    Honeysuckles (*Lonicera* spp.)

    Lilac (*Syringa vulgaris*)

    Privets (*Ligustrum* spp.)

    Roses (*Rosa* spp.)

Flowers

    Bee balm (*Monarda didyma*)

    Dahlias (*Dahlia hybrids*)

    Delphinium (*Delphinium* x *elatum*)

    Phlox (*Phlox paniculata*)

    Zinnia (*Zinnia elegans*)

Spray Away Brown Patch in Lawns

If your lovely green lawn develops brown or yellow rings or patches that die out, brown patch may be the culprit. A variety of Rhizoctonia fungi causes this disease; some species thrive in cool weather, while others affect grasses in warm weather.

If brown patch plagues your lawn, fight back with this formula from John Dromgoole, owner of Garden-Ville in Austin, Texas. Follow up with John's suggestions for correcting water and fertilizer problems or the disease will return.

Ingredients and Supplies

    1 rounded tablespoon baking soda or potassium bicarbonate

    1 tablespoon horticultural oil

    1 gallon water

Directions

1. Mix all ingredients thoroughly.

2. Spray lightly on your lawn. Avoid overuse or drenching the soil with baking soda.

Yield: About 1 gallon of spray for battling brown patch

Note: John says potassium bicarbonate, available in garden centers, is the best choice for this spray. Unlike baking soda, potassium bicarbonate leaves no salt residue in the soil.

COMPOST STOPS BROWN PATCH COLD

How can you tell if your lawn has brown patch? Take a look at your lawn care techniques. John Dromgoole says, "the disease is generally caused by poor drainage, too much rain or irrigation, and/or too much nitrogen fertilizer. Another symptom is that the leaves easily pull loose from the runners."

Aerate to improve the movement of air, nutrients, and water through the soil. And fix drainage problems by filling in low spots or installing drain

tiles in your yard. To permanently solve brown patch problems, John suggests applying a half-inch layer of finished compost to your lawn. The microbe trichoderma, which exists in compost, is a powerful deterrent to brown patch.

Lawn Fungus Fighter

If your lawn develops 2- to 6-inch-diameter reddish-brown spots during the hot, sticky days of summer, it may have a fungal disease called Fusarium blight. Rather than watch those spots turn tan and then yellow as the grass roots die, follow the lead of Robert Redmon, a director of grounds management for the University of Alabama in Huntsville.

When part of the lawn Robert tends became diseased and developed unstoppable brown patches, he made a concoction with two fungus-busting agents: bleach and oil. This mix will help you get temporary control of a fungus-infested lawn during high stress periods. Then you can use cultural controls for a long-term solution. Robert says that he has used this spray primarily for fescues, but adds that it should work equally well for other cool-season grasses.

Ingredients and Supplies

    1 ounce household bleach

    2 ounces horticultural oil or a surfactant (the amount according to the label)

    4 gallons water

    Pump spray bottle or hose-end sprayer

    White Dutch clover seed

    Goggles

    Rubber gloves

Directions

1. Mix the bleach and oil with water in the sprayer. (This mix will cover about 1,000 square feet of lawn.) Be very careful when you handle bleach. Wear goggles, rubber gloves, and long sleeves and take care to avoid splashing when you pour the bleach.

2. Spray the mix on affected areas starting when temperatures consistently reach the mid-60s at night.

3. Fusarium blight is a disease that migrates from the soil to plant parts and then spreads as the temperature and humidity increase. You'll need to reapply the spray monthly to keep the blight under control.

4. When you reseed the area in the fall with fescue or other grass seed, include some clover—¼ to ⅓ pound of clover per 50 pounds of fescue seed, Robert says. That's enough for approximately ½ acre of overseeding.

Note: This recipe should work where fungicides have failed, Robert claims. "I had used a fungicide in another spot that didn't seem to be doing the job, but the bleach-and-oil mixture seemed to take care of it," he states.

Variation: If you want a bleachless control for fusarium blight and other diseases, use compost. Adding compost to your lawn may control some diseases because organic matter increases the number of beneficial microorganisms in the soil. A healthy population of beneficial microorganisms can crowd out disease microorganisms or, in some cases, even kill them.

To add compost to your lawn, screen it first to remove any large pieces, then apply it using a cyclone or drop-type spreader. If you prefer to use a sprayer, mix up a hearty compost tea solution and spray it on.

Continued →

LAWN CARE PRESCRIPTION

Robert Redmon has more advice for a healthy lawn. Follow these tips and you won't have to worry about finding cures for fungal diseases.

- Plant resistant grass varieties.
- Once your grass is growing, make sure that it gets enough water (1 inch per week).
- Don't water your lawn at night, when it is sure to stay damp, because wet conditions help fungi spread.
- Mow your lawn when it's dry, and leave it alone when it's wet to avoid spreading fungi.
- Fertilize with an organic fertilizer.
- Aerate your lawn so that water and air can move easily through the soil.

Dr. H. Arthur Lamey, a plant pathologist at North Dakota State University Extension Service in Fargo, also suggests that you avoid evening watering. He adds these precautions to ward off the fungal spores that, he says, plant themselves almost like seeds.

- Don't mow grass too short.
- Remove excess thatch.

Dual-Purpose Garden Spray

A garden product that you may already have can help your plants fight off fungal diseases. Antidesiccants (or antitranspirants) are best known as the stuff you spray on Christmas trees or wreaths to hold in moisture and make them last longer. But studies show that the sprays can also fight off rust and powdery mildew, says landscape consultant Mark Whitelaw, a consulting rosarian for the American Rose Society.

Ingredients and Supplies

    Antitranspirant or antidesiccant
    Backpack or pump sprayer

Directions

1. Antitranspirants are sold at nurseries under various commercial names as a ready-to-use spray or as a concentrate that you'll need to mix up. Buy whichever is most useful to you. And don't let those long words scare you off—antitranspirants are virtually nontoxic and biodegradable. They work by creating a film on a plant's leaves.

2. When you spray, be sure to coat the tops and bottoms of leaves. Application techniques depend on which form you buy, Mark says, so read and follow label directions. By coating the leaves and stems, you block fungi from the leaves and/or give any fungal spores that are already there a coat, which prevents them from spreading. The film will not protect new growth, so reapply as needed, according to the label.

Note: Gardeners in cool, humid climates, like the Pacific Northwest and New England, boast success with anti desiccants in fighting the dreaded rose rust which thrives in their area, Mark says. At the same time, antidesiccants are popular with some in southern California's dry inland areas. "Antitranspirants are particularly effective against powdery mildew in areas where hot, dry conditions prevail during the day, but high humidity conditions exist at night and early morning," he explains.

WATER FIRST

Whether you're feeding your plants, using a foliar (leaf) spray, insecticidal soap, or any other man-made interference, getting out your hose or watering can should always be step number one.

"Always, always irrigate before applying any chemical, of any sort, for any purpose!" Mark Whitelaw insists. "This puts less stress on the roots and foliage of the plant." If you don't water, you'll create conditions that can injure the leaves.

Fishy Foliar Spray

You can feed your plants and slow the spread of fungal diseases at the same time when you combine two ocean-going ingredients in a foliar (leaf) spray. Rick Estes, president of the New Hampshire chapter of the Northeast Organic Farming Association, uses this nutrient-rich seaweed and fish emulsion "soup" when plants show the first symptom of disease. He also uses it during the growing season and at transplanting time to give plants an energy boost.

Ingredients and Supplies

    2–4 tablespoons liquid seaweed
    2–4 tablespoons liquid fish emulsion (sold at most garden centers and some discount chain stores)
    1 gallon water
    Backpack, pump, or hose-end sprayer

Directions

1. Before you get started, take note: You may have to set your alarm clock. "You should get up before the sun hits the leaves to foliar-feed," Rick says. "Then the stomata (pore-like openings) of the leaves are open, taking in their moisture" for the day ahead.

2. Mix the liquids with 1 gallon of water in the sprayer and shake to blend thoroughly.

3. Spray generously, coating tops and bottoms of leaves. Stretch out your treatments. Don't spray more often than every 5 days, Rick suggests, even if plants show symptoms of a fungus or other ailment. "Always give the plants time to put the extra nutrients to work," he says. Rick recommends a dose of "nutrient and mineral soup" at transplanting time to help reduce shock and give plants a boost. For the squeamish (or those with curious cats): You can buy odorless fish emulsion.

Yield: About 1 gallon of Fishy Foliar Spray

SEAWEED STRAIGHT

For a last-ditch effort, when a treasured plant is nearly dead, Rose Marie Nichols McGee reaches for the liquid seaweed—a magical tip that she cherishes but hesitates to share. "I love liquid seaweed, but I'm always nervous about making too many claims for something. It's a tip we kind of pass on to friends," says the president of Nichols Garden Nursery.

So consider this a tip from a friend: To try to save a dying plant, make a circle of liquid seaweed around the trunk or stem and water it in. "If there's still something there, the seaweed gives it a booster."

Stick It to 'Em Molasses Spray

Molasses is anything but slow in fighting fungal disease in the garden, says organic gardener Andy Lopez, founder of the Invisible Gardeners of America. Don't worry about bugs, he says. "The plants absorb the molasses instantly. There's nothing left for the bugs!" Andy often mixes sulfured molasses with other organic garden sprays because, he says, the sugar feeds the plants and the sulfur is a natural fungicide.

Ingredients and Supplies

    1 cup molasses
    1 cup seaweed powder (optional)
    1 cup powdered milk (optional)
    1 cup rock powder (optional)
    1 gallon warm water
    Backpack or pump sprayer
    Old panty hose
    Fine-meshed strainer

Directions

1. If you are using only molasses, stir thoroughly into warm water, and spray (skip steps 2 and 3). If you have any or all of the optional ingredients, mix the molasses and powders into a thick paste and follow steps 2 and 3.

2. Wrap about 1 cup of the paste in the panty hose and tie it into a ball. Place the ball in water and let it sit for 2 to 4 hours.

3. Strain the liquid and mist plants every few weeks. You can use it to stop the spread of fungal diseases or as a preventive.

Yield: About 1 gallon of molasses spray

Note: Pick the right sprayer for your garden's size. For a few plants or a small garden, a hand-held pump spray bottle will do the job. For a medium-size garden, a 1½-gallon pump sprayer will speed up the application. For bigger gardens, a backpack model not only holds more spray, but is easier to haul around.

Wash Away Fungi with Garrett's Spray

For a natural fungicide for ornamental plants, horticulturist and organic gardener Howard Garrett recommends his own homemade spray. Garrett spray packs a punch because it contains four fungus-fighting ingredients. You can add even more antifungal power with additives like baking soda (see the variations below).

Ingredients and Supplies

    1–2 cups compost tea (see "Compost Tea Cure-All for Plants" on page 000)
    1 tablespoon liquid seaweed
    1 tablespoon blackstrap molasses
    1 tablespoon apple cider vinegar
    1 gallon water
    Backpack or pump sprayer

Directions

1. Mix the ingredients in the sprayer. The acidity of the vinegar helps to kill black spot on roses, powdery mildew, brown patch, and other nasty fungi, Howard says. And the manure-based compost tea has natural fungus-fighting abilities.

2. Spray during the cool part of the day. As tempting as it is to blast away, don't overdo it, Howard cautions. To avoid damage to leaves, mist plant lightly and be sure not to drip vinegar on the soil.

3. Clean your sprayer thoroughly after use.

Variations: To give your fungus-fighting spray even more "umph," add baking soda, potassium bicarbonate, or ¼ cup garlic tea. To make garlic tea, liquefy 3 bulbs of garlic in a blender and strain out the solids. Pour the garlic juice into a 1-gallon container and fill with water. Shake the garlic juice well before using.

Continued ➡

COMPOST TEA KEEPS ORNAMENTALS FUNGUS FREE

Compost is an effective fungus fighter that can help control any fungal problems that your ornamental plants might have. Compost teas made from manure are more effective at fighting fungi than compost teas made from only vegetable matter. But don't use compost teas made from manure on edible plants. Animal manure may contain E. coli bacteria which could be transferred to your fruits, vegetables, and herbs if you spray them with the tea.

Making compost for compost tea is easy. Any mix of vegetable matter and animal manure (from herbivores or poultry) will do, but for the best results, make a compost pile that's about 80 percent plant matter and 20 percent chicken, cow, goat, horse, or sheep manure. Use whatever materials you have available for the plant matter, including leaves, hay, grass clippings, tree trimmings, food scraps, bark, sawdust, rice hulls, and weeds (before they set seed).

Oil on the Offense Spray

To prevent fungal diseases from taking hold in late winter and early spring when wet, rainy weather can mean trouble, spray your plants with diluted oil, suggests Andy Lopez, founder of the Invisible Gardeners of America. Andy uses oil on fruit trees, vegetables, roses, and most flowers. However, he cautions, oil benefits only shiny-leaf plants. Do not spray oil on fuzzy-leaf plants, which are vulnerable to burning.

Ingredients and Supplies

1 teaspoon oil (plant-based oil such as castor, coconut, or a light salad oil)

1 teaspoon liquid soap (any biodegradable dishwashing liquid or Dr. Bronner's Peppermint 18-in-1 Soap)

1 gallon water (with chamomile tea or compost tea, optional)

Backpack or pump sprayer

Directions

1. Mix the oil, soap, and water in the sprayer. Water is easiest, but if you've got it, substitute a few cups of chamomile tea or compost tea, both of which help inhibit disease, Andy suggests.

2. Spray a fine mist on plants as often as needed, "usually daily the first week, then weekly, and, if it holds out, then monthly."

Yield: About 1 gallon of preventive oil spray

Note: Andy is picky about the types of oil he will use in the garden. Plant-based oils, such as castor oil or coconut oil, are his favorites, but he is also fond of fish oils, which have minerals that can help strengthen plants against disease. Because it contains peppermint oil (which acts as an insect repellent), he likes to use Dr. Bronner's peppermint soap when mixing any garden spray with a liquid soap.

Variation: Because it's a cheap, easy, and effective alternative, many gardeners prefer plain old salad oil for disease prevention, says Marion Hess, special contributor for Prodigy's on-line gardening newsletter, *Prodigy Gardens Newsletter*. "You mix 1 teaspoon of a light salad oil, like canola or safflower, and 1 teaspoon of liquid soap in 1 gallon of water. It seems to prevent disease."

Even when they're made with vegetable oil instead of petroleum oil, oil sprays can injure your plants if you don't apply them properly. Avoid using an oil spray when temperatures are expected to go above 85°F or below freezing. It's always best to test an oil spray on a few leaves and then wait and watch for a few days before dousing an entire plant.

Fire-Away Rust Removal

If you're fond of old-fashioned hollyhocks, odds are that you're familiar with rust, the ugly orange fungus that can quickly disfigure an entire garden. "Even if you stayed on it every single day with a chemical, you would not get all of the spores," says Mary Lou Heard, owner of Heard's Country Gardens in Westminster, California. So she devised the "fire method." She just makes a tiny fire beneath the hollyhock (with safety precautions!) to kill spores. It works for roses and snapdragons, too.

Ingredients and Supplies

¼ cup shredded paper or paper scraps

Matches

Jug of water and/or fire extinguisher

Directions

1. First, remember that you are lighting a fire; although it's small, use precautions. Have a jug of water or a fire extinguisher nearby. Make sure that there is no dry material nearby that could catch a flame and be sure to completely extinguish any remaining sparks.

2. Begin by placing a thin layer of the paper at the base of the plant. "You make a little circle of fire around the stem," Mary Lou says. She explains that the fire makes an instant flash of heat in a full circle around the base of the plant. Mary Lou emphasizes that you want to make sure that the area of heat extends to the outermost leaf, however far away that farthest leaf is. That way, you can be sure that you're hitting all the rust spores.

3. Light the fire. Expect a quick flame for 5 to 10 seconds. It should extinguish on its own; if not, use the water to douse it. You may lose some lower leaves in the process, Mary Lou cautions. But she adds, "When the plant recovers from this little bitty heat, it comes back so gorgeous."

Note: If more than one plant shows symptoms of rust, repeat the process individually, for each plant. In 2 weeks, check to be sure that the plant is clean. If there are any diseased leaves, remove them. If the fungus reappears, treat that plant again. Mary Lou says she's never had any problems past that point.

Deter Disease with Disinfectant Dips for Tools

Clean your tools! You've heard that advice before, but now it's time to take it seriously. Using bleach or another disinfectant for tools is a must, says Dr. Cheryl Smith, a specialist in plant health with the University of New Hampshire Cooperative Extension. "If you're going to do pruning or any type of cutting, cut diseased areas of a plant last, and make sure that cutting tools, even scissors, get thoroughly cleaned prior to next use," Cheryl says. Otherwise, an isolated problem could become a full-scale plague.

Ingredients and Supplies

1½ cups household bleach

1 gallon water

Clean bucket

New steel wool pad

Motor oil or other oil used to condition tools

Directions

1. Mix the bleach and water to produce a 10 percent solution. This works fine for most cleaning.

2. Dip tools in the disinfectant after each use. For plants or trees that are already suffering symptoms, dip tools as you go along, cautions landscape consultant Mark Whitelaw. "If you are pruning severely diseased shrubs, or shrubs with highly infectious diseases, I recommend dipping the 'business end' of the pruners between making each cut."

3. After disinfecting, your tools need tender loving care to prevent discoloration or corrosion. Rinse thoroughly, then rub them lightly with a clean steel wool pad.

4. Sharpen the edges if you'd like, and oil the tools before storing them for the next outing.

Yield: About 1 gallon of tool-disinfecting dip

Variation: To destroy fire blight bacteria that afflicts apple and crabapple trees, use 3 cups of bleach in 1 gallon of water (a 20 percent solution), says Dr. H. Arthur Lamey, a plant pathologist with the North Dakota State University Extension Service in Fargo. Or you may use pine cleaner at full strength, he says; just be sure that the label lists 19.9 percent pine oil.

WASH UP

Don't forget to clean your shovel, hand tools, gloves, and even gardening shoes to prevent diseases from spreading, especially if you suspect a soil-borne disease. After you are finished working in the garden, wash your gloves and shoe soles in warm, soapy water and hang them out to dry.

CUT OUT DISEASE PROBLEMS WITH PROPER PRUNING

To prevent diseases on fruit and other trees, start with sharp shears, says landscape consultant Mark Whitelaw. "Clean cuts reduce the likelihood of rot and disease." Never leave a stump or stub. Cut limbs close to, but not flush with, the trunk—where the branch and branch collar (swollen area) meet. Prune so that branches grow outward; inward growth reduces air circulation, which helps diseases grow. Prune when leaves are dry.

FOILED AGAIN

As a shimmery mulch, aluminum foil can help foil viruses that afflict your vegetables, says Dr. Frank Killebrew, extension plant pathologist at Mississippi State University. And if you wrap it around plant stems, foil can also deter fungal diseases.

Ingredients and Supplies

Aluminum foil or other light-reflective material

Directions

1. For a mulch, spread a 30-inch-wide light-reflective material on the soil surrounding squash or tomatoes, Dr. Killebrew suggests. The shimmer scares away aphids and thrips, which carry disfiguring, crop-reducing viruses.

2. To deter southern blight on tomatoes and peppers, wrap aluminum foil around plant stems, from 2 inches below the soil surface to 2 inches above the soil surface. The foil serves as a physical barrier against the fungus.

Herbal Soap Spray

Keeping plants clean and disease-free is the backbone of Donna Carrier's job as owner of Organic Plant Care, an interior landscaping company based in East Swanzey, New Hampshire. Soap sprays are a crucial part of her strictly organic regimen, but they don't have to smell bad to work, she says. Donna concocted her own soap spray that's scented with fragrant herbs.

Continued ➡

Ingredients and Supplies

- 1 cup wormwood or tansy
- 1 cup lavender
- 1 cup sage
- 1-quart heat-resistant canning jar
- 2 cups water
- 1 teaspoon liquid, nondetergent soap, like castile soap or Murphy's Oil Soap
- Pump spray bottle

Directions

1. Place the wormwood or tansy, lavender, and sage in the canning jar and fill the jar with boiling water.

2. Let the mix sit until it cools to room temperature. Then drain off and reserve the liquid.

3. Combine 1/8 cup of the herbal liquid with 2 cups water and 1 teaspoon liquid nondetergent soap.

4. Fill the pump spray bottle and spray the mixture on plants. Repeat once a month.

Yield: About 2 cups of herbal soap spray

Note: If your plants are very dirty or dusty, saturate a cotton cloth with the liquid and wipe the leaves clean.

Soapy Indoor Plant Spray

For indoor plants that are exposed to pollutants from heaters or stoves, a cleaning spray can boost health and deter diseases, says Donna Carrier, owner of Organic Plant Care, East Swanzey, New Hampshire. This gentle spray cleans dust and dirt from plants and does not pose any risks to plants or animals, she adds. You can use it in your outdoor garden, too.

Ingredients and Supplies

- 1 tablespoon liquid, nondetergent soap
- 1 tablespoon liquid seaweed (optional)
- 1 quart lukewarm water
- Pump spray bottle
- Clean cloth

Directions

1. Mix soap, seaweed, and water together in the spray bottle.

2. Spray plants liberally and wipe off excess moisture with a clean cloth. Use monthly.

Yield: About 1 quart of soapy plant spray

Plant Mixing Plan

To save cucumbers and squash from one of their greatest enemies—bacterial wilt—try companion planting, suggests Dennis Glowniak, president of the California Organic Garden Club. Dennis says you can't beat this combination of tansy and radishes for a healthy summer-long feast of cucumbers and squash.

Like many bacterial diseases, wilt is carried by an insect pest. In this case, it's the cucumber beetle, which injects the wilt disease as it feeds. In this planting plan, the pungent aroma of tansy confuses and repels the beetles, while the radishes lure them away from the vine crops.

Ingredients and Supplies

- Squash or cucumber transplants
- Radish seeds
- Tansy plants

Directions

1. Plant the squash or cucumber transplants in your garden, and tuck radish seeds into the soil in a circle around each transplant. The radishes should pop up within a day or two.

2. Check the radishes daily for cucumber beetles and squish any that you find. If you're squeamish about squishing them, drop the beetles into a jar or bag and throw it into the trash.

3. Plant the tansy the same day you plant your vegetable transplants. Tansy can be invasive, so set it in a plastic pot with the bottom cut out and set the plant in the soil, pot and all, to contain it. If you plant tansy directly into the soil, check it regularly and pull up any underground shoots that wander away from the planting area. Plant a 4-inch clump of tansy for every 2 vegetable plants. Anecdotal evidence suggests that the tansy encourages overall healthy growth in cucumbers, Dennis says.

4. Divide unpotted tansy with a shovel at least annually. "You don't walk away from tansy," Dennis warns.

ANOTHER FRIENDLY MIX

Some herbs have a reputation for helping their neighbors fight off disease. "Try basil, for tomatoes," for instance, Dennis Glowniak recommends. "People think of basil and tomato as going well together in sauces, but actually a number of tests have shown that when they're planted together, both plants are more vigorous." Dennis explains that a vigorous plant repels diseases and insects more easily than one that's unthrifty. To give your tomatoes the benefits of basil (and vice versa), simply plant one basil plant inside each tomato cage, on the sunny side.

Keep 'Em Moving

To give your vegetable plants an added edge against diseases, enter them in a witness relocation program of sorts. That is, move them around each season so that the diseases are less likely to find them. If you always plant in the same spot, "it's inevitable that you're going to build up disease-causing microbes in the soil," says Dr. Frank Killebrew, extension plant pathologist at Mississippi State University. "Sooner or later, you're going to get zapped."

Ingredients and Supplies

- Notebook (for keeping garden records)
- Chart (for reference)
- Disease-resistant vegetable seeds or plants

Directions

1. "Crop rotation does require some record keeping," Dr. Killebrew says. If you've kept a garden diary in the past few years, all the better. If not, now's the time to start. Begin by making a record of what you grow where.

2. Rotate your crops as best you can, for a minimum of 3 years. If you have a small garden, you may not be able to rotate crops effectively. In that case, consider moving the location of your garden every few years.

Note: For an easy rotation, group members of the same plant family together so that you can move them together. If you have plenty of space, split family members apart to confuse insects in addition to disrupting diseases. Then make sure that you rotate all of the individuals to new locations where no members of the same family have grown in the previous 2 years. Ideally, you should move crops to new ground after just 1 season, but certainly after 2 seasons, Dr. Killebrew says.

MORE DISEASE-STOPPING METHODS

Crop rotation goes a long way toward reducing disease (and insect) problems, but like any other garden technique, it's not a complete solution. "Crop rotation in itself does not mean that you've walked away from the problem," Dr. Frank Killebrew says. You still need to take other steps, like mulching and planting disease-resistant vegetable varieties. Mulch helps tomatoes and other vegetables avoid being splashed by rain or irrigation water—on its own, the water is harmless, but it gives diseases a medium for spreading. Planting disease-resistant varieties is a great way to combat wilts and other diseases which are willing to wait in the soil. Fusarium wilt, for instance, will not disappear from the soil just because you've moved its favorite meal away for a few years.

Disease Glossary

Acervulus A shallow, saucer-shaped mass of hyphae with a depression in the center that bears conidiophores—stalk-like filaments that have conidia (asexual spores) at the tips. Spores are released when the acervulus grows and ruptures cells of the host plant. Plural is *acervuli.*

Alternate host One of two plants upon which a parasitic fungus must live.

Anthracnose A disease characterized by lesions that show on the epidermis. Caused by fungi that produce asexual spores in acervuli.

Ascomycetes A fungal group characterized by a membranous sac, or ascus, in which the cells divide to form ascospores. Yeasts, molds, and mildews are ascomycetes. Ascospores are sexual.

Bacteria One-celled microorganisms that reproduce by division. Bacteria are dependent on either dead or living organic matter for food.

Bacteriophage A virus-like organism that destroys bacteria.

Baisidiomycetes A group of fungi characterized by mycelium with cross walls and the production of sexual spores on club-shaped filaments called basidia. Rusts, smuts, and mushrooms are basidiomycetes.

Blasting Failure to produce fruit or seeds.

Blight General description of diseases that cause sudden leaf, flower, or stem death.

Blotch A superficial spot or necrotic area.

Canker A diseased or dying area on a stem. Most commonly applied to woody plants.

Carrier A plant or animal bearing an infectious disease agent without showing symptoms. Carriers can transmit the disease to other organisms. Most bear the disease agent internally, although the term can be used when the agent is carried externally.

Causal organism The organism responsible for causing a disease.

Certified seed Seed monitored to ensure varietal purity and freedom from disease organisms.

Chlamydospore An asexual spore formed by a mycelial cell. Thick-walled, chlamydospores are resting spores that can remain dormant until conditions are correct for development.

Chlorosis Yellowing caused by partial failure of chlorophyll development. Symptomatic of many diseases.

Coalesce To grow together to form one spot or splotch.

Conidia Asexual spores formed at the tips of conidiophores. Produced most numerously during the height of the growing season, conidia are wind- or rain-borne.

Continued ➡

Conidiophore Hyphae on which conidia are produced.

Damping-off Used to describe the death of seedlings, emerged or not, caused by a number of organisms.

Defoliate To cause most leaves on a plant to die and drop.

Dieback Progressive death of branches or stems from the tip backwards toward the main stem or trunk.

Enzyme A chemical produced by cells which brings about changes in processes such as ripening or digestion. Some pathogenic bacteria produce enzymes that damage host plants.

Epidermis The outermost layer of cells of a plant part.

Epinasty An abnormal growth pattern of leaves caused by rapid growth of cells on the upper surface, resulting in a downward cupping of the leaf.

Escape Applied to plants that are not resistant to a particular pathogen but do not acquire it.

Exudate Any substance produced within a plant that is then released or discharged through natural openings or injuries.

Facultative parasite An organism that can grow on either living or dead organic matter.

Fasciation Plant distortion caused by injury or infection resulting in flattened or curved shoots. Stems may look fused.

Flagellum A whiplike filament of a cell enabling it to swim through liquids.

Fruiting body A plant that lacks chlorophyll and is dependent upon either dead or living organic matter for food supplies. Fungi reproduce by both sexual and asexual spores and are composed of a body of filaments called hyphae that form branched systems called mycelia.

Gall A localized swelling composed of unorganized cells. Caused by bacteria, fungi, or insects.

Gamete A mature sex cell.

Girdle A lesion that encircles the stem or root, causing death.

Haustorium A specialized fungal hypha that penetrates the cells of a host plant and absorbs food from them.

Host A plant infected or parasitized by a pathogen.

Hyperplasia Abnormal increase in resulting in formation of galls and tumors.

Hyphae Threads or filaments of a fungal mycelium or body.

Lesion A spot or area of diseased tissue.

Mildew A fungus that grows on the surface of plant parts.

Mold A fungus that produces a woolly growth on the surface of plant parts.

Mosaic A disease caused by a virus, characterized by mottled patterns of yellow and green on the leaves.

Mycelium The vegetative body of a fungus, composed of many hyphae.

Necrotic Dead. (Necrosis is death.)

Nematode Nonsegmented, microscopic roundworms that live in soil, water, plants, animals, and dead organic matter. Some nematodes are plant parasites.

Nodule A lump or knot.

Obligate parasite A parasite that can live only on living matter.

Parasite An organism that obtains its nutrients from a secondary organism.

Pathogen An organism capable of causing disease in other organisms.

Penetration peg A strong hypha anchored to the host surface with a sticky substance. Produced in order to bore into a host.

Perfect stage The period of a fungal life cycle when spores are produced sexually.

Phloem The vessels in the plant that carry dissolved sugars from leaves to the rest of the plant. One of the two vessels in the vascular bundle.

Phycomycetes One group of fungi. Characterized by sexual reproduction and few cross walls in the hyphae.

Primary infection The first infection by a fungus after a resting period.

Pustule A blisterlike structure.

Pycnidium A flask-shaped, fruiting body of a fungus that contains asexual spores. Usually located near the surface of the host.

Pycnium The flask-shaped, fruiting body of a rust fungus that contains pycniospores. These spores are unisexual and are usually fertilized by insects feeding on the nectar produced in the pycnium.

Resistance Ability of a plant to remain relatively healthy despite infection by a pathogen. Resistance is an inborn quality and is not caused by environmental factors.

Resting spore A spore that can remain for long periods of time before germinating. Most resting spores are very thick-walled.

Ring spot Symptomatic of some diseases. Ring spots are brownish yellow on the margin and green in the center.

Rogue To remove a plant. Plants infected with some diseases are normally rogued to prevent the spread of the disease.

Rosette Formation of short-stalked leaves that radiate from a central stem. Some diseases produce an unnatural rosette in their hosts.

Russet A corky, roughened area on the skin surface. Russeting can be caused by pathogens, insects, or cultural techniques.

Rust The disease caused by a rust fungus, or the fungus itself. Rusts may have one or more hosts through their life cycles and, in some cases, have as many as five types of spores.

Saprophyte An organism that feeds on dead organic matter.

Scab A disease that is characterized by rough, scaly tissue on the skin surface.

Sclerotium A resting mass of fungal hyphae that does not contain spores but that is capable of becoming dormant and remaining so for many years before resuming growth.

Scorch A burning of tissue caused by a pathogen or by environmental conditions.

Secondary infection A disease caused by infectious material following a primary infection or produced by reproductive material that has not undergone a resting period.

Shothole A disease symptom in which small round holes die and drop out of leaves.

Sign Any visible portion of a pathogen. Signs can include mycelia, spores, fruiting bodies, or even a mass of bacteria.

Smut A disease caused by a smut fungus, or the fungus itself. Smuts are characterized by the formation of dark masses of resting spores.

Sporangium A fungal fruiting body that produces asexual spores.

Spore A single cell or multicelled reproductive unit. Fungi produce sexual and asexual spores. The resting structures of some bacteria are also called spores.

Strain Synonym for race when describing plant pathogens. A strain, or race, is a subgroup within a species that differs in host range or effect from other members of the species.

Summer spore A spore that proliferates during the best growing conditions and that does not rest between release and germination.

Susceptible Without inherent resistance to a pathogen.

Systemic Applied to a pathogen or chemical that travels throughout the plant body. Many systemics travel through the vascular system.

Thallus The vegetative body of a thallophyte, a simple plant, including fungi, algae, bacteria, slime molds, and lichens.

Tolerant Capable of sustaining an infection by a pathogen, or of enduring environmental stress or injury without much damage.

Toxin A poison.

Vascular Applied to the vessels in the plant that carry water or nutrients. Respectively, these are the xylem and phloem vessels.

Vector An organism or agent that transmits diseases. Many insects are vectors of plant diseases.

Vein-banding A symptom of some viral diseases in which regions along the veins are a darker green color than regions between veins.

Virulent Strongly capable of producing disease.

Virus An obligate parasite composed of genetic materials and protein that is capable of reproducing within living materials.

Wilt Drooping plant tissue as a consequence of insufficient water supply. Some diseases cause wilt by plugging the vascular system.

Xylem The vessels that carry water in the plant.

Yellows Disease that causes abnormal yellowing of leaves and stems.

Zoospore A spore that swims.

BIBLIOGRAPHY

Works Excerpted and/or Reprinted in this Book

Ball, Jeff, *Flower Garden Problem Solver*, Rodale Press, 1997

Ball, Jeff, *Landscape Problem Solver*, Rodale Press, 1989

Benjamin, Joan, *Great Garden Formulas*, Rodale Press, 2000

Bradley, Fern Marshall, *Expert's Book of Garden Hints*, Rodale Press, 1993

Bradley, Fern Marshall, *Vegetable Garden Problem Solver*, Rodale Press, 2001

Bradley, Fern Marshall, *Gardening with Perennials*, Rodale Press, 2000

Bubel, Nancy, *New Seed Starters Handbook*, Rodale Press, 1988

Cox, Jeff, *Your Organic Garden*, Rodale Press, 1994

Cunningham, Sally Jean, *Great Garden Companions*, Rodale Press, 2000

Ellis, Barbara, *Rodale's Illustrated Encyclopedia of Gardening and Landscaping Techniques*, Rodale Press, 1997

Ellis, Barbara W., *Rodale's Low-Maintenance Gardening Techniques*, Rodale Press, 1995

Erler, Catriona Tudor, *The Frugal Gardener*, Rodale Press, 2001

Gilkeson, Linda, *Insect, Disease, and Weed ID Guide*, Rodale Press, 2001

The Editors of Organic Gardening Magazine, *Compost: Organic Gardening Basics*, Rodale Press, 2001

The Editors of Organic Gardening Magazine, *Herbs: Organic Gardening Basics Volume 5*, Rodale Press, 2001

The Editors of Organic Gardening Magazine, *Lawns: Organic Gardening Basics*, Rodale Press, 2001

The Editors of Organic Gardening Magazine, *Perennials: Organic Gardening Basics*, Rodale Press, 2001

The Editors of Organic Gardening Magazine, *Pests: Organic Gardening Basics*, Rodale Press, 2001

The Editors of Organic Gardening Magazine, *Roses: Organic Gardening Basics*, Rodale Press, 2001

The Editors of Organic Gardening Magazine, *Soil: Organic Gardening Basics*, Rodale Press, 2001

The Editors of Organic Gardening Magazine, *Vegetables: Organic Gardening Basics*, Rodale, 2001

Hodgson, Larry, *Annuals for Every Purpose*, Rodale Press, 2003

Hodgson, Larry, *Making the Most of Shade*, Rodale Press, 2005

Hodgson, Larry, *Perennials for Every Purpose*, Rodale Press, 2003

Kowalchik, Claire, *Rodale's Encyclopedia of Herbs*, Rodale Press, 1998

Martin, Deborah, *Rodale Book of Composting*, Rodale Press, 1992

Martin, Deborah L., *1001 Ingenious Gardening Ideas*, Rodale Press, 2007

Mattern, Vicki, *Gardener-to-Gardener Seed-Starting Primer and Almanac*, Rodale Press, 2002

Phillips, Ellen, *Rodale's Illustrated Encyclopedia of Perennials*, Rodale Press, 2004

Pleasant, Barbara, *Easy Garden Projects to Make Build, and Grow*, Rodale Press, 2006

Roth, Sally, *Natural Landscaping*, Rodale Press, 2002

Yepsen, Roger, *Newspaper, Pennies, Cardboard, and Eggs*, Rodale Press, 2007

INDEX

Continued ➡

Continued ➡

Continued ➡

Continued ➤

Continued ➤

Continued ➡